AIRLINE FLEETS
2011

Edited by Pete Webber

in collaboration with Colin Frost, Ken Marshall, Terry Smith, Barrie Towey,
Tony Wheeler and John Wilkinson

Published by Air-Britain (Historians) Ltd

Sales Department   41 Penshurst Road, Leigh
                                                            Tonbridge, Kent TN11 8HL

Membership Enquiries   1 Rose Cottages, 179 Penn Road
                                                            Hazlemere,Bucks HP15 7NE

Further information is available on our website: http://www.air-britain.co.uk

PHOTO CAPTIONS
Front cover: Boeing 737-7M2 D2-TBJ of TAAG Angola at Johannesburg, 9.10 (Tony Best)

Rear cover: Top: SAAB SF.340B VH-ZLW of REX – Regional Express at Sydney-Mascot
15.3.09 (Stewart Kedar)
Centre: Egyptair Boeing 777-36NER SU-GDL on approach at London-Heathrow
on 8.4.10 (Roger Birchall)
Bottom: PR-IOC, Boeing 727-264 FedEx 3 freighter of Rio Linhas Aereas at Rio
de Janeiro-Santos Dumont on 9.11.10 (Vito Cedrini)

© Air-Britain (Historians) Ltd 2011

ISBN 978-0-85130-433-5   ISSN 0262-1657

Printed by Bell & Bain Ltd, Glasgow

2

Air-Britain supports the fight against terrorism and the efforts of the Police and other Authorities in protecting airports and airfields from criminal activity. If you see anything suspicious do not hesitate to call the
Anti-Terrorist Hotline 0800 789321
or alert a Police Officer.

INTRODUCTION

Information and Changes for the 2010 Edition

This my third and last edition of this book and time to hand over the reins to a new incumbent. Following on from last year I have introduced a few more changes which I hope will be seen as enhancements. Please take the time to look at the section at the end of these notes that details the use of abreviations and symbols, Clear understanding of this will help you better to use the book. For example the new symbol ♦ is used to highlight a change to the entry for an aircraft.

Once again this year I have made space available for deliveries expected through the year. I very much doubt that every potentional delivery has been allowed for, but you should be able to update the book through the year and keep it up to date for as long as possible.

Last year saw the merger of Delta and Northwest completed. We know that resulted in a mega carrier, but it is nothing compared to the new 'United'. The joining of Continental and United to form the new United has resulted in a huge carrier, although no doubt it will shrink a little over the year as some of the older types are retired.

The merger mania continues to spread and AirTran and Southwest should be one airline by the next edition.

Looking at the industry prospects have continued to improve.

Airbus has now booked its 10,000th order.

The A320 'family' (A318/319/320/321) continues to sell well, the smaller models also booking regular sales in the corporate market. The 320NEO has started to take its first orders in the final weeks before this edition.

The A330 is still attracting orders and is benefitting from the time lapse before the A350 and B787 are available. Production of the A330 is also boosted by military tanker orders and the soon to enter service A330F. The A340 is effectivly only made to special order now, though still available.

The A380 fleet continues to grow, more carriers will be getting their first aircraft this year and other new carriers are placing their first orders.

Boeing is still having 'fun' with the 787. I have included the 787 deliveries as they were expected to be in 2011 prior to the latest delay. First delivery is now scheduled for September 2011, all the examples shown in this book will probably not make it into service before the next edition appears.

Likewise the 747-800 deliveries shown in this edition are the planned 2011 ones, we will wait and see what happens.....

The 737 line goes on and on. Established operators continue to expand their fleets. Older generation 737s are finding a good second-hand market in the old Soviet states. Boeing have not yet decided if they are to offer a newer 737 model with new engines.

The 767 line is still continuing slowly and 2011 should see line number 1000 flown and delivered.

The 777 does well as a result of the on-going 787 delays.

Embraer are finding strong sales for their 170 and 190 family aircraft. The smaller 145 line is mostly taken up with Legacy corporate aircraft, with new models being intoduced to the existing strong line up.

In Canada Bombardier is still busy with CRJ700 and CRJ900 production, the CRJ1000 has now joined the other models in airline service with the first deliveries to Europe. The C Series is still being marketed to airlines looking to replace A320 and B737NG, but orders continue to be hard to find.

DHC are busy with the DHC-8-400 with regular deliveries worldwide and new orders.

The Russian industry continues to make a small number of new deliveries, the An148 making its entry into commercial service. The Sukhoi Superjet is now certified and the first deliveries are expected any time. Older Soviet era aircraft are fast becoming rare.

4

Details included
Details are included for around 2,800 operators in 200 countries – also included in the main text are those airlines whose fleets have been deleted this year, along with the reason.   As a general guideline, the complete fleets of operators with an IATA two- or three-letter code are included, (unless they only operate corporate flights) , together with non-IATA coded operators of regular services where fleets are known.   Many of the world's helicopter fleets down to Bell 206 size are included, with the large majority of all twin-engined aircraft and many single-engined aircraft down to Piper Cherokee Six that are also operated on passenger or express freight services.

The larger fleets are shown in type and registration order, with a space separating types. For reasons of saving space this is not done for smaller fleets and those with a large number of types but only one or two aircraft of each type. These fleets are in registration order. This format is being developed all the time and I hope it has resulted in as clean a presentation of the data as is possible within sensible boundaries.

Civil registered jet and turboprop airliners in non-airline use, i.e. those owned and operated by the manufacturers or used in executive or special purpose roles, are again included in this year's edition. This section **does not** include details of the stored ex-airline aircraft.

The component parts of the US majors have again been grouped together under the airline heading and cross-referenced to the individual feeder carriers although this is becoming increasingly difficult as more and more operators provide feeder services to a range of airlines including, in some cases, regionals owned by one US major operating services for a competitor.   As a result some of the feeders are listed separately for at least part of their fleets although they are cross-referenced to the majors as appropriate.

Credits
I am indebted to the following for contributions, corrections, assistance and the use of information, Ian Burnett, Colin Frost, Peter Gerhadt, Ken Marshall, Terry Smith, Chris Swan, Barrie Towey, John Wilkinson, all contributors to the Commercial Scene section of Air-Britain News edited by Tony Wheeler; Aviation Letter, and the various Air-Britain publications as well as relevant web-sites.

Update Information
For readers who are not already members of Air-Britain, this edition can be kept up to date by reading Commercial Scene in Air-Britain News and other sections of our regular publications.   Details of the many benefits of membership are included at the end of this book.

Where possible, information received up to **26th January 2011** has been incorporated in the main text. Naturally, in a work of this complexity and scope, some errors and omissions will occur, and any reader who can add to, amend or correct the information included in this publication is invited to write to the address below.

Users are advised that the information in this publication cannot be reproduced, stored in a retrieval system or transmitted in the form in which it appears, by any means electronic, photocopying, recording or otherwise, without the express prior permission of the Copyright owner.   Individual items of information may be used in other publications with due acknowledgement to Air-Britain (Historians).

As I mentioned in my introductory notes, this is my last edition of the book. Updates and corrections should be sent to the following address and all will be forwarded to the new editor:

airlinefleets@air-britain.co.uk

Pete Webber
26Jan2011

EXPLANATORY NOTES

1 Noise Regulations

With effect from 01Jan85 FAR Part 36 Stage 2 regulations came into force with respect to four-engined aircraft. These prevented any further civil operations of Boeing 707/720 and DC-8 (except -70 series) aircraft to or from US airports unless they were fitted with hushkits so that they conformed to the new noise standards. Similar regulations applied in the UK from 01Jan88. Stage 3 requirements are now implemented with all non-compliant aircraft required to be hush-kitted or re-engined; this applies to 707s, 727s, 737s (srs-100/200s), DC-8/9s, 1-11s, Tu-134/154s and Il-62/76s. Many of these aircraft are being withdrawn from service as the economic situation makes it uneconomic to undertake the costly conversions (indeed some of the planned hush-kitting schemes have been abandoned). In the main text of the book reference is made, where known, to the type of hush-kit fitted to Boeing 707, 727, early 737s and Douglas DC-8s and 9s and whether it is Stage 2 or Stage 3 compliant. (For example, FedEx 3 means a 727 fitted with a Stage 3 compliant FedEx hush-kit). Stage 4 hush-kits are now available for MD-80 series and the first ones are included in this volume.

2 Chapter 11

In the US section of this book, reference is sometimes made to 'Chapter 11'. This refers to a section of the US bankruptcy code designed to give a company protection from its creditors while it attempts a financial reorganisation. Plans for such a reorganisation have to be submitted to and approved by the bankruptcy court. A Chapter 11 filing may or may not be accompanied by a cessation of operations. If operations do continue, then it is usually at a very much reduced level. If they are suspended, then it is possible that they may be restarted in some form at a future date. If the reorganisation plan fails, then an application for liquidation under Chapter 7 will be made.

Since a Chapter 11 filing does not automatically result in a permanent cessation of operations, airlines are only deleted from this book if at the time of writing it appears that resumption of operations in the near future is unlikely.

3 Boeing 747 Suffixes

An M suffix after Boeing 747-200s indicates that the aircraft is a Combi (Mixed) version fitted with a Side Cargo Door. While not used officially in national registers, the M suffix convention is used in Boeing official literature and is therefore adopted in this publication. Suffixes SCD and EUD indicate converted Side Cargo Door and Extended Upper Deck versions. SF indicates that the aircraft is a 'Special Freighter' conversion and BCF a Boeing Converted Freighter and BDSF is similar but converted by IAI without Boeing support (for 747-400 passenger to freight conversions).

4 Boeing 737 Test Registrations and Winglets

Several Boeing 737s complete their first flights from Renton (PAE) to Boeing Field (BFI) with the registration N1786B or other test registration and these are shown when known. In the book the suffix /W indicates the aircraft is fitted with Aviation Partner Boeing winglets.

5 German Spellings

German place names appear in anglicised form for operator bases but in the native German spelling for aircraft names (e.g. in the Lufthansa fleet).

6 Description of Entries

Countries are listed in alphabetical order of nationality prefix, with the airlines in each country also in alphabetical order. Fleets are listed in alphabetical order of aircraft manufacturer where five or more of the same type occur, otherwise they are listed in registration order. Aircraft type descriptions generally quote the manufacturer currently considered responsible for producing the aircraft. The immediate previous identity appears after the constructor's number and helps determine the source of newly acquired aircraft.

Each Country is identified in bold and italics and enclosed in a shadowed box; followed by airlines in alphabetical order, again enclosed in a box. The details listed for each airline are its name (and any trading or alternative name where appropriate); airline callsign; the two letter IATA designator and three-letter ICAO codes in brackets (where allocated and known); and their main operating base(s), again with the recognised three letter code in brackets (where allocated).

6

Each individual entry, from the left, lists current registration (or that known to be reserved and likely to be taken up with that operator in brackets), followed by type. The next column lists the construction number, followed, for Boeing and McDonnell-Douglas types, by the line number separated by a slash (/). There then appears the immediate past identity (where known) followed by any fleet number or name. The final entry indicates any lease arrangements or other comments. Any three-letter designation refers to another airline and these codes will be found indexed later in the book. Aircraft on order are listed where either delivery is due in the year following the date of publication or where details of the aircraft are known. Otherwise details of aircraft on order for delivery in subsequent years are listed at the bottom of the aircraft type or airline entry; also listed there are any alliances, franchises or ownership details of interest.

Leased (lsd) aircraft will be found in the owner's fleet as well as that of the leasing airline. Where it is known that an aircraft is due to change operator during the currency of this book, it is shown in both fleets with a suitable note. Aircraft that have been withdrawn from service (wfs) are listed unless they are known to have been broken up or are beyond repair. Likewise, aircraft that have been involved in accidents but not confirmed as written off are still included.

7 Abbreviations

Abbreviations and symbols used in the text have the following meanings:

♦	Any entry that is a new delivery, new aircraft in the fleet, addition of winglets, storage or lease.
[xxx]	Any 3 letter code in square brackets indicates a storage location
<	Leased in from
>	Leased out to
c/s	Colour Scheme
FP	Floatplane
Frtr	Freighter
o/o	On Order and expected to be delivered before the next edition
SPB	Seaplane Base
WS	Wheels/Skis

AP-   PAKISTAN (Islamic Republic of Pakistan)

AIRBLUE   Pakblue (ED/ABQ)   Karachi (KHI)

☐ AP-BIE	Airbus A319-112	3385	ex EI-DZY	
☐ AP-BIF	Airbus A319-112	3388	ex EI-DZZ	
☐ AP-EDB	Airbus A319-111	3364	ex D-AHIH	◆
☐ AP-EDC	Airbus A319-111	3403	ex D-AHII	◆
☐ AP-BGW	Airbus A320-232	0760	ex F-OHLO	
☐ AP-EDA	Airbus A320-214	3974	ex F-WWIT	◆
☐ AP-BJA	Airbus A321-231	1199	ex D-ARFB	
☐ AP-BRJ	Airbus A321-231	1008	ex (TC-IEI)	

JS FOCUS AIR   JS Charters (JSJ)   Karachi (KHI)

☐ AP-BHZ	Fokker F.27 Friendship 500	10686	ex D-ADUP
☐ AP-BJC	Beech 1900C-1	UC-119	ex N119YV
☐ AP-BJS	Beech 1900C-1	UC-145	ex ZS-PCD

PAKISTAN INTERNATIONAL AIRLINES   Pakistan (PK/PIA)   Karachi (KHI)

☐ AP-BDZ	Airbus A310-308	585	ex F-WWCH	
☐ AP-BEB	Airbus A310-308	587	ex F-WWCT	
☐ AP-BEC	Airbus A310-308	590	ex F-WWCX	Nowshera-Defenders of the Land
☐ AP-BEG	Airbus A310-308	653	ex F-WWCZ	Gilgit-The Silk Route
☐ AP-BEQ	Airbus A310-308	656	ex F-WWCB	
☐ AP-BEU	Airbus A310-308	691	ex F-WWCD	Peshawar- Gateway to the East
☐ AP-BGN	Airbus A310-324ET	676	ex F-WQTG	Taxila-The Exquisite Ghandhara
☐ AP-BGO	Airbus A310-324ET	678	ex F-WQTC	Gwadar-The New Port City
☐ AP-BGP	Airbus A310-324ET	682	ex F-WQTF	Murree-Songs of the Pines
☐ AP-BGQ	Airbus A310-325ET	660	ex F-OGYT	Sialkot-The Diligence of Industry
☐ AP-BGR	Airbus A310-325ET	687	ex F-OGYU	Mohenjodaro-Indus Valley Civilization
☐ AP-BGS	Airbus A310-325ET	689	ex F-OGYV	Ziarat-The City of Flowers
☐ AP-BHH	ATR 42-500	645	ex F-WWLE	Gwadar-The New Port City
☐ AP-BHI	ATR 42-500	653	ex F-WWLK	Ziarat-The City of Flowers
☐ AP-BHJ	ATR 42-500	657	ex F-WWLO	Mohenjodaro-IndusValley Civilization
☐ AP-BHM	ATR 42-500	659	ex F-WWLQ	Hala-Shades of Ash and Azure
☐ AP-BHN	ATR 42-500	661	ex F-WWLS	Chitral-Mysteries of the Kalash
☐ AP-BHO	ATR 42-500	663	ex F-WWLU	Hansanabdal-The Gurdwara Glory
☐ AP-BHP	ATR 42-500	665	ex F-WWLW	Gilgit-The Silk Route
☐ AP-BCA	Boeing 737-340	23294/1114		Gilgit-The Silk Route
☐ AP-BCB	Boeing 737-340	23295/1116		Multan-City of Saints
☐ AP-BCC	Boeing 737-340	23296/1121		Quetta-Nature's Orchard
☐ AP-BCD	Boeing 737-340	23297/1122		Turbat-Romantic Interludes
☐ AP-BCF	Boeing 737-340	23299/1235		Sukkur
☐ AP-BEH	Boeing 737-33A	25504/2341		Chitral-Mysteries of the Kalash
☐ AP-BFT	Boeing 737-340	23298/1123	ex AP-BCE	Bahawalpur-The Splendour and Majesty
☐ AP-BAK	Boeing 747-240M	21825/383		Thar-Colours of the Desert
☐ AP-BAT	Boeing 747-240M	22077/429		Quetta-Nature's Orchard
☐ AP-BFU	Boeing 747-367	23392/634	ex B-HIJ	Islamabad-The Margalla Magic
☐ AP-BFV	Boeing 747-367	23534/659	ex B-HIK	
☐ AP-BFW	Boeing 747-367	23221/615	ex B-HII	Lahore-Garden of the Mughals
☐ AP-BFX	Boeing 747-367	23709/671	ex B-HOL	Karachi-Green Turtle Waters
☐ AP-BFY	Boeing 747-367	23920/690	ex B-HOM	Ziarat-The City of Flowers
☐ AP-BGG	Boeing 747-367	24215/709	ex B-HON	Kaghan-Mountain Paradise
☐ AP-BGJ	Boeing 777-240ER	33775/467		
☐ AP-BGK	Boeing 777-240ER	33776/469		
☐ AP-BGL	Boeing 777-240ER	33777/473		
☐ AP-BGY	Boeing 777-240LR	33781/504	ex N5022E	
☐ AP-BGZ	Boeing 777-240LR	33782/519	ex N6066Z	
☐ AP-BHV	Boeing 777-340ER	33778/601		Thar-Colours of the Desert
☐ AP-BHW	Boeing 777-340ER	33779/611		Lahore-Garden of the Mughal
☐ AP-BHX	Boeing 777-340ER	35296/613		Quetta-Nature's Orchard
☐ AP-BID	Boeing 777-340ER	33780/705		

RAYYAN AIR   Karachi (KHI)

☐ AP-BIB	Boeing 747-21AC	23652/669	ex N652AP

ROYAL AIRLINES		Royal Pakistan (RO/RPK)		Karachi (KHI)
☐ AP-BHS	Cessna 402C	402C0415	ex ZS-MNA	

SHAHEEN AIR CARGO		Shaheen Cargo (SEE)		Islamabad (ISB)

Operate freight flights with Boeing 707-320Cs leased from Pakistan Air Force, and Ilyushin Il-76s leased from other operators, as required.

SHAHEEN AIR INTERNATIONAL		Shaheen Air (NL/SAI)		Karachi (KHI)
☐ AP-BHA	Boeing 737-277 (Nordam 3)	22645/768	ex N178AW	Yaz
☐ AP-BHB	Boeing 737-277 (Nordam 3)	22655/872	ex N188AW	Chundam
☐ AP-BHC	Boeing 737-291 (Nordam 3)	21509/521	ex EX-040	
☐ AP-BHG	Boeing 737-201 (Nordam 3)	21666/547	ex N224JT	
☐ AP-BIK	Boeing 737-2B7 (Nordam 3)	23114/997	ex N281AU	
☐ AP-BIP	Boeing 737-230 (Nordam 3)	22634/840	ex ZS-OIV	
☐ AP-BIQ	Boeing 737-258 (Nordam 3)	22857/919	ex ZS-OOD	
☐ AP-BIR	Boeing 737-228	23006/944	ex ZS-OVE	
☐ AP-BIS	Boeing 737-228	23008/952	ex ZS-OVF	◆
☐ AP-BIT	Boeing 737-236	21803/677	ex ZS-OKD	
☐ AP-BIU	Boeing 737-236	21807/710	ex ZS-OKE	
☐ AP-BJI	Boeing 737-201 (Nordam 3)	22444/800	ex N242US	

STAR AIR AVIATION		(6S/URJ)		Karachi (KHI)
☐ AP-URJ	Boeing 727-224F	20660/985	ex N895AJ	

VISION AIR INTERNATIONAL		(VIS)		Karachi (KHI)
☐ AP-BIA	Boeing 737-2H3	22625/776	ex UP-B3705	

A2-   BOTSWANA (Republic of Botswana)

AIR BOTSWANA		Botswana (BP/BOT)		Gaborone (GBE)
☐ A2-ABD	British Aerospace 146 Srs.100	E1101	ex (G-CBAE)	
☐ A2-ABN	ATR 42-500	507	ex F-WQNG	Chobe
☐ A2-ABO	ATR 42-500	511	ex F-WQNC	Okavango
☐ A2-ABP	ATR 42-500	512	ex F-WQNI	Makgadikgadi
☐ A2-ABR	ATR 72-212A	786	ex F-WWEE	
☐ A2-ABS	ATR 72-212A	788	ex F-WWEG	
☐ A2-NAC	Beech 1900D	UE-325	ex ZS-OYM	<NAC Executive

DELTA AIR				Maun (MUB)
☐ A2-AGR	Cessna U206F Stationair	U20601837	ex ZS-OCC	
☐ A2-AHN	Cessna U206G Stationair 6 II	U20606432	ex ZS-LKX	
☐ A2-AID	Cessna U206G Stationair 6 II	U20605755	ex N9353Z	
☐ A2-AIW	Cessna 210N Centurion II	21064163	ex ZS-MYC	
☐ A2-AJA	Britten-Norman BN-2A Islander	271	ex ZS-LKE	
☐ A2-AJJ	Cessna 210L Centurion II	21061533	ex ZS-KPV	

KALAHARI AIR SERVICES AND CHARTER				Gaborone (GBE)
☐ A2-AFK	Cessna 210N Centurion II	21064203	ex N5427Y	
☐ A2-AHZ	Beech 200 Super King Air	BB-95	ex ZS-JPD	
☐ A2-DBH	Beech C90 King Air	LJ-988	ex ZS-LUU	
☐ A2-KAB	Beech 1900C-1	UC-150	ex ZS-PCE	
☐ A2-KAS	Beech 200 Super King Air	BB-614	ex ZS-LKA	

MACK AIR				Maun (MUB)
☐ A2-AIC	Cessna U206G Stationair 6 II	U20606419	ex N9353Z	
☐ A2-AJI	Cessna U206G Stationair 6 II	U20606842	ex ZS-NSS	
☐ A2-AKB	Cessna U206F Stationair	U20601889	ex A2-ZHJ	
☐ A2-AKI	Cessna 208B Caravan I	208B0552	ex 5Y-VIJ	
☐ A2-FMD	Cessna U206G Stationair 6 II	U20606005	ex ZS-KSM	
☐ A2-ZFF	Cessna U206D Super Skywagon	U206-1263	ex ZS-FPD	
☐ A2-AJZ	Gippsland GA-8 Airvan	GA8-04-059	ex VH-CRQ	
☐ A2-MAC	Cessna 210N Centurion II	21063337	ex V5-MRW	
☐ A2-MEG	Cessna 208B Caravan I	208B0944	ex N4085S	

MOREMI AIR SERVICES				Maun (MUB)
☐ A2-AEI	Cessna U206F Stationair	U20602470	ex ZS-LDJ	

☐ A2-AKD	Cessna 208B Caravan I	208B0582	ex ZS-JML	
☐ A2-TEN	Cessna 210L Centurion II	21061141	ex A2-AIY	
☐ A2-ZED	Britten-Norman BN-2A-21 Islander	736	ex ZS-XGF	

NAC EXECUTIVE CHARTER — *Gaborone (GBE)*

☐ A2-AJO	Beech 58 Baron	TH-614	ex ZS-OGB	
☐ A2-MXI	Beech 200T Super King Air	BT-5	ex N205EC	
☐ A2-NAC	Beech 1900D	UE-325	ex ZS-OYM	<BOT

NORTHERN AIR — *Maun (MUB)*

☐ A2-ADK	Cessna U206G Stationair 6 II	U20606056	ex ZS-KUO
☐ A2-AER	Cessna U206G Stationair 6 II	U20606324	ex ZS-KXE
☐ A2-NAB	Cessna U206G Stationair 6 II	U20605439	ex ZS-KDA

SAFARI AIR — *Maun (MUB)*

☐ A2-AIX	Cessna U206F Stationair	U20601944	ex ZS-MAD
☐ A2-AJQ	Gippsland GA-8 Airvan	GA8-02-023	ex VH-DTA
☐ A2-AJS	Gippsland GA-8 Airvan	GA8-04-047	ex VH-LED
☐ A2-CEX	Cessna 207 Skywagon	20700154	ex ZS-IDG

SEFOFANE AIR CHARTER — *Maun (MUB)*

☐ A2-AIV	Cessna U206G Stationair 6 II	U20606410	ex ZS-LUA	
☐ A2-ANT	Cessna U206G Stationair 6 II	U20606237	ex ZS-ANT	
☐ A2-BEE	Cessna U206G Stationair 6 II	U20605665	ex ZS-KUL	
☐ A2-JET	Cessna 206H Stationair	20608027	ex ZS-OIA	
☐ A2-OWL	Cessna U206G Stationair 6 II	U20606978	ex ZS-NXR	
☐ A2-XIG	Cessna U206G Stationair 6 II	U20605528	ex ZS-NSU	
☐ A2-BUF	Cessna 208B Caravan I	208B0815	ex ZS-BUF	Kwatale
☐ A2-EGL	Cessna 208B Caravan I	208B1158	ex ZS-ABR	
☐ A2-GNU	Cessna 208B Caravan I	208B0848	ex N1287Y	
☐ A2-LEO	Cessna 208B Caravan I	208B0820	ex N1307A	
☐ A2-NAS	Cessna 208B Caravan I	208B0704	ex ZS-TSW	
☐ A2-ZEB	Cessna 208B Caravan I	208B0750	ex N750LK	

XUGANA AIR — *Maun (MUB)*

☐ A2-AKH	Cessna 208 Caravan I	20800288	ex C-FWTK
☐ A2-AKK	Cessna 208B Caravan I	208B0441	ex ZS-OAR
☐ A2-AKO	Cessna 208B Caravan I	208B0736	ex ZS-OWW

A3-   TONGA (Kingdom of Tonga)

AIRLINES TONGA — *Tongatapu-Fua'amotu International (TBU)*

| ☐ DQ-FHC | Harbin Y-12 II | 0056 | | Save our Oceans | Op by FAJ |
| ☐ DQ-FHF | Harbin Y-12 II | 0047 | ex B-531L | | Op by FAJ |

PEAU VAVA'U AIR *(30/PVU)* — *Tongatapu-Fua'amotu International (TBU)*

| ☐ A3-AWP | Douglas DC-3C | 16387/33135 | ex ZK-AWP | Lucille | |
| ☐ A3-FEW | Beech 65-80 Queen Air | LC-168 | ex DQ-FEW | | Queenaire 8800 conversion |

A4O-   OMAN (Sultanate of Oman)

OMANAIR — *Khanjar (WY/OMA)* — *Muscat-Seeb Intl (MCT)*

☐ A4O-DA	Airbus A330-243	1038	ex F-WWYM	
☐ A4O-DB	Airbus A330-343X	1044	ex F-WWKA	
☐ A4O-DC	Airbus A330-243	1049	ex F-WWKL	
☐ A4O-DD	Airbus A330-343X	1063	ex F-WWYN	
☐ A4O-DE	Airbus A330-343X	1093	ex F-WWYM	♦
☐ A4O-DF	Airbus A330-243	1120	ex F-WWYA	♦
☐ A4O-	Airbus A330-243		ex	o/o♦
☐ A4O-BA	Boeing 737-8BK/W	29685/2457	ex N1786B	Fahud
☐ A4O-BB	Boeing 737-8Q8/W	30721/2255		
☐ A4O-BC	Boeing 737-81M/W	35284/2738	ex N1786B	Ras Al Had
☐ A4O-BD	Boeing 737-81M/W	35287/2804	ex N1786B	
☐ A4O-BE	Boeing 737-81M/W	37161/2919	ex N1786B	
☐ A4O-BF	Boeing 737-8FZ/W	29637/3051		

10

☐ A4O-BG	Boeing 737-8FZ/W	29664/3060	ex N1787B	
☐ A4O-BJ	Boeing 737-81M/W	34242/1674		
☐ A4O-BM	Boeing 737-8FZ/W	29682/2853		
☐ A4O-BN	Boeing 737-8Q8/W	30652/1018	ex N1795B	Muscat
☐ A4O-BO	Boeing 737-71M	33103/1154	ex N6066Z	
☐ A4O-BP	Boeing 737-8Q8/W	35272/2537	ex N1786B	
☐ A4O-BR	Boeing 737-81M/W	33104/1337		
☐ A4O-BS	Boeing 737-7Q8	30649/1048		
☐ A4O-BU	Boeing 737-81M/W	35108/2554	ex N1786B	
☐ A4O-	Boeing 737-8			o/o♦
☐ A4O-	Boeing 737-8			o/o♦
☐ A4O-AS	ATR 42-500	574	ex VT-ADL	
☐ A4O-AT	ATR 42-500	576	ex F-WWEP	>DKN
☐ A4O-	Embraer ERJ-175LR			o/o♦
☐ A4O-	Embraer ERJ-175LR			o/o♦
☐ A4O-	Embraer ERJ-175LR			o/o♦

A5-   BHUTAN (Kingdom of Bhutan)

DRUKAIR		Royal Bhutan (KB/DRK)		Paro (PBH)
☐ A5-RGF	Airbus A319-115	2306	ex D-AVYA	
☐ A5-RGG	Airbus A319-115	2346	ex D-AVWO	

A6-   UNITED ARAB EMIRATES (Al Imarat al-Arabiya al-Muttahida)

ABU DHABI AVIATION				Abu Dhabi-Bateen (AZI)
☐ A6-AWA	Agusta AW139	31044	ex I-EASJ	
☐ A6-AWB	Agusta AW139	31053		
☐ A6-AWC	Agusta AW139	31058		
☐ A6-AWF	Agusta AW139	31118		
☐ A6-AWH	Agusta AW139	41011		
☐ A6-AWK	Agusta AW139	31150		
☐ A6-AWL	Agusta AW139	31153		
☐ A6-BBB	Agusta AW139	31028	ex I-RAIP	Royal Jet colours
☐ A6-BCE	Bell 206B JetRanger III	2185		
☐ A6-BCF	Bell 206B JetRanger III	2423		
☐ A6-BCK	Bell 206B JetRanger III	2426		
☐ A6-BCL	Bell 206B JetRanger III	2720		
☐ A6-BAB	Bell 212	31227		
☐ A6-BAM	Bell 212	31165	ex C-GTHQ	
☐ A6-BBC	Bell 212	30777		
☐ A6-BBE	Bell 212	30783	ex N9937K	
☐ A6-BBK	Bell 212	30802		
☐ A6-BBL	Bell 212	30822		
☐ A6-BBO	Bell 212	30903		
☐ A6-BBP	Bell 212	30917		
☐ A6-BBQ	Bell 212	30942		
☐ A6-BBR	Bell 212	30976		
☐ A6-BBS	Bell 212	30977		
☐ A6-BBU	Bell 212	31183		
☐ A6-BBV	Bell 212	31189		
☐ A6-BBY	Bell 212	32125		
☐ A6-BBZ	Bell 212	32141		
☐ A6-	Bell 212	30891	ex C-FRUT	
☐ A6-BAE	Bell 412HP	36072		
☐ A6-BAF	Bell 412HP	36082		
☐ A6-BAH	Bell 412HP	36119	ex C-GBUP	
☐ A6-BAI	Bell 412HP	36122		
☐ A6-BAK	Bell 412HP	36123		
☐ A6-BAL	Bell 412HP	36150		
☐ A6-BAO	Bell 412HP	36152		
☐ A6-BAP	Bell 412HP	36189	ex N52091	
☐ A6-BAQ	Bell 412EP	36190		
☐ A6-BAS	Bell 412EP	36215		
☐ A6-BAT	Bell 412EP	36216		
☐ A6-BAV	Bell 412EP	36319	ex N70791	

☐ A6-BAZ	Bell 412	33107	ex PK-HMU		
☐ A6-HBM	Bell 412EP	36280	ex C-GJCO		
☐ A6-ADA	de Havilland DHC-8Q-202	471	ex C-GLOT		
☐ A6-ADB	de Havilland DHC-8Q-315	650	ex C-FLUJ		
☐ A6-ADC	de Havilland DHC-8Q-202	473	ex C-GFRP		
☐ A6-ADD	de Havilland DHC-8Q-315	627	ex V2-LGL		
☐ A6-ADE	de Havilland DHC-8Q-315	628	ex V2-LGM		
☐ A6-ADF	de Havilland DHC-8Q-315	610	ex V2-LGJ		
☐ A6-ADG	de Havilland DHC-8Q-315	624	ex V2-LGK		
☐ A6-ADK	de Havilland DHC-8-402Q	4222	ex C-FTIA		

AEROGULF SERVICES · Aerogulf · Dubai (DXB)

☐ A6-ALO	Bell 206L-3 LongRanger III	51435	ex PT-YBK		
☐ A6-ALP	Bell 206B JetRanger III	2495	ex (A6-BCJ)		
☐ A6-ALA	Bell 212	30664	ex N71AL		
☐ A6-ALC	Bell 212	30790	ex N2781A		
☐ A6-ALD	Bell 212	30809	ex N143AL		
☐ A6-ALU	Bell 212	30729	ex C-GBKC		
☐ A6-ALV	Bell 212	30703	ex A6-HMR		
☐ A6-ALW	Bell 212	35065	ex N62200		
☐ A6-ALX	Bell 212	30888	ex YV-191CP		

AIR ARABIA · Arabia (G9/ABY) · Sharjah (SHJ)

☐ A6-ABA	Airbus A320-214	2158	ex F-WWDF	Al Bdee'a	
☐ A6-ABB	Airbus A320-214	2166	ex F-WWDR	Waset	
☐ A6-ABC	Airbus A320-214	2278	ex F-WWDM	Al Riqa'a	
☐ A6-ABD	Airbus A320-214	2349	ex F-WWBP	Sharjah	
☐ A6-ABE	Airbus A320-214	2712	ex F-WWBB	Al Heera	
☐ A6-ABG	Airbus A320-214	2930	ex F-WWBU		
☐ A6-ABH	Airbus A320-214	2964	ex F-WWDA		
☐ A6-ABI	Airbus A320-214	3044	ex F-WWDP		
☐ A6-ABJ	Airbus A320-214	3218	ex F-WWBB	Kalba	
☐ A6-ABK	Airbus A320-214	3444	ex F-WWIF		
☐ A6-ABL	Airbus A320-214	3476	ex F-WWDG		
☐ A6-ABO	Airbus A320-214	3626	ex F-WWIR		
☐ A6-ABP	Airbus A320-214	3802	ex F-WWBV		
☐ A6-ABQ	Airbus A320-214	3840	ex F-WWBM		
☐ A6-ABR	Airbus A320-214	3925	ex F-WWBP		
☐ A6-ABS	Airbus A320-214	4061	ex F-WWBE		
☐ A6-ABT	Airbus A320-214	4243	ex F-WWDO		♦
☐ A6-ANA	Airbus A320-214	4468	ex D-AXAD		♦
☐ A6-ANB	Airbus A320-214	4524	ex F-WWDK		♦
☐ A6-ANC	Airbus A320-214	4539	ex F-WWIN		♦
☐ A6-	Airbus A320-214		ex		o/o♦
☐ A6-	Airbus A320-214		ex		o/o♦
☐ A6-	Airbus A320-214		ex		o/o♦
☐ A6-	Airbus A320-214		ex		o/o♦
☐ A6-	Airbus A320-214		ex		o/o♦
☐ A6-	Airbus A320-214		ex		o/o♦
☐ A6-	Airbus A320-214		ex		o/o♦

AVE.COM · Phoenix Sharjah (2E/PHW) · Sharjah (SHJ)

☐ A6-PHA	Boeing 737-2T4	23444/1154	ex EX-027		
☐ A6-PHC	Boeing 737-33A	23626/1284	ex EC-JJV		
☐ A6-PHD	Boeing 737-2T5 (Nordam 3)	22395/729	ex EX-048		
☐ A6-PHF	Boeing 737-219	21645/535	ex EX-012		
☐ A6-PHG	Boeing 737-3Q8	24986/2192	ex N431LF		
☐ A6-PHH	Boeing 737-3Q8	26314/2707	ex G-THOF		
☐ EX-077	Boeing 737-268	21277/469	ex HZ-AGJ		stored

DOLPHIN AIR · Dolphin (ZD/FDN) · Sharjah (SHJ)

☐ A6-ZYA	Boeing 737-2S2C	21926/597	ex N720A		[RKT]
☐ A6-ZYC	Boeing 737-2X2	22679/807	ex N719A		[RKT]

EASTERN SKYJETS · (ESJ) · Dubai (DXB)

☐ A6-ESA	Douglas DC-9-51 (ABS 3)	48136/993	ex TG-JII		
☐ A6-ESC	Douglas DC-9-32	48150/1014	ex TG-URY		
☐ A6-ESF	Boeing 737-4Y0	25177/2176	ex EI-EMY		♦
☐ A6-ESK	British Aerospace Jetstream 41	41090	ex G-CEDS		

12

EASTOK AVIA		**(EAA)**	**Sharjah (SHJ)**
☐ EY-621	Airbus A320-231	0386	ex N386BV ♦
☐ EX-532	Boeing 737-247 (Nordam 3)	23605/1371	ex N378DL
☐ EX-734	Boeing 737-25A (Nordam 3)	23791/1486	ex 5N-BID >East Air

EMIRATES		**Emirates (EK/UAE)**	**Dubai (DXB)**
☐ A6-EAA	Airbus A330-243	348	ex F-WWYK
☐ A6-EAD	Airbus A330-243	382	ex F-WWYR
☐ A6-EAE	Airbus A330-243	384	ex F-WWYS
☐ A6-EAF	Airbus A330-243	392	ex F-WWYX
☐ A6-EAG	Airbus A330-243	396	ex F-WWKJ
☐ A6-EAH	Airbus A330-243	409	ex F-WWKT
☐ A6-EAI	Airbus A330-243	437	ex F-WWYI
☐ A6-EAJ	Airbus A330-243	451	ex F-WWKE
☐ A6-EAK	Airbus A330-243	452	ex F-WWKF
☐ A6-EAL	Airbus A330-243	462	ex F-WWKK
☐ A6-EAM	Airbus A330-243	491	ex F-WWYO
☐ A6-EAN	Airbus A330-243	494	ex F-WWKJ
☐ A6-EAO	Airbus A330-243	509	ex F-WWYX
☐ A6-EAP	Airbus A330-243	525	ex F-WWKV
☐ A6-EAQ	Airbus A330-243	518	ex F-WWKT
☐ A6-EAR	Airbus A330-243	536	ex F-WWYF
☐ A6-EAS	Airbus A330-243	455	ex F-WWKH
☐ A6-EKQ	Airbus A330-243	248	ex F-WWYX
☐ A6-EKR	Airbus A330-243	251	ex F-WWKO
☐ A6-EKS	Airbus A330-243	283	ex F-WWKH
☐ A6-EKT	Airbus A330-243	293	ex F-WWKR
☐ A6-EKU	Airbus A330-243	295	ex F-WWYF
☐ A6-EKV	Airbus A330-243	314	ex F-WWYR
☐ A6-EKW	Airbus A330-243	316	ex F-WWYS
☐ A6-EKX	Airbus A330-243	326	ex F-WWYV
☐ A6-EKY	Airbus A330-243	328	ex F-WWYX
☐ A6-EKZ	Airbus A330-243	345	ex F-WWYI
☐ A6-ERA	Airbus A340-541	457	ex F-WWTI
☐ A6-ERB	Airbus A340-541	471	ex F-WWTK
☐ A6-ERC	Airbus A340-541	485	ex F-WWTL
☐ A6-ERD	Airbus A340-541	520	ex F-WWTS
☐ A6-ERE	Airbus A340-541	572	ex F-WWTV
☐ A6-ERF	Airbus A340-541	394	ex F-WWTE
☐ A6-ERG	Airbus A340-541	608	ex F-WWTX
☐ A6-ERH	Airbus A340-541	611	ex F-WWTY
☐ A6-ERI	Airbus A340-541	685	ex F-WWTP
☐ A6-ERJ	Airbus A340-541	694	ex F-WWTQ
☐ A6-ERM	Airbus A340-313X	236	ex D-AIFL
☐ A6-ERN	Airbus A340-313X	166	ex D-ASIC
☐ A6-ERO	Airbus A340-313X	163	ex D-ASIB
☐ A6-ERP	Airbus A340-313X	185	ex D-AGBM
☐ A6-ERQ	Airbus A340-313X	190	ex D-AJGP
☐ A6-ERR	Airbus A340-313X	202	ex D-ASID
☐ A6-ERS	Airbus A340-313X	139	ex D-ASIM
☐ A6-ERT	Airbus A340-313X	149	ex D-ASIN
☐ A6-EDA	Airbus A380-861	011	ex D-AXXA
☐ A6-EDB	Airbus A380-861	013	ex F-WWSJ
☐ A6-EDC	Airbus A380-861	016	ex D-AXAC
☐ A6-EDD	Airbus A380-861	020	ex F-WWSS
☐ A6-EDE	Airbus A380-861	017	ex D-AXAE
☐ A6-EDF	Airbus A380-861	007	ex F-WWJB
☐ A6-EDG	Airbus A380-861	023	ex F-WWST
☐ A6-EDH	Airbus A380-861	025	ex F-WWSV
☐ A6-EDI	Airbus A380-861	028	ex F-WWSZ ♦
☐ A6-EDJ	Airbus A380-861	009	ex F-WWSF ♦
☐ A6-EDK	Airbus A380-861	030	ex F-WWSD ♦
☐ A6-EDL	Airbus A380-861	046	ex F-WWAG ♦
☐ A6-EDM	Airbus A380-861	042	ex F-WWAO ♦
☐ A6-EDN	Airbus A380-861	056	ex F-WWAR ♦
☐ A6-EDO	Airbus A380-861	057	ex F-WWAS ♦
☐ A6-EDP	Airbus A380-861		ex F-WW o/o♦
☐ A6-EDQ	Airbus A380-861		ex F-WW o/o♦
☐ A6-EDR	Airbus A380-861		ex F-WW o/o♦
☐ A6-EDS	Airbus A380-861		ex F-WW o/o♦
☐ A6-EDT	Airbus A380-861		ex F-WW o/o♦
☐ A6-EBA	Boeing 777-31HER	32706/506	

	Reg	Type	c/n	ex	
☐	A6-EBB	Boeing 777-36NER	32789/508		
☐	A6-EBC	Boeing 777-36NER	32790/512		
☐	A6-EBD	Boeing 777-31HER	33501/516	ex N5022E	
☐	A6-EBE	Boeing 777-36NER	32788/532		
☐	A6-EBF	Boeing 777-31HER	32708/536		
☐	A6-EBG	Boeing 777-36NER	33862/535		
☐	A6-EBH	Boeing 777-31HER	32707/539		
☐	A6-EBI	Boeing 777-36NER	32785/540		
☐	A6-EBJ	Boeing 777-36NER	32787/542		
☐	A6-EBK	Boeing 777-31HER	34481/549	ex N5020K	
☐	A6-EBL	Boeing 777-31HER	32709/551	ex N5017V	
☐	A6-EBM	Boeing 777-31HER	34482/556		
☐	A6-EBN	Boeing 777-36NER	32791/560		
☐	A6-EBO	Boeing 777-36NER	32792/568		
☐	A6-EBP	Boeing 777-31HER	32710/569	ex N5017V	
☐	A6-EBQ	Boeing 777-36NER	33863/576	ex N5017V	
☐	A6-EBR	Boeing 777-31HER	34483/578		
☐	A6-EBS	Boeing 777-31HER	32715/582		
☐	A6-EBT	Boeing 777-31HER	32730/585		
☐	A6-EBU	Boeing 777-31HER	34484/590		
☐	A6-EBV	Boeing 777-31HER	32728/594		
☐	A6-EBW	Boeing 777-36NER	32793/598		
☐	A6-EBX	Boeing 777-31HER	32729/619	ex N5017V	
☐	A6-EBY	Boeing 777-36NER	33864/622	ex N5017V	
☐	A6-EBZ	Boeing 777-31HER	32713/628		
☐	A6-ECA	Boeing 777-36NER	32794/632	ex N5017B	
☐	A6-ECB	Boeing 777-31HER	32714/641	ex N5016R	
☐	A6-ECC	Boeing 777-36NER	33865/664	ex N5020K	
☐	A6-ECD	Boeing 777-36NER	32795/669	ex N5017V	
☐	A6-ECE	Boeing 777-31HER	35575/681		
☐	A6-ECF	Boeing 777-31HER	35574/690		
☐	A6-ECG	Boeing 777-31HER	35579/709		
☐	A6-ECH	Boeing 777-31HER	35581/714		
☐	A6-ECI	Boeing 777-31HER	35580/728	ex N1785B	
☐	A6-ECJ	Boeing 777-31HER	35583/734		
☐	A6-ECK	Boeing 777-31HER	35584/743		
☐	A6-ECL	Boeing 777-31HER	37704/748		
☐	A6-ECM	Boeing 777-31HER	37703/755	ex N5017V	
☐	A6-ECN	Boeing 777-31HER	37705/761		
☐	A6-ECO	Boeing 777-31HER	37706/765		
☐	A6-ECP	Boeing 777-31HER	37707/768		
☐	A6-ECQ	Boeing 777-31HER	35588/779		
☐	A6-ECR	Boeing 777-31HER	35592/794	ex N5017V	
☐	A6-ECS	Boeing 777-31HER	38980/803	ex N5017V	
☐	A6-ECT	Boeing 777-31HER	35591/808		
☐	A6-ECU	Boeing 777-31HER	35593/817		
☐	A6-ECV	Boeing 777-31HER	35594/824		
☐	A6-ECW	Boeing 777-31HER	38981/828		
☐	A6-ECX	Boeing 777-31HER	38982/830		
☐	A6-ECY	Boeing 777-31HER	35595/840		
☐	A6-ECZ	Boeing 777-31HER	38983/847		
☐	A6-EFD	Boeing 777-F1H	35606/766		
☐	A6-EFE	Boeing 777-F1H	35607/788	ex N5017V	
☐	A6-	Boeing 777-F1H			o/o ♦
☐	A6-EGA	Boeing 777-31HER	38984/861		♦
☐	A6-	Boeing 777-31HER			o/o ♦
☐	A6-	Boeing 777-31HER			o/o ♦
☐	A6-	Boeing 777-31HER			o/o ♦
☐	A6-	Boeing 777-31HER			o/o ♦
☐	A6-	Boeing 777-31HER			o/o ♦
☐	A6-	Boeing 777-31HER			o/o ♦
☐	A6-EMD	Boeing 777-21H	27247/30		
☐	A6-EME	Boeing 777-21H	27248/33		
☐	A6-EMF	Boeing 777-21H	27249/42		
☐	A6-EMG	Boeing 777-21HER	27252/63	ex N5020K	
☐	A6-EMH	Boeing 777-21HER	27251/54		
☐	A6-EMI	Boeing 777-21HER	27250/47	ex N5028Y	
☐	A6-EMJ	Boeing 777-21HER	27253/91		
☐	A6-EMK	Boeing 777-21HER	29324/171		
☐	A6-EML	Boeing 777-21HER	29325/176		
☐	A6-EMM	Boeing 777-31H	29062/256		
☐	A6-EMN	Boeing 777-31H	29063/262		
☐	A6-EMO	Boeing 777-31H	28680/300		
☐	A6-EMP	Boeing 777-31H	29395/326	ex N50281	
☐	A6-EMQ	Boeing 777-31H	32697/396		
☐	A6-EMR	Boeing 777-31H	29396/402		
☐	A6-EMS	Boeing 777-31H	29067/408	ex N50281	

☐ A6-EMT	Boeing 777-31H	32699/414	ex N5014K	
☐ A6-EMU	Boeing 777-31H	29064/418		
☐ A6-EMV	Boeing 777-31H	28687/432		
☐ A6-EMW	Boeing 777-31H	32700/434		
☐ A6-EMX	Boeing 777-31H	32702/444		
☐ A6-EWA	Boeing 777-21HLR	35572/654		
☐ A6-EWB	Boeing 777-21HLR	35573/662	ex N5573S	
☐ A6-EWC	Boeing 777-21HLR	35576/677		
☐ A6-EWD	Boeing 777-21HLR	35577/688		
☐ A6-EWE	Boeing 777-21HLR	35582/725		
☐ A6-EWF	Boeing 777-21HLR	35586/739	ex N5017V	
☐ A6-EWG	Boeing 777-21HLR	35578/741	ex N6018N	
☐ A6-EWH	Boeing 777-21HLR	35587/747		
☐ A6-EWI	Boeing 777-21HLR	35589/757	ex N5017V	
☐ A6-EWJ	Boeing 777-21HLR	35590/775	ex N5017V	
☐ A6-EFI	Boeing 747-81HF	37451		o/o
☐ A6-	Boeing 747-81HF			o/o
☐ N408MC	Boeing 747-47UF	29261/1192	ex (N495MC)	<GTI
☐ N415MC	Boeing 747-47UF	32837/1304		<GTI
☐ N497MC	Boeing 747-47UF	29258/1220		<GTI
☐ OO-THC	Boeing 747-4HAERF	35235/1389	ex N50217	<TAY
☐ OO-THD	Boeing 747-4HAERF	35236/1399		<TAY

ETIHAD AIRWAYS — Etihad (EY/ETD) — Abu Dhabi (AUH)

☐ A6-EID	Airbus A319-132	1947	ex D-APAA	
☐ A6-EIE	Airbus A319-132	1955	ex D-APAB	
☐ A6-EIA	Airbus A320-232	1944	ex PH-MPD	
☐ A6-EIB	Airbus A320-232	1945	ex PH-MPE	Abu Dhabi Grand Prix colours
☐ A6-EIC	Airbus A320-232	2167	ex PH-MPF	
☐ A6-EIF	Airbus A320-232	3004	ex EI-EAO	
☐ A6-EIG	Airbus A320-232	3050	ex EI-EAN	
☐ A6-EIH	Airbus A320-232	3693	ex F-WWBH	
☐ A6-EII	Airbus A320-232	3713	ex F-WWIX	
☐ A6-EIJ	Airbus A320-232	3902	ex F-WWIA	
☐ A6-EIK	Airbus A320-232	3676	ex VT-INW	
☐ A6-EIL	Airbus A320-232	4066	ex F-WWBH	
☐ A6-EIM	Airbus A320-232	4077	ex F-WWBO	
☐ A6-EIN	Airbus A320-232	4124	ex F-WWIN	
☐ A6-EIZ	Airbus A320-211	0350	ex 9H-AFE	
☐ A6-AFA	Airbus A330-343X	1071	ex F-WWYP	
☐ A6-AFB	Airbus A330-343X	1081	ex F-WWYL	
☐ A6-AFC	Airbus A330-343X	1167	ex F-WWYR	♦
☐ A6-	Airbus A330-343X		ex	o/o♦
☐ A6-	Airbus A330-343X		ex	o/o♦
☐ A6-	Airbus A330-343X		ex	o/o♦
☐ A6-EYD	Airbus A330-243	658	ex F-WWYN	
☐ A6-EYE	Airbus A330-243	688	ex F-WWYJ	
☐ A6-EYF	Airbus A330-243	717	ex F-WWYN	
☐ A6-EYG	Airbus A330-243	724	ex F-WWKN	
☐ A6-EYH	Airbus A330-243	729	ex F-WWKR	
☐ A6-EYI	Airbus A330-243	730	ex F-WWKS	
☐ A6-EYJ	Airbus A330-243	737	ex F-WWYB	
☐ A6-EYK	Airbus A330-243	788	ex F-WWKM	
☐ A6-EYL	Airbus A330-243	809	ex F-WWYB	
☐ A6-EYM	Airbus A330-243	824	ex F-WWKD	
☐ A6-EYN	Airbus A330-243	832	ex F-WWKN	
☐ A6-EYO	Airbus A330-243	852	ex F-WWKT	
☐ A6-EYP	Airbus A330-243	854	ex F-WWYY	
☐ A6-EYQ	Airbus A330-243	868	ex F-WWYQ	
☐ A6-EYR	Airbus A330-243	975	ex F-WWKS	
☐ A6-EYS	Airbus A330-243	991	ex F-WWKM	
☐ A6-DCA	Airbus A330-243F	1032	ex F-WWKG	♦
☐ A6-DCB	Airbus A330-243F	1070	ex F-WWYF	♦
☐ A6-EHA	Airbus A340-541	748	ex F-WWTS	
☐ A6-EHB	Airbus A340-541	757	ex F-WWTU	
☐ A6-EHC	Airbus A340-541	761	ex F-WWTV	
☐ A6-EHD	Airbus A340-541	783	ex F-WWTY	
☐ A6-EHE	Airbus A340-642HGW	829	ex F-WWCG	
☐ A6-EHF	Airbus A340-642HGW	837	ex F-WWCB	
☐ A6-EHH	Airbus A340-642HGW	870	ex F-WWCK	
☐ A6-EHI	Airbus A340-642HGW	929	ex F-WWCB	
☐ A6-EHJ	Airbus A340-642HGW	933	ex F-WWCF	

☐ A6-EHK	Airbus A340-642HGW	1030	ex F-WWCX		
☐ A6-EHL	Airbus A340-642HGW	1040	ex F-WWCH		
☐ A6-ETA	Boeing 777-3FXER	34597/538	ex N6018N		
☐ A6-ETB	Boeing 777-3FXER	34598/543	ex N5020K		
☐ A6-ETC	Boeing 777-3FXER	34599/544			
☐ A6-ETD	Boeing 777-3FXER	34600/547			
☐ A6-ETE	Boeing 777-3FXER	34601/548			
☐ A6-ETF	Boeing 777-3FXER	39700/832	ex N1794B		♦
☐ A6-ETG	Boeing 777-3FXER				o/o♦
☐ A6-ETH	Boeing 777-3FXER				o/o♦
☐ A6-EYZ	Boeing 767-341ER	30341/768	ex A6-SUL		<AUH
☐ TF-ELK	Airbus A300B4-622RF	557	ex EI-DGU	Crystal Cargo	<ABD

FALCON EXPRESS CARGO AIRLINES (FC/FVS) Dubai (DXB)

☐ A6-FCA	Beech 1900C-1	UC-57	ex OY-GED		
☐ A6-FCB	Beech 1900C-1	UC-66	ex OY-GEI		
☐ A6-FCC	Beech 1900C-1	UC-68	ex OY-GEJ		
☐ A6-FCD	Beech 1900C-1	UC-71	ex OY-GEK		
☐ A6-FCY	Fokker F.27 Friendship 500	10370	ex HA-FAB		♦
☐ A6-FCZ	Fokker F.27 Friendship 500	10448	ex HB-ITY		

FLYDUBAI (FZ/FCB) Dubai (DXB)

☐ A6-FDA	Boeing 737-8KN/W	35794/2794			
☐ A6-FDB	Boeing 737-8KN/W	35795/2829			
☐ A6-FDC	Boeing 737-8KN/W	40233/2952	ex N1786B		
☐ A6-FDD	Boeing 737-8KN/W	40234/2966			
☐ A6-FDE	Boeing 737-8KN/W	40235/3053			
☐ A6-FDF	Boeing 737-8KN/W	40236/3110			
☐ A6-FDG	Boeing 737-8KN/W	29636/3197			♦
☐ A6-FDH	Boeing 737-8KN/W	31716/3270			♦
☐ A6-FDI	Boeing 737-8KN/W	31765/3302			♦
☐ A6-FDJ	Boeing 737-8KN/W	40237/3356	ex N6046P		♦
☐ A6-FDK	Boeing 737-8KN/W	40238/3391			♦
☐ A6-FDL	Boeing 737-8KN/W	40239/3460			♦
☐ A6-FDM	Boeing 737-8KN/W	40240/3485			♦
☐ A6-	Boeing 737-8KN/W				o/o♦
☐ A6-	Boeing 737-8KN/W				o/o♦
☐ A6-	Boeing 737-8KN/W				o/o♦
☐ A6-	Boeing 737-8KN/W				o/o♦
☐ A6-	Boeing 737-8KN/W				o/o♦
☐ A6-	Boeing 737-8KN/W				o/o♦
☐ A6-	Boeing 737-8KN/W				o/o♦
☐ A6-	Boeing 737-8KN/W				o/o♦
☐ A6-	Boeing 737-8KN/W				o/o♦

HEAVYLIFT INTERNATIONAL (HVL) Sharjah (SHJ)

☐ A6-HLC	Douglas DC-8-63AF (BAC 3)	46126/524	ex N812AX	
☐ A6-HLG	Boeing 737-3G7F	24710/1825	ex N308AW	
☐ A6-HLH	Boeing 737-3G7F	24711/1843	ex N309AW	

MAXIMUS AIR CARGO Cargo Max (MXU) Abu Dhabi (AUH)

☐ A6-MAC	Lockheed L-382G-44K-30 Hercules	5024	ex 1215		<UAE AF
☐ A6-MAX	Lockheed L-382G-44K-30 Hercules	4895	ex 1216		<UAE AF
☐ A6-MXA	Airbus A300B4-622RF	788	ex TF-ELA		<ABD
☐ A6-MXB	Airbus A300B4-622RF	767	ex TF-ELE		<ABD
☐ UR-BXQ	Ilyushin Il-76TD	1023410360	ex EX-832		<UKL
☐ UR-BXR	Ilyushin Il-76TD	1023411384	ex EX-411		<UKL
☐ UR-BXS	Ilyushin Il-76TD	1023411368	ex EX-436		<UKL
☐ UR-ZYD	Antonov An-124 Ruslan	19530502843	ex UR-CCX		<UAK

MIDEX AIRLINES (MG/MIX) Al Ain (AAN)

☐ A6-MDA	Airbus A300B4-203F	157	ex N371PC	Midex 1	
☐ A6-MDB	Airbus A300B4-203F	196	ex N372PC	Midex 2	
☐ A6-MDC	Airbus A300B4-203F	218	ex N373PC	Midex 3	
☐ A6-MDD	Airbus A300B4-203F	203	ex N473AS		
☐ A6-MDE	Airbus A300B4-203F	125	ex N472AS		
☐ A6-MDF	Airbus A300B4-203F	134	ex N370PC		
☐ A6-MDG	Boeing 747-228F	25266/878	ex PH-MCN		
☐ A6-MDH	Boeing 747-228F	24735/772	ex F-WCZX		♦

16

☐ A6-MDI	Boeing 747-228F	24879/822	ex F-WZCY	♦

RAK AIRWAYS — Rakair (RT/RKM) — Ras Al Khaimah (RKT)

☐ A6-AAM	Airbus A318-112	1599	ex D-AIJA	
☐ A6-RKA	Boeing 757-256	29311/940	ex EC-HIU	

SEAWINGS

☐ A6-SEA	Cessna 208 Caravan I	20800118	ex TF-SEA	FP
☐ A6-SEB	Cessna 208 Caravan I	20800401	ex N1000X	FP
☐ A6-SEC	Cessna 208 Caravan I	20800355	ex N444GH	FP

SILVER AIR

☐ A6-JUD	Boeing 737-306	23541/1309	ex PH-BDE	

SKYLINK ARABIA — Dubai (DXB)

☐ ER-AVB	Antonov An-26B-100	57303204	ex UR-26556	♦
☐ ER-AZN	Antonov An-24RV	37308801	ex	
☐ RDPL-34157	Ilyushin Il-76T	093418556	ex ER-IBP	
☐ UP-I7611	Ilyushin Il-76T	093418548	ex UN-76031	
☐ UP-I7630	Ilyushin Il-76T	0023441189	ex RA-76823	
☐ UP-AN203	Antonov An-12AP	00347408	ex UN-11021	
☐ ZS-MAD	Fokker F.28 Fellowship 4000	11225	ex 5H-ZAS	
☐ 4L-GLT	Antonov An-12BK	7345305	ex EX-130	
	Also quoted as Skylink Airlines			

A7- QATAR (State of Qatar)

GULF HELICOPTERS — Doha (DOH)

☐ A7-GHA	Agusta AW139	31132		
☐ A7-GHB	Agusta AW139	31140		
☐ A7-GHC	Agusta AW139	31225		
☐ A7-GHD	Agusta AW139	31233		
☐ A7-GHE	Agusta AW139	31235		
☐ A7-GHF	Agusta AW139	31242		
☐ A7-GHJ	Agusta AW139	41241		
☐ A7-HBT	Agusta AW139	31068	ex I-EASO	♦
☐ A7-HBN	Bell 212	31130	ex VT-HGE	
☐ A7-HBO	Bell 212	30911	ex EP-HUE	
☐ A7-HAV	Bell 412SP	33205	ex D-HHNN	
☐ A7-HAW	Bell 412HP	36046	ex N9142N	
☐ A7-HAY	Bell 412EP	36126	ex N2045S	
☐ A7-HAZ	Bell 412HP	36041	ex N92801	
☐ A7-HBB	Bell 412EP	36259	ex N9026K	
☐ A7-HBC	Bell 412EP	36276	ex N9154J	
☐ A7-HBD	Bell 412EP	36088	ex N4324X	
☐ A7-HBH	Bell 412EP	36326	ex N8067Q	
☐ A7-HBI	Bell 412EP	36270	ex PP-MBE	
☐ A7-HBJ	Bell 412EP	36370	ex N43939	
☐ A7-HBL	Bell 412SP	33117	ex EP-HUC	
☐ A7-HBM	Bell 412EP	36400	ex N2116N	
☐ A7-HBP	Bell 412SP	36016	ex EP-HUF	
☐ A7-HBQ	Bell 412EP	36412	ex N7512Z	
☐ A7-HBR	Bell 412SP	36017	ex EP-HUG	
☐ A7-HBS	Bell 412SP	33116	ex A7-HBK	
☐ VT-HGF	Bell 412EP	36206	ex A7-HBE	>United Helicharters
☐ A7-HAO	Agusta-Bell 206B JetRanger II	8044	ex A4O-DC	
☐ A7-HBF	Bell 230	23015	ex N236X	
☐ A7-HHT	Sikorsky S-92A	920031	ex N7113U	

QATAR AIRWAYS — Qatari (QR/QTR) — Doha (DOH)

☐ A7-ABX	Airbus A300B4-622RF	554	ex HL7537	Al Dawha
☐ A7-ABY	Airbus A300B4-622RF	560	ex HL7294	Fuwairit
☐ A7-AFB	Airbus A300B4-622RF	614	ex HL7298	Al'ArishCargo titles
☐ A7-CJA	Airbus A319-133LR	1656	ex D-AVYT	Al Hilal
☐ A7-CJB	Airbus A319-133LR	2341	ex D-AVWK	Al Jasra
☐ A7-MED	Airbus A319-133LR	4114	ex D-AVWA	♦
☐ A7-ADA	Airbus A320-232	1566	ex F-WWBG	Al Zubara

☐ A7-ADB	Airbus A320-232	1648	ex F-WWDU	Dukhan		
☐ A7-ADC	Airbus A320-232	1773	ex F-WWDG	Mesaieed		
☐ A7-ADD	Airbus A320-232	1895	ex F-WWBT	Halul		
☐ A7-ADE	Airbus A320-232	1957	ex F-WWIG	Al Gharafa		
☐ A7-ADF	Airbus A320-232	2097	ex F-WWIP	Al Wukeir		
☐ A7-ADG	Airbus A320-232	2121	ex F-WWIT	Al Ghuweriyah		
☐ A7-ADH	Airbus A320-232	2138	ex F-WWBI	Al Jumeilliyah		
☐ A7-ADI	Airbus A320-232	2161	ex F-WWBK	Al Khuraytiyat		
☐ A7-ADJ	Airbus A320-232	2288	ex F-WWBS	Al Samriya		
☐ A7-ADU	Airbus A320-232	3071	ex F-WWIM			
☐ A7-AHA	Airbus A320-232	4110	ex F-WWDT			
☐ A7-AHB	Airbus A320-232	4130	ex F-WWIR			
☐ A7-AHC	Airbus A320-232	4183	ex F-WWIB			
☐ A7-AHD	Airbus A320-232	4436	ex D-AVVW			♦
☐ A7-AHE	Airbus A320-232	4479	ex D-AUBC			♦
☐ A7-AHF	Airbus A320-232	4496	ex F-WWIJ			♦
☐ A7-	Airbus A320-232		ex		o/o	♦
☐ A7-	Airbus A320-232		ex		o/o	♦
☐ A7-	Airbus A320-232		ex		o/o	♦
☐ A7-	Airbus A320-232		ex		o/o	♦
☐ A7-	Airbus A320-232		ex		o/o	♦
☐ A7-	Airbus A320-232		ex		o/o	♦
☐ A7-	Airbus A320-232		ex		o/o	♦
☐ A7-	Airbus A320-232		ex		o/o	♦
☐ A7-MBK	Airbus A320-232CJ	4170	ex F-WWDF			♦
☐ A7-ADK	Airbus A321-231	1487	ex OE-LOS			
☐ A7-ADS	Airbus A321-231	1928	ex D-AVXA	Al Aaliyah		
☐ A7-ADT	Airbus A321-231	2107	ex D-AVXD	Al Saffiyah		
☐ A7-ADV	Airbus A321-231	3274	ex D-AVZM			
☐ A7-ADW	Airbus A321-231	3369	ex D-AVZJ			
☐ A7-ADX	Airbus A321-231	3397	ex D-AVZP			
☐ A7-ADY	Airbus A321-231	3636	ex D-AVZK			
☐ A7-ADZ	Airbus A321-231	3669	ex D-AVZY			
☐ A7-AIA	Airbus A321-231	4173	ex D-AZAB			♦
☐ A7-AIB	Airbus A321-231	4382	ex D-AVZY			♦
☐ A7-AIC	Airbus A321-231	4406	ex D-AZAD			♦
☐ A7-ACA	Airbus A330-202	473	ex F-WWKR	Al Wajbah		
☐ A7-ACB	Airbus A330-202	489	ex F-WWYN	Al Majida		
☐ A7-ACC	Airbus A330-202	511	ex F-WWKR	Al Shahaniya		
☐ A7-ACD	Airbus A330-202	521	ex F-WWKU	Al Wuseil		
☐ A7-ACE	Airbus A330-202	571	ex F-WWKF	Al Dhakira		
☐ A7-ACF	Airbus A330-202	638	ex F-WWYQ	Al Kara'anah		
☐ A7-ACG	Airbus A330-202	743	ex F-WWKV	Al Wabra		
☐ A7-ACH	Airbus A330-202	441	ex F-WWYK	Al Mafjar		
☐ A7-ACI	Airbus A330-202	746	ex F-WWKV	Muathier		
☐ A7-ACJ	Airbus A330-202	760	ex F-WWYO	Zikreet		
☐ A7-ACK	Airbus A330-202	792	ex F-WWKP			
☐ A7-ACL	Airbus A330-202	820	ex F-WWKA			
☐ A7-ACM	Airbus A330-202	849	ex F-WWKP			
☐ A7-ACN	Airbus A330-202	893	ex F-WWYK			
☐ A7-AFL	Airbus A330-202	612	ex F-WWKZ	Al Messila		
☐ A7-AFM	Airbus A330-202	616	ex F-WWKT	Al-Udaid		
☐ A7-AFP	Airbus A330-202	684	ex F-WWYG	Al Shamal		
☐ A7-AEA	Airbus A330-302	623	ex F-WWYC	Al Muntazah		
☐ A7-AEB	Airbus A330-302	637	ex F-WWYP	Al Sayliyah		
☐ A7-AEC	Airbus A330-302	659	ex F-WWYX	Al Markhiya		
☐ A7-AED	Airbus A330-302	680	ex F-WWYD	Al Nu'uman		
☐ A7-AEE	Airbus A330-302	711	ex F-WWYK	Semaisma		
☐ A7-AEF	Airbus A330-302	721	ex F-WWKJ	Al Rumellah		
☐ A7-AEG	Airbus A330-302	734	ex F-WWYU	Al Duhell		
☐ A7-AEH	Airbus A330-302	789	ex F-WWKN			
☐ A7-AEI	Airbus A330-302	813	ex F-WWYI			
☐ A7-AEJ	Airbus A330-302	826	ex F-WWKF			
☐ A7-AEM	Airbus A330-302	893	ex F-WWYK			
☐ A7-AEN	Airbus A330-302	907	ex F-WWYE			
☐ A7-AEO	Airbus A330-302	918	ex F-WWYQ			
☐ A7-AGA	Airbus A340-642HGW	740	ex F-WWCP			
☐ A7-AGB	Airbus A340-642HGW	715	ex F-WWCR	Ras Dukhan		
☐ A7-AGC	Airbus A340-642HGW	766	ex F-WWCM	Ras Ushainij		
☐ A7-AGD	Airbus A340-642HGW	798	ex F-WWCL			
☐ A7-BBA	Boeing 777-2DZLR	36012/753	ex N1788B	Alhuwaila		
☐ A7-BBB	Boeing 777-2DZLR	36013/762	ex N50281	Gaza		

☐ A7-BBC	Boeing 777-2DZLR	36015/825	ex N5023Q		
☐ A7-BBD	Boeing 777-2DZLR	36016/831	ex N5573S		
☐ A7-BBE	Boeing 777-2DZLR	36017/837			
☐ A7-BBF	Boeing 777-2DZLR	36018/842			
☐ A7-BBG	Boeing 777-2DZLR	36101/883			♦
☐ A7-BBH	Boeing 777-2DZLR	36102/885			♦
☐ A7-	Boeing 777-2DZLR				♦
☐ A7-BFA	Boeing 777-FDZ	36098/865			o/o♦
☐ A7-BFB	Boeing 777-FDZ	36100/874			♦
☐ A7-BAA	Boeing 777-3DZER	36009/676			
☐ A7-BAB	Boeing 777-3DZER	36103/686		Um-Alamad	
☐ A7-BAC	Boeing 777-3DZER	36010/731	ex N5016R		
☐ A7-BAE	Boeing 777-3DZER	36104/769		Almas-Habia	
☐ A7-BAF	Boeing 777-3DZER	37661/815			
☐ A7-BAG	Boeing 777-3DZER	36014/819	ex N5017Q	Littoriya	
☐ A7-BAH	Boeing 777-3DZER	37662/849			♦
☐ A7-BAI	Boeing 777-3DZER	36095/742	ex N5028Y		
☐ A7-BAJ	Boeing 777-3DZER	36096/851			♦
☐ A7-BAK	Boeing 777-3DZER	36097/859			♦
☐ A7-BAL	Boeing 777-3DZER	38244/893	ex N52081		♦
☐ A7-BAM	Boeing 777-3DZER				o/o♦
☐ A7-BAN	Boeing 777-3DZER				o/o♦
☐ A7-BAO	Boeing 777-3DZER	36011/750			
☐ A7-BAP	Boeing 777-3DZER				o/o♦
☐ A7-BAQ	Boeing 777-3DZER	38247/910			
☐ A7-	Boeing 787-8				o/o♦
☐ A7-	Boeing 787-8				o/o♦
☐ A7-	Boeing 787-8				o/o♦
☐ A7-	Boeing 787-8				o/o♦

A9C- BAHRAIN (State of Bahrain)

BAHRAIN AIR   (2B/BAB)   Bahrain (BAH)

☐ A9C-BAW	Airbus A319-111	2763	ex N946FR	
☐ A9C-BAX	Airbus A319-111	2700	ex N944FR	
☐ A9C-BAU	Airbus A320-214	4055	ex F-WWBB	
☐ A9C-BAV	Airbus A320-214	3861	ex F-WWDP	
☐ A9C-BAY	Airbus A320-212	0579	ex D-AKNY	
☐ A9C-BAZ	Airbus A320-212	0645	ex D-AKNZ	

DHL INTERNATIONAL AVIATION   Dilmun (ES/DHX)   Bahrain (BAH)

☐ A9C-DHB	Swearingen SA.227AT Merlin IVC	AT-434	ex HZ-SN8	Frtr SNAS c/s	
☐ HZ-SNA	Boeing 727-264F (FedEx 3)	20896/1051	ex A9C-SNA	all-white	Joint ops with RSE
☐ HZ-SNB	Boeing 727-223F (FedEx 3)	21084/1199	ex EC-HAH	all-white	Joint ops with RSE
☐ HZ-SNC	Boeing 727-230F (FedEx 3)	20905/1091	ex EC-IVF		Joint ops with RSE
☐ HZ-SND	Boeing 727-223F (FedEx 3)	20994/1190	ex EC-IVE	all-white	Joint ops with RSE
☐ HZ-SNF	Boeing 727-277F (FedEx 3)	22643/1762	ex ZS-DPE		Joint ops with RSE

GULF AIR   Gulf Air (GF/GFA)   Bahrain (BAH)

☐ A9C-EU	Airbus A319-112	1884	ex C-GTDT		
☐ A9C-EV	Airbus A319-112	1901	ex C-GTDS		
☐ A9C-AA	Airbus A320-214	3706	ex F-WJKJ		
☐ A9C-AB	Airbus A320-214	4030	ex F-WWIB		
☐ A9C-AC	Airbus A320-214	4059	ex F-WWBD		
☐ A9C-AD	Airbus A320-214	4083	ex F-WWBT		
☐ A9C-AE	Airbus A320-214	4146	ex D-AVVG		
☐ A9C-AF	Airbus A320-214	4158	ex F-WWBQ		
☐ A9C-AG	Airbus A320-214	4188	ex F-WWIG		
☐ A9C-AH	Airbus A320-214	4218	ex F-WWBH		♦
☐ A9C-AI	Airbus A320-214	4255	ex F-WWIO		♦
☐ A9C-AJ	Airbus A320-214	4502	ex F-WWIU		♦
☐ A9C-AK	Airbus A320-214	4541	ex D-AXAM		♦
☐ A9C-	Airbus A320-214		ex		o/o♦
☐ A9C-	Airbus A320-214		ex		o/o♦
☐ A9C-	Airbus A320-214		ex		o/o♦
☐ A9C-	Airbus A320-214		ex		o/o♦
☐ A9C-	Airbus A320-214		ex		o/o♦
☐ A9C-EE	Airbus A320-212	0419	ex A4O-EE	805 Al-Rumaitha	
☐ A9C-EL	Airbus A320-212	0497	ex A4O-EL	812	

☐ A9C-EN	Airbus A320-212	0537	ex A4O-EN	814
☐ A9C-ES	Airbus A321-211	0675	ex F-OHGU	
☐ A9C-ET	Airbus A321-211	0761	ex F-GTAF	
☐ A9C-KA	Airbus A330-243	276	ex A4O-KA	501
☐ A9C-KB	Airbus A330-243	281	ex A4O-KB	502
☐ A9C-KC	Airbus A330-243	286	ex A4O-KC	503
☐ A9C-KD	Airbus A330-243	287	ex A4O-KD	504
☐ A9C-KE	Airbus A330-243	334	ex A4O-KE	505
☐ A9C-KF	Airbus A330-243	340	ex A4O-KF	506 Aldafra
☐ A9C-KG	Airbus A330-243	527	ex F-OMEA	
☐ A9C-KH	Airbus A330-243	529	ex F-OMEB	
☐ A9C-KI	Airbus A330-243	532	ex F-OMEC	
☐ A9C-KJ	Airbus A330-243	992	ex F-WWKN	
☐ A9C-LF	Airbus A340-312	133	ex A4O-LF	406
☐ A9C-LG	Airbus A340-313X	212	ex A4O-LG	407
☐ A9C-LH	Airbus A340-313X	215	ex A4O-LH	408
☐ A9C-LI	Airbus A340-313X	554	ex A4O-LI	409
☐ A9C-LJ	Airbus A340-313X	282	ex A4O-LL	410
☐ A9C-MA	Embraer ERJ170LR	17000292	ex PT-TQT	
☐ A9C-MB	Embraer ERJ170LR	17000278	ex PT-TQE	
☐ A9C-MC	Embraer ERJ-190AR	19000372	ex PT-XNJ	♦
☐ A9C-MD	Embraer ERJ-190AR	19000373	ex PT-XNK	♦

B- CHINA (People's Republic Of China)

AIR CHINA   Air China (CA/CCA)   Beijing-Capital (PEK)

Member of Star Alliance

☐ B-2223	Airbus A319-111	1679	ex D-AVWI
☐ B-2225	Airbus A319-111	1654	ex D-AVYS
☐ B-2339	Airbus A319-111	1753	ex D-AVYJ
☐ B-2364	Airbus A319-115	2499	ex D-AVWB
☐ B-2404	Airbus A319-131	2454	ex D-AVWE
☐ B-6004	Airbus A319-115	2508	ex D-AVWO
☐ B-6014	Airbus A319-115	2525	ex D-AVWE
☐ B-6022	Airbus A319-131	2000	ex D-AVYZ
☐ B-6023	Airbus A319-131	2007	ex D-AVWM
☐ B-6024	Airbus A319-131	2015	ex D-AVWT
☐ B-6031	Airbus A319-131	2172	ex D-AVWW
☐ B-6032	Airbus A319-131	2202	ex D-AVYF
☐ B-6033	Airbus A319-131	2205	ex D-AVYJ
☐ B-6034	Airbus A319-115	2237	ex D-AVWL
☐ B-6035	Airbus A319-115	2269	ex D-AVWX
☐ B-6036	Airbus A319-115	2285	ex D-AVYS
☐ B-6037	Airbus A319-115	2293	ex D-AVYY
☐ B-6038	Airbus A319-115	2298	ex D-AVWF
☐ B-6044	Airbus A319-115	2532	ex D-AVWL
☐ B-6046	Airbus A319-115	2545	ex D-AVWW
☐ B-6047	Airbus A319-115	2551	ex D-AVYJ
☐ B-6048	Airbus A319-131	2559	ex D-AVYU
☐ B-6213	Airbus A319-131	2614	ex D-AVXS
☐ B-6216	Airbus A319-131	2643	ex D-AVWO
☐ B-6223	Airbus A319-115	2805	ex D-AVWV
☐ B-6225	Airbus A319-115	2819	ex D-AVXB
☐ B-6226	Airbus A319-115	2839	ex D-AVYI
☐ B-6227	Airbus A319-115	2847	ex D-AVXG
☐ B-6228	Airbus A319-115	2890	ex D-AVYI
☐ B-6235	Airbus A319-131	3195	ex D-AVWC
☐ B-6236	Airbus A319-131	3200	ex D-AVWG
☐ B-6237	Airbus A319-131	3226	ex D-AVYJ
☐ B-6238	Airbus A319-115	3250	ex D-AVWO
☐ B-2210	Airbus A320-214	1296	ex F-WWBG
☐ B-2354	Airbus A320-214	0707	ex F-WWIN
☐ B-2355	Airbus A320-214	0724	ex F-WWBN
☐ B-2376	Airbus A320-214	0876	ex F-WWIF
☐ B-2377	Airbus A320-214	0921	ex F-WWDY
☐ B-6606	Airbus A320-214	3337	ex B-6350
☐ B-6607	Airbus A320-214	3461	ex B-6390

☐ B-6608	Airbus A320-214	3601	ex B-6393		
☐ B-6676	Airbus A320-232	4317	ex F-WWBR		♦
☐ B-6677	Airbus A320-232	4348	ex F-WWBU		♦
☐ B-	Airbus A320-232				o/o♦
☐ B-	Airbus A320-232				o/o♦
☐ B-	Airbus A320-232				o/o♦
☐ B-	Airbus A320-232				o/o♦
☐ B-	Airbus A320-232				o/o♦
☐ B-	Airbus A320-232				o/o♦
☐ B-	Airbus A320-232				o/o♦
☐ B-6326	Airbus A321-213	3329	ex D-AVZX		
☐ B-6327	Airbus A321-213	3307	ex D-AVZT		
☐ B-6361	Airbus A321-213	3523	ex D-AVZX	Beautiful Sichuan c/s	
☐ B-6362	Airbus A321-213	3623	ex D-AVZG		
☐ B-6363	Airbus A321-213	3653	ex D-AVZV		
☐ B-6365	Airbus A321-213	3655	ex D-AVZW		
☐ B-6382	Airbus A321-213	3665	ex D-AVZX		
☐ B-6383	Airbus A321-213	3678	ex D-AZAE		
☐ B-6385	Airbus A321-213	3722	ex D-AZAH		
☐ B-6386	Airbus A321-213	3725	ex D-AZVS		
☐ B-6555	Airbus A321-213	3766	ex D-AZAO		
☐ B-6556	Airbus A321-213	3806	ex D-AVZD		
☐ B-6593	Airbus A321-213	3973	ex D-AVZS		
☐ B-6595	Airbus A321-213	4022	ex D-AVZG		
☐ B-6596	Airbus A321-213	4031	ex D-AVZI		
☐ B-6597	Airbus A321-213	4062	ex D-AVZO		
☐ B-6599	Airbus A321-213	3940	ex D-AZAI		
☐ B-6603	Airbus A321-213	4131	ex D-AZAJ		
☐ B-6605	Airbus A321-213	4091	ex D-AVZX		
☐ B-6631	Airbus A321-213	4180	ex D-AZAM		
☐ B-6632	Airbus A321-213	4221	ex D-AVZJ		♦
☐ B-6633	Airbus A321-213	4283	ex D-AZAQ		♦
☐ B-6665	Airbus A321-213	4318	ex D-AVZW		♦
☐ B-6675	Airbus A321-213	4377	ex D-AZAA		♦
☐ B-6701	Airbus A321-213	4472	ex D-AVZE		♦
☐ B-6711	Airbus A321-213	4494	ex D-AVZF		♦
☐ B-	Airbus A321-213		ex D-		o/o♦
☐ B-	Airbus A321-213		ex D-		o/o♦
☐ B-	Airbus A321-213		ex D-		o/o♦
☐ B-	Airbus A321-213		ex D-		o/o♦
☐ B-	Airbus A321-213		ex D-		o/o♦
☐ B-	Airbus A321-213		ex D-		o/o♦
☐ B-	Airbus A321-213		ex D-		o/o♦
☐ B-6070	Airbus A330-243	750	ex F-WWKA		
☐ B-6071	Airbus A330-243	756	ex F-WWYQ		
☐ B-6072	Airbus A330-243	759	ex F-WWYK		
☐ B-6073	Airbus A330-243	780	ex F-WWKY		
☐ B-6075	Airbus A330-243	785	ex F-WWYY		
☐ B-6076	Airbus A330-243	797	ex F-WWKU		
☐ B-6079	Airbus A330-243	810	ex F-WWYF		
☐ B-6080	Airbus A330-243	815	ex F-WWYL		
☐ B-6081	Airbus A330-243	839	ex F-WWYO		
☐ B-6090	Airbus A330-243	860	ex F-WWYN		
☐ B-6091	Airbus A330-243	867	ex F-WWYP	Star Alliance colours	
☐ B-6092	Airbus A330-243	873	ex F-WWKV		
☐ B-6093	Airbus A330-243	884	ex F-WWKO	Star Alliance colours	
☐ B-6113	Airbus A330-243	890	ex F-WWYM		
☐ B-6115	Airbus A330-243	909	ex F-WWYG		
☐ B-6117	Airbus A330-243	903	ex F-WWKR		
☐ B-6130	Airbus A330-243	930	ex F-WWKS		
☐ B-6131	Airbus A330-243	941	ex F-WWKO		
☐ B-6132	Airbus A330-243	944	ex F-WWYT		
☐ B-6505	Airbus A330-243	957	ex F-WWYC		
☐ B-6511	Airbus A330-243	1110	ex F-WWYG		♦
☐ B-6512	Airbus A330-243	1087	ex F-WWKD		♦
☐ B-6513	Airbus A330-243	1130	ex F-WWKN		♦
☐ B-	Airbus A330-243				o/o♦
☐ B-	Airbus A330-243				o/o♦
☐ B-	Airbus A330-243				o/o♦
☐ B-	Airbus A330-343				o/o♦
☐ B-	Airbus A330-343				o/o♦
☐ B-	Airbus A330-343				o/o♦
☐ B-2385	Airbus A340-313X	192	ex B-HMX		

☐ B-2386	Airbus A340-313X	199	ex B-HMY	
☐ B-2387	Airbus A340-313X	201	ex B-HMZ	
☐ B-2388	Airbus A340-313X	242	ex F-WWJD	
☐ B-2389	Airbus A340-313X	243	ex F-WWJE	
☐ B-2390	Airbus A340-313X	264	ex F-WWJY	
☐ B-2522	Boeing 737-3Z0	23451/1240	ex N5573K	For Okair as Frtr
☐ B-2530	Boeing 737-3Z0	27046/2252		
☐ B-2533	Boeing 737-3Z0	27138/2436		
☐ B-2535	Boeing 737-3J6	25078/2002		
☐ B-2580	Boeing 737-3J6	25080/2254		
☐ B-2581	Boeing 737-3J6	25081/2263		
☐ B-2584	Boeing 737-3J6	25891/2385		
☐ B-2585	Boeing 737-3J6	27045/2384		
☐ B-2586	Boeing 737-3Z0	27047/2357		
☐ B-2587	Boeing 737-3J6	25892/2396		
☐ B-2588	Boeing 737-3J6	25893/2489		
☐ B-2590	Boeing 737-3Z0	27126/2370		
☐ B-2597	Boeing 737-3Z0	27176/2495		
☐ B-2598	Boeing 737-3J6	27128/2493		
☐ B-2599	Boeing 737-3Z0	25896/2558		
☐ B-2600	Boeing 737-36N	28554/2835	ex G-ECAS	
☐ B-2627	Boeing 737-36E	26315/2706	ex N141LF	
☐ B-2630	Boeing 737-36E	26317/2719	ex N151LF	
☐ B-2905	Boeing 737-33A	25506/2360	ex N403AW	
☐ B-2906	Boeing 737-33A	25507/2373	ex N404AW	
☐ B-2907	Boeing 737-33A	25508/2414	ex N405AW	
☐ B-2947	Boeing 737-33A	25511/2599		
☐ B-2948	Boeing 737-3J6	27361/2631		
☐ B-2949	Boeing 737-3J6	27372/2650		
☐ B-2950	Boeing 737-3Z0	27374/2647		
☐ B-2951	Boeing 737-3Z0	27373/2658		
☐ B-2953	Boeing 737-3J6	27523/2710		
☐ B-2954	Boeing 737-3J6	27518/2768		
☐ B-2957	Boeing 737-3Z0	27521/2738		
☐ B-5035	Boeing 737-36N	28672/2976	ex F-GRFA	
☐ B-5036	Boeing 737-36N	28673/2995	ex F-GRFB	
☐ B-2161	Boeing 737-86N	28655/965	ex N1786B	
☐ B-2509	Boeing 737-8Z0	30072/466	ex N1787B	
☐ B-2510	Boeing 737-8Z0	30071/381	ex N1786B	
☐ B-2511	Boeing 737-8Z0	30073/487	ex N1786B	
☐ B-2612	Boeing 737-79L	33411/1538		
☐ B-2613	Boeing 737-79L	33412/1544	ex N1786B	
☐ B-2641	Boeing 737-89L	29876/337		
☐ B-2642	Boeing 737-89L	29877/359		
☐ B-2643	Boeing 737-89L	29878/379	ex N1786B	
☐ B-2645	Boeing 737-89L	29879/427	ex N1786B	
☐ B-2648	Boeing 737-89L	29880/511	ex N1786B	
☐ B-2649	Boeing 737-89L	30159/572	ex N1784B	
☐ B-2650	Boeing 737-89L	30160/594		
☐ B-2657	Boeing 737-89L	30517/1224		
☐ B-2670	Boeing 737-89L	30514/1055		
☐ B-2671	Boeing 737-89L	30515/1165		
☐ B-2672	Boeing 737-89L	30516/1168		
☐ B-2673	Boeing 737-86N	29888/1133	ex N1786B	
☐ B-2690	Boeing 737-86N	29889/1153		
☐ B-2700	Boeing 737-79L	33413/1560		
☐ B-5043	Boeing 737-79L	33408/1331		
☐ B-5044	Boeing 737-79L	33409/1351		
☐ B-5045	Boeing 737-79L	33410/1354		
☐ B-5063	Boeing 737-7BX	30736/658	ex G-STRC	
☐ B-5064	Boeing 737-7BX	30737/687	ex G-STRD	
☐ B-5167	Boeing 737-808	34701/1887	ex N1787B	
☐ B-5168	Boeing 737-808	34702/1917		
☐ B-5169	Boeing 737-808	34703/1941	ex N1795B	
☐ B-5170	Boeing 737-808	34705/1998		
☐ B-5171	Boeing 737-808	34706/2014	ex N1786B	
☐ B-5172	Boeing 737-8Q8	30704/1985		
☐ B-5173	Boeing 737-8Q8	30705/2001		
☐ B-5175	Boeing 737-86N	35209/2067		
☐ B-5176	Boeing 737-86N	34258/2096		Olympic mascot c/s
☐ B-5177	Boeing 737-86N	35210/2127		Olympic mascot c/s
☐ B-5178	Boeing 737-86N	32682/2117	ex N1787B	Olympic mascot c/s
☐ B-5179	Boeing 737-86N	35211/2146		
☐ B-5196	Boeing 737-86N	36810/2699		
☐ B-5197	Boeing 737-86N/W	36811/2777		

☐ B-5198	Boeing 737-89L/W	36491/2759		
☐ B-5201	Boeing 737-79L/W	34023/1795	ex N1786B	
☐ B-5202	Boeing 737-79L/W	34537/1837	ex N1786B	
☐ B-5203	Boeing 737-79L/W	34538/1853		
☐ B-5211	Boeing 737-79L	34019/1749		
☐ B-5213	Boeing 737-79L/W	34020/1769	ex N1786B	
☐ B-5214	Boeing 737-79L/W	34021/1774		
☐ B-5217	Boeing 737-79L/W	34022/1786		
☐ B-5220	Boeing 737-79L/W	34539/1856	ex (B-5204)	
☐ B-5226	Boeing 737-79L/W	34540/1877	ex N1787B	
☐ B-5227	Boeing 737-79L/W	34541/1937		
☐ B-5228	Boeing 737-79L/W	34542/1993		
☐ B-5229	Boeing 737-79L/W	34543/2006		
☐ B-5311	Boeing 737-8Q8	29373/2171		
☐ B-5312	Boeing 737-8Q8	29374/2203	ex N1786B	
☐ B-5313	Boeing 737-8Q8	30716/2210	ex N1786B	
☐ B-5325	Boeing 737-86N	32692/2275	ex N1786B	
☐ B-5326	Boeing 737-86N	35214/2308		
☐ B-5327	Boeing 737-86N	35219/2371	ex N1779B	
☐ B-5328	Boeing 737-86N	35221/2444	ex N1786B	
☐ B-5329	Boeing 737-86N	35222/2463		
☐ B-5341	Boeing 737-89L/W	36483/2403	ex N1786B	
☐ B-5342	Boeing 737-89L/W	36484/2441	ex N1786B	
☐ B-5343	Boeing 737-89L/W	36485/2470		
☐ B-5387	Boeing 737-89L/W	36492/2828		
☐ B-5390	Boeing 737-89L/W	36486/2606		
☐ B-5391	Boeing 737-89L/W	36487/2664		
☐ B-5392	Boeing 737-89L/W	36488/2674		
☐ B-5397	Boeing 737-89L/W	36489/2704	ex N1787B	
☐ B-5398	Boeing 737-89L/W	36490/2715		
☐ B-5422	Boeing 737-89L/W	36741/2845	ex N1787B	
☐ B-5423	Boeing 737-89L/W	36742/2877		
☐ B-5425	Boeing 737-89L/W	36743/2896		
☐ B-5426	Boeing 737-89L/W	36744/2969		
☐ B-5431	Boeing 737-86N	36812/2918	ex N1787B	
☐ B-5436	Boeing 737-86N	36813/2976		
☐ B-5437	Boeing 737-86N/W	36815/3020		
☐ B-5438	Boeing 737-86N/W	36816/3032		
☐ B-5442	Boeing 737-86N/W	36745/3049		
☐ B-5443	Boeing 737-86N/W	36746/3072	ex N1786B	
☐ B-5447	Boeing 737-89L/W	40015/3509		♦
☐ B-5455	Boeing 737-86N/W	36774/2944		
☐ B-5457	Boeing 737-86N/W	36775/2951	ex N1787B	
☐ B-5477	Boeing 737-89L/W	36755/3387		♦
☐ B-5485	Boeing 737-89L/W	36747/3124	ex N1796B	
☐ B-5486	Boeing 737-89L/W	36748/3127	ex N1786B	
☐ B-5495	Boeing 737-89L/W	36749/3145		
☐ B-5496	Boeing 737-89L/W	36750/3155		
☐ B-5497	Boeing 737-89L/W	36751/3167		♦
☐ B-5500	Boeing 737-89L/W	36752/3188	ex N1786B	♦
☐ B-5507	Boeing 737-89L/W	36753/3247	ex N1796B	♦
☐ B-5508	Boeing 737-89L/W	36545/3275		♦
☐ B-5509	Boeing 737-89L/W	36547/3300		♦
☐ B-5510	Boeing 737-89L/W	36548/3312	ex N1795B	♦
☐ B-5518	Boeing 737-89L/W	36754/3336	ex N1786B	♦
☐ B-5519	Boeing 737-86N	36802/3350	ex N1787B	♦
☐ B-5525	Boeing 737-86N	37886/3436		♦
☐ B-	Boeing 737-8			o/o♦
☐ B-	Boeing 737-8			o/o♦
☐ B-	Boeing 737-8			o/o♦
☐ B-	Boeing 737-8			o/o♦
☐ B-	Boeing 737-8			o/o♦
☐ B-	Boeing 737-8			o/o♦
☐ B-	Boeing 737-8			o/o♦
☐ B-	Boeing 737-8			o/o♦
☐ B-2443	Boeing 747-4J6	25881/957		
☐ B-2445	Boeing 747-4J6	25882/1021		
☐ B-2447	Boeing 747-4J6	25883/1054		
☐ B-2460	Boeing 747-4J6M	24348/792		
☐ B-2467	Boeing 747-4J6M	28754/1119		
☐ B-2468	Boeing 747-4J6M	28755/1128		
☐ B-2469	Boeing 747-4J6M	28756/1175		
☐ B-2470	Boeing 747-4J6M	29070/1181		
☐ B-2471	Boeing 747-4J6M	29071/1229		
☐ B-2472	Boeing 747-4J6	30158/1243		

☐ B-2820	Boeing 757-2Z0	25885/476		
☐ B-2821	Boeing 757-2Z0	25886/480		
☐ B-2826	Boeing 757-2Y0	26155/495		
☐ B-2832	Boeing 757-2Z0	25887/554		
☐ B-2836	Boeing 757-2Z0	27258/595		
☐ B-2837	Boeing 757-2Z0	27259/609		
☐ B-2839	Boeing 757-2Z0	27269/615		
☐ B-2840	Boeing 757-2Z0	27270/622		
☐ B-2841	Boeing 757-2Z0	27367/624		
☐ B-2844	Boeing 757-2Z0	27511/669		
☐ B-2845	Boeing 757-2Z0	27512/674		
☐ B-2855	Boeing 757-2Z0	29792/822		
☐ B-2856	Boeing 757-2Z0	29793/833		
☐ B-2499	Boeing 767-332ER	30597/797	ex B-4025	
☐ B-2553	Boeing 767-2J6ER	23744/155	ex N60659	
☐ B-2557	Boeing 767-3J6	25875/429		
☐ B-2558	Boeing 767-3J6	25876/478		
☐ B-2559	Boeing 767-3J6	25877/530		
☐ B-2560	Boeing 767-3J6	25878/569		
☐ B-2059	Boeing 777-2J6	29153/168		
☐ B-2060	Boeing 777-2J6	29154/173		
☐ B-2061	Boeing 777-2J6	29155/179		
☐ B-2063	Boeing 777-2J6	29156/214		
☐ B-2064	Boeing 777-2J6	29157/240		
☐ B-2065	Boeing 777-2J6	29744/280		
☐ B-2066	Boeing 777-2J6	29745/290		
☐ B-2067	Boeing 777-2J6	29746/338		
☐ B-2068	Boeing 777-2J6	29747/344		
☐ B-2069	Boeing 777-2J6	29748/349		
☐ B-	Boeing 777-3J6			o/o♦
☐ B-	Boeing 777-3J6			o/o♦
☐ B-	Boeing 777-3J6			o/o♦
☐ B-	Boeing 777-3J6			o/o♦

AIR CHINA CARGO		**AirChina Freight (CA/CAO)**		**Beijing-Capital (PEK)**
☐ B-2409	Boeing 747-412 (SF)	26560/1052	ex 9V-SFC	<SQC
☐ B-2455	Boeing 747-412BCF	27070/1049	ex B-HKS	♦
☐ B-2456	Boeing 747-4J6BCF	24346/743		
☐ B-2458	Boeing 747-4J6BCF	24347/775		
☐ B-2462	Boeing 747-2J6F	24960/814		
☐ B-2475	Boeing 747-4FTF	34239/1367		
☐ B-2476	Boeing 747-4FTF	34240/1373		
☐ B-2477	Boeing 747-433BCF	24998/840	ex N998GP	
☐ B-2478	Boeing 747-433BCF	25075/868	ex N575GP	
☐ B-2871	Tupolev Tu-204-120SE	1450743664030		
☐ B-2872	Tupolev Tu-204-120SE	145074..64031		o/o♦
☐ B-2872	Tupolev Tu-204-120SE	145074..64031		o/o♦
☐ B-	Tupolev Tu-204-120SE			o/o♦
☐ B-	Tupolev Tu-204-120SE			o/o♦

CAPITAL AIRLINES		**(JD/DRA)**		**Beijing-Capital (PEK)**
☐ B-6156	Airbus A319-112	2849	ex D-AVXJ	<CHH
☐ B-6157	Airbus A319-112	2891	ex D-AVYS	<CHH
☐ B-6169	Airbus A319-112	2985	ex D-AVXJ	<CHH
☐ B-6177	Airbus A319-112	3285	ex D-AVYY	<CHH
☐ B-6178	Airbus A319-132	3548	ex D-AVWK	<CHH
☐ B-6179	Airbus A319-132	3561	ex D-AVWR	<CHH
☐ B-6180	Airbus A319-132	3578	ex D-AVYA	
☐ B-6181	Airbus A319-132	3580	ex D-AVYB	
☐ B-6182	Airbus A319-132	3520	ex D-AVWA	
☐ B-6192	Airbus A319-132	3768	ex D-AVXG	<CHH
☐ B-6193	Airbus A319-133	3849	ex D-AVYV	
☐ B-6198	Airbus A319-112	2617	ex D-AVYI	
☐ B-6199	Airbus A319-112	2644	ex D-AVWP	
☐ B-6212	Airbus A319-115	2581	ex D-AVXG	<CGN
☐ B-6215	Airbus A319-112	2611	ex D-AVXR	<CGN
☐ B-6221	Airbus A319-112	2746	ex D-AVYL	
☐ B-6222	Airbus A319-112	2733	ex D-AVXL	
☐ B-6245	Airbus A319-133	3851	ex D-AVYW	
☐ B-6400	Airbus A319-132	3638	ex B-502L	
☐ B-6401	Airbus A319-133	3842	ex B-510L	

☐ B-6402	Airbus A319-132	3914	ex B-507L	
☐ B-6403	Airbus A319-132	3958	ex B-509L	
☐ B-6405	Airbus A319-132	3982	ex B-511L	
☐ B-6417	Airbus A319-133	4522	ex D-AVYJ	<CHH♦
☐ B-	Airbus A319-133X	4042	ex F-WWDA	o/o
☐ B-6709	Airbus A320-232	4412	ex D-AVVH	<CHH♦
☐ B-6710	Airbus A320-232	4440	ex F-WWDT	<CHH♦
☐ B-6723	Airbus A320-232	4483	ex D-AUBE	<CHH♦
☐ B-6726	Airbus A320-232	4505	ex F-WWBC	<CHH♦
☐ B-2112	Boeing 737-36N	28599/3115	ex EI-DRS	<CHH
☐ B-2113	Boeing 737-36N	28602/3118	ex EI-DRY	<CHH
☐ B-2115	Boeing 737-36N	28606/3124	ex EI-DRZ	<CHH
☐ B-2608	Boeing 737-36Q	28662/2914	ex N305FA	<CHH
☐ B-3000	Boeing 737-36Q	29326/3020	ex N932HA	<CHH

CHANG AN AIRLINES · Changan (HU/CGN) · Xi'an (SIA)

☐ B-6210	Airbus A319-115	2557	ex D-AVYK	<CHH
☐ B-6211	Airbus A319-115	2561	ex D-AVYO	<CHH
☐ B-6212	Airbus A319-115	2581	ex D-AVXG	>DRA
☐ B-6215	Airbus A319-112	2611	ex D-AVXR	>DRA
☐ B-3444	AVIC I Y7-100C	09701		
☐ B-3445	AVIC I Y7-100C	09705		
☐ B-3475	AVIC I Y7-100C	06703		
☐ B-3707	AVIC I Y7-100C	12701		
☐ B-3708	AVIC I Y7-100C	11705		
☐ B-5092	Boeing 737-705	29092/260	ex VH-VBX	<CHH
☐ B-5115	Boeing 737-8FH/W	29640/1649		<CHH
☐ B-5116	Boeing 737-8FH/W	29672/1745	ex N1786B	<CHH
☐ B-5180	Boeing 737-8FH/W	35089/2042		<CHH
☐ B-5181	Boeing 737-8FH/W	35090/2073		<CHH

CHENGDU AIRLINES · (EU) · Chengdu (CTU)

☐ B-6151	Airbus A319-112	1263	ex N739US	
☐ B-6152	Airbus A319-112	0946	ex N706US	
☐ B-6155	Airbus A319-112	0949	ex N707UW	
☐ B-6163	Airbus A319-112	3024	ex D-AVXR	
☐ B-6229	Airbus A319-112	2762	ex B-1136L	♦
☐ B-6230	Airbus A319-112	2774	ex D-AVYF	
☐ B-	Airbus A320-214	2820	ex D-ABDF	o/o♦

CHINA CARGO AIRLINES · Cargo King (CK/CKK) · Shanghai-Pu Dong Intl (PVG)

☐ B-2308	Airbus A300B4-605RF	532	ex F-WWAH	
☐ B-2425	Boeing 747-40BERF	35207/1377		
☐ B-2426	Boeing 747-40BERF	35208/1392		
☐ B-2076	Boeing 777-F6N	37711/846	ex N5573S	♦
☐ B-2077	Boeing 777-F6N	37713/856		♦
☐ B-2078	Boeing 777-F6N	37714/869		♦
☐ B-2079	Boeing 777-F6N	37715/876		♦
☐ B-2082	Boeing 777-F6N			o/o♦
☐ B-2083	Boeing 777-F6N			o/o♦
☐ B-2170	McDonnell-Douglas MD-11F	48461/475		
☐ B-2171	McDonnell-Douglas MD-11F	48495/461		
☐ B-2172	McDonnell-Douglas MD-11F	48496/496		
☐ B-2174	McDonnell-Douglas MD-11F	48498/522		
☐ B-2175	McDonnell-Douglas MD-11F	48520/541	ex N9134D	
☐ B-	Tupolev Tu-204-120SE	145074..64041	o/o	

CHINA EASTERN AIRLINES · China Eastern (MU/CES) · Shanghai-Pu Dong Intl (PVG)

☐ B-2306	Airbus A300B4-605RF	521	ex F-WWAF	
☐ B-2307	Airbus A300B4-605RF	525	ex F-WWAJ	
☐ B-2317	Airbus A300B4-605R	741	ex F-WWAY	
☐ B-2318	Airbus A300B4-605R	707	ex F-WWAU	
☐ B-2319	Airbus A300B4-605R	732	ex F-WWAT	
☐ B-2324	Airbus A300B4-622R	725	ex F-WWAR	
☐ B-2325	Airbus A300B4-605R	746	ex F-WWAA	
☐ B-2326	Airbus A300B4-605R	754	ex F-WWAY	

☐ B-2330	Airbus A300B4-605R	763	ex F-WWAH	
☐ B-2215	Airbus A319-112	1541	ex D-AVWI	
☐ B-2216	Airbus A319-112	1551	ex D-AVWN	
☐ B-2217	Airbus A319-112	1601	ex D-AVWX	
☐ B-2222	Airbus A319-112	1603	ex D-AVWY	
☐ B-2226	Airbus A319-112	1786	ex D-AVYP	
☐ B-2227	Airbus A319-112	1778	ex D-AVYE	
☐ B-2331	Airbus A319-112	1285	ex D-AVYT	
☐ B-2332	Airbus A319-112	1303	ex D-AVWN	
☐ B-2333	Airbus A319-112	1377	ex D-AVWE	
☐ B-2334	Airbus A319-112	1386	ex D-AVWC	
☐ B-6167	Airbus A319-115	3168	ex D-AVWB	
☐ B-6172	Airbus A319-115	3186	ex D-AVYG	
☐ B-6217	Airbus A319-115	2693	ex D-AVXC	
☐ B-6218	Airbus A319-115	2757	ex D-AVWH	
☐ B-6231	Airbus A319-115	2825	ex D-AVXD	
☐ B-6332	Airbus A319-115	3262	ex D-AVZB	
☐ B-2201	Airbus A320-214	0914	ex F-WWDV	
☐ B-2202	Airbus A320-214	0925	ex F-WWID	
☐ B-2203	Airbus A320-214	1005	ex F-WWDL	
☐ B-2205	Airbus A320-214	0984	ex F-WWDI	
☐ B-2206	Airbus A320-214	0986	ex F-WWDJ	
☐ B-2207	Airbus A320-214	1028	ex F-WWDG	
☐ B-2208	Airbus A320-214	1070	ex F-WWBH	
☐ B-2209	Airbus A320-214	1030	ex F-WWDU	
☐ B-2211	Airbus A320-214	1041	ex F-WWID	
☐ B-2212	Airbus A320-214	1316	ex F-WWDG	
☐ B-2213	Airbus A320-214	1345	ex F-WWDX	
☐ B-2219	Airbus A320-214	1532	ex F-WWIP	
☐ B-2220	Airbus A320-214	1542	ex F-WWIV	
☐ B-2221	Airbus A320-214	1639	ex F-WWDZ	
☐ B-2228	Airbus A320-214	1906	ex F-WWDK	
☐ B-2229	Airbus A320-214	1911	ex F-WWDT	
☐ B-2230	Airbus A320-214	1964	ex F-WWDR	
☐ B-2335	Airbus A320-214	1312	ex F-WWBZ	
☐ B-2336	Airbus A320-214	1330	ex F-WWDV	
☐ B-2337	Airbus A320-214	1357	ex F-WWBF	
☐ B-2338	Airbus A320-214	1361	ex F-WWBU	
☐ B-2356	Airbus A320-214	0665	ex F-WWBB	
☐ B-2357	Airbus A320-214	0754	ex F-WWIY	
☐ B-2358	Airbus A320-214	0838	ex F-WWBB	
☐ B-2359	Airbus A320-214	0854	ex F-WWBK	
☐ B-2362	Airbus A320-214	0828	ex F-WWIM	
☐ B-2363	Airbus A320-214	0883	ex F-WWDC	
☐ B-2372	Airbus A320-214	0897	ex F-WWDK	
☐ B-2375	Airbus A320-214	0909	ex F-WWDS	
☐ B-2378	Airbus A320-214	0939	ex F-WWIQ	
☐ B-2379	Airbus A320-214	0967	ex F-WWBN	
☐ B-2398	Airbus A320-214	1108	ex F-WWDH	
☐ B-2399	Airbus A320-214	1093	ex F-WWIZ	
☐ B-2400	Airbus A320-214	1072	ex F-WWBI	
☐ B-2410	Airbus A320-214	2437	ex F-WWIX	
☐ B-2411	Airbus A320-214	2451	ex F-WWDF	
☐ B-2412	Airbus A320-214	2478	ex F-WWDV	
☐ B-2413	Airbus A320-214	2493	ex F-WWDZ	
☐ B-2415	Airbus A320-214	2498	ex F-WWIL	
☐ B-6001	Airbus A320-214	1981	ex F-WWDL	
☐ B-6002	Airbus A320-214	2022	ex F-WWDG	
☐ B-6003	Airbus A320-214	2034	ex F-WWIF	
☐ B-6005	Airbus A320-214	2036	ex F-WWIZ	
☐ B-6006	Airbus A320-214	2068	ex F-WWIL	
☐ B-6007	Airbus A320-214	2056	ex F-WWIR	
☐ B-6008	Airbus A320-214	2049	ex F-WWII	
☐ B-6009	Airbus A320-214	2219	ex F-WWDN	
☐ B-6010	Airbus A320-214	2221	ex F-WWIU	
☐ B-6011	Airbus A320-214	2235	ex F-WWBY	
☐ B-6012	Airbus A320-214	2239	ex F-WWDP	
☐ B-6013	Airbus A320-214	2244	ex F-WWIR	
☐ B-6015	Airbus A320-214	2212	ex F-WWBF	
☐ B-6016	Airbus A320-214	2155	ex F-WWDU	
☐ B-6017	Airbus A320-214	2274	ex F-WWIJ	
☐ B-6028	Airbus A320-214	2171	ex F-WWDG	
☐ B-6029	Airbus A320-214	2182	ex F-WWIO	
☐ B-6030	Airbus A320-214	2199	ex F-WWDX	
☐ B-6259	Airbus A320-214	2562	ex F-WWIZ	

☐	B-6260	Airbus A320-214	2591	ex F-WWDT	
☐	B-6261	Airbus A320-214	2606	ex F-WWBR Young Pioneers c/s	
☐	B-6262	Airbus A320-214	2627	ex F-WWDV	
☐	B-6333	Airbus A320-214	3170	ex F-WWIN	
☐	B-6335	Airbus A320-214	3197	ex F-WWIX	
☐	B-6346	Airbus A320-232	3481	ex F-WWDL	
☐	B-6370	Airbus A320-214	3559	ex F-WWBF	
☐	B-6371	Airbus A320-214	3611	ex D-AVVF	
☐	B-6372	Airbus A320-232	3613	ex F-WWIH	
☐	B-6373	Airbus A320-232	3650	ex F-WWDP	
☐	B-6375	Airbus A320-232	3677	ex F-WWBC	
☐	B-6376	Airbus A320-232	3692	ex F-WWBF	
☐	B-6399	Airbus A320-232	3716	ex F-WWBJ	
☐	B-6558	Airbus A320-232	3793	ex F-WWBH	
☐	B-6559	Airbus A320-232	3904	ex F-WWIB	
☐	B-6560	Airbus A320-232	3937	ex F-WWDQ	
☐	B-6585	Airbus A320-232	3965	ex F-WWIE	
☐	B-6586	Airbus A320-232	3775	ex B-504L	
☐	B-6587	Airbus A320-232	3797	ex B-505L	
☐	B-6600	Airbus A320-232	3870	ex B-506L	
☐	B-6601	Airbus A320-232	4037	ex F-WWIL	
☐	B-6616	Airbus A320-232	3929	ex B-508L	
☐	B-6617	Airbus A320-232	4144	ex D-AVVC	
☐	B-6635	Airbus A320-232	4027	ex B-513L	
☐	B-6638	Airbus A320-232	4240	ex F-WWDI	♦
☐	B-6639	Airbus A320-232	4252	ex F-WWIN	♦
☐	B-6653	Airbus A320-232	4232	ex B-503L	o/o
☐	B-6671	Airbus A320-232	4186	ex B-520L	♦
☐	B-6672	Airbus A320-232	4220	ex B-502L	o/o
☐	B-6673	Airbus A320-232	4340	ex F-WWBF	♦
☐	B-6695	Airbus A320-232	4297	ex B-508L	♦
☐	B-6715	Airbus A320-232	4355	ex B-512L	♦
☐	B-	Airbus A320-232		ex	o/o♦
☐	B-	Airbus A320-232		ex	o/o♦
☐	B-	Airbus A320-232		ex	o/o♦
☐	B-	Airbus A320-232		ex	o/o♦
☐	B-	Airbus A320-232		ex	o/o♦
☐	B-	Airbus A320-232		ex	o/o♦
☐	B-	Airbus A320-232		ex	o/o♦
☐	B-	Airbus A320-232		ex	o/o♦
☐	B-	Airbus A320-232		ex	o/o♦
☐	B-	Airbus A320-232		ex	o/o♦
☐	B-	Airbus A320-232		ex	o/o♦
☐	B-2289	Airbus A321-211	2309	ex D-AVZD	
☐	B-2290	Airbus A321-211	2315	ex D-AVZM	
☐	B-2291	Airbus A321-211	2543	ex D-AVZF	
☐	B-2292	Airbus A321-211	2549	ex D-AVZI	
☐	B-2419	Airbus A321-211	2882	ex D-AVZJ	
☐	B-2420	Airbus A321-211	2895	ex D-AVZA	
☐	B-6329	Airbus A321-211	3233	ex D-AVZH	
☐	B-6330	Airbus A321-211	3247	ex D-AVZK	
☐	B-6331	Airbus A321-211	3249	ex D-AVZO	
☐	B-6332	Airbus A321-211	3262	ex D-AVZB	
☐	B-6345	Airbus A321-211	3471	ex D-AVZV	
☐	B-6366	Airbus A321-211	3593	ex D-AZAB	
☐	B-6367	Airbus A321-211	3612	ex D-AZAD	
☐	B-6368	Airbus A321-211	3639	ex D-AVZT	
☐	B-6369	Airbus A321-211	3682	ex D-AVZB	
☐	B-	Airbus A321-211		ex	o/o♦
☐	B-	Airbus A321-211		ex	o/o♦
☐	B-6082	Airbus A330-243	821	ex F-WWKB	
☐	B-6083	Airbus A330-343E	830	ex F-WWKK	
☐	B-6085	Airbus A330-343E	836	ex F-WWYK	
☐	B-6095	Airbus A330-343E	851	ex F-WWKR	
☐	B-6096	Airbus A330-343E	862	ex F-WWYG	
☐	B-6097	Airbus A330-343E	866	ex F-WWYL	
☐	B-6099	Airbus A330-243	916	ex F-WWYP	
☐	B-6100	Airbus A330-343E	928	ex F-WWKJ	
☐	B-6119	Airbus A330-343	713	ex F-WWYT	
☐	B-6120	Airbus A330-343	720	ex F-WWYZ	
☐	B-6121	Airbus A330-243	728	ex F-WWKQ	
☐	B-6122	Airbus A330-243	732	ex F-WWKT	
☐	B-6123	Airbus A330-243	735	ex F-WWYA	
☐	B-6125	Airbus A330-343	773	ex F-WWKF	

☐	B-6126	Airbus A330-343	777	ex F-WWKK	
☐	B-6127	Airbus A330-343	781	ex F-WWYT	
☐	B-6128	Airbus A330-343	782	ex F-WWYV	
☐	B-6129	Airbus A330-343	791	ex F-WWKO	
☐	B-6506	Airbus A330-343E	936	ex F-WWKG	
☐	B-6507	Airbus A330-343E	942	ex F-WWYK	
☐	B-	Airbus A330-343E		ex	o/o♦
☐	B-	Airbus A330-343E		ex	o/o♦
☐	B-	Airbus A330-343E		ex	o/o♦
☐	B-2380	Airbus A340-313X	129	ex F-WWJQ	
☐	B-2381	Airbus A340-313X	131	ex F-WWJO	
☐	B-2382	Airbus A340-313X	141	ex F-WWJC	
☐	B-2383	Airbus A340-313X	161	ex F-WWJQ	
☐	B-2384	Airbus A340-313X	182	ex F-WWJM	
☐	B-6050	Airbus A340-642	468	ex F-WWCP	
☐	B-6051	Airbus A340-642	488	ex F-WWCT	
☐	B-6052	Airbus A340-642	514	ex F-WWCU	
☐	B-6053	Airbus A340-642	577	ex F-WWCM	
☐	B-6055	Airbus A340-642	586	ex F-WWCR Expo 2010 colours	
☐	B-2538	Boeing 737-3W0	25090/2040		
☐	B-2571	Boeing 737-39P	29410/3053		
☐	B-2572	Boeing 737-39P	29411/3071		
☐	B-2573	Boeing 737-39P	29412/3080	ex N1786B	
☐	B-2589	Boeing 737-3W0	27127/2377		
☐	B-2594	Boeing 737-341	26853/2275	ex (PP-VPB)	
☐	B-2955	Boeing 737-33A	27453/2687		
☐	B-2956	Boeing 737-33A	27907/2690		
☐	B-2958	Boeing 737-3W0	27522/2727		
☐	B-2966	Boeing 737-33A	27462/2765		
☐	B-2969	Boeing 737-36R	30102/3108	ex N1787B	
☐	B-2981	Boeing 737-3W0	28972/2919		
☐	B-2983	Boeing 737-3W0	28973/2941		
☐	B-2985	Boeing 737-3W0	29068/2945		
☐	B-2986	Boeing 737-3W0	29069/2951		
☐	B-2988	Boeing 737-36R	29087/2970		
☐	B-2502	Boeing 737-7W0	30075/311		
☐	B-2503	Boeing 737-7W0	30074/292	ex N1786B	
☐	B-2639	Boeing 737-7W0	29912/140	ex N1787B	
☐	B-2640	Boeing 737-7W0	29913/148	ex N1800B	
☐	B-2665	Boeing 737-86R	30495/876		
☐	B-2680	Boeing 737-76Q	30282/1143	ex N706BA	
☐	B-2681	Boeing 737-79P	33037/1198		
☐	B-2682	Boeing 737-79P	33038/1219		
☐	B-2683	Boeing 737-79P	28253/1247		
☐	B-2684	Boeing 737-79P	33039/1227		
☐	B-2685	Boeing 737-79P	33040/1244		
☐	B-5030	Boeing 737-79P	30651/1267		
☐	B-5031	Boeing 737-79P	28255/1284		
☐	B-5032	Boeing 737-79P	30035/1288		
☐	B-5033	Boeing 737-79P	30657/1319		
☐	B-5034	Boeing 737-79P	30036/1336		
☐	B-5054	Boeing 737-79P	29365/1841	ex N1784B	
☐	B-5074	Boeing 737-79P	33008/1718	ex N1786B	
☐	B-5084	Boeing 737-79P	33009/1728	ex N1786B	
☐	B-5085	Boeing 737-89P/W	30691/1702		
☐	B-5086	Boeing 737-89P/W	32800/1681		
☐	B-5087	Boeing 737-89P/W	32802/1725		
☐	B-5093	Boeing 737-79P/W	29357/1630		
☐	B-5094	Boeing 737-79P/W	29358/1651		
☐	B-5095	Boeing 737-79P/W	29361/1694		
☐	B-5096	Boeing 737-79P/W	29362/1713		
☐	B-5097	Boeing 737-79P	29364/1823	ex N6067E	
☐	B-5100	Boeing 737-89P/W	30681/1645	ex N1786B	
☐	B-5101	Boeing 737-89P/W	30682/1673		
☐	B-5199	Boeing 737-89P/W	36272/2753		
☐	B-5208	Boeing 737-79P/W	33041/1902	ex N1787B	
☐	B-5209	Boeing 737-79P/W	33042/1947	ex N1779B	
☐	B-5210	Boeing 737-79P/W	33043/1976		
☐	B-5223	Boeing 737-79P/W	33044/1987		
☐	B-5225	Boeing 737-79P/W	33045/1999		
☐	B-5231	Boeing 737-79P/W	33046/2034		
☐	B-5242	Boeing 737-79P/W	36269/2357		
☐	B-5243	Boeing 737-79P/W	36270/2398		
☐	B-5245	Boeing 737-79P/W	36271/2697		

☐ B-5255	Boeing 737-79P/W	36757/2902	ex N1786B	
☐ B-5256	Boeing 737-79P/W	36758/2949		
☐ B-5257	Boeing 737-79P/W	33759/2968	ex N1786B	
☐ B-5258	Boeing 737-79P/W	36760/3009		
☐ B-5259	Boeing 737-79P/W	36762/3046		
☐ B-5262	Boeing 737-79P/W	36764/3067	ex N1787B	
☐ B-5263	Boeing 737-79P/W	36766/3086	ex N1796B	
☐ B-5265	Boeing 737-79P/W	36767/3239	ex N1786B	
☐ B-5267	Boeing 737-79P/W	36768/3269		♦
☐ B-5271	Boeing 737-79P/W	36772/3444	ex N1787B	♦
☐ B-5376	Boeing 737-86N/W	35226/2641		♦
☐ B-5472	Boeing 737-89P/W	36761/3001	ex N1779B	
☐ B-5473	Boeing 737-89P/W	36763/3036	ex N1786B	
☐ B-5475	Boeing 737-89P/W	36765/3065		
☐ B-5492	Boeing 737-89P/W	29661/3083	ex N1787B	
☐ B-5493	Boeing 737-89P/W	29652/3121		
☐ B-5501	Boeing 737-89P/W	39388/3204		♦
☐ B-5515	Boeing 737-89P/W	36769/3311		♦
☐ B-5516	Boeing 737-89P/W	39389/3304	ex N1787B	♦
☐ B-5517	Boeing 737-89P/W	29653/3294	ex N1786B	♦
☐ B-5527	Boeing 737-89P/W	36771/3343		♦
☐ B-5530	Boeing 737-89P/W	29655/3351	ex N1786B	♦
☐ B-2568	Boeing 767-3W0ER	28148/620		
☐ B-2569	Boeing 767-3W0ER	28149/627		
☐ B-5001	Boeing 767-3W0ER	28264/644		
☐ B-3013	Canadair CRJ-200LR	7571	ex C-FVAZ	
☐ B-3019	Canadair CRJ-200LR	7581	ex C-FMMX	
☐ B-3021	Canadair CRJ-200LR	7596	ex C-FMNW	
☐ B-3070	Canadair CRJ-200LR	7647	ex C-FMLB	
☐ B-3071	Canadair CRJ-200LR	7684	ex C-FMMT	
☐ B-3049	Embraer ERJ-145LI	14500839	ex PT-SOA	
☐ B-3050	Embraer ERJ-145LI	14500848	ex PT-SOB	
☐ B-3051	Embraer ERJ-145LI	14500898	ex PT-SOD	
☐ B-3052	Embraer ERJ-145LI	14500905	ex PT-SOE	
☐ B-3053	Embraer ERJ-145LI	14500882	ex PT-SOC	
☐ B-3055	Embraer ERJ-145LI	14500921	ex PT-S	
☐ B-3056	Embraer ERJ-145LI	14500928	ex PT-S	
☐ B-3057	Embraer ERJ-145LI	14500932	ex PT-S	
☐ B-3058	Embraer ERJ-145LI	14500958		
☐ B-3059	Embraer ERJ-145LI	14500949		

CHINA EXPRESS AIRLINES — China Express (G5/HXA) — Guiyang (KWE)

☐ B-3001	Canadair CRJ-200LR	7565	ex B-KBJ	<CDG
☐ B-3012	Canadair CRJ-200LR	7557	ex C-FMLB	<CDG
☐ B-3016	Canadair CRJ-200LR	7614	ex C-FMKV	
☐ B-7700	Canadair CRJ-200LR	7704	ex N387DF	♦

CHINA FLYING DRAGON AVIATION CO — Feilong (CFA) — Harbin - Ping Fang

☐ B-7420	Aérospatiale AS350B2 Ecureuil	2522	ex F-WYMH	
☐ B-7421	Aérospatiale AS350B2 Ecureuil	2523	ex F-WYMG	
☐ B-7422	Aérospatiale AS350B2 Ecureuil	2534	ex F-WYMB	
☐ B-7423	Aérospatiale AS350B2 Ecureuil	2538	ex F-WYMF	
☐ B-7424	Aérospatiale AS350B2 Ecureuil	2547	ex F-WYME	
☐ B-7425	Aérospatiale AS350B2 Ecureuil	2554	ex F-WYMF	
☐ B-7427	Aérospatiale AS350B2 Ecureuil	2566		
☐ B-3201	AVIC II Y-11B	003	prototype, status?	
☐ B-3862	AVIC II Y-11	(11)0407		
☐ B-3863	AVIC II Y-11	(11)0408		
☐ B-3864	AVIC II Y-11	(11)0409		
☐ B-3874	AVIC II Y-11	(11)0102		
☐ B-3875	AVIC II Y-11	(11)0105		
☐ B-3876	AVIC II Y-11	(11)0106		
☐ B-3877	AVIC II Y-11	(11)0107		
☐ B-3878	AVIC II Y-11	(11)0110		
☐ B-3879	AVIC II Y-11	(11)0201		
☐ B-3880	AVIC II Y-11	(11)0202		
☐ B-3881	AVIC II Y-11	(11)0203		
☐ B-3882	AVIC II Y-11	(11)0204		
☐ B-3883	AVIC II Y-11	(11)0205		
☐ B-3884	AVIC II Y-11	(11)0210		

☐ B-3801	Harbin Y-12 II	0006		Frtr
☐ B-3802	Harbin Y-12 II	0002		Surveyor
☐ B-3803	Harbin Y-12 II	0003		Surveyor
☐ B-3804	Harbin Y-12 II	0011		Surveyor
☐ B-3805	Harbin Y-12 II	0005		Surveyor
☐ B-3806	Harbin Y-12 II	0008		Frtr
☐ B-3807	Harbin Y-12 II	0016		Op for Maritime Service
☐ B-3808	Harbin Y-12 II	0017		Op for Maritime Service
☐ B-3819	Harbin Y-12 II	0004		Frtr
☐ B-7109	AVIC II Z-9A Haitun (SA365N)	045		Op for Ministry of Forestry
☐ B-7110	AVIC II Z-9A Haitun (SA365N)	047		Op for Ministry of Forestry
☐ B-7112	AVIC II Z-9A Haitun (SA365N)			

CHINA POSTAL AIRLINES	**China Post (8Y/CYZ)**			**Nanjing-Lukou (NKG)**

☐ B-3101	AVIC II Y-8F-100	10(08)01		
☐ B-3102	AVIC II Y-8F-100	10(08)02		
☐ B-3103	AVIC II Y-8F-100	10(08)05		
☐ B-3109	AVIC II Y-8F-100	13(08)03		
☐ B-3110	AVIC II Y-8F-100	13(08)04		c/n not confirmed
☐ B-2135	Boeing 737-45R(SF)	29035/3046	ex N202BK	
☐ B-2513	Boeing 737-45R (SF)	29034/3015	ex N653AC	♦
☐ B-2526	Boeing 737-3Y0 (SF)	25172/2089		
☐ B-2527	Boeing 737-3Y0 (SF)	25173/2097		
☐ B-2528	Boeing 737-3Y0 (SF)	25174/2168		
☐ B-2656	Boeing 737-3Q8 (SF)	26292/2519	ex N141LF	
☐ B-2661	Boeing 737-3Q8 (SF)	26284/2418	ex N379BC	
☐ B-2662	Boeing 737-3Q8 (SF)	24988/2466	ex N441LF	
☐ B-2881	Boeing 737-45R (SF)	29032/2943	ex N651AC	
☐ B-2882	Boeing 737-45R (SF)	29033/2963	ex N652AC	
☐ B-2891	Boeing 737-46J (SF)	28334/2802	ex N212BF	
☐ B-2892	Boeing 737-46J (SF)	28271/2801	ex N211BF	
☐ B-5046	Boeing 737-341 (SF)	24276/1645	ex N276HE	
☐ B-5047	Boeing 737-341 (SF)	24278/1660	ex N278HE	
☐ B-5071	Boeing 737-341 (QC)	24277/1658	ex N277HE	
☐ B-5072	Boeing 737-341 (QC)	24279/1673	ex N279HE	

CHINA SOUTHERN AIRLINES	**China Southern (CZ/CSN)**			**Guangzhou (CAN)**

Member of Skyteam

☐ B-2315	Airbus A300B4-622RF	733	ex F-WWAU	
☐ B-2316	Airbus A300B4-622R	734	ex F-WWAE	
☐ B-2323	Airbus A300B4-622R	739	ex F-WWAB	
☐ B-2328	Airbus A300B4-622RF	756	ex HL7580	
☐ B-2294	Airbus A319-132	2371	ex D-AVWL	
☐ B-2295	Airbus A319-132	2408	ex D-AVWB	
☐ B-2296	Airbus A319-132	2426	ex D-AVYZ	
☐ B-2297	Airbus A319-132	2435	ex D-AVYH	
☐ B-6018	Airbus A319-132	1971	ex D-AVYC	
☐ B-6019	Airbus A319-132	1986	ex D-AVYJ	
☐ B-6020	Airbus A319-133	2004	ex D-AVWB	
☐ B-6021	Airbus A319-133	2008	ex D-AVWN	
☐ B-6039	Airbus A319-132	2200	ex D-AVYE	
☐ B-6040	Airbus A319-132	2203	ex D-AVYG	
☐ B-6041	Airbus A319-132	2232	ex D-AVWI	
☐ B-6042	Airbus A319-132	2273	ex D-AVWZ	
☐ B-6158	Airbus A319-132	2901	ex D-AVWP	
☐ B-6160	Airbus A319-132	2940	ex D-AVWW	
☐ B-6161	Airbus A319-132	2948	ex D-AVXB	
☐ B-6162	Airbus A319-132	2969	ex D-AVYT	
☐ B-6168	Airbus A319-132	3020	ex D-AVXN	
☐ B-6183	Airbus A319-115	3828	ex D-AVYK	
☐ B-6187	Airbus A319-115	3903	ex D-AVWQ	
☐ B-6190	Airbus A319-132	3860	ex D-AVWC	
☐ B-6191	Airbus A319-132	3890	ex D-AVWJ	
☐ B-6195	Airbus A319-112	3983	ex D-AVYF	
☐ B-6200	Airbus A319-115	2519	ex D-AVYX	
☐ B-6201	Airbus A319-115	2541	ex D-AVWV	
☐ B-6202	Airbus A319-115	2546	ex D-AVWX	
☐ B-6203	Airbus A319-112	2554	ex D-AVYS	
☐ B-6205	Airbus A319-132	2505	ex D-AVWG	
☐ B-6206	Airbus A319-132	2574	ex D-AVXD	
☐ B-6207	Airbus A319-132	2579	ex D-AVXF	

☐ B-6208	Airbus A319-112	2555	ex D-AVWU	
☐ B-6209	Airbus A319-112	2558	ex D-AVYP	
☐ B-6219	Airbus A319-132	2667	ex D-AVYG	
☐ B-6220	Airbus A319-132	2815	ex D-AVWX	
☐ B-6239	Airbus A319-132	3144	ex D-AVXT	
☐ B-6240	Airbus A319-132	3258	ex D-AVXM	
☐ B-6241	Airbus A319-132	3269	ex D-AVYA	
☐ B-6242	Airbus A319-132	3311	ex D-AVYR	
☐ B-6243	Airbus A319-132	3342	ex D-AVYJ	
☐ B-6407	Airbus A319-132	4036	ex D-AVYK	
☐ B-6408	Airbus A319-112	4038	ex D-AVYL	
☐ B-6409	Airbus A319-112	4071	ex D-AVYU	
☐ B-2347	Airbus A320-233	0705	ex F-WWIL	
☐ B-2350	Airbus A320-232	0712	ex F-WWDI	
☐ B-2351	Airbus A320-233	0718	ex F-WWBI	
☐ B-2352	Airbus A320-232	0720	ex F-WWBU	
☐ B-2353	Airbus A320-232	0722	ex F-WWBM	
☐ B-2365	Airbus A320-232	0849	ex F-WWBI	
☐ B-2366	Airbus A320-232	0859	ex F-WWBO	
☐ B-2367	Airbus A320-232	0881	ex F-WWDB	
☐ B-2368	Airbus A320-232	0895	ex F-WWDJ	
☐ B-2369	Airbus A320-232	0900	ex F-WWDM	
☐ B-2374	Airbus A320-232	2345	ex F-WWBC	
☐ B-2391	Airbus A320-232	0950	ex F-WWIZ	
☐ B-2392	Airbus A320-232	0966	ex F-WWBK	
☐ B-2393	Airbus A320-232	1035	ex F-WWDX	
☐ B-2395	Airbus A320-232	1039	ex F-WWDZ	
☐ B-2396	Airbus A320-232	1057	ex F-WWIO	
☐ B-2405	Airbus A320-232	2343	ex F-WWIV	
☐ B-2406	Airbus A320-214	2354	ex F-WWIP	
☐ B-2407	Airbus A320-232	2334	ex F-WWIM	
☐ B-2408	Airbus A320-214	2361	ex F-WWBM	
☐ B-2459	Airbus A320-214	0709	ex F-OHCX	
☐ B-6251	Airbus A320-214	2484	ex F-WWIO	
☐ B-6252	Airbus A320-214	2506	ex F-WWBP	
☐ B-6253	Airbus A320-214	2511	ex F-WWIT	
☐ B-6255	Airbus A320-214	2637	ex F-WWBX	
☐ B-6263	Airbus A320-214	2708	ex F-WWIU	
☐ B-6269	Airbus A320-232	2743	ex F-WWBK	
☐ B-6272	Airbus A320-214	2770	ex F-WWDM	
☐ B-6275	Airbus A320-232	2680	ex F-WWIY	
☐ B-6276	Airbus A320-232	2689	ex F-WWIG	
☐ B-6277	Airbus A320-232	2701	ex F-WWIR	
☐ B-6278	Airbus A320-232	2714	ex F-WWBD	
☐ B-6279	Airbus A320-232	2772	ex F-WWDR	
☐ B-6281	Airbus A320-214	2796	ex F-WWIC	
☐ B-6282	Airbus A320-214	2824	ex F-WWDF	
☐ B-6283	Airbus A320-214	2834	ex F-WWBP	
☐ B-6287	Airbus A320-214	2899	ex F-WWDB	
☐ B-6288	Airbus A320-214	2855	ex F-WWIS	
☐ B-6289	Airbus A320-214	2861	ex F-WWIY	
☐ B-6290	Airbus A320-214	2877	ex F-WWBK	
☐ B-6291	Airbus A320-214	2915	ex F-WWDM	
☐ B-6292	Airbus A320-214	2960	ex F-WWBN	
☐ B-6293	Airbus A320-214	2986	ex F-WWIG	
☐ B-6303	Airbus A320-214	2950	ex F-WWIL	
☐ B-6575	Airbus A320-232	3910	ex F-WWIS	
☐ B-6576	Airbus A320-232	3941	ex F-WWDS	
☐ B-6577	Airbus A320-232	3959	ex F-WWDJ	
☐ B-6582	Airbus A320-232	3999	ex F-WWDK	
☐ B-6583	Airbus A320-232	4003	ex F-WWDP	
☐ B-6588	Airbus A320-232	4017	ex F-WWBX	
☐ B-6620	Airbus A320-214	4172	ex F-WWDM	
☐ B-6623	Airbus A320-214	4205	ex D-AVVZ	♦
☐ B-6627	Airbus A320-232	4225	ex F-WWBO	♦
☐ B-6641	Airbus A320-232	4140	ex B-518L	♦
☐ B-6651	Airbus A320-232	4260	ex F-WWBC	♦
☐ B-6652	Airbus A320-232	4290	ex F-WWIX	♦
☐ B-6655	Airbus A320-214	4350	ex D-AXAU	♦
☐ B-6656	Airbus A320-214	4322	ex D-AXAN	♦
☐ B-6681	Airbus A320-214	4365	ex F-WWDQ	♦
☐ B-6703	Airbus A320-214	4396	ex B-515L	♦
☐ B-	Airbus A320-214		ex	o/o♦
☐ B-	Airbus A320-214		ex	o/o♦
☐ B-	Airbus A320-214		ex	o/o♦
☐ B-	Airbus A320-214		ex	o/o♦

☐ B-2280	Airbus A321-231	1596	ex D-AVZL		
☐ B-2281	Airbus A321-231	1614	ex D-AVZA		
☐ B-2282	Airbus A321-231	1776	ex D-AVZC		
☐ B-2283	Airbus A321-231	1788	ex D-AVZE		
☐ B-2284	Airbus A321-231	1974	ex D-AVZN		
☐ B-2285	Airbus A321-231	1995	ex D-AVZZ		
☐ B-2287	Airbus A321-231	2080	ex D-AVZW		
☐ B-2288	Airbus A321-231	2067	ex D-AVZP		
☐ B-2417	Airbus A321-231	2521	ex D-AVZC		
☐ B-2418	Airbus A321-231	2530	ex D-AVZD		
☐ B-6265	Airbus A321-231	2713	ex D-AVZI		
☐ B-6267	Airbus A321-231	2741	ex D-AVZK		
☐ B-6270	Airbus A321-231	2759	ex D-AVZL		
☐ B-6271	Airbus A321-231	2767	ex D-AVZM		
☐ B-6273	Airbus A321-231	2809	ex D-AVZC		
☐ B-6302	Airbus A321-231	2936	ex D-AVZT		
☐ B-6305	Airbus A321-231	2971	ex D-AVZM		
☐ B-6306	Airbus A321-231	3067	ex D-AVZJ		
☐ B-6307	Airbus A321-231	3075	ex D-AVZB		
☐ B-6308	Airbus A321-231	3112	ex D-AVZE		
☐ B-6317	Airbus A321-231	3217	ex D-AVZD		
☐ B-6318	Airbus A321-231	3251	ex D-AVZP		
☐ B-6319	Airbus A321-231	3241	ex D-AVZJ		
☐ B-6339	Airbus A321-231	3507	ex D-AVZJ		
☐ B-6342	Airbus A321-231	3459	ex D-AVZT		
☐ B-6343	Airbus A321-231	3493	ex D-AVZF		
☐ B-6345	Airbus A321-231	3471	ex D-AVZY		
☐ B-6353	Airbus A321-231	3552	ex D-AVZP		
☐ B-6355	Airbus A321-231	3566	ex D-AVZS		
☐ B-6356	Airbus A321-231	3587	ex D-AVZR		
☐ B-6378	Airbus A321-231	3645	ex D-AVZU		
☐ B-6379	Airbus A321-231	3681	ex D-AZAF		
☐ B-6389	Airbus A321-231	3764	ex D-AZAN		
☐ B-6397	Airbus A321-231	3784	ex D-AZAQ		
☐ B-6398	Airbus A321-231	3847	ex D-AVZH		
☐ B-6552	Airbus A321-231	3867	ex D-AVZL		
☐ B-6553	Airbus A321-231	3920	ex D-AVZY		
☐ B-6578	Airbus A321-231	3934	ex D-AZAE		
☐ B-6579	Airbus A321-231	3938	ex D-AZAH		
☐ B-6580	Airbus A321-231	3951	ex D-AZAT		
☐ B-6581	Airbus A321-231	3981	ex D-AZAM		
☐ B-6622	Airbus A321-231	4194	ex D-AVZD		◆
☐ B-6625	Airbus A321-231	4184	ex D-AZAN		◆
☐ B-6626	Airbus A321-231	4189	ex D-AVZB		◆
☐ B-6628	Airbus A321-231	4217	ex D-AVZI		◆
☐ B-6629	Airbus A321-231	4224	ex D-AVZL		◆
☐ B-6630	Airbus A321-231	4230	ex D-AVZQ		◆
☐ B-6657	Airbus A321-231	4266	ex D-AVZH		◆
☐ B-6659	Airbus A321-231	4292	ex D-AZAV		◆
☐ B-6660	Airbus A321-231	4299	ex D-AZAX		◆
☐ B-6661	Airbus A321-231	4341	ex D-AZAS		◆
☐ B-6663	Airbus A321-231	4338	ex D-AZAR		◆
☐ B-6683	Airbus A321-231	4369	ex D-AVZS		◆
☐ B-6685	Airbus A321-231	4416	ex D-AZAE		◆
☐ B-6686	Airbus A321-231	4387	ex D-AZAC		◆
☐ B-6687	Airbus A321-231	4430	ex D-AZAI		◆
☐ B-6056	Airbus A330-243	649	ex F-WWKI		
☐ B-6057	Airbus A330-243	652	ex F-WWKL		
☐ B-6058	Airbus A330-243	656	ex F-WWYV		
☐ B-6059	Airbus A330-243	664	ex F-WWKP		
☐ B-6077	Airbus A330-243	818	ex F-WWYQ		
☐ B-6078	Airbus A330-243	840	ex F-WWYS		
☐ B-6086	Airbus A330-343E	879	ex F-WWKG		
☐ B-6087	Airbus A330-343E	889	ex F-WWKZ		
☐ B-6098	Airbus A330-343E	908	ex F-WWYF		
☐ B-6111	Airbus A330-343E	935	ex F-WWKF		
☐ B-6112	Airbus A330-343E	937	ex F-WWKI		
☐ B-6135	Airbus A330-343E	1096	ex F-WWYT	◆	
☐ B-6500	Airbus A330-343E	954	ex F-WWKT		
☐ B-6501	Airbus A330-343E	964	ex F-WWYK		
☐ B-6502	Airbus A330-343E	958	ex F-WWYD		
☐ B-6515	Airbus A330-343E	1116	ex F-WWKJ		◆
☐ B-6516	Airbus A330-343E	1129	ex F-WWKE		◆
☐ B-	Airbus A330-343E		ex F-WW	o/o◆	
☐ B-	Airbus A330-343E		ex F-WW	o/o◆	
☐ B-	Airbus A330-343E		ex F-WW	o/o◆	

☐ B-	Airbus A330-343E		ex F-WW	o/o♦
☐ B-	Airbus A380-841	054	ex F-WWAX	o/o ♦
☐ B-3022	ATR 72-212A	521	ex F-WWED	
☐ B-3023	ATR 72-212A	531	ex F-WWLK	
☐ B-3025	ATR 72-212A	547	ex F-WWLO	
☐ B-3026	ATR 72-212A	552	ex F-WWLP	
☐ B-3027	ATR 72-212A	555	ex F-WWLL	
☐ B-2539	Boeing 737-3Y0	26068/2306		
☐ B-2574	Boeing 737-37K	29407/3100	ex N1786B	
☐ B-2575	Boeing 737-37K	29408/3104	ex N1800B	
☐ B-2582	Boeing 737-31B	25895/2499		
☐ B-2583	Boeing 737-31B	25897/2554		
☐ B-2596	Boeing 737-31B	27151/2437		
☐ B-2909	Boeing 737-3Y0	26082/2456		
☐ B-2910	Boeing 737-3Y0	26083/2459		
☐ B-2911	Boeing 737-3Y0	26084/2460		
☐ B-2920	Boeing 737-3Q8	27271/2523		
☐ B-2921	Boeing 737-3Q8	27286/2528		
☐ B-2922	Boeing 737-31B	27272/2555		
☐ B-2923	Boeing 737-31B	27275/2565		
☐ B-2924	Boeing 737-31B	27287/2575		
☐ B-2926	Boeing 737-31B	27289/2593		
☐ B-2927	Boeing 737-31B	27290/2595		
☐ B-2929	Boeing 737-31B	27343/2619		
☐ B-2930	Boeing 737-31L	27273/2556		
☐ B-2931	Boeing 737-31L	27276/2567		
☐ B-2935	Boeing 737-37K	27283/2547		
☐ B-2936	Boeing 737-37K	27335/2609		
☐ B-2941	Boeing 737-31B	27344/2622		
☐ B-2946	Boeing 737-37K	27375/2655		
☐ B-2952	Boeing 737-31B	27519/2678		
☐ B-2959	Boeing 737-31B	27520/2775		
☐ B-2162	Boeing 737-7K9	30041/909	ex N1786B	
☐ B-2163	Boeing 737-7K9	30042/931	ex N1786B	
☐ B-2169	Boeing 737-71B	32936/1531		
☐ B-2620	Boeing 737-71B	32937/1569		
☐ B-2622	Boeing 737-71B	32938/1603		
☐ B-2698	Boeing 737-76N	32583/994	ex N583SF	
☐ B-2699	Boeing 737-76N	32596/1028	ex N1786B	
☐ B-2916	Boeing 737-71B	32939/1607		
☐ B-2917	Boeing 737-71B	32940/1624		
☐ B-5068	Boeing 737-71B	32933/1430		
☐ B-5069	Boeing 737-71B	32934/1465		
☐ B-5070	Boeing 737-71B	32935/1507		
☐ B-5107	Boeing 737-7K9	34320/1763		
☐ B-5108	Boeing 737-7K9	34321/1802	ex N1786B	
☐ B-5221	Boeing 737-71B	29366/1872	ex N1795B	
☐ B-5222	Boeing 737-71B	29367/1896	ex N1784B	
☐ B-5230	Boeing 737-71B	29371/2064		
☐ B-5232	Boeing 737-71B	35360/2051		
☐ B-5233	Boeing 737-71B	35361/2077		
☐ B-5235	Boeing 737-71B	29370/2137		
☐ B-5236	Boeing 737-71B	35362/2102		
☐ B-5237	Boeing 737-71B	29372/2131	ex N1786B	
☐ B-5238	Boeing 737-71B	35363/2066		
☐ B-5239	Boeing 737-71B	35364/2156		
☐ B-5240	Boeing 737-71B	35368/2264		
☐ B-5241	Boeing 737-71B	35372/2291		
☐ B-5247	Boeing 737-71B	35377/2980	ex N1786B	
☐ B-5250	Boeing 737-71B	35378/2346		
☐ B-5251	Boeing 737-71B	35384/2446		
☐ B-5252	Boeing 737-71B	35382/3034	ex N1786B	
☐ B-5253	Boeing 737-71B	35383/3005		
☐ B-	Boeing 737-71B			o/o♦
☐ B-	Boeing 737-71B			o/o♦
☐ B-	Boeing 737-71B			o/o♦
☐ B-	Boeing 737-71B			o/o♦
☐ B-	Boeing 737-71B			o/o♦
☐ B-2693	Boeing 737-81B	32921/1187	ex N6065Y	
☐ B-2694	Boeing 737-81B	32922/1199		
☐ B-2695	Boeing 737-81B	32923/1213		
☐ B-2696	Boeing 737-81B	32924/1230		

☐ B-2697	Boeing 737-81B	32925/1250		
☐ B-5020	Boeing 737-81B	32926/1268		
☐ B-5021	Boeing 737-81B	32927/1290		
☐ B-5022	Boeing 737-81B	32928/1323		
☐ B-5040	Boeing 737-81B	32929/1348		
☐ B-5041	Boeing 737-81B	32930/1355		
☐ B-5042	Boeing 737-81B	32931/1362		
☐ B-5067	Boeing 737-81B	32932/1395		
☐ B-5112	Boeing 737-86N	34248/1806		
☐ B-5113	Boeing 737-81B	34250/1784		
☐ B-5120	Boeing 737-83N/W	32580/1024	ex N313TZ	
☐ B-5121	Boeing 737-83N/W	32609/1059	ex N316TZ	
☐ B-5122	Boeing 737-83N/W	32610/1110	ex N320TZ	
☐ B-5123	Boeing 737-83N/W	32611/1135	ex N322TZ	
☐ B-5125	Boeing 737-83N/W	32612/1184	ex N326TZ	
☐ B-5126	Boeing 737-83N/W	32613/1197	ex N327TZ	
☐ B-5127	Boeing 737-83N/W	32615/1207	ex N329TZ	
☐ B-5128	Boeing 737-83N/W	32882/1163	ex N324TZ	
☐ B-5129	Boeing 737-83N/W	32884/1181	ex N325TZ	
☐ B-5133	Boeing 737-86N	34252/1851	ex N1787B	
☐ B-5147	Boeing 737-81B	30697/1915	ex N1786B	
☐ B-5149	Boeing 737-81B	30699/1933		
☐ B-5155	Boeing 737-8K5/W	30783/804	ex N307TA	
☐ B-5156	Boeing 737-81Q/W	30786/1138	ex N786TA	
☐ B-5157	Boeing 737-81Q/W	30787/1234	ex N787TM	
☐ B-5163	Boeing 737-81B	30708/2087		
☐ B-5165	Boeing 737-81B	30709/1961		
☐ B-5166	Boeing 737-81B	33006/1983		
☐ B-5189	Boeing 737-81B	35365/2191		
☐ B-5190	Boeing 737-81B	35366/2223		
☐ B-5191	Boeing 737-81B	35367/2237	ex N1786B	
☐ B-5192	Boeing 737-81B	35369/2272		
☐ B-5193	Boeing 737-81B	35370/2299		
☐ B-5195	Boeing 737-81B	35371/2302		
☐ B-5300	Boeing 737-81B	35375/2314		
☐ B-5310	Boeing 737-81B	35376/2329		
☐ B-5339	Boeing 737-81B	35380/2372	ex N1782B	
☐ B-5340	Boeing 737-81B	35381/2402		
☐ B-5356	Boeing 737-81B	35385/2486	ex N1787B	
☐ B-5419	Boeing 737-81B	35379/2957	ex N1787B	
☐ B-5420	Boeing 737-81B	35374/2940		
☐ B-5421	Boeing 737-81B	35373/2881		
☐ B-5445	Boeing 737-81B	35388/3154		
☐ B-5446	Boeing 737-81B	35389/3144		
☐ B-5468	Boeing 737-81B	35386/3068	ex N1786B	
☐ B-5469	Boeing 737-81B	35387/3041		
☐ B-	Boeing 737-8			o/o♦
☐ B-	Boeing 737-8			o/o♦
☐ B-	Boeing 737-8			o/o♦
☐ B-2461	Boeing 747-41BF	32804/1312		
☐ B-2473	Boeing 747-41BF	32803/1306	ex N1788B	
☐ B-2812	Boeing 757-28S	32341/961		
☐ B-2813	Boeing 757-28S	32342/966		
☐ B-2816	Boeing 757-21B	25083/359		
☐ B-2817	Boeing 757-21B	25258/389		
☐ B-2818	Boeing 757-21B	25259/392		
☐ B-2822	Boeing 757-21B	25884/461		
☐ B-2823	Boeing 757-21B	25888/575		
☐ B-2824	Boeing 757-21B	25889/583		
☐ B-2825	Boeing 757-21B	25890/585		
☐ B-2827	Boeing 757-2Y0	26156/503		
☐ B-2830	Boeing 757-28S	32343/1015	ex N60668	
☐ B-2831	Boeing 757-2Y0	26153/482		
☐ B-2835	Boeing 757-236	25598/445	ex N5573P	
☐ B-2838	Boeing 757-2Z0	27260/613		
☐ B-2851	Boeing 757-28S	29215/797		
☐ B-2853	Boeing 757-28S	29216/811		
☐ B-2859	Boeing 757-28S	29217/868		
☐ B-2860	Boeing 757-236	29945/873	ex N546NA	
☐ B-2051	Boeing 777-21B	27357/20		Toyota Camry c/s
☐ B-2052	Boeing 777-21B	27358/24	ex N5017V	
☐ B-2053	Boeing 777-21B	27359/46		
☐ B-2054	Boeing 777-21B	27360/48		
☐ B-2055	Boeing 777-21BER	27524/55		

☐ B-2056	Boeing 777-21BER	27525/66				
☐ B-2057	Boeing 777-21BER	27604/106	ex N5022E	Pearl of The South		
☐ B-2058	Boeing 777-21BER	27605/110	ex N5028Y			
☐ B-2062	Boeing 777-21BER	27606/121	ex N688CZ			
☐ B-2070	Boeing 777-21BER	32703/472				
☐ B-2071	Boeing 777-F1B	37309/760	ex N447BA			♦
☐ B-2072	Boeing 777-F1B	37310/770	ex N448BA			♦
☐ B-2073	Boeing 777-F1B	37311/811	ex N553BA			
☐ B-2075	Boeing 777-F1B	37312/820	ex N554BA			
☐ B-2081	Boeing 777-F1B	37313/888				♦
☐ B-	Boeing 777-F1B					o/o♦
☐ B-	Boeing 787-8					o/o♦
☐ B-	Boeing 787-8					o/o♦
☐ B-	Boeing 787-8					o/o♦
☐ B-3060	Embraer ERJ-145LI	145701	ex PT-SGF			
☐ B-3061	Embraer ERJ-145LI	145755	ex PT-SNA			
☐ B-3062	Embraer ERJ-145LI	145781	ex PT-SNB			
☐ B-3063	Embraer ERJ-145LI	14500804	ex PT-S			
☐ B-3065	Embraer ERJ-145LI	14500815	ex PT-S			
☐ B-3066	Embraer ERJ-145LI	14500823	ex PT-SXL			
☐ B-2132	McDonnell-Douglas MD-82	49516/1622				SAIC c/n 17
☐ B-2136	McDonnell-Douglas MD-82	49520/1671				SAIC c/n 21
☐ B-2143	McDonnell-Douglas MD-82	49851/1807				SAIC c/n 28
☐ B-2145	McDonnell-Douglas MD-82	49853/1981				SAIC c/n 35
☐ B-2152	McDonnell-Douglas MD-82	53164/2041	ex N833AU			[HRB]
☐ B-2100	McDonnell-Douglas MD-90-30	60001/4001		AVIC II assembled		
☐ B-2103	McDonnell-Douglas MD-90-30	60002/4002		AVIC II assembled		
☐ B-2251	McDonnell-Douglas MD-90-30	53524/2146				
☐ B-2252	McDonnell-Douglas MD-90-30	53525/2150				
☐ B-2254	McDonnell-Douglas MD-90-30	53527/2175				
☐ B-2255	McDonnell-Douglas MD-90-30	53528/2177				
☐ B-2259	McDonnell-Douglas MD-90-30	53529/2220				
☐ B-2260	McDonnell-Douglas MD-90-30	53530/2222				
☐ B-2261	McDonnell-Douglas MD-90-30	53531/2228				
☐ B-2266	McDonnell-Douglas MD-90-30	53532/2253				
☐ B-2267	McDonnell-Douglas MD-90-30	53533/2258				
☐ B-7303	Sikorsky S-76A	760289				
☐ B-7304	Sikorsky S-76A	760293				
☐ B-7306	Sikorsky S-76A	760106	ex VH-XHA			
☐ B-7307	Sikorsky S-76C+	760478				
☐ B-7308	Sikorsky S-76C+	760480				
☐ B-7311	Sikorsky S-76C+	760192				
☐ B-7320	Sikorsky S-76C+	760263				
☐ B-7329	Sikorsky S-76C++	760769				♦
☐ B-7330	Sikorsky S-76C++	760771				♦
☐ B-7331	Sikorsky S-76C++	760715	ex N2557H			

CHINA UNITED AIRLINES — Lianhang (KN/CUA) — Beijing-Nanyuan (NAY)

☐ B-4008	Boeing 737-3T0	23839/1507	ex N19357		Op for Govt
☐ B-4009	Boeing 737-3T0	23840/1516	ex N27358		Op for Govt
☐ B-4018	Boeing 737-33A	25502/2310			Op for Govt
☐ B-4019	Boeing 737-33A	25503/2313			Op for Govt
☐ B-4020	Boeing 737-34N	28081/2746			Op for Govt
☐ B-4021	Boeing 737-34N	28082/2747			Op for Govt
☐ B-4052	Boeing 737-3Q8	24701/1957	ex PK-GWI		Op for Govt
☐ B-4053	Boeing 737-3Q8	24702/1994	ex PK-GWJ		Op for Govt
☐ B-2663	Boeing 737-7AD	28437/72	ex N701EW		<CSH
☐ B-2997	Boeing 737-7Q8	28223/272			<CSH
☐ B-4025	Boeing 737-76D	33470/1334	ex B-5048		Op for Govt
☐ B-4026	Boeing 737-76D	33472/1343	ex B-2689		Op for Govt
☐ B-5183	Boeing 737-8Q8/W	30711/2159	ex N1787B		<CSH
☐ B-5323	Boeing 737-8Q8/W	30725/2292			<CSH
☐ B-5399	Boeing 737-86N/W	35224/2617			<CSH
☐ B-5547	Boeing 737-86N/W	36806/3448			♦
☐ B-4005	Canadair CRJ-200LR	7138	ex C-FZAT	Op for Govt	
☐ B-4006	Canadair CRJ-200LR	7149	ex C-FZIS	Op for Govt	
☐ B-4007	Canadair CRJ-200LR	7180	ex C-GATM	Op for Govt	
☐ B-4010	Canadair CRJ-200LR	7189	ex C-GATY	Op for Govt	
☐ B-4011	Canadair CRJ-200LR	7193	ex C-GBFR	Op for Govt	

☐ B-4701	Canadair CRJ-200LR	7639	ex C-GKAK	Op for China Maritime Service
☐ B-4702	Canadair CRJ-200LR	7455	ex C-GHUT	Op for China Maritime Service
☐ B-4060	Canadair CRJ-701ER	10164	ex C-FBNI	
☐ B-4061	Canadair CRJ-701ER	10183	ex C-FCRA	
☐ B-4062	Canadair CRJ-701ER	10187	ex C-FCRF	
☐ B-4063	Canadair CRJ-701ER	10204	ex C-FEHT	
☐ B-4064	Canadair CRJ-701ER	10206	ex C-FEHU	
☐ B-4016	Tupolev Tu-154M	91A872		
☐ B-4017	Tupolev Tu-154M	91A873		
☐ B-4028	Tupolev Tu-154M	93A967		VIP
☐ B-4012	Yakovlev Yak-42D	4520424914375		Op for Chinese Navy
☐ B-4013	Yakovlev Yak-42D	45204249144..?		Op for Chinese Navy

CHINA XINHUA AIRLINES — Xinhua (HU/CXH) — Tianjin (TSN)

☐ B-2908	Boeing 737-341	26854/2303	ex PP-VPC	<CHH
☐ B-2934	Boeing 737-39K	27274/2559		<CHH
☐ B-2942	Boeing 737-332	25997/2506	ex N304DE	<CHH
☐ B-2943	Boeing 737-332	25998/2510	ex N305DE	<CHH
☐ B-2945	Boeing 737-39K	27362/2639		<CHH
☐ B-2982	Boeing 737-36Q	28657/2859	ex N211BF	
☐ B-2987	Boeing 737-46Q	28663/2922		<CHH
☐ B-2989	Boeing 737-46Q	28758/2939		<CHH
☐ B-2993	Boeing 737-46Q	28759/2981		<CHH
☐ B-5080	Boeing 737-86N	28614/477	ex N614LS	<CHH
☐ B-5081	Boeing 737-86N	30231/515	ex N302LS	<CHH
☐ B-5082	Boeing 737-883	30193/587	ex LN-RCS	<CHH
☐ B-5138	Boeing 737-84P/W	32607/1832		<CHH
☐ B-5139	Boeing 737-84P/W	32608/1855		<CHH
☐ B-5141	Boeing 737-84P/W	34030/1800		<CHH
☐ B-5153	Boeing 737-84P/W	34029/1921		<CHH

CHONGQING AIRLINES — Chongqing (OQ/CQN) — Chongqing (CKG)

☐ B-2343	Airbus A320-233	0696	ex F-WWII	<CSN
☐ B-2345	Airbus A320-233	0698	ex F-WWBT	<CSN
☐ B-2346	Airbus A320-233	0704	ex F-WWDY	<CSN
☐ B-6246	Airbus A319-133	3836	ex D-AVYO	
☐ B-6247	Airbus A319-133	3876	ex D-AVWG	
☐ B-6248	Airbus A319-133	3901	ex D-AVWP	

CITIC OFFSHORE HELICOPTERS — China Helicopter (CHC) — Shenzhen Heliport

☐ B-7127	Eurocopter EC225LP	2676		
☐ B-7128	Eurocopter EC225LP	2687		
☐ B-7951	Aérospatiale AS.332L	2165		
☐ B-7956	Aérospatiale AS.332L1	2356	ex HL9202	
☐ B-7957	Aérospatiale AS.332L1	9000		
☐ B-7958	Aérospatiale AS.332L1	9001	ex F-WQDT	
☐ B-7959	Aérospatiale AS.332L1	2087	ex F-WYMR	
☐ B-7961	Aérospatiale AS.332L1	2641		
☐ B-7962	Aérospatiale AS.332L1	2644		
☐ B-7005	Eurocopter EC155B	6639		
☐ B-7006	Eurocopter EC155B	6641		
☐ B-7007	Eurocopter EC135T2	0246		
☐ B-7008	Eurocopter EC155B	6623		
☐ B-7101	Aérospatiale AS365N	6012		
☐ B-7102	Aérospatiale AS365N	6013		
☐ B-7103	Aérospatiale AS365N	6041		
☐ B-7105	Aérospatiale AS365N	6046		
☐ B-7106	Aérospatiale AS365N	6047		
☐ B-7107	Aérospatiale AS365N	6027		
☐ B-7120	Eurocopter EC155B1	6717	ex F-WWOU	
☐ B-7132	Eurocopter EC155B1	6904		♦
☐ B-7133	Eurocopter EC155B1	6912		♦
☐ B-7429	Aérospatiale AS.350B3	4627		♦
☐ B-7772	Agusta A.109E Power	11136		

DONGHAI AIRLINES — Donghai Air (J5/EPA) — Shenzhen Bao'an (SZX)

☐ B-2517	Boeing 737-3W0 (SF)	23396/1166	ex N5573K	
☐ B-2518	Boeing 737-3W0 (SF)	23397/1193	ex N1791B	

☐ B-2897	Boeing 737-3B7F	24902/1973	ex N108KH
☐ B-2898	Boeing 737-3Y0F	24916/2066	ex N106KH

DONGHUA AIRLINES — Jinjiang (JJN)

☐ B-3889	AVIC II Y-11	(11)0305

GRAND CHINA AIRLINES — Grand China (CN/GDC) — Haikou (HAK)

☐ B-2637	Boeing 737-86N	28576/103	ex N576GE	
☐ B-2652	Boeing 737-84P	30475/731	Jin Sui Piao Xiang special c/s	
☐ B-5337	Boeing 737-84P/W	35747/2433		<CHH

GRANDSTAR CARGO INTERNATIONAL — (GD/GSC)

☐ B-2427	Boeing 747-4B5F	26401/1087	ex HL7497

GREAT WALL AIRLINES — G-W Air (IJ/GWL) — Shanghai-Pu Dong Intl (PVG)

☐ B-2428	Boeing 747-412F	28263/1094	ex 9V-SFE
☐ B-2430	Boeing 747-412BCF	27137/990	ex N137GP
☐ B-2433	Boeing 747-412F	28027/1256	ex 9V-SFI

HAINAN AIRLINES — Hainan (HU/CHH) — Haikou (HAK)

☐ B-6156	Airbus A319-112	2849	ex D-AVXJ	>DRA
☐ B-6157	Airbus A319-112	2891	ex D-AVYS	>DRA
☐ B-6169	Airbus A319-112	2985	ex D-AVXJ	>DRA
☐ B-6177	Airbus A319-112	3285	ex D-AVYY	>DRA
☐ B-6178	Airbus A319-132	3548	ex D-AVWK	>DRA
☐ B-6179	Airbus A319-132	3561	ex D-AVWR	>DRA
☐ B-6192	Airbus A319-132	3768	ex D-AVXG	>DRA
☐ B-6210	Airbus A319-115	2557	ex D-AVYK	Op by CGN
☐ B-6211	Airbus A319-115	2561	ex D-AVYO	Op by CGN
☐ B-6212	Airbus A319-115	2581	ex D-AVXG	Op by CGN
☐ B-6215	Airbus A319-112	2611	ex D-AVXR	
☐ B-6221	Airbus A319-112	2746	ex D-AVYL	
☐ B-6222	Airbus A319-112	2733	ex D-AVXL	
☐ B-6412	Airbus A319-132	4262	ex B-506L	>CHB♦
☐ B-6413	Airbus A319-132	4452	ex D-AVYB	>CHB♦
☐ B-6417	Airbus A319-133	4522	ex D-AVYJ	>DRA♦
☐ B-	Airbus A319-133		ex	o/o♦
☐ B-6709	Airbus A320-232	4412	ex D-AVVH	>DRA♦
☐ B-6710	Airbus A320-232	4440	ex F-WWDT	>DRA♦
☐ B-6723	Airbus A320-232	4483	ex D-AUBE	>DRA♦
☐ B-6726	Airbus A320-232	4505	ex F-WWBC	>DRA♦
☐ B-	Airbus A320-232		ex	o/o♦
☐ B-	Airbus A320-232		ex	o/o♦
☐ B-	Airbus A320-232		ex	o/o♦
☐ B-	Airbus A320-232		ex	o/o♦
☐ B-	Airbus A320-232		ex	o/o♦
☐ B-	Airbus A320-232		ex	o/o♦
☐ B-	Airbus A320-232		ex	o/o♦
☐ B-	Airbus A320-232		ex	o/o♦
☐ B-6088	Airbus A330-243	906	ex F-WWYD	
☐ B-6089	Airbus A330-243	919	ex F-WWYS	
☐ B-6116	Airbus A330-243	875	ex F-WWKB	
☐ B-6118	Airbus A330-243	881	ex F-WWKI	
☐ B-6133	Airbus A330-243	982	ex F-WWYY	
☐ B-6519	Airbus A330-243	1159	ex F-WWKF	
☐ B-6520	Airbus A330-343X	1168	ex F-WWYJ	♦
☐ B-6527	Airbus A330-343X	1178	ex F-WWKE	♦
☐ B-	Airbus A330-		ex	o/o♦
☐ B-6508	Airbus A340-642	436	ex B-HQA	
☐ B-6509	Airbus A340-642	453	ex B-HQB	
☐ B-6510	Airbus A340-642	475	ex B-HQC	
☐ B-2112	Boeing 737-36N	28599/3115	ex EI-DRS	>DRA
☐ B-2113	Boeing 737-36N	28602/3118	ex EI-DRY	>DRA
☐ B-2115	Boeing 737-36N	28606/3124	ex EI-DRZ	>DRA
☐ B-2501	Boeing 737-44P	29914/3067	ex N1786B	
☐ B-2576	Boeing 737-44P	29915/3106	ex N1786B	special flower c/s
☐ B-2578	Boeing 737-33A	25603/2333	ex N401AW	special flower c/s
☐ B-2579	Boeing 737-33A	25505/2342	ex N402AW	special flower c/s

☐ B-2608	Boeing 737-36Q	28662/2914	ex N305FA		>DRA
☐ B-2934	Boeing 737-39K	27274/2559			>CXH
☐ B-2942	Boeing 737-332	25997/2506	ex N304DE		>CXH
☐ B-2943	Boeing 737-332	25998/2510	ex N305DE		>CXH
☐ B-2945	Boeing 737-39K	27362/2639			>CXH
☐ B-2960	Boeing 737-4Q8	24332/1866	ex N191LF		
☐ B-2963	Boeing 737-3Q8	26325/2772			
☐ B-2965	Boeing 737-4Q8	26334/2782			
☐ B-2967	Boeing 737-4Q8	26335/2793			
☐ B-2970	Boeing 737-4Q8	26337/2811			
☐ B-2987	Boeing 737-46Q	28663/2922			>CXH
☐ B-2989	Boeing 737-46Q	28758/2939			>CXH
☐ B-2993	Boeing 737-46Q	28759/2981			>CXH
☐ B-3000	Boeing 737-36Q	29326/3020	ex N932HA		>DRA
☐ B-5053	Boeing 737-322F	24378/1704	ex N357UA		>YZR
☐ B-5055	Boeing 737-330 (QC)	24283/1677	ex N283A		>YZR
☐ B-5056	Boeing 737-330 (QC)	23836/1508	ex N836Y		>YZR
☐ B-5057	Boeing 737-330 (QC)	23837/1514	ex N837Y		>YZR
☐ B-5058	Boeing 737-330 (QC)	23835/1465	ex N835A		>YZR
☐ B-5059	Boeing 737-322F	24362/1696	ex N356UA		>YZR
☐ B-5060	Boeing 737-76N	28582/154	ex N582HE		>CXI
☐ B-5061	Boeing 737-76N	28583/163	ex N583HE		>CXI
☐ B-5062	Boeing 737-76N	28585/173	ex N585HE		>CXI
☐ B-5091	Boeing 737-705	29091/230	ex VH-VBW		>LKE
☐ B-5092	Boeing 737-705	29092/260	ex VH-VBX		>CGN
☐ B-5248	Boeing 737-790/W	30626/1273	ex N629AS		>LKE
☐ B-5249	Boeing 737-790	33011/1291	ex N645AS		>LKE
☐ B-2157	Boeing 737-84P/W	32600/1015	ex N1786B		
☐ B-2158	Boeing 737-84P/W	32601/1033			
☐ B-2159	Boeing 737-84P/W	32599/972	ex N1787B		
☐ B-2636	Boeing 737-86N	28574/67	ex N574GE		
☐ B-2638	Boeing 737-8Q8	28220/212	ex N361LF	special palm c/s	
☐ B-2646	Boeing 737-8Q8	28056/273	ex N371LF	special orchid c/s	
☐ B-2647	Boeing 737-84P	29947/345	ex N1787B	special Happy Sea Wave c/s	
☐ B-2651	Boeing 737-84P	30474/607	ex N1787B		
☐ B-2675	Boeing 737-86Q/W	32885/1147			
☐ B-2676	Boeing 737-84P/W	32602/1170			
☐ B-2677	Boeing 737-84P/W	32604/1191			
☐ B-5080	Boeing 737-86N	28614/477	ex N614LS		>CXH
☐ B-5081	Boeing 737-86N	30231/515	ex N302LS		>CXH
☐ B-5082	Boeing 737-883	30193/587	ex LN-RCS		>CXH
☐ B-5083	Boeing 737-883	28319/548	ex LN-RCO		
☐ B-5089	Boeing 737-883	28320/551	ex OY-KKU		
☐ B-5090	Boeing 737-883	28321/577	ex LN-RCR		
☐ B-5115	Boeing 737-8FH/W	29640/1649			>CGN
☐ B-5116	Boeing 737-8FH/W	29672/1745	ex N1786B		>CGN
☐ B-5135	Boeing 737-84P/W	32603/1766	ex N1786B		
☐ B-5136	Boeing 737-84P/W	32605/1796	ex B-KBE		
☐ B-5137	Boeing 737-84P/W	32606/1805	ex B-KBF		
☐ B-5138	Boeing 737-84P/W	32607/1832			>CXH
☐ B-5139	Boeing 737-84P/W	32608/1855			>CXH
☐ B-5141	Boeing 737-84P/W	34030/1800			>CXH
☐ B-5153	Boeing 737-84P/W	34029/1921			>CXH
☐ B-5180	Boeing 737-8FH/W	35089/2042			>CGN
☐ B-5181	Boeing 737-8FH/W	35090/2073			>CGN
☐ B-5182	Boeing 737-808/W	34708/2097			
☐ B-5337	Boeing 737-84P/W	35747/2433			>GDC
☐ B-5338	Boeing 737-84P/W	35749/2330			
☐ B-5346	Boeing 737-8BK/W	29673/2373	ex N1786B		
☐ B-5358	Boeing 737-84P/W	35077/2419	ex N1787B		
☐ B-5359	Boeing 737-8FH/W	35101/2459	ex N1786B		
☐ B-5371	Boeing 737-84P/W	35752/2556	ex N1787B		
☐ B-5372	Boeing 737-84P/W	35758/2593			
☐ B-5373	Boeing 737-84P/W	35754/2618	ex N1787B		
☐ B-5375	Boeing 737-84P/W	35762/2648			
☐ B-5403	Boeing 737-84P/W	35756/2691			
☐ B-5405	Boeing 737-84P/W	35759/2668			
☐ B-5406	Boeing 737-84P/W	35760/2678			
☐ B-5407	Boeing 737-808/W	34967/2239	ex B-HXF		
☐ B-5408	Boeing 737-84P/W	35764/2778	ex N1786B		
☐ B-5409	Boeing 737-808/W	34968/2265	ex B-KXG		
☐ B-5416	Boeing 737-84P/W	34031/2801	ex N1780B		
☐ B-5417	Boeing 737-86N/W	35639/2821			
☐ B-5418	Boeing 737-86N/W	36541/2769	ex N1786B		
☐ B-5427	Boeing 737-8Q8/W	35285/2772	ex N1787B		

☐ B-5428	Boeing 737-86N/W	36542/2806	ex N1796B	
☐ B-5429	Boeing 737-86N/W	36543/2831	ex N1796B	
☐ B-5430	Boeing 737-84P/W	34032/2827	ex N1787B	
☐ B-5439	Boeing 737-808/W	34707/2046	ex B-KBH	
☐ B-5449	Boeing 737-808/W	34971/2400	ex B-KXH	
☐ B-5462	Boeing 737-84P/W	36780/3095	ex N1796B	
☐ B-5465	Boeing 737-84P/W	34033/2854	ex N1787B	
☐ B-5466	Boeing 737-84P/W	34034/2912		
☐ B-5467	Boeing 737-84P/W	36779/2885		
☐ B-5478	Boeing 737-84P/W	35751/3038	ex N1786B	
☐ B-5479	Boeing 737-84P/W	35753/3066	ex N1786B	
☐ B-5480	Boeing 737-86N/W	35648/2973		
☐ B-5481	Boeing 737-86N/W	35649/2981		
☐ B-5482	Boeing 737-84P/W	35748/2938	ex N1786B	
☐ B-5483	Boeing 737-84P/W	35750/3007		
☐ B-5502	Boeing 737-84P/W	35757/3192	ex N1786B	♦
☐ B-5503	Boeing 737-84P/W	36782/3186		♦
☐ B-5520	Boeing 737-84P/W	35765/3344		♦
☐ B-5521	Boeing 737-84P/W	35766/3313		♦
☐ B-5522	Boeing 737-84P/W	36781/3278	ex N1786B	♦
☐ B-5538	Boeing 737-84P/W	36783/3382		♦
☐ B-5539	Boeing 737-84P/W	35763/3378		♦
☐ B-	Boeing 737-84P/W			o/o
☐ B-	Boeing 737-84P/W			o/o
☐ B-	Boeing 737-84P/W			o/o
☐ B-	Boeing 737-84P/W			o/o
☐ B-	Boeing 737-84P/W			o/o
☐ B-KBI	Boeing 737-808/W	34709/2121	ex N1787B	>CRK
☐ B-KBK	Boeing 737-84P/W	35072/2155	ex N1786B	>CRK
☐ B-KBM	Boeing 737-84P/W	35076/2380		>CRK
☐ B-KBQ	Boeing 737-84P/W	35274/2570		>HKE
☐ B-KBR	Boeing 737-84P/W	35276/2611		>HKE
☐ B-KBT	Boeing 737-84P/W	37422/3241		>CRK♦
☐ B-KXE	Boeing 737-808/W	34710/2144		>HKE
☐ B-2490	Boeing 767-34PER	33047/889		
☐ B-2491	Boeing 767-34PER	33048/891		
☐ B-2492	Boeing 767-34PER	33049/893		

HEBEI AIRLINES (NS/DBH) Shenyang

☐ B-3040	Embraer ERJ-145LR	145317	ex PT-SMI	<CSC
☐ B-3041	Embraer ERJ-145LR	145349	ex PT-SNP	<CSC
☐ B-6170	Airbus A319-132	2396	ex N101LF	<CSC

HENAN AIRLINES (VD/KPA) Xian

☐ B-7691	Canadair CRJ-200LR	7218	ex N37218	
☐ B-3126	Embraer ERJ-190LR	19000201	ex PT-SGJ	
☐ B-3131	Embraer ERJ-190LR	19000220	ex PT-SIB	
☐ B-3132	Embraer ERJ-190LR	19000263	ex PT-	
☐ B-3133	Embraer ERJ-190LR	19000264	ex PT-TLE	

JADE CARGO INTERNATIONAL Jade Cargo (JI/JAE) Shenzhen (SZX)

☐ B-2421	Boeing 747-4EVERF	35169/1391	ex N1794B	
☐ B-2422	Boeing 747-4EVERF	35173/1387		
☐ B-2423	Boeing 747-4EVERF	35174/1398		
☐ B-2439	Boeing 747-4EVERF	35170/1376		
☐ B-2440	Boeing 747-4EVERF	35171/1380		
☐ B-2441	Boeing 747-4EVERF	35172/1383		

JIANGNAN UNIVERSAL AVIATION Changzhou-West Suburbs (CZX)

☐ B-3865	AVIC II Y-11	(11)0410		
☐ B-3866	AVIC II Y-11	(11)0104		
☐ B-3867	AVIC II Y-11	(11)0206		
☐ B-3868	AVIC II Y-11	(11)0109		
☐ B-3821	Harbin Y-12 II	0032	ex (JU-1019)	
☐ B-3823	Harbin Y-12 II	0068	ex (JU-1021)	

JUNEYAO AIRLINES Air Juneyao (HO/DKH) Shanghai-Hongqiao (SHA)

☐ B-6232	Airbus A319-112	2879	ex D-AVXN	
☐ B-6233	Airbus A319-112	2913	ex D-AVWZ	
☐ B-6298	Airbus A320-214	2975	ex F-WWDO	
☐ B-6311	Airbus A320-214	3027	ex F-WWBM	

☐ B-6338	Airbus A320-214	3368	ex F-WWDE	
☐ B-6340	Airbus A320-214	3234	ex F-WWBH	
☐ B-6341	Airbus A320-214	3268	ex F-WWBU	
☐ B-6381	Airbus A320-214	3485	ex F-WWIG	
☐ B-6395	Airbus A320-214	3596	ex F-WWDI	
☐ B-6396	Airbus A320-214	3605	ex F-WWDN	
☐ B-6572	Airbus A320-214	3967	ex F-WWIF	
☐ B-6602	Airbus A320-214	3984	ex F-WWBJ	
☐ B-6618	Airbus A320-214	4102	ex F-WWDO	
☐ B-6619	Airbus A320-214	4154	ex F-WWBK	
☐ B-6640	Airbus A320-214	4064	ex B-515L	
☐ B-6670	Airbus A320-214	4276	ex F-WWDU	♦
☐ B-6717	Airbus A320-214	4401	ex F-WWBK	♦
☐ B-6735	Airbus A320-214	4429	ex B-	♦
☐ B-	Airbus A320-214		ex	o/o♦
☐ B-	Airbus A320-214		ex	o/o♦
☐ B-	Airbus A320-214		ex	o/o♦
☐ B-	Airbus A320-214		ex	o/o♦
☐ B-	Airbus A320-214		ex	o/o♦

KUNMING AIRLINES — (KY/KNA) — Kunming (KMG)

☐ B-2635	Boeing 737-79K	29191/127	ex N1786B	<CSZ♦
☐ B-2668	Boeing 737-78S	30171/681	ex N1786B	<CSZ♦
☐ B-2678	Boeing 737-76N	32244/895	ex N315ML	
☐ B-2679	Boeing 737-76N	29893/710	ex N313ML	

LUCKY AIRLINES — Lucky Air (8L/LKE) — Dali City (DLU)

☐ B-5060	Boeing 737-76N	28582/154	ex N582HE	<CXI
☐ B-5061	Boeing 737-76N	28583/163	ex N583HE	<CXI
☐ B-5091	Boeing 737-705	29091/230	ex VH-VBW	<CHH
☐ B-5246	Boeing 737-7Q8/W	30674/1511	ex N751AL	
☐ B-5248	Boeing 737-790/W	30626/1273	ex N629AS	<CHH
☐ B-5249	Boeing 737-790	33011/1291	ex N645AS	<CHH
☐ B-5268	Boeing 737-790/W	30662/1382	ex N648AS	♦
☐ B-5272	Boeing 737-790/W	30663/1386	ex N649AS	♦

OK AIRWAYS — Okayjet (BK/OKA) — Tianjin (TSN)

☐ B-2117	Boeing 737-3Q8 (SF)	24961/2133	ex N141LF	
☐ B-2863	Boeing 737-83N/W	30673/1500	ex N333TZ	
☐ B-2865	Boeing 737-83N/W	30679/1404	ex N332TZ	
☐ B-5367	Boeing 737-8Q8/W	30733/2452	ex N1786B	
☐ B-5562	Boeing 737-8HO/W	37934/3491		♦
☐ B-5571	Boeing 737-86N/W	35643/2884	ex N546MS	♦
☐ B-5573	Boeing 737-8HO/W	37932/3498		♦
☐ B-5575	Boeing 737-8AS/W	33554/1418	ex N598MS	♦
☐ B-	Boeing 737-8HO/W			o/o♦
☐ B-	Boeing 737-8HO/W			o/o♦
☐ B-	Boeing 737-8HO/W			o/o♦
☐ B-	Boeing 737-8HO/W			o/o♦

RAINBOW JET — Cai Hong (RBW) — Jinan (TNA)

☐ B-3630	Cessna 208B Caravan I	208B0883	ex N12285	
☐ B-3631	Cessna 208 Caravan I	20800333	ex N1228V	FP
☐ B-3632	Cessna 208 Caravan I	20800332	ex N1284F	FP
☐ B-3636	Cessna 208 Caravan I	20800338	ex N1321L	FP
☐ B-3639	Cessna 208 Caravan I	20800354	ex N5283U	FP

SF AIRLINES

☐ B-2899	Boeing 757-21B(SF)	24401/232	ex N401AN	

SHAN XI AIRLINES — Shanxi (CXI) — Taiyuan-Wusu (TYN)

☐ B-3701	AVIC I Y7-100C	12705		[TYN]
☐ B-3702	AVIC I Y7-100C	12707		[TYN]
☐ B-3703	AVIC I Y7-100C	12708		[TYN]
☐ B-5060	Boeing 737-76N	28582/154	ex N582HE	>LKE
☐ B-5061	Boeing 737-76N	28583/163	ex N583HE	>LKE
☐ B-5062	Boeing 737-76N	28585/173	ex N585HE	<CHH

SHANDONG AIRLINES — Shandong (SC/CDG) — Jinan (TNA)

☐ B-2111	Boeing 737-36Q	29405/3047	ex N405GT	
☐ B-2877	Boeing 737-33V	29331/3062	ex G-EZYG	
☐ B-2878	Boeing 737-36Q	28760/2989	ex N307FL	

☐ B-2961	Boeing 737-35N	28156/2774		
☐ B-2962	Boeing 737-35N	28157/2778		
☐ B-2968	Boeing 737-35N	28158/2818		
☐ B-2995	Boeing 737-35N	29315/3054		
☐ B-2996	Boeing 737-35N	29316/3065		
☐ B-5065	Boeing 737-36Q	28664/2940	ex N287CH	
☐ B-5066	Boeing 737-36Q	28761/3011	ex N286CH	
☐ B-5098	Boeing 737-36Q	29140/3013	ex N914CH	
☐ B-5099	Boeing 737-36Q	29189/3057	ex N918CH	
☐ B-5111	Boeing 737-85N/W	33660/1752		
☐ B-5117	Boeing 737-85N/W	33661/1770		
☐ B-5118	Boeing 737-85N/W	33664/1726		
☐ B-5119	Boeing 737-85N/W	33665/1775	ex N1781B	
☐ B-5205	Boeing 737-75N/W	33654/1790		
☐ B-5206	Boeing 737-75N/W	33666/1742	ex N1779B	
☐ B-5207	Boeing 737-75N/W	33663/1838	ex N1787B	
☐ B-5321	Boeing 737-8AL/W	35073/2197		
☐ B-5331	Boeing 737-8AL/W	35075/2287		
☐ B-5332	Boeing 737-8FH/W	35095/2295		
☐ B-5333	Boeing 737-8FH/W	35096/2336	ex N1782B	
☐ B-5335	Boeing 737-8FH/W	35097/2345	ex N1787B	
☐ B-5336	Boeing 737-8FH/W	35098/2361		
☐ B-5347	Boeing 737-85N/W	36190/2429		
☐ B-5348	Boeing 737-85N/W	36191/2453	ex N1786B	
☐ B-5349	Boeing 737-85N/W	36192/2642		
☐ B-5350	Boeing 737-85N/W	36193/2669	ex N1786B	
☐ B-5351	Boeing 737-85N/W	36194/2684		
☐ B-5352	Boeing 737-85N/W	36195/2823		
☐ B-5450	Boeing 737-85N/W	36773/2874	ex N1786B	
☐ B-5451	Boeing 737-85N/W	36776/2998		
☐ B-5452	Boeing 737-85N/W	36777/3045	ex N1796B	
☐ B-5453	Boeing 737-85N/W	36778/3277		◆
☐ B-5513	Boeing 737-86N/W	36546/3293	ex N1796B	◆
☐ B-5526	Boeing 737-8FZ/W	31717/3237	ex N1796B	◆
☐ B-5536	Boeing 737-8AL/W	37424/3342	ex N1786B	◆
☐ B-5541	Boeing 737-85N/W	40882/3368	ex N1789B	◆
☐ B-5542	Boeing 737-85N/W	40883/3383	ex N1786B	◆
☐ B-5543	Boeing 737-86N/W	39392/3447	ex N1786B	◆
☐ B-3001	Canadair CRJ-200LR	7565	ex C-FMNH	>HXA
☐ B-3005	Canadair CRJ-200LR	7435	ex C-FMKW	
☐ B-3006	Canadair CRJ-200LR	7443	ex C-FMLV	
☐ B-3007	Canadair CRJ-200LR	7498	ex C-FMLF	
☐ B-3008	Canadair CRJ-200LR	7512	ex B-604L	
☐ B-3009	Canadair CRJ-200LR	7522	ex C-FMMY	
☐ B-3012	Canadair CRJ-200LR	7557	ex C-FMLB	>HXA
☐ B-3079	Canadair CRJ-701ER	10118	ex C-	
☐ B-3080	Canadair CRJ-701ER	10120	ex C-	

SHANGHAI AIRLINES	**Shanghai Air (FM/CSH)**	**Shanghai-Hongqiao (SHA)**

Member of Star Alliance, merging with China Eastern

☐ B-6591	Airbus A321-231	3969	ex D-AVZM	
☐ B-6592	Airbus A321-231	4045	ex D-AVZL	
☐ B-6642	Airbus A321-231	4198	ex D-AVZE	◆
☐ B-6643	Airbus A321-231	4209	ex D-AVZF	◆
☐ B-6668	Airbus A321-231	4378	ex D-AVZX	◆
☐ B-2153	Boeing 737-8Q8	28242/942	ex N1786B	
☐ B-2167	Boeing 737-8Q8	30631/1047		
☐ B-2168	Boeing 737-8Q8	30632/1086		
☐ B-2577	Boeing 737-76D	30168/600	ex N1786B	
☐ B-2631	Boeing 737-7Q8	28212/35	ex N301LF	
☐ B-2632	Boeing 737-7Q8	28216/122	ex N1795B	
☐ B-2663	Boeing 737-7AD	28437/72	ex N701EW	>CUA
☐ B-2686	Boeing 737-8Q8	28251/1200		
☐ B-2688	Boeing 737-86D/W	33471/1192	ex N60668	
☐ B-2913	Boeing 737-76D	30167/550	ex N1786B	
☐ B-2997	Boeing 737-7Q8	28223/272	ex N1786B	>CUA
☐ B-5076	Boeing 737-86N	32739/1434		
☐ B-5077	Boeing 737-86N	32742/1464		
☐ B-5088	Boeing 737-82R	30666/1460	ex N171LF	
☐ B-5130	Boeing 737-8Q8	32801/1666		
☐ B-5131	Boeing 737-8Q8	30686/1704	ex N1784B	

☐ B-5132	Boeing 737-8Q8	30685/1789		
☐ B-5140	Boeing 737-8Q8	30698/1911		
☐ B-5142	Boeing 737-8Q8	30700/1942	ex N1782B	
☐ B-5143	Boeing 737-86N/W	32691/2033		
☐ B-5145	Boeing 737-8Q8	33007/1986		
☐ B-5148	Boeing 737-86N/W	34254/1897		
☐ B-5183	Boeing 737-8Q8/W	30711/2159	ex N1787B	>CUA
☐ B-5185	Boeing 737-8Q8/W	30715/2230		
☐ B-5260	Boeing 737-76D/W	35777/3037		
☐ B-5261	Boeing 737-76D/W	35778/3064	ex N1786B	
☐ B-5315	Boeing 737-86D	35767/2316		
☐ B-5316	Boeing 737-86D	35768/2362		
☐ B-5320	Boeing 737-8Q8/W	30718/2251	ex N1786B	
☐ B-5323	Boeing 737-8Q8/W	30725/2292		>CUA
☐ B-5330	Boeing 737-86N/W	35212/2277	ex N1786B	
☐ B-5353	Boeing 737-8Q8	30728/2386		
☐ B-5368	Boeing 737-8Q8	35273/2567		
☐ B-5369	Boeing 737-8Q8/W	35281/2709		
☐ B-5370	Boeing 737-8Q8/W	35271/2551	ex N1786B	
☐ B-5393	Boeing 737-86D/W	35769/2632		
☐ B-5395	Boeing 737-86D/W	35770/2698	ex N1786B	
☐ B-5396	Boeing 737-86D/W	35771/2740	ex N1786B	
☐ B-5399	Boeing 737-86D/W	35224/2617		>CUA
☐ B-5460	Boeing 737-86D/W	35772/3047		
☐ B-5461	Boeing 737-86D/W	35773/2939	ex N1787B	
☐ B-5470	Boeing 737-86D/W	35774/3010	ex N1786B	
☐ B-5471	Boeing 737-86D/W	35775/3098	ex N1796B	
☐ B-5523	Boeing 737-86D/W	35776/3360		♦
☐ B-5545	Boeing 737-86N/W	36803/3376		♦
☐ B-5546	Boeing 737-86N/W	39391/3431	ex N1786B	♦
☐ B-5548	Boeing 737-86N/W	36807/3479	ex N1795B	♦
☐ B-5549	Boeing 737-86N/W	37888/3470	ex N1796B	♦
☐ B-5550	Boeing 737-86N/W	39393/3483		♦
☐ B-2833	Boeing 757-26D	27152/560		
☐ B-2834	Boeing 757-26D	27183/576		
☐ B-2842	Boeing 757-26D	27342/626		
☐ B-2843	Boeing 757-26D	27681/684		
☐ B-2850	Boeing 757-231	30338/891	ex N725TW	
☐ B-2857	Boeing 757-26D	33959/1044		
☐ B-2858	Boeing 757-26D	33960/1045		
☐ B-2875	Boeing 757-26D	33966/1049	ex N1795B	
☐ B-2876	Boeing 757-26D	33967/1050		last 757 built
☐ B-2880	Boeing 757-26D	33961/1046	ex N1795B	
☐ B-2498	Boeing 767-36D	27684/849		
☐ B-2500	Boeing 767-36DER	35155/946		
☐ B-2563	Boeing 767-36D	27309/546		
☐ B-2566	Boeing 767-36DER	35156/950		
☐ B-2567	Boeing 767-36D	27685/686		
☐ B-2570	Boeing 767-36D	27941/770		Star Alliance Colours
☐ B-5018	Boeing 767-3Q8ER	28207/695	ex N635TW	
☐ B-3011	Canadair CRJ-200ER	7556	ex C-FMKZ	
☐ B-3018	Canadair CRJ-200ER	7453	ex C-FMNQ	
☐ B-3020	Canadair CRJ-200ER	7459	ex C-FMMQ	
☐ B-3075	Canadair CRJ-200ER	7226	ex G-DUOF	
☐ B-7698	Canadair CRJ-200ER	7247	ex G-DUOG	

SHANGHAI CARGO | | | (F4/SHQ) | Shanghai-Pu Dong Intl (PVG) |

☐ B-2176	McDonnell-Douglas MD-11F	48415/576	ex N103EV	
☐ B-2177	McDonnell-Douglas MD-11F	48544/580	ex N105EV	
☐ B-2178	McDonnell-Douglas MD-11F	48543/572	ex N7821B	
☐ B-2179	McDonnell-Douglas MD-11F	48545/587	ex N106BV	
☐ B-2808	Boeing 757-26D (PCF)	24471/231	ex N1792B	Frtr
☐ B-2809	Boeing 757-26D (PCF)	24472/235	ex N5573B	Frtr

SHENZHEN AIRLINES | | Shenzhen Air (ZH/CSZ) | | Shenzhen (SZX) |

☐ B-6153	Airbus A319-115	2841	ex D-AVYM	
☐ B-6159	Airbus A319-115	2905	ex D-AVWQ	
☐ B-6165	Airbus A319-115X	2935	ex D-AVWM	VIP [CJ]
☐ B-6196	Airbus A319-115	2672	ex D-AVYK	
☐ B-6197	Airbus A319-115	2684	ex D-AVWM	
☐ B-	Airbus A319-115		ex D-AV	o/o

☐ B-2416	Airbus A320-214	0994	ex EC-HAB		
☐ B-6286	Airbus A320-214	2909	ex F-WWDU		
☐ B-6296	Airbus A320-214	2973	ex F-WWDN		
☐ B-6297	Airbus A320-214	2980	ex F-WWBP		
☐ B-6312	Airbus A320-214	3131	ex F-WWBK		
☐ B-6313	Airbus A320-214	3132	ex F-WWBP		
☐ B-6315	Airbus A320-214	3153	ex F-WWBZ		
☐ B-6316	Airbus A320-214	3206	ex F-WWII		
☐ B-6351	Airbus A320-214	3366	ex F-WWIU		
☐ B-6352	Airbus A320-214	3383	ex F-WWDN		
☐ B-6357	Airbus A320-214	3440	ex F-WWDZ		
☐ B-6358	Airbus A320-214	3435	ex F-WWDV		
☐ B-6359	Airbus A320-214	3456	ex D-AVVA		
☐ B-6360	Airbus A320-214	3528	ex F-WWDV		
☐ B-6377	Airbus A320-214	3599	ex F-WWDK		
☐ B-6392	Airbus A320-214	3696	ex D-AVVA		
☐ B-6563	Airbus A320-214	3698	ex B-503L		
☐ B-6565	Airbus A320-214	3971	ex F-WWIO		
☐ B-6566	Airbus A320-214	3855	ex F-WWDK		
☐ B-6567	Airbus A320-214	3887	ex F-WWBS		
☐ B-6568	Airbus A320-214	3898	ex F-WWDN		
☐ B-6569	Airbus A320-214	3848	ex F-WWDE		
☐ B-6570	Airbus A320-214	4010	ex B-512L		
☐ B-6571	Airbus A320-232	3935	ex F-WWDO		
☐ B-6589	Airbus A320-214	4028	ex F-WWIA		
☐ B-6613	Airbus A320-232	4176	ex F-WWDY		
☐ B-6615	Airbus A320-232	4214	ex F-WWIM		♦
☐ B-6647	Airbus A320-214	4226	ex F-WWBT		♦
☐ B-6648	Airbus A320-214	4159	ex B-519L		♦
☐ B-6650	Airbus A320-232	4300	ex F-WWBQ		♦
☐ B-6690	Airbus A320-232	4359	ex F-WWDL		♦
☐ B-6691	Airbus A320-232	4409	ex D-AVVE		♦
☐ B-6720	Airbus A320-232	4474	ex F-WWDC		♦
☐ B-6721	Airbus A320-232	4515	ex D-AXAF		♦
☐ B-6722	Airbus A320-232	4531	ex F-WWDQ		♦
☐ B-	Airbus A320-232		ex		o/o♦
☐ B-	Airbus A320-232		ex		o/o♦
☐ B-	Airbus A320-232		ex		o/o♦
☐ B-	Airbus A320-232		ex		o/o♦
☐ B-	Airbus A320-232		ex		o/o♦
☐ B-	Airbus A320-232		ex		o/o♦
☐ B-	Airbus A320-232		ex		o/o♦
☐ B-	Airbus A320-232		ex		o/o♦
☐ B-	Airbus A320-232		ex		o/o♦
☐ B-	Airbus A320-232		ex		o/o♦
☐ B-2601	Boeing 737-36N	28559/2882	ex EI-CUL		
☐ B-2602	Boeing 737-36N	28573/3041	ex N573LS		
☐ B-2687	Boeing 737-36N	28555/2846	ex B-2610		
☐ B-2932	Boeing 737-3K9	25787/2302	ex N41069		
☐ B-2933	Boeing 737-3K9	25788/2331	ex N4113D		
☐ B-2939	Boeing 737-31L	27345/2625			
☐ B-2940	Boeing 737-31L	27346/2636			
☐ B-2971	Boeing 737-3Q8	25373/2290	ex N221LF		
☐ B-2972	Boeing 737-33A	27463/2831			
☐ B-2633	Boeing 737-79K	29190/110	ex N1786B		
☐ B-2635	Boeing 737-79K	29191/127	ex N1786B		>KMG
☐ B-2666	Boeing 737-78S	30169/631	ex N1786B		
☐ B-2667	Boeing 737-78S	30170/654			
☐ B-2668	Boeing 737-78S	30171/681	ex N1786B		>KMG
☐ B-2669	Boeing 737-77L	32722/1023	ex N1786B		
☐ B-2691	Boeing 737-8Q8	30628/808	ex N802SY		
☐ B-2692	Boeing 737-8Q8	28241/841	ex N803SY		
☐ B-5025	Boeing 737-7BX	30742/864	ex N366ML		
☐ B-5026	Boeing 737-7BX	30741/823	ex N367ML		
☐ B-5049	Boeing 737-86N	28639/772	ex N639SH		
☐ B-5050	Boeing 737-86N	28643/828	ex N643SH		
☐ B-5073	Boeing 737-8Q8/W	30680/1402			
☐ B-5075	Boeing 737-8Q8	30692/1410			
☐ B-5078	Boeing 737-8Q8	30690/1414	ex N1779B		
☐ B-5079	Boeing 737-8Q8	30693/1422			
☐ B-5102	Boeing 737-97L	33644/1750			
☐ B-5103	Boeing 737-97L	33645/1760			
☐ B-5105	Boeing 737-97L	33646/1764	ex N1784B		
☐ B-5106	Boeing 737-97L	33648/1722			
☐ B-5109	Boeing 737-97L	33649/1755			

☐ B-5186	Boeing 737-8BK	33020/2103			
☐ B-5187	Boeing 737-8BK	33828/2124			
☐ B-5317	Boeing 737-86N/W	32686/2175	ex N1781B		
☐ B-5322	Boeing 737-86N/W	32688/2218			
☐ B-5345	Boeing 737-86N/W	35215/2306	ex N1780B		
☐ B-5357	Boeing 737-8AL/W	35081/2519	ex N1787B		
☐ B-5360	Boeing 737-86J/W	30062/485	ex D-ABAW		<BER
☐ B-5361	Boeing 737-86J/W	30063/517	ex D-ABAX		<BER
☐ B-5362	Boeing 737-86J/W	30499/567	ex D-ABAY		<BER
☐ B-5363	Boeing 737-86J/W	30500/593	ex D-ABAZ		<BER
☐ B-5365	Boeing 737-86J/W	30501/619	ex D-ABAC		<BER
☐ B-5377	Boeing 737-8AL/W	35079/2555	ex N1786B		
☐ B-5378	Boeing 737-8AL/W	35085/2563	ex N1787B		
☐ B-5379	Boeing 737-8AL/W	35087/2605	ex N1786B		
☐ B-5380	Boeing 737-87L/W	35527/2616			
☐ B-5381	Boeing 737-87L/W	35528/2631		City of Hohhot	
☐ B-5400	Boeing 737-87L/W	35529/2677			
☐ B-5401	Boeing 737-87L/W	35530/2703	ex N1786B		
☐ B-5402	Boeing 737-87L/W	35531/2726	ex N1786B		
☐ B-5410	Boeing 737-8AL/W	35088/2771			
☐ B-5411	Boeing 737-87L/W	35532/2851			
☐ B-5412	Boeing 737-87L/W	35533/2900			
☐ B-5413	Boeing 737-87L/W	35535/2895	· ex N1786B		
☐ B-5440	Boeing 737-87L/W	35534/3003			
☐ B-5441	Boeing 737-87L/W	35536/3019	ex N1786B		

SHUANGYANG AVIATION — Shuangyang (CSY) — Anshun (AOG)

☐ B-3811	Harbin Y-12 II	0012	Combi
☐ B-3812	Harbin Y-12 II	0024	Sprayer
☐ B-3813	Harbin Y-12 II	0025	Sprayer
☐ B-3814	Harbin Y-12 II	0026	Sprayer
☐ B-3895	AVIC II Y-11	(11)0401	
☐ B-3896	AVIC II Y-11	(11)0402	
☐ B-3897	AVIC II Y-11	(11)0403	
☐ B-3898	AVIC II Y-11	(11)0404	

SICHUAN AIRLINES — Chuanhang (3U/CSC) — Chengdu (CTU)

☐ B-2298	Airbus A319-133	2534	ex D-AVYM	
☐ B-2299	Airbus A319-133	2597	ex D-AVXN	
☐ B-2300	Airbus A319-133	2639	ex D-AVWK	
☐ B-6043	Airbus A319-133	2313	ex D-AVYI	
☐ B-6045	Airbus A319-133	2348	ex D-AVYH	
☐ B-6054	Airbus A319-133	2510	ex D-AVWC	
☐ B-6170	Airbus A319-132	2396	ex N101LF	>DBH
☐ B-6171	Airbus A319-132	2431	ex N112CG	<ACG
☐ B-6173	Airbus A319-133	3114	ex D-AYYA	
☐ B-6175	Airbus A319-133	3116	ex D-AYYB	
☐ B-6176	Airbus A319-133	3124	ex D-AYYC	
☐ B-6185	Airbus A319-133	3680	ex D-AVYY	
☐ B-6406	Airbus A319-133	3962	ex D-AVXP	
☐ B-6410	Airbus A319-133	4018	ex D-AVYG	
☐ B-	Airbus A319-133		ex	o/o♦
☐ B-2340	Airbus A320-233	0540	ex F-WWDK	
☐ B-2341	Airbus A320-232	0551	ex F-WWBI	
☐ B-2342	Airbus A320-232	0556	ex F-WWIL	
☐ B-2348	Airbus A320-233	0912	ex EI-TAA	
☐ B-2373	Airbus A320-233	0919	ex F-WWIC	
☐ B-2397	Airbus A320-233	1013	ex F-WWDP	
☐ B-6025	Airbus A320-232	0573	ex B-MAD	
☐ B-6026	Airbus A320-232	0582	ex B-MAE	
☐ B-6027	Airbus A320-233	1007	ex N460TA	
☐ B-6049	Airbus A320-233	0902	ex (D-ANNI)	
☐ B-6256	Airbus A320-232	0872	ex N872CV	
☐ B-6257	Airbus A320-232	0874	ex EI-TAE	
☐ B-6295	Airbus A320-233	1500	ex N481TA	
☐ B-6321	Airbus A320-232	3210	ex F-WWIK	
☐ B-6322	Airbus A320-232	3158	ex F-WWDP	
☐ B-6323	Airbus A320-232	3167	ex F-WWIM	
☐ B-6325	Airbus A320-232	3196	ex F-WWIE	
☐ B-6347	Airbus A320-232	3386	ex F-WWDP	
☐ B-6348	Airbus A320-232	3449	ex F-WWIY	
☐ B-6388	Airbus A320-232	3591	ex B-501L	
☐ B-6621	Airbus A320-232	4068	ex F-WWBI	
☐ B-6697	Airbus A320-232	4288	ex F-WWIS	♦

☐ B-6700	Airbus A320-232	4326	ex F-WWIA		♦
☐ B-6718	Airbus A320-232	4420	ex D-AZAF		♦
☐ B-6719	Airbus A320-232	4424	ex F-WWBD		♦
☐ B-	Airbus A320-232		ex	o/o♦	
☐ B-	Airbus A320-232		ex	o/o♦	
☐ B-	Airbus A320-232		ex	o/o♦	
☐ B-	Airbus A320-232		ex	o/o♦	
☐ B-	Airbus A320-232		ex	o/o♦	
☐ B-	Airbus A320-232		ex	o/o♦	
☐ B-2286	Airbus A321-131	0550	ex N550BR		
☐ B-2293	Airbus A321-131	0591	ex N451LF		
☐ B-2370	Airbus A321-231	0878	ex D-AVZF		
☐ B-2371	Airbus A321-231	0915	ex D-AVZM		
☐ B-6285	Airbus A321-231	1060	ex HL7590		
☐ B-6300	Airbus A321-231	1293	ex HL7549		
☐ B-6387	Airbus A321-231	3583	ex D-AVZE		
☐ B-6551	Airbus A321-231	3730	ex D-AZAI		
☐ B-6590	Airbus A321-231	3893	ex D-AVZV		
☐ B-6598	Airbus A321-231	3996	ex D-AZAQ		
☐ B-	Airbus A321-231		ex	o/o♦	
☐ B-	Airbus A321-231		ex	o/o♦	
☐ B-	Airbus A321-231		ex	o/o♦	
☐ B-6517	Airbus A330-240	1138	ex F-WWYZ		♦
☐ B-6518	Airbus A330-240	1082	ex F-WWYZ		♦
☐ B-	Airbus A330-240		ex	o/o♦	
☐ B-3040	Embraer ERJ-145LR	145317	ex PT-SMI	>DBH	
☐ B-3041	Embraer ERJ-145LR	145349	ex PT-SNP	>DBH	
☐ B-3042	Embraer ERJ-145LR	145352	ex PT-SNR		
☐ B-3043	Embraer ERJ-145LR	145377	ex PT-SQB		
☐ B-3045	Embraer ERJ-145LR	145470	ex PT-SVP		

SICHUAN AOLIN GENERAL AVIATION   Chengdu (CTU)

☐ B-3637	Cessna 208B Caravan I	208B0919	ex N1294D	
☐ B-3640	Cessna 208B Caravan I	208B0952	ex N1132X	
☐ B-3641	Cessna 208B Caravan I	208B0953	ex N1133B	

SPRING AIRLINES   Air Spring (9S/CQH)   Shanghai-Hongqiao (SHA)

☐ B-6250	Airbus A320-214	1372	ex EI-DKS		
☐ B-6280	Airbus A320-214	1286	ex N120US		
☐ B-6301	Airbus A320-214	2939	ex F-WWIO		
☐ B-6309	Airbus A320-214	3014	ex F-WWBO		
☐ B-6310	Airbus A320-214	3023	ex F-WWBZ		
☐ B-6320	Airbus A320-214	1686	ex N686RL		
☐ B-6328	Airbus A320-214	0978	ex N888CQ		
☐ B-6349	Airbus A320-214	1852	ex I-EEZC		
☐ B-6380	Airbus A320-214	1769	ex EC-JDK		
☐ B-6561	Airbus A320-214	3819	ex F-WWIO		
☐ B-6562	Airbus A320-214	3747	ex F-WWIL		
☐ B-6573	Airbus A320-214	1920	ex I-EEZD		
☐ B-6612	Airbus A320-214	4072	ex F-WWBM		
☐ B-6645	Airbus A320-214	4168	ex D-AVVQ		
☐ B-6646	Airbus A320-214	4093	ex B-516L		♦
☐ B-6667	Airbus A320-214	4244	ex F-WWDP		♦
☐ B-6705	Airbus A320-214	4331	ex D-AXAQ		♦
☐ B-6706	Airbus A320-214	4366	ex D-AXAX		♦
☐ B-6707	Airbus A320-214	4373	ex F-WWBO		♦
☐ B-6708	Airbus A320-214	4375	ex D-AVVB		♦
☐ B-	Airbus A320-214		ex	o/o♦	
☐ B-	Airbus A320-214		ex	o/o♦	
☐ B-	Airbus A320-214		ex	o/o♦	
☐ B-	Airbus A320-214		ex	o/o♦	
☐ B-	Airbus A320-214		ex	o/o♦	
☐ B-	Airbus A320-214		ex	o/o♦	
☐ B-	Airbus A320-214		ex	o/o♦	

TIANJIN AIRLINES   (GS/GCR)   Tianjin (TSN)

☐ B-3873	Dornier 328-300 (328JET)	3201	ex D-BAUU	
☐ B-3892	Dornier 328-300 (328JET)	3212	ex D-BGUU	
☐ B-3946	Dornier 328-300 (328JET)	3208	ex D-BDXI	
☐ B-3947	Dornier 328-300 (328JET)	3203	ex D-BXXX	
☐ B-3948	Dornier 328-300 (328JET)	3204	ex D-BDXT	
☐ B-3949	Dornier 328-300 (328JET)	3198	ex N328AB	

☐ B-3960	Dornier 328-300 (328JET)	3123	ex D-BDXJ	
☐ B-3961	Dornier 328-300 (328JET)	3128	ex D-BDXK	
☐ B-3962	Dornier 328-300 (328JET)	3143	ex D-BDXX	
☐ B-3963	Dornier 328-300 (328JET)	3138	ex D-BDXT	
☐ B-3965	Dornier 328-300 (328JET)	3140	ex D-BDXW	
☐ B-3966	Dornier 328-300 (328JET)	3135	ex D-BDXQ	
☐ B-3967	Dornier 328-300 (328JET)	3144	ex D-BDXB	
☐ B-3968	Dornier 328-300 (328JET)	3148	ex D-BDXE	
☐ B-3969	Dornier 328-300 (328JET)	3153	ex D-BDXN	
☐ B-3970	Dornier 328-300 (328JET)	3154	ex D-BDXP	
☐ B-3971	Dornier 328-300 (328JET)	3172	ex D-BDXJ	
☐ B-3972	Dornier 328-300 (328JET)	3175	ex D-BDXK	
☐ B-3973	Dornier 328-300 (328JET)	3158	ex D-BDXQ	
☐ B-3975	Dornier 328-300 (328JET)	3159	ex D-BDXU	
☐ B-3976	Dornier 328-300 (328JET)	3177	ex D-BDXY	
☐ B-3977	Dornier 328-300 (328JET)	3182	ex D-BDXD	
☐ B-3978	Dornier 328-300 (328JET)	3187	ex D-BDXP	
☐ B-3979	Dornier 328-300 (328JET)	3191	ex D-BDXJ	
☐ B-3982	Dornier 328-300 (328JET)	3195	ex D-BDXJ	
☐ B-3983	Dornier 328-300 (328JET)	3211	ex D-BEUU	
☐ B-3985	Dornier 328-300 (328JET)	3215	ex D-BHUU	
☐ B-3986	Dornier 328-300 (328JET)	3217	ex D-BJUU	
☐ B-3987	Dornier 328-300 (328JET)	3218	ex D-BKUU	
☐ B-3030	Embraer ERJ-145LI	14501009	ex PT-SOX	
☐ B-3031	Embraer ERJ-145LI	14501013	ex PT-SOY	
☐ B-3032	Embraer ERJ-145LI	14501019	ex PT-SOZ	
☐ B-3033	Embraer ERJ-145LI	14501022		
☐ B-3035	Embraer ERJ-145LI	14500996	ex PT-SOU	
☐ B-3036	Embraer ERJ-145LI	14501000	ex PT-S	
☐ B-3037	Embraer ERJ-145LI	14501005	ex PT-S	
☐ B-3038	Embraer ERJ-145LI	14501024		
☐ B-3039	Embraer ERJ-145LI	14500992	ex PT-SOT	
☐ B-3067	Embraer ERJ-145LI	14501036		
☐ B-3068	Embraer ERJ-145LI	14501040		
☐ B-3069	Embraer ERJ-145LI	14501043		
☐ B-3081	Embraer ERJ-145LI	14501027		
☐ B-3082	Embraer ERJ-145LI	14501030	ex PT-SZP	
☐ B-3083	Embraer ERJ-145LI	14501033		
☐ B-3085	Embraer ERJ-145LI	14501047		
☐ B-3086	Embraer ERJ-145LI	14501050		
☐ B-3087	Embraer ERJ-145LI	14501053		♦
☐ B-3088	Embraer ERJ-145LI	14501056		♦
☐ B-3089	Embraer ERJ-145LI	14501063		♦
☐ B-3091	Embraer ERJ-145LI	14501065		♦
☐ B-3092	Embraer ERJ-145LI	14501068		♦
☐ B-	Embraer ERJ-145LI	14501028		o/o♦
☐ B-	Embraer ERJ-145LI	14501059		o/o♦
☐ B-	Embraer ERJ-145LI	14501068		o/o♦
☐ B-	Embraer ERJ-145LI	14501070		o/o♦
☐ B-	Embraer ERJ-145LI	14501073		o/o♦
☐ B-3120	Embraer ERJ-190LR	19000171	ex PT-SDG	
☐ B-3121	Embraer ERJ-190LR	19000181	ex PT-SDP	
☐ B-3122	Embraer ERJ-190LR	19000186	ex PT-SDU	
☐ B-3123	Embraer ERJ-190LR	19000192	ex PT-SGA	
☐ B-3125	Embraer ERJ-190LR	19000194	ex PT-SGC	
☐ B-3127	Embraer ERJ-190LR	19000207	ex PT-SGQ	
☐ B-3128	Embraer ERJ-190LR	19000229	ex PT-SIA	
☐ B-3129	Embraer ERJ-190LR	19000246	ex PT-SIR	
☐ B-3150	Embraer ERJ-190LR	19000253	ex PT-SIY	
☐ B-3151	Embraer ERJ-190LR	19000268	ex PT-TLI	
☐ B-3152	Embraer ERJ-190LR	19000274	ex PT-TLO	
☐ B-3153	Embraer ERJ-190LR	19000284	ex PT-TLY	
☐ B-3155	Embraer ERJ-190LR	19000293	ex PT-TZH	
☐ B-3156	Embraer ERJ-190LR	19000299	ex PT-TZN	
☐ B-3157	Embraer ERJ-190LR	19000306	ex PT-TZU	
☐ B-3158	Embraer ERJ-190LR	19000313	ex PT-TXB	
☐ B-3159	Embraer ERJ-190LR	19000318	ex PT-TXG	
☐ B-3160	Embraer ERJ-190LR	19000325	ex PT-TXL	
☐ B-3161	Embraer ERJ-190LR	19000328	ex PT-TXQ	
☐ B-3162	Embraer ERJ-190LR	19000331	ex PT-TXR	
☐ B-3163	Embraer ERJ-190LR	19000335	ex PT-TXV	
☐ B-3165	Embraer ERJ-190LR	19000340	ex PT-TXZ	♦
☐ B-3166	Embraer ERJ-190LR	19000348	ex PT-XQO	♦
☐ B-3167	Embraer ERJ-190LR	19000352	ex PT-XQS	♦
☐ B-3168	Embraer ERJ-190LR	19000355	ex PT-XQU	♦

☐ B-3169	Embraer ERJ-190LR	19000369	ex PT-XNH		♦
☐ B-3170	Embraer ERJ-190LR	19000371	ex PT-XNI		♦
☐ B-3171	Embraer ERJ-190LR	19000379	ex PT-XNO		♦
☐ B-3172	Embraer ERJ-190LR	19000385	ex PT-XNT		♦
☐ B-3173	Embraer ERJ-190LR	19000394	ex PT-XUA		♦
☐ B-3175	Embraer ERJ-190LR	19000405	ex PT-TYY		♦
☐ B-3176	Embraer ERJ-190LR	19000406	ex PT-		♦
☐ B-	Embraer ERJ-190LR	190	ex PT-		o/o♦
☐ B-	Embraer ERJ-190LR	190	ex PT-		o/o♦
☐ B-	Embraer ERJ-190LR	190	ex PT-		o/o♦
☐ B-	Embraer ERJ-190LR	190	ex PT-		o/o♦
☐ B-	Embraer ERJ-190LR	190	ex PT-		o/o♦
☐ B-	Embraer ERJ-190LR	190	ex PT-		o/o♦

UNI-TOP AIRLINES (UW)

☐ B-2448	Boeing 747-2J6B (SF)	23461/628	ex N60668		[WUH]
☐ B-2450	Boeing 747-2J6B (SF)	23746/670	ex N6018N		[PEK]

WEST AIR (PN/CHB)   Chongqing (CKG)

☐ B-6412	Airbus A319-132	4262	ex B-506L		<CHH♦
☐ B-6413	Airbus A319-132	4452	ex D-AVYB		<CHH♦
☐ B-2963	Boeing 737-3Q8	26325/2772			<CHH

XIAMEN AIRLINES   Xiamen Air (MF/CXA)   Xiamen (XMN)

☐ B-2658	Boeing 737-75C	30512/637	ex N1786B		
☐ B-2659	Boeing 737-75C	30513/676			
☐ B-2991	Boeing 737-75C	29085/90			
☐ B-2992	Boeing 737-75C	29086/108	ex N1786B		
☐ B-2998	Boeing 737-75C	29042/73	ex N1786B		
☐ B-2999	Boeing 737-75C	29084/86	ex N1796B		
☐ B-5028	Boeing 737-75C	30034/1275			
☐ B-5029	Boeing 737-75C	30634/1229			
☐ B-5038	Boeing 737-7Q8	30656/1304	ex N1787B		
☐ B-5039	Boeing 737-75C	28258/1315			
☐ B-5146	Boeing 737-86N/W	34253/1866			
☐ B-5151	Boeing 737-86N/W	34255/1975			
☐ B-5152	Boeing 737-86N/W	34256/1990			
☐ B-5159	Boeing 737-85C/W	35044/2018	ex N1784B		
☐ B-5160	Boeing 737-85C/W	35045/2050			
☐ B-5161	Boeing 737-85C/W	35046/2105			
☐ B-5162	Boeing 737-85C/W	35047/2130	ex N1787B		
☐ B-5212	Boeing 737-75C	34024/1703			
☐ B-5215	Boeing 737-75C	34025/1724			
☐ B-5216	Boeing 737-75C	34026/1733			
☐ B-5218	Boeing 737-75C	34027/1767	ex N1786B		
☐ B-5219	Boeing 737-75C	34028/1771			
☐ B-5301	Boeing 737-85C/W	35048/2194			
☐ B-5302	Boeing 737-85C/W	35049/2271			
☐ B-5303	Boeing 737-85C/W	35050/2305	ex N1780B		
☐ B-5305	Boeing 737-85C/W	35051/2364			
☐ B-5306	Boeing 737-85C/W	35052/2418	ex N1786B		
☐ B-5307	Boeing 737-85C/W	35053/2447			
☐ B-5308	Boeing 737-86N/W	32687/2229			
☐ B-5309	Boeing 737-86N/W	32689/2254			
☐ B-5318	Boeing 737-85C/W	30723/2283			
☐ B-5319	Boeing 737-8FH/W	35102/2471	ex N1796B		
☐ B-5355	Boeing 737-8FH/W	35104/2495	ex N1780B		
☐ B-5382	Boeing 737-86N/W	36540/2681			
☐ B-5383	Boeing 737-86N/W	35631/2693			
☐ B-5385	Boeing 737-86N/W	35633/2741			
☐ B-5386	Boeing 737-86N/W	35634/2732			
☐ B-5388	Boeing 737-86N/W	35635/2764			
☐ B-5389	Boeing 737-86N/W	35636/2775	ex N1786B		
☐ B-5432	Boeing 737-86N/W	35641/2852			
☐ B-5433	Boeing 737-86N/W	35642/2855	ex N1796B		
☐ B-5435	Boeing 737-86N/W	35644/2922			
☐ B-5456	Boeing 737-85C/W	35054/2914	ex N1786B		
☐ B-5458	Boeing 737-85C/W	35055/3016	ex N1786B		
☐ B-5459	Boeing 737-85C/W	35057/2992			
☐ B-5476	Boeing 737-85C/W	35056/3091			
☐ B-5487	Boeing 737-85C/W	35058/3150			
☐ B-5488	Boeing 737-85C/W	37148/3104			
☐ B-5489	Boeing 737-85C/W	37149/3142			
☐ B-5498	Boeing 737-85C/W	37574/3160			
☐ B-5499	Boeing 737-85C/W	37575/3190	ex N1786B		♦

☐ B-5511	Boeing 737-85C/W	37576/3245	ex N1787B	♦
☐ B-5512	Boeing 737-85C/W	37577/3255		♦
☐ B-5529	Boeing 737-85C/W	37150/3386		♦
☐ B-5532	Boeing 737-85C/W	37151/3397		♦
☐ B-5535	Boeing 737-85C/W	37579/3424		♦
☐ B-5551	Boeing 737-84P/W	36697/3443	ex N1786B	♦
☐ B-5552	Boeing 737-84P/W	37425/3408		♦
☐ B-	Boeing 737-			o/o♦
☐ B-	Boeing 737-			o/o♦
☐ B-	Boeing 737-			o/o♦
☐ B-	Boeing 737-			o/o♦
☐ B-	Boeing 737-			o/o♦
☐ B-	Boeing 737-			o/o♦
☐ B-	Boeing 737-			o/o♦
☐ B-	Boeing 737-			o/o♦
☐ B-	Boeing 737-			o/o♦
☐ B-	Boeing 737-			o/o♦
☐ B-	Boeing 737-			o/o♦
☐ B-	Boeing 737-			o/o♦
☐ B-	Boeing 737-			o/o♦
☐ B-	Boeing 737-			o/o♦
☐ B-	Boeing 737-			o/o♦
☐ B-2828	Boeing 757-25C	25899/565		
☐ B-2829	Boeing 757-25C	25900/574		
☐ B-2848	Boeing 757-25C	27513/685		
☐ B-2849	Boeing 757-25C	27517/698		
☐ B-2862	Boeing 757-25C	34008/1047		
☐ B-2866	Boeing 757-25C	34009/1048		
☐ B-2868	Boeing 757-25C	32941/993		
☐ B-2869	Boeing 757-25C	32942/1009		

XINJIANG GENERAL AVIATION — Shihezi

☐ B-3869	AVIC II Y-11	(11)0501	
☐ B-3870	AVIC II Y-11	(11)0502	
☐ B-3885	AVIC II Y-11	(11)0301	
☐ B-3887	AVIC II Y-11	(11)0303	
☐ B-3888	AVIC II Y-11	(11)0304	
☐ B-3890	AVIC II Y-11	(11)0306	
☐ B-3891	AVIC II Y-11	(11)0307	
☐ B-3894	AVIC II Y-11	(11)0310	
☐ B-3815	Harbin Y-12 II	0023	Geological survey
☐ B-3817	Harbin Y-12 II	0029	Photographic survey
☐ B-3818	Harbin Y-12 II	0030	Photographic survey

YANGTZE RIVER EXPRESS — Yangtze River (Y8/YZR) — Shanghai-Hongqiao (SHA)

☐ B-5053	Boeing 737-322F	24378/1704	ex N357UA	<CHH
☐ B-5055	Boeing 737-330(QC)	24283/1677	ex N283A	<CHH
☐ B-5056	Boeing 737-330(QC)	23836/1508	ex N836Y	<CHH
☐ B-5057	Boeing 737-330(QC)	23837/1514	ex N837Y	<CHH
☐ B-5058	Boeing 737-330(QC)	23835/1465	ex N835A	<CHH
☐ B-5059	Boeing 737-322F	24362/1696	ex N356UA	<CHH
☐ B-2431	Boeing 747-409F	30761/1254	ex N703CL	<CAL
☐ B-2432	Boeing 747-481(SF)	28283/1142	ex N200FQ	
☐ B-2435	Boeing 747-481(SF)	28282/1133	ex N483YR	

ZHONGFEI AIRLINES — Zhongfei (CFZ) — Xi'an-Yanliang

☐ B-3820	Harbin Y-12 II	0031	
☐ B-4103	Cessna 550 Citation II	550-0301	Calibrator
☐ B-4104	Cessna 550 Citation II	550-0297	Calibrator
☐ B-4105	Cessna 550 Citation II	550-0305	Calibrator

B-H/K/L   CHINA - HONG KONG

AIR HONG KONG — Air Hong Kong (LD/AHK) — Hong Kong (HKG)

☐ B-LDA	Airbus A300F4-605R	855	ex F-WWAN
☐ B-LDB	Airbus A300F4-605R	856	ex F-WWAP
☐ B-LDC	Airbus A300F4-605R	857	ex F-WWAQ
☐ B-LDD	Airbus A300F4-605R	858	ex F-WWAR
☐ B-LDE	Airbus A300F4-605R	859	ex F-WWAS

☐ B-LDF	Airbus A300F4-605R	860	ex F-WWAT		
☐ B-LDG	Airbus A300F4-605R	870	ex F-WWAJ		
☐ B-LDH	Airbus A300F4-605R	871	ex F-WWAK		
☐ TC-AGK	Airbus A300B4-203F	117	ex G-CEXH	Siirt 5	<KZU
☐ TC-KZU	Airbus A300B4-203	173	ex (TC-ORK)	Siirt 2	<KZU

CATHAY PACIFIC AIRWAYS   Cathay (CX/CPA)   Hong Kong (HKG)

Member of Oneworld

☐ B-HLA	Airbus A330-342	071	ex VR-HLA		
☐ B-HLB	Airbus A330-342	083	ex VR-HLB		
☐ B-HLC	Airbus A330-342	099	ex VR-HLC		
☐ B-HLD	Airbus A330-342	102	ex VR-HLD		
☐ B-HLE	Airbus A330-342	109	ex VR-HLE		
☐ B-HLF	Airbus A330-342	113	ex VR-HLF		
☐ B-HLG	Airbus A330-342	118	ex VR-HLG		
☐ B-HLH	Airbus A330-342	121	ex VR-HLH		
☐ B-HLI	Airbus A330-342	155	ex VR-HLI		
☐ B-HLJ	Airbus A330-342	012	ex VR-HLJ		
☐ B-HLK	Airbus A330-342	017	ex VR-HLK		
☐ B-HLL	Airbus A330-342	244	ex F-WWKG		
☐ B-HLM	Airbus A330-343X	386	ex F-WWYT		
☐ B-HLN	Airbus A330-343X	389	ex F-WWYV		
☐ B-HLO	Airbus A330-343X	393	ex F-WWYY		
☐ B-HLP	Airbus A330-343X	418	ex F-WWKV		
☐ B-HLQ	Airbus A330-343X	420	ex F-WWYB		
☐ B-HLR	Airbus A330-343X	421	ex F-WWYC		
☐ B-HLS	Airbus A330-343X	423	ex F-WWYD		
☐ B-HLT	Airbus A330-343X	439	ex F-WWYJ		
☐ B-HLU	Airbus A330-343X	539	ex F-WWYG		
☐ B-HLV	Airbus A330-343X	548	ex F-WWYI		
☐ B-HLW	Airbus A330-343X	565	ex F-WWYR		
☐ B-LAA	Airbus A330-342E	669	ex F-WWKS	Asia's World City titles	
☐ B-LAB	Airbus A330-342E	673	ex F-WWKZ	Asia's World City titles	
☐ B-LAC	Airbus A330-342E	679	ex F-WWYC		
☐ B-LAD	Airbus A330-342E	776	ex F-WWKI	Progress Hong Kong c/s	
☐ B-LAE	Airbus A330-342E	850	ex F-WWKQ		
☐ B-LAF	Airbus A330-342E	855	ex F-WWYC		
☐ B-LAG	Airbus A330-342E	895	ex F-WWYV		
☐ B-LAH	Airbus A330-342E	915	ex F-WWYN		
☐ B-LAI	Airbus A330-342E	959	ex F-WWYE		
☐ B-LAJ	Airbus A330-343X	1163	ex F-WWKR		♦
☐ B-	Airbus A330-343X		ex		o/o♦
☐ B-	Airbus A330-343X		ex		o/o♦
☐ B-	Airbus A330-343X		ex		o/o♦
☐ B-HXA	Airbus A340-313X	136	ex VR-HXA		
☐ B-HXB	Airbus A340-313X	137	ex VR-HXB		
☐ B-HXC	Airbus A340-313X	142	ex VR-HXC		
☐ B-HXD	Airbus A340-313X	147	ex VR-HXD		
☐ B-HXE	Airbus A340-313X	157	ex VR-HXE		
☐ B-HXF	Airbus A340-313X	160	ex VR-HXF		
☐ B-HXG	Airbus A340-313X	208	ex F-WWJC		
☐ B-HXH	Airbus A340-313X	218	ex F-WWJT		
☐ B-HXI	Airbus A340-313X	220	ex F-WWJO		
☐ B-HXJ	Airbus A340-313X	227	ex F-WWJL		
☐ B-HXK	Airbus A340-313X	228	ex F-WWJI		
☐ B-HXL	Airbus A340-313X	381	ex F-WWJB		
☐ B-HXM	Airbus A340-313X	123	ex 9V-SJA		[VCV]
☐ B-HXN	Airbus A340-313X	126	ex 9V-SJB		[VCV]
☐ B-HXO	Airbus A340-313X	128	ex 9V-SJC		[VCV]
☐ B-HKE	Boeing 747-412	25127/859	ex N127LC		
☐ B-HKF	Boeing 747-412	25128/860	ex 9V-SML		
☐ B-HKH	Boeing 747-412BCF	24227/831	ex 9V-SMH		
☐ B-HKJ	Boeing 747-412BCF	27133/962	ex 9V-SMR		
☐ B-HKT	Boeing 747-412	27132/955	ex 4X-ELS		
☐ B-HKU	Boeing 747-412	27069/1010	ex 9V-SMV		
☐ B-HKV	Boeing 747-412	26552/1056	ex 9V-SPD		
☐ B-HKX	Boeing 747-412BCF	26557/1101	ex 9V-SPL		
☐ B-HMD	Boeing 747-2L5B(SF)	22105/435	ex VR-HMD		[VCV]
☐ B-HME	Boeing 747-2L5B(SF)	22106/443	ex VR-HME		[VCV]
☐ B-HOP	Boeing 747-467	23815/728	ex VR-HOP		
☐ B-HOR	Boeing 747-467	24631/771	ex VR-HOR		
☐ B-HOS	Boeing 747-467	24850/788	ex VR-HOS		
☐ B-HOT	Boeing 747-467	24851/813	ex VR-HOT		

	Registration	Type	Line	ex	Notes	
☐	B-HOU	Boeing 747-467BCF	24925/834	ex VR-HOU		◆
☐	B-HOV	Boeing 747-467	25082/849	ex VR-HOV		
☐	B-HOW	Boeing 747-467	25211/873	ex VR-HOW		
☐	B-HOX+	Boeing 747-467	24955/877	ex VR-HOX		
☐	B-HOY	Boeing 747-467	25351/887	ex VR-HOY	Asia's World City c/s	
☐	B-HOZ	Boeing 747-467BCF	25871/925	ex VR-HOZ		
☐	B-HUA	Boeing 747-467	25872/930	ex VR-HUA		
☐	B-HUB	Boeing 747-467	25873/937	ex VR-HUB		
☐	B-HUD	Boeing 747-467	25874/949	ex VR-HUD		
☐	B-HUE	Boeing 747-467	27117/970	ex VR-HUE		
☐	B-HUF	Boeing 747-467	25869/993	ex VR-HUF		
☐	B-HUG	Boeing 747-467	25870/1007	ex VR-HUG		
☐	B-HUH	Boeing 747-467F	27175/1020	ex VR-HUH		
☐	B-HUI	Boeing 747-467	27230/1033	ex VR-HUI		
☐	B-HUJ	Boeing 747-467	27595/1061	ex VR-HUJ		
☐	B-HUK	Boeing 747-467F	27503/1065	ex VR-HUK		
☐	B-HUL	Boeing 747-467F	30804/1255			
☐	B-HUO	Boeing 747-467F	32571/1271	ex B-HUM		
☐	B-HUP	Boeing 747-467F	30805/1282	ex (B-HUN)		
☐	B-HUQ	Boeing 747-467F	34150/1356			
☐	B-HUR	Boeing 747-444BCF	24976/827	ex ZS-SAV		◆
☐	B-HUS	Boeing 747-444BCF	25152/861	ex ZS-SAW		◆
☐	B-HVX	Boeing 747-267F	24568/776	ex VR-HVX	[VCV]	
☐	B-HVZ	Boeing 747-267F	23864/687	ex VR-HVZ	[VCV]	
☐	B-KAA	Boeing 747-312M	23769/666	ex 9V-SKP	Frtr	
☐	B-KAB	Boeing 747-312M	23409/637	ex 9V-SKM	[VCV]	
☐	B-KAC	Boeing 747-3H6M	23600/650	ex N73741	[VCV]	
☐	B-KAD	Boeing 747-209F	24308/752	ex B-18771	[VCV]	
☐	B-KAE	Boeing 747-412BCF	25068/852	ex 9V-SMJ	[VCV]	
☐	B-KAF	Boeing 747-412BCF	26547/921	ex 9V-SMM	[VCV]	
☐	B-KAG	Boeing 747-412BCF	27067/953	ex 9V-SMP		
☐	B-KAH	Boeing 747-412BCF	27134/981	ex 9V-SMS		
☐	B-KAI	Boeing 747-412BCF	27217/1023	ex 9V-SMY		◆
☐	B-LIA	Boeing 747-467ERF	37299/1404			
☐	B-LIB	Boeing 747-467ERF	36867/1409	ex N5014K		
☐	B-LIC	Boeing 747-467ERF	36868/1413	ex N5014K		
☐	B-LID	Boeing 747-467ERF	36869/1414			
☐	B-LIE	Boeing 747-467ERF	36870/1415	ex N5022E		
☐	B-LIF	Boeing 747-467ERF	36871/1417			
☐	B-LJA	Boeing 747-867F	39238/1427			o/o◆
☐	B-LJB	Boeing 747-867F	39239/1428			o/o◆
☐	B-LJC	Boeing 747-867F	39240/1433			o/o◆
☐	B-	Boeing 747-867F				o/o◆
☐	B-	Boeing 747-867F				o/o◆
☐	B-	Boeing 747-867F				o/o◆
☐	B-HNA	Boeing 777-267	27265/14	ex VR-HNA		
☐	B-HNB	Boeing 777-267	27266/18	ex VR-HNB		
☐	B-HNC	Boeing 777-267	27263/28	ex VR-HNC		
☐	B-HND	Boeing 777-267	27264/31	ex VR-HND		
☐	B-HNE	Boeing 777-367	27507/94	ex N5014K		
☐	B-HNF	Boeing 777-367	27506/102	ex N5016R		
☐	B-HNG	Boeing 777-367	27505/118	ex N5017V		
☐	B-HNH	Boeing 777-367	27504/136			
☐	B-HNI	Boeing 777-367	27508/204			
☐	B-HNJ	Boeing 777-367	27509/224			
☐	B-HNK	Boeing 777-367	27510/248			
☐	B-HNL	Boeing 777-267	27116/1	ex N7771		
☐	B-HNM	Boeing 777-367	33702/456			
☐	B-HNN	Boeing 777-367	33703/462			
☐	B-HNO	Boeing 777-367	33704/470			
☐	B-HNP	Boeing 777-367	34243/513			
☐	B-HNQ	Boeing 777-367	34244/567	ex N6009F		
☐	B-KPA	Boeing 777-367ER	36154/661	ex N1788B		
☐	B-KPB	Boeing 777-367ER	35299/670			
☐	B-KPC	Boeing 777-367ER	34432/674			
☐	B-KPD	Boeing 777-367ER	36155/680			
☐	B-KPE	Boeing 777-367ER	36156/685			
☐	B-KPF	Boeing 777-367ER	36832/692		Asia World City c/s	
☐	B-KPG	Boeing 777-367ER	35300/700			
☐	B-KPH	Boeing 777-367ER	35301/720	ex N50281		
☐	B-KPI	Boeing 777-367ER	36833/746			
☐	B-KPJ	Boeing 777-367ER	36157/754	ex N5016R		
☐	B-KPK	Boeing 777-367ER	36158/783	ex N5023Q		
☐	B-KPL	Boeing 777-367ER	36161/818			
☐	B-KPM	Boeing 777-367ER	36159/835			
☐	B-KPN	Boeing 777-367ER	36165/839			

50

☐ B-KPO	Boeing 777-367ER	36160/843			◆
☐ B-KPP	Boeing 777-367ER	36164/845	ex N1785B		◆
☐ B-KPQ	Boeing 777-367ER	36162/860	ex N5016R		◆
☐ B-KPR	Boeing 777-367ER	36163/877			◆
☐ B-	Boeing 777-367ER				o/o◆
☐ B-	Boeing 777-367ER				o/o◆
☐ B-	Boeing 777-367ER				o/o◆
☐ B-	Boeing 777-367ER				o/o◆
☐ B-	Boeing 777-367ER				o/o◆
☐ B-	Boeing 777-367ER				o/o◆
☐ B-	Boeing 777-367ER				o/o◆

DRAGONAIR — Dragon (KA/HDA) — Hong Kong (HKG)

☐ B-HSD	Airbus A320-232	0756	ex F-WWBC		
☐ B-HSE	Airbus A320-232	0784	ex F-WWDL		
☐ B-HSG	Airbus A320-232	0812	ex B-22315		
☐ B-HSI	Airbus A320-232	0930	ex F-WWIE		
☐ B-HSJ	Airbus A320-232	1253	ex F-WWIU		
☐ B-HSK	Airbus A320-232	1721	ex F-WWDF		
☐ B-HSL	Airbus A320-232	2229	ex F-WWIE		
☐ B-HSM	Airbus A320-232	2238	ex F-WWDG		
☐ B-HSN	Airbus A320-232	2428	ex F-WWBI		
☐ B-HSO	Airbus A320-232	4023	ex F-WWDN		
☐ B-HSP	Airbus A320-232	4247	ex F-WWDV		◆
☐ B-HTD	Airbus A321-231	0993	ex D-AVZF		
☐ B-HTE	Airbus A321-231	1024	ex D-AVZD		
☐ B-HTF	Airbus A321-231	0633	ex G-OZBC		
☐ B-HTG	Airbus A321-231	1695	ex D-AVZA		
☐ B-HTH	Airbus A321-231	1984	ex D-AVZX		
☐ B-HTI	Airbus A321-231	2021	ex D-AVXJ		
☐ B-HWF	Airbus A330-343	654	ex F-WWYM		
☐ B-HWG	Airbus A330-343	662	ex F-WWYZ	The Way of the Dragon	
☐ B-HWH	Airbus A330-343	692	ex F-WWYO		
☐ B-HWI	Airbus A330-343	716	ex F-WWYX		
☐ B-HWJ	Airbus A330-343	741	ex F-WWYE		
☐ B-HWK	Airbus A330-343	786	ex F-WWYZ		
☐ B-HYB	Airbus A330-342	106	ex VR-HYB		
☐ B-HYD	Airbus A330-342	132	ex VR-HYD		
☐ B-HYF	Airbus A330-342	234	ex F-WWKF		
☐ B-HYG	Airbus A330-343	405	ex F-WWKQ		
☐ B-HYI	Airbus A330-343	479	ex F-WWKU		
☐ B-HYJ	Airbus A330-343	512	ex F-WWYR		
☐ B-HYQ	Airbus A330-343	581	ex F-WWKK		

HONG KONG AIRLINES — Bauhina (HX/CRK) — Hong Kong (HKG)

☐ B-LNC	Airbus A330-223	1031	ex F-WWKF	◆
☐ B-LND	Airbus A330-223	1042	ex F-WWKK	◆
☐ B-LNE	Airbus A330-223	1039	ex F-WWYO	◆
☐ B-LNF	Airbus A330-223	1059	ex F-WWKV	◆
☐ B-LNG	Airbus A330-223	1054	ex F-WWYC	◆
☐ B-	Airbus A330-223			o/o◆
☐ B-	Airbus A330-223			o/o◆
☐ B-	Airbus A330-223			o/o◆
☐ B-LNY	Airbus A330-243F	1062	ex F-WWKD	◆
☐ B-LNZ	Airbus A330-243F	1051	ex F-WWKU	◆
☐ B-KBI	Boeing 737-808/W	34709/2121	ex N1787B	<CHH
☐ B-KBK	Boeing 737-84P/W	35072/2155	ex N1786B	<CHH
☐ B-KBM	Boeing 737-84P/W	35076/2380		<CHH
☐ B-KBT	Boeing 737-84P/W	37422/3241		<CHH◆
☐ B-KBU	Boeing 737-84P/W	37953/3299		<CHH◆

HONG KONG EXPRESS AIRWAYS — Hong Kong Shuttle (UO/HKE) — Hong Kong (HKG)

☐ B-KBQ	Boeing 737-84P/W	35274/2570	<CHH
☐ B-KBR	Boeing 737-84P/W	35276/2611	<CHH
☐ B-KXE	Boeing 737-808/W	34710/2144	<CHH

SKY SHUTTLE HELICOPTERS — Heli Hong Kong (UO/HHK) — HK / Macau Heliport

☐ B-KHM	Agusta AW139	31238
☐ B-KHN	Agusta AW139	31243
☐ B-MHI	Agusta AW139	31220
☐ B-MHK	Agusta AW139	31229

☐ B-MHL	Agusta AW139	31230		
☐ B-HJR	Sikorsky S-76C+	760497		
☐ B-MHF	Sikorsky S-76C+	760474	ex CS-MHF	
☐ B-MHG	Sikorsky S-76C+	760475	ex CS-MHG	
☐ B-MHH	Sikorsky S-76C+	760476	ex CS-MHH	

B-M   CHINA - MACAU

AIR MACAU — Air Macau (NX/AMU) — Macau (MFM)

☐ B-MAS	Airbus A300B4-622RF	743	ex N221LF	Cargo titles
☐ B-MBJ	Airbus A300B4-622RF	677	ex TC-OAY	
☐ B-MAK	Airbus A319-132	1758	ex D-AVYF	Rio Yangtze
☐ B-MAL	Airbus A319-132	1790	ex D-AVYR	Rio Amarelo
☐ B-MAM	Airbus A319-112	1893	ex D-AVYJ	Lago Sul Lua
☐ B-MAN	Airbus A319-132	1912	ex D-AVWZ	Rio Huang Pu
☐ B-MAO	Airbus A319-132	1962	ex D-AVWU	Rio Yaluzangbu
☐ B-MAH	Airbus A320-232	0805	ex CS-MAH	Ilha da Madeira
☐ B-MAX	Airbus A320-232	0928	ex N928MD	
☐ B-MAB	Airbus A321-131	0557	ex VN-A341	Lotus
☐ B-MAF	Airbus A321-131	0620	ex CS-MAF	Acores
☐ B-MAG	Airbus A321-131	0631	ex CS-MAG	Ilha de Coloane
☐ B-MAJ	Airbus A321-231	0908	ex CS-MAJ	Farol da Guia
☐ B-MAP	Airbus A321-231	1850	ex D-AVZX	Rio das Perolas
☐ B-MAQ	Airbus A321-231	1926	ex D-AVZS	Lago Tai
☐ B-MAR	Airbus A321-131	0597	ex VN-A346	Hao Jiang

VIVA MACAU — Jackpot (ZG/VVM) — Macau (MFM)

Ceased operations 06/Apr/2010

B-   CHINA – TAIWAN (Republic of China)

CHINA AIRLINES   China Airlines/Dynasty (CI/CAL)   Taipei-Chiang Kai Shek/Sung Shan (TPE/TSA)

☐ B-18301	Airbus A330-302	602	ex F-WWYM	
☐ B-18302	Airbus A330-302	607	ex F-WWYY	
☐ B-18303	Airbus A330-302	641	ex F-WWYS	
☐ B-18305	Airbus A330-302	671	ex F-WWKN	orchid colours
☐ B-18306	Airbus A330-302	675	ex F-WWYU	
☐ B-18307	Airbus A330-302	691	ex F-WWYL	
☐ B-18308	Airbus A330-302	699	ex F-WWKA	
☐ B-18309	Airbus A330-302	707	ex F-WWKI	
☐ B-18310	Airbus A330-302	714	ex F-WWYV	
☐ B-18311	Airbus A330-302	752	ex F-WWKZ	Taiwanese Fruits c/s
☐ B-18312	Airbus A330-302	769	ex F-WWYS	
☐ B-18315	Airbus A330-302	823	ex F-WWKS	
☐ B-18316	Airbus A330-302	838	ex F-WWYM	
☐ B-18317	Airbus A330-302	861	ex F-WWYA	
☐ B-18351	Airbus A330-302	725	ex F-WWKO	
☐ B-18352	Airbus A330-302	805	ex F-WWYG	
☐ B-18353	Airbus A330-302	920	ex F-WWYU	
☐ B-18355	Airbus A330-302	1177	ex F-WWYI	♦
☐ B-18801	Airbus A340-313X	402	ex F-WWJC	
☐ B-18802	Airbus A340-313X	406	ex F-WWJK	
☐ B-18803	Airbus A340-313X	411	ex F-WWJL	
☐ B-18805	Airbus A340-313X	415	ex F-WWJO	
☐ B-18806	Airbus A340-313X	433	ex F-WWJS	
☐ B-18807	Airbus A340-313X	541	ex F-WWJK	
☐ B-18601	Boeing 737-809/W	28402/113	ex N1787B	
☐ B-18605	Boeing 737-809/W	28404/130	ex N1784B	
☐ B-18606	Boeing 737-809/W	28405/132		
☐ B-18607	Boeing 737-809/W	29104/139		
☐ B-18608	Boeing 737-809/W	28406/141		
☐ B-18609	Boeing 737-809/W	28407/161		
☐ B-18610	Boeing 737-809/W	29105/295		
☐ B-18612	Boeing 737-809/W	30173/695	ex N1785B	

☐ B-18615	Boeing 737-809/W	30174/1175	ex N6067E	
☐ B-16817	Boeing 737-809/W	29106/302	ex B-18611	
☐ B-18201	Boeing 747-409	28709/1114		
☐ B-18202	Boeing 747-409	28710/1132		
☐ B-18203	Boeing 747-409	28711/1136		
☐ B-18205	Boeing 747-409	28712/1137		
☐ B-18206	Boeing 747-409	29030/1145		
☐ B-18207	Boeing 747-409	29219/1176		
☐ B-18208	Boeing 747-409	29031/1186		
☐ B-18210	Boeing 747-409	33734/1353		Dreamliner c/s
☐ B-18211	Boeing 747-409	33735/1354		
☐ B-18212	Boeing 747-409	33736/1357		
☐ B-18215	Boeing 747-409	33737/1358		
☐ B-18251	Boeing 747-409	27965/1063	ex B-16801	
☐ B-18701	Boeing 747-409F	30759/1249		
☐ B-18702	Boeing 747-409F	30760/1252		
☐ B-18705	Boeing 747-409F	30762/1263		
☐ B-18706	Boeing 747-409F	30763/1267		
☐ B-18707	Boeing 747-409F	30764/1269		
☐ B-18708	Boeing 747-409F	30765/1288		
☐ B-18709	Boeing 747-409F	30766/1294		
☐ B-18710	Boeing 747-409F	30767/1300		a
☐ B-18711	Boeing 747-409F	30768/1314		
☐ B-18712	Boeing 747-409F	33729/1332		
☐ B-18715	Boeing 747-409F	33731/1334		
☐ B-18716	Boeing 747-409F	33732/1339		
☐ B-18717	Boeing 747-409F	30769/1346		
☐ B-18718	Boeing 747-409F	30770/1348		
☐ B-18719	Boeing 747-409F	33739/1355		
☐ B-18720	Boeing 747-409F	33733/1359		
☐ B-18721	Boeing 747-409F	33738/1362		
☐ B-18722	Boeing 747-409F	34265/1372		all-white
☐ B-18723	Boeing 747-409F	34266/1379		
☐ B-18725	Boeing 747-409F	30771/1385		
☐ N168CL	Boeing 747-409	29906/1219	ex B-18209	

DAILY AIR   Taipei-Sung Shan (TSA)

☐ B-55561	Dornier 228-212	8215	ex B-12253	
☐ B-55563	Dornier 228-212	8224	ex B-12259	
☐ B-55565	Dornier 228-212	8234	ex B-11152	
☐ B-55567	Dornier 228-212	8235	ex B-11156	

EVA AIRWAYS   Eva (BR/EVA)   Taipei-Chiang Kai Shek (TPE)

☐ B-16301	Airbus A330-203	530	ex F-WWYA	
☐ B-16302	Airbus A330-203	535	ex F-WWYE	
☐ B-16303	Airbus A330-203	555	ex F-WWYL	
☐ B-16305	Airbus A330-203	573	ex F-WWYP	
☐ B-16306	Airbus A330-203	587	ex F-WWKL	
☐ B-16307	Airbus A330-203	634	ex F-WWYJ	
☐ B-16308	Airbus A330-203	655	ex F-WWYT	
☐ B-16309	Airbus A330-203	661	ex F-WWYY	
☐ B-16310	Airbus A330-203	678	ex F-WWYB	
☐ B-16311	Airbus A330-203	693	ex F-WWYP	
☐ B-16312	Airbus A330-203	755	ex F-WWYP	
☐ B-16401	Boeing 747-45E	27062/942		
☐ B-16402	Boeing 747-45EBDSF	27063/947		
☐ B-16403	Boeing 747-45EM	27141/976	ex N403EV	
☐ B-16405	Boeing 747-45EM	27142/982	ex N405EV	
☐ B-16406	Boeing 747-45EMBDSF	27898/1051	ex N406EV	
☐ B-16407	Boeing 747-45EMSF	27899/1053	ex N407EV	
☐ B-16408	Boeing 747-45EM	28092/1076	ex N408EV	
☐ B-16409	Boeing 747-45EM	28093/1077	ex N409EV	
☐ B-16410	Boeing 747-45E	29061/1140		
☐ B-16411	Boeing 747-45E	29111/1151		
☐ B-16412	Boeing 747-45E	29112/1159		
☐ B-16462	Boeing 747-45EMBDSF	27173/998		
☐ B-16463	Boeing 747-45EMBDSF	27174/1004		
☐ B-16481	Boeing 747-45EF	30607/1251		
☐ B-16482	Boeing 747-45EF	30608/1279		
☐ B-16483	Boeing 747-45EF	30609/1309		
☐ B-16701	Boeing 777-35EER	32639/524		
☐ B-16702	Boeing 777-35EER	32640/531		

☐ B-16703	Boeing 777-35EER	32643/572		
☐ B-16705	Boeing 777-35EER	32645/597	ex N6009F	
☐ B-16706	Boeing 777-35EER	33750/612		
☐ B-16707	Boeing 777-35EER	33751/634		
☐ B-16708	Boeing 777-35EER	33752/658		
☐ B-16709	Boeing 777-35EER	33753/683		
☐ B-16710	Boeing 777-35EER	32641/707		
☐ B-16711	Boeing 777-35EER	33754/721	ex N5028Y	
☐ B-16712	Boeing 777-35EER	33755/735		
☐ B-16713	Boeing 777-35EER	33756/758		
☐ B-16715	Boeing 777-35EER	33757/810		
☐ B-16716	Boeing 777-35EER	32642/822		♦
☐ B-16717	Boeing 777-35EER	32644/863	ex N559BA	♦
☐ B-16101	McDonnell-Douglas MD-11F	48542/570		
☐ B-16107	McDonnell-Douglas MD-11F	48546/589		
☐ B-16108	McDonnell-Douglas MD-11F	48778/619		
☐ B-16109	McDonnell-Douglas MD-11F	48779/620		
☐ B-16110	McDonnell-Douglas MD-11F	48786/630		
☐ B-16111	McDonnell-Douglas MD-11F	48787/631		
☐ B-16112	McDonnell-Douglas MD-11F	48789/633	ex N90178	
☐ B-16113	McDonnell-Douglas MD-11F	48790/634	ex N9030Q	
☐ B-17913	McDonnell-Douglas MD-90-30	53537/2162		<UIA
☐ B-17917	McDonnell-Douglas MD-90-30ER	53572/2217		<UIA
☐ B-17923	McDonnell-Douglas MD-90-30ER	53534/2153	ex B-16901	<UIA
☐ B-17925	McDonnell-Douglas MD-90-30ER	53568/2171	ex B-16902	<UIA
☐ B-17926	McDonnell-Douglas MD-90-30ER	53567/2169	ex B-15301	<UIA

GREAT WING AIRLINES

Taichung

☐ B-69832	Britten-Norman BN-2A-26 Islander	2039	ex B-12232

MANDARIN AIRLINES

Mandarin Air (AE/MDA)   *Taipei-Sung Shan (TSA)*

☐ B-16821	Embraer ERJ-190AR	19000087	ex PT-SNF
☐ B-16822	Embraer ERJ-190AR	19000091	ex PT-SNK
☐ B-16823	Embraer ERJ-190AR	19000099	ex PT-SNT
☐ B-16825	Embraer ERJ-190AR	19000167	ex PT-SAZ
☐ B-16826	Embraer ERJ-190AR	19000175	ex PT-SDK
☐ B-16827	Embraer ERJ-190AR	19000182	ex PT-SDQ
☐ B-16828	Embraer ERJ-190AR	19000190	ex PT-SDY
☐ B-16829	Embraer ERJ-190AR	19000302	ex PT-TZQ

ROC AVIATION

Taipei-Sung Shan (TSA)

☐ B-68801	Britten-Norman BN-2B-26 Islander	2255	ex G-BTVI
☐ B-68802	Britten-Norman BN-2B-20 Islander	2241	ex G-BSPU

TRANSASIA AIRWAYS

Transasia (GE/TNA)   *Taipei-Sung Shan (TSA)*

☐ B-22310	Airbus A320-232	0791	ex F-WWDR
☐ B-22311	Airbus A320-232	0822	ex F-WWBY
☐ B-22601	Airbus A321-131	0538	ex F-WGYZ
☐ B-22602	Airbus A321-131	0555	ex F-WFYZ
☐ B-22605	Airbus A321-131	0606	ex F-WGYY
☐ B-22606	Airbus A321-131	0731	ex F-WQGL
☐ B-22607	Airbus A321-131	0746	ex F-WQGM
☐ B-22801	ATR 72-212A	517	ex F-WWLK
☐ B-22802	ATR 72-212A	525	ex F-WWLB
☐ B-22803	ATR 72-212A	527	ex F-WWLC
☐ B-22805	ATR 72-212A	558	ex F-WQIU
☐ B-22806	ATR 72-212A	560	ex F-WQIY
☐ B-22807	ATR 72-212A	567	ex F-WQIZ
☐ B-22810	ATR 72-212A	642	ex F-WQMF
☐ B-22811	ATR 72-212A	749	ex F-WQNC
☐ B-22812	ATR 72-212A	774	ex F-WWEM

UNI AIR

Glory (B7/UIA)   *Taipei-Sung Shan (TSA)*

☐ B-15217	de Havilland DHC-8-311A	379	ex C-GEOA
☐ B-15219	de Havilland DHC-8-311A	381	ex C-FDHD
☐ B-15225	de Havilland DHC-8-311B	405	ex C-GFHZ
☐ B-15231	de Havilland DHC-8-311B	414	ex C-GFBW
☐ B-15233	de Havilland DHC-8-311B	402	ex C-GDFT
☐ B-15235	de Havilland DHC-8Q-311B	443	ex C-FWBB
☐ B-15237	de Havilland DHC-8Q-311B	467	ex C-GELN

54

☐ B-15239	de Havilland DHC-8Q-311B	571	ex C-GEWI

☐ B-17911	McDonnell-Douglas MD-90-30	53535/2158		
☐ B-17913	McDonnell-Douglas MD-90-30	53537/2162		>EVA
☐ B-17917	McDonnell-Douglas MD-90-30ER	53572/2217		>EVA
☐ B-17918	McDonnell-Douglas MD-90-30ER	53571/2193	ex B-16903	
☐ B-17919	McDonnell-Douglas MD-90-30	53569/2173	ex N6206F	
☐ B-17920	McDonnell-Douglas MD-90-30	53574/2186		
☐ B-17921	McDonnell-Douglas MD-90-30	53554/2166	ex SU-BNN	
☐ B-17922	McDonnell-Douglas MD-90-30	53601/2243	ex SU-BMT	
☐ B-17923	McDonnell-Douglas MD-90-30ER	53534/2153	ex B-16901	>EVA
☐ B-17925	McDonnell-Douglas MD-90-30ER	53568/2171	ex B-16902	>EVA
☐ B-17926	McDonnell-Douglas MD-90-30ER	53567/2169	ex B-15301	>EVA

C- CANADA

ABITIBI HELICOPTERS — La Sarre, QC/Calgary-Springbank, AB (SSQ/-)

☐ C-FHAK	Aérospatiale AS350BA+ AStar	1545	ex N517WW
☐ C-FHAP	Aérospatiale AS350B2 AStar	3292	
☐ C-FHAU	Aérospatiale AS350BA AStar	2778	
☐ C-FIYM	Aérospatiale AS350B1 AStar	1881	ex LN-OPT
☐ C-FNJY	Aérospatiale AS350BA AStar	2546	
☐ C-FSOZ	Aérospatiale AS350B2 AStar	2129	ex N141MB
☐ C-FSPE	Aérospatiale AS350BA AStar	2787	
☐ C-FXAH	Aérospatiale AS350BA AStar	2509	ex N905BK
☐ C-FXBP	Aérospatiale AS350BA AStar	1553	ex I-VBIT
☐ C-FXDM	Aérospatiale AS350BA AStar	1548	ex N798JH
☐ C-FXED	Aérospatiale AS350BA AStar	3087	
☐ C-FXEJ	Aérospatiale AS350BA AStar	1031	
☐ C-FXHP	Aérospatiale AS350BA AStar	3100	
☐ C-FXND	Aérospatiale AS350BA AStar	2168	ex G-COPT
☐ C-FXPM	Aérospatiale AS350BA AStar	1428	ex C-FBHX
☐ C-GAVQ	Aérospatiale AS350B2 AStar	2781	ex N350PD
☐ C-GHSM	Aérospatiale AS350BA+ AStar	1468	ex N700WW
☐ C-GHUM	Bell 205A-1	30252	ex HI-733SP

AC JETZ — Montreal-Mirabel/Montreal-Trudeau, QC (YMX/YUL)

Specialist sports charter and VIP division of Air Canada.

ADLAIR AVIATION — Cambridge Bay, NT/Yellowknife, NT (YCB/YZF)

☐ C-FGYN	de Havilland DHC-2 Beaver	134	ex CF-GYN	FP or skis
☐ C-GBFP	Learjet 25B	25B-167	ex N664CL	Ernie Lyall	EMS
☐ C-GBYN	Beech B200 Super King Air	BB-1232	ex N209CM	EMS
☐ C-GCYN	Beech 200 Super King Air	BB-710	ex C-GXHW	
☐ C-GFYN	de Havilland DHC-6 Twin Otter 200	209	ex N915SA	Wheels or skis

ADLER AVIATION — Shockwave (SWH) — Kitchener-Waterloo, ON (YKF)

☐ C-GBWB	Piper PA-31 Navajo C	31-7612025	ex N108DR
☐ C-GTGR	Cessna 421C Golden Eagle II	421C0061	ex N15LW

ADVENTURE AIR — Lac du Bonnet, MB (YAX)

☐ CF-JFA	de Havilland DHC-2 Beaver	1581	ex N5563	FP
☐ C-FKLR	Cessna 208 Caravan I	20800223	ex N899A	FP
☐ C-FQZH	Piper PA-31-350 Chieftain	31-7952070	ex N105TT	
☐ C-FVQD	de Havilland DHC-3 Turbo Otter	466	ex CF-VQD	FP
☐ C-FXPC	de Havilland DHC-2 Beaver	1196	ex CF-XPC	FP
☐ C-GAAX	Cessna 208B Caravan I	208B0348	ex N32JA	
☐ C-GGRJ	Cessna A185F Skywagon	18502745	ex (N1090F)	FP
☐ C-GKYG	de Havilland DHC-3 Otter	261	ex N2750	FP
☐ C-GMGV	de Havilland DHC-2 Beaver	432	ex N62278	FP
☐ C-GSUV	de Havilland DHC-3 Otter	376	ex N445FD	FP
☐ C-GUEH	Piper PA-31 Turbo Navajo C	31-7712057	ex N27255	
☐ C-GWQE	Cessna 337F Super Skymaster II	33701459	ex N1859M	

AEROPRO — Aeropro (APO) — Montreal-Trudeau, QC (YUL)

Suspended operations 15/Jul/2010

AEROSMITH — Gander, NL (YQX)

☐ C-GAAM	Cessna A185F Skywagon	18502675	ex C-GMNM	FP/WS
☐ C-GAAZ	Cessna A185F Skywagon	18502735	ex C-GAEH	FP/WS

☐ C-GSND	Beech 80-A65 Queen Air	LC-299	ex N122Y	Queenaire 8200 conversion

AIR BRAVO — Thunder Bay, ON (YQT)

☐ C-FAJV	Pilatus PC-12/45	234	ex HB-FRE	
☐ C-FKPA	Pilatus PC-12/45	275	ex N275PC	
☐ C-FKSL	Pilatus PC-12/45	324	ex N324PC	
☐ C-FPCI	Pilatus PC-12/45	399	ex N399PB	
☐ C-FPCN	Pilatus PC-12/45	258	ex N258WC	
☐ C-FTAB	Pilatus PC-12/45	229	ex C-FMPO	♦
☐ C-GFIL	Pilatus PC-12/45	268	ex N268PC	
☐ C-GVKC	Pilatus PC-12/45	207	ex ZS-OEV	
☐ C-GBCM	Rockwell Commander 700	70027	ex N700DL	
☐ C-GVWX	Rockwell Commander 700	70005	ex N9905S	

AIR CAB — Vancouver-Coal Harbour, BC (CXH)

☐ C-FBMO	Cessna A185E Skywagon	18501627	ex N1934U	FP
☐ C-FQGZ	Cessna A185E Skywagon	18501691	ex N1967U	FP
☐ C-FOES	de Havilland DHC-2 Turbo Beaver	1673/TB43	ex CF-OES	FP
☐ C-FRJG	de Havilland DHC-2 Beaver	1550	ex CF-RJG	FP
☐ C-GAXE	de Havilland DHC-2 Beaver	841	ex 54-1698	FP
☐ C-GJGC	de Havilland DHC-2 Beaver	88	ex CF-GQM	FP
☐ C-GJZE	de Havilland DHC-2 Beaver	1276	ex N87780	FP

AIR CANADA — Air Canada (AC/ACA) — Montreal-Mirabel/Montreal-Trudeau, QC (YMX/YUL)

Member of Star Alliance

☐ C-FBLJ	Airbus A319-112	1630	ex XA-MXG		♦
☐ C-FYIY	Airbus A319-114	0634	ex D-AVYP	252	
☐ C-FYJE	Airbus A319-114	0656	ex D-AVYZ	255	
☐ C-FYJG	Airbus A319-114	0670	ex D-AVYE	256	
☐ C-FYJH	Airbus A319-114	0672	ex D-AVYF	257	
☐ C-FYJI	Airbus A319-114	0682	ex D-AVYH	258	
☐ C-FYJP	Airbus A319-114	0688	ex D-AVYJ	259	
☐ C-FYKC	Airbus A319-114	0691	ex D-AVYP	260	
☐ C-FYKR	Airbus A319-114	0693	ex D-AVYQ	261	
☐ C-FYKW	Airbus A319-114	0695	ex D-AVYS	262	
☐ C-FYNS	Airbus A319-114	0572	ex D-AVYK	251	
☐ C-FZUG	Airbus A319-114	0697	ex D-AVYT	263	
☐ C-FZUH	Airbus A319-114	0711	ex D-AVYV	264	TCA retro c/s
☐ C-FZUJ	Airbus A319-114	0719	ex D-AVYW	265	
☐ C-FZUL	Airbus A319-114	0721	ex D-AVYY	266	
☐ C-GAPY	Airbus A319-114	0728	ex D-AVYE	267	
☐ C-GAQL	Airbus A319-114	0732	ex D-AVYX	268	
☐ C-GAQX	Airbus A319-114	0736	ex D-AVYG	269	
☐ C-GAQZ	Airbus A319-114	0740	ex D-AVYH	270	
☐ C-GARG	Airbus A319-114	0742	ex D-AVYM	271	
☐ C-GARJ	Airbus A319-114	0752	ex D-AVYP	272	
☐ C-GARO	Airbus A319-114	0757	ex D-AVYQ	273	
☐ C-GBHM	Airbus A319-114	0769	ex D-AVYB	274	
☐ C-GBHN	Airbus A319-114	0773	ex D-AVYK	275	
☐ C-GBHO	Airbus A319-114	0779	ex D-AVYT	276	
☐ C-GBHR	Airbus A319-114	0785	ex D-AVYU	277	
☐ C-GBHY	Airbus A319-114	0800	ex D-AVYE	278	
☐ C-GBHZ	Airbus A319-114	0813	ex D-AVYG	279	
☐ C-GBIA	Airbus A319-114	0817	ex D-AVYM	280	
☐ C-GBIJ	Airbus A319-114	0829	ex D-AVYH	281	
☐ C-GBIK	Airbus A319-114	0831	ex D-AVYI	282	
☐ C-GBIM	Airbus A319-114	0840	ex D-AVYQ	283	
☐ C-GBIN	Airbus A319-114	0845	ex D-AVYA	284	
☐ C-GBIP	Airbus A319-114	0546	ex D-AVYV	285	
☐ C-GITP	Airbus A319-112	1562	ex D-AVYR	286	
☐ C-GITR	Airbus A319-112	1577	ex D-AVWR	287	
☐ C-GKNW	Airbus A319-112	1805	ex XA-MXJ		♦
☐ C-GKOB	Airbus A319-112	1853	ex N571SX	296	ACJetz♦
☐ C-FDCA	Airbus A320-211	0232	ex F-WWIY	405	ACJetz
☐ C-FDQQ	Airbus A320-211	0059	ex F-WWDI	201	
☐ C-FDQV	Airbus A320-211	0068	ex F-WWDO	202	
☐ C-FDRH	Airbus A320-211	0073	ex F-WWDC	203	
☐ C-FDRK	Airbus A320-211	0084	ex F-WWDP	204	
☐ C-FDRP	Airbus A320-211	0122	ex F-WWIP	205	
☐ C-FDSN	Airbus A320-211	0126	ex F-WWIU	206	
☐ C-FDST	Airbus A320-211	0127	ex F-WWIV	207	

☐ C-FDSU	Airbus A320-211	0141	ex F-WWDH	208	
☐ C-FFWI	Airbus A320-211	0149	ex F-WWDP	209	
☐ C-FFWJ	Airbus A320-211	0150	ex F-WWDQ	210	
☐ C-FFWM	Airbus A320-211	0154	ex F-WWDY	211	
☐ C-FFWN	Airbus A320-211	0159	ex F-WWIG	212	65th colours
☐ C-FGYL	Airbus A320-211	0254	ex F-WWBF	218	
☐ C-FGYS	Airbus A320-211	0255	ex F-WWBG	219	
☐ C-FKCK	Airbus A320-211	0265	ex 'G-FKCK'	220	
☐ C-FKCO	Airbus A320-211	0277	ex F-WWDX	221	
☐ C-FKCR	Airbus A320-211	0290	ex F-WWBY	222	
☐ C-FKOJ	Airbus A320-211	0330	ex F-WWIB	226	
☐ C-FKPT	Airbus A320-211	0324	ex F-WWDC	225	
☐ C-FLSS	Airbus A320-211	0284	ex F-WWBU	408	
☐ C-FLSU	Airbus A320-211	0309	ex F-WWIJ	411	
☐ C-FMSX	Airbus A320-211	0378	ex 'C-FMSK'	232	
☐ C-FNVU	Airbus A320-211	0403	ex F-WWBO	415	
☐ C-FNVV	Airbus A320-211	0404	ex F-WWDF	416	
☐ C-FPDN	Airbus A320-211	0341	ex F-WWBR	228	
☐ C-FPWD	Airbus A320-211	0231	ex F-WWDV	404	AC Jetz
☐ C-FPWE	Airbus A320-211	0175	ex F-WWIN	402	AC Jetz
☐ C-FTJO	Airbus A320-211	0183	ex F-WWIX	213	
☐ C-FTJP	Airbus A320-211	0233	ex F-WWIQ	214	
☐ C-FTJQ	Airbus A320-211	0242	ex F-WWDJ	215	
☐ C-FTJR	Airbus A320-211	0248	ex F-WWDT	216	
☐ C-FTJS	Airbus A320-211	0253	ex F-WWBE	217	
☐ C-FXCD	Airbus A320-214	2018	ex F-WWBV	239	
☐ C-FZQS	Airbus A320-214	2145	ex F-WWDI	240	
☐ C-FZUB	Airbus A320-214	1940	ex F-WWIP	238	
☐ C-GJVT	Airbus A320-214	1719	ex F-WWBC	235	
☐ C-GKOD	Airbus A320-214	1864	ex F-WWIE	236	
☐ C-GKOE	Airbus A320-214	1874	ex F-WWBN	237	
☐ C-GPWG	Airbus A320-211	0174	ex F-WWIM	401	
☐ C-GQCA	Airbus A320-211	0210	ex F-WWIC	403	AC Jetz
☐ C-GITU	Airbus A321-211	1602	ex D-AMTA	451	
☐ C-GITY	Airbus A321-211	1611	ex D-AVAV	452	
☐ C-GIUB	Airbus A321-211	1623	ex D-AMTB	453	70th Anniversary colours
☐ C-GIUE	Airbus A321-211	1632	ex D-AMTC	454	
☐ C-GIUF	Airbus A321-211	1638	ex D-AMTD	455	
☐ C-GJVX	Airbus A321-211	1726	ex D-AVXC	456	
☐ C-GJWD	Airbus A321-211	1748	ex D-AVXE	457	
☐ C-GJWI	Airbus A321-211	1772	ex D-AVZA	458	
☐ C-GJWN	Airbus A321-211	1783	ex D-AVZD	459	
☐ C-GJWO	Airbus A321-211	1811	ex D-AVZI	460	
☐ C-GFAF	Airbus A330-343X	277	ex F-WWKO	931	
☐ C-GFAH	Airbus A330-343X	279	ex F-WWYB	932	
☐ C-GFAJ	Airbus A330-343X	284	ex F-WWYA	933	
☐ C-GFUR	Airbus A330-343X	344	ex F-WWYC	934	
☐ C-GHKR	Airbus A330-343X	400	ex F-WWKM	935	
☐ C-GHKW	Airbus A330-343X	408	ex F-WWKS	936	
☐ C-GHKX	Airbus A330-343X	412	ex F-WWKU	937	
☐ C-GHLM	Airbus A330-343X	419	ex F-WWYA	938	Star Alliance c/s
☐ C-FBEF	Boeing 767-233ER	24323/250	ex N6009F	617	[ROW]
☐ C-FBEG	Boeing 767-233ER	24324/252	ex N6009F	618	[ROW]
☐ C-FBEM	Boeing 767-233ER	24325/254	ex N6038E	619	[ROW]
☐ C-FCAB	Boeing 767-375ER	24082/213	ex N6055X	681	
☐ C-FCAE	Boeing 767-375ER	24083/215	ex N6046P	682	70th colours
☐ C-FCAF	Boeing 767-375ER	24084/219	ex N6038E	683	
☐ C-FCAG	Boeing 767-375ER	24085/220	ex N6009F	684	
☐ C-FMWP	Boeing 767-333ER	25583/508		631	
☐ C-FMWQ	Boeing 767-333ER	25584/596		632	
☐ C-FMWU	Boeing 767-333ER	25585/597		633	
☐ C-FMWV	Boeing 767-333ER	25586/599		634	
☐ C-FMWY	Boeing 767-333ER	25587/604		635	10 Year Star Alliance colours
☐ C-FMXC	Boeing 767-333ER	25588/606		636	
☐ C-FOCA	Boeing 767-375ER	24575/311		640	
☐ C-FPCA	Boeing 767-375ER	24306/258		637	
☐ C-FTCA	Boeing 767-375ER	24307/259		638	
☐ C-FVNM	Boeing 767-209ER	22681/18	ex ZK-NBF	621	[ROW]
☐ C-FXCA	Boeing 767-375ER	24574/302		639	
☐ C-GAUE	Boeing 767-233	22518/22		602	[MZJ]
☐ C-GAUW	Boeing 767-233	22524/88	ex N6038E	608	[MHV]
☐ C-GAVC	Boeing 767-233ER	22527/102	ex N1783B	611	[ROW]
☐ C-GBZR	Boeing 767-38EER	25404/411	ex HL7267	645 Free Spirit c/s	
☐ C-GDSP	Boeing 767-233ER	24142/229	ex N6009F	613 all-silver fuselage	[ROW]
☐ C-GDSS	Boeing 767-233ER	24143/233	ex N6005C	614	[MHV]

☐ C-GDSU	Boeing 767-233ER	24144/234	ex N6018N	615		[ROW]
☐ C-GDSY	Boeing 767-233ER	24145/236	ex N6005C	616		[ROW]
☐ C-GDUZ	Boeing 767-38EER	25347/399	ex HL7266	646		
☐ C-GEOQ	Boeing 767-375ER	30112/765		647		
☐ C-GEOU	Boeing 767-375ER	30108/771		648		
☐ C-GHLA	Boeing 767-35HER	26387/445	ex VH-BZL	656		
☐ C-GHLK	Boeing 767-35HER	26388/456	ex VH-BZM	657		
☐ C-GHLQ	Boeing 767-333ER	30846/832	ex N6009F	658		
☐ C-GHLT	Boeing 767-333ER	30850/835	ex N6018N	659		
☐ C-GHLU	Boeing 767-333ER	30851/836	ex N6046P	660		
☐ C-GHLV	Boeing 767-333ER	30852/843	ex N6055X	661		
☐ C-GHOZ	Boeing 767-375ER	24087/249	ex N487CT	685		
☐ C-GHPD	Boeing 767-3Y0ER	24999/354	ex N25034	687		
☐ C-GHPF	Boeing 767-3Y0ER	26206/487	ex N226MT	689		
☐ C-GHPH	Boeing 767-3Y0ER	26207/503	ex N227MT	690		
☐ C-GLCA	Boeing 767-375ER	25120/361		641		
☐ C-GSCA	Boeing 767-375ER	25121/372	ex B-2564	642		
☐ C-FIUA	Boeing 777-233LR	35239/640		701		
☐ C-FIUF	Boeing 777-233LR	35243/651	ex N1788B	702		
☐ C-FIUJ	Boeing 777-233LR	35244/679		703		
☐ C-FIVK	Boeing 777-233LR	35245/689		704		
☐ C-FNND	Boeing 777-233LR	35246/695		705		
☐ C-FNNH	Boeing 777-233LR	35247/699		706		
☐ C-FITL	Boeing 777-333ER	35256/620		731		
☐ C-FITU	Boeing 777-333ER	35254/626		732		
☐ C-FITW	Boeing 777-333ER	35298/638		733		
☐ C-FIUL	Boeing 777-333ER	35255/642		734		
☐ C-FIUR	Boeing 777-333ER	35242/649		735		
☐ C-FIUV	Boeing 777-333ER	35248/702		736		
☐ C-FIUW	Boeing 777-333ER	35249/712		737		
☐ C-FIVM	Boeing 777-333ER	35251/717		738		
☐ C-FIVQ	Boeing 777-333ER	35240/749		740		
☐ C-FIVR	Boeing 777-333ER	35241/763		741		
☐ C-FIVS	Boeing 777-333ER	35784/797		742		
☐ C-FRAM	Boeing 777-333ER	35250/726		739		
☐ C-FEIQ	Embraer ERJ-175SU	17000083	ex PT-SZI	371		
☐ C-FEIX	Embraer ERJ-175SU	17000085	ex PT-SZK	372		
☐ C-FEJB	Embraer ERJ-175SU	17000086	ex PT-SZL	373		
☐ C-FEJC	Embraer ERJ-175SU	17000089	ex PT-SZP	374		
☐ C-FEJD	Embraer ERJ-175SU	17000090	ex PT-SZQ	375		
☐ C-FEJF	Embraer ERJ-175SU	17000091	ex PT-SZR	376		
☐ C-FEJL	Embraer ERJ-175SU	17000095	ex PT-SZV	377		
☐ C-FEJP	Embraer ERJ-175SU	17000096	ex PT-SZW	378		
☐ C-FEJY	Embraer ERJ-175SU	17000097	ex PT-SZX	379		
☐ C-FEKD	Embraer ERJ-175SU	17000101	ex PT-SAC	380		
☐ C-FEKH	Embraer ERJ-175SU	17000102	ex PT-SAH	381		
☐ C-FEKI	Embraer ERJ-175SU	17000103	ex PT-SAI	382		
☐ C-FEKJ	Embraer ERJ-175SU	17000109	ex PT-SAR	383		
☐ C-FEKS	Embraer ERJ-175SU	17000110	ex PT-SAS	384		
☐ C-FFYG	Embraer ERJ-175SU	17000116	ex PT-SDD	385		
☐ C-FFYJ	Embraer ERJ-190AR	19000013	ex PT-STM	302		
☐ C-FFYM	Embraer ERJ-190AR	19000015	ex PT-STP	303		
☐ C-FFYT	Embraer ERJ-190AR	19000018	ex PT-STS	304		
☐ C-FGLW	Embraer ERJ-190AR	19000022	ex PT-STW	306		
☐ C-FGLX	Embraer ERJ-190AR	19000024	ex PT-STY	307		
☐ C-FGLY	Embraer ERJ-190AR	19000028	ex PT-SGC	308		
☐ C-FGMF	Embraer ERJ-190AR	19000019	ex PT-STT	305		
☐ C-FHIQ	Embraer ERJ-190AR	19000031	ex PT-SGF	309		
☐ C-FHIS	Embraer ERJ-190AR	19000036	ex PT-SGK	310		
☐ C-FHIU	Embraer ERJ-190AR	19000037	ex PT-SGL	311		
☐ C-FHJJ	Embraer ERJ-190AR	19000041	ex PT-SGQ	312		
☐ C-FHJT	Embraer ERJ-190AR	19000043	ex PT-SGS	313		
☐ C-FHJU	Embraer ERJ-190AR	19000044	ex PT-SGT	314		
☐ C-FHKA	Embraer ERJ-190AR	19000046	ex PT-SGV	315		
☐ C-FHKE	Embraer ERJ-190AR	19000048	ex PT-SGX	316		
☐ C-FHKI	Embraer ERJ-190AR	19000052	ex PT-SIB	317		
☐ C-FHKP	Embraer ERJ-190AR	19000055	ex PT-SIE	318		
☐ C-FHKS	Embraer ERJ-190AR	19000064	ex PT-SJC	319		
☐ C-FHLH	Embraer ERJ-190AR	19000068	ex PT-SJH	320		
☐ C-FHNL	Embraer ERJ-190AR	19000070	ex PT-SJJ	321		
☐ C-FHNP	Embraer ERJ-190AR	19000071	ex PT-SJK	322		
☐ C-FHNV	Embraer ERJ-190AR	19000075	ex PT-SJP	323		
☐ C-FHNW	Embraer ERJ-190AR	19000077	ex PT-SJS	324		

☐ C-FHNX	Embraer ERJ-190AR	19000083	ex PT-SNA	325	
☐ C-FHNY	Embraer ERJ-190AR	19000085	ex PT-SND	326	
☐ C-FHON	Embraer ERJ-190AR	19000097	ex PT-SNR	330	
☐ C-FHOS	Embraer ERJ-190AR	19000101	ex PT-SNV	331	
☐ C-FHOY	Embraer ERJ-190AR	19000105	ex PT-SNZ	332	
☐ C-FLWE	Embraer ERJ-190AR	19000092	ex PT-SNL	327	
☐ C-FLWH	Embraer ERJ-190AR	19000094	ex PT-SNO	328	
☐ C-FLWK	Embraer ERJ-190AR	19000096	ex PT-SNQ	329	
☐ C-FMYV	Embraer ERJ-190AR	19000108	ex PT-SQC	333	
☐ C-FMZB	Embraer ERJ-190AR	19000111	ex PT-SQF	334	
☐ C-FMZD	Embraer ERJ-190AR	19000115	ex PT-SQJ	335	
☐ C-FMZR	Embraer ERJ-190AR	19000116	ex PT-SQK	336	
☐ C-FMZU	Embraer ERJ-190AR	19000118	ex PT-SQM	337	
☐ C-FMZW	Embraer ERJ-190AR	19000124	ex PT-SQT	338	
☐ C-FNAI	Embraer ERJ-190AR	19000132	ex PT-SYK	339	
☐ C-FNAJ	Embraer ERJ-190AR	19000134	ex PT-SYM	340	
☐ C-FNAN	Embraer ERJ-190AR	19000136	ex PT-SYO	341	
☐ C-FNAP	Embraer ERJ-190AR	19000142	ex PT-SYU	342	
☐ C-FNAQ	Embraer ERJ-190AR	19000146	ex PT-SYY	343	
☐ C-FNAW	Embraer ERJ-190AR	19000149	ex PT-SAC	344	
☐ C-FNAX	Embraer ERJ-190AR	19000151	ex PT-SAG	345	
☐ C-GWEN	Embraer ERJ-190AR	19000010	ex PT-STJ	301	
☐ CF-TCC	Lockheed L-10A	1116	ex N3749	Trans Canada Airlines colours	

AIR CANADA JAZZ   **Jazz (QK/JZA)**
Halifax, NS/Calgary, AB/London, ON/Vancouver, BC (YHZ/YYC/YXU/YVR)

Note: Fleet is being repainted into mainline Air Canada c/s, colours will be replaced…..

☐ C-GJZB	Boeing 757-28AER	28203/802	ex G-TCBA		♦
☐ C-GJZD	Boeing 757-25F	30757/928	ex G-JMCD		♦
☐ C-GJZH	Boeing 757-25F	30758/932	ex G-JMCE		♦
☐ C-GJZS	Boeing 757-21K	28674/746	ex G-WJAN		♦
☐ C-GJZT	Boeing 757-28A	28835/858	ex G-FCLF		♦
☐ C-FDJA	Canadair CRJ-200ER	7979	ex C-FMLI	162 green	
☐ C-FEJA	Canadair CRJ-200ER	7983	ex C-FMLV	163 yellow	
☐ C-FFJA	Canadair CRJ-200ER	7985	ex C-FMNH	164 orange	
☐ C-FIJA	Canadair CRJ-200ER	7987	ex C-FMNX	165 red	
☐ C-FRIA	Canadair CRJ-100ER	7045	ex C-FMLQ	101 red	
☐ C-FRIB	Canadair CRJ-100ER	7047	ex C-FMLT	102 green	
☐ C-FRID	Canadair CRJ-100ER	7049	ex C-FMLV	103 yellow	
☐ C-FSJF	Canadair CRJ-100ER	7054	ex C-FMMT	105 orange	
☐ C-FSJJ	Canadair CRJ-100ER	7058	ex C-FMNB	106 orange	
☐ C-FSJU	Canadair CRJ-100ER	7060	ex C-FMNH	107 orange	
☐ C-FSKE	Canadair CRJ-100ER	7065	ex C-FMOI	108 red	
☐ C-FSKM	Canadair CRJ-100ER	7071	ex C-FMKZ	110 orange	
☐ C-FVKM	Canadair CRJ-100ER	7074	ex C-FMLI	111 green	
☐ C-FVKN	Canadair CRJ-100ER	7078	ex C-FMLU	112 orange	
☐ C-FVKR	Canadair CRJ-100ER	7083	ex C-FMNQ	114 green	
☐ C-FVMD	Canadair CRJ-100ER	7082		113 orange	
☐ C-FWJB	Canadair CRJ-100ER	7087		115 green	
☐ C-FWJF	Canadair CRJ-100ER	7095		116 orange	
☐ C-FWJI	Canadair CRJ-100ER	7096		117 red	
☐ C-FWJS	Canadair CRJ-100ER	7097		118 red	
☐ C-FWJT	Canadair CRJ-100ER	7098		119 green	
☐ C-FWRR	Canadair CRJ-100ER	7107		120 red	
☐ C-FWRS	Canadair CRJ-100ER	7112		121 red	
☐ C-FWRT	Canadair CRJ-100ER	7118		122 red	
☐ C-FWSC	Canadair CRJ-100ER	7120		123 green	
☐ C-FXMY	Canadair CRJ-100ER	7124		124 yellow	
☐ C-FZJA	Canadair CRJ-200ER	7988	ex C-FMNY	166 green	
☐ C-GGJA	Canadair CRJ-200ER	8002	ex C-FMMY	167 yellow	
☐ C-GJZD	Canadair CRJ-200ER	7544	ex N668BR	155 green	
☐ C-GJZJ	Canadair CRJ-200ER	7553	ex N706BR	157 orange	
☐ C-GJZZ	Canadair CRJ-200ER	7978	ex C-FMLF	161 red	
☐ C-GKEJ	Canadair CRJ-200ER	7269	ex N577ML	180 red	
☐ C-GKEK	Canadair CRJ-200ER	7270	ex N578ML	181 green	
☐ C-GKEM	Canadair CRJ-200ER	7277	ex N579ML	182 yellow	
☐ C-GKEP	Canadair CRJ-200ER	7303	ex N581ML	183 orange	
☐ C-GKER	Canadair CRJ-200ER	7368	ex N588ML	184 red	
☐ C-GKEU	Canadair CRJ-200ER	7376	ex N589ML	185 green	
☐ C-GKEW	Canadair CRJ-200ER	7385	ex N590ML	186 yellow	
☐ C-GKEZ	Canadair CRJ-200ER	7327	ex N583ML	187 orange	
☐ C-GKFR	Canadair CRJ-200ER	7330	ex N584ML	188 red	
☐ C-GKGC	Canadair CRJ-200ER	7334	ex N585ML	189 green	

☐	C-GMJA	Canadair CRJ-200ER	8003	ex C-FMNB	168 orange
☐	C-GNJA	Canadair CRJ-200ER	8004	ex C-FMKV	169 red
☐	C-GOJA	Canadair CRJ-200ER	8009	ex C-FMLI	170 yellow
☐	C-GQJA	Canadair CRJ-200ER	7963	ex C-FCGX	171 Star Alliance c/s
☐	C-GTJA	Canadair CRJ-200ER	7966	ex C-FCLV	172 green
☐	C-GUJA	Canadair CRJ-200ER	8011	ex C-FMLS	173 orange
☐	C-GXJA	Canadair CRJ-200ER	8017	ex C-FMNX	174 yellow
☐	C-GZJA	Canadair CRJ-200ER	8018	ex C-FMNY	175 orange
☐	C-FBJZ	Canadair CRJ-705ER	15037		702 green
☐	C-FCJZ	Canadair CRJ-705ER	15040		703 orange
☐	C-FDJZ	Canadair CRJ-705ER	15041		704 yellow
☐	C-FJJZ	Canadair CRJ-705ER	15043		705 red
☐	C-FKJZ	Canadair CRJ-705ER	15044		706 green
☐	C-FLJZ	Canadair CRJ-705ER	15045		707 yellow
☐	C-FNJZ	Canadair CRJ-705ER	15046		708 orange
☐	C-FTJZ	Canadair CRJ-705ER	15047		709 red
☐	C-FUJZ	Canadair CRJ-705ER	15048		710 Star Alliance c/s
☐	C-GDJZ	Canadair CRJ-705ER	15049		711 green
☐	C-GFJZ	Canadair CRJ-705ER	15050		712 yellow
☐	C-GJAZ	Canadair CRJ-705ER	15036		701 red
☐	C-GLJZ	Canadair CRJ-705ER	15051		713 orange
☐	C-GNJZ	Canadair CRJ-705ER	15052		714 red
☐	C-GOJZ	Canadair CRJ-705ER	15053		715 green
☐	C-GPJZ	Canadair CRJ-705ER	15055	ex C-FGND	716 red
☐	C-FABA	de Havilland DHC-8-102	92		805 orange
☐	C-FABN	de Havilland DHC-8-102	44		803 red
☐	C-FABT	de Havilland DHC-8-102	49		848 green
☐	C-FABW	de Havilland DHC-8-102	97		806 green
☐	C-FACD	de Havilland DHC-8-102	150		808 yellow
☐	C-FACF	de Havilland DHC-8-311A	259		308 yellow
☐	C-FACT	de Havilland DHC-8-311A	262		309 green
☐	C-FACV	de Havilland DHC-8-311A	278		311 red
☐	C-FADF	de Havilland DHC-8-311A	272	ex C-FACU	310 red
☐	C-FGQK	de Havilland DHC-8-102	193		819 yellow
☐	C-FGRC	de Havilland DHC-8-102	195		821 green
☐	C-FGRM	de Havilland DHC-8-102	199		820 red
☐	C-FGRP	de Havilland DHC-8-102	207		822 green
☐	C-FGRY	de Havilland DHC-8-102	212		844 red
☐	C-FJFM	de Havilland DHC-8-311A	240		324 yellow
☐	C-FJMG	de Havilland DHC-8-102A	255		824 orange
☐	C-FJVV	de Havilland DHC-8-311A	271		306 red
☐	C-FJXZ	de Havilland DHC-8-311A	264	ex C-FTAQ	326 red
☐	C-FMDW	de Havilland DHC-8-311A	269		305 green
☐	C-FPON	de Havilland DHC-8-102	171		836 orange
☐	C-FRUZ	de Havilland DHC-8-311	293	ex N2492B	327 red
☐	C-FSOU	de Havilland DHC-8-311A	342	ex LN-WFA	328 green
☐	C-FTAK	de Havilland DHC-8-311A	246		323 red
☐	C-GABF	de Havilland DHC-8-102	25		816 green
☐	C-GABO	de Havilland DHC-8-311A	248		312 orange
☐	C-GABP	de Havilland DHC-8-311A	257		307 green
☐	C-GANF	de Havilland DHC-8-102	42		802 orange
☐	C-GANI	de Havilland DHC-8-102	64		830 green
☐	C-GANK	de Havilland DHC-8-102	87		831 yellow
☐	C-GANQ	de Havilland DHC-8-102	96		833 yellow
☐	C-GANS	de Havilland DHC-8-102	57		828 green
☐	C-GCTC	de Havilland DHC-8-102	65	ex V2-LEE	846 orange
☐	C-GETA	de Havilland DHC-8-301	186		321 red
☐	C-GEWQ	de Havilland DHC-8-311A	202		325 red
☐	C-GHTA	de Havilland DHC-8-301	198		316 orange
☐	C-GION	de Havilland DHC-8-102	127		832 yellow
☐	C-GJIG	de Havilland DHC-8-102	68		826 orange
☐	C-GJMI	de Havilland DHC-8-102	77		825 yellow
☐	C-GJMO	de Havilland DHC-8-102	79		834 yellow
☐	C-GJSV	de Havilland DHC-8-102	85		814 green
☐	C-GJSX	de Havilland DHC-8-102	88		835 red
☐	C-GKON	de Havilland DHC-8-102	130		815 red
☐	C-GKTA	de Havilland DHC-8-301	124		317 green
☐	C-GLTA	de Havilland DHC-8-301	154		318 green
☐	C-GMON	de Havilland DHC-8-301	131		301 orange
☐	C-GMTA	de Havilland DHC-8-301	174		319 yellow
☐	C-GNON	de Havilland DHC-8-301	137		302 green
☐	C-GOND	de Havilland DHC-8-102	90		840 red
☐	C-GONJ	de Havilland DHC-8-102	95		839 orange
☐	C-GONN	de Havilland DHC-8-102	101		898 yellow
☐	C-GONO	de Havilland DHC-8-102	102		807 orange

☐ C-GONR	de Havilland DHC-8-102	109		841 green
☐ C-GONW	de Havilland DHC-8-102	112		843 green
☐ C-GONX	de Havilland DHC-8-102	118		829 red
☐ C-GONY	de Havilland DHC-8-102	115		827 yellow
☐ C-GSTA	de Havilland DHC-8-301	182		320 yellow
☐ C-GTAG	de Havilland DHC-8-301	200		315 orange
☐ C-GTAI	de Havilland DHC-8-102	78		853 yellow
☐ C-GTAQ	de Havilland DHC-8-301	180	ex C-FGVK	313 red
☐ C-GTAT	de Havilland DHC-8-301	188	ex C-FGVT	314 red
☐ C-GTBP	de Havilland DHC-8-102	66		855 green
☐ C-GUON	de Havilland DHC-8-301	143		303 green
☐ C-GVON	de Havilland DHC-8-301	149		304 orange
☐ C-GVTA	de Havilland DHC-8-301	190		322 red
☐ C-	de Havilland DHC-8-402Q			o/o♦
☐ C-	de Havilland DHC-8-402Q			o/o♦
☐ C-	de Havilland DHC-8-402Q			o/o♦
☐ C-	de Havilland DHC-8-402Q			o/o♦
☐ C-	de Havilland DHC-8-402Q			o/o♦

AIR CREEBEC · Cree (YN/CRQ) · Val d'Or, QC / Timmins, ON (YVO/YTS)

☐ C-FHGG	Beech A100 King Air	B-207	ex N727LE	
☐ C-FTQR	Beech 1900D	UE-129		
☐ C-GIZX	Beech A100 King Air	B-172	ex N753DB	
☐ C-FCLS	de Havilland DHC-8-102	249	ex N841EX	
☐ C-FCSK	de Havilland DHC-8-102	122		
☐ C-FDWO	de Havilland DHC-8-106	277	ex N880CC	
☐ C-GAIS	de Havilland DHC-8-102	138	ex C-FCIZ	
☐ C-GJOP	de Havilland DHC-8-102	121	ex N381BC	
☐ C-GTCO	de Havilland DHC-8-102	119		
☐ C-GYWX	de Havilland DHC-8-102	175	ex N283BC	
☐ C-GZEW	de Havilland DHC-8-314	393	ex N801SA	
☐ C-FPCM	Embraer EMB.110P1 Bandeirante	110340	ex LN-TDI	
☐ C-FPCU	Embraer EMB.110P1 Bandeirante	110445	ex LN-TDA	
☐ C-FYRH	Embraer EMB.110P1 Bandeirante	110259	ex N91PB	
☐ C-FLIY	Hawker Siddeley HS.748 Srs.2A/244	1723	ex SE-LEG	Frtr
☐ C-FPJR	Hawker Siddeley HS.748 Srs.2A/244	1725	ex SE-LEK	Frtr

AIR-DALE FLYING SERVICE · Ranger Lake SPB, ON/Wawa Hawk Junction SPB, ON

☐ C-FGYT	de Havilland DHC-2 Beaver	182	ex CF-GYT	FP
☐ CF-ODE	de Havilland DHC-2 Beaver	131		FP
☐ C-GELP	de Havilland DHC-2 Beaver	780	ex N5318G	FP
☐ C-GQXI	de Havilland DHC-2 Beaver	427	ex N1059	FP

AIR GEORGIAN · Georgian (ZX/GGN) · Toronto-Pearson Intl, ON (YYZ)

☐ C-GAAR	Beech 1900D	UE-207	ex N10625	964 Baie-Saint Laurent
☐ C-GAAS	Beech 1900D	UE-209	ex N10659	965 Iles de la Madelaine
☐ C-GAAU	Beech 1900D	UE-232	ex N10705	904 Baie Comeau
☐ C-GAAV	Beech 1900D	UE-235	ex N10708	967
☐ C-GGGA	Beech 1900D	UE-291	ex N20704	951
☐ C-GHGA	Beech 1900D	UE-293	ex N21063	953
☐ C-GMGA	Beech 1900D	UE-315	ex N22890	956 Baie Comeau
☐ C-GORA	Beech 1900D	UE-326	ex N23164	957
☐ C-GORC	Beech 1900D	UE-320	ex N22976	959
☐ C-GORF	Beech 1900D	UE-330	ex N23222	958
☐ C-GORI	Beech 1900D	UE-47	ex N84502	970
☐ C-GORZ	Beech 1900D	UE-134	ex N860CA	973
☐ C-GVGA	Beech 1900D	UE-292	ex N20707	952
☐ C-GWGA	Beech 1900D	UE-309	ex N22874	955
☐ C-GZGA	Beech 1900D	UE-306	ex N22700	954

AIR INUIT · Air Inuit (3H/AIE) · Kuujjuaq, QC (YVP)

☐ C-FAIY	de Havilland DHC-6 Twin Otter 300	362	ex C-FASS	FP/WS
☐ C-FJFR	de Havilland DHC-6 Twin Otter 300	784	ex HK-2762	
☐ C-FTJJ	de Havilland DHC-6 Twin Otter 300	325	ex 8Q-MAJ	N93NC res
☐ C-GKCJ	de Havilland DHC-6 Twin Otter 300	698	ex A6-AMM	dbr 11Feb07?
☐ C-GMDC	de Havilland DHC-6 Twin Otter 300	763		
☐ C-GNDO	de Havilland DHC-6 Twin Otter 300	430		
☐ C-GTYX	de Havilland DHC-6 Twin Otter 300	631		
☐ C-FAIV	de Havilland DHC-8-102	235	ex N828EX	

☐ C-FCJD	de Havilland DHC-8-102	158		
☐ C-FDAO	de Havilland DHC-8-102	123		
☐ C-FDND	de Havilland DHC-8-102	129		
☐ C-GAII	de Havilland DHC-8-102	160	ex N831EX	
☐ C-GAIW	de Havilland DHC-8-102	155	ex N830EX	
☐ C-GRAI	de Havilland DHC-8Q-314	483	ex OE-LTK	
☐ C-GUAI	de Havilland DHC-8Q-314	423	ex OE-LTF	
☐ C-FAIO	Beech A100 King Air	B-132	ex C-GXHP	
☐ C-FAIP	Beech A100 King Air	B-193	ex F-GXAB	
☐ C-FDOX	Hawker Siddeley HS.748 Srs.2A/310LFD	1749	ex TJ-CCD	Frtr
☐ C-FGET	Hawker Siddeley HS.748 Srs.2A/244	1724	ex D-AFSG	
☐ C-GAIG	Boeing 737-2S2C	21928/603	ex A6-ZYB	
☐ C-GCUK	Hawker Siddeley HS.748 Srs.2A/343LFD	1762	ex V2-LAZ	Frtr
☐ C-GAIK	Beech A100 King Air	B-104	ex C-GCFD	
☐ C-GEGJ	Hawker Siddeley HS.748 Srs.2A/244	1711	ex TF-GMB	
☐ C-GMAI	Boeing 737-2Q2C	21467/515	ex TN-AHW	♦

AIR IVANHOE   Foleyet-Ivanhoe Lake, ON

| ☐ C-GERE | de Havilland DHC-2 Beaver | 352 | ex N62784 | FP |
| ☐ C-GPUS | de Havilland DHC-2 Beaver | 624 | ex 53-2824 | FP |

AIR KIPAWA   Kipawa, QC

| ☐ C-FODA | de Havilland DHC-2 Beaver | 112 | ex CF-ODA | FP |

AIR LABRADOR   Lab Air (WJ/LAL)   Goose Bay, NL (YYR)

☐ C-FGON	de Havilland DHC-6 Twin Otter 300	369	ex CF-GON	FP/WS
☐ C-GLAI	de Havilland DHC-6 Twin Otter 300	296	ex N5377G	FP/WS
☐ C-GNQY	de Havilland DHC-6 Twin Otter 300	450	ex N965HA	FP/WS
☐ C-FXON	de Havilland DHC-8-102	183	ex V2-LDZ	
☐ C-GLHO	Beech 1900D	UE-266	ex N10950	
☐ C-GLON	de Havilland DHC-8-102	133		
☐ C-GTMB	Beech 1900D	UE-345	ex N23388	
☐ C-GUYR	Cessna 208 Caravan I	20800031	ex N604MA	

AIR MECATINA   La Romaine, QC

☐ C-FJDP	Cessna A185E Skywagon	185-1425	ex CF-JDP	FP
☐ C-FSKQ	Beech 200 Super King Air	BB-99	ex 5Y-SEL	
☐ C-GNBB	Beech 200 Super King Air	BB-479	ex N200UQ	
☐ C-GZIJ	Piper PA-31-350 Navajo Chieftain	31-7552041	ex N901FA	

AIR MELANCON   St Anne-du-Lac, QC

☐ C-FBPB	de Havilland DHC-2 Beaver	1434	ex VH-IDF	FP/WS
☐ C-FQQD	de Havilland DHC-2 Beaver	1580	ex FAP 64-374	FP/WS
☐ C-FZVP	de Havilland DHC-2 Beaver	1033	ex N564	FP/WS
☐ C-GQXH	de Havilland DHC-2 Beaver	536	ex N1579	FP/WS

AIR MIKISEW   Air Mikisew (V8)   Fort McMurray, AB (YMM)

☐ C-FAMB	Beech B200 Super King Air	BB-1281	ex N865TC	
☐ C-FKAM	British Aerospace Jetstream 31	724	ex N852JS	
☐ C-FKEY	Cessna 208 Caravan I	20800307	ex N5264A	FP
☐ C-FMCN	Beech 1900D	UE-20	ex N220CJ	
☐ C-FUAM	British Aerospace Jetstream 31	746	ex N404UE	
☐ C-FVGT	Piper PA-31-350 Navajo Chieftain	31-7405133	ex N74981	
☐ C-GDIR	Cessna A185F Skylane	18503973	ex (N6552E)	
☐ C-GFJN	Cessna 207A Stationair 7	20700592	ex (N73446)	
☐ C-GURM	Piper PA-31-350 Navajo Chieftain	31-7752184	ex N273RH	
☐ C-GVAM	Cessna U206G Stationair 6	U20606177	ex N918WJ	
☐ C-GVQU	Cessna A185F Skylane	18503648	ex N8206Q	

AIR MONT-LAURIER   Ste-Veronique, QC

☐ CF-GQA	de Havilland DHC-2 Beaver	72	ex CF-GQA	FP
☐ C-FQQC	de Havilland DHC-2 Beaver	56	ex CF-QQC	FP
☐ C-FSUB	de Havilland DHC-3 Otter	8	ex RCAF 3662	FP
☐ C-FTUR	de Havilland DHC-2 Beaver	1529	ex CF-TUR	FP
☐ C-GGSC	de Havilland DHC-3 Otter	366	ex N5072F	FP
☐ C-GMGP	Cessna A185F Skywagon	18502077	ex N9054F	FP
☐ C-GUML	de Havilland DHC-2 Beaver	307	ex N1402Z	FP
☐ C-GVLK	Cessna U206G Stationair 6 II	U20604329	ex N756SW	FP

AIR MONTMAGNY — Montmagny, QC

☐ C-GBFU	Britten-Norman BN-2A-27 Islander	535	ex N70JA
☐ C-GCTM	Cessna U206G Stationair	U20603794	ex N8920G
☐ C-GGJG	Britten-Norman BN-2B-26 Islander	2219	ex F-ODUP
☐ C-GTMQ	Cessna 206H Stationair	20608038	ex N7255B

AIR NOOTKA — Gold River, BC

☐ C-FIBR	Cessna 180K Skywagon	18052788	ex N818BR	FP
☐ C-FOXD	de Havilland DHC-2 Beaver	807	ex N90723	FP
☐ C-GIUR	Cessna A185F Skywagon	18503290	ex (N94214)	FP
☐ C-GPVB	de Havilland DHC-2 Beaver	871	ex N9253Z	FP

AIR NORTH — Air North (4N/ANT) — Whitehorse, YT (YXY)

☐ C-FANB	Boeing 737-48E	25764/2314	ex N764TA	♦
☐ C-FJLB	Boeing 737-201 (Nordam 3)	22273/680	ex N233US	
☐ C-GANH	Boeing 737-505/W	27153/2516	ex VP-BOQ	♦
☐ C-GANV	Boeing 737-2X6C	23122/1036	ex N816AL	
☐ C-GNAU	Boeing 737-201 (Nordam 3)	21817/602	ex N228US	
☐ C-FAID	de Havilland DHC-8Q-314	400	ex OE-LTD	
☐ C-FAGI	Hawker Siddeley HS.748 Srs.2A/276	1699	ex G-11-6	
☐ C-FCSE	Hawker Siddeley HS.748 Srs 2A/269	1679	ex G-AYFL	
☐ C-FYDU	Hawker Siddeley HS.748 Srs.2A/273	1694	ex ZK-MCP	
☐ C-FYDY	Hawker Siddeley HS.748 Srs.2A/233	1661	ex ZK-MCJ	Frtr
☐ C-GLIZ	Cessna 206 Super Skywagon	206-0156	ex N5156U	

AIR NUNAVUT — Air Baffin (BFF) — Iqaluit, NT (YFB)

☐ C-FCGW	Beech 200 Super King Air	BB-207	ex N111WH	CatPass 200 conversion
☐ C-FZNQ	Beech 200 Super King Air	BB-264	ex N465CJ	CatPass 200 conversion
☐ C-GZYO	Beech 200 Super King Air	BB-383	ex N384DB	

AIR OPTIMA — Miramichi, NB (YCH)

☐ C-FIML	Cessna 310Q	310Q0758	ex CF-IML
☐ C-GABL	Cessna 310R II	310R0927	ex N3840G

AIR QUASAR — (QAT) — Montreal-St Hubert, QC (YHU)

☐ C-FCFC	Piper PA-23-150	23-312	ex CF-CFC
☐ C-FDTF	Cessna 210L Centurion II	21060291	ex N93168
☐ C-FVEI	Cessna 210L Centurion II	21059550	ex N4650Q
☐ C-GNEL	Cessna 210L Centurion II	21060004	ex N35636

AIR ROBERVAL

☐ C-FDGW	Cessna 208 Caravan I	20800272	ex C-FCPW	
☐ C-FNFI	de Havilland DHC-3 Turbo Otter	379		FP/WS
☐ C-FVVY	de Havilland DHC-3 Turbo Otter	410	ex RCAF 9427	FP/WS
☐ C-GFZT	Cessna U206F Stationair II	U20603406	ex (N8550Q)	FP/WS
☐ C-GJEM	Cessna 208 Caravan	20800152	ex N9728F	FP/WS
☐ C-GSMA	Cessna 310Q	310Q1008	ex N313SK	

AIR SAGUENAY — Lac St-Sebastien, QC

☐ C-FIUS	de Havilland DHC-2 Beaver	901	ex CF-IUS	FP/WS
☐ C-FJAC	de Havilland DHC-2 Beaver	937	ex CF-JAC	FP/WS
☐ C-FJKI	de Havilland DHC-2 Beaver	992	ex CF-JKI	FP/WS
☐ C-FKRJ	de Havilland DHC-2 Beaver	1210	ex CF-KRJ	FP/WS
☐ C-GAEF	de Havilland DHC-2 Beaver	372	ex 51-16830	FP/WS
☐ C-GAXL	de Havilland DHC-2 Beaver	1032	ex 56-537	FP/WS
☐ C-GPUO	de Havilland DHC-2 Beaver	810	ex 54-1677	FP/WS
☐ C-GUJI	de Havilland DHC-2 Beaver	1141	ex N68013	FP/WS
☐ C-FDAK	de Havilland DHC-3 Otter	157	ex CF-DAK	FP/WS
☐ C-FODT	de Havilland DHC-3 Otter	218	ex CF-ODT	FP/WS
☐ C-GLFL	de Havilland DHC-3 Turbo Otter	329	ex 58-1712	FP/WS
☐ C-GLMT	de Havilland DHC-3 Otter	216	ex IM-1716	FP/WS
☐ C-GQDU	de Havilland DHC-3 Turbo Otter	43	ex N94472	FP/WS
☐ C-GUTQ	de Havilland DHC-3 Otter	402	ex HK-3049X	FP/WS
☐ C-FYAO	Cessna A185E Skywagon	18501472	ex (N2722J)	FP/WS

☐ C-GTBY	Cessna 208 Caravan I	20800261	ex C-GFLN		FP/WS

AIR SATELLITE — Satellite (6O/ASJ) — Baie Comeau, QC (YBC)

☐ C-GSSW	Piper PA-34-200 Seneca	34-7450046	ex N56995		

AIR-SPRAY — Air Spray (ASB) — Edmonton-Municipal/Red Deer, AB (YEG/YQF)

☐ CF-CBK	Douglas B-26C Invader	28940	ex N9996Z	11	
☐ CF-CUI	Douglas B-26C Invader	28803	ex N9401Z	12	
☐ C-FKBM	Douglas A-26B Invader	27415	ex N8017E	20	
☐ C-FOVC	Douglas B-26C Invader	28776	ex N3426G	56	
☐ C-FPGF	Douglas A-26B Invader	29154	ex 44-35875	1	
☐ CF-ZTC	Douglas B-26C Invader	29136	ex N9300R	13 Lucky Jack	
☐ C-GHZM	Douglas A-26B Invader	27400	ex N4805E	5 Fire Eater	
☐ C-GTOX	Douglas A-26B Invader	27802	ex N9174Z	14	
☐ C-FLJO	Lockheed L-188C Electra	1103	ex N429NA	82	
☐ C-FLXT	Lockheed L-188C Electra	1130	ex N308D		
☐ C-FVFH	Lockheed L-188A Electra	1006	ex PK-RLF	89	
☐ C-FVFI	Lockheed L-188C Electra	1082	ex PK-RLD		[YQF]
☐ C-FZCS	Lockheed L-188C Electra	1060	ex HR-SHN	87	
☐ C-GHZI	Lockheed L-188C Electra	2007	ex N1968R	84	
☐ C-GYVI	Lockheed L-188CF Electra	1112	ex N360Q	83	
☐ C-GZCF	Lockheed L-188CF Electra	1091	ex G-CEXS	90	
☐ C-GZVM	Lockheed L-188A Electra	1036	ex N351Q	85	
☐ C-GZYH	Lockheed L-188A Electra	1124	ex HR-AMM		[YQF]
☐ C-FAKP	Rockwell 690 Turbo Commander	11040	ex N690DC	56	
☐ C-FIIL	Rockwell 690A Turbo Commander	11167	ex N85AB		
☐ C-FMCX	Rockwell 690B Turbo Commander	11446	ex N137BW		
☐ C-FZRQ	Rockwell 690 Turbo Commander	11025	ex N100LS	51	
☐ C-GFPP	Rockwell 690 Turbo Commander	11032	ex N349AC	52	
☐ C-GJFO	Rockwell 690 Turbo Commander	11035	ex N15VZ	53	
☐ C-GKDZ	Rockwell 690 Turbo Commander	11016	ex N428SJ	54	
☐ C-GZON	Rockwell 690 Turbo Commander	11020	ex N14CV	55	
☐ C-FEHK	Ted Smith Aerostar 600A	60-0400-140	ex N17LH	307	
☐ C-FGWE	Cessna 310Q II	310Q0920	ex (N69686)	302	for sale
☐ C-FJCF	Ted Smith Aerostar 600A	60-0153-067	ex N37HA	308	
☐ C-GXJP	Cessna 310P	310P0073	ex N101QC	305	for sale
☐ C-GXXN	Cessna T310P	310P0002	ex N5702M	306	for sale

AIR TINDI — Air Tindi (8T) — Yellowknife, NT (YZF)

☐ C-FASG	de Havilland DHC-6 Twin Otter 300	373		FP/WS
☐ C-FATM	de Havilland DHC-6 Twin Otter 300	265	ex PJ-ATL	FP/WS
☐ C-FATN	de Havilland DHC-6 Twin Otter 300	226	ex N153BU	FP/WS
☐ C-FATO	de Havilland DHC-6 Twin Otter 310	674	ex A6-MRM	FP/WS
☐ C-FATW	de Havilland DHC-6 Twin Otter 300	525	ex PK-BRA	FP/WS
☐ C-GMAS	de Havilland DHC-6 Twin Otter 300	438	ex N546N	FP/WS
☐ C-GNPS	de Havilland DHC-6 Twin Otter 300	558		FP/WS
☐ C-FATA	Beech 200 Super King Air	BB-283	ex N283JP	
☐ C-FCGU	Beech 200B Super King Air	BB-301	ex N611SW	CatPass 200 conversion
☐ C-FKAY	Cessna 208B Caravan I	208B0470	ex N1294N	
☐ C-FWZV	de Havilland DHC-7-103	81	ex P2-ANP	
☐ C-FXUY	de Havilland DHC-3 Turbo Otter	142	ex N214L	FP/WS
☐ C-FZDV	de Havilland DHC-3 Otter	349	ex N28NC	
☐ C-GATH	Cessna 208B Caravan I	208B1244	ex N5225K	
☐ C-GATV	Cessna 208B Caravan I	208B0308		
☐ C-GATY	Cessna 208 Caravan I	20800305	ex N52627	FP/WS
☐ C-GCEV	de Havilland DHC-7-102	63	ex HB-IVY	
☐ C-GDPB	Beech 200C Super King Air	BL-44	ex N18379	EMS
☐ C-GFFL	de Havilland DHC-7-102	74	ex HB-IVY	
☐ C-GHUE	Beech 1900D	UE-52	ex N152MJ	♦
☐ C-GPHO	Cessna A185F Skywagon	18503099	ex (N80151)	FP/WS
☐ C-GTUC	Beech 200 Super King Air	BB-268	ex N565RA	
☐ C-GWXI	Cessna A185F Skywagon	18502818	ex (N1298F)	FP/WS
☐ C-GXHF	Beech 200 Super King Air	BB-1343	ex 5Y-ECO	Beech 1300 conversion
☐ C-GZIX	Cessna A185F Skywagon	18504182	ex N46CR	FP/WS

AIR TRANSAT — Transat (TS/TSC) — Montreal-Trudeau, QC (YUL)

☐ C-FDAT	Airbus A310-308	658	ex A6-EKK	305
☐ C-GFAT	Airbus A310-304	545	ex A6-EKG	301
☐ C-GLAT	Airbus A310-308	588	ex A6-EKI	302
☐ C-GPAT	Airbus A310-308	597	ex A6-EKJ	303

64

☐ C-GSAT	Airbus A310-308	600	ex 5Y-KQM	304
☐ C-GTSF	Airbus A310-304	472	ex CS-TEZ	345
☐ C-GTSH	Airbus A310-308	599	ex D-AIDN	343
☐ C-GTSK	Airbus A310-304	541	ex CS-TEW	
☐ C-GTSW	Airbus A310-304	483	ex CS-TEH	
☐ C-GTSX	Airbus A310-304	527	ex D-AIDH	346
☐ C-GTSY	Airbus A310-304	447	ex N447DN	344
☐ C-GVAT	Airbus A310-304	485	ex D-AIDC	321
☐ C-GCTS	Airbus A330-342	177	ex B-HYE	
☐ C-GGTS	Airbus A330-243	250	ex F-WWKK	101
☐ C-GITS	Airbus A330-243	271	ex F-WWKY	102
☐ C-GKTS	Airbus A330-342	111	ex B-HYC	100
☐ C-GPTS	Airbus A330-243	480	ex F-WWKV	103
☐ C-GTSN	Airbus A330-243	369	ex HB-IQZ	♦
☐ C-	Airbus A330-243		ex	o/o♦
☐ C-	Airbus A330-243		ex	o/o♦

AIR TUNILIK — *Schefferville-Squaw Lake, QC (YKL)*

☐ C-FLLX	de Havilland DHC-2 Beaver	1293	ex CF-LLX	FP/WS
☐ C-GNKR	de Havilland DHC-2 Beaver	331	ex N5698	

AIRBORNE ENERGY SOLUTIONS — *Whitecourt, AB (YZU)*

☐ C-FPKM	Aérospatiale AS350B2 AStar	2426	ex JA6045
☐ C-FWKM	Aérospatiale AS350B2 AStar	2427	ex JA6044
☐ C-GREV	Aérospatiale AS350BA AStar	1039	ex N98TV
☐ C-GTKM	Aérospatiale AS350BA AStar	2515	ex JA6095
☐ C-FARJ	Bell 206B JetRanger	741	ex N700BH
☐ C-FBKH	Bell 206B JetRanger	575	ex N100FW
☐ C-GJEL	Bell 206B JetRanger	116	ex N855NR
☐ C-GKRH	Bell 206B JetRanger II	2109	ex N354AC
☐ C-GTEZ	Bell 206B JetRanger	746	ex N2926W
☐ C-GTQU	Bell 206B JetRanger	766	ex N8199J
☐ C-GXAG	Bell 206B JetRanger	150	ex N6283N
☐ C-GXBY	Bell 206B JetRanger	477	ex N72HP
☐ C-FARQ	Cessna 208B Caravan I	208B0765	ex N5174W
☐ C-FHHA	Bell 206L-1 LongRanger	45662	ex C-GBPO
☐ C-FNCI	Piper PA-31 Navajo C	31-8112007	ex N9149Z
☐ C-FZGP	Bell 206B JetRanger II	940	ex N888LH
☐ C-FZHG	Piper PA-31 Turbo Navajo B	31-753	ex N103DE
☐ C-GAEO	Beech 300 Super King Air	FL-479	ex N3179V
☐ C-GEAH	Bell 205A-1	30096	ex LX-HAH
☐ C-GFYK	Cessna U206F Stationair II	U20603350	ex (N8492Q)
☐ C-GLRR	Piper PA-31-325 Navajo C/R	31-7812044	ex N824AB
☐ C-GQLG	Bell 205A-1	30008	ex A7-HAF

AIRCO AIRCRAFT CHARTERS — *Edmonton-Municipal, AB (YXD)*

☐ C-FTOW	Beech 1900D	UE-130	
☐ C-FWPG	Beech 100 King Air	B-67	ex N26KW
☐ C-FWYF	Beech 100 King Air	B-89	ex N169RA
☐ C-FWYN	Beech 100 King Air	B-47	ex C-GNAX
☐ C-FWYO	Beech 100 King Air	B-28	ex N27JJ
☐ C-GBMI	Piper PA-31-350 Chieftain	31-8352007	ex N23NP
☐ C-GZNB	Piper PA-31-350 Navajo Chieftain	31-7752079	ex N6654B

AIREXPRESS ONTARIO — *Oshawa, ON (YOO)*

☐ C-FSKX	Beech 200 Super King Air	BB-1126	ex N650JW
☐ C-FTIU	Beech 350 Super King Air	FL-584	ex N33984
☐ C-GBBS	Beech 200 Super King Air	BB-757	ex N948MB

AIRSPAN HELICOPTERS — *Sechelt, BC (YHS)*

☐ C-FBKS	Bell 206LR+ LongRanger	45033	ex N206ML
☐ C-FJPI	Aérospatiale AS350BA AStar	1260	ex N350NH
☐ C-FVSP	Bell 206B JetRanger	899	ex N83070
☐ C-GHHI	Bell 206L-3 LongRanger III	51037	ex N30EA
☐ C-GJKN	Bell 205A-1	30091	ex CS-HEA
☐ C-GVIW	Bell 206L-1 LongRanger III	45410	

ALBERTA CENTRAL AIRWAYS — *Lac la Biche, AB (YLB)*

☐ C-FJWU	Beech 65-E90 King Air	LW-332	ex N636GW

☐ C-FNED	Beech 65-C90 King Air	LJ-680	ex N928RD	
☐ C-FTSU	de Havilland DHC-6 Twin Otter 300	451	ex C-FINM	
☐ C-FTWU	de Havilland DHC-6 Twin Otter 300	372	ex N17GL	
☐ C-FWPN	Beech 100 King Air	B-51	ex N16SW	
☐ C-GACA	Beech 200 Super King Air	BB-1309	ex N4277C	Beech 1300 conversion
☐ C-GACN	Beech 200 Super King Air	BB-1384	ex N575T	Beech 1300 conversion
☐ C-GEUA	Piper PA-31 Turbo Navajo	31-187	ex N64JK	
☐ C-GGBZ	Cessna U206G Stationair 6 II	U20605637		
☐ C-GUWO	Piper PA-31 Turbo Navajo	31-203	ex N9154Y	
☐ C-GWFF	Piper PA-31 Turbo Navajo C	31-7512063	ex N61390	
☐ C-GYUW	Cessna U206G Stationair 6	U20603738		

ALBERTA CITYLINK   Alberta Citylink (ABK)   Calgary-Intl/Medicine Hat, AB (YYC/YXH)

☐ C-FBID	British Aerospace Jetstream 31	802	ex G-31-802
☐ C-FZVY	British Aerospace Jetstream 31	833	ex N833JX
☐ C-GZOS	British Aerospace Jetstream 31	796	ex N424UE

ALKAN AIR   Alkan Air (AKN)   Whitehorse, YT (YXY)

☐ C-FAKN	Beech 200 Super King Air	BB-216	ex LN-VIU	
☐ C-FAKW	Beech 300 Super King Air	FA-183	ex N19NC	
☐ C-FAKZ	Cessna 208B Caravan I	208B0666	ex N939JL	
☐ C-FCPV	de Havilland DHC-6 Twin Otter 300	371	ex HC-CES	◆
☐ C-FSKF	Cessna 208B Caravan I	208B0673	ex N5268M	
☐ C-FTBI	Short SC.7 Skyvan	SH1847	ex N64HB	
☐ C-GLCS	de Havilland DHC-3 Otter	428	ex N17685	
☐ C-GMOC	Beech 200 Super King Air	BB-513	ex N513SA	
☐ C-GSDT	Piper PA-31-350 Chieftain	31-8152102	ex N120FL	
☐ C-GYTB	Cessna U206G Stationair	U20603685	ex (N7579N)	

ALLEN AIRWAYS   Sioux Lookout, ON (YXL)

☐ C-FERZ	Cessna 180K	18053071	ex N2799K	FP
☐ C-FYCK	Cessna A185E Skywagon	185-1478	ex CF-YCK	FP/WS
☐ C-GQDO	Cessna A185F Skywagon	18503745	ex (N8585Q)	FP/WS

ALPEN HELICOPTERS   Langley, BC (YNJ)

☐ C-GAHL	Bell 206B JetRanger III	2600	ex N8264U
☐ C-GJSG	Bell 206B JetRanger III	326	ex N1545V
☐ C-GPCX	Bell 206L-1 LongRanger II	45554	
☐ C-GRBO	Cessna A185F Skywagon	18503414	ex N903TH

ALPINE AVIATION   Whitehorse, YT (YXY)

☐ C-FGSI	Cessna U206F Stationair	U20602165	ex CF-GSI	
☐ C-GMGD	de Havilland DHC-2 Beaver	519	ex N67091	FP

ALPINE HELICOPTERS   Kelowna, BC (YLW)

☐ C-FALU	Bell 206B JetRanger III	1072	
☐ C-GALR	Bell 206B JetRanger III	1892	ex N100YB
☐ C-GALX	Bell 206B JetRanger	1046	ex N58096
☐ C-FJCH	Bell 206L-1 LongRanger	45737	ex N144JD
☐ C-GALH	Bell 206L-3 LongRanger III	51297	ex N753HL
☐ C-GALJ	Bell 206L-3 LongRanger III	51010	ex N22654
☐ C-GALL	Bell 206L-3 LongRanger III	51015	ex N22660
☐ C-GRLK	Bell 206L-3 LongRanger III	51028	ex N42814
☐ C-FAHB	Bell 212	30794	ex A6-BBH
☐ C-FAHC	Bell 212	31246	ex N212HT
☐ C-FAHG	Bell 212	30940	ex N8530F
☐ C-FAHK	Bell 212	30852	ex XA-SSE
☐ C-FAHL	Bell 212	30588	ex XA-SSJ
☐ C-FAHP	Bell 212	30933	ex D-HELL
☐ C-FAHR	Bell 212	30789	ex A6-BBI
☐ C-FAHZ	Bell 212	30562	ex XA-SSI
☐ C-FALK	Bell 212	30982	ex N212EL
☐ C-FALV	Bell 212	30816	ex N74AL
☐ C-GAHO	Bell 212	30937	
☐ C-GAHV	Bell 212	30699	ex N90221
☐ C-GALI	Bell 212	30525	ex JA9510
☐ C-GIRZ	Bell 212	30622	ex RP-C1677
☐ C-GRNR	Bell 212	30999	

66

☐ C-FAHI	Bell 407	53016	ex N409KA	
☐ C-FALA	Bell 407	53115		
☐ C-FALF	Bell 407	53271	ex CC-CWS	
☐ C-FALM	Bell 407	53018	ex N409KA	
☐ C-FNOB	Bell 407	53070	ex N57416	
☐ C-GALG	Bell 407	53059	ex N409PH	
☐ C-GYAA	Bell 407	53152	ex N407RH	

ALTA FLIGHTS Alta Flights (ALZ) Edmonton-Intl/Calgary-Intl/Fort McMurray, AB (YEG/YYC/YMM)

☐ C-FAFI	Swearingen SA.227DC Metro 23	DC-868B	ex ZK-JSV	Frtr
☐ C-FTNY	Piper PA-31-350 Chieftain	31-7952245	ex N2169X	
☐ C-FVVS	Piper PA-31-350 Chieftain	31-7952199	ex N35347	
☐ C-GAAF	Swearingen SA.227DC Metro 23	DC-891B	ex B-3956	
☐ C-GSAF	Swearingen SA.227DC Metro 23	DC-866B	ex B-3951	
☐ C-GGKJ	Beech B100 King Air	BE-49	ex N400RK	

AMIGO AIRWAYS Nanaimo-Harbour SPB, BC

☐ C-GGGF	Beech D18S	CA-267	ex N1042H	FP

ARCTIC SUNWEST CHARTERS Yellowknife, NT (YZF)

☐ C-FASC	de Havilland DHC-8-102	038	ex C-GJUZ	
☐ C-FASN	Beech B100 King Air	BE-17	ex N178NC	
☐ C-FASQ	de Havilland DHC-6 Twin Otter 100	78	ex C-FAKM	FP/WS
☐ C-FASV	de Havilland DHC-5A Buffalo	95A	ex 5Y-GBA	
☐ C-FASY	de Havilland DHC-5A Buffalo	107A	ex 5Y-GAA	
☐ C-FKCL	Piper PA-31-350 Navajo Chieftain	31-7752134	ex C-GJET	
☐ C-FOEV	de Havilland DHC-2 Turbo Beaver III	1680/TB48	ex CF-OEV	FP/WS
☐ C-FOPE	de Havilland DHC-2 Turbo Beaver III	1691/TB59	ex CF-OPE	FP/WS
☐ C-FSWN	Piper PA-31-350 Chieftain	31-7952182	ex C-GREP	
☐ C-FTFX	de Havilland DHC-6 Twin Otter 300	340	ex CF-TFX	FP/WS
☐ C-FTXQ	de Havilland DHC-6 Twin Otter 300	308	ex N776A	<FAB
☐ C-GARW	de Havilland DHC-6 Twin Otter 300	367	ex N200DA	FP/WS
☐ C-GASB	de Havilland DHC-8-102	013	ex N802MX	
☐ C-GASW	Beech 99	U-39	ex N99LP	
☐ C-GOZG	Piper PA-32-300 Cherokee Six	32-7540034		
☐ C-GRTA	Eurocopter EC120B Colibri	1076		
☐ C-GSDJ	Cessna A185F Skywagon	18504212	ex N31079	FP/WS

ATIKOKAN AERO SERVICE Atikokan-Municipal, ON (YIB)

☐ CF-IPL	de Havilland DHC-2 Beaver	132		FP/WS
☐ C-GDZH	de Havilland DHC-2 Beaver	356	ex 51-16555	FP/WS

ATLEO RIVER AIR SERVICE Tofino, BC (YTP)

☐ C-GIYQ	Cessna A185F Skywagon II	18503618	ex (N7582Q)	FP/WS
☐ C-GYJX	Cessna A185F Skywagon	18503187	ex (N93161)	FP

ATLIN AIR CHARTERS Atlin, BC

☐ C-GGEK	Cessna 207A Stationair 8 II	20700731	ex N63AK	
☐ C-GOZR	de Havilland DHC-2 Beaver	800	ex 54-1670	

AVIABEC La Tuque SPB, QC (YLQ)

☐ C-FMPT	de Havilland DHC-2 Beaver	1260	ex CF-MPT	FP
☐ C-GSJO	Cessna U206G Stationair 6	U20606827	ex (N9276R)	FP

AVIATION COMMERCIAL AVIATION Access (CMS) Hearst, ON (YHF)

☐ C-FGSX	Piper PA-31T-2 Cheyenne II XL	31T-8166048	ex N600XL	
☐ C-GBFO	Piper PA-31T-2 Cheyenne II XL	31T-8166069	ex N511SC	

AVIATION MAURICIE Lac à la Tortue/Lac Sept-Iles, QC

☐ C-FASO	Cessna U206F Stationair	U20602081	ex N70558	FP/WS
☐ C-FIDG	de Havilland DHC-2 Beaver	718	ex N99872	FP/WS
☐ C-FVDG	Cessna U206B Super Skywagon	U206-0666	ex CF-VDG	FP/WS
☐ C-GOER	de Havilland DHC-2 Beaver	514	ex N99830	FP/WS
☐ C-GYXE	Cessna U206F Stationair	U20603801		FP/WS

BAILEY HELICOPTERS Boundary Bay, BC (YDT)

☐ C-FBHC	Aérospatiale AS350B2 AStar	2850	ex C-FWCH	
☐ C-FBHD	Aérospatiale AS350BA AStar	2166	ex PT-HSE	
☐ C-FBHN	Aérospatiale AS350B2 AStar	3763		

☐ C-FBHX	Aérospatiale AS350BA AStar	2311	ex N787KR		
☐ C-GAVL	Aérospatiale AS350BA AStar	2258	ex N350AH		
☐ C-GKKH	Aérospatiale AS350B AStar	2008	ex JA9481		
☐ C-FBYD	Bell 206B JetRanger III	2519	ex N5008L		
☐ C-FCQD	Bell 206B JetRanger III	534	ex N8146J		
☐ C-FHTM	Bell 206B JetRanger	1017	ex CF-HTM		
☐ C-FHTR	Bell 206B JetRanger	1036	ex CF-HTR		
☐ C-FKOD	Bell 206B JetRanger	1228	ex CF-DOK		
☐ C-FPRB	Bell 206B JetRanger III	3232	ex N20EA		
☐ C-FZWC	Bell 206B JetRanger II	2064	ex N16706		
☐ C-GAXB	Bell 206B JetRanger III	3527	ex N226EC		
☐ C-GBHB	Bell 206B JetRanger III	2415	ex N5001U		
☐ C-GDRH	Bell 206B JetRanger II	2452	ex N37EA		
☐ C-GHHE	Bell 206B JetRanger III	1979	ex N9906K		
☐ C-GJXB	Bell 206B JetRanger II	2208	ex N220CH		
☐ C-GTEK	Bell 206B JetRanger III	1684	ex N222ML		
☐ C-FBHV	Bell 206LR+ LongRanger	45113	ex N403EH		
☐ C-FBHW	Bell 205A-1	30286	ex N224HT		
☐ C-GNMD	Bell 206LR+ LongRanger	45080			

BAKERS NARROWS AIR SERVICE — Flin Flon Athapapuskow Lake SPB, MN

| ☐ C-FNMN | Cessna U206G Stationair | U20604070 | ex N756GB | | FP/WS |

BAMAJI AIR — Sioux Lookout, ON (YXL)

☐ C-FHEP	de Havilland DHC-2 Beaver	69	ex C-FIOB		FP/WS
☐ C-FKAC	Found FBA-2C1 Bush Hawk XP	42			FP/WS
☐ C-GAJU	de Havilland DHC-2 Beaver	1169	ex 56-0415		FP/WS
☐ C-GBKA	Cessna A185F Skywagon	18502375	ex N53099		FP/WS
☐ C-GFDS	de Havilland DHC-2 Beaver	1269	ex 31343		FP/WS
☐ C-GIPR	Cessna 208 Caravan I	20800343			FP/WS

BAR XH AIR — Palliser (BXH) — Medicine Hat, AB (YXH)

☐ C-FCGB	Beech 200 Super King Air	BB-24	ex N183MC	035	CatPass 200 conversion EMS
☐ C-GXHD	Beech 200 Super King Air	BB-1338	ex N915YW		Beech 1300 conversion
☐ C-GXHG	Beech 200 Super King Air	BB-1383	ex N913YW		Beech 1300 conversion
☐ C-GXHN	Beech 200 Super King Air	BB-693	ex N245JS		
☐ C-GXHR	Beech 200 Super King Air	BB-1305	ex 5Y-EOB		Beech 1300 conversion
☐ C-GXHS	Beech 200 Super King Air	BB-1302	ex PP-WYY		Beech 1300 conversion
☐ C-FBHO	Piper PA-31-350 Navajo Chieftain	31-7405466	ex N61439		
☐ C-GMDF	Piper PA-31T Cheyenne	31T-7620019	ex N82000		
☐ C-GXHK	Piper PA-31-350 Navajo Chieftain	31-7752108	ex N115SC		

BC YUKON AIR SERVICE — Dease Lake, BC (YDL)

| ☐ C-FHGZ | de Havilland DHC-2 Beaver | 759 | ex CF-HGZ | | FP/WS |

BEARSKIN AIRLINES — Bearskin (JV/BLS) — Sioux Lookout, ON (YXL)

☐ C-FAMC	Swearingen SA.227AC Metro III	AC-719B	ex N436MA		
☐ C-FFZN	Swearingen SA.227AC Metro III	AC-785B	ex N30019	Spirit of Service	
☐ C-FXUS	Swearingen SA.227CC Metro 23	CC-841B	ex N456LA		
☐ C-FYAG	Swearingen SA.227AC Metro III	AC-670B	ex N670VG	Spirit of Fort Frances	
☐ C-FYWG	Swearingen SA.227AC Metro III	AC-782B	ex N3000S	Spirit of Winnipeg	
☐ C-GAFQ	Swearingen SA.227DC Metro 23	DC-890B	ex N211SA		
☐ C-GJVB	Swearingen SA.227DC Metro 23	DC-902B	ex N902WB		
☐ C-GJVC	Swearingen SA.227DC Metro 23	DC-885B	ex N885ML		
☐ C-GJVH	Swearingen SA.227DC Metro 23	DC-898B	ex N898ML		
☐ C-GYHD	Swearingen SA.227AC Metro III	AC-739B	ex N227JH	Spirit of Dryden	
☐ C-GYQT	Swearingen SA.227AC Metro III	AC-644B	ex N644VG	Spirit of Thunder Bay	
☐ C-GYRL	Swearingen SA.227AC Metro III	AC-706B	ex G-BUKA		
☐ C-GYTL	Swearingen SA.227CC Metro 23	CC-829B	ex N30154	Spirit of Big Trout Lake	
☐ C-GYXL	Swearingen SA.227AC Metro III	AC-725B	ex N227FA		
☐ C-GEHY	Piper PA-23-250 Aztec C	27-3843	ex N6548Y		
☐ C-GFVY	Cessna A185F Skywagon	18503056	ex (N21319)		FP/WS

BIG SALMON AIR — Whitehorse, YT (YXY)

☐ C-FZNL	Cessna A185E Skywagon	18501826	ex (N1602M)		FP/WS
☐ C-GJSR	Cessna U206C Super Skywagon	U206-1106	ex N29136		FP/WS
☐ C-GUAL	Cessna 207A Stationair 8	20700733	ex (N9806M)		FP/WS

BLACK SHEEP AVIATION   Whitehorse, YT (YXY)

☐ C-GDJW	de Havilland DHC-3 Otter	10	ex C-FGTL	FP/WS
☐ C-GMCW	de Havilland DHC-3 Otter	108	ex N5339G	FP/WS
☐ C-GZTQ	Cessna A185F Skywagon II	18503491	ex (N1824Q)	FP/WS

BLACK TUSK HELICOPTER   Squamish, BC (YSE)

☐ C-FSAI	Aérospatiale AS350B2 AStar	2176	ex N121KR
☐ C-FWQU	Bell 214B-1	28029	ex N3999N
☐ C-FZVT	Bell 214B-1	28016	ex LN-OSG
☐ C-GLOG	Bell 206B JetRanger III	3186	ex N801H
☐ C-GSEE	Bell 206B JetRanger	451	ex N95SB

BLACKCOMB HELICOPTERS   Whistler Heliport, BC

☐ C-FHRX	Cessna A185F Skywagon	18502185	ex CF-HRX
☐ C-FKKM	Bell 206B JetRanger II	883	ex N14854
☐ C-FXBC	Aérospatiale AS355F2 Twin Star	5274	ex C-FDNW
☐ C-GJPN	Aérospatiale AS350B2 AStar	4473	
☐ C-GJTH	Bell 205A-1	30036	ex PK-UHC
☐ C-GPGP	Bell 206B JetRanger	2244	
☐ C-GSKI	Aérospatiale AS350B2 AStar	3377	ex C-GILU
☐ C-GSRF	Aérospatiale AS350B2 AStar	2480	ex C-FLHA
☐ C-GYYR	Aérospatiale AS350BA AStar	1675	ex ZK-HBT

BLUE WATER AVIATION SERVICES   Silver Falls, MB

☐ C-FCUW	Cessna 337 Super Skymaster	337-0009	ex N2109X	
☐ C-GBTU	de Havilland DHC-3 Turbo Otter	209	ex IM-1711	FP/WS
☐ C-GFVZ	Cessna A185F Skywagon	18503058	ex (N21451)	FP/WS
☐ C-GGGD	Cessna TU206G Stationair 8	U20605664	ex (N5348X)	FP/WS
☐ C-GHYB	de Havilland DHC-3 Otter	386	ex UB656	FP/WS

BOLTON LAKE AIR SERVICES   Winnipeg-St Andrews, MB (YAV)

☐ C-GYXM	Cessna A185E Skywagon	185-1171	ex N4717Q	FP

BRUCELANDAIR INTERNATIONAL   Wiarton, ON (YVV)

☐ C-FDME	Piper PA-31 Navajo C	31-7812107	ex N21PJ	
☐ C-GBTS	Socata TBM-700	19	ex N635DS	
☐ C-GGNA	Piper PA-23-250 Aztec C	27-3757	ex N6463Y	
☐ C-GPVN	Piper PA-31 Turbo Navajo B	31-7400979	ex TF-EGT	Photo/Survey

BUFFALO AIRWAYS   Buffalo (J4/BFL)   Hay River, NT/Yellowknife (YHY/YZF)

☐ C-GBPD	Canadair CL215	1084		291	Op for NWT Govt	
☐ C-GBYU	Canadair CL215	1083	ex C-GKEA	290	Op for NWT Govt	
☐ C-GCSX	Canadair CL215	1088	ex c-GKEA	295	Op for NWT Govt	
☐ C-GDHN	Canadair CL215	1089	ex C-GKEE	296	Op for NWT Govt	
☐ C-FCUE	Douglas DC-3	12983	ex NC41407			
☐ C-FDTB	Douglas DC-3	12597	ex CF-TEC			[YQF]
☐ C-FDTH	Douglas DC-3	12591	ex CF-TEB			[YQF]
☐ C-FFAY	Douglas DC-3	4785	ex CF-FAY			[YQF]
☐ C-FLFR	Douglas DC-3	13155	ex CF-LFR			
☐ C-GJKM	Douglas DC-3	13580	ex CAF 12946			
☐ C-GPNR	Douglas DC-3	13333	ex CAF 12932			
☐ C-GWIR	Douglas DC-3	9371	ex N18262			
☐ C-GWZS	Douglas DC-3	12327	ex CAF 12913			
☐ C-FBAA	Douglas C-54D-DC	10653	ex N4994H	12	Arctic Expeditor	[YZF]
☐ C-FBAJ	Douglas C-54A-DC	3088	ex N11712	02		[YHY]
☐ C-FBAK	Douglas C-54D-DC	10613	ex N62342			[YHY]
☐ C-FBAM	Douglas C-54G-DC	36009	ex N4958M			[YHY]
☐ C-FBAP	Douglas C-54A-DC	36089	ex N2742G	15		[YHY]
☐ C-FIQM	Douglas C-54G-DC	36088	ex N4218S	57	Arctic Trader	Tanker
☐ C-GBAJ	Douglas C-54A-DC	27328	ex N62297			Tanker
☐ C-GBNV	Douglas C-54G-DC	35988	ex N3303F	56		Tanker
☐ C-GBPA	Douglas C-54D-DC	10673	ex N87591	16		[YZF]
☐ C-GCTF	Douglas C-54E-DC	27281	ex N51819	58		Tanker
☐ C-GPSH	Douglas C-54A-DC	7458	ex N7171H	1	Arctic Distributor	
☐ C-FAVO	Curtiss C-46D Commando	33242	ex N9891Z	Arctic Thunder		
☐ C-FBAQ	Lockheed L-188AF Electra	1039	ex OE-ILB			
☐ C-FCGE	Beech 65-A90 King Air	LJ-118	ex CF-CGE	Birddog 1		
☐ C-FCGH	Beech 65-A90 King Air	LJ-203	ex CF-CGH	Birddog 4		

☐ C-FIJX	Lockheed L-188CF Electra	2010	ex N2RK		♦
☐ C-FNJE	Consolidated PBY-5A Catalina	CV-437	ex CF-NJE		
☐ C-FPQM	Consolidated PBY-5A Catalina	CV-425	ex CF-GMS	714	
☐ CF-SAN	Noorduyn Norseman V	N29-29	ex CF-SAN		FP
☐ C-FUAW	Consolidated PBY-5A Catalina	CV-201	ex (CF-NTK)	708	
☐ C-FULX	Beech 95-C55 Baron	TE-147	ex CF-ULX	Birddog 3	
☐ C-FUPT	Cessna A185E Skywagon	185-1075	ex (N4568F)	141	
☐ C-GBAU	Beech 95-D55 Baron	TE-701	ex N7907R	3	
☐ C-GIWJ	Beech 95 Travel Air	TD-32	ex N2707Y		
☐ C-GLBA	Lockheed L-188AF Electra	1145	ex OE-ILA		
☐ C-GTFC	Consolidated Vultee	279	ex N152PA		
☐ C-GTXW	Curtiss C-46A Commando	30386	ex 5Y-TXW		[YZF]
☐ C-GWCB	Beech B95 Travel Air	TD-369	ex N9914R	140	
☐ C-GYFM	Beech 95 Travel Air	TD-202	ex N654Q		

BUSHLAND AIRWAYS   Moosonee, ON (YMO)

☐ C-FBGB	Cessna U206E Super Skywagon	U20601514	ex (N9114M)		FP
☐ C-FYJR	Cessna A185E Skywagon	185-1520	ex (N2770J)		FP
☐ C-GSNU	Cessna 207A Stationair 7	20700491	ex N6DF		
☐ C-GYWE	Piper PA-32-260 Cherokee Six	32-141	ex N3305W		

CALM AIR   Calm Air (MO/CAV)   Thompson, MB (YTH)

☐ C-FCIJ	ATR 42-300	139	ex ZS-OSN		
☐ C-FECI	ATR 42-320	203	ex F-WNUG		♦
☐ C-FJYV	ATR 42-300	216	ex N216AT	421	
☐ C-FJYW	ATR 42-300	235	ex N233RM	422	
☐ C-FMAK	ATR 42-300	142	ex N142GP		
☐ C-FCRZ	ATR 72-202	357	ex F-WDHA		♦
☐ C-FULE	ATR 72-212	215	ex F-WNUE		
☐ C-FSKS	Cessna 208B Caravan I	208B0722	ex N5268M		
☐ C-FAMO	Hawker Siddeley HS.748 Srs.2A/258LFD 1669		ex CF-AMO	746	Frtr
☐ C-GDOP	Hawker Siddeley HS.748 Srs.2A/283 1745		ex F-ODQQ	744	[YTH]
☐ C-GEPB	Hawker Siddeley HS.748 Srs.2A/254 1686		ex 9G-ABX	743	[YTH]
☐ C-GHSC	Hawker Siddeley HS.748 Srs.2B/FAALFD 1790		ex G-BJTL	745	Frtr
☐ C-GSBF	Hawker Siddeley HS.748 Srs.2A/210 1662		ex G-BCDZ		
☐ C-FSPB	SAAB SF.340B	340B-351	ex B-3656	345	
☐ C-FTJV	SAAB SF.340B	340B-366	ex SE-C66	341	Combi
☐ C-FTJW	SAAB SF.340B	340B-377	ex SE-C77	342	Combi
☐ C-FTLW	SAAB SF.340B	340B-336	ex SE-C36	346	
☐ C-GMNM	SAAB SF.340B	340B-364	ex SE-LHO	344	
☐ C-GTJY	SAAB SF.340B	340B-166	ex N587MA	343	

CAMERON AIR SERVICE   Toronto-City Centre, ON (YTZ)

☐ C-FKCA	Cessna 208 Caravan I	20800211	ex N211PA	
☐ C-FXWH	Cessna U206C Super Skywagon	U206-1170	ex CF-XWH	
☐ C-GCGA	Cessna 208 Caravan I	20800242	ex (A6-CGA)	
☐ C-GGSG	Cessna TU206G Stationair 6	U20605852	ex (N6281X)	

CAMPBELL HELICOPTERS   Abbotsford, BC (YXX)

☐ C-FBEP	Bell 212	30746	ex 4X-BJN	
☐ C-FJUR	Bell 212	30728	ex N8233V	
☐ C-FJUT	Bell 212	30808	ex N8233V	
☐ C-FJUU	Bell 212	30795	ex N8233V	
☐ C-FMPZ	Bell 212	30528	ex HC-BOI	
☐ C-GCVP	Bell 212	30542	ex G-BALZ	
☐ C-GFDV	Bell 212	30842	ex N291B	
☐ C-GFQN	Bell 212	30571	ex N554CR	

CANADIAN AIR CRANE   Delta, BC (DJN)

☐ C-FCRN	Erickson/Sikorsky S-64E Skycrane	64061	ex N172AC	747	
☐ C-GJRY	Erickson/Sikorsky S-64E Skycrane	64052	ex N247AC		♦
☐ C-GJZK	Erickson/Sikorsky S-64E Skycrane	64003	ex N176AC		

CANADIAN HELICOPTERS   Canadian (CDN)   Montreal-Les Cedres, QC /Edmonton, AB

☐ C-FCCA	Aérospatiale AS350BA AStar	2900		
☐ C-FCHN	Aérospatiale AS350BA AStar	2921		
☐ C-FETA	Aérospatiale AS350D AStar	1085	ex N137BH	
☐ C-FFBU	Aérospatiale AS350BA AStar	1215	ex N3605B	

	Registration	Type	Serial	Ex
☐	C-FHVH	Aérospatiale AS350BA AStar	1256	ex N36075
☐	C-FPBA	Aérospatiale AS350B2 AStar	2492	ex JA6091
☐	C-FPER	Aérospatiale AS350BA AStar	2552	ex F-WYMK
☐	C-FPLJ	Aérospatiale AS350D AStar	1060	ex C-FQNS
☐	C-FQNS	Aérospatiale AS350B2 AStar	1423	ex N5783Y
☐	C-FSHV	Aérospatiale AS350B AStar	1287	ex N5143R
☐	C-FSLB	Aérospatiale AS350B AStar	2142	ex JA9786
☐	C-FVVH	Aérospatiale AS350BA AStar	2612	
☐	C-FYCO	Aérospatiale AS350BA AStar	2899	
☐	C-GAHH	Aérospatiale AS350B AStar	1036	ex XA-…
☐	C-GAHI	Aérospatiale AS350B2 AStar	1086	
☐	C-GALD	Aérospatiale AS350BA AStar	1146	
☐	C-GALE	Aérospatiale AS350B AStar	1350	
☐	C-GATX	Aérospatiale AS350BA AStar	1221	
☐	C-GAYX	Aérospatiale AS350BA AStar	1179	
☐	C-GBCZ	Aérospatiale AS350B2 AStar	1159	ex N3600W
☐	C-GBPS	Aérospatiale AS350BA AStar	1277	ex N3610R
☐	C-GCEC	Aérospatiale AS350B AStar	1431	ex N666JK
☐	C-GCHH	Aérospatiale AS350B-2 AStar	2461	ex ZK-HND
☐	C-GCKP	Aérospatiale AS350D AStar	1138	ex N140BH
☐	C-GCWD	Aérospatiale AS350BA AStar	2047	ex N844BP
☐	C-GCWW	Aérospatiale AS350B2 AStar	1435	ex N340DF
☐	C-GDKD	Aérospatiale AS350BA AStar	1432	ex N5785H
☐	C-GDSX	Aérospatiale AS350BA AStar	1134	ex N35972
☐	C-GDUF	Aérospatiale AS350BA AStar	1309	
☐	C-GEPH	Aérospatiale AS350BA AStar	1193	ex ZK-HET
☐	C-GEVH	Aérospatiale AS350BA AStar	2620	ex F-WYMN
☐	C-GFHS	Aérospatiale AS350B AStar	1401	
☐	C-GGIE	Aérospatiale AS350B2 AStar	3280	
☐	C-GLNE	Aérospatiale AS350BA AStar	1128	ex N3599N
☐	C-GLNK	Aérospatiale AS350D AStar	1261	ex N3608C
☐	C-GLNM	Aérospatiale AS350D AStar	1262	ex N3608D
☐	C-GLNO	Aérospatiale AS350D AStar	1264	ex N3608N
☐	C-GMEY	Aérospatiale AS350B AStar	1004	ex N350AS
☐	C-GMIZ	Aérospatiale AS350B2 AStar	1170	
☐	C-GNMN	Aérospatiale AS350BA AStar	1315	ex XA-SNA
☐	C-GOVH	Aérospatiale AS350BA AStar	1286	ex N224GA
☐	C-GRBT	Aérospatiale AS350B2 AStar	1246	ex N877JM
☐	C-GRGJ	Aérospatiale AS350B AStar	1171	ex N3600G
☐	C-GRGU	Aérospatiale AS350BA AStar	1213	ex N7172H
☐	C-GSLF	Aérospatiale AS350D AStar	1310	
☐	C-GTPF	Aérospatiale AS350BA AStar	2932	
☐	C-GTVH	Aérospatiale AS350BA AStar	2611	ex N600CH
☐	C-GVHC	Aérospatiale AS355F2 Twin Star	5195	ex N5801T
☐	C-GVHK	Aérospatiale AS355F1 Twin Star	5098	ex N60031
☐	C-FAHW	Bell 206B JetRanger II	785	ex CF-AHW
☐	C-FBQH	Bell 206B JetRanger II	745	ex CF-BQH
☐	C-FCQE	Bell 206B JetRanger II	535	ex N8147J
☐	C-FHTP	Bell 206B JetRanger II	1024	ex CF-HTP
☐	C-FHTS	Bell 206B JetRanger II	1037	ex CF-HTS
☐	C-FKNX	Bell 206B JetRanger III	2440	ex N5003X
☐	C-FOAN	Bell 206B JetRanger II	791	ex CF-OAN
☐	C-FPOD	Bell 206B JetRanger II	696	ex CF-POD
☐	C-GAHC	Bell 206B JetRanger II	468	ex N2959W
☐	C-GAHR	Bell 206B JetRanger II	873	ex N1488B
☐	C-GBHE	Bell 206B JetRanger II	1335	
☐	C-GBHI	Bell 206B JetRanger III	1758	ex N49584
☐	C-GCIR	Bell 206B JetRanger III	3029	
☐	C-GDBA	Bell 206B JetRanger III	2232	ex N16821
☐	C-GETF	Bell 206B JetRanger III	3036	
☐	C-GFQH	Bell 206B JetRanger II	1090	ex N100JG
☐	C-GHUQ	Bell 206B JetRanger II	1721	ex N3199G
☐	C-GIFY	Bell 206B JetRanger II	2008	
☐	C-GIXS	Bell 206B JetRanger III	2304	ex N272RM
☐	C-GMKT	Bell 206B JetRanger II	774	ex N101PN
☐	C-GNLD	Bell 206B JetRanger III	2357	ex N57PH
☐	C-GNLE	Bell 206B JetRanger III	2358	ex N56PH
☐	C-GNLG	Bell 206B JetRanger III	2360	
☐	C-GNPH	Bell 206B JetRanger III	2352	ex N58148
☐	C-GOKE	Bell 206B JetRanger III	1830	ex N49655
☐	C-GRGN	Bell 206B JetRanger II	1824	ex N333WW
☐	C-GSHP	Bell 206B JetRanger II	1259	ex N259CH
☐	C-GXHC	Bell 206B JetRanger II	395	ex N28956
☐	C-GYQH	Bell 206B JetRanger III	1394	ex N111BH
☐	C-GZQH	Bell 206B JetRanger II	1055	ex N58148

☐ C-FNYQ	Bell 206L LongRanger	45047	ex N20LT	
☐ C-GGZQ	Bell 206L LongRanger	45006	ex N49637	
☐ C-GLMV	Bell 206L-1 LongRanger II	45430	ex N454CH	
☐ C-GLQY	Bell 206L LongRanger	45146		
☐ C-GMHT	Bell 206L LongRanger	45127	ex N16847	
☐ C-GMHY	Bell 206L LongRanger	45145	ex N16924	
☐ C-GNLC	Bell 206L LongRanger	45055	ex N9978K	
☐ C-GNLK	Bell 206L LongRanger	46601	ex N16939	
☐ C-GNMC	Bell 206L LongRanger	45067		
☐ C-GNZR	Bell 206L LongRanger	45118	ex N16809	
☐ C-GQEZ	Bell 206L LongRanger	45038	ex N9942K	
☐ C-GTLB	Bell 206L LongRanger	45031	ex N9927K	
☐ C-GTOM	Bell 206L LongRanger	45010		
☐ C-GVHX	Bell 206L LongRanger	45138	ex N90AC	
☐ C-FBHF	Bell 212	30509	ex N7072J	
☐ C-FCAD	Bell 212	30923	ex HC-CFF	
☐ C-FNJJ	Bell 212	30944	ex N2093S	
☐ C-FOKV	Bell 212	30819	ex N16787	
☐ C-GAHD	Bell 212	30570	ex N7034J	
☐ C-GFQP	Bell 212	30578	ex N58120	
☐ C-GHVH	Bell 212	30877	ex N8555V	
☐ C-GICH	Bell 212	30950	ex N507EH	
☐ C-GKCH	Bell 212	31213	ex N360EH	
☐ C-GOKG	Bell 212	30843		
☐ C-GOKL	Bell 212	30597	ex N2990W	
☐ C-GOKX	Bell 212	30680	ex VH-LHX	
☐ C-GOKY	Bell 212	30698	ex (5H-)	
☐ C-FFAB	Eurocopter EC120B	1486		
☐ C-FLCN	Eurocopter EC120B	1055		
☐ C-FOCH	Eurocopter EC120B	1547		
☐ C-FDCH	Sikorsky S-61N	61773	ex ZS-PWR	
☐ C-FIBN	Sikorsky S-61N	61811	ex PT-HPV	
☐ C-GIMN	Sikorsky S-76A	760110	ex G-BIAV	EMS
☐ C-GIMR	Sikorsky S-76A	760079	ex G-BHYB	
☐ C-GLFO	Sikorsky S-76A	760149	ex N76LA	

CANADIAN NORTH — Norterra (5T/ANX) — Yellowknife, NT (YZF)

☐ C-GCNO	Boeing 737-25A	23790/1422	ex N790CC	
☐ C-GCNS	Boeing 737-275	23283/1109	ex C9-BAN	
☐ C-GCNV	Boeing 737-232	23074/993	ex N302DL	586
☐ C-GDPA	Boeing 737-2T2C (AvAero 3)	22056/655		584 Spirit of Yellowknife
☐ C-GFPW	Boeing 737-275C (AvAero 3)	21294/481		552
☐ C-GKCP	Boeing 737-217 (AvAero 3)	22729/915		523
☐ C-GNDU	Boeing 737-242C (AvAero 3)	22877/880		562
☐ C-GOPW	Boeing 737-275C (AvAero 3)	22160/688	ex N8288V	582 Spirit of Nunavut
☐ C-GSPW	Boeing 737-275C (AvAero 3)	22618/813		583
☐ C-FTAY	Fokker F.28 Fellowship 1000	11084	ex VH-ATG	158
☐ C-GECN	de Havilland DHC-8-106	324	ex C-FSQY	
☐ C-GRGI	de Havilland DHC-8-106	304	ex N829PH	
☐ C-GRGO	de Havilland DHC-8-106	258	ex N735AG	
☐ C-GXCN	de Havilland DHC-8-106	345	ex RA-67255	

CANJET — Canjet (C6/CJA) — Halifax-Intl, NS (YHZ)

☐ C-FTCX	Boeing 737-8AS/W	29921/560	ex EI-CSF	801
☐ C-FTCZ	Boeing 737-8AS/W	29923/576	ex EI-CSH	802
☐ C-FXGG	Boeing 737-81Q/W	29051/479	ex N290AN	
☐ C-FYQN	Boeing 737-8AS/W	29933/1038	ex EI-CST	
☐ C-FYQO	Boeing 737-8AS/W	29934/1050	ex EI-CSV	
☐ C-GDGQ	Boeing 737-8FH/W	35093/2176	ex D-AXLD	♦
☐ C-GDGY	Boeing 737-8Q8/W	28218/160	ex D-AXLF	♦

CAN-WEST CORPORATE AIR CHARTER — Slave Lake, AB (YZH)

☐ C-FCWW	Piper PA-31-350 Chieftain	31-8152192	ex N4097L
☐ C-FKCW	Beech 200 Super King Air	BB-973	ex C-FEVC
☐ C-FOOS	Cessna U206E Stationair	U20601698	ex (N9498G)
☐ C-FSAO	Beech 200 Super King Air	BB-1610	ex N713TA
☐ C-FSAT	Beech 200 Super King Air	BB-1526	ex N417MC
☐ C-GAYZ	Cessna A185F Skywagon	18504040	ex (N6416E)
☐ C-GKOX	Beech 200 Super King Air	BB-389	ex C-GKOS

☐ C-GLGD	Cessna U206G Stationair 6	U20606261	ex (N6388Z)	
☐ C-GNCW	Beech Baron 58	TH-1313	ex N6138C	
☐ C-GSAZ	Piper PA-31 Navajo C	31-8112063	ex N4094Y	
☐ C-GXNL	Cessna 210L Centurion II	21060909	ex N5327V	
☐ C-GYDD	Cessna A185F Skywagon	18503124	ex (N80516)	

CARAVAN AIRLINES — Lloydminster, AB (YLL)

| ☐ C-GBIT | Cessna 208 Caravan I | 20800135 | ex N9706F | FP or wheels |

CARGAIR — Ste Michel-des-Saints/Montreal-St.Hubert, QC (-/YHU)

☐ C-FDMP	Piper PA-23-250 Aztec C	27-3560	ex N6306Y	
☐ CF-GQA	de Havilland DHC-2 Beaver	72	ex CF-GQA	
☐ C-FTSJ	Piper PA-23-250 Aztec D	27-4387	ex N9652N	
☐ C-GMRG	Piper PA-31 Navajo C	31-7812051	ex N27563	
☐ C-GSYH	Piper PA-23-250 Aztec D	27-4214	ex N28EA	

CARGOJET AIRWAYS — Cargojet (W8/CJT) — Winnipeg-Intl, MB/Toronto-Pearson Intl, QC (YWG/YYZ)

☐ C-FCJF	Boeing 727-223F (FedEx 3)	22011/1653	ex C-GACG	
☐ C-FCJI	Boeing 727-225F (FedEx 3)	22435/1674	ex N804MA	[YHM]
☐ C-FCJP	Boeing 727-223F (FedEx 3)	22012/1655	ex C-FUAC	
☐ C-FCJU	Boeing 727-260F (FedEx 3)	22759/1789	ex C-FACM	
☐ C-GCJB	Boeing 727-225F (FedEx 3)	21855/1535	ex N886MA	<Flagship Intl
☐ C-GCJD	Boeing 727-231F (FedEx 3)	21988/1586	ex N808MA	<Flagship Intl
☐ C-GCJN	Boeing 727-225F (FedEx 3)	21451/1310	ex N610PA	
☐ C-GCJQ	Boeing 727-225F (FedEx 3)	22437/1682	ex N806MA	<Flagship Intl
☐ C-GCJY	Boeing 727-223F/W (Duganair 3)	22460/1746	ex N702NE	
☐ C-GCJZ	Boeing 727-225F (FedEx 3)	21854/1532	ex N889MA	
☐ C-GUJC	Boeing 727-260F (FedEx 3)	21979/1534	ex C-FACJ	
☐ C-FKCJ	Boeing 757-236F	24792/279	ex SE-DUO	
☐ C-FGAJ	Boeing 767-223F	22319/112	ex N317AA	
☐ C-FMCJ	Boeing 767-223F	22316/95	ex N313AA	

CARSON AIR — Kelowna, BC (YLW)

☐ C-FAFR	Swearingen SA.227AC Metro III	AC-684	ex N585MA	
☐ C-FBWQ	Swearingen SA.226TC Metro II	TC-379	ex N1011U	
☐ C-FCAW	Swearingen SA.26AT Merlin IIB	T26-172E	ex N135SR	
☐ C-FJKK	Swearingen SA.227AC Metro III	AC-713B	ex N2719H	
☐ C-FKKR	Swearingen SA.226TC Metro II	TC-308	ex N300GL	
☐ C-FTJC	Swearingen SA.226TC Metro II	TC-274	ex N7774H	
☐ C-FTSK	Swearingen SA.227AC Metro III	AC-674B	ex C-FAFM	Frtr
☐ C-GAMI	Swearingen SA.227AC Metro III	AC-587	ex N3115T	
☐ C-GCAU	Swearingen SA.226TC Metro II	TC-331E	ex N255AM	Frtr
☐ C-GCAW	Swearingen SA.226TC Metro II	TC-358	ex N1009R	no titles
☐ C-GDLK	Swearingen SA.226TC Metro II	TC-302	ex N151SA	
☐ C-GKKC	Swearingen SA.226TC Metro II	TC-370	ex N125AV	
☐ C-GKLJ	Swearingen SA.226TC Metro II	TC-380	ex C-GMET	
☐ C-GKLK	Swearingen SA.227AC Metro III	AC-741B	ex N41NE	♦
☐ C-GKLN	Swearingen SA.226TC Metro II	TC-253	ex N328BA	
☐ C-GLSC	Swearingen SA.226TC Metro II	TC-325	ex N162SW	
☐ C-GSKC	Swearingen SA.226TC Metro II	TC-235	ex N235BA	
☐ C-FAFF	Beech B300 Super King Air	FL-112	ex N405J	
☐ C-FCAV	Piper PA-42 Cheyenne III	42-8001006	ex N131RC	
☐ C-FRLD	Beech B300 Super King Air	FL-33	ex N15WS	
☐ C-FVKC	Beech B300 Super King Air	FL-273	ex OY-JVL	
☐ C-FWPR	Beech B300 Super King Air	FL-125	ex N32KC	
☐ C-GJLK	Beech B300 Super King Air	FL-13	ex C-FWXR	EMS, for BC Ambulance Service

CC HELICOPTERS — Chilcotin (DES) — Lillooet, BC

☐ C-FGYQ	Bell 206B JetRanger III	1357	ex CF-GYQ	
☐ C-FHTQ	Bell 206B JetRanger III	1030	ex CF-HTQ	
☐ C-FUNF	Bell 407	53225	ex N80709	
☐ C-FWCE	Bell 206L-1 LongRanger	45172	ex C-FHNN	
☐ C-GPIH	Bell 407	53426	ex N407WS	
☐ C-GSQM	Bell 212	31160	ex VH-LHL	
☐ C-GTRH	Bell 212	30778	ex N9937K	
☐ C-GWCF	Bell 206L-1 LongRanger	45448	ex N31LA	

CENTRAL FLYWAY AIR — Thompson, MB (YTH)

| ☐ C-FBJA | Beech 95-B55 Baron | TC-71 | ex N1238Z | |
| ☐ C-FJOF | de Havilland DHC-2 Beaver | 1053 | ex CF-JOF | FP |

☐ C-FPEN	de Havilland DHC-3 Otter	439	ex CF-PEN	FP
☐ C-FRHW	de Havilland DHC-3 Otter	445	ex 5N-ABN	FP
☐ C-GICM	Beech 95-C55 Baron	TE-64	ex N171M	
☐ C-GYOK	de Havilland DHC-2 Beaver	677	ex N5152G	FP

CENTRAL MOUNTAIN AIR — Glacier (9M/GLR) — Smithers, BC (YYD)

☐ C-FCMB	Beech 1900D	UE-278		916	
☐ C-FCME	Beech 1900D	UE-277		915	
☐ C-FCMN	Beech 1900D	UE-276		914	
☐ C-FCMO	Beech 1900D	UE-281		917	
☐ C-FCMP	Beech 1900D	UE-271	ex N11037	912	
☐ C-FCMR	Beech 1900D	UE-283	ex N21872	918	
☐ C-FCMU	Beech 1900D	UE-285		919	
☐ C-FCMV	Beech 1900D	UE-272	ex N11079	913	
☐ C-FDTR	Beech 1900D	UE-76	ex N76ZV		
☐ C-GCMA	Beech 1900D	UE-289		920	
☐ C-GCML	Beech 1900D	UE-243	ex N10879	925	
☐ C-GCMY	Beech 1900D	UE-287		921	>NTA
☐ C-GFSV	Beech 1900D	UE-346	ex N23424	922	
☐ C-GGBY	Beech 1900D	UE-351	ex N23517	923	
☐ C-GGCA	Beech 1900D	UE-359	ex N31559	924	

☐ C-FDYN	Dornier 328-110	3096	ex D-CMUC
☐ C-FGQN	de Havilland DHC-2 Beaver	96	
☐ C-GWRN	Piper PA-31 Navajo Chieftain	31-7852062	

CHC HELICOPTERS INTERNATIONAL — Vancouver-International, BC (YVR)

☐ C-FYPO	Aérospatiale AS.332L	2077	ex LN-OMK	
☐ C-FYZD	Aérospatiale AS.332L	2007	ex OY-HEO	
☐ C-GOSE	Aérospatiale AS.332L	2048	ex C-GTCH	
☐ C-GOSI	Aérospatiale AS.332L	2074	ex C-GVCH	
☐ C-FYQC	Aérospatiale SA365N Dauphin 2	6419	ex 5N-BJF	
☐ C-GDVO	Aérospatiale AS365N2 Dauphin 2	6424	ex G-BTUX	♦
☐ C-FRWF	Bell 212	30894	ex ZS-RXB	
☐ PR-MEX	Sikorsky S-61N	61753	ex PH-NZG	
☐ C-	Sikorsky S-76A++	760032	ex HS-HTR	
☐ C-	Sikorsky S-76A++	760148	ex HS-HTI	
☐ C-FGDO	Sikorsky S-76C+	760602	ex 5N-BIV	
☐ C-FRHM	Sikorsky S-76C++	760689	ex N25042	
☐ C-FRSA	Sikorsky S-76C++	760691	ex 9M-AIS	
☐ C-FUVS	Sikorsky S-76C+	760547	ex ZS-RRX	
☐ C-FUVU	Sikorsky S-76C+	760548	ex ZS-RRY	
☐ C-FXXV	Sikorsky S-76C+	760468	ex 5N-BGN	
☐ C-FZSZ	Sikorsky S-76C++	760731	ex N781X	
☐ C-FZUT	Sikorsky S-76C++	760764	ex N764L	
☐ C-FZUY	Sikorsky S-76C++	760765	ex N765L	
☐ C-GBVZ	Sikorsky S-76A+	760183	ex G-BVCX	
☐ C-GBWC	Sikorsky S-76A+	760201	ex G-DRNT	
☐ C-GHRE	Sikorsky S-76C+	760575	ex N7100C	
☐ C-GIHO	Sikorsky S-76A++	760015	ex HS-HTO	
☐ C-GIMJ	Sikorsky S-76A++	760009	ex D2-EXZ	
☐ C-GIMQ	Sikorsky S-76A++	760102	ex HS-HTQ	
☐ C-GKWS	Sikorsky S-76A++	760297	ex EP-HCS	
☐ C-GKWT	Sikorsky S-76A++	760295	ex B-HZD	based Yangon
☐ C-GMNB	Sikorsky S-76C+	760490	ex VT-HGH	

CHIMO AIR SERVICE — Red Lake SPB, ON (YRL)

☐ CF-HZA	Beech D18S	A-111		FP
☐ CF-JIN	Noorduyn Norseman V	CCF-55	ex CF-LFR	FP
☐ CF-KAO	Noorduyn Norseman VI	636	ex 44-70371	FP
☐ C-FODQ	de Havilland DHC-3 Otter	111	ex CF-ODQ	FP

CLEARWATER AIRWAYS — Burditt Lake SPB, ON

☐ C-FGUE	Beech C-18S	8107	ex N480DB	FP
☐ C-GESW	Beech C-18S	7911	ex N4858V	FP

COCHRANE AIR SERVICES — Cochrane-Lillabelle Lake, ON (YCN)

☐ C-FEYQ	de Havilland DHC-2 Beaver	465	ex CF-EYQ	FP
☐ C-FGBF	de Havilland DHC-2 Beaver	168	ex CF-GBF	FP

CONAIR AVIATION		Conair Canada (CRC)			Abbotsford, BC (YXX)
☐ C-FDHK	Air Tractor AT-802A	802A-0198		80	
☐ C-FDHL	Air Tractor AT-802A	802A-0199			
☐ C-FDHN	Air Tractor AT-802A	802A-0200			
☐ C-FLSI	Air Tractor AT-802A	802A-0173		82	
☐ C-FXVF	Air Tractor AT-802A	802A-0033		78	
☐ C-FXVL	Air Tractor AT-802A	802A-0034		79	
☐ C-GAAG	Air Tractor AT-802A	802A-0174		91	
☐ C-GBWF	Air Tractor AT-802A	802A-0303			
☐ C-GSJB	Air Tractor AT-802A	802A-0148		06	
☐ C-GWNL	Air Tractor AT-802A	802A-0299			
☐ C-FEFK	Conair Firecat	G-360/014	ex F-ZBEH	574	
☐ C-FEFX	Conair Firecat	G-527/031	ex N425DF	575	
☐ C-FJOH	Conair Firecat	G-254/034	ex N424DF	576	
☐ C-FOPU	Conair Firecat	DHC-38/007	ex RCN1539	564	
☐ C-FOPV	Conair Firecat	DHC-34/006	ex RCN1535	566	
☐ C-FOPY	Conair Firecat	DHC-24/019	ex CF-IOF	569	
☐ C-GABC	Conair Firecat	DHC-90/011	ex RCAF12191		567
☐ C-GHDY	Conair Firecat	G-374/029	ex Bu136465	573	
☐ C-GHPJ	Conair Firecat	G-509/022	ex Bu136600	571	
☐ C-GWHK	Conair Firecat	DHC-37/016	ex CAF12138	2	Tanker
☐ C-GWUO	Conair Firecat	DHC-39/003	ex N99261	563	
☐ C-GWUP	Conair Firecat	DHC-19/012	ex RCN12120	568	
☐ C-FEKF	Convair 580	80	ex C-GEVB	445	Tanker 45
☐ C-FFKF	Convair 580	179	ex C-GEVC	444	Tanker 44
☐ C-FHKF	Convair 580	374	ex C-GEUZ	455	Tanker 55
☐ C-FJVD	Convair 580	478	ex N8099S		
☐ C-FKFA	Convair 580	100	ex C-FLVY	452	Tanker 52
☐ C-FKFB	Convair 580	57	ex N568JA	447	Tanker 47
☐ C-FKFL	Convair 580	465	ex C-FZQS	449	Tanker 49
☐ C-FKFM	Convair 580	70	ex N73133	454	Tanker 54
☐ C-GKFO	Convair 580	78	ex N5815	453	Tanker 53
☐ C-GYXC	Convair 580	507	ex VH-PDV		
☐ C-GYXS	Convair 580	501	ex VH-PAL`		
☐ C-FFIF	Piper PA-60 Aerostar 600A	60-0702-7961218	ex N6073K	122	
☐ C-GLVG	Piper PA-60 Aerostar 600A	60-0695-7961217	ex N6072U	111	
☐ C-GMGZ	Piper PA-60 Aerostar 600A	60-0708-7961220	ex N6075C	112	
☐ C-GOSX	Piper PA-60 Aerostar 600A	60-0863-8161246	ex N3647B	110	
☐ C-GRIK	Piper PA-60 Aerostar 600A	60-0563-7961183	ex N8040J	108	
☐ C-GSXX	Ted Smith Aerostar 600A	60-0430-146	ex N9795Q	109	
☐ C-GUHK	Piper PA-60 Aerostar 600A	60-0761-8061230	ex N8EA	119	
☐ C-GUSZ	Piper PA-60 Aerostar 600A	60-0894-8161253	ex N6893Q	118	
☐ C-FCZZ	Rockwell 690A Turbo Commander	11106	ex N57106	135	
☐ C-FNWD	Rockwell 690B Turbo Commander	11497	ex N81831		
☐ C-GAAL	Rockwell 690A Turbo Commander	11104	ex N690AZ	131	
☐ C-GDCL	Rockwell 690A Turbo Commander	11192	ex N57192	134	
☐ C-GHWF	Rockwell 690A Turbo Commander	11134	ex N45VT	132	
☐ C-GWEW	Rockwell 690 Turbo Commander	11057	ex N376TC	133	
☐ C-GFSK	Canadair CL215	1085	ex C-GKDN	201	
☐ C-GFSL	Canadair CL215	1086	ex C-GKDP	202	
☐ C-GFSM	Canadair CL215	1098		203	
☐ C-GFSN	Canadair CL215	1099		204	
☐ C-GSDG	Cessna 208B Caravan I	208B0376	ex N1118P	127	
☐ C-GHLY	Douglas DC-6B	45501/953	ex OO-VGE	446	Tanker
☐ C-GIBS	Douglas DC-6A/C	45531/1015	ex HB-IBS	451	Tanker
☐ C-GKUG	Douglas DC-6A/B	45177/859	ex N863TA	450	Tanker
☐ C-FYYJ	Lockheed L-188AC Electra	1143	ex G-LOFD		♦
☐ C-GYCG	Lockheed L-188PF Electra	1138	ex C-FIJR		♦
CORILAIR CHARTERS					**Campbell River, BC**
☐ C-FEWP	Cessna U206D Skylane	U206-1344	ex CF-EWP		
☐ C-FJPB	de Havilland DHC-2 Beaver	1319	ex N1019T		FP
☐ C-FNEQ	Cessna U206G Stationair 6	U20605036	ex N4660U		
☐ C-GACK	de Havilland DHC-2 Beaver	711	ex 53-7903		FP
☐ C-GTNE	Cessna A185E Skywagon	18501889	ex CF-QLN		FP

CORPORATE EXPRESS AIRLINE — Penta (CPB) — Calgary-Intl, AB (YYC)

Reg	Type	S/N	Notes
C-GEXI	Canadair CRJ-200	7186	ex N621BR
C-GEXM	Canadair CRJ-200	7187	ex N622BR
C-GPII	Piaggio P.180 Avanti	1133	ex N139PA
C-GXPS	SAAB SF.340A	340A-075	ex N75UW

COUGAR HELICOPTERS — Cougar (CHI) — Halifax-Waterfront Heliport, NS (YWF)

Reg	Type	S/N	Notes	
C-GIHS	Sikorsky S-76A++	760150	ex HS-HTS	
C-GDKN	Sikorsky S-92A	920111	ex N21278	
C-GEKN	Sikorsky S-92A	920114	ex N7633A	♦
C-GGKN	Sikorsky S-92A	920124		♦
C-GIKN	Sikorsky S-92A	920126	ex N2183N	♦
C-GMCH	Sikorsky S-92A	920023	ex N8016B	
C-GQCH	Sikorsky S-92A	920074	ex N2581T	
C-GSCH	Sikorsky S-92A	920010	ex N7108J	
C-GVCH	Sikorsky S-92A	920080	ex N25837	
N920VH	Sikorsky S-92A	920061	ex C-GTCH	♦
C-FHCH	Sikorsky S-61N	61761	ex N613RM	
C-FNCH	Sikorsky S-61N	61757	ex N461AL	
C-FTIG	Sikorsky S-61N	61491	ex N613RM	
C-GYCH	Sikorsky S-61N	61762	ex PH-NZI	

COULSON AIRCRANE — Port Alberni, BC (YPB)

Reg	Type	S/N	Notes		
C-FCLM	Sikorsky S-61N	61492	ex N265F		
C-FDYK	Bell 206B JetRanger II	972	ex CF-DYK		
C-FLYK	Martin JRM-3 Mars	76820	ex Bu76820	Philippine Mars	Tanker
C-FLYL	Martin JRM-3 Mars	76823	ex Bu76823	Hawaii Mars	Tanker
C-FMAY	Sikorsky S-61N	61363	ex N306V		
C-FXEC	Sikorsky S-61N	61821	ex N264F		
C-GXOH	Bell 206B JetRanger II	865	ex N14844		

COURTESY AIR — Buffalo Narrows, SK (YVT)

Reg	Type	S/N	Notes
C-FCAK	Beech A100 King Air	B-96	ex N116RJ
C-FJDF	Beech 1900C	UB-68	ex N68GH
C-FJMF	Beech 99	U-180	ex OY-PAG
C-FLMF	Beech C99	U-189	ex N189AV
C-FNMF	Beech C99	U-167	ex N167EE
C-GDVD	Beech 58 Baron	TH-668	ex N4557S
C-GKLO	Piper PA-31-350 Chieftain	31-8152118	ex N4505N
C-GKNL	Piper PA-31-350 Chieftain	31-7852083	ex N27607
C-GMFV	Cessna U206G Stationair 6 II	U20604714	ex N732RY
C-GNRM	Piper PA-31-350 Navajo Chieftain	31-7752145	ex N27315

CUSTOM HELICOPTERS — Winnipeg-St Andrews, MB (YAV)

Reg	Type	S/N	Notes	
C-FCHJ	Aérospatiale AS350B2 AStar	2603	ex XC-JAK	
C-GCHX	Aérospatiale AS350BA AStar	2517	ex CP-2335	
C-GGSP	Aérospatiale AS350B1 AStar	2126	ex N213LA	♦
C-FCHD	Bell 205A-1	30014	ex N5598M	
C-FCHE	Bell 205A-1	30167	ex XA-SSR	
C-GRWK	Bell 205A-1	30005	ex N3764U	
C-FJMH	Bell 206B JetRanger II	1331	ex N70711	
C-FKBV	Bell 206B JetRanger II	364	ex N465CC	
C-FSVG	Bell 206B JetRanger III	2865	ex N1074G	
C-FZSJ	Bell 206B JetRanger II	648	ex CF-ZSJ	
C-GBWN	Bell 206B JetRanger II	2204		
C-GFIV	Bell 206B JetRanger II	424	ex N1481W	
C-GGZS	Bell 206B JetRanger II	1885		
C-GKBU	Bell 206B JetRanger II	386	ex N1448W	
C-GQQO	Bell 206B JetRanger II	1096	ex N83182	
C-GQQT	Bell 206B JetRanger II	1657	ex N90218	
C-GSHJ	Bell 206B JetRanger II	114	ex N125GW	
C-FYHN	Bell 206L LongRanger	45050	ex N600FB	
C-GAVH	Bell 206L-1 LongRanger III	45740	ex N385FP	
C-GCHG	Bell 206L-1 LongRanger II	51508	ex N8592X	
C-GCHI	Bell 206L-1 LongRanger II	45516	ex N141VG	
C-GCHZ	Bell 206L-1 LongRanger III	45314	ex N210AH	
C-GIPG	Bell 206L-1 LongRanger II	45592	ex N3895K	

DELTA HELICOPTERS   High Level, AB (YOJ)

☐ C-FDHW	Aérospatiale AS350BA AStar	2211	ex ZK-HKZ
☐ C-FDKH	Aérospatiale AS350B-2 AStar	2226	ex ZK-HEE
☐ C-FKDS	Aérospatiale AS350BA AStar	2802	ex N6101U
☐ C-FRUQ	Aérospatiale AS350B-2 AStar	2596	ex EC-FUF
☐ C-FWCL	Aérospatiale AS350BA AStar	2869	ex C-FWAW
☐ C-GDLD	Aérospatiale AS350B AStar	1369	ex N5771C
☐ C-GUPH	Aérospatiale AS350B AStar	1368	ex N99PS
☐ C-GVIV	Aérospatiale AS350B2 AStar	3419	
☐ C-GVXA	Aérospatiale AS350BA AStar	1278	ex N78EW
☐ C-FAHO	Bell 204B	2060	ex CF-AHO
☐ C-GDUK	Bell 204B	2034	ex N636
☐ C-GJLV	Bell 204B	2064	ex Thai 918
☐ C-GRGA	Bell 204B	2026	ex N1177W
☐ C-GTNP	Bell 204B	2028	ex OY-HBS
☐ C-GVEX	Bell 204B	2031	ex OY-HBV
☐ C-FCQJ	Bell 206B JetRanger	540	ex N8152J
☐ C-FDYO	Bell 206B JetRanger	994	ex CF-DYO
☐ C-GDBN	Bell 206B JetRanger III	2467	ex C-GDEN
☐ C-GDJW	Bell 206B JetRanger III	2909	ex N353E
☐ C-GGOZ	Bell 206B JetRanger	443	ex N2162L
☐ C-GNMI	Bell 206B JetRanger III	2602	ex N5014F
☐ C-GPEZ	Bell 206B JetRanger	1130	ex N9JJ
☐ C-GSHN	Bell 206B JetRanger	616	ex N101TF
☐ C-GTIS	Bell 206B JetRanger	827	ex N3YE
☐ C-GWML	Bell 206B JetRanger	269	ex N30AL
☐ C-GEOM	Bell 206L-1 LongRanger II	45625	
☐ C-GERI	Bell 206L-1 LongRanger II	45668	
☐ C-GPGO	Bell 206L-1 LongRanger II	45475	ex N57416

DYNAMIC FLIGHT SERVICES   Calgary, AB (YYC)

☐ C-GTJJ	Piper PA-31 Navajo C	31-7712062	ex N27271
☐ C-GZOC	Piper PA-31 Navajo C	31-7512018	ex N59934

EAGLE AIR SERVICES   Port Hardy, BC (YZT)

☐ C-FEAZ	Piper PA-31-350 Navajo Chieftain	31-7652088	ex N88MG
☐ C-GITW	Piper PA-31-350 Navajo Chieftain	31-7652114	

EAGLE COPTERS   Calgary, AB (YYC)

☐ C-FDEF	Bell 205A	30038	ex CS-HET	
☐ C-GEAG	Bell 205A-1	30262	ex XC-CIC	
☐ C-FWZI	Bell 206L-1 LongRanger II	45447	ex N202EC	
☐ C-FZXH	Bell 206B JetRanger II	622		
☐ C-GBHF	Bell 206B JetRanger II	1028		
☐ C-GQKU	Bell 206B JetRanger II	2173		
☐ C-FBHY	Bell 212	31194		
☐ C-FBUA	Bell 212	30826		
☐ C-FNOS	Bell 212	30866		
☐ C-FNOU	Bell 212	30787	ex 5N-AXX	
☐ C-GAZF	Bell 212	30640	ex HK-4518X	♦
☐ C-GBBP	Bell 212	30934	ex OB-1847P	
☐ C-GXXH	Bell 407	53197	ex N782FS	♦
☐ N142EC	Bell 412	36142	ex N512PD	♦
☐ N6233	Bell 412	36233	ex N514PD	♦
☐ C-FTIW	Sikorsky S-76A+	760186		
☐ C-GIYO	Aérospatiale AS350BA AStar	2274		

EAST-WEST TRANSPORTATION   Salmon Arm, BC (YSN)

☐ C-FXNI	Bell 214B-1	28022	ex N214GL

ELBOW RIVER HELICOPTERS   Calgary-Springbank, AB (YBW)

☐ C-FGAV	Bell 206L-1 LongRanger II	45156	
☐ C-FPMR	Bell 212	31115	ex N48ZP
☐ C-GERB	Bell 206L-3 LongRanger III	51008	
☐ C-GERW	Bell 212	30814	ex C-FRWM
☐ C-GKCA	Bell 206L-3 LongRanger III	51341	
☐ C-GZAV	Bell 407	53002	

77

ENERJET		**(ENJ)**		

☐ C-GOEJ	Boeing 737-7BD/W	33920/1753	ex PH-OEJ	

ENTERPRISE AIR

☐ C-FCLO	Beech E-18S	BA-143	ex N31M	

EXACT AIR — *Chicoutimi-St Honore, QC*

☐ C-FDOS	Beech A100 King Air	B-106	ex CF-DOS
☐ C-FLTS	Beech A100 King Air	B-149	ex N883CA
☐ C-FQQB	Piper PA-31 Turbo Navajo	31-310	ex N9239Y
☐ C-FTYZ	Beech 100 King Air	B-86	ex N53MD
☐ C-FUPQ	Beech A100 King Air	B-162	ex N224LB
☐ C-FVTL	Piper PA-31-325 Navajo C/R	31-7912091	ex N3532U
☐ C-FVYW	Piper PA-31-325 Navajo C/R	31-7612026	ex N22AU
☐ C-FXDE	Beech A100 King Air	B-176	ex N3076W
☐ C-GGTF	Cessna 310R	310R0550	ex N87409
☐ C-GIAS	Cessna 402B	402B0545	ex N678CM
☐ C-GPTU	Piper PA-31 Navajo C	31-7712005	ex N62986
☐ C-GZAS	Cessna 402B	402B0626	ex N2083K

EXPLOITS VALLEY AIR SERVICES — *Gander, NL (YQX)*

☐ C-FEVA	Beech 1900D	UE-126	ex N126YV	♦
☐ C-GAAT	Beech 1900D	UE-217	ex N1564J	963
☐ C-GZUZ	Beech A100 King Air	B-143	ex C-GNVB	

EXPRESS AIR — *Expressair (WEW)* — *Ottawa, ON (YOW)*

☐ C-FKAZ	Cessna 208 Caravan I	20800236		FP
☐ C-GAWP	Pilatus PC-12/45	187	ex N187PC	

FAR WEST HELICOPTERS — *Chilliwack, BC (YCW)*

☐ C-FJSL	Bell 206B JetRanger III	1154	ex N59384
☐ C-GCQT	Bell 206B JetRanger II	492	ex N15FD
☐ C-GGQL	Bell 206B JetRanger II	2117	ex N16723
☐ C-GVTM	Bell 206B JetRanger II	194	ex N4038G

FAST AIR — *Winnipeg-Intl, MB (YWG)*

☐ C-FDEB	Beech 200 Super King Air	BB-55	ex N200BC	
☐ C-FFAR	Beech 200 Super King Air	BB-864	ex N847TS	
☐ C-GDHF	Beech B200 Super King Air	BB-1129	ex CS-DDF	CatPass 250 conversion
☐ C-GFAD	Beech B200 Super King Air	BB-1428	ex N660MW	
☐ C-GFSB	Beech 200 Super King Air	BB-84		
☐ C-GWGI	Beech B200 Super King Air	BB-1022	ex C-FDGP	
☐ C-FJAL	Piper PA-31-350 Navajo Chieftain	31-7752160	ex N19LA	
☐ C-GMDL	Piper PA-31-325 Navajo C/R	31-7512033	ex N775WM	
☐ C-GMOB	Piper PA-31-350 Chieftain	31-7852072	ex N27596	
☐ C-GNDI	Piper PA-31T Cheyenne	31T-7620036	ex N73TB	
☐ C-GPNP	Piper PA-31T Cheyenne	31T-7520024	ex N431AC	

FIREWEED HELICOPTERS — *Whitehorse, YT (YXY)*

☐ C-FAVT	Bell 206L-1 LongRanger II	45207	ex N302CK
☐ C-FFWH	Bell 206B JetRanger III	2464	ex N1974T
☐ C-GFWE	Bell 206L-4 LongRanger IV	52036	ex C-FMPK
☐ C-GFWI	Bell 204C	2070	ex C-GEAI
☐ C-GFWZ	Bell 206B JetRanger III	1900	ex C-GBJZ
☐ C-GLAV	Bell 206L-1 LongRanger II	45414	ex C-GMPV
☐ C-GMNW	Bell 206L-1 LongRanger II	45512	

FIRST AIR — *Firstair (7F/FAB)* — *Carp, ON/Iqaluit, NT/Yellowknife, NT (YRP/YFB/YZF)*

☐ C-FIQR	ATR 42-300 (QC)	133	ex F-WWEE
☐ C-FIQU	ATR 42-300 (QC)	138	ex F-WWEK
☐ C-FTCP	ATR 42-300 (QC)	143	ex F-WWEO
☐ C-FTJB	ATR 42-300 (QC)	119	ex N423TE
☐ C-GHCP	ATR 42-300 (QC)	123	ex F-WWET
☐ C-GKLB	ATR 42-310	331	ex G-CDFF
☐ C-GSRR	ATR 42-300 (QC)	125	ex OY-MUH
☐ C-GULU	ATR 42-310	155	ex 5R-MJD
☐ C-GUNO	ATR 42-310	132	ex 5R-MJC

☐ C-FACP	Boeing 737-2L9 (AvAero 3)	22072/623	ex C2-RN9		
☐ C-FNVK	Boeing 737-2R4C	23130/1040	ex JY-JAF		Frtr
☐ C-FNVT	Boeing 737-248C (AvAero 3)	21011/411	ex F-GKTK	Snowy Owl c/s	
☐ C-GCPT	Boeing 737-217 (AvAero 3)	22258/770		Inukshuk tail logo	
☐ C-GNDC	Boeing 737-242C (AvAero 3)	21728/580			
☐ C-GNWN	Boeing 737-210C (AvAero 3)	21067/414	ex N4952W		
☐ C-FUFA	Boeing 727-233F (FedEx 3)	20941/1128	ex N727LS		
☐ C-GFNW	Hawker Siddeley HS.748 Srs.2A /335LFD	1758	ex 9Y-TFX		405
☐ C-GHPW	Lockheed L-382G-42C Hercules	4799		Capt Harry Sorenson	
☐ C-GKLY	Boeing 767-223 (SCD)	22314/73	ex N714AX		
☐ C-GUSI	Lockheed L-328G-31C Hercules	4600	ex ZS-RSI	EARL titles	
☐ C-GXFA	Boeing 727-233F (Raisbeck 3)	20938/1105	ex C-GAAG		

FLAIR AIRLINES — Flair (FLE) — Kelowna, BC (YLW)

☐ C-FLEJ	Boeing 737-4B3	24751/2107	ex CN-RPB
☐ C-FLEN	Boeing 737-4K5	24769/1839	ex OK-VGZ
☐ C-FLER	Boeing 737-46B	24573/1844	ex N41XA

FORDE LAKE AIR SERVICES — Hearst, ON (YHF)

☐ C-FLUA	de Havilland DHC-2 Beaver	1318	ex CF-LUA	
☐ C-GGNM	Cessna A185F Skywagon	18502807	ex (N1283F)	FP
☐ C-GRAP	de Havilland DHC-2 Beaver	829	ex 54-1690	FP

FOREST PATROL — St John, NB (YSJ)

☐ C-FBEJ	Ayres S-2R	1768R	ex CF-BEJ
☐ C-FZTE	Ayres S-2R	1578R	ex CF-ZTE
☐ C-GMQA	Ayres S-2R-T34	T34-013DC	ex N4020H
☐ C-GMQB	Ayres S-2R-T34	T34-014DC	ex N4020S
☐ C-GMQC	Ayres S-2R-T34	T34-015DC	ex N4020U
☐ C-FESS	Bell 407	53129	
☐ C-FXZU	Bell 206L-4 LongRanger IV	52164	
☐ C-GVDI	Cessna TU206G Stationair 6	U20606490	ex C-GJDI

FOREST PROTECTION — Fredericton / Miramichi, NB (YFC/YCH)

☐ C-FFPL	Air Tractor AT-802	802-0110		620	Sprayer/Tanker
☐ C-FZPV	Air Tractor AT-802	802-0141	ex N8507T	622	Sprayer
☐ C-GJJK	Air Tractor AT-802	802-0120	ex N85071	621	Sprayer/Tanker
☐ C-GJJX	Air Tractor AT-802	802-0121		624	Tanker
☐ C-GZRH	Air Tractor AT-802	802-0143		623	Sprayer
☐ C-GZUE	Air Tractor AT-802	802-0147		625	Sprayer
☐ C-FIMR	Grumman TBM-3 Avenger	53610	ex RCN303	23	
☐ C-GJDF	Cessna 337G Super Skymaster	33701516	ex N72488		
☐ C-GLEL	Grumman TBM-3 Avenger	53200	ex N9010C	13	
☐ C-GLFA	Cessna A188B AgTruck	18802222T	ex (N9296R)		Sprayer
☐ C-GMEK	Cessna U206F Stationair II	U20603083	ex N3755C		
☐ C-GXJI	Cessna 210J Centurion II	21059155	ex N3355S		
☐ C-GXMA	Cessna 337G Super Skymaster	33701644	ex N53468		

FORT FRANCES SPORTSMEN AIRWAYS — Fort Frances, ON (YAG)

☐ C-GBQC	de Havilland DHC-3 Otter	401	ex RCAF 9420	FP/WS
☐ C-GMDG	de Havilland DHC-3 Turbo Otter	302	ex N90575	FP/WS
☐ C-GUTL	de Havilland DHC-3 Otter	365	ex HK-3048X	FP/WS

FOUR SEASONS AVIATION — Toronto-Pearson International, ON (YYZ)

☐ C-FHNB	Aérospatiale AS355F1 Twin Star	5174	ex N5798B
☐ C-FWZZ	Aérospatiale AS350B2 AStar	3931	ex C-FFIQ
☐ C-GGAZ	Bell 206B JetRanger	2156	

FUGRO AVIATION CANADA — Ottawa-Rockcliffe, ON (YRO)

☐ C-FDKM	CASA 212 Srs 200	CC40-2-196	ex PR-FAB	Nose & tail magnetometer
☐ C-FYAU	Cessna 404 Titan II	404-0431	ex N408EX	Tail magnetometer
☐ C-FZLK	Cessna 208B Caravan I	208B0569	ex N1210N	Tail magnetometer
☐ C-GDPP	CASA 212 Srs 200	CC50-3-265	ex N430CA	Nose & tail magnetometer
☐ C-GFAV	Cessna 208 Caravan I	20800251	ex N1251V	Tail magnetometer
☐ C-GGRD	Cessna 208B Caravan I	208B1150	ex N208ML	
☐ C-GNCA	Cessna 208B Caravan I	208B0764	ex N208KC	Tail magnetometer

GATEWAY HELICOPTERS — North Bay, ON (YYB)

☐ C-FBTW	Aérospatiale AS350B2 AStar	3289	
☐ C-FDEV	Aérospatiale AS350B2 AStar	2970	ex TG-RAJ
☐ C-FGEO	Aérospatiale AS350B3 AStar	4368	
☐ C-GBGH	Aérospatiale AS350B2 AStar	4398	ex N398EC
☐ C-GEOY	Aérospatiale AS350B3 AStar	4316	
☐ C-GEOZ	Aérospatiale AS350B3 AStar	4223	ex F-GURR
☐ C-GENL	Bell 206B JetRanger III	2505	ex N5008F
☐ C-GINF	Bell 206B JetRanger III	3294	ex N39108
☐ C-GTPG	Bell 206B JetRanger II	1233	ex C-FHZL
☐ C-GUIK	Bell 206B JetRanger II	1908	
☐ C-GDQH	Bell 206LR LongRanger	45046	ex N663JB
☐ C-GHUG	Bell 206LR+ LongRanger	45142	ex N286CP
☐ C-GKCW	Bell 206L LongRanger	45122	ex N6139U
☐ C-GKMJ	Bell 206LR+ LongRanger	45096	ex C-GJBC
☐ C-GMHK	Bell 206L-1 LongRanger II	45286	ex N29EA
☐ C-GRYS	Bell 206L LongRanger	45097	ex N16783
☐ C-GZCD	Bell 206L-1 LongRanger II	45688	ex N80KA
☐ C-GMVU	Cessna 185E Skywagon	18503432	ex N9373H
☐ C-GRGY	Bell 204B	2022	ex CF-OKZ

GEFFAIR CANADA — Montreal-Trudeau, QC (YUL)

☐ C-GMHZ	Piper PA-31 Turbo Navajo	31-434	ex N712NT

GEMINI HELICOPTERS — High Level/Footner Lake, AB (YOJ)

☐ C-FETD	Aérospatiale AS350BA AStar	1025	ex N135BH
☐ C-FXLD	Aérospatiale AS350B AStar	1438	ex N817CF
☐ C-GAVA	Bell 205A-1	30187	ex N222HT
☐ C-GEAP	Bell 204B	2063	ex Thai 917
☐ C-GEMJ	Aérospatiale AS350B2 AStar	2064	ex N203TB
☐ C-GEMK	Eurocopter EC120B	1427	
☐ C-GEMN	Eurocopter EC120B	1423	
☐ C-GEMU	Eurocopter EC120B	1057	ex VH-AZH
☐ C-GVYI	Aérospatiale AS350D AStar	1041	ex F-WZFK

GEOGRAPHIC AIR SURVEY — Edmonton-City Centre, AL (YXD)

☐ C-GEOG	Aero Commander 680F	1120-73	ex N444UB	Surveyor
☐ C-GEOS	Rockwell 690A Turbo Commander	11279	ex N57180	Surveyor

GEORGIAN BAY AIRWAYS — Parry Sound, ON (YPD)

☐ CF-IJG	Noorduyn Norseman VI	139	FP

GILLAM AIR SERVICES — Gillam, MB (YGX)

☐ C-FSDY	de Havilland DHC-2 Beaver	897	ex N64273
☐ C-GOXI	Piper PA-23-250 Aztec E	27-7405484	
☐ C-GPPP	Britten-Norman BN-2A-27 Islander	423	ex (N93JA)
☐ C-GSAD	Britten-Norman BN-2A-26 Islander	7	ex N32JC
☐ C-GXQV	Cessna A185F Skywagon	18503375	

GOGAL AIR SERVICES — Snow Lake, MB

☐ CF-ECG	Noorduyn Norseman V	N29-43		FP/WS
☐ CF-GLI	Noorduyn Norseman VI	365	ex N88719	FP/WS
☐ C-GBAO	Piper PA-31-350 Navajo Chieftain	31-7405234	ex N54309	
☐ C-GCWO	Cessna A185F Skywagon	18503207	ex N93275	FP/WS

GOLDAK AIRBORNE SURVEYS — Saskatoon, SK (YXE)

☐ C-GJBA	Piper PA-31 Turbo Navajo	31-159	ex N9119Y	Surveyor, tail magnetometer
☐ C-GJBB	Piper PA-31 Turbo Navajo	31-519	ex N310DS	Surveyor
☐ C-GJBG	Piper PA-31 Navajo C	31-7612003	ex N59718	Surveyor
☐ C-GLDX	Cessna 208 Caravan I	20800366	ex C-FFCL	

GOVERNMENT OF QUEBEC — Quebec (QUE) — Quebec, QC (YQB)

☐ C-FASE	Canadair CL215T	1114	ex Greece 1114	238
☐ C-FAWQ	Canadair CL215T	1115	ex Greece 1115	239
☐ C-FTXG	Canadair CL215	1014	ex CF-TXG 228	
☐ C-FTXJ	Canadair CL215	1017	ex CF-TXJ 230	

☐	C-FTXK	Canadair CL215	1018		ex CF-TXK	231	
☐	C-GFQB	Canadair CL215	1092		ex C-GKDP	237	
☐	C-GQBA	Canadair CL415	2005		ex C-GKDN	240	
☐	C-GQBC	Canadair CL415	2012		ex C-GKET	241	
☐	C-GQBD	Canadair CL415	2016		ex C-GBPU	242	
☐	C-GQBE	Canadair CL415	2017		ex C-GKEA	243	
☐	C-GQBF	Canadair CL415	2019		ex C-FVKV	244	
☐	C-GQBG	Canadair CL415	2022		ex C-FVLW	245	
☐	C-GQBI	Canadair CL415	2023		ex C-FVLI	246	
☐	C-GQBK	Canadair CL415	2026		ex C-FVLY	247	
☐	C-GBPQ	Bell 206B JetRanger III	2897		ex YU-HLL		
☐	C-GQBQ	Canadair CL-600-2B16 (Challenger 604)		5051	ex N300KC		EMS
☐	C-GQBT	de Havilland DHC-8Q-202	470		ex P2-ANL		EMS/VIP
☐	C-GSQA	Bell 206LT TwinRanger	52060				Police
☐	C-GSQL	Bell 412EP	36262		ex N6077U		

GREAT SLAVE HELICOPTERS   Yellowknife, NT (YZF)

☐	C-FGSC	Aérospatiale AS350BA AStar	3067		
☐	C-FHAF	Aérospatiale AS350BA AStar	1543	ex N516WW	
☐	C-FIDA	Aérospatiale AS350B3 AStar	4375		
☐	C-FQDA	Aérospatiale AS350BA AStar	4179		
☐	C-FYDA	Aérospatiale AS350B3 AStar	4157		
☐	C-FYKD	Aérospatiale AS350B2 AStar	4053	ex F-WQDE	
☐	C-FYZF	Aérospatiale AS350B3 AStar	3823		
☐	C-GABX	Aérospatiale AS350BA AStar	2438	ex HC-CBU	
☐	C-GAVO	Aérospatiale AS350B3 AStar	3139	ex F-WWOG	
☐	C-GBDA	Aérospatiale AS350B3 AStar	4065	ex PR-TDA	
☐	C-GDCV	Aérospatiale AS350B2 AStar	4422		
☐	C-GFHN	Aérospatiale AS350B2 AStar	2128	ex EC-ELN	
☐	C-GGSW	Aérospatiale AS350B2 AStar	2675		
☐	C-GGSY	Aérospatiale AS350B2 AStar	3591		
☐	C-GHMZ	Aérospatiale AS350BA AStar	2325		
☐	C-GIUX	Aérospatiale AS350BA AStar	1240	ex C-GHRD	
☐	C-GJGK	Aérospatiale AS350B2 AStar	2127	ex F-GHFJ	
☐	C-GNGK	Aérospatiale AS350B2 AStar	2539	ex N392BK	
☐	C-GRTM	Aérospatiale AS350BA AStar	1402	ex C-GAHE	
☐	C-GYFS	Aérospatiale AS350B2 AStar	3868		
☐	C-FAFL	Bell 206B JetRanger	1256		
☐	C-FALP	Bell 206B JetRanger II	2090	ex N214EL	
☐	C-FGSD	Bell 206B JetRanger	427	ex N83TA	
☐	C-FHBH	Bell 206B JetRanger III	3258	ex N904R	
☐	C-FHZP	Bell 206B JetRanger	1238	ex CF-HZP	
☐	C-FTWM	Bell 206B JetRanger	712	ex CF-TWM	
☐	C-GAHP	Bell 206B JetRanger	805	ex N2959W	
☐	C-GAHX	Bell 206B JetRanger	187	ex N4014G	
☐	C-GGRC	Bell 206B JetRanger III	3623		
☐	C-GHPO	Bell 206B JetRanger II	2151	ex HR-AFT	
☐	C-GOKA	Bell 206B JetRanger	156	ex N4052G	
☐	C-GOMK	Bell 206B JetRanger	1889		
☐	C-GTYU	Bell 206B JetRanger II	2144	ex N16627	
☐	C-GUYM	Bell 206B JetRanger	1687	ex N90191	
☐	C-GVTK	Bell 206B JetRanger II	104	ex N6200N	
☐	C-FBFH	Bell 206L-1 LongRanger II	45178	ex N5005G	
☐	C-FGSG	Bell 206LR+ LongRanger	45115	ex N405EH	
☐	C-GACG	Bell 206L-3 LongRanger III	51046	ex N53096	
☐	C-GFEG	Bell 206L LongRanger	45150	ex N38Q	
☐	C-GHBY	Bell 206LR+ LongRanger	45109	ex N402EH	
☐	C-GHRR	Bell 206L-4 LongRanger IV	52017	ex C-GMPA	
☐	C-GMSX	Bell 206L-3 LongRanger III	51474	ex N42489	
☐	C-GRFZ	Bell 206L-1 LongRanger II	45610		
☐	C-GSHF	Bell 206L-3 LongRanger III	51349	ex C-GHHY	
☐	C-GSHL	Bell 206L LongRanger	45092	ex N16751	
☐	C-GSHQ	Bell 206L-4 LongRanger IV	52226	ex XC-LFC	
☐	C-GSHW	Bell 206L-3 LongRanger III	51602	ex OK-XIS	
☐	C-FBUC	Bell 212	30687	ex XA-TQG	
☐	C-FJAD	Bell 212	30966	ex C-GZNA	
☐	C-GEEC	Bell 212	30931	ex EC-GOR	
☐	C-GEZO	Bell 212	30576	ex N4367Z	
☐	C-GGSM	Bell 212	30741	ex N49676	
☐	C-GKTL	Bell 212	32124	ex A6-BBX	
☐	C-GJDA	Eurocopter EC130B4	4192		

☐ C-GSDA	Eurocopter EC130B4	4041	ex F-WWXI	
☐ C-GSHD	Bell 205A-1	30058	ex C-FNMQ	
☐ C-GSHG	Bell 205A-1	30165	ex C-GENZ	

GREEN AIRWAYS — Red Lake, ON (YRL)

☐ C-FLEA	de Havilland DHC-3 Otter	286	ex CF-LEA	FP/WS
☐ C-FOBE	Noorduyn UC-64A Norseman	480	ex 43-35406	FP/WS
☐ C-FODJ	de Havilland DHC-3 Otter	14	ex CF-ODJ	FP/WS
☐ C-FVIA	de Havilland DHC-2 Beaver	714	ex N9047U	FP/WS
☐ C-GEZU	de Havilland DHC-2 Beaver	647	ex 53-8159	FP/WS
☐ C-GEZW	de Havilland DHC-2 Beaver	1217	ex 57-6138	FP/WS
☐ C-GYUY	Cessna A185F Skywagon II	18503731	ex (N8550Q)	FP/WS

GRONDAIR — St Frederic du Beauce, QC

☐ C-FNNM	Cessna TR182RG Skylane	R18200946	ex N738NR	
☐ C-FQTA	Cessna R182RG Skylane	R18200324	ex N4107C	
☐ C-FQTC	Cessna R182RG Skylane	R18201717	ex N4608T	
☐ C-FRGN	Cessna R182RG Skylane	R18200394	ex N9083C	
☐ C-FRYF	Cessna R182RG Skylane	R18201001	ex N65ET	
☐ C-FRYP	Cessna R182RG Skylane	R18200479	ex N9879C	
☐ C-FRZE	Cessna R182RG Skylane	R18200197	ex N2657C	
☐ C-GCJA	Cessna R182RG Skylane	R18201219	ex (N757DM)	
☐ C-GHVC	Cessna R182RG Skylane	R18201886	ex N5532T	
☐ C-GRUA	Cessna R182RG Skylane	R18200077	ex N7325X	
☐ C-GSCF	Cessna R182RG Skylane	R18201257	ex N757QM	
☐ C-GVCV	Cessna R182RG Skylane	R18200030	ex N7343T	
☐ C-FONY	Beech A100 King Air	B-154	ex N46JK	
☐ C-GAST	Cessna 310R	310R0730	ex N5009J	
☐ C-GBRC	Cessna 310R	310R1284	ex N6116X	
☐ C-GIGB	Cessna 337G Super Skymaster II	33701599	ex N72478	
☐ C-GJGW	Cessna 310R	310R0960	ex N37200	
☐ C-GSRW	Piper PA-31 Turbo Navajo	31-262	ex N707FR	
☐ C-GUMQ	Piper PA-31 Turbo Navajo	31-84	ex N777GS	

GUARDIAN HELICOPTERS — Calgary-Springbank, AL/Fort Nelson, BC (YBW/YYE)

☐ C-FFJY	Bell 205A-1	30002	ex VH-NGM	
☐ C-FJGK	Bell 206B JetRanger II	1940	ex N16HR	
☐ C-FKNT	Bell 206L LongRanger	45028	ex N2494L	
☐ C-FKOX	Bell 206B JetRanger	1261	ex CF-KOX	
☐ C-FMGK	Bell 206L-1 LongRanger	45402	ex N723SH	
☐ C-FOGK	Aérospatiale AS350BA Astar	1603	ex ZK-ICY	
☐ C-FRDJ	Bell 206B JetRanger	63	ex N206WE	
☐ C-FTGK	Bell 205A-1	30009	ex N4750R	
☐ C-GLGK	Piper PA-31P Pressurised Navajo	31P-7300117	ex N777JP	
☐ C-GLQI	Bell 206B JetRanger II	1964	ex N49694	
☐ C-GRTL	Aérospatiale AS350BA AStar	1377	ex N577DL	
☐ C-GTVA	Bell 206B JetRanger II	2133		
☐ C-GWGK	Aérospatiale AS350B3 AStar	3350	ex N335MB	
☐ C-GXLE	Aérospatiale AS350BA AStar	1337	ex N2069B	
☐ C-GZGK	Aérospatiale AS350BA AStar	2277	ex N391MA	

HARBOUR AIR SEAPLANES — Harbour Air (H3) — Vancouver-Coal Harbour, BC (CXH)

☐ C-FAXI	de Havilland DHC-2 Beaver	1514	ex N6535D	205	FP
☐ C-FFHQ	de Havilland DHC-2 Beaver	42	ex CF-FHQ	203	FP
☐ C-FJFQ	de Havilland DHC-2 Beaver	963	ex CF-JFQ	206	FP
☐ C-FMXS	de Havilland DHC-2 Beaver	1010	ex N43882	202	FP
☐ C-FOCJ	de Havilland DHC-2 Beaver	39	ex CF-OCJ		FP
☐ C-FOCN	de Havilland DHC-2 Beaver	44	ex CF-OCN	208	FP
☐ C-FOCY	de Havilland DHC-2 Beaver	79	ex CF-OCY	204	FP
☐ C-FOSP	de Havilland DHC-2 Beaver	1501	ex N2961	207	FP
☐ C-GCYM	de Havilland DHC-2 Beaver	354	ex N63PS		FP
☐ C-FHAA	de Havilland DHC-3 Turbo Otter	357	ex C-GIWT	309	FP
☐ C-FHAD	de Havilland DHC-3 Turbo Otter	119	ex N81FW	315	FP
☐ C-FHAX	de Havilland DHC-3 Turbo Otter	339	ex N41755	313	FP
☐ C-FITF	de Havilland DHC-3 Turbo Otter	89	ex CF-ITF	303	FP
☐ C-FIUZ	de Havilland DHC-3 Turbo Otter	135	ex F-OAKK	306	FP
☐ C-FJHA	de Havilland DHC-3 Turbo Otter	393	ex 4R-ARB		FP
☐ C-FODH	de Havilland DHC-3 Turbo Otter	3	ex CF-ODH	307	FP
☐ C-FRNO	de Havilland DHC-3 Turbo Otter	21	ex N128F	301	FP
☐ C-GHAR	de Havilland DHC-3 Turbo Otter	42	ex N234KA	308	FP
☐ C-GHAS	de Havilland DHC-3 Turbo Otter	284	ex N84SF	310	FP

82

☐ C-GHAZ	de Havilland DHC-3 Turbo Otter	19	ex C-FEYY		FP
☐ C-GLCP	de Havilland DHC-3 Turbo Otter	422	ex N17682		FP
☐ C-GOPP	de Havilland DHC-3 Turbo Otter	355	ex N53KA	305	FP
☐ C-GUTW	de Havilland DHC-3 Turbo Otter	405	ex CAF 9423	302	FP
☐ C-GVNL	de Havilland DHC-3 Turbo Otter	105	ex N5341G	304	FP
☐ C-GCRE	Cessna A185F Skywagon	18502522	ex (N1807R)		FP
☐ C-GZSH	Cessna A185F Skywagon	18503482	ex (N1463Q)		FP

HAUTS-MONTS — Quebec, QC / Jackson, MS (YQB/JAN)

☐ C-GPSP	Cessna 441 Conquest II	441-0058	ex OY-BHM	Photo/survey
☐ C-GPSQ	Cessna 441 Conquest II	441-0076	ex N441RC	Photo/survey
☐ C-GPSR	Cessna 441 Conquest II	441-0143	ex N26PK	Photo/survey
☐ N454EA	Cessna 441 Conquest II	441-0054	ex C-GRSL	Photo/survey
☐ N8970N	Cessna 441 Conquest II	441-0092		Photo/survey
☐ C-GHMN	Piper PA-23-250 Aztec C	27-3893	ex N6590Y	Photo/survey
☐ C-GNZQ	Piper PA-23-250 Aztec E	27-7554067	ex N54755	Photo/survey
☐ C-GPSZ	Cessna 421C Golden Eagle II	421C0148	ex N303HC	Photo/survey

HAWK AIR — Wawa-Hawk Junction, ON (YXZ)

☐ C-FBBG	de Havilland DHC-2 Beaver	358-173	ex N2848D	FP
☐ C-FQMN	de Havilland DHC-3 Otter	184	ex N2959W	FP

HAWKAIR AVIATION SERVICE — Hawkair (BH) — Terrace, BC (YXT)

☐ C-FABG	de Havilland DHC-8-102	147	
☐ C-FCJE	de Havilland DHC-8-102	165	
☐ C-FDNG	de Havilland DHC-8-102	166	
☐ C-FIDL	de Havilland DHC-8-311	305	ex V2-LFW

HAYES HELICOPTER SERVICES — Duncan, BC (DUQ)

☐ C-FBHG	Bell 206B JetRanger II	713	ex CF-BHG
☐ C-GHHF	Bell 206B JetRanger III	3311	ex C-FNHL
☐ C-GPCT	Bell 206B JetRanger III	3085	

HEARST AIR SERVICE — Hearst, ON (YHF)

☐ C-FBTU	de Havilland DHC-2 Beaver	1564	ex CF-BTU	FP/WS
☐ C-FDDX	de Havilland DHC-3 Turbo Otter	165	ex CF-DDX	FP/WS
☐ C-FDPM	de Havilland DHC-2 Beaver	1247	ex N87878	FP/WS

HELI-EXCEL — Sept-Iles, QC (YZV)

☐ C-FAEF	Aérospatiale AS350BA AStar	2152	ex N700YH
☐ C-FHEI	Aérospatiale AS350BA AStar	2969	
☐ C-FJYL	Aérospatiale AS350BA AStar	2959	
☐ C-FOZT	Aérospatiale AS350BA AStar	2644	
☐ C-FQHC	Aérospatiale AS350BA AStar	1011	ex N49561
☐ C-FSPF	Aérospatiale AS350BA AStar	2785	
☐ C-FVRT	Aérospatiale AS350BA AStar	2849	
☐ C-GAWV	Aérospatiale AS350B2 AStar	2998	
☐ C-GGPF	Aérospatiale AS350BA AStar	1313	ex N900BA
☐ C-GIEQ	Aérospatiale AS350B2 AStar	3349	ex N686CC
☐ C-GVEI	Aérospatiale AS350B2 AStar	2671	ex N682CC
☐ C-FBYU	Bell 205A-1	30168	ex LX-HFZ
☐ C-FDDG	Bell 205A-1	30019	ex LX-HRI
☐ C-FXKL	Aérospatiale AS355F2 Twin Star	5148	ex N5797P
☐ C-GLHE	Bell 205A-1	30092	ex F-GHHQ
☐ C-GLHH	Bell 205A-1	30223	ex F-GHHR

HELI-EXPRESS — Quebec, QC (YQB)

☐ C-FCCI	Aérospatiale AS350BA AStar	1303	ex N5768Y
☐ C-GDEH	Aérospatiale AS350BA AStar	1348	ex N905DB
☐ C-GHEX	Aérospatiale AS350B2 AStar	2867	ex CP-2392
☐ C-GIMG	Aérospatiale AS350D AStar	1382	ex ZK-HZZ
☐ C-GJPC	Aérospatiale AS350BA AStar	1398	ex N269JM
☐ C-GRDI	Aérospatiale AS350B2 AStar	2866	ex C-FWAU
☐ C-GVEM	Aérospatiale AS350BA AStar	2510	ex N752BH
☐ C-GADA	Bell 205A-1	30031	ex PK-UHJ

HELI-INTER
Val d'Or/Chicoutimi-St Honore, QC

☐ C-FMGB	Aérospatiale AS350BA+ AStar	1292	ex N350SS
☐ C-FMHI	Aérospatiale AS350BA AStar	9037	ex EI-MYO
☐ C-FMOZ	Aérospatiale AS350BA AStar	1374	ex F-GHFR
☐ C-FONZ	Aérospatiale AS350BA AStar	1400	ex HR-ANU
☐ C-FPOO	Aérospatiale AS350BA AStar	2508	ex N370WM
☐ C-FZSU	Aérospatiale AS350B2 AStar	2481	ex XA-TMJ
☐ C-FZXY	Aérospatiale AS350BA AStar	2082	ex N6102E
☐ C-GGHA	Aérospatiale AS350BA AStar	2624	ex F-GHYK
☐ C-GGIS	Aérospatiale AS350BA AStar	1110	ex N40445
☐ C-GILZ	Aérospatiale AS350B2 AStar	3386	
☐ C-GJPA	Aérospatiale AS350BA AStar	1075	ex C-FHAH
☐ C-GMQM	Aérospatiale AS350D AStar	1380	ex N108SH
☐ C-GZGM	Aérospatiale AS350B2 AStar	9056	
☐ C-FCNV	Bell 205A-1	30288	ex LX-HXU
☐ C-FSMI	Bell 205A-1	30263	ex (N205HT)
☐ C-GFHW	Bell 205A-1	30115	ex VH-NGI
☐ C-GHNQ	Bell 206L LongRanger	45014	ex N259MH
☐ C-GVHP	Bell 205A-1	30119	ex N688CC

HELI-LIFT INTERNATIONAL
Yorkton, SK (YQV)

☐ C-GHLE	Bell 205A-1	30195	ex HL9150
☐ C-GHLJ	Bell 206L-3 LongRanger III	51280	ex N60992
☐ C-GHLX	Aérospatiale AS350B AStar	1589	ex N85PB
☐ C-GIYN	Aérospatiale AS350BA AStar	1776	ex JA9368
☐ C-GMOR	Bell 205A-1	30159	ex LX-HOR
☐ C-GQCW	Aérospatiale AS350BA AStar	1255	ex N3607T
☐ C-GSHK	Bell 204B	2067	ex Thai 920

HELICOPTER TRANSPORT SERVICES
Carp, ON (YRP)

☐ C-FMIE	Aérospatiale AS350B2 AStar	4216	
☐ C-FVVQ	Aérospatiale AS350BA AStar	1210	ex N350LW
☐ C-FVVR	Aérospatiale AS350B AStar	1353	ex N9101N
☐ C-GHAV	Aérospatiale AS350B2 AStar	2758	
☐ C-GZCN	Aérospatiale AS350B1 AStar	2207	ex LN-OCD
☐ C-FCYW	Bell 204B	2004	ex N8588F
☐ C-FDZE	Bell 204B	2055	ex N7932S
☐ C-GFFY	Bell 205A-1	30123	ex N1084C
☐ C-GMHE	Bell 205A-1	30212	ex PT-HHZ
☐ C-GQLL	Bell 205A-1	30018	ex A7-HAG
☐ C-FMAO	Bell 206B JetRanger	407	ex CF-MAO
☐ C-FWGN	Bell 206B JetRanger	690	ex C-FCTV
☐ C-GQMR	Bell 206B JetRanger II	2207	
☐ C-GZPF	Bell 206B JetRanger	3490	ex N2168S
☐ C-GZPG	Bell 206B JetRanger	867	ex N28EE
☐ C-GZPH	Bell 206B JetRanger	3162	ex N70523
☐ C-GZRQ	Bell 206B JetRanger II	1981	ex N206YP
☐ C-FARV	Bell 206L LongRanger	45117	
☐ C-FKEP	Bell 206L LongRanger	45024	ex N111AL
☐ C-FLTX	Bell 206LR+ LongRanger	45043	ex N96AT
☐ C-FOVL	Bell 206L-3 LongRanger III	51041	ex N282BH
☐ C-FPOQ	Bell 206L-4 LongRanger IV	52363	
☐ C-GZPE	Bell 206L-4 LongRanger IV	52334	
☐ C-GZPI	Bell 206L-4 LongRanger IV	52351	
☐ C-GZPJ	Bell 206L-4 LongRanger IV	52353	
☐ C-GZRS	Bell 206L-3 LongRanger III	51146	ex N3193U
☐ C-FMLT	Bell 212	30889	ex JA9532
☐ C-GAHZ	Bell 212	30758	ex N5306T
☐ C-GHTK	Bell 212	30904	ex JA9538
☐ C-GXTF	Bell 212	30825	ex N212RT
☐ C-GDYZ	Bell 214ST	28109	ex N727HT	♦
☐ C-GPNC	Beech B300C Super King Air	FM-15	ex N415KA

HELICRAFT 2000
Montreal-St.Hubert, QC (YHC)

☐ C-FHVV	Aérospatiale AS350BA AStar	1225	ex N215EH
☐ C-FIFL	Aérospatiale AS350D AStar	1453	ex F-GCTM
☐ C-FLIZ	Aérospatiale AS350BA AStar	2484	ex F-GHRD

☐ C-FLOO	Aérospatiale AS350BA AStar	2739	ex JA6133
☐ C-FPHY	Aérospatiale AS350BA AStar	1496	ex N5805B
☐ C-GIYJ	Aérospatiale AS350BA AStar	1407	ex JA9273
☐ C-GMAN	Aérospatiale AS350B2 AStar	3073	
☐ C-GMIM	Aérospatiale AS350BA AStar	1257	ex F-GCJC
☐ C-GMYG	Aérospatiale AS350D AStar	1201	ex N3604X
☐ C-GPHN	Aérospatiale AS350BA AStar	1251	
☐ C-FGDT	Bell 206B JetRanger	2993	ex N993RM
☐ C-FXHA	Aérospatiale AS355F2 Twin Star	5426	ex N684CC
☐ C-FXHE	Aérospatiale AS355F2 Twin Star	5074	ex N685CC
☐ C-GARE	Bell 206B JetRanger	1852	
☐ C-GKHX	Bell 206L-2 LongRanger	46612	ex N373MH
☐ C-GYHZ	Bell 206L LongRanger	45126	ex N16840

HELIFOR INDUSTRIES   Campbell River, BC (YBL)

☐ C-FHCN	Boeing Vertol 107 II	404	ex N194CH	♦
☐ C-FHFB	Boeing Vertol 234UT Chinook	MJ-005	ex N238CH	<WCO
☐ C-GHCD	Boeing Vertol 107 II	101	ex N6682D	<WCO
☐ C-GHFF	Boeing Vertol 107 II	406	ex N195CH	<WCO
☐ C-GHFY	Boeing Vertol 107 II	2002	ex N190CH	<WCO

HELIJET INTERNATIONAL   Helijet (JB/JBA)   Vancouver-Intl, BC (YVR)

☐ C-GHJL	Sikorsky S-76A II	760214	ex N101PB	EMS
☐ C-GHJP	Sikorsky S-76A II	760065	ex (C-GHJT)	
☐ C-GHJT	Sikorsky S-76A	760052	ex VH-XHZ	
☐ C-GHJV	Sikorsky S-76A	760167	ex N5426U	
☐ C-GHJW	Sikorsky S-76A II	760074	ex N586C	
☐ C-GBSF	Sikorsky S-61N	61222	ex C-GROV	
☐ C-GHJJ	Learjet 31A	102	ex N681AF	EMS
☐ C-GHJU	Learjet 31A	120	ex N200TJ	EMS
☐ C-GLMX	Bell 206L-1 LongRanger	45439	ex N92ZT	
☐ C-GHJF	Beech 200 Super King Air	BB-1493	ex N3015Q	
☐ C-GXHJ	Bell 206L-1 LongRanger	45741	ex N3174P	

HELIQWEST AVIATION   Edmonton-Municipal, AB (YXD)

☐ C-FETK	Bell 205A-1	30299	ex OE-XEH
☐ C-FHQK	Bell 205A-1	30142	ex C-GXLF
☐ C-FIAN	Bell 206A JetRanger	32	ex CF-IAN
☐ C-FSXX	Bell 205A-1	30172	ex PP-EOU
☐ C-FXFT	Kaman K-1200 K-Max	A94-0007	ex N135KA
☐ C-FZQB	Bell 212	30629	ex PK-HCF
☐ C-GEAK	Bell 205A-1	30183	ex N393EH
☐ C-GEAT	Bell 205A-1	30088	ex G-BKGH

HICKS & LAWRENCE   St Thomas, ON (YQS)

☐ C-FBME	Cessna 337G Super Skymaster II	33701734	ex N146HA
☐ C-FBNX	Cessna 337G Super Skymaster II	33701738	ex N53614
☐ C-FBRG	Cessna 337G Super Skymaster II	33701695	ex N26286
☐ C-FBRH	Cessna 337G Super Skymaster II	33701662	ex N53496
☐ C-FBRK	Cessna 337H Super Skymaster II	33701884	ex N75BP
☐ C-FIGS	Cessna 337G Super Skymaster II	33701728	ex N714GP
☐ C-FIKM	Cessna 337G Super Skymaster	33701588	ex N72448
☐ C-FIXO	Cessna 337H Super Skymaster II	33701820	ex N1328L
☐ CF-JIP	Cessna 337G Super Skymaster	33701534	ex N72177
☐ C-FNHL	Cessna 337D Super Skymaster	337-1035	ex C-FPWB
☐ C-FSIW	Cessna 337G Super Skymaster	33701571	ex N72377
☐ C-FSIY	Cessna 337G Super Skymaster II	33701949	ex N959CC
☐ C-FSIZ	Cessna 337G Super Skymaster II	33701632	ex N53450
☐ C-GDQU	Cessna 337G Super Skymaster II	33701607	ex N53413
☐ C-GEOR	Cessna 337G Super Skymaster II	33701730	ex (N53595)
☐ C-GFSC	Cessna 337G Super Skymaster II	33701793	ex N53699
☐ C-GIOG	Cessna 337G Super Skymaster II	33701746	ex (N53638)
☐ C-GNRO	Cessna 337D Super Skymaster	337-1101	ex N68169
☐ C-GWDU	Cessna 337B Super Skymaster	337-0665	ex N2365S
☐ C-FMUM	Rockwell 500S Shrike Commander	3103	ex N37GW
☐ C-GETH	Rockwell 500S Shrike Commander	1800-15	ex N732
☐ C-GETJ	Rockwell 500S Shrike Commander	3275	ex N81450
☐ C-GIZV	Aero Commander 500B	1440-155	ex N678GH
☐ C-GJLO	Rockwell 500S Shrike Commander	1796-11	ex N5009E
☐ C-GJMA	Aero Commander 500B	1319-128	ex N330U

☐ C-FKJI	Beech 200 Super King Air	BB-105	ex N71TZ
☐ C-GJBZ	Piper PA-36-375 Pawnee Brave	36-7902036	ex N3989E
☐ C-GJLI	Beech 200 Super King Air	BB-347	ex N424CR
☐ C-GQNJ	Beech 200 Super King Air	BB-275	
☐ C-GTWW	Beech 65-C90 King Air	LJ-657	ex N9030R

HIGHLAND HELICOPTERS — Vancouver-Intl, BC (YVR)

☐ C-FHHC	Aérospatiale AS350B2 AStar	2569	ex N2PW
☐ C-FHHU	Aérospatiale AS350B2 AStar	2790	ex C-FSQY
☐ C-FHHY	Aérospatiale AS350BA AStar	1650	ex C-GSKI
☐ C-FJHH	Aérospatiale AS350B2 AStar	3279	
☐ C-FKHH	Aérospatiale AS350B2 AStar	2736	
☐ C-FYYA	Aérospatiale AS350BA AStar	2295	ex ZK-HOU
☐ C-GBHH	Aérospatiale AS350B2 AStar	3180	
☐ C-GDHH	Aérospatiale AS350B2 AStar	4103	
☐ C-GGTO	Aérospatiale AS350B2 AStar	4393	
☐ C-GHHH	Aérospatiale AS350B2 AStar	3270	
☐ C-GHHV	Aérospatiale AS350B2 AStar	2918	ex N4034Q
☐ C-GHHW	Aérospatiale AS350B2 AStar	3039	
☐ C-GHHZ	Aérospatiale AS350B2 AStar	3054	
☐ C-GNHH	Aérospatiale AS350B2 AStar	2737	ex N9446H
☐ C-GRHH	Aérospatiale AS350B2 AStar	3315	ex N37PT
☐ C-GRJO	Aérospatiale AS350B2 AStar	4277	
☐ C-GTIA	Aérospatiale AS350B2 AStar	4328	ex F-WWPZ
☐ C-GXHH	Aérospatiale AS350B2 AStar	4058	ex F-WQDF
☐ C-FCDL	Bell 206B JetRanger III	3852	ex N93AJ
☐ C-FCOY	Bell 206B JetRanger III	3280	ex N7023J
☐ C-FETC	Bell 206B JetRanger III	3515	ex C-GTIA
☐ C-FHHB	Bell 206B JetRanger	519	ex CF-HHB
☐ C-FHHI	Bell 206B JetRanger III	2310	ex N101CD
☐ C-GHHD	Bell 206B JetRanger	1566	ex N90003
☐ C-GHHG	Bell 206B JetRanger	1396	ex N918TR
☐ C-GHHM	Bell 206B JetRanger III	2712	
☐ C-GHHO	Bell 206B JetRanger	1690	
☐ C-GHHR	Bell 206B JetRanger II	1963	
☐ C-GHHX	Bell 206B JetRanger III	2714	
☐ C-GHXJ	Bell 206B JetRanger	1832	
☐ C-GIZO	Bell 206B JetRanger III	2715	
☐ C-GJJA	Bell 206B JetRanger II	2032	ex N9958K
☐ C-GJMJ	Bell 206B JetRanger	620	ex N7112J
☐ C-GKDG	Bell 206B JetRanger III	2969	
☐ C-GKGI	Bell 206B JetRanger	1790	ex N49629
☐ C-GKJL	Bell 206B JetRanger III	3005	
☐ C-GMDX	Bell 206B JetRanger III	3032	
☐ C-GMZH	Bell 206B JetRanger III	3203	
☐ C-GNLT	Bell 206B JetRanger III	2973	
☐ C-GNSQ	Bell 206B JetRanger III	3274	
☐ C-GOPF	Bell 206B JetRanger III	3227	
☐ C-GOPK	Bell 206B JetRanger III	3247	
☐ C-GAXW	Bell 206L-3 LongRanger III	51395	ex N6501S
☐ C-GFHH	Bell 206L-3 LongRanger III	51362	ex C-FPCL

HORNE AIR — Hornepayne, ON (YHN)

☐ C-FFHP	de Havilland DHC-2 Beaver	57	ex CF-FHP	FP
☐ C-FIDM	de Havilland DHC-2 Beaver	1323	ex N99871	FP
☐ C-GEWG	de Havilland DHC-2 Beaver	842	ex N87572	FP

HURON AIR AND OUTFITTERS — Armstrong, ON (YYW)

☐ C-FDPW	de Havilland DHC-2 Beaver	1339	ex 58-2011	FP/WS
☐ C-FGSR	Noorduyn Norseman V	N29-47	ex CF-GSR	FP
☐ C-FIOF	de Havilland DHC-3 Otter	24	ex LN-SUV	FP/WS

HYDRO-QUEBEC (SERVICE TRANSPORT AERIEN) — Hydro (HYD) — Montreal-Trudeau, QC (YUL)

☐ C-GHQL	de Havilland DHC-8-402Q	4115		Op by AIE
☐ C-GHQP	de Havilland DHC-8-402Q	4004	ex C-GIHK	Op by AIE
☐ C-GJNL	de Havilland DHC-8-311	422	ex G-BXPZ	Op by AIE

ICARUS FLYING SERVICE — Ile de la Madelaine, QC (YGR)

☐ C-GFBF	Britten-Norman BN-2B-27 Islander	2125	ex VP-FBF

IGNACE AIRWAYS — Ignace/Thunder Bay, ON (ZUC/YQT)

☐ C-FAPR	de Havilland DHC-3 Otter	31	ex LN-LMM	FP
☐ CF-TTL	Cessna U206C Super Skywagon	U206-1062	ex N29088	FP
☐ C-GZBR	de Havilland DHC-2 Beaver	1272	ex N434GR	FP

INFINITY FLIGHT SERVICES — Edmonton-Municipal, AB (YXD)

☐ C-GSWF	Beech B100 King Air	BE-129	ex LV-VCU

INLAND AIR CHARTERS — Prince Rupert, BC (YPR)

☐ C-FFRL	de Havilland DHC-2 Beaver	482	ex CF-FRL	FP
☐ C-FGQC	de Havilland DHC-2 Beaver	75	ex CF-GQC	FP
☐ C-FIAX	de Havilland DHC-2 Beaver	140	ex VH-AAD	FP
☐ C-FJOM	de Havilland DHC-2 Beaver	1024	ex CF-JOM	FP
☐ C-FJPX	de Havilland DHC-2 Beaver	1076	ex CF-JPX	FP

INTEGRA AIR — Lethbridge, AB (YQL)

☐ C-FFIA	British Aerospace Jetstream 31	779	ex C-FSAS
☐ C-FFNV	Piper PA-31T Cheyenne	31T-7720058	ex N167DA
☐ C-GGIA	British Aerospace Jetstream 31	778	ex C-FMIP

JACKSON AIR SERVICES — Jackson (JCK) — Flin Flon, MB (YFO)

☐ C-FMAJ	de Havilland DHC-3 Otter	383	ex 4655	FP/WS
☐ C-GDYR	Cessna A185F Skywagon	18503018		FP/WS
☐ C-GISX	Cessna A185F Skywagon II	18503836	ex N4669E	FP/WS
☐ C-GJMZ	Partenavia P.68B Observer	369-27/OB		

JOHNNY MAY'S AIR CHARTERS — Kuujjuaq, QC (YVP)

☐ C-FCEE	de Havilland DHC-3 Otter	282	ex 57-6134		FP/WS
☐ C-GMAY	de Havilland DHC-2 Beaver	1123	ex 56-0393	Pengo Palee	FP/WS

KABEELO AIRWAYS — Confederation Lake, ON (YMY)

☐ C-GDYT	de Havilland DHC-2 Beaver	1109	ex 56-4403	FP
☐ C-GLSA	de Havilland DHC-2 Beaver	1389	ex N94471	FP

KALUSAIR — North Lancaster, ON

☐ C-FSYF	Piper PA-34-200	34-7450202	ex N44159
☐ C-GKSB	Piper PA-31 Turbo Navajo	31-268	ex N370RC
☐ C-GKSI	Piper PA-31-325 Navajo C/R	31-7912008	ex N27791

KASABA AIR SERVICE — Kasba Lake, NT (YDU)

☐ CF-MAS	de Havilland DHC-2 Beaver	38	ex C-FMAS	FP

KAYAIR — Ear Falls, ON (YMY)

☐ CF-TBH	Beech 3T	6226	43-35671	FP

KD AIR — Kay Dee (XC/KDC) — Port Alberni, BC (YPB)

☐ C-GPCA	Piper PA-31 Turbo Navajo	31-42	ex N333DG
☐ C-GXEY	Piper PA-31-350 Navajo Chieftain	31-7305044	ex N74910

KECHIKA VALLEY AIR — Fort St John, BC (YXJ)

☐ C-GOSC	Cessna U206G Stationair 6	U20603757	ex (N5649G)	FP/WS

KEEWATIN AIR — (FK) — Churchill, MB/Rankin Inlet, NU (YYQ /YRT)

☐ C-FBPK	Beech 1900D	UE-128	ex N128EU	
☐ C-FCGT	Beech 200 Super King Air	BB-159	ex N47FH	EMS
☐ C-FJXO	Beech 1900C	UC-124	ex N124CU	
☐ C-FRMV	Beech B200 Super King Air	BB-979	ex N22TP	
☐ C-FSKN	Beech B200 Super King Air	BB-1109	ex F-GLLH	
☐ C-FSKO	Beech B200 Super King Air	BB-1007	ex N514MA	EMS
☐ C-FZPW	Beech B200 Super King Air	BB-940	ex N519SA	EMS

KELOWNA FLIGHTCRAFT AIR CHARTER — Flightcraft (KW/KFA) — Kelowna, BC (YLW)

☐ C-GACU	Boeing 727-225F/W (Duganair 3)	20152/775	ex N8833E	710	Op for Purolator Courier
☐ C-GGKF	Boeing 727-223F (FedEx 3)	21523/1467	ex C-FMKF	718	Op for Purolator Courier
☐ C-GIKF	Boeing 727-227F (FedEx 3)	20772/982	ex N99763	721	Op for Purolator Courier

Reg	Type	C/n	Ex	Fleet	Notes
C-GJKF	Boeing 727-227F (FedEx 3)	21042/1106	ex N10756	722	Op for Purolator Courier
C-GKFJ	Boeing 727-281F (Raisbeck 3)	21455/1316	ex C-FLHJ	715	Op for Purolator Courier
C-GKKF	Boeing 727-227F (FedEx 3)	21043/1113	ex N16758	723	Op for Purolator Courier
C-GLKF	Boeing 727-227F (FedEx 3)	21118/1167	ex N14760	724	Op for Purolator Courier
C-GMKF	Boeing 727-227F (FedEx 3)	21119/1175	ex N16761	725	Op for Purolator Courier
C-GNKF	Boeing 727-227F (FedEx 3)	20839/1031	ex N88770	726	Op for Purolator Courier
C-GQKF	Boeing 727-243F (FedEx 3)	21265/1226	ex N17402	720	Op for Purolator Courier
C-GTKF	Boeing 727-225F (FedEx 3)	21580/1435	ex N8883Z	728	Op for Purolator Courier
C-GWKF	Boeing 727-243F/W (Duganair 3)	21270/1231	ex N17407	719	Op for Purolator Courier
C-GXKF	Boeing 727-243F/W (Duganair 3)	21663/1438	ex N17410	716	Op for Purolator Courier
C-FKFZ	Convair 580F	151	ex N11151	510	Op for Purolator Courier
C-GKFF	Convair 580F	160	ex N9067R	511	Op for Purolator Courier
C-GKFG	Convair 580F	22	ex N32KA	516	[YLW]
C-GKFU	Convair 580F	82	ex N90857	501	Op for Purolator Courier
C-GKFA	Douglas DC-10-30F	46921/214	ex N811SL	101	
C-GKFB	Douglas DC-10-30F	46949/179	ex N949PL	102	
C-GKFD	Douglas DC-10-30F	47928/192	ex N304WL	103	◆
C-	Douglas DC-10-30F	46917/211	ex N303WL		[YHM]◆
C-GJRH	Cessna 340	340-0058	ex N340BD		
C-GKFX	Beech A60 Duke	P-235	ex N60GF		

KENN BOREK AIR

Borek Air (4K/KBA)

Calgary-Intl, AB/Edmonton-Intl, AB/ Iqaluit, NT/Resolute Bay, NT (YYC/YEG/YFB/YRB)

Reg	Type	C/n	Ex	Notes	
C-FMKB	Basler BT-67TP	47/19560	ex N57NA	Frtr; dam Dec07	
C-GAWI	Basler BT-67	19227	ex N79017	Lidia;	>Alfred Wegener Institute
C-GEAI	Basler BT-67	16305/33053	ex N200AN		
C-GJKB	Basler BT-67	13383	ex N167BT		
C-GVKB	Basler BT-67	12300	ex N907Z		
C-GKBA	Beech B99	U-164	ex SE-GRB		
C-GKBB	Beech 65-C90 King Air	LJ-607	ex N48DA		
C-FMWM	Beech A100 King Air	B-59	ex N702JL		
C-FRKB	Beech 100 King Air	B-72	ex C-GTLF		
C-FTUA	Beech 100 King Air	B-61	ex C-GSYN		
C-GAVI	Beech A100 King Air	B-201	ex G-BBVM		
C-GKBQ	Beech 100 King Air	B-62	ex LN-NLB		
C-GKBZ	Beech 100 King Air	B-85	ex LN-PAJ		
C-GWWA	Beech 100 King Air	B-27	ex G-BOFN		
C-FBCN	Beech 200 Super King Air	BB-7			
C-FEKB	Beech 200 Super King Air	BB-468	ex N9UT	Beech 1300 conversion	
C-FKBU	Beech 200 Super King Air	BB-285	ex C-GQXF		
C-GKBN	Beech 200 Super King Air	BB-29	ex LN-ASG		
C-GKBP	Beech 200 Super King Air	BB-505	ex HP-1083P		
C-FBBA	de Havilland DHC-6 Twin Otter 300	276	ex 8Q-MAK		
C-FBBV	de Havilland DHC-6 Twin Otter 300	311	ex C-FMPC		
C-FBBW	de Havilland DHC-6 Twin Otter 300	588	ex 8Q-KBA		
C-FDHB	de Havilland DHC-6 Twin Otter 300	338	ex CF-DHB		
C-FGOG	de Havilland DHC-6 Twin Otter 300	348	ex CF-GOG	FP/WS	
C-FHKB	de Havilland DHC-6 Twin Otter 300	402	ex N204SA	◆	
C-GBPE	de Havilland DHC-6 Twin Otter 100	21	ex 8Q-QHC		
C-GCKB	de Havilland DHC-6 Twin Otter 300	312	ex C-FMPF		
C-GDHC	de Havilland DHC-6 Twin Otter 300	494			
C-GIKB	de Havilland DHC-6 Twin Otter 100	64	ex 8Q-CSL		
C-GKBC	de Havilland DHC-6 Twin Otter 300	650	ex N55921		
C-GKBG	de Havilland DHC-6 Twin Otter 300	733			
C-GKBH	de Havilland DHC-6 Twin Otter 300	732	ex 8Q-MAV		
C-GKBO	de Havilland DHC-6 Twin Otter 300	725	ex HP-1273APP		
C-GKBR	de Havilland DHC-6 Twin Otter 300	617	ex 8Q-MAU		
C-GSKB	de Havilland DHC-6 Twin Otter 100	99	ex 8Q-QBU		
C-GTKB	de Havilland DHC-6 Twin Otter 100	60	ex 8Q-MAC		
C-GXXB	de Havilland DHC-6 Twin Otter 300	426	ex 8Q-MAN		
C-FLKB	Embraer EMB.110P1 Bandeirante	110397	ex N903LE		
C-GANR	Embraer EMB.110P1 Bandeirante	110373	ex HP-931APP		
C-GBBR	Embraer EMB.110P1 Bandeirante	110444	ex HP-1177AP		
C-GFKB	Embraer EMB.110P1 Bandeirante	110400	ex 9N-AFF		

KENORA AIR SERVICE

Kenora SPB, ON (YQK)

Reg	Type	C/n	Ex	Notes
CF-CBA	de Havilland DHC-3 Otter	230	ex C-FCBA	FP

88

					FP
☐ CF-JEI	de Havilland DHC-2 Beaver	1020			FP
☐ C-FNOT	de Havilland DHC-2 Beaver	1067	ex N4193A		FP
☐ C-FODO	de Havilland DHC-2 Beaver	822	ex CF-ODO		FP
☐ CF-TBX	Beech D18S	A-479	ex N841B		FP
☐ C-FWDB	Cessna A185E Skywagon	185-1250	ex (N4783Q)		FP
☐ C-FWMM	Cessna A185F Skywagon	18502238	ex N4361Q		FP
☐ C-GAQJ	de Havilland DHC-2 Beaver	1130	ex 56-4411		FP
☐ C-GEHX	Beech 3NM	CA-112	ex CF-ZNF		FP
☐ C-GOTD	Cessna A185F Skywagon	18502445	ex (N1724R)		FP
☐ C-GPVC	de Havilland DHC-2 Beaver	290	ex N9257Z		FP
☐ C-GYJY	Cessna A185F Skywagon	18502468	ex N1748R		FP

KEYSTONE AIR SERVICE   *Keystone (BZ/KEE)*   *Swan River, MB (YSE)*

☐ C-FAFT	Beech 200 Super King Air	BB-57	ex N121DA
☐ C-FPCD	Beech B99	U-151	ex C-FBRO
☐ C-FSPN	Beech 200 Super King Air	BB-745	ex N428P
☐ C-FXLO	Piper PA-31-350 Chieftain	31-8052022	ex N3547N
☐ C-GBDN	Piper PA-31-350 Navajo Chieftain	31-7652035	ex N59763
☐ C-GCJH	Piper PA-31-350 Chieftain	31-7952109	ex N42FL
☐ C-GFOL	Beech 200 Super King Air	BB-27	ex N120DP
☐ C-GGQU	Piper PA-31 Turbo Navajo	31-155	ex N9116Y
☐ C-GOSU	Piper PA-31-350 Navajo Chieftain	31-7752148	ex N27327

KISSISSING AIR   *Kississing Lake/Pine Falls, MB*

☐ C-FENB	Noorduyn UC-64A Norseman	324	ex 43-5384	FP
☐ CF-FAQ	de Havilland DHC-2 Beaver	94	ex C-FFAQ	FP
☐ C-FIDF	de Havilland DHC-2 Beaver	1321	ex N99870	FP
☐ C-FIKP	de Havilland DHC-2 Beaver	890	ex CF-IKP	FP
☐ C-FKIX	Cessna 185A Skywagon	18503794	ex N9866Q	FP
☐ C-FOBR	Noorduyn Norseman V	N29-35	ex CF-OBR	FP
☐ C-FYMV	de Havilland DHC-2 Beaver	1589	ex CF-YMV	FP
☐ C-GADE	de Havilland DHC-2 Beaver	730	ex 53-7919	FP
☐ C-GDLO	Cessna TU206B Super Skywagon	U206-0690	ex N4990F	FP

KIVALLIQ AIR   *Kivalliq(FK)*   *Winnipeg-Intl, MB/Rankin Inlet, NU (YWG/YRT)*

☐ C-FJXL	Beech 1900C	UC-102	ex N15479

KLUANE AIRWAYS   *Whitehorse, YT (YXY)*

☐ C-FMPS	de Havilland DHC-2 Beaver	1114	ex CF-MPS	FP

L AND A AVIATION   *Hay River, NT (YHY)*

☐ C-FYFJ	Cessna A185F Skywagon II	18503797	ex N9913Q	FP/WS
☐ CF-ZEB	Cessna 337F Super Skymaster	33701428	ex N1828M	
☐ C-GHYT	Beech A100 King Air	B-98	ex N998RC	
☐ C-GJHM	Cessna A185F Skywagon II	18504203		FP/WS

LABRADOR AIR SAFARI   *Baie Comeau, QC (YBC)*

☐ C-FJGV	de Havilland DHC-2 Beaver	977	ex CF-JGV	FP/WS
☐ C-FOCU	de Havilland DHC-2 Beaver	73	ex CF-OCU	FP/WS
☐ C-FPQC	de Havilland DHC-2 Beaver	873	ex CF-IKQ	FP/WS
☐ C-FUWJ	de Havilland DHC-2 Beaver	453	ex N7691	FP/WS
☐ C-FYYT	de Havilland DHC-2 Beaver	1569	ex VH-IDZ	FP/WS
☐ C-GUJU	de Havilland DHC-2 Beaver	1639	ex N4600Y	FP/WS
☐ C-GWAE	de Havilland DHC-2 Beaver	1094	ex N93434	FP/WS
☐ C-FAZW	de Havilland DHC-3 Otter	451	ex JW-9101	FP/WS
☐ C-FJZN	de Havilland DHC-3 Otter	205	ex CF-JZN	FP/WS
☐ C-GLCO	de Havilland DHC-3 Otter	420	ex N17681	FP/WS
☐ C-GLJI	de Havilland DHC-3 Otter	150	ex 55-3297	FP/WS
☐ C-GVNX	de Havilland DHC-3 Otter	353	ex N5335G	FP/WS
☐ C-FTBC	Cessna U206F Stationair	U20602047	ex CF-TBC	FP/WS
☐ C-GUBN	Cessna U206F Stationair II	U20602860	ex (N1185Q)	FP/WS

LAC LA CROIX QUETICO AIR SERVICE   *Lac la Croix, ON/Crane Lake, MB*

☐ C-FHAN	de Havilland DHC-2 Beaver	316	ex N11255	FP
☐ C-FVSF	Cessna A185E Skywagon	185-1223	ex CF-VSF	FP
☐ C-GDZD	de Havilland DHC-2 Beaver	496	ex 52-6116	FP
☐ C-GUEC	Cessna A185F Skywagon	18503986	ex N5513E	FP

LAC SEUL AIRWAYS — Ear Falls, ON (YMY)

☐ CF-HXY	de Havilland DHC-3 Otter	67		FP
☐ C-GLLO	Cessna U206F Stationair II	U20602913	ex N1602Q	FP

LAKELAND AIRWAYS — Temagami, ON

☐ C-FJKT	de Havilland DHC-2 Beaver	1023	ex CF-JKT	
☐ C-GUFH	Cessna A185F Skywagon	18502857	ex (N1488F)	

LAKELSE AIR — Terrace, BC (YXT)

☐ C-FHQT	Bell 204B	2024	ex C-GEAV	
☐ C-FMGM	Kaman K-1200 K-MAX	A94-0013	ex N163KA	
☐ C-FNBR	Aérospatiale AS350B2 AStar	2565	ex N60618	
☐ C-GALU	Bell 206B JetRanger III	2511	ex N50071	
☐ C-GBCN	Aérospatiale AS350B2 AStar	2609	ex F-GLHP	
☐ C-GHQW	Bell 206B JetRanger III	1708		
☐ C-GJUP	Aérospatiale AS350B AStar	2155	ex JA9793	
☐ C-GPTC	Aérospatiale AS350B2 AStar	2092	ex OY-HDY	
☐ C-GWHO	Bell 206L LongRanger	45013	ex N3GH	

LAKES DISTRICT AIR SERVICES — Burns Lake, BC (YPZ)

☐ C-FFHS	de Havilland DHC-2 Beaver	51	ex CF-HHS	FP/WS
☐ C-FVXQ	Cessna A185E Skywagon	185-1198	ex CF-XVQ	FP/WS

LAUZON AVIATION — Elliot Lake, ON (YEL)

☐ C-FRUY	de Havilland DHC-2 Beaver	687	ex N74157	FP

LAWRENCE BAY AIRWAYS — Southend-Reindeer Lake, SK

☐ C-GUJX	de Havilland DHC-2 Beaver	1132	ex 56-4412	FP

LEUENBERGER AIR SERVICE — Nakina SPB, ON (YQN)

☐ C-FSOX	de Havilland DHC-3 Turbo Otter	437	ex CF-SOX	FP
☐ C-GLCW	de Havilland DHC-3 Turbo Otter	172	ex 55-3310	FP

LIARD AIR — Muncho Lake, BC

☐ C-GNNP	de Havilland DHC-3 Turbo Otter	465	ex N342KA	FP
☐ C-GUDK	de Havilland DHC-2 Beaver	708	ex 53-7900	FP
☐ C-GUGE	Cessna A185F Skywagon	18502904	ex N8730Z	FP/WS

LITTLE RED AIR SERVICE — Little Red (LRA) — Fort Vermilion, AB

☐ C-FGWR	Beech B200 Super King Air	BB-1599	ex C-FGWD	
☐ C-FLRB	Beech A100 King Air	B-131	ex N102FG	
☐ C-FLRD	Beech A100 King Air	B-243	ex PT-OFZ	
☐ C-FLTC	Beech 65-C90 King Air	LJ-631	ex N103FG	
☐ C-FPQQ	Beech B200 Super King Air	BB-1304	ex N3173K	
☐ C-GGUH	Cessna 208B Caravan I	208B0827	ex N51478	
☐ C-GICJ	Cessna U206F Stationair	U20603044	ex N4318Q	
☐ C-GWVT	Cessna U206F Stationair	U20602918	ex (N1721Q)	

LOCKHART AIR SERVICES — Sioux Lookout, ON (YXL)

☐ C-FKQM	Cessna 404 Titan II	404-0108	ex N37102	
☐ G-GFIT	Cessna 310R	310R1865	ex (N3173M)	
☐ C-GIJF	Cessna 310R	310R1875	ex N3208M	
☐ C-GOGP	Cessna 402C	402C0516	ex N401SA	

MANITOBA GOVERNMENT AIR SERVICES — Winnipeg-Intl/Thompson, MB (YWG/YTH)

☐ C-FTUV	Canadair CL215	1020	ex CF-TUV	256	
☐ C-FTXI	Canadair CL215	1016	ex CF-TXI	255	
☐ C-GBOW	Canadair CL215	1087	ex C-GKDY	253	
☐ C-GMAF	Canadair CL215	1044	ex C-GUMW	250	
☐ C-GMAK	Canadair CL215	1107		254	
☐ C-GUMW	Canadair CL215	1065		251	
☐ C-GYJB	Canadair CL215	1068		252	
☐ C-FEMA	Cessna S550 Citation S/11	S550-0040			EMS
☐ C-FMAX	de Havilland DHC-3 Otter	267	ex CF-MAX		FP/WS
☐ C-FODY	de Havilland DHC-3 Otter	429	ex CF-ODY		FP/WS
☐ C-FWAH	de Havilland DHC-6 Twin Otter 300	240	ex CF-WAH		
☐ C-GBNX	Cessna 560 Citation V	0074	ex N593MD		EMS
☐ C-GDAT	Cessna 310R	310R1883	ex N315U		

□ C-GMLN	Cessna 310R	310R1884	ex N316U
□ C-GRNE	Piper PA-31-350 Chieftain	31-7952224	ex N91834
□ C-GYNE	Cessna 310R	310R1367	ex N4086C

MARITIME AIR CHARTER — Halifax, NS (YHZ)

□ C-FCAI	Piper PA-31 Turbo Navajo	31-475	ex N22DC
□ C-FDOR	Beech A100 King Air	B-103	ex CF-DOR
□ C-FYKQ	Piper PA-31 Turbo Navajo	31-399	ex CF-YKQ
□ C-GILS	Britten-Norman BN-2A-21 Islander	0416	ex N92JA
□ C-GXUG	Piper PA-31 Turbo Navajo	31-665	ex N1GY

MARTINI AVIATION — Fort Langley, BC

□ C-GMNT	de Havilland DHC-2 Turbo Beaver	1653-TB30	ex N4478
□ C-GPLT	Pilatus PC-12/45	566	ex HB-FPX
□ C-GUWF	de Havilland DHC-2 Beaver	287	ex N91364

MAX AVIATION — Max Aviation (MAX) — Montreal-St Hubert, QC (YHU)

□ C-FOGP	Beech B100 King Air	BE-134	ex N363EA
□ C-GPJL	Beech B100 King Air	BE-107	ex N3699B
□ C-GPRU	Beech B100 King Air	BE-26	ex N36WH
□ C-GSWG	Beech B100 King Air	BE-131	ex N6354H
□ C-GVIK	Beech A100 King Air	BE-7	ex N57HT

McMURRAY AVIATION — Fort McMurray, AB (YMM)

□ C-GHJB	Cessna U206E Stationair	U20601677	ex N9477G
□ C-GHGT	Cessna U206G Stationair	U20605874	
□ C-GHLI	Cessna 208B Caravan I	208B0565	ex N5858J
□ C-GKOM	Cessna 208 Caravan	20800365	ex N675TF
□ C-GRKO	Cessna U206G Stationair	U20606617	ex N9707Z
□ C-GWKO	Cessna 208B Caravan I	208B1245	ex N52591
□ C-GZZD	Cessna U206F Stationair	U20601957	ex N50946

MEADOW AIR — Meadow Lake, SK (YLJ)

□ C-GBGR	Cessna 337 Super Skymaster	337-0398	ex N6398F
□ C-GETG	Cessna 337 Super Skymaster	337-0921	ex N2621S
□ C-GGFA	Cessna 337 Super Skymaster	337-1263	ex N1263M
□ C-GYHW	Cessna 337 Super Skymaster	337-1111	ex N86204

MELAIRE — Fort Frances, ON (YAG)

| □ C-FOMJ | de Havilland DHC-2 Turbo Beaver | 1683/TB51 | ex CF-OMJ | FP/WS |

MINIPI AVIATION — Goose Bay, NL (YYR)

| □ C-FCOO | de Havilland DHC-2 Beaver | 314 | ex N377JW | FP |

MISSINIPPI AIRWAYS — The Pas, MB/Pukatawagan, MB (YQD/XPK)

□ C-FIXS	Cessna 208B Caravan I	208B1209	
□ C-FJKM	Piper PA-31-350 Chieftain	31-7952089	ex N764A
□ C-FMCB	Cessna 208B Caravan I	208B1114	ex N1274B
□ C-FTYO	Beech 200 Super King Air	BB-1222	ex N126KA
□ C-FWXI	Beech 200 Super King Air	BB-1224	ex C-GTLA	EMS
□ C-GADW	Piper PA-31-350 Navajo Chieftain	31-7752078	ex N27191
□ C-GGGT	Cessna TU206G Stationair	U20604170	ex N756LF
□ C-GHQF	Piper PA-31-350 Chieftain	31-8052050	ex N633WA
□ C-GMKO	Piper PA-31-350 Chieftain	31-7952063	ex N932LA
□ C-GOCN	Cessna 208B Caravan I	208B0780	ex N308KC
□ C-GOGT	Beech B200 Super King Air	BB-535	
□ C-GWHW	Piper PA-31-350 Chieftain	31-8052060	ex N223CH
□ C-GYQD	Piper PA-31-350 Chieftain	31-8152039	ex N4075T

MISSIONAIR — Winnipeg-Intl, MB/Sachigo Lake, ON (YWG/ZPB)

| □ C-FSHA | Piper PA-31-350 Navajo Chieftain | 31-7752062 | ex PH-NTB |
| □ C-GCJX | Piper PA-31-350 Navajo Chieftain | 31-7552064 | ex N4WE |

MOLSON AIR — Wabowden, MB

| □ C-FBQY | de Havilland DHC-2 Beaver | 1496 | ex N147Q | FP/WS |
| □ C-GYBQ | Cessna A185F Skywagon | 18503568 | ex N4014Q | FP/WS |

MONTAIR AVIATION — Boundary Bay, BC (YDT)

| □ C-GRSL | Beech 65-90B King Air | LJ-609 | ex Z-WSG |
| □ C-GYPD | Piper PA-34-220T Seneca | 34-7870025 | ex N47991 |

MORGAN AIR SERVICES — Calgary-Intl, AB (YYC)

☐ C-FCCM	Piper PA-30-160 Twin Comanche	30-1632	ex CF-CCM	
☐ C-FNRM	Gulfstream Commander 690C	11692	ex N152X	
☐ C-FRQS	Piper PA-30-160 Twin Comanche	30-934	ex N7854Y	
☐ C-GOMA	Beech 200 Super King Air	BB-262	ex EC-HHO	
☐ C-GSQD	Cessna 401	401-0300	ex (176TC)	

MORNINGSTAR AIR EXPRESS — Morningstar (MAL) — Edmonton-Intl, AB (YEG)

☐ C-FEXB	Cessna 208B Caravan I	208B0539	ex N758FX		Lsd fr/op for FDX
☐ C-FEXE	Cessna 208B Caravan I	208B0244	ex N750FE		Lsd fr/op for FDX
☐ C-FEXF	Cessna 208B Caravan I	208B0508	ex N749FX		Lsd fr/op for FDX
☐ C-FEXV	Cessna 208B Caravan I	208B0482	ex N738FX		Lsd fr/op for FDX
☐ C-FEXX	Cessna 208B Caravan I	208B0209	ex (N877FE)		Lsd fr/op for FDX
☐ C-FEXY	Cessna 208B Caravan I	208B0226	ex N896FE		Lsd fr/op for FDX
☐ C-FMES	Boeing 727-225F (FedEx 3)	22548/1734	ex N461FE	Carolina	Lsd fr/op for FDX
☐ C-FMEY	Boeing 727-247F (FedEx 3)	21328/1251	ex N234FE		Lsd fr/op for FDX
☐ C-FMAI	Boeing 757-2B7SF	27199/586	ex N908FD		Lsd fr/op for FDX ♦
☐ C-FMEP	Boeing 757-2B7SF	27144/544	ex N904FD		Lsd fr/op for FDX ♦
☐ C-FMFG	Boeing 757-2B7	27198/584	ex N904FD		Lsd fr/op for FDX ♦
☐ C-GATK	ATR 42-310F	135	ex N923FX		Lsd fr/op for FDX

MUSTANG HELICOPTERS — Red Deer, AB (YQF)

☐ C-FAOV	Aérospatiale AS350B2 AStar	9066		
☐ C-FAOX	Aérospatiale AS350B2 AStar	9067		
☐ C-FAOZ	Aérospatiale AS350B2 AStar	9068	ex N68CQ	
☐ C-FMNE	Aérospatiale AS350B2 AStar	9082		
☐ C-FNWE	Aérospatiale AS350B2 AStar	9086		
☐ C-FNYE	Aérospatiale AS350B2 AStar	9091		
☐ C-FNYF	Aérospatiale AS350B2 AStar	9092		
☐ C-FNYK	Aérospatiale AS350B2 AStar	9088		
☐ C-GJHC	Aérospatiale AS350B2 AStar	3412		
☐ C-GXTO	Aérospatiale AS350B2 AStar	9061	ex N681CC	
☐ C-GZGN	Aérospatiale AS350B2 AStar	9062	ex N680CC	
☐ C-FFHB	Bell 205A-1	30294	ex VH-HHW	
☐ C-GFRE	Bell 205A-1	30185	ex EC-FYX	
☐ C-GHUF	Bell 205A-1	30106	ex N687CC	
☐ C-GIVV	Bell 206B JetRanger III	2823	ex N2757C	
☐ C-GVHQ	Bell 205A-1	30110	ex N689CC	
☐ C-FUMN	Piper PA-31 Navajo C	31-8112076	ex N4095F	

NAKINA OUTPOST CAMPS AND AIR SERVICE — (T2) — Nakina, ON (YQN)

☐ C-FDGV	de Havilland DHC-6 Twin Otter 200	154	ex TF-JMD	
☐ CF-MIQ	de Havilland DHC-3 Turbo Otter	336		FP/WS
☐ C-FMPY	de Havilland DHC-3 Turbo Otter	324	ex CF-MPY	FP/WS
☐ C-FNQB	Cessna 208 Caravan	20800387		
☐ C-FTIN	Cessna A185F Skywagon	18503362	ex N7325H	FP/WS
☐ C-FUYC	Cessna 208B Caravan I	208B1204		
☐ C-FZRJ	Cessna 208B Caravan I	208B0597	ex N52609	
☐ C-GEOW	Pilatus PC-12/45	244	ex HB-FRO	
☐ C-GMVB	Cessna 208B Caravan I	208B0317		

NATIONAL HELICOPTERS — Toronto, ON

☐ C-FFUJ	Bell 206B JetRanger III	2982	ex N525W	
☐ C-FLYC	Bell 206L-1 LongRanger II	45478	ex XA-SPN	
☐ C-FNHB	Bell 206L-1 LongRanger II	45661	ex N166BH	
☐ C-FNHG	Bell 206L-1 LongRanger II	45784	ex N220HC	
☐ C-FTCH	Bell 206B JetRanger	860	ex N809JA	
☐ C-GIGS	Bell 206B JetRanger	1434	ex N59474	
☐ C-GMUR	Eurocopter EC120B	1438		
☐ C-GSZZ	Bell 206B JetRanger III	2319	ex XA-TCU	

NESTOR FALLS FLY-IN OUTPOSTS — Nestor Falls SPB, ON

☐ C-FMDB	de Havilland DHC-2 Beaver	268	ex N2104X	FP
☐ C-FODK	de Havilland DHC-3 Otter	13	ex CF-ODK	FP
☐ C-FSOR	de Havilland DHC-3 Otter	239	ex IM 1725	FP
☐ C-FWWV	Beech 3N	CA-18	ex RCAF 1443	FP
☐ C-GDWB	Cessna U206G Stationair	U20604460	ex N756YJ	FP
☐ C-GYGL	Cessna A185F Skywagon	18503298	ex (N94269)	FP

NEWFOUNDLAND & LABRADOR AIR SERVICES — St John's, NL (YYT)

☐ C-FAYN	Canadair CL215	1105		282	
☐ C-FAYU	Canadair CL215	1106		283	
☐ C-FTXA	Canadair CL215	1006	ex CF-TXA	284	
☐ C-FYWP	Canadair CL215	1002	ex CF-YWP	285	
☐ C-GDKW	Canadair CL215	1095		280	
☐ C-GDKY	Canadair CL215	1096		281	
☐ C-FIZU	Canadair CL415	2076			♦
☐ C-FNJC	Canadair CL415	2077			♦
☐ C-GMFY	Canadair CL415	2078			♦
☐ C-GLFY	Cessna 337G Super Skymaster	33701700	ex (N53557)		
☐ C-GNLA	Beech B300 Super King Air	FL-26	ex N59TF		

NOLINOR AVIATION — Nolinor (NRL) — Montreal-Trudeau, QC (YUL)

☐ C-FAWV	Convair 580F	154	ex C-FMGB	Frtr
☐ C-FHNM	Convair 580F	454	ex N583P	>GV
☐ C-FTAP	Convair 580	334	ex N580N	
☐ C-GKFP	Convair 580	446	ex N589PL	
☐ C-GNRL	Convair 580F	375	ex CS-TMM	Frtr
☐ C-GQHB	Convair 580	376	ex ZS-KRX	
☐ C-GRLQ	Convair 580	347	ex N580TA	
☐ C-GNLN	Boeing 737-2B6C (Nordam 3)	23050/975	ex CN-RMN	Frtr
☐ C-GTUK	Boeing 737-2B6C (Nordam 3)	23049/951	ex CN-RMM	Frtr

NORDAIR QUEBEC 2000 — La Grande Riviere, QC (YGL)

☐ C-FGYK	de Havilland DHC-2 Beaver	123	ex CF-GYK	
☐ C-FKLC	de Havilland DHC-3 Otter	255	ex CF-KLC	FP/WS
☐ C-FSVP	de Havilland DHC-3 Turbo Otter	28	ex N252KA	FP/WS

NORDPLUS — Schefferville-Squaw Lake, QC (YKL)

☐ C-FLAP	de Havilland DHC-3 Otter	289	ex CF-LAP	FP
☐ C-FODG	de Havilland DHC-2 Beaver	205		FP
☐ C-FFYK	Cessna A185F Skywagon	18502174	ex CF-FYK	FP
☐ C-GFUT	de Havilland DHC-3 Otter	404	ex CAF9422	FP

NORTH CARIBOO AIR — North Caribou (NCB) — Fort St John, BC (YXJ)

☐ C-FDAM	Beech 100 King Air	B-8	ex N59T	
☐ C-FIDN	Beech 100 King Air	B-3	ex N128RC	
☐ C-FMXY	Beech 100 King Air	B-40	ex N923K	
☐ C-FSKA	Beech A100 King Air	B-239	ex N154TC	
☐ C-GBVX	Beech B100 King Air	BE-99	ex N524BA	
☐ C-GNCV	Beech 100 King Air	B-23	ex N701RJ	
☐ C-GPCB	Beech A100 King Air	B-45	ex N704S	
☐ C-GTLS	Beech 100 King Air	B-35	ex N178WM	
☐ C-FCGC	Beech 200 Super King Air	BB-236	ex N46KA	CatPass 200 conversion
☐ C-FCGM	Beech 200 Super King Air	BB-217	ex N200CD	CatPass 200 conversion
☐ C-FRRQ	Beech 200 Super King Air	BB-560	ex F-GTEF	
☐ C-GDFN	Beech 200 Super King Air	BB-359	ex N351MA	
☐ C-GDFT	Beech 200 Super King Air	BB-354	ex N221BG	
☐ C-GZRX	Beech 200 Super King Air	BB-574	ex N75WL	
☐ C-FCWP	de Havilland DHC-8-102	111	ex N925CA	
☐ C-FLSX	de Havilland DHC-8-102	285	ex N834EX	
☐ C-FNCG	de Havilland DHC-8-102	211	ex C-GABH	
☐ C-FODL	de Havilland DHC-8-102	294	ex N881CC	
☐ C-GAQN	de Havilland DHC-8-311	548	ex 5N-BHW	
☐ C-GNCF	de Havilland DHC-8-311A	244	ex PH-ABQ	♦
☐ C-FMKD	Beech 65-B90 King Air	LJ-376	ex N300RV	
☐ C-FNCL	Beech 1900D	UE-11	ex C-FSKT	
☐ C-FNCP	Beech 1900D	UE-58	ex C-GSKY	
☐ CF-QSX	Cessna A185F Skywagon	18502116	ex (N70334)	
☐ C-FVAX	Cessna 425 Conquest	425-0178	ex (N90GM)	
☐ C-GZTU	Beech 1900C-1	UC-103	ex N15031	
☐ C-GCFM	Beech 65-C90 King Air	LJ-886	ex N15SL	
☐ C-GELD	Piper PA-31 Turbo Navajo	31-555	ex N6621L	
☐ C-GIGK	de Havilland DHC-6 Twin Otter 300	492	ex N300BC	

| ☐ C-GLAC | Beech 58 Baron | TH-339 | ex N6YC | |
| ☐ C-GMWO | Piper PA-31 Navajo C | 31-8112042 | ex N4086Y | |

NORTH PACIFIC SEAPLANES   Prince Rupert, BC (YPR)

☐ C-FIFQ	de Havilland DHC-2 Beaver	825	ex CF-IFQ	FP
☐ C-FJOS	de Havilland DHC-2 Beaver	1030	ex CF-JOS	FP
☐ C-FKDC	de Havilland DHC-2 Beaver	1080	ex CF-KDC	FP
☐ C-FOCZ	de Havilland DHC-2 Beaver	100	ex N254BD	FP
☐ C-FTCW	de Havilland DHC-2 Beaver	646	ex VH-SMH	FP
☐ C-FHAS	de Havilland DHC-3 Turbo Otter	382	ex N382BH	FP

NORTH WRIGHT AIRWAYS   Northwright (HW/NWL)
Norman Wells/Good Hope/Deline, NT (YVQ/YGH/YWJ)

☐ C-FBAX	Cessna 207 Skywagon	20700355	ex N1755U	
☐ C-FKHD	Beech 99	U-11	ex F-BRUN	
☐ C-FNWL	de Havilland DHC-6 Twin Otter 300	596	ex N16NG	
☐ C-FVCE	Beech 99A	U-118	ex N918BB	
☐ CF-WHP	Cessna 337C Super Skymaster	337-0895	ex (N2595S)	
☐ CF-ZIZ	Fairchild PC-6/B1-H2 Turbo Porter	2009	ex N353F	FP
☐ C-GAAP	Pilatus PC-6/B1-H2 Turbo Porter	569	ex N2851T	FP
☐ C-GALF	Cessna 207A Stationair 8 II	20700674	ex N9118M	
☐ C-GDBI	Cessna 207 Skywagon	20700039	ex N91052	
☐ C-GDLC	Cessna 208B Caravan I	208B0767	ex N5151D	
☐ C-GFCV	Cessna U206C Super Skywagon	U206-1213	ex N4345E	
☐ C-GHDT	Helio 295 Super Courier	1401	ex N6327V	
☐ C-GJGZ	Cessna A185F Skwagon II	18503856	ex (N4750E)	
☐ C-GMOK	Cessna 207A Stationair 8 II	20700673	ex N6373D	
☐ C-GNWA	Cessna A185F Skwagon II	18503345	ex C-GFJC	
☐ C-GRDD	de Havilland DHC-6 Twin Otter 100	54	ex N8081N	FP/WS
☐ C-GWUY	Beech 200 Super King Air	BB-77	ex N300CP	
☐ C-GZGO	Britten-Norman BN-2A-26 Islander	2017	ex N59360	
☐ C-GZIZ	Cessna 208B Caravan I	208B0546	ex N5262W	
☐ C-GZVX	Cessna U206G Stationair 6	U20604110	ex (N756HT)	

NORTHERN AIR CARE   Edmonton-City Centre, AB

| ☐ C-GNAA | Beech 100 King Air | B-24 | ex N382WC | |

NORTHERN AIR CHARTER   Peace River, AB (YPE)

☐ C-GIRG	Cessna A185F Skywagon II	18504181	ex (N61424)	
☐ C-GNAC	Piper PA-31 Navajo C	31-7812106	ex N27707	
☐ C-GNAJ	Beech A100 King Air	B-107	ex LN-AAH	
☐ C-GNAK	Beech B200 Super King Air	BB-1376	ex HK-3990X	Catpass 200 conversion
☐ C-GNAM	Beech B200 Super King Air	BB-1339	ex N252AF	EMS, Beech 1300 conversion
☐ C-GNAP	Piper PA-23-250 Aztec F	27-8054002	ex C-GTGS	
☐ C-GNAR	Beech 1900D	UE-252	ex JA017A	
☐ C-GNAX	Beech B200 Super King Air	BB-1419	ex N146SB	

NORTHERN AIR SOLUTIONS   Bracebridge, ON

| ☐ C-FLDC | Cessna 208 Caravan I | 20800319 | ex N208JN | |

NORTHERN LIGHTS AIR   Lynn Lake SPB, MB (YYL)

| ☐ C-GNLL | Cessna 206B Super Skywagon | 206-0192 | ex N5192U | FP |

NORTHSTAR AIR   Pickle Lake, ON (YPL)

☐ C-FLNB	Cessna 208B Caravan I	208B0799	ex N799B	
☐ C-FVPC	Pilatus PC-12/45	358	ex N358PC	
☐ C-GCQA	de Havilland DHC-3 Otter	77	ex N129JH	FP/WS
☐ C-GJAS	Cessna 208 Caravan I	20800322	ex N51869	FP/WS

NORTHWARD AIR   Dawson Creek, BC (YDQ)

| ☐ C-FOMF | Cessna A185A Skywagon | 185-0423 | ex (N1623Z) | |
| ☐ CF-SLV | Cessna U206 Super Skywagon | U206-0412 | ex N8012Z | |

NORTHWAY AVIATION   Northway (NAL)   Arnes, MB (YNR)

☐ C-FBHP	Cessna 207A Stationair 8	20700647	ex N73857	
☐ C-FHDL	Cessna 180	18030430	ex N1730G	
☐ C-GNWG	Cessna 208 Caravan I	20800412	ex N52136	
☐ C-GNWV	Cessna 208B Caravan I	208B1115	ex N5093D	

NORTHWEST FLYING   Nestor Falls SPB, ON

☐ CF-NKL	Beech C-45H	AF-378	ex N9864Z	FP
☐ C-GEBL	de Havilland DHC-2 Beaver	1068	ex N33466	FP
☐ C-GYYS	de Havilland DHC-3 Otter	276	ex N1UW	FP

NORTHWESTERN AIR   Polaris (J3/PLR)   Fort Smith, NT (YSM)

☐ C-FCPE	British Aerospace Jetstream 31	825	ex G-31-825	
☐ C-FNAE	British Aerospace Jetstream 31	881	ex N431AM	
☐ C-FNAF	British Aerospace Jetstream 31	789	ex N411UE	
☐ C-FNAM	British Aerospace Jetstream 31	767	ex N767JX	
☐ C-FNAY	British Aerospace Jetstream 31	768	ex N159PC	
☐ C-FNAZ	British Aerospace Jetstream 32	843	ex C-GEAZ	
☐ C-GNAQ	British Aerospace Jetstream 32EP	837	ex C-FZYB	
☐ C-GNGI	British Aerospace Jetstream 31	739	ex N855JS	
☐ C-FCGI	Beech 65-A90 King Air	LJ-220	ex CF-CGI	
☐ C-GNAH	Beech 99	U-107	ex N207BH	
☐ C-GNAL	Beech 99	U-57	ex TF-ELD	

NT AIR   Thunderbird (NTA)   Prince George/Smithers, BC (YXS/YYD)

☐ CF-GWM	Cessna U206F Stationair	U20601802	ex CF-BZO		FP/WS
☐ C-FEYT	Beech A100 King Air	B-210	ex N75GR		
☐ C-FHVX	Dornier 328-100	3094	ex D-CMTM		
☐ C-GAVY	Piper PA-31-350 Navajo Chieftain	31-7752165	ex N27409		
☐ C-GCMT	Beech 1900C-1	UC-120	ex N15683		
☐ C-GCMY	Beech 1900D	UE-287		921	<GLR
☐ C-GCMZ	Beech 1900C-1	UC-61	ex N1568L	929	
☐ C-GCYA	Cessna A185F Skywagon	18502578	ex (N4515C)		FP
☐ C-GDOX	Cessna 208B Caravan I	208B0541	ex N621BB		
☐ C-GEFA	Beech 1900C-1	UC-94	ex N80346	927	
☐ C-GJSU	Beech 100 King Air	B-88	ex N100ZM		
☐ C-GYIS	Cessna A185F Skywagon	18502895	ex N8679Z		FP/WS

NUELTIN LAKE AIR SERVICE   Nueltin Lake, MB

☐ C-FDBR	Found FBA-2C1 Bush Hawk XP	34	ex C-GDWS	FP
☐ C-FDCL	Cessna U206G Stationair	U20603542	ex N8790Q	FP
☐ C-FSAP	Noorduyn Norseman VI	231	ex 43-5240	FP
☐ C-GVDQ	Piper PA-31-350 Chieftain	31-8152119	ex N40869	

OMEGA AIR   Richmond, BC

☐ C-FMCL	Aérospatiale AS355F1 Twin Star	5255	ex C-FUHF
☐ C-GBFH	Bell 206B JetRanger	2171	
☐ C-GDHD	Eurocopter EC120B Colibri	1116	ex C-GOWC
☐ C-GHMH	Bell 206B JetRanger	1582	ex N116PC

ONTARIO MINISTRY OF NATURAL RESOURCES AVIATION SERVICES
Trillium (TRI)   Sault Ste Marie, ON (YAM)

☐ C-GOGD	Canadair CL415	2028	ex C-GAOI	270	
☐ C-GOGE	Canadair CL415	2031	ex C-GAUR	271	
☐ C-GOGF	Canadair CL415	2032	ex C-GBGE	272	
☐ C-GOGG	Canadair CL415	2033	ex C-GBFY	273	
☐ C-GOGH	Canadair CL415	2034	ex C-GCNO	274	
☐ C-GOGW	Canadair CL415	2037	ex C-GBPM	275	
☐ C-GOGX	Canadair CL415	2038	ex C-GBPU	276	
☐ C-GOGY	Canadair CL415	2040		277	
☐ C-GOGZ	Canadair CL415	2043		278	
☐ C-FOEH	de Havilland DHC-2 Turbo Beaver	1644/TB24	ex CF-OEH		FP/WS
☐ C-FOER	de Havilland DHC-2 Turbo Beaver	1671/TB41	ex CF-OER		FP/WS
☐ C-FOEU	de Havilland DHC-2 Turbo Beaver	1678/TB46	ex CF-OEU		FP/WS
☐ C-FOEW	de Havilland DHC-2 Turbo Beaver	1682/TB50	ex CF-OEW		FP/WS
☐ C-FOPA	de Havilland DHC-2 Turbo Beaver	1688/TB56	ex CF-OPA		FP/WS
☐ C-FOPG	de Havilland DHC-6 Twin Otter 300	232	ex CF-OPG		FP/WS
☐ C-FOPI	de Havilland DHC-6 Twin Otter 300	243	ex CF-OPI		FP/WS
☐ C-FOPJ	de Havilland DHC-6 Twin Otter 300	344	ex CF-OPJ		FP/WS
☐ C-GOGA	de Havilland DHC-6 Twin Otter 300	739			FP/WS
☐ C-GOGB	de Havilland DHC-6 Twin Otter 300	761			FP/WS
☐ C-GOGC	de Havilland DHC-6 Twin Otter 300	750			FP/WS
☐ C-FATR	Eurocopter EC130B4	3759			

☐ C-FMNR	Eurocopter EC130B4	4391		
☐ C-GOFH	Bell 206L-1 LongRanger II	45359	ex N100U	
☐ C-GOFI	Bell 206L-1 LongRanger II	45342	ex N167CP	
☐ C-GOGJ	Aérospatiale AS350B2 AStar	2749		
☐ C-GOGL	Aérospatiale AS350B2 AStar	2738		
☐ C-GOGQ	Aérospatiale AS350B2 AStar	3196		
☐ C-GOGS	Beech B300 Super King Air	FL-269	ex N3169N	
☐ C-GOIC	Beech B300 Super King Air	FL-272	ex N3172N	
☐ C-GONT	Eurocopter EC130B4	4423		

OOTSA AIR — Burns Lake, BC (YPZ)

☐ C-FCDT	de Havilland DHC-2 Beaver	390	ex CF-CDT	
☐ C-FYSI	Cessna A185E Skywagon	185-1524	ex CF-YSI	
☐ C-GZXV	de Havilland DHC-2 Beaver	1079	ex N49771	

ORCA AIR — Richmond, BC (YVR)

☐ C-FLRA	Piper PA-31-350 Navajo Chieftain	31-7752091	ex N52MS	
☐ C-GPAK	Piper PA-31-350 Chieftain	31-8052070	ex N3558S	
☐ C-GPMP	Piper PA-31-350 Chieftain	31-7852024	ex C-GWTT	
☐ C-GPWP	Piper PA-31-350 Chieftain	31-7952090	ex N35164	
☐ C-GWXL	Piper PA-31-350 Chieftain	31-7952036	ex C-GLYG	
☐ C-GZBO	Piper PA-31-350 Chieftain	31-8252048	ex N430S	

ORNGE

☐ C-GYNF	Agusta AW139	41226		EMS♦
☐ C-GYNG	Agusta AW139	41227		EMS♦
☐ C-GYNH	Agusta AW139	41230		EMS♦
☐ C-GYNJ	Agusta AW139	41232	ex N454SM	EMS♦
☐ C-GYNK	Agusta AW139	41236		EMS♦
☐ C-GYNL	Agusta AW139	41238		EMS♦
☐ C-GYNM	Agusta AW139	41245		EMS♦
☐ C-GRXA	Pilatus PC-12NG	1083	ex N983NG	EMS
☐ C-GRXB	Pilatus PC-12NG	1094	ex N994NG	EMS
☐ C-GRXD	Pilatus PC-12NG	1106	ex N106PC	EMS
☐ C-GRXE	Pilatus PC-12NG	1117	ex N117PZ	EMS
☐ C-GRXH	Pilatus PC-12NG	1163	ex N163NP	EMS
☐ C-GRXM	Pilatus PC-12NG	1169	ex N169NP	EMS
☐ C-GRXN	Pilatus PC-12NG	1224	ex N224NG	EMS♦
☐ C-GRXO	Pilatus PC-12NG	1225	ex N225NG	EMS♦
☐ C-GRXP	Pilatus PC-12NG	1249	ex N249NG	EMS♦
☐ C-GRXR	Pilatus PC-12NG	1255	ex N255NG	EMS♦
☐ C-FABH	Sikorsky S-76A II	760271	ex C-GHJV	EMS
☐ C-FSBH	Sikorsky S-76A	760168	ex N5427S	EMS
☐ C-GFFJ	Sikorsky S-76A	760138	ex VH-HUD	EMS
☐ C-GIMA	Sikorsky S-76A	760018	ex G-BZAC	EMS
☐ C-GIMB	Sikorsky S-76A	760111	ex G-BIAW	EMS
☐ C-GIMM	Sikorsky S-76A	760044	ex HS-HTM	EMS
☐ C-GIMT	Sikorsky S-76A	760130	ex N1548S	EMS
☐ C-GIMV	Sikorsky S-76A	760005	ex VH-WXE	EMS
☐ C-GIMW	Sikorsky S-76A	760226	ex N76FB	EMS
☐ C-GIMY	Sikorsky S-76A	760055	ex N376LL	EMS
☐ C-GIMZ	Sikorsky S-76A	760169	ex N399PK	EMS

OSNABURGH AIRWAYS — Pickle Lake, ON (YPL)

☐ C-FCZO	de Havilland DHC-3 Otter	71	ex CF-CZO	FP/WS
☐ C-FFQX	Noorduyn Norseman VI	625	ex N51131	FP/WS
☐ C-GMAU	de Havilland DHC-2 Beaver	1134	ex N775E	FP/WS

OSPREY WINGS — La Ronge, SK (YVC)

☐ C-FTCT	de Havilland DHC-2 Beaver	962	ex FAP-0205	FP/WS
☐ C-FZCO	de Havilland DHC-2 Beaver	1027	ex N8034J	FP/WS
☐ C-GAIJ	de Havilland DHC-2 Beaver	1373	ex N5334G	FP/WS
☐ C-GQKS	de Havilland DHC-2 Beaver	1096	ex N690	FP/WS
☐ C-GUWL	de Havilland DHC-2 Beaver	1223	ex 67-6140	FP/WS
☐ C-FASZ	de Havilland DHC-3 Otter	463	ex IM672	FP/WS
☐ CF-DIZ	de Havilland DHC-3 Otter	460	ex JW-9107	FP/WS
☐ C-FXRI	de Havilland DHC-3 Otter	258	ex VH-SBT	FP/WS
☐ C-GPHD	de Havilland DHC-3 Otter	113	ex 55-3267	FP/WS
☐ C-FLXP	de Havilland DHC-6 Twin Otter 200	217	ex N201EH	FP/WS

☐ C-FVEG	de Havilland DHC-6 Twin Otter 300	260	ex OH-SLK	FP/WS
☐ C-GCIM	Cessna A185F Skywagon II	18503953	ex (N5308E)	FP/WS
☐ C-GQOQ	de Havilland DHC-6 Twin Otter 200	155	ex EC-BPE	FP/WS

PACIFIC COASTAL AIRLINES   Pasco (8P/PCO)   Port Hardy, BC (YZT)

☐ C-FPCO	Beech 1900C	UB-52	ex C-GKHB		
☐ C-FPCV	Beech 1900C	UB-9	ex N189GA	302	
☐ C-FPCX	Beech 1900C	UB-66	ex OY-JRF		
☐ C-GBPC	Beech 1900C	UB-43	ex N565M		
☐ C-GCPZ	Beech 1900C	UB-71	ex C-GNPG		♦
☐ C-GIPC	Beech 1900C-1	UC-110	ex N210CU	Special colours	
☐ C-GPCY	Beech 1900C	UB-45	ex C-FYZD	301	
☐ C-FHUZ	Grumman G-21A Goose	B-83	ex BuA37830		
☐ C-FIOL	Grumman G-21A Goose	B-107	ex RCN 397		
☐ C-FUAZ	Grumman G-21A Goose	1077	ex N95400		
☐ C-GDDJ	Grumman G-21A Goose	1184	ex N1257A		
☐ C-GCPU	SAAB SF.340A	340A-140	ex N140CQ		
☐ C-GPCE	SAAB SF.340A	340A-004	ex N340SZ	Trawler c/s	
☐ C-GPCG	SAAB SF.340A	340A-094	ex N107EA		
☐ C-GPCJ	SAAB SF.340A	340A-006	ex N360SZ	Sailing boat c/s	
☐ C-GPCN	SAAB SF.340A	340A-027	ex N27XJ		o/o
☐ C-GPCQ	SAAB SF.340A	340A-043	ex N43SZ		
☐ C-FDSG	de Havilland DHC-2 Beaver	892	ex 54-1737		FP
☐ C-FMAZ	de Havilland DHC-2 Beaver	1413	ex CF-MAZ		FP
☐ C-GASF	de Havilland DHC-2 Beaver	1202	ex 57-2561		FP
☐ C-GPCF	Short SD.3-60	SH3620	ex (N366AC)	706	
☐ C-GPCP	Beech 200 Super King Air	BB-140		302	Catpass 200 conversion
☐ C-GPCW	Short SD.3-60	SH3622	ex 8Q-OCA	703	

PACIFIC EAGLE AVIATION   Port McNeil, BC (YMP)

☐ C-FEYN	de Havilland DHC-2 Beaver	508	ex N6167K	FP
☐ C-FICK	de Havilland DHC-2 Beaver	796	ex CF-ICK	FP
☐ C-FMXR	de Havilland DHC-2 Beaver	374	ex N7160C	FP
☐ C-GIDE	Republic RC-3 Seabee	355	ex N6167K	Amphibian

PACIFIC WESTERN HELICOPTERS   Prince George, BC (YXS)

☐ C-GPWE	Aérospatiale AS350B2 AStar	3027	ex C-GBKV
☐ C-GPWK	Aérospatiale AS350B AStar	1559	ex N29TV
☐ C-GPWL	Aérospatiale AS350B2 AStar	2956	ex C-GVXT
☐ C-GPWQ	Aérospatiale AS350B AStar	1099	ex N3596B
☐ C-GPWV	Aérospatiale AS350B AStar	1637	ex ZK-HRQ
☐ C-GPWZ	Aérospatiale AS350B2 AStar	2314	ex JA9863
☐ C-GPGM	Bell 206B JetRanger III	3178	ex N38902
☐ C-GPWH	Bell 206B JetRanger III	3131	ex N81AJ
☐ C-GPWJ	Bell 206B JetRanger III	2240	ex C-GNMM
☐ C-GPWR	Bell 206B JetRanger III	2989	ex N577AH
☐ C-GPWY	Bell 206B JetRanger III	3790	ex C-GIYD
☐ C-GTES	Bell 206B JetRanger III	2292	ex N16877
☐ C-GPWC	Cessna TU206F Stationair II	U20602644	ex N59290
☐ C-GPWT	Bell 205A-1	30231	ex N57954
☐ C-GPWX	Bell 212	30535	ex C-FAHX

PACIFIC WINGS AIRLINES   Sechelt, BC (YLT)

☐ C-GSUE	de Havilland DHC-2 Beaver	1199	ex N37AT	FP

PANORAMA HELICOPTERS   Alma, QC (YTF)

☐ C-FDYS	Aérospatiale AS350B AStar	1057	ex N211TV
☐ C-FETG	Aérospatiale AS350BA AStar	1378	ex N353LN
☐ C-GOVD	Aérospatiale AS350D AStar	1621	ex N3604X
☐ C-GRFM	Aérospatiale AS350B2 AStar	2601	ex N15234
☐ C-GSOX	Aérospatiale AS350B2 AStar	9022	ex N301TH
☐ C-GVED	Aérospatiale AS350BA AStar	1527	ex N597M
☐ C-FOKY	Bell 204B	2043	ex CF-OKY
☐ C-FSZX	Bell 206B JetRanger	2333	ex N206RM
☐ C-GBKH	Bell 206L-3 LongRanger III	51261	

PASCAN AVIATION — Pascan (PSC) — Quebec, QC (YQB)

☐ C-FHQA	British Aerospace Jetstream 32	876	ex N876CP
☐ C-FHSC	Beech B100 King Air	BE-105	ex N87XX
☐ C-FIDC	Beech B100 King Air	BE-27	ex N87JE
☐ C-FKQA	British Aerospace Jetstream 32	877	ex N877CP
☐ C-FODC	Beech B100 King Air	BE-59	ex N777DQ
☐ C-FYUT	Pilatus PC-12/45	254	ex N254PC
☐ C-GBTL	Pilatus PC-12/45	159	ex N159PB
☐ C-GNSC	Beech B100 King Air	BE-102	ex N57TJ
☐ C-GQJT	British Aerospace Jetstream 32EP	886	ex N886CP
☐ C-GRDC	Pilatus PC-12/45	214	ex PT-XTG
☐ C-GUSC	British Aerospace Jetstream 32	902	ex N242BM

PELICAN NARROWS AIR SERVICES — Pelican Narrows, SK

☐ C-GFZA	Cessna A185F Skywagon	18503084	FP/WS
☐ C-GTBC	de Havilland DHC-2 Beaver	1364	ex 58-2032

PERIMETER AVIATION — Perimeter (4B/PAG) — Winnipeg-Intl, MB (YWG)

☐ C-FBTL	Swearingen SA.226TC Metro II	TC-385	ex XA-TGG	
☐ C-FFDB	Swearingen SA.226TC Metro II	TC-249	ex N327BA	
☐ C-FIHB	Swearingen SA.226TC Metro II	TC-361	ex N166SW	
☐ C-FIHE	Swearingen SA.226TC Metro II	TC-373	ex N1010Z	
☐ C-FIIA	Swearingen SA.226TC Metro II	TC-329	ex N236AM	
☐ C-FJNW	Swearingen SA.226TC Metro IIA	TC-352	ex N167MA	
☐ C-FSLZ	Swearingen SA.226TC Metro II	TC-222EE	ex N104GS	
☐ C-FSWT	Swearingen SA.226TC Metro II	TC-382	ex N1011N	
☐ C-FUZY	Swearingen SA.226TC Metro II	TC-343	ex VH-UZY	
☐ C-GIQF	Swearingen SA.226TC Metro II	TC-279	ex F-GFGE	
☐ C-GIQG	Swearingen SA.226TC Metro II	TC-285	ex F-GFGD	
☐ C-GIQK	Swearingen SA.226TC Metro II	TC-288	ex F-GFGF	
☐ C-GPCL	Swearingen SA.226AT Merlin IV	AT-017	ex N511M	Frtr
☐ C-GQAJ	Swearingen SA.226TC Metro II	TC-295	ex C-FUIF	EMS, Aeromed titles
☐ C-GQAP	Swearingen SA.226TC Metro II	TC-263	ex N103UR	
☐ C-GYRD	Swearingen SA.226TC Metro II	TC-278	ex N5493M	Jt ops with Dene Cree Air
☐ C-FFJM	Swearingen SA.227AC Metro III	AC-700	ex N459AM	
☐ C-FMAV	Swearingen SA.227AC Metro III	AC-616	ex VH-UUF	
☐ C-GFWX	Swearingen SA.227AC Metro III	AC-650B	ex N26863	
☐ C-GWVH	Swearingen SA.227AC Metro IIIA	AC-714	ex VH-UUQ	
☐ C-FOFR	de Havilland DHC-8-106	317	ex N288DH	
☐ C-FPPW	de Havilland DHC-8-102A	390	ex N827EX	◆
☐ C-GWPS	de Havilland DHC-8-102	120	ex N928HA	
☐ C-FAMF	Swearingen SA.226T Merlin IIIA	T-274	ex I-SWAA	
☐ C-FCMJ	Rockwell Commander 681B	6054	ex N21HC	
☐ C-FDMX	Beech D95A Travel Air	TD-587	ex N5663K	
☐ C-FEQK	Beech 95-B55 Baron	TC-1374	ex CF-EQK	
☐ C-FKMZ	Beech E95 Travel Air	TD-708	ex N6223V	
☐ C-FRQI	Beech 99	U-124	ex TF-ELB	
☐ C-GEUJ	Beech B60 Duke	P-498	ex N36RR	
☐ C-GFQC	Beech B99	U-120	ex N47156	
☐ C-GQQC	Beech D95A Travel Air	TD-676	ex N7874L	

PHOENIX HELI-FLIGHT — Fort McMurray, AB (YMM)

☐ C-FANK	Eurocopter EC120B Colibri	1498	
☐ C-FAVX	Aérospatiale AS350B2 AStar	4242	
☐ C-FHLF	Aérospatiale AS350D AStar	1074	ex N35934
☐ C-FHLO	Aérospatiale AS350B3 AStar	4480	
☐ C-FNFU	Aérospatiale AS350B2 AStar	2467	ex C-GNIX
☐ C-GFHF	Eurocopter EC120B Colibri	1417	
☐ C-GPHF	Eurocopter EC130B4	3862	ex F-WWXM
☐ C-GTWN	Aérospatiale AS355N Twin Star	5673	ex 9M-JBG
☐ C-GXNP	Aérospatiale AS355N Twin Star	5757	ex F-WWXA

PORTER AIRLINES — (PD/POE) — Toronto-City Centre, ON (YTZ)

☐ C-FLQY	de Havilland DHC-8-402Q	4306	◆
☐ C-GLQB	de Havilland DHC-8-402Q	4130	
☐ C-GLQC	de Havilland DHC-8-402Q	4134	
☐ C-GLQD	de Havilland DHC-8-402Q	4138	
☐ C-GLQE	de Havilland DHC-8-402Q	4140	

☐ C-GLQF	de Havilland DHC-8-402Q	4193		
☐ C-GLQG	de Havilland DHC-8-402Q	4194		
☐ C-GLQH	de Havilland DHC-8-402Q	4225		
☐ C-GLQJ	de Havilland DHC-8-402Q	4228		
☐ C-GLQK	de Havilland DHC-8-402Q	4247		
☐ C-GLQL	de Havilland DHC-8-402Q	4249		
☐ C-GLQM	de Havilland DHC-8-402Q	4252		
☐ C-GLQN	de Havilland DHC-8-402Q	4254		
☐ C-GLQO	de Havilland DHC-8-402Q	4270		
☐ C-GLQP	de Havilland DHC-8-402Q	4271		
☐ C-GLQQ	de Havilland DHC-8-402Q	4272		
☐ C-GLQR	de Havilland DHC-8-402Q	4278		
☐ C-GLQV	de Havilland DHC-8-402Q	4279		
☐ C-GLQX	de Havilland DHC-8-402Q	4282		
☐ C-GLQZ	de Havilland DHC-8-402Q	4308		◆
☐ C-	de Havilland DHC-8-402Q			o/o◆
☐ C-	de Havilland DHC-8-402Q			o/o◆
☐ C-	de Havilland DHC-8-402Q			o/o◆
☐ C-	de Havilland DHC-8-402Q			o/o◆

PRINCE EDWARD AIR — Comet (CME) — Charlottetown, PE (YYG)

☐ C-FKAX	Beech 1900C	UB-67	ex N3067X	Frtr
☐ C-GKGA	Beech 1900C-1	UC-117	ex N117ZR	Frtr
☐ C-GSKA	Beech 1900C	UB-32	ex N317BH	
☐ C-GSKG	Beech 1900C-1	UC-22	ex N19016	
☐ C-GSKM	Beech 1900C	UB-21	ex N61MK	
☐ C-GSKN	Beech 1900C-1	UC-54	ex N31729	
☐ C-GSKU	Beech 1900C	UB-35	ex N735GL	
☐ C-GSKW	Beech 1900C	UB-33	ex N318BH	
☐ C-GTGA	Beech 1900C-1	UC-62	ex N62YV	Frtr
☐ C-FFGA	Cessna 208B Caravan I	208B0662	ex N5264E	026
☐ C-FHGA	Cessna 208B Caravan I	208B0047	ex C-FESH	024
☐ C-GEGA	Cessna 208B Caravan I	208B0379	ex N1119A	
☐ C-GLGA	Cessna 208B Caravan I	208B0350	ex N64AP	
☐ C-GSKS	Cessna 208B Caravan I	208B0762	ex N52623	
☐ C-GSKV	Cessna 208B Caravan I	208B0847		
☐ C-FFFH	Piper PA-31-350 Navajo Chieftain	31-7552130	ex N54CG	
☐ C-GATD	Piper PA-31-350 Navajo Chieftain	31-7405143	ex N74986	
☐ C-GGQM	Piper PA-31-350 Navajo Chieftain	31-7952033	ex TF-EGU	
☐ C-GIIZ	Piper PA-31-350 Navajo Chieftain	31-7552099	ex N29TW	
☐ C-GILJ	Piper PA-31-350 Navajo Chieftain	31-7552010	ex N374SA	
☐ C-GRFA	Piper PA-31-350 Navajo Chieftain	31-7405228	ex N54292	
☐ C-GYYJ	Piper PA-31-350 Navajo Chieftain	31-7652086	ex N59833	
☐ C-GPEA	Beech 200 Super King Air	BB-170	ex N869MA	CatPass 250 conversion
☐ N340AQ	SAAB SF.340AF	340A-019	ex C-GYQM	

PROPAIR — Propair (PRO) — Rouyn-Noranda, QC (YUY)

☐ C-FDJX	Beech A100 King Air	B-165	ex N811CU	
☐ C-FDOU	Beech A100 King Air	B-112	ex CF-DOU	
☐ C-FPAJ	Beech A100 King Air	B-151	ex N324B	
☐ C-FWRM	Beech A100 King Air	B-125	ex N89JM	
☐ C-GJLJ	Beech A100 King Air	B-235	ex N23517	
☐ C-GJLP	Beech A100 King Air	B-148	ex N67V	
☐ C-FAWE	Grumman G.159 Gulfstream 1	188	ex HB-LDT	
☐ C-FLEO	de Havilland DHC-2 Beaver	1270	ex N8700R	FP/WS
☐ C-FOGY	Beech 200 Super King Air	BB-168	ex N10VW	
☐ C-GLPJ	Beech 1900C-1	UC-139	ex N253RM	
☐ C-GLPM	de Havilland DHC-3 Turbo Otter	147	ex C-FJFJ	FP/WS
☐ C-GQAB	Cessna A185F Skywagon	18502766	ex (N1203F)	FP/WS
☐ C-GUGQ	de Havilland DHC-2 Beaver	400	ex 51-16485	FP/WS

PROVINCE OF ALBERTA — Alberta (GOA) — Edmonton-Municipal, AB (YXD)

☐ C-GFSA	Beech B300 Super King Air	FL-174		Op by Air Transportation Services
☐ C-GFSD	Beech B200 Super King Air	BB-1962	ex N7162V	
☐ C-GFSE	Beech B200 Super King Air	BB-1963	ex N7063F	
☐ C-GFSJ	de Havilland DHC-8-103	017		Op by Air Transportation Services

PROVINCIAL AIRLINES — (PB/SPR) — St Johns, NL (YYT)

☐ C-FGFZ	Beech 200 Super King Air	BB-403	ex N147K	
☐ C-GGAO	Beech 200 Super King Air	BB-659	ex N77QX	

☐ C-GGJF	Beech B200 Super King Air	BB-939	ex N125KW	
☐ C-GMRS	Beech 200 Super King Air	BB-187	ex N630DB	Maritime Patrol
☐ C-GMWR	Beech 200 Super King Air	BB-68	ex N844N	Maritime Patrol
☐ C-GTJZ	Beech 200 Super King Air	BB-499	ex N499TT	
☐ C-FUMY	de Havilland DHC-6 Twin Otter 300	675	ex PJ-TOD	
☐ C-FWLG	de Havilland DHC-6 Twin Otter 300	731	ex N915MA	
☐ C-GIED	de Havilland DHC-6 Twin Otter 300	600	ex N604NA	
☐ C-GJDE	de Havilland DHC-6 Twin Otter 300	471	ex C-GMPK	FP/WS
☐ C-FHRC	de Havilland DHC-8-102	209	ex TR-LGL	
☐ C-GPAB	de Havilland DHC-8-106MPA	275	ex N827PH	
☐ C-GPAL	de Havilland DHC-8-102	157	ex N824PH	
☐ C-GPAU	de Havilland DHC-8-106	282	ex N833EX	
☐ C-GRNN	de Havilland DHC-8-106MPA	314	ex N830PH	
☐ C-FMPV	de Havilland DHC-2 Beaver	1304	ex CF-MPV	FP
☐ C-FPAG	SAAB SF.340A	340A-028	ex N336BE	
☐ C-FPAI	SAAB SF.340A	340A-047	ex N337BE	
☐ C-GMEW	Swearingen SA.227AC Metro III	AC-668B	ex N668JS	
☐ C-GOFB	de Havilland DHC-3 Otter	39	ex 3681	

PROVINCIAL HELICOPTERS — Lac du Bonnet, MB

☐ C-FOGV	Bell 206L-3 LongRanger III	51121	ex V2-LGE	
☐ C-FPHB	Bell 206B JetRanger	1213	ex N62SH	
☐ C-FPMK	Bell 206B JetRanger III	3611	ex N8BG	
☐ C-FXTO	Aérospatiale AS355F Twin Star	5087	ex N260MH	
☐ C-FZYH	Bell 206B JetRanger II	1967	ex G-CRPS	
☐ C-GSZY	Bell 206B JetRanger III	2313	ex V2-LFA	

QUANTUM HELICOPTERS — Terrace, BC (YXT)

☐ C-FFHK	Bell 206B JetRanger	1065	ex CF-FHK	
☐ C-FHKJ	Bell 206L LongRanger	45116	ex N222CD	
☐ C-FNTR	Bell 205B	30297	ex OE-XBT	
☐ C-FQHB	Bell 206L LongRanger	45095	ex 5N-AJC	
☐ C-FRCL	Bell 206LR+ LongRanger	45019	ex SE-HUD	
☐ C-GMQH	Bell 206L LongRanger	45103	ex PH-HXH	
☐ C-GQNS	Bell 206LR+ LongRanger	45134		
☐ C-GSLV	Bell 206B JetRanger III	4199	ex N3202G	
☐ C-GSML	Bell 206LR+ LongRanger	45056	ex ZK-HRA	
☐ C-GTVL	Bell 206B JetRanger II	2166		

QWEST HELICOPTERS — Fort Nelson, BC (YYE)

☐ C-FMSZ	Aérospatiale AS350BA AStar	1101	ex N152AD	
☐ C-FUOQ	Aérospatiale AS350BA AStar	2180	ex N102FX	
☐ C-FSPR	Aérospatiale AS350B AStar	1814	ex ZK-HHY	
☐ C-FWII	Aérospatiale AS350BA AStar	1746	ex N433EW	
☐ C-GERL	Aérospatiale AS350B AStar	1645	ex JA9340	
☐ C-GTHJ	Aérospatiale AS350B AStar	1540	ex N4454Y	
☐ C-FMCH	Bell 206B-2 JetRanger	2132	ex N306CK	
☐ C-GIOB	Bell 206B JetRanger III	603	ex N678KG	
☐ C-GLCD	Bell 206B JetRanger	1284		
☐ C-GNMB	Bell 206B JetRanger	1631	ex N90171	
☐ C-GNNH	Bell 206B JetRanger	1632		
☐ C-GTDQ	Bell 206B JetRanger	1503	ex C-GOXX	
☐ C-GTVE	Bell 206B JetRanger	2163		

RAINBOW AIRWAYS — Dunchurch, ON

| ☐ C-GMOI | de Havilland DHC-2 Beaver | 1236 | ex N6083 | FP |

RCMP - GRC AIR SERVICES — Ottawa, ON

☐ C-FGSB	Aérospatiale AS350B3 AStar	3796		
☐ C-FMPG	Aérospatiale AS350B3 AStar	3082		
☐ C-FMPH	Aérospatiale AS350B3 AStar	3683		
☐ C-FMPP	Aérospatiale AS350B3 AStar	4124		
☐ C-FRPQ	Aérospatiale AS350B3 AStar	3636	ex F-WQDZ	
☐ C-GMPF	Aérospatiale AS350B3 AStar	4229		
☐ C-GMPK	Aérospatiale AS350B3 AStar	3923		
☐ C-GMPN	Aérospatiale AS350B3 AStar	3072		
☐ C-FGMQ	Pilatus PC-12/47E	1107		♦
☐ C-FMPA	Pilatus PC-12/47E	1216	ex HB-FQO	♦

☐ C-FMPB	Pilatus PC-12/45	283	ex N283PC		
☐ C-FMPE	Pilatus PC-12/45	314	ex HB-FQZ		
☐ C-FMPF	Pilatus PC-12/45	768	ex HB-FSY		
☐ C-FMPK	Pilatus PC-12/47E	1092			◆
☐ C-FMPW	Pilatus PC-12/45	315	ex HB-FRA		
☐ C-GMPE	Pilatus PC-12/47E	1073			◆
☐ C-GMPM	Pilatus PC-12/47E	1011	ex N911NG		
☐ C-GMPO	Pilatus PC-12/47E	1197	ex N197PE		◆
☐ C-GMPP	Pilatus PC-12/45	374	ex N374PC		
☐ C-GMPV	Pilatus PC-12/47E	1181	ex N181PE		◆
☐ C-GMPW	Pilatus PC-12/45	274	ex N274PC		
☐ C-GMPX	Pilatus PC-12/47E	1017			
☐ C-GMPY	Pilatus PC-12/45	311	ex N311PB		
☐ C-GMPZ	Pilatus PC-12/45	272	ex N272PC		
☐ C-FDGM	Cessna U206G Stationair 6 II	U20606864	ex N9450R	Soloy conversion	
☐ C-FDTM	Cessna T206H Stationair 6	T20608476	ex (N6199U)		
☐ C-FMPL	de Havilland DHC-6 Twin Otter 300	320	ex CF-MPL		
☐ C-FMPQ	Eurocopter EC120B Colibri	1533			
☐ C-FRPH	Cessna 208B Caravan I	208B0377	ex N1118B		
☐ C-FSUJ	Cessna 208B Caravan I	208B0373	ex N973CC		
☐ C-FSWC	Cessna T206H Stationair	T20608438			
☐ C-GFOX	Piaggio P.180 Avanti	1065	ex N126PA		
☐ C-GMPJ	de Havilland DHC-6 Twin Otter 300	534			
☐ C-GMPR	Cessna 208 Caravan I	20800253	ex N208CF		
☐ C-GMPT	Eurocopter EC120B Colibri	1355			
☐ C-GTJN	Cessna T206H Stationair	T20608443			

RED SUCKER LAKE AIR SERVICES — Red Sucker Lake, MB

☐ C-FTHE	Piper PA-31 Navajo C	31-7512005	ex N121L		
☐ C-GMAM	de Havilland DHC-2 Beaver	1558	ex G-AZLU	FP/WS	

REGIONAL 1 AIRLINES — Transcanada (TSH) — Calgary-Intl, AB (YYC)

☐ C-FJFW	de Havilland DHC-8-311	315	ex N315SN	
☐ C-FYDH	de Havilland DHC-8-102	083	ex N809LR	
☐ C-GRGK	de Havilland DHC-8Q-202	522	ex B-17201	

REMOTE HELICOPTERS — Slave Lake, NT (YZH)

☐ C-GRHJ	Aérospatiale AS350BA AStar	2149		
☐ C-GRHK	Aérospatiale AS350B Ecureuil	2305	ex F-GGPE	
☐ C-GRHL	Aérospatiale AS350B2 AStar	3018	ex C-GIRL	
☐ C-GRHN	Aérospatiale AS350BA AStar	1683	ex N13TV	
☐ C-GTAM	Aérospatiale AS350BA Ecureuil	1232	ex G-MAGI	
☐ C-GRHA	Bell 212	30791	ex N82283I	
☐ C-GRHS	Bell 212	30785	ex N8228R	
☐ C-GRHW	Bell 204B	2056	ex N204FB	
☐ C-GRHY	Bell 206B JetRanger	1087	ex C-FBJV	
☐ C-GRHZ	Bell 206B JetRanger	2691	ex C-GSKX	
☐ C-GRMH	Bell 206L-3 LongRanger III	51003	ex N2123X	

RESOURCE HELICOPTERS — Vancouver-Intl, BC (YVR)

☐ C-FRSR	Bell 204B	2020	ex CF-RSR	
☐ C-GSHB	Bell 204B	2038	ex 9Y-TDZ	

RIVER AIR — Kenora/Menaki, ON (YQK/-)

☐ C-FAYM	Cessna U206E Skywagon	U20601541	ex (N9141M)	FP
☐ C-FFYC	Cessna 208 Caravan I	20800111	ex N9647F	FP
☐ C-FMAQ	de Havilland DHC-2 Beaver	14	ex CF-MAQ	FP/WS
☐ C-FRSW	Beech 3NM	CA-105	ex CF-RSW	
☐ C-GIAT	Cessna A185F Skywagon	18502619	ex N4851C	FP
☐ C-GPDS	de Havilland DHC-2 Beaver	1349	ex N62352	FP
☐ C-GYKO	de Havilland DHC-3 Otter	287	ex N22UT	FP

ROSS AIR — Clearwater Lake SPB, ON

☐ CF-PFC	Beech C-45H	AF-199	ex N9942Z	
☐ C-GCIZ	Cessna A185F Skywagon	18503316	ex N1614H	FP
☐ C-GDCN	de Havilland DHC-2 Turbo Beaver	1661/TB35	ex N8PE	FP

ROSS AIR SERVICE — Sandy Bay, SK

☐ C-FWXV	Cessna A185E Skywagon	185-1355	ex CF-WXV	FP/WS

RUSTY MYERS FLYING SERVICE   Fort Frances, ON (YAG)

☐ C-FERM	Beech 3N	CA-62	ex CAF 1487	FP
☐ C-FKSJ	Cessna 208 Caravan I	20800035	ex N9382F	FP
☐ C-FOBT	de Havilland DHC-2 Beaver	3	ex CF-OBT	FP
☐ C-FOBY	de Havilland DHC-2 Beaver	13	ex CF-OBY	FP
☐ C-FRPL	Beech 3NM	CA-225	ex CAF 2346	FP
☐ C-FRVL	Beech 3T	7835	ex CAF 1396	FP
☐ CF-ZRI	Beech D18S	A-940	ex N164U	FP
☐ C-GAGK	Cessna 208 Caravan I	20800342	ex N51744	FP

SABOURIN LAKE LODGE   Sabourin Lake, MB

☐ C-FSJX	de Havilland DHC-2 Beaver	1592	ex CF-SJX	FP
☐ C-GYER	Cessna U206F Stationair	U20603503	ex N8750Q	FP

SALTSPRING ISLAND AIR   Saltspring Island, BC

☐ C-FAOP	de Havilland DHC-2 Beaver	1249	ex CF-AOP	FP
☐ C-FEGE	de Havilland DHC-2 Beaver	1539	ex CF-EGE	FP
☐ C-FJFL	de Havilland DHC-2 Beaver	898	ex CF-JFL	FP
☐ CF-ZZJ	de Havilland DHC-2 Beaver	1019	ex 5H-TCP	FP

SALTWATER WEST ENTERPRISES   Smithers, BC (YYD)

☐ C-GFTZ	de Havilland DHC-3 Otter	174	ex N90574	

SANDY LAKE SEAPLANE SERVICE   Sandy Lake, ON (ZSI)

☐ C-GBBZ	Cessna U206G Stationair	U20605712	ex (N5396X)	FP/WS
☐ C-GBGJ	Cessna U206G Stationair	U20605249	ex N5368U	FP/WS
☐ C-GDYD	de Havilland DHC-2 Beaver	1461	ex VH-IMH	FP/WS
☐ C-GEBZ	Cessna 207 Skywagon	20700303	ex N1703U	FP/WS
☐ C-GTCC	Cessna U206F Stationair	U20602167	ex N7303Q	FP/WS

SAPAWE AIR   Eva Lake, QC

☐ C-FEYR	de Havilland DHC-2 Beaver	497	ex CF-EYR	FP
☐ C-FOCC	de Havilland DHC-2 Beaver	23	ex CF-OOC	FP
☐ C-GKBW	de Havilland DHC-2 Beaver	310	ex N1441Z	FP

SASAIR   Quebec City, QC (YQB)

☐ C-FADL	Cessna 310R II	310R1867	ex N44NC	
☐ C-FFJL	Cessna 310R II	310R1616	ex N2631A	
☐ C-GAWN	Cessna 310R II	310R0957	ex N37211	
☐ C-GAWT	Cessna 310R II	310R1600	ex N36846	
☐ C-GMCR	Cessna 310R II	310R1424	ex N5149C	
☐ C-GSVI	Cessna 310R II	310R0833	ex N58JB	
☐ C-GYOT	Cessna 310R II	310R0912		
☐ CF-DPQ	Cessna 337G Super Skymaster	33701519	ex N72091	
☐ C-GILW	Cessna 337G Super Skymaster II	33701781	ex 6Y-JNF	
☐ C-GJOD	Cessna 337G Super Skymaster II	33701694	ex N53551	
☐ C-GTEL	Cessna 337G Super Skymaster II	33701659	ex C-FKTN	
☐ C-GYOB	Cessna 337G Super Skymaster II	33701780		
☐ C-GZIS	Piper PA-31-300 Navajo	31-316	ex N9243Y	FP/WS

SASKATCHEWAN GOVERNMENT NORTHERN AIR OPERATIONS
Saskatchewan (SGS)   La Ronge/Saskatoon, SK (YVC/YXE)

☐ C-GSAO	Beech 95-B55 Baron	TC-2149	ex N4974M		
☐ C-GSPG	Beech 95-B55 Baron	TC-2213	ex N2064A		
☐ C-GVSE	Beech 95-B55 Baron	TC-2270	ex N717BC		
☐ C-FAFN	Canadair CL215	1093	ex C-GKDY	216	
☐ C-FAFO	Canadair CL215	1094	ex C-GKBO	217	
☐ C-FAFP	Canadair CL215	1100	ex C-GKEA	218	
☐ C-FAFQ	Canadair CL215	1101	ex C-GKEE	219	
☐ C-FYWO	Canadair CL215	1003	ex CF-YWO	214	
☐ C-FYXG	Canadair CL215	1009	ex CF-YXG	215	
☐ C-GEHP	Grumman CS2F-2 Tracker	DHC-97	ex CAF12198 1		Tanker
☐ C-GEHR	Grumman CS2F-2 Tracker	DHC-51	ex CAF12185 3		Tanker
☐ C-GEQC	Grumman CS2F-2 Tracker	DHC-53	ex CAF12187 4		Tanker
☐ C-GEQD	Grumman CS2F-2 Tracker	DHC-98	ex CAF12199 5		Tanker
☐ C-GEQE	Grumman CS2F-2 Tracker	DHC-92	ex CAF12193 6		Tanker

☐ C-FMFP	Rockwell 690A Turbo Commander	11307	ex N690TD		
☐ C-FNAO	Gulfstream Commander 690C	11731	ex N815BC		
☐ C-FSPM	Gulfstream Commander 690D	15002	ex N721ML		
☐ C-GEAS	Beech 350 Super King Air	FL-17	ex N56872		
☐ C-GLLS	Beech B200 Super King Air	BB-1601	ex N2303F		
☐ C-GOVT	Gulfstream Commander 695A	15020	ex N600CM		
☐ C-GSAE	Beech B200 Super King Air	BB-1748	ex N50848		EMS
☐ C-GSAH	Beech B200 Super King Air	BB-1972	ex N7022F		EMS
☐ C-GSAU	Beech B200 Super King Air	BB-1974	ex N7074N		EMS
☐ C-GSAV	Beech B200 Super King Air	BB-1790	ex N4470T		EMS
☐ C-GSKJ	Convair 580	202	ex N30EG		Tanker
☐ C-GSKR	Convair 580	509	ex N57RD	471	Tanker
☐ C-GSKQ	Convair 580	217	ex N723ES		Tanker
☐ C-GVSK	Convair 580	238	ex N43938		Tanker
☐ C-GYSK	Convair 580	234	ex N131SF		Tanker

SEAIR SEAPLANES   Vancouver-International SPB, BC

☐ C-FDHC	de Havilland DHC-2 Turbo Beaver	1677/TB45	ex N164WC	FP
☐ C-FPCG	de Havilland DHC-2 Beaver	1000	ex N188JM	FP
☐ C-FPMA	de Havilland DHC-2 Turbo Beaver	1625/TB15	ex N1454T	FP
☐ C-GOBC	de Havilland DHC-2 Beaver	1560	ex N159M	FP
☐ C-FJOE	Cessna 208 Caravan I	20800390	ex N5254Y	FP
☐ C-FLAC	Cessna 208 Caravan I	20800357	ex N5267J	FP
☐ C-GSAS	Cessna 208 Caravan I	20800341	ex N5154J	FP
☐ C-GURL	Cessna 208 Caravan I	20800501		FP
☐ C-GYIX	Cessna A185F Skywagon	18503162	ex (N93021)	FP

SELKIRK AIR   Selkirk, MB

☐ C-GCKZ	Cessna A185F Skywagon	18502665	ex (N4949C)	FP/WS
☐ C-GFIQ	de Havilland DHC-2 Beaver	632	ex N90525	FP/WS
☐ C-GPHI	de Havilland DHC-2 Beaver	838	ex N67687	FP/WS

SEQUOIA HELICOPTERS   Abbotsford, BC (YXX)

☐ C-GTHK	Bell 212	30641	ex N708H	

SHARP WINGS   Williams Lake, BC

☐ C-FMQG	Cessna TU206G Turbo Skywagon	U206-1101	ex CF-MQG	
☐ C-GKMN	de Havilland DHC-2 Beaver	348	ex N9755Z	

SHOWALTER'S FLY-IN SERVICE   Ear Falls SPB, ON (YMY)

☐ C-FXUO	Beech D18S	CA-208	ex RCAF 2329	FP
☐ C-FZNG	Beech D18S	CA-182	ex RCAF 2309	FP
☐ C-FZYE	de Havilland DHC-2 Beaver	192	ex CF-ZYE	FP

SIFTON AIR YUKON   Haines Junction, YK (YHT)

☐ C-FRKA	Cessna 206 Super Skywagon	206-0200	ex N5200U	FP
☐ C-GEXT	Cessna U206F Stationair	U20603249	ex (N8338Q)	FP
☐ C-GVCJ	Britten-Norman BN-2A Islander	90	ex N871JA	
☐ C-GVKJ	Cessna 205 (210-5)	205-0092	ex N1892Z	FP

SIMPSON AIR COMMUTER CANADA   (NCS)   Fort Simpson, NT (YFS)

☐ CF-FHZ	de Havilland DHC-2 Beaver	66	ex C-FFHZ	
☐ C-FNML	Piper PA-23-250 Aztec	27-7554075	ex N8VV	
☐ C-GGHU	Cessna U206G Stationair 6 II	U20605723	ex (N5407X)	
☐ C-GPMS	Cessna U206G Stationair 6 II	U20604207	ex (N756MU)	

SIOUX AIR   Sioux Lookout, ON (YXL)

☐ C-GGRU	Cessna U206G Stationair 6 II	U20605838	ex N5373X	FP/WS

SIOUX NARROWS AIRWAYS   Great Bear Lake, NT (DAS)

☐ CF-GTP	Noorduyn UC-64A Norseman	423	43-35349	
☐ CF-KOA	de Havilland DHC-3 Otter	130	ex N88753	FP
☐ C-GBDW	de Havilland DHC-2 Beaver	954	ex C9-AGS	FP
☐ C-GMXS	de Havilland DHC-2 Beaver	1213	ex N5382G	FP
☐ C-GSMG	de Havilland DHC-3 Otter	363	ex CAF 9405	FP
☐ C-GUJY	de Havilland DHC-2 Beaver	393	ex C-GVMH	FP

SKYLINE HELICOPTERS   Kelowna, BC (YLW)

☐ C-GSLH	Bell 212	30565	ex N94W
☐ C-GSLI	Bell 212	30519	ex C-FNHB
☐ C-GSLJ	Agusta A.119 Koala	14526	ex N56TG
☐ C-GSLR	Agusta A.119 Koala	14511	ex N5UQ
☐ C-GSLT	Bell 212	30851	ex JA9527

SKYNORTH AIR   Winnipeg International, MB (YWG)

☐ C-FSDA	Piper PA-31-350 Navajo Chieftain	31-7752167	ex N27413
☐ C-GKAJ	Beech A100 King Air	B-232	ex N9192S
☐ C-GRTG	Piper PA-31-350 Navajo Chieftain	31-7652004	ex N180RM
☐ C-GTZK	Piper PA-31 Turbo Navajo	31-381	ex N9SG
☐ C-GYQK	Beech A100 King Air	B-153	ex N120AS

SKY REGIONAL AIRLINES   Toronto-Island (YTZ)

☐ C-FSRJ	de Havilland DHC-8-402Q	4165	ex N501LX	♦
☐ C-FSRN	de Havilland DHC-8-402Q	4170	ex N503LX	♦
☐ C-FSRW	de Havilland DHC-8-402Q	4172	ex N504LX	♦
☐ C-	de Havilland DHC-8-402Q	4174	ex N505LX	o/o♦
☐ C-	de Havilland DHC-8-402Q	4181	ex N507LX	o/o♦
☐ C-	de Havilland DHC-8-402Q	4182	ex N508LX	o/o♦
☐ C-	de Havilland DHC-8-402Q	4184	ex N509LX	o/o♦

SKYSERVICE AIRLINES   Skytour (5G/SSV)   Montreal-Trudeau, QC (YUL)

Ceased operations 31/Mar/2010

SLATE FALLS AIRWAYS   (SYJ)   Sioux Lookout, ON (YXL)

☐ CF-DIN	de Havilland DHC-2 Beaver	68		FP/WS
☐ C-FCZP	de Havilland DHC-3 Otter	69	ex CF-CZP	FP/WS
☐ C-FNWX	de Havilland DHC-3 Turbo Otter	412	ex CF-NWX	FP/WS
☐ C-GGRW	Cessna U206G Stationair 6 II	U20605689	ex N5373X	FP/WS
☐ C-GPCR	Cessna U206G Stationair 6 II	U20605082	ex N206JW	FP/WS

SONTAIR   Sontair (STI)   Chatham, ON (XCM)

☐ C-GSKT	Cessna 208B Caravan I	208B0759	ex N5262W

SOUTH MORESBY AIR CHARTERS   Queen Charlotte, BC (ZQS)

☐ C-GHAO	Cessna A185F Skywagon	18502370	ex N53088	FP/WS

SOUTHERN AVIATION   Regina, SK (YQR)

☐ C-GKKL	Cessna 414A Chancellor III	414A0301	ex N579CD

STARLINK AVIATION   Avionair (ANU)   Montreal-Trudeau, QC (YUL)

☐ C-GCCN	British Aerospace Jetstream 31	704	ex N333PX	
☐ C-GCCZ	British Aerospace Jetstream 31	712	ex N335PX	
☐ C-GDFW	British Aerospace Jetstream 31	720	ex G-HDGS	
☐ C-GEMQ	British Aerospace Jetstream 31	747	ex N103XV	
☐ C-GNRG	British Aerospace Jetstream 31	791	ex N791JX	
☐ C-GOAD	Embraer EMB.120ER Brasilia	120086	ex N19704	GoAir Citylink colours

STRAIT AIR   L'Anse au Clair, NL

☐ C-FVTQ	Piper PA-31-350 Chieftain	31-7853034	ex N300DT
☐ C-GZBQ	de Havilland DHC-2 Beaver	919	ex 55-0697

SUDBURY AVIATION   Whitewater Lake, ON

☐ C-FHVT	de Havilland DHC-2 Beaver I	284	ex VP-PAT	FP/WS
☐ C-FIUU	de Havilland DHC-2 Beaver I	945	ex CF-IUU	FP/WS
☐ C-GQVG	Cessna A185F Skywagon	18503818	ex N4619E	FP/WS

SUMMIT AIR CHARTERS   Yellowknife, NT/Atlin, BC/Whitehorse, YT (YZF/YSQ/YXY)

☐ C-FEQV	Dornier 228-202	8126	ex P2-MBR	[OBF]
☐ C-FEQX	Dornier 228-202	8101	ex P2-MBP	♦
☐ C-FPSA	Dornier 228-202	8122	ex D-CLUU	
☐ C-FPSH	Dornier 228-202	8071	ex N253MC	
☐ C-FUCN	Dornier 228-202	8109	ex N276MC	
☐ C-GJPY	Dornier 228-202	8088	ex 6Y-JQM	

104

☐ C-GSAX	Dornier 228-202	8153	ex P2-MBV	
☐ C-FYSQ	Short SC.7 Skyvan	SH1968	ex N491AS	Frtr
☐ C-GJGS	Short SC.7 Skyvan	SH1909	ex N56NS	Frtr
☐ C-GKOA	Short SC.7 Skyvan	SH1905	ex N52NS	Frtr

SUNWEST AVIATION — Chinook (CNK) — Calgary-Intl, AB (YYC)

☐ C-FAFJ	Cessna 208B Caravan I	208B0641	ex N52655	
☐ C-FDOI	Piper PA-31-350 Chieftain	31-8152150	ex N40901	
☐ C-FGEW	Swearingen SA.226TC Metro II	TC-347	ex N330BA	
☐ C-FJVR	Cessna 441 Conquest II	441-0096	ex N451WS	
☐ C-FNOC	Cessna 208 Caravan I	20800090	ex N9536F	
☐ C-FPCP	Beech B300 Super King Air	FL-317	ex N3217V	
☐ C-GHOP	Beech 200 Super King Air	BB-120	ex N6773S	
☐ C-GJFY	Beech 200 Super King Air	BB-812	ex C-GYUI	
☐ C-GMOZ	Piper PA-31-350 Chieftain	31-8052067	ex N3556B	
☐ C-GMWW	Swearingen SA.227DC Metro 23	DC-852B	ex N453LA	
☐ C-GOHO	Piper PA-31-350 Chieftain	31-8152167	ex N38SL	
☐ C-GRWN	Piper PA-31-350 Chieftain	31-8152044	ex N4076J	
☐ C-GSBC	Beech B200 Super King Air	BB-1780	ex N46TF	
☐ C-GSHV	Swearingen SA.227DC Metro 23	DC-900B	ex D-CJKO	
☐ C-GSHY	Swearingen SA.227DC Metro 23	DC-897B	ex N3051Q	
☐ C-GSHZ	Swearingen SA.227DC Metro 23	DC-887B	ex N3007C	
☐ C-GSLX	Beech 1900D	UE-264	ex C-GSLB	
☐ C-GSWB	Beech 1900D	UE-386	ex N847CA	
☐ C-GSWK	Swearingen SA.226TC Metro II	TC-368	ex F-GEBU	The Spirit of Medicine Hat
☐ C-GSWO	Cessna 208 Caravan I	20800153	ex N1016M	
☐ C-GSWV	Beech 1900D	UE-141	ex N17354	all-white
☐ C-GSWX	Beech 1900D	UE-63	ex N166K	
☐ C-GSWZ	Beech 1900D	UE-337	ex N23159	
☐ C-GVAG	Piper PA-31-350 Navajo Chieftain	31-7752166	ex N27411	

SUNWING AIRLINES — Sunwing (WG/SWG) — Toronto-Pearson Intl, ON (YYZ)

☐ C-FEAK	Boeing 737-86Q/W	30292/1451	ex N292AG	
☐ C-FLSW	Boeing 737-8HX/W	36552/2658		
☐ C-FRZG	Boeing 737-8K5/W	35139/2538	ex G-FDZG	
☐ C-FTAE	Boeing 737-8Q8/W	30637/800	ex SE-RHR	
☐ C-FTAH	Boeing 737-8Q8/W	29351/1471	ex OK-TVJ	
☐ C-FTDW	Boeing 737-808/W	34704/1958	ex N1786B	Joan Maria
☐ C-FTJH	Boeing 737-8BK	29642/2247	ex N1786B	
☐ C-FTOH	Boeing 737-8HX/W	29647/2865		
☐ C-FYLC	Boeing 737-8BK/W	33029/1945	ex G-OXLC	
☐ C-GLBW	Boeing 737-8Q8/W	30671/1307	ex 5B-DBW	<ECA
☐ C-GTVG	Boeing 737-8Q8/W	30719/2257	ex OK-TVG	♦

SUPERIOR AIRWAYS — Sioux Lookout, ON (YXL)

☐ C-FVWY	Piper PA-31-350 Chieftain	31-8252063	ex N4110N	
☐ C-GAGT	Cessna T206H Stationair 6	T20608158	ex N1965	
☐ C-GAJT	Piper PA-31-350 Chieftain	31-8152012	ex N900SA	
☐ C-GAJW	Piper PA-31-350 Chieftain	31-8152157	ex N700TS	

SUPERIOR HELICOPTERS — Longlac, ON

☐ C-GSHF	Bell 206L-3 LongRanger III	51349	ex C-GHHY	
☐ C-GSHG	Bell 205A-1	30165	ex C-GENZ	
☐ C-GSHQ	Bell 206L-4 LongRanger IV	52226	ex XC-LFC	
☐ C-GSHW	Bell 206L-3 LongRanger III	51602	ex OK-XIS	

SUSTUT AIR — Smithers, BC (YYD)

☐ C-FAFV	Cessna 208B Caravan I	208B0528	ex N9510W	
☐ C-FUMC	Short SC.7 Skyvan	SH1844	ex N430NA	Frtr

SWANBERG AIR — Grande Prairie, AB (YQU)

☐ C-GCTH	Piper PA-31-350 Navajo Chieftain	31-7752063	ex N37620	
☐ C-GPSB	Piper PA-42 Cheyenne III	42-8001030	ex N855GA	
☐ C-GPSN	British Aerospace Jetstream 31	783	ex C-GHGI	
☐ C-GPSO	British Aerospace Jetstream 31	756	ex C-GJPX	
☐ C-GPSV	British Aerospace Jetstream 31	816	ex C-FBII	
☐ C-GPSW	British Aerospace Jetstream 31	735	ex N854JS	
☐ C-GPSX	Piper PA-31P Pressurised Navajo	31P-7300113	ex N100MC	

TASMAN HELICOPTERS — Vancouver-Intl, BC (YVR)

☐ C-FKGT	Bell 212	30901	ex HC-CBW

☐ C-FTHD	Bell 407	53134	ex C-GFNR
☐ C-FTVL	Bell 212	30551	ex XC-UHE
☐ C-FVTS	Bell 212	30546	ex N2164Z
☐ C-GFHA	Bell 205A-1	30086	ex VH-NHA

THUNDER AIRLINES — Air Thunder (THU) — Thunder Bay, ON (YQT)

☐ C-FASB	Beech A100 King Air	B-163	ex SE-ING
☐ C-FFFG	Mitsubishi MU-2L	662	ex N5191B
☐ C-FJEL	Mitsubishi MU-2N	706SA	ex N866MA
☐ C-FRWK	Mitsubishi MU-2L	1521SA	ex N437MA
☐ C-FWVR	Cessna 208B Caravan I	208B0483	ex N51426
☐ C-GAMC	Mitsubishi MU-2L	785SA	ex N273MA
☐ C-GASI	Beech A100 King Air	B-126	ex N23BW
☐ C-GNEX	Beech A100 King Air	B-211	ex N9194F
☐ C-GUPP	Beech A100 King Air	B-157	ex N123CS
☐ C-GZNS	Mitsubishi MU-2L	1550SA	ex N64WB

THUNDERBIRD AVIATION — Stony Rapids, SK (YSF)

☐ CF-PEM	de Havilland DHC-3 Otter	438		FP

TIMBERLAND HELICOPTERS — Courtenay, BC (YCA)

☐ C-FHDX	Aérospatiale AS.330J Puma	1355	ex JA9955

TLI CHO AIR — Yellowknife, NT (YZF)

☐ C-FATN	de Havilland DHC-6 Twin Otter 300	226	ex N153BU	FP/WS

TOFINO AIR LINES — Tofino, BC (YTP)

☐ C-FGCY	de Havilland DHC-2 Beaver	216	ex CF-GCY	FP
☐ C-FHRT	de Havilland DHC-2 Beaver	1203	ex N64390	FP
☐ C-FITS	de Havilland DHC-3 Otter	90	ex CF-ITS	FP
☐ C-FJIM	de Havilland DHC-2 Beaver	461	ex N66035	FP
☐ C-GFLT	de Havilland DHC-2 Beaver	279	ex N5149G	FP
☐ C-GHBX	Cessna 180J	18052449	ex (N52029)	FP
☐ C-GHZR	Cessna 180J	18052667	ex (N7542K)	FP
☐ C-GIDX	Cessna 180J	18052709	ex (N7716K)	FP
☐ C-GYFO	Cessna 180J	18052759	ex (N7825K)	FP

TRANS CAPITAL AIR — Toronto-City Centre, ON (YTZ)

☐ C-FJHQ	de Havilland DHC-7-103	11	ex PK-TVS	Op for UN
☐ C-FWYU	de Havilland DHC-7-103	12	ex N678MA	Op for UN. UN-234
☐ C-GCPP	de Havilland DHC-7-102	87	ex HK-3111W	[YTZ]
☐ C-GGXS	de Havilland DHC-7-102	64	ex 4X-AHB	
☐ C-GVPP	de Havilland DHC-7-102	72	ex N272EP	Op for UN
☐ C-GVWD	de Havilland DHC-7-102	108	ex HK-3340W	Op for UN. UN-311

TRANS NORTH HELICOPTERS — Trans North (TNT) — Whitehorse, YT (YXY)

☐ C-FCHU	Bell 206B JetRanger III	2213	ex N70TT	
☐ C-FDRZ	Bell 206B JetRanger II	764	ex CF-DRZ	
☐ C-FGGC	Bell 206B JetRanger II	1080	ex N58113	
☐ C-GMIG	Bell 206B JetRanger II	2186		
☐ C-GMYQ	Bell 206B JetRanger III	2628	ex N5016Q	
☐ C-GPGH	Bell 206B JetRanger III	4022		
☐ C-GPWI	Bell 206B JetRanger III	2234	ex N347BB	
☐ C-GTNY	Bell 206B JetRanger II	990	ex CF-KNY	
☐ C-GTNT	Aérospatiale AS350B2 AStar	3327		
☐ C-GTNU	Aérospatiale AS350B2 AStar	3046	ex N318SA	
☐ C-GTNV	Aérospatiale AS350B2 AStar	1655	ex N627LH	

TRANSPORT CANADA — Various

☐ C-FGXE	Beech 65-C90A King Air	LJ-1179	ex N179RC
☐ C-FGXG	Beech 65-C90A King Air	LJ-1139	ex N212RL
☐ C-FGXH	Beech 65-C90A King Air	LJ-1162	ex N477JA
☐ C-FGXJ	Beech 65-C90A King Air	LJ-1178	ex N357CY
☐ C-FGXL	Beech 65-C90A King Air	LJ-1189	ex N200SL
☐ C-FGXO	Beech 65-C90A King Air	LJ-1200	ex N68TW
☐ C-FGXQ	Beech 65-C90A King Air	LJ-1192	ex N616SC
☐ C-FGXS	Beech 65-C90A King Air	LJ-1207	ex N207RC
☐ C-FGXT	Beech 65-C90A King Air	LJ-1230	ex N1564P
☐ C-FGXU	Beech 65-C90A King Air	LJ-1140	ex N8841

☐ C-FGXX	Beech 65-C90A King Air	LJ-1151	ex N126RL	
☐ C-FGXZ	Beech 65-C90A King Air	LJ-1177	ex N479JA	
☐ C-GCFB	Beech 65-C90A King Air	LJ-929	ex N81DD	
☐ C-GCFZ	Beech 65-C90A King Air	LJ-849	ex N6647P	
☐ C-FCGK	Bell 206B JetRanger	24		
☐ C-FCGO	Bell 206B JetRanger	140		
☐ C-FCGQ	Bell 206B JetRanger	182		
☐ C-FCGR	Bell 206B JetRanger	189		
☐ C-FDOC	Bell 206B JetRanger	349		
☐ C-FDOD	Bell 206B JetRanger	379		
☐ C-FDOE	Bell 206B JetRanger	381		
☐ C-FDOF	Bell 212	30536		
☐ C-FDOP	Bell 212	30567		
☐ C-GCGB	Bell 212	30930	ex N241LG	◆
☐ C-GCHF	Bell 212	30617		
☐ C-GCHT	Bell 212	30910		
☐ C-FJCZ	Cessna C550 Citation II	550-0700		
☐ C-FJWZ	Cessna C550 Citation II	550-0685		
☐ C-FJXN	Cessna C550 Citation II	550-0684	ex N6778L	
☐ C-FKCE	Cessna C550 Citation II	550-0686		
☐ C-FKDX	Cessna C550 Citation II	550-0687	ex N6778Y	
☐ C-FKEB	Cessna C550 Citation II	550-0688		
☐ C-FKLB	Cessna C550 Citation II	550-0699		
☐ C-FLZA	Cessna C550 Citation II	550-0701		
☐ C-FMFM	Cessna C550 Citation II	550-0702		
☐ C-FCSW	de Havilland DHC-6 Twin Otter 300	355	ex CF-CSW	
☐ C-FCSX	de Havilland DHC-6 Twin Otter 300	35&	ex CF-CSX	
☐ C-GCFR	de Havilland DHC-7-102	102		
☐ C-GCFJ	de Havilland DHC-8-100	20		
☐ C-GCFN	MBB 105CBS-4	S-682		
☐ C-GCFO	MBB 105CBS-4	S-715		
☐ C-GCFQ	MBB 105CBS-4	S-716		
☐ C-GCFS	MBB 105CBS-4	S-725		
☐ C-GCFT	MBB 105CBS-4	S-726		
☐ C-GCFU	MBB 105CBS-4	S-727		
☐ C-GCFV	MBB 105CBS-4	S-728		
☐ C-GCFX	MBB 105CBS-4	S-730		
☐ C-GCFY	MBB 105CBS-4	S-733		
☐ C-GCHW	MBB 105CBS-4	S-681		
☐ C-GCHU	MBB 105CBS-4	S-696		
☐ C-GCHY	MBB 105CBS-4	S-729		
☐ C-GGGM	MBB 105CBS-4	S-618		
☐ C-FDOH	Sikorsky S-61N	61703		

TRANSWEST AIR — Athabaska(9T/ABS) La Ronge/Stony Rapids, SK (YVC/YSF)

☐ C-GALM	Cessna A185F Skywagon	18503711	ex N783A	FP/WS
☐ C-GCJM	Cessna A185F Skywagon	18503955	ex (N5330E)	FP/WS
☐ C-GXZA	Cessna A185F Skywagon	18503019	ex N5211R	FP/WS
☐ C-GZVF	Cessna A185F Skywagon	18503202	ex N93256	FP/WS
☐ C-FGHY	de Havilland DHC-2 Beaver	1344	ex 58-2015	FP/WS
☐ C-FGQD	de Havilland DHC-2 Beaver	76	ex CF-QGD	FP/WS
☐ C-FIFJ	de Havilland DHC-2 Beaver	831	ex CF-IFJ	FP/WS
☐ C-FOED	de Havilland DHC-2 Turbo Beaver	1591/TB9	ex CF-OED	FP/WS
☐ C-GAEB	de Havilland DHC-2 Beaver	703	ex 53-7895	FP/WS
☐ C-GHGN	de Havilland DHC-2 Beaver	80	ex N115LA	FP/WS
☐ C-GMAQ	de Havilland DHC-2 Beaver	234	ex 51-16784	FP/WS
☐ C-FCCE	de Havilland DHC-6 Twin Otter 100	8	ex CF-CCE	FP/WS
☐ C-FGLF	de Havilland DHC-6 Twin Otter 200	138	ex LV-APT	FP/WS
☐ C-FPGE	de Havilland DHC-6 Twin Otter 200	197	ex CF-PGE	FP/WS
☐ C-FSCA	de Havilland DHC-6 Twin Otter 100	17	ex CF-SCA	FP/WS
☐ C-FVOG	de Havilland DHC-6 Twin Otter 100	35	ex CF-VOG	FP/WS
☐ C-FAAF	Piper PA-31-350 Navajo Chieftain	31-7752096	ex N27229	
☐ C-FNVH	Piper PA-31-350 Navajo Chieftain	31-7305098	ex N98BJ	
☐ C-FQWP	Piper PA-31-325 Navajo C/R	31-7400990	ex N7082Y	
☐ C-FZPJ	Piper PA-31-350 Navajo Chieftain	31-7752185	ex N27359	
☐ C-GAYY	Piper PA-31 Navajo C	31-8012006		
☐ C-GCTG	Piper PA-31-350 Navajo Chieftain	31-7552087	ex N72ET	
☐ C-GGIQ	Piper PA-31-350 Navajo Chieftain	31-7552082	ex N59989	

☐ C-GNOV	Piper PA-31 Navajo C	31-7812087		
☐ C-GQHV	Piper PA-31-350 Navajo Chieftain	31-7405230	ex N54293	
☐ C-GQXX	Piper PA-31-350 Chieftain	31-7852009		
☐ C-GUNP	Piper PA-31-350 Chieftain	31-8052048	ex N3554D	
☐ C-GWUM	Piper PA-31-350 Navajo Chieftain	31-7405404	ex N66878	
☐ C-FEYP	Beech A100 King Air	B-206	ex N86BM	
☐ C-FHPE	de Havilland DHC-3 Turbo Otter	273	ex Burma 4651	FP/WS
☐ C-FJTG	Bell 205A-1	30104	ex N8138J	
☐ C-FOHG	Bell 407	53187	ex N478WN	
☐ C-FOKD	Bell 407	53193	ex N407NR	
☐ C-FSGD	de Havilland DHC-3 Turbo Otter	316	ex N521BK	FP/WS
☐ C-FTMC	Bell 206L-4 LongRanger IV	52223	ex XC-CJS	
☐ C-FYID	Bell 206L-1 LongRanger II	45206	ex N78CF	
☐ C-GAON	Cessna 310R II	310R1627	ex N2632Y	
☐ C-GCNC	Bell 206B JetRanger II	1142	ex N58152	
☐ C-GELT	Bell 206B JetRanger III	2994	ex N5744V	
☐ C-GFSG	Beech 200 Super King Air	BB-671		
☐ C-GJHW	Beech A100 King Air	B-175	ex N92DL	
☐ C-GKCY	SAAB SF.340A	340A-133	ex SE-ISM	
☐ C-GPNO	Beech 95-B55 Baron	TC-734	ex N174E	
☐ C-GTJX	SAAB SF.340B	340B-165	ex N586MA	
☐ C-GTWG	Beech 1900D	UE-79	ex N79SK	
☐ C-GTWK	SAAB SF.340B	340B-190	ex XA-TUQ	
☐ C-GYHY	Bell 206B JetRanger III	2317	ex N16825	

TRANSWEST HELICOPTERS   Chilliwack, BC (YCW)

☐ C-GIGG	Bell 206B JetRanger	155	ex N6295N
☐ C-GTWF	Bell 214B-1	28014	ex C-FQTJ
☐ C-GTWH	Bell 214B-1	28017	ex N214MV
☐ C-GTWI	Bell 214B-1	28011	ex LN-OSW

TRIUMPH AIRWAYS   Oshawa, ON (YOO)

☐ C-FOOW	Douglas DC-3	13342	ex 8P-OOW	painted as CF-OOW

TSAYTA AVIATION   Fort St James, BC (YXJ)

☐ C-GHNH	Cessna A185F Skywagon	18502705	ex (N1048F)	FP/WS
☐ C-GKAW	Britten-Norman BN-2A-8 Islander	128	ex N158MA	
☐ C-GWDW	de Havilland DHC-2 Beaver	306	ex N311N	FP
☐ C-GWKX	Cessna A185E Skywagon	18502032	ex N70167	FP/WS

TUDHOPE AIRWAYS   Hudson, ON

☐ C-FOCP	de Havilland DHC-2 Beaver	49	ex CF-OCP	FP/WS
☐ C-FSDC	Found FBA-2C	17	ex CF-SDC	FP/WS

TWEEDSMUIR AIR SERVICES   Nimpo Lake, BC

☐ C-FFHT	de Havilland DHC-2 Beaver	55	ex CF-FHT	FP
☐ C-GFRJ	Cessna A185F Skywagon II	18504011		FP
☐ C-GNPO	de Havilland DHC-2 Beaver	773	ex C-GMOJ	FP

TYAX AIR SERVICE   Gold Bridge, BC

☐ C-GIYV	de Havilland DHC-2 Beaver	1488	ex XP823	FP/WS

ULTRA HELICOPTERS   Grimshaw, AB

☐ C-FALE	Bell 206B JetRanger III	1074	ex N83160
☐ C-GBPB	Bell 206B JetRanger	321	ex N6285N
☐ C-GHHK	Bell 206B JetRanger	1588	
☐ C-GMXU	Bell 206B JetRanger	1520	ex N15DW
☐ C-GUHM	Bell 206B JetRanger	2439	ex C-GPQW
☐ C-FXMJ	Aérospatiale AS350BA AStar	1436	ex N816CF
☐ C-GAHM	Bell 205A-1	30215	ex N59607
☐ C-GEWR	Bell 206L-1 LongRanger II	45594	ex N3892R
☐ C-GNMP	Aérospatiale AS350B AStar	1040	ex C-GSKI
☐ C-GUHB	Bell 206L-3 LongRanger III	51026	ex N5741X
☐ C-GUHZ	Bell 206L-3 LongRanger III	51014	ex N752HL

UNIVAIR AVIATION   Montreal-St Hubert, QC (YHU)

☐ C-FDCY	Piper PA-31 Navajo C	31-7912007	ex N27768
☐ C-GRTC	Piper PA-44-180 Seminole	44-7995077	ex N180TL

108

UNIVERSAL HELICOPTERS — Goose Bay, NL (YYR)

☐ C-FCNG	Bell 206L LongRanger	45149	ex C-GMPT
☐ C-FCWR	Bell 206L LongRanger	45086	ex C-GMPM
☐ C-FLIA	Bell 206L-4 LongRanger IV	52149	ex N9221U
☐ C-FPHO	Bell 206L LongRanger	45147	ex N3247K
☐ C-GAHS	Bell 206LR+ LongRanger	45048	ex D-HMHS
☐ C-GDCA	Bell 206LR+ LongRanger	45021	ex N31DM
☐ C-GIZY	Bell 206LR+ LongRanger	45027	ex N176KH
☐ C-GLSH	Bell 206LR+ LongRanger	45018	
☐ C-GQIX	Bell 206L LongRanger	45008	ex N8EL
☐ C-GVYO	Bell 206LR+ LongRanger	46609	ex N16950
☐ C-FAPN	Aérospatiale AS350BA AStar	2201	ex N891SA
☐ C-FHHH	Aérospatiale AS350BA AStar	1421	ex N5782X
☐ C-FXAL	Aérospatiale AS350B AStar	1816	ex SE-HNP
☐ C-GNAI	Aérospatiale AS350B AStar	1685	ex N380NA
☐ C-FTJU	Bell 407	53331	ex G-CEOA
☐ C-FXYF	Bell 407	53022	
☐ C-GEPA	Bell 407	53739	ex C-FLPA
☐ C-GOFL	Bell 407	53130	

VALHALLA HELICOPTERS — Kelowna, BC (YLW)

☐ C-FPSZ	Bell 205A-1	30230	ex N30091
☐ C-GLFT	Bell 212	30713	ex N20851

VALLEY HELICOPTERS — Hope & Merritt, BC

☐ C-FAVY	Bell 407	53120	ex N30EH
☐ C-FCHV	Bell 206B JetRanger	1541	ex N59620
☐ C-FHHJ	Bell 206L LongRanger III	51382	
☐ C-FVLY	Bell 407	53816	ex N234BH
☐ C-GTTR	Bell 206B JetRanger	1538	
☐ C-GTYV	Bell 206B JetRanger II	1976	ex N49741
☐ C-GXVS	Bell 206B JetRanger II	1893	ex N90266

VANCOUVER ISLAND AIR — Campbell River, BC (YBL)

☐ C-FCSN	Beech D18S	CA-16	ex RCAF1441	FP
☐ C-FGNR	Beech 3NM	CA-191	ex (CF-SIK)	FP
☐ C-FIZB	Cessna 180J	18052409	ex N46262	FP
☐ C-FUVQ	de Havilland DHC-2 Beaver	696	ex N34M	FP
☐ C-FWCA	de Havilland DHC-2 Beaver	1285	ex C-GUDB	FP
☐ C-GAIV	Beech TC-45G	AF-80	ex N711KP	FP
☐ C-GHAG	de Havilland DHC-3 Turbo Otter	214	ex 4R-ARA	FP

VIH HELICOPTERS — Victoria, BC (YYJ)

☐ C-FDUB	Aérospatiale AS350BA AStar	3041	ex N4073S
☐ C-FVIG	Aérospatiale AS350B2 AStar	2893	ex N333AS
☐ C-FVIT	Aérospatiale AS350B2 AStar	2890	ex N544AS
☐ C-FXHS	Aérospatiale AS350B1 AStar	2248	
☐ C-GEYN	Aérospatiale AS350B2 AStar	2732	ex VP-BBB
☐ C-GNME	Aérospatiale AS350B2 AStar	2826	ex N351WW
☐ C-GNMJ	Aérospatiale AS350BA AStar	2829	
☐ C-GOLV	Aérospatiale AS350BA AStar	1108	ex N3595N
☐ C-GPHM	Aérospatiale AS350B2 AStar	2488	
☐ C-GPHQ	Aérospatiale AS350B1 AStar	2017	ex N855NM
☐ C-GPHR	Aérospatiale AS350B1 AStar	2268	
☐ C-GPTL	Aérospatiale AS350B2 AStar	2103	ex OY-HEH
☐ C-GPWO	Aérospatiale AS350BA AStar	2236	ex N2BQ
☐ C-GVIA	Aérospatiale AS350B1 AStar	2297	ex N442BV
☐ C-GAYB	Bell 205A-1	30295	
☐ C-GKVI	Bell 205A-1	30182	ex C-GOLE
☐ C-GLVI	Bell 205A-1	30209	ex C-GPET
☐ C-GVIE	Bell 205B	30188	ex JA9854
☐ C-GVIJ	Bell 205A-1	30105	ex C-FOAR
☐ C-FANC	Bell 206B JetRanger II	1283	
☐ C-FBER	Bell 206B JetRanger III	2648	ex N5018L
☐ C-FBHQ	Bell 206B JetRanger II	970	ex CF-BHQ
☐ C-FHSO	Bell 206B JetRanger	165	ex CF-HSO
☐ C-GHCQ	Bell 206B JetRanger II	1302	
☐ C-GISE	Bell 206B JetRanger II	839	ex N300FH
☐ C-GNMT	Bell 206B JetRanger III	2295	ex N722CH

☐ C-GORO	Bell 206B JetRanger II	2086	ex N15558
☐ C-GWGS	Bell 206B JetRanger	447	ex N2230W
☐ C-FCTD	Bell 206L-1 LongRanger II	45159	ex N2943A
☐ C-FGSL	Bell 206L LongRanger	45759	ex N3174L
☐ C-FJTO	Bell 206L LongRanger	45085	ex SE-HOP
☐ C-FVIX	Bell 206L LongRanger	45139	ex SE-HTL
☐ C-GENT	Bell 206L LongRanger	45041	ex ZK-HYV
☐ C-GMJS	Bell 206L LongRanger	46608	ex N120RM
☐ C-GVIQ	Bell 206L-1 LongRanger II	45492	ex N83MT
☐ C-GVIZ	Bell 206L-1 LongRanger	45346	ex N26SH
☐ C-FNMD	Bell 212	30730	ex PT-HRK
☐ C-FVIK	Bell 212	30990	ex YV-O-CVG-8
☐ C-FWDV	Bell 212	30973	ex N2768N
☐ C-GGSO	Bell 212	30696	ex N90220
☐ C-GCVI	Bell 407	53854	
☐ C-GGVI	Bell 407	53834	
☐ C-GJVI	Bell 407	53866	
☐ C-GNVI	Bell 407	53847	
☐ C-GVIB	Bell 407	53826	ex C-FTLZ
☐ C-GVIU	Bell 407	53789	ex C-FPNX
☐ C-FIGR	Kamov Ka-32-IIBC	(31585)8707/05	ex B-77299
☐ C-FLIE	Eurocopter EC135P2+	0479	ex D-HECN
☐ C-FPZR	Sikorsky S-61L	61362	ex N305V
☐ C-FQNG	Sikorsky S-61N Helipro Short	61032	ex N301Y
☐ C-FTVI	Sikorsky S-61N Helipro Short	61818	ex N4240S
☐ C-GKHL	Kamov Ka-32-IIBC	(31594)8801/03	ex RA-31594
☐ C-GVIY	Bell 222UT	47562	ex JA9665

VILLERS AIR SERVICES   Fort Nelson, BC (YYE)

☐ C-FGAQ	Britten-Norman BN-2A-27 Islander	212	ex G-51-212
☐ C-FJBD	Beech 58 Baron	TH-260	ex N518SW
☐ C-FTUP	Piper PA-31-350 Navajo Chieftain	31-7652101	ex N76DE
☐ C-FTVP	Cessna 208B Caravan I	208B1264	ex N5090Y
☐ C-GEBH	Cessna U206E Stationair	U20601697	ex N8232Q
☐ C-GPMV	Piper PA-31 Navajo C	31-7712081	ex N273PE

VOYAGE AIR   Fort McMurray, AB (ZFM)

☐ C-GBNA	de Havilland DHC-3 Otter	125	ex N5368G	FP/WS
☐ C-GDOB	de Havilland DHC-2 Beaver	774	ex C-GEZR	FP/WS
☐ C-GOLB	Cessna A185F Skywagon	18503188	ex N93173	FP/WS
☐ C-GOZP	Cessna A185F Skywagon	18503258	ex (N93874)	FP/WS
☐ C-GQQJ	de Havilland DHC-2 Beaver	719	ex N202PS	FP/WS
☐ C-GUJW	de Havilland DHC-2 Beaver	1657	ex 305	FP/WS
☐ C-GZSI	de Havilland DHC-2 Beaver	1003	ex N5327	FP/WS

VOYAGEUR AIRWAYS   Voyageur (VC/VAL)   Sudbury/North Bay, ON (YSB/YYB)

☐ C-FAPP	Beech A100 King Air	B-169	ex N305TZ	
☐ C-FBGS	Beech A100 King Air	B-204	ex N108JL	
☐ C-GDPI	Beech A100 King Air	B-156	ex N21RX	
☐ C-GISH	Beech A100 King Air	B-152	ex N67LC	
☐ C-GJBV	Beech A100 King Air	B-100	ex N100S	
☐ C-GJJF	Beech A100 King Air	B-123	ex N741EB	
☐ C-FZKM	de Havilland DHC-7-102	61	ex N903HA	
☐ C-GFOF	de Havilland DHC-7-102	37	ex N67RM	Op for UN
☐ C-GGUL	de Havilland DHC-7-102	70	ex N905HA	Op for RNethAF
☐ C-GGUN	de Havilland DHC-7-110	66	ex N66SU	[YYB]
☐ C-GJPI	de Havilland DHC-7-102	36	ex N702GW	Op for Fugro Airborne Surveys
☐ C-GLOL	de Havilland DHC-7-102	39	ex HB-IVW	Op for UN
☐ C-FEXZ	de Havilland DHC-8-314	319	ex G-BRYJ	
☐ C-FEYG	de Havilland DHC-8-311	320	ex N320BC	Op for UN
☐ C-FEZD	de Havilland DHC-8-314	385	ex LN-WFR	
☐ C-FIQT	de Havilland DHC-8-314	395	ex N342EN	
☐ C-FNCU	de Havilland DHC-8-314	517	ex G-NVSB	Op for UN?
☐ C-GHQZ	de Havilland DHC-8-314	370	ex OE-LLY	Op for UN
☐ C-FMCY	Canadair CRJ-200	7064	ex D-ACLP	
☐ C-FMUV	Canadair CRJ-200	7073	ex D-ACLQ	
☐ C-FTYS	Canadair CRJ-200LR	7039	ex N653ML	
☐ C-FWWU	Canadair CRJ-200LR	7299	ex N299BS	
☐ C-FXHC	Canadair CRJ-200ER	7329	ex N329BS	

☐ C-FXLH	Canadair CRJ-200LR	7283	ex G-MKSA	
☐ C-FZVW	Beech 200 Super King Air	BB-787	ex N26G	
☐ C-FZVX	Beech 200 Super King Air	BB-231	ex N200FH	
☐ C-GIND	Beech 200C Super King Air B	BL-42	ex N819CD	
☐ C-GJJT	Beech 200 Super King Air	BB-828	ex N62GA	

WAASHESHKUN AIRWAYS — Baie du Poste (Mistassini Lake), ON

☐ C-FDIO	de Havilland DHC-3 Otter	452	ex TAF 9102	FP/WS

WABAKIMI AIR — Armstrong, ON (YYW)

☐ CF-BJY	de Havilland DHC-2 Beaver	173	ex N4792C	FP/WS
☐ C-FBPC	de Havilland DHC-2 Beaver	144	ex VH-AAS	FP/WS
☐ C-FYLZ	de Havilland DHC-3 Otter	247	ex VH-SBR	FP/WS

WABUSK AIR SERVICE — Moosonee, ON (YMO)

☐ C-GKMW	Piper PA-31 Turbo Navajo B	31-725	ex N231CD	
☐ C-GLEW	Piper PA-31 Turbo Navajo	31-685	ex N6775L	
☐ C-GMNX	Piper PA-31 Turbo Navajo	31-528	ex N6601L	
☐ C-GWLW	Piper PA-31-350 Navajo Chieftain	31-7405221	ex N54277	
☐ C-FDOY	Beech 100 King Air	B-120	ex CF-DOY	

WAHKASH CONTRACTING — Campbell River, BC (YBL)

☐ C-FIGF	de Havilland DHC-2 Beaver	834	ex CF-IGF	
☐ C-GVHT	de Havilland DHC-2 Beaver	257	ex 51-16797	

WALSTEN AIR SERVICE — Walsten (WAS) — Kenora, ON (YQK)

☐ C-GFZQ	Cessna U206E Super Skywagon	U20601543	ex N9143M	FP
☐ C-GJLI	Beech 200 Super King Air	BB-347	ex N424CR	
Current status uncertain				

WAMAIR SERVICE & OUTFITTING — Matheson Island, MB

☐ C-FLXY	Cessna 208 Caravan I	20800297	ex N208LA	
☐ C-FXOQ	Piper PA-31 Turbo Navajo	31-440	ex N6478L	
☐ C-GDCJ	de Havilland DHC-2 Beaver	1055	ex N4411F	FP/WS
☐ C-GEIF	Cessna U206F Stationair 6	U20602938		FP/WS
☐ C-GJPX	Cessna 208 Caravan I	20800302	ex N1284N	Amphibian
☐ C-GKCK	Cessna U206E Super Skywagon	U20601487	ex N1487M	FP/WS
☐ C-GRNK	Piper PA-31-350 Navajo Chieftain	31-7652112	ex N59888	
☐ C-GWAB	Cessna A185F Skywagon	18502399	ex N1676R	FP/WS

WASAYA AIRWAYS — Wasaya (WT/WSG) — Thunder Bay, ON (YQT)

☐ C-FKPI	Pilatus PC-12/45	250	ex N250PB		
☐ C-FKRB	Pilatus PC-12/45	233	ex HB-FRD		
☐ C-FKUL	Pilatus PC-12/45	204	ex ZS-PAY		
☐ C-FPCL	Pilatus PC-12/45	276	ex N276CN		
☐ C-FSRK	Pilatus PC-12/45	202	ex ZS-SRK		
☐ C-FWAV	Pilatus PC-12/45	280	ex N280PC		
☐ C-FYZS	Pilatus PC-12/45	227	ex N227PC		
☐ C-GBJV	Pilatus PC-12/45	237	ex HB-FRH		
☐ C-GBXW	Pilatus PC-12/45	170	ex N170PD		
☐ C-GKAY	Pilatus PC-12/45	178	ex N178PC		
☐ C-GPAI	Pilatus PC-12/45	491	ex N491VA		
☐ C-FFFS	Hawker Siddeley HS.748 Srs.2A/209LFD	1663	ex G-BHCJ	806	Frtr
☐ C-FTTW	Hawker Siddeley HS.748 Srs.2A/264	1681	ex G-AYIR	805	Frtr
☐ C-GLTC	Hawker Siddeley HS.748 Srs.2A/244LFD	1656	ex N57910	801	Super Tanker
☐ C-GMAA	Hawker Siddeley HS.748 Srs.2A/214LFD	1576	ex TR-LQY	807	Frtr
☐ C-FKAD	Cessna 208B Caravan I	208B0327			
☐ C-FKDL	Cessna 208B Caravan I	208B0240	ex (N5127B)		
☐ C-FPCC	Cessna 208B Caravan I	208B0840	ex N52623		
☐ C-FWAW	Cessna 208B Caravan I	208B0895	ex N5265B		
☐ C-FQWA	Beech 1900D	UE-75	ex N175MH		
☐ C-FWAU	Beech 1900D	UE-164	ex N861CA		
☐ C-FWAX	Beech 1900D	UE-297	ex N21679		
☐ C-FWZK	Beech 1900D	UE-8	ex D-CBSF		
☐ C-GSWA	Beech 1900D	UE-34	ex N83801		
☐ C-GZVJ	Beech 1900D	UE-223	ex N1123J		

WATSON'S SKYWAYS — Wawa-Hawk Junction, ON (YXZ)

☐ C-FAZQ	Cessna U206 Super Skywagon	U206-0337	ex CF-AZQ		FP or wheels
☐ C-GIKP	Cessna 208 Caravan I	20800141	ex C-GHGV		FP

WEAGAMOW AIR — Weagamow-Round Lake, ON (ZRJ)

☐ C-FLIN	Piper PA-31-350 Chieftain	31-8152013	ex N81TT		
☐ C-FOCD	de Havilland DHC-2 Beaver	24	ex CF-OCD		FP/WS
☐ C-GNNO	Cessna A185F Skywagon	18502685	ex (N1016F)		FP

WEST COAST AIR — (8O) — Vancouver-Coal Harbor, BC (CXH)

☐ C-FAWA	de Havilland DHC-2 Beaver	1430	ex VH-IDR		FP
☐ C-FEBE	de Havilland DHC-2 Beaver	792	ex N9983B		FP
☐ C-FJBP	de Havilland DHC-2 Beaver	942	ex CF-JBP		FP
☐ C-FGQZ	de Havilland DHC-2 Beaver	118	ex CF-GQZ		FP
☐ C-FWAC	de Havilland DHC-2 Beaver	1356	ex N68089		FP
☐ C-GEZS	de Havilland DHC-2 Beaver	1277	ex 57-6170		FP
☐ C-GFDI	de Havilland DHC-2 Beaver	606	ex 53-2810		FP
☐ C-GHMI	de Havilland DHC-2 Beaver	1215	ex ZA-CAJ	205	FP
☐ C-GMKP	de Havilland DHC-2 Beaver	1374	ex N87775		FP
☐ C-GOLC	de Havilland DHC-2 Beaver	1392	ex N62354		FP
☐ C-GTBQ	de Havilland DHC-2 Beaver	1316	ex N9036		FP
☐ C-GVPB	de Havilland DHC-2 Beaver	1551	ex SE-KKR		FP
☐ C-FGQE	de Havilland DHC-6 Twin Otter 100	40	ex CF-GQE	609	FP
☐ C-FGQH	de Havilland DHC-6 Twin Otter 100	106	ex 8Q-MAF	604	FP
☐ C-FMHR	de Havilland DHC-6 Twin Otter 100	51	ex CF-MHR	605	FP
☐ C-FWTE	de Havilland DHC-6 Twin Otter 100	96	ex CF-WTE	603	FP
☐ C-GJAW	de Havilland DHC-6 Twin Otter 200	176	ex N2261L	607	FP
☐ C-GQKN	de Havilland DHC-6 Twin Otter 100	94	ex PZ-TAV	606	FP

WEST COAST HELICOPTERS — Port McNeill, BC (YMP)

☐ C-FWCD	Aérospatiale AS350B AStar	1854	ex C-FQCD	
☐ C-FWCH	Aérospatiale AS350B AStar	1696	ex C-FSUL	
☐ C-FWCO	Aérospatiale AS350BA AStar	2868	ex C-FVTM	
☐ C-FWCR	Aérospatiale AS350B2 AStar	2204	ex F-GMBZ	
☐ C-FWCS	Aérospatiale AS350B2 AStar	1990	ex C-FSWH	
☐ C-FWCW	Aérospatiale AS350B2 AStar	3651		
☐ C-FWEC	Aérospatiale AS350B2 AStar	3221	ex C-FWCN	
☐ C-FYWC	Aérospatiale AS350B AStar	1356	ex C-FNTA	
☐ C-GQSW	Aérospatiale AS350BA AStar	2091	ex JA9744	
☐ C-GMEP	Bell 206B JetRanger III	3055		

WEST WIND AVIATION — Westwind (WEW) — Regina, SK (YQR)

☐ C-FCPD	British Aerospace Jetstream 31	822	ex G-31-822		
☐ C-FDAD	Cessna 401A	401A0058	ex N6601L		
☐ C-FWWF	Beech 200 Super King Air	BB-374	ex N111UR		
☐ C-FWWQ	Beech 200 Super King Air	BB-667	ex N667NA		
☐ C-FZJE	Cessna 401B	401B0032	ex (N7931Q)		
☐ C-GAXR	Cessna 401B	401B0050	ex N1250C		
☐ C-GEUY	Cessna 414 II	414-0821			
☐ C-GHGK	British Aerospace Jetstream 31	786	ex N786SC		
☐ C-GMAG	Beech 100A King Air	B-229	ex N100HC		
☐ C-GGPX	Cessna 402C II	402C0280	ex C-GGSN		
☐ C-GPRT	Beech 1900C	UC-140	ex N140YV	Pronto A/w colours	
☐ C-GPRZ	Beech 1900C-1	UC-76	ex ZS-PJM		
☐ C-GRSY	Cessna 401	401-0248	ex N8400F		
☐ C-GWWB	Cessna 414	414-0514	ex N414DM		
☐ C-GWWC	ATR 42-300	209	ex N209AT		
☐ C-GWWD	ATR 42-300	211	ex N213AT		
☐ C-GWWN	Beech 200 Super King Air	BB-14	ex N418CS		
☐ C-GWWR	ATR 42-300	238	ex G-RHUM		
☐ C-GWWV	Beech 200 Super King Air	BB-287	ex N498AC		
☐ C-GWWX	Beech 1900C-1	UC-44	ex OY-JRI		
☐ C-GWWY	Beech 1900C-1	UC-63	ex ZS-PDI		

WESTAIR AVIATION — Northen Life (NLF) — Kamloops, BC (YKA)

☐ C-FRJE	Piper PA-31T Cheyenne II	31T-7820002	ex C-GCUL	
☐ C-GPIM	Piper PA-31T Cheyenne II	31T-8020065	ex C-GNAM	
☐ C-GVKA	Piper PA-31T Cheyenne II	31T-7920008	ex N9715N	
☐ C-GWCA	Piper PA-42-720 Cheyenne IIIA	42-5501057	ex C-GSAA	
☐ C-GXAJ	Cessna U206F Stationair II	U20602810	ex N35935	

WESTJET		Westjet (WS/WJA)			Calgary-Intl, AB (YYC)

☐ C-FAWJ	Boeing 737-8CT/W	35502/2323		807	
☐ C-FBWJ	Boeing 737-7CT/W	32767/1629	ex (C-GWSA)	230	
☐ C-FBWS	Boeing 737-7CT/W	37088/3080	ex N1786B	255	
☐ C-FCWJ	Boeing 737-7CT/W	35086/2613		250	
☐ C-FEWJ	Boeing 737-7CT/W	32769/1665		232	
☐ C-FGWJ	Boeing 737-7CT/W	32764/1553		226	
☐ C-FIWJ	Boeing 737-7CT/W	30712/2185		240	
☐ C-FIWS	Boeing 737-76N/W	32404/851		001	
☐ C-FJWS	Boeing 737-76N/W	28651/872		002	
☐ C-FKWJ	Boeing 737-8CT/W	36435/3469		815	♦
☐ C-FKWS	Boeing 737-76N/W	30134/905	ex N1787B	003	
☐ C-FLWJ	Boeing 737-7CT/W	38096/3520		262	♦
☐ C-FMWJ	Boeing 737-7CT/W	32771/1754		233	
☐ C-FTWJ	Boeing 737-7CT/W	30713/2220	ex N1786B	241	
☐ C-FUWS	Boeing 737-7CT/W	32765/1574		228	
☐ C-FWAD	Boeing 737-7CT/W	32753/1222		201	
☐ C-FWAF	Boeing 737-7CT/W	32747/1239		202	
☐ C-FWAI	Boeing 737-7CT/W	33656/1246		203	
☐ C-FWAO	Boeing 737-7CT/W	33657/1254		205	
☐ C-FWAQ	Boeing 737-7CT/W	32748/1266		206	
☐ C-FWBG	Boeing 737-7CT/W	32749/1281		207	
☐ C-FWBL	Boeing 737-7CT/W	32750/1286		208	
☐ C-FWBW	Boeing 737-7CT/W	33697/1303		209	
☐ C-FWBX	Boeing 737-7CT/W	32751/1333		210	
☐ C-FWCC	Boeing 737-7CT/W	32752/1339		211	
☐ C-FWCN	Boeing 737-7CT/W	33698/1346		212	
☐ C-FWSE	Boeing 737-8CT/W	36690/2987		811	
☐ C-FWSF	Boeing 737-7CT/W	32758/1431		218	
☐ C-FWSI	Boeing 737-7CT/W	36691/2983		253	
☐ C-FWSK	Boeing 737-7CT/W	36420/2671		251	
☐ C-FWSO	Boeing 737-7CT/W	32759/1445		219	
☐ C-FWSV	Boeing 737-7CT/W	32760/1472		220	
☐ C-FWSX	Boeing 737-7CT/W	32761/1493		221	
☐ C-FWSY	Boeing 737-7CT/W	32762/1501		222	
☐ C-FXWJ	Boeing 737-7CT/W	32768/1648	ex (C-GZWS)	231	
☐ C-FZWS	Boeing 737-76N/W	32731/1044		006	
☐ C-GBWS	Boeing 737-6CT	34288/1931		608	
☐ C-GCWJ	Boeing 737-7CT/W	33970/1556		227	
☐ C-GEWJ	Boeing 737-6CT	35571/2045		615	
☐ C-GGWJ	Boeing 737-7CT/W	35503/2334		242	
☐ C-GJWS	Boeing 737-8CT/W	34152/1714		802	
☐ C-GKWJ	Boeing 737-8CT/W	34151/1684		801	
☐ C-GLWS	Boeing 737-76N/W	32581/1009	ex N1787B	005	
☐ C-GMWJ	Boeing 737-7CT/W	35985/2135	ex N1779B	239	
☐ C-GPWS	Boeing 737-6CT	34284/1759		601	
☐ C-GQWJ	Boeing 737-7CT/W	35505/2436	ex N1786B	246	
☐ C-GRWS	Boeing 737-76N/W	32881/1155		007	
☐ C-GSWJ	Boeing 737-7CT/W	37423/3347		261	♦
☐ C-GTWS	Boeing 737-76N/W	32883/1179		008	
☐ C-GUWJ	Boeing 737-7CT/W	36422/2497	ex N1786B	248	
☐ C-GUWS	Boeing 737-76N/W	33378/1206		009	
☐ C-GVWJ	Boeing 737-7CT/W	36421/2484	ex N1786B	247	
☐ C-GWAZ	Boeing 737-7CT/W	32763/1522		223	
☐ C-GWBF	Boeing 737-7CT/W	32757/1370		213	
☐ C-GWBJ	Boeing 737-7CT/W	32754/1385	ex N1787B	215	
☐ C-GWBL	Boeing 737-8CT	34154/1734		806	
☐ C-GWBN	Boeing 737-7CT/W	34155/1772		235	
☐ C-GWBT	Boeing 737-7CT/W	32755/1396		216	
☐ C-GWBX	Boeing 737-7CT/W	34156/1793		236	
☐ C-GWCM	Boeing 737-7CT/W	32756/1413		217	
☐ C-GWCN	Boeing 737-7CT/W	34157/1818	ex N1784B	237	
☐ C-GWCQ	Boeing 737-6CT	35111/2004		610	
☐ C-GWCT	Boeing 737-6CT	35112/2016		611	
☐ C-GWCY	Boeing 737-6CT	35113/2022		612	
☐ C-GWJE	Boeing 737-7CT/W	35078/2431		245	
☐ C-GWJF	Boeing 737-7CT/W	32766/1599		229	
☐ C-GWJG	Boeing 737-7CT/W	35504/2366	ex N1786B	243	
☐ C-GWJK	Boeing 737-7CT/W	35084/2564	ex N1786B	249	
☐ C-GWJO	Boeing 737-7CT/W	33969/1527		225	
☐ C-GWJU	Boeing 737-6CT	34289/1956		609	
☐ C-GWSA	Boeing 737-8CT/W	34153/1731		805	
☐ C-GWSB	Boeing 737-6CT	34285/1797		602	
☐ C-GWSE	Boeing 737-76N/W	33379/1216		010	
☐ C-GWSH	Boeing 737-76N/W	29886/1258		011	

☐ C-GWSI	Boeing 737-6CT	34286/1816		603	
☐ C-GWSJ	Boeing 737-6CT	34621/1862		605	
☐ C-GWSK	Boeing 737-6CT	34287/1912	ex N1787B	607	
☐ C-GWSL	Boeing 737-6CT	34633/1884		606	
☐ C-GWSN	Boeing 737-7CT/W	37089/3090	ex N1796B	256	
☐ C-GWSO	Boeing 737-7CT/W	37090/3092	ex N1796B	257	
☐ C-GWSP	Boeing 737-7CT/W	36693/3108		258	
☐ C-GWSQ	Boeing 737-7CT/W	37091/3134		259	
☐ C-GWSR	Boeing 737-8CT/W	35288/2802		809	
☐ C-GWSU	Boeing 737-7CT/W	36689/2860	ex N1787B	252	
☐ C-GWSV	Boeing 737-8CT/W	37158/2841		810	
☐ C-GWSX	Boeing 737-8CT/W	36696/3314		813	
☐ C-GWSY	Boeing 737-7CT/W	37421/3184	ex N1786B	260	♦
☐ C-GWSZ	Boeing 737-7CT/W	37092/3164	ex N1787B	812	♦
☐ C-GWWJ	Boeing 737-8CT/W	35080/2524	ex N1786B	808	
☐ C-GXWJ	Boeing 737-6CT	35570/2032		613	
☐ C-GYWJ	Boeing 737-7CT/W	32772/1879		238	
☐ C-GZWS	Boeing 737-8CT/W	32770/1719		803	
☐ C-	Boeing 737-				o/o♦
☐ C-	Boeing 737-				o/o♦
☐ C-	Boeing 737-				o/o♦
☐ C-	Boeing 737-				o/o♦
☐ C-	Boeing 737-				o/o♦
☐ C-	Boeing 737-				o/o♦
☐ C-	Boeing 737-				o/o♦

WESTLAND HELICOPTERS — Houston, BC

☐ C-GQKT	Bell 206 JetRanger II	2148

WHISTLER AIR SERVICES — Whistler, BC (YWS)

☐ C-FSKZ	de Havilland DHC-2 Beaver	1594	ex CF-SKZ	FP
☐ C-GEND	de Havilland DHC-3 Turbo Otter	371	ex N83U	FP
☐ C-GSFA	Cessna 208 Caravan	20800212	ex 8Q-MAT	FP

WHITE RIVER AIR — White River, ON (YWR)

☐ CF-FHR	de Havilland DHC-2 Beaver	46	
☐ C-FWRA	de Havilland DHC-3 Otter	213	ex India IM1714

WILDCAT HELICOPTERS — Penticton, BC (YYF)

☐ C-FCAN	Bell 212	30919	ex XA-IOW
☐ C-GGAT	Bell 212	30846	ex N16796
☐ C-GSGT	Bell 212	30771	ex C-FSAT
☐ C-GSRH	Bell 212	30895	ex N751HL

WILDERNESS AIR — Vermilion Bay, ON (YVG)

☐ C-FGMK	de Havilland DHC-2 Beaver	1329	ex 58-2003	FP
☐ C-FODV	de Havilland DHC-3 Otter	411	ex CF-ODV	FP
☐ C-GFZF	Cessna A185E Skywagon	18502002	ex N70118	FP
☐ C-GLAB	de Havilland DHC-3 Otter	348	ex 59-2210	FP
☐ C-GNFN	Cessna 208 Caravan	20800502		

WILDERNESS HELICOPTERS — Wawa-Hawk Junction, ON (YXZ)

☐ C-FALS	Bell 206L LongRanger	45061	ex N56DE
☐ C-GMCJ	Bell 206L-3 LongRanger III	51459	
☐ C-GWHA	Bell 206L-1 LongRanger II	45694	ex N82KA
☐ C-GWHM	Bell 206L-3 LongRanger III	51009	ex N22621

WILLISTON LAKE AIR SERVICES — Mackenzie, BC (YZY)

☐ C-FBAD	Piper PA-31-350 Navajo Chieftain	31-7752101	ex N6196C
☐ C-GRWP	Piper PA-31-350 Chieftain	31-7952095	

WINDWARD AIR SERVICES — Toronto, ON

☐ C-GAGE	Cessna 441 Conquest	441-0214	ex N792KC

WINGS OVER KISSISSING

☐ C-FFVZ	de Havilland DHC-3 Turbo Otter	145	ex N80944	FP/WS
☐ C-FODW	de Havilland DHC-3 Turbo Otter	403	ex CF-ODW	FP/WS
☐ C-FWEJ	de Havilland DHC-3 Turbo Otter	208	ex IM1710	FP/WS
☐ C-GEWP	de Havilland DHC-2 Turbo Beaver	1543/TB2	ex ET-AKI	FP
☐ C-GGOR	de Havilland DHC-3 Turbo Otter	97	ex TI-SPE	FP

WOLVERINE AIR — Fort Simpson, NT (YFS)

☐ C-FTQB	Cessna A185F Skywagon	18501655	ex (N1948U)
☐ C-GHKB	Cessna 207 Skywagon	20700228	ex N1628U
☐ C-GIHF	Britten-Norman BN-2A-26 Islander	475	ex G-BDJU
☐ C-GQOA	Cessna U206G Stationair 6	U20604993	ex (N4600U)
☐ C-GTUG	Cessna U206G Stationair 6	U20606214	ex (N6282Z)

YELLOWHEAD HELICOPTERS — Valemount, BC

☐ C-FPQX	Bell 206B JetRanger	1330	
☐ C-FYHB	Bell 206B JetRanger	1655	ex C-GCHH
☐ C-FYHJ	Bell 206B JetRanger III	2900	ex N344P
☐ C-GDGH	Bell 206B JetRanger	2476	ex N352E
☐ C-GXYH	Bell 206B JetRanger III	2267	ex N130VG
☐ C-GYHL	Bell 206B JetRanger III	1702	
☐ C-GYHR	Bell 206B JetRanger III	2571	ex N5015A
☐ C-GYHT	Bell 206B JetRanger III	4104	ex HL9107
☐ C-GYHP	Bell 206L-1 LongRanger	45400	ex N2621
☐ C-GYHQ	Bell 206L-1 LongRanger	45419	ex N2629
☐ C-GYHX	Bell 206L-3 LongRanger III	51545	ex N206AC
☐ C-FYHD	Bell 205A-1	30128	ex C-FNMO
☐ C-FGYH	Bell 407	53641	
☐ C-FYHY	Bell 407	53945	◆
☐ C-GJWC	Cessna T210L Turbo Centurion II	21060438	ex N93858

ZIMMER AIR SERVICES — Blenheim, ON

☐ C-FIHC	Aérospatiale AS355F1 Twin Star	5191	ex N355TD
☐ C-GBCL	Bell 206B JetRanger II	3458	ex N2145R
☐ C-GFEC	Bell 206B JetRanger II	1611	
☐ C-GHSW	Aérospatiale AS350D AStar	1082	ex N4268V
☐ C-GMLO	Bell 206B JetRanger	957	ex N809JA

CC- CHILE (Republic of Chile)

AEROCARDAL

☐ CC-AAQ	Dornier 228-202	8119	ex CS-TGO	
☐ CC-ACG	Dornier 328-110	3063	ex OE-LKE	◆
☐ CC-CWC	Dornier 228-202K	8162	ex D-CLUE	◆
☐ CC-CWX	Dornier 228-101	7027	ex CC-CSA	◆

AEROLINEA PRINCIPAL CHILE (PCP) — Santiago-Benitez Intl (SCL)

☐ CC-ACD	Boeing 737-2K9	23404/1176	ex C9-BAK	◆
☐ CC-ACE	Boeing 737-322	24669/1907	ex N394UA	◆
☐ CC-CZK	Boeing 737-236	21804/686	ex G-BGDP	
☐ CC-CZO	Boeing 737-236	22030/693	ex G-BGJI	

AEROSERVICIO

☐ CC-CEI	Cessna 421C Golden Eagle III	421C0655	ex CC-PFM

AEROVIAS DAP — Dap (DAP) — Punta Arenas (PUQ)

☐ CC-ACO	British Aerospace 146 Srs.200	E2094	ex OY-RCB	◆
☐ CC-CHV	de Havilland DHC-6 Twin Otter 300	709	ex (G-BHUY)	
☐ CC-CLT	CASA C.212-100	A10-1-103	ex E-210	[PUQ]
☐ CC-CLV	Cessna 402C	402C0073	ex CC-CDU	
☐ CC-CLY	Beech 100 King Air	B-79	ex CC-PIE	
☐ CC-COV	Cessna 402C	402C0282	ex CC-CDS	
☐ CC-CZP	British Aerospace 146 Srs.200	E2042	ex G-FLTD	

BOSQUES ARAUCO

☐ CC-CBB	Bell UH-1H	5162	ex N647F
☐ CC-CBH	Bell UH-1H	5843	ex N49KP
☐ CC-CBL	Bell UH-1H	9495	ex N97KP
☐ CC-CBO	Bell UH-1H	4133	ex N3149N
☐ CC-CBU	Bell UH-1H	4060	ex N768MC
☐ CC-CBW	Bell UH-1H	10810	ex N45401
☐ CC-CBY	Bell UH-1H	9445	ex N62615
☐ CC-CBZ	Bell UH-1H	10091	ex N6259T

COPTERS — Copters (KOP) — Rancagua (QRC)

☐ CC-CLE	Bell UH-1H	8535	ex N46666	
☐ CC-CLI	Aérospatiale AS355N Ecureuil 2	5700	ex PR-YHE	
☐ CC-CLK	Bell UH-1H	4902	ex N38CF	

DAP HELICOPTEROS — HeliDap (DHE) — Punta Arenas (PUQ)

☐ CC-CHK	MBB 105CB-4-2	S-687	ex H-62	EMS
☐ CC-CHM	MBB 105CB-4-2	S-688	ex H-63	EMS
☐ CC-CHN	MBB 105CB-4-2	S-689	ex H-64	EMS
☐ CC-CHQ	MBB 105CB-4-2	S-708	ex H-65	EMS
☐ CC-CHR	MBB 105CB-4-2	S-710	ex H-66	EMS
☐ CC-CCA	Eurocopter EC135T1	0122	ex N214TD	
☐ CC-CIB	Aérospatiale AS355F2 Twin Star	5371	ex XA-MDE	
☐ CC-CIK	Aérospatiale AS355F2 Twin Star	5413	ex N710KM	
☐ CC-CIN	Aérospatiale AS355F1 Twin Star	5147	ex N22TS	
☐ CC-CMV	Aérospatiale AS355F2 Twin Star	5372	ex N225CC	

EAGLE COPTERS

☐ CC-ABK	Bell 407	53961	ex C-FZXC	♦
☐ CC-CAF	Bell 204B	2010	ex CC-CLI	
☐ CC-CIS	Bell 212	30932	ex CS-HFY	>INAER
☐ CC-CIY	Bell 212	30685	ex CS-HFW	>INAER

EMPRESSA AERO - SERVICIOS PARRAGUE — Aspar (PRG) — Santiago

☐ CC-CDT	Canadian Vickers PBY-5A Catalina	CV-332	ex F-YCHB	32
☐ CC-CNP	Consolidated PBY-6A Catalina	2029	ex EC-FXN	35

HELICOPTEROS DEL PACIFICO — Temuco

☐ CC-CLO	Bell UH-1H	5057	ex EC-GOC	
☐ CC-COW	Bell UH-1H	5844	ex N7232K	
☐ CC-CPT	Garlick-Bell UH-1D	8001	ex 70+01	
☐ CC-CPU	Garlick-Bell UH-1D	8115	ex 70+55	
☐ CC-CPY	Garlick-Bell UH-1D	8205	ex 71+45	
☐ CC-CPZ	Garlick-Bell UH-1D	8221	ex 71+61	

HELICOPTERS CHILE — Machali Heliport

☐ CC-CLB	Bell UH-1H	5892	ex N28BC	
☐ CC-CLF	Bell AH-1S	24060	ex N82277	

HELIWORKS — Heliworks (HLW) — Concepcion (CCP)

☐ CC-CHU	Lockheed P2V-7S Neptune	726-7217	ex N703AU	03

INAER HELICOPTER CHILE

☐ CC-CIQ	Bell 205A-1	30134	ex EC-GAA	<Helisureste
☐ CC-CIS	Bell 212	30932	ex CS-HFY	<Eagle Copters
☐ CC-CIU	Bell 407	53727	ex C-FLFC	
☐ CC-CIY	Bell 212	30685	ex CS-HFW	<Eagle Copters

LAN AIRLINES — LAN (LA/LAN) — Santiago-Benitez Intl (SCL)

Member of Oneworld

☐ CC-CVA	Airbus A318-121	3001	ex D-AUAI	
☐ CC-CVB	Airbus A318-121	3030	ex D-AUAK	
☐ CC-CVF	Airbus A318-121	3062	ex D-AUAM	
☐ CC-CVH	Airbus A318-121	3214	ex D-AUAD	
☐ CC-CVN	Airbus A318-121	3216	ex D-AUAE	
☐ CC-CVP	Airbus A318-121	3371	ex D-AUAC	
☐ CC-CVR	Airbus A318-121	3390	ex D-AUAH	
☐ CC-CVS	Airbus A318-121	3438	ex D-AUAA	
☐ CC-CVU	Airbus A318-121	3469	ex D-AUAD	
☐ CC-CVV	Airbus A318-121	3509	ex D-AUAE	
☐ CC-CZJ	Airbus A318-121	3585	ex D-AUAB	
☐ CC-CZN	Airbus A318-121	3602	ex D-AUAF	
☐ CC-CZQ	Airbus A318-121	3606	ex D-AUAG	
☐ CC-CZR	Airbus A318-121	3635	ex D-AUAI	
☐ CC-CZS	Airbus A318-121	3642	ex D-AUAJ	
☐ CC-BCA	Airbus A319-132	4563	ex D-AVWB	o/o♦

☐ CC-BCB	Airbus A319-132	4598	ex D-AVWG	o/o♦
☐ CC-	Airbus A319-132		ex	o/o♦
☐ CC-	Airbus A319-132		ex	o/o♦
☐ CC-COU	Airbus A319-132	2089	ex D-AVWL	>LPE
☐ CC-COX	Airbus A319-132	2096	ex D-AVYN	>LPE
☐ CC-COY	Airbus A319-132	2295	ex D-AVWA	>LPE
☐ CC-COZ	Airbus A319-132	2304	ex D-AVWN	>LPE
☐ CC-CPE	Airbus A319-132	2321	ex D-AVYO	>LPE
☐ CC-CPF	Airbus A319-132	2572	ex D-AVXC	>LPE
☐ CC-CPI	Airbus A319-132	2585	ex D-AVXH	>LPE
☐ CC-CPJ	Airbus A319-132	2845	ex D-AVYX	
☐ CC-CPL	Airbus A319-132	2858	ex D-AVYB	
☐ CC-CPM	Airbus A319-132	2864	ex D-AVWC	>LPE
☐ CC-CPO	Airbus A319-132	2872	ex D-AVWJ	>LPE
☐ CC-CPQ	Airbus A319-132	2886	ex D-AVXP	>LPE
☐ CC-CPX	Airbus A319-132	2887	ex D-AVYF	>LPE
☐ CC-CQK	Airbus A319-132	2892	ex D-AVYV	>LPE
☐ CC-CQL	Airbus A319-132	2894	ex D-AVWE	>LPE
☐ CC-CYE	Airbus A319-132	3663	ex D-AVYV	
☐ CC-CYF	Airbus A319-132	3671	ex D-AVYW	
☐ CC-CYI	Airbus A319-132	3770	ex D-AVXE	
☐ CC-CYJ	Airbus A319-132	3772	ex D-AVXH	
☐ CC-CYL	Airbus A319-132	3779	ex D-AVXJ	
☐ CC-BAA	Airbus A320-233	4383	ex D-AVVF	♦
☐ CC-BAB	Airbus A320-233	4400	ex D-AVVD	♦
☐ CC-BAC	Airbus A320-233	4439	ex D-AVVX	♦
☐ CC-BAD	Airbus A320-233	4476	ex D-AUBB	♦
☐ CC-BAE	Airbus A320-233	4509	ex D-AUBO	♦
☐ CC-BAF	Airbus A320-233	4516	ex D-AXAG	♦
☐ CC-BAG	Airbus A320-233	4546	ex D-AXAO	♦
☐ CC-BAH	Airbus A320-233	4549	ex D-AUBQ	♦
☐ CC-BAI	Airbus A320-233	4543	ex F-WWIS	♦
☐ CC-BAJ	Airbus A320-233	4576	ex F-WWBX	o/o♦
☐ CC-BAK	Airbus A320-233	4597	ex D-AVVH	o/o♦
☐ CC-	Airbus A320-2		ex	o/o♦
☐ CC-	Airbus A320-2		ex	o/o♦
☐ CC-	Airbus A320-2		ex	o/o♦
☐ CC-	Airbus A320-2		ex	o/o♦
☐ CC-	Airbus A320-2		ex	o/o♦
☐ CC-	Airbus A320-2		ex	o/o♦
☐ CC-	Airbus A320-2		ex	o/o♦
☐ CC-	Airbus A320-2		ex	o/o♦
☐ CC-COF	Airbus A320-233	1355	ex F-WWBE	
☐ CC-COI	Airbus A320-233	1526	ex F-WWIM	
☐ CC-COL	Airbus A320-233	1568	ex VP-BCK	
☐ CC-COM	Airbus A320-233	1626	ex F-WWDL	
☐ CC-CQM	Airbus A320-233	3280	ex F-WWDM	>LPE
☐ CC-CQN	Airbus A320-233	3319	ex F-WWBC	
☐ CC-CQO	Airbus A320-233	3535	ex F-WWDZ	
☐ CC-CQP	Airbus A320-233	3556	ex F-WWBC	
☐ CC-CQA	Airbus A340-313X	359	ex F-WWJY	
☐ CC-CQC	Airbus A340-313X	363	ex F-WWJZ	
☐ CC-CQE	Airbus A340-313X	429	ex F-WWJQ	
☐ CC-CQF	Airbus A340-313X	442	ex F-WWJY	
☐ CC-CQG	Airbus A340-313X	167	ex C-FYLC	
☐ CC-BJA	Boeing 767-316ER/W	26329/641	ex LV-BMR	♦
☐ CC-CDM	Boeing 767-352ER	26261/575	ex VN-A763	
☐ CC-CDP	Boeing 767-316ER/W	27597/602		
☐ CC-CEB	Boeing 767-316ER/W	26327/621		
☐ CC-CRG	Boeing 767-375ER/W	25865/430	ex LV-BTE	♦
☐ CC-CRH	Boeing 767-375ER	25864/426	ex B-2562	
☐ CC-CRV	Boeing 767-316ER/W	27615/681	ex LV-BFU	
☐ CC-CWF	Boeing 767-316ER/W	34626/940		
☐ CC-CWG	Boeing 767-316ER/W	34629/944		
☐ CC-CWH	Boeing 767-316ER/W	34628/945		
☐ CC-CWV	Boeing 767-316ER/W	35230/955		
☐ CC-CWY	Boeing 767-316ER/W	35231/961		
☐ CC-CXC	Boeing 767-316ER/W	36710/962		
☐ CC-CXE	Boeing 767-316ER/W	35696/968		
☐ CC-CXG	Boeing 767-316ER/W	36712/972	ex N5020K	
☐ CC-CXI	Boeing 767-316ER/W	37800/984		
☐ CC-CXJ	Boeing 767-316ER/W	37801/985		
☐ CC-CXK	Boeing 767-316ER/W	37802/987		♦
☐ CC-CXL	Boeing 767-31BER	26265/570	ex LV-BFD	

☐ CC-CZT	Boeing 767-316ER/W	29228/699		
☐ CC-CZU	Boeing 767-316ER/W	29229/729		
☐ CC-CZW	Boeing 767-316ER/W	29227/698		
☐ CC-	Boeing 767-316ER/W			o/o♦
☐ CC-	Boeing 767-316ER/W			o/o♦
☐ CC-	Boeing 787-816	38464/10		o/o♦
☐ CC-	Boeing 787-816	38475/16		o/o♦

LAN CARGO — LAN Cargo (UC/LCO) — Santiago-Benitez Intl (SCL)

☐ CC-CSD	Boeing 737-204F	20417/255	ex TF-ABD	<LAN
☐ CC-CZZ	Boeing 767-316F/W	25756/712		
☐ N314LA	Boeing 767-316F/W	32573/848		op by MAA
☐ N316LA	Boeing 767-316F/W	30842/860		op by FWL
☐ N420LA	Boeing 767-316F/W	34627/948		>MAA
☐ N524LA	Boeing 767-346F	35816/956	ex JA631J	♦
☐ PR-ABD	Boeing 767-316F/W	34245/935		>TUS
☐ N772LA	Boeing 777-F6N	37708/774		
☐ N774LA	Boeing 777-F6N	37710/782		o/o

LAN EXPRESS — LANExpres (LU/LXP) — Santiago-Benitez Intl (SCL)

99.4% owned subsidiary of LAN Airlines and operates aircraft leased from the parent.

LASSA - LINEAS DE AEROSERVICIOS — (LSE) — Santiago-Tobalaba

☐ CC-CIZ	Bell UH-1B	1124	ex EC-EOH
☐ CC-CME	Bell UH-1H	8800	ex EC-GDO
☐ CC-CMF	Bell UH-1H	5398	ex EC-GDM
☐ CC-CNF	Bell UH-1H	5949	ex N1214B
☐ CC-CNH	Bell UH-1H	10484	ex EC-GOH
☐ CC-CNL	Garrick-Bell UH-1B	318	ex LV-WNR
☐ CC-CNM	Bell UH-1H	4609	ex N1216Y
☐ CC-CFY	Piper PA-31 Turbo Navajo	31-600	ex E-203
☐ CC-CNW	Dornier 228-202K	8063	ex G-BMMR

LINEA AEREA COSTA NORTE — Costa Norte (NOT) — Iquique (IQQ)

☐ CC-CAJ	Cessna 337H Super Skymaster II	33701860	ex N1368L	
☐ CC-CFU	Rockwell 500S Shrike Commander	3320	ex N348TT	
☐ CC-CFW	Rockwell 500S Shrike Commander	3230	ex N567PT	
☐ CC-CGB	Cessna 337H Super Skymaster II	33701941	ex N123YM	
☐ CC-CGK	Cessna 337H Super Skymaster II	33701818	ex N1326L	
☐ CC-CGX	Rockwell 500S Shrike Commander	3306	ex N10PP	<S/A Aeropecsa
☐ CC-CHG	Rockwell 500S Shrike Commander	3293	ex N916AC	<S/A Aeropecsa

PATAGONIA AIRLINES — Puerto Montt (PMC)

☐ CC-CDR	Cessna 208B Caravan I	208B1202	ex N13194
☐ CC-CFF	Cessna 402C	402C0405	ex CC-CMI
☐ CC-CTS	Cessna 208B Caravan I	208B1316	ex N21424

SKY AIRLINE — Aerosky (H2/SKU) — Santiago-Benitez Intl (SCL)

☐ CC-ABW	Airbus A320-233	1523	ex N484TA	♦
☐ CC-ADP	Airbus A320-231	0406	ex N406PR	♦
☐ CC-AAG	Boeing 737-247	23608/1399	ex LV-BIF	♦
☐ CC-CAP	Boeing 737-236	22027/654	ex CC-CZM	[SCL]
☐ CC-CDB	Boeing 737-230 (Nordam 3)	22120/715	ex N122NJ	
☐ CC-CTB	Boeing 737-2Q3	23481/1241	ex N381AC	
☐ CC-CTD	Boeing 737-2Q3	23117/1033	ex N380AC	
☐ CC-CTF	Boeing 737-230 (Nordam 3)	22122/721	ex LV-BCD	
☐ CC-CTH	Boeing 737-230 (Nordam 3)	22636/808	ex N271LR	[SCL]
☐ CC-CTK	Boeing 737-230 (Nordam 3)	22402/744	ex N261LR	
☐ CC-CTM	Boeing 737-230	22139/791	ex LV-BBO	
☐ CC-CTO	Boeing 737-230	22114/657	ex LV-BBI	
☐ CC-CTX	Boeing 737-2T4 (AvAero 3)	22698/823	ex N722WN	

TRANSPORTES AEREOS DON CARLOS — Don Carlos (DCL) — Coyhaique-Teniente Vidal (GXQ)

☐ CC-CCB	Cessna 402B	402B1089	ex N82930
☐ CC-CCI	Beech 95-E55 Baron	TE-1008	ex CC-PDL
☐ CC-CRU	Piper PA-23-250 Aztec C	27-3726	ex CC-PRX

118

TRANSPORTES AEREOS SAN RAFAEL	San Rafael (SRF)	Coyhaique-Teniente Vidal (GXQ)	
☐ CC-CEZ	Piper PA-31 Navajo C	31-7612035	ex CC-PVM
☐ CC-CHI	Piper PA-23-250 Aztec F	27-8054054	ex N805BC
☐ CC-CPN	Piper PA-31 Navajo C	31-7712052	ex CC-PVB
☐ CC-CSE	Piper PA-31 Turbo Navajo B	31-731	ex CC-CKW

CN- MOROCCO (Kingdom of Morocco)

AIR ARABIA MAROC		(3O/MAC)		
☐ CN-NMA	Airbus A320-214	3809	ex F-WWDV	
☐ CN-NMB	Airbus A320-214	3833	ex D-ABDV	
☐ CN-NMC	Airbus A320-214	3246	ex A6-ABM	
☐ CN-NMD	Airbus A320-214	4310	ex AB-ABU	♦

ATLAS BLUE		Atlas Blue (8A/BMM)		Marrakech (RAK)
☐ CN-RMF	Boeing 737-4B6	24807/1880		<RAM
☐ CN-RMG	Boeing 737-4B6	24808/1888		<RAM
☐ CN-RMX	Boeing 737-4B6	26526/2219		<RAM
☐ CN-RNC	Boeing 737-4B6	26529/2584		<RAM
☐ CN-RND	Boeing 737-4B6	26530/2588		<RAM
☐ CN-RNX	Airbus A321-211	2064	ex D-AVZO	<RAM
☐ CN-RNY	Airbus A321-211	2076	ex D-AVZS	<RAM
☐ CN-ROM	Airbus A321-211	3070	ex D-AVZA	<RAM

JET4YOU		Argan (8J/JFU)		Casablanca-Mohamed V (CMN)
☐ CN-RPA	Boeing 737-4B3	24750/1916	ex OO-TUM	<CRL
☐ CN-RPC	Boeing 737-4K5	24125/1687	ex OO-TUI	
☐ CN-RPE	Boeing 737-8K5/W	27990/246	ex D-AHFJ	<HLF
☐ CN-RPF	Boeing 737-8K5/W	34691/2246	ex G-FDZO	
☐ CN-RPG	Boeing 737-8K5/W	34692/2249	ex G-FDZP	
☐ CN-RPH	Boeing 737-46J	28867/2879	ex OO-JAM	

REGIONAL AIR LINES		Maroc Regional (FN/RGL)		Casablanca-Anfa (CAS)
☐ CN-CDU	ATR 42-300	134	ex F-WWEF	[NTE]<RAM♦
☐ CN-CDV	ATR 42-300	137	ex F-WWEI	[CMN]<RAM♦
☐ CN-RLA	Beech 1900D	UE-259	ex N10863	
☐ CN-RLD	Beech 1900D	UE-267	ex N10999	
☐ CN-RLF	ATR 42-320	208	ex F-WQNL	
☐ CN-RLG	ATR 42-320	366	ex F-WQNM	

ROYAL AIR MAROC		Royalair Maroc (AT/RAM)	Casablanca-Mohamed V (CMN)	
☐ CN-RNX	Airbus A321-211	2064	ex D-AVZO	>BMM
☐ CN-RNY	Airbus A321-211	2076	ex D-AVZS	>BMM
☐ CN-ROF	Airbus A321-211	2726	ex D-AVZO	
☐ CN-ROM	Airbus A321-211	3070	ex D-AVZA all-white	>BMM
☐ CN-CDU	ATR 42-300	134	ex F-WWEF	>RGL
☐ CN-CDV	ATR 42-300	137	ex F-WWEI	> RGL
☐ CN-COA	ATR 72-201	441	ex F-WKVB	
☐ CN-COB	ATR 72-202	444	ex F-WKVD	
☐ CN-COC	ATR 72-201	470	ex F-WKVI	
☐ CN-COD	ATR 72-202	483	ex F-WKVC	
☐ CN-RMF	Boeing 737-4B6	24807/1880		Lsd BMM
☐ CN-RMG	Boeing 737-4B6	24808/1888		Lsd BMM
☐ CN-RMI	Boeing 737-2B6 (Nordam 3)	21214/449	El Ayoun	[CAS]
☐ CN-RMJ	Boeing 737-2B6 (Nordam 3)	21215/452	Oujda	[CAS]
☐ CN-RMK	Boeing 737-2B6 (Nordam 3)	21216/456	Smara	[CAS]
☐ CN-RML	Boeing 737-2B6 (Nordam 3)	22767/851	ex 6V-AHK	[CMN]
☐ CN-RMV	Boeing 737-5B6	25317/2157		
☐ CN-RMW	Boeing 737-5B6	25364/2166		
☐ CN-RMX	Boeing 737-4B6	26526/2219		>BMM
☐ CN-RMY	Boeing 737-5B6	26525/2209		
☐ CN-RNB	Boeing 737-5B6	26527/2472		
☐ CN-RNC	Boeing 737-4B6	26529/2584		>BMM
☐ CN-RND	Boeing 737-4B6	26530/2588		>BMM
☐ CN-RNG	Boeing 737-5B6	27679/2734	ex (CN-RNF)	
☐ CN-RNH	Boeing 737-5B6	27680/2855		
☐ CN-ROX	Boeing 737-3M8F	24020/1614	ex N240MT	

☐ CN-RNL	Boeing 737-7B6/W	28982/236	ex N1786B	
☐ CN-RNM	Boeing 737-7B6/W	28984/294	ex N1786B	
☐ CN-RNQ	Boeing 737-7B6/W	28985/501	ex N1786B	
☐ CN-RNR	Boeing 737-7B6/W	28986/519	ex N1787B	
☐ CN-RNV	Boeing 737-7B6/W	28988/1261		
☐ CN-RNJ	Boeing 737-8B6/W	28980/55		
☐ CN-RNK	Boeing 737-8B6/W	28981/60		
☐ CN-RNP	Boeing 737-8B6/W	28983/492	ex N1786B	
☐ CN-RNU	Boeing 737-8B6/W	28987/1095		
☐ CN-RNW	Boeing 737-8B6/W	33057/1347	ex N1787B	
☐ CN-RNZ	Boeing 737-8B6/W	33058/1432		
☐ CN-ROA	Boeing 737-8B6/W	33059/1457		
☐ CN-ROB	Boeing 737-8B6/W	33060/1646		
☐ CN-ROC	Boeing 737-8B6/W	33061/1661		
☐ CN-ROD	Boeing 737-7B6/W	33062/1883		
☐ CN-ROE	Boeing 737-8B6/W	33063/1913	ex N1781B	
☐ CN-ROH	Boeing 737-85P	33978/1957		
☐ CN-ROJ	Boeing 737-85P	33979/1963		
☐ CN-ROK	Boeing 737-8B6/W	33064/2180	ex N1786B	
☐ CN-ROL	Boeing 737-8B6/W	33065/2206	ex N1787B	
☐ CN-ROP	Boeing 737-8B6/W	33066/2506	ex N1782B	
☐ CN-ROR	Boeing 737-8B6/W	33067/2527	ex N1786B	
☐ CN-ROS	Boeing 737-8B6/W	37718/2773		
☐ CN-ROT	Boeing 737-8B6/W	33068/2883		
☐ CN-ROU	Boeing 737-8B6/W	33069/2911		
☐ CN-ROY	Boeing 737-8B6/W	33070/3233		
☐ CN-ROZ	Boeing 737-8B6/W	33071/3258	ex N1786B	♦
☐ CN-	Boeing 737-8B6/W			o/o♦
☐ CN-	Boeing 737-8B6/W			o/o♦
☐ CN-	Boeing 737-8B6/W			o/o♦
☐ CN-	Boeing 737-8B6/W			o/o♦
☐ CN-	Boeing 737-8B6/W			o/o♦
☐ CN-	Boeing 737-8B6/W			o/o♦
☐ CN-RGA	Boeing 747-428	25629/956	ex F-OGTG	
☐ CN-RMT	Boeing 757-2B6	23686/103	ex N32831	
☐ CN-RMZ	Boeing 757-2B6	23687/106		
☐ CN-RNS	Boeing 767-36NER	30115/863		
☐ CN-RNT	Boeing 767-36NER	30843/867		
☐ CN-ROG	Boeing 767-328ER	27212/531	ex HL7200	
☐ CN-ROV	Boeing 767-3Q8ER	27686/793	ex N201LF	
☐ CN-ROW	Boeing 767-343ER	30008/743	ex N768MT	
☐ CN-	Boeing 787-8B6	35507/17		o/o♦
☐ CN-	Boeing 787-8B6	35508/19		o/o♦
☐ CN-CDF	Beech 200 Super King Air	BB-577		Trainer
☐ CN-CDN	Beech 200 Super King Air	BB-713	ex N36741	Trainer

CP-   BOLIVIA (Republic of Bolivia)

AEROCON
Aerocon (AEK) Trinidad (TDD)

☐ CP-2176	Dornier Do.228-202K	8163	ex D-CIKI
☐ CP-2459	Swearingen SA.227DC Metro 23	DC-847B	ex N847LS
☐ CP-2477	Swearingen SA.227DC Metro 23	DC-830B	ex N1119K
☐ CP-2485	Swearingen SA.227DC Metro 23	DC-817B	ex VH-UUD
☐ CP-2500	Swearingen SA.227AC Metro III	AC-733B	ex N160MC
☐ CP-2527	Swearingen SA.227DC Metro 23	DC-824B	ex N471Z
☐ CP-2548	Swearingen SA.227BC Metro 23	BC-768B	ex N768ML
☐ CP-2563	Swearingen SA.227BC Metro 23	BC-783B	ex N783ML
☐ CP-2590	Swearingen SA.227BC Metro 23	BC-773B	ex N773US
☐ CP-2602	Swearingen SA.227BC Metro 23	BC-780B	ex N780AL
☐ CP-	Swearingen SA.227BC Metro 23	BC-781B	ex N781AL

AEROESTE
Aeroeste (ROE) Santa Cruz-El Trompillo (SRZ)

☐ CP-2266	Rockwell 690B Turbo Commander	11395	ex N816PC
☐ CP-2328	LET L-410UVP-E20	912536	ex S9-TAY
☐ CP-2349	LET L-410UVP-E20	912530	ex S9-TBM
☐ CP-2382	LET L-410UVP-E9	861727	ex S9-TBH

120

AEROLINEAS SUD AMERICANAS				Santa Cruz-Viru Viru (VVI)
☐ CP-2499	Boeing 727-224 (FedEx 3)	22449/1756	ex N296SC	

AEROSUR		Aerosur (5L/RSU)		Santa Cruz-Viru Viru (VVI)
☐ CP-2377	Boeing 727-23	20044/592	ex N1969	[VVI]
☐ CP-2422	Boeing 727-264 (FedEx 3)	21617/1416	ex XA-HON	
☐ CP-2423	Boeing 727-264 (FedEx 3)	21638/1457	ex XA-HOX	
☐ CP-2424	Boeing 727-264 (FedEx 3)	22156/1607	ex XA-MED	[CBB]
☐ CP-2431	Boeing 727-264 (FedEx 3)	22411/1696	ex XA-MEJ	[VVI]
☐ CP-2447	Boeing 727-264 (FedEx 3)	22409/1676	ex XA-MEH	
☐ CP-2455	Boeing 727-287 (FedEx 3)	22606/1812	ex N910PG	stored
☐ CP-2462	Boeing 727-264 (FedEx 3)	22158/1642	ex XA-MEF	
☐ CP-2498	Boeing 727-223 (FedEx 3)	22463/1755	ex CP-2463	
☐ CP-2515	Boeing 727-222	21904/1528	ex N346PA	
☐ CP-2438	Boeing 737-201 (Nordam 3)	21815/589	ex C-FNAX	
☐ CP-2476	Boeing 737-281 (AvAero 3)	21771/594	ex N751AA	
☐ CP-2484	Boeing 737-281	21768/586	ex N749AP	
☐ CP-2486	Boeing 737-281	21769/587	ex N752AP	
☐ CP-2561	Boeing 737-2P6	21613/530	ex N835AL	
☐ CP-2595	Boeing 737-33A	24790/1955	ex N790AW	
☐ CP-2603	Boeing 747-443	32339/1275	ex G-VROM	
☐ CP-2521	Boeing 767-260ER	23107/93	ex ET-AIF	
☐ CP-2659	Boeing 767-284ER	24742/303	ex N988AN	♦

ALAS DEL SUR				
☐ CP-2479	Fairchild F-27	99	ex CX-BRT	[VVI]♦

AMAZONAS TRANSPORTES AEREOS		Amazonas (Z8)		La Paz (LPB)
☐ CP-2413	Cessna 208B Caravan I	208B0838	ex N3039G	
☐ CP-2473	Swearingen SA.227DC Metro 23	DC-842B	ex N510FS	

BOLIVIANA DE AVIACION		(OB/BOV)		La Paz (LPB)
☐ CP-2550	Boeing 737-33A	25118/2065	ex N401LF	
☐ CP-2551	Boeing 737-382	24449/1857	ex N449AN	
☐ CP-2552	Boeing 737-3M8	25041/2024	ex D-ADIJ	
☐ CP-2553	Boeing 737-382	24450/1873	ex N460XS	

ECO EXPRESS				La Paz (LPB)
☐ CP-2026	Convair 340-70	249	ex 53-7797	

HELIBOL				Santa Cruz-El Trompillo (SRZ)
☐ CP-	Bell 212	30596	ex N212SJ	♦

LAB AIRLINES		LloydAereo (LB/LLB)		Cochabamba (CBB)
☐ CP-1366	Boeing 727-2K3/W (Duganair 3)	21494/1373		
☐ CP-1367	Boeing 727-2K3/W (Duganair 3)	21495/1403		
☐ CP-	Boeing 727-2S7 (FedEx 3)	22492/1729	ex N685CA	[CBB]

LINEAS AEREAS CANEDO		(LCN)		Cochabamba (CBB)
☐ CP-744	Aero Commander 680	680341-34	ex OB-M-573	Juan Salvador Gaviota
☐ CP-896	Aero Commander 680	680-548-216	ex N316E	Jose Fernando Gaviota
☐ CP-973	Curtiss C-46C Commando	32941	ex N32227	
☐ CP-1080	Curtiss C-46A Commando	26771	ex TAM61	[LPB]
☐ CP-1093	Aero Commander 680F	680F-1035-51	ex N6197X	
☐ CP-1128	Douglas DC-3D	1998	ex N15M	stored CBB, on rebuild
☐ CP-1960	Douglas DC-3C	18993	ex PT-KVN	[TDD]
☐ CP-2421	Douglas C-117D	12979/43365	ex N545CT	>RSU

TAB CARGO		Bol (BOL)		La Paz (LPB)
☐ CP-1376	Lockheed 382C-72D Hercules	4759	ex TAM-91	
☐ CP-2184	Lockheed 182A-2A Hercules	3228	ex TAM-69	
☐ CP-2489	Douglas DC-10-10F	46903/43	ex N68044	
☐ CP-2555	Douglas DC-10-30F	46937/152	ex N833LA	

TAM - TRANSPORTES AEREO MILITAR — La Paz (LPB)

☐ FAB-61	Lockheed 282-1B Hercules	3549	ex 58-0750	
☐ FAB-65	Lockheed 282-1B Hercules	3588	ex 59-1536	
☐ FAB-66	Lockheed 282-1B Hercules	3560	ex TAM-66	
☐ FAB-90	Fokker F.27M Troopship 400M	10578	ex TAM-90	
☐ FAB-93	Fokker F.27M Troopship 400M	10599	ex TAM-93	
☐ FAB-96	CAIC MA60	0411	ex B-850L	
☐ FAB-97	CAIC MA60	0412	ex B-858L	
☐ FAB-99	British Aerospace 146 Srs.100	E1081	ex N81HN	
☐ FAB-100	British Aerospace 146 Srs.200	E2080	ex N290UE	
☐ FAB-101	British Aerospace 146 Srs.200	E2041	ex OY-RCZ	
☐ FAB-102	British Aerospace 146 Srs.200	E2023	ex G-CLHD	
☐ FAB-103	British Aerospace 146 Srs.200	E2040	ex EI-DJJ	
☐ FAB-104	British Aerospace 146 Srs.200	E2024	ex G-FLTB	[CBB]

CS- PORTUGAL (Republic of Portugal)

AEROVIP — Cascais-Tires

☐ CS-AYT	Dornier 228-200	8084	ex VP-FBK	
☐ CS-TGG	Dornier 228-202K	8160	ex D-CORA	
☐ CS-TLJ	Short SD.3-60	SH3692	ex OY-MUD	std Cascais

EURO ATLANTIC AIRWAYS — EuroAtlantic (MM/MMZ) — Lisbon (LIS)

☐ CS-TEB	Lockheed L-1011-500 Tristar	293A-1240	ex V2-LEO	Naughton Simao	[AMM]
☐ CS-TFK	Boeing 757-2G5	23983/161	ex N983MQ		
☐ CS-TFM	Boeing 777-212ER	28513/144	ex 9V-SRA		>BBG
☐ CS-TFS	Boeing 767-3Y0ER	25411/408	ex S9-DBW		
☐ CS-TFT	Boeing 767-3Y0ER	26208/505	ex S9-DBY		
☐ CS-TLO	Boeing 767-383ER	24318/257	ex N318SR		
☐ CS-TLX	Boeing 757-2G5	24176/173	ex TC-OGD		
☐ CS-TLZ	Boeing 767-375ERF	24086/248	ex N240LD		

HELIBRAVO AVIACAO — HeliBravo (HIB) — Cascais-Tires

☐ CS-HED	Aérospatiale AS350B2 Ecureuil	2669	ex D-HJOE	
☐ CS-HFK	Aérospatiale AS350B2 Ecureuil	3223	ex LX-HDS	
☐ CS-HFM	Aérospatiale AS350B2 Ecureuil	1690	ex D-HFSF	
☐ CS-HFN	Aérospatiale AS350B2 Ecureuil	2437	ex D-HHWW	
☐ EC-	Aérospatiale AS350B2 Ecureuil	2097	ex I-FLAO	
☐ EC-JPM	Aérospatiale AS350B2 Ecureuil	3547	ex I-PAMR	
☐ CS-DIQ	Pilatus PC-12/45	625	ex HB-FPU	
☐ CS-HFQ	Eurocopter EC130B4	3541	ex HB-ZEY	
☐ SP-SSL	PZL Swidnik W-3A2 Sokol	370508	ex SP-PSL	<PZL Swidnik
☐ SP-SWA	PZL Swidnik W-3A2 Sokol	310319	ex SP-SUP	<PZL Swindik

HELIPORTUGAL — Heliportugal (HPL) — Cascais-Tires

☐ CS-HDK	Aérospatiale AS350B2 Ecureuil	1871	ex D-HHFZ	>CJR as 5N-BHS
☐ CS-HEL	Aérospatiale AS350B2 Ecureuil	2594	ex D-HEPB	
☐ CS-HEO	Aérospatiale AS350B2 Ecureuil	1222	ex RP-C8880	>CJR as 5N-BHT
☐ CS-HFI	Aérospatiale AS350B2 Ecureuil	1216	ex PT-YJC	
☐ CS-HFO	Aérospatiale AS350B2 Ecureuil	1824	ex F-GFDL	
☐ CS-HFX	Aérospatiale AS350B2 Ecureuil	4081	ex F-WWXD	
☐ CS-HGG	Aérospatiale AS350B2 Ecureuil	9085		
☐ CS-HFV	Aérospatiale SA365N Dauphin 2	6338	ex N661ME	
☐ CS-HGA	Aérospatiale SA365N Dauphin 2	6336	ex JA9978	
☐ CS-HGD	Aérospatiale SA365N Dauphin 2	6218	ex F-ONVU	
☐ CS-HGV	Aérospatiale SA365N Dauphin 2	6829		
☐ CS-HGW	Aérospatiale SA365N Dauphin 2	6830		
☐ F-OIBJ	Aérospatiale SA365N Dauphin 3	6089	ex N2XJ	
☐ F-OJTU	Aérospatiale SA365N Dauphin 2	6841		
☐ 5N-BIK	Aérospatiale SA365N Dauphin 3	6138	ex F-GNVS	>CJR
☐ CS-HEX	Eurocopter EC120B Colibri	1183	ex F-WQDV	
☐ CS-HFP	Eurocopter EC130B4	4033	ex F-WQDB	
☐ CS-HGQ	Agusta AW139	31057	ex N915DH	
☐ CS-HGU	Agusta AW139	31143		
☐ CS-HMF	Kamov Ka-32A11BC	9907		

HELISUL	Sul (HSU)				Cascais-Tires
☐ CS-HEN	Aérospatiale AS350BA Ecureuil	1845	ex LN-OPC		
☐ CS-HEZ	Bell 212	30557	ex EC-GHP		<HSE
☐ CS-HFB	Bell 206B JetRanger III	3640	ex D-HSBA		
☐ CS-HFJ	Bell 212	30684	ex EC-IEM		
☐ EC-HFD	Bell 412EP	36183	ex N52247		EMS <HSE
☐ EC-JLH	Bell 412EP	36374	ex N3119U		EMS <HSE

HI FLY	Sky Flyer (5K/HFY)				Lisbon (LIS)
☐ CS-TEI	Airbus A310-304	495	ex F-WWCO		>PFL♦
☐ CS-TEX	Airbus A310-304	565	ex F-WWCC		
☐ CS-TFZ	Airbus A330-243	1008	ex F-WW		
☐ CS-TMT	Airbus A330-322	096	ex F-WQSA		Op for Belgium AF
☐ CS-TQM	Airbus A340-313X	117	ex A6-EYC		
☐ OY-KBM	Airbus A340-313X	450	ex F-WWJD		♦

HTA HELICOPTERES	Heliapra (AHT)				Loulé-Morgado de Apre
☐ CS-HEE	Aérospatiale AS355F1 Ecureuil 2	5006	ex F-WQEA		
☐ CS-HEY	Aérospatiale AS350B2 Ecureuil	9027	ex D-HXST		
☐ CS-HFR	Aérospatiale AS350B2 Ecureuil	9054	ex D-HHTA		
☐ CS-HFZ	Aérospatiale AS350B3 Ecureuil	9090	ex LN-OCR		

LUZAIR	Lisbon Jet (LUZ)				Lisbon (LIS)
☐ CS-TFY	Airbus A320-232	1868	ex N548JB		
☐ CS-TMP	Lockheed L-1011-500 Tristar	293A-1248	ex SE-DVI		
☐ CS-TMR	Lockheed L-1011-500 Tristar	293B-1241	ex SE-DVF		[VCV]
☐ CS-TQI	Boeing 767-3S1ER	25221/384	ex N237W		

OMNI - AVIACAO E TECNOLOGIA	Omni (OC/OAV)				Cascais-Tires
☐ CS-DDU	Beech 200 Super King Air	BB-640	ex N47CF		
☐ CS-HCO	Agusta-Bell 206B JetRanger III	8678	ex I-BDPL		
☐ CS-HDS	Bell 222	47028	ex G-META	EMS	
☐ CS-TLU	Airbus A319-133X	1256	ex F-GSVU		[CJ]
☐ CS-TMU	Beech 1900D	UE-335	ex N23269	Castor	Op for PGA Express
☐ CS-TMV	Beech 1900D	UE-341	ex N23309	Esquilio	Op for PGA Express
☐ CS-	Piper PA-31P-350 Mojave	31P-8414023	ex N684B		

ORBEST	Orbest (OBS)				Lisbon (LIS)
☐ CS-TRA	Airbus A330-243	461	ex EC-IDB		

PGA EXPRESS					Lisbon (LIS)
☐ CS-TMU	Beech 1900D	UE-335	ex N23269	Castor	Op by OAV
☐ CS-TMV	Beech 1900D	UE-341	ex N23309	Esquilio	Op by OAV

PORTUGALIA AIRLINES	Portugalia (NI/PGA)				Lisbon (LIS)
☐ CS-TPG	Embraer ERJ-145EP	145014	ex PT-SYK	Melro	
☐ CS-TPH	Embraer ERJ-145EP	145017	ex PT-SYN	Pardal	
☐ CS-TPI	Embraer ERJ-145EP	145031	ex PT-SYZ	Cuco	
☐ CS-TPJ	Embraer ERJ-145EP	145036	ex PT-SZC	Chapim	
☐ CS-TPK	Embraer ERJ-145EP	145041	ex PT-SZG	Gaio	
☐ CS-TPL	Embraer ERJ-145EP	145051	ex PT-SZQ	Pisco	
☐ CS-TPM	Embraer ERJ-145EP	145095	ex PT-SBR	Rola	
☐ CS-TPN	Embraer ERJ-145EP	145099	ex PT-SBV	Brigao	
☐ CS-TPA	Fokker 100	11257	ex PH-LMF	Albatroz	
☐ CS-TPB	Fokker 100	11262	ex PH-EZE	Pelicano	
☐ CS-TPC	Fokker 100	11287	ex PH-LML	Flamingo	
☐ CS-TPD	Fokker 100	11317	ex EP-IDK	Condor	
☐ CS-TPE	Fokker 100	11342	ex PH-LNJ	Gaviao	
☐ CS-TPF	Fokker 100	11258	ex PH-EZD	Grifo	

SATA AIR ACORES	SATA (SP/SAT)				Ponta Delgada (PDL)
☐ CS-TRB	de Havilland DHC-8Q-202	476	ex C-FXBX	Graciosa	
☐ CS-TRC	de Havilland DHC-8Q-202	480	ex C-FXBZ	Faial	
☐ CS-TRD	de Havilland DHC-8-402Q	4291	ex C-GAUA		
☐ CS-TRE	de Havilland DHC-8-402Q	4295	ex C-GBIY		
☐ CS-TRF	de Havilland DHC-8-402Q	4297	ex C-GBJE		
☐ CS-TRG	de Havilland DHC-8-402Q	4298	ex C-GBJF		

SATA INTERNACIONAL		Air Azores (S4/RZO)			Ponta Delgada (PDL)
☐ CS-TGU	Airbus A310-304	571	ex F-GJKQ	Terceira	
☐ CS-TGV	Airbus A310-304	651	ex F-WQKR	Sao Miguel	
☐ CS-TKJ	Airbus A320-212	0795	ex C-FTDA	Pico	
☐ CS-TKK	Airbus A320-214	2390	ex F-WWII	Corvo	
☐ CS-TKL	Airbus A320-214	2425	ex F-WWBH	Sao Jorge	
☐ CS-TKM	Airbus A310-304	661	ex JY-AGL	Autonomia	
☐ CS-TKN	Airbus A310-325ET	624	ex TF-ELR	Macaronesia	<AUA
☐ CS-TKO	Airbus A320-214	3891	ex F-WWDC	Diaspora	

TAP AIR PORTUGAL		Air Portugal (TP/TAP)			Lisbon (LIS)
Member of Star Alliance					
☐ CS-TTA	Airbus A319-111	0750	ex D-AVYO	Vieira da Silva	
☐ CS-TTB	Airbus A319-111	0755	ex D-AVYJ	Gago Coutinho	
☐ CS-TTC	Airbus A319-111	0763	ex D-AVYS	Fernando Pessoa	
☐ CS-TTD	Airbus A319-111	0790	ex D-AVYC	Amadeo de Souza-Cardoso	
☐ CS-TTE	Airbus A319-111	0821	ex D-AVYN	Francisco d'Ollanda	
☐ CS-TTF	Airbus A319-111	0837	ex D-AVYL	Calouste Gulbenkian	
☐ CS-TTG	Airbus A319-111	0906	ex D-AVYN	Humberto Delgado	
☐ CS-TTH	Airbus A319-111	0917	ex D-AVYJ	Antonio Sergio	
☐ CS-TTI	Airbus A319-111	0933	ex D-AVYP	Eça de Queirós	
☐ CS-TTJ	Airbus A319-111	0979	ex D-AVYM	Eusébio	
☐ CS-TTK	Airbus A319-111	1034	ex D-AVYL	Miguel Torga	
☐ CS-TTL	Airbus A319-111	1100	ex D-AVYX	Almeida Garrett	
☐ CS-TTM	Airbus A319-111	1106	ex D-AVWR	Alexandre Herculano	
☐ CS-TTN	Airbus A319-111	1120	ex D-AVYI	Camilo Castelo Branco	
☐ CS-TTO	Airbus A319-111	1127	ex D-AVYH	Antero de Quental	
☐ CS-TTP	Airbus A319-111	1165	ex D-AVWV	Josefa d'Obidos	
☐ CS-TTQ	Airbus A319-112	0629	ex SU-LBF	Agostinho da Silva	
☐ CS-TTR	Airbus A319-112	1756	ex C-GJWE	Soares dos Reis	
☐ CS-TTS	Airbus A319-112	1765	ex C-GJWF	Guilhermina Suggia	
☐ CS-TMW	Airbus A320-214	1667	ex F-WWII	Luisa Todi	
☐ CS-TNB	Airbus A320-211	0191	ex F-WWDH	Sophia de Mello Breyner	
☐ CS-TNG	Airbus A320-214	0945	ex F-WWIX	Mouzinho de Silveira	
☐ CS-TNH	Airbus A320-214	0960	ex F-WWBH	Almada Negreiros	
☐ CS-TNI	Airbus A320-214	0982	ex F-WWDF	Aquilino Ribeiro	
☐ CS-TNJ	Airbus A320-214	1181	ex F-WWDS	Florbela Espanca	
☐ CS-TNK	Airbus A320-214	1206	ex F-WWIL	Teofilo Braga	
☐ CS-TNL	Airbus A320-214	1231	ex F-WWIJ	Vitorino Nemésio	
☐ CS-TNM	Airbus A320-214	1799	ex F-WWIF	Natalia Correia	
☐ CS-TNN	Airbus A320-214	1816	ex F-WWID	Gil Vicente	
☐ CS-TNP	Airbus A320-214	2178	ex 9H-AER	Alexandre O'NeillStar Alliance c/s	
☐ CS-TNQ	Airbus A320-214	3769	ex F-WWDQ	Jose Regio	
☐ CS-TNR	Airbus A320-214	3883	ex F-WWIU	Luis De Freitas Branco	
☐ CS-TNS	Airbus A320-214	4021	ex F-WWDM	D Afonso Henriques	
☐ CS-TNT	Airbus A320-214	4095	ex F-WWDI	Rafael Bordalo Pinheiro	
☐ CS-TNU	Airbus A320-214	4106	ex F-WWDR	Columbano Bordalo Pinheiro	
☐ CS-TNV	Airbus A320-214	4145	ex F-WWIY	Grao Vasco	
☐ CS-TQD	Airbus A320-214	0870	ex HB-IJT	Eugénio de Andrade	
☐ CS-TJE	Airbus A321-211	1307	ex D-AVZM	Pero Vaz de Caminha	
☐ CS-TJF	Airbus A321-211	1399	ex D-AVZI	Luis Vaz de Camões	
☐ CS-TJG	Airbus A321-211	1713	ex D-AVZS	Amalia Rodrigues	
☐ CS-TOE	Airbus A330-223	305	ex D-AXEL	Pedro Alvares Cabral	
☐ CS-TOF	Airbus A330-223	308	ex D-ARND	Infante D Henrique	
☐ CS-TOG	Airbus A330-223	312	ex D-ARNO	Bartolomeu de Gusmão	
☐ CS-TOH	Airbus A330-223	181	ex OE-LAO	Nuno GonçalvesStar Alliance c/s	
☐ CS-TOI	Airbus A330-223	195	ex OE-LAN	Damião de Góis	
☐ CS-TOJ	Airbus A330-223	223	ex OE-LAM	D João II 'O Príncipe Perfeito'	
☐ CS-TOK	Airbus A330-223	317	ex OE-LAP	Padre António Vieira	
☐ CS-TOL	Airbus A330-223	877	ex F-WWKF	Joao Goncalves Zarco	
☐ CS-TOM	Airbus A330-202	899	ex F-WWKN	Vasco da Gama	
☐ CS-TON	Airbus A330-202	904	ex F-WWKT	Joao XXI	
☐ CS-TOO	Airbus A330-202	914	ex F-WWYL	Fernao de Magalhaes	
☐ CS-TOP	Airbus A330-202	934	ex F-WWKZ	Pedro Nunes	
☐ CS-TOA	Airbus A340-312	041	ex F-WWJB	Fernao Mendes Pinto	
☐ CS-TOB	Airbus A340-312	044	ex F-WWJN	D. Joao de Castro	
☐ CS-TOC	Airbus A340-312	079	ex F-WWJS	Wenceslao de Moraes	
☐ CS-TOD	Airbus A340-312	091	ex F-WWJA	D. Francisco de Almeida	

WHITE		Young Sky (WHT)		Lisbon (LIS)
☐ CS-TDI	Airbus A310-308	573	ex JY-AGK	
☐ CS-TKI	Airbus A310-304	448	ex C-GRYA	
☐ CS-TQK	Airbus A320-232	2204	ex 9V-TAA Flypurple	
☐ CS-TQO	Airbus A320-214	0548	ex F-GYFL	◆

CU-   CUBA (Republic of Cuba)

AEROCARIBBEAN		AeroCaribbean (7L/CRN)		Havana (HAV)
☐ CU-T1509	ATR 42-300	009	ex CU-T1296	
☐ CU-T1512	ATR 42-300	136	ex CU-T1298	
☐ CU-T1544	ATR 72-212	472	ex F-WQNG	
☐ CU-T1545	ATR 72-212	473	ex F-WQNI	
☐ CU-T1547	ATR 72-212	485	ex F-WQNB	
☐ CU-T1550	ATR 42-300	014	ex PP-PTE	<Trip L/A
☐ CU-T1506	Antonov An-26	87306710	ex CU-T110	
☐ CU-C1515	Ilyushin Il-18GrM	188010805	ex CU-C132	Frtr
☐ CU-T1532	Ilyushin Il-18D	188010904	ex CU-T131	stored Holguin
☐ CU-T1534	Yakovlev Yak-40	9731754	ex CU-T1212	stored
☐ CU-T1537	Yakovlev Yak-40	9021360	ex CU-T1450	
☐ CU-T1538	Yakovlev Yak-40	9021260	ex CU-T1449	
☐ CU-T1551	Embraer EMB.110P1 Bandeirante	110132	ex PT-GKV	

AEROGAVIOTA		Gaviota (KG/GTV)		Havana (HAV)
☐ CU-T1402	Antonov An-26B	12605	ex 14-02	
☐ CU-T1403	Antonov An-26B	12905	ex 14-03	
☐ CU-T1404	Antonov An-26B	12906	ex 14-04	
☐ CU-T1406	Antonov An-26B	13502	ex 14-06	
☐ CU-T1408	Antonov An-26	6903	ex 14-28	
☐ CU-T1417	Antonov An-26			
☐ CU-T1420	Antonov An-26	87306607	ex 14-20	
☐ CU-T1421	Antonov An-26	6610	ex 14-21	status uncertain
☐ CU-T1425	Antonov An-26	6904	ex 14-25	
☐ CU-T1426	Antonov An-26	5603	ex 14-26	
☐ CU-T1428	Antonov An-26B	11303	ex 14-28	
☐ CU-T1429	Antonov An-26	7006	ex 14-29	
☐ CU-T1432	Antonov An-26	7306	ex 14-32	status uncertain
☐ CU-T1433	Antonov An-26	7309	ex 14-33	status uncertain
☐ CU-T1434	Antonov An-26	7701	ex 14-34	
☐ CU-T1435	Antonov An-26	7702	ex 14-35	
☐ CU-T1240	ATR 42-500	617	ex F-WWLB	VIP lsd to/ op in CUB c/s
☐ CU-T1454	ATR 42-500	616	ex F-WWLA	
☐ CU-T1455	ATR 42-500	618	ex F-WWLC	
☐ CU-T1456	ATR 42-500	619	ex F-WWLD	
☐ CU-H1423	Mil Mi-8T			
☐ CU-H1424	Mil Mi-8P			
☐ CU-H1427	Mil Mi-8PS			
☐ CU-H1429	Mil Mi-17 (Mi-8MTV-1)			
☐ CU-H1430	Mil Mi-17 (Mi-8MTV-1)			
☐ CU-H1431	Mil Mi-8P			
☐ CU-H1436	Mil Mi-8T			

AEROTAXI		Seraer (CNI)		Havana (HAV)
☐ CU-T1540	Embraer EMB.110C Bandeirante	110091	ex CU-T1108	
☐ CU-T1541	Embraer EMB.110C Bandeirante	110116	ex CU-T1109	
☐ CU-T1542	Embraer EMB.110C Bandeirante	110136	ex PT-GKY	

CUBANA DE AVIACION		Cubana (CU/CUB)		Havana (HAV)
☐ CU-T1214	Antonov An-24RV	47309404	ex CU-T923	
☐ CU-T1223	Antonov An-24RV	47309405	ex CU-T924	
☐ CU-T1244	Antonov An-24RV	57310301	ex JU-1011	
☐ CU-T1257	Antonov An-24RV	37309104	ex CU-T1536	
☐ CU-T1260	Antonov An-24RV	57310307	ex CCCP-47307	La Pinta
☐ CU-T1263	Antonov An-24RV	47309610	ex RA-46678	
☐ CU-T1267	Antonov An-24RV	47309907	ex CCCP-46696	
☐ CU-T1228	Antonov An-26B	12604	ex CU-T1401	

☐ CU-T1229	Antonov An-26B	13501	ex CU-T1405		
☐ CU-T1240	ATR 42-500	617	ex F-WWLB		VIP Lsd fr/ op by GTV
☐ CU-T1280	Ilyushin Il-62M	3749648		15 de Febrero	stored?
☐ CU-T1282	Ilyushin Il-62M	2052456			[HAV]
☐ CU-T1284	Ilyushin Il-62M	4053732			
☐ CU-T1250	Ilyushin Il-96-300	74393202015			
☐ CU-T1251	Ilyushin Il-96-300	74393202016			
☐ CU-T1254	Ilyushin Il-96-300	74393202017			
☐ CU-	Ilyushin Il-96-300				o/o
☐ CU-C1700	Tupolev Tu-204-100SE	1450744664036	ex RA-64035		
☐ CU-T1701	Tupolev Tu-204-100E	1450743164035	ex RA-64036		
☐ CU-T1702	Tupolev Tu-204-100E	1450743164042	ex RA-64042		
☐ CU-C1703	Tupolev Tu-204-100SE	1450744664037			
☐ CU-T1247	Yakovlev Yak-42D	4520424309017	ex UN-42712		
☐ CU-T1255	Yakovlev Yak-42D	4520424116664	ex RA-42443		
☐ CU-T1704	Yakovlev Yak-42D	4520424711397	ex CU-T1246		
☐ CU-T1707	Yakovlev Yak-42D	4520423016269	ex UR-CFA		◆
☐ CU-T1708	Yakovlev Yak-42D	4520423606235	ex UR-CFH		◆
☐ CU-T1709	Yakovlev Yak-42D	4520424811442	ex RA-42364		◆

CX-   URUGUAY (Republic of Uruguay)

AEROMAS   Aeromas Express (MSM)   Montevideo-Carrasco (MVD)

☐ CX-BDI	Piper PA-23-250 Aztec B	27-2265	ex N5217Y		
☐ CX-BRM	Beech A80 Queen Air	LD-200	ex N326JB	Excalibur Queenaire conv	[MVD]
☐ CX-MAS	Embraer EMB.110P1 Bandeirante	110393	ex N91DA		
☐ CX-MAX	Cessna 208A Caravan I	20800042	ex ZP-TYT		
☐ LV-LHO	Beech 65-B90 King Air	LJ-428	ex N74GR		

AIR CLASS   Acla (QD/QCL)   Montevideo-Carrasco (MVD)

☐ CX-CAF	British Aerospace Jetstream 41	41101	ex N333UE		
☐ CX-CLA	Swearingen SA.227AC Metro III	AC-736	ex N339LC		Op for DHL
☐ CX-CLS	Swearingen SA.227AC Metro III	AC-755B	ex N27465		
☐ CX-CSS	Swearingen SA.227AC Metro III	AC-642	ex N821BC		
☐ CX-LAS	Swearingen SA.227AC Metro III	AC-482	ex N784C		

BQB LINEAS AÉREAS   Montevideo-Carrasco (MVD)

☐ CX-JCL	ATR 72-212A	805	ex F-WWEQ	Jean Mermoz	◆
☐ CX-JPL	ATR 72-212A	816	ex F-WWEF	Antoine de Saint-Expurey	◆

PLUNA LINEAS AÉREAS URUGUAYAS   Pluna (PU/PUA)   Montevideo-Carrasco (MVD)

☐ CX-BON	Boeing 737-2A3	22737/830	ex PH-TSI	Gen Jose Artigas	[MVD]
☐ CX-BOO	Boeing 737-2A3	22738/834	ex PH-TSA	Brig Gen Juan A Lavalleja	[MVD]
☐ CX-BOP	Boeing 737-2A3	22739/844	ex PH-TSB	Gen Fructuoso Rivera	[MVD]
☐ CX-PUF	Boeing 737-230	22135/781	ex LV-BBM		
☐ CX-CRA	Canadair CRJ-900	15165	ex C-FTMF		Blue c/s
☐ CX-CRB	Canadair CRJ-900	15169	ex C-		Turquoise c/s
☐ CX-CRC	Canadair CRJ-900	15175	ex C-		Red c/s
☐ CX-CRD	Canadair CRJ-900	15180	ex C-		Purple c/s
☐ CX-CRE	Canadair CRJ-900	15185	ex C-		Red c/s
☐ CX-CRF	Canadair CRJ-900	15204	ex C-		Blue c/s
☐ CX-CRH	Canadair CRJ-900	15233	ex C-		
☐ CX-CRI	Canadair CRJ-900	15234	ex C-		Purple c/s
☐ CX-CRK	Canadair CRJ-900	15239	ex C-		

C2-   NAURU (Republic of Nauru)

OUR AIRLINE   Air Nauru (ON/RON)   Brisbane, QLD (BNE)

☐ VH-INU	Boeing 737-3Y0	23684/1353	ex N323AW		<Govt of Nauru

C3- ANDORRA (Principality of Andorra)

HELIAND				La Massana Heliport
☐ F-GYDJ	Aérospatiale AS350B3 Ecureuil	3719	ex N5219F	Lsd to/op by SHP

HELITRANS	Grau Roig Heliport

Leases Aérospatiale Ecureuil helicopters from Heliswiss Iberica when required

C5- GAMBIA (Republic of The Gambia)

SLOK AIR INTERNATIONAL		Slok Gambia (S0/OKS)			Banjul (BJL)
☐ C5-EUN	Boeing 737-201 (Nordam 3)	22798/924	ex 5N-EUN	Ibrahim Babangida	
☐ C5-IFY	Boeing 737-201 (Nordam 3)	22797/916	ex 5N-IFY	Olusegun Obasanjo	
☐ C5-NYA	Boeing 737-201 (Nordam 3)	22799/932	ex 5N-NYA	John Kuffour	[PGF]
☐ C5-OBJ	Boeing 737-201 (Nordam 3)	22795/912	ex N253AU	Atiku Abubakar	
☐ C5-OUK	Boeing 737-201 (Nordam 3)	22796/914	ex N254AU	Yahya Jammeh	
☐ C5-ZNA	Boeing 737-201 (Nordam 3)	22806/938	ex 5N-ZNA	Ahmadu Bello	

C6- BAHAMAS (Commonwealth of the Bahamas)

ABACO AIR				Marsh Harbour (MHH)
☐ C6-BAA	Britten-Norman BN-2A-21 Islander	214	ex N214TL	
☐ C6-BFQ	Britten-Norman BN-2A-8 Islander	347	ex N69HA	
☐ C6-BFR	Aero Commander 500	825	ex N846VK	
☐ C6-BFS	Aero Commander 500	685	ex N6285B	
☐ C6-BHH	Britten-Norman BN-2B-26 Islander	2021	ex N599MS	
☐ C6-BHY	Aero Commander 500	834	ex N521SQ	

BAHAMASAIR		Bahamas (UP/BHS)		Nassau (NAS)
☐ C6-BFG	de Havilland DHC-8-311A	288	ex C-GESR	
☐ C6-BFH	de Havilland DHC-8-311A	291	ex C-GFOD	
☐ C6-BFJ	de Havilland DHC-8Q-311	323	ex N583DS	
☐ C6-BFO	de Havilland DHC-8-301	164	ex N802XV	
☐ C6-BFP	de Havilland DHC-8Q-311	309	ex N994DC	
☐ C6-BFM	Boeing 737-2K5 (Nordam 3)	22596/763	ex N231TA	
☐ C6-BFW	Boeing 737-2K5 (Nordam 3)	22601/833	ex N233TA	
☐ C6-BGK	Boeing 737-275	22086/667	ex C-GLPW	
☐ C6-BGL	Boeing 737-275 (AvAero 3)	22087/673	ex C-GMPW	

CAT ISLAND AIR				Nassau (NAS)
☐ C6-CAA	SAAB SF.340A	340A-122	ex N379KB	
☐ C6-CAH	Embraer EMB.110P1 Bandeirante	110249	ex C6-BHA	[NAS]
☐ C6-CAP	Embraer EMB.110P1 Bandeirante	110304	ex J8-VAZ	
☐ C6-CAT	Piper PA-23-250 Aztec E	27-7554083	ex N54779	

CHEROKEE AIR				Marsh Harbour (MHH)
☐ C6-BGS	Piper PA-23-250 Aztec F	27-7854067	ex N17MR	
☐ C6-SBH	Cessna 208B Caravan I	208B0822	ex N822SA	

FLAMINGO AIR				Nassau (NAS)
☐ C6-BGI	Piper PA-23-250 Aztec E	27-7405469	ex N4443W	
☐ C6-BGZ	Piper PA-23-250 Aztec D	27-4246	ex C-FINU	

ISLAND WINGS				Stella Maris (SML)
☐ C6-FLY	Piper PA-23-250 Aztec E	27-4622	ex N140FR	
☐ C6-FOX	Piper PA-23-250 Aztec D	27-4535	ex N139BP	

LEAIR CHARTER SERVICES				Nassau (NAS)
☐ C6-BGJ	Cessna 402C II	402C0106	ex VQ-THC	
☐ C6-CAB	Embraer EMB.110P1 Bandeirante	110198	ex G-ONEW	Dam 25/02/2008
☐ C6-LEE	Piper PA-23-250 Aztec F	27-7654049	ex N62568	
☐ C6-PDX	Embraer EMB.110P1 Bandeirante	110288	ex OO-SKU	[NAS]

2

MAJOR'S AIR SERVICES — Freeport (FPO)

☐ C6-RRM	Beech C99	U-231	ex N141RM

PINEAPPLE AIR — Pineapple (PNP) — Nassau (NAS)

☐ N60MJ	Beech 1900D	UE-60	ex N85445
☐ N157PA	Beech 1900C	UB-56	ex N505RH
☐ N381CR	Beech 1900C	UB-69	ex N331CR
☐ C6-HAN	Beech C99	U-165	ex N42517

REGIONAL AIR — Nassau (NAS)

☐ C6-RAL	Cessna 208B Caravan I	208B0841	ex N1295G
☐ C6-RAS	Cessna 208B Caravan I	208B0693	ex N90HE

SALAMIS AVIATION — Nassau (NAS)

☐ N75X	Swearingen SA.227TT Merlin IIIC	TT-421	ex N90BJ
☐ N81WS	Swearingen SA.227TT Merlin IIIC	TT-480	ex N500DB

SEAIR AIRWAYS — Seair (DYL) — Nassau (NAS)

☐ C6-BGT	Piper PA-23-250 Aztec E	27-7305051	ex N89BB
☐ C6-BUS	Britten-Norman BN-2A-26 Islander	2040	ex N23US

SKY BAHAMAS — Sky Bahamas (SBM) — Nassau (NAS)

☐ C6-SBB	SAAB SF.340A	340A-149	ex N779SB	
☐ C6-SBC	SAAB SF.340A	340A-023	ex N778SB	
☐ C6-SBD	SAAB SF.340A	340A-021	ex N776SB	
☐ C6-SGB	SAAB SF.340A	340A-110	ex N110XJ	♦
☐ C6-SFB	Beech 1900D	UE-2	ex N2YV	♦

SOUTHERN AIR CHARTER — Southern (PL/SOA) — Nassau (NAS)

☐ C6-BGY	Piper PA-23-250 Aztec E	27-7554044	ex N166PG
☐ N70JL	Beech 100 King Air	B-87	ex N125DB
☐ N376SA	Beech 1900C	UB-72	ex N504RH
☐ N378SA	Beech 1900C	UB-31	ex N196GA

STELLA MARIS AVIATION — Stella Maris (SML)

☐ C6-	Aero Commander 500B	500B-1520-184	ex N175AC
☐ C6-	Piper PA-31-350 Chieftain	31-7952234	ex N750SC

VISION AIR — Freeport (FPO)

☐ N888MX	Beech 1900C	UB-39	ex N502CG

WESTERN AIR — (WST) — Freeport (FPO)

☐ C6-FPO	Swearingen SA.227AC Metro III	AC-652	ex N26877	
☐ C6-JER	Swearingen SA.227AC Metro III	AC-588	ex N892MA	
☐ C6-KER	Swearingen SA.227AC Metro III	AC-595	ex N385PH	
☐ C6-REX	Swearingen SA.227AC Metro III	AC-649	ex N26861	[REX]
☐ C6-SAD	Swearingen SA.227AC Metro III	AC-746B	ex N46NE	
☐ C6-SAR	Swearingen SA.227AC Metro III	AC-598	ex N3116Z	
☐ C6-HBW	SAAB SF.340A	340A-067	ex N712MG	
☐ C6-JAY	SAAB SF.340A	340A-120	ex N418MW	
☐ C6-RMW	SAAB SF.340A	340A-121	ex N121CQ	
☐ C6-SLR	SAAB SF.340B	340B-248	ex XA-TUB	
☐ C6-VIP	SAAB SF.340A	340A-098	ex N98XJ	♦
☐ C6-WAL	Piper PA-31-350 Navajo Chieftain	31-7652129	ex N70FS	
☐ N900MX	Beech 1900C	UB-55	ex N155GA	

C9- MOZAMBIQUE (Republic of Mozambique)

LAM - LINHAS AEREAS DE MOCAMBIQUE — Mozambique (TM/LAM) — Maputo (MPM)

☐ C9-AUL	de Havilland DHC-8-402Q	4019	ex LN-RDC	
☐ C9-AUM	de Havilland DHC-8-402Q	4020	ex LN-RDE	
☐ C9-BAJ	Boeing 737-205	23464/1223	ex N464BA	Pemba
☐ C9-BAO	Boeing 737-205 (Nordam 3)	23467/1245	ex XA-ABC	Quirimbas
☐ C9-EMA	Embraer ERJ-190AR	19000301	ex PT-TZP	Cobue
☐ C9-EMB	Embraer ERJ-190AR	19000309	ex PT-TZX	Chiloane

MOCAMBIQUE EXPRESSO		Mozambique Express (MXE)		Maputo / Beira (MPM/BEW)
☐ C9-ASV	Beech 200C Super King Air	BL-21	ex N3831T	
☐ C9-AUK	British Aerospace Jetstream 41	41044	ex ZS-NUO	
☐ ZS-AAB	Embraer EMB.120RT Brasilia	120228	ex N248CA	

STA - SOCIEDADE DE TRANSPORTS AÉREOS			Maputo (MPM)

Operates services with Islanders leased from sister company TTA and other aircraft as required

TRANSAIRWAYS		(TWM)		Maputo/Beira (MPM/BEW)
☐ 3D-BCI	Embraer EMB.120ER Brasilia	120139	ex N283UE	
☐ 3D-BEE	Beech 1900C-1	UC-148	ex N148YV	
☐ 3D-NVA	LET L-410UVP-E3	882035	ex 3D-ZZM	
☐ 3D-NVC	LET L-410UVP	831033	ex 5Y-BLC	Sluffy

TTA – SOCIEDADE DE TRANSPORTE E TRABALHO AEREO		Kanimanbo (TTA)		Maputo (MPM)
☐ C9-AMH	Piper PA-32-300 Cherokee Six C	32-40682	ex ZS-IGO	[MPM]
☐ C9-AOV	Britten-Norman BN-2A-3 Islander	624	ex G-AYJF	
☐ C9-APD	Britten-Norman BN-2A-9 Islander	683	ex G-AZXO	

D-   GERMANY (Federal Republic of Germany)

ADVANCED AVIATION			Bad Saulgau / Bangui (-/BGF)
☐ D-CAAL	Dornier 228-202K	8152	ex CS-TGH	
☐ D-FINA	Cessna 208B Caravan I	208B0475	ex N1202D	
☐ D-FISH	Cessna 208 Caravan I	20800363	ex N41145	
☐ D-FLIP	Cessna 208B Caravan I	208B0331	ex N3331	
☐ D-ISIS	Dornier 228-200	8007	ex RP-C2817	
☐ D4-CBK	Dornier 228-212	8222	ex 7Q-YKS	Op for Guardia Costiera

AEROLINE		Sylt-Air (7E/AWU)		Westerland (GWT)
☐ D-GFPG	Partenavia P.68B	170		
☐ D-IOLB	Cessna 404 Titan II	404-0691	ex SE-IVG	

AEROLOGIC		(BOX)	Leipzig-Halle (LEJ)
☐ D-AALA	Boeing 777-FZN	36001/780	
☐ D-AALB	Boeing 777-FZN	36002/799	ex N5017Q
☐ D-AALC	Boeing 777-FZN	36003/836	
☐ D-AALD	Boeing 777-FZN	36004/838	
☐ D-AALE	Boeing 777-FZN	36198/872	♦
☐ D-AALF	Boeing 777-FZN	36201/881	♦
☐ D-AALG	Boeing 777-FZN	36199/894	♦
☐ D-AALH	Boeing 777-FZN	36200/904	♦

AIR CARGO GERMANY		(6U/ACX)	Frankfurt Hahn (HHN)
☐ D-ACGA	Boeing 747-409(BDSF)	24311/869	ex N481AT
☐ D-ACGB	Boeing 747-409(BDSF)	24312/954	ex N482AT
☐ D-ACGC	Boeing 747-412BCF	24975/838	ex PH-MPQ ♦

AIR HAMBURG			Uetersen (QSM)
☐ D-IAEB	Britten-Norman BN-2A-6 Islander	218	ex OH-BNB

AIR SERVICE BERLIN			Berlin-Schonefeld (SXF)
☐ D-CXXX	Douglas DC-3	16124/32872	ex G-AMPZ Jack Bennett

AIR SERVICE WILDGRUBER			Friedrichshafen-Loewental (FDH)
☐ D-IEXE	Beech 99	U-46	ex LN-SAX Op for Skydive Portugal

AIRBERLIN		AirBerlin (AB/BER)		Berlin-Tegel (TXL)
☐ D-ABGA	Airbus A319-132	2383	ex N807BR	
☐ D-ABGC	Airbus A319-132	2468	ex N815BR	
☐ D-ABGH	Airbus A319-112	3245	ex D-AVWE	
☐ D-ABGI	Airbus A319-112	3346	ex D-AVYU	
☐ D-ABGJ	Airbus A319-112	3415	ex D-AVYI	
☐ D-ABGK	Airbus A319-112	3447	ex D-AVYS	
☐ D-ABGL	Airbus A319-112	3586	ex D-AVYF	

☐	D-ABGN	Airbus A319-112	3661	ex D-AVYU	
☐	D-ABGO	Airbus A319-112	3689	ex D-AVWF	
☐	D-ABGP	Airbus A319-112	3728	ex D-AVWF	
☐	D-ABGQ	Airbus A319-112	3700	ex D-AVWM	
☐	D-ABGR	Airbus A319-112	3704	ex D-AVWJ	
☐	D-ABGS	Airbus A319-112	3865	ex D-AVWD	
☐	D-ABDA	Airbus A320-214	2539	ex F-WWIR	
☐	D-ABDB	Airbus A320-214	2619	ex F-WWDK	
☐	D-ABDC	Airbus A320-214	2654	ex F-WWIN	
☐	D-ABDD	Airbus A320-214	2685	ex F-WWIB	
☐	D-ABDE	Airbus A320-214	2696	ex F-WWDI	
☐	D-ABDG	Airbus A320-214	2835	ex F-WWIB	
☐	D-ABDI	Airbus A320-214	2853	ex F-WWIR	[PAD]♦
☐	D-ABDJ	Airbus A320-214	2865	ex F-WWBB	[DUS]♦
☐	D-ABDP	Airbus A320-214	3093	ex F-WWIT	
☐	D-ABDQ	Airbus A320-214	3121	ex F-WWBD	
☐	D-ABDR	Airbus A320-214	3242	ex F-WWBP	
☐	D-ABDS	Airbus A320-214	3289	ex F-WWDS	
☐	D-ABDU	Airbus A320-214	3516	ex D-AVVC	
☐	D-ABDW	Airbus A320-214	3945	ex F-WWDX	
☐	D-ABDX	Airbus A320-214	3995	ex F-WWDG	
☐	D-ABDY	Airbus A320-214	4013	ex F-WWIG	
☐	D-ABFA	Airbus A320-214	4101	ex D-AVVK	
☐	D-ABFB	Airbus A320-214	4128	ex F-WWIQ	
☐	D-ABFC	Airbus A320-214	4161	ex D-AVVP	
☐	D-ABFD	Airbus A320-214	4187	ex D-AVVY	♦
☐	D-ABFE	Airbus A320-214	4269	ex D-AXAE	♦
☐	D-ABFF	Airbus A320-214	4329	ex D-AXAP	♦
☐	D-ABFG	Airbus A320-214	4291	ex D-AXAG	♦
☐	D-ABFK	Airbus A320-214	4433	ex D-AVVQ	♦
☐	D-ABFL	Airbus A320-214	4463	ex D-AXAC	♦
☐	D-ABFM	Airbus A320-214	4478	ex F-WWDJ	♦
☐	D-ABFN	Airbus A320-214	4510	ex F-WWBK	♦
☐	D-ABFO	Airbus A320-214	4565	ex D-AVVA	♦
☐	D-ABFP	Airbus A320-214	4506	ex D-AXAS	o/o♦
☐	D-	Airbus A320-214		ex	o/o♦
☐	D-	Airbus A320-214		ex	o/o♦
☐	D-	Airbus A320-214		ex	o/o♦
☐	D-	Airbus A320-214		ex	o/o♦
☐	D-	Airbus A320-214		ex	o/o♦
☐	D-	Airbus A320-214		ex	o/o♦
☐	D-ALTB	Airbus A320-214	1385	ex F-WWIT	[DUS]♦
☐	D-ALTC	Airbus A320-214	1441	ex F-WWBQ	[DUB]♦
☐	D-ALTD	Airbus A320-214	1493	ex F-WWDY	
☐	D-ALTE	Airbus A320-214	1504	ex OE-LTU	
☐	D-ALTF	Airbus A320-214	1553	ex OE-LTV	
☐	D-ALTH	Airbus A320-214	1797	ex F-WWDV	
☐	D-ALTJ	Airbus A320-214	1838	ex F-WWBM	
☐	D-ALTK	Airbus A320-214	1931	ex F-WWIH	
☐	D-ALTL	Airbus A320-214	2009	ex F-WWBO	
☐	D-ABCA	Airbus A321-211	3708	ex D-AVZO	
☐	D-ABCB	Airbus A321-211	3749	ex D-AVZC	
☐	D-ABCF	Airbus A321-211	1966	ex N221LF	
☐	D-ABCG	Airbus A321-211	1988	ex N341LF	
☐	D-ALSA	Airbus A321-211	1629	ex D-AVZC	
☐	D-ALSB	Airbus A321-211	1994	ex D-AVZR	
☐	D-ALSC	Airbus A321-211	2005	ex D-AVXI	
☐	D-ALSD	Airbus A321-211	1607	ex I-PEKN	
☐	D-AERK	Airbus A330-322	120	ex F-WWKN	
☐	D-AERQ	Airbus A330-322	127	ex F-WWKO	
☐	D-AERS	Airbus A330-322	171	ex C-FRAV	
☐	D-ALPA	Airbus A330-223	403	ex F-WWKO	
☐	D-ALPB	Airbus A330-223	432	ex F-WWYG	
☐	D-ALPC	Airbus A330-223	444	ex F-WWKD	
☐	D-ALPD	Airbus A330-223	454	ex F-WWKG	
☐	D-ALPE	Airbus A330-223	469	ex F-WWKO	
☐	D-ALPF	Airbus A330-223	476	ex F-WWKT	
☐	D-ALPG	Airbus A330-223	493	ex F-WWKI	
☐	D-ALPH	Airbus A330-223	739	ex F-WWYD	
☐	D-ALPI	Airbus A330-223	828	ex F-WWKI	
☐	D-ALPJ	Airbus A330-223	911	ex F-WWYA	
☐	D-ADIH	Boeing 737-3Y0	23921/1513	ex N921NB	
☐	D-AGEB	Boeing 737-322	24320/1670	ex N352UA	Spirit of Hinrich Bischoff

	Reg	Type	c/n	ex	Name	Status
☐	D-ABAA	Boeing 737-76Q	30271/740	ex N271CH		
☐	D-ABAB	Boeing 737-76Q	30277/947	ex N277CH		
☐	D-ABBS	Boeing 737-76N/W	28654/986	ex N743AL		
☐	D-ABBT	Boeing 737-76N/W	32582/1013	ex N744AL		
☐	D-ABBV	Boeing 737-7Q8	30629/1011	ex P4-CAS		
☐	D-ABBW	Boeing 737-7Q8	30642/1097	ex P4-DAS		
☐	D-ABLA	Boeing 737-76J/W	36114/2421	ex N1786B		
☐	D-ABLB	Boeing 737-76J/W	36115/2692			
☐	D-ABLC	Boeing 737-76J/W	36116/2730			
☐	D-ABLD	Boeing 737-76J/W	36117/2776	ex N1787B		
☐	D-ABLE	Boeing 737-76J/W	36873/3496	ex N1786B		♦
☐	D-ABLF	Boeing 737-76J/W	36874/3488			o/o♦
☐	D-	Boeing 737-76J/W				o/o♦
☐	D-	Boeing 737-76J/W				o/o♦
☐	D-	Boeing 737-76J/W				o/o♦
☐	D-	Boeing 737-76J/W				o/o♦
☐	D-	Boeing 737-76J/W				o/o♦
☐	D-AGEC	Boeing 737-76J/W	36118/2832	ex D-ABLE		>GMI
☐	D-AGEL	Boeing 737-75B	28110/5	ex N1791B		Lsd to GMI
☐	D-AGEN	Boeing 737-75B	28100/16	ex N1789B		>GMI
☐	D-AGEP	Boeing 737-75B	28102/18	ex N5573B		>GMI
☐	D-AGER	Boeing 737-75B	28107/27	ex N1002R		>GMI
☐	D-AGES	Boeing 737-75B	28108/28			>GMI
☐	D-AGEU	Boeing 737-75B	28104/39			>GMI
☐	D-AHIA	Boeing 737-73S	29082/229	ex D-ASKH		<HLX
☐	D-AHIA	Boeing 737-73S	29082/229	ex D-ASKH		<TUI
☐	D-AHXA	Boeing 737-7K5/W	30714/2202	ex N1786B		<TUI
☐	D-AHXB	Boeing 737-7K5/W	30717/2228			♦
☐	D-AHXC	Boeing 737-7K5/W	34693/2260			♦
☐	D-AHXD	Boeing 737-7K5/W	30726/2298			<TUI
☐	D-AHXE	Boeing 737-7K5/W	35135/2451		Robinson Club Piz Buin	<TUI
☐	D-AHXF	Boeing 737-7K5/W	35136/2465		Robinson Club Arosa	<TUI
☐	D-AHXH	Boeing 737-7K5/W	35282/2585			<TUI
☐	D-AHXG	Boeing 737-7K5/W	35140/2575			♦
☐	D-AHXJ	Boeing 737-7K5/W	35277/2609			♦
☐	D-ABAF	Boeing 737-86J/W	30878/844	ex N1787B		
☐	D-ABAG	Boeing 737-86J/W	30879/871	ex N1786B		
☐	D-ABAP	Boeing 737-86J/W	28070/106			
☐	D-ABAQ	Boeing 737-86J/W	28071/133			
☐	D-ABAR	Boeing 737-86J/W	28072/147	ex N1786B		
☐	D-ABAS	Boeing 737-86J/W	28073/200	ex N1795B		
☐	D-ABAV	Boeing 737-86J/W	30498/450	ex N1787B		
☐	D-ABBA	Boeing 737-86J/W	30570/879	ex N1786B		
☐	D-ABBB	Boeing 737-86J/W	32624/961	ex N1798B		
☐	D-ABBC	Boeing 737-86J/W	32625/995	ex N1786B		
☐	D-ABBD	Boeing 737-86J/W	30880/1043			
☐	D-ABBE	Boeing 737-86J/W	30881/1067			
☐	D-ABBF	Boeing 737-86J/W	32917/1210			
☐	D-ABBG	Boeing 737-86J/W	32918/1255			
☐	D-ABBH	Boeing 737-86J/W	32919/1279			
☐	D-ABBI	Boeing 737-86J/W	32920/1293			
☐	D-ABBJ	Boeing 737-86Q/W	30286/1280	ex N1787B		
☐	D-ABBK	Boeing 737-8BK/W	33013/1317			
☐	D-ABBU	Boeing 737-8Q8	30627/752	ex P4-BAS		
☐	D-ABBX	Boeing 737-808	34969/2293			
☐	D-ABBY	Boeing 737-808	34970/2379	ex N1787B		
☐	D-ABBZ	Boeing 737-85F	30478/997	ex TC-SKC		
☐	D-ABKA	Boeing 737-82R	29329/224	ex TC-APG		
☐	D-ABKD	Boeing 737-86J/W	37742/2796			
☐	D-ABKE	Boeing 737-86J/W	37743/2834	ex N1787B		
☐	D-ABKF	Boeing 737-86J/W	37745/3044	ex N1787B		
☐	D-ABKG	Boeing 737-86J/W	37746/3109	ex N1786B		
☐	D-ABKH	Boeing 737-86J/W	37747/3120	ex N1786B		
☐	D-ABKI	Boeing 737-86J/W	37748/3157			
☐	D-ABKJ	Boeing 737-86J/W	37749/3176	ex N1786B		♦
☐	D-ABKK	Boeing 737-86J/W	37753/3261	ex N1787B		♦
☐	D-ABKL	Boeing 737-86J/W	37754/3306			♦
☐	D-ABKM	Boeing 737-86J/W	37755/3349	ex N1769B		♦
☐	D-ABKN	Boeing 737-86J/W	37756/3371			♦
☐	D-ABKO	Boeing 737-86J/W	37757/3377	ex N1786B		♦
☐	D-ABKP	Boeing 737-86J/W	37758/3439	ex N1787B		♦
☐	D-	Boeing 737-86J/W				o/o♦
☐	D-	Boeing 737-86J/W				o/o♦
☐	D-	Boeing 737-86J/W				o/o♦
☐	D-	Boeing 737-86J/W				o/o♦
☐	D-	Boeing 737-86J/W				o/o♦

☐ D-	Boeing 737-86J/W			o/o♦
☐ D-	Boeing 737-86J/W			o/o♦
☐ D-	Boeing 737-86J/W			o/o♦
☐ D-	Boeing 737-86J/W			o/o♦
☐ D-	Boeing 737-86J/W			o/o♦
☐ D-ABQA	de Havilland DHC-8-402Q	4223	ex C-FTID	
☐ D-ABQB	de Havilland DHC-8-402Q	4226	ex C-FTUM	
☐ D-ABQC	de Havilland DHC-8-402Q	4231	ex C-FUCI	
☐ D-ABQD	de Havilland DHC-8-402Q	4234	ex C-FUCS	
☐ D-ABQE	de Havilland DHC-8-402Q	4239	ex C-FURQ	
☐ D-ABQF	de Havilland DHC-8-402Q	4245	ex C-FVGV	
☐ D-ABQG	de Havilland DHC-8-402Q	4250	ex C-FVUN	
☐ D-ABQH	de Havilland DHC-8-402Q	4256	ex C-FWGO	
☐ D-ABQI	de Havilland DHC-8-402Q	4264	ex C-FXIW	
☐ D-ABQJ	de Havilland DHC-8-402Q	4274	ex C-FYGN	

ARCUS AIR		**Arcus Air (ZE/AZE)**		**Mannheim (MHG)**
☐ D-CAAM	Dornier 228-212	8205	ex D-CBDH	
☐ D-CAAR	Dornier 228-212	8211	ex 57+02	
☐ D-CAAZ	Dornier 228-212	8212	ex 57+03	
☐ D-CUTT	Dornier 228-212	8200	ex D-CBDC	

AUGSBURG AIRWAYS		**Augsburg Air (IQ/AUB)**		**Munich (MUC)**
☐ D-ADHA	de Havilland DHC-8-402Q	4028	ex C-GFBW	
☐ D-ADHB	de Havilland DHC-8-402Q	4029	ex C-GFCA	
☐ D-ADHC	de Havilland DHC-8-402Q	4045	ex C-GDIW	
☐ D-ADHD	de Havilland DHC-8-402Q	4056	ex C-GFYI	
☐ D-ADHE	de Havilland DHC-8-402Q	4066	ex C-GEOA	
☐ D-ADHP	de Havilland DHC-8-402Q	4003	ex C-FHUP	
☐ D-ADHQ	de Havilland DHC-8-402Q	4016	ex C-FSPV	
☐ D-ADHR	de Havilland DHC-8-402Q	4041	ex C-FRGT	
☐ D-ADHS	de Havilland DHC-8-402Q	4044	ex C-FRBO	
☐ D-ADHT	de Havilland DHC-8-402Q	4281	ex C-FYMQ	
☐ D-AEMA	Embraer ERJ-190LR	19000290	ex PT-TZE	
☐ D-AEMB	Embraer ERJ-190LR	19000297	ex PT-TZL	
☐ D-AEMC	Embraer ERJ-190LR	19000300	ex PT-TZO	
☐ D-AEMD	Embraer ERJ-190LR	19000305	ex PT-TZT	
☐ D-AEME	Embraer ERJ-190LR	19000308	ex PT-TXH	
☐ D-AEMF	Embraer ERJ-190LR	19000310	ex PT-TZY	
☐ D-AEMG	Embraer ERJ-190LR	19000404	ex PT-TYX	♦

AVANTI AIR		**Euroexpress (EEX)**		**Frankfurt (FRA)**
☐ D-ANFC	ATR 72-202	237	ex F-WWEG	
☐ D-BCRN	ATR 42-300	329	ex G-WLSH	
☐ D-BCRP	ATR 42-300 (QC)	158	ex F-WWEE	

BINAIR		**Binair (BID)**		**Munich (MUC)**
☐ D-CBIN	Swearingen SA.226AT Expediter IV	AT-440B	ex I-FSAD	
☐ D-CCCC	Swearingen SA.227AT Merlin IVC	AT-511	ex N600N	
☐ D-CKPP	Swearingen SA.227DC Metro 23	DC-805B	ex N715MQ	
☐ D-CPSW	Swearingen SA.227AC Metro III	AC-757B	ex F-GJPN	
☐ D-IBIN	Swearingen SA.226TC Metro II	TC-252	ex PH-RAZ	
☐ D-ICRK	Swearingen SA.226TC Metro II	TC-333	ex 4X-CSD	

BREMENFLY				**Bremen (BRE)**
☐ D-ABRF	Boeing 737-4Q8	26281/2380	ex N164LF	[SXF]♦

BUSINESSWINGS				**Kassel-Calden (KSF)**
☐ D-CUKT	Dornier 228-212	8192	ex LN-BER	
☐ D-FALK	Cessna 208 Caravan I	20800023	ex N9354F	
☐ D-FAST	Cessna 208 Caravan I	20800207	ex N208MC	
☐ D-IROL	Dornier 228-100	7003	ex SE-KHL	
☐ D-IVER	de Havilland DHC-6 Twin Otter 300	411	ex SE-IYP	

CIRRUS AIRLINES		**Cirrus (C9/RUS)**		**Saarbrücken-Ensheim (SCN)**
☐ D-BGAE	Dornier 328-300 (328JET)	3146	ex D-BDXC	
☐ D-BGAL	Dornier 328-300 (328JET)	3131	ex D-BDXN	
☐ D-BGAQ	Dornier 328-300 (328JET)	3130	ex D-BDXL	

☐ D-CCIR	Dornier 328-130	3100	ex D-CDXA		
☐ D-CIRA	Dornier 328-120	3077	ex HB-AEJ		
☐ D-CIRB	Dornier 328-110	3017	ex HB-AEF		
☐ D-CIRC	Dornier 328-100	3041	ex HB-AEI		
☐ D-CIRD	Dornier 328-110	3011	ex HB-AEG		
☐ D-CIRG	Dornier 328-110	3040	ex N340LS		o/o
☐ D-CIRI	Dornier 328-110	3005	ex TF-CSC		
☐ D-CIRJ	Dornier 328-110	3035	ex N335LS		o/o
☐ D-CIRK	Dornier 328-110	3050	ex N350AD		
☐ D-CIRL	Dornier 328-110	3075	ex N461PS		
☐ D-CIRM	Dornier 328-110	3068	ex N458PS		o/o
☐ D-CIRO	Dornier 328-110	3025	ex N328LS		o/o
☐ D-CIRP	Dornier 328-110	3006	ex TF-CSD		
☐ D-CIRT	Dornier 328-110	3093	ex TF-CSB		
☐ D-CIRU	Dornier 328-110	3033	ex N424JS		o/o
☐ D-CIRW	Dornier 328-110	3044	ex N430JS		o/o
☐ D-COSA	Dornier 328-110	3085	ex D-CDXR		
☐ D-CPRP	Dornier 328-110	3066	ex D-CDXL	Maximillian	
☐ D-CPRW	Dornier 328-110	3097	ex D-CDXY		
☐ D-CTOB	Dornier 328-110	3107	ex OE-LKH		Damaged 19/3/2008
☐ D-ALIA	Embraer ERJ-170LR	17000006	ex PT-SVD		
☐ D-ALIE	Embraer ERJ-170LR	17000059	ex PT-SVI		

CONDOR   *Condor (DE/CFG)*   *Frankfurt (FRA)*

☐ D-ABOA	Boeing 757-330/W	29016/804	ex N757X		
☐ D-ABOB	Boeing 757-330/W	29017/810	ex N6067B		
☐ D-ABOC	Boeing 757-330/W	29015/818	ex N6069B		
☐ D-ABOE	Boeing 757-330/W	29012/839	ex N1012N		
☐ D-ABOF	Boeing 757-330/W	29013/846			
☐ D-ABOG	Boeing 757-330/W	29014/849			
☐ D-ABOH	Boeing 757-330/W	30030/855	ex N1787B		
☐ D-ABOI	Boeing 757-330/W	29018/909	ex N1002R		
☐ D-ABOJ	Boeing 757-330/W	29019/915			
☐ D-ABOK	Boeing 757-330/W	29020/918	ex N1795B		♦
☐ D-ABOL	Boeing 757-330/W	29021/923			♦
☐ D-ABOM	Boeing 757-330/W	29022/926			
☐ D-ABON	Boeing 757-330/W	29023/929	ex N1003M		
☐					
☐ D-ABUA	Boeing 767-330ER/W	26991/455			
☐ D-ABUB	Boeing 767-330ER/W	26987/466			
☐ D-ABUC	Boeing 767-330ER/W	26992/470			
☐ D-ABUD	Boeing 767-330ER/W	26983/471			
☐ D-ABUE	Boeing 767-330ER/W	26984/518	ex N1788B		
☐ D-ABUF	Boeing 767-330ER/W	26985/537			
☐ D-ABUH	Boeing 767-330ER/W	26986/553	ex N6046P		
☐ D-ABUI	Boeing 767-330ER/W	26988/562			
☐ D-ABUZ	Boeing 767-330ER/W	25209/382	ex (N634TW)		

CONDOR BERLIN   *Condor Berlin (CIB)*   *Berlin-Schönefeld (SXF)*

☐ D-AICA	Airbus A320-212	0774	ex F-WWDN	
☐ D-AICC	Airbus A320-212	0809	ex F-WWIE	
☐ D-AICD	Airbus A320-212	0884	ex F-WWDE	
☐ D-AICE	Airbus A320-212	0894	ex F-WWDI	
☐ D-AICF	Airbus A320-212	0905	ex F-WWDP	
☐ D-AICG	Airbus A320-212	0957	ex F-WWBE	
☐ D-AICH	Airbus A320-212	0971	ex F-WWBY	
☐ D-AICI	Airbus A320-212	1381	ex F-WWIP	
☐ D-AICJ	Airbus A320-212	1402	ex F-WWDB	
☐ D-AICK	Airbus A320-212	1416	ex F-WWDZ	
☐ D-AICL	Airbus A320-212	1437	ex F-WWBG	
☐ D-AICN	Airbus A320-214	1968	ex G-TCKE	

CONTACT AIR   *Contactair (KIS)*   *Stuttgart (STR)*

☐ D-BMMM	ATR 42-500	546	ex F-WWLE	<EWG
☐ D-BPPP	ATR 42-500	581	ex F-WWLE	<EWG
☐ D-BQQQ	ATR 42-500	584	ex F-WWEP	<EWG [SCN]♦
☐ D-BSSS	ATR 42-500	602	ex F-WWLA	<EWG
☐ D-BTTT	ATR 42-500	603	ex F-WWLD	<EWG
☐ D-AFKA	Fokker 100	11517	ex B-12293	
☐ D-AFKB	Fokker 100	11527	ex PH-MJL	
☐ D-AFKC	Fokker 100	11496	ex PH-MJQ	
☐ D-AFKD	Fokker 100	11500	ex PH-MJR	
☐ D-AFKE	Fokker 100	11505	ex PH-MJP	

133

☐ D-AFKF	Fokker 100	11470	ex PH-MJK	
☐ D-AGPH	Fokker 100	11308	ex PH-CXH	
☐ D-AGPK	Fokker 100	11313	ex PH-CXK	>SWR

EAT LEIPZIG (BCS) Leipzig-Halle (LEJ)

☐ D-ALEA	Boeing 757-236 (SF)	22172/9	ex OO-DLN	♦
☐ D-ALEB	Boeing 757-236 (SF)	22173/10	ex OO-DPF	♦
☐ D-ALEC	Boeing 757-236 (SF)	22175/13	ex OO-DLQ	♦
☐ D-ALED	Boeing 757-236 (SF)	22179/24	ex OO-DLP	♦
☐ D-ALEE	Boeing 757-236 (SF)	22183/32	ex OO-DPB	♦
☐ D-ALEF	Boeing 757-236 (SF)	22189/58	ex OO-DPM	♦
☐ D-ALEG	Boeing 757-236 (SF)	23398/77	ex OO-DPO	♦
☐ D-ALEH	Boeing 757-236 (SF)	23492/89	ex OO-DPK	♦
☐ D-ALEI	Boeing 757-236 (SF)	23493/90	ex OO-DPJ	♦
☐ D-AELJ	Boeing 757-23APF	24971/340	ex OO-DLJ	♦
☐ D-ALEK	Boeing 757-236 (SF)	23533/93	ex OO-DPN	♦

EUROWINGS Eurowings (EW/EWG) Dortmund/Nuremberg (DTM/NUE)

☐ D-BMMM	ATR 42-500	546	ex F-WWLE	>KIS
☐ D-BPPP	ATR 42-500	581	ex F-WWLE	>KIS
☐ D-BQQQ	ATR 42-500	584	ex F-WWEP	>KIS [SCN]♦
☐ D-BSSS	ATR 42-500	602	ex F-WWLA	>KIS
☐ D-BTTT	ATR 42-500	603	ex F-WWLD	>KIS
☐ D-ACRA	Canadair CRJ-200LR	7567	ex C-FMNX	
☐ D-ACRB	Canadair CRJ-200LR	7570	ex C-FMOW	
☐ D-ACRC	Canadair CRJ-200LR	7573	ex C-FMNQ	
☐ D-ACRD	Canadair CRJ-200LR	7583	ex C-FMNB	
☐ D-ACRE	Canadair CRJ-200LR	7607	ex C-FMML	
☐ D-ACRF	Canadair CRJ-200LR	7619	ex C-FMLI	Goch
☐ D-ACRG	Canadair CRJ-200LR	7630	ex C-FMOW	
☐ D-ACRH	Canadair CRJ-200LR	7738	ex C-FMLF	Herzogenaurach
☐ D-ACRI	Canadair CRJ-200ER	7862	ex C-GZPA	
☐ D-ACRJ	Canadair CRJ-200LR	7864	ex C-GZOZ	
☐ D-ACRK	Canadair CRJ-200LR	7901	ex C-FVAZ	
☐ D-ACRL	Canadair CRJ-200LR	7902	ex C-FMND	
☐ D-ACRM	Canadair CRJ-200LR	7478	ex I-ADJA	
☐ D-ACRN	Canadair CRJ-200LR	7486	ex I-ADJB	
☐ D-ACRO	Canadair CRJ-200LR	7494	ex I-ADJC	
☐ D-ACRP	Canadair CRJ-200LR	7625	ex I-ADJD	
☐ D-ACRQ	Canadair CRJ-200LR	7629	ex I-ADJE	
☐ D-ACNA	Canadair CRJ-900NG	15229	ex C-GZQA	Amberg
☐ D-ACNB	Canadair CRJ-900NG	15230	ex C-GZQM	Wermelskirchen
☐ D-ACNC	Canadair CRJ-900NG	15236	ex C-GIBO	
☐ D-ACND	Canadair CRJ-900NG	15238	ex C-GIBT	
☐ D-ACNE	Canadair CRJ-900NG	15241	ex C-GICL	
☐ D-ACNF	Canadair CRJ-900NG	15243	ex C-GIAU	
☐ D-ACNG	Canadair CRJ-900NG	15245	ex C-GZQF	
☐ D-ACNH	Canadair CRJ-900NG	15247	ex C-GZQK	
☐ D-ACNI	Canadair CRJ-900NG	15248		
☐ D-ACNJ	Canadair CRJ-900NG	15249	ex C-GZQX	
☐ D-ACNK	Canadair CRJ-900NG	15251	ex C-GIBL	
☐ D-ACNL	Canadair CRJ-900NG	15252		♦
☐ D-ACNM	Canadair CRJ-900NG	15253		♦
☐ D-ACNN	Canadair CRJ-900NG	15254		♦
☐ D-ACNO	Canadair CRJ-900NG	15255		♦
☐ D-ACNP	Canadair CRJ-900NG	15259	ex C-GZQV	♦
☐ D-ACNQ	Canadair CRJ-900NG	15260	ex C-	♦

EXCELLENT AIR Excellent Air (GZA) Münster-Osnabruck

☐ D-IFUN	Beech 200 Super King Air	BB-575	ex D-ISJP	
☐ D-IICE	Beech 200 Super King Air	BB-269	ex N269D	EMS

FLM AVIATION FLM (FKI) Hamburg/ Kiel/ Parchim (HAM/KEL/-)

☐ D-CNAG	Swearingen SA.227DC Metro 23	DC-893B	ex N3032A	Op for Manx2
☐ D-CSAL	Swearingen SA.227AC Metro III	AC-601	ex I-FSAH	Op for Manx2
☐ D-GBRD	Partenavia P.68B	14	ex OY-DZR	
☐ D-IFFB	Beech 300LW Super King Air	FA-224	ex N56449	
☐ D-IHBL	Swearingen SA.227TT Merlin 300	TT-512A	ex N123GM	

134

FLUGDIENST FEHLHABER		Witchcraft (FFG)			Cologne (CGN)
☐ D-ISHY	Reims Cessna F406 Caravan II	F406-0027	ex PH-FWH		Frtr
☐ D-INUS	Reims Cessna F406 Caravan II	F406-0043	ex F-WQUD		Frtr

FRISIA LUFTVERKEHR				Norden-Norddeich (NOE)	
☐ D-IFKU	Britten-Norman BN-2B-20 Islander	2290	ex G-BVXY	Norderney	
☐ D-IFTI	Britten-Norman BN-2B-20 Islander	2299	ex G-BWYY	Norddeich	
☐ D-IFUT	Britten-Norman BN-2B-20 Islander	2300	ex G-OBNG	Juist	

GERMANIA		Germania (ST/GMI)			Cologne (CGN)
☐ D-	Airbus A319-1		ex		o/o♦
☐ D-	Airbus A319-1		ex		o/o♦
☐ D-	Airbus A319-1		ex		o/o♦
☐ D-	Airbus A319-1		ex		o/o♦
☐ D-	Airbus A319-1		ex		o/o♦
☐ D-ADII	Boeing 737-329	23775/1412	ex N775AA		
☐ D-AGEE	Boeing 737-35B	24238/1626	ex UR-GAG	Handel/Bach c/s	
☐ D-AGEG	Boeing 737-35B	24237/1624	ex UR-GAF		
☐ D-AGEJ	Boeing 737-3L9	24221/1604	ex OO-SEJ	Handel/Bach c/s	
☐ D-AGEK	Boeing 737-3M8	25015/1991	ex N799BB	Spirit of Peter Kiessling	
☐ D-AGEC	Boeing 737-76J/W	36118/2832	ex D-ABLE		<BER
☐ D-AGEL	Boeing 737-75B	28110/5	ex N1791B		<BER
☐ D-AGEN	Boeing 737-75B	28100/16	ex N1789B		<BER
☐ D-AGEP	Boeing 737-75B	28102/18	ex N5573B		<BER
☐ D-AGEQ	Boeing 737-75B	28103/23	ex N1787B		
☐ D-AGER	Boeing 737-75B	28107/27	ex N1002R		<BER
☐ D-AGES	Boeing 737-75B	28108/28			<BER
☐ D-AGET	Boeing 737-75B	28109/31			
☐ D-AGEU	Boeing 737-75B	28104/39			<BER
☐ D-AGPC	Fokker 100	11280	ex PH-CXC		[WOE]
☐ D-AGPD	Fokker 100	11281	ex PH-CXD		[WOE]

GERMANWINGS		German Wings (4U/GWI)			Cologne (CGN)
☐ D-AGWA	Airbus A319-132	2813	ex D-AVWM		
☐ D-AGWB	Airbus A319-132	2833	ex D-AVXI		
☐ D-AGWC	Airbus A319-132	2976	ex D-AVYX		
☐ D-AGWD	Airbus A319-132	3011	ex D-AVWB		
☐ D-AGWE	Airbus A319-132	3128	ex D-AVXB		
☐ D-AGWF	Airbus A319-132	3172	ex D-AVXG		
☐ D-AGWG	Airbus A319-132	3193	ex D-AVYS		
☐ D-AGWH	Airbus A319-132	3352	ex D-AVYX		
☐ D-AGWI	Airbus A319-132	3358	ex D-AVYZ		
☐ D-AGWJ	Airbus A319-132	3375	ex D-AVWB		
☐ D-AGWK	Airbus A319-132	3500	ex D-AVYW		
☐ D-AGWL	Airbus A319-132	3534	ex D-AVWB		
☐ D-AGWM	Airbus A319-132	3839	ex D-AVYQ		
☐ D-AGWN	Airbus A319-132	3841	ex D-AVYS		
☐ D-AGWO	Airbus A319-132	4166	ex D-AVWH		
☐ D-AGWP	Airbus A319-132	4227	ex D-AVYK		♦
☐ D-AGWQ	Airbus A319-132	4256	ex D-AVYP		♦
☐ D-AGWR	Airbus A319-132	4285	ex D-AVWS		♦
☐ D-AKNK	Airbus A319-112	1077	ex N718UW		
☐ D-AKNL	Airbus A319-112	1084	ex N719US		
☐ D-AKNM	Airbus A319-112	1089	ex N720US	Baden-Wurttemberg colours	
☐ D-AKNN	Airbus A319-112	1136	ex N726US		
☐ D-AKNO	Airbus A319-112	1147	ex N727UW	Berlin Bearbus	
☐ D-AKNP	Airbus A319-112	1155	ex N728UW		
☐ D-AKNQ	Airbus A319-112	1170	ex N729US		
☐ D-AKNR	Airbus A319-112	1209	ex N736US		
☐ D-AKNS	Airbus A319-112	1277	ex N743UW	Insel Rugen	
☐ D-AKNT	Airbus A319-112	2607	ex D-AVXQ		
☐ D-AKNU	Airbus A319-112	2628	ex D-AVWB		
☐ D-AKNV	Airbus A319-112	2632	ex D-AVWE		

GERMAN SKY AIRLINES		(GHY)			Dusseldorf (DUS)
☐ D-AGSA	Boeing 737-883	28323/625	ex OY-CJS		♦

HAMBURG INTERNATIONAL		Hamburg Jet (4R/HHI)			Hamburg (HAM)

Suspended operation 20/Oct/2010

HELOG LUFTTRANSPORT — Ainring / Salzburg

☐ D-HAXH	Aérospatiale SA.330J Puma	1410		Op for UN
☐ D-HAXI	Aérospatiale SA.330J Puma	1429		Op for UN
☐ D-HAXK	Aérospatiale SA.330J Puma	1442		Op for UN
☐ D-HAXL	Aérospatiale SA.330J Puma	1454		Op for UN
☐ D-HAXR	Aérospatiale SA.330J Puma	1553		Op for UN
☐ D-HAXS	Aérospatiale SA.330J Puma	1573		Op for UN
☐ D-HAXW	Aérospatiale SA.330J Puma	1594		Op for UN
☐ D-HMAX	Kaman K-1200 K-Max	A94-0021	ex OE-XKM	

LGW - LUFTFAHRTGESELLSCHAFT WALTER — Walter (HE/LGW)Dortmund (DTM)

☐ D-IKBA	Dornier 228-200	8066	ex D-CBDR
☐ D-ILWB	Dornier 228-200	8035	ex D-CDIZ
☐ D-ILWD	Dornier 228-200	8069	ex D-CHOF
☐ D-ILWS	Dornier 228-200	8002	ex D-CBDU
☐ D-IMIK	Dornier 228-200	8058	ex D-CMIC

LUFTHANSA — Lufthansa (LH/DLH) — Frankfurt (FRA)

Member of Star Alliance

☐ D-AIBA	Airbus A319-114	4141	ex D-AVWG		
☐ D-AIBB	Airbus A319-112	4182	ex D-AVWK		♦
☐ D-AIBC	Airbus A319-112	4332	ex D-AVXF		♦
☐ D-AIBD	Airbus A319-112	4455	ex D-AVYC		♦
☐ D-AIBE	Airbus A319-112	4511	ex D-AVYH		♦
☐ D-	Airbus A319-112		ex D-AV		o/o♦
☐ D-	Airbus A319-112		ex D-AV		o/o♦
☐ D-AILA	Airbus A319-114	0609	ex D-AVYF	Frankfurt an der Oder	
☐ D-AILB	Airbus A319-114	0610	ex D-AVYG	Lutherstadt Wittenberg	
☐ D-AILC	Airbus A319-114	0616	ex D-AVYI	Rüsselsheim	
☐ D-AILD	Airbus A319-114	0623	ex D-AVYL	Dinkelsbühl	
☐ D-AILE	Airbus A319-114	0627	ex D-AVYO	Kelsterbach	
☐ D-AILF	Airbus A319-114	0636	ex D-AVYS	Trier	
☐ D-AILH	Airbus A319-114	0641	ex D-AVYV	Norderstedt	
☐ D-AILK	Airbus A319-114	0679	ex D-AVYG	Aschaffenburg	
☐ D-AILL	Airbus A319-114	0689	ex D-AVYL	Marburg	
☐ D-AILM	Airbus A319-114	0694	ex D-AVYR	Friedrichshafen	
☐ D-AILN	Airbus A319-114	0700	ex D-AVYU	Idar-Oberstein	
☐ D-AILP	Airbus A319-114	0717	ex D-AVYA	Tübingen	
☐ D-AILR	Airbus A319-114	0723	ex D-AVYD	Tegernsee	
☐ D-AILS	Airbus A319-114	0729	ex D-AVYF	Heide	
☐ D-AILT	Airbus A319-114	0738	ex D-AVYN	Straubing	
☐ D-AILU	Airbus A319-114	0744	ex D-AVYI	Verden	
☐ D-AILW	Airbus A319-114	0853	ex D-AVYO	Donaueschingen	
☐ D-AILX	Airbus A319-114	0860	ex D-AVYS	Fellbach	
☐ D-AILY	Airbus A319-114	0875	ex D-AVYC	Schweinfurt	
☐ D-AIPA	Airbus A320-211	0069	ex F-WWII	Buxtehude	
☐ D-AIPB	Airbus A320-211	0070	ex F-WWIJ	Heidelberg	
☐ D-AIPC	Airbus A320-211	0071	ex F-WWIO	Braunschweig	
☐ D-AIPD	Airbus A320-211	0072	ex F-WWIP	Freiburg	
☐ D-AIPE	Airbus A320-211	0078	ex F-WWIU	Kassel	
☐ D-AIPF	Airbus A320-211	0083	ex F-WWDE	Deggendorf	
☐ D-AIPH	Airbus A320-211	0086	ex F-WWDJ	Münster	
☐ D-AIPK	Airbus A320-211	0093	ex F-WWDQ	Wiesbaden	
☐ D-AIPL	Airbus A320-211	0094	ex 7T-VKO	Ludwigshafen am Rhein	
☐ D-AIPM	Airbus A320-211	0104	ex F-WWIG	Troisdorf	
☐ D-AIPP	Airbus A320-211	0110	ex F-WWID	Starnberg	
☐ D-AIPR	Airbus A320-211	0111	ex F-WWIE	Kaufbeuren	
☐ D-AIPS	Airbus A320-211	0116	ex F-WWIK	Augsburg	
☐ D-AIPT	Airbus A320-211	0117	ex F-WWIL	Cottbus	
☐ D-AIPU	Airbus A320-211	0135	ex F-WWDB		
☐ D-AIPW	Airbus A320-211	0137	ex F-WWDD	Schwerin	
☐ D-AIPX	Airbus A320-211	0147	ex F-WWDN	Mannheim	
☐ D-AIPY	Airbus A320-211	0161	ex F-WWIA	Magdeburg	
☐ D-AIPZ	Airbus A320-211	0162	ex F-WWDS		
☐ D-AIQA	Airbus A320-211	0172	ex F-WWIK		
☐ D-AIQB	Airbus A320-211	0200	ex F-WWDJ	Bielefeld	
☐ D-AIQC	Airbus A320-211	0201	ex F-WWDL	Zwickau	
☐ D-AIQD	Airbus A320-211	0202	ex F-WWDM	Jena	
☐ D-AIQE	Airbus A320-211	0209	ex F-WWDY	Gera	
☐ D-AIQF	Airbus A320-211	0216	ex F-WWDR	Halle a.d.Saale	
☐ D-AIQH	Airbus A320-211	0217	ex F-WWDS	Dessau	

☐ D-AIQK	Airbus A320-211	0218	ex F-WWDX	Rostock		
☐ D-AIQL	Airbus A320-211	0267	ex F-WWDY	Stralsund		
☐ D-AIQM	Airbus A320-211	0268	ex F-WWIB	Nordenham		
☐ D-AIQN	Airbus A320-211	0269	ex F-WWIC	Laupheim		
☐ D-AIQP	Airbus A320-211	0346	ex F-WWDX	Suhl		
☐ D-AIQR	Airbus A320-211	0382	ex F-WWIZ	Lahr/Schwarzwald		
☐ D-AIQS	Airbus A320-211	0401	ex F-WWBD	Eisenach		
☐ D-AIQT	Airbus A320-211	1337	ex F-WWDO	Gotha		
☐ D-AIQU	Airbus A320-211	1365	ex F-WWIG	Backnang		
☐ D-AIQW	Airbus A320-211	1367	ex F-WWIH	Kleve		
☐ D-AIZA	Airbus A320-214	4097	ex D-AVVF			
☐ D-AIZB	Airbus A320-214	4120	ex D-AVVV			
☐ D-AIZC	Airbus A320-214	4153	ex D-AVVL	Budingen		
☐ D-AIZD	Airbus A320-214	4191	ex D-AVVD			♦
☐ D-AIZE	Airbus A320-214	4261	ex D-AXAC			♦
☐ D-AIZF	Airbus A320-214	4289	ex D-AXAF			♦
☐ D-AIZG	Airbus A320-214	4324	ex D-AXAO			♦
☐ D-AIZH	Airbus A320-214	4363	ex D-AXAW			♦
☐ D-AIZI	Airbus A320-214	4398	ex D-AVVL			♦
☐ D-AIZJ	Airbus A320-214	4449	ex D-AVVM			♦
☐ D-AIZK	Airbus A320-214		ex			o/o
☐ D-AIDA	Airbus A321-231	4360	ex D-AVZM			♦
☐ D-AIDB	Airbus A321-231	4545	ex D-AVZZ			♦
☐ D-AIDC	Airbus A321-231	4560	ex D-AZAB			♦
☐ D-AIDD	Airbus A321-231	4585	ex D-AVZC			o/o♦
☐ D-AIDE	Airbus A321-231	4607	ex			o/o♦
☐ D-AIDF	Airbus A321-231	4626	ex			o/o♦
☐ D-AIDG	Airbus A321-231	4672	ex			o/o♦
☐ D-AIDH	Airbus A321-231	4710	ex			o/o♦
☐ D-	Airbus A321-231		ex			o/o♦
☐ D-	Airbus A321-231		ex			o/o♦
☐ D-	Airbus A321-231		ex			o/o♦
☐ D-	Airbus A321-231		ex			o/o♦
☐ D-AIRA	Airbus A321-131	0458	ex F-WWIQ	Finkenwerder		
☐ D-AIRB	Airbus A321-131	0468	ex F-WWIS	Baden-Baden		
☐ D-AIRC	Airbus A321-131	0473	ex D-AVZC	Erlangen		
☐ D-AIRD	Airbus A321-131	0474	ex D-AVZD	Coburg		
☐ D-AIRE	Airbus A321-131	0484	ex D-AVZF	Osnabrück		
☐ D-AIRF	Airbus A321-131	0493	ex D-AVZH	Kempten		
☐ D-AIRH	Airbus A321-131	0412	ex D-AVZA	Garmisch-Partenkirchen		
☐ D-AIRK	Airbus A321-131	0502	ex D-AVZL	Freudenstadt/Schwarzwald		
☐ D-AIRL	Airbus A321-131	0505	ex D-AVZM	Kulmbach		
☐ D-AIRM	Airbus A321-131	0518	ex D-AVZT	Darmstadt		
☐ D-AIRN	Airbus A321-131	0560	ex D-AVZK	Kaiserslautern		
☐ D-AIRO	Airbus A321-131	0563	ex D-AVZN	Konstanz		
☐ D-AIRP	Airbus A321-131	0564	ex D-AVZL	Lunenburg		
☐ D-AIRR	Airbus A321-131	0567	ex D-AVZM	Wismar		
☐ D-AIRS	Airbus A321-131	0595	ex D-AVZX	Husum		
☐ D-AIRT	Airbus A321-131	0652	ex D-AVZI	Regensburg		
☐ D-AIRU	Airbus A321-131	0692	ex D-AVZT	Würzburg		
☐ D-AIRW	Airbus A321-131	0699	ex D-AVZY	Heilbronn		
☐ D-AIRX	Airbus A321-131	0887	ex D-AVZI	Weimar	retro colours	
☐ D-AIRY	Airbus A321-131	0901	ex D-AVZK	Flensburg		
☐ D-AISB	Airbus A321-231	1080	ex D-AVZP	Hameln		
☐ D-AISC	Airbus A321-231	1161	ex D-AVZG	Speyer		
☐ D-AISD	Airbus A321-231	1188	ex F-WWDD	Chemnitz		
☐ D-AISE	Airbus A321-231	1214	ex D-AVZS	Neudstadt an der Weinstrasse		
☐ D-AISF	Airbus A321-231	1260	ex D-AVZI	Lippstadt		
☐ D-AISG	Airbus A321-231	1273	ex D-AVZU	Dormagen		
☐ D-AISH	Airbus A321-231	3265	ex D-AVZL			
☐ D-AISI	Airbus A321-231	3339	ex D-AVZD	Bergheim		
☐ D-AISJ	Airbus A321-231	3360	ex D-AVZF	Gutersloh		
☐ D-AISK	Airbus A321-231	3387	ex D-AVZO	Emden		
☐ D-AISL	Airbus A321-231	3434	ex D-AVZD	Arnsberg		
☐ D-AISN	Airbus A321-231	3592	ex D-AZAA	Goppingen		
☐ D-AISO	Airbus A321-231	3625	ex D-AVZH	Bocholt		
☐ D-AISP	Airbus A321-231	3864	ex D-AVZK	Rosenheim		
☐ D-AISQ	Airbus A321-231	3936	ex D-AZAF	Lindau		
☐ D-AISR	Airbus A321-231	3987	ex D-AZAN	Donauworth		
☐ D-AIST	Airbus A321-231	4005	ex D-AVZD	Erbach		
☐ D-AISU	Airbus A321-231	4016	ex D-AVZF	Nordlingen		
☐ D-AISV	Airbus A321-231	4047	ex D-AZAG	Bingen		
☐ D-AISW	Airbus A321-231	4054	ex D-AZAR	Stade		
☐ D-AISX	Airbus A321-231	4073	ex D-AVZR			
☐ D-AISZ	Airbus A321-231	4085	ex D-AVZW			

☐	D-AIKA	Airbus A330-343X	570	ex F-WWYV	Minden	
☐	D-AIKB	Airbus A330-343X	576	ex F-WWKN	Cuxhaven	
☐	D-AIKC	Airbus A330-343X	579	ex F-WWKG	Hamm	
☐	D-AIKD	Airbus A330-343X	629	ex F-WWYF	Siegen	
☐	D-AIKE	Airbus A330-343X	636	ex F-WWYL	Landshut	
☐	D-AIKF	Airbus A330-343X	642	ex F-WWKV	Witten	
☐	D-AIKG	Airbus A330-343X	645	ex F-WWKE	Ludwigsburg	
☐	D-AIKH	Airbus A330-343X	648	ex F-WWKG		
☐	D-AIKI	Airbus A330-343X	687	ex F-WWYI		
☐	D-AIKJ	Airbus A330-343X	701	ex F-WWKD	Furth	
☐	D-AIKK	Airbus A330-343X	896	ex F-WWYX		
☐	D-AIKL	Airbus A330-343X	905	ex F-WWYC	Ingolstadt	
☐	D-AIKM	Airbus A330-343X	913	ex F-WWYJ		
☐	D-AIKN	Airbus A330-343X	922	ex F-WWYY		
☐	D-AIKO	Airbus A330-343X	989	ex F-WWKJ		
☐	D-AIFA	Airbus A340-313X	352	ex F-WWJU	Dorsten	
☐	D-AIFB	Airbus A340-313X	355	ex F-WWJX	Gummersbach	
☐	D-AIFC	Airbus A340-313X	379	ex F-WWJJ	Gander & Halifax	
☐	D-AIFD	Airbus A340-313X	390	ex F-WWJE	Giessen	
☐	D-AIFE	Airbus A340-313X	434	ex F-WWJT	Passau	
☐	D-AIFF	Airbus A340-313X	447	ex F-WWJB	Delmenhorst	
☐	D-AIGA	Airbus A340-311	020	ex F-WWJK	Oldenburg	
☐	D-AIGB	Airbus A340-311	024	ex F-WWJO	Recklinghausen	
☐	D-AIGC	Airbus A340-311	027	ex F-WWJR	Wilhelmshaven	Star Alliance c/s
☐	D-AIGD	Airbus A340-311	028	ex F-WWJS	Remscheid	
☐	D-AIGF	Airbus A340-311	035	ex F-WWJV	Göttingen	
☐	D-AIGH	Airbus A340-311	052	ex F-WWJQ	Koblenz	
☐	D-AIGI	Airbus A340-311	053	ex F-WWJJ	Worms	
☐	D-AIGK	Airbus A340-311	056	ex F-WWJK	Bayreuth	
☐	D-AIGL	Airbus A340-313X	135	ex F-WWJS	Herne	
☐	D-AIGM	Airbus A340-313X	158	ex F-WWJN	Görlitz	
☐	D-AIGN	Airbus A340-313X	213	ex F-WWJM	Solingen	
☐	D-AIGO	Airbus A340-313X	233	ex F-WWJJ	Offenbach	
☐	D-AIGP	Airbus A340-313X	252	ex F-WWJM	Paderborn	
☐	D-AIGS	Airbus A340-313X	297	ex F-WWJK	Bergisch-Gladbach	
☐	D-AIGT	Airbus A340-313X	304	ex F-WWJY	Viersen	
☐	D-AIGU	Airbus A340-313X	321	ex F-WWJM	Castrop-Rauxel	
☐	D-AIGV	Airbus A340-313X	325	ex F-WWJN	Dinslaken	
☐	D-AIGW	Airbus A340-313X	327	ex F-WWJO	Gladbeck	
☐	D-AIGX	Airbus A340-313X	354	ex F-WWJV	Düren	
☐	D-AIGY	Airbus A340-313X	335	ex F-WWJS	Lünen	
☐	D-AIGZ	Airbus A340-313X	347	ex F-WWJT	Villingen-Schwenningen	
☐	D-AIHA	Airbus A340-642	482	ex F-WWCS	Nürnberg	Star Alliance c/s
☐	D-AIHB	Airbus A340-642	517	ex F-WWCR	Bremerhaven	
☐	D-AIHC	Airbus A340-642	523	ex F-WWCV	Essen	
☐	D-AIHD	Airbus A340-642	537	ex F-WWCZ	Stuttgart	
☐	D-AIHE	Airbus A340-642	540	ex F-WWCF	Leverkusen	
☐	D-AIHF	Airbus A340-642	543	ex F-WWCE	Lübeck	
☐	D-AIHH	Airbus A340-642	566	ex F-WWCJ	Wiesbaden	
☐	D-AIHI	Airbus A340-642	569	ex F-WWCB	Monchengladbach	
☐	D-AIHK	Airbus A340-642	580	ex F-WWCN	Mainz	
☐	D-AIHL	Airbus A340-642	583	ex F-WWCQ		
☐	D-AIHM	Airbus A340-642	762	ex F-WWCI	Wuppertal	
☐	D-AIHN	Airbus A340-642	763	ex F-WWCJ		
☐	D-AIHO	Airbus A340-642	767	ex F-WWCN		
☐	D-AIHP	Airbus A340-642	771	ex F-WWCQ		
☐	D-AIHQ	Airbus A340-642	790	ex F-WWCE		
☐	D-AIHR	Airbus A340-642	794	ex F-WWCF		
☐	D-AIHS	Airbus A340-642	812	ex F-WWCX		
☐	D-AIHT	Airbus A340-642	846	ex F-WWCH		
☐	D-AIHU	Airbus A340-642	848	ex F-WWCI		
☐	D-AIHV	Airbus A340-642	897	ex F-WWTI		
☐	D-AIHW	Airbus A340-642	972	ex F-WWCL		
☐	D-AIHX	Airbus A340-642	981	ex F-WWCN		
☐	D-AIHY	Airbus A340-642	987	ex F-WWCQ		
☐	D-AIHZ	Airbus A340-642	1005	ex F-WWCR		
☐	D-AIMA	Airbus A380-841	038	ex F-WWSH	Frankfurt am Main	♦
☐	D-AIMB	Airbus A380-841	041	ex F-WWAF	Munchen	♦
☐	D-AIMC	Airbus A380-841	044	ex F-WWAJ	Peking	♦
☐	D-AIMD	Airbus A380-841	048	ex F-WWAK	Tokio	♦
☐	D-AIME	Airbus A380-841	061	ex F-WW		o/o♦
☐	D-AIMF	Airbus A380-841	066	ex F-WW		o/o♦
☐	D-AIMG	Airbus A380-841	069	ex F-WW		o/o♦
☐	D-AIMH	Airbus A380-841	070	ex F-WW		o/o♦
☐	D-	Airbus A380-841		ex		o/o♦

☐ D-	Airbus A380-841		ex		o/o♦
☐ D-ABEA	Boeing 737-330	24565/1818		Saarbrucken	
☐ D-ABEB	Boeing 737-330	25148/2077		Xanten	
☐ D-ABEC	Boeing 737-330	25149/2081		Karlsruhe	
☐ D-ABED	Boeing 737-330	25215/2082		Hagen	
☐ D-ABEE	Boeing 737-330	25216/2084		Ulm	
☐ D-ABEF	Boeing 737-330	25217/2094		Weiden i.d.Opf	
☐ D-ABEH	Boeing 737-330	25242/2102		Bad Kissingen	
☐ D-ABEI	Boeing 737-330	25359/2158	ex (D-ABJK)	Bamberg	
☐ D-ABEK	Boeing 737-330	25414/2164	ex (D-ABJL)		
☐ D-ABEL	Boeing 737-330	25415/2175	ex (D-ABJM)	Pforzheim	
☐ D-ABEM	Boeing 737-330	25416/2182	ex (D-ABJN)	Eberswalde-Finow	
☐ D-ABEN	Boeing 737-330	26428/2196	ex (D-ABJP)	Neubrandenburg	
☐ D-ABEO	Boeing 737-330	26429/2207	ex (D-ABJR)	Plauen	
☐ D-ABEP	Boeing 737-330	26430/2216	ex (D-ABJS)	Naumburg/Saale	
☐ D-ABER	Boeing 737-330	26431/2242	ex TC-SUK	Merseburg	
☐ D-ABES	Boeing 737-330	26432/2247	ex (D-ABJU)	Köthen/Anhalt	
☐ D-ABET	Boeing 737-330	27903/2682		Gelsenkirchen	
☐ D-ABEU	Boeing 737-330	27904/2691		Goslar	
☐ D-ABEW	Boeing 737-330	27905/2705		Detmold	
☐ D-ABIA	Boeing 737-530	24815/1933	ex OK-SWY	Greifswald	
☐ D-ABIB	Boeing 737-530	24816/1958	ex OK-SWZ	Esslingen	
☐ D-ABIC	Boeing 737-530	24817/1967		Krefeld	
☐ D-ABID	Boeing 737-530	24818/1974		Aachen	
☐ D-ABIE	Boeing 737-530	24819/1979		Hildesheim	
☐ D-ABIF	Boeing 737-530	24820/1985		Landau	
☐ D-ABIH	Boeing 737-530	24821/1993		Bruchsal	
☐ D-ABII	Boeing 737-530	24822/1997		Lörrach	
☐ D-ABIK	Boeing 737-530	24823/2000		Rastatt	
☐ D-ABIL	Boeing 737-530	24824/2006		Memmingen	
☐ D-ABIM	Boeing 737-530	24937/2011		Salzgitter	
☐ D-ABIN	Boeing 737-530	24938/2023		Langenhagen	
☐ D-ABIO	Boeing 737-530	24939/2031		Wesel	
☐ D-ABIP	Boeing 737-530	24940/2034		Oberhausen	
☐ D-ABIR	Boeing 737-530	24941/2042		Anklam	
☐ D-ABIS	Boeing 737-530	24942/2048		Rendsburg	
☐ D-ABIT	Boeing 737-530	24943/2049		Neumünster	
☐ D-ABIU	Boeing 737-530	24944/2051		Limburg	
☐ D-ABIW	Boeing 737-530	24945/2063		Bad Nauheim	
☐ D-ABIX	Boeing 737-530	24946/2070		Iserlohn	
☐ D-ABIY	Boeing 737-530	25243/2086		Lingen	
☐ D-ABIZ	Boeing 737-530	25244/2098		Kirchheim unter Teck	
☐ D-ABJA	Boeing 737-530	25270/2116		Bad Segeberg	
☐ D-ABJB	Boeing 737-530	25271/2117		Rheine	
☐ D-ABJC	Boeing 737-530	25272/2118		Erding	
☐ D-ABJD	Boeing 737-530	25309/2122		Freising	
☐ D-ABJE	Boeing 737-530	25310/2126		Ingelheim am Rhein	
☐ D-ABJF	Boeing 737-530	25311/2128	ex LZ-BOI	Aalen	
☐ D-ABJH	Boeing 737-530	25357/2141		Heppenheim/Bergstrasse	
☐ D-ABJI	Boeing 737-530	25358/2151		Siegburg	
☐ D-ABWH	Boeing 737-330 (QC)	24284/1685		Rothenburg o.d. Tauber	
☐ D-ABXL	Boeing 737-330	23531/1307		Neuss	
☐ D-ABXM	Boeing 737-330	23871/1433		Herford	
☐ D-ABXN	Boeing 737-330	23872/1447		Böblingen	
☐ D-ABXO	Boeing 737-330	23873/1489		Schwäbisch Gmünd	
☐ D-ABXP	Boeing 737-330	23874/1495		Fulda	
☐ D-ABXR	Boeing 737-330	23875/1500		Celle	
☐ D-ABXS	Boeing 737-330	24280/1656		Sindelfingen	
☐ D-ABXT	Boeing 737-330	24281/1664		Reutlingen	
☐ D-ABXU	Boeing 737-330	24282/1671		Seeheim-Jugenheim	
☐ D-ABXW	Boeing 737-330	24561/1785		Hanau	
☐ D-ABXX	Boeing 737-330	24562/1787		Bad Homburg v d Höhe	
☐ D-ABXY	Boeing 737-330	24563/1801		Hof	
☐ D-ABXZ	Boeing 737-330	24564/1807		Bad Mergentheim	
☐ D-ABTA	Boeing 747-430M	24285/747		Sachsen	[HAM]
☐ D-ABTB	Boeing 747-430M	24286/749		Brandenburg	
☐ D-ABTC	Boeing 747-430M	24287/754		Mecklenburg-Vorpommern	
☐ D-ABTD	Boeing 747-430M	24715/785		Hamburg	
☐ D-ABTE	Boeing 747-430M	24966/846	ex N6046P	Sachsen-Anhalt	
☐ D-ABTF	Boeing 747-430M	24967/848		Thüringen	
☐ D-ABTH	Boeing 747-430M	25047/856		Duisburg	
☐ D-ABTK	Boeing 747-430	29871/1293	ex (D-ABVI)	Kiel	
☐ D-ABTL	Boeing 747-430	29872/1299	ex (D-ABVG)	Dresden	
☐ D-ABVA	Boeing 747-430	23816/723	ex N6055X	Berlin	
☐ D-ABVB	Boeing 747-430	23817/700	ex N5573S	Bonn	

☐ D-ABVC	Boeing 747-430	24288/757		Baden-Württemberg
☐ D-ABVD	Boeing 747-430	24740/786	ex N60668	Bochum
☐ D-ABVE	Boeing 747-430	24741/787		Potsdam
☐ D-ABVF	Boeing 747-430	24761/796	ex N6018N	Frankfurt am Main
☐ D-ABVH	Boeing 747-430	25045/845	ex N6018N	Düsseldorf
☐ D-ABVK	Boeing 747-430	25046/847	ex N6009F	Hannover
☐ D-ABVL	Boeing 747-430	26425/898	ex N60659	München
☐ D-ABVM	Boeing 747-430	29101/1143	ex (V8-AC2)	Hessen
☐ D-ABVN	Boeing 747-430	26427/915		Dortmund
☐ D-ABVO	Boeing 747-430	28086/1080		Mülheim an der Ruhr
☐ D-ABVP	Boeing 747-430	28284/1103		Bremen
☐ D-ABVR	Boeing 747-430	28285/1106		Köln
☐ D-ABVS	Boeing 747-430	28286/1109		Saarland
☐ D-ABVT	Boeing 747-430	28287/1110		Rheinland-Pfalz
☐ D-ABVU	Boeing 747-430	29492/1191		Bayern
☐ D-ABVW	Boeing 747-430	29493/1205		Wolfsburg
☐ D-ABVX	Boeing 747-430	29868/1237		Schleswig-Holstein
☐ D-ABVY	Boeing 747-430	29869/1261		Nordrhein-Westfalen
☐ D-ABVZ	Boeing 747-430	29870/1264		Niedersachsen
☐ D-CDLH☐	Junkers Ju52/3m g8e	130714	ex N52JU	Tempelhof ☐Painted as D-AQUI

LUFTHANSA CARGO — Lufthansa Cargo (LH/GEC) — Frankfurt (FRA)

☐ D-ALCA	McDonnell-Douglas MD-11F	48781/625	ex N9020Q	Wilhelm Althen
☐ D-ALCB	McDonnell-Douglas MD-11F	48782/626	ex N9166N	
☐ D-ALCC	McDonnell-Douglas MD-11F	48783/627		Karl-Ulrich Garnadt
☐ D-ALCD	McDonnell-Douglas MD-11F	48784/628		
☐ D-ALCE	McDonnell-Douglas MD-11F	48785/629		
☐ D-ALCF	McDonnell-Douglas MD-11F	48798/637		
☐ D-ALCG	McDonnell-Douglas MD-11F	48799/639		
☐ D-ALCH	McDonnell-Douglas MD-11F	48801/640		
☐ D-ALCI	McDonnell-Douglas MD-11F	48800/641		
☐ D-ALCJ	McDonnell-Douglas MD-11F	48802/642		
☐ D-ALCK	McDonnell-Douglas MD-11F	48803/643	ex N9166N	
☐ D-ALCL	McDonnell-Douglas MD-11F	48804/644		
☐ D-ALCM	McDonnell-Douglas MD-11F	48805/645	ex N6069R	
☐ D-ALCN	McDonnell-Douglas MD-11F	48806/646		
☐ D-ALCO	McDonnell-Douglas MD-11F	48413/488	ex N413LT	light green
☐ D-ALCP	McDonnell-Douglas MD-11F	48414/491	ex N414LT	purple ♦
☐ D-ALCR	McDonnell-Douglas MD-11F	48581/565	ex N581LT	dark blue ♦
☐ D-ALCS	McDonnell-Douglas MD-11F	48630/567	ex N630LT	orange ♦

LUFTHANSA CITYLINE — Hansaline (CL/CLH) — Frankfurt/Cologne (FRA/CGN)

☐ D-AVRA	Avro 146-RJ85	E2256	ex G-6-256	
☐ D-AVRB	Avro 146-RJ85	E2253	ex G-BVWD	
☐ D-AVRG	Avro 146-RJ85	E2266	ex G-6-266	
☐ D-AVRH	Avro 146-RJ85	E2268	ex G-OCLH	
☐ D-AVRI	Avro 146-RJ85	E2270	ex G-CLHX	
☐ D-AVRJ	Avro 146-RJ85	E2277	ex G-BWKY	
☐ D-AVRK	Avro 146-RJ85	E2278	ex G-6-278	
☐ D-AVRM	Avro 146-RJ85	E2288	ex G-6-288	
☐ D-AVRN	Avro 146-RJ85	E2293	ex G-6-293	
☐ D-AVRO	Avro 146-RJ85	E2246	ex G-6-246	
☐ D-AVRP	Avro 146-RJ85	E2303	ex G-6-303	
☐ D-AVRQ	Avro 146-RJ85	E2304	ex G-6-304	
☐ D-AVRR	Avro 146-RJ85	E2317	ex G-6-317	
☐ D-ACHA	Canadair CRJ-200LR	7378	ex C-FMLF	Murrhardt
☐ D-ACHD	Canadair CRJ-200LR	7403	ex C-FMNB	Lutherstadt Eisleben
☐ D-ACHE	Canadair CRJ-200LR	7407	ex C-FMLB	Meissen [CGN]♦
☐ D-ACHF	Canadair CRJ-200LR	7431	ex C-FMLI	Montabaur
☐ D-ACHI	Canadair CRJ-200LR	7464	ex C-FMKV	Deidesheim [CGN]♦
☐ D-ACHK	Canadair CRJ-200LR	7499	ex C-FMLI	Schkeuditz
☐ D-ACJB	Canadair CRJ-200LR	7128	ex C-FMMQ	
☐ D-ACJC	Canadair CRJ-200LR	7130	ex C-FMMW	
☐ D-ACLY	Canadair CRJ-200LR	7119	ex C-FMND	
☐ D-ACLZ	Canadair CRJ-200LR	7121	ex C-FMNQ	
☐ D-ACPA	Canadair CRJ-701ER	10012	ex C-GHZV	Westerland/Sylt
☐ D-ACPB	Canadair CRJ-701ER	10013	ex C-GHZY	Rüdesheim am Rhein
☐ D-ACPC	Canadair CRJ-701ER	10014	ex C-GISW	Espelkamp
☐ D-ACPD	Canadair CRJ-701ER	10015	ex C-GISZ	Vilshofen an der Donau
☐ D-ACPE	Canadair CRJ-701ER	10027	ex C-GIAZ	Belzig
☐ D-ACPF	Canadair CRJ-701ER	10030	ex C-GIBI	Uhingen
☐ D-ACPG	Canadair CRJ-701ER	10034	ex C-GIBO	Leinfelden-Echterdingen

☐ D-ACPH	Canadair CRJ-701ER	10043	ex C-GHZY	Eschwege	
☐ D-ACPI	Canadair CRJ-701ER	10046	ex C-GIAE	Viernheim	
☐ D-ACPJ	Canadair CRJ-701ER	10040	ex C-GKCO	Neumarkt in der Oberpfalz	
☐ D-ACPK	Canadair CRJ-701ER	10063	ex C-GIBN	Besigheim	
☐ D-ACPL	Canadair CRJ-701ER	10076	ex C-GIAE	Halberstadt	
☐ D-ACPM	Canadair CRJ-701ER	10080	ex C-GIAO	Heidenheim an der Brenz	
☐ D-ACPN	Canadair CRJ-701ER	10083	ex C-GIAU	Quedlinburg	
☐ D-ACPO	Canadair CRJ-701ER	10085	ex C-FZYS	Spaichingen	
☐ D-ACPP	Canadair CRJ-701ER	10086	ex C-GIGJ	Torgau	
☐ D-ACPQ	Canadair CRJ-701ER	10091	ex C-GZJA	Lubbecke	Star Alliance c/s
☐ D-ACPR	Canadair CRJ-701ER	10098	ex C-	Weinheim an der Bergstrasse	
☐ D-ACPS	Canadair CRJ-701ER	10100	ex C-	Berchtesgaden	Star Alliance c/s
☐ D-ACPT	Canadair CRJ-701ER	10103	ex C-GJLZ	Altötting	Star Alliance c/s
☐ D-ACKA	Canadair CRJ-900LR	15072	ex C-	Pfaffenhofen a.d.Ilm	
☐ D-ACKB	Canadair CRJ-900LR	15073	ex C-FJVT	Schliersee	
☐ D-ACKC	Canadair CRJ-900LR	15078	ex C-	Mettman	
☐ D-ACKD	Canadair CRJ-900LR	15080	ex C-	Wittlich	
☐ D-ACKE	Canadair CRJ-900LR	15081	ex C-	Wernigerode	
☐ D-ACKF	Canadair CRJ-900LR	15083	ex C-FJVR	Prenzlau	
☐ D-ACKG	Canadair CRJ-900LR	15084	ex C-GIAO	Glücksburg	
☐ D-ACKH	Canadair CRJ-900LR	15085	ex C-GICL	Radebeul	
☐ D-ACKI	Canadair CRJ-900LR	15088	ex C-GIAP	Tuttlingen	
☐ D-ACKJ	Canadair CRJ-900LR	15089	ex C-	Ilmenau	
☐ D-ACKK	Canadair CRJ-900LR	15094	ex C-	Fürstenwalde	
☐ D-ACKL	Canadair CRJ-900LR	15095	ex C-	Bad Bergzabern	
☐ D-	Canadair CRJ-900LR		ex C-		o/o♦
☐ D-	Canadair CRJ-900LR		ex C-		o/o♦
☐ D-	Canadair CRJ-900LR		ex C-		o/o♦
☐ D-	Canadair CRJ-900LR		ex C-		o/o♦
☐ D-AEBA	Embraer ERJ-195LR	19000314	ex PT-TXC		
☐ D-AEBB	Embraer ERJ-195LR	19000316	ex PT-TXE		
☐ D-AEBC	Embraer ERJ-195LR	19000320	ex PT-TXI		
☐ D-AEBD	Embraer ERJ-195LR	19000324	ex PT-TXM		
☐ D-AEBE	Embraer ERJ-195LR	19000350	ex PT-XQQ		♦
☐ D-	Embraer ERJ-195LR		ex PT-		o/o♦
☐ D-	Embraer ERJ-195LR		ex PT-		o/o♦
☐ D-	Embraer ERJ-195LR		ex PT-		o/o♦
☐ D-AECA	Embraer ERJ-190LR	19000327	ex PT-TXP		
☐ D-AECB	Embraer ERJ-190LR	19000332	ex PT-TXS		
☐ D-AECC	Embraer ERJ-190LR	19000333	ex PT-TXT		
☐ D-AECD	Embraer ERJ-190LR	19000337	ex PT-TXW		♦
☐ D-AECE	Embraer ERJ-190LR	19000341	ex PT-XQI		♦
☐ D-AECF	Embraer ERJ-190LR	19000359	ex PT-XNA		♦
☐ D-AECG	Embraer ERJ-190LR	19000368	ex PT-XNG	Kronberg/Taunus	♦
☐ D-AECH	Embraer ERJ-190LR	19000376	ex PT-XNM		♦
☐ D-AECI	Embraer ERJ-190LR	19000381	ex PT-XNQ		♦

LUFTVERKEHR FRIESLAND HARLE — Harle

☐ D-IADE	Cessna 340A	340A0607	ex OE-FSK		
☐ D-ILFA	Britten-Norman BN-2B-26 Islander	2243	ex G-BSWO		
☐ D-ILFC	Britten-Norman BN-2B-20 Islander	2272	ex JA5321		
☐ D-ILFD	Britten-Norman BN-2B-20 Islander	2296	ex JA02TY		
☐ D-ILFH	Britten-Norman BN-2B-26 Islander	2212	ex G-BPXS		
☐ D-IORF	Britten-Norman BN-2A-26 Islander	2020	ex N100DA		<Ostseeflug

NIGHTEXPRESS — Executive (EXT) — Frankfurt (FRA)

☐ D-CCAS	Short SD.3-60	SH3737	ex G-OLBA	
☐ D-CRAS	Short SD.3-60	SH3744	ex N825BE	
☐ D-IEXB	Beech 99	U-70	ex G-NUIT	

OCA INTERNATIONAL — Munster (FMO)

☐ D-COPS	SAAB SF.340A	340A-087	ex OK-CCB	<CCB

OLT - OSTFRIESISCHE LUFTTRANSPORT — Oltra (OL/OLT) — Emden/Bremen (EME/BRE)

☐ D-AOLG	Fokker 100	11452	ex PH-RRN	Toulouse
☐ D-AOLH	Fokker 100	11265	ex PH-SEM	
☐ D-AOLB	SAAB 2000	2000-005	ex SE-005	
☐ D-AOLC	SAAB 2000	2000-016	ex SE-016	
☐ D-AOLT	SAAB 2000	2000-037	ex HB-IZU	Emden
☐ D-CASB	SAAB SF.340B	340B-223	ex SE-KSI	
☐ D-COLE	SAAB SF.340A	340A-144	ex LV-WTF	Bremen

☐ D-COLB	Swearingen SA.227AC Metro III	AC-754B	ex N54NE		
☐ D-COLD	Swearingen SA.227AC Metro III	AC-421B	ex SE-LIM		
☐ D-COLT	Swearingen SA.227AC Metro III	AC-690	ex N715C		
☐ D-CSWF	Swearingen SA.227DC Metro III	DC-896B			♦
☐ D-ECDJ	Cessna 207 Skywagon	20700176	ex N1576U		
☐ D-EOLF	Gippsland GA-8 Airvan	GA8-05-080	ex VH-IMI	Borkum	
☐ D-FOLE	Cessna 208B Caravan I	208B0523	ex N5197A		
☐ D-IFBN	Britten-Norman BN-2B-26 Islander	2185	ex G-BLNF	Juist	
☐ D-IOLK	Britten-Norman BN-2B-26 Islander	2306	ex G-CEUB		
☐ D-IOLO	Britten-Norman BN-2B-26 Islander	2305	ex G-CEUA		

OSTSEEFLUG   Rostock-Laage (RLG)

☐ D-IORF	Britten-Norman BN-2A-26 Islander	2020	ex N100DA		>L Friesland Harle

PRIVATAIR   PrivatJet (PTG)   Düsseldorf (DUS)

☐ D-APBB	Boeing 737-8Q8/W	35278/2625	ex N812SY	
☐ D-APBC	Boeing 737-8BK/W	33016/1588	ex N807SY	
☐ D-APBD	Boeing 737-8BK/W	33021/1667	ex N808SY	

PRIVATE WINGS   Private Wings (8W/PWF)   Berlin-Schönefeld (SXF)

☐ D-BIRD	Dornier 328-300 (328JET)	3180	ex N422FJ	
☐ D-BJET	Dornier 328-300 (328JET)	3207	ex N328FG	
☐ D-CATZ	Dornier 328-110	3090	ex N404SS	
☐ D-COCA	Beech 1900D	UE-224	ex N224YV	
☐ D-COLA	Beech B300 Super King Air	FL-75	ex HB-GJB	
☐ D-CPWF	Dornier 328-110	3112	ex D-CFWF	
☐ D-CREW	Dornier 328-110	3113	ex D-CGAO	>SUS

PTL LUFTFAHRTUNTERNEHMEN   King Star (KST)   Landshut (QLG)

☐ D-IBAD	Beech B200 Super King Air	BB-1229	

REGIO-AIR   German Link (RAG)   Trollenhagen

☐ D-IBIJ	Cessna 402B	402B0327	ex YU-BIJ	<Goller
☐ D-IESS	Swearingen SA.226TC Metro II	TC-338	ex N90141	

TUIFLY   Tuifly (X3/HLF, HLX)   Hanover (HAJ)

☐ D-AGEQ	Boeing 737-75B	28103/23	ex N1787B		Lsd fr/op by GMI
☐ D-AGET	Boeing 737-75B	28109/31			Lsd fr/op by GMI
☐ D-AHIA	Boeing 737-73S	29082/229	ex D-ASKH		>BER
☐ D-AHXA	Boeing 737-7K5/W	30714/2202	ex N1786B		>BER
☐ D-AHXD	Boeing 737-7K5/W	30726/2298			>BER
☐ D-AHXE	Boeing 737-7K5/W	35135/2451		Robinson Club Piz Buin	>BER
☐ D-AHXF	Boeing 737-7K5/W	35136/2465		Robinson Club Arosa	>BER
☐ D-AHXH	Boeing 737-7K5/W	35282/2585			>BER
☐ D-AHFA	Boeing 737-8K5/W	27981/7	ex C-GCQS	Robinson Club Pamfilya	
☐ D-AHFB	Boeing 737-8K5/W	27982/8	ex N35030	Robinson Club Nobilis	
☐ D-AHFH	Boeing 737-8K5/W	27983/218	ex N1786B	Robinson Club Fleesensee	
☐ D-AHFI	Boeing 737-8K5/W	27984/220	ex N1787B		
☐ D-AHFK	Boeing 737-8K5/W	27991/248	ex HA-LKC		
☐ D-AHFL	Boeing 737-8K5/W	27985/470	ex HA-LKD		
☐ D-AHFM	Boeing 737-8K5/W	27986/474		Goldbair	
☐ D-AHFO	Boeing 737-8K5/W	27987/499			
☐ D-AHFP	Boeing 737-8K5/W	27988/508	ex N1786B		
☐ D-AHFR	Boeing 737-8K5/W	30593/528	ex N1787B	Robinson Club Agadir	
☐ D-AHFS	Boeing 737-8K5/W	28623/556			
☐ D-AHFT	Boeing 737-8K5/W	30413/636	ex N1015B		
☐ D-AHFU	Boeing 737-8K5/W	30414/703	ex N1787B	Robinson Club Soma Bay	
☐ D-AHFV	Boeing 737-8K5/W	30415/719	ex N1786B		
☐ D-AHFW	Boeing 737-8K5/W	30882/760	ex N1786B		
☐ D-AHFX	Boeing 737-8K5/W	30416/778	ex N1786B		
☐ D-AHFY	Boeing 737-8K5/W	30417/781	ex N1787B		
☐ D-AHFZ	Boeing 737-8K5/W	30883/783	ex N1786B	Robinson Club Cala Serena	
☐ D-AHLK	Boeing 737-8K5/W	35143/2763			
☐ D-ATUA	Boeing 737-8K5/W	37245/3486			♦
☐ D-ATUB	Boeing 737-8K5/W	37247/3497	ex N1786B		♦
☐ D-ATUC	Boeing 737-8K5/W	34684/1870	ex N1786B		
☐ D-ATUD	Boeing 737-8K5/W	34685/1901			
☐ D-ATUE	Boeing 737-8K5/W	34686/1903			
☐ D-ATUF	Boeing 737-8K5/W	34687/1907	ex N1786B		Retro c/s

☐ D-ATUG	Boeing 737-8K5/W	34688/1909	
☐ D-ATUH	Boeing 737-8K5/W	34689/1935	
☐ D-	Boeing 737-8K5/W		o/o♦
☐ D-	Boeing 737-8K5/W		o/o♦
☐ D-	Boeing 737-8K5/W		o/o♦
☐ D-	Boeing 737-8K5/W		o/o♦

WDL AVIATION		WDL (WE/WDL)			Cologne (CGN)
☐ D-ALIN	British Aerospace 146 Srs.300	E3142	ex EI-DEW		[CGN]
☐ D-AMAJ	British Aerospace 146 Srs.200	E2028	ex G-BZBA		
☐ D-AMAX	British Aerospace 146 Srs.300	E3157	ex EI-DEX		[CGN]
☐ D-AMGL	British Aerospace 146 Srs.200	E2055	ex G-CBFL	all-white	
☐ D-AWBA	British Aerospace 146 Srs.300A	E3134	ex ZK-NZF		
☐ D-AWUE	British Aerospace 146 Srs.200	E2050	ex PK-PJP		
☐ D-ADEP	Fokker F.27 Friendship 600	10318	ex OY-CCK		
☐ D-ADOP	Fokker F.27 Friendship 600	10316	ex OY-BVF	Babs	[CGN]
☐ D-AELG	Fokker F.27 Friendship 600	10338	ex VR-BLZ		[CGN]
☐ D-AELH	Fokker F.27 Friendship 400	10340	ex VR-BLX	Jude[CGN]	
☐ D-AELJ	Fokker F.27 Friendship 600	10342	ex F-BYAB	Flying Dutchman	[CGN]
☐ D-AELK	Fokker F.27 Friendship 600	10361	ex F-GCJV	Petra	
☐ D-AELM	Fokker F.27 Friendship 600	10450	ex OY-CCL	Dietmar Rabe von Papenheim	[CGN]
☐ D-AISY	Fokker F.27 Friendship 600	10391	ex OY-CCR		[CGN]
☐ D-BAKB	Fokker F.27 Friendship 600	10261	ex F-GHRC	Hully Gully	
☐ D-BAKC	Fokker F.27 Friendship 600	10195	ex F-GFJS		[CGN]
☐ D-BAKD	Fokker F.27 Friendship 600	10179	ex SP-FNF		[CGN]

XL AIRWAYS GERMANY		(GV/GXL)			Frankfurt (FRA)
☐ D-AXLD	Boeing 737-8FH/W	35093/2176	ex C-FYLD		
☐ D-AXLE	Boeing 737-8Q8/W	30724/2286			
☐ D-AXLF	Boeing 737-8Q8/W	28218/160	ex G-XLAB	Tinks	
☐ D-AXLG	Boeing 737-8Q8	28226/77	ex G-XLAA		

DQ- FIJI (Republic of Fiji)

AIR FIJI		Fijiair (PC/FAJ)			Suva-Nausori (SUV)
☐ DQ-AFR	AVIC II Y-12	013	ex B-744L		
☐ DQ-AFS	AVIC II Y-12	015	ex B-745L		
☐ DQ-FHC	Harbin Y-12 II	0056		Op for Airlines Tonga	
☐ DQ-FHF	Harbin Y-12 II	0047	ex B-531L	Op for Airlines Tonga	
☐ DQ-AFO	Embraer EMB.110P1 Bandeirante	110419	ex EI-BVX		
☐ DQ-FET	Britten-Norman BN-2A-21 Islander	661	ex ZK-NNE		[SUV]
☐ DQ-FIC	Britten-Norman BN-2A-21 Islander	511	ex ZK-KHB	Island Shuttle titles	
☐ DQ-MUM	Embraer EMB.120ER Brasilia	120079	ex VH-XFH	Pacific Link titles	
☐ DQ-TLC	Embraer EMB.110P1 Bandeirante	110417	ex VH-TLD	Op for Airlines Tonga	
☐ DQ-YES	Embraer EMB.110P1 Bandeirante	110307	ex VH-FNR		
☐ DQ-	AVIC I MA-60				o/o
☐ ZK-CIF	Convair 580	381	ex N566EA		<CVA

AIR KATAFANGA				Suva-Nausori (SUV)
☐ DQ-FIK	Piper PA-31-350 Navajo Chieftain	31-7752090	ex N7088C	

AIR PACIFIC		Pacific (FJ/FJI)			Nadi (NAN)
☐ DQ-FJC	Boeing 767-3X2ER	26260/552		Island of Taveuni	
☐ DQ-FJF	Boeing 737-7X2/W	28878/96	ex N1786B	Island of Koro	
☐ DQ-FJG	Boeing 737-8X2/W	29968/275	ex N1786B	Island of Kadavu	
☐ DQ-FJH	Boeing 737-8X2/W	29969/339	ex N1786B	Island of Gau	
☐ DQ-FJK	Boeing 747-412	24064/755	ex 9V-SMD	Island of Vanua Levu	<SIA
☐ DQ-FJL	Boeing 747-412	24062/722	ex 9V-SMB	Island of Viti Levu	<SIA

AIR WAKAYA				Suva-Nausori (SUV)
☐ DQ-DHG	Cessna 208B Caravan I	208B1120	ex N1274X	
☐ DQ-FHG	Britten-Norman BN-2B-26 Islander	2230	ex G-BSAC	

NORTHERN AIR SERVICES				Suva-Nausori (SUV)
☐ DQ-JJS	Britten-Norman BN-2A-26 Islander	856	ex VH-IFA	

PACIFIC ISLAND AIR — Nadi (NAN)

☐ DQ-GEE	de Havilland DHC-2 Beaver	1358	ex C-GSKY	FP
☐ DQ-SLM	Britten-Norman BN-2A-26 Islander	605	ex VH-XFI	
☐ DQ-YIR	Britten-Norman BN-2A-26 Islander	845	ex VH-FCOI	

PACIFIC SUN — Sunflower (PI/SUF) — Nadi (NAN)

☐ DQ-FCX	Britten-Norman BN-2A-27 Islander	833	ex G-BEMJ	Adi Yasawa	
☐ DQ-FDV	Britten-Norman BN-2A-26 Islander	41	ex 9M-MDA	Bui Nigone	[NAN]
☐ DQ-FDW	Britten-Norman BN-2A-26 Islander	602	ex 9M-MDC	Adi Makutu	
☐ DQ-FEY	de Havilland DHC-6 Twin Otter 100	87	ex N64NB	Spirit of the North	
☐ DQ-FEZ	de Havilland DHC-6 Twin Otter 100	9	ex F-OCFJ	Spirit of the West	
☐ DQ-FIE	de Havilland DHC-6 Twin Otter 300	660	ex N933CL	Spirit of Nadi	
☐ DQ-FIN	Britten-Norman BN-2A-26 Islander	159	ex VH-ISA		
☐ DQ-PSA	ATR 42-500	554	ex 3B-NBB		
☐ DQ-PSB	ATR 42-500	534	ex 3B-NBA		

TURTLE AIRWAYS — Turtle (TLT) — Nadi-Newtown Beach

☐ DQ-FEX	Cessna U206G Stationair 6 II	U20605706	ex ZK-FHE	FP
☐ DQ-TAL	de Havilland DHC-2 Beaver	1255	ex C-GLED	FP
☐ DQ-TAM	de Havilland DHC-2 Beaver	1433	ex VH-IME	FP
☐ DQ-TAN	Cessna U206G Stationair 6 II	U20605574	ex VH-HBX	FP

D2- ANGOLA (Republic of Angola)

AEROJET — Mabeco (MBC) — Luanda (LAD)

☐ D2-EDE	Embraer EMB.120ER Brasilia	120039	ex N188SW	
☐ D2-EDF	Embraer EMB.120ER Brasilia	120037	ex N187SW	
☐ D2-FDK	Embraer EMB.120ER Brasilia	120281	ex N215SW	
☐ D2-FET	Embraer EMB.120ER Brasilia	120175	ex OM-SKY	♦
☐ D2-FER	Yakovlev Yak-40	9541844	ex RA-87994	

AIR 26 — Air 26 (DCD) — Luanda (LAD)

☐ D2-EYN	Embraer EMB.120ER Brasilia	120165	ex N264AS	Nova Erce
☐ D2-EYO	Embraer EMB.120RT Brasilia	120210	ex N269AS	
☐ D2-EYP	Embraer EMB.120RT Brasilia	120146	ex N262AS	
☐ D2-EYQ	Embraer EMB.120ER Brasilia	120062	ex F-GFEO	
☐ D2-EZC	Embraer EMB.120ER Brasilia	120200	ex N652CT	
☐ D2-EZZ	Embraer EMB.120FC Brasilia	120102	ex N126AM	Frtr

AIR GEMINI — Twins (GLL) — Luanda (LAD)

☐ D2-ERJ	Douglas DC-9-32 (ABS 3)	47765/900	ex N924LG	
☐ D2-ERL	Douglas DC-9-32 (ABS 3)	47788/901	ex N925LG	
☐ D2-ERN	Boeing 727-25C (FedEx 3)	19358/367	ex S9-BAU	
☐ D2-ERS	Douglas DC-9-32	47110/167	ex N923LG	
☐ D2-ERU	Boeing 727-2S7	22020/1592	ex N681CA	
☐ S9-BAR	Boeing 727-22C	19098/318	ex N832RV	[LAD]
☐ S9-BOE	Boeing 727-22C (FedEx 3)	19192/388	ex N706DH	[LAD]

ALADA — Air Alada (RAD) — Luanda (LAD)

☐ D2-FAX	Antonov An-32A	1510	ex RA-48115 Kimoka	
☐ D2-FFR	Ilyushin Il-18D	0393607150	ex UR-75896	converted Il-22
☐ D2-FRB	Antonov An-32	2208	ex Hungary 208	

ANGOLA AIR CHARTER — Angola Charter (AGO) — Luanda (LAD)

☐ D2-FCO	Ilyushin Il-76MD	0043454615	ex ER-IBE	
☐ D2-FCP	Boeing 727-77C (FedEx 3)	20370/821	ex N526PC	
☐ D2-FDO	Embraer EMB.120RT Brasilia	120082	ex N102SK	
☐ D2-FDT	Embraer EMB.120RT Brasilia	120081	ex N103SK	
☐ D2-MBV	Antonov An-12BP	5343208	ex ER-AXH	

ANGOLA AIRSERVICES — Luanda (LAD)

☐ ZS-NYK	British Aerospace Jetstream 4121	41095	G-4-095	
☐ ZS-PCA	Beech 1900C-1	UC-138	ex N138GA	
☐ D2-FHE	British Aerospace Jetstream 4101	41046	ex N146KM	
☐ D2-FHF	British Aerospace Jetstream 4101	41049	ex N149KM	

DIEXIM EXPRESS   Luanda (LAD)

☐ D2-FFE	Embraer EMB.120ER Brasilia	120242	ex N8078V	
☐ D2-FFO	Beech B300 Super King Air	FL-10	ex N350FH	
☐ D2-FFP	Embraer EMB.120RT Brasilia	120235	ex F-GJTF	
☐ D2-FFU	Embraer EMB.120ER Brasilia	120244	ex F-GTBH	
☐ D2-FFW	Embraer ERJ-145MP	145360	ex F-OIJE	Il Aladia
☐ D2-FFY	Embraer EMB.120RT Brasilia	120171	ex N221CR	

GIRA GLOBO   Gira Globo (GGL)   Luanda (LAD)

☐ D2-FCN	Ilyushin Il-76TD	0053462872	ex UR-76651	Op for Angolan Air Force, T-900
☐ D2-FDG	Antonov An-32B	2201	ex RA-48116 Mulanda	
☐ D2-FEM	Ilyushin Il-76TD	0063469062	ex UR-76688 Rei-Ekuikui	T-905
☐ D2-FEW	Ilyushin Il-76TD	0073475239	ex UR-76721	Op for Angolan Air Force, T-904

HM AIRWAYS   Luanda (LAD)

☐ D2-EYA	Bell 427	56037	ex N51804	
☐ D2-EYB	Bell 427	56046	ex N427MM	
☐ D2-EYC	Bell 427	56048	ex N804RM	
☐ D2-EYD	Bell 427	56049	ex N88PQ	
☐ D2-EYE	Bell 427	56050	ex N918RB	
☐ D2-EYF	Bell 427	56051	ex N96EA	
☐ D2-EYG	Bell 427	56052	ex N97EA	
☐ D2-EYH	Bell 427	56053	ex N97TZ	
☐ D2-EYI	Bell 430	49102	ex N41786	
☐ D2-EYJ	Bell 430	49108	ex N767MM	
☐ D2-EYK	Bell 430	49109	ex N825GB	
☐ D2-EUO	de Havilland DHC-8-402NG	4312	ex C-GDCQ	♦
☐ D2-EUP	de Havilland DHC-8-402NG	4315	ex C-GDFF	♦
☐ D2-	de Havilland DHC-8-402NG	4322	ex C-GEVB	o/o♦
☐ D2-	de Havilland DHC-8-402NG	4325	ex C-GEZN	o/o♦
☐ D2-EYL	de Havilland DHC-8-315	613	ex C-FDGW	
☐ D2-EYM	de Havilland DHC-8-315	614	ex C-FDHE	
☐ D2-EYU	de Havilland DHC-8-315	645	ex C-FLKI	
☐ D2-EYV	Embraer EMB.120ER Brasilia	120145	ex N284UE	

SAL - SOCIEDADE DE AVIACAO LIGEIRA   Luanda (LAD)

☐ D2-ECN	Cessna F406 Caravan II	F406-0002	ex PH-MNS	
☐ D2-ECO	Cessna F406 Caravan II	F406-0011	ex D-IDAA	
☐ D2-ECP	Cessna F406 Caravan II	F406-0016	ex PH-LAS	
☐ D2-ECQ	Cessna F406 Caravan II	F406-0019	ex G-CVAN	
☐ D2-ECW	Beech B300 Super King Air	FL-102	ex S9-TAP	
☐ D2-ECX	Beech B200 Super King Air	BB-1362	ex N1565F	
☐ D2-ECY	Beech B200C Super King Air	BL-135	ex S9-NAP	
☐ D2-EDA	Cessna 208B Caravan I	208B0568	ex N1215K	
☐ D2-EDB	Cessna 208B Caravan I	208B0665	ex N1256G	
☐ D2-EOD	Short SC.7 Skyvan 3	SH1938	ex CR-LOD	[LAD]

SERVISAIR   Luanda (LAD)

☐ D2-FGJ	McDonnell-Douglas MD-82	53220/2073	ex I-DATU	♦

SONAIR   Sonair (SOR)   Luanda (LAD)

☐ D2-EQD	Aérospatiale SA365N2 Dauphin 2	6521	ex F-GJIA	
☐ D2-EQE	Aérospatiale SA365N2 Dauphin 2	6531	ex F-WQSR	
☐ D2-EUO	Aérospatiale SA365N Dauphin 2	9000		
☐ D2-EVE	Aérospatiale SA365N2 Dauphin 2	6418	ex F-WQSR	
☐ D2-EVF	Aérospatiale SA365N2 Dauphin 2	6410	ex F-GHRX	
☐ D2-EXX	Aérospatiale SA365N2 Dauphin 2	6439	ex F-WQSR	
☐ D2-ERQ	Beech 1900D	UE-274	ex N11015	
☐ D2-EVJ	Beech 1900D	UE-111	ex N3119U	
☐ D2-EVK	Beech 1900D	UE-121	ex N3221A	
☐ D2-EVL	Beech 1900D	UE-312	ex N312RC	
☐ D2-EVN	Beech 1900D	UE-370	ex N30539	
☐ D2-EVR	Beech 1900D	UE-280	ex N11284	
☐ D2-EVX	Beech 1900D	UE-340	ex N23317	
☐ D2-EVY	Beech 1900D	UE-249	ex N249GL	
☐ D2-EWW	Beech 1900D	UE-399	ex N854CA	
☐ D2-EWX	Beech 1900D	UE-405	ex N856CA	
☐ D2-EWY	Beech 1900D	UE-401	ex N840CA	
☐ D2-FFJ	Beech 1900D	UE-412	ex N44828	

☐ D2-EVA	de Havilland DHC-6 Twin Otter 310	728	ex V2-LDD		
☐ D2-EVB	de Havilland DHC-6 Twin Otter 310	810	ex V2-LDH		
☐ D2-EVC	de Havilland DHC-6 Twin Otter 310	809	ex V2-LDG		
☐ D2-EVH	de Havilland DHC-6 Twin Otter 300	511	ex HB-LOM		
☐ D2-EVM	de Havilland DHC-6 Twin Otter 310	794	ex HB-LRF		
☐ D2-FVN	de Havilland DHC-6 Twin Otter 310	817	ex N817L		
☐ D2-FVO	de Havilland DHC-6 Twin Otter 310	821	ex N821L		
☐ D2-FVP	de Havilland DHC-6 Twin Otter 310	743	ex 5Y-TMF		
☐ D2-FVQ	de Havilland DHC-6 Twin Otter 310	704	ex 5N-ASP		
☐ D2-EVS	Sikorsky S-76C	760603	ex C-GHRI		<CHC Helicopters Intl
☐ D2-EXG	Sikorsky S-76A	760042	ex ZS-RKE		<Heli-Union
☐ D2-EXH	Sikorsky S-76A	760268	ex ZS-RBE		<CHC Helicopter (Africa)
☐ D2-EXK	Sikorsky S-76C	760525	ex N9017U		
☐ D2-EXL	Sikorsky S-76C	760526	ex N9007U		
☐ D2-EXO	Sikorsky S-76C	760543	ex N2040S		
☐ D2-EXP	Sikorsky S-76C	760544	ex N2048K		
☐ D2-EQH	Eurocopter EC.225LP	2743			◆
☐ D2-EQI	Eurocopter EC.225LP	2746			◆
☐ D2-ESN	Fokker F.27 Friendship 500	10610	ex PH-FTY	Kwanda	
☐ D2-ESR	Fokker 50	20240	ex PH-RPK	Lombo Este	
☐ D2-ESU	Boeing 727-23F	19431/372	ex N516FE		
☐ D2-ESW	Fokker 50	20241	ex PH-RRM		<Golfo Intl
☐ D2-ESZ	Aérospatiale AS.332L2 II	2503	ex F-WQPA		
☐ D2-EVD	Boeing 727-29C	19403/435	ex CB-02		
☐ D2-EVG	Boeing 727-29C	19402/415	ex N70PA		
☐ D2-EVP	Aérospatiale AS.332L2 II	2398	ex F-WQEA		<CHC Helicopter (Africa)
☐ D2-EVT	Eurocopter EC.225LP		ex F-WQDI		
☐ D2-EVW	Boeing 737-7HB	35954/2310			
☐ D2-EVZ	Boeing 737-7HBC/W	35955/2531			
☐ D2-EWS	Boeing 737-7HBC/W	35956/2536			
☐ D2-EXN	Aérospatiale AS.332L2 II	2590			
☐ D2-FSA	Boeing 727-29C	19987/634	ex HZ-HE4		Frtr
☐ S9-CAM	Beech B300 Super King Air	FL-163	ex N1057Q		<Golfo Intl
☐ S9-CAN	Beech B300 Super King Air	FL-294	ex N3214J		<Golfo Intl
☐ N262SG	Boeing 747-481	29262/1199	ex JA403A		[KUL]
☐ N263SG	Boeing 747-481	29263/1204	ex B-LFC		
☐ N322SG	Boeing 747-481	30322/1250	ex B-LFD		

TAAG ANGOLA AIRLINES		**DTA (DT/DTA)**			**Luanda (LAD)**
☐ D2-TBC	Boeing 737-2M2C	21173/447	ex D2-TAB		
☐ D2-TBF	Boeing 737-7M2/W	34559/2013	ex N6067U		
☐ D2-TBG	Boeing 737-7M2/W	34560/2036			
☐ D2-TBH	Boeing 737-7M2/W	34561/2043			
☐ D2-TBJ	Boeing 737-7M2/W	34562/2149			
☐ D2-TBO	Boeing 737-2M2	22776/891	ex N1782B		[BBU]
☐ D2-TBX	Boeing 737-2M2	23351/1117			
☐ D2-TEA	Boeing 747-312M	23410/653	ex 9V-SKN	Cidade de Kuito	
☐ D2-TEB	Boeing 747-357M	23751/686	ex N375TC		
☐ D2-TED	Boeing 777-2M2ER	34565/581			
☐ D2-TEE	Boeing 777-2M2ER	34566/587		Kuitu Kuanavale	
☐ D2-TEF	Boeing 777-2M2ER	34567/687			
☐ D2-	Boeing 777-3M2ER				o/o◆
☐ D2-	Boeing 777-3M2ER				o/o◆

TRANSTECO		**Transteco (TTC)**			**Luanda (LAD)**
☐ D2-FEI	Beech 200 King Air	BB-620	ex ZS-OGV		

TROPICANA					**Luanda (LAD)**
☐ D2-EBF	Beech B200 Super King Air	BB-836	ex S9-NAQ		
☐ D2-FFK	Beech B200 Super King Air	BB-1026	ex N153D	Aeronautica titles	
☐ D2-FFL	Beech 200 Super King Air	BB-126	ex N777XZ	Capembe	
☐ D2-FFM	Beech 1900D	UE-108	ex N118SK	Mavinga	

D4-   CAPE VERDE ISLANDS (Republic of Cape Verde)

CABO VERDE EXPRESS		**(CVE)**		**Sal (SID)**
☐ D4-CBL	LET L-410UVP-E10	902511	ex 9Q-CUM	) D4-CBL, -CBR identities
☐ D4-CBR	LET L-410UVP-E20	912533	ex D-CLED	) may be reversed
☐ D4-JCA	LET L-410UVP-E20	912604	ex OY-PEY	

HALCYON AIR				**Praia (RAI)**
☐ D4-CBQ	ATR 42-320	296	ex J5-GZZ	Santa Maria
☐ D4-CBW	ATR 42-500	532	ex N532FA	◆

TACV - TRANSPORTES AEREOS DE CABO VERDE / CAPE VERDE AIRLINES

		Cabo Verde (VR/TCV)		Praia (RAI)
☐ D4-CBP	Boeing 757-2Q8	30045/957	ex N301AM	Emigranti
☐ D4-CBT	ATR 72-212A	747	ex F-WWEH	Jorge Barbosa
☐ D4-CBU	ATR 72-212A	755	ex F-WWEP	Baltizar Lopes
☐ D4-CBV	ATR 42-512	669	ex F-WWLC	

D6- COMOROS (Federal Islamic Republic of the Comores)

COMORES AIR SERVICE				**Moroni (YVA)**
☐ D6-CAM	LET L-410UVP	851336	ex D6-GDH	
☐ D6-CAN	LET L-410UVP	841331	ex 9L-LCZ	

COMORES AVIATION		**Comores (KR/KMZ)**		**Moroni (YVA)**
☐ ZS-AAY	British Aerospace 146 Srs.200	E2044	ex TN-AIC	◆
☐ D6-CAK	LET L-410UVP	841219	ex D2-TGH	dbr 09Apr07?
☐ D6-CAL	LET L-410UVP	800526	ex HA-LAB	

COMORO ISLAND AIRWAYS				**Moroni (YVA)**
☐ D6-CAS	Airbus A320-214	3040	ex EC-KAX	>SUD

HERITAGE AVIATION				**Moroni (YVA)**
☐ D6-CAQ	LET L-410UVP			
	Status uncertain			

EC- SPAIN (Kingdom of Spain)

AERONOVA		**Aeronova (OVA)**		**Valencia (VLC)**
☐ EC-GVE	Swearingen SA.227AC Metro III	AC-669B	ex N2702Z	
☐ EC-HCH	Swearingen SA.227AC Metro III	AC-658B	ex N2692P	
☐ EC-HZH	Swearingen SA.227AC Metro III	AC-720	ex N2724S	
☐ EC-IXL	Swearingen SA.227AC Metro III	AC-689B	ex D-COLC	
☐ EC-JCU	Swearingen SA.227AC Metro III	AC-679B	ex N6UB	

AIR EUROPA		**Europa (UX/AEA)**		**Palma de Mallorca (PMI)**
Associate member of Skyteam				
☐ EC-JPF	Airbus A330-202	733	ex F-WWKU	
☐ EC-JQG	Airbus A330-202	745	ex F-WWYG	Estepona-Costa del Sol
☐ EC-JQQ	Airbus A330-202	749	ex F-WWYJ	
☐ EC-JZL	Airbus A330-202	814	ex F-WWYJ	David Bisbal
☐ EC-KOM	Airbus A330-202	931	ex F-WWKU	
☐ EC-KTG	Airbus A330-202	950	ex F-WWKQ	
☐ EC-LKE	Airbus A330-243	461	ex CS-TRA	◆
☐ EC-HBL	Boeing 737-85P	28381/250	ex N1787B	
☐ EC-HBM	Boeing 737-85P	28382/256	ex N1787B	
☐ EC-HGO	Boeing 737-85P	28384/420	ex N1786B	
☐ EC-HGP	Boeing 737-85P	28385/421	ex N1786B	Marbella
☐ EC-HGQ	Boeing 737-85P	28386/426	ex N1786B	El Mundo titles
☐ EC-HJP	Boeing 737-85P	28535/480	ex N1800B	
☐ EC-HJQ	Boeing 737-85P	28387/522	ex N1786B	
☐ EC-HKQ	Boeing 737-85P/W	28388/533		San Pedro Alcantara
☐ EC-HKR	Boeing 737-85P/W	28536/540	ex N1787B	
☐ EC-HZS	Boeing 737-86Q/W	30276/920	ex N747BX	
☐ EC-IDA	Boeing 737-86Q/W	32773/1051	ex N73792	
☐ EC-IDT	Boeing 737-86Q/W	30281/1076	ex N73793	
☐ EC-III	Boeing 737-86Q/W	30284/1233		
☐ EC-ISE	Boeing 737-86Q/W	30290/1406	ex N1786B	
☐ EC-ISN	Boeing 737-86Q/W	30291/1435		
☐ EC-JAP	Boeing 737-85P/W	33971/1580		
☐ EC-JBJ	Boeing 737-85P/W	33972/1598		Salamanca

☐ EC-JBK	Boeing 737-85P/W	33973/1606		
☐ EC-JBL	Boeing 737-85P/W	33974/1610		
☐ EC-JHK	Boeing 737-85P/W	33975/1716	ex N1787B	
☐ EC-JHL	Boeing 737-85P/W	33976/1740		
☐ EC-JNF	Boeing 737-85P/W	33977/1878	Mutua Madrileqa	
☐ EC-KBV	Boeing 737-85P/W	33980/2245	ex N1786B	
☐ EC-KCG	Boeing 737-85P/W	33981/2269		
☐ EC-KEO	Boeing 737-85P/W	33982/2338		
☐ EC-	Boeing 737-85P			o/o
☐ EC-	Boeing 737-85P			o/o
☐ EC-	Boeing 737-85P			o/o
☐ EC-HPU	Boeing 767-3Q8ER	30048/828		
☐ EC-HSV	Boeing 767-3Q8ER	29387/840		
☐ SP-LPF	Boeing 767-319ER	24876/413	ex ZK-NCF	<LOT
☐ EC-KRJ	Embraer ERJ-195LR	19000196	ex PT-SGE	
☐ EC-KXD	Embraer ERJ-195LR	19000244	ex PT-SIP	
☐ EC-KYO	Embraer ERJ-195LR	19000276	ex PT-TLQ	
☐ EC-KYP	Embraer ERJ-195LR	19000281	ex PT-TLV	
☐ EC-LCQ	Embraer ERJ-195LR	19000303	ex PT-TZR	
☐ EC-LEK	Embraer ERJ-195LR	19000344	ex PT-XQG	♦
☐ EC-LFZ	Embraer ERJ-195LR	19000357	ex PT-XQV	♦
☐ EC-LIN	Embraer ERJ-195LR	19000401	ex PT-XUG	♦
☐ EC-	Embraer ERJ-195LR			o/o♦
☐ EC-	Embraer ERJ-195LR			o/o♦

AIR NOSTRUM — Nostrum Air (YW/ANE) — Valencia (VLC)

☐ EC-HBY	ATR 72-212A	578	ex F-WWEA	Abeto
☐ EC-HCG	ATR 72-212A	580	ex F-WWEC	Castano
☐ EC-HEI	ATR 72-212A	570	ex F-WWEG	Eucalipto
☐ EC-HEJ	ATR 72-212A	565	ex F-WWEE	Carrasca
☐ EC-HJI	ATR 72-212A	562	ex F-WWLZ	Sauce
☐ EC-	ATR 72-600		ex	o/o♦
☐ EC-	ATR 72-600		ex	o/o♦
☐ EC-	ATR 72-600		ex	o/o♦
☐ EC-	ATR 72-600		ex	o/o♦
☐ EC-GYI	Canadair CRJ-200ER	7249	ex C-GDDM	Pinazo
☐ EC-GZA	Canadair CRJ-200ER	7252	ex C-GDDO	Beniliure
☐ EC-HEK	Canadair CRJ-200ER	7320	ex C-GFCN	Cecilio Pla
☐ EC-HHI	Canadair CRJ-200ER	7343	ex C-GFKQ	Genaro Lahuerta Lopez
☐ EC-HHV	Canadair CRJ-200ER	7350	ex C-GFKR	Sorolla
☐ EC-HPR	Canadair CRJ-200ER	7430	ex C-GHDM	Mompo
☐ EC-HSH	Canadair CRJ-200ER	7466	ex C-GHWD	J Michavilla
☐ EC-HTZ	Canadair CRJ-200ER	7493	ex C-GIHJ	Ricardo Verde
☐ EC-HXM	Canadair CRJ-200ER	7514	ex C-GIQL	Francisco Dominguez
☐ EC-HYG	Canadair CRJ-200ER	7529	ex C-GIXG	E Sales Frances
☐ EC-HZR	Canadair CRJ-200ER	7547	ex C-GJFR	José Ribera
☐ EC-IAA	Canadair CRJ-200ER	7563	ex C-GJIZ	A Munoz Degrain
☐ EC-IBM	Canadair CRJ-200ER	7591	ex C-GJQZ	J Navarro Llorens
☐ EC-IDC	Canadair CRJ-200ER	7622	ex C-GJYV	Francisco Ribalta
☐ EC-IGO	Canadair CRJ-200ER	7661	ex C-FVAZ	Juan de Juanes
☐ EC-IJE	Canadair CRJ-200ER	7700	ex C-GZJZ	Josquin Agrasot
☐ EC-IJF	Canadair CRJ-200ER	7705	ex C-GZKC	Vicente Magip
☐ EC-IJS	Canadair CRJ-200ER	7706	ex C-GZKD	Manuel Benedito
☐ EC-IKZ	Canadair CRJ-200ER	7732	ex C-GZUR	Tomas Yepes
☐ EC-ILF	Canadair CRJ-200ER	7746	ex C-FZQR	Vincente Lopez
☐ EC-INF	Canadair CRJ-200ER	7785	ex C-GYVM	Pedro de Valencia
☐ EC-IRI	Canadair CRJ-200ER	7851	ex C-GZNF	Benjamin Palencia
☐ EC-ITU	Canadair CRJ-200ER	7866	ex C-GZSQ	Pons Arnau
☐ EC-IVH	Canadair CRJ-200ER	7915	ex C-FADU	José Mongrell
☐ EC-IZP	Canadair CRJ-200ER	7950	ex C-FBFI	Enriqe Martinez Cubells
☐ EC-JCG	Canadair CRJ-200ER	7973	ex C-FCEU	José Vergara
☐ EC-JCL	Canadair CRJ-200ER	7975	ex C-FCID	
☐ EC-JCM	Canadair CRJ-200ER	7981	ex C-FCNN	Beato de Liebana
☐ EC-JCO	Canadair CRJ-200ER	7984	ex C-FCRX	
☐ EC-JEE	Canadair CRJ-200ER	7989	ex C-FCZD	Juan Ignacio Pombo
☐ EC-JEF	Canadair CRJ-200ER	8008	ex C-FDKH	José Monleon
☐ EC-JEN	Canadair CRJ-200ER	7958	ex C-FBQO	
☐ EC-JNX	Canadair CRJ-200ER	8058	ex C-FGEP	Catedral de Leon
☐ EC-JOD	Canadair CRJ-200ER	8061	ex C-FGYE	
☐ EC-JOY	Canadair CRJ-200ER	8064	ex C-FHCW	Catedral de Leon
☐ EC-JNB	Canadair CRJ-900ER	15057	ex C-	
☐ EC-JTS	Canadair CRJ-900ER	15071	ex C-FJTF	

☐ EC-JTT	Canadair CRJ-900ER	15074	ex C-FJTJ		
☐ EC-JTU	Canadair CRJ-900ER	15079	ex C-FJTE		
☐ EC-JXZ	Canadair CRJ-900ER	15087	ex C-FLGI		
☐ EC-JYA	Canadair CRJ-900ER	15090	ex C-FLIX		
☐ EC-JYV	Canadair CRJ-900ER	15106	ex C-FLMJ		
☐ EC-JZS	Canadair CRJ-900ER	15111	ex C-FLMK		
☐ EC-JZT	Canadair CRJ-900ER	15113	ex C-FLMN		
☐ EC-JZU	Canadair CRJ-900ER	15115	ex C-FLMQ		
☐ EC-JZV	Canadair CRJ-900ER	15117	ex C-FLMS		
☐ EC-LJR	Canadair CRJ-1000	19002	ex C-GCBN		♦
☐ EC-LJS	Canadair CRJ-1000	19003	ex C-GIZJ		♦
☐ EC-LJT	Canadair CRJ-1000	19005	ex C-	o/o	♦
☐ EC-	Canadair CRJ-1000		ex C-	o/o	♦
☐ EC-	Canadair CRJ-1000		ex C-	o/o	♦
☐ EC-	Canadair CRJ-1000		ex C-	o/o	♦
☐ EC-	Canadair CRJ-1000		ex C-	o/o	♦
☐ EC-	Canadair CRJ-1000		ex C-	o/o	♦
☐ EC-	Canadair CRJ-1000		ex C-	o/o	♦
☐ EC-	Canadair CRJ-1000		ex C-	o/o	♦
☐ EC-	Canadair CRJ-1000		ex C-	o/o	♦
☐ EC-IBS	de Havilland DHC-8Q-315	560	ex PH-DME	Cerezo	
☐ EC-IGE	de Havilland DHC-8Q-315	576	ex PH-DMY	Alamo	
☐ EC-IIA	de Havilland DHC-8Q-315	587	ex C-GDIU	Palmera	
☐ EC-IIB	de Havilland DHC-8Q-315	588	ex C-GDIW	Nogal	
☐ EC-IOV	de Havilland DHC-8Q-315	581	ex PH-DEJ	Cedro	
☐ EC-LFE	de Havilland DHC-8Q-315	589	ex PH-DXB		♦
☐ EC-LFG	de Havilland DHC-8Q-315	582	ex PH-DMZ		♦
☐ EC-LFH	de Havilland DHC-8Q-315	586	ex PH-DXA		♦
☐ EC-LFU	de Havilland DHC-8Q-315	574	ex PH-DMX		♦

ALBA STAR *(LAV)*

☐ EC-LAV	Boeing 737-408	24352/1705	ex EC-KTM	♦

ANDALUS LINEAS AEREAS *Malaga*

☐ EC-LCP	Embraer ERJ-145MP	145408	ex EI-EEJ	

AUDELI *Audeli (ADI)* *Madrid-Barajas (MAD)*

☐ EC-IDF	Airbus A340-313X	474	ex F-WWJG	Mariana Pineda	Op by IBE
☐ EC-IIH	Airbus A340-313X	483	ex F-WWJI	Maria Barbara de Braganza	Op by IBE
☐ EC-KCL	Airbus A340-311	005	ex F-GLZA		Op by IBE

BINTER CANARIAS *(NT/IBB)* *Las Palmas-Gran Canaria/Tenerife-Sur, Reine Sofia (LPA/TFS)*

☐ EC-GQF	ATR 72-202	489	ex F-WWLJ		Lsd fr/op for NAY
☐ EC-GRP	ATR 72-202	488	ex F-WWLI		Lsd fr/op for NAY
☐ EC-GRU	ATR 72-202	493	ex F-WWLN		Lsd fr/op for NAY
☐ EC-HEZ	ATR 72-212A	582	ex F-WWEL	Montana del Fuego	op for NAY
☐ EC-IYC	ATR 72-212A	709	ex F-WWEI		
☐ EC-IZO	ATR 72-212A	711	ex F-WWEK		
☐ EC-JAH	ATR 72-212A	712	ex F-WWEL		
☐ EC-JBI	ATR 72-212A	713	ex F-WWEM		
☐ EC-JEH	ATR 72-212A	716	ex F-WWEP		
☐ EC-JEV	ATR 72-212A	717	ex F-WWER		
☐ EC-JQL	ATR 72-212A	726	ex F-WWEG		
☐ EC-KGI	ATR 72-212A	752	ex F-WWEM		Lsd fr/op for NAY
☐ EC-KGJ	ATR 72-212A	753	ex F-WWEN		Lsd fr/op for NAY
☐ EC-KRY	ATR 72-212A	795	ex F-WWEV	Azero	Lsd fr/op for NAY
☐ EC-KSG	ATR 72-212A	796	ex F-WWEW	Malvasla Volcanica	Lsd fr/op for NAY
☐ EC-KYI	ATR 72-212A	850	ex F-WWET	Guarapo	Lsd fr/op for NAY
☐ EC-LAD	ATR 72-212A	864	ex F-WWEJ	Baifo	Lsd fr/op for NAY
☐ EC-LFA	ATR 72-212A	902	ex F-WWER		♦
☐ EC-LGF	ATR 72-212A	907	ex F-WWEX		♦
☐ EC-IJO	Beech 1900D	UE-300	ex F-GRPM		Lsd fr/op by NAY

BKS AIR *Cosmos (CKM)* *Bilbao (BIO)*

☐ EC-JGB	Beech B200 Super King Air	BB-1478	ex D-IHAN	

CALIMA AVIACION *(CMV)* *Las Palmas (LPA)*

☐ EC-LDN	Boeing 737-448	24474/1742	ex N474EA	♦
☐ EC-LKO	Boeing 737-85F	28821/151	ex D-ABBL	♦

CEGISA — Salamanca-Matacan (SLM)

☐ EC-GBP	Canadair CL-215	1031	ex EC-957	Tanker op for DGCN
☐ EC-GBQ	Canadair CL-215	1033	ex EC-958	Tanker op for DGCN
☐ EC-GBR	Canadair CL-215	1051	ex EC-983	Tanker op for DGCN
☐ EC-GBS	Canadair CL-215	1052	ex EC-984	Tanker op for DGCN
☐ EC-GBT	Canadair CL-215	1054	ex EC-985	Tanker op for DGCN
☐ EC-HET	Canadair CL-215	1034	ex I-SISB	Tanker op for Hisporavia
☐ EC-HEU	Canadair CL-215	1038	ex I-SISC	Tanker op for Hisporavia
☐ EC-IQC	Air Tractor AT-802A	802A-0155	ex N8512Q	Tanker
☐ EC-IUJ	Air Tractor AT-802A	802A-0154	ex C-GYZB	Tanker

CLICKAIR

Merged with Vueling

EURO CONTINENTAL AIR — Euro Continental (ECN) — Barcelona (BCN)

☐ EC-GPS	Swearingen SA.227AC Metro III	AC-722	ex N439MA		Frtr Lsd to/op for EAL
☐ EC-JIP	Swearingen SA.226TC Metro II	TC-301	ex N5FY	Viatauro titles	
☐ EC-JQC	Swearingen SA.226AC Merlin IVA	AT-066	ex N5FY		

FAASA AVIACION — FAASA (FAM) — Cordoba-Palma del Rio (ODB)

☐ EC-HNJ	Air Tractor AT-802	802-0096	ex N9075U	
☐ EC-IVL	Air Tractor AT-802A	802A-0159	ex N85152	based Chile as CC-CII
☐ EC-JLD	Air Tractor AT-802A	802A-0210	ex N41810	
☐ EC-JTF	Air Tractor AT-802A	802A-0219		
☐ EC-JTG	Air Tractor AT-802A	802A-0220	ex N8522M	based Chile as CC-CIP
☐ EC-EOI	Bell UH-1B	408	ex N5023U	
☐ EC-EOX	Bell UH-1B	1214	ex N90632	
☐ EC-GAS	Bell 205A-1	30081	ex EC-844	based Chile as CC-CID
☐ EC-GIV	Bell UH-1H	12481	ex N11UH	based Chile as CC-CEN
☐ EC-GKY	Bell UH-1H	13274	ex HE.10B-37	
☐ EC-GKZ	Bell UH-1H	13275	ex HE.10B-38	
☐ EC-GOE	Bell UH-1H	5272	ex N19UH	based Chile as CC-CEL
☐ EC-GOG	Bell UH-1H	9960	ex N17UH	based Chile as CC-CEO
☐ EC-HDD	Bell UH-1H	13551	ex HE.10B-51	
☐ EC-IXU	Bell 412	33037	ex N177EH	
☐ EC-IXV	Bell 412	33068	ex N422EH	
☐ EC-JIM	Bell 412EP	36191	ex N70722	
☐ EC-JRY	Agusta-Bell 412HP	25803	ex SE-JIY	
☐ EC-JTD	Agusta-Bell 412HP	25801	ex SE-JIX	
☐ EC-DVR	Agusta A.109A	7231		EMS
☐ EC-FGL	Bell 206L-3 LongRanger III	51379	ex N65108	EMS
☐ EC-HBJ	Agusta A.109C	7646	ex D-HBRK	EMS
☐ EC-HFV	Bell 212	30818	ex N25UH	
☐ EC-HXL	Bell 222UT	47570	ex TC-HLS	
☐ EC-IFB	Bell 222UT	47572	ex TC-HKL	
☐ EC-IOM	Agusta-Bell 212	5504	ex D-HAFV	
☐ EC-KED	Agusta A.119 Koala	14015	ex N119LF	<ERA Helicopters
☐ EC-KEF	Agusta A.119 Koala	14048	ex N325BC	
☐ EC-KEG	Agusta A.119 Koala	14520	ex N119JA	<ERA Helicopters
☐ EC-KFZ	Kamov Ka.32A-11BC	9804		
☐ EC-KGA	Kamov Ka.32A-11BC	9805		

FLIGHTLINE — Flight-Avia (FTL) — Barcelona (BCN)

☐ EC-GFK	Swearingen SA.226AT Merlin IVA	AT-062	ex EC-125	
☐ EC-HBF	Swearingen SA.226AT Merlin IVA	AT-074	ex EC-GDR	MRW Courier titles
☐ EC-HHN	Embraer EMB.120RT Brasilia	120103	ex N127AM	all-white
☐ EC-LFT	Embraer EMB.120ER Brasilia	120014	ex F-GVBR	

FLYSUR — Cordoba-Palma del Rio (ODB)

☐ EC-IDG	ATR 42-320	003	ex F-WQNE	<TLY

GESTAIR CARGO — (RGN) — Madrid-Barajas (MAD)

☐ EC-FTR	Boeing 757-256 (PCF)	26239/553	ex EC-420	
☐ EC-KLD	Boeing 757-256 (PCF)	24121/183	ex N28AT	
☐ EC-LKI	Boeing 767-383ER (BDSF)	26544/412	ex N767FF	◆
☐ EC-	Boeing 767-383ER (BDSF)	24729/358	ex N767NF	o/o◆

HELI DUERO   *Valladolid (VLL)*

☐ EC-HOX	Bell 212	32254	ex 4X-BCF	
☐ EC-HOY	Bell 212	32225	ex 4X-BCN	
☐ EC-HPJ	Bell 212	32217	ex 4X-BCJ	
☐ EC-HXV	Bell 212	30647	ex FAP 74-614	
☐ EC-HZG	Bell 212	32224	ex 4X-BCO	
☐ EC-IXX	Bell 412	33043	ex N419EH	

HELICSA HELICOPTEROS   *Helicsa (HHH)*   *Albacete-Helicsa Heliport/Madrid*

☐ EC-DXM	Aérospatiale SA365C2 Dauphin 2	5007	ex PH-SSL	
☐ EC-FOX	Aérospatiale SA365C2 Dauphin 2	5024	ex EC-136	EMS
☐ EC-GCZ	Aérospatiale SA365C2 Dauphin 2	5037	ex EC-887	EMS
☐ EC-GXY	Aérospatiale SA365N1 Dauphin 2	6242	ex N12AE	EMS
☐ EC-HCL	Aérospatiale AS365N2 Dauphin 2	6416	ex SE-JAE	SAR
☐ EC-HIM	Aérospatiale AS365N2 Dauphin 2	6478	ex SE-JCE	SAR
☐ EC-HRL	Aérospatiale AS365C2 Dauphin 2	5055	ex PH-SSY	EMS
☐ EC-IEL	Aérospatiale SA365C3 Dauphin 2	5017	ex F-GHXF	EMS
☐ EC-IGM	Aérospatiale SA365N3 Dauphin 2	6616	ex F-WQDA	Survey
☐ EC-ILN	Aérospatiale SA365N1 Dauphin 2	6234	ex LV-WLU	EMS
☐ EC-JDQ	Aérospatiale SA365N3 Dauphin 2	6679	ex EC-IZQ	Survey
☐ EC-JLV	Aérospatiale SA365N1 Dauphin 2	6264	ex LN-OPM	EMS
☐ EC-JLX	Aérospatiale SA365N1 Dauphin 2	6346	ex LN-OPL	EMS
☐ EC-JVG	Aérospatiale AS365N3 Dauphin 2	6718	ex F-WWOQ	
☐ EC-EEQ	Bell 212	30612	ex D-HOBB	EMS
☐ EC-FBM	Bell 212	30574	ex EC-552	SAR
☐ EC-GIC	Bell 212	30775	ex LN-OQD	SAR
☐ EC-GID	Bell 212	31150	ex OY-HCS	SAR
☐ EC-GLS	Bell 212	31155	ex OY-HCU	SAR
☐ EC-GVP	Bell 212	30572	ex LN-OQG	SAR
☐ EC-GXA	Bell 212	30812	ex LN-OQJ	SAR
☐ EC-HFX	Bell 212	30639	ex G-BCMC	SAR
☐ EC-HTJ	Bell 212	30648	ex PK-HMC	SAR
☐ EC-INN	Bell 212	31146	ex SE-JLP	
☐ EC-IKY	Eurocopter EC135T2	0255	ex D-HECO	EMS
☐ EC-ION	Eurocopter EC135T2	0272		EMS
☐ EC-ITJ	Eurocopter EC135T2	0306		EMS
☐ EC-IUN	Eurocopter EC135T2	0317		EMS
☐ EC-JDG	Eurocopter EC135T2	0354		EMS
☐ EC-JHT	Eurocopter EC135T2	0396		EMS
☐ EC-JUE	Eurocopter EC135T2	0345	ex EC-067	EMS
☐ EC-DVK	MBB Bo.105CB	S-630	ex D-HDSZ	Argos I
☐ EC-DVL	MBB Bo.105CB	S-631	ex D-HDTA	Argos II
☐ EC-ESX	MBB BK-117B-1	7176	ex D-HBHS	
☐ EC-FFV	MBB Bo.105CBS	S-852	ex D-HFHJ	
☐ EC-FMZ	Sikorsky S-61N	61361	ex LN-ORH	Op for SASEMAR
☐ EC-FTB	Sikorsky S-61N	61741	ex LN-OSY	Op for SASEMAR
☐ EC-FVO	Sikorsky S-61N	61756	ex EC-575	Op for SASEMAR
☐ EC-FZJ	Sikorsky S-61N	61758	ex EC-717	Op for SASEMAR
☐ EC-GHY	Aérospatiale AS355F1 Ecureuil 2	5089	ex EC-293	EMS
☐ EC-GSK	Bell 412	33092	ex SE-HVL	
☐ EC-HEE	Aérospatiale AS355N Ecureuil 2	5645	ex F-OHVD	
☐ EC-HXZ	Bell 412	33106	ex PK-HMT	EMS
☐ EC-JTO	Aérospatiale AS350B3 Ecureuil	3091	ex LN-OPK	
☐ EC-JTP	Aérospatiale AS350B3 Ecureuil	3445	ex SE-JHK	
☐ EC-JYE	Aérospatiale SA.330J Puma	1241	ex D-HAXC	
☐ EC-JYF	Aérospatiale SA.330J Puma	1285	ex D-HAXD	
☐ EC-KDO	Aérospatiale AS350B3 Ecureuil	3667	ex LN-OMA	
☐ EC-LCH	Agusta AW139	31257		

HELIMAR   *Valencia-Heliport*

☐ EC-DNU	Aérospatiale AS350B Ecureuil	1475	ex F-WZFH	
☐ EC-DYK	Aérospatiale AS350B Ecureuil	1863		
☐ EC-FME	Aérospatiale AS350B2 Ecureuil	2448	ex F-GKLR	
☐ EC-GDL	Aérospatiale AS350B2 Ecureuil	2879		op for Policia Foral de Navarra
☐ EC-GDP	Aérospatiale AS350B2 Ecureuil	2886		op for Policia Foral de Navarra
☐ EC-GIY	Aérospatiale AS350B2 Ecureuil	2175	ex JA9809	
☐ EC-EVS	Bell UH-1B	893	ex EC-463	
☐ EC-EXO	Bell UH-1B	202	ex EC-436	
☐ EC-GIZ	Bell UH-1H	5631	ex EC-297	
☐ EC-GJA	Bell UH-1H	5387	ex EC-298	

☐	EC-GJB	Bell UH-1H	9262	ex EC-299		
☐	EC-GSP	Bell UH-1H	8853	ex N1206P		
☐	EC-IGP	Bell 212	30915	ex N5009N		
☐	EC-IGQ	Bell 212	30936	ex N5010F		

HELISURESTE	**Helisureste (UV/HSE)**	**Alicante-San Vincente Heliport**

☐	EC-DNM	Agusta A.109A	7222	ex N4210X		EMS
☐	EC-DZT	Agusta A.109A	7159	ex HB-XIU		EMS
☐	EC-FUY	Agusta A.109C	7670	ex EC-453		Fishery Patrol
☐	EC-GCQ	Agusta A.109C	7665	ex EC-895		Fishery Patrol
☐	EC-GRA	Agusta A.109C	7676	ex EC-GJD		
☐	EC-HAO	Agusta A.109C Max	7642	ex D-HAAC		EMS
☐	EC-HBQ	Agusta A.109A II	7399	ex I-SOCC		EMS
☐	EC-HHQ	Agusta A.109E Power	11058			EMS
☐	EC-IJR	Agusta A.109E Power	11137			EMS
☐	EC-IKN	Agusta A.109A II	7391	ex I-AGSL		EMS
☐	EC-ILA	Agusta A.109E Power	11028	ex F-GSMP		
☐	EC-IRQ	Agusta A.109E Power	11205			
☐	EC-IUS	Agusta A.109E Power	11229			
☐	EC-JGC	Agusta A.109E Power	11622			
☐	EC-JKP	Agusta A.109E Power	11637			>EDO
☐	EC-JPP	Agusta A.109S Grand	22005	ex I-RAIP		
☐	EC-JUS	Agusta A.109E Power	11675			
☐	EC-KJU	Agusta A.109S Grand	11709			
☐	I-REMS	Agusta A.109S Grand	22024			
☐	EC-JOU	Agusta AW139	31034	ex I-RAII		
☐	EC-KHV	Agusta AW139	31089			
☐	EC-KJT	Agusta AW139	31104	ex I-EASK		
☐	EC-KLM	Agusta AW139	31201	ex I-EASB	201	o/o Op for SASEMAR
☐	EC-KLN	Agusta AW139	31202		202	Op for SASEMAR
☐	EC-KXE	Agusta AW139	31219			
☐	EC-LBM	Agusta AW139	31226			
☐	EC-EUT	Bell 206L-3 LongRanger III	51337	ex N8212U		
☐	EC-FCO	Bell 206L-3 LongRanger III	51179	ex N52CH		
☐	EC-FFQ	Bell 206L-3 LongRanger III	51463	ex N6635Y		
☐	EC-FOL	Bell 206L-3 LongRanger III	51417	ex N6605R		
☐	EC-FRY	Bell 206L-3 LongRanger III	51330	ex N43904		
☐	EC-GCU	Bell 206LT TwinRanger	52105	ex EC-843		EMS
☐	EC-JKG	Bell 206L-4 LongRanger IV	52068	ex OK-YIP		
☐	EC-FBL	Bell 212	30558	ex EC-553		
☐	EC-GXG	Bell 212	30759	ex N21601		
☐	EC-IFA	Bell 212	30689	ex N1074C		
☐	EC-IYO	Bell 212	30946	ex C-GZMZ		
☐	EC-IYP	Bell 212	30533	ex C-FZPX		
☐	EC-IMZ	Bell 407	53547	ex C-GLZA		
☐	EC-IYZ	Bell 407	53599			
☐	EC-IZB	Bell 407	53601			
☐	EC-JAR	Bell 407	53370	ex N54LM		
☐	EC-JBU	Bell 407	53241	ex I-FREC		
☐	EC-JBV	Bell 407	53613	ex C-FBXL		
☐	EC-JSD	Bell 407	53687	ex C-FHYS		
☐	EC-FEL	Agusta-Bell 412SP	25576	ex EC-607		
☐	EC-GOP	Bell 412HP	36031	ex N4603T		
☐	EC-GPA	Bell 412HP	36071	ex N7238Y		
☐	EC-HFD	Bell 412EP	36183	ex N52247		>HSU
☐	EC-HXX	Bell 412	33062	ex N4014U		
☐	EC-HYM	Bell 412	33045	ex C-FTDM		
☐	EC-HZD	Bell 412	33056	ex N4031F		
☐	EC-IPM	Bell 412	33050	ex C-GJKT		
☐	EC-JJE	Bell 412EP	33004	ex N164EH		
☐	EC-JJQ	Bell 412EP	36376	ex N46372		
☐	EC-JLH	Bell 412EP	36374	ex N3119U		>HSU
☐	EC-JXQ	Bell 412EP	36091	ex N5087V		
☐	EC-KBB	Bell 412EP	36426	ex N94479		
☐	EC-KBT	Bell 412EP	36423	ex C-FLOX		
☐	EC-KGZ	Bell 412EP	36434	ex C-FMQC		
☐	EC-KUV	Agusta-Bell 412	25602	ex I-MAGM		
☐	EC-LBL	Agusta-Bell 412SP	25600	ex I-CGCL		
☐	EC-JAK	Kamov Ka.32A-11BC	9624/8811/11			based Chile

☐ EC-JAL	Kamov Ka-32A-11BC	9625/8812/12			
☐ EC-JGV	Kamov Ka.32A-11BC	97-08/23			Based Chile
☐ EC-JGX	Kamov Ka.32A-11BC	97-09/24			Based Chile
☐ EC-JSP	Kamov Ka.32A-11BC	9710			
☐ EC-JSQ	Kamov Ka.32A-11BC	9712			
☐ EC-JUZ	Kamov Ka.32A-11BC	9713			
☐ EC-JVA	Kamov Ka.32A-11BC	9714			
☐ EC-JXG	Kamov Ka.32A-11BC	9715			
☐ EC-KFZ	Kamov Ka.32A-11BC	9804			
☐ EC-KGA	Kamov Ka.32A-11BC	9805			
☐ EC-KSH	Kamov Ka.32A-11BC	9814			
☐ EC-DYQ	Agusta-Bell 206B JetRanger III	8677	ex HB-XML		
☐ EC-KEL	CASA CN-235-300MPA	169	ex EC-027		Op for SASEMAR
☐ EC-KEM	CASA CN-235-300MPA	171	ex EC-021	103	Op for SASEMAR
☐ EC-KIJ	Eurocopter EC135T2i	0579			
☐ EC-KJP	Aérospatiale AS355NP Ecureuil 2	5752			

HELISWISS IBERICA — Iberswiss (HSW) — Barcelona-Sabadell / Baqueira-Beret

☐ EC-FRU	Bell 206B JetRanger III	4268	ex EC-339	
☐ EC-GQH	Bell 206B JetRanger	578	ex HB-XDH	
☐ EC-IUO	Aérospatiale AS350B2 Ecureuil	2393	ex EC-HYV	
☐ EC-JFS	Aérospatiale AS350B3 Ecureuil	3785	ex N18HX	
☐ EC-JID	Aérospatiale AS350BA Ecureuil	1452	ex F-GKCF	

IBERIA LINEAS AEREAS DE ESPANA — Iberia (IB/IBE) — Madrid-Barajas (MAD)

Member of Oneworld

☐ EC-HGR	Airbus A319-111	1154	ex D-AVYY	Ribeira Sacra	
☐ EC-HGS	Airbus A319-111	1180	ex D-AVWR	Bardenas Reales	
☐ EC-HGT	Airbus A319-111	1247	ex D-AVYV	Ignitas de Enciso	
☐ EC-HKO	Airbus A319-111	1362	ex D-AVWJ	Gorbea	
☐ EC-JAZ	Airbus A319-111	2264	ex D-AVWQ	Las Medulas	
☐ EC-JDL	Airbus A319-111	2365	ex D-AVYN	Los Llanos de Aridane	
☐ EC-JEI	Airbus A319-111	2311	ex D-AVYG	Xativa	
☐ EC-JVE	Airbus A319-111	2843	ex D-AVYT	Puerto de la Cruz	
☐ EC-JXA	Airbus A319-111	2870	ex D-AVWG	Ciudad de Ubeda	
☐ EC-JXJ	Airbus A319-111	2889	ex D-AVYH	Ciudad de Baeza	
☐ EC-JXV	Airbus A319-111	2897	ex D-AVWH	Concejo de Cabrales	
☐ EC-KBJ	Airbus A319-111	3054	ex D-AVYS	Lince Iberico	
☐ EC-KBX	Airbus A319-111	3078	ex D-AVYH	Oso Pardo	
☐ EC-KDI	Airbus A319-111	3102	ex D-AVYA	Cigüeña Negra	
☐ EC-KEV	Airbus A319-111	3169	ex D-AVXD	Urogallo	
☐ EC-KFT	Airbus A319-111	3179	ex D-AVXK	Nutria	
☐ EC-KHM	Airbus A319-111	3209	ex D-AVWL	Búho Real	
☐ EC-KJC	Airbus A319-111	3255	ex D-AVXL	Avutarda	
☐ EC-KKS	Airbus A319-111	3320	ex D-AVYF	Halcón Peregrino	retro colours
☐ EC-KMD	Airbus A319-111	3380	ex D-AVWE		
☐ EC-KME	Airbus A319-111	3377	ex D-AVWC	Grulla	
☐ EC-KOY	Airbus A319-111	3443	ex D-AVYN		
☐ EC-KUB	Airbus A319-111	3651	ex D-AVYR		
☐ EC-LEI	Airbus A319-111	3744	ex D-AVWZ	Vison Europeo	♦
☐ EC-FDA	Airbus A320-211	0176	ex EC-581	Lagunas de Ruidera	
☐ EC-FDB	Airbus A320-211	0173	ex EC-580	Lago de Sanabria	
☐ EC-FGR	Airbus A320-211	0224	ex EC-586	Dehesa de Moncayo	[MAD]
☐ EC-FGV	Airbus A320-211	0207	ex EC-584	Monfrague	[MAD]
☐ EC-FLP	Airbus A320-211	0266	ex EC-881	Torcal de Antequera	[MAD]
☐ EC-FLQ	Airbus A320-211	0274	ex EC-882	Dunas de Liencres	[MAD]
☐ EC-FNR	Airbus A320-211	0323	ex EC-885	Monte el Valle	
☐ EC-FQY	Airbus A320-211	0356	ex EC-886	Juan Miro	
☐ EC-HAF	Airbus A320-214	1047	ex F-WWIE	Santiago de Compostela	
☐ EC-HAG	Airbus A320-214	1059	ex F-WWIP	Senorio de Bertiz	
☐ EC-HDK	Airbus A320-214	1067	ex F-WWBF	Mar Ortigola	
☐ EC-HDT	Airbus A320-214	1119	ex F-WWBO	Museo Guggenheim Bilbao	
☐ EC-HGZ	Airbus A320-214	1208	ex F-WWIM	Boi Taull	
☐ EC-HQG	Airbus A320-214	1379	ex F-WWIO	Las Hurdes	[MAD]
☐ EC-HSF	Airbus A320-214	1255	ex EC-HHC	Mar Menor	
☐ EC-HTA	Airbus A320-214	1516	ex F-WWIK	Cadaques	
☐ EC-HTB	Airbus A320-214	1530	ex F-WWIO	Playa de las Americas	
☐ EC-HTC	Airbus A320-214	1540	ex F-WWIU	Alpujarra	For VLE
☐ EC-HUJ	Airbus A320-214	1292	ex EC-HKL	Getaria	
☐ EC-HUK	Airbus A320-214	1318	ex EC-HKM	Laguna Negra	
☐ EC-HUL	Airbus A320-214	1347	ex EC-HKN	Monasterio de Rueda	
☐ EC-HYC	Airbus A320-214	1262	ex EC-HKI	Ciudad de Ceuta	

☐	EC-HYD	Airbus A320-214	1288	ex EC-HKX	Maspalomas	
☐	EC-IEF	Airbus A320-214	1655	ex F-WWDY	Castillo de Loarre	
☐	EC-IEG	Airbus A320-214	1674	ex F-WWIL	Costa Brava	
☐	EC-IEI	Airbus A320-214	1694	ex F-WWBT	Monasterio de Valldigna	
☐	EC-ILQ	Airbus A320-214	1736	ex F-WWDJ	La Padrera	
☐	EC-ILR	Airbus A320-214	1793	ex F-WWIM	San Juan de la Pena	
☐	EC-ILS	Airbus A320-214	1809	ex F-WWBC	Sierra de Cameros	
☐	EC-IZH	Airbus A320-214	2225	ex F-WWID	San Pere de Roda	
☐	EC-IZR	Airbus A320-214	2242	ex F-WWDA	Urkiola	
☐	EC-JFG	Airbus A320-214	2143	ex F-WWBV	Valle de Ricote	
☐	EC-JFH	Airbus A320-214	2104	ex F-WWBE	Trujillo	
☐	EC-JFN	Airbus A320-214	2391	ex F-WWDB	Sierra de las Nieves	
☐	EC-JSB	Airbus A320-214	2776	ex F-WWDV	Benalmadena	
☐	EC-JSK	Airbus A320-214	2807	ex F-WWIN	Ciudad Encantada	
☐	EC-KHJ	Airbus A320-214	2347	ex XA-UDT	Muralla de Lugo	
☐	EC-KNM	Airbus A320-214	1229	ex XA-MXD	Hoces de Gabriel	
☐	EC-KOH	Airbus A320-214	2248	ex XA-UDU	Fontibre	
☐	EC-LEA	Airbus A320-214	1099	ex EC-HDO	Formentera	◆
☐	EC-LKH	Airbus A320-214	1101	ex EC-HDP	Parque de Cabarceno	◆
☐	EC-	Airbus A320-214		ex		o/o◆
☐	EC-	Airbus A320-214		ex		o/o◆
☐	EC-	Airbus A320-214		ex		o/o◆
☐	EC-HUH	Airbus A321-211	1021	ex EC-HAC	Benidorm	
☐	EC-HUI	Airbus A321-211	1027	ex EC-HAE	Comunidad Autonoma de la Rioja	
☐	EC-IGK	Airbus A321-211	1572	ex EC-HTF	Costa Calida	
☐	EC-IIG	Airbus A321-211	1554	ex EC-HTE	Ciudad de Siguenza	
☐	EC-IJN	Airbus A321-211	1836	ex D-AVZN	Merida	
☐	EC-ILO	Airbus A321-211	1681	ex D-AVZW	Cueva de Nerja	
☐	EC-ILP	Airbus A321-211	1716	ex D-AVZT	Peniscola	
☐	EC-ITN	Airbus A321-211	2115	ex D-AVXG	Empuries	
☐	EC-IXD	Airbus A321-211	2220	ex D-AVZR	Valle de Aran	
☐	EC-JDM	Airbus A321-211	2357	ex D-AVZV	Cantabria	
☐	EC-JDR	Airbus A321-211	2488	ex D-AVXD	Sierra Cebollera	
☐	EC-JEJ	Airbus A321-211	2381	ex D-AVZI	Riofrio	
☐	EC-JGS	Airbus A321-211	2472	ex D-AVXA	Guadalupe	
☐	EC-JLI	Airbus A321-211	2563	ex D-AVZB	Delta Del Llobregat	
☐	EC-JMR	Airbus A321-211	2599	ex D-AVZL	Aranjuez	
☐	EC-JNI	Airbus A321-211	2270	ex D-AVZA	Palmeral de Elche	
☐	EC-JQZ	Airbus A321-211	2736	ex D-AVZJ	Generalife	
☐	EC-JRE	Airbus A321-211	2756	ex D-AVZA	Villa de Uncastillo	
☐	EC-JZM	Airbus A321-211	2996	ex D-AVZP	Aquila Imperial	
☐	EC-	Airbus A330-341	144	ex PK-GPD		o/o
☐	EC-GGS	Airbus A340-313	125	ex EC-154	Concha Espina	
☐	EC-GHX	Airbus A340-313	134	ex EC-155	Rosalia de Castro	
☐	EC-GJT	Airbus A340-313	145	ex EC-156	Rosa Chacel	
☐	EC-GLE	Airbus A340-313	146	ex EC-157	Concepcion Arenal	
☐	EC-GPB	Airbus A340-313X	193	ex F-WWJR	Teresa de Avila	
☐	EC-GQK	Airbus A340-313X	197	ex F-WWJL	Emelia Pardo Bazan	[CHR]
☐	EC-GUP	Airbus A340-313X	217	ex F-WWJG	Agustina de Aragon	
☐	EC-GUQ	Airbus A340-313X	221	ex F-WWJA	Beatriz Galindo	
☐	EC-HDQ	Airbus A340-313X	302	ex F-WWJU	Sor Juana Ines de la Cruz	
☐	EC-HGU	Airbus A340-313X	318	ex F-WWJL	Maria de Molina	
☐	EC-HGV	Airbus A340-313X	329	ex F-WWJP	Maria Guerrero	
☐	EC-HGX	Airbus A340-313X	332	ex F-WWJR	Maria Pita	
☐	EC-HQN	Airbus A340-313X	414	ex F-WWJN	Luisa Carvajal y Mendoza	
☐	EC-ICF	Airbus A340-313X	459	ex F-WWJU	Maria Zambrano	
☐	EC-IDF	Airbus A340-313X	474	ex F-WWJG	Mariana Pineda	Op for ADI
☐	EC-IIH	Airbus A340-313X	483	ex F-WWJI	Maria Barbara de Braganza	Op for ADI
☐	EC-KCL	Airbus A340-311	005	ex F-GLZA		Op for ADI
☐	EC-KOU	Airbus A340-313	088	ex C-FTNQ		
☐	EC-KSE	Airbus A340-313X	170	ex C-FYLD		
☐	EC-LHM	Airbus A340-313X	387	ex F-WJKK		◆
☐	EC-INO	Airbus A340-642	431	ex F-WWCI	Gaudi	
☐	EC-IOB	Airbus A340-642	440	ex F-WWCL	Julio Romero de Torres	
☐	EC-IQR	Airbus A340-642	460	ex F-WWCO	Salvador Dali	
☐	EC-IZX	Airbus A340-642	601	ex F-WWCS	Mariano Benlliure	
☐	EC-IZY	Airbus A340-642	604	ex F-WWCH	Ignacio de Zuloaga	
☐	EC-JBA	Airbus A340-642	606	ex F-WWCV	Joaquin Rodrigo	
☐	EC-JCY	Airbus A340-642	617	ex F-WWCL	Andres Segovia	
☐	EC-JCZ	Airbus A340-642	619	ex F-WWCP	Vincente Aleixandre	
☐	EC-JFX	Airbus A340-642	672	ex F-WWCB	Jacinto Benavente	
☐	EC-JLE	Airbus A340-642	702	ex F-WWCM	Santiago Ramon y Cajal	
☐	EC-JNQ	Airbus A340-642	727	ex F-WWCV	Antonio Machado	

154

☐ EC-JPU	Airbus A340-642	744	ex F-WWCF	Pio Baroja	
☐ EC-KZI	Airbus A340-642	1017	ex F-WWCS		♦
☐ EC-LCZ	Airbus A340-642	993	ex F-WWCK		[MAD]♦
☐ EC-LEU	Airbus A340-642	960	ex F-WWCG	Virgen de Montsserat	♦
☐ EC-LEV	Airbus A340-642	1079	ex F-WWCE		♦
☐ EC-LFS	Airbus A340-642	1122	ex F-WW		o/o♦
☐ EC-EXG	McDonnell-Douglas MD-87	49833/1706	ex EC-296	Ciudad de Almeria	
☐ EC-EXM	McDonnell-Douglas MD-87	49835/1717	ex EC-298	Ciudad de Zaragoza	[MAD]
☐ EC-FHD	McDonnell-Douglas MD-87	53212/1877	ex EC-638	Ciudad de Leon	
☐ EC-FIG	McDonnell-Douglas MD-88	53195/1929	ex EC-753	Penon de Ifach	[MAD]
☐ EC-FJE	McDonnell-Douglas MD-88	53197/1940	ex EC-755	Gibraltaro	[MAD]
☐ EC-FLN	McDonnell-Douglas MD-88	53303/1974	ex EC-945	Puerta de Tierra	
☐ EC-FOF	McDonnell-Douglas MD-88	53307/2015	ex EC-966	Puerta de Alcala	
☐ EC-FOZ	McDonnell-Douglas MD-88	53308/2022	ex EC-987	Montjuic	
☐ EC-FPD	McDonnell-Douglas MD-88	53309/2023	ex EC-988	Lago de Coradonga	[MAD]

IBERWORLD AIRLINES   *Iberworld (TY/IWD)*   **Palma de Mallorca (PMI)**

☐ EC-INZ	Airbus A320-214	2011	ex F-WWBR		
☐ EC-JQP	Airbus A320-214	2745	ex F-WWBO		
☐ EC-KYZ	Airbus A320-214	3758	ex F-WWBZ		
☐ EC-KZG	Airbus A320-214	3868	ex F-WWIC		
☐ EC-LAJ	Airbus A320-214	3889	ex F-WWBX		
☐ EC-LAQ	Airbus A320-214	3933	ex F-WWBU		
☐ EC-IJH	Airbus A330-322	072	ex D-AERG	Gloria Fluxa	
☐ EC-JHP	Airbus A330-343X	670	ex F-WWKU		
☐ EC-KCP	Airbus A330-343E	833	ex F-WWKO		
☐ EC-LEQ	Airbus A330-343E	1097	ex F-WWKL		>XLF♦

ISLAS AIRWAYS   *Pintadera (IF/ISW)*   **Tenerife Norte (TNR)**

☐ EC-IKQ	ATR 72-202	477	ex F-WQNM	La Palma	
☐ EC-JCD	ATR 72-202	452	ex F-WQND		
☐ EC-KKZ	ATR 72-212	766	ex F-WWEE	Isla de Fuerteventura	
☐ EC-KNO	ATR 72-212	770	ex F-WWEI	Isla de Palma	
☐ EC-KUR	ATR 72-212A	808	ex F-WWES	Isla de Lanzarote	
☐ EC-LKK	ATR 72-212	461	ex F-GVZF		♦
☐ EC-	ATR 72-500		ex		o/o♦
☐ EC-	ATR 72-500		ex		o/o♦
☐ EC-	ATR 72-500		ex		o/o♦

LANZAROTE AEROCARGO   *Baraka (LZT)*   **Lanzarote-Arrecife (ACE)**

☐ EC-IKM	Cessna 208B Caravan I	208B0948	ex D-FMCG		

MINT AIRWAYS

☐ EC-LBC	Boeing 757-28A	26276/704	ex G-CEJM	Tato Goya	
☐ EC-LHL	Boeing 757-28A	24544/280	ex OM-ASG	David Summers	♦

NAYSA AEROTAXIS   *Naysa (ZN/NAY)*   **Las Palmas-Gran Canaria (LPA)**

☐ EC-GQF	ATR 72-202	489	ex F-WWLJ		Lsd to/op for IBB
☐ EC-GRP	ATR 72-202	488	ex F-WWLI		Lsd to/op for IBB
☐ EC-GRU	ATR 72-202	493	ex F-WWLN		Lsd to/op for IBB
☐ EC-HEZ	ATR 72-212A	582	ex F-WWEL	Montana del Fuego	op for IBB
☐ EC-IPJ	ATR 72-202	307	ex F-GKOC		Lsd to/op for IBB
☐ EC-KGI	ATR 72-212A	752	ex F-WWEM		Lsd to/op for IBB
☐ EC-KGJ	ATR 72-212A	753	ex F-WWEN		Lsd to/op for IBB
☐ EC-KRY	ATR 72-212A	795	ex F-WWEV	Azero	Lsd to/op for IBB
☐ EC-KSG	ATR 72-212A	796	ex F-WW		Lsd to/op for IBB
☐ EC-KYI	ATR 72-212A	850	ex F-WWET	Guarapo	Lsd to/op for IBB
☐ EC-LAD	ATR 72-212A	864	ex F-WWEJ	Baifo	Lsd to/op for IBB
☐ EC-IJO	Beech 1900D	UE-300	ex F-GRPM	Garajonal	

PANAIR LINEAS AEREAS   *Skyjet (PV/PNR)*   **Madrid-Barajas (MAD)**

☐ EC-ELT	British Aerospace 146 Srs.200QT	E2102	ex EC-198		
☐ EC-FVY	British Aerospace 146 Srs.200QT	E2117	ex EC-615		
☐ EC-FZE	British Aerospace 146 Srs.200QT	E2105	ex EC-719		
☐ EC-GQO	British Aerospace 146 Srs.200QT	E2086	ex D-ADEI		
☐ EC-HDH	British Aerospace 146 Srs.200QT	E2056	ex G-TNTA		
☐ EC-HJH	British Aerospace 146 Srs.200QT	E2112	ex G-BOMK		
☐ EC-HQT	Airbus A300B4-103F	124	ex G-TNTS		[MHV]

PIRINAIR EXPRESS — Pirinair Express (PRN) — Zaragoza (ZAZ)

☐ EC-FZB	Swearingen SA.226TC Metro II	TC-221	ex EC-666
☐ EC-JCV	Swearingen SA.226AT Merlin IVA	AT-038	ex SX-BGT

PRIVALEGE STYLE — (PVG)

☐ EC-HDS	Boeing 757-256	26252/900		Milagros Diaz
☐ EC-ISY	Boeing 757-256	26241/572	ex N26ND	<Bristol Assoc

PRONAIR AIRLINES — Valencia (VLC)

☐ EC-KJI	McDonnell-Douglas MD-87	49836/1721	ex EC-EXN	Ciudad de Torretallada
☐ EC-KRP	Boeing 747-245F	20826/242	ex EC-KMR	
☐ EC-KRV	McDonnell-Douglas MD-87	49843/1771	ex EC-EZS	

PULLMANTUR AIR — Pullmantur (PLM) — Madrid-Barajas (MAD)

☐ EC-KQC	Boeing 747-412	26549/1030	ex 9V-SMZ	
☐ EC-KSM	Boeing 747-412	27178/1015	ex 9V-SMW	
☐ EC-KXN	Boeing 747-4H6	25703/1025	ex N703AC	
☐ EC-LGL	Boeing 747-412	26555/1075	ex 9V-SPH	◆

RYJET — Malaga (AGP)

☐ EC-JHE	SAAB SF.340A	340A-018	ex SE-LMV

SAESA — Saesa (SSS) — Madrid-Cuatro Vientos

☐ EC-IEU	Bell 205A-1	30083	ex PT-HCR

SAICUS AIR — (FYA) — Palma de Mallorca (PMI)

☐ EC-JUV	Boeing 737-301 (SF)	23741/1498	ex N576US
☐ EC-KKJ	Boeing 737-4B7 (SF)	24559/1847	ex N437US

SERAIR — Cargopress (SEV) — Las Palmas-Gran Canaria (LPA)

☐ EC-GTM	Beech 1900C	UB-30	ex N7210R
☐ EC-GUD	Beech 1900C-1	UC-156	ex N156YV
☐ EC-GZG	Beech 1900C-1	UC-161	ex N55635
☐ EC-JDY	Beech 1900C-1	UC-91	ex N91YV

SPANAIR — Spanair (JK/JKK) — Palma de Mallorca (PMI)

Member of Star Alliance

☐ EC-HPM	Airbus A321-231	1276	ex D-AVZO	Camilo Jose Cela
☐ EC-HQZ	Airbus A321-231	1333	ex D-AVZB	
☐ EC-HRG	Airbus A321-231	1366	ex D-AVZC	Placido Domingo
☐ EC-HRP	Airbus A320-232	1349	ex F-WWBD	Juan de Avalos
☐ EC-HXA	Airbus A320-232	1497	ex F-WWID	
☐ EC-IAZ	Airbus A320-232	1631	ex F-WWDP	
☐ EC-ICL	Airbus A320-232	1682	ex F-WWBD	
☐ EC-IEJ	Airbus A320-232	1749	ex F-WWBO	
☐ EC-IIZ	Airbus A320-232	1862	ex F-WWDZ	Club Vacaciones titles
☐ EC-IJU	Airbus A321-231	1843	ex D-AVZR	
☐ EC-ILH	Airbus A320-232	1914	ex F-WWDU	Star Alliance c/s
☐ EC-IMB	Airbus A320-232	1933	ex F-WWII	Vodafone Passport titles
☐ EC-INB	Airbus A321-231	1946	ex D-AVXD	
☐ EC-INM	Airbus A320-232	1979	ex F-WWBE	Star Alliance c/s
☐ EC-IOH	Airbus A320-232	1998	ex F-WWIV	Star Alliance c/s
☐ EC-IPI	Airbus A320-232	2027	ex F-WWDP	Star Alliance c/s
☐ EC-IVG	Airbus A320-232	2168	ex F-WWDA	
☐ EC-IYG	Airbus A320-232	2210	ex F-WWBG	
☐ EC-IZK	Airbus A320-232	2223	ex F-WWDO	Reyno de Navarra titles
☐ EC-JJD	Airbus A320-232	2479	ex F-WWIM	Costa Brava titles
☐ EC-JNC	Airbus A320-232	2589	ex F-WWDP	Juan Antonio Samaranch
☐ EC-KEC	Airbus A320-232	1183	ex G-MIDW	
☐ EC-KOX	Airbus A320-232	1383	ex G-MIDV	
☐ EC-KPX	Airbus A320-232	1407	ex G-MIDU	
☐ EC-FTS	McDonnell-Douglas MD-83	49621/1495	ex EC-479	Sunbird
☐ EC-GCV	McDonnell-Douglas MD-82	53165/2042	ex EC-894	Sunburst
☐ EC-GNY	McDonnell-Douglas MD-83	49396/1305	ex N396GE	Sunflash
☐ EC-GQG	McDonnell-Douglas MD-83	49577/1454	ex EC-FSY	Star Alliance c/s
☐ EC-GVO	McDonnell-Douglas MD-83	49642/1421	ex N462GE	Sunspot
☐ EC-GXU	McDonnell-Douglas MD-83	49622/1498	ex EC-FTT	Star Alliance c/s

☐ EC-KAZ	McDonnell-Douglas MD-87	49614/1556	ex OY-KHI	Star Alliance c/s	<SAS
☐ EC-KCZ	McDonnell-Douglas MD-87	49609/1517	ex OY-KHF	Star Alliance c/s	<SAS
☐ EC-KHA	McDonnell-Douglas MD-87	49611/1522	ex LN-RMG	Star Alliance c/s	<SAS
☐ EC-KJE	McDonnell-Douglas MD-87	49606/1569	ex SE-DIF	Star Alliance c/s	<SAS
☐ EC-KVA	McDonnell-Douglas MD-87	53208/1865	ex EC-FEY		[MAD]

SWIFTAIR — Swift (SWT) — Madrid-Barajas (MAD)

☐ EC-INV	ATR 72-201	274	ex N274AT	Frtr
☐ EC-ISX	ATR 42-320	242	ex N242AT	Frtr; no titles
☐ EC-IVP	ATR 42-300	231	ex F-GKND	Frtr
☐ EC-IYH	ATR 72-212	330	ex F-WQUI	Frtr
☐ EC-JAD	ATR 42-300	321	ex F-GHPY	
☐ EC-JBN	ATR 42-300 (QC)	218	ex F-GHPK	all-white
☐ EC-JBX	ATR 42-300	254	ex N255AE	Frtr
☐ EC-JDX	ATR 72-201	234	ex F-GHPV	Frtr; all-white
☐ EC-JQF	ATR 72-201F	147	ex SE-LVK	
☐ EC-JRP	ATR 72-212	446	ex D-AEWK	
☐ EC-JXF	ATR 72-201F	150	ex OY-CIV	
☐ EC-KAD	ATR 72-202F	171	ex F-GKPC	
☐ EC-KAE	ATR 72-202F	192	ex F-GKPE	
☐ EC-KAI	ATR 42-300F	141	ex EI-FXF	
☐ EC-KIZ	ATR 72-202F	204	ex F-GPOA	<FPO
☐ EC-KJA	ATR 72-202F	207	ex F-GPOB	<FPO
☐ EC-KKQ	ATR 72-212A	763	ex F-WWEB	
☐ EC-KUL	ATR 72-212A	809	ex F-WWET	
☐ EC-KVI	ATR 72-212A	824	ex F-WWEM	>AEE
☐ EC-IMY	Boeing 727-225 (FedEx 3)	21293/1241	ex N8875Z	pax aircraft
☐ EC-JHU	Boeing 727-230F (FedEx 3)	21442/1326	ex N302FV	
☐ EC-KDY	Boeing 737-3S3F	23811/1445	ex N811AN	
☐ EC-KLR	Boeing 737-3Q8 (SF)	23766/1375	ex N237CP	
☐ EC-KRA	Boeing 737-3Y0F	24679/1897	ex SX-BGK	
☐ EC-KTZ	Boeing 737-375F	23708/1395	ex N111KH	
☐ EC-KVD	Boeing 737-306F	23538/1288	ex N102KH	
☐ EC-LAC	Boeing 737-3M8F	24022/1662	ex N107KH	
☐ EC-LJI	Boeing 737-301 (SF)	23512/1291	ex OO-TNI	♦
☐ EC-GQA	Embraer EMB-120ER Brasilia	120027	ex EC-GMT	Frtr
☐ EC-HAK	Embraer EMB-120ER Brasilia	120008	ex N212AS	Frtr
☐ EC-HCF	Embraer EMB-120ER Brasilia	120007	ex N211AS	Frtr
☐ EC-HFK	Embraer EMB.120ER Brasilia	120063	ex N7215U	Frtr
☐ EC-HMY	Embraer EMB-120ER Brasilia	120009	ex N214AS	Frtr, all-white
☐ EC-HTS	Embraer EMB.120ER Brasilia	120168	ex N168CA	Frtr
☐ EC-IMX	Embraer EMB-120ER Brasilia	120158	ex N312FV	Frtr
☐ EC-JBD	Embraer EMB.120ER Brasilia	120012	ex D-CAOB	Frtr
☐ EC-JBE	Embraer EMB.120ER Brasilia	120013	ex D-CAOA	Frtr
☐ EC-JKH	Embraer EMB.120ER Brasilia	120092	ex OM-SPY	
☐ EC-JJS	McDonnell-Douglas MD-83	49793/1656	ex N827NK	>UN
☐ EC-JQV	McDonnell-Douglas MD-83	49526/1342	ex N14879	Real Madrid c/s
☐ EC-JUF	McDonnell-Douglas MD-83	53168/2061	ex N802NK	Op for UN
☐ EC-JUG	McDonnell-Douglas MD-83	49847/1585	ex N834NK	Op for UN
☐ EC-KCX	McDonnell-Douglas MD-83	49619/1483	ex N814NK	
☐ EC-LEY	McDonnell-Douglas MD-83	53182/2068	ex I-SMED	

TAF HELICOPTERS — Helitaf (HET) — Barcelona (BCN)

☐ EC-DRG	Aérospatiale AS350B Ecureuil	1597		
☐ EC-ERD	Aérospatiale AS350B Ecureuil	1530	ex G-JORR	EMS
☐ EC-EZP	Aérospatiale AS350B Ecureuil	2413	ex EC-562	
☐ EC-FOA	Aérospatiale AS350BA Ecureuil	2626	ex EC-990	
☐ EC-FOQ	Aérospatiale AS350BA Ecureuil	2639	ex EC-906	
☐ EC-IHX	Aérospatiale AS350B3 Ecureuil	3587	ex F-WQRN 06	EMS
☐ EC-IOI	Aérospatiale AS350B3 Ecureuil	3640	ex F-WQDH	
☐ EC-IPC	Aérospatiale AS350B3 Ecureuil	3710		
☐ EC-JEA	Aérospatiale AS350B3 Ecureuil	3819	ex SE-JHX	
☐ EC-KFU	Aérospatiale AS350B3 Ecureuil	4251	ex SE-JJO	
☐ EC-KJF	Aérospatiale AS350B3 Ecureuil	4088	ex SE-JJJ	
☐ EC-IFU	Eurocopter EC135P2	0223		EMS
☐ EC-IQZ	Eurocopter EC135P2	0293		EMS
☐ EC-JJI	Eurocopter EC135P2	0383		
☐ EC-JVS	Eurocopter EC135P2	0436		
☐ EC-KDA	Eurocopter EC135P2+	0538		
☐ EC-DSU	MBB Bo.105CBS-5	S-623	ex D-HDSS 02	EMS

☐ EC-FYV	MBB Bo.105CBS-5	S-896	ex EC-705	01		EMS
☐ EC-HNT	MBB Bo.105CBS-4	S-414	ex D-HDMA			EMS
☐ EC-HPB	MBB Bo.105CBS-4	S-672	ex D-HEIM			EMS
☐ EC-IKO	MBB Bo.105CBS-4	S-661	ex D-HGYN			EMS
☐ EC-IKT	MBB Bo.105CBS	S-615	ex D-HEMS			EMS
☐ EC-GUH	Aérospatiale AS355F2 Twin Star	5474	ex N6040U			EMS
☐ EC-GUZ	Aérospatiale AS355F2 Twin Star	5454	ex N26ET			
☐ EC-IKV	Eurocopter EC130B4	3753				

TAS TRANSPORTES AEREOS DEL SUR

☐ EC-KEK	CASA CN-235-300MPA	C166	ex EC-101	Op for SASEMA
☐ EC-KEL	CASA CN-235-300MPA	169	ex EC-027	Op for SASEMA
☐ EC-KEM	CASA CN-235-300MPA	171	ex EC-021	Op for SASEMA

TAVASA — Tavasa (TVH) — Bilbao (BIO)

☐ EC-EBB	Aérospatiale SA365C3 Dauphin 2	5013	ex F-GBOU
☐ EC-EGV	Aérospatiale SA365C3 Dauphin 2	5032	ex F-GBTB
☐ EC-ERY	Sikorsky S-76A+	760037	ex EC-364
☐ EC-ERZ	Aérospatiale AS350B2 Ecureuil	2261	
☐ EC-GMZ	Eurocopter EC135T1	0016	ex D-HECG
☐ EC-GNA	Eurocopter EC135T1	0017	ex D-HECH

TOP-FLY — Topfly (TLY) — Barcelona (BCN)

☐ EC-EYV	Piper PA-34-220T Seneca III	34-8233109	ex OE-FYB	
☐ EC-GJM	Swearingen SA.227AC Metro III	BC-772B	ex N439MA	
☐ EC-HZM	Piper PA-34-200 Seneca	34-7250169	ex F-GFJE	
☐ EC-IDG	ATR 42-320	003	ex F-WQNE	all-white
☐ EC-IRS	Swearingen SA.227BC Metro III	BC-786B	ex N61AJ	
☐ EC-ITP	Swearingen SA.227BC Metro III	BC-789B	ex ZS-PDW	
☐ EC-JYJ	Aérospatiale AS355F2 Twin Star	5425	ex N225NR	

TRAGSA MEDIOS AEREOS — Tragsa (TRG) — Madrid-Cuatro Vientos/Toledo

☐ EC-HTV	Bell 212	30665	ex N212HS
☐ EC-HTX	Bell 212	31151	ex N8169Q
☐ EC-HUS	Bell 212	30655	ex D-HAFS
☐ EC-HXR	Agusta-Bell 212	5522	ex D-HAFG
☐ EC-IAV	Bell 212	30534	ex N7964J
☐ EC-IGR	Bell 212	30989	ex N1074C
☐ EC-ERK	Bell 204 (UH-1E)	6069	ex N151LC
☐ EC-GSO	Bell UH-1H	5466	ex N1217A
☐ EC-GUT	Bell UH-1H	13367	ex N21UH
☐ EC-GXF	Bell UH-1H	12604	ex N22UH

TRANPORTES AEREOS DEL SUR — TAS (HSS) — Seville (SVQ)

☐ EC-GHS	Partenavia P.68 Observer	329-20-OB	ex G-OBSV		
☐ EC-GSQ	Beech B300 Super King Air	FL-128	ex N128FL		
☐ EC-HAP	CASA C.212-300MPA	465	ex EC-011		Maritime Patrol
☐ EC-HTU	CASA C.212-300MPA	470			Maritime Patrol
☐ EC-IFL	Partenavia P.68C	412	ex N412VR		
☐ EC-ILE	Beech B200 Super King Air	BB-1792	ex N5092K	Muxtamel	EMS
☐ EC-INX	CASA C.212-300MPA	472			Maritime Patrol
☐ EC-IUX	Beech B200 Super King Air	BB-1840	ex N816LD		

VUELING AIRLINES — Vueling (VY/VLG) — Barcelona (BCN)

☐ EC-FCB	Airbus A320-211	0158	ex EC-579	Montana de Covadonga	♦
☐ EC-GRG	Airbus A320-211	0143	ex EC-FBS		
☐ EC-GRH	Airbus A320-211	0146	ex EC-FBR		
☐ EC-GRI	Airbus A320-211	0177	ex EC-FEO		
☐ EC-HHA	Airbus A320-214	1221	ex F-WWBF		
☐ EC-HQI	Airbus A320-214	1396	ex F-WWIX		
☐ EC-HQJ	Airbus A320-214	1430	ex F-WWBR		
☐ EC-HQL	Airbus A320-214	1461	ex F-WWDD	Click on Vueling	
☐ EC-HTD	Airbus A320-214	1550	ex F-WWDC	Unos vuelan, ostros Vueling	
☐ EC-ICQ	Airbus A320-211	0199	ex EC-FGU		
☐ EC-ICR	Airbus A320-211	0240	ex EC-FIA		
☐ EC-ICS	Airbus A320-211	0241	ex EC-FIC		
☐ EC-ICT	Airbus A320-211	0264	ex EC-FKD		
☐ EC-IZD	Airbus A320-214	2207	ex F-WWDS	Barceloning	
☐ EC-JFF	Airbus A320-214	2388	ex F-WWIH	Vueling the world	
☐ EC-JGM	Airbus A320-214	2407	ex F-WWDC	The joy of Vueling	

☐ EC-JSY	Airbus A320-214	2785	ex F-WWBU	Connie Baraja	
☐ EC-JTQ	Airbus A320-214	2794	ex F-WWBN	Vueling, que es gerundio	
☐ EC-JTR	Airbus A320-214	2798	ex F-WWIF	no Vueling, no party	
☐ EC-JYX	Airbus A320-214	2962	ex F-WWDJ	Elisenda Masana	
☐ EC-JZI	Airbus A320-214	2988	ex F-WWII	Vueling in love	
☐ EC-JZQ	Airbus A320-214	0992	ex TC-JLE	I Want to Vueling	
☐ EC-KBU	Airbus A320-214	1413	ex TC-JLF	Be Vueling my friend	
☐ EC-KCU	Airbus A320-216	3109	ex F-WWIR	My name is Ling. Vue Ling	
☐ EC-KDG	Airbus A320-214	3095	ex F-WWIY		
☐ EC-KDH	Airbus A320-214	3083	ex F-WWIX	Ain't no Vueling high enough	
☐ EC-KDT	Airbus A320-216	3145	ex F-WWBM	Ready, steady, Vueling	
☐ EC-KDX	Airbus A320-216	3151	ex F-WWBU		
☐ EC-KFI	Airbus A320-216	3174	ex F-WWIP		
☐ EC-KHN	Airbus A320-216	3203	ex F-WWIG		
☐ EC-KJD	Airbus A320-216	3237	ex F-WWBJ		
☐ EC-KKT	Airbus A320-214	3293	ex F-WWDU	Vueling Together	
☐ EC-KLB	Airbus A320-214	3321	ex F-WWBY	Vuela y punto	
☐ EC-KLT	Airbus A320-216	3376	ex F-WWDI		
☐ EC-KMI	Airbus A320-216	3400	ex F-WWBT	How are you? I'm Vueling!	
☐ EC-KRH	Airbus A320-214	3529	ex D-AVVD		
☐ EC-LAA	Airbus A320-214	2678	ex A6-ABZ		
☐ EC-LAB	Airbus A320-214	2761	ex OE-LEV		
☐ EC-	Airbus A320-214		ex		o/o♦
☐ EC-	Airbus A320-214		ex		o/o♦
☐ EC-	Airbus A320-214		ex		o/o♦
☐ EC-	Airbus A320-214		ex		o/o♦
☐ EC-	Airbus A320-214		ex		o/o♦
☐ EC-	Airbus A320-214		ex		o/o♦

VUELOS MEDITERRANEO — Vuelos Mediterraneo (VMM) — Valencia (VLC)

☐ EC-FCC	Cessna 402B II	402B1013	ex EC-614
☐ EC-HCU	Swearingen SA.226TC Metro II	TC-390	ex N19WP

ZOREX — Zorex (ORZ) — Madrid-Barajas (MAD)

☐ EC-HJC	Swearingen SA.226TC Metro II	TC-318	ex OY-JEO
☐ EC-JYC	Swearingen SA.226TC Metro II	TC-303	ex N117AR

EI-   IRELAND (Eire)

AER ARANN — Aer Arann (RE/REA) — Dublin (DUB)

☐ EI-BYO	ATR 42-310	161	ex OY-CIS	
☐ EI-CBK	ATR 42-310	199	ex F-WWEM	
☐ EI-CPT	ATR 42-300	191	ex (SE-KCX)	
☐ EI-CVR	ATR 42-310	022	ex F-GGLK	
☐ EI-EHH	ATR 42-300	196	ex G-SSEA	
☐ EI-REH	ATR 72-202	260	ex OY-RTA	
☐ EI-REI	ATR 72-202	267	ex OY-RTB	
☐ EI-REL	ATR 72-212A	748	ex F-WWEI	
☐ EI-REM	ATR 72-212A	760	ex F-WWEW	
☐ EI-REO	ATR 72-212A	787	ex F-WWEF	
☐ EI-REP	ATR 72-212A	797	ex F-WWEZ	
☐ EI-RES	ATR 72-212A		ex F-WW	o/o
☐ EI-RET	ATR 72-212A		ex F-WW	o/o
☐ EI-REU	ATR 72-212A		ex F-WW	o/o
☐ EI-REV	ATR 72-212A		ex F-WW	o/o

AER ARANN ISLANDS — Galway (GWY)

☐ EI-AYN	Britten-Norman BN-2A-8 Islander	704	ex G-BBFJ
☐ EI-BCE	Britten-Norman BN-2A-26 Islander	519	ex G-BDUV
☐ EI-CUW	Britten-Norman BN-2B-26 Islander	2293	ex G-BWYW

AER LINGUS — Shamrock (EI/EIN) — Dublin (DUB)

☐ EI-CVA	Airbus A320-214	1242	ex F-WWIT	St Schira/Scire
☐ EI-CVB	Airbus A320-214	1394	ex F-WWIV	St Mobhi/Mobhi
☐ EI-CVC	Airbus A320-214	1443	ex F-WWBS	St Kealin/Caolfhionn
☐ EI-CVD	Airbus A320-214	1467	ex F-WWDG	St Kevin/Caoimhin
☐ EI-DEA	Airbus A320-214	2191	ex F-WWBX	St Fidelma/Fiedeilme
☐ EI-DEB	Airbus A320-214	2206	ex F-WWBP	St Nathy/Naithi
☐ EI-DEC	Airbus A320-214	2217	ex F-WWBH	St Fergal/Fearghal
☐ EI-DEE	Airbus A320-214	2250	ex F-WWBE	St Ultan/Ultan

☐ EI-DEF	Airbus A320-214	2256	ex F-WWBK	St Declan/Deaglan	
☐ EI-DEG	Airbus A320-214	2272	ex F-WWIB	St Fachtna/Fachtna	
☐ EI-DEH	Airbus A320-214	2294	ex F-WWBX	St Conleth/Connlaodh	
☐ EI-DEI	Airbus A320-214	2374	ex F-WWDU	St Oliver Plunkett/Oilibh Plunceid	
☐ EI-DEJ	Airbus A320-214	2364	ex F-WWDI	St Kilian/Cillian	
☐ EI-DEK	Airbus A320-214	2399	ex F-WWIZ	St Eunan/Eunan	
☐ EI-DEL	Airbus A320-214	2409	ex F-WWDE	St Canice/Cainneach	
☐ EI-DEM	Airbus A320-214	2411	ex F-WWDG	St Ibar/Ibhar	
☐ EI-DEN	Airbus A320-214	2432	ex F-WWBK	St Kieran/Ciaran	
☐ EI-DEO	Airbus A320-214	2486	ex F-WWIV	St Senan/Seanan	
☐ EI-DEP	Airbus A320-214	2542	ex F-WWIU	St Eugene/Eoghan	
☐ EI-DER	Airbus A320-214	2583	ex F-WWDE	St Mel/Mel	
☐ EI-DES	Airbus A320-214	2635	ex F-WWDZ	St Pappin/Paipan	
☐ EI-DET	Airbus A320-214	2810	ex F-WWIP	St Brendan/Breandan	
☐ EI-DVE	Airbus A320-214	3129	ex F-WWBJ	St Aideen/Etaoin	
☐ EI-DVF	Airbus A320-214	3136	ex F-WWDF	St Jarlath/Iarfhlaith	
☐ EI-DVG	Airbus A320-214	3318	ex F-WWIV	St Flannan/Flannan	
☐ EI-DVH	Airbus A320-214	3345	ex F-WWBP		
☐ EI-DVI	Airbus A320-214	3501	ex F-WWBQ	St Emer/Eimaer	
☐ EI-DVJ	Airbus A320-214	3857	ex F-WWDL	St Macarthan/Macarthain	
☐ EI-DVK	Airbus A320-214	4572	ex D-AUBY		♦
☐ EI-	Airbus A320-214		ex F-WWDV		o/o♦
☐ EI-	Airbus A320-214		ex		o/o♦
☐ EI-	Airbus A320-214		ex		o/o♦
☐ EI-EDP	Airbus A320-214	3781	ex F-WWIR		
☐ EI-EDS	Airbus A320-214	3755	ex F-WWBU	St Malachy/Maolmhaodhog	
☐ EI-CPC	Airbus A321-211	0815	ex D-AVZT	St Fergus/Feargus	
☐ EI-CPD	Airbus A321-211	0841	ex D-AVZA	St Davnet/Damhnat	
☐ EI-CPE	Airbus A321-211	0926	ex D-AVZQ	St Enda/Eanna	
☐ EI-CPF	Airbus A321-211	0991	ex D-AVZE	St Ida/Ide	
☐ EI-CPG	Airbus A321-211	1023	ex D-AVZR	St Aidan/Aodhan	
☐ EI-CPH	Airbus A321-211	1094	ex F-WWDD	St Dervilla/Dearbhile	
☐ EI-DAA	Airbus A330-202	397	ex F-WWKK	St Keeva/Caoimhe	
☐ EI-DUO	Airbus A330-202	841	ex F-WWYT	St Columba/Colum	
☐ EI-DUZ	Airbus A330-302	847	ex F-WWKM	St Aoife/Aoife	
☐ EI-EAV	Airbus A330-302	985	ex F-WWKF	Ronan	
☐ EI-EDY	Airbus A330-302	1025	ex F-WWYU	Maincin	
☐ EI-ELA	Airbus A330-302X	1106	ex F-WWYH	St Patrick/Padraig	♦
☐ EI-LAX	Airbus A330-202	269	ex F-WWKV	St Mella/Mella	
☐ EI-ORD	Airbus A330-301	059	ex F-GMDD	St Maeve/Maedbh	

AIR CONTRACTORS   *Contract / Rapex (AG/ABR)*   **Dublin (DUB)**

☐ EI-DHL	Airbus A300B4-203F	274	ex OO-DIB		
☐ EI-EAB	Airbus A300B4-203F	199	ex OO-DLW		♦
☐ EI-EAC	Airbus A300B4-203F	250	ex OO-DLT		
☐ EI-EAD	Airbus A300B4-203F	289	ex OO-DLU		
☐ EI-OZB	Airbus A300B4-103F	184	ex OO-DIH		
☐ EI-OZC	Airbus A300B4-103F	189	ex OO-DIJ		
☐ EI-OZD	Airbus A300B4-203F	236	ex OO-DLE		
☐ EI-OZE	Airbus A300B4-203F	152	ex OO-DLC		♦
☐ EI-OZF	Airbus A300B4-203F	259	ex OO-DLD		
☐ EI-OZG	Airbus A300B4-203F	208	ex OO-DLG		♦
☐ EI-OZH	Airbus A300B4-203F	234	ex OO-DLI		
☐ EI-OZI	Airbus A300B4-203F	219	ex OO-DLZ		♦
☐ EI-SAF	Airbus A300B4-203F	220	ex OO-DIC		
☐ EI-FXA	ATR 42-320F	282	ex N282AT	Lsd fr/op for FDX	
☐ EI-FXB	ATR 42-320F	243	ex (N924FX)	Lsd fr/op for FDX	
☐ EI-FXC	ATR 42-320F	310	ex (N925FX)	Lsd fr/op for FDX	
☐ EI-FXD	ATR 42-300F	273	ex (N927FX)	Lsd fr/op for FDX	
☐ EI-FXE	ATR 42-320F	327	ex (N926FX)	Lsd fr/op for FDX	
☐ EI-FXG	ATR 72-202F	224	ex (N814FX)	Lsd fr/op for FDX	
☐ EI-FXH	ATR 72-202F	229	ex N815FX	Lsd fr/op for FDX	
☐ EI-FXI	ATR 72-202F	294	ex N818FX	Lsd fr/op for FDX	
☐ EI-FXJ	ATR 72-202F	292	ex N813FX	Lsd fr/op for FDX	
☐ EI-FXK	ATR 72-202F	256	ex N817FX	Lsd fr/op for FDX	
☐ EI-REJ	ATR 72-202F	126	ex ES-KRA		
☐ EI-SLA	ATR 42-300F	149	ex SE-LST	>MSA	
☐ EI-SLC	ATR 42-300F	082	ex OY-CIE	>MSA	
☐ EI-SLF	ATR 72-202F	210	ex OY-RUA		
☐ EI-SLG	ATR 72-202F	183	ex F-WQNI		
☐ EI-SLH	ATR 72-202F	157	ex OY-RTG		
☐ EI-SLI	ATR 42-320	115	ex F-WWEL		
☐ EI-SLJ	ATR 72-201	324	ex LY-PTK		

☐ EI-SLK	ATR 72-212	395	ex N642AS	
☐ EI-SLL	ATR 72-212	387	ex N641AS	
☐ EI-SLM	ATR 72-212	413	ex N643AS	
☐ EI-SLN	ATR 72-212	405	ex N640AS	♦
☐ EI-JIV	Lockheed L-382G-35C Hercules	4673	ex ZS-JIV	<SFR

CHC IRELAND   Dublin (DUB)

☐ EI-CXS	Sikorsky S-61N	61816	ex IAC 257	IMES Rescue based Sligo
☐ EI-CZN	Sikorsky S-61N	61740	ex G-CBWC	IMES Rescue standby
☐ EI-GCE	Sikorsky S-61N	61817	ex LN-ORC	IMES Rescue based Shannon
☐ EI-MES	Sikorsky S-61N	61776	ex G-BXAE	IMES Rescue based Dublin
☐ EI-RCG	Sikorsky S-61N	61807	ex G-87-1	IMES Rescue based Shannon
☐ EI-SAR	Sikorsky S-61N	61143	ex G-AYOM	IMES Rescue based Waterford
☐ EI-MIP	Aérospatiale SA365N2 Dauphin 2	6119	ex G-BLEY	

CITYJET   City-Ireland (WX/BCY)   Dublin (DUB)

☐ EI-RJA	Avro 146-RJ85	E2329	ex G-CDYK	Rathlin Island	
☐ EI-RJB	Avro 146-RJ85	E2330	ex G-CEBS	Bere Island	
☐ EI-RJC	Avro 146-RJ85	E2333	ex G-CEHA	Achill Island	
☐ EI-RJD	Avro 146-RJ85	E2334	ex G-CEFL	Valentia Island	
☐ EI-RJE	Avro 146-RJ85	E2335	ex G-CEBU	St MacDara's Island	
☐ EI-RJF	Avro 146-RJ85	E2337	ex G-CEFN	Great Blasket Island	
☐ EI-RJG	Avro 146-RJ85	E2344	ex G-CEHB	Sherkin Island	
☐ EI-RJH	Avro 146-RJ85	E2345	ex G-CEIC	Inishturko/o	
☐ EI-RJI	Avro 146-RJ85	E2346	ex (G-CDZP)	Skellig Michael	
☐ EI-RJJ	Avro 146-RJ85	E2347	ex G-CEIF	Hare Island	
☐ EI-RJK	Avro 146-RJ85	E2348	ex N523XJ	Collanmore Island	
☐ EI-RJL	Avro 146-RJ85	E2349	ex OH-SAQ		[NWI]♦
☐ EI-RJM	Avro 146-RJ85	E2350	ex OH-SAR		[NWI]♦
☐ EI-RJN	Avro 146-RJ85	E2351	ex N526XJ	Lake Isle of Inisheer	CityJet c/s
☐ EI-RJO	Avro 146-RJ85	E2352	ex N527XJ	Inis Mor	
☐ EI-RJP	Avro 146-RJ85	E2363	ex N529XJ	Clare Island	
☐ EI-RJR	Avro 146-RJ85	E2364	ex N530XJ	Tory Island	
☐ EI-RJS	Avro 146-RJ85	E2365	ex N531XJ	Dursey Island	CityJet c/s
☐ EI-RJT	Avro 146-RJ85	E2366	ex N532XJ	Inishbofin	CityJet c/s
☐ EI-RJU	Avro 146-RJ85	E2367	ex N533XJ	Cape Clear	
☐ EI-RJV	Avro 146-RJ85	E2370	ex N534XJ	Lambay Island	
☐ EI-RJW	Avro 146-RJ85	E2371	ex N535XJ	Garinish Island	
☐ EI-RJX	Avro 146-RJ85	E2372	ex N536XJ	Scattery Island	
☐ EI-RJY	Avro 146-RJ85	E2307	ex N502XJ	Inishcealtra	
☐ EI-RJZ	Avro 146-RJ85	E2326	ex N512XJ		
☐ EI-WXA	Avro 146-RJ85	E2310	ex N503XJ		
☐ EI-WXB	Avro 146-RJ85	E2311	ex N504XJ		[NWI]

IRISH HELICOPTERS   Dublin/Cork (DUB/ORK)

☐ EI-BLD	MBB Bo.105DB	S-381	ex D-HDLQ
☐ EI-LIT	MBB Bo.105CBS	S-434	ex A6-DBH
☐ EI-FAC	Aérospatiale AS350B1 Ecureuil	1991	ex G-BVJE

PREMIER HELICOPTERS   Dublin (DUB)

☐ EI-CGQ	Aérospatiale AS350B Ecureuil	2076	ex G-BUPK
☐ EI-ECA	Agusta A.109A II	7387	ex N109RP
☐ EI-LKS	Eurocopter EC130B4	3643	ex F-WQDQ
☐ EI-LNX	Eurocopter EC130B4	3498	ex N460AE
☐ EI-MLN	Agusta A.109E Power	11115	ex G-ECMM
☐ EI-MSG	Agusta A.109E Power	11692	
☐ EI-PKS	Bell 206B JetRanger III	4480	ex OE-XAC
☐ EI-SQG	Agusta A.109E Power	11084	
☐ EI-TWO	Agusta A.109E Power	11131	ex D-HARY

RYANAIR   Ryanair (FR/RYR)   Dublin (DUB)

☐ EI-DAC	Boeing 737-8AS/W	29938/1240
☐ EI-DAD	Boeing 737-8AS/W	33544/1249
☐ EI-DAE	Boeing 737-8AS/W	33545/1252
☐ EI-DAF	Boeing 737-8AS/W	29939/1262
☐ EI-DAG	Boeing 737-8AS/W	29940/1265
☐ EI-DAH	Boeing 737-8AS/W	33546/1269
☐ EI-DAI	Boeing 737-8AS/W	33547/1271
☐ EI-DAJ	Boeing 737-8AS/W	33548/1274
☐ EI-DAK	Boeing 737-8AS/W	33717/1310
☐ EI-DAL	Boeing 737-8AS/W	33718/1311

☐ EI-DAM	Boeing 737-8AS/W	33719/1312		
☐ EI-DAN	Boeing 737-8AS/W	33549/1361		
☐ EI-DAO	Boeing 737-8AS/W	33550/1366	ex N1800B	
☐ EI-DAP	Boeing 737-8AS/W	33551/1368	ex N6066U	
☐ EI-DAR	Boeing 737-8AS/W	33552/1371	ex EI-DAQ	
☐ EI-DAS	Boeing 737-8AS/W	33553/1372	ex EI-DAR	
☐ EI-DAX	Boeing 737-8AS/W	33557/1438		
☐ EI-DAY	Boeing 737-8AS/W	33558/1441		
☐ EI-DAZ	Boeing 737-8AS/W	33559/1443		
☐ EI-DCB	Boeing 737-8AS/W	33560/1447		
☐ EI-DCC	Boeing 737-8AS/W	33561/1463		
☐ EI-DCD	Boeing 737-8AS/W	33562/1466		
☐ EI-DCE	Boeing 737-8AS/W	33563/1473		
☐ EI-DCF	Boeing 737-8AS/W	33804/1529		
☐ EI-DCG	Boeing 737-8AS/W	33806/1530		
☐ EI-DCH	Boeing 737-8AS/W	33566/1546		
☐ EI-DCI	Boeing 737-8AS/W	33567/1547		
☐ EI-DCJ	Boeing 737-8AS/W	33564/1562		
☐ EI-DCK	Boeing 737-8AS/W	33565/1563		
☐ EI-DCL	Boeing 737-8AS/W	33806/1576	ex N1786B	Dreamliner colours
☐ EI-DCM	Boeing 737-8AS/W	33807/1578		
☐ EI-DCN	Boeing 737-8AS/W	33808/1590	ex N60436	
☐ EI-DCO	Boeing 737-8AS/W	33809/1592		
☐ EI-DCP	Boeing 737-8AS/W	33810/1595		
☐ EI-DCR	Boeing 737-8AS/W	33811/1613		
☐ EI-DCS	Boeing 737-8AS/W	33812/1615		
☐ EI-DCT	Boeing 737-8AS/W	33813/1617		
☐ EI-DCV	Boeing 737-8AS/W	33814/1618		
☐ EI-DCW	Boeing 737-8AS/W	33568/1631		
☐ EI-DCX	Boeing 737-8AS/W	33569/1635		
☐ EI-DCY	Boeing 737-8AS/W	33670/1637		
☐ EI-DCZ	Boeing 737-8AS/W	33815/1638		
☐ EI-DHA	Boeing 737-8AS/W	33571/1642		
☐ EI-DHB	Boeing 737-8AS/W	33572/1652		
☐ EI-DHC	Boeing 737-8AS/W	33573/1655		
☐ EI-DHD	Boeing 737-8AS/W	33816/1657	ex N1784B	
☐ EI-DHE	Boeing 737-8AS/W	33574/1658	ex N1786B	
☐ EI-DHF	Boeing 737-8AS/W	33575/1660	ex N1782B	
☐ EI-DHG	Boeing 737-8AS/W	33576/1670	ex N1787B	
☐ EI-DHH	Boeing 737-8AS/W	33817/1677		
☐ EI-DHI	Boeing 737-8AS/W	33818/1685		
☐ EI-DHJ	Boeing 737-8AS/W	33819/1691		
☐ EI-DHK	Boeing 737-8AS/W	33820/1696		
☐ EI-DHM	Boeing 737-8AS/W	33821/1698		
☐ EI-DHN	Boeing 737-8AS/W	33577/1782		
☐ EI-DHO	Boeing 737-8AS/W	33578/1792	ex N1786B	
☐ EI-DHP	Boeing 737-8AS/W	33579/1794		
☐ EI-DHR	Boeing 737-8AS/W	33822/1798		
☐ EI-DHS	Boeing 737-8AS/W	33580/1807		
☐ EI-DHT	Boeing 737-8AS/W	33581/1809		
☐ EI-DHV	Boeing 737-8AS/W	33582/1811		
☐ EI-DHW	Boeing 737-8AS/W	33823/1819	ex N1786B	
☐ EI-DHX	Boeing 737-8AS/W	33585/1824	ex N60436	
☐ EI-DHY	Boeing 737-8AS/W	33824/1826	ex N1781B	
☐ EI-DHZ	Boeing 737-8AS/W	33583/1834		
☐ EI-DLB	Boeing 737-8AS/W	33584/1836	ex N5573L	
☐ EI-DLC	Boeing 737-8AS/W	33586/1844	ex N1786B	
☐ EI-DLD	Boeing 737-8AS/W	33825/1847		
☐ EI-DLE	Boeing 737-8AS/W	33587/1864		
☐ EI-DLF	Boeing 737-8AS/W	33588/1867		
☐ EI-DLG	Boeing 737-8AS/W	33589/1869	ex N1786B	
☐ EI-DLH	Boeing 737-8AS/W	33590/1886		
☐ EI-DLI	Boeing 737-8AS/W	33591/1894	ex N1786B	
☐ EI-DLJ	Boeing 737-8AS/W	34177/1899		
☐ EI-DLK	Boeing 737-8AS/W	33592/1904	ex N1786B	
☐ EI-DLL	Boeing 737-8AS/W	33593/1914		
☐ EI-DLM	Boeing 737-8AS/W	33694/1923		
☐ EI-DLN	Boeing 737-8AS/W	33595/1926		
☐ EI-DLO	Boeing 737-8AS/W	34178/1929		
☐ EI-DLR	Boeing 737-8AS/W	33596/2057		
☐ EI-DLS	Boeing 737-8AS/W	33621/2058		
☐ EI-DLT	Boeing 737-8AS/W	33597/2060		
☐ EI-DLV	Boeing 737-8AS/W	33598/2063		
☐ EI-DLW	Boeing 737-8AS/W	33599/2078		
☐ EI-DLX	Boeing 737-8AS/W	33600/2082		
☐ EI-DLY	Boeing 737-8AS/W	33601/2088		
☐ EI-DLZ	Boeing 737-8AS/W	33622/2101		

☐ EI-DPA	Boeing 737-8AS/W	33602/2109	
☐ EI-DPB	Boeing 737-8AS/W	33603/2112	ex N1787B
☐ EI-DPC	Boeing 737-8AS/W	33604/2120	ex N1786B
☐ EI-DPD	Boeing 737-8AS/W	33623/2123	ex N1786B
☐ EI-DPE	Boeing 737-8AS/W	33605/2140	ex N1787B
☐ EI-DPF	Boeing 737-8AS/W	33606/2158	
☐ EI-DPG	Boeing 737-8AS/W	33607/2163	
☐ EI-DPH	Boeing 737-8AS/W	33624/2168	
☐ EI-DPI	Boeing 737-8AS/W	33608/2173	
☐ EI-DPJ	Boeing 737-8AS/W	33609/2179	
☐ EI-DPK	Boeing 737-8AS/W	33610/2183	
☐ EI-DPL	Boeing 737-8AS/W	33611/2189	
☐ EI-DPM	Boeing 737-8AS/W	33640/2198	
☐ EI-DPN	Boeing 737-8AS/W	35549/2200	ex N1787B
☐ EI-DPO	Boeing 737-8AS/W	33612/2207	ex N1786B
☐ EI-DPP	Boeing 737-8AS/W	33613/2213	
☐ EI-DPR	Boeing 737-8AS/W	33614/2219	ex N1786B
☐ EI-DPS	Boeing 737-8AS/W	33641/2222	
☐ EI-DPT	Boeing 737-8AS/W	35550/2227	ex N1787B
☐ EI-DPV	Boeing 737-8AS/W	35551/2236	ex N1779B
☐ EI-DPW	Boeing 737-8AS/W	35552/2263	
☐ EI-DPX	Boeing 737-8AS/W	35553/2279	
☐ EI-DPY	Boeing 737-8AS/W	33615/2375	ex N1781B
☐ EI-DPZ	Boeing 737-8AS/W	33616/2376	
☐ EI-DWA	Boeing 737-8AS/W	33617/2377	
☐ EI-DWB	Boeing 737-8AS/W	36075/2382	
☐ EI-DWC	Boeing 737-8AS/W	36076/2384	
☐ EI-DWD	Boeing 737-8AS/W	33642/2389	ex N1781B
☐ EI-DWE	Boeing 737-8AS/W	36074/2391	
☐ EI-DWF	Boeing 737-8AS/W	33619/2396	
☐ EI-DWG	Boeing 737-8AS/W	33620/2397	
☐ EI-DWH	Boeing 737-8AS/W	33637/2408	ex N1787B
☐ EI-DWI	Boeing 737-8AS/W	33643/2410	
☐ EI-DWJ	Boeing 737-8AS/W	36077/2411	
☐ EI-DWK	Boeing 737-8AS/W	36078/2415	ex N1786B
☐ EI-DWL	Boeing 737-8AS/W	33618/2416	ex N1787B
☐ EI-DWM	Boeing 737-8AS/W	36080/2430	
☐ EI-DWO	Boeing 737-8AS/W	36079/2440	
☐ EI-DWP	Boeing 737-8AS/W	36082/2443	
☐ EI-DWR	Boeing 737-8AS/W	36081/2448	ex N1786B
☐ EI-DWS	Boeing 737-8AS/W	33625/2472	ex N1786B
☐ EI-DWT	Boeing 737-8AS/W	33626/2489	
☐ EI-DWV	Boeing 737-8AS/W	33627/2492	
☐ EI-DWW	Boeing 737-8AS/W	33629/2507	ex N1781B
☐ EI-DWX	Boeing 737-8AS/W	33630/2508	
☐ EI-DWY	Boeing 737-8AS/W	33638/2518	ex N1781B
☐ EI-DWZ	Boeing 737-8AS/W	33628/2520	ex N1796B
☐ EI-DYA	Boeing 737-8AS/W	33631/2529	ex N1786B
☐ EI-DYB	Boeing 737-8AS/W	33633/2542	
☐ EI-DYC	Boeing 737-8AS/W	36567/2543	ex N1787B
☐ EI-DYD	Boeing 737-8AS/W	33632/2544	ex N1786B
☐ EI-DYE	Boeing 737-8AS/W	36568/2548	
☐ EI-DYF	Boeing 737-8AS/W	36569/2549	ex N1786B
☐ EI-DYH	Boeing 737-8AS/W	36570/2573	
☐ EI-DYI	Boeing 737-8AS/W	36571/2574	
☐ EI-DYJ	Boeing 737-8AS/W	36572/2580	
☐ EI-DYK	Boeing 737-8AS/W	36573/2581	
☐ EI-DYL	Boeing 737-8AS/W	36574/2635	
☐ EI-DYM	Boeing 737-8AS/W	36575/2636	
☐ EI-DYN	Boeing 737-8AS/W	36576/2367	
☐ EI-DYO	Boeing 737-8AS/W	33636/2728	
☐ EI-DYP	Boeing 737-8AS/W	37515/2729	
☐ EI-DYR	Boeing 737-8AS/W	37513/2734	
☐ EI-DYS	Boeing 737-8AS/W	37514/2735	
☐ EI-DYT	Boeing 737-8AS/W	33634/2745	
☐ EI-DYV	Boeing 737-8AS/W	37512/2746	
☐ EI-DYW	Boeing 737-8AS/W	33635/2747	
☐ EI-DYX	Boeing 737-8AS/W	37517/2754	
☐ EI-DYY	Boeing 737-8AS/W	37521/2755	ex N1787B
☐ EI-DYZ	Boeing 737-8AS/W	37518/2760	
☐ EI-EBA	Boeing 737-8AS/W	37516/2761	
☐ EI-EBB	Boeing 737-8AS/W	37519/2779	ex N1787B
☐ EI-EBC	Boeing 737-8AS/W	37520/2780	ex N1795B
☐ EI-EBD	Boeing 737-8AS/W	37522/2781	ex N1796B
☐ EI-EBE	Boeing 737-8AS/W	37523/2788	
☐ EI-EBF	Boeing 737-8AS/W	37524/2791	ex N1796B
☐ EI-EBG	Boeing 737-8AS/W	37525/2792	

☐ EI-EBH	Boeing 737-8AS/W	37526/2797		
☐ EI-EBI	Boeing 737-8AS/W	37527/2798		
☐ EI-EBK	Boeing 737-8AS/W	37528/2807		
☐ EI-EBL	Boeing 737-8AS/W	37529/2808	ex N1796B	
☐ EI-EBM	Boeing 737-8AS/W	35002/2839	ex N1787B	
☐ EI-EBN	Boeing 737-8AS/W	35003/2840		
☐ EI-EBO	Boeing 737-8AS/W	35004/2843	ex N1796B	
☐ EI-EBP	Boeing 737-8AS/W	37531/2844		
☐ EI-EBR	Boeing 737-8AS/W	37530/2856	ex N1779B	
☐ EI-EBS	Boeing 737-8AS/W	35001/2857	ex N1786B	
☐ EI-EBT	Boeing 737-8AS/W	35000/2858		
☐ EI-EBV	Boeing 737-8AS/W	35009/2872		
☐ EI-EBW	Boeing 737-8AS/W	35010/2873		
☐ EI-EBX	Boeing 737-8AS/W	35007/2882		
☐ EI-EBY	Boeing 737-8AS/W	35006/2886		
☐ EI-EBZ	Boeing 737-8AS/W	35008/2887		
☐ EI-EFA	Boeing 737-8AS/W	35005/2892	ex N1786B	
☐ EI-EFB	Boeing 737-8AS/W	37532/2893		
☐ EI-EFC	Boeing 737-8AS/W	35015/2901		
☐ EI-EFD	Boeing 737-8AS/W	35011/2903	ex N1787B	
☐ EI-EFE	Boeing 737-8AS/W	37533/2905		
☐ EI-EFF	Boeing 737-8AS/W	35016/2917	ex N1786B	
☐ EI-EFG	Boeing 737-8AS/W	35014/2921	ex N1786B	
☐ EI-EFH	Boeing 737-8AS/W	35012/2923	ex N1787B	
☐ EI-EFI	Boeing 737-8AS/W	35013/2924	ex N1786B	
☐ EI-EFJ	Boeing 737-8AS/W	37536/2936	ex N1786B	
☐ EI-EFK	Boeing 737-8AS/W	37537/2948	ex N1786B	
☐ EI-EFL	Boeing 737-8AS/W	37534/2958		
☐ EI-EFM	Boeing 737-8AS/W	37535/2960	ex N1787B	
☐ EI-EFN	Boeing 737-8AS/W	37538/2967	ex N1787B	
☐ EI-EFO	Boeing 737-8AS/W	37539/2978		
☐ EI-EFP	Boeing 737-8AS/W	37540/2979		
☐ EI-EFR	Boeing 737-8AS/W	37541/3012	ex N1786B	
☐ EI-EFS	Boeing 737-8AS/W	37542/3021		
☐ EI-EFT	Boeing 737-8AS/W	37543/3023	ex N1787B	
☐ EI-EFV	Boeing 737-8AS/W	35017/3052	ex N60659	
☐ EI-EFW	Boeing 737-8AS/W	35018/3078	ex N1786B	
☐ EI-EFX	Boeing 737-8AS/W	35019/3079	ex N1787B	
☐ EI-EFY	Boeing 737-8AS/W	35020/3084	ex N1786B	
☐ EI-EFZ	Boeing 737-8AS/W	38489/3089	ex N1787B	
☐ EI-EGA	Boeing 737-8AS/W	38490/3096	ex N1787B	
☐ EI-EGB	Boeing 737-8AS/W	38491/3097	ex N1787B	
☐ EI-EGC	Boeing 737-8AS/W	38492/3099	ex N1786B	
☐ EI-EGD	Boeing 737-8AS/W	34981/3420		♦
☐ EI-EKA	Boeing 737-8AS/W	35022/3139		
☐ EI-EKB	Boeing 737-8AS/W	38494/3141		
☐ EI-EKC	Boeing 737-8AS/W	38495/3143		
☐ EI-EKD	Boeing 737-8AS/W	35024/3146		
☐ EI-EKE	Boeing 737-8AS/W	35023/3148		
☐ EI-EKF	Boeing 737-8AS/W	35025/3152		
☐ EI-EKG	Boeing 737-8AS/W	35021/3161		
☐ EI-EKH	Boeing 737-8AS/W	38493/3162		
☐ EI-EKI	Boeing 737-8AS/W	38496/3169	ex N1786B	
☐ EI-EKJ	Boeing 737-8AS/W	38497/3173	ex N1796B	
☐ EI-EKK	Boeing 737-8AS/W	38500/3174	ex N1787B	
☐ EI-EKL	Boeing 737-8AS/W	38498/3179	ex N1796B	
☐ EI-EKM	Boeing 737-8AS/W	38499/3181	ex N1786B	
☐ EI-EKN	Boeing 737-8AS/W	35026/3187	ex N1787B	
☐ EI-EKO	Boeing 737-8AS/W	35027/3198	ex N1795B	
☐ EI-EKP	Boeing 737-8AS/W	35028/3199	ex N1786B	
☐ EI-EKR	Boeing 737-8AS/W	38503/3202	ex N1786B	
☐ EI-EKS	Boeing 737-8AS/W	38504/3203	ex N1796B	
☐ EI-EKT	Boeing 737-8AS/W	38505/3206	ex N1786B	
☐ EI-EKV	Boeing 737-8AS/W	38507/3211		
☐ EI-EKW	Boeing 737-8AS/W	38506/3221	ex N1786B	♦
☐ EI-EKX	Boeing 737-8AS/W	35030/3218	ex N1787B	♦
☐ EI-EKY	Boeing 737-8AS/W	35031/3230		♦
☐ EI-EKZ	Boeing 737-8AS/W	38508/3234		♦
☐ EI-EMA	Boeing 737-8AS/W	35032/3240		♦
☐ EI-EMB	Boeing 737-8AS/W	35811/3241	ex N1796B	♦
☐ EI-EMC	Boeing 737-8AS/W	38510/3246		♦
☐ EI-EMD	Boeing 737-8AS/W	38509/3248	ex N1786B	♦
☐ EI-EME	Boeing 737-8AS/W	35029/3254		♦
☐ EI-EMF	Boeing 737-8AS/W	34978/3256	ex N1786B	♦
☐ EI-EMH	Boeing 737-8AS/W	34974/3262		♦
☐ EI-EMI	Boeing 737-8AS/W	34979/3263		♦
☐ EI-EMJ	Boeing 737-8AS/W	34975/3271	ex N1786B	♦

☐ EI-EMK	Boeing 737-8AS/W	38512/3272	ex N1786B	♦
☐ EI-EML	Boeing 737-8AS/W	38513/3283	ex N1786B	♦
☐ EI-EMM	Boeing 737-8AS/W	35814/3284	ex N1786B	♦
☐ EI-EMN	Boeing 737-8AS/W	35815/3285		♦
☐ EI-EMO	Boeing 737-8AS/W	40283/3318		♦
☐ EI-EMP	Boeing 737-8AS/W	40285/3322	ex N1787B	♦
☐ EI-EMR	Boeing 737-8AS/W	40284/3323		♦
☐ EI-ENA	Boeing 737-8AS/W	34983/3416	ex N1796B	♦
☐ EI-ENB	Boeing 737-8AS/W	40289/3418		♦
☐ EI-ENC	Boeing 737-8AS/W	34980/3419		♦
☐ EI-ENE	Boeing 737-8AS/W	34976/3428		♦
☐ EI-ENF	Boeing 737-8AS/W	35034/3451		♦
☐ EI-ENG	Boeing 737-8AS/W	34977/3453	ex N1787B	♦
☐ EI-ENH	Boeing 737-8AS/W	35033/3454	ex N1796B	♦
☐ EI-ENI	Boeing 737-8AS/W	40300/3514		♦
☐ EI-ENJ	Boeing 737-8AS/W	40301/3514	ex N1796B	♦
☐ EI-ENK	Boeing 737-8AS/W	40303/3524		o/o♦
☐ EI-ENL	Boeing 737-8AS/W	35037/3527		o/o♦
☐ EI-ENM	Boeing 737-8AS/W	35038/3528		o/o♦
☐ EI-ENN	Boeing 737-8AS/W	35036/3533		o/o♦
☐ EI-ENO	Boeing 737-8AS/W	40302/3534		o/o♦
☐ EI-ENP	Boeing 737-8AS/W	40304/3535		o/o♦
☐ EI-ENR	Boeing 737-8AS/W			o/o♦
☐ EI-ENS	Boeing 737-8AS/W			o/o♦
☐ EI-ENT	Boeing 737-8AS/W			o/o♦
☐ EI-ENU	Boeing 737-8AS/W			o/o♦
☐ EI-ENV	Boeing 737-8AS/W			o/o♦
☐ EI-ENW	Boeing 737-8AS/W			o/o♦
☐ EI-ENX	Boeing 737-8AS/W			o/o♦
☐ EI-ENY	Boeing 737-8AS/W			o/o♦
☐ EI-ENZ	Boeing 737-8AS/W			o/o♦
☐ EI-EPA	Boeing 737-8AS/W			o/o♦
☐ EI-EPB	Boeing 737-8AS/W			o/o♦
☐ EI-EPC	Boeing 737-8AS/W			o/o♦
☐ EI-EPD	Boeing 737-8AS/W			o/o♦
☐ EI-EPE	Boeing 737-8AS/W			o/o♦
☐ EI-EPF	Boeing 737-8AS/W			o/o♦
☐ EI-EPG	Boeing 737-8AS/W			o/o♦
☐ EI-EPH	Boeing 737-8AS/W			o/o♦
☐ EI-	Boeing 737-8AS/W			o/o♦
☐ EI-	Boeing 737-8AS/W			o/o♦
☐ EI-	Boeing 737-8AS/W			o/o♦
☐ EI-	Boeing 737-8AS/W			o/o♦
☐ EI-	Boeing 737-8AS/W			o/o♦
☐ EI-	Boeing 737-8AS/W			o/o♦

VISION AIR	Vision (VAT)	Dublin (DUB)

☐ EI-DIF	Piper PA-31-350 Navajo Chieftain	31-7752105	ex G-OAMT

EK-   ARMENIA (Republic of Armenia)

AIR ARMENIA	Air Armenia (QN/ARR)	Yerevan-Zvartnots (EVN)

☐ EK-11001	Antonov An-12TBK	8346107	ex CCCP-11244	
☐ EK-12104	Antonov An-12BK	8346104	ex CCCP-12110	Cargo titles
☐ EK-32500	Antonov An-32B	2009	ex 9L-LFP	

AIR ARMENIA CARGO		

☐ EK-11810	Antonov An-12BP	5342908	ex UR-11810

AIR HIGHNESSES	(HNS)	Yerevan-Zvartnots (EVN)

☐ EK-12006	Antonov An-12B	01348006	ex UR-CGR	
☐ EK-12908	Antonov An-12B	7344908	ex EK-11029	
☐ EK-76300	Ilyushin Il-76TD	083410300	ex TN-AHT	
☐ EK-76310	Ilyushin Il-76T	1013409310	ex RDPL-34148	♦

ARARAT INTERNATIONAL AIRLINES		Yerevan-Zvartnots (EVN)

☐ EK-82224	McDonnell-Douglas MD-82	53224/2084	ex LZ-LDB	>IRK♦
☐ EK-82852	McDonnell-Douglas MD-82	49852/1959	ex B-2151	

ARK AIRWAYS

☐ EK-76555	Ilyushin Il-76TD	1033416515	ex UP-I7616	♦

ARMAVIA — Armavia (U8/RNV) — Yerevan-Zvartnots (EVN)

☐ EK-RA01	Airbus A319-132	0913	ex HZ-NAS		Op for Govt
☐ EK-32007	Airbus A319-111	3834	ex D-AVYM	Victor Hambardzumyan	
☐ EK-32011	Airbus A319-132	2277	ex N803BR	Mika	
☐ EK-32012	Airbus A319-132	2362	ex N806BR	Air Marshal S Khidiakov	
☐ EK-32005	Airbus A320-211	3492	ex F-WWIU		
☐ EK-32006	Airbus A320-214	0772	ex M-ABCQ		♦
☐ EK-32008	Airbus A320-211	0229	ex N229AN	Aram Khachatryan	
☐ EK-20014	Canadair CRJ-200LR	7282	ex D-ACJI	Sergey Mergelyan	
☐ EK-86118	Ilyushin Il-86	51483209086	ex CCCP-86118		
☐ EK-95015	Sukhoi Superjet 100	95007		Yuri Gagarin	o/o♦
☐ EK-	Sukhoi Superjet 100	95009			o/o♦
☐ EK-65072	Tupolev Tu-134A-3	49972	ex CCCP-65072		Op for Govt
☐ EK-42362	Yakovlev Yak-42D	4520424811431	ex UR-CDU		
☐ EK-42417	Yakovlev Yak-42D	4520423219110	ex RA-42417	all-white	
☐ EK-42470	Yakovlev Yak-42D	4520424116677	ex RA-42444		

AYK AVIA — Yerevan-Zvartnots (EVN)

☐ EK-32410	Antonov An-32	2416	ex 9L-LFU	
☐ EK-74027	Antonov An-74-200	36547096920	ex RA-74027	
☐ EK-74043	Antonov An-74-200	36547096923	ex RA-74043	

BLUE SKY — Blue Armenia (BLM) — Yerevan-Zvartnots (EVN)

☐ EK-30044	Airbus A300B2K-3C	244	ex N142RF	>IRM
☐ EK-30060	Airbus A300B2K-3C	160	ex N141RF	>IRM
☐ EP-MNC	Boeing 747-422	26879/973	ex EK-74779	>IRM

CENTRAL AIRWAYS

☐ EK-26443	Antonov An-26	17311705	ex ER-AFL

MIAPET AVIA — Miapet (MPT) — Yerevan-Zvartnots (EVN)

☐ EK-11660	Antonov An-12BP	5343209	ex RA-11660	dam PNR 25Jan08

NAVIGATOR AIRLINES

☐ EK-26440	Antonov An-26	57303504	ex RA-26640

PHOENIX AVIA — Phoenix Armenia (PHY) — Yerevan-Zvartnote (EVN)

☐ EK-11007	Antonov An-12	5343506	ex RA-11995		
☐ EK-12148	Antonov An-12BK	4341906	ex military	Vasili Pro Kho Renko titles	
☐ EK-12803	Antonov An-12B	01347803	ex XU-395		
☐ EK-46419	Antonov An-24B	87303704	ex RA-46419		
☐ EK-46741	Antonov An-12BK	8345408	ex RA-46741	White Bird	
☐ EK-46839	Antonov An-24T	7910201	ex RA-46839	Ali	
☐ EK-76464	Ilyushin Il-76TD	0023437090	ex RA-76464		♦
☐ EK-76787	Ilyushin Il-76TD	0093495854	ex RA-76787		

SOUTH AIRLINES — South (STH) — Sharjah (SHJ)

☐ EK-11112	Antonov An-12BP	5343307	ex EK-11132
☐ EK-11779	Antonov An-12BP	5343402	ex RA-11401
☐ EK-12122	Antonov An-12BP	5343507	ex RA-11786
☐ EK-12305	Antonov An-12BP	00347305	ex EK-12777
☐ EK-26441	Antonov An-26	57303009	ex ER-AZS
☐ EK-46507	Antonov An-24RV	37308403	ex RA-46507
☐ EK-46656	Antonov An-24RV	47309302	ex RA-46656
☐ EK-47828	Antonov An-24B	17307209	ex UN-47828
☐ EK-72101	Antonov An-72-100	36572040548	ex 4L-VAS
☐ EK-74045	Antonov An-74-200	36547098966	ex RA-74060
☐ EK-76707	Ilyushin Il-76TD	073410292	ex RA-76495
☐ EK-76717	Ilyushin Il-76TD	0043450484	ex UR-76581
☐ EK-76727	Ilyushin Il-76TD	0063467021	ex UR-76681
☐ EK-76737	Ilyushin Il-76MD	0083483502	ex UR-76778

166

TARON AVIA			*(TRV)*	
☐ EK-12005	Antonov An-12BP	5343005	ex XU-U4C	
☐ EK-12704	Antonov An-12BP	01347704	ex EK-11102	
☐ EK-12129	Antonov An-12BP	5342903	ex EK-11772	
☐ EK-76643	Ilyushin Il-76TD	0083488643	ex UR-UCD	♦

VERTIR			*(VRZ)*	
☐ EK-31095	Airbus A310-304	595	ex C-GTSI	
☐ EK-74711	Boeing 747-SR81	22711/559	ex SX-DCB	♦

VETERAN AIRLINE		*Veteran (RVT)*		*Yerevan-Zvartnots (EVN)*
☐ EK-46513	Antonov An-24RV	37308409	ex UR-46513	
☐ EK-74798	Boeing 747-281BSF	23698/667	ex N288RF	♦
☐ EK-76381	Ilyushin Il-76MD	1033418596	ex ST-ATI	♦

EP-   IRAN (Islamic Republic of Iran)

ARIA AIR		*Aria (IRX)*		*Lar/Bandar Abbas (LRR/BND)*
☐ EP-EAF	Fokker 50	20235	ex D-AFKP	
☐ EP-EAH	Fokker 50	20234	ex D-AFKO	

ATA AIR				
☐ UR-CDN	McDonnell-Douglas MD-83	53520/2137	ex TC-OAV	<KHO
☐ UR-CHM	McDonnell-Douglas MD-83	53465/2093	ex TC-OAS	<KHO
☐ UR-CHP	McDonnell-Douglas MD-83	53466/2101	ex TC-OAT	<KHO
☐ UR-CHQ	McDonnell-Douglas MD-83	53488/2134	ex TC-OAU	<KHO

CASPIAN AIRLINES		*Caspian (RV/CPN)*		*Rasht (RAS)*
☐ EP-CPN	Tupolev Tu-154M	91A898	ex EP-JAZ	
☐ EP-CPO	Tupolev Tu-154M	91A899	ex EP-ARG	
☐ EP-CPS	Tupolev Tu-154M	93A957	ex UN-85775	
☐ UR-BHJ	McDonnell-Douglas MD-83	53184/2088	ex TC-AKL	<UKM
☐ UR-CHN	McDonnell-Douglas MD-83	49938/1785	ex N938MD	<UKM

CHABAHAR AIR		*Chabahar (IRU)*		*Tehran-Mehrabad (THR)*
☐ EP-CFM	Fokker 100	11394	ex PT-MQL	>IRA
☐ EP-CFN	Fokker 100	11423	ex PT-MQO	>IRA
☐ EP-CFO	Fokker 100	11389	ex PT-MQE	>IRA
☐ EP-CFP	Fokker 100	11409	ex PT-MQN	>IRA
☐ EP-CFQ	Fokker 100	11429	ex PT-MQT	>IRA
☐ EP-CFR	Fokker 100	11383	ex PT-MQD	>IRA

ERAM AIR		*Eram Air (YE/IRY)*		*Tabriz (TBZ)*
☐ EP-EKA	Tupolev Tu-154M	92A912	ex RA-85730	<OMS
☐ EP-EKB	Tupolev Tu-154M	92A946	ex RA-85763	<OMS
☐ EP-EKC	Tupolev Tu-154M	89A799	ex EP-MCE	
☐ EP-EKE	Tupolev Tu-154M	92A940	ex EP-MCK	<NKZ

FARS AIR		*(QFZ)*		*Qeshm-Dayrestan (GSM)*
☐ EP-QFA	Yakovlev Yak-42D	4520422007018	ex ER-YCE	
☐ EP-QFB	Yakovlev Yak-42D	4520422003019	ex ER-YCF	

HELICOPTER SERVICES				*Tehran*
☐ EP-HEB	Aérospatiale AS350B2 Ecureuil	3050	ex F-WQDA	
☐ EP-HEC	Aérospatiale AS350B3 Ecureuil	3621	ex F-WQDD	
☐ EP-HED	Aérospatiale AS350B3 Ecureuil	3629	ex F-WQDJ	
☐ EP-HEE	Aérospatiale AS350B3 Ecureuil	3644	ex F-WQDK	
☐ EP-HEF	Aérospatiale AS350B3 Ecureuil	3655		
☐ EP-HEG	Aérospatiale AS350B3 Ecureuil	3658		
☐ EP-HEH	Aérospatiale AS350B3 Ecureuil	3668		
☐ EP-HBJ	Bell 212	30504	ex N8112J	
☐ EP-HDV	Aérospatiale AS365N2 Dauphin 2	6467	ex F-GLMZ	
☐ EP-HTN	Bell 212	30885	ex N5009K	
☐ EP-HTO	Bell 205A-1	30163	ex N64743	
☐ EP-HTQ	Bell 205A-1	30189	ex N90039	
☐ EP-HUA	Bell 212	31176	ex HB-XPO	

IRAN AIR		*Iranair (IR/IRA)*		*Tehran-Mehrabad (THR)*
☐ EP-IBA	Airbus A300B4-605R	723	ex F-WWAL	
☐ EP-IBB	Airbus A300B4-605R	727	ex F-WWAZ	
☐ EP-IBC	Airbus A300B4-605R	632	ex SX-BEK	
☐ EP-IBD	Airbus A300B4-605R	696	ex SX-BEL	
☐ EP-IBG	Airbus A300B4-203F	299	ex EP-MDA	
☐ EP-IBH	Airbus A300B4-203F	302	ex EP-MDB	
☐ EP-IBI	Airbus A300B4-2C	151	ex TC-FLK	
☐ EP-IBJ	Airbus A300B4-2C	256	ex TC-FLL	
☐ EP-IBS	Airbus A300B2-203	080	ex F-WZEO	
☐ EP-IBT	Airbus A300B2-203	185	ex F-WZMB	
☐ EP-IBV	Airbus A300B2-203	187	ex F-WZMD	
☐ EP-IBZ	Airbus A300B2-203	226	ex F-WZME	
☐ EP-ICE	Airbus A300B4-203F	139	ex TC-KZT	
☐ EP-IBK	Airbus A310-304	671	ex SU-MWB	
☐ EP-IBL	Airbus A310-304	436	ex A6-EKB	
☐ EP-IBM	Airbus A310-203	338	ex TC-JCL	
☐ EP-IBN	Airbus A310-203	375	ex TC-JCM	
☐ EP-IBP	Airbus A310-203	370	ex TC-JCR	
☐ EP-IBQ	Airbus A310-203	389	ex TC-JCS	
☐ EP-IBX	Airbus A310-203	390	ex TC-JCU	
☐ EP-IEA	Airbus A320-232	0530	ex EP-MHK	
☐ EP-IEB	Airbus A320-232	0575	ex EP-MHN	
☐ EP-IEC	Airbus A320-232	0857	ex EP-MHJ	
☐ EP-IED	Airbus A320-212	0345	ex VP-CBZ	
☐ EP-IEE	Airbus A320-211	0303	ex EK-32303	
☐ EP-IEF	Airbus A320-211	0312	ex EK-32312	
☐ EP-IEG	Airbus A320-211	2054	ex EK-32054	
☐ EP-IRR	Boeing 727-286	20946/1052		
☐ EP-IRS	Boeing 727-286	20947/1070		
☐ EP-IRT	Boeing 727-286	21078/1114		
☐ EP-IAA	Boeing 747SP-86	20998/275		
☐ EP-IAB	Boeing 747SP-86	20999/278	Khorasan	
☐ EP-IAC	Boeing 747SP-86	21093/307	Fars	
☐ EP-IAD	Boeing 747SP-86	21758/371	ex N1800B Khorasan	
☐ EP-IAG	Boeing 747-286M	21217/291	Azarabadegan	
☐ EP-IAH	Boeing 747-286M	21218/300	Khuzestan	
☐ EP-IAI	Boeing 747-230M	22670/550	ex EP-AUA	
☐ EP-IAM	Boeing 747-186B	21759/381	ex N5573P	
☐ EP-ICD	Boeing 747-21AC	24134/712	ex TC-AKZ	
☐ EP-AWZ	Fokker 100	11497	ex PH-AFO	
☐ EP-CFD	Fokker 100	11442	ex PT-MRI	
☐ EP-CFE	Fokker 100	11422	ex F-GRMV	
☐ EP-CFH	Fokker 100	11443	ex F-GSTG	
☐ EP-CFI	Fokker 100	11511	ex PT-MRU	
☐ EP-CFJ	Fokker 100	11516	ex PT-MRV	
☐ EP-CFK	Fokker 100	11518	ex PT-MRW	
☐ EP-CFL	Fokker 100	11343	ex PT-MRY	
☐ EP-CFM	Fokker 100	11394	ex PT-MQL	<IRU
☐ EP-CFN	Fokker 100	11423	ex PT-MQO	<IRU
☐ EP-CFO	Fokker 100	11389	ex PT-MQE	<IRU
☐ EP-CFP	Fokker 100	11409	ex PT-MQN	<IRU
☐ EP-CFQ	Fokker 100	11429	ex PT-MQT	<IRU
☐ EP-IDA	Fokker 100	11292	ex PH-LMG	
☐ EP-IDD	Fokker 100	11294	ex PH-LMM	
☐ EP-IDF	Fokker 100	11298	ex PH-LMN	
☐ EP-IDG	Fokker 100	11302	ex PH-LMW	
☐ UR-CHW	McDonnell-Douglas MD-82	49510/1514	ex S5-ACY	
☐ UR-CHX	McDonnell-Douglas MD-82	53162/2010	ex S5-ACZ	

IRAN AIR TOUR AIRLINE		*Iran Air Tour (B9/IRB)*		*Tehran-Mehrabad/Mashad (THR/MHD)*
☐ UR-BXM	McDonnell-Douglas MD-82	49505/1381	ex G-CEPD	♦
☐ EP-MBQ	Tupolev Tu-154M	92A931	ex RA-85747	<NKZ
☐ EP-MBT	Tupolev Tu-154M	92A930	ex RA-85749	<NKZ
☐ EP-MCJ	Tupolev Tu-154M	89A800	ex EP-MBP	
☐ EP-MCL	Tupolev Tu-154M	91A880	ex RA-85705	
☐ EP-MCM	Tupolev Tu-154M	90A855	ex RA-85085	
☐ EP-MCN	Tupolev Tu-154M	88A792	ex RA-85847	

☐ EP-MCO	Tupolev Tu-154M	88A774	ex RA-85831	
☐ EP-MCP	Tupolev Tu-154M	85A724	ex RA-85146	
☐ EP-MCS	Tupolev Tu-154M	88A795	ex RA-85653	
☐ EP-MCT	Tupolev Tu-154M	90A860	ex RA-85689	
☐ EP-MCU	Tupolev Tu-154M	93A977	ex RA-85793	
☐ EP-MCV	Tupolev Tu-154M	85A706	ex RA-85037	
☐ EP-MCX	Tupolev Tu-154M	85A707	ex LZ-HMW	
☐ EP-	Tupolev Tu-204-100			o/o
☐ EP-	Tupolev Tu-204-100			o/o

IRAN ASEMAN AIRLINES — (EP/IRC) — Tehran-Mehrabad (THR)

☐ EP-ATA	ATR 72-212	334	ex F-WWLQ	
☐ EP-ATH	ATR 72-212	339	ex F-WWLU	
☐ EP-ATS	ATR 72-212	391	ex F-WWED	
☐ EP-ATU	ATR 72-212A	697	ex F-OIRA	
☐ EP-ATX	ATR 72-212A	573	ex F-OIRB	
☐ EP-ATZ	ATR 72-212	398	ex F-WWEK	
☐ EP-ASG	Fokker 100	11438	ex HL7210	
☐ EP-ASI	Fokker 100	11519	ex HL7215	
☐ EP-ASJ	Fokker 100	11378	ex HL7206	
☐ EP-ASK	Fokker 100	11388	ex HL7208	
☐ EP-ASM	Fokker 100	11433	ex F-GIOI	
☐ EP-ASO	Fokker 100	11454	ex F-GIOJ	
☐ EP-ASP	Fokker 100	11504	ex HL7213	
☐ EP-ASQ	Fokker 100	11513	ex HL7214	
☐ EP-ASR	Fokker 100	11522	ex HL7216	
☐ EP-AST	Fokker 100	11523	ex HL7217	
☐ EP-ASU	Fokker 100	11430	ex PT-MQP	
☐ EP-ASX	Fokker 100	11431	ex PT-MQS	>IRK
☐ EP-ASZ	Fokker 100	11421	ex PT-MQR	
☐ EP-ATB	Fokker 100	11401	ex PT-MQF	
☐ EP-ATC	Fokker 100	11296	ex F-GPXM	♦
☐ EP-ATD	Fokker 100	11387	ex F-GPXG	♦
☐ EP-ATF	Fokker 100	11476	ex F-GPXH	♦
☐ EP-ATG	Fokker 100	11329	ex F-GPXK	♦
☐ EP-ASA	Boeing 727-228	22081/1594	ex LX-IRA	
☐ EP-ASB	Boeing 727-228	22082/1603	ex LX-IRB	
☐ EP-ASC	Boeing 727-228	22084/1638	ex LX-IRC	
☐ EP-ASD	Boeing 727-228	22085/1665	ex LX-IRD	

KISH AIR — Kishair (Y9/IRK) — Tehran-Mehrabad (THR)

☐ EP-LBV	Fokker 50	20158	ex VP-CSE	
☐ EP-LCB	Fokker 50	20274	ex EC-GKV	
☐ EP-LCC	Fokker 50	20275	ex EC-GKX	
☐ EP-LCE	Fokker 50	20265	ex PH-LXF	
☐ EP-LCF	Fokker 50	20263	ex PH-LXE	
☐ EP-LCG	Fokker 50	20236	ex PH-JXL	
☐ EP-ASX	Fokker 100	11431	ex PT-MQS	<IRC
☐ EK-82224	McDonnell-Douglas MD-82	53224/2084	ex LZ-LDB	♦
☐ EP-LCI	McDonnell-Douglas MD-83	49844/1579	ex UR-CHR	<KHO
☐ UR-BXN	McDonnell-Douglas MD-83	49569/1405	ex LZ-LDV	<KHO
☐ UR-CHS	McDonnell-Douglas MD-83	49572/1468	ex LZ-LDA	<KHO
☐ EP-LBR	Tupolev Tu-154M	90A838	ex RA-85089	
☐ EP-LBS	Tupolev Tu-154M	91A901	ex UN-85719	

MAHAN AIR — Mahan Air (W5/IRM) — Kerman (KER)

☐ EK-30044	Airbus A300B2K-3C	244	ex N142RF	<Blue Sky
☐ EK-30060	Airbus A300B2K-3C	160	ex N141RF	<Blue Sky
☐ EP-MHF	Airbus A300B4-103	055	ex S7-AAZ	
☐ EP-MHG	Airbus A300B4-203	204	ex AP-BFL	
☐ EP-MHL	Airbus A300B4-203	175	ex SU-BMM	
☐ EP-MHM	Airbus A300B2K-3C	090	ex TC-SGA	<SGX
☐ EP-MNG	Airbus A300B4-603	401	ex D-AIAK	♦
☐ EP-MNI	Airbus A300B4-603	405	ex D-AIAL	♦
☐ EP-MNJ	Airbus A300B4-603	380	ex D-AIAH	♦
☐ EP-MNK	Airbus A300B4-603	618	ex D-AIAT	♦
☐ EP-MNM	Airbus A300B4-605R	773	ex D-AIAX	♦
☐ EP-MNN	Airbus A300B4-605R	701	ex D-AIAZ	♦
☐ EP-MNQ	Airbus A300B4-603	553	ex EX-35010	
☐ EP-MNR	Airbus A300B4-603	411	ex EX-35009	
☐ EP-MNS	Airbus A300B4-603	414	ex EX-35008	

☐ EP-MNT	Airbus A300B4-603	546	ex EX-35007	
☐ EP-MNU	Airbus A300B4-605R	608	ex EX-35006	
☐ EP-	Airbus A300B4-601	368	ex EK-30068	o/o♦
☐ EP-MHO	Airbus A310-304	488	ex EK-31088	<Blue Sky
☐ EP-MNX	Airbus A310-304	564	ex EX-35005	
☐ EX-301	Airbus A310-304	524	ex D-AIDF	<KTC
☐ EX-35003	Airbus A310-304	567	ex OK-WAB	<KTC
☐ EX-35004	Airbus A310-308	620	ex D-AHLC	<KTC
☐ F-OJHH	Airbus A310-304ER	586	ex EP-MHH	
☐ F-OJHI	Airbus A310-304ER	537	ex EP-MHI	
☐ EP-MNA	Boeing 747-422	24383/811	ex EK-74783	
☐ EP-MNB	Boeing 747-422	24363/740	ex EK-74763	<Blue Sky
☐ EP-MNC	Boeing 747-422	26879/973	ex EK-74779	<Blue Sky
☐ EP-MND	Boeing 747-3B3 (SCD)	23413/632	ex EK-74713	<Blue Sky
☐ EP-MNE	Boeing 747-3B3 (SCD)	23480/641	ex EK-74780	
☐ EX-27000	British Aerospace 146 Srs.300	E3216	ex B-2717	
☐ EX-27001	British Aerospace 146 Srs.300	E3212	ex B-2712	

NAFT AIR — NAFT (IRG) — Ahwaz (AWZ)

☐ EP-GAS	Fokker 50	20224	ex PH-JXA	
☐ EP-IOD	de Havilland DHC-6 Twin Otter 300	460		
☐ EP-IOE	de Havilland DHC-6 Twin Otter 300	425		
☐ EP-IOP	de Havilland DHC-6 Twin Otter 300	577		
☐ EP-MIS	Fokker 100	11503	ex F-GPXI	
☐ EP-NFT	Fokker 50	20220	ex PH-RRF	
☐ EP-OIL	Fokker 50	20222	ex PH-LNZ	
☐ EP-OPI	Fokker 100	11509	ex F-GLIR	
☐ EP-PET	Fokker 50	20283	ex PH-MXF	
☐ EP-SUS	Fokker 100	11487	ex F-GPXA	

NAVID AIR — Navid (IRI) — Karaj-Payam (QKC)

☐ EP-NAA	Mil Mi-17I	59489602238	ex RA-25520	
☐ EP-NAB	Mil Mi-8MTV-1	95932	ex RA-27108	
☐ EP-NAC	Mil Mi-8T	99254442	ex RA-27024	
☐ EP-NAD	Mil Mi-8T	99254471	ex RA-27025	
☐ EP-NAF	Bell 212	31231	ex A6-BAC	<Abu Dhabi Avn

PAYAM INTERNATIONAL AIR — Payamair (2F/IRP) — Karaj-Payam (QKC)

☐ EP-TPH	Embraer EMB.110P1A Bandeirante	110453	ex EP-TPM	Tehran
☐ EP-TPI	Embraer EMB.110P1 Bandeirante	110438	ex EP-TPA	Kerrian
☐ EP-TPJ	Embraer EMB.110P1 Bandeirante	110442	ex EP-TPT	Kashan
☐ EP-TPK	Embraer EMB.110P1 Bandeirante	110386	ex EP-TPG	Esfahan
☐ EP-TPL	Embraer EMB.110P1 Bandeirante	110423	ex EP-TPS	Semnan
☐ EP-TPC	Bell 212	30516	ex 6-9202	
☐ EP-TPN	Bell 212	30517	ex 6-9203	
☐ EP-	Boeing 727-222F (FedEx 3)	21920/1634	ex A6-RCA	
☐ EP-	Boeing 727-222F (FedEx 3)	21917/1616	ex A6-RCB	

QESHM AIR — Faraz Air (IRQ) — Qeshm-Dayrestan (GSM)

| ☐ JY-JRF | Boeing 767-233 | 22526/92 | ex J2-KCN | |
| ☐ JY-RFF | Boeing 737-4K5 | 27831/2677 | ex OO-TUB | |

SAFAT AIRLINES — (IRV)

| ☐ EP-SAJ | Antonov An-26 | 57314002 | ex RA-26592 | |
| ☐ EP-SAK | Antonov An-26 | 57314001 | ex RA-26591 | |

SAFIRAN AIRLINES — Safiran (SFN) — Tehran-Mehrabad (THR)

☐ EP-SFD	Ir.An-140	9001	ex HESA-01	
☐ EP-SFE	Ir.An-140	9002		Op by Police Avn
☐ EP-SFF	Ir.An-140	9003		Op by Police Avn as HESA 90-03
☐ EP-	Ir.An-140			o/o

SAHA AIRLINE — Saha (IRZ) — Tehran-Mehrabad (THR)

☐ EP-SIF	Airbus A300B4-622R	762	ex ZS-TSA	♦
☐ EP-SIG	Airbus A300B4-622R	750	ex B-2327	♦
☐ EP-SHG	Boeing 707-3J9C	20830/876	ex 5-8301	
☐ EP-SHK	Boeing 707-3J9C	21128/917	ex 5-8312	

| ☐ EP-SHU | Boeing 707-3J9C | 21126/914 | ex 5-8310 | [THR] |
| ☐ EP-SHV | Boeing 707-3J9C | 21125/912 | ex 5-8309 | |

TABAN AIR		**Taban (TBM)**		**Mashad (MHD)**
☐ LZ-HBD	British Aerospace 146 Srs.300	E3141	ex N615AW	<HMS
☐ LZ-HBZ	British Aerospace 146 Srs.200	E2103	ex G-JEAK	<HMS
☐ EK-85523	McDonnell-Douglas MD-82	49523/1724	ex B-2139	
☐ EK-82524	McDonnell-Douglas MD-82	49524/1746	ex B-2140	
☐ EP-TBA	Tupolev Tu-154M	97A1008	ex RA-85819	
☐ RA-85761	Tupolev Tu-154M	93A944		<KGL

TARA AIRLINES		**Tarair (IRR)**		**Bandar Abbas (BND)**
☐ EP-TRA	Kamov Ka-32	8902	ex RA-31071	
☐ EP-TRB	Agusta A.109E Power	11007	ex D-HOBM	
☐ EP-TRH	MBB Bo.105CB	S-66	ex A6-ALS	
☐ EP-TRK	Agusta A.109E Power	11023	ex I-MALL	
☐ EP-TRM	Kamov Ka-32	8604	ex RA-31582	
☐ EP-TRT	MBB Bo.105CB	S-100	ex A6-ALQ	
☐ EP-TRZ	Kamov Ka-32	8901	ex RA-31070	

YAS AIR				**Tehran-Mehrabad (THR)**
☐ EP-GOL	Ilyushin Il-76	1013409297	ex EP-PCC	
☐ EP-GOM	Ilyushin Il-76TD	1023409321	ex EP-PCB	
☐ EP-GOQ	Antonov An-74-200	365470991021	ex 15-2250	

ZAGROS AIRLINES		**(IZG)**		
☐ SX-BTM	McDonnell-Douglas MD-83	49627/1580	ex TF-JXC	
☐ UR-CDQ	McDonnell-Douglas MD-82	49372/1252	ex SX-BSQ	<KHO

ER-   MOLDOVA (Republic of Moldova)

AERIANTUR-M AIRLINES		**Aerem (MBV)**		**Kishinev-Chisinau (KIV)**
☐ ER-AXI	Antonov An-12B	6344310	ex RA-11339	

AIR MOLDOVA		**Air Moldova (9U/MLD)**		**Kishinev-Chisinau (KIV)**
☐ ER-AXP	Airbus A320-233	0741	ex N452TA	
☐ ER-AXV	Airbus A320-211	0622	ex F-WQSG	
☐ ER-EMA	Embraer EMB.120RT Brasilia	120223	ex N246CA	>TDM
☐ F-HBBB	Embraer EMB.120ER Brasilia	120209	ex EC-HUP	
☐ ER-ECB	Embraer ERJ-190LR	19000325	ex PT-TXN	♦
☐ ER-YGD	Yakovlev Yak-40D	9831458	ex RA-87970	Op for Govt
☐ ER-65140	Tupolev Tu-134A-3	60932	ex CCCP-65140	Op for Govt

AIRLINK ARABIA				**Kishinev-Chisinau (KIV)**
☐ ER-AZX	Antonov An-24RV	47309804	ex RA-46687	

GRIXONA				
☐ ER-ICS	Ilyushin IL-18D	187009903	ex UR-CEO	

MOLDAVIAN AIRLINES		**Moldavian (2M/MDV)**		**Kishinev-Chisinau (KIV)**
☐ ER-FZA	Fokker 100	11395	ex F-WQVS	
☐ ER-SFA	SAAB 2000	2000-056	ex HB-IYA	<SWR
☐ ER-SFB	SAAB 2000	2000-022	ex HB-IZL	

TEPAVIA TRANS AIRLINE		**Tepavia (TET)**		**Kishinev-Chisinau (KIV)**
☐ ER-AJC	WSK-PZL/Antonov An-28	1AJ003-12	ex RA-28748	
☐ ER-AWM	Antonov An-32B	3009	ex HA-TCL	
☐ ER-AZW	Antonov An-32A	2109	ex S9-BOI	
☐ ER-LIC	LET L-410UVP	820904	ex EW-215KB	

ES-   ESTONIA (Republic of Estonia)

AIREST		**Elka (AIT)**		**Tallinn-Ylemiste (TLL)**
☐ ES-LLC	LET L-410UVP-E20C	912609	ex OK-WDH	

AVIES AIR COMPANY		Avies (U3/AIA)		Tallinn-Ylemiste (TLL)
☐ ES-PAH	Piper PA-31-350 Navajo Chieftain	31-7405156	ex SE-GDI	
☐ ES-PJG	British Aerospace Jetstream 31	701	ex ES-LJD	Tooru
☐ ES-PJR	British Aerospace Jetstream 32EP	949	ex SE-LNU	
☐ ES-PLB	LET L-410UVP	851413	ex LY-AVY	
☐ LY-PCL	LET L-410UVP-E	892335	ex LY-AVV	

ENIMEX		Enimex (ENI)		Tallinn-Ylemiste (TLL)
☐ ES-NOB	Antonov An-72-100	36572070695	ex CCCP-72931	>UN as UNO-215
☐ ES-NOH	Antonov An-72-100	36572095909	ex EL-ALX	Op for UN
☐ ES-NOI	Antonov An-72-100	36572096914	ex 3C-QQO	
☐ ES-NOK	Antonov An-72-100	36572090780	ex RA-72939	Op for UN

ESTONIAN AIR		Estonian (OV/ELL)		Tallinn-Ylemiste (TLL)
☐ ES-ABJ	Boeing 737-33R	28873/2975	ex ZK-NGA	
☐ ES-ABK	Boeing 737-36N	28572/3031	ex G-STRE	Kalev
☐ ES-ABL	Boeing 737-5L9	28997/3008	ex OK-DGB	
☐ ES-ABO	Boeing 737-505	24646/2138	ex YL-BBA	♦
☐ ES-ABP	Boeing 737-528	27425/2730	ex G-GFFI	♦
☐ ES-	Canadair CRJ-900		ex	o/o♦
☐ ES-	Canadair CRJ-900		ex	o/o♦

ESTONIAN AIR REGIONAL		Estonian (OV/ELL)		Tallinn-Ylemiste (TLL)
☐ ES-ASM	SAAB SF.340A	340A-132	ex SE-LMT	
☐ ES-ASN	SAAB SF.340A	340A-151	ex SE-KUU	

FLYLAL CHATERS EESTI				Tallinn-Ylemiste (TLL)
☐ ES-LBD	Boeing 737-35B	25069/2053	ex LY-AQV	

JP AIR CARGO				Tallinn-Ylemiste (TLL)
☐ ES-JFA	Swearingen SA.227AC Metro III	AC-657	ex SX-BBX	Jussi

ET-   ETHIOPIA (Federal Democratic Republic of Ethiopia)

ABYSSINIAN FLIGHT SERVICES				Addis Ababa (ADD)
☐ ET-ALD	Cessna 208 Caravan I	208B00172	ex N9750F	
☐ ET-ALF	Cessna TU206F Turbo Stationair II	U20602598	ex N206AM	

ETHIOPIAN AIRLINES		Ethiopian (ET/ETH)		Addis Ababa (ADD)
☐ ET-ALK	Boeing 737-760/W	33764/1408		
☐ ET-ALM	Boeing 737-760/W	33765/1539		
☐ ET-ALN	Boeing 737-760/W	33766/1757		
☐ ET-ALQ	Boeing 737-76N/W	33420/1459		
☐ ET-ALU	Boeing 737-76N/W	32741/1487		
☐ ET-AMZ	Boeing 737-8BK/W	29646/2282	ex G-CEJP	
☐ ET-ANA	Boeing 737-86R/W	30494/786	ex B-2660	
☐ ET-ANG	Boeing 737-7K9/W	34401/2216	ex OY-MRP	>SKK♦
☐ ET-ANH	Boeing 737-7K9/W	34402/2270	ex OY-MRR	>SKK♦
☐ ET-ANZ	Boeing 737-8HO/W	37933/3437		♦
☐ ET-AOA	Boeing 737-8HO/W	37936/3459	ex N1786B	♦
☐ ET-AOB	Boeing 737-8HO/W	37937/3467	ex N1796B	♦
☐ ET-	Boeing 737-8HO/W			o/o♦
☐ ET-AOK	Boeing 737-790/W	33012/1306	ex M-ABDH	>SKK♦
☐ ET-AJS	Boeing 757-260PF	24845/300	ex N3519L	
☐ ET-AJX	Boeing 757-260 (PCF)	25014/348		
☐ ET-AKC	Boeing 757-260	25353/408		
☐ ET-AKE	Boeing 757-260ER	26057/444		
☐ ET-AKF	Boeing 757-260ER	26058/496		
☐ ET-ALY	Boeing 757-231	28480/750	ex N708TW	
☐ ET-ALZ	Boeing 757-231	30319/883	ex N720TW	
☐ ET-AMK	Boeing 757-23N	32449/974	ex C-GMYE	
☐ ET-AMT	Boeing 757-23N	27976/814	ex N520AT	
☐ ET-AMU	Boeing 757-23N	27975/779	ex N519AT	
☐ ET-ALC	Boeing 767-33AER	28043/734		
☐ ET-ALH	Boeing 767-3BGER	30565/802	ex HB-IHW	
☐ ET-ALJ	Boeing 767-360ER	33767/918	ex N5020K	

172

☐ ET-ALL	Boeing 767-3BGER	30564/798	ex OO-IHV		
☐ ET-ALO	Boeing 767-360ER	33768/922			
☐ ET-ALP	Boeing 767-360ER	33769/933			
☐ ET-AME	Boeing 767-306ER	27611/633	ex PH-BZH		
☐ ET-AMF	Boeing 767-3BGER	30563/786	ex B-2561		
☐ ET-AMG	Boeing 767-3BGER	30566/817	ex B-2562		
☐ ET-AMQ	Boeing 767-33AER	27909/591	ex PR-VAA		
☐ ET-ANN	Boeing 777-260LR	40770/900		The Blue Nile	♦
☐ ET-ANO	Boeing 777-260LR	40771/908			♦
☐ ET-	Boeing 777-260LR				o/o♦
☐ ET-	Boeing 777-260LR				o/o♦
☐ ET-	Boeing 777-260LR				o/o♦
☐ ET-	Boeing 787-860				o/o♦
☐ ET-	Boeing 787-860				o/o♦
☐ ET-	Boeing 787-860				o/o♦
☐ ET-	Boeing 787-860				o/o♦
☐ ET-AIT	de Havilland DHC-6 Twin Otter 310	820	ex C-GDNG		
☐ ET-AIX	de Havilland DHC-6 Twin Otter 300	835	ex C-GDFT		
☐ ET-ANI	de Havilland DHC-8-402Q	4299	ex C-GBKC		♦
☐ ET-ANJ	de Havilland DHC-8-402Q	4303	ex C-GCLU		♦
☐ ET-ANK	de Havilland DHC-8-402Q	4304	ex C-GCPF		♦
☐ ET-ANL	de Havilland DHC-8-402Q	4307	ex C-GCPY		♦
☐ ET-ANV	de Havilland DHC-8-402Q	4317	ex C-GEHI		♦
☐ ET-ANW	de Havilland DHC-8-402Q	4320	ex C-GEUN		>SKK♦
☐ ET-ANX	de Havilland DHC-8-402Q	4330	ex C-GSNH		♦
☐ ET-AKR	Fokker 50	20313	ex PH-LOP		
☐ ET-AKS	Fokker 50	20328	ex PH-EXB	all-white	
☐ ET-AKT	Fokker 50	20331	ex PH-EXC	all-white	
☐ ET-AKU	Fokker 50	20333	ex PH-EXD	all-white	
☐ ET-AKV	Fokker 50	20335	ex PH-EXE		
☐ ET-AML	McDonnell-Douglas MD-11ERF	48758/615	ex N742BC		
☐ ET-AND	McDonnell-Douglas MD-11BCF	48780/624	ex N588BC		

TRANS NATION AIRWAYS   *Trans Nation (TNW)*   **Addis Ababa/Jeddah (ADD/JED)**

☐ ET-AKZ	de Havilland DHC-8-202	469	ex C-GLOT		>ETC
☐ ET-ALX	de Havilland DHC-8-202	475	ex ZK-ECR		>RWD
☐ ET-AMR	Bell 222UT	47554	ex N111DS		

EW-   BELARUS (Republic of Belarus)

BELAVIA BELARUSSIAN AIRLINES   *Belarus Avia (B2/BRU)*   **Minsk 1 (MHP)**

☐ EW-250PA	Boeing 737-524	26319/2748	ex N427LF		
☐ EW-251PA	Boeing 737-5Q8	27634/2889	ex PT-SSC		
☐ EW-252PA	Boeing 737-524	26340/2777	ex LY-AGZ		
☐ EW-253PA	Boeing 737-524	26339/2771	ex LY-AGQ		
☐ EW-254PA	Boeing 737-3Q8	26294/2550	ex N201LF		
☐ EW-282PA	Boeing 737-3Q8	26321/2764	ex B-5024		
☐ EW-283PA	Boeing 737-3Q8	26333/2786	ex B-2604		
☐ EW-290PA	Boeing 737-5Q8	27629/2834	ex N381LF		
☐ EW-294PA	Boeing 737-505	26338/2822	ex B-2975		♦
☐ EW-001PA	Boeing 737-8EV/W	33079/1075	ex N375BC	Op for Govt BBJ2	
☐ EW-100PJ	Canadair CRJ-200LR	7309	ex N400MJ		
☐ EW-276PJ	Canadair CRJ-200ER	7799	ex N698BR		
☐ EW-277PJ	Canadair CRJ-200ER	7852	ex N710BR		
☐ EW-85703	Tupolev Tu-154M	91A878	ex CCCP-85703		
☐ EW-85706	Tupolev Tu-154M	91A881	ex CCCP-85706		
☐ EW-85741	Tupolev Tu-154M	91A896	ex ES-LTC		
☐ EW-85748	Tupolev Tu-154M	92A924			
☐ EW-85815	Tupolev Tu-154M	95A1010		VIP	
☐ EW-88187	Yakovlev Yak-40	9620748	ex CCCP-88187	Op for Govt	

GENEX

☐ EW-246TG	Antonov An-26B	67314403	ex UR-26214	Op by Airest	

| ☐ EW-259TG | Antonov An-26B | 27312706 | ex UR-26094 | |
| ☐ EW-278TG | Antonov An-26 | 13306 | ex HA-TCZ | |

GOMELAVIA		*Gomel (YD/GOM)*		*Gomel (GME)*
☐ EW-245TI	Antonov An-12BP	6344608	ex EX-096	
☐ EW-46250	Antonov An-24B	77303208	ex CCCP-46250	[GME]
☐ EW-46304	Antonov An-24B	97305304	ex CCCP-46304	[GME]
☐ EW-46631	Antonov An-24RV	37308810	ex CCCP-46631	
☐ EW-47697	Antonov An-24RV	27307604	ex CCCP-47697	

RUBYSTAR		*RubyStar (RSB)*		*Minsk-Machulishchy*
☐ EW-275TI	Antonov An-12BK	00347210	ex RA--13392	
☐ EW-47808	Antonov An-24RV	17306910	ex CCCP-47808	

TRANS AVIA EXPORT CARGO AIRLINES		*Transexport (AL/TXC)*		*Minsk-Machulishchy*
☐ EW-269TI	Antonov An-12BP	1340106	ex UN-11018	
☐ EW-76710	Ilyushin Il-76TD	0063473182	ex RA-76710	
☐ EW-76711	Ilyushin Il-76TD	0063473187	ex CCCP-76711	
☐ EW-76712	Ilyushin Il-76TD	0063473190	ex CCCP-76712	
☐ EW-76735	Ilyushin Il-76TD	0073476314	ex CCCP-76735	
☐ EW-76737	Ilyushin Il-76TD	0073477323	ex CCCP-76737	>AYZ
☐ EW-78769	Ilyushin Il-76MD	0083487607	ex CCCP-78769	
☐ EW-78779	Ilyushin Il-76TD	0083489662	ex CCCP-78779	>AYZ
☐ EW-78787	Ilyushin Il-76MD	0083490698	ex CCCP-78787	
☐ EW-78792	Ilyushin Il-76TD	0093490718	ex EP-CFA	all-white
☐ EW-78799	Ilyushin Il-76TD	0093491754	ex CCCP-78799	
☐ EW-78801	Ilyushin Il-76TD	0093492763	ex CCCP-78801	
☐ EW-78808	Ilyushin Il-76TD	0093493794	ex CCCP-78808	
☐ EW-78819	Ilyushin Il-76TD	0093495883	ex CCCP-78819	
☐ EW-78827	Ilyushin Il-76TD	1003499997	ex CCCP-78827	
☐ EW-78828	Ilyushin Il-76TD	1003401004	ex RA-78828	
☐ EW-78836	Ilyushin Il-76TD	0093499986	ex CCCP-78836	
☐ EW-78839	Ilyushin Il-76TD	1003402047	ex CCCP-78839	
☐ EW-78848	Ilyushin Il-76TD	1003405159	ex CCCP-78848	

EX-   KYRGYZSTAN (Republic of Kyrgyzstan)

AEROVISTA AIRLINES		*Aerovista Group (AAP)*		*Sharjah (SHJ)*
☐ EX-87250	Yakovlev Yak-40	9310726	ex CCCP-87250	<TLR
☐ EX-87664	Yakovlev Yak-40	9240825	ex CCCP-87664	>TLR
☐ EX-88207	Yakovlev Yak-40K	9631149	ex EY-87207	>TLR
☐ EX-88270	Yakovlev Yak-40	9720853	ex RA-88270	>TLR

AIR MANAS		*Air Manas (MBB)*		*Bishkek-Manas (FRU)*
☐ EX-00002	Tupolev Tu-154M	91A904	ex RA-85722	VIP Op for Government

ANIKAY AIR		*Anikay (AKF)*		*Bishkek-Manas/Sharjah (FRU/SHJ)*
☐ EX-405	Ilyushin Il-18D	184007405	ex T9-ABB	no titles
☐ EX-601	Ilyushin Il-18E	185008601	ex EL-ALD	National Paints titles

AVIA TRAFFIC COMPANY		*Atomic (AVJ)*		*Bishkek-Manas (FRU)*
☐ EX-051	Antonov An-24RV	57310105	ex ER-AZG	
☐ EX-076	Boeing 737-268	20882/356	ex HZ-AGF	<ESD
☐ EX-777	Boeing 737-268	21654/532	ex HZ-AGS	<ESD
☐ EX-27002	British Aerospace 146 Srs.200	E2172	ex OO-DJH	♦
☐ EX-27007	British Aerospace 146 Srs.200	E2180	ex OO-DJG	♦

BOTIR-AVIA		*Botir-Avia (B8/BTR)*		*Bishkek-Manas (FRU)*
☐ EX-89616	Ilyushin Il-76T	0023438120	ex UR-86916	[SHJ]

BRITISH GULF INTERNATIONAL AIRLINES		*Gulf Inter (BGK)*		*Bishkek-Manas/Sharjah (FRU/SHJ)*
☐ S9-SAE	Antonov An-12B	402408	ex LZ-BRP	
☐ S9-SAH	Antonov An-12B	5343703	ex EX-164	Alex
☐ S9-SAJ	Antonov An-12TB	401901	ex EX-160	Irenal
☐ S9-SAM	Antonov An-12BP	3341408	ex EX-162	Akula	[SHJ]
☐ S9-SAP	Antonov An-12BP	5343305	ex EX-161	Fatima
☐ S9-SAR	Antonov An-12TA	2340801	ex EX-085	
☐ S9-SAV	Antonov An-12AP	2340602	ex EX-045	Igor

CLICK AIRWAYS — Click (4C/CGK) — Sharjah (SHJ)

☐ EK-11418	Antonov An-12BP	7344705	ex EX-166	Regd to Click Airways International
☐ EX-029	Antonov An-12BP	8345607	ex EX-12555	
☐ EX-169	Antonov An-12BP	01348005	ex EX-034	
☐ EX-401	Antonov An-12			
☐ EX-402	Antonov An-12			
☐ EX-403	Antonov An-12			
☐ EY-402	Antonov An-12B	8346006	ex EX-031	no titles
☐ EK-76400	Ilyushin Il-76TD	1023413438	ex JY-JIB	
☐ EX-033	Ilyushin Il-76TD	0033446235	ex RA-76788	
☐ EX-035	Ilyushin Il-76TD	0093498962	ex RA-76795	
☐ EX-036	Ilyushin Il-76TD	0093495863	ex RA-76785	>Ababeel
☐ EY-604	Ilyushin Il-76TD	1023410355	ex ST-WTA	

ESEN AIR — Essen (ESD)

☐ EX-076	Boeing 737-268	20882/356	ex HZ-AGF	>AVJ
☐ EX-777	Boeing 737-268	21654/532	ex HZ-AGS	>AVJ

GALAXY AIRLINES — Kackar (GAL) — Bishkek-Manas (FRU)

☐ EX-786	Ilyushin Il-18V	188011201	ex RA-74268	op by 'Osh Avia'
☐ EX-75466	Ilyushin Il-18	187010403	ex RA-75466 National Paints titles	

GARINCO AIRWAYS

☐ EX-87820	Yakovlev Yak-40	9231224	ex RA-87820

INTAL AIR — Intal (INL) — Bishkek-Manas/Sharjah (FRU/SHJ)

☐ EX-050	Boeing 737-229C (Nordam 3)	21139/437	ex TJ-AIO	
☐ EX-061	Boeing 737-2S2C (Nordam 3)	21927/600	ex N806AL	
☐ EX-081	Boeing 737-268	21283/477	ex HZ-AGN	
☐ EX-201	Ilyushin Il-18D	188011201	ex EX-74268 no titles	

ITEK AIR — Itek Air (GI/IKA) — Bishkek-Manas (FRU)

☐ EX-127	Boeing 737-275 (AvAero 3)	21819/627	ex AP-BHU
☐ EX-25003	Boeing 737-2T5	22632/847	ex UP-B3703

KYRGHYZSTAN — Altyn Avia (QH/LYN) — Bishkek-Manas (FRU)

☐ EX-014	Antonov An-24RV	77310807	ex 4R-SEL	
☐ EX-020	Tupolev Tu-134A-3	61042	ex 4L-65750	
☐ EX-24805	Antonov An-24RV	77310805	ex S9-CBA all-white	
☐ EX-85718	Tupolev Tu-154M	91A900	ex CCCP-85718	

KYRGHYZSTAN AIRLINES — Kyrgyz (R8/KGA) — Bishkek-Manas / Karakol / Osh (FRU/-/OSS)

☐ EX-25004	Boeing 737-247 (Nordam 3)	23516/1257	ex EY-531
☐ EX-85257	Tupolev Tu-154B-2	78A257	ex CCCP-85257
☐ EX-85590	Tupolev Tu-154B-2	84A590	ex CCCP-85590
☐ EX-85762	Tupolev Tu-154M	92A945	ex RA-85762
☐ EX-87538	Yakovlev Yak-40	9530342	ex CCCP-87538
☐ EX-87571	Yakovlev Yak-40	9221521	ex CCCP-87571
☐ EX-87589	Yakovlev Yak-40	9220123	ex CCCP-87589

KYRGHYZ AIRWAYS — (EAV) — Bishkek-Manas (FRU)

☐ EX-736	Boeing 737-247 (Nordam 3)	23517/1261	ex N243WA	♦
☐ EX-32001	Airbus A320-212	0445	ex N187AT	♦
☐ EX-37001	Boeing 737-301	23937/1587	ex E7-BBA	♦
☐ EX-	ATR 42-320	213	ex OY-PCD	o/o♦

KYRGYZ TRANS AIR — Dinafra (KTC) — Bishkek-Manas (FRU)

☐ EX-301	Airbus A310-304	524	ex D-AIDF	>IRM
☐ EX-35003	Airbus A310-304	567	ex OK-WAB	>IRM
☐ EX-35004	Airbus A310-308	620	ex D-AHLC	>IRM

SKY WAY AIR — Sky Worker (SAB) — Dubai (DXB)

☐ EX-016	Antonov An-26	17311207	ex RA-26065
☐ EX-126	Antonov An-26B	11508	ex UN-26075

TENIR AIRLINES		*Tenir Air (TEB)*		*Sharjah (SHJ)*
☐ EK-11032	Antonov An-12V	7345004	ex 11032	
☐ EX-075	Ilyushin Il-76TD	0053463908	ex ER-IBL	all-white

TRANS AIR				
☐ EX-24103	Antonov An-24B	07306103	ex TN-AFL	

TRAST AERO		*Trast Aero (S5/TSJ)*		*Sharjah (SHJ)*
☐ EK-46581	Antonov An-24B	97304910	ex RA-46581	
☐ EX-103	ROMBAC One-Eleven 561RC	403	ex YR-BRC	
☐ TN-AGB	Antonov An-26B-100	87307210		
☐ 3X-GET	Antonov An-26B	67304104	ex S9-KAV	
☐ 4L-BKA	Antonov An-26B	87306407	ex LZ-MNH	
☐ 4L-GAS	Boeing 707-379C	19821/718	ex EX-120	
☐ 4L-OVA	Antonov An-32	1408	ex 3X-GES	

EY-   TAJIKISTAN (Republic of Tajikistan)

EAST AIR		*(EG)*		*Dushanbe (DYU)*
☐ EY-321	ATR 42-320	213	ex OY-PCD	◆
☐ EY-532	Boeing 737-25A	23791/1486	ex EX-734	
☐ EY-538	Boeing 737-4Y0	23980/1667	ex N239DT	

RUS AVIATION				*Sharjah (SHJ)*
☐ EY-403	Antonov An-12BP	00347107	ex EX-042	

SOMON AIR		*(4J / SMR)*		*Dushanbe (DYU)*
☐ EY-777	Boeing 737-8GJ/W	34960/2765	ex N960BB	Sadriddin Ayni
☐ EY-787	Boeing 737-8GJ/W	34955/2512	ex N349FD	Ismoil Somoni
☐ OK-TVH	Boeing 737-8Q8/W	35275/2604		<TVS◆

TAJIK AIR		*Tajikistan (7J/TJK)*	*Dushanbe/Khudzhand (DYU/LBD)*	
☐ EY-46365	Antonov An-24B	07305906	ex CCCP-46365	
☐ EY-45595	Antonov An-24B	97305105	ex UR-45595	
☐ EY-47693	Antonov An-24RV	27307510	ex CCCP-47693	>DAO
☐ EY-47802	Antonov An-24RV	17306901	ex UN-47802	
☐ EY-24404	Mil Mi-8T	98625146	ex CCCP-24404	
☐ EY-25149	Mil Mi-8MTV-1	95190	ex CCCP-25149	
☐ EY-25167	Mil Mi-8MTV-1	95378	ex CCCP-25167	
☐ EY-25169	Mil Mi-8MTV-1	95380	ex CCCP-25169	>UN
☐ EY-25438	Mil Mi-8MTV-1	95549	ex CCCP-25438	
☐ EY-65763	Tupolev Tu-134A-3	62299	ex CCCP-65763	
☐ EY-65788	Tupolev Tu-134A-3	62835	ex CCCP-65788	
☐ EY-85651	Tupolev Tu-154M	88A793	ex RA-85651	
☐ EY-85691	Tupolev Tu-154M	90A864	ex EP-EAB	>IRX
☐ EY-85692	Tupolev Tu-154M	90A865	ex EP-TUE	
☐ EY-85717	Tupolev Tu-154M	91A897	ex EP-EAA	
☐ EY-87214	Yakovlev Yak-40K	9640851	ex HA-LJB	
☐ EY-87217	Yakovlev Yak-40	9510340	ex EP-EAL	
☐ EY-87434	Yakovlev Yak-40	9431035	ex EP-TUF	
☐ EY-87922	Yakovlev Yak-40K	9731355	ex EP-EAM	
☐ EY-87963	Yakovlev Yak-40K	9831058	ex EP-EAK	>KMF
☐ EY-87967	Yakovlev Yak-40K	9831158	ex EP-CPI	
☐ EY-88267	Yakovlev Yak-40K	9720553	ex CCP-66267	
☐ EY-536	Boeing 737-3B7	23700/1461	ex N514AU	
☐ LY-AWF	Boeing 737-522	26707/2512	ex C-FDCZ	
☐ LY-AWG	Boeing 737-522	26700/2490	ex C-FDCH	
☐ EY-751	Boeing 757-2Q8	24964/424	ex N926JS	
☐ EY-26205	Antonov An-26B	14107	ex CCCP-26205	
☐ EY-26658	Antonov An-26	7904	ex 26658	
☐ EY-28736	WSK-PZL/Antonov An-28	1AJ007-24	ex CCCP-28736	
☐ EY-28921	WSK-PZL/Antonov An-28	1AJ008-07	ex CCCP-28921	

176

EZ- TURKMENISTAN (Republic of Turkmenistan)

TURKMENISTAN AIRLINES		Turkmenistan (T5/TUA)		Askhabad (ASB)
☐ EZ-A101	Boeing 717-22K	55153/5072	ex N6202S	
☐ EZ-A102	Boeing 717-22K	55154/5078		
☐ EZ-A103	Boeing 717-22K	55155/5086		
☐ EZ-A104	Boeing 717-22K	55195/5130		
☐ EZ-A105	Boeing 717-22K	55196/5133		
☐ EZ-A106	Boeing 717-22K	55186/5146		
☐ EZ-A107	Boeing 717-22K	55187/5147		
☐ EZ-A001	Boeing 737-341	26855/2305	ex EK-A001	
☐ EZ-A002	Boeing 737-332	25994/2439	ex N301DE	
☐ EZ-A003	Boeing 737-332	25995/2455	ex N302DE	
☐ EZ-A004	Boeing 737-82K	36088/2181	ex N1795B	
☐ EZ-A005	Boeing 737-82K	36089/2233		
☐ EZ-A006	Boeing 737-7GL/W	37236/2986	ex N1786B	
☐ EZ-A007	Boeing 737-7GL/W	37234/2682		
☐ EZ-A008	Boeing 737-7GL/W	37237/2988	ex N1787B	
☐ EZ-A009	Boeing 737-7GL/W	37235/2993	ex N3134C	
☐ EZ-	Boeing 737-9			o/o♦
☐ EZ-	Boeing 737-9			o/o♦
☐ EZ-A010	Boeing 757-23A	25345/412	ex N58AW	
☐ EZ-A011	Boeing 757-22K	28336/725		
☐ EZ-A012	Boeing 757-22K	28337/726		
☐ EZ-A014	Boeing 757-22K	30863/952		
☐ EZ-A700	Boeing 767-32KER	33968/926		op for Govt
☐ EZ-A777	Boeing 777-22KLR	39548/889		op for Govt
☐ EZ-L482	Mil Mi-8MTV-1	96144		
☐ EZ-L483	Mil Mi-8MTV-1	96145		
☐ EZ-22763	Mil Mi-8T	9831150	ex CCCP-22763	
☐ EZ-24624	Mil Mi-8T	8253	ex CCCP-24624	
☐ EZ-24701	Mil Mi-8T	98103235	ex CCCP-24701	
☐ EZ-F426	Ilyushin Il-76TD	1033418609		
☐ EZ-F427	Ilyushin Il-76TD	1033418620		
☐ EZ-F428	Ilyushin Il-76TD	1043418624		
☐ EZ-P710	Aérospatiale AS.332L2	2577	ex F-WQDJ	op for Govt
☐ EZ-P711	Aérospatiale AS.332L2	2578	ex F-WWOU	op for Govt
☐ EZ-S701	Sikorsky S-76C+	760463		op for Govt
☐ EZ-S702	Sikorsky S-76C+	760461		
☐ EZ-S703	Sikorsky S-76A+	760294	ex VH-XHL	
☐ EZ-S720	Sikorsky S-92	920017	ex N7118Z	op for Govt
☐ EZ-S721	Sikorsky S-92	920026	ex N8103U	op for Govt

E3- ERITREA (State of Eritrea)

ERITREAN AIRLINES		Eritrean (B8/ERT)		Asmara (ASM)
☐ E3-AAQ	Boeing 767-238ER	23309/129	ex N771WD	

NAS AIR				Asmara (ASM)
☐ E3-NAD	Boeing 737-268	21276/468	ex 4L-EUL	
☐ E3-NAS	Boeing 737-2T5	21960/642	ex EX-214 Dalia	

E5- COOK ISLANDS

AIR RAROTONGA		Air Rarotonga (GZ)		Rarotonga (RAR)
☐ E5-EFS	SAAB SF.340A	340A-049	ex ZK-EFS	
☐ E5-FTS	Embraer EMB.110P1 Bandeirante	110239	ex ZK-FTS	
☐ E5-TAK	Embraer EMB.110P1 Bandeirante	110448	ex ZK-TAK	

E7- BOSNIA-HERZEGOVINA (Republic of Bosnia-Herzegovina)

BH AIRLINES		Air Bosna (JA/BON)			Banja Luka
☐ E7-AAD	ATR 72-212	464	ex T9-AAD	Sarajevo	
☐ E7-AAE	ATR 72-212	465	ex T9-AAE	Mostar	
☐ TC-JLR	Airbus A319-132	3142	ex SX-OAV		<BON♦

ICAR				
☐ E7-AAK	LET L-410UVP-E	892321	ex T9-AAK	

F- FRANCE (French Republic)

AERO SOTRAVIA				Nangis les Loges
☐ F-GCPO	Piper PA-34-200T Seneca II	34-8070358	ex N8266V	
☐ F-GDHD	Britten-Norman BN-2A-9 Islander	591	ex 9Q-CMJ	
☐ F-GMLJ	Cessna 414	414-0635	ex I-CCEE	

AIGLE AZUR		Aigle Azur (ZI/AAF)		Paris-Orly/Charles de Gaulle (ORY/CDG)
☐ F-GXAH	Airbus A319-112	1846	ex C-GTDX	
☐ F-HBMI	Airbus A319-114	0639	ex N573SX	
☐ F-GJVF	Airbus A320-211	0244		
☐ F-HBAC	Airbus A320-214	0888	ex EC-GZE	
☐ F-HBII	Airbus A320-214	3852	ex F-WWDH	
☐ F-	Airbus A320-214		ex	o/o♦
☐ F-GUAA	Airbus A321-211	0808	ex G-JSJX	
☐ F-HBAB	Airbus A321-211	0823	ex F-WBAB	
☐ F-HBAF	Airbus A321-211	1006	ex EC-IXY	
☐ F-HCAI	Airbus A321-211	1451	ex TC-KTC	

AIR CORSICA		Corsica (XK/CCM)		Ajaccio (AJA)
☐ F-GYFK	Airbus A320-214	0533	ex F-WQSY	
☐ F-GYFM	Airbus A319-112	1068	ex F-WQRR	
☐ F-GYJM	Airbus A319-112	1145	ex F-WQRT	
☐ F-HBEV	Airbus A320-216	3952	ex F-WWBI	Calanche de Piana
☐ F-HBSA	Airbus A320-216	3882	ex F-WWIP	Scala di Santa Regina
☐ F-GRPI	ATR 42-500	722	ex F-WWEC	
☐ F-GRPJ	ATR 42-500	724	ex F-WWEI	
☐ F-GRPK	ATR 72-212A	727	ex F-WWEH	
☐ F-GRPX	ATR 72-212A	734	ex F-WWEO	
☐ F-GRPY	ATR 72-212A	742	ex F-WWEC	
☐ F-GRPZ	ATR 72-212A	745	ex F-WWEF	
☐ F-HAPL	ATR 72-212A	654	ex F-OIJG	♦

AIR FRANCE		Airfrans (AF/AFR)		Paris Charles de Gaulle/Orly (CDG/ORY)

Member of Skyteam

☐ F-GUGA	Airbus A318-111	2035	ex D-AUAD	
☐ F-GUGB	Airbus A318-111	2059	ex D-AUAF	
☐ F-GUGC	Airbus A318-111	2071	ex D-AUAG	
☐ F-GUGD	Airbus A318-111	2081	ex D-AUAH	
☐ F-GUGE	Airbus A318-111	2100	ex D-AUAI	
☐ F-GUGF	Airbus A318-111	2109	ex D-AUAJ	
☐ F-GUGG	Airbus A318-111	2317	ex D-AUAA	
☐ F-GUGH	Airbus A318-111	2344	ex D-AUAF	
☐ F-GUGI	Airbus A318-111	2350	ex D-AUAG	
☐ F-GUGJ	Airbus A318-111	2582	ex D-AUAE	
☐ F-GUGK	Airbus A318-111	2601	ex D-AUAF	
☐ F-GUGL	Airbus A318-111	2686	ex D-AUAA	
☐ F-GUGM	Airbus A318-111	2750	ex D-AUAB	
☐ F-GUGN	Airbus A318-111	2918	ex D-AUAB	
☐ F-GUGO	Airbus A318-111	2951	ex D-AUAD	
☐ F-GUGP	Airbus A318-111	2967	ex D-AUAF	
☐ F-GUGQ	Airbus A318-111	2972	ex D-AUAG	
☐ F-GUGR	Airbus A318-111	3009	ex D-AUAJ	
☐ F-GPMA	Airbus A319-113	0598	ex D-AVYD	

☐ F-GPMB	Airbus A319-113	0600	ex D-AVYC	
☐ F-GPMC	Airbus A319-113	0608	ex D-AVYE	
☐ F-GPMD	Airbus A319-113	0618	ex D-AVYJ	
☐ F-GPME	Airbus A319-113	0625	ex D-AVYQ	
☐ F-GPMF	Airbus A319-113	0637	ex D-AVYT	
☐ F-GRHA	Airbus A319-111	0938	ex D-AVYS	
☐ F-GRHB	Airbus A319-111	0985	ex D-AVYO	
☐ F-GRHC	Airbus A319-111	0998	ex D-AVYW	
☐ F-GRHD	Airbus A319-111	1000	ex D-AVYP	
☐ F-GRHE	Airbus A319-111	1020	ex D-AVYX	
☐ F-GRHF	Airbus A319-111	1025	ex D-AVYE	
☐ F-GRHG	Airbus A319-111	1036	ex D-AVYS	
☐ F-GRHH	Airbus A319-111	1151	ex D-AVWK	
☐ F-GRHI	Airbus A319-111	1169	ex D-AVYX	
☐ F-GRHJ	Airbus A319-111	1176	ex D-AVWN	
☐ F-GRHK	Airbus A319-111	1190	ex D-AVYQ	
☐ F-GRHL	Airbus A319-111	1201	ex D-AVWT	
☐ F-GRHM	Airbus A319-111	1216	ex D-AVYF	
☐ F-GRHN	Airbus A319-111	1267	ex D-AVWB	
☐ F-GRHO	Airbus A319-111	1271	ex D-AVWC	
☐ F-GRHP	Airbus A319-111	1344	ex D-AVYQ	
☐ F-GRHQ	Airbus A319-111	1404	ex D-AVYB	
☐ F-GRHR	Airbus A319-111	1415	ex D-AVYF	
☐ F-GRHS	Airbus A319-111	1444	ex D-AVWA	
☐ F-GRHT	Airbus A319-111	1449	ex D-AVWD	
☐ F-GRHU	Airbus A319-111	1471	ex D-AVYR	
☐ F-GRHV	Airbus A319-111	1505	ex D-AVYF	
☐ F-GRHX	Airbus A319-111	1524	ex D-AVWC	
☐ F-GRHY	Airbus A319-111	1616	ex D-AVWG	
☐ F-GRHZ	Airbus A319-111	1622	ex D-AVYO	
☐ F-GRXA	Airbus A319-111	1640	ex D-AVYJ	
☐ F-GRXB	Airbus A319-111	1645	ex D-AVYC	
☐ F-GRXC	Airbus A319-111	1677	ex D-AVWF	
☐ F-GRXD	Airbus A319-111	1699	ex D-AVYG	
☐ F-GRXE	Airbus A319-111	1733	ex D-AVWT	
☐ F-GRXF	Airbus A319-111	1938	ex D-AVWG	
☐ F-GRXG	Airbus A319-115LR	2213	ex D-AVYM	Dedicate
☐ F-GRXH	Airbus A319-115LR	2228	ex D-AVWC	Dedicate
☐ F-GRXI	Airbus A319-115LR	2279	ex D-AVYF	Dedicate
☐ F-GRXJ	Airbus A319-115LR	2456	ex D-AVYX	Dedicate
☐ F-GRXK	Airbus A319-115LR	2716	ex D-AVYX	Dedicate
☐ F-GRXL	Airbus A319-111	2938	ex D-AVWV	
☐ F-GRXM	Airbus A319-111	2961	ex D-AVYI	
☐ F-GRXN	Airbus A319-115LR	3065	ex D-AVWP	Dedicate
☐ F-GFKH	Airbus A320-211	0061		Ville de Bruxelles
☐ F-GFKI	Airbus A320-211	0062		Ville de Lisbonne
☐ F-GFKJ	Airbus A320-211	0063		Ville de Copenhague — Retro c/s
☐ F-GFKM	Airbus A320-211	0102		Ville de Luxembourg
☐ F-GFKR	Airbus A320-211	0186		Ville de Barcelonne
☐ F-GFKS	Airbus A320-211	0187		
☐ F-GFKV	Airbus A320-211	0227		Ville de Bordeaux
☐ F-GFKX	Airbus A320-211	0228		Ville de Francfort
☐ F-GFKY	Airbus A320-211	0285		Ville de Toulouse
☐ F-GFKZ	Airbus A320-211	0286		Ville de Turin
☐ F-GHQC	Airbus A320-211	0044	ex F-GGEH	
☐ F-GHQE	Airbus A320-211	0115		
☐ F-GHQG	Airbus A320-211	0155		
☐ F-GHQH	Airbus A320-211	0156		
☐ F-GHQJ	Airbus A320-211	0214		
☐ F-GHQK	Airbus A320-211	0236		
☐ F-GHQL	Airbus A320-211	0239		
☐ F-GHQM	Airbus A320-211	0237		
☐ F-GHQO	Airbus A320-211	0278		
☐ F-GHQP	Airbus A320-211	0337		
☐ F-GHQQ	Airbus A320-211	0352		
☐ F-GHQR	Airbus A320-211	0377		
☐ F-GJVA	Airbus A320-211	0144	ex F-WWDK	
☐ F-GJVB	Airbus A320-211	0145	ex F-WWDL	
☐ F-GJVG	Airbus A320-211	0270		
☐ F-GJVW	Airbus A320-211	0491		
☐ F-GKXA	Airbus A320-211	0287		Ville de Nantes
☐ F-GKXC	Airbus A320-214	1502	ex F-WWIG	
☐ F-GKXD	Airbus A320-214	1873	ex F-WWDV	
☐ F-GKXE	Airbus A320-214	1879	ex F-WWDX	
☐ F-GKXF	Airbus A320-214	1885		
☐ F-GKXG	Airbus A320-214	1894	ex F-WWDV	

179

☐ F-GKXH	Airbus A320-214	1924		
☐ F-GKXI	Airbus A320-214	1949		
☐ F-GKXJ	Airbus A320-214	1900		
☐ F-GKXK	Airbus A320-214	2140	ex F-WWBR	
☐ F-GKXL	Airbus A320-214	2705		
☐ F-GKXM	Airbus A320-214	2721	ex F-WWXM	
☐ F-GKXN	Airbus A320-214	3008	ex F-WWBH	
☐ F-GKXO	Airbus A320-214	3420	ex F-WWIP	
☐ F-GKXP	Airbus A320-214	3470	ex F-WWBP	
☐ F-GKXQ	Airbus A320-214	3777	ex D-AVVH	
☐ F-GKXR	Airbus A320-214	3795	ex F-WWBM	
☐ F-GKXS	Airbus A320-214	3825	ex F-WWIV	
☐ F-GKXT	Airbus A320-214	3859	ex F-WWDM	
☐ F-GKXU	Airbus A320-214	4063	ex F-WWBF	
☐ F-GKXV	Airbus A320-214	4084	ex D-AVVA	
☐ F-GKXY	Airbus A320-214	4105	ex D-AVVR	
☐ F-GKXZ	Airbus A320-214	4137	ex F-WWIZ	
☐ F-HBNA	Airbus A320-214	4335	ex F-WWIU	◆
☐ F-HEPA	Airbus A320-214	4139	ex F-WWIX	
☐ F-HEPB	Airbus A320-214	4241	ex F-WWDK	◆
☐ F-HEPC	Airbus A320-214	4267	ex F-WWBM	◆
☐ F-HEPD	Airbus A320-214	4295	ex F-WWIZ	◆
☐ F-HEPE	Airbus A320-214	4298	ex F-WWDF	◆
☐ F-	Airbus A320-214			o/o
☐ F-	Airbus A320-214			o/o
☐ F-	Airbus A320-214			o/o
☐ F-	Airbus A320-214			o/o
☐ F-	Airbus A320-214			o/o
☐ F-	Airbus A320-214			o/o
☐ F-	Airbus A320-214			o/o
☐ F-	Airbus A320-214			o/o
☐ F-	Airbus A320-214			o/o
☐ F-	Airbus A320-214			o/o
☐ F-	Airbus A320-214			o/o
☐ F-	Airbus A320-214			o/o
☐ F-GMZA	Airbus A321-111	0498	ex D-AVZK	
☐ F-GMZB	Airbus A321-111	0509	ex D-AVZN	
☐ F-GMZC	Airbus A321-111	0521	ex D-AVZW	
☐ F-GMZD	Airbus A321-111	0529	ex D-AVZA	
☐ F-GMZE	Airbus A321-111	0544	ex D-AVZF	
☐ F-GTAD	Airbus A321-212	0777	ex D-AVZI	
☐ F-GTAE	Airbus A321-212	0796	ex D-AVZN	
☐ F-GTAH	Airbus A321-212	1133	ex D-AVZD	
☐ F-GTAI	Airbus A321-212	1299	ex D-AVZP	
☐ F-GTAJ	Airbus A321-212	1476	ex D-AVZF	
☐ F-GTAK	Airbus A321-212	1658	ex D-AVZP	
☐ F-GTAL	Airbus A321-212	1691	ex D-AVZY	
☐ F-GTAM	Airbus A321-212	1859	ex D-AVZY	
☐ F-GTAN	Airbus A321-212	3051	ex D-AVZD	
☐ F-GTAO	Airbus A321-212	3098	ex D-AVZQ	
☐ F-GTAP	Airbus A321-212	3372	ex D-AVZK	
☐ F-GTAQ	Airbus A321-212	3399	ex D-AVZQ	
☐ F-GTAR	Airbus A321-212	3401	ex D-AVZR	
☐ F-GTAS	Airbus A321-212	3419	ex D-AVZE	
☐ F-GTAT	Airbus A321-212	3441	ex D-AVZH	
☐ F-GTAU	Airbus A321-212	3814	ex D-AVZE	
☐ F-GTAV	Airbus A321-212	3884	ex D-AVZU	
☐ F-GTAX	Airbus A321-212	3930	ex D-AZAD	
☐ F-GTAY	Airbus A321-212	4251	ex D-AZAG	◆
☐ F-	Airbus A321-212			o/o ◆
☐ F-GZCA	Airbus A330-203	422		
☐ F-GZCB	Airbus A330-203	443		
☐ F-GZCC	Airbus A330-203	448		
☐ F-GZCD	Airbus A330-203	458	ex (F-WWJH)	
☐ F-GZCE	Airbus A330-203	465	ex F-WWKM	
☐ F-GZCF	Airbus A330-203	481		
☐ F-GZCG	Airbus A330-203	498	ex F-WWKI	
☐ F-GZCH	Airbus A330-203	500		
☐ F-GZCI	Airbus A330-203	502	ex F-WWKJ	
☐ F-GZCJ	Airbus A330-203	503		
☐ F-GZCK	Airbus A330-203	516		
☐ F-GZCL	Airbus A330-203	519		
☐ F-GZCM	Airbus A330-203	567	ex (F-WWYT)	
☐ F-GZCN	Airbus A330-203	584		
☐ F-GZCO	Airbus A330-203	657		

☐ F-GLZC	Airbus A340-311	029				
☐ F-GLZH	Airbus A340-311	078				
☐ F-GLZI	Airbus A340-311	084				
☐ F-GLZJ	Airbus A340-313X	186				
☐ F-GLZK	Airbus A340-313X	207				
☐ F-GLZL	Airbus A340-313X	210				
☐ F-GLZM	Airbus A340-313X	237				
☐ F-GLZN	Airbus A340-313X	245				
☐ F-GLZO	Airbus A340-313X	246				
☐ F-GLZP	Airbus A340-313X	260				
☐ F-GLZR	Airbus A340-313X	307				
☐ F-GLZS	Airbus A340-313X	310				
☐ F-GLZT	Airbus A340-313X	319				
☐ F-GLZU	Airbus A340-313X	377				
☐ F-GNIG	Airbus A340-313X	174				
☐ F-GNIH	Airbus A340-313X	373				
☐ F-GNII	Airbus A340-313X	399				
☐ F-HPJA	Airbus A380-861	033	ex F-WWSB			
☐ F-HPJB	Airbus A380-861	040	ex F-WWSE			
☐ F-HPJC	Airbus A380-861	043	ex F-WWAB			♦
☐ F-HPJD	Airbus A380-861	049	ex F-WWAL			♦
☐ F-HPJE	Airbus A380-861	052	ex F-WWAN		o/o♦	
☐ F-HPJF	Airbus A380-861	064	ex F-WWAU		o/o♦	
☐ F-HPJG	Airbus A380-861	067	ex F-WW		o/o♦	
☐ F-HPJH	Airbus A380-861	077	ex F-WW		o/o♦	
☐ F-GCBG	Boeing 747-228F	22939/569	ex N4544F	Air France Cargo	[XCR]	
☐ F-GEXA	Boeing 747-4B3	24154/741				
☐ F-GEXB	Boeing 747-4B3M	24155/864				
☐ F-GISB	Boeing 747-428MBCF	25302/884			[XCR]	
☐ F-GISC	Boeing 747-428M	25599/899			[XCR]	
☐ F-GISD	Boeing 747-428M	25628/934				
☐ F-GISE	Boeing 747-428BCF	25630/960			[XCR]	
☐ F-GITD	Boeing 747-428	25600/901				
☐ F-GITE	Boeing 747-428	25601/906				
☐ F-GITF	Boeing 747-428	25602/909				
☐ F-GITH	Boeing 747-428	32868/1325				
☐ F-GITI	Boeing 747-428	32869/1327				
☐ F-GITJ	Boeing 747-428	32871/1343				
☐ F-GIUA	Boeing 747-428ERF	32866/1315	ex N5017Q			
☐ F-GIUC	Boeing 747-428ERF	32867/1318				
☐ F-GIUD	Boeing 747-428ERF	32870/1344				
☐ F-GSPA	Boeing 777-228ER	29002/129				
☐ F-GSPB	Boeing 777-228ER	29003/133				
☐ F-GSPC	Boeing 777-228ER	29004/138				
☐ F-GSPD	Boeing 777-228ER	29005/187				
☐ F-GSPE	Boeing 777-228ER	29006/189				
☐ F-GSPF	Boeing 777-228ER	29007/201				
☐ F-GSPG	Boeing 777-228ER	27609/195				
☐ F-GSPH	Boeing 777-228ER	28675/210				
☐ F-GSPI	Boeing 777-228ER	29008/258				
☐ F-GSPJ	Boeing 777-228ER	29009/263				
☐ F-GSPK	Boeing 777-228ER	29010/267				
☐ F-GSPL	Boeing 777-228ER	30457/284	ex N50281			
☐ F-GSPM	Boeing 777-228ER	30456/307				
☐ F-GSPN	Boeing 777-228ER	29011/314				
☐ F-GSPO	Boeing 777-228ER	30614/320				
☐ F-GSPP	Boeing 777-228ER	30615/327				
☐ F-GSPQ	Boeing 777-228ER	28682/331				
☐ F-GSPR	Boeing 777-228ER	28683/367				
☐ F-GSPS	Boeing 777-228ER	32306/370				
☐ F-GSPT	Boeing 777-228ER	32308/382				
☐ F-GSPU	Boeing 777-228ER	32309/383				
☐ F-GSPV	Boeing 777-228ER	28684/385				
☐ F-GSPX	Boeing 777-228ER	32698/392				
☐ F-GSPY	Boeing 777-228ER	32305/395				
☐ F-GSPZ	Boeing 777-228ER	32310/401				
☐ F-GSQA	Boeing 777-328ER	32723/466	ex N5017Q			
☐ F-GSQB	Boeing 777-328ER	32724/478				
☐ F-GSQC	Boeing 777-328ER	32727/480				
☐ F-GSQD	Boeing 777-328ER	32726/490				
☐ F-GSQE	Boeing 777-328ER	32851/492				
☐ F-GSQF	Boeing 777-328ER	32849/494	ex N50217			
☐ F-GSQG	Boeing 777-328ER	32850/500	ex N5028Y			
☐ F-GSQH	Boeing 777-328ER	32711/501				

☐ F-GSQI	Boeing 777-328ER	32725/502	ex N60697		
☐ F-GSQJ	Boeing 777-328ER	32852/510			
☐ F-GSQK	Boeing 777-328ER	32845/530	ex N5017Q		
☐ F-GSQL	Boeing 777-328ER	32853/545			
☐ F-GSQM	Boeing 777-328ER	32848/558			
☐ F-GSQN	Boeing 777-328ER	32960/565			
☐ F-GSQO	Boeing 777-328ER	32961/570			
☐ F-GSQP	Boeing 777-328ER	35676/573			
☐ F-GSQR	Boeing 777-328ER	35677/579			
☐ F-GSQS	Boeing 777-328ER	32962/608			
☐ F-GSQT	Boeing 777-328ER	32846/616			
☐ F-GSQU	Boeing 777-328ER	32847/624	ex N5022E		
☐ F-GSQV	Boeing 777-328ER	32854/636			
☐ F-GSQX	Boeing 777-328ER	32963/645	ex N5014K		
☐ F-GSQY	Boeing 777-328ER	35678/647			
☐ F-GUOB	Boeing 777-F28	32965/732	ex N5023Q		
☐ F-GUOC	Boeing 777-F28	32966/752			
☐ F-GZNA	Boeing 777-328ER	35297/671	ex N50217		
☐ F-GZNB	Boeing 777-328ER	32964/715			
☐ F-GZNC	Boeing 777-328ER	35542/723		Gille Dehove	
☐ F-GZND	Boeing 777-328ER	35543/777	ex N1785B		
☐ F-GZNE	Boeing 777-328ER	37432/790			
☐ F-GZNF	Boeing 777-328ER	37433/792	ex N50281		
☐ F-GZNG	Boeing 777-328ER	32968/795			
☐ F-GZNH	Boeing 777-328ER	35544/905	ex N5017V		♦
☐ F-	Boeing 777-328ER				o/o♦
☐ F-	Boeing 777-328ER				o/o♦
☐ F-	Boeing 777-328ER				o/o♦
☐ F-	Boeing 777-328ER				o/o♦
☐ F-	Boeing 777-328ER				o/o♦

AIR FRANCE REGIONAL — *Various*

The majority of services are operated in full Air France colours with titles 'Air France by' the appropriate airline, Airlinair, Brit'Air, CCM Airlines, Regional and Cityjet.

AIR MEDITERRANÉE — *Mediterranée (BIE)* — *Tarbes (LDE)*

☐ F-GYAI	Airbus A320-211	0293	ex 9H-ABQ		
☐ F-GYAJ	Airbus A321-211	2707	ex D-AVZF		
☐ F-GYAN	Airbus A321-111	0535	ex F-WQQU		
☐ F-GYAO	Airbus A321-111	0642	ex F-WQQV		
☐ F-GYAP	Airbus A321-111	0517	ex HB-IOA		
☐ F-GYAQ	Airbus A321-211	0827	ex HB-IOI		
☐ F-GYAR	Airbus A321-211	0891	ex HB-IOJ	FRAM colours	
☐ F-GYAZ	Airbus A321-111	0519	ex D-ANJA		
☐ F-HCOA	Boeing 737-5L9	28084/2788	ex OY-APB		♦

AIRBUS TRANSPORT INTERNATIONAL — *Super Transport (4Y/BGA)* — *Toulouse-Blagnac (TLS)*

☐ F-GSTA	Airbus A300B4-608ST Beluga	655/001	ex F-WAST	Super Transporter 1	
☐ F-GSTB	Airbus A300B4-608ST Beluga	751/002	ex F-WSTB	Super Transporter 2	
☐ F-GSTC	Airbus A300B4-608ST Beluga	765/003	ex F-WSTC	Super Transporter 3	
☐ F-GSTD	Airbus A300B4-608ST Beluga	776/004	ex F-WSTD	Super Transporter 4	
☐ F-GSTF	Airbus A300B4-608ST Beluga	796/005	ex F-WSTF	Super Transporter 5	

AIRLEC AIR ESPACE — *AirLec (ARL)* — *Bordeaux (BOD)*

☐ F-GGRV	Piper PA-31T Cheyenne	31T-7720036	ex N41RC	
☐ F-GGVG	Swearingen SA.226T Merlin IIIB	T-293	ex D-IBBB	
☐ F-GLPT	Swearingen SA.226T Merlin IIIB	T-298	ex VH-AWU	
☐ F-GRNT	Swearingen SA.226T Merlin IIIB	T-312	ex N84GA	

AIRLINAIR — *Airlinair (A5/RLA)* — *Paris-Orly (ORY)*

☐ F-GKNB	ATR 42-300	226		
☐ F-GKNC	ATR 42-300	230		
☐ F-GKYN	ATR 42-300	095	ex F-ODUL	
☐ F-GPYA	ATR 42-500	457	ex F-WWET	
☐ F-GPYB	ATR 42-500	480	ex F-WWLZ	
☐ F-GPYC	ATR 42-500	484	ex F-WWEB	
☐ F-GPYD	ATR 42-500	490	ex F-WWLJ	
☐ F-GPYF	ATR 42-500	495	ex F-WWLM	op for AFR
☐ F-GPYK	ATR 42-500	537	ex F-WWLC	op for AFR
☐ F-GPYL	ATR 42-500	542	ex F-WWLH	op for AFR
☐ F-GPYM	ATR 42-500	520	ex F-WWLR	op for AFR
☐ F-GPYN	ATR 42-500	539	ex F-WWLO	op for AFR

☐ F-GPYO	ATR 42-500	544	ex F-WWLH		
☐ F-GVZB	ATR 42-500	524	ex F-OHQL		
☐ F-GVZJ	ATR 42-320	093	ex F-WQNO		
☐ F-GVZO	ATR 42-320	080	ex OY-PCG		◆
☐ F-GVZZ	ATR 42-300	055	ex F-WVZZ		
☐ F-GKPD	ATR 72-202	177	ex F-WWE	all-white	
☐ F-GPOC	ATR 72-202 (QC)	311	ex B-22707		op for AFR
☐ F-GPOD	ATR 72-202 (QC)	361	ex B-22711		op for AFR
☐ F-GVZG	ATR 72-201	145	ex G-HERM		
☐ F-GVZL	ATR 72-212A	553	ex F-OHJO		
☐ F-GVZM	ATR 72-212A	590	ex F-OHJT		
☐ F-GVZN	ATR 72-212A	563	ex F-OHJU		

ALSAIR		*Alsair (AL/LSR)*		*Colmar (CMR)*

☐ F-GEOU	Beech 65-C90 King Air	LJ-941	ex N3804C

ATLANTIQUE AIR ASSISTANCE		*Triple A (TLB)*		*Nantes (NTE)*

☐ F-GIZB	Beech C90 King Air	LJ-955	ex N786SB
☐ F-GNBR	Beech 1900D	UE-327	ex N23154
☐ F-GPYY	Beech 1900C-1	UC-115	ex N115YV
☐ F-GTVA	Embraer EMB.120ER Brasilia	120253	ex F-GJTG
☐ F-HAAV	ATR 42-320	019	ex F-WKVB
☐ F-HBSO	ATR 42-320	066	ex D4-CBS

BLUE LINE		*Blue Berry (BLE)*		*Paris-Charles de Gaulle (CDG)*

☐ F-GMLI	McDonnell-Douglas MD-83	53014/1740	ex F-WMLI	VIP
☐ F-GMLK	McDonnell-Douglas MD-83	49672/1494	ex F-WMLK	
☐ F-GMLX	McDonnell-Douglas MD-83	49823/1540	ex OE-LMI	
☐ F-HBOS	Airbus A310-325ET	674	ex F-WHUR	◆

BRIT'AIR		*Brit Air (DB/BZH)*		*Morlaix (MXN)*

☐ F-GRJE	Canadair CRJ-100ER	7106	ex C-FMNQ	
☐ F-GRJF	Canadair CRJ-100ER	7108	ex C-FMLU	
☐ F-GRJG	Canadair CRJ-100ER	7143	ex C-FMMQ	
☐ F-GRJI	Canadair CRJ-100ER	7147	ex C-FZAL	
☐ F-GRJJ	Canadair CRJ-100ER	7190	ex C-GBFF	
☐ F-GRJK	Canadair CRJ-100ER	7219	ex C-FMMQ	
☐ F-GRJL	Canadair CRJ-100ER	7221	ex C-FMNX	
☐ F-GRJM	Canadair CRJ-100ER	7222	ex C-FMMY	
☐ F-GRJN	Canadair CRJ-100ER	7262	ex C-FMLT	
☐ F-GRJO	Canadair CRJ-100ER	7296	ex C-FMNW	
☐ F-GRJP	Canadair CRJ-100ER	7301	ex C-FVAZ	
☐ F-GRJQ	Canadair CRJ-100ER	7321	ex C-FMLS	
☐ F-GRJR	Canadair CRJ-100ER	7375	ex C-FMKW	
☐ F-GRJT	Canadair CRJ-100ER	7389	ex C-FMOS	
☐ F-GRZA	Canadair CRJ-701	10006	ex C-GHCE	
☐ F-GRZB	Canadair CRJ-701	10007	ex C-GHCF	
☐ F-GRZC	Canadair CRJ-701	10008	ex C-GHCO	
☐ F-GRZD	Canadair CRJ-701	10016	ex C-GJEZ	
☐ F-GRZE	Canadair CRJ-701	10032	ex C-GIBL	
☐ F-GRZF	Canadair CRJ-701	10036	ex C-GIBQ	
☐ F-GRZG	Canadair CRJ-701	10037	ex C-GIBT	
☐ F-GRZH	Canadair CRJ-701	10089	ex C-GIBI	
☐ F-GRZI	Canadair CRJ-701	10093	ex C-	
☐ F-GRZJ	Canadair CRJ-701	10096	ex C-	
☐ F-GRZK	Canadair CRJ-701	10198	ex C-	
☐ F-GRZL	Canadair CRJ-701	10245	ex C-	
☐ F-GRZM	Canadair CRJ-701	10263	ex C-	
☐ F-GRZN	Canadair CRJ-701	10264	ex C-	
☐ F-GRZO	Canadair CRJ-701	10265	ex C-	
☐ F-HDTA	Canadair CRJ-900ER	15001	ex C-FZTU	◆
☐ F-HMLA	Canadair CRJ-1000	19004	ex C-GELU	◆
☐ F-HMLC	Canadair CRJ-1000	19006	ex C-GHKA	◆
☐ F-HMLD	Canadair CRJ-1000	19007	ex C-	◆
☐ F-	Canadair CRJ-1000		ex C-	o/o ◆
☐ F-	Canadair CRJ-1000		ex C-	o/o ◆
☐ F-	Canadair CRJ-1000		ex C-	o/o ◆
☐ F-	Canadair CRJ-1000		ex C-	o/o ◆
☐ F-GKHD	Fokker 100	11381	ex HB-IVI	
☐ F-GKHE	Fokker 100	11386	ex HB-IVK	

☐ F-GPXB	Fokker 100	11492	ex PH-EZK
☐ F-GPXC	Fokker 100	11493	ex PH-EZY
☐ F-GPXD	Fokker 100	11494	ex PH-EZO
☐ F-GPXE	Fokker 100	11495	ex PH-EZP
☐ F-GPXF	Fokker 100	11330	ex F-WQJX
☐ F-GPXJ	Fokker 100	11323	ex EI-DBR

CHALAIR AVIATION — Chalar (CLG) — Caen-Carpiquet (CFR)

☐ F-BXPY	Beech 65-C90 King Air	LJ-684	
☐ F-GHVV	Beech 200 Super King Air	BB-676	ex N1362B
☐ F-GIJB	Beech 200 Super King Air	BB-13	ex N83MA
☐ F-GOOB	Beech 1900C-1	UC-153	ex N153YV
☐ F-GPAS	Beech 200 Super King Air	BB-209	ex D-IACS
☐ F-HBCA	Beech 1900D	UE-188	ex SE-KXV
☐ F-HBCB	Beech 1900D	UE-390	ex 3B-VTL
☐ F-HBCC	Beech 1900D	UE-350	ex 3B-VIP
☐ F-HBCE	Beech 1900D	UE-323	ex OY-CHU

CORSAIR — Corsair (SS/CRL) — Ajaccio (AJA)

☐ F-GTUI	Boeing 747-422	26875/931	ex N186UA
☐ F-HKIS	Boeing 747-422	25380/913	ex F-WKIS
☐ F-HSEA	Boeing 747-422	26877/944	ex F-WSEA
☐ F-HSEX	Boeing 747-422	26878/966	ex F-WSEX
☐ F-HSUN	Boeing 747-422	26880/984	ex F-WSUN
☐ F-HLOV	Boeing 747-422	25379/911	ex F-WLOV
☐ F-HBIL	Airbus A330-243	320	
☐ F-HCAT	Airbus A330-243	285	ex F-WWKB

EUROPE AIRPOST — French Post (5O/FPO) — Paris-Charles de Gaulle (CDG)

☐ EI-STA	Boeing 737-31S	29057/2942	ex G-THOG	♦
☐ F-GFUE	Boeing 737-3B3 (QC)	24387/1693		
☐ F-GFUF	Boeing 737-3B3 (QC)	24388/1725		
☐ F-GIXB	Boeing 737-33A (QC)	24789/1953	ex F-OGSD	
☐ F-GIXC	Boeing 737-38B (QC)	25124/2047	ex F-OGSS	Saint-Louis
☐ F-GIXD	Boeing 737-33A (QC)	25744/2198	ex N3213T	
☐ F-GIXE	Boeing 737-3B3 (QC)	26850/2235	ex N854WT	
☐ F-GIXF	Boeing 737-3B3 (QC)	26851/2267	ex N4361V	
☐ F-GIXH	Boeing 737-3S3 (QC)	23788/1393	ex N271LF	
☐ F-GIXI	Boeing 737-348 (QC)	23809/1458	ex F-OGSY	
☐ F-GIXJ	Boeing 737-3Y0 (QC)	23685/1357	ex G-MONH	
☐ F-GIXL	Boeing 737-348 (QC)	23810/1474	ex F-OHCS	
☐ F-GIXO	Boeing 737-3Q8 (QC)	24132/1555	ex N241LF	
☐ F-GIXR	Boeing 737-3H6 (SF)	27125/2415	ex 9M-MZA	
☐ F-GIXS	Boeing 737-3H6 (SF)	27347/2615	ex 9M-MZB	
☐ F-GIXT	Boeing 737-39M (QC)	28898/2906	ex F-ODZZ	
☐ F-GZTA	Boeing 737-33V (QC)	29333/3084	ex HA-LKV	
☐ F-GZTB	Boeing 737-33VF	29336/3102	ex HA-LKU	
☐ F-GZTC	Boeing 737-73V	32414/1214	ex G-EZJS	
☐ F-GZTD	Boeing 737-73V	32418/1300	ex G-EZJW	♦
☐ F-GPOA	ATR 72-202 (QC)	204	ex F-ORAC	op by SWT
☐ F-GPOB	ATR 72-202 (QC)	207	ex F-ORAN	op by SWT
☐ F-GPOC	ATR 72-202 (QC)	311	ex B-22707	>RLA
☐ F-GPOD	ATR 72-202 (QC)	361	ex B-22711	>RLA

FINIST'AIR — Finistair (FTR) — Brest (BES)

☐ F-GHGZ	Cessna 208A Caravan I	20800188	ex (N9769F)	
☐ F-GJFI	Cessna 208B Caravan I	208B0230	ex N208GC	
☐ F-GNYR	Cessna 208B Caravan I	208B1039	ex D-FOXI	Op for Atlantic Air Lift

HELI-UNION — Heli Union (HLU) — Paris-Heliport/Toussus-le-Noble (JDP/TNF)

☐ F-GEPN	Aérospatiale SA365C3 Dauphin 2	5073	ex D-HELY	based PNR
☐ F-GERJ	Aérospatiale SA365N Dauphin 2	6066	ex F-ODRA	based Gabon
☐ F-GFCH	Aérospatiale SA365C2 Dauphin 2	5072	ex F-OCCD	
☐ F-GFEC	Aérospatiale SA365C2 Dauphin 2	5071	ex F-ODBV	
☐ F-GFPA	Aérospatiale SA365C2 Dauphin 2	5063	ex LV-AIE	
☐ F-GJPZ	Aérospatiale SA365N Dauphin 2	6115	ex LN-OLN	
☐ F-GKCU	Aérospatiale SA365N Dauphin 2	6011	ex PH-SEC	based PNR
☐ F-GMAY	Aérospatiale SA365N Dauphin 2	6137		
☐ F-GRCF	Aérospatiale AS365N3 Dauphin 2	9000		♦
☐ F-GSYA	Aérospatiale SA365N Dauphin 2	6220	ex JA9913	
☐ F-GTCH	Aérospatiale AS365N3 Dauphin 2	6710	ex F-WWOR	

☐ F-GVGV	Aérospatiale AS365N3 Dauphin 2	6724	ex F-WWOL	
☐ F-HMLB	Aérospatiale AS365N3 Dauphin 2	6726	ex F-WWOS	
☐ TJ-SAH	Aérospatiale SA365N Dauphin 2	6037	ex F-GMHI	
☐ F-GHOY	Aérospatiale AS.332L1	9005	ex F-WQEB	
☐ F-GJTU	Aérospatiale AS350B3 Ecureuil	3449	ex EP-HEU	based Cayenne
☐ F-GYSH	Aérospatiale AS.332L1	9006	ex F-WQEE	o/o

HEX'AIR — Hex Airline (UD/HER) — Le Puy (LPY)

| ☐ F-GOPE | Beech 1900D | UE-103 | ex N82930 | |
| ☐ F-GUPE | Beech 1900D | UE-248 | ex N10882 | >PEA |

OPENSKIES — (BOS) — Paris-Orly (ORY)

☐ F-GPEJ	Boeing 757-236/W	25807/610	ex G-BPEJ	Penny	♦
☐ F-GPEK	Boeing 757-236/W	25808/665	ex G-BPEK	Lauren	♦
☐ F-HAVI	Boeing 757-26D/W	24473/301	ex N473AP	Violetta	
☐ F-HAVN	Boeing 757-230/W	25140/382	ex D-ABNF	Gloria	

PAN EUROPÉENE AIR SERVICE — Pan Euro (PEA) — Chambéry (CMF)

☐ F-GUPE	Beech 1900D	UE-248	ex N10882	<HER
☐ F-GYPE	Embraer ERJ-135LR	145492	ex PT-SXL	
☐ F-GZPE	Piaggio P.180 Avanti	1064		
☐ F-HAPE	Beech 1900D	UE-367	ex N30515	
☐ F-HBPE	Embraer ERJ-145LR	145106	ex PH-RXC	

RÉGIONAL — Régional Europe (YS/RAE) — Nantes (NTE)

☐ F-GOHA	Embraer ERJ-135ER	145189	ex PT-SFM	
☐ F-GOHC	Embraer ERJ-135ER	145243	ex PT-SJF	
☐ F-GOHD	Embraer ERJ-135ER	145252	ex PT-SJJ	
☐ F-GOHE	Embraer ERJ-135ER	145335	ex PT-SNB	
☐ F-GOHF	Embraer ERJ-135ER	145347	ex PT-SNN	
☐ F-GRGP	Embraer ERJ-135ER	145188	ex PT-SFL	
☐ F-GRGQ	Embraer ERJ-135ER	145233	ex PT-SJB	
☐ F-GRGR	Embraer ERJ-135ER	145236	ex PT-SJE	
☐ F-GRGA	Embraer ERJ-145EP	145008	ex PT-SYE	
☐ F-GRGB	Embraer ERJ-145EP	145010	ex PT-SYG	
☐ F-GRGC	Embraer ERJ-145EP	145012	ex PT-SYI	
☐ F-GRGD	Embraer ERJ-145EP	145043	ex PT-SZI	
☐ F-GRGE	Embraer ERJ-145EP	145047	ex PT-SZM	
☐ F-GRGF	Embraer ERJ-145EP	145050	ex PT-SZP	
☐ F-GRGG	Embraer ERJ-145EP	145118	ex PT-SCT	
☐ F-GRGH	Embraer ERJ-145EP	145120	ex PT-SCW	
☐ F-GRGI	Embraer ERJ-145EP	145152	ex PT-SED	
☐ F-GRGJ	Embraer ERJ-145EP	145297	ex PT-SKO	
☐ F-GRGK	Embraer ERJ-145EP	145324	ex PT-SMQ	
☐ F-GRGL	Embraer ERJ-145EP	145375	ex PT-SOZ	
☐ F-GRGM	Embraer ERJ-145EP	145418	ex PT-STP	
☐ F-GUAM	Embraer ERJ-145MP	145266	ex PT-SIY	
☐ F-GUBA	Embraer ERJ-145MP	145398	ex PT-SQV	
☐ F-GUBB	Embraer ERJ-145MP	145419	ex PT-STQ	
☐ F-GUBC	Embraer ERJ-145MP	145556	ex PT-SZR	
☐ F-GUBD	Embraer ERJ-145MP	145333	ex PT-SMZ	
☐ F-GUBE	Embraer ERJ-145MP	145668	ex PT-SFC	
☐ F-GUBF	Embraer ERJ-145MP	145669	ex PT-SFD	
☐ F-GUBG	Embraer ERJ-145MP	14500890	ex PT-SYD	
☐ F-GUEA	Embraer ERJ-145MP	145342	ex PT-SNI	
☐ F-GUFD	Embraer ERJ-145MP	145197	ex PT-SGN	
☐ F-GUMA	Embraer ERJ-145MP	145405	ex PT-STC	
☐ F-GUPT	Embraer ERJ-145MP	145294	ex PT-SKL	
☐ F-GVGS	Embraer ERJ-145MP	145385	ex PT-SQJ	
☐ F-GVHD	Embraer ERJ-145MP	145178	ex PT-SEZ	
☐ F-HBXA	Embraer ERJ-170STD	17000237	ex PT-SFN	
☐ F-HBXB	Embraer ERJ-170STD	17000250	ex PT-SJB	
☐ F-HBXC	Embraer ERJ-170STD	17000263	ex PT-SJR	
☐ F-HBXD	Embraer ERJ-170STD	17000281	ex PT-TQH	
☐ F-HBXE	Embraer ERJ-170STD	17000286	ex PT-TQM	
☐ F-HBXF	Embraer ERJ-170STD	17000292	ex PT-TQS	
☐ F-HBXG	Embraer ERJ-170STD	17000301	ex PT-XQA	♦
☐ F-HBXH	Embraer ERJ-170STD	17000307	ex PT-XQH	♦
☐ F-HBXI	Embraer ERJ-170STD	17000310	ex PT-XQX	♦
☐ F-HBXJ	Embraer ERJ-170STD	17000312	ex PT-XQZ	♦

☐ F-HBLA	Embraer ERJ-190LR	19000051	ex PT-SIA	
☐ F-HBLB	Embraer ERJ-190LR	19000060	ex PT-SIN	
☐ F-HBLC	Embraer ERJ-190LR	19000080	ex PT-SJW	
☐ F-HBLD	Embraer ERJ-190LR	19000113	ex PT-SQH	
☐ F-HBLE	Embraer ERJ-190LR	19000123	ex PT-SQS	
☐ F-HBLF	Embraer ERJ-190LR	19000158	ex PT-SAO	
☐ F-HBLG	Embraer ERJ-190LR	19000254	ex PT-SIZ	
☐ F-HBLH	Embraer ERJ-190LR	19000266	ex PT-TLG	
☐ F-HBLI	Embraer ERJ-190STD	19000298	ex PT-TZM	
☐ F-HBLJ	Embraer ERJ-190STD	19000311	ex PT-	

REGOURD AVIATION

☐ F-GTSK	Embraer EMB.120RT Brasilia	120213	ex OO-MTD	no titles

SECURITÉ CIVILE Marseille (MRS)

☐ F-ZBEU	Canadair CL415	2024	ex C-FZDE	42
☐ F-ZBFN	Canadair CL415	2006	ex C-FVUK	33
☐ F-ZBFP	Canadair CL415	2002	ex C-FBET	31
☐ F-ZBFS	Canadair CL415	2001	ex C-GSCT	32
☐ F-ZBFV	Canadair CL415	2013	ex C-FWPE	37
☐ F-ZBFW	Canadair CL415	2014	ex C-FWZH	38
☐ F-ZBFX	Canadair CL415	2007	ex C-FVUJ	34
☐ F-ZBFY	Canadair CL415	2010	ex C-FVDY	35
☐ F-ZBME	Canadair CL415	2057	ex C-GILN	44
☐ F-ZBMF	Canadair CL415	2063	ex C-FGZT	45
☐ F-ZBMG	Canadair CL415	2065	ex C-FLFW	48
☐ F-ZBAA	Conair Turbo Firecat	456/027	ex F-WEOL	22
☐ F-ZBAP	Conair Turbo Firecat	567/026	ex F-ZBDA	12
☐ F-ZBAZ	Conair Turbo Firecat	DHC-57/008	ex F-WEOL	01
☐ F-ZBCZ	Conair Turbo Firecat	DHC-94/036	ex F-ZBCA	23
☐ F-ZBEH	Conair Turbo Firecat	410/035	ex F-WEOJ	20
☐ F-ZBET	Conair Turbo Firecat	703/028	ex F-WEOJ	15
☐ F-ZBEW	Conair Turbo Firecat	621/025	ex F-WEOL	11
☐ F-ZBEY	Conair Turbo Firecat	400/017	ex F-WEOK	07
☐ F-ZBMA	Conair Turbo Firecat	461/021	ex C-GFZG	24
☐ F-ZBFJ	Beech B200 Super King Air	BB-1102	ex D-IWAN	98
☐ F-ZBFK	Beech B200 Super King Air	BB-876	ex F-GHSC	96
☐ F-ZBMB	Beech B200 Super King Air	BB-1379	ex F-GJFD	97
☐ F-ZBMC	de Havilland DHC-8-402QMRT	4040	ex C-FBAM	73
☐ F-ZBMD	de Havilland DHC-8-402QMRT	4043	ex C-FBSG	74

TAXI AIR FRET Paris-Le Bourget (LBG)

☐ F-BTME	Beech 99	U-79	ex N551GP	
☐ F-GFDJ	Beech 65-E90 King Air	LW-86	ex N410PB	

TRANSAVIA FRANCE Transavia (TO/TVF) Paris-Orly (ORY)

☐ F-GZHA	Boeing 737-8GJ/W	34901/2267	ex (VT-SPN)	
☐ F-GZHB	Boeing 737-8GJ/W	34902/2309	ex (VT-SPO)	
☐ F-GZHC	Boeing 737-8K2/W	29651/2534		
☐ F-GZHD	Boeing 737-8K2/W	29650/2583		
☐ F-GZHE	Boeing 737-8K2/W	29678/2615	ex N1787B	
☐ F-GZHF	Boeing 737-8HX/W	29677/2946	ex PH-ZOM	◆
☐ F-GZHN	Boeing 737-85H/W	29445/186	ex OY-SEI	
☐ F-GZHV	Boeing 737-85H/W	29444/178	ex OY-SEH	

TWIN JET Twin Jet (T7/TJT) Marseille (MRS)

☐ F-GLND	Beech 1900D	UE-196	ex N3234G	
☐ F-GLNE	Beech 1900D	UE-197	ex N3234U	
☐ F-GLNF	Beech 1900D	UE-69	ex YR-RLA	
☐ F-GLNH	Beech 1900D	UE-73	ex YR-BLB	
☐ F-GLNK	Beech 1900D	UE-269	ex N11017	
☐ F-GLPL	Beech 1900C-1	UC-92	ex N15382	
☐ F-GRYL	Beech 1900D	UE-301	ex N22161	
☐ F-GTKJ	Beech 1900D	UE-348	ex N23406	
☐ F-GTVC	Beech 1900D	UE-349	ex N23430	Op for Ministère de l'Interieur

XL AIRWAYS FRANCE Starway (SE/XLF) Paris-Orly (ORY)

☐ F-GKHK	Airbus A320-212	0343	ex OO-TCK	
☐ F-GRSI	Airbus A320-214	0973	ex F-WWBR	
☐ F-GTHL	Airbus A320-212	0189	ex F-OHFR	

☐ F-GRSQ	Airbus A330-243	501	ex F-WWKG	
☐ F-GSEU	Airbus A330-243	635	ex F-WWYO	
☐ EC-LEQ	Airbus A330-343E	1097	ex F-WWKL	>IWD♦
☐ F-HAXL	Boeing 737-8Q8	35279	ex G-XLFR	

F-O PACIFIC TERRITORIES (French Polynesia and New Caledonia)

AIR ARCHIPELS		Archipels (RHL)		Papeete (PPT)
☐ F-OIQK	Beech B200C Super King Air	BL-149	ex N36949	
☐ F-OIQL	Beech B200C Super King Air	BL-148	ex N36948	

AIR CALÉDONIE		AirCal (TY/TPC)		Nouméa (NOU)
☐ F-OIAQ	de Havilland DHC-6 Twin Otter 300	381	ex VH-RPZ	
☐ F-OIPI	ATR 42-500	647	ex F-WWLE	
☐ F-OIPN	ATR 72-212A	735	ex F-WWEP	
☐ F-OIPS	ATR 72-212A	764	ex F-WWEC	

AIR LOYAUTÉ		Iazur (VZR)		Nouméa (NOU)
☐ F-OIAY	de Havilland DHC-6 Twin Otter 300	507	ex P2-KSR	

AIR MOOREA		Air Moorea (QE/TAH)		Papeete (PPT)
☐ F-ODBN	de Havilland DHC-6 Twin Otter 300	470		
☐ F-OHJG	de Havilland DHC-6 Twin Otter 300	603	ex Fr AF 603	
☐ F-OIQF	de Havilland DHC-6 Twin Otter 300	815	ex N45KH	
☐ F-OIQP	de Havilland DHC-6 Twin Otter 300	715	ex 5Y-SKL	

AIR TAHITI		Air Tahiti (VT/VTA)		Papeete (PPT)
☐ F-OIQB	ATR 42-500	621	ex F-WWLB	
☐ F-OIQC	ATR 42-500	627	ex F-WWLH	
☐ F-OIQD	ATR 42-500	631	ex F-WWLL	
☐ F-O	ATR 42-500		ex F-WW	o/o♦
☐ F-OHJS	ATR 72-212A	696	ex F-WWES	
☐ F-OIQN	ATR 72-212A	719	ex F-WWET	
☐ F-OIQO	ATR 72-212A	731	ex F-WWEL	
☐ F-OIQR	ATR 72-212A	862	ex F-WWEJ	
☐ F-OIQU	ATR 72-212A	751	ex F-WWEL	
☐ F-OIQT	ATR 72-212A	829	ex F-WWEW	
☐ F-OIQV	ATR 72-212A	806	ex F-WWER	

AIR TAHITI NUI		Tahiti Airlines (TN/THT)		Papeete (PPT)
☐ F-OJGF	Airbus A340-313X	385	ex F-WWJC	Mangareva
☐ F-OJTN	Airbus A340-313X	395	ex C-GZIA	Bora Bora
☐ F-OLOV	Airbus A340-313E	668	ex F-WWJD	Nuku Hiva
☐ F-OSEA	Airbus A340-313X	438	ex F-WWJV	Rangiroa
☐ F-OSUN	Airbus A340-313X	446	ex F-WWJA	Moorea

AIRCALIN		AirCalin (SB/ACI)		Nouméa (NOU)
☐ F-OCQZ	de Havilland DHC-6 Twin Otter 300	412		
☐ F-OHSD	Airbus A330-202	507	ex F-WWYS	
☐ F-OJSB	Airbus A320-232	2152		
☐ F-OJSE	Airbus A330-202	510	ex F-WWYT	

F-O ATLANTIC / INDIAN OCEAN TERRITORIES (St Pierre & Miquelon and Réunion)

AIR AUSTRAL		Réunion (UU/REU)		St Denis-Gilot (RUN)
☐ F-OHSF	ATR 72-212A	650	ex F-WWEC	
☐ F-OMRU	ATR 72-212A	855	ex F-WWEI	
☐ F-OZSE	ATR 72-212A	813	ex F-WWEC	
☐ F-ODZJ	Boeing 737-53A	24877/1943	ex F-GHXN	[DNR]♦
☐ F-ODZY	Boeing 737-33A	27452/2679		[DNR]♦
☐ F-ONGA	Boeing 737-89M/W	40910/3484		♦
☐ F-ONGB	Boeing 737-89M/W	40911/3504	ex N1786B	♦
☐ F-OMAY	Boeing 777-2Q8ER	29402/517		

☐ F-ONOU	Boeing 777-3Q8ER	35783/786	ex N5573S	Leon Dierx	
☐ F-OPAR	Boeing 777-2Q8ER	29908/229	ex EI-CRS	Marcel Goulette	
☐ F-OREU	Boeing 777-39MER	37434/912			♦
☐ F-ORUN	Boeing 777-2Q8ER	28676/246	ex EI-CRT	Pierre Legourque	
☐ F-OSYD	Boeing 777-3Q8ER	35782/778	ex N5014K	C. Leconte de Lisle	
☐ F-	Boeing 777-2				o/o♦

| **AIR ST-PIERRE** | | *Saint-Pierre (PJ/SPM)* | | *St-Pierre et Miquelon (FSP)* | |

☐ F-OFSP	ATR 42-500	801	ex F-WWLT
☐ F-OSPJ	Reims Cessna F406 Caravan II	F406-0091	

F-O FRENCH CARIBBEAN (Guadeloupe & Saint-Barthélemy, Martinique and French Guyana)

| **AIR ANTILLES EXPRESS** | | *(3S)* | | *Pointe-à-Pitre (PTP)* |

☐ F-OIJB	ATR 42-500	579	ex F-WWLF	<GUY
☐ F-OIXD	ATR 42-500	695	ex F-WWLQ	
☐ F-OIXE	ATR 42-500	807	ex F-WWLX	
☐ F-OIXH	ATR 42-500	831	ex F-WWLD	♦

| **AIR CARAIBES** | | *French West (TX/FWI)* |

Pointe-à-Pitre/Fort-de-France/St Barthélemy/St Martin (PTP/FDF/SBH/SFG)

☐ F-OGVE	Dornier 228-212	8237	ex D-CBDD	>Take A/l
☐ F-OHQM	Cessna 208B Caravan I	208B0726		>Take A/l
☐ F-OIJH	ATR 72-212A	682	ex F-WWEE	
☐ F-OIJK	ATR 72-212A	736	ex F-WWEQ	
☐ F-OIXL	ATR 72-212A	888	ex F-WWES	
☐ F-OSUD	Embraer ERJ-190LR	19000130	ex PT-SQZ	

| **AIR CARAIBES ATLANTIQUE** | | *Car Line (TX/CAJ)* | | *Pointe-à-Pitre (PTP)* |

☐ F-GOTO	Airbus A330-323E	1021	ex F-WWYN	
☐ F-OFDF	Airbus A330-223	253	ex HB-IQD	
☐ F-OONE	Airbus A330-323E	965	ex F-WWYL	Region Guyane
☐ F-ORLY	Airbus A330-323X	758	ex F-WWYR	
☐ F-	Airbus A330-323X		ex	o/o♦

| **AIR GUYANE EXPRESS** | | *Green Bird (3S/GUY)* | | *Cayenne (CAY)* |

☐ F-OIJB	ATR 42-500	579	ex F-WWLF	>Air Antilles Express
☐ F-OIJI	de Havilland DHC-6 Twin Otter 300	277	ex HB-LSU	
☐ F-OIJL	de Havilland DHC-6 Twin Otter 300	281	ex HB-LSV	
☐ F-OIJY	de Havilland DHC-6 Twin Otter 300	797	ex D-IFLY	

| **AIRAWAK** | | | *Fort-de-France (FDF)* |

☐ F-OGXA	Britten-Norman BN-2A-26 Islander	788	ex D-IHUG
☐ F-OIXB	Cessna 402B II	402B1220	ex V2-LEW

| **ST BARTH COMMUTER** | | *Black Fin (PV/SBU)* | | *St Barthélemy (SBH)* |

☐ F-OGXB	Britten-Norman BN-2A-2 Islander	303	ex D-IHVH	stored
☐ F-OHQX	Britten-Norman BN-2A-26 Islander	3009	ex F-OHQW	
☐ F-OHQY	Britten-Norman BN-2B-20 Islander	2251	ex V2-LFE	
☐ F-OIJS	Britten-Norman BN-2B-20 Islander	2294	ex VH-CSS	
☐ F-OIJU	Britten-Norman BN-2B-20 Islander	2291	ex G-BVYD	
☐ F-OSBC	Cessna 208B Caravan	208B2188		♦
☐ F-OSBH	Cessna 208B Caravan	208B2117	ex N6137Y	♦

| **TAKE AIR LINES** | | | *Fort-de-France (FDF)* |

☐ F-OGVE	Dornier 228-212	8237	ex D-CBDD	<FWI
☐ F-OHQM	Cessna 208B Caravan I	208B0726		<FWI
☐ F-OTKE	LET L-410UVP-E	902409	ex OK-VDV	

| **TROPICAL AIRLINES** | | | *Pointe-à-Pitre (PTP)* |

☐ F-OHQN	Cessna 208B Caravan I	208B0715	ex N1285H
☐ F-OHQU	Cessna 208B Caravan I	208B0725	ex N12326
☐ F-OIJO	Cessna 208B Caravan I	208B0961	ex N4109K

G- UNITED KINGDOM (United Kingdom of Great Britain and Northern Ireland)

AIR ATLANTIQUE		Atlantic (7M/AAG)		Coventry (CVT)
☐ G-APSA	Douglas DC-6A	45497/995	ex 4W-ABQ	

AIR SOUTHWEST		Swallow (WOW)		Plymouth (PLH)
☐ G-WOWA	de Havilland DHC-8-311	296	ex C-GZOF	
☐ G-WOWB	de Havilland DHC-8-311	334	ex C-GZOU	
☐ G-WOWC	de Havilland DHC-8-311	311	ex N784BC	
☐ G-WOWD	de Havilland DHC-8-311	286	ex C-FDIY	
☐ G-WOWE	de Havilland DHC-8-311	256	ex C-FFBG	Cloud Surfer

ASTRAEUS		Flystar (5W/AEU)		London-Gatwick (LGW)
☐ G-STRP	Airbus A320-211	0136	ex EC-GRF	
☐ G-PJPJ	Boeing 737-5H6	27355/2646	ex G-GFFJ	
☐ G-STRF	Boeing 737-76N/W	29885/1120	ex EI-CXD	
☐ G-STRI	Boeing 737-33A	25011/2012	ex OM-HLB	
☐ G-STRJ	Boeing 737-33A	25119/2069	ex OM-HLC	
☐ G-STRN	Boeing 737-7L9/W	28007/136	ex D-AABH	
☐ G-OJIB	Boeing 757-23AER	24292/219	ex G-OOOG	
☐ G-STRW	Boeing 757-28A	24543/286	ex C-GTSN	
☐ G-STRX	Boeing 757-2Q8	25621/457	ex N459AX	
☐ G-STRY	Boeing 757-2Q8	28161/723	ex N369AX	>BMI
☐ G-STRZ	Boeing 757-258	27622/745	ex 4X-EBI	

ATLANTIC RECONNAISSANCE		Atlantic (AAG)		Coventry (CVT)
☐ G-BCEN	Britten-Norman BN-2A-26 Islander	403	ex 4X-AYG	Maritime & Coastguard Agency
☐ G-EXEX	Cessna 404 Titan	404-0037	ex SE-GZF	Maritime & Coastguard Agency
☐ G-MIND	Cessna 404 Titan	404-0004	ex G-SKKC	Op for Enviroment Agency
☐ G-NOSE	Cessna 402B	402B0823	ex N98AR	Pollution control
☐ G-SOUL	Cessna 310R II	310R0140	ex N5020J	Op for OSRL
☐ G-TASK	Cessna 404 Titan	404-0829	ex PH-MPC	Maritime & Coastguard Agency
☐ G-TURF	Reims Cessna F406 Caravan II	F406-0020	ex PH-FWF	Maritime & Coastguard Agency

AURIGNY AIR SERVICES		Ayline (GR/AUR)		Guernsey (GCI)
☐ G-BWDB	ATR 72-202	449	ex F-WQNI	
☐ G-COBO	ATR 72-212A	852	ex F-WWEV	
☐ G-VZON	ATR 72-212A	853	ex F-WWEW	
☐ G-BDTO	Britten-Norman BN-2A Mk.III-2 Trislander	1027	ex G-RBSI	
☐ G-BEVT	Britten-Norman BN-2A Mk.III-2 Trislander	1057		
☐ G-FTSE	Britten-Norman BN-2A Mk.III-2 Trislander	1053	ex G-BEPI	
☐ G-JOEY	Britten-Norman BN-2A Mk.III-2 Trislander	1016	ex G-BDGG	Joey
☐ G-RBCI	Britten-Norman BN-2A Mk.III-2 Trislander	1035	ex G-BDWV	
☐ G-RLON	Britten-Norman BN-2A Mk.III-2 Trislander	1008	ex G-ITEX	Royal London Asset Mgt c/s
☐ G-XTOR	Britten-Norman BN-2A Mk.III-2 Trislander	359	ex G-BAXD	

BA CITYFLYER		Flyer (CJ/CFE)		London City (LCY)
☐ G-LCYD	Embraer ERJ-170STD	17000294	ex PT-TQU	
☐ G-LCYE	Embraer ERJ-170STD	17000296	ex PT-TQW	
☐ G-LCYF	Embraer ERJ-170STD	17000298	ex PT-TQR	
☐ G-LCYG	Embraer ERJ-170STD	17000300	ex PT-TQZ	
☐ G-LCYH	Embraer ERJ-170STD	17000302	ex PT-XQB	
☐ G-LCYI	Embraer ERJ-170STD	17000305	ex PT-XQE	
☐ G-LCYJ	Embraer ERJ-190SR	19000339	ex PT-TXY	♦
☐ G-LCYK	Embraer ERJ-190SR	19000343	ex PT-XQK	♦
☐ G-LCYL	Embraer ERJ-190SR	19000346	ex PT-XQM	♦
☐ G-LCYM	Embraer ERJ-190SR	19000351	ex PT-XQR	♦
☐ G-LCYN	Embraer ERJ-190SR	19000392	ex PT-XNY	♦
☐ G-	Embraer ERJ-190SR		ex	o/o♦
☐ G-	Embraer ERJ-190SR		ex	o/o♦

BLUE ISLANDS		Blue Island (XA/BCI)		Jersey (JER)
☐ G-BEDP	Britten-Norman BN-2A Mk.III-2 Trislander	1039	ex ZS-SFG	
☐ G-DRFC	ATR 42-320	007	ex OY-CIB	
☐ G-ISLB	British Aerospace Jetstream 32	871	ex N871JX	
☐ G-ISLC	British Aerospace Jetstream 32	873	ex N873JX	
☐ G-ISLD	British Aerospace Jetstream 32EP	915	ex N915AE	

☐ G-LCOC	Britten-Norman BN-2A Mk.III-1 Trislander		366	ex G-BCCU
☐ G-XAXA	Britten-Norman BN-2A-26 Islander	530	ex G-LOTO
☐ LN-FAN	British Aerospace Jetstream 32	864	ex SE-LHK	<HTA

BMI BRITISH MIDLAND INTERNATIONAL Midland (BD/BMA)
East Midland-Nottingham/London-Heathrow (EMA/LHR)

Member of Star Alliance

☐ G-DBCA	Airbus A319-131	2098	ex D-AVYV	
☐ G-DBCB	Airbus A319-131	2188	ex D-AVYA	
☐ G-DBCC	Airbus A319-131	2194	ex D-AVYT	
☐ G-DBCD	Airbus A319-131	2389	ex D-AVYJ	
☐ G-DBCE	Airbus A319-131	2429	ex D-AVWG	
☐ G-DBCF	Airbus A319-131	2466	ex D-AVYA	
☐ G-DBCG	Airbus A319-131	2694	ex D-AVXD	
☐ G-DBCH	Airbus A319-131	2697	ex D-AVXE	
☐ G-DBCI	Airbus A319-131	2720	ex D-AVWC	
☐ G-DBCJ	Airbus A319-131	2981	ex D-AVXG	
☐ G-DBCK	Airbus A319-131	3049	ex D-AVYG	
☐ G-MEDH	Airbus A320-232	1922	ex F-WWBX	
☐ G-MEDK	Airbus A320-232	2441	ex F-WWBQ	
☐ G-MIDO	Airbus A320-232	1987	ex F-WWIR	
☐ G-MIDP	Airbus A320-232	1732	ex F-WWBK	
☐ G-MIDS	Airbus A320-232	1424	ex F-WWBO	
☐ G-MIDT	Airbus A320-232	1418	ex F-WWBI	
☐ G-MIDX	Airbus A320-232	1177	ex F-WWDP	Star Alliance c/s
☐ G-MIDY	Airbus A320-232	1014	ex F-WWDQ	
☐ G-MEDF	Airbus A321-231	1690	ex D-AVZX	
☐ G-MEDG	Airbus A321-231	1711	ex D-AVZK	
☐ G-MEDJ	Airbus A321-231	2190	ex D-AVZD	
☐ G-MEDL	Airbus A321-231	2653	ex D-AVZC	
☐ G-MEDM	Airbus A321-231	2799	ex D-AVZP	
☐ G-MEDN	Airbus A321-231	3512	ex D-AVZK	
☐ G-MEDU	Airbus A321-231	3926	ex D-AZAB	
☐ G-WWBD	Airbus A330-243	401	ex F-WWKN	Star Alliance c/s
☐ G-WWBM	Airbus A330-243	398	ex F-WWKL	>THY
☐ G-STRY	Boeing 757-2Q8	28161/723	ex N369AX	<AEU

BMI REGIONAL Granite (BD/BMR) Aberdeen/East Midlands-Nottingham (ABZ/EMA)

☐ G-EMBI	Embraer ERJ-145EP	145126	ex PT-SDG	
☐ G-EMBJ	Embraer ERJ-145MP	145134	ex PT-SDL	
☐ G-EMBN	Embraer ERJ-145EP	145201	ex PT-SGQ	
☐ G-RJXA	Embraer ERJ-145EP	145136	ex PT-SDP	
☐ G-RJXB	Embraer ERJ-145EP	145142	ex PT-SDS	
☐ G-RJXC	Embraer ERJ-145EP	145153	ex PT-SEE	
☐ G-RJXD	Embraer ERJ-145EP	145207	ex PT-SGX	
☐ G-RJXE	Embraer ERJ-145EP	145245	ex PT-SIJ	
☐ G-RJXF	Embraer ERJ-145EP	145280	ex PT-SJW	
☐ G-RJXG	Embraer ERJ-145EP	145390	ex PT-SQO	
☐ G-RJXH	Embraer ERJ-145EP	145442	ex PT-SUN	
☐ G-RJXI	Embraer ERJ-145EP	145454	ex PT-SUZ	Star Alliance c/s
☐ G-RJXJ	Embraer ERJ-135ER	145473	ex PT-SVS	
☐ G-RJXK	Embraer ERJ-135ER	145494	ex PT-SXN	Star Alliance c/s
☐ G-RJXL	Embraer ERJ-135ER	145376	ex PT-SQA	
☐ G-RJXM	Embraer ERJ-145MP	145216	ex PH-RXA	
☐ G-RJXN	Embraer ERJ-145MP	145336	ex SP-LGI	
☐ G-RJXP	Embraer ERJ-135ER	145431	ex G-CDFS	
☐ G-RJXR	Embraer ERJ-145EP	145070	ex G-CCYH	

BMIBABY Baby (WW/BMI) East Midlands-Nottingham (EMA)

☐ G-BVKB	Boeing 737-59D	27268/2592	ex SE-DNM	foxy baby
☐ G-BVKD	Boeing 737-59D	26421/2279	ex SE-DNK	Ice Ice baby
☐ G-BVZE	Boeing 737-59D	26422/2412	ex SE-DNL	little costa baby
☐ G-OBMP	Boeing 737-3Q8	24963/2193		robin hood baby
☐ G-ODSK	Boeing 737-37Q	28537/2904		baby dragon fly
☐ G-OGBD	Boeing 737-3L9	27833/2688	ex OY-MAR	
☐ G-TOYD	Boeing 737-3Q8	26307/2664	ex G-EZYT	
☐ G-TOYF	Boeing 737-36N	28557/2862	ex G-IGOO	Rainbow baby
☐ G-TOYG	Boeing 737-36N	28872/3082	ex G-IGOJ	Butterfly baby
☐ G-TOYH	Boeing 737-36N	28570/3010	ex G-IGOY	Baby of the north

190

☐ G-TOYI	Boeing 737-3Q8	28054/3016	ex YJ-AV18	Geordie baby	
☐ G-TOYJ	Boeing 737-36M	28332/2809	ex PK-GGW		
☐ G-TOYK	Boeing 737-33R	28870/2899	ex N870GX		
☐ G-TOYM	Boeing 737-36Q	29141/3035	ex VT-SJD	Groovy baby	

BOND AIR SERVICES — *Red Head (RHD)* — *Gloucestershire (GLO)*

☐ G-BZRS	Eurocopter EC135T2	0166	ex D-HECL	back-up
☐ G-DAAT	Eurocopter EC135T2	0312		EMS Devon
☐ G-DORS	Eurocopter EC135T2+	0517		EMS Dorset & Somerset
☐ G-EMAA	Eurocopter EC135T2	0448		EMS
☐ G-HBOB	Eurocopter EC135T2+	0664		Thames Valley Air Ambulance
☐ G-HWAA	Eurocopter EC135T2	0375		EMS
☐ G-KRNW	Eurocopter EC135T2	0175		EMS Cornwall Air Ambulance
☐ G-NWAA	Eurocopter EC135T2	0427		EMS North West Air Ambulance
☐ G-SASA	Eurocopter EC135T2	0147		EMS Scottish Ambulance Service
☐ G-SASB	Eurocopter EC135T2	0151		EMS Scottish Ambulance Service
☐ G-SPAO	Eurocopter EC135T2+	0546		Strathclyde Police
☐ G-SPHU	Eurocopter EC135T2	0245	ex D-HKBA	Great Western Air Ambulance
☐ G-SSXX	Eurocopter EC135T2	0270	ex G-SSSX	EMS Essex Air Ambulance
☐ G-WMAS	Eurocopter EC135T2	0174		EMS County Air Ambulance
☐ G-WONN	Eurocopter EC135T2+	0597		Strathclyde Police
☐ G-	Eurocopter EC135T2+		o/o	South & East Wales Police
☐ G-BATC	MBB Bo.105DB	S-45	ex D-HDAW	EMS North Wales Air Ambulance
☐ G-BTHV	MBB Bo.105DBS-4	S-855	ex D-HMBV	EMS
☐ G-BUXS	MBB Bo.105DBS-4	S-41/913	ex G-PASA	Northern Lighthouse
☐ G-CDBS	MBB Bo.105DBS-4	S-738	ex D-HDRZ	EMS
☐ G-NAAA	MBB Bo.105DBS-4	S-34/912	ex G-BUTN	EMS
☐ G-NAAB	MBB Bo.105DBS-4	S-416	ex D-HDMO	EMS
☐ G-NDAA	MBB Bo.105DBS-4	S-135/914	ex G-WMAA	EMS Devon Air Ambulance
☐ G-TVAM	MBB Bo.105DBS-4	S-392	ex G-SPOL	EMS Thames Valley Air Ambulance
☐ G-WAAS	MBB Bo.105DBS-4	S-138/911	ex G-ESAM	EMS Welsh Air Ambulance

BOND OFFSHORE HELICOPTERS — *Bond (BND)* — *Gloucestershire/Aberdeen (GLO/ABZ)*

☐ G-REDJ	Aérospatiale AS.332L2 II	2608	ex F-WWOJ
☐ G-REDK	Aérospatiale AS.332L2 II	2610	ex F-WWOM
☐ G-REDM	Aérospatiale AS.332L2 II	2614	ex F-WWOF
☐ G-REDN	Aérospatiale AS.332L2 II	2616	ex F-WQDH
☐ G-REDO	Aérospatiale AS.332L2 II	2622	ex F-WWOH
☐ G-REDP	Aérospatiale AS.332L2 II	2634	ex F-WWOB
☐ G-REDR	Eurocopter EC225LP	2699	
☐ G-REDT	Eurocopter EC225LP	2701	
☐ G-REDV	Eurocopter EC225LP	2732	
☐ G-REDW	Eurocopter EC225LP	2734	

BRISTOW HELICOPTERS — *Bristow (BHL)* — *Redhill/Aberdeen (KRH/ABZ)*

☐ G-BLXR	Aérospatiale AS.332L	2154		Cromarty	
☐ G-BMCW	Aérospatiale AS.332L	2161	ex F-WYMG	Monifieth	
☐ G-BMCX	Aérospatiale AS.332L	2164		Lossiemouth	
☐ G-BWWI	Aérospatiale AS.332L	2040	ex OY-HMF	Johnshaven	
☐ G-BWZX	Aérospatiale AS.332L	2120	ex F-WQDE	Muchalls	
☐ G-TIGC	Aérospatiale AS.332L	2024	ex (G-BJYH)	Royal Burgh of Montrose	
☐ G-TIGE	Aérospatiale AS.332L	2028	ex (G-BJYJ)	City of Dundee	
☐ G-TIGF	Aérospatiale AS.332L	2030	ex F-WKQJ	Peterhead	
☐ G-TIGG	Aérospatiale AS.332L	2032	ex F-WXFT	Macduff	
☐ G-TIGJ	Aérospatiale AS.332L	2042	ex VH-BHT	Rosehearty	
☐ G-TIGS	Aérospatiale AS.332L	2086		Findochty	
☐ G-TIGV	Aérospatiale AS.332L	2099	ex LN-ONC	Burghead	
☐ G-CGSN	Agusta AW139	31312			♦
☐ G-ZZSA	Eurocopter EC225LP	2603	ex F-WWOJ		
☐ G-ZZSB	Eurocopter EC225LP	2615	ex F-WWOG		
☐ G-ZZSC	Eurocopter EC225LP	2654	ex F-WWOG		
☐ G-ZZSD	Eurocopter EC225LP	2658	ex F-WWOQ		
☐ G-ZZSE	Eurocopter EC225LP	2660	ex F-WWOJ		
☐ G-ZZSF	Eurocopter EC225LP	2662	ex F-WWOR		
☐ G-ZZSG	Eurocopter EC225LP	2714			
☐ G-ZZSI	Eurocopter EC225LP	2736	ex G-CGES		
☐ G-BIMU	Sikorsky S-61N II	61752	ex N8511Z	Stac Pollaidh	SAR
☐ G-BPWB	Sikorsky S-61N II	61822	ex EI-BHO	Portland Castle	SAR
☐ G-BIEJ	Sikorsky S-76A+	760097		Glen Lossie	
☐ G-BISZ	Sikorsky S-76A+	760156			

☐ G-BJFL	Sikorsky S-76A+	760056	ex EZ-S704	
☐ G-BJGX	Sikorsky S-76A+	760026	ex N103BH	Glen Elgin
☐ G-CEYZ	Sikorsky S-76C++	760669	ex N4514R	
☐ G-CFDV	Sikorsky S-76C++	760666	ex N45140	
☐ G-CFJC	Sikorsky S-76C++	760708	ex N415Y	
☐ G-CFPZ	Sikorsky S-76C+	760744	ex N2039J	
☐ G-CGIW	Sikorsky S-76C+	760773	ex N773L	◆
☐ G-CGOP	Sikorsky S-76C+	760778	ex N778T	◆
☐ G-CGOU	Sikorsky S-76C+	760780	ex N20868	◆
☐ G-CGRK	Sikorsky S-76C+	760768	ex N889BG	◆
☐ G-CGRU	Sikorsky S-76C	760656	ex N76TZ	◆
☐ G-KAZA	Sikorsky S-76C+	760615	ex N81085	
☐ G-KAZB	Sikorsky S-76C+	760614	ex N8094S	
☐ G-IACA	Sikorsky S-92A	920050	ex N81254	
☐ G-IACB	Sikorsky S-92A	920062	ex N4516G	
☐ G-IACC	Sikorsky S-92A	920063	ex N45158	
☐ G-IACD	Sikorsky S-92A	920065	ex N4515G	
☐ G-IACE	Sikorsky S-92A	920066	ex N45148	
☐ G-IACF	Sikorsky S-92A	920068	ex N4509G	
☐ G-ISST	Eurocopter EC155 B1	6778		
☐ G-ISSU	Eurocopter EC155 B1	6762		
☐ G-ISSV	Eurocopter EC155 B1	6757		
☐ G-ISSW	Eurocopter EC155 B1	6755		

BRITISH AIRWAYS — Speedbird & Shuttle (BA/BAW/SHT)
London-Heathrow/Gatwick & Manchester (LHR/LGW/MAN)

Member of Oneworld

☐ G-EUNA	Airbus A318-112	4007	ex D-AUAC	
☐ G-EUNB	Airbus A318-112	4039	ex D-AUAF	
☐ G-EUOA	Airbus A319-131	1513	ex D-AVYE	
☐ G-EUOB	Airbus A319-131	1529	ex D-AVWH	
☐ G-EUOC	Airbus A319-131	1537	ex D-AVYP	
☐ G-EUOD	Airbus A319-131	1558	ex D-AVYJ	
☐ G-EUOE	Airbus A319-131	1574	ex D-AVWF	
☐ G-EUOF	Airbus A319-131	1590	ex D-AVYW	
☐ G-EUOG	Airbus A319-131	1594	ex D-AVWU	
☐ G-EUOH	Airbus A319-131	1604	ex D-AVYM	
☐ G-EUOI	Airbus A319-131	1606	ex D-AVYN	
☐ G-EUPA	Airbus A319-131	1082	ex D-AVYK	
☐ G-EUPB	Airbus A319-131	1115	ex D-AVYT	
☐ G-EUPC	Airbus A319-131	1118	ex D-AVYU	
☐ G-EUPD	Airbus A319-131	1142	ex D-AVWG	
☐ G-EUPE	Airbus A319-131	1193	ex D-AVYT	
☐ G-EUPF	Airbus A319-131	1197	ex D-AVWS	
☐ G-EUPG	Airbus A319-131	1222	ex D-AVYG	
☐ G-EUPH	Airbus A319-131	1225	ex D-AVYK	
☐ G-EUPJ	Airbus A319-131	1232	ex D-AVYJ	
☐ G-EUPK	Airbus A319-131	1236	ex D-AVYO	
☐ G-EUPL	Airbus A319-131	1239	ex D-AVYP	
☐ G-EUPM	Airbus A319-131	1258	ex D-AVYR	
☐ G-EUPN	Airbus A319-131	1261	ex D-AVWA	
☐ G-EUPO	Airbus A319-131	1279	ex D-AVYU	
☐ G-EUPP	Airbus A319-131	1295	ex D-AVWU	
☐ G-EUPR	Airbus A319-131	1329	ex D-AVYH	
☐ G-EUPS	Airbus A319-131	1338	ex D-AVYM	
☐ G-EUPT	Airbus A319-131	1380	ex D-AVWH	
☐ G-EUPU	Airbus A319-131	1384	ex D-AVWP	
☐ G-EUPV	Airbus A319-131	1423	ex D-AVYE	
☐ G-EUPW	Airbus A319-131	1440	ex D-AVYP	
☐ G-EUPX	Airbus A319-131	1445	ex D-AVWB	
☐ G-EUPY	Airbus A319-131	1466	ex D-AVYU	
☐ G-EUPZ	Airbus A319-131	1510	ex D-AVYY	
☐ G-BUSI	Airbus A320-211	0103	ex F-WWDB	[LDE]◆
☐ G-BUSJ	Airbus A320-211	0109	ex F-WWIC	
☐ G-BUSK	Airbus A320-211	0120	ex F-WWIN	
☐ G-EUUA	Airbus A320-232	1661	ex F-WWIH	
☐ G-EUUB	Airbus A320-232	1689	ex F-WWBE	
☐ G-EUUC	Airbus A320-232	1696	ex F-WWIO	
☐ G-EUUD	Airbus A320-232	1760	ex F-WWBN	
☐ G-EUUE	Airbus A320-232	1782	ex F-WWDO	
☐ G-EUUF	Airbus A320-232	1814	ex F-WWIY	

☐ G-EUUG	Airbus A320-232	1829	ex F-WWIU	
☐ G-EUUH	Airbus A320-232	1665	ex F-WWIG	
☐ G-EUUI	Airbus A320-232	1871	ex F-WWBI	
☐ G-EUUJ	Airbus A320-232	1883	ex F-WWBQ	
☐ G-EUUK	Airbus A320-232	1899	ex F-WWDO	
☐ G-EUUL	Airbus A320-232	1708	ex F-WWIV	
☐ G-EUUM	Airbus A320-232	1907	ex F-WWDN	
☐ G-EUUN	Airbus A320-232	1910	ex F-WWDP	
☐ G-EUUO	Airbus A320-232	1958	ex F-WWIT	
☐ G-EUUP	Airbus A320-232	2038	ex F-WWDB	
☐ G-EUUR	Airbus A320-232	2040	ex F-WWID	
☐ G-EUUS	Airbus A320-232	3301	ex F-WWIF	
☐ G-EUUT	Airbus A320-232	3314	ex F-WWIT	
☐ G-EUUU	Airbus A320-232	3351	ex F-WWID	
☐ G-EUUV	Airbus A320-232	3468	ex F-WWBO	
☐ G-EUUW	Airbus A320-232	3499	ex F-WWIN	
☐ G-EUUX	Airbus A320-232	3550	ex F-WWDM	
☐ G-EUUY	Airbus A320-232	3607	ex F-WWIC	
☐ G-EUUZ	Airbus A320-232	3649	ex F-WWDO	
☐ G-EUYA	Airbus A320-232	3697	ex F-WWBM	
☐ G-EUYB	Airbus A320-232	3703	ex F-WWBV	
☐ G-EUYC	Airbus A320-232	3721	ex F-WWBY	
☐ G-EUYD	Airbus A320-232	3726	ex F-WWDH	
☐ G-EUYE	Airbus A320-232	3912	ex F-WWBB	
☐ G-EUYF	Airbus A320-232	4185	ex F-WWIC	
☐ G-EUYG	Airbus A320-232	4238	ex F-WWDH	♦
☐ G-EUYH	Airbus A320-232	4265	ex F-WWBK	♦
☐ G-EUYI	Airbus A320-232	4306	ex F-WWIC	♦
☐ G-EUYJ	Airbus A320-232	4464	ex F-WWBQ	♦
☐ G-EUYK	Airbus A320-232	4551	ex F-WWBE	♦
☐ G-EUYL	Airbus A320-232		ex	o/o♦
☐ G-EUYM	Airbus A320-232		ex	o/o♦
☐ G-EUYN	Airbus A320-232		ex	o/o♦
☐ G-TTOB	Airbus A320-232	1687	ex F-WWIM	
☐ G-TTOE	Airbus A320-232	1754	ex F-WWDH	
☐ G-EUXC	Airbus A321-231	2305	ex D-AVZE	
☐ G-EUXD	Airbus A321-231	2320	ex D-AVZO	
☐ G-EUXE	Airbus A321-231	2323	ex D-AVZP	
☐ G-EUXF	Airbus A321-231	2324	ex D-AVZQ	
☐ G-EUXG	Airbus A321-231	2351	ex D-AVZU	
☐ G-EUXH	Airbus A321-231	2363	ex D-AVZW	
☐ G-EUXI	Airbus A321-231	2536	ex D-AVZE	
☐ G-EUXJ	Airbus A321-231	3081	ex D-AVZL	
☐ G-EUXK	Airbus A321-231	3235	ex D-AVZI	
☐ G-EUXL	Airbus A321-231	3254	ex D-AVZV	
☐ G-EUXM	Airbus A321-231	3290	ex D-AVZC	
☐ G-DOCA	Boeing 737-436	25267/2131		
☐ G-DOCB	Boeing 737-436	25304/2144		
☐ G-DOCE	Boeing 737-436	25350/2167		
☐ G-DOCF	Boeing 737-436	25407/2178		
☐ G-DOCG	Boeing 737-436	25408/2183		
☐ G-DOCH	Boeing 737-436	25428/2185		
☐ G-DOCL	Boeing 737-436	25842/2228		
☐ G-DOCN	Boeing 737-436	25848/2379		
☐ G-DOCO	Boeing 737-436	25849/2381		
☐ G-DOCS	Boeing 737-436	25852/2390		
☐ G-DOCT	Boeing 737-436	25853/2409		
☐ G-DOCU	Boeing 737-436	25854/2417		
☐ G-DOCV	Boeing 737-436	25855/2420		
☐ G-DOCW	Boeing 737-436	25856/2422		
☐ G-DOCX	Boeing 737-436	25857/2451		
☐ G-DOCY	Boeing 737-436	25844/2514	ex OO-LTQ	
☐ G-DOCZ	Boeing 737-436	25858/2522	ex EC-FXJ	
☐ G-GBTA	Boeing 737-436	25859/2532	ex G-BVHA	
☐ G-GBTB	Boeing 737-436	25860/2545	ex OO-LTS	
☐ G-BNLA	Boeing 747-436	23908/727	ex N60665	[VCV]
☐ G-BNLB	Boeing 747-436	23909/730		[VCV]
☐ G-BNLC	Boeing 747-436	23910/734		[VCV]
☐ G-BNLD	Boeing 747-436	23911/744	ex N6018N	[VCV]
☐ G-BNLE	Boeing 747-436	24047/753		
☐ G-BNLF	Boeing 747-436	24048/773		
☐ G-BNLG	Boeing 747-436	24049/774		[VCV]
☐ G-BNLH	Boeing 747-436	24050/779	ex VH-NLH	[VCV]
☐ G-BNLI	Boeing 747-436	24051/784		

☐ G-BNLJ	Boeing 747-436	24052/789	ex N60668
☐ G-BNLK	Boeing 747-436	24053/790	ex N6009F
☐ G-BNLL	Boeing 747-436	24054/794	
☐ G-BNLM	Boeing 747-436	24055/795	ex N6009F
☐ G-BNLN	Boeing 747-436	24056/802	
☐ G-BNLO	Boeing 747-436	24057/817	
☐ G-BNLP	Boeing 747-436	24058/828	
☐ G-BNLR	Boeing 747-436	24447/829	ex N6005C
☐ G-BNLS	Boeing 747-436	24629/841	
☐ G-BNLT	Boeing 747-436	24630/842	
☐ G-BNLU	Boeing 747-436	25406/895	[VCV]
☐ G-BNLV	Boeing 747-436	25427/900	
☐ G-BNLW	Boeing 747-436	25432/903	
☐ G-BNLX	Boeing 747-436	25435/908	
☐ G-BNLY	Boeing 747-436	27090/959	ex N60659
☐ G-BNLZ	Boeing 747-436	27091/964	
☐ G-BYGA	Boeing 747-436	28855/1190	
☐ G-BYGB	Boeing 747-436	28856/1194	
☐ G-BYGC	Boeing 747-436	25823/1195	
☐ G-BYGD	Boeing 747-436	28857/1196	
☐ G-BYGE	Boeing 747-436	28858/1198	
☐ G-BYGF	Boeing 747-436	25824/1200	
☐ G-BYGG	Boeing 747-436	28859/1212	
☐ G-CIVA	Boeing 747-436	27092/967	
☐ G-CIVB	Boeing 747-436	25811/1018	
☐ G-CIVC	Boeing 747-436	25812/1022	
☐ G-CIVD	Boeing 747-436	27349/1048	
☐ G-CIVE	Boeing 747-436	27350/1050	
☐ G-CIVF	Boeing 747-436	25434/1058	ex (G-BNLY)
☐ G-CIVG	Boeing 747-436	25813/1059	ex N6009F
☐ G-CIVH	Boeing 747-436	25809/1078	
☐ G-CIVI	Boeing 747-436	25814/1079	
☐ G-CIVJ	Boeing 747-436	25817/1102	
☐ G-CIVK	Boeing 747-436	25818/1104	
☐ G-CIVL	Boeing 747-436	27478/1108	
☐ G-CIVM	Boeing 747-436	28700/1116	
☐ G-CIVN	Boeing 747-436	28848/1129	
☐ G-CIVO	Boeing 747-436	28849/1135	ex N6046P
☐ G-CIVP	Boeing 747-436	28850/1144	
☐ G-CIVR	Boeing 747-436	25820/1146	
☐ G-CIVS	Boeing 747-436	28851/1148	
☐ G-CIVT	Boeing 747-436	25821/1149	
☐ G-CIVU	Boeing 747-436	25810/1154	
☐ G-CIVV	Boeing 747-436	25819/1156	ex N6009F
☐ G-CIVW	Boeing 747-436	25822/1157	
☐ G-CIVX	Boeing 747-436	28852/1172	
☐ G-CIVY	Boeing 747-436	28853/1178	
☐ G-CIVZ	Boeing 747-436	28854/1183	
☐ G-CPEM	Boeing 757-236	28665/747	
☐ G-CPEN	Boeing 757-236	28666/751	
☐ G-CPEO	Boeing 757-236	28667/762	
☐ G-CPET	Boeing 757-236	29115/798	
☐ G-BNWA	Boeing 767-336ER	24333/265	ex N6009F
☐ G-BNWB	Boeing 767-336ER	24334/281	ex N6046P
☐ G-BNWC	Boeing 767-336ER	24335/284	
☐ G-BNWD	Boeing 767-336ER	24336/286	ex N6018N
☐ G-BNWH	Boeing 767-336ER	24340/335	ex N6005C
☐ G-BNWI	Boeing 767-336ER	24341/342	
☐ G-BNWM	Boeing 767-336ER	25204/376	
☐ G-BNWN	Boeing 767-336ER	25444/398	
☐ G-BNWO	Boeing 767-336ER	25442/418	
☐ G-BNWR	Boeing 767-336ER	25732/421	
☐ G-BNWS	Boeing 767-336ER	25826/473	ex N6018N
☐ G-BNWT	Boeing 767-336ER	25828/476	
☐ G-BNWU	Boeing 767-336ER	25829/483	
☐ G-BNWV	Boeing 767-336ER	27140/490	
☐ G-BNWW	Boeing 767-336ER	25831/526	
☐ G-BNWX	Boeing 767-336ER	25832/529	
☐ G-BNWY	Boeing 767-336ER	25834/608	ex N5005C
☐ G-BNWZ	Boeing 767-336ER	25733/648	
☐ G-BZHA	Boeing 767-336ER	29230/702	
☐ G-BZHB	Boeing 767-336ER	29231/704	
☐ G-BZHC	Boeing 767-336ER	29232/708	
☐ G-RAES	Boeing 777-236ER	27491/76	ex (G-ZZZP)

194

☐ G-VIIA	Boeing 777-236ER	27483/41	ex N5022E		
☐ G-VIIB	Boeing 777-236ER	27484/49	ex (G-ZZZG)		
☐ G-VIIC	Boeing 777-236ER	27485/53	ex (G-ZZZH)		
☐ G-VIID	Boeing 777-236ER	27486/56	ex (G-ZZZI)		
☐ G-VIIE	Boeing 777-236ER	27487/58	ex (G-ZZZJ)		
☐ G-VIIF	Boeing 777-236ER	27488/61	ex (G-ZZZK)		
☐ G-VIIG	Boeing 777-236ER	27489/65	ex (G-ZZZL)		
☐ G-VIIH	Boeing 777-236ER	27490/70	ex (G-ZZZM)		
☐ G-VIIJ	Boeing 777-236ER	27492/111	ex (G-ZZZN)		
☐ G-VIIK	Boeing 777-236ER	28840/117			
☐ G-VIIL	Boeing 777-236ER	27493/127			
☐ G-VIIM	Boeing 777-236ER	28841/130			
☐ G-VIIN	Boeing 777-236ER	29319/157			
☐ G-VIIO	Boeing 777-236ER	29320/182			
☐ G-VIIP	Boeing 777-236ER	29321/193			
☐ G-VIIR	Boeing 777-236ER	29322/203			
☐ G-VIIS	Boeing 777-236ER	29323/206			
☐ G-VIIT	Boeing 777-236ER	29962/217			
☐ G-VIIU	Boeing 777-236ER	29963/221			
☐ G-VIIV	Boeing 777-236ER	29964/228			
☐ G-VIIW	Boeing 777-236ER	29965/233			
☐ G-VIIX	Boeing 777-236ER	29966/236			
☐ G-VIIY	Boeing 777-236ER	29967/251			
☐ G-YMMA	Boeing 777-236ER	30302/242	ex N5017Q		
☐ G-YMMB	Boeing 777-236ER	30303/265			
☐ G-YMMC	Boeing 777-236ER	30304/268			
☐ G-YMMD	Boeing 777-236ER	30305/269			
☐ G-YMME	Boeing 777-236ER	30306/275			
☐ G-YMMF	Boeing 777-236ER	30307/281			
☐ G-YMMG	Boeing 777-236ER	30308/301			
☐ G-YMMH	Boeing 777-236ER	30309/303			
☐ G-YMMI	Boeing 777-236ER	30310/308			
☐ G-YMMJ	Boeing 777-236ER	30311/311			
☐ G-YMMK	Boeing 777-236ER	30312/312			
☐ G-YMML	Boeing 777-236ER	30313/334			
☐ G-YMMN	Boeing 777-236ER	30316/346			
☐ G-YMMO	Boeing 777-236ER	30317/361			
☐ G-YMMP	Boeing 777-236ER	30315/369			
☐ G-YMMR	Boeing 777-236ER	36516/771	ex N5014K		
☐ G-YMMS	Boeing 777-236ER	36517/784			
☐ G-YMMT	Boeing 777-236ER	36518/791			
☐ G-YMMU	Boeing 777-236ER	36519/796	ex N6009F		
☐ G-ZZZA	Boeing 777-236	27105/6	ex N77779		
☐ G-ZZZB	Boeing 777-236	27106/10	ex N77771		
☐ G-ZZZC	Boeing 777-236	27107/15	ex N5014K		
☐ G-STBA	Boeing 777-336ER	40542/879			◆
☐ G-STBB	Boeing 777-336ER	39286/887			◆
☐ G-STBC	Boeing 777-336ER	39287/901	ex N6018N		◆
☐ G-STBD	Boeing 777-336ER				o/o◆
☐ G-STBE	Boeing 777-336ER				o/o◆

BRITISH GLOBAL	**Kruger Air (7G/MKA)**	**Ostend (OST)**

Ceased operations 09/Apr/2010

BRITISH INTERNATIONAL	**Brintel (BS/VRA)**	**Cardiff, Penzance & Plymouth (CWL/PZE/PLH)**

☐ G-ATBJ	Sikorsky S-61N	61269	ex N10043		
☐ G-ATFM	Sikorsky S-61N	61270	ex CF-OKY		based Falklands Islands
☐ G-AYOY	Sikorsky S-61N	61476			
☐ G-BCEA	Sikorsky S-61N	61721			based Falklands Islands
☐ G-BCEB	Sikorsky S-61N	61454	ex N4023S	The Isles of Scilly	
☐ G-BFFJ	Sikorsky S-61N	61777	ex N6231	Tresco	
☐ G-BFRI	Sikorsky S-61N II	61809			
☐ G-BHOG	Sikorsky S-61N II	61825	ex PT-YEK		
☐ G-VIPZ	Sikorsky S-61N	61824	ex G-DAWS		

CHC SCOTIA HELICOPTERS	**Helibus (SHZ)**	**Aberdeen (ABZ)**

☐ G-BKZE	Aérospatiale AS.332L	2102	ex F-WKQE	<Heliworld Lsg	
☐ G-BKZG	Aérospatiale AS.332L	2106	ex HB-ZBT		
☐ G-BUZD	Aérospatiale AS.332L	2069	ex C-GSLJ		
☐ G-CHCF	Aérospatiale AS.332L2	2567			
☐ G-CHCG	Aérospatiale AS.332L2	2592			
☐ G-CHCH	Aérospatiale AS.332L2	2601			
☐ G-CHCI	Aérospatiale AS.322L	2395	ex LN-OHD		
☐ G-CHCJ	Eurocopter EC225LP	2745			◆

□	G-CHCL	Eurocopter EC225LP	2674		
□	G-CHCM	Eurocopter EC225LP	2675		
□	G-CHCN	Eurocopter EC225LP	2679		
□	G-NNCY	Eurocopter EC225LP	2773	ex G-LCAS	◆
□	G-PUMA	Aérospatiale AS.332L	2038	ex F-WMHB	
□	G-PUMB	Aérospatiale AS.332L	2075		
□	G-PUME	Aérospatiale AS.332L	2091		
□	G-PUMN	Aérospatiale AS.332L2	2484	ex LN-OHF	<HKS
□	G-PUMO	Aérospatiale AS.332L2	2467		
□	G-PUMS	Aérospatiale AS.332L2	2504		
□	G-BKXD	Aérospatiale SA365N Dauphin 2	6088	ex F-WMHD	
□	G-BLEZ	Aérospatiale SA365N Dauphin 2	6131		
□	G-BLUM	Aérospatiale SA365N Dauphin 2	6101		
□	G-BTEU	Aérospatiale SA365N2 Dauphin 2	6392		
□	G-BTNC	Aérospatiale SA365N2 Dauphin 2	6409		
□	G-CHCO	Aérospatiale AS365N2 Dauphin 2	6358	ex LN-ODB	
□	G-CGIJ	Agusta AW139	31203		Op for HM Coastguard
□	G-CGRG	Agusta AW139	31319		◆
□	G-CGRH	Agusta AW139	31320		◆
□	G-CGWB	Agusta AW139	31209		Op for HM Coastguard
□	G-CHCP	Agusta AW139	31046	ex PH-IEH	
□	G-CHCT	Agusta AW139	31042	ex PH-TRH	
□	G-CHCV	Agusta AW139	41005	ex N106AW	
□	G-CHCW	Agusta AW139	31072	ex PH-EUA	
□	G-JEZA	Agusta AW139	31255		
□	G-SARD	Agusta AW139	31208		Op for HM Coastguard
□	G-SNSA	Agusta AW139	31308		◆
□	G-BMAL	Sikorsky S-76A+	760120	ex F-WZSA	
□	G-CHCD	Sikorsky S-76A+	760101	ex (ZS-RNH)	
□	G-SSSC	Sikorsky S-76C	760408		
□	G-SSSD	Sikorsky S-76C	760415		
□	G-SSSE	Sikorsky S-76C	760417		
□	G-CGMU	Sikorsky S-92A	920034	ex N8010S	o/o Op for HM Coastguard
□	G-CGOC	Sikorsky S-92A	920051	ex N45165	
□	G-CHCK	Sikorsky S-92A	920030	ex N8001N	
□	G-CHCS	Sikorsky S-92A	920125		◆
□	G-SARB	Sikorsky S-92A	920045	ex N80562	Op for HM Coastguard
□	G-SARC	Sikorsky S-92A	920052	ex N45168	o/o Op for HM Coastguard

DHL AIR *World Express (D0/DHK)* **EastMidlands-Nottingham/Brussels (EMA/BRU)**

□	G-BIKC	Boeing 757-236 (SF)	22174/11		
□	G-BIKF	Boeing 757-236 (SF)	22177/16		
□	G-BIKG	Boeing 757-236 (SF)	22178/23		
□	G-BIKI	Boeing 757-236 (SF)	22180/25	ex OO-DLO	
□	G-BIKJ	Boeing 757-236 (SF)	22181/29		
□	G-BIKK	Boeing 757-236 (SF)	22182/30		
□	G-BIKM	Boeing 757-236 (SF)	22184/33	ex N8293V	
□	G-BIKN	Boeing 757-236 (SF)	22186/50		
□	G-BIKO	Boeing 757-236 (SF)	22187/52		
□	G-BIKP	Boeing 757-236 (SF)	22188/54		
□	G-BIKS	Boeing 757-236 (SF)	22190/63		
□	G-BIKU	Boeing 757-236 (SF)	23399/78		
□	G-BIKV	Boeing 757-236 (SF)	23400/81		
□	G-BIKZ	Boeing 757-236 (SF)	23532/98		
□	G-BMRA	Boeing 757-236 (SF)	23710/123		
□	G-BMRB	Boeing 757-236 (SF)	23975/145		
□	G-BMRC	Boeing 757-236 (SF)	24072/160		
□	G-BMRD	Boeing 757-236 (SF)	24073/166		
□	G-BMRE	Boeing 757-236 (SF)	24074/168		
□	G-BMRF	Boeing 757-236 (SF)	24101/175		
□	G-BMRH	Boeing 757-236 (SF)	24266/210		
□	G-BMRJ	Boeing 757-236 (SF)	24268/214		>AXF◆
□	G-DHLE	Boeing 767-3JHF/W	37805/980		
□	G-DHLF	Boeing 767-3JHF/W	37806/981		
□	G-DHLG	Boeing 767-3JHF/W	37807/982		

DIRECTFLIGHT *Metman/Watchdog (DCT)* **Cranfield/Exeter (-/EXT)**

□	G-LUXE	British Aerospace 146 Srs.301	E3001	ex G-5-300	Atmospheric Research, op for FAAM
□	G-MAFA	Reims Cessna F406 Caravan II	F406-0036	ex G-DFLT	Op for DEFRA
□	G-MAFB	Reims Cessna F406 Caravan II	F406-0080	ex F-WWSR	Op for DEFRA

196

☐ G-SICA	Britten-Norman BN-2B-20 Islander	2304	ex G-SLAP	Op for Shetland Islands Council
☐ G-SICB	Britten-Norman BN-2B-20 Islander	2260	ex G-NESU	Op for Shetland Islands Council

EASTERN AIRWAYS — Eastflight (T3/EZE) — Humberside (HUY)

☐ G-CDYI	British Aerospace Jetstream 41	41019	ex N305UE	
☐ G-MAJA	British Aerospace Jetstream 41	41032	ex G-4-032	
☐ G-MAJB	British Aerospace Jetstream 41	41018	ex G-BVKT	
☐ G-MAJC	British Aerospace Jetstream 41	41005	ex G-LOGJ	
☐ G-MAJD	British Aerospace Jetstream 41	41006	ex G-WAWR	
☐ G-MAJE	British Aerospace Jetstream 41	41007	ex G-LOGK	
☐ G-MAJF	British Aerospace Jetstream 41	41008	ex G-WAWL	
☐ G-MAJG	British Aerospace Jetstream 41	41009	ex G-LOGL	
☐ G-MAJH	British Aerospace Jetstream 41	41010	ex G-WAYR	
☐ G-MAJI	British Aerospace Jetstream 41	41011	ex G-WAND	
☐ G-MAJJ	British Aerospace Jetstream 41	41024	ex G-WAFT	
☐ G-MAJL	British Aerospace Jetstream 41	41087	ex G-4-087	
☐ G-MAJP	British Aerospace Jetstream 41	41039	ex N550HK	
☐ G-MAJU	British Aerospace Jetstream 41	41071	ex N558HK	
☐ G-MAJV	British Aerospace Jetstream 41	41074	ex N557HK	
☐ G-MAJW	British Aerospace Jetstream 41	41015	ex N303UE	
☐ G-MAJX	British Aerospace Jetstream 41	41098	ex N330UE	
☐ G-MAJY	British Aerospace Jetstream 41	41099	ex N331UE	
☐ G-MAJZ	British Aerospace Jetstream 41	41100	ex N332UE	
☐ G-CGMC	Embraer ERJ-135ER	145198	ex F-GOHB	♦
☐ G-CDEA	SAAB 2000	2000-009	ex SE-009	
☐ G-CDEB	SAAB 2000	2000-036	ex SE-036	
☐ G-CDKA	SAAB 2000	2000-006	ex SE-006	
☐ G-CDKB	SAAB 2000	2000-032	ex SE-032	
☐ G-CERY	SAAB 2000	2000-008	ex D-AOLA	
☐ G-CERZ	SAAB 2000	2000-042	ex SE-LSA	
☐ G-CFLU	SAAB 2000	2000-055	ex SE-LSG	
☐ G-CFLV	SAAB 2000	2000-023	ex SE-023	

EASYJET AIRLINES — Easy (U2/EZY) — London-Luton (LTN)

☐ G-EJAR	Airbus A319-111	2412	ex D-AVWH	
☐ G-EJJB	Airbus A319-111	2380	ex D-AVWV	
☐ G-EZAA	Airbus A319-111	2677	ex D-AVYU	
☐ G-EZAB	Airbus A319-111	2681	ex D-AVYY	
☐ G-EZAC	Airbus A319-111	2691	ex D-AVXB	
☐ G-EZAD	Airbus A319-111	2702	ex D-AVXI	
☐ G-EZAF	Airbus A319-111	2715	ex D-AVYT	
☐ G-EZAG	Airbus A319-111	2727	ex D-AVXG	
☐ G-EZAI	Airbus A319-111	2735	ex D-AVXM	
☐ G-EZAJ	Airbus A319-111	2742	ex D-AVXP	
☐ G-EZAK	Airbus A319-111	2744	ex D-AVXQ	
☐ G-EZAL	Airbus A319-111	2754	ex D-AVWG	
☐ G-EZAM	Airbus A319-111	2037	ex HB-JZA	
☐ G-EZAN	Airbus A319-111	2765	ex D-AVWL	
☐ G-EZAO	Airbus A319-111	2769	ex D-AVWO	
☐ G-EZAP	Airbus A319-111	2777	ex D-AVYG	
☐ G-EZAS	Airbus A319-111	2779	ex D-AVYH	
☐ G-EZAT	Airbus A319-111	2782	ex D-AVYO	
☐ G-EZAU	Airbus A319-111	2795	ex D-AVWQ	
☐ G-EZAV	Airbus A319-111	2803	ex D-AVWV	
☐ G-EZAW	Airbus A319-111	2812	ex D-AVYU	
☐ G-EZAX	Airbus A319-111	2818	ex D-AVXA	
☐ G-EZAY	Airbus A319-111	2827	ex D-AVXE	
☐ G-EZAZ	Airbus A319-111	2829	ex D-AVXF	
☐ G-EZBA	Airbus A319-111	2860	ex D-AVWB	
☐ G-EZBB	Airbus A319-111	2854	ex D-AVXM	
☐ G-EZBC	Airbus A319-111	2866	ex D-AVWD	
☐ G-EZBD	Airbus A319-111	2873	ex D-AVWK	
☐ G-EZBE	Airbus A319-111	2884	ex D-AVXO	
☐ G-EZBF	Airbus A319-111	2923	ex D-AVYK	
☐ G-EZBG	Airbus A319-111	2946	ex D-AVXA	
☐ G-EZBH	Airbus A319-111	2959	ex D-AVXH	
☐ G-EZBI	Airbus A319-111	3003	ex D-AVYB	Madrid
☐ G-EZBJ	Airbus A319-111	3036	ex D-AVWJ	
☐ G-EZBK	Airbus A319-111	3041	ex D-AVWK	
☐ G-EZBL	Airbus A319-111	3053	ex D-AVYJ	
☐ G-EZBM	Airbus A319-111	3059	ex D-AVWE	Edinburgh
☐ G-EZBN	Airbus A319-111	3061	ex D-AVWH	
☐ G-EZBO	Airbus A319-111	3082	ex D-AVYK	

	Reg	Type	c/n	Ex	Notes	
☐	G-EZBR	Airbus A319-111	3088	ex D-AVYY	100th Airbus titles	
☐	G-EZBT	Airbus A319-111	3090	ex D-AVWM		
☐	G-EZBU	Airbus A319-111	3118	ex D-AVWW		
☐	G-EZBV	Airbus A319-111	3122	ex D-AVWX		
☐	G-EZBW	Airbus A319-111	3134	ex D-AVXE		
☐	G-EZBX	Airbus A319-111	3137	ex D-AVXH		
☐	G-EZBY	Airbus A319-111	3176	ex D-AVXJ		
☐	G-EZBZ	Airbus A319-111	3184	ex D-AVYF		
☐	G-EZDA	Airbus A319-111	3413	ex D-AVYH		
☐	G-EZDB	Airbus A319-111	3411	ex D-AVYF		
☐	G-EZDC	Airbus A319-111	2043	ex HB-JZB		
☐	G-EZDD	Airbus A319-111	3442	ex D-AVYL		
☐	G-EZDE	Airbus A319-111	3426	ex D-AVYP		
☐	G-EZDF	Airbus A319-111	3432	ex D-AVYG		
☐	G-EZDH	Airbus A319-111	3466	ex D-AVWM		
☐	G-EZDI	Airbus A319-111	3537	ex D-AVWC		
☐	G-EZDJ	Airbus A319-111	3544	ex D-AVWJ	I Love Malpensa	
☐	G-EZDK	Airbus A319-111	3555	ex D-AVWP		
☐	G-EZDL	Airbus A319-111	3569	ex D-AVWT		
☐	G-EZDM	Airbus A319-111	3571	ex D-AVWU		
☐	G-EZDN	Airbus A319-111	3608	ex D-AVYJ		
☐	G-EZDO	Airbus A319-111	3634	ex D-AVYP		
☐	G-EZDP	Airbus A319-111	3675	ex D-AVYX		
☐	G-EZDR	Airbus A319-111	3683	ex D-AVYZ		
☐	G-EZDS	Airbus A319-111	3702	ex D-AVWP		
☐	G-EZDT	Airbus A319-111	3720	ex D-AVWR		
☐	G-EZDU	Airbus A319-111	3735	ex D-AVWX		
☐	G-EZDV	Airbus A319-111	3742	ex D-AVWY		
☐	G-EZDW	Airbus A319-111	3746	ex D-AVXA		
☐	G-EZDX	Airbus A319-111	3754	ex D-AVXB		
☐	G-EZDY	Airbus A319-111	3763	ex D-AVXF		
☐	G-EZDZ	Airbus A319-111	3774	ex D-AVXI		
☐	G-EZEA	Airbus A319-111	2119	ex D-AVWZ		
☐	G-EZEB	Airbus A319-111	2120	ex D-AVYK		
☐	G-EZEC	Airbus A319-111	2129	ex D-AVWR		
☐	G-EZED	Airbus A319-111	2170	ex D-AVWT		
☐	G-EZEF	Airbus A319-111	2176	ex D-AVYS		
☐	G-EZEG	Airbus A319-111	2181	ex D-AVWF		
☐	G-EZEJ	Airbus A319-111	2214	ex D-AVYO		
☐	G-EZEK	Airbus A319-111	2224	ex D-AVYZ		
☐	G-EZEO	Airbus A319-111	2249	ex D-AVYN		
☐	G-EZEP	Airbus A319-111	2251	ex D-AVYQ		
☐	G-EZET	Airbus A319-111	2271	ex D-AVWY		
☐	G-EZEU	Airbus A319-111	2283	ex D-AVYP		
☐	G-EZEV	Airbus A319-111	2289	ex D-AVYV		
☐	G-EZEW	Airbus A319-111	2300	ex D-AVWH		
☐	G-EZEZ	Airbus A319-111	2360	ex D-AVWP		
☐	G-EZFA	Airbus A319-111	3788	ex D-AVXK		
☐	G-EZFB	Airbus A319-111	3799	ex D-AVXN		
☐	G-EZFC	Airbus A319-111	3808	ex D-AVYC		
☐	G-EZFD	Airbus A319-111	3810	ex D-AVYF		
☐	G-EZFE	Airbus A319-111	3824	ex D-AVYI		
☐	G-EZFF	Airbus A319-111	3844	ex D-AVYT		
☐	G-EZFG	Airbus A319-111	3845	ex D-AVYU		
☐	G-EZFH	Airbus A319-111	3854	ex D-AVWA		
☐	G-EZFI	Airbus A319-111	3888	ex D-AVWH		
☐	G-EZFJ	Airbus A319-111	4040	ex D-AVYM		
☐	G-EZFK	Airbus A319-111	4048	ex D-AVYP		
☐	G-EZFL	Airbus A319-111	4056	ex D-AVYS		
☐	G-EZFM	Airbus A319-111	4069	ex D-AVYT		
☐	G-EZFN	Airbus A319-111	4076	ex D-AVYV		
☐	G-EZFO	Airbus A319-111	4080	ex D-AVYW		
☐	G-EZFP	Airbus A319-111	4087	ex D-AVYX		
☐	G-EZFR	Airbus A319-111	4125	ex D-AVWC		
☐	G-EZFS	Airbus A319-111	4129	ex D-AVWE		
☐	G-EZFT	Airbus A319-111	4132	ex D-AVWF	Sir George White	
☐	G-EZFU	Airbus A319-111	4313	ex D-AVXC		♦
☐	G-EZFV	Airbus A319-111	4327	ex D-AVXE		♦
☐	G-EZFW	Airbus A319-111	4380	ex D-AVYQ		♦
☐	G-EZFX	Airbus A319-111	4385	ex D-AVYS		♦
☐	G-EZFY	Airbus A319-111	4418	ex D-AVXJ		♦
☐	G-EZFZ	Airbus A319-111	4425	ex D-AVXL		♦
☐	G-EZGA	Airbus A319-111	4427	ex D-AVXM		♦
☐	G-EZGB	Airbus A319-111	4437	ex D-AVXO		♦
☐	G-EZGC	Airbus A319-111	4444	ex D-AVXP		♦
☐	G-EZGD	Airbus A319-111	4451	ex D-AVYA		♦
☐	G-	Airbus A319-111		ex		o/o♦

☐ G-	Airbus A319-111		ex		o/o♦
☐ G-	Airbus A319-111		ex		o/o♦
☐ G-	Airbus A319-111		ex		o/o♦
☐ G-	Airbus A319-111		ex		o/o♦
☐ G-	Airbus A319-111		ex		o/o♦
☐ G-	Airbus A319-111		ex		o/o♦
☐ G-	Airbus A319-111		ex		o/o♦
☐ G-	Airbus A319-111		ex		o/o♦
☐ G-	Airbus A319-111		ex		o/o♦
☐ G-	Airbus A319-111		ex		o/o♦
☐ G-	Airbus A319-111		ex		o/o♦
☐ G-	Airbus A319-111		ex		o/o♦
☐ G-EZIA	Airbus A319-111	2420	ex D-AVYL		
☐ G-EZIC	Airbus A319-111	2436	ex D-AVWC		
☐ G-EZID	Airbus A319-111	2442	ex D-AVWT	'100' titles	
☐ G-EZIE	Airbus A319-111	2446	ex D-AVWQ		
☐ G-EZIG	Airbus A319-111	2460	ex D-AVYM		
☐ G-EZIH	Airbus A319-111	2463	ex D-AVWV		
☐ G-EZII	Airbus A319-111	2471	ex D-AVYK		
☐ G-EZIJ	Airbus A319-111	2477	ex D-AVYU		
☐ G-EZIK	Airbus A319-111	2481	ex D-AVYV		
☐ G-EZIL	Airbus A319-111	2492	ex D-AVWM		
☐ G-EZIM	Airbus A319-111	2495	ex D-AVYO		
☐ G-EZIN	Airbus A319-111	2503	ex D-AVYZ		
☐ G-EZIO	Airbus A319-111	2512	ex D-AVWP		
☐ G-EZIP	Airbus A319-111	2514	ex D-AVWQ		
☐ G-EZIR	Airbus A319-111	2527	ex D-AVWK		
☐ G-EZIS	Airbus A319-111	2528	ex D-AVWJ		
☐ G-EZIT	Airbus A319-111	2538	ex D-AVYN		
☐ G-EZIU	Airbus A319-111	2548	ex D-AVYF		
☐ G-EZIV	Airbus A319-111	2565	ex D-AVYY		
☐ G-EZIW	Airbus A319-111	2578	ex D-AVXE		
☐ G-EZIX	Airbus A319-111	2605	ex D-AVXP		
☐ G-EZIY	Airbus A319-111	2636	ex D-AVWH		
☐ G-EZIZ	Airbus A319-111	2646	ex D-AVWQ		
☐ G-EZMH	Airbus A319-111	2053	ex HB-JZD		
☐ G-EZMS	Airbus A319-111	2378	ex D-AVWS		
☐ G-EZNC	Airbus A319-111	2050	ex HB-JZC		
☐ G-EZPG	Airbus A319-111	2385	ex D-AVYD		
☐ G-EZSM	Airbus A319-111	2062	ex HB-JZE		
☐ G-EZTA	Airbus A320-214	3805	ex D-AVVD		
☐ G-EZTB	Airbus A320-214	3843	ex F-WWBO		
☐ G-EZTC	Airbus A320-214	3871	ex F-WWIG		
☐ G-EZTD	Airbus A320-214	3909	ex D-AVVB		
☐ G-EZTE	Airbus A320-214	3913	ex D-AVVF		
☐ G-EZTF	Airbus A320-214	3922	ex D-AVVG		
☐ G-EZTG	Airbus A320-214	3946	ex D-AVVJ		
☐ G-EZTH	Airbus A320-214	3953	ex D-AVVM		
☐ G-EZTI	Airbus A320-214	3975	ex D-AVVN		
☐ G-EZTJ	Airbus A320-214	3979	ex D-AVVO		
☐ G-EZTK	Airbus A320-214	3991	ex D-AVVP		
☐ G-EZTL	Airbus A320-214	4012	ex D-AVVC		
☐ G-EZTM	Airbus A320-214	4014	ex D-AVVD		
☐ G-EZTN	Airbus A320-214	4006	ex F-WWDY		
☐ G-EZTP	Airbus A320-214	4157	ex D-AVVN		
☐ G-EZTR	Airbus A320-214	4179	ex D-AVVX		
☐ G-EZTS	Airbus A320-214	4196	ex D-AVVE		
☐ G-EZTT	Airbus A320-214	4219	ex D-AVVM		
☐ G-EZTU	Airbus A320-214	4233	ex F-WWBV		♦
☐ G-EZTV	Airbus A320-214	4234	ex F-WWBZ		♦
☐ G-EZTW	Airbus A320-214	4250	ex F-WWIF		♦
☐ G-EZTX	Airbus A320-214	4286	ex F-WWIR		♦
☐ G-EZTY	Airbus A320-214	4543	ex D-AUBS		♦
☐ G-EZTZ	Airbus A320-214	4556	ex D-AUBW		♦
☐ G-EZUA	Airbus A320-214	4588	ex D-AVVE		♦
☐ G-	Airbus A320-214		ex		o/o♦
☐ G-	Airbus A320-214		ex		o/o♦
☐ G-	Airbus A320-214		ex		o/o♦
☐ G-	Airbus A320-214		ex		o/o♦
☐ G-	Airbus A320-214		ex		o/o♦
☐ G-	Airbus A320-214		ex		o/o♦
☐ G-	Airbus A320-214		ex		o/o♦
☐ G-	Airbus A320-214		ex		o/o♦
☐ G-	Airbus A320-214		ex		o/o♦
☐ G-TTOG	Airbus A320-232	1969	ex F-WWDZ		

	Reg	Type	Serial	ex	Name	
☐	G-TTOJ	Airbus A320-232	2157	ex F-WWDE		
☐	G-EZJZ	Boeing 737-73V	32421/1357		Ray Webster	
☐	G-EZKA	Boeing 737-73V	32422/1363	ex (G-ESYA)		
☐	G-EZKB	Boeing 737-73V	32423/1433	ex (G-ESYB)		
☐	G-EZKC	Boeing 737-73V	32424/1450	ex (G-ESYC)		
☐	G-EZKD	Boeing 737-73V	32425/1453	ex N1787B		
☐	G-EZKE	Boeing 737-73V	32426/1474	ex (G-ESYE)	Daniel Swaddle	
☐	G-EZKF	Boeing 737-73V	32427/1489	ex (G-ESYF)		
☐	G-EZKG	Boeing 737-73V	32428/1495	ex (G-ESYG)		

FLYBE   Jersey (BE/BEE)   Jersey/Exeter (JER/EXT)

	Reg	Type	Serial	ex	Name	
☐	G-ECOA	de Havilland DHC-8-402Q	4180	ex C-FMUE		
☐	G-ECOB	de Havilland DHC-8-402Q	4185	ex LN-WDT		
☐	G-ECOC	de Havilland DHC-8-402Q	4197	ex LN-WDU		
☐	G-ECOD	de Havilland DHC-8-402Q	4206	ex C-FPEX		
☐	G-ECOE	de Havilland DHC-8-402Q	4212	ex LN-WDV		
☐	G-ECOF	de Havilland DHC-8-402Q	4216	ex LN-WDW		♦
☐	G-ECOG	de Havilland DHC-8-402Q	4220	ex C-FSRQ		
☐	G-ECOH	de Havilland DHC-8-402Q	4221	ex C-FSRW		
☐	G-ECOI	de Havilland DHC-8-402Q	4224	ex C-FTIE		
☐	G-ECOJ	de Havilland DHC-8-402Q	4229	ex C-FTUS		
☐	G-ECOK	de Havilland DHC-8-402Q	4230	ex C-FTUT		
☐	G-ECOM	de Havilland DHC-8-402Q	4233	ex C-FUCR		
☐	G-ECOO	de Havilland DHC-8-402Q	4237	ex C-FUOH		
☐	G-ECOP	de Havilland DHC-8-402Q	4242	ex C-FUTG		
☐	G-ECOR	de Havilland DHC-8-402Q	4248	ex C-FVUJ		
☐	G-ECOT	de Havilland DHC-8-402Q	4251	ex C-FVUV		
☐	G-ECOV	de Havilland DHC-8-402Q	4033	ex LN-RDM		
☐	G-ECOY	de Havilland DHC-8-402Q	4022	ex LN-RDG		
☐	G-ECOZ	de Havilland DHC-8-402Q	4034	ex LN-RDR		
☐	G-FLBA	de Havilland DHC-8-402Q	4253	ex C-FVVB		
☐	G-FLBB	de Havilland DHC-8-402Q	4255	ex C-FWGE		
☐	G-FLBC	de Havilland DHC-8-402Q	4257	ex C-FWGY		
☐	G-FLBD	de Havilland DHC-8-402Q	4259	ex C-FWZN		
☐	G-FLBE	de Havilland DHC-8-402Q	4261	ex C-FXAB		♦
☐	G-FLBF	de Havilland DHC-8-402Q	4344	ex C-		o/o♦
☐	G-FLBG	de Havilland DHC-8-402Q	4350	ex C-		o/o♦
☐	G-FLBH	de Havilland DHC-8-402Q	4366	ex C-		o/o♦
☐	G-FLBI	de Havilland DHC-8-402Q	4370	ex C-		o/o♦
☐	G-JECE	de Havilland DHC-8-402Q	4094	ex C-FDHU	The Wembley Grecians	
☐	G-JECF	de Havilland DHC-8-402Q	4095	ex C-FDHV		
☐	G-JECG	de Havilland DHC-8-402Q	4098	ex C-FAQH		
☐	G-JECH	de Havilland DHC-8-402Q	4103	ex C-FCQC		
☐	G-JECI	de Havilland DHC-8-402Q	4105	ex C-FCQK		
☐	G-JECJ	de Havilland DHC-8-402Q	4110	ex C-FCVN		
☐	G-JECK	de Havilland DHC-8-402Q	4113	ex C-FDRL		
☐	G-JECL	de Havilland DHC-8-402Q	4114	ex C-FDRN	The George Best	
☐	G-JECM	de Havilland DHC-8-402Q	4118	ex C-FFCE		
☐	G-JECN	de Havilland DHC-8-402Q	4120	ex C-FFCL		
☐	G-JECO	de Havilland DHC-8-402Q	4126	ex C-FFPT		
☐	G-JECP	de Havilland DHC-8-402Q	4136	ex C-FHEL		
☐	G-JECR	de Havilland DHC-8-402Q	4139	ex C-FHQM		
☐	G-JECS	de Havilland DHC-8-402Q	4142	ex C-FHQV		
☐	G-JECT	de Havilland DHC-8-402Q	4144	ex C-FHQY	Matt le Tissier	
☐	G-JECU	de Havilland DHC-8-402Q	4146	ex C-FJKY		
☐	G-JECX	de Havilland DHC-8-402Q	4155	ex C-FLKO		
☐	G-JECY	de Havilland DHC-8-402Q	4157	ex C-FLKV		
☐	G-JECZ	de Havilland DHC-8-402Q	4179	ex C-FMTY		
☐	G-JEDI	de Havilland DHC-8-402Q	4052	ex C-GFOD		
☐	G-JEDJ	de Havilland DHC-8-402Q	4058	ex C-FDHZ		
☐	G-JEDK	de Havilland DHC-8-402Q	4065	ex C-GEMU	Vignoble de Bergerac	
☐	G-JEDL	de Havilland DHC-8-402Q	4067	ex C-GEOZ		
☐	G-JEDM	de Havilland DHC-8-402Q	4077	ex C-FGNP		
☐	G-JEDN	de Havilland DHC-8-402Q	4078	ex C-FNGB		
☐	G-JEDO	de Havilland DHC-8-402Q	4079	ex C-GDFT		
☐	G-JEDP	de Havilland DHC-8-402Q	4085	ex C-FDHO	Special colours	
☐	G-JEDR	de Havilland DHC-8-402Q	4087	ex C-FDHI		
☐	G-JEDT	de Havilland DHC-8-402Q	4088	ex C-FDHP		
☐	G-JEDU	de Havilland DHC-8-402Q	4089	ex C-GEMU	Pride of Exeter	
☐	G-JEDV	de Havilland DHC-8-402Q	4090	ex C-FDHX		
☐	G-JEDW	de Havilland DHC-8-402Q	4093	ex C-GFBW		
☐	G-KKEV	de Havilland DHC-8-402Q	4201	ex C-FOUU	Kevin Keegan	
☐	G-	Embraer ERJ-175LR				o/o♦
☐	G-	Embraer ERJ-175LR				o/o♦

☐ G-	Embraer ERJ-175LR				o/o♦
☐ G-	Embraer ERJ-175LR				o/o♦

☐ G-FBEA	Embraer ERJ-195LR	19000029	ex PT-SGD	Wings of the Community	
☐ G-FBEB	Embraer ERJ-195LR	19000057	ex PT-SII		
☐ G-FBEC	Embraer ERJ-195LR	19000069	ex PT-SJI		
☐ G-FBED	Embraer ERJ-195LR	19000084	ex PT-SNB		
☐ G-FBEE	Embraer ERJ-195LR	19000093	ex PT-SNN		
☐ G-FBEF	Embraer ERJ-195LR	19000104	ex PT-SNY		
☐ G-FBEG	Embraer ERJ-195LR	19000120	ex PT-SQO		
☐ G-FBEH	Embraer ERJ-195LR	19000128	ex PT-SQX		
☐ G-FBEI	Embraer ERJ-195LR	19000143	ex PT-SYV		
☐ G-FBEJ	Embraer ERJ-195LR	19000155	ex PT-SAK		
☐ G-FBEK	Embraer ERJ-195LR	19000168	ex PT-SDC		
☐ G-FBEL	Embraer ERJ-195LR	19000184	ex PT-SDS		
☐ G-FBEM	Embraer ERJ-195LR	19000204	ex PT-SGN		
☐ G-FBEN	Embraer ERJ-195LR	19000213	ex PT-SGW		

GLOBAL SUPPLY SYSTEMS — JetLift (GSS) — London-Stansted (STN)

☐ G-GSSA	Boeing 747-47UF	29256/1213	ex N495MC		Lsd fr/op by GTI
☐ G-GSSB	Boeing 747-47UF	29252/1165	ex N491MC	Louise Jane	Lsd fr/op by GTI
☐ G-GSSC	Boeing 747-47UF	29255/1184	ex N494MC		Lsd fr/op by GTI
☐ G-GSSD	Boeing 747-87UF	37562/1429			o/o♦
☐ G-GSSE	Boeing 747-87UF	37563/1432			o/o♦

HD AIR — (RPX) — Southend (SEN)

☐ G-CLAS	Short SD.3-60	SH3635	ex EI-BEK	

HEBRIDEAN AIR SERVICES — Cumbernauld

☐ G-BSPT	Britten-Norman BN-2B-20 Islander	2240	ex TF-VEG	
☐ G-HEBS	Britten-Norman BN-2B-26 Islander	2267	ex G-BUBJ	

HIGHLAND AIRWAYS — HiWay (8H/HWY) — Inverness (INV)

Ceased operations 24/Mar/2010

ISLES OF SCILLY SKYBUS — Scillonia (5Y/IOS) — Lands End-St Just (LEQ)

☐ G-BIHO	de Havilland DHC-6 Twin Otter 310	738	ex A6-ADB	
☐ G-BUBN	Britten-Norman BN-2B-26 Islander	2270		
☐ G-CBML	de Havilland DHC-6 Twin Otter 310	695	ex C-FZSP	
☐ G-CEWM	de Havilland DHC-6 Twin Otter 300	656	ex N70551	
☐ G-SBUS	Britten-Norman BN-2A-26 Islander	3013	ex G-BMMH	
☐ G-SSKY	Britten-Norman BN-2B-26 Islander	2247	ex G-BSWT	

JANES AVIATION — Southend (SEN)

☐ G-AYIM	Hawker Siddeley HS.748 Srs.2A/270	1687	ex G-11-687	[SEN]
☐ G-OSOE	Hawker Siddeley HS.748 Srs.2A/270	1697	ex G-AYYG	[SEN]

JET2 — Channex (LS/EXS) — Leeds-Bradford /Manchester (LBA/MAN)

☐ G-CELA	Boeing 737-377	23663/1323	ex VH-CZK	Jet2 Newcastle	
☐ G-CELB	Boeing 737-377	23664/1326	ex VH-CZL	Jet2 Yorkshire	
☐ G-CELC	Boeing 737-33A	23831/1471	ex N190FH	Jet2 Tunisia	
☐ G-CELD	Boeing 737-33A	23832/1473	ex N191FH	Jet2 Espana	
☐ G-CELE	Boeing 737-33A	24029/1601	ex VH-CZX	Jet2 Belfast	
☐ G-CELF	Boeing 737-377	24302/1618	ex S7-ABB	Jet2 Sardinia	
☐ G-CELG	Boeing 737-377	24303/1620	ex S7-ABD	HelenNormington	
☐ G-CELH	Boeing 737-330 (QC)	23525/1278	ex D-ABXD	Jet2 Faro	
☐ G-CELI	Boeing 737-330	23526/1282	ex D-ABXE	Jet2 Manchester	
☐ G-CELJ	Boeing 737-330	23529/1293	ex LZ-BOG	Jet2 Italia	
☐ G-CELK	Boeing 737-330	23530/1297	ex LZ-BOH	Jet2 Edinburgh	
☐ G-CELO	Boeing 737-33A (QC)	24028/1599	ex TF-ELO	Jet2 Faro	
☐ G-CELP	Boeing 737-330 (QC)	23522/1246	ex TF-ELP	Jet2 Private Charter	
☐ G-CELR	Boeing 737-330 (QC)	23523/1271	ex TF-ELR	Jet2 Corfu	
☐ G-CELS	Boeing 737-377	23660/1294	ex VH-CZH	Jet2 Leeds-Bradford	
☐ G-CELU	Boeing 737-377	23657/1280	ex VH-CZE	Jet2 Barcelona	
☐ G-CELV	Boeing 737-377	23661/1314	ex VH-CZI	Jet2 Amsterdam	
☐ G-CELW	Boeing 737-377F	23659/1292	ex N659DG		
☐ G-CELX	Boeing 737-377	23654/1273	ex VH-CZB	Jet2 Malaga	
☐ G-CELY	Boeing 737-377F	23662/1316	ex N622DG	Jet2 Ireland	
☐ G-CELZ	Boeing 737-377F	23658/1281	ex VH-CZF	Jet2 Paris	
☐ G-CGET	Boeing 737-33A	27455/2709	ex G-TOYE		
☐ G-GDFA	Boeing 737-3G7	24011/1608	ex OE-IAD		
☐ G-GDFB	Boeing 737-33A	25743/2206	ex SX-BBU		♦

☐ G-GDFC	Boeing 737-8K2/W	28375/85	ex PH-HZC	♦

☐ G-LSAA	Boeing 757-236	24122/187	ex N241CV	Jet2 Tenerife
☐ G-LSAB	Boeing 757-27B/W	24136/169	ex N136CV	Jet2 Menorca
☐ G-LSAC	Boeing 757-23A/W	25488/471	ex N254DG	Jet2 Lanzarote
☐ G-LSAD	Boeing 757-236	24397/221	ex SX-BLW	
☐ G-LSAE	Boeing 757-27B/W	24135/165	ex OM-SNA	Jet2 Murcia
☐ G-LSAG	Boeing 757-21B	24014/144	ex B-2801	
☐ G-LSAH	Boeing 757-21B	24015/148	ex B-2802	
☐ G-LSAI	Boeing 757-21B	24016/150	ex B-2803	
☐ G-LSAJ	Boeing 757-236	24793/292	ex G-CDUP	Jet2 New York
☐ G-LSAK	Boeing 757-23N	27973/735	ex N517AT	

LOCH LOMOND SEAPLANES · Luss

☐ G-MDJE	Cessna 208 Caravan I	20800336	ex N208FM

LOGANAIR · Logan (LOG) · Glasgow (GLA)

☐ G-GNTB	SAAB SF.340A (QC)	340A-082	ex HB-AHL	
☐ G-GNTF	SAAB SF.340A (QC)	340A-113	ex SE-F13	all-white
☐ G-LGNA	SAAB SF.340B	340B-199	ex N592MA	Flybe c/s
☐ G-LGNB	SAAB SF.340B	340B-216	ex N595MA	Flybe c/s
☐ G-LGNC	SAAB SF.340B	340B-318	ex SE-KXC	Flybe c/s
☐ G-LGND	SAAB SF.340B	340B-169	ex G-GNTH	Flybe c/s
☐ G-LGNE	SAAB SF.340B	340B-172	ex G-GNTI	Flybe c/s
☐ G-LGNF	SAAB SF.340B	340B-192	ex N192JE	Flybe c/s
☐ G-LGNG	SAAB SF.340B	340B-327	ex SE-C27	Flybe c/s
☐ G-LGNH	SAAB SF.340B	340B-333	ex SE-C33	Flybe c/s
☐ G-LGNI	SAAB SF.340B	340B-160	ex SE-F60	Flybe c/s
☐ G-LGNJ	SAAB SF.340B	340B-173	ex SE-F73	Flybe c/s
☐ G-LGNK	SAAB SF.340B	340B-185	ex SE-F85	Flybe c/s
☐ G-LGNL	SAAB SF.340B	340B-246	ex SE-G46	Flybe c/s
☐ G-LGNM	SAAB SF.340B	340B-187	ex SE-F47	Flybe c/s
☐ G-LGNN	SAAB SF.340B	340B-197	ex SE-F97	
☐ G-BJOP	Britten-Norman BN-2B-26 Islander	2132		Capt EE Fresson
☐ G-BLDV	Britten-Norman BN-2B-26 Islander	2179	ex D-INEY	
☐ G-BPCA	Britten-Norman BN-2B-26 Islander	2198	ex G-BLNX	Capt David Barclay MBE
☐ G-BVVK	de Havilland DHC-6 Twin Otter 310	666	ex LN-BEZ	Flybe c/s
☐ G-BZFP	de Havilland DHC-6 Twin Otter 310	696	ex C-GGNF	Flybe c/s

LYDD AIR · Lyddair (LYD) · Lydd (LYX)

☐ G-LYDB	Piper PA-31-350 Chieftain	31-8052107	ex TI-PAI
☐ G-LYDC	Piper PA-31-350 Navajo Chieftain	31-7652110	ex N210PM
☐ G-LYDF	Piper PA-31-350 Chieftain	31-7952031	ex N12CD
☐ G-OJAV	Britten-Norman BN-2A Mk.III-2 Trislander	1024	ex G-BDOS

MANX2 AIRLINES · Manx2 (MX) · Ronaldsway (IOM)

☐ D-CMNX	Dornier 228-202K	8065	ex TF-CSG	
☐ D-IFLM	Dornier 228-201	8046	ex TF-CSF	
☐ D-ILKA	Dornier 228-100	7005	ex LN-HTB	
☐ OK-ASA	LET L-410UVP-E	902439	ex SP-KPY	Lsd fr/op by Van Air
☐ OK-TCA	LET L-410UVP-E	902431	ex SP-KPZ	Lsd fr/op by Van Air
☐ OK-UBA	LET L-410UVP-E	892319	ex SP-TXA	Lsd fr/op by Van Air

MONARCH AIRLINES · Monarch (ZB/MON) · London-Luton (LTN)

☐ G-MAJS	Airbus A300B4-605R	604	ex F-WWAX
☐ G-MONR	Airbus A300B4-605R	540	ex VH-YMJ
☐ G-MONS	Airbus A300B4-605R	556	ex VH-YMK
☐ G-OJMR	Airbus A300B4-605R	605	ex F-WWAY
☐ G-MONX	Airbus A320-212	0392	ex F-WWDR
☐ G-MPCD	Airbus A320-212	0379	ex C-GZCD
☐ G-MRJK	Airbus A320-214	1081	ex PH-BMC
☐ G-OZBB	Airbus A320-212	0389	ex C-GZUM
☐ G-OZBK	Airbus A320-214	1370	ex PH-BMD
☐ G-MARA	Airbus A321-231	0983	ex D-AVZB
☐ G-OJEG	Airbus A321-231	1015	ex D-AVZN
☐ G-OZBE	Airbus A321-231	1707	ex D-AVZH
☐ G-OZBF	Airbus A321-231	1763	ex D-AVZB
☐ G-OZBG	Airbus A321-231	1941	ex D-AVXC
☐ G-OZBH	Airbus A321-231	2105	ex D-AVXB

☐ G-OZBI	Airbus A321-231	2234	ex D-AVZV	
☐ G-OZBL	Airbus A321-231	0864	ex G-MIDE	
☐ G-OZBM	Airbus A321-231	1045	ex G-MIDJ	
☐ G-OZBN	Airbus A321-231	1153	ex G-MIDK	
☐ G-OZBO	Airbus A321-231	1207	ex G-MIDM	
☐ G-OZBP	Airbus A321-231	1433	ex G-TTIB	
☐ G-OZBR	Airbus A321-231	1794	ex N586NK	
☐ G-OZBS	Airbus A321-231	1428	ex G-TTIA	
☐ G-OZBT	Airbus A321-231	3546	ex G-TTIH	
☐ G-OZBU	Airbus A321-231	3575	ex G-TTII	
☐ G-EOMA	Airbus A330-243	265	ex F-WWKU	
☐ G-SMAN	Airbus A330-243	261	ex F-WWKR	
☐ G-DAJB	Boeing 757-2T7ER	23770/125		
☐ G-MONJ	Boeing 757-2T7ER	24104/170		
☐ G-MONK	Boeing 757-2T7ER	24105/172		

PDG HELICOPTERS   *Osprey (PDG)*   *Inverness / Glasgow (INV/GLA)*

☐ G-BXGA	Aérospatiale AS350B2 Ecureuil	2493	ex OO-RCH	
☐ G-PDGF	Aérospatiale AS350B2 Ecureuil	9024	ex G-FROH	
☐ G-PDGR	Aérospatiale AS350B2 Ecureuil	2559	ex G-RICC	
☐ G-PLMB	Aérospatiale AS350B Ecureuil	1207	ex G-BMMB	
☐ G-PLMH	Aérospatiale AS350B2 Ecureuil	2156	ex F-WQDJ	
☐ G-BPRJ	Aérospatiale AS355F1 Twin Star	5201	ex N368E	
☐ G-BVLG	Aérospatiale AS355F1 Twin Star	5011	ex N57745	
☐ G-NETR	Aérospatiale AS355F2 Ecureuil 2	5164	ex G-JARV	Op for Network Rail
☐ G-NTWK	Aérospatiale AS355F2 Ecureuil 2	5347	ex G-FTWO	Op for Network Rail
☐ G-PDGT	Aérospatiale AS355F2 Twin Star	5374	ex N325SC	
☐ G-HEMS	Aérospatiale AS365N Dauphin 2	6009	ex 8P-BHD	
☐ G-PDGN	Aérospatiale SA365N Dauphin 2	6074	ex PH-SSU	
☐ G-PLMI	Aérospatiale SA365C1 Dauphin 2	5001	ex F-GFYH	
☐ G-WAAN	MBB Bo.105DB	S-20	ex G-AZOR	Op for Great North Air Ambulance

POLICE AVIATION SERVICES   *Special (PLC)*   *Gloucestershire (GLO)*

☐ G-BXZK	MD Helicopters MD902 Explorer	900-00057	ex N9238T	Op for Dorset Police
☐ G-CEMS	MD Helicopters MD902 Explorer	900-00089	ex PK-OCR	Op for Yorkshire Air Ambulance
☐ G-GNAA	MD Helicopters MD902 Explorer	900-00079	ex PH-RVD	Op for Lincs & Notts Air Ambulance
☐ G-KAAT	MD Helicopters MD902 Explorer	900-00056	ex G-PASS	Op for Kent Air Ambulance
☐ G-KSSH	MD Helicopters MD902 Explorer	900-00062	ex G-WMID	Op for Surrey Air Ambulance
☐ G-LNAA	MD Helicopters MD902 Explorer	900-00074	ex G-76-074	Op for Lincs & Notts Air Ambulance
☐ G-SASH	MD Helicopters MD902 Explorer	900-00080	ex PH-SHF	Op for Yorkshire Air Ambulance
☐ G-SUSX	MD Helicopters MD902 Explorer	900-00065	ex N3065W	Op for Sussex Police
☐ G-WPAS	MD Helicopters MD902 Explorer	900-00053	ex N92237	Op for Wiltshire Police
☐ G-YPOL	MD Helicopters MD902 Explorer	900-00078	ex N7038S	Op for West Yorkshire Police
☐ G-CHEZ	Britten-Norman BN-2B-20 Islander	2234	ex 9M-TAM	Op for Cheshire Police
☐ G-PASV	Britten-Norman BN-2B-21 Islander	2157	ex G-BKJH	
☐ G-PASX	MBB Bo.105DBS-4	S-814	ex D-HDZX	
☐ G-WCAO	Eurocopter EC135T2	0204	ex D-HECU	Op for Western Counties Police
☐ G-WMAO	Eurocopter EC135P2+	0501		Op for West Midlands Police
☐ G-WYPA	MBB Bo.105DBS-4	S-815	ex D-HDZY	

PREMIAIR AVIATION SERVICES   *Premiere (PGL)*   *Denham*

☐ G-DANZ	Aérospatiale AS355N Ecureuil 2	5658		
☐ G-VONE	Aérospatiale AS355N Ecureuil 2	5572	ex G-LCON	
☐ G-VONF	Aérospatiale AS355F1 Ecureuil 2	5262	ex G-BXBT	
☐ G-VONG	Aérospatiale AS355F1 Ecureuil 2	5327	ex G-OILX	
☐ G-VONH	Aérospatiale AS355F1 Ecureuil 2	5303	ex G-BKUL	
☐ G-VONK	Aérospatiale AS355F1 Ecureuil 2	5325	ex G-BLRI	
☐ G-XOIL	Aérospatiale AS355N Ecureuil 2	5627	ex G-LOUN	
☐ G-BOYF	Sikorsky S-76B	760343		
☐ G-BURS	Sikorsky S-76A+	760040	ex G-OHTL	
☐ G-VONA	Sikorsky S-76A	760086	ex G-BUXB	
☐ G-VONB	Sikorsky S-76B	760339	ex G-POAH	
☐ G-VONC	Sikorsky S-76B	760354	ex N966PR	
☐ G-XXEA	Sikorsky S-76C+	760492		Op for Royal Travel Office
☐ VP-BIR	Sikorsky S-76B	760430	ex N9HM	
☐ G-CCAU	Eurocopter EC135T1	0040	ex G-79-01	Op for West Mercia Constabulary
☐ G-HAAT	MD Helicopters MD902 Explorer	900-00081	ex G-GMPS	Op for Hertfordshire Air Ambulance
☐ G-VOND	Bell 222	47041	ex G-OWCG	

SCOTAIRWAYS		Suckling (CB/SAY)		Cambridge (CBG)
☐ G-BWIR	Dornier 328-100	3023	ex D-CDXF	
☐ G-BWWT	Dornier 328-110	3022	ex D-CDXO	
☐ G-BYHG	Dornier 328-110	3098	ex D-CDAE	
☐ G-BYMK	Dornier 328-110	3062	ex LN-ASK	
☐ G-BZOG	Dornier 328-110	3088	ex D-CDXI	
☐ G-CCGS	Dornier 328-110	3101	ex D-CPRX	

SKYSOUTH		Skydrift (SDL)		Norwich / Shoreham (NWI /)
☐ G-OETV	Piper PA-31-350 Chieftain	31-7852073	ex N27597	
☐ G-STHA	Piper PA-31-350 Chieftain	31-8052077	ex G-GLUG	
☐ G-TABS	Embraer EMB.110P1 Bandeirante	110212	ex G-PBAC	

STERLING AVIATION		Silver (SVH)		Norwich (NWI)
☐ G-BFYA	MBB Bo.105DB	S-321	ex D-HJET	Op for Norfolk Police
☐ G-BMTC	Aérospatiale AS355F2 Ecureuil 2	5302	ex G-EPOL	
☐ G-BXNS	Bell 206B JetRanger III	2385	ex N16822	
☐ G-BXNT	Bell 206B JetRanger III	2398	ex N94CA	
☐ G-EYNL	MBB Bo.105DBS-5	S-382	ex LN-OTJ	Op for East Anglian Air Ambulance
☐ G-FFRI	Aérospatiale AS355F1 Ecureuil 2	5120	ex G-GLOW	
☐ G-OEMT	MBB BK-117C-1	7538	ex D-HMEC	Op for East Anglian Air Ambulance
☐ G-RESC	MBB BK-117C-1	7504	ex D-HELW	
☐ G-TOPS	Aérospatiale AS355F1 Ecureuil 2	5151	ex G-BPRH	

THOMAS COOK AIRLINES		Top Jet (MT/TCX)		Manchester (MAN)
☐ G-CRPH	Airbus A320-231	0424	ex C-GJUU	
☐ G-DHJZ	Airbus A320-214	1965	ex C-FOJZ	
☐ G-DHRG	Airbus A320-214	1942	ex C-GHRG	>SSV
☐ G-FTDF	Airbus A320-231	0437	ex C-FTDF	<SSV
☐ G-GTDL	Airbus A320-231	0476	ex C-GTDL	
☐ G-KKAZ	Airbus A320-214	2003	ex C-FZAZ	
☐ G-OMYA	Airbus A320-214	0716	ex G-BXKB	
☐ G-SUEW	Airbus A320-214	1961	ex C-GUEW	
☐ G-TCAC	Airbus A320-232	1411	ex C-FRAA	
☐ G-TCAD	Airbus A320-214	2114	ex EC-JDO	
☐ G-DHJH	Airbus A321-211	1238	ex D-AVZL	
☐ G-NIKO	Airbus A321-211	1250	ex D-AVZF	
☐ G-OMYJ	Airbus A321-211	0677	ex G-OOAF	
☐ G-TCDA	Airbus A321-211	2060	ex TC-JMG	
☐ G-MDBD	Airbus A330-243	266	ex F-WWKG	
☐ G-MLJL	Airbus A330-243	254	ex F-WWKT	
☐ G-OJMB	Airbus A330-243	427	ex F-WWYH	
☐ G-OJMC	Airbus A330-243	456	ex F-WWKI	
☐ G-OMYT	Airbus A330-243	301	ex G-MOJO	
☐ G-TCXA	Airbus A330-243	795	ex F-WWKR	
☐ G-FCLA	Boeing 757-28A	27621/738	ex N1789B	
☐ G-FCLB	Boeing 757-28A	28164/749	ex N751NA	
☐ G-FCLC	Boeing 757-28A	28166/756		
☐ G-FCLD	Boeing 757-25F	28718/752	ex C-FULD	
☐ G-FCLE	Boeing 757-28A	28171/805		
☐ G-FCLF	Boeing 757-28A	28835/858	ex N1787B	
☐ G-FCLH	Boeing 757-28A	26274/676	ex N751LF	
☐ G-FCLI	Boeing 757-28A	26275/672	ex N161LF	
☐ G-FCLJ	Boeing 757-2Y0	26160/555	ex N160GE	
☐ G-FCLK	Boeing 757-2Y0	26161/557	ex EI-CJY	
☐ G-JMAA	Boeing 757-3CQ	32241/960	ex N5002K	
☐ G-JMAB	Boeing 757-3CQ	32242/963	ex N1795B	
☐ G-JMCD	Boeing 757-25F	30757/928	ex C-FCLD	
☐ G-JMCE	Boeing 757-25F	30758/932	ex XA-JPB	
☐ G-JMCG	Boeing 757-2G5	26278/671	ex SX-BLV	
☐ G-TCBA	Boeing 757-28AER	28203/802	ex G-OOOY	
☐ G-TCBB	Boeing 757-236	29945/873	ex N945BB	♦
☐ G-WJAN	Boeing 757-21K	28674/746	ex C-FFAN	
☐ G-DAJC	Boeing 767-31KER/W	27206/533	ex C-GJJC	
☐ G-TCCA	Boeing 767-31KER/W	27205/528	ex G-SJMC	♦
☐ G-TCCB	Boeing 767-31KER/W	28865/657	ex G-DIMB	♦

THOMSONFLY.COM		Thomson (BY/TOM)	London-Luton/Coventry (LTN/CVT)	
☐ G-OOAR	Airbus A320-214	1320	ex F-WWDT	
☐ G-OOPP	Airbus A320-214	1571	ex C-GTDG	
☐ G-OOPT	Airbus A320-214	1605	ex C-GTDH	
☐ G-OOPU	Airbus A320-214	1637	ex G-OOAU	
☐ G-OOPX	Airbus A320-214	2180	ex G-OOAX	
☐ G-OOPE	Airbus A321-211	0852	ex G-OOAE	
☐ G-OOPH	Airbus A321-211	0781	ex G-OOAH	
☐ G-THOL	Boeing 737-36N	28594/3107	ex G-IGOK	
☐ G-THON	Boeing 737-36N	28596/3112	ex G-IGOL	
☐ G-THOO	Boeing 737-33V	29335/3094	ex HA-LKT	
☐ G-THOP	Boeing 737-3U3	28740/3003	ex N335AW	
☐ G-CDZH	Boeing 737-804	28227/452	ex SE-DZH	
☐ G-CDZI	Boeing 737-804	28229/478	ex SE-DZI	
☐ G-CDZL	Boeing 737-804	30465/502	ex D-ATUA	
☐ G-CDZM	Boeing 737-804	30466/505	ex D-ATUB	
☐ G-FDZA	Boeing 737-8K5/W	35134/2152		
☐ G-FDZB	Boeing 737-8K5/W	35131/2242	r	
☐ G-FDZD	Boeing 737-8K5/W	35132/2276		
☐ G-FDZE	Boeing 737-8K5/W	35137/2482	ex N1786B	
☐ G-FDZF	Boeing 737-8K5/W	35138/2499	ex N1786B	
☐ G-FDZG	Boeing 737-8K5/W	35139/2538		
☐ G-FDZJ	Boeing 737-8K5/W	34690/2184	ex D-ATUI	<HLX
☐ G-FDZR	Boeing 737-8K5/W	35145/2849	ex N1786B	
☐ G-FDZS	Boeing 737-8K5/W	35147/2866	ex N1786B	
☐ G-FDZT	Boeing 737-8K5/W	37248/3532		o/o♦
☐ G-FDZU	Boeing 737-8K5/W			o/o♦
☐ G-FDZW	Boeing 737-8K5/W			o/o♦
☐ G-FDZX	Boeing 737-8K5/W			o/o♦
☐ G-FDZY	Boeing 737-8K5/W			o/o♦
☐ G-FDZZ	Boeing 737-8K5/W			o/o♦
☐ G-BYAI	Boeing 757-204	26967/522		
☐ G-BYAL	Boeing 757-204	25626/549		
☐ G-BYAO	Boeing 757-204	27235/598	Eric Morecombe	
☐ G-BYAP	Boeing 757-204	27236/600	John Lennon	
☐ G-BYAT	Boeing 757-204	27208/606	Becky Davey	
☐ G-BYAU	Boeing 757-204	27220/618		
☐ G-BYAW	Boeing 757-204	27234/663	Philip Stanley	
☐ G-BYAX	Boeing 757-204/W	28834/850		
☐ G-BYAY	Boeing 757-204/W	28836/861	ex N1786B	
☐ G-CPEP	Boeing 757-2Y0	25268/400	ex C-GTSU	
☐ G-CPEU	Boeing 757-236/W	29941/864	ex C-FLEU	
☐ G-CPEV	Boeing 757-236/W	29943/871	ex C-GOEV	
☐ G-OOBA	Boeing 757-28A/W	32446/950	ex C-GUBA	
☐ G-OOBB	Boeing 757-28A/W	32447/951	ex C-GTBB	
☐ G-OOBC	Boeing 757-28A/W	33098/1026		♦
☐ G-OOBD	Boeing 757-28A/W	33099/1028		
☐ G-OOBE	Boeing 757-28A/W	33100/1029		
☐ G-OOBF	Boeing 757-28A/W	33101/1041		
☐ G-OOBG	Boeing 757-236/W	29942/867	ex C-FUBG	
☐ G-OOBH	Boeing 757-236/W	29944/872	ex C-FOBH	
☐ G-OOBI	Boeing 757-2B7	27146/551	ex N615AU	
☐ G-OOBJ	Boeing 757-2B7	27147/552	ex N616AU	
☐ G-OOBN	Boeing 757-2Q8ER	29379/919	ex HB-IHR	♦
☐ G-OOBP	Boeing 757-2Q8ER	30394/922	ex HB-IHS	♦
☐ G-OOOX	Boeing 757-2Y0ER	26158/526	ex C-FLOX	
☐ G-DBLA	Boeing 767-35EER/W	26063/434	ex B-16603	
☐ G-OOAN	Boeing 767-39HER/W	26256/484	ex G-UKLH	Caribbean Star	♦
☐ G-OOBK	Boeing 767-324ER/W	27392/568	ex VN-A762	
☐ G-OOBL	Boeing 767-324ER/W	27393/571	ex VN-A764	
☐ G-OOBM	Boeing 767-324ER/W	27568/593	ex VN-A765	
☐ G-OBYD	Boeing 767-304ER/W	28042/649	ex SE-DZG	Bill Travers
☐ G-OBYE	Boeing 767-304ER/W	28979/691	ex D-AGYE	
☐ G-OBYF	Boeing 767-304ER/W	28208/705	ex D-AGYF	
☐ G-OBYG	Boeing 767-304ER/W	29137/733		
☐ G-OBYH	Boeing 767-304ER/W	28883/737	ex SE-DZO	
☐ G-OBYJ	Boeing 767-304ER/W	29384/784		
☐ G-PJLO	Boeing 767-35EER	26064/438	ex B-16605	

TITAN AIRWAYS		Zap (ZT/AWC)		London-Stansted (STN)
☐ G-POWF	Avro 146-RJ100	E3373	ex G-CFAA	♦
☐ G-ZAPK	British Aerospace 146 Srs.200 (QC)	E2148	ex G-BTIA	
☐ G-ZAPN	British Aerospace 146 Srs.200 (QC)	E2119	ex ZK-NZC	
☐ G-ZAPO	British Aerospace 146 Srs.200 (QC)	E2176	ex F-GMMP	
☐ G-ZAPR	British Aerospace 146 Srs.200QT	E2114	ex VH-JJZ	
☐ G-POWC	Boeing 737-33A (QC)	25402/2159	ex SE-DPB	
☐ G-ZAPV	Boeing 737-3Y0 (SF)	24546/1811	ex G-IGOC	Royal Mail
☐ G-ZAPW	Boeing 737-3L9 (QC)	24219/1600	ex G-IGOX	Crystal Holidays
☐ G-ZAPZ	Boeing 737-33A (QC)	25401/2067	ex SE-DPA	
☐ G-ZAPX	Boeing 757-256	29309/936	ex EC-HIS	
☐ G-POWD	Boeing 767-36NER	30847/902	ex N308TL	
☐ G-POWB	Beech B300 Super King Air	FL-506	ex N7106L	
☐ G-WELY	Agusta A.109E Power	11710		

VIRGIN ATLANTIC AIRWAYS		Virgin (VS/VIR)		London-Gatwick/Heathrow (LGW/LHR)
☐ G-VGEM	Airbus A330-3	1215		o/o♦
☐ G-VINE	Airbus A330-3	1231		o/o♦
☐ G-VKSS	Airbus A330-3	1201		o/o♦
☐ G-VLUV	Airbus A330-3	1206		o/o♦
☐ G-VSXY	Airbus A330-3	1195		o/o♦
☐ G-VAIR	Airbus A340-313X	164	ex F-WWJA	Maiden Tokyo
☐ G-VELD	Airbus A340-313X	214	ex F-WWJY	African Queen
☐ G-VFAR	Airbus A340-313X	225	ex F-WWJZ	Diana
☐ G-VHOL	Airbus A340-311	002	ex F-WWAS	Jetstreamer
☐ G-VSEA	Airbus A340-311	003	ex F-WWDA	Plane Sailing
☐ G-VSUN	Airbus A340-313	114	ex F-WWJI	Rainbow Lady
☐ G-VATL	Airbus A340-642	376	ex F-WWCC	Miss Kitty
☐ G-VBLU	Airbus A340-642	723	ex F-WWCS	Soul Sister
☐ G-VBUG	Airbus A340-642HGW	804	ex F-WWCV	Lady Bird
☐ G-VEIL	Airbus A340-642	575	ex F-WWCK	Queen of the Skies
☐ G-VFIT	Airbus A340-642	753	ex F-WWCG	Dancing Queen
☐ G-VFIZ	Airbus A340-642	764	ex F-WWCB	Bubbles
☐ G-VFOX	Airbus A340-642	449	ex F-WWCM	Silver Lady
☐ G-VFUN	Airbus A340-642		ex F-WW	Party Girl	o/o
☐ G-VGAS	Airbus A340-642	639	ex F-WWCI	Varga Girl
☐ G-VGOA	Airbus A340-642	371	ex F-WWCB	Indian Princess
☐ G-VMEG	Airbus A340-642	391	ex F-WWCK	Mystic Maiden
☐ G-VNAP	Airbus A340-642	622	ex F-WWCE	Sleeping Beauty
☐ G-VOGE	Airbus A340-642	416	ex F-WWCF	Cover Girl
☐ G-VRED	Airbus A340-642	768	ex F-WWCH	Scarlet Lady
☐ G-VSHY	Airbus A340-642	383	ex F-WWCD	Madam Butterfly
☐ G-VSSH	Airbus A340-642	615	ex F-WWCZ	Sweet Dreamer
☐ G-VWEB	Airbus A340-642	787	ex F-WWCZ	Surfer Girl
☐ G-VWIN	Airbus A340-642	736	ex F-WWCL	Lady Luck
☐ G-VWKD	Airbus A340-642	706	ex F-WWCQ	Miss Behavin'
☐ G-VYOU	Airbus A340-642	765	ex F-WWCK	Emmeline Heansy
☐ G-VAST	Boeing 747-41R	28757/1117		Ladybird
☐ G-VBIG	Boeing 747-4Q8	26255/1081		Tinker Belle
☐ G-VFAB	Boeing 747-4Q8	24958/1028		Lady Penelope
☐ G-VGAL	Boeing 747-443	32337/1272	ex (EI-CVH)	Jersey Girl
☐ G-VHOT	Boeing 747-4Q8	26326/1043		Tubular Belle
☐ G-VLIP	Boeing 747-443	32338/1274	ex (EI-CVI)	Hot Lips
☐ G-VROC	Boeing 747-41R	32746/1336		Mustang Sally
☐ G-VROS	Boeing 747-443	30885/1268	ex (EI-CVG)	English Rose
☐ G-VROY	Boeing 747-443	32340/1277	ex (EI-CVK)	Pretty Woman
☐ G-VTOP	Boeing 747-4Q8	28194/1100		Virginia Plain
☐ G-VWOW	Boeing 747-41R	32745/1287		Cosmic Girl
☐ G-VXLG	Boeing 747-41R	29406/1177		Ruby Tuesday

WEST ATLANTIC		Neptune (NPT)		Coventry (CVT)
☐ G-BTPA	British Aerospace ATP (LFD)	2007	ex EC-HGC	
☐ G-BTPE	British Aerospace ATP (LFD)	2012	ex EC-HGE	
☐ G-BTPF	British Aerospace ATP (LFD)	2013	ex EC-HCY	
☐ G-BTPG	British Aerospace ATP (LFD)	2014	ex (G-JEMF)	[CVT]
☐ G-BTPH	British Aerospace ATP (LFD)	2015	ex (G-JEMH)	
☐ G-BTPJ	British Aerospace ATP (LFD)	2016	ex EC-HFR	[CVT]
☐ G-BTPL	British Aerospace ATP	2042	ex EC-HES	[CVT]

☐ G-BTTO	British Aerospace ATP (LFD)	2033	ex EC-HNA	
☐ G-BUUP	British Aerospace ATP (LFD)	2008	ex G-MANU	
☐ G-BUUR	British Aerospace ATP (LFD)	2024	ex EC-GUX	
☐ G-MANC	British Aerospace ATP	2054	ex VT-FFA	[CVT]
☐ G-MANH	British Aerospace ATP (LFD)	2017	ex G-LOGC	
☐ G-OAAF	British Aerospace ATP	2029	ex G-JEMB	
☐ G-OBWP	British Aerospace ATP	2051	ex VT-FFC	[CVT]
☐ G-FIZU	Lockheed L-188CF Electra	2014	ex EI-CHY	
☐ G-LOFC	Lockheed L-188CF Electra	1100	ex N665F	
☐ G-LOFE	Lockheed L-188CF Electra	1144	ex EI-CET	
☐ G-JMCL	Boeing 737-322F	23951/1532	ex D-AGEA	

WOODGATE EXECUTIVE AIR SERVICES — Woodair (CWY) — Belfast-Aldergrove (BFS)

☐ G-JAJK	Piper PA-31-350 Chieftain	31-8152014	ex G-OLDB	

HA-   HUNGARY (Hungarian Republic)

ABC AIR HUNGARY — ABC Hungary (AHU) — Budapest (BUD)

☐ HA-LAD	LET L-410UVP-E	902516		
☐ HA-LAS	LET L-410UVP-E4	871924	ex 9A-BAL	
☐ HA-LAZ	LET L-410UVP-E	902504	ex SP-KTZ	<BPS

ATLANT HUNGARY — Atlant-Hungary (ATU) — Budapest (BUD)

☐ HA-TCK	Ilyushin Il-76TD	1023409280	ex T-902	

BUDAPEST AIR SERVICES — Base (BPS) — Budapest (BUD)

☐ HA-FAI	Embraer EMB.120ER Brasilia	120123	ex F-GTSI	
☐ HA-FAL	Embraer EMB.120RT Brasilia	120176	ex F-GTSJ	
☐ HA-FAN	Embraer EMB.120ER Brasilia	120104	ex F-GTSH	
☐ HA-LAF	LET L-410UVP-E8A	902518		Flight Inspection Services
☐ HA-LAV	LET L-410UVP-E	892215	ex SP-KTA	>AHU
☐ HA-LAZ	LET L-410UVP-E	902504	ex SP-KTZ no titles	>AHU
☐ HA-TCT	Antonov An-26B	13505	ex UR-ELA	
☐ HA-TCY	Antonov An-26B	97308205	ex ER-AZR	<MJL
☐ HA-YFD	LET L-410UVP-E17	892324	Op for Hungarian Air Ambulance	

CITYLINE HUNGARY — Cityhun (ZM/CNB) — Budapest (BUD)

☐ HA-TCM	Antonov An-26	14009	ex UR-ELI	
☐ HA-TCN	Antonov An-26	7705	ex UR-26244 for sale	
☐ HA-TCO	Antonov An-26	2208	ex UR-CEP	<Hegedus

FARNAIR HUNGARY — Blue Strip (FAH) — Budapest (BUD)

☐ HA-FAD	Fokker F.27 Friendship 500	10449	ex PH-JLN	
☐ HA-FAF	Fokker F.27 Friendship 500F	10632	ex PH-FYC	
☐ HA-FAH	Fokker F.27 Friendship 500F	10634	ex PH-FHL	
☐ HA-FAJ	Beech 1900C-1	UC-79	ex A6-FCE	
☐ HA-FAM	Beech 1900D	UE-16	ex N16UE	
☐ HA-LAQ	LET L-410UVP-E4	841332	ex HAF-332	based UK for skydiving
☐ HA-YFC	LET L-410FG	851528		based UK for skydiving

FLEET AIR INTERNATIONAL

☐ HA-TAB	SAAB SF.340A	340A-083	ex EC-IUP	
☐ HA-TAD	SAAB SF.340A	340A-126	ex SE-LSP	

HEGEDUS

☐ HA-TCO	Antonov An-26	2208	ex UR-CEP	>CNB

MALEV – HUNGARIAN AIRLINES — Malev (MA/MAH) — Budapest (BUD)

Member of Oneworld

☐ HA-LOA	Boeing 737-7Q8	28254/1283	
☐ HA-LOB	Boeing 737-7Q8	29346/1264	ex N5573L
☐ HA-LOC	Boeing 737-8Q8	32797/1287	
☐ HA-LOD	Boeing 737-6Q8	28259/1378	
☐ HA-LOE	Boeing 737-6Q8	28260/1400	
☐ HA-LOF	Boeing 737-6Q8	29348/1415	
☐ HA-LOG	Boeing 737-6Q8	28261/1437	

☐ HA-LOH	Boeing 737-8Q8	30667/1448		
☐ HA-LOI	Boeing 737-7Q8	29350/1452		
☐ HA-LOJ	Boeing 737-6Q8	29349/1455		
☐ HA-LOK	Boeing 737-8Q8	30669/1479		
☐ HA-LOL	Boeing 737-7Q8	29352/1491		
☐ HA-LOM	Boeing 737-8Q8	30672/1497	Charter Services	
☐ HA-LON	Boeing 737-6Q8	29353/1508		
☐ HA-LOP	Boeing 737-7Q8	29354/1581		
☐ HA-LOR	Boeing 737-7Q8	29355/1609		
☐ HA-LOS	Boeing 737-7Q8	29359/1659		
☐ HA-LOU	Boeing 737-8Q8	30684/1689	ex (HA-LOT)	
☐ HA-LHB	Boeing 767-27GER	27049/482	ex N60668	[BUD]
☐ HA-LNA	Canadair CRJ-200ER	7676	ex C-FMKZ	[BUD]
☐ HA-LQA	de Havilland DHC-8-402Q	4054	ex OY-KCD	
☐ HA-LQB	de Havilland DHC-8-402Q	4057	ex OY-KCE	
☐ HA-LQC	de Havilland DHC-8-402Q	4062	ex OY-KCF	
☐ HA-LQD	de Havilland DHC-8-402Q	4063	ex OY-KCG	

TRAVEL SERVICE HUNGARY — Traveller (TVL) — Budapest (BUD)

☐ HA-LKB	Boeing 737-86Q/W	30294/1469	ex OK-TVI
☐ HA-LKE	Boeing 737-86Q/W	30278/963	ex OK-TVC

WIZZ AIR — (W6/WZZ) — Budapest (BUD)

☐ HA-LPA	Airbus A320-233	0839	ex EI-DFV	
☐ HA-LPB	Airbus A320-233	1635	ex EI-DFT	
☐ HA-LPC	Airbus A320-233	0892	ex EI-DGF	
☐ HA-LPD	Airbus A320-233	1902	ex EI-DGB	
☐ HA-LPE	Airbus A320-233	1892	ex EI-DFU	
☐ HA-LPF	Airbus A320-233	1834	ex EI-DGC	
☐ HA-LPH	Airbus A320-232	2688	ex F-WWIE	
☐ HA-LPI	Airbus A320-232	2752	ex F-WWDE	
☐ HA-LPJ	Airbus A320-232	3127	ex F-WWBH	
☐ HA-LPK	Airbus A320-232	3143	ex F-WWBI	
☐ HA-LPL	Airbus A320-232	3166	ex F-WWIL	
☐ HA-LPM	Airbus A320-232	3177	ex F-WWDG	
☐ HA-LPN	Airbus A320-232	3354	ex F-WWIG	
☐ HA-LPO	Airbus A320-232	3384	ex F-WWDO	
☐ HA-LPQ	Airbus A320-232	3409	ex F-WWIC	
☐ HA-LPR	Airbus A320-232	3430	ex F-WWBC	
☐ HA-LPS	Airbus A320-232	3771	ex F-WWDS	
☐ HA-LPT	Airbus A320-232	3807	ex F-WWDR	
☐ HA-LPU	Airbus A320-232	3877	ex F-WWIJ	
☐ HA-LPV	Airbus A320-232	3927	ex F-WWBR	
☐ HA-LPW	Airbus A320-232	3947	ex F-WWBD	
☐ HA-LPX	Airbus A320-232	3968	ex F-WWIN	
☐ HA-LPY	Airbus A320-232	4109	ex D-AVVS	
☐ HA-LPZ	Airbus A320-232	4174	ex F-WWDU	
☐ HA-LWA	Airbus A320-232	4223	ex F-WWBI	♦
☐ HA-LWB	Airbus A320-232	4246	ex F-WWDR	♦
☐ HA-LWC	Airbus A320-232	4323	ex F-WWDT	♦
☐ HA-LWD	Airbus A320-232	4351	ex F-WWBZ	♦
☐ HA-LWE	Airbus A320-232	4372	ex F-WWBM	♦
☐ HA-	Airbus A320-232		ex	o/o♦
☐ HA-	Airbus A320-232		ex	o/o♦
☐ HA-	Airbus A320-232		ex	o/o♦
☐ HA-	Airbus A320-232		ex	o/o♦
☐ HA-	Airbus A320-232		ex	o/o♦
☐ HA-	Airbus A320-232		ex	o/o♦

HB-   SWITZERLAND & LIECHSTENSTEIN (Swiss Confederation)

AIR ENGIADINA — St Moritz

☐ HB-AEU	Dornier 328-310 (328JET)	3199	ex OE-HCM	Lsd fr/op by Swiss Jet

AIR GLACIERS — Air Glaciers (7T/AGV) — Sion (SIR)

☐ HB-CGW	Cessna U206G Stationair 6	U20604822	ex D-ELML
☐ HB-FCT	Pilatus PC-6/B2-H2 Turbo Porter	637	
☐ HB-FDU	Pilatus PC-6/B1-H2 Turbo Porter	663	
☐ HB-FFW	Pilatus PC-6/B2-H2 Turbo Porter	735	
☐ HB-GIL	Beech 200 Super King Air	BB-194	ex N502EB
☐ HB-GJI	Beech 200 Super King Air	BB-451	ex D-IBOW

☐ HB-GJM	Beech 200 Super King Air	BB-255	ex N32KD	
☐ HB-ZCZ	Aérospatiale AS350B3 Ecureuil	3434	ex F-WQDG	
☐ HB-ZEP	Eurocopter EC120B Colibri	1336	ex F-WWPO	
☐ HB-ZFB	Eurocopter EC130B4	3536	ex F-GNLD	

AIR ZERMATT — Air Zermatt (AZF) — Zermatt Heliport

☐ HB-XSU	Aérospatiale AS350B2 Ecureuil	2115		
☐ HB-ZCC	Aérospatiale AS350B2 Ecureuil	2107	ex I-REGL	
☐ HB-ZCX	Aérospatiale AS350B2 Ecureuil	3105	ex I-AOLA	
☐ HB-ZEF	Eurocopter EC135T2	0259	ex D-HECA	

BABOO — Baboo (F7/BBO) — Geneva (GVA)

☐ HB-JQA	de Havilland DHC-8-402Q	4017	ex C-FJJG	
☐ HB-JQB	de Havilland DHC-8-402Q	4175	ex C-FMKK	

BELAIR AIRLINES — Belair (4T/BHP) — Zurich (ZRH)

☐ HB-IOX	Airbus A319-112	3604	ex D-ABGM	
☐ HB-IOY	Airbus A319-112	3202	ex D-ABGG	♦
☐ HB-IOP	Airbus A320-214	4187	ex D-AVVY	♦
☐ HB-IOQ	Airbus A320-214	3422	ex D-ABDT	♦
☐ HB-IOR	Airbus A320-214	4033	ex D-ABDZ	
☐ HB-IOS	Airbus A320-214	2968	ex D-ABDK	
☐ HB-IOT	Airbus A320-214	2991	ex D-ABDL	
☐ HB-IOU	Airbus A320-214	3006	ex D-ABDM	
☐ HB-IOW	Airbus A320-214	3055	ex D-ABDO	
☐ HB-IOZ	Airbus A320-214	4294	ex D-ABFH	♦

DARWIN AIRLINE — Darwin (0D/DWT) — Geneva (GVA)

☐ HB-IYD	SAAB 2000	2000-059	ex VP-BPP	
☐ HB-IZG	SAAB 2000	2000-010	ex SE-010	Insubria
☐ HB-IZH	SAAB 2000	2000-011	ex SE-011	Ticino
☐ HB-IZJ	SAAB 2000	2000-015	ex (F-GOZJ)	Verbano
☐ HB-IZZ	SAAB 2000	2000-048	ex SE-048	Ceresio

EASYJET SWITZERLAND — Topswiss (DS/EZS) — Geneva (GVA)

☐ HB-JZF	Airbus A319-111	2184	ex G-EZEH	<EZY
☐ HB-JZG	Airbus A319-111	2196	ex G-EZEI	<EZY
☐ HB-JZH	Airbus A319-111	2230	ex G-EZEM	<EZY
☐ HB-JZI	Airbus A319-111	2245	ex G-EZEN	<EZY
☐ HB-JZJ	Airbus A319-111	2265	ex G-EZES	<EZY
☐ HB-JZK	Airbus A319-111	2319	ex G-EZEX	<EZY
☐ HB-JZL	Airbus A319-111	2353	ex G-EZEY	<EZY
☐ HB-JZM	Airbus A319-111	2370	ex G-EZMK	<EZY
☐ HB-JZN	Airbus A319-111	2387	ex G-EZBS	<EZY
☐ HB-JZO	Airbus A319-111	2398	ex G-HMCC	<EZY
☐ HB-JZP	Airbus A319-111	2427	ex G-EZIB	<EZY
☐ HB-JZQ	Airbus A319-111	2450	ex G-EZIF	<EZY
☐ HB-JZR	Airbus A320-214	4034	ex G-EZTO	<EZY
☐ HB-JZS	Airbus A319-111	3084	ex G-EZBP	<EZY
☐ HB-JZU	Airbus A319-111	2402	ex G-EZNM	<EZY♦
☐ HB-JZV	Airbus A319-111	2709	ex G-EZAE	<EZY♦
☐ HB-JZW	Airbus A319-111	2729	ex G-EZAH	<EZY♦

EDELWEISS AIR — Edelweiss (WK/EDW) — Zurich (ZRH)

☐ HB-IHX	Airbus A320-214	0942	ex F-WWIU	Calvaro	<Alp Air
☐ HB-IHY	Airbus A320-214	0947	ex F-WWIY	Upali	<Alp Air
☐ HB-IHZ	Airbus A320-214	1026	ex F-WWDD	Viktoria	

FARNAIR SWITZERLAND — Farner (FAT) — Basle (BSL)

☐ HB-AFC	ATR 42-320F	087	ex F-WQLF	
☐ HB-AFD	ATR 42-320	121	ex F-WQNA	
☐ HB-AFF	ATR 42-320	264	ex F-GOBK	
☐ HB-AFG	ATR 72-201F	108	ex F-WQNA	
☐ HB-AFH	ATR 72-202F	313	ex F-GJKP	
☐ HB-AFJ	ATR 72-202F	154	ex OY-RTE	
☐ HB-AFK	ATR 72-202F	232	ex F-GKOB	
☐ HB-AFL	ATR 72-202F	222	ex F-GKPF	
☐ HB-AFM	ATR 72-202F	364	ex B-22712	
☐ HB-AFN	ATR 72-202F	389	ex B-22716	

☐ HB-AFP	ATR 72-201F	381	ex B-22715	
☐ HB-AFR	ATR 72-201F	195	ex F-WKVC	
☐ HB-AFS	ATR 72-201F	198	ex F-WKVJ	
☐ HB-AFV	ATR 72-201F	341	ex F-WKVJ	♦
☐ HB-AFW	ATR 72-201F	419	ex F-WNUD	♦

HELISWISS		*Heliswiss (HSI)*		*Bern (BRN)*
☐ HB-XKE	Kamov Ka-32A	8709/02	ex RA-31587	
☐ HB-ZFX	Kamov Ka-32A12	8809/09	ex RA-31599	

HELLO		*Fly Hello (HW/FHE)*		*Basle (BSL)*
☐ HB-JIY	Airbus A320-214	1171	ex RP-C3230	♦
☐ HB-JIZ	Airbus A320-214	0936	ex RP-C3229	♦
☐ HB-JID	McDonnell-Douglas MD-90-30	53460/2142	ex OY-KIM	
☐ HB-JIE	McDonnell-Douglas MD-90-30	53461/2147	ex SE-DMG	
☐ HB-JIF	McDonnell-Douglas MD-90-30	53462/2149	ex LN-ROB	

HELOG		*Helog (HLG)*		*Küssnacht*
☐ HB-XVY	Aérospatiale AS.332C	2033	ex N5795P	Op for UN

HELVETIC AIRWAYS		*Helvetic (2L/OAW)*		*Zurich (ZRH)*
☐ HB-JVC	Fokker 100	11501	ex N1468A	
☐ HB-JVE	Fokker 100	11459	ex N1450A	
☐ HB-JVF	Fokker 100	11466	ex N1454D	
☐ HB-JVG	Fokker 100	11478	ex N1458H	
☐ HB-JVH	Fokker 100	11324	ex F-GPNK	♦
☐ HB-JVI	Fokker 100	11325	ex F-GPNL	♦

PRIVATAIR		*PrivatAir (PTI)*		*Geneva (GVA)*
☐ D-APBB	Boeing 737-8Q8/W	35278/2625	ex N812SY	
☐ HB-IEE	Boeing 757-23A/W	24527/249	ex HB-IHU	
☐ HB-IIQ	Boeing 737-7CN/W	30752/451	ex N1026G	[BBJ] [AMM]
☐ HB-IIR	Boeing 737-86Q/W	30295/1600		
☐ HB-JJA	Boeing 737-7AK/W	34303/1758	ex N1780B	[BBJ] >KLM
☐ HB-JJG	Boeing 767-306ER	30393/781	ex PH-BZO	

SKYWORK AIRLINES		*Skyfox (SRK)*		*Bern (BRP)*
☐ HB-AES	Dornier 328-110	3021	ex D-CHIC	
☐ HB-JGA	de Havilland DHC-8-402Q	4198	ex C-FOKB	

SWISS EUROPEAN AIR LINES		*Euroswiss (SWU)*		
		Basle, Lugano, Geneva, Zurich (BSL/LUG/GVA/ZRH)		
☐ HB-IXN	Avro 146-RJ100	E3286	ex G-6-286	Balmhorn
☐ HB-IXO	Avro 146-RJ100	E3284	ex G-6-284	Brisen
☐ HB-IXP	Avro 146-RJ100	E3283	ex G-6-283	Chestenberg
☐ HB-IXQ	Avro 146-RJ100	E3282	ex G-6-282	Corno Gries
☐ HB-IXR	Avro 146-RJ100	E3281	ex G-6-281	Hohe Winde
☐ HB-IXS	Avro 146-RJ100	E3280	ex G-6-280	Mont Velan
☐ HB-IXT	Avro 146-RJ100	E3259	ex G-BVYS	Ottenberg
☐ HB-IXU	Avro 146-RJ100	E3276	ex G-6-276	Pfannenstiel
☐ HB-IXV	Avro 146-RJ100	E3274	ex G-6-274	Saxer First
☐ HB-IXW	Avro 146-RJ100	E3272	ex G-6-272	Schafarnisch
☐ HB-IXX	Avro 146-RJ100	E3262	ex G-6-262	Siberen
☐ HB-IYQ	Avro 146-RJ100	E3384	ex G-CFAH	Piz Bruin
☐ HB-IYR	Avro 146-RJ100	E3382	ex G-CFAF	Vrenelisgärtli
☐ HB-IYS	Avro 146-RJ100	E3381	ex G-CFAE	Churfirstenspecial c/s
☐ HB-IYT	Avro 146-RJ100	E3380	ex G-CFAD	Bluemlisalp
☐ HB-IYU	Avro 146-RJ100	E3379	ex G-CFAC	Rot TurmStar Alliance c/s
☐ HB-IYV	Avro 146-RJ100	E3377	ex G-CFAB	Pizzo BaroneStar Alliance c/s
☐ HB-IYW	Avro 146-RJ100	E3359	ex G-6-359	Spitzmeilen
☐ HB-IYY	Avro 146-RJ100	E3339	ex G-6-339	Titlis
☐ HB-IYZ	Avro 146-RJ100	E3338	ex G-6-338	Tour d'Ai

SWISS INTERNATIONAL AIRLINES		*Swiss (LX/SWR)*		*Zurich (ZRH)*

Member of Star Alliance

☐ HB-IPR	Airbus A319-112	1018	ex D-AVYQ	Piz Morteratsch
☐ HB-IPS	Airbus A319-112	0734	ex D-AVYZ	Clariden
☐ HB-IPT	Airbus A319-112	0727	ex D-AVYC	Rotsandnollen
☐ HB-IPU	Airbus A319-112	0713	ex D-AVYB	Schrattenflue

☐ HB-IPV	Airbus A319-112	0578	ex D-AVYA	Castelegns		
☐ HB-IPX	Airbus A319-112	0612	ex D-AVYH	Mont Racine		
☐ HB-IPY	Airbus A319-112	0621	ex D-AVYK	Les Ordons		
☐ HB-IJB	Airbus A320-214	0545	ex TC-JLA			
☐ HB-IJD	Airbus A320-214	0553	ex TC-JLH			
☐ HB-IJE	Airbus A320-214	0559	ex TC-JLI	Arosa		
☐ HB-IJF	Airbus A320-214	0562	ex TC-JLB			
☐ HB-IJH	Airbus A320-214	0574	ex TC-JLD			
☐ HB-IJI	Airbus A320-214	0577	ex F-WWDT	Basodino		
☐ HB-IJJ	Airbus A320-214	0585	ex F-WWIV	Les Diablerets		
☐ HB-IJK	Airbus A320-214	0596	ex F-WWBH	Wissigstock		
☐ HB-IJL	Airbus A320-214	0603	ex F-WWBK	Pizol		
☐ HB-IJM	Airbus A320-214	0635	ex F-WWDD	Schilthorn		
☐ HB-IJN	Airbus A320-214	0643	ex F-WWDI	Vanil Noir		
☐ HB-IJO	Airbus A320-214	0673	ex F-WWBF	Lisengrat		
☐ HB-IJP	Airbus A320-214	0681	ex F-WWBH	Nollen		
☐ HB-IJQ	Airbus A320-214	0701	ex F-WWDL	Locarno		
☐ HB-IJR	Airbus A320-214	0703	ex F-WWDS	Dammastock		
☐ HB-IJS	Airbus A320-214	0782	ex F-WWDS	Creux du Van		
☐ HB-IJU	Airbus A320-214	1951	ex F-WWIQ	Bietschhorn		
☐ HB-IJV	Airbus A320-214	2024	ex F-WWDK	Wildspitz		
☐ HB-IJW	Airbus A320-214	2134	ex F-WWBO	Bachtel		
☐ HB-IJX	Airbus A320-214	1762	ex D-ALTG	Davos		
☐ HB-	Airbus A320-214		ex		o/o♦	
☐ HB-	Airbus A320-214		ex		o/o♦	
☐ HB-IOC	Airbus A321-111	0520	ex D-AVZV	Eiger		
☐ HB-IOD	Airbus A321-111	0522	ex TC-JMA			
☐ HB-IOF	Airbus A321-111	0541	ex TC-JMB			
☐ HB-IOH	Airbus A321-111	0664	ex D-AVZL	Pitz Palu		
☐ HB-IOK	Airbus A321-111	0987	ex D-AVZC	Biefertenstock		
☐ HB-IOL	Airbus A321-111	1144	ex D-AVZE	Kaiseregg		
☐ HB-IOM	Airbus A321-212	4534	ex D-AVZL		♦	
☐ HB-IQA	Airbus A330-223	229	ex F-WWKS	Lauteraarhorn		
☐ HB-IQC	Airbus A330-223	249	ex F-WWKI	Breithorn		
☐ HB-IQH	Airbus A330-223	288	ex F-WWKX	Allainhorn		
☐ HB-IQI	Airbus A330-223	291	ex F-WWKS	Piz Bernina		
☐ HB-IQQ	Airbus A330-223	322	ex D-AIMD	Bern		
☐ HB-JHA	Airbus A330-343E	1000	ex F-WWYX	Schwyz		
☐ HB-JHB	Airbus A330-343E	1018	ex F-WWYJ	Sion		
☐ HB-JHC	Airbus A330-343E	1029	ex F-WWYY	Bellinzona		
☐ HB-JHD	Airbus A330-343E	1026	ex F-WWKE	St. Gallen		
☐ HB-JHE	Airbus A330-343E	1084	ex F-WWKE	Fribourg		
☐ HB-JHF	Airbus A330-343E	1089	ex F-WWKI	Bern		♦
☐ HB-JHG	Airbus A330-343E	1101	ex F-WWYI	Glarus		♦
☐ HB-JHH	Airbus A330-343E	1145	ex F-WWYD	Neuchatel		♦
☐ HB-JHI	Airbus A330-343E	1181	ex F-WWKM			♦
☐ HB-JHJ	Airbus A330-343E	1188	ex F-WWYQ			♦
☐ HB-	Airbus A330-343E		ex		o/o♦	
☐ HB-JMA	Airbus A340-313X	538	ex F-WWJJ	Matterhorn		
☐ HB-JMB	Airbus A340-313X	545	ex F-WWJL	Zurich		
☐ HB-JMC	Airbus A340-313X	546	ex F-WWJM	Basel		
☐ HB-JMD	Airbus A340-313X	556	ex F-WWJN	Liestal		
☐ HB-JME	Airbus A340-313X	559	ex F-WWJP	Dom		
☐ HB-JMF	Airbus A340-313X	561	ex F-WWJQ	Liskamm		
☐ HB-JMG	Airbus A340-313X	562	ex F-WWJR	Luzern		
☐ HB-JMH	Airbus A340-313E	585	ex F-WWJV	Chur		
☐ HB-JMI	Airbus A340-313E	598	ex F-WWJX	Schaffhausen		
☐ HB-JMJ	Airbus A340-313X	150	ex C-FYKX	City of Basel		
☐ HB-JMK	Airbus A340-313X	169	ex OE-LAK			
☐ HB-JML	Airbus A340-313X	263	ex OE-LAL		<AUA	
☐ HB-JMM	Airbus A340-313X	154	ex C-FYKZ			
☐ HB-JMN	Airbus A340-313X	175	ex C-FYLG			
☐ HB-JMO	Airbus A340-313X	179	ex C-FYLU			
☐ HB-IIR	Boeing 737-86Q/W	1600/30295			<PTI	
☐ D-AGPK	Fokker 100	11313	ex PH-CXK		<KIS	

ZIMEX AVIATION		*Zimex (C4/IMX)*			*Zurich (ZRH)*
☐ HB-LOK	de Havilland DHC-6 Twin Otter 300	658	ex D-IASL		
☐ HB-LQV	de Havilland DHC-6 Twin Otter 300	643	ex 5Y-LQV		
☐ HB-LRO	de Havilland DHC-6 Twin Otter 300	523	ex F-GKTO		
☐ HB-LRR	de Havilland DHC-6 Twin Otter 300	505	ex 5Y-KZT		

☐ HB-LTG	de Havilland DHC-6 Twin Otter 300	628	ex D-IFLY		
☐ HB-LTR	de Havilland DHC-6 Twin Otter 300	238	ex C-GHTO		
☐ HB-LUC	de Havilland DHC-6 Twin Otter 300	351	ex N353PM		
☐ HB-LUE	de Havilland DHC-6 Twin Otter 300	233	ex PK-LTX		
☐ HB-LUM	de Havilland DHC-6 Twin Otter 300	420	ex PK-TWG		
☐ ST-LRN	de Havilland DHC-6 Twin Otter 310	636	ex HB-LRN		
☐ HB-AEK	Beech 1900D	UE-296	ex D-CBCB		
☐ HB-AEL	Beech 1900D	UE-385	ex N839CA	<Arab Wings	
☐ HB-AEM	Beech 1900D	UE-379	ex F-HALS		
☐ HB-GJD	Beech 200C Super King Air	BL-7	ex F-GJBJ		
☐ HB-GJX	Beech B200 Super King Air	BB-932	ex SE-KKM		

HC- ECUADOR (Republic of Ecuador)

AEROGAL		Aerogal (2K/GLG)		Shell-Mera/Quito (-/UIO)
☐ HC-CKL	Airbus A319-112	1866	ex N866MX	◆
☐ HC-	Airbus A319-112		ex	o/o◆
☐ HC-	Airbus A319-112		ex	o/o◆
☐ HC-	Airbus A319-112		ex	o/o◆
☐ HC-	Airbus A319-112		ex	o/o◆
☐ HC-CJM	Airbus A320-214	4379	ex F-WWIF	◆
☐ HC-CJV	Airbus A320-214	4547	ex D-AUBP	◆
☐ HC-CJW	Airbus A320-214	4487	ex D-AUBG	◆
☐ HC-CDJ	Boeing 727-227	21246/1216	ex N14GA	Piquero
☐ HC-CED	Boeing 737-2B7 (Nordam 3)	22887/976	ex N275AU	
☐ HC-CEQ	Boeing 737-2Y5 (Nordam 3)	23848/1418	ex N342CA	Iguana
☐ HC-CER	Boeing 737-2Y5 (Nordam 3)	23847/1414	ex N341CA	
☐ HC-CFG	Boeing 737-281 (AvAero 3)	21770/588	ex N746AP	
☐ HC-CFH	Boeing 737-2T5 (Nordam 3)	22979/950	ex N120NJ	Nescafe titles
☐ HC-CFM	Boeing 737-244	22589/843	ex ZS-SIJ	
☐ HC-CFO	Boeing 737-2E3 (AvAero 3)	22703/811	ex N324JM	
☐ HC-CFR	Boeing 737-244	22581/796	ex ZS-SIB	
☐ HC-CHC	Boeing 757-236	25592/453	ex N521NA	
☐ HC-CIY	Boeing 757-2K2/W	26635/608	ex N635AV	◆
☐ HC-CIJ	Boeing 767-322ER	25287/449	ex N287AV	

AEROMASTER AIRWAYS				Quito (UIO)
☐ HC-BXT	Rockwell Commander 690C	11615	ex N811EC	
☐ HC-CBH	Bell 206L-1 LongRanger III	45354	ex N213HC	
☐ HC-CBT	Bell 427	56028	ex N40560	
☐ HC-CHG	Sikorsky S-64F Skycrane	64075	ex N722HT	◆
☐ HC-	de Havilland DHC-6 Twin Otter 200	120	ex N120AA	o/o [FLL]

AEROPACSA		Aeropacsa (RPC)		Guayaquil (GYE)
☐ HC-BDV	Cessna TU206F Turbo Stationair II	U20603439		
☐ HC-CBD	Dornier 28D-2 Skyservant	4182	ex HK-4004	
☐ HC-CDI	Dornier 28D-2 Skyservant	4152	ex 58+77	

AIR CUENCA				Cuenca (CUE)
☐ HC-CJB	Boeing 737-548	26287/2427	ex EI-CDS	◆

ATESA		Atesa (TXU)		Quito (UIO)
☐ HC-BLP	Cessna TU206G Turbo Stationair 6 II	U20606449	ex N9383Z	

ATUR		(TUR)		Quito (UIO)
☐ HC-BYL	Cessna TU206G Turbo Centurion	U20606628	ex N9727Z	Soloy conv

EMETEBE TAXI AEREO		Emetebe (EMT)		Puerto Baquerizo Moreno
☐ HC-BDX	Britten-Norman BN-2A-27 Islander	51	ex F-OGEB	
☐ HC-BNE	Piper PA-23-250 Aztec D	27-3959	ex N6742Y	
☐ HC-BZF	Britten-Norman BN-2A-27 Islander	200	ex F-BTGO	

ICARO EXPRESS		Icaro (X8/ICD)		Quito (UIO)
☐ HC-CDK	Aérospatiale AS350B Ecureuil	3001	ex N444LH	
☐ HC-CEC	Aérospatiale AS350B Ecureuil	3009	ex N483AE	

☐ HC-CFD	Boeing 737-236 (Stage 3)	21801/669	ex ZS-SIS		<SFR
☐ HC-CFL	Boeing 737-236	22026/644	ex ZS-SIU		<SFR
☐ HC-CFY	Boeing 737-290QC	22577/760	ex N730AS		
☐ HC-CJI	Boeing 737-205	22022/616	ex N771LS		♦

LAN ECUADOR — Aerolane (XL/LNE) — Quito (UIO)

☐ HC-CGZ	Boeing 767-3Q8ER/W	28206/694	ex CC-CML		
☐ HC-CHA	Boeing 767-316ER/W	27613/652	ex CC-CBJ		
☐ HC-CIZ	Boeing 767-316ER/W	36711/970	ex CC-CXF		♦
☐ HC-CJA	Boeing 767-316ER/W	35698/973	ex CC-CXH		♦
☐ HC-CJX	Boeing 767-316ER/W	35697/967	ex CC-CXD		♦

SAEREO — Saereo (SRO) — Quito (UIO)

☐ HC-BUD	Gulfstream Commander 6b-90C	11669	ex N844MA	
☐ HC-BVN	Beech 1900C	UB-53	ex N814BE	
☐ HC-BYH	Cessna T207A Stationair 8 II	20700749	ex N9905M	
☐ HC-BZO	Bell 407	53302	ex N8226A	
☐ HC-CBC	Beech 1900D	UE-17	ex N17YV	[UIO]
☐ HC-CDM	Embraer EMB.120ER Brasilia	120088	ex N193SW	
☐ HC-CEM	Embraer EMB.120ER Brasilia	120227	ex N198SW	

TAME — Tame (EQ/TAE) — Quito (UIO)

☐ HC-CGT	Airbus A319-132	2659	ex N511NK		
☐ HC-CGW	Airbus A320-233	2084	ex N487TA	Ciudad de Quito	
☐ HC-CDY	Airbus A320-233	2014	ex F-WWBT		
☐ HC-CGJ	Airbus A320-214	0657	ex F-GRSE		
☐ HC-CID	Airbus A320-232	0934	ex N934BV		
☐ HC-BHM	Boeing 727-2T3 (Raisbeck 3)	22078/1644	ex N1293E	Cotopaxi	Also FAE-078
☐ HC-BZS	Boeing 727-230 (Raisbeck 3)	21620/1419	ex TC-AFO	Imbabura	Also FAE-620
☐ HC-CEX	Embraer ERJ-170LR	17000087	ex PT-SZM	Francisco de Orellana	
☐ HC-CEY	Embraer ERJ-170LR	17000092	ex PT-SZS	Puerto Baquerizo Moreno	
☐ HC-CEZ	Embraer ERJ-190LR	19000027	ex PT-SGB	Ciudad de Cuenca	
☐ HC-CGF	Embraer ERJ-190LR	19000137	ex PT-SYQ	Ciudad de Loja	
☐ HC-CGG	Embraer ERJ-190LR	19000141	ex PT-SYT	Ciudad de Manta	
☐ HC-BZU	Fokker F.28 Fellowship 4000	11112	ex SE-DGE	Morona Santiago	Also FAE-112
☐ HC-CEH	Fokker F.28 Fellowship 4000	11228	ex N479AU	Ciudad de Loja	Also FAE-228

TRANS AM — Aero Transam (7T/RTM) — Guayaquil (GYE)

| ☐ HC-CDX | ATR 42-300F | 081 | ex YV-914C | Op for DHL |

VIP-VUELOS INTERNOS PRIVADOS — Vipec (V6/VUR) — Quito (UIO)

☐ HC-CFC	Dornier 328-110	3018	ex N422JS
☐ HC-CFI	Dornier 328-110	3084	ex N462JS
☐ HC-CFS	Dornier 328-110	3039	ex N427JS

HH- HAITI (Republic of Haiti)

CARIBINTAIR — Caribintair (CRT) — Port-au-Prince (PAP)

☐ HH-CRB	LET L-410UVP	800413	ex HI-671CT
☐ HH-CRT	LET L-410UVP-E	861721	ex LY-AZF
☐ HH-DMX	British Aerospace Jetstream 31	753	ex N842JS

HANAIR

| ☐ HH- | Britten-Norman BN-2A-26 Islander | 150 | ex 4X-CAH |

NATION AIR

| ☐ HH-NAT | LET L-410UVP | 851439 | ex HI-693CT |

TORTUG'AIR — Port-au-Prince (PAP)

☐ HH-AET	LET L-410UVP-E3	871816	ex 3D-CCE
☐ HH-BET	LET L-410UVP	851403	ex 3D-DSI
☐ HH-JET	British Aerospace Jetstream 32	883	ex N883CH
☐ HH-LOG	LET L-410UVP-E3	871827	ex S9-DIV
☐ HH-TOR	LET L-410UVP-E	871930	ex S9-BAO
☐ HH-YET	British Aerospace Jetstream 32	914	ex N914AE

VISION AIR

☐ HH-RPL	Britten-Norman BN-2A Mk.III-2 Trislander	1040	ex XA-TYU

HI- DOMINICAN REPUBLIC (Republica Dominicana)

ACSA — Santo Domingo-Herrara (HEX)

☐ HI-744CT	Cessna 401B	401B0214	ex N7995Q
☐ HI-772CT	British Aerospace Jetstream 3101	660	ex N411MX
☐ HI-816	British Aerospace Jetstream 31	694	ex N694AM
☐ HI-840	British Aerospace Jetstream 32EP	819	ex N148JH

AERODOMCA — Santo Domingo-Herrara (HEX)

☐ HI761	LET L-410UVP-E	871938	ex HI-761CT

AIR SANTO DOMINGO — Aero Domingo (EX/SDO) — Santo Domingo-Herrara (HEX)

☐ HI-657CT	Short SD.3-60	SH3672	ex 8P-SCD
☐ HI-679CT	LET L-410UVP-E	882023	ex HI-679CA
☐ HI-688CT	LET L-410UVP-E	861616	ex HI-688CA
☐ HI-695CT	LET L-410UVP-E	861615	ex HI-695CA
☐ HI-760CT	Cessna 208B Caravan I	208B0802	ex N1326D

CARIBAIR — Caribair (CBC) — Santo Domingo-Herrara (HEX)

☐ HI-569CT	Piper PA-31 Turbo Navajo B	31-700	ex HI-569CA	
☐ HI-585CA	Piper PA-31 Turbo Navajo B	31-850	ex N333GT	
☐ HI-653CA	Britten-Norman BN-2A-26 Islander	8	ex N28BN	
☐ HI-666CT	LET L-410UVP	851517	ex TG-TJV	
☐ HI-697CT	LET L-410UVP-E9A	882040	ex S9-TAV	
☐ HI-698CT	LET L-410UVP-E9A	882039	ex S9-TAU	status?
☐ HI-713CT	LET L-410UVP	851340	ex HI-713CA	
☐ HI-746CT	British Aerospace Jetstream 3101	692	ex HI-746CA	no titles
☐ HI-830	British Aerospace Jetstream 3101	780	ex HI-830CT	
☐ HI-848	SAAB SF.340A	340A-128	ex N128CH	
☐ HI-866	SAAB SF.340A	340A-138	ex N138SD	o/o

PAN AM DOMINICA — (7Q) — Santo Domingo-Herrara (HEX)

☐ HI-817CT	British Aerospace Jetstream 31	673	ex N507PA
☐ HI-841CT	British Aerospace Jetstream 31	674	ex N508PA
☐ HI869	Douglas DC-9-32	47566/691	ex N949N
☐ HI876	Douglas DC-9-32	47046/168	ex N602NW
☐ N206ZT	Bell 206B JetRanger III	2906	ex N330B

SAPAIR — Proservicios (5S/PSV) — Santo Domingo-Herrara (HEX)

☐ HI-691CT	LET L-410UVP	831107	ex S9-TAW
☐ HI-722CT	LET L-410UVP-E	861729	ex LY-AZH
☐ HI-724CT	LET L-410UVP-E	882032	ex LY-AZN

☐ HI-644	de Havilland DHC-6 Twin Otter 200	46	ex CS-TFG
☐ HI-658CT	Short SD.3-60	SH3674	ex 8P-SCE
☐ HI-720CT	Embraer EMB.120RT Brasilia	120038	ex N332JS
☐ HI-819	British Aerospace Jetstream 31	811	ex TG-TAK
☐ HI-851	British Aerospace Jetstream 32EP	940	ex N940AE
☐ HI-856	British Aerospace Jetstream 32EP	919	ex N919AE
☐ HI-858	British Aerospace Jetstream 32EP	938	ex N938AE
☐ HI-	British Aerospace Jetstream 32EP	972	ex N972JX

VOL AIR — Santo Domingo-Herrara (HEX)

☐ HI-785CT	Piper PA-31-350 Navajo Chieftain	31-7305066	ex N74923
☐ HI-787CA	Britten-Norman BN-2A-8 Islander	5429	ex HI-787SP
☐ HI-789CA	Britten-Norman BN-2A-21 Islander	849	ex HI-640CA
☐ HI862	British Aerospace Jetstream 31	826	ex N16EX

HK- COLOMBIA (Republic of Colombia)

ADA – AEROLINEAS DE ANTIOQUIA — Antioquia (ANQ) — Medellin-Olaya Herrera (MDE)

☐ HK-4364	British Aerospace Jetstream 32EP	897	ex N482UE
☐ HK-4381	British Aerospace Jetstream 32EP	898	ex N483UE

214

☐ HK-4398	British Aerospace Jetstream 32EP	828	ex N473UE	
☐ HK-4515	British Aerospace Jetstream 32EP	900	ex N496UE	
☐ HK-4548	British Aerospace Jetstream 32EP	893	ex N479UE	
☐ HK-4	British Aerospace Jetstream 32EP	890	ex N477UE	
☐ HK-2548	de Havilland DHC-6 Twin Otter 300	718	ex C-GDIW	
☐ HK-2603	de Havilland DHC-6 Twin Otter 300	749		
☐ HK-2669	de Havilland DHC-6 Twin Otter 300	760		Arcangel Rafael
☐ HK-3972	Dornier 28D-2 Skyservant	4156	ex YS-400P	
☐ HK-4000	Dornier 28D-2 Skyservant	4177	ex YS-404P	
☐ HK-4042	Cessna T303 Crusader	T30300155	ex N6421C	
☐ HK-4073	Dornier 28D-2 Skyservant	4114	ex N952	

ADES COLOMBIA · Villavicencio (VVC)

| ☐ HK-2279 | Cessna U206G Stationair 6 II | U20604885 | ex (N734WH) |
| ☐ HK-2430 | Cessna TU206G Stationair 6 II | U20605166 | ex (N4926U) |

AERCARIBE

| ☐ HK-4427 | Antonov An-32 | 1909 | ex HK-4427X | identity not confirmed |
| ☐ HK-4257 | Antonov An-32B | 3203 | ex OB-1699 | |

AEROASIS · Bogota-Eldorado (BOG)

| ☐ HK-4738 | Airbus A320-232 | 3330 | ex N330SU | ◆ |
| ☐ HK-4740 | Airbus A320-232 | 3264 | ex N326SU | ◆ |

AEROLINEAS DE LA PAZ · Villavicencio (VVC)

☐ HK-1663	Cessna U206F Stationair	U20601962	ex N50961	
☐ HK-3035	Cessna T303 Crusader	T30300191		
☐ HK-4189	Douglas DC-3	4319	ex HK-3994	
☐ HK-4292X	Douglas DC-3	17061/34328	ex OB-1756	status?

AEROREPUBLICA COLOMBIA · Aerorepublica (P5/RPB) · Bogota-Eldorado (BOG)

☐ HK-3928X	Douglas DC-9-32	47311/398	ex N286AW	Miguel Angel
☐ HK-3963	Douglas DC-9-32	47437/544	ex I-RIZL	
☐ HK-4155	Douglas DC-9-32	47524/632	ex N27522	
☐ HK-4453X	Embraer ERJ-190LR	19000063	ex PT-SJB	
☐ HK-4454X	Embraer ERJ-190LR	19000061	ex PT-SIO	
☐ HK-4455X	Embraer ERJ-190LR	19000076	ex PT-SJR	dam 17Jly07
☐ HK-4456X	Embraer ERJ-190LR	19000074	ex PT-SJN	
☐ HK-4505X	Embraer ERJ-190LR	19000114	ex PT-SQI	
☐ HK-4506X	Embraer ERJ-190LR	19000110	ex PT-SQE	
☐ HK-4507X	Embraer ERJ-190LR	19000122	ex PT-SQQ	
☐ HK-4508X	Embraer ERJ-190LR	19000138	ex PT-SYR	
☐ HK-4559X	Embraer ERJ-190LR	19000200	ex PT-SGI	
☐ HK-4560X	Embraer ERJ-190LR	19000208	ex PT-SGR	
☐ HK-4599	Embraer ERJ-190LR	19000269	ex PT-TLJ	
☐ HK-4601	Embraer ERJ-190LR	19000251	ex PT-SIW	
☐ HP-1562CMP	Embraer ERJ-190AR	19000095	ex PT-SNP	<CMP
☐ HK-4238X	McDonnell-Douglas MD-81	48009/985	ex N489NC	[BOG]
☐ HK-4259	McDonnell-Douglas MD-81	48005/957	ex N835F	stored
☐ HK-4265	McDonnell-Douglas MD-81	48002/938	ex N832F	
☐ HK-4408X	McDonnell-Douglas MD-83	53124/1991	ex N726BC	[VCV]◆

AEROSUCRE · Aerosucre (6N/KRE) · Barranquilla (BAQ)

☐ HK-727	Boeing 727-59F	19127/243	
☐ HK-3985	Boeing 727-224F (FedEx 3)	20465/814	ex N32723
☐ HK-4216	Boeing 737-230C (Nordam 3)	20253/223	ex HP-1408PVI
☐ HK-4253X	Boeing 737-2H6C (Nordam 3)	21109/436	ex HP-1311CMP
☐ HK-4328	Boeing 737-2S5C (Nordam 3)	22148/663	ex N802AL
☐ HK-4465	Boeing 727-222F (FedEx 3)	19915/681	ex N7642U
☐ HK-4504	Boeing 727-2J0F (FedEx 3)	21108/1174	ex N284KH
☐ HK-4544	Boeing 727-2J0F (FedEx 3)	21105/1158	ex N281KH

AEROVANGUARDIA · Villavicencio (VVC)

| ☐ HK-3199 | Douglas DC-3 | 14599/26044 | ex FAC1123 El Viejo |

AERUPIA · Villavicencio (VVC)

| ☐ HK-2713 | Piper PA-34-220T Seneca III | 34-8133241 | |
| ☐ HK-2822 | Britten-Norman BN-2B-27 Islander | 2109 | ex N2643X |

AIR COLOMBIA — Villavicencio (VVC)

☐ HK-3292	Douglas DC-3	19661	ex N9101S
☐ HK-3293X	Douglas DC-3	9186	ex N46877

AIRES — Aires (4C/ARE) — Bogota-Eldorado (BOG)

☐ HK-3951	de Havilland DHC-8-301	184	ex N184CL	Gustavo Artunduaga	<AGES
☐ HK-3952	de Havilland DHC-8-301	169	ex N169CL		<AGES
☐ HK-4030	de Havilland DHC-8-301	100	ex N100CQ		<AGES
☐ HK-4107X	de Havilland DHC-8Q-311	224	ex D-BELT		<AGES
☐ HK-4345	de Havilland DHC-8-102	63	ex N820PH		<AGES
☐ HK-4432X	de Havilland DHC-8-201	428	ex N990HA		
☐ HK-4473	de Havilland DHC-8Q-201	479	ex N985HA		id not confirmed
☐ HK-4480	de Havilland DHC-8Q-201	509	ex N998HA		
☐ HK-4491	de Havilland DHC-8Q-201	478	ex N983HA		
☐ HK-4495	de Havilland DHC-8Q-201	497	ex N996HA		
☐ HK-4509	de Havilland DHC-8Q-201	507	ex N997HA		
☐ HK-4513X	de Havilland DHC-8Q-201	468	ex N969HA		
☐ HK-4520	de Havilland DHC-8Q-201	465	ex N968HA		
☐ HK-4539	de Havilland DHC-8Q-201	452	ex N966HA		
☐ HK-4554X	de Havilland DHC-8Q-201	450	ex N965HA		
☐ HK-4618	de Havilland DHC-8-201	432	ex HC-CFK		
☐ HK-4724X	de Havilland DHC-8-402Q	4137	ex HL5255		◆
☐ HK-4725X	de Havilland DHC-8-402Q	4124	ex HL5252		◆
☐ HK-4726	de Havilland DHC-8-402Q	4119	ex HL5251		◆
☐ HK-4727X	de Havilland DHC-8-402Q	4129	ex HL5254		◆
☐ HK-4608	Boeing 737-73S/W	29080/211	ex D-AHID		
☐ HK-4623	Boeing 737-73S/W	29081/215	ex D-AHIE		
☐ HK-4627	Boeing 737-73S/W	29078/187	ex OY-MLW		
☐ HK-4635	Boeing 737-73V/W	30249/1128	ex G-EZJN		
☐ HK-4641	Boeing 737-73V/W	30244/1148	ex G-EZJO		
☐ HK-4660X	Boeing 737-752/W	34296/1783	ex XA-WAM		
☐ HK-4675X	Boeing 737-73V/W	32415/1260	ex G-EZJT		
☐ HK-4694	Boeing 737-7Q8/W	30687/2252	ex N171LF		◆
☐ HK-4695	Boeing 737-7Q8/W	30710/2188	ex N225LF		◆

ALIANSA — Villavicencio (VVC)

☐ HK-122	Douglas DC-3	4414	ex C-122	Frtr
☐ HK-2820	Douglas DC-3	20171	ex N151D	Frtr
☐ HK-3215	Douglas DC-3	14666/26111	ex N124SF	Frtr status?

APSA - AEROEXPRESO BOGOTA — Aeroexpreso (ABO) — Bogota-Guayamaral

☐ HK-3736X	Bell 212	31144	ex N3895P
☐ HK-4222X	Bell 212	30815	ex N24HL

ARALL - AEROLINEAS LLANERAS — Villavicencio (VVC)

☐ HK-1018	de Havilland DHC-2 Beaver	93	ex HK-240
☐ HK-1231	Cessna TU206D Skywagon	U206-1391	ex (N72389)
☐ HK-2257	Cessna U206G Stationair 6	U20604600	ex (N9950M)
☐ HK-2373	de Havilland DHC-2 Beaver	61	ex HK-84
☐ HK-2868	Cessna TU206G Stationair 6	U20606626	ex (N9724Z)

ARKAS

☐ HK-4492X	ATR 42-300	015	ex PR-TTA
☐ HK-4493X	ATR 42-300F	018	ex F-GPIA

AVIANCA — Avianca (AV/AVA) — Bogota-Eldorado (BOG)

☐ N590EL	Airbus A318-111	2328	ex XA-UBQ	◆
☐ N591EL	Airbus A318-111	2333	ex XA-UBR	◆
☐ N592EL	Airbus A318-111	2358	ex XA-UBS	◆
☐ N593EL	Airbus A318-111	2367	ex XA-UBT	◆
☐ N594EL	Airbus A318-111	2377	ex XA-UBU	◆
☐ N595EL	Airbus A318-111	2394	ex XA-UBV	◆
☐ N596EL	Airbus A318-111	2523	ex XA-UBW	◆
☐ N597EL	Airbus A318-111	2544	ex XA-UBX	◆
☐ N598EL	Airbus A318-111	2552	ex XA-UBY	◆
☐ N599EL	Airbus A318-111	2575	ex XA-UBZ	◆
☐ HK-4553	Airbus A319-112	3467	ex D-AVWN	
☐ HK-4552	Airbus A319-112	3518	ex D-AVYZ	
☐ N422AV	Airbus A319-115	4200	ex D-AVYC	◆

☐ N647AV	Airbus A319-115	3647	ex D-AVYQ	
☐ N691AV	Airbus A319-115	3691	ex D-AVWG	
☐ N	Airbus A319-115		ex	o/o♦
☐ N	Airbus A319-115		ex	o/o♦
☐ N	Airbus A319-115		ex	o/o♦
☐ HK-4549	Airbus A320-214	3408	ex F-WWBZ	
☐ HK-4659	Airbus A320-214	4100	ex F-WWDK	
☐ N281AV	Airbus A320-214	4281	ex F-WWIH	♦
☐ N284AV	Airbus A320-214	4284	ex F-WWIP	♦
☐ N345AV	Airbus A320-214	4345	ex F-WWBI	♦
☐ N398AV	Airbus A320-214	3988	ex F-WWBO	
☐ N401AV	Airbus A320-214	4001	ex F-WWDL	
☐ N411AV	Airbus A320-214	4011	ex F-WWIC	
☐ N416AV	Airbus A320-214	4167	ex F-WWBY	
☐ N417AV	Airbus A320-214	4175	ex D-AVVT	♦
☐ N426AV	Airbus A320-214	4026	ex F-WWDU	
☐ N446AV	Airbus A320-214	4046	ex D-AVVI	
☐ N451AV	Airbus A320-214	4051	ex F-WWIP	
☐ N481AV	Airbus A320-214	4381	ex F-WWBB	♦
☐ N664AV	Airbus A320-214	3664	ex F-WWDX	
☐ N961AV	Airbus A320-214	3961	ex F-WWDV	
☐ N980AV	Airbus A320-214	3980	ex F-WWIZ	
☐ N992AV	Airbus A320-214	3992	ex F-WWDE	
☐	Airbus A320-214		ex	o/o♦
☐	Airbus A320-214		ex	o/o♦
☐	Airbus A320-214		ex	o/o♦
☐	Airbus A320-214		ex	o/o♦
☐ N948AC	Airbus A330-243	948	ex F-WWKN	
☐ N967CG	Airbus A330-243	967	ex F-WWYI	
☐ N968AV	Airbus A330-243	1009	ex F-WWYE	
☐ N969AV	Airbus A330-243	1016	ex F-WWYI	
☐ N973AV	Airbus A330-243	1073	ex F-WWKZ	
☐ N	Airbus A330-243		ex	o/o♦
☐ N421AV	Boeing 767-2B1ER	25421/407	ex PT-TAK	
☐ N728CG	Boeing 767-283ER	24728/305	ex XA-TNS	special c/s
☐ N984AN	Boeing 767-383ER	24357/262	ex LN-RCB	
☐ N986AN	Boeing 767-259ER	24835/321		Amerigo Vespucio
☐ HK-4467	Fokker 50	20301	ex PH-MXZ	
☐ HK-4468X	Fokker 50	20300	ex PH-MXT	>SAM
☐ HK-4469X	Fokker 50	20285	ex PH-AVJ	>SAM
☐ HK-4470	Fokker 50	20297	ex PH-AVO	
☐ HK-4487X	Fokker 50	20266	ex PH-LXW	>SAM
☐ HK-4496X	Fokker 50	20278	ex PH-AVG	
☐ HK-4497X	Fokker 50	20288	ex PH-MXJ	>SAM
☐ HK-4501X	Fokker 50	20299	ex PH-MXS	
☐ HK-4580	Fokker 50	20296	ex PR-OAX	
☐ HK-4581	Fokker 50	20281	ex PR-OAW	
☐ EI-CBY	McDonnell-Douglas MD-83	49944/1888		Ciudad de Barranquilla
☐ EI-CBZ	McDonnell-Douglas MD-83	49945/1889	ex N6206F	Ciudad de Santiago de Cali
☐ EI-CCE	McDonnell-Douglas MD-83	49947/1900		Ciudad de Medellin
☐ EI-CEQ	McDonnell-Douglas MD-83	53123/1987		Ciudad de LeticiaJuan Valdez c/s
☐ HK-4590X	McDonnell-Douglas MD-83	49942/1799	ex EI-CBS	
☐ HK-4592X	McDonnell-Douglas MD-83	53122/1984	ex EI-CEP	
☐ N632CT	McDonnell-Douglas MD-83	49632/1603	ex 9Y-THV	Retro c/s

AVIHECO   Bogota-Eldorado/Ibague (BOG/IBE)

☐ HK-3039	Bell 206L-2 LongRanger III	51052		
☐ HK-4142	LET L-410UVP-E	861703	ex N5957J	for sale
☐ HK-4267	Bell 206L-2 LongRanger III	51252	ex N37CA	
☐ HK-4306	Bell 206L-2 LongRanger III	51606	ex HC-BXA	
☐ HK-4334	Convair 580F	176	ex N631MB	Used by CIA/DAC

COSMOS AIR CARGO   Bogota-Eldorado (BOG)

☐ HK-4386X	Boeing 727-82C/W (FedEx 3)	19968/660	ex N709DH	
☐ HK-4407X	Boeing 727-30C/W (Duganair 3)	19011/387	ex N701DH	

EASYFLY   (ESY)   Bogota-Eldorado (BOG)

☐ HK-4502	British Aerospace Jetstream 4101	41091	ex N572HK	
☐ HK-4503	British Aerospace Jetstream 4101	41093	ex N574HK	
☐ HK-4521	British Aerospace Jetstream 4101	41092	ex N573HK	

☐ HK-4522	British Aerospace Jetstream 4101	41086	ex N568HK
☐ HK-4551	British Aerospace Jetstream 4101	41089	ex N570HK
☐ HK-4568	British Aerospace Jetstream 4101	41057	ex N552HK
☐ HK-4584X	British Aerospace Jetstream 4101	41073	ex N556HK
☐ HK-4585X	British Aerospace Jetstream 4101	41067	ex N554HK
☐ HK-4596X	British Aerospace Jetstream 4101	41079	ex N563HK

HELIANDES · Medellin-Olaya Herrara (MDE)

☐ HK-3898X	Mil Mi-17 (Mi-8MTV-1)	96156	
☐ HK-4160X	Mil Mi-17 (Mi-8MTV-1)	95585	ex RA-25446
☐ HK-4164	Mil Mi-17 (Mi-8MTV-1)	95875	ex HK-3890X
☐ HK-4187X	LET L-410UVP-E	902432	ex HA-LAT
☐ HK-4223	Bell 206B JetRanger	303	ex HP-1321HC

HELICARGO · Medellin-Olaya Herrera (MDE)

☐ HK-2610	Aérospatiale AS350B Ecureuil	1339	ex F-WZFO
☐ HK-2967	Aérospatiale AS350B Ecureuil	1688	
☐ HK-3553	Bell 206L-3 LongRanger III	51177	ex N300WJ
☐ HK-3561	Rockwell Turbo Commander 690B	11365	ex LV-LZS
☐ HK-4215	Aérospatiale AS350BA Ecureuil	1495	ex N64050
☐ HK-4236	Beech 200 Super King Air	BB-135	ex N402RG
☐ HK-4301	Aérospatiale AS355F2 Twin Star	5420	ex N1074P
☐ HK-4370	Gulfstream Commander 695B	96080	ex N960AC
☐ HK-4375	Aérospatiale AS355F2 Twin Star	5384	ex N9040V

HELICOL · Helicol (HEL) · Bogota-Eldorado (BOG)

☐ HK-3303X	Bell 212	30654	ex N59608
☐ HK-3336X	Bell 212	31207	ex N2180J
☐ HK-3578G	Bell 412	33203	
☐ HK-3633X	Bell 206L-1 LongRanger II	45510	ex N57497
☐ HK-4031X	Bell 212	31203	ex HK-3184X
☐ HK-4213G	Bell 407	53405	ex (N2382Z)

HELITEC · Cali (CLO)

☐ HK-3341	Bell 212	31287	ex N3204H
☐ HK-3742	Bell 212	30847	
☐ HK-4025	Bell 212	31143	ex HC-BSQ
☐ HK-4231X	Kamov Ka-32S	9101	ex N40475

HELIVALLE · Palmira (QPI)

☐ HK-3693	Piper PA-42 Cheyenne III	42-8001075	ex N4998M
☐ HK-3978X	Bell 206L-3 LongRanger III	51446	ex N6643K
☐ HK-4015X	Bell 206L-4 LongRanger IV	52092	ex N4268G
☐ HK-4026X	Bell 212	35055	ex N4354J
☐ HK-4129X	Bell 212	30926	ex N412AX

LAN CARGO COLOMBIA · Bogota-Eldorado (BOG)

| ☐ N312LA | Boeing 767-316F/W | 32572/846 | |
| ☐ N418LA | Boeing 767-316F/W | 34246/936 | |

LAP - LINEAS AÉREAS PETROLERAS · LAP (APT) · Bogota-Eldorado (BOG)

| ☐ HK-2503 | Piper PA-31 Navajo C | 31-8012056 | |

LATINA DE AVIACION · Villavicencio (VVC)

| ☐ HK-4173X | Beech 1900C-1 | UC-14 | ex N38015 |
| ☐ HK-2006 | Douglas DC-3C | 43086 | ex N43A |

LINEAS AÉREAS SURAMERICANAS COLOMBIA · Suramericano (LAU) · Bogota-Eldorado (BOG)

☐ HK-1271	Boeing 727-24C (Raisbeck 3)	19524/428	ex N1781B	
☐ HK-1273	Boeing 727-24C (Raisbeck 3)	19526/442	ex N8320	Voyager
☐ HK-3814X	Boeing 727-25F (Raisbeck 3)	18270/79	ex N5111Y	Skipper
☐ HK-4154	Boeing 727-51F (Raisbeck 3)	18804/162	ex N5607	Orion
☐ HK-4261	Boeing 727-251F (FedEx 3)	21156/1170	ex N296AJ	<Flying Cargo
☐ HK-4262	Boeing 727-2F9F/W (Duganair 3)	21427/1291	ex N299AJ	<Flying Cargo
☐ HK-4354	Boeing 727-2X3F (FedEx 3)	22608/1727	ex N397AJ	<Flying Cargo
☐ HK-4401	Boeing 727-2X3F (FedEx 3)	22609/1731	ex N797AJ	
☐ HK-4607	Boeing 727-259F (FedEx 3)	22476/1747	ex N901LF	
☐ HK-4636	Boeing 727-2S2F (FedEx 3)	22927/1821	ex N129FB	
☐ HK-4637	Boeing 727-2S2F (FedEx 3)	22928/1822	ex N131FB	

SADELCA		Sadelca (SDK)			Neiva (NVA)
☐ HK-1514	Douglas DC-3	11741	ex N100RW		
☐ HK-2494	Douglas DC-3	16357/33105	ex N87611		
☐ HK-2664	Douglas DC-3	19433	ex HK-2665	Angela Sofia	
☐ HK-3286	Douglas DC-3	6144	ex HP-86	Liliana	
☐ HK-4136X	Antonov An-32B	2509	ex (YV-1089CP)		

SADI				Ibagué (IBE)
☐ HK-3154	Cessna TU206G Stationair 6	U20606836	ex (N9330R)	
☐ HK-3829	Bell 222	47076	ex N50RX	
☐ HK-4013	LET L-410UVP-E	861601	ex TG-TJS	
☐ HK-4109	LET L-410UVP	912529	ex S9-TBB	
☐ HK-4226	Bell 206B JetRanger III	2684	ex N2753E	

SAEP		SAEP (KSP)		Bogota-Eldorado (BOG)
☐ HK-4296X	Antonov An-32A	1704	ex ER-AXF	

SAM		SAM (MM/SAM)		Medellin-Olaya Herrara (MDE)
☐ HK-4469X	Fokker 50	20285	ex PH-AVJ	
☐ HK-4487X	Fokker 50	20266	ex PH-LXW	
☐ HK-4497X	Fokker 50	20288	ex PH-MXJ	
☐ HK-4419	Fokker 100	11457	ex N1448A	
☐ HK-4420	Fokker 100	11482	ex N1462C	
☐ HK-4430	Fokker 100	11465	ex N1453D	
☐ HK-4431	Fokker 100	11506	ex N1470K	
☐ HK-4437	Fokker 100	11469	ex N1457B	
☐ HK-4438	Fokker 100	11514	ex N1472B	
☐ HK-4443	Fokker 100	11479	ex N1459A	
☐ HK-4444	Fokker 100	11458	ex N1449D	
☐ HK-4445	Fokker 100	11449	ex N1446A	
☐ HK-4451	Fokker 100	11464	ex N1452B	
☐ HK-4486	Fokker 100	11414	ex OB-1831-P	
☐ HK-4488	Fokker 100	11376	ex OB-1821-P	
☐ HK-4489	Fokker 100	11377	ex OB-1816-P	
☐ HK-4578	Fokker 100	11413	ex PR-OAH	
☐ HK-4579	Fokker 100	11419	ex PR-OAV	

SARPA				Medellin-Olaya Herrara (MDE)
☐ HK-4099	Agusta-Bell 212	5630		
☐ HK-4100	Agusta-Bell 212	5631		
☐ HK-4124	Bell 212	30844	ex N405RA	
☐ HK-4232	Bell 212	30993	ex XA-SRZ	
☐ HK-4233	Bell 212	31164	ex XA-LAM	
☐ HK-4350	British Aerospace Jetstream 32EP	836	ex G-OEST	
☐ HK-4362	British Aerospace Jetstream 32EP	840	ex G-BYMA	
☐ HK-4394E	British Aerospace Jetstream 32EP	905	ex N486UE	EMS
☐ HK-4405E	British Aerospace Jetstream 32EP	849	ex N474UE	
☐ HK-4540X	British Aerospace Jetstream 32EP	933	ex N933CX	
☐ HK-4541	British Aerospace Jetstream 32EP	937	ex N937AE	

SATENA		Satena (9N/NSE)		Bogota-Eldorado (BOG)
☐ FAC-1182	ATR 42-500	526	ex SP-EDC	♦
☐ FAC-1183	ATR 42-500	522	ex OY-PCB	♦
☐ FAC-1160	Dornier 328-120	3079	ex D-CDXB	El Cafetero
☐ FAC-1161	Dornier 328-120	3080	ex D-CDXH	La Macarena
☐ FAC-1162	Dornier 328-120	3082	ex D-CDXP	Bahia Solano
☐ FAC-1163	Dornier 328-120	3081	ex D-CDXM	El Antioqueño
☐ FAC-1164	Dornier 328-120	3092	ex D-CDXO	El Casanereno
☐ FAC-1165	Dornier 328-120	3103	ex D-CDXW	El Guambiano
☐ FAC-1171	Embraer ERJ-145LR	145774	ex PT-SME	Milenium I
☐ FAC-1172	Embraer ERJ-145LR	145776	ex PT-SMG	Milenium II
☐ FAC-1176	Embraer ERJ-145EP	145165	ex EI-DMV	
☐ FAC-1177	Embraer ERJ-145EP	145227	ex EI-DMW	
☐ FAC-1103	LET L-410UVP-E	902420	ex HK-4224	Lsd fr/op by SRC
☐ FAC-1104	LET L-410UVP-E	861707	ex HK-4094X	Lsd to/op for NSE
☐ FAC-1180	Embraer ERJ-170LR	17000151	ex PT-SEP	

219

SEARCA COLOMBIA — Searca (SRC) — Medellin-Olaya Herrara (MDE)

Reg	Type	c/n	ex
HK-4266X	Beech 1900C-1	UC-64	ex N1568W
HK-4282	Beech 1900C-1	UC-60	ex N901SC
HK-4392	Beech 1900C-1	UC-38	ex N38SU
HK-4476	Beech 1900D	UE-123	ex N123YV
HK-4499	Beech 1900D	UE-110	ex N110YV
HK-4512	Beech 1900D	UE-105	ex N105YV
HK-4537	Beech 1900D	UE-95	ex N95YV
HK-4558	Beech 1900D	UE-156	ex N156E
HK-4563	Beech 1900D	UE-113	ex N113YV
HK-4598	Beech 1900D	UE-183	ex N48544
HK-4600	Beech 1900D	UE-99	ex N99YV
HK-4630	Beech 1900D	UE-93	ex N93ZV
HK-4673	Beech 1900D	UE-104	ex N104YV
HK-4681	Beech 1900D	UE-213	ex N3199Q
HK-4038X	LET L-410UVP	851323	ex TG-TJT
HK-4048	LET L-410UVP-E	912626	ex OM-111
HK-4105	LET L-410UVP-E	861613	ex N5957N
HK-4147	LET L-410UVP-E	892341	ex YV-986C
HK-4161	LET L-410UVP-E	861612	ex N6968L
HK-4196	LET L-410UVP-E	861617	ex CCCP-67577
HK-4235	LET L-410UVP-E	902423	ex S9-BAD
FAC-1103	LET L-410UVP-E	902420	ex HK-4224 — Lsd to/op for NSE
FAC-1104	LET L-410UVP-E	861707	ex HK-4094X — Lsd to/op for NSE
HK-4108X	Beech 200 Super King Air	BB-60	ex N530JA

SELVA

Reg	Type	c/n	ex	
HK-4052	Antonov An-32	1805	ex YN-CBU	
HK-4240	Antonov An-32B	3204	ex UR-48131 Juan Pabla	
HK-4295	Antonov An-26	67304702	ex LZ-NHA	
HK-4356	Antonov An-26B-100	77305109	ex YN-CGC	
HK-4369	Antonov An-32	2510	ex ER-AWA	stored
HK-4388	Antonov An-26B-100	27312402	ex LZ-NHE	
HK-4706	Antonov An-26B-100	27312203	ex 3X-GFB	◆

TAMPA AIRLINES — Tampa (QT/TPA) — Medellin-Olaya Herrara (MDE)

Reg	Type	c/n	ex	
N767QT	Boeing 767-241ER (SF)	23804/178	ex PP-VNQ	<767 Leasing
N768QT	Boeing 767-241ER (SF)	23803/161	ex N803HE	
N769QT	Boeing 767-241ER (SF)	23801/170	ex PP-VNO	
N770QT	Boeing 767-241ER (SF)	23802/172	ex PP-VNP	

TAP LINEAS AEREAS

Reg	Type	c/n	ex
HK-	Boeing 727-151C	19868/529	ex N433EX

TAS - TRANSPORTE AEREO DE SANTANDER — Bucaramanga (BGA)

Reg	Type	c/n	ex
HK-4102	Dornier 28D-2 Skyservant	4187	ex D-IDES
HK-4104	Dornier 28D-2 Skyservant	4193	ex D-IDRV
HK-4139	Dornier 28D-2 Skyservant	4153	ex D-IDRF
HK-4290X	Cessna 402C	402C0427	ex N717A

TAXI AÉREO CUSIANA — Bogota-Eldorado (BOG)

Reg	Type	c/n	ex
HK-2522	Cessna 402C II	402C0322	ex N2522P
HK-3916	Cessna 208B Caravan I	208B0372	ex N1117P
HK-4225X	LET L-410UVP	871929	ex S9-CBB
HK-4367	LET L-410UVP-E20	851334	ex CP-2252

TRANS ORIENTE — Villavicencio (VVC)

Reg	Type	c/n	ex
HK-3981	Dornier 28D-2 Skyservant	4162	ex D-IDND
HK-3982	Dornier 28D-2 Skyservant	4169	ex D-IDNC
HK-3991X	Dornier 28D-2 Skyservant	4148	ex D-IDNF
HK-3992X	Dornier 28D-2 Skyservant	4161	ex D-IDNE
HK-4053X	Dornier 28D-1 Skyservant	4105	ex D-IDNH

VERTICAL DE AVIACION — Bogota-Guaymaral

Reg	Type	c/n	ex
HK-3730X	Mil Mi-8TV-1	95728	ex CCCP-25112
HK-3731X	Mil Mi-8TV-1	95586	ex CCCP-25447
HK-3732X	Mil Mi-8TV-1	95729	ex CCCP-25113
HK-3758X	Mil Mi-8TV-1	95908	ex HC-BSG

☐ HK-3779X	Mil Mi-8TV-1	95645	ex CCCP-25500
☐ HK-3780X	Mil Mi-8TV-1	95909	ex RA-27068
☐ HK-3862	Mil Mi-8TV-1	95923	ex CCCP-27087
☐ HK-3863	Mil Mi-8TV-1	95894	ex CCCP-27060
☐ HK-3864	Mil Mi-8TV-1	95893	ex CCCP-27059
☐ HK-3865	Mil Mi-8TV-1	95892	ex CCCP-27058
☐ HK-3882X	Mil Mi-8TV-1	96018	
☐ HK-3888X	Mil Mi-8TV-1	95838	
☐ HK-3908X	Mil Mi-8TV-1	95823	
☐ HK-3910X	Mil Mi-8TV-1	96008	ex RA-27185
☐ HK-3911X	Mil Mi-8TV-1	96124	ex RA-25768
☐ HK-3250	Bell 212	31219	ex HC-BSI
☐ HK-3723	Bell 212	32122	ex N1080V
☐ HK-4208X	Beech 1900C-1	UC-152	ex N152GL

VIARCO   Villavicencio (VVC)

☐ HK-1315	Douglas DC-3	4307	ex PP-ANG
☐ HK-1842	Cessna U206F Stationair II	U20603487	ex (N8734Q)
☐ HK-3349X	Douglas DC-3	11825	ex FAE 92066/HC-AVC

HL-   SOUTH KOREA (Republic of Korea)

AIR BUSAN   (BX/ABL)   Busan-Gimhae (PVS)

☐ HL8213	Airbus A321-231	1970	ex EI-LVB ♦
☐ HL7232	Boeing 737-58E	25767/2614	
☐ HL7233	Boeing 737-58E	25768/2724	
☐ HL7250	Boeing 737-58E	25769/2737	
☐ HL7510	Boeing 737-48E	25771/2816	
☐ HL7517	Boeing 737-48E	25774/2909	

ASIANA AIRLINES   Asiana (OZ/AAR)   Seoul-Incheon/Kimpo (ICN/SEL)

Member of Star Alliance

☐ HL7737	Airbus A320-232	2397	ex F-WWIU
☐ HL7738	Airbus A320-232	2459	ex F-WWDM
☐ HL7744	Airbus A320-232	2808	ex F-WWIO
☐ HL7745	Airbus A320-232	2840	ex F-WWIE
☐ HL7753	Airbus A320-232	2943	ex F-WWIM
☐ HL7762	Airbus A320-232	3244	ex F-WWBQ
☐ HL7769	Airbus A320-232	3437	ex F-WWDX
☐ HL7772	Airbus A320-232	3483	ex F-WWDN
☐ HL7773	Airbus A320-232	3496	ex F-WWIL
☐ HL7776	Airbus A320-232	3641	ex F-WWBS
☐ HL7788	Airbus A320-232	3873	ex F-WWIH
☐ HL7594	Airbus A321-231	1356	ex D-AVZA
☐ HL7703	Airbus A321-231	1511	ex D-AVZA
☐ HL7711	Airbus A321-231	1636	ex D-AVZG
☐ HL7713	Airbus A321-231	1734	ex D-AVXD
☐ HL7722	Airbus A321-231	2041	ex D-AVZA
☐ HL7723	Airbus A321-231	2045	ex D-AVZC
☐ HL7729	Airbus A321-231	2110	ex D-AVXF
☐ HL7730	Airbus A321-231	2226	ex D-AVZU
☐ HL7731	Airbus A321-231	2247	ex D-AVZG
☐ HL7735	Airbus A321-231	2290	ex D-AVZB
☐ HL7761	Airbus A321-231	1227	ex N127AG
☐ HL7763	Airbus A321-231	3297	ex D-AVZR
☐ HL7767	Airbus A321-231	0802	ex N802BV
☐ HL7789	Airbus A321-231	4112	ex D-AZAE
☐ HL7790	Airbus A321-231	4142	ex D-AVZM
☐ HL7736	Airbus A330-323X	640	ex F-WWYR
☐ HL7740	Airbus A330-323X	676	ex F-WWYA
☐ HL7741	Airbus A330-323X	708	ex F-WWKL
☐ HL7746	Airbus A330-323X	772	ex F-WWKE
☐ HL7747	Airbus A330-323X	803	ex F-WWYE
☐ HL7754	Airbus A330-323X	845	ex F-WWYZ
☐ HL7792	Airbus A330-323X	1001	ex F-WWKL
☐ HL7793	Airbus A330-323X	1055	ex F-WWYD
☐ HL7794	Airbus A330-323X	1151	ex F-WWYS ♦
☐ HL	Airbus A330-323X		ex o/o♦

☐ HL7508	Boeing 737-48E	25772/2791			
☐ HL7511	Boeing 737-48E	27630/2848			
☐ HL7513	Boeing 737-48E	25776/2860			
☐ HL7413	Boeing 747-48EM (SF)	25405/880			
☐ HL7414	Boeing 747-48EM (SF)	25452/892			
☐ HL7415	Boeing 747-48EM (SF)	25777/946			
☐ HL7616	Boeing 747-446F	33748/1351	ex N401AL		♦
☐ HL7417	Boeing 747-48EM	25779/1006			
☐ HL7418	Boeing 747-48E	25780/1035	ex N6018N		
☐ HL7419	Boeing 747-48EF	25781/1044			
☐ HL7420	Boeing 747-48EF	25783/1064			
☐ HL7421	Boeing 747-48EM	25784/1086			
☐ HL7423	Boeing 747-48EM	25782/1115			
☐ HL7428	Boeing 747-48E	28552/1160	ex N6018N		
☐ HL7436	Boeing 747-48EF	29170/1305	ex N1785B		
☐ HL7604	Boeing 747-48EF	29907/1370			
☐ HL7247	Boeing 767-38E	25757/523			
☐ HL7248	Boeing 767-38E	25758/582			
☐ HL7506	Boeing 767-38E	25760/639			
☐ HL7507	Boeing 767-38EF	25761/616	ex N6005C		
☐ HL7514	Boeing 767-38E	25763/656		Tea Changum colours	
☐ HL7515	Boeing 767-38E	25762/658	ex N6055X		
☐ HL7516	Boeing 767-38E	25759/668		Star Alliance colours	
☐ HL7528	Boeing 767-38E	29129/693	ex N6005C		
☐ HL7500	Boeing 777-28EER	28685/400			
☐ HL7596	Boeing 777-28EER	28681/322			
☐ HL7597	Boeing 777-28EER	28686/359			
☐ HL7700	Boeing 777-28EER	30859/403	ex N5014K		
☐ HL7732	Boeing 777-28EER	29174/481			
☐ HL7739	Boeing 777-28EER	29175/526			
☐ HL7742	Boeing 777-28EER	29171/553			
☐ HL7755	Boeing 777-28EER	30861/646			
☐ HL7756	Boeing 777-28EER	30860/659			
☐ HL7775	Boeing 777-28EER	30862/738			
☐ HL7791	Boeing 777-28EER	35525/853			♦

EASTARJET		***(ZE/ESR)***		***Seoul-Gimpo (GMP/SEL)***

☐ HL7781	Boeing 737-683	28302/243	ex G-CDKD	
☐ HL7797	Boeing 737-73V	30240/974	ex N240CL	
☐ HL8204	Boeing 737-73V	30248/1118	ex G-EZJM	
☐ HL8205	Boeing 737-73V	32412/1151	ex G-EZJP	
☐ HL8207	Boeing 737-73V	32413/1202	ex G-EZJR	
☐ HL8215	Boeing 737-73V	32417/1285	ex G-EZJV	♦

JEJU AIR		***(7C/JJA)***		***Cheju International (CJU)***

☐ HL7779	Boeing 737-85F	28824/180	ex VT-SPC	
☐ HL7780	Boeing 737-85F	28827/467	ex VT-SPD	
☐ HL7796	Boeing 737-86N/W	28628/573	ex N372LZ	
☐ HL8206	Boeing 737-86J/W	30877/782	ex D-ABAE	
☐ HL8214	Boeing 737-86N/W	28608/410	ex D-ABBQ	♦
☐ HL8232	Boeing 737-8K5/W	27979/44	ex D-AHFE	♦
☐ HL8233	Boeing 737-85P/W	28383/266	ex EC-HBN	♦
☐ HL8234	Boeing 737-86Q/W	30285/1237	ex OO-VAS	♦

JIN AIR		***(LJ/JNA)***		***Seoul-Incheon/Kimpo (ICN/SEL)***

☐ HL7555	Boeing 737-86N	30230/460	ex N1786B	
☐ HL7558	Boeing 737-86N	28625/590	ex N1786B	
☐ HL7564	Boeing 737-86N	28638/765		
☐ HL7798	Boeing 737-809/W	28236/739	ex B-16802	

KOREAN AIR		***Koreanair (KE/KAL)***	***Seoul-Incheon/Kimpo (ICN/SEL)***

Member of Skyteam

☐ HL7239	Airbus A300B4-622R	627	ex F-WWAD	
☐ HL7240	Airbus A300B4-622R	631	ex F-WWAB	
☐ HL7241	Airbus A300B4-622R	662	ex F-WWAT	
☐ HL7242	Airbus A300B4-622R	685	ex F-WWAG	Jeju colours
☐ HL7243	Airbus A300B4-622R	692	ex F-WWAR	
☐ HL7245	Airbus A300B4-622R	731	ex F-WWAK	
☐ HL7295	Airbus A300B4-622R	582	ex F-WWAM	
☐ HL7297	Airbus A300B4-622R	609	ex F-WWAE	

☐ HL7524	Airbus A330-322	206	ex HL7552	
☐ HL7525	Airbus A330-322	219	ex F-WWKO	
☐ HL7538	Airbus A330-223	222	ex F-WWKP	
☐ HL7539	Airbus A330-223	226	ex F-WWKR	
☐ HL7540	Airbus A330-322	241	ex F-WWKF	
☐ HL7550	Airbus A330-322	162	ex F-WWKK	
☐ HL7551	Airbus A330-322	172	ex F-WWKI	
☐ HL7552	Airbus A330-223	258	ex F-WWKQ	
☐ HL7553	Airbus A330-323X	267	ex F-WWKZ	
☐ HL7554	Airbus A330-323X	256	ex F-WWKN	
☐ HL7584	Airbus A330-323X	338	ex F-WWKP	
☐ HL7585	Airbus A330-323X	350	ex F-WWYF	
☐ HL7586	Airbus A330-323X	351	ex F-WWYH	
☐ HL7587	Airbus A330-323X	368	ex F-WWKF	
☐ HL7701	Airbus A330-323	425	ex F-WWYE	
☐ HL7702	Airbus A330-323	428	ex F-WWYF	
☐ HL7709	Airbus A330-323	484	ex F-WWKD	
☐ HL7710	Airbus A330-323	490	ex F-WWKF	
☐ HL7720	Airbus A330-323	550	ex F-WWKP	
☐ HL8211	Airbus A330-223	1133	ex F-WWKA	♦
☐ HL8212	Airbus A330-223	1155	ex F-WWKI	♦
☐ HL	Airbus A330-223		ex	o/o♦
☐ HL	Airbus A330-223		ex	o/o♦
☐ HL7611	Airbus A380-861	035	ex F-WWAT	o/o♦
☐ HL	Airbus A380-861		ex F-WW	o/o♦
☐ HL	Airbus A380-861		ex F-WW	o/o♦
☐ HL	Airbus A380-861		ex F-WW	o/o♦
☐ HL	Airbus A380-861		ex F-WW	o/o♦
☐ HL7556	Boeing 737-86N	28615/482	ex N1787B	
☐ HL7557	Boeing 737-86N	28622/562	ex N1786B	
☐ HL7559	Boeing 737-86N	28626/611		
☐ HL7560	Boeing 737-8B5/W	29981/622		
☐ HL7561	Boeing 737-8B5/W	29982/663		
☐ HL7562	Boeing 737-8B5	29983/678		
☐ HL7563	Boeing 737-86N	28636/756		
☐ HL7565	Boeing 737-8B5/W	29984/848		
☐ HL7566	Boeing 737-8B5/W	29985/852		
☐ HL7567	Boeing 737-86N	28647/878		
☐ HL7568	Boeing 737-8B5/W	29986/891		
☐ HL7757	Boeing 737-8GQ/W	35790/2119		
☐ HL7758	Boeing 737-8GQ/W	35791/2150		
☐ HL7785	Boeing 737-8GQ/W	37162/2906	ex N1795B	
☐ HL7786	Boeing 737-8GQ/W	37163/2955	ex N1786B	
☐ HL	Boeing 737-8			o/o♦
☐ HL	Boeing 737-8			o/o♦
☐ HL	Boeing 737-8			o/o♦
☐ HL	Boeing 737-8			o/o♦
☐ HL7569	Boeing 737-9B5	29987/999	ex B-5110	
☐ HL7599	Boeing 737-9B5	29988/1026	ex N1795B	
☐ HL7704	Boeing 737-9B5	29989/1082	ex N1786B	
☐ HL7705	Boeing 737-9B5	29990/1162		
☐ HL7706	Boeing 737-9B5	29991/1188		
☐ HL7707	Boeing 737-9B5	29992/1190		
☐ HL7708	Boeing 737-9B5	29993/1208	ex N60659	
☐ HL7716	Boeing 737-9B5	29994/1320		
☐ HL7717	Boeing 737-9B5	29995/1332		
☐ HL7718	Boeing 737-9B5	29996/1338		
☐ HL7719	Boeing 737-9B5	29997/1416		
☐ HL7724	Boeing 737-9B5	29998/1494		
☐ HL7725	Boeing 737-9B5	29999/1512		
☐ HL7726	Boeing 737-9B5	30001/1729	ex N1786B	
☐ HL7727	Boeing 737-9B5	30000/1536	ex N6066U	
☐ HL7728	Boeing 737-9B5	30002/1620		
☐ HL	Boeing 737-9B5			o/o♦
☐ HL	Boeing 737-9B5			o/o♦
☐ HL7400	Boeing 747-4B5F	26414/1295		
☐ HL7402	Boeing 747-4B5	26407/1155	ex N6038E	
☐ HL7403	Boeing 747-4B5F	26408/1163	ex N60659	
☐ HL7404	Boeing 747-4B5	26409/1170	ex N6009F	
☐ HL7434	Boeing 747-4B5F	32809/1316		
☐ HL7437	Boeing 747-4B5F	32808/1323		
☐ HL7438	Boeing 747-4B5ERF	33515/1329	ex N6005X	
☐ HL7439	Boeing 747-4B5ERF	33516/1338		

☐ HL7443	Boeing 747-2B5B	21772/363		
☐ HL7448	Boeing 747-4B5F	26416/1246		
☐ HL7449	Boeing 747-4B5F	26411/1248		
☐ HL7460	Boeing 747-4B5	26404/1107		
☐ HL7461	Boeing 747-4B5	26405/1118		
☐ HL7462	Boeing 747-4B5F	26406/1123		
☐ HL7465	Boeing 747-4B5	26412/1284		
☐ HL7466	Boeing 747-4B5F	26413/1286		
☐ HL7467	Boeing 747-4B5F	27073/1291		
☐ HL7472	Boeing 747-4B5	26403/1095		
☐ HL7473	Boeing 747-4B5	28335/1098		
☐ HL7480	Boeing 747-4B5M	24619/793	ex N6009F	
☐ HL7482	Boeing 747-4B5BCF	25205/853		
☐ HL7483	Boeing 747-4B5BCF	25275/874		
☐ HL7484	Boeing 747-4B5	26392/893		
☐ HL7485	Boeing 747-4B5	26395/922		
☐ HL7486	Boeing 747-4B5	26396/951		
☐ HL7487	Boeing 747-4B5	26393/958		
☐ HL7488	Boeing 747-4B5	26394/986		
☐ HL7489	Boeing 747-4B5	27072/1013		
☐ HL7490	Boeing 747-4B5	27177/1019		
☐ HL7491	Boeing 747-4B5	27341/1037		
☐ HL7492	Boeing 747-4B5	26397/1055		
☐ HL7493	Boeing 747-4B5	26398/1057		
☐ HL7494	Boeing 747-4B5	27662/1067		
☐ HL7495	Boeing 747-4B5	28096/1073		
☐ HL7498	Boeing 747-4B5	26402/1092		
☐ HL7499	Boeing 747-4B5ERF	33517/1340		
☐ HL7600	Boeing 747-4B5ERF	33945/1347		
☐ HL7601	Boeing 747-4B5ERF	33946/1350		
☐ HL7602	Boeing 747-4B5ERF	34301/1365		
☐ HL7603	Boeing 747-4B5ERF	34302/1368		
☐ HL7605	Boeing 747-4B5ERF	35526/1375		
☐ HL7606	Boeing 747-4B5BCF	24199/739	ex VT-EVJ	
☐ HL7607	Boeing 747-4B5	24198/729	ex VT-AIC	
☐ HL7608	Boeing 747-4B5BCF	24621/830	ex VT-AID	
☐ HL7609	Boeing 747-8HTF	37132/1425		o/o♦
☐ HL7610	Boeing 747-8HTF	37133/1426		o/o♦
☐ HL7526	Boeing 777-2B5ER	27947/148	ex N50217	
☐ HL7530	Boeing 777-2B5ER	27945/59		
☐ HL7531	Boeing 777-2B5ER	27946/62		
☐ HL7574	Boeing 777-2B5ER	28444/305		
☐ HL7575	Boeing 777-2B5ER	28445/309		
☐ HL7598	Boeing 777-2B5ER	27949/356		
☐ HL7714	Boeing 777-2B5ER	27951/411		
☐ HL7715	Boeing 777-2B5ER	28372/416		
☐ HL7721	Boeing 777-2B5ER	33727/452		
☐ HL7733	Boeing 777-2B5ER	34206/520	ex N5023Q	
☐ HL7734	Boeing 777-2B5ER	34207/528		
☐ HL7743	Boeing 777-2B5ER	34208/584		
☐ HL7750	Boeing 777-2B5ER	34209/633		
☐ HL7751	Boeing 777-2B5ER	34210/657	ex N6018N	
☐ HL7752	Boeing 777-2B5ER	34211/682		
☐ HL7764	Boeing 777-2B5ER	34214/684	ex N50281	
☐ HL7765	Boeing 777-2B5ER	34212/711		
☐ HL7766	Boeing 777-2B5ER	34213/730		
☐ HL7532	Boeing 777-3B5	28371/162		
☐ HL7533	Boeing 777-3B5	27948/178		
☐ HL7534	Boeing 777-3B5	27950/120	ex N5020K	
☐ HL7573	Boeing 777-3B5	27952/288		
☐ HL7782	Boeing 777-3B5ER	37643/785		
☐ HL7783	Boeing 777-3B5ER	37644/806	ex N5020K	
☐ HL7784	Boeing 777-3B5ER	37136/823		
☐ HL8208	Boeing 777-3B5ER	37645/867		♦
☐ HL8209	Boeing 777-3B5ER	37646/875		♦
☐ HL8210	Boeing 777-3B5ER	40377/882	ex N5106R	♦
☐ HL	Boeing 777-3B5ER			o/o♦
☐ HL	Boeing 777-3B5ER			o/o♦
☐ HL	Boeing 777-3B5ER			o/o♦

YEONGNAM AIR

☐ HL7774	Fokker 100	11293	ex G-MAMH	

HP-   PANAMA (Republic of Panama)

AEROPERLAS		Aeroperlas (WL/APP)		Panama City-Albrook (BLB)
☐ HP-1251APP	Short SD.3-60	SH3610	ex N715NC	
☐ HP-1315APP	Short SD.3-60	SH3614	ex N363MQ	[PAC]
☐ HP-1319APP	Short SD.3-60	SH3607	ex N361MQ	
☐ HP-1326APP	Short SD.3-60	SH3631	ex N360MM	[BLB]
☐ HP-004APP	ATR 42-300	004	ex TG-IAX	<ISV
☐ HP-1281APP	de Havilland DHC-6 Twin Otter 300	407	ex C-FVFK	
☐ HP-1283APP	de Havilland DHC-6 Twin Otter 300	269	ex C-GKBO	
☐ HP-1336APP	Beech A100 King Air	B-173	ex C-GAST	
☐ HP-1359APP	Cessna 208B Caravan I	208B0711	ex TI-BAO	
☐ HP-1445APP	Canadair CL-66B Cosmopolitan	CL66B-7	ex N4FY	
☐ TG-MYH	ATR 42-300	113	ex G-ZAPJ	<TSP

AIR PANAMA		Turismo Aereo (PST)		Panama City-Albrook (BLB)
☐ HP-1542PST	Fokker F.27 Friendship 500F	10560	ex HP-1542PS	
☐ HP-1543PST	Fokker F.27 Friendship 400	10268	ex C-GWXC	
☐ HP-1604PST	Fokker F.27 Friendship 500F	10471	ex N716FE	<NPTC
☐ HP-1631PST	Fokker F.27 Friendship 500	10658	ex N725FE	[PAC]
☐ HP-639PS	Britten-Norman BN-2A-8 Islander	60	ex HP-639KN	
☐ HP-1153PS	Britten-Norman BN-2A-26 Islander	672	ex HP-1153XI	
☐ HP-1345PS	Cessna 208B Caravan I	208B0380	ex HP-1354AR	
☐ HP-1494PS	Britten-Norman BN-2A-3 Islander	673	ex CN-TCC	
☐ HP-1507PS	de Havilland DHC-6 Twin Otter 300	532	ex C-GQKZ	
☐ HP-1509PS	de Havilland DHC-6 Twin Otter 300	360	ex HP-1509APP	
☐ HP-1625PST	de Havilland DHC-8-311	519	ex G-BRYY	
☐ HP-1670PST	SAAB SF.340B	340B-299	ex N299CJ	
☐ HP-1671PST	SAAB SF.340B	340B-294	ex N294CJ	

ARROW PANAMA		Arrow Panama (8A/WAP) Panama City-Tocumen Intl (PTY)
☐ HP-441WAP	Douglas DC-8-63CF (BAC 3)	45988/416 ex N441J

COPA AIRLINES		Copa (CM/CMP)		Panama City-Tocumen Intl (PTY)
☐ HP-1369CMP	Boeing 737-71Q/W	29047/235	ex N8251R	669
☐ HP-1370CMP	Boeing 737-71Q/W	29048/288	ex N82521	670
☐ HP-1371CMP	Boeing 737-7V3/W	30049/388	ex N1787B	671
☐ HP-1372CMP	Boeing 737-7V3/W	28607/399		672
☐ HP-1373CMP	Boeing 737-7V3/W	30458/459		673
☐ HP-1374CMP	Boeing 737-7V3/W	30459/494	ex N1787B	674
☐ HP-1375CMP	Boeing 737-7V3/W	30460/558	ex N1787B	675
☐ HP-1376CMP	Boeing 737-7V3/W	30497/574		676
☐ HP-1377CMP	Boeing 737-7V3/W	30462/1161		677
☐ HP-1378CMP	Boeing 737-7V3/W	30461/1173		678
☐ HP-1379CMP	Boeing 737-7V3/W	30463/1221		679
☐ HP-1380CMP	Boeing 737-7V3/W	30464/1241		680
☐ HP-1520CMP	Boeing 737-7V3/W	33707/1376		681
☐ HP-1521CMP	Boeing 737-7V3/W	33708/1379		682
☐ HP-1522CMP	Boeing 737-8V3/W	33709/1387		480
☐ HP-1523CMP	Boeing 737-8V3/W	33710/1397		481
☐ HP-1524CMP	Boeing 737-7V3/W	33705/1505		683
☐ HP-1525CMP	Boeing 737-7V3/W	33706/1518		684
☐ HP-1526CMP	Boeing 737-7V3/W	34006/1585	ex N1782B	482
☐ HP-1527CMP	Boeing 737-7V3/W	30676/1619		685
☐ HP-1528CMP	Boeing 737-7V3/W	29360/1644		686
☐ HP-1529CMP	Boeing 737-7V3/W	29670/1711		483
☐ HP-1530CMP	Boeing 737-7V3/W	34535/1962		687
☐ HP-1531CMP	Boeing 737-7V3/W	34536/1995		688
☐ HP-1532CMP	Boeing 737-8V3/W	35068/2343		484
☐ HP-1533CMP	Boeing 737-8V3/W	35067/2423		485
☐ HP-1534CMP	Boeing 737-8V3/W	35125/2624		486
☐ HP-1535CMP	Boeing 737-8V3/W	35126/2805	ex N1786B	487
☐ HP-1536CMP	Boeing 737-8V3/W	35127/2963		488
☐ HP-1537CMP	Boeing 737-8V3/W	36550/3114		489
☐ HP-1538CMP	Boeing 737-8V3/W	36554/3130		490
☐ HP-1539CMP	Boeing 737-8V3/W	29667/3151	ex N1786B	491
☐ HP-1711CMP	Boeing 737-8V3/W	40663/3265		492 ♦
☐ HP-1712CMP	Boeing 737-8V3/W	40664/3267	ex N1796B	493 ♦
☐ HP-1713CMP	Boeing 737-8V3/W	40890/3455		494 ♦
☐ HP-1714CMP	Boeing 737-8V3/W	40891/3476		495 ♦
☐ HP-1715CMP	Boeing 737-8V3/W	40361/3500		496 ♦

☐ HP-	Boeing 737-8V3/W			o/o♦
☐ HP-	Boeing 737-8V3/W			o/o♦
☐ HP-	Boeing 737-8V3/W			o/o♦
☐ HP-	Boeing 737-8V3/W			o/o♦
☐ HP-	Boeing 737-8V3/W			o/o♦
☐ HP-	Boeing 737-8V3/W			o/o♦
☐ HP-	Boeing 737-8V3/W			o/o♦
☐ HP-	Boeing 737-8V3/W			o/o♦
☐ HP-	Boeing 737-8V3/W			o/o♦
☐ HP-	Boeing 737-8V3/W			o/o♦

☐ HP-1540CMP	Embraer ERJ-190AR	19000012	ex PT-STL	
☐ HP-1556CMP	Embraer ERJ-190AR	19000016	ex PT-STQ	
☐ HP-1557CMP	Embraer ERJ-190AR	19000034	ex PT-SGI	
☐ HP-1558CMP	Embraer ERJ-190AR	19000038	ex PT-SGN	
☐ HP-1559CMP	Embraer ERJ-190AR	19000053	ex PT-SIC	
☐ HP-1560CMP	Embraer ERJ-190AR	19000056	ex PT-SIF	
☐ HP-1561CMP	Embraer ERJ-190AR	19000089	ex PT-SNI	
☐ HP-1562CMP	Embraer ERJ-190AR	19000095	ex PT-SNP	>RMB
☐ HP-1563CMP	Embraer ERJ-190AR	19000098	ex PT-SNS	
☐ HP-1564CMP	Embraer ERJ-190AR	19000100	ex PT-SNU	
☐ HP-1565CMP	Embraer ERJ-190AR	19000126	ex PT-SQV	
☐ HP-1566CMP	Embraer ERJ-190AR	19000165	ex PT-SAX	
☐ HP-1567CMP	Embraer ERJ-190AR	19000174	ex PT-SDJ	
☐ HP-1568CMP	Embraer ERJ-190AR	19000212	ex PT-SGV	
☐ HP-1569CMP	Embraer ERJ-190AR	19000222	ex PT-SHG	

DHL AERO EXPRESSO — Yellow (D5/DAE) — Panama City-Tocumen Intl (PTY)

☐ HP-1510DAE	Boeing 727-264F (FedEx 3)	20709/950	ex N624DH	[ROW]
☐ HP-1610DAE	Boeing 727-264F (FedEx 3)	20780/986	ex N625DH	
☐ HP-1710DAE	Boeing 727-2Q4F (FedEx 3)	22424/1683	ex OO-DHZ	
☐ HP-1810DAE	Boeing 757-27APCF	29611/910	ex N646AL	♦
☐ HP-1910DAE	Boeing 757-27APCF	29607/832	ex N644AL	♦
☐ HP-	Boeing 757-27APCF	29610/904	ex N645AL	♦

PANAIR CARGO — Panama City-Tocumen Intl (PTY)

| ☐ HP-1653CTW | Boeing 727-277F (FedEx 3) | 21695/1481 | ex N982JM | |

PANAVIA CARGO AIRLINES — Panavia (6Z/PVI) — Panama City-Tocumen Intl (PTY)

| ☐ HP-1261PVI | Boeing 727-25F/W (Duganair 3) | 18965/205 | ex N8141N | [PTY] |
| ☐ HP-1585PVI | Boeing 727-224F (FedEx 3) | 20662/1072 | ex N334FV | |

HR-   HONDURAS (Republic of Honduras)

AERO CARIBE

| ☐ HR-AWA | LET L-410UVP-E | 882025 | ex HI-681CT | ♦ |

AEROLINEAS SOSA — Sosa (P4/VSO) — La Ceiba (LCE)

☐ HR-AIH	Britten-Norman BN-2A-21 Islander	513	ex C-GVZY	
☐ HR-AQR	LET L-410UVP	851516	ex S9-TBD	
☐ HR-ARE	LET L-410UVP	841312	ex S9-TBL	
☐ HR-ARJ	Nord 262A-14	15	ex N417SA	stored
☐ HR-ARP	Nord 262A-27	33	ex N274A	stored
☐ HR-ARU	Nord 262A-21	21	ex TG-ANP	stored
☐ HR-ASI	LET L-410UVP-E	871925	ex N888LT	
☐ HR-ASR	Fairchild F-27F	84	ex 3C-QQA	
☐ HR-ASZ	LET L-410UVP	851530	ex HR-AQO	
☐ HR-ATA	British Aerospace Jetstream 31	725	ex N833JS	
☐ HR-ATB	British Aerospace Jetstream 31	726	ex N834JS	
☐ HR-ATE	British Aerospace Jetstream 31	757	ex N843JS	
☐ HR-AUE	LET L-410UVP			

ATLANTIC AIRLINES — Atlantic Honduras (ZF/HHA) — La Ceiba (LCE)

☐ HR-ASD	LET L-410UVP-E	882034	ex YS-15C	
☐ HR-ASE	LET L-410UVP-E	861611	ex YS-10C	
☐ HR-ASG	LET L-410UVP-E	861710	ex HR-AJG	
☐ HR-ASH	LET L-410UVP-E	861716	ex YS-14C	
☐ HR-ASJ	LET L-410UVP-E	861724	ex YS-12C	
☐ HR-ASM	LET L-410UVP-E	861711	ex YS-05C	

☐ HR-ASN	LET L-410UVP-E	861701	ex YS-06C	
☐ HR-ASW	LET L-410UVP-E	871910	ex CU-T1193	
☐ HR-ASX	LET L-410UVP-E	871915	ex CU-T1194	
☐ HR-ATC	Hawker Siddeley HS.748 Srs 2B/424	1801	ex C-GBCS	
☐ HR-ATI	Fairchild F-27F	95	ex N19FF	
☐ HR-ATL	Fokker F.27 Friendship 500F	10522	ex N283EA	
☐ HR-ATN	Boeing 737-2Y5 (Nordam 3)	23040/955	ex N118RW	

CENTRAL AMERICAN AIRWAYS — La Ceiba (LCE)

| ☐ HR-AUQ | LET L-410UVP | 912603 | ex HH-AVP | |

ISLENA AIRLINES — (WC/ISV) — La Ceiba (LCE)

☐ HR-AUX	ATR 42-320 (QC)	394	ex 9A-CTU	
☐ HR-AVA	ATR 42-320	388	ex F-WQNC	
☐ HR-IAP	Short SD.3-60	SH3616	ex N345MV	
☐ HR-IAW	Short SD.3-60	SH3669	ex N361PA	
☐ HR-IAY	ATR 42-300	120	ex F-WQHM	
☐ HR-IBH	Cessna 208B Caravan I			

ROLLINS AIR — La Ceiba (LCE)

☐ HR-ASC	Yakovlev Yak-40	9332029	ex`RA-87321	
☐ HR-AVN	Lockheed L-1011-500 Tristar	293B-1242	ex TL-ADW	◆
☐ HR-AWG	British Aerospace Jetstream 31	764	ex C-FSEW	◆
☐ HR-AWH	British Aerospace Jetstream 31	766	ex C-GPDC	◆
☐ HR-AWM	Lockheed L1011-500 Tristar	193C-1229	ex N163AT	◆
☐ HR-	GAF N.22 Nomad			
☐ HR-	LET L-410UVP			

SETCO — Tegucigalpa (TGU)

☐ HR-AFB	Rockwell 500S Shrike Commander	3268	ex HR-315	[TGU]
☐ HR-AFC	Rockwell 500S Shrike Commander	3271	ex HR-317	[TGU]
☐ HR-AJY	Douglas DC-3	6068	ex HP-685	[TGU]
☐ HR-AKM	Rockwell 500S Shrike Commander	3098	ex HR-CNA	
☐ HR-ALU	Douglas DC-3			[TGU]
☐ HR-ATH	Douglas DC-3	6102	ex HR-SAH	no titles

HS- THAILAND (Kingdom of Thailand)

BANGKOK AIRWAYS — Bangkok Air (PG/BKP) — Bangkok-Suvarnabhumi (BKK)

☐ HS-PGN	Airbus A319-132	3759	ex D-AVXD	Luang Prabang	
☐ HS-PGT	Airbus A319-132	3421	ex D-AVYM	Sukhothai	
☐ HS-PGX	Airbus A319-132	3424	ex D-AVYO	Hirsoshima	
☐ HS-PGY	Airbus A319-132	3454	ex D-AVWH	Angkor Wat	
☐ HS-PGZ	Airbus A319-132	3694	ex D-AVWH	Phnom Penh	
☐ HS-PPA	Airbus A319-132	3911	ex D-AVYN	Si Satchanali	
☐ HS-PGU	Airbus A320-232	2254	ex F-WWDC	Guilin	
☐ HS-PGV	Airbus A320-232	2310	ex F-WWDS	Krabi	
☐ HS-PGW	Airbus A320-232	2509	ex F-WWIQ	Samui	
☐ HS-PGA	ATR 72-212A	710	ex F-WWEJ	Kut	
☐ HS-PGB	ATR 72-212A	708	ex F-WWEH	Phuket	
☐ HS-PGC	ATR 72-212A	715	ex F-WWEO	Nangyuan	
☐ HS-PGD	ATR 72-212A	833	ex F-WWEZ		
☐ HS-PGF	ATR 72-212A	700	ex F-WWEW	Hua Hin	
☐ HS-PGG	ATR 72-212A	692	ex F-WWEO	Chang	
☐ HS-PGK	ATR 72-212A	680	ex F-WWEV	Apsara	
☐ HS-PGM	ATR 72-212A	704	ex F-WWEC	Tao	
☐ HS-	ATR 72-600		ex		o/o◆
☐ HS-	ATR 72-600		ex		o/o◆

BUSINESS AIR — Bangkok-Suvarnabhumi (BKK)

☐ HS-BIA	Boeing 767-222ER	21868/10	ex HS-SSC	
☐ HS-BIB	Boeing 767-341ER	24753/291	ex N753SJ	◆
☐ HS-BIC	Boeing 767-341ER	24752/289	ex N752SJ	◆

DESTINATION AIR — Phuket (HKT)

| ☐ HS-DAA | Cessna 208 Caravan I | 20800321 | ex N122KW | FP |
| ☐ HS-DAB | Cessna 206H Stationair 6 | 20608046 | ex N2312V | FP |

227

HAPPY AIR		(HPY)		Phuket (HKT)
☐ HS-HPY	SAAB SF.340A	340A-115	ex SE-F15	

K-MILE AIR		(8K/KMI)		Bangkok-Suvarnabhumi (BKK)
☐ HS-SCH	Boeing 727-247F (FedEx 3)	21700/1489	ex 9M-TGJ	<TSE
☐ HS-SCJ	Boeing 727-247F (FedEx 3)	21392/1305	ex 9M-TGK	<TSE

NOK AIR		Nok Air (DD/NOK)		Bangkok Don Muang (BMK)
☐ HS-DDL	Boeing 737-4Y0	24917/2071	ex TC-JDF	
☐ HS-DDM	Boeing 737-4Y0	26065/2284	ex TC-JDY	
☐ HS-DDN	Boeing 737-4Q8	24707/2057	ex VT-SIE	
☐ HS-DDO	Boeing 737-4Y0	26081/2442	ex UR-GAR	◆
☐ HS-DDP	Boeing 737-406	25355/2132	ex PH-BDZ	◆
☐ HS-DDQ	Boeing 737-4M0	29204/3051	ex PK-GZI	◆
☐ HS-TDA	Boeing 737-4D7	24830/1899	Songkhla	
☐ HS-TDB	Boeing 737-4D7	24831/1922	Phuket	
☐ HS-TDE	Boeing 737-4D7	26612/2330	Surin	
☐ HS-	Boeing 737-800		ex	o/o
☐ HS-	Boeing 737-800		ex	o/o

ONE-TWO-GO		Orient Express (OG/QTG)		Bangkok-Suvarnabhumi (BKK)
☐ HS-OMA	McDonnell-Douglas MD-82	49439/1318	ex N18835	[DMK]
☐ HS-OMB	McDonnell-Douglas MD-82	49441/1322	ex N35836	
☐ HS-OMC	McDonnell-Douglas MD-82	49479/1297	ex N819NY	[DMK]
☐ HS-OMD	McDonnell-Douglas MD-82	49485/1316	ex N72825	
☐ HS-OME	McDonnell-Douglas MD-82	49182/1128	ex N911TW	
☐ HS-OMI	McDonnell-Douglas MD-87	49464/1476	ex JA8278	[DMK]
☐ HS-OMJ	McDonnell-Douglas MD-87	49465/1604	ex JA8279	[DMK]
☐	McDonnell-Douglas MD-87	53040/1897	ex JA8372	o/o
☐	McDonnell-Douglas MD-81	53297/2040	ex N821TH	o/o
☐	McDonnell-Douglas MD-81	53298/2045	ex N822TH	o/o
☐ HS-UTN	Boeing 747-346	23149/599	ex JA8163	

ORIENT THAI AIRLINES		Orient Express (OX/OEA)		Bangkok-Suvarnabhumi (BKK)
☐ HS-	Boeing 737-324/W	23374/1204	ex N10323	o/o◆
☐ HS-STC	Boeing 747-412	26548/923	ex N584MD	◆
☐ HS-UTD	Boeing 747-146A	21029/259	ex JA8128	>QTG
☐ HS-UTM	Boeing 747-346SR	23637/655	ex JA8176	
☐ HS-UTO	Boeing 747-346	23639/664	ex JA8178	all-white
☐ HS-UTV	Boeing 747-346	23151/607	ex JA8166	
☐ HS-UTW	Boeing 747-346	23067/588	ex JA812J	

PHUKET AIRLINES				Phuket (HKT)
☐ HS-AGN	Boeing 747-422	26474/988	ex N106UA	◆
☐ HS-AKS	Boeing 747-422	26881/989	ex N192UA	◆
☐ HS-VAC	Boeing 747-306	23056/587	ex (HS-TSA)	
☐ HS-VAN	Boeing 747-312	23245/626	ex (HS-TSB)	

SGA AIRLINES		(5E)		Bangkok-Suvarnabhumi (BKK)
☐ HS-GAA	Cessna 208B Caravan I	208B0643	ex N522GM	Ops in Nok Air colours
☐ HS-GAB	Cessna 208B Caravan I	208B1196	ex N208WD	Ops in Nok Air colours
☐ HS-SKR	Cessna 208B Caravan I	208B1241	ex N208AE	

SKY EYES AVIATION		Sky Eyes (I6/SEQ)		Bangkok-Suvarnabhumi (BKK)
☐ HS-SEC	Lockheed L-1011-200F Tristar	193N-1212	ex 9L-LDZ	[FJR]

SKYSTAR AIRWAYS		(XT/SKT)		Bangkok-Suvarnabhumi (BKK)
☐ HS-SSA	Boeing 767-222ER	21871/15	ex N610UA	Pattana	[ICN]
☐ HS-SSB	Boeing 767-222ER	21872/20	ex N611UA	Suphahon	[ICN]
☐ HS-SSD	Boeing 767-222	21880/50	ex N620UA		[CAN]

SUVARNABHUMI AIRLINES				Phuket (HKT)
☐ HS-AKU	Boeing 737-2B7 (Nordam 3)	23115/998	ex N282AU	Kavida-Urawan	[CGK]

THAI AIRASIA		(FD/AIQ)		Bangkok-Suvarnabhumi (BKK)
☐ HS-ABA	Airbus A320-216	3277	ex F-WWDH	
☐ HS-ABB	Airbus A320-216	3299	ex F-WWDZ	

☐ HS-ABC	Airbus A320-216	3338	ex F-WWBM		
☐ HS-ABD	Airbus A320-216	3394	ex F-WWBQ		
☐ HS-ABE	Airbus A320-216	3489	ex F-WWIR		
☐ HS-ABF	Airbus A320-216	3505	ex F-WWBS		
☐ HS-ABG	Airbus A320-216	3576	ex F-WWBN		
☐ HS-ABH	Airbus A320-216	3679	ex F-WWBD		
☐ HS-ABI	Airbus A320-216	3729	ex F-WWDK		
☐ HS-ABJ	Airbus A320-216	4019	ex F-WWDF		
☐ HS-ABK	Airbus A320-216	4088	ex F-WWBV		
☐ HS-ABL	Airbus A320-216	4126	ex F-WWIO		
☐ HS-ABM	Airbus A320-216	4278	ex F-WWID		♦
☐ HS-ABN	Airbus A320-216	4302	ex F-WWDM		♦
☐ HS-ABO	Airbus A320-216	4333	ex F-WWIM		♦
☐ HS-ABP	Airbus A320-216	4367	ex F-WWDR		♦
☐ HS-ABQ	Airbus A320-216	4386	ex F-WWDE		♦
☐ HS-ABR	Airbus A320-216	4390	ex F-WWDK		♦
☐ HS-ABS	Airbus A320-216	4426	ex F-WWBP		♦
☐ HS-ABT	Airbus A320-216	4557	ex F-WWDT		♦
☐ HS-	Airbus A320-216		ex		o/o♦

THAI AIRWAYS INTERNATIONAL — Thai (TG/THA) — Bangkok-Suvarnabhumi (BKK)

Member of Star Alliance

☐ HS-TAF	Airbus A300B4-601	398	ex F-WWAN	Ratchasima	
☐ HS-TAG	Airbus A300B4-605R	464	ex F-WWAL	Srinapha	
☐ HS-TAH	Airbus A300B4-605R	518	ex F-WWAE	Napachinda	
☐ HS-TAK	Airbus A300B4-622R	566	ex F-WWAB	Phaya Thai	
☐ HS-TAL	Airbus A300B4-622R	569	ex F-WWAD	Sri Trang	
☐ HS-TAM	Airbus A300B4-622R	577	ex F-WWAG	Chiang Mai	
☐ HS-TAN	Airbus A300B4-622R	628	ex F-WWAE	Chiang Rai	
☐ HS-TAO	Airbus A300B4-622R	629	ex F-WWAF	Chanthaburi	Star Alliance c/s
☐ HS-TAP	Airbus A300B4-622R	635	ex F-WWAP	Pathum Thani	
☐ HS-TAR	Airbus A300B4-622R	681	ex F-WWAB	Yasothon	
☐ HS-TAS	Airbus A300B4-622R	705	ex F-WWAT	Yala	
☐ HS-TAT	Airbus A300B4-622R	782	ex F-WWAY	Srimuang	
☐ HS-TAW	Airbus A300B4-622R	784	ex F-WWAL	Suranaree	
☐ HS-TAX	Airbus A300B4-622R	785	ex F-WWAO	Thepsatri	
☐ HS-TAY	Airbus A300B4-622R	786	ex F-WWAQ	Srisoonthorn	
☐ HS-TAZ	Airbus A300B4-622R	787	ex F-WWAB	Srisubhan	
☐ HS-TEA	Airbus A330-321	050	ex F-WWKI	Manorom	
☐ HS-TEB	Airbus A330-321	060	ex F-WWKQ	Sri Sakhon	
☐ HS-TEC	Airbus A330-321	062	ex F-WWKR	Bang Rachan	
☐ HS-TED	Airbus A330-321	064	ex F-WWKS	Donchedi	
☐ HS-TEE	Airbus A330-321	065	ex F-WWKT	Kusuman	
☐ HS-TEF	Airbus A330-321	066	ex F-WWKJ	Song Dao	
☐ HS-TEG	Airbus A330-321	112	ex F-WWKM	Lam Plai Mat	
☐ HS-TEH	Airbus A330-321	122	ex F-WWKG	Sai Buri	
☐ HS-TEJ	Airbus A330-322	209	ex F-WWKN	Sudawadi	
☐ HS-TEK	Airbus A330-322	224	ex F-WWKD	Srichulalak	Royal Barge c/s
☐ HS-TEL	Airbus A330-322	231	ex F-WWKU	Thepamart	Star Alliance c/s
☐ HS-TEM	Airbus A330-323X	346	ex F-WWYE	Jiraprabha	
☐ HS-TEN	Airbus A330-343E	990	ex F-WWKK	Suchada	
☐ HS-TEO	Airbus A330-343E	1003	ex F-WWKR	Chutamas	
☐ HS-TEP	Airbus A330-343E	1035	ex F-WWKS	Srianocha	
☐ HS-TEQ	Airbus A330-343E	1037	ex F-WWYA	Si Ayutthaya	[BOD]
☐ HS-TER	Airbus A330-343E	1060	ex F-WWYQ	U Thong	[BOD]
☐ HS-TES	Airbus A330-343E	1074	ex F-WWKJ		[BOD]
☐ HS-TET	Airbus A330-343E	1086	ex F-WWYV		[BOD]♦
☐ HS-TEU	Airbus A330-343E	1090	ex F-WWYB		[BOD]♦
☐ HS-TLA	Airbus A340-541	624	ex F-WWTN	Chiang Kham	
☐ HS-TLB	Airbus A340-541	628	ex F-WWTO	Uttaradit	
☐ HS-TLC	Airbus A340-541	698	ex F-WWTR	Phitsanulok	
☐ HS-TLD	Airbus A340-541HGW	775	ex F-WWTX		
☐ HS-TNA	Airbus A340-642	677	ex F-WWCJ	Watthana Nakhon	
☐ HS-TNB	Airbus A340-642	681	ex F-WWCK	Saraburi	
☐ HS-TNC	Airbus A340-642	689	ex F-WWCN	Chon Buri	
☐ HS-TND	Airbus A340-642	710	ex F-WWCX	Phetchaburi	
☐ HS-TNE	Airbus A340-642	719	ex F-WWCH		
☐ HS-TNF	Airbus A340-642	953	ex F-WWCM	Mae Hong Son	
☐ HS-	Airbus A380-841	070	ex F-WW		o/o
☐ HS-	Airbus A380-841	075	ex F-WW		o/o
☐ HS-TDF	Boeing 737-4D7	26613/2338		Si Sa Ket	

☐ HS-TDG	Boeing 737-4D7	26614/2481		Kalasin	
☐ HS-TDH	Boeing 737-4D7	28703/2962		Lopburi	
☐ HS-TDJ	Boeing 737-4D7	28704/2968		Nakhon Chaisi	
☐ HS-TDK	Boeing 737-4D7	28701/2977		Sri Surat	
☐ HS-TYS	Boeing 737-8Z6/W	35478/1955	ex N369BJ	Also carries 55-555	BBJ2
☐ HS-TGA	Boeing 747-4D7	32369/1273		Srisuriyothai	
☐ HS-TGB	Boeing 747-4D7	32370/1278		Si Satchanalai	
☐ HS-TGF	Boeing 747-4D7	33770/1335		Sri Ubon	
☐ HS-TGG	Boeing 747-4D7	33771/1337		Pathoomawadi	
☐ HS-TGH	Boeing 747-4D7	24458/769		Chaiprakarn	
☐ HS-TGJ	Boeing 747-4D7	24459/777		Hariphunchai	
☐ HS-TGK	Boeing 747-4D7	24993/833		Alongkorn	
☐ HS-TGL	Boeing 747-4D7	25366/890		Theparat	
☐ HS-TGM	Boeing 747-4D7	27093/945		Chao Phraya	
☐ HS-TGN	Boeing 747-4D7	26615/950		Simongkhon	
☐ HS-TGO	Boeing 747-4D7	26609/1001		Bowonrangsi	
☐ HS-TGP	Boeing 747-4D7	26610/1047		Thepprasit	
☐ HS-TGR	Boeing 747-4D7	27723/1071		Siriwatthna	
☐ HS-TGT	Boeing 747-4D7	26616/1097		Watthanothai	
☐ HS-TGW	Boeing 747-4D7	27724/1111		Visuthakasatriya	
☐ HS-TGX	Boeing 747-4D7	27725/1134		Sirisobhakya	
☐ HS-TGY	Boeing 747-4D7	28705/1164	ex N60697	Dararasmi	
☐ HS-TGZ	Boeing 747-4D7	28706/1214		Phimara	
☐ HS-TJA	Boeing 777-2D7	27726/25		Lamphun	
☐ HS-TJB	Boeing 777-2D7	27727/32		U Thaithani	
☐ HS-TJC	Boeing 777-2D7	27728/44		Nakhon Nayok	
☐ HS-TJD	Boeing 777-2D7	27729/51		Mukdahan	
☐ HS-TJE	Boeing 777-2D7	27730/89		Chaiyaphum	
☐ HS-TJF	Boeing 777-2D7	27731/95		Phanom Sarakham	
☐ HS-TJG	Boeing 777-2D7	27732/100		Pattani	
☐ HS-TJH	Boeing 777-2D7	27733/113		Suphan Buri	
☐ HS-TJR	Boeing 777-2D7ER	34586/588		Nakhon Sawan	
☐ HS-TJS	Boeing 777-2D7ER	34587/595		Phra Nakhon	
☐ HS-TJT	Boeing 777-2D7ER	34588/596		Pathum Wan	
☐ HS-TJU	Boeing 777-2D7ER	34589/599		Phichit	
☐ HS-TJV	Boeing 777-2D7ER	34590/665		Nakhon Pathom	
☐ HS-TJW	Boeing 777-2D7ER	34591/672		Phetchabun	
☐ HS-TKA	Boeing 777-3D7	29150/156	ex N5028Y	Sriwanna	
☐ HS-TKB	Boeing 777-3D7	29151/170		Chainarai	
☐ HS-TKC	Boeing 777-3D7	29211/250		Kwanmuang	
☐ HS-TKD	Boeing 777-3D7	29212/260		Thepalai	
☐ HS-TKE	Boeing 777-3D7	29213/304		Sukhirin	
☐ HS-TKF	Boeing 777-3D7	29214/310		Chutamai	
☐ N774SA	Boeing 777-FZB	37986/844	ex N5023Q		Op by SOO
☐ N775SA	Boeing 777-FZB	37987/852			Op by SOO
☐ HS-TRA	ATR 72-201	164	ex F-WWEO	Hummingbird/Lampang	
☐ HS-TRB	ATR 72-201	167	ex F-WWEU	Chai Nat	

THAI AVIATION SERVICES   Songkhla (SGZ)

☐ HS-HTE	Sikorsky S-76A++	760706	ex N2584R	<CHC Helicopters
☐ HS-HTJ	Sikorsky S-76A++	760720	ex N720G	<CHC Helicopters
☐ HS-HTK	Sikorsky S-76C+	760546	ex C-FCHC	<CHC Helicopters
☐ HS-HTM	Sikorsky S-76C+	760537	ex VT-HGI	<CHC Helicopters
☐ HS-HTP	Sikorsky S-76A++	760697	ex N25811	<CHC Helicopters
☐ HS-HTU	Sikorsky S-76A++	760010	ex VH-HUB	<CHC Helicopters
☐ HS-HTW	Sikorsky S-76C++	760724	ex C-FUWP	<CHC Helicopters
☐ HS-HTY	Sikorsky S-76A	760011	ex C-GIHY	<CHC Helicopters
☐ HS-HTZ	Sikorsky S-76C+	760561	ex C-GHRZ	<CHC Helicopters
☐ HS-HTA	Sikorsky S-61N	61815	ex C-GOLH	<CHC Helicopters Intl
☐ HS-HTC	Sikorsky S-61N	61722	ex C-GARC	<CHC Helicopters Intl

THAI FLYING SERVICE   Thai Flying (TFT)   Bangkok-Don Muang (DMK)

☐ HS-ITD	Beech 200 350	FL-151	ex N10817
☐ HS-TFG	Rockwell Turbo Commander 690B	11482	ex N745T

HZ- SAUDI ARABIA (Kingdom of Saudi Arabia)

AL KHAYALA

Wholly owned by National Air Services and operates business class services between Jeddah and Riyadh

230

ALWAFEER AIR		(AW/WFR)		Jeddah (JED)
☐ HZ-AWA1	Boeing 747-4H6	27672/1091	ex 9M-MPI	
☐ HZ-AWA2	Boeing 747-4H6	28426/1130	ex 9M-MPJ	
☐ HZ-AWA3	Boeing 747-4H6	25701/997	ex 9M-MPD	

NAS AIR		(2N/KNE)		Jeddah (JED)
☐ VP-CAN	Airbus A319-112	1886	ex C-GKOC	
☐ HZ-XY7	Airbus A320-214	2165	ex (VP-BBQ)	
☐ VP-CXR	Airbus A320-214	3894	ex F-WWDF	
☐ VP-CXS	Airbus A320-214	3787	ex F-WWBB	
☐ VP-CXT	Airbus A320-214	3817	ex F-WWIN	
☐ VP-CXW	Airbus A320-214	3475	ex F-WWDF	
☐ VP-CXX	Airbus A320-214	3425	ex F-WWIZ	
☐ VP-CXY	Airbus A320-214	3396	ex F-WWBR	
☐ VP-CXZ	Airbus A320-214	3361	ex F-WWIK	
☐ VP-CQV	Embraer ERJ-190LR	19000367	ex PT-XNF	♦
☐ VP-CQW	Embraer ERJ-190LR	19000232	ex PT-SID	
☐ VP-CQX	Embraer ERJ-190LR	19000233	ex PT-SIE	
☐ VP-CQY	Embraer ERJ-190LR	19000227	ex PT-SHQ	
☐ VP-CQZ	Embraer ERJ-190LR	19000217	ex PT-SHA	
☐	Embraer ERJ-190LR		ex PT-	o/o♦
☐	Embraer ERJ-190LR		ex PT-	o/o♦
☐	Embraer ERJ-190LR		ex PT-	o/o♦
☐	Embraer ERJ-190LR		ex PT-	o/o♦
☐	Embraer ERJ-190LR		ex PT-	o/o♦
☐	Embraer ERJ-190LR		ex PT-	o/o♦
☐	Embraer ERJ-190LR		ex PT-	o/o♦
☐	Embraer ERJ-190LR		ex PT-	o/o♦

SAMA AIRLINES	(ZS)	Jeddah (JED)

Ceased operations 24/Aug/2010

SAUDI ARABIAN AIRLINES		Saudia (SV/SVA)		Jeddah (JED)
☐ HZ-ASA	Airbus A320-214	4081	ex F-WWBR	
☐ HZ-ASB	Airbus A320-214	4090	ex F-WWBZ	
☐ HZ-ASC	Airbus A320-214	4337	ex F-WWIV	♦
☐ HZ-ASD	Airbus A320-214	4364	ex F-WWDI	♦
☐ HZ-ASE	Airbus A320-214	4408	ex F-WWIE	♦
☐ HZ-AS11	Airbus A320-214	4015	ex F-WWBS	
☐ HZ-AS12	Airbus A320-214	4057	ex F-WWBC	
☐ HZ-AS13	Airbus A320-214	4104	ex F-WWDQ	
☐ HZ-AS14	Airbus A320-214	4115	ex F-WWDX	
☐ HZ-AS15	Airbus A320-214	4122	ex F-WWIF	
☐ HZ-AS16	Airbus A320-214	4135	ex F-WWIU	
☐ HZ-AS17	Airbus A320-214	4349	ex F-WWBV	♦
☐ HZ-AS18	Airbus A320-214	4357	ex F-WWDH	♦
☐ HZ-AS19	Airbus A320-214	4376	ex F-WWIN	♦
☐ HZ-AS20	Airbus A320-214	4392	ex F-WWDO	♦
☐ HZ-AS21	Airbus A320-214	4414	ex D-AVVI	♦
☐ HZ-AS22	Airbus A320-214	4484	ex F-WWDN	♦
☐ HZ-AS23	Airbus A320-214	4519	ex F-WWDE	♦
☐ HZ-AS31	Airbus A320-214	4092	ex F-WWDE	
☐ HZ-AS32	Airbus A320-214	4273	ex F-WWBY	♦
☐ HZ-AS33	Airbus A320-214	4314	ex F-WWBP	♦
☐ HZ-AS34	Airbus A320-214	4397	ex F-WWIL	♦
☐ HZ-AS35	Airbus A320-214	4391	ex D-AVVG	♦
☐ HZ-AS36	Airbus A320-214	4393	ex D-AVVJ	♦
☐ HZ-AS37	Airbus A320-214	4394	ex F-WWDX	♦
☐ HZ-AS38	Airbus A320-214	4432	ex D-AVVP	♦
☐ HZ-AS39	Airbus A320-214	4442	ex F-WWIA	♦
☐ HZ-AS40	Airbus A320-214	4419	ex F-WWDU	♦
☐ HZ-AS41	Airbus A320-214	4454	ex F-WWBE	♦
☐ HZ-AS42	Airbus A320-214	4501	ex F-WWIM	♦
☐ HZ-AS43	Airbus A320-214	4517	ex F-WWBO	♦
☐ HZ-AS44	Airbus A320-214	4564	ex F-WWBD	♦
☐ HZ-	Airbus A320-214		ex	o/o♦
☐ HZ-	Airbus A320-214		ex	o/o♦
☐ HZ-	Airbus A320-214		ex	o/o♦
☐ HZ-	Airbus A320-214		ex	o/o♦
☐ HZ-	Airbus A320-214		ex	o/o♦

Reg	Type	c/n	ex	note
☐ HZ-	Airbus A320-214		ex	o/o♦
☐ HZ-ASH	Airbus A321-211	4467	ex D-AVZD	♦
☐ HZ-ASI	Airbus A321-211	4542	ex D-AVZR	♦
☐ HZ-ASJ	Airbus A321-211	4577	ex D-AZAG	o/o♦
☐ HZ-ASK	Airbus A321-211	4590	ex D-AZAJ	o/o♦
☐ HZ-AQA	Airbus A330-343X	1108	ex F-WWKZ	♦
☐ HZ-AQB	Airbus A330-343X	1127	ex F-WWYP	♦
☐ HZ-AQC	Airbus A330-343X	1137	ex F-WWKM	♦
☐ HZ-AQD	Airbus A330-343X	1141	ex F-WWKL	♦
☐ HZ-AQE	Airbus A330-343X	1147	ex F-WWYB	♦
☐ HZ-AQF	Airbus A330-343X	1153	ex F-WWYT	♦
☐ HZ-AQG	Airbus A330-343X	1192	ex F-WWKO	♦
☐ HZ-AQH	Airbus A330-343X	1189	ex F-WWKA	♦
☐ TC-ETK	Airbus A330-223	358	ex I-EEZA	<KKK
☐ TC-ETL	Airbus A330-223	364	ex I-EEZB	<KKK
☐ HZ-AIB	Boeing 747-168B	22499/517		[JED]
☐ HZ-AIC	Boeing 747-168B	22500/522		
☐ HZ-AID	Boeing 747-168B	22501/525		
☐ HZ-AIE	Boeing 747-168B	22502/530	ex N8284V	
☐ HZ-AII	Boeing 747-168B	22749/557		
☐ HZ-AIK	Boeing 747-368	23262/616	ex N6005C	
☐ HZ-AIL	Boeing 747-368	23263/619	ex N6009F	
☐ HZ-AIM	Boeing 747-368	23264/620	ex N6046P	
☐ HZ-AIN	Boeing 747-368	23265/622	ex N6046P	
☐ HZ-AIP	Boeing 747-368	23267/630	ex N6055X	
☐ HZ-AIQ	Boeing 747-368	23268/631	ex N6005C	
☐ HZ-AIR	Boeing 747-368	23269/643	ex N6038E	
☐ HZ-AIS	Boeing 747-368	23270/645	ex N6046P	
☐ HZ-AIT	Boeing 747-368	23271/652	ex N6038N	
☐ HZ-AIU	Boeing 747-268F	24359/724	ex N6018N	
☐ HZ-AIV	Boeing 747-468	28339/1122	ex N6005C	
☐ HZ-AIW	Boeing 747-468	28340/1138		
☐ HZ-AIX	Boeing 747-468	28341/1182		
☐ HZ-AIY	Boeing 747-468	28342/1216	ex N6009F	
☐ TF-AMI	Boeing 747-412 (SF)	27066/940	ex N706RB	<ABD
☐ TF-AMS	Boeing 747-481	24920/832	ex JA8096	<ABD
☐ TF-AMT	Boeing 747-481	25135/863	ex JA8097	<ABD
☐ TF-AMU	Boeing 747-48EF	27603/1210	ex HL7426	<ABD
☐ TF-AMV	Boeing 747-412	28022/1082	ex 9V-SPI	<ABD
☐ TF-ARU	Boeing 747-344	22970/577	ex ZS-SAT	<ABD
☐ HZ-AKA	Boeing 777-268ER	28344/98	ex N50217	
☐ HZ-AKB	Boeing 777-268ER	28345/99	ex N5023Q	
☐ HZ-AKC	Boeing 777-268ER	28346/101		
☐ HZ-AKD	Boeing 777-268ER	28347/103		
☐ HZ-AKE	Boeing 777-268ER	28348/109		
☐ HZ-AKF	Boeing 777-268ER	28349/114		
☐ HZ-AKG	Boeing 777-268ER	28350/119		
☐ HZ-AKH	Boeing 777-268ER	28351/124		
☐ HZ-AKI	Boeing 777-268ER	28352/143		
☐ HZ-AKJ	Boeing 777-268ER	28353/147		
☐ HZ-AKK	Boeing 777-268ER	28354/154		
☐ HZ-AKL	Boeing 777-268ER	28355/166		
☐ HZ-AKM	Boeing 777-268ER	28356/175		
☐ HZ-AKN	Boeing 777-268ER	28357/181		
☐ HZ-AKO	Boeing 777-268ER	28358/186		
☐ HZ-AKP	Boeing 777-268ER	28359/194		
☐ HZ-AKQ	Boeing 777-268ER	28360/219	ex N5016R	
☐ HZ-AKR	Boeing 777-268ER	28361/230	ex N5017V	
☐ HZ-AKS	Boeing 777-268ER	28362/255		
☐ HZ-AKT	Boeing 777-268ER	28363/298		
☐ HZ-AKU	Boeing 777-268ER	28364/306		
☐ HZ-AKV	Boeing 777-268ER	28365/323		
☐ HZ-AKW	Boeing 777-268ER	28366/351		
☐ HZ-	Boeing 777-368			o/o♦
☐ HZ-	Boeing 777-368			o/o♦
☐ HZ-AEA	Embraer ERJ-170LR	17000108	ex PT-SAQ	
☐ HZ-AEB	Embraer ERJ-170LR	17000114	ex PT-SAZ	
☐ HZ-AEC	Embraer ERJ-170LR	17000118	ex PT-SDF	
☐ HZ-AED	Embraer ERJ-170LR	17000119	ex PT-SDG	
☐ HZ-AEE	Embraer ERJ-170LR	17000121	ex PT-SDJ	
☐ HZ-AEF	Embraer ERJ-170LR	17000123	ex PT-SDM	

☐ HZ-AEG	Embraer ERJ-170LR	17000124	ex PT-SDN	
☐ HZ-AEH	Embraer ERJ-170LR	17000135	ex PT-SDY	
☐ HZ-AEI	Embraer ERJ-170LR	17000142	ex PT-SEG	
☐ HZ-AEJ	Embraer ERJ-170LR	17000145	ex PT-SEJ	
☐ HZ-AEK	Embraer ERJ-170LR	17000149	ex PT-SEN	
☐ HZ-AEL	Embraer ERJ-170LR	17000152	ex PT-SEQ	
☐ HZ-AEM	Embraer ERJ-170LR	17000155	ex PT-SES	
☐ HZ-AEN	Embraer ERJ-170LR	17000158	ex PT-SEW	
☐ HZ-AEO	Embraer ERJ-170LR	17000161	ex PT-SMB	
☐ HZ-APA	McDonnell-Douglas MD-90-30	53491/2191		
☐ HZ-APB	McDonnell-Douglas MD-90-30	53492/2205	ex N9012S	
☐ HZ-APC	McDonnell-Douglas MD-90-30	53493/2209	ex N9014S	
☐ HZ-APD	McDonnell-Douglas MD-90-30	53494/2213	ex N9010L	
☐ HZ-APE	McDonnell-Douglas MD-90-30	53495/2215	ex N6203D	
☐ HZ-APF	McDonnell-Douglas MD-90-30	53496/2216	ex N9012S	
☐ HZ-APG	McDonnell-Douglas MD-90-30	53497/2219		
☐ HZ-APH	McDonnell-Douglas MD-90-30	53498/2221	ex N6202D	
☐ HZ-API	McDonnell-Douglas MD-90-30	53499/2223		
☐ HZ-APJ	McDonnell-Douglas MD-90-30	53500/2225		
☐ HZ-APK	McDonnell-Douglas MD-90-30	53501/2226		
☐ HZ-APL	McDonnell-Douglas MD-90-30	53502/2227		
☐ HZ-APM	McDonnell-Douglas MD-90-30	53503/2229		
☐ HZ-APN	McDonnell-Douglas MD-90-30	53504/2230		
☐ HZ-APO	McDonnell-Douglas MD-90-30	53505/2231	ex N9012S	
☐ HZ-APP	McDonnell-Douglas MD-90-30	53506/2232		
☐ HZ-APQ	McDonnell-Douglas MD-90-30	53507/2235		
☐ HZ-APR	McDonnell-Douglas MD-90-30	53508/2237		
☐ HZ-APS	McDonnell-Douglas MD-90-30	53509/2250	ex N6203D	
☐ HZ-APT	McDonnell-Douglas MD-90-30	53510/2251	ex N6203U	
☐ HZ-APU	McDonnell-Douglas MD-90-30	53511/2255		
☐ HZ-APV	McDonnell-Douglas MD-90-30	53512/2256		
☐ HZ-APX	McDonnell-Douglas MD-90-30	53514/2260	ex N6200N	
☐ HZ-APY	McDonnell-Douglas MD-90-30	53515/2262	ex N9014S	
☐ HZ-APZ	McDonnell-Douglas MD-90-30	53516/2263	ex N9075H	
☐ HZ-AP3	McDonnell-Douglas MD-90-30	53518/2289	ex N6203D	
☐ HZ-AP4	McDonnell-Douglas MD-90-30	53519/2290	ex N9075H	
☐ HZ-AP7	McDonnell-Douglas MD-90-30	53517/2288	ex HZ-AP2	
☐ HZ-ANA	McDonnell-Douglas MD-11F	48773/609	ex N90187	
☐ HZ-ANB	McDonnell-Douglas MD-11F	48775/616	ex N91566	
☐ HZ-ANC	McDonnell-Douglas MD-11F	48776/617	ex N91078	
☐ HZ-AND	McDonnell-Douglas MD-11F	48777/618	ex N9166N	
☐ HZ-AGG	Boeing 737-268	20883/366		
☐ TC-OAH	Airbus A300B4-605R	584	ex S7-RGO	<OHY
☐ TC-OAZ	Airbus A300B4-605R	603	ex SX-BEM	<OHY
☐ TC-ETF	Airbus A321-231	1438	ex N585NK	<KKK
☐ TC-ETG	Boeing 757-256	26254/905	ex EC-HDV	<KKK
☐ TC-OGS	Boeing 757-256	29307/924	ex EC-HIQ	<KKK
☐ TC-OGT	Boeing 757-256	29308/935	ex EC-HIR	<KKK

SILVERWING

☐ HZ-AJW	Airbus A319-112	1494	ex N320NP	

SNAS AVIATION		**Red Sea (RSE)**		**Riyadh/Bahrain (RUH/BAH)**

☐ HZ-SNA	Boeing 727-264F (FedEx 3)	20896/1051	ex EC-HLP	all-white	
☐ HZ-SNB	Boeing 727-223F (FedEx 3)	21084/1199	ex EC-HAH	all-white	
☐ HZ-SNC	Boeing 727-230F (FedEx 3)	20905/1091	ex EC-IVF		<BCS
☐ HZ-SND	Boeing 727-223F (FedEx 3)	20994/1190	ex EC-IVE	all-white	<BCS
☐ HZ-SNF	Boeing 727-230F (FedEx 3)	22643/1762	ex ZS-DPE		

H4- SOLOMON ISLANDS

PACIFIC AIR EXPRESS	**Solpac (PAQ)**	**Honiara / Brisbane, QLD (HIR/BNE)**

Operates cargo flights using aircraft leased from HeavyLift Cargo as required

SOLOMONS	**Solomon (IE/SOL)**	**Honiara (HIR)**

☐ H4-AAI	Britten-Norman BN-2A-9 Islander	355	ex N355BN
☐ H4-HNP	de Havilland DHC-6 Twin Otter 300	491	ex YJ-RV1
☐ H4-SID	de Havilland DHC-6 Twin Otter 300	442	ex VH-XFE

I-ITALY (Italian Republic)

AIR DOLOMITI — Dolomiti (EN/DLA) — Trieste (TRS)

☐ I-ADLL	ATR 42-500	518	ex F-OHFP	La Rondine di Giacomo Puccini	
☐ I-ADLQ	ATR 42-500	606	ex F-WQMA	L'Elisir d'Amore de Gaetano	[MGL]♦
☐ I-ADCA	ATR 72-212A	658	ex D-ANFG		
☐ I-ADCB	ATR 72-212A	660	ex D-ANFH		
☐ I-ADCC	ATR 72-212A	662	ex D-ANFI		
☐ I-ADCD	ATR 72-212A	664	ex D-ANFJ		♦
☐ I-ADCE	ATR 72-212A	668	ex D-ANFL		♦
☐ I-ADLJ	ATR 72-212A	686	ex F-WQMO	Il Trovatore di Giuseppe Verdi	
☐ I-ADLK	ATR 72-212A	706	ex F-WWEF	Il Barbiere de Siviglia di Gioacchino Rossini	
☐ I-ADLN	ATR 72-212A	557	ex F-WWLV	Turandot di Giacomo Puccini	
☐ I-ADLO	ATR 72-212A	585	ex F-WQJH	La Bohème di Giacomo Puccini	
☐ I-ADLS	ATR 72-212A	634	ex F-WQMB	Ernani di Giuseppe Verdi	
☐ I-ADLT	ATR 72-212A	638	ex F-WQME	Otello di Giuseppe Verdi	
☐ I-ADLW	ATR 72-212A	707	ex F-WWEG	La Gazza Ladra di Gioacchino Rossini Donizzetti	
☐ I-ADJK	Embraer ERJ-195LR	19000245	ex PT-SIQ		
☐ I-ADJL	Embraer ERJ-195LR	19000256	ex PT-STE		
☐ I-ADJM	Embraer ERJ-195LR	19000258	ex PT-STG		
☐ I-ADJN	Embraer ERJ-195LR	19000270	ex PT-TLKja		
☐ I-ADJO	Embraer ERJ-195LR	19000280	ex PT-TLU		

AIR EUROPE ITALY — Air Europe (VA/VLE) — Milan-Malpensa (MXP)

Wholly owned subsidiary of Volare Group, parent of Volareweb

AIR ITALY — Air Italy (I9/AEY) — Milan-Malpensa (MXP)

☐ EI-IGR	Boeing 737-36N/W	28561/2896	ex N561SM	♦
☐ EI-IGS	Boeing 737-36N/W	28562/2908	ex N562SM	♦
☐ I-AIGL	Boeing 737-33A	23636/1438	ex N636AN	
☐ I-AIGM	Boeing 737-33A	24299/1598	ex SE-RCS	
☐ I-AIGN	Boeing 737-84P/W	35074/2217	ex N574TC	
☐ I-AIGP	Boeing 737-76N/W	37233/2578	ex OM-NGQ	
☐ I-AIGG	Boeing 767-304ER	28041/614	ex G-OBYC	
☐ I-AIGH	Boeing 767-23BER	23973/208	ex N252MY	
☐ I-AIGI	Boeing 767-23BER	23974/214	ex N253MY	
☐ I-AIGJ	Boeing 767-304ER	28039/610	ex N769NA	

AIR VALLÉE — Air Vallée (DO/RVL) — Aosta (AOT)

☐ I-AIRJ	Dornier 328-300 (328JET)	3186		
☐ I-AIRX	Dornier 328-300 (328JET)	3142	ex D-BDXS	Casino de la Vallée c/s

ALIDAUNIA — Lid (D4/LID) — Foggia (FOG)

☐ I-AGSE	Agusta A.109A II	7354		
☐ I-AGSH	Agusta A.109A II	7384		
☐ I-LIDC	MBB BK-117C-1	7529	ex D-HMB.	
☐ I-LIDD	Agusta A.109E Power	11107		
☐ I-MSTR	Agusta A.109A	7227	ex N4256P	
☐ I-RMDV	Sikorsky S-76A	760235	ex (N721CD)	
☐ I-	Agusta AW139			o/o
☐ I-	Agusta AW139			o/o

ALITALIA — Alitalia (AZ/AZA) — Rome-Fiumicino (FCO)

Member of Skyteam

☐ EI-IMC	Airbus A319-112	2057	ex I-BIMC	Isola di Lipari	♦
☐ EI-IME	Airbus A319-112	1740	ex I-BIME	Isola di Panarea	♦
☐ EI-IMF	Airbus A319-112	2083	ex I-BIMF	Isola Tremiti	♦
☐ EI-IMG	Airbus A319-112	2086	ex I-BIMG	Isola di Pantelleria	♦
☐ EI-IMH	Airbus A319-112	2101	ex I-BIMH	Isola di Ventotene	♦
☐ EI-IMI	Airbus A319-112	1745	ex I-BIMI	Isola di Ponza	♦
☐ EI-IMJ	Airbus A319-112	1779	ex I-BIMJ	Isola di Caprera	♦
☐ EI-IML	Airbus A319-112	2127	ex I-BIML	Isola La Maddalena	♦
☐ EI-IMO	Airbus A319-112	1770	ex I-BIMO	Isola d'Ischia	♦
☐ I-BIMA	Airbus A319-112	1722	ex D-AVWP	Isola d'Elba	
☐ I-BIMB	Airbus A319-112	2033	ex D-AVYP	Isola del Giglio	
☐ I-BIMD	Airbus A319-112	2074	ex D-AVYM	Isola di Capri	

☐ EI-DSA	Airbus A320-216	2869	ex F-WWBE		
☐ EI-DSB	Airbus A320-216	2932	ex F-WWBX		
☐ EI-DSC	Airbus A320-216	2995	ex F-WWIY		
☐ EI-DSD	Airbus A320-216	3076	ex F-WWIP		
☐ EI-DSE	Airbus A320-216	3079	ex F-WWIL		
☐ EI-DSF	Airbus A320-216	3080	ex F-WWIV		
☐ EI-DSG	Airbus A320-216	3115	ex F-WWIZ		
☐ EI-DSH	Airbus A320-216	3178	ex F-WWDS		
☐ EI-DSI	Airbus A320-216	3213	ex F-WWIU		
☐ EI-DSJ	Airbus A320-216	3295	ex F-WWDV		
☐ EI-DSK	Airbus A320-216	3328	ex F-WWIX		
☐ EI-DSL	Airbus A320-216	3343	ex F-WWBO		
☐ EI-DSM	Airbus A320-216	3362	ex F-WWIR		
☐ EI-DSN	Airbus A320-216	3412	ex F-WWIL		
☐ EI-DSO	Airbus A320-216	3464	ex F-WWBM		
☐ EI-DSP	Airbus A320-216	3482	ex F-WWDM		
☐ EI-DSR	Airbus A320-216	3502	ex F-WWBR		
☐ EI-DSS	Airbus A320-216	3515	ex F-WWDP		
☐ EI-DST	Airbus A320-216	3532	ex F-WWDY		
☐ EI-DSU	Airbus A320-216	3563	ex F-WWBI		
☐ EI-DSV	Airbus A320-216	3598	ex F-WWDJ		
☐ EI-DSW	Airbus A320-216	3609	ex F-WWIE		
☐ EI-DSX	Airbus A320-216	3643	ex F-WWBT		
☐ EI-DSY	Airbus A320-216	3666	ex F-WWDY		
☐ EI-DSZ	Airbus A320-216	3695	ex F-WWBI		
☐ EI-DTA	Airbus A320-216	3732	ex F-WWDM		
☐ EI-DTB	Airbus A320-216	3815	ex F-WWIF	Giacomo Leopardi	
☐ EI-DTC	Airbus A320-216	3831	ex F-WWBD		
☐ EI-DTD	Airbus A320-216	3846	ex F-WWBY		
☐ EI-DTE	Airbus A320-216	3885	ex F-WWIY	Francesco Petrarca	
☐ EI-DTF	Airbus A320-216	3906	ex F-WWIM	Giovanni Boccaccio	
☐ EI-DTG	Airbus A320-216	3921	ex F-WWBK	Ludovico Ariosto	
☐ EI-DTH	Airbus A320-216	3956	ex F-WWBZ	Torquato Tasso	
☐ EI-DTI	Airbus A320-216	3976	ex F-WWIV	Niccolo Machiavelli	
☐ EI-DTJ	Airbus A320-216	3978	ex F-WWIX	Giovani Pascoli	
☐ EI-DTK	Airbus A320-216	4075	ex F-WWBN	Giovanni Verga	
☐ EI-DTL	Airbus A320-216	4108	ex F-WWDS		
☐ EI-DTM	Airbus A320-216	4119	ex F-WWIE		
☐ EI-DTN	Airbus A320-216	4143	ex F-WWBB		
☐ EI-DTO	Airbus A320-216	4152	ex F-WWBJ		
☐ EI-EIA	Airbus A320-216	4195	ex F-WWIL	Elsa Morante	◆
☐ EI-EIB	Airbus A320-216	4249	ex F-WWDX		◆
☐ EI-EIC	Airbus A320-216	4520	ex D-AXAI		◆
☐ EI-EID	Airbus A320-216	4523	ex D-AUBU		◆
☐ EI-EIE	Airbus A320-216	4536	ex D-AXAL		◆
☐ EI-	Airbus A320-216		ex		o/o◆
☐ EI-	Airbus A320-216		ex		o/o◆
☐ EI-	Airbus A320-216		ex		o/o◆
☐ EI-	Airbus A320-216		ex		o/o◆
☐ EI-	Airbus A320-216		ex		o/o◆
☐ EI-	Airbus A320-216		ex		o/o◆
☐ EI-	Airbus A320-216		ex		o/o◆
☐ EI-	Airbus A320-216		ex		o/o◆
☐ EI-	Airbus A320-216		ex		o/o◆
☐ EI-	Airbus A320-216		ex		o/o◆
☐ EI-	Airbus A320-216		ex		o/o◆
☐ EI-	Airbus A320-216		ex		o/o◆
☐ EI-	Airbus A320-216		ex		o/o◆
☐ EI-	Airbus A320-216		ex		o/o◆
☐ EI-	Airbus A320-216		ex		o/o◆
☐ EI-	Airbus A320-216		ex		o/o◆
☐ EI-	Airbus A320-216		ex		o/o◆
☐ EI-	Airbus A320-216		ex		o/o◆
☐ EI-	Airbus A320-216		ex		o/o◆
☐ EI-IKB	Airbus A320-214	1226	ex I-BIKB	Wolfgang Amadeus Mozart	◆
☐ EI-IKL	Airbus A320-214	1489	ex I-BIKL	Libeccio	◆
☐ EI-IKU	Airbus A320-214	1217	ex I-BIKU	Fryderyk Chopin	◆
☐ I-BIKA	Airbus A320-214	0951	ex F-WWBT	Johann Sebastian Bach	
☐ I-BIKC	Airbus A320-214	1448	ex F-WWBV	Torre di Pisa	
☐ I-BIKD	Airbus A320-214	1457	ex F-WWDE	Maschio Angioino Napoli	
☐ I-BIKE	Airbus A320-214	0999	ex F-WWBZ	Franz Liszt	
☐ I-BIKF	Airbus A320-214	1473	ex F-WWDP	Mole Antonelliana	
☐ I-BIKG	Airbus A320-214	1480	ex F-WWDT	Scirocco	
☐ I-BIKI	Airbus A320-214	1138	ex F-WWDJ	Girolamo Frescobaldi	

☐	I-BIKO	Airbus A320-214	1168	ex F-WWDL	George Bizet	
☐	I-WEBA	Airbus A320-214	3138	ex F-WWDI		
☐	I-WEBB	Airbus A320-214	3161	ex F-WWIC		
☐	EI-IXC	Airbus A321-112	0526	ex I-BIXC	Piazza del Campo-Siena	♦
☐	EI-IXG	Airbus A321-112	0516	ex I-BIXG	Piazza del Miracoli-Pisa	♦
☐	EI-IXH	Airbus A321-112	0940	ex I-BIXH	Piazza della Signoria-Gubbio	♦
☐	EI-IXI	Airbus A321-112	0494	ex I-BIXI	Piazza San Marco-Venezia	♦
☐	EI-IXJ	Airbus A321-112	0959	ex I-BIXJ	Piazza del Municipio-Noto	♦
☐	EI-IXV	Airbus A321-112	0819	ex I-BIXV	Piazza del Rinascimento-Urbino	♦
☐	EI-IXZ	Airbus A321-112	0848	ex I-BIXZ	Piazza del Duomo Orvieto	♦
☐	I-BIXA	Airbus A321-112	0477	ex D-AVZE	Piazza del Duomo-Milano	
☐	I-BIXB	Airbus A321-112	0524	ex D-AVZY	Piazza Castello-Torino	
☐	I-BIXD	Airbus A321-112	0532	ex D-AVZB	Piazza Pretoria-Palermo	
☐	I-BIXE	Airbus A321-112	0488	ex D-AVZG	Piazza di Spagna-Roma	
☐	I-BIXF	Airbus A321-112	0515	ex D-AVZQ	Piazza Maggiore-Bologna	
☐	I-BIXK	Airbus A321-112	1220	ex D-AVZC	Piazza Ducale Vigevano	
☐	I-BIXL	Airbus A321-112	0513	ex D-AVZO	Piazza del Duomo-Lecce	
☐	I-BIXM	Airbus A321-112	0514	ex D-AVZP	Piazza di San Francesco-Assisi	
☐	I-BIXN	Airbus A321-112	0576	ex D-AVZR	Piazza del Duomo-Catania	
☐	I-BIXO	Airbus A321-112	0495	ex D-AVZJ	Piazza Plebiscito-Napoli	
☐	I-BIXP	Airbus A321-112	0583	ex D-AVZT	Carlo Morelli	
☐	I-BIXQ	Airbus A321-112	0586	ex D-AVZU	Domenico Colapietro	
☐	I-BIXR	Airbus A321-112	0593	ex D-AVZW	Piazza del Campidoglio-Roma	
☐	I-BIXS	Airbus A321-112	0599	ex D-AVZZ	Piazza San Martino-Lucca	
☐	I-BIXT	Airbus A321-112	0765	ex D-AVZW	Piazza del Signori-Vicenza	
☐	I-BIXU	Airbus A321-112	0434	ex D-AVZB	Piazza della Signoria-Firenze	
☐	EI-DIP	Airbus A330-202	339	ex A6-EYW		
☐	EI-DIR	Airbus A330-202	272	ex A6-EYV		
☐	EI-EJG	Airbus A330-202	1123	ex F-WWKY	Raffaello Sanzio	♦
☐	EI-EJH	Airbus A330-202	1135	ex F-WWYU	Sandro Botticelli	♦
☐	EI-	Airbus A330-202		ex		o/o♦
☐	EI-	Airbus A330-202		ex		o/o♦
☐	EI-	Airbus A330-202		ex		o/o♦
☐	EI-	Airbus A330-202		ex		o/o♦
☐	EI-	Airbus A330-202		ex		o/o♦
☐	EI-	Airbus A330-202		ex		o/o♦
☐	D-AGMR	Boeing 737-430	27007/2367	ex TC-SUS		
☐	EI-COI	Boeing 737-430	27002/2323	ex D-ABKC		
☐	EI-CWE	Boeing 737-42C	24232/2060	ex N941PG		
☐	EI-CWF	Boeing 737-42C	24814/2270	ex PH-BPG		
☐	EI-CWW	Boeing 737-4Y0	24906/2009	ex EC-GAZ		
☐	EI-CWX	Boeing 737-4Y0	24912/2064	ex EC-GBN		
☐	EI-DMR	Boeing 737-436	25851/2387	ex G-DOCR		
☐	EI-DOH	Boeing 737-31S	29056/2928	ex VT-SAX		
☐	EI-DOS	Boeing 737-49R	28881/2833	ex PK-GWZ		
☐	EI-DOV	Boeing 737-48E	27632/2857	ex HL7512		
☐	F-GKTA	Boeing 737-3M8	24413/1884	ex (OO-LTH)		
☐	EI-CRD	Boeing 767-31BER	26259/534	ex B-2565		
☐	EI-CRF	Boeing 767-31BER	25170/542	ex B-2566		
☐	EI-CRM	Boeing 767-343ER	30009/746	ex (I-DEIB)	Amerigo Vespucci	
☐	EI-DBP	Boeing 767-35HER	26389/459	ex C-GGBJ	Duca degli Abruzzi	
☐	EI-DDW	Boeing 767-3S1ER	26608/559	ex N979PG	Sebastiano Caboto	
☐	I-DEIG	Boeing 767-33AER	27918/603	ex G-OITG	Francesco Agello	
☐	EI-DBK	Boeing 777-243ER	32783/455		Ostuni	
☐	EI-DBL	Boeing 777-243ER	32781/459		Sestriere	
☐	EI-DBM	Boeing 777-243ER	32782/463		Argentario	
☐	EI-DDH	Boeing 777-243ER	32784/477		Tropea	
☐	I-DISA	Boeing 777-243ER	32855/413		Taormina	
☐	I-DISB	Boeing 777-243ER	32859/426		Porto Rotondo	
☐	I-DISD	Boeing 777-243ER	32860/439		Cortina d'Ampezzo	
☐	I-DISE	Boeing 777-243ER	32856/421		Portofino	
☐	I-DISO	Boeing 777-243ER	32857/424	ex N5014K	Positano	
☐	I-DISU	Boeing 777-243ER	32858/425		Madonna de Campiglio	
☐	I-DACQ	McDonnell-Douglas MD-82	49974/1774		Taranto	[FCO]
☐	I-DACR	McDonnell-Douglas MD-82	49975/1775		Carrara	
☐	I-DACS	McDonnell-Douglas MD-82	53053/1806		Maratea	
☐	I-DACT	McDonnell-Douglas MD-82	53054/1856		Valtellina	
☐	I-DACU	McDonnell-Douglas MD-82	53055/1857		Brindisi	[NAP]
☐	I-DACV	McDonnell-Douglas MD-82	53056/1880		Riccione	
☐	I-DACW	McDonnell-Douglas MD-82	53057/1894		Vieste	[FCO]
☐	I-DACX	McDonnell-Douglas MD-82	53060/1944		Piacenza	[FCO]

☐ I-DACY	McDonnell-Douglas MD-82	53059/1942		Novara	[FCO]
☐ I-DACZ	McDonnell-Douglas MD-82	53058/1927		Castelfidardo	
☐ I-DAND	McDonnell-Douglas MD-82	53061/1957		Trani	
☐ I-DANF	McDonnell-Douglas MD-82	53062/1960		Sassari	
☐ I-DANG	McDonnell-Douglas MD-82	53176/1972		Benevento	
☐ I-DANH	McDonnell-Douglas MD-82	53177/1973		Messina	
☐ I-DANL	McDonnell-Douglas MD-82	53178/1994		Cosenza	[FCO]
☐ I-DANM	McDonnell-Douglas MD-82	53179/1997		Vicenza	[FCO]
☐ I-DANP	McDonnell-Douglas MD-82	53180/2002		Fabriano	[FCO]
☐ I-DANQ	McDonnell-Douglas MD-82	53181/2005		Lecce	
☐ I-DANR	McDonnell-Douglas MD-82	53203/2007		Matera	[FCO]
☐ I-DANU	McDonnell-Douglas MD-82	53204/2009		Trapani	
☐ I-DANV	McDonnell-Douglas MD-82	53205/2028		Forte dei Marmi	[FCO]
☐ I-DANW	McDonnell-Douglas MD-82	53206/2034		Siena	
☐ I-DATA	McDonnell-Douglas MD-82	53216/2048		Gubbio	[FCO]
☐ I-DATC	McDonnell-Douglas MD-82	53222/2080		Foggia	
☐ I-DATD	McDonnell-Douglas MD-82	53223/2081		Savona	[FCO]
☐ I-DATE	McDonnell-Douglas MD-82	53217/2053		Grosseto	
☐ I-DATG	McDonnell-Douglas MD-82	53225/2086		Arezzo	
☐ I-DATH	McDonnell-Douglas MD-82	53226/2087		Pescara	[FCO]
☐ I-DATI	McDonnell-Douglas MD-82	53218/2060		Siracusa	
☐ I-DATJ	McDonnell-Douglas MD-82	53227/2103		Lunigiana	[FCO]
☐ I-DATM	McDonnell-Douglas MD-82	53230/2106		Cividale del Friuli	
☐ I-DATO	McDonnell-Douglas MD-82	53219/2062		Reggio Emilia	[FCO]
☐ I-DATQ	McDonnell-Douglas MD-82	53233/2110		Modena	
☐ I-DATR	McDonnell-Douglas MD-82	53234/2111		Livorno	[FCO]
☐ I-DATS	McDonnell-Douglas MD-82	53235/2113	ex N9021J	Foligno	[FCO]
☐ I-DAVB	McDonnell-Douglas MD-82	49216/1262		Ferrara	
☐ I-DAVJ	McDonnell-Douglas MD-82	49431/1377		Parma	
☐ I-DAVR	McDonnell-Douglas MD-82	49550/1584		Pisa	[FCO]
☐ I-DAVT	McDonnell-Douglas MD-82	49552/1597		Como	

ALITALIA EXPRESS		**Ali Express (XM/SMX)**		**Rome-Fiumicino (FCO)**

☐ EI-DOT	Canadair CRJ-900ER	15066	ex C-	
☐ EI-DOU	Canadair CRJ-900ER	15068	ex C-	
☐ EI-DRI	Canadair CRJ-900ER	15076	ex C-	
☐ EI-DRJ	Canadair CRJ-900ER	15077	ex C-	
☐ EI-DRK	Canadair CRJ-900ER	15075	ex C-	
☐ EI-DUK	Canadair CRJ-900ER	15104	ex C-	
☐ EI-DVP	Canadair CRJ-900ER	15116	ex C-	
☐ EI-DVR	Canadair CRJ-900ER	15118	ex C-	
☐ EI-DVS	Canadair CRJ-900ER	15119	ex C-	
☐ EI-DVT	Canadair CRJ-900ER	15123	ex C-	
☐ EI-DFG	Embraer ERJ-170LR	17000008	ex PT-SKA	Via Appia
☐ EI-DFH	Embraer ERJ-170LR	17000009	ex PT-SKB	Via Aurélia
☐ EI-DFI	Embraer ERJ-170LR	17000010	ex PT-SKC	Via Cassia
☐ EI-DFJ	Embraer ERJ-170LR	17000011	ex PT-SKD	Via Flaminia
☐ EI-DFK	Embraer ERJ-170LR	17000032	ex PT-SUA	Via Salaria
☐ EI-DFL	Embraer ERJ-170LR	17000036	ex PT-SUF	Via Tiburtina Valeria

AQUA AIRLINES				**Como**

☐ I-SEAB	Cessna 208 Caravan I	20800225	ex N225WA	FP

BELLE AIR EUROPE				**Bergamo (AOI)**

☐ I-LZAN	ATR 72-212A	908	ex F-ORAB	<LBY♦

BLU EXPRESS.COM		**(BV/BPA)**		**Rome-Fiumicino (FCO)**

☐ EI-CUA	Boeing 737-4K5	24901/1854	ex D-AHLR		<BPA
☐ EI-CUD	Boeing 737-4Q8	26298/2564	ex TC-JEI		<BPA
☐ EI-CUN	Boeing 737-4K5	27074/2281	ex D-AHLS		<BPA
☐ EI-DVY	Boeing 737-31S	29059/2967	ex LZ-BOM	Citta di Palermo	<BPA
☐ EI-DXB	Boeing 737-31S	29060/2979	ex LZ-BON	Citta di Roma	<BPA
☐ EI-EEW	Boeing 737-375	23808/1434	ex N238PL		
☐ EI-ERD	Boeing 737-36N	28563/2921	ex N557MS		♦
☐ I-LLAG	Boeing 767-330ER	25137/377	ex N691LF		

BLUE PANORAMA AIRLINES		**Blue Panorama (BV/BPA)**		**Rome-Fiumicino (FCO)**

☐ EI-CUA	Boeing 737-4K5	24901/1854	ex D-AHLR	
☐ EI-CUD	Boeing 737-4Q8	26298/2564	ex TC-JEI	
☐ EI-CUN	Boeing 737-4K5	27074/2281	ex D-AHLS	
☐ EI-DVY	Boeing 737-31S	29059/2967	ex LZ-BOM	Citta di Palermo
☐ EI-DXB	Boeing 737-31S	29060/2979	ex LZ-BON	Citta di Roma

237

☐ EI-DXC	Boeing 737-4Q8	26300/2604	ex TC-JKA			◆
☐ EI-DKL	Boeing 757-231	28482/770	ex N714P			
☐ EI-DNA	Boeing 757-231	28483/777	ex N715TW			
☐ EI-CXO	Boeing 767-3G5ER	28111/612	ex (I-BPAB)			
☐ EI-CZH	Boeing 767-3G5ER	29435/720	ex (I-BPAD)			
☐ EI-EED	Boeing 767-31AER	27619/595	ex N281LF			

CARGOITALIA — White Pelican (2G/CRG) — Milan-Malpensa (MXP)

☐ EI-EMS	McDonnell-Douglas MD-11BCF	48766/600	ex OH-LGF			◆
☐ EI-UPE	McDonnell-Douglas MD-11C	48427/471	ex I-DUPE			◆
☐ EI-UPI	McDonnell-Douglas MD-11C	48428/474	ex I-DUPI			
☐ I-CGIA	Douglas DC-10-30F	47843/335	ex N331FV	Amarone della Valpolicella	[FNI]	

CARGOLUX ITALIA — (C8 / ICV) — Milan-Malpensa (MXP)

☐ LX-KCV	Boeing 747-4R7F	25868/1125	Lombardia	

CITYFLY — City Fly (CII) — Rome-Urbe (ROM)

☐ I-DEPE	Britten-Norman BN-2B-26 Islander	2253	ex G-BTLY	
☐ I-LACO	Britten-Norman BN-2A-6 Islander	17	ex G-AWBY	

CORPO FORESTALE DELLO STATO — Rome-Ciampino (CIA)

☐ I-CFAA	Agusta-Bell 412SP	25610		CFS-20	
☐ I-CFAB	Agusta-Bell 412SP	25614		CFS-21	
☐ I-CFAC	Agusta-Bell 412SP	25615		CFS-22	
☐ I-CFAD	Agusta-Bell 412SP	25618		CFS-23	
☐ I-CFAE	Agusta-Bell 412EP	25918		CFS-24	
☐ I-CFAF	Agusta-Bell 412EP	25919		CFS-25	
☐ I-CFAK	Agusta-Bell 412EP	25926		CFS-26	
☐ I-CFAL	Agusta-Bell 412EP	25978		CFS-27	
☐ I-CFSJ	Agusta-Bell 412	25561		CFS-14	
☐ I-CFSO	Agusta-Bell 412	25562		CFS-15	
☐ I-CFSP	Agusta-Bell 412	25563		CFS-16	
☐ I-CFSW	Agusta-Bell 412	25564		CFS-18	
☐ I-CFSX	Agusta-Bell 412	25572		CFS-19	
☐ I-CFAG	Erickson/Sikorsky S-64E Skycrane	64088	ex N213AC	CFS-100	Op by European Air-Crane
☐ I-CFAH	Erickson/Sikorsky S-64E Skycrane	64080	ex N174AC	CFS-101	Op by European Air-Crane
☐ I-CFAI	Erickson/Sikorsky S-64E Skycrane	64067	ex N197AC	CFS-102	Op by European Air-Crane
☐ I-CFAJ	Erickson/Sikorsky S-64E Skycrane	64078	ex N227AC	CFS-103	Op by European Air-Crane

EAGLE AIRLINES — E3/EGS — Venice (VCE)

☐ I-GIOA	Fokker 100	11315	ex F-GNLI		◆
☐ I-GIOB	Fokker 100	11364	ex F-GIOG		o/o◆
☐ I-GIOI	Fokker 100	11307	ex F-GNLK		◆

ELBAFLY — Elba-Island de Campo (EBA)

☐ S5-BAF	LET L-410UVP-E8C	912540	ex OM-WDA	FedEx colours	Lsd fr/op by SOP

ELIDOLOMITI — Elidolomiti (EDO) — Belluno (BLX)

☐ EC-JKP	Agusta A.109E Power	11637		EMS <HSE
☐ I-AGKL	Agusta A.109K2	10020		EMS
☐ I-REMJ	Agusta A.109S Grand	22041		EMS
☐ I-REMR	Agusta A.109E Power	11133		EMS
☐ I-REMV	Agusta A.109E Power	11119		EMS

ELIFRIULA — Elifriula (EFG) — Trieste (TRS)

☐ I-HBLU	Aérospatiale AS350B3 Ecureuil	3940	ex F-WWPE	
☐ I-HOLD	Aérospatiale AS350B3 Ecureuil	3566		
☐ I-HORT	Aérospatiale AS350B Ecureuil	3699		
☐ I-HPLC	Aérospatiale AS350B Ecureuil	3702		
☐ I-HALP	Eurocopter EC135T2	0469	ex D-HDOL	
☐ I-HIFI	Eurocopter EC135T1	0085		EMS
☐ I-HSAR	Agusta A.109E Power	11125		EMS
☐ I-ORAO	Aérospatiale AS355N Ecureuil 2	5583		

ELILARIO ITALIA — Lario (ELH) — Colico/Bergamo-Orio al Serio(-/BGY)

☐ I-EITB	Agusta-Bell 412SP	25972		
☐ I-MAGM	Agusta-Bell 412SP	25602	ex Fv11338	

☐ I-NUBJ	Agusta-Bell 412EP	25913			
☐ I-RMTI	Agusta-Bell 412EP	25923			
☐ I-RNBR	Agusta-Bell 412EP	25921			
☐ I-EITC	Agusta A.109S Grand	22007			
☐ I-ESUE	Agusta A.109E Power	11124			
☐ I-FLAK	Agusta A.109E Power	11076			
☐ I-GEMI	Agusta A.109E Power	11085			
☐ I-NIGI	Agusta A.109E Power	11619			
☐ I-RCPM	Agusta A.109E Power Elite	11172			
☐ I-AICO	MBB BK-117C-1	7542	ex D-HZBV		
☐ I-AVJF	MBB BK-117C-1	7525	ex D-HMBI		
☐ I-DENI	MBB BK-117C-1	7539			
☐ I-EITF	MBB BK-117C-1	9082	ex D-HMBI		
☐ I-EITG	MBB BK-117C-1	9086	ex D-HMBN		
☐ I-EITH	MBB BK-117C-1	9093	ex D-HMBB		
☐ I-HBHG	MBB BK-117B-2	7164	ex D-HBHG		
☐ I-HECD	MBB BK-117C-1	7500	ex D-HECD	EMS	
☐ I-HVEN	MBB BK-117C-1	7526	ex D-HVEN	EMS	
☐ I-MESO	MBB BK-117C-1	7532	ex D-HMB.		
☐ I-DAMS	Aérospatiale AS365N3 Dauphin 2	6700	ex F-WWQX		
☐ I-EITD	Agusta AW139	31054	ex I-RAIC		
☐ I-HMED	Aérospatiale EC.135T1	0082	ex D-HBYI	EMS	
☐ I-LOBE	Aérospatiale AS365N3 Dauphin 2	6699	ex F-WWQX		
☐ I-ROCS	Agusta AW139	31005		EMS	
☐ I-VRVR	Aérospatiale AS355F1 Ecureuil 2	5180			

ELILOMBARDA		(EQA)		Calcinate del Pesce

☐ I-CEPA	Agusta AW139	31050	
☐ I-CESR	Agusta A.109S Grand	22033	
☐ I-HELO	Agusta A.109E Power	11605	
☐ I-MALF	Agusta-Bell 412EP	25975	EMS
☐ I-MECE	Agusta-Bell 412EP	25976	EMS
☐ I-PAXE	Agusta A.109E Power	11127	

EUROPEAN AIR CRANE	Florence (FLR)

European Air Crane is a subsidiary of Erikson Air Craneoperates Erickson/Sikorsky S-64E Skycranes for CFDS

HELI-ITALIA	Helitalia (HIT)	Florence (FLR)

☐ I-HBHA	Agusta A.109K2	10023	ex I-ECAM	EMS
☐ I-HBHB	Agusta A.109K2	10025	ex N109TA	EMS
☐ I-HDPR	Agusta A.109E	11625		EMS
☐ I-MAFP	Agusta A.109E Power	11121		EMS
☐ I-RRMM	Agusta A.109E Power	11667		EMS
☐ D-HDNO	MBB BK-117C-1	7548		EMS
☐ D-HDSR	MBB BK-117C-1	7545		EMS
☐ I-HBHC	MBB BK-117B-1	7251	ex D-HITZ	EMS
☐ I-HBMC	MBB BK-117C-1	7528	ex D-HBMC	EMS
☐ I-HBMS	MBB BK-117C-1	7531	ex D-HMBB	EMS
☐ I-HDBX	MBB BK-117C-1	7546	ex D-HDBX	EMS
☐ I-HDBZ	MBB BK-117C-1	7547	ex D-HDBZ	EMS
☐ I-HKAV	MBB BK-117C-1	7540	ex D-HKAV	EMS

ITALI AIRLINES	Itali (9X/ACL)	Pescara (PSR)

☐ I-ACLG	Dornier 328-310 (328JET)	3133	ex D-BGAG	
☐ I-ACLH	Dornier 328-310 (328JET)	3152	ex D-BGAR	
☐ I-BSTI	Swearingen SA.227AC Metro III	AC-470	ex N581BT	
☐ I-BSTS	Swearingen SA.227AC Metro III	AC-603	ex N3117S	
☐ I-DAVA	McDonnell-Douglas MD-82	49215/1253		
☐ I-DAWW	McDonnell-Douglas MD-82	49212/1233		
☐ I-DAWZ	McDonnell-Douglas MD-82	49214/1245		
☐ I-	ATR 72-		ex	o/o

ITALIATOUR AIRLINES		

☐ I-CLBA	Avro 146-RJ85	E2300	ex EI-CNJ	[BSL]

LIVINGSTON	Livingston (LM/LVG)	Milan-Malpensa (MXP)

Suspended operations October 2010

LUFTHANSA ITALIA

☐ D-AILI	Airbus A319-114	0651	ex D-AVYY	Roma
☐ D-AKNF	Airbus A319-112	0646	ex D-AVYB	Torino
☐ D-AKNG	Airbus A319-112	0654	ex D-AVYX	Varese
☐ D-AKNH	Airbus A319-112	0794	ex D-AVYD	Bologna
☐ D-AKNI	Airbus A319-112	1016	ex D-AVYK	Genova
☐ D-AKNJ	Airbus A319-112	1172	ex D-AVWF	

MERIDIANA FLY — Merair (IG/EEZ) — Olbia (OLB)

☐ EI-DEZ	Airbus A319-112	1283	ex F-WQQE	Capo Gallo	
☐ EI-DFA	Airbus A319-112	1305	ex D-ANDI	Capo Carbonara	
☐ EI-DFP	Airbus A319-112	1048	ex F-OHJV	Capo Caccia	
☐ I-EEZQ	Airbus A319-112	0518	ex F-OOUA		♦
☐ EI-EZO	Airbus A320-232	1723	ex I-EEZO		♦
☐ EI-EZR	Airbus A320-214	1198	ex N267AV		♦
☐ I-EEZE	Airbus A320-214	1937	ex F-WWIO		
☐ I-EEZF	Airbus A320-214	1983	ex F-WWDM		
☐ I-EEZG	Airbus A320-214	2001	ex F-WWBB	Domina titles	
☐ I-EEZH	Airbus A320-214	0737	ex F-GRSG		
☐ I-EEZI	Airbus A320-214	0749	ex F-GRSH		
☐ I-EEZK	Airbus A320-214	1125	ex I-VLEA		
☐ I-EEZN	Airbus A320-232	1715	ex G-TTOC		
☐ I-EEZP	Airbus A320-233	2102	ex N489TA		
☐ EI-EZL	Airbus A330-223	802	ex I-EEZL		
☐ I-EEZJ	Airbus A330-223	665	ex F-WWKO	Campari titles	
☐ I-EEZM	Airbus A330-223	822	ex 4X-ABE		
☐ EI-CIW	McDonnell-Douglas MD-83	49785/1628	ex HL7271	Isola Tremiti	
☐ EI-CKM	McDonnell-Douglas MD-83	49792/1655	ex TC-INC	Isola dell'Asinara	
☐ EI-CNR	McDonnell-Douglas MD-83	53199/1968	ex N531LS		
☐ EI-CRE	McDonnell-Douglas MD-83	49854/1601	ex D-ALLL	Tavolara-Punta Coda Cavallo	
☐ EI-CRH	McDonnell-Douglas MD-83	49935/1773	ex HB-IKM	Torre Guaceto	
☐ EI-CRW	McDonnell-Douglas MD-83	49951/1915	ex HB-IKN	Portofino	
☐ I-SMEB	McDonnell-Douglas MD-82	53064/1908	ex B-28001	Parco di Baia	
☐ I-SMEC	McDonnell-Douglas MD-83	49808/1836	ex N183NA	Porto Cesareo	
☐ I-SMEL	McDonnell-Douglas MD-82	49247/1151	ex HB-IKK	Parco Gaiola	
☐ I-SMEM	McDonnell-Douglas MD-82	49248/1152	ex HB-IKL	Penisola del sinis	
☐ I-SMEN	McDonnell-Douglas MD-83	53013/1738	ex EI-CRJ	Isole Egadi	
☐ I-SMEP	McDonnell-Douglas MD-82	49740/1618		Punta Campanella	
☐ I-SMER	McDonnell-Douglas MD-82	49901/1766	ex N6202S	Cinque Terre	
☐ I-SMES	McDonnell-Douglas MD-82	49902/1948		Isole Pelagie	
☐ I-SMET	McDonnell-Douglas MD-82	49531/1362		Miramare nel Golfo di Trieste	
☐ I-SMEV	McDonnell-Douglas MD-82	49669/1493		Isole di Ventotene e Santo Stefano	
☐ I-SMEZ	McDonnell-Douglas MD-82	49903/1949	ex PH-SEZ	Secche di Tor Paterno	

MINILINER — Miniliner (MNL) — Bergamo-Orio al Serio (BGY)

☐ I-MLGT	Fokker F.27 Friendship 500	10379	ex F-BPUG		
☐ I-MLHT	Fokker F.27 Friendship 500	10382	ex F-BPUH		
☐ I-MLQT	Fokker F.27 Friendship 400	10295	ex HB-ITQ		
☐ I-MLRT	Fokker F.27 Friendship 500	10377	ex F-BPUE		
☐ I-MLTT	Fokker F.27 Friendship 500	10378	ex F-BPUF		
☐ I-MLUT	Fokker F.27 Friendship 500	10369	ex F-BPUA		
☐ I-MLVT	Fokker F.27 Friendship 500	10373	ex F-BPUC		
☐ I-MLXT	Fokker F.27 Friendship 500	10374	ex F-BPUD		
☐ I-MLCT	Fokker 50	20191	ex PH-KVC	Frtr	
☐ I-MLDT	Fokker 50	20197	ex PH-KVD	Frtr	
☐ PH-LMA	Fokker 50	20118	ex (PH-LCA)	Frtr	>APF
☐ PH-LMB	Fokker 50	20119	ex (PH-LCD)	Frtr	>APF

MISTRAL AIR — Airmerci (MSA) — Rome-Ciampino (CIA)

☐ EI-DUS	Boeing 737-3M8 (QC)	24021/1630	ex TF-ELM	Maestrale	
☐ EI-DVA	Boeing 737-36E (QC)	25159/2068	ex F-GIXM		
☐ EI-DVC	Boeing 737-33A (QC)	25426/2172	ex SE-DPC	Libeccio	
☐ EI-ELY	Boeing 737-4S3	25595/2233	ex SX-BGJ		♦
☐ EI-ELZ	Boeing 737-4Q8	26308/2665	ex SX-BGV		♦
☐ EI-SLA	ATR 42-300F	149	ex SE-LST		<ABR
☐ EI-SLC	ATR 42-300F	082	ex OY-CIE		<ABR

240

NEOS		Moonflower (NO/NOS)			Milan-Malpensa (MXP)
☐ I-NDMJ	Boeing 767-306ER/W	27958/589	ex EI-DMJ	Ciudad de la Habana	♦
☐ I-NDOF	Boeing 767-306ER	27610/605	ex EI-DOF		♦
☐ I-NEOS	Boeing 737-86N/W	32733/1078		Citta di Milano	
☐ I-NEOT	Boeing 737-86N/W	33004/1144		Citta di Torino	
☐ I-NEOU	Boeing 737-86N/W	29887/1263		Citta di Verona	
☐ I-NEOW	Boeing 737-86N/W	32685/2186	ex G-XLAN	Lago Maggiore	
☐ I-NEOX	Boeing 737-86N/W	33677/1486		Citta di Bologna	
☐ I-NEOZ	Boeing 737-86N/W	34257/2024	ex SU-BPH		o/o♦

SKYBRIDGE AIROPS				Rome-Ciampano (CIA)
☐ I-SKYB	Embraer EMB.120RT Brasilia	120087	ex F-GTSG	

SOREM				Rome-Ciampano/Urbe (CIA/ROM)
☐ I-CFST	Canadair CL215	1072	ex MM62019	1
☐ I-SRMA	Canadair CL215	1004	ex I-SMRA	A1
☐ I-SRMC	Canadair CL215	1076	ex C-GBXQ	S2
☐ I-SRMD	Canadair CL215	1097	ex C-GOFN	S3
☐ I-SRME	Canadair CL215	1049	ex C-GUKM	S4
☐ I-DPCC	Canadair CL415	2066	ex C-FNLH	27
☐ I-DPCD	Canadair CL415	2003	ex C-FTUA	7
☐ I-DPCE	Canadair CL415	2004	ex C-FTUS	8
☐ I-DPCF	Canadair CL415	2059	ex C-GIWU	23
☐ I-DPCG	Canadair CL415	2060	ex C-GJHU	24
☐ I-DPCH	Canadair CL415	2062	ex C-GJLB	25
☐ I-DPCI	Canadair CL415	2058	ex C-GISM	26
☐ I-DPCN	Canadair CL415	2070	ex C-FUEP	28
☐ I-DPCO	Canadair CL415	2009	ex C-FVRA	10
☐ I-DPCP	Canadair CL415	2020	ex C-FYCY	11
☐ I-DPCQ	Canadair CL415	2021	ex C-FYDA	12
☐ I-DPCR	Canadair CL415	2074	ex C-FZTY	♦
☐ I-DPCS	Canadair CL415	2073	ex C-FZEG	♦
☐ I-DPCT	Canadair CL415	2029	ex C-FZYS	18
☐ I-DPCU	Canadair CL415	2030	ex C-GALV	14
☐ I-DPCV	Canadair CL415	2035	ex C-GCXG	15
☐ I-DPCW	Canadair CL415	2036	ex C-GDHW	6
☐ I-DPCY	Canadair CL415	2047	ex C-GFUS	20
☐ I-DPCZ	Canadair CL415	2048	ex C-GGCW	21

VOLIAMO				
☐ HA-LEW	Boeing 737-2K2C (AvAero 3)	20836/354	ex F-GIXA	

WINDJET		Ghibli (IV/JET)		Catania (CTA)
☐ EI-DVD	Airbus A319-113	0647	ex F-GPMH	
☐ EI-DVU	Airbus A319-113	0660	ex F-GPMI	
☐ EI-ECX	Airbus A319-132	2698	ex N515NK	
☐ EI-ECY	Airbus A319-132	2723	ex N519NK	
☐ EI-CUM	Airbus A320-232	0542	ex N721LF	
☐ EI-DFO	Airbus A320-211	0371	ex A6-ABX	
☐ EI-DNP	Airbus A320-212	0421	ex A4O-EF	
☐ EI-DOE	Airbus A320-211	0215	ex F-GJVE	
☐ EI-DOP	Airbus A320-232	0816	ex B-HSF	
☐ EI-ELG	Airbus A320-232	0877	ex B-HSH	
☐ F-GJVC	Airbus A320-211	0204	ex EI-DFN	
☐ I-LINH	Airbus A320-231	0163	ex G-RDVE	

JA   JAPAN

AIR CENTRAL		(NV/CRF)		Nagoya-Chubu (NGO)
☐ JA841A	de Havilland DHC-8-402Q	4080	ex C-GDLK	
☐ JA853A	de Havilland DHC-8-402Q	4135	ex C-FGKN	>AKX
☐ JA854A	de Havilland DHC-8-402Q	4151	ex C-FJLH	>AKX

AIR DO		Air Do (HD/ADO)		Sapporo-New Chitose (CTS)
☐ JA300K	Boeing 737-54K	27434/2872		<ANA
☐ JA8404	Boeing 737-54K	27381/2708	ex N35108	<ANA
☐ JA8504	Boeing 737-54K	27432/2783		

☐ JA8595	Boeing 737-54K	28461/2850		

☐ JA01HD	Boeing 767-33AER	28159/689	ex OO-CTQ	
☐ JA98AD	Boeing 767-33AER	27476/687	ex N767AN	
☐ JA8258	Boeing 767-381	23758/179	ex N6055X	<ANA

AIR DOLPHIN   Okinawa-Naha (OKA)

☐ JA21EG	Beech 65-C90A King Air	LJ-1591	ex N400TG	
☐ JA3428	Cessna P206C Super Skylane	P206-0517	ex N1610C	
☐ JA5320	Britten-Norman BN-2B-20 Islander	2269	ex G-BUBM	

AIR JAPAN   Air Japan (NQ/AJX)   Osaka-Itami/Kansi (ITM/KIX)

☐ JA55DZ	Cessna 208B Caravan I	208B0530	ex N164SA

AIR NEXT   Blue Dolphin (7A/NXA)   Fukuoka (FUK)

☐ JA302K	Boeing 737-54K	28990/3002	ex N1787B	<ANA
☐ JA304K	Boeing 737-54K	28992/3030		<ANA
☐ JA306K	Boeing 737-54K	29794/3109	ex N1786B	<ANA
☐ JA307K	Boeing 737-54K	29795/3116	ex N60436	<ANA
☐ JA351K	Boeing 737-5Y0	25189/2240	ex N189NK	<ANA
☐ JA352K	Boeing 737-5Y0	26097/2534	ex N97NK	<ANA
☐ JA353K	Boeing 737-5Y0	26104/2552	ex N104NK	<ANA
☐ JA354K	Boeing 737-5Y0	26105/2553	ex N105NK	<ANA
☐ JA359K	Boeing 737-5L9	28128/2817	ex N8128R	<ANA

AIR NIPPON   ANK Air (EL/ANK)   Tokyo-Haneda (HND)

☐ JA301K	Boeing 737-54K	27435/2875		<ANA
☐ JA303K	Boeing 737-54K	28991/3017		<ANA
☐ JA305K	Boeing 737-54K	28993/3075	ex N1781B	<ANA
☐ JA355K	Boeing 737-5L9	28129/2823	ex N8129L	<ANA
☐ JA356K	Boeing 737-5L9	28083/2784	ex N8083N	<ANA
☐ JA357K	Boeing 737-5L9	28131/2828	ex N88131	<ANA
☐ JA358K	Boeing 737-5L9	28130/2825	ex N8130J	<ANA
☐ JA392K	Boeing 737-46M	28550/2847	ex N8550F	>ADO
☐ JA8195	Boeing 737-54K	27433/2815		<ANA
☐ JA8196	Boeing 737-54K	27966/2824		<ANA
☐ JA8404	Boeing 737-54K	27381/2708	ex N35108	>ADO
☐ JA8500	Boeing 737-54K	27431/2751		<ANA
☐ JA8596	Boeing 737-54K	28462/2853		<ANA
☐ JA01AN	Boeing 737-781/W	33916/1781	ex N6066U	Gold titles/cheatlines	<ANA
☐ JA02AN	Boeing 737-781/W	33872/1850		Gold titles/cheatlines	<ANA
☐ JA03AN	Boeing 737-781/W	33873/1871	ex N1787B		<ANA
☐ JA04AN	Boeing 737-781/W	33874/1890	ex N1781B		<ANA
☐ JA05AN	Boeing 737-781/W	33875/1971			<ANA
☐ JA06AN	Boeing 737-781/W	33876/1992			<ANA
☐ JA07AN	Boeing 737-781/W	33900/2071			<ANA
☐ JA08AN	Boeing 737-781/W	33877/2086			<ANA
☐ JA09AN	Boeing 737-781/W	33878/2145			<ANA
☐ JA10AN	Boeing 737-781ER/W	33879/2157	ex N716BA	ANA Business Jet	<ANA
☐ JA11AN	Boeing 737-781/W	33882/2268			<ANA
☐ JA12AN	Boeing 737-781/W	33881/2301			<ANA
☐ JA13AN	Boeing 737-781ER/W	33880/2232	ex N717BA	ANA Business Jet	<ANA
☐ JA14AN	Boeing 737-781/W	33883/2370	ex N1787B		<ANA
☐ JA15AN	Boeing 737-781/W	33888/2394	ex N6063S		<ANA
☐ JA16AN	Boeing 737-781/W	33889/2488	ex N721BA		<ANA
☐ JA17AN	Boeing 737-781/W	33884/2513	ex N1779B		<ANA
☐ JA18AN	Boeing 737-781/W	33885/2582			<ANA
☐ JA51AN	Boeing 737-881/W	33886/2607	ex N1766B	<ANA
☐ JA52AN	Boeing 737-881/W	33887/2643		<ANA
☐ JA53AN	Boeing 737-881/W	33891/2739		<ANA
☐ JA54AN	Boeing 737-881/W	33890/2833		<ANA
☐ JA55AN	Boeing 737-881/W	33892/2889		<ANA
☐ JA56AN	Boeing 737-881/W	33893/2926		<ANA
☐ JA57AN	Boeing 737-881/W	33894/2975	ex N1787B	<ANA
☐ JA58AN	Boeing 737-881/W	33895/3029	ex N1796B	<ANA
☐ JA59AN	Boeing 737-881/W	33886/3073		<ANA
☐ JA60AN	Boeing 737-881/W	33897/3126		<ANA
☐ JA61AN	Boeing 737-881/W	33906/3379		<ANA♦
☐ JA62AN	Boeing 737-881/W	33899/3414		<ANA♦
☐ JA63AN	Boeing 737-881/W	33901/3449	ex N1787B	<ANA♦
☐ JA64AN	Boeing 737-881/W	33902/3478	ex N1787B	<ANA♦
☐ JA65AN	Boeing 737-881/W	33903/3502	ex N1786B	<ANA♦

☐ JA801K	de Havilland DHC-8Q-314	565	ex C-GDFT	
☐ JA802K	de Havilland DHC-8Q-314	577	ex C-FDHD	
☐ JA803K	de Havilland DHC-8Q-314	583	ex C-FDHW	
☐ JA804K	de Havilland DHC-8Q-314	591	ex C-GFUM	
☐ JA805K	de Havilland DHC-8Q-314	592	ex C-GFYI	

AIR NIPPON NETWORK · Alfa Wing (EH/ANA) · Sapporo-Okadama (OKD)

☐ JA801K	de Havilland DHC-8Q-314	565	ex C-GDFT	<ANK
☐ JA802K	de Havilland DHC-8Q-314	577	ex C-FDHD	<ANK
☐ JA803K	de Havilland DHC-8Q-314	583	ex C-FDHW	<ANK
☐ JA804K	de Havilland DHC-8Q-314	591	ex C-GFUM	<ANK
☐ JA805K	de Havilland DHC-8Q-314	592	ex C-GFYI	<ANK
☐ JA841A	de Havilland DHC-8-402Q	4080	ex C-GDLK	<ANA
☐ JA842A	de Havilland DHC-8-402Q	4082	ex C-GFOD	<ANA
☐ JA843A	de Havilland DHC-8-402Q	4084	ex C-GFQL	<ANA
☐ JA844A	de Havilland DHC-8-402Q	4091	ex C-GHRI	<ANA
☐ JA845A	de Havilland DHC-8-402Q	4096	ex C-FAQB	<ANA
☐ JA846A	de Havilland DHC-8-402Q	4097	ex C-FAQD	<ANA
☐ JA847A	de Havilland DHC-8-402Q	4099	ex C-FAQK	<ANA
☐ JA848A	de Havilland DHC-8-402Q	4102	ex C-FCQA	<ANA
☐ JA849A	de Havilland DHC-8-402Q	4106	ex C-FCVE	<ANA
☐ JA850A	de Havilland DHC-8-402Q	4108	ex C-FCVJ	<ANA
☐ JA851A	de Havilland DHC-8-402Q	4109	ex C-FCVK	<ANA
☐ JA852A	de Havilland DHC-8-402Q	4131	ex C-FGKC	<ANA
☐ JA853A	de Havilland DHC-8-402Q	4135	ex C-FGKN	<ANA
☐ JA854A	de Havilland DHC-8-402Q	4151	ex C-FJLH	<ANA
☐ JA855A	de Havilland DHC-8-402Q	4292	ex C-GAUB	<ANA
☐ JA856A	de Havilland DHC-8-402Q	4335	ex C-GGHS	<ANA♦
☐ JA	de Havilland DHC-8-402Q		ex C-	o/o♦
☐ JA	de Havilland DHC-8-402Q		ex C-	o/o♦
☐ JA	de Havilland DHC-8-402Q		ex C-	o/o♦

AMAKUSA AIRLINES · (AHX) · Kumamoto (KMJ)

☐ JA81AM	de Havilland DHC-8Q-103	537	ex C-FCSG	

ANA - ALL NIPPON AIRWAYS · All Nippon (NH/ANA) · Tokyo-Haneda (HND)

Member of Star Alliance

☐ JA203A	Airbus A320-214	2061	ex F-WWDC	
☐ JA204A	Airbus A320-214	2998	ex F-WWIZ	
☐ JA205A	Airbus A320-214	3099	ex F-WWIE	
☐ JA206A	Airbus A320-214	3147	ex F-WWBQ	
☐ JA207A	Airbus A320-214	3148	ex F-WWBR	
☐ JA208A	Airbus A320-214	3189	ex F-WWDZ	
☐ JA8300	Airbus A320-211	0549	ex F-WWIT	
☐ JA8304	Airbus A320-211	0531	ex F-WWDY	
☐ JA8313	Airbus A320-211	0534	ex F-WWBC	
☐ JA8382	Airbus A320-211	0139	ex F-WWDF	wfs 30Nov07
☐ JA8384	Airbus A320-211	0151	ex F-WWDR	D-ALLD resd
☐ JA8385	Airbus A320-211	0167	ex F-WWIE	D-ALLE resd
☐ JA8386	Airbus A320-211	0170	ex F-WWII	
☐ JA8387	Airbus A320-211	0196	ex F-WWDE	
☐ JA8388	Airbus A320-211	0212	ex F-WWIG	
☐ JA8389	Airbus A320-211	0219	ex F-WWDZ	
☐ JA8390	Airbus A320-211	0245	ex F-WWDE	D-ALLF resd
☐ JA8391	Airbus A320-211	0300	ex F-WWDD	D-ALLG resd
☐ JA8392	Airbus A320-211	0328	ex F-WWDR	D-ALLH resd
☐ JA8393	Airbus A320-211	0365	ex F-WWBZ	D-ALLI resd
☐ JA8394	Airbus A320-211	0383	ex F-WWBF	
☐ JA8395	Airbus A320-211	0413	ex F-WWIM	
☐ JA8396	Airbus A320-211	0482	ex F-WWIO	D-ALLJ resd
☐ JA8400	Airbus A320-211	0554	ex F-WWIG	
☐ JA8609	Airbus A320-211	0501	ex F-WWIN	
☐ JA8654	Airbus A320-211	0507	ex F-WWBT	
☐ JA8946	Airbus A320-211	0669	ex F-WWBD	
☐ JA8947	Airbus A320-211	0685	ex F-WWDR	
☐ JA8997	Airbus A320-211	0658	ex F-WWIU	
☐ JA	Airbus A320-214		ex F-WW	o/o
☐ JA	Airbus A320-214		ex F-WW	o/o
☐ JA	Airbus A320-214		ex F-WW	o/o

☐ JA300K	Boeing 737-54K	27434/2872		>ADO
☐ JA301K	Boeing 737-54K	27435/2875		>ANK
☐ JA302K	Boeing 737-54K	28990/3002	ex N1787B	>NXA
☐ JA303K	Boeing 737-54K	28991/3017		>ANK

☐	JA304K	Boeing 737-54K	28992/3030	ex N1786B	>NXA
☐	JA305K	Boeing 737-54K	28993/3075	ex N1781B	>ANK
☐	JA306K	Boeing 737-54K	29794/3109		>NXA
☐	JA307K	Boeing 737-54K	29795/3116	ex N60436	>NXA
☐	JA351K	Boeing 737-5Y0	25189/2240	ex N189NK	>NXA
☐	JA352K	Boeing 737-5Y0	26097/2534	ex N97NK	>NXA
☐	JA353K	Boeing 737-5Y0	26104/2552	ex N104NK	>NXA
☐	JA354K	Boeing 737-5Y0	26105/2553	ex N105NK	>NXA
☐	JA355K	Boeing 737-5L9	28129/2823	ex N8129L	>ANK
☐	JA356K	Boeing 737-5L9	28083/2784	ex N8083N	>ANK
☐	JA357K	Boeing 737-5L9	28131/2828	ex N88131	>ANK
☐	JA358K	Boeing 737-5L9	28130/2825	ex N8130J	>ANK
☐	JA359K	Boeing 737-5L9	28128/2817	ex N8128R	>ANK
☐	JA392K	Boeing 737-46M	28550/2847	ex N8550F	>NXA
☐	JA8195	Boeing 737-54K	27433/2815		>ANK
☐	JA8196	Boeing 737-54K	27966/2824		>ANK
☐	JA8404	Boeing 737-54K	27381/2708	ex N35108	>ANK
☐	JA8419	Boeing 737-54K	27430/2723		
☐	JA8500	Boeing 737-54K	27431/2751		>ANK
☐	JA8596	Boeing 737-54K	28462/2853		>ANK
☐	JA01AN	Boeing 737-781/W	33916/1781	ex N6066U	>ANK
☐	JA02AN	Boeing 737-781/W	33872/1850		>ANK
☐	JA03AN	Boeing 737-781/W	33873/1871	ex N1787B	>ANK
☐	JA04AN	Boeing 737-781/W	33874/1890	ex N1781B	>ANK
☐	JA05AN	Boeing 737-781/W	33875/1971		>ANK
☐	JA06AN	Boeing 737-781/W	33876/1992		>ANK
☐	JA07AN	Boeing 737-781/W	33900/2071		>ANK
☐	JA08AN	Boeing 737-781/W	33877/2086		>ANK
☐	JA09AN	Boeing 737-781/W	33878/2145		>ANK
☐	JA10AN	Boeing 737-781ER/W	33879/2157	ex N716BA	>ANK
☐	JA11AN	Boeing 737-781/W	33882/2268		>ANK
☐	JA12AN	Boeing 737-781/W	33881/2301		>ANK
☐	JA13AN	Boeing 737-781ER/W	33880/2232	ex N717BA	>ANK
☐	JA14AN	Boeing 737-781/W	33883/2370		>ANK
☐	JA15AN	Boeing 737-781/W	33888/2394		>ANK
☐	JA16AN	Boeing 737-781/W	33889/2488		>ANK
☐	JA17AN	Boeing 737-781/W	33884/2513		>ANK
☐	JA18AN	Boeing 737-781/W	33885/2582		>ANK
☐	JA	Boeing 737-781/W			o/o♦
☐	JA	Boeing 737-781/W			o/o♦
☐	JA	Boeing 737-781/W			o/o♦
☐	JA	Boeing 737-781/W			o/o♦
☐	JA	Boeing 737-781/W			o/o♦
☐	JA51AN	Boeing 737-881/W	33886/2607	ex N1766B	>ANK
☐	JA52AN	Boeing 737-881/W	33887/2643		>ANK
☐	JA53AN	Boeing 737-881/W	33891/2739		>ANK
☐	JA54AN	Boeing 737-881/W	33890/2833		>ANK
☐	JA55AN	Boeing 737-881/W	33892/2889		>ANK
☐	JA56AN	Boeing 737-881/W	33893/2926		>ANK
☐	JA57AN	Boeing 737-881/W	33894/2975	ex N1787B	>ANK
☐	JA58AN	Boeing 737-881/W	33895/3029	ex N1796B	>ANK
☐	JA59AN	Boeing 737-881/W	33886/3073		>ANK
☐	JA60AN	Boeing 737-881/W	33897/3126		>ANK
☐	JA61AN	Boeing 737-881/W	33906/3379		>ANK♦
☐	JA62AN	Boeing 737-881/W	33899/3414		>ANK♦
☐	JA63AN	Boeing 737-881/W	33901/3449	ex N1787B	>ANK♦
☐	JA64AN	Boeing 737-881/W	33902/3478	ex N1787B	>ANK♦
☐	JA65AN	Boeing 737-881/W	33903/3502	ex N1786B	>ANK♦
☐	JA66AN	Boeing 737-881/W	33909		o/o♦
☐	JA67AN	Boeing 737-881/W	33911		o/o♦
☐	JA8099	Boeing 747-481D	25292/891		
☐	JA8956	Boeing 747-481D	25640/920		Pocket Monsters 2004 colours
☐	JA8957	Boeing 747-481D	25642/927		Pocket Monsters colours
☐	JA8958	Boeing 747-481	25641/928	ex N6009F	
☐	JA8959	Boeing 747-481D	25646/952		
☐	JA8960	Boeing 747-481D	25643/972		
☐	JA8961	Boeing 747-481D	25644/975		
☐	JA8962	Boeing 747-481	25645/979		
☐	JA8963	Boeing 747-481D	25647/991	ex N6055X	
☐	JA8964	Boeing 747-481D	27163/996	ex N5573S	
☐	JA8965	Boeing 747-481D	27436/1060		
☐	JA8966	Boeing 747-481D	27442/1066		
☐	JA601A	Boeing 767-381	27943/669		

☐ JA601F	Boeing 767-381F	33404/885	ex N6055X		>AJV
☐ JA602A	Boeing 767-381	27944/684			
☐ JA602F	Boeing 767-381F	33509/937			>AJV
☐ JA603A☐	Boeing 767-381ER	32972/877	ex N6046P		
☐ JA604A☐	Boeing 767-381ER	32973/881			
☐ JA604F	Boeing 767-381F	35709/947			>AJV
☐ JA605A☐	Boeing 767-381ER	32974/882			
☐ JA606A☐	Boeing 767-381ER	32975/883		Fly Panda c/s	
☐ JA607A☐	Boeing 767-381ER	32976/884			
☐ JA608A☐	Boeing 767-381ER	32977/886			
☐ JA609A☐	Boeing 767-381ER	32978/888			
☐ JA610A☐	Boeing 767-381ER	32979/895			
☐ JA611A☐	Boeing 767-381ER	32980/914		Star Cluster	
☐ JA612A☐	Boeing 767-381ER	33506/920			
☐ JA613A☐	Boeing 767-381ER	33507/924			
☐ JA614A	Boeing 767-381ER	33508/931		Star Alliance colours	
☐ JA615A	Boeing 767-381ER	35877/951			
☐ JA616A	Boeing 767-381ER	35876/953			
☐ JA617A	Boeing 767-381ER	37719/971			
☐ JA618A	Boeing 767-381ER	37720/976			
☐ JA619A	Boeing 767-381ER	40564/993			♦
☐ JA620A	Boeing 767-381ER	40565/996			♦
☐ JA621A	Boeing 767-381ER	40566/998			♦
☐ JA	Boeing 767-381ER				o/o♦
☐ JA	Boeing 767-381ER				o/o♦
☐ JA	Boeing 767-381ER				o/o♦
☐ JA	Boeing 767-381ER				o/o♦
☐ JA8256	Boeing 767-381	23756/176	ex N6005C		
☐ JA8257	Boeing 767-381	23757/177	ex N6038E		
☐ JA8258	Boeing 767-381	23758/179	ex N6055X		>ADO
☐ JA8259	Boeing 767-381	23759/185	ex N6038E		
☐ JA8271	Boeing 767-381	24002/199	ex N60668		
☐ JA8272	Boeing 767-381	24003/212	ex N6038E		
☐ JA8273	Boeing 767-381	24004/218	ex N6055X		
☐ JA8274	Boeing 767-381	24005/222	ex N6046P		
☐ JA8275	Boeing 767-381	24006/223	ex N6018N		
☐ JA8285	Boeing 767-381	24350/245	ex N1789B		
☐ JA8286	Boeing 767-381ERBCF	24400/269			
☐ JA8287	Boeing 767-381	24351/271			
☐ JA8288	Boeing 767-381	24415/276			
☐ JA8289	Boeing 767-381	24416/280			
☐ JA8290	Boeing 767-381	24417/290			
☐ JA8291	Boeing 767-381	24755/295			
☐ JA8322	Boeing 767-381	25618/458			
☐ JA8323	Boeing 767-381ERBCF	25654/463			
☐ JA8324	Boeing 767-381	25655/465			
☐ JA8342	Boeing 767-381	27445/573			
☐ JA8356	Boeing 767-381ERBCF	25136/379			
☐ JA8357	Boeing 767-381	25293/401			
☐ JA8358	Boeing 767-381ERBCF	25616/432			
☐ JA8359	Boeing 767-381	25617/439			
☐ JA8360	Boeing 767-381	25055/352			
☐ JA8362	Boeing 767-381ERBCF	24632/285			
☐ JA8363	Boeing 767-381	24756/300			
☐ JA8368	Boeing 767-381	24880/336			
☐ JA8567	Boeing 767-381	25656/510			
☐ JA8568	Boeing 767-381	25657/515			
☐ JA8569	Boeing 767-381	27050/516			
☐ JA8578	Boeing 767-381	25658/519			
☐ JA8579	Boeing 767-381	25659/520			
☐ JA8664	Boeing 767-381ER	27339/556			
☐ JA8669	Boeing 767-381	27444/567			
☐ JA8670	Boeing 767-381	25660/539			
☐ JA8674	Boeing 767-381	25661/543			
☐ JA8677	Boeing 767-381	25662/551			
☐ JA8970	Boeing 767-381ER	25619/645			
☐ JA8971	Boeing 767-381ER	27942/651			
☐ N742AX	Boeing 767-232 (SCD)	22217/27	ex N105DA		<ABX
☐ N744AX	Boeing 767-232 (SCD)	22221/53	ex N109DL		<ABX
☐ JA701A	Boeing 777-281	27938/77			
☐ JA702A	Boeing 777-281	27033/75			
☐ JA703A	Boeing 777-281	27034/81	ex N50217		
☐ JA704A	Boeing 777-281	27035/131			
☐ JA705A	Boeing 777-281	29029/137			
☐ JA706A	Boeing 777-281	27036/141			
☐ JA707A	Boeing 777-281ER	27037/247			

☐ JA708A	Boeing 777-281ER	28277/278			
☐ JA709A	Boeing 777-281ER	28278/286			
☐ JA710A	Boeing 777-281ER	28279/302			
☐ JA711A	Boeing 777-281	33406/482		Star Alliance c/s	
☐ JA712A	Boeing 777-281	33407/495		Star Alliance c/s	
☐ JA713A	Boeing 777-281	32647/509			
☐ JA714A	Boeing 777-281	28276/523			
☐ JA715A	Boeing 777-281ER	32646/563			
☐ JA716A	Boeing 777-281ER	33414/574			
☐ JA717A	Boeing 777-281ER	33415/580			
☐ JA731A	Boeing 777-381ER	28281/488	ex N240BA	Star Alliance colours	
☐ JA732A	Boeing 777-381ER	27038/511			
☐ JA733A	Boeing 777-381ER	32648/529	ex N5014K		
☐ JA734A	Boeing 777-381ER	32649/557			
☐ JA735A	Boeing 777-381ER	34892/571			
☐ JA736A	Boeing 777-381ER	34893/589			
☐ JA751A	Boeing 777-381	28272/142	ex N5017Q		
☐ JA752A	Boeing 777-381	28274/160			
☐ JA753A	Boeing 777-381	28273/132			Sky Blue
☐ JA754A	Boeing 777-381	27939/172			Sky Lark
☐ JA755A	Boeing 777-381	28275/104	ex N5017Q		
☐ JA756A	Boeing 777-381	27039/440			
☐ JA757A	Boeing 777-381	27040/442			
☐ JA777A	Boeing 777-381ER	32650/593			
☐ JA778A	Boeing 777-381ER	32651/606			
☐ JA779A	Boeing 777-381ER	34894/631			
☐ JA780A	Boeing 777-381ER	34895/639			
☐ JA781A	Boeing 777-381ER	27041/667			
☐ JA782A	Boeing 777-381ER	33416/691			
☐ JA783A	Boeing 777-381ER	27940/737			
☐ JA784A	Boeing 777-381ER	37950/833			
☐ JA785A	Boeing 777-381ER	37951/855			♦
☐ JA786A	Boeing 777-381ER	37948/866			♦
☐ JA787A	Boeing 777-381ER	37949/870			♦
☐ JA788A	Boeing 777-381ER	40686/873			♦
☐ JA789A	Boeing 777-381ER	40687/878			♦
☐ JA8197	Boeing 777-281	27027/16	ex N5016R		
☐ JA8198	Boeing 777-281	27028/21			
☐ JA8199	Boeing 777-281	27029/29			
☐ JA8967	Boeing 777-281	27030/37			
☐ JA8968	Boeing 777-281	27031/38			
☐ JA8969	Boeing 777-281	27032/50			
☐ JA801A	Boeing 787-881	34485/7			o/o♦
☐ JA802A	Boeing 787-881	34486/9			o/o♦
☐ JA803A	Boeing 787-881	34488/8			o/o♦
☐ JA804A	Boeing 787-881	34497/11			o/o♦
☐ JA805A	Boeing 787-881	34508/12			o/o♦
☐ JA806A	Boeing 787-881	34490/13			o/o♦
☐ JA807A	Boeing 787-881	34510/22			o/o♦
☐ JA808A	Boeing 787-881	34514/24			o/o♦
☐ JA809A	Boeing 787-881	34498/14			o/o♦
☐ JA810A	Boeing 787-881	34491/15			o/o♦
☐ JA811A	Boeing 787-881				o/o♦
☐ JA812A	Boeing 787-881				o/o♦
☐ JA813A	Boeing 787-881				o/o♦
☐ JA814A	Boeing 787-881				o/o♦
☐ JA815A	Boeing 787-881				o/o♦

FUJI DREAM AIRLINES — (JH / FDA)

☐ JA01FJ	Embraer ERJ-170STD	17000271	ex PT-SNB		
☐ JA02FJ	Embraer ERJ-170STD	17000289	ex PT-TQP		
☐ JA03FJ	Embraer ERJ-175STD	17000304	ex PT-XQD		
☐ JA04FJ	Embraer ERJ-170SU	17000129	ex N866RW		♦
☐ JA05FJ	Embraer ERJ-175STD	17000317	ex PT-XUL		

HOKKAIDO AIR SYSTEM — North Air (NTH) — Sapporo-Chitose (CTS)

☐ JA01HC	SAAB SF.340B	340B-432	ex SE-B32	
☐ JA02HC	SAAB SF.340B	340B-440	ex SE-B40	
☐ JA03HC	SAAB SF.340B	340B-458	ex SE-B58	

IBEX AIRLINES — Fair (FW/IBX) — Sendai (SDJ)

☐ JA01RJ	Canadair CRJ-100ER	7052	ex OE-LRD	
☐ JA02RJ	Canadair CRJ-100ER	7033	ex OE-LRB	

☐ JA03RJ	Canadair CRJ-200ER	7624	ex C-GJZF	
☐ JA04RJ	Canadair CRJ-200ER	7798	ex C-FMLF	
☐ JA05RJ	Canadair CRJ-702NG	10279	ex C-FYDI	
☐ JA06RJ	Canadair CRJ-702NG	10303	ex C-GFFK	♦

J-AIR   (JL/JAL)   Nagoya-Komaki (NKM)

☐ JA201J	Canadair CRJ-200ER	7452	ex C-FMND	
☐ JA202J	Canadair CRJ-200ER	7484	ex C-FMLU	
☐ JA203J	Canadair CRJ-200ER	7626	ex C-FMNW	
☐ JA204J	Canadair CRJ-200ER	7643	ex C-FMNB	
☐ JA205J	Canadair CRJ-200ER	7767	ex C-FMLB	
☐ JA206J	Canadair CRJ-200ER	7834	ex C-FMMT	
☐ JA207J	Canadair CRJ-200ER	8050	ex C-FFVJ	
☐ JA208J	Canadair CRJ-200ER	8059	ex C-FMOW	
☐ JA209J	Canadair CRJ-200ER	8062	ex C-FMNQ	
☐ JA211J	Embraer ERJ-170STD	17000251	ex PT-SJC	
☐ JA212J	Embraer ERJ-170STD	17000268	ex PT-SJW	
☐ JA213J	Embraer ERJ-170STD	17000285	ex PT-TQL	
☐ JA214J	Embraer ERJ-170STD	17000295	ex PT-TQV	
☐ JA215J	Embraer ERJ-170STD	17000297	ex PT-TQX	
☐ JA216J	Embraer ERJ-170STD	17000299	ex PT-TQY	
☐ JA217J	Embraer ERJ-170STD	17000308	ex PT-XQW	♦
☐ JA218J	Embraer ERJ-170STD	17000314	ex PT-XUI	♦
☐ JA219J	Embraer ERJ-170STD	17000315	ex PT-XUJ	♦
☐ JA	Embraer ERJ-170STD		ex PT-	o/o♦

JAL EXPRESS   Janex (JC/JEX)   Osaka-Kansai (KIX)

☐ JA8991	Boeing 737-446	27916/2718		
☐ JA8992	Boeing 737-446	27917/2729	ex N1792B	
☐ JA8993	Boeing 737-446	28087/2812		<JAL
☐ JA8994	Boeing 737-446	28097/2907	ex N1786B	<JAL
☐ JA8995	Boeing 737-446	28831/2911		<JAL
☐ JA8996	Boeing 737-446	28832/2953	ex N1786B	<JAL
☐ JA8998	Boeing 737-446	28994/3044		<JAL
☐ JA8999	Boeing 737-446	29864/3111	ex N1786B	<JAL
☐ JA307J	Boeing 737-846/W	35336/2450		<JAL
☐ JA308J	Boeing 737-846/W	35337/2479	ex N1786B	<JAL
☐ JA309J	Boeing 737-846/W	35338/2522		<JAL
☐ JA311J	Boeing 737-846/W	35340/2571		<JAL
☐ JA313J	Boeing 737-846/W	35342/2633		<JAL
☐ JA314J	Boeing 737-846/W	35343/2701		<JAL
☐ JA316J	Boeing 737-846/W	35345/2762		<JAL
☐ JA319J	Boeing 737-846/W	35348/2867	ex N1795B	<JAL
☐ JA322J	Boeing 737-846/W	35351/3002		<JAL
☐ JA323J	Boeing 737-846/W	35352/3057	ex N1787B	<JAL
☐ JA324J	Boeing 737-846/W	35353/3105	ex N1786B	<JAL
☐ JA325J	Boeing 737-846/W	35354/3117	ex N1787B	<JAL
☐ JA326J	Boeing 737-846/W	35355/3159	ex N1787B	<JAL
☐ JA327J	Boeing 737-846/W	35356/3201	ex N1796B	<JAL
☐ JA328J	Boeing 737-846/W	35357/3279	ex N1786B	<JAL♦
☐ JA329J	Boeing 737-846/W	35358/3315	ex N1796B	<JAL♦
☐ JA330J	Boeing 737-846/W	35359/3341		<JAL♦
☐ JA331J	Boeing 737-846/W	40346/3366	ex N1795B	<JAL♦
☐ JA332J	Boeing 737-846/W	40347/3385		<JAL♦
☐ JA333J	Boeing 737-846/W	40348/3465	ex N1799B	<JAL♦
☐ JA334J	Boeing 737-846/W	40349/3489	ex N1786B	<JAL♦
☐ JA	Boeing 737-846/W			o/o
☐ JA8262	McDonnell-Douglas MD-81	49463/1488		<JAL
☐ JA8374	McDonnell-Douglas MD-81	53043/1982		<JAL
☐ JA8556	McDonnell-Douglas MD-81	53301/2082		<JAL

JAL WAYS   Jalways (JO/JAZ)   Tokyo-Narita (NRT)

Wholly owned by Japan Airlines and leases aircraft from the parent as required.

JAPAN AIR COMMUTER   Commuter (3X/JAC)   Amami (ASJ)

☐ JA841C	de Havilland DHC-8-402Q	4072	ex C-GEWI	
☐ JA842C	de Havilland DHC-8-402Q	4073	ex C-GFCA	
☐ JA843C	de Havilland DHC-8-402Q	4076	ex C-FDHZ	
☐ JA844C	de Havilland DHC-8-402Q	4092	ex C-GFEN	
☐ JA845C	de Havilland DHC-8-402Q	4101	ex C-FCPZ	
☐ JA846C	de Havilland DHC-8-402Q	4107	ex C-FCVI	

☐ JA847C	de Havilland DHC-8-402Q	4111	ex C-FCVS	
☐ JA848C	de Havilland DHC-8-402Q	4121	ex C-FFCO	
☐ JA849C	de Havilland DHC-8-402Q	4133	ex C-FGKJ	
☐ JA850C	de Havilland DHC-8-402Q	4158	ex C-FLKW	
☐ JA851C	de Havilland DHC-8-402Q	4177	ex C-FMTK	
☐ JA001C	SAAB SF.340B	340B-419	ex SE-B19	
☐ JA002C	SAAB SF.340B	340B-459	ex SE-B59	
☐ JA8594	SAAB SF.340B	340B-399	ex SE-C99	
☐ JA8642	SAAB SF.340B	340B-365	ex SE-C65	
☐ JA8649	SAAB SF.340B	340B-368	ex SE-C68	
☐ JA8703	SAAB SF.340B	340B-355	ex SE-C55	
☐ JA8704	SAAB SF.340B	340B-361	ex SE-C61	
☐ JA8886	SAAB SF.340B	340B-281	ex SE-G81	
☐ JA8887	SAAB SF.340B	340B-308	ex SE-C08	
☐ JA8888	SAAB SF.340B	340B-331	ex SE-C31	
☐ JA8900	SAAB SF.340B	340B-378	ex SE-C78	

JAPAN AIRLINES — Japanair (JL/JAL) — Tokyo-Haneda (HND)

Member of Oneworld

☐ JA011D	Airbus A300B4-622R	783	ex F-WWAA	
☐ JA012D	Airbus A300B4-622R	797	ex F-WWAQ	
☐ JA014D	Airbus A300B4-622R	836	ex F-WWAF	
☐ JA015D	Airbus A300B4-622R	837	ex F-WWAK	
☐ JA016D	Airbus A300B4-622R	838	ex F-WWAL	
☐ JA8375	Airbus A300B4-622R	602	ex F-WWAT	
☐ JA8376	Airbus A300B4-622R	617	ex F-WWAK	
☐ JA8377	Airbus A300B4-622R	621	ex F-WWAA	
☐ JA8527	Airbus A300B4-622R	724	ex F-WWAQ	
☐ JA8529	Airbus A300B4-622R	729	ex F-WWAM	
☐ JA8559	Airbus A300B4-622R	641	ex F-WWAM	
☐ JA8561	Airbus A300B4-622R	670	ex F-WWAD	
☐ JA8562	Airbus A300B4-622R	679	ex F-WWAL	
☐ JA8563	Airbus A300B4-622R	683	ex F-WWAJ	
☐ JA8564	Airbus A300B4-622R	703	ex F-WWAO	
☐ JA8566	Airbus A300B4-622R	730	ex F-WWAV	
☐ JA8573	Airbus A300B4-622R	737	ex F-WWAF	
☐ JA8657	Airbus A300B4-622R	753	ex F-WWAD	
☐ JA8659	Airbus A300B4-622R	770	ex F-WWAQ	
☐ JA8993	Boeing 737-446	28087/2812		>JEX
☐ JA8994	Boeing 737-446	28097/2907	ex N1786B	>JEX
☐ JA8995	Boeing 737-446	28831/2911		>JEX
☐ JA8996	Boeing 737-446	28832/2953	ex N1786B	>JEX
☐ JA8998	Boeing 737-446	28994/3044		>JEX
☐ JA8999	Boeing 737-446	29864/3111	ex N1786B	>JEX
☐ JA301J	Boeing 737-846/W	35330/2095		
☐ JA302J	Boeing 737-846/W	35331/2162		
☐ JA303J	Boeing 737-846/W	35332/2225	ex N6066U	
☐ JA304J	Boeing 737-846/W	35333/2253		
☐ JA305J	Boeing 737-846/W	35334/2289		
☐ JA306J	Boeing 737-846/W	35335/2395	ex N6065Y	
☐ JA307J	Boeing 737-846/W	35336/2450		>JEX
☐ JA308J	Boeing 737-846/W	35337/2479	ex N1786B	>JEX
☐ JA309J	Boeing 737-846/W	35338/2522		>JEX
☐ JA310J	Boeing 737-846/W	35339/2510		
☐ JA311J	Boeing 737-846/W	35340/2571		>JEX
☐ JA312J	Boeing 737-846/W	35341/2584	ex N1786B	
☐ JA313J	Boeing 737-846/W	35342/2633		>JEX
☐ JA314J	Boeing 737-846/W	35343/2701		>JEX
☐ JA315J	Boeing 737-846/W	35344/2731		
☐ JA316J	Boeing 737-846/W	35345/2762		>JEX
☐ JA317J	Boeing 737-846/W	35346/2824		
☐ JA318J	Boeing 737-846/W	35347/2830	ex N1784B	
☐ JA319J	Boeing 737-846/W	35348/2867	ex N1795B	>JEX
☐ JA320J	Boeing 737-846/W	35349/2953	ex N1786B	
☐ JA321J	Boeing 737-846/W	35350/2977		
☐ JA322J	Boeing 737-846/W	35351/3002		>JEX
☐ JA323J	Boeing 737-846/W	35352/3057	ex N1787B	>JEX
☐ JA324J	Boeing 737-846/W	35353/3105	ex N1786B	>JEX
☐ JA325J	Boeing 737-846/W	35354/3117	ex N1787B	>JEX
☐ JA326J	Boeing 737-846/W	35355/3159	ex N1787B	>JEX
☐ JA327J	Boeing 737-846/W	35356/3201	ex N1796B	>JEX
☐ JA328J	Boeing 737-846/W	35357/3279	ex N1786B	>JEX♦

☐ JA329J	Boeing 737-846/W	35358/3315	ex N1796B		>JEX♦
☐ JA330J	Boeing 737-846/W	35359/3341			>JEX♦
☐ JA331J	Boeing 737-846/W	40346/3366	ex N1795B		>JEX♦
☐ JA332J	Boeing 737-846/W	40347/3385			>JEX♦
☐ JA333J	Boeing 737-846/W	40348/3465	ex N1799B		>JEX♦
☐ JA334J	Boeing 737-846/W	40349/3489	ex N1786B		>JEX♦
☐ JA	Boeing 737-846/W				o/o
☐ JA8074	Boeing 747-446	24426/768			
☐ JA8075	Boeing 747-446	24427/780			[VCV]
☐ JA8076	Boeing 747-446	24777/797	ex N6046P		
☐ JA8077	Boeing 747-446	24784/798			
☐ JA8078	Boeing 747-446	24870/821	ex N60697		
☐ JA8080	Boeing 747-446	24886/825			
☐ JA8081	Boeing 747-446	25064/851			
☐ JA8084	Boeing 747-446D	25214/879			
☐ JA8086	Boeing 747-446	25308/885			
☐ JA8087	Boeing 747-446	26346/897			
☐ JA8088	Boeing 747-446	26341/902			
☐ JA8089	Boeing 747-446	26342/905			
☐ JA8090	Boeing 747-446D	26347/907			
☐ JA8902	Boeing 747-446BCF	26344/929	ex N6018N		[VCV]♦
☐ JA8904	Boeing 747-446D	26348/941		Tamagocchi colours	
☐ JA8907	Boeing 747-446D	26351/963			
☐ JA8911	Boeing 747-446BCF	26356/1026			[VCV]♦
☐ JA8916	Boeing 747-446	26362/1202		Yokoso Japan	
☐ JA8917	Boeing 747-446	29899/1208	ex N6009F		
☐ JA8918	Boeing 747-446	27650/1234			
☐ JA8920	Boeing 747-446	27648/1253			
☐ JA8921	Boeing 747-446	27645/1262	ex N747BA		
☐ JA8922	Boeing 747-446	27646/1280	ex N747BJ		[VCV]♦
☐ JA601J	Boeing 767-346ER	32886/875	ex N60697		
☐ JA602J	Boeing 767-346ER	32887/879			
☐ JA603J	Boeing 767-346ER	32888/880	ex N1794B		
☐ JA604J	Boeing 767-346ER	33493/905			
☐ JA605J	Boeing 767-346ER	33494/911			
☐ JA606J	Boeing 767-346ER	33495/915			
☐ JA607J	Boeing 767-346ER	33496/917			
☐ JA608J	Boeing 767-346ER	33497/919			
☐ JA609J	Boeing 767-346ER	33845/921			
☐ JA610J	Boeing 767-346ER	33846/925			
☐ JA611J	Boeing 767-346ER	33847/927			
☐ JA612J	Boeing 767-346ER	33848/929			
☐ JA613J	Boeing 767-346ER	33849/935			
☐ JA614J	Boeing 767-346ER	33851/938			
☐ JA615J	Boeing 767-346ER	33850/942	ex N50217		
☐ JA616J	Boeing 767-346ER	35813/954			
☐ JA617J	Boeing 767-346ER	35814/957	ex N5023Q		
☐ JA618J	Boeing 767-346ER	35815/964			
☐ JA619J	Boeing 767-346ER	37550/969			
☐ JA620J	Boeing 767-346ER	37547/974			
☐ JA621J	Boeing 767-346ER	37548/975			
☐ JA622J	Boeing 767-346ER	37549/977			
☐ JA623J	Boeing 767-346ER	36131/978	ex N1794B		
☐ JA651J	Boeing 767-346ER	40363/994			♦
☐ JA652J	Boeing 767-346ER	40364/995			♦
☐ JA653J	Boeing 767-346ER	40365/997			♦
☐ JA654J	Boeing 767-346ER	40366/999			o/o♦
☐ JA	Boeing 767-346ER				o/o♦
☐ JA	Boeing 767-346ER				o/o♦
☐ JA	Boeing 767-346ER				o/o♦
☐ JA	Boeing 767-346ER				o/o♦
☐ JA8231	Boeing 767-246	23212/117	ex N6046P		
☐ JA8233	Boeing 767-246	23214/122	ex N6038E		[VCV]♦
☐ JA8264	Boeing 767-346	23965/186	ex N6018N		
☐ JA8265	Boeing 767-346	23961/192	ex N6005C		
☐ JA8266	Boeing 767-346	23966/191	ex N6018N		
☐ JA8267	Boeing 767-346	23962/193	ex N6038E		
☐ JA8268	Boeing 767-346	23963/224	ex N6055X		
☐ JA8269	Boeing 767-346	23964/225	ex N6046P		
☐ JA8299	Boeing 767-346	24498/277	ex N6055X		
☐ JA8364	Boeing 767-346	24782/327			
☐ JA8365	Boeing 767-346	24783/329			
☐ JA8397	Boeing 767-346	27311/547			
☐ JA8398	Boeing 767-346	27312/548			
☐ JA8399	Boeing 767-346	27313/554			

☐ JA8975	Boeing 767-346	27658/581		
☐ JA8976	Boeing 767-346	27659/667		
☐ JA8980	Boeing 767-346	28837/673		
☐ JA8986	Boeing 767-346	28838/680		
☐ JA8987	Boeing 767-346	28553/688		
☐ JA8988	Boeing 767-346	29863/772		
☐ JA007D	Boeing 777-289	27639/134		
☐ JA008D	Boeing 777-289	27640/146		
☐ JA009D	Boeing 777-289	27641/159	ex N5017V	
☐ JA010D	Boeing 777-289	27642/213		
☐ JA701J	Boeing 777-246ER	32889/410	ex (JA8989)	
☐ JA702J	Boeing 777-246ER	32890/417	ex (JA8990)	
☐ JA703J	Boeing 777-246ER	32891/427	ex N5023Q	
☐ JA704J	Boeing 777-246ER	32892/435	ex N50281	oneworld c/s
☐ JA705J	Boeing 777-246ER	32893/446		
☐ JA706J	Boeing 777-246ER	33394/464		
☐ JA707J	Boeing 777-246ER	32894/475		
☐ JA708J	Boeing 777-246ER	32895/483		
☐ JA709J	Boeing 777-246ER	32896/489		
☐ JA710J	Boeing 777-246ER	33395/525		
☐ JA711J	Boeing 777-246ER	33396/533		
☐ JA712J	Boeing 777-246ER	37879		o/o
☐ JA713J	Boeing 777-246ER	37880		o/o
☐ JA714J	Boeing 777-246ER	37881		o/o
☐ JA715J	Boeing 777-246ER	37882		o/o
☐ JA716J	Boeing 777-246ER	37883		o/o
☐ JA731J	Boeing 777-346ER	32431/429	ex N5016R	
☐ JA732J	Boeing 777-346ER	32430/423	ex N5017V	
☐ JA733J	Boeing 777-346ER	32432/521		
☐ JA734J	Boeing 777-346ER	32433/527		
☐ JA735J	Boeing 777-346ER	32434/577		
☐ JA736J	Boeing 777-346ER	32435/583		
☐ JA737J	Boeing 777-346ER	36126/668		
☐ JA738J	Boeing 777-346ER	32436/724		
☐ JA739J	Boeing 777-346ER	32437/736		
☐ JA740J	Boeing 777-346ER	36127/744		
☐ JA741J	Boeing 777-346ER	36128/812	ex N50281	
☐ JA742J	Boeing 777-346ER	36129/816	ex N1788B	
☐ JA743J	Boeing 777-346ER	36130/821	ex N6009F	
☐ JA751J	Boeing 777-346	27654/458		
☐ JA752J	Boeing 777-346	27655/460		
☐ JA771J	Boeing 777-246	27656/437	ex (JA711J)	
☐ JA772J	Boeing 777-246	27657/507		
☐ JA773J	Boeing 777-246	27653/635		
☐ JA8941	Boeing 777-346	28393/152		
☐ JA8942	Boeing 777-346	28394/158	ex N50284	
☐ JA8943	Boeing 777-346	28395/196		
☐ JA8944	Boeing 777-346	28396/212		
☐ JA8945	Boeing 777-346	28397/238		
☐ JA8977	Boeing 777-289	27636/45		
☐ JA8978	Boeing 777-289	27637/79		
☐ JA8979	Boeing 777-289	27638/107		
☐ JA8981	Boeing 777-246	27364/23	ex (JA8195)	
☐ JA8982	Boeing 777-246	27365/26	ex (JA8196)	
☐ JA8983	Boeing 777-246	27366/39		
☐ JA8984	Boeing 777-246	27651/68		
☐ JA8985	Boeing 777-246	27652/72		
☐ JA	Boeing 777-			o/o
☐ JA821A	Boeing 787-846	34831/20		o/o♦
☐ JA	Boeing 787-846	34833/21		o/o♦
☐ JA	Boeing 787-846	34832/23		o/o♦
☐ JA	Boeing 787-846	34834/27		o/o♦
☐ JA	Boeing 787-846			o/o♦
☐ JA	Boeing 787-846			o/o♦
☐ JA	Boeing 787-846			o/o♦
☐ JA	Boeing 787-846			o/o♦
☐ JA8262	McDonnell-Douglas MD-81	49463/1488		>JEX
☐ JA8374	McDonnell-Douglas MD-81	53043/1982		>JEX
☐ JA8497	McDonnell-Douglas MD-81	49281/1200		
☐ JA8554	McDonnell-Douglas MD-81	53299/2075		
☐ JA8556	McDonnell-Douglas MD-81	53301/2082		>JEX
☐ JA8557	McDonnell-Douglas MD-81	53302/2085		

250

☐ JA001D	McDonnell-Douglas MD-90-30	53555/2207		
☐ JA002D	McDonnell-Douglas MD-90-30	53556/2210		
☐ JA003D	McDonnell-Douglas MD-90-30	53557/2211		
☐ JA004D	McDonnell-Douglas MD-90-30	53558/2212		
☐ JA005D	McDonnell-Douglas MD-90-30	53559/2236		
☐ JA006D	McDonnell-Douglas MD-90-30	53560/2245		
☐ JA8004	McDonnell-Douglas MD-90-30	53359/2164		
☐ JA8020	McDonnell-Douglas MD-90-30	53360/2190		
☐ JA8029	McDonnell-Douglas MD-90-30	53361/2202		
☐ JA8062	McDonnell-Douglas MD-90-30	53352/2098		
☐ JA8063	McDonnell-Douglas MD-90-30	53353/2120		
☐ JA8064	McDonnell-Douglas MD-90-30	53354/2125		
☐ JA8065	McDonnell-Douglas MD-90-30	53355/2131		
☐ JA8066	McDonnell-Douglas MD-90-30	53356/2157		
☐ JA8069	McDonnell-Douglas MD-90-30	53357/2164		
☐ JA8070	McDonnell-Douglas MD-90-30	53358/2179		

JAPAN TRANSOCEAN AIR — JAI Ocean (NU/JTA) — Okinawa-Naha (OKA)

☐ JA8523	Boeing 737-4Q3	26603/2618		
☐ JA8524	Boeing 737-4Q3	26604/2684		
☐ JA8525	Boeing 737-4Q3	26605/2752		
☐ JA8526	Boeing 737-4Q3	26606/2898		
☐ JA8597	Boeing 737-4Q3	27660/3043		
☐ JA8930	Boeing 737-4K5	27102/2394	ex D-AHLM	
☐ JA8931	Boeing 737-429	25247/2106	ex N931NU	
☐ JA8932	Boeing 737-429	25248/2120	ex N932NU	
☐ JA8933	Boeing 737-429	25226/2104	ex N933NU	
☐ JA8934	Boeing 737-4K5	27830/2670	ex N934NU	
☐ JA8938	Boeing 737-4Q3	29485/3085		
☐ JA8939	Boeing 737-4Q3	29486/3088	ex N1800B	
☐ JA8940	Boeing 737-4Q3	29487/3122		

JP EXPRESS — (9N/AJV)

☐ JA601F	Boeing 767-381F	33404/885	ex N6055X	<ANA
☐ JA602F	Boeing 767-381F	33509/937		<ANA
☐ JA604F	Boeing 767-381F	35709/947		<ANA

NEW CENTRAL AVIATION — Tokyo-Chofu

☐ JA31CA	Dornier 228-212	8242	ex D-CBDO	
☐ JA32CA	Dornier 228-212	8243	ex D-CBDP	
☐ JA34CA	Dornier 228-200NG	8300	ex D-CRAQ	♦
☐ JA3453	Cessna TU206C Super Skywagon	U206-1218	ex N1775C	
☐ JA3669	Cessna TU206F Turbo Stationair	U20601964	ex N1704C	
☐ JA5305	Britten-Norman BN-2B-20 Islander	2239	ex G-BSPS	
☐ JA5319	Britten-Norman BN-2B-20 Islander	2268	ex G-BUBK	

NIPPON CARGO AIRLINES — Nippon Cargo (KZ/NCA) — Tokyo-Narita (NRT)

☐ JA01KZ	Boeing 747-481F	34016/1360	NCA Pleiades	
☐ JA02KZ	Boeing 747-481F	34017/1363	NCA Progress	
☐ JA03KZ	Boeing 747-4KZF	34018/1378	NCA Phoenix	
☐ JA04KZ	Boeing 747-4KZF	34283/1384	NCA Pegasus	
☐ JA05KZ	Boeing 747-4KZF	36132/1394	NCA Apollo	
☐ JA06KZ	Boeing 747-4KZF	36133/1397	NCA Antares	
☐ JA07KZ	Boeing 747-4KZF	36134/1405	NCA Andromeda	
☐ JA08KZ	Boeing 747-4KZF	36135/1408	NCA Aries	
☐ JA11KZ	Boeing 747-8KZF	36136/1421		o/o
☐ JA12KZ	Boeing 747-8KZF	36137/1422		o/o
☐ JA13KZ	Boeing 747-6KZF	36138/1431		o/o

ORIENTAL AIR BRIDGE — Oriental Bridge (NGK) — Nagasaki (NGS)

☐ JA801B	de Havilland DHC-8Q-201	566	ex C-GDNG
☐ JA802B	de Havilland DHC-8Q-201	579	ex C-FDHO

RYUKYU AIR COMMUTER — (RAC) — Okinawa-Naha (OKA)

☐ JA5324	Britten-Norman BN-2B-20 Islander	2297	ex G-BWNG
☐ JA5325	Britten-Norman BN-2B-20 Islander	2298	ex G-BWYX
☐ JA8935	de Havilland DHC-8Q-103B	593	ex C-GSAH
☐ JA8936	de Havilland DHC-8Q-314	635	ex C-FIOX
☐ JA8972	de Havilland DHC-8Q-103	472	ex C-GDKL
☐ JA8973	de Havilland DHC-8Q-103	501	ex C-GDLD
☐ JA8974	de Havilland DHC-8Q-103B	540	ex C-FDHP

SKYMARK AIRLINES		Skymark (BC/SKY)		Osaka-Itami (ITM)
☐ JA73NA	Boeing 737-8HX/W	36849/3372		♦
☐ JA73NB	Boeing 737-8HX/W	36848/3394		♦
☐ JA73NC	Boeing 737-8FZ/W	31743/3450	ex N1787B	♦
☐ JA73ND	Boeing 737-8FZ/W	33440/3474		♦
☐ JA73NE	Boeing 737-82Y/W	40713/3501	ex N1787B	♦
☐ JA	Boeing 737-8			o/o♦
☐ JA	Boeing 737-8			o/o♦
☐ JA737H	Boeing 737-86N	34247/1830	ex N1787B	
☐ JA737K	Boeing 737-86N	34249/1857	ex N1786B	
☐ JA737L	Boeing 737-86N	32694/1960		
☐ JA737M	Boeing 737-86N	32683/2136		
☐ JA737N	Boeing 737-8HX	36845/2339		
☐ JA737P	Boeing 737-8HX	29681/2493	ex N1795B	
☐ JA737Q	Boeing 737-86N/W	35228/2630		
☐ JA737R	Boeing 737-86N/W	35630/2666		
☐ JA737T	Boeing 737-8Q8/W	35290/2818		
☐ JA737U	Boeing 737-8FZ/W	29680/2888		
☐ JA737X	Boeing 737-8AL/W	36692/3088	ex N1786B	
☐ JA737Y	Boeing 737-8FZ/W	29663/3113	ex N1786B	
☐ JA737Z	Boeing 737-82Y/W	40712/3308	ex N1786B	♦

SKYNET ASIA AIRWAYS		Newsky (6J/SNJ)		Miyazaki (KMI)
☐ JA391K	Boeing 737-4Y0	24545/1805	ex N545NK	
☐ JA737A	Boeing 737-46Q	29000/3033	ex N56CD	Miyazaki Intl c/s
☐ JA737B	Boeing 737-46Q	29001/3040	ex N89CD	
☐ JA737E	Boeing 737-4Y0	26069/2352	ex N869DC	
☐ JA737F	Boeing 737-43Q	28492/2837	ex N284CH	
☐ JA737G	Boeing 737-43Q	28491/2832	ex N491MT	
☐ JA737V	Boeing 737-4M0	29201/3018	ex N391LS	
☐ JA737W	Boeing 737-4M0	29202/3025	ex N392LS	

STARFLYER		Starflyer (7G/SFJ)		Kitakyushu (KKJ)
☐ JA01MC	Airbus A320-214	2620	ex F-WWDM	
☐ JA02MC	Airbus A320-214	2658	ex F-WWIP	
☐ JA03MC	Airbus A320-214	2695	ex F-WWII	
☐ JA04MC	Airbus A320-214	3025	ex F-WWBI	

JU - MONGOLIA (State of Mongolia)

AERO MONGOLIA		Aero Mongolia (MNG)		Ulan Bator (ULN)
☐ JU-8251	Fokker 50	20251	ex PH-WXH	
☐ JU-8257	Fokker 50	20257	ex OY-PCI	♦
☐ JU-8258	Fokker 50	20258	ex PH-KXU	
☐ JU-8428	Fokker 100	11428	ex C-GKZG	
☐ JU-8452	Fokker 100	11352	ex C-GKZB	

CENTRAL MONGOLIAN AIRWAYS		Central Mongolia (CEM)		Ulan Bator (ULN)
☐ JU-5444	Mil Mi-8T	20409	ex JU-1024	
☐ JU-5445	Mil Mi-8T	98103227	ex JU-1025	
☐ JU-5446	Mil Mi-8T	20411	ex JU-1026	

EZNIS AIRWAYS		(EZA)		Ulan Bator (ULN)
☐ JU-9901	SAAB SF.340B	340B-259	ex N259AE	
☐ JU-9903	SAAB SF.340B	340B-297	ex N297AE	
☐ JU-9905	SAAB SF.340B	340B-359	ex LY-ESK	
☐ JU-9907	SAAB SF.340B	340B-425	ex N425XJ	♦

MIAT - MONGOLIAN AIRLINES		Mongol Air (OM/MGL)		Ulan Bator (ULN)
☐ EI-CSG	Boeing 737-8AS/W	29922/571	Ogedei Khaan	
☐ EI-CXV	Boeing 737-8CX/W	32364/1166	Khubelai Khaan	
☐ JU-1004	Antonov An-24RV	17306807	ex MT-1004	[ULN]
☐ JU-1006	Antonov An-24RV	47309807	ex MT-1006	[ULN]
☐ JU-1009	Antonov An-24RV	57310104	ex MT-1009	[ULN]
☐ JU-1010	Airbus A310-304	526	ex F-OHPT	Chinggis Khan
☐ JU-1014	Antonov An-26B-100	14101	ex MT-1014	

SKY HORSE AVIATION		Sky Horse (TNL)		Ulan Bator (ULN)
☐ JU-2030	LET L-410UVP-E1	861801	ex OK-RDE	
☐ JU-2032	LET L-410UVP-E1	810602	ex UR-67001	♦

JY-   JORDAN (Hashemite Kingdom of Jordan)

BARQ AVIATION				Amman (AMM)
☐ N162AT	Lockheed L-1011-500 Tristar	193B-1220	ex JY-AGC	[VCV]
☐ N164AT	Lockheed L-1011-500 Tristar	193B-1238	ex JY-AGE	[FJR]
☐ N194AT	Lockheed L-1011-100 Tristar	193B-1230	ex N8034T	[FJR]

JORDAN AVIATION		Jordan Aviation (R5/JAV)		Amman-Marka (ADJ)
☐ JY-JAH	Airbus A310-304	481	ex VT-EVH	
☐ JY-JAV	Airbus A310-222	357	ex 3B-STK Zuhair	op for UN
☐ JY-JAC	Airbus A320-211	0029	ex N290SE	
☐ JY-JAE	Boeing 727-2N4	21846/1549	ex 7O-ACX hanaviation.jo titles	
☐ JY-JAB	Boeing 737-33A	23630/1312	ex N169AW Noor	
☐ JY-JAD	Boeing 737-322	24662/1862	ex N387UA	
☐ JY-JAN	Boeing 737-322	23956/1564	ex N324UA Amman	
☐ JY-JAO	Boeing 737-322	24672/1915	ex N672RY	
☐ JY-JAP	Boeing 737-46B	24124/1679	ex SX-BGX	
☐ JY-JAQ	Boeing 737-46J	27826/2694	ex D-ABRE	♦
☐ JY-JAX	Boeing 737-322	23955/1550	ex N323UA	
☐ JY-JAY	Boeing 737-3S3	29244/3059	ex N244SJ	♦
☐ JY-JAG	Boeing 767-204ER	24757/299	ex G-SLVR	
☐ JY-JAI	Boeing 767-204ER	24736/296	ex G-SILC	
☐ JY-JAL	Boeing 767-204ER	24239/243	ex G-BOPB	

JORDAN INTERNATIONAL AIR CARGO		(J4/JCI)		Amman-Marka (ADJ)
☐ JY-JIA	Ilyushin Il-76TD	0023437093	ex EX-86911	

PETRA AIRLINES				Amman-Marka (ADJ)
☐ JY-PTA	Airbus A320-212	0459	ex A9C-EI	♦

ROYAL FALCON				Amman-Marka (ADJ)
☐ JY-JRE	Airbus A319-112	1124	ex F-OHJY	♦
☐ JY-RFF	Boeing 737-4K5	27831/2677	ex OO-TUB	
☐ JY-JRD	Boeing 767-3P6ER	26237/544	ex N90GZ	
☐ JY-JRF	Boeing 767-233	22526/92	ex J2-KCN	>IRQ

ROYAL JORDANIAN		Jordanian (RJ/RJA)		Amman (AMM)
Member of Oneworld				
☐ JY-AGM	Airbus A310-304	491	ex F-ODVH	Prince Hamzeh
☐ JY-AGN	Airbus A310-304	531	ex F-ODVI	Princess Haya
☐ JY-AGQ	Airbus A310-304F	445	ex F-ODVF	Princess Raiyah
☐ JY-AGR	Airbus A310-304F	490	ex F-ODVG	Prince Faisal
☐ JY-AYL	Airbus A319-132	3428	ex D-AVYQ	Mafraq
☐ JY-AYM	Airbus A319-132	3685	ex D-AVWC	Ma'an
☐ JY-AYN	Airbus A319-132	3803	ex D-AVYB	Shobak
☐ JY-AYP	Airbus A319-132	3832	ex D-AVYL	Ajloun
☐ F-OHGV	Airbus A320-232	2649	ex F-WWIL	Irbid
☐ F-OHGX	Airbus A320-231	2953	ex F-WWIX	Madaba
☐ JY-AYD	Airbus A320-232	2598	ex F-WWBJ	Amman
☐ JY-AYF	Airbus A320-232	2692	ex F-WWIH	Aqaba
☐ JY-AYI	Airbus A320-212	0569	ex F-OGYC	>RYW
☐ JY-AYG	Airbus A321-231	2730	ex D-AVZB	As-Salt
☐ JY-AYH	Airbus A321-231	2793	ex D-AVZN	Karak
☐ JY-AYJ	Airbus A321-231	3458	ex D-AVZM	Ramtha
☐ JY-AYK	Airbus A321-231	3522	ex D-AVZW	Tafila

☐ JY-AY	Airbus A321-231		ex D-AV		o/o
☐ JY-AIE	Airbus A330-223	970	ex EI-EJY	Jordan River	♦
☐ JY-AIF	Airbus A330-223	979	ex EI-EJZ	Prince Ali Ibn Al Hussain	♦
☐ JY-AIA	Airbus A340-212	038	ex F-GLZE	Prince Hussein bin Abdullah	
☐ JY-AIB	Airbus A340-212	043	ex F-GLZF	Princess Iman Bint Abdullah	
☐ JY-AIC	Airbus A340-212	014	ex F-OHLP	Princess Salma Bint Abdullah	
☐ JY-AID	Airbus A340-212	022	ex F-OHLQ	Queen Rania Alabdulah	
☐ JY-EMA	Embraer ERJ-195LR	19000107	ex PT-SQB		
☐ JY-EMB	Embraer ERJ-195LR	19000131	ex PT-SYJ		
☐ JY-EMC	Embraer ERJ-175LR	17000223	ex PT-SCZ	Zay	
☐ JY-EMD	Embraer ERJ-175LR	17000232	ex PT-SFI	Dana	
☐ JY-EME	Embraer ERJ-195LR	19000050	ex PT-SGZ	Jerash	
☐ JY-EMF	Embraer ERJ-195LR	19000067	ex PT-SJG	Petra	
☐ JY-EMG	Embraer ERJ-195LR	19000088	ex PT-SNG		
☐ JY-EMH	Embraer ERJ-175LR	17000316	ex PT-XUK		♦

ROYAL JORDANIAN XPRESS — Amman (AMM)

Wholly owned subsidiary of Royal Jordanianleases aircraft from the parent as required.

ROYAL WINGS AIRLINES — Royal Wings (RY/RYW) — Amman (AMM)

☐ JY-AYI	Airbus A320-212	0569	ex F-OGYC		<RJA

SKYGATE INTERNATIONAL — Air Bishkek (SGD) — Amman/Sharjah (AMM/SHJ)

☐ (EX-058)	Lockheed L1011-250 Tristar	193C-1228	ex N737D		[VCV]
☐ JY-SGI	Lockheed L1011-250 Tristar	193C-1234	ex N1738D	Al Saafa	[AMM]

SOLITAIRE AIR

☐ JY-SOA	Boeing 737-4Q8	25109/2561	ex N776AS		♦

STARJET — (MBM) — Abu Dhabi (AUH)

☐ A6-BSM	Lockheed L-1011-500 Tristar	193G-1222	ex 9L-LED		[CDG]
☐ EX-088	Lockheed L-1011-500 Tristar	193G-1179	ex 9L-LDR	Saif	

TRANSWORLD AVIATION — Aqaba (AQJ)

☐ JY-TWB	Antonov An-26			
☐ JY-TWC	Boeing 737-2T4C	23065/989	ex N110ER	

J2- DJIBOUTI (Republic of Djibouti)

DAALLO AIRLINES — Dalo Airlines (D3/DAO) — Djibouti/Dubai (JIB/DAB)

☐ (J2-KCV)	Boeing 747-212B	21938/436	ex N938GA	[OPF], for IRA?
☐ J2-SHE	Antonov An-24RV	67310505	ex EK-47318	
☐ J2-SHF	Boeing 747SP-09	21300/304	ex 9Q-CWY	[SHJ]
☐ UP-I1802	Ilyushin Il-18E	185008603	ex UN-75002	<MGK

DJIBOUTI AIRLINES — Djibouti Air (D8/DJB) — Djibouti (JIB)

Leases aircraft from other operators as required

SILVER AIR — (SVJ) — Djibouti / Dubai (JIB/DAB)

☐ J2-KCC	Boeing 737-268	20576/297	ex HZ-AGC	[ADD]
☐ J2-KCE	Boeing 737-268	21360/485	ex HZ-AGO	
☐ J2-SRH	Boeing 737-268	21280/471	ex HZ-AGK	[ADD]
☐ J2-SRS	Boeing 737-268	21361/488	ex HZ-AGP	

TEEBAH AIRLINES — Teebah (TBN) — Amman (AMM)

☐ 9L-LEL	Boeing 727-247 (FedEx 3)	21483/1350	ex N831WA	Lsd to/op for IAW

J8- ST. VINCENT & GRENADINES (State of St. Vincent & Grenadines)

MUSTIQUE AIRWAYS — Mustique (MAW) — Mustique (MQS)

☐ J8-CIW	Britten-Norman BN-2B-26 Islander	2018	ex J8-VAH
☐ J8-KIM	Rockwell 500S Shrike Commander	3253	ex J8-VBE

☐ J8-MQS	Aero Commander 500B	1400-144	ex J8-SJK	
☐ J8-PUG	Aero Commander 500U	1670-18	ex J8-VBD	
☐ J6-SLU	Aero Commander 500B	1146-80	ex N6275X	
☐ J8-UVF	Britten-Norman BN-2B-26 Islander	2165	ex J8-VAM	

SVG AIR		*Grenadines (SVD)*		*Kingston, St Vincent (SVD)*
☐ J8-SUN	de Havilland DHC-6 Twin Otter 300	477	ex 8P-MLK	all-white
☐ J8-VAQ	Cessna 402B II STOL	402B1038	ex N400XY	
☐ J8-VAY	Aero Commander 500U	1637-2	ex N6531V	
☐ J8-VBG	Aero Commander 500U	1660-13	ex C-FWPR	
☐ J8-VBI	Britten-Norman BN-2B-26 Islander	2025	ex J3-GAF	
☐ J8-VBJ	Britten-Norman BN-2A Islander	163	ex J3-GAG	
☐ J8-VBK	Britten-Norman BN-2A-26 Islander	570	ex J3-GAH	
☐ J8-VBL	Cessna 402C II	402C0640	ex N404MN	
☐ J8-VBQ	de Havilland DHC-6 Twin Otter 300	604	ex 8P-BGC	all-white
☐ J8-VBS	de Havilland DHC-6 Twin Otter 300	249	ex 8P-ERK	Trans Island 2000 colours

LN-   NORWAY (Kingdom of Norway)

AIRLIFT				*Førde (FDE)*
☐ LN-OCW	Aérospatiale AS350B3 Ecureuil	3942		
☐ LN-OMB	Aérospatiale AS350B2 Ecureuil	2514	ex F-WYMO	
☐ LN-OPF	Aérospatiale AS350B3 Ecureuil	3679		
☐ LN-OPG	Aérospatiale AS350B3 Ecureuil	3712		
☐ LN-OPN	Aérospatiale AS350B3 Ecureuil	4116	ex F-WWXC	
☐ LN-OPP	Aérospatiale AS350B2 Ecureuil	2020	ex SE-HRT	
☐ LN-OPU	Aérospatiale AS350B3 Ecureuil	3563	ex SE-JGR	
☐ LN-OPV	Aérospatiale AS350B2 Ecureuil	2378	ex HB-XUS	
☐ LN-OPW	Aérospatiale AS350B3 Ecureuil	4117	ex F-WWPH	
☐ LN-OPZ	Aérospatiale AS350B3 Ecureuil	3064	ex SE-JCV	
☐ LN-OXA	Aérospatiale AS350B3 Ecureuil	4255		
☐ LN-OXB	Aérospatiale AS350B3 Ecureuil	4258	ex F-WWXP	
☐ LN-OXC	Aérospatiale AS350B3 Ecureuil	4260	ex F-WWXQ	
☐ LN-OXD	Aérospatiale AS350B3 Ecureuil	4278		
☐ LN-OBX	Aérospatiale AS.332C	2001	ex I-EMEB	
☐ LN-OCO	Aérospatiale AS365N Dauphin 2	6420	ex OY-HLL	
☐ LN-OMX	Aérospatiale AS.332L1	2351	ex G-BTNZ	

AIRWING				*Oslo-Gardermoen (OSL)*
☐ LN-AWA	Beech A100 King Air	B-213	ex SE-LDL	
☐ LN-AWD	Beech 350 Super King Air	FL-256	ex D-CSKF	
☐ LN-FIX	Beech B200 Super King Air	BB-1898	ex N199GA	♦
☐ LN-SEA	Cessna 208 Caravan I	20800383	ex N7890C	♦

BENAIR	*Scoop (HAX)*			*Oslo-Gardermoen (OSL)*
☐ LN-PBF	Cessna 208B Caravan I	208B0584	ex OY-PBF	
☐ LN-PBK	Cessna 208B Caravan I	208B0914	ex N5196U	
☐ LN-PBO	Cessna 208B Caravan I	208B1128		

BERGEN AIR TRANSPORT		*Bergen Air (BGT)*		*Bergen (BGO)*
☐ LN-BAA	Beech B200 Super King Air	BB-1327	ex N67SD	
☐ LN-BAB	Beech 350 Super King Air	FL-590	ex N590EU	
☐ LN-TWL	Beech B200 Super King Air	BB-1144	ex N120AJ	

BRISTOW NORWAY		*Norske (NOR)*		*Stavanger (SVG)*
☐ LN-OBA	Aérospatiale AS.332L1	2384		
☐ LN-OMI	Aérospatiale AS.332L	2123	ex G-BLZJ	
☐ LN-ONH	Aérospatiale AS.332L2	2488	ex F-WQDB	
☐ LN-ONF	Eurocopter EC225LP 2	2750		♦
☐ LN-ONG	Eurocopter EC225LP 2	2755		♦
☐ LN-ONN	Sikorsky S-92	920011	ex N7107S	Mona Lisa
☐ LN-ONO	Sikorsky S-92	920012	ex N7108Z	Madonna
☐ LN-ONP	Sikorsky S-92A	920025	ex N8011N	
☐ LN-ONQ	Sikorsky S-92A	920032	ex N8036Q	
☐ LN-ONR	Sikorsky S-92A	920033	ex N8021R	
☐ LN-ONS	Sikorsky S-92A	920043	ex N8061E	
☐ LN-ONT	Sikorsky S-92A	920070	ex N4510G	

☐ LN-ONU	Sikorsky S-92A	920091	ex N2000Q		
☐ LN-ONV	Sikorsky S-92A	920092	ex N2010H		
☐ LN-ONW	Sikorsky S-92A	920090	ex N921AL		♦
☐ LN-ONX	Sikorsky S-92A	920137	ex N1133W		♦

CHC HELIKOPTER SERVICE · Helibus (L5/HKS) · Stavanger/Bergen (SVG/BGO)

☐ LN-OAW	Aérospatiale AS.332L	2053	ex VH-LHD
☐ LN-OHA	Aérospatiale AS.332L	2396	ex F-WYMS
☐ LN-OHC	Aérospatiale AS.332L	2393	
☐ LN-OHE	Aérospatiale AS.332L2 2	2474	
☐ LN-OHG	Aérospatiale AS.332L2 2	2493	
☐ LN-OHI	Aérospatiale AS.332L2 2	2582	ex F-WW
☐ LN-OHJ	Aérospatiale AS.332L2 2	2594	
☐ LN-OHK	Aérospatiale AS.332L2 2	2613	
☐ LN-OHL	Aérospatiale AS.332L2 2	2617	
☐ LN-OHM	Aérospatiale AS.332L2 2	2477	ex PR-HPG
☐ LN-OHW	Eurocopter EC225LP 2	2715	ex F-WJXV
☐ LN-OHZ	Eurocopter EC225LP 2	2691	
☐ LN-OJA	Eurocopter EC225LP 2	2692	
☐ LN-OJB	Eurocopter EC225LP 2	2725	
☐ LN-OJC	Eurocopter EC225LP 2	2739	
☐ LN-OJD	Eurocopter EC225LP 2	2744	ex F-WWOY
☐ LN-OJE	Eurocopter EC225LP 2	2716	
☐ LN-OJF	Eurocopter EC225LP 2	2721	ex F-WJXT
☐ LN-OJG	Eurocopter EC225LP 2	2747	
☐ LN-OLB	Aérospatiale AS.332L	2082	ex OY-HMJ
☐ LN-OLD	Aérospatiale AS.332L	2103	ex OY-HMI
☐ LN-OME	Aérospatiale AS.332L	2139	ex C-GQCH
☐ LN-OMF	Aérospatiale AS.332L	2067	ex G-PUMK
☐ LN-OMH	Aérospatiale AS.332L	2113	ex HZ-RH4
☐ LN-OPH	Aérospatiale AS.332L1	2347	
☐ LN-OPX	Aérospatiale AS.332L1	9009	

☐ LN-OQA	Sikorsky S-92A	920013	ex (LN-ONO)	
☐ LN-OQB	Sikorsky S-92A	920014	ex (LN-OQA)	
☐ LN-OQC	Sikorsky S-92A	920018	ex N7118N	
☐ LN-OQD	Sikorsky S-92A	920022	ex N8016T	
☐ LN-OQE	Sikorsky S-92A	920047	ex N80071	
☐ LN-OQF	Sikorsky S-92A	920056	ex N4502R	
☐ LN-OQG	Sikorsky S-92A	920095	ex N20168	
☐ LN-OQH	Sikorsky S-92A	920097	ex N2021Y	
☐ LN-OQI	Sikorsky S-92A	920098	ex N2055A	
☐ LN-OQJ	Sikorsky S-92A	920110	ex N2126Z	
☐ LN-OQK	Sikorsky S-92A	920117	ex N21285	♦
☐ LN-OQL	Sikorsky S-92A	920132	ex N132GN	♦

CLASSIC NORWAY AIR · Molde (MOL)

| ☐ LN-SVZ | British Aerospace Jetstream 31 | 641 | ex OY-SVZ |

FONNAFLY · Fonna (NOF) · Rosendal / Bergen / Oslo-Gardermoen / Voss (-/BGN/OSL/-)

☐ LN-FFF	Cessna U206G Stationair 6 II	U20604497	ex SE-GXB	Fonna 19	FP
☐ LN-HAI	Cessna U206F Stationair 6 II	U20603058			FP
☐ LN-HOO	Cessna TU206F Turbo Stationair 6 II	U20605490		Fonna 10	FP
☐ LN-IKA	Cessna TU206F Turbo Stationair 6 II	U20606251	ex N6356Z	Fonna 11	FP

HELITRANS · Scanbird (HTA) · Trondheim (TRD)

☐ LN-OAK	Aérospatiale AS350B3 Ecureuil	3212		
☐ LN-OEB	Aérospatiale AS350B3 Ecureuil	3312		♦
☐ LN-OFB	Aérospatiale AS350B3 Ecureuil	4691		♦
☐ LN-OGL	Aérospatiale AS350B3 Ecureuil	3792	ex F-WQDD	
☐ LN-OGN	Aérospatiale AS350B3 Ecureuil	3570		♦
☐ LN-OMD	Aérospatiale AS350B3 Ecureuil	3303	ex HB-ZCL	
☐ LN-OMY	Aérospatiale AS350BA Ecureuil	1017	ex SE-HIA	
☐ LN-OPA	Aérospatiale AS350B3 Ecureuil	3589		

☐ LN-ABO	Cessna 185A Skywagon	185-0439	ex SE-EEM	
☐ LN-FAN	British Aerospace Jetstream 32	864	ex SE-LHK	>BCI
☐ LN-FAQ	British Aerospace Jetstream 32EP	953	ex UR-CET	
☐ LN-HTB	British Aerospace Jetstream 32EP	795	ex G-OAKJ	
☐ LN-HTD	Swearingen SA.226T Merlin III	T-294	ex PH-DYB	Op for Baltic Air Svs
☐ LN-OPO	Bell 214B	28053	ex N18091	
☐ LN-ORM	Bell 214B-1	28054	ex SE-HLE	

LUFTTRANSPORT — Luft Transport (L5/LTR) — Bardufoss (BDU)

☐ LN-OLE	Aérospatiale SA365N2 Dauphin 2	6405	ex VT-CKR	
☐ LN-OLM	Aérospatiale AS365N3 Dauphin 2	6725	ex F-WWOT	
☐ LN-OLN	Aérospatiale AS365N3 Dauphin 2	6721	ex F-WWOF	
☐ LN-OLF	Agusta AW139	31148		
☐ LN-OLO	Agusta AW139	31139		
☐ LN-OLS	Agusta AW139	31136		
☐ LN-OLU	Agusta AW139	31135		
☐ LN-OLV	Agusta AW139	31023	ex I-RAIB	Vaeroy
☐ LN-LTA	Beech B200 Super King Air	BB-1868	ex N954RM	
☐ LN-LTB	Beech B200 Super King Air	BB-2001	ex N3501D	
☐ LN-LTC	Beech B200 Super King Air	BB-2002	ex N60102	
☐ LN-LTD	Beech B200 Super King Air	BB-2006	ex N61806	
☐ LN-LTE	Beech B200 Super King Air	BB-2007	ex N63007	
☐ LN-LTG	Beech B200 Super King Air	BB-2009		
☐ LN-LTI	Beech B200 Super King Air	BB-2010		◆
☐ LN-LTJ	Beech B200 Super King Air	BB-2011		◆
☐ LN-LTK	Beech B200 Super King Air	BB-2004		◆
☐ LN-LTL	Beech B200 Super King Air	BB-2005		◆
☐ LN-MOD	Beech B200 Super King Air	BB-1459	ex N8163R	
☐ LN-MOF	Beech B200 Super King Air	BB-1461	ex N8261E	
☐ LN-MOG	Beech B200 Super King Air	BB-1465	ex N8214T	
☐ LN-MOJ	Beech B200 Super King Air	BB-1334	ex TC-SKO	
☐ LN-MOT	Beech B200 Super King Air	BB-1590	ex D-IHUT	
☐ LN-LTS	Dornier 228-200NG	8301		◆
☐ LN-LYR	Dornier 228-202K	8166	ex D-CICA	Kings Bay
☐ LN-MOL	Dornier 228-202K	8156	ex TF-ELA	
☐ LN-OLA	Agusta A.109E Power	11117		
☐ LN-OLI	Agusta A.109E Power	11204		

NORSK LUFTAMBULANCE — Helidoc (DOC) — Oslo/Dröbak (OSL/-)

☐ LN-OOC	Eurocopter EC135P2+	0350	ex D-HECH	EMS
☐ LN-OOD	Eurocopter EC135P2+	0356	ex D-HECL	EMS
☐ LN-OOE	Eurocopter EC135P2+	0357	ex D-HECA	EMS
☐ LN-OOF	Eurocopter EC135P2+	0390	ex D-HECH	EMS
☐ LN-OOG	Eurocopter EC135P2+	0393	ex D-HECM	EMS
☐ LN-OOH	Eurocopter EC135P2+	0399	ex D-HECG	EMS
☐ LN-OOI	Eurocopter EC135P2+	0580		EMS
☐ LN-OOJ	Eurocopter EC135P2+	0588		EMS
☐ LN-OOK	Eurocopter EC135P2+	0669	ex D-HTSH	EMS
☐ LN-OOL	Eurocopter EC135P2+	0736		EMS
☐ LN-OOM	MBB BK-117C-2	9074	ex D-HMBB	

NORWEGIAN — Nor Shuttle (DY/NAX) — Oslo-Gardermoen (OSL)

☐ LN-KHA	Boeing 737-31S/W	29100/2984	ex SX-BGY		
☐ LN-KHB	Boeing 737-31S/W	29264/3070	ex SX-BGW		
☐ LN-KHC	Boeing 737-31S/W	29265/3073	ex SX-BGX		
☐ LN-KKA	Boeing 737-33A	25033/2025	ex SX-BTO		
☐ LN-KKB	Boeing 737-33A	27457/2756	ex N457AN		
☐ LN-KKC	Boeing 737-3Y5	25615/2478	ex 9H-ABT		
☐ LN-KKD	Boeing 737-33V	29339/3119	ex 5N-VNB		
☐ LN-KKE	Boeing 737-33A	27285/2608	ex G-ZAPM		
☐ LN-KKF	Boeing 737-3K2	24326/1683	ex N730BC		[OSL]
☐ LN-KKG	Boeing 737-3K2	24327/1712	ex PH-HVN	Gidsken Jakobsen	
☐ LN-KKH	Boeing 737-3K2	24328/1856	ex PH-HVT	Otto Sverdrup	
☐ LN-KKI	Boeing 737-3K2	24329/1858	ex PH-HVV	Helge Ingstad	
☐ LN-KKJ	Boeing 737-36N	28564/2936	ex N564SR	Sonja Henie	
☐ LN-KKL	Boeing 737-36N	28671/2955	ex N671SR	Roald Amundsen	[OSL]
☐ LN-KKM	Boeing 737-3Y0	24676/1829	ex HA-LES	Thor Heyerdahl	
☐ LN-KKN	Boeing 737-3Y0	24910/2030	ex HA-LET	Sigrid Undset	
☐ LN-KKO	Boeing 737-3Y0	24909/2021	ex HA-LED	Henrik Ibsen	
☐ LN-KKP	Boeing 737-3M8	25040/2017	ex OO-SBX	Kirsten Flagstad	
☐ LN-KKQ	Boeing 737-36Q	28658/2865	ex EC-GMY	Alf Proysen	
☐ LN-KKR	Boeing 737-3Y0	24256/1629	ex OM-AAA		
☐ LN-KKS	Boeing 737-33A	24094/1729	ex ZK-PLU		
☐ LN-KKT	Boeing 737-3L9	27336/2587	ex G-IGOS		
☐ LN-KKU	Boeing 737-3L9	27337/2594	ex G-IGOU		
☐ LN-KKV	Boeing 737-3Y5	25613/2446	ex 9H-ABR	Niels Henrik Abel	
☐ LN-KKW	Boeing 737-3K9	24213/1794	ex CS-TLL		
☐ LN-KKX	Boeing 737-33S/W	29072/3012	ex ZK-NGN		

☐ LN-KKY	Boeing 737-3S3	29245/3061	ex N292SZ			
☐ LN-KKZ	Boeing 737-33A	27458/2959	ex N458AN			
☐ LN-DYA	Boeing 737-8JP/W	39162/2994	ex N1786B			
☐ LN-DYB	Boeing 737-8JP/W	39163/3054				
☐ LN-DYC	Boeing 737-8JP/W	39164/3196	ex N1787B			♦
☐ LN-DYD	Boeing 737-8JP/W	39002/3231	ex N1787B			♦
☐ LN-DYE	Boeing 737-8JP/W	39003/3401	ex N1787B	Arne Jacbobsen		♦
☐ LN-DYF	Boeing 737-8JP/W	39004/3482	ex N1787B			♦
☐ LN-DYG	Boeing 737-8JP/W	39165/3507	ex N1786B			♦
☐ LN-DYH	Boeing 737-8JP/W	40865/3410		Soren Kierkegaard		♦
☐ LN-DYI	Boeing 737-8JP/W	40866/3432	ex N1787B	Aasmund Olavson Vinje		♦
☐ LN-DYJ	Boeing 737-8JP/W	39045/3530			o/o	♦
☐ LN-	Boeing 737-8JP/W				o/o	♦
☐ LN-	Boeing 737-8JP/W				o/o	♦
☐ LN-	Boeing 737-8JP/W				o/o	♦
☐ LN-	Boeing 737-8JP/W				o/o	♦
☐ LN-	Boeing 737-8JP/W				o/o	♦
☐ LN-	Boeing 737-8JP/W				o/o	♦
☐ LN-	Boeing 737-8JP/W				o/o	♦
☐ LN-	Boeing 737-8JP/W				o/o	♦
☐ LN-	Boeing 737-8JP/W				o/o	♦
☐ LN-	Boeing 737-8JP/W				o/o	♦
☐ LN-NOB	Boeing 737-8FZ/W	34954/2483	ex N1786B	Edvard Grieg		
☐ LN-NOC	Boeing 737-81Q/W	30785/1007	ex EC-ICD			
☐ LN-NOD	Boeing 737-8Q8/W	35280/2629		Sonja Henie		
☐ LN-NOE	Boeing 737-8Q8/W	35283/2742	ex N1787B			
☐ LN-NOF	Boeing 737-86N/W	36809/2647				
☐ LN-NOG	Boeing 737-86N/W	35647/2927	ex N1786B			
☐ LN-NOH	Boeing 737-86N/W	36814/3015	ex N1779B			
☐ LN-NOI	Boeing 737-86N/W	36820/3131				
☐ LN-NOJ	Boeing 737-86N/W	37884/3223	ex N1796B			♦
☐ LN-NOL	Boeing 737-8Q8/W	37159/2868				
☐ LN-NOM	Boeing 737-86N/W	28642/813	ex SE-RHA			
☐ LN-NON	Boeing 737-86N/W	28620/542	ex SE-RHB			
☐ LN-NOO	Boeing 737-86Q/W	30289/1399	ex N289CG			
☐ LN-NOP	Boeing 737-86N/W	32655/1662	ex EI-ECL			
☐ LN-NOQ	Boeing 737-86N/W	32658/1695	ex EI-ECM			
☐ LN-NOS	Boeing 737-8BK/W	33018/1488	ex EI-EDL			
☐ LN-NOT	Boeing 737-8JP/W	37816/3194	ex N1796B			♦
☐ LN-NOU	Boeing 737-8FZ/W	29674/3140	ex N1787B			
☐ LN-NOV	Boeing 737-8FZ/W	31713/3215				♦
☐ LN-NOW	Boeing 737-8FZ/W	37817/3364	ex N1796B	Oda Krohg		♦

SCANDINAVIAN AIRLINE SYSTEM — Scandinavian (SK/SAS) — Copenhagen-Kastrup (CPH)

For details see under Sweden (SE-)

WIDERØE'S FLYVESELSKAP — Widerøe (WF/WIF) — Bodo (BOO)

☐ LN-ILS	de Havilland DHC-8-103	396	ex C-GHRI		
☐ LN-WDE	de Havilland DHC-8-402Q	4183	ex C-FNEC		
☐ LN-WDF	de Havilland DHC-8-402Q	4244	ex C-FUTZ		
☐ LN-WDG	de Havilland DHC-8-402Q	4266	ex C-FXJF		
☐ LN-WDH	de Havilland DHC-8-402Q	4273	ex C-FYGI		
☐ LN-WDI	de Havilland DHC-8-402Q	4286	ex C-FZFX		
☐ LN-WDJ	de Havilland DHC-8-402Q	4290	ex C-GARX		
☐ LN-WDK	de Havilland DHC-8-402Q	4337	ex C-GGIR		♦
☐ LN-WFC	de Havilland DHC-8-311A	236	ex D-BEYT		
☐ LN-WFD	de Havilland DHC-8-311	407	ex C-FSIJ		
☐ LN-WFH	de Havilland DHC-8-311A	238	ex C-FZOH	all-white	
☐ LN-WFO	de Havilland DHC-8Q-311	493	ex C-GERC		
☐ LN-WFP	de Havilland DHC-8Q-311	495	ex C-GFUM		
☐ LN-WFS	de Havilland DHC-8Q-311	535	ex C-GEWI		
☐ LN-WFT	de Havilland DHC-8Q-311	532	ex C-FATN		
☐ LN-WIA	de Havilland DHC-8-103B	359	ex C-GHRI	Nordland	
☐ LN-WIB	de Havilland DHC-8-103B	360	ex C-GFBW	Finnmark	
☐ LN-WIC	de Havilland DHC-8-103B	367	ex C-GDNG	Sogn og Fjordane	
☐ LN-WID	de Havilland DHC-8-103B	369	ex C-FDHD	More og Romsdal	
☐ LN-WIE	de Havilland DHC-8-103B	371	ex C-GFYI	Hordaland	
☐ LN-WIF	de Havilland DHC-8-103B	372	ex C-GFOD	Nord-Tröndelag	
☐ LN-WIG	de Havilland DHC-8-103B	382	ex C-GLOT	Troms	
☐ LN-WIH	de Havilland DHC-8-103B	383	ex C-GFYI	Oslo	
☐ LN-WII	de Havilland DHC-8-103B	384	ex C-GFOD	Nordkapp	
☐ LN-WIJ	de Havilland DHC-8-103B	386	ex C-GFQL	Hammerfest	
☐ LN-WIL	de Havilland DHC-8-103B	398	ex C-GFCF	Narvik	

☐ LN-WIM	de Havilland DHC-8-103B	403	ex C-GDIU	Vesterälen	
☐ LN-WIN	de Havilland DHC-8-103B	409	ex C-GDNG	Alstadhaug/Lofoten	
☐ LN-WIO	de Havilland DHC-8-103B	417	ex C-GFQL	Rost/Akershus	
☐ LN-WIP	de Havilland DHC-8-103A	239	ex C-FXNE	Alstahaug	
☐ LN-WIR	de Havilland DHC-8-103A	273	ex C-FZNU	Nordkyn	
☐ LN-WIT	de Havilland DHC-8-103	310	ex D-BIER		
☐ LN-WIU	de Havilland DHC-8-103	378	ex C-FZKQ		

ARGENTINA (Republic of Argentina)

AEROCHACO

☐ LV-BSC	McDonnell-Douglas MD-87	49727/1621	ex N755RA	
☐ LV-BZH	McDonnell-Douglas MD-87	49780/1674	ex N572SH	
☐ LV-ZPZ	British Aerospace Jetstream 32EP	931	ex N931AE	

AEROLINEAS ARGENTINAS — Argentina (AR/ARG) — Buenos Aires-Ezeiza (EZE)

☐ LV-BIT	Airbus A340-313	093	ex 9Y-TJN	
☐ LV-BMT	Airbus A340-312	048	ex C-FDRO	
☐ LV-CEK	Airbus A340-343	094	ex EI-EHZ	♦
☐ LV-ZPJ	Airbus A340-211	074	ex F-OHPG	
☐ LV-ZPO	Airbus A340-211	063	ex F-OHPF	
☐ LV-ZPX	Airbus A340-211	080	ex F-OHPH	
☐ LV-ZRA	Airbus A340-211	085	ex F-OHPI	[EZE]
☐ LV-AYE	Boeing 737-5H6	26456/2527	ex F-GJNY	
☐ LV-AYI	Boeing 737-528	25234/2411	ex F-GJNI	
☐ LV-AZU	Boeing 737-528	25235/2428	ex F-GJNJ	
☐ LV-BAR	Boeing 737-528	26450/2503	ex F-GJNZ	
☐ LV-BAT	Boeing 737-5H6	27356/2654	ex F-GJNP	
☐ LV-BAX	Boeing 737-5H6	26448/2484	ex F-GJNL	
☐ LV-BBN	Boeing 737-5H6	26454/2511	ex F-GJNX	
☐ LV-BBW	Boeing 737-5Y0	24897/2003	ex B-2542	
☐ LV-BDD	Boeing 737-5Y0	24899/2093	ex B-2544	
☐ LV-BDV	Boeing 737-5Y0	24900/2095	ex B-2545	
☐ LV-BEO	Boeing 737-5Y0	25176/2155	ex B-2547	
☐ LV-BIH	Boeing 737-53A	24786/1898	ex N786AW	
☐ LV-BIM	Boeing 737-53A	25425/2177	ex N425AN	
☐ LV-BIX	Boeing 737-53A	24788/1921	ex N233BC	
☐ LV-BNM	Boeing 737-5K5	24926/1966	ex D-AHLD	
☐ LV-BNS	Boeing 737-5K5	24776/1848	ex D-AHLG	
☐ LV-BOT	Boeing 737-505	24652/1917	ex N650TC	
☐ LV-BYY	Boeing 737-7BD/W	33938/2863	ex N357AT	
☐ LV-BZA	Boeing 737-76N/W	32674/1952	ex OK-GCA	
☐ LV-BZO	Boeing 737-76N/W	32676/1974	ex OK-GCB	
☐ LV-CAD	Boeing 737-76N/W	32680/2089	ex OK-GCC	
☐ LV-CAM	Boeing 737-73V/W	30243/919	ex N243CL	
☐ LV-CAP	Boeing 737-76N/W	32695/1919	ex OK-GCD	
☐ LV-CBF	Boeing 737-76N/W	32696/1922	ex OK-GCE	
☐ LV-CBG	Boeing 737-73V/W	30235/672	ex N384DF	
☐ LV-CBS	Boeing 737-73V/W	30236/715	ex N385DF	
☐ LV-CBT	Boeing 737-76N/W	34756/2208	ex OK-GCF	
☐ LV-CCR	Boeing 737-73V/W	30237/730	ex N386DF	
☐ LV-GOO	Boeing 737-7BD	35962/2932	ex N358AT	
☐ LV-WSY	Boeing 737-281	20562/293	ex JA8416	>DLU
☐ LV-WTX	Boeing 737-281	20561/292	ex LV-PMI	stored
☐ LV-ZRO	Boeing 737-236	23164/1060	ex N925PG	[EZE]
☐ LV-ZSW	Boeing 737-236	23170/1086	ex N937PG	stored
☐ LV-ZTT	Boeing 737-236	21806/699	ex N947PG	[EZE]
☐ LV-ZTY	Boeing 737-236	23159/1047	ex N949PG	
☐ LV-ZXC	Boeing 737-236	23160/1053	ex N950PG	
☐ LV-ZXP	Boeing 737-228	23003/939	ex LV-PIV	[EZE]
☐ LV-ZXU	Boeing 737-236	23226/1105	ex N952PG	
☐ LV-ZYG	Boeing 737-236	21795/645	ex N954PG	[EZE]
☐ LV-ZYI	Boeing 737-228	23010/959	ex LV-PJC	
☐ LV-ZYN	Boeing 737-236	21794/643	ex N900PG	
☐ LV-ZZD	Boeing 737-228	23011/971	ex LV-PJD	
☐ LV-ZZI	Boeing 737-236	23166/1067	ex N956PG	
☐ LV-ALJ	Boeing 747-475	25422/912	ex N971PG	
☐ LV-AXF	Boeing 747-475	24895/837	ex N895NC	
☐ LV-BBU	Boeing 747-475	24883/823	ex N987PG	
☐ LV-MLP	Boeing 747-287B	21726/403		
☐ LV-MLR	Boeing 747-287B	21727/404		[EZE]

☐ LV-OEP	Boeing 747-287B	22297/487			
☐ LV-OPA	Boeing 747-287B	22593/552	ex EC-JJG		[EZE]
☐ LV-VBX	McDonnell-Douglas MD-88	53047/2016		Parque Nacional Lanin	
☐ LV-VBZ	McDonnell-Douglas MD-88	53049/2031		Parque Baritu	
☐ LV-VCB	McDonnell-Douglas MD-88	53351/2043	ex EC-JKC	Parque Iguazu	[AEP]
☐ LV-VGB	McDonnell-Douglas MD-88	53446/2046	ex EC-JOI	Parque Nahuel Huapi	[AEP]

AERO VIP (AOG) Buenos Aires-Aeroparque (AEP)

☐ LV-BYW	Canadair CRJ-900	15209	ex CX-CRG	

AIR TANGO Buenos Aires-Aeroparque (AEP)

☐ LV-WEO	Swearingen SA.226TC Metro II	TC-346	ex N52EA	

AMERICAN JET Buenos Aires-Aeroparque (AEP)

☐ LV-BYJ	Swearingen SA.227DC Metro 23	DC-889B	ex N889AJ	
☐ LV-BYL	Swearingen SA.227DC Metro 23	DC-819B	ex N819SK	
☐ LV-BYM	Swearingen SA.227DC Metro 23	DC-856B	ex N3027B	
☐ LV-BYN	Swearingen SA.227DC Metro 23	DC-888B	ex N332AJ	
☐ LV-WTD	Dornier 228-200	8094	ex D-CBDR	
☐ LV-WTV	Dornier 228-200	8093	ex N228AM	
☐ LV-ZXA	Swearingen SA.227DC Metro 23	DC-901B	ex LV-PIR	no titles

ANDES LINEAS AEREAS Aeroandes (ANS) Salta International (SLA)

☐ LV-CFD	Canadair CRJ-900ER	15064	ex C-GEFX		♦
☐ LV-BHF	McDonnell-Douglas MD-82	49508/1449	ex N821NK		
☐ LV-BTH	McDonnell-Douglas MD-83	49952/1934	ex N995AC		
☐ LV-BZR	McDonnell-Douglas MD-87	49706/1614	ex XA-TWT		
☐ LV-CDD	McDonnell-Douglas MD-83	49579/1465	ex EC-GOM		♦

AUSTRAL LINEAS AEREAS Austral (AU/AUT) Buenos Aires-Aeroparque (AEP)

☐ LV-ZTE	Boeing 737-228	23349/1135	ex LV-PIJ		[AEP]
☐ LV-ZTX	Boeing 737-228	23504/1267	ex LV-PIP		[EZE]
☐ LV-ZXB	Boeing 737-228	23009/958	ex LV-PIS		
☐ LV-ZXH	Boeing 737-228	23503/1256	ex LV-PIU		[AEP]
☐ LV-ZXV	Boeing 737-228	23793/1426	ex LV-PIX		[EZE]
☐ LV-CET	Embraer ERJ-190AR	19000383	ex PT-XNR		♦
☐ LV-CEU	Embraer ERJ-190AR	19000389	ex PT-XNW		♦
☐ LV-CEV	Embraer ERJ-190AR	19000390	ex PT-XNX		♦
☐ LV-CHO	Embraer ERJ-190AR	19000395	ex PT-XUB		♦
☐ LV-CHQ	Embraer ERJ-190AR	19000397	ex PT-XUC		♦
☐ LV-CHR	Embraer ERJ-190AR	19000400	ex PT-TYF		♦
☐ LV-CHS	Embraer ERJ-190AR	19000402	ex PT-TYV		♦
☐ LV-CID	Embraer ERJ-190AR	19000409	ex PT-TBH		♦
☐ LV-CIE	Embraer ERJ-190AR	19000414	ex PT-TBL		♦
☐ LV-	Embraer ERJ-190AR	19000	ex PT-		o/o♦
☐ LV-	Embraer ERJ-190AR	19000	ex PT-		o/o♦
☐ LV-	Embraer ERJ-190AR	19000	ex PT-		o/o♦
☐ LV-	Embraer ERJ-190AR	19000	ex PT-		o/o♦
☐ LV-ARF	McDonnell-Douglas MD-83	49252/1169	ex LV-PJH		
☐ LV-AYD	McDonnell-Douglas MD-83	53015/1818	ex N824NK		[Palomar]
☐ LV-BAY	McDonnell-Douglas MD-83	49284/1209	ex LV-PJJ		
☐ LV-BDE	McDonnell-Douglas MD-83	49943/1887	ex N943MT		[AEP]
☐ LV-BDO	McDonnell-Douglas MD-83	49941/1793	ex N941MT		
☐ LV-BEG	McDonnell-Douglas MD-83	49630/1591	ex N320FV		[AEP]
☐ LV-BGV	McDonnell-Douglas MD-83	49904/1680	ex N960PG		[AEP]
☐ LV-BGZ	McDonnell-Douglas MD-82	49906/1786	ex EC-JZA		
☐ LV-BHH	McDonnell-Douglas MD-82	49741/1630	ex N959PG		
☐ LV-BHN	McDonnell-Douglas MD-83	53190/2148	ex N190AN		
☐ LV-VAG	McDonnell-Douglas MD-83	53117/1951	ex N6202D		
☐ LV-WFN	McDonnell-Douglas MD-81	48025/952	ex N10027		[AEP]
☐ LV-WGM	McDonnell-Douglas MD-83	49784/1627	ex N509MD		
☐ LV-WGN	McDonnell-Douglas MD-83	49934/1764	ex N907MD		
☐ LV-BOA	McDonnell-Douglas MD-88	53174/1854	ex N168PL		
☐ LV-BOH	McDonnell-Douglas MD-88	53175/1868	ex N169PL		
☐ LV-BOR	McDonnell-Douglas MD-88	49929/1741	ex XA-AMV		[AEP]
☐ LV-BTI	McDonnell-Douglas MD-88	49927/1716	ex XA-AMT		
☐ LV-BTW	McDonnell-Douglas MD-88	49926/1715	ex XA-AMS		
☐ LV-BXA	McDonnell-Douglas MD-88	49928/1732	ex XA-AMU		

BAIRES FLY   Buenos Aires-Aeroparque (AEP)

☐ LV-VDJ	Swearingen SA.227AC Metro III	AC-729	ex N27823
☐ LV-WHG	Swearingen SA.226TC Metro II	TC-344	ex N44CS
☐ LV-WJT	Swearingen SA.227AC Metro III	AC-776B	ex N776NE
☐ LV-WTE	Swearingen SA.227AC Metro III	AC-584	ex LV-PMF
☐ LV-ZMG	Swearingen SA.227AC Metro III	AC-425	ex N721MA

FLYING AMERICA   Buenos Aires-Aeroparque (AEP)

☐ LV-BGH	Swearingen SA.227AC Metro III	AC-467	ex TF-JMK
☐ LV-BGR	Swearingen SA.227AC Metro III	AC-461B	ex EC-HXY
☐ LV-YIC	Swearingen SA.227AC Metro III	AC-448	ex LV-PNF

HANGAR UNO   Buenos Aires-Don Torcuato

| ☐ LV-WFR | Britten-Norman BN-2B-26 Islander | 2263 | ex G-BUBF | Puerto Carmelo titles |

HAWK AIR   Air Hawk (HKR)   Buenos Aires-Aeroparque (AEP)

☐ LV-WHX	Piper PA-31 Turbo Navajo	31-353	ex N716DR	
☐ LV-WIR	Swearingen SA.226T Merlin III	T-232	ex N56TA	Frtr
☐ LV-WNC	Swearingen SA.226AT Merlin IVA	AT-036	ex N642TS	Frtr
☐ LV-WXW	Swearingen SA.226TC Metro II	TC-419	ex N7205L	Frtr

LADE - LINEAS AEREAS DEL ESTADO   Lade (5U/LDE)   Comodoro Rivadavia (CRD)

| ☐ TC-91 | Boeing 707-387B | 21070/897 | ex T-91 | |

☐ T-81	de Havilland DHC-6 Twin Otter 200	165		
☐ T-82	de Havilland DHC-6 Twin Otter 200	167		
☐ T-85	de Havilland DHC-6 Twin Otter 200	173		
☐ T-86	de Havilland DHC-6 Twin Otter 200	225		Antarctic red colours
☐ T-88	de Havilland DHC-6 Twin Otter 200	158	ex LV-JMP	
☐ T-89	de Havilland DHC-6 Twin Otter 200	185	ex LV-JPX	
☐ T-90	de Havilland DHC-6 Twin Otter 200	178	ex LV-JMR	

☐ T-44	Fokker F.27 Friendship 600	10454	ex PH-EXB	
☐ T-45	Fokker F.27 Friendship 600	10368	ex TC-79	
☐ TC-71	Fokker F.27 Friendship 400M	10403	ex PH-FOB	
☐ TC-74	Fokker F.27 Friendship 400M	10408	ex PH-FOG	
☐ TC-75	Fokker F.27 Friendship 500	10621	ex PH-EXM	
☐ TC-79	Fokker F.27 Friendship 400M	10575	ex PH-EXG	

☐ TC-52	Fokker F.28 Fellowship 1000C	11074	ex LV-RCS	[El Palomar]
☐ TC-53	Fokker F.28 Fellowship 1000C	11020	ex PH-EXX	
☐ TC-55	Fokker F.28 Fellowship 1000C	11024	ex PH-EXZ	stored

☐ T-31	SAAB SF.340B	340B-270	ex N284DC	
☐ T-32	SAAB SF.340B	340B-226	ex N285DC	
☐ T-33	SAAB SF.340B	340B-288	ex N288JJ	
☐ T-34	SAAB SF.340B	340B-217	ex N217JJ	

LAN ARGENTINA   LAN Ar (4M/DSM)   Buenos Aires-Aeroparque (AEP)

☐ LV-BET	Airbus A320-233	1854	ex CC-COO	<LAN
☐ LV-BFO	Airbus A320-233	1877	ex CC-COQ	<LAN
☐ LV-BFY	Airbus A320-233	1858	ex CC-COP	<LAN
☐ LV-BGI	Airbus A320-233	1903	ex CC-COT	<LAN
☐ LV-BHU	Airbus A320-233	1512	ex CC-COH	<LAN
☐ LV-BOI	Airbus A320-233	1491	ex CC-COG	<LAN
☐ LV-BRA	Airbus A320-233	1304	ex CC-COC	<LAN
☐ LV-BRY	Airbus A320-233	1351	ex CC-COE	<LAN
☐ LV-BSJ	Airbus A320-233	1332	ex CC-COD	<LAN
☐ LV-BTA	Airbus A320-233	1548	ex CC-COK	<LAN

| ☐ LV-CDQ | Boeing 767-316ER/W | 35229/949 | ex CC-CWN | <LAN♦ |

MACAIR JET   Buenos Aires-Aeroparque (AEP)

☐ LV-ZOW	British Aerospace Jetstream 32EP	869	ex N869AE
☐ LV-ZPW	British Aerospace Jetstream 32EP	861	ex N861AE
☐ LV-ZRL	British Aerospace Jetstream 32EP	928	ex N928AE
☐ LV-ZSB	British Aerospace Jetstream 32EP	942	ex N942AE
☐ LV-ZST	British Aerospace Jetstream 32EP	941	ex N941AE

SOL LINEAS AEREAS		Flight Sol (8R/OLS)		Rosario-Fisherton (ROS)
☐ LV-BEW	SAAB SF.340A	340A-150	ex N150CN	
☐ LV-BEX	SAAB SF.340A	340A-014	ex N14XS	
☐ LV-BMD	SAAB SF.340A	340A-123	ex N123XS	
☐ LV-BTP	SAAB SF.340A	340A-131	ex VH-KDI	

TAPSA AVIACION		Tapsa (TPS)		Buenos Aires-Aeroparque (AEP)
☐ LV-LSI	de Havilland DHC-6 Twin Otter 300	456	ex LV-PTW	

TRANSPORTES BRAGADO				Buenos Aires-Aeroparque (AEP)
☐ LV-MGD	Piper PA-31T Cheyenne	31T-7720059	ex LV-PXD	
☐ LV-ZNU	Cessna 208B Caravan I	208B0718	ex LV-POC	

LX-   LUXEMBOURG (Grand Duchy of Luxembourg)

CARGOLUX AIRLINES INTERNATIONAL		Cargolux (CV/CLX)			Luxembourg (LUX)
☐ LX-LCV	Boeing 747-4R7F	29053/1139		Grevenmacher	
☐ LX-NCV	Boeing 747-4R7F	29730/1203		Vianden	
☐ LX-OCV	Boeing 747-4R7F	29731/1222		Differdange	
☐ LX-PCV	Boeing 747-4R7F	29732/1231		Diekirch	
☐ LX-RCV	Boeing 747-4R7F	30400/1235		Schengen	
☐ LX-SCV	Boeing 747-4R7F	29733/1281		Niederanven	
☐ LX-TCV	Boeing 747-4R7F	30401/1311	ex N6046P	Sandweiler	
☐ LX-UCV	Boeing 747-4R7F	33827/1345		Bertrange	
☐ LX-VCA	Boeing 747-8R7F	35808/1420	ex N747EX		o/o♦
☐ LX-VCB	Boeing 747-8R7F	35806/1423			o/o♦
☐ LX-VCC	Boeing 747-8R7F	35807/1424			o/o♦
☐ LX-VCD	Boeing 747-8R7F	35809/			o/o♦
☐ LX-VCV	Boeing 747-4R7F	34235/1366		Walferdange	
☐ LX-WCV	Boeing 747-4R7F	35804/1390	ex N5022E	Pétange	
☐ LX-YCV	Boeing 747-4R7F	35805/1407		City of Contern	
☐ LX-ZCV	Boeing 747-481BDSF	24801/805	ex F-GISF		♦
☐ N741WA	Boeing 747-4H6 (BDSF)	25702/999	ex 9V-SPR		<WOA♦

LUXAIR		Luxair (LG/LGL)			Luxembourg (LUX)
☐ LX-LGQ	Boeing 737-7C9/W	33802/1442		Chateau de Berg	
☐ LX-LGR	Boeing 737-7C9/W	33803/1468		Chateau de Fischbach	
☐ LX-LGS	Boeing 737-7C9/W	33956/1634		Chateau de Senningen	
☐ LX-LGT	Boeing 737-8K5/W	28228/484	ex D-AHFN		
☐ LX-LGA	de Havilland DHC-8-402Q	4159	ex C-FLKX		
☐ LX-LGC	de Havilland DHC-8-402Q	4162	ex C-FLTY		
☐ LX-LGD	de Havilland DHC-8-402Q	4171	ex C-FMJC		
☐ LX-LGE	de Havilland DHC-8-402Q	4284	ex C-FXYV		
☐ LX-	de Havilland DHC-8-402Q	4349	ex C-		o/o♦
☐ LX-LGI	Embraer ERJ-145LU	145369	ex PT-SOU		
☐ LX-LGJ	Embraer ERJ-145LU	145395	ex PT-SQS		
☐ LX-LGK	Embraer ERJ-135LR	14500886	ex PT-SXY		
☐ LX-LGL	Embraer ERJ-135LR	14500893	ex PT-SYF	900th titles	
☐ LX-LGW	Embraer ERJ-145LU	145135	ex PT-SDM		
☐ LX-LGX	Embraer ERJ-145LU	145147	ex PT-SDX		
☐ LX-LGY	Embraer ERJ-145LU	145242	ex PT-SIH		
☐ LX-LGZ	Embraer ERJ-145LU	145258	ex PT-SIR		

WEST AIR EUROPE		West Lux (WLX)			Luxembourg (LUX)
☐ LX-WAL	British Aerospace ATPF	2059	ex SE-LHZ		<SWN
☐ LX-WAO	British Aerospace ATP (LFD)	2043	ex SE-LPS		<SWN
☐ LX-WAP	British Aerospace ATPF	2057	ex SE-LPR		<SWN
☐ LX-WAS	British Aerospace ATP	2058	ex SE-LPT		<SWN
☐ LX-WAT	British Aerospace ATP (LFD)	2011	ex SE-MAO		<SWN
☐ LX-WAV	British Aerospace ATP (LFD)	2041	ex SE-LPV		<SWN
☐ LX-WAW	British Aerospace ATP (LFD)	2021	ex SE-LGZ		
☐ LX-WAB	ATR 72-201F	227	ex OY-RUC		

LY-   LITHUANIA (Republic of Lithuania)

APATAS		Apatas (LYT)		Kaunus-Karmelava (KUN)
☐ LY-AVA	LET L-410UVP-E3	882036	ex Soviet AF 2036	
☐ LY-AVT	LET L-410UVP-E3	882033	ex Soviet AF 2033	

AURELA		Aurela (LSK)		Vilnius (VNO)
☐ LY-SKA	Boeing 737-35B	23972/1537	ex N223DZ	
☐ LY-SKW	Boeing 737-382	25162/2241	ex N161LF	

AVIAVILSA		Aviavilsa (LVR)		Vilnius (VNO)
☐ LY-APK	Antonov An-26B	27312201	ex RA-26114	<GZP
☐ LY-APN	Antonov An-26B	27312010	ex UR-BXF	
☐ LY-ETM	ATR 42-300F	067	ex (SE-MAS)	

AVION EXPRESS				
☐ LY-ISA	SAAB SF.340A	340A-056	ex SE-LMX	

DANU ORO TRANSPORTAS		Danu (R6/DNU)		Vilnius (VNO)
☐ LY-ARI	ATR 42-300	012A	ex F-WQBT	
☐ LY-DAT	ATR 42-500	445	ex F-WKVF	♦
☐ LY-LWH	ATR 42-300	148	ex LN-FAO	
☐ LY-OOV	ATR 42-300F	005	ex EI-SLD	
☐ LY-RUM	ATR 42-300	010	ex OY-RUM	<DTR
☐ LY-RUN	SAAB SF.340A	340A-086	ex G-RUNG	<DTR
☐ LY-RUS	SAAB SF.340A	340A-074	ex SE-LTO	

NORDIC SOLUTIONS AIR SERVICES		Nordvind (N9/NVD)		Vilnius (VNO)
☐ LY-NSA	SAAB SF.340AF	340A-055	ex SE-KPE	
☐ LY-NSB	SAAB SF.340AF	340A-045	ex SE-ISV	
☐ LY-NSC	SAAB SF.340AF	340A-037	ex SE-KPD	

SMALL PLANET AIRLINES		(LLC)		Vilnius (VNO)
☐ LY-AWD	Boeing 737-522	26739/2494	ex C-FDCU	
☐ LY-AWE	Boeing 737-522	26684/2388	ex C-FCFR	
☐ LY-AWH	Boeing 737-3Y0	23924/1542	ex N924RM	
☐ LY-BSD	Boeing 737-2T4	22701/886	ex N4569N	Steponas Darius	[VNO]
☐ LY-FLC	Boeing 737-31S	29055/2923	ex EI-DNX	
☐ LY-FLD	Boeing 737-322	24664/1877	ex ES-LBC	
☐ LY-FLE	Boeing 737-3L9	27061/2347	ex PK-AWG	♦
☐ LY-FLH	Boeing 737-382	25161/2226	ex N161AN	♦
☐ LY-FLA	Boeing 757-29J/W	27203/588	ex N703AM	
☐ LY-FLG	Boeing 757-204	27237/602	ex G-BYAR	

STAR1 AIRLINES		(HCW)		Vilnius (VNO)
☐ LY-STG	Boeing 737-73S	29083/392	ex D-AHIB	

LZ-   BULGARIA (Republic of Bulgaria)

AIR MAX		Aeromax (RMX)		Plovdiv (PDV)
☐ LZ-RMK	LET L-410UVP	851406	ex UR-67502	
☐ LZ-RMV	LET L-410UVP-E	892215	ex HA-LAV	♦
☐ LZ-RMW	LET L-410UVP-E	902517	ex HA-LAE	

AIR SCORPIO		Scorpio Univers (SCU)		Sofia (SOF)
☐ LZ-CCB	Cessna 402B	402B0581	ex EC-HDF	
☐ LZ-MNR	Antonov An-26b-	87307504	ex LZ-NHC	
☐ LZ-MNT	Antonov An-26	2209	ex HAF-209	
☐ LZ-RMC	LET L-410UVP-E12	882207	ex LZ-LSC	

AIRGO AIRLINES OF SOFIA				
☐ LZ-BPS	British Aerospace ATP (LFD)	2005	ex SX-BPS	♦

BH AIR		Balkan Holidays (BGH)		Sofia (SOF)
☐ LZ-BHB	Airbus A320-212	0294	ex OY-CNP	
☐ LZ-BHC	Airbus A320-212	0349	ex OY-CNR	
☐ LZ-BHD	Airbus A320-212	0221	ex CS-TQE	
☐ LZ-BHE	Airbus A320-211	0305	ex EI-DNK	
☐ TC-OAN	Airbus A321-231	1421	ex D-ALAP	<OHY

BULGARIA AIR		Flying Bulgaria (FB/LZB)		Sofia (SOF)
☐ LZ-FBE	Airbus A320-214	3780	ex D-AVVI	
☐ LZ-FBF	Airbus A319-111	3028	ex N950FR	
☐ LZ-BOQ	Boeing 737-522	26687/2402	ex N946UA	
☐ LZ-BOU	Boeing 737-3L9	23717/1365	ex N231DN	
☐ LZ-BOV	Boeing 737-330	23833/1439	ex N241DL	
☐ LZ-BOW	Boeing 737-330	23834/1454	ex N242DL	

BULGARIAN AIR CHARTER		Bulgarian Charter (BUC)		Sofia (SOF)
☐ LZ-LDC	McDonnell-Douglas MD-82	49217/1268	ex I-DAVC	
☐ LZ-LDE	McDonnell-Douglas MD-82	53221/2079	ex I-DATB	♦
☐ LZ-LDF	McDonnell-Douglas MD-82	49219/1310	ex I-DAVF	
☐ LZ-LDG	McDonnell-Douglas MD-83	53149/1817	ex TC-FLN	
☐ LZ-LDH	McDonnell-Douglas MD-83	53150/1831	ex TC-FLO	
☐ LZ-LDK	McDonnell-Douglas MD-82	49432/1378	ex I-DAVK	
☐ LZ-LDL	McDonnell-Douglas MD-82	53229/2105	ex I-DATL	♦
☐ LZ-LDM	McDonnell-Douglas MD-82	53228/2104	ex I-DATK	♦
☐ LZ-LDP	McDonnell-Douglas MD-82	49973/1762	ex I-DACP	♦
☐ LZ-LDR	McDonnell-Douglas MD-82	49277/1181	ex HB-INR	
☐ LZ-LDW	McDonnell-Douglas MD-82	49795/1639	ex I-DAVV	♦
☐ LZ-LDY	McDonnell-Douglas MD-82	49213/1243	ex I-DAWY	
☐ LZ-LDZ	McDonnell-Douglas MD-83	49930/1720	ex HB-ISZ	

CARGO AIR		Vega Airlines (VEA)		Sofia (SOF)
☐ LZ-CGO	Boeing 737-301F	23237/1222	ex N503UW	
☐ LZ-CGP	Boeing 737-35BF	23970/1467	ex N221DL	♦

HELI AIR		Heli Bulgaria (HLR)		Sofia (SOF)
☐ LZ-CBG	Antonov An-12A	2340804	ex RA-11370	[SOF]
☐ LZ-CCE	LET L-410UVP-E	871816	ex 1816	
☐ LZ-CCF	LET L-410UVP-E	861722	ex 1722	Op for UN
☐ LZ-CCG	LET L-410UVP-E	902503	ex S5-BAE	
☐ LZ-CCP	LET L-410UVP-E20	912540	ex OK-WDA	
☐ LZ-CCR	LET L-410UVP-E10	892301	ex SP-FTX	
☐ LZ-CCS	LET L-410UVP-E	902425	ex 3D-EER	Op for UN
☐ LZ-CCT	LET L-410UVP-E10	912528	ex ST-DND	Op for UN
☐ LZ-LSB	LET L-410UVP-E2	861802	no titles	Op for UN

HEMUS AIR		Hemus Air (DU/HMS)		Sofia (SOF)
☐ LZ-HBA	British Aerospace 146 Srs.200	E2072	ex VH-NJQ	
☐ LZ-HBB	British Aerospace 146 Srs.200	E2073	ex VH-NJU	
☐ LZ-HBC	British Aerospace 146 Srs.200	E2093	ex VH-JJS	
☐ LZ-HBD	British Aerospace 146 Srs.300	E3141	ex N615AW	>TBM
☐ LZ-HBE	British Aerospace 146 Srs.300	E3131	ex EI-CLG	
☐ LZ-HBF	British Aerospace 146 Srs.300	E3159	ex EI-CLI	
☐ LZ-HBG	British Aerospace 146 Srs.300	E3146	ex EI-CLH	
☐ LZ-HBZ	British Aerospace 146 Srs.200	E2103	ex G-JEAK	>TBM
☐ LZ-TIM	Avro 146-RJ70	E1258	ex EI-CPJ	Op for Bulgarian Govt
☐ LZ-FBA	Airbus A319-112	3564	ex D-AVWS	
☐ LZ-FBB	Airbus A319-112	3309	ex EI-DZW	
☐ LZ-FBC	Airbus A320-214	2540	ex EC-JMB	
☐ LZ-FBD	Airbus A320-214	2596	ex EC-JNA	
☐ LZ-ATR	ATR 42-300	151	ex F-WQNC	>LBY
☐ LZ-ATS	ATR 42-300	130	ex F-WQNO	

VIA - AIR VIA		(VL/VIM)		Varna (VAR)
☐ LZ-MDA	Airbus A320-232	2732	ex F-WWBE	
☐ LZ-MDB	Airbus A320-232	3125	ex F-WWBF	
☐ LZ-MDC	Airbus A320-232	4270	ex F-WWBS	♦
☐ LZ-MDD	Airbus A320-232	4305	ex F-WWDZ	♦
☐ LZ-MDM	Airbus A320-232	2804	ex F-WWIM	

☐ LZ-	Airbus A320-232		ex	o/o♦
☐ LZ-	Airbus A320-232		ex	o/o♦

WIZZ AIR BULGARIA AIRLINES	**(8Z/WVL)**			**Sofia (SOF)**
☐ LZ-WZA	Airbus A320-232	2571	ex HA-LPG	<WZZ
☐ LZ-WZB	Airbus A320-232	3562	ex F-WWBH	<WZZ
☐ LZ-WZC	Airbus A320-232	4308	ex F-WWIG	<WZZ♦

N   UNITED STATES OF AMERICA

ABX AIR		**Abex (GB/ABX)**	**Wilmington-Airborne Airpark, OH (ILN)**	
☐ N312AA	Boeing 767-223SF	22315/94		
☐ N702AX	Boeing 767-231ER	22566/29	ex N603TW	
☐ N707AX	Boeing 767-231ER	22570/63	ex N607TW	
☐ N708AX	Boeing 767-231ER	22571/64	ex N608TW	
☐ N709AX	Boeing 767-231ER	22572/65	ex N609TW	
☐ N713AX	Boeing 767-205ER	23058/101	ex N651TW	
☐ N739AX	Boeing 767-232 (SCD)	22216/26	ex N104DA	
☐ N740AX	Boeing 767-232 (SCD)	22213/6	ex N101DA	
☐ N741AX	Boeing 767-232 (SCD)	22215/17	ex N103DA	for conv to Frtr
☐ N742AX	Boeing 767-232 (SCD)	22217/27	ex N105DA	>ANA
☐ N743AX	Boeing 767-232 (SCD)	22218/31	ex N106DA	
☐ N744AX	Boeing 767-232 (SCD)	22221/53	ex N109DL	>ANA
☐ N745AX	Boeing 767-232 (SCD)	22222/56	ex N110DL	
☐ N747AX	Boeing 767-232 (SCD)	22224/56	ex N112DL	
☐ N749AX	Boeing 767-232	22226/78	ex N114DL	for conv to Frtr
☐ N750AX	Boeing 767-232 (SCD)	22227/83	ex N115DA	
☐ N752AX	Boeing 767-281	23434/171	ex JA8255	
☐ N767AX	Boeing 767-281	22785/51	ex JA8479	
☐ N768AX	Boeing 767-281	22786/54	ex JA8480	
☐ N769AX	Boeing 767-281F	22787/58	ex JA8481	
☐ N773AX	Boeing 767-281	22788/61	ex JA8482	
☐ N774AX	Boeing 767-281	22789/67	ex JA8483	
☐ N775AX	Boeing 767-281	22790/69	ex JA8484	
☐ N783AX	Boeing 767-281	23016/80	ex JA8485	
☐ N784AX	Boeing 767-281	23017/82	ex JA8486	
☐ N785AX	Boeing 767-281	23018/84	ex JA8487	
☐ N786AX	Boeing 767-281	23019/85	ex JA8488	
☐ N787AX	Boeing 767-281F	23020/96	ex JA8489	
☐ N788AX	Boeing 767-281	23021/103	ex JA8490	
☐ N790AX	Boeing 767-281	23140/106	ex JA8238	
☐ N791AX	Boeing 767-281	23141/108	ex JA8239	
☐ N792AX	Boeing 767-281 (SCD)	23142/110	ex JA8240	
☐ N793AX	Boeing 767-281	23143/114	ex JA8241	
☐ N794AX	Boeing 767-281	23144/115	ex JA8242	
☐ N795AX	Boeing 767-281F	23145/116	ex JA8243	
☐ N796AX	Boeing 767-281	23146/121	ex JA8244	
☐ N797AX	Boeing 767-281	23147/123	ex JA8245	
☐ N798AX	Boeing 767-281 (SCD)	23431/143	ex JA8251	DHL colours

ACADEMY AIRLINES		**Academy (ACD)**	**Hampton-Clayton Co/Tara Field, GA**	
☐ N17WT	Beech 65-90 King Air	LJ-86	ex N60RJ	<Jeffair

ACTION AIRLINES		**Action Air (AXQ)**	**Groton-New London, CT (GON)**	
☐ N660RA	Piper PA-34-200T Seneca II	34-7870354	ex N36708	<Griswold Air Service

ADIRONDACK FLYING SERVICE			**Lake Placid, NY (LKP)**	
☐ N83D	Cessna 414A Chancellor II	414A0615	ex C-FACF	
☐ N8091Q	Cessna 402B	402B0369	ex F-OGFL	
☐ N33247	Cessna U206F Stationair	U20602692		

ADVANCED AIRWAYS			**West Palm Beach-Lantana County Park, FL (LNA)**	
☐ N89M	Aero Commander 500	500-659	ex N4300S	dbr Oct05?
☐ N312EC	Aero Commander 500	500-782	ex N123RK	
☐ N3836C	Aero Commander 500	500-791	ex N8447C	
☐ N3841C	Aero Commander 500	500-707		

AERO CHARTER	**Char Tran (CTA)**		**Albuquerque-International Sunport, NM (ABQ)**	
☐ N38CJ	Cessna 402C II	402C0023	ex N38CC	
☐ N593DM	Cessna 402B II	402B1228	ex N25BH	

☐ N596DM	Cessna 402C II	402C0255	ex N7011X	
☐ N598DM	Cessna 402C II	402C0114	ex N81970	
☐ N635MA	Cessna 402C II	402C0634	ex 5H-TGA	
☐ N775RC	Cessna 402C II	402C0311	ex 5Y-BKK	
☐ N588DM	Cessna 310Q	310Q0624	ex C-GYLZ	
☐ N589DM	Cessna 310Q II	310Q1048	ex C-GONG	
☐ N590DM	Cessna 310Q	310Q0059	ex N212TA	

AERO FLITE · Kingman, AZ (IGM)

☐ N262NR	Canadair CL215	1081	ex C-GDRS	262	op for Minnesota DNR
☐ N263NR	Canadair CL215	1082	ex C-GENU	263	Lsd fr/op for Minnesota DNR
☐ N264V	Canadair CL215	1090	ex C-GOFM	264	
☐ N266NR	Canadair CL215	1102	ex C-GOFO	266	Lsd fr/op for Minnesota DNR
☐ N267V	Canadair CL215	1103	ex C-GOFP	267	

AERO INDUSTRIES · Wabash (WAB) · Richmond, VA (RIC)

☐ N3521S	Piper PA-31-350 Chieftain	31-7952107	
☐ N27508	Piper PA-31-350 Chieftain	31-7852031	

AERO UNION · Chico-Municipal, CA (CIC)

☐ N900AU	Lockheed P-3A Orion	185-5104	ex N406TP	00	Tanker
☐ N920AU	Lockheed P-3A Orion	185-5039	ex Bu150513	20	Tanker
☐ N921AU	Lockheed P-3A Orion	185-5098	ex Bu151385	21	Tanker
☐ N922AU	Lockheed P-3A Orion	185-5100	ex N181AU	22	Tanker
☐ N923AU	Lockheed P-3A Orion	185-5085	ex N185AU	23	Tanker
☐ N925AU	Lockheed P-3A Orion	185-5074	ex N183AU	25	Tanker
☐ N927AU	Lockheed P-3A Orion	185-5082	ex N182AU	27	Tanker
☐ N4096W	Piper PA-32-300 Cherokee Six	32-40159			
☐ N5938Y	Piper PA-23-250 Aztec C	27-3103			

AEX AIR · Desert (DST) · Phoenix-Sky Harbor, AZ/La Verne, CA (PHX/POC)

☐ N14FB	Piper PA-31 Turbo Navajo	31-351	ex N93H
☐ N57AS	Piper PA-31 Turbo Navajo	31-113	ex N585HW
☐ N300WA	Piper PA-31 Turbo Navajo	31-294	ex N9227Y
☐ N49SA	Piper PA-34-200 Seneca	34-7350057	ex C-FDRW
☐ N86PP	Piper PA-34-200 Seneca	34-7250358	ex N15054
☐ N1080U	Piper PA-34-200 Seneca	34-7250083	
☐ N1656H	Piper PA-34-200T Seneca II	34-7770131	
☐ N2817T	Piper PA-34-200 Seneca	34-7250170	
☐ N4581T	Piper PA-34-200 Seneca	34-7250139	
☐ N41298	Piper PA-34-200 Seneca	34-7450106	
☐ N55549	Piper PA-34-200 Seneca	34-7350228	
☐ N56795	Piper PA-34-200 Seneca	34-7450032	
☐ N56974	Piper PA-34-200 Seneca	34-7450044	
☐ N57368	Piper PA-34-200 Seneca	34-7450054	
☐ N75053	Piper PA-34-200T Seneca II	34-7670233	

AIR AMERICA · San Juan –Luis Munoz Marin Intl, PR (SJU)

☐ N21WW	Piper PA-23-250 Aztec E	27-7554066	ex N54754
☐ N30PT	Cessna 421C Golden Eagle	421C0157	ex N5284J
☐ N2395Z	Piper PA-23-250 Aztec F	27-7954107	ex (AN-LAS)
☐ N7049T	Britten-Norman BN-2A-21 Islander	643	ex C-GPAB
☐ N62749	Piper PA-23-250 Aztec F	27-7654198	

AIR ARCTIC · Fairbanks-Intl, AK (FAI)

☐ N234CE	Piper PA-31-350 Chieftain	31-8052203	<Northern Alaska
☐ N820FS	Piper PA-31-350 Chieftain	31-7952185	ex TF-VLA
☐ N7164D	Piper PA-31-350 Chieftain	31-8052013	ex C-GBGI
☐ N3589B	Piper PA-31-350 Chieftain	31-8052134	
☐ N59826	Piper PA-31-350 Navajo Chieftain	31-7652077	

AIR CARGO CARRIERS · Night Cargo (2Q/SNC) · Milwaukee-General Mitchell Intl, WI (MKE)

☐ N58DD	Short SD.3-30	SH3008	ex TG-TJA
☐ N167RC	Short SD.3-30	SH3038	ex N690RA
☐ N330AC	Short SD.3-30	SH3007	ex C-GSKW
☐ N334AC	Short SD.3-30	SH3029	ex VH-LSI
☐ N336MV	Short SD.3-30	SH3018	ex PJ-DDB
☐ N390GA	Short SD.3-30	SH3077	ex 4X-CSP
☐ N936MA	Short SD.3-30	SH3036	ex G-BGNI
☐ N2629P	Short SD.3-30	SH3079	ex G-BJLL

☐ N124CA	Short SD.3-60	SH3652	ex G-BLJS
☐ N136LR	Short SD.3-60	SH3752	ex VH-SUL all-white
☐ N151CA	Short SD.3-60	SH3653	ex G-BLJT
☐ N360AB	Short SD.3-60	SH3756	ex G-BPKZ
☐ N360RW	Short SD.3-60	SH3613	ex C-FCRB
☐ N360SA	Short SD.3-60	SH3601	ex G-WIDE
☐ N367AC	Short SD.3-60	SH3626	ex VH-MVW
☐ N368AC	Short SD.3-60	SH3651	ex VH-BWO
☐ N376AC	Short SD.3-60	SH3736	ex G-VBAC
☐ N601CA	Short SD.3-60	SH3623	ex G-BKWM
☐ N617FB	Short SD.3-60	SH3617	ex G-BKUF
☐ N688AN	Short SD.3-60	SH3633	ex C-GPCJ
☐ N701A	Short SD.3-60	SH3627	ex G-BKZP
☐ N742CC	Short SD.3-60	SH3742	ex D-CFXH
☐ N764JR	Short SD.3-60	SH3764	ex VH-SUF
☐ N972AA	Short SD.3-60	SH3754	ex N263GA
☐ N973AA	Short SD.3-60	SH3749	ex N749JT
☐ N3732X	Short SD.3-60	SH3732	ex PK-DSN
☐ N4498Y	Short SD.3-60	SH3625	ex G-BKZN
☐ N960AA	AMD Falcon 20C	144	ex N385AC
☐ N961AA	AMD Falcon 20D	205	ex N585AC

AIR CHOICE ONE — Weber (WBR) — Farmington Regional, MD (FAM)

☐ N86SJ	Beech Baron 58	TH-656	ex N4184S
☐ N45038	Piper PA-31-350 Chieftain	31-8052202	

AIR DIRECT — Rhinelander-Oneida County, WI (RHI)

☐ N213JD	Cessna 310R II	310R0136	ex N102CT
☐ N800L	Piper PA-31 Turbo Navajo	31-426	ex C-GSGA
☐ N87395	Cessna 310R	310R0543	

AIR EVAC

☐ N12AE	Bell 206L-1 LongRanger	45649	ex N46SG
☐ N19AE	Bell 206L-1 LongRanger	45691	ex N2025V
☐ N24AE	Bell 206L-1 LongRanger	45646	ex N2124Z
☐ N27AE	Bell 206L-1 LongRanger	45192	ex N5007Y
☐ N28AE	Bell 206L-3 LongRanger III	51077	ex N10UB
☐ N29AE	Bell 206L-3 LongRanger III	51191	ex N804SB
☐ N32AE	Bell 206L-1 LongRanger	45327	ex N1067C
☐ N43AE	Bell 206L-1 LongRanger	45187	ex N5007Q
☐ N48AE	Bell 206L-1 LongRanger	45562	ex N206AH
☐ N51AE	Bell 206L-1 LongRanger	45165	ex N119SD
☐ N52AE	Bell 206L-1 LongRanger	45758	ex N2253E
☐ N53AE	Bell 206L-1 LongRanger	45300	ex N27702
☐ N54AE	Bell 206L-1 LongRanger	45157	ex N16938
☐ N59AE	Bell 206L-1 LongRanger	45291	ex N522MT
☐ N61AE	Bell 206L-1 LongRanger	45470	ex N9900M
☐ N63AE	Bell 206L-1 LongRanger	45499	ex N5748Q
☐ N68AE	Bell 206L-1 LongRanger	45647	ex N21240
☐ N74AE	Bell 206L-1 LongRanger	45765	ex N3178K
☐ N79AE	Bell 206L-1 LongRanger	45436	ex N1068S
☐ N83AE	Bell 206L-1 LongRanger	45272	ex N2759U
☐ N88AE	Bell 206L-1 LongRanger	45263	ex N119TA
☐ N89AE	Bell 206L-1 LongRanger	45433	ex N1084Y
☐ N96AE	Bell 206L-1 LongRanger	45751	ex N2245Y
☐ N101AE	Bell 206L-1 LongRanger	45454	ex N5737T
☐ N103AE	Bell 206L-1 LongRanger	45597	ex N3904L
☐ N105AE	Bell 206L-1 LongRanger	45297	ex N2275A
☐ N106AE	Bell 206L-1 LongRanger	45566	ex N677M
☐ N108AE	Bell 206L-1 LongRanger	45730	ex N2070Z
☐ N113AE	Bell 206L-1 LongRanger	45371	ex N719RR
☐ N114AE	Bell 206L-1 LongRanger	45507	ex HK-3823X
☐ N116AE	Bell 206L-1 LongRanger	45632	ex HK-3619X
☐ N117AE	Bell 206L-1 LongRanger	45627	ex HK-3581
☐ N118AE	Bell 206L-1 LongRanger	45724	ex HK-3582
☐ N119AE	Bell 206L-3 LongRanger III	51201	ex HK-3725X
☐ N121AE	Bell 206L-1 LongRanger	45690	ex N2025G
☐ N122AE	Bell 206L-1 LongRanger	45276	ex N60WJ
☐ N124AE	Bell 206L-3 LongRanger III	51591	ex HK-3754X
☐ N127AE	Bell 206L-3 LongRanger III	51592	ex HK-3972P
☐ N129AE	Bell 206L-1 LongRanger	45547	ex N4753T
☐ N130AE	Bell 206L-1 LongRanger	45467	ex N5741Y
☐ N132AE	Bell 206L-1 LongRanger	45491	ex N5745S
☐ N133AE	Bell 206L-1 LongRanger	45280	ex N2762D

☐ N134AE	Bell 206L-1 LongRanger	45593	ex N38958
☐ N138AE	Bell 206L-1 LongRanger	45782	ex N3197V
☐ N139AE	Bell 206L-1 LongRanger	45546	ex N5756N
☐ N176AE	Bell 206L-1 LongRanger	45224	ex N911QC
☐ N192AE	Bell 206L-1 LongRanger	45660	ex N194H
☐ N209S	Bell 206B JetRanger III	3511	ex N713TV
☐ N216S	Bell 206L-1 LongRanger	45669	ex C-FJRG
☐ N225AE	Bell 206L-1 LongRanger	45577	ex N577E
☐ N228AE	Bell 206L-1 LongRanger	45697	ex XA-TKU
☐ N229AE	Bell 206L-1 LongRanger	45256	ex N2756A
☐ N230AE	Bell 206L-3 LongRanger III	51331	ex N941SL
☐ N233AE	Bell 206L-3 LongRanger III	51453	ex N6643T
☐ N239AE	Bell 206L-1 LongRanger	45367	ex 5N-BAS
☐ N242AE	Bell 206L-1 LongRanger	45506	ex 5N-AQB
☐ N248AE	Bell 206L-3 LongRanger III	51129	ex N206AH
☐ N249AE	Bell 206L-1 LongRanger	45459	ex N5740L
☐ N258AE	Bell 206L-1 LongRanger	45578	ex N805KA
☐ N267AE	Bell 206L-1 LongRanger	45582	ex C-GKCX
☐ N269AE	Bell 206L-3 LongRanger III	51530	ex N3116P
☐ N271AE	Bell 206L-3 LongRanger III	51351	ex N792CA
☐ N274AE	Bell 206L-1 LongRanger	45762	ex N676M
☐ N275AE	Bell 206L-3 LongRanger III	51186	ex N708M
☐ N277AE	Bell 206L-3 LongRanger III	51421	ex N9107G
☐ N279AE	Bell 206L-1 LongRanger	45682	ex N258LH
☐ N281AE	Bell 206L-3 LongRanger III	51451	ex N719H
☐ N282AE	Bell 206L-3 LongRanger III	51452	ex N722H
☐ N285AE	Bell 206L-3 LongRanger III	51550	ex N727H
☐ N287AE	Bell 206L-3 LongRanger III	51404	ex N6251V
☐ N288AE	Bell 206L-3 LongRanger III	51327	ex N165SB
☐ N290AE	Bell 206L-3 LongRanger III	51192	ex N805SB
☐ N292AE	Bell 206L-1 LongRanger	45780	ex N3192P
☐ N293AE	Bell 206L-3 LongRanger III	51476	ex N793CA
☐ N295AE	Bell 206L-3 LongRanger III	51455	ex N791CA
☐ N296AE	Bell 206L-1 LongRanger	45398	ex N1078G
☐ N299AE	Bell 206L-1 LongRanger	45621	ex N911WA
☐ N302AE	Bell 206L-1 LongRanger	45435	ex N1067D
☐ N303AE	Bell 206L-1 LongRanger	45348	ex N1075P
☐ N311AE	Bell 206L-1 LongRanger	45572	ex N87TV
☐ N314AE	Bell 206L-4 LongRanger IV	52222	ex XC-CUU
☐ N315AE	Bell 206L-1 LongRanger	45482	ex N2654
☐ N318AE	Bell 206L-3 LongRanger III	51160	ex N911NS
☐ N319AE	Bell 206L-4 LongRanger IV	52040	ex N96AP
☐ N322AE	Bell 206L-3 LongRanger III	51387	ex P2-HLT
☐ N325AE	Bell 206L-4 LongRanger IV	52009	ex N203UT
☐ N327AE	Bell 206L-3 LongRanger III	51365	ex N203M
☐ N334AE	Bell 206L-3 LongRanger III	51326	ex N401CJ
☐ N395AE	Bell 206L-1 LongRanger	45551	ex N5749J
☐ N402AE	Bell 206L-4 LongRanger IV	52393	
☐ N493AE	Bell 407	53275	ex N406LS	♦
☐ N495AE	Bell 407	53363	ex N407LS	♦
☐ N496AE	Bell 407	53328	ex N408LS	♦
☐ N595AE	Bell 206L-1 LongRanger	45244	ex N5019F
☐ N600CE	Bell 407	53347	
☐ N911SA	Bell 206L-1 LongRanger	45383	ex N1080A
☐ N162GC	Beech B200	BB-1238	ex N212JB
☐ N300MT	Beech E-90	LW-143	ex N300BA

AIR FLAMENCO — San Juan-Fernando Luis Ribas Dominici, PR (SIG)

☐ N821RR	Britten-Norman BN-2A-9 Islander	338	ex N146A
☐ N901GD	Britten-Norman BN-2A-26 Islander	855	ex XA-JEK The Spirit of Culebra
☐ N903GD	Britten-Norman BN-2A-6 Islander	625	ex HI-636CT
☐ N904GD	Britten-Norman BN-2B-26 Islander	2128	ex N902VL
☐ N905GD	Britten-Norman BN-2A-9 Islander	339	ex C-FTAM
☐ N906GD	Britten-Norman BN-2A-26 Islander	3008	ex VP-AAB
☐ N907GD	Britten-Norman BN-2A-9 Islander	340	ex N161A
☐ N908GD	Britten-Norman BN-2A-26 Islander	2040	ex C6-BUS
☐ N909GD	Britten-Norman BN-2A-6 Islander	239	ex N143BW

AIR GRAND CANYON — Grand Canyon-National Park, AZ (GCN)

☐ N803AN	Cessna T207A Stationair 7	20700570	ex N73204
☐ N6308H	Cessna T207A Stationair 7	20700476	
☐ N6491H	Cessna T207A Stationair 7	20700543	
☐ N7311U	Cessna T207A Turbo Skywagon	20700395	
☐ N7351U	Cessna T207A Stationair 7	20700415	

☐ N94LG	Aérospatiale AS350B2 AStar	2728	ex N60928	EMS
☐ N103HN	Aérospatiale AS350B2 AStar	2575	ex N92LG	EMS
☐ N108LN	Aérospatiale AS350B3 AStar	3959		
☐ N111LN	Aérospatiale AS350B AStar	1602	ex N58045	
☐ N152AC	Aérospatiale AS350B2 AStar	3574	ex N471AE	
☐ N197AM	Aérospatiale AS350B2 AStar	2917	ex N97LG	EMS♦
☐ N220CF	Aérospatiale AS350B2 AStar	3411	ex N436AE	
☐ N350AM	Aérospatiale AS350B3 AStar	3996	ex N203AE	
☐ N350RM	Aérospatiale AS350D AStar	1024		
☐ N379AM	Aérospatiale AS350B2 AStar	3474	ex N779LF	
☐ N392LG	Aérospatiale AS350B3 AStar	3252	ex N5229Y	EMS
☐ N394LG	Aérospatiale AS350B3 AStar	3134	ex N104LG	EMS
☐ N396LG	Aérospatiale AS350B3 AStar	3336	ex N415AE	
☐ N397LG	Aérospatiale AS350B3 AStar	3268	ex N404AE	EMS
☐ N781LF	Aérospatiale AS350B AStar	1178	ex N1113H	
☐ N792LF	Aérospatiale AS350B AStar	1035	ex N9004M	
☐ N852HW	Aérospatiale AS350B2 AStar	2630	ex N352HW	
☐ N902CF	Aérospatiale AS350B3 AStar	3630	ex N477AE	
☐ N903CF	Aérospatiale AS350B3 AStar	3645	ex N481AE	
☐ N904CF	Aérospatiale AS350B3 AStar	3676	ex N484AE	
☐ N916AM	Aérospatiale AS350B2 AStar	2404	ex N911LM	EMS
☐ N937AM	Aérospatiale AS350B2 AStar	2654	ex N93LG	EMS
☐ N5797T	Aérospatiale AS350D AStar	1472	ex N3944S	
☐ N1VH	Agusta A109A-II	7273		♦
☐ N2MF	Agusta A109A-II	7277		♦
☐ N206AL	Bell 206L-1 LongRanger II	45446	ex N5735M	
☐ N206UH	Bell 206L-3 LongRanger III	51167		
☐ N220LL	Bell 206L-3 LongRanger III	51039	ex N3175R	EMS
☐ N222AM	Bell 222U	47547	ex N221HX	
☐ N222LL	Bell 222	47060	ex N222LG	EMS
☐ N226LL	Bell 222UT	47537	ex N781SA	EMS
☐ N227AM	Bell 222U	47542	ex N820AM	
☐ N911NM	Bell 222U	47569	ex N4181X	
☐ N247SM	Bell 407	53176	ex N911WB	
☐ N406LL	Bell 407	53279	ex N407CX	EMS
☐ N407AM	Bell 407	53309		EMS Lsd fr/op for Guardian Air
☐ N407LL	Bell 407	53561	ex N386T	EMS
☐ N407UH	Bell 407	53345		EMS
☐ N407VV	Bell 407	53476		EMS Lsd fr/op for Guardian Air
☐ N408AM	Bell 407	53445	ex N61002	
☐ N408GA	Bell 407	53392		EMS Guardian Air titles
☐ N772AL	Bell 407	53040		EMS
☐ N773AL	Bell 407	53160	ex N176PA	EMS
☐ N905HA	Bell 407	53497	ex N200LN	
☐ N911AL	Bell 407	53144	ex N70829	EMS
☐ N101HN	Eurocopter EC135P1	0162	ex N427AE	EMS
☐ N102HN	Eurocopter EC135P1	0159	ex N426AE	EMS
☐ N135DH	Eurocopter EC135P1	0133	ex N5233N	EMS
☐ N135ED	Eurocopter EC135P2	0335		
☐ N135LN	Eurocopter EC135P1	0322	ex N135BF	
☐ N135N	Eurocopter EC135P1	0086	ex N52268	EMS <Memorial Mission H/c
☐ N135SJ	Eurocopter EC135P1	0054	ex N4056V	
☐ N137LN	Eurocopter EC135P2	0339		
☐ N138LN	Eurocopter EC135P2	0352	ex N135BF	
☐ N64UP	MBB BK-117B-1	7143	ex N204UP	EMS♦
☐ N101VU	MBB BK-117C-2	9039		EMS
☐ N102VU	MBB BK-117C-2	9044		EMS
☐ N117AM	MBB BK-117B-1	7140	ex N90620	
☐ N117CW	MBB BK-117A-4	7125	ex N9021D	
☐ N117MV	MBB BK-117A-3	7089	ex N492MB	
☐ N118NY	MBB BK-117A-4	7115	ex N202HN	
☐ N125EC	MBB BK-117A-4	7065	ex N155SC	
☐ N138HH	MBB BK-117A-3	7060	ex N127HH	
☐ N156AM	MBB BK-117A-3	7173	ex N155SC	
☐ N158BK	MBB BK-117A-3	7058	ex D-HBNF	
☐ N163BK	MBB BK-117A-3	7063	ex D-HBNK	
☐ N164AM	MBB BK-117B-2	7229	ex N104VU	
☐ N420MB	MBB BK-117A-3	7077	ex D-HBNY	

☐ N424MB	MBB BK-117A-4	7082	ex D-HBPC	
☐ N485UH	MBB BK-117A-1	7036	ex N128HH	
☐ N485UM	MBB BK-117A-1	7129	ex N586BH	
☐ N528SF	MBB BK-117A-3	7104	ex N528MB	
☐ N612AM	MBB BK-117B-1	7230	ex N61LF	
☐ N911BY	MBB BK-117A-4	7127	ex N11UM	
☐ N990SL	MBB BK-117B-2	7057	ex N911KD	
☐ N299AM	Pilatus PC-12/45	236	ex HB-FRG	EMS
☐ N399AM	Pilatus PC-12/45	249	ex HB-FRT	EMS
☐ N852AL	Pilatus PC-12/45	213	ex N213WA	EMS
☐ N853AL	Pilatus PC-12/45	168	ex N168WA	EMS
☐ N854AL	Pilatus PC-12/45	397	ex N397WA	EMS
☐ N912NM	Pilatus PC-12/45	169	ex N661DT	EMS
☐ N28MS	Beech 65-E90 King Air	LW-100	ex N31FN	
☐ N30LG	Aérospatiale AS355F1 Twin Star	5065	ex N5787B	
☐ N92DV	Beech 65-E90 King Air	LW-292	ex N7MA	EMS Air 4 Lsd fr/op for Guardian Air
☐ N105LC	MBB Bo.105CBS-4	S-789	ex N5414F	Op for LEC Medical Center
☐ N151AC	Eurocopter EC130B4	3732		
☐ N206CM	Bell 430	49041	ex N430RX	EMS
☐ N208CM	Bell 430	49010	ex N151MH	EMS
☐ N220TB	Beech B200 Super King Air	BB-1057	ex F-GILY	
☐ N412LG	Bell 412SP	33209		
☐ N430Q	Bell 430	49002	ex N430U	
☐ N430UH	Bell 430	49056	ex N430UM	EMS
☐ N554AL	Bell 412	33017	ex N20703	
☐ N778AM	Bell 412	33033	ex N565AC	
☐ N791DC	Beech B200 Super King Air	BB-1402	ex N91CD	EMS
☐ N793DC	Beech B200 Super King Air	BB-1404	ex N93CD	EMS
☐ N825LF	MBB Bo.105CBS-4	S-796	ex N5417E	
☐ N910U	Eurocopter EC130B4	3470	ex N452AE	
☐ N920U	Eurocopter EC130B4	3453	ex N451AE	
☐ N15460	Sikorsky S-76C+	760477	ex N176AE	

AIR MIDWEST — Air Midwest (ZV/AMW) — Wichita-Mid Continent, KS (ICT)

☐ N135YV	Beech 1900D	UE-135	Mesa Airlines	<ASH
☐ N138YV	Beech 1900D	UE-138	Mesa Airlines	<ASH
☐ N142ZV	Beech 1900D	UE-142	all-white	<ASH
☐ N10675	Beech 1900D	UE-229	Mesa Airlines	<ASH

AIR ST THOMAS — Paradise (ZP/STT) — St Thomas-Cyril E King, VI (STT)

☐ N5623Y	Piper PA-23-250 Aztec C	27-2733		<Virgin Air
☐ N6389Y	Piper PA-23-250 Aztec C	27-3675		
☐ N8125F	Cessna 402	402-0231	ex LV-PLC	

AIR SUNSHINE — Air Sunshine (YI/RSI) — Fort Lauderdale-Hollywood Intl, FL (FLL)

☐ N220RS	Cessna 402C	402C0220	ex N2716L	
☐ N347AB	Cessna 402C	402C0347	ex N26548	
☐ N351AB	Cessna 402C	402C0351	ex N26629	
☐ N402RS	Cessna 402C	402C0402	ex N2663N	
☐ N603AB	Cessna 402C	402C0603	ex N84PB	
☐ N123HY	Embraer EMB.110P1 Bandeirante	110321	ex N619KC	
☐ N744BA	SAAB SF.340A	340A-105	ex SE-F05	
☐ N792BA	SAAB SF.340A	340A-092	ex N742BA	[FLL]♦
☐ N793BA	SAAB SF.340A	340A-093	ex N743BA	[FLL]♦

AIR TAHOMA — Tahoma (5C/HMA) — Columbus-Rickenbacker, OH (LCK)

☐ N581P	Convair 580	29	ex C-FBHW	
☐ N582P	Convair 580	475	ex N969N	[LCK]
☐ N584E	Convair 580	24	ex C-FAUF	
☐ N585P	Convair 580	163	ex N718RA	
☐ N588X	Convair 580	52	ex EC-HLD	
☐ N590X	Convair 580	130	ex EC-GSJ	[LCK]
☐ N150PA	Convair 240-27	278	ex N99377	no titles	<Cool Air
☐ N156PA	Convair 240-27	324	ex N9016L	[LCK] <Cool Air
☐ N99380	Convair 240-27 (T-29B)	249	ex 51-5118	<Cool Air

AIR TEJAS — Gainesville-Municipal, TX (GLE)

☐ N141JR	Douglas DC-3	19366	ex CF-CUC	
☐ N472AF	Douglas DC-3	13485	ex XA-SYN	
☐ N941AT	Douglas DC-3	12907	ex N6666A	Vera Lynn II

AIR WISCONSIN	Air Wisconsin (ZW/AWI)	Appleton-Outagamie Co, WI (ATW)

Operates Canadair CRJ-200LRs for US Airways Express, for details see that listing

AIRBORNE SUPPORT				Houma-Terrebonne, LA (HUM)

☐ N38WA	Rockwell 690A Turbo Commander	11169	ex XB-FLF	
☐ N64766	Douglas DC-3	27218	ex CAF12910	Sprayer
☐ N64767	Douglas DC-3	10199	ex CAF12941	Sprayer
☐ N67024	Douglas DC-4	10550	ex Bu50871	Sprayer

AIRNET SYSTEMS	StarCheck(USC)
	Columbus-Port Columbus Intl, OH / Dallas-Love Field, TX (CMH/DAL)

☐ N4AW	Beech 58 Baron	TH-450	ex N228TA
☐ N21ES	Beech 58 Baron	TH-1123	ex N6744V
☐ N26CC	Beech 58 Baron	TH-136	
☐ N27MT	Beech 58 Baron	TH-1120	ex F-GDJY
☐ N33DK	Beech 58 Baron	TH-372	ex N2CF
☐ N33WC	Beech 58 Baron	TH-170	
☐ N58WA	Beech 58 Baron	TH-201	ex N58TC
☐ N65FS	Beech 58 Baron	TH-1084	ex N6681Y
☐ N78DM	Beech 58 Baron	TH-281	ex N78MM
☐ N78RE	Beech 58 Baron	TH-371	ex N904AJ
☐ N95BB	Beech 58 Baron	TH-333	ex N95BD
☐ N140S	Beech 58 Baron	TH-1155	ex N3677N
☐ N297AT	Beech 58 Baron	TH-1349	ex F-GOGA
☐ N367S	Beech 58 Baron	TH-1393	ex N158EB
☐ N400RP	Beech 58 Baron	TH-319	ex N1036W
☐ N456WW	Beech 58 Baron	TH-444	ex N444TE
☐ N525GW	Beech 58 Baron	TH-557	ex N52WP
☐ N696BD	Beech 58 Baron	TH-352	ex N43HK
☐ N858LG	Beech 58 Baron	TH-518	ex N555GP
☐ N882MT	Beech 58 Baron	TH-1343	ex F-WQFG
☐ N1653W	Beech 58 Baron	TH-252	
☐ N1814W	Beech 58 Baron	TH-287	
☐ N1847F	Beech 58 Baron	TH-1291	
☐ N1859K	Beech 58 Baron	TH-1299	
☐ N2027V	Beech 58 Baron	TH-965	
☐ N2064V	Beech 58 Baron	TH-1004	
☐ N2892W	Beech 58 Baron	TH-389	
☐ N3695V	Beech 58 Baron	TH-1183	
☐ N3703Q	Beech 58 Baron	TH-1189	
☐ N4098S	Beech 58 Baron	TH-600	
☐ N6573K	Beech 58 Baron	TH-1369	
☐ N6650D	Beech 58 Baron	TH-1375	
☐ N6758C	Beech 58 Baron	TH-1080	
☐ N7383R	Beech 58 Baron	TH-502	
☐ N9044V	Beech 58 Baron	TH-216	
☐ N9189Q	Beech 58 Baron	TH-148	
☐ N9367Q	Beech 58 Baron	TH-192	
☐ N17708	Beech 58 Baron	TH-813	
☐ N36673	Beech 58 Baron	TH-1143	
☐ N36901	Beech 58 Baron	TH-1173	
☐ N62500	Beech 58 Baron	TH-1347	
☐ N3RY	Cessna 208B Caravan I	208B0436	ex C-GSKR
☐ N102AN	Cessna 208B Caravan I	208B0906	ex N51666
☐ N103AN	Cessna 208B Caravan I	208B0928	
☐ N104AN	Cessna 208B Caravan I	208B0918	
☐ N105AN	Cessna 208B Caravan I	208B0956	
☐ N106AN	Cessna 208B Caravan I	208B0917	ex N5207V
☐ N107AN	Cessna 208B Caravan I	208B0993	
☐ N108AN	Cessna 208B Caravan I	208B0975	
☐ N1026V	Cessna 208B Caravan I	208B0319	
☐ N1115M	Cessna 208B Caravan I	208B0356	
☐ N9514F	Cessna 208 Caravan I	20800079	
☐ N9539F	Cessna 208 Caravan I	20800092	
☐ N9642F	Cessna 208 Caravan I	20800110	
☐ N3597G	Cessna 310R	310R0875	
☐ N5238J	Cessna 310R	310R0810	
☐ N6121C	Cessna 310R	310R1288	
☐ N6122C	Cessna 310R	310R1290	
☐ N6160X	Cessna 310R	310R1305	
☐ N8521G	Cessna 310R	310R0931	

☐ N37223	Cessna 310R	310R0963	
☐ N37575	Cessna 310R	310R1207	

☐ N15WH	Learjet 35A	35A-085	
☐ N25AN	Learjet 35A	35A-259	ex HK-3983X
☐ N27BL	Learjet 35A	35A-163	ex YV-173CP
☐ N27TT	Learjet 35A	35A-122	ex OE-GMP
☐ N31WR	Learjet 35A	35A-313	ex TR-LZI
☐ N39DK	Learjet 35A	35A-480	ex (N35FH)
☐ N51LC	Learjet 35A	35A-302	ex N631CW
☐ N56EM	Learjet 35A	35A-144	ex N56HF
☐ N64CP	Learjet 35A	35A-264	ex VR-CDI
☐ N72JF	Learjet 35A	35A-088	ex OE-GBR
☐ N81FR	Learjet 35A	35A-081	ex N118DA
☐ N88BG	Learjet 35A	35A-090	ex I-FIMI
☐ N98LC	Learjet 35A	35A-077	ex ZS-NRZ
☐ N122JW	Learjet 35A	35A-217	ex N111RF
☐ N130F	Learjet 35	35-044	ex N44VW
☐ N400JE	Learjet 35A	35A-120	
☐ N684HA	Learjet 35A	35A-113	ex N684LA
☐ N700SJ	Learjet 35A	35A-082	ex N700GB
☐ N701AS	Learjet 35A	35A-047	ex N13MJ
☐ N813AS	Learjet 35A	35A-167	ex N725P
☐ N900JC	Learjet 35	35-178	ex N35GG
☐ N959SA	Learjet 35A	35A-076	
☐ N1140A	Learjet 35	35-045	ex N304AT
☐ N8040A	Learjet 35	35-048	ex F-GHMP

☐ N2KC	Piper PA-31-350 Chieftain	31-7952217	ex N3540X
☐ N4UE	Piper PA-31-350 Chieftain	31-8152061	ex N4U
☐ N42HD	Piper PA-31-350 Chieftain	31-8152031	ex N42ND
☐ N106TG	Piper PA-31-350 Chieftain	31-8052002	ex N106FC
☐ N225TM	Piper PA-31-350 Chieftain	31-8152165	ex XA-MAU
☐ N525AA	Piper PA-31-350 Chieftain	31-8052111	ex N3583U
☐ N711LH	Piper PA-31-350 Chieftain	31-8152174	ex N711BH
☐ N3547C	Piper PA-31-350 Chieftain	31-8052018	
☐ N3587P	Piper PA-31-350 Chieftain	31-8052120	
☐ N3590D	Piper PA-31-350 Chieftain	31-8052144	
☐ N4079Y	Piper PA-31-350 Chieftain	31-8152079	ex (N479MG)
☐ N22427	Piper PA-31-350 Chieftain	31-8152065	ex (N4078S)
☐ N35453	Piper PA-31-350 Chieftain	31-8052006	ex (N900GF)
☐ N35551	Piper PA-31-350 Chieftain	31-8052063	
☐ N35584	Piper PA-31-350 Chieftain	31-8052076	
☐ N35871	Piper PA-31-350 Chieftain	31-8052123	ex (N191VF)
☐ N40919	Piper PA-31-350 Chieftain	31-8152162	
☐ N6892R	Piper PA-60	60-0887-8161251	
All are Frtrs.			

AIRNOW — Sky Courier (RLR) — Burlington-Intl, VT (BTV)

☐ N804TH	Cessna 208B Caravan I	208B0421	ex N9551F
☐ N805TH	Cessna 208B Caravan I	208B0609	ex N9551F
☐ N929TG	Cessna 208B Caravan I	208B0371	ex N207TA
☐ N9339B	Cessna 208B Caravan I	208B0057	
☐ N9612B	Cessna 208B Caravan I	208B0136	

☐ N24AN	Embraer EMB.110P1 Bandeirante	110318	ex F-GBRM
☐ N31AN	Embraer EMB.110P1 Bandeirante	110372	ex C-FSXR
☐ N36AN	Embraer EMB.110P1 Bandeirante	110451	ex C-GDCQ
☐ N42AN	Embraer EMB.110P1 Bandeirante	110456	ex C-GHCA
☐ N51BA	Embraer EMB.110P1 Bandeirante	110404	ex N903FB
☐ N62CZ	Embraer EMB.110P1 Bandeirante	110388	ex PT-SFF
☐ N64CZ	Embraer EMB.110P1 Bandeirante	110399	ex PT-SFQ
☐ N83BA	Embraer EMB.110P1 Bandeirante	110351	ex N405AS
☐ N97BA	Embraer EMB.110P1 Bandeirante	110322	ex N403AS
☐ N621KC	Embraer EMB.110P1 Bandeirante	110335	ex PT-SDL
☐ N710NH	Embraer EMB.110P1 Bandeirante	110250	ex PT-SAQ
☐ N830AC	Embraer EMB.110P1 Bandeirante	110205	ex N524MW

AIRPAC AIRLINES — Airpac (APC) — Seattle-Boeing Field, WA (BFI)

☐ N36PB	Piper PA-31-350 Navajo Chieftain	31-7405128	
☐ N627HA	Piper PA-31-350 Chieftain	31-7952241	
☐ N777KT	Piper PA-31-350 Navajo Chieftain	31-7552053	ex N1TW
☐ N3582X	Piper PA-31-350 Chieftain	31-8052105	
☐ N27594	Piper PA-31-350 Chieftain	31-7852070	

☐ N41SA	Cessna 404 Titan	404-0023	ex N5271J		
☐ N2117V	Piper PA-34-200T Seneca II	34-7970160			
☐ N2880A	Beech 99	U-109			
☐ N4490F	Piper PA-34-200T Seneca II	34-7670339			
☐ N8107D	Piper PA-34-200T Seneca II	34-8070010			
☐ N36319	Piper PA-34-200T Seneca II	34-7870318			

AIRSERV INTERNATIONAL
Warrenton, VA

☐ N8HZ	Cessna 208B Caravan I	208B0980			
☐ N715BT	Cessna 208B Caravan I	208B0835			
☐ N719BT	Cessna 208B Caravan I	208B0898			
☐ N899AS	de Havilland DHC-6 Twin Otter 300	347	ex LN-FKB		Op for UN

AIRTRAN AIRWAYS
Citrus (FL/TRS) — *Orlando-Intl, FL/Atlanta-Hartsfield Intl, GA (MCO/ATL)*

Has agreed a merger with Southwest

☐ N603AT	Boeing 717-22A	55127/5074	ex N482HA	771
☐ N717JL	Boeing 717-2BD	55042/5115	ex N983AT	740
☐ N891AT	Boeing 717-2BD	55043/5131	ex (N984AT)	741
☐ N892AT	Boeing 717-2BD	55044/5134	ex N7071U	742
☐ N893AT	Boeing 717-2BD	55045/5136		743
☐ N894AT	Boeing 717-2BD	55046/5137		744
☐ N895AT	Boeing 717-2BD	55047/5139		745
☐ N896AT	Boeing 717-2BD	55048/5141		746
☐ N899AT	Boeing 717-2BD	55049/5143		747
☐ N906AT	Boeing 717-231	55087/5060	ex N420TW	795
☐ N910AT	Boeing 717-231	55086/5056	ex N2419C	794
☐ N915AT	Boeing 717-231	55085/5055	ex N418TW	793
☐ N919AT	Boeing 717-231	55084/5052	ex N2417F	792
☐ N920AT	Boeing 717-231	55083/5049	ex N416TW	791
☐ N921AT	Boeing 717-231	55082/5046	ex N415TW	790
☐ N922AT	Boeing 717-2BD	55050/5144		748
☐ N923AT	Boeing 717-2BD	55051/5148		749
☐ N924AT	Boeing 717-231	55080/5043	ex N413TW	789
☐ N925AT	Boeing 717-231	55079/5042	ex N412TW	788
☐ N926AT	Boeing 717-231	55078/5039	ex N411TW	787
☐ N927AT	Boeing 717-231	55077/5038	ex N2410W	786
☐ N928AT	Boeing 717-231	55076/5035	ex N409TW	785
☐ N929AT	Boeing 717-231	55075/5032	ex N408TW	784
☐ N930AT	Boeing 717-231	55072/5025	ex N405TW	782
☐ N932AT	Boeing 717-231	55073/5028	ex N406TW	783
☐ N933AT	Boeing 717-231	55071/5024	ex N2404A	781
☐ N934AT	Boeing 717-231	55070/5022	ex N403TW	780
☐ N935AT	Boeing 717-231	55069/5019	ex N402TW	779
☐ N936AT	Boeing 717-231	55058/5017	ex N401TW	778
☐ N937AT	Boeing 717-231	55091/5075	ex N424TW	799
☐ N938AT	Boeing 717-2BD	55098/5155		751
☐ N939AT	Boeing 717-2BD	55099/5156		752
☐ N940AT	Boeing 717-2BD	55004/5005	ex N717XE	702
☐ N942AT	Boeing 717-2BD	55005/5006		703
☐ N943AT	Boeing 717-2BD	55006/5007		704
☐ N944AT	Boeing 717-2BD	55007/5008		705
☐ N945AT	Boeing 717-2BD	55008/5009		706
☐ N946AT	Boeing 717-2BD	55009/5010		707
☐ N947AT	Boeing 717-2BD	55010/5011		708
☐ N948AT	Boeing 717-2BD	55011/5012		709
☐ N949AT	Boeing 717-2BD	55003/5004	ex N717XD	701
☐ N950AT	Boeing 717-2BD	55012/5018		710
☐ N951AT	Boeing 717-2BD	55013/5021		711
☐ N952AT	Boeing 717-2BD	55014/5027		712
☐ N953AT	Boeing 717-2BD	55015/5033		713
☐ N954AT	Boeing 717-2BD	55016/5036		714
☐ N955AT	Boeing 717-2BD	55017/5040		715
☐ N956AT	Boeing 717-2BD	55018/5044		716
☐ N957AT	Boeing 717-2BD	55019/5047		717
☐ N958AT	Boeing 717-2BD	55020/5051		718
☐ N959AT	Boeing 717-2BD	55021/5057		719
☐ N960AT	Boeing 717-2BD	55022/5058		720
☐ N961AT	Boeing 717-2BD	55023/5062		721
☐ N963AT	Boeing 717-2BD	55024/5066		722
☐ N964AT	Boeing 717-2BD	55025/5071		723
☐ N965AT	Boeing 717-2BD	55026/5076		724
☐ N966AT	Boeing 717-2BD	55027/5081		725
☐ N967AT	Boeing 717-2BD	55028/5082		726
☐ N968AT	Boeing 717-2BD	55029/5091		727

☐	N969AT	Boeing 717-2BD	55030/5094		728
☐	N970AT	Boeing 717-2BD	55031/5096		729
☐	N971AT	Boeing 717-2BD	55032/5097		730
☐	N972AT	Boeing 717-2BD	55033/5099		731
☐	N974AT	Boeing 717-2BD	55034/5101		732
☐	N975AT	Boeing 717-2BD	55035/5102		733
☐	N977AT	Boeing 717-2BD	55036/5106		734
☐	N978AT	Boeing 717-2BD	55037/5108		735
☐	N979AT	Boeing 717-2BD	55038/5109		736
☐	N980AT	Boeing 717-2BD	55039/5111		737
☐	N981AT	Boeing 717-2BD	55040/5113		738
☐	N982AT	Boeing 717-2BD	55041/5114		739
☐	N983AT	Boeing 717-2BD	55052/5150		750
☐	N985AT	Boeing 717-231	55090/5068	ex N423TW	798
☐	N986AT	Boeing 717-231	55089/5067	ex N422TW	797
☐	N987AT	Boeing 717-231	55088/5063	ex N2421A	796
☐	N988AT	Boeing 717-23S	55068/5065	ex (EI-CWJ)	760
☐	N989AT	Boeing 717-23S	55152/5085	ex (EI-CWK)	761
☐	N990AT	Boeing 717-23S	55134/5088	ex (EI-CWM)	762
☐	N991AT	Boeing 717-23S	55135/5090	ex N6202S	763
☐	N992AT	Boeing 717-2BD	55136/5100	ex N6202D	764
☐	N993AT	Boeing 717-2BD	55137/5103		765
☐	N994AT	Boeing 717-2BD	55138/5104	ex N6206F	766
☐	N995AT	Boeing 717-2BD	55139/5105		767
☐	N996AT	Boeing 717-2BD	55140/5107		768
☐	N997AT	Boeing 717-2BD	55141/5110		769
☐	N998AT	Boeing 717-2BD	55142/5112		770
☐	N126AT	Boeing 737-76N/W	32679/1514		300
☐	N149AT	Boeing 737-76N/W	32681/1526		301
☐	N166AT	Boeing 737-7BD/W	33917/1550		302
☐	N167AT	Boeing 737-7BD/W	33918/1572		304
☐	N168AT	Boeing 737-76N/W	32653/1566		303
☐	N169AT	Boeing 737-76N/W	32744/1584		305
☐	N173AT	Boeing 737-76N/W	32661/1593		306
☐	N174AT	Boeing 737-76N/W	32667/1623	ex N1787B	307
☐	N175AT	Boeing 737-76N/W	32652/1627		308
☐	N176AT	Boeing 737-76N/W	32654/1641		309
☐	N184AT	Boeing 737-76N/W	32656/1671		310
☐	N240AT	Boeing 737-76N/W	32657/1687		311
☐	N261AT	Boeing 737-76N/W	32660/1710		312
☐	N267AT	Boeing 737-76N/W	33919/1730		313
☐	N272AT	Boeing 737-7BD/W	33921/1778	ex N1784B	315
☐	N273AT	Boeing 737-76N/W	32662/1788		316
☐	N276AT	Boeing 737-76N/W	32664/1804		317
☐	N278AT	Boeing 737-76N/W	32665/1827		318
☐	N279AT	Boeing 737-76N/W	32666/1833		319
☐	N281AT	Boeing 737-7BD/W	33922/1845		320
☐	N283AT	Boeing 737-7BD/W	34479/1874		321
☐	N284AT	Boeing 737-76N/W	32668/1876		322
☐	N285AT	Boeing 737-76N/W	32670/1898	ex N5573L	323
☐	N287AT	Boeing 737-76N/W	32671/1925		325
☐	N288AT	Boeing 737-7BD/W	33924/1940		326
☐	N289AT	Boeing 737-76N/W	32673/1943	ex N1787B	327
☐	N290AT	Boeing 737-7BD/W	33925/1967		328
☐	N291AT	Boeing 737-76N/W	32675/1970		329
☐	N292AT	Boeing 737-7BD/W	33926/1997		330
☐	N295AT	Boeing 737-76N/W	32677/2002		331
☐	N296AT	Boeing 737-7BD/W	34861/2041		332
☐	N299AT	Boeing 737-76N/W	32678/2055		333
☐	N300AT	Boeing 737-7BD/W	33923/2083		334
☐	N307AT	Boeing 737-7BD/W	34862/2094		335
☐	N308AT	Boeing 737-7BD/W	35109/2126	ex N1787B	336
☐	N309AT	Boeing 737-7BD/W	33929/2129		337
☐	N311AT	Boeing 737-7BD/W	33930/2143		338
☐	N312AT	Boeing 737-7BD/W	35110/2147		339
☐	N313AT	Boeing 737-7BD/W	33927/2169		340
☐	N315AT	Boeing 737-7BD/W	35788/2178		341
☐	N316AT	Boeing 737-7BD/W	33928/2190		342
☐	N318AT	Boeing 737-7BD/W	33931/2214		344
☐	N326AT	Boeing 737-7BD/W	33933/2278	ex N1786B	345
☐	N328AT	Boeing 737-7BD/W	33934/2296		346
☐	N329AT	Boeing 737-7BD/W	36091/2304		347
☐	N330AT	Boeing 737-7BD/W	36399/2312		348
☐	N336AT	Boeing 737-7BD/W	36716/2505	ex N1787B	350
☐	N337AT	Boeing 737-7BD/W	36717/2526	ex N1786B	351
☐	N338AT	Boeing 737-7BD/W	33943/2552		352

274

☐ N344AT	Boeing 737-7BD/W	36718/2568	ex N1786B	353
☐ N353AT	Boeing 737-7BD/W	36724/2813	ex N1787B	
☐ N354AT	Boeing 737-7BD/W	36725/2815	ex N1787B	
☐ N	Boeing 737-7BD/W		ex	o/o♦
☐ N	Boeing 737-7BD/W		ex	o/o♦
☐ N	Boeing 737-7BD/W		ex	o/o♦
☐ N	Boeing 737-7BD/W		ex	o/o♦
☐ N480AC	Boeing 737-7BD/W	34480/1900	ex C-GBEJ	♦

AK AIR — Anchorage Intl, AK / Palmer Municipal, AK (ANC/PAQ)

☐ N90KH	Beech 65-C90 King Air	LJ-542	ex N9442Q	
☐ N98UP	Aero Commander 680FL	680FL-1475	ex N30321	previously c/n 680FLP-1475-4
☐ N210HD	Aero Commander 500S Shrike	1841-33	ex N9016N	
☐ N222ME	Rockwell 690A Turbo Commander	11338	ex N46906	
☐ N340AH	Cessna 340	340-0100	ex N123S	
☐ N634CT	Rockwell 500S Shrike Commander	3121	ex N803AC	
☐ N9116N	Rockwell 500S Shrike Commander	3086		

ALASKA AIRLINES — Alaska (AS/ASA) — Seattle-Tacoma Intl, WA (SEA)

☐ N703AS	Boeing 737-490	28893/3039	ex (N747AS)	
☐ N705AS	Boeing 737-490	29318/3042	ex (N748AS)	
☐ N706AS	Boeing 737-490	28894/3050	ex (N749AS)	Disneyworld titles
☐ N708AS	Boeing 737-490	28895/3098		
☐ N709AS	Boeing 737-490 (SF)	28896/3099	ex N1787B	
☐ N713AS	Boeing 737-490	30161/3110	ex N1787B	
☐ N754AS	Boeing 737-4Q8	25095/2265		Spirit of Alaska
☐ N755AS	Boeing 737-4Q8	25096/2278		
☐ N756AS	Boeing 737-4Q8	25097/2299		
☐ N760AS	Boeing 737-4Q8	25098/2320		
☐ N762AS	Boeing 737-4Q8F	25099/2334		
☐ N763AS	Boeing 737-4Q8F	25100/2346		
☐ N764AS	Boeing 737-4Q8F	25101/2348		
☐ N765AS	Boeing 737-4Q8F	25102/2350		
☐ N767AS	Boeing 737-490	27081/2354		
☐ N768AS	Boeing 737-490F	27082/2356		
☐ N769AS	Boeing 737-4Q8	25103/2452		
☐ N771AS	Boeing 737-4Q8	25104/2476		
☐ N772AS	Boeing 737-4Q8	25105/2505		
☐ N773AS	Boeing 737-4Q8	25106/2518		[VCV]♦
☐ N778AS	Boeing 737-4Q8	25110/2586		
☐ N779AS	Boeing 737-4Q8	25111/2605		
☐ N786AS	Boeing 737-4S3	24795/1870	ex TF-FIE	
☐ N788AS	Boeing 737-490	28885/2891		
☐ N791AS	Boeing 737-490	28886/2902		
☐ N792AS	Boeing 737-490	28887/2903		Salmon Thirty Seven
☐ N793AS	Boeing 737-490	28888/2990		
☐ N794AS	Boeing 737-490	28889/3000		
☐ N795AS	Boeing 737-490	28890/3006		
☐ N796AS	Boeing 737-490	28891/3027		
☐ N797AS	Boeing 737-490	28892/3036		
☐ N799AS	Boeing 737-490	29270/3038		
☐ N607AS	Boeing 737-790/W	29751/313		
☐ N609AS	Boeing 737-790/W	29752/350		
☐ N611AS	Boeing 737-790/W	29753/385		
☐ N612AS	Boeing 737-790/W	30162/406	ex N1787B	
☐ N613AS	Boeing 737-790/W	30163/430		
☐ N614AS	Boeing 737-790/W	30343/439		
☐ N615AS	Boeing 737-790/W	30344/472	ex N1787B	
☐ N617AS	Boeing 737-790/W	30542/532		
☐ N618AS	Boeing 737-790/W	30543/536	ex N1787B	
☐ N619AS	Boeing 737-790/W	30164/597		
☐ N622AS	Boeing 737-790/W	30165/661		
☐ N623AS	Boeing 737-790/W	30166/700		
☐ N624AS	Boeing 737-790/W	30778/724		
☐ N625AS	Boeing 737-790/W	30792/754	ex N1795B	
☐ N626AS	Boeing 737-790/W	30793/763		
☐ N627AS	Boeing 737-790/W	30794/796	ex N1787B	
☐ N644AS	Boeing 737-790/W	30795/1277		
☐ N506AS	Boeing 737-890/W	35690/2627		
☐ N508AS	Boeing 737-890/W	35691/2662	ex N1786B	
☐ N512AS	Boeing 737-890/W	39043/2711		
☐ N513AS	Boeing 737-890/W	35192/2721	ex N1786B	
☐ N514AS	Boeing 737-890/W	35193/2727	ex N1786B	
☐ N516AS	Boeing 737-890/W	39044/2751		

☐ N517AS	Boeing 737-890/W	35197/2770			
☐ N518AS	Boeing 737-890/W	35693/2785			
☐ N519AS	Boeing 737-890/W	36482/2800	ex N1795B		
☐ N520AS	Boeing 737-890/W	36481/2812	ex N1786B		
☐ N523AS	Boeing 737-890/W	35194/2816			
☐ N524AS	Boeing 737-890/W	35195/2850	ex N1796B		
☐ N525AS	Boeing 737-890/W	35692/2859	ex N1786B		
☐ N526AS	Boeing 737-890/W	35196/2862	ex N1796B		
☐ N527AS	Boeing 737-890/W	35694/2913	ex N1796B		
☐ N528AS	Boeing 737-890/W	35695/2930			
☐ N529AS	Boeing 737-890/W	35198/3229	ex N1796B		♦
☐ N530AS	Boeing 737-890/W	36578/3257	ex N1786B		♦
☐ N531AS	Boeing 737-890/W	35199/3287	ex N1787B		♦
☐ N532AS	Boeing 737-890/W	36346/3317			♦
☐ N533AS	Boeing 737-890/W	35201/3511	ex N1786B		♦
☐ N	Boeing 737-890/W				o/o♦
☐ N	Boeing 737-890/W				o/o♦
☐ N	Boeing 737-890/W				o/o♦
☐ N546AS	Boeing 737-890/W	30022/1640			
☐ N548AS	Boeing 737-890/W	30020/1738			
☐ N549AS	Boeing 737-8FH/W	30824/1664			
☐ N551AS	Boeing 737-890/W	34593/1860			
☐ N552AS	Boeing 737-890/W	34595/1882	ex N1795B		
☐ N553AS	Boeing 737-890/W	34594/1906			
☐ N556AS	Boeing 737-890/W	35175/1980			
☐ N557AS	Boeing 737-890/W	35176/2010			
☐ N558AS	Boeing 737-890/W	35177/2031			
☐ N559AS	Boeing 737-890/W	35178/2026	ex N6067E	ETOPS test aircraft	
☐ N560AS	Boeing 737-890/W	35179/2072			
☐ N562AS	Boeing 737-890/W	35091/2084			
☐ N563AS	Boeing 737-890/W	35180/2090			
☐ N564AS	Boeing 737-890/W	35103/2099			
☐ N565AS	Boeing 737-890/W	35181/2134			
☐ N566AS	Boeing 737-890/W	35182/2164			
☐ N568AS	Boeing 737-890/W	35183/2166			
☐ N569AS	Boeing 737-890/W	35184/2192		75th anniversary colours	
☐ N570AS	Boeing 737-890/W	35185/2212			
☐ N577AS	Boeing 737-890/W	35186/2221	ex N1787B		
☐ N579AS	Boeing 737-890/W	35187/2226			
☐ N581AS	Boeing 737-890/W	35188/2259			
☐ N583AS	Boeing 737-890/W	35681/2333			
☐ N584AS	Boeing 737-890/W	35682/2365			
☐ N585AS	Boeing 737-890/W	35683/2385			
☐ N586AS	Boeing 737-890/W	35189/2393			
☐ N587AS	Boeing 737-890/W	35684/2422	ex N1786B		
☐ N588AS	Boeing 737-890/W	35685/2454	ex N1786B		
☐ N589AS	Boeing 737-890/W	35686/2458	ex N1786B		
☐ N590AS	Boeing 737-890/W	35687/2478			
☐ N592AS	Boeing 737-890/W	35190/2511	ex N1786B		
☐ N593AS	Boeing 737-890/W	35107/2545	ex N1786B		
☐ N594AS	Boeing 737-890/W	35191/2560	ex N1786B		
☐ N596AS	Boeing 737-890/W	35688/2587			
☐ N597AS	Boeing 737-890/W	35689/2601			
☐ N302AS	Boeing 737-990/W	30017/596	ex N737X		
☐ N303AS	Boeing 737-990/W	30016/683	ex N672AS		
☐ N305AS	Boeing 737-990/W	30013/774	ex (N673AS)		
☐ N306AS	Boeing 737-990/W	30014/802	ex (N674AS)		
☐ N307AS	Boeing 737-990/W	30015/838	ex N1786B		
☐ N309AS	Boeing 737-990/W	30857/902	ex N1786B		
☐ N315AS	Boeing 737-990/W	30019/1218			
☐ N317AS	Boeing 737-990/W	30856/1296	ex N1786B		
☐ N318AS	Boeing 737-990/W	30018/1326			
☐ N319AS	Boeing 737-990/W	33679/1344			
☐ N320AS	Boeing 737-990/W	33680/1380			
☐ N323AS	Boeing 737-990/W	30021/1454			

ALASKA CENTRAL EXPRESS — *Ace Air (KO/AER)* — Anchorage-Intl, AK (ANC)

☐ N111AX	Beech 1900C-1	UC-81	ex N5632C		
☐ N113AX	Beech 1900C-1	UC-41	ex N41UE		
☐ N114AX	Beech 1900C-1	UC-36	ex N1566C		
☐ N115AX	Beech 1900C-1	UC-2	ex N19NG		
☐ N117AX	Beech 1900C-1	UC-17	ex N17ZV		♦
☐ N9874M	Cessna 207A Stationair 8 II	20700745			
☐ N9957M	Cessna 207A Stationair 8 II	20700764			

ALASKA SEAPLANE SERVICE (J5)   Juneau-Int'l, AK (JNU)

☐ N777DH	de Havilland DHC-2 Beaver	47	ex CF-FHN	FP
☐ N4794C	de Havilland DHC-2 Beaver	342	ex 51-16545	FP
☐ N60077	de Havilland DHC-2 Beaver	1419	ex LV-GLJ	FP

ALASKA WEST AIR   Kenai Island Lake, AK (ENA)

☐ N49AW	de Havilland DHC-3 Otter	310	ex N21PG	
☐ N87AW	de Havilland DHC-3 Otter	52	ex C-FMPO	
☐ N222RL	de Havilland DHC-2 Turbo Beaver	1570/TB5	ex C-FOEB	FP
☐ N1432Z	de Havilland DHC-2 Beaver	797	ex 54-1668	FP

ALLEGIANT AIR   Allegiant (G4/AAY)   Las Vegas-McCarran Int'l, NV (LAS)

☐ N901NV	Boeing 757-204	26963/450	ex N963BV	♦
☐ N902NV	Boeing 757-204	26964/452	ex N964BV	♦
☐ N903NV	Boeing 757-204	26966/520	ex G-BYAH	o/o♦
☐ N399NV	McDonnell-Douglas MD-87	49413/1681	ex XA-TXH	[MHV]
☐ N401NV	McDonnell-Douglas MD-88	49761/1623	ex N158PL	
☐ N402NV	McDonnell-Douglas MD-88	49763/1626	ex N160PL	
☐ N403NV	McDonnell-Douglas MD-88	49764/1632	ex N161PL	
☐ N404NV	McDonnell-Douglas MD-88	49765/1645	ex N162PL	
☐ N405NV	McDonnell-Douglas MD-83	49623/1499	ex SE-RFA	
☐ N406NV	McDonnell-Douglas MD-82	49900/1765	ex SE-RFC	
☐ N407NV	McDonnell-Douglas MD-82	53244/1901	ex SE-RFD	
☐ N408NV	McDonnell-Douglas MD-82	53246/1918	ex SE-RFB	
☐ N409NV	McDonnell-Douglas MD-83	49574/1413	ex SE-RDV	
☐ N410NV	McDonnell-Douglas MD-83	49965/2044	ex SE-DLV	
☐ N411NV	McDonnell-Douglas MD-82	53245/1978	ex HK-4413	
☐ N412NV	McDonnell-Douglas MD-88	49759/1606	ex N822ME	
☐ N414NV	McDonnell-Douglas MD-88	49766/1657	ex N823ME	
☐ N415NV	McDonnell-Douglas MD-82	49909/1625	ex SE-DII	♦
☐ N416NV	McDonnell-Douglas MD-82	49555/1402	ex SE-DIO	♦
☐ N418NV	McDonnell-Douglas MD-82	49615/1543	ex SE-DID	♦
☐ N419NV	McDonnell-Douglas MD-82	53366/1999	ex LN-ROO	♦
☐ N422NV	McDonnell-Douglas MD-82	49381/1231	ex OY-KGZ	♦
☐ N423NV	McDonnell-Douglas MD-82	53008/1895	ex SE-DIY	[IGM]♦
☐ N428NV	McDonnell-Douglas MD-82	49420/1254	ex OY-KGY	[IGM]♦
☐ N429NV	McDonnell-Douglas MD-82	49385/1244	ex SE-DFT	♦
☐ N515PT	McDonnell-Douglas MD-87	49612/1827	ex EC-JRR	[IGM]♦
☐ N860GA	McDonnell-Douglas MD-83	49786/1631	ex 9Y-THW	
☐ N861GA	McDonnell-Douglas MD-83	49557/1436	ex SE-DPI	
☐ N862GA	McDonnell-Douglas MD-83	49556/1415	ex LN-RMF	
☐ N863GA	McDonnell-Douglas MD-83	49911/1653	ex OY-KHL	
☐ N864GA	McDonnell-Douglas MD-83	49912/1659	ex LN-RMJ	
☐ N865GA	McDonnell-Douglas MD-83	49998/1800	ex SE-DIX	
☐ N866GA	McDonnell-Douglas MD-83	49910/1638	ex OY-KHK	
☐ N868GA	McDonnell-Douglas MD-83	49554/1379	ex LN-RMA	
☐ N869GA	McDonnell-Douglas MD-83	53294/1917	ex SE-DIZ	
☐ N871GA	McDonnell-Douglas MD-83	53296/1937	ex OY-KHT	
☐ N872GA	McDonnell-Douglas MD-83	53295/1922	ex LN-RMN	
☐ N873GA	McDonnell-Douglas MD-83	49658/1461	ex N946AS	
☐ N874GA	McDonnell-Douglas MD-83	49643/1423	ex N945AS	
☐ N875GA	McDonnell-Douglas MD-83	53468/2130	ex C-GKLN	
☐ N876GA	McDonnell-Douglas MD-83	53469/2116	ex C-GKLR	
☐ N877GA	McDonnell-Douglas MD-83	53467/2102	ex C-GKLJ	
☐ N878GA	McDonnell-Douglas MD-83	53487/2132	ex C-GKLQ	
☐ N879GA	McDonnell-Douglas MD-83	53486/2130	ex C-GKLN	
☐ N880GA	McDonnell-Douglas MD-83	49625/1503	ex OH-LMG	
☐ N881GA	McDonnell-Douglas MD-83	49708/1561	ex SE-RGO	
☐ N883GA	McDonnell-Douglas MD-83	49710/1547	ex SE-RGP	
☐ N884GA	McDonnell-Douglas MD-83	49401/1357	ex SE-RDS	
☐ N886GA	McDonnell-Douglas MD-82	49931/1754	ex N829NK	
☐ N887GA	McDonnell-Douglas MD-82	49932/1756	ex N830NK	
☐ N891GA	McDonnell-Douglas MD-83	49423/1283	ex LN-RLG	
☐ N892GA	McDonnell-Douglas MD-83	49826/1578	ex N861LF	
☐ N893GA	McDonnell-Douglas MD-83	53051/1718	ex N881LF	
☐ N894GA	McDonnell-Douglas MD-82	49660/1445	ex EI-BTX	
☐ N895GA	McDonnell-Douglas MD-82	49667/1466	ex EI-BTY	
☐ N945MA	McDonnell-Douglas MD-87	49725/1552	ex VP-BOP	
☐ N948MA	McDonnell-Douglas MD-87	49778/1646	ex VP-BOO	
☐ N949MA	McDonnell-Douglas MD-87	49779/1670	ex N751RA	
☐ N952MA	McDonnell-Douglas MD-87	49673/1508	ex N673HC	

ALLWEST FREIGHT — Kenai-Municipal, AK (ENA)

☐ N549WB	Short SC.7 Skyvan	SH1911	ex XA-SRD	Frtr

ALOHA AIR CARGO — Honolulu-Intl, HI (HNL)

☐ N826AL	Boeing 737-282C	23051/1002	ex CS-TEQ	
☐ N840AL	Boeing 737-2X6C	23124/1046	ex N747AS	
☐ N841AL	Boeing 737-2X6C	23123/1042	ex N746AS	
☐ N842AL	Boeing 737-290QC	23136/1032	ex N742AS	
☐ N843KH	SAAB SF.340A	340A-046	ex XA-STX	◆

ALPINE AIR EXPRESS — Alpine Air (5A/AIP) — Provo-Municipal, UT (PVU)

☐ N14MV	Beech 99	U-59	ex C-FGJT	
☐ N24BH	Beech 99	U-67	ex C-GVNQ	
☐ N95WA	Beech 99	U-6	ex N19RA	
☐ N99CA	Beech 99A	U-127	ex N22AT	
☐ N99GH	Beech 99A	U-112	ex N86569	
☐ N216CS	Beech C99	U-216	ex C-GGPP	based HNL
☐ N236AL	Beech C99	U-236	ex RP-C2317	based HNL
☐ N237SL	Beech C99	U-237	ex RP-C2370	based HNL
☐ N238AL	Beech C99	U-238	ex RP-C2380	based HNL
☐ N239AL	Beech C99	U-239	ex RP-C2390	based HNL
☐ N326CA	Beech B99	U-135	ex N10RA	
☐ N950AA	Beech B99	U-159	ex C-FCBU	
☐ N955AA	Beech 99A	U-128	ex J6-AAE	
☐ N4381Y	Beech 99	U-71	ex N216BH	
☐ N125BA	Beech 1900C	UB-6	ex N125GP	
☐ N127BA	Beech 1900C	UB-7	ex N126GP	
☐ N153GA	Beech 1900C	UB-34	ex N734GL	based HNL
☐ N154GA	Beech 1900C	UB-25	ex N315BH	
☐ N155CJ	Beech 1900D	UE-55	ex N85230	
☐ N172GA	Beech 1900C	UB-11	ex N11ZR	
☐ N190GA	Beech 1900C	UB-1	ex N1YW	
☐ N192GA	Beech 1900C	UB-17	ex N17ZR	based HNL
☐ N194GA	Beech 1900C	UB-8	ex CC-CAF	
☐ N197GA	Beech 1900C	UB-16	ex N16ZR	
☐ N198GA	Beech 1900C	UB-5	ex CC-CAS	

AMERICAN AIRLINES — American (AA/AAL) — Dallas-Fort Worth, TX (DFW)

Member of Oneworld

☐ N800NN	Boeing 737-823/W	29564/2964		3DY	
☐ N801NN	Boeing 737-823/W	29565/2972		3EA	
☐ N802NN	Boeing 737-823/W	31073/2982		3EB	
☐ N803NN	Boeing 737-823/W	29566/2995		3EC	
☐ N804NN	Boeing 737-823/W	29567/3004		3ED	
☐ N805NN	Boeing 737-823/W	31075/3013		3EE	
☐ N806NN	Boeing 737-823/W	29561/3028		3EF	
☐ N807NN	Boeing 737-823/W	31077/3035		3EF	
☐ N808NN	Boeing 737-823/W	33206/3042		3EH	
☐ N809NN	Boeing 737-823/W	33519/3050		3EJ	
☐ N810NN	Boeing 737-823/W	33207/3056		3EK	
☐ N811NN	Boeing 737-823/W	31079/3063		3EL	
☐ N812NN	Boeing 737-823/W	33520/3070		3EM	
☐ N813NN	Boeing 737-823/W	30918/3077		3EN	
☐ N814NN	Boeing 737-823/W	29562/3085		3EP	
☐ N815NN	Boeing 737-823/W	33208/3094		3ER	
☐ N816NN	Boeing 737-823/W	31081/3102		3ES	
☐ N817NN	Boeing 737-823/W	29558/3107		3ET	
☐ N818NN	Boeing 737-823/W	30910/3112		3EU	
☐ N819NN	Boeing 737-823/W	31083/3118		3EV	
☐ N820NN	Boeing 737-823/W	29559/3125		3EW	
☐ N821NN	Boeing 737-823/W	30912/3137		3EX	
☐ N822NN	Boeing 737-823/W	31085/3149		3EY	
☐ N823NN	Boeing 737-823/W	29560/3156		3FA	
☐ N824NN	Boeing 737-823/W	30916/3170		3FB	◆
☐ N825NN	Boeing 737-823/W	31087/3178		3FC	◆
☐ N826NN	Boeing 737-823/W	31089/3185		3FD	◆
☐ N827NN	Boeing 737-823/W	33209/3193	ex N1786B	3FE	◆
☐ N829NN	Boeing 737-823/W	33210/3200	ex N1787B	3FF	◆
☐ N830NN	Boeing 737-823/W	31091/3209	ex N1786B	3FG	◆
☐ N831NN	Boeing 737-823/W	33211/3217	ex N1796B	3FH	◆
☐ N832NN	Boeing 737-823/W	33521/3228	ex N1786B	3FJ	◆

☐ N833NN	Boeing 737-823/W	31093/3236	ex N1786B	3FK		♦
☐ N834NN	Boeing 737-823/W	29576/3244	ex N1787B	3FL		♦
☐ N835NN	Boeing 737-823/W	29577/3252	ex N1796B	3FM		♦
☐ N836NN	Boeing 737-823/W	31095/3260	ex N1786B	3FN		♦
☐ N837NN	Boeing 737-823/W	30908/3268	ex N1786B	3FP		♦
☐ N838NN	Boeing 737-823/W	31097/3276		3FR		♦
☐ N839NN	Boeing 737-823/W	29557/3282	ex N1786B	3FS		♦
☐ N840NN	Boeing 737-823/W	33518/3291	ex N1786B	3FT		♦
☐ N841NN	Boeing 737-823/W	30914/3298		3FU		♦
☐ N842NN	Boeing 737-823/W	31099/3307	ex N1786B	3FV		♦
☐ N843NN	Boeing 737-823/W	30906/3328	ex N1787B	3FW		♦
☐ N844NN	Boeing 737-823/W	33212/3334		3FX		♦
☐ N845NN	Boeing 737-823/W	40579/3340	ex N1786B	3FY		♦
☐ N846NN	Boeing 737-823/W	31101/3347		3GA		♦
☐ N847NN	Boeing 737-823/W	29575/3361		3GB		♦
☐ N848NN	Boeing 737-823/W	31103/3367		3GC		♦
☐ N849NN	Boeing 737-823/W	33213/3373		3GD		♦
☐ N850NN	Boeing 737-823/W	40580/3380		3GE		♦
☐ N851NN	Boeing 737-823/W	29556/3390		3GF		♦
☐ N852NN	Boeing 737-823/W	40581/3396		3GG		♦
☐ N853NN	Boeing 737-823/W	31105/3404		3GH		♦
☐ N854NN	Boeing 737-823/W	33214/3412		3GJ		♦
☐ N855NN	Boeing 737-823/W	40852/3422		3GK		♦
☐ N856NN	Boeing 737-823/W	31107/3427		3GL		♦
☐ N857NN	Boeing 737-823/W	30907/3434		3GM		♦
☐ N858NN	Boeing 737-823/W	30904/3440		3GN		♦
☐ N859NN	Boeing 737-823/W	29555/3456		3GP		♦
☐ N860NN	Boeing 737-823/W	40583/3462		3GR		♦
☐ N861NN	Boeing 737-823/W	31109/3468		3GS		♦
☐ N862NN	Boeing 737-823/W	30905/3475		3GT		♦
☐ N863NN	Boeing 737-823/W	30903/3481		3GU		♦
☐ N864NN	Boeing 737-823/W	31111/3487		3GV		♦
☐ N865NN	Boeing 737-823/W	29554/3493	ex N1787B	3GW		♦
☐ N866NN	Boeing 737-823/W	40584/3499		3GX		♦
☐	Boeing 737-823/W				o/o	♦
☐	Boeing 737-823/W				o/o	♦
☐	Boeing 737-823/W				o/o	♦
☐	Boeing 737-823/W				o/o	♦
☐	Boeing 737-823/W				o/o	♦
☐	Boeing 737-823/W				o/o	♦
☐	Boeing 737-823/W				o/o	♦
☐	Boeing 737-823/W				o/o	♦
☐	Boeing 737-823/W				o/o	♦
☐	Boeing 737-823/W				o/o	♦
☐	Boeing 737-823/W				o/o	♦
☐	Boeing 737-823/W				o/o	♦
☐	Boeing 737-823/W				o/o	♦
☐	Boeing 737-823/W				o/o	♦
☐	Boeing 737-823/W				o/o	♦
☐ N901AN	Boeing 737-823/W	29503/184		3AA		
☐ N902AN	Boeing 737-823/W	29504/190		3AB		
☐ N903AN	Boeing 737-823/W	29505/196		3AC		
☐ N904AN	Boeing 737-823/W	29506/207		3AD		
☐ N905AN	Boeing 737-823/W	29507/231		3AE		
☐ N906AN	Boeing 737-823/W	29508/240		3AF		
☐ N907AN	Boeing 737-823/W	29509/254		3AG		
☐ N908AN	Boeing 737-823/W	29510/263		3AH		
☐ N909AN	Boeing 737-823/W	29511/267	ex (N909AM)	3AJ		
☐ N910AN	Boeing 737-823/W	29512/271		3AK		
☐ N912AN	Boeing 737-823/W	29513/289		3AL		
☐ N913AN	Boeing 737-823/W	29514/293		3AM		
☐ N914AN	Boeing 737-823/W	29515/316		3AN		
☐ N915AN	Boeing 737-823/W	29516/322		3AP		
☐ N916AN	Boeing 737-823/W	29517/332		3AR		
☐ N917AN	Boeing 737-823/W	29518/344		3AS		
☐ N918AN	Boeing 737-823/W	29519/353		3AT		
☐ N919AN	Boeing 737-823/W	29520/363		3AU		
☐ N920AN	Boeing 737-823/W	29521/378		3AV		
☐ N921AN	Boeing 737-823/W	29522/383		3AW		
☐ N922AN	Boeing 737-823/W	29523/398		3AX		
☐ N923AN	Boeing 737-823/W	29524/405		3AY		
☐ N924AN	Boeing 737-823/W	29525/434		3BA		
☐ N925AN	Boeing 737-823/W	29526/440		3BB		
☐ N926AN	Boeing 737-823/W	29527/453		3BC		
☐ N927AN	Boeing 737-823/W	30077/462		3BD		
☐ N928AN	Boeing 737-823/W	29528/473		3BE		

☐ N929AN	Boeing 737-823/W	30078/488		3BF
☐ N930AN	Boeing 737-823/W	29529/503		3BG
☐ N931AN	Boeing 737-823/W	30079/509		3BH
☐ N932AN	Boeing 737-823/W	29530/527		3BJ
☐ N933AN	Boeing 737-823/W	30080/531		3BK
☐ N934AN	Boeing 737-823/W	29531/553		3BL
☐ N935AN	Boeing 737-823/W	30081/559		3BM
☐ N936AN	Boeing 737-823/W	29532/575		3BN
☐ N937AN	Boeing 737-823/W	30082/579		3BP
☐ N938AN	Boeing 737-823/W	29533/608		3BR
☐ N939AN	Boeing 737-823/W	30083/612		3BS
☐ N940AN	Boeing 737-823/W	30598/616		3BT
☐ N941AN	Boeing 737-823/W	29534/624		3BU
☐ N942AN	Boeing 737-823/W	30084/629		3BV
☐ N943AN	Boeing 737-823/W	30599/635		3BW
☐ N944AN	Boeing 737-823/W	29535/645		3BX
☐ N945AN	Boeing 737-823/W	30085/649		3BY
☐ N946AN	Boeing 737-823/W	30600/655		3CA
☐ N947AN	Boeing 737-823/W	29536/671	ex (N2292Z)	3CB
☐ N948AN	Boeing 737-823/W	30086/679	ex (N2294B)	3CC
☐ N949AN	Boeing 737-823/W	29537/699		3CD
☐ N950AN	Boeing 737-823/W	30087/704		3CE
☐ N951AA	Boeing 737-823/W	29538/720		3CF Astrojet c/s
☐ N952AA	Boeing 737-823/W	30088/726		3CG
☐ N953AN	Boeing 737-823/W	29539/741		3CH
☐ N954AN	Boeing 737-823/W	30089/745		3CJ
☐ N955AN	Boeing 737-823/W	29540/762		3CK
☐ N956AN	Boeing 737-823/W	30090/764		3CL
☐ N957AN	Boeing 737-823/W	29541/788		3CM
☐ N958AN	Boeing 737-823/W	30091/797		3CN
☐ N959AN	Boeing 737-823/W	30828/801		3CP
☐ N960AN	Boeing 737-823/W	29542/818		3CR
☐ N961AN	Boeing 737-823/W	30092/822		3CS
☐ N962AN	Boeing 737-823/W	30858/825		3CT
☐ N963AN	Boeing 737-823/W	29543/834		3CU
☐ N964AN	Boeing 737-823/W	30093/837		3CV
☐ N965AN	Boeing 737-823/W	29544/860		3CW
☐ N966AN	Boeing 737-823/W	30094/863		3CX
☐ N967AN	Boeing 737-823/W	29545/883		3CY
☐ N968AN	Boeing 737-823/W	30095/886		3DA
☐ N969AN	Boeing 737-823/W	29546/910		3DB
☐ N970AN	Boeing 737-823/W	30096/915		3DC
☐ N971AN	Boeing 737-823/W	29547/937		3DD
☐ N972AN	Boeing 737-823/W	30097/941		3DE
☐ N973AN	Boeing 737-823/W	29548/971		3DF
☐ N974AN	Boeing 737-823/W	30098/977		3DG
☐ N975AN	Boeing 737-823/W	29549/992		3DH
☐ N976AN	Boeing 737-823/W	30099/1001		3DJ
☐ N978AN	Boeing 737-823/W	30100/1022		3DL
☐ N979AN	Boeing 737-823/W	29568/2838		3DM
☐ N980AN	Boeing 737-823/W	33203/2846		3DN
☐ N981AN	Boeing 737-823/W	29569/2870		3DP
☐ N982AN	Boeing 737-823/W	31067/2876		3DR
☐ N983AN	Boeing 737-823/W	29570/2899		3DS
☐ N987AN	Boeing 737-823/W	31069/2907		3DT
☐ N989AN	Boeing 737-823/W	33205/2915		3DU
☐ N990AN	Boeing 737-823/W	29563/2935		3DV
☐ N991AN	Boeing 737-823/W	30920/2945		3DW
☐ N992AN	Boeing 737-823/W	31071/2954		3DX
☐ N172AJ	Boeing 757-223/W	32400/1012		5FT
☐ N173AN	Boeing 757-223/W	32399/1005		5FS
☐ N174AA	Boeing 757-223/W	31308/998		5FR
☐ N175AN	Boeing 757-223/W	32394/992		5FK
☐ N176AA	Boeing 757-223/W	32395/994		5FL
☐ N177AN	Boeing 757-223/W	32396/996		5FM
☐ N178AA	Boeing 757-223/W	32398/1002	ex (N20171)	5FN
☐ N179AA	Boeing 757-223/W	32397/1000	ex (N20140)	5FP
☐ N181AN	Boeing 757-223/W	29591/852	ex N5573L	5EN
☐ N182AN	Boeing 757-223/W	29592/853		5EP
☐ N183AN	Boeing 757-223ER/W	29593/862		5ER
☐ N184AN	Boeing 757-223ER/W	29594/866	ex N1787B	5ES
☐ N185AN	Boeing 757-223/W	32379/962		5ET
☐ N186AN	Boeing 757-223/W	32380/964		5EU
☐ N187AN	Boeing 757-223/W	32381/965		5EV
☐ N188AN	Boeing 757-223/W	32382/969		5EW
☐ N189AN	Boeing 757-223/W	32383/970		5EX

☐ N190AA	Boeing 757-223/W	32384/973	5EY
☐ N191AN	Boeing 757-223/W	32385/977	5FA
☐ N192AN	Boeing 757-223/W	32386/979	5FB
☐ N193AN	Boeing 757-223/W	32387/981	5FC
☐ N194AA	Boeing 757-223/W	32388/983	5FD
☐ N195AN	Boeing 757-223/W	32389/984	5FE
☐ N196AA	Boeing 757-223/W	32390/986	5FF
☐ N197AN	Boeing 757-223/W	32391/988	5FG
☐ N198AA	Boeing 757-223/W	32392/989	5FH
☐ N199AN	Boeing 757-223/W	32393/991	5FJ
☐ N601AN	Boeing 757-223/W	27052/661	5DU
☐ N602AN	Boeing 757-223/W	27053/664	5DV
☐ N603AA	Boeing 757-223/W	27054/670	5DW
☐ N604AA	Boeing 757-223/W	27055/677	5DX
☐ N605AA	Boeing 757-223/W	27056/680	5DY
☐ N606AA	Boeing 757-223/W	27057/707	5EA
☐ N607AM	Boeing 757-223/W	27058/712	5EB
☐ N608AA	Boeing 757-223ER/W	27446/720	5EC
☐ N609AA	Boeing 757-223ER/W	27447/722	5ED
☐ N610AA	Boeing 757-223/W	24486/234	610
☐ N611AM	Boeing 757-223/W	24487/236	611
☐ N612AA	Boeing 757-223/W	24488/240	612
☐ N613AA	Boeing 757-223/W	24489/242	613
☐ N614AA	Boeing 757-223/W	24490/243	614
☐ N615AM	Boeing 757-223/W	24491/245	615
☐ N616AA	Boeing 757-223/W	24524/248	616
☐ N617AM	Boeing 757-223/W	24525/253	617
☐ N618AA	Boeing 757-223/W	24526/260	618
☐ N619AA	Boeing 757-223/W	24577/269	619
☐ N620AA	Boeing 757-223/W	24578/276	620
☐ N621AM	Boeing 757-223/W	24579/283	621
☐ N622AA	Boeing 757-223/W	24580/289	622
☐ N623AA	Boeing 757-223/W	24581/296	623
☐ N624AA	Boeing 757-223/W	24582/297	624
☐ N625AA	Boeing 757-223/W	24583/303	625
☐ N626AA	Boeing 757-223/W	24584/304	626
☐ N627AA	Boeing 757-223/W	24585/308	627
☐ N628AA	Boeing 757-223/W	24586/309	628
☐ N629AA	Boeing 757-223/W	24587/315	629
☐ N630AA	Boeing 757-223/W	24588/316	630
☐ N631AA	Boeing 757-223/W	24589/317	631
☐ N632AA	Boeing 757-223/W	24590/321	632
☐ N633AA	Boeing 757-223/W	24591/324	633
☐ N634AA	Boeing 757-223/W	24592/327	634
☐ N635AA	Boeing 757-223/W	24593/328	635
☐ N636AM	Boeing 757-223/W	24594/336	636
☐ N637AM	Boeing 757-223/W	24595/337	637
☐ N638AA	Boeing 757-223/W	24596/344	638
☐ N639AA	Boeing 757-223/W	24597/345	639
☐ N640A	Boeing 757-223/W	24598/350	640
☐ N641AA	Boeing 757-223/W	24599/351	641
☐ N642AA	Boeing 757-223/W	24600/357	642
☐ N643AA	Boeing 757-223/W	24601/360	643
☐ N645AA	Boeing 757-223/W	24603/370	5BR
☐ N646AA	Boeing 757-223/W	24604/375	5BS
☐ N647AM	Boeing 757-223/W	24605/378	5BT
☐ N648AA	Boeing 757-223/W	24606/379	5BU
☐ N649AA	Boeing 757-223/W	24607/383	5BV
☐ N650AA	Boeing 757-223/W	24608/384	5BW
☐ N652AA	Boeing 757-223/W	24610/391	5BY
☐ N653A	Boeing 757-223/W	24611/397	5CA
☐ N654A	Boeing 757-223/W	24612/398	5CB
☐ N655AA	Boeing 757-223/W	24613/402	5CC
☐ N656AA	Boeing 757-223/W	24614/404	5CD
☐ N657AM	Boeing 757-223/W	24615/409	5CE
☐ N658AA	Boeing 757-223/W	24616/410	5CF
☐ N659AA	Boeing 757-223/W	24617/417	5CG Pride of American
☐ N660AM	Boeing 757-223/W	25294/418	5CH
☐ N661AA	Boeing 757-223/W	25295/423	5CJ
☐ N662AA	Boeing 757-223/W	25296/425	5CK
☐ N663AM	Boeing 757-223/W	25297/432	5CL
☐ N664AA	Boeing 757-223/W	25298/433	5CM
☐ N665AA	Boeing 757-223/W	25299/436	5CN
☐ N666A	Boeing 757-223/W	25300/451	5CP
☐ N668AA	Boeing 757-223/W	25333/460	5CS
☐ N669AA	Boeing 757-223/W	25334/463	5CT
☐ N670AA	Boeing 757-223/W	25335/468	5CU

☐ N671AA	Boeing 757-223/W	25336/473		5CV	
☐ N672AA	Boeing 757-223/W	25337/474		5CW	
☐ N673AN	Boeing 757-223/W	29423/812		5EE	
☐ N674AN	Boeing 757-223/W	29424/816		5EF	
☐ N675AN	Boeing 757-223/W	29425/817		5EG	
☐ N676AN	Boeing 757-223/W	29426/827	ex N1798B	5EH	
☐ N677AN	Boeing 757-223/W	29427/828		5EJ	
☐ N678AN	Boeing 757-223/W	29428/837	ex N1787B	5EK	
☐ N679AN	Boeing 757-223/W	29589/842	ex N1800B	5EL	Astrojet c/s
☐ N680AN	Boeing 757-223/W	29590/847		5EM	
☐ N681AA	Boeing 757-223/W	25338/483		5CX	
☐ N682AA	Boeing 757-223/W	25339/484		5CY	
☐ N683A	Boeing 757-223/W	25340/491		5DA	
☐ N684AA	Boeing 757-223/W	25341/504		5DB	
☐ N685AA	Boeing 757-223/W	25342/507		5DC	
☐ N686AA	Boeing 757-223/W	25343/509		5DD	
☐ N687AA	Boeing 757-223ER/W	25695/536		5DE	
☐ N688AA	Boeing 757-223ER/W	25730/548		5DF	
☐ N689AA	Boeing 757-223ER/W	25731/562		5DG	
☐ N690AA	Boeing 757-223ER/W	25696/566		5DH	
☐ N691AA	Boeing 757-223ER/W	25697/568		5DJ	
☐ N692AA	Boeing 757-223/W	26972/578		5DK	
☐ N693AA	Boeing 757-223/W	26973/580		5DL	
☐ N694AN	Boeing 757-223/W	26974/582		5DM	
☐ N695AN	Boeing 757-223/W	26975/621		5DN	
☐ N696AN	Boeing 757-223/W	26976/627		5DP	
☐ N697AN	Boeing 757-223/W	26977/633		5DR	
☐ N698AN	Boeing 757-223/W	26980/635		5DS	
☐ N699AN	Boeing 757-223/W	27051/660		5DT	
☐ N7667A	Boeing 757-223/W	25301/459		5CR	
☐ N319AA	Boeing 767-223ER	22320/128		319	
☐ N320AA	Boeing 767-223ER	22321/130		320	
☐ N321AA	Boeing 767-223ER	22322/139		321	
☐ N322AA	Boeing 767-223ER	22323/140		322	
☐ N323AA	Boeing 767-223ER	22324/146		323	
☐ N324AA	Boeing 767-223ER	22325/147		324	
☐ N325AA	Boeing 767-223ER	22326/157		325	
☐ N327AA	Boeing 767-223ER	22327/159		327	
☐ N328AA	Boeing 767-223ER	22328/160		328	
☐ N329AA	Boeing 767-223ER	22329/164		329	
☐ N332AA	Boeing 767-223ER	22331/168		332	
☐ N335AA	Boeing 767-223ER	22333/194		335	
☐ N336AA	Boeing 767-223ER	22334/195		336	
☐ N338AA	Boeing 767-223ER	22335/196		338	
☐ N339AA	Boeing 767-223ER	22336/198		339	
☐ N342AN	Boeing 767-323ER	33081/896		342	
☐ N343AN	Boeing 767-323ER	33082/899		343	
☐ N344AN	Boeing 767-323ER	33083/900		344	
☐ N345AN	Boeing 767-323ER/W	33084/906		345	
☐ N346AN	Boeing 767-323ER	33085/907		346	
☐ N347AN	Boeing 767-323ER	33086/908		347	
☐ N348AN	Boeing 767-323ER	33087/910		348	
☐ N349AN	Boeing 767-323ER	33088/913		349	
☐ N350AN	Boeing 767-323ER	33089/916		350	
☐ N351AA	Boeing 767-323ER	24032/202		351	
☐ N352AA	Boeing 767-323ER	24033/205		352	
☐ N353AA	Boeing 767-323ER	24034/206		353	
☐ N354AA	Boeing 767-323ER	24035/211		354	
☐ N355AA	Boeing 767-323ER	24036/221		355	
☐ N357AA	Boeing 767-323ER	24038/227		357	
☐ N358AA	Boeing 767-323ER	24039/228		358	
☐ N359AA	Boeing 767-323ER	24040/230		359	
☐ N360AA	Boeing 767-323ER	24041/232		360	
☐ N361AA	Boeing 767-323ER	24042/235		361	
☐ N362AA	Boeing 767-323ER	24043/237		362	
☐ N363AA	Boeing 767-323ER	24044/238		363	
☐ N366AA	Boeing 767-323ER	25193/388		366	
☐ N368AA	Boeing 767-323ER	25195/404		368	
☐ N369AA	Boeing 767-323ER	25196/422		369	
☐ N370AA	Boeing 767-323ER	25197/425		370	
☐ N371AA	Boeing 767-323ER	25198/431		371	
☐ N372AA	Boeing 767-323ER	25199/433		372	
☐ N373AA	Boeing 767-323ER/W	25200/435		373	
☐ N374AA	Boeing 767-323ER	25201/437		374	
☐ N376AN	Boeing 767-323ER	25445/447		376	
☐ N377AN	Boeing 767-323ER/W	25446/453		377	

☐ N378AN	Boeing 767-323ER	25447/469		378	
☐ N379AA	Boeing 767-323ER	25448/481		379	
☐ N380AN	Boeing 767-323ER/W	25449/489		380	
☐ N381AN	Boeing 767-323ER/W	25450/495		381	
☐ N382AN	Boeing 767-323ER/W	25451/498		382	
☐ N383AN	Boeing 767-323ER	26995/500		383	
☐ N384AA	Boeing 767-323ER	26996/512		384	
☐ N385AM	Boeing 767-323ER/W	27059/536		385	
☐ N386AA	Boeing 767-323ER	27060/540		386	
☐ N387AM	Boeing 767-323ER/W	27184/541		387	
☐ N388AA	Boeing 767-323ER	27448/563		388	
☐ N389AA	Boeing 767-323ER/W	27449/564		389	
☐ N390AA	Boeing 767-323ER	27450/565		390	
☐ N391AA	Boeing 767-323ER	27451/566		391	
☐ N392AN	Boeing 767-323ER	29429/700		392	
☐ N393AN	Boeing 767-323ER	29430/701		393	
☐ N394AN	Boeing 767-323ER	29431/703		394	
☐ N395AN	Boeing 767-323ER	29432/709		395	
☐ N396AN	Boeing 767-323ER	29603/739		396	
☐ N397AN	Boeing 767-323ER	29604/744		397	
☐ N398AN	Boeing 767-323ER	29605/748		398	
☐ N399AN	Boeing 767-323ER/W	29606/752		399	
☐ N7375A	Boeing 767-323ER	25202/441		375	
☐ N39356	Boeing 767-323ER	24037/226		356	
☐ N39364	Boeing 767-323ER/W	24045/240		364	
☐ N39365	Boeing 767-323ER	24046/241		365	
☐ N39367	Boeing 767-323ER	25194/394		367	
☐ N750AN	Boeing 777-223ER	30259/332	ex (N798AN)	7BJ	
☐ N751AN	Boeing 777-223ER	30798/333		7BK	
☐ N752AN	Boeing 777-223ER	30260/339	ex (N799AN)	7BL	
☐ N753AN	Boeing 777-223ER	30261/341	ex (N750AN)	7BM	
☐ N754AN	Boeing 777-223ER	30262/345		7BN	
☐ N755AN	Boeing 777-223ER	30263/354		7BP	
☐ N756AM	Boeing 777-223ER	30264/358		7BR	
☐ N757AN	Boeing 777-223ER	32636/363		7BS	
☐ N758AN	Boeing 777-223ER	32637/371		7BT	
☐ N759AN	Boeing 777-223ER	32638/376		7BU	Pink Ribbon c/s
☐ N760AN	Boeing 777-223ER	31477/379		7BV	
☐ N761AJ	Boeing 777-223ER	31478/393		7BW	
☐ N762AN	Boeing 777-223ER	31479/399		7BX	
☐ N765AN	Boeing 777-223ER	32879/433		7BY	
☐ N766AN	Boeing 777-223ER	32880/445		7CA	
☐ N767AJ	Boeing 777-223ER	33539/555		7CB	
☐ N768AA	Boeing 777-223ER	33540/566		7CC	
☐ N770AN	Boeing 777-223ER	29578/185		7AA	
☐ N771AN	Boeing 777-223ER	29579/190		7AB	
☐ N772AN	Boeing 777-223ER	29580/198		7AC	
☐ N773AN	Boeing 777-223ER	29583/199		7AD	
☐ N774AN	Boeing 777-223ER	29581/208		7AE	
☐ N775AN	Boeing 777-223ER	29584/209		7AF	
☐ N776AN	Boeing 777-223ER	29582/215		7AG	
☐ N777AN	Boeing 777-223ER	29585/218		7AH	
☐ N778AN	Boeing 777-223ER	29587/223		7AJ	
☐ N779AN	Boeing 777-223ER	29955/225		7AK	
☐ N780AN	Boeing 777-223ER	29956/241	ex N6055X	7AL	
☐ N781AN	Boeing 777-223ER	29586/266		7AM	
☐ N782AN	Boeing 777-223ER	30003/270		7AN	
☐ N783AN	Boeing 777-223ER	30004/271		7AP	
☐ N784AN	Boeing 777-223ER	29588/272		7AR	
☐ N785AN	Boeing 777-223ER	30005/274		7AS	
☐ N786AN	Boeing 777-223ER	30250/276		7AT	
☐ N787AL	Boeing 777-223ER	30010/277		7AU	
☐ N788AN	Boeing 777-223ER	30011/283		7AV	
☐ N789AN	Boeing 777-223ER	30252/285		7AW	
☐ N790AN	Boeing 777-223ER	30251/287		7AX	
☐ N791AN	Boeing 777-223ER	30254/289		7AY	
☐ N792AN	Boeing 777-223ER	30253/292		7BA	
☐ N793AN	Boeing 777-223ER	30255/299		7BB	
☐ N794AN	Boeing 777-223ER	30256/313		7BC	
☐ N795AN	Boeing 777-223ER	30257/315		7BD	
☐ N796AN	Boeing 777-223ER	30796/316		7BE	
☐ N797AN	Boeing 777-223ER	30012/321	ex (N796AN)	7BF American Spirit	
☐ N798AN	Boeing 777-223ER	30797/324		7BG	
☐ N799AN	Boeing 777-223ER	30258/328	ex (N797AN)	7BH	

☐	N110HM	McDonnell-Douglas MD-83	49787/1636	ex HL7274	4WU	
☐	N208AA	McDonnell-Douglas MD-82	49159/1107		208	
☐	N218AA	McDonnell-Douglas MD-82	49168/1100		218	[ROW]
☐	N219AA	McDonnell-Douglas MD-82	49171/1112		219	[ROW]
☐	N223AA	McDonnell-Douglas MD-82	49173/1114		223	[ROW]
☐	N227AA	McDonnell-Douglas MD-82	49177/1121		227	
☐	N232AA	McDonnell-Douglas MD-82	49179/1123		232	[ROW]
☐	N233AA	McDonnell-Douglas MD-82	49180/1124		233	[ROW]
☐	N245AA	McDonnell-Douglas MD-82	49257/1160		245	
☐	N249AA	McDonnell-Douglas MD-82	49269/1164		249	
☐	N251AA	McDonnell-Douglas MD-82	49270/1165		251	
☐	N253AA	McDonnell-Douglas MD-82	49286/1175		253	
☐	N255AA	McDonnell-Douglas MD-82	49287/1176		255	
☐	N258AA	McDonnell-Douglas MD-82	49288/1187		258	
☐	N259AA	McDonnell-Douglas MD-82	49289/1193		269	
☐	N262AA	McDonnell-Douglas MD-82	49290/1195		262	
☐	N266AA	McDonnell-Douglas MD-82	49291/1210		266	
☐	N271AA	McDonnell-Douglas MD-82	49293/1212		271	
☐	N274AA	McDonnell-Douglas MD-82	49271/1166		274	
☐	N278AA	McDonnell-Douglas MD-82	49294/1213		278	
☐	N279AA	McDonnell-Douglas MD-82	49295/1214		279	[ROW]
☐	N283AA	McDonnell-Douglas MD-82	49296/1215		283	[ROW]
☐	N287AA	McDonnell-Douglas MD-82	49299/1218		287	[ROW]
☐	N290AA	McDonnell-Douglas MD-82	49302/1221		290	
☐	N291AA	McDonnell-Douglas MD-82	49303/1222		291	
☐	N292AA	McDonnell-Douglas MD-82	49304/1223		292	
☐	N293AA	McDonnell-Douglas MD-82	49305/1226		293	
☐	N298AA	McDonnell-Douglas MD-82	49310/1247		298	
☐	N403A	McDonnell-Douglas MD-82	49314/1256		403	
☐	N408AA	McDonnell-Douglas MD-82	49319/1266		408	[ROW]
☐	N410AA	McDonnell-Douglas MD-82	49321/1273		410	[ROW]
☐	N411AA	McDonnell-Douglas MD-82	49322/1280		411	[ROW]
☐	N412AA	McDonnell-Douglas MD-82	49323/1281		412	
☐	N413AA	McDonnell-Douglas MD-82	49324/1289		413	[ROW]
☐	N415AA	McDonnell-Douglas MD-82	49326/1295		415	[ROW]
☐	N416AA	McDonnell-Douglas MD-82	49327/1296		416	[ROW]
☐	N417AA	McDonnell-Douglas MD-82	49328/1301		417	[ROW]
☐	N418AA	McDonnell-Douglas MD-82	49329/1302		418	[ROW]
☐	N419AA	McDonnell-Douglas MD-82	49331/1306		419	[ROW]
☐	N420AA	McDonnell-Douglas MD-82	49332/1307		420	
☐	N422AA	McDonnell-Douglas MD-82	49334/1312		422	
☐	N423AA	McDonnell-Douglas MD-82	49335/1320		423	
☐	N424AA	McDonnell-Douglas MD-82	49336/1321		424	
☐	N426AA	McDonnell-Douglas MD-82	49338/1327		426	
☐	N427AA	McDonnell-Douglas MD-82	49339/1328		427	[ROW]
☐	N429AA	McDonnell-Douglas MD-82	49341/1336		429	[ROW]
☐	N430AA	McDonnell-Douglas MD-82	49342/1337		430	[ROW]
☐	N431AA	McDonnell-Douglas MD-82	49343/1339		431	
☐	N432AA	McDonnell-Douglas MD-82	49350/1376		432	
☐	N433AA	McDonnell-Douglas MD-83	49451/1388		433	
☐	N434AA	McDonnell-Douglas MD-83	49452/1389		434	
☐	N435AA	McDonnell-Douglas MD-83	49453/1390		435	
☐	N436AA	McDonnell-Douglas MD-83	49454/1391		436	
☐	N437AA	McDonnell-Douglas MD-83	49455/1392		437	
☐	N438AA	McDonnell-Douglas MD-83	49456/1393		438	
☐	N439AA	McDonnell-Douglas MD-83	49457/1398		439	
☐	N440AA	McDonnell-Douglas MD-82	49459/1407		440	
☐	N441AA	McDonnell-Douglas MD-82	49460/1408		441	
☐	N442AA	McDonnell-Douglas MD-82	49468/1409		442	
☐	N446AA	McDonnell-Douglas MD-82	49472/1426		446	
☐	N447AA	McDonnell-Douglas MD-82	49473/1427		447	
☐	N448AA	McDonnell-Douglas MD-82	49474/1431		448	
☐	N449AA	McDonnell-Douglas MD-82	49475/1432		449	
☐	N450AA	McDonnell-Douglas MD-82	49476/1439		450	
☐	N451AA	McDonnell-Douglas MD-82	49477/1441		451	
☐	N452AA	McDonnell-Douglas MD-82	49553/1450		452	
☐	N453AA	McDonnell-Douglas MD-82	49558/1451		453	
☐	N454AA	McDonnell-Douglas MD-82	49559/1460		454	
☐	N455AA	McDonnell-Douglas MD-82	49560/1462		455	
☐	N456AA	McDonnell-Douglas MD-82	49561/1474		456	
☐	N457AA	McDonnell-Douglas MD-82	49562/1475		457	
☐	N458AA	McDonnell-Douglas MD-82	49563/1485		458	
☐	N459AA	McDonnell-Douglas MD-82	49564/1486		459	
☐	N460AA	McDonnell-Douglas MD-82	49565/1496		460	
☐	N461AA	McDonnell-Douglas MD-82	49566/1497		461	
☐	N462AA	McDonnell-Douglas MD-82	49592/1505		462	
☐	N463AA	McDonnell-Douglas MD-82	49593/1506		463	

☐ N464AA	McDonnell-Douglas MD-82	49594/1507	464
☐ N465A	McDonnell-Douglas MD-82	49595/1509	465
☐ N466AA	McDonnell-Douglas MD-82	49596/1510	466
☐ N467AA	McDonnell-Douglas MD-82	49597/1511	467
☐ N468AA	McDonnell-Douglas MD-82	49598/1513	468
☐ N469AA	McDonnell-Douglas MD-82	49599/1515	469
☐ N470AA	McDonnell-Douglas MD-82	49600/1516	470
☐ N471AA	McDonnell-Douglas MD-82	49601/1518	471
☐ N472AA	McDonnell-Douglas MD-82	49647/1520	472
☐ N473AA	McDonnell-Douglas MD-82	49648/1521	473
☐ N474	McDonnell-Douglas MD-82	49649/1526	474
☐ N475AA	McDonnell-Douglas MD-82	49650/1527	475
☐ N476AA	McDonnell-Douglas MD-82	49651/1528	476
☐ N477AA	McDonnell-Douglas MD-82	49652/1529	477
☐ N478AA	McDonnell-Douglas MD-82	49653/1534	478
☐ N479AA	McDonnell-Douglas MD-82	49654/1535	479
☐ N480AA	McDonnell-Douglas MD-82	49655/1536	480
☐ N481AA	McDonnell-Douglas MD-82	49656/1545	481
☐ N482AA	McDonnell-Douglas MD-82	49675/1546	482
☐ N483A	McDonnell-Douglas MD-82	49676/1550	483
☐ N484AA	McDonnell-Douglas MD-82	49677/1551	484
☐ N485AA	McDonnell-Douglas MD-82	49678/1555	485
☐ N486AA	McDonnell-Douglas MD-82	49679/1557	486
☐ N487AA	McDonnell-Douglas MD-82	49680/1558	487
☐ N488AA	McDonnell-Douglas MD-82	49681/1560	488
☐ N489AA	McDonnell-Douglas MD-82	49682/1562	489
☐ N490AA	McDonnell-Douglas MD-82	49683/1563	490
☐ N491AA	McDonnell-Douglas MD-82	49684/1564	491
☐ N492AA	McDonnell-Douglas MD-82	49730/1565	492
☐ N493AA	McDonnell-Douglas MD-82	49731/1566	493
☐ N494AA	McDonnell-Douglas MD-82	49732/1567	494
☐ N495AA	McDonnell-Douglas MD-82	49733/1607	495
☐ N496AA	McDonnell-Douglas MD-82	49734/1619	496
☐ N497AA	McDonnell-Douglas MD-82	49735/1635	497
☐ N498AA	McDonnell-Douglas MD-82	49736/1640	498
☐ N499AA	McDonnell-Douglas MD-82	49737/1641	499
☐ N501AA	McDonnell-Douglas MD-82	49738/1648	501
☐ N505AA	McDonnell-Douglas MD-82	49799/1652	505
☐ N510AM	McDonnell-Douglas MD-82	49804/1669	510
☐ N513AA	McDonnell-Douglas MD-82	49890/1686	513
☐ N516AM	McDonnell-Douglas MD-82	49893/1696	516
☐ N552AA	McDonnell-Douglas MD-82	53034/1826	552
☐ N553AA	McDonnell-Douglas MD-82	53083/1828	553
☐ N554AA	McDonnell-Douglas MD-82	53084/1830	554
☐ N555AN	McDonnell-Douglas MD-82	53085/1839	555
☐ N556AA	McDonnell-Douglas MD-82	53086/1840	556
☐ N557AN	McDonnell-Douglas MD-82	53087/1841	557
☐ N558AA	McDonnell-Douglas MD-82	53088/1852	558
☐ N559AA	McDonnell-Douglas MD-82	53089/1853	559
☐ N560AA	McDonnell-Douglas MD-82	53090/1858	560
☐ N561AA	McDonnell-Douglas MD-82	53091/1863	561
☐ N562AA	McDonnell-Douglas MD-83	49344/1370	562
☐ N563AA	McDonnell-Douglas MD-83	49345/1371	563
☐ N564AA	McDonnell-Douglas MD-83	49346/1372	564
☐ N565AA	McDonnell-Douglas MD-83	49347/1373	565
☐ N566AA	McDonnell-Douglas MD-83	49348/1374	566
☐ N567AM	McDonnell-Douglas MD-83	53293/2021	567
☐ N568AA	McDonnell-Douglas MD-83	49349/1375	568
☐ N569AA	McDonnell-Douglas MD-83	49351/1385	569
☐ N570AA	McDonnell-Douglas MD-83	49352/1386	570
☐ N571AA	McDonnell-Douglas MD-83	49353/1387	571
☐ N572AA	McDonnell-Douglas MD-83	49458/1406	572
☐ N573AA	McDonnell-Douglas MD-82	53092/1864	573
☐ N574AA	McDonnell-Douglas MD-82	53151/1866	574
☐ N575AM	McDonnell-Douglas MD-82	53152/1875	575
☐ N576AA	McDonnell-Douglas MD-82	53153/1876	576
☐ N577AA	McDonnell-Douglas MD-82	53154/1878	577
☐ N578AA	McDonnell-Douglas MD-82	53155/1883	578
☐ N579AA	McDonnell-Douglas MD-82	53156/1884	579
☐ N580AA	McDonnell-Douglas MD-82	53157/1885	580
☐ N581AA	McDonnell-Douglas MD-82	53158/1891	581
☐ N582AA	McDonnell-Douglas MD-82	53159/1892	582
☐ N583AA	McDonnell-Douglas MD-82	53160/1893	583
☐ N584AA	McDonnell-Douglas MD-82	53247/1902	584
☐ N585AA	McDonnell-Douglas MD-82	53248/1903	585
☐ N586AA	McDonnell-Douglas MD-82	53249/1904	586
☐ N587AA	McDonnell-Douglas MD-82	53250/1907	587

	Registration	Type	Serial	ex	Code	Name	Note
☐	N588AA	McDonnell-Douglas MD-83	53251/1909		588		
☐	N589AA	McDonnell-Douglas MD-83	53252/1910		589		
☐	N590AA	McDonnell-Douglas MD-83	53253/1919		590		
☐	N591AA	McDonnell-Douglas MD-83	53254/1920		591		
☐	N592AA	McDonnell-Douglas MD-83	53255/1932		592		
☐	N593AA	McDonnell-Douglas MD-83	53256/1933		593		
☐	N594AA	McDonnell-Douglas MD-83	53284/1966		594		
☐	N595AA	McDonnell-Douglas MD-83	53285/1989		595		
☐	N596AA	McDonnell-Douglas MD-83	53286/2000		596		
☐	N597AA	McDonnell-Douglas MD-83	53287/2006		597		
☐	N598AA	McDonnell-Douglas MD-83	53288/2011		598		
☐	N599AA	McDonnell-Douglas MD-83	53289/2012		599		
☐	N919TW	McDonnell-Douglas MD-82	49368/1198		4TU		[ROW]
☐	N923TW	McDonnell-Douglas MD-82	49379/1205	ex D-ALLS	4UN		[ROW]
☐	N931TW	McDonnell-Douglas MD-82	49527/1382		4WA		
☐	N940AS	McDonnell-Douglas MD-83	49825/1577		4UJ		[ROW]
☐	N941AS	McDonnell-Douglas MD-83	49925/1616		4UK		[ROW]
☐	N948TW	McDonnell-Douglas MD-83	49575/1414	ex EI-BWD	4WS	Wings of Pride	
☐	N951TW	McDonnell-Douglas MD-83	53470/2135	ex N978AS	4XA		
☐	N953U	McDonnell-Douglas MD-82	49267/1239		4UA		[ROW]
☐	N954U	McDonnell-Douglas MD-82	49426/1399	ex N786JA	4UB		
☐	N955U	McDonnell-Douglas MD-82	49427/1401	ex N787JA	4UC		
☐	N961TW	McDonnell-Douglas MD-83	53611/2264		4XT		
☐	N962TW	McDonnell-Douglas MD-83	53612/2265		4XU		
☐	N963TW	McDonnell-Douglas MD-83	53613/2266		4XV		
☐	N964TW	McDonnell-Douglas MD-83	53614/2267		4XW		
☐	N965TW	McDonnell-Douglas MD-83	53615/2268		4XX		
☐	N966TW	McDonnell-Douglas MD-83	53616/2269		4XY		
☐	N967TW	McDonnell-Douglas MD-83	53617/2270		4YA		
☐	N968TW	McDonnell-Douglas MD-83	53618/2271		4YB		
☐	N969TW	McDonnell-Douglas MD-83	53619/2272		4YC		
☐	N970TW	McDonnell-Douglas MD-83	53620/2273		4YD		[TUL]
☐	N971TW	McDonnell-Douglas MD-83	53621/2274		4YE		[TUL]
☐	N972TW	McDonnell-Douglas MD-83	53622/2275		4YF		
☐	N973TW	McDonnell-Douglas MD-83	53623/2276		4YG		
☐	N974TW	McDonnell-Douglas MD-83	53624/2277		4YH		
☐	N975TW	McDonnell-Douglas MD-83	53625/2278		4YJ		
☐	N976TW	McDonnell-Douglas MD-83	53626/2279		4YK		
☐	N978TW	McDonnell-Douglas MD-83	53628/2281		4YM		
☐	N979TW	McDonnell-Douglas MD-83	53629/2282		4YN		
☐	N980TW	McDonnell-Douglas MD-83	53630/2283		4YP		
☐	N982TW	McDonnell-Douglas MD-83	53632/2285		4YR		
☐	N983TW	McDonnell-Douglas MD-83	53633/2286		4YS		
☐	N984TW+	McDonnell-Douglas MD-83	53634/2287		4YT	Spirit of Long Beach	
☐	N3507A	McDonnell-Douglas MD-82	49801/1661		507		
☐	N3515	McDonnell-Douglas MD-82	49892/1695		515		
☐	N7506	McDonnell-Douglas MD-82	49800/1660		506		
☐	N7508	McDonnell-Douglas MD-82	49802/1662		508		
☐	N7509	McDonnell-Douglas MD-82	49803/1663		509		
☐	N7512A	McDonnell-Douglas MD-82	49806/1673		512		
☐	N7514A	McDonnell-Douglas MD-82	49891/1694		514		
☐	N7517A	McDonnell-Douglas MD-82	49894/1697		517		
☐	N7518A	McDonnell-Douglas MD-82	49895/1698		518		
☐	N7519A	McDonnell-Douglas MD-82	49896/1707		519		
☐	N7520A	McDonnell-Douglas MD-82	49897/1708		520		
☐	N7521A	McDonnell-Douglas MD-82	49898/1709		521		
☐	N7522A	McDonnell-Douglas MD-82	49899/1722		522		
☐	N7525A	McDonnell-Douglas MD-82	49917/1735		525		
☐	N7526A	McDonnell-Douglas MD-82	49918/1743		526		
☐	N7527A	McDonnell-Douglas MD-82	49919/1744		527		
☐	N7528A	McDonnell-Douglas MD-82	49920/1750		528		
☐	N7530	McDonnell-Douglas MD-82	49922/1753		530		
☐	N7531A	McDonnell-Douglas MD-82	49923/1758		531		
☐	N7532A	McDonnell-Douglas MD-82	49924/1759		532		
☐	N7533A	McDonnell-Douglas MD-82	49987/1760		533		
☐	N7534A	McDonnell-Douglas MD-82	49988/1768		534		
☐	N7535A	McDonnell-Douglas MD-82	49989/1769		535		
☐	N7536A	McDonnell-Douglas MD-82	49990/1770		536		
☐	N7537A	McDonnell-Douglas MD-82	49991/1780		537		
☐	N7538A	McDonnell-Douglas MD-82	49992/1781		538		
☐	N7539A	McDonnell-Douglas MD-82	49993/1782		539		
☐	N7540A	McDonnell-Douglas MD-82	49994/1790		540		
☐	N7541A	McDonnell-Douglas MD-82	49995/1791		541		
☐	N7542A	McDonnell-Douglas MD-82	49996/1792		542		
☐	N7543A	McDonnell-Douglas MD-82	53025/1802		543		
☐	N7544A	McDonnell-Douglas MD-82	53026/1804		544		
☐	N7546A	McDonnell-Douglas MD-82	53028/1813		546		

☐ N7547A	McDonnell-Douglas MD-82	53029/1814		547	
☐ N7548A	McDonnell-Douglas MD-82	53030/1816		548	
☐ N7549A	McDonnell-Douglas MD-82	53031/1819		549	
☐ N7550	McDonnell-Douglas MD-82	53032/1820		550	
☐ N9302B	McDonnell-Douglas MD-83	49528/1383		4WB	
☐ N9304C	McDonnell-Douglas MD-83	49530/1397		4WD	
☐ N9307R	McDonnell-Douglas MD-83	49663/1437	ex SE-DPH	4WG	[ROW]
☐ N9401W	McDonnell-Douglas MD-83	53137/1872	ex N9001L	4WJ	
☐ N9402W	McDonnell-Douglas MD-83	53138/1886	ex N9001D	4WK	
☐ N9403W	McDonnell-Douglas MD-83	53139/1899	ex N9035C	4WL	
☐ N9404V	McDonnell-Douglas MD-83	53140/1923	ex N9075H	4WM	
☐ N9405T	McDonnell-Douglas MD-83	53141/1935		4WN	
☐ N9406W	McDonnell-Douglas MD-83	53126/2026	ex N6203U	4WP	
☐ N9407R	McDonnell-Douglas MD-83	49400/1356	ex EI-CKB	4WR	
☐ N9409F	McDonnell-Douglas MD-83	53121/1971	ex N532MD	4WT	
☐ N9412W	McDonnell-Douglas MD-83	53187/2118		4WU	
☐ N9413T	McDonnell-Douglas MD-83	53188/2119		4WW	
☐ N9414W	McDonnell-Douglas MD-83	53189/2121		4WX	
☐ N9420D	McDonnell-Douglas MD-83	49824/1554	ex 9Y-THU	4WY	
☐ N9615W	McDonnell-Douglas MD-83	53562/2192		4XB	
☐ N9616G	McDonnell-Douglas MD-83	53563/2196		4XC	
☐ N9617R	McDonnell-Douglas MD-83	53564/2199		4XD	
☐ N9618A	McDonnell-Douglas MD-83	53565/2201		4XE	
☐ N9619V	McDonnell-Douglas MD-83	53566/2206		4XF	
☐ N9620D	McDonnell-Douglas MD-83	53591/2208		4XG	
☐ N9621A	McDonnell-Douglas MD-83	53592/2234		4XH	
☐ N9622A	McDonnell-Douglas MD-83	53593/2239		4XJ	
☐ N9624T	McDonnell-Douglas MD-83	53594/2241		4XK	
☐ N9625W	McDonnell-Douglas MD-83	53595/2244		4XL	
☐ N9626F	McDonnell-Douglas MD-83	53596//2247		4XM	
☐ N9627R	McDonnell-Douglas MD-83	53597/2249		4XN	
☐ N9628W	McDonnell-Douglas MD-83	53598/2252		4XP	
☐ N9629H	McDonnell-Douglas MD-83	53599/2254		4XR	
☐ N9630A	McDonnell-Douglas MD-83	53561/2174	ex N90126	4XS	
☐ N9677W	McDonnell-Douglas MD-83	53627/2280		4YL	
☐ N9681B	McDonnell-Douglas MD-83	53631/2284	ex (N981TW)	4XT	
☐ N14551	McDonnell-Douglas MD-82	53033/1822		551	
☐ N16545	McDonnell-Douglas MD-82	53027/1805		545	
☐ N33414	McDonnell-Douglas MD-82	49325/1290		414	
☐ N33502	McDonnell-Douglas MD-82	49739/1649		502	
☐ N44503	McDonnell-Douglas MD-82	49797/1650		503	
☐ N59523	McDonnell-Douglas MD-82	49915/1723		523	
☐ N70401	McDonnell-Douglas MD-82	49312/1249		401	
☐ N70425	McDonnell-Douglas MD-82	49337/1325		425	
☐ N70504	McDonnell-Douglas MD-82	49798/1651		504	
☐ N70524	McDonnell-Douglas MD-82	49916/1729		524	
☐ N70529	McDonnell-Douglas MD-82	49921/1752		529	
☐ N73444	McDonnell-Douglas MD-82	49470/1417		444 Working Together titles	
☐ N76200	McDonnell-Douglas MD-83	53290/2013		200	
☐ N76201	McDonnell-Douglas MD-83	53291/2019		201	
☐ N76202	McDonnell-Douglas MD-83	53292/2020		202	
☐ N77421	McDonnell-Douglas MD-82	49333/1311		421	
☐ N90511	McDonnell-Douglas MD-82	49805/1672		511	

AMERICAN CONNECTION   Waterski (AX/LOF)   Indianapolis, IN/St Louis-Lambert Intl, MO (IND/STL)

☐ N295SK	Embraer ERJ-140LR	145513	ex PT-SYF	Chautauqua
☐ N297SK	Embraer ERJ-140LR	145522	ex PT-SYN	Chautauqua
☐ N299SK	Embraer ERJ-140LR	145532	ex PT-STW	Chautauqua
☐ N371SK	Embraer ERJ-140LR	145535	ex PT-STZ	Chautauqua
☐ N372SK	Embraer ERJ-140LR	145538	ex PT-SZC	Chautauqua
☐ N373SK	Embraer ERJ-140LR	145543	ex PT-SZG	Chautauqua
☐ N374SK	Embraer ERJ-140LR	145544	ex PT-SZH	Chautauqua
☐ N375SK	Embraer ERJ-140LR	145569	ex PT-SBF	Chautauqua
☐ N376SK	Embraer ERJ-140LR	145578	ex PT-SBO	Chautauqua
☐ N377SK	Embraer ERJ-140LR	145579	ex PT-SBP	Chautauqua
☐ N378SK	Embraer ERJ-140LR	145593	ex PT-SCC	Chautauqua
☐ N379SK	Embraer ERJ-140LR	145606	ex PT-SCP	Chautauqua
☐ N380SK	Embraer ERJ-140LR	145613	ex PT-SCX	Chautauqua
☐ N381SK	Embraer ERJ-140LR	145619	ex PT-SDH	Chautauqua
☐ N382SK	Embraer ERJ-140LR	145624	ex PT-SDM	Chautauqua
☐ N811HK	Embraer ERJ-145ER	145256	ex PT-SIQ	Trans State

AMERICAN EAGLE		Eagle Flight (MQ/EGF)	Dallas-Fort Worth, TX (DFW)	
☐ N4AE	ATR 72-212	244	ex N244AT	
☐ N260AE	ATR 72-201	263	ex N263AT	
☐ N270AT	ATR 72-212	270	ex F-WWEL	
☐ N288AM	ATR 72-212	288	ex F-WWLP	
☐ N308AE	ATR 72-212	309	ex N309AM	
☐ N322AC	ATR 72-212	320	ex N320AT	
☐ N342AT	ATR 72-212	345	ex N345AT	
☐ N348AE	ATR 72-212	349	ex N349AT	
☐ N355AT	ATR 72-212	355	ex F-WWEQ	
☐ N369AT	ATR 72-212	369	ex F-WWEC	
☐ N377AT	ATR 72-212	377	ex F-WWLA	
☐ N399AT	ATR 72-212	399	ex F-WWLK	
☐ N407AT	ATR 72-212	407	ex F-WWEL	
☐ N408AT	ATR 72-212	408	ex F-WWEM	
☐ N410AT	ATR 72-212	410	ex F-WWLS	
☐ N414WF	ATR 72-212	414	ex F-WWLD	
☐ N417AT	ATR 72-212	417	ex F-WWIT	
☐ N420AT	ATR 72-212	420	ex F-WWLY	
☐ N425MJ	ATR 72-212	425	ex F-WWEC	
☐ N426AT	ATR 72-212	426	ex F-WWED	
☐ N429AT	ATR 72-212	429	ex F-WWEH	
☐ N431AT	ATR 72-212	431	ex F-WWEI	
☐ N434AT	ATR 72-212	434	ex F-WWEM	
☐ N440AM	ATR 72-212	440	ex F-WWEP	
☐ N447AM	ATR 72-212	447	ex F-WWEC	
☐ N448AM	ATR 72-212	448	ex F-WWED	
☐ N451AT	ATR 72-212	451	ex F-WWES	
☐ N494AE	ATR 72-212A	494	ex F-WWLS	
☐ N498AT	ATR 72-212A	498	ex F-WWLW	
☐ N499AT	ATR 72-212A	499	ex F-WWLY	
☐ N529AM	ATR 72-212A	529	ex F-WWLR	
☐ N533AT	ATR 72-212A	533	ex F-WWLO	
☐ N536AT	ATR 72-212A	536	ex F-WWLZ	
☐ N538AT	ATR 72-212A	538	ex F-WWEA	
☐ N540AM	ATR 72-212A	540	ex F-WWLJ	
☐ N541AT	ATR 72-212	541	ex F-WWLA	
☐ N545AT	ATR 72-212A	545	ex F-WWLE	
☐ N548AT	ATR 72-212A	548	ex F-WWLI	
☐ N550LL	ATR 72-212A	550	ex F-WWLK	
☐ N500AE	Canadair CRJ-701ER	10025	ex C-GJEX	
☐ N501BG	Canadair CRJ-701ER	10017	ex C-GIAH	
☐ N502AE	Canadair CRJ-701ER	10018	ex C-GJUI	
☐ N503AE	Canadair CRJ-701ER	10021	ex C-GIAP	
☐ N504AE	Canadair CRJ-701ER	10044	ex C-GHZZ	
☐ N505AE	Canadair CRJ-701ER	10053	ex C-GIAU	
☐ N506AE	Canadair CRJ-701ER	10056	ex C-GIAX	
☐ N507AE	Canadair CRJ-701ER	10059	ex C-GIBH	
☐ N508AE	Canadair CRJ-701ER	10072	ex C-GHZV	
☐ N509AE	Canadair CRJ-701ER	10078	ex C-GZUC	
☐ N510AE	Canadair CRJ-701ER	10105	ex C-	
☐ N511AE	Canadair CRJ-701ER	10107	ex C-	
☐ N512AE	Canadair CRJ-701ER	10110	ex C-	
☐ N513AE	Canadair CRJ-701ER	10114	ex C-	
☐ N514AE	Canadair CRJ-701ER	10119	ex C-	
☐ N515AE	Canadair CRJ-701ER	10121	ex C-	
☐ N516AE	Canadair CRJ-701ER	10123	ex C-	
☐ N517AE	Canadair CRJ-701ER	10124	ex C-	
☐ N518AE	Canadair CRJ-701ER	10126	ex C-	
☐ N519AE	Canadair CRJ-701ER	10131	ex C-	
☐ N520DC	Canadair CRJ-701ER	10140	ex C-	
☐ N521AE	Canadair CRJ-701ER	10142	ex C-	
☐ N522AE	Canadair CRJ-701ER	10147	ex C-	
☐ N523AE	Canadair CRJ-701ER	10152	ex C-	
☐ N524AE	Canadair CRJ-701ER	10154	ex C-	
☐ N525AE	Canadair CRJ-702ER NG	10302	ex C-	♦
☐ N526EA	Canadair CRJ-702ER NG	10304	ex C-	♦
☐ N527EA	Canadair CRJ-702ER NG	10305	ex C-	♦
☐ N528EG	Canadair CRJ-702ER NG	10306	ex C-	♦
☐ N529EA	Canadair CRJ-702ER NG	10307	ex C-	♦
☐ N530EA	Canadair CRJ-702ER NG	10308	ex C-	♦
☐ N531EG	Canadair CRJ-702ER NG	10309	ex C-	♦
☐ N532EA	Canadair CRJ-702ER NG	10310	ex C-	♦
☐ N533AE	Canadair CRJ-702ER NG	10311	ex C-	♦
☐ N534AE	Canadair CRJ-702ER NG	10312	ex C-	♦

☐ N535EA	Canadair CRJ-702ER NG	10313	ex C-			♦
☐ N536EA	Canadair CRJ-702ER NG	10315	ex C-			♦
☐ N537EA	Canadair CRJ-702ER NG	10316	ex C-GIAP			♦
☐ N538EG	Canadair CRJ-702ER NG	10317	ex C-			♦
☐ N539EA	Canadair CRJ-702ER NG	10318	ex C-			♦
☐ N540EG	Canadair CRJ-702ER NG	10319	ex C-			♦
☐ N	Canadair CRJ-702ER NG					o/o♦
☐ N	Canadair CRJ-702ER NG					o/o♦
☐ N	Canadair CRJ-702ER NG					o/o♦
☐ N	Canadair CRJ-702ER NG					o/o♦
☐ N	Canadair CRJ-702ER NG					o/o♦
☐ N	Canadair CRJ-702ER NG					o/o♦
☐ N700LE	Embraer ERJ-135LR	145156	ex PT-SFC			
☐ N701MH	Embraer ERJ-135LR	145162	ex PT-SFD			
☐ N702AE	Embraer ERJ-135LR	145164	ex PT-SFE			[IGM]
☐ N703MR	Embraer ERJ-135LR	145173	ex PT-SFG			[IGM]
☐ N704PG	Embraer ERJ-135LR	145174	ex PT-SFH			[IGM]
☐ N705AE	Embraer ERJ-135LR	145184	ex PT-SFJ			[IGM]
☐ N706RG	Embraer ERJ-135LR	145194	ex PT-SFO			[IGM]
☐ N707EB	Embraer ERJ-135LR	145195	ex PT-SFP			[CMI]
☐ N708AE	Embraer ERJ-135LR	145205	ex PT-SFR			
☐ N709GB	Embraer ERJ-135LR	145211	ex PT-SFV			[IGM]
☐ N710TB	Embraer ERJ-135LR	145224	ex PT-SFZ			[IGM]
☐ N711PH	Embraer ERJ-135LR	145235	ex PT-SJC			
☐ N712AE	Embraer ERJ-135LR	145247	ex PT-SJG			
☐ N713AE	Embraer ERJ-135LR	145249	ex PT-SJH			
☐ N715AE	Embraer ERJ-135LR	145262	ex PT-SIV			[IGM]
☐ N716AE	Embraer ERJ-135LR	145264	ex PT-SIW			
☐ N717AE	Embraer ERJ-135LR	145272	ex PT-SJO			
☐ N718AE	Embraer ERJ-135LR	145275	ex PT-SJR			[IGM]
☐ N719AE	Embraer ERJ-135LR	145276	ex PT-SJS			
☐ N720AE	Embraer ERJ-135LR	145279	ex PT-SJV			
☐ N721HS	Embraer ERJ-135LR	145283	ex PT-S JZ			
☐ N722AE	Embraer ERJ-135LR	145287	ex PT-SKE			
☐ N723AE	Embraer ERJ-135LR	145288	ex PT-SKF			
☐ N724AE	Embraer ERJ-135LR	145301	ex PT-SKS			
☐ N725AE	Embraer ERJ-135LR	145312	ex PT-SMD			
☐ N726AE	Embraer ERJ-135LR	145314	ex PT-SMF			[IGM]
☐ N727AE	Embraer ERJ-135LR	145326	ex PT-SMS			[IGM]
☐ N728AE	Embraer ERJ-135LR	145328	ex PT-SMU			
☐ N729AE	Embraer ERJ-135LR	145343	ex PT-SNJ			[IGM]
☐ N730KW	Embraer ERJ-135LR	145346	ex PT-SNM			
☐ N731BE	Embraer ERJ-135LR	145356	ex PT-SNV			[IGM]
☐ N732DH	Embraer ERJ-135LR	145358	ex PT-SNX			[ABI]
☐ N733KR	Embraer ERJ-135LR	145368	ex PT-SOT			
☐ N734EK	Embraer ERJ-135LR	145371	ex PT-SOW			
☐ N735TS	Embraer ERJ-135LR	145386	ex PT-SQK			
☐ N736DT	Embraer ERJ-135LR	145388	ex PT-SQM			
☐ N737MW	Embraer ERJ-135LR	145396	ex PT-SQT			
☐ N738NR	Embraer ERJ-135LR	145401	ex PT-SQY			
☐ N739AE	Embraer ERJ-135LR	145402	ex PT-SQZ			
☐ N800AE	Embraer ERJ-140LR	145425	ex PT-XGF			
☐ N801AE	Embraer ERJ-140LR	145469	ex PT-SVO			
☐ N802AE	Embraer ERJ-140LR	145471	ex PT-SVQ			
☐ N803AE	Embraer ERJ-140LR	145483	ex PT-SXC	100th RJ Spirit of Eagle titles		
☐ N804AE	Embraer ERJ-140LR	145487	ex PT-SXG			
☐ N805AE	Embraer ERJ-140LR	145489	ex PT-SXI			
☐ N806AE	Embraer ERJ-140LR	145503	ex PT-SXW			
☐ N807AE	Embraer ERJ-140LR	145506	ex PT-SXZ	Make A Wish colours		
☐ N808AE	Embraer ERJ-140LR	145519	ex PT-SYK			
☐ N809AE	Embraer ERJ-140LR	145521	ex PT-SYM			
☐ N810AE	Embraer ERJ-140LR	145525	ex PT-SYQ			
☐ N811AE	Embraer ERJ-140LR	145529	ex PT-STT			
☐ N812AE	Embraer ERJ-140LR	145531	ex PT-STV			
☐ N813AE	Embraer ERJ-140LR	145539	ex PT-SZD			
☐ N814AE	Embraer ERJ-140LR	145541	ex PT-SZF			
☐ N815AE	Embraer ERJ-140LR	145545	ex PT-SZI			
☐ N816AE	Embraer ERJ-140LR	145552	ex PT-SZO			
☐ N817AE	Embraer ERJ-140LR	145554	ex PT-SZQ			
☐ N818AE	Embraer ERJ-140LR	145561	ex PT-SZW			
☐ N819AE	Embraer ERJ-140LR	145566	ex PT-SBC			
☐ N820AE	Embraer ERJ-140LR	145576	ex PT-SBM			
☐ N821AE	Embraer ERJ-140LR	145577	ex PT-SBN			
☐ N822AE	Embraer ERJ-140LR	145581	ex PT-SBS			
☐ N823AE	Embraer ERJ-140LR	145582	ex PT-SBT			

☐ N824AE	Embraer ERJ-140LR	145584	ex PT-SBV
☐ N825AE	Embraer ERJ-140LR	145589	ex PT-SBZ
☐ N826AE	Embraer ERJ-140LR	145592	ex PT-SCA
☐ N827AE	Embraer ERJ-140LR	145602	ex PT-SCL
☐ N828AE	Embraer ERJ-140LR	145604	ex PT-SCN
☐ N829AE	Embraer ERJ-140LR	145609	ex PT-SCS
☐ N830AE	Embraer ERJ-140LR	145615	ex PT-SDD
☐ N831AE	Embraer ERJ-140LR	145616	ex PT-SDE
☐ N832AE	Embraer ERJ-140LR	145627	ex PT-SDP
☐ N833AE	Embraer ERJ-140LR	145629	ex PT-SDR
☐ N834AE	Embraer ERJ-140LR	145631	ex PT-SDT
☐ N835AE	Embraer ERJ-140LR	145634	ex PT-SDW
☐ N836AE	Embraer ERJ-140LR	145635	ex PT-SDX
☐ N837AE	Embraer ERJ-140LR	145647	ex PT-SEH
☐ N838AE	Embraer ERJ-140LR	145651	ex PT-SEL
☐ N839AE	Embraer ERJ-140LR	145653	ex PT-SEN
☐ N840AE	Embraer ERJ-140LR	145656	ex PT-SEQ
☐ N841AE	Embraer ERJ-140LR	145667	ex PT-SFB
☐ N842AE	Embraer ERJ-140LR	145673	ex PT-SFG
☐ N843AE	Embraer ERJ-140LR	145680	ex PT-SFM
☐ N844AE	Embraer ERJ-140LR	145682	ex PT-SFO
☐ N845AE	Embraer ERJ-140LR	145685	ex PT-SFR
☐ N846AE	Embraer ERJ-140LR	145692	ex PT-SFY
☐ N847AE	Embraer ERJ-140LR	145707	ex PT-SGK
☐ N848AE	Embraer ERJ-140LR	145710	ex PT-SGO
☐ N849AE	Embraer ERJ-140LR	145716	ex PT-SGT
☐ N850AE	Embraer ERJ-140LR	145722	ex PT-SGY
☐ N851AE	Embraer ERJ-140LR	145734	ex PT-SHK
☐ N852AE	Embraer ERJ-140LR	145736	ex PT-SHM
☐ N853AE	Embraer ERJ-140LR	145742	ex PT-SJB
☐ N854AE	Embraer ERJ-140LR	145743	ex PT-SJC
☐ N855AE	Embraer ERJ-140LR	145747	ex PT-SJG
☐ N856AE	Embraer ERJ-140LR	145748	ex PT-SJH
☐ N857AE	Embraer ERJ-140LR	145752	ex PT-SJL
☐ N858AE	Embraer ERJ-140LR	145754	ex PT-SJN
☐ N600BP	Embraer ERJ-145LR	145044	ex N813HK
☐ N601DW	Embraer ERJ-145LR	145046	ex N814HK
☐ N602AE	Embraer ERJ-145LR	145048	ex N815HK [IGM]
☐ N603KC	Embraer ERJ-145LR	145055	ex N816HK
☐ N604AE	Embraer ERJ-145LR	145058	ex N604DG
☐ N605KS	Embraer ERJ-145LR	145059	ex N818HK
☐ N606AE	Embraer ERJ-145LR	145062	ex N819HK
☐ N607AE	Embraer ERJ-145LR	145064	ex N820HK
☐ N608LM	Embraer ERJ-145LR	145068	ex N821HK
☐ N609DP	Embraer ERJ-145LR	145069	ex N822HK
☐ N610AE	Embraer ERJ-145LR	145073	ex PT-SAR
☐ N611AE	Embraer ERJ-145LR	145074	ex PT-SAS
☐ N612AE	Embraer ERJ-145LR	145079	ex PT-SAX
☐ N613AE	Embraer ERJ-145LR	145081	ex PT-S
☐ N614AE	Embraer ERJ-145LR	145086	ex PT-S
☐ N615AE	Embraer ERJ-145LR	145087	ex PT-S
☐ N616AE	Embraer ERJ-145LR	145092	ex PT-S
☐ N617AE	Embraer ERJ-145LR	145093	ex PT-SBP
☐ N618AE	Embraer ERJ-145LR	145097	ex PT-SBT
☐ N619AE	Embraer ERJ-145LR	145101	ex PT-S
☐ N620AE	Embraer ERJ-145LR	145102	ex PT-S
☐ N621AE	Embraer ERJ-145LR	145105	ex PT-S
☐ N622AE	Embraer ERJ-145LR	145108	ex PT-S
☐ N623AE	Embraer ERJ-145LR	145109	ex PT-S
☐ N624AE	Embraer ERJ-145LR	145111	ex PT-S
☐ N625AE	Embraer ERJ-145LR	145115	ex PT-SCR
☐ N626AE	Embraer ERJ-145LR	145117	ex PT-SCT
☐ N627AE	Embraer ERJ-145LR	145121	ex PT-SCX
☐ N628AE	Embraer ERJ-145LR	145124	ex PT-SDA
☐ N629AE	Embraer ERJ-145LR	145130	ex PT-SDH
☐ N630AE	Embraer ERJ-145LR	145132	ex PT-SDJ
☐ N631AE	Embraer ERJ-145LR	145139	ex PT-SDQ
☐ N632AE	Embraer ERJ-145LR	145143	ex PT-SDT
☐ N633AE	Embraer ERJ-145LR	145148	ex PT-SDY
☐ N634AE	Embraer ERJ-145LR	145150	ex PT-SEB
☐ N635AE	Embraer ERJ-145LR	145158	ex PT-S
☐ N636AE	Embraer ERJ-145LR	145160	ex PT-S
☐ N637AE	Embraer ERJ-145LR	145170	ex PT-S
☐ N638AE	Embraer ERJ-145LR	145172	ex PT-S
☐ N639AE	Embraer ERJ-145LR	145182	ex PT-SGE
☐ N640AE	Embraer ERJ-145LR	145183	ex PT-SGF

☐	N641AE	Embraer ERJ-145LR	145191	ex PT-SGJ	
☐	N642AE	Embraer ERJ-145LR	145193	ex PT-SGK	
☐	N643AE	Embraer ERJ-145LR	145200	ex PT-S	200th titles
☐	N644AE	Embraer ERJ-145LR	145204	ex PT-SGW	
☐	N645AE	Embraer ERJ-145LR	145212	ex PT-SGZ	
☐	N646AE	Embraer ERJ-145LR	145213	ex PT-SHA	
☐	N647AE	Embraer ERJ-145LR	145222	ex PT-SHH	
☐	N648AE	Embraer ERJ-145LR	145225	ex PT-SHJ	
☐	N649PP	Embraer ERJ-145LR	145234	ex PT-SIB	
☐	N650AE	Embraer ERJ-145LR	145417	ex PT-STO	
☐	N651AE	Embraer ERJ-145LR	145422	ex PT-STT	
☐	N652RS	Embraer ERJ-145LR	145432	ex PT-SUD	
☐	N653AE	Embraer ERJ-145LR	145433	ex PT-SUE	
☐	N654AE	Embraer ERJ-145LR	145437	ex PT-SUI	
☐	N655AE	Embraer ERJ-145LR	145452	ex PT-SUX	
☐	N656AE	Embraer ERJ-145LR	145740	ex PT-SHV	
☐	N657AE	Embraer ERJ-145LR	145744	ex PT-SJD	
☐	N658AE	Embraer ERJ-145LR	145760	ex PT-SJO	
☐	N659AE	Embraer ERJ-145LR	145762	ex PT-SJT	
☐	N660CL	Embraer ERJ-145LR	145764	ex PT-SJV	
☐	N661JA	Embraer ERJ-145LR	145766	ex PT-SJX	
☐	N662EH	Embraer ERJ-145LR	145777	ex PT-SMG	
☐	N663AR	Embraer ERJ-145LR	145778	ex PT-SMH	
☐	N664MS	Embraer ERJ-145LR	145779	ex PT-SMI	
☐	N665BC	Embraer ERJ-145LR	145783	ex PT-SMK	
☐	N667GB	Embraer ERJ-145LR	145784	ex PT-SML	
☐	N668HH	Embraer ERJ-145LR	145785	ex PT-SMM	
☐	N669MB	Embraer ERJ-145LR	145788	ex PT-SMQ	
☐	N670AE	Embraer ERJ-145LR	145790	ex PT-SMR	
☐	N671AE	Embraer ERJ-145LR	145793	ex PT-SMU	
☐	N672AE	Embraer ERJ-145LR	145794	ex PT-SMV	
☐	N673AE	Embraer ERJ-145LR	145797	ex PT-SMX	
☐	N674RJ	Embraer ERJ-145LR	14500801	ex PT-SNF	
☐	N675AE	Embraer ERJ-145LR	14500806	ex PT-SNI	
☐	N676AE	Embraer ERJ-145LR	14500807	ex PT-SNJ	
☐	N677AE	Embraer ERJ-145LR	14500810	ex PT-SNL	
☐	N678AE	Embraer ERJ-145LR	14500813	ex PT-SNP	
☐	N679AE	Embraer ERJ-145LR	14500814	ex PT-SNQ	
☐	N680AE	Embraer ERJ-145LR	14500820	ex PT-SNU	
☐	N681AE	Embraer ERJ-145LR	14500824	ex PT-SNX	
☐	N682AE	Embraer ERJ-145LR	14500826	ex PT-SNY	
☐	N683AE	Embraer ERJ-145LR	14500833	ex PT-SQF	
☐	N684JW	Embraer ERJ-145LR	14500835	ex PT-SQH	
☐	N685AE	Embraer ERJ-145LR	14500836	ex PT-SQI	
☐	N686AE	Embraer ERJ-145LR	14500843	ex PT-SQN	
☐	N687JS	Embraer ERJ-145LR	14500846	ex PT-SQQ	
☐	N688AE	Embraer ERJ-145LR	14500849	ex PT-SQS	
☐	N689EC	Embraer ERJ-145LR	14500853	ex PT-SQV	
☐	N690AE	Embraer ERJ-145LR	14500858	ex PT-SXM	
☐	N691AE	Embraer ERJ-145LR	14500860	ex PT-SXA	
☐	N692AE	Embraer ERJ-145LR	14500866	ex PT-SXF	
☐	N693AE	Embraer ERJ-145LR	14500868	ex PT-SXG	
☐	N694AE	Embraer ERJ-145LR	14500869	ex PT-SXN	
☐	N695AE	Embraer ERJ-145LR	14500870	ex PT-SXH	
☐	N696AE	Embraer ERJ-145LR	14500874	ex PT-SXO	
☐	N697AB	Embraer ERJ-145LR	14500875	ex PT-SXQ	
☐	N698CB	Embraer ERJ-145LR	14500877	ex PT-SXS	
☐	N699AE	Embraer ERJ-145LR	14500883	ex PT-SXW	
☐	N900AE	Embraer ERJ-145LR	14500885	ex PT-SXX	
☐	N902BC	Embraer ERJ-145LR	14500887	ex PT-SXZ	
☐	N905JH	Embraer ERJ-145LR	14500892	ex PT-SYE	
☐	N906AE	Embraer ERJ-145LR	14500894	ex PT-SYG	
☐	N907AE	Embraer ERJ-145LR	14500895	ex PT-SYH	
☐	N908AE	Embraer ERJ-145LR	14500897	ex PT-SYJ	
☐	N909AE	Embraer ERJ-145LR	14500899	ex PT-SYK	
☐	N918AE	Embraer ERJ-145LR	14500902	ex PT-SYM	
☐	N922AE	Embraer ERJ-145LR	14500906	ex PT-SYO	
☐	N923AE	Embraer ERJ-145LR	14500907	ex PT-SYQ	
☐	N925AE	Embraer ERJ-145LR	14500908	ex PT-SYR	
☐	N928AE	Embraer ERJ-145LR	14500911	ex PT-SYT	
☐	N931AE	Embraer ERJ-145LR	14500912	ex PT-SYU	
☐	N932AE	Embraer ERJ-145LR	14500915	ex PT-SYW	
☐	N933JN	Embraer ERJ-145LR	14500918	ex PT-SYY	
☐	N935AE	Embraer ERJ-145LR	14500920	ex PT-SYZ	
☐	N939AE	Embraer ERJ-145LR	14500923	ex PT-SOU	
☐	N941LT	Embraer ERJ-145LR	14500926	ex PT-SOW	
☐	N942LL	Embraer ERJ-145LR	14500930	ex PT-SOZ	

AMERIFLIGHT		Ameriflight (AMF)	Burbank Glendale-Pasadena, CA (BUR)
☐ N20FW	Beech 99A	U-111	
☐ N21FW	Beech 99A	U-117	
☐ N34AK	Beech 99A	U-105	ex N4099A
☐ N51RP	Beech C99	U-212	
☐ N52RP	Beech C99	U-210	ex N66305
☐ N53RP	Beech C99	U-195	ex N64997
☐ N55RP	Beech C99	U-198	ex N64002
☐ N68TA	Beech C99	U-177	ex N177EE
☐ N96AV	Beech C99	U-201	
☐ N102GP	Beech C99	U-208	ex N6628K
☐ N104BE	Beech C99	U-221	ex N7203L
☐ N106SX	Beech C99	U-166	
☐ N107SX	Beech C99	U-176	
☐ N108SX	Beech C99	U-184	ex N6787P
☐ N130GP	Beech C99	U-222	ex N818FL
☐ N131GP	Beech C99	U-225	ex J6-AAF
☐ N134PM	Beech B99	U-34	ex N852SA
☐ N164HA	Beech B99	U-60	ex N72TC
☐ N174AV	Beech C99	U-174	ex N99CJ
☐ N191AV	Beech C99	U-191	ex VR-CIB
☐ N193SU	Beech C99	U-193	ex C-GFAT
☐ N199AF	Beech B99	U-161	ex N12AK
☐ N204AF	Beech C99	U-204	ex N575W
☐ N213AV	Beech C99	U-213	ex N6656N
☐ N221BH	Beech C99	U-168	ex N18AK
☐ N223BH	Beech C99	U-173	ex N6460D
☐ N225BH	Beech C99	U-181	ex N62936
☐ N226BH	Beech C99	U-182	ex N6263D
☐ N228BH	Beech C99	U-229	ex N3067L
☐ N235AV	Beech C99	U-235	ex N235BH
☐ N261SW	Beech C99	U-202	
☐ N802BA	Beech 99	U-29	ex N800BE
☐ N805BA	Beech 99A	U-147	ex N803BE
☐ N949K	Beech 99A	U-36	
☐ N990AF	Beech C99	U-211	ex N113GP
☐ N991AF	Beech C99	U-214	ex N112GP
☐ N992AF	Beech C99	U-203	ex N541JC
☐ N997SB	Beech C99	U-192	ex N6534A
☐ N1924T	Beech 99A	U-115	ex N24AT
☐ N4199C	Beech C99	U-50	ex N7940
☐ N4299A	Beech B99	U-146	
☐ N6199D	Beech C99	U-169	
☐ N6724D	Beech C99	U-215	
☐ N7200Z	Beech C99	U-219	
☐ N7209W	Beech C99	U-224	
☐ N7862R	Beech 99A	U-85	
☐ N8226Z	Beech C99	U-190	ex 6Y-JVB
☐ N8227P	Beech C99	U-194	ex 6Y-JVA
☐ N62989	Beech C99	U-183	
☐ N63978	Beech C99	U-171	
☐ N81820	Beech C99	U-232	ex N232BH
☐ N19RZ	Beech 1900C-1	UC-75	ex JA190C
☐ N21RZ	Beech 1900C-1	UC-106	ex JA190B
☐ N26RZ	Beech 1900C-1	UC-134	ex JA190D
☐ N34RZ	Beech 1900C-1	UC-151	ex JA190A
☐ N49UC	Beech 1900C-1	UC-49	ex C-GCMJ
☐ N111YV	Beech 1900C-1	UC-111	ex F-GPYX
☐ N112YV	Beech 1900C-1	UC-112	ex VH-AFR
☐ N330AF	Beech 1900C	UB-38	ex N805BE
☐ N331AF	Beech 1900C	UB-44	ex N807BE
☐ N1568G	Beech 1900C-1	UC-58	ex F-GNAD
☐ N2049K	Beech 1900C-1	UC-164	ex J6-AAJ
☐ N3052K	Beech 1900C	UB-70	
☐ N3071A	Beech 1900C	UB-46	ex N10RA
☐ N3229A	Beech 1900C	UB-51	
☐ N7203C	Beech 1900C	UB-28	
☐ N31701	Beech 1900C	UB-2	ex N121CZ
☐ N31702	Beech 1900C	UB-3	ex N122CZ
☐ N31703	Beech 1900C	UB-10	ex N123CZ
☐ N31704	Beech 1900C	UB-12	ex N124CZ
☐ N31705	Beech 1900C	UB-60	
☐ N179CA	Embraer EMB.120ER Brasilia	120179	ex PT-SQR

☐ N189CA	Embraer EMB.120ER Brasilia	120189	ex PT-SRC
☐ N201YW	Embraer EMB.120RT Brasilia	120201	ex N142EB
☐ N246AS	Embraer EMB.120ER Brasilia	120100	ex PP-SMS
☐ N247CA	Embraer EMB.120ER Brasilia	120225	ex PT-SSU
☐ N257AS	Embraer EMB.120ER Brasilia	120126	ex PT-SNS
☐ N258AS	Embraer EMB.120ER Brasilia	120131	ex PT-SNX
☐ N94AF	Learjet 35A	35A-094	ex (N35PF)
☐ N128CA	Learjet 35A	35A-248	ex C-GBFA
☐ N237AF	Learjet 35A	35A-262	ex N237GA
☐ N535AF	Learjet 35A	35A-191	ex N35SE
☐ N754WS	Learjet 35A	35A-197	ex N754GL
☐ N199DS	Piper PA-31 Turbo Navajo B	31-7400980	ex N7588L
☐ N500CF	Piper PA-31 Turbo Navajo	31-425	ex N6467L
☐ N6480L	Piper PA-31 Turbo Navajo	31-443	
☐ N6733L	Piper PA-31 Turbo Navajo	31-636	
☐ N6759L	Piper PA-31 Turbo Navajo	31-661	ex N479SJ
☐ N7434L	Piper PA-31 Turbo Navajo B	31-822	
☐ N7441L	Piper PA-31 Turbo Navajo B	31-844	
☐ N9132Y	Piper PA-31 Turbo Navajo	31-178	
☐ N27275	Piper PA-31 Navajo C	31-7712066	
☐ N3BT	Piper PA-31-350 Navajo Chieftain	31-7752172	ex N27422
☐ N29UM	Piper PA-31-350 Navajo Chieftain	31-7652127	ex N29JM
☐ N555RG	Piper PA-31-350 Navajo Chieftain	31-7305103	ex N555RC
☐ N600TS	Piper PA-31-350 Navajo Chieftain	31-7305047	ex N537N
☐ N777MP	Piper PA-31-350 Navajo Chieftain	31-7552072	ex N59983
☐ N961CA	Piper PA-31-350 Navajo Chieftain	31-7652014	ex N961PS
☐ N3525G	Piper PA-31-350 Chieftain	31-7952123	
☐ N3527D	Piper PA-31-350 Chieftain	31-7952137	
☐ N3540N	Piper PA-31-350 Chieftain	31-7952214	
☐ N3548B	Piper PA-31-350 Chieftain	31-8052025	
☐ N3553F	Piper PA-31-350 Chieftain	31-8052044	
☐ N3555D	Piper PA-31-350 Chieftain	31-8052059	
☐ N4044P	Piper PA-31-350 Chieftain	31-8152004	
☐ N4078B	Piper PA-31-350 Chieftain	31-8152055	
☐ N4087J	Piper PA-31-350 Chieftain	31-8152128	
☐ N4098A	Piper PA-31-350 Chieftain	31-8152200	
☐ N4502Y	Piper PA-31-350 Chieftain	31-8052189	
☐ N27426	Piper PA-31-350 Navajo Chieftain	31-7752175	
☐ N27579	Piper PA-31-350 Chieftain	31-7852063	
☐ N27677	Piper PA-31-350 Chieftain	31-7852101	
☐ N35336	Piper PA-31-350 Chieftain	31-7952189	
☐ N35805	Piper PA-31-350 Chieftain	31-8052090	
☐ N42076	Piper PA-31-350 Navajo Chieftain	31-7405209	ex G-OSPT
☐ N42079	Piper PA-31-350 Navajo Chieftain	31-7405488	ex G-BCOD
☐ N45004	Piper PA-31-350 Chieftain	31-8052163	
☐ N45014	Piper PA-31-350 Chieftain	31-8052171	
☐ N59820	Piper PA-31-350 Navajo Chieftain	31-7652073	
☐ N59973	Piper PA-31-350 Navajo Chieftain	31-7552079	
☐ N62858	Piper PA-31-350 Navajo Chieftain	31-7652115	
☐ N62959	Piper PA-31-350 Navajo Chieftain	31-7752008	
☐ N66859	Piper PA-31-350 Navajo Chieftain	31-7405168	
☐ N123KC	Piper PA-32R-300 Lance	32R-7680431	
☐ N188SP	Piper PA-32R-300 Lance	32R-7780309	
☐ N1333H	Piper PA-32R-300 Lance	32R-7780154	
☐ N5363F	Piper PA-32R-300 Lance	32R-7680510	
☐ N7838C	Piper PA-32R-300 Lance	32R-7680064	
☐ N8456F	Piper PA-32R-300 Lance	32R-7780100	
☐ N9226K	Piper PA-32R-300 Lance	32R-7680199	
☐ N75195	Piper PA-32R-300 Lance	32R-7680277	
☐ N75397	Piper PA-32R-300 Lance	32R-7680301	
☐ N152AF	Swearingen SA.227AC Metro III	AC-520	ex TG-DHL
☐ N155AF	Swearingen SA.227AC Metro III	AC-455	ex N356AE
☐ N191AF	Swearingen SA.227AC Metro III	AC-491	ex N209CA
☐ N240DH	Swearingen SA.227AT Expediter	AT-602B	ex N3117P
☐ N241DH	Swearingen SA.227AT Expediter	AT-607B	ex N3118A
☐ N242DH	Swearingen SA.227AT Expediter	AT-608B	ex N3118G
☐ N243DH	Swearingen SA.227AT Expediter	AT-609B	ex N3118H
☐ N244DH	Swearingen SA.227AT Expediter	AT-618B	
☐ N245DH	Swearingen SA.227AT Expediter	AT-624B	
☐ N246DH	Swearingen SA.227AT Expediter	AT-625B	
☐ N247DH	Swearingen SA.227AT Expediter	AT-626B	
☐ N248DH	Swearingen SA.227AT Expediter	AT-630B	
☐ N249DH	Swearingen SA.227AT Expediter	AT-631B	

☐ N360AE	Swearingen SA.227AC Metro III	AC-675	
☐ N362AE	Swearingen SA.227AC Metro III	AC-677B	
☐ N377PH	Swearingen SA.227AC Metro III	AC-574	ex (D-CABG)
☐ N421MA	Swearingen SA.227AC Metro III	AC-634	ex N3119Q
☐ N422MA	Swearingen SA.227AC Metro III	AC-635	ex N3119T
☐ N423MA	Swearingen SA.227AC Metro III	AC-636	ex N26823
☐ N424MA	Swearingen SA.227AC Metro III	AC-639	
☐ N426MA	Swearingen SA.227AC Metro III	AC-645	
☐ N428MA	Swearingen SA.227AC Metro III	AC-646	
☐ N443AF	Swearingen SA.227AC Metro III	AC-443	ex N443NE
☐ N473AF	Swearingen SA.227AC Metro III	AC-473	ex N473NE
☐ N475AF	Swearingen SA.227AC Metro III	AC-475	ex N475NE
☐ N476AF	Swearingen SA.227AC Metro III	AC-476	ex N476NE
☐ N488AF	Swearingen SA.227AC Metro III	AC-488	ex N488NE
☐ N529AF	Swearingen SA.227AC Metro III	AC-752	ex XA-TML
☐ N544UP	Swearingen SA.227AT Expediter	AT-544	ex N68TA
☐ N548UP	Swearingen SA.227AT Expediter	AT-548	ex N548SA
☐ N556UP	Swearingen SA.227AT Expediter	AT-556	ex N3113B
☐ N560UP	Swearingen SA.227AT Expediter	AT-560	ex N3113A
☐ N561UP	Swearingen SA.227AT Expediter	AT-561	ex N3113F
☐ N566UP	Swearingen SA.227AT Expediter	AT-566	ex N3113N
☐ N569UP	Swearingen SA.227AT Expediter	AT-569	ex N31134
☐ N573G	Swearingen SA.227AT Merlin IVC	AT-446B	ex N3008L
☐ N578AF	Swearingen SA.227AC Metro III	AC-578	ex C-FJLE
☐ N671AV	Swearingen SA.227AC Metro III	AC-671	
☐ N672AV	Swearingen SA.227AC Metro III	AC-672	
☐ N673AV	Swearingen SA.227AC Metro III	AC-673	
☐ N698AF	Swearingen SA.227AC Metro III	AC-698	ex N698FA
☐ N801AF	Swearingen SA.227AC Metro III	AC-701	ex C-GWXZ
☐ N807M	Swearingen SA.227AT Merlin IVC	AT-454B	ex N3013T
☐ N838AF	Swearingen SA.227AC Metro III	AC-738	ex C-GWXX
☐ N200AF	Beech 200 Super King Air	BB-102	ex N997MA

AMERIJET INTERNATIONAL — Amerijet (M6/AJT) — Fort Lauderdale-Hollywood Intl, FL (FLL)

☐ N199AJ	Boeing 727-2F9F/W (Duganair 3)	21426/1285	ex N83428	
☐ N395AJ	Boeing 727-233F/W (Duganair 3)	21100/1148	ex N727SN	
☐ N495AJ	Boeing 727-233F/W (Duganair 3)	20937/1103	ex C-GAAD	
☐ N598AJ	Boeing 727-212F/W (Duganair 3)	21947/1506	ex N86430	
☐ N794AJ	Boeing 727-227F/W (Duganair 3)	21243/1197	ex N567PE	Nogravity.com 'G-Force-One'
☐ N804AJ	Boeing 727-2D3F/W (Super 27)	21021/1082	ex N8883Z	[GYR]
☐ N909PG	Boeing 727-2K5F (FedEx 3)	21852/1553	ex XA-SXL	
☐ N994AJ	Boeing 727-233F/W (Duganair 3)	20942/1130	ex N727JH	

AMERISTAR JET CHARTER — Ameristar (AJI) — Dallas-Addison, TX (ADS)

☐ N148TW	AMD Falcon 20C	148	ex N148WC
☐ N158TW	AMD Falcon 20C	158	ex N450MA
☐ N204TW	AMD Falcon 20DC	204	ex EC-EGM
☐ N221TW	AMD Falcon 20DC	221	ex EC-EIV
☐ N223TW	AMD Falcon 20C	123	ex N45MR
☐ N232TW	AMD Falcon 20C	32	ex F-GIVT
☐ N236TW	AMD Falcon 20D	236	ex N936NW
☐ N240TW	AMD Falcon 20C	40	ex C-GSKQ
☐ N285TW	AMD Falcon 20EF	285	ex N285AP
☐ N295TW	AMD Falcon 20C	5	ex F-GJPR
☐ N314TW	AMD Falcon 20E	314	ex F-GDLU
☐ N699TW	AMD Falcon 20DC	50	ex EC-EDO
☐ N977TW	AMD Falcon 20C	13	ex F-BTCY
☐ N147TW	Learjet 25	25-023	ex N767SC
☐ N157TW	Learjet 24	24-157	ex N659AT
☐ N222TW	Learjet 24	24-161	ex N24KF
☐ N233TW	Learjet 24B	24B-221	ex N59JG
☐ N237TW	Learjet 24D	24D-237	ex N825DM
☐ N265TW	Learjet 25D	25D-265	ex N69GF
☐ N266TW	Learjet 24D	24D-266	ex N266BS
☐ N277TW	Learjet 24D	24D-277	ex N57BC
☐ N299TW	Learjet 24D	24D-299	ex XB-GJS
☐ N324TW	Learjet 24D	24D-324	ex XA-SCY
☐ N330TW	Learjet 24E	24E-330	ex N511AT
☐ N333TW	Learjet 24	24-168	ex N155BT
☐ N525TW	Learjet 25	25-011	ex N108GA
☐ N888TW	Learjet 24D	24D-292	ex N800PC
☐ N176TW	Beech 65-E90 King Air	LW-76	ex ZS-LJF

☐ N732TW	Boeing 737-2H4 (AvAero 3)	22731/864	ex N82SW	[ELP]
☐ N733TW	Boeing 737-2H4 (AvAero 3)	22732/877	ex N83SW	
☐ N783TW	Douglas DC-9-15F (ABS 3)	47010/97	ex N916R	
☐ N784TW	Douglas DC-9-15F (ABS 3)	47014/141	ex N923R	
☐ N785TW	Douglas DC-9-15F (ABS 3)	47015/156	ex N5373G	

ANDREW AIRWAYS Kodiak-Municipal, AK (KDK)

☐ N1544	de Havilland DHC-2 Beaver	1230	ex N67686	FP/WS
☐ N1545	de Havilland DHC-2 Beaver	1493	ex N123UA	FP/WS
☐ N5303X	Cessna U206G Stationair 6 II	U20605622		FP/WS

ANOKA AIR CHARTER Red Zone (RZZ) Minneapolis-Anoka County / Blaine, MN (-/BWS)

☐ N200VW	Piper PA-31-350 Chieftain	31-8052011	ex N200NC
☐ N633D	Piper PA-31-350 Chieftain	31-7852098	ex N63ND
☐ N646DR	Beech 200 Super King Air	BB-646	ex N646BM
☐ N700RF	Beech 65-C90A King Air	LJ-1262	ex N200HV

ARCTIC CIRCLE AIR SERVICE Air Arctic (5F/CIR)
Aniak/Bethel/Dillingham-Municipal/Fairbanks-Intl, AK (ANI/BET/DLG/FAI)

☐ N300SN	Cessna 402C II	402C0060	ex N5871C
☐ N402ET	Cessna 402C II	402C0054	ex C-GTKJ
☐ N4630N	Cessna 402C II	402C0001	

☐ N168LM	Short SD.3-30	SH3104	ex N174Z	Frtr
☐ N261AG	Short SD.3-30	SH3117	ex 84-0470	Frtr
☐ N7721C	Piper PA-32R-300 Lance	32R-7680060		

ARCTIC TRANSPORTATION SERVICES Arctic Transport (7S/RCT)
Unalakleet-Municipal, AK (UNK)

☐ N26TA	Cessna 207A Stationair 8	20700725	ex N9759M
☐ N624DR	Cessna 207A Stationair 7 II	20700517	ex N917AC
☐ N624ER	Cessna 207A Stationair 8 II	20700752	ex N9936M
☐ N7305U	Cessna 207A Skywagon	20700392	
☐ N7605U	Cessna 207A Stationair 7	20700443	
☐ N9475M	Cessna 207A Stationair 8	20700695	
☐ N9736M	Cessna 207A Stationair 8	20700722	
☐ N9829M	Cessna 207A Stationair 8	20700741	
☐ N9956M	Cessna 207A Stationair 8	20700763	
☐ N73217	Cessna 207A Stationair 8	20700572	
☐ N73467	Cessna 207A Stationair 8 II	20700594	
☐ N73503	Cessna 207A Stationair 8	20700599	
☐ N73789	Cessna 207A Stationair 8	20700629	

☐ N424CA	CASA 212-200	CC20-7-242		
☐ N437RA	CASA 212-200	CC21-2-166	ex N437CA	
☐ N439RA	CASA 212-200	CC50-9-287	ex N287MA	
☐ N440RA	CASA 212-200	CC20-6-174	ex N687MA	Frtr
☐ N1906	Short SC.7 Skyvan 3A	SH1906	ex HS-DCC	Frtr
☐ N2719A	Cessna 402C	402C0233		

ARIS HELICOPTERS San Jose-Intl, CA (SJC)

☐ N58AH	Sikorsky S-58ET	58-328	ex N39790

ARROW CARGO Big A (JW/APW) Miami-Intl, FL (MIA)

Ceased operations 30/June/2010

ASIA PACIFIC AIRLINES Magellan (MGE) Guam (GUM)

☐ N319NE	Boeing 727-212F/W (Duganair 3)	21349/1289	ex N591DB
☐ N705AA	Boeing 727-223F/W (Super 27)	22462/1751	
☐ N86425	Boeing 727-212F/W (Duganair 3)	21459/1329	ex N296AS

ASPEN HELICOPTERS Aspen (AHF) Oxnard, CA (OXR)

☐ N212AH	Bell 212	30959	ex C-FYMJ
☐ N383SH	Bell 206L-3 LongRanger III	51073	ex N333SH
☐ N1085T	Bell 206L-1 LongRanger III	45376	
☐ N3832K	Partenavia P.68C	272	
☐ N5006Y	Bell 206B JetRanger III	2485	
☐ N5012F	Bell 206B JetRanger III	2559	
☐ N6602L	Partenavia P.68 Observer	326-19-OB	ex VH-OBS
☐ N8131	Piper PA-31-350 Chieftain	31-8152032	ex LN-REM

| ☐ N39049 | Bell 206B JetRanger III | 3101 |
| ☐ N49643 | Bell 206B JetRanger | 1813 |

ASTAR AIR CARGO   DHL (ER/DHL)   Cincinnati-Northern Kentucky Intl, OH (CVG)

☐ N362DH	Airbus A300B4-103F	084	ex HS-THP		[IGM]
☐ N363DH	Airbus A300B4-103F	085	ex HS-THR		[IGM]
☐ N364DH	Airbus A300B4-203F	141	ex HS-THT		[IGM]
☐ N365DH	Airbus A300B4-203F	149	ex HS-THW		[IGM]
☐ N366DH	Airbus A300B4-203F	249	ex F-WIHZ		[IGM]
☐ N367DH	Airbus A300B4-203F	265	ex F-WIHY		[IGM]
☐ N741DH	Boeing 727-2Q9F (FedEx 3)	21931/1531	ex N202AV		[IGM]
☐ N742DH	Boeing 727-225F (FedEx 3)	21290/1238	ex N8872Z		[IGM]
☐ N745DH	Boeing 727-224F (FedEx 3)	20665/1149	ex N69736		[IGM]
☐ N747DH	Boeing 727-224F (FedEx 3)	22253/1702	ex N79744		[IGM]
☐ N748DH	Boeing 727-225F (FedEx 3)	22440/1692	ex XA-TCX		[IGM]
☐ N749DH	Boeing 727-223F (FedEx 3)	22013/1659	ex N897AA		[IGM]
☐ N751DH	Boeing 727-264 (FedEx 3)	22982/1802	ex A7-ABD		[IGM]
☐ N752DH	Boeing 727-223F (FedEx 3)	22466/1763	ex N709AA		[IGM]
☐ N753DH	Boeing 727-223F (FedEx 3)	22468/1766	ex N712AA		[IGM]
☐ N754DH	Boeing 727-223F (FedEx 3)	22008/1646	ex N892AA		[IGM]
☐ N760AT	Boeing 727-2B7F (FedEx 3)	21954/1525	ex N760US		[IGM]
☐ N770AT	Boeing 727-2B7F (FedEx 3)	21953/1516	ex N755US		[IGM]
☐ N780DH	Boeing 727-223F (FedEx 3)	22006/1636	ex N890AA		[IGM]
☐ N782DH	Boeing 727-227F (FedEx 3)	21998/1577	ex N769AT		[IGM]
☐ N783DH	Boeing 727-227F (FedEx 3)	21999/1581	ex N766AT		[IGM]
☐ N784DH	Boeing 727-227F (FedEx 3)	22001/1585	ex N767AT		[IGM]
☐ N785AT	Boeing 727-214F (FedEx 3)	21691/1480	ex N752US		[IGM]
☐ N786AT	Boeing 727-214F (FedEx 3)	21692/1482	ex N753US		[IGM]
☐ N788AT	Boeing 727-214F (FedEx 3)	21958/1533	ex N754US		[IGM]
☐ N793DH	Boeing 727-247F (FedEx 3)	21393/1307	ex N784AT		[IGM]
☐ N801DH	Douglas DC-8-73AF	46033/431	ex C-FTIK		
☐ N802DH	Douglas DC-8-73AF	46076/451	ex C-FTIO		
☐ N804DH	Douglas DC-8-73AF	46124/511	ex C-FTIR		
☐ N805DH	Douglas DC-8-73AF	46125/515	ex C-FTIS		
☐ N806DH	Douglas DC-8-73CF	46002/394	ex N815UP		
☐ N807DH	Douglas DC-8-73CF	45990/375	ex N816UP		
☐ N873SJ	Douglas DC-8-73F	46091/519	ex F-GESM	Billy J Benson	

ATI-AIR TRANSPORT INTERNATIONAL   Air Transport (8C/ATN)   Little Rock-Adams Field, AR (LIT)

☐ N761CX	Boeing 767-223 (SCD)	22318/111	ex N316AA		
☐ N762CX	Boeing 767-232 (SCD)	22225/77	ex N748AX		♦
☐ N763CX	Boeing 767-232 (SCD)	22223/74	ex N746AX		♦
☐ N41CX	Douglas DC-8-62CF (BAC 3)	46129/523	ex N798AL		
☐ N71CX	Douglas DC-8-62F (BAC 3)	45961/361	ex N818CK		
☐ N602AL	Douglas DC-8-73F	45991/380	ex D-ADUI		
☐ N603AL	Douglas DC-8-73F	46003/401	ex D-ADUA		
☐ N604BX	Douglas DC-8-73CF	46046/444	ex N792FT		
☐ N605AL	Douglas DC-8-73F	46106/490	ex D-ADUC		
☐ N606AL	Douglas DC-8-73F	46044/432	ex D-ADUE		
☐ N721CX	Douglas DC-8-72CF	46013/427	ex 46013		
☐ N722CX	Douglas DC-8-72CF	46130/542	ex 46130		
☐ N728PL	Douglas DC-8-62F (BAC 3)	45918/353	ex F-BOLF	Jerry 'Pete' Zerkel	
☐ N799AL	Douglas DC-8-62F (BAC 3)	45922/335	ex RTAF 60112		<BAX Global
☐ N820BX+	Douglas DC-8-71F	46065/460	ex N8098U	Larry LJ Johnston'	
☐ N821BX	Douglas DC-8-71F	45811/262	ex N8071U		
☐ N822BX	Douglas DC-8-71F	45813/284	ex N8073U		
☐ N823BX	Douglas DC-8-71F	46064/459	ex N8097U		
☐ N825BX	Douglas DC-8-71F	45978/381	ex N8088U		[MHV]♦
☐ N826BX	Douglas DC-8-71F	45998/399	ex N8094U		[ROW]
☐ N828BX	Douglas DC-8-71F	45993/392	ex N8089U		
☐ N829BX	Douglas DC-8-71F	45994/387	ex N501SR		[MHV]
☐ N830BX	Douglas DC-8-71F	45973/358	ex N783UP		

ATLANTIC AIR CARGO   Miami-Intl, FL (MIA)

| ☐ N437GB | Douglas DC-3 | 19999 | ex HR-LAD | | Frtr |
| ☐ N705GB | Douglas DC-3 | 13854 | ex TG-SAA | | Frtr |

ATLANTIC SOUTHEAST AIRLINES   Candler(EV/CAA)
Atlanta-Hartsfield Intl, GA/Orlando-Intl, FL (ATL/MCO)

Wholly owned subsidiary of SkyWest Airlines, and operates as Delta Connection

ATLAS AIR | Giant (5Y/GTI) | New York-JFK Intl, NY (JFK)

☐ N355MC	Boeing 747-341 (SF)	23395/629	ex PP-VNI	>PAC
☐ N408MC	Boeing 747-47UF	29261/1192	ex (N495MC)	>UAE
☐ N409MC	Boeing 747-47UF	30558/1242		
☐ N412MC	Boeing 747-47UF	30559/1244		
☐ N415MC	Boeing 747-47UF	32837/1304		>UAE
☐ N416MC	Boeing 747-47UF	32838/1307		>PAC
☐ N418MC	Boeing 747-47UF	32840/1319		
☐ N419MC	Boeing 747-48EF	28367/1096	ex TF-AMO	
☐ N429MC	Boeing 747-481BCF	24833/812	ex JA8095	
☐ N492MC	Boeing 747-47UF	29253/1169		
☐ N493MC	Boeing 747-47UF	29254/1179		
☐ N496MC	Boeing 747-47UF	29257/1217		
☐ N497MC	Boeing 747-47UF	29258/1220		> UAE
☐ N498MC	Boeing 747-47UF	29259/1227		
☐ N499MC	Boeing 747-47UF	29260/1240		
☐ N508MC	Boeing 747-230M	21644/256	ex D-ABYS	stored
☐ N512MC	Boeing 747-230M	21220/294	ex D-ABYJ	[ROW]
☐ N516MC	Boeing 747-243M	22507/497	ex I-DEMD	[ROW]
☐ N517MC	Boeing 747-243B (SF)	23300/613	ex I-DEMT	
☐ N522MC	Boeing 747-2D7B (SF)	21783/417	ex HS-TGB	
☐ N523MC	Boeing 747-2D7B (SF)	21782/402	ex N323MC	
☐ N524MC	Boeing 747-2D7B (SF)	21784/424	ex HS-TGC	
☐ N526MC	Boeing 747-2D7B (SF)	22337/479	ex HS-TGF	all-white
☐ N528MC	Boeing 747-2D7B (SF)	22472/597	ex HS-TGS	[ROW]
☐ N537MC	Boeing 747-271C	22403/524	ex LX-BCV	all-white [ROW]
☐ N540MC	Boeing 747-243M	22508/499	ex I-DEMF	

BAKER AVIATION | Baker Aviation (8Q/BAJ) Kotzebue-Wien Memorial, AK (OTZ)

☐ N6908M	Cessna 207A Stationair 8	20700672	
☐ N9942M	Cessna 207A Stationair 8	20700756	

BALD MOUNTAIN AIR SERVICE | Homer, AK

☐ N104BM	de Havilland DHC-3 Turbo Otter	118	ex CF-BEP	FP/WS
☐ N413JP	de Havilland DHC-3 Otter	314	ex C-GCDX	FP/WS
☐ N564DH	de Havilland DHC-6 Twin Otter 300	564	ex B-3504	
☐ N716JP	de Havilland DHC-6 Twin Otter 300	527	ex TI-AZV	

BALTIA AIRLINES | (BTL)

☐ N705BL	Boeing 747-282B	21035/256	ex N559EV	o/o♦
☐ N706BL	Boeing 747-251B	21705/374	ex N623US	o/o♦

BANKAIR | Bankair (B4/BKA) | Columbia-Owens Field, SC (CUB)

☐ N33PT	Learjet 25D	25D-240	ex N83EA	
☐ N58EM	Learjet 35	35-046	ex VH-LJL	
☐ N58HC	Learjet 25D	25D-341	ex XA-SAE	
☐ N67PA	Learjet 35A	35A-208	ex (N39DJ)	
☐ N90WR	Learjet 35	35-022	ex OY-BLG	
☐ N135AG	Learjet 35A	35A-132	ex N37TJ	
☐ N155AM	Learjet 35A	35A-131	ex N26GD	
☐ N326DD	Learjet 35A	35A-173	ex YU-BPY	
☐ N369BA	Learjet 35A	35A-312	ex LV-OFV	
☐ N399BA	Learjet 35A	35A-371	ex LV-ALF	
☐ N465NW	Learjet 35A	35A-465		
☐ N500ED	Learjet 35A	35A-241	ex N500EX	
☐ N900BJ	Learjet 35A	35A-123	ex N900JE	
☐ N21CJ	Mitsubishi MU-2L	789SA	ex N278MA	
☐ N21JA	Mitsubishi MU-2J	614	ex N998CA	
☐ N44KU	Mitsubishi MU-2J	647	ex N44KS	
☐ N174MA	Mitsubishi MU-2B	753SA	ex N100BY	
☐ N334EB	Mitsubishi MU-2J	568	ex N99SL	
☐ N535WM	Mitsubishi MU-2J	655	ex N535MA	
☐ N610CA	Mitsubishi MU-2B	788SA	ex N277MA	
☐ N637WG	Mitsubishi MU-2J	637	ex N951MS	
☐ N942ST	Mitsubishi MU-2B	745SA	ex N942MA	

BARON AVIATION SERVICES | Show-Me (BVN) | Rolla-Vichy-National, MO (VIH)

Operates Cessna 208/208B Caravans on behalf of Federal Express

BASLER AIRLINES   Basler (BFC)   Oshkosh-Wittman Regional, WI (OSH)

☐ N300BF	Basler BT-67	15299/26744	ex N300TX	Turbo-Express

BAY AIR   Dillingham & Shannons Pond SPB, AK (DLG/-)

☐ N364RA	de Havilland DHC-2 Beaver	364	ex N62300	FP

BEMIDJI AIRLINES   Bemidji (CH/BMJ)   Bemidji, MN (BJI)

☐ N55SA	Beech 65-A80 Queen Air	LD-243	ex N794A	Queenaire 8800 conversion
☐ N80RR	Beech 65-B80 Queen Air	LD-296		Queenaire 8800 conversion
☐ N95LL	Beech 65-A80 Queen Air	LD-235	ex N33TX	Queenaire 8800 conversion
☐ N103BA	Beech 65-B80 Queen Air	LD-435	ex N103EE	Queenaire 8800 conversion
☐ N104BA	Beech 65-B80 Queen Air	LD-411	ex N4258S	
☐ N106BA	Beech 65-B80 Queen Air	LD-409	ex N1338T	Queenaire 8800 conversion
☐ N107BA	Beech 65-B80 Queen Air	LD-358	ex N7838L	Queenaire 8800 conversion
☐ N110BA	Beech 65-B80 Queen Air	LD-279	ex N102KK	Queenaire 8800 conversion
☐ N111AR	Beech 65-80 Queen Air	LF-68	ex 62-3780	
☐ N131BA	Beech 65-B80 Queen Air	LD-297	ex N1555M	Queenaire 8800 conversion
☐ N132BA	Beech 65-B80 Queen Air	LD-331	ex C-GRID	Queenaire 8800 conversion
☐ N134BA	Beech 65-A80 Queen Air	LD-202	ex N848S	Queenaire 8800 conversion
☐ N135BA	Beech 65-80 Queen Air	LD-68	ex N29RG	Queenaire 8800 conversion
☐ N138BA	Beech 65-80 Queen Air	LD-361	ex N3344Z	
☐ N306D	Beech 65-80 Queen Air	LD-439	ex N4258S	
☐ N5078E	Beech 65-80 Queen Air	LF-76	ex 63-13637	
☐ N5078N	Beech 65-80 Queen Air	LF-16	ex 60-3467	
☐ N5078U	Beech 65-80 Queen Air	LF-32	ex 62-3834	
☐ N5079E	Beech 65-80 Queen Air	LF-52	ex 62-3854	
☐ N5080L	Beech 65-80 Queen Air	LF-59	ex 62-3861	
☐ N5080H	Beech 65-80 Queen Air	LF-27		
☐ N70NP	Beech 99	U-14	ex N914Y	
☐ N108BA	Beech 99	U-40	ex C-GQFD	
☐ N125DP	Beech 99	U-12	ex C-GPCE	
☐ N130BA	Beech 99A	U-80	ex N51PA	Frtr
☐ N137BA	Beech 99	U-137	ex C-GAWW	
☐ N172EE	Beech C99	U-172	ex N993SB	
☐ N175EE	Beech C99	U-175	ex N994SB	
☐ N223CA	Beech C99	U-200	ex SE-IZX	Frtr
☐ N6645K	Beech C99	U-209		
☐ N7207E	Beech C99	U-223		
☐ N7212P	Beech C-99	U-220		
☐ N60BA	Beech 65-E90 King Air	LW-79	ex N12AK	
☐ N70DD	Beech 58 Baron	TH-370	ex N25660	
☐ N4016A	Beech 58 Baron	TH-9		

BERING AIR   Bering Air (8E/BRG)   Nome, AK (OME)

☐ N205BA	Cessna 208B Caravan I	208B0890		
☐ N806BA	Cessna 208B Caravan I	208B0943		
☐ N1128L	Cessna 208B Caravan I	208B0536		
☐ N141ME	Piper PA-31-350 Chieftain	31-8152117	ex N4086L	
☐ N4112D	Piper PA-31-350 T-1020	31-8353004		
☐ N4112E	Piper PA-31-350 T-1020	31-8353005		
☐ N4118G	Piper PA-31-350 T-1020	31-8453001		
☐ N41189	Piper PA-31-350 T-1020	31-8553002		
☐ N45052	Piper PA-31-350 Chieftain	31-8152063		
☐ N15GA	Beech 1900D	UE-37	Ex F-HCHA	
☐ N79CF	Beech 200 Super King Air	BB-441		CatPass 250 conversion
☐ N148SK	Beech 1900D	UE-148		
☐ N326KW	Beech 200 Super King Air	BB-1360	ex HK-3703X	CatPass 250 conversion
☐ N349TA	CASA 212-200	CC60-9-349	ex N316CA	Frtr
☐ N9964M	Cessna 207A Stationair 8	20700766		
☐ N9988M	Cessna 207A Stationair 8	20700776		

BERRY AVIATION   Berry (BYA)   San Marcos-Municipal, TX (HYI)

☐ N335PH	Dornier 328-100	3013	ex D-CALT	
☐ N339PH	Dornier 328-100	3015	ex D-CARR	
☐ N473PS	Dornier 328-100	3010	ex HB-AEG	
☐ N900LH	Dornier 328-100	3014	ex N336PH	
☐ N165BA	Swearingen SA.226TC Metro II	TC-215	ex N911HF	

☐ N226BA	Swearingen SA.226TC Metro II	TC-321	ex N105UR		
☐ N323BA	Swearingen SA.226TC Metro II	TC-280	ex N303TL		Frtr
☐ N373PH	Swearingen SA.227AC Metro III	AC-538	ex N732C		
☐ N589BA	Swearingen SA.227AC Metro III	AC-589	ex XA-TSF		[HYI]
☐ N590BA	Swearingen SA.227AC Metro III	AC-590	ex XA-TSG		[HYI]
☐ N680AX	Swearingen SA.227AC Metro III	AC-680	ex N365AE		
☐ N691AX	Swearingen SA.227AC Metro III	AC-691	ex N367AE		
☐ N697AX	Swearingen SA.227AC Metro III	AC-697	ex N730C		
☐ N729C	Swearingen SA.227AC Metro III	AC-571	ex N374PH		
☐ N789C	Swearingen SA.227AC Metro III	AC-540	ex N389PH		
☐ N26959	Swearingen SA.227AC Metro III	AC-662B			
☐ N27442	Swearingen SA.227AC Metro III	AC-750B			

BIG ISLAND AIR — Big Isle (BIG) — Kailua-Keahole Kona Intl, HI (KOA)

☐ N281A	Cessna 208 Caravan I	20800271	ex LV-WYX	

BIGHORN AIRWAYS — Bighorn Air (BHR)
Sheridan-County, WY/Casper-Natrona Co, WY (SHR/CPR)

☐ N107BH	CASA C.212-200	CC20-4-165	ex N212TH	
☐ N112BH	CASA C.212-200	CC50-11-292	ex N311ST	
☐ N114BH	Cessna 340A	340A1230	ex N6228X	
☐ N115BH	Cessna 340A	340A1531	ex N2688Q	
☐ N117BH	CASA C.212-200	CC23-1-171	ex N349CA	
☐ N118BH	Cessna 340A	340A0003	ex N5168J	
☐ N257MC	Dornier 228-202	8102	ex YV-648C	
☐ N263MC	Dornier 228-202	8141	ex N116DN	
☐ N266MC	Dornier 228-202	8150	ex D-CBDL	
☐ N414PG	Cessna 414A Chancellor III	414A0811	ex D-ICAC	
☐ N543CC	Bell 206B JetRanger III	3593	ex N2295W	
☐ N700WJ	Cessna 425 Conquest I	425-0036	ex F-GCQN	
☐ N6266C	Cessna T210N Turbo Centurion II	21063849		

BIMINI ISLAND AIR — (BMY) — Fort Lauderdale-Executive, FL (FXE)

☐ N46ZP	Cessna 402B II	402B1004	ex N87159	
☐ N325SV	SAAB SF.340A	340A-072	ex N72VN	
☐ N460BA	SAAB SF.340A	340A-033	ex N441EA	

BORINQUEN AIR — San Juan-Munoz Marin Intl, PR (SJU)

☐ N1019B	Beech E-18S	BA-254		Frtr
☐ N86553	Douglas DC-3	4715	ex 41-18590	Frtr

BOSTON-MAINE AIRWAYS — Clipper Express (E9/CXS) — Portsmouth-Pease Intl, NH (PSM)

☐ N342PA	Boeing 727-222 (FedEx 3)	21893/1503	ex N7298U	Clipper Guilford
☐ N525PA	British Aerospace Jetstream 31	666	ex N305PX	Clipper Tay
☐ N529PA	British Aerospace Jetstream 31	771	ex N846JS	Clipper Shenandoah
☐ N530PA	British Aerospace Jetstream 31	732	ex N836JS	Clipper Allagash
☐ N531PA	British Aerospace Jetstream 31	748	ex N839JS	Clipper Missouri
☐ N538PA	British Aerospace Jetstream 31	751	ex N841JS	Clipper Isar
☐ N539PA	British Aerospace Jetstream 31	741	ex N838JS	

BRAVO AIRLINES — Miami-Opa Locka, FL (OPF)

☐ N701AU	Lockheed P2V-7 Neptune Firestar	726-7190	ex N920AU	01	Tanker
☐ N716AU	Lockheed P2V-7 Neptune Firestar	726-7065	ex N90YY	16	Tanker
☐ N718AU	Lockheed P2V-7 Neptune Firestar	726-7214	ex N964L	18	Tanker

BRISTOW US — Airlog (ALG) — New Iberia-Air Logistics Heliport, LA (-)

☐ N139TZ	Agusta AW139	41202		
☐ N239BG	Agusta AW139	41221		♦
☐ N339BG	Agusta AW139	41234	ex N208YS	♦
☐ N206XS	Bell 206B JetRanger III	3040		Op by Bristow Academy
☐ N5008N	Bell 206B JetRanger III	2518		Op by Bristow Academy
☐ N69AL	Bell 206L-4 LongRanger IV	52139	ex PT-YBH	
☐ N76AL	Bell 206L-4 LongRanger IV	52165	ex N15EW	
☐ N133AL	Bell 206L-3 LongRanger III	51133		based Alaska
☐ N176AL	Bell 206L-4 LongRanger IV	52146	ex C-FOFE	
☐ N177AL	Bell 206L-4 LongRanger IV	52157	ex C-GLZU	
☐ N182AL	Bell 206L-3 LongRanger III	52057	ex D-HSDA	
☐ N188AL	Bell 206L-4 LongRanger IV	52082	ex N84TV	

☐ N189AL	Bell 206L-4 LongRanger IV	52340		
☐ N192AL	Bell 206L-4 LongRanger IV	52342		
☐ N193AL	Bell 206L-4 LongRanger IV	52344		
☐ N194AL	Bell 206L-4 LongRanger IV	52148	ex XA-TFI	
☐ N196AL	Bell 206L-4 LongRanger IV	52380	ex N218K	
☐ N206DB	Bell 206L-4 LongRanger IV	52127		
☐ N265AL	Bell 206L-4 LongRanger IV	52280	ex C-GFNY	
☐ N266AL	Bell 206L-4 LongRanger IV	52281		
☐ N267AL	Bell 206L-4 LongRanger IV	52282	ex C-GAXE	
☐ N268AL	Bell 206L-4 LongRanger IV	52283		
☐ N269AL	Bell 206L-4 LongRanger IV	52284		
☐ N271AL	Bell 206L-4 LongRanger IV	52287		
☐ N272AL	Bell 206L-4 LongRanger IV	52288		
☐ N275AL	Bell 206L-4 LongRanger IV	52285		
☐ N276AL	Bell 206L-4 LongRanger IV	52312		
☐ N278AL	Bell 206L-4 LongRanger IV	52313		
☐ N279AL	Bell 206L-4 LongRanger IV	52314	ex C-GAEP	
☐ N280AL	Bell 206L-4 LongRanger IV	52315		
☐ N281AL	Bell 206L-4 LongRanger IV	52319		
☐ N330P	Bell 206L-3 LongRanger III	51295		
☐ N346AL	Bell 206L-3 LongRanger III	51378		based Alaska
☐ N358AL	Bell 206L-3 LongRanger III	51460		based Alaska
☐ N360AL	Bell 206L-3 LongRanger III	51462		based Alaska
☐ N363AL	Bell 206L-3 LongRanger III	51472	ex C-GLZE	based Alaska
☐ N3174Y	Bell 206L-3 LongRanger III	51038		
☐ N403AL	Bell 407	53478	ex N4041F	
☐ N404AL	Bell 407	53479	ex N40410	
☐ N405AL	Bell 407	53480	ex N40414	
☐ N406AL	Bell 407	53481	ex N6146J	
☐ N407AL	Bell 407	53044		
☐ N407TZ	Bell 407	53204	ex N487AL	
☐ N408AL	Bell 407	53491	ex N6148U	
☐ N409AL	Bell 407	53494	ex N9182V	
☐ N410AL	Bell 407	53482	ex N388RT	
☐ N415AL	Bell 407	53182	ex N415AG	
☐ N431AL	Bell 407	53923	ex C-FYPN	
☐ N436AL	Bell 407	53069	ex N58236	
☐ N447AL	Bell 407	53126	ex PT-YNM	
☐ N457AL	Bell 407	53151		
☐ N477AL	Bell 407	53203		
☐ N497AL	Bell 407	53172		
☐ N507AL	Bell 407	53103	ex N407ST	
☐ N527AL	Bell 407	53211		
☐ N537AL	Bell 407	53230		
☐ N547AL	Bell 407	53240		
☐ N557AL	Bell 407	53243		
☐ N577AL	Bell 407	53247		
☐ N587AL	Bell 407	53248		
☐ N597AL	Bell 407	53091	ex N427AL	
☐ N607AL	Bell 407	53264		
☐ N617AL	Bell 407	53265		
☐ N627AL	Bell 407	53284		
☐ N637AL	Bell 407	53293	ex PT-YUW	
☐ N647AL	Bell 407	53357	ex N60321	
☐ N657AL	Bell 407	53413	ex N155ZS	
☐ N667AL	Bell 407	53624	ex XA-SKY	
☐ N687AL	Bell 407	53366	ex N6302B	
☐ N697AL	Bell 407	53374	ex N6112Q	
☐ N727AL	Bell 407	53227	ex N298RS	
☐ N796RV	Bell 407	53037	ex RP-C2468	
☐ N847AL	Bell 407	53150	ex N407XS	
☐ N937AL	Bell 407	53383	ex N63894	
☐ N335BG	Eurocopter EC135P2+	0793		♦
☐ N535AL	Eurocopter EC135P2+	0716		
☐ N635AL	Eurocopter EC135P2+	0758		
☐ N935AL	Eurocopter EC135P2+	0817		
☐ N519AL	Sikorsky S-76A	760058	ex G-EWEL	
☐ N522AL	Sikorsky S-76A	760236	ex N202SR	
☐ N701AL	Sikorsky S-76A	760238		
☐ N702AL	Sikorsky S-76A	760243		
☐ N707AL	Sikorsky S-76A	760189	ex N989QS	
☐ N709AL	Sikorsky S-76A	760278		
☐ N802E	Sikorsky S-76C+	760802		♦
☐ N803K	Sikorsky S-76C+	760803		♦

☐ N804I	Sikorsky S-76C+	760804			◆
☐ N860AL	Sikorsky S-76C+	760527	ex N9024W		
☐ N861AL	Sikorsky S-76C+	760529	ex N2032W		
☐ N862AL	Sikorsky S-76C+	760531	ex N2021W		
☐ N863AL	Sikorsky S-76C+	760536	ex N5009K		
☐ N864AL	Sikorsky S-76C+	760557	ex N50093		
☐ N865AL	Sikorsky S-76C	760564	ex N70089		
☐ N866AL	Sikorsky S-76C	760562	ex N50085		
☐ N867AL	Sikorsky S-76C	760579	ex N7104Q		
☐ N868AL	Sikorsky S-76C+	760580	ex N7102S		
☐ N870AL	Sikorsky S-76C+	760606	ex N8119N		
☐ N871AL	Sikorsky S-76C+	760627	ex N80907		
☐ N877AL	Sikorsky S-76C+	760618	ex N81081		
☐ N879AL	Sikorsky S-76C+	760652	ex 9M-SPU		
☐ N881AL	Sikorsky S-76C+	760673	ex N4512G		
☐ N883AL	Sikorsky S-76C	760677	ex N4514G		
☐ N884AL	Sikorsky S-76C	760721			
☐ N31211	Sikorsky S-76A	760225			
☐ N150AL	Sikorsky S-92A	920150			◆
☐ N920AL	Sikorsky S-92A	920088	ex N2577X		
☐ N29AL	Bell 212	30569			based Alaska
☐ N390AL	Bell 214ST	28198			
☐ N392AL	Bell 214ST	28114	ex G-BKJD		
☐ N393AL	Bell 214ST	28117	ex N214EV		
☐ N397AL	Bell 412	36012	ex XA-TLO		
☐ N412BG	Bell 412SP	33210	ex XA-TYQ		◆
☐ N492HL	MBB Bo.105CBS-4	S-803	ex N124PW		based Alaska
☐ N494HL	MBB Bo.105CBS-4	S-813	ex N494HL		

BROOKS AVIATION · Douglas-Municipal, GA (DQH)

☐ N99FS	Douglas DC-3	12425	ex (N89BF)	

BROOKS FUEL · Fairbanks-Intl, AK (FAI)

☐ N708Z	Douglas C-54G	36067	ex USCG 5614		
☐ N3054V	Douglas DC-4	10547	ex N76AU	162	Tanker
☐ N51802	Douglas C-54G	35930	ex 45-0477		[FAI]
☐ N96358	Douglas C-54E	27284	ex Bu90398		

BUSINESS AVIATION COURIER · Dakota (DKT) · Sioux Falls-Joe Foss Field, SD (FSD)

☐ N76MD	Cessna 402B II	402B1055	ex N987PF	
☐ N402BP	Cessna 402B	402B0353	ex N5419M	
☐ N402SS	Cessna 402B	402B0562	ex N402CC	
☐ N624CA	Cessna 402B	402B0876	ex D-IJOS	
☐ N780MB	Cessna 402B	402B0249	ex N402RT	
☐ N1048	Cessna 402B	402B0628	ex N104WM	
☐ N3729C	Cessna 402B	402B0589	ex XB-EAC	
☐ N3796C	Cessna 402B	402B0803		
☐ N3813	Cessna 402B	402B0807	ex PK-VCE	
☐ N366AE	Swearingen SA.227AC Metro III	AC-681B		
☐ N371PH	Swearingen SA.227AC Metro III	AC-576	ex N3119W	
☐ N387PH	Swearingen SA.227AC Metro III	AC-531	ex N31094	
☐ N685BA	Swearingen SA.227AC Metro III	AC-685	ex N685AV	
☐ N3108B	Swearingen SA.227AC Metro III	AC-509	ex XA-TAK	
☐ N3116N	Swearingen SA.227AC Metro III	AC-596		
☐ N80BS	Cessna 404 Titan II	404-0048	ex G-ZAPB	
☐ N500FS	Cessna 310R II	310R0630		
☐ N1533T	Cessna 310R II	310R0111		
☐ N3482G	Cessna 310R II	310R0850		

BUTLER AIRCRAFT · Redmond, OR (RDM)

☐ N401US	Douglas DC-7	45145/767	ex N6331C	62	Tanker
☐ N531BA	Lockheed 182-1A Hercules (C-130A)	3139	ex 56-0531	67	Tanker
☐ N838D	Douglas DC-7	45347/936		60	Tanker
☐ N6353C	Douglas DC-7	45486/964		66	Tanker
☐ N60018	Cessna TU206F Stationair	U20602002			

C&M AIRWAYS · Red Wing (RWG) · El Paso-Intl, TX (ELP)

☐ N640CM	Convair 640	104	ex C-GCWY	[ELP]

☐ N3420	Convair 640	64	[ELP]
☐ N563PC	Douglas DC-9-15RC (ABS 3)	47055/194	ex N1305T

CAPE AIR — Cair (9K/KAP)
Hyannis-Barnstable Municipal, MA/Naples-Municipal, FL (HYA/APF)

☐ N14834	ATR 42-320	193	ex F-WWEG
☐ N42836	ATR 42-320	200	ex F-WWEN 836
☐ N69SC	Cessna 402C II	402C0041	ex N5778C
☐ N83PB	Cessna 402C II	402C0350	ex N26627
☐ N106CA	Cessna 402C III	402C1020	ex TJ-AHQ
☐ N120PC	Cessna 402C II	402C0079	ex N2612L
☐ N121PB	Cessna 402C II	402C0507	ex N6874X
☐ N161TA	Cessna 402C II	402C0070	ex N2611A
☐ N223PB	Cessna 402C II	402C0105	ex N261PB
☐ N247GS	Cessna 402C II	402C0637	ex N404BK
☐ N401TJ	Cessna 402C II	402C0109	ex TJ-AFV
☐ N402VN	Cessna 402C II	402C0488	ex (N6840D)
☐ N406GA	Cessna 402C II	402C0329	ex N2642D
☐ N494BC	Cessna 402C II	402C0308	ex N67PB
☐ N514NC	Cessna 402C II	402C0514	ex N125PB
☐ N524CA	Cessna 402C II	402C0522	ex C-GSKG
☐ N525RH	Cessna 402C II	402C0525	ex N68761
☐ N548GA	Cessna 402C II	402C0653	ex N6773T
☐ N618CA	Cessna 402C II	402C0620	ex VH-RGK
☐ N660CA	Cessna 402C II	402C0406	ex C-GHMI
☐ N747WS	Cessna 402C II	402C0080	ex C-GHYZ
☐ N762EA	Cessna 402C II	402C0061	ex N5872C
☐ N763EA	Cessna 402C II	402C0497	ex N763AN
☐ N764EA	Cessna 402C II	402C0237	ex N2719T
☐ N769EA	Cessna 402C II	402C0303	ex N3283M
☐ N771EA	Cessna 402C II	402C0046	ex N5809C
☐ N781EA	Cessna 402C II	402C0310	ex N822AN
☐ N812AN	Cessna 402C II	402C0229	ex N2718P
☐ N818AN	Cessna 402C II	402C0501	ex N6842Q
☐ N991AA	Cessna 402C II	402C0317	ex N36916
☐ N1361G	Cessna 402C II	402C0270	
☐ N1376G	Cessna 402C II	402C0271	ex N156PB special landscape c/s
☐ N2611X	Cessna 402C II	402C0072	
☐ N2615G	Cessna 402C II	402C0101	ex C-GHGM
☐ N2649Z	Cessna 402C II	402C0333	
☐ N2651S	Cessna 402C II	402C0342	
☐ N2714B	Cessna 402C II	402C0210	
☐ N2714M	Cessna 402C II	402C0211	
☐ N3292M	Cessna 402C II	402C0304	
☐ N4652N	Cessna 402C II	402C0011	
☐ N6813J	Cessna 402C II	402C0641	
☐ N6875D	Cessna 402C II	402C0511	special Flagship Whalers c/s
☐ N6879R	Cessna 402C II	402C0611	ex C-GJVC
☐ N7037E	Cessna 402C II	402C0471	ex C-GGXH
☐ N26156	Cessna 402C II	402C0112	
☐ N26514	Cessna 402C II	402C0344	
☐ N26632	Cessna 402C II	402C0404	
☐ N36911	Cessna 402C II	402C0314	
☐ N67786	Cessna 402C II	402C0631	special Key West Express c/s
☐ N67886	Cessna 402C II	402C0435	
☐ N68391	Cessna 402C II	402C0483	
☐ N68752	Cessna 402C II	402C0518	
☐ N88833	Cessna 402C II	402C0265	special flowers c/s

CAPITAL CARGO INTERNATIONAL AIRLINES — Cappy (PT/CCI) — Orlando-Intl, FL (MCO)

☐ N286SC	Boeing 727-2A1F (FedEx 3)	21601/1694	ex N328AS	Beth
☐ N287SC	Boeing 727-2A1F (FedEx 3)	21345/1673	ex N327AS	Florence
☐ N308AS	Boeing 727-227F (FedEx 3)	22002/1627	ex N479BN	Eloise
☐ N357KP	Boeing 727-230F (FedEx 3)	20675/924	ex G-BPNY	Princess Kendall
☐ N708AA	Boeing 727-223F (FedEx 3)	22465/1761		
☐ N713AA	Boeing 727-223F (FedEx 3)	22469/1769		Jessica
☐ N715AA	Boeing 727-223F (FedEx 3)	22470/1771		
☐ N755DH	Boeing 727-225F (FedEx 3)	21857/1539	ex N887MA	
☐ N801EA	Boeing 727-225F (FedEx 3)	22432/1658		Miss Ashley
☐ N808EA	Boeing 727-225F (FedEx 3)	22439/1689	ex TC-DEL	Yvonne [JAX]
☐ N815EA	Boeing 727-225F (FedEx 3)	22552/1773		Gudrund
☐ N898AA	Boeing 727-223F (FedEx 3)	22014/1663		Roberta
☐ N899AA	Boeing 727-223F (FedEx 3)	22015/1666		Angie

302

☐ N89427	Boeing 727-227F (FedEx 3)	21365/1273	ex N323AS	Carol

☐ N605DL	Boeing 757-232F	22812/46	
☐ N620DL	Boeing 757-232F	22910/111	
☐ N315AA	Boeing 767-223F	22317/109	

CAPITAL CITY AIR CARRIER — Cap City (CCQ) — Pierre-Regional, SD (PIR)

☐ N300VF	Piper PA-31-350 Chieftain	31-7852050	ex N27532
☐ N305SK	Piper PA-31-350 Navajo Chieftain	31-7652039	ex N59769
☐ N400RA	Piper PA-31-350 Navajo Chieftain	31-7405167	ex N22AE
☐ N777ZM	Piper PA-31-350 Chieftain	31-8052193	ex N45027
☐ N984PA	Piper PA-31-350 Navajo Chieftain	31-7305104	ex N74995
☐ N27537	Piper PA-31-350 Chieftain	31-7852053	

☐ N13PB	Piper PA-34-200T Seneca II	34-7870003
☐ N6597F	Piper PA-34-200T Seneca II	34-7770032
☐ N8017C	Piper PA-34-220T Seneca III	34-8133200
☐ N8180G	Piper PA-34-200T Seneca II	34-8070174
☐ N9638K	Piper PA-34-200T Seneca II	34-7670212
☐ N36369	Piper PA-34-200T Seneca II	34-7870323

☐ N126BP	Cessna 414A Chancellor	414A0214	ex N5660C
☐ N402RM	Cessna 402B	402B0607	ex C-FEAG
☐ N75156	Piper PA-32R-300 Lance	32R-7680272	

CARIBBEAN SUN AIRLINES — (WAL)

☐ N802WA	McDonnell-Douglas MD-83	53052/1731	ex N751LF

CARSON HELICOPTERS — Perkasie-Heliport, PA/Jackonsville Heliport, OR

☐ N103WF	Sikorsky S-61N	61766	ex 9M-AVO	
☐ N116AZ	Sikorsky S-61N	61242	ex VH-BHO	
☐ N302Y	Sikorsky S-61N	61472	ex YV-323C	
☐ N349FC	Sikorsky S-61 (UH-3H)	61239		
☐ N349RH	Sikorsky S-61 (UH-3H)	61117	ex Bu149702	
☐ N350DA	Sikorsky S-61 (SH-3H)	61187		
☐ N352DH	Sikorsky S-61 (SH-3H)	61161	ex N1048Y	
☐ N364DZ	Sikorsky S-61N II	61819	ex G-BGWJ	
☐ N364FH	Sikorsky S-61N II	61718	ex G-BBVA	
☐ N364HH	Sikorsky S-61N II	61712	ex G-BBHL	
☐ N410GH	Sikorsky S-61N	61749	ex V8-BSP	
☐ N420SC	Sikorsky S-61N	61745	ex PP-MNL	♦
☐ N502SC	Sikorsky S-61N	61737	ex G-BCLC	
☐ N561EH	Sikorsky S-61N	61471	ex ZS-RAX	
☐ N561SC	Sikorsky S-61A	61272	ex N81661	
☐ N612RM	Sikorsky S-61N	61744	ex C-FSYH	
☐ N617HM	Sikorsky S-61N	61754	ex C-GSBL	
☐ N618PA	Sikorsky S-61L	61426	ex	
☐ N725JH	Sikorsky S-61N	61775	ex V8-SAV	
☐ N905AL	Sikorsky S-61N	61717	ex V8-UDZ	
☐ N3173U	Sikorsky S-61A	61186	ex 149916	
☐ N4263A	Sikorsky S-61R	61551	ex 65-5700	
☐ N4263F	Sikorsky S-61R	61533	ex 64-14230	
☐ N6981R	Sikorsky S-61N	61453	ex	
☐ N8167B	Sikorsky S-61A	61137	ex Bu149720	
☐ N8170V	Sikorsky S-61A	61232	ex	
☐ N8174J	Sikorsky S-61R	61584	ex 66-13286	stored
☐ N9260A	Sikorsky S-61D	61442	ex Bu156496	
☐ N9271A	Sikorsky S-61D	61449	ex Bu156486	
☐ N13491	Sikorsky S-61A	61129		
☐ N42626	Sikorsky S-61R	61522	ex 63-9690	
☐ N81664	Sikorsky S-61A	61063	ex Bu148989	
☐ N81692	Sikorsky S-61A	61074	ex Bu149000	
☐ N81701	Sikorsky S-61R	61529	ex 64-14226	stored
☐ N81702	Sikorsky S-61R	61608	ex 64-14706	stored
☐ N81743	Sikorsky S-61R	61575	ex 65-12800	stored
☐ N82702	Sikorsky S-61D	61432	ex N92592	
☐ N92590	Sikorsky S-61D	61351	ex Bu152691	

☐ N239Z	de Havilland DHC-6 Twin Otter 300	239	ex N15239	Based Argentina
☐ N920R	de Havilland DHC-6 Twin Otter 100	45	ex HC-BYK	Based Argentina

CASCADE AIR — Ephrata-Municipal, WA (EPH)

☐ N272R	Douglas DC-3	13678	ex NC88824
☐ N91314	Douglas DC-3	4538	ex NC17884

CASTLE AVIATION		Castle (CSJ)		Akron-Canton Regional, OH (CAK)
☐ N24MG	Cessna 208B Caravan I	208B0850	ex N5261R	Frtr
☐ N27MG	Cessna 208B Caravan I	208B0650	ex N5262Z	Frtr
☐ N29MG	Cessna 208B Caravan I	208B0812	ex N52229	Frtr
☐ N31MG	Cessna 208B Caravan I	208B1065		Frtr
☐ N1029Y	Cessna 208B Caravan I	208B0325		Frtr
☐ N49MG	Piper PA-60 Aerostar 600	60-0634-7961201	ex N8232J	
☐ N52MG	Ted Smith Aerostar 600A	60-0530-172	ex N8047J	

CATALINA FLYING BOATS		Catalina Air (CBT)		Long Beach-Daugherty Field, CA (LGB)
☐ N18R	Beech E-18S	BA-312		>PPG
☐ N103AF	Beech G-18S	BA-526	ex N277S	>PPG
☐ N166H	Beech E-18S	BA-253		
☐ N403JB	Douglas DC-3	16943/34202	ex N17778	
☐ N2298C	Douglas DC-3	16453/33201	ex (N352SA)	
☐ N9375Y	Beech G-18S	BA-564		>PPG
☐ N9680B	Cessna 208B Caravan I	208B0150		

CDF AVIATION				Sacramento-Mather, CA (MHR)
☐ N481DF	Bell UH-1H	13318	ex 72-21019 104	
☐ N489DF	Bell UH-1H	12224	ex 69-15936 901	standby
☐ N490DF	Bell UH-1H	12375	ex 70-15765 205	
☐ N491DF	Bell UH-1H	12146	ex 69-15858 301	
☐ N492DF	Bell UH-1H	11433	ex 69-15145	standby
☐ N493DF	Bell UH-1H	12001	ex 69-15713	standby
☐ N494DF	Bell UH-1H	11303	ex 69-15015 404	
☐ N495DF	Bell UH-1H	12218	ex 69-15930 106	
☐ N496DF	Bell UH-1H	11964	ex 69-15676 102	
☐ N497DF	Bell UH-1H	11553	ex 69-15265 202	
☐ N498DF	Bell UH-1H	12153	ex 69-15865 406	
☐ N499DF	Bell UH-1H	12846	ex 71-20022 101	
☐ N417DF	Grumman S-2A Tracker	061	ex Bu133090 76	
☐ N443DF	Grumman S-2A Tracker	195	ex Bu133224 72	
☐ N422DF	Marsh S-2T Turbo Tracker	286C	ex N518DF 82	
☐ N424DF	Marsh S-2T Turbo Tracker	289C	ex N519DF 83	
☐ N425DF	Marsh S-2T Turbo Tracker	294C	ex N522DF 89	
☐ N426DF	Marsh S-2T Turbo Tracker	293C	ex N520DF 88	
☐ N427DF	Marsh S-2T Turbo Tracker	326C	ex N524DF 70	
☐ N428DF	Marsh S-2T Turbo Tracker	137C	ex N511DF 91	
☐ N431DF	Marsh S-2T Turbo Tracker	109C	ex N504DF 78	
☐ N432DF	Marsh S-2T Turbo Tracker	112C	ex N505DF 71	
☐ N433DF	Marsh S-2T Turbo Tracker	130C	ex N510DF 86	
☐ N434DF	Marsh S-2T Turbo Tracker	335C	ex N527DF 90	
☐ N435DF	Marsh S-2T Turbo Tracker	329C	ex N526DF 76	
☐ N437DF	Marsh S-2T Turbo Tracker	123C	ex N507DF 73	
☐ N438DF	Marsh S-2T Turbo Tracker	173C	ex N513DF 85	
☐ N439DF	Marsh S-2T Turbo Tracker	129C	ex N509DF 74	
☐ N440DF	Marsh S-2T Turbo Tracker	148C	ex N512DF 96	
☐ N441DF	Marsh S-2T Turbo Tracker	277C	ex N517DF 100	
☐ N442DF	Marsh S-2T Turbo Tracker	295C	ex Bu152826 94	
☐ N444DF	Marsh S-2T Turbo Tracker	187C	ex N515DF 75	
☐ N445DF	Marsh S-2T Turbo Tracker	232C	ex N516DF 80	
☐ N449DF	Marsh S-2T Turbo Tracker	307C	ex N523DF 81	
☐ N450DF	Marsh S-2T Turbo Tracker	228C	ex Bu152341	
☐ N400DF	Rockwell OV-10A Bronco	305-122M-65	ex Bu155454 440	
☐ N401DF	Rockwell OV-10A Bronco	305-128M-68	ex Bu155457 310	standby
☐ N402DF	Rockwell OV-10A Bronco	305-132M-70	ex Bu155459 210	
☐ N403DF	Rockwell OV-10A Bronco	305-148M-78	ex Bu155467 240	standby
☐ N407DF	Rockwell OV-10A Bronco	305-164M-86	ex Bu155475 430	
☐ N408DF	Rockwell OV-10A Bronco	305-178M-90	ex Bu155480 230	
☐ N409DF	Rockwell OV-10A Bronco	305-18M-12	ex Bu155401 330	
☐ N410DF	Rockwell OV-10A Bronco	305-158M-82	ex Bu155471 110	
☐ N413DF	Rockwell OV-10A Bronco	305-20M-13	ex Bu155402 120	
☐ N414DF	Rockwell OV-10A Bronco	305-26M-16	ex Bu155415 140	
☐ N415DF	Rockwell OV-10A Bronco	305-68M-38	ex Bu155427 460	
☐ N418DF	Rockwell OV-10A Bronco	305-70M-39	ex Bu155428 340	
☐ N421DF	Rockwell OV-10A Bronco	305-206M-107	ex Bu155496 240	
☐ N429DF	Rockwell OV-10A Bronco	305A-17M-11	ex Bu155400 310	

304

CENTRAL AIR SOUTHWEST — Central Commuter (CTL) — Kansas City-Downtown, KS/Cushing-Municipal, OK (MKC/CUH)

☐ N23BQ	Aero Commander 500B	1065-46	ex N6196X
☐ N30MB	Aero Commander 500B	1453-160	ex N6376U
☐ N107DF	Aero Commander 500B	1191-97	ex N88PC
☐ N127KH	Aero Commander 500B	1027-38	ex N801TC
☐ N261ER	Aero Commander 500B	1362-133	ex N780SP
☐ N272CA	Aero Commander 500B	1409-146	ex N635BC
☐ N304JT	Aero Commander 500B	1494-175	ex N222AV
☐ N324RR	Aero Commander 500B	1386-139	ex N471A
☐ N411ET	Aero Commander 500B	1621-214	ex N445CA
☐ N411JF	Aero Commander 500B	1014-35	ex N6178X
☐ N411PT	Aero Commander 500B	1207-99	ex N291CA
☐ N415BH	Aero Commander 500B	918-5	ex N6129X
☐ N443WA	Aero Commander 500B	1315-124	ex N553RA
☐ N444CA	Aero Commander 500B	1458-162	ex N6326U
☐ N444CB	Aero Commander 500B	1119-69	ex N6229X
☐ N446AE	Aero Commander 500B	1613-211	ex N724LH
☐ N477CC	Aero Commander 500B	1480-172	ex N477CA
☐ N516DT	Aero Commander 500B	1574-200	ex N134X
☐ N518TM	Aero Commander 500B	995-26	ex N6156X
☐ N524HW	Aero Commander 500B	1533-191	ex N324MA
☐ N607MM	Aero Commander 500U Shrike	1712-25	ex N252LD
☐ N610BW	Aero Commander 500B	1523-185	ex N159BM
☐ N615MT	Aero Commander 500B	911-2	ex N193CA
☐ N626DS	Aero Commander 500B	1460-163	ex N315TG
☐ N630KC	Aero Commander 500B	997-28	ex N6163X
☐ N662MW	Aero Commander 500B	1235-106	ex N106CA
☐ N667CA	Aero Commander 500B	1468-166	ex C-FRJU
☐ N690RR	Aero Commander 500B	1169-88	ex N6289X
☐ N716TC	Aero Commander 500B	1225-102	ex N192CA
☐ N777CM	Aero Commander 500B	1412-147	ex N120EL
☐ N888CA	Aero Commander 500B	1318-127	ex N621RM
☐ N917GT	Aero Commander 500B	1137-77	ex N177CA
☐ N922BS	Aero Commander 500B	1598-207	ex N1193Z
☐ N6154X	Aero Commander 500B	983-24	
☐ N6324U	Aero Commander 500B	1363-134	
☐ N690AT	Rockwell 690A Turbo Commander	11202	ex N600PB

CENTURION II AIR CARGO — Challenge Cargo (WE/CWC) — Miami-Intl, FL (MIA)

☐ N612GC	Douglas DC-10-30F	47840/337	ex G-BHDJ
☐ N984AR	McDonnell-Douglas MD-11BCF	48429/500	ex N429AN
☐ N988AR	McDonnell-Douglas MD-11F	48434/476	ex N701GC ♦

CHAMPLAIN AIR — Plattsburg-Clinton County, NY (PLB)

☐ N59NA	Douglas DC-3	9043	ex G-AKNB	
☐ N700CA	Douglas DC-3	12438	ex N107AD	Mary Ann

CHANNEL ISLANDS AVIATION — Channel (CHN) — Camarillo, CA (CMA)

☐ N55JA	Britten-Norman BN-2A-8 Islander	295	ex G-51-295
☐ N2722D	Cessna 441 Conquest II	441-0168	
☐ N6844O	Cessna 425 Conquest I	425-0062	

CHAUTAUQUA AIRLINES — Chautauqua (RP/CHQ) — Indianapolis-Intl, IN (IND)

Operates as US Airways Express from Boston, ME, Indianapolis, IN, Pittsburgh, PA and New York-La Guardia, NY. Also operates as American Connection from St Louis, MO, as Delta Connection from Orlando, FL, as United Express from Chicago, IL and Washington, DC and as Continental Express from Cleveland, OH, Houston, TX and Newark, NJ.
Wholly owned subsidiary of Republic Airways Holdings.

CHERRY-AIR — Cherry (CCY) — Dallas-Addison, TX (ADS)

☐ N209CA	AMD Falcon 20C	71	ex N195AS
☐ N216CA	AMD Falcon 20C	11	ex N983AJ
☐ N217CA	AMD Falcon 20C	75	ex UR-EFB
☐ N218CA	AMD Falcon 20D	218	ex EC-EEU
☐ N220CA	AMD Falcon 20D	220	ex EC-EDL
☐ N234CA	AMD Falcon 20C	17	ex N55TH
☐ N235CA	AMD Falcon 20C	139	ex N900WB
☐ N151WW	Learjet 24	24-170	ex N200DH
☐ N233CA	Learjet 25B	25B-133	ex XA-RZY

☐ N236CA	Learjet 25B	25B-161	ex N61EW	[ADS]
☐ N238CA	Learjet 25	25-040	ex N23FN	
☐ N343CA	Learjet 25B	25B-202	ex YU-BRA	

CIMARRON AIRE   *Cimmaron Aire (CMN)*   **McAlester-Regional, OK (MLC)**

| ☐ N737SW | Beech E-18S | BA-402 | ex N388W | Frtr |

COASTAL AIR TRANSPORT   *Coastal (DQ/CXT)*   **St Croix-Alexander Hamilton, VI (STX)**

| ☐ N676MF | Cessna 402B | 402B0106 | ex N7856Q | Cruzan Queen |
| ☐ N677MF | Cessna 404 Titan | 404-0421 | ex N96889 | |

COASTAL HELICOPTER   **Juneau-Intl, AK (JNU)**

☐ N178CH	Aérospatiale AS350B2 AStar	2042	ex N910TV
☐ N203CH	Aérospatiale AS350BA AStar	1430	ex N57843
☐ N204CH	Aérospatiale AS350B1 AStar	2054	ex N6080D
☐ N205CH	Aérospatiale AS350BA AStar	1254	ex N3607S
☐ N207CH	Aérospatiale AS350B1 AStar	2027	ex C-FUAM
☐ N209CH	Aérospatiale AS350BA AStar	2494	ex N532BH
☐ N216CH	Aérospatiale AS350B2 AStar	3619	ex N67PT
☐ N655TV	Aérospatiale AS350B AStar	1590	ex N38TH
☐ N57717	Aérospatiale AS350A+ AStar	1334	ex N112SH
☐ N53AG	Bell UH-1H	13827	ex 72-21588
☐ N371AH	Bell 206B JetRanger	1660	ex N450AS
☐ N496CH	Bell 206B JetRanger	1905	ex N49686

COLGAN AIR   *Colgan (9L/CJC)*   **Manassas-Regional, VA (MNZ)**

☐ N202SR	SAAB SF.340B	340B-202	ex N305CE
☐ N210CJ	SAAB SF.340B	340B-210	ex N308CE
☐ N251CJ	SAAB SF.340B	340B-251	ex XA-TQO

COLUMBIA HELICOPTERS   *Columbia Heli (WCO)*
         Aurora-State, OR/Lake Charles-Regional, LA (UAO/LCH)

☐ C-GHFF	Boeing Vertol 107 II	406	ex N195CH	>Helifor
☐ C-GHFY	Boeing Vertol 107 II	2002	ex N190CH	>Helifor
☐ N184CH	Kawasaki KV107-II	4001	ex Thai 4001	
☐ N185CH	Kawasaki KV107-II	4003	ex Thai 4003	
☐ N186CH	Kawasaki KV107-II	4005	ex P2-CHA	
☐ N187CH	Kawasaki KV107-II	4012	ex HC-BZP	
☐ N188CH	Boeing Vertol 107 II	107	ex C-FHFW	♦
☐ N191CH	Boeing Vertol 107 II	2003	ex P2-CHD	
☐ N192CH	Kawasaki KV107-II	4011	ex JA9505	
☐ N6672D	Boeing Vertol 107 II	2		
☐ N6674D	Boeing Vertol 107 II	4	ex C-FHFV	
☐ N6676D	Boeing Vertol 107 II	6		
☐ C-FHFB	Boeing Vertol 234UT Chinook	MJ-005	ex N238CH	>Helifor
☐ N235CH	Boeing Vertol 234UT Chinook	MJ-002	ex G-BISO	
☐ N239CH	Boeing Vertol 234UT Chinook	MJ-006	ex C-FHFJ	
☐ N241CH	Boeing Vertol 234UT Chinook	MJ-016	ex HC-CEN	
☐ N242CH	Boeing Vertol 234UT Chinook	MJ-023	ex HC-BYF	
☐ N245CH	Boeing Vertol 234UT Chinook	MJ-022	ex P2-CHJ	
☐ N246CH	Boeing Vertol 234UT Chinook	MJ-017	ex LN-OMK	
☐ P2-CHI	Boeing Vertol 234UT Chinook	MJ-003	ex N237CH	>TOK
☐ N111NS	Beech 200C Super King Air	BL-36		
☐ N3697F	Beech 200C Super King Air	BL-14		

COMAIR   *Comair (OH/COM)*   **Cincinnati-Northern Kentucky Intl, OH (CVG)**

Wholly owned subsidiary of Delta Air Lines operates as Delta Connection in full colours and using DL flight numbers from Cincinnati, OH and Orlando, FL.

COMMUTAIR   *Commutair (C5/UCA)*   **Plattsburgh-Clinton County, NY (PLB)**

Operates as Continental Connection in full colours and using CO flight numbers. Commutair is a trading name of Champlain Enterprises. Lease sixteen de Havilland DHC-8Q-200s from Horizon Airlines for service from Cleveland.

COMPASS AIRLINES   *(CP/CPZ)*   **Washington-Dulles-Intl, DC (IAD)**

Wholly owned subsidiary of Northwest Airlines (nwa) and operates as nwa airlink (Northwest Airlink).

CORPJET — Beewee (CPJ) — Baltimore-Martin State, MD (MTN)

☐ N208HF	Cessna 208 Caravan I	20800116	ex C-GMPR	
☐ N716BT	Cessna 208B Caravan I	208B0843	ex N5260Y	Frtr
☐ N801TH	Cessna 208 Caravan I	20800123	ex N9680F	
☐ N801FL	Cessna 208B Caravan I	208B0809	ex N5264E	
☐ N5YV	Beech 1900D	UE-5		

CORPORATE AIR — Air Spur (CPT) — Billings-Logan Intl, MT (BIL)

☐ N210AS	Embraer EMB.120FC Brasilia	120006	ex PT-SIA	Frtr
☐ N319BH	Beech 1900C	UB-36	ex N19RA	Frtr
☐ N330SB	Short SD.3-30	SH3013	ex N241CA	Frtr
☐ N331SB	Short SD.3-30	SH3015	ex N331CA	Frtr; [HNL]
☐ N7254R	Beech 1900C	UB-22		Frtr

CORPORATE FLIGHT MANAGEMENT — Volunteer (VTE) — Smyrna, TN (MQY)

☐ N10UP	British Aerospace Jetstream 31	635	ex N635JX
☐ N643JX	British Aerospace Jetstream 31	643	ex N421MX
☐ N657BA	British Aerospace Jetstream 31	657	ex N412MX

CSA AIR — Iron Air (IRO) — Iron Mountain--Ford, MI (IMT)

Operates Cessna Caravans leased from and on behalf of Federal Express

CUSTOM AIR TRANSPORT — Catt (5R/CTT) — Fort Lauderdale-Hollywood Intl, FL (FLL)

☐ N511PE	Boeing 727-232F (FedEx 3)	20634/917	ex N452DA	
☐ N902PG	Boeing 727-281F (FedEx 3)	20725/958	ex OY-TNT	[ROW]
☐ N7635U	Boeing 727-222F (FedEx 3)	19908/653		
☐ N7644U	Boeing 727-222F (FedEx 3)	20038/716		[ROW]
☐ N7645U	Boeing 727-222F (FedEx 3)	20039/720		
☐ N24343	Boeing 727-231F (Super 27)	21630/1458		

DELTA AIR LINES — Delta (DL/DAL) — Atlanta-Hartsfield Intl, GA (ATL)

Member of Skyteam

☐ N301NB	Airbus A319-114	1058	ex D-AVYP	3101City of Duluth
☐ N302NB	Airbus A319-114	1062	ex D-AVWA	3102
☐ N314NB	Airbus A319-114	1191	ex D-AVWO	3114
☐ N315NB	Airbus A319-114	1230	ex D-AVYM	3115
☐ N316NB	Airbus A319-114	1249	ex D-AVYW	3116
☐ N317NB	Airbus A319-114	1324	ex D-AVWT	3117
☐ N318NB	Airbus A319-114	1325	ex D-AVYF	3118
☐ N319NB	Airbus A319-114	1346	ex D-AVYR	3119
☐ N320NB	Airbus A319-114	1392	ex D-AVYT	3120
☐ N321NB	Airbus A319-114	1414	ex D-AVYL	3121
☐ N322NB	Airbus A319-114	1434	ex D-AVYO	3122
☐ N323NB	Airbus A319-114	1453	ex D-AVWE	3123
☐ N324NB	Airbus A319-114	1456	ex D-AVWF	3124
☐ N325NB	Airbus A319-114	1483	ex D-AVYU	3125
☐ N326NB	Airbus A319-114	1498	ex D-AVYC	3126
☐ N327NB	Airbus A319-114	1501	ex D-AVYD	3127
☐ N328NB	Airbus A319-114	1520	ex D-AVYN	3128
☐ N329NB	Airbus A319-114	1543	ex D-AVWJ	3129
☐ N330NB	Airbus A319-114	1549	ex D-AVWM	3130
☐ N331NB	Airbus A319-114	1567	ex D-AVYU	3131
☐ N332NB	Airbus A319-114	1570	ex D-AVWD	3132
☐ N333NB	Airbus A319-114	1582	ex D-AVYA	3133
☐ N334NB	Airbus A319-114	1659	ex D-AVYU	3134
☐ N335NB	Airbus A319-114	1662	ex D-AVYW	3135
☐ N336NB	Airbus A319-114	1683	ex D-AVWJ	3136
☐ N337NB	Airbus A319-114	1685	ex D-AVWL	3137
☐ N338NB	Airbus A319-114	1693	ex D-AVYD	3138
☐ N339NB	Airbus A319-114	1709	ex D-AVWG	3139
☐ N340NB	Airbus A319-114	1714	ex D-AVWN	3140
☐ N341NB	Airbus A319-114	1738	ex D-AVWV	3141
☐ N342NB	Airbus A319-114	1746	ex D-AVYA	3142
☐ N343NB	Airbus A319-114	1752	ex D-AVYH	3143
☐ N344NB	Airbus A319-114	1766	ex D-AVYU	3144
☐ N345NB	Airbus A319-114	1774	ex D-AVYD	3145
☐ N346NB	Airbus A319-114	1796	ex D-AVYX	3146
☐ N347NB	Airbus A319-114	1800	ex D-AVYZ	3147
☐ N348NB	Airbus A319-114	1810	ex D-AVWH	3148
☐ N349NB	Airbus A319-114	1815	ex D-AVWI	3149

☐	N351NB	Airbus A319-114	1820	ex D-AVWL	3151
☐	N352NB	Airbus A319-114	1824	ex D-AVWM	3152
☐	N353NB	Airbus A319-114	1828	ex D-AVWO	3153
☐	N354NB	Airbus A319-114	1833	ex D-AVWS	3154
☐	N355NB	Airbus A319-114	1839	ex D-AVWA	3155
☐	N357NB	Airbus A319-114	1875	ex D-AVYH	3157
☐	N358NB	Airbus A319-114	1897	ex D-AVYK	3158
☐	N359NB	Airbus A319-114	1923	ex D-AVWC	3159
☐	N360NB	Airbus A319-114	1959	ex D-AVWL	3160
☐	N361NB	Airbus A319-114	1976	ex D-AVYB	3161
☐	N362NB	Airbus A319-114	1982	ex D-AVYF	3162
☐	N363NB	Airbus A319-114	1990	ex D-AVYL	3163
☐	N364NB	Airbus A319-114	2002	ex D-AVWA	3164
☐	N365NB	Airbus A319-114	2013	ex D-AVWS	3165
☐	N366NB	Airbus A319-114	2026	ex D-AVWX	3166
☐	N368NB	Airbus A319-114	2039	ex D-AVYT	3168
☐	N369NB	Airbus A319-114	2047	ex D-AVWC	3169
☐	N370NB	Airbus A319-114	2087	ex D-AVWI	3170
☐	N371NB	Airbus A319-114	2095	ex D-AVYI	3171
☐	N309US	Airbus A320-211	0118	ex F-WWIM	3209
☐	N310NW	Airbus A320-211	0121	ex F-WWIO	3210
☐	N311US	Airbus A320-211	0125	ex F-WWIT	3211
☐	N312US	Airbus A320-211	0152	ex F-WWDT	3212
☐	N313US	Airbus A320-211	0153	ex F-WWDX	3213
☐	N314US	Airbus A320-211	0160	ex F-WWDZ	3214
☐	N315US	Airbus A320-211	0171	ex F-WWIJ	3215
☐	N316US	Airbus A320-211	0192	ex F-WWIY	3216
☐	N317US	Airbus A320-211	0197	ex F-WWDF	3217
☐	N318US	Airbus A320-211	0206	ex F-WWDK	3218
☐	N319US	Airbus A320-211	0208	ex F-WWDT	3219
☐	N320US	Airbus A320-211	0213	ex F-WWIB	3220
☐	N321US	Airbus A320-211	0262	ex F-WWDI	3221
☐	N322US	Airbus A320-211	0263	ex F-WWDQ	3222
☐	N323US	Airbus A320-211	0272	ex F-WWBP	3223
☐	N324US	Airbus A320-211	0273	ex F-WWDS	3224
☐	N325US	Airbus A320-211	0281	ex F-WWBS	3225
☐	N326US	Airbus A320-211	0282	ex F-WWIA	3226
☐	N327NW	Airbus A320-211	0297	ex F-WWIO	3227
☐	N328NW	Airbus A320-211	0298	ex F-WWIP	3228
☐	N329NW	Airbus A320-211	0306	ex F-WWDG	3229
☐	N330NW	Airbus A320-211	0307	ex F-WWDJ	3230
☐	N331NW	Airbus A320-211	0318	ex F-WWBF	3231
☐	N332NW	Airbus A320-211	0319	ex F-WWBG	3232
☐	N333NW	Airbus A320-211	0329	ex F-WWDY	3233
☐	N334NW	Airbus A320-212	0339	ex F-WWBP	3234
☐	N335NW	Airbus A320-212	0340	ex F-WWBQ	3235
☐	N336NW	Airbus A320-212	0355	ex F-WWIE	3236
☐	N337NW	Airbus A320-212	0358	ex F-WWIO	3237
☐	N338NW	Airbus A320-212	0360	ex F-WWBY	3238
☐	N339NW	Airbus A320-212	0367	ex F-WWDG	3239
☐	N340NW	Airbus A320-212	0372	ex F-WWIX	3240
☐	N341NW	Airbus A320-212	0380	ex F-WWIS	3241
☐	N342NW	Airbus A320-212	0381	ex F-WWIJ	3242
☐	N343NW	Airbus A320-212	0387	ex F-WWBV	3243
☐	N344NW	Airbus A320-212	0388	ex F-WWDC	3244
☐	N345NW	Airbus A320-212	0399	ex F-WWIG	3245
☐	N347NW	Airbus A320-212	0408	ex F-WWDN	3247
☐	N348NW	Airbus A320-212	0410	ex F-WWDV	3248
☐	N349NW	Airbus A320-212	0417	ex F-WWBR	3249
☐	N350NA	Airbus A320-212	0418	ex F-WWDG	3250
☐	N351NW	Airbus A320-212	0766	ex F-WWDG	3251
☐	N352NW	Airbus A320-212	0778	ex F-WWDO	3252
☐	N353NW	Airbus A320-212	0786	ex F-WWDP	3253
☐	N354NW	Airbus A320-212	0801	ex F-WWDY	3254
☐	N355NW	Airbus A320-212	0807	ex F-WWIC	3255
☐	N356NW	Airbus A320-212	0818	ex F-WWBD	3256
☐	N357NW	Airbus A320-212	0830	ex F-WWIN	3257
☐	N358NW	Airbus A320-212	0832	ex F-WWIO	3258
☐	N359NW	Airbus A320-212	0846	ex F-WWBH	3259
☐	N360NW	Airbus A320-212	0903	ex F-WWDO	3260
☐	N361NW	Airbus A320-212	0907	ex F-WWDQ	3261
☐	N362NW	Airbus A320-212	0911	ex F-WWDT	3262
☐	N363NW	Airbus A320-212	0923	ex F-WWDZ	3263
☐	N364NW	Airbus A320-212	0962	ex F-WWBF	3264
☐	N365NW	Airbus A320-212	0964	ex F-WWBJ	3265
☐	N366NW	Airbus A320-212	0981	ex F-WWDE	3266

Delta c/s

☐	N367NW	Airbus A320-212	0988	ex F-WWIH	3267
☐	N368NW	Airbus A320-212	0996	ex F-WWBV	3268
☐	N369NW	Airbus A320-212	1011	ex F-WWDO	3269
☐	N370NW	Airbus A320-212	1037	ex F-WWDY	3270
☐	N371NW	Airbus A320-212	1535	ex F-WWIS	3271
☐	N372NW	Airbus A320-212	1633	ex F-WWDO	3272
☐	N373NW	Airbus A320-212	1641	ex F-WWIR	3273
☐	N374NW	Airbus A320-212	1646	ex F-WWDS	3274
☐	N375NC	Airbus A320-212	1789	ex F-WWDU	3275
☐	N376NW	Airbus A320-212	1812	ex F-WWBB	3276
☐	N377NW	Airbus A320-212	2082	ex F-WWIU	3277
☐	N378NW	Airbus A320-212	2092	ex F-WWBP	3278
☐	N801NW	Airbus A330-323E	524	ex F-WWYZ	3301
☐	N802NW	Airbus A330-323E	533	ex F-WWYD	3302
☐	N803NW	Airbus A330-323E	542	ex F-WWYH	3303
☐	N804NW	Airbus A330-323E	549	ex F-WWYJ	3304
☐	N805NW	Airbus A330-323E	552	ex F-WWKQ	3305
☐	N806NW	Airbus A330-323E	578	ex F-WWKD	3306
☐	N807NW	Airbus A330-323E	588	ex F-WWKM	3307
☐	N808NW	Airbus A330-323E	591	ex F-WWKO	3308
☐	N809NW	Airbus A330-323E	663	ex F-WWKM	3309
☐	N810NW	Airbus A330-323E	674	ex F-WWKT	3310
☐	N811NW	Airbus A330-323E	690	ex F-WWKV	3311
☐	N812NW	Airbus A330-323E	784	ex F-WWYX	3312
☐	N813NW	Airbus A330-323E	799	ex F-WWKV	3313
☐	N814NW	Airbus A330-323E	806	ex F-WWYN	3314
☐	N815NW	Airbus A330-323E	817	ex F-WWYP	3315
☐	N816NW	Airbus A330-323E	827	ex F-WWKG	3316
☐	N817NW	Airbus A330-323E	843	ex F-WWYX	3317
☐	N818NW	Airbus A330-323E	857	ex F-WWYD	3318
☐	N819NW	Airbus A330-323E	858	ex F-WWYE	3319
☐	N820NW	Airbus A330-323E	859	ex F-WWYF	3320
☐	N821NW	Airbus A330-323E	865	ex F-WWYJ	3321
☐	N851NW	Airbus A330-223	609	ex F-WWYZ	3351
☐	N852NW	Airbus A330-223	614	ex F-WWKU	3352
☐	N853NW	Airbus A330-223	618	ex F-WWKN	3353
☐	N854NW	Airbus A330-223	620	ex F-WWYA	3354
☐	N855NW	Airbus A330-223	621	ex F-WWYB	3355
☐	N856NW	Airbus A330-223	631	ex F-WWYG	3356
☐	N857NW	Airbus A330-223	633	ex F-WWYI	3357
☐	N858NW	Airbus A330-223	718	ex F-WWYY	3358
☐	N859NW	Airbus A330-223	722	ex F-WWKM	3359
☐	N860NW	Airbus A330-223	778	ex F-WWKL	3360
☐	N861NW	Airbus A330-223	796	ex F-WWKT	3361
☐	N301DQ	Boeing 737-732/W	29687/2667	ex N1795B	3601
☐	N302DQ	Boeing 737-732/W	29648/2683		3602
☐	N303DQ	Boeing 737-732/W	29688/2720	ex N1786B	3603
☐	N304DQ	Boeing 737-732/W	29683/2724	ex N1787B	3604
☐	N305DQ	Boeing 737-732/W	29645/2743		3605
☐	N306DQ	Boeing 737-732/W	29633/2758		3606
☐	N307DQ	Boeing 737-732/W	29679/2767		3607
☐	N308DE	Boeing 737-732/W	29656/3022	ex N1786B	3608
☐	N309DE	Boeing 737-732/W	29634/3031	ex N1796B	3609
☐	N310DE	Boeing 737-732/W	29665/3058	ex N1786B	3610
☐	N371DA	Boeing 737-832/W	29619/115	ex N1787B	3701
☐	N372DA	Boeing 737-832/W	29620/118	ex N1782B	3702
☐	N373DA	Boeing 737-832/W	29621/123	ex N1800B	3703
☐	N374DA	Boeing 737-832/W	29622/128	ex N1787B	3704
☐	N375DA	Boeing 737-832/W	29623/145		3705
☐	N376DA	Boeing 737-832/W	29624/176		3706
☐	N377DA	Boeing 737-832/W	29625/264		3707
☐	N378DA	Boeing 737-832/W	30265/340		3708
☐	N379DA	Boeing 737-832/W	30349/351		3709
☐	N380DA	Boeing 737-832/W	30266/361		3710
☐	N381DN	Boeing 737-832/W	30350/365	ex (N381DA)	3711
☐	N382DA	Boeing 737-832/W	30345/389		3712
☐	N383DN	Boeing 737-832/W	30346/393	ex (N383DA)	3713
☐	N384DA	Boeing 737-832/W	30347/412		3714
☐	N385DN	Boeing 737-832/W	30348/418		3715
☐	N386DA	Boeing 737-832/W	30373/446	ex N1780B	3716
☐	N387DA	Boeing 737-832/W	30374/457	ex N1795B	3717
☐	N388DA	Boeing 737-832/W	30375/469		3718
☐	N389DA	Boeing 737-832/W	30376/513	ex N1787B	3719

	Registration	Type	MSN/Line	Ex	Fleet	Notes
☐	N390DA	Boeing 737-832/W	30536/518	ex N6063S	3720	
☐	N391DA	Boeing 737-832/W	30560/535	ex N1787B	3721	
☐	N392DA	Boeing 737-832/W	30561/564		3722	
☐	N393DA	Boeing 737-832/W	30377/584	ex N1782B	3723	
☐	N394DA	Boeing 737-832/W	30562/589		3724	
☐	N395DN	Boeing 737-832/W	30773/604		3725	
☐	N396DA	Boeing 737-832/W	30378/632	ex N1795B	3726	Delta Shuttle♦
☐	N397DA	Boeing 737-832/W	30537/638		3727	Delta Shuttle
☐	N398DA	Boeing 737-832/W	30774/641		3728	Delta Shuttle
☐	N399DA	Boeing 737-832/W	30379/657		3729	Delta Shuttle
☐	N3730B	Boeing 737-832	30538/662		3730	Delta Shuttle
☐	N3731T	Boeing 737-832/W	30775/665		3731	Delta Shuttle
☐	N3732J	Boeing 737-832/W	30380/674		3732	Delta Shuttle
☐	N3733Z	Boeing 737-832/W	30539/685		3733	Delta Shuttle
☐	N3734B	Boeing 737-832/W	30776/689		3734	Delta Shuttle
☐	N3735D	Boeing 737-832/W	30381/694	ex (N3735J)	3735	Delta Shuttle
☐	N3736C	Boeing 737-832/W	30540/709		3736	Delta Shuttle
☐	N3737C	Boeing 737-832/W	30799/712		3737	
☐	N3738B	Boeing 737-832/W	30382/723		3738	
☐	N3739P	Boeing 737-832/W	30541/729		3739	
☐	N3740C	Boeing 737-832/W	30800/732		3740	
☐	N3741S	Boeing 737-832/W	30487/750		3741	
☐	N3742C	Boeing 737-832/W	30835/755	ex N1781B	3742	
☐	N3743H	Boeing 737-832/W	30836/770	ex N1795B	3743	
☐	N3744F	Boeing 737-832/W	30837/805		3744	
☐	N3745B	Boeing 737-832/W	32373/831		3745	
☐	N3746H	Boeing 737-832/W	30488/842		3746	
☐	N3747D	Boeing 737-832/W	32374/846	ex N1787B	3747	
☐	N3748Y	Boeing 737-832/W	30489/865		3748	
☐	N3749D	Boeing 737-832/W	30490/867		3749	
☐	N3750D	Boeing 737-832/W	32375/870	ex N1787B	3750	
☐	N3751B	Boeing 737-832/W	30491/892		3751	
☐	N3752	Boeing 737-832/W	30492/894		3752	
☐	N3753	Boeing 737-832/W	32626/899		3753	
☐	N3754A	Boeing 737-832/W	29626/907		3754	
☐	N3755D	Boeing 737-832/W	29627/914		3755	
☐	N3756	Boeing 737-832/W	30493/917	ex N1799B	3756	
☐	N3757D	Boeing 737-832/W	30813/921		3757	
☐	N3758Y	Boeing 737-832/W	30814/923		3758	
☐	N3759	Boeing 737-832/W	30815/949		3759	
☐	N3760C	Boeing 737-832/W	30816/952	ex N1787B	3760	
☐	N3761R	Boeing 737-832/W	29628/964	ex N1784B	3761	
☐	N3762Y	Boeing 737-832/W	30817/968		3762	
☐	N3763D	Boeing 737-832/W	29629/1003	ex N1787B	3763	
☐	N3764D	Boeing 737-832/W	30818/1006		3764	
☐	N3765	Boeing 737-832/W	30819/1008	ex N1795B	3765	
☐	N3766	Boeing 737-832/W	30820/1029		3766	
☐	N3767	Boeing 737-832/W	30821/1031		3767	
☐	N3768	Boeing 737-832/W	29630/1053		3768	
☐	N3769L	Boeing 737-832/W	30822/1057		3769	
☐	N3771K	Boeing 737-832/W	29632/1103		3771	
☐	N3772H	Boeing 737-832/W	30823/3274		3772	♦
☐	N3773D	Boeing 737-832/W	30825/3338	ex N1796B	3773	♦
☐	N37700	Boeing 737-832/W	29631/1074		3770	
☐	N661US	Boeing 747-451	23719/696	ex N401PW	6301	
☐	N662US	Boeing 747-451	23720/708	ex (N302US)	6302	
☐	N663US	Boeing 747-451	23818/715	ex (N303US)	6303	
☐	N664US	Boeing 747-451	23819/721	ex (N304US)	6304	The Spirit of Beijing
☐	N665US	Boeing 747-451	23820/726	ex (N305US)	6305	
☐	N666US	Boeing 747-451	23821/742	ex (N306US)	6306	
☐	N667US	Boeing 747-451	24222/799	ex (N307US)	6307	
☐	N668US	Boeing 747-451	24223/800	ex (N308US)	6308	
☐	N669US	Boeing 747-451	24224/803	ex (N309US)	6309	
☐	N670US	Boeing 747-451	24225/804	ex (N311US)	6310	Alliance Spirit
☐	N671US	Boeing 747-451	26477/1206		6311	
☐	N672US	Boeing 747-451	30267/1223		6312	
☐	N673US	Boeing 747-451	30268/1226		6313	
☐	N674US	Boeing 747-451	30269/1232		6314	
☐	N675NW	Boeing 747-451	33001/1297		6315	
☐	N676NW	Boeing 747-451	33002/1303		6316	
☐	N501US	Boeing 757-251	23190/53		5501	St Paul
☐	N502US	Boeing 757-251	23191/55		5502	Minneapolis
☐	N503US	Boeing 757-251	23192/59		5503	Detroit
☐	N507US	Boeing 757-251	23196/68		5507	Seattle
☐	N508US	Boeing 757-251	23197/69		5508	Washington DC [MZJ]

☐ N513US	Boeing 757-251	23201/83		5513 Orlando	[MZJ]
☐ N514US	Boeing 757-251	23202/86		5514 San Francisco	
☐ N516US	Boeing 757-251	23204/104		5516 San Diego	
☐ N517US	Boeing 757-251	23205/105		5517 Portland	
☐ N518US	Boeing 757-251	23206/107		5518 Milwaukee	
☐ N519US	Boeing 757-251	23207/108		5519 Cleveland	
☐ N520US	Boeing 757-251	23208/109		5520 Philadelphia	
☐ N521US	Boeing 757-251	23209/110		5521 Denver	
☐ N522US	Boeing 757-251	23616/119		5522	[MZJ]
☐ N523US	Boeing 757-251	23617/121		5523 Dallas	
☐ N525US	Boeing 757-251	23619/124		5525 Miami	[MZJ]
☐ N526US	Boeing 757-251	23620/131		5526 Memphis	
☐ N528US	Boeing 757-251	23843/137		5528	
☐ N529US	Boeing 757-251	23844/140		5529 New Orleans	
☐ N530US	Boeing 757-251	23845/188		5530 Omaha	
☐ N531US	Boeing 757-251	23846/190		5531 Newark	
☐ N532US	Boeing 757-251	24263/192		5532 Fort Myers	[MZJ]
☐ N533US	Boeing 757-251	24264/194		5533 Orange County	
☐ N534US	Boeing 757-251	24265/196		5534 Winnipeg	
☐ N535US	Boeing 757-251/W	26482/693		5635	
☐ N536US	Boeing 757-251/W	26483/695		5636	
☐ N537US	Boeing 757-251/W	26484/697		5637	
☐ N538US	Boeing 757-251/W	26485/699		5638	
☐ N539US	Boeing 757-251/W	26486/700		5639	Delta c/s
☐ N540US	Boeing 757-251/W	26487/701		5640	
☐ N541US	Boeing 757-251	26488/703		5641	
☐ N542US	Boeing 757-251	26489/705		5642	
☐ N543US	Boeing 757-251	26490/709		5643	
☐ N544US	Boeing 757-251/W	26491/710		5644	
☐ N545US	Boeing 757-251/W	26492/711		5645	
☐ N546US	Boeing 757-251/W	26493/713		5646	
☐ N547US	Boeing 757-251/W	26494/714		5647	
☐ N548US	Boeing 757-251/W	26495/715		5648	
☐ N549US	Boeing 757-251/W	26496/716		5649	
☐ N550NW	Boeing 757-251	26497/968		5550	
☐ N551NW	Boeing 757-251	26498/971		5551	
☐ N552NW	Boeing 757-251/W	26499/975		5552	
☐ N553NW	Boeing 757-251/W	26500/982		5553	
☐ N554NW	Boeing 757-251/W	26501/987		5554	
☐ N555NW	Boeing 757-251/W	33391/1011		5555	
☐ N556NW	Boeing 757-251/W	33392/1013		5556	
☐ N557NW	Boeing 757-251/W	33393/1016		5557	

names prefixed 'City of'

☐ N581NW	Boeing 757-351	32982/1001	ex N753JM	5801	
☐ N582NW	Boeing 757-351	32981/1014		5802, The Bernie Epple	
☐ N583NW	Boeing 757-351	32983/1019		5803	
☐ N584NW	Boeing 757-351	32984/1020		5804	
☐ N585NW	Boeing 757-351	32985/1021		5805	
☐ N586NW	Boeing 757-351	32987/1022		5806	
☐ N587NW	Boeing 757-351	32986/1023		5807	
☐ N588NW	Boeing 757-351	32988/1024		5808	
☐ N589NW	Boeing 757-351	32989/1025		5809	
☐ N590NW	Boeing 757-351	32990/1027	ex N1795B	5810	
☐ N591NW	Boeing 757-351	32991/1030		5811	
☐ N592NW	Boeing 757-351	32992/1033		5812	
☐ N593NW	Boeing 757-351	32993/1034	ex N1795B	5813	
☐ N594NW	Boeing 757-351	32994/1035		5814	
☐ N595NW	Boeing 757-351	32995/1036	ex N1795B	5815	
☐ N596NW	Boeing 757-351	32996/1037		5816	

☐ N602DL	Boeing 757-232	22809/39		602	
☐ N603DL	Boeing 757-232	22810/41		603	
☐ N604DL	Boeing 757-232	22811/43		604	
☐ N608DA	Boeing 757-232	22815/64		608	
☐ N609DL	Boeing 757-232	22816/65		609	
☐ N610DL	Boeing 757-232	22817/66		610	pink c/s
☐ N612DL	Boeing 757-232	22819/73		612	
☐ N613DL	Boeing 757-232	22820/84		613	
☐ N614DL	Boeing 757-232	22821/85		614	
☐ N615DL	Boeing 757-232	22822/87		615	
☐ N616DL	Boeing 757-232	22823/91		616	[SAT]
☐ N617DL	Boeing 757-232	22907/92		617	[MZJ]
☐ N618DL	Boeing 757-232	22908/95		618	[MZJ]
☐ N619DL	Boeing 757-232	22909/101		619	
☐ N620DL	Boeing 757-232	22910/111		620	for CCI
☐ N621DL	Boeing 757-232	22911/112		621	

☐	N622DL	Boeing 757-232	22912/113	622	[MZJ]
☐	N623DL	Boeing 757-232	22913/118	623	
☐	N624DL	Boeing 757-232	22914/120	624	
☐	N625DL	Boeing 757-232	22915/126	625	
☐	N626DL	Boeing 757-232	22916/128	626	
☐	N627DL	Boeing 757-232	22917/129	627	
☐	N628DL	Boeing 757-232	22918/133	628	
☐	N629DL	Boeing 757-232	22919/134	629	
☐	N630DL	Boeing 757-232	22920/135	630	
☐	N631DL	Boeing 757-232	23612/138	631	
☐	N632DL	Boeing 757-232	23613/154	632	
☐	N633DL	Boeing 757-232	23614/157	633	
☐	N634DL	Boeing 757-232	23615/158	634	
☐	N635DL	Boeing 757-232	23762/159	ex 'N635DA'	635	
☐	N636DL	Boeing 757-232	23763/164	636	
☐	N637DL	Boeing 757-232	23760/171	637	
☐	N638DL	Boeing 757-232/W	23761/177	638	
☐	N639DL	Boeing 757-232	23993/198	639	
☐	N640DL	Boeing 757-232/W	23994/201	640	
☐	N641DL	Boeing 757-232/W	23995/202	641	
☐	N642DL	Boeing 757-232	23996/205	642	
☐	N643DL	Boeing 757-232	23997/206	643	
☐	N644DL	Boeing 757-232	23998/207	644	
☐	N645DL	Boeing 757-232	24216/216	645	
☐	N646DL	Boeing 757-232	24217/217	646	[VCV]
☐	N647DL	Boeing 757-232	24218/222	647	
☐	N648DL	Boeing 757-232/W	24372/223	648	
☐	N649DL	Boeing 757-232/W	24389/229	649	
☐	N650DL	Boeing 757-232/W	24390/230	650	
☐	N651DL	Boeing 757-232	24391/238	651	
☐	N652DL	Boeing 757-232	24392/239	652	
☐	N653DL	Boeing 757-232	24393/261	653	
☐	N654DL	Boeing 757-232	24394/264	654	
☐	N655DL	Boeing 757-232	24395/265	655	
☐	N656DL	Boeing 757-232	24396/266	656	
☐	N657DL	Boeing 757-232	24419/286	657	
☐	N658DL	Boeing 757-232	24420/287	658	[MZJ]
☐	N659DL	Boeing 757-232	24421/293	659	[MZJ]
☐	N660DL	Boeing 757-232	24422/294	660	
☐	N661DN	Boeing 757-232	24972/335	661	[MZJ]
☐	N662DN	Boeing 757-232	24991/342	662	
☐	N663DN	Boeing 757-232/W	24992/343	663	
☐	N664DN	Boeing 757-232	25012/347	664	
☐	N665DN	Boeing 757-232/W	25013/349	665	
☐	N666DN	Boeing 757-232/W	25034/354	666	
☐	N667DN	Boeing 757-232	25035/355	667	
☐	N668DN	Boeing 757-232	25141/376	668	
☐	N669DN	Boeing 757-232	25142/377	669	
☐	N670DN	Boeing 757-232	25331/415	670	
☐	N671DN	Boeing 757-232	25332/416	671	
☐	N672DL	Boeing 757-232	25977/429	672	
☐	N673DL	Boeing 757-232	25978/430	673	
☐	N674DL	Boeing 757-232	25979/439	674	
☐	N675DL	Boeing 757-232	25980/448	675	
☐	N676DL	Boeing 757-232	25981/455	676	
☐	N677DL	Boeing 757-232	25982/456	677	
☐	N678DL	Boeing 757-232	25983/465	678	
☐	N679DA	Boeing 757-232	26955/500	679	
☐	N680DA	Boeing 757-232	26956/502	680	
☐	N681DA	Boeing 757-232	26957/516	681	
☐	N682DA	Boeing 757-232	26958/518	682	
☐	N683DA	Boeing 757-232	27103/533	683	
☐	N684DA	Boeing 757-232	27104/535	684	
☐	N685DA	Boeing 757-232	27588/667	685	
☐	N686DA	Boeing 757-232	27589/689	686	
☐	N687DL	Boeing 757-232	27586/800	687	
☐	N688DL	Boeing 757-232	27587/803	688	
☐	N689DL	Boeing 757-232	27172/807	689	
☐	N690DL	Boeing 757-232	27585/808	690	
☐	N692DL	Boeing 757-232/W	29724/820	ex N1799B	692	
☐	N693DL	Boeing 757-232	29725/826	ex N1799B	693	
☐	N694DL	Boeing 757-232	29726/831	694	
☐	N695DL	Boeing 757-232	29727/838	ex N1795B	695	
☐	N696DL	Boeing 757-232	29728/845	ex N1795B	696	
☐	N697DL	Boeing 757-232	30318/880	ex N1795B	697	
☐	N698DL	Boeing 757-232	29911/885	698	
☐	N699DL	Boeing 757-232	29970/887	ex N1795B	699	

	Registration	Type	MSN/Line	Ex	Fleet	Notes
☐	N702TW	Boeing 757-2Q8/W	28162/732		6801	
☐	N703TW	Boeing 757-2Q8ER/W	27620/736		6802	
☐	N704X	Boeing 757-2Q8/W	28163/741		6803	
☐	N705TW	Boeing 757-231/W	28479/742		6811	
☐	N706TW	Boeing 757-2Q8/W	28165/743		6804	
☐	N707TW	Boeing 757-2Q8ER/W	27625/744		6805	
☐	N709TW	Boeing 757-2Q8/W	28168/754		6806	
☐	N710TW	Boeing 757-2Q8/W	28169/757		6807	
☐	N711ZX	Boeing 757-231/W	28481/758		6814	
☐	N712TW	Boeing 757-2Q8ER/W	27624/760		6808	
☐	N713TW	Boeing 757-2Q8/W	28173/764		6809	
☐	N717TW	Boeing 757-231/W	28485/854		6812	
☐	N718TW	Boeing 757-231/W	28486/869		6815	
☐	N721TW	Boeing 757-231/W	29954/874		6810	
☐	N722TW	Boeing 757-231/W	29385/893	ex N1795B	6816	
☐	N723TW	Boeing 757-231/W	29378/907		6817	
☐	N727TW	Boeing 757-231/W	30340/901		6813	
☐	N750AT	Boeing 757-212ER	23126/45	ex 9V-SGL	6902	
☐	N751AT	Boeing 757-212ER	23125/44	ex 9V-SGK	6901	
☐	N752AT	Boeing 757-212ER	23128/48	ex 9V-SGN	6904	
☐	N757AT	Boeing 757-212ER	23127/47	ex 9V-SGM	6903	
☐	N900PC	Boeing 757-26D	28446/740		691	
☐	N6700	Boeing 757-232	30337/890		6700	
☐	N6701	Boeing 757-232	30187/892		6701	
☐	N6702	Boeing 757-232	30188/898		6702	
☐	N6703D	Boeing 757-232	30234/908	ex N1795B	6703	
☐	N6704Z	Boeing 757-232	30396/914	ex N1795B	6704	
☐	N6705Y	Boeing 757-232	30397/917		6705	
☐	N6706Q	Boeing 757-232	30422/921		6706	
☐	N6707A	Boeing 757-232	30395/927		6707	
☐	N6708D	Boeing 757-232	30480/934		6708	
☐	N6709	Boeing 757-232	30481/937		6709	
☐	N6710E	Boeing 757-232	30482/939		6710	
☐	N6711M	Boeing 757-232	30483/941		6711	
☐	N6712B	Boeing 757-232	30484/942		6712	
☐	N6713Y	Boeing 757-232	30777/944		6713	
☐	N6714Q	Boeing 757-232	30485/949		6714	
☐	N6715C	Boeing 757-232	30486/953		6715	
☐	N6716C	Boeing 757-232	30838/955		6716	
☐	N67171	Boeing 757-232	30839/959		6717	
☐	N121DE	Boeing 767-332	23435/162		121	[VCV]
☐	N124DE	Boeing 767-332	23438/189		124	[VCV]
☐	N125DL	Boeing 767-332	24075/200		125	
☐	N126DL	Boeing 767-332	24076/201		126	
☐	N127DL	Boeing 767-332	24077/203		127	
☐	N128DL	Boeing 767-332	24078/207		128	
☐	N129DL	Boeing 767-332	24079/209		129	
☐	N130DL	Boeing 767-332	24080/216		130	
☐	N131DN	Boeing 767-332	24852/320		131	[MZJ]
☐	N132DN	Boeing 767-332	24981/345		132	[VCV]
☐	N133DN	Boeing 767-332	24982/348		133	[VCV]
☐	N134DL	Boeing 767-332	25123/353		134	[VCV]
☐	N135DL	Boeing 767-332	25145/356		135	[VCV]
☐	N136DL	Boeing 767-332	25146/374		136	
☐	N137DL	Boeing 767-332	25306/392		137	
☐	N138DL	Boeing 767-332	25409/410		138	
☐	N139DL	Boeing 767-332	25984/427		139	
☐	N140LL	Boeing 767-332	25988/499		1401	
☐	N143DA	Boeing 767-332	25991/721		1403	
☐	N144DA	Boeing 767-332	27584/751		1404	
☐	N152DL	Boeing 767-3P6ER	24984/339	ex A4O-GM	1502	
☐	N153DL	Boeing 767-3P6ER	24985/340	ex A4O-GN	1503	
☐	N154DL	Boeing 767-3P6ER	25241/389	ex A4O-GO	1504	
☐	N155DL	Boeing 767-3P6ER	25269/390	ex A4O-GP	1505	[VCV]♦
☐	N156DL	Boeing 767-3P6ER	25354/406	ex A4O-GR	1506	
☐	N169DZ	Boeing 767-332ER	29689/706		1601	
☐	N171DN	Boeing 767-332ER	24759/304		171	
☐	N171DZ	Boeing 767-332ER	29690/717		1701	Habitat for Humanity c/s
☐	N172DN	Boeing 767-332ER	24775/312		172	[VCV]
☐	N172DZ	Boeing 767-332ER	29691/719		1702	
☐	N173DN	Boeing 767-332ER	24800/313		173	[VCV]
☐	N173DZ	Boeing 767-332ER	29692/723		1703	
☐	N174DN	Boeing 767-332ER/W	24802/317		174	
☐	N174DZ	Boeing 767-332ER	29693/725		1704	
☐	N175DN	Boeing 767-332ER	24803/318		175	
☐	N175DZ	Boeing 767-332ER	29696/740		1705	

☐ N176DN	Boeing 767-332ER	25061/341		176	
☐ N176DZ	Boeing 767-332ER	29697/745		1706	
☐ N177DN	Boeing 767-332ER/W	25122/346		177	
☐ N177DZ	Boeing 767-332ER	29698/750		1707	
☐ N178DN	Boeing 767-332ER	25143/349		178	
☐ N178DZ	Boeing 767-332ER	30596/795		1708	
☐ N179DN	Boeing 767-332ER/W	25144/350		179	
☐ N180DN	Boeing 767-332ER	25985/428		180	
☐ N181DN	Boeing 767-332ER	25986/446		181	
☐ N182DN	Boeing 767-332ER	25987/461		182	
☐ N183DN	Boeing 767-332ER	27110/492		183	
☐ N184DN	Boeing 767-332ER	27111/496		184	
☐ N185DN	Boeing 767-332ER/W	27961/576		185	
☐ N186DN	Boeing 767-332ER/W	27962/585		186	♦
☐ N187DN	Boeing 767-332ER/W	27582/617		187	
☐ N188DN	Boeing 767-332ER	27583/631		188	
☐ N189DN	Boeing 767-332ER	25990/646		189	
☐ N190DN	Boeing 767-332ER	28447/653		190	
☐ N191DN	Boeing 767-332ER/W	28448/654		191	
☐ N192DN	Boeing 767-332ER/W	28449/664		192	
☐ N193DN	Boeing 767-332ER	28450/671		193	
☐ N194DN	Boeing 767-332ER/W	28451/675		194	[MZJ]
☐ N195DN	Boeing 767-332ER	28452/676		195	
☐ N196DN	Boeing 767-332ER	28453/679		196	
☐ N197DN	Boeing 767-332ER	28454/683		197	
☐ N198DN	Boeing 767-332ER	28455/685		198	
☐ N199DN	Boeing 767-332ER	28456/690		199	
☐ N394DL	Boeing 767-324ER	27394/572	ex HL7505	1521	
☐ N1200K	Boeing 767-332ER	28457/696		1200	
☐ N1201P	Boeing 767-332ER	28458/697		1201	
☐ N1402A	Boeing 767-332	25989/506		1402	
☐ N1501P	Boeing 767-3P6ER	24983/334	ex A4O-GL	1501	
☐ N1602	Boeing 767-332ER	29694/735		1602	
☐ N1603	Boeing 767-332ER	29695/736		1603	
☐ N1604R	Boeing 767-332ER	30180/749		1604	
☐ N1605	Boeing 767-332ER	30198/753		1605	
☐ N1607B	Boeing 767-332ER/W	30388/787		1607	
☐ N1608	Boeing 767-332ER/W	30573/788		1608	
☐ N1609	Boeing 767-332ER/W	30574/789		1609	
☐ N1610D	Boeing 767-332ER/W	30594/790		1610	
☐ N1611B	Boeing 767-332ER	30595/794		1611	
☐ N1612T	Boeing 767-332ER/W	30575/838		1612	
☐ N1613B	Boeing 767-332ER/W	32776/847		1613	
☐ N16065	Boeing 767-332ER	30199/755		1606	
☐ N825MH	Boeing 767-432ER	29703/758	ex N6067U	1801	
☐ N826MH	Boeing 767-432ER	29713/769		1802	
☐ N827MH	Boeing 767-432ER	29705/773	ex N76400	1803	
☐ N828MH	Boeing 767-432ER	29699/791		1804	
☐ N829MH	Boeing 767-432ER	29700/801		1805	
☐ N830MH	Boeing 767-432ER	29701/803		1806	
☐ N831MH	Boeing 767-432ER	29702/804		1807	
☐ N832MH	Boeing 767-432ER	29704/807		1808	
☐ N833MH	Boeing 767-432ER	29706/810		1809	
☐ N834MH	Boeing 767-432ER	29707/813		1810	
☐ N835MH	Boeing 767-432ER	29708/814		1811	
☐ N836MH	Boeing 767-432ER	29709/818		1812	
☐ N837MH	Boeing 767-432ER	29710/820		1813	
☐ N838MH	Boeing 767-432ER	29711/821		1814	
☐ N839MH	Boeing 767-432ER	29712/824		1815	
☐ N840MH	Boeing 767-432ER	29718/830		1816	
☐ N841MH	Boeing 767-432ER	29714/855		1817	
☐ N842MH	Boeing 767-432ER	29715/856		1818	
☐ N843MH	Boeing 767-432ER	29716/865		1819	
☐ N844MH	Boeing 767-432ER	29717/871		1820	
☐ N845MH	Boeing 767-432ER	29719/874		1821	
☐ N701DN	Boeing 777-232LR	29740/697	ex N5016R	7101	
☐ N702DN	Boeing 777-232LR	29741/704		7102	
☐ N703DN	Boeing 777-232LR	32222/767		7103	
☐ N704DK	Boeing 777-232LR	29739/772	ex N5016R	7104	
☐ N705DN	Boeing 777-232LR	29742/773		7105	
☐ N706DN	Boeing 777-232LR	30440/776	ex N5023Q	7106	
☐ N707DN	Boeing 777-232LR	39091/782		7107	
☐ N708DN	Boeing 777-232LR	39254/789		7108	
☐ N709DN	Boeing 777-232LR	40559/854		7109	♦
☐ N710DN	Boeing 777-232LR	40560/857		7110	♦

☐ N860DA	Boeing 777-232ER	29951/202		7001	
☐ N861DA	Boeing 777-232ER	29952/207		7002	
☐ N862DA	Boeing 777-232ER	29734/235	ex N5022E	7003	
☐ N863DA	Boeing 777-232ER	29735/245	ex N5014K	7004	
☐ N864DA	Boeing 777-232ER	29736/249	ex N50217	7005	
☐ N865DA	Boeing 777-232ER	29737/257		7006	
☐ N866DA	Boeing 777-232ER	29738/261		7007	
☐ N867DA	Boeing 777-232ER	29743/387		7008	
☐ N90S	Douglas DC-9-31	47244/498		9931	[MZJ]
☐ N401EA	Douglas DC-9-51	47682/788	ex N920VJ	9885	
☐ N600TR	Douglas DC-9-51	47783/899	ex YV-40C	9886	
☐ N623NW	Douglas DC-9-32	47591/706	ex I-RIFT	9623	[MZJ]
☐ N670MC	Douglas DC-9-51	47659/807	ex HB-ISP	9882	
☐ N671MC	Douglas DC-9-51	47660/810	ex HB-ISR	9883	
☐ N675MC	Douglas DC-9-51	47651/780	ex OE-LDK	9880	[MZJ]
☐ N676MC	Douglas DC-9-51	47652/798	ex OE-LDL	9881	
☐ N677MC	Douglas DC-9-51	47756/873	ex OE-LDO	9884	
☐ N750NW	Douglas DC-9-41	47114/218	ex SE-DBX	9750	[MZJ]
☐ N751NW	Douglas DC-9-41	47115/261	ex OY-KGA	9751	
☐ N752NW	Douglas DC-9-41	47116/308	ex LN-RLK	9752	
☐ N753NW	Douglas DC-9-41	47117/319	ex SE-DBW	9753	[MZJ]
☐ N754NW	Douglas DC-9-41	47178/323	ex OY-KGB	9754	[MZJ]
☐ N755NW	Douglas DC-9-41	47179/335	ex LN-RLC	9755	
☐ N756NW	Douglas DC-9-41	47180/354	ex SE-DBU	9756	[MZJ]
☐ N758NW	Douglas DC-9-41	47286/359	ex OY-KGC	9758	[MZJ]
☐ N760NC	Douglas DC-9-51	47708/813		9851	
☐ N760NW	Douglas DC-9-41	47288/369	ex SE-DBT	9760	
☐ N761NC	Douglas DC-9-51	47709/814		9852	
☐ N762NC	Douglas DC-9-51	47710/818		9853	
☐ N762NW	Douglas DC-9-41	47395/555	ex OY-KGG	9762	
☐ N763NW	Douglas DC-9-41	47396/557	ex LN-RLD	9763	
☐ N764NC	Douglas DC-9-51	47717/833		9855	
☐ N765NC	Douglas DC-9-51	47718/834		9856	
☐ N766NC	Douglas DC-9-51	47739/852		9857	
☐ N767NC	Douglas DC-9-51	47724/853		9858	
☐ N768NC	Douglas DC-9-51	47729/854		9859	
☐ N769NC	Douglas DC-9-51	47757/877		9860	
☐ N770NC	Douglas DC-9-51	47758/880		9861	
☐ N771NC	Douglas DC-9-51	47769/881		9862	
☐ N772NC	Douglas DC-9-51	47774/884		9863	
☐ N773NC	Douglas DC-9-51	47775/888		9864	
☐ N774NC	Douglas DC-9-51	47776/889		9865	
☐ N775NC	Douglas DC-9-51	47785/904		9866	
☐ N776NC	Douglas DC-9-51	47786/905		9867	Delta c/s
☐ N777NC	Douglas DC-9-51	47787/912		9868	
☐ N778NC	Douglas DC-9-51	48100/927		9869	
☐ N779NC	Douglas DC-9-51	48101/931		9870	
☐ N780NC	Douglas DC-9-51	48102/932		9871	
☐ N781NC	Douglas DC-9-51	48121/935		9872	
☐ N782NC	Douglas DC-9-51	48107/936		9873	
☐ N783NC	Douglas DC-9-51	48108/937		9874	
☐ N784NC	Douglas DC-9-51	48109/939		9875	
☐ N785NC	Douglas DC-9-51	48110/945		9876	
☐ N786NC	Douglas DC-9-51	48148/984		9877	
☐ N787NC	Douglas DC-9-51	48149/990		9878	
☐ N914RW	Douglas DC-9-31	47362/492	ex N907H	9962	[MZJ]
☐ N915RW	Douglas DC-9-31	47139/169	ex N8930E	9957	[MZJ]
☐ N921RW	Douglas DC-9-31	47164/259	ex N8941E	9954	[MZJ]
☐ N923RW	Douglas DC-9-31	47183/272	ex N8947E	9956	[MZJ]
☐ N940N	Douglas DC-9-32	47572/708		9918	[MZJ]
☐ N943N	Douglas DC-9-32	47647/773		9921	[MZJ]
☐ N964N	Douglas DC-9-31	47416/512		9914	[MZJ]
☐ N965N	Douglas DC-9-31	47417/518		9915	[MZJ]
☐ N984US	Douglas DC-9-32	47383/538	ex HB-IFV	9984	[MZJ]
☐ N987US	Douglas DC-9-32	47458/646	ex OE-LDF	9987	[MZJ]
☐ N994Z	Douglas DC-9-32	47097/193	ex N979NE	9981	[MZJ]
☐ N1309T	Douglas DC-9-31	47316/439		9944	[MZJ]
☐ N1334U	Douglas DC-9-31	47280/597		9933	[MZJ]
☐ N3324L	Douglas DC-9-32	47103/205	ex YV-70C	9941	[MZJ]
☐ N8920E	Douglas DC-9-31	45835/95		9927	[MZJ]
☐ N8921E	Douglas DC-9-31	45836/96		9928	[MZJ]
☐ N8929E	Douglas DC-9-31	45866/138		9948	[MZJ]
☐ N8932E	Douglas DC-9-31	47141/227		9996	[MZJ]
☐ N8938E	Douglas DC-9-31	47161/249	ex 5N-GIN	9947	[MZJ]
☐ N8944E	Douglas DC-9-31	47167/266		9988	[MZJ]
☐ N8960E	Douglas DC-9-31	45869/331		9992	[MZJ]

☐ N8986E	Douglas DC-9-31	47402/482	ex 5N-INZ	9993	[MZJ]
☐ N9332	Douglas DC-9-31	47264/329	ex (N9107)	9968	[MZJ]
☐ N9341	Douglas DC-9-31	47390/490		9977	[MZJ]
☐ N9343	Douglas DC-9-31	47439/501		9979	[MZJ]
☐ N9344	Douglas DC-9-31	47440/502		9980	[MZJ]
☐ N9346	Douglas DC-9-32	47376/517	ex N394PA	9950	[MZJ]
☐ N9347	Douglas DC-9-32	45827/135	ex HL7201	9951	[MZJ]
☐ N900DE	McDonnell-Douglas MD-88	53372/1970		9000	
☐ N901DE	McDonnell-Douglas MD-88	53378/1980		9001	
☐ N902DE	McDonnell-Douglas MD-88	53379/1983		9002	
☐ N903DE	McDonnell-Douglas MD-88	53380/1986		9003	
☐ N904DE	McDonnell-Douglas MD-88	53409/1990		9004	
☐ N904DL	McDonnell-Douglas MD-88	49535/1347		904	
☐ N905DE	McDonnell-Douglas MD-88	53410/1992		9005	
☐ N905DL	McDonnell-Douglas MD-88	49536/1348		905	
☐ N906DE	McDonnell-Douglas MD-88	53415/2027		9006	
☐ N906DL	McDonnell-Douglas MD-88	49537/1355		906	
☐ N907DE	McDonnell-Douglas MD-88	53416/2029		9007	
☐ N907DL	McDonnell-Douglas MD-88	49538/1365		907	
☐ N908DE	McDonnell-Douglas MD-88	53417/2032		9008	
☐ N908DL	McDonnell-Douglas MD-88	49539/1366		908	
☐ N909DE	McDonnell-Douglas MD-88	53418/2033		9009	
☐ N909DL	McDonnell-Douglas MD-88	49540/1395		909	
☐ N910DE	McDonnell-Douglas MD-88	53419/2036		9010	
☐ N910DL	McDonnell-Douglas MD-88	49541/1416		910	
☐ N911DE	McDonnell-Douglas MD-88	49967/2037		9011	
☐ N911DL	McDonnell-Douglas MD-88	49542/1433		911	
☐ N912DE	McDonnell-Douglas MD-88	49997/2038		9012	
☐ N912DL	McDonnell-Douglas MD-88	49543/1434		912	
☐ N913DE	McDonnell-Douglas MD-88	49956/2039		9013	
☐ N913DL	McDonnell-Douglas MD-88	49544/1443		913	
☐ N914DE	McDonnell-Douglas MD-88	49957/2049		9014	
☐ N914DL	McDonnell-Douglas MD-88	49545/1444		914	
☐ N915DE	McDonnell-Douglas MD-88	53420/2050		9015	Delta Shuttle
☐ N915DL	McDonnell-Douglas MD-88	49546/1447		915	
☐ N916DE	McDonnell-Douglas MD-88	53421/2051		9016	
☐ N916DL	McDonnell-Douglas MD-88	49591/1448		916	
☐ N917DE	McDonnell-Douglas MD-88	49958/2054		9017	
☐ N917DL	McDonnell-Douglas MD-88	49573/1469		917	
☐ N918DE	McDonnell-Douglas MD-88	49959/2055		9018	
☐ N918DL	McDonnell-Douglas MD-88	49583/1470		918	[VCV]
☐ N919DE	McDonnell-Douglas MD-88	53422/2058		9019	
☐ N919DL	McDonnell-Douglas MD-88	49584/1471		919	
☐ N920DE	McDonnell-Douglas MD-88	53423/2059		9020	
☐ N920DL	McDonnell-Douglas MD-88	49644/1473		920	
☐ N921DL	McDonnell-Douglas MD-88	49645/1480		921	
☐ N922DL	McDonnell-Douglas MD-88	49646/1481		922	
☐ N923DL	McDonnell-Douglas MD-88	49705/1491		923	
☐ N924DL	McDonnell-Douglas MD-88	49711/1492		924	[VCV]
☐ N925DL	McDonnell-Douglas MD-88	49712/1500		925	
☐ N926DL	McDonnell-Douglas MD-88	49713/1523		926	
☐ N927DA	McDonnell-Douglas MD-88	49714/1524		927	
☐ N928DL	McDonnell-Douglas MD-88	49715/1530		928	
☐ N929DL	McDonnell-Douglas MD-88	49716/1531		929	
☐ N930DL	McDonnell-Douglas MD-88	49717/1532		930	
☐ N931DL	McDonnell-Douglas MD-88	49718/1533		931	
☐ N932DL	McDonnell-Douglas MD-88	49719/1570		932	
☐ N933DL	McDonnell-Douglas MD-88	49720/1571		933	
☐ N934DL	McDonnell-Douglas MD-88	49721/1574		934	
☐ N935DL	McDonnell-Douglas MD-88	49722/1575		935	
☐ N936DL	McDonnell-Douglas MD-88	49723/1576		936	
☐ N937DL	McDonnell-Douglas MD-88	49810/1588		937	
☐ N938DL	McDonnell-Douglas MD-88	49811/1590		938	
☐ N939DL	McDonnell-Douglas MD-88	49812/1593		939	
☐ N940DL	McDonnell-Douglas MD-88	49813/1599		940	
☐ N941DL	McDonnell-Douglas MD-88	49814/1602		941	
☐ N942DL	McDonnell-Douglas MD-88	49815/1605		942	
☐ N943DL	McDonnell-Douglas MD-88	49816/1608		943	
☐ N944DL	McDonnell-Douglas MD-88	49817/1612		944	
☐ N945DL	McDonnell-Douglas MD-88	49818/1613		945	
☐ N946DL	McDonnell-Douglas MD-88	49819/1629		946	
☐ N947DL	McDonnell-Douglas MD-88	49878/1664		947	
☐ N948DL	McDonnell-Douglas MD-88	49879/1666		948	
☐ N949DL	McDonnell-Douglas MD-88	49880/1676		949	
☐ N950DL	McDonnell-Douglas MD-88	49881/1677		950	
☐ N951DL	McDonnell-Douglas MD-88	49882/1679		951	

☐ N952DL	McDonnell-Douglas MD-88	49883/1683		952	
☐ N953DL	McDonnell-Douglas MD-88	49884/1685		953	
☐ N954DL	McDonnell-Douglas MD-88	49885/1689		954	
☐ N955DL	McDonnell-Douglas MD-88	49886/1691		955	
☐ N956DL	McDonnell-Douglas MD-88	49887/1699		956	
☐ N957DL	McDonnell-Douglas MD-88	49976/1700		957	
☐ N958DL	McDonnell-Douglas MD-88	49977/1701		958	
☐ N959DL	McDonnell-Douglas MD-88	49978/1710		959	
☐ N960DL	McDonnell-Douglas MD-88	49979/1711		960	
☐ N961DL	McDonnell-Douglas MD-88	49980/1712		961	
☐ N962DL	McDonnell-Douglas MD-88	49981/1725		962	
☐ N963DL	McDonnell-Douglas MD-88	49982/1726		963	
☐ N964DL	McDonnell-Douglas MD-88	49983/1747		964	
☐ N965DL	McDonnell-Douglas MD-88	49984/1748		965	
☐ N966DL	McDonnell-Douglas MD-88	53115/1795		966	
☐ N967DL	McDonnell-Douglas MD-88	53116/1796		967	
☐ N968DL	McDonnell-Douglas MD-88	53161/1808		968	
☐ N969DL	McDonnell-Douglas MD-88	53172/1810		969	
☐ N970DL	McDonnell-Douglas MD-88	53173/1811		970	
☐ N971DL	McDonnell-Douglas MD-88	53214/1823		971	
☐ N972DL	McDonnell-Douglas MD-88	53215/1824		972	
☐ N973DL	McDonnell-Douglas MD-88	53241/1832		973	
☐ N974DL	McDonnell-Douglas MD-88	53242/1833		974	
☐ N975DL	McDonnell-Douglas MD-88	53243/1834		975	
☐ N976DL	McDonnell-Douglas MD-88	53257/1845		976	
☐ N977DL	McDonnell-Douglas MD-88	53258/1848		977	
☐ N978DL	McDonnell-Douglas MD-88	53259/1849		978	
☐ N979DL	McDonnell-Douglas MD-88	53266/1859		979	
☐ N980DL	McDonnell-Douglas MD-88	53267/1860		980	
☐ N981DL	McDonnell-Douglas MD-88	53268/1861		981	
☐ N982DL	McDonnell-Douglas MD-88	53273/1870		982	
☐ N983DL	McDonnell-Douglas MD-88	53274/1873		983	
☐ N984DL	McDonnell-Douglas MD-88	53311/1912		984	
☐ N985DL	McDonnell-Douglas MD-88	53312/1914		985	
☐ N986DL	McDonnell-Douglas MD-88	53313/1924		986	
☐ N987DL	McDonnell-Douglas MD-88	53338/1926		987	
☐ N988DL	McDonnell-Douglas MD-88	53339/1928		988	
☐ N989DL	McDonnell-Douglas MD-88	53341/1936		989	
☐ N990DL	McDonnell-Douglas MD-88	53342/1939		990	
☐ N991DL	McDonnell-Douglas MD-88	53343/1941		991	
☐ N992DL	McDonnell-Douglas MD-88	53344/1943		992	
☐ N993DL	McDonnell-Douglas MD-88	53345/1950		993	
☐ N994DL	McDonnell-Douglas MD-88	53346/1952		994	
☐ N995DL	McDonnell-Douglas MD-88	53362/1955		995	
☐ N996DL	McDonnell-Douglas MD-88	53363/1958		996	
☐ N997DL	McDonnell-Douglas MD-88	53364/1961		997	
☐ N998DL	McDonnell-Douglas MD-88	53370/1963		998	
☐ N999DN	McDonnell-Douglas MD-88	53371/1965		999	
☐ N901DA	McDonnell-Douglas MD-90-30	53381/2100	ex N902DC	9201	
☐ N902DA	McDonnell-Douglas MD-90-30	53382/2094		9202	
☐ N903DA	McDonnell-Douglas MD-90-30	53383/2095		9203	
☐ N904DA	McDonnell-Douglas MD-90-30	53384/2096		9204	
☐ N905DA	McDonnell-Douglas MD-90-30	53385/2097		9205	
☐ N906DA	McDonnell-Douglas MD-90-30	53386/2099		9206	
☐ N907DA	McDonnell-Douglas MD-90-30	53387/2115		9207	
☐ N908DA	McDonnell-Douglas MD-90-30	53388/2117		9208	
☐ N909DA	McDonnell-Douglas MD-90-30	53389/2122		9209	
☐ N910DN	McDonnell-Douglas MD-90-30	53390/2123		9210	
☐ N911DA	McDonnell-Douglas MD-90-30	53391/2126		9211	
☐ N912DN	McDonnell-Douglas MD-90-30	53392/2136		9212	
☐ N913DN	McDonnell-Douglas MD-90-30	53393/2154		9213	
☐ N914DN	McDonnell-Douglas MD-90-30	53394/2156		9214	
☐ N915DN	McDonnell-Douglas MD-90-30	53395/2159		9215	
☐ N916DN	McDonnell-Douglas MD-90-30	53396/2161		9216	
☐ N917DN	McDonnell-Douglas MD-90-30	53552/2163	ex N593BC		
☐ N918DH	McDonnell-Douglas MD-90-30ER	53576/2195	ex HB-JIC		
☐ N919DN	McDonnell-Douglas MD-90-30	53553/2165	ex HB-JIB		
☐ N920DN	McDonnell-Douglas MD-90-30	53582/2198	ex B-2256		[GSO]♦
☐ N921DN	McDonnell-Douglas MD-90-30	53583/2200	ex B-2257		[MIA]♦
☐ N922DX	McDonnell-Douglas MD-90-30	53584/2203	ex B-2258		[MHV]♦
☐ N923DN	McDonnell-Douglas MD-90-30	53585/2224	ex B-2262		[MIA]♦
☐ N924DN	McDonnell-Douglas MD-90-30	53586/2233	ex B-2263		[VCV]♦
☐ N925DN	McDonnell-Douglas MD-90-30	53587/2240	ex B-2265		[MIA]♦
☐ N926DH	McDonnell-Douglas MD-90-30	53588/2248	ex B-2268		[ATL]♦
☐ N927DN	McDonnell-Douglas MD-90-30	53589/2259	ex B-2269		[MZJ]♦
☐ N928DN	McDonnell-Douglas MD-90-30	53590/2261	ex B-2270		[MZJ]♦

☐ N929DN	McDonnell-Douglas MD-90-30	53459/2141	ex OH-BLC	[MZJ]♦
☐ N930DN	McDonnell-Douglas MD-90-30	53458/2140	ex OH-BLU	[VCV]♦
☐ N953DN	McDonnell-Douglas MD-90-30	53523/2143	ex B-2250	[MZJ]♦
☐ N956DN	McDonnell-Douglas MD-90-30	53526/2170	ex B-2253	[MZJ]♦

DELTA CONNECTION (DL/DAL)
Cincinnati-Northern Kentucky Intl, OH/Atlanta-Hartsfield Intl, GA/Orlando-Intl, FL (CVG/ATL/MCO)

☐ N403CA	Canadair CRJ-200ER	7428	ex N896AS	7428	[VCV]
☐ N405SW	Canadair CRJ-200ER	7029	ex C-FMND	7029	SkyWest
☐ N406SW	Canadair CRJ-200ER	7030	ex C-FMNH	7030	SkyWest
☐ N408CA	Canadair CRJ-200ER	7440	ex C-FMLQ	7440	Comair
☐ N408SW	Canadair CRJ-200ER	7055	ex C-FMMW	7055	SkyWest
☐ N409CA	Canadair CRJ-200ER	7441	ex C-FMLS	7441	Comair
☐ N409SW	Canadair CRJ-200ER	7056	ex C-FMMX	7056	SkyWest
☐ N410SW	Canadair CRJ-200ER	7066	ex C-FMOL	7066	SkyWest
☐ N411SW	Canadair CRJ-200ER	7067	ex C-FMOS	7067	SkyWest
☐ N412SW	Canadair CRJ-200ER	7101	ex C-FMMX	7101	SkyWest
					SkyWest 30th anniversary c/s
☐ N416SW	Canadair CRJ-200ER	7089	ex N60SR	7089	SkyWest
☐ N417SW	Canadair CRJ-200ER	7400	ex C-FMMW	7400	SkyWest
☐ N418SW	Canadair CRJ-200ER	7446	ex C-FMNW	7446	SkyWest
☐ N420CA	Canadair CRJ-200ER	7451	ex C-FVAZ	7451	Comair
☐ N423SW	Canadair CRJ-200ER	7456	ex C-FMMB	7456	SkyWest
☐ N426SW	Canadair CRJ-200ER	7468	ex C-FMLF	7468	SkyWest
☐ N427CA	Canadair CRJ-200ER	7460	ex N897AS	7460	Comair
☐ N427SW	Canadair CRJ-200ER	7497	ex C-FMLB	7497	SkyWest
☐ N429SW	Canadair CRJ-200ER	7518	ex C-FMMN	7518	SkyWest
☐ N430CA	Canadair CRJ-200ER	7461	ex N898AS	7461	Comair
☐ N430SW	Canadair CRJ-200ER	7523	ex C-FMNB	7523	SkyWest
☐ N431SW	Canadair CRJ-200ER	7536	ex C-FMNW	7536	SkyWest
☐ N432SW	Canadair CRJ-200ER	7548	ex C-GJFG	7548	SkyWest
☐ N433SW	Canadair CRJ-200ER	7550	ex C-GJFH	7550	SkyWest
☐ N435CA	Canadair CRJ-200ER	7473	ex N496SW	7473	Comair
☐ N435SW	Canadair CRJ-200ER	7555	ex C-GJHK	7555	SkyWest
☐ N436CA	Canadair CRJ-200ER	7482	ex N497SW	7482	Comair
☐ N437SW	Canadair CRJ-200ER	7564	ex C-GJIA	7564	SkyWest
☐ N438SW	Canadair CRJ-200ER	7574	ex C-FMLU	7574	SkyWest
☐ N439SW	Canadair CRJ-200ER	7578	ex C-FMMN	7578	SkyWest
☐ N440SW	Canadair CRJ-200ER	7589	ex C-FMLI	7589	SkyWest
☐ N441SW	Canadair CRJ-200ER	7602	ex C-FMND	7602	SkyWest
☐ N442CA	Canadair CRJ-200ER	7483	ex N498SW	7483	Comair
☐ N442SW	Canadair CRJ-200ER	7609	ex C-FMMQ	7609	SkyWest
☐ N443CA	Canadair CRJ-200ER	7539	ex C-GJJH	7539	Comair
☐ N443SW	Canadair CRJ-200ER	7638	ex C-FMMN	7638	SkyWest
☐ N445SW	Canadair CRJ-200ER	7651	ex C-FMLS	7651	SkyWest
☐ N446CA	Canadair CRJ-200ER	7546	ex C-GJLH	7546	Comair
☐ N446SW	Canadair CRJ-200ER	7666	ex C-FMMB	7666	SkyWest
☐ N447CA	Canadair CRJ-200ER	7552	ex C-GJLL	7552	Comair
☐ N447SW	Canadair CRJ-200ER	7677	ex C-FMLB	7677	SkyWest
☐ N448SW	Canadair CRJ-200ER	7678	ex C-FMLF	7678	SkyWest
☐ N449SW	Canadair CRJ-200ER	7699	ex C-FMMQ	7699	SkyWest
☐ N451CA	Canadair CRJ-200ER	7562	ex C-GJVH	7562	Comair
☐ N452SW	Canadair CRJ-200ER	7716	ex C-FMNW	7716	SkyWest
☐ N453SW	Canadair CRJ-200ER	7743	ex C-FMLV	7743	SkyWest
☐ N454SW	Canadair CRJ-200ER	7749	ex C-FMOS	7749	SkyWest
☐ N455CA	Canadair CRJ-200ER	7592	ex C-FMLT	7592	Pinnacle
☐ N455SW	Canadair CRJ-200ER	7760	ex C-FMMW	7760	SkyWest
☐ N457SW	Canadair CRJ-200ER	7773	ex C-FMLV	7773	SkyWest
☐ N459SW	Canadair CRJ-200ER	7782	ex C-FMND	7782	SkyWest
☐ N460SW	Canadair CRJ-200ER	7803	ex C-FMLV	7803	SkyWest
☐ N461SW	Canadair CRJ-200ER	7811	ex C-FVAZ	7811	SkyWest
☐ N463SW	Canadair CRJ-200ER	7820	ex C-FMMW	7820	SkyWest
☐ N464SW	Canadair CRJ-200ER	7827	ex C-FMLB	7827	SkyWest
☐ N465SW	Canadair CRJ-200ER	7845	ex C-FMOI	7845	SkyWest
☐ N466SW	Canadair CRJ-200ER	7856	ex C-FMKZ	7856	SkyWest
☐ N477CA	Canadair CRJ-200ER	7670	ex C-FMMW	7670	Mesaba
☐ N487CA	Canadair CRJ-200ER	7729	ex C-FMMQ	7729	Mesaba
☐ N492SW	Canadair CRJ-100ER	7168	ex N982CA	7168	SkyWest
☐ N528CA	Canadair CRJ-100ER	7841	ex C-FVAZ	7841	Comair
☐ N587SW	Canadair CRJ-100ER	7062	ex N943CA	7062	SkyWest
☐ N588SW	Canadair CRJ-100ER	7069	ex N945CA	7069	Comair
☐ N589SW	Canadair CRJ-100ER	7072	ex N946CA	7072	Comair
☐ N590SW	Canadair CRJ-100ER	7077	ex N947CA	7077	Comair
☐ N591SW	Canadair CRJ-100ER	7079	ex N948CA	7079	SkyWest
☐ N594SW	Canadair CRJ-100ER	7285	ex N767CA	7285	Comair <DAL
☐ N595SW	Canadair CRJ-100ER	7292	ex N769CA	7292	Comair <DAL

	Registration	Type	Serial	Ex		Operator
☐	N597SW	Canadair CRJ-100ER	7293	ex N776CA	7293	Comair <DAL
☐	N601XJ	Canadair CRJ-200LR	8044	ex C-FFHW		
☐	N602XJ	Canadair CRJ-200LR	8045	ex C-FMKZ		
☐	N629BR	Canadair CRJ-200ER	7251	ex (N533CA)	7251	Comair
☐	N659BR	Canadair CRJ-200ER	7509	ex C-FMOS	7509	Comair
☐	N675BR	Canadair CRJ-200ER	7635	ex (N536CA)	7635	Comair
☐	N680BR	Canadair CRJ-200ER	7679	ex C-FMLI		Atlantic Southeast
☐	N681BR	Canadair CRJ-200ER	7680	ex C-FMLQ		Atlantic Southeast
☐	N682BR	Canadair CRJ-200ER	7691	ex C-FVAZ		Atlantic Southeast
☐	N683BR	Canadair CRJ-200ER	7692	ex C-FMND		Atlantic Southeast
☐	N684BR	Canadair CRJ-200ER	7708	ex C-FMLF		Atlantic Southeast
☐	N685BR	Canadair CRJ-200ER	7712	ex (N532CA)	7712	Comair
☐	N686BR	Canadair CRJ-200ER	7715	ex C-FMNH		Atlantic Southeast
☐	N710CA	Canadair CRJ-100ER	7241	ex C-FVAZ	7241	Comair
☐	N712CA	Canadair CRJ-100ER	7244	ex C-FMLU	7244	Comair
☐	N713CA	Canadair CRJ-100ER	7245	ex C-FMOI	7245	Comair
☐	N716CA	Canadair CRJ-100ER	7250	ex C-FMMW	7250	Comair
☐	N720SW	Canadair CRJ-200ER	7297	ex N778CA	7297	SkyWest <DAL
☐	N721CA	Canadair CRJ-100ER	7259	ex C-FMLI	7259	Comair
☐	N739CA	Canadair CRJ-100ER	7273	ex C-FMNQ	7273	Comair
☐	N779CA	Canadair CRJ-100ER	7306	ex C-FMMB	7306	Comair
☐	N781CA	Canadair CRJ-100ER	7312	ex C-FMMY	7312	Comair
☐	N783CA	Canadair CRJ-100ER	7315	ex C-FMKW	7315	Comair
☐	N784CA	Canadair CRJ-100ER	7319	ex C-FMLI	7319	Comair
☐	N785CA	Canadair CRJ-100ER	7326	ex C-FMNW	7326	Comair
☐	N786CA	Canadair CRJ-100ER	7333	ex C-FMNQ	7333	Comair
☐	N797CA	Canadair CRJ-100ER	7344	ex C-FMKV	7344	Comair
☐	N800AY	Canadair CRJ-200LR	8000	ex C-FMMW	8000	
☐	N801AY	Canadair CRJ-200LR	8001	ex C-FMMX	8001	
☐	N804CA	Canadair CRJ-100ER	7352	ex C-FMLT	7352	Comair
☐	N805AY	Canadair CRJ-200LR	8005	ex C-FDQP	8005	
☐	N807CA	Canadair CRJ-100ER	7364	ex C-FMLU	7364	Comair
☐	N809CA	Canadair CRJ-100ER	7366	ex C-FMMB	7366	Comair
☐	N810CA	Canadair CRJ-200ER	7370	ex C-FMMW	7370	Comair
☐	N811CA	Canadair CRJ-200ER	7380	ex C-FMLQ	7380	Comair
☐	N812AY	Canadair CRJ-200LR	8012	ex C-	8012	
☐	N812CA	Canadair CRJ-200ER	7381	ex C-FMLS	7381	Comair
☐	N813AY	Canadair CRJ-200LR	8013	ex C-	8013	
☐	N814CA	Canadair CRJ-200ER	7387	ex C-GFVM	7387	Comair
☐	N815CA	Canadair CRJ-200ER	7397	ex C-FMML	7397	Comair
☐	N818CA	Canadair CRJ-200ER	7408	ex C-FMLF	7408	Comair
☐	N819AY	Canadair CRJ-200LR	8019	ex C-FMLQ	8019	
☐	N819CA	Canadair CRJ-200ER	7415	ex C-FMNH	7415	Comair
☐	N820AS	Canadair CRJ-200ER	7188	ex C-FMMQ	820	Atlantic Southeast
☐	N820AY	Canadair CRJ-200LR	8020	ex C-FMLS	8020	
☐	N821AS	Canadair CRJ-200ER	7194	ex C-FMKV	821	Atlantic Southeast
☐	N821AY	Canadair CRJ-200LR	8021	ex C-FMLT	8021	
☐	N823AS	Canadair CRJ-200ER	7196	ex C-FMKZ	823	Atlantic Southeast
☐	N823AY	Canadair CRJ-200LR	8023	ex C-FMMT	8023	
☐	N824AS	Canadair CRJ-200ER	7203	ex C-FMLB	824	Atlantic Southeast
☐	N824AY	Canadair CRJ-200LR	8024	ex C-FMNH	8024	
☐	N825AS	Canadair CRJ-200ER	7207	ex C-FMNX	825	Atlantic Southeast
☐	N825AY	Canadair CRJ-200LR	8025	ex C-FMNW	8025	
☐	N826AS	Canadair CRJ-200ER	7210	ex C-FMOW	826	Atlantic Southeast
☐	N826AY	Canadair CRJ-200LR	8026	ex C-FMNX	8026	
☐	N827AS	Canadair CRJ-200ER	7212	ex C-FMND	827	Atlantic Southeast
☐	N827AY	Canadair CRJ-200LR	8027	ex C-FMNY	8027	
☐	N828AS	Canadair CRJ-200ER	7213	ex C-FMNQ	828	Atlantic Southeast
☐	N829AS	Canadair CRJ-200ER	7232	ex C-FMLT	829	Atlantic Southeast
☐	N829AY	Canadair CRJ-200LR	8029	ex C-FMOW	8029	
☐	N830AY	Canadair CRJ-200LR	8030	ex C-FVAZ	8030	
☐	N831AY	Canadair CRJ-200LR	8031	ex C-FETZ	8031	
☐	N832AY	Canadair CRJ-200LR	8032	ex C-FMNQ	8032	
☐	N833AS	Canadair CRJ-200ER	7246	ex C-FMMB	833	Atlantic Southeast
☐	N833AY	Canadair CRJ-200LR	8033	ex C-FMLU	8033	
☐	N834AY	Canadair CRJ-200LR	8034	ex C-FEXV	8034	
☐	N835AS	Canadair CRJ-200ER	7258	ex C-FMLF	835	Atlantic Southeast
☐	N835AY	Canadair CRJ-200LR	8035	ex C-FMMB	8035	
☐	N836AY	Canadair CRJ-200LR	8036	ex C-FMML	8036	
☐	N837AS	Canadair CRJ-200ER	7271	ex C-FVAZ	837	Atlantic Southeast
☐	N838AS	Canadair CRJ-200ER	7276	ex C-FMMB	838	Atlantic Southeast
☐	N839AS	Canadair CRJ-200ER	7284	ex C-FMKV	839	Atlantic Southeast
☐	N839AY	Canadair CRJ-200LR	8039	ex C-FMMW	8039	
☐	N840AS	Canadair CRJ-200ER	7290	ex C-FMLQ	840	Atlantic Southeast
☐	N840AY	Canadair CRJ-200LR	8040	ex C-FEZX	8040	
☐	N841AS	Canadair CRJ-200ER	7300	ex C-FMOW	841	Atlantic Southeast
☐	N841AY	Canadair CRJ-200LR	8041	ex C-FMMY	8041	

☐ N842AS	Canadair CRJ-200ER	7304	ex C-FMLU 842	Atlantic Southeast
☐ N843AS	Canadair CRJ-200ER	7310	ex C-FMMW 843	Atlantic Southeast
☐ N844AS	Canadair CRJ-200ER	7317	ex C-FMLB 844	Atlantic Southeast
☐ N845AS	Canadair CRJ-200ER	7324	ex C-FMMT 845	Atlantic Southeast
☐ N846AS	Canadair CRJ-200ER	7328	ex C-FMNY 846	Atlantic Southeast
☐ N847AS	Canadair CRJ-200ER	7335	ex C-FMOI 847	Atlantic Southeast
☐ N848AS	Canadair CRJ-200ER	7339	ex C-FMMQ 848	Atlantic Southeast
☐ N849AS	Canadair CRJ-200ER	7347	ex C-FMLB 849	Atlantic Southeast
☐ N850AS	Canadair CRJ-200ER	7355	ex C-FMNH 850	Atlantic Southeast
☐ N851AS	Canadair CRJ-200ER	7360	ex C-FMOW 851	Atlantic Southeast
☐ N852AS	Canadair CRJ-200ER	7369	ex C-FMMQ 852	Atlantic Southeast
☐ N853AS	Canadair CRJ-200ER	7374	ex C-FMKV 853	Atlantic Southeast
☐ N854AS	Canadair CRJ-200ER	7382	ex C-FMLT 854	Atlantic Southeast
☐ N855AS	Canadair CRJ-200ER	7395	ex C-GGKY 855	Atlantic Southeast
☐ N856AS	Canadair CRJ-200ER	7404	ex C-FMKV 856	Atlantic Southeast
☐ N857AS	Canadair CRJ-200ER	7411	ex C-FMLS 857	Atlantic Southeast
☐ N858AS	Canadair CRJ-200ER	7417	ex C-FMNX 858	Atlantic Southeast
☐ N859AS	Canadair CRJ-200ER	7421	ex C-FVAZ 859	Atlantic Southeast
☐ N860AS	Canadair CRJ-200ER	7433	ex C-FMNB 860	Atlantic Southeast
☐ N861AS	Canadair CRJ-200ER	7445	ex C-FMNH 861	Atlantic Southeast
☐ N862AS	Canadair CRJ-200ER	7476	ex C-FMNW 7476	SkyWest
☐ N863AS	Canadair CRJ-200ER	7487	ex C-FMML 7487	SkyWest
☐ N864AS	Canadair CRJ-200ER	7502	ex C-FMLT 864	SkyWest
☐ N865AS	Canadair CRJ-200ER	7507	ex C-FMNX 865	Comair
☐ N866AS	Canadair CRJ-200ER	7517	ex C-FMML 7517	SkyWest
☐ N867AS	Canadair CRJ-200ER	7463	ex C-FMNB 867	Atlantic Southeast
☐ N868AS	Canadair CRJ-200ER	7474	ex C-FMMT 868	Atlantic Southeast
				Texas Bluebonnet c/s
☐ N868CA	Canadair CRJ-200ER	7427	ex C-FMML 7427	Comair
☐ N869AS	Canadair CRJ-200ER	7479	ex C-FMOS 869	SkyWest
☐ N870AS	Canadair CRJ-200ER	7530	ex C-FMLQ 870	Atlantic Southeast
☐ N871AS	Canadair CRJ-200ER	7537	ex C-FMNX 871	Atlantic Southeast
☐ N872AS	Canadair CRJ-200ER	7542	ex C-FMND 872	Atlantic Southeast
☐ N873AS	Canadair CRJ-200ER	7549	ex C-GJLI 873	Atlantic Southeast
☐ N874AS	Canadair CRJ-200ER	7551	ex C-GJLK 874	Atlantic Southeast
☐ N875AS	Canadair CRJ-200ER	7559	ex C-GJLQ 875	Atlantic Southeast
☐ N876AS	Canadair CRJ-200ER	7576	ex C-FMMB 876	Atlantic Southeast
☐ N877AS	Canadair CRJ-200ER	7579	ex C-FMMQ 877	Atlantic Southeast
☐ N878AS	Canadair CRJ-200ER	7590	ex C-FMLQ 878	Atlantic Southeast
☐ N879AS	Canadair CRJ-200ER	7600	ex C-FMOW 879	Atlantic Southeast
☐ N880AS	Canadair CRJ-200ER	7606	ex C-FMMB 880	Atlantic Southeast
☐ N881AS	Canadair CRJ-200ER	7496	ex C-GIXF 881	Atlantic Southeast
☐ N882AS	Canadair CRJ-200ER	7503	ex C-GJAO 882	Atlantic Southeast
☐ N883AS	Canadair CRJ-200ER	7504	ex C-GIZD 883	Atlantic Southeast
☐ N884AS	Canadair CRJ-200ER	7513	ex C-GIZF 884	Atlantic Southeast
☐ N885AS	Canadair CRJ-200ER	7521	ex C-GJDX 885	Atlantic Southeast
☐ N886AS	Canadair CRJ-200ER	7531	ex C-GJJC 886	Atlantic Southeast
☐ N889AS	Canadair CRJ-200ER	7538	ex C-GJJG 889	Atlantic Southeast
☐ N900EV	Canadair CRJ-200ER	7608	ex C-FMMN 900	Atlantic Southeast
☐ N901EV	Canadair CRJ-200ER	7616	ex C-FMKZ 901	Atlantic Southeast
☐ N902EV	Canadair CRJ-200ER	7620	ex C-FMLQ 902	Atlantic Southeast
☐ N903EV	Canadair CRJ-200ER	7621	ex C-FMLS 903	Atlantic Southeast
☐ N904EV	Canadair CRJ-200ER	7628	ex C-FMNY 904	Atlantic Southeast
☐ N905EV	Canadair CRJ-200ER	7632	ex C-FMND 905	Atlantic Southeast
☐ N906EV	Canadair CRJ-200ER	7642	ex C-FMMY 906	Atlantic Southeast
☐ N907EV	Canadair CRJ-200ER	7648	ex C-FMLF 907	Atlantic Southeast
☐ N908EV	Canadair CRJ-200ER	7654	ex C-FMMT 908	Atlantic Southeast
☐ N909EV	Canadair CRJ-200ER	7658	ex C-FMNY 909	Atlantic Southeast
☐ N910EV	Canadair CRJ-200ER	7727	ex C-FMML 7727	SkyWest
☐ N912EV	Canadair CRJ-200ER	7728	ex C-FMMN 7728	SkyWest
☐ N913EV	Canadair CRJ-200ER	7731	ex C-FMMX 7731	SkyWest
☐ N914CA	Canadair CRJ-100ER	7012	ex C-FMLB 7012	Comair
☐ N914EV	Canadair CRJ-200ER	7752	ex C-FMND 914	Atlantic Southeast
☐ N915CA	Canadair CRJ-100ER	7013	ex C-FMLQ 7013	Comair
☐ N915EV	Canadair CRJ-200ER	7754	ex C-FMLU 7754	SkyWest
☐ N916CA	Canadair CRJ-100ER	7014	ex C-FMLI 7014	Comair
☐ N916EV	Canadair CRJ-200ER	7757	ex C-FMML 916	Atlantic Southeast
☐ N917CA	Canadair CRJ-100ER	7017	ex C-FMLT 7017	Comair
☐ N917EV	Canadair CRJ-200ER	7769	ex C-FMLI 917	Atlantic Southeast
☐ N918CA	Canadair CRJ-100ER	7018	ex C-FMLU 7018	Comair
☐ N919EV	Canadair CRJ-200ER	7780	ex C-FMOW 919	Atlantic Southeast
☐ N920EV	Canadair CRJ-200ER	7810	ex C-FMOW 920	Atlantic Southeast
☐ N921EV	Canadair CRJ-200ER	7819	ex C-FMMQ 921	Atlantic Southeast
☐ N922EV	Canadair CRJ-200ER	7822	ex C-FMMY 922	Atlantic Southeast
☐ N923EV	Canadair CRJ-200ER	7826	ex C-FMKZ 923	Atlantic Southeast
☐ N924CA	Canadair CRJ-100ER	7026	ex C-FMMX 7026	Comair
☐ N924EV	Canadair CRJ-200ER	7830	ex C-FMLQ 924	Atlantic Southeast

☐	N925EV	Canadair CRJ-200ER	7831	ex C-FMLS	925	Atlantic Southeast
☐	N926EV	Canadair CRJ-200ER	7843	ex C-FMNQ	926	Atlantic Southeast
☐	N927CA	Canadair CRJ-100ER	7031	ex C-FMNQ	7031	Comair
☐	N927EV	Canadair CRJ-200ER	7844	ex C-FMLU	927	Atlantic Southeast
☐	N928EV	Canadair CRJ-200ER	8006	ex C-FMMB	928	Atlantic Southeast <DAL
☐	N929CA	Canadair CRJ-100ER	7035	ex C-FMOI	7035	Comair
☐	N929EV	Canadair CRJ-200ER	8007	ex C-FMMN	929	Atlantic Southeast <DAL
☐	N930EV	Canadair CRJ-200ER	8014	ex C-FMKW	930	Atlantic Southeast <DAL
☐	N931CA	Canadair CRJ-100ER	7037	ex C-FMOS	7037	Comair
☐	N931EV	Canadair CRJ-200ER	8015	ex C-FMKZ	931	Atlantic Southeast <DAL
☐	N932CA	Canadair CRJ-100ER	7038	ex C-FMOW	7038	Comair
☐	N932EV	Canadair CRJ-200ER	8016	ex C-FMLB	932	Atlantic Southeast <DAL
☐	N933CA	Canadair CRJ-100ER	7040	ex C-FMKW	7040	Comair
☐	N933EV	Canadair CRJ-200ER	8022	ex C-FEHV	933	Atlantic Southeast <DAL
☐	N934CA	Canadair CRJ-100ER	7042	ex C-FMLB	7042	Comair
☐	N934EV	Canadair CRJ-200ER	8028	ex C-FMOS	934	Atlantic Southeast <DAL
☐	N935EV	Canadair CRJ-200ER	8037	ex C-FMMN	935	Atlantic Southeast <DAL
☐	N936CA	Canadair CRJ-100ER	7043	ex C-FMLF	7043	Comair
☐	N936EV	Canadair CRJ-200ER	8038	ex C-FEZT	936	Atlantic Southeast <DAL
☐	N937CA	Canadair CRJ-100ER	7044	ex C-FMLI	7044	Comair
☐	N937EV	Canadair CRJ-200ER	8042	ex C-FFAB	937	Atlantic Southeast <DAL
☐	N938CA	Canadair CRJ-100ER	7046	ex C-FMLS	7046	Comair
☐	N940CA	Canadair CRJ-100ER	7048	ex C-FMLU	7048	Comair
☐	N941CA	Canadair CRJ-100ER	7050	ex C-FMMB	7050	Comair
☐	N954CA	Canadair CRJ-100ER	7100	ex C-FXFB	7100	Comair <DAL
☐	N956CA	Canadair CRJ-100ER	7105	ex C-FMNH	7105	Comair <DAL
☐	N957CA	Canadair CRJ-100ER	7109	ex C-FMLV	7109	Comair <DAL
☐	N958CA	Canadair CRJ-100ER	7111	ex C-FMML	7111	Comair <DAL
☐	N959CA	Canadair CRJ-100ER	7116	ex C-FMMX	7116	Comair <DAL
☐	N960CA	Canadair CRJ-100ER	7117	ex C-FMMY	7117	Comair
☐	N962CA	Canadair CRJ-100ER	7123	ex C-FMLU	7123	Comair
☐	N963CA	Canadair CRJ-100ER	7127	ex C-FMMN	7127	Comair
☐	N964CA	Canadair CRJ-100ER	7129	ex C-FMMT	7129	Comair <DAL
☐	N965CA	Canadair CRJ-100ER	7131	ex C-FMMX	7131	Comair stored
☐	N966CA	Canadair CRJ-100ER	7132	ex C-FMMY	7132	Comair <DAL
☐	N967CA	Canadair CRJ-100ER	7134	ex C-FMND	7134	Comair
☐	N969CA	Canadair CRJ-100ER	7141	ex C-FMML	7141	Comair
☐	N970EV	Canadair CRJ-200ER	7527	ex N663BR	970	Atlantic Southeast <DAL
☐	N971CA	Canadair CRJ-100ER	7145	ex C-FMMW	7145	Comair
☐	N971EV	Canadair CRJ-200ER	7528	ex N664BR	971	Atlantic Southeast <DAL
☐	N972EV	Canadair CRJ-200ER	7534	ex N665BR	972	Atlantic Southeast <DAL
☐	N973CA	Canadair CRJ-100ER	7146	ex C-FMMX	7146	Comair
☐	N973EV	Canadair CRJ-200ER	7575	ex N708BR	973	Atlantic Southeast <DAL
☐	N974EV	Canadair CRJ-200ER	7594	ex N672BR	974	Atlantic Southeast <DAL
☐	N975EV	Canadair CRJ-200ER	7599	ex N673BR	975	Atlantic Southeast <DAL
☐	N976EV	Canadair CRJ-200ER	7601	ex N674BR	976	Atlantic Southeast <DAL
☐	N977EV	Canadair CRJ-200ER	7720	ex N687BR	977	Atlantic Southeast <DAL
☐	N978EV	Canadair CRJ-200ER	7723	ex N688BR	978	Atlantic Southeast <DAL
☐	N979EV	Canadair CRJ-200ER	7737	ex N689BR	979	Atlantic Southeast <DAL
☐	N980EV	Canadair CRJ-200ER	7759	ex N692BR	980	Atlantic Southeast <DAL
☐	N981EV	Canadair CRJ-200ER	7768	ex N694BR	981	Atlantic Southeast <DAL
☐	N989CA	Canadair CRJ-100ER	7215	ex C-FMOI	7215	Comair <DAL
☐	N8390A	Canadair CRJ-200LR	7390	ex C-FMOW	8390	Spirit of 'Memphis Belle'
☐	N8409N	Canadair CRJ-200LR	7409	ex C-FMLI	8409	
☐	N8412F	Canadair CRJ-200LR	7412	ex C-FMLT	8412	
☐	N8416B	Canadair CRJ-200LR	7416	ex C-FMNW	8416	
☐	N8423C	Canadair CRJ-200LR	7423	ex C-FMNQ	8423	
☐	N8432A	Canadair CRJ-200LR	7432	ex C-GHRR	8432	
☐	N8444F	Canadair CRJ-200LR	7444	ex C-FMMT	8444	
☐	N8458A	Canadair CRJ-200LR	7458	ex C-FMMN	8458	
☐	N8475B	Canadair CRJ-200LR	7475	ex C-FMNH	8475	
☐	N8477R	Canadair CRJ-200LR	7477	ex C-FMNX	8477	
☐	N8488D	Canadair CRJ-200LR	7488	ex C-FMMN	8488	
☐	N8492C	Canadair CRJ-200LR	7492	ex C-FMMY	8492	
☐	N8495B	Canadair CRJ-200LR	7495	ex C-FMKW	8495	
☐	N8501F	Canadair CRJ-200LR	7501	ex C-FMLS	8501	
☐	N8505Q	Canadair CRJ-200LR	7505	ex C-FMNH	8505	
☐	N8506C	Canadair CRJ-200LR	7506	ex C-FMNW	8506	
☐	N8515F	Canadair CRJ-200LR	7515	ex C-FMOI	8515	
☐	N8516C	Canadair CRJ-200LR	7516	ex C-FMMB	8516	
☐	N8524A	Canadair CRJ-200LR	7524	ex C-FMKV	8524	
☐	N8525B	Canadair CRJ-200LR	7525	ex C-FMKW	8525	
☐	N8532G	Canadair CRJ-200LR	7532	ex C-FMLT	8532	
☐	N8533D	Canadair CRJ-200LR	7533	ex C-FMLV	8533	
☐	N8541D	Canadair CRJ-200LR	7541	ex C-FVAZ	8541	
☐	N8543F	Canadair CRJ-200LR	7543	ex C-FMNQ	8543	
☐	N8554A	Canadair CRJ-200LR	7554	ex C-FMKV	8554	

☐	N8560F	Canadair CRJ-200LR	7560	ex C-FMLQ	8560	
☐	N8577D	Canadair CRJ-200LR	7577	ex C-FMML	8577	
☐	N8580A	Canadair CRJ-200LR	7580	ex C-FMMW	8580	
☐	N8587E	Canadair CRJ-200LR	7587	ex C-FMLB	8587	
☐	N8588D	Canadair CRJ-200LR	7588	ex C-GJSZ	8588	
☐	N8598B	Canadair CRJ-200LR	7598	ex C-FMNY	8598	
☐	N8604C	Canadair CRJ-200LR	7604	ex C-FMLU	8604	
☐	N8611A	Canadair CRJ-200LR	7611	ex C-FMMX	8611	
☐	N8623A	Canadair CRJ-200LR	7623	ex C-FMLV	8623	
☐	N8631E	Canadair CRJ-200LR	7631	ex C-FVAZ	8631	
☐	N8646A	Canadair CRJ-200LR	7646	ex C-FMKZ	8646	
☐	N8659B	Canadair CRJ-200LR	7659	ex C-FMOS	8659	
☐	N8665A	Canadair CRJ-200LR	7665	ex C-FMOI	8665	
☐	N8672A	Canadair CRJ-200LR	7672	ex C-FMMY	8672	
☐	N8673D	Canadair CRJ-200LR	7673	ex C-FMNB	8673	
☐	N8674A	Canadair CRJ-200LR	7674	ex C-FMKV	8674	
☐	N8683B	Canadair CRJ-200LR	7683	ex C-FMLV	8683	
☐	N8688C	Canadair CRJ-200LR	7688	ex C-FMNY	6888	
☐	N8694A	Canadair CRJ-200LR	7694	ex C-FMLU	8694	
☐	N8696C	Canadair CRJ-200LR	7696	ex C-FMMB	8696	
☐	N8698A	Canadair CRJ-200LR	7698	ex C-FMMN	8698	
☐	N8709A	Canadair CRJ-200LR	7709	ex C-FMLI	8709	
☐	N8710A	Canadair CRJ-200LR	7710	ex C-FMLQ	8710	
☐	N8718E	Canadair CRJ-200LR	7718	ex C-FMNY	8718	
☐	N8721B	Canadair CRJ-200LR	7721	ex C-FVAZ	8721	
☐	N8733G	Canadair CRJ-200LR	7733	ex C-FMNB	8733	
☐	N8736A	Canadair CRJ-200LR	7736	ex C-FMKZ	8736	
☐	N8745B	Canadair CRJ-200LR	7745	ex C-FMNH	8745	
☐	N8747B	Canadair CRJ-200LR	7747	ex C-FMNX	8747	
☐	N8751D	Canadair CRJ-200LR	7751	ex C-FVAZ	8751	
☐	N8758D	Canadair CRJ-200LR	7758	ex C-FMMN	8758	
☐	N8771A	Canadair CRJ-200LR	7771	ex C-FMLS	8771	
☐	N8775A	Canadair CRJ-200LR	7775	ex C-FMNH	8775	
☐	N8783E	Canadair CRJ-200LR	7783	ex C-FMNQ	8783	
☐	N8790A	Canadair CRJ-200LR	7790	ex C-FMMW	8790	
☐	N8794B	Canadair CRJ-200LR	7794	ex C-FMKV	8794	
☐	N8797A	Canadair CRJ-200LR	7797	ex C-FMLB	8797	
☐	N8800G	Canadair CRJ-200LR	7800	ex C-FMLQ	8800	
☐	N8808H	Canadair CRJ-200LR	7808	ex C-FMNY	8808	
☐	N8828D	Canadair CRJ-200LR	7828	ex C-FMLF	8828	
☐	N8836A	Canadair CRJ-200LR	7836	ex C-FMNW	8836	
☐	N8837B	Canadair CRJ-200LR	7837	ex C-FMNX	8837	
☐	N8839E	Canadair CRJ-200LR	7839	ex C-FMOS	8839	
☐	N8847A	Canadair CRJ-200LR	7847	ex C-FMML	8847	
☐	N8855A	Canadair CRJ-200LR	7855	ex C-FMKW	8855	
☐	N8869B	Canadair CRJ-200LR	7869	ex C-FMOS	8869	
☐	N8877A	Canadair CRJ-200LR	7877	ex C-FMML	8877	
☐	N8883E	Canadair CRJ-200LR	7883	ex C-FMNB	8883	
☐	N8884E	Canadair CRJ-200LR	7884	ex C-FMKV	8884	
☐	N8886A	Canadair CRJ-200LR	7886	ex C-FMKZ	8886	
☐	N8888D	Canadair CRJ-200LR	7888	ex C-FMLF	8888	
☐	N8891A	Canadair CRJ-200LR	7891	ex C-FMLS	8891	
☐	N8894A	Canadair CRJ-200LR	7894	ex C-FMMT	8894	
☐	N8896A	Canadair CRJ-200LR	7896	ex C-FMNW	8896	
☐	N8903A	Canadair CRJ-200LR	7903	ex C-FMNQ	8903	
☐	N8907A	Canadair CRJ-200LR	7907	ex C-FMML	8907	
☐	N8908D	Canadair CRJ-200LR	7908	ex C-FMMN	8908	
☐	N8913A	Canadair CRJ-200LR	7913	ex C-FMNB	8913	
☐	N8914A	Canadair CRJ-200LR	7914	ex C-FMKV	8914	
☐	N8918B	Canadair CRJ-200LR	7918	ex C-FMLF	8918	
☐	N8921B	Canadair CRJ-200LR	7921	ex C-FMLS	8921	
☐	N8923A	Canadair CRJ-200LR	7923	ex C-FMLV	8923	
☐	N8924B	Canadair CRJ-200LR	7924	ex C-FMMT	8924	
☐	N8928A	Canadair CRJ-200LR	7928	ex C-FMNY	8928	
☐	N8930E	Canadair CRJ-200LR	7930	ex C-FMOW	8930	
☐	N8932C	Canadair CRJ-200LR	7932	ex C-FMND	8932	
☐	N8933B	Canadair CRJ-200LR	7933	ex C-FMNQ	8933	
☐	N8936A	Canadair CRJ-200LR	7936	ex C-FMMB	8936	
☐	N8938A	Canadair CRJ-200LR	7938	ex C-FMMN	8938	
☐	N8940E	Canadair CRJ-200LR	7940	ex C-FMMW	8940	
☐	N8942A	Canadair CRJ-200LR	7942	ex C-FMMY	8942	
☐	N8943A	Canadair CRJ-200LR	7943	ex C-FMNB	8943	
☐	N8944B	Canadair CRJ-200LR	7944	ex C-FMKV	8944 Spirit of Beale St
☐	N8946A	Canadair CRJ-200LR	7946	ex C-FMKZ	8946	
☐	N8948B	Canadair CRJ-200LR	7948	ex C-FMLF	8948	
☐	N8960A	Canadair CRJ-200LR	7960	ex C-FMOW	8960	
☐	N8964E	Canadair CRJ-200LR	7964	ex C-FMLU	8964	

☐ N8965E"	Canadair CRJ-200LR	7965	ex C-FMOI	8965	
☐ N8968E	Canadair CRJ-200LR	7968	ex C-FMMN	8968	
☐ N8969A	Canadair CRJ-200LR	7969	ex C-FMMQ	8969	
☐ N8970D	Canadair CRJ-200LR	7970	ex C-FMMW	8970	
☐ N8971A	Canadair CRJ-200LR	7971	ex C-FMMX	8971	
☐ N8972E	Canadair CRJ-200LR	7972	ex C-FMMY	8972	
☐ N8974C"	Canadair CRJ-200LR	7974	ex C-FMKV	8974	
☐ N8976E"	Canadair CRJ-200LR	7976	ex C-FMKZ	8976	
☐ N8977A	Canadair CRJ-200LR	7977	ex C-FMLB	8977	
☐ N8980A	Canadair CRJ-200LR	7980	ex C-FMLQ	8980	
☐ N8982A	Canadair CRJ-200LR	7982	ex C-FMLT	8982	
☐ N8986B	Canadair CRJ-200LR	7986	ex C-FMNW	8986	

Operated by Pinnacle Airlines except those marked " which are operated by Mesaba.

☐ N317CA	Canadair CRJ-701ER	10055	ex C-GZXI	10055	Atlantic Southeast <DAL
☐ N331CA	Canadair CRJ-701ER	10061	ex C-GIBJ	10061	SkyWest <DAL
☐ N340CA	Canadair CRJ-701ER	10062	ex C-GIBL	10062	SkyWest <DAL
☐ N354CA	Canadair CRJ-701ER	10064	ex C-GIBO	10064	Atlantic Southeast <DAL
☐ N355CA	Canadair CRJ-701ER	10067	ex C-GIBT	10067	Atlantic Southeast <DAL
☐ N367CA	Canadair CRJ-701ER	10069	ex C-GICL	10069	SkyWest <DAL
☐ N368CA	Canadair CRJ-701ER	10075	ex C-GIAD	10075	SkyWest <DAL
☐ N369CA	Canadair CRJ-701ER	10079	ex C-GZUD	10079	Comair
☐ N371CA	Canadair CRJ-701ER	10082	ex C-GIAR	10082	Comair
☐ N374CA	Canadair CRJ-701ER	10090	ex C-	10090	Comair
☐ N376CA	Canadair CRJ-701ER	10092	ex C-	10092	Atlantic Southeast <DAL
☐ N378CA	Canadair CRJ-701ER	10097	ex C-GIAJ	10097	Comair
☐ N379CA	Canadair CRJ-701ER	10102	ex C-	10102	Atlantic Southeast <DAL
☐ N390CA	Canadair CRJ-701ER	10106	ex C-	10106	Atlantic Southeast <DAL
☐ N391CA	Canadair CRJ-701ER	10108	ex C-	10108	Comair
☐ N398CA	Canadair CRJ-701ER	10112	ex C-	10112	Comair
☐ N603SK	Canadair CRJ-702ER	10248	ex C-FHUC	10248	SkyWest
☐ N604SK	Canadair CRJ-702ER	10249	ex C-	10239	SkyWest
☐ N606SK	Canadair CRJ-702ER	10250	ex C-	10250	SkyWest
☐ N607SK	Canadair CRJ-702ER	10251	ex C-FIBQ	10251	SkyWest
☐ N608SK	Canadair CRJ-702ER	10252	ex C-	10252	SkyWest
☐ N609SK	Canadair CRJ-701ER	10020	ex N701EV	10020	SkyWest
☐ N611SK	Canadair CRJ-701ER	10035	ex N702EV	10035	SkyWest
☐ N613SK	Canadair CRJ-701ER	10038	ex N703EV	10038	SkyWest
☐ N614SK	Canadair CRJ-701ER	10051	ex N705EV	10051	SkyWest
☐ N625CA	Canadair CRJ-701ER	10113	ex C-	10113	Comair
☐ N641CA	Canadair CRJ-701ER	10122	ex C-	10122	Comair
☐ N642CA	Canadair CRJ-701ER	10125	ex C-	10125	Comair
☐ N653CA	Canadair CRJ-701ER	10129	ex C-GZUC	10129	Comair
☐ N655CA	Canadair CRJ-701ER	10134	ex C-	10134	Comair
☐ N656CA	Canadair CRJ-701ER	10143	ex C-GIAU	10143	Comair
☐ N658CA	Canadair CRJ-701ER	10148	ex C-GIAU	10148	Comair
☐ N659CA	Canadair CRJ-701ER	10153	ex C-	10153	Atlantic Southeast <DAL
☐ N668CA	Canadair CRJ-701ER	10162	ex C-	10162	SkyWest <DAL
☐ N669CA	Canadair CRJ-701ER	10176	ex C-	10176	Comair
☐ N690CA	Canadair CRJ-701ER	10182	ex C-	10182	Comair o/o
☐ N707EV	Canadair CRJ-701ER	10057	ex C-GIAZ		Atlantic Southeast
☐ N708EV	Canadair CRJ-701ER	10060	ex C-GIBI		Atlantic Southeast
☐ N709EV	Canadair CRJ-701ER	10068	ex C-GICB		Atlantic Southeast
☐ N710EV	Canadair CRJ-701ER	10071	ex C-GICP		Atlantic Southeast
☐ N712EV	Canadair CRJ-701ER	10074	ex C-GHZZ		Atlantic Southeast
☐ N713EV	Canadair CRJ-701ER	10081	ex C-GIAP		Atlantic Southeast
☐ N716EV	Canadair CRJ-701ER	10084	ex C-GIAV		Atlantic Southeast
☐ N717EV	Canadair CRJ-701ER	10088	ex C-GIBH		Atlantic Southeast
☐ N718EV	Canadair CRJ-701ER	10095	ex C-		Atlantic Southeast
☐ N719EV	Canadair CRJ-701ER	10099	ex C-GICL		Atlantic Southeast
☐ N720EV	Canadair CRJ-701ER	10115	ex C-GIAW		Atlantic Southeast
☐ N722EV	Canadair CRJ-701ER	10127	ex C-		Atlantic Southeast
☐ N723EV	Canadair CRJ-701ER	10132	ex C-		Atlantic Southeast
☐ N724EV	Canadair CRJ-701ER	10138	ex C-GIBT		Atlantic Southeast
☐ N730EV	Canadair CRJ-701ER	10141	ex C-GIAP		Atlantic Southeast
☐ N738EV	Canadair CRJ-701ER	10146	ex C-		Atlantic Southeast
☐ N740EV	Canadair CRJ-701ER	10151	ex C-		Atlantic Southeast
☐ N741EV	Canadair CRJ-701ER	10155	ex C-FBQS		Atlantic Southeast
☐ N744EV	Canadair CRJ-701ER	10157	ex C-		Atlantic Southeast
☐ N748EV	Canadair CRJ-701ER	10158	ex C-		Atlantic Southeast
☐ N750EV	Canadair CRJ-701ER	10161	ex C-		Atlantic Southeast
☐ N751EV	Canadair CRJ-701ER	10163	ex C-		Atlantic Southeast
☐ N752EV	Canadair CRJ-701ER	10166	ex C-		Atlantic Southeast
☐ N753EV	Canadair CRJ-701ER	10169	ex C-		Atlantic Southeast
☐ N754EV	Canadair CRJ-701ER	10173	ex C-FCRJ		Atlantic Southeast
☐ N755EV	Canadair CRJ-701ER	10185	ex C-		Atlantic Southeast
☐ N758EV	Canadair CRJ-701ER	10210	ex C-		Atlantic Southeast

☐ N759EV	Canadair CRJ-701ER	10211	ex C-		Atlantic Southeast
☐ N760EV	Canadair CRJ-701ER	10212	ex C-		Atlantic Southeast
☐ N761ND	Canadair CRJ-701ER	10213	ex C-		Atlantic Southeast
☐ N131EV	Canadair CRJ-900ER	15217	ex C-		Atlantic Southeast
☐ N132EV	Canadair CRJ-900ER	15219	ex C-		Atlantic Southeast
☐ N133EV	Canadair CRJ-900ER	15222	ex C-		Atlantic Southeast
☐ N134EV	Canadair CRJ-900ER	15223	ex C-		Atlantic Southeast
☐ N135EV	Canadair CRJ-900ER	15225	ex C-GIBI		Atlantic Southeast
☐ N136EV	Canadair CRJ-900ER	15226	ex C-		Atlantic Southeast
☐ N137EV	Canadair CRJ-900ER	15227	ex C-		Atlantic Southeast
☐ N138EV	Canadair CRJ-900ER	15235	ex C-GZQW		Atlantic Southeast
☐ N146PQ	Canadair CRJ-900ER	15146	ex C-		Pinnacle
☐ N147PQ	Canadair CRJ-900ER	15147	ex C-		Pinnacle
☐ N153PQ	Canadair CRJ-900ER	15153	ex C-		Pinnacle
☐ N161PQ	Canadair CRJ-900ER	15161	ex C-		Pinnacle
☐ N162PQ	Canadair CRJ-900ER	15162	ex C-		Pinnacle
☐ N166PQ	Canadair CRJ-900ER	15166	ex C-		Pinnacle
☐ N170PQ	Canadair CRJ-900ER	15170	ex C-		Pinnacle
☐ N176PQ	Canadair CRJ-900ER	15176	ex C-		Pinnacle
☐ N181PQ	Canadair CRJ-900ER	15181	ex C-		Pinnacle
☐ N186PQ	Canadair CRJ-900ER	15186	ex C-		Pinnacle
☐ N187PQ	Canadair CRJ-900ER	15187	ex C-		Pinnacle
☐ N195PQ	Canadair CRJ-900ER	15195	ex C-FVWD		Pinnacle
☐ N197PQ	Canadair CRJ-900ER	15197	ex C-GZQV		Pinnacle
☐ N200PQ	Canadair CRJ-900ER	15200	ex C-GWVU		Pinnacle
☐ N228PQ	Canadair CRJ-900ER	15228	ex C-		Pinnacle
☐ N232PQ	Canadair CRJ-900ER	15232	ex C-GZQR		Pinnacle
☐ N538CA	Canadair CRJ-900ER	15157	ex C-		Comair <DAL
☐ N548CA	Canadair CRJ-900ER	15159	ex C-		Comair
☐ N549CA	Canadair CRJ-900ER	15164	ex C-		Comair
☐ N554CA	Canadair CRJ-900ER	15168	ex C-		Comair
☐ N582CA	Canadair CRJ-900ER	15171	ex C-		Comair
☐ N600LR	Canadair CRJ-900ER	15142	ex C-		Mesaba
☐ N601LR	Canadair CRJ-900ER	15145	ex C-		Mesaba
☐ N602LR	Canadair CRJ-900ER	15151	ex C-		Mesaba
☐ N604LR	Canadair CRJ-900ER	15152	ex C-		Mesaba <DAL
☐ N605LR	Canadair CRJ-900ER	15160	ex C-		Mesaba <DAL
☐ N606LR	Canadair CRJ-900ER	15173	ex C-		Pinnacle <DAL
☐ N607LR	Canadair CRJ-900ER	15178	ex C-		Atlantic Southeast <DAL
☐ N676CA	Canadair CRJ-900ER	15127	ex C-		Comair
☐ N678CA	Canadair CRJ-900ER	15125	ex C-		Comair
☐ N679CA	Canadair CRJ-900ER	15132	ex C-		Comair
☐ N689CA	Canadair CRJ-900ER	15133	ex C-		Comair
☐ N691CA	Canadair CRJ-900ER	15136	ex C-		Comair
☐ N692CA	Canadair CRJ-900ER	15092	ex C-		Comair
☐ N693CA	Canadair CRJ-900ER	15096	ex C-		Comair
☐ N695CA	Canadair CRJ-900ER	15097	ex C-	30th Anniversary c/s	Comair
☐ N800SK	Canadair CRJ-900ER	15060	ex C-		SkyWest
☐ N802SK	Canadair CRJ-900ER	15061	ex C-		SkyWest
☐ N803SK	Canadair CRJ-900ER	15062	ex C-FJTQ		SkyWest
☐ N804SK	Canadair CRJ-900ER	15067	ex C-		SkyWest
☐ N805SK	Canadair CRJ-900ER	15069	ex C-GZQT		SkyWest
☐ N806SK	Canadair CRJ-900ER	15070	ex C-GZQV		SkyWest
☐ N807SK	Canadair CRJ-900ER	15082	ex C-		SkyWest
☐ N809SK	Canadair CRJ-900ER	15086	ex C-FLCX		SkyWest
☐ N810SK	Canadair CRJ-900ER	15093	ex C-		SkyWest
☐ N812SK	Canadair CRJ-900ER	15098	ex C-		SkyWest
☐ N813SK	Canadair CRJ-900ER	15099	ex C-		SkyWest
☐ N814SK	Canadair CRJ-900ER	15100	ex C-		SkyWest
☐ N815SK	Canadair CRJ-900ER	15101	ex C-		SkyWest
☐ N816SK	Canadair CRJ-900ER	15105	ex C-		SkyWest
☐ N817SK	Canadair CRJ-900ER	15107	ex C-		SkyWest
☐ N820SK	Canadair CRJ-900ER	15108	ex C-		SkyWest
☐ N821SK	Canadair CRJ-900ER	15109	ex C-	35th Anniversary c/s	SkyWest
☐ N822SK	Canadair CRJ-900ER	15203	ex C-		SkyWest
☐ N823SK	Canadair CRJ-900ER	15205	ex C-		SkyWest
☐ N824SK	Canadair CRJ-900ER	15208	ex C-		SkyWest
☐ N825SK	Canadair CRJ-900ER	15212	ex C-		SkyWest
☐ N901XJ	Canadair CRJ-900	15130	ex C-		Mesaba
☐ N902XJ	Canadair CRJ-900	15131	ex C-FNWB		Mesaba
☐ N903XJ	Canadair CRJ-900	15134	ex C-FOFO		Mesaba
☐ N904XJ	Canadair CRJ-900	15135	ex C-		Mesaba
☐ N905XJ	Canadair CRJ-900	15137	ex C-		Mesaba
☐ N906XJ	Canadair CRJ-900	15138	ex C-		Mesaba
☐ N907XJ	Canadair CRJ-900	15139	ex C-FOVM		Mesaba
☐ N908XJ	Canadair CRJ-900	15140	ex C-FOWF		Mesaba

☐	N909XJ	Canadair CRJ-900	15141	ex C-		Mesaba
☐	N910XJ	Canadair CRJ-900	15143	ex C-		Mesaba
☐	N912XJ	Canadair CRJ-900	15144	ex C-		Mesaba
☐	N913XJ	Canadair CRJ-900	15148	ex C-FQYX		Mesaba
☐	N914XJ	Canadair CRJ-900	15149	ex C-		Mesaba
☐	N915XJ	Canadair CRJ-900	15150	ex C-		Mesaba
☐	N916XJ	Canadair CRJ-900	15154	ex C-		Mesaba
☐	N917XJ	Canadair CRJ-900	15155	ex C-		Mesaba
☐	N918XJ	Canadair CRJ-900	15156	ex C-		Mesaba
☐	N919XJ	Canadair CRJ-900	15163	ex C-		Mesaba
☐	N920XJ	Canadair CRJ-900	15167	ex C-		Mesaba
☐	N921XJ	Canadair CRJ-900	15172	ex C-		Mesaba
☐	N922XJ	Canadair CRJ-900	15174	ex C-FTTY		Mesaba
☐	N923XJ	Canadair CRJ-900	15177	ex C-		Mesaba
☐	N924XJ	Canadair CRJ-900	15179	ex C-		Mesaba
☐	N925XJ	Canadair CRJ-900	15183	ex C-		Mesaba
☐	N926XJ	Canadair CRJ-900	15184	ex C-		Mesaba
☐	N927XJ	Canadair CRJ-900	15188	ex C-		Mesaba
☐	N928XJ	Canadair CRJ-900	15190	ex C-		Mesaba
☐	N929XJ	Canadair CRJ-900	15191	ex C-		Mesaba
☐	N930XJ	Canadair CRJ-900	15192	ex C-		Mesaba
☐	N931XJ	Canadair CRJ-900	15193	ex C-		Mesaba
☐	N932XJ	Canadair CRJ-900	15194	ex C-		Mesaba
☐	N933XJ	Canadair CRJ-900	15196	ex C-		Mesaba
☐	N934XJ	Canadair CRJ-900	15198	ex C-		Mesaba
☐	N935XJ	Canadair CRJ-900	15199	ex C-		Mesaba
☐	N936XJ	Canadair CRJ-900	15201	ex C-		Mesaba
☐	N937XJ	Canadair CRJ-900	15210	ex C-		Mesaba
☐	N272SK	Embraer ERJ-145LR	145306	ex PT-SKX	8272	Chautauqua
☐	N273SK	Embraer ERJ-145LR	145331	ex PT-SMX	8273	Chautauqua
☐	N274SK	Embraer ERJ-145LR	145344	ex PT-SNK	8274	Chautauqua
☐	N561RP	Embraer ERJ-145LR	145447	ex PT-SUS	8561	Chautauqua
☐	N562RP	Embraer ERJ-145LR	145451	ex PT-SUW	8562	Chautauqua
☐	N563RP	Embraer ERJ-145LR	145509	ex PT-SYB	8563	Chautauqua
☐	N564RP	Embraer ERJ-145LR	145524	ex PT-SYP	8564	Chautauqua
☐	N565RP	Embraer ERJ-145LR	145679	ex PT-SFL	8565	Chautauqua
☐	N566RP	Embraer ERJ-145LR	145691	ex PT-SFX	8566	Chautauqua
☐	N567RP	Embraer ERJ-145LR	145698	ex PT-SGD	8567	Chautauqua
☐	N568RP	Embraer ERJ-145LR	145800	ex PT-SNE	8568	Chautauqua
☐	N569RP	Embraer ERJ-145LR	14500816	ex PT-SNR	8569	Chautauqua
☐	N570RP	Embraer ERJ-145LR	14500821	ex PT-SNV	8570	Chautauqua
☐	N571RP	Embraer ERJ-145LR	14500827	ex PT-SNZ	8571	Chautauqua
☐	N572RP	Embraer ERJ-145LR	14500828	ex PT-SQB	8572	Chautauqua
☐	N573RP	Embraer ERJ-145LR	14500837	ex PT-SQJ	8573	Chautauqua
☐	N574RP	Embraer ERJ-145LR	14500845	ex PT-SQP	8574	Chautauqua
☐	N575RP	Embraer ERJ-145LR	14500847	ex PT-SQR	8575	Chautauqua
☐	N576RP	Embraer ERJ-145LR	14500856	ex PT-SQX	8576	Chautauqua
☐	N577RP	Embraer ERJ-145LR	14500862	ex PT-SXC	8577	Chautauqua
☐	N578RP	Embraer ERJ-145LR	14500865	ex PT-SXE	8578	Chautauqua
☐	N579RP	Embraer ERJ-145LR	14500871	ex PT-SXI	8579	Chautauqua
☐	N825MJ	Embraer ERJ-145LR	145179	ex PT-SGB		Mesa
☐	N826MJ	Embraer ERJ-145LR	145214	ex PT-SHB		Freedom
☐	N827MJ	Embraer ERJ-145LR	145217	ex PT-SHD		Mesa
☐	N828MJ	Embraer ERJ-145LR	145218	ex PT-SHE		Mesa
☐	N829MJ	Embraer ERJ-145LR	145228	ex PT-SHQ		Freedom
☐	N830MJ	Embraer ERJ-145LR	145259	ex PT-SIS		Freedom
☐	N831MJ	Embraer ERJ-145LR	145273	ex PT-SJP		Mesa
☐	N832MJ	Embraer ERJ-145LR	145310	ex PT-SMB		Freedom
☐	N833MJ	Embraer ERJ-145LR	145327	ex PT-SMT		Mesa
☐	N836MJ	Embraer ERJ-145LR	145359	ex PT-SNY		Freedom
☐	N837MJ	Embraer ERJ-145LR	145367	ex PT-SOR		Freedom
☐	N838MJ	Embraer ERJ-145LR	145384	ex PT-SQI		Freedom
☐	N841MJ	Embraer ERJ-145LR	145448	ex PT-SUT		Mesa
☐	N842MJ	Embraer ERJ-145LR	145457	ex PT-SVC		Freedom
☐	N844MJ	Embraer ERJ-145LR	145481	ex PT-SXA		Mesa
☐	N845MJ	Embraer ERJ-145LR	145502	ex PT-SXV		Freedom
☐	N847MJ	Embraer ERJ-145LR	145517	ex PT-SYI		Mesa
☐	N848MJ	Embraer ERJ-145LR	145530	ex PT-STU		Mesa
☐	N849MJ	Embraer ERJ-145LR	145534	ex PT-STY		Mesa
☐	N850MJ	Embraer ERJ-145LR	145568	ex PT-SBE		Mesa
☐	N851MJ	Embraer ERJ-145LR	145572	ex PT-SBI		Freedom
☐	N852MJ	Embraer ERJ-145LR	145567	ex PT-SBD		Mesa
☐	N853MJ	Embraer ERJ-145LR	145464	ex PT-SVJ		Freedom
☐	N854MJ	Embraer ERJ-145LR	145490	ex PT-SXJ		Mesa
☐	N855MJ	Embraer ERJ-145LR	145614	ex PT-SCZ		Mesa
☐	N856MJ	Embraer ERJ-145LR	145626	ex PT-SDO		Freedom

☐ N857MJ	Embraer ERJ-145LR	145765	ex PT-SJW	Mesa
☐ N860MJ	Embraer ERJ-145LR	145773	ex PT-SMD	Mesa
☐ N10575	Embraer ERJ-145LR	145640	ex PT-SEC	ExpressJet
☐ N12569	Embraer ERJ-145LR	145630	ex PT-SDS	ExpressJet
☐ N14570	Embraer ERJ-145LR	145632	ex PT-SDU	ExpressJet
☐ N22909	Embraer ERJ-145LR	145459	ex PT-SVE	ExpressJet
☐ N11137	Embraer ERJ-145XR	145721	ex PT-SGX	ExpressJet
☐ N11165	Embraer ERJ-145XR	14500819	ex PT-SNT	ExpressJet
☐ N11176	Embraer ERJ-145XR	14500881	ex PT-SXV	ExpressJet
☐ N11181	Embraer ERJ-145XR	14500904	ex PT-SYN	ExpressJet
☐ N11184	Embraer ERJ-145XR	14500917	ex PT-SVX	ExpressJet
☐ N11193	Embraer ERJ-145XR	14500938	ex PT-SCJ	ExpressJet
☐ N12167	Embraer ERJ-145XR	14500834	ex PT-SQG	ExpressJet
☐ N14168	Embraer ERJ-145XR	14500840	ex PT-SQL	ExpressJet
☐ N14171	Embraer ERJ-145XR	14500859	ex PT-SQZ	ExpressJet
☐ N14173	Embraer ERJ-145XR	14500872	ex PT-SXK	ExpressJet
☐ N14179	Embraer ERJ-145XR	14500896	ex PT-SYI	ExpressJet
☐ N16170	Embraer ERJ-145XR	14500850	ex PT-SQT	ExpressJet
☐ N16183	Embraer ERJ-145XR	14500914	ex PT-SYV	ExpressJet
☐ N33182	Embraer ERJ-145XR	14500909	ex PT-SYS	ExpressJet
☐ N201JQ	Embraer ERJ-175LR	17000235	ex PT-SFL	Shuttle America
☐ N202JQ	Embraer ERJ-175LR	17000240	ex PT-SFQ	Shuttle America
☐ N203JQ	Embraer ERJ-175LR	17000242	ex PT-SFT	Shuttle America
☐ N204JQ	Embraer ERJ-175LR	17000243	ex PT-SFU	Shuttle America
☐ N206JQ	Embraer ERJ-175LR	17000249	ex PT-SJA	Shuttle America
☐ N207JQ	Embraer ERJ-175LR	17000254	ex PT-SJG	Shuttle America
☐ N208JQ	Embraer ERJ-175LR	17000257	ex PT-SJJ	Shuttle America
☐ N209JQ	Embraer ERJ-175LR	17000258	ex PT-SJK	Shuttle America
☐ N210JQ	Embraer ERJ-175LR	17000260	ex PT-SJN	Shuttle America
☐ N211JQ	Embraer ERJ-175LR	17000261	ex PT-SJO	Shuttle America
☐ N212JQ	Embraer ERJ-175LR	17000264	ex PT-SJS	Shuttle America
☐ N213JQ	Embraer ERJ-175LR	17000265	ex PT-SJT	Shuttle America
☐ N214JQ	Embraer ERJ-175LR	17000267	ex PT-SJV	Shuttle America
☐ N215JQ	Embraer ERJ-175LR	17000270	ex PT-SNA	Shuttle America
☐ N216JQ	Embraer ERJ-175LR	17000273	ex PT-SNH	Shuttle America
☐ N602CZ	Embraer ERJ-175LR	17000171	ex PT-SMN	Compass
☐ N603CZ	Embraer ERJ-175LR	17000176	ex PT-SMT	Compass
☐ N604CZ	Embraer ERJ-175LR	17000181	ex PT-SMY	Compass
☐ N605CZ	Embraer ERJ-175LR	17000186	ex PT-SUD	Compass
☐ N606CZ	Embraer ERJ-175LR	17000188	ex PT-SUH	Compass
☐ N607CZ	Embraer ERJ-175LR	17000192	ex PT-SUT	Compass
☐ N608CZ	Embraer ERJ-175LR	17000195	ex PT-SXA	Compass
☐ N609CZ	Embraer ERJ-175LR	17000197	ex PT-SXJ	Compass
☐ N610CZ	Embraer ERJ-175LR	17000198	ex PT-SXK	Compass
☐ N612CZ	Embraer ERJ-175LR	17000201	ex PT-SXQ	Compass
☐ N613CZ	Embraer ERJ-175AR	17000203	ex PT-SXS	Compass
☐ N614CZ	Embraer ERJ-175LR	17000205	ex PT-SCA	Compass
☐ N615CZ	Embraer ERJ-175LR	17000207	ex PT-SCC	Compass
☐ N616CZ	Embraer ERJ-175LR	17000209	ex PT-SCG	Compass
☐ N617CZ	Embraer ERJ-175LR	17000210	ex PT-SCH	Compass
☐ N619CZ	Embraer ERJ-175LR	17000213	ex PT-SCK	Compass
☐ N620CZ	Embraer ERJ-175LR	17000214	ex PT-SCL	Compass
☐ N621CZ	Embraer ERJ-175LR	17000218	ex PT-SCP	Compass
☐ N622CZ	Embraer ERJ-175LR	17000219	ex PT-SCQ	Compass
☐ N623CZ	Embraer ERJ-175LR	17000221	ex PT-SCT	Compass
☐ N624CZ	Embraer ERJ-175LR	17000222	ex PT-SCX	Compass
☐ N625CZ	Embraer ERJ-175AR	17000225	ex PT-SFB	Compass
☐ N626CZ	Embraer ERJ-175AR	17000226	ex PT-SFC	Compass
☐ N627CZ	Embraer ERJ-175AR	17000229	ex PT-SFF	Compass
☐ N628CZ	Embraer ERJ-175AR	17000233	ex PT-SFJ	Compass
☐ N629CZ	Embraer ERJ-175AR	17000236	ex PT-SFM	Compass
☐ N630CZ	Embraer ERJ-175AR	17000238	ex PT-SFO	Compass
☐ N631CZ	Embraer ERJ-175AR	17000239	ex PT-SFP	Compass
☐ N632CZ	Embraer ERJ-175AR	17000244	ex PT-SFV	Compass
☐ N633CZ	Embraer ERJ-175AR	17000245	ex PT-SFW	Compass
☐ N634CZ	Embraer ERJ-175AR	17000246	ex PT-SFX	Compass
☐ N635CZ	Embraer ERJ-175AR	17000252	ex PT-SJD	Compass
☐ N636CZ	Embraer ERJ-175AR	17000253	ex PT-SJE	Compass
☐ N637CZ	Embraer ERJ-175AR	17000256	ex PT-SJI	Compass
☐ N638CZ	Embraer ERJ-175AR	17000259	ex PT-SJL	Compass
☐ N639CZ	Embraer ERJ-175AR	17000262	ex PT-SJP	Compass
☐ N855RW	Embraer ERJ-170SE	17000077	ex PT-SZC	Shuttle America
☐ N859RW	Embraer ERJ-170SE	17000082	ex PT-SZH	Shuttle America
☐ N860RW	Embraer ERJ-170SE	17000084	ex PT-SZJ	Shuttle America
☐ N862RW	Embraer ERJ-170SE	17000098	ex PT-SZY	Shuttle America

326

☐ N867RW	Embraer ERJ-170SU	17000130	ex PT-SDT		Shuttle America
☐ N868RW	Embraer ERJ-170SU	17000131	ex PT-SDU		Republic
☐ N869RW	Embraer ERJ-170SE	17000133	ex PT-SDW		Shuttle America
☐ N870RW	Embraer ERJ-170SE	17000138	ex PT-SEC		Republic
☐ N958WH	Embraer ERJ-175LR	17000248	ex PT-SFZ	8205	Shuttle America
☐ N365PX	SAAB SF.340B	340B-265	ex SE-G65		Mesaba; [BGR]
☐ N408XJ	SAAB SF.340B	340B-408	ex SE-B08		Mesaba
☐ N410XJ	SAAB SF.340B	340B-410	ex SE-B10		Mesaba
☐ N411XJ	SAAB SF.340B	340B-411	ex SE-B11		Mesaba
☐ N412XJ	SAAB SF.340B	340B-412	ex SE-B12		Mesaba
☐ N413XJ	SAAB SF.340B	340B-413	ex SE-B13		Mesaba
☐ N415XJ	SAAB SF.340B	340B-415	ex SE-B15		Mesaba
☐ N416XJ	SAAB SF.340B	340B-416	ex SE-B16		Mesaba
☐ N417XJ	SAAB SF.340B	340B-417	ex SE-B17		Mesaba
☐ N418XJ	SAAB SF.340B	340B-418	ex SE-B18		Mesaba
☐ N420XJ	SAAB SF.340B	340B-420	ex SE-B20		Mesaba
☐ N421XJ	SAAB SF.340B	340B-421	ex SE-B21		Mesaba
☐ N422XJ	SAAB SF.340B	340B-422	ex SE-B22		Mesaba
☐ N423XJ	SAAB SF.340B	340B-423	ex SE-B23		Mesaba
☐ N424XJ	SAAB SF.340B	340B-424	ex SE-B24		Mesaba
☐ N426XJ	SAAB SF.340B	340B-426	ex SE-B26		Mesaba
☐ N427XJ	SAAB SF.340B	340B-427	ex SE-B27		Mesaba
☐ N428XJ	SAAB SF.340B	340B-428	ex SE-B28		Mesaba
☐ N429XJ	SAAB SF.340B	340B-429	ex SE-B29		Mesaba
☐ N430XJ	SAAB SF.340B	340B-430	ex SE-B30		Mesaba
☐ N433XJ	SAAB SF.340B	340B-433	ex SE-B33		Mesaba
☐ N434XJ	SAAB SF.340B	340B-434	ex SE-B34		Mesaba
☐ N435XJ	SAAB SF.340B	340B-435	ex SE-B35		Mesaba
☐ N436XJ	SAAB SF.340B	340B-436	ex SE-B36		Mesaba
☐ N437XJ	SAAB SF.340B	340B-437	ex SE-B37		Mesaba
☐ N438XJ	SAAB SF.340B	340B-438	ex SE-B38		Mesaba
☐ N439XJ	SAAB SF.340B	340B-439	ex SE-B39		Mesaba
☐ N441XJ	SAAB SF.340B	340B-441	ex SE-B41	25th Anniversary c/s	Mesaba
☐ N442XJ	SAAB SF.340B	340B-442	ex SE-B42		Mesaba
☐ N443XJ	SAAB SF.340B	340B-443	ex SE-B43		Mesaba
☐ N444XJ	SAAB SF.340B	340B-444	ex SE-B44		Mesaba
☐ N445XJ	SAAB SF.340B	340B-445	ex SE-B45		Mesaba
☐ N446XJ	SAAB SF.340B	340B-446	ex SE-B46		Mesaba
☐ N447XJ	SAAB SF.340B	340B-447	ex SE-B47		Mesaba
☐ N448XJ	SAAB SF.340B	340B-448	ex SE-B48		Mesaba
☐ N449XJ	SAAB SF.340B	340B-449	ex SE-B49		Mesaba
☐ N450XJ	SAAB SF.340B	340B-450	ex SE-B50		Mesaba
☐ N451XJ	SAAB SF.340B	340B-451	ex SE-B51		Mesaba
☐ N452XJ	SAAB SF.340B	340B-452	ex SE-B52		Mesaba
☐ N453XJ	SAAB SF.340B	340B-453	ex SE-B53		Mesaba
☐ N454XJ	SAAB SF.340B	340B-454	ex SE-B54		Mesaba
☐ N456XJ	SAAB SF.340B	340B-456	ex SE-B56		Mesaba
☐ N457XJ	SAAB SF.340B	340B-457	ex SE-B57		Mesaba

DESERT AIR   *Anchorage, AK (ANC)*

☐ N105CA	Douglas DC-3	14275/25720	ex N85FA		[CLK]
☐ N153PA	Convair 240-27	304	ex 51-7892		
☐ N19906	Douglas DC-3	4747	ex 41-38644		[ANC]
☐ N44587	Douglas DC-3	12857	ex N353SA		[ANC]

DODITA AIR CARGO   *San Juan-Munoz Marin Intl, PR (SJU)*

☐ N912AL	Convair 440-78	353	ex PZ-TGA		[SJU]
☐ N31325	Convair 240-52	52-8	ex 52-1183		[SJU]

DYNAMIC AIRWAYS

☐ N880DA	McDonnell-Douglas MD-88	49760/1620	ex N701ME		♦

EASTERN CARIBBEAN AIR   *(JI)*   *San Juan-Munoz Marin Intl, PR (SJU)*

☐ N288RA	Beech 100 King Air	B-5	ex N280RA	

EDWARDS JET CENTER OF MONTANA   *Edwards (EDJ)*   *Billings-Logan Intl, MT (BIL)*

☐ N90EJ	Beech C90 King Air	LJ-749	ex N552R	
☐ N102LF	Beech 100 King Air	B-65	ex N102RS	
☐ N265EJ	Beech 200 Super King Air	BB-911	ex N411CC	
☐ N2703U	Cessna 340A	340A0914		
☐ N6316X	Cessna 340A	340A0487		
☐ N9781S	Cessna 414A Chancellor III	414A0515	ex D-IFLO	

EG & G

☐ N20RA	Beech 1900C	UB-42	
☐ N623RA	Beech 1900C-1	UC-163	ex N3043L
☐ N273RH	Boeing 737-66N	29890/1276	ex N824SR
☐ N288DP	Boeing 737-66N	29892/1305	ex N892SR
☐ N319BD	Boeing 737-66N	28649/887	ex N649MT
☐ N365SR	Boeing 737-66N	29891/1294	ex N891RD
☐ N859WP	Boeing 737-66N	28652/938	ex N645DM
☐ N869HH	Boeing 737-66N	28650/932	ex N628SR

EMPIRE AIRLINES — Empire Air (EM/CFS) — Coeur d'Alene, ID/Spokane-Intl, WA (COE/GEG)

Operates Cessna 208 Caravans and ATR 42/72s plus Fokker F.27 Friendship 500s leased from, and operated on behalf of, FedEx

EPPS AVIATION CHARTER — Epps Air (EPS) — Atlanta-De Kalb-Peachtree, GA (PDK)

☐ N10HT	Mitsubishi MU-2B-60	778SA	ex N264MA
☐ N46AK	Mitsubishi MU-2B-60	754SA	ex N942ST
☐ N888RH	Mitsubishi MU-2B-60	737SA	ex N315MA
☐ N888SE	Mitsubishi MU-2B-60	1549SA	ex N475MA
☐ N941MA	Mitsubishi MU-2B-60	744SA	
☐ N984RE	Mitsubishi MU-2B-60	787SA	ex N267PC
☐ N1164F	Mitsubishi MU-2B-60	1562SA	ex D-ICDG
☐ N8083A	Mitsubishi MU-2B-60	739SA	ex N707EZ
☐ N23WJ	Beech 200 Super King Air	BB-1297	ex N21VF
☐ N57GA	Beech 200 Super King Air	BB-477	ex F-GILB
☐ N109DT	Beech 65-C90A King Air	LJ-1102	ex N682TA
☐ N795CA	Beech 200 Super King Air	BB-559	ex N559BM

ERA AVIATION — Erah (7H/ERH) — Anchorage-Intl South, AK (ANC)

☐ N881EA	de Havilland DHC-8-106	233	ex C-GFOD
☐ N882EA	de Havilland DHC-8-103	98	ex D-BERT
☐ N883EA	de Havilland DHC-8-106	260	ex C-GGEW
☐ N971EA	Beech 1900D	UE-387	ex N848CA
☐ N972EA	Beech 1900D	UE-389	ex N852CA
☐ N973EA	Beech 1900D	UE-391	ex N841CA

ERA HELICOPTERS — Anchorage-Intl South, AK/Lake Charles-Regional, LA (ANC/LCH)

☐ N108TA	Aérospatiale AS350BA AStar	3080	
☐ N109TA	Aérospatiale AS350B2 AStar	3103	
☐ N118TA	Aérospatiale AS350B2 AStar	3110	
☐ N147BH	Aérospatiale AS350BA AStar	1273	ex N3610G
☐ N152TA	Aérospatiale AS350B1 AStar	2241	ex N60321
☐ N159JK	Aérospatiale AS350B2 AStar	3253	
☐ N161EH	Aérospatiale AS350B2 AStar	2144	
☐ N162EH	Aérospatiale AS350B2 AStar	2147	
☐ N165EH	Aérospatiale AS350B1 AStar	2185	
☐ N166EH	Aérospatiale AS350B2 AStar	2194	
☐ N178EH	Aérospatiale AS350B2 AStar	2264	
☐ N181EH	Aérospatiale AS350B2 AStar	2680	
☐ N182EH	Aérospatiale AS350B2 AStar	2681	
☐ N183EH	Aérospatiale AS350B2 AStar	2752	
☐ N185EH	Aérospatiale AS350B2 AStar	2823	
☐ N186EH	Aérospatiale AS350B2 AStar	2844	
☐ N187EH	Aérospatiale AS350B2 AStar	2839	
☐ N188EH	Aérospatiale AS350B2 AStar	2954	
☐ N190EH	Aérospatiale AS350B2 AStar	2974	
☐ N191EH	Aérospatiale AS350B2 AStar	2505	
☐ N192EH	Aérospatiale AS350B2 AStar	2582	
☐ N193EH	Aérospatiale AS350B2 AStar	2599	
☐ N194EH	Aérospatiale AS350B2 AStar	2608	
☐ N195EH	Aérospatiale AS350B2 AStar	2615	
☐ N196EH	Aérospatiale AS350B2 AStar	2976	
☐ N212EH	Aérospatiale AS350B2 AStar	3151	
☐ N214EH	Aérospatiale AS350B2 AStar	3163	
☐ N215EH	Aérospatiale AS350B2 AStar	3172	
☐ N216EH	Aérospatiale AS350B2 AStar	3184	
☐ N217EH	Aérospatiale AS350B2 AStar	3197	
☐ N217FD	Aérospatiale AS350B2 AStar	4221	ex N646PT
☐ N328BF	Aérospatiale AS350B2 AStar	4284	
☐ N420JA	Aérospatiale AS350B2 AStar	4212	

☐ N603WB	Aérospatiale AS350B2 AStar	4225	
☐ N747WB	Aérospatiale AS350B2 AStar	2768	
☐ N906BA	Aérospatiale AS350B AStar	1479	ex N5786Y
☐ N4061G	Aérospatiale AS350BA AStar	3051	ex F-OHVB
☐ N40584	Aérospatiale AS350B2 AStar	2924	ex F-OHNT
☐ N18EA	Agusta A.109E Power	11210	ex N261CF
☐ N530KS	Agusta A.109E Power	11694	
☐ N820FT	Agusta A.109E Power	11701	
☐ N903RW	Agusta A.109E Power	11601	ex N3ZJ
☐ N910LB	Agusta A.109E Power	11682	
☐ N108AG	Agusta A.119 Koala	14053	ex N911AM
☐ N126RD	Agusta A.119 Koala	14504	ex N6QY
☐ N149JM	Agusta A.119 Koala	14533	
☐ N203JP	Agusta A.119 Koala	14535	
☐ N330JN	Agusta A.119 Koala	14510	
☐ N514RE	Agusta A.119 Koala II	14701	
☐ N602FB	Agusta A.119 Koala	14528	
☐ N626JP	Agusta A.119 Koala II	14716	
☐ N628RL	Agusta A.119 Koala II	14713	
☐ N709CG	Agusta A.119 Koala	14052	ex N18YC
☐ N715RT	Agusta A.119 Koala	14516	
☐ N802SM	Agusta A.119 Koala II	14711	
☐ N803EB	Agusta A.119 Koala	14033	ex N7KN
☐ N822MM	Agusta A.119 Koala	14055	ex N6QX
☐ N907AG	Agusta A.119 Koala	14045	ex N119MW
☐ N915BE	Agusta A.119 Koala	14519	
☐ N927JK	Agusta A.119 Koala	14517	
☐ N109DR	Agusta AW139	31309	♦
☐ N116YS	Agusta AW139	41206	♦
☐ N149DH	Agusta AW139	41004	
☐ N156JS	Agusta AW139	41003	ex I-EASH
☐ N339DF	Agusta AW139	41021	
☐ N339JR	Agusta AW139	41015	
☐ N603PW	Agusta AW139	31311	♦
☐ N813DG	Agusta AW139	31032	
☐ N829SN	Agusta AW139	41244	♦
☐ N125TA	Bell 206B JetRanger III	1315	ex N302SH
☐ N297CA	Bell 206B JetRanger III	1453	ex N117V
☐ N707HJ	Bell 206B JetRanger III	3173	ex N707TV
☐ N39114	Bell 206B JetRanger III	3293	
☐ N59582	Bell 206B JetRanger III	1460	
☐ N357EH	Bell 212	31209	
☐ N358EH	Bell 212	31211	
☐ N359EH	Bell 212	31212	ex C-GRVN
☐ N361EH	Bell 212	30554	ex XA-TRY
☐ N362EH	Bell 212	30853	ex XA-TRX
☐ N370EH	Bell 212	30624	
☐ N399EH	Bell 212	30810	ex XA-AAM
☐ N500EH	Bell 212	30945	
☐ N508EH	Bell 212	30908	
☐ N509EH	Bell 212	30925	
☐ N510EH	Bell 212	31113	ex C-GNCH ♦
☐ N511EH	Bell 212	31118	
☐ N522EH	Bell 212	31199	ex XA-TRZ
☐ N523EH	Bell 212	31214	ex C-GRWX
☐ N167EH	Bell 412	33089	ex VH-NSO
☐ N168EH	Bell 412	33058	ex VH-NSI
☐ N169EH	Bell 412	33064	ex XA-BDD
☐ N417EH	Bell 412	33031	ex N3911E
☐ N421EH	Bell 412	33067	ex N57413
☐ N116KG	Eurocopter EC120B Colibri	1152	ex N413AE
☐ N120GB	Eurocopter EC120B Colibri	1063	
☐ N120TX	Eurocopter EC120B Colibri	1029	
☐ N131MB	Eurocopter EC120B Colibri	1070	
☐ N517SS	Eurocopter EC120B Colibri	1080	ex N5234N
☐ N89EM	Eurocopter EC135P1	0049	ex N94387
☐ N320TV	Eurocopter EC135P2	0467	
☐ N357TC	Eurocopter EC135P2+	0626	
☐ N551BA	Eurocopter EC135P2	0188	

☐ N605SS	Eurocopter EC135P2	0461		
☐ N611LS	Eurocopter EC135P2	0472		
☐ N812LV	Eurocopter EC135P2+	0614		
☐ N109RR	Eurocopter EC225LP	2777		◆
☐ N124EH	MBB Bo.105CBS	S-559	ex 9Y-TJE	
☐ N125EH	MBB Bo.105CBS	S-562	ex N9376Y	
☐ N129EH	MBB Bo.105CBS	S-580	ex N29077	
☐ N130EH	MBB Bo.105CBS	S-588	ex N2910H	
☐ N131EH	MBB Bo.105CBS	S-595	ex N3129U	
☐ N135EH	MBB Bo.105CBS	S-675	ex N4573D	
☐ N149EH	MBB Bo.105CBS	S-705	ex N968MB	
☐ N152EH	MBB Bo.105CBS	S-701	ex N954MB	
☐ N153EH	MBB Bo.105CBS	S-702	ex PH-NZY	
☐ N290EH	MBB Bo.105CBS-4	S-850	ex N6554Y	
☐ N291EH	MBB Bo.105CBS-4	S-842	ex N65962	
☐ N293EH	MBB Bo.105CBS-4	S-844	ex N6612K	
☐ N294EH	MBB Bo.105CBS-4	S-846	ex N6559A	
☐ N296EH	MBB Bo.105CBS-4	S-849	ex N65385	
☐ N298EH	MBB Bo.105CBS-4	S-845	ex N4186F	
☐ N423EH	MBB Bo.105CBS	S-543	ex N42018	
☐ N424EH	MBB Bo.105CBS	S-548	ex N42001	
☐ N426EH	MBB Bo.105CBS	S-552	ex N93173	
☐ N427EH	MBB Bo.105CBS	S-554	ex N93205	
☐ N562EH	Sikorsky S-61N	61257	ex PH-NZA	
☐ N564EH	Sikorsky S-61N	61365	ex C-GBSF	
☐ N547WM	Sikorsky S-76C++	760722	ex N2579P	
☐ N573EH	Sikorsky S-76A++	760373	ex B-	
☐ N574EH	Sikorsky S-76A++	760369	ex N369AG	
☐ N575EH	Sikorsky S-76A++	760366	ex N621LH	
☐ N576EH	Sikorsky S-76A++	760212	ex N15458	
☐ N577EH	Sikorsky S-76A++	760222	ex N15459	
☐ N578EH	Sikorsky S-76A++	760099	ex N223BF	
☐ N761EH	Sikorsky S-76C++	760736	ex N20302	
☐ N905RD	Sikorsky S-76C+	760610	ex N8109K	

ERICKSON AIR CRANE   Central Point, OR

☐ N154AC	Erickson/Sikorsky S-64E Skycrane	64037	ex 68-18435	733 Georgia Peach
☐ N158AC	Erickson/Sikorsky S-64F Skycrane	64081	ex HL9260	744 Goliath
☐ N159AC	Erickson/Sikorsky S-64F Skycrane	64084	ex 68-18476	741
☐ N163AC	Erickson/Sikorsky S-64E Skycrane	64093	ex 70-18485	738 Hurricane Bubba
☐ N164AC	Erickson/Sikorsky S-64E Skycrane	64034	ex C-FCRN	730 The Incredible Hulk
☐ N171AC	Erickson/Sikorsky S-64F Skycrane	64090	ex 69-18482	[Central Point]
☐ N173AC	Erickson/Sikorsky S-64E Skycrane	64015	ex 68-18413	736 Christina
☐ N178AC	Erickson/Sikorsky S-64E Skycrane	64097	ex 70-18489	748 Isabelle
☐ N179AC	Erickson/Sikorsky S-64E Skycrane	64091	ex C-GFAH	733 Elvis
☐ N194AC	Erickson/Sikorsky S-64E Skycrane	64017	ex C-GFLH	746
☐ N217AC	Erickson/Sikorsky S-64E Skycrane	64064	ex N542SB	732 Malcolm
☐ N218AC	Erickson/Sikorsky S-64E Skycrane	64033	ex N545SB	749 Elsie
☐ N237AC	Erickson/Sikorsky S-64E Skycrane	64095	ex 69-18487	[Central Point]
☐ N243AC	Erickson/Sikorsky S-64E Skycrane	64022	ex N544CH	[Central Point]
☐ N543CH	Erickson/Sikorsky S-64E Skycrane	64016	ex N4409U	[Central Point]
☐ N957AC	Erickson/Sikorsky S-64E Skycrane	64065	ex C-GESG	745
☐ N4099M	Erickson/Sikorsky S-64E Skycrane	64028	ex 67-18426	[Central Point]
☐ N6962R	Erickson/Sikorsky S-64E Skycrane	64058	ex HC-CAT	741 Olga
☐ N7073C	Erickson/Sikorsky S-64E Skycrane	64042	ex 68-18440	[Central Point]

EVERGREEN HELICOPTERS   (7E)
McMinnville, OR/Anchorage-Merrill, AK/ Galveston, TX (RNC/MRI/GLS)

☐ N351EV	Aérospatiale AS350B2 AStar	2930	ex SE-JCX	<GC Air
☐ N352EV	Aérospatiale AS350B2 AStar	2555	ex JA6112	
☐ N353EV	Aérospatiale AS350B2 AStar	2444	ex C-GJVG	
☐ N354EV	Aérospatiale AS350B3 AStar	3664	ex SE-JHG	
☐ N355EV	Aérospatiale AS350B3 AStar	3550	ex F-GYDE	
☐ N356EV	Aérospatiale AS350B3 AStar	3649	ex SE-JHF	
☐ N359EV	Aérospatiale AS350B3 AStar	3797	ex I-BALO	
☐ N917JT	Aérospatiale AS350B2 AStar	2759	ex N6096P	
☐ N300EV	Aérospatiale SA.330J Puma	1301	ex F-GSYF	
☐ N330J	Aérospatiale SA.330J Puma	1647	ex XA-SKT	
☐ N330JF	Aérospatiale SA.330J Puma	1514	ex 9M-SSD	
☐ N366EV	Aérospatiale SA.330J Puma	1201	ex D-HAXA	◆

| ☐ N367EV | Aérospatiale SA.330J Puma | 1332 | ex D-HAXG | ♦ |
| ☐ N405R | Aérospatiale SA.330J Puma | 1475 | ex PP-MGB | |

| ☐ N139EV | Agusta AW139 | 31006 | ex UAE 4003 |
| ☐ N140EV | Agusta AW139 | 31025 | ex UAE 4004 |

☐ N33AZ	Bell 206L-3 LongRanger III	51110	
☐ N206EV	Bell 206L-4 LongRanger IV	52311	ex N46340
☐ N3195S	Bell 206L-3 LongRanger III	51136	
☐ N5007F	Bell 206L-1 LongRanger III	45186	

☐ N212EV	Bell 212	30881	ex HK-4064X
☐ N398EH	Bell 212	30766	ex HK-4059X
☐ N5410N	Bell 212	31206	ex VH-CUZ
☐ N16973	Bell 212	30882	ex VH-CRO
☐ N59633	Bell 212	30676	

| ☐ N419EV | Bell 412EP | 36464 | ex C-FSOD |

☐ N348CA	CASA C.212-200	CC20-7-175		
☐ N352CA	CASA C.212-200	CC40-1-190		>US Air Force
☐ N422CA	CASA C.212-200	CC40-5-238		
☐ N423CA	CASA C.212-200	S1-1-240		>US Air Force

☐ N22MS	Learjet 35A	35A-209	ex N711DS
☐ N352HS	Learjet 35A	35A-596	ex N826CP
☐ N405PC	Learjet 35A	35A-651	ex HB-VJK

☐ N60EV	Sikorsky S-61 (H-3E)	61643	ex 69-5799
☐ N61EV	Sikorsky S-61 (H-3E)	61566	ex 65-12791
☐ N62EV	Sikorsky S-61 (HH-3F)	61670	ex USCG 1493
☐ N63EV	Sikorsky S-61 (HH-3F)	61674	ex USCG 1497

☐ N70DB	Bell 206B JetRanger	1730		
☐ N134WJ	Beech B200C Super King Air	BL-134	ex SE-LMP	
☐ N191EV	Beech 1900D	UE-114	ex N114YV	
☐ N202EV	Lockheed P2V-5 Neptune	726-5387	ex Bu131502 141	Tanker
☐ N204BB	MBB B0.105C	S-57	ex D-HDBH	
☐ N500KM	MBB Bo.105C	S-76	ex N500KV	
☐ N6979R	Sikorsky S-64E	64079		
☐ N9688G	Cessna U206F Stationair	U20601888		
☐ N10729	Bell 206B JetRanger III	2876		

EVERGREEN INTERNATIONAL AIRLINES — Evergreen (EZ/EIA)
McMinnville, OR/Marana-Pinal Airpark, AZ (RNC/MZJ)

☐ N470EV	Boeing 747-273C	20653/237	ex N749WA	947 Super Tanker
☐ N471EV	Boeing 747-273C	20651/209	ex N747WR	
☐ N478EV	Boeing 747SR-46 (SCD)	21033/254	ex PT-TDE	[MZJ]
☐ N479EV	Boeing 747-132 (SCD)	19898/94	ex N725PA	Water Bomber 979
☐ N480EV	Boeing 747-121 (SCD)	20348/106	ex N690UP	[MZJ]
☐ N482EV	Boeing 747-212B (SCD)	20713/219	ex N729PA	
☐ N485EV	Boeing 747-212B (SCD)	20712/218	ex N728PA	
☐ N486EV	Boeing 747-212B (SCD)	20888/240	ex N745SJ	
☐ N487EV	Boeing 747-230B (SCD)	23286/614	ex TF-AMF	
☐ N488EV	Boeing 747-230B (SCD)	23287/617	ex D-ABZA	
☐ N489EV	Boeing 747-230B (SF)	23393/633	ex TF-AMH	
☐ N490EV	Boeing 747-230F	24138/706	ex TF-ARV	
☐ N491EV	Boeing 747-412F	26561/1042	ex 9V-SFB	♦

☐ N249BA	Boeing 747-409LCF	24309/766	ex B-18271	Op for Boeing
☐ N718BA	Boeing 747-4H6LCF	27042/932	ex N74713	Op for Boeing
☐ N747BC	Boeing 747-4J6LCF	25879/904	ex B-2464	Op for Boeing
☐ N780BA	Boeing 747-409LCF	24310/778	ex B-18272	Op for Boeing

☐ N915F	Douglas DC-9-15RC (ABS 3)	47061/207	ex EC-EYS	[MZJ]
☐ N916F	Douglas DC-9-15RC (ABS 3)	47044/265	ex OH-LYH	[MZJ]
☐ N933F	Douglas DC-9-33RC (ABS 3)	47191/280	ex N33UA	[MZJ]
☐ N941F	Douglas DC-9-33F (ABS 3)	47193/311	ex VH-IPC	[MZJ]

EVERTS AIR ALASKA — Everts (3Z/VTS) — Fairbanks-Intl, AK (FAI)

☐ N108NS	Piper PA-32R-300 Lance	32R-7680288	
☐ N148RF	Piper PA-32R-300 Lance	32R-7680076	
☐ N575JD	Cessna 208B Caravan I	208B0595	ex N5268V
☐ N1063H	Piper PA-32R-300 Lance	32R-7780129	
☐ N6969J	Piper PA-32R-300 Lance	32R-7680398	

EVERTS AIR CARGO — Everts (3K/VTS) — Fairbanks-Intl, AK (FAI)

☐ N151	Douglas DC-6B	45496/992	ex C-GICD		
☐ N251CE	Douglas C-118A	44612/532	ex Bu153693		
☐ N351CE	Douglas C-118A	44599/505	ex 53-3228		
☐ N400UA	Douglas DC-6A	44258/467	ex YV-296C		
☐ N555SQ	Douglas DC-6B	45137/830	ex N37585		
☐ N1036F	Douglas C-118A	43581/295	ex 51-3834		[FAI]
☐ N1377K	Douglas C-118A	44596/499	ex 53-3225		[FAI]
☐ N6174C	Douglas DC-6A	44075/451	ex C-GBYN		
☐ N6586C	Douglas DC-6BF	45222/849			
☐ N9056R	Douglas DC-6A/B	45498/1005	ex C-FCZZ		
☐ N99330	Douglas C-118A	43576/275	ex C-GPEG		[FAI]
☐ N932AX	Douglas DC-9-33RC (ABS 3)	47465/584	ex N7465B		♦
☐ N1105G	Embraer EMB.120FC Brasilia	120105	ex PT-SMX		
☐ N1110J	Embraer EMB.120FC Brasilia	120110	ex PT-SNC		
☐ N7848B	Curtiss C-46R Commando	273	ex HP-238	Dumbo	
☐ N12703	Embraer EMB.120FC Brasilia	120084	ex PT-SMB		[FAI]
☐ N54514	Curtiss C-46D Commando	33285	ex 51-1122	Maid in Japan	

EVERTS AIR FUEL — Fairbanks-Intl, AK (FAI)

☐ N100CE	Douglas C-118A	44662/629	ex N51599		♦
☐ N444CE	Douglas DC-6B	45478/962	ex C-GHLZ	Spirit of America	
☐ N451CE	Douglas C-118B	43712/358	ex N840CS		
☐ N747CE	Douglas C-118A	44661/628	ex N233HP		
☐ N1822M	Curtiss C-46F Commando	22521	ex 44-18698	Salmon Ella	
☐ N1837M	Curtiss C-46F Commando	22388	ex CF-FNC	Hot Stuff	
☐ N7780B	Douglas DC-6A	45372/875			

EXECUTIVE AIRLINES — Executive Eagle (OW/EXK)
San Juan-Luis Munoz Marin Intl, PR / Miami Intl, FL (SJU/MIA)

A wholly owned subsidiary of American Eagle Airlines and operates as American Eagle

EXPRESSJET AIRLINES — Jet Link (CO/BTA)
Cleveland, OH/Houston- Intercontinental, TX/Newark, NJ (CLE/IAH/EWR)

☐ N11544	Embraer ERJ-145LR	145557	ex PT-SZS
☐ N11551	Embraer ERJ-145LR	145411	ex PT-STI
☐ N14907	Embraer ERJ-145LR	145468	ex PT-SVN
☐ N18557	Embraer ERJ-145LR	145596	ex PT-SCF
☐ N19554	Embraer ERJ-145LR	145587	ex PT-SBX
☐ N11189	Embraer ERJ-145XR	14500931	ex PT-SCA
☐ N11192	Embraer ERJ-145XR	14500936	ex PT-SCI
☐ N11199	Embraer ERJ-145XR	14500953	ex PT-SFA
☐ N12163	Embraer ERJ-145XR	14500811	ex PT-SNN
☐ N12175	Embraer ERJ-145XR	14500878	ex PT-SXT
☐ N12201	Embraer ERJ-145XR	14500959	ex PT-SFG
☐ N14162	Embraer ERJ-145XR	14500808	ex PT-SNK
☐ N14174	Embraer ERJ-145XR	14500876	ex PT-SXR
☐ N14188	Embraer ERJ-145XR	14500929	ex PT-SOY
☐ N14198	Embraer ERJ-145XR	14500951	ex PT-SCZ
☐ N16178	Embraer ERJ-145XR	14500889	ex PT-SYC

FEDERICO HELICOPTERS (FDE) — Fresno-Air Terminal, CA/Mariposa-Yosemite, CA (FAT/OYS)

☐ N205JG	Bell UH-1H (205)	9884	ex 67-17686
☐ N752A	Sikorsky S-55A	55981	ex C-GRXA
☐ N1386L	Bell UH-1B (204)	652	ex 62-4592

FEDEX EXPRESS — FedEx (FX/FDX) — Memphis-Intl, TN (MEM)

☐ N650FE	Airbus A300F4-605R	726	ex F-WWAP	Molly Mickler
☐ N651FE	Airbus A300F4-605R	728	ex F-WWAJ	Diane Kathleen
☐ N652FE	Airbus A300F4-605R	735	ex F-WWAN	Rachel Patricia
☐ N653FE	Airbus A300F4-605R	736	ex F-WWAD	Samantha Massey
☐ N654FE	Airbus A300F4-605R	738	ex F-WWAX	Richard
☐ N655FE	Airbus A300F4-605R	742	ex F-WWAJ	Dion
☐ N656FE	Airbus A300F4-605R	745	ex F-WWAP	Devin
☐ N657FE	Airbus A300F4-605R	748	ex F-WWAM	Lizzie
☐ N658FE	Airbus A300F4-605R	752	ex F-WWAE	Tristian
☐ N659FE	Airbus A300F4-605R	757	ex F-WWAF	Calvin
☐ N660FE	Airbus A300F4-605R	759	ex F-WWAG	Zack
☐ N661FE	Airbus A300F4-605R	760	ex F-WWAL	Whitney

☐ N662FE	Airbus A300F4-605R	761	ex F-WWAK	Tessa
☐ N663FE	Airbus A300F4-605R	766	ex F-WWAO	Domenick
☐ N664FE	Airbus A300F4-605R	768	ex F-WWAA	Amanda
☐ N665FE	Airbus A300F4-605R	769	ex F-WWAM	Ethan
☐ N667FE	Airbus A300F4-605R	771	ex F-WWAF	Sean
☐ N668FE	Airbus A300F4-605R	772	ex F-WWAP	Tianna
☐ N669FE	Airbus A300F4-605R	774	ex F-WWAE	Kaitlyn
☐ N670FE	Airbus A300F4-605R	777	ex F-WWAQ	Amrit
☐ N671FE	Airbus A300F4-605R	778	ex F-WWAV	Drew
☐ N672FE	Airbus A300F4-605R	779	ex F-WWAZ	Young Joe
☐ N673FE	Airbus A300F4-605R	780	ex F-WWAU	Mark
☐ N674FE	Airbus A300F4-605R	781	ex F-WWAN	Thea
☐ N675FE	Airbus A300F4-605R	789	ex F-WWAZ	Byron
☐ N676FE	Airbus A300F4-605R	790	ex F-WWAV	Jade
☐ N677FE	Airbus A300F4-605R	791	ex F-WWAD	Clifford
☐ N678FE	Airbus A300F4-605R	792	ex F-WWAF	Allison
☐ N679FE	Airbus A300F4-605R	793	ex F-WWAG	Ty
☐ N680FE	Airbus A300F4-605R	794	ex F-WWAH	Tierney
☐ N681FE	Airbus A300F4-605R	799	ex F-WWAJ	Kaci
☐ N682FE	Airbus A300F4-605R	800	ex F-WWAK	Gabrial
☐ N683FE	Airbus A300F4-605R	801	ex F-WWAL	Xenophon
☐ N684FE	Airbus A300F4-605R	802	ex F-WWAM	Daniel
☐ N685FE	Airbus A300F4-605R	803	ex F-WWAB	Landon Ostlie
☐ N686FE	Airbus A300F4-605R	804	ex F-WWAO	Alex
☐ N687FE	Airbus A300F4-605R	873	ex F-WWAO	
☐ N688FE	Airbus A300F4-605R	874	ex F-WWAP	
☐ N689FE	Airbus A300F4-605R	875	ex F-WWAQ	
☐ N690FE	Airbus A300F4-605R	876	ex F-WWAR	
☐ N691FE	Airbus A300F4-605R	877	ex F-WWAS	
☐ N692FE	Airbus A300F4-605R	878	ex F-WWAT	Gabriel
☐ N716FD	Airbus A300B4-622F	358	ex HL7287	Halle
☐ N717FD	Airbus A300B4-622F	361	ex HL7280	Roben
☐ N718FD	Airbus A300B4-622F	365	ex HL7281	Anna
☐ N719FD	Airbus A300B4-622F	388	ex HL7290	Cale
☐ N720FD	Airbus A300B4-622F	417	ex HL7291	Kristin Marie
☐ N721FD	Airbus A300B4-622RF	477	ex D-ASAE	Kathryn
☐ N722FD	Airbus A300B4-622RF	479	ex HL7535	Terry
☐ N723FD	Airbus A300B4-622RF	543	ex HL7536	Cody
☐ N724FD	Airbus A300B4-622RF	530	ex F-OIHA	Anacarina
☐ N725FD	Airbus A300B4-622RF	572	ex SU-GAT	Zebradedra
☐ N726FD	Airbus A300B4-622RF	575	ex SU-GAU	
☐ N727FD	Airbus A300B4-622RF	579	ex SU-GAV	Mira
☐ N728FD	Airbus A300B4-622RF	581	ex SU-GAW	Cassie
☐ N729FD	Airbus A300B4-622RF	657	ex TF-ELU	Kaylee
☐ N730FD	Airbus A300B4-622RF	659	ex TF-ELB	Kailey
☐ N731FD	Airbus A300B4-605RF	709	ex B-2320	
☐ N732FD	Airbus A300B4-605RF	713	ex B-2321	
☐ N733FD	Airbus A300B4-605RF	715	ex B-2322	
☐ N740FD	Airbus A300B4-622RF	559	ex F-WQTD	
☐ N741FD	Airbus A300B4-622RF	611	ex A7-AFC	
☐ N742FD	Airbus A300B4-622RF	613	ex A7-AFD	
☐ N743FD	Airbus A300B4-622RF	630	ex A7-AFA	
☐ N744FD	Airbus A300B4-622RF	664	ex A7-ABN	
☐ N745FD	Airbus A300B4-622RF	668	ex A7-ABO	
☐ N746FD	Airbus A300B4-622RF	688	ex A7-ABW	
☐ N748FD	Airbus A300B4-622RF	633	ex N633AN	
☐ N749FD	Airbus A300B4-622RF	536	ex TF-ELD	
☐ N750FD	Airbus A300B4-622RF	555	ex F-HEEE	
☐ N751FD	Airbus A300B4-622RF	625	ex F-HDDD	
☐ N401FE	Airbus A310-203F	191	ex D-AICA	David	[VCV]
☐ N402FE	Airbus A310-203F	201	ex D-AICB	Carlye	
☐ N403FE	Airbus A310-203F	230	ex D-AICC	Maddison	
☐ N404FE	Airbus A310-203F	233	ex D-AICD	Collin	
☐ N405FE	Airbus A310-203F	237	ex D-AICF	Mariah	
☐ N407FE	Airbus A310-203F	254	ex D-AICH	Stacey Denise	[VCV]
☐ N408FE	Airbus A310-203F	257	ex D-AICK	Kealoha	[VCV]
☐ N409FE	Airbus A310-203F	273	ex D-AICL	Jake	[VCV]
☐ N410FE	Airbus A310-203F	356	ex D-AICM	Carolyn	♦
☐ N411FE	Airbus A310-203F	359	ex D-AICN	Barbra	[VCV]
☐ N412FE	Airbus A310-203F	360	ex D-AICP	Corina	[VCV]
☐ N414FE	Airbus A310-203F	400	ex D-AICS	Tanner	[VCV]
☐ N416FE	Airbus A310-222F	288	ex F-WGYR	Patrick	[VCV]
☐ N417FE	Airbus A310-222F	333	ex N802PA	Kyle	
☐ N418FE	Airbus A310-222F	343	ex N803PA	Rachel	
☐ N419FE	Airbus A310-222F	345	ex N804PA	Krystle	[VCV]
☐ N421FE	Airbus A310-222F	342	ex N806PA	Caitlin	

☐	N423FE	Airbus A310-203F	281	ex PH-MCA	Trey	
☐	N425FE	Airbus A310-203F	264	ex PH-AGD	Jerome	
☐	N426FE	Airbus A310-203F	245	ex PH-AGB	Shana	
☐	N427FE	Airbus A310-203F	362	ex PH-AGH	Zackary	
☐	N428FE	Airbus A310-203F	248	ex PH-AGC	Kristina	
☐	N429FE	Airbus A310-203F	364	ex PH-AGI	Conner	
☐	N430FE	Airbus A310-203F	394	ex PH-AGK	Kelleen	
☐	N431FE	Airbus A310-203F	316	ex F-WWAD	Asumi	
☐	N435FE	Airbus A310-203F	369	ex F-GEME	Ceara	
☐	N436FE	Airbus A310-203F	454	ex F-GEMG	Gillian	
☐	N443FE	Airbus A310-203F	283	ex PH-AGE	Katelin	
☐	N445FE	Airbus A310-203F	297	ex PH-AGF	Nicholas	
☐	N446FE	Airbus A310-222F	224	ex HB-IPA	Makenna	[VCV]♦
☐	N447FE	Airbus A310-222F	251	ex HB-IPB	Shaunna	
☐	N448FE	Airbus A310-222F	260	ex HB-IPD	Augustine	
☐	N450FE	Airbus A310-222F	162	ex F-GPDJ	Selna	
☐	N451FE	Airbus A310-222F	303	ex OO-SCA	Reis	
☐	N453FE	Airbus A310-222F	267	ex D-ASAL	Rush	
☐	N454FE	Airbus A310-222F	278	ex D-ASAK	Marissa	
☐	N455FE	Airbus A310-222F	331	ex F-WWAH	Sara	
☐	N456FE	Airbus A310-222F	318	ex F-OHPQ	Simon	
☐	N801FD	Airbus A310-324F	539	ex D-ASAD	Amos	
☐	N802FD	Airbus A310-324F	542	ex D-ASAD	Saeed	
☐	N803FD	Airbus A310-324F	378	ex N853CH	Rylan	
☐	N804FD	Airbus A310-324F	549	ex N101MP	Paige	
☐	N805FD	Airbus A310-324F	456	ex F-OGYR	Fernando	
☐	N806FD	Airbus A310-324F	458	ex F-OGYN	Addisyn	
☐	N807FD	Airbus A310-324F	492	ex F-WQTA	Joshua	
☐	N808FD	Airbus A310-324F	439	ex F-OHPU	Berkeley	
☐	N809FD	Airbus A310-324F	449	ex F-OHPV	Gavin	
☐	N810FD	Airbus A310-324F	452	ex F-OHPY	Sebastian	
☐	N811FD	Airbus A310-324F	457	ex F-OGYM		
☐	N812FD	Airbus A310-324F	467	ex F-OGYS	Agyei	
☐	N813FD	Airbus A310-324F	500	ex N501RR		
☐	N814FD	Airbus A310-324F	534	ex N534RR		
☐	N815FD	Airbus A310-324F	638	ex F-OJAF	Tommy	
☐	N816FD	Airbus A310-304F	593	ex F-OGQR		
☐	N817FD	Airbus A310-304F	552	ex TF-ELS		
☐	N68096	Airbus A310-324	589	ex N285BA		[VCV]
☐	C-GATK	ATR 42-310F	135	ex N923FX		>MAL
☐	EC-KAI	ATR 42-300F	141	ex EI-FXF		>SWT
☐	N900FX	ATR 42-320F	170	ex N14825		Op by CFS
☐	N901FX	ATR 42-320F	172	ex N26826		Op by CFS
☐	N903FX	ATR 42-320F	179	ex N14828		Op by CFS
☐	N906FX	ATR 42-320F	280	ex N97841		Op by MTN
☐	N907FX	ATR 42-320F	286	ex N86842		Op by MTN
☐	N908FX	ATR 42-300F	023	ex N972NA		Op by CFS
☐	N909FX	ATR 42-300F	275	ex N275BC		Op by MTN
☐	N910FX	ATR 42-300F	277	ex N277AT		Op by MTN
☐	N911FX	ATR 42-300F	045	ex N424MQ		Op by CFS
☐	N912FX	ATR 42-300F	047	ex N47AE		Op by CFS
☐	N913FX	ATR 42-320F	250	ex N251AE		Op by CFS
☐	N914FX	ATR 42-300F	293	ex N293AT		Op by CFS
☐	N915FX	ATR 42-320F	269	ex N269AT		Op by MTN
☐	N916FX	ATR 42-300F	314	ex N314AM		Op by MTN
☐	N917FX	ATR 42-320F	354	ex N351AT		Op by CFS
☐	N918FX	ATR 42-300F	262	ex N262AT		Op by MTN
☐	N919FX	ATR 42-320F	266	ex N265AE		Op by CFS
☐	N920FX	ATR 42-320F	325	ex N325AT		Op by MTN
☐	N921FX	ATR 42-300F	319	ex N319AM		Op by CFS
☐	EI-FXG	ATR 72-202F	224	ex (N814FX)		>ABR
☐	EI-FXH	ATR 72-202F	229	ex N815FX		>ABR
☐	EI-FXI	ATR 72-202F	294	ex N818FX		>ABR
☐	EI-FXJ	ATR 72-202F	292	ex N813FX		>ABR
☐	EI-FXK	ATR 72-202F	256	ex N817FX		>ABR
☐	N800FX	ATR 72-212	336	ex N630AS		♦
☐	N801FX	ATR 72-212	338	ex N632AS		♦
☐	N802FX	ATR 72-212	344	ex N633AS		♦
☐	N803FX	ATR 72-212	362	ex N631AS		♦
☐	N804FX	ATR 72-212	370	ex N634AS		♦
☐	N805FX	ATR 72-212	372	ex N635AS		♦
☐	N806FX	ATR 72-212	375	ex N636AS		♦
☐	N807FX	ATR 72-212	383	ex N637AS		♦
☐	N809FX	ATR 72-202F	217	ex N721TE		Op by MTN
☐	N810FX	ATR 72-202F	220	ex N722TE		Op by MTN [COE]

☐ N811FX	ATR 72-202F	283	ex N723TE		Op by MTN
☐ N812FX	ATR 72-212F	404	ex D-AEWI		Op by CFS
☐ N816FX	ATR 72-212F	347	ex D-AEWG		Op by CFS
☐ N819FX	ATR 72-212F	359	ex D-AEWH		Op by CFS
☐ N820FX	ATR 72-212F	248	ex N248AT		
☐ N821FX	ATR 72-212F	253	ex N252AM		
☐ N203FE	Boeing 727-2S2F (FedEx 3)	22925/1819		Jonathan	
☐ N204FE	Boeing 727-2S2F (FedEx 3)	22926/1820		Rebecca	
☐ N207FE	Boeing 727-2S2F (Super 27)	22929/1823		Vivian	
☐ N211FE	Boeing 727-2S2F (FedEx 3)	22933/1827		Bobby	
☐ N213FE	Boeing 727-2S2F (FedEx 3)	22935/1829		Cagen	
☐ N215FE	Boeing 727-2S2F (FedEx 3)	22936/1830		Billy	
☐ N216FE	Boeing 727-2S2F (Super 27)	22937/1831		Wade	
☐ N217FE	Boeing 727-2S2F (Super 27)	22938/1832		Sonja	
☐ N218FE	Boeing 727-233F (FedEx 3)	21101/1150	ex C-GAAM	Christin	[VCV]♦
☐ N220FE	Boeing 727-233F (FedEx 3)	20934/1074	ex C-GAAC	Emily	
☐ N221FE	Boeing 727-233F (FedEx 3)	20932/1069	ex C-GAAA	Megan Nicole	
☐ N222FE	Boeing 727-233F (FedEx 3)	20933/1071	ex C-GAAB	Michael	[VCV]
☐ N223FE	Boeing 727-233F (FedEx 3)	20935/1076	ex C-GAAD	Dustin	
☐ N233FE	Boeing 727-247F (FedEx 3)	21327/1249	ex C-FMEI		♦
☐ N235FE	Boeing 727-247F (FedEx 3)	21329/1254	ex C-FMEA	Stephanie	♦
☐ N236FE	Boeing 727-247F (FedEx 3)	21330/1260	ex C-FMEE		♦
☐ N237FE	Boeing 727-247F (FedEx 3)	21331/1266	ex N2826W	Tristan	
☐ N240FE	Boeing 727-277F (FedEx 3)	20978/1083	ex VH-RMY	Baron	
☐ N241FE	Boeing 727-277F (FedEx 3)	20979/1098	ex VH-RMZ	Jill	
☐ N243FE	Boeing 727-277F (FedEx 3)	21480/1352	ex VH-RML	Braden	[VCV]
☐ N244FE	Boeing 727-277F (FedEx 3)	21647/1436	ex VH-RMM	Crystal	
☐ N245FE	Boeing 727-277F (FedEx 3)	22016/1566	ex VH-RMO	Kelsey	
☐ N254FE	Boeing 727-233F (FedEx 3)	20936/1078	ex C-GAAE	Courtney	[VCV]♦
☐ N257FE	Boeing 727-233F (FedEx 3)	20939/1112	ex C-GAAH	Felicia	
☐ N258FE	Boeing 727-233F (FedEx 3)	20940/1120	ex C-GAAI	Lacey	
☐ N262FE	Boeing 727-233F (FedEx 3)	21624/1468	ex C-GAAO	Betsy	
☐ N263FE	Boeing 727-233F (FedEx 3)	21625/1470	ex C-GAAP	Marc	
☐ N264FE	Boeing 727-233F (FedEx 3)	21626/1472	ex C-GAAQ	Brennan	
☐ N265FE	Boeing 727-233F (FedEx 3)	21671/1523	ex C-GBZB	Paul	
☐ N266FE	Boeing 727-233F (FedEx 3)	21672/1538	ex C-GAAS	Steven	
☐ N267FE	Boeing 727-233F (FedEx 3)	21673/1541	ex C-GMSX	Jolene	
☐ N268FE	Boeing 727-233F (FedEx 3)	21674/1543	ex C-GAAU	Ginger	
☐ N269FE	Boeing 727-233F (FedEx 3)	21675/1555	ex C-GAAV	Alexander	
☐ N271FE	Boeing 727-233F (FedEx 3)	22036/1596	ex C-GAAX	Andrew	[VCV]☐
☐ N273FE	Boeing 727-233F (FedEx 3)	22038/1612	ex C-GAAZ	Samantha	
☐ N274FE	Boeing 727-233F (FedEx 3)	22039/1614	ex C-GYNA	Jessica	
☐ N275FE	Boeing 727-233F (FedEx 3)	22040/1626	ex C-GYNB	Skylar	
☐ N276FE	Boeing 727-233F (FedEx 3)	22041/1628	ex C-GYNC	Devan	
☐ N277FE	Boeing 727-233F (FedEx 3)	22042/1630	ex C-GYND	Hutch	
☐ N278FE	Boeing 727-233F (FedEx 3)	22345/1699	ex C-GYNE	Jeffrey	
☐ N279FE	Boeing 727-233F (FedEx 3)	22346/1704	ex C-GYNF	Ryan	
☐ N280FE	Boeing 727-223F (FedEx 3)	22347/1708	ex C-GYNG	Chad	
☐ N281FE	Boeing 727-233F (FedEx 3)	22348/1714	ex C-GYNH	Ivie	
☐ N282FE	Boeing 727-233F (FedEx 3)	22349/1722	ex C-GYNI	Dominique	
☐ N283FE	Boeing 727-233F (FedEx 3)	22350/1745	ex C-GYNJ	Randall	
☐ N284FE	Boeing 727-233F (FedEx 3)	22621/1791	ex C-GYNK	Victoria	
☐ N285FE	Boeing 727-233F (FedEx 3)	22622/1792	ex C-GYNL	Jordann	
☐ N286FE	Boeing 727-233F (FedEx 3)	22623/1803	ex C-GYNM	Charlsi	
☐ N287FE	Boeing 727-2D4F (FedEx 3)	21849/1527	ex N361PA	Alexa	
☐ N288FE	Boeing 727-2D4F (FedEx 3)	21850/1536	ex N362PA	Michelle	
☐ N462FE	Boeing 727-225F (FedEx 3)	22550/1739	ex N813EA	Daven	
☐ N463FE	Boeing 727-225F (FedEx 3)	22551/1744	ex N814EA	Tonga	
☐ N464FE	Boeing 727-225F (FedEx 3)	21288/1234	ex N8870Z	Blake	
☐ N465FE	Boeing 727-225F (FedEx 3)	21289/1235	ex N8871Z	Nathan	
☐ N466FE	Boeing 727-225F (FedEx 3)	21292/1240	ex N8874Z	Gideon	
☐ N467FE	Boeing 727-225F (FedEx 3)	21449/1306	ex N8876Z	Joy	
☐ N468FE	Boeing 727-225F (FedEx 3)	21452/1312	ex N8879Z	Chad	
☐ N469FE	Boeing 727-225F (FedEx 3)	21581/1437	ex N8884Z	Ray	
☐ N479FE	Boeing 727-227F (FedEx 3)	21461/1337	ex N455BN	Norah	
☐ N480FE	Boeing 727-227F (FedEx 3)	21462/1342	ex N456BN	Warren	[VCV]
☐ N481FE	Boeing 727-227F (FedEx 3)	21463/1353	ex N457BN	Tiffany	
☐ N482FE	Boeing 727-227F (FedEx 3)	21464/1355	ex N458BN	Natalie	
☐ N483FE	Boeing 727-227F (FedEx 3)	21465/1363	ex N459BN	David	
☐ N484FE	Boeing 727-227F (FedEx 3)	21466/1372	ex N460BN	Hallie	
☐ N485FE	Boeing 727-227F (FedEx 3)	21488/1388	ex N461BN	Kristen	
☐ N486FE	Boeing 727-227F (FedEx 3)	21489/1390	ex N462BN	Hunter	
☐ N487FE	Boeing 727-227F (FedEx 3)	21490/1396	ex N463BN	Britney	
☐ N488FE	Boeing 727-227F (FedEx 3)	21491/1402	ex N464BN	Olivia	
☐ N489FE	Boeing 727-227F (FedEx 3)	21492/1440	ex N465BN	Timothy	
☐ N490FE	Boeing 727-227F (FedEx 3)	21493/1442	ex N466BN	Chase	

☐	N491FE	Boeing 727-227F (FedEx 3)	21529/1444	ex N467BN	Noel	
☐	N492FE	Boeing 727-227F (FedEx 3)	21530/1446	ex N468BN	Two Bears	
☐	N493FE	Boeing 727-227F (FedEx 3)	21531/1450	ex N469BN	Maxx	
☐	N494FE	Boeing 727-227F (FedEx 3)	21532/1453	ex N470BN	Ebony	
☐	N495FE	Boeing 727-227F (FedEx 3)	21669/1484	ex N471BN	Leslie	
☐	N498FE	Boeing 727-232F (FedEx 3)	20867/1068	ex CS-TCI	Aidan	
☐	N499FE	Boeing 727-232F (FedEx 3)	21018/1095	ex CS-TCJ	Sierra	
☐	N226CL	Boeing 757-225	22612/114	ex G-VKND		[VCV]
☐	N240MQ	Boeing 757-2Y0	25240/388	ex XA-MTY		[VCV]
☐	N901FD	Boeing 757-2B7F	27122/525	ex N610AU		
☐	N902FD	Boeing 757-2B7SF	27123/534	ex N927UW		[VCV]
☐	N903FD	Boeing 757-2B7SF	27124/540	ex N928UW		
☐	N905FD	Boeing 757-2B7	27145/546	ex N930UW		[VCV]
☐	N906FD	Boeing 757-2B7SF	27148/564	ex N931UW		
☐	N909FD	Boeing 757-2B7	27200/589	ex N934UW		[VCV]
☐	N910FD	Boeing 757-236SF	25054/362	ex G-OOOK		under conv
☐	N912FD	Boeing 757-28ASF	24260/204	ex N517NA		
☐	N913FD	Boeing 757-28ASF	24017/162	ex C-FTDV		under conv
☐	N914FD	Boeing 757-28A	24367/208	ex C-FCLG		under conv
☐	N915FD	Boeing 757-236SF	24120/174	ex 4X-EBO		under conv
☐	N916FD	Boeing 757-27BSF	24137/178	ex 4X-EBY		
☐	N917FD	Boeing 757-23A	24291/215	ex CX-PUD		under conv
☐	N918FD	Boeing 757-23AER	24290/212	ex N290AN		under conv
☐	N919FD	Boeing 757-23ASF	24636/259	ex G-FJEA		
☐	N920FD	Boeing 757-23AER	24289/209	ex G-OAVB		under conv
☐	N921FD	Boeing 757-23AF	24924/333	ex N924AW		[VCV]
☐	N922FD	Boeing 757-23A	24293/220	ex N293AW		[VCV]
☐	N923FD	Boeing 757-204F	26266/514	ex G-BYAF		
☐	N924FD	Boeing 757-204	26267/538	ex G-BYAK		[VCV]
☐	N925FD	Boeing 757-204	27238/604	ex G-BYAS		[VCV]
☐	N928FD	Boeing 757-28A	24369/226	ex G-JMCF		[VCV]♦
☐	N933FD	Boeing 757-21BSF	24330/200	ex B-2804		
☐	N934FD	Boeing 757-21B	24331/203	ex B-2805		[HKG]
☐	N935FD	Boeing 757-2T7ER	22780/15	ex G-MONB		[VCV]
☐	N936FD	Boeing 757-2T7ER	23293/56	ex G-MONE		[VCV]
☐	N937FD	Boeing 757-2T7	23895/132	ex N513NA		[VCV]♦
☐	N939FD	Boeing 757-23A	24528/250	ex N549AX		♦
☐	N941FD	Boeing 757-225	22691/155	ex TF-LLY		[VCV]
☐	N946FD	Boeing 757-236	24398/224	ex G-CPEL		[VCV]♦
☐	N947FD	Boeing 757-236ER	24882/323	ex G-BPEC		[VCV]♦
☐	N948FD	Boeing 757-236ER	25059/363	ex G-BPED		[VCV]♦
☐	N949FD	Boeing 757-236ER	25060/364	ex G-BPEE		[VCV]♦
☐	N950FD	Boeing 757-236	25806/601	ex G-BPEI		[VCV]♦
☐	N954FD	Boeing 757-236	29113/784	ex G-CPER		o/o[LGW]♦
☐	N955FD	Boeing 757-236	29114/793	ex G-CPES		o/o[LGW]♦
☐	N957FD	Boeing 757-21B	24774/288	ex N802PG		[VCV]♦
☐	N960FD	Boeing 757-236	25593/466	ex G-OOOZ		♦
☐	N993FD	Boeing 757-2Q8	24965/438	ex SU-BPY		[VCV]
☐	N994FD	Boeing 757-23A	25490/510	ex N490AN		[VCV]
☐	N850FD	Boeing 777-FS2	37721/813		Saad	
☐	N851FD	Boeing 777-FS2	37722/834			♦
☐	N852FD	Boeing 777-FS2	37723/848			♦
☐	N853FD	Boeing 777-FS2	37724/829		Talon	
☐	N854FD	Boeing 777-FS2	37725/890		Faith	
☐	N855FD	Boeing 777-FS2	37726/892			♦
☐	N856FD	Boeing 777-FS2	37727/884		Shae	♦
☐	N857FD	Boeing 777-FS2	37728/886		Braydon	♦
☐	N880FD	Boeing 777-F28	32967/718	ex F-GUOA		♦
☐	N882FD	Boeing 777-F28	32969/827	ex N449BA		♦
☐	N883FD	Boeing 777-FHT	39285/897	ex N5022E	Abbi	♦
☐	N	Boeing 777-FS2				o/o♦
☐	N	Boeing 777-FS2				o/o♦
☐	N	Boeing 777-FS2				o/o♦
☐	N	Boeing 777-FS2				o/o♦
☐	C-FEXB	Cessna 208B Caravan I	208B0539	ex N758FX		>MAL
☐	C-FEXF	Cessna 208B Caravan I	208B0508	ex N749FX		>MAL
☐	C-FEXV	Cessna 208B Caravan I	208B0482	ex N738FX		>MAL
☐	C-FEXY	Cessna 208B Caravan I	208B0226	ex N896FE		>MAL
☐	N700FX	Cessna 208B Caravan I	208B0419			Op by CFS
☐	N701FX	Cessna 208B Caravan I	208B0420			Op by WIG
☐	N702FX	Cessna 208B Caravan I	208B0422			Op by BVN
☐	N703FX	Cessna 208B Caravan I	208B0423			Op by IRO
☐	N705FX	Cessna 208B Caravan I	208B0425			Op by CFS
☐	N706FX	Cessna 208B Caravan I	208B0426			Op by IRO

☐ N707FX	Cessna 208B Caravan I	208B0427	Op by PCM
☐ N709FX	Cessna 208B Caravan I	208B0430	Op by CFS
☐ N710FX	Cessna 208B Caravan I	208B0431	Op by CPT
☐ N711FX	Cessna 208B Caravan I	208B0433	Op by CFS
☐ N712FX	Cessna 208B Caravan I	208B0435	Op by IRO
☐ N713FX	Cessna 208B Caravan I	208B0438	Op by PCM
☐ N715FX	Cessna 208B Caravan I	208B0440	Op by MTN
☐ N716FX	Cessna 208B Caravan I	208B0442	Op by CPT
☐ N717FX	Cessna 208B Caravan I	208B0445	Op by IRO
☐ N718FX	Cessna 208B Caravan I	208B0448	Op by BVN
☐ N719FX	Cessna 208B Caravan I	208B0450	Op by BVN
☐ N720FX	Cessna 208B Caravan I	208B0452	Op by CFS
☐ N721FX	Cessna 208B Caravan I	208B0453	Op by MTN
☐ N722FX	Cessna 208B Caravan I	208B0454	Op by PCM
☐ N723FX	Cessna 208B Caravan I	208B0456	Op by BVN
☐ N724FX	Cessna 208B Caravan I	208B0458	Op by CPT
☐ N725FX	Cessna 208B Caravan I	208B0460	Op by WIG
☐ N726FX	Cessna 208B Caravan I	208B0465	Op by PCM
☐ N727FX	Cessna 208B Caravan I	208B0468	Op by IRO
☐ N728FX	Cessna 208B Caravan I	208B0471	Op by CFS
☐ N729FX	Cessna 208B Caravan I	208B0474	Op by MTN
☐ N730FX	Cessna 208B Caravan I	208B0477	Op by CPT
☐ N731FX	Cessna 208B Caravan I	208B0480	Op by WIG
☐ N740FX	Cessna 208B Caravan I	208B0484	Op by MTN
☐ N741FX	Cessna 208B Caravan I	208B0486	Op by BVN
☐ N742FX	Cessna 208B Caravan I	208B0489	Op by MTN
☐ N744FX	Cessna 208B Caravan I	208B0492	Op by PCM
☐ N745FX	Cessna 208B Caravan I	208B0495	Op by BVN
☐ N746FX	Cessna 208B Caravan I	208B0498	Op by CFS
☐ N747FE	Cessna 208B Caravan I	208B0238	Op by MTN
☐ N747FX	Cessna 208B Caravan I	208B0501	Op by MTN
☐ N748FE	Cessna 208B Caravan I	208B0241	Op by WIG
☐ N748FX	Cessna 208B Caravan I	208B0503	Op by PCM
☐ N749FE	Cessna 208B Caravan I	208B0242	Op by BVN
☐ N750FX	Cessna 208B Caravan I	208B0511	Op by PCM
☐ N751FE	Cessna 208B Caravan I	208B0245	Op by CPT
☐ N751FX	Cessna 208B Caravan I	208B0514	Op by BVN
☐ N752FE	Cessna 208B Caravan I	208B0247	Op by IRO
☐ N752FX	Cessna 208B Caravan I	208B0517	Op by CFS
☐ N753FX	Cessna 208B Caravan I	208B0520	Op by BVN
☐ N754FX	Cessna 208B Caravan I	208B0526	Op by PCM
☐ N755FE	Cessna 208B Caravan I	208B0250	Op by MTN
☐ N755FX	Cessna 208B Caravan I	208B0529	Op by WIG
☐ N756FE	Cessna 208B Caravan I	208B0251	Op by BVN
☐ N756FX	Cessna 208B Caravan I	208B0532	Op by CFS
☐ N757FX	Cessna 208B Caravan I	208B0535	Op by WIG
☐ N760FE	Cessna 208B Caravan I	208B0252	Op by CPT
☐ N761FE	Cessna 208B Caravan I	208B0254	Op by IRO
☐ N762FE	Cessna 208B Caravan I	208B0255	Op by PCM
☐ N763FE	Cessna 208B Caravan I	208B0256	Op by PCM
☐ N764FE	Cessna 208B Caravan I	208B0258	Op by MTN
☐ N765FE	Cessna 208B Caravan I	208B0259	Op by BVN
☐ N766FE	Cessna 208B Caravan I	208B0260	Op by CPT
☐ N767FE	Cessna 208B Caravan I	208B0262	Op by IRO
☐ N768FE	Cessna 208B Caravan I	208B0263	Op by PCM
☐ N769FE	Cessna 208B Caravan I	208B0264	Op by MTN
☐ N770FE	Cessna 208B Caravan I	208B0265	Op by BVN
☐ N771FE	Cessna 208B Caravan I	208B0267	Op by PCM
☐ N772FE	Cessna 208B Caravan I	208B0268	Op by PCM
☐ N773FE	Cessna 208B Caravan I	208B0269	Op by BVN
☐ N774FE	Cessna 208B Caravan I	208B0271	Op by BVN
☐ N775FE	Cessna 208B Caravan I	208B0272	Op by CFS
☐ N776FE	Cessna 208B Caravan I	208B0273	Op by MTN
☐ N778FE	Cessna 208B Caravan I	208B0275	Op by CFS
☐ N779FE	Cessna 208B Caravan I	208B0276	Op by CFS
☐ N780FE	Cessna 208B Caravan I	208B0277	Op by WIG
☐ N781FE	Cessna 208B Caravan I	208B0278	Op by PCM
☐ N782FE	Cessna 208B Caravan I	208B0280	Op by PCM
☐ N783FE	Cessna 208B Caravan I	208B0281	Op by WIG
☐ N784FE	Cessna 208B Caravan I	208B0282	Op by IRO
☐ N785FE	Cessna 208B Caravan I	208B0283	Op by PCM
☐ N786FE	Cessna 208B Caravan I	208B0284	Op by BVN
☐ N787FE	Cessna 208B Caravan I	208B0285	Op by MTN
☐ N788FE	Cessna 208B Caravan I	208B0286	Op by CFS
☐ N789FE	Cessna 208B Caravan I	208B0287	Op by WIG
☐ N790FE	Cessna 208B Caravan I	208B0288	Op by PCM
☐ N792FE	Cessna 208B Caravan I	208B0290	Op by MTN

☐	N793FE	Cessna 208B Caravan I	208B0291		Op by BVN
☐	N794FE	Cessna 208B Caravan I	208B0292		Op by CPT
☐	N795FE	Cessna 208B Caravan I	208B0293		Op by IRO
☐	N796FE	Cessna 208B Caravan I	208B0212	ex C-FEXY	Op by CPT
☐	N797FE	Cessna 208B Caravan I	208B0042	ex C-FEXH	Op by CPT
☐	N798FE	Cessna 208B Caravan I	208B0174	ex C-FEDY	Op by CPT
☐	N799FE	Cessna 208A Caravan I	20800065	ex C-FEXF	Op by CPT
☐	N800FE	Cessna 208A Caravan I	20800007	ex (N9300F)	Op by CPT
☐	N801FE	Cessna 208A Caravan I	20800009	ex (N9305F)	Op by MTN
☐	N804FE	Cessna 208B Caravan I	208B0039	ex F-GETN	Op by WIG
☐	N807FE	Cessna 208B Caravan I	208B0041	ex F-GETO	Op by WIG
☐	N812FE	Cessna 208A Caravan I	20800040	ex (N9401F)	Op by CPT
☐	N819FE	Cessna 208A Caravan I	20800056	ex (N9451F)	Op by MTN
☐	N820FE	Cessna 208B Caravan I	208B0111	ex F-GHHC	Op by MTN
☐	N827FE	Cessna 208A Caravan I	20800072	ex (N9491F)	Op by CPT
☐	N828FE	Cessna 208B Caravan I	208B0122	ex F-GHHD	Op by IRO
☐	N830FE	Cessna 208A Caravan I	20800075	ex (N9502F)	Op by IRO
☐	N831FE	Cessna 208B Caravan I	208B0225	ex F-GHHE	Op by MTN
☐	N832FE	Cessna 208 Caravan I	20800081	ex (N9518F)	Op by BVN
☐	N833FE	Cessna 208A Caravan I	20800084	ex EI-FDX	Op by CFS
☐	N835FE	Cessna 208A Caravan I	20800016	ex EI-FEX	Op by WIG
☐	N841FE	Cessna 208B Caravan I	208B0144		Op by BVN
☐	N842FE	Cessna 208B Caravan I	208B0146		Op by MTN
☐	N843FE	Cessna 208B Caravan I	208B0147		Op by IRO
☐	N844FE	Cessna 208B Caravan I	208B0149		Op by PCM
☐	N845FE	Cessna 208B Caravan I	208B0152		Op by BVN
☐	N846FE	Cessna 208B Caravan I	208B0154		Op by CPT
☐	N847FE	Cessna 208B Caravan I	208B0156		Op by MTN
☐	N848FE	Cessna 208B Caravan I	208B0158		Op by MTN
☐	N849FE	Cessna 208B Caravan I	208B0162		Op by MTN
☐	N850FE	Cessna 208B Caravan I	208B0164		Op by CFS
☐	N851FE	Cessna 208B Caravan I	208B0166		Op by CPT
☐	N852FE	Cessna 208B Caravan I	208B0168		Op by MTN
☐	N853FE	Cessna 208B Caravan I	208B0170		Op by MTN
☐	N855FE	Cessna 208B Caravan I	208B0203		Op by MTN
☐	N856FE	Cessna 208B Caravan I	208B0176		Op by CFS
☐	N857FE	Cessna 208B Caravan I	208B0177		Op by PCM
☐	N858FE	Cessna 208B Caravan I	208B0178		Op by IRO
☐	N859FE	Cessna 208B Caravan I	208B0181		Op by CFS
☐	N860FE	Cessna 208B Caravan I	208B0182		Op by CPT
☐	N861FE	Cessna 208B Caravan I	208B0183		Op by BVN
☐	N862FE	Cessna 208B Caravan I	208B0184		Op by MTN
☐	N863FE	Cessna 208B Caravan I	208B0186		Op by CPT
☐	N864FE	Cessna 208B Caravan I	208B0187		Op by CPT
☐	N865FE	Cessna 208B Caravan I	208B0188		Op by WIG
☐	N866FE	Cessna 208B Caravan I	208B0189	ex HK-3924X	Op by BVN
☐	N867FE	Cessna 208B Caravan I	208B0191		Op by CPT
☐	N869FE	Cessna 208B Caravan I	208B0195		Op by MTN
☐	N870FE	Cessna 208B Caravan I	208B0196		Op by WIG
☐	N871FE	Cessna 208B Caravan I	208B0198		Op by IRO
☐	N872FE	Cessna 208B Caravan I	208B0200		Op by PCM
☐	N873FE	Cessna 208B Caravan I	208B0202		Op by CFS
☐	N874FE	Cessna 208B Caravan I	208B0205		Op by MTN
☐	N875FE	Cessna 208B Caravan I	208B0206		Op by CFS
☐	N876FE	Cessna 208B Caravan I	208B0207		Op by CFS
☐	N877FE	Cessna 208B Caravan I	208B0232		Op by CPT
☐	N878FE	Cessna 208B Caravan I	208B0211		Op by MTN
☐	N879FE	Cessna 208B Caravan I	208B0213		Op by PCM
☐	N880FE	Cessna 208B Caravan I	208B0215		Op by CFS
☐	N881FE	Cessna 208B Caravan I	208B0204		Op by MTN
☐	N882FE	Cessna 208B Caravan I	208B0208		Op by CFS
☐	N883FE	Cessna 208B Caravan I	208B0210		Op by IRO
☐	N884FE	Cessna 208B Caravan I	208B0233		Op by IRO
☐	N885FE	Cessna 208B Caravan I	208B0185		Op by CPT
☐	N886FE	Cessna 208B Caravan I	208B0190		Op by PCM
☐	N887FE	Cessna 208B Caravan I	208B0216		Op by MTN
☐	N888FE	Cessna 208B Caravan I	208B0217		Op by WIG
☐	N889FE	Cessna 208B Caravan I	208B0218		Op by BVN
☐	N890FE	Cessna 208B Caravan I	208B0219		Op by CPT
☐	N891FE	Cessna 208B Caravan I	208B0221		Op by PCM
☐	N892FE	Cessna 208B Caravan I	208B0222		Op by PCM
☐	N894FE	Cessna 208B Caravan I	208B0224		Op by BVN
☐	N895FE	Cessna 208B Caravan I	208B0015	ex C-FEXG	Op by CFS
☐	N897FE	Cessna 208B Caravan I	208B0227		Op by CFS
☐	N898FE	Cessna 208B Caravan I	208B0228		Op by WIG
☐	N899FE	Cessna 208B Caravan I	208B0235		Op by CFS
☐	N900FE	Cessna 208B Caravan I	208B0054	ex SE-KLX	Op by BVN

☐ N901FE	Cessna 208B Caravan I	208B0001	ex N9767F		Op by WIG
☐ N902FE	Cessna 208B Caravan I	208B0002			Op by BVN
☐ N903FE	Cessna 208B Caravan I	208B0003			Op by CPT
☐ N904FE	Cessna 208B Caravan I	208B0004			Op by CPT
☐ N905FE	Cessna 208B Caravan I	208B0005			Op by MTN
☐ N906FE	Cessna 208B Caravan I	208B0006			Op by IRO
☐ N907FE	Cessna 208B Caravan I	208B0007			Op by IRO
☐ N908FE	Cessna 208B Caravan I	208B0008			Op by PCM
☐ N909FE	Cessna 208B Caravan I	208B0009			Op by WIG
☐ N910FE	Cessna 208B Caravan I	208B0010			Op by CPT
☐ N911FE	Cessna 208B Caravan I	208B0011			Op by WIG
☐ N912FE	Cessna 208B Caravan I	208B0012			Op by BVN
☐ N914FE	Cessna 208B Caravan I	208B0014			Op by IRO
☐ N916FE	Cessna 208B Caravan I	208B0016			Op by CPT
☐ N917FE	Cessna 208B Caravan I	208B0017			Op by MTN
☐ N918FE	Cessna 208B Caravan I	208B0018			Op by CFS
☐ N919FE	Cessna 208B Caravan I	208B0019			Op by WIG
☐ N920FE	Cessna 208B Caravan I	208B0020			Op by PCM
☐ N921FE	Cessna 208B Caravan I	208B0021			Op by MTN
☐ N922FE	Cessna 208B Caravan I	208B0022			Op by BVN
☐ N923FE	Cessna 208B Caravan I	208B0023			Op by IRO
☐ N924FE	Cessna 208B Caravan I	208B0024			Op by CPT
☐ N925FE	Cessna 208B Caravan I	208B0025			Op by IRO
☐ N926FE	Cessna 208B Caravan I	208B0026			Op by CPT
☐ N927FE	Cessna 208B Caravan I	208B0027			Op by IRO
☐ N928FE	Cessna 208B Caravan I	208B0028			Op by BVN
☐ N929FE	Cessna 208B Caravan I	208B0029			Op by BVN
☐ N930FE	Cessna 208B Caravan I	208B0030			Op by PCM
☐ N931FE	Cessna 208B Caravan I	208B0031			Op by WIG
☐ N933FE	Cessna 208B Caravan I	208B0033			Op by CPT
☐ N934FE	Cessna 208B Caravan I	208B0034			Op by BVN
☐ N935FE	Cessna 208B Caravan I	208B0035			Op by WIG
☐ N936FE	Cessna 208B Caravan I	208B0036			Op by CPT
☐ N937FE	Cessna 208B Caravan I	208B0037			Op by WIG
☐ N938FE	Cessna 208B Caravan I	208B0038			Op by MTN
☐ N939FE	Cessna 208B Caravan I	208B0180			Op by BVN
☐ N940FE	Cessna 208B Caravan I	208B0040			Op by CFS
☐ N943FE	Cessna 208B Caravan I	208B0043			Op by MTN
☐ N946FE	Cessna 208B Caravan I	208B0048	ex (N948FE)		Op by IRO
☐ N947FE	Cessna 208B Caravan I	208B0050	ex (N950FE)		Op by WIG
☐ N950FE	Cessna 208B Caravan I	208B0056	ex (N956FE)		Op by BVN
☐ N952FE	Cessna 208B Caravan I	208B0060	ex (N960FE)		Op by CPT
☐ N953FE	Cessna 208B Caravan I	208B0062	ex (N962FE)		Op by CFS
☐ N954FE	Cessna 208B Caravan I	208B0064	ex (N964FE)		Op by IRO
☐ N955FE	Cessna 208B Caravan I	208B0066	ex (N966FE)		Op by MTN
☐ N956FE	Cessna 208B Caravan I	208B0068	ex (N968FE)		Op by CFS
☐ N957FE	Cessna 208B Caravan I	208B0070	ex (N970FE)		Op by BVN
☐ N958FE	Cessna 208B Caravan I	208B0071			Op by WIG
☐ N959FE	Cessna 208B Caravan I	208B0073			Op by WIG
☐ N960FE	Cessna 208B Caravan I	208B0075			Op by CFS
☐ N961FE	Cessna 208B Caravan I	208B0077			Op by BVN
☐ N962FE	Cessna 208B Caravan I	208B0078			Op by MTN
☐ N963FE	Cessna 208B Caravan I	208B0080			Op by WIG
☐ N964FE	Cessna 208B Caravan I	208B0083			Op by CPT
☐ N965FE	Cessna 208B Caravan I	208B0084			Op by CFS
☐ N966FE	Cessna 208B Caravan I	208B0086			Op by WIG
☐ N967FE	Cessna 208B Caravan I	208B0088			Op by MTN
☐ N968FE	Cessna 208B Caravan I	208B0090			Op by PCM
☐ N969FE	Cessna 208B Caravan I	208B0092			Op by PCM
☐ N970FE	Cessna 208B Caravan I	208B0093			Op by BVN
☐ N971FE	Cessna 208B Caravan I	208B0094			Op by CPT
☐ N972FE	Cessna 208B Caravan I	208B0096			Op by CPT
☐ N973FE	Cessna 208B Caravan I	208B0098			Op by MTN
☐ N975FE	Cessna 208B Caravan I	208B0101			Op by MTN
☐ N976FE	Cessna 208B Caravan I	208B0103			Op by CFS
☐ N977FE	Cessna 208B Caravan I	208B0104			Op by CPT
☐ N979FE	Cessna 208B Caravan I	208B0106			Op by MTN
☐ N980FE	Cessna 208B Caravan I	208B0108			Op by CPT
☐ N981FE	Cessna 208B Caravan I	208B0110			Op by WIG
☐ N983FE	Cessna 208B Caravan I	208B0113			Op by CFS
☐ N984FE	Cessna 208B Caravan I	208B0115			Op by PCM
☐ N985FE	Cessna 208B Caravan I	208B0117			Op by PCM
☐ N986FE	Cessna 208B Caravan I	208B0194			Op by IRO
☐ N987FE	Cessna 208B Caravan I	208B0201			Op by PCM
☐ N989FE	Cessna 208B Caravan I	208B0124			Op by WIG
☐ N990FE	Cessna 208B Caravan I	208B0125			Op by CPT
☐ N991FE	Cessna 208B Caravan I	208B0127			Op by CPT

	Reg	Type	c/n	ex	Name	Notes
☐	N992FE	Cessna 208B Caravan I	208B0128			Op by CFS
☐	N993FE	Cessna 208B Caravan I	208B0130			Op by IRO
☐	N994FE	Cessna 208B Caravan I	208B0132			Op by BVN
☐	N995FE	Cessna 208B Caravan I	208B0133			Op by PCM
☐	N996FE	Cessna 208B Caravan I	208B0135			Op by WIG
☐	N997FE	Cessna 208B Caravan I	208B0197			Op by CPT
☐	N998FE	Cessna 208B Caravan I	208B0139			Op by WIG
☐	N999FE	Cessna 208B Caravan I	208B0231			Op by MTN
☐	N301FE	McDonnell-Douglas MD-10-30CF	46800/96	ex N101TV	Braun	
☐	N302FE	McDonnell-Douglas MD-10-30CF	46801/103	ex N102TV	Cori	
☐	N303FE	McDonnell-Douglas MD-10-30CF	46802/110	ex N103TV	Amanda	
☐	N304FE	McDonnell-Douglas MD-10-30CF	46992/257	ex EC-DSF	Claire	
☐	N306FE	McDonnell-Douglas MD-10-30F	48287/409		John	
☐	N307FE	McDonnell-Douglas MD-10-30F	48291/412		Erin Lee	
☐	N308FE	McDonnell-Douglas MD-10-30F	48297/416		Ann	
☐	N311FE	McDonnell-Douglas MD-10-30CF	46871/219	ex LN-RKB	Abraham	
☐	N312FE	McDonnell-Douglas MD-10-30CF	48300/433		Angela	
☐	N313FE	McDonnell-Douglas MD-10-30F	48311/440		Ameyali	
☐	N314FE	McDonnell-Douglas MD-10-30F	48312/442		Caitlan	
☐	N315FE	McDonnell-Douglas MD-10-30F	48313/443		Kevin	[VCE]
☐	N316FE	McDonnell-Douglas MD-10-30F	48314/444		Brandon	
☐	N317FE	McDonnell-Douglas MD-10-30CF	46835/277	ex N106WA	Madison	
☐	N318FE	McDonnell-Douglas MD-10-30CF	46837/282	ex N108WA	Mason	
☐	N319FE	McDonnell-Douglas MD-10-30CF	47820/317	ex N112WA	Sheridan	
☐	N320FE	McDonnell-Douglas MD-10-30F	47835/326	ex OO-SLD	Maura	[VCV]
☐	N321FE	McDonnell-Douglas MD-10-30F	47836/330	ex OO-SLE	Athena	
☐	N357FE	McDonnell-Douglas MD-10-10F	46939/203	ex N1849U	Channelle	
☐	N358FE	McDonnell-Douglas MD-10-10F	46633/297	ex N1839U	Kurt	
☐	N359FE	McDonnell-Douglas MD-10-10F	46635/307	ex N1842U	Michaela	
☐	N360FE	McDonnell-Douglas MD-10-10F	46636/309	ex N1843U	Phillip	
☐	N361FE	McDonnell-Douglas MD-10-10F	48260/344	ex N1844U	Lucas	
☐	N362FE	McDonnell-Douglas MD-10-10F	48261/347	ex N1845U	Cole	
☐	N363FE	McDonnell-Douglas MD-10-10F	48263/353	ex N1847U	Carter	
☐	N365FE	McDonnell-Douglas MD-10-10F	46601/6	ex N1802U	Joey	♦
☐	N366FE	McDonnell-Douglas MD-10-10F	46602/8	ex N1803U	Gretchen	
☐	N367FE	McDonnell-Douglas MD-10-10F	46605/15	ex N1806U	Lathan	
☐	N368FE	McDonnell-Douglas MD-10-10F	46606/17	ex N1807U	Cindy	
☐	N369FE	McDonnell-Douglas MD-10-10F	46607/25	ex N1808U	Jessie	[VCV]♦
☐	N370FE	McDonnell-Douglas MD-10-10F	46608/26	ex N1809U	Jay	♦
☐	N371FE	McDonnell-Douglas MD-10-10F	46609/27	ex N1810U	Vincent	
☐	N372FE	McDonnell-Douglas MD-10-10F	46610/32	ex N1811U	Gus	
☐	N373FE	McDonnell-Douglas MD-10-10F	46611/35	ex N1812U		
☐	N374FE	McDonnell-Douglas MD-10-10F	46612/39	ex N1813U	Brittnie	[VCV]
☐	N375FE	McDonnell-Douglas MD-10-10F	46613/42	ex N1814U		
☐	N377FE	McDonnell-Douglas MD-10-10F	47965/59	ex N1833U	Shelby	[VCV]
☐	N381FE	McDonnell-Douglas MD-10-10F	46615/76	ex N1816U	Duval	♦
☐	N383FE	McDonnell-Douglas MD-10-10F	46616/86	ex N1817U	Cody	
☐	N384FE	McDonnell-Douglas MD-10-10F	46617/89	ex N1818U	Kelly	
☐	N385FE	McDonnell-Douglas MD-10-10F	46619/119	ex N1820U	Lindsay	
☐	N386FE	McDonnell-Douglas MD-10-10F	46620/138	ex N1821U	TJ	first MD-10 conversion
☐	N387FE	McDonnell-Douglas MD-10-10F	46621/140	ex N1822U	Joel	
☐	N388FE	McDonnell-Douglas MD-10-10F	46622/144	ex N1823U	Izzul	
☐	N389FE	McDonnell-Douglas MD-10-10F	46623/154	ex N1824U	Kayla	
☐	N390FE	McDonnell-Douglas MD-10-10F	46624/155	ex N1825U	Rasik	
☐	N392FE	McDonnell-Douglas MD-10-10F	46626/198	ex N1827U	Axton	
☐	N394FE	McDonnell-Douglas MD-10-10F	46628/207	ex N1829U	Parker	
☐	N395FE	McDonnell-Douglas MD-10-10F	46629/208	ex N1830U	Audreon	
☐	N396FE	McDonnell-Douglas MD-10-10F	46630/209	ex N1831U	Adrienne	
☐	N397FE	McDonnell-Douglas MD-10-10F	46631/210	ex N1832U	Stefani	
☐	N398FE	McDonnell-Douglas MD-10-10F	46634/298	ex N1841U	Kacie	
☐	N399FE	McDonnell-Douglas MD-10-10F	48262/351	ex N1846U	Tariq	
☐	N550FE	McDonnell-Douglas MD-10-10F	46521/55	ex N121AA	Adam	
☐	N554FE	McDonnell-Douglas MD-10-10F	46708/62	ex N153AA		
☐	N556FE	McDonnell-Douglas MD-10-10F	46710/70	ex N160AA	Kirsten	
☐	N559FE	McDonnell-Douglas MD-10-10F	46930/112	ex N167AA	Francesca	
☐	N560FE	McDonnell-Douglas MD-10-10F	46938/153	ex N168AA	Deonna	
☐	N562FE	McDonnell-Douglas MD-10-10F	46947/247	ex N126AA	Janai	
☐	N563FE	McDonnell-Douglas MD-10-10F	46948/249	ex N127AA	Kristine	
☐	N564FE	McDonnell-Douglas MD-10-10F	46984/250	ex N128AA	Ava	
☐	N566FE	McDonnell-Douglas MD-10-10F	46989/271	ex N130AA	Ben	
☐	N567FE	McDonnell-Douglas MD-10-10F	46994/273	ex N131AA		[VCV]♦
☐	N569FE	McDonnell-Douglas MD-10-10F	47828/319	ex N133AA	Stas	
☐	N570FE	McDonnell-Douglas MD-10-10F	47829/321	ex N134AA	Joelle	
☐	N571FE	McDonnell-Douglas MD-10-10F	47830/323	ex N135AA	Ella	
☐	N10060	McDonnell-Douglas MD-10-10F	46970/269	ex N581LF	Haylee	
☐	N40061	McDonnell-Douglas MD-10-10F	46973/272	ex N591LF	Garrett	

☐ N68049	McDonnell-Douglas MD-10-10CF	47803/139		Dusty
☐ N68050	McDonnell-Douglas MD-10-10CF	47804/142		Merideth Allison
☐ N68051	McDonnell-Douglas MD-10-10CF	47805/145		Todd
☐ N68052	McDonnell-Douglas MD-10-10CF	47806/148		Brock
☐ N68053	McDonnell-Douglas MD-10-10CF	47807/173		Chayne
☐ N68054	McDonnell-Douglas MD-10-10CF	47808/177		Eren
☐ N68057	McDonnell-Douglas MD-10-10CF	48264/379	ex N1848U	Nelson
☐ N68059	McDonnell-Douglas MD-10-10F	46907/78	ex TC-JAY	Mary Rea
☐ N521FE	McDonnell-Douglas MD-11F	48478/514	ex N807DE	
☐ N522FE	McDonnell-Douglas MD-11F	48476/510	ex N805DE	
☐ N523FE	McDonnell-Douglas MD-11F	48479/536	ex N808DE	
☐ N524FE	McDonnell-Douglas MD-11F	48480/538	ex N809DE	
☐ N525FE	McDonnell-Douglas MD-11F	48565/542	ex N810DE	
☐ N526FE	McDonnell-Douglas MD-11F	48600/560	ex N813DE	
☐ N527FE	McDonnell-Douglas MD-11F	48601/562	ex N812DE	
☐ N528FE	McDonnell-Douglas MD-11F	48623/605	ex N814DE	
☐ N529FE	McDonnell-Douglas MD-11F	48624/622	ex N815DE	
☐ N572FE	McDonnell-Douglas MD-11ER	48755/613	ex N730BC	
☐ N573FE	McDonnell-Douglas MD-11BCF	48769/603	ex N746BC	
☐ N574FE	McDonnell-Douglas MD-11F	48499/486	ex N499HE	
☐ N575FE	McDonnell-Douglas MD-11F	48500/493	ex N485LS	Sonni
☐ N576FE	McDonnell-Douglas MD-11F	48501/513	ex N501FR	Keeley
☐ N577FE	McDonnell-Douglas MD-11F	48469/519	ex B-18172	Tobias
☐ N578FE	McDonnell-Douglas MD-11F	48458/449	ex N489GX	Stephen
☐ N579FE	McDonnell-Douglas MD-11F	48470/546	ex B-18151	Nash
☐ N580FE	McDonnell-Douglas MD-11F	48471/558	ex B-18152	Ashton
☐ N582FE	McDonnell-Douglas MD-11F	48420/451	ex N1751A	Jamie
☐ N583FE	McDonnell-Douglas MD-11F	48421/452	ex N1752K	Nnacy
☐ N584FE	McDonnell-Douglas MD-11F	48436/483	ex N1768D	Jeffrey Wellington
☐ N585FE	McDonnell-Douglas MD-11F	48481/482	ex N1759	Katherine
☐ N586FE	McDonnell-Douglas MD-11F	48487/469	ex N1753	Dylan
☐ N587FE	McDonnell-Douglas MD-11F	48489/492	ex N1754	Jeanno
☐ N588FE	McDonnell-Douglas MD-11F	48490/499	ex N1755	Kendra
☐ N589FE	McDonnell-Douglas MD-11F	48491/503	ex N1756	Shaun
☐ N590FE	McDonnell-Douglas MD-11F	48505/462	ex N1757A	Stan
☐ N591FE	McDonnell-Douglas MD-11F	48527/504	ex N1758B	Giovanni
☐ N592FE	McDonnell-Douglas MD-11F	48550/526	ex N1760A	Joshua
☐ N593FE	McDonnell-Douglas MD-11F	48551/527	ex N1761R	Harrison
☐ N594FE	McDonnell-Douglas MD-11F	48552/530	ex N1762B	Derek
☐ N595FE	McDonnell-Douglas MD-11F	48553/531	ex N1763	Avery
☐ N596FE	McDonnell-Douglas MD-11F	48554/535	ex N1764B	Peyton
☐ N597FE	McDonnell-Douglas MD-11F	48596/537	ex N1765B	Corbin
☐ N598FE	McDonnell-Douglas MD-11F	48597/540	ex N1766A	Kate
☐ N599FE	McDonnell-Douglas MD-11F	48598/550	ex N1767A	Mariana
☐ N601FE	McDonnell-Douglas MD-11F	48401/447	ex N111MD	Jim Riedmeyer
☐ N602FE	McDonnell-Douglas MD-11F	48402/448	ex N211MD	Malcolm Baldrige 1990
☐ N603FE	McDonnell-Douglas MD-11F	48459/470		Elizabeth
☐ N604FE	McDonnell-Douglas MD-11F	48460/497		Hollis
☐ N605FE	McDonnell-Douglas MD-11F	48514/515		April Star
☐ N606FE	McDonnell-Douglas MD-11F	48602/549		Charles & Teresa
☐ N607FE	McDonnell-Douglas MD-11F	48547/517		Christina
☐ N608FE	McDonnell-Douglas MD-11F	48548/521		Colton
☐ N609FE	McDonnell-Douglas MD-11F	48549/545		Scott
☐ N610FE	McDonnell-Douglas MD-11F	48603/551		Marisa
☐ N612FE	McDonnell-Douglas MD-11F	48605/555		Alyssa
☐ N613FE	McDonnell-Douglas MD-11F	48749/598		Krista
☐ N614FE	McDonnell-Douglas MD-11F	48528/507		Cristy
☐ N615FE	McDonnell-Douglas MD-11F	48767/602		Max
☐ N616FE	McDonnell-Douglas MD-11F	48747/594		Shanita
☐ N617FE	McDonnell-Douglas MD-11F	48748/595		Travis
☐ N618FE	McDonnell-Douglas MD-11F	48754/604		Justin
☐ N619FE	McDonnell-Douglas MD-11F	48770/607		Lyndon
☐ N620FE	McDonnell-Douglas MD-11F	48791/635		Grady
☐ N621FE	McDonnell-Douglas MD-11F	48792/636		Connor
☐ N623FE	McDonnell-Douglas MD-11F	48794/638		Meghan
☐ N624FE	McDonnell-Douglas MD-11F	48443/458	ex HB-IWA	Corinne
☐ N625FE	McDonnell-Douglas MD-11BCF	48753/608	ex N785BC	◆
☐ N628FE	McDonnell-Douglas MD-11F	48447/464	ex HB-IWE	Noah
☐ N631FE	McDonnell-Douglas MD-11F	48454/477	ex HB-IWI	

FLIGHT ALASKA		**Tundra (4Y/UYA)**	**Dillingham-Memorial, AK (DLG)**

☐ N755AB	Cessna 207A Stationair 8 II	20700622	ex HP-916
☐ N1704U	Cessna 207 Skywagon	20700304	
☐ N6470H	Cessna 207A Stationair 7 II	20700534	
☐ N7336U	Cessna 207A Skywagon	20700405	

	FLIGHT EXPRESS		Flight Express (FLX)	Orlando-Executive, FL (ORL)
☐	N6BW	Beech 58 Baron	TH-292	
☐	N31T	Beech 58 Baron	TH-121	ex N9146Q
☐	N46US	Beech 58 Baron	TH-294	ex N220DC
☐	N80AC	Beech 58 Baron	TH-56	ex N949SR
☐	N103GA	Beech 58 Baron	TH-213	ex N72TM
☐	N112BS	Beech 58 Baron	TH-628	ex N4075S
☐	N112KB	Beech 58 Baron	TH-1007	ex N20663
☐	N159TH	Beech 58 Baron	TH-159	ex N270K
☐	N225TA	Beech 58 Baron	TH-64	ex N225TC
☐	N258TJ	Beech 58 Baron	TH-988	ex N12WZ
☐	N329H	Beech 58 Baron	TH-219	ex N1529W
☐	N703MC	Beech 95-E55 Baron	TE-974	ex N18BL
☐	N752P	Beech 58 Baron	TH-422	ex YV-52P
☐	N796Q	Beech 58 Baron	TH-43	
☐	N950JP	Beech 58 Baron	TH-432	ex (N982DC)
☐	N955HE	Beech 58 Baron	TH-230	ex N955HF
☐	N1888W	Beech 58 Baron	TH-340	
☐	N4099S	Beech 95-E55 Baron	TE-1037	
☐	N4174S	Beech 58 Baron	TH-621	
☐	N4492F	Beech 95-E55 Baron	TE-1097	ex YV-1229P
☐	N4626A	Beech 58 Baron	TH-39	
☐	N4675S	Beech 58 Baron	TH-689	
☐	N8195R	Beech 58 Baron	TH-529	
☐	N9098Q	Beech 58 Baron	TH-109	
☐	N18447	Beech 58 Baron	TH-883	
☐	N8WE	Cessna 210L Centurion II	21060766	ex N1745X
☐	N70TC	Cessna 210M Centurion II	21061707	
☐	N102CR	Cessna T210N Turbo Centurion II	21064745	
☐	N210CT	Cessna 210L Centurion II	21060356	
☐	N221AT	Cessna 210N Centurion II	21064567	ex N9637V
☐	N274CS	Cessna 210L Centurion II	21060148	
☐	N300EW	Cessna 210L Centurion II	21061219	
☐	N318JP	Cessna 210L Centurion II	21060770	
☐	N732CQ	Cessna 210L Centurion II	21061413	
☐	N732HN	Cessna T210L Turbo Centurion II	21061527	
☐	N732LW	Cessna 210M Centurion II	21061606	
☐	N732ST	Cessna 210M Centurion II	21061744	
☐	N732YA	Cessna 210M Centurion II	21061870	
☐	N761AT	Cessna 210M Centurion II	21062108	
☐	N761AY	Cessna 210M Centurion II	21062113	
☐	N761BQ	Cessna 210M Centurion II	21062129	
☐	N761DW	Cessna T210M Turbo Centurion II	21062183	
☐	N777BK	Cessna 210L Centurion II	21060560	
☐	N778VK	Cessna 210M Centurion II	21062895	
☐	N965B	Cessna 210M Centurion II	21061580	ex N732KU
☐	N1666X	Cessna 210L Centurion II	21060701	
☐	N2013S	Cessna 210L Centurion II	21060981	
☐	N2110S	Cessna 210L Centurion II	21061074	
☐	N2137S	Cessna 210L Centurion II	21061098	
☐	N2145U	Cessna T210N Turbo Centurion II	21064776	
☐	N2255S	Cessna 210L Centurion II	21061199	
☐	N2263S	Cessna 210L Centurion II	21061207	
☐	N2280S	Cessna 210L Centurion II	21061223	
☐	N2437S	Cessna 210L Centurion II	21061281	
☐	N2495S	Cessna 210L Centurion II	21061304	
☐	N2667S	Cessna 210L Centurion II	21061347	
☐	N4637Y	Cessna 210N Centurion II	21063965	
☐	N4673C	Cessna 210N Centurion II	21063586	
☐	N4702C	Cessna T210N Turbo Centurion II	21063591	
☐	N4781C	Cessna 210N Centurion II	21063624	
☐	N5171V	Cessna 210L Centurion II	21060846	
☐	N5229A	Cessna 210N Centurion II	21063320	
☐	N5307A	Cessna 210N Centurion II	21063360	
☐	N5489V	Cessna 210L Centurion II	21060961	
☐	N6149B	Cessna T210M Turbo Centurion II	21062694	
☐	N6195N	Cessna 210N Centurion II	21062966	
☐	N6490N	Cessna 210N Centurion II	21063064	
☐	N6598Y	Cessna T210N Turbo Centurion II	21064451	
☐	N6611C	Cessna T210N Turbo Centurion II	21063930	
☐	N6622N	Cessna 210N Centurion II	21063125	
☐	N7398M	Cessna 210M Centurion II	21062018	
☐	N7660E	Cessna 210M Centurion II	21062692	
☐	N7874J	Cessna 210L Centurion II	21060597	ex YV-644CP

☐ N8427M	Cessna 210M Centurion II	21062043		
☐ N9073M	Cessna 210M Centurion II	21062058		
☐ N9489M	Cessna 210M Centurion II	21062081		
☐ N29209	Cessna 210L Centurion II	21059832		
☐ N29278	Cessna 210L Centurion II	21059852		
☐ N30326	Cessna 210L Centurion II	21059914		
☐ N59130	Cessna 210L Centurion II	21060110		
☐ N59141	Cessna 210L Centurion II	21060118		
☐ N59240	Cessna 210L Centurion II	21060174		
☐ N59299	Cessna 210L Centurion II	21060199		
☐ N93111	Cessna 210L Centurion II	21060266		
☐ N93887	Cessna 210L Centurion II	21060445		

FLIGHT INTERNATIONAL AVIATION — Flight International (FNT) — Newport News-Williamsburg Intl, VA (PHF)

☐ N10FN	Learjet 36	36-015	ex N14CF
☐ N12FN	Learjet 36	36-016	ex N616DJ
☐ N16FN	Learjet 36A	36A-027	ex N27MJ
☐ N26FN	Learjet 36	36-011	ex N26MJ
☐ N39FN	Learjet 35	35-006	ex N39DM
☐ N50FN	Learjet 35A	35A-070	ex N543PA
☐ N51FN	Learjet 35A	35A-069	ex N48GP
☐ N52FN	Learjet 35A	35A-424	ex N508GP
☐ N54FN	Learjet 25C	25C-083	ex N200MH
☐ N55FN	Learjet 35A	35A-202	ex D-CGPD
☐ N83FN	Learjet 36	36-007	ex N83DM
☐ N84FN	Learjet 36	36-002	ex N84DM
☐ N96FN	Learjet 35A	35A-186	ex (N317JD)
☐ N118FN	Learjet 35A	35A-118	ex N88JA
☐ N710GS	Learjet 35	35-032	ex N711MA
☐ N175SW	Swearingen SA.227AC Metro III	AC-621B	
☐ N766C	Swearingen SA.227AC Metro III	AC-559	ex N170SW
☐ N781C	Swearingen SA.227AC Metro III	AC-535	ex N3110J
☐ N782C	Swearingen SA.227AC Metro III	AC-525	ex N31078
☐ N26974	Swearingen SA.227AC Metro III	AC-664	
☐ N707ML	Piper PA-31T Cheyenne	31T-7520017	ex N502RH

FLIGHT LINE — American Check (ACT) — Denver-Centennial, CO/Salt Lake City, UT (DEN/SLC)

☐ N6KF	Mitsubishi MU-2B-36	659	ex N5JE
☐ N34AL	Mitsubishi MU-2B-60	792SA	ex N66LA
☐ N35RR	Mitsubishi MU-2B-60	1525SA	ex N442MA
☐ N60FL	Mitsubishi MU-2B-60	1512SA	ex HB-LQB
☐ N132BK	Mitsubishi MU-2B-60	1529SA	ex N818R
☐ N157CA	Mitsubishi MU-2B-60	1558SA	ex N5PQ
☐ N361JA	Mitsubishi MU-2B-36	681	ex C-GJWM
☐ N740PB	Mitsubishi MU-2B-36	657	ex N740PC
☐ N103BU	Piper PA-31-350 Navajo Chieftain	31-7405202	ex N999DW
☐ N350FL	Piper PA-31-350 Navajo Chieftain	31-7752182	ex N5SL

FLORIDA AIR CARGO — Miami-Opa Locka, FL (OPF)

☐ N15MA	Douglas DC-3	19286	ex F-WSGV	no titles

FLORIDA AIR TRANSPORT — Fort Lauderdale-Executive, FL (FXE)

☐ N70BF	Douglas C-118B	43720/373	ex XA-SCZ	dam June 2007
☐ N381AA	Douglas DC-7BF	44921/666	ex N101LM	[OPF] Jt ops with Turks Air
☐ N406WA	Douglas C-54G	35944	ex N460WA	[OPF]

FLORIDA COASTAL AIRLINES — Florida Coastal (PA/FCL) — Fort Pierce-St Lucie, FL (FPR)

☐ N77FC	Cessna 402C II	402C0044	ex N440RC
☐ N78FC	Cessna 402C II	402C0496	ex C-FFCH
☐ N567JS	Cessna 402B II	402B1090	ex N87216
☐ N856D	Cessna 402B II	402B1339	ex N40EM

FLORIDA WEST INTERNATIONAL AIRLINES — Flo West (RF/FWL) — Miami-Intl, FL (MIA)

☐ N316LA	Boeing 767-316F	30842/860		<LCO
☐ N422LA	Boeing 767-346F	35818/960	ex JA633J	♦
☐ N526LA	Boeing 767-346F	35817/959	ex JA632J	♦

FOCUS AIR — Focus (F2/FKS) — Fort Lauderdale-Hollywood Intl, FL (FLL)

Focus Air is a subsidiary of Omega Air Holdings

40 MILE AIR — Mile-Air (Q5/MLA) — Tok-Junction, AK (TKJ)

☐ N87TS	Piper PA-31 Turbo Navajo B	31-7300969	ex N4426Y
☐ N207DG	Cessna T207 Turbo Skywagon	20700070	ex N91902
☐ N734GW	Cessna U206G Stationair 6	U20604832	
☐ N1541F	Cessna 185D Skywagon	185-0896	

FOUR STAR AIR CARGO — Four Star (HK/FSC) — St Thomas-Cyril E King, VI (STT)

☐ N131FS	Douglas DC-3	16172/32920	ex N67PA	Frtr
☐ N132FS	Douglas DC-3	14333/25778	ex N333EF	Frtr
☐ N133FS	Douglas DC-3	15757/27202	ex N53NA	Frtr
☐ N135FS	Douglas DC-3	20063	ex NC63107	Frtr
☐ N138FS	Douglas DC-3	9967	ex N303SF	Frtr

FREEDOM AIR — Freedom (FP/FRE) — Guam, GU (GUM)

☐ N4168R	Piper PA-32-300 Cherokee Six C	32-40484	
☐ N4171R	Piper PA-32-300 Cherokee Six C	32-40504	
☐ N8628N	Piper PA-32-300 Cherokee Six	32-7140021	
☐ N8938N	Piper PA-32-300 Cherokee Six C	32-40736	
☐ N8969N	Piper PA-32-300 Cherokee Six	32-40769	
☐ N44FA	Cessna 207A Stationair 8	20700659	ex N75975
☐ N72FA	Piper PA-31 Navajo C	31-7812023	ex JA5278
☐ N74NF	Short SD.3-60	SH3721	ex N121PC
☐ N131FA	Piper PA-23-250 Aztec D	27-4097	ex N234SP
☐ N330FA	Short SD.3-30	SH3112	ex N188LM
☐ N2843F	Short SD.3-60	SH3739	ex SX-BFW

FREEDOM AIRLINES — (FRL) — New York-JFK, NY/Orlando, FL (JFK/MCO)

A division of Mesa Airlines; provides Delta Connection services from Orlando-MCO, FL and New York, NY

FREIGHT RUNNERS EXPRESS — Freight Runners (FRG) — Milwaukee-General Mitchell Intl, WI (MKE)

☐ N199CZ	Beech 99	U-30	ex N3RP	Frtr
☐ N299CZ	Beech 99	U-74	ex C-FCVJ	Frtr
☐ N399CZ	Beech B99	U-91	ex N195WA	Frtr
☐ N499CZ	Beech 99A	U-81	ex N36AK	Frtr
☐ N599CZ	Beech B99	U-89	ex 5Y-BJW	Frtr
☐ N799CZ	Beech 99	U-68	ex N196WA	Frtr dbr 23Dec06?
☐ N899CZ	Beech 99A	U-96	ex N199CA	Frtr
☐ N999CZ	Beech 99A	U-116	ex C-GZAM	♦
☐ N75GB	Cessna 402B	402B0912		
☐ N191CZ	Beech 1900C	UB-59	ex D-CARA	
☐ N727CA	Cessna 402A	402A0102	ex N7802Q	Frtr
☐ N1517U	Cessna 207 Skywagon	20700117		Frtr
☐ N1518U	Cessna 207 Skywagon	20700118		Frtr
☐ N4504B	Cessna 402B	402B1370	ex C-GSMN	

FRONTIER AIRLINES — Frontier Flight (F9/FFT) — Denver-International, CO (DEN)

☐ N801FR	Airbus A318-111	1939	ex D-AUAA	Grizzly Bear
☐ N802FR	Airbus A318-111	1991	ex D-AUAB	Elk
☐ N803FR	Airbus A318-111	2017	ex D-AUAC	Hare 'Bugs'
☐ N804FR	Airbus A318-111	2051	ex D-AUAE	Kit Fox Pups
☐ N805FR	Airbus A318-111	1660	ex D-AUAA	Great Grey Owl
☐ N807FR	Airbus A318-111	2276	ex D-AUAC	Cougar
☐ N902FR	Airbus A319-111	1515	ex D-AVYM	
☐ N904FR	Airbus A319-111	1579	ex D-AVWS	Trumpeter Swan
☐ N905FR	Airbus A319-111	1583	ex D-AVYC	Seal
☐ N906FR	Airbus A319-111	1684	ex D-AVWK	Pronghorn Antelope
☐ N908FR	Airbus A319-111	1759	ex D-AVYL	Blue Heron
☐ N910FR	Airbus A319-112	1781	ex D-AVYK	Cougar
☐ N912FR	Airbus A319-111	1803	ex D-AVWE	Red Fox Pup
☐ N914FR	Airbus A319-111	1841	ex D-AVWT	Great Egret
☐ N918FR	Airbus A319-111	1943	ex D-AVWH	Whitetail Deer
☐ N919FR	Airbus A319-111	1980	ex D-AVYD	Ocelot
☐ N920FR	Airbus A319-111	1997	ex D-AVYO	Coyote
☐ N921FR	Airbus A319-111	2010	ex D-AVWO	Mountain Goat

☐ N922FR	Airbus A319-111	2012	ex D-AVWR	Red Fox
☐ N923FR	Airbus A319-111	2019	ex D-AVWV	Racoon
☐ N924FR	Airbus A319-111	2030	ex D-AVYG	Polar Bear Cubs
☐ N925FR	Airbus A319-111	2103	ex D-AVWH	Dall's Sheep
☐ N926FR	Airbus A319-111	2198	ex D-AVYD	Black-tailed Deer Fawn
☐ N927FR	Airbus A319-111	2209	ex D-AVYL	Bottle-nosed Dolphin
☐ N928FR	Airbus A319-111	2236	ex D-AVWK	Bobcat
☐ N929FR	Airbus A319-111	2240	ex D-AVWP	Lynx
☐ N930FR	Airbus A319-111	2241	ex D-AVWU	Cougar & cub
☐ N931FR	Airbus A319-111	2253	ex D-AVYR	Bear cub
☐ N932FR	Airbus A319-111	2258	ex D-AVYK	Bald Eagle
☐ N933FR	Airbus A319-111	2260	ex D-AVYX	Hawk
☐ N934FR	Airbus A319-111	2287	ex D-AVYU	Lynx pup
☐ N935FR	Airbus A319-111	2318	ex D-AVYJ	Sea Otter
☐ N936FR	Airbus A319-111	2392	ex D-AVYK	Walrus
☐ N937FR	Airbus A319-111	2400	ex D-AVYU	Blue crowned conure
☐ N938FR	Airbus A319-111	2406	ex D-AVWA	Arctic Fox
☐ N939FR	Airbus A319-111	2448	ex D-AVWL	Emperor Penguins
☐ N940FR	Airbus A319-111	2465	ex D-AVWW	Snow Hare
☐ N941FR	Airbus A319-112	2483	ex D-AVYY	Gray Wolf
☐ N942FR	Airbus A319-111	2497	ex D-AVYT	Bighorn
☐ N943FR	Airbus A319-112	2518	ex D-AVWT	Fawn
☐ N945FR	Airbus A319-112	2751	ex D-AVWD	Bull Moose
☐ N947FR	Airbus A319-111	2806	ex D-AVYK	Leopard
☐ N948FR	Airbus A319-112	2836	ex D-AVXR	Pelican
☐ N949FR	Airbus A319-112	2857	ex D-AVYL	White Ermine
☐ N951FR	Airbus A319-112	4127	ex N412MX	♦
☐ N952FR	Airbus A319-112	4204	ex N204MX	♦
☐ N953FR	Airbus A319-112	4254	ex N254MX	♦
☐ N201FR	Airbus A320-214	3389	ex F-WWDQ	Elk
☐ N202FR	Airbus A320-214	3431	ex F-WWDT	Named 'Colorado'
☐ N203FR	Airbus A320-214	1806	ex D-ALTI	
☐ N204FR	Airbus A320-214	2325	ex N270AV	
☐ N205FR	Airbus A320-214	4253	ex D-AXAB	Killer Whale ♦
☐ N206FR	Airbus A320-214	4272	ex F-WWBX	Polar Bear ♦
☐ N207FR	Airbus A320-214	4307	ex D-AXAK	♦
☐ N208FR	Airbus A320-214	4562	ex D-AUBX	♦
☐	Airbus A320-214		ex	o/o♦
☐	Airbus A320-214		ex	o/o♦
☐	Airbus A320-214		ex	o/o♦
☐	Airbus A320-214		ex	o/o♦
☐	Airbus A320-214		ex	o/o♦
☐	Airbus A320-214		ex	o/o♦
☐	Airbus A320-214		ex	o/o♦
☐	Airbus A320-214		ex	o/o♦
☐ N502LX	de Havilland DHC-8-402Q	4168	ex C-FMIU	Wolf Cubs
☐ N506LX	de Havilland DHC-8-402Q	4176	ex C-FMKN	Raccoon
☐ N510LX	de Havilland DHC-8-402Q	4186	ex C-FNER	Bobcat
☐ N511LX	de Havilland DHC-8-402Q	4265	ex C-FXJC	Snowy Owl

FRONTIER FLYING SERVICE   Frontier-Air (2F/FTA)   Fairbanks-Intl, AK (FAI)

☐ N575A	Beech 1900C-1	UC-83	ex N80334
☐ N575F	Beech 1900C-1	UC-99	ex N80598
☐ N575G	Beech 1900C-1	UC-155	ex N155YV
☐ N575P	Beech 1900C-1	UC-95	ex N80532
☐ N575Q	Beech 1900C-1	UC-160	ex N160AM
☐ N575X	Beech 1900C-1	UC-149	ex N149YV
☐ N575Z	Beech 1900C-1	UC-136	ex N21493
☐ N44AC	Piper PA-31-350 Chieftain	31-8052147	ex N3590M
☐ N137CS	Piper PA-31-350 Chieftain	31-8152137	ex C-GVPP
☐ N200AK	Piper PA-31-350 Chieftain	31-8052180	ex N8529T
☐ N3516A	Piper PA-31-350 Chieftain	31-7952106	
☐ N3535F	Piper PA-31-350 Chieftain	31-7952200	
☐ N3536B	Piper PA-31-350 Chieftain	31-7952205	
☐ N4112K	Piper PA-31-350 T-1020	31-8353006	
☐ N4301C	Piper PA-31-350 T-1020	31-8353001	ex C-FKGX
☐ N4501B	Piper PA-31-350 Chieftain	31-8052168	
☐ N4585U	Piper PA-31-350 Chieftain	31-8052198	ex C-GPIJ
☐ N190WA	Beech C99	U-207	ex N207CS
☐ N196WA	Beech C99	U-179	ex N995SB
☐ N9620M	Cessna 207A Stationair 8	20700711	
☐ N73100	Cessna 207A Stationair 7	20700559	

GALLUP FLYING SERVICES — Gallup-Municipal, NM (GUP)

☐ N41BG	Cessna 340A	340A0305	ex N4134G
☐ N986GM	Cessna 414A Chancellor	414A0089	ex N612CB
☐ N6640C	Cessna 414A Chancellor	414A0044	
☐ N7909Q	Cessna T310Q	310Q0620	
☐ N8840K	Cessna 414A Chancellor	414A0236	
☐ N29359	Cessna 210L Centurion II	21059858	
☐ N68149	Cessna 414A Chancellor	414A0642	

GB AIRLINK — Island Tiger (GBX) — Fort Lauderdale-Hollywood Intl, FL (FLL)

☐ N80GB	Short SC.7 Skyvan 3	SH1888	ex LX-ABC	Frtr
☐ N911E	Beech E-18S	BA-10	ex N501J	Frtr

GO! — Honolulu-Intl, HI (HNL)

☐ N591ML	Canadair CRJ-200LR	7388	ex B-7699
☐ N27318	Canadair CRJ-200LR	7318	ex C-FMLF
☐ N37342	Canadair CRJ-200LR	7342	ex C-FMMY
☐ N77302	Canadair CRJ-200LR	7302	ex C-FMND

GO! EXPRESS — Honolulu-Intl, HI (HNL)

Operated by Mokulele Airlines.

GOJET AIRLINES — Gateway (G7/GJS) — St Louis-Lambert Intl, MO (STL)

GoJet Airlines is a wholly owned subsidiary of Trans State Airlines and operates feeder services for United Express.

GRAND CANYON AIRLINES — Canyon View (CVU)
Grand Canyon-National Park, AZ/Valle-J Robidoux, AZ (GCN/VLE)

☐ N72GC	de Havilland DHC-6 Twin Otter 300	264	ex N264Z
☐ N74GC	de Havilland DHC-6 Twin Otter 300	559	ex J6-AAK
☐ N171GC	de Havilland DHC-6 Twin Otter 300	406	ex J8-VBR
☐ N173GC	de Havilland DHC-6 Twin Otter 300	295	ex C-GLAZ
☐ N177GC	de Havilland DHC-6 Twin Otter 300	263	ex N102AC
☐ N178GC	de Havilland DHC-6 Twin Otter 300	697	ex TI-AZD

GRANT AVIATION — (GV/GUN) — Emmonak, AK (EMK)

☐ N8NZ	Cessna 207A Stationair 7 II	20700421	ex VH-XXL
☐ N48CF	Cessna T207A Turbo Skywagon	20700366	
☐ N54GV	Cessna 207A Stationair 7 II	20700447	
☐ N207DF	Cessna 207A Stationair 8 II	20700728	ex ZK-EAL
☐ N562CT	Cessna 207A Stationair 7 II	20700487	ex HI-562CT
☐ N2162C	Cessna 207A Stationair 8 II	20700575	ex HI-346
☐ N9651M	Cessna 207A Stationair 8 II	20700715	
☐ N9728M	Cessna 207A Stationair 8 II	20700721	
☐ N9973M	Cessna 207A Stationair 8 II	20700771	
☐ N77HV	Piper PA-31-350 Chieftain	31-8152193	ex C-GLCN
☐ N78GA	Piper PA-31-350 Chieftain	31-8352030	ex XA-DAM
☐ N90PB	Beech 200 Super King Air	BB-125	ex TG-UGA
☐ N162GA	Cessna 208B Caravan I	208B0667	ex C-FPNG
☐ N417PM	Piper PA-31-350 Chieftain	31-8052051	ex N357CT
☐ N454SF	Cessna 208B Caravan I	208B0797	ex N5180C
☐ N4105D	Piper PA-31-350 Chieftain	31-8252027	
☐ N27739	Piper PA-31-350 Chieftain	31-7852135	ex SE-KKS

GREAT LAKES AIRLINES — Lakes Air (ZK/GLA) — Cheyenne, WY (CYS)

☐ N100UX	Beech 1900D	UE-100		Fly Telluride
☐ N122UX	Beech 1900D	UE-122	ex N122YV	
☐ N153GL	Beech 1900D	UE-153	ex N153ZV	
☐ N154GL	Beech 1900D	UE-154	ex N154ZV	Sierra Vista
☐ N169GL	Beech 1900D	UE-169		
☐ N170GL	Beech 1900D	UE-170	ex N170YV	Garden City, NE
☐ N173YV	Beech 1900D	UE-173		
☐ N182YV	Beech 1900D	UE-182		
☐ N184UX	Beech 1900D	UE-184	ex N184YV	
☐ N192GL	Beech 1900D	UE-192	ex N192YV	Telluride, CO
☐ N195GL	Beech 1900D	UE-195	ex N195YV	Miles City, MT
☐ N201GL	Beech 1900D	UE-201	ex N201YQ	Ponca City, OK
☐ N202UX	Beech 1900D	UE-202	ex (N202GV)	
☐ N208GL	Beech 1900D	UE-208	ex N208YV	Fly Telluride

☐ N210GL	Beech 1900D	UE-210	ex N210UX	
☐ N211GL	Beech 1900D	UE-211	ex N211UX	Laramie, WY
☐ N218YV	Beech 1900D	UE-218		
☐ N219GL	Beech 1900D	UE-219	ex N219YV	
☐ N220GL	Beech 1900D	UE-220	ex N220UX	Hays, KS
☐ N231YV	Beech 1900D	UE-231		
☐ N237YV	Beech 1900D	UE-237		
☐ N240GL	Beech 1900D	UE-240	ex N240YV	Devil's Tower, WY
☐ N245GL	Beech 1900D	UE-245	ex N245YV	
☐ N247GL	Beech 1900D	UE-247	ex N247YV	
☐ N251GL	Beech 1900D	UE-251	ex N251ZV	Grand Tetons
☐ N253GL	Beech 1900D	UE-253	ex N253YV	
☐ N254GL	Beech 1900D	UE-254	ex N10840	Grand Island, NE
☐ N255GL	Beech 1900D	UE-255	ex N10860	
☐ N257GL	Beech 1900D	UE-257	ex N257YV	
☐ N261GL	Beech 1900D	UE-261	ex N261YV	Scotts Bluff, NE
☐ N71GL	Embraer EMB.120ER Brasilia	120071	ex N267UE	
☐ N96ZK	Embraer EMB.120ER Brasilia	120096	ex N452UE	
☐ N108UX	Embraer EMB.120ER Brasilia	120108	ex N451UE	
☐ N293UX	Embraer EMB.120ER Brasilia	120293	ex PT-SVN	
☐ N297UX	Embraer EMB.120ER Brasilia	120297	ex PT-SVQ	
☐ N299UX	Embraer EMB.120ER Brasilia	120299	ex PT-SVT	

GREAT NORTHERN AIR   *Anchorage-Lake Hood SPB, AK (LHD)*

| ☐ N36GB | Cessna U206F Stationair | U20601854 | ex N9654G | FP |

GRIFFING FLYING SERVICE   *Sandusky-Griffing, OH (SKY)*

☐ N426S	Piper PA-31-350 Chieftain	31-8152190	ex N426SC	
☐ N428S	Piper PA-32-301 Saratoga	32-8106021		
☐ N442S	Britten-Norman BN-2A-20 Islander	770	ex N6863G	

GRIZZLY MOUNTAIN AVIATION   *Prineville Heliport, OR*

| ☐ N22753 | Bell UH-1B | 1109 | ex 64-13985 | |

GUARDIAN AIR   *Flagstaff, AZ / Bullhead City, AZ (FLG/IFP)*

☐ N62GA	Pilatus PC-12/45	259	ex N259WA	EMS	op by Air Methods
☐ N92DV	Beech 65-E90 King Air	LW-292	ex N7MA	EMS Air 4	op by Air Methods
☐ N407AM	Bell 407	53309		EMS	op by Air Methods
☐ N407VV	Bell 407	53476		EMS	op by Air Methods
☐ N408GA	Bell 407	53392		EMS	op by Air Methods
☐ N987GM	Beech 65-E90 King Air	LW-65	ex N3065W	EMS Air 2	op by Air Methods

GULF AND CARIBBEAN AIR   *Trans Auto (TSU)*   Fort Lauderdale-Hollywood Intl, FL (FLL)

☐ N471FL	AMD Falcon 20	163	ex N258PE	
☐ N481FL	AMD Falcon 20C-5	27	ex N326VW	
☐ N511FL	AMD Falcon 20C-5	122	ex N302TT	
☐ N521FL	AMD Falcon 20C-5	68	ex N458SW	
☐ N531FL	AMD Falcon 20	113	ex N22WJ	
☐ N541FL	AMD Falcon 20	48	ex N23ND	
☐ N221FL	Boeing 727-22C (FedEx 3)	19805/543	ex C-GKFW	709	
☐ N251FL	Boeing 727-277F/W (Duganair 3)	20551/1054	ex C-GYKF		♦
☐ N281FL	Boeing 727-225F/W (Duganair 3)	20153/779	ex C-GKFH	711	
☐ N131FL	Convair 580	155	ex N5804	13	Frtr
☐ N141FL	Convair 580	111	ex N302K	14	Frtr
☐ N151FL	Convair 580	51	ex N5810	15	Frtr
☐ N171FL	Convair 580	318	ex N300K	17	Frtr
☐ N181FL	Convair 580	387	ex N301K	18	Frtr
☐ N191FL	Convair 580	326	ex N923DR	19	Frtr
☐ N361FL	Convair 5800	343	ex C-FKFS		
☐ N371FL	Convair 5800	309	ex C-FMKF		Frtr
☐ N381FL	Convair 5800	276	ex C-FKFS		Frtr
☐ N391FL	Convair 5800	278	ex C-GKFD		Frtr
☐ N991FL	Convair 580	508	ex C-GTTG		Frtr
☐ N7813B	Convair 340-70	265	ex 53-7813		stored

GULFSTREAM INTERNATIONAL   *Gulf Flight (3M/GFT)*   Fort Lauderdale-Hollwood, FL (FLL)

☐ N45AR	Beech 1900D	UE-12	ex N138MA	Lsd fm CSC
☐ N46AR	Beech 1900D	UE-27		Lsd fm CSC
☐ N266AS	Embraer EMB.120ER Brasilia	120188	ex PT-SRB	201	[SGF]

☐ N614HR	Piper PA-31-350 Navajo Chieftain	31-7305121	ex N74HP		>Gulfstream Air Charter
☐ N27319	Piper PA-31-350 Chieftain	31-7852137			>Gulfstream Air Charter

HAGELAND AVIATION SERVICES — Hageland (H6/HAG) — St Mary's, Bethel, AK (KSM)

☐ N17GN	Cessna 207A Stationair 8 II	20700693	ex C-GDFK
☐ N104K	Cessna 207 Skywagon	20700122	ex C-GUHZ
☐ N327CT	Cessna 207A Stationair 7 II	20700535	ex N6475H
☐ N747SQ	Cessna 207A Skywagon	20700387	ex N1787U
☐ N1668U	Cessna 207 Skywagon	20700268	
☐ N5277J	Cessna 207A Stationair 8 II	20700772	ex N9975M
☐ N6207H	Cessna 207A Stationair 7 II	20700551	ex C-FSEE
☐ N6314H	Cessna 207A Stationair 7 II	20700478	
☐ N7320U	Cessna 207A Skywagon	20700397	
☐ N7384U	Cessna 207A Stationair 7 II	20700431	
☐ N7389U	Cessna 207A Stationair 7 II	20700432	
☐ N9399M	Cessna 207A Stationair 8 II	20700652	ex VH-UAA
☐ N9400M	Cessna 207A Stationair 8 II	20700687	
☐ N9869M	Cessna 207A Stationair 8 II	20700744	
☐ N9996M	Cessna 207A Stationair 8 II	20700779	
☐ N73067	Cessna 207A Stationair 7 II	20700558	
☐ N126AR	Cessna 208B Caravan I	208B1004	ex N5163K
☐ N169LJ	Cessna 208B Caravan I	208B0599	ex N169BJ
☐ N208SD	Cessna 208B Caravan I	208B0491	
☐ N215MC	Cessna 208B Caravan I	208B0730	ex N12328
☐ N303GV	Cessna 208B Caravan I	208B0581	
☐ N407GV	Cessna 208B Caravan I	208B0616	ex N5262X
☐ N410GV	Cessna 208B Caravan I	208B0632	ex N5264U
☐ N411GV	Cessna 208B Caravan I	208B0672	
☐ N715HE	Cessna 208B Caravan I	208B0603	ex N715HL
☐ N717PA	Cessna 208B Caravan I	208B0804	ex N12890
☐ N1232Y	Cessna 208B Caravan I	208B0566	ex N5246Z
☐ N1275N	Cessna 208B Caravan I	208B0756	
☐ N12373	Cessna 208B Caravan I	208B0697	ex N5268Z
☐ N404GV	Beech 1900C-1	UC-154	ex N154YV
☐ N406GV	Reims Cessna F406 Caravan II	F406-0049	ex 9M-PMS
☐ N1553C	Beech 1900C-1	UC-24	ex N31226
☐ N6590Y	Reims Cessna F406 Caravan II	F406-0052	
☐ N6591R	Reims Cessna F406 Caravan II	F406-0054	
☐ N9575G	Cessna U206F Stationair	U20601775	
☐ N91361	Cessna 180H	180-52045	
☐ N15503	Beech 1900C-1	UC-72	

HAWAIIAN AIRLINES — Hawaiian (HA/HAL) — Honolulu-Intl, HI (HNL)

☐ N380HA	Airbus A330-243	1104	ex F-WWYZ	◆
☐ N381HA	Airbus A330-243	1114	ex F-WWYN	◆
☐ N382HA	Airbus A330-243	1171	ex F-WWYA	◆
☐ N	Airbus A330-243		ex	o/o◆
☐ N	Airbus A330-243		ex	o/o◆
☐ N475HA	Boeing 717-22A	55121/5050	I'Iwi	
☐ N476HA	Boeing 717-22A	55118/5053	Elepaio	
☐ N477HA	Boeing 717-22A	55122/5061	Apapane	
☐ N478HA	Boeing 717-22A	55123/5064	Amakihi	
☐ N479HA	Boeing 717-22A	55124/5069	Akepa	
☐ N480HA	Boeing 717-22A	55125/5070	Pueo	
☐ N481HA	Boeing 717-22A	55126/5073	Alauahio	
☐ N483HA	Boeing 717-22A	55128/5079	ex N604AT	
☐ N484HA	Boeing 717-22A	55129/5080	Oma'o	
☐ N485HA	Boeing 717-22A	55130/5089	Palila	
☐ N486HA	Boeing 717-22A	55131/5092	Akiki	
☐ N487HA	Boeing 717-22A	55132/5098	Lo	
☐ N488HA	Boeing 717-23S	55001/5002	ex VH-NXF	
☐ N489HA	Boeing 717-23S	55002/5003	ex VH-NXB	
☐ N490HA	Boeing 717-23S	55151/5041	ex VH-NXC	
☐ N580HA	Boeing 767-33AER/W	28140/850	Kolea	
☐ N581HA	Boeing 767-33AER/W	28141/853	Manu o Ku	
☐ N582HA	Boeing 767-33AER/W	28139/857	Ake Ake	
☐ N583HA	Boeing 767-33AER	25531/423	ex D-AMUP	A
☐ N584HA	Boeing 767-3G5ER	24258/255	ex D-AMUS	Kioea
☐ N585HA	Boeing 767-3G5ER	24257/251	ex D-AMUR	Noio
☐ N586HA	Boeing 767-3G5ER	24259/268	ex D-AMUN	Ou
☐ N587HA	Boeing 767-33AER/W	33421/887	Pakalakala	

☐ N588HA	Boeing 767-3CBER/W	33466/890	Iwa	◆
☐ N589HA	Boeing 767-33AER/W	33422/892	Moli	◆
☐ N590HA	Boeing 767-3CBER/W	33467/894	Koa'e Ula	◆
☐ N591HA	Boeing 767-33AER	33423/897	Ake keke	
☐ N592HA	Boeing 767-3CBER/W	33468/898	Hunakai	
☐ N593HA	Boeing 767-33AER	33424/901	Nene	
☐ N594HA	Boeing 767-332	23275/136	ex N116DL	
☐ N596HA	Boeing 767-332	23276/151	ex N117DL	
☐ N597HA	Boeing 767-332	23277/152	ex N118DL	
☐ N598HA	Boeing 767-332	23278/153	ex N119DL	

HEARTLAND AVIATION
Night Chase (NTC)
Eau Claire-Chippewa Valley Regional, WI (EAU)

☐ N310JZ	Cessna 310R II	310R1623	ex N310JD
☐ N3286M	Cessna 310R II	310R1894	

HEAVY LIFT HELICOPTERS
Apple Valley, CA/Ketchikan, AK (APV/KTN)

☐ N53HL	Sikorsky CH-53D Fire Stallion		ex 156668	
☐ N68HL	Sikorsky CH-53D Fire Stallion		ex 156674	
☐ N6156U	Sikorsky S-64 Skycrane	64012	ex 66-18410	790 Pegasus
☐ N44094	Sikorsky S-64 Skycrane	64023	ex 67-18421	794

HELI-FLITE
Corona-Municipal, CA (AJO)

☐ N1078Q	Bell 206B JetRanger III	2425	ex N5002X
☐ N9043N	Sikorsky S-58F (SH-34G)	58761	ex Bu143957
☐ N87717	Sikorsky S-58F (SH-34J)	581269	ex Bu148011

HELI-JET
Eugene-Private Heliport, OR

☐ N28HJ	Bell 205A-1	30006	ex PK-UHI
☐ N58HJ	Bell 205A-1	30314	
☐ N66HJ	Bell 205A-1	30239	ex N49766
☐ N73HJ	Bell 212	30552	ex XC-EDM
☐ N97HJ	Bell 205A-1	30173	ex C-GFHG

HELICOPTER TRANSPORT SERVICES
Baltimore-Martin State, MD (MTN)

☐ N715HT	Sikorsky S-64F Skycrane	64077	ex N470KG	715
☐ N716HT	Sikorsky S-64F Skycrane	64092	ex N484KG	716
☐ N718HT	Sikorsky S-64F Skycrane	64074	ex N467KG	718
☐ N719HT	Sikorsky S-64F Skycrane	64076	ex N469KG	719
☐ N721HT	Sikorsky S-64F Skycrane	64073	ex N466KG	721
☐ N47B	Sikorsky S-58BT	58-530	ex EC-CYJ	
☐ N72B	Sikorsky S-58ET	58-1626	ex EC-DJN	
☐ N664Y	Sikorsky S-61R	61501		
☐ N724HT	Bell 214ST	28123	ex FAP634	
☐ N725HT	Bell 214ST	28128	ex N241WJ	
☐ N91158	Sikorsky S-61N Helipro Short	61424	ex G-AZDC	

HELIFLIGHT
Fort Lauderdale-Executive, FL (FLE)

☐ N58HF	Sikorsky S-58J		ex 57-1692

HOMER AIR
Homer, AK (HOM)

☐ N206DC	Cessna U206F Stationair II	U20603198	ex N8337Q
☐ N522HA	Cessna U206B Super Skywagon	U206-0755	ex N3455L
☐ N7138Q	Cessna U206F Stationair II	U20603074	
☐ N9815M	Cessna U206G Stationair 6 II	U20604572	

HORIZON AIR
Horizon Air (QX/QXE)   **Seattle-Tacoma Intl, WA (SEA)**

☐ N600QX	Canadair CRJ-701	10005	ex C-GCRA	600
☐ N601QX	Canadair CRJ-701	10009	ex C-GHCS	601
☐ N603QX	Canadair CRJ-701	10011	ex C-GHCZ	603
☐ N604QX	Canadair CRJ-701	10019	ex C-GIAJ	604
☐ N605QX	Canadair CRJ-701	10022	ex C-GIAR	605
☐ N606QX	Canadair CRJ-701	10023	ex C-GISU	606
☐ N608QX	Canadair CRJ-701	10026	ex C-GIAX	608
☐ N609QX	Canadair CRJ-701	10031	ex C-GIBJ	609
☐ N611QX	Canadair CRJ-701	10041	ex C-GICP	611
☐ N612QX	Canadair CRJ-701	10042	ex C-GHZV	612
☐ N613QX	Canadair CRJ-701	10045	ex C-GIAD	613
☐ N614QX	Canadair CRJ-701	10049	ex C-GIAJ	614
☐ N615QX	Canadair CRJ-701	10065	ex C-GIBQ	615

349

☐ N616QX	Canadair CRJ-701	10128	ex C-	616	WSU Cougars c/s	
☐ N617QX	Canadair CRJ-701	10130	ex C-	617		
☐ N618QX	Canadair CRJ-701	10205	ex C-	618		
☐ N619QX	Canadair CRJ-701	10246	ex C-	619		
☐ N353PH	de Havilland DHC-8Q-202	496	ex C-GFRP			
☐ N354PH	de Havilland DHC-8Q-202	498	ex C-FCSG	City of North Bend/Coos Bay		
☐ N358PH	de Havilland DHC-8Q-202	506	ex C-FWBB			
☐ N359PH	de Havilland DHC-8Q-202	514	ex C-GEOA	City of Kelowna	>UCA	
☐ N360PH	de Havilland DHC-8Q-202	515	ex C-GEWI	City of Medford	>UCA	
☐ N361PH	de Havilland DHC-8Q-202	516	ex C-GFOD	City of Sun Valley	>UCA	
☐ N362PH	de Havilland DHC-8Q-202	518	ex C-FDHI		>UCA	
☐ N363PH	de Havilland DHC-8Q-202	520	ex C-FDHP	City of Boise	>UCA	
☐ N364PH	de Havilland DHC-8Q-202	524	ex C-FDHX	Cities of Seattle/Tacoma	>UCA	
☐ N365PH	de Havilland DHC-8Q-202	526	ex C-FDHZ	City of Pocatello	>UCA	
☐ N366PH	de Havilland DHC-8Q-202	510	ex C-GELN	City of Redding	>UCA	
☐ N367PH	de Havilland DHC-8Q-202	511	ex C-GDLD		>UCA	
☐ N368PH	de Havilland DHC-8Q-202	512	ex C-GDFT	City of Idaho Falls	>UCA	
☐ N369PH	de Havilland DHC-8Q-202	513	ex C-FWBB			
☐ N374PH	de Havilland DHC-8Q-202	528	ex C-GDIU			
☐ N375PH	de Havilland DHC-8Q-202	529	ex C-GDKL		>UCA	
☐ N379PH	de Havilland DHC-8Q-202	530	ex C-GDLK		>UCA	
☐ N400QX	de Havilland DHC-8-402Q	4030	ex C-GFCF			
☐ N401QX	de Havilland DHC-8-402Q	4031	ex C-GFCW			
☐ N402QX	de Havilland DHC-8-402Q	4032	ex C-GFOD			
☐ N403QX	de Havilland DHC-8-402Q	4037	ex C-FDHP			
☐ N404QX	de Havilland DHC-8-402Q	4046	ex C-GDKL			
☐ N405QX	de Havilland DHC-8-402Q	4047	ex C-GDLD			
☐ N406QX	de Havilland DHC-8-402Q	4048	ex C-GDLK			
☐ N407QX	de Havilland DHC-8-402Q	4049	ex C-GDNK			
☐ N408QX	de Havilland DHC-8-402Q	4050	ex C-GFCA			
☐ N409QX	de Havilland DHC-8-402Q	4051	ex C-GFCW			
☐ N410QX	de Havilland DHC-8-402Q	4053	ex C-GFQL			
☐ N411QX	de Havilland DHC-8-402Q	4055	ex C-GFUM			
☐ N412QX	de Havilland DHC-8-402Q	4059	ex C-FGNP			
☐ N413QX	de Havilland DHC-8-402Q	4060	ex C-FNGB			
☐ N414QX	de Havilland DHC-8-402Q	4061	ex C-GDFT			
☐ N415QX	de Havilland DHC-8-402Q	4081	ex C-GELN			
☐ N416QX	de Havilland DHC-8-402Q	4083	ex C-GDNK			
☐ N417QX	de Havilland DHC-8-402Q	4086	ex C-FCSG			
☐ N418QX	de Havilland DHC-8-402Q	4143	ex C-FHQX			
☐ N419QX	de Havilland DHC-8-402Q	4145	ex C-FHRD			
☐ N420QX	de Havilland DHC-8-402Q	4147	ex C-FJLA			
☐ N421QX	de Havilland DHC-8-402Q	4149	ex C-FJLF			
☐ N422QX	de Havilland DHC-8-402Q	4150	ex C-FJLG			
☐ N423QX	de Havilland DHC-8-402Q	4153	ex C-FJLO			
☐ N424QX	de Havilland DHC-8-402Q	4006	ex B-3568			
☐ N425QX	de Havilland DHC-8-402Q	4039	ex B-3569	25 Years Jubilee c/s		
☐ N426QX	de Havilland DHC-8-402Q	4154	ex C-FJLX			
☐ N427QX	de Havilland DHC-8-402Q	4156	ex C-FLKU			
☐ N428QX	de Havilland DHC-8-402Q	4160	ex C-FLTL			
☐ N429QX	de Havilland DHC-8-402Q	4161	ex C-FLTT			
☐ N430QX	de Havilland DHC-8-402Q	4163	ex C-FMES			
☐ N431QX	de Havilland DHC-8-402Q	4164	ex C-FMEU			
☐ N432QX	de Havilland DHC-8-402Q	4166	ex C-FMFH			
☐ N433QX	de Havilland DHC-8-402Q	4210	ex C-FPQB			
☐ N434MK	de Havilland DHC-8-402Q	4227	ex C-FTUQ	Milton G Koult II		
☐ N435QX	de Havilland DHC-8-402Q	4232	ex C-FUCO			
☐ N436QX	de Havilland DHC-8-402Q	4236	ex C-FUOF			
☐ N437QX	de Havilland DHC-8-402Q	4240	ex C-FUSM			
☐ N438QX	de Havilland DHC-8-402Q	4243	ex C-FUTP			
☐ N439QX	de Havilland DHC-8-402Q	4246	ex C-FVGY			
☐ N	de Havilland DHC-8-402Q		ex C-		o/o♦	
☐ N	de Havilland DHC-8-402Q		ex C-		o/o♦	
☐ N	de Havilland DHC-8-402Q		ex C-		o/o♦	
☐ N	de Havilland DHC-8-402Q		ex C-		o/o♦	
☐ N	de Havilland DHC-8-402Q		ex C-		o/o♦	
☐ N	de Havilland DHC-8-402Q		ex C-		o/o♦	
☐ N	de Havilland DHC-8-402Q		ex C-		o/o♦	
☐ N	de Havilland DHC-8-402Q		ex C-		o/o♦	

IBC AIRWAYS — Chasqui (II/CSQ) — Miami-Intl, FL (MIA)

☐ N431BC	SAAB SF.340B	340B-260	ex N363PX	
☐ N481BC	SAAB SF.340B	340B-274	ex N368PX	
☐ N541BC	SAAB SF.340A	340A-029	ex N184K	

☐ N611BC	SAAB SF.340A		340A-060	ex N403BH	Frtr
☐ N631BC	SAAB SF.340A		340A-061	ex N404BH	Frtr
☐ N641BC	SAAB SF.340A		340A-069	ex N340SL	Frtr
☐ N651BC	SAAB SF.340A		340A-076	ex N76XJ	Frtr
☐ N661BC	SAAB SF.340A		340A-125	ex N125CH	Frtr
☐ N671BC	SAAB SF.340A		340A-084	ex N163PW	Frtr
☐ N691BC	SAAB SF.340A		340A-041	ex XA-BML	Frtr
☐ N831BC	Swearingen SA.227AC Metro III		AC-654B	ex N26906	
☐ N841BC	Swearingen SA.227TC Metro II		TC-282	ex N248AM	
☐ N851BC	Swearingen SA.227AT Merlin IVC		AT-495B	ex N9UA	
☐ N861BC	Swearingen SA.227AC Metro III		AC-487B	ex N550TD	
☐ N871BC	Swearingen SA.227AC Metro III		AC-659B	ex N2693C	
☐ N891BC	Swearingen SA.227AC Metro III		AC-709B	ex N2708D	

ILIAMNA AIR TAXI   Iliamna Air (V8/IAR)   Iliamna, AK (ILI)

☐ N38KC	Piper PA-31-350 Chieftain	31-8352033	ex N35AT		
☐ N715HL	Pilatus PC-12/45	292	ex N292PB		
☐ N715TL	Pilatus PC-12/45	548	ex HB-FST		
☐ N3682Z	Beech 58 Baron	TH-1159			
☐ N1748U	Cessna 207 Skywagon	20700348			
☐ N7379U	Cessna 207A Stationair 7 II	20700427			
☐ N9720M	Cessna 207A Stationair 8 II	20700720			
☐ N62230	de Havilland DHC-2 Beaver	707	ex 53-7899		FP
☐ N68088	de Havilland DHC-2 Beaver	1197	ex 56-4447		FP

INLAND AVIATION SERVICES   (7N)   Aniak, AK (ANI)

☐ N1673U	Cessna 207 Skywagon	20700273	
☐ N1701U	Cessna 207 Skywagon	20700301	
☐ N1754U	Cessna T207 Turbo Skywagon	20700354	
☐ N91002	Cessna 207 Skywagon	20700003	
☐ N91099	Cessna 207 Skywagon	20700073	

INTER ISLAND AIR   Pago Pago International (PPG)

☐ N27BN	Britten-Norman BN-2B-26 Islander	2220	ex ZK-JOC	
☐ N228ST	Dornier 228-212	8240	ex D-CBDJ	Islands of Manu'a

INTERMOUNTAIN HELICOPTERS   Columbia, CA (COA)

☐ N9122Z	Bell 212	30716	ex C-GFRS

INTERNATIONAL AIR RESPONSE   Coolidge-Municipal, AZ(CHD)

☐ N117TG	Lockheed C-130A-1A Hercules	3018	ex 54-1631	31 Iron Butterfly	
☐ N118TG	Lockheed C-130A-1A Hercules	3219	ex 57-0512	32	
☐ N119TG	Lockheed C-130A Hercules	3227	ex N138FF		[CHD]
☐ N121TG	Lockheed C-130A Hercules	3119	ex N132FF		
☐ N125TG	Lockheed C-130A Hercules	3138	ex N131FF		[CHD]
☐ N126TG	Lockheed C-130A-1A Hercules	3142	ex N131HP		[CHD]♦
☐ N133HP	Lockheed C-130A-1A Hercules	3189	ex N8026J		
☐ N797AL	Douglas DC-8-63F (BAC 3)	46163/556	ex SE-DBL		[VCV]
☐ N995CF	Douglas DC-8-62F (BAC 3)	46024/428	ex N815ZA		[VCV]
☐ N4887C	Douglas DC-7B	45351/903	33		

ISLAND AIR   Moku (WP/MKU   Honolulu-Intl, HI (HNL)

☐ N805WP	de Havilland DHC-8-103	353	ex N853MA	
☐ N806WP	de Havilland DHC-8-103	357	ex N854MA	
☐ N808WP	de Havilland DHC-8-103	026	ex N812PH	[HNL]♦
☐ N809WP	de Havilland DHC-8-103	032	ex N813SN	
☐ N829EX	de Havilland DHC-8-103	146	ex N805AW	
☐ N979HA	de Havilland DHC-8-103	373	ex C-GFQL	

ISLAND AIR CHARTERS   Barracuda (ILF)   Fort Lauderdale-Hollywood Intl, FL (FLL)

☐ N138LW	Britten-Norman BN-2A-27 Islander	138	ex YR-BNF
☐ N779KS	Britten-Norman BN-2A-27 Islander	779	ex YR-BNE

ISLAND AIR SERVICE   (2O)   Kodiak-Municipal, AK (ADQ)

☐ N27MR	Britten-Norman BN-2A-26 Islander	884	ex XC-DUN	dam 18Jun07
☐ N1162W	Beech B80 Queen Air	LD-350		
☐ N2233Z	Britten-Norman BN-2A-26 Islander	23	ex C-FXYK	
☐ N3941W	Piper PA-32-260 Cherokee Six	32-890		
☐ N4875X	Cessna U206G Stationair 6 II	U20605559		FP or wheels

☐ N5891V	Britten-Norman BN-2A-26 Islander	3011	ex J8-VAN	
☐ N8152Z	Piper PA-32-301 Saratoga	32-8006004		

ISLAND AIRLINES   Island (IS/ISA)   Nantucket-Memorial, MA (ACK)

☐ N401BK	Cessna 402C II	402C0297	ex N3252M
☐ N402BK	Cessna 402C II	689	ex N550CQ
☐ N403BK	Cessna 402C II	402C0330	ex N26436
☐ N406BK	Cessna 402C III	402C0807	ex N1235A
☐ N407BK	Cessna 402C II	402C0238	ex N279CB
☐ N409BK	Cessna 402C II	402C0651	ex N67220
☐ N410BK	Cessna 402C II	402C1006	ex N175TT

ISLAND AIRWAYS   Charlevoix-Municipal, MI (CVX)

☐ N19WA	Britten-Norman BN-2A-8 Islander	524	ex N307SK
☐ N80KM	Britten-Norman BN-2A Islander	80	ex G-BNXA
☐ N95BN	Britten-Norman BN-2A-8 Islander	95	ex G-AXKB
☐ N137MW	Britten-Norman BN-2A Islander	137	ex G-AXWH
☐ N866JA	Britten-Norman BN-2A-6 islander	185	ex G-31-185

ISLAND SEAPLANE SERVICE   Honolulu-Keehi Lagoon SPB, HI

☐ N110AW	de Havilland DHC-2 Beaver	690	ex N11015	Fantasy Islands c/sFP

ISLAND WINGS AIR SERVICE   Ketchikan-Waterfront SPB, AK (WFB)

☐ N1117F	de Havilland DHC-2 Beaver	1369	ex N6783L	FP

JETBLUE AIRWAYS   JetBlue (B6/JBU)   New York-JFK Intl, NY (JFK)

☐ N503JB	Airbus A320-232	1123	ex F-WWBR	Blue Bird	
☐ N504JB	Airbus A320-232	1156	ex F-WWBV	Shades Of Blue	
☐ N505JB	Airbus A320-232	1173	ex F-WWDN	Blue Skies	
☐ N506JB	Airbus A320-232	1235	ex F-WWIN	Wild Blue Yonder	
☐ N509JB	Airbus A320-232	1270	ex F-WWDF	True Blue	
☐ N510JB	Airbus A320-232	1280	ex F-WWBA	Out Of The Blue	
☐ N516JB	Airbus A320-232	1302	ex F-WWBQ	Royal Blue	
☐ N517JB	Airbus A320-232	1327	ex F-WWDU	Blue Moon	
☐ N519JB	Airbus A320-232	1398	ex F-WWIY	It Had To Be Blue	
☐ N520JB	Airbus A320-232	1446	ex F-WWBT	Blue Velvet	
☐ N521JB	Airbus A320-232	1452	ex F-WWBY	Baby Blue	
☐ N523JB	Airbus A320-232	1506	ex F-WWII	Born To Be Blue	
☐ N524JB	Airbus A320-232	1528	ex F-WWIN	Blue Belle	
☐ N527JL	Airbus A320-232	1557	ex D-ANNE		◆
☐ N529JB	Airbus A320-232	1610	ex F-WWDE	Ole Blue Eyes	
☐ N534JB	Airbus A320-232	1705	ex F-WWIU	Bada Bing, Bada Blue	
☐ N535JB	Airbus A320-232	1739	ex F-WWBQ	Estrella Azul	
☐ N536JB	Airbus A320-232	1784	ex F-WWDS	Canyon Blue	
☐ N537JT	Airbus A320-232	1785	ex D-ANNI		◆
☐ N547JB	Airbus A320-232	1849	ex F-WWDF	Forever Blue	
☐ N552JB	Airbus A320-232	1861	ex F-WWDM	Blue Jay	
☐ N554JB	Airbus A320-232	1898	ex F-WWBK	Sacre' Bleu!	
☐ N556JB	Airbus A320-232	1904	ex F-WWDD	Betty Blue	
☐ N558JB	Airbus A320-232	1915	ex F-WWIF	Song Sung Blue	
☐ N559JB	Airbus A320-232	1917	ex F-WWIR	Here's Looking At Blue, Kid	
☐ N561JB	Airbus A320-232	1927	ex F-WWIC	La Vie En Blue	
☐ N562JB	Airbus A320-232	1948	ex F-WWDF	The Name Is Blue, jetBlue	
☐ N563JB	Airbus A320-232	2006	ex F-WWBY	Blue Chip	
☐ N564JB	Airbus A320-232	2020	ex F-WWBZ	Absolute Blue	
☐ N565JB	Airbus A320-232	2031	ex F-WWDT	Bippity Boppity Blue	
☐ N566JB	Airbus A320-232	2042	ex F-WWDU	Blue Suede Shoes	
☐ N568JB	Airbus A320-232	2063	ex F-WWDE	Blue Sapphire	
☐ N569JB	Airbus A320-232	2075	ex F-WWDF	Blues Brothers	
☐ N570JB	Airbus A320-232	2099	ex F-WWBD	Devil With A Blue Dress On	
☐ N571JB	Airbus A320-232	2125	ex F-WWIX	Blue Monday	
☐ N579JB	Airbus A320-232	2132	ex F-WWDB	Can't Stop Lovin' Blue	
☐ N580JB	Airbus A320-232	2136	ex F-WWBB	Mo Better Blue	
☐ N583JB	Airbus A320-232	2150	ex F-WWII	Bluesville	
☐ N584JB	Airbus A320-232	2149	ex F-WWID	Blue Fox	
☐ N585JB	Airbus A320-232	2159	ex F-WWIC	I Got Blue Babe	
☐ N586JB	Airbus A320-232	2160	ex F-WWIN	Blue Flight Special	
☐ N587JB	Airbus A320-232	2177	ex F-WWIL	Blue Kid In Town	
☐ N588JB	Airbus A320-232	2201	ex F-WWIT	Hopelessly Devoted To Blue	
☐ N589JB	Airbus A320-232	2215	ex F-WWBJ	Blue Skies Ahead	
☐ N590JB	Airbus A320-232	2231	ex F-WWIH	Liberty Blue	
☐ N591JB	Airbus A320-232	2246	ex F-WWIS	Tale Of Blue Cities	
☐ N592JB	Airbus A320-232	2259	ex F-WWBI	American Blue	

☐ N593JB	Airbus A320-232	2280	ex F-WWDT	I Only Have Eyes For Blue
☐ N594JB	Airbus A320-232	2284	ex F-WWBQ	Whole Lotta Blue
☐ N595JB	Airbus A320-232	2286	ex F-WWBR	Rhythm & Blues
☐ N597JB	Airbus A320-232	2307	ex F-WWIC	For The Love Of Blue
☐ N598JB	Airbus A320-232	2314	ex F-WWDK	Me & You & A Plane Named Blue
☐ N599JB	Airbus A320-232	2336	ex F-WWIN	If The Blue Fits
☐ N603JB	Airbus A320-232	2352	ex F-WWIL	Viva La Blue
☐ N605JB	Airbus A320-232	2368	ex F-WWDO	Blue Yorker
☐ N606JB	Airbus A320-232	2384	ex F-WWIE	Idlewild Blue
☐ N607JB	Airbus A320-232	2386	ex F-WWIG	Beantown Blue
☐ N608JB	Airbus A320-232	2415	ex F-WWDP	..And Along Came Blue
☐ N612JB	Airbus A320-232	2447	ex F-WWBU	Blue Look Maaahvelous
☐ N613JB	Airbus A320-232	2449	ex F-WWBX	Bahama Blue
☐ N615JB	Airbus A320-232	2461	ex F-WWDR	I Love Blue
☐ N618JB	Airbus A320-232	2489	ex F-WWDX	Can't Get Enough Of Blue
☐ N621JB	Airbus A320-232	2491	ex F-WWDY	Do-be-do-be Blue
☐ N623JB	Airbus A320-232	2504	ex F-WWBM	All We Need Is Blue
☐ N624JB	Airbus A320-232	2520	ex F-WWBN	Blue-T-Ful
☐ N625JB	Airbus A320-232	2535	ex F-WWII	CompanyBlue
☐ N627JB	Airbus A320-232	2577	ex F-WWDB	A Friend Like Blue
☐ N629JB	Airbus A320-232	2580	ex F-WWBH	Bright Lights, Blue City
☐ N630JB	Airbus A320-232	2640	ex F-WWBY	Honk If You love Blue
☐ N632JB	Airbus A320-232	2647	ex F-WWIF	Clear Blue Sky
☐ N633JB	Airbus A320-232	2671	ex F-WWDZ	Major Blue
☐ N634JB	Airbus A320-232	2710	ex F-WWIZ	B☐L☐U☐E
☐ N635JB	Airbus A320-232	2725	ex F-WWDQ	All Because of Blue
☐ N636JB	Airbus A320-232	2755	ex F-WWDL	All Wrapped Up In Blue
☐ N637JB	Airbus A320-232	2781	ex F-WWDY	Big Blue Bus
☐ N638JB	Airbus A320-232	2802	ex F-WWIL	Blue begins with you
☐ N639JB	Airbus A320-232	2814	ex F-WWIV	A Little Blue Will Do
☐ N640JB	Airbus A320-232	2832	ex F-WWBD	Blue Better Believe It
☐ N641JB	Airbus A320-232	2848	ex F-WWIK	Blue Come Back Now Ya Hear
☐ N643JB	Airbus A320-232	2871	ex F-WWBF	Blue Jersey
☐ N644JB	Airbus A320-232	2880	ex F-WWBO	Blue Loves Ya, Baby
☐ N645JB	Airbus A320-232	2900	ex F-WWDE	Blues Have More Fun
☐ N646JB	Airbus A320-232	2945	ex F-WWIP	Bravo Lima Uniform Echo
☐ N648JB	Airbus A320-232	2970	ex F-WWDI	That's What I Like About Blue
☐ N649JB	Airbus A320-232	2977	ex F-WWBD	Fancy Meeting Blue Here
☐ N651JB	Airbus A320-232	2992	ex F-WWIS	BetaBlue
☐ N652JB	Airbus A320-232	3029	ex F-WWBT	Out With The Old, In With The Blue
☐ N653JB	Airbus A320-232	3039	ex F-WWDH	Breath of Fresh Blue
☐ N655JB	Airbus A320-232	3072	ex F-WWIN	special colours, Blue 100
☐ N656JB	Airbus A320-232	3091	ex F-WWIQ	California Blue
☐ N657JB	Airbus A320-232	3119	ex F-WWBC	Denim Blue
☐ N658JB	Airbus A320-232	3150	ex F-WWBT	Woo-Hoo JetBlue
☐ N659JB	Airbus A320-232	3190	ex F-WWIQ	Simply Blue
☐ N661JB	Airbus A320-232	3228	ex F-WWBD	Let the Blue Times Roll
☐ N662JB	Airbus A320-232	3263	ex F-WWDO	Glad to be Blue
☐ N663JB	Airbus A320-232	3287	ex F-WWDG	Paint the town blue
☐ N665JB	Airbus A320-232	3348	ex F-WWBV	Something about blue
☐ N703JB	Airbus A320-232	3381	ex F-WWDM	It's up to blue, New York, New York
☐ N705JB	Airbus A320-232	3416	ex F-WWIN	Big Blue People Seater
☐ N706JB	Airbus A320-232	3451	ex F-WWBE	As blue as it gets
☐ N708JB	Airbus A320-232	3479	ex F-WWDJ	All that and a bag of blue chips
☐ N709JB	Airbus A320-232	3488	ex F-WWIK	Brand Spanking Blue
☐ N712JB	Airbus A320-232	3517	ex F-WWDQ	Enough about me..Let's talk about Blue
☐ N715JB	Airbus A320-232	3554	ex F-WWBB	How's My Flying? Call 1-800-JetBlue
☐ N729JB	Airbus A320-232	3572	ex F-WWBJ	If You Can Read This, Your Blue Close
☐ N746JB	Airbus A320-232	3622	ex F-WWIL	Some Like It Blue
☐ N760JB	Airbus A320-232	3659	ex F-WWDU	The Blues Were Made For Flying
☐ N763JB	Airbus A320-232	3707	ex F-WWIQ	Unforgetably blue
☐ N766JB	Airbus A320-232	3724	ex F-WWDG	Etjay Luebay
☐ N768JB	Airbus A320-232	3760	ex F-WWDC	Blue Crew
☐ N775JB	Airbus A320-232	3800	ex F-WWBT	Canard Bleu
☐ N779JB	Airbus A320-232	3811	ex F-WWID	Real Blue
☐ N	Airbus A320-232		ex	o/o♦
☐ N	Airbus A320-232		ex	o/o♦
☐ N	Airbus A320-232		ex	o/o♦
☐ N	Airbus A320-232		ex	o/o♦
☐ N178JB	Embraer ERJ-190-AR	19000004	ex PT-STD	It's A Blue Thing
☐ N179JB	Embraer ERJ-190-AR	19000006	ex PT-STF	Come Fly With Blue
☐ N183JB	Embraer ERJ-190-AR	19000007	ex PT-STG	Azul Brasileiro
☐ N184JB	Embraer ERJ-190-AR	19000008	ex PT-STH	Outta the Blue
☐ N187JB	Embraer ERJ-190-AR	19000009	ex PT-STI	Dream Come Blue
☐ N190JB	Embraer ERJ-190-AR	19000011	ex PT-STK	Luiz F Kahl
☐ N192JB	Embraer ERJ-190-AR	19000014	ex PT-STO	Yes, I'm A Natural Blue

☐ N193JB	Embraer ERJ-190AR	19000017	ex PT-STR	Peek-a-Blue	
☐ N197JB	Embraer ERJ-190AR	19000020	ex PT-STU	Color Me Blue	
☐ N198JB	Embraer ERJ-190AR	19000021	ex PT-STV	Big Apple Blue	
☐ N203JB	Embraer ERJ-190AR	19000023	ex PT-STX	Look at Blue now	
☐ N206JB	Embraer ERJ-190AR	19000025	ex PT-STZ	Blue-It's the New Black	
☐ N216JB	Embraer ERJ-190AR	19000026	ex PT-SGA	Blue Getaway	
☐ N228JB	Embraer ERJ-190AR	19000030	ex PT-SGE	Blue 4 You	
☐ N229JB	Embraer ERJ-190AR	19000032	ex PT-SGG	Blue Amigo	
☐ N231JB	Embraer ERJ-190AR	19000033	ex PT-SGH	Blue Bonnet	
☐ N236JB	Embraer ERJ-190AR	19000035	ex PT-SGJ	Blue by Design	
☐ N238JB	Embraer ERJ-190AR	19000039	ex PT-SGO	Blue Clipper	
☐ N239JB	Embraer ERJ-190AR	19000040	ex PT-SGP	Blissfully Blue	
☐ N247JB	Embraer ERJ-190AR	19000042	ex PT-SGR	Blue is so You	
☐ N249JB	Embraer ERJ-190AR	19000045	ex PT-SGU	Blueprint	
☐ N258JB	Embraer ERJ-190AR	19000047	ex PT-SGW	Blue Send Me	
☐ N265JB	Embraer ERJ-190AR	19000049	ex PT-SGY	Blue Streak	
☐ N266JB	Embraer ERJ-190AR	19000054	ex PT-SID	Blue Sweet Blue	
☐ N267JB	Embraer ERJ-190AR	19000065	ex PT-SJD	Bluesmobile	
☐ N273JB	Embraer ERJ-190AR	19000073	ex PT-SJM	Carribean Blue	
☐ N274JB	Embraer ERJ-190AR	19000082	ex PT-SJY	Good, Better, Blue	
☐ N279JB	Embraer ERJ-190AR	19000090	ex PT-SNJ	Indigo Blue	
☐ N281JB	Embraer ERJ-190AR	19000103	ex PT-SNX	Lady in Blue	
☐ N283JB	Embraer ERJ-190AR	19000125	ex PT-SQU	Pretty in Blue	
☐ N284JB	Embraer ERJ-190AR	19000144	ex PT-SVY	Sincerely Blue	
☐ N289JB	Embraer ERJ-190AR	19000002	ex PT-XMB	Blue Complete Me	
☐ N292JB	Embraer ERJ-190AR	19000179	ex PT-SDN	Parlez-Blue?	
☐ N294JB	Embraer ERJ-190AR	19000185	ex PT-SDT	Room with a blue	
☐ N296JB	Embraer ERJ-190AR	19000219	ex PT-SHC	Blue's your daddy	
☐ N298JB	Embraer ERJ-190AR	19000249	ex PT-SIT	Cool Blue	
☐ N304JB	Embraer ERJ-190AR	19000257	ex PT-STF	Midnight Blue	
☐ N306JB	Embraer ERJ-190AR	19000272	ex PT-TLM	Blue Orleans	
☐ N307JB	Embraer ERJ-190AR	19000286	ex PT-TZA	Mi Corazon Azul	
☐ N309JB	Embraer ERJ-190AR	19000289	ex PT-TZD	Rhapsodyin Blue	
☐ N316JB	Embraer ERJ-190AR	19000292	ex PT-TZG	Usto Schulz	
☐ N317JB	Embraer ERJ-190AR	19000363	ex PT-XNC	Deja Blue	♦
☐ N318JB	Embraer ERJ-190AR	19000364	ex PT-XND	Blue Jean Baby	♦
☐ N323JB	Embraer ERJ-190AR	19000384	ex PT-XNS	Only Blue	♦
☐ N324JB	Embraer ERJ-190AR	19000388	ex PT-XNV	Blue Traveller	♦
☐ N	Embraer ERJ-190AR		ex PT-		o/o♦
☐ N	Embraer ERJ-190AR		ex PT-		o/o♦
☐ N	Embraer ERJ-190AR		ex PT-		o/o♦
☐ N	Embraer ERJ-190AR		ex PT-		o/o♦
☐ N	Embraer ERJ-190AR		ex PT-		o/o♦

JIM HANKINS AIR SERVICE — Hankins (HKN) — Jackson-Hawkins Field, MS (JAN)

☐ N22BR	Beech H-18	BA-729	ex N402AP	Frtr
☐ N81CK	Volpar Turboliner	BA-509	ex F-ODHJ	Frtr
☐ N231SK	Volpar Turboliner	AF-856	ex N346V	Frtr
☐ N404CK	Volpar Turboliner	AF-297	ex N404TH	Frtr
☐ N4209V	Volpar Turboliner	AF-884	ex HB-GFX	Frtr
☐ N92756	Beech H-18	BA-728	ex JA5133	Frtr
☐ N3BA	Douglas DC-3	12172	ex N94530	Frtr
☐ N40XL	Beech 58 Baron	TH-400	ex N80LM	
☐ N366MQ	Short SD.3-60	SH3639	ex G-BLEH	
☐ N899DD	Beech 58 Baron	TH-899	ex VH-BWJ	
☐ N958JH	Beech 65-C90A King Air	LJ-1108	ex N438SP	
☐ N3106W	Beech 58 Baron	TH-408		
☐ N6652A	Beech 58 Baron	TH-1045		
☐ N8061A	Douglas DC-3	6085	ex (N351SA)	Frtr

KACHINA AVIATION — Boise-Air Terminal, ID (BOI)

☐ N171KA	Bell 206L-1 LongRanger III	45607	ex C-GZPZ
☐ N212KA	Bell 212	30776	ex C-FAHI
☐ N213KA	Bell 212	31172	ex C-FNOB
☐ N214KA	Bell 212	30827	ex C-FAHC
☐ N215KA	Bell 212	30651	ex C-FAHZ

KALITTA AIR — Connie (K4/CKS) — Detroit-Willow Run, MI (YIP)

☐ N616US	Boeing 747-251F	21120/258		[OSC]♦
☐ N619US	Boeing 747-251F	21321/308		[OSC]♦
☐ N629US	Boeing 747-251F	22388/444		[OSC]♦
☐ N630US	Boeing 747-2J9F	21668/400	ex N1288E	[OSC]♦
☐ N631NW	Boeing 747-251B (SF)	23111/594	ex N631US	[OSC]♦
☐ N646NW	Boeing 747-222B (SF)	23737/675	ex N152UA	[OSC]♦

☐ N700CK	Boeing 747-246B (SF)	22990/579	ex JA8161	
☐ N701CK	Boeing 747-259B (SCD)	21730/372	ex N924FT	
☐ N703CK	Boeing 747-212B (SF)	21939/449	ex N319FV	
☐ N704CK	Boeing 747-246F	23391/654	ex JA8171	
☐ N705CK	Boeing 747-246B (SCD)	21034/243	ex JA8123	
☐ N706CK	Boeing 747-249F	21827/406	ex N806FT	
☐ N707CK	Boeing 747-246F	21681/382	ex JA8132	
☐ N708CK	Boeing 747-212B (SF)	21937/419	ex N526UP	
☐ N709CK	Boeing 747-132 (SCD)	20247/159	ex N625PL	
☐ N710CK	Boeing 747-2B4M	21097/262	ex N204AE	
☐ N712CK	Boeing 747-122 (SCD)	19754/60	ex N854FT	
☐ N713CK	Boeing 747-2B4M	21099/264	ex OD-AGH	
☐ N715CK	Boeing 747-209B (SF)	22447/556	ex B-18755	
☐ N716CK	Boeing 747-122 (SCD)	19753/52	ex N853FT	
☐ N717CK	Boeing 747-123 (SCD)	20325/125	ex N673UP	
☐ N740CK	Boeing 747-4H6FCF	24405/745	ex N73714	
☐ N741CK	Boeing 747-4H6FCF	24315/738	ex N73713	
☐ N742CK	Boeing 747-446BCF	24424/760	ex JA8072	
☐ N743CK	Boeing 747-446BCF	26350/961	ex JA8906	♦
☐ N744CK	Boeing 747-446BCF	26353/980	ex JA8909	♦
☐ N745CK	Boeing 747-446BCF	26361/1188	ex JA8915	♦
☐ N746CK	Boeing 747-246F	22989/571	ex JA811J	
☐ N747CK	Boeing 747-221F	21743/384	ex JA8165	
☐ N748CK	Boeing 747-221F	21744/392	ex JA8160	
☐ N768CK	Boeing 747-346	23969/691	ex JA8185	[OSC]
☐ N790CK	Boeing 747-251B (SF)	23112/595	ex N632NW	♦
☐ N791CK	Boeing 747-251F	23888/682	ex N640US	♦
☐ N792CK	Boeing 747-212F	24177/710	ex N644NW	♦
☐ N793CK	Boeing 747-222B (SF)	23736/673	ex N645NW	[OSC]♦

KALITTA CHARTERS II		**Kalitta (KFS)**	**Detroit-Willow Run, MI (YIP)**	
☐ N720CK	Boeing 727-2B6F (Raisbeck 3)	21298/1246	ex N721SK	
☐ N722CK	Boeing 727-2H3F (Raisbeck 3)	20948/1084	ex N722SK	
☐ N723CK	Boeing 727-2H3F (Raisbeck 3)	20545/877	ex N723SK	
☐ N724CK	Boeing 727-225F (Raisbeck 3)	20383/831	ex N8840E	
☐ N725CK	Boeing 727-224F (Raisbeck 3)	22252/1697	ex N746DH	
☐ N726CK	Boeing 727-2M7 (FedEx 3)	21951/1680	ex N750DH	♦
☐ N915CK	Douglas DC-9-15RC	47086/219	ex N915R	

KALITTA FLYING SERVICES		**Kalitta (KFS)**		
		Detroit-Willow Run, MI/Morristown, TN/El Paso, TX (YIP/MRX/ESP)		
☐ N70CK	AMD Falcon 20C	128	ex N228CK	
☐ N108R	AMD Falcon 20DC	108	ex N101ZE	
☐ N192CK	AMD Falcon 20C	192	ex N192R	
☐ N212R	AMD Falcon 20DC	212	ex N31FE	
☐ N226CK	AMD Falcon 20DC	226	ex N226R	
☐ N227CK	AMD Falcon 20DC	227	ex N227R	
☐ N229CK	AMD Falcon 20DC	229	ex N229R	
☐ N230RA	AMD Falcon 20DC	230	ex N26EV	
☐ N240CK	AMD Falcon 20C-5	24	ex N240TJ	
☐ N301R	AMD Falcon 20C	3	ex N92MH	
☐ N560RA	AMD Falcon 20C	56	ex N388AJ	[YIP]
☐ N810RA	AMD Falcon 20C	81	ex N93RS	
☐ N995CK	AMD Falcon 20C	95	ex N950RA	
☐ N998CK	AMD Falcon 20C	98	ex N980R	
☐ N39CK	Learjet 25	25-005	ex XA-SDQ	
☐ N50CK	Learjet 25B	25B-157	ex N57CK	
☐ N71CK	Learjet 36A	36A-035	ex VH-BIB	
☐ N72CK	Learjet 35A	35A-165	ex N16BJ	
☐ N73CK	Learjet 35A	35A-092	ex N39WA	
☐ N75CK	Learjet 25D	25D-256	ex N6LL	
☐ N76CK	Learjet 25	25-020	ex N500JS	
☐ N83CK	Learjet 25B	25B-183	ex N5LL	
☐ N130CK	Learjet 25	25-038	ex N813JW	
☐ N150CK	Learjet 25D	25D-150	ex N251JA	
☐ N222B	Learjet 25	25-047		
☐ N248CK	Learjet 25D	25D-248	ex (N248LJ)	
☐ N536KN	Learjet 35A	35A-073	ex N610GA	
☐ N588CG	Learjet 24D	24D-304	ex N500CG	
☐ N818CK	Learjet 25B	25B-118	ex N118MB	
☐ N905CK	Learjet 36	36-005	ex N9108Z	
☐ N913CK	Learjet 35	35-013	ex N535TA	

All Frtrs. A sister company of Kalitta Charters II

KAMAKA AIR · Honolulu-Intl, HI (HNL)

☐ N231H	Beech E-18S	BA-281	ex N23Y
☐ N933T	Beech Super H-18	BA-665	
☐ N9796N	Douglas C-117D	43375	ex C-FLED

KATMAI AIR · King Salmon, AK / Anchorage-Lake Hood SPB, AK (AKN/LHD)

☐ N31TN	Beech B99	U-49	ex N98RZ	
☐ N491K	de Havilland DHC-3 Otter	434	ex N49KA	FP
☐ N492K	Piper PA-31-350 Chieftain	31-8052176	ex C-GAWL	
☐ N495K	Cessna U206F Stationair II	U20602549	ex N1274V	FP
☐ N496K	Cessna U206G Stationair	U20603953	ex N756BE	FP
☐ N498K	Cessna T207A Stationair 8	20700624	ex N73762	FP
☐ N499K	Cessna T207A Stationair 8	20700632	ex N73835	FP
☐ N9644G	Cessna U206F Stationair	U20601844		FP

KENMORE AIR · Kenmore (M5/KEN) · Kenmore SPB, WA (KEH)

☐ N74KA	Cessna 208B Caravan I	208B0770	ex N36SJ		FP
☐ N426KM	Cessna 208 Caravan I	20800306	ex N12656		FP
☐ N518KM	Cessna 208 Caravan I	20800279	ex C-FWCS		FP
☐ N694MA	Cessna 208B Caravan I	208B0694			FP
☐ N41F	de Havilland DHC-2 Beaver	1352	ex 58-2022		FP
☐ N900KA	de Havilland DHC-2 Beaver	1676	ex LN-BFH	Maggie Evening Magazine	FP
☐ N1018F	de Havilland DHC-2 Beaver	710	ex N62SJ		FP
☐ N1455T	de Havilland DHC-2 Turbo Beaver III	1647/TB26	ex CF-OEI		FP
☐ N6781L	de Havilland DHC-2 Beaver	788	ex N10LU		FP
☐ N9744T	de Havilland DHC-2 Turbo Beaver III	1692/TB60	ex N1944		FP
☐ N9766Z	de Havilland DHC-2 Beaver	504	ex N13454		FP
☐ N17598	de Havilland DHC-2 Beaver	1129	ex VP-FAH		FP
☐ N57576	de Havilland DHC-2 Beaver	1168	ex C-GNPQ		FP
☐ N72355	de Havilland DHC-2 Beaver	1164	ex N62355		FP
☐ N50KA	de Havilland DHC-3 Turbo Otter	221	ex C-GLMT	K5 Evening c/s	FP
☐ N58JH	de Havilland DHC-3 Turbo Otter	131	ex N8510Q		FP
☐ N87KA	de Havilland DHC-3 Turbo Otter	11	ex N8262V		FP
☐ N606KA	de Havilland DHC-3 Turbo Otter	37	ex N8260L		FP
☐ N707KA	de Havilland DHC-3 Turbo Otter	106	ex N888KA		FP
☐ N3125S	de Havilland DHC-3 Turbo Otter	407	ex RCAF 9424	Seattle Hospital c/s FP
☐ N90422	de Havilland DHC-3 Turbo Otter	152	ex 55-3296	Expedia.com titles	FP

KEY LIME AIR · Key Lime (LYM) · Denver-International, CO (DEN)

☐ N313RA	Piper PA-31-350 Chieftain	31-8052069	ex N333BM
☐ N411BJ	Piper PA-31-350 Chieftain	31-7952043	ex C-GPQR
☐ N3549X	Piper PA-31-350 Chieftain	31-8052034	ex C-FAWT
☐ N9247L	Piper PA-31-350 Chieftain	31-8152160	ex G-BWAS
☐ N27989	Piper PA-31-350 Chieftain	31-7952077	
☐ N66906	Piper PA-31-350 Navajo Chieftain	31-7405197	
☐ N74952	Piper PA-31-350 Navajo Chieftain	31-7305100	
☐ N62Z	Swearingen SA.226TC Metro II	TC-237	ex N5437M
☐ N184SW	Swearingen SA.227AC Metro III	AC-647	ex CX-TAA
☐ N340AE	Swearingen SA.227AC Metro III	AC-510	ex N3108E
☐ N425MA	Swearingen SA.227AC Metro III	AC-640	
☐ N508FA	Swearingen SA.227AC Metro III	AC-508	ex ZK-NSW
☐ N509SS	Swearingen SA.226TC Metro II	TC-206	ex N261S
☐ N542FA	Swearingen SA.227AC Metro III	AC-542	ex ZK-NSX
☐ N765FA	Swearingen SA.227AC Metro III	AC-765	ex ZK-NSI
☐ N769KL	Swearingen SA.227AC Metro III	AC-769B	ex HZ-SN10
☐ N770S	Swearingen SA.226TC Metro II	TC-248	
☐ N779BC	Swearingen SA.227AC Metro III	BC-779B	ex XA-RXW
☐ N787KL	Swearingen SA.227BC Metro III	BC-787B	ex XA-SAQ
☐ N820DC	Swearingen SA.227DC Metro 23	DC-820B	ex XA-SHD
☐ N882DC	Swearingen SA.227DC Metro 23	DC-882B	ex C-GAFQ
☐ N2691W	Swearingen SA.227AC Metro III	AC-655B	
☐ N2728G	Swearingen SA.227AC Metro III	AC-731	
☐ N81418	Swearingen SA.226TC Metro II	TC-223	ex EC-GNM
☐ N27BJ	Learjet 24B	24B-227	ex N28AT
☐ N404MG	Cessna 404 Titan	404-0813	ex 3X-GCF
☐ N37127	Cessna 404 Titan	404-0114	

KING AIRELINES   Las Vegas-Henderson Executive, NV (HSH)

☐ N8564Q	Cessna U206F Stationair	U20603420	
☐ N1570U	Cessna 207 Skywagon	20700170	ex N67TA
☐ N3156X	Cessna T207 Turbo Skywagon	20700376	
☐ N3728B	Cessna T207 Turbo Skywagon	20700298	ex JA3728
☐ N70437	Cessna 207A Stationair 7	20700552	
☐ N73320	Cessna T207A Stationair 7	20700577	
☐ N57SA	Cessna 402A	402A0101	ex N7801Q
☐ N69PB	Cessna 402B II	402B1248	
☐ N82TA	Cessna 402	402-0156	ex N402DK
☐ N402SW	Cessna 402	402-0036	ex N8236Q
☐ N2966Q	Cessna 402B	402B0321	ex RP-C1998
☐ N5098G	Cessna 402A	402A0056	ex C-FPDH
☐ N9901F	Cessna 402B	402B0402	ex C-GXHC

KING FLYING SERVICE   Naknek, AK (NNK)

| ☐ N38186 | Piper PA-32-300 Cherokee Six | 32-7740077 |
| ☐ N44851 | Piper PA-32-300 Cherokee Six | 32-7740107 |

KITTY HAWK AIRCARGO   Air Kittyhawk (KR/KHA)   Fort Wayne-International, IN (FWA)

☐ N90AX	Boeing 727-222F (FedEx 3)	20040/729	ex N7646U	[ROW]
☐ N855AA	Boeing 727-223F (FedEx 3)	20996/1193		[ROW]
☐ N858AA	Boeing 727-223F (FedEx 3)	21085/1200		[ROW]
☐ N6808	Boeing 727-223F (FedEx 3)	19483/558	ex (N744CK)	[ROW]
☐ N6809	Boeing 727-223F (FedEx 3)	19484/560		[ROW]
☐ N6827	Boeing 727-223F (FedEx 3)	20180/698		[ROW]
☐ N6831	Boeing 727-223F (FedEx 3)	20184/707		[ROW]
☐ N6833	Boeing 727-223F (FedEx 3)	20186/721		[ROW]
☐ N69740	Boeing 727-224F (FedEx 3)	20668/1154		[ROW]
☐ N77780	Boeing 727-232F (FedEx 3)	20635/918	ex N13780	store

Filed Chapter 11 bankruptcy protection 15Oct07, operations continued for a short period but then they terminated scheduled operations and returned some of the fleet to lessors. Plans to continue to fly cargo charters but current status uncertain.

KOLOB CANYONS AIR SERVICES   Cedar City, UT (CDC)

☐ N2BZ	Aero Commander 500S Shrike	3227	ex N57150	
☐ N57RS	Rockwell 690A Turbo Commander	11149	ex N5KW	
☐ N66GW	Rockwell 690A Turbo Commander	11174	ex N6B	
☐ N90AT	Rockwell 690A Turbo Commander	11272	ex N888PB	
☐ N98PJ	Rockwell 690A Turbo Commander	11320	ex N220HC	
☐ N900DT	Aero Commander 500S Shrike	3056	ex N9008N	
☐ N481UE	British Aerospace Jetstream 32	895	ex G-31-895	
☐ N894KA	British Aerospace Jetstream 32	894	ex N480UE	Cargo conversion

K2 AVIATION   Talkeetna, AK (TKA)

☐ N121KT	de Havilland DHC-2 Beaver	1407	ex N692F	Wheels or skis
☐ N122KT	Piper PA-32-300 Cherokee Six	32-7940190	ex N2898W	
☐ N125KT	Cessna A185F Skywagon II	18503494	ex N1855Q	Wheels or skis
☐ N323KT	de Havilland DHC-2 Beaver	1022	ex N10RM	Wheels or skis
☐ N727KT	de Havilland DHC-3 Turbo Otter	419	ex N427PM	Wheels or skis
☐ N828KT	Piper PA-32-350 Chieftain	31-8052098	ex SE-KDB	
☐ M929KT	de Havilland DHC-3 Turbo Otter	461	ex N271PA	Wheels or skis
☐ N1292F	Cessna A185F Skywagon	18502668	ex N3263C	Wheels or skis

LAB FLYING SERVICE   LAB (JF/LAB)   Juneau-Intl, AK/Haines-Municipal, AK (JNU/HNS)

☐ N54KA	Piper PA-32-300 Cherokee Six	32-7840197	
☐ N666EB	Piper PA-32-300 Six	32-7940115	ex N2116G
☐ N2181Z	Piper PA-32-300 Six	32-7940104	
☐ N2897X	Piper PA-32-300 Six	32-7940187	
☐ N2930Q	Piper PA-32R-300 Lance	32R-7780269	
☐ N3957X	Piper PA-32-300 Cherokee Six	32-7640003	
☐ N4485X	Piper PA-32-300 Cherokee Six	32-7640026	
☐ N5686V	Piper PA-32R-300 Lance	32R-7780361	
☐ N6117J	Piper PA-32-300 Cherokee Six	32-7640095	
☐ N6968J	Piper PA-32R-300 Lance	32R-7680397	
☐ N7718C	Piper PA-32-300 Cherokee Six	32-7640049	
☐ N8127Q	Piper PA-32-300 Six	32-7940269	
☐ N8493C	Piper PA-32R-300 Lance	32R-7680118	
☐ N9795C	Piper PA-32-300 Cherokee Six	32-7840118	
☐ N39636	Piper PA-32-300 Cherokee Six	32-7840172	

☐ N3523Y	Piper PA-31-350 Chieftain	31-7952115	
☐ N3835Z	Britten-Norman BN-2A-26 Islander	2010	ex G-BEJW
☐ N6314V	Helio H-295 Courier II	2534	
☐ N7333L	Piper PA-34-200T Seneca II	34-7670099	
☐ N27513	Piper PA-31-350 Chieftain	31-7852033	
☐ N29884	Britten-Norman BN-2A-26 Islander	847	ex G-HMCG
☐ N54732	Piper PA-31-350 Navajo Chieftain	31-7405254	

LAKE & PENINSULA AIRLINES — Port Alsworth, AK (PTA)

☐ N756BW	Cessna U206G Stationair	U20603969	FP/Wheels or skis
☐ N9530F	Cessna 208 Caravan I	20800088	
☐ N9602F	Cessna 208 Caravan I	20800103	
☐ N9909Z	Cessna U206G Stationair 6	U20606740	FP/Wheels or skis

LAKE CLARK AIR — Port Alsworth, AK (PTA)

☐ N76RA	Piper PA-31-350 Navajo Chieftain	31-7752089	ex N27212	
☐ N200VF	Piper PA-31-350 Navajo Chieftain	31-7405445	ex N61402	
☐ N733KD	Cessna U206G Stationair 6 II	U20604772		FP
☐ N991AK	Beech 99	U-28	ex N33TN	
☐ N8300Q	Cessna U206F Stationair II	U20603161		FP
☐ N27231	Piper PA-31-350 Navajo Chieftain	31-7752106		
☐ N70076	Cessna 207A Stationair 7 II	20700547		
☐ N91028	Cessna 207 Skywagon	20700019		

LAS VEGAS HELICOPTERS — Las Vegas NV (LAS)

☐ N701LV	Aérospatiale AS350BA	1546	ex N73MH
☐ N702LV	Eurocopter EC130B4	3845	ex N325MP
☐ N705LV	Aérospatiale AS350BA	1878	
☐ N707LV	Eurocopter EC130B4	4388	ex N578AM

LINDSAY AVIATION — Lindsay Air (LSY) — Buffalo-Intl, NY (BUF)

☐ N85DS	Cessna 310Q	310Q0080	ex N7580Q
☐ N3376G	Cessna 310R II	310R0818	
☐ N8669G	Cessna 310R II	310R0948	

LOGISTIC AIR — Reno, NV (RNO)

☐ N303TW	Boeing 747-257B	20116/112	ex LV-YSB	[MZJ]
☐ N741LA	Boeing 747-246B	19824/122	ex TF-ATB	[MZJ]
☐ 5U-ACE	Boeing 747-230B	20527/179	ex N745LA	[ROW]
☐ 5U-ACF	Boeing 747-146B	23150/601	ex (CP-2480)	
☐ 5U-ACG	Boeing 747-146B	22067/427	ex N553SW	
☐ N735LA	Boeing 737-268	20574/294	ex HZ-AGA	[RKT]
☐ N2409N	Boeing 737-242C (AvAero 3)	20496/268	ex C-FNAP	[QUE]
☐ N24089	Boeing 737-242C (AvAero 3)	20455/254	ex C-FNAQ	[MZJ]

LYNDEN AIR CARGO — Lynden (L2/LYC) — Anchorage-Intl, AK (ANC)

☐ N401LC	Lockheed L-382G-31C Hercules	4606	ex ZS-RSJ
☐ N402LC	Lockheed L-382G-35C Hercules	4698	ex ZS-JJA
☐ N403LC	Lockheed L-382G-31C Hercules	4590	ex N903SJ
☐ N404LC	Lockheed L-382G-38C Hercules	4763	ex N909SJ
☐ N405LC	Lockheed L-382G-69C Hercules	5025	ex ZS-OLG
☐ N406LC	Lockheed L-382G-35C Hercules	4676	ex ZS-JVL

LYNX AIR INTERNATIONAL — Lynx Flight (LXF) — Fort Lauderdale-Executive, FL (FXE)

| ☐ N61NE | Swearingen SA.227AC Metro III | AC-761B | | |
| ☐ N158SD | SAAB SF.340A | 340A-158 | ex N158CQ | [FLL] |

LYNX AVIATION — (SHA) — Denver, CO (DEN)

Operates de Havilland DHC-8-402Qs on behalf of Frontier Airlines, of which it is a wholly owned subsidiary.

M & N AVIATION — (W4) — San Juan-Munoz Marin Intl, PR (SJU)

☐ N409MN	Cessna 208B Caravan I	208B0846	ex N51666
☐ N410MN	Beech 1900C	UC-167	ex N167GL
☐ N787RA	Cessna 208B Caravan I	208B1019	ex N52144
☐ N1131G	Cessna 208B Caravan I	208B0661	
☐ N1241X	Cessna 208B Caravan I	208B0657	ex N52601

MARTINAIRE		**Martex (MRA)**		**Dallas-Addison, TX (ADS)**
☐ N78SA	Cessna 208B Caravan I	208B0467	ex N5058J	
☐ N162SA	Cessna 208B Caravan I	208B0548	ex N1219N	
☐ N1031P	Cessna 208B Caravan I	208B0404		
☐ N1037N	Cessna 208B Caravan I	208B0334	ex (C-GWFN)	
☐ N1116W	Cessna 208B Caravan I	208B0411		
☐ N1119V	Cessna 208B Caravan I	208B0383		
☐ N1120N	Cessna 208B Caravan I	208B0386		
☐ N1120W	Cessna 208B Caravan I	208B0388		
☐ N1324G	Cessna 208B Caravan I	208B0777	ex N5262Z	
☐ N4591B	Cessna 208B Caravan I	208B0137	ex (N997FE)	
☐ N4602B	Cessna 208B Caravan I	208B0140	ex (N999FE)	
☐ N4625B	Cessna 208B Caravan I	208B0159		
☐ N4655B	Cessna 208B Caravan I	208B0160		
☐ N4662B	Cessna 208B Caravan I	208B0161		
☐ N4687B	Cessna 208B Caravan I	208B0167		
☐ N4698B	Cessna 208B Caravan I	208B0175		
☐ N7580B	Cessna 208B Caravan I	208B0051	ex (N951FE)	
☐ N9331B	Cessna 208B Caravan I	208B0055	ex (N995FE)	
☐ N9471B	Cessna 208B Caravan I	208B0081		
☐ N9505B	Cessna 208B Caravan I	208B0085		
☐ N9525B	Cessna 208B Caravan I	208B0087		
☐ N9546B	Cessna 208B Caravan I	208B0126		
☐ N9594B	Cessna 208B Caravan I	208B0131		
☐ N9623B	Cessna 208B Caravan I	208B0138		
☐ N9634B	Cessna 208B Caravan I	208B0141		
☐ N9714B	Cessna 208B Caravan I	208B0153		
☐ N9738B	Cessna 208B Caravan I	208B0097		
☐ N9760B	Cessna 208B Caravan I	208B0102		
☐ N9761B	Cessna 208B Caravan I	208B0107		
☐ N9762B	Cessna 208B Caravan I	208B0109		
☐ N9766B	Cessna 208B Caravan I	208B0112		
☐ N9829B	Cessna 208B Caravan I	208B0116		
☐ N9956B	Cessna 208B Caravan I	208B0119		
☐ N354AE	Swearingen SA.227AC Metro III	AC-633	ex N3113C	
☐ N370AE	Swearingen SA.227AC Metro III	AC-506	ex N87FM	
☐ N592BA	Swearingen SA.227AC Metro III	AC-592	ex N384PH	
☐ N26932	Swearingen SA.227AC Metro III	AC-660	ex (N660AV)	

MAVERICK HELICOPTERS		**Las Vegas-McCarran Intl / Grand Canyon-National Park (LAS/GCN)**
☐ N801MH	Eurocopter EC130B4	3654
☐ N802MH	Eurocopter EC130B4	3707
☐ N803MH	Eurocopter EC130B4	3735
☐ N804MH	Eurocopter EC130B4	3750
☐ N805MH	Eurocopter EC130B4	3799
☐ N806MH	Eurocopter EC130B4	3833
☐ N807MH	Eurocopter EC130B4	3912
☐ N808MH	Eurocopter EC130B4	3914
☐ N809MH	Eurocopter EC130B4	3927
☐ N810MH	Eurocopter EC130B4	3949
☐ N812MH	Eurocopter EC130B4	3956
☐ N813MH	Eurocopter EC130B4	3967
☐ N814MH	Eurocopter EC130B4	4020
☐ N815MH	Eurocopter EC130B4	4022
☐ N816MH	Eurocopter EC130B4	4038
☐ N817MH	Eurocopter EC130B4	4125
☐ N818MH	Eurocopter EC130B4	4131
☐ N821MH	Eurocopter EC130B4	4134
☐ N822MH	Eurocopter EC130B4	4142
☐ N823MH	Eurocopter EC130B4	4158
☐ N824MH	Eurocopter EC130B4	4173
☐ N846MH	Eurocopter EC130B4	4248
☐ N847MH	Eurocopter EC130B4	4266
☐ N848MH	Eurocopter EC130B4	4290
☐ N849MH	Eurocopter EC130B4	4313
☐ N850MH	Eurocopter EC130B4	4327
☐ N851MH	Eurocopter EC130B4	4340
☐ N852MH	Eurocopter EC130B4	4356
☐ N853MH	Eurocopter EC130B4	4417
☐ N854MH	Eurocopter EC130B4	4433
☐ N856MH	Eurocopter EC130B4	4437
☐ N857MH	Eurocopter EC130B4	4457
☐ N858MH	Eurocopter EC130B4	4503
☐ N862MH	Eurocopter EC130B4	4545

☐ N567MA	Beech 1900D	UE-67	ex N67YV	
☐ N886MA	Beech 1900D	UE-86	ex N86YV	

MCCALL AVIATION   Mccall, ID (MYL)

☐ N848MA	Britten-Norman BN-2B-20 Islander	2210	ex 8P-TAJ	
☐ N7520N	Cessna TU206G Stationair	U20603663		

MCNEELY CHARTER SERVICE   Mid-South (MDS)
West Memphis-Municipal, AR/Malden, MO (AWM/MAW)

☐ N106GA	Beech Baron 58	TH-437	ex N4379W	
☐ N120SC	Swearingen SA.226TC Merlin IVA	AT-067	ex C-FJTL	
☐ N212SA	Cessna 208B Caravan I	208B0466		
☐ N262AG	Short SD.3-30	SH3120	ex 84-0473	
☐ N866D	Mitsubishi MU-2B-36 (MU-2L)	656	ex N666D	
☐ N2699Y	Swearingen SA.227AC Metro III	AC-666		

MESA AIRLINES   Air Shuttle (YV/ASH)   Phoenix-Sky Harbor Intl, AZ/Albuquerque-Intl, NM (PHX/ABQ)

☐ N138YV	Beech 1900D	UE-138		>AMW
☐ N139ZV	Beech 1900D	UE-139		>BSY
☐ N142ZV	Beech 1900D	UE-142		>AMW
☐ N144ZV	Beech 1900D	UE-144		>AMW
☐ N155ZV	Beech 1900D	UE-155		>AMW
☐ N161YV	Beech 1900D	UE-161		>AMW
☐ N162ZV	Beech 1900D	UE-162		>AMW
☐ N165YV	Beech 1900D	UE-165		>BSY
☐ N166YV	Beech 1900D	UE-166		>AMW
☐ N167YV	Beech 1900D	UE-167		>AMW
☐ N171ZV	Beech 1900D	UE-171		>BSY
☐ N174YV	Beech 1900D	UE-174	ex N17541	[ABQ]
☐ N176YV	Beech 1900D	UE-176		>AMW
☐ N237YV	Beech 1900D	UE-237		>BSY
☐ N242YV	Beech 1900D	UE-242		>AMW
☐ N244YV	Beech 1900D	UE-244		>AMW
☐ N10675	Beech 1900D	UE-229		>AMW

MESABA AIRLINES   Mesaba (XJ/MES)   Minneapolis-St Paul Intl, MN (MSP)

Operates services as part of the Delta Connection network, using flight numbers in the range 3000-3439.

MIAMI AIR INTERNATIONAL   Biscayne (LL/BSK)   Miami-Intl, FL (MIA)

☐ N732MA	Boeing 737-81Q/W	30618/830	ex D-AXLI	
☐ N733MA	Boeing 737-81Q/W	30619/856	ex G-OXLA	
☐ N734MA	Boeing 737-8Q8/W	30039/701	ex 5W-SAM	Billie
☐ N737KA	Boeing 737-7BX	30740/776	ex VH-VBT	
☐ N738MA	Boeing 737-8Q8/W	32799/1467		Diane
☐ N739MA	Boeing 737-8Q8/W	30670/1481		Ely
☐ N740EH	Boeing 737-8DC/W	34596/1875		
☐ N742MA	Boeing 737-83N/W	30675/898	ex N304TZ	
☐ N752MA	Boeing 737-48E	28198/2806	ex HL7509	
☐ N753MA	Boeing 737-48E	28053/2954	ex HL7518	Miami Heat c/s

MIAMI AIR LEASE   Miami-Opa Locka, FL (OPF)

☐ N41527	Convair 440-72	346	ex C-FPUM	

MID-ATLANTIC FREIGHT   (MDC)   Greensboro-Piedmont Triad Intl, NC (GSO)

☐ N1041L	Cessna 208B Caravan I	208B0337		
☐ N4698B	Cessna 208B Caravan I	208B0175	ex XC-AA35	
☐ N9525B	Cessna 208B Caravan I	208B0087		

MIDWEST AIRLINES   Midex (YX/MEP)
Appleton-Outagamie County, WI / Milwaukee-General Mitchell Intl, WI (ATW/MKE)

☐ N907ME	Boeing 717-2BL	55171/5121		[VCV]
☐ N922ME	Boeing 717-2BL	55184/5142		[VCV]
☐ N601ME	McDonnell-Douglas MD-88	49762/1624	ex (N159PL)	[BYH]
☐ N804ME	McDonnell-Douglas MD-81	48030/962	ex JA8459	[BYH]
☐ N808ME	McDonnell-Douglas MD-82	48070/999	ex JA8468	
☐ N809ME	McDonnell-Douglas MD-82	48071/1004	ex JA8469	[BYH]
☐ N812ME	McDonnell-Douglas MD-81	48006/966	ex OY-KIG	[BYH]
☐ N813ME	McDonnell-Douglas MD-81	48007/971	ex OY-KIH	[GSP]
☐ N814ME	McDonnell-Douglas MD-81	48010/992	ex SE-DMY	[BYH]

MIDWEST AVIATION — Midwest (MWT) — Marshall-Ryan Field, MN (MML)

☐ N185MV	Beech 200 Super King Air	BB-1034	ex N185MC	
☐ N382JM	Piper PA-32R-301T Saratoga SP	32R-8229026	ex D-EHJE	
☐ N727SC	Piper PA-31-350 Navajo Chieftain	31-7305110	ex G-BBZB	
☐ N3558X	Piper PA-31-350 Chieftain	31-8052073		
☐ N6894G	Piper PA-60 Aerostar 600	60-0905-8161256		
☐ N43305	Piper PA-32R-301 Saratoga	32R-8413002		

MIDWEST CONNECT — Skyway-Ex (AL/SYX) — Milwaukee-General Mitchell Intl, WI (MKE)

☐ N403SW	Canadair CRJ-200ER	7028	ex C-FMNB	SkyWest
☐ N407SW	Canadair CRJ-200ER	7034	ex C-FMNY	SkyWest
☐ N468CA	Canadair CRJ-200ER	7649	ex C-FMLI	SkyWest
☐ N471CA	Canadair CRJ-200ER	7655	ex C-FMNH	SkyWest
☐ N472CA	Canadair CRJ-200ER	7667	ex C-FMML	SkyWest
☐ N479CA	Canadair CRJ-200ER	7675	ex C-FMKW	SkyWest
☐ N494CA	Canadair CRJ-200ER	7765	ex C-FMKW	SkyWest
☐ N495CA	Canadair CRJ-200ER	7774	ex C-FMMT	SkyWest
☐ N496CA	Canadair CRJ-200ER	7791	ex C-FMMX	SkyWest
☐ N498CA	Canadair CRJ-200ER	7792	ex C-FMMY	SkyWest
☐ N506CA	Canadair CRJ-200ER	7793	ex C-FMNB	SkyWest
☐ N507CA	Canadair CRJ-200ER	7796	ex C-GZFC	SkyWest
☐ N699BR	Canadair CRJ-200ER	7801	ex C-FMLS	SkyWest
☐ N709BR	Canadair CRJ-200ER	7850	ex C-FMMW	SkyWest
☐ N983CA	Canadair CRJ-100ER	7169	ex C-FMNX	SkyWest
☐ N984CA	Canadair CRJ-100ER	7171	ex C-FMML	SkyWest
☐ N986CA	Canadair CRJ-100ER	7174	ex C-FMNX	SkyWest
☐ N988CA	Canadair CRJ-100ER	7204	ex C-FMMT	SkyWest
☐ N836RP	Embraer ERJ-135LR	145713	ex PT-SGQ	Chautauqua

MIDWEST HELICOPTER AIRWAYS — Hinsdale-Midwest Heliport, IL

☐ N129NH	Sikorsky S-58ET	58555	ex N47781
☐ N827MW	Sikorsky S-58ET	58827	ex C-GLOG
☐ N2256Z	Sikorsky S-58JT	58867	ex 57-1707
☐ N4247V	Sikorsky S-58ET	581547	
☐ N90561	Sikorsky S-58JT	581332	ex Bu148777

MINDEN AIR — Minden, NV (MEV)

☐ N446MA	British Aerospace 146 Srs.200	E2111	ex C-FBAO		Tanker
☐ N556MA	British Aerospace 146 Srs.200	E2106	ex C-GRNZ		Tanker
☐ N355MA	Lockheed P2V-7 Neptune (P-2H)	726-7229	ex 148344	55	Tanker - red colours
☐ N4692A	Lockheed P2V-7 Neptune (P-2H)	726-7247	ex 148357	48	Tanker - yellow colours

MOKULELE AIRLINES — Kailua/Kona-Keahole-Kona Intl, HI (KOA)

☐ N861MA	Cessna 208B Caravan I	208B0825	ex N98RR
☐ N862MA	Cessna 208B Caravan I	208B1138	ex N115KW
☐ N863MA	Cessna 208B Caravan I	208B1049	ex N208LR
☐ N864MA	Cessna 208B Caravan I	208B1275	ex N4115J

MOUNTAIN AIR CARGO — Mountain (MTN) — Kinston-Regional Jetport, NC (ISO)

☐ N2679U	Short SD.3-30	SH3071	ex (N330AE)
☐ N26288	Short SD.3-30	SH3074	ex G-BIYF

MOUNTAIN WEST HELICOPTERS — Provo-Municipal, UT (PVU)

☐ N317KA	Kaman K-1200 K-Max	A94-0025	

NATIONAL AIRLINES — (5M/MUA) — Detroit-Willow Run, MI (YIP)

☐ N919CA	Boeing 747-428BCF	25302/884	ex F-GISB		◆
☐ TF-NAC	Boeing 747-428MBCF	25238/872	ex N952CA		◆
☐ N259CA	Boeing 757-2Y0ER	26152/478	ex EI-CEY		◆
☐ N763CA	Boeing 757-2Y0ERCF	26154/486	ex EI-CEZ		◆
☐ N290MA	British Aerospace Jetstream 32EP	800	ex N370MT		
☐ N339TE	British Aerospace Jetstream 32	935	ex G-31-935		
☐ N343TE	British Aerospace Jetstream 32	955	ex G-31-955		
☐ N695MA	British Aerospace Jetstream 31	695	ex N169PC		
☐ N743PE	British Aerospace Jetstream 31	755	ex N755SP		
☐ N155CA	Douglas DC-8-73CF	46073/485	ex N803UP		

☐ N865F	Douglas DC-8-63F (BAC 3)	46088/464	ex TF-FLC		
☐ N872SJ	Douglas DC-8-71F	46040/449	ex HK-4294		
☐ N921R	Douglas DC-8-63F (BAC 3)	46145/548	ex N806WA		

NATIVE AMERICAN AIR SERVICES — Phoenix-Williams Gateway, AZ (CHD)

☐ N617LH	Aérospatiale AS350B2 AStar	2140			EMS
☐ N827NA	Aérospatiale AS350B3 AStar	3144			EMS
☐ N3819	Aérospatiale AS350B3 AStar	3877			EMS
☐ N41299	Aérospatiale AS350B3 AStar	3806			EMS
☐ N44925	Aérospatiale AS350B3 AStar	3838			EMS
☐ N317NA	Pilatus PC-12/45	223	ex N223PD		Air Ambulance
☐ N562NA	Pilatus PC-12/45	174	ex N174PC		Air Ambulance
☐ N613NA	Pilatus PC-12/45	197	ex N197PC		Air Ambulance
☐ N970NA	Pilatus PC-12/45	226	ex N308NA		Air Ambulance

NAVAIR — Minneapolis-Flying Cloud, MN (FCM)

☐ N16U	Beech E-18S	BA-394	ex N5660D		Frtr

NEPTUNE AVIATION SERVICES — Missoula-Intl, MT (MSO)

☐ N146FF	British Aerospace 146 Srs.200	E2048	ex N608AW		Tanker
☐ N122HP	Lockheed P2V-7 Neptune	726-7226	ex Bu148341		
☐ N128HP	Lockheed P2V-7 Neptune	726-7074	ex Bu140972		
☐ N443NA	Lockheed P2V-7 Neptune	726-7168	ex N139HP		
☐ N445NA	Lockheed P2V-7 Neptune	726-7102	ex N140HP		
☐ N807NA	Lockheed P2V-5 Neptune	426-5305	ex N1386K		07
☐ N1386C	Lockheed P2V-5 Neptune	426-5268	ex Bu128422		44
☐ N4235N	Lockheed SP-2H Neptune	726-7158	ex Bu144681		10
☐ N2216S	Lockheed P2V-7 Neptune	726-7231	ex Bu148346		
☐ N2218E	Lockheed P2V-7 Neptune	726-7246	ex Bu148356		
☐ N2218Q	Lockheed P2V-7 Neptune	726-7255	ex Bu148359		
☐ N9855F	Lockheed P2V-5 Neptune	426-5326	ex Bu131445		06
☐ N14447	Lockheed P2V-7 Neptune	826-8010	ex RCAF 24110		11
☐ N96264	Lockheed P2V-5 Neptune	426-5192	ex Bu128346		12
☐ N96278	Lockheed P2V-5 Neptune	426-5340	ex Bu131459		05

NEW ENGLAND AIRLINES — New England (EJ/NEA) — Westerly-State, RI (WST)

☐ N123NE	Britten-Norman BN-2A-26 Islander	46	ex G-BJSA		
☐ N404WB	Britten-Norman BN-2A-26 Islander	564	ex N304SK		
☐ N345CS	Piper PA-32-300 Cherokee Six	32-7640043	ex N345ES		
☐ N406WB	Piper PA-32-300 Cherokee Six	32-7640058	ex N8303C		
☐ N408WB	Piper PA-32-300 Cherokee Six	32-7240092	ex N4885T		
☐ N598JA	Britten-Norman BN-2A Islander	66			

NEW MEXICO AIRLINES

☐ N306PW	Cessna 208B Caravan I	208B1240	ex N208TD		

NORD AVIATION — Santa Teresa-Dona Ana County, NM (EPZ)

☐ N321L	Douglas C-117D	43345	ex N307SF	Frtr	
☐ N620NA	Douglas DC-6A	44677/527	ex N32RU	Frtr	
☐ N738WB	Beech D50C Twin Bonanza	DH-286		Frtr	
☐ N57626	Douglas DC-3	4564	ex NC57626	Frtr	

NORTH AMERICAN AIRLINES — North American (NA/NAO) — New York-JFK Intl, NY (JFK)

☐ N750NA	Boeing 757-28A	26277/658		Deidre Stiehm	
☐ N752NA	Boeing 757-28A	28174/865	ex N1795B	Alisa Ferrara	
☐ N754NA	Boeing 757-28A	29381/958			
☐ N755NA	Boeing 757-28A	30043/925	ex N523NA	John Plueger	
☐ N756NA	Boeing 757-28A	32448/967		Claudette Abrahams	
☐ N760NA	Boeing 767-39HER	26257/488	ex N164LF	Tom Cygan	
☐ N764NA	Boeing 767-328ER	27135/493	ex N135EL		
☐ N765NA	Boeing 767-306ER	28098/607	ex PH-BZE		
☐ N767NA	Boeing 767-324ER	27569/601	ex N569NB	Janice M	
☐ N768NA	Boeing 767-36NER	29898/754	ex N898GE	Lisa Caroline	

NORTH STAR AIR CARGO — Sky Box (SBX) — Milwaukee-General Mitchell Intl, WI (MKE)

☐ N50NS	Short SC.7 Skyvan	SH1856	ex N50GA		Frtr
☐ N51NS	Short SC.7 Skyvan	SH1843	ex N20DA		Frtr
☐ N101WA	Short SC.7 Skyvan	SH1859	ex (PH-DAF)		Frtr
☐ N731E	Short SC.7 Skyvan	SH1853	ex N80JJ		Frtr

NORTH STAR AVIATION — Boca Raton, FL (BCT)

☐ N153KM	British Aerospace Jetstream 4101	41053	ex ZK-JSN	
☐ N308UE	British Aerospace Jetstream 4101	41023	ex G-4-023	
☐ N679AS	British Aerospace Jetstream 4101	41056	ex N156KM	
☐ N680AS	British Aerospace Jetstream 4101	41030	ex N410JA	

NORTHERN AIR CARGO — Yukon (NC/NAC) — Anchorage-Intl, AK (ANC)

☐ N779TA	Douglas DC-6A	45529/1035	ex PP-LFC	[FAI]
☐ N2907F	Douglas C-118A	44636/574	ex 53-3265	[FAI]
☐ N310DL	Boeing 737-232	23082/1006	ex OD-LMB	◆
☐ N320DL	Boeing 737-232F (Nordam 3)	23092/1023		<JetGlobal
☐ N321DL	Boeing 737-232F (Nordam 3)	23093/1024		<JetGlobal
☐ N322DL	Boeing 737-232F (Nordam 3)	23094/1026		<JetGlobal

NORTHWEST HELICOPTERS — Olympia, WA (OLM)

☐ N64NH	Bell UH-1H	4379	ex 64-13672
☐ N65NH	Bell UH-1H	5078	ex 65-10034
☐ N66NH	Bell UH-1H	5624	ex 66-1141
☐ N67NH	Bell UH-1H	9486	ex 67-17282
☐ N71NH	Bell UH-1H	11682	ex 69-16267
☐ N78NW	Bell UH-1H	9266	ex N342WN
☐ N79NW	Bell UH-1H	4417	ex 64-13710
☐ N111DR	Bell UH-1H	4406	ex N83NW
☐ N114DR	Bell UH-1H	5275	ex N85NW
☐ N117DR	Bell UH-1H	5204	ex N95NW
☐ N166DR	Bell UH-1H	9143	ex N86NW
☐ N175SF	Bell EH-1H	12290	ex 69-16713
☐ N176SF	Bell EH-1H	11757	ex 69-15469
☐ N313B	Bell UH-1H	4057	ex 63-08765
☐ N602WA	Bell UH-1H	4746	ex 65-9702
☐ N5517N	Bell UH-1H	9589	ex 67-17391
☐ N6165X	Bell UH-1K	6307	ex 157183
☐ N7515S	Bell UH-1H		ex 69-15328
☐ N7515Z	Bell UH-1H		ex 70-16336

NORTHWEST SEAPLANES — Mariner (2G/MRR) — Seattle-Lake Union, WA/Seattle-Renton (LKS/RNT)

☐ N90YC	de Havilland DHC-2 Beaver	1338	ex N127WA	FP
☐ N67681	de Havilland DHC-2 Beaver	1158	ex N215LU	FP
☐ N67684	de Havilland DHC-2 Beaver	1208	ex N67894	FP
☐ N67685	de Havilland DHC-2 Beaver	1250	ex N128WA	FP
☐ N67689	de Havilland DHC-2 Beaver	1242	ex N67675	FP

OMNI AIR INTERNATIONAL — Omni (OY/OAE) — Tulsa-Intl, OK (TUL)

☐ N558AX	Boeing 757-23N	27971/690	ex N514AT	
☐ N639AX	Boeing 757-28A	24368/213	ex N368CG	
☐ N342AX	Boeing 767-328ER	27136/497	ex N225LF	
☐ N351AX	Boeing 767-33AER	27908/578	ex I-DEIF	
☐ N378AX	Boeing 767-33AER	28147/622	ex I-DEIL	
☐ N396AX	Boeing 767-319ER	26264/555	ex N411LF	◆
☐ N108AX	Douglas MD-10-30	47927/190	ex N49082	
☐ N270AX	Douglas DC-10-30	48318/446	ex N353WL	
☐ N522AX	Douglas DC-10-30ER	48315/436	ex N243NW	
☐ N531AX	Douglas DC-10-30ERF	48316/437	ex N244NW	
☐ N540AX	Douglas DC-10-30	46595/299	ex D-ADPO	[VCV]
☐ N603AX	Douglas DC-10-30	48267/434	ex N238NW	
☐ N612AX	Douglas DC-10-30ER	48290/435	ex N239NW	
☐ N621AX	Douglas DC-10-30ER	48319/438	ex N240NW	
☐ N630AX	Douglas DC-10-30	46596/301	ex D-ADQO	[VCV]
☐ N720AX	Douglas DC-10-30	48252/342	ex D-ADSO	
☐ N810AX	Douglas DC-10-30ER	48265/345	ex F-GPVC	
☐ N59083	Douglas DC-10-30	47926/170	ex OO-SLG	[VCV]

OMNIFLIGHT HELICOPTERS — Dallas-Addison, TX (ADS)

☐ N93CH	Bell 206L-3 LongRanger III	51314		
☐ N94CH	Bell 206L-4 LongRanger IV	52070		
☐ N95CH	Bell 206L-4 LongRanger IV	52195		
☐ N154MW	Bell 206L-4 LongRanger IV	52154	ex PT-YBQ	
☐ N206AZ	Bell 206L-3 LongRanger III	51007	ex N725RE	
☐ N224LF	Bell 206L-1 LongRanger II	45199	ex N5013Y	EMS

☐ N314LS	Bell 206L-3 LongRanger III	51006	ex N2210H	EMS
☐ N112LL	MBB BK-117A-3	7038	ex N4493X	
☐ N117AP	MBB BK-117B-1	7144	ex N311LS	
☐ N117M	MBB BK-117A-3	7023	ex N39251	EMS
☐ N117MH	MBB BK-117A-3	7112	ex N627MB	EMS
☐ N117MK	MBB BK-117B-2	7196	ex N117BK	EMS
☐ N117NG	MBB BK-117A-4	7083	ex N312LF	EMS
☐ N117UC	MBB BK-117B-1	7206	ex N214AE	EMS
☐ N117VU	MBB BK-117B-1	7211	ex N8194S	
☐ N118LL	MBB BK-117A-3	7097	ex N117SJ	
☐ N170MC	MBB BK-117B-1	7217	ex N7161S	
☐ N171MU	MBB BK-117A-4	7138	ex N313LF	
☐ N217MC	MBB BK-117B-1	7195	ex N54113	EMS Op for Mayo Foundation
☐ N317MC	MBB BK-117C-1	7505	ex N117AE	EMS Op for Mayo Foundation
☐ N460H	MBB BK-117B-1	7142	ex N90266	EMS
☐ N504LH	MBB BK-117A-3	7061	ex N312LS	
☐ N527MB	MBB BK-117A-3	7103	ex D-HBPX	
☐ N711FC	MBB BK-117A-4	7070	ex N311LF	EMS
☐ N909LC	MBB BK-117B-1	7013	ex N113LL	♦
☐ N911MZ	MBB BK-117A-3	7098	ex N117UC	
☐ N1140H	MBB BK-117A-3	7078	ex N212AE	
☐ N75LV	Beech B200 Super King Air	BB-1075	ex C-GTDY	EMS
☐ N222HX	Bell 222UT	47533	ex N3201W	
☐ N277LF	Bell 222UT	47520	ex N911LW	EMS
☐ N350AZ	Aérospatiale AS350B2 AStar	3127	ex N4073A	
☐ N350GR	Aérospatiale AS350B AStar	3140	ex N911GF	EMS
☐ N40751	Aérospatiale AS350B2 AStar	3154		

PACE AIRLINES *Pace (Y5/PCE)* **Winston-Salem/Smith Reynolds, NC (INT)**

☐ N373PA	Boeing 737-3Y0	23749/1389	ex N749AP	The Steffie Pacemaker
☐ N583CC	Boeing 737-291 (Nordam 3)	21069/415	ex N15255	
☐ N737DX	Boeing 737-408	24804/1851	ex TF-FIC	
☐ N801DM	Boeing 757-256/W	26240/561	ex N286CD	Op for Dallas Mavericks

PACIFIC AIRWAYS *(3F)* **Ketchikan-Harbor SPB, AK (WFB)**

☐ N12UA	de Havilland DHC-2 Beaver	700	ex C-GSIN	FP
☐ N96DG	de Havilland DHC-2 Beaver	702	ex N99132	FP
☐ N264P	de Havilland DHC-2 Beaver	464	ex N23RF	FP
☐ N5595M	de Havilland DHC-2 Beaver	1571	ex 105	FP
☐ N9290Z	de Havilland DHC-2 Beaver	1387	ex 58-2055	FP
☐ N9294Z	de Havilland DHC-2 Beaver	1379	ex 58-2047	FP

PACIFIC HELICOPTERS **Kahului-International, HI (OGG)**

☐ N1076C	Bell TH-1F	6436	ex N64F	
☐ N4963F	Bell TH-1L	6404	ex Bu157809	
☐ N6131P	Bell UH-1H	5787	ex 66-16093	
☐ N6226H	Bell UH-1B	3115	ex 66-14420	
☐ N8079E	Bell UH-1H	4762	ex 65-9718	
☐ N80780	Bell UH-1H	4527	ex 64-13820	
☐ N64F	Bell 204B	2027	ex N103CR	
☐ N261F	Sikorsky S-61N	61771	ex G-BEOO	
☐ N262F	Sikorsky S-61N	61364	ex V8-UDU	
☐ N263F	Sikorsky S-61N	61488	ex V8-UDQ	
☐ N503AH	Bell 206B JetRanger	686	ex C-FAOL	
☐ N622F	Bell 222U	47543	ex C-GIVU	
☐ N866JH	Ted Smith Aerostar 601	61-0042-83	ex N7471S	
☐ N5743H	Bell 206B JetRanger III	3042		
☐ N6651H	Bell 206L-1 LongRanger II	45211		
☐ N8649Z	Cessna TP206C Super Skylane	P206-0449		

PACIFIC WINGS *Tsunami (LW/NMI)* **Kahului-Intl, HI (OGG)**

☐ N301PW	Cessna 208B Caravan I	208B0983	
☐ N302PW	Cessna 208B Caravan I	208B0984	
☐ N303PW	Cessna 208B Caravan I	208B0985	
☐ N304PW	Cessna 208B Caravan I	208B0833	ex N699BA
☐ N305PW	Cessna 208B Caravan I	208B0828	ex N297DF

PAPILLON GRAND CANYON AIRWAYS *(HI)* **Grand Canyon-National Park, AZ, (GCN)**

☐ N197AE	Aérospatiale AS350B2 AStar	3909	36
☐ N425EH	Aérospatiale AS350B2 AStar	4197	35

☐ N890PA	Aérospatiale AS350B2 AStar	4554		37
☐ N891PA	Aérospatiale AS350B2 AStar	4557		33
☐ N177PA	Bell 206L-1 LongRanger III	45194	ex N992PA	17
☐ N178PA	Bell 206L-1 LongRanger III	45319	ex F-ODUB	8
☐ N333ER	Bell 206L-1 LongRanger III	45203		12
☐ N1075S	Bell 206L-1 LongRanger III	45366		10
☐ N2072M	Bell 206L-1 LongRanger II	45720		2
☐ N3893U	Bell 206L-3 LongRanger III	51020		9
☐ N3895D	Bell 206L-1 LongRanger II	45590		1
☐ N4227E	Bell 206L-1 LongRanger III	45702	ex N725RE	18
☐ N5743C	Bell 206L-1 LongRanger II	45474		23
☐ N5745Y	Bell 206L-1 LongRanger III	45531		11
☐ N10761	Bell 206L-1 LongRanger II	45381		27
☐ N20316	Bell 206L-1 LongRanger II	45687		21
☐ N22425	Bell 206L-1 LongRanger II	45743		29
☐ N27694	Bell 206L-1 LongRanger II	45282		4
☐ N38885	Bell 206L-1 LongRanger II	45726		20
☐ N50046	Bell 206L-1 LongRanger II	45173		28
☐ N57491	Bell 206L-1 LongRanger II	45505		15
☐ N130GC	Eurocopter EC130B4	3562		41
☐ N130PH	Eurocopter EC130B4	3670		38
☐ N132GC	Eurocopter EC130B4	3756		43
☐ N133GC	Eurocopter EC130B4	3883		48
☐ N133PH	Eurocopter EC130B4	3939		49
☐ N135PH	Eurocopter EC130B4	3695		39
☐ N136PH	Eurocopter EC130B4	3896		46
☐ N137PH	Eurocopter EC130B4	3775		40
☐ N138PH	Eurocopter EC130B4	3790		44
☐ N151GC	Eurocopter EC130B4	4402		51
☐ N152GC	Eurocopter EC130B4	4448		52
☐ N175PA	Bell 407	53154		
☐ N368PA	MD Helicopters MD900 Explorer	900-00012	ex N901CF	
☐ N407PA	Bell 407	53567	ex N16FR	
☐ N616AC	Bell 407	53354	ex N407BR	

PARAGON AIR EXPRESS — Paragon Express (PGX) — Nashville-Intl, TN (BNA)

☐ N703PA	Cessna 208B Caravan I	208B0776	ex N5262B	Frtr

PARAMOUNT JET — Little Rock-Adams Field, AR (LIT)

☐ N406BN	Boeing 727-291F (Raisbeck 3)	19991/521	ex HI-630CA	no titles

PENAIR — Peninsula(KS/PEN) — Anchorage-Intl, AK (ANC)

☐ N4327P	Piper PA-32-301 Saratoga	32-8406002		
☐ N8212H	Piper PA-32-301 Saratoga	32-8006046		
☐ N8305H	Piper PA-32-301 Saratoga	32-8106017		
☐ N8402S	Piper PA-32-301 Saratoga	32-8106075		
☐ N8470Y	Piper PA-32-301 Saratoga	32-8206012		
☐ N81052	Piper PA-32-301 Saratoga	32-8206023		
☐ N81844	Piper PA-32-301 Saratoga	32-8006012		
☐ N82455	Piper PA-32-301 Saratoga	32-8006079		
☐ N109XJ	SAAB SF.340A	340A-109	ex N109AE	
☐ N665PA	SAAB SF.340B	340B-181	ex N590MA	
☐ N675PA	SAAB SF.340B	340B-206	ex N593MA	Spirit of Bristol Bay
☐ N676PA	SAAB SF.340B	340B-316	ex VH-LIH	
☐ N677PA	SAAB SF.340B	340B-328	ex VH-XDZ	
☐ N679PA	SAAB SF.340B	340B-345	ex N345CV	
☐ N685PA	SAAB SF.340B	340B-212	ex N594MA	Spirit of the Aleutians
☐ N640PA	Swearingen SA.227AC Metro III	AC-759B	ex N306NE	Spirit of the Aleutians
☐ N892DC	Swearingen SA.227DC Metro 23	DC-892B	ex C-GAFO	
☐ N15PR	Piper PA-31-350 Chieftain	31-8352011	ex SE-KPC	
☐ N28KE	Piper PA-31-350 Chieftain	31-8152049	ex C-GVSX	
☐ N700RD	Piper PA-31T3 T-1040	31T-5575001	ex HP-1101P	
☐ N741	Grumman G-21A Goose	B-97		
☐ N750PA	Cessna 208B Caravan I	208B0628		
☐ N7811	Grumman G-21A Goose	B-122		
☐ N9304F	Cessna 208 Caravan I	20800008		
☐ N9481F	Cessna 208 Caravan I	20800070		
☐ N22932	Grumman G-21A Goose	B-139	ex CF-WCP	

PHI - PETROLEUM HELICOPTERS   *Petroleum (PHM)*   Lafayette-Regional, LA (LFT)

☐ N151AE	Aérospatiale AS350B3 AStar	3814		
☐ N153AE	Aérospatiale AS350B3 AStar	3829		
☐ N350LG	Aérospatiale AS350B3 AStar	3690	ex N499AE	
☐ N351LG	Aérospatiale AS350B3 AStar	3722	ex N580AE	
☐ N352LG	Aérospatiale AS350B3 AStar	3777	ex N142AE	
☐ N353P	Aérospatiale AS350B2 AStar	3885	ex N194AE	
☐ N354P	Aérospatiale AS350B2 AStar	3886	ex N196AE	
☐ N498AE	Aérospatiale AS350B3 AStar	3687		
☐ N585AE	Aérospatiale AS350B3 AStar	3736		
☐ N587AE	Aérospatiale AS350B3 AStar	3730		
☐ N590AE	Aérospatiale AS350B3 AStar	3733		
☐ N732AE	Aérospatiale AS350B2 AStar	2873	ex N4000L	EMS
☐ N946AE	Aérospatiale AS350B2 AStar	3351	ex N855PH	EMS
☐ N945AE	Aérospatiale AS350B2 AStar	3004	ex N40466	EMS
☐ N954AE	Aérospatiale AS350B2 AStar	3248	ex N854PH	EMS
☐ N956AE	Aérospatiale AS350B2 AStar	3352	ex N856PH	
☐ N972AE	Aérospatiale AS350B3 AStar	3234		EMS
☐ N973AE	Aérospatiale AS350B3 AStar	3229	ex C-GFIH	EMS
☐ N974AE	Aérospatiale AS350B2 AStar	2653	ex N350BZ	
☐ N975AE	Aérospatiale AS350B2 AStar	2777	ex N6095S	
☐ N4031L	Aérospatiale AS350B2 AStar	2907		Based Antarctica
☐ N4036H	Aérospatiale AS350B2 AStar	2919		Based Antarctica
☐ N139PH	Agusta AW139	31121		◆
☐ N379SH	Agusta AW139	41253		◆
☐ N380SH	Agusta AW139	41254		◆
☐ N30KH	Bell 206L-3 LongRanger III	51527	ex HK-3726X	
☐ N45RP	Bell 206L-1 LongRanger II	45521	ex HC-BXS	
☐ N49EA	Bell 206L-3 LongRanger III	51507	ex D-HHSG	
☐ N92MT	Bell 206L-3 LongRanger III	51175	ex CC-ETG	
☐ N202PH	Bell 206L-3 LongRanger III	51076	ex N31821	
☐ N203PH	Bell 206L-3 LongRanger III	51520	ex N31077	
☐ N204PH	Bell 206L-3 LongRanger III	51465	ex N41791	
☐ N205FC	Bell 206L-3 LongRanger III	51130		
☐ N206FS	Bell 206L-3 LongRanger III	51506	ex C-FLNW	
☐ N209PH	Bell 206L-3 LongRanger III	51531	ex N8594X	◆
☐ N214PH	Bell 206L-3 LongRanger III	51131	ex N4835	
☐ N215PH	Bell 206L-3 LongRanger III	51575	ex N53119	
☐ N219PH	Bell 206L-3 LongRanger III	51509	ex N8593X	
☐ N221PH	Bell 206L-3 LongRanger III	51494	ex N8590X	◆
☐ N266P	Bell 206L-4 LongRanger IV	52271	ex N3020J	
☐ N269AE	Bell 206L-3 LongRanger III	51530	ex N3116P	
☐ N306PH	Bell 206L-1 LongRanger II	45411	ex N11027	
☐ N363BH	Bell 206L-3 LongRanger III	51345	ex N997PT	
☐ N436PH	Bell 206L-3 LongRanger III	51436	ex EI-CIO	
☐ N593AE	Bell 206L-2 LongRanger II	45421	ex N513EH	
☐ N595AE	Bell 206L-1 LongRanger II	45244	ex N5019F	EMS
☐ N668PH	Bell 206L-3 LongRanger III	51487	ex N8589X	
☐ N979BH	Bell 206L-3 LongRanger III	51403	ex N998PT	
☐ N2249Z	Bell 206L-1 LongRanger II	45753		
☐ N3107N	Bell 206L-3 LongRanger III	51512		
☐ N3108E	Bell 206L-3 LongRanger III	51498		
☐ N3116L	Bell 206L-3 LongRanger III	51529		
☐ N3207Q	Bell 206L-3 LongRanger III	51540	ex C-FLYD	
☐ N4180F	Bell 206L-3 LongRanger III	51469		
☐ N4282Z	Bell 206L-3 LongRanger III	51499		
☐ N5014V	Bell 206L-1 LongRanger II	45217		
☐ N6160Y	Bell 206L-3 LongRanger III	51609	ex C-FOYN	
☐ N6160Z	Bell 206L-3 LongRanger III	51610		
☐ N6251Y	Bell 206L-3 LongRanger III	51556	ex C-FLYG	
☐ N6603X	Bell 206L-3 LongRanger III	51412		
☐ N6610C	Bell 206L-3 LongRanger III	51425		
☐ N6748D	Bell 206L-3 LongRanger III	51106	ex HC-BVB	
☐ N7074W	Bell 206L-4 LongRanger IV	52033		
☐ N7077F	Bell 206L-4 LongRanger IV	52038		
☐ N8587X	Bell 206L-3 LongRanger III	51464		
☐ N8588X	Bell 206L-3 LongRanger III	51486		
☐ N8591X	Bell 206L-3 LongRanger III	51495		
☐ N21497	Bell 206L-3 LongRanger III	51518		
☐ N32041	Bell 206L-3 LongRanger III	51539	ex C-FLXL	
☐ N54641	Bell 206L-3 LongRanger III	51184	ex JA9471	
☐ N62127	Bell 206L-4 LongRanger IV	52023		

☐ N401PH	Bell 407	53615	ex N407MD	
☐ N402PH	Bell 407	53159		
☐ N403PH	Bell 407	53267	ex N8595X	
☐ N404PH	Bell 407	53188		
☐ N406PH	Bell 407	53198		
☐ N407H	Bell 407	53464	ex N407XM	
☐ N407PH	Bell 407	53003	ex C-FWRD	
☐ N408PH	Bell 407	53228		
☐ N409PH	Bell 407	53626	ex N45655	
☐ N410PH	Bell 407	53636	ex C-FDXK	
☐ N411PH	Bell 407	53637		
☐ N415PH	Bell 407	53390	ex N492PH	
☐ N417PH	Bell 407	53038		
☐ N418PH	Bell 407	53640	ex N418PH	
☐ N420PH	Bell 407	53747	ex C-FLZR	
☐ N421PH	Bell 407	53749	ex C-FLZP	
☐ N422PH	Bell 407	53675		
☐ N424PH	Bell 407	53682		
☐ N426PH	Bell 407	53751		
☐ N428PH	Bell 407	53754		
☐ N429PH	Bell 407	53772		
☐ N432PH	Bell 407	53681	ex N431P	
☐ N433PH	Bell 407	53679	ex N433P	
☐ N434PH	Bell 407	53773		
☐ N447PH	Bell 407	53114		
☐ N467PH	Bell 407	53142		
☐ N490PH	Bell 407	53378	ex N6387C	
☐ N491PH	Bell 407	53386	ex N6390Y	
☐ N493PH	Bell 407	53393		
☐ N494PH	Bell 407	53396		
☐ N495PH	Bell 407	53397		
☐ N496PH	Bell 407	53398		
☐ N498PH	Bell 407	53399		
☐ N501PH	Bell 407	53401		
☐ N510PH	Bell 407	53209		
☐ N612PH	Bell 407	53199		
☐ N719PH	Bell 407	53266		
☐ N720PH	Bell 407	53277		
☐ N721PH	Bell 407	53278		
☐ N722PH	Bell 407	53288		
☐ N723PH	Bell 407	53283		
☐ N724PH	Bell 407	53327		
☐ N740PH	Bell 407	53435	ex N6077V	
☐ N741PH	Bell 407	53457		
☐ N742PH	Bell 407	53461		
☐ N807PH	Bell 407	53656	ex C-FFQS	
☐ N4999	Bell 407	53323		
☐ N107X	Bell 412SP	33113		
☐ N108X	Bell 412SP	33115		
☐ N126PA	Bell 412	33168		
☐ N142PH	Bell 412SP	33150	ex HL9236	
☐ N143PH	Bell 412SP	33134	ex N800Y	
☐ N412SM	Bell 412EP	36213	ex N426DR	EMS
☐ N412UM	Bell 412SP	33023	ex N3911L	
☐ N413UM	Bell 412	33012	ex N3893P	
☐ N1202T	Bell 412SP	33112	ex D-HHOF	
☐ N2014K	Bell 412	33020	ex YV-922C	
☐ N2148K	Bell 412SP	36001		
☐ N2149S	Bell 412SP	36002		
☐ N2258F	Bell 412	33073	ex YV-1030C	
☐ N2261D	Bell 412SP	33076		
☐ N3893L	Bell 412	33006	ex C-FOQL	
☐ N3893N	Bell 412	33010		
☐ N6559Z	Bell 412SP	36019		
☐ N7128R	Bell 412SP	36007		
☐ N21498	Bell 412SP	36003		
☐ N22347	Bell 412SP	36005	ex XA-RSL	
☐ N22608	Bell 412	33075		
☐ N33008	Bell 412SP	36004		
☐ N301PH	Eurocopter EC135P2	0355		
☐ N302PH	Eurocopter EC135P2	0364	EMS	
☐ N303PH	Eurocopter EC135P2	0372		
☐ N304PH	Eurocopter EC135P2	0386		
☐ N305PH	Eurocopter EC135P2	0395		
☐ N307PH	Eurocopter EC135P2	0398		

☐ N308PH	Eurocopter EC135P2	0401		
☐ N309PH	Eurocopter EC135P2	0403		
☐ N311PH	Eurocopter EC135P2	0413		
☐ N312PH	Eurocopter EC135P2	0404		PHi Air Medical
☐ N314PH	Eurocopter EC135P2	0409		
☐ N317PH	Eurocopter EC135P2	0423		
☐ N320PH	Eurocopter EC135P2	0430		
☐ N323PH	Eurocopter EC135P2	0434		
☐ N324PH	Eurocopter EC135P2	0571		
☐ N327PH	Eurocopter EC135P2	0445	ex D-HECB	
☐ N328PH	Eurocopter EC135P2	0450	ex D-HECG	
☐ N330PH	Eurocopter EC135P2	0514		
☐ N332PH	Eurocopter EC135P2	0519		
☐ N343PH	Eurocopter EC135P2	0456		
☐ N344PH	Eurocopter EC135P2	0459		
☐ N376PH	Eurocopter EC135P2	0523		
☐ N380PH	Eurocopter EC135P2	0593		
☐ N381PH	Eurocopter EC135P2	0611		
☐ N382PH	Eurocopter EC135P2	0618		
☐ N383PH	Eurocopter EC135P2	0622		
☐ N800PH	MBB Bo.105CBS-4	S-800	ex N133AE	
☐ N851PH	MBB Bo.105CBS-4	S-851	ex N137AE	
☐ N868PH	MBB Bo.105CB	S-668	ex N205UC	
☐ N4573B	MBB Bo.105S	S-673		
☐ N5421E	MBB Bo.105CBS-4	S-806		
☐ N6607K	MBB Bo.105CBS-4	S-841		
☐ N8199J	MBB Bo.105CBS-4	S-826		
☐ N9190Y	MBB Bo.105CB	S-669		
☐ N54191	MBB Bo.105CBS-4	S-804		
☐ N81832	MBB Bo.105CBS-4	S-828		
☐ N81992	MBB Bo.105CBS-4	S-827		
☐ N89H	Sikorsky S-76C	760406		
☐ N127FH	Sikorsky S-76A	760063	ex N402M	
☐ N274X	Sikorsky S-76C+	760440	ex N278X	
☐ N276X	Sikorsky S-76C	760405		
☐ N478X	Sikorsky S-76C	760493		
☐ N709P	Sikorsky S-76C-2	760716		
☐ N718P	Sikorsky S-76C-2	760686		
☐ N725P	Sikorsky S-76C-2	760688		
☐ N734P	Sikorsky S-76C	760600	ex N70936	
☐ N738P	Sikorsky S-76C-2	760668		
☐ N745P	Sikorsky S-76C	760619		
☐ N746P	Sikorsky S-76C	760623		
☐ N759P	Sikorsky S-76C-2	760690		
☐ N760PH	Sikorsky S-76A	760078	ex VH-BJR	
☐ N761PH	Sikorsky S-76A	760224	ex VH-BJS	
☐ N762P	Sikorsky S-76A	760060	ex N76NY	
☐ N763P	Sikorsky S-76A	760166	ex C-GHJT	
☐ N764P	Sikorsky S-76A	760276	ex N913UK	
☐ N766P	Sikorsky S-76C	760594		
☐ N767P	Sikorsky S-76C++	760599		
☐ N769P	Sikorsky S-76C	760671		
☐ N776P	Sikorsky S-76A	760275	ex N911UK	
☐ N776PH	Sikorsky S-76C	760505	ex N505PH	
☐ N778P	Sikorsky S-76A	760035	ex N4253S	
☐ N779P	Sikorsky S-76C+	760655	ex N4501G	
☐ N784P	Sikorsky S-76C	760634		
☐ N785P	Sikorsky S-76C	760635		
☐ N786P	Sikorsky S-76C	760643		
☐ N787P	Sikorsky S-76C-2	760692		
☐ N790P	Sikorsky S-76C	760675	ex N45138	
☐ N792P	Sikorsky S-76A	760193	ex N792CH	
☐ N796P	Sikorsky S-76C-2	760681		
☐ N798P	Sikorsky S-76C-2	760685		
☐ N911MJ	Sikorsky S-76A	760231	ex N3122D	
☐ N1545K	Sikorsky S-76A	760047		
☐ N1545X	Sikorsky S-76A	760050		
☐ N1546G	Sikorsky S-76A	760076		
☐ N1546K	Sikorsky S-76A	760082		
☐ N5435V	Sikorsky S-76A	760158		
☐ PP-MCS	Sikorsky S-76A	760077	ex N1547D	Based Brazil
☐ PR-CHG	Sikorsky S-76C+	760658	ex N658A	Based Brazil
☐ PR-CHI	Sikorsky S-76C+	760670	ex N4514K	Based Brazil
☐ N192PH	Sikorsky S-92	920006		

☐ N292PH	Sikorsky S-92	920008	
☐ N392PH	Sikorsky S-92	920015	
☐ N492PH	Sikorsky S-92	920016	ex N592PH
☐ N592PH	Sikorsky S-92A	920027	
☐ N692PH	Sikorsky S-92A	920028	
☐ N925PH	Sikorsky S-92A	920118	
☐ N992PH	Sikorsky S-92A	920055	ex N4502G

☐ N217AE	MBB BK-117B-2	7152	ex N217UC	
☐ N217PH	MBB BK-117A-4	7092	ex N911RZ	
☐ N226PH	Bell 212	31106	ex N27805	
☐ N227PH	Bell 212	30953	ex N3131S	
☐ N230H	Bell 230	23004	ex N500HG	◆
☐ N241PH	Beech B200 Super King Air	BB-1182	ex N416CS	
☐ N393AA	Bell 230	23028	ex N14UH	◆
☐ N430X	Bell 430	49058		
☐ N430XM	Bell 430	49073	ex N9125G	
☐ N911TL	MBB BK-117B-1	7198	ex N911AF	
☐ N2275Y	Bell 206B JetRanger III	3626		
☐ N2753F	Bell 206B JetRanger III	2729		
☐ N3208H	Bell 212	31304		
☐ N3897N	Bell 214ST	28106		
☐ N5736J	Bell 212	31140		
☐ N5748M	Bell 214ST	28102	ex VH-LHU	
☐ N6992	Bell 222U	47521	ex N911WY	
☐ N8045T	Bell 214ST	28101	ex VH-LHQ	
☐ N8765J	MBB BK-117A-3	7054	ex ZS-HRP	
☐ N59806	Bell 214ST	28140	ex B-7723	

PHILLIPS AIR CHARTER		Beachball (BCH)		Del Rio Intl, TX (DRT)

☐ N666AK	Beech E-18S	BA-18	ex N3602B	Frtr

PHOENIX AIR		Gray Bird (PHA)		Cartersville, GA (VPC)

☐ N164PA	Grumman G-159 Gulfstream I	54	ex N26AJ	
☐ N167PA	Grumman G-159 Gulfstream I	199	ex N183PA	
☐ N171PA	Grumman G-159 Gulfstream I	192	ex YV-76CP	
☐ N185PA	Grumman G-159 Gulfstream I	26	ex YV-82CP	
☐ N190PA	Grumman G-159 Gulfstream I (LFD)	195	ex N1900W	Frtr
☐ N192PA	Grumman G-159 Gulfstream I	149	ex N684FM	[VPC]
☐ N193PA	Grumman G-159 Gulfstream I (LFD)	125	ex N5NA	Frtr
☐ N195PA	Grumman G-159C Gulfstream I	88	ex C-GPTN	
☐ N196PA	Grumman G-159 Gulfstream I	139	ex C-FRTU	
☐ N198PA	Grumman G-159C Gulfstream I	27	ex N415CA	

☐ N32PA	Learjet 36A	36A-025	ex N800BL	
☐ N56PA	Learjet 36A	36A-023	ex N6YY	
☐ N62PG	Learjet 36A	36A-031	ex N20UG	
☐ N71PG	Learjet 36	36-013	ex D-CBRD	
☐ N80PG	Learjet 35	35-063	ex N663CA	
☐ N524PA	Learjet 35	35-033	ex N31FN	
☐ N527PA	Learjet 36A	36A-019	ex N540PA	
☐ N541PA	Learjet 35	35-053	ex N53FN	
☐ N542PA	Learjet 35	35-030	ex C-GKPE	
☐ N544PA	Learjet 35A	35A-247	ex N523PA	coded NY
☐ N545PA	Learjet 36A	36A-028	ex N75TD	coded HI
☐ N547PA	Learjet 36	36-012	ex N712JE	coded AK
☐ N549PA	Learjet 35A	35A-119	ex (N64DH)	coded GA
☐ N568PA	Learjet 35A	35A-205	ex N59FN	

☐ N163PA	Gulfstream G-1159A Gulfstream III-SMA	249	ex F-249
☐ N173PA	Gulfstream G-1159A Gulfstream III-SMA	313	ex F-313

PHOENIX AIRTRANSPORT		Papago (PPG)	Phoenix-Sky Harbor Intl, AZ (PHX)

☐ N18R	Beech E-18S	BA-312		<CBT
☐ N103AF	Beech G-18S	BA-526	ex N277S	<CBT

PIEDMONT AIRLINES	Piedmont (US/PDT)	Salisbury-Wicomico Regional, MD (SBY)

A wholly owned subsidiary of US Airways and uses US Airways Express flight numbers in the range US3000-3399.

PINNACLE AIRLINES	Flagship (9E/FLG)	Memphis-Intl, TN/Minneapolis-St Paul Intl, MN (MEM/MSP)

Operates for Delta Connection: Colgan Air is a wholly owned subsidiary.

PLANEMASTERS — Planemaster (PMS) — Chicago-Du Page, IL (DPA)

☐ N274PM	Cessna 208B Caravan I	208B0705		
☐ N279PM	Cessna 208B Caravan I	208B0623	ex N104VE	Frtr
☐ N281PM	Cessna 208B Caravan I	208B0902		
☐ N282PM	Cessna 208B Caravan I	208B0981		
☐ N286PM	Cessna 208B Caravan I	208B0631		
☐ N1114A	Cessna 208B Caravan I	208B0309		Frtr
☐ N1256P	Cessna 208B Caravan I	208B0564		

PLATINUM AIRLINES — Miami-Opa Locka, FL (OPF)

☐ N727PL	Boeing 727-232 (Raisbeck 3)	20643/951	ex N17789	Poliana, std OPF

PLAYERS AIR Players Air (PYZ) — Atlanta-de Kalb Peachtree, GA (PDK)

☐ N650CT	Embraer EMB.120RT	120198	ex N267AS
☐ N651CT	Embraer EMB.120RT	120197	ex N58733
☐ N653CT	Embraer EMB.120ER	120243	ex N204SW

POLAR AIR CARGO — Polar (PO/PAC) — New York-JFK Intl, NY (JFK)

☐ N355MC	Boeing 747-341 (SF)	23395/629	ex PP-VNI	<GTI
☐ N416MC	Boeing 747-47UF	32838/1307		<GTI
☐ N450PA	Boeing 747-46NF	30808/1257	The Spirit of Long Beach	
☐ N451PA	Boeing 747-46NF	30809/1259	Wings of Change	
☐ N452PA	Boeing 747-46NF	30810/1260	Polar Spirit	
☐ N453PA	Boeing 747-46NF	30811/1283		
☐ N454PA	Boeing 747-46NF	30812/1310		

PONDEROSA AIRLINES — Taylor, AZ (TYZ)

☐ N3UV	Rockwell 500S Shrike Commander	3146	ex N3U
☐ N4QS	Aero Commander 500S Shrike	1755-1	ex N4GS
☐ N17DL	Aero Commander 500S Shrike	1866-42	ex N9029N
☐ N40TC	Rockwell 500S Shrike Commander	3091	ex SE-EWH
☐ N88CB	Rockwell 500S Shrike Commander	3067	ex N9081N
☐ N519WA	Rockwell 500S Shrike Commander	3081	ex N222GS
☐ N999GB	Aero Commander 500U Shrike	1717-27	ex CF-YGP

PRESIDENTIAL AIRWAYS — Melbourne-Intl, FL (MLB)

☐ N961BW	CASA C.212-200	CC40-8-248	ex N202FN		
☐ N962BW	CASA C.212-200	CC44-1-290	ex N439CA		
☐ N963BW	CASA C.212-200	CC60-3-320	ex N204FN		
☐ N966BW	CASA C.212-200	CC50-10-289	ex N316ST		
☐ N967BW	CASA C.212-200	CD51-2-304	ex N203PA		
☐ N969BW	CASA C.212-200	CD51-1-262	ex N262MA	Frtr	
☐ N2357G	CASA C.212-200	CD51-2-309	ex N968BW		
☐ N4399T	CASA C.212-300	DF-1-393	ex N965BW		
☐ N6369C	CASA C.212-200	MS03-08-379	ex M964BW		
☐ N150RN	de Havilland DHC-8-103	086	ex N986BW		
☐ N511AV	de Havilland DHC-8-102	051	ex C-GAAN		♦
☐ N955BW	Swearingen SA.227DC Metro 23	DC-821B	ex N821JB		
☐ N956BW	Swearingen SA.227DC Metro 23	DC-864B	ex C-GKAF		
☐ N982BW	CASA CN-235-100	010	ex ZS-OGE	[JNB] as ZS-OGE	
☐ N990AV	de Havilland DHC-8-102	99	ex C-GZTC		♦

PRIORITY AIR — New Orleans-Lakefront, LA (NEW)

☐ N46SA	Swearingen SA.226T Merlin III	T-231	ex N20QN	EMS

PRIORITY AIR CHARTER — Priority Air (PRY) — Kidron-Stolzfus Airfield, OH

☐ N208TF	Cessna 208B Caravan I	208B0592	
☐ N218PA	Cessna 208B Caravan I	208B0306	ex N218PF
☐ N228PA	Cessna 208B Caravan I	208B0930	ex N2418W
☐ N248PA	Cessna 208B Caravan I	208B0134	ex N208JL
☐ N719BT	Cessna 208B Caravan I	208B0898	
☐ N820B	Cessna 340A II	340A0328	ex YV-1268P

PROFESSIONAL AIR CHARTER — Fort Lauderdale Executive, FL (FXE)

☐ N4633P	Beech 95-B55 Baron	TC-1560
☐ N27888	Piper PA-31-350 Chieftain	31-7952025

PROMECH AIR		(Z3)		Ketchikan-Harbor SPB, AK (WFB)
☐ N1108Q	de Havilland DHC-2 Beaver	416	ex 51-16851	FP
☐ N4787C	de Havilland DHC-2 Beaver	1330	ex C-FGMK	FP
☐ N64393	de Havilland DHC-2 Beaver	845	ex 54-1701	FP
☐ N64397	de Havilland DHC-2 Beaver	760	ex 53-7943	FP
☐ N270PA	de Havilland DHC-3 Turbo Otter	270	ex N51KA	FP
☐ N409PA	de Havilland DHC-3 Turbo Otter	409	ex C-FLDD	FP
☐ N435B	de Havilland DHC-3 Turbo Otter	183	ex C-GIGZ	FP
☐ N959PA	de Havilland DHC-3 Turbo Otter	159	ex N67KA	FP
☐ N3952B	de Havilland DHC-3 Turbo Otter	225	ex C-GGON	FP
☐ N444BA	Cessna A185E Skywagon	185-1433		FP
☐ N531H	Cessna A185E Skywagon	185-1348		FP

PSA AIRLINES	Blue Streak (JIA)	Dayton-Cox Intl, OH (DAY)

A wholly owned subsidiary of US Airways, operates services as a US Airways Express commuter using US flight numbers in the range 4000-4299. All aircraft officially leased to US Airways from AFS Investments and sub-leased to PSA Airlines.

PUERTO RICO AIR MANAGEMENT SERVICES(2P)			San Juan-Munoz Marin Intl, PR (SJU)
☐ N75LA	Beech 100 King Air	B-75	ex C-F (SCD)

QUICK AIR			Danville-Vermillion County, IL (DNV)
☐ N16BE	Beech Baron 58	TH-946	
☐ N233H	Beech G-18S	BA-481	ex (N584MS)	Frtr

RAM AIR FREIGHT		RAM Express (REX)	Raleigh-Durham-Intl, NC (RDU)
☐ N7351R	Beech 58 Baron	TH-481	
☐ N401NA	Cessna 402B	402B0035	ex SE-FXI
☐ N884RC	Cessna 402B	402B0884	ex TF-JVC
☐ N130BW	Piper PA-32-300 Cherokee Six	32-40963	ex D-EBOK
☐ N169BW	Piper PA-32RT-300 Lance II	32R-7885080	ex N30006
☐ N221MC	Piper PA-32RT-300 Lance II	32R-7885032	
☐ N333TG	Piper PA-32R-300 Lance	32R-7680320	ex N202SW
☐ N631BW	Piper PA-32-300 Cherokee Six	32-7340041	ex N4GQ
☐ N833WC	Piper PA-32-300 Cherokee Six	32-7640059	
☐ N1061Q	Piper PA-32-260 Cherokee Six E	32-7200015	ex SE-FLD
☐ N4498F	Piper PA-32R-300 Lance	32R-7680453	
☐ N4817S	Piper PA-32-260 Cherokee Six	32-1277	
☐ N5454F	Piper PA-32R-300 Lance	32R-7780012	
☐ N6291J	Piper PA-32R-300 Lance	32R-7680350	
☐ N6934J	Piper PA-32R-300 Lance	32R-7680389	
☐ N8209C	Piper PA-32R-300 Lance	32R-7680082	
☐ N8954C	Piper PA-32R-300 Lance	32R-7680146	
☐ N8985C	Piper PA-32R-300 Lance	32R-7680147	
☐ N9392K	Piper PA-32R-300 Lance	32R-7680219	
☐ N38305	Piper PA-32R-300 Lance	32R-7780413	
☐ N87619	Piper PA-32-300 Cherokee Six C	32-40752	
☐ N48LJ	Piper PA-34-200T Seneca II	34-7770030	ex C-GQET
☐ N86BW	Piper PA-34-200T Seneca II	34-7770340	ex C-GZAQ
☐ N88WA	Piper PA-34-200T Seneca II	34-7570274	
☐ N286BW	Piper PA-34-200T Seneca II	34-7970182	ex N341DK
☐ N553DM	Piper PA-34-200T Seneca II	34-7670330	ex C-GXHY
☐ N1063X	Piper PA-34-200T Seneca II	34-7570198	
☐ N3570M	Piper PA-34-200T Seneca II	34-7870117	
☐ N4358X	Piper PA-34-200T Seneca II	34-7670027	
☐ N6935C	Piper PA-34-200T Seneca II	34-7870167	
☐ N7633C	Piper PA-34-200T Seneca II	34-7670098	
☐ N8076N	Piper PA-34-200T Seneca II	34-7970487	
☐ N8793E	Piper PA-34-200T Seneca II	34-7670180	
☐ N21407	Piper PA-34-200T Seneca II	34-7870435	
☐ N39545	Piper PA-34-200T Seneca II	34-7870389	ex C-FWFJ

RAM AIR SERVICES			
☐ N702RS	SAAB SF.340B	340B-233	ex N233CJ
☐ N703RS	SAAB SF.340B	340B-252	ex N252CJ

RAMP 66	Pelican (PPK)	North Myrtle Beach-Grand Strand, NC (CRE)
☐ N6656C	Beech 58 Baron	TH-1060

RAPID AIR — Grand Rapids-Kent County Intl, MI (GRR)

☐ N4084L	Cessna 310Q	310Q0493	

REDDING AERO ENTERPRISES — Boxer (BXR) — Redding-Municipal, CA (RDD)

☐ N2610G	Cessna 402C II	402C0064	
☐ N2613B	Cessna 402C II	402C0083	
☐ N2712F	Cessna 402C II	402C0121	
☐ N5826C	Cessna 402C II	402C0050	
☐ N5849C	Cessna 402C II	402C0052	
☐ N36908	Cessna 402C II	402C0313	
☐ N48SA	Cessna 404A Titan II	404-0417	ex C-GSPG
☐ N932C	Cessna 208B Caravan I	208B0032	ex N932FE
☐ N6072V	Piper Aerostar 601P	61P-0696-7963332	

REPUBLIC AIRWAYS — Brickyard (RW/RPA) — Chicago-O'Hare, IL/Washington-Dulles, DC (ORD/DUL)

☐ N810MD	Embraer ERJ-170SU	17000026	ex PT-SKT
☐ N813MA	Embraer ERJ-170SU	17000031	ex PT-SKZ
☐ N815MD	Embraer ERJ-170SU	17000034	ex PT-SUD
☐ N818MD	Embraer ERJ-170SU	17000039	ex PT-SUI
☐ N821MD	Embraer ERJ-170SU	17000042	ex PT-SUL
☐ N823MD	Embraer ERJ-170SU	17000044	ex PT-SUO
☐ N824MD	Embraer ERJ-170SU	17000045	ex PT-SUO
☐ N826MD	Embraer ERJ-170SU	17000046	ex PT-SUP
☐ N871RW	Embraer ERJ-170SU	17000140	ex PT-SEE
☐ N872RW	Embraer ERJ-170SU	17000143	ex PT-SEH
☐ N873RW	Embraer ERJ-170SU	17000144	ex PT-SEI
☐ N874RW	Embraer ERJ-170SU	17000148	ex PT-SEM
☐ N161HL	Embraer ERJ-190AR	19000154	ex N161HQ
☐ N162HL	Embraer ERJ-190AR	19000231	ex N162HQ
☐ N163HQ	Embraer ERJ-190AR	19000255	ex PT-STD
☐ N164HQ	Embraer ERJ-190AR	19000275	ex PT-TLP
☐ N165HQ	Embraer ERJ-190AR	19000291	ex PT-TZF
☐ N166HQ	Embraer ERJ-190AR	19000166	ex N959UW
☐ N167HQ	Embraer ERJ-190AR	19000173	ex N960UW
☐ N168HQ	Embraer ERJ-190AR	19000183	ex N961UW
☐ N169HQ	Embraer ERJ-190AR	19000188	ex N962UW
☐ N170HQ	Embraer ERJ-190AR	19000191	ex N963UW
☐ N171HQ	Embraer ERJ-190AR	19000197	ex N964UW
☐ N172HQ	Embraer ERJ-190AR	19000198	ex N965UW
☐ N173HQ	Embraer ERJ-190AR	19000206	ex N966UW
☐ N174HQ	Embraer ERJ-190AR	19000211	ex N967UW
☐ N175HQ	Embraer ERJ-190AR	19000216	ex N968UW
☐ N	Embraer ERJ-190AR		o/o♦
☐ N	Embraer ERJ-190AR		o/o♦
☐ N	Embraer ERJ-190AR		o/o♦
☐ N	Embraer ERJ-190AR		o/o♦
☐ N	Embraer ERJ-190AR		o/o♦
☐ N	Embraer ERJ-190AR		o/o♦

RHOADES INTERNATIONAL — Rhoades Express (RDS) — Columbus-Municipal, IN (CLU)

☐ N132JR	Cessna 402B	402B1363	ex (N4606N)	
☐ N134JR	Cessna 310R	310R2117	ex N6831X	Frtr
☐ N376AS	AMI Turbo DC-3-65TP	15602/27047	ex ZS-OBU	Frtr
☐ N587CA	Convair 640	463	ex C-FPWO	Frtr

ROBLEX AVIATION — Roblex (ROX) — Isla Grande, PR (SIG)

☐ N151PR	Short SD.3-60	SH3725	ex N162DD	The Warrior
☐ N165DD	Short SD.3-60	SH3740	ex D-CFXF	
☐ N377AR	Short SD.3-60	SH3755	ex SE-LHY	
☐ N411ER	Short SD.3-60	SH3726	ex G-BNMW	
☐ N875RR	Short SD.3-60	SH3741	ex G-ZAPD	
☐ N948RR	Short SD.3-60	SH3751	ex G-BVMX	
☐ N821RR	Britten-Norman BN-2A-9 Islander	338	ex N146A	El Beb

ROGERS HELICOPTERS — Fresno, CA

☐ N505WW	Aérospatiale AS350B2 AStar	2442	ex JA6046
☐ N910VR	Aérospatiale AS350B2 AStar	3213	ex I-VINO
☐ N911EW	Aérospatiale AS350B2 AStar	2657	ex I-MUSY
☐ N3609J	Aérospatiale AS350D AStar	1245	

372

☐ N2292W	Bell 206B JetRanger III	505		
☐ N2762P	Bell 206B JetRanger III	2711		
☐ N2763M	Bell 206B JetRanger III	2646		
☐ N16832	Bell 206B JetRanger III	2243		
☐ N20395	Bell 206B JetRanger III	3301		
☐ N58140	Bell 206B JetRanger III	1108		
☐ N59564	Bell 206B JetRanger III	1389		
☐ N59571	Bell 206B JetRanger III	1433	ex XA-SVF	
☐ N91AL	Bell 212	30821		
☐ N212HL	Bell 212	30621	ex XA-VVM	
☐ N811KA	Bell 212	30656	ex N59630	
☐ N873HL	Bell 212	30873	ex N910KW	
☐ N911HW	Bell 212	31101	ex N703H	
☐ N911KW	Bell 212	30592	ex N50EW	
☐ N911VR	Bell 212	30998	ex N701H	
☐ N24GT	Rockwell 690A Turbo Commander	11254	ex XA-RMZ	
☐ N101MZ	Aérospatiale AS355F1 Twin Star	5045		
☐ N102UM	Aérospatiale AS355F1 Twin Star	5075	ex N130US	
☐ N313DH	Bell 206L LongRanger II	45630	ex A6-CAC	
☐ N700PQ	Rockwell 690B Turbo Commander	11389	ex N700PC	
☐ N712M	Bell 206L-3 LongRanger III	51072		
☐ N896SB	Beech A100 King Air	B-160	ex OY-CCS	
☐ N912VR	Agusta A.109K2	10028	ex JA111D	EMS
☐ N10864	Bell 206L-1 LongRanger III	45434		
☐ N27472	Piper PA-31-350 Chieftain	31-7852019		
☐ N29176	Cessna T210L Turbo Centurion II	21059828		

ROSS AVIATION   Energy (NRG)   Albuquerque-Kirkland AFB, NM

☐ N148DE	de Havilland DHC-6 Twin Otter 300	493	ex N72348
☐ N162DE	de Havilland DHC-6 Twin Otter 300	429	ex N35062
☐ N166DE	Douglas DC-9-15RC (ABS 3)	47152/170	ex N66AF
☐ N229DE	Douglas DC-9-15RC (ABS 3)	45826/79	ex N29AF
☐ N7232R	Beech B200C Super King Air	BL-69	ex N2811B

ROTORCRAFT   Broussard-Heliport, LA / Patterson-HPW Memorial, LA (-/PTN)

☐ N3RL	Bell 206B JetRanger	396	ex N99NW
☐ N21RT	Bell 206B JetRanger III	2659	ex C-GFSE
☐ N37AJ	Bell 206B JetRanger	1877	ex N999GC
☐ N65DD	Bell 206B JetRanger	1235	ex N66677
☐ N72Z	Bell 206B JetRanger III	3537	ex N22181
☐ N113RL	Bell 206B JetRanger III	3306	ex N97BL
☐ N203RL	Bell 206B JetRanger III	3337	ex N2033J
☐ N275RL	Bell 206B JetRanger	1601	ex N90115
☐ N277RL	Bell 206B JetRanger III	3277	ex N181AA
☐ N314RT	Bell 206B JetRanger III	3014	ex N223HA
☐ N496RL	Bell 206B JetRanger III	3496	ex N2163Y
☐ N742RT	Bell 206B JetRanger III	2742	ex N921RB
☐ N913RL	Bell 206B JetRanger III	2913	ex B-66061
☐ N969RL	Bell 206B JetRanger III	3969	ex N187AA
☐ N2043B	Bell 206B JetRanger III	3355	
☐ N3187D	Bell 206B JetRanger	1326	ex C-GOKC
☐ N104RT	Bell 206L-3 LongRanger III	51364	ex LV-WCF
☐ N157H	Bell 206L-4 LongRanger IV	52320	
☐ N204RL	Bell 206L-1 LongRanger II	45204	ex N73FA
☐ N207RT	Bell 206L-4 LongRanger IV	52207	ex HC-BYQ
☐ N283RL	Bell 206L-1 LongRanger II	45283	ex N2761X
☐ N303RL	Bell 206L-3 LongRanger III	51202	ex N303MP
☐ N317RL	Bell 206L-4 LongRanger IV	52317	ex C-FFRB
☐ N318RL	Bell 206L-4 LongRanger IV	52318	
☐ N322RL	Bell 206L-4 LongRanger IV	52322	
☐ N370RL	Bell 206L-1 LongRanger II	45370	ex N618DE
☐ N396RL	Bell 206L-1 LongRanger II	45396	ex N396RT
☐ N397RL	Bell 206L-1 LongRanger II	45397	ex N1078D
☐ N405RL	Bell 206L-3 LongRanger III	51405	ex N253EV
☐ N410RL	Bell 206L-4 LongRanger IV	52310	
☐ N468RL	Bell 206L-3 LongRanger III	51155	ex N468AG
☐ N473RT	Bell 206L-3 LongRanger III	51473	ex CX-SCX
☐ N505RL	Bell 206L-1 LongRanger II	45176	ex N5005F
☐ N510RT	Bell 206L-3 LongRanger II	51078	ex N946L
☐ N514RL	Bell 206L-3 LongRanger III	51514	ex N206MY
☐ N516EH	Bell 206L-1 LongRanger II	45416	
☐ N518RL	Bell 206L-1 LongRanger II	45183	ex N406EH

☐ N520RL	Bell 206L-4 LongRanger IV	52052	ex N802D	
☐ N523RL	Bell 206L-4 LongRanger IV	52321	ex N194H	
☐ N598RL	Bell 206L-1 LongRanger II	45598	ex N264AA	
☐ N709RL	Bell 206L-3 LongRanger III	51101	ex N709M	
☐ N720RL	Bell 206L-4 LongRanger IV	52027	ex XA-FJM	
☐ N772RL	Bell 206L-1 LongRanger II	45311	ex N2772A	
☐ N801RL	Bell 206L-3 LongRanger III	51081	ex N704M	
☐ N5019G	Bell 206L-1 LongRanger II	45247		
☐ N5750Y	Bell 206L-1 LongRanger II	45517		
☐ N52192	Bell 206L-4 LongRanger IV	52192		
☐ N163RL	Bell 407	53163	ex N972AA	
☐ N164RL	Bell 407	53140	ex N407MT	
☐ N167RL	Bell 407	53167	ex N973AA	
☐ N309RL	Bell 407	53092	ex N407HX	
☐ N594RL	Bell 407	53594	ex C-GAFF	
☐ N595RL	Bell 407	53595	ex C-GAFI	
☐ N83T	Sikorsky S-76A	760117		
☐ N293CA	Bell 412	33005	ex N3912Y	
☐ N4125C	Bell 412	33103	ex N412AC	

ROYAL AIR FREIGHT   Air Royal (RAX)   Pontiac-Oakland, MI (PTK)

☐ N120RA	AMD Falcon 20DC	211	ex N764LA	
☐ N123RA	AMD Falcon 20C	30	ex N514SA	
☐ N277RA	AMD Falcon 20C	8	ex N612GA	
☐ N900RA	AMD Falcon 20C	59	ex N159MV	
☐ N22DM	Cessna 310R	310R0069	ex N7593Q	
☐ N22LE	Cessna 310R	310R0033	ex N1398G	
☐ N310KS	Cessna 310R	310R1501		
☐ N1591T	Cessna 310R	310R0112		
☐ N2643D	Cessna 310R	310R1686		
☐ N87309	Cessna 310R	310R0510		
☐ N87341	Cessna 310R	310R0520		
☐ N34A	Embraer EMB.110P1 Bandeirante	110350	ex N4361Q	
☐ N49RA	Embraer EMB.110P1 Bandeirante	110424	ex C-GPRV	
☐ N64DA	Embraer EMB.110P1 Bandeirante	110385	ex PT-SFC	
☐ N72RA	Embraer EMB.110P1 Bandeirante	110377	ex C-GHOV	[PTK]
☐ N73RA	Embraer EMB.110P1 Bandeirante	110413	ex C-GPNW	
☐ N9RA	Learjet 25D	25D-277	ex N81MW	
☐ N16KK	Learjet 25B	25B-174	ex N412SP	
☐ N25FM	Learjet 25	25-063	ex N24LT	
☐ N25MD	Learjet 25	25-054	ex N509G	
☐ N48L	Learjet 24A	24A-107		
☐ N110RA	Learjet 25	25-025	ex (N111LM)	
☐ N688GS	Learjet 25B	25B-123	ex N906SU	
☐ N710TV	Learjet 24	24-159	ex N66MR	N269AL resd
☐ N876MC	Learjet 24B	24B-217	ex C-FZHT	
☐ N2094L	Learjet 25B	25B-095	ex C-GRCO	
☐ N160PB	Cessna 402C	402C0493	ex N6841M	
☐ N200AJ	Beech A100 King Air	B-146	ex N410SB	
☐ N305CW	Mitsubishi MU-2B-36 (MU-2L)	667	ex N300CW	
☐ N717PS	Mitsubishi MU-2B-36 (MU-2L)	686	ex N23RA	
☐ N5279J	Cessna 402B	402B1202	ex N6841M	
☐ N5373J	Cessna 402B	402B0367	ex C-GCXI	

RUSTS FLYING SERVICE   Anchorage-Lake Hood SPB, AK (LHD)

☐ N626KT	Cessna U206G Stationair 6 II	U20604426	ex N756WY	FP
☐ N2740X	de Havilland DHC-2 Beaver	579	ex C-GIJO	FP
☐ N2899J	de Havilland DHC-3 Turbo Otter	425	ex C-GLCR	FP
☐ N4444Z	de Havilland DHC-2 Beaver	1307	ex N123PG	FP
☐ N4596U	Cessna U206G Stationair 6 II	U20604990		FP
☐ N4661Z	Cessna U206G Stationair 6 II	U20605998		FP
☐ N4891Z	Cessna U206G Stationair 6 II	U20606044		FP
☐ N68083	de Havilland DHC-2 Beaver	1254	ex 57-2580	FP

RYAN INTERNATIONAL AIRLINES   Ryan International (RD/RYN)   Wichita-Mid Continent, KS (ICT)

☐ N120DL	Boeing 767-332	23279/154		>LAV
☐ N123DN	Boeing 767-332	23437/188		
☐ N125RD	Boeing 767-383ER	24849/330	ex XA-MIR	
☐ N151GX	Boeing 757-2G5	24451/227	ex OB-1788-P	[VCV]♦

☐ N526NA	Boeing 757-236	24794/278	ex EC-HDG	
☐ N637TW	Boeing 767-33AER	25403/409	ex PR-BRW	
☐ N763BK	Boeing 767-3Z9ER	23765/165	ex G-VKNG	
☐ N764RD	Boeing 767-3Y0ER	26204/464	ex PR-VAD	
☐ N932RD	McDonnell-Douglas MD-83	49233/1203	ex N932AS	
☐ N964AS	McDonnell-Douglas MD-83	53078/1996		
☐ N969NS	McDonnell-Douglas MD-83	53063/1851	ex N969AS	
☐ N976AS	McDonnell-Douglas MD-83	53452/2109		

SAFEWING AVIATION — Swiftwing (SFF) — Kansas City-Downtown, MO (MKC)

☐ N33MP	Piper PA-23-250 Aztec F	27-7654194	ex N62746	
☐ N63798	Piper PA-23-250 Aztec F	27-7754124		

SAINT LOUIS HELICOPTER — Chesterfield-Spirit of St Louis, MO (SUS)

☐ N1078T	Sikorsky S-58HT	581016	ex C-FOHA	
☐ N6488	Sikorsky S-58D	581573		
☐ N45726	Sikorsky S-58 (H-34A)	58675	ex 56-4037	

SALMON AIR — Mountain Bird (S6/MBI) — Salmon-Lemhi County, ID (SMN)

☐ N80GV	Piper PA-31-350 Navajo Chieftain	31-7552003	ex N61487	
☐ N3528Y	Piper PA-31-350 Chieftain	31-7952149		
☐ N4237D	Piper PA-31-350 Navajo Chieftain	31-7305055	ex N800MW	
☐ N31932	Piper PA-31-350 Navajo Chieftain	31-7405144	ex N888TV	
☐ N84859	Piper PA-31-350 Navajo Chieftain	31-7305043	ex N804PC	
☐ N6561B	Britten-Norman BN-2A-20 Islander	520	ex YV-0-GSF-6	dam 15Jly07
☐ N7067Z	Cessna T210M Turbo Centurion II	21062572	ex C-GPTX	
☐ N8514C	Piper PA-34-200T Seneca II	34-7670147		

SAN JUAN AIRLINES — West Isle Air (2G/MRR) — Anacortes, WA (OTS)

☐ N63SJ	Cessna U206F Stationair	U20603521	ex N8768Q	
☐ N1584U	Cessna 207 Skywagon	20700184		
☐ N7405	Cessna T207 Turbo Skywagon	20700147	ex V3-HNO	

SAPPHIRE AVIATION — Sapphire (SPP) — West Palm Beach, FL (LNA)

☐ N57EB	Aero Commander 500A	500A-1245-71	ex N357TK	
☐ N78343	Aero Commander 500A	500A-1264-87		

SB AIR — S-Bar (SBF) — Albuquerque-Intl, NM/Dallas-Love Field, TX (ABQ/DAL)

☐ N17NM	Beech 65-E90 King Air	LW-237	ex N5NM	EMS
☐ N21NM	Beech 65-E90 King Air	LW-336	ex N675J	EMS
☐ N44GK	Beech 65-E90 King Air	LW-298	ex N2029X	EMS N118SB resd
☐ N304LG	Beech 65-E90 King Air	LW-231	ex N4954S	EMS
☐ N11692	Beech 65-C90 King Air	LJ-772	ex F-GFBO	EMS
☐ N114SB	Beech 200 Super King Air	BB-161	ex N131PA	

SCENIC AIRLINES — Scenic (YR/SCE) — Las Vegas-North, NV/Page, AZ (VGT/PGA)

☐ N142SA	de Havilland DHC-6 Twin Otter 300	241	ex N385EX	
☐ N146SA	de Havilland DHC-6 Twin Otter 300	514	ex N27RA	
☐ N148SA	de Havilland DHC-6 Twin Otter 300	409	ex N548N	
☐ N226SA	de Havilland DHC-6 Twin Otter 300	585	ex Chile 934	
☐ N227SA	de Havilland DHC-6 Twin Otter 300	517	ex N43SP	
☐ N228SA	de Havilland DHC-6 Twin Otter 300	253	ex N103AC	
☐ N241SA	de Havilland DHC-6 Twin Otter 300	556	ex N97RA	
☐ N297SA	de Havilland DHC-6 Twin Otter 300	297	ex N852TB	
☐ N359AR	de Havilland DHC-6 Twin Otter 300	359	ex N148SA	
☐ N692AR	de Havilland DHC-6 Twin Otter 300	692	ex N230SA	

SCENIC AVIATION — Blanding Municipal, UT (BDG)

☐ N13GZ	Beech 65-C90B King Air	LJ-1590	ex PT-WXH	
☐ N588SA	Beech 65-C90B King Air	LJ-1588		
☐ N590GM	Beech 65-C90B King Air	LJ-1594		
☐ N1083S	Beech 65-C90B King Air	LJ-1443		
☐ N47744	Piper PA-34-200T Seneca II	34-7870026		

SEABORNE AIRLINES — Seaborne (BB) — St Thomas-SPB, VI (SPB)

☐ N224SA	de Havilland DHC-6 Twin Otter 300	247	ex C-GOES	VistaLiner
☐ N288SA	de Havilland DHC-6 Twin Otter 300	389	ex V2-LEY	VistaLiner
☐ N562CP	de Havilland DHC-6 Twin Otter 300	562	ex TI-BAL	
☐ N888PV	de Havilland DHC-6 Twin Otter 300	620	ex CF-TWW	

SERVANT AIR(8D) — Kodiak-Municipal, AK (KDK)

☐ N1658U	Cessna 207 Skywagon	20700258	
☐ N1750U	Cessna 207 Skywagon	20700350	
☐ N75311	Piper PA-32R-300 Lance	32R-7680291	

SHUTTLE AMERICA — Shuttlecraft (S5/TCF) — Wilmington-Newcastle, DE/Windsor Locks-Bradley Intl, CT (ILG/BDL)

Operates aircraft for Delta Connection and United Express in full colours. Wholly owned by Republic Airlines.

SIERRA PACIFIC AIRLINES — Sierra Pacific (SI/SPA) — Tucson-Intl, AZ (TUS)

☐ N703S	Boeing 737-2T4 (AvAero 3)	22529/750	ex N703ML
☐ N712S	Boeing 737-2Y5 (AvAero 3)	23038/949	ex ZK-NAF

SIERRA WEST AIRLINES — Platinum West (PKW) — Oakdale, CA (SCK)

☐ N63NE	Swearingen SA.227AC Metro III	AC-763B		Frtr
☐ N221TR	Learjet 35A	35A-221	ex VH-FSY	Frtr
☐ N242DR	Learjet 35A	35A-242	ex VH-FSZ	Frtr
☐ N283SA	AMD Falcon 20	83	ex (N82SR)	Frtr
☐ N681TR	Swearingen SA.227AC Metro III	AC-682	ex N921BC	Frtr
☐ N8897Y	Swearingen SA.226AT Merlin IVC	AT-492	ex C-FJTA	Frtr

SILLER AVIATION — Yuba City-Sutter County, CA (MYV)

☐ N4196Z	Sikorsky S-61R	61567	ex 65-12792
☐ N4197R	Sikorsky S-61R	61571	ex 65-12796
☐ N5193J	Sikorsky S-61A	61014	ex Bu148036
☐ N8170V	Sikorsky S-61A	61232	
☐ N15456	Sikorsky S-61N	61826	
☐ N45917	Sikorsky S-61V-1	61271	
☐ N51953	Sikorsky S-61A	61172	ex Bu149903
☐ N429C	Sikorsky CH-54A	64031	ex 67-18429
☐ N2268L	Sikorsky CH-54A	64013	ex 66-18411
☐ N4035S	Sikorsky S-64E Skycrane	64099	ex 70-18491
☐ N4037S	Sikorsky S-64E Skycrane	64101	ex 70-18493
☐ N7095B	Sikorsky CH-54A	64032	ex 67-18430
☐ N9125M	Sikorsky CH-54A	64057	ex 68-18455

SKAGWAY AIR SERVICE — Skagway Air (N5/SGY) — Skagway, AK (SGY)

☐ N1132Q	Piper PA-32-300 Cherokee Six	32-7740046	
☐ N2884M	Piper PA-32-300 Cherokee Six	32-7840058	
☐ N8127K	Piper PA-32-300 Six	32-7940268	
☐ N31589	Piper PA-32-300 Cherokee Six	32-7840135	
☐ N40698	Piper PA-32-300 Cherokee Six	32-7440056	
☐ N8216T	Piper PA-32-301 Saratoga	32-8206037	
☐ N9540K	Piper PA-34-200T Seneca II	34-7670208	

SKY CASTLE AVIATION — New Castle-Henry County, IN (MIE)

☐ N38W	Beech H18	BA-580	ex N616T	Frtr
☐ N4231V	Piper PA-31-350 Navajo Chieftain	31-7652162	ex C-GBHM	
☐ N6685S	Beech 58 Baron	TH-718		

SKY KING — Songbird (F3/SGB) — Sacramento-Metropolitan, CA (SMF)

☐ N147AW	Boeing 737-297 (Nordam 3)	22630/860	ex N729AL	no titles
☐ N249TR	Boeing 737-2K5 (Nordam 3)	22598/792	ex F-GFLX	
☐ N251TR	Boeing 737-228 (Nordam 3)	23792/1397	ex F-GBYP	♦
☐ N252TR	Boeing 737-228 (Nordam 3)	23001/936	ex F-GBYB	Boni Belle
☐ N464AT	Boeing 737-2L9 (AvAero 3)	21278/479	ex N358AS	no titles
☐ N465AT	Boeing 737-2L9 (AvAero 3)	21528/517	ex N359AS	no titles
☐ N916SK	Boeing 737-4Q8	24706/1996	ex SP-LLI	
☐ N977UA	Boeing 737-2L9 (AvAero 3)	21508/518	ex N7391F	no titles

SKYLEASE AIR CARGO — (WI/TDX) — Greensboro-Piedmont Triad Intl, NC (GSO)

☐ N501TR	Airbus A300B4-203F	053	ex N6254X	>MST♦
☐ N504TA	Airbus A300B4-203F	216	ex N861PA	
☐ N952AR	McDonnell-Douglas MD-11F	48497/512	ex B-2173	♦
☐ N985AR	McDonnell-Douglas MD-11C	48430/508	ex EI-UPU	Frank Fine
☐ N986AR	McDonnell-Douglas MD-11C	48426/468	ex EI-UPA	

SKYWAY ENTERPRISES   Skyway Inc (SKZ)   Orlando-Kissimmee, FL/Detroit-Willow Run, IL (ISM/YIP)

☐ N366MQ	Short SD.3-60	SH3639	ex G-14-3639
☐ N367MQ	Short SD.3-60	SH3640	ex G-BLGA
☐ N377MQ	Short SD.3-60	SH3699	ex G-BMUY
☐ N378MQ	Short SD.3-60	SH3700	ex G-BMXP
☐ N380MQ	Short SD.3-60	SH3702	ex (G-BMXS)
☐ N381MQ	Short SD.3-60	SH3703	ex G-14-3703
☐ N383MQ	Short SD.3-60	SH3706	ex (G-BNBB)
☐ N384MQ	Short SD.3-60	SH3711	ex G-BNBG
☐ N385MQ	Short SD.3-60	SH3707	ex G-BNBC
☐ N387MQ	Short SD.3-60	SH3710	ex G-BNBF
☐ N112PS	Douglas DC-9-15F (ABS 3)	47013/129	ex N557AS
☐ N118SW	Short SD.3-30	SH3100	ex 83-0512

SKYWEST AIRLINES   SkyWest (OO/SKW)   Salt Lake City-Intl, UT/Los Angeles-Intl, CA (SLC/LAX)

☐ N947SW	Canadair CRJ-200ER	7786	ex C-FMMB	7786
☐ N216SW	Embraer EMB.120ER Brasilia	120285	ex PT-SVF	
☐ N217SW	Embraer EMB.120ER Brasilia	120286	ex PT-SVG	
☐ N224SW	Embraer EMB.120ER Brasilia	120294	ex PT-SVO	
☐ N271YV	Embraer EMB.120ER Brasilia	120271	ex PT-SUS	
☐ N296SW	Embraer EMB.120ER Brasilia	120325	ex PT-SXR	
☐ N299SW	Embraer EMB.120ER Brasilia	120329	ex PT-SXV	
☐ N301YV	Embraer EMB.120ER Brasilia	120301	ex PT-SVV	
☐ N576SW	Embraer EMB.120ER Brasilia	120345	ex PT-SBZ	

SMITHAIR   Smithair (SMH)   Hampton-Clayton County, GA

☐ N351N	Learjet 23	23-054	ex N351NR	Frtr
☐ N900NA	Learjet 24A	24A-111	ex N44WD	EMS
☐ N7200K	Learjet 23	23-099		Frtr

SMOKEY BAY AIR   (2E)   Homer, AK (HOM)

☐ N35860	Cessna U206G Super Skywagon	U20602764
☐ N72067	Cessna U206D Super Skywagon	U206-1273

SNOW AVIATION   Columbus-Rickenbacker, OH (LCK)

☐ N130SA	Lockheed C-130A Hercules	3035	ex N2127W	Development aircraft
☐ N307SA	Lockheed C-130E Hercules	3688	ex N131EV	Development aircraft

SOUTH AERO   Albuquerque-Intl, NM (ABQ)

☐ N42MG	Cessna 402C II	402C0320	ex N36992
☐ N57PB	Cessna 402C II	402C0300	ex N3628M
☐ N305AT	Cessna 402C II	402C0030	ex C-GZVM
☐ N402MQ	Cessna 402C II	402C0095	ex N81PB
☐ N2711X	Cessna 402C II	402C0116	
☐ N2713X	Cessna 402C II	402C0207	
☐ N4643N	Cessna 402C II	402C0006	ex C-GIKA
☐ N5820C	Cessna 402C II	402C0047	
☐ N6880A	Cessna 402C II	402C0616	
☐ N54ZP	Cessna 404 Titan II	404-0694	ex N6764X
☐ N165SA	Cessna 404 Titan II	404-0622	
☐ N5388J	Cessna 404 Titan II	404-0666	
☐ N6479N	Cessna T210N Turbo Centurion II	21063053	
☐ N7213N	Cessna T210N Turbo Centurion II	21063207	

SOUTH PACIFIC EXPRESS   Pago Pago International (PPG)

☐ N711MP	Short SD.3-60	SH3698	ex G-BMUX

SOUTHEAST AVIATION   Ketchikan-SPB, AK (WFB)

☐ N82SF	de Havilland DHC-2 Beaver	839	ex N44CD	FP
☐ N9279Z	de Havilland DHC-2 Beaver	345	ex 51-16821	FP

SOUTHERN AIR   Southern Air (9S/SOO)   Columbus-Rickenbacker, OH (LCK)

☐ N704SA	Boeing 747-2B5F	24195/718	ex N298JD	
☐ N708SA	Boeing 747-2B5F	24196/720	ex N299JD	
☐ N723SA	Boeing 747-246F	23641/684	ex JA8180	[MHV]
☐ N740SA	Boeing 747-230B (SF)	21380/320	ex N507MC	[MHV]

☐ N746SA	Boeing 747-206M (EUD)	21111/276	ex PH-BUI	Wilbur Wright	[MHV]♦
☐ N748SA	Boeing 747-206M (EUD/(SF))	21110/271	ex PH-BUH		[MHV]
☐ N749SA	Boeing 747-3n12B5F	24194/713	ex N301JD		
☐ N751SA	Boeing 747-228F	22678/535	ex F-GCBE		[CGK]
☐ N752SA	Boeing 747-228F	21255/295	ex F-BPVR	William Neff	
☐ N753SA	Boeing 747-228F	21787/398	ex F-BPVZ	Southern Dreams	
☐ N754SA	Boeing 747-228F	21576/334	ex N536MC		
☐ N758SA	Boeing 747-281F	23138/604	ex JA8167		
☐ N760SA	Boeing 747-230M	21221/299	ex N509MC		
☐ N761SA	Boeing 747-2F6SF	21832/421	ex N534MC		
☐ N765SA	Boeing 747-2F6B (SCD)	21833/423	ex N535FC		
☐ N783SA	Boeing 747-281F	23919/689	ex JA8188		
☐ N789SA	Boeing 747-341 (SF)	23394/627	ex N354FC		
☐ N795SA	Boeing 747-243M	22506/492	ex VP-BIB		
☐ N798SA	Boeing 747-246B (SF)	23389/635	ex JA8169		[MHV]
☐ N815SA	Boeing 747-2L5B(SF)	22107/469	ex B-HMF		[MHV]
☐ N818SA	Boeing 747-346	23068/589	ex JA813J		[VCV]
☐ N774SA	Boeing 777-FZB	37986/844	ex N5023Q		Op for THA
☐ N775SA	Boeing 777-FZB	37987/852			Op for THA

SOUTHERN SEAPLANE — Southern Skies (SSC) — Belle Chase-Southern Seaplane SPB, LA (BCS)

☐ N2272X	Cessna U206E Skywagon	U20601556			FP
☐ N21058	de Havilland DHC-2 Beaver	630	ex CF-HOE		FP
☐ N61301	Cessna A185F Skywagon	18504144			FP
☐ N61441	Cessna A185F Skywagon	18504191			FP
☐ N70822	Cessna U206F Stationair	U20602099			FP

SOUTHWEST AIRLINES — Southwest (WN/SWA) — Dallas-Love Field, TX (DAL)

☐ N300SW	Boeing 737-3H4	22940/1037		The Spirit of Kitty Hawk	
☐ N302SW	Boeing 737-3H4	22942/1052		The Spirit of Kitty Hawk	
☐ N303SW	Boeing 737-3H4	22943/1101			
☐ N304SW	Boeing 737-3H4	22944/1138			
☐ N305SW	Boeing 737-3H4	22945/1139			[MHV]♦
☐ N306SW	Boeing 737-3H4	22946/1148			[MHV]♦
☐ N307SW	Boeing 737-3H4	22947/1156			[GYR]♦
☐ N308SA	Boeing 737-3Y0	23498/1233	ex G-EZYA		
☐ N310SW	Boeing 737-3H4	22949/1161			
☐ N311SW	Boeing 737-3H4	23333/1183			
☐ N312SW	Boeing 737-3H4	23334/1185			
☐ N313SW	Boeing 737-3H4	23335/1201			
☐ N314SW	Boeing 737-3H4	23336/1229			
☐ N315SW	Boeing 737-3H4	23337/1231			
☐ N316SW	Boeing 737-3H4	23338/1232			
☐ N317WN	Boeing 737-3Q8	24068/1506	ex G-EZYE		
☐ N318SW	Boeing 737-3H4	23339/1255			
☐ N323SW	Boeing 737-3H4	23344/1378			
☐ N325SW	Boeing 737-3H4	23689/1398			
☐ N326SW	Boeing 737-3H4	23690/1400			
☐ N327SW	Boeing 737-3H4	23691/1407			
☐ N328SW	Boeing 737-3H4	23692/1521			
☐ N329SW	Boeing 737-3H4	23693/1525			
☐ N330SW	Boeing 737-3H4	23694/1529			
☐ N331SW	Boeing 737-3H4	23695/1536			
☐ N332SW	Boeing 737-3H4	23696/1545			
☐ N333SW	Boeing 737-3H4	23697/1547			
☐ N334SW	Boeing 737-3H4	23938/1549		Shamu	
☐ N335SW	Boeing 737-3H4	23939/1553			
☐ N336SW	Boeing 737-3H4	23940/1557			
☐ N337SW	Boeing 737-3H4	23959/1567			
☐ N338SW	Boeing 737-3H4	23960/1571			
☐ N339SW	Boeing 737-3H4	24090/1591			
☐ N340LV	Boeing 737-3K2	23738/1360	ex PH-HVJ		
☐ N341SW	Boeing 737-3H4	24091/1593			
☐ N342SW	Boeing 737-3H4	24133/1682			
☐ N343SW	Boeing 737-3H4	24151/1686			
☐ N344SW	Boeing 737-3H4	24152/1688			
☐ N345SA	Boeing 737-3K2	23786/1386	ex PH-HVK		
☐ N346SW	Boeing 737-3H4	24153/1690			
☐ N347SW	Boeing 737-3H4	24374/1708			
☐ N348SW	Boeing 737-3H4	24375/1710			
☐ N349SW	Boeing 737-3H4	24408/1734			
☐ N350SW	Boeing 737-3H4	24409/1748			
☐ N351SW	Boeing 737-3H4	24572/1790			
☐ N352SW	Boeing 737-3H4/W	24888/1942		Lone Star One	

☐ N353SW	Boeing 737-3H4	24889/1947		
☐ N354SW	Boeing 737-3H4	25219/2092		
☐ N355SW	Boeing 737-3H4/W	25250/2103		
☐ N356SW	Boeing 737-3H4	25251/2105		
☐ N357SW	Boeing 737-3H4	26594/2294		
☐ N358SW	Boeing 737-3H4	26595/2295		
☐ N359SW	Boeing 737-3H4/W	26596/2297		
☐ N360SW	Boeing 737-3H4/W	26571/2307		
☐ N361SW	Boeing 737-3H4/W	26572/2309		
☐ N362SW	Boeing 737-3H4/W	26573/2322		
☐ N363SW	Boeing 737-3H4/W	26574/2429	Heroes of the Heart	
☐ N364SW	Boeing 737-3H4/W	26575/2430		
☐ N365SW	Boeing 737-3H4/W	26576/2433		
☐ N366SW	Boeing 737-3H4/W	26577/2469		
☐ N367SW	Boeing 737-3H4/W	26578/2470		
☐ N368SW	Boeing 737-3H4/W	26579/2473		
☐ N369SW	Boeing 737-3H4/W	26580/2477		
☐ N370SW	Boeing 737-3H4/W	26597/2497		
☐ N371SW	Boeing 737-3H4/W	26598/2500		
☐ N372SW	Boeing 737-3H4/W	26599/2504		
☐ N373SW	Boeing 737-3H4/W	26581/2509		
☐ N374SW	Boeing 737-3H4/W	26582/2515		
☐ N375SW	Boeing 737-3H4/W	26583/2520		
☐ N376SW	Boeing 737-3H4/W	26584/2570		
☐ N378SW	Boeing 737-3H4/W	26585/2579		
☐ N379SW	Boeing 737-3H4/W	26586/2580		
☐ N380SW	Boeing 737-3H4/W	26587/2610		
☐ N382SW	Boeing 737-3H4/W	26588/2611		
☐ N383SW	Boeing 737-3H4/W	26589/2612	Arizona One	
☐ N384SW	Boeing 737-3H4/W	26590/2613		
☐ N385SW	Boeing 737-3H4/W	26600/2617		
☐ N386SW	Boeing 737-3H4/W	26601/2626		
☐ N387SW	Boeing 737-3H4/W	26602/2627		
☐ N388SW	Boeing 737-3H4	26591/2628		
☐ N389SW	Boeing 737-3H4	26592/2629		
☐ N390SW	Boeing 737-3H4/W	26593/2642		
☐ N391SW	Boeing 737-3H4/W	27378/2643		
☐ N392SW	Boeing 737-3H4/W	27379/2644		
☐ N394SW	Boeing 737-3H4/W	27380/2645		
☐ N395SW	Boeing 737-3H4/W	27689/2667		
☐ N396SW	Boeing 737-3H4/W	27690/2668		
☐ N397SW	Boeing 737-3H4/W	27691/2695		
☐ N398SW	Boeing 737-3H4/W	27692/2696		
☐ N399WN	Boeing 737-3H4/W	27693/2697		
☐ N600WN	Boeing 737-3H4	27694/2699		
☐ N601WN	Boeing 737-3H4/W	27695/2702	Jack Vidal	
☐ N602SW	Boeing 737-3H4/W	27953/2713		
☐ N603SW	Boeing 737-3H4/W	27954/2714		
☐ N604SW	Boeing 737-3H4/W	27955/2715		
☐ N605SW	Boeing 737-3H4	27956/2716		
☐ N606SW	Boeing 737-3H4/W	27926/2740		
☐ N607SW	Boeing 737-3H4/W	27927/2741	June M Morris	
☐ N608SW	Boeing 737-3H4/W	27928/2742		
☐ N609SW	Boeing 737-3H4/W	27929/2744	California One	♦
☐ N610WN	Boeing 737-3H4/W	27696/2745		
☐ N611SW	Boeing 737-3H4/W	27697/2750		
☐ N612SW	Boeing 737-3H4/W	27930/2753		
☐ N613SW	Boeing 737-3H4	27931/2754		
☐ N614SW	Boeing 737-3H4/W	28033/2755		
☐ N615SW	Boeing 737-3H4/W	27698/2757		
☐ N616SW	Boeing 737-3H4/W	27699/2758		
☐ N617SW	Boeing 737-3H4/W	27700/2759	ex N1786B	
☐ N618WN	Boeing 737-3H4	28034/2761		
☐ N619SW	Boeing 737-3H4/W	28035/2762		
☐ N620SW	Boeing 737-3H4/W	28036/2766		
☐ N621SW	Boeing 737-3H4	28037/2767		
☐ N622SW	Boeing 737-3H4/W	27932/2779		
☐ N623SW	Boeing 737-3H4/W	27933/2780		
☐ N624SW	Boeing 737-3H4/W	27934/2781		
☐ N625SW	Boeing 737-3H4/W	27701/2787		
☐ N626SW	Boeing 737-3H4/W	27702/2789		
☐ N627SW	Boeing 737-3H4/W	27935/2790		
☐ N628SW	Boeing 737-3H4/W	27703/2795		
☐ N629SW	Boeing 737-3H4/W	27704/2796	25 Silver One	
☐ N630WN	Boeing 737-3H4/W	27705/2797		
☐ N631SW	Boeing 737-3H4/W	27706/2798		
☐ N632SW	Boeing 737-3H4/W	27707/2799		

☐ N633SW	Boeing 737-3H4/W	27936/2807		
☐ N634SW	Boeing 737-3H4/W	27937/2808		
☐ N635SW	Boeing 737-3H4/W	27708/2813		
☐ N636WN	Boeing 737-3H4/W	27709/2814		
☐ N637SW	Boeing 737-3H4/W	27710/2819		
☐ N638SW	Boeing 737-3H4/W	27711/2820		
☐ N639SW	Boeing 737-3H4/W	27712/2821		
☐ N640SW	Boeing 737-3H4/W	27713/2840		
☐ N641SW	Boeing 737-3H4/W	27714/2841		
☐ N642WN	Boeing 737-3H4/W	27715/2842		
☐ N643SW	Boeing 737-3H4/W	27716/2843		
☐ N644SW	Boeing 737-3H4/W	28329/2869		
☐ N645SW	Boeing 737-3H4/W	28330/2870		
☐ N646SW	Boeing 737-3H4/W	28331/2871		
☐ N647SW	Boeing 737-3H4/W	27717/2892	Triple Crown c/s	
☐ N648SW	Boeing 737-3H4/W	27718/2893		
☐ N649SW	Boeing 737-3H4/W	27719/2894		
☐ N650SW	Boeing 737-3H4/W	27720/2901		
☐ N651SW	Boeing 737-3H4/W	27721/2915		♦
☐ N652SW	Boeing 737-3H4/W	27722/2916		
☐ N653SW	Boeing 737-3H4/W	28398/2917		
☐ N654SW	Boeing 737-3H4/W	28399/2918		
☐ N655WN	Boeing 737-3H4/W	28400/2931		
☐ N656SW	Boeing 737-3H4/W	28401/2932		
☐ N657SW	Boeing 737-3L9	23331/1111	ex N960WP	
☐ N658SW	Boeing 737-3L9	23332/1118	ex N961WP	
☐ N659SW	Boeing 737-301	23229/1112	ex N950WP	
☐ N660SW	Boeing 737-301	23230/1115	ex N949WP	
☐ N661SW	Boeing 737-317	23173/1098	ex N946WP	
☐ N662SW	Boeing 737-3Q8	23255/1125	ex N327US	
☐ N663SW	Boeing 737-3Q8	23256/1128	ex N329US	
☐ N664WN	Boeing 737-3Y0	23495/1206	ex EC-FVT	
☐ N665WN	Boeing 737-3Y0	23497/1227	ex G-MONF	
☐ N669SW	Boeing 737-3A4	23752/1484	ex N758MA	
☐ N670SW	Boeing 737-3G7	23784/1533	ex N779MA	
☐ N671SW	Boeing 737-3G7	23785/1535	ex N778MA	
☐ N676SW	Boeing 737-3A4	23288/1100	ex N742MA	[MHV]♦
☐ N679AA	Boeing 737-3A4	23291/1211	ex N306AC	[MHV]♦
☐ N682SW	Boeing 737-3Y0	23496/1217	ex N67AB	
☐ N683SW	Boeing 737-3G7	24008/1576	ex N301AW	
☐ N684WN	Boeing 737-3T0	23941/1520	ex EC-EID	
☐ N685SW	Boeing 737-3Q8	23401/1209	ex G-BOWR	
☐ N686SW	Boeing 737-317	23175/1110	ex EI-CHU	
☐ N687SW	Boeing 737-3Q8	23388/1187	ex N103GU	
☐ N688SW	Boeing 737-3Q8	23254/1107	ex N780MA	
☐ N689SW	Boeing 737-3Q8	23387/1163	ex N734MA	
☐ N690SW	Boeing 737-3G7	23783/1531	ex N785MA	
☐ N691WN	Boeing 737-3G7	23781/1494	ex N784MA	
☐ N692SW	Boeing 737-3T5	23062/1083	ex N733MA	
☐ N693SW	Boeing 737-317	23174/1104	ex N775MA	
☐ N694SW	Boeing 737-3T5	23061/1080	ex N744MA	
☐ N697SW	Boeing 737-3T0	23838/1505	ex N764MA	
☐ N698SW	Boeing 737-317	23176/1213	ex EI-CHD	
☐ N699SW	Boeing 737-3Y0	23826/1372	ex EI-CHE	
☐ N501SW	Boeing 737-5H4	24178/1718	ex N73700	
☐ N502SW	Boeing 737-5H4	24179/1744		
☐ N503SW	Boeing 737-5H4	24180/1766		
☐ N504SW	Boeing 737-5H4	24181/1804		
☐ N505SW	Boeing 737-5H4	24182/1826		
☐ N506SW	Boeing 737-5H4	24183/1852		
☐ N507SW	Boeing 737-5H4	24184/1864		
☐ N508SW	Boeing 737-5H4	24185/1932		
☐ N509SW	Boeing 737-5H4	24186/1934		
☐ N510SW	Boeing 737-5H4	24187/1940		
☐ N511SW	Boeing 737-5H4	24188/2029		
☐ N512SW	Boeing 737-5H4	24189/2056		
☐ N513SW	Boeing 737-5H4	24190/2058		
☐ N514SW	Boeing 737-5H4	25153/2078		
☐ N515SW	Boeing 737-5H4	25154/2080		
☐ N519SW	Boeing 737-5H4	25318/2121		
☐ N520SW	Boeing 737-5H4	25319/2134		
☐ N521SW	Boeing 737-5H4	25320/2136		
☐ N522SW	Boeing 737-5H4	26564/2202		
☐ N523SW	Boeing 737-5H4	26565/2204		
☐ N524SW	Boeing 737-5H4	26566/2224		
☐ N525SW	Boeing 737-5H4	26567/2283		

☐	N526SW	Boeing 737-5H4	26568/2285		
☐	N527SW	Boeing 737-5H4	26569/2287		
☐	N528SW	Boeing 737-5H4	26570/2292		
☐	N200WN	Boeing 737-7H4/W	32482/1638	ex N1795B	
☐	N201LV	Boeing 737-7H4/W	29854/1650		Fred J Jones
☐	N202WN	Boeing 737-7H4/W	33999/1653		
☐	N203WN	Boeing 737-7H4/W	32483/1656		
☐	N204WN	Boeing 737-7H4/W	29855/1663		
☐	N205WN	Boeing 737-7H4/W	34010/1668	ex N1784B	
☐	N206WN	Boeing 737-7H4/W	34011/1675		
☐	N207WN	Boeing 737-7H4/W	34012/1678		
☐	N208WN	Boeing 737-7H4/W	29856/1679		
☐	N209WN	Boeing 737-7H4/W	32484/1683	ex N1787B	
☐	N210WN	Boeing 737-7H4/W	34162/1690		
☐	N211WN	Boeing 737-7H4/W	34163/1699		
☐	N212WN	Boeing 737-7H4/W	32485/1708		
☐	N213WN	Boeing 737-7H4/W	34217/1717		
☐	N214WN	Boeing 737-7H4/W	32486/1721		Maryland One
☐	N215WN	Boeing 737-7H4/W	32487/1723		Ron Chapman
☐	N216WR	Boeing 737-7H4/W	32488/1735	ex N1784B	
☐	N217JC	Boeing 737-7H4/W	34232/1737	ex (N217WN)	
☐	N218WN	Boeing 737-7H4/W	32489/1741		
☐	N219WN	Boeing 737-7H4/W	32490/1744	ex N1786B	
☐	N220WN	Boeing 737-7H4/W	32491/1756		
☐	N221WN	Boeing 737-7H4/W	34259/1776	ex N1786B	
☐	N222WN	Boeing 737-7H4/W	34290/1780		
☐	N223WN	Boeing 737-7H4/W	32492/1799	ex N1795B	
☐	N224WN	Boeing 737-7H4/W	32493/1801	ex N1786B	Slam Dunk One
☐	N225WN	Boeing 737-7H4/W	34333/1820		
☐	N226WN	Boeing 737-7H4/W	32494/1822	ex N1786B	
☐	N227WN	Boeing 737-7H4/W	34450/1831	ex N1786B	
☐	N228WN	Boeing 737-7H4/W	32496/1835	ex N1780B	
☐	N229WN	Boeing 737-7H4/W	32498/1858		
☐	N230WN	Boeing 737-7H4/W	34592/1868		5000th 737 built
☐	N231WN	Boeing 737-7H4/W	32499/1881	ex N1787B	
☐	N232WN	Boeing 737-7H4/W	32500/1888		
☐	N233LV	Boeing 737-7H4/W	32501/1893		
☐	N234WN	Boeing 737-7H4/W	32502/1905		
☐	N235WN	Boeing 737-7H4/W	34630/1916	ex N1787B	
☐	N236WN	Boeing 737-7H4/W	34631/1928	ex N1786B	
☐	N237WN	Boeing 737-7H4/W	34632/1930		
☐	N238WN	Boeing 737-7H4/W	34713/1950		Spreading the LUV
☐	N239WN	Boeing 737-7H4/W	34714/1954	ex N1786B	
☐	N240WN	Boeing 737-7H4/W	32503/1959	ex N1786B	
☐	N241WN	Boeing 737-7H4/W	32504/1965		
☐	N242WN	Boeing 737-7H4/W	32505/1969		
☐	N243WN	Boeing 737-7H4/W	34863/1973		
☐	N244WN	Boeing 737-7H4/W	34864/1977		
☐	N245WN	Boeing 737-7H4/W	32506/1982		
☐	N246LV	Boeing 737-7H4/W	32507/1984	ex N1786B	
☐	N247WN	Boeing 737-7H4/W	32508/1989		
☐	N248WN	Boeing 737-7H4/W	32509/2000		
☐	N249WN	Boeing 737-7H4/W	34951/2005		
☐	N250WN	Boeing 737-7H4/W	34972/2019		
☐	N251WN	Boeing 737-7H4/W	32510/2025		
☐	N252WN	Boeing 737-7H4/W	34973/2027		
☐	N253WN	Boeing 737-7H4/W	32511/2038		
☐	N254WN	Boeing 737-7H4/W	32512/2040		
☐	N255WN	Boeing 737-7H4/W	32513/2049		
☐	N256WN	Boeing 737-7H4/W	32514/2059		
☐	N257WN	Boeing 737-7H4/W	32515/2062		
☐	N258WN	Boeing 737-7H4/W	32516/2076		
☐	N259WN	Boeing 737-7H4/W	35554/2092		
☐	N260WN	Boeing 737-7H4/W	32518/2114	ex N1786B	
☐	N261WN	Boeing 737-7H4/W	32517/2133	ex N1787B	
☐	N262WN	Boeing 737-7H4/W	32519/2139	ex N1786B	
☐	N263WN	Boeing 737-7H4/W	32520/2153		
☐	N264LV	Boeing 737-7H4/W	32521/2161		
☐	N265WN	Boeing 737-7H4/W	32522/2174		
☐	N266WN	Boeing 737-7H4/W	32523/2182	ex N1787B	Colleen Barrett
☐	N267WN	Boeing 737-7H4/W	32525/2193		
☐	N268WN	Boeing 737-7H4/W	32524/2199		
☐	N269WN	Boeing 737-7H4/W	32526/2204		
☐	N270WN	Boeing 737-705/W	29089/83	ex VP-BBT	
☐	N271LV	Boeing 737-705/W	29090/109	ex VP-BBU	
☐	N272WN	Boeing 737-7H4/W	32527/2224	ex N1786B	

☐ N273WN	Boeing 737-7H4/W	32528/2238		
☐ N274WN	Boeing 737-7H4/W	32529/2244		
☐ N275WN	Boeing 737-7H4/W	36153/2256		
☐ N276WN	Boeing 737-7H4/W	32530/2262		
☐ N277WN	Boeing 737-7H4/W	32531/2274		
☐ N278WN	Boeing 737-7H4/W	36441/2281	ex N1787B	
☐ N279WN	Boeing 737-7H4/W	32532/2284	ex N1786B	
☐ N280WN	Boeing 737-7H4/W	32533/2294		
☐ N281WN	Boeing 737-7H4/W	36528/2307		Southwest's 500th Boeing 737
☐ N282WN	Boeing 737-7H4/W	32534/2318		
☐ N283WN	Boeing 737-7H4/W	36610/2322		
☐ N284WN	Boeing 737-7H4/W	32535/2328	ex N1786B	
☐ N285WN	Boeing 737-7H4/W	32536/2337		
☐ N286WN	Boeing 737-7H4/W	32471/1535	ex N471WN	
☐ N287WN	Boeing 737-7H4/W	32537/2344	ex N1786B	
☐ N288WN	Boeing 737-7H4/W	36611/2350	ex N1786B	
☐ N289CT	Boeing 737-7H4/W	36633/2354	ex N1786B	
☐ N290WN	Boeing 737-7H4/W	36632/2363		
☐ N291WN	Boeing 737-7H4/W	32539/2378		
☐ N292WN	Boeing 737-7H4/W	32538/2383		
☐ N293WN	Boeing 737-7H4/W	36612/2387		
☐ N294WN	Boeing 737-7H4/W	32540/2390	ex N1786B	
☐ N295WN	Boeing 737-7H4/W	32541/2409		
☐ N296WN	Boeing 737-7H4/W	36613/2413		
☐ N297WN	Boeing 737-7H4/W	32542/2417		
☐ N298WN	Boeing 737-7H4/W	32543/2438		
☐ N299WN	Boeing 737-7H4/W	36614/2442		
☐ N400WN	Boeing 737-7H4/W	27891/806		
☐ N401WN	Boeing 737-7H4/W	29813/810		
☐ N402WN	Boeing 737-7H4/W	29814/811	ex N1786B	
☐ N403WN	Boeing 737-7H4/W	29815/821	ex N1786B	
☐ N404WN	Boeing 737-7H4/W	27892/880	ex N1787B	
☐ N405WN	Boeing 737-7H4/W	27893/881	ex N1786B	
☐ N406WN	Boeing 737-7H4/W	27894/885	ex N1786B	
☐ N407WN	Boeing 737-7H4/W	29817/903	ex N1786B	
☐ N408WN	Boeing 737-7H4/W	27895/934	ex N1786B	
☐ N409WN	Boeing 737-7H4/W	27896/945	ex N1787B	
☐ N410WN	Boeing 737-7H4/W	27897/946	ex N1786B	
☐ N411WN	Boeing 737-7H4/W	29821/950	ex N1786B	
☐ N412WN	Boeing 737-7H4/W	29818/956	ex N1795B	
☐ N413WN	Boeing 737-7H4/W	29819/960		
☐ N414WN	Boeing 737-7H4/W	29820/967	ex N1795B	
☐ N415WN	Boeing 737-7H4/W	29836/980	ex N1787B	
☐ N416WN	Boeing 737-7H4/W	32453/990	ex N1786B	
☐ N417WN	Boeing 737-7H4/W	29822/993	ex N1786B	The Rollin W King
☐ N418WN	Boeing 737-7H4/W	29823/1000		The Winning Spirit
☐ N419WN	Boeing 737-7H4/W	29824/1017	ex N1786B	
☐ N420WN	Boeing 737-7H4/W	29825/1039		
☐ N421LV	Boeing 737-7H4/W	32452/1040		
☐ N422WN	Boeing 737-7H4/W	29826/1093		
☐ N423WN	Boeing 737-7H4/W	29827/1101		
☐ N424WN	Boeing 737-7H4/W	29828/1105		
☐ N425LV	Boeing 737-7H4/W	29829/1109		
☐ N426WN	Boeing 737-7H4/W	29830/1114		
☐ N427WN	Boeing 737-7H4/W	29831/1119		
☐ N428WN	Boeing 737-7H4/W	29844/1243		
☐ N429WN	Boeing 737-7H4/W	33658/1256		
☐ N430WN	Boeing 737-7H4/W	33659/1257		
☐ N431WN	Boeing 737-7H4/W	29845/1259		
☐ N432WN	Boeing 737-7H4/W	33715/1297	ex N1786B	
☐ N433LV	Boeing 737-7H4/W	33716/1301		
☐ N434WN	Boeing 737-7H4/W	32454/1313		
☐ N435WN	Boeing 737-7H4/W	32455/1328		
☐ N436WN	Boeing 737-7H4/W	32456/1342		
☐ N437WN	Boeing 737-7H4/W	29832/1349		
☐ N438WN	Boeing 737-7H4/W	29833/1353		
☐ N439WN	Boeing 737-7H4/W	29834/1356		The Donald G Ogden
☐ N440LV	Boeing 737-7H4/W	29835/1358		
☐ N441WN	Boeing 737-7H4/W	29837/1360		
☐ N442WN	Boeing 737-7H4/W	32459/1365	ex (N442LV)	
☐ N443WN	Boeing 737-7H4/W	29838/1369		The Spirit of Hope
☐ N444WN	Boeing 737-7H4/W	29839/1374	ex N1786B	
☐ N445WN	Boeing 737-7H4/W	29841/1388		
☐ N446WN	Boeing 737-7H4/W	29842/1401	ex N1787B	
☐ N447WN	Boeing 737-7H4/W	33720/1405		
☐ N448WN	Boeing 737-7H4/W	33721/1409		The Spirit of Kitty Hawk
☐ N449WN	Boeing 737-7H4/W	32469/1427		

☐ N450WN	Boeing 737-7H4/W	32470/1429	ex N60668		
☐ N451WN	Boeing 737-7H4/W	32495/1458			
☐ N452WN	Boeing 737-7H4/W	29846/1461			
☐ N453WN	Boeing 737-7H4/W	29847/1476			
☐ N454WN	Boeing 737-7H4/W	29851/1477			
☐ N455WN	Boeing 737-7H4/W	32462/1480			
☐ N456WN	Boeing 737-7H4/W	32463/1484			
☐ N457WN	Boeing 737-7H4/W	33856/1485			
☐ N458WN	Boeing 737-7H4/W	33857/1490			
☐ N459WN	Boeing 737-7H4/W	32497/1492			
☐ N460WN	Boeing 737-7H4/W	32464/1499			
☐ N461WN	Boeing 737-7H4/W	32465/1510			
☐ N462WN	Boeing 737-7H4/W	32466/1513			
☐ N463WN	Boeing 737-7H4/W	32467/1515			
☐ N464WN	Boeing 737-7H4/W	32468/1517			
☐ N465WN	Boeing 737-7H4/W	33829/1519			
☐ N466WN	Boeing 737-7H4/W	30677/1520			
☐ N467WN	Boeing 737-7H4/W	33830/1521			
☐ N468WN	Boeing 737-7H4/W	33858/1523			
☐ N469WN	Boeing 737-7H4/W	33859/1525			
☐ N470WN	Boeing 737-7H4/W	33860/1528			
☐ N472WN	Boeing 737-7H4/W	33831/1537			
☐ N473WN	Boeing 737-7H4/W	33832/1541			
☐ N474WN	Boeing 737-7H4/W	33861/1543	ex N1786B		
☐ N475WN	Boeing 737-7H4/W	32474/1545			
☐ N476WN	Boeing 737-7H4/W	32475/1549			
☐ N477WN	Boeing 737-7H4/W	33988/1552			
☐ N478WN	Boeing 737-7H4/W	33989/1555			
☐ N479WN	Boeing 737-7H4/W	33990/1558			
☐ N480WN	Boeing 737-7H4/W	33998/1561			
☐ N481WN	Boeing 737-7H4/W	29853/1564			
☐ N482WN	Boeing 737-7H4/W	29852/1568			
☐ N483WN	Boeing 737-7H4/W	32472/1570			
☐ N484WN	Boeing 737-7H4/W	33841/1575	ex N1786B		
☐ N485WN	Boeing 737-7H4/W	32473/1577	ex N1786B		
☐ N486WN	Boeing 737-7H4/W	33852/1579			
☐ N487WN	Boeing 737-7H4/W	33854/1583			
☐ N488WN	Boeing 737-7H4/W	33853/1587			
☐ N489WN	Boeing 737-7H4/W	33855/1589	ex N1780B		
☐ N490WN	Boeing 737-7H4/W	32476/1591		100 H-E-B titles	
☐ N491WN	Boeing 737-7H4/W	33867/1598			
☐ N492WN	Boeing 737-7H4/W	33866/1605			
☐ N493WN	Boeing 737-7H4/W	32477/1616			
☐ N494WN	Boeing 737-7H4/W	33868/1621			
☐ N495WN	Boeing 737-7H4/W	33869/1625			
☐ N496WN	Boeing 737-7H4/W	32478/1626			
☐ N497WN	Boeing 737-7H4/W	32479/1628			
☐ N498WN	Boeing 737-7H4/W	32480/1633			
☐ N499WN	Boeing 737-7H4/W	32481/1636			
☐ N550WN	Boeing 737-76Q/W	30279/1010	ex VT-SIR		
☐ N551WN	Boeing 737-76Q/W	30280/1025	ex VT-SIS		
☐ N554WN	Boeing 737-7BX/W	30746/1085	ex VH-VBS		o/o♦
☐ N555LV	Boeing 737-7H4/W	36726			o/o♦
☐ N556WN	Boeing 737-7H4/W	33936			o/o♦
☐ N700GS	Boeing 737-7H4/W	27835/4			
☐ N701GS	Boeing 737-7H4/W	27836/6	ex N35108		
☐ N703SW	Boeing 737-7H4/W	27837/12	ex N1792B		
☐ N704SW	Boeing 737-7H4/W	27838/15			
☐ N705SW	Boeing 737-7H4/W	27839/20			
☐ N706SW	Boeing 737-7H4/W	27840/24			
☐ N707SA	Boeing 737-7H4/W	27841/1	ex N737X		
☐ N708SW	Boeing 737-7H4/W	27842/2			
☐ N709SW	Boeing 737-7H4/W	27843/3			
☐ N710SW	Boeing 737-7H4/W	27844/34	ex N1787B		
☐ N711HK	Boeing 737-7H4/W	27845/38		The Herbert D Kelleher	
☐ N712SW	Boeing 737-7H4/W	27846/53			
☐ N713SW	Boeing 737-7H4/W	27847/54		Shamu c/s	
☐ N714CB	Boeing 737-7H4/W	27848/61		Southwest Classic colours	
☐ N715SW	Boeing 737-7H4/W	27849/62		Shamu c/s	
☐ N716SW	Boeing 737-7H4/W	27850/64			
☐ N717SA	Boeing 737-7H4/W	27851/70	ex N1799B		
☐ N718SW	Boeing 737-7H4/W	27852/71	ex N3134C		
☐ N719SW	Boeing 737-7H4/W	27853/82			
☐ N720WN	Boeing 737-7H4/W	27854/121	ex N1787B		
☐ N723SW	Boeing 737-7H4/W	27855/199	ex N1787B		
☐ N724SW	Boeing 737-7H4/W	27856/201	ex N1787B		
☐ N725SW	Boeing 737-7H4/W	27857/208	ex N1786B		

☐ N726SW	Boeing 737-7H4/W	27858/213			
☐ N727SW	Boeing 737-7H4/W	27859/274	ex N1786B	Nevada One c/s	
☐ N728SW	Boeing 737-7H4/W	27860/276	ex N1787B		
☐ N729SW	Boeing 737-7H4/W	27861/278	ex N1786B		
☐ N730SW	Boeing 737-7H4/W	27862/284	ex N1795B		
☐ N731SA	Boeing 737-7H4/W	27863/318	ex N1786B		
☐ N732SW	Boeing 737-7H4/W	27864/319	ex N1787B		
☐ N733SA	Boeing 737-7H4/W	27865/320	ex N1787B		
☐ N734SA	Boeing 737-7H4/W	27866/324	ex N1795B		
☐ N735SA	Boeing 737-7H4/W	27867/354	ex N1786B		
☐ N736SA	Boeing 737-7H4/W	27868/357	ex N1786B		
☐ N737JW	Boeing 737-7H4/W	27869/358			
☐ N738CB	Boeing 737-7H4/W	27870/360	ex N1786B		
☐ N739GB	Boeing 737-7H4/W	29275/144	ex N1786B		
☐ N740SW	Boeing 737-7H4/W	29276/155			
☐ N741SA	Boeing 737-7H4/W	29277/157			
☐ N742SW	Boeing 737-7H4/W	29278/172		Nolan Ryan Express	
☐ N743SW	Boeing 737-7H4/W	29279/175	ex N60436		
☐ N744SW	Boeing 737-7H4/W	29490/232	ex N1781B		
☐ N745SW	Boeing 737-7H4/W	29491/237	ex "N728SW"		
☐ N746SW	Boeing 737-7H4/W	29798/299	ex N1786B		
☐ N747SA	Boeing 737-7H4/W	29799/306			
☐ N748SW	Boeing 737-7H4/W	29800/331	ex N1786B		
☐ N749SW	Boeing 737-7H4/W	29801/343	ex N1786B		
☐ N750SA	Boeing 737-7H4/W	29802/366			
☐ N751SW	Boeing 737-7H4/W	29803/373	ex N1786B		
☐ N752SW	Boeing 737-7H4/W	29804/387			
☐ N753SW	Boeing 737-7H4/W	29848/400	ex N1787B		
☐ N754SW	Boeing 737-7H4/W	29849/416	ex N1787B		
☐ N755SA	Boeing 737-7H4/W	27871/419	ex N1787B		
☐ N756SA	Boeing 737-7H4/W	27872/422	ex N1786B		
☐ N757LV	Boeing 737-7H4/W	29850/425	ex N1786B		
☐ N758SW	Boeing 737-7H4/W	27873/437	ex N1786B		
☐ N759GS	Boeing 737-7H4/W	30544/448	ex N1786B		
☐ N760SW	Boeing 737-7H4/W	27874/468	ex N1786B		
☐ N761RR	Boeing 737-7H4/W	27875/495			
☐ N762SW	Boeing 737-7H4/W	27876/512	ex N1786B		
☐ N763SW	Boeing 737-7H4/W	27877/520	ex N1786B		
☐ N764SW	Boeing 737-7H4/W	27878/521	ex N1787B		
☐ N765SW	Boeing 737-7H4/W	29805/525	ex N1786B		
☐ N766SW	Boeing 737-7H4/W	29806/537	ex N1786B		
☐ N767SW	Boeing 737-7H4/W	29807/541	ex N1787B		
☐ N768SW	Boeing 737-7H4/W	30587/580	ex N1002R		
☐ N769SW	Boeing 737-7H4/W	30588/592			
☐ N770SA	Boeing 737-7H4/W	30589/595			
☐ N771SA	Boeing 737-7H4/W	27879/599			
☐ N772SW	Boeing 737-7H4/W	27880/601			
☐ N773SA	Boeing 737-7H4/W	27881/603	ex N1786B		
☐ N774SW	Boeing 737-7H4/W	27882/609	ex N1786B		
☐ N775SW	Boeing 737-7H4/W	30590/617	ex N1786B		
☐ N776WN	Boeing 737-7H4/W	30591/620	ex N1786B		
☐ N777QC	Boeing 737-7H4/W	30592/621	ex N1786B		
☐ N778SW	Boeing 737-7H4/W	27883/626	ex N1786B		
☐ N779SW	Boeing 737-7H4/W	27884/628	ex N1786B		
☐ N780SW	Boeing 737-7H4/W	27885/643	ex N1786B		
☐ N781WN	Boeing 737-7H4/W	30601/646		New Mexico One	
☐ N782SA	Boeing 737-7H4/W	29808/670	ex N1787B		
☐ N783SW	Boeing 737-7H4/W	29809/675	ex N1785B		
☐ N784SW	Boeing 737-7H4/W	29810/677	ex N1786B		
☐ N785SW	Boeing 737-7H4/W	30602/693	ex N1786B		
☐ N786SW	Boeing 737-7H4/W	29811/698	ex N1787B		
☐ N787SA	Boeing 737-7H4/W	29812/705	ex N1786B		
☐ N788SA	Boeing 737-7H4/W	30603/707	ex N1786B		
☐ N789SW	Boeing 737-7H4/W	29816/718	ex N1786B		
☐ N790SW	Boeing 737-7H4/W	30604/721	ex N1786B		
☐ N791SW	Boeing 737-7H4/W	27886/736	ex N1786B		
☐ N792SW	Boeing 737-7H4/W	27887/737			
☐ N793SA	Boeing 737-7H4/W	27888/744	ex N1786B	Spirit One	
☐ N794SW	Boeing 737-7H4/W	30605/748	ex N1781B		
☐ N795SW	Boeing 737-7H4/W	30606/780	ex N1786B		
☐ N796SW	Boeing 737-7H4/W	27889/784	ex N1786B		
☐ N797MX	Boeing 737-7H4/W	27890/803			
☐ N798SW	Boeing 737-7AD/W	28436/41	ex N700EW		
☐ N799SW	Boeing 737-7Q8/W	28209/14	ex 9Y-TJI		
☐ N900WN	Boeing 737-7H4/W	32544/2460			
☐ N901WN	Boeing 737-7H4/W	32545/2462			
☐ N902WN	Boeing 737-7H4/W	36615/2469			

☐ N903WN	Boeing 737-7H4/W	32457/2473		
☐ N904WN	Boeing 737-7H4/W	36616/2480	ex N1780B	
☐ N905WN	Boeing 737-7H4/W	36617/2491	ex N1786B	
☐ N906WN	Boeing 737-7H4/W	36887/2494		
☐ N907WN	Boeing 737-7H4/W	36619/2500		
☐ N908WN	Boeing 737-7H4/W	36620/2509	ex N1786B	
☐ N909WN	Boeing 737-7H4/W	32458/2517		
☐ N910WN	Boeing 737-7H4/W	36618/2521	ex N1786B	
☐ N912WN	Boeing 737-7H4/W	36621/2532	ex N1786B	
☐ N913WN	Boeing 737-7H4/W	29840/2536	ex N1787B	
☐ N914WN	Boeing 737-7H4/W	36622/2540	ex N1787B	
☐ N915WN	Boeing 737-7H4/W	36888/2546		
☐ N916WN	Boeing 737-7H4/W	36623/2558		
☐ N917WN	Boeing 737-7H4/W	36624/2562	ex N1787B	
☐ N918WN	Boeing 737-7H4/W	29843/2572		
☐ N919WN	Boeing 737-7H4/W	36625/2591		
☐ N920WN	Boeing 737-7H4/W	32460/2597	ex N1796B	
☐ N921WN	Boeing 737-7H4/W	36626/2600		
☐ N922WN	Boeing 737-7H4/W	32461/2620		
☐ N923WN	Boeing 737-7H4/W	36627/2634		
☐ N924WN	Boeing 737-7H4/W	36628/2640		
☐ N925WN	Boeing 737-7H4/W	36630/2656	ex N1786B	
☐ N926WN	Boeing 737-7H4/W	36629/2663	ex N1786B	
☐ N927WN	Boeing 737-7H4/W	36889/2679		
☐ N928WN	Boeing 737-7H4/W	36890/2687		
☐ N929WN	Boeing 737-7H4/W	36631/2689		
☐ N930WN	Boeing 737-7H4/W	36636/2784	ex N1786B	
☐ N931WN	Boeing 737-7H4/W	36637/2799	ex N1799B	
☐ N932WN	Boeing 737-7H4/W	36639/2837	ex N1786B	
☐ N933WN	Boeing 737-7H4/W	36640/2847		
☐ N934WN	Boeing 737-7H4/W	36642/2878		
☐ N935WN	Boeing 737-7H4/W	36641/2894		
☐ N936WN	Boeing 737-7H4/W	36643/2909	ex N1787B	
☐ N937WN	Boeing 737-7H4/W	36644/2925	ex N1787B	
☐ N938WN	Boeing 737-7H4/W	36645/2929	ex N1786B	
☐ N939WN	Boeing 737-7H4/W	36646/2933	ex N1787B	
☐ N940WN	Boeing 737-7H4/W	36900/2943	ex N1786B	
☐ N941WN	Boeing 737-7H4/W	36647/2961	ex N1796B	
☐ N942WN	Boeing 737-7H4/W	36648/2985	ex N1787B	
☐ N943WN	Boeing 737-7H4/W	36913/3195	ex N1786B	◆
☐ N944WN	Boeing 737-7H4/W	36659/3220		◆
☐ N945WN	Boeing 737-7H4/W	36660/3226	ex N1787B	◆
☐ N946WN	Boeing 737-7H4/W	36918/3251		◆
☐ N947WN	Boeing 737-7H4/W	36924/3290	ex N1787B	◆
☐ N948WN	Boeing 737-7H4/W	36662/3296		◆
☐ N949WN	Boeing 737-7H4/W	36663/3358	ex N1786B	◆
☐ N950WN	Boeing 737-7H4/W	36664/3365	ex N1799B	◆
☐ N951WN	Boeing 737-7H4/W	36665/3388		◆
☐ N952WN	Boeing 737-7H4/W	36667/3477		◆
☐ N953WN	Boeing 737-7H4/W	36668/3510	ex N1786B	◆
☐ N954WN	Boeing 737-7H4/W	36669/		o/o◆
☐ N955WN	Boeing 737-7H4/W	36671/		o/o◆
☐ N956WN	Boeing 737-7H4/W	36672/		o/o◆
☐ N958WN	Boeing 737-7H4/W	36673/		o/o◆
☐ N959WN	Boeing 737-7H4/W	36674/		o/o◆
☐ N960WN	Boeing 737-7H4/W	36675/		o/o◆
☐ N961WN	Boeing 737-7H4/W	36962/		o/o◆
☐ N962WN	Boeing 737-7H4/W	36963/		o/o◆
☐ N963WN	Boeing 737-7H4/W	36676/		o/o◆
☐ N964WN	Boeing 737-7H4/W	36965/		o/o◆
☐ N965WN	Boeing 737-7H4/W	36677/		o/o◆
☐ N966WN	Boeing 737-7H4/W	36966/		o/o◆
☐ N967WN	Boeing 737-7H4/W	36967/		o/o◆

SPERNAK AIRWAYS   Anchorage-Merrill, AK (MRI)

☐ N29CF	Cessna 207 Skywagon	20700353	
☐ N6492H	Cessna 207A Stationair 7 II	20700544	
☐ N7392U	Cessna 207A Stationair 7 II	20700435	
☐ N73047	Cessna 207A Stationair 7 II	20700556	ex XB-EXR

SPIRIT AIRLINES   Spirit Wings (NK/NKS)   Fort Lauderdale-Hollywood Intl, FL (FLL)

☐ N502NK	Airbus A319-132	2433	ex D-AVWX	St Maarten/St Martin
☐ N503NK	Airbus A319-132	2470	ex D-AVYJ	The Caribbean
☐ N504NK	Airbus A319-132	2473	ex D-AVYP	The Bahamas
☐ N505NK	Airbus A319-132	2485	ex D-AVYI	

☐ N506NK	Airbus A319-132	2490	ex D-AVWH	
☐ N507NK	Airbus A319-132	2560	ex D-AVYV	
☐ N508NK	Airbus A319-132	2567	ex D-AVWM	
☐ N509NK	Airbus A319-132	2603	ex D-AVXO	
☐ N510NK	Airbus A319-132	2622	ex D-AVYT	Fort Lauderdale
☐ N512NK	Airbus A319-132	2673	ex D-AVYO	Turks & Caicos Islands
☐ N514NK	Airbus A319-132	2679	ex D-AVYV	Cayman Islands
☐ N516NK	Airbus A319-132	2704	ex D-AVXJ	Cancun
☐ N517NK	Airbus A319-132	2711	ex D-AVYM	Orlando
☐ N522NK	Airbus A319-132	2893	ex D-AVYY	Las Vegas
☐ N523NK	Airbus A319-132	2898	ex D-AVWN	Tampa
☐ N524NK	Airbus A319-132	2929	ex D-AVYU	Suncatcher
☐ N525NK	Airbus A319-132	2942	ex D-AVWX	The Americas
☐ N526NK	Airbus A319-132	2963	ex D-AVYM	
☐ N527NK	Airbus A319-132	2978	ex D-AVXD	
☐ N528NK	Airbus A319-132	2983	ex D-AVXI	
☐ N529NK	Airbus A319-132	3007	ex D-AVYL	
☐ N530NK	Airbus A319-132	3017	ex D-AVXL	
☐ N531NK	Airbus A319-132	3026	ex D-AVWC	
☐ N532NK	Airbus A319-132	3165	ex D-AVYX	
☐ N533NK	Airbus A319-132	3393	ex D-AVWJ	
☐ N534NK	Airbus A319-132	3395	ex D-AVWK	
☐	Airbus A319-132		ex	o/o♦

All names prefixed 'Spirit of'

☐ N601NK	Airbus A320-232	4206	ex D-AVVI	♦
☐ N602NK	Airbus A320-232	4264	ex D-AXAD	♦
☐ N603NK	Airbus A320-232	4321	ex D-AXAM	♦
☐ N604NK	Airbus A320-232	4431	ex D-AVVO	♦
☐ N605NK	Airbus A320-232	4548	ex F-WWIV	♦
☐ N606NK	Airbus A320-232	4592	ex F-WWIR	o/o♦
☐ N607NK	Airbus A320-232	4595	ex F-WWIZ	o/o♦

☐ N587NK	Airbus A321-231	2476	ex D-AVXB	Jamaica
☐ N588NK	Airbus A321-231	2590	ex D-AVZK	

SPUR AVIATION   Twin Falls, ID (TWF)

☐ N531SA	Rockwell 500S Shrike Commander	3059	ex N9027N
☐ N532SA	Aero Commander 500S Shrike	1868-44	ex N9032N
☐ N533SA	Aero Commander 500S Shrike	1786-9	ex N4664E
☐ N534SA	Aero Commander 500S Shrike	1816-22	ex N8485P
☐ N535SA	Rockwell 500S Shrike Commander	3138	ex N1BK
☐ N536SA	Rockwell 500S Shrike Commander	3169	ex N54LW
☐ N50655	Rockwell Turbo Commander 680V	1714-88	ex XB-CED
☐ N54163	Rockwell Turbo Commander 680W	1774-12	ex N5416

STARS AND STRIPES AIR TOURS   Boulder City, AZ

☐ N208WF	Cessna 208B Caravan I	208B1042	ex N208JF
☐ N1242Y	Cessna 208B Caravan I	208B0939	ex N124LA

Helicopter flights operated by Las Vegas Helicopters

SUBURBAN AIR FREIGHT   Sub Air (SUB)   Omaha-Eppley Airfield, NE (OMA)

☐ N114MN	Aero Commander 680FL	1553-107	ex (N2611L)
☐ N290MP	Aero Commander 680FL	1535-104	
☐ N309VS	Aero Commander 680FL	1659-128	ex N6626V
☐ N2828S	Aero Commander 680FL	1329-14	
☐ N4983S	Aero Commander 680FL	1427-70	ex CF-LAC
☐ N5035E	Aero Commander 680FL	1764-147	
☐ N9011N	Aero Commander 680FL	1836-153	
☐ N118SF	Beech C99	U-32	ex C-FESU
☐ N124GP	Beech 1900C	UB-23	ex N23VK
☐ N128SF	Beech 99	U-87	ex N59CA
☐ N147SF	Beech 99	U-47	ex N204BH
☐ N208QC	Cessna 208B Caravan I	208B0774	ex N5261R
☐ N253SF	Beech 1900C-1	UC-53	ex N31764 ♦
☐ N398A	Cessna 208B Caravan I	208B0390	ex LN-TWE
☐ N719GL	Beech 1900C	UB-19	ex N314BH
☐ N864SF	Cessna 208B Caravan I	208B0864	
☐ N895SF	Cessna 208B Caravan I	208B0095	ex N9662B
☐ N7994R	Beech C99	U-103	

SUN COUNTRY AIRLINES   Sun Country (SY/SCX)   Minneapolis/St Paul Intl, MN (MSP)

☐ N710SY	Boeing 737-73V	30241/1034	ex N241CL
☐ N711SY	Boeing 737-73V	30245/1058	ex G-EZJJ

☐ N712SY	Boeing 737-7Q8	28219/183	ex PR-GOU	◆
☐ N801SY	Boeing 737-8Q8/W	30332/777	ex N1787B	The Phoenix
☐ N804SY	Boeing 737-8Q8/W	30689/908		Laughlin Luck
☐ N805SY	Boeing 737-8Q8/W	30032/985	ex N1781B	The Spirit of Minnesota
☐ N806SY	Boeing 737-8Q8/W	28215/75	ex N800NA	
☐ N809SY	Boeing 737-8Q8/W	30683/1669		
☐ N813SY	Boeing 737-8Q8	28237/769	ex OY-SED	

SUPERIOR AVIATION   Spend Air (SO/HKA)   Iron Mountain-Kingsford, MI (IMT)

☐ N6851X	Cessna 441 Conquest II	441-0212

SUPERIOR HELICOPTERS   Glendale-Heliport, OR

☐ N161KA	Kaman K-1200 K-Max	A94-0016
☐ N312KA	Kaman K-1200 K-Max	A94-0024

TALKEETNA AIR TAXI   Talkeetna, AK (TKA)

☐ N144Q	de Havilland DHC-2 Beaver	1465		Wheels or skis
☐ N185FK	Cessna A185F Skywagon	18502513	ex N1796R	Wheels or skis
☐ N561TA	de Havilland DHC-2 Beaver	581	ex CF-HGV	Wheels or skis
☐ N565TA	de Havilland DHC-3 Otter	46	ex C-FQOQ	Wheels or skis
☐ N1694M	Cessna A185F Skywagon	18501879		Wheels or skis
☐ N8190Y	de Havilland DHC-2 Beaver	824	ex C-GPUP	Wheels or skis

TANANA AIR SERVICE   Tan Air (4E/TNR)   Ruby, AK (RBY)

☐ N97CR	Piper PA-32R-300 Lance	32R-7780078	ex JA3776
☐ N4352F	Piper PA-32R-300 Lance	32R-7680441	
☐ N4803S	Piper PA-32-260 Cherokee Six B	32-1188	
☐ N31606	Piper PA-32-260 Cherokee Six E	32-7840137	
☐ N75387	Piper PA-32R-300 Lance	32R-7680298	
☐ N101LJ	Piper PA-31 Turbo Navajo	31-267	ex N9204Y

TAQUAN AIR SERVICE   Taquan (K3)   Metlakatla/Ketchikan-Waterfront SPB, AK (MTM/WFB)

☐ N1018A	de Havilland DHC-2 Beaver	178	ex N52409	FP
☐ N5160G	de Havilland DHC-2 Beaver	236	ex 51-16483	FP
☐ N37756	de Havilland DHC-2 Beaver	1456	ex G-203	FP
☐ N67673	de Havilland DHC-2 Beaver	1284	ex 57-2586	FP
☐ N67676	de Havilland DHC-2 Beaver	809	ex N93AK	FP
☐ N68010	de Havilland DHC-2 Beaver	1243	ex 57-6150	FP

TBM   Tulare-Mefford Field, CA/Visalia-Municipal, CA (TLR/VIS)

☐ N466TM	Lockheed C-130A-1A Hercules	3173	ex 57-0466	64	Tanker
☐ N473TM	Lockheed C-130A-1A Hercules	3081	ex 56-0473	63	Tanker [TLR]

TELESIS TRANSAIR   Telesis (TLX)   Dallas-Love Field, TX (DAL)

☐ N403TE	Cessna 401	401-0008	ex N4080Q
☐ N405TE	Cessna 401	401-0121	ex N3208Q
☐ N408TE	Cessna 401	401-0269	ex N4021Q
☐ N409TE	Cessna 401A	401A0118	ex N217BA
☐ N3220Q	Cessna 401	401-0020	
☐ N301TE	Piper PA-32-300 Cherokee Six	32-40216	ex N4146W
☐ N406TE	Cessna 402B	402B1366	ex N110KS
☐ N602TE	Piper PA-60-601P Aerostar	61P-0583-7962134	ex N942TJ
☐ N603TE	Ted Smith Aerostar 600	60-0320-118	ex N90609
☐ N604TE	Ted Smith Aerostar 600	60-0206-091	ex N7544S

TEMSCO HELICOPTERS   Temsco (TMS)   Ketchikan-Temsco Heliport, AK

☐ N94TH	Aérospatiale AS350B AStar	2548	
☐ N141TH	Aérospatiale AS350B2 AStar	1167	ex N98MB
☐ N143TH	Aérospatiale AS350B2 AStar	9043	
☐ N145TH	Aérospatiale AS350B2 AStar	9060	
☐ N147TH	Aérospatiale AS350B2 AStar	9070	
☐ N149TH	Aérospatiale AS350B2 AStar	9071	
☐ N403AE	Aérospatiale AS350B3 AStar	3281	
☐ N405AE	Aérospatiale AS350B3 AStar	3286	
☐ N802TH	Aérospatiale AS350B2 AStar	9023	
☐ N911CV	Aérospatiale AS350B3 AStar	3142	ex N40729
☐ N913LP	Aérospatiale AS350B2 AStar	2383	
☐ N970TH	Aérospatiale AS350BA AStar	9011	
☐ N4022D	Aérospatiale AS350B2 AStar	2891	

☐ N6015S　Aérospatiale AS350BA AStar　1884
☐ N6080R　Aérospatiale AS350BA AStar　2685
☐ N6094E　Aérospatiale AS350BA AStar　2750
☐ N6094U　Aérospatiale AS350BA AStar　2751
☐ N6302Y　Aérospatiale AS350B2 AStar　9007
☐ N57954　Aérospatiale AS350B AStar　1127　ex N35977
☐ N57958　Aérospatiale AS350B AStar　1512

☐ N214TH　Bell 214B-1　28031　ex N4374D
☐ N502TH　Bell 205A-1　30030　ex C-FKHQ
☐ N16920　Bell 212　30865
☐ N83230　Bell 212　30560

TEPPER AVIATION　　　Crestview-Bob Sikes, FL (CEW)

☐ N2679C　Lockheed L-382G-69C Hercules　4796　ex N8183J
☐ N2731G　Lockheed L-382G-30C Hercules　4582　ex N2189M
☐ N3796B　Lockheed L-382G-39C Hercules　5027　ex N4557C
Operates for various US Government agencies

TIMBERLINE AIR SERVICE　　　Alpine Heliport, OR

☐ N154TL　Bell UH-IE　6155　ex Bu154770
☐ N155TL　Bell UH-IE　6164　ex Bu154779
☐ N457CC　Bell UH-IL　6401　ex N204FW

TOLAIR SERVICES　　Tol Air (TI/TOL)　San Juan-Munoz Marin Intl, PR (SJU)

☐ N728T　Beech E-18S　BA-130　ex N28V　Frtr
☐ N732T　Beech E-18S　BA-114　ex N52A　Frtr
☐ N748T　Beech E-18S　BA-329　ex N398B　Frtr
☐ N749T　Beech E-18S　BA-55　ex N4641A　Frtr
☐ N779T　Beech H-18　BA-618　ex N220WH　Frtr

☐ N87T　Douglas DC-3　6148　ex N31MC　Frtr
☐ N147JR　Convair 240-57 (T-29C)　403　ex N154PA　[OPF]
☐ N783T　Douglas DC-3　4219　ex N783V　Frtr
☐ N840T　Cessna 402B　402B1099　ex N87280

TRANS NORTH AVIATION　　(HX)　　Eagle River, WI (EGV)

☐ N4599F　Cessna 340A　340A0652
☐ N59773　Piper PA-31-350 Navajo Chieftain　31-7652044

TRANS STATES AIRLINES　　Waterski (AX/LOF)　St Louis-Lambert Intl, MO (STL)

Operates commuter services for American Airlines as American Connection, US Airways as US Airways Express and United Air Lines as United Express from St Louis, MO, Baltimore-Washington, MD, Newark, NJ, Chicago, IL and Pittsburgh, PA.
　Go Jet Airlines is a wholly owned subsidiary based in St Louis, MO operating CRJ-700s for United Express.

TRANSAIR　Maui (P6/MUI)　　Honolulu-Intl, HI (HNL)

☐ N221LM　Short SD.3-60　SH3722　ex N722PC
☐ N351TA　Short SD.3-60　SH3759　ex N159CC
☐ N729PC　Short SD.3-60　SH3729　ex 6Y-JMY
☐ N808KR　Short SD.3-60　SH3734　ex D-CFAO　Frtr
☐ N808TR　Short SD.3-60　SH3718　ex VQ-TSK　Frtr
☐ N827BE　Short SD.3-60　SH3746　ex N746SA　Frtr
☐ N4476F　Short SD.3-60　SH3731　ex 5N-BFT

TRANSNORTHERN AVIATION　　Transnorthern (TNV)　Talkeetna / Fairbanks, AK (TKA/FAI)

☐ N27TN　Douglas C-117D　43332　ex N99857　♦
☐ N30TN　Douglas C-117D　43159　ex N53315　Passenger
☐ N39TN　Beech 99　U-2　ex TI-AYM
☐ N3114G　Swearingen SA.227AC Metro III　AC-583

TRICOASTAL AIR　　Grand Express (GAE)　Toledo Express, OH (TOL)

☐ N168GA　Swearingen SA.226TC Metro　TC-207　ex N501AB
☐ N589DC　AMD Falcon 20　45　ex N175GA　[TOL]

TROPIC AIR CHARTERS　　Fort Lauderdale Executive, FL (FXE)

☐ N131JL　Britten-Norman BN-2A-6 Islander　225　ex G-51-225
☐ N200MU　Britten-Norman BN-2A-27 Islander　78　ex 6Y-JSX
☐ N296TA　Britten-Norman BN-2A-26 Islander　384　ex J8-VBN
☐ N297TA　Britten-Norman BN-2A-26 Islander　741　ex N196TA

388

TWIN CITIES AIR SERVICE		Twin City (TCY)	Auburn-Lewiston Municipal, ME (LEW)

☐ N18VV	Cessna 402C	402C0619	ex N180PB
☐ N196TC	Cessna 310R	310R1801	
☐ N401SX	Cessna 402C	402C0447	ex 9A-BPV
☐ N402SX	Cessna 402C	402C0606	ex 9A-BPX
☐ N3249M	Cessna 402C	402C0296	

UFLY AIRWAYS		(6F/FAO)	Miami, FL (MIA)

☐ N836NK	McDonnell-Douglas MD-83	53045/1777	ex N833RA
☐ N836RA	McDonnell-Douglas MD-83	53046/1794	ex YV-44C

UNION FLIGHTS		Union Flights (UNF)	Dayton-Carson City, NV (CSN)

☐ N127HA	Cessna 208B Caravan I	208B0148	
☐ N208N	Cessna 208B Caravan I	208B0279	ex F-OGRU
☐ N1116N	Cessna 208B Caravan I	208B0417	
☐ N9655B	Cessna 208B Caravan I	208B0145	
☐ N6654Z	Piper PA-31-350 Navajo Chieftain	31-7752143	ex C-GSUY	Frtr

UNITED AIR LINES	United (UA/UAL)		Chicago-O'Hare Intl, IL/San Francisco-Intl, CA (ORD/SFO)

Member of Star Alliance. Ex 'Continental' aircraft are listed by last 3 within types.

☐ N801UA	Airbus A319-131	0686	ex D-AVYI	4001
☐ N802UA	Airbus A319-131	0690	ex D-AVYO	4002
☐ N803UA	Airbus A319-131	0748	ex D-AVYL	4003
☐ N804UA	Airbus A319-131	0759	ex D-AVYR	4004
☐ N805UA	Airbus A319-131	0783	ex D-AVYY	4005
☐ N806UA	Airbus A319-131	0788	ex D-AVYW	4006
☐ N807UA	Airbus A319-131	0798	ex D-AVYX	4007
☐ N808UA	Airbus A319-131	0804	ex D-AVYF	4008
☐ N809UA	Airbus A319-131	0825	ex D-AVYZ	4009
☐ N810UA	Airbus A319-131	0843	ex D-AVYR	4010
☐ N811UA	Airbus A319-131	0847	ex D-AVYB	4011
☐ N812UA	Airbus A319-131	0850	ex D-AVYK	4012
☐ N813UA	Airbus A319-131	0858	ex D-AVYP	4013
☐ N814UA	Airbus A319-131	0862	ex D-AVYT	4014
☐ N815UA	Airbus A319-131	0867	ex D-AVYU	4015
☐ N816UA	Airbus A319-131	0871	ex D-AVYY	4016
☐ N817UA	Airbus A319-131	0873	ex D-AVYX	4017
☐ N818UA	Airbus A319-131	0882	ex D-AVYE	4018
☐ N819UA	Airbus A319-131	0893	ex D-AVYV	4019
☐ N820UA	Airbus A319-131	0898	ex D-AVYZ	4020
☐ N821UA	Airbus A319-131	0944	ex D-AVYC	4021
☐ N822UA	Airbus A319-131	0948	ex D-AVYE	4022
☐ N823UA	Airbus A319-131	0952	ex D-AVYF	4023
☐ N824UA	Airbus A319-131	0965	ex D-AVYH	4024
☐ N825UA	Airbus A319-131	0980	ex D-AVYN	4025
☐ N826UA	Airbus A319-131	0989	ex D-AVYU	4026
☐ N827UA	Airbus A319-131	1022	ex D-AVYD	4027
☐ N828UA	Airbus A319-131	1031	ex D-AVYF	4028
☐ N829UA	Airbus A319-131	1211	ex D-AVYC	4029
☐ N830UA	Airbus A319-131	1243	ex D-AVWI	4030
☐ N831UA	Airbus A319-131	1291	ex D-AVWF	4031
☐ N832UA	Airbus A319-131	1321	ex D-AVWQ	4032
☐ N833UA	Airbus A319-131	1401	ex D-AVYA	4033
☐ N834UA	Airbus A319-131	1420	ex D-AVYM	4034
☐ N835UA	Airbus A319-131	1426	ex D-AVYN	4035
☐ N836UA	Airbus A319-131	1460	ex D-AVYI	4036
☐ N837UA	Airbus A319-131	1474	ex D-AVYS	4037
☐ N838UA	Airbus A319-131	1477	ex D-AVYG	4038
☐ N839UA	Airbus A319-131	1507	ex D-AVYX	4039
☐ N840UA	Airbus A319-131	1522	ex D-AVYZ	4040
☐ N841UA	Airbus A319-131	1545	ex D-AVWK	4041
☐ N842UA	Airbus A319-131	1569	ex D-AVWA	4042
☐ N843UA	Airbus A319-131	1573	ex D-AVWE	4043
☐ N844UA	Airbus A319-131	1581	ex D-AVWT	4044
☐ N845UA	Airbus A319-131	1585	ex D-AVYD	4045
☐ N846UA	Airbus A319-131	1600	ex D-AVWW	4046
☐ N847UA	Airbus A319-131	1627	ex D-AVYB	4047
☐ N848UA	Airbus A319-131	1647	ex D-AVYK	4048
☐ N849UA	Airbus A319-131	1649	ex D-AVYP	4049
☐ N850UA	Airbus A319-131	1653	ex D-AVYR	4050
☐ N851UA	Airbus A319-131	1664	ex D-AVYX	4051
☐ N852UA	Airbus A319-131	1671	ex D-AVWD	4052

☐ N853UA	Airbus A319-131	1688	ex D-AVWM	4053
☐ N854UA	Airbus A319-131	1731	ex D-AVWS	4054
☐ N855UA	Airbus A319-131	1737	ex D-AVWU	4055
☐ N401UA	Airbus A320-232	0435	ex F-WWDD	4501
☐ N402UA	Airbus A320-232	0439	ex F-WWIJ	4502
☐ N403UA	Airbus A320-232	0442	ex F-WWIY	4703
☐ N404UA	Airbus A320-232	0450	ex F-WWII	4704
☐ N405UA	Airbus A320-232	0452	ex F-WWBF	4705
☐ N406UA	Airbus A320-232	0454	ex F-WWBJ	4506
☐ N407UA	Airbus A320-232	0456	ex F-WWDB	4507
☐ N408UA	Airbus A320-232	0457	ex F-WWDG	4508
☐ N409UA	Airbus A320-232	0462	ex F-WWDQ	4709
☐ N410UA	Airbus A320-232	0463	ex F-WWDV	4910
☐ N411UA	Airbus A320-232	0464	ex F-WWDX	4711
☐ N412UA	Airbus A320-232	0465	ex F-WWIM	4712
☐ N413UA	Airbus A320-232	0470	ex F-WWBM	4713
☐ N414UA	Airbus A320-232	0472	ex F-WWIU	4814
☐ N415UA	Airbus A320-232	0475	ex F-WWBP	4615
☐ N416UA	Airbus A320-232	0479	ex F-WWDH	4616
☐ N417UA	Airbus A320-232	0483	ex F-WWIT	4617
☐ N418UA	Airbus A320-232	0485	ex F-WWIZ	4618
☐ N419UA	Airbus A320-232	0487	ex F-WWDJ	4619
☐ N420UA	Airbus A320-232	0489	ex F-WWDM	4620
☐ N421UA	Airbus A320-232	0500	ex F-WWDZ	4621
☐ N422UA	Airbus A320-232	0503	ex F-WWIV	4622
☐ N423UA	Airbus A320-232	0504	ex F-WWBO	4623
☐ N424UA	Airbus A320-232	0506	ex F-WWBQ	4624
☐ N425UA	Airbus A320-232	0508	ex F-WWBY	4625
☐ N426UA	Airbus A320-232	0510	ex F-WWBZ	4626
☐ N427UA	Airbus A320-232	0512	ex F-WWDD	4627
☐ N428UA	Airbus A320-232	0523	ex F-WWDE	4628
☐ N429UA	Airbus A320-232	0539	ex F-WWIX	4629
☐ N430UA	Airbus A320-232	0568	ex F-WWDC	4630
☐ N431UA	Airbus A320-232	0571	ex F-WWDH	4631
☐ N432UA	Airbus A320-232	0587	ex F-WWBB	4632
☐ N433UA	Airbus A320-232	0589	ex F-WWBD	4633
☐ N434UA	Airbus A320-232	0592	ex F-WWBF	4634
☐ N435UA	Airbus A320-232	0613	ex F-WWBQ	4635
☐ N436UA	Airbus A320-232	0638	ex F-WWDE	4636
☐ N437UA	Airbus A320-232	0655	ex F-WWIK	4637
☐ N438UA	Airbus A320-232	0678	ex F-WWBJ	4838
☐ N439UA	Airbus A320-232	0683	ex F-WWDQ	4839
☐ N440UA	Airbus A320-232	0702	ex F-WWDP	4840
☐ N441UA	Airbus A320-232	0751	ex F-WWIU	4841
☐ N442UA	Airbus A320-232	0780	ex F-WWDQ	4842
☐ N443UA	Airbus A320-232	0820	ex F-WWBT	4643
☐ N444UA	Airbus A320-232	0824	ex F-WWBZ	4844
☐ N445UA	Airbus A320-232	0826	ex F-WWIL	4845
☐ N446UA	Airbus A320-232	0834	ex F-WWIP	4846
☐ N447UA	Airbus A320-232	0836	ex F-WWIR	4847
☐ N448UA	Airbus A320-232	0842	ex F-WWBF	4848
☐ N449UA	Airbus A320-232	0851	ex F-WWBJ	4849
☐ N451UA	Airbus A320-232	0865	ex F-WWBR	4851
☐ N452UA	Airbus A320-232	0955	ex F-WWBD	4852
☐ N453UA	Airbus A320-232	1001	ex F-WWBH	4853
☐ N454UA	Airbus A320-232	1104	ex F-WWDC	4654
☐ N455UA	Airbus A320-232	1105	ex F-WWDE	4655
☐ N456UA	Airbus A320-232	1128	ex F-WWIJ	4656
☐ N457UA	Airbus A320-232	1146	ex F-WWBM	4857
☐ N458UA	Airbus A320-232	1163	ex F-WWDK	4858
☐ N459UA	Airbus A320-232	1192	ex F-WWDX	4859
☐ N460UA	Airbus A320-232	1248	ex F-WWIS	4860
☐ N461UA	Airbus A320-232	1266	ex F-WWDC	4661
☐ N462UA	Airbus A320-232	1272	ex F-WWDI	4962
☐ N463UA	Airbus A320-232	1282	ex F-WWBJ	4663 Jim Briggs
☐ N464UA	Airbus A320-232	1290	ex F-WWBR	4664
☐ N465UA	Airbus A320-232	1341	ex F-WWDP	4865
☐ N466UA	Airbus A320-232	1343	ex F-WWDQ	4666
☐ N467UA	Airbus A320-232	1359	ex F-WWBH	4867
☐ N468UA	Airbus A320-232	1363	ex F-WWIE	4668
☐ N469UA	Airbus A320-232	1409	ex F-WWDF	4869
☐ N470UA	Airbus A320-232	1427	ex F-WWBN	4870
☐ N471UA	Airbus A320-232	1432	ex F-WWBA	4871
☐ N472UA	Airbus A320-232	1435	ex F-WWBC	4872
☐ N473UA	Airbus A320-232	1469	ex F-WWDL	4873
☐ N474UA	Airbus A320-232	1475	ex F-WWDQ	4874

☐ N475UA	Airbus A320-232	1495	ex F-WWIC	4875	
☐ N476UA	Airbus A320-232	1508	ex F-WWBB	4876	
☐ N477UA	Airbus A320-232	1514	ex F-WWBF	4877	
☐ N478UA	Airbus A320-232	1533	ex F-WWIQ	4878	
☐ N479UA	Airbus A320-232	1538	ex F-WWIT	4879	
☐ N480UA	Airbus A320-232	1555	ex F-WWBP	4880	
☐ N481UA	Airbus A320-232	1559	ex F-WWDH	4881	
☐ N482UA	Airbus A320-232	1584	ex F-WWBN	4882	
☐ N483UA	Airbus A320-232	1586	ex F-WWBR	4883	
☐ N484UA	Airbus A320-232	1609	ex F-WWBZ	4884	
☐ N485UA	Airbus A320-232	1617	ex F-WWDD	4885	
☐ N486UA	Airbus A320-232	1620	ex F-WWDG	4886	
☐ N487UA	Airbus A320-232	1669	ex F-WWIJ	4887	
☐ N488UA	Airbus A320-232	1680	ex F-WWBF	4888	
☐ N489UA	Airbus A320-232	1702	ex F-WWIT	4889	
☐ N490UA	Airbus A320-232	1728	ex F-WWBI	4890	
☐ N491UA	Airbus A320-232	1741	ex F-WWBU	4891	
☐ N492UA	Airbus A320-232	1755	ex F-WWDZ	4892	
☐ N493UA	Airbus A320-232	1821	ex F-WWIO	4893	
☐ N494UA	Airbus A320-232	1840	ex F-WWDC	4894	
☐ N495UA	Airbus A320-232	1842	ex F-WWBP	4895	
☐ N496UA	Airbus A320-232	1845	ex F-WWDR	4896	
☐ N497UA	Airbus A320-232	1847	ex F-WWDE	4897	
☐ N498UA	Airbus A320-232	1865	ex F-WWIK	4898	
☐ N14604	Boeing 737-524/W	27317/2576		604	♦
☐ N58606	Boeing 737-524/W	27319/2590		606	[GYR]
☐ N27610	Boeing 737-524/W	27323/2616		610	♦
☐ N11612	Boeing 737-524/W	27325/2630		612	[GYR]
☐ N14613	Boeing 737-524/W	27326/2633		613	[GYR]
☐ N17614	Boeing 737-524/W	27327/2634		614	♦
☐ N16617	Boeing 737-524/W	27330/2648		617	
☐ N17619	Boeing 737-524/W	27332/2659		0619	
☐ N17620	Boeing 737-524/W	27333/2660	ex N1790B	620	
☐ N19621	Boeing 737-524/W	27334/2661		0621	
☐ N18622	Boeing 737-524/W	27526/2669		0622	
☐ N19623	Boeing 737-524/W	27527/2672		623	
☐ N13624	Boeing 737-524/W	27528/2675		624	
☐ N46625	Boeing 737-524/W	27529/2683		625	
☐ N32626	Boeing 737-524/W	27530/2686		626	
☐ N17627	Boeing 737-524/W	27531/2700		627	
☐ N14628	Boeing 737-524/W	27532/2712		628	
☐ N14629	Boeing 737-524/W	27533/2725		629	
☐ N59630	Boeing 737-524/W	27534/2726		630	
☐ N62631	Boeing 737-524/W	27535/2728		631	
☐ N16632	Boeing 737-524/W	27900/2736		632	
☐ N24633	Boeing 737-524/W	27901/2743		0633	
☐ N19638	Boeing 737-524/W	28899/2912		638	
☐ N14639	Boeing 737-524/W	28900/2913		639	
☐ N17640	Boeing 737-524/W	28901/2924		640	
☐ N11641	Boeing 737-524/W	28902/2926		641	
☐ N16642	Boeing 737-524/W	28903/2927		0642	
☐ N17644	Boeing 737-524/W	28905/2934	ex N1786B	0644	
☐ N14645	Boeing 737-524/W	28906/2935	ex N1786B	645	
☐ N16646	Boeing 737-524/W	28907/2956	ex N1786B	0646	
☐ N16647	Boeing 737-524/W	28908/2958		647	
☐ N16648	Boeing 737-524/W	28909/2960		0648	
☐ N16649	Boeing 737-524/W	28910/2972		649	
☐ N16650	Boeing 737-524/W	28911/2973		0650	
☐ N11651	Boeing 737-524/W	28912/2980	ex (N16651)	0651	
☐ N14652	Boeing 737-524/W	28913/2985		0652	
☐ N14653	Boeing 737-524/W	28914/2986		653	
☐ N14655	Boeing 737-524/W	28916/2994		655	[GYR]
☐ N16701	Boeing 737-724/W	28762/29	ex N1786B	701	
☐ N24702	Boeing 737-724/W	28763/32		702	
☐ N16703	Boeing 737-724/W	28764/37		703	
☐ N14704	Boeing 737-724/W	28765/43		704	
☐ N25705	Boeing 737-724/W	28766/46		705	
☐ N24706	Boeing 737-724/W	28767/47		706	
☐ N23707	Boeing 737-724/W	28768/48	ex N1787B	707	
☐ N23708	Boeing 737-724/W	28769/52		708	
☐ N16709	Boeing 737-724/W	28779/93		709	
☐ N15710	Boeing 737-724/W	28780/94		710	
☐ N54711	Boeing 737-724/W	28782/97	ex N1786B	711	
☐ N15712	Boeing 737-724/W	28783/105	ex N1786B	712	
☐ N16713	Boeing 737-724/W	28784/107	ex N1786B	713	

☐ N33714	Boeing 737-724/W	28785/119	ex N1786B	714
☐ N24715	Boeing 737-724/W	28786/125	ex N1795B	715
☐ N13716	Boeing 737-724/W	28787/156	ex N1782B	716
☐ N29717	Boeing 737-724/W	28936/182	ex N1786B	717
☐ N13718	Boeing 737-724/W	28937/185	ex N1786B	718
☐ N17719	Boeing 737-724/W	28938/195	ex N1786B	719
☐ N13720	Boeing 737-724/W	28939/214	ex N1786B	720
☐ N23721	Boeing 737-724/W	28940/219		721
☐ N27722	Boeing 737-724/W	28789/247	ex N1786B	722
☐ N21723	Boeing 737-724/W	28790/253	ex N1787B	723
☐ N27724	Boeing 737-724/W	28791/283	ex N1787B	724
☐ N39726	Boeing 737-724/W	28796/315	ex N1787B	726
☐ N38727	Boeing 737-724/W	28797/317	ex N1786B	727
☐ N39728	Boeing 737-724/W	28944/321	ex N1786B	728
☐ N24729	Boeing 737-724/W	28945/325	ex N1784B	729
☐ N17730	Boeing 737-724/W	28798/338	ex N1786B	730
☐ N14731	Boeing 737-724/W	28799/346	ex N1786B	731
☐ N16732	Boeing 737-724/W	28948/352	ex N60436	732
☐ N27733	Boeing 737-724/W	28800/364	ex N1786B	733 Sir Samuel J LeFrak
☐ N27734	Boeing 737-724/W	28949/371	ex N1786B	734
☐ N14735	Boeing 737-724/W	28950/376	ex N1786B	735
☐ N24736	Boeing 737-724/W	28803/380	ex N1786B	736
☐ N13750	Boeing 737-724/W	28941/286		750
☐ N25201	Boeing 737-824/W	28958/443	ex N1786B	201
☐ N24202	Boeing 737-824/W	30429/581	ex N1786B	202
☐ N33203	Boeing 737-824/W	30613/591	ex N1786B	203
☐ N35204	Boeing 737-824/W	30576/606	ex N1795B	204
☐ N27205	Boeing 737-824/W	30577/615	ex N1786B	205
☐ N11206	Boeing 737-824/W	30578/618	ex N1786B	206
☐ N36207	Boeing 737-824/W	30579/627	ex N1786B	207
☐ N26208	Boeing 737-824/W	30580/644	ex N1786B	208
☐ N33209	Boeing 737-824/W	30581/647	ex N1786B	209
☐ N26210	Boeing 737-824/W	28770/56		210
☐ N24211	Boeing 737-824/W	28771/58		211
☐ N24212	Boeing 737-824/W	28772/63		0212
☐ N27213	Boeing 737-824/W	28773/65		213
☐ N14214	Boeing 737-824/W	28774/74		214
☐ N26215	Boeing 737-824/W	28775/76		215
☐ N12216	Boeing 737-824/W	28776/79		216
☐ N16217	Boeing 737-824/W	28777/81		217
☐ N12218	Boeing 737-824/W	28778/84		218
☐ N14219	Boeing 737-824/W	28781/88		0219
☐ N18220	Boeing 737-824/W	28929/134	ex N60436	220
☐ N12221	Boeing 737-824/W	28930/153	ex N1796B	221
☐ N34222	Boeing 737-824/W	28931/159		0222
☐ N18223	Boeing 737-824/W	28932/162	ex N1786B	0223
☐ N24224	Boeing 737-824/W	28933/165	ex N1782B	224
☐ N12225	Boeing 737-824/W	28934/168	ex N1782B	225
☐ N26226	Boeing 737-824/W	28935/171	ex N1787B	226
☐ N13227	Boeing 737-824/W	28788/262	ex N1787B	227
☐ N14228	Boeing 737-824/W	28792/281	ex N1787B	228
☐ N17229	Boeing 737-824/W	28793/287	ex N1786B	229
☐ N14230	Boeing 737-824/W	28794/296	ex N1787B	230
☐ N14231	Boeing 737-824/W	28795/300	ex N1787B	231
☐ N26232	Boeing 737-824/W	28942/304		232
☐ N17233	Boeing 737-824/W	28943/328	ex N1787B	233
☐ N16234	Boeing 737-824/W	28946/334	ex N1787B	234
☐ N14235	Boeing 737-824/W	28947/342		235
☐ N35236	Boeing 737-824/W	28801/367	ex N1786B	236
☐ N14237	Boeing 737-824/W	28802/374		237
☐ N12238	Boeing 737-824/W	28804/386	ex N1786B	238
☐ N27239	Boeing 737-824/W	28951/391	ex N1787B	239
☐ N14240	Boeing 737-824/W	28952/394	ex N1786B	240
☐ N54241	Boeing 737-824/W	28953/395	ex N1787B	241
☐ N14242	Boeing 737-824/W	28805/402	ex N1786B	242
☐ N18243	Boeing 737-824/W	28806/403	ex N1786B	243
☐ N17244	Boeing 737-824/W	28954/409	ex N1787B	244
☐ N17245	Boeing 737-824/W	28955/411	ex N1786B	245
☐ N27246	Boeing 737-824/W	28956/413	ex N1786B	246
☐ N36247	Boeing 737-824/W	28807/431	ex N1786B	247
☐ N13248	Boeing 737-824/W	28808/435	ex N1786B	248
☐ N14249	Boeing 737-824/W	28809/438	ex N1786B	249
☐ N14250	Boeing 737-824/W	28957/441	ex N1786B	250
☐ N73251	Boeing 737-824/W	30582/650	ex N1786B	251
☐ N37252	Boeing 737-824/W	30583/656	ex N1787B	252
☐ N37253	Boeing 737-824/W	30584/660		253

☐	N76254	Boeing 737-824/W	30779/667	ex N1786B	254
☐	N37255	Boeing 737-824/W	30610/686	ex N1787B	255
☐	N73256	Boeing 737-824/W	30611/692	ex N1787B	256
☐	N38257	Boeing 737-824/W	30612/706	ex N1786B	257
☐	N77258	Boeing 737-824/W	30802/708	ex N1786B	258
☐	N73259	Boeing 737-824/W	30803/854	ex N1786B	259
☐	N35260	Boeing 737-824/W	30855/862	ex N1786B	260
☐	N77261	Boeing 737-824/W	31582/897	ex N1786B	261
☐	N33262	Boeing 737-824/W	32402/901	ex N1786B	262
☐	N37263	Boeing 737-824/W	31583/906	ex N1786B	263
☐	N33264	Boeing 737-824/W	31584/916	ex N1786B	264
☐	N76265	Boeing 737-824/W	31585/928	ex N1786B	265
☐	N33266	Boeing 737-824/W	32403/930		266
☐	N37267	Boeing 737-824/W	31586/939	ex N1786B	267
☐	N38268	Boeing 737-824/W	31587/957	ex N1786B	268
☐	N76269	Boeing 737-824/W	31588/966	ex N1786B	269
☐	N73270	Boeing 737-824/W	31632/970	ex N1787B	270
☐	N35271	Boeing 737-824/W	31589/982	ex N1786B	271
☐	N36272	Boeing 737-824/W	31590/987	ex N1795B	272
☐	N37273	Boeing 737-824/W	31591/1012	ex N1787B	273
☐	N37274	Boeing 737-824/W	31592/1062		274
☐	N73275	Boeing 737-824/W	31593/1077		275
☐	N73276	Boeing 737-824/W	31594/1079		0276
☐	N37277	Boeing 737-824/W	31595/1099		277
☐	N73278	Boeing 737-824/W	31596/1390		278
☐	N79279	Boeing 737-824/W	31597/1411	ex N1787B	0279
☐	N36280	Boeing 737-824/W	31598/1423		280
☐	N37281	Boeing 737-824/W	31599/1425		0281
☐	N34282	Boeing 737-824/W	31634/1440		282
☐	N73283	Boeing 737-824/W	31606/1456		283
☐	N33284	Boeing 737-824/W	31635/1475		284
☐	N78285	Boeing 737-824/W	33452/1540		0285
☐	N33286	Boeing 737-824/W	31600/1506		286
☐	N37287	Boeing 737-824/W	31636/1509		287
☐	N76288	Boeing 737-824/W	33451/1516		288
☐	N33289	Boeing 737-824/W	31607/1542	ex N1786B	0289
☐	N37290	Boeing 737-824/W	31601/1567		290
☐	N73291	Boeing 737-824/W	33454/1611		291
☐	N33292	Boeing 737-824/W	33455/1622		292
☐	N37293	Boeing 737-824/W	33453/1743		293
☐	N33294	Boeing 737-824/W	34000/1762		294
☐	N77295	Boeing 737-824/W	34001/1779		295
☐	N77296	Boeing 737-824/W	34002/1787		296
☐	N39297	Boeing 737-824/W	34003/1791		297
☐	N37298	Boeing 737-824/W	34004/1813		298
☐	N73299	Boeing 737-824/W	34005/1821	ex N1786B	299
☐	N78501	Boeing 737-824/W	31602/1994	ex N1786B	501
☐	N76502	Boeing 737-824/W	31603/2017		502
☐	N76503	Boeing 737-824/W	33461/2023		503
☐	N76504	Boeing 737-824/W	31604/2035		504
☐	N76505	Boeing 737-824/W	32834/2048	ex N1786B	505
☐	N78506	Boeing 737-824/W	32832/2065		506
☐	N87507	Boeing 737-824/W	31637/2487	ex N1786B	0507
☐	N76508	Boeing 737-824/W	31639/2514		0508
☐	N78509	Boeing 737-824/W	31638/2523	ex N1787B	0509
☐	N77510	Boeing 737-824/W	32828/2579		0510
☐	N78511	Boeing 737-824/W	33459/2598		0511
☐	N87512	Boeing 737-824/W	33458/2602		512
☐	N87513	Boeing 737-824/W	31621/2655		0513
☐	N76514	Boeing 737-824/W	31626/2680		0514
☐	N76515	Boeing 737-824/W	31623/2713		515
☐	N76516	Boeing 737-824/W	37096/2718		0516
☐	N76517	Boeing 737-824/W	31628/2723		0517
☐	N77518	Boeing 737-824/W	31605/2768		0518 Capt Marlon Green
☐	N76519	Boeing 737-824/W	30132/3138	ex N1796B	0519 ♦
☐	N77520	Boeing 737-824/W	31658/3158	ex N1786B	0520 ♦
☐	N79521	Boeing 737-824/W	31662/3169	ex N1786B	0521 ♦
☐	N76522	Boeing 737-824/W	31660/3175	ex N1786B	0522 ♦
☐	N76523	Boeing 737-824/W	37101/3216	ex N1786B	0523 ♦
☐	N78524	Boeing 737-824/W	31642/3224		0524 ♦
☐	N77525	Boeing 737-824/W	31659/3253	ex N1787B	0525 ♦
☐	N76526	Boeing 737-824/W	38700/3289		0526 ♦
☐	N87527	Boeing 737-824/W	38701/3305		0527 ♦
☐	N76528	Boeing 737-824/W	31663/3464		0528 ♦
☐	N76529	Boeing 737-824/W	31652/3490		0529 ♦
☐	N	Boeing 737-824/W			o/o ♦
☐	N	Boeing 737-824/W			o/o ♦

☐ N	Boeing 737-824/W				o/o♦
☐ N	Boeing 737-824/W				o/o♦
☐ N30401	Boeing 737-924/W	30118/820		401	
☐ N79402	Boeing 737-924/W	30119/857		402	
☐ N38403	Boeing 737-924/W	30120/884	ex N1786B	403	
☐ N32404	Boeing 737-924/W	30121/893	ex N1787B	404	
☐ N72405	Boeing 737-924/W	30122/911	ex N1786B	405	
☐ N73406	Boeing 737-924/W	30123/943	ex N1786B	406	
☐ N35407	Boeing 737-924/W	30124/951	ex N1786B	407	
☐ N37408	Boeing 737-924/W	30125/962	ex N1787B	408	
☐ N37409	Boeing 737-924/W	30126/1004	ex N1787B	409	
☐ N75410	Boeing 737-924/W	30127/1021	ex N1786B	410	
☐ N71411	Boeing 737-924/W	30128/1052		411	
☐ N31412	Boeing 737-924/W	30129/1112		412	
☐ N37413	Boeing 737-924ER/W	31664/2474		0413	
☐ N47414	Boeing 737-924ER/W	32827/2490	ex N1787B	0414	
☐ N39415	Boeing 737-924ER/W	32826/2516		0415	
☐ N39416	Boeing 737-924ER/W	37093/2528		416	
☐ N38417	Boeing 737-924ER/W	31665/2541		417	
☐ N39418	Boeing 737-924ER/W	33456/2547		418	
☐ N37419	Boeing 737-924ER/W	31666/2553		419	
☐ N37420	Boeing 737-924ER/W	33457/2565		420	
☐ N27421	Boeing 737-924ER/W	37094/2577		421	
☐ N37422	Boeing 737-924ER/W	31620/2614		422	
☐ N39423	Boeing 737-924ER/W	32829/2645		423	
☐ N38424	Boeing 737-924ER/W	37095/2651		424	
☐ N75425	Boeing 737-924ER/W	33460/2657		425	
☐ N75426	Boeing 737-924ER/W	31622/2676		426	
☐ N37427	Boeing 737-924ER/W	37097/2707		427	
☐ N75428	Boeing 737-924ER/W	31633/2737		428	
☐ N75429	Boeing 737-924ER/W	30130/2750		429	
☐ N77430	Boeing 737-924ER/W	37098/2774	ex N1786B	430	
☐ N77431	Boeing 737-924ER/W	32833/2787		431	
☐ N75432	Boeing 737-924ER/W	32835/2817		432	
☐ N75433	Boeing 737-924ER/W	33527/2842		0433	
☐ N37434	Boeing 737-924ER/W	33528/2891		434	
☐ N75435	Boeing 737-924ER/W	33529/2916		435	
☐ N75436	Boeing 737-924ER/W	33531/2947		436	
☐ N37437	Boeing 737-924ER/W	33532/2959		437	
☐ N78438	Boeing 737-924ER/W	33533/2971		438	
☐ N57439	Boeing 737-924ER/W	33534/2990	ex N1786B	439	
☐ N45440	Boeing 737-924ER/W	33535/2996		440	
☐ N53441	Boeing 737-924ER/W	30131/3014	ex N1787B	441	
☐ N53442	Boeing 737-924ER/W	33536/3027		0442	
☐ N38443	Boeing 737-924ER/W	31655/3393	ex N1786B	0443	♦
☐ N36444	Boeing 737-924ER/W	31643/3417	ex N1786B	0444	♦
☐ N104UA	Boeing 747-422	26902/1141		8104	
☐ N105UA	Boeing 747-451	26473/985	ex N60659	8105	
☐ N107UA	Boeing 747-422	26900/1168		8107	
☐ N116UA	Boeing 747-422	26908/1193		8116	
☐ N117UA	Boeing 747-422	28810/1197		8117	
☐ N118UA	Boeing 747-422	28811/1201		8118	
☐ N119UA	Boeing 747-422	28812/1207		8119	
☐ N120UA	Boeing 747-422	29166/1209		8120	
☐ N121UA	Boeing 747-422	29167/1211		8121	
☐ N122UA	Boeing 747-422	29168/1218		8122	
☐ N127UA	Boeing 747-422	28813/1221		8127	
☐ N128UA	Boeing 747-422	30023/1245		8128	
☐ N171UA	Boeing 747-422	24322/733		8171	
☐ N173UA	Boeing 747-422	24380/759		8173	
☐ N174UA	Boeing 747-422	24381/762		8174	
☐ N175UA	Boeing 747-422	24382/806		8175	
☐ N177UA	Boeing 747-422	24384/819		8177	
☐ N178UA	Boeing 747-422	24385/820		8178	
☐ N179UA	Boeing 747-422	25158/866		8179	
☐ N180UA	Boeing 747-422	25224/867		8180	
☐ N181UA	Boeing 747-422	25278/881	ex N6005C	8181	
☐ N182UA	Boeing 747-422	25279/882		8182	
☐ N187UA	Boeing 747-422	26876/939		8187	
☐ N193UA	Boeing 747-422	26890/1085		8193	[VCV]
☐ N194UA	Boeing 747-422	26892/1088		8194	[VCV]
☐ N195UA	Boeing 747-422	26899/1113		8195	[VCV]
☐ N196UA	Boeing 747-422	28715/1120		8196	[VCV]
☐ N197UA	Boeing 747-422	26901/1121		8197	
☐ N198UA	Boeing 747-422	28716/1124		8198	[VCV]

☐ N199UA	Boeing 747-422	28717/1126	8199
☐ N501UA	Boeing 757-222	24622/241	5401
☐ N502UA	Boeing 757-222/W	24623/246	5702
☐ N503UA	Boeing 757-222	24624/247	5403
☐ N504UA	Boeing 757-222	24625/251	5404
☐ N505UA	Boeing 757-222	24626/254	5705
☐ N506UA	Boeing 757-222	24627/263	5406
☐ N507UA	Boeing 757-222	24743/270	5407
☐ N508UA	Boeing 757-222	24744/277	5708
☐ N509UA	Boeing 757-222	24763/284	5409
☐ N510UA	Boeing 757-222/W	24780/290	5710
☐ N511UA	Boeing 757-222	24799/291	5411
☐ N512UA	Boeing 757-222/W	24809/298	5712
☐ N513UA	Boeing 757-222	24810/299	5413
☐ N514UA	Boeing 757-222	24839/305	5414
☐ N515UA	Boeing 757-222	24840/306	5415
☐ N516UA	Boeing 757-222	24860/307	5416
☐ N517UA	Boeing 757-222/W	24861/310	5717
☐ N518UA	Boeing 757-222/W	24871/311	5718
☐ N519UA	Boeing 757-222	24872/312	5419
☐ N520UA	Boeing 757-222	24890/313	5420
☐ N521UA	Boeing 757-222	24891/319	5421
☐ N522UA	Boeing 757-222	24931/320	5422
☐ N523UA	Boeing 757-222	24932/329	5423
☐ N524UA	Boeing 757-222	24977/331	5424
☐ N525UA	Boeing 757-222/W	24978/338	5725
☐ N526UA	Boeing 757-222	24994/339	5426
☐ N527UA	Boeing 757-222	24995/341	5427
☐ N528UA	Boeing 757-222	25018/346	5428
☐ N529UA	Boeing 757-222	25019/352	5429
☐ N530UA	Boeing 757-222	25043/353	5430
☐ N532UA	Boeing 757-222/W	25072/366	5732
☐ N533UA	Boeing 757-222	25073/367	5433
☐ N534UA	Boeing 757-222	25129/372	5434
☐ N535UA	Boeing 757-222	25130/373	5435
☐ N536UA	Boeing 757-222	25156/380	5436
☐ N537UA	Boeing 757-222	25157/381	5437
☐ N538UA	Boeing 757-222	25222/385	5438
☐ N539UA	Boeing 757-222	25223/386	5439
☐ N540UA	Boeing 757-222	25252/393	5440
☐ N541UA	Boeing 757-222	25253/394	5441
☐ N542UA	Boeing 757-222	25276/396	5442
☐ N543UA	Boeing 757-222ER/W	25698/401	5543
☐ N544UA	Boeing 757-222ER/W	25322/405	5544
☐ N545UA	Boeing 757-222ER/W	25323/406	5545
☐ N546UA	Boeing 757-222ER/W	25367/413	5546
☐ N547UA	Boeing 757-222ER	25368/414	5547
☐ N548UA	Boeing 757-222ER	25396/420	5548
☐ N549UA	Boeing 757-222ER/W	25397/421	5549
☐ N550UA	Boeing 757-222ER	25398/426	5550
☐ N551UA	Boeing 757-222ER	25399/427	5551
☐ N552UA	Boeing 757-222ER	26641/431	5552
☐ N553UA	Boeing 757-222	25277/434	5453
☐ N554UA	Boeing 757-222/W	26644/435	5754
☐ N555UA	Boeing 757-222/W	26647/442	5755
☐ N556UA	Boeing 757-222	26650/447	5456
☐ N557UA	Boeing 757-222	26653/454	5757
☐ N558UA	Boeing 757-222	26654/462	5458
☐ N559UA	Boeing 757-222	26657/467	5459
☐ N560UA	Boeing 757-222	26660/469	5760
☐ N561UA	Boeing 757-222	26661/479	5461
☐ N562UA	Boeing 757-222	26664/487	5462
☐ N563UA	Boeing 757-222	26665/488	5463
☐ N564UA	Boeing 757-222	26666/490	5464
☐ N565UA	Boeing 757-222	26669/492	5465
☐ N566UA	Boeing 757-222	26670/494	5466
☐ N567UA	Boeing 757-222	26673/497	5467
☐ N568UA	Boeing 757-222	26674/498	5468
☐ N569UA	Boeing 757-222	26677/499	5469
☐ N570UA	Boeing 757-222	26678/501	5470
☐ N571UA	Boeing 757-222	26681/506	5471
☐ N572UA	Boeing 757-222	26682/508	5472
☐ N573UA	Boeing 757-222	26685/512	5473
☐ N574UA	Boeing 757-222	26686/513	5474
☐ N575UA	Boeing 757-222	26689/515	5475
☐ N576UA	Boeing 757-222	26690/524	5676

☐ N577UA	Boeing 757-222	26693/527		5677
☐ N578UA	Boeing 757-222	26694/531		5678
☐ N579UA	Boeing 757-222	26697/539		5679
☐ N580UA	Boeing 757-222	26698/542		5680
☐ N581UA	Boeing 757-222	26701/543		5681
☐ N582UA	Boeing 757-222	26702/550		5682
☐ N583UA	Boeing 757-222	26705/556		5683
☐ N584UA	Boeing 757-222	26706/559		5684
☐ N585UA	Boeing 757-222	26709/563		5685
☐ N586UA	Boeing 757-222	26710/567		5686
☐ N587UA	Boeing 757-222	26713/570		5687
☐ N588UA	Boeing 757-222	26717/571		5688
☐ N589UA	Boeing 757-222ER	28707/773	ex N3509J	5589
☐ N590UA	Boeing 757-222ER/W	28708/785		5590
☐ N592UA	Boeing 757-222	28143/719		5492 Richard Damron, Captain
☐ N593UA	Boeing 757-222	28144/724		5493
☐ N594UA	Boeing 757-222	28145/727		5494
☐ N595UA	Boeing 757-222ER	28748/789		5595
☐ N596UA	Boeing 757-222ER/W	28749/794		5596
☐ N597UA	Boeing 757-222ER	28750/841		5597
☐ N598UA	Boeing 757-222ER	28751/844	ex N1787B	5598
☐ N58101	Boeing 757-224/W	27291/614		0101
☐ N14102	Boeing 757-224/W	27292/619		0102
☐ N33103	Boeing 757-224/W	27293/623		0103
☐ N17104	Boeing 757-224/W	27294/629		104
☐ N17105	Boeing 757-224/W	27295/632		0105
☐ N14106	Boeing 757-224/W	27296/637		0106 Sam E Ashmore
☐ N14107	Boeing 757-224/W	27297/641		107
☐ N21108	Boeing 757-224/W	27298/645		0108
☐ N12109	Boeing 757-224/W	27299/648		0109
☐ N13110	Boeing 757-224/W	27300/650		110
☐ N57111	Boeing 757-224/W	27301/652		0111
☐ N18112	Boeing 757-224/W	27302/653		0112
☐ N13113	Boeing 757-224/W	27555/668		0113
☐ N12114	Boeing 757-224/W	27556/682		0114
☐ N14115	Boeing 757-224/W	27557/686		0115
☐ N12116	Boeing 757-224/W	27558/702		0116
☐ N19117	Boeing 757-224/W	27559/706		0117
☐ N14118	Boeing 757-224/W	27560/748	ex (N19118)	0118
☐ N18119	Boeing 757-224/W	27561/753		0119
☐ N14120	Boeing 757-224/W	27562/761		0120
☐ N14121	Boeing 757-224/W	27563/766		121
☐ N17122	Boeing 757-224/W	27564/768		0122
☐ N26123	Boeing 757-224/W	28966/781		123
☐ N29124	Boeing 757-224/W	27565/786		0124
☐ N12125	Boeing 757-224/W	28967/788	ex N1787B	0125
☐ N17126	Boeing 757-224/W	27566/790		126
☐ N48127	Boeing 757-224/W	28968/791		0127
☐ N17128	Boeing 757-224/W	27567/795		128
☐ N29129	Boeing 757-224/W	28969/796		129
☐ N19130	Boeing 757-224/W	28970/799		0130
☐ N34131	Boeing 757-224/W	28971/806		131
☐ N33132	Boeing 757-224/W	29281/809		132
☐ N17133	Boeing 757-224/W	29282/840		133
☐ N67134	Boeing 757-224/W	29283/848	ex N1800B	134
☐ N41135	Boeing 757-224/W	29284/851		0135
☐ N19136	Boeing 757-224/W	29285/856		0136
☐ N34137	Boeing 757-224/W	30229/899		0137
☐ N13138	Boeing 757-224/W	30351/903	ex N1795B	0138
☐ N17139	Boeing 757-224/W	30352/911		0139
☐ N41140	Boeing 757-224/W	30353/913		0140
☐ N19141	Boeing 757-224/W	30354/933		0141
☐ N75851	Boeing 757-324/W	32810/990		0851
☐ N57852	Boeing 757-324/W	32811/995		852
☐ N75853	Boeing 757-324/W	32812/997		853
☐ N75854	Boeing 757-324/W	32813/999		854
☐ N57855	Boeing 757-324/W	32814/1038		855 ♦
☐ N74856	Boeing 757-324/W	32815/1039		0856 ♦
☐ N57857	Boeing 757-324/W	32816/1040		0857
☐ N75858	Boeing 757-324/W	32817/1042		0858
☐ N56859	Boeing 757-324/W	32818/1043		859 last 757-300 built
☐ N73860	Boeing 757-33N/W	32584/972	ex N550TZ	860
☐ N75861	Boeing 757-33N/W	32585/976	ex N551TZ	861
☐ N57862	Boeing 757-33N/W	32586/978	ex N552TZ	863
☐ N57863	Boeing 757-33N/W	32587/980	ex N553TZ	863 ♦
☐ N57864	Boeing 757-33N/W	32588/985	ex N554TZ	864

☐ N77865	Boeing 757-33N/W	32589/1003	ex N555TZ	865	
☐ N78866	Boeing 757-33N/W	32591/1007	ex N557TZ	866	♦
☐ N77867	Boeing 757-33N/W	32592/1008	ex N558TZ	867	
☐ N57868	Boeing 757-33N/W	32590/1017	ex N556TZ	868	♦
☐ N57869	Boeing 757-33N/W	32593/1018	ex N559TZ	869	♦
☐ N57870	Boeing 757-33N/W	33525/1031	ex N560TZ	0870	♦
☐ N77871	Boeing 757-33N/W	33526/1032	ex N561TZ	871	
☐ N641UA	Boeing 767-322ER	25091/360		6341	
☐ N642UA	Boeing 767-322ER	25092/367		6342	
☐ N643UA	Boeing 767-322ER	25093/368		6343	
☐ N644UA	Boeing 767-322ER	25094/369		6344	
☐ N646UA	Boeing 767-322ER	25283/420		6346	
☐ N647UA	Boeing 767-322ER	25284/424		6347	
☐ N648UA	Boeing 767-322ER	25285/443		6348	[MZJ]
☐ N649UA	Boeing 767-322ER	25286/444		6349	
☐ N651UA	Boeing 767-322ER	25389/452		6351	
☐ N652UA	Boeing 767-322ER	25390/457		6352	
☐ N653UA	Boeing 767-322ER	25391/460		6353 Star Alliance c/s	
☐ N654UA	Boeing 767-322ER	25392/462		6354	
☐ N655UA	Boeing 767-322ER	25393/468		6355	
☐ N656UA	Boeing 767-322ER	25394/472		6356	
☐ N657UA	Boeing 767-322ER	27112/479		6357	
☐ N658UA	Boeing 767-322ER	27113/480		6358	
☐ N659UA	Boeing 767-322ER	27114/485		6359	
☐ N660UA	Boeing 767-322ER	27115/494		6360	
☐ N661UA	Boeing 767-322ER	27158/507		6361	
☐ N662UA	Boeing 767-322ER	27159/513		6362	
☐ N663UA	Boeing 767-322ER	27160/514		6363	
☐ N664UA	Boeing 767-322ER	29236/707		6764	
☐ N665UA	Boeing 767-322ER	29237/711		6765	
☐ N666UA	Boeing 767-322ER	29238/715		6766	
☐ N667UA	Boeing 767-322ER	29239/716		6767	
☐ N668UA	Boeing 767-322ER	30024/742		6768	
☐ N669UA	Boeing 767-322ER	30025/757		6769	
☐ N670UA	Boeing 767-322ER	29240/763		6770	
☐ N671UA	Boeing 767-322ER	30026/766		6771	
☐ N672UA	Boeing 767-322ER	30027/773		6772	
☐ N673UA	Boeing 767-322ER	29241/779		6773	
☐ N674UA	Boeing 767-322ER	29242/782		6774	
☐ N675UA	Boeing 767-322ER	29243/800		6775	
☐ N676UA	Boeing 767-322ER	30028/834		6776	
☐ N677UA	Boeing 767-322ER	30029/852		6777	
☐ N76151	Boeing 767-224ER	30430/811	ex (N37165)	151	
☐ N73152	Boeing 767-224ER	30431/815	ex (N37166)	152	
☐ N76153	Boeing 767-224ER	30432/819	ex (N37167)	153	
☐ N69154	Boeing 767-224ER	30433/823	ex (N37168)	154	
☐ N68155	Boeing 767-224ER	30434/825	ex (N37169)	155	
☐ N76156	Boeing 767-224ER	30435/827	ex (N37170)	156	
☐ N67157	Boeing 767-224ER	30436/833		157	
☐ N67158	Boeing 767-224ER	30437/839		158	
☐ N68159	Boeing 767-224ER	30438/845		159	
☐ N68160	Boeing 767-224ER	30439/851		160	
☐ N66051	Boeing 767-424ER	29446/799	ex (N76401)	051	
☐ N67052	Boeing 767-424ER	29447/805	ex (N87402)	052	
☐ N59053	Boeing 767-424ER	29448/809	ex (N47403)	053	
☐ N76054	Boeing 767-424ER	29449/816	ex (N87404)	054	
☐ N76055	Boeing 767-424ER	29450/826		0055	
☐ N66056	Boeing 767-424ER	29451/842		056	
☐ N66057	Boeing 767-424ER	29452/859		057	
☐ N67058	Boeing 767-424ER	29453/862		058	
☐ N69059	Boeing 767-424ER	29454/864		0059	
☐ N78060	Boeing 767-424ER	29455/866		060	
☐ N68061	Boeing 767-424ER	29456/868		061	
☐ N76062	Boeing 767-424ER	29457/869		062	
☐ N69063	Boeing 767-424ER	29458/872		063	
☐ N76064	Boeing 767-424ER	29459/873		064	
☐ N76065	Boeing 767-424ER	29460/876		065	
☐ N77066	Boeing 767-424ER	29461/878		066	
☐ N204UA	Boeing 777-222ER	28713/191		2904	
☐ N206UA	Boeing 777-222ER	30212/216		2906	
☐ N209UA	Boeing 777-222ER	30215/259		2609	
☐ N210UA	Boeing 777-222ER	30216/264		2510	
☐ N211UA	Boeing 777-222	30217/282		2511	
☐ N212UA	Boeing 777-222	30218/293		2512	

☐ N213UA	Boeing 777-222	30219/295		2513
☐ N214UA	Boeing 777-222	30220/296		2514
☐ N215UA	Boeing 777-222	30221/297		2515
☐ N216UA	Boeing 777-222ER	30549/291		2616
☐ N217UA	Boeing 777-222ER	30550/294		2617
☐ N218UA	Boeing 777-222ER	30222/317		2618 10 Years Star Alliance c/s
☐ N219UA	Boeing 777-222ER	30551/318		2619
☐ N220UA	Boeing 777-222ER	30223/340		2620
☐ N221UA	Boeing 777-222ER	30552/347		2621
☐ N222UA	Boeing 777-222ER	30553/352		2622
☐ N223UA	Boeing 777-222ER	30224/357		2623
☐ N224UA	Boeing 777-222ER	30225/375		2624
☐ N225UA	Boeing 777-222ER	30554/377		2625 Spirit of United
☐ N226UA	Boeing 777-222ER	30226/380		2626
☐ N227UA	Boeing 777-222ER	30555/381		2627
☐ N228UA	Boeing 777-222ER	30556/384		2628
☐ N229UA	Boeing 777-222ER	30557/388		2629
☐ N768UA	Boeing 777-222	26919/11		2368
☐ N769UA	Boeing 777-222	26921/12		2369
☐ N771UA	Boeing 777-222	26932/3	ex N7773	2371
☐ N772UA	Boeing 777-222	26930/5	ex (N77775)	2372
☐ N773UA	Boeing 777-222	26929/4	ex N7774	2373 Richard H Leung, Customer
☐ N774UA	Boeing 777-222	26936/2	ex N7772	2374
☐ N775UA	Boeing 777-222	26947/22		2375
☐ N776UA	Boeing 777-222	26937/27		2376
☐ N777UA	Boeing 777-222	26916/7		2377
☐ N778UA	Boeing 777-222	26940/34		2378
☐ N779UA	Boeing 777-222	26941/35		2379
☐ N780UA	Boeing 777-222	26944/36		2380
☐ N781UA	Boeing 777-222	26945/40		2381
☐ N782UA	Boeing 777-222ER	26948/57		2982
☐ N783UA	Boeing 777-222ER	26950/60		2983
☐ N784UA	Boeing 777-222ER	26951/69		2984
☐ N785UA	Boeing 777-222ER	26954/73		2985
☐ N786UA	Boeing 777-222ER	26938/52		2986
☐ N787UA	Boeing 777-222ER	26939/43		2987
☐ N788UA	Boeing 777-222ER	26942/82		2988
☐ N791UA	Boeing 777-222ER	26933/93		2991
☐ N792UA	Boeing 777-222ER	26934/96		2992
☐ N793UA	Boeing 777-222ER	26946/97		2993
☐ N794UA	Boeing 777-222ER	26953/105		2994
☐ N795UA	Boeing 777-222ER	26927/108		2995
☐ N796UA	Boeing 777-222ER	26931/112		2996
☐ N797UA	Boeing 777-222ER	26924/116		2997
☐ N798UA	Boeing 777-222ER	26928/123		2998
☐ N799UA	Boeing 777-222ER	26926/139		2999
☐ N78001	Boeing 777-224ER	27577/161		0001 Gordon M Bethune
☐ N78002	Boeing 777-224ER	27578/165		002
☐ N78003	Boeing 777-224ER	27579/167		003
☐ N78004	Boeing 777-224ER	27580/169		004
☐ N78005	Boeing 777-224ER	27581/177		005
☐ N77006	Boeing 777-224ER	29476/183		006 Robert F Six
☐ N74007	Boeing 777-224ER	29477/197		0007
☐ N78008	Boeing 777-224ER	29478/200		0008
☐ N78009	Boeing 777-224ER	29479/211		0009
☐ N76010	Boeing 777-224ER	29480/220		010
☐ N79011	Boeing 777-224ER	29859/227		0011
☐ N77012	Boeing 777-224ER	29860/234		0012
☐ N78013	Boeing 777-224ER	29861/243		013
☐ N77014	Boeing 777-224ER	29862/253		014
☐ N27015	Boeing 777-224ER	28678/273		015
☐ N57016	Boeing 777-224ER	28679/279		016
☐ N78017	Boeing 777-224ER	31679/391		017
☐ N37018	Boeing 777-224ER	31680/397		0018
☐ N77019	Boeing 777-224ER	35547/617		0019
☐ N69020	Boeing 777-224ER	31687/625		0020
☐ N76021	Boeing 777-224ER	39776/858		021 ♦
☐ N77022	Boeing 777-224ER	39777/868		022 ♦
☐ N	Boeing 787-8			o/o♦
☐ N	Boeing 787-8			o/o♦
☐ N	Boeing 787-8			o/o♦
☐ N	Boeing 787-8			o/o♦
☐ N	Boeing 787-8			o/o♦
☐ N	Boeing 787-8			o/o♦

UNITED EXPRESS		United (UA)				
		Chicago-O'Hare Intl, IL/San Francisco-Intl, CA/Denver, CO (ORD/SFO/DEN)				

☐ N81533	Beech 1900D	UE-137	ex N137ZV			Gulfstream Intl
☐ N81535	Beech 1900D	UE-147				Gulfstream Intl
☐ N81536	Beech 1900D	UE-152				Gulfstream Intl
☐ N38537	Beech 1900D	UE-158				Gulfstream Intl
☐ N81538	Beech 1900D	UE-199				Gulfstream Intl
☐ N82539	Beech 1900D	UE-168				Gulfstream Intl
☐ N16540	Beech 1900D	UE-172				Gulfstream Intl
☐ N17541	Beech 1900D	UE-203				Gulfstream Intl
☐ N47542	Beech 1900D	UE-198				Gulfstream Intl
☐ N49543	Beech 1900D	UE-181				Gulfstream Intl
☐ N53545	Beech 1900D	UE-185				Gulfstream Intl
☐ N81546	Beech 1900D	UE-187				Gulfstream Intl
☐ N69547	Beech 1900D	UE-189				Gulfstream Intl
☐ N69549	Beech 1900D	UE-194				Gulfstream Intl
☐ N87550	Beech 1900D	UE-205				Gulfstream Intl
☐ N87551	Beech 1900D	UE-206				Gulfstream Intl
☐ N87552	Beech 1900D	UE-216				Gulfstream Intl
☐ N87554	Beech 1900D	UE-227				Gulfstream Intl
☐ N87555	Beech 1900D	UE-234				Gulfstream Intl
☐ N81556	Beech 1900D	UE-239				Gulfstream Intl
☐ N87557	Beech 1900D	UE-246				Gulfstream Intl
☐ N154SF	Canadair CRJ-200LR	7154	ex LV-WSB	154		Mesa
☐ N473CA	Canadair CRJ-200ER	7668	ex C-FMMN	472		Chautauqua
☐ N571ML	Canadair CRJ-200LR	7209	ex C-GBNW			Mesa
☐ N592ML	Canadair CRJ-200LR	7410	ex C-FMLQ			Mesa
☐ N645BR	Canadair CRJ-200ER	7383	ex C-FMLV	462		Chautauqua
☐ N647BR	Canadair CRJ-200ER	7399	ex C-FMNQ	463		Chautauqua
☐ N648BR	Canadair CRJ-200ER	7406	ex C-FMKZ			Chautauqua
☐ N650ML	Canadair CRJ-200LR	7137	ex N261BD			Mesa
☐ N652BR	Canadair CRJ-200ER	7429	ex C-FMMQ	458		Chautauqua
☐ N653BR	Canadair CRJ-200ER	7438	ex C-FMLF	460		Chautauqua
☐ N667BR	Canadair CRJ-200ER	7535	ex C-FMNH	461		Chautauqua
☐ N702BR	Canadair CRJ-200ER	7462	ex N851FJ	459		Chautauqua
☐ N715SF	Canadair CRJ-200LR	7115	ex LV-WPF			Mesa
☐ N830AS	Canadair CRJ-200ER	7236	ex C-FMNW			Atlantic Southeast♦
☐ N832AS	Canadair CRJ-200ER	7243	ex C-FMNQ			Atlantic Southeast♦
☐ N834AS	Canadair CRJ-200ER	7254	ex C-FMKV			Atlantic Southeast♦
☐ N836AS	Canadair CRJ-200ER	7263	ex C-FMLU			Atlantic Southeast♦
☐ N903SW	Canadair CRJ-200ER	7425	ex C-FMOI	7425		SkyWest
☐ N905SW	Canadair CRJ-200ER	7437	ex C-FMLB	7437		SkyWest
☐ N906SW	Canadair CRJ-200ER	7510	ex C-FMOW	7510		SkyWest
☐ N907SW	Canadair CRJ-200ER	7511	ex C-FVAZ	7511		SkyWest
☐ N908SW	Canadair CRJ-200ER	7540	ex C-FMOW	7540		SkyWest
☐ N909SW	Canadair CRJ-200ER	7558	ex C-GJHL	7558		SkyWest
☐ N910SW	Canadair CRJ-200ER	7566	ex C-GJHY	7566		SkyWest
☐ N912SW	Canadair CRJ-200ER	7595	ex C-FMNH	7595		SkyWest
☐ N913SW	Canadair CRJ-200ER	7597	ex C-FMNX	7597		SkyWest
☐ N915SW	Canadair CRJ-200ER	7615	ex C-GKJQ	7615		SkyWest
☐ N916SW	Canadair CRJ-200ER	7634	ex C-FMLU	7634		SkyWest
☐ N917SW	Canadair CRJ-200ER	7641	ex C-FMMX	7641		SkyWest
☐ N918SW	Canadair CRJ-200ER	7645	ex C-FMKW	7645		SkyWest
☐ N919SW	Canadair CRJ-200ER	7657	ex C-FMNX	7657		SkyWest
☐ N920SW	Canadair CRJ-200ER	7660	ex C-FMOW	7660		SkyWest
☐ N923SW	Canadair CRJ-200ER	7664	ex C-FMLU	7664		SkyWest
☐ N924SW	Canadair CRJ-200ER	7681	ex C-FMLS	7681		SkyWest
☐ N925SW	Canadair CRJ-200ER	7682	ex C-FMLT	7682		SkyWest
☐ N926SW	Canadair CRJ-200ER	7687	ex C-FMNX	7687		SkyWest
☐ N927SW	Canadair CRJ-200ER	7693	ex C-FMNQ	7693		SkyWest
☐ N928SW	Canadair CRJ-200ER	7701	ex C-FMMX	7701		SkyWest
☐ N929SW	Canadair CRJ-200ER	7703	ex C-FMNB	7703		SkyWest
☐ N930SW	Canadair CRJ-200ER	7713	ex C-FMLV	7713		SkyWest
☐ N932SW	Canadair CRJ-200ER	7714	ex C-FMMT	7714		SkyWest
☐ N934SW	Canadair CRJ-200ER	7722	ex C-FMND	7722		SkyWest
☐ N935SW	Canadair CRJ-200ER	7725	ex C-FMOI	7725		SkyWest
☐ N936SW	Canadair CRJ-200ER	7726	ex C-FMMB	7726		SkyWest
☐ N937SW	Canadair CRJ-200ER	7735	ex C-FMKW	7735		SkyWest
☐ N938SW	Canadair CRJ-200ER	7741	ex C-FMLS	7741		SkyWest
☐ N939SW	Canadair CRJ-200ER	7742	ex C-FMLT	7742		SkyWest
☐ N941SW	Canadair CRJ-200ER	7750	ex C-FMOW	7750		SkyWest
☐ N943SW	Canadair CRJ-200ER	7762	ex C-FMMY	7762		SkyWest
☐ N944SW	Canadair CRJ-200ER	7764	ex C-FMKV	7764		SkyWest
☐ N945SW	Canadair CRJ-200ER	7770	ex C-FMLQ	7770		SkyWest

☐ N946SW	Canadair CRJ-200ER	7776	ex C-FMNW	7776	SkyWest
☐ N948SW	Canadair CRJ-200ER	7789	ex C-GXTU	7789	SkyWest
☐ N951SW	Canadair CRJ-200ER	7795	ex C-FMKW	7795 30th anniversary c/s	SkyWest
☐ N952SW	Canadair CRJ-200ER	7805	ex C-FMNH	7805	SkyWest
☐ N953SW	Canadair CRJ-200ER	7813	ex C-GZGP	7813	SkyWest
☐ N954SW	Canadair CRJ-200ER	7815	ex C-FMOI	7815	SkyWest
☐ N955SW	Canadair CRJ-200ER	7817	ex C-FMML	7817	SkyWest
☐ N956SW	Canadair CRJ-200ER	7825	ex C-FMKW	7825	SkyWest
☐ N957SW	Canadair CRJ-200ER	7829	ex C-FMLI	7829	SkyWest
☐ N958SW	Canadair CRJ-200ER	7833	ex C-FMLV	7833	SkyWest
☐ N959SW	Canadair CRJ-200ER	7840	ex C-FMOW	7840	SkyWest
☐ N960SW	Canadair CRJ-200ER	7853	ex C-FMNB	7853	SkyWest
☐ N961SW	Canadair CRJ-200ER	7857	ex C-FMLB	7857	SkyWest
☐ N962SW	Canadair CRJ-200ER	7859	ex C-FMLI	7859	SkyWest
☐ N963SW	Canadair CRJ-200ER	7865	ex C-FMNH	7865	SkyWest
☐ N964SW	Canadair CRJ-200ER	7868	ex C-GZTD	7867	SkyWest
☐ N965SW	Canadair CRJ-200ER	7871	ex C-FVAZ	7871	SkyWest
☐ N967SW	Canadair CRJ-200ER	7872	ex C-FMND	7872	SkyWest
☐ N969SW	Canadair CRJ-200ER	7876	ex C-FMMB	7876	SkyWest
☐ N970SW	Canadair CRJ-200ER	7881	ex C-GZUJ	7881	SkyWest
☐ N971SW	Canadair CRJ-200ER	7947	ex C-FMLB	7947	SkyWest
☐ N973SW	Canadair CRJ-200ER	7949	ex C-FMLI	7949	SkyWest
☐ N975SW	Canadair CRJ-200ER	7951	ex C-FMLS	7951	SkyWest
☐ N976SW	Canadair CRJ-200ER	7952	ex C-FMLT	7952	SkyWest
☐ N978SW	Canadair CRJ-200ER	7953	ex C-FMLV	7953	SkyWest
☐ N979SW	Canadair CRJ-200ER	7954	ex C-FMMT	7954	SkyWest
☐ N980SW	Canadair CRJ-200ER	7955	ex C-FMNH	7955	SkyWest
☐ N982SW	Canadair CRJ-200ER	7956	ex C-FMNW	7956	SkyWest
☐ N983SW	Canadair CRJ-200ER	7961	ex C-FVAZ	7961	SkyWest
☐ N986SW	Canadair CRJ-200ER	7967	ex C-FMML	7967	SkyWest
☐ N17156	Canadair CRJ-200LR	7156	ex C-FZSC		Mesa
☐ N17175	Canadair CRJ-200LR	7175	ex LV-WXB		Mesa
☐ N27172	Canadair CRJ-200LR	7172	ex C-FMMN		Mesa
☐ N27185	Canadair CRJ-200LR	7185	ex C-FMMB		Mesa
☐ N37208	Canadair CRJ-200LR	7208	ex C-FMNY		Mesa
☐ N37228	Canadair CRJ-200LR	7228	ex B-7692		Mesa
☐ N47202	Canadair CRJ-200LR	7202	ex C-FMLT		Mesa
☐ N75994	Canadair CRJ-200LR	7367	ex C-FZTY		Mesa
☐ N75995	Canadair CRJ-200LR	7361	ex C-FZTW		Mesa
☐ N77181	Canadair CRJ-200LR	7181	ex C-FMNQ		Mesa
☐ N77195	Canadair CRJ-200LR	7195	ex C-FMKW		Mesa
☐ N151GJ	Canadair CRJ-702ER	10216	ex C-		GoJet
☐ N152GJ	Canadair CRJ-702ER	10218	ex C-		GoJet
☐ N153GJ	Canadair CRJ-702ER	10219	ex C-		GoJet
☐ N154GJ	Canadair CRJ-702ER	10224	ex C-		GoJet
☐ N155GJ	Canadair CRJ-702ER	10225	ex C-		GoJet
☐ N156GJ	Canadair CRJ-702ER	10227	ex C-		GoJet
☐ N157GJ	Canadair CRJ-702ER	10230	ex C-		GoJet
☐ N158GJ	Canadair CRJ-702ER	10237	ex C-		GoJet
☐ N159GJ	Canadair CRJ-702ER	10238	ex C-		GoJet
☐ N160GJ	Canadair CRJ-702ER	10239	ex C-		GoJet
☐ N161GJ	Canadair CRJ-702ER	10253	ex C-		GoJet
☐ N162GJ	Canadair CRJ-702ER	10254	ex C-		GoJet
☐ N163GJ	Canadair CRJ-702ER	10255	ex C-		GoJet
☐ N164GJ	Canadair CRJ-702ER	10256	ex C-		GoJet
☐ N165GJ	Canadair CRJ-702ER	10257	ex C-		GoJet
☐ N166GJ	Canadair CRJ-702ER	10266	ex C-		GoJet
☐ N167GJ	Canadair CRJ-702ER	10269	ex C-		GoJet
☐ N168GJ	Canadair CRJ-702ER	10272	ex C-GHZZ		GoJet
☐ N169GJ	Canadair CRJ-702ER	10273	ex C-		GoJet
☐ N170GJ	Canadair CRJ-702ER	10280	ex C-GICN		GoJet
☐ N171GJ	Canadair CRJ-702ER	10282	ex C-GIAR		GoJet
☐ N172GJ	Canadair CRJ-702ER	10283	ex C-		GoJet
☐ N173GJ	Canadair CRJ-702ER	10287	ex C-		GoJet
☐ N174GJ	Canadair CRJ-702ER	10296	ex C-		GoJet
☐ N175GJ	Canadair CRJ-702ER	10297	ex C-		GoJet
☐ N501MJ	Canadair CRJ-701ER	10047	ex C-FZVM		Mesa
☐ N502MJ	Canadair CRJ-701ER	10050	ex C-GIAI		Mesa
☐ N503MJ	Canadair CRJ-701ER	10058	ex C-GIBG		Mesa
☐ N504MJ	Canadair CRJ-701ER	10066	ex C-GIBR		Mesa
☐ N505MJ	Canadair CRJ-701ER	10070	ex C-GICN		Mesa
☐ N506MJ	Canadair CRJ-701ER	10073	ex C-GHZY		Mesa
☐ N507MJ	Canadair CRJ-701ER	10077	ex C-GIAH		Mesa
☐ N508MJ	Canadair CRJ-701ER	10087	ex C-FZZE		Mesa
☐ N509MJ	Canadair CRJ-701ER	10094	ex C-		Mesa
☐ N510MJ	Canadair CRJ-701ER	10101	ex C-		Mesa

☐ N511MJ	Canadair CRJ-701ER	10104	ex C-			Mesa
☐ N512MJ	Canadair CRJ-701ER	10109	ex C-			Mesa
☐ N513MJ	Canadair CRJ-701ER	10111	ex C-			Mesa
☐ N514MJ	Canadair CRJ-701ER	10116	ex C-			Mesa
☐ N515MJ	Canadair CRJ-701ER	10117	ex C-			Mesa
☐ N516LR	Canadair CRJ-701ER	10258	ex C-			Mesa
☐ N518LR	Canadair CRJ-701ER	10259	ex C-			Mesa
☐ N519LR	Canadair CRJ-701ER	10260	ex C-FLGD			Mesa
☐ N521LR	Canadair CRJ-701ER	10261	ex C-FMHJ			Mesa
☐ N522LR	Canadair CRJ-701ER	10262	ex C-			Mesa
☐ N701SK	Canadair CRJ-701ER	10133	ex C-	10133	SkyWest
☐ N702SK	Canadair CRJ-701ER	10136	ex C-	10136	SkyWest
☐ N703SK	Canadair CRJ-701ER	10139	ex C-	10139	SkyWest
☐ N705SK	Canadair CRJ-701ER	10145	ex C-	10145	SkyWest
☐ N706SK	Canadair CRJ-701ER	10149	ex C-	10149	SkyWest
☐ N707SK	Canadair CRJ-701ER	10003	ex C-FBKA	10003	SkyWest
☐ N708SK	Canadair CRJ-701ER	10156	ex C-	10156	SkyWest
☐ N709SK	Canadair CRJ-701ER	10159	ex C-	10159	SkyWest
☐ N710SK	Canadair CRJ-701ER	10170	ex C-	10170	SkyWest
☐ N712SK	Canadair CRJ-701ER	10172	ex C-GIAR	10172	SkyWest
☐ N713SK	Canadair CRJ-701ER	10174	ex C-	10174	SkyWest
☐ N715SK	Canadair CRJ-701ER	10179	ex C-	10179	SkyWest
☐ N716SK	Canadair CRJ-701ER	10180	ex C-	10180	SkyWest
☐ N718SK	Canadair CRJ-701ER	10184	ex C-	10184	SkyWest
☐ N719SK	Canadair CRJ-701ER	10188	ex C-	10188	SkyWest
☐ N724SK	Canadair CRJ-701ER	10189	ex C-	10189	SkyWest
☐ N726SK	Canadair CRJ-701ER	10190	ex C-	10190	SkyWest
☐ N727SK	Canadair CRJ-701ER	10191	ex C-	10191	SkyWest
☐ N728SK	Canadair CRJ-701ER	10192	ex C-	10192	SkyWest
☐ N730SK	Canadair CRJ-701ER	10193	ex C-	10193	SkyWest
☐ N732SK	Canadair CRJ-701ER	10194	ex C-	10194	SkyWest
☐ N738SK	Canadair CRJ-701ER	10195	ex C-	10195	SkyWVst
☐ N740SK	Canadair CRJ-701ER	10196	ex C-	10196	SkyWest
☐ N742SK	Canadair CRJ-701ER	10197	ex C-	10197	SkyWest
☐ N743SK	Canadair CRJ-701ER	10199	ex C-	10199	SkyWest
☐ N744SK	Canadair CRJ-701ER	10200	ex C-	10200	SkyWest
☐ N745SK	Canadair CRJ-701ER	10201	ex C-	10201	SkyWest
☐ N746SK	Canadair CRJ-701ER	10202	ex C-FEUP	10202	SkyWest
☐ N748SK	Canadair CRJ-701ER	10203	ex C-	10203	SkyWest
☐ N750SK	Canadair CRJ-701ER	10207	ex C-	10207	SkyWest
☐ N751SK	Canadair CRJ-701ER	10208	ex C-	10208	SkyWest
☐ N752SK	Canadair CRJ-701ER	10209	ex C-	10209	SkyWest
☐ N753SK	Canadair CRJ-701ER	10214	ex C-FEVZ	10214	SkyWest
☐ N754SK	Canadair CRJ-701ER	10215	ex C-	10215	SkyWest
☐ N755SK	Canadair CRJ-701ER	10220	ex C-FFVZ	10220	SkyWest
☐ N756SK	Canadair CRJ-701ER	10221	ex C-	10221	SkyWest
☐ N758SK	Canadair CRJ-701ER	10222	ex C-	10222	SkyWest
☐ N760SK	Canadair CRJ-701ER	10223	ex C-	10223	SkyWest
☐ N762SK	Canadair CRJ-702ER	10226	ex C-	10226	SkyWest
☐ N763SK	Canadair CRJ-702ER	10228	ex C-	10228	SkyWest
☐ N764SK	Canadair CRJ-702ER	10229	ex C-FGRE	10229	SkyWest
☐ N765SK	Canadair CRJ-702ER	10231	ex C-	10231	SkyWest
☐ N766SK	Canadair CRJ-702ER	10232	ex C-	10232	SkyWest
☐ N767SK	Canadair CRJ-702ER	10233	ex C-	10233	SkyWest
☐ N768SK	Canadair CRJ-702ER	10234	ex C-	10234	SkyWest
☐ N770SK	Canadair CRJ-702ER	10243	ex C-	10243	SkyWest
☐ N771SK	Canadair CRJ-702ER	10244	ex C-	10244	SkyWest
☐ N772SK	Canadair CRJ-702ER	10235	ex C-	10235	SkyWest
☐ N773SK	Canadair CRJ-702ER	10236	ex C-	10236	SkyWest
☐ N774SK	Canadair CRJ-702ER	10240	ex C-	10240	SkyWest
☐ N776SK	Canadair CRJ-702ER	10241	ex C-	10241	SkyWest
☐ N778SK	Canadair CRJ-702ER	10242	ex C-	10242	SkyWest
☐ N779SK	Canadair CRJ-702ER	10276	ex C-	10276	SkyWest
☐ N780SK	Canadair CRJ-702ER	10277	ex C-	10277	SkyWest
☐ N782SK	Canadair CRJ-702ER	10278	ex C-	10278	SkyWest
☐ N783SK	Canadair CRJ-702ER	10281	ex C-GICP	10281	SkyWest
☐ N784SK	Canadair CRJ-702ER	10284	ex C-	10284	SkyWest
☐ N785SK	Canadair CRJ-702ER	10285	ex C-	10285	SkyWest
☐ N786SK	Canadair CRJ-702ER	10286	ex C-	10286	SkyWest
☐ N787SK	Canadair CRJ-702ER	10288	ex C-	10288	SkyWest
☐ N788SK	Canadair CRJ-702ER	10290	ex C-	10290	SkyWest
☐ N789SK	Canadair CRJ-702ER	10291	ex C-	10291	SkyWest
☐ N790SK	Canadair CRJ-702ER	10292	ex C-	10292	SkyWest
☐ N791SK	Canadair CRJ-702ER	10293	ex C-	10293	SkyWest
☐ N792SK	Canadair CRJ-702ER	10294	ex C-	10294	SkyWest
☐ N793SK	Canadair CRJ-702ER	10295	ex C-	10295	SkyWest
☐ N794SK	Canadair CRJ-702ER	10298	ex C-	10298	SkyWest

	Registration	Type		ex		Operator
☐	N795SK	Canadair CRJ-702ER	10299	ex C-	10299	SkyWest
☐	N796SK	Canadair CRJ-702ER	10300	ex C-	10300	SkyWest
☐	N	Canadair CRJ-702ER		ex C-		SkyWest
☐	N	Canadair CRJ-702ER		ex C-		SkyWest
☐	N	Canadair CRJ-702ER		ex C-		SkyWest
☐	N	Canadair CRJ-702ER		ex C-		SkyWest
☐	N	Canadair CRJ-702ER		ex C-		SkyWest
☐	N	Canadair CRJ-702ER		ex C-		SkyWest
☐	N	Canadair CRJ-702ER		ex C-		SkyWest
☐	N	Canadair CRJ-702ER		ex C-		SkyWest
☐	N	Canadair CRJ-702ER		ex C-		SkyWest
☐	N	Canadair CRJ-702ER		ex C-		SkyWest
☐	N	Canadair CRJ-702ER		ex C-		SkyWest
☐	N	Canadair CRJ-702ER		ex C-		SkyWest
☐	N	Canadair CRJ-702ER		ex C-		SkyWest
☐	N	Canadair CRJ-702ER		ex C-		SkyWest
☐	N	Canadair CRJ-702ER		ex C-		SkyWest
☐	N	Canadair CRJ-702ER		ex C-		SkyWest
☐	N	Canadair CRJ-702ER		ex C-		SkyWest
☐	N	Canadair CRJ-702ER		ex C-		SkyWest
☐	N	Canadair CRJ-702ER		ex C-		SkyWest
☐	N	Canadair CRJ-702ER		ex C-		SkyWest
☐	N	Canadair CRJ-702ER		ex C-		SkyWest
☐	N	Canadair CRJ-702ER		ex C-		SkyWest
☐	N	Canadair CRJ-702ER		ex C-		SkyWest
☐	N351PH	de Havilland DHC-8Q-202	490	ex C-GFUM	763	Commutair <QXE
☐	N358PH	de Havilland DHC-8Q-202	506	ex C-FWBB	775	Commutair <QXE
☐	N359PH	de Havilland DHC-8Q-202	514	ex C-GEOA	764	Commutair <QXE
☐	N360PH	de Havilland DHC-8Q-202	515	ex C-GEWI	762	Commutair <QXE
☐	N361PH	de Havilland DHC-8Q-202	516	ex C-GFOD	767	Commutair <QXE
☐	N362PH	de Havilland DHC-8Q-202	518	ex C-FDHI	766	Commutair <QXE
☐	N363PH	de Havilland DHC-8Q-202	520	ex C-FDHP	760	Commutair <QXE
☐	N364PH	de Havilland DHC-8Q-202	524	ex C-FDHX	765	Commutair <QXE
☐	N365PH	de Havilland DHC-8Q-202	526		773	Commutair <QXE
☐	N366PH	de Havilland DHC-8Q-202	510	ex C-GELN	769	Commutair <QXE
☐	N367PH	de Havilland DHC-8Q-202	511	ex C-GDLD	774	Commutair <QXE
☐	N368PH	de Havilland DHC-8Q-202	512	ex C-GDFT	768	Commutair <QXE
☐	N369PH	de Havilland DHC-8Q-202	513	ex C-FWBB	770	Commutair <QXE
☐	N374PH	de Havilland DHC-8Q-202	528	ex C-GDIU	771	Commutair <QXE
☐	N375PH	de Havilland DHC-8Q-202	529	ex C-GDKL	761	Commutair <QXE
☐	N379PH	de Havilland DHC-8Q-202	530	ex C-GDLK		Commutair <QXE
☐	N436YV	de Havilland DHC-8Q-202	436	ex C-GDNG		Mesa
☐	N444YV	de Havilland DHC-8Q-202	444	ex C-GFRP	all-white	Mesa
☐	N445YV	de Havilland DHC-8Q-202	445	ex C-GFEN		Mesa
☐	N446YV	de Havilland DHC-8Q-202	446	ex C-GEOA		Mesa
☐	N454YV	de Havilland DHC-8Q-202	454	ex C-GEOA		Mesa
☐	N455YV	de Havilland DHC-8Q-202	455	ex C-GFRP		Mesa
☐	N456YV	de Havilland DHC-8Q-202	456	ex C-GFOD		Mesa
☐	N34NG	de Havilland DHC-8-402Q	4340	ex C-GGSI		Colgan Air♦
☐	N187WQ	de Havilland DHC-8-402Q	4187	ex C-FNQG	777	Colgan Air
☐	N188WQ	de Havilland DHC-8-402Q	4188	ex C-FNQH	778	Colgan Air
☐	N190WQ	de Havilland DHC-8-402Q	4190	ex C-FNQN	779	Colgan Air
☐	N191WQ	de Havilland DHC-8-402Q	4191	ex C-FNQQ	780	Colgan Air
☐	N195WQ	de Havilland DHC-8-402Q	4195	ex C-FOJM	781	Colgan Air
☐	N196WQ	de Havilland DHC-8-402Q	4196	ex C-FOJT	782	Colgan Air
☐	N199WQ	de Havilland DHC-8-402Q	4199	ex C-FOUO	783	Colgan Air
☐	N202WQ	de Havilland DHC-8-402Q	4202	ex C-FOUY	785	Colgan Air
☐	N203WQ	de Havilland DHC-8-402Q	4203	ex C-FPDY	786	Colgan Air
☐	N204WQ	de Havilland DHC-8-402Q	4204	ex C-FPEF	787	Colgan Air
☐	N208WQ	de Havilland DHC-8-402Q	4208	ex C-FPPW	788	Colgan Air
☐	N209WQ	de Havilland DHC-8-402Q	4209	ex C-FPQA	789	Colgan Air
☐	N213WQ	de Havilland DHC-8-402Q	4213	ex C-FQXO	790	Colgan Air
☐	N214WQ	de Havilland DHC-8-402Q	4214	ex C-FQXP	791	Colgan Air
☐	N323NG	de Havilland DHC-8-402Q	4323	ex C-GEVP		Colgan Air♦
☐	N328NG	de Havilland DHC-8-402Q	4328	ex C-GPNN		Colgan Air♦
☐	N332NG	de Havilland DHC-8-402Q	4332	ex C-GFKK		Colgan Air♦
☐	N333NG	de Havilland DHC-8-402Q	4333	ex C-GGFI		Colgan Air♦
☐	N336NG	de Havilland DHC-8-402Q	4336	ex C-GGIF		Colgan Air♦
☐	N338NG	de Havilland DHC-8-402Q	4338	ex C-GGQY		Colgan Air♦
☐	N339NG	de Havilland DHC-8-402Q	4339	ex C-GGRI		Colgan Air♦
☐	N341NG	de Havilland DHC-8-402Q	4341	ex C-GGSV		Colgan Air♦
☐	N342NG	de Havilland DHC-8-402Q	4342	ex C-GGUB		Colgan Air♦
☐	N346NG	de Havilland DHC-8-402Q	4346	ex C-GHCO		Colgan Air♦

☐ N351NG	de Havilland DHC-8-402Q	4351	ex C-GHVS		o/o♦
☐ N354NG	de Havilland DHC-8-402Q	4354	ex		o/o♦
☐ N	de Havilland DHC-8-402Q		ex		o/o♦
☐ N	de Havilland DHC-8-402Q		ex		o/o♦
☐ N	de Havilland DHC-8-402Q		ex		o/o♦
☐ N	de Havilland DHC-8-402Q		ex		o/o♦
☐ N	de Havilland DHC-8-402Q		ex		o/o♦
☐ N221SW	Embraer EMB.120ER Brasilia	120290	ex PT-SVK		SkyWest
☐ N223SW	Embraer EMB.120ER Brasilia	120291	ex PT-SVL		SkyWest
☐ N226SW	Embraer EMB.120ER Brasilia	120296	ex PT-SVQ		SkyWest
☐ N229SW	Embraer EMB.120ER Brasilia	120305	ex PT-SVX		SkyWest
☐ N233SW	Embraer EMB.120ER Brasilia	120307	ex PT-SVZ		SkyWest
☐ N234SW	Embraer EMB.120ER Brasilia	120308	ex PT-SXA		SkyWest
☐ N235SW	Embraer EMB.120ER Brasilia	120310	ex PT-SXC		SkyWest
☐ N236SW	Embraer EMB.120ER Brasilia	120312	ex PT-SXE		SkyWest
☐ N237SW	Embraer EMB.120ER Brasilia	120314	ex PT-SXG		SkyWest
☐ N251YV	Embraer EMB.120ER Brasilia	120251	ex PT-STX		SkyWest
☐ N270YV	Embraer EMB.120ER Brasilia	120270	ex PT-SUR		SkyWest
☐ N284YV	Embraer EMB.120ER Brasilia	120284	ex PT-SVE		SkyWest
☐ N288SW	Embraer EMB.120ER Brasilia	120316	ex PT-SXI		SkyWest
☐ N290SW	Embraer EMB.120ER Brasilia	120317	ex PT-SXJ		SkyWest
☐ N291SW	Embraer EMB.120ER Brasilia	120318	ex PT-SXK		SkyWest
☐ N292SW	Embraer EMB.120ER Brasilia	120319	ex PT-SXL		SkyWest
☐ N292UX	Embraer EMB.120ER Brasilia	120292	ex PT-SVM		SkyWest
☐ N294SW	Embraer EMB.120ER Brasilia	120321	ex PT-SXN		SkyWest
☐ N295SW	Embraer EMB.120ER Brasilia	120322	ex PT-SXO		SkyWest
☐ N297SW	Embraer EMB.120ER Brasilia	120327	ex PT-SXT		SkyWest
☐ N298SW	Embraer EMB.120ER Brasilia	120328	ex PT-SXU		SkyWest
☐ N308SW	Embraer EMB.120ER Brasilia	120326	ex PT-SXS		SkyWest
☐ N393SW	Embraer EMB.120ER Brasilia	120330	ex PT-SXW		SkyWest
☐ N560SW	Embraer EMB.120ER Brasilia	120334	ex PT-SXX		SkyWest
☐ N561SW	Embraer EMB.120ER Brasilia	120335	ex PT-SXY		SkyWest
☐ N562SW	Embraer EMB.120ER Brasilia	120336	ex PT-SXZ		SkyWest
☐ N564SW	Embraer EMB.120ER Brasilia	120339	ex PT-SAC		SkyWest
☐ N565SW	Embraer EMB.120ER Brasilia	120340	ex PT-SAI		SkyWest
☐ N566SW	Embraer EMB.120ER Brasilia	120341	ex PT-SAF		SkyWest
☐ N567SW	Embraer EMB.120ER Brasilia	120342	ex PT-SAL		SkyWest
☐ N568SW	Embraer EMB.120ER Brasilia	120343	ex PT-SAZ		SkyWest
☐ N569SW	Embraer EMB.120ER Brasilia	120344	ex PT-SBY		SkyWest
☐ N578SW	Embraer EMB.120ER Brasilia	120346	ex PT-SCA		SkyWest
☐ N579SW	Embraer EMB.120ER Brasilia	120347	ex PT-SCB		SkyWest
☐ N580SW	Embraer EMB.120ER Brasilia	120348	ex PT-SCC		SkyWest
☐ N581SW	Embraer EMB.120ER Brasilia	120349	ex PT-SCZ		SkyWest
☐ N582SW	Embraer EMB.120ER Brasilia	120350	ex PT-SDC		SkyWest
☐ N583SW	Embraer EMB.120ER Brasilia	120351	ex PT-SEF		SkyWest
☐ N584SW	Embraer EMB.120ER Brasilia	120352	ex PT-SEG		SkyWest
☐ N585SW	Embraer EMB.120ER Brasilia	120353	ex PT-SEH		SkyWest
☐ N586SW	Embraer EMB.120ER Brasilia	120354	ex PT-SEJ		SkyWest
☐ N16501	Embraer ERJ-135ER	145145	ex PT-SDV	501	[IGM]
☐ N16502	Embraer ERJ-135ER	145166	ex PT-SFF	502	[IGM]
☐ N19503	Embraer ERJ-135ER	145176	ex PT-SFI	503	[IGM]
☐ N25504	Embraer ERJ-135ER	145186	ex PT-SFK	504	[CLE]
☐ N14505	Embraer ERJ-135ER	145192	ex PT-SFN	505	[IGM]
☐ N27506	Embraer ERJ-135ER	145206	ex PT-SFT	506	[IGM]
☐ N17507	Embraer ERJ-135ER	145215	ex PT-SFW	507	[IGM]
☐ N14508	Embraer ERJ-135ER	145220	ex PT-SFY	508	[IGM]
☐ N15509	Embraer ERJ-135ER	145238	ex PT-SID	509	[IGM]
☐ N16510	Embraer ERJ-135ER	145251	ex PT-SJI	510	[IGM]
☐ N16511	Embraer ERJ-135ER	145267	ex PT-SIZ	511	[IGM]
☐ N27512	Embraer ERJ-135ER	145274	ex PT-SJQ	512	[IGM]
☐ N17513	Embraer ERJ-135LR	145292	ex PT-SKJ	513	[IGM]
☐ N14514	Embraer ERJ-135LR	145303	ex PT-SKU	514	[IGM]
☐ N29515	Embraer ERJ-135LR	145309	ex PT-SMA	515	[IGM]
☐ N14516	Embraer ERJ-135LR	145323	ex PT-SMP	516	[IGM]
☐ N24517	Embraer ERJ-135LR	145332	ex PT-SMY	517	[IGM]
☐ N28518	Embraer ERJ-135LR	145334	ex PT-SNA	518	[IGM]
☐ N12519	Embraer ERJ-135LR	145366	ex PT-SOQ	519	[IGM]
☐ N16520	Embraer ERJ-135LR	145372	ex PT-SOX	520	[IGM]
☐ N17521	Embraer ERJ-135LR	145378	ex PT-SQC	521	[IGM]
☐ N14522	Embraer ERJ-135LR	145383	ex PT-SQH	522	[IGM]
☐ N27523	Embraer ERJ-135LR	145389	ex PT-SQN	523	[IGM]
☐ N17524	Embraer ERJ-135LR	145399	ex PT-SQW	524	[IGM]
☐ N16525	Embraer ERJ-135LR	145403	ex PT-STA	525	[IGM]
☐ N11526	Embraer ERJ-135LR	145410	ex PT-STH	526	Republic
☐ N15527	Embraer ERJ-135LR	145413	ex PT-STJ	527	Republic

	Registration	Type	MSN	Ex	No.	Operator
☐	N12528	Embraer ERJ-135LR	145504	ex PT-SXX	528	Republic
☐	N28529	Embraer ERJ-135LR	145512	ex PT-SYE	529	Republic
☐	N12530	Embraer ERJ-135LR	145533	ex PT-STX	530	Republic
☐	N269SK	Embraer ERJ-145LR	145293	ex PT-SYG		Chautauqua
☐	N270SK	Embraer ERJ-145LR	145304	ex PT-SKV		Chautauqua
☐	N271SK	Embraer ERJ-145LR	145305	ex PT-SKW		Chautauqua
☐	N265SK	Embraer ERJ-145LR	145226	ex PT-SHL		Chautauqua
☐	N266SK	Embraer ERJ-145LR	145241	ex PT-SIG	436	Chautauqua
☐	N267SK	Embraer ERJ-145LR	145268	ex PT-SJK	437	Chautauqua
☐	N268SK	Embraer ERJ-145LR	145270	ex PT-SJM		Chautauqua
☐	N275SK	Embraer ERJ-145LR	145345	ex PT-SNL	439	Chautauqua
☐	N276SK	Embraer ERJ-145LR	145348	ex PT-SNO		Chautauqua
☐	N277SK	Embraer ERJ-145LR	145355	ex PT-SNU	440	Chautauqua
☐	N278SK	Embraer ERJ-145LR	145370	ex PT-		Chautauqua
☐	N279SK	Embraer ERJ-145LR	145379	ex PT-SQD		Chautauqua
☐	N281SK	Embraer ERJ-145LR	145391	ex PT-		Chautauqua
☐	N283SK	Embraer ERJ-145LR	145424	ex PT-STV	442	Chautauqua
☐	N284SK	Embraer ERJ-145LR	145427	ex PT-STY		Chautauqua
☐	N285SK	Embraer ERJ-145LR	145435	ex PT-SUG	444	Chautauqua
☐	N286SK	Embraer ERJ-145LR	145443	ex PT-SUO		Chautauqua
☐	N287SK	Embraer ERJ-145LR	145460	ex PT-SVF		Chautauqua
☐	N288SK	Embraer ERJ-145LR	145461	ex PT-SVG		Chautauqua
☐	N289SK	Embraer ERJ-145LR	145463	ex PT-SVI		Chautauqua
☐	N290SK	Embraer ERJ-145LR	145474	ex PT-SVT		Chautauqua
☐	N292SK	Embraer ERJ-145LR	145488	ex PT-SXH		Chautauqua
☐	N294SK	Embraer ERJ-145LR	145497	ex PT-SXQ		Chautauqua
☐	N296SK	Embraer ERJ-145LR	145514	ex PT-SYG		Chautauqua
☐	N806HK	Embraer ERJ-145ER	145112	ex PT-SCO		Trans State
☐	N807HK	Embraer ERJ-145ER	145119	ex PT-SCV		Trans State
☐	N810HK	Embraer ERJ-145LR	145231	ex PT-SHV		Trans State
☐	N833HK	Embraer ERJ-145LR	145240	ex HB-JAB		Trans State
☐	N835HK	Embraer ERJ-145LR	145670	ex PT-SFE		Trans Stare
☐	N836HK	Embraer ERJ-145LR	145695	ex PT-SGA		Trans State
☐	N838HK	Embraer ERJ-145LR	145321	ex HB-JAG		Trans State
☐	N839HK	Embraer ERJ-145LR	14500829	ex PT-SQC		Trans State
☐	N840HK	Embraer ERJ-145LR	145341	ex HB-JAH		Trans State
☐	N841HK	Embraer ERJ-145LR	145382	ex HB-JAJ		Trans State
☐	N842HK	Embraer ERJ-145LR	14500830	ex PT-SQD		Trans State
☐	N843HK	Embraer ERJ-145LR	14500822	ex PT-SNW		Trans State
☐	N844HK	Embraer ERJ-145LR	14500838	ex PT-SQK		Trans State
☐	N845HK	Embraer ERJ-145LR	14500842	ex PT-SQM		Trans State
☐	N846HK	Embraer ERJ-145LR	14500855	ex PT-SQW		Trans State
☐	N847HK	Embraer ERJ-145LR	14500857	ex PT-SQY		Trans State
☐	N851HK	Embraer ERJ-145LR	145340	ex N834MJ		Trans State
☐	N852HK	Embraer ERJ-145LR	145353	ex N835MJ		Trans State
☐	N858MJ	Embraer ERJ-145LR	145767	ex PT-SJY		Mesa
☐	N859MJ	Embraer ERJ-145LR	145769	ex PT-SMA		Mesa
☐	N11535	Embraer ERJ-145LR	145518	ex PT-SYJ	535	ExpressJet
☐	N11536	Embraer ERJ-145LR	145520	ex PT-SYL	536	ExpressJet
☐	N21537	Embraer ERJ-145LR	145523	ex PT-SYO	537	ExpressJet
☐	N13538	Embraer ERJ-145LR	145527	ex PT-STS	538	ExpressJet
☐	N11539	Embraer ERJ-145LR	145536	ex PT-SZA	539	ExpressJet
☐	N12540	Embraer ERJ-145LR	145537	ex PT-SZB	540	ExpressJet
☐	N16541	Embraer ERJ-145LR	145542	ex PT-SZF	541	ExpressJet
☐	N14542	Embraer ERJ-145LR	145547	ex PT-SZK	542	ExpressJet
☐	N14543	Embraer ERJ-145LR	145553	ex PT-SZP	543	ExpressJet
☐	N26545	Embraer ERJ-145LR	145558	ex PT-SZT	545	ExpressJet
☐	N16546	Embraer ERJ-145LR	145562	ex PT-SZX	546	ExpressJet
☐	N11547	Embraer ERJ-145LR	145563	ex PT-SZY	547	ExpressJet
☐	N11548	Embraer ERJ-145LR	145565	ex PT-SBB	548	ExpressJet
☐	N26549	Embraer ERJ-145LR	145571	ex PT-SBH	549	ExpressJet
☐	N13550	Embraer ERJ-145LR	145575	ex PT-SBL	550	ExpressJet
☐	N12552	Embraer ERJ-145LR	145583	ex PT-SBU	552	ExpressJet
☐	N13553	Embraer ERJ-145LR	145585	ex PT-SBW	553	ExpressJet
☐	N15555	Embraer ERJ-145LR	145594	ex PT- (SCD)	555	ExpressJet
☐	N18556	Embraer ERJ-145LR	145595	ex PT-SCE	556	ExpressJet
☐	N14558	Embraer ERJ-145LR	145598	ex PT-SCG	558	ExpressJet
☐	N16559	Embraer ERJ-145LR	145603	ex PT-SCM	559	ExpressJet
☐	N17560	Embraer ERJ-145LR	145605	ex PT-SCO	560	ExpressJet
☐	N16561	Embraer ERJ-145LR	145610	ex PT-SCT	561	ExpressJet
☐	N14562	Embraer ERJ-145LR	145611	ex PT-SCV	562	ExpressJet
☐	N12563	Embraer ERJ-145LR	145612	ex PT-SCW	563	ExpressJet
☐	N12564	Embraer ERJ-145LR	145618	ex PT-SDG	564	ExpressJet
☐	N11565	Embraer ERJ-145LR	145621	ex PT-SDJ	565	ExpressJet
☐	N13566	Embraer ERJ-145LR	145622	ex PT-SDK	566	ExpressJet

☐ N12567	Embraer ERJ-145LR	145623	ex PT-SDL	567		ExpressJet
☐ N14568	Embraer ERJ-145LR	145628	ex PT-SDQ	568		ExpressJet
☐ N16571	Embraer ERJ-145LR	145633	ex PT-SDV	571		ExpressJet
☐ N15572	Embraer ERJ-145LR	145636	ex PT-SDY	572		ExpressJet
☐ N14573	Embraer ERJ-145LR	145638	ex PT-SDZ	573		ExpressJet
☐ N15574	Embraer ERJ-145LR	145639	ex PT-SEB	574		ExpressJet
☐ N12900	Embraer ERJ-145LR	145511	ex PT-SYD	900		ExpressJet
☐ N48901	Embraer ERJ-145LR	145501	ex PT-SXU	901		ExpressJet
☐ N14902	Embraer ERJ-145LR	145496	ex PT-SXO	902		ExpressJet
☐ N13903	Embraer ERJ-145LR	145479	ex PT-SVY	903		ExpressJet
☐ N14904	Embraer ERJ-145LR	145477	ex PT-SVW	904		ExpressJet
☐ N14905	Embraer ERJ-145LR	145476	ex PT-SVV	905		ExpressJet
☐ N29906	Embraer ERJ-145LR	145472	ex PT-SVR	906		ExpressJet
☐ N13908	Embraer ERJ-145LR	145465	ex PT-SVK	908		ExpressJet
☐ N15910	Embraer ERJ-145LR	145455	ex PT-SVA	910		ExpressJet
☐ N16911	Embraer ERJ-145LR	145446	ex PT-SUR	911		ExpressJet
☐ N15912	Embraer ERJ-145LR	145439	ex PT-SUK	912		ExpressJet
☐ N13913	Embraer ERJ-145LR	145438	ex PT-SUJ	913		ExpressJet
☐ N13914	Embraer ERJ-145LR	145430	ex PT-SUB	914		ExpressJet
☐ N36915	Embraer ERJ-145LR	145421	ex PT-STS	915		ExpressJet
☐ N14916	Embraer ERJ-145LR	145415	ex PT-STL	916		ExpressJet
☐ N29917	Embraer ERJ-145LR	145414	ex PT-STK	917		ExpressJet
☐ N16918	Embraer ERJ-145LR	145397	ex PT-SQU	918		ExpressJet
☐ N16919	Embraer ERJ-145LR	145393	ex PT-SQQ	919		ExpressJet
☐ N14920	Embraer ERJ-145LR	145380	ex PT-SQE	920		ExpressJet
☐ N12921	Embraer ERJ-145LR	145354	ex PT-SNT	921		ExpressJet
☐ N12922	Embraer ERJ-145LR	145338	ex PT-SNE	922		ExpressJet
☐ N14923	Embraer ERJ-145LR	145318	ex PT-SMJ	923		ExpressJet
☐ N12924	Embraer ERJ-145LR	145311	ex PT-SMC	924		ExpressJet
☐ N14925	Embraer ERJ-145EP	145004	ex PT-SYA	925		ExpressJet
☐ N15926	Embraer ERJ-145EP	145005	ex PT-SYB	926		ExpressJet
☐ N16927	Embraer ERJ-145EP	145006	ex PT-SYC	927		ExpressJet
☐ N17928	Embraer ERJ-145EP	145007	ex PT-SYD	928		ExpressJet
☐ N13929	Embraer ERJ-145EP	145009	ex PT-SYF	929		ExpressJet
☐ N14930	Embraer ERJ-145EP	145011	ex PT-SYH	930		ExpressJet
☐ N15932	Embraer ERJ-145EP	145015	ex PT-SYL	932		ExpressJet
☐ N14933	Embraer ERJ-145EP	145018	ex PT-SYO	933		ExpressJet
☐ N12934	Embraer ERJ-145EP	145019	ex PT-SYP	934		ExpressJet
☐ N13935	Embraer ERJ-145EP	145022	ex PT-SYS	935		ExpressJet
☐ N13936	Embraer ERJ-145EP	145025	ex PT-SYV	936		ExpressJet
☐ N14937	Embraer ERJ-145EP	145026	ex PT-SYW	937		ExpressJet
☐ N14938	Embraer ERJ-145EP	145029	ex PT-SYX	938		ExpressJet
☐ N14939	Embraer ERJ-145EP	145030	ex PT-SYY	939		ExpressJet
☐ N14940	Embraer ERJ-145EP	145033	ex PT-SZA	940		ExpressJet
☐ N15941	Embraer ERJ-145EP	145035	ex PT-SZB	941		ExpressJet
☐ N14942	Embraer ERJ-145EP	145037	ex PT-SZD	942		ExpressJet
☐ N14943	Embraer ERJ-145EP	145040	ex PT-SZF	943		ExpressJet
☐ N16944	Embraer ERJ-145EP	145045	ex PT-SZK	944		ExpressJet
☐ N14945	Embraer ERJ-145EP	145049	ex PT-SZO	945		ExpressJet
☐ N12946	Embraer ERJ-145EP	145052	ex PT-SZR	946		ExpressJet
☐ N14947	Embraer ERJ-145EP	145054	ex PT-SZT	947		ExpressJet
☐ N15948	Embraer ERJ-145EP	145056	ex PT-SZV	948		ExpressJet
☐ N13949	Embraer ERJ-145LR	145057	ex PT-SZW	949		ExpressJet
☐ N14950	Embraer ERJ-145LR	145061	ex PT-SAE	950		ExpressJet
☐ N16951	Embraer ERJ-145LR	145063	ex PT-SAG	951		ExpressJet
☐ N14952	Embraer ERJ-145LR	145067	ex PT-SAL	952		ExpressJet
☐ N14953	Embraer ERJ-145LR	145071	ex PT-SAP	953		ExpressJet
☐ N16954	Embraer ERJ-145LR	145072	ex PT-SAQ	954		ExpressJet
☐ N13955	Embraer ERJ-145LR	145075	ex PT-SAT	955		ExpressJet
☐ N13956	Embraer ERJ-145LR	145078	ex PT-S	956		ExpressJet
☐ N12957	Embraer ERJ-145LR	145080	ex PT-S	957		ExpressJet
☐ N13958	Embraer ERJ-145LR	145085	ex PT-S	958		ExpressJet
☐ N14959	Embraer ERJ-145LR	145091	ex PT-S	959		ExpressJet
☐ N14960	Embraer ERJ-145LR	145100	ex PT-SBW	960 100th c/s		ExpressJet
☐ N16961	Embraer ERJ-145LR	145103	ex PT-S	961		ExpressJet
☐ N27962	Embraer ERJ-145LR	145110	ex PT-S	962		ExpressJet
☐ N16963	Embraer ERJ-145LR	145116	ex PT-SCS	963		ExpressJet
☐ N13964	Embraer ERJ-145LR	145123	ex PT-SCZ	964		ExpressJet
☐ N13965	Embraer ERJ-145LR	145125	ex PT-SDC	965		ExpressJet
☐ N19966	Embraer ERJ-145LR	145131	ex PT-SDI	966		ExpressJet
☐ N12967	Embraer ERJ-145LR	145133	ex PT-SDK	967		ExpressJet
☐ N13968	Embraer ERJ-145LR	145138	ex PT-SDP	968		ExpressJet
☐ N13969	Embraer ERJ-145LR	145141	ex PT-SDR	969		ExpressJet
☐ N13970	Embraer ERJ-145LR	145146	ex PT-SDW	970		ExpressJet
☐ N22971	Embraer ERJ-145LR	145149	ex PT-SDZ	971		ExpressJet
☐ N14972	Embraer ERJ-145LR	145151	ex PT-SEC	972		ExpressJet
☐ N15973	Embraer ERJ-145LR	145159	ex PT-S	973		ExpressJet

☐ N14974	Embraer ERJ-145LR	145161	ex PT-S	974		ExpressJet
☐ N13975	Embraer ERJ-145LR	145163	ex PT-S	975		ExpressJet
☐ N16976	Embraer ERJ-145LR	145171	ex PT-SEV	976		ExpressJet
☐ N14977	Embraer ERJ-145LR	145175	ex PT-SEX	977		ExpressJet
☐ N13978	Embraer ERJ-145LR	145180	ex PT-SGC	978		ExpressJet
☐ N13979	Embraer ERJ-145LR	145181	ex PT-SGD	979		ExpressJet
☐ N15980	Embraer ERJ-145LR	145202	ex PT-SGT	980		ExpressJet
☐ N16981	Embraer ERJ-145LR	145208	ex PT-SGY	981		ExpressJet
☐ N18982	Embraer ERJ-145LR	145223	ex PT-SHI	982		ExpressJet
☐ N15983	Embraer ERJ-145LR	145239	ex PT-SIE	983		ExpressJet
☐ N17984	Embraer ERJ-145LR	145246	ex PT-SIK	984		ExpressJet
☐ N15985	Embraer ERJ-145LR	145248	ex PT-SIL	985		ExpressJet
☐ N15986	Embraer ERJ-145LR	145254	ex PT-SIO	986		ExpressJet
☐ N16987	Embraer ERJ-145LR	145261	ex PT-SIU	987		ExpressJet
☐ N13988	Embraer ERJ-145LR	145265	ex PT-SIX	988		ExpressJet
☐ N13989	Embraer ERJ-145LR	145271	ex PT-SJN	989		ExpressJet
☐ N13990	Embraer ERJ-145LR	145277	ex PT-SJT	990		ExpressJet
☐ N14991	Embraer ERJ-145LR	145278	ex PT-SJU	991		ExpressJet
☐ N13992	Embraer ERJ-145LR	145284	ex PT-SKB	992		ExpressJet
☐ N14993	Embraer ERJ-145LR	145289	ex PT-SKG	993		ExpressJet
☐ N13994	Embraer ERJ-145LR	145291	ex PT-SKI	994		ExpressJet
☐ N13995	Embraer ERJ-145LR	145295	ex PT-SKM	995		ExpressJet
☐ N12996	Embraer ERJ-145LR	145296	ex PT-SKN	996		ExpressJet
☐ N13997	Embraer ERJ-145LR	145298	ex PT-SKP	997		ExpressJet
☐ N14998	Embraer ERJ-145LR	145302	ex PT-SKT	998		ExpressJet
☐ N16999	Embraer ERJ-145LR	145307	ex PT-SKY	999		ExpressJet
☐ N18101	Embraer ERJ-145XR	145590	ex PT-SDC	101		ExpressJet
☐ N18102	Embraer ERJ-145XR	145643	ex PT-SEE	102		ExpressJet
☐ N24103	Embraer ERJ-145XR	145645	ex PT-SEF	103		ExpressJet
☐ N41104	Embraer ERJ-145XR	145646	ex PT-SEG	104		ExpressJet
☐ N14105	Embraer ERJ-145XR	145649	ex PT-SEJ	105		ExpressJet
☐ N11106	Embraer ERJ-145XR	145650	ex PT-SEK	106		ExpressJet
☐ N11107	Embraer ERJ-145XR	145654	ex PT-SEO	107		ExpressJet
☐ N17108	Embraer ERJ-145XR	145655	ex PT-SEP	108		ExpressJet
☐ N11109	Embraer ERJ-145XR	145657	ex PT-SER	109		ExpressJet
☐ N34110	Embraer ERJ-145XR	145658	ex PT-SES	110		ExpressJet
☐ N34111	Embraer ERJ-145XR	145659	ex PT-SET	111		ExpressJet
☐ N16112	Embraer ERJ-145XR	145660	ex PT-SEU	112		ExpressJet
☐ N11113	Embraer ERJ-145XR	145662	ex PT-SEW	113		ExpressJet
☐ N18114	Embraer ERJ-145XR	145664	ex PT-SEY	114		ExpressJet
☐ N17115	Embraer ERJ-145XR	145666	ex PT-SFA	115		ExpressJet
☐ N14116	Embraer ERJ-145XR	145672	ex PT-SFF	116		ExpressJet
☐ N14117	Embraer ERJ-145XR	145674	ex PT-SFH	117		ExpressJet
☐ N13118	Embraer ERJ-145XR	145675	ex PT-SFI	118		ExpressJet
☐ N11119	Embraer ERJ-145XR	145677	ex PT-SFK	119		ExpressJet
☐ N18120	Embraer ERJ-145XR	145681	ex PT-SFN	120		ExpressJet
☐ N11121	Embraer ERJ-145XR	145683	ex PT-SFP	121		ExpressJet
☐ N12122	Embraer ERJ-145XR	145684	ex PT-SFQ	122		ExpressJet
☐ N13123	Embraer ERJ-145XR	145688	ex PT-SFU	123		ExpressJet
☐ N13124	Embraer ERJ-145XR	145689	ex PT-SFV	124		ExpressJet
☐ N14125	Embraer ERJ-145XR	145690	ex PT-SFW	125		ExpressJet
☐ N12126	Embraer ERJ-145XR	145693	ex PT-SFZ	126		ExpressJet
☐ N11127	Embraer ERJ-145XR	145697	ex PT-SGC	127		ExpressJet
☐ N24128	Embraer ERJ-145XR	145700	ex PT-SGE	128		ExpressJet
☐ N21129	Embraer ERJ-145XR	145703	ex PT-SGH	129		ExpressJet
☐ N21130	Embraer ERJ-145XR	145704	ex PT-SGI	130		ExpressJet
☐ N31131	Embraer ERJ-145XR	145705	ex PT-SGJ	131		ExpressJet
☐ N13132	Embraer ERJ-145XR	145708	ex PT-SGL	132		ExpressJet
☐ N13133	Embraer ERJ-145XR	145712	ex PT-SGP	133		ExpressJet
☐ N25134	Embraer ERJ-145XR	145714	ex PT-SGR	134		ExpressJet
☐ N12135	Embraer ERJ-145XR	145718	ex PT-SGU	135		ExpressJet
☐ N12136	Embraer ERJ-145XR	145719	ex PT-SGV	136		ExpressJet
☐ N17138	Embraer ERJ-145XR	145727	ex PT-SHD	138		ExpressJet
☐ N23139	Embraer ERJ-145XR	145731	ex PT-SHH	139		ExpressJet
☐ N11140	Embraer ERJ-145XR	145732	ex PT-SHI	140		ExpressJet
☐ N26141	Embraer ERJ-145XR	145733	ex PT-SHJ	141		ExpressJet
☐ N12142	Embraer ERJ-145XR	145735	ex PT-SHL	142		ExpressJet
☐ N14143	Embraer ERJ-145XR	145739	ex PT-SHT	143		ExpressJet
☐ N21144	Embraer ERJ-145XR	145741	ex PT-SJA	144		ExpressJet
☐ N12145	Embraer ERJ-145XR	145745	ex PT-SJE	145		ExpressJet
☐ N17146	Embraer ERJ-145XR	145746	ex PT-SJF	146		ExpressJet
☐ N16147	Embraer ERJ-145XR	145749	ex PT-SJI	147		ExpressJet
☐ N14148	Embraer ERJ-145XR	145751	ex PT-SJK	148		ExpressJet
☐ N16149	Embraer ERJ-145XR	145753	ex PT-SJM	149		ExpressJet
☐ N11150	Embraer ERJ-145XR	145756	ex PT-SJP	150		ExpressJet
☐ N16151	Embraer ERJ-145XR	145758	ex PT-SJQ	151		ExpressJet

☐ N27152	Embraer ERJ-145XR	145759	ex PT-SJR	152	ExpressJet
☐ N14153	Embraer ERJ-145XR	145761	ex PT-SJS	153	ExpressJet
☐ N21154	Embraer ERJ-145XR	145772	ex PT-SMC	154	ExpressJet
☐ N11155	Embraer ERJ-145XR	145782	ex PT-SMJ	155	ExpressJet
☐ N10156	Embraer ERJ-145XR	145786	ex PT-SMN	156	ExpressJet
☐ N12157	Embraer ERJ-145XR	145787	ex PT-SMP	157	ExpressJet
☐ N14158	Embraer ERJ-145XR	145791	ex PT-SMS	158	ExpressJet
☐ N17159	Embraer ERJ-145XR	145792	ex PT-SMT	159	ExpressJet
☐ N12160	Embraer ERJ-145XR	145799	ex PT-SMZ	160	ExpressJet
☐ N13161	Embraer ERJ-145XR	14500805	ex PT-SNH	161	ExpressJet
☐ N11164	Embraer ERJ-145XR	14500817	ex PT-SNS	164	ExpressJet
☐ N12166	Embraer ERJ-145XR	14500831	ex PT-SQE	166	ExpressJet
☐ N17169	Embraer ERJ-145XR	14500844	ex PT-SQO	169	ExpressJet
☐ N12172	Embraer ERJ-145XR	14500864	ex PT-SXD	172	ExpressJet
☐ N14177	Embraer ERJ-145XR	14500888	ex PT-SYA	177	ExpressJet
☐ N14180	Embraer ERJ-145XR	14500900	ex PT-SYL	180	ExpressJet
☐ N17185	Embraer ERJ-145XR	14500922	ex PT-SOT	185	ExpressJet
☐ N14186	Embraer ERJ-145XR	14500924	ex PT-SOV	186	ExpressJet
☐ N11187	Embraer ERJ-145XR	14500927	ex PT-SOX	187	ExpressJet
☐ N27190	Embraer ERJ-145XR	14500934	ex PT-SCC	190	ExpressJet
☐ N11191	Embraer ERJ-145XR	14500935	ex PT-SCH	191	ExpressJet
☐ N11194	Embraer ERJ-145XR	14500940	ex PT-SCL		ExpressJet
☐ N12195	Embraer ERJ-145XR	14500943	ex PT-SCO	195	ExpressJet
☐ N17196	Embraer ERJ-145XR	14500945	ex PT-SCQ	196	ExpressJet
☐ N21197	Embraer ERJ-145XR	14500947	ex PT-SCS	197	ExpressJet
☐ N27200	Embraer ERJ-145XR	14500956	ex PT-SFE	200	ExpressJet
☐ N13202	Embraer ERJ-145XR	14500962	ex PT-SFJ	202	ExpressJet
☐ N14203	Embraer ERJ-145XR	14500964	ex PT-SFL	203	ExpressJet
☐ N14204	Embraer ERJ-145XR	14500968	ex PT-	204	ExpressJet
☐ N631RW	Embraer ERJ-170SE	17000007	ex PT-SKX		Shuttle America
☐ N632RW	Embraer ERJ-170SE	17000050	ex PT-SUU		Shuttle America
☐ N633RW	Embraer ERJ-170SE	17000054	ex PT-SUZ		Shuttle America
☐ N634RW	Embraer ERJ-170SE	17000055	ex PT-SVE		Shuttle America
☐ N635RW	Embraer ERJ-170SE	17000056	ex PT-SVF		Shuttle America
☐ N636RW	Embraer ERJ-170SE	17000052	ex PT-SVK		Shuttle America
☐ N637RW	Embraer ERJ-170SE	17000051	ex PT-SUV		Shuttle America
☐ N638RW	Embraer ERJ-170SE	17000053	ex PT-SUY		Shuttle America
☐ N639RW	Embraer ERJ-170SE	17000057	ex PT-SVG		Shuttle America
☐ N640RW	Embraer ERJ-170SE	17000058	ex PT-SVH		Shuttle America
☐ N641RW	Embraer ERJ-170SE	17000062	ex PT-SVN		Shuttle America
☐ N642RW	Embraer ERJ-170SE	17000063	ex PT-SVO		Shuttle America
☐ N643RW	Embraer ERJ-170SE	17000060	ex PT-SVL		Shuttle America
☐ N644RW	Embraer ERJ-170SE	17000061	ex PT-SVM		Shuttle America
☐ N645RW	Embraer ERJ-170SE	17000064	ex PT-SVP		Shuttle America
☐ N646RW	Embraer ERJ-170SE	17000066	ex PT-SVR		Shuttle America
☐ N647RW	Embraer ERJ-170SE	17000067	ex PT-SVS		Shuttle America
☐ N648RW	Embraer ERJ-170SE	17000068	ex PT-SVT		Shuttle America
☐ N649RW	Embraer ERJ-170SE	17000070	ex PT-SVV		Shuttle America
☐ N650RW	Embraer ERJ-170SE	17000071	ex PT-SVW		Shuttle America
☐ N651RW	Embraer ERJ-170SE	17000072	ex PT-SVX		Shuttle America
☐ N652RW	Embraer ERJ-170SE	17000075	ex PT-SZA		Shuttle America
☐ N653RW	Embraer ERJ-170SE	17000076	ex PT-SZB		Shuttle America
☐ N654RW	Embraer ERJ-170SE	17000104	ex PT-SAK		Shuttle America
☐ N655RW	Embraer ERJ-170SE	17000105	ex PT-SAM		Shuttle America
☐ N656RW	Embraer ERJ-170SE	17000113	ex PT-SAY		Shuttle America
☐ N657RW	Embraer ERJ-170SE	17000115	ex PT-SDC		Shuttle America
☐ N856RW	Embraer ERJ-170SE	17000078	ex PT-SZD		Shuttle America
☐ N857RW	Embraer ERJ-170SE	17000079	ex PT-SZE		Shuttle America
☐ N858RW	Embraer ERJ-170SE	17000080	ex PT-SZF		Shuttle America
☐ N861RW	Embraer ERJ-170SE	17000094	ex PT-SZU		Shuttle America
☐ N863RW	Embraer ERJ-170SE	17000100	ex PT-SAB		Shuttle America
☐ N864RW	Embraer ERJ-170SE	17000117	ex PT-SDE		Shuttle America
☐ N865RW	Embraer ERJ-170SE	17000122	ex PT-SDK		Shuttle America
☐ N184CJ	SAAB SF.340B	340B-184	ex N300CE		Colgan Air
☐ N191MJ	SAAB SF.340B	340B-191	ex N301AE		Colgan Air
☐ N193CJ	SAAB SF.340B	340B-193	ex N302CE		Colgan Air
☐ N194CJ	SAAB SF.340B	340B-194	ex N303CE		Colgan Air
☐ N196CJ	SAAB SF.340B	340B-196	ex N196JW		Colgan Air
☐ N198CJ	SAAB SF.340B	340B-198	ex N304CE		Colgan Air
☐ N204CJ	SAAB SF.340B	340B-204	ex N307CE		Colgan Air
☐ N220MJ	SAAB SF.340B	340B-220	ex N360PX		Colgan Air
☐ N237MJ	SAAB SF.340B	340B-237	ex N351BE		Colgan Air
☐ N239CJ	SAAB SF.340B	340B-239	ex N352BE		Colgan Air
☐ N242CJ	SAAB SF.340B	340B-242	ex N353BE		Colgan Air
☐ N277MJ	SAAB SF.340B	340B-277	ex N357BE		Colgan Air

☐ N309CE	SAAB SF.340B	340B-201	ex N201AE	Colgan Air
☐ N311CE	SAAB SF.340B	340B-214	ex SE-G14	Colgan Air
☐ N314CE	SAAB SF.340B	340B-335	ex N335AE	Colgan Air
☐ N334CJ	SAAB SF.340B	340B-334	ex N312CE	Colgan Air
☐ N343CJ	SAAB SF.340B	340B-343	ex N315CE	Colgan Air
☐ N352CJ	SAAB SF.340B	340B-352	ex N317CE	Colgan Air
☐ N356CJ	SAAB SF.340B	340B-356	ex N356SB	Colgan Air

UNIVERSAL AIRLINES — Pacific Northern (PNA) — Victoria-Regional, TX (VCT)

☐ N170UA	Douglas DC-6A	45518/998	ex N870TA
☐ N500UA	Douglas DC-6A	44597/501	ex N766WC
☐ N600UA	Douglas DC-6BF	44894/651	ex N37570

UPS AIRLINES — UPS (5X/UPS) — Louisville-Intl, KY (SDF)

☐ N120UP	Airbus A300F4-622R	805	ex F-WWAR	
☐ N121UP	Airbus A300F4-622R	806	ex F-WWAP	
☐ N122UP	Airbus A300F4-622R	807	ex F-WWAX	
☐ N124UP	Airbus A300F4-622R	808	ex F-WWAT	
☐ N125UP	Airbus A300F4-622R	809	ex F-WWAU	
☐ N126UP	Airbus A300F4-622R	810	ex F-WWAB	
☐ N127UP	Airbus A300F4-622R	811	ex F-WWAD	
☐ N128UP	Airbus A300F4-622R	812	ex F-WWAE	
☐ N129UP	Airbus A300F4-622R	813	ex F-WWAF	
☐ N130UP	Airbus A300F4-622R	814	ex F-WWAG	
☐ N131UP	Airbus A300F4-622R	815	ex F-WWAH	
☐ N133UP	Airbus A300F4-622R	816	ex F-WWAJ	
☐ N134UP	Airbus A300F4-622R	817	ex F-WWAL	
☐ N135UP	Airbus A300F4-622R	818	ex F-WWAM	
☐ N136UP	Airbus A300F4-622R	819	ex F-WWAN	
☐ N137UP	Airbus A300F4-622R	820	ex F-WWAO	
☐ N138UP	Airbus A300F4-622R	821	ex F-WWAQ	
☐ N139UP	Airbus A300F4-622R	822	ex F-WWAS	
☐ N140UP	Airbus A300F4-622R	823	ex F-WWAV	
☐ N141UP	Airbus A300F4-622R	824	ex F-WWAY	
☐ N142UP	Airbus A300F4-622R	825	ex F-WWAA	
☐ N143UP	Airbus A300F4-622R	826	ex F-WWAB	
☐ N144UP	Airbus A300F4-622R	827	ex F-WWAD	
☐ N145UP	Airbus A300F4-622R	828	ex F-WWAE	
☐ N146UP	Airbus A300F4-622R	829	ex F-WWAG	
☐ N147UP	Airbus A300F4-622R	830	ex F-WWAJ	
☐ N148UP	Airbus A300F4-622R	831	ex F-WWAM	
☐ N149UP	Airbus A300F4-622R	832	ex F-WWAN	
☐ N150UP	Airbus A300F4-622R	833	ex F-WWAO	
☐ N151UP	Airbus A300F4-622R	834	ex F-WWAP	
☐ N152UP	Airbus A300F4-622R	835	ex F-WWAQ	
☐ N153UP	Airbus A300F4-622R	839	ex F-WWAR	
☐ N154UP	Airbus A300F4-622R	840	ex F-WWAS	
☐ N155UP	Airbus A300F4-622R	841	ex F-WWAT	
☐ N156UP	Airbus A300F4-622R	845	ex F-WWAU	
☐ N157UP	Airbus A300F4-622R	846	ex F-WWAV	
☐ N158UP	Airbus A300F4-622R	847	ex F-WWAX	
☐ N159UP	Airbus A300F4-622R	848	ex F-WWAZ	
☐ N160UP	Airbus A300F4-622R	849	ex F-WWAF	
☐ N161UP	Airbus A300F4-622R	850	ex F-WWAG	
☐ N162UP	Airbus A300F4-622R	851	ex F-WWAJ	
☐ N163UP	Airbus A300F4-622R	852	ex F-WWAK	
☐ N164UP	Airbus A300F4-622R	853	ex F-WWAL	
☐ N165UP	Airbus A300F4-622R	854	ex F-WWAM	
☐ N166UP	Airbus A300F4-622R	861	ex F-WWAU	
☐ N167UP	Airbus A300F4-622R	862	ex F-WWAH	
☐ N168UP	Airbus A300F4-622R	863	ex F-WWAV	
☐ N169UP	Airbus A300F4-622R	864	ex F-WWAX	
☐ N170UP	Airbus A300F4-622R	865	ex F-WWAZ	
☐ N171UP	Airbus A300F4-622R	866	ex F-WWAE	
☐ N172UP	Airbus A300F4-622R	867	ex F-WWAF	
☐ N173UP	Airbus A300F4-622R	868	ex F-WWAG	
☐ N174UP	Airbus A300F4-622R	869	ex F-WWAN	
☐ N676UP	Boeing 747-123 (SF)	20101/57	ex N9676	[ROW]
☐ N677UP	Boeing 747-123 (SF)	20391/143	ex N629FE	[ROW]
☐ N681UP	Boeing 747-121 (SF)	19661/70	ex N628FE	[ROW]
☐ N682UP	Boeing 747-121 (SF)	20349/110	ex N626FE	[ROW]
☐ N683UP	Boeing 747-121 (SF)	20353/131	ex N627FE	United Way titles
☐ N570UP	Boeing 747-44AF	35667/1388		
☐ N572UP	Boeing 747-44AF	35669/1396		

☐ N573UP	Boeing 747-44AF	35662/1401	
☐ N574UP	Boeing 747-44AF	35663/1403	
☐ N575UP	Boeing 747-44AF	35664/1406	
☐ N576UP	Boeing 747-44AF	35665/1410	
☐ N577UP	Boeing 747-44AF	35666/1412	
☐ N578UP	Boeing 747-45EM	27154/994	ex B-16461
☐ N579UP	Boeing 747-45EM	26062/1016	ex B-16465
☐ N580UP	Boeing 747-428F	25632/968	ex LX-ICV
☐ N581UP	Boeing 747-4R7F	25866/1002	ex LX-FCV
☐ N583UP	Boeing 747-4R7F	25867/1008	ex LX-GCV ♦
☐ N401UP	Boeing 757-24APF	23723/139	
☐ N402UP	Boeing 757-24APF	23724/141	
☐ N403UP	Boeing 757-24APF	23725/143	
☐ N404UP	Boeing 757-24APF	23726/147	
☐ N405UP	Boeing 757-24APF	23727/149	
☐ N406UP	Boeing 757-24APF	23728/176	
☐ N407UP	Boeing 757-24APF	23729/181	
☐ N408UP	Boeing 757-24APF	23730/184	
☐ N409UP	Boeing 757-24APF	23731/186	
☐ N410UP	Boeing 757-24APF	23732/189	
☐ N411UP	Boeing 757-24APF	23851/191	
☐ N412UP	Boeing 757-24APF	23852/193	
☐ N413UP	Boeing 757-24APF	23853/195	
☐ N414UP	Boeing 757-24APF	23854/197	
☐ N415UP	Boeing 757-24APF	23855/199	
☐ N416UP	Boeing 757-24APF	23903/318	
☐ N417UP	Boeing 757-24APF	23904/322	
☐ N418UP	Boeing 757-24APF	23905/326	
☐ N419UP	Boeing 757-24APF	23906/330	
☐ N420UP	Boeing 757-24APF	23907/334	
☐ N421UP	Boeing 757-24APF	25281/395	
☐ N422UP	Boeing 757-24APF	25324/399	
☐ N423UP	Boeing 757-24APF	25325/403	
☐ N424UP	Boeing 757-24APF	25369/407	
☐ N425UP	Boeing 757-24APF	25370/411	
☐ N426UP	Boeing 757-24APF	25457/477	
☐ N427UP	Boeing 757-24APF	25458/481	
☐ N428UP	Boeing 757-24APF	25459/485	
☐ N429UP	Boeing 757-24APF	25460/489	
☐ N430UP	Boeing 757-24APF	25461/493	
☐ N431UP	Boeing 757-24APF	25462/569	ex OY-USA
☐ N432UP	Boeing 757-24APF	25463/573	ex OY-USB
☐ N433UP	Boeing 757-24APF	25464/577	ex OY-USC
☐ N434UP	Boeing 757-24APF	25465/579	ex OY-USD
☐ N435UP	Boeing 757-24APF	25466/581	
☐ N436UP	Boeing 757-24APF	25467/625	
☐ N437UP	Boeing 757-24APF	25468/628	
☐ N438UP	Boeing 757-24APF	25469/631	
☐ N439UP	Boeing 757-24APF	25470/634	
☐ N440UP	Boeing 757-24APF	25471/636	
☐ N441UP	Boeing 757-24APF	27386/638	
☐ N442UP	Boeing 757-24APF	27387/640	
☐ N443UP	Boeing 757-24APF	27388/642	
☐ N444UP	Boeing 757-24APF	27389/644	
☐ N445UP	Boeing 757-24APF	27390/646	
☐ N446UP	Boeing 757-24APF	27735/649	
☐ N447UP	Boeing 757-24APF	27736/651	
☐ N448UP	Boeing 757-24APF	27737/654	
☐ N449UP	Boeing 757-24APF	27738/656	
☐ N450UP	Boeing 757-24APF	25472/659	
☐ N451UP	Boeing 757-24APF	27739/675	
☐ N452UP	Boeing 757-24APF	25473/679	
☐ N453UP	Boeing 757-24APF	25474/683	
☐ N454UP	Boeing 757-24APF	25475/687	
☐ N455UP	Boeing 757-24APF	25476/691	
☐ N456UP	Boeing 757-24APF	25477/728	
☐ N457UP	Boeing 757-24APF	25478/729	
☐ N458UP	Boeing 757-24APF	25479/730	
☐ N459UP	Boeing 757-24APF	25480/733	
☐ N460UP	Boeing 757-24APF	25481/734	
☐ N461UP	Boeing 757-24APF	28265/755	
☐ N462UP	Boeing 757-24APF	28266/759	
☐ N463UP	Boeing 757-24APF	28267/763	
☐ N464UP	Boeing 757-24APF	28268/765	
☐ N465UP	Boeing 757-24APF	28269/767	
☐ N466UP	Boeing 757-24APF	25482/769	

☐ N467UP	Boeing 757-24APF	25483/771		
☐ N468UP	Boeing 757-24APF	25484/774		
☐ N469UP	Boeing 757-24APF	25485/776		
☐ N470UP	Boeing 757-24APF	25486/778		
☐ N471UP	Boeing 757-24APF	28842/813		
☐ N472UP	Boeing 757-24APF	28843/815		
☐ N473UP	Boeing 757-24APF	28846/823	ex N5573L	
☐ N474UP	Boeing 757-24APF	28844/879		
☐ N475UP	Boeing 757-24APF	28845/882		
☐ N301UP	Boeing 767-34AF	27239/580		
☐ N302UP	Boeing 767-34AF	27240/590		
☐ N303UP	Boeing 767-34AF	27241/594		
☐ N304UP	Boeing 767-34AF	27242/598		
☐ N305UP	Boeing 767-34AF	27243/600		
☐ N306UP	Boeing 767-34AF	27759/622		
☐ N307UP	Boeing 767-34AF	27760/624		
☐ N308UP	Boeing 767-34AF	27761/626		
☐ N309UP	Boeing 767-34AF	27740/628		
☐ N310UP	Boeing 767-34AF	27762/630		
☐ N311UP	Boeing 767-34AF	27741/632		
☐ N312UP	Boeing 767-34AF	27763/634		
☐ N313UP	Boeing 767-34AF	27764/636		
☐ N314UP	Boeing 767-34AF	27742/638		
☐ N315UP	Boeing 767-34AF	27743/640		
☐ N316UP	Boeing 767-34AF	27744/660		
☐ N317UP	Boeing 767-34AF	27745/666		
☐ N318UP	Boeing 767-34AF	27746/670		
☐ N319UP	Boeing 767-34AF	27758/672		
☐ N320UP	Boeing 767-34AF	27747/674		
☐ N322UP	Boeing 767-34AF	27748/678		
☐ N323UP	Boeing 767-34AF	27749/682		
☐ N324UP	Boeing 767-34AF	27750/724		
☐ N325UP	Boeing 767-34AF	27751/726		
☐ N326UP	Boeing 767-34AF	27752/728		
☐ N327UP	Boeing 767-34AF	27753/730		
☐ N328UP	Boeing 767-34AF	27754/732		
☐ N329UP	Boeing 767-34AF	27755/756		
☐ N330UP	Boeing 767-34AF	27756/760		
☐ N331UP	Boeing 767-34AF	27757/764		
☐ N332UP	Boeing 767-34AF	32843/854		
☐ N334UP	Boeing 767-34AF	32844/858		
☐ N335UP	Boeing 767-34AF	37856/979	ex N5023Q	
☐ N336UP	Boeing 767-34AF	37857/983		
☐ N337UP	Boeing 767-34AF	37858/986		
☐ N338UP	Boeing 767-34AF	37944/988		
☐ N339UP	Boeing 767-34AF	37859/989		♦
☐ N340UP	Boeing 767-34AF	37860/991		♦
☐ N341UP	Boeing 767-34AF	37861/992		♦
☐	Boeing 767-34AF			o/o♦
☐	Boeing 767-34AF			o/o♦
☐	Boeing 767-34AF			o/o♦
☐	Boeing 767-34AF			o/o♦
☐	Boeing 767-34AF			o/o♦
☐	Boeing 767-34AF			o/o♦
☐	Boeing 767-34AF			o/o♦
☐	Boeing 767-34AF			o/o♦
☐	Boeing 767-34AF			o/o♦
☐	Boeing 767-34AF			o/o♦
☐	Boeing 767-34AF			o/o♦
☐	Boeing 767-34AF			o/o♦
☐	Boeing 767-34AF			o/o♦
☐	Boeing 767-34AF			o/o♦
☐ N700UP	Douglas DC-8-71CF	45900/316	ex N861FT	[ROW]
☐ N702UP	Douglas DC-8-71CF	45902/294	ex N810EV	
☐ N715UP	Douglas DC-8-71F	45915/295	ex N824E	[ROW]
☐ N718UP	Douglas DC-8-71F	46018/420	ex N1301L	[ROW]
☐ N729UP	Douglas DC-8-71F	46029/425	ex N1302L	[ROW]
☐ N752UP	Douglas DC-8-71CF	45952/338	ex N864FT	[ROW]
☐ N811UP	Douglas DC-8-73CF	46089/501	ex N407FE	[ROW]
☐ N812UP	Douglas DC-8-73CF	46112/520	ex N776FT	[ROW]
☐ N814UP	Douglas DC-8-73CF	46090/504	ex N405FE	[ROW]
☐ N819UP	Douglas DC-8-73F	46019/411	ex TF-VLY	
☐ N840UP	Douglas DC-8-73CF	46140/528	ex N797FT	
☐ N851UP	Douglas DC-8-73CF	46051/440	ex N811EV	[ROW]
☐ N852UP	Douglas DC-8-73CF	46052/442	ex N31EK	

☐ N866UP	Douglas DC-8-73CF	45966/393	ex N773FT	[ROW]
☐ N867UP	Douglas DC-8-73CF	45967/385	ex N907CL	[ROW]
☐ N868UP	Douglas DC-8-73CF	45968/389	ex N871TV	[ROW]
☐ N874UP	Douglas DC-8-73PF	46074/468	ex HB-IDZ	[ROW]
☐ N880UP	Douglas DC-8-73F	46080/466	ex TF-VLZ	
☐ N894UP	Douglas DC-8-73CF	46094/482	ex N910CL	[ROW]
☐ N250UP	McDonnell-Douglas MD-11F	48745/596	ex N798BA	
☐ N251UP	McDonnell-Douglas MD-11F	48744/592	ex N797BA	
☐ N252UP	McDonnell-Douglas MD-11F	48768/601	ex PP-SFA	
☐ N253UP	McDonnell-Douglas MD-11F	48439/554	ex PP-VPM	
☐ N254UP	McDonnell-Douglas MD-11F	48406/547	ex PP-VPL	
☐ N255UP	McDonnell-Douglas MD-11F	48404/523	ex PP-VPJ	
☐ N256UP	McDonnell-Douglas MD-11F	48405/524	ex PP-VPK	
☐ N257UP	McDonnell-Douglas MD-11F	48451/505	ex HS-TMG	
☐ N258UP	McDonnell-Douglas MD-11F	48416/466	ex HS-TMD	
☐ N259UP	McDonnell-Douglas MD-11F	48417/467	ex HS-TME	
☐ N260UP	McDonnell-Douglas MD-11F	48418/501	ex HS-TMF	
☐ N270UP	McDonnell-Douglas MD-11F	48576/574	ex JA8585	
☐ N271UP	McDonnell-Douglas MD-11F	48572/556	ex JA8581	
☐ N272UP	McDonnell-Douglas MD-11F	48571/552	ex JA8580	
☐ N273UP	McDonnell-Douglas MD-11F	48574/566	ex JA8583	
☐ N274UP	McDonnell-Douglas MD-11F	48575/568	ex JA8584	
☐ N275UP	McDonnell-Douglas MD-11F	48774/610	ex JA8589	
☐ N276UP	McDonnell-Douglas MD-11F	48579/599	ex JA8588	
☐ N277UP	McDonnell-Douglas MD-11F	48578/588	ex JA8587	
☐ N278UP	McDonnell-Douglas MD-11F	48577/583	ex JA8586	
☐ N279UP	McDonnell-Douglas MD-11F	48573/559	ex JA8582	
☐ N280UP	McDonnell-Douglas MD-11F	48634/614	ex N38WF	
☐ N281UP	McDonnell-Douglas MD-11F	48538/533	ex N48WF	
☐ N282UP	McDonnell-Douglas MD-11F	48452/472	ex N74WF	
☐ N283UP	McDonnell-Douglas MD-11F	48484/484	ex V5-NMC	
☐ N284UP	McDonnell-Douglas MD-11F	48541/621	ex PP-VTU	
☐ N285UP	McDonnell-Douglas MD-11F	48457/498	ex PP-VTH	
☐ N286UP	McDonnell-Douglas MD-11F	48453/473	ex V5-NMD	
☐ N287UP	McDonnell-Douglas MD-11	48539/571	ex PP-VTP	
☐ N288UP	McDonnell-Douglas MD-11F	48540/611	ex PP-VTK	
☐ N289UP	McDonnell-Douglas MD-11	48455/487	ex PP-VTJ	
☐ N290UP	McDonnell-Douglas MD-11F	48456/494	ex PP-VTI	
☐ N291UP	McDonnell-Douglas MD-11F	48477/511	ex N806DE	
☐ N292UP	McDonnell-Douglas MD-11F	48566/543	ex N811DE	
☐ N293UP	McDonnell-Douglas MD-11F	48473/481	ex N802DE	
☐ N294UP	McDonnell-Douglas MD-11F	48472/480	ex N801DE	
☐ N295UP	McDonnell-Douglas MD-11F	48475/489	ex N804DE	
☐ N296UP	McDonnell-Douglas MD-11F	48474/485	ex N803DE	

US AIRWAYS — U S Air (US/USA)
Pittsburgh-Greater Pittsburgh Intl, PA/Phoenix-Sky Harbor Intl, AZ (PIT/PHX)

Member of Star Alliance

☐ N700UW	Airbus A319-112	0885	ex D-AVYF	Star Alliance c/s
☐ N701UW	Airbus A319-112	0890	ex D-AVYG	Star Alliance c/s
☐ N702UW	Airbus A319-112	0896	ex D-AVYH	Star Alliance c/s
☐ N703UW	Airbus A319-112	0904	ex D-AVYI	Star Alliance c/s
☐ N704US	Airbus A319-112	0922	ex D-AVYQ	
☐ N705UW	Airbus A319-112	0929	ex D-AVYA	
☐ N708UW	Airbus A319-112	0972	ex D-AVYT	
☐ N709UW	Airbus A319-112	0997	ex D-AVYV	Philadelphia Eagles c/s
☐ N710UW	Airbus A319-112	1019	ex D-AVYR	
☐ N711UW	Airbus A319-112	1033	ex D-AVYG	
☐ N712US	Airbus A319-112	1038	ex D-AVYW	
☐ N713UW	Airbus A319-112	1040	ex D-AVYH	
☐ N714US	Airbus A319-112	1046	ex D-AVYZ	
☐ N715UW	Airbus A319-112	1051	ex D-AVYV	
☐ N716UW	Airbus A319-112	1055	ex D-AVYM	
☐ N717UW	Airbus A319-112	1069	ex D-AVWC	Carolina Panthers c/s
☐ N721UW	Airbus A319-112	1095	ex D-AVYQ	
☐ N722US	Airbus A319-112	1097	ex D-AVYS	
☐ N723UW	Airbus A319-112	1109	ex D-AVWP	
☐ N724UW	Airbus A319-112	1122	ex D-AVYA	
☐ N725UW	Airbus A319-112	1135	ex D-AVWC	
☐ N730US	Airbus A319-112	1182	ex D-AVYD	
☐ N732US	Airbus A319-112	1203	ex D-AVYA	
☐ N733UW	Airbus A319-112	1205	ex D-AVYB	Pittsburgh Steelers c/s
☐ N737US	Airbus A319-112	1245	ex D-AVYN	
☐ N738US	Airbus A319-112	1254	ex D-AVYQ	

☐ N740UW	Airbus A319-112	1265	ex D-AVWO	
☐ N741UW	Airbus A319-112	1269	ex D-AVWP	
☐ N742PS	Airbus A319-112	1275	ex N742US	PSA c/s
☐ N744P	Airbus A319-112	1287	ex N744US	Piedmont c/s
☐ N745VJ	Airbus A319-112	1289	ex N745UW	Allegheny c/s 'Vistajet'
☐ N746UW	Airbus A319-112	1297	ex D-AVWV	
☐ N747UW	Airbus A319-112	1301	ex D-AVWM	
☐ N748UW	Airbus A319-112	1311	ex D-AVYA	
☐ N749US	Airbus A319-112	1313	ex D-AVWG	
☐ N750UW	Airbus A319-112	1315	ex D-AVWH	
☐ N751UW	Airbus A319-112	1317	ex D-AVWK	
☐ N752US	Airbus A319-112	1319	ex D-AVWS	
☐ N753US	Airbus A319-112	1326	ex D-AVYG	
☐ N754UW	Airbus A319-112	1328	ex D-AVYJ	
☐ N755US	Airbus A319-112	1331	ex D-AVYN	
☐ N756US	Airbus A319-112	1340	ex D-AVYO	
☐ N757UW	Airbus A319-112	1342	ex D-AVYP	
☐ N758US	Airbus A319-112	1348	ex D-AVYS	
☐ N760US	Airbus A319-112	1354	ex D-AVWI	
☐ N762US	Airbus A319-112	1358	ex D-AVWD	
☐ N763US	Airbus A319-112	1360	ex D-AVWF	
☐ N764US	Airbus A319-112	1369	ex D-AVWM	
☐ N765US	Airbus A319-112	1371	ex D-AVWO	
☐ N766US	Airbus A319-112	1378	ex D-AVWG	
☐ N767UW	Airbus A319-112	1382	ex D-AVWN	
☐ N768US	Airbus A319-112	1389	ex D-AVYI	
☐ N769US	Airbus A319-112	1391	ex D-AVYJ	
☐ N770UW	Airbus A319-112	1393	ex D-AVYU	
☐ N801AW	Airbus A319-132	0889	ex D-AVYM	
☐ N802AW	Airbus A319-132	0924	ex D-AVYR	
☐ N803AW	Airbus A319-132	0931	ex D-AVYK	
☐ N804AW	Airbus A319-132	1043	ex D-AVYY	
☐ N805AW	Airbus A319-132	1049	ex D-AVYU	
☐ N806AW	Airbus A319-132	1056	ex D-AVYO	
☐ N807AW	Airbus A319-132	1064	ex D-AVWB	
☐ N808AW	Airbus A319-132	1088	ex D-AVWM	
☐ N809AW	Airbus A319-132	1111	ex D-AVWT	
☐ N810AW	Airbus A319-132	1116	ex D-AVWV	
☐ N812AW	Airbus A319-132	1178	ex D-AVWP	
☐ N813AW	Airbus A319-132	1223	ex D-AVYH	
☐ N814AW	Airbus A319-132	1281	ex D-AVYC	
☐ N815AW	Airbus A319-132	1323	ex D-AVWW	
☐ N816AW	Airbus A319-132	1350	ex D-AVYV	
☐ N817AW	Airbus A319-132	1373	ex D-AVWA	
☐ N818AW	Airbus A319-132	1375	ex D-AVWB	
☐ N819AW	Airbus A319-132	1395	ex D-AVYX	
☐ N820AW	Airbus A319-132	1397	ex D-AVWQ	
☐ N821AW	Airbus A319-132	1406	ex D-AVYC	
☐ N822AW	Airbus A319-132	1410	ex D-AVYD	Nevada flag c/s
☐ N823AW	Airbus A319-132	1463	ex D-AVYJ	
☐ N824AW	Airbus A319-132	1490	ex D-AVYA	
☐ N825AW	Airbus A319-132	1527	ex D-AVWG	
☐ N826AW	Airbus A319-132	1534	ex D-AVYO	Arizona flag c/s
☐ N827AW	Airbus A319-132	1547	ex D-AVWL	
☐ N828AW	Airbus A319-132	1552	ex D-AVWO	America West Heritage c/s
☐ N829AW	Airbus A319-132	1563	ex D-AVYS	
☐ N830AW	Airbus A319-132	1565	ex D-AVYT	
☐ N831AW	Airbus A319-132	1576	ex D-AVWQ	
☐ N832AW	Airbus A319-132	1643	ex D-AVYA	
☐ N833AW	Airbus A319-132	1844	ex D-AVWV	
☐ N834AW	Airbus A319-132	2302	ex D-AVWM	
☐ N835AW	Airbus A319-132	2458	ex D-AVYN	
☐ N836AW	Airbus A319-132	2570	ex D-AVXB	
☐ N837AW	Airbus A319-132	2595	ex D-AVXM	Arizona Cardinals c/s
☐ N838AW	Airbus A319-132	2615	ex D-AVXT	America West Heritage c/s
☐ N839AW	Airbus A319-132	2669	ex D-AVYH	dam
☐ N840AW	Airbus A319-132	2690	ex D-AVXA	
☐ N102UW	Airbus A320-214	0844	ex F-WWBG	
☐ N103US	Airbus A320-214	0861	ex F-WWBP	
☐ N104UW	Airbus A320-214	0863	ex F-WWBQ	
☐ N105UW	Airbus A320-214	0868	ex F-WWBU	
☐ N107US	Airbus A320-214	1052	ex F-WWIM	
☐ N108UW	Airbus A320-214	1061	ex F-WWBB	
☐ N109UW	Airbus A320-214	1065	ex F-WWBD	
☐ N110UW	Airbus A320-214	1112	ex F-WWBJ	
☐ N111US	Airbus A320-214	1114	ex F-WWBK	

☐ N112US	Airbus A320-214	1134	ex F-WWIV		
☐ N113UW	Airbus A320-214	1141	ex F-WWBC		
☐ N114UW	Airbus A320-214	1148	ex F-WWBQ		
☐ N117UW	Airbus A320-214	1224	ex F-WWBH		
☐ N118US	Airbus A320-214	1264	ex F-WWDE		
☐ N119US	Airbus A320-214	1268	ex F-WWDH		
☐ N121UW	Airbus A320-214	1294	ex F-WWBC		
☐ N122US	Airbus A320-214	1298	ex F-WWBM		
☐ N123UW	Airbus A320-214	1310	ex F-WWBX		
☐ N124US	Airbus A320-214	1314	ex F-WWDJ		
☐ N125UW	Airbus A320-214	4086	ex F-WWBU		
☐ N126UW	Airbus A320-214	4149	ex D-AVVJ		
☐ N127UW	Airbus A320-214	4202	ex D-AVVH		♦
☐ N128UW	Airbus A320-214	4242	ex F-WWDL		♦
☐ N601AW	Airbus A320-232	1935	ex D-ALAU		
☐ N602AW	Airbus A320-232	0565	ex D-ALAA		
☐ N604AW	Airbus A320-232	1196	ex F-WWDZ		
☐ N620AW	Airbus A320-231	0052	ex N901BN		
☐ N621AW	Airbus A320-231	0053	ex N902BN		
☐ N622AW	Airbus A320-231	0054	ex N903BN		
☐ N624AW	Airbus A320-231	0055	ex N904BN		
☐ N625AW	Airbus A320-231	0064	ex N905BN		
☐ N626AW	Airbus A320-231	0065	ex N906BN		
☐ N627AW	Airbus A320-231	0066	ex N907GP		
☐ N628AW	Airbus A320-231	0067	ex N908GP		
☐ N629AW	Airbus A320-231	0076	ex N910GP		
☐ N631AW	Airbus A320-231	0077	ex N911GP		
☐ N632AW	Airbus A320-231	0081	ex N912GP		
☐ N633AW	Airbus A320-231	0082	ex N913GP		
☐ N637AW	Airbus A320-231	0099	ex N917GP	Arizona Cardinals c/s	
☐ N640AW	Airbus A320-232	0448	ex N931LF		
☐ N642AW	Airbus A320-232	0584	ex F-WWDZ		
☐ N644AW	Airbus A320-231	0317	ex N300ML		
☐ N647AW	Airbus A320-232	0762	ex F-WWDE		
☐ N648AW	Airbus A320-232	0770	ex F-WWDJ		
☐ N649AW	Airbus A320-232	0803	ex F-WWDZ		
☐ N650AW	Airbus A320-232	0856	ex F-WWBM		
☐ N651AW	Airbus A320-232	0866	ex F-WWBS		
☐ N652AW	Airbus A320-232	0953	ex F-WWDR		
☐ N653AW	Airbus A320-232	1003	ex F-WWDK		
☐ N654AW	Airbus A320-232	1050	ex F-WWIL		
☐ N655AW	Airbus A320-232	1075	ex F-WWIG		
☐ N656AW	Airbus A320-232	1079	ex F-WWIQ		
☐ N657AW	Airbus A320-232	1083	ex F-WWIU		
☐ N658AW	Airbus A320-232	1110	ex F-WWDI		
☐ N659AW	Airbus A320-232	1166	ex F-WWDG		
☐ N660AW	Airbus A320-232	1234	ex F-WWIO		
☐ N661AW	Airbus A320-232	1284	ex F-WWBK		
☐ N662AW	Airbus A320-232	1274	ex F-WWDR		
☐ N663AW	Airbus A320-232	1419	ex F-WWBJ		
☐ N664AW	Airbus A320-232	1621	ex F-WWDK		
☐ N665AW	Airbus A320-232	1644	ex F-WWDN		
☐ N667AW	Airbus A320-232	1710	ex F-WWIX		
☐ N668AW	Airbus A320-232	1764	ex F-WWBZ		
☐ N669AW	Airbus A320-232	1792	ex F-WWDX		
☐ N672AW	Airbus A320-232	2193	ex F-WWDZ		
☐ N673AW	Airbus A320-232	2312	ex F-WWDJ		
☐ N675AW	Airbus A320-232	2405	ex F-WWDA	N233UW resd	
☐ N676AW	Airbus A320-232	2422	ex F-WWBB		
☐ N677AW	Airbus A320-232	2430	ex F-WWBJ		
☐ N678AW	Airbus A320-232	2482	ex F-WWIN	N236UW resd	
☐ N679AW	Airbus A320-232	2613	ex F-WWIX		
☐ N680AW	Airbus A320-232	2630	ex F-WWDX		
☐	Airbus A320-232		ex		o/o♦
☐	Airbus A320-232		ex		o/o♦
☐	Airbus A320-232		ex		o/o♦
☐	Airbus A320-232		ex		o/o♦
☐	Airbus A320-232		ex		o/o♦
☐	Airbus A320-232		ex		o/o♦
☐ N161UW	Airbus A321-211	1403	ex D-AVZD		
☐ N162UW	Airbus A321-211	1412	ex D-AVZF		
☐ N163US	Airbus A321-211	1417	ex D-AVZG		
☐ N165US	Airbus A321-211	1431	ex D-AVZB		
☐ N167US	Airbus A321-211	1442	ex D-AVXA		
☐ N169UW	Airbus A321-211	1455	ex D-AVXD		
☐ N170US	Airbus A321-211	1462	ex D-AVZM		

	Registration	Type	c/n	ex	notes
☐	N171US	Airbus A321-211	1465	ex D-AVZN	
☐	N172US	Airbus A321-211	1472	ex D-AVZO	
☐	N173US	Airbus A321-211	1481	ex D-AVZI	
☐	N174US	Airbus A321-211	1492	ex D-AVZR	
☐	N176UW	Airbus A321-211	1499	ex D-AVZT	
☐	N177US	Airbus A321-211	1517	ex D-AVZF	
☐	N178US	Airbus A321-211	1519	ex D-AVZH	
☐	N179UW	Airbus A321-211	1521	ex D-AVZJ	
☐	N180US	Airbus A321-211	1525	ex D-AVZV	
☐	N181UW	Airbus A321-211	1531	ex D-AVZW	
☐	N182UW	Airbus A321-211	1536	ex D-AVZB	
☐	N183UW	Airbus A321-211	1539	ex D-AVZC	
☐	N184US	Airbus A321-211	1651	ex D-AVZQ	
☐	N185UW	Airbus A321-211	1666	ex D-AVZI	
☐	N186US	Airbus A321-211	1701	ex D-AVZD	
☐	N187US	Airbus A321-211	1704	ex D-AVZE	
☐	N188US	Airbus A321-211	1724	ex D-AVXB	
☐	N189UW	Airbus A321-211	1425	ex N164UW	
☐	N190UW	Airbus A321-211	1436	ex N166US	
☐	N191UW	Airbus A321-211	1447	ex N168US	
☐	N192UW	Airbus A321-211	1496	ex N175US	
☐	N193UW	Airbus A321-211	3584	ex D-AVZL	
☐	N194UW	Airbus A321-211	3629	ex D-AVZI	
☐	N195UW	Airbus A321-211	3633	ex D-AVZJ	
☐	N196UW	Airbus A321-211	3879	ex D-AVZR	
☐	N197UW	Airbus A321-211	3928	ex D-AZAC	
☐	N507AY	Airbus A321-231	3712	ex D-AVZP	
☐	N508AY	Airbus A321-231	3740	ex D-AZAL	
☐	N509AY	Airbus A321-231	3796	ex D-AZAS	
☐	N510UW	Airbus A321-231	3858	ex D-AVZI	
☐	N519UW	Airbus A321-231	3881	ex D-AVZT	
☐	N520UW	Airbus A321-231	3924	ex D-AZAA	
☐	N521UW	Airbus A321-231	3944	ex D-AZAJ	
☐	N523UW	Airbus A321-231	3960	ex D-AZAV	
☐	N524UW	Airbus A321-231	3977	ex F-WWIX	
☐	N534UW	Airbus A321-231	3989	ex D-AZAO	
☐	N535UW	Airbus A321-231	3993	ex D-AZAP	
☐	N536UW	Airbus A321-231	4025	ex D-AVZH	
☐	N537UW	Airbus A321-231	4041	ex D-AVZJ	
☐	N538UW	Airbus A321-231	4050	ex D-AZAK	
☐	N539UW	Airbus A321-231	4082	ex D-AVZV	
☐	N540UW	Airbus A321-231	4107	ex D-AZAD	
☐	N541UW	Airbus A321-231	4123	ex D-AZAI	
☐	N542UW	Airbus A321-231	4134	ex D-AZAL	
☐		Airbus A321-231		ex	o/o♦
☐		Airbus A321-231		ex	o/o♦
☐		Airbus A321-231		ex	o/o♦
☐		Airbus A321-231		ex	o/o♦
☐		Airbus A321-231		ex	o/o♦
☐	N270AY	Airbus A330-323X	315	ex N670UW	
☐	N271AY	Airbus A330-323X	323	ex N671UW	
☐	N272AY	Airbus A330-323X	333	ex N672UW	
☐	N273AY	Airbus A330-323X	337	ex N673UW	
☐	N274AY	Airbus A330-323X	342	ex N674UW	
☐	N275AY	Airbus A330-323X	370	ex N675US	
☐	N276AY	Airbus A330-323X	375	ex N676UW	
☐	N277AY	Airbus A330-323X	380	ex N677UW	
☐	N278AY	Airbus A330-323X	388	ex N678US	
☐	N279AY	Airbus A330-243	1011	ex F-WWYG	
☐	N280AY	Airbus A330-243	1022	ex F-WWYP	
☐	N281AY	Airbus A330-243	1041	ex F-WWYT	
☐	N282AY	Airbus A330-243	1069	ex F-WWYG	
☐	N283AY	Airbus A330-243	1076	ex F-WWKP	
☐	N284AY	Airbus A330-243	1095	ex F-WWYS	
☐	N285AY	Airbus A330-243	1100	ex F-WWYF	♦
☐	N154AW	Boeing 737-3G7	23776/1417		
☐	N155AW	Boeing 737-3G7	23777/1419		
☐	N156AW	Boeing 737-3G7	23778/1455		
☐	N157AW	Boeing 737-3G7	23779/1457		
☐	N158AW	Boeing 737-3G7	23780/1459		
☐	N302AW	Boeing 737-3G7	24009/1578		
☐	N303AW	Boeing 737-3G7	24010/1606		
☐	N305AW	Boeing 737-3G7	24012/1612		
☐	N313AW	Boeing 737-3S3	23712/1336	ex EC-EBZ	
☐	N314AW	Boeing 737-3S3	23733/1345	ex G-BMTG	

☐ N315AW	Boeing 737-3S3	23734/1359	ex G-BMTH	
☐ N316AW	Boeing 737-3S3	23713/1341	ex G-BMTF	
☐ N332AW	Boeing 737-3B7	23384/1427	ex N953WP	
☐ N334AW	Boeing 737-3Y0	23748/1381	ex N962WP	
☐ N516AU	Boeing 737-3B7	23702/1475	ex N385AU	
☐ N529AU	Boeing 737-3B7	24411/1713		
☐ N530AU	Boeing 737-3B7	24412/1735		
☐ N531AU	Boeing 737-3B7	24478/1743		
☐ N532AU	Boeing 737-3B7	24479/1745		
☐ N533AU	Boeing 737-3B7	24515/1767		
☐ N574US	Boeing 737-301	23739/1469	ex N358US	
☐ N588US	Boeing 737-301	23933/1559	ex (N360P)	[GYR]
☐ N404US	Boeing 737-401	23886/1487	ex (N402P)	
☐ N405US	Boeing 737-401	23885/1512	ex (N403P)	
☐ N406US	Boeing 737-401	23876/1528	ex (N404P)	
☐ N409US	Boeing 737-401	23879/1573	ex (N407P)	
☐ N417US	Boeing 737-401	23984/1674		
☐ N418US	Boeing 737-401	23985/1676		
☐ N419US	Boeing 737-401	23986/1684		
☐ N420US	Boeing 737-401	23987/1698		
☐ N421US	Boeing 737-401	23988/1714		
☐ N422US	Boeing 737-401	23989/1716		
☐ N423US	Boeing 737-401	23990/1732		
☐ N424US	Boeing 737-401	23991/1746		
☐ N425US	Boeing 737-401	23992/1764		
☐ N426US	Boeing 737-4B7	24548/1789		
☐ N427US	Boeing 737-4B7	24549/1791		
☐ N430US	Boeing 737-4B7	24552/1797		
☐ N432US	Boeing 737-4B7	24554/1817		
☐ N433US	Boeing 737-4B7	24555/1819		
☐ N434US	Boeing 737-4B7	24556/1821		
☐ N435US	Boeing 737-4B7	24557/1835		
☐ N438US	Boeing 737-4B7	24560/1849		
☐ N439US	Boeing 737-4B7	24781/1874		
☐ N440US	Boeing 737-4B7	24811/1890		stored
☐ N441US	Boeing 737-4B7	24812/1892		
☐ N442US	Boeing 737-4B7	24841/1906		
☐ N443US	Boeing 737-4B7	24842/1908		
☐ N444US	Boeing 737-4B7	24862/1910		
☐ N445US	Boeing 737-4B7	24863/1914		
☐ N449US	Boeing 737-4B7	24893/1946		
☐ N450UW	Boeing 737-4B7	24933/1954	ex N775AU	
☐ N451UW	Boeing 737-4B7	24934/1956	ex N776AU	
☐ N452UW	Boeing 737-4B7	24979/1980	ex N777AU	
☐ N453UW	Boeing 737-4B7	24980/1982	ex N778AU	
☐ N454UW	Boeing 737-4B7	24996/1986	ex N779AU	
☐ N455UW	Boeing 737-4B7	24997/1990	ex N780AU	
☐ N456UW	Boeing 737-4B7	25020/1992	ex N781AU	
☐ N457UW	Boeing 737-4B7	25021/1995	ex N782AU	
☐ N458UW	Boeing 737-4B7	25022/2010	ex N783AU	
☐ N459UW	Boeing 737-4B7	25023/2020	ex N784AU	
☐ N460UW	Boeing 737-4B7	25024/2026	ex N785AU	
☐ N200UU	Boeing 757-2B7/W	27809/673	ex N631AU	
☐ N201UU	Boeing 757-2B7/W	27810/678	ex N632AU	
☐ N202UW	Boeing 757-2B7/W	27811/681	ex N633AU	
☐ N203UW	Boeing 757-23N/W	30548/930	ex N642UW	
☐ N204UW	Boeing 757-23N/W	30886/945	ex N643UW	
☐ N205UW	Boeing 757-23N/W	30887/946	ex N644UW	
☐ N206UW	Boeing 757-2B7/W	27808/666	ex N630AU	
☐ N901AW	Boeing 757-2S7	23321/76	ex N601RC	
☐ N902AW	Boeing 757-2S7	23322/79	ex N602RC	
☐ N903AW	Boeing 757-2S7	23323/80	ex N603RC	
☐ N904AW	Boeing 757-2S7	23566/96	ex N604RC	
☐ N905AW	Boeing 757-2S7	23567/97	ex N605RC	
☐ N906AW	Boeing 757-2S7	23568/99	ex N606RC	
☐ N908AW	Boeing 757-2G7/W	24233/244		
☐ N909AW	Boeing 757-2G7/W	24522/252		
☐ N910AW	Boeing 757-2G7/W	24523/256		
☐ N923UW	Boeing 757-225	22203/26	ex N607AU	[VCV]
☐ N925UW	Boeing 757-225	22205/28	ex N609AU	
☐ N935UW	Boeing 757-2B7/W	27201/605	ex N622AU	Star Alliance c/s
☐ N936UW	Boeing 757-2B7	27244/607	ex N623AU	
☐ N937UW	Boeing 757-2B7/W	27245/630	ex N624AU	
☐ N938UW	Boeing 757-2B7/W	27246/643	ex N625VJ	
☐ N939UW	Boeing 757-2B7/W	27303/647	ex N626AU	

☐ N940UW	Boeing 757-2B7/W	27805/655	ex N627AU		
☐ N941UW	Boeing 757-2B7/W	27806/657	ex N628AU		
☐ N942UW	Boeing 757-2B7/W	27807/662	ex N629AU		
☐ N245AY	Boeing 767-201ER	23897/173	ex N645US		
☐ N246AY	Boeing 767-201ER	23898/175	ex N646US		
☐ N248AY	Boeing 767-201ER	23900/190	ex N648UA		
☐ N249AU	Boeing 767-201ER	23901/197	ex N649US		
☐ N250AY	Boeing 767-201ER	23902/217	ex N650US		
☐ N251AY	Boeing 767-201ER	24764/306	ex N651US		
☐ N252AU	Boeing 767-2B7ER	24765/308	ex N652US		
☐ N253AY	Boeing 767-2B7ER	24894/338	ex N653US		
☐ N255AY	Boeing 767-2B7ER	25257/383	ex N655US		
☐ N256AY	Boeing 767-2B7ER	26847/486	ex N656US		

US AIRWAYS EXPRESS

Air Express (USX)
Charlotte, NC,/Philadelphia. PA/Pittsburgh, PA (CLT/PHL/PIT)

☐ N124CJ	Beech 1900D	UE-24	ex N575D	LVA	Colgan Air
☐ N171CJ	Beech 1900D	UE-71	ex N85704	LVU	Colgan Air
☐ N172MJ	Beech 1900D	UE-72	ex N85804	LVI	Colgan Air
☐ N191CJ	Beech 1900D	UE-19	ex N83005	LVI	Colgan Air
☐ N221CJ	Beech 1900D	UE-221		LVG	Colgan Air
☐ N202PS	Canadair CRJ-200ER	7858	ex C-FMLF	202	PSA Airlines
☐ N206PS	Canadair CRJ-200ER	7860	ex C-FMLQ	206	PSA Airlines
☐ N207PS	Canadair CRJ-200ER	7873	ex C-FMNQ	207	PSA Airlines
☐ N209PS	Canadair CRJ-200ER	7874	ex C-FMLU	209	PSA Airlines
☐ N213PS	Canadair CRJ-200ER	7879	ex C-FMMQ	213	PSA Airlines
☐ N215PS	Canadair CRJ-200ER	7880	ex C-FMMW	215	PSA Airlines
☐ N216PS	Canadair CRJ-200ER	7882	ex C-FMMY	216	PSA Airlines
☐ N218PS	Canadair CRJ-200ER	7885	ex C-FMKW	218	PSA Airlines
☐ N220PS	Canadair CRJ-200ER	7887	ex C-FMLB	220	PSA Airlines
☐ N221PS	Canadair CRJ-200ER	7889	ex C-FMLI	221	PSA Airlines
☐ N223JS	Canadair CRJ-200ER	7892	ex C-FMLT	223	PSA Airlines
☐ N226JS	Canadair CRJ-200ER	7895	ex C-FMNH	226	PSA Airlines
☐ N228PS	Canadair CRJ-200ER	7897	ex C-FMNX	228	PSA Airlines
☐ N229PS	Canadair CRJ-200ER	7898	ex C-FMNY	229	PSA Airlines
☐ N230PS	Canadair CRJ-200ER	7904	ex C-FMLU	230	PSA Airlines
☐ N237PS	Canadair CRJ-200ER	7906	ex C-FMMB	237	PSA Airlines
☐ N241PS	Canadair CRJ-200ER	7909	ex C-FMMQ	241	PSA Airlines
☐ N242JS	Canadair CRJ-200ER	7911	ex C-FMMX	242	PSA Airlines
☐ N244PS	Canadair CRJ-200ER	7912	ex C-FMMY	244	PSA Airlines
☐ N245PS	Canadair CRJ-200ER	7919	ex C-FMLI	245	PSA Airlines
☐ N246PS	Canadair CRJ-200ER	7920	ex C-FMLQ	246	PSA Airlines
☐ N247JS	Canadair CRJ-200ER	7922	ex C-FMLT	247	PSA Airlines
☐ N248PS	Canadair CRJ-200ER	7925	ex C-FMNH	248	PSA Airlines
☐ N249PS	Canadair CRJ-200ER	7926	ex C-FMNW	249	PSA Airlines
☐ N250PS	Canadair CRJ-200ER	7929	ex C-FMOS	250	PSA Airlines
☐ N251PS	Canadair CRJ-200ER	7931	ex C-FVAZ	251	PSA Airlines
☐ N253PS	Canadair CRJ-200ER	7934	ex C-FMLU	253	PSA Airlines
☐ N254PS	Canadair CRJ-200ER	7935	ex C-FMOI	254	PSA Airlines
☐ N256PS	Canadair CRJ-200ER	7937	ex C-FMML	256	PSA Airlines
☐ N257PS	Canadair CRJ-200ER	7939	ex C-FMMQ	257	PSA Airlines
☐ N258PS	Canadair CRJ-200ER	7941	ex C-FMMX	258	PSA Airlines
☐ N259PS	Canadair CRJ-200ER	7945	ex C-FMKW	259	PSA Airlines
☐ N260JS	Canadair CRJ-200ER	7957	ex C-FMNX	260	PSA Airlines
☐ N261PS	Canadair CRJ-200ER	7959	ex C-FMOS	261	PSA Airlines
☐ N262PS	Canadair CRJ-200ER	7962	ex C-FMND	262	PSA Airlines
☐ N401AW	Canadair CRJ-200LR	7280	ex C-FMLQ	401	Air Wisconsin
☐ N403AW	Canadair CRJ-200LR	7288	ex C-FMLF	403	Air Wisconsin
☐ N404AW	Canadair CRJ-200LR	7294	ex C-FMMT	404	Air Wisconsin
☐ N405AW	Canadair CRJ-200LR	7362	ex C-FMND	405	Air Wisconsin
☐ N406AW	Canadair CRJ-200LR	7402	ex C-FMMY	406	Air Wisconsin
☐ N407AW	Canadair CRJ-200LR	7424	ex C-FMLU	407	Air Wisconsin
☐ N408AW	Canadair CRJ-200LR	7568	ex C-FMNY	408	Air Wisconsin
☐ N409AW	Canadair CRJ-200LR	7447	ex C-FMNX	409	Air Wisconsin
☐ N410AW	Canadair CRJ-200LR	7490	ex C-FMMW	410	Air Wisconsin
☐ N411ZW	Canadair CRJ-200LR	7569	ex C-FMNZ	411	Air Wisconsin
☐ N412AW	Canadair CRJ-200LR	7582	ex C-FMMY	412	Air Wisconsin
☐ N413AW	Canadair CRJ-200LR	7585	ex C-FMKW	413	Air Wisconsin
☐ N414ZW	Canadair CRJ-200LR	7586	ex C-FMKZ	414	Air Wisconsin
☐ N415AW	Canadair CRJ-200LR	7593	ex C-FMLV	415	Air Wisconsin
☐ N416AW	Canadair CRJ-200LR	7603	ex C-FMNQ	416	Air Wisconsin
☐ N417AW	Canadair CRJ-200LR	7610	ex C-FMMW	417	Air Wisconsin
☐ N418AW	Canadair CRJ-200LR	7618	ex C-FMLF	418	Air Wisconsin
☐ N419AW	Canadair CRJ-200LR	7633	ex C-FMNQ	419	Air Wisconsin

☐	N420AW	Canadair CRJ-200LR	7640	ex C-FMMW	420		Air Wisconsin
☐	N421ZW	Canadair CRJ-200LR	7346	ex N587ML	421		Air Wisconsin
☐	N422AW	Canadair CRJ-200LR	7341	ex N586ML	422		Air Wisconsin
☐	N423AW	Canadair CRJ-200LR	7636	ex C-FMMB	423		Air Wisconsin
☐	N424AW	Canadair CRJ-200LR	7656	ex C-FMNW	424		Air Wisconsin
☐	N425AW	Canadair CRJ-200LR	7663	ex C-FMNQ	425		Air Wisconsin
☐	N426AW	Canadair CRJ-200LR	7669	ex C-FMMQ	426		Air Wisconsin
☐	N427ZW	Canadair CRJ-200LR	7685	ex C-FMNH	427		Air Wisconsin
☐	N428AW	Canadair CRJ-200LR	7695	ex C-FMOI	428		Air Wisconsin
☐	N429AW	Canadair CRJ-200LR	7711	ex CFMLS	429		Air Wisconsin
☐	N430AW	Canadair CRJ-200LR	7719	ex C-FMOS	430		Air Wisconsin
☐	N431AW	Canadair CRJ-200LR	7256	ex N575ML	431		Air Wisconsin
☐	N432AW	Canadair CRJ-200LR	7257	ex N576ML	432		Air Wisconsin
☐	N433AW	Canadair CRJ-200LR	7289	ex N580ML	433		Air Wisconsin
☐	N434AW	Canadair CRJ-200LR	7322	ex N582ML	434		Air Wisconsin
☐	N435AW	Canadair CRJ-200LR	7724	ex C-FMLU	435		Air Wisconsin
☐	N436AW	Canadair CRJ-200LR	7734	ex C-FMKV	436		Air Wisconsin
☐	N437AW	Canadair CRJ-200LR	7744	ex C-FMMT	437		Air Wisconsin
☐	N438AW	Canadair CRJ-200LR	7748	ex C-GFAX	438		Air Wisconsin
☐	N439AW	Canadair CRJ-200LR	7753	ex C-FZZO	439		Air Wisconsin
☐	N440AW	Canadair CRJ-200LR	7766	ex C-FMKZ	440		Air Wisconsin
☐	N441ZW	Canadair CRJ-200LR	7777	ex C-FMNX	441		Air Wisconsin
☐	N442AW	Canadair CRJ-200LR	7778	ex C-FMNY	442		Air Wisconsin
☐	N443AW	Canadair CRJ-200LR	7781	ex C-FVAZ	443		Air Wisconsin
☐	N444ZW	Canadair CRJ-200LR	7788	ex C-FMMN	444		Air Wisconsin
☐	N445AW	Canadair CRJ-200LR	7804	ex C-FMMT	445		Air Wisconsin
☐	N446AW	Canadair CRJ-200LR	7806	ex C-FMNW	446		Air Wisconsin
☐	N447AW	Canadair CRJ-200LR	7812	ex C-FMND	447		Air Wisconsin
☐	N448AW	Canadair CRJ-200LR	7814	ex C-FMLU	448		Air Wisconsin
☐	N449AW	Canadair CRJ-200LR	7818	ex C-FMMN	449		Air Wisconsin
☐	N450AW	Canadair CRJ-200LR	7823	ex C-FMNB	450		Air Wisconsin
☐	N451AW	Canadair CRJ-200LR	7832	ex C-FMLT	451		Air Wisconsin
☐	N452AW	Canadair CRJ-200LR	7835	ex C-FMNH	452		Air Wisconsin
☐	N453AW	Canadair CRJ-200LR	7838	ex C-FMNY	453		Air Wisconsin
☐	N454AW	Canadair CRJ-200LR	7842	ex C-FMND	454		Air Wisconsin
☐	N455AW	Canadair CRJ-200LR	7848	ex C-FMMN	455		Air Wisconsin
☐	N456ZW	Canadair CRJ-200LR	7849	ex C-FMMQ	456		Air Wisconsin
☐	N457AW	Canadair CRJ-200LR	7854	ex C-FMKV	457		Air Wisconsin
☐	N458AW	Canadair CRJ-200LR	7861	ex C-FMLS	458		Air Wisconsin
☐	N459AW	Canadair CRJ-200LR	7863	ex C-FMLV	459		Air Wisconsin
☐	N460AW	Canadair CRJ-200LR	7867	ex C-GZTD	460		Air Wisconsin
☐	N461AW	Canadair CRJ-200LR	7870	ex C-FMOW	461		Air Wisconsin
☐	N462AW	Canadair CRJ-200LR	7875	ex C-FMOI	462		Air Wisconsin
☐	N463AW	Canadair CRJ-200LR	7878	ex C-FMMN	463		Air Wisconsin
☐	N464AW	Canadair CRJ-200LR	7890	ex C-FMLQ	464		Air Wisconsin
☐	N465AW	Canadair CRJ-200LR	7893	ex C-FMLV	465		Air Wisconsin
☐	N466AW	Canadair CRJ-200LR	7899	ex C-FMOS	466		Air Wisconsin
☐	N467AW	Canadair CRJ-200LR	7900	ex C-FMOW	467		Air Wisconsin
☐	N468AW	Canadair CRJ-200LR	7916	ex C-FMKZ	468		Air Wisconsin
☐	N469AW	Canadair CRJ-200LR	7917	ex C-FMLB	469		Air Wisconsin
☐	N470AW	Canadair CRJ-200LR	7927	ex C-FMNX	470		Air Wisconsin
☐	N570ML	Canadair CRJ-200LR	7206	ex C-GBNO	YJX		Mesa
☐	N651ML	Canadair CRJ-200LR	7139	ex N787BC	YCD		Mesa
☐	N7264V	Canadair CRJ-200LR	7264	ex C-FMMT			Mesa
☐	N7291Z	Canadair CRJ-200LR	7291	ex C-FMLS			Mesa
☐	N7305V	Canadair CRJ-200LR	7305	ex C-F			Mesa
☐	N17231	Canadair CRJ-200LR	7231	ex C-FMLS			Mesa
☐	N17275	Canadair CRJ-200LR	7275	ex C-FMOI			Mesa
☐	N17337	Canadair CRJ-200LR	7337	ex C-FMML			Mesa
☐	N17358	Canadair CRJ-200LR	7358	ex C-FMNY			Mesa
☐	N27173	Canadair CRJ-200LR	7173	ex C-FMMQ			Mesa
☐	N27314	Canadair CRJ-200LR	7314	ex C-FMKV			Mesa
☐	N37178	Canadair CRJ-200LR	7178	ex C-GAVO			Mesa
☐	N75984	Canadair CRJ-200LR	7489	ex C-GZGX	YJW		Mesa
☐	N77260	Canadair CRJ-200LR	7260	ex C-FMLQ			Mesa
☐	N77286	Canadair CRJ-200LR	7286	ex C-FMKZ			Mesa
☐	N97325	Canadair CRJ-200LR	7325	ex C-FMNH			Mesa
☐	N702PS	Canadair CRJ-701ER	10135	ex C-	702		PSA Airlines
☐	N703PS	Canadair CRJ-701ER	10137	ex C-	703		PSA Airlines
☐	N705PS	Canadair CRJ-701ER	10144	ex C-	705		PSA Airlines
☐	N706PS	Canadair CRJ-701ER	10150	ex C-FBLQ	706		PSA Airlines
☐	N708PS	Canadair CRJ-701ER	10160	ex C-	708	Star Alliance c/s	PSA Airlines
☐	N709PS	Canadair CRJ-701ER	10165	ex N165MD	709		PSA Airlines
☐	N710PS	Canadair CRJ-701ER	10167	ex N167MD	710		PSA Airlines
☐	N712PS	Canadair CRJ-701ER	10168	ex N168MD	712		PSA Airlines
☐	N716PS	Canadair CRJ-701ER	10171	ex N171MD	716		PSA Airlines

☐ N718PS	Canadair CRJ-701ER	10175	ex C-FCQX	718		PSA Airlines
☐ N719PS	Canadair CRJ-701ER	10177	ex N177MD	719		PSA Airlines
☐ N720PS	Canadair CRJ-701ER	10178	ex N175MD	720		PSA Airlines
☐ N723PS	Canadair CRJ-701ER	10181	ex C-FCRE	723		PSA Airlines
☐ N725PS	Canadair CRJ-701ER	10186	ex C-	725		PSA Airlines
☐ N726PS	Canadair CRJ-701ER		ex C-	726	o/o	PSA Airlines
☐ N728PS	Canadair CRJ-701ER		ex C-	728	o/o	PSA Airlines
☐ N729PS	Canadair CRJ-701ER		ex C-	729	o/o	PSA Airlines
☐ N730PS	Canadair CRJ-701ER		ex C-	730	o/o	PSA Airlines
☐ N736PS	Canadair CRJ-701ER		ex C-	736	o/o	PSA Airlines
☐ N740PS	Canadair CRJ-701ER		ex C-	740	o/o	PSA Airlines
☐ N741PS	Canadair CRJ-701ER		ex C-	741	o/o	PSA Airlines
☐ N743PS	Canadair CRJ-701ER		ex C-	743	o/o	PSA Airlines
☐ N744PS	Canadair CRJ-701ER		ex C-		o/o	PSA Airlines
☐ N745PS	Canadair CRJ-701ER		ex C-		o/o	PSA Airlines
☐ N746PS	Canadair CRJ-701ER		ex C-		o/o	PSA Airlines
☐ N748PS	Canadair CRJ-701ER		ex C-		o/o	PSA Airlines
☐ N749PS	Canadair CRJ-701ER		ex C-		o/o	PSA Airlines
☐ N750PS	Canadair CRJ-701ER		ex C-		o/o	PSA Airlines
☐ N751PS	Canadair CRJ-701ER		ex C-		o/o	PSA Airlines
☐ N752PS	Canadair CRJ-701ER		ex C-		o/o	PSA Airlines
☐ N753PS	Canadair CRJ-701ER		ex C-		o/o	PSA Airlines
☐ N754PS	Canadair CRJ-701ER		ex C-		o/o	PSA Airlines
☐ N755PS	Canadair CRJ-701ER		ex C-		o/o	PSA Airlines
☐ N756PS	Canadair CRJ-701ER		ex C-		o/o	PSA Airlines
☐ N	Canadair CRJ-701ER		ex C-		o/o	PSA Airlines
☐ N	Canadair CRJ-701ER		ex C-		o/o	Mesa
☐ N	Canadair CRJ-701ER		ex C-		o/o	Mesa
☐ N	Canadair CRJ-701ER		ex C-		o/o	Mesa
☐ N	Canadair CRJ-701ER		ex C-		o/o	Mesa
☐ N	Canadair CRJ-701ER		ex C-		o/o	Mesa
☐ N	Canadair CRJ-701ER		ex C-		o/o	Mesa
☐ N	Canadair CRJ-701ER		ex C-		o/o	Mesa
☐ N	Canadair CRJ-701ER		ex C-		o/o	Mesa
☐ N	Canadair CRJ-701ER		ex C-		o/o	Mesa
☐ N902FJ	Canadair CRJ-900ER	15002	ex C-GDNH			Mesa
☐ N903FJ	Canadair CRJ-900ER	15003	ex C-GZQA			Mesa
☐ N904FJ	Canadair CRJ-900ER	15004	ex C-GZQB			Mesa
☐ N905J	Canadair CRJ-900ER	15005	ex C-GZQC			Mesa
☐ N906FJ	Canadair CRJ-900ER	15006	ex C-GZQE			Mesa
☐ N907FJ	Canadair CRJ-900ER	15007	ex C-GZQF			Mesa
☐ N908FJ	Canadair CRJ-900ER	15008	ex C-GZQG			Mesa
☐ N909FJ	Canadair CRJ-900ER	15009	ex C-GZQI			Mesa
☐ N910FJ	Canadair CRJ-900ER	15010	ex C-GZQJ			Mesa
☐ N911FJ	Canadair CRJ-900ER	15011	ex C-GZQK			Mesa
☐ N912FJ	Canadair CRJ-900ER	15012	ex C-GZQL			Mesa
☐ N913FJ	Canadair CRJ-900ER	15013	ex C-GZQM			Mesa
☐ N914FJ	Canadair CRJ-900ER	15014	ex C-GZQO			Mesa
☐ N915FJ	Canadair CRJ-900ER	15015	ex C-GZQP			Mesa
☐ N916FJ	Canadair CRJ-900ER	15016	ex C-GZQQ			Mesa
☐ N917FJ	Canadair CRJ-900ER	15017	ex C-GZQR			Mesa
☐ N918FJ	Canadair CRJ-900ER	15018	ex C-			Mesa
☐ N919FJ	Canadair CRJ-900ER	15019	ex C-			Mesa
☐ N920FJ	Canadair CRJ-900ER	15020	ex C-			Mesa
☐ N921FJ	Canadair CRJ-900ER	15021	ex C-			Mesa
☐ N922FJ	Canadair CRJ-900ER	15022	ex C-			Mesa
☐ N923FJ	Canadair CRJ-900ER	15023	ex C-			Mesa
☐ N924FJ	Canadair CRJ-900ER	15024	ex C-			Mesa
☐ N925FJ	Canadair CRJ-900ER	15025	ex C-			Mesa
☐ N926LR	Canadair CRJ-900ER	15026	ex C-			Mesa
☐ N927LR	Canadair CRJ-900ER	15027	ex C-			Mesa
☐ N928LR	Canadair CRJ-900ER	15028	ex C-			Mesa
☐ N929LR	Canadair CRJ-900ER	15029	ex C-			Mesa
☐ N930LR	Canadair CRJ-900ER	15030	ex C-			Mesa
☐ N931LR	Canadair CRJ-900ER	15031	ex C-			Mesa
☐ N932LR	Canadair CRJ-900ER	15032	ex C-			Mesa
☐ N933LR	Canadair CRJ-900ER	15033	ex C-			Mesa
☐ N934FJ	Canadair CRJ-900ER	15034	ex C-			Mesa
☐ N935LR	Canadair CRJ-900ER	15035	ex C-			Mesa
☐ N938LR	Canadair CRJ-900ER	15038	ex C-			Mesa
☐ N939LR	Canadair CRJ-900ER	15039	ex C-			Mesa
☐ N942LR	Canadair CRJ-900ER	15042	ex C-			Mesa
☐ N956LR	Canadair CRJ-900ER	15056	ex C-			Mesa
☐ N326EN	de Havilland DHC-8-311	234	ex N386DC	HDF		Piedmont

☐	N327EN	de Havilland DHC-8-311A	261	ex N379DC	HDD	Piedmont
☐	N328EN	de Havilland DHC-8-311A	281	ex N380DC	HDC	Piedmont
☐	N329EN	de Havilland DHC-8-311	290	ex SU-UAD	HDG	Piedmont
☐	N330EN	de Havilland DHC-8-311A	274	ex N805SA	HDI	Piedmont
☐	N331EN	de Havilland DHC-8-311A	279	ex N806SA	HDJ	Piedmont
☐	N333EN	de Havilland DHC-8-311	221	ex N803SA	HDK	Piedmont
☐	N335EN	de Havilland DHC-8-311	375	ex N804SA	HDN	Piedmont
☐	N336EN	de Havilland DHC-8-311A	336	ex N284BC	HAD	Piedmont
☐	N337EN	de Havilland DHC-8-311A	284	ex SU-UAE	HDH	Piedmont
☐	N343EN	de Havilland DHC-8-311A	340	ex OE-LLZ	HDE	Piedmont
☐	N437YV	de Havilland DHC-8-202	437	ex C-FDHD		Mesa
☐	N449YV	de Havilland DHC-8Q-202	449	ex C-GFHZ		Mesa
☐	N804EX	de Havilland DHC-8-102A	227	ex C-GFYI	ESA	Piedmont
☐	N805EX	de Havilland DHC-8-102A	228	ex C-GLOT	ESB	Piedmont
☐	N806EX	de Havilland DHC-8-102A	263	ex C-GEVP	ESC	Piedmont
☐	N807EX	de Havilland DHC-8-102A	292	ex C-GFQL	ESD	Piedmont
☐	N808EX	de Havilland DHC-8-102A	299	ex C-GDKL	ESE	Piedmont
☐	N809EX	de Havilland DHC-8-102A	302	ex PT-MFI	ESF	Piedmont
☐	N810EX	de Havilland DHC-8-102A	308	ex C-GDKL	ESG	Piedmont
☐	N812EX	de Havilland DHC-8-102A	312	ex C-GDNG	ESH	Piedmont
☐	N814EX	de Havilland DHC-8-102A	318	ex C-GDNG	ESI	Piedmont
☐	N815EX	de Havilland DHC-8-102A	321	ex C-GDFT	ESJ	Piedmont
☐	N816EX	de Havilland DHC-8-102A	329	ex C-GEVP	ESK	Piedmont
☐	N837EX	de Havilland DHC-8-102A	217	ex N976HA	ERH	Piedmont
☐	N838EX	de Havilland DHC-8-102A	220	ex N977HA	ERK	Piedmont
☐	N906HA	de Havilland DHC-8-102	9	ex C-GHRI	HAS	Piedmont
☐	N907HA	de Havilland DHC-8-102	11	ex C-GESR	HSB	Piedmont
☐	N908HA	de Havilland DHC-8-102	15	ex C-GIBQ	HSC	Piedmont
☐	N911HA	de Havilland DHC-8-102	34	ex C-GEOA	HSF	Piedmont
☐	N912HA	de Havilland DHC-8-102	40	ex C-GEOA	HSG	Piedmont
☐	N914HA	de Havilland DHC-8-102	53	ex C-GETI	HSH	Piedmont
☐	N930HA	de Havilland DHC-8-102	126	ex C-GFQL	HSW	Piedmont
☐	N931HA	de Havilland DHC-8-102	132	ex C-GFOD	HSZ	Piedmont
☐	N933HA	de Havilland DHC-8-102	134	ex C-GFUM	HBA	Piedmont
☐	N934HA	de Havilland DHC-8-102	139	ex C-GETI	HBB	Piedmont
☐	N935HA	de Havilland DHC-8-102	142	ex C-GLOT	HBC	Piedmont
☐	N936HA	de Havilland DHC-8-102	145	ex C-GFQL	HRA	Piedmont
☐	N937HA	de Havilland DHC-8-102	148	ex C-GLOT	HRB	Piedmont
☐	N938HA	de Havilland DHC-8-102	152	ex C-GFUM	HRC	Piedmont
☐	N940HA	de Havilland DHC-8-102	156	ex C-GLOT	HRE	Piedmont
☐	N941HA	de Havilland DHC-8-102	161	ex C-GETI	HRF	Piedmont
☐	N942HA	de Havilland DHC-8-102	163	ex C-GFUM	HRG	Piedmont
☐	N943HA	de Havilland DHC-8-102	167	ex C-GFOD	HRH	Piedmont
☐	N987HA	de Havilland DHC-8-201	425	ex C-GFHZ		Mesa
☐	N988HA	de Havilland DHC-8-201	426	ex C-FDHD		Mesa
☐	N989HA	de Havilland DHC-8-201	427	ex C-GFEN		Mesa
☐	N991HA	de Havilland DHC-8-201	431	ex C-GLOT		Mesa
☐	N257JQ	Embraer ERJ-145LR	14500812	ex PT-SNO	JBJ	Chautauqua
☐	N258JQ	Embraer ERJ-145LR	145768	ex PT-SJZ	JBI	Chautauqua
☐	N259JQ	Embraer ERJ-145LR	145763	ex PT-SJU	JBH	Chautauqua
☐	N280SK	Embraer ERJ-145LR	145381	ex PT-SQF	JRM	Chautauqua
☐	N291SK	Embraer ERJ-145LR	145486	ex PT-SXF	JRX	Chautauqua
☐	N293SK	Embraer ERJ-145LR	145500	ex PT-SXT	JRY	Chautauqua
☐	N298SK	Embraer ERJ-145LR	145508	ex PT-SYA	JRZ	Chautauqua
☐	N370SK	Embraer ERJ-145LR	145515	ex PT-SYH	JBA	Chautauqua
☐	N801HK	Embraer ERJ-145ER	145053	ex PT-SZS	TRK	Trans State
☐	N802HK	Embraer ERJ-145ER	145066	ex PT-SAJ	TRL	Trans State
☐	N803HK	Embraer ERJ-145ER	145077	ex PT-S	TRM	Trans State
☐	N804HK	Embraer ERJ-145ER	145082	ex PT-S	TRA	Trans State
☐	N805HK	Embraer ERJ-145ER	145096	ex PT-SBS	TRB	Trans State
☐	N808HK	Embraer ERJ-145ER	145157	ex PT-SEK	TRD	Trans State
☐	N809HK	Embraer ERJ-145ER	145187	ex PT-SGH	TRE	Trans State
☐	N812HK	Embraer ERJ-145ER	145373	ex PT-SOY	TRG	Trans State
☐	N839MJ	Embraer ERJ-145LR	145416	ex PT-STM	YRO	Mesa
☐	N840MJ	Embraer ERJ-145LR	145429	ex PT-SUA	YRP	Mesa
☐	N843MJ	Embraer ERJ-145LR	145478	ex PT-SVX	YRT	Mesa
☐	N846MJ	Embraer ERJ-145LR	145507	ex PT-SXZ	YRW	Mesa
☐	N977RP	Embraer ERJ-145MP	145185	ex SE-DZD	JBH	Chautauqua <SKX
☐	N978RP	Embraer ERJ-145LR	145169	ex G-CCLD	JBX	Chautauqua <SKX
☐	N801MA	Embraer ERJ-170SU	17000012	ex PT-SKE	801	Republic
☐	N802MD	Embraer ERJ-170SU	17000013	ex PT-SKF	802	Republic
☐	N803MD	Embraer ERJ-170SU	17000015	ex PT-SKI	803	Republic
☐	N805MD	Embraer ERJ-170SU	17000018	ex PT-SKL	805	Republic
☐	N806MD	Embraer ERJ-170SU	17000019	ex PT-SKM	806	Republic
☐	N807MD	Embraer ERJ-170SU	17000020	ex PT-SKN	807	Republic

☐ N808MD	Embraer ERJ-170SU	17000021	ex PT-SKO	808	Republic
☐ N809MD	Embraer ERJ-170SU	17000022	ex PT-SKP	809	Republic
☐ N811MD	Embraer ERJ-170SU	17000028	ex PT-SKV	811	Republic
☐ N812MD	Embraer ERJ-170SU	17000030	ex PT-SKY	812	Republic
☐ N814MD	Embraer ERJ-170SU	17000033	ex PT-SUB	814	Republic
☐ N816MA	Embraer ERJ-170SU	17000037	ex PT-SUG	816	Republic
☐ N817MD	Embraer ERJ-170SU	17000038	ex PT-SUH	817	Republic
☐ N819MD	Embraer ERJ-170SU	17000040	ex PT-SUJ	819	Republic
☐ N820MD	Embraer ERJ-170SU	17000041	ex PT-SUK	820	Republic
☐ N822MD	Embraer ERJ-170SU	17000043	ex PT-SUM	822	Republic
☐ N827MD	Embraer ERJ-170SU	17000047	ex PT-SUQ	827	Republic
☐ N828MD	Embraer ERJ-170SU	17000048	ex PT-SUR	828	Republic
☐ N829MD	Embraer ERJ-170SU	17000049	ex PT-SUT	829	Republic
☐ N101HQ	Embraer ERJ-175LR	17000156	ex PT-SEU		Republic
☐ N102HQ	Embraer ERJ-175LR	17000157	ex PT-SEV		Republic
☐ N103HQ	Embraer ERJ-175LR	17000159	ex PT-SEX		Republic
☐ N104HQ	Embraer ERJ-175LR	17000160	ex PT-SMA		Republic
☐ N105HQ	Embraer ERJ-175LR	17000163	ex PT-SMF		Republic
☐ N106HQ	Embraer ERJ-175LR	17000164	ex PT-SMG		Republic
☐ N107HQ	Embraer ERJ-175LR	17000165	ex PT-SMH		Republic
☐ N108HQ	Embraer ERJ-175LR	17000166	ex PT-SMI		Republic
☐ N109HQ	Embraer ERJ-175LR	17000168	ex PT-SMK		Republic
☐ N110HQ	Embraer ERJ-175LR	17000172	ex PT-SMP		Republic
☐ N111HQ	Embraer ERJ-175LR	17000173	ex PT-SMQ		Republic
☐ N112HQ	Embraer ERJ-175LR	17000174	ex PT-SMR		Republic
☐ N113HQ	Embraer ERJ-175LR	17000177	ex PT-SMU		Republic
☐ N114HQ	Embraer ERJ-175LR	17000179	ex PT-SMW		Republic
☐ N115HQ	Embraer ERJ-175LR	17000182	ex PT-SMZ		Republic
☐ N116HQ	Embraer ERJ-175LR	17000183	ex PT-SUA		Republic
☐ N117HQ	Embraer ERJ-175LR	17000184	ex PT-SUB		Republic
☐ N118HQ	Embraer ERJ-175LR	17000189	ex PT-SUI		Republic
☐ N119HQ	Embraer ERJ-175LR	17000190	ex PT-SUQ		Republic
☐ N120HQ	Embraer ERJ-175LR	17000193	ex PT-SUV		Republic
☐ N121HQ	Embraer ERJ-175LR	17000194	ex PT-SUY		Republic
☐ N122HQ	Embraer ERJ-175LR	17000196	ex PT-SXF		Republic
☐ N123HQ	Embraer ERJ-175LR	17000199	ex PT-SXM		Republic
☐ N124HQ	Embraer ERJ-175LR	17000200	ex PT-SXO		Republic
☐ N125HQ	Embraer ERJ-175LR	17000202	ex PT-SXR		Republic
☐ N126HQ	Embraer ERJ-175LR	17000204	ex PT-SXU		Republic
☐ N127HQ	Embraer ERJ-175LR	17000206	ex PT-SCB		Republic
☐ N128HQ	Embraer ERJ-175LR	17000208	ex PT-SCF		Republic
☐ N129HQ	Embraer ERJ-175LR	17000211	ex PT-SCI		Republic
☐ N130HQ	Embraer ERJ-175LR	17000212	ex PT-SCJ		Republic
☐ N131HQ	Embraer ERJ-175LR	17000215	ex PT-SCM		Republic
☐ N132HQ	Embraer ERJ-175LR	17000216	ex PT-SCN		Republic
☐ N133HQ	Embraer ERJ-175LR	17000217	ex PT-SCO		Republic
☐ N134HQ	Embraer ERJ-175LR	17000220	ex PT-SCS		Republic
☐ N135HQ	Embraer ERJ-175LR	17000224	ex PT-SFA		Republic
☐ N136HQ	Embraer ERJ-170LR	17000228	ex PT-SFE		Republic
☐ N137HQ	Embraer ERJ-170LR	17000231	ex PT-SFH		Republic
☐ N138HQ	Embraer ERJ-170LR	17000234	ex PT-SFK		Republic
☐ N944UW	Embraer ERJ-190AR	19000058	ex PT-SIL		Republic
☐ N945UW	Embraer ERJ-190AR	19000062	ex PT-SJA		Republic
☐ N946UW	Embraer ERJ-190AR	19000072	ex PT-SJL		Republic
☐ N947UW	Embraer ERJ-190AR	19000078	ex PT-SJU		Republic
☐ N948UW	Embraer ERJ-190AR	19000081	ex PT-SJX		Republic
☐ N949UW	Embraer ERJ-190AR	19000102	ex PT-SNW		Republic
☐ N950UW	Embraer ERJ-190AR	19000106	ex PT-SQA		Republic
☐ N951UW	Embraer ERJ-190AR	19000112	ex PT-SQG		Republic
☐ N952UW	Embraer ERJ-190AR	19000119	ex PT-SQN		Republic
☐ N953UW	Embraer ERJ-190AR	19000133	ex PT-		Republic
☐ N954UW	Embraer ERJ-190AR	19000139	ex PT-SYS		Republic
☐ N955UW	Embraer ERJ-190AR	19000152	ex PT-SAH		Republic
☐ N956UW	Embraer ERJ-190AR	19000156	ex PT-SAM		
☐ N957UW	Embraer ERJ-190AR	19000161	ex PT-SAQ		
☐ N958UW	Embraer ERJ-190AR	19000164	ex PT-SAT		
☐ N9CJ	SAAB SF.340B	340B-224	ex N224TH	LVE	Colgan Air
☐ N203CJ	SAAB SF.340B	340B-203	ex N306CE	LNI	Colgan Air
☐ N249CJ	SAAB SF.340B	340B-249	ex N361PX		Colgan Air
☐ N321CJ	SAAB SF.340B	340B-321	ex XA-TQX	LVH	Colgan Air
☐ N338CJ	SAAB SF.340B	340B-338	ex N338SB	LNG	Colgan Air
☐ N339CJ	SAAB SF.340B	340B-339	ex N339SB	LNA	Colgan Air
☐ N341CJ	SAAB SF.340B	340B-341	ex N341SB	LND	Colgan Air
☐ N344CJ	SAAB SF.340B	340B-344	ex N344SB	LNF	Colgan Air

☐ N346CJ	SAAB SF.340B	340B-346	ex N346SB	LNB	Colgan Air
☐ N347CJ	SAAB SF.340B	340B-347	ex N347SB	LNH	Colgan Air
☐ N350CJ	SAAB SF.340B	340B-350	ex N350CF	LNE	Colgan Air
☐ N362PX	SAAB SF.340B	340B-258	ex SE-G58		ColganAir

US FOREST SERVICE Boise, ID (BOI)

☐ N106Z	Bell 206B JetRanger	508	ex N950NS
☐ N109Z	Bell UH-I (CobraLifter)	20854	ex 69-16422
☐ N111Z	Cessna TU206F Stationair	U20602919	
☐ N115Z	Basler Turbo-67 (DC-3TP)	16819/33567	ex N146Z
☐ N126Z	Cessna TU206F Stationair	U20602367	ex N2399U
☐ N127Z	Beech A100 King Air	B-179	ex N20EG
☐ N136Z	Cessna TU206G Stationair 6	U20606923	ex N9659R
☐ N141Z	de Havilland DHC-6 Twin Otter 300	803	ex C-GDNG
☐ N142Z	Basler Turbo-67 (DC-3TP)	20494	ex N100Z
☐ N143Z	de Havilland DHC-6 Twin Otter 300	437	ex 87-0802
☐ N144Z	Cessna 550 Citation Bravo	550-0926	ex N100Z
☐ N147Z	Aero Commander 500B	1432-152	
☐ N148Z	Beech 65-B90 King Air	LJ-472	ex N104Z
☐ N149Z	Beech B200C Super King Air	BL-124	ex N107Z
☐ N173Z	Short SD.3-30	SH3116	ex 84-0469
☐ N175Z	Short SD.3-30	SH3115	ex 84-0468
☐ N178Z	Short SD.3-30	SH3119	ex 84-0472
☐ N179Z	Short SD.3-30	SH3109	ex 84-0462
☐ N181Z	Beech 65-E90 King Air	LW-52	ex N74171
☐ N182Z	Beech 200 Super King Air	BB-402	ex N318W
☐ N191Z	de Havilland DHC-2 Beaver	1006	
☐ N192Z	de Havilland DHC-2 Beaver	1347	
☐ N193Z	de Havilland DHC-2 Beaver	11627	ex N197Z

US HELICOPTERS Wingate-US Heliport, NC

☐ N36TV	Aérospatiale AS350B AStar	1858	ex N69TL	
☐ N119TV	Aérospatiale AS350B AStar	2122	ex N477HD	♦
☐ N129TV	Aérospatiale AS350BA AStar	2897		
☐ N311TV	Aérospatiale AS350BA AStar	2922		
☐ N355TV	Aérospatiale AS350B AStar	2647	ex TG-JBG	
☐ N357TV	Aérospatiale AS350B AStar	2376	ex N795WC	
☐ N915HD	Aérospatiale AS350B2 AStar	3583	ex N311SJ	
☐ N73DP	Bell 206B JetRanger II	2513		
☐ N79TV	Bell 206L-1 LongRanger III	45718	ex N84PC	
☐ N116TV	Bell 206L-3 LongRanger III	51199	ex N45MH	
☐ N141TV	Bell 206B JetRanger III	4148	ex N748M	
☐ N212TV	Bell 206B JetRanger II	2048	ex N97CW	
☐ N316TV	Bell 206B JetRanger III	2704	ex N188TV	♦

USA 3000 AIRLINES Getaway (U5/GWY) Philadelphia-Intl, PA (PHL)

☐ N260AV	Airbus A320-214	1564	ex D-AXLC	
☐ N261AV	Airbus A320-214	1615	ex F-WWDR	
☐ N262AV	Airbus A320-214	1725	ex F-WWBP	Miss Doreen
☐ N263AV	Airbus A320-214	1860	ex D-AXLB	Chicago
☐ N264AV	Airbus A320-214	1867	ex F-WWIL	Bermuda

USA JET AIRLINES Jet USA (JUS) Detroit-Willow Run, MI (YIP)

☐ N505AJ	AMD Falcon 20C	89	ex N71CP	[YIP]
☐ N822AA	AMD Falcon 20D	195	ex N195MP	
☐ N823AA	AMD Falcon 20D	228	ex OE-GRU	
☐ N826AA	AMD Falcon 20C	67	ex N821AA	
☐ N827AA	AMD Falcon 20E	298	ex OE-GNN	
☐ N192US	Douglas DC-9-15RC	47156/228	ex N9357	VIP
☐ N194US	Douglas DC-9-15RC (ABS 3)	47016/173	ex N9349	[YIP]
☐ N195US	Douglas DC-9-15RC (ABS 3)	47017/186	ex N9352	VIP
☐ N205US	Douglas DC-9-32CF	47690/843	ex N724HB	
☐ N208US	Douglas DC-9-32F (ABS 3)	47220/296	ex N935F	[YIP]
☐ N215US	Douglas DC-9-32 (ABS 3)	47480/607	ex N986US	
☐ N231US	Douglas DC-9-32 (ABS 3)	48114/919	ex XA-TXG	
☐ N327US	Douglas DC-9-33F (ABS 3)	47414/536	ex N940F	
☐ N949NS	McDonnell-Douglas MD-83	53022/1809	ex N949AS	♦
☐ N829AA	LearJet 25B	25B-100	ex N25TK	

VIEQUES AIR LINK		Vieques (V4/VES)			Vieques, PR (VQS)
☐ N663VL	Britten-Norman BN-2B-26 Islander	2110	ex N663J		
☐ N861VL	Britten-Norman BN-2B-26 Islander	2155	ex N861JA		
☐ N902VL	Britten-Norman BN-2A-20 Islander	685	ex N148ES		
☐ N903VL	Britten-Norman BN-2A-26 Islander	2019	ex N2159X		
☐ N904VL	Britten-Norman BN-2A-26 Islander	3014	ex HK-3813	no titles	
☐ N335VL	Cessna 208B Caravan I	208B0964	ex N5260Y		
☐ N741VL	Cessna 208B Caravan I	208B1091	ex N1272N		
☐ N742VL	Cessna 208B Caravan I	208B1100	ex N12727		
☐ N905VL	Britten-Norman BN-2A Mk.III-2 Trislander	1048	ex N905GD		
☐ N906VL	Britten-Norman BN-2A Mk.III-2 Trislander	1060	ex N906GD		

VINTAGE PROPS AND JETS		(VQ)		New Smyrna Beach-Municipal, FL
☐ N211VP	Beech 100 King Air	B-2	ex N11JJ	
☐ N219VP	Beech 1900C	UB-14	ex N188GA	
☐ N431R	Beech 100 King Air	B-71	ex N431CH	
☐ N577D	Beech 100 King Air	B-22	ex N577L	
☐ N5727	Beech 100 King Air	B-48	ex N572	

VIRGIN AMERICA		(VX/VRD)		San Francisco, CA (SFO)	
☐ N521VA	Airbus A319-112	2773	ex D-AVWZ	let there be flight	
☐ N522VA	Airbus A319-112	2811	ex D-AVYP		
☐ N523VA	Airbus A319-112	3181	ex D-AVYB		
☐ N524VA	Airbus A319-112	3204	ex D-AVWK	dark horse	
☐ N525VA	Airbus A319-112	3324	ex D-AVYG		
☐ N526VA	Airbus A319-112	3347	ex D-AVYW		
☐ N527VA	Airbus A319-112	3417	ex D-AVYK	tubular belle	
☐ N528VA	Airbus A319-112	3445	ex D-AVYR	fog cutter	
☐ N529VA	Airbus A319-112	3684	ex D-AVWB	moodlights, camera, action	
☐ N530VA	Airbus A319-112	3686	ex D-AVWD	gogo dancer	
☐ N621VA	Airbus A320-214	2616	ex F-WWDJ	air colbert	
☐ N622VA	Airbus A320-214	2674	ex F-WWID	California Dreaming	
☐ N623VA	Airbus A320-214	2740	ex PR-MHH	three if by air	
☐ N624VA	Airbus A320-214	2778	ex F-WWDX	red, white & blue	
☐ N625VA	Airbus A320-214	2800	ex F-WWIJ	Jefferson Airplane	
☐ N626VA	Airbus A320-214	2830	ex F-WWDO	unicorn chaser	
☐ N627VA	Airbus A320-214	2851	ex F-WWIQ		
☐ N628VA	Airbus A320-214	2993	ex F-WWIT		
☐ N629VA	Airbus A320-214	3037	ex PR-MHL	Midnight Ride	
☐ N630VA	Airbus A320-214	3101	ex F-WWIG	superfly	
☐ N631VA	Airbus A320-214	3135	ex F-WWDL	chic mobile	
☐ N632VA	Airbus A320-214	3155	ex F-WWDH	youtube air	
☐ N633VA	Airbus A320-214	3230	ex F-WWBE	the tim clark express	
☐ N634VA	Airbus A320-214	3359	ex F-WWII	mach daddy	
☐ N635VA	Airbus A320-214	3398	ex F-WWBS	my other ride's a spaceship	
☐ N636VA	Airbus A320-214	3460	ex F-WWBJ		
☐ N637VA	Airbus A320-214	3465	ex F-WWBN	an airplane named desire	
☐ N638VA	Airbus A320-214	3503	ex D-AVVB	san francisco pride	
☐ N639VA	Airbus A320-214	3016	ex 9K-CAE		♦
☐ N640VA	Airbus A320-214	3349	ex 9K-CAF		♦
☐ N641VA	Airbus A320-214	3656	ex 9K-CAG		♦
☐ N642VA	Airbus A320-214	3670	ex 9K-CAH		♦
☐ N835VA	Airbus A320-214	4448	ex D-AVVZ		♦
☐ N836VA	Airbus A320-214	4480	ex D-AUBD		♦
☐ N837VA	Airbus A320-214	4558	ex D-AUBT		♦
☐ N838VA	Airbus A320-214	4559	ex		o/o♦
☐ N839VA	Airbus A320-214	4610	ex		o/o♦
☐ N840VA	Airbus A320-214	4616	ex		o/o♦
☐ N	Airbus A320-214		ex		o/o♦
☐ N	Airbus A320-214		ex		o/o♦

VISION AIRLINES				Las Vegas North, NV (VGT)
☐ N732VA	Boeing 737-3T0	23366/1174	ex N34315	
☐ N742VA	Boeing 737-448	24773/1850	ex TC-MNH	
☐ N743VA	Boeing 737-4B6	25262/2088	ex N252MQ	
☐ N781VA	Boeing 737-8Q8/W	28214/78	ex OY-SEB	
☐ N766VA	Boeing 767-2Q8ER	24448/272	ex EI-DMP	
☐ N767VA	Boeing 767-222ER	21870/13	ex N609UA	
☐ N768VA	Boeing 767-222ER	21869/11	ex N608UA	
☐ N769VA	Boeing 767-222ER	21866/7	ex N605UA	

☐ N801VA	de Havilland DHC-8Q-202	494	ex N352PH	◆
☐ N402VA	Dornier 228-202K	8085	ex G-BWEX	
☐ N403VA	Dornier 228-202K	8171	ex 9M-BAS	
☐ N404VA	Dornier 228-203F	8120	ex N279MC	
☐ N405VA	Dornier 228-203F	8144	ex N264MC	
☐ N409VA	Dornier 228-201	8097	ex N228ME	
☐ N38VP	Dornier 328-310 (328JET)	3174	ex N417FJ	
☐ N328DA	Dornier 328-310 (328JET)	3171	ex N416FJ	[VGT]
☐ N329MX	Dornier 328-100	3049	ex D-CAOS	
☐ N330MX	Dornier 328-100	3067	ex D-CDXN	
☐ N331MX	Dornier 328-100	3074	ex D-CDXA	
☐ N431JS	Dornier 328-110	3028	ex D-CDHN	o/o
☐ N905HB	Dornier 328-310 (328JET)	3178	ex N420FJ	[VGT]
☐ N906HB	Dornier 328-310 (328JET)	3179	ex N421FJ	

WARBELOW'S AIR · Ventaire (4W/WAV) · Fairbanks-Intl, AK (FAI)

☐ N42WP	Piper PA-31-350 Chieftain	31-8252038	ex N41063
☐ N300ED	Piper PA-31-350 Chieftain	31-7852008	ex N27457
☐ N3527U	Piper PA-31-350 Chieftain	31-7952141	
☐ N3582P	Piper PA-31-350 Chieftain	31-8052103	
☐ N4082T	Piper PA-31-350 Chieftain	31-8152089	
☐ N4434D	Piper PA-31-350 Navajo Chieftain	31-7552020	ex PH-ASC
☐ N27755	Piper PA-31-350 Chieftain	31-7852148	
☐ N59764	Piper PA-31-350 Navajo Chieftain	31-7652037	
☐ N59829	Piper PA-31-350 Navajo Chieftain	31-7652081	
☐ N121WV	Beech 1900C-1	UC-78	ex N503RH
☐ N756DJ	Cessna U206G Stationair	U20604005	
☐ N767DM	Piper PA-31-T2 Cheyenne II XL	31T-8166042	ex N500XL
☐ N5200X	Cessna U206G Stationair 6 II	U20605591	
☐ N7380U	Cessna 207A Stationair 7	20700428	

WARD AIR · Juneau-Intl, AK (JNU)

☐ N767RR	Cessna 310Q	310Q0455		
☐ N8295Q	Cessna U206F Stationair II	U20603156		FP
☐ N62353	de Havilland DHC-2 Beaver	1363	ex 58-2031	FP
☐ N62355	de Havilland DHC-2 Beaver	1045	ex N67897	FP
☐ N62357	de Havilland DHC-2 Beaver	1145	ex N64391	FP
☐ N63354	de Havilland DHC-3 Otter	30	ex C-FWAF	FP
☐ N93025	Cessna A185F Skywagon	18503163		FP
☐ N93356	de Havilland DHC-3 Otter	144	ex N62KA	FP

WEST AIR · PAC Valley (PCM) · Fresno-Air Terminal, CA / Chico-Municipal, CA (FAT/CIC)

Operates Cessna Caravans leased from, and operated on behalf of, FedEx

WESTERN AIR EXPRESS · Western Express (WAE) · Boise, ID (BOI)

☐ N167WA	Cessna 402B II	402B1044	ex N98680
☐ N6367X	Cessna 402B II	402B1330	
☐ N7947Q	Cessna 402B	402B0397	
☐ N158WA	Swearingen SA.226TC Metro II	TC-411	ex N5974V
☐ N159WA	Swearingen SA.226TC Metro II	TC-334	ex N341PL
☐ N160WA	Swearingen SA.226TC Metro IIA	TC-399	ex N56EA
☐ N162WA	Swearingen SA.226TC Metro IIA	TC-418	ex C-GRET

WESTERN AIR EXPRESS · Lubbock-Intl, TX (LBB)

☐ N6AQ	Beech 65-A80 Queen Air	LD-214	ex N699WW	Frtr
☐ N20NP	Beech 65-B80 Queen Air	LD-433	ex N3289A	Frtr
☐ N5376M	Beech 65-B80 Queen Air	LD-301	ex CF-HOA	Frtr
☐ N7817L	Beech 65-B80 Queen Air	LD-340		Frtr
☐ N8071R	Beech 65-B80 Queen Air	LD-420		Frtr

WESTERN AVIATORS · Westavia (WTV) · Grand Junction-Walker Field, CO (GJT)

☐ N106RE	Piper PA-31-350 Navajo Chieftain	31-7752056	
☐ N159SW	Piper PA-31-350 Navajo Chieftain	31-7405229	ex N400AA
☐ N494SC	Piper PA-31-350 Navajo Chieftain	31-7752099	ex N27199
☐ N495SC	Piper PA-31-350 Chieftain	31-8052062	ex N3555Y

WESTWIND AVIATION · Phoenix-Deer Valley, AZ (DVT)

☐ N9317M	Cessna T207A Stationair 8 II	20700680

☐ N9482M	Cessna T207A Stationair 8 II	20700698		
☐ N122JB	Cessna 208B Caravan I	208B1025	ex N5090V	
☐ N208WW	Cessna 208B Caravan I	208B0721		
☐ N785WW	Cessna 208B Caravan I	208B0792	ex N5267T	
☐ N786WW	Cessna 208B Caravan I	208B1099	ex N12744	
☐ N1129G	Cessna 208B Caravan I	208B0924	ex N5262X	

WIGGINS AIRWAYS — Wiggins (WIG) — Norwood-Memorial, MA (OWD)

☐ N190WA	Beech C99	U-207	ex N207CS	
☐ N191WA	Beech C99	U-136	ex C-GCPF	
☐ N192WA	Beech C99	U-152	ex C-GEOI	
☐ N193WA	Beech 99	U-17	ex N10MV	
☐ N194WA	Beech 99	U-64	ex C-FAWX	
☐ N195WA	Beech 99	U-38	ex N202BH	
☐ N196WA	Beech C99	U-179	ex N995SB	
☐ N197WA	Beech 99A	U-130	ex C-FOZU	
☐ N198WA	Beech 99A	U-142	ex N133BA	
☐ N199WA	Beech B99	U-154	ex N99CH	
☐ N91RK	Beech A100 King Air	B-226	ex N9126S	

WILLOW AIR — Willow-Lake SPB, AK (WOW)

☐ N98JH	de Havilland DHC-2 Beaver	953	ex 5-3 RNAF	FP

WINGS OF ALASKA — Wings Alaska (K5/WAK) — Juneau-Intl, AK (JNU)

☐ N335AK	de Havilland DHC-3 Turbo Otter	263	ex C-FOMS	FP
☐ N336AK	de Havilland DHC-3 Turbo Otter	333	ex N567KA	FP
☐ N337AK	de Havilland DHC-3 Turbo Otter	418	ex N2783J	FP
☐ N338AK	de Havilland DHC-3 Turbo Otter	262	ex N62355	FP
☐ N339AK	de Havilland DHC-3 Turbo Otter	454	ex N28TH	FP
☐ N753AK	de Havilland DHC-3 Turbo Otter	7	ex N342AK	FP
☐ N39AK	Cessna 207A Stationair 8 II	20700597	ex N73482	FP/WS
☐ N62AK	Cessna 207A Stationair 8 II	20700780	ex N9997M	FP/WS
☐ N72KA	Cessna 208B Caravan I	208B0326	ex N1030N	FP
☐ N92AK	de Havilland DHC-2 Beaver	1031	ex C-GFNR	FP/WS
☐ N96AK	Cessna 207A Stationair 8 II	20700782	ex N1347Q	FP/WS
☐ N331AK	Cessna 208B Caravan I	208B0739	ex N5264S	
☐ N332AK	Cessna 208B Caravan I	208B0779	ex N5264S	FP/WS

WORLD AIRWAYS — World (WO/WOA) — Charleston-Intl, SC (CHS)

☐ N136WA	Douglas DC-10-30	47844/336	ex N237NW		[MZJ]♦
☐ N137WA	Douglas DC-10-30	48282/355	ex N241NW		
☐ N138WA	Douglas DC-10-30	47845/356	ex N242NW		[CEW]
☐ N223NW	Douglas DC-10-30	46580/183	ex HB-IHF		[MZJ]
☐ N224NW	Douglas DC-10-30	46581/184	ex HB-IHG		[MZJ]
☐ N303WL	Douglas DC-10-30F	46917/211	ex N13086	303	[MZJ]
☐ N702TZ	Douglas DC-10-30	46912/188	ex N234NW		[MZJ]
☐ N705TZ	Douglas DC-10-30	46915/199	ex N235NW		
☐ N269WA	McDonnell-Douglas MD-11	48450/479	ex OH-LGB		♦
☐ N270WA	McDonnell-Douglas MD-11	48449/455	ex OH-LGA		
☐ N271WA	McDonnell-Douglas MD-11	48518/525		271	
☐ N272WA	McDonnell-Douglas MD-11	48437/506		272	
☐ N273WA	McDonnell-Douglas MD-11	48519/539		273	
☐ N274WA	McDonnell-Douglas MD-11F	48633/563		274	
☐ N275WA	McDonnell-Douglas MD-11CF	48631/579		275	
☐ N276WA	McDonnell-Douglas MD-11CF	48632/582		276	
☐ N277WA	McDonnell-Douglas MD-11ER	48743/590	ex N6203D	277	
☐ N278WA	McDonnell-Douglas MD-11ER	48746/597	ex N9020Q	278	
☐ N279WA	McDonnell-Douglas MD-11F	48756/623	ex P4-TKA	279	
☐ N380WA	McDonnell-Douglas MD-11F	48407/456	ex HL7371	380	♦
☐ N381WA	McDonnell-Douglas MD-11F	48523/516	ex HL7375	381	
☐ N382WA	McDonnell-Douglas MD-11F	48411/453	ex N703GC		
☐ N383WA	McDonnell-Douglas MD-11F	48412/454	ex N705GC		
☐ N384WA	McDonnell-Douglas MD-11F	48435/478	ex N702GC		
☐ N740WA	Boeing 747-4H6 (BDSF)	25700/974	ex 9V-SPS		
☐ N741WA	Boeing 747-4H6 (BDSF)	25702/999	ex 9V-SPR		>CLX♦
☐ N742WA	Boeing 747-412BCF	27071/1072	ex N270RP		♦
☐ N743WA	Boeing 747-412SF	26562/1074	ex 9V-SPG		♦

WRIGHT AIR SERVICE		Wright Air (8V/WRT)		Fairbanks-Intl, AK (FAI)
☐ N32WA	Cessna 208B Caravan I	208B0234	ex C-FKEL	
☐ N540ME	Cessna 208B Caravan I	208B0540		
☐ N900WA	Cessna 208B Caravan I	208B0659	ex N52613	
☐ N976E	Cessna 208B Caravan I	208B0976	ex N5263D	
☐ N1323R	Cessna 208B Caravan I	208B0745		
☐ N4365U	Cessna 208B Caravan I	208B0253	ex N208CC	
☐ N9FW	Piper PA-31-350 Navajo Chieftain	31-7405468	ex N61441	
☐ N54WA	Piper PA-31-350 Navajo Chieftain	31-7652067	ex N942LU	
☐ N7426L	Piper PA-31 Turbo Navajo B	31-812		
☐ N91027	Cessna 207 Skywagon	20700018		

XTRA AIRWAYS		Casino Express (XP/CXP)		Elko-JC Harris Field, NV (EKO)
☐ N42XA	Boeing 737-429	25729/2217	ex TF-ELP	
☐ N43XA	Boeing 737-4S3	24796/1887	ex TF-ELV	
☐ N188AQ	Boeing 737-322	24670/1909	ex PR-GLM	♦
☐ N279AD	Boeing 737-4Q8	26279/2221	ex SX-BGS	

YUKON AVIATION				Bethel, AK (BET)
☐ N150HH	Bell 206B JetRanger III	701		
☐ N205WA	Bell UH-1H	12261	ex 69-16663	
☐ N1322F	Cessna A185F Skywagon	18502825		
☐ N1653U	Cessna 207 Super Skywagon	20700253		
☐ N4237V	Bell 204 (UH-1B)	261	ex 60-0315	
☐ N7318U	Cessna 207A Skywagon	20700396		
☐ N24165	Beech Baron 58TC	TK-78		
☐ N29970	Cessna A185F Skywagon II	18504292	ex (C-GMTU)	
☐ N91060	Cessna T207 Turbo Skywagon	20700047		

OB- PERU (Republic of Peru)

AERO TRANSPORTE		ATSA (AMP)		Lima-Jorge Chavez Intl (LIM)
☐ OB-1629	Piper PA-42 Cheyenne III	42-8001067	ex N183CC	
☐ OB-1630	Piper PA-42 Cheyenne III	42-8001022	ex N145CA	
☐ OB-1633	Piper PA-42 Cheyenne III	42-7801003	ex N134KM	
☐ OB-1687	Piper PA-42 Cheyenne III	42-8001016	ex N69PC	
☐ OB-1803	Piper PA-42 Cheyenne III	42-7800002	ex N911VJ	
☐ OB-1667-P	Beech 1900C	UB-54	ex N815BE	
☐ OB-1778-P	Antonov An-26B-100	14205	ex OB-1777-T	
☐ OB-1869-T	Antonov An-32B	3305	ex ER-AFM	
☐ OB-1875	Beech 1900D	UE-68	ex N168AZ	

AEROCONDOR		Condor (Q6/CDP)		Lima-Jorge Chavez Intl (LIM)
☐ OB-1192	Cessna U206G Stationair 6	U20605538		
☐ OB-1204	Cessna U206G Stationair 6	U20605800		
☐ OB-1297	Beech 65-B90 King Air	LJ-326	ex N7702	Fray GregorioTaurus conversion
☐ OB-1594	Beech 65-B90 King Air	LJ-322	ex N45SC	Taurus conversion
☐ OB-1616	Cessna U206B Super Skywagon	U206-0878	ex N3878G	
☐ OB-1627	Fokker F.27 Friendship 100	10116	ex YV-929C	
☐ OB-1650-P	Antonov An-24RV	37308802	ex OB-1562	
☐ OB-1693-P	Fokker F.27 Friendship 200	10181	ex N863MA	[LIM]
☐ OB-1740-P	Cessna 208B Caravan I	208B0735	ex N12652	
☐ OB-1741	Cessna 208B Caravan I	208B0670	ex N1132D	
☐ OB-1770-P	Fokker 50	20280	ex PH-LXU	
☐ OB-1793-P	Boeing 737-2H6 (Nordam 3)	20583/303	ex N121GU	
☐ OB-1797-P	Cessna 208B Caravan I	208B1068	ex OB-1797-T	
☐ OB-1815-P	Cessna 208B Caravan I	208B1129	ex N1282M	
☐ OB-1828	Antonov An-26	87307409	ex RA-26647	
☐ OB-1829-P	Fokker 50	20260	ex SE-LLN	

AIR MAJORO				Lima-Jorge Chavez Intl (LIM)
☐ OB-1920-P	Cessna 402C II	402C0442	ex N6790B	
☐ OB-1921-P	Cessna 402C II	402C0419	ex N419RC	

AMAZON SKY				Lima-Jorge Chavez Intl (LIM)
☐ OB-1859-P	Antonov An-26B-100	6209	ex UR-VYV	

425

AVIASUR Iquitos (IQT)

☐ OB-1663	Mil Mi-17 (Mi-8MTV-1)	94704	ex OB-1725
☐ OB-1760	Mil Mi-17 (Mi-8MTV-1)	93823	
☐ OB-1761	Mil Mi-17 (Mi-8MTV-1)	93477	

CIELOS AIRLINES — Cielos (A2/CIU) — Lima-Jorge Chavez Intl (LIM)

☐ N609GC	Douglas DC-10-30F	46932/158	ex G-NIUK	Petete VIII
☐ N614GC	Douglas DC-10-30F	46931/137	ex N832LA	Petete V
☐ OB-1749	Douglas DC-10-30CF	46891/127	ex N105AM	Petete
☐ OB-1812-P	Douglas DC-10-30CF	46975/248	ex N1856U	

HELICOPTEROS MERCOSUR Lima

| ☐ OB-1856-P | Bell 212 | 31225 | ex 9Y-BPT |

HELISUR Iquitos (IQT)

☐ OB-1584	Mil Mi-17 (Mi-8MTV-1)	95432	ex CCCP-70879
☐ OB-1585	Mil Mi-17 (Mi-8MTV-1)	223M103	ex RA-70951
☐ OB-1586	Mil Mi-17 (Mi-8MTV-1)	223M104	
☐ OB-1691	Mil Mi-17 (Mi-8MTV-1)	96153	ex RA-27193
☐ OB-1826	Mil Mi-8MTV-1	93281	

HELITAXI SERVICES

| ☐ OB-1842P | Mil Mi-8T | 9785572 | ex RA-27099 |

LAN PERU — Linea Peru (LP/LPE) — Lima-Jorge Chavez Intl (LIM)

☐ CC-COU	Airbus A319-132	2089	ex D-AVWL	<LAN
☐ CC-COX	Airbus A319-132	2096	ex D-AVYN	<LAN
☐ CC-COY	Airbus A319-132	2295	ex D-AVWA	<LAN
☐ CC-COZ	Airbus A319-132	2304	ex D-AVWN	<LAN
☐ CC-CPE	Airbus A319-132	2321	ex D-AVYO	<LAN
☐ CC-CPF	Airbus A319-132	2572	ex D-AVXC	<LAN
☐ CC-CPI	Airbus A319-132	2585	ex D-AVXH	<LAN
☐ CC-CPM	Airbus A319-132	2864	ex D-AVWC	<LAN
☐ CC-CPO	Airbus A319-132	2872	ex D-AVWJ	<LAN
☐ CC-CPQ	Airbus A319-132	2886	ex D-AVXP	<LAN
☐ CC-CPX	Airbus A319-132	2887	ex D-AVYF	<LAN
☐ CC-CQK	Airbus A319-132	2892	ex D-AVYV	<LAN
☐ CC-CQL	Airbus A319-132	2894	ex D-AVWE	<LAN
☐ CC-CQM	Airbus A320-233	3280	ex F-WWDM	<LAN

LC BUSRE — Busre (LCB) — Lima-Jorge Chavez Intl (LIM)

☐ N139LC	Swearingen SA.227TC Metro III	AC-732	ex XA-ACT	
☐ N239LC	Swearingen SA.227TC Metro III	AC-735	ex N523WA	<Pacific Coast Grp
☐ N386PH	Swearingen SA.227TC Metro III	AC-597	ex N3116T	

PERUVIAN AIRLINES — (PVN)

☐ OB-1954-P	Boeing 737-247 (Nordam 3)	23188/1071	ex HC-CGA	♦
☐ OB-1955	Boeing 737-2T7	22761/850	ex N763SH	♦
☐ OB-1956	Boeing 737-2T7	22762/856	ex N762SH	♦
☐ OB-	Boeing 737-217	21716/560	ex N716SH	
☐ OB-	Boeing 737-33A	23627/1302	ex N166AW	♦

SERVICIOS AEREOS DE LOS ANDES Miraflores, Lima

☐ OB-1864	de Havilland DHC-6 Twin Otter 200	282	ex CC-PCI	
☐ OB-1866	Bell 204B	2197	ex C-GVEL	
☐ OB-1897-P	de Havilland DHC-6 Twin Otter 300	521	ex C-FSXF	
☐ OB-1910-P	Bell 212	30798	ex C-GSLL	
☐ OB-1912-P	Bell 212	30820	ex C-GZMQ	
☐ OB-1913-P	de Havilland DHC-6 Twin Otter 300	391	ex C-GHVV	
☐ OB-	Bell 204B	2044	ex C-GAHN	♦
☐ OB-	Bell 205A-1	30136	ex C-GCZG	♦
☐ OB-	Bell 212	30615	ex C-GAZX	♦

STAR PERU — Star Up (2I/SRU) — Lima-Jorge Chavez Intl (LIM)

☐ OB-1794-P	Boeing 737-2Y5 (Nordam 3)	23039/954	ex HR-ATM	Best of Peru c/s
☐ OB-1800-P	Boeing 737-291 (Nordam 3)	21641/537	ex HR-ATR	Machu Picchu c/s
☐ OB-1823-P	Boeing 737-2T2 (Nordam 3)	22793/892	ex LY-BSG	Lord of Sipan c/s
☐ OB-1839-P	Boeing 737-204	22640/867	ex N640AD	
☐ OB-1841-P	Boeing 737-204	22058/629	ex N58AD	

☐ OB-1851-P	Boeing 737-230 (Nordam 3)	22133/772	ex N133AD	

☐ OB-1051-P	Cessna 208B Caravan I			
☐ OB-1717	Antonov An-24RV	27308010	ex ER-AFU	Anna
☐ OB-1734-P	Antonov An-24RV	17307006	ex ER-AFC	
☐ OB-1769	Antonov An-24RV	57310110	ex ER-AWX	Leonid
☐ OB-1772-P	Antonov An-26B-100	10704	ex UR-26216	
☐ OB-1877-P	British Aerospace 146 Srs.100	E1199	ex A5-RGE	
☐ OB-1879-P	British Aerospace 146 Srs.100	E1095	ex A5-RGD	
☐ OB-1885-P	British Aerospace 146 Srs.200	E2087	ex N292UE	
☐ OB-1914-P	British Aerospace 146 Srs.300	E3181	ex G-JEBE	
☐ OB-1923-P	British Aerospace 146 Srs.300	E3185	ex G-JEBB	
☐ OB-1930-P	British Aerospace 146 Srs.200	E2201	ex D-AJET	♦
☐ OB-1943-P	British Aerospace 146 Srs.200	E2133	ex C-GRNV	♦
☐ OB-1948-P	British Aerospace 146 Srs.200	E2156	ex N156TR	♦

TACA PERU		*Trans Peru (T0/TPU)*	*Lima-Jorge Chavez Intl (LIM)*

☐ N471TA	Airbus A319-132	1066	ex D-AVWE	<TAI
☐ N472TA	Airbus A319-132	1113	ex D-AVWU	<TAI

TRANSPORTES AEREOS CIELOS ANDINOS	*(NDN)*		*Lima-Jorge Chavez Intl (LIM)*

☐ OB-1651	Antonov An-24RV	27308303	ex OB-1571	
☐ OB-1859-P	Antonov An-26			
☐ OB-1876-T	Antonov An-26B-100	17311506	ex EX-063	
☐ OB-1887-P	Antonov An-26-100	87306606	ex UR-VIG	
☐ OB-1893-P	Antonov An-26-100	8401		

OD-   LEBANON (Republic of Lebanon)

BERYTOS AIRWAYS	*(BYR)*	*Beirut (BEY)*

Operates charter flights with Airbus A320 and Douglas DC-9-51 aircraft wet leased from UM Air as required

CIRRUS MIDDLE EAST	*Beirut (BEY)*

☐ OD-NOR	Boeing 737-247 (Nordam 3)	22754/870	ex N247US	

FLYING CARPET AIR TRANSPORT SERVICES	*Flying Carpet (7Y/FCR)*	*Beirut (BEY)*

☐ OD-AMB	Boeing 737-2H4 (AvAero 3)	23109/1016	ex N103SW	
☐ OD-MAB	Swearingen SA.227AC Metro III	AC-604	ex C-FNAL	

MIDDLE EAST AIRLINES		*Cedar Jet (ME/MEA)*	*Beirut (BEY)*

☐ F-OMRN	Airbus A320-232	4339	ex D-AXAR	♦
☐ F-OMRO	Airbus A320-232	4296	ex D-AXAI	♦
☐ OD-MRR	Airbus A320-232	3837	ex F-WWBJ	
☐ OD-MRS	Airbus A320-232	3804	ex F-WWDJ	
☐ OD-MRT	Airbus A320-232	3736	ex F-ORMK	
☐	Airbus A320-232		ex	o/o♦
☐ F-ORME	Airbus A321-231	1878	ex D-AVZA	
☐ F-ORMF	Airbus A321-231	1953	ex D-AVXF	
☐ F-ORMG	Airbus A321-231	1956	ex D-AVZE	
☐ F-ORMH	Airbus A321-231	1967	ex D-AVZI	
☐ F-ORMI	Airbus A321-231	1977	ex D-AVZU	
☐ F-ORMJ	Airbus A321-231	2055	ex D-AVZE	
☐ F-ORMA	Airbus A330-243	926	ex F-WWKD	
☐ OD-MEA	Airbus A330-243	984	ex F-WWKE	
☐ OD-MEB	Airbus A330-243	998	ex F-WWYT	
☐ OD-MEC	Airbus A330-243	995	ex F-WWKQ	

TMA	*(TMA)*	*Beirut (BEY)*

☐ OD-TMA	Airbus A300F4-622RF	872	ex N140MN	♦

WINGS OF LEBANON AVIATION	*Wings Lebanon (WLB)*	*Beirut (BEY)*

☐ OD-HAJ	Boeing 737-3Q8	26313/2704	ex G-THOE	
☐ OD-WOL	Boeing 737-232 (AvAero 3)	23083/1008	ex N311DL	>THE

427

OE- AUSTRIA (Republic of Austria)

AIR ALPS AVIATION — Alpav (A6/LPV) — Innsbruck (INN)

☐ OE-LKA	Dornier 328-110	3110	ex D-COXI	Igls-Innsbruck
☐ OE-LKB	Dornier 328-110	3036	ex HB-AEH	Sudtirol colours
☐ OE-LKC	Dornier 328-110	3119	ex D-CDXK	Regio Bodensee
☐ OE-LKD	Dornier 328-110	3072	ex HS-PBB	Riviera di Rimini

AMERER AIR — Amer Air (AMK) — Linz (LNZ)

☐ OE-ILW	Fokker F.27 Friendship 500	10681	ex N505AW	Sissy	Frtr

AUSTRIAN AIRLINES — Austrian (OS/AUA) — Vienna-Schwechat (VIE)

Member of Star Alliance

☐ OE-LDA	Airbus A319-112	2131	ex D-AVWS	Sofia	
☐ OE-LDB	Airbus A319-112	2174	ex D-AVYP	Bucharest	
☐ OE-LDC	Airbus A319-112	2262	ex D-AVWE	Kiev	
☐ OE-LDD	Airbus A319-112	2416	ex D-AVWN	Moscow	
☐ OE-LDE	Airbus A319-112	2494	ex D-AVYL	Baku	
☐ OE-LDF	Airbus A319-112	2547	ex D-AVYA	Sarajevo	
☐ OE-LDG	Airbus A319-112	2652	ex D-AVYF	Tbilisi	
☐ OE-LBN	Airbus A320-214	0768	ex F-WWDH		
☐ OE-LBO	Airbus A320-214	0776	ex F-WWDM	Pyhrn-Eisenwürzen	
☐ OE-LBP	Airbus A320-214	0797	ex F-WWDV	Neusiedlersee	Retro c/s
☐ OE-LBQ	Airbus A320-214	1137	ex F-WWDF	Ray Charles	
☐ OE-LBR	Airbus A320-214	1150	ex F-WWBP	Frida Kahlo	
☐ OE-LBS	Airbus A320-214	1189	ex F-WWDV	Waldviertel	
☐ OE-LBT	Airbus A320-214	1387	ex F-WWIS	Wörthersee	
☐ OE-LBU	Airbus A320-214	1478	ex F-WWDS	Mühlvierter	
☐ OE-LBA	Airbus A321-111	0552	ex D-AVZH	Salzkammergut	
☐ OE-LBB	Airbus A321-111	0570	ex D-AVZQ	Pinzgau	
☐ OE-LBC	Airbus A321-111	0581	ex D-AVZS	Südtirol	
☐ OE-LBD	Airbus A321-211	0920	ex D-AVZN	Steirisches Weinland	
☐ OE-LBE	Airbus A321-211	0935	ex D-AVZR	Wachau	
☐ OE-LBF	Airbus A321-211	1458	ex D-AVXE	Wien	
☐ OE-LNJ	Boeing 737-8Z9/W	28177/69		Wildspitze	
☐ OE-LNK	Boeing 737-8Z9/W	28178/222		Freddie Mercury	
☐ OE-LNL	Boeing 737-6Z9	30137/526	ex N743NV	Kahlenberg	
☐ OE-LNM	Boeing 737-6Z9	30138/546	ex N1795B	Albert Einstein	
☐ OE-LNN	Boeing 737-7Z9/W	30418/815		Maria Callas	
☐ OE-LNO	Boeing 737-7Z9/W	30419/874		Greta Garbo	
☐ OE-LNP	Boeing 737-8Z9/W	30420/1100		Grossglockner	
☐ OE-LNQ	Boeing 737-8Z9/W	30421/1345		Grossvenediger	
☐ OE-LNR	Boeing 737-8Z9/W	33833/1680		Piz Buin	
☐ OE-LNS	Boeing 737-8Z9/W	34262/1720		Geshriebenstein	
☐ OE-LNT	Boeing 737-8Z9/W	33834/1938		Gerlitzen	
☐ OE-LAE	Boeing 767-3Z9ER/W	30383/812		Wiener Sangerknaben	
☐ OE-LAT	Boeing 767-31AER	25273/393	ex PH-MCK	Thailand	
☐ OE-LAW	Boeing 767-3Z9ER	26417/448		China	
☐ OE-LAX	Boeing 767-3Z9ER/W	27095/467		Salzburger Festspiele	
☐ OE-LAY	Boeing 767-3Z9ER/W	29867/731	ex D-ABUV	Japan	
☐ OE-LAZ	Boeing 767-3Z9ER/W	30331/759	ex D-ABUW	India	
☐ OE-LPA	Boeing 777-2Z9ER	28698/87	ex N5022E	Melbourne	
☐ OE-LPB	Boeing 777-2Z9ER	28699/163		Sydney	
☐ OE-LPC	Boeing 777-2Z9ER	29313/386		Don Bradman	
☐ OE-LPD	Boeing 777-2Z9ER	35960/607		America	

AUSTRIAN ARROWS — Vienna-Schwechat (VIE)

☐ OE-LCJ	Canadair CRJ-200LR	7142	ex B-3017	Stadt Hannover
☐ OE-LCN	Canadair CRJ-200LR	7365	ex C-FMOI	Stadt Bremen
☐ OE-LCR	Canadair CRJ-200LR	7910	ex C-FMMW	Stadt Baden
☐ OE-LGA	de Havilland DHC-8-402Q	4014	ex C-GDNG	Kärnten
☐ OE-LGB	de Havilland DHC-8-402Q	4015	ex C-GDOE	Tirol
☐ OE-LGC	de Havilland DHC-8-402Q	4026	ex C-GEVP	Salzburg
☐ OE-LGD	de Havilland DHC-8-402Q	4027	ex C-GEWI	Land Steiermark
☐ OE-LGE	de Havilland DHC-8-402Q	4042	ex C-FNGB	Land Oberösterreich
☐ OE-LGF	de Havilland DHC-8-402Q	4068	ex C-GERC	Land Niederösterreich

☐ OE-LGG	de Havilland DHC-8-402Q	4074	ex C-GFCF	Stadt Budapest	
☐ OE-LGH	de Havilland DHC-8-402Q	4075	ex C-GFCW	Vorarlberg	
☐ OE-LGI	de Havilland DHC-8-402Q	4100	ex C-FAQR	Eisenstadt	
☐ OE-LGJ	de Havilland DHC-8-402Q	4104	ex C-FCQH	St Pölten	
☐ OE-LGK	de Havilland DHC-8-402Q	4280	ex C-FYMK	Burgenland	
☐ OE-LGL	de Havilland DHC-8-402Q	4310	ex C-GCQB	Altenrhein	♦
☐ OE-LGM	de Havilland DHC-8-402Q	4319	ex C-GEII	Villach	♦
☐ OE-LGN	de Havilland DHC-8-402Q	4326	ex C-GEZY	Gmunden	♦
☐ OE-LTG	de Havilland DHC-8Q-314	438	ex C-GDFT	Hall in Tirol	
☐ OE-LTH	de Havilland DHC-8Q-314	442	ex C-GFUM	Stadt Kitzbühel	
☐ OE-LTM	de Havilland DHC-8Q-314	527	ex C-FDHW	Achensee	
☐ OE-LTN	de Havilland DHC-8Q-314	531	ex C-GDNK	St Anton am Arlberg	[LNZ]♦
☐ OE-LTO	de Havilland DHC-8Q-314	553	ex C-FWBB	Kufstein	
☐ OE-LTP	de Havilland DHC-8Q-314	554	ex C-GDLK	Lienz	[LNZ]♦
☐ OE-LFG	Fokker 70	11549	ex PH-EZW	Innsbruck	
☐ OE-LFH	Fokker 70	11554	ex PH-EZN	Stadt Salzburg	
☐ OE-LFI	Fokker 70	11529	ex PH-WXF	Stadt Klagenfurt	
☐ OE-LFJ	Fokker 70	11532	ex PH-WXG	Stadt Graz	
☐ OE-LFK	Fokker 70	11555	ex PH-EZP	Krems	
☐ OE-LFL	Fokker 70	11573	ex PH-WXE	Stadt Linz	
☐ OE-LFP	Fokker 70	11560	ex PH-EZW	Wels	
☐ OE-LFQ	Fokker 70	11568	ex PH-EZC	Dornbirn	
☐ OE-LFR	Fokker 70	11572	ex PH-EZD	Steyr	
☐ OE-LVA	Fokker 100	11490	ex PH-ZFB	Riga	
☐ OE-LVB	Fokker 100	11502	ex PH-ZFE	Vilnius	
☐ OE-LVC	Fokker 100	11446	ex PH-ZFF	Tirana	
☐ OE-LVD	Fokker 100	11515	ex PH-ZFG	Skopje	
☐ OE-LVE	Fokker 100	11499	ex PH-ZFH	Zagreb	
☐ OE-LVF	Fokker 100	11483	ex PH-ZFI	Yerevan	
☐ OE-LVG	Fokker 100	11520	ex PH-ZFJ	Krakow Star Alliance c/s	
☐ OE-LVH	Fokker 100	11456	ex PH-ZFK	Minsk	
☐ OE-LVI	Fokker 100	11468	ex PH-ZFL	Prague	
☐ OE-LVJ	Fokker 100	11359	ex PH-ZFM	Bratislava	
☐ OE-LVK	Fokker 100	11397	ex PH-ZFQ	Burgenland	
☐ OE-LVL	Fokker 100	11404	ex PH-ZFR	Odessa	
☐ OE-LVM	Fokker 100	11361	ex PH-ZFN	Krasnodar	
☐ OE-LVN	Fokker 100	11367	ex PH-ZFO	Dniepropetrovsk	
☐ OE-LVO	Fokker 100	11460	ex PH-ZFS	Chisinau	

FLYING BULLS   Salzburg (SZG)

☐ OE-EDM	Cessna 208 Caravan I	20800257	ex N666CS	Amphibian
☐ N996DM	Douglas DC-6B	45563/1034	ex V5-NCF	Red Bull
☐ N6123C	North American B-25J Mitchell	108-47647	ex 44-86893A	

Operate some pleasure flights as well as airshow appearances

GROSSMANN AIR TRANSPORT   Grossman (HTG)   Vienna-Schwechat (VIE)

☐ OE-HTG	Dornier 328-300 (Envoy 3)	3162	ex D-BDXG

INTERSKY   Intersky (3L/ISK)   Freidrichschafen-Lowental (FDH)

☐ OE-LIA	de Havilland DHC-8Q-311	505	ex D-BHAT	
☐ OE-LIC	de Havilland DHC-8Q-314	503	ex D-BHAS	
☐ OE-LIE	de Havilland DHC-8Q-315	546	ex HB-JEJ	
☐ OE-LSB	de Havilland DHC-8Q-314	525	ex C-FDHY	Espace Mittelland

LAUDA AIR   Lauda Air (NG/LDA)   Vienna-Schwechat (VIE)

Operates leisure services for Austrian Airlines using OS/AUA designators as 'Lauda Air-the Austrian way to holidays'. Leases aircraft as required from Austrian. Member of Star Alliance.

MAPJET   MapJet (MPJ)   Vienna-Schwechat (VIE)

☐ OE-IKB	McDonnell-Douglas MD-83	49448/1313	ex N990PG	
☐ OE-LOG	McDonnell-Douglas MD-83	49359/1349	ex HB-INV	
☐ OE-LRW	McDonnell-Douglas MD-83	49629/1583	ex EC-HBP	all-white
☐ OE-LMP	Airbus A310-322	410	ex N410AN	[BRU]

NIKI   FlyNiki (HG/NLY)   Vienna-Schwecat (VIE)

☐ OE-LED	Airbus A319-112	3407	ex D-AVYC	
☐ OE-LEK	Airbus A319-112	3019	ex D-AVXM	Tango
☐ OE-LEA	Airbus A320-214	2529	ex F-WWID	Rock'n Roll

☐ OE-LEB	Airbus A320-214	4231	ex D-AXAA	Polka	♦
☐ OE-LEC	Airbus A320-214	4316	ex D-AXAL		♦
☐ OE-LEE	Airbus A320-214	2749	ex F-WWDB		
☐ OE-LEF	Airbus A320-214	4368	ex D-AXAY		♦
☐ OE-LEO	Airbus A320-214	2668	ex F-WWBP	Soul	
☐ OE-LEU	Airbus A320-214	2902	ex F-WWDH		
☐ OE-LEX	Airbus A320-214	2867	ex F-WWBC	Jazz	
☐ OE-	Airbus A320-214		ex		o/o♦
☐ OE-	Airbus A320-214		ex		o/o♦
☐ OE-	Airbus A320-214		ex		o/o♦
☐ OE-	Airbus A320-214		ex		o/o♦
☐ OE-	Airbus A320-214		ex		o/o♦
☐ OE-	Airbus A320-214		ex		o/o♦
☐ OE-	Airbus A320-214		ex		o/o♦
☐ OE-LES	Airbus A321-211	3504	ex D-AVZI	Boogie Woogie	
☐ OE-LET	Airbus A321-211	3830	ex D-AVZG	Heavy Metal	
☐ OE-	Airbus A321-211		ex		o/o♦
☐ OE-	Airbus A321-211		ex		o/o♦
☐ OE-IHA	Embraer ERJ-190LR	19000285	ex PT-TLZ		
☐ OE-IHB	Embraer ERJ-190LR	19000294	ex PT-TZI		
☐ OE-IHC	Embraer ERJ-190LR	19000349	ex PT-XQP		♦
☐ OE-IHD	Embraer ERJ-190LR	19000354	ex PT-XQT		♦
☐ OE-	Embraer ERJ-190LR		ex PT-		o/o♦
☐ OE-	Embraer ERJ-190LR		ex PT-		o/o♦

ROBIN HOOD AVIATION — (RH/RHA) — Graz (GRZ)

☐ OE-GIR	SAAB SF.340A	340A-134	ex SE-F34	Graz-Zurich titles
☐ OE-GOD	SAAB SF.340A	340A-153	ex ZK-NLO	

TYROLEAN AIRWAYS — Tyrolean (VO/TYR) — Innsbruck (INN)

Wholly owned by Austrian Airlines. Operates scheduled services as 'Austrian Arrows, operated by Tyrolean' using OS/ AUA designators in 5000 range and in full Austrian colours.

TYROLEAN JET SERVICE — Tyroljet (TJS) — Innsbruck (INN)

☐ OE-HMS	Dornier 328-300 (328JET)	3121	ex D-BDXI
☐ OE-HTJ	Dornier 328-300 (328JET)	3114	ex D-BDXA

WELCOME AIR — Welcomeair (2W/WLC) — Innsbruck (INN)

☐ OE-GBB	Dornier 328-110	3078	ex D-CDXG	Rotterdam
☐ OE-LIR	Dornier 328-110	3115	ex D-CDXG	Phönix
☐ OE-LJR	Dornier 328-310 (328JET)	3213	ex D-BDX.	Aurora

OH-   FINLAND (Republic of Finland)

AIR ALAND — Mariehamn (MHQ)

☐ LY-RIK	SAAB SF.340A	340A-112	ex SE-F12

AIR FINLAND — Air Finland (OF/FIF) — Helsinki-Vantaa (HEL)

☐ OH-AFI	Boeing 757-2K2/W	26330/717	ex PH-TKD
☐ OH-AFJ	Boeing 757-28A	26269/612	ex N321LF
☐ OH-AFK	Boeing 757-28A	25622/530	ex N364LF

BLUE1 — Bluefin (KF/BLF) — Helsinki-Vantaa (HEL)

Member of Star Alliance

☐ OH-SAJ	Avro 146-RJ85	E2388	ex G-6-388	Pyhaselka	
☐ OH-SAK	Avro 146-RJ85	E2389	ex G-6-389	Nasijarvi	
☐ OH-SAL	Avro 146-RJ85	E2392	ex G-6-390	Orivesi	
☐ OH-SAO	Avro 146-RJ85	E2393	ex G-CBMG	Oulujärvi	
☐ OH-SAP	Avro 146-RJ85	E2394	ex G-CBMH	Pielinen	
☐ OH-BLG	Boeing 717-23S	55059/5023	ex SE-REN	Blue Flow	♦
☐ OH-BLH	Boeing 717-23S	55060/5026	ex SE-REO	Summer Spring	♦
☐ OH-BLI	Boeing 717-23S	55061/5029	ex SE-REP	Sky Trickle	♦
☐ OH-BLJ	Boeing 717-23S	55065/5048	ex SE-REL		♦
☐ OH-BLM	Boeing 717-23S	55056/5054	ex SE-REM	Spring Rain	♦
☐ OH-BLP	Boeing 717-23S	55064/5037	ex EC-KNE		♦

430

COPTERLINE		*Copterline (AAQ)*		*Helsinki-Malmi (HEM)*
☐ OH-HCH	Eurocopter EC135P1	0008	ex D-HPOZ	
☐ OH-HCK	Eurocopter EC135P2	0378		
☐ OH-HCL	Eurocopter EC135P2	0379		
☐ OH-HCM	Eurocopter EC135P2	0414		
☐ OH-HCN	Eurocopter EC135P2	0415		
☐ OH-HCO	Eurocopter EC135P2	0418	ex D-HECT	
☐ OH-HCP	Eurocopter EC135P2	0419		
☐ OH-HCD	MBB Bo.105CBS-4	S-547	ex AB-7	
☐ OH-HKI	MBB Bo.105CBS-4	S-731	ex D-HECB	

FINNAIR		*Finnair (AY/FIN)*		*Helsinki-Vantaa (HEL)*

Member of Oneworld

☐ OH-LVA	Airbus A319-112	1073	ex F-WWID	
☐ OH-LVB	Airbus A319-112	1107	ex D-AVWS	
☐ OH-LVC	Airbus A319-112	1309	ex D-AVWY	
☐ OH-LVD	Airbus A319-112	1352	ex D-AVYW	
☐ OH-LVE	Airbus A319-112	1791	ex D-AVYS	Retro c/s
☐ OH-LVF	Airbus A319-112	1808	ex D-AVWG	
☐ OH-LVG	Airbus A319-112	1916	ex D-AVYG	
☐ OH-LVH	Airbus A319-112	1184	ex EI-CZE	
☐ OH-LVI	Airbus A319-112	1364	ex F-WQQZ	
☐ OH-LVK	Airbus A319-112	2124	ex D-AVWB	
☐ OH-LVL	Airbus A319-112	2266	ex D-AVWS	
☐ OH-LXA	Airbus A320-214	1405	ex F-WWDH	
☐ OH-LXB	Airbus A320-214	1470	ex F-WWDO	
☐ OH-LXC	Airbus A320-214	1544	ex F-WWIX	
☐ OH-LXD	Airbus A320-214	1588	ex F-WWBQ	
☐ OH-LXE	Airbus A320-214	1678	ex F-WWIF	
☐ OH-LXF	Airbus A320-214	1712	ex F-WWIY	
☐ OH-LXG	Airbus A320-214	1735	ex F-WWBM	
☐ OH-LXH	Airbus A320-214	1913	ex F-WWIZ	
☐ OH-LXI	Airbus A320-214	1989	ex F-WWDN	
☐ OH-LXK	Airbus A320-214	2065	ex F-WWIQ	
☐ OH-LXL	Airbus A320-214	2146	ex F-WWDN	
☐ OH-LXM	Airbus A320-214	2154	ex F-WWDP	
☐ OH-LZA	Airbus A321-211	0941	ex D-AVZT	
☐ OH-LZB	Airbus A321-211	0961	ex D-AVZU	
☐ OH-LZC	Airbus A321-211	1185	ex D-AVZI	
☐ OH-LZD	Airbus A321-211	1241	ex D-AVZG	
☐ OH-LZE	Airbus A321-211	1978	ex D-AVZV	
☐ OH-LZF	Airbus A321-211	2208	ex D-AVZI	
☐ OH-LTM	Airbus A330-302E	994	ex F-WWKO	
☐ OH-LTN	Airbus A330-302E	1007	ex F-WWYC	
☐ OH-LTO	Airbus A330-302E	1013	ex F-WW	
☐ OH-LTP	Airbus A330-302E	1023	ex F-WW	
☐ OH-LTR	Airbus A330-302E	1067	ex F-WWKY	
☐ OH-LTS	Airbus A330-302E	1078	ex F-WWYU	♦
☐ OH-LTT	Airbus A330-302E	1088	ex F-WWKH	♦
☐ OH-LTU	Airbus A330-302E	1173	ex F-WWYN	♦
☐ OH-LQA	Airbus A340-311	058	ex G-VFLY	
☐ OH-LQB	Airbus A340-313E	835	ex F-WWJG	
☐ OH-LQC	Airbus A340-313E	844	ex F-WWJI	
☐ OH-LQD	Airbus A340-313E	921	ex F-WWJK	
☐ OH-LQE	Airbus A340-313E	938	ex F-WWJL	
☐ OH-LQF	Airbus A340-313X	168	ex F-GNIF	<AFR♦
☐ OH-LBO	Boeing 757-2Q8/W	28172/772	ex N1789B	
☐ OH-LBR	Boeing 757-2Q8/W	28167/775		
☐ OH-LBS	Boeing 757-2Q8/W	27623/792	ex N5573K	
☐ OH-LBT	Boeing 757-2Q8/W	28170/801		
☐ OH-LEE	Embraer ERJ-170STD	17000093	ex PT-SZT	
☐ OH-LEF	Embraer ERJ-170STD	17000106	ex PT-SAO	
☐ OH-LEG	Embraer ERJ-170STD	17000107	ex PT-SAP	
☐ OH-LEH	Embraer ERJ-170STD	17000112	ex PT-SAX	
☐ OH-LEI	Embraer ERJ-170STD	17000120	ex PT-SDI	
☐ OH-LEK	Embraer ERJ-170STD	17000127	ex PT-SDQ	
☐ OH-LEL	Embraer ERJ-170STD	17000139	ex PT-SED	

☐ OH-LEO	Embraer ERJ-170STD	17000150	ex PT-SEO	
☐ OH-LKE	Embraer ERJ-190LR	19000059	ex PT-SEW	
☐ OH-LKF	Embraer ERJ-190LR	19000066	ex PT-SJE	
☐ OH-LKG	Embraer ERJ-190LR	19000079	ex PT-SJV	
☐ OH-LKH	Embraer ERJ-190LR	19000086	ex PT-SNE	
☐ OH-LKI	Embraer ERJ-190LR	19000117	ex PT-SQL	
☐ OH-LKK	Embraer ERJ-190LR	19000127	ex PT-SQW	
☐ OH-LKL	Embraer ERJ-190LR	19000153	ex PT-SAI	
☐ OH-LKM	Embraer ERJ-190LR	19000160	ex PT-SAP	
☐ OH-LKN	Embraer ERJ-190LR	19000252	ex PT-SIX	
☐ OH-LKO	Embraer ERJ-190LR	19000267	ex PT-	
☐ OH-	Embraer ERJ-190LR		ex PT-	o/o♦
☐ OH-	Embraer ERJ-190LR		ex PT-	o/o♦
☐ OH-LGC	McDonnell-Douglas MD-11F	48512/529	ex N512SU	
☐ N513AY	McDonnell-Douglas MD-11BCF	48513/564	ex OH-LGD	parked for cargo conversion [QPG]♦

FINNCOMM AIRLINES — Westbird (FC/WBA) — Helsinki-Vantaa (HEL)

☐ OH-ATA	ATR 42-500	641	ex F-WWLV	
☐ OH-ATB	ATR 42-500	643	ex F-WWLA	
☐ OH-ATC	ATR 42-500	651	ex F-WWLI	
☐ OH-ATD	ATR 42-500	655	ex F-WWLM	
☐ OH-ATE	ATR 72-212A	741	ex F-WWEB	
☐ OH-ATF	ATR 72-212A	744	ex F-WWEE	
☐ OH-ATG	ATR 72-212A	757	ex F-WWER	
☐ OH-ATH	ATR 72-212A	769	ex F-WWEH	
☐ OH-ATI	ATR 72-212A	783	ex F-WWEB	
☐ OH-ATJ	ATR 72-212A	792	ex F-WWEM	
☐ OH-ATK	ATR 72-212A	848	ex F-WWEN	
☐ OH-ATL	ATR 72-212A	851	ex F-WWEU	
☐ OH-	ATR 72-212A		ex	o/o♦
☐ OH-	ATR 72-212A		ex	o/o♦
☐ OH-	ATR 72-212A		ex	o/o♦
☐ OH-	ATR 72-212A		ex	o/o♦

SCANWINGS — Skywings (ABF) — Helsinki-Vantaa (HEL)

☐ OH-BAX	Beech 65-C90 King Air	LJ-948	ex N4495U	
☐ OH-BEX	Beech 65-C90 King Air	LJ-978	ex N725KR	

TURKU AIR — Turku (TKU)

☐ OH-KYC	Piper PA-31-350 Chieftain	31-8052186	ex SE-KYC	
☐ OH-PNU	Piper PA-31-350 Navajo Chieftain	31-7752027	ex N62993	
☐ OH-PNX	Piper PA-31-350 Chieftain	31-8052040	ex ES-PAG	
☐ OH-PNY	Piper PA-31-350 Navajo Chieftain	31-7652079	ex LN-SAB	

UTIN LENTO — Utti

☐ OH-SIS	Cessna 208 Caravan I	20800105	ex LN-PBD	
☐ OH-USI	Cessna 208 Caravan I	20800275	ex N52639	

OK- CZECH REPUBLIC

CENTRAL CONNECT AIRLINES — (3B/CCG) — Ostrava (OSR)

☐ OK-CCC	SAAB SF.340B	340B-208	ex YR-VGM	
☐ OK-CCD	SAAB SF.340B	340A-161	ex SE-KXH	
☐ OK-CCE	SAAB SF.340A	340A-108	ex N108CQ	Frtr; Op for UPS
☐ OK-CCF	SAAB SF.340A	340A-101	ex N101CN	Frtr; Op for UPS
☐ OK-CCG	SAAB SF.340A	340A-104	ex N104CQ	Frtr; Op for UPS
☐ OK-CCK	SAAB SF.340A	340A-078	ex SE-LSR	
☐ OK-CCL	SAAB SF.340A	340A-159	ex LY-NSD	Frtr
☐ OK-CCN	SAAB SF.340B	340B-230	ex SE-KTE	
☐ OK-CCO	SAAB SF.340B	340B-188	ex XA-TJI	

CSA CZECH AIRLINES — CSA Lines (OK/CSA) — Prague-Ruzyne (PRG)

Member of Skyteam

☐ OK-MEK	Airbus A319-112	3043	ex D-AVWL	
☐ OK-MEL	Airbus A319-112	3094	ex D-AVWN	
☐ OK-NEM	Airbus A319-112	3406	ex D-AVYB	
☐ OK-NEN	Airbus A319-112	3436	ex D-AVYJ	

432

☐ OK-NEO	Airbus A319-112	3452	ex D-AVYY		
☐ OK-NEP	Airbus A319-112	3660	ex D-AVYT		
☐ OK-OER	Airbus A319-112	3892	ex D-AVWK		
☐ OK-PET	Airbus A319-112	4258	ex D-AVWM		♦
☐ OK-	Airbus A319-112		ex		o/o♦
☐ OK-	Airbus A319-112		ex		o/o♦
☐ OK-	Airbus A319-112		ex		o/o♦
☐ OK-	Airbus A319-112		ex		o/o♦
☐ OK-GEA	Airbus A320-214	1439	ex CS-TQA	Roznov pod Radhostem	
☐ OK-GEB	Airbus A320-214	1450	ex CS-TQB	Strakonice	
☐ OK-LEE	Airbus A320-214	2719	ex F-WWDC		
☐ OK-LEF	Airbus A320-214	2758	ex F-WWDP		
☐ OK-LEG	Airbus A320-214	2789	ex F-WWBX		
☐ OK-MEH	Airbus A320-214	3031	ex F-WWBU		
☐ OK-MEI	Airbus A320-214	3060	ex F-WWDY		
☐ OK-MEJ	Airbus A320-214	3097	ex F-WWID		
☐ OK-CEC	Airbus A321-211	0674	ex C-GKOH	Nove mesto nad Metuji	
☐ OK-CED	Airbus A321-211	0684	ex C-GKOJ	Havlickuv Brod	
☐ OK-JFJ	ATR 42-500	623	ex F-WWLD	Namest nad Oslavou	
☐ OK-JFK	ATR 42-500	625	ex F-WWLF	Slavkov u Brna	
☐ OK-JFL	ATR 42-500	629	ex F-WWLJ	Susice	
☐ OK-KFM	ATR 42-500	635	ex F-WWLP	Benesov	
☐ OK-KFN	ATR 42-500	637	ex F-WWLR	Prerov	
☐ OK-KFO	ATR 42-500	633	ex F-WWLN	Sokolov	
☐ OK-KFP	ATR 42-500	639	ex F-WWLT	Svitavy	
☐ OK-VFI	ATR 42-320	173	ex F-WQNE	Nebesky jezdec/Sky Rider	
☐ OK-XFA	ATR 72-202	285	ex F-WWLO	Cesky Krumlov	
☐ OK-XFB	ATR 72-202	297	ex F-WWLW	Znojmo	
☐ OK-XFC	ATR 72-202	299	ex F-WWLX	Nitra	
☐ OK-XFD	ATR 72-202	303	ex F-WWLB	Mlada Boleslav	
☐ OK-CGK	Boeing 737-55S	28471/2885		Pardubice	
☐ OK-DGL	Boeing 737-55S	28472/3004		Tabor	
☐ OK-EGO	Boeing 737-55S	28475/3096		Jindrichuv Hradec	
☐ OK-WGX	Boeing 737-436	25349/2156	ex G-DOCD	Unicov	
☐ OK-WGY	Boeing 737-436	25839/2188	ex G-DOCI	Roudnice nad Labem	
☐ OK-XGA	Boeing 737-55S	26539/2300	ex (OO-SYL)	Plzen	
☐ OK-XGB	Boeing 737-55S	26540/2317	ex (OO-SYM)	Olomouc	
☐ OK-XGC	Boeing 737-55S	26541/2319	ex (OO-SYN)	Ceske Budejovice	
☐ OK-XGD	Boeing 737-55S	26542/2337	ex (OO-SYO)	Poprad	
☐ OK-XGE	Boeing 737-55S	26543/2339	ex (OO-SYP)	Kosice	

CZECH CHARTER AIRLINES

| ☐ OK-CCA | Boeing 737-31S | 29058/2946 | ex G-THOH | | o/o♦ |

LR AIRLINES — *Lady Racine (LRB)* — *Ostrava (OSR)*

| ☐ OK-LRA | LET L-410UVP-E | 892216 | ex CCCP-67605 | Lady Racine |

SILVER AIR — *Solid (SLD)* — *Prague-Ruzyne (PRG)*

☐ OK-SLD	LET L-410UVP-E9	022634	Ceska Posta titles	
☐ OK-WDC	LET L-410UVP-E	912531		
☐ OK-WDT	LET L-410UVP-E	912615	ex CCCP-67684	DHL c/s

SKYDIVE & AIR SERVICE — *Pribram-Dlouha Lhota*

| ☐ OK-ASA | LET L-410UVP-E | 902439 | ex RA-67646 |
| ☐ OK-SAS | LET L-410UVP | 831040 | ex RA-67412 |

SMARTWINGS — *Skytravel (QS/TVS)* — *Prague-Ruzyne (PRG)*

| ☐ OK-SWU | Boeing 737-522 | 26703/2498 | ex N955UA |
| ☐ OK-SWV | Boeing 737-522 | 26696/2440 | ex N951UA |

TIME AIR

| ☐ OK-GTJ | Beech 300 Super King Air | FA-223 | ex D-IHHB | |
| ☐ OK-SUR | Cessna 421C Golden Eagle III | 421C0861 | ex D-IOAA | Op for Pony Express |

TRAVEL SERVICE AIRLINES — *Skytravel (QS/TVS)* — *Prague-Ruzyne (PRG)*

| ☐ OK-TVB | Boeing 737-8CX/W | 32362/1125 | | |
| ☐ OK-TVD | Boeing 737-86N | 28595/285 | ex CN-RNO | Prague Airport |

☐ OK-TVF	Boeing 737-8FH/W	29669/1692		
☐ OK-TVG	Boeing 737-8Q8/W	30719/2257		
☐ OK-TVH	Boeing 737-8Q8/W	35275/2604		>SMR♦
☐ OK-TVJ	Boeing 737-8Q8/W	29351/1471	ex C-FTAH	
☐ OK-TVK	Boeing 737-86N/W	32740/1444	ex N977RY	
☐ OK-TVL	Boeing 737-8FN/W	37076/3147		
☐ OK-TVM	Boeing 737-8FN/W	37077/3163		
☐ OK-TVN	Boeing 737-8BK/W	29643/2303	ex G-CEJO	♦
☐ OK-TVO	Boeing 737-8CX/W	32360/1084	ex PR-GOK	♦
☐ OK-TVP	Boeing 737-8K5/W	32907/1117	ex D-AHLR	♦
☐ OK-	Boeing 737-8			o/o♦
☐ OK-	Boeing 737-8			o/o♦

VAN AIR EUROPE		**(6Z/VAA)**		**Brno-Turany**
☐ OK-RDA	LET L-410UVP-E9	861813	ex HA-YFG	Op for Manx2
☐ OK-TCA	LET L-410UVP-E	902431	ex SP-KPZ	Op for Manx2
☐ OK-UBA	LET L-410UVP-E19	892319	ex SP-TXA	Op for Manx2

OM-   SLOVAKIA (Slovak Republic)

AIREXPLORE

☐ OM-AEX	Boeing 737-4Y0	25178/2199	ex D-AEFL	♦

AIR SLOVAKIA	**Slovakia (GM/SVK)**	**Bratislava-MR Stefanik (BTS)**

Ceased operations 25/May/2010

CENTRAL CHARTER AIRLINES SLOVAKIA		**Bratislava-MR Stefanik (BTS)**

☐ OM-CCA	Boeing 737-36M	28333/2810	ex OE-IAK	♦

DANUBE WINGS	**(V5)**	**Bratislava-MR Stefanik (BTS)**

☐ OM-VRA	ATR 72-201	373	ex F-WAGR
☐ OM-VRB	ATR 72-202	367	ex EI-REG
☐ OM-VRC	ATR 72-202	307	ex F-WKVB

DUBNICA AIR		**Slavnica**

☐ OM-ODQ	LET L-410UVP	841320	ex OK-ODQ
☐ OM-PGA	LET L-410UVP-T	820909	ex OM-DAA
☐ OM-SAB	LET L-410MA	750405	ex 0405 Slovak AF

SEAGLE AIR	**Seagle (CGL)**	**Trencin**

Ceased operations 23/Feb/2010

SLOVAK GOVERNMENT FLYING SERVICE	**Slovak Government (SSG)**	**Bratislava-MR Stefanik (BTS)**

☐ OM-BYE	Yakovlev Yak-40	9440338	ex OK-BYE	VIP
☐ OM-BYL	Yakovlev Yak-40	9940560	ex OK-BYL	VIP
☐ OM-BYO	Tupolev Tu-154M	89A803	ex OK-BYO	
☐ OM-BYR	Tupolev Tu-154M	98A1012		VIP

TRAVEL SERVICE SLOVAKIA

☐ OM-TVA	Boeing 737-86N/W	32243/869	ex OK-TVA	♦

OO-   BELGIUM (Kingdom of Belgium)

AIR SERVICE LIEGE		**Liege (LGG)**

☐ OO-ASL	Beech B200C Super King Air	BL-49	ex OK-LFB	
☐ OO-GMJ	Beech B300 Super King Air	FL-460	ex D-CGMJ	
☐ OO-LET	Beech B200 Super King Air	BB-1473	ex N8210X	
☐ OO-PHB	Beech 1900D	UE-106	ex N106UE	Mr Blue Sky

AIRVENTURE	**Venture Liner (RVE)**	**Antwerp-Deurne (ANR)**

☐ OO-SXC	Embraer EMB.121A Xingu	121042	ex PT-MBJ	MS

BRUSSELS AIRLINES		*Estail (TV/DAT)*		**Brussels-National (BRU)**

Member of Star Alliance

☐ OO-SSC	Airbus A319-112	1086	ex F-OHJX	◆
☐ OO-SSD	Airbus A319-112	1102	ex EI-DEY	◆
☐ OO-SSG	Airbus A319-112	1160	ex EI-CZF	
☐ OO-SSK	Airbus A319-112	1336	ex F-WQRU	
☐ OO-SSM	Airbus A319-112	1388	ex F-WQRV	
☐ OO-SSP	Airbus A319-113	0644	ex F-GPMG	
☐ OO-SSR	Airbus A319-112	4275	ex N275MX	◆
☐ OO-SNA	Airbus A320-214	1441	ex D-ALTC	o/o◆
☐ OO-SFM	Airbus A330-301	030	ex F-GMDA	
☐ OO-SFN	Airbus A330-301	037	ex F-GMDB	
☐ OO-SFO	Airbus A330-301	045	ex F-GMDC	
☐ OO-SFV	Airbus A330-322	095	ex 9M-MKR	◆
☐ OO-SFW	Airbus A330-322	082	ex EI-DVB	
☐ OO-DJK	Avro 146-RJ85	E2271	ex G-6-271	
☐ OO-DJL	Avro 146-RJ85	E2273	ex G-6-273	
☐ OO-DJN	Avro 146-RJ85	E2275	ex G-6-275	
☐ OO-DJO	Avro 146-RJ85	E2279	ex G-6-279	
☐ OO-DJP	Avro 146-RJ85	E2287	ex G-6-287	
☐ OO-DJQ	Avro 146-RJ85	E2289	ex G-6-289	
☐ OO-DJR	Avro 146-RJ85	E2290	ex G-6-290	
☐ OO-DJS	Avro 146-RJ85	E2292	ex G-6-292	
☐ OO-DJT	Avro 146-RJ85	E2294	ex G-6-294	
☐ OO-DJV	Avro 146-RJ85	E2295	ex G-6-295	
☐ OO-DJW	Avro 146-RJ85	E2296	ex G-6-296	
☐ OO-DJX	Avro 146-RJ85	E2297	ex G-6-297	
☐ OO-DJY	Avro 146-RJ85	E2302	ex G-6-302	
☐ OO-DJZ	Avro 146-RJ85	E2305	ex G-6-305	
☐ OO-DWA	Avro 146-RJ100	E3308	ex G-BXEU	
☐ OO-DWB	Avro 146-RJ100	E3315	ex G-6-315	
☐ OO-DWC	Avro 146-RJ100	E3322	ex G-6-322	
☐ OO-DWD	Avro 146-RJ100	E3324	ex G-6-324	
☐ OO-DWE	Avro 146-RJ100	E3327	ex G-6-327	
☐ OO-DWF	Avro 146-RJ100	E3332	ex G-6-332	
☐ OO-DWG	Avro 146-RJ100	E3336	ex G-6-336	
☐ OO-DWH	Avro 146-RJ100	E3340	ex G-6-340	
☐ OO-DWI	Avro 146-RJ100	E3342	ex G-6-342	
☐ OO-DWJ	Avro 146-RJ100	E3355	ex G-6-355	
☐ OO-DWK	Avro 146-RJ100	E3360	ex G-6-360	
☐ OO-DWL	Avro 146-RJ100	E3361	ex G-6-361	
☐ OO-LTM	Boeing 737-3M8	25070/2037	ex F-GMTM	
☐ OO-VEG	Boeing 737-36N/W	28568/2987	ex EI-TVQ	
☐ OO-VEH	Boeing 737-36N/W	28571/3022	ex EI-TVR	
☐ OO-VEK	Boeing 737-405	24270/1726	ex LN-BRA	
☐ OO-VEN	Boeing 737-36N	28586/3090	ex EI-TVN	
☐ OO-VEP	Boeing 737-43Q	28489/2827	ex VH-VGA	
☐ OO-VES	Boeing 737-43Q	28493/2838	ex VH-VGE	
☐ OO-VET	Boeing 737-4Q8	28202/3009	ex VT-SJB	
☐ OO-VEX	Boeing 737-36N/W	28670/2948	ex EI-TVS	
☐ OO-DJE	British Aerospace 146 Srs.200	E2164	ex G-6-164	[BRU]
☐ OO-DJJ	British Aerospace 146 Srs.200	E2196	ex SE-DRM	[BRU]
☐ OO-MJE	British Aerospace 146 Srs.200	E2192	ex G-6-192	[BRU]

JETAIRFLY		*Beauty (TB/JAF)*		**Brussels-National (BRU)**

☐ OO-JAA	Boeing 737-8BK/W	29660/2355	ex N811SY		◆
☐ OO-JAF	Boeing 737-8K5	35133/2313	ex N1780B	Smile	
☐ OO-JAN	Boeing 737-76N/W	28609/417	ex VT-JNT	Revelation	
☐ OO-JAO	Boeing 737-7K5/W	35141/2603	ex D-AHXI	Playing to Win	◆
☐ OO-JAQ	Boeing 737-8K5/W	35148/2790	ex N1786B	Vision	
☐ OO-JAR	Boeing 737-7K5/W	35150/2825		Enjoy	
☐ OO-JAS	Boeing 737-7K5/W	35144/2652	ex D-AHXK		
☐ OO-JAT	Boeing 737-5K5	24927/1968	ex D-AHLF		
☐ OO-JAX	Boeing 737-8K5/W	37238/3452	ex N1787B	Brightness	◆
☐ OO-JBG	Boeing 737-8K5/W	35142/2660		Gerard Brackx	
☐ OO-TUA	Boeing 737-4K5	24127/1707	ex D-AHLL	Passion	
☐ OO-VAC	Boeing 737-8BK/W	33014/1367	ex N334CT	Rising Sun	
☐ OO-JAP	Boeing 767-38EER	30840/829	ex N308MT	Crystal	
☐ OO-TUC	Boeing 767-341ER	24844/324	ex N484TC	Discover	

435

NOORDZEE HELIKOPTERS VLAANDEREN — Ostend /Antwerp-Deurne/Kortrijk-Wevelgem (OST/ANR/KJK)

☐ OO-NHE	Aérospatiale AS365N3 Dauphin 2	6843			
☐ OO-NHG	Aérospatiale AS365N3 Dauphin 2	6881			
☐ OO-NHH	Aérospatiale AS365N3 Dauphin 2	6891			
☐ OO-NHK	Aérospatiale AS365N3 Dauphin 2	6876			
☐ OO-NHM	Aérospatiale SA365N Dauphin 3	6740	ex C-FYRC		♦
☐ OO-NHU	Aérospatiale AS365SR Dauphin	6665	ex F-WWOS	Flipper 2	
☐ OO-NHX	Aérospatiale AS365N3 Dauphin 2	6706	ex OY-HMO		
☐ OO-NHY	Aérospatiale AS365N3 Dauphin 2	6754			
☐ OO-NHZ	Aérospatiale AS365N2 Dauphin 2	6450	ex N4H	Flipper 3	EMS
☐ OO-ECB	Eurocopter EC120B Colibri	1096	ex F-WQDK		
☐ OO-EMS	MD Helicopters MD900 Explorer	900-00020	ex SE-JCG		EMS
☐ OO-NHB	Eurocopter EC145B	9083	ex D-HMBG		EMS
☐ OO-NHF	MD Helicopters MD900 Explorer	900-00015	ex N9015P		EMS

SKY SERVICE — Sky Service (SKS) — Kortrijk-Wevelgem (KJK)

☐ OO-LAC	Beech 200C Super King Air	BL-16	ex F-GLTX	
☐ OO-SKL	Beech B200 Super King Air	BB-1348	ex D2-EST	
☐ OO-SKM	Beech B200 Super King Air	BB-1407	ex D2-ESQ	
☐ OO-VHV	Beech 65-E90 King Air	LW-316	ex N77WZ	

THOMAS COOK AIRLINES BELGIUM — Thomas Cook (FQ/TCW) — Brussels-National (BRU)

☐ OO-TCH	Airbus A320-214	1929	ex D-AICM	Experience	
☐ OO-TCI	Airbus A320-214	1975	ex EI-DBD	Mega Mindy	
☐ OO-TCJ	Airbus A320-214	1787	ex EI-DBC	inspire	
☐ OO-TCN	Airbus A320-232	0425	ex SX-BVA		
☐ OO-TCO	Airbus A320-214	1306	ex G-OOAP	sensation	
☐ OO-TCP	Airbus A320-214	0653	ex F-GRSD		
☐ OO-TCR	Airbus A320-214	0453	ex OE-IAE		♦

TNT AIRWAYS — Quality (3V/TAY) — Liege (LGG)

☐ EC-HQT	Airbus A300B4-203F	124	ex G-TNTS		[MHV]
☐ OO-TZB	Airbus A300B4-203F	261	ex N229KW		
☐ TF-ELF	Airbus A300B4-622RF	529	ex EI-DJN		<ABD
☐ OO-TNA	Boeing 737-3T0 (SF)	23569/1258	ex N13331		
☐ OO-TNB	Boeing 737-3T0 (SF)	23578/1358	ex N39340		
☐ OO-TNC	Boeing 737-301 (SF)	23513/1327	ex N559AU		
☐ OO-TNE	Boeing 737-3Q8 (SF)	23535/1301	ex TF-ELQ		
☐ OO-TNF	Boeing 737-3Q8 (QC)	24131/1541	ex N241MT		
☐ OO-TNG	Boeing 737-3Y0 (QC)	24255/1625	ex N255CF		
☐ OO-TNH	Boeing 737-301 (SF)	23930/1539	ex N585US		
☐ OO-TNJ	Boeing 737-301 (SF)	23260/1146	ex N325AW		
☐ OO-TNK	Boeing 737-301 (SF)	23258/1126	ex N326AW		
☐ OO-TNL	Boeing 737-34S (SF)	29109/3001	ex N132MN		♦
☐ OO-THA	Boeing 747-4HAERF	35232/1381		Peter Abeles 1924-1999	
☐ OO-THB	Boeing 747-4HAERF	35234/1386		Ken Thomas 1913-1997	
☐ OO-THC	Boeing 747-4HAERF	35235/1389	ex N50217		op for UAE
☐ OO-THD	Boeing 747-4HAERF	35236/1399			op for UAE
☐ OO-TSA	Boeing 777-FHT	38969			o/o♦
☐ OO-	Boeing 777-FHT				o/o♦
☐ OO-	Boeing 777-FHT				o/o♦
☐ OO-TAA	British Aerospace 146 Srs.300QT	E3151	ex G-TNTR		
☐ OO-TAD	British Aerospace 146 Srs.300QT	E3166	ex G-TNTM		
☐ OO-TAE	British Aerospace 146 Srs.300QT	E3182	ex G-TNTG		
☐ OO-TAF	British Aerospace 146 Srs.300QT	E3186	ex G-TNTK		
☐ OO-TAH	British Aerospace 146 Srs.300QT	E3168	ex G-TNTL		
☐ OO-TAJ	British Aerospace 146 Srs.300QT	E3153	ex G-TNTE		
☐ OO-TAK	British Aerospace 146 Srs.300QT	E3150	ex G-TJPM		
☐ OO-TAQ	British Aerospace 146 Srs.200QT	E2078	ex G-BNPJ		♦
☐ OO-TAR	British Aerospace 146 Srs.200QT	E2067	ex G-TNTB		
☐ OO-TAS	British Aerospace 146 Srs.300QT	E3154	ex EC-FFY		
☐ OO-TAU	British Aerospace 146 Srs.200QT	E2100	ex EC-GQP		
☐ OO-TAW	British Aerospace 146 Srs.200QT	E2089	ex EC-EPA		
☐ OO-TAY	British Aerospace 146 Srs.200 (QC)	E2211	ex F-GOMA		
☐ OO-TAZ	British Aerospace 146 Srs.200 (QC)	E2188	ex F-GLNI		

436

VLM AIRLINES — Rubens (VG/VLM) — Antwerp-Deurne (ANR)

	Reg	Type	MSN	ex	Name
☐	OO-VLE	Fokker 50	20132	ex PH-ARG	City of Southampton
☐	OO-VLF	Fokker 50	20208	ex PH-DMT	Panamarenko
☐	OO-VLI	Fokker 50	20226	ex PH-JXC	
☐	OO-VLJ	Fokker 50	20105	ex PH-ARE	Isle of Man
☐	OO-VLL	Fokker 50	20144	ex TF-JMG	City of Groningen
☐	OO-VLM	Fokker 50	20135	ex PH-VLM	Ville de Nantes
☐	OO-VLN	Fokker 50	20145	ex PH-VLN	City of Reenstar
☐	OO-VLO	Fokker 50	20127	ex ES-AFL	Angela Dirkin
☐	OO-VLP	Fokker 50	20209	ex PH-DMS	
☐	OO-VLQ	Fokker 50	20159	ex EC-GBH	City of Manchester
☐	OO-VLR	Fokker 50	20121	ex PH-ARF	City of Brussels
☐	OO-VLS	Fokker 50	20109	ex EC-GBG	City of Hamburg
☐	OO-VLT	Fokker 50	20237	ex PH-JXM	City of Eindhoven
☐	OO-VLV	Fokker 50	20160	ex EC-GDD	Island of Jersey
☐	OO-VLX	Fokker 50	20177	ex PH-ZFD	City of Luxembourg
☐	OO-VLY	Fokker 50	20181	ex PH-ZFC	City of Liverpool
☐	OO-VLZ	Fokker 50	20264	ex TF-JMU	City of Rotterdam

OY-   DENMARK (Kingdom of Denmark)

AIR ALPHA GREENLAND — Air Alpha (GD/AHA) — NuUK Godthaab (GOH)

	Reg	Type	MSN	ex	Name
☐	OY-HIC	Bell 222U	47522	ex PT-HXC	

AIR GREENLAND — Greenlandair (GL/GRL) — NuUK Godthaab (GOH)

	Reg	Type	MSN	ex	Name
☐	OY-HGA	Aérospatiale AS350B2 Ecureuil	2600		
☐	OY-HGK	Aérospatiale AS350B2 Ecureuil	2570	ex C-FNJW	
☐	OY-HGO	Aérospatiale AS350B3 Ecureuil	3919		
☐	OY-HGP	Aérospatiale AS350B3 Ecureuil	4062		
☐	OY-HGS	Aérospatiale AS350B3 Ecureuil	4226		
☐	OY-HIZ	Aérospatiale AS350B3 Ecureuil	3727	ex LN-ODM	
☐	OY-HCY	Bell 212	31166		Piseeq 2
☐	OY-HDM	Bell 212	31142	ex N57545	
☐	OY-HDN	Bell 212	31136	ex N5752K	Miteq
☐	OY-HMD	Bell 212	31125	ex LN-ORI	
☐	OY-HIA	Bell 222UT	47529	ex TC-HCS	
☐	OY-HID	Bell 222U	47548	ex D-HCAN	
☐	OY-HIE	Bell 222U	47501	ex D-HUKM	
☐	OY-HIF	Bell 222UT	47512	ex N256SP	
☐	OY-POF	de Havilland DHC-6 Twin Otter 300	235	ex N6868	
☐	OY-CBT	de Havilland DHC-7-103	10	ex C-GRQB-X	Papikkaaq
☐	OY-CBU	de Havilland DHC-7-103	20		Nipiki
☐	OY-CTC	de Havilland DHC-7-102	101	ex G-BNDC	Minniki
☐	OY-GRD	de Havilland DHC-7-103	9	ex A6-ALM	Sapangaq
☐	OY-GRE	de Havilland DHC-7-103	106	ex N54026	Taateraaq
☐	OY-GRF	de Havilland DHC-7-102	113	ex OE-LLU	Sululik
☐	OY-GRG	de Havilland DHC-8Q-202	504	ex C-FXBO	♦
☐	OY-GRH	de Havilland DHC-8Q-202	488	ex C-GCTX	♦
☐	OY-GRL	Boeing 757-236	25620/449	ex TF-GRL	Kunuunnguaq
☐	OY-GRN	Airbus A330-223	230	ex F-WIHL	Norsaq
☐	OY-HAF	Sikorsky S-61N	61267	ex N10045	Nattoralik
☐	OY-HAG	Sikorsky S-61N	61268	ex N10046	Kussak
☐	OY-PCL	Beech 200 Super King Air	BB-1675	ex N2355Z	

ATLANTIC AIRWAYS — Faroeline (RC/FLI) — Vagar (FAE)

	Reg	Type	MSN	ex
☐	OY-HMB	Bell 212	30686	ex LN-OSR
☐	OY-HSJ	Bell 412	36069	ex N412SX
☐	OY-HSR	Bell 412EP	36133	ex N62734
☐	OY-RCC	Avro 146-RJ100	E3357	ex HB-IYX
☐	OY-RCD	Avro 146-RJ85	E2235	ex HB-IXK
☐	OY-RCE	Avro 146-RJ85	E2233	ex HB-IXH

BEL AIR — Holsted

	Reg	Type	MSN
☐	OY-HJL	Agusta AW139	31245

BENAIR AIR SERVICE — Birdie (BDI) — Stauning (STA)

☐ OY-ARJ	Cessna 414	414-0614	ex D-IAWM	
☐ OY-BJP	Swearingen SA.227AC Metro III	AC-499	ex F-GHVG	
☐ OY-HDD	Bell 206B JetRanger III	3649	ex N130S	
☐ OY-MUG	Short SD.3-60	SH3716	ex G-BNDM	all-white
☐ OY-PBH	LET L-410UVP-E20	972736	ex OK-EDA	
☐ OY-PBI	LET L-410UVP-E20	871936	ex OK-SDM	
☐ OY-PBV	Short SD.3-60	SH3747	ex G-GPBV	
☐ OY-PBW	Short SD.3-60	SH3760	ex VH-SEG	

CHC DENMARK — Helibird (HBI) — Esbjerg (EBJ)

☐ OY-HDT	Aérospatiale AS.332L	2017	ex G-BWHN	<CHC Helicopters Intl
☐ OY-HKA	Sikorsky S-92A	920046	ex N8052Z	
☐ OY-HKB	Sikorsky S-92A	920058	ex N4502X	
☐ OY-HKC	Sikorsky S-92A	920060	ex N4503U	

CIMBER AIR — Cimber (QI/CIM) — Sonderborg (SGD)

☐ OY-CIJ	ATR 42-500	497	ex F-WWLR	
☐ OY-CIK	ATR 42-500	501	ex F-WWEE	>OMA
☐ OY-CIL	ATR 42-500	514	ex F-WWLO	
☐ OY-CIM	ATR 72-212A	468	ex EC-JCR	♦
☐ OY-CIN	ATR 72-212A	568	ex F-WWEH	
☐ OY-CIO	ATR 72-212A	595	ex EC-JCF	>MAU
☐ OY-RTC	ATR 72-202	508	ex F-WQNK	
☐ OY-RTD	ATR 72-211	509	ex F-OHFQ	
☐ OY-RTF	ATR 72-202	496	ex F-WQNL	
☐ OY-RTH	ATR 42-500	549	ex D-BLLL	<EWG
☐ OY-MBI	Canadair CRJ-200LR	7436	ex G-MSKT	
☐ OY-MBT	Canadair CRJ-200LR	7617	ex C-GKDI	
☐ OY-RJA	Canadair CRJ-200LR	7413	ex D-ACIM	
☐ OY-RJB	Canadair CRJ-200LR	7419	ex D-ACIN	
☐ OY-RJC	Canadair CRJ-200LR	7015	ex D-ACLF	
☐ OY-RJD	Canadair CRJ-200LR	7007	ex D-ACLH	
☐ OY-RJE	Canadair CRJ-200LR	7009	ex C-FMUQ	
☐ OY-RJF	Canadair CRJ-200LR	7019	ex C-FMUR	
☐ OY-RJG	Canadair CRJ-200LR	7104	ex D-ACLU	
☐ OY-RJH	Canadair CRJ-200LR	7090	ex D-ACLS	
☐ OY-RJI	Canadair CRJ-200LR	7093	ex D-ACLT	
☐ OY-RJJ	Canadair CRJ-200ER	7784	ex HA-LNC	

CIMBER STERLING

☐ OY-MRE	Boeing 737-7L9/W	28008/203		
☐ OY-MRF	Boeing 737-7L9/W	28009/221		
☐ OY-MRG	Boeing 737-7L9/W	28010/396		
☐ OY-MRH	Boeing 737-7L9/W	28013/682		
☐ OY-MRS	Boeing 737-76N/W	32737/1130	ex G-STRH	
☐ OY-MRU	Boeing 737-73S/W	29079/194		

COPENHAGEN AIRTAXI — Aircat (CAT) — Copenhagen-Roskilde (RKE)

☐ OY-CAC	Partenavia P.68B	179		
☐ OY-CAT	Britten-Norman BN-2B-26 Islander	2224	ex EC-FFZ	
☐ OY-CDC	Partenavia P.68C	211	ex D-GEMD	

DANCOPTER — Holsted Heliport & Esbjerg (-/EBJ)

☐ OY-HJA	Eurocopter EC155B1	6828	
☐ OY-HJP	Eurocopter EC155B1	6655	ex F-WWOI
☐ OY-HSK	Eurocopter EC155B1	6660	ex N155EW
☐ OY-HSL	Eurocopter EC155B1	6658	

DANISH AIR TRANSPORT — Danish (DX/DTR) — Kolding-Vamdrup

☐ LY-RUM	ATR 42-300	010	ex OY-RUM	>DNU
☐ OY-CIR	ATR 42-310	107	ex F-GHPX	
☐ OY-CIU	ATR 42-310	112	ex C-FIQB	
☐ OY-JRJ	ATR 42-320	036	ex F-WQIS	based BSG
☐ OY-JRY	ATR 42-300	063	ex F-WQOC	
☐ OY-RUB	ATR 72-202	301	ex F-WQNS	
☐ OY-RUD	ATR 72-201	162	ex LY-ATR	
☐ OY-JRU	McDonnell-Douglas MD-87	49403/1404	ex SE-RBA	
☐ OY-RUE	McDonnell-Douglas MD-83	49936/1778	ex YR-HBZ	

JETTIME		*Jettime (JTG)*		*Copenhagen-Kastrup (CPH)*
☐ OY-JTA	Boeing 737-33A	23631/1337	ex N371FA	
☐ OY-JTB	Boeing 737-3Y0	24464/1753	ex RP-C4010	
☐ OY-JTC	Boeing 737-3L9/W	23718/1402	ex 9M-AAB	
☐ OY-JTD	Boeing 737-3Y0/W	24678/1853	ex 9M-AAY	
☐ OY-JTE	Boeing 737-3L9	27834/2692	ex G-OGBE	
☐ OY-JTF	Boeing 737-382QC	24364/1657	ex OK-GCG	◆

NORTH FLYING		*North Flying (M3/NFA)*		*Aalborg (AAL)*
☐ OY-DLY	Piper PA-31 Turbo Navajo	31-229	ex G-AWOW	
☐ OY-FRE	Piper PA-31 Turbo Navajo	31-632	ex G-AXYA	
☐ OY-NPB	Swearingen SA.227AC Metro III	AC-420	ex N67TC	>Air Norway
☐ OY-NPD	Swearingen SA.227DC Metro 23	DC-865B	ex 9M-BCH	
☐ OY-NPE	Swearingen SA.227DC Metro 23	DC-867B	ex N23VJ	
☐ OY-NPF	Swearingen SA.227DC Metro 23	DC-880B	ex TF-JME	

PRIMERA AIR SCANDINAVIA		*(PF)*		
☐ OY-PSA	Boeing 737-8Q8/W	30688/2280	ex TF-JXD	
☐ OY-PSB	Boeing 737-8Q8/W	30722/2261	ex TF-JXE	
☐ OY-PSC	Boeing 737-86N/W	33419/1251	ex TF-JXF	
☐ OY-PSD	Boeing 737-86N/W	28618/514	ex TF-JXH	
☐ OY-PSE	Boeing 737-8Q8/W	30664/743	ex TF-JXI	
☐ OY-PSF	Boeing 737-7Q8/W	28210/22	ex TF-JXG	

SCANDINAVIAN AIRLINE SYSTEM	*Scandinavian (SK/SAS)*	*Copenhagen-Kastrup (CPH)*

For details see under Sweden (SE-)

STAR AIR		*Whitestar (S6/SRR)*		*Copenhagen-Kastrup (CPH)*
☐ OY-SRF	Boeing 767-219ER (SF)	23327/134	ex N327MR	
☐ OY-SRG	Boeing 767-219ER (SF)	23328/149	ex N328MT	
☐ OY-SRH	Boeing 767-204ER (SF)	24457/256	ex N457GE	
☐ OY-SRI	Boeing 767-25E (SF)	27193/527	ex N622EV	
☐ OY-SRJ	Boeing 767-25E (SF)	27195/535	ex N625EV	
☐ OY-SRK	Boeing 767-204ER (SF)	23072/107	ex N307MT	
☐ OY-SRL	Boeing 767-232 (SF)	22219/37	ex N107DL	
☐ OY-SRM	Boeing 767-25E (SF)	27192/524	ex N621EV	
☐ OY-SRN	Boeing 767-219ER (SF)	23326/124	ex N326MR	
☐ OY-SRO	Boeing 767-25E (SF)	27194/532	ex N623EV	
☐ OY-SRP	Boeing 767-232 (SF)	22220/38	ex N108DL	

STENBERG AVIATION				*Thisted (TED)*
☐ OY-ASY	Embraer EMB.110P1 Bandeirante	110308	ex EI-BPI	flying.dk titles	Op by Flyvsmart
☐ OY-BHT	Embraer EMB.110P2 Bandeirante	110161	ex N4942S	flying dk titles	Op by Flyvsmart

SUN-AIR OF SCANDINAVIA		*Sunscan (EZ/SUS)*		*Billund (BLL)*
☐ OY-NCA	Dornier 328-110	3047	ex N433JS	
☐ OY-NCC	Dornier 328-110	3083	ex D-CIAC	all-white
☐ OY-NCD	Dornier 328-120	3104	ex D-CIAA	
☐ OY-NCG	Dornier 328-110	3055	ex N437JS	
☐ OY-NCK	Dornier 328-110	3061	ex N460PS	
☐ OY-NCL	Dornier 328-300 (328JET)	3192	ex N427FJ	
☐ OY-NCM	Dornier 328-310 (328JET)	3190	ex N426FJ	
☐ OY-NCN	Dornier 328-310 (328JET)	3193	ex N428FJ	
☐ OY-NCO	Dornier 328-310 (328JET)	3210	ex OE-HAB	
☐ OY-NCP	Dornier 328-310 (328JET)	3132	ex N328AC	◆
☐ OY-NCS	Dornier 328-110	3070	ex N459PS	
☐ OY-SVB	British Aerospace Jetstream 31	985	ex JA8591	
☐ OY-SVF	British Aerospace Jetstream 31	686	ex G-BSFG	Skien

THOMAS COOK SCANDINAVIA		*(DK/VKG)*		*Copenhagen-Kastrup (CPH)*
☐ OY-VKA	Airbus A321-211	1881	ex D-AVZO	
☐ OY-VKB	Airbus A321-211	1921	ex D-AVZQ	
☐ OY-VKC	Airbus A321-211	1932	ex D-AVXB	
☐ OY-VKD	Airbus A321-211	1960	ex G-EFPA	<MYT
☐ OY-VKE	Airbus A321-211	1887	ex G-CTLA	<MYT
☐ OY-VKM	Airbus A320-214	1889	ex F-WWBV	
☐ OY-VKS	Airbus A320-214	1954	ex G-YLBM	
☐ OY-VKT	Airbus A321-211	1972	ex G-SMTJ	

□ OY-VKF	Airbus A330-243	309	ex G-CSJS
□ OY-VKG	Airbus A330-343X	349	ex F-WWYG
□ OY-VKH	Airbus A330-343X	356	ex F-WWYJ
□ OY-VKI	Airbus A330-343X	357	ex C-GVKI

TRANSAVIA DENMARK — (PH/TDK)

□ OY-TDA	Boeing 737-8K2/W	30646/1122	ex PH-HZY
□ OY-TDB	Boeing 737-8K2/W	30650/1158	ex PH-HZV

P- KOREA (Democratic People's Republic of Korea)

AIR KORYO — Air Koryo (JS/KOR) — Pyongyang (FNJ)

□ P-527	Antonov An-24B	67302207		
□ P-532	Antonov An-24RV	47309707		
□ P-533	Antonov An-24RV	47309708		
□ P-534	Antonov An-24RV	47309802		
□ P-537	Antonov An-24B	67302408		
□ P-551	Tupolev Tu-154B	75A129	ex 551	
□ P-552	Tupolev Tu-154B	76A143	ex 552	
□ P-553	Tupolev Tu-154B	77A191	ex 553	
□ P-561	Tupolev Tu-154B-2	83A573		
□ P-618	Ilyushin Il-62M	2546624	no titles	Op for Govt
□ P-632	Tupolev Tu-204-300	1450742364012	ex RA-64012	
□ P-633	Tupolev Tu-204-100	64048	ex RA-64048	♦
□ P-813	Tupolev Tu-134B-3	66215		
□ P-814	Tupolev Tu-134B-3	66368		
□ P-835	Ilyushin Il-18D	188011205	ex 835	
□ P-836	Ilyushin Il-18V	185008204	ex 836	
□ P-881	Ilyushin Il-62M	3647853		
□ P-882	Ilyushin Il-62M	2850236	no titles	Op for Govt
□ P-885	Ilyushin Il-62M	3933913	ex 885	
□ P-912	Ilyushin Il-76MD	1003403104		
□ P-913	Ilyushin Il-76MD	1003404126		
□ P-914	Ilyushin Il-76MD	1003404146		
□ P-	Tupolev Tu-204-300			o/o

PH- NETHERLANDS (Kingdom of the Netherlands)

AMSTERDAM AIRLINES — Amstel (WD/AAN) — Amsterdam-Schiphol (AMS)

□ PH-AAX	Airbus A320-231	0430	ex XA-TXT
□ PH-AAY	Airbus A320-232	0527	ex N619AW

ARKEFLY/ TUI NETHERLANDS — (OR/TFL) — Amsterdam-Schiphol (AMS)

□ PH-TFA	Boeing 737-8FH/W	35100/2424	ex N1786B	Ferdinand Fransen
□ PH-TFB	Boeing 737-8K5/W	35149/2820	ex N1781B	
□ PH-TFC	Boeing 737-8K5/W	35146/2875	ex N1787B	
□ PH-AHQ	Boeing 767-383ER	24477/337	ex OY-KDL	
□ PH-AHX	Boeing 767-383ER	24847/315	ex LN-RCD	
□ PH-AHY	Boeing 767-383ER	24848/325	ex OY-KDN	
□ PH-OYI	Boeing 767-304ER/W	29138/783	ex G-OBYI	♦

CHC AIRWAYS — Schreiner (AW/SCH) — Rotterdam (RTM)

□ 5A-DLX	de Havilland DHC-8-311A	254	ex PH-SDK	Op for Waha Oil

CHC HELICOPTERS NETHERLANDS — den Helder (DHR)

□ PH-NZS	Sikorsky S-76B	760325	ex G-UKLS
□ PH-NZT	Sikorsky S-76B	760326	ex G-UKLT
□ PH-NZU	Sikorsky S-76B	760329	ex G-UKLU
□ PH-NZV	Sikorsky S-76B	760336	ex G-UKLM
□ PH-NZW	Sikorsky S-76B	760381	ex G-OKLE
□ PH-NZZ	Sikorsky S-76B	760316	ex N373G
□ PH-NZD	Sikorsky S-61N	61489	ex EI-CTK
□ PH-EAA	Agusta AW139	31141	
□ PH-EUC	Agusta AW139	41210	ex N246SM	♦
□ PH-EUD	Agusta AW139	31295		♦

☐ PH-SHK	Agusta AW139	31030	ex I-RAIA	
☐ PH-SHL	Agusta AW139	31041		
☐ PH-SHN	Eurocopter EC155B1	6755	ex F-WQVV	
☐ PH-SHO	Eurocopter EC155B1	6739	ex F-WWOV	
☐ PH-SHP	Agusta AW139	31099		

DENIM AIR		*Denim (3D/DNM)*	**Amsterdam-Schiphol (AMS)**

Ceased operations 18/Feb/2010

KLM CITYHOPPER		*City (WA/KLC)*	**Amsterdam-Schiphol (AMS)**

☐ PH-EZA	Embraer E190STD	19000224	ex PT-SHI		
☐ PH-EZB	Embraer E190STD	19000235	ex PT-SIG		
☐ PH-EZC	Embraer E190STD	19000250	ex PT-SIU		
☐ PH-EZD	Embraer E190STD	19000279	ex PT-TLT		
☐ PH-EZE	Embraer E190STD	19000288	ex PT-TZC		
☐ PH-EZF	Embraer E190STD	19000304	ex PT-TZS		
☐ PH-EZG	Embraer E190STD	19000315	ex PT-TXD		
☐ PH-EZH	Embraer E190STD	19000319	ex PT-TXH		
☐ PH-EZI	Embraer E190STD	19000322	ex PT-TXK		
☐ PH-EZK	Embraer E190STD	19000326	ex PT-TXO		
☐ PH-EZL	Embraer E190STD	19000334	ex PT-TXU		♦
☐ PH-EZM	Embraer E190STD	19000338	ex PT-TXX		♦
☐ PH-EZN	Embraer E190STD	19000342	ex PT-XQJ		♦
☐ PH-EZO	Embraer E190STD	19000347	ex PT-XQL		♦
☐ PH-EZP	Embraer E190STD	19000348	ex PT-XQN		♦
☐ PH-EZR	Embraer E190STD	19000375	ex PT-XNL		♦
☐ PH-EZS	Embraer E190STD	19000380	ex PT-XNP		♦
☐ PH-KVG	Fokker 50	20211		City of Stuttgart	[NWI]♦
☐ PH-KVH	Fokker 50	20217		City of Hanover	[NWI]♦
☐ PH-KVI	Fokker 50	20218		City of Bordeaux	[NWI]♦
☐ PH-KVK	Fokker 50	20219		City of London	[NWI]♦
☐ PH-LXP	Fokker 50	20276	ex G-UKTG	City of Durham	
☐ PH-LXR	Fokker 50	20277	ex G-UKTH	City of Amsterdam	
☐ PH-LXT	Fokker 50	20279	ex G-UKTI	City of Stavanger	[AMS]
☐ PH-JCH	Fokker 70	11528	ex OE-LFS		
☐ PH-JCT	Fokker 70	11537	ex OE-LFT		
☐ PH-KBX	Fokker 70	11547			
☐ PH-KZA	Fokker 70	11567			
☐ PH-KZB	Fokker 70	11562			
☐ PH-KZC	Fokker 70	11566			
☐ PH-KZD	Fokker 70	11582			
☐ PH-KZE	Fokker 70	11576			
☐ PH-KZF	Fokker 70	11577	ex (G-BVTH)		
☐ PH-KZG	Fokker 70	11578	ex (G-BWTI)		
☐ PH-KZH	Fokker 70	11583			
☐ PH-KZI	Fokker 70	11579	ex (I-REJC)		
☐ PH-KZK	Fokker 70	11581	ex (I-REJD)		
☐ PH-KZL	Fokker 70	11536	ex 9V-SLK		
☐ PH-KZM	Fokker 70	11561	ex 9V-SLL		
☐ PH-KZN	Fokker 70	11553	ex PK-PFE		
☐ PH-KZO	Fokker 70	11538	ex G-BVTE		
☐ PH-KZP	Fokker 70	11539	ex G-BVTF		
☐ PH-KZR	Fokker 70	11551	ex G-BVTG		
☐ PH-KZS	Fokker 70	11540	ex F-GLIS		
☐ PH-KZT	Fokker 70	11541	ex F-GLIT		
☐ PH-KZU	Fokker 70	11543	ex F-GLIU		
☐ PH-KZV	Fokker 70	11556	ex F-GLIV		
☐ PH-KZW	Fokker 70	11558	ex F-GLIX		
☐ PH-WXA	Fokker 70	11570	ex I-REJO		
☐ PH-WXC	Fokker 70	11574	ex I-REJI		
☐ PH-WXD	Fokker 70	11563	ex HA-LMD		
☐ PH-KLD	Fokker 100	11269	ex G-UKFM	[WOE]	
☐ PH-OFC	Fokker 100	11263	ex G-UKFC	[WOE]	
☐ PH-OFE	Fokker 100	11260	ex G-UKFE		
☐ PH-OFF	Fokker 100	11274	ex G-UKFF	[WOE]	
☐ PH-OFH	Fokker 100	11277	ex G-UKFH	[WOE]	
☐ PH-OFI	Fokker 100	11279	ex G-UKFI		
☐ PH-OFL	Fokker 100	11444	ex F-OORG		
☐ PH-OFM	Fokker 100	11475	ex F-OFRG		
☐ PH-OFN	Fokker 100	11477	ex F-OHXA		
☐ PH-OFO	Fokker 100	11462	ex PT-MRS		
☐ PH-OFP	Fokker 100	11472	ex PT-MRP		

KLM ROYAL DUTCH AIRLINES   **KLM (KL/KLM)**   **Amsterdam-Schiphol (AMS)**

Member of Skyteam

☐ PH-AOA	Airbus A330-203	682	ex F-WWYE	dam-Amsterdam
☐ PH-AOB	Airbus A330-203	686	ex F-WWYH	Potsdamer Platz-Berlin
☐ PH-AOC	Airbus A330-203	703	ex F-WWKE	Place de la Concorde-Paris
☐ PH-AOD	Airbus A330-203	738	ex F-WWYC	Piazza del Duomo-Milano
☐ PH-AOE	Airbus A330-203	770	ex F-WWKD	Parliament Square-Edinburgh
☐ PH-AOF	Airbus A330-203	801	ex F-WWYC	Federation Square-Melbourne
☐ PH-AOH	Airbus A330-203	811	ex F-WWYH	Senaatintori/Senate Square-Helsinki
☐ PH-AOI	Airbus A330-203	819	ex F-WWYR	Plaza de la Independencia-Madrid
☐ PH-AOK	Airbus A330-203	834	ex F-WWKZ	Radhuspladsen-Kobenhavn
☐ PH-AOL	Airbus A330-203	900	ex F-WWKP	Piccadilly Circus-London
☐ PH-AOM	Airbus A330-203	1161	ex F-WWKP	Piazza San Marco-Venezia ◆
☐ PH-BDO	Boeing 737-306	24262/1642		Jacob van Heemskerck
☐ PH-BDP	Boeing 737-306	24404/1681		Jacob Roggeveen [NWI]◆
☐ PH-BDT	Boeing 737-406	24530/1772		Gerrit de Veer
☐ PH-BDW	Boeing 737-406	24858/1903		Leifur Eiriksson
☐ PH-BPB	Boeing 737-4Y0	24344/1723	ex G-UKLB	Jan Tinbergen
☐ PH-BPC	Boeing 737-4Y0	24468/1747	ex G-UKLE	Ernest Hemingway
☐ PH-BTA	Boeing 737-406	25412/2161		Fernao de Magelhaes
☐ PH-BTB	Boeing 737-406	25423/2184		Henry Hudson
☐ PH-BTD	Boeing 737-306	27420/2406		James Cook
☐ PH-BTE	Boeing 737-306	27421/2438		Roald Amundsen
☐ PH-BTF	Boeing 737-406	27232/2591		Alexander von Humboldt
☐ PH-BTG	Boeing 737-406	27233/2601		Sir Henry Morton Stanley
☐ PH-BTH	Boeing 737-306	28719/2930		Heike Kamerling-Onnes
☐ HB-JJA+	Boeing 737-7AK/W	34303/1758	ex N1780B	[BBJ] <PTI
☐ PH-BGD	Boeing 737-7K2/W	30366/2675		Goldcrest/Goadhaantje
☐ PH-BGE	Boeing 737-7K2/W	30371/2705		Ortolan Bunting/Ortolaan
☐ PH-BGF	Boeing 737-7K2/W	30365/2714		Great White Heron/Grote Zilverreiger
☐ PH-BGG	Boeing 737-7K2/W	30367/2835		King Eider/Koeningseider
☐ PH-BGH	Boeing 737-7K2/W	38053/3119		Godwit/Grutto
☐ PH-BGI	Boeing 737-7K2/W	30364/3172	ex N1786B	Finch/Vink ◆
☐ PH-BGK	Boeing 737-7K2/W	38054/3292	ex N1786B	Fulmar/Noordse Stormvogel ◆
☐ PH-BGL	Boeing 737-7K2/W	30369/3407		Tjiftjaf/Warbler ◆
☐ PH-	Boeing 737-			o/o◆
☐ PH-	Boeing 737-			o/o◆
☐ PH-	Boeing 737-			o/o◆
☐ PH-	Boeing 737-			o/o◆
☐ PH-	Boeing 737-			o/o◆
☐ PH-	Boeing 737-			o/o◆
☐ PH-	Boeing 737-			o/o◆
☐ PH-	Boeing 737-			o/o◆
☐ PH-	Boeing 737-			o/o◆
☐ PH-	Boeing 737-			o/o◆
☐ PH-BCA	Boeing 737-8K2/W	37820/3480		Flamingo ◆
☐ PH-BGA	Boeing 737-8K2/W	37593/2569	ex N1786B	
☐ PH-BGB	Boeing 737-8K2/W	37594/2594		Whimbiel/Regenwulp
☐ PH-BGC	Boeing 737-8K2/W	30361/2619		Pintail/Pijlstaart
☐ PH-BXA	Boeing 737-8K2/W	29131/198	ex N1786B	Zwann/Swan Retro c/s
☐ PH-BXB	Boeing 737-8K2/W	29132/261	ex N1786B	Valk/Falcon
☐ PH-BXC	Boeing 737-8K2/W	29133/305		Karhoen/Grouse
☐ PH-BXD	Boeing 737-8K2/W	29134/355	ex N1784B	Arend/Eagle
☐ PH-BXE	Boeing 737-8K2/W	29595/552	ex N1787B	Havik/Hawk
☐ PH-BXF	Boeing 737-8K2/W	29596/583	ex N1787B	Zwalluw/Swallow
☐ PH-BXG	Boeing 737-8K2/W	30357/605	ex N1787B	Kraanvogel/Crane
☐ PH-BXH	Boeing 737-8K2/W	29597/630	ex N1786B	Gans/Goose
☐ PH-BXI	Boeing 737-8K2/W	30358/633	ex N1787B	Zilvermeeuw/Herring Gull
☐ PH-BXK	Boeing 737-8K2/W	29598/639	ex N1015G	Gierzwalluw/Swift
☐ PH-BXL	Boeing 737-8K2/W	30359/659		Sperwer/Sparrow Hawk
☐ PH-BXM	Boeing 737-8K2/W	30355/714	ex N1786B	Kluut/Avocet
☐ PH-BXN	Boeing 737-8K2/W	30356/728	ex N1787B	Merel/Blackbird
☐ PH-BXU	Boeing 737-8BK/W	33028/1936		Albatross
☐ PH-BXV	Boeing 737-8K2/W	30370/2205	ex N1786B	Roodborstje/Robin
☐ PH-BXW	Boeing 737-8K2/W	30360/2467	ex N1784B	Partridge
☐ PH-BXY	Boeing 737-8K2/W	30372/2503		Grebe/Fuut
☐ PH-BXZ	Boeing 737-8K2/W	30368/2533	ex N1786B	
☐ PH-BXO	Boeing 737-9K2/W	29599/866	ex N1786B	Plevier/Plover
☐ PH-BXP	Boeing 737-9K2/W	29600/924	ex N1786B	Merkroet/Crested Coot
☐ PH-BXR	Boeing 737-9K2/W	29601/959	ex N1786B	Nachtegaal/Nightingale

☐ PH-BXS	Boeing 737-9K2/W	29602/981	ex N1786B	Buizard/Buzzard	
☐ PH-BXT	Boeing 737-9K2/W	32944/1498		Zeestern/Sea Tern	
☐ PH-BFA	Boeing 747-406	23999/725	ex N6018N	City of Atlanta	
☐ PH-BFB	Boeing 747-406	24000/732		City of Bangkok	
☐ PH-BFC	Boeing 747-406M	23982/735	ex N6038E	City of Calgary	
☐ PH-BFD	Boeing 747-406M	24001/737		City of Dubai/Doebai	
☐ PH-BFE	Boeing 747-406M	24201/763	ex N6046P	City of Melbourne	Lsd ORIX
☐ PH-BFF	Boeing 747-406M	24202/770	ex N6046P	City of Freetown	Lsd ORIX
☐ PH-BFG	Boeing 747-406	24517/782		City of Guayaquil	
☐ PH-BFH	Boeing 747-406M	24518/783	ex N60668	City of Hong Kong	
☐ PH-BFI	Boeing 747-406M	25086/850		City of Jakarta	
☐ PH-BFK	Boeing 747-406	25087/854		City of Karachi	
☐ PH-BFL	Boeing 747-406	25356/888		City of Lima	
☐ PH-BFM	Boeing 747-406M	26373/896		City of Mexico	
☐ PH-BFN	Boeing 747-406	26372/969		City of Nairobi	
☐ PH-BFO	Boeing 747-406M	25413/938		City of Orlando	
☐ PH-BFP	Boeing 747-406M	26374/992		City of Paramaribo	
☐ PH-BFR	Boeing 747-406M	27202/1014		City of Rio de Janeiro	
☐ PH-BFS	Boeing 747-406	28195/1090		City of Seoul	
☐ PH-BFT	Boeing 747-406	28459/1112		City of Tokyo	
☐ PH-BFU	Boeing 747-406	28196/1127		City of Beijing	
☐ PH-BFV	Boeing 747-406	28460/1225		City of Vancouver	
☐ PH-BFW	Boeing 747-406	30454/1258		City of Shanghai	
☐ PH-BFY	Boeing 747-406	30455/1302		City of Johannesburg	
☐ PH-CKA	Boeing 747-406ERF	33694/1326		EendrachtKLM Cargo	
☐ PH-CKB	Boeing 747-406ERF	33695/1328		LeeuwinKLM Cargo	
☐ PH-CKC	Boeing 747-406ERF	33696/1341		OranjeKLM Cargo	
☐ PH-CKD	Boeing 747-406ERF	35233/1382			
☐ PH-BQA	Boeing 777-206ER	33711/454	ex N5014K	Albert Plesman	
☐ PH-BQB	Boeing 777-206ER	33712/457		Borobudur	
☐ PH-BQC	Boeing 777-206ER	29397/461		Chichen-Itza	
☐ PH-BQD	Boeing 777-206ER	33713/465		Darjeeling Highway	
☐ PH-BQE	Boeing 777-206ER	28691/468		Epidaurus	
☐ PH-BQF	Boeing 777-206ER	29398/474		Ferrara City	
☐ PH-BQG	Boeing 777-206ER	32704/476		Galapagos Islands	
☐ PH-BQH	Boeing 777-206ER	32705/493	ex N5016R	Hadrian's Wall	
☐ PH-BQI	Boeing 777-206ER	33714/497		Iguazu Falls	
☐ PH-BQK	Boeing 777-206ER	29399/499		Mount Kilimanjaro	
☐ PH-BQL	Boeing 777-206ER	34711/552		Litomyšl Castle	
☐ PH-BQM	Boeing 777-206ER	34712/559		Machu Picchu	
☐ PH-BQN	Boeing 777-206ER	32720/561		Nahanni National Park	
☐ PH-BQO	Boeing 777-206ER	35295/609		Old Rauma	
☐ PH-BQP	Boeing 777-206ER	32721/630		Pont du Gard	
☐ PH-BVA	Boeing 777-306ER	35671/694	(ex PH-BQR)	De Hoge Veluwe National Park	
☐ PH-BVB	Boeing 777-306ER	36145/706		Fulufjallet National Park	
☐ PH-BVC	Boeing 777-306ER	37582/787		Sian Ka'an National Park	
☐ PH-BVD	Boeing 777-306ER	35979/807		National Park Amboseli	
☐ PH-	Boeing 777-306ER				o/o♦
☐ PH-	Boeing 777-306ER				o/o♦
☐ PH-KCA	McDonnell-Douglas MD-11	48555/557	ex N6202D	Amy Johnson	
☐ PH-KCB	McDonnell-Douglas MD-11	48556/561		Maria Montessori	
☐ PH-KCC	McDonnell-Douglas MD-11	48557/569		Marie Curie	
☐ PH-KCD	McDonnell-Douglas MD-11	48558/573		Florence Nightingale	
☐ PH-KCE	McDonnell-Douglas MD-11	48559/575	ex N91566	Audrey Hepburn	
☐ PH-KCF	McDonnell-Douglas MD-11	48560/578		Annie Romein	
☐ PH-KCG	McDonnell-Douglas MD-11	48561/585		Maria Callas	
☐ PH-KCH	McDonnell-Douglas MD-11	48562/591		Anna Pavlova	
☐ PH-KCI	McDonnell-Douglas MD-11	48563/593	ex PP-SPM	Mother Theresa	
☐ PH-KCK	McDonnell-Douglas MD-11	48564/612		Ingrid Bergman	

MARTINAIR — *Martinair (MP/MPH)* — **Amsterdam-Schiphol (AMS)**

☐ PH-MPP	Boeing 747-412BCF	24061/717	ex N733BA		[AMS] ♦
☐ PH-MPR	Boeing 747-412BCF	24226/809	ex N242BA		
☐ PH-MPS	Boeing 747-412BCF	24066/791	ex N728BA		[MZJ]
☐ PH-MCI	Boeing 767-31AER	25312/400		Prins Pieter-Christiaan	
☐ PH-MCJ	Boeing 767-31AER	25535/491	ex CS-TLM		
☐ PH-MCL	Boeing 767-31AER	26469/415		Koningin Beatrix	Retro c/s
☐ PH-MCM	Boeing 767-31AER	26470/416		Prins Floris	
☐ PH-MCP	McDonnell-Douglas MD-11CF	48616/577	ex N90187		
☐ PH-MCR	McDonnell-Douglas MD-11CF	48617/581		Cargo	

☐ PH-MCS	McDonnell-Douglas MD-11CF	48618/584		
☐ PH-MCT	McDonnell-Douglas MD-11CF	48629/486		
☐ PH-MCU	McDonnell-Douglas MD-11F	48757/606		Prinses Maxima
☐ PH-MCW	McDonnell-Douglas MD-11CF	48788/632		
☐ PH-MCY	McDonnell-Douglas MD-11F	48445/460	ex N626FE	

ORANGE AIRCRAFT LEASING	**Orange (RNG)**			**Lelystad (LEY)**
☐ PH-RAQ	ATR 42-300	139	ex ZS-OSN	[MST]
☐ PH-RNG	Beech 1900D	UE-70	ex ZS-PZH	

TRANSAVIA AIRLINES	**Transavia (HV/TRA)**			**Amsterdam-Schiphol (AMS)**
☐ PH-XRA	Boeing 737-7K2/W	30784/873	ex N1786B	Leontien van Moorsel
☐ PH-XRB	Boeing 737-7K2/W	28256/1298		
☐ PH-XRC	Boeing 737-7K2/W	29347/1318	ex OY-TDZ	♦
☐ PH-XRD	Boeing 737-7K2/W	30659/1329		
☐ PH-XRE	Boeing 737-7K2/W	30668/1482		
☐ PH-XRV	Boeing 737-7K2/W	34170/1701		Rotterdam The Hague Airport
☐ PH-XRW	Boeing 737-7K2/W	33465/1316		
☐ PH-XRX	Boeing 737-7K2/W	33464/1299		Stadprins Akkedeer
☐ PH-XRY	Boeing 737-7K2/W	33463/1292		
☐ PH-XRZ	Boeing 737-7K2/W	33462/1278		
☐ PH-HSA	Boeing 737-8K2/W	34171/2950	ex N1786B	
☐ PH-HSB	Boeing 737-8K2/W	34172/3242	ex N1786B	♦
☐ PH-HSC	Boeing 737-8K2/W	34173/3266		♦
☐ PH-	Boeing 737-8K2/W			o/o♦
☐ PH-	Boeing 737-8K2/W			o/o♦
☐ PH-HSW	Boeing 737-8K2/W	37160/2880	ex 9Y-TJR	
☐ PH-HZD	Boeing 737-8K2/W	28376/252	ex N1786B	
☐ PH-HZE	Boeing 737-8K2/W	28377/277	ex N1786B	City of Rhodos
☐ PH-HZF	Boeing 737-8K2/W	28378/291	ex N1796B	
☐ PH-HZG	Boeing 737-8K2/W	28379/498	ex N1786B	
☐ PH-HZI	Boeing 737-8K2/W	28380/524		
☐ PH-HZJ	Boeing 737-8K2/W	30389/549	ex N1796B	
☐ PH-HZK	Boeing 737-8K2/W	30390/555	ex N1786B	
☐ PH-HZL	Boeing 737-8K2/W	30391/814	ex N1786B	
☐ PH-HZM	Boeing 737-8K2/W	30392/833	ex N1786B	
☐ PH-HZN	Boeing 737-8K2/W	32943/1478		
☐ PH-HZO	Boeing 737-8K2/W	34169/2243		
☐ PH-HZW	Boeing 737-8K2/W	29345/1132	ex VT-SPZ	Jumbo Supermarket

PJ-   NETHERLANDS ANTILLES

DIVI DIVI AIR	**Divi divi (DVR)**			**Curacao (CUR)**
☐ PJ-BMV	Cessna 402B	402B0865	ex C-GCKB	
☐ PJ-DVA	Dornier 228-202	8100	ex ZK-VIR	
☐ PJ-SEA	Britten-Norman BN-2A-26 Islander	311	ex C-FFXS	FlyDivi.com titles
☐ PJ-SKY	Britten-Norman BN-2A-26 Islander	885	ex C-FDYT	

DUTCH ANTILLES AIRLINES				**Curacao (CUR)**
☐ PJ-DAA	Fokker 100	11310	ex D-AGPI	FlyDAE titles
☐ PJ-DAB	Fokker 100	11331	ex D-AGPM	

DUTCH ANTILLES EXPRESS	**BonExpress (9H/DNL)**			**Kralendijk (BON)**
☐ PJ-SLH	ATR 42-320	090	ex F-WQNN	all-white
☐ PJ-XLM	ATR 42-320	378	ex PH-XLM	
☐ PJ-XLN	ATR 42-500	513	ex PH-XLN	

INSEL AIR INTERNATIONAL	**Inselair (7I/INC)**			**Curacao (CUR)**
☐ PJ-MDA	McDonnell-Douglas MD-83	49449/1354	ex 9A-CBJ	
☐ PJ-MDB	McDonnell-Douglas MD-82	48021/1078	ex N812NK	<SFR
☐ PJ-MDC	McDonnell-Douglas MD-82	49434/1446	ex N434AG	
☐ PJ-MDD	McDonnell-Douglas MD-82	49972/1757	ex N972AG	
☐ PJ-VIA	Embraer EMB.110P1 Bandeirante	110387	ex E5-TAI	
☐ PJ-VIP	Embraer EMB.110P1 Bandeirante	110382	ex YV-249C	Curacao

WINAIR	**Windward (WM/WIA)**			**St. Maarten (SXM)**
☐ PJ-AIW	Britten-Norman BN-2A-26 Islander	2038	ex C-GZKG	
☐ PJ-CIW	Britten-Norman BN-2B-26 Islander	876	ex C-GZTP	

☐ PJ-WIH	de Havilland DHC-6 Twin Otter 300	766	ex N304CH	Spirit of Freddy Johnson
☐ PJ-WIL	de Havilland DHC-6 Twin Otter 300	358	ex C-FCSY	
☐ PJ-WIN	de Havilland DHC-6 Twin Otter 300	518	ex 5Y-SKA	

WINDWARD EXPRESS AIRWAYS — St Maarten (SXM)

☐ PJ-WEA	Britten-Norman BN-2A-27 Islander	659	ex N659CM
☐ PJ-WEB	Britten-Norman BN-2A-26 Islander	2208	ex 8P-TAG

PK- INDONESIA (Republic of Indonesia)

AIR MALEO

☐ PK-VKD	British Aerospace 146 Srs.100	E1104	ex RP-C5255	[Clark]

AIR MARK INDONESIA AVIATION — Jakarta-Halim (HLP)

☐ EW-262TK	Antonov An-32A	2103	ex ER-AWY
☐ PK-AIY	Fokker 50	20227	ex OY-EBG

AIRFAST INDONESIA — Airfast (AFE) — Balikpapan/Jayapura (BPN/DJJ)

☐ PK-OAT	Agusta-Bell 204B	3169	ex PK-LBC	
☐ PK-OAW	Beech 65-B80 Queen Air	LD-308	ex PK-JBF	
☐ PK-OBA	Bell 204B	2050	ex VH-UTW	
☐ PK-OCA	ITPN Bell 412	34009/NB09	ex PK-XFJ	
☐ PK-OCB	ITPN Bell 412	34007/NB07	ex PK-XFH	
☐ PK-OCC	CASA-Nurtanio C.212	50N/CC4-2-210	ex PK-NZJ	
☐ PK-OCE	Bell 212	30981	ex PK-VBZ	
☐ PK-OCJ	de Havilland DHC-6 Twin Otter 300	522	ex A6-MBM	
☐ PK-OCK	de Havilland DHC-6 Twin Otter 310	616	ex 9Q-CLE	all-white
☐ PK-OCL	de Havilland DHC-6 Twin Otter 300	689	ex N689WJ	Santigi
☐ PK-OCP	Boeing 737-27A	23794/1424	ex B-2625	
☐ PK-OCT	McDonnell-Douglas MD-82	49889/1761	ex N823RA	
☐ PK-OCU	McDonnell-Douglas MD-82	53017/1797	ex N824RA	
☐ PK-OCY	Beech 1900D	UE-393	ex N830CA	
☐ PK-OSP	British Aerospace 146 Srs.100	E1124	ex G-CBXY	Op for Metro TV

AVIASI UPATA RAKSA INDONESIA — Jakarta-Halim (HLP)

☐ PK-AFE	Pilatus PC-6/B2-H2 Turbo Porter	799	ex ST-0604
☐ PK-AGD	Cessna 402B	402B0398	ex VH-WNE
☐ PK-AGE	Cessna 402B	402B0046	ex L-4021
☐ PK-AGF	Cessna 402B	402B0047	ex L-4022

AVIASTAR MANDIRI — Banjarmasin (BDJ)

☐ PK-BRE	British Aerospace 146 Srs.200	E2139	ex C-GRNU	
☐ PK-BRF	British Aerospace 146 Srs.200	E2210	ex PK-LNJ	
☐ PK-BRM	CASA-Nurtanio C.212	91N/411	ex PK-VSD	
☐ PK-BRN	CASA-Nurtanio C.212	90N/410	ex PK-VSC	dam 11Jan07
☐ PK-BRP	de Havilland DHC-6 Twin Otter 300	356	ex N972SW	
☐ PK-BRQ	de Havilland DHC-6 Twin Otter 300	702	ex N702PV	
☐ PK-BRS	de Havilland DHC-6 Twin Otter 300	756	ex C-FPNZ	
☐ PK-BRT	de Havilland DHC-6 Twin Otter 300	380	ex C-GHBP	
☐ PK-BRW	Fokker 50	20307	ex OY-PCJ	♦

BATAVIA AIR — Batavia (7P/BTV) — Jakarta-Soekarno Hatta (CGK)

☐ PK-YVA	Airbus A319-132	2648	ex D-AVWT	
☐ PK-YVC	Airbus A319-132	2660	ex D-AVWU	
☐ PK-	Airbus A319-132		ex D-AV	o/o ♦
☐ PK-YUC	Airbus A320-233	0460	ex N951LF	♦
☐ PK-YUE	Airbus A320-233	0461	ex N941LF	♦
☐ PK-YVD	Airbus A320-231	0449	ex G-JOEM	
☐ PK-YVE	Airbus A320-231	0441	ex B-22306	
☐ PK-YVF	Airbus A320-233	1676	ex N206CT	
☐ PK-YVG	Airbus A320-231	0168	ex N168BN	
☐ PK-YVH	Airbus A320-232	0710	ex B-2401	♦
☐ PK-YVI	Airbus A330-202	330	ex EI-EWR	
☐ PK-YVJ	Airbus A330-202	205	ex N271LF	
☐ PK-	Airbus A330-202	211	ex N272LF	o/o
☐ PK-	ATR 72-212A		ex F-WW	o/o
☐ PK-	ATR 72-212A		ex F-WW	o/o

445

☐ PK-YTA	Boeing 737-266	21192/451	ex N201YT		
☐ PK-YTC	Boeing 737-2M8	22090/664	ex N220LS		
☐ PK-YTD	Boeing 737-2T4	22802/901	ex N203YT		[CGK]
☐ PK-YTE	Boeing 737-405	25303/2137	ex LN-BRP		
☐ PK-YTG	Boeing 737-2Q8	22453/748	ex N453LS		[CGK]
☐ PK-YTH	Boeing 737-204	20806/338	ex N806YT		[CGK]
☐ PK-YTI	Boeing 737-2L9	22407/698	ex N30AU		[CGK]
☐ PK-YTJ	Boeing 737-204	21693/541	ex N693YT		
☐ PK-YTK	Boeing 737-4Y0	24687/1865	ex TC-APT		
☐ PK-YTL	Boeing 737-2P5	23113/1010	ex N113YT		[CGK]
☐ PK-YTM	Boeing 737-3B7	22957/1127	ex N384US		[CGK]
☐ PK-YTN	Boeing 737-217 (AvAero 3)	22659/874	ex N986PG		
☐ PK-YTP	Boeing 737-4Y0	24345/1731	ex TC-APC		
☐ PK-YTQ	Boeing 737-281 (AvAero 3)	21767/585	ex N745AP		[CGK]
☐ PK-YTR	Boeing 737-281 (AvAero 3)	21766/583	ex N738AP		
☐ PK-YTS	Boeing 737-2T4 (AvAero 3)	22055/633	ex N739AA		stored
☐ PK-YTU	Boeing 737-3Y9	25604/2405	ex N999CZ		
☐ PK-YTV	Boeing 737-2M8 (AvAero 3)	21955/659	ex N742AP		
☐ PK-YTW	Boeing 737-3B7	23318/1234	ex N396US		[CGK]
☐ PK-YTX	Boeing 737-3B7	22953/1022	ex N374US		
☐ PK-YTY	Boeing 737-3B7	22955/1043	ex N376US		[CGK]
☐ PK-YTZ	Boeing 737-4Y0	23869/1639	ex N869AP		[CGK]
☐ PK-YVK	Boeing 737-301	23233/1200	ex N232AP		
☐ PK-YVL	Boeing 737-322	24638/1784	ex N373UA		
☐ PK-YVM	Boeing 737-322	24253/1650	ex N349UA		
☐ PK-YVN	Boeing 737-48E	25766/2543	ex N766SJ		
☐ PK-YVO	Boeing 737-4Y0	23868/1616	ex PK-RIH		
☐ PK-YVP	Boeing 737-4Y0	23979/1661	ex PK-RIT		
☐ PK-YVQ	Boeing 737-4S3	25594/2223	ex N594AB		
☐ PK-YVR	Boeing 737-4Y0	24494/1757	ex N494AC		
☐ PK-YVS	Boeing 737-4H6	27352/2624	ex HS-DDJ		
☐ PK-YVT	Boeing 737-4H6	27191/2676	ex HS-DDH		
☐ PK-YVU	Boeing 737-33A	24097/1741	ex N497AN		
☐ PK-YVV	Boeing 737-3B7	23316/1212	ex N394US		
☐ PK-YVW	Boeing 737-3B7	23319/1250	ex N397US		
☐ PK-YVX	Boeing 737-33A	24093/1727	ex N493AN		
☐ PK-YVY	Boeing 737-3B7	22952/1015	ex N373US		[CGK]
☐ PK-YVZ	Boeing 737-3B7	23317/1221	ex N395US		[CGK]
☐ PK-YCM	Fokker F.28 Fellowship 4000	11168	ex PK-KFD		[CGK]

CARDIG AIR

☐ PK-BBA	Boeing 737-347SF	23597/1287	ex N311WA	Motivation	
☐ PK-BBB	Boeing 737-347SF	23598/1289	ex N312WA	Creativity	

CITILINK Jakarta-Halim (HLP)

☐ PK-GHV	Boeing 737-3Y0	24914/2054	ex HA-LEF	[CGK]

DERAYA AIR TAXI Deraya (DRY) Jakarta-Halim (HLP)

☐ PK-DCC	Cessna 402C II	402C0250	ex N444DS	
☐ PK-DCJ	Cessna 402B	402B0615	ex N3759C	
☐ PK-DCO	CASA-Nurtanio C.212-A4	13N/A4-11-93	ex PK-XCL	[HLP]
☐ PK-DCP	CASA-Nurtanio C.212-A4	14N/A4-11-101	ex PK-XCM	
☐ PK-DCQ	CASA-Nurtanio C.212-A4	16N/A4-13-112	ex PK-XCO	
☐ PK-DCZ	Cessna 402B	402B0890	ex N5203J	
☐ PK-DGA	British Aerospace ATP(F)	2026	ex G-JEMD	
☐ PK-DGI	British Aerospace ATP(F)	2027	ex G-JEME	
☐ PK-DSB	Short SD.3-30	SH3056	ex DQ-SUN	
☐ PK-DSF	Short SC.7 Skyvan 3	SH1881	ex AF-702	
☐ PK-DSH	Short SD.3-60	SH3757	ex N350TA	
☐ PK-DSR	Short SD.3-30	SH3060	ex DQ-FIJ	
☐ PK-DSS	Short SD.3-60	SH3743	ex N743RW	
☐ PK-DYR	Piper PA-31T Cheyenne II	31T-7820054	ex VH-MWT	
☐ PK-LPN	Cessna U206F Stationair II	U20602789	ex PK-UFO	

DIRGANTARA AIR SERVICE Dirgantara (AW/DIR)
Jakarta-Halim/Bandarmasin/Pontianak (HLP/BDJ/PNK)

☐ PK-VIB	Britten-Norman BN-2A-21 Islander	545	ex PK-TRC	
☐ PK-VIM	Britten-Norman BN-2A-3 Islander	634	ex 9V-BEB	
☐ PK-VIN	Britten-Norman BN-2A-3 Islander	351	ex G-BBJA	
☐ PK-VIS	Britten-Norman BN-2A-21 Islander	485	ex G-BEGB	
☐ PK-VIU	Britten-Norman BN-2A-21 Islander	781	ex PK-KNH	
☐ PK-VIW	Britten-Norman BN-2A-21 Islander	2026	ex G-BIPD	
☐ PK-VIX	Britten-Norman BN-2A-21 Islander	2027	ex G-BIUF	

☐ PK-VIY	Britten-Norman BN-2A-21 Islander	2133	ex G-BJOR

☐ PK-VSA	CASA-Nurtanio C.212	87N/CC4-38-282	ex PK-HJA
☐ PK-VSB	CASA-Nurtanio C.212	88N/CC4-39-283	ex PK-HJB
☐ PK-VSF	CASA Nurtanio C.212	93N/4-413	ex PK-HJI
☐ PK-VSN	CASA-Nurtanio C.212	22N/A4-19-136	ex PK-XCU

☐ PK-VMB	Gippsland GA-8 Airvan	GA8-03-031	ex VH-BOI
☐ PK-VMC	Gippsland GA-8 Airvan	GA8-03-033	ex VH-BNL
☐ PK-VMD	Gippsland GA-8 Airvan	GA8-03-041	ex VH-FDR
☐ PK-VME	Gippsland GA-8 Airvan	GA8-03-042	ex VH-JYN

EASTINDO   Jakarta-Halim (HLP)

☐ PK-RGA	Beech 1900D	UE-376	ex N31425
☐ PK-RGE	Fokker 100	11445	ex F-WQVP
☐ PK-RGI	Beech B200 Super King Air	BB-1732	ex N23268
☐ PK-RGP	Britten-Norman BN-2B-20 Islander	2249	ex PK-HNG

GADING SARI AVIATION SERVICES

☐ 9M-PMM	Boeing 737-205C	20458/278	ex RP-C2906 Frtr	<TSE

GARUDA INDONESIA   Indonesia (GA/GIA)   Jakarta-Soekarno Hatta (CGK)

☐ PK-GPA	Airbus A330-341	138	ex F-WWKH	
☐ PK-GPC	Airbus A330-341	140	ex F-WWKU	
☐ PK-GPD	Airbus A330-341	144	ex F-WWKG	for IBE
☐ PK-GPE	Airbus A330-341	148	ex F-WWKD	
☐ PK-GPF	Airbus A330-341	153	ex F-WWKY	
☐ PK-GPG	Airbus A330-341	165	ex F-WWKL	
☐ PK-GPH	Airbus A330-243	1020	ex F-WWYL	
☐ PK-GPI	Airbus A330-243	1052	ex F-WWKQ	
☐ PK-GPJ	Airbus A330-243	988	ex F-WWKI	
☐ PK-GPK	Airbus A330-243	1028	ex F-WWYZ	
☐ PK-GPL	Airbus A330-243	1184	ex F-WWKT	♦

☐ PK-GCA	Boeing 737-3L9	24569/1775	ex N569AG
☐ PK-GCC	Boeing 737-3Q8	28200/2854	ex 9M-AAC
☐ PK-GGA	Boeing 737-5U3	28726/2920	
☐ PK-GGC	Boeing 737-5U3	28727/2937	ex N1786B
☐ PK-GGD	Boeing 737-5U3	28728/2938	ex N1786B
☐ PK-GGE	Boeing 737-5U3	28729/2950	ex N60436
☐ PK-GGF	Boeing 737-5U3	28730/2952	
☐ PK-GGG	Boeing 737-3U3	28731/2949	
☐ PK-GGN	Boeing 737-3U3	28735/3029	ex N5573K
☐ PK-GGO	Boeing 737-3U3	28736/3032	ex N3134C
☐ PK-GGP	Boeing 737-3U3	28737/3037	ex N1020L
☐ PK-GGQ	Boeing 737-3U3	28739/3064	ex N1024A
☐ PK-GGR	Boeing 737-3U3	28741/3079	ex N1026G
☐ PK-GGV	Boeing 737-3Q8	26293/2541	ex N318FL
☐ PK-GHQ	Boeing 737-34S	29108/2983	ex (PK-GHA)
☐ PK-GHW	Boeing 737-3M8	25039/2007	ex N303FL
☐ PK-GHX	Boeing 737-3L9	26440/2234	ex N310FL
☐ PK-GWK	Boeing 737-4U3	25713/2531	
☐ PK-GWL	Boeing 737-4U3	25714/2535	ex N6067B
☐ PK-GWM	Boeing 737-4U3	25715/2537	
☐ PK-GWN	Boeing 737-4U3	25716/2540	
☐ PK-GWO	Boeing 737-4U3	25717/2546	
☐ PK-GWP	Boeing 737-4U3	25718/2548	
☐ PK-GWQ	Boeing 737-4U3	25719/2549	
☐ PK-GWT	Boeing 737-4K5	26316/2711	ex D-AHLG
☐ PK-GWU	Boeing 737-4Q8	24708/2076	ex N708KS
☐ PK-GZA	Boeing 737-497	25663/2382	ex N663AL
☐ PK-GZH	Boeing 737-4M0	29203/3049	ex VP-BAJ
☐ PK-GZJ	Boeing 737-4M0	29205/3056	ex VP-BAM
☐ PK-GZK	Boeing 737-4M0	29206/3058	ex VP-BAN
☐ PK-GZL	Boeing 737-4M0	29207/3078	ex VP-BAO
☐ PK-GZM	Boeing 737-4M0	29208/3081	ex VP-BAP
☐ PK-GZN	Boeing 737-4M0	29209/3087	ex VP-BAQ
☐ PK-GZO	Boeing 737-4M0	29210/3091	ex VP-BAR
☐ PK-GZP	Boeing 737-46Q	28661/2910	ex EI-CXI
☐ PK-GZQ	Boeing 737-4S3	25134/2083	ex N534AG

☐ PK-GEE	Boeing 737-8CX/W	32361/1098	ex TC-IEA
☐ PK-GEF	Boeing 737-8CX/W	32363/1139	ex N236GX
☐ PK-GEG	Boeing 737-83N/W	30033/1149	ex N323TZ
☐ PK-GEH	Boeing 737-83N/W	30643/1106	ex N319TZ

☐ PK-GEI	Boeing 737-86N/W	29883/1083	ex N29883	
☐ PK-GEJ	Boeing 737-86N/W	33003/1121	ex G-XLAG	
☐ PK-GEK	Boeing 737-85F/W	30568/793	ex N568MQ	
☐ PK-GEL	Boeing 737-8AS/W	29927/727	ex EI-CSN	
☐ PK-GEM	Boeing 737-8AS/W	29928/735	ex EI-CSO	
☐ PK-GEN	Boeing 737-8AS/W	29929/753	ex EI-CSP	
☐ PK-GEO	Boeing 737-8AS/W	29930/757	ex EI-CSQ	
☐ PK-GEP	Boeing 737-8AS/W	29931/1020	ex EI-CSR	
☐ PK-GEQ	Boeing 737-86N/W	32659/1709	ex EC-JEX	
☐ PK-GER	Boeing 737-86J/W	30876/759	ex D-ABAD	
☐ PK-GFA	Boeing 737-86N/W	36549/3331		♦
☐ PK-GFC	Boeing 737-86N/W	39390/3348		♦
☐ PK-GFD	Boeing 737-8U3/W	40807/3337		♦
☐ PK-GFE	Boeing 737-86N/W	36804/3374		♦
☐ PK-GFF	Boeing 737-8U3/W	36436/3370		♦
☐ PK-GFG	Boeing 737-8BK/W	37819/3402	ex N1786B	♦
☐ PK-GFH	Boeing 737-8U3/W	36850/3389		♦
☐ PK-GFI	Boeing 737-86N/W	36805/3438		♦
☐ PK-GFJ	Boeing 737-86N/W	37885/3445	ex N1796B	♦
☐ PK-GFK	Boeing 737-86N/W	37887/3463		♦
☐ PK-GFL	Boeing 737-86N/W	36808/3505	ex N1786B	♦
☐ PK-GFM	Boeing 737-8U3/W	39920/3518		♦
☐ PK-	Boeing 737-8			o/o♦
☐ PK-	Boeing 737-8			o/o♦
☐ PK-	Boeing 737-8			o/o♦
☐ PK-	Boeing 737-8			o/o♦
☐ PK-	Boeing 737-8			o/o♦
☐ PK-	Boeing 737-8			o/o♦
☐ PK-	Boeing 737-8			o/o♦
☐ PK-	Boeing 737-8			o/o♦
☐ PK-	Boeing 737-8			o/o♦
☐ PK-	Boeing 737-8			o/o♦
☐ PK-GMA	Boeing 737-8U3/W	30151/2942	ex N1784B	
☐ PK-GMC	Boeing 737-8U3/W	30155/3081	ex N1786B	
☐ PK-GMD	Boeing 737-8U3/W	30156/3100		
☐ PK-GME	Boeing 737-8U3/W	30157/3123		
☐ PK-GMF	Boeing 737-8U3/W	30140/3129		
☐ PK-GMG	Boeing 737-8U3/W	30141/3166	ex N1796B	♦
☐ PK-GMH	Boeing 737-8U3/W	30142/3213	ex N1786B	♦
☐ PK-GMI	Boeing 737-8U3/W	30143/3243	ex N1786B	♦
☐ PK-GMJ	Boeing 737-8U3/W	30144/3249	ex N1787B	♦
☐ PK-GMK	Boeing 737-8U3/W	30145/3171	ex N1787B	♦
☐ PK-GML	Boeing 737-8U3/W	31763/3177	ex N1787B	♦
☐ PK-GMM	Boeing 737-8U3/W	30147/3285		♦
☐ PK-GMN	Boeing 737-8U3/W	30146/3303		♦
☐ PK-GMO	Boeing 737-8U3/W	30147/3327	ex N1786B	♦
☐ PK-GMP	Boeing 737-8U3/W	30148/3353	ex N1787B	♦
☐ PK-GMQ	Boeing 737-8U3/W	30149/3405	ex N1787B	♦
☐ PK-GMR	Boeing 737-8U3/W	30150/3429		♦
☐ PK-	Boeing 737-8			o/o♦
☐ PK-	Boeing 737-8			o/o♦
☐ PK-	Boeing 737-8			o/o♦
☐ PK-GSG	Boeing 747-4U3	25704/1011		
☐ PK-GSH	Boeing 747-4U3	25705/1029	ex N6038E	
☐ PK-GSI	Boeing 747-441	24956/917	ex N791LF	
☐ PK-	Boeing 777-3U3ER			o/o
☐ PK-	Boeing 777-3U3ER			o/o
☐ PK-	Boeing 777-3U3ER			o/o
☐ PK-	Boeing 777-3U3ER			o/o

GATARI AIR SERVICE — Gatari (GHS) — Jakarta-Halim (HLP)

☐ PK-HMB	Bell 212	30502	ex PK-DBY	
☐ PK-HMM	Bell 212	30958	ex PK-PGF	
☐ PK-HNH	Fokker F.28 Fellowship 4000	11218	ex PK-GQB	
☐ PK-HNJ	Fokker F.28 Fellowship 3000RC	11134	ex PK-GFW	[HLP]
☐ PK-HNN	Fokker F.28 Fellowship 3000R	11119	ex PK-GFS	[HLP]
☐ PK-HNP	Fokker F.28 Fellowship 4000	11216	ex PK-GKZ	[HLP]
☐ PK-HNS	ATR 42-500	601	ex PK-TSQ	
☐ PK-HNT	ATR 42-500	614	ex OY-EDE	♦
☐ PK-HNY	Kawasaki/MBB BK-117B-1	1052	ex JA6614	

448

GT AIR   Jakarta-Halim (HLP)

☐ PK-LTP	Fokker F.27 Friendship 500	10398	ex PH-FNW	Syaloom	[HLP]
☐ PK-LTQ	Fokker F.27 Friendship 500	10389/10528	ex HB-ILQ	stored HLP	
☐ PK-LTT	Dornier 28D-1 Skyservant	4031	ex PK-VRB		
☐ PK-LTU	Dornier 28D-1 Skyservant	4026	ex PK-VRA		
☐ PK-LTY	de Havilland DHC-6 Twin Otter 300	831	ex B-3512	Anugrah	

INDONESIA AIR TRANSPORT   Intra (IDA)   Jakarta-Halim (HLP)

☐ PK-TRD	Aérospatiale SA365C Dauphin 2	5058	ex N3606Q		
☐ PK-TRE	Aérospatiale SA365C Dauphin 2	5004	ex N3604G		
☐ PK-TSH	Aérospatiale SA365N Dauphin 2	6008	ex N801BA		
☐ PK-TSI	Aérospatiale SA365N Dauphin 2	6026	ex N87SV		
☐ PK-TSW	Aérospatiale AS365N2 Dauphin 2	6470	ex HL9204		
☐ PK-TSX	Aérospatiale AS365N2 Dauphin 2	6472	ex HL9206		
☐ PK-THT	ATR 42-500	611	ex I-ADLZ		♦
☐ PK-TSY	ATR 42-300	118	ex LY-ARY		
☐ PK-TSZ	ATR 42-300	059	ex LY-ARJ		
☐ PK-TRU	BAC One-Eleven 492GM	262	ex G-BLDH		[AOR]
☐ PK-TST	BAC One-Eleven 423ET	118	ex G-BEJM		VIP [AOR]
☐ PK-TRW	Beech 1900D	UE-177	ex N3237H		
☐ PK-TRX	Beech 1900D	UE-186	ex N3233J		
☐ PK-TSF	Bell 212	30974	ex N27664		
☐ PK-TSG	Bell 212	30753	ex N81FC		
☐ PK-TSJ	Fokker F.27 Friendship 500RFC	10525	ex N702A		
☐ PK-TSO	Fokker 50	20186	ex PH-ZDB		
☐ PK-TSP	Fokker 50	20316	ex PK-TWJ		

INDONESIA AIRASIA   Wagon Air (QZ/AWQ)   Jakarta-Soekarno Hatta (CGK)

☐ PK-AXA	Airbus A320-216	3610	ex F-WWIG		
☐ PK-AXC	Airbus A320-216	3648	ex F-WWBZ		
☐ PK-AXD	Airbus A320-216	3182	ex 9M-AFX		
☐ PK-AXE	Airbus A320-216	3715	ex F-WWIZ		
☐ PK-AXF	Airbus A320-216	3765	ex F-WWDO		
☐ PK-AXG	Airbus A320-216	3813	ex F-WWIE		
☐ PK-AXH	Airbus A320-216	3875	ex F-WWII		
☐ PK-AXI	Airbus A320-216	3963	ex F-WWID		
☐ PK-AXJ	Airbus A320-216	4035	ex F-WWIJ		
☐ PK-AXK	Airbus A320-216	4147	ex F-WWBC		
☐ PK-AXL	Airbus A320-216	4346	ex F-WWBT		
☐ PK-AXM	Airbus A320-216	4462	ex F-WWBI		♦
☐ PK-AXN	Airbus A320-216	4477	ex F-WWDH		♦
☐ PK-AXO	Airbus A320-216	4486	ex F-WWDP		♦
☐ PK-AWO	Boeing 737-322	24659/1836	ex 9M-AEA		
☐ PK-AWP	Boeing 737-3Y0	24905/2001	ex 9M-AAD		
☐ PK-AWQ	Boeing 737-3B7	23376/1308	ex N947WP		<AXM
☐ PK-AWT	Boeing 737-3B7	23345/1170	ex N304WA		<AXM
☐ PK-AWU	Boeing 737-301	23257/1124	ex 9M-AAU		
☐ PK-AWX	Boeing 737-3Y0	24547/1813	ex 9M-AEC		

ISLAND SEAPLANES   Bali-Benoa Harbour

☐ PK-SDL	de Havilland DHC-2 Beaver	413	ex C-GIPL		FP

JATAYU AIR   Jatayu (VJ/JTY)   Jakarta-Soekarno Hatta (CGK)

☐ PK-JAC	Boeing 727-232 (FedEx 3)	21587/1492	ex PK-RIZ		[CGK]
☐ PK-JAG	Boeing 727-232 (FedEx 3)	21306/1270	ex PK-MBW		
☐ PK-JGN	Boeing 727-223 (Raisbeck 3)	21384/1328	ex N872AA		[CGK]
☐ PK-JGP	Boeing 737-204 (Nordam 3)	22364/696	ex PK-AIG		[CGK]
☐ PK-JGS	Boeing 737-222	19949/197	ex N199NA		[PCB]
☐ PK-JGW	Boeing 737-2N7	21226/458	ex N119SW		[MES]
☐ PK-LIA	Boeing 737-2P5	21440/502	ex N440GB		[CGK]

KALSTAR   Serpong

☐ PK-KSE	ATR 42-320	415	ex N415AN	
☐ PK-KSI	ATR 42-320	348	ex N38AN	

KARTIKA AIRLINES — Kartika (3Y/KAE) — Jakarta-Soekarno Hatta (CGK)

☐ PK-KAD	Boeing 737-284	22338/691	ex PK-IJQ	
☐ PK-KAO	Boeing 737-284	22339/692	ex PK-IJP	<Aero Nusantara

KURA KURA AVIATION — Semarang (SRG)

☐ PK-WLW	Cessna 402B	402B0555	ex VH-ASL
☐ PK-WLX	Cessna 402B	402B0549	ex VH-AAP
☐ PK-WLY	Cessna 402B	402B0541	ex VH-PEK

LION AIRLINES — Lion Inter (JT/LNI) — Jakarta-Soekarno Hatta (CGK)

☐ PK-LIF	Boeing 737-4Y0	24467/1733	ex PK-MBL	
☐ PK-LIG	Boeing 737-4Y0	24513/1779	ex PK-MBM	[CGK]
☐ PK-LIH	Boeing 737-4Y0	24520/1803	ex HL7260	
☐ PK-LII	Boeing 737-46B	24123/1663	ex EC-GRX	
☐ PK-LIQ	Boeing 737-4Y0	24911/2033	ex OK-TVS	[PNK]♦
☐ PK-LIR	Boeing 737-4Y0	24692/1963	ex EC-IRA	
☐ PK-LIS	Boeing 737-4Y0	24693/1972	ex OK-WGG	
☐ PK-LIT	Boeing 737-4Y0	24512/1777	ex PK-GWV	
☐ PK-LIU	Boeing 737-3G7	23218/1076	ex N380WL	
☐ PK-LIV	Boeing 737-3G7	23219/1090	ex N390WL	
☐ PK-LIW	Boeing 737-4Y0	24684/1841	ex EI-CVN	
☐ PK-LFF	Boeing 737-9GPER/W	35679/2093	ex N6055X	
☐ PK-LFG	Boeing 737-9GPER/W	35680/1981	ex N900ER	
☐ PK-LFH	Boeing 737-9GPER/W	35710/2285	ex N1786B	
☐ PK-LFI	Boeing 737-9GPER/W	35711/2319	ex N1780B	
☐ PK-LFJ	Boeing 737-9GPER/W	35712/2349	ex (PK-LAJ)	
☐ PK-LFK	Boeing 737-9GPER/W	35713/2437	ex N1781B	
☐ PK-LFL	Boeing 737-9GPER/W	35714/2461	ex (PK-LAL)	
☐ PK-LFM	Boeing 737-9GPER/W	35715/2485	ex N1786B	
☐ PK-LFO	Boeing 737-9GPER/W	35716/2504	ex N1786B	
☐ PK-LFP	Boeing 737-9GPER/W	35717/2455		
☐ PK-LFQ	Boeing 737-9GPER/W	35718/2670		
☐ PK-LFR	Boeing 737-9GPER/W	35719/2694		
☐ PK-LFS	Boeing 737-9GPER/W	35720/2756		
☐ PK-LFT	Boeing 737-9GPER/W	35721/2793		
☐ PK-LFU	Boeing 737-9GPER/W	35722/2836	ex N1784B	
☐ PK-LFV	Boeing 737-9GPER/W	35723/2848	ex N1787B	
☐ PK-LFW	Boeing 737-9GPER/W	35724/2879		
☐ PK-LFY	Boeing 737-9GPER/W	35725/2897	ex N1786B	
☐ PK-LFZ	Boeing 737-9GPER/W	35726/2904		
☐ PK-LGF	Boeing 737-96NER/W	35223/2559	ex N223MT	
☐ PK-LGG	Boeing 737-96NER/W	35225/2590	ex N225MT	
☐ PK-LGH	Boeing 737-96NER/W	35227/2621	ex G-XLAR	
☐ PK-LGI	Boeing 737-96NER/W	36539/2596	ex G-XLAP	
☐ PK-LGJ	Boeing 737-9GPER/W	35727/2934	ex N1796B	
☐ PK-LGK	Boeing 737-9GPER/W	35728/2984	ex N1786B	
☐ PK-LGL	Boeing 737-9GPER/W	35729/3008		
☐ PK-LGM	Boeing 737-9GPER/W	35730/3075		
☐ PK-LGO	Boeing 737-9GPER/W	35731/3093		
☐ PK-LGP	Boeing 737-9GPER/W	35732/3111		
☐ PK-LGQ	Boeing 737-9GPER/W	35733/3135		
☐ PK-LGR	Boeing 737-9GPER/W	35734/3153		
☐ PK-LGS	Boeing 737-9GPER/W	35735/3183		♦
☐ PK-LGT	Boeing 737-9GPER/W	35736/3207	ex N1787B	♦
☐ PK-LGU	Boeing 737-9GPER/W	35737/3225	ex N1787B	♦
☐ PK-LGV	Boeing 737-9GPER/W	37268/3297		♦
☐ PK-LGW	Boeing 737-9GPER/W	37269/3321		♦
☐ PK-LGY	Boeing 737-9GPER/W	37270/3333		♦
☐ PK-LGZ	Boeing 737-9GPER/W	37271/3345	ex N1786B	♦
☐ PK-LHH	Boeing 737-9GPER/W	37275/3375		♦
☐ PK-LHI	Boeing 737-9GPER/W	37276/3381		♦
☐ PK-LHJ	Boeing 737-9GPER/W	37272/3411		♦
☐ PK-LHK	Boeing 737-9GPER/W	37273/3423	ex N1787B	♦
☐ PK-LHL	Boeing 737-9GPER/W	37274/3441		♦
☐ PK-	Boeing 737-9GPER/W			o/o♦
☐ PK-	Boeing 737-9GPER/W			o/o♦
☐ PK-	Boeing 737-9GPER/W			o/o♦
☐ PK-	Boeing 737-9GPER/W			o/o♦
☐ PK-	Boeing 737-9GPER/W			o/o♦
☐ PK-	Boeing 737-9GPER/W			o/o♦
☐ PK-	Boeing 737-9GPER/W			o/o♦
☐ PK-	Boeing 737-9GPER/W			o/o♦
☐ PK-	Boeing 737-9GPER/W			o/o♦

☐ PK-	Boeing 737-9GPER/W			o/o♦
☐ PK-	Boeing 737-9GPER/W			o/o♦
☐ PK-	Boeing 737-9GPER/W			o/o♦
☐ PK-	Boeing 737-9GPER/W			o/o♦
☐ PK-LHF	Boeing 747-412	24063/736	ex N240BA	
☐ PK-LHG	Boeing 747-412	24065/761	ex N465BB	
☐ PK-LMI	McDonnell-Douglas MD-82	49263/1163	ex N809NY	
☐ PK-LMM	McDonnell-Douglas MD-82	48069/1032	ex N480CT	[CGK]
☐ PK-LMO	McDonnell-Douglas MD-82	49373/1201	ex N493AP	
☐ PK-LMR	McDonnell-Douglas MD-82	49116/1061	ex N16887	[CGK]
☐ PK-LMW	McDonnell-Douglas MD-82	49443/1291	ex N830US	dbr 04Mar06?
☐ PK-LMY	McDonnell-Douglas MD-82	49250/1186	ex N17812	Lsd UBA
☐ PK-LIK	McDonnell-Douglas MD-90-30	53570/2181	ex N904RA	
☐ PK-LIL	McDonnell-Douglas MD-90-30	53573/2182	ex N905RA	
☐ PK-LIM	McDonnell-Douglas MD-90-30	53489/2129	ex N901RA	
☐ PK-LIO	McDonnell-Douglas MD-90-30	53490/2133	ex N902RA	
☐ PK-LIP	McDonnell-Douglas MD-90-30	53551/2144	ex N903RA	

MANDALA AIRLINES   Mandala (RI/MDL)   Jakarta-Soekarno Hatta (CGK)

Suspended operations 13/Jan/2011

☐ PK-RMH	Airbus A319-132	2797	ex N521NK	
☐ PK-RMI	Airbus A319-132	2784	ex N520NK	
☐ PK-RMC	Airbus A320-212	0391	ex EI-DIJ	
☐ PK-RMK	Airbus A320-232	3524	ex VT-DNU	
☐ PK-RML	Airbus A320-232	3543	ex VT-DNT	
☐ PK-RIA	Boeing 737-2P6	21357/497	ex LV-WFX	
☐ PK-RII	Boeing 737-2E7	22876/922	ex G-BLDE gold colours	[SUB]
☐ PK-RIJ	Boeing 737-210	21820/578	ex G-BKNH	stored
☐ PK-RIL	Boeing 737-230	22137/788	ex D-ABHL	
☐ PK-RIN	Boeing 737-2H6	21732/559	ex PK-KJM	[CGK]
☐ PK-RIQ	Boeing 737-291	23023/957	ex TF-ABI	[CGK]
☐ PK-RIY	Boeing 727-232 (FedEx 3)	21585/1479	ex N525DA	

MANUNGGAL AIR   Jakarta-Halim (HLP)

☐ PK-VTA	British Aerospace 146 Srs.100	E1015	ex N146AP	
☐ PK-VTM	British Aerospace 146 Srs.100	E1009	ex RP-C2999	
☐ PK-VTR	Aérospatiale/MBB Transall C-160NG	233	ex PK-PTO	[HLP]
☐ PK-VTS	Aérospatiale/MBB Transall C-160P	207	ex PK-PTY	[HLP]

MERPATI NUSANTARA AIRLINES   Merpati (MZ/MNA)   Jakarta-Soekarno Hatta/Surabaya (CGK/SUB)

☐ PK-MFA	ATR 72-212	379	ex N379FA	♦
☐ PK-	ATR 72-212	385	ex N385FA	o/o♦
☐ PK-MBC	Boeing 737-230	22129/754	ex D-ABFY	[SUB]
☐ PK-MBE	Boeing 737-230	22142/797	ex D-ABHS Batanta	
☐ PK-MBH	Boeing 737-2S3	22279/650	ex N279AD	
☐ PK-MBJ	Boeing 737-2U4	22576/761	ex N576DF	
☐ PK-MBN	Boeing 737-377	24304/1622	ex S2-AEA	
☐ PK-MBO	Boeing 737-377	24305/1641	ex S2-AEB	
☐ PK-MBP	Boeing 737-33A	23632/1344	ex N173AW	
☐ PK-MBQ	Boeing 737-217 (AvAero 3)	22260/784	ex N285TR	
☐ PK-MBS	Boeing 737-217 (AvAero 3)	22342/810	ex N288TR	[SUB]
☐ PK-MBU	Boeing 737-217 (AvAero 3)	22259/771	ex N284TR	[SUB]
☐ PK-MBX	Boeing 737-228 (Nordam 3)	23005/943	ex N253TR	[SUB]
☐ PK-MBY	Boeing 737-228 (Nordam 3)	23004/941	ex N234TR	[SUB]
☐ PK-MBZ	Boeing 737-228 (Nordam 3)	23007/948	ex N237TR	[SUB]
☐ PK-MDC	Boeing 737-2L9	21685	ex PK-RIF	
☐ PK-MDD	Boeing 737-2S3	22278/646	ex PK-RIC	
☐ PK-MDE	Boeing 737-322	24660/1838	ex N385UA	
☐ PK-MDF	Boeing 737-3S1	24856/1911	ex PK-AWS	
☐ PK-MDG	Boeing 737-3Q8	26296/2581	ex N296AG	
☐ PK-MDH	Boeing 737-301	23932/1554	ex N587US	
☐ PK-MDJ	Boeing 737-301	23931/1552	ex N586US	
☐ PK-MDK	Boeing 737-3B7	23858/1509	ex N140CT	
☐ PK-MDO	Boeing 737-4Q8	24069/1635	ex N240AD	
☐ PK-MDQ	Boeing 737-3Q8	24300/1666	ex N243AD	
☐ PK-MDZ	Boeing 737-4Q8	26280/2239	ex N129AC	
☐ PK-MZA	CAIC MA60	0407		

☐ PK-MZB	CAIC MA60	0406			
☐ PK-MZC	CAIC MA60	0409			
☐ PK-MZD	CAIC MA60	0410			o/o
☐ PK-MZE	CAIC MA60	0501			o/o
☐ PK-MZF	CAIC MA60	0502			o/o
☐ PK-MZG	CAIC MA60	0505			o/o
☐ PK-MZI	CAIC MA60	0506			o/o
☐ PK-MZJ	CAIC MA60	0601			o/o
☐ PK-MZK	CAIC MA60	0602			o/o
☐ PK-MZL	CAIC MA60	0603			o/o
☐ PK-MZM	CAIC MA60	0604			o/o
☐ PK-NCH	CASA-Nurtanio C.212-AB4	30N/AB4-2-173	ex PK-XAD	Weh	
☐ PK-NCN	CASA-Nurtanio C.212-AB4	36N/AB4-8-191	ex PK-XAJ	Seribu	
☐ PK-NCU	CASA-Nurtanio C.212-C4	74N/CC4-24-254	ex PK-XDW	Pantar	
☐ PK-NCV	CASA-Nurtanio C.212-C4	75N/CC4-26-255	ex PK-XDX	Misool	
☐ PK-NCX	CASA-Nurtanio C.212-C4	77N/CC4-28-257	ex PK-XDZ	Batudata	
☐ PK-NCZ	CASA-Nurtanio C.212-C4	79N/CC4-30-274	ex PK-XEC	Tanah Massa	
☐ PK-MNC	CASA-Nurtanio CN-235	5/N002	ex PK-XND	Wokam	
☐ PK-MND	CASA-Nurtanio CN-235	7/N003	ex PK-XNE	Sermata	[SUB]
☐ PK-MNE	CASA-Nurtanio CN-235	9/N004	ex PK-XNF	Letiall-white	
☐ PK-MNF	CASA-Nurtanio CN-235-200	10/N005	ex PK-XNG	Wowoni	[SUB]
☐ PK-MNG	CASA-Nurtanio CN-235	14/N006	ex PK-XNH	Timorall-white	
☐ PK-MNI	CASA-Nurtanio CN-235	16/N007	ex PK-XNI	Babarall-white	
☐ PK-MNJ	CASA-Nurtanio CN-235	19/N009	ex PK-XNK	Damar	[SUB]
☐ PK-MNK	CASA-Nurtanio CN-235	20/N010	ex PK-XNL	Kobroor	
☐ PK-MNM	CASA-Nurtanio CN-235	26/N012	ex PK-XNN	Moa	
☐ PK-MNP	CASA-Nurtanio CN-235	30/N015	ex PK-XNQ	Kaledupo	
☐ PK-NUH	de Havilland DHC-6 Twin Otter 300	383		Natuna	
☐ PK-NUO	de Havilland DHC-6 Twin Otter 300	487		Singkep	[BIK]
☐ PK-NUR	de Havilland DHC-6 Twin Otter 300	484		Muna	[BIK]
☐ PK-NUS	de Havilland DHC-6 Twin Otter 300	481		Peleng	
☐ PK-NUV	de Havilland DHC-6 Twin Otter 300	472		Tanimbar	
☐ PK-NUZ	de Havilland DHC-6 Twin Otter 300	443	ex PK-NUM	Alor	
☐ PK-NVA	de Havilland DHC-6 Twin Otter 300	551	ex VH-UQY		
☐ PK-MFF	Fokker F.27 Friendship 500	10551	ex ZK-NFA	Tanah Bela	[SUB]
☐ PK-MFG	Fokker F.27 Friendship 500	10552	ex ZK-NFB	Lingga	[SUB]
☐ PK-MFJ	Fokker F.27 Friendship 500	10598	ex ZK-NFE	Adonara	[SUB]
☐ PK-MFK	Fokker F.27 Friendship 500	10607	ex ZK-NFF	Wangi-Wangi	[SUB]
☐ PK-MFQ	Fokker F.27 Friendship 500	10623	ex PK-GRF	Bintan	[SUB]
☐ PK-MFV	Fokker F.27 Friendship 500	10625	ex PK-GRH	Kabia	[SUB]
☐ PK-MFW	Fokker F.27 Friendship 500	10626	ex PK-GRI	Maja	[SUB]
☐ PK-MFY	Fokker F.27 Friendship 500	10629	ex PK-GRK	Halmahera	
☐ PK-MJA	Fokker 100	11453	ex PH-MXO	Bawal	[SUB]
☐ PK-MJC	Fokker 100	11463	ex PH-EZV	Sabu	
☐ PK-MJD	Fokker 100	11474	ex PH-EZW	Rupat	

NUSANTARA AIR CHARTER   Jakarta-Halim (HLP)

☐ PK-JKC	British Aerospace 146 Srs.200	E2113	ex SE-DRN		
☐ PK-JKM	Fokker F.28 Fellowship 4000	11116	ex PK-YHK		
☐ PK-JKW	British Aerospace 146 Srs.200	E2204	ex PK-LNI		

PELITA AIR   Pelita (6D/PAS)   Jakarta-Halim/Pondok Cabe (HLP/PCB)

☐ PK-PDT	Aérospatiale SA.330G Puma	1264	ex F-WTNB		
☐ PK-PDY	Aérospatiale SA.330G Puma	1160			
☐ PK-PEI	Aérospatiale SA.330J Puma	1299			
☐ PK-PEK	Aérospatiale SA.330G Puma	1283			
☐ PK-PEO	Aérospatiale SA.330J Puma	1261			
☐ PK-PHW	Aérospatiale SA.330G Puma	1082	ex F-OCRQ		
☐ PK-PUG	Aérospatiale AS.332C	NSP2/2020	ex PK-XSB		
☐ PK-PUH	Aérospatiale AS.332C	NSP3/2021	ex PK-XSC		
☐ PK-PCN	CASA-Nurtanio C.212-A4	56N/CC4-8-216	ex PK-XDE		[PCB]
☐ PK-PCO	CASA-Nurtanio C.212-A4	55N/CC4-8-215	ex PK-XDD		
☐ PK-PCP	CASA-Nurtanio C.212-A4	48N/AB4-20-208	ex PK-XAV		
☐ PK-PCQ	CASA-Nurtanio C.212-A4	47N/AB4-18-207	ex PK-XDE		[PCB]
☐ PK-PCR	CASA-Nurtanio C.212-A4	46N/AB4-18-206	ex PK-XAT		
☐ PK-PCS	CASA-Nurtanio C.212-A4	45N/AB4-17-205	ex PK-XAS		
☐ PK-PCT	CASA-Nurtanio C.212-A4	44N/AB4-16-204	ex PK-XAR		
☐ PK-PCU	CASA-Nurtanio C.212-A4	43N/AB4-15-203	ex PK-XAQ		

☐ PK-PKT	de Havilland DHC-7-110	54	ex C-FYXV		
☐ PK-PSV	de Havilland DHC-7-103	105	ex C-GFOD		
☐ PK-PSW	de Havilland DHC-7-103	100	ex C-GFCF		
☐ PK-PSX	de Havilland DHC-7-103	94	ex C-GFYI		
☐ PK-PSY	de Havilland DHC-7-103	86	ex C-GFUM		
☐ PK-PSZ	de Havilland DHC-7-103	75	ex C-GFCF		
☐ PK-PFZ	Fokker 100	11486	ex PH-ZFA		
☐ PK-PJK	Fokker F.28 Fellowship 4000	11192	ex PH-EXW	Lengguru	[PCB]
☐ PK-PJL	Fokker F.28 Fellowship 4000	11111	ex PH-EZA	Kurau	
☐ PK-PJM	Fokker F.28 Fellowship 4000	11178	ex PH-EXW	Matak	[PCB]
☐ PK-PJN	Fokker 100	11288	ex PH-LMU	Minas	
☐ PK-PJY	Fokker F.28 Fellowship 4000	11146	ex PH-EXN	Aceh	
☐ PK-PGQ	Nurtanio/MBB Bo.105CB	N60/S-458			
☐ PK-PGR	Nurtanio/MBB Bo.105CB	N62/S-460			
☐ PK-PGU	Nurtanio/MBB Bo.105C	N12/S-218	ex PK-XZJ		
☐ PK-PGZ	Nurtanio/MBB Bo.105CB	N65/S-553			
☐ PK-PIH	Nurtanio/MBB Bo.105CB	N68/S-556			
☐ PK-PIJ	Nurtanio/MBB Bo.105CB	N70/S-558	ex PK-XYN		
☐ PK-PIM	Nurtanio/MBB Bo.105CB	N72/S-560	ex PK-XYP		
☐ PK-PJJ	Avro 146-RJ85	E2239	ex G-6-239	Wamena	
☐ PK-PUA	Sikorsky S-76A	76-0179	ex N5446U		>Travira
☐ PK-PUD	Sikorsky S-76A	76-0195	ex N3121A		>Travira
☐ PK-PUE	Sikorsky S-76A	76-0200			>Travira
☐ PK-PUJ	Bell 412EP	36282	ex N2012Y		
☐ PK-PUK	Bell 412EP	36288	ex N2028L		
☐ PK-PUL	Bell 430	49088	ex N3005J		

PENAS   *Penas (PNS)*   *Jakarta-Halim (HLP)*

☐ PK-VCD	Cessna 402B	402B0024	ex N5242M	

PREMIAIR   *Jakarta-Halim (HLP)*

☐ PK-RJC	Embraer EMB.120ER Brasilia	120214	ex VH-ANV		
☐ PK-RJI	Fokker 100	11328	ex G-BXWF	Imanuel	VIP

RIAU AIRLINES   *Riau (RIU)*   *Pekanbaru (PKU)*

☐ PK-RAL	Fokker 50	20282	ex PH-MXE	Bengkalis	
☐ PK-RAS	Fokker 50	20261	ex PT-SRA	Kampat	

RPX AIRLINES   *Public Express (RH/RPH)*   *Jakarta-Soekarno Hatta (CGK)*

☐ PK-RPH	Boeing 737-2K2C (AvAero 3)	20943/405	ex F-GGVP	
☐ PK-RPI	Boeing 737-2K2C (AvAero 3)	20944/408	ex F-GGVQ	

SABANG MERAUKE RAYA AIR CHARTER   *Samer (SMC)*   *Medan (MES)*

☐ PK-ZAE	Britten-Norman BN-2A-21 Islander	565	ex G-BEGH	
☐ PK-ZAF	Fokker F27 Friendship 200	10222	ex PK-MFA	
☐ PK-ZAK	Piper PA-31 Turbo Navajo	31-407	ex PK-FJA	
☐ PK-ZAN	CASA-Nurtanio C.212-A4	5N/A4-3-60	ex A-2102	
☐ PK-ZAO	CASA-Nurtanio C.212-A4	6N/A4-3-64	ex A-2101	
☐ PK-ZAQ	CASA-Nurtanio C.212-A4	82N/277	ex PK-JSR	
☐ PK-ZAV	CASA-Nurtanio C.212-A4	81N/276	ex PK-JSS	
☐ PK-ZAY	Fokker F27 Friendship 200	10223	ex PK-CFY	

SRIWIJAYA AIR   *Sriwijaya (SJ/SJY)*   *Jakarta-Soekarno Hatta (CGK)*

☐ PK-CJA	Boeing 737-284	22301/683	ex PK-IJS	Brenda	
☐ PK-CJC	Boeing 737-33A	24025/1556	ex SE-RCP		I
☐ PK-CJD	Boeing 737-204 (Nordam 3)	22057/621	ex 9L-LFI	Emilio	
☐ PK-CJE	Boeing 737-2T4	23446/1165	ex ET-ALE	Citra	
☐ PK-CJF	Boeing 737-284	22343/695	ex SX-BCI		
☐ PK-CJG	Boeing 737-2H6	23320/1120	ex PK-ALC	Serumpun Sebalai	
☐ PK-CJH	Boeing 737-2B7 (Nordam 3)	22883/935	ex N271AU		
☐ PK-CJI	Boeing 737-2B7 (Nordam 3)	23135/1054	ex PK-ALV	Membalong	[CGK]
☐ PK-CJJ	Boeing 737-2B7 (Nordam 3)	22880/927	ex N268AU		
☐ PK-CJK	Boeing 737-236	22032/742	ex PK-ALK		
☐ PK-CJL	Boeing 737-284	21301/474	ex PK-TXE		
☐ PK-CJM	Boeing 737-2B7 (Nordam 3)	22884/956	ex PK-TXC		
☐ PK-CJN	Boeing 737-2B7 (Nordam 3)	23134/1050	ex PK-TXA	Sherly	[CGK]
☐ PK-CJO	Boeing 737-284	22300/674	ex PK-IJR	Lomasasta	
☐ PK-CJP	Boeing 737-2B7 (Nordam 3)	23132/1044	ex PK-ALN	Lenggang	[CGK]
☐ PK-CJR	Boeing 737-284	21225/464	ex SX-BCB	Perkasa	

☐ PK-CJS	Boeing 737-3L9	27925/2763	ex N104VR	
☐ PK-CJT	Boeing 737-33A	24791/1984	ex N791AW	
☐ PK-CJU	Boeing 737-4Q8	24234/1627	ex N234AN	
☐ PK-CJV	Boeing 737-4Y0	24689/1883	ex N689MD	
☐ PK-CJW	Boeing 737-4Y0	24690/1885	ex N690MD	
☐ PK-CJY	Boeing 737-3Q8	24698/1846	ex PK-GHS	◆
☐ PK-CKA	Boeing 737-4Q8	25169/2237	ex N483JC	
☐ PK-CKC	Boeing 737-4Q8	26285/2416	ex N587BC	
☐ PK-CKD	Boeing 737-4Y0	25180/2201	ex N251MD	
☐ PK-	Boeing 737-3Q8	24987/2268	ex N596BC	

SUSI AIR   Medan (MES)

☐ PK-BVA	Cessna 208B Caravan I	208B2126	ex N61905	
☐ PK-BVD	Cessna 208B Caravan I	208B2141	ex N61932	
☐ PK-BVE	Cessna 208B Caravan I	208B2142	ex N6194X	
☐ PK-BVF	Cessna 208B Caravan I	208B2143	ex N61983	
☐ PK-BVG	Cessna 208B Caravan I	208B2146	ex N6203C	
☐ PK-BVH	Cessna 208B Caravan I	208B2151	ex N6204C	
☐ PK-BVJ	Cessna 208B Caravan I	208B2177	ex N1015J	◆
☐ PK-BVK	Cessna 208B Caravan I	208B2198	ex N10200	◆
☐ PK-BVL	Cessna 208B Caravan I	208B2206		◆
☐ PK-VVA	Cessna 208B Caravan I	208B1066	ex N12690	
☐ PK-VVB	Cessna 208B Caravan I	208B1285	ex N4117B	
☐ PK-VVD	Cessna 208B Caravan I	208B1303	ex N20722	
☐ PK-VVE	Cessna 208B Caravan I	208B1287	ex N41176	
☐ PK-VVF	Cessna 208B Caravan I	208B1177	ex OB-1844-T	
☐ PK-VVG	Cessna 208B Caravan I	208B1308	ex N20840	
☐ PK-VVH	Cessna 208B Caravan I	208B1078	ex N278ST	
☐ PK-VVI	Cessna 208B Caravan I	208B1205	ex RP-C2929	
☐ PK-VVJ	Cessna 208B Caravan I	208B2086	ex N2232Y	
☐ PK-VVM	Cessna 208B Caravan I	208B2093	ex N2154L	
☐ PK-VVO	Cessna 208B Caravan I	208B2111	ex N61611	
☐ PK-VVR	Cessna 208B Caravan I	208B1085	ex N12722	
☐ PK-VVS	Cessna 208B Caravan I	208B1117	ex N12775	
☐ PK-VVT	Cessna 208B Caravan I	208B2068	ex N61413	
☐ PK-BVM	Pilatus PC-6/B2-H4 Turbo Porter	975		◆
☐ PK-BVT	Pilatus PC-6/B2-H4 Turbo Porter	968		◆
☐ PK-BVY	Pilatus PC-6/B2-H4 Turbo Porter	973		◆
☐ PK-VVK	Pilatus PC-6/B2-H4 Turbo Porter	958		
☐ PK-VVP	Pilatus PC-6/B2-H4 Turbo Porter	957		
☐ PK-VVQ	Pilatus PC-6/B2-H4 Turbo Porter	965		
☐ PK-VVU	Pilatus PC-6/B2-H4 Turbo Porter	967		

TIMAX CARGO AIRLINES

☐ PK-YGZ	Boeing 727-31F (FedEx 3)	20112/700	ex OO-DHO	<TMG

TRANSWISATA AIR   Jakarta-Halim (HLP)

☐ PK-TWA	Fokker F.28 Fellowship 4000	11234	ex N484US	
☐ PK-TWC	Fokker 50	20272	ex D-AFFI	
☐ PK-TWF	Fokker 50	20142	ex D-AFFX	
☐ PK-TWM	Fokker F.28 Fellowship 4000	11183	ex ZS-JAV	
☐ PK-TWN	Fokker 100	11335	ex PH-SXI	
☐ PK-TWR	Fokker 50	20317	ex B-12279	

TRAVIRA AIR   Denpasar (DPS)

☐ PK-TVE	Beech 1900D	UE-338	ex N338RH	
☐ PK-TVH	Beech 1900D	UE-364	ex N30469	
☐ PK-TVJ	Beech 1900D	UE-352	ex N352RA	
☐ PK-TVK	Beech 1900D	UE-375	ex PK-TVK	Air Ambulance
☐ PK-TVL	Beech 1900D	UE-360	ex VH-FOZ	
☐ PK-PUA	Sikorsky S-76A	760179	ex N5446U	<PAS
☐ PK-PUD	Sikorsky S-76A	760195	ex N3121A	<PAS
☐ PK-PUE	Sikorsky S-76A	760200		<PAS
☐ PK-TVF	Sikorsky S-76A	760154	ex VH-CPH	
☐ PK-TVP	Sikorsky S-76C	760421	ex N899KK	
☐ PK-TVQ	Sikorsky S-76A	760286	ex N30DJ	
☐ PK-TVP	Sikorsky S-76C	760436	ex N476X	
☐ PK-TVU	Sikorsky S-76C	760298	ex N520AL	
☐ PK-NZU	IPTN/MBB Bo.105CB	N121/S-719	ex PK-IWJ	
☐ PK-TUB	de Havilland DHC-8Q-315	590	ex EC-LFF	o/o◆
☐ PK-TVA	IPTN/MBB Bo.105CB	N1/S-124	ex PK-PEE	

☐ PK-TVB	IPTN/MBB Bo.105CB	N6/S-177	ex PK-PGV		
☐ PK-TVI	Cessna 208 Caravan I	20800313	ex C-FAMB		FP
☐ PK-TVN	Cessna 208 Caravan I	20800358	ex N1229N		FP
☐ PK-TVW	Cessna 208 Caravan I	20800418	ex N20869		
☐ PK-TVX	Cessna 208 Caravan I	20800421	ex N2098U		
☐ PK-TVY	de Havilland DHC-8-315	549	ex VH-AAY		
☐ PK-TVZ	Boeing 737-5L9	28996/2998	ex N737RH		VIP

TRIGANA AIR SERVICE · Trigana (TGN) · Jakarta-Halim (HLP)

☐ PK-YRE	ATR 42-300	027	ex F-GPZB	<Martinique Aero Lease
☐ PK-YRH	ATR 42-300	097	ex F-ODGN	
☐ PK-YRI	ATR 72-202	326	ex F-WQUF	
☐ PK-YRK	ATR 42-300	106	ex N422TE	
☐ PK-YRN	ATR 42-300	102	ex N421TE	
☐ PK-YRR	ATR 42-310	214	ex F-GHPI	
☐ PK-YRV	ATR 42-300	190	ex G-BYHA	
☐ PK-YRX	ATR 72-202	342	ex F-WQRY	
☐ PK-YRY	ATR 72-202	201	ex F-WQAL	
☐ PK-YPX	de Havilland DHC-6 Twin Otter 300	684	ex HB-LTF	
☐ PK-YRC	Cessna TU206D Skywagon	U206-1269	ex PK-MCA	
☐ PK-YRF	de Havilland DHC-6 Twin Otter 300	462	ex D-ISKY	
☐ PK-YRG	Fokker F.27 Friendship 500	10397	ex PH-FNV	
☐ PK-YRJ	de Havilland DHC-4A Caribou	27	ex N666NC	
☐ PK-YRQ	Bell 206L-4 LongRanger IV	52069	ex F-GPGC	
☐ PK-YRT	Boeing 737-2K5	22599/814	ex PK-KJN	
☐ PK-YRU	de Havilland DHC-6 Twin Otter 300	685	ex VH-VHP	

TRI-MG INTRA-ASIA AIRLINES · Trilines (GY/TMG) · Jakarta-Halim (HLP)

☐ PK-YGL	LET L-410UVP-E	892342	ex RP-C748		
☐ PK-YGR	Boeing 727-223F (FedEx 3)	20893/1189	ex N117JB	Zenith	
☐ PK-YGZ	Boeing 727-31F (FedEx 3)	20112/700	ex OO-DHO	Noble Witness	>Timax Cargo

WINGS AIR · Wings Abadi (IW/WON) · Jakarta-Soekarno Hatta (CGK)

☐ PK-WFF	ATR 72-212A	869	ex F-WWET		
☐ PK-WFG	ATR 72-212A	882	ex F-WWEL		
☐ PK-WFH	ATR 72-212A	883	ex F-WWEM		
☐ PK-WFI	ATR 72-212A	871	ex F-WWEV		
☐ PK-WFJ	ATR 72-212A	898	ex F-WWEI		
☐ PK-WFK	ATR 72-212A	905	ex F-WWEV		♦
☐ PK-WFL	ATR 72-212A	915	ex F-WWEM		♦
☐ PK-WFM	ATR 72-212A	922	ex F-WWEV		♦
☐ PK-WFO	ATR 72-212A	936	ex F-WWEL		♦
☐ PK-WFP	ATR 72-212A	937	ex F-WWEM		♦
☐ PK-	ATR 72-212A		ex		o/o♦
☐ PK-	ATR 72-212A		ex		o/o♦
☐ PK-	ATR 72-212A		ex		o/o♦
☐ PK-	ATR 72-212A		ex		o/o♦
☐ PK-	ATR 72-212A		ex		o/o♦
☐ PK-WIA	de Havilland DHC-8-301	194	ex N194TY		
☐ PK-WID	de Havilland DHC-8-301	116	ex N116TY		
☐ PK-WIE	de Havilland DHC-8-301	108	ex N108TY		
☐ PK-LMG	McDonnell-Douglas MD-82	49417/1278	ex N417GE		[CGK], <LNI
☐ PK-LMP	McDonnell-Douglas MD-82	49117/1063	ex N35888		<LNI
☐ PK-LMS	McDonnell-Douglas MD-82	49114/1066	ex N14890		[CGK], <LNI
☐ PK-LMT	McDonnell-Douglas MD-82	49118/1065	ex N14889		<LNI
☐ PK-LMU	McDonnell-Douglas MD-82	49429/1242	ex N829US		[CGK], <LNI
☐ PK-WIF	McDonnell-Douglas MD-82	49481/1308	ex N72821		<LNI
☐ PK-WIG	McDonnell-Douglas MD-82	49489/1351	ex N72829		[CGK], <LNI
☐ PK-WIH	McDonnell-Douglas MD-82	49582/1411	ex N57837		<LNI
☐ PK-WIK	McDonnell-Douglas MD-82	49788/1637	ex PK-LMK		<LNI
☐ PK-WIL	McDonnell-Douglas MD-82	48083/1043	ex PK-LML		<LNI
☐ PK-WIO	McDonnell-Douglas MD-82	49102/1076	ex PK-LMQ		[CGK], <LNI
☐ PK-WIP	McDonnell-Douglas MD-82	49190/1180	ex PK-LMV		[CGK], <LNI

XPRESS AIR · (XN/XAR) · Ujung Pandang

☐ PK-TXD	Boeing 737-284	22400/766	ex SX-BCK	Grace	
☐ PK-TXF	Boeing 737-284	21302/475	ex SX-BCD		
☐ PK-TXG	Boeing 737-5L9	25066/2038	ex OY-MAE		
☐ PK-TXM	Dornier 328-110	3032	ex N423JS		
☐ PK-TXN	Dornier 328-110	3030	ex N328CH		
☐ PK-TXP	Dornier 328-110	3043	ex N429JS		

| ☐ PK-TXQ | Dornier 328-110 | 3038 | ex N426JS |
| ☐ PK-YGN | LET L-410UVP-E | 902434 | ex RP-C728 |

PP-, PR-, PT- BRAZIL (Federative Republic of Brazil)

ABAETE AEROTAXI Salvador, BA (SSA)

☐ PT-OGK	Cessna 208A Caravan I	20800078	ex N65575	
☐ PT-OGP	Cessna 208A Caravan I	20800050	ex N817FE	
☐ PT-OGR	Cessna 208A Caravan I	20800100	ex N838FE	
☐ PT-OGS	Cessna 208A Caravan I	20800034	ex N811FE	
☐ PT-OGT	Cessna 208A Caravan I	20800038	ex N815FE	
☐ PT-OGU	Cessna 208A Caravan I	20800066	ex N826FE	
☐ PT-OZA	Cessna 208B Caravan I	208B0157	ex N4615B	
☐ PP-ATT	Cessna 402B	402B0631	ex N3786C	
☐ PT-JBD	Cessna 402B	402B0404		
☐ PT-JRT	Cessna 402B	402B0552	ex N1634T	
☐ PT-JTZ	Cessna 402B	402B0532		
☐ PT-LKZ	Cessna 402B	402B1074	ex N1554G	
☐ PT-RGV	Embraer EMB.821 Caraja	820136	ex PT-ZNA	
☐ PT-VCH	Embraer EMB.821 Caraja	821012		
☐ PT-VCI	Embraer EMB.821 Caraja	820144		
☐ PT-VKD	Embraer EMB.821 Caraja	820159		
☐ PT-WFL	Embraer EMB.821 Caraja	820150		
☐ PT-ACM	Embraer EMB.121A Xingu	121021	ex PT-MAN	
☐ PT-MCA	Embraer EMB.121A1 Xingu	121058		

ABAETE LINHAS AEREAS (ABJ) Salvador, BA (SSA)

☐ PT-GKO	Embraer EMB.110P Bandeirante	110119	
☐ PT-MFO	Embraer EMB.110C Bandeirante	110058	ex FAB2158
☐ PT-MFP	Embraer EMB.110C Bandeirante	110105	ex FAB2181
☐ PT-MFQ	Embraer EMB.110C Bandeirante	110121	ex FAB2188
☐ PT-MFS	Embraer EMB.110C Bandeirante	110054	ex FAB2160

ABSA CARGO Absa Cargo (M3/TUS) Sao Paulo-Viracopos, SP (VCP)

☐ PR-ABB	Boeing 767-316F/W	29881/778	ex CC-CZX	<LAN♦
☐ PR-ABD	Boeing 767-316F/W	34245/934		<LAN
☐ PR-ACG	Boeing 767-316F/W	30780/806	ex CC-CZY	<LAN♦

AEB TAXI AERO Porto Alegre, RS (POA)

☐ PT-EVP	Embraer EMB.810C Seneca II	810250	
☐ PT-IUD	Piper PA-31-350 Navajo Chieftain	31-7305037	ex N74915
☐ PT-JEH	Piper PA-31-350 Navajo Chieftain	31-7305057	ex N74928

AERO STAR TAXI AEREO Salvador, BA (SSA)

☐ PT-EDF	Embraer EMB-820C Navajo	820014	
☐ PT-EZN	Embraer EMB-820C Navajo	820106	
☐ PT-KRO	Britten-Norman BN-2A-21 Islander	742	ex G-BCVL
☐ PT-KTR	Britten-Norman BN-2A-27 Islander	495	ex G-BDNN

AEROLEO TAXI AERO Rio de Janeiro-Santos Dumont, RJ / Macae & Sao Tome, RJ (SDU/MEA)

☐ PR-FNT	Aérospatiale AS.332L1	2468	ex LN-OMT	
☐ PR-GDR	Aérospatiale AS.332L1	2381	ex LN-OBF	
☐ PR-AEL	Sikorsky S-61N	61808	ex N563EH	
☐ PR-CHL	Sikorsky S-76A++	760160	ex D2-EXF	
☐ PR-CHP	Sikorsky S-76C+	760743	ex C-FYDD	
☐ PR-EDA	Sikorsky S-76A	760279	ex N710AL	<ALG
☐ PR-GPC	Sikorsky S-76A	760266	ex N703AL	<ALG
☐ PR-LBA	Sikorsky S-76C+	760705	ex N2584Q	<ALG
☐ PR-LCT	Sikorsky S-76C+	760723	ex N723Y	<ALG
☐ PR-LCL	Sikorsky S-76A	760280	ex N712AL	<ALG
☐ PR-LCV	Sikorsky S-76C+	760672	ex N4508N	<ALG
☐ PR-LCX	Sikorsky S-76C+	760704	ex N231Y	<ALG
☐ PR-LCZ	Sikorsky S-76C+	760707	ex N415Y	<ALG
☐ PR-LDA	Sikorsky S-76C+	760756	ex N756N	<ALG

☐ PR-LDB	Sikorsky S-76C+	760759	ex N759L	<ALG
☐ PR-LDC	Sikorsky S-76C+	760783		♦
☐ PR-LDD	Sikorsky S-76C+	760679	ex N882AL	<ALG
☐ PR-LDE	Sikorsky S-76C+	760784		♦
☐ PR-LDG	Sikorsky S-76C+	760785		♦
☐ PR-LDH	Sikorsky S-76C+	760777	ex N777LQ	♦
☐ PR-NLF	Sikorsky S-76A	760085	ex N1547K	<ALG
☐ PT-HOR	Sikorsky S-76A	760003	ex N476AL	<ALG
☐ PT-YAY	Sikorsky S-76A	760277	ex N708AL	<ALG
☐ PR-JAA	Sikorsky S-92A	920099	ex N2059J	
☐ PR-JAE	Sikorsky S-92A	920105	ex N2082Q	♦
☐ PR-JAF	Sikorsky S-92A	920093	ex N922AL	♦

AIR BRASIL CARGO (BSL)   Sao Paulo-Guarulhos, SP (GRU)

☐ PR-AIB	Boeing 727-227F (FedEx 3)	21363/1258	ex N79754	<Flightstar Group

AIR MINAS (6M)   Belo Horizonte, MG (CNF)

☐ PR-GDC	Embraer EMB.120ER Brasilia	120150	ex N789TX
☐ PR-MDP	Embraer EMB.120ER Brasilia	120250	ex N250YV
☐ PR-MGE	Embraer EMB.120RT Brasilia	120130	ex N130G
☐ PR-TUH	Embraer EMB.120ER Brasilia	120276	ex N212SW
☐ PR-UHT	Embraer EMB.120ER Brasilia	120280	ex N214SW

AMAZONAVES TAXI AEREO   Tefe / Manaus, AM (-/MAO)

☐ PP-ITZ	Cessna 208B Caravan I	208B0499	ex N5188N
☐ PT-EUS	Embraer EMB.810C Seneca	810230	
☐ PT-MET	Cessna 208B Caravan I	208B0509	ex N5073G
☐ PT-OLJ	Embraer EMB.810C Seneca	810330	
☐ PT-WIG	Embraer EMB.810C Seneca	810433	

APUI TAXI AEREO   Manaus-Ponta Pelada, AM (PLL)

☐ PT-GKX	Embraer EMB.110P Bandeirante	110129	
☐ PT-LRR	Embraer EMB.110P1 Bandeirante	110315	ex N695RA
☐ PT-ODJ	Embraer EMB.110 Bandeirante	110034	ex FAB 2144
☐ PT-ODY	Embraer EMB.110 Bandeirante	110039	ex FAB 2147
☐ PT-RCV	Embraer EMB.810C Seneca	810333	

ATA BRASIL   ATA Brasil (ABZ)   Fortaleza, CE (FOR)

☐ PR-GMA	Boeing 727-224F (FedEx 3)	20659/979	ex OY-SEY	[GYN]
☐ PR-LSW	Boeing 737-248C	20219/208	ex CC-CEI	
☐ PR-MGA	Boeing 737-204C	20282/245	ex N282AD	

AVIANCA BRAZIL (ONE)   Rio de Janeiro-Santos Dumont, RJ (SDU)

☐ PR-AVB	Airbus A319-115	4222	ex D-AVYJ		♦
☐ PR-AVC	Airbus A319-115	4287	ex D-AVWT		♦
☐ PR-AVD	Airbus A319-115	4336	ex D-AVXG		♦
☐ PR-BRB	Boeing 737-3Q4	24210/1577	ex PT-TEH		
☐ PR-BRD	Boeing 737-3M8	24376/1717	ex EC-GGO		
☐ PR-OAO	Embraer EMB.120RT Brasilia	120057	ex N239AS	Grey c/s	
☐ PR-OAP	Embraer EMB.120RT Brasilia	120060	ex N240AS	Magenta c/s	
☐ PT-SLC	Embraer EMB.120ER Brasilia	120094	ex PT-SML	Red c/s	
☐ PT-SRF	Embraer EMB.120ER Brasilia	120192		White c/s	
☐ PR-OAD	Fokker 100	11370	ex N1412A		
☐ PR-OAE	Fokker 100	11426	ex N1436A		
☐ PR-OAF	Fokker 100	11415	ex N1430D		
☐ PR-OAG	Fokker 100	11412	ex N1427A		
☐ PR-OAI	Fokker 100	11417	ex N1432A		
☐ PR-OAJ	Fokker 100	11418	ex N1433B		
☐ PR-OAK	Fokker 100	11425	ex N1435D		
☐ PR-OAL	Fokker 100	11435	ex N1440A		
☐ PR-OAM	Fokker 100	11436	ex N1441A		
☐ PR-OAQ	Fokker 100	11467	ex N1455K		
☐ PR-OAR	Fokker 100	11481	ex N1461C		
☐ PR-OAS	Fokker 100	11405	ex N1422J		
☐ PR-OAT	Fokker 100	11411	ex N1426A		
☐ PR-OAU	Fokker 100	11427	ex N1437B		

AZUL (AD / AZU) Sao Paulo-Viracopos, SP (VCP)

☐ PR-AZR	ATR 72-202QC	519	ex F-WKVB		♦
☐ PR-	ATR 72-				o/o♦
☐ PR-	ATR 72-				o/o♦
☐ PR-	ATR 72-				o/o♦
☐ PR-	ATR 72-				o/o♦
☐ PR-AYA	Embraer ERJ-195AR	19000237	ex PT-SIK	Azul e Brasil	
☐ PR-AYB	Embraer ERJ-195AR	19000239		Tudo Azul	
☐ PR-AYC	Embraer ERJ-195AR	19000240		A Liberdade e Azul	
☐ PR-AYD	Embraer ERJ-195AR	19000247		Azalou	
☐ PR-AYE	Embraer ERJ-195AR	19000260	ex PT-STI	Azul do Cor da Mar	
☐ PR-AYF	Embraer ERJ-195AR	19000353		Tripulante Azul	♦
☐ PR-AYG	Embraer ERJ-195AR	19000356		Tudo Novo, Tudo Azul	♦
☐ PR-AYH	Embraer ERJ-195AR	19000361		Céu, Sol, Sul, Azul	♦
☐ PR-AYI	Embraer ERJ-195AR	19000366		Azul Celeste	♦
☐ PR-AYJ	Embraer ERJ-195AR	19000370		Azul Real	♦
☐ PR-AYK	Embraer ERJ-195AR	19000374		Diamante Azul	♦
☐ PR-AYL	Embraer ERJ-195AR	19000378		Amazonia Azul	♦
☐ PR-AYM	Embraer ERJ-195AR	19000382		Cada Vez mais Azul	♦
☐ PR-AYN	Embraer ERJ-195AR	19000386		Blue Angels	♦
☐ PR-AYO	Embraer ERJ-195AR	19000391		Rosa e Azul	♦
☐ PR-AYP	Embraer ERJ-195AR	19000396		Arara Azul	♦
☐ PR-AYQ	Embraer ERJ-195AR	19000407			o/o♦
☐ PR-	Embraer ERJ-195AR				o/o♦
☐ PR-	Embraer ERJ-195AR				o/o♦
☐ PR-	Embraer ERJ-195AR				o/o♦
☐ PR-	Embraer ERJ-195AR				o/o♦
☐ PR-	Embraer ERJ-195AR				o/o♦
☐ PR-	Embraer ERJ-195AR				o/o♦
☐ PR-	Embraer ERJ-195AR				o/o♦
☐ PR-	Embraer ERJ-195AR				o/o♦
☐ PR-	Embraer ERJ-195AR				o/o♦
☐ PR-	Embraer ERJ-195AR				o/o♦
☐ PR-AZA	Embraer ERJ-190AR	19000150	ex N290JB	Azulville	
☐ PR-AZB	Embraer ERJ-190AR	19000241	ex N840JE	Azul Paulista	
☐ PR-AZC	Embraer ERJ-190AR	19000242	ex N841JS	Ceu Azul	
☐ PR-AZD	Embraer ERJ-190AR	19000271	ex PT-TLL	Passaro Azul	
☐ PR-AZE	Embraer ERJ-190AR	19000282	ex PT-TLW	Verda, Amarelo e Azul	
☐ PR-AZF	Embraer ERJ-190AR	19000295		Voce que e Feito de Azul	
☐ PR-AZG	Embraer ERJ-190AR	19000329		A Terra e Azul	
☐ PR-AZH	Embraer ERJ-190AR	19000330		Azulcenter	
☐ PR-AZI	Embraer ERJ-190AR	19000336		Adorinha Azul	
☐ PR-AZL	Embraer ERJ-190AR	19000147	ex N288JB	O Rio de Janeiro continua Azul	

BAHIA TAXI AEREO – BATA Salvador, BA (SSA)

☐ PT-EPY	Embraer EMB.820C Navajo	820077	

BETA CARGO AIR Beta Cargo (BET) Sao Paulo-Guarulhos, SP (GRU)

☐ PP-BEL	Douglas DC-8-73AF	46047/447	ex N809DH	
☐ PP-BEM	Douglas DC-8-73F	46086/478	ex N870TV	
☐ PP-BET	Douglas DC-8-73CF	46103/483	ex N795FT	
☐ PP-BEX	Douglas DC-8-73F	46104/488	ex N796FT	
☐ PP-BRR	Boeing 707-323C (Comtran 2)	20088/727	ex PT-TCN	[GRU]

BHS - BRAZILIAN HELICOPTER SERVICES TAXI AEREO
Sao Paulo-Marte, SP, Farol de Sao Tome, SP, Macae& Sao Tome, RJ

☐ PP-MEM	Sikorsky S-76A+	760092	ex N176PA	
☐ PP-MET	Sikorsky S-76A	760229	ex N31217	
☐ PP-MHM	Sikorsky S-76C	760376	ex N776AB	
☐ PP-MPM	Sikorsky S-76C	760375	ex N775AB	
☐ PR-CHA	Sikorsky S-76C+	760625	ex C-GBQE	
☐ PR-CHB	Sikorsky S-76A++	760004	ex C-GIME	
☐ PR-CHC	Sikorsky S-76C+	760632	ex C-GBQF	
☐ PR-CHD	Sikorsky S-76C+	760636	ex C-GBQG	
☐ PR-CHE	Sikorsky S-76C+	760642	ex C-GBQH	
☐ PR-CHF	Sikorsky S-76C+	760657	ex N4505G	
☐ PR-CHK	Sikorsky S-76C+	760687	ex C-FRHF	<CHC Helicopters Intl
☐ PR-CJK	Sikorsky S-76C+	760674	ex N4513G	<CHC Helicopters Intl
☐ PR-CHN	Sikorsky S-76A++	760187	ex C-FIHD	
☐ PR-CHP	Sikorsky S-76C++	760743	ex C-FYDD	
☐ PR-CHQ	Sikorsky S-76C++	760734	ex C-FXFK	

☐ PR-MCH	Sikorsky S-76A++	760213	ex C-GIMX	
☐ PT-YGM	Sikorsky S-76A	760067	ex ZS-RJK	<CHC Helicopters Africa
☐ PT-YIM	Sikorsky S-76A	760144	ex XA-SRS	
☐ PT-YQM	Sikorsky S-76A	760051	ex ZS-RGZ	<CHC Helicopters Africa
☐ PR-CHR	Sikorsky S-92A	920112	ex C-FRWL	
☐ PR-CHS	Sikorsky S-92A	920113	ex C-FPKW	
☐ PR-CHT	Sikorsky S-92A	920119	ex C-GDHU	
☐ PR-CHU	Sikorsky S-92A	920127	ex C-GFHO	♦
☐ PP-MTM	Aérospatiale AS.332L2	2599		
☐ PP-MZM	Aérospatiale AS.332L2	2572	ex F-WQDJ	
☐ PR-BGB	Eurocopter EC225LP	2768		♦
☐ PR-CHW	Eurocopter EC225LP	2740	ex G-DRIT	
☐ PR-CHX	Eurocopter EC225LP	2729	ex G-CLAR	
☐ PR-CHY	Eurocopter EC225LP	2722	ex G-LJAM	
☐ PR-CHZ	Aérospatiale AS.332L	2015	ex OY-HHA	<CHC Helicopters Intl
☐ PR-PLL	Eurocopter EC225LP	2680	ex N225EH	
☐ PR-VLL	Eurocopter EC225LP	2685	ex N247CF	
☐ PR-YCL	Eurocopter EC225LP 2	2708	ex LN-OHY	
☐ PR-MEK	Aérospatiale SA365N Dauphin 2	6030	ex PH-SSX	
☐ PT-HNZ	Helibras HS.350B Esquilo	B-1151-2486		

CRUISER TAXI AEREO BRASIL   (J6)   Curitiba, PR (CWB)

☐ PR-CRA	LET L-410UVP-E20	902514	ex OK-VDP
☐ PR-CRX	LET L-410UVP-E20	912617	ex OK-2617
☐ PT-WBR	Embraer EMB.110C Bandeirante	110045	ex FAB 2153

FRETAX TAXI AEREO

☐ PR-JOH	Cessna 208B Caravan I	208B0323	ex N465BA	♦
☐ PR-JOS	Cessna 208B Caravan I	208B0067	ex N126HA	♦
☐ PR-MSH	Cessna 208B Caravan I	208B0700	ex N700RH	♦
☐ PR-SMM	Cessna 208B Caravan I	208B1224		♦
☐ PT-OGE	Cessna 208 Caravan	2080184	ex N9765F	♦
☐ PT-OGQ	Cessna 208 Caravan	2080032	ex N809FE	♦

GENSA   Gensa Brasil (GEN)   Campo Grande, MS (CGR)

☐ PR-GSA	Embraer EMB.120ER Brasilia	120119	ex 5N-TCE
☐ PR-GSB	Embraer EMB.120ER Brasilia	120127	ex 5N-LCE
☐ PT-SHN	Embraer EMB.110P1A Bandeirante	110460	
☐ PT-SOG	Embraer EMB.110P1 Bandeirante	110490	

GIRASSOL AEROTAXI   Manaus-Eduardo Gomes, AM (MAO)

☐ PT-DKO	Beech 95-B55 Baron	TC-1335	
☐ PT-EAA	Embraer EMB.810C Seneca	810001	
☐ PT-EBN	Embraer EMB.820C Navajo	820001	
☐ PT-JBT	Piper PA-31-350 Navajo Chieftain	31-7305101	ex N74953
☐ PT-KXV	Rockwell 500S Shrike Commander	3104	ex PT-FRA
☐ PT-LYH	Piper PA-31-350 Navajo Chieftain	31-7305124	ex PP-EFS

GOL TRANSPORTES AEREOS   Gol Transporte (G3/GLO)   Sao Paulo-Congonhas, SP (CGH)

☐ PR-GID	Boeing 737-76N/W	29904/347	ex N745AL	
☐ PR-GIF	Boeing 737-73S	29076/98	ex OY-MLY	
☐ PR-GIG	Boeing 737-73S	29077/104	ex OY-MLZ	
☐ PR-GIH	Boeing 737-76N/W	32743/1503	ex N750AL	
☐ PR-GII	Boeing 737-7L9	28011/1203	ex OY-MRL	
☐ PR-GIJ	Boeing 737-7L9	28012/1092	ex OY-MRK	>SNB
☐ PR-GIK	Boeing 737-7Q8	28224/369	ex N161LF	
☐ PR-GIL	Boeing 737-7Q8	30635/713	ex N151LF	
☐ PR-GIM	Boeing 737-73V	30238/913	ex G-EZJE	
☐ PR-GIN	Boeing 737-73V	30242/690	ex G-EZJD	
☐ PR-GOA	Boeing 737-7L9	28005/11	ex OY-MRB	special c/s
☐ PR-GOB	Boeing 737-75B	28099/13	ex D-AGEM	
☐ PR-GOC	Boeing 737-75B	28101/17	ex D-AGEO	
☐ PR-GOD	Boeing 737-75B	28105/66	ex D-AGEV	
☐ PR-GOE	Boeing 737-75B	28106/68	ex D-AGEW	
☐ PR-GOF	Boeing 737-76Q	30273/843	ex N1786B Aurea	
☐ PR-GOG	Boeing 737-76Q	30275/900	ex N795BA	
☐ PR-GOH	Boeing 737-76N	32440/954	ex N1786B	
☐ PR-GOI	Boeing 737-76N	32574/983	ex N1786B	
☐ PR-GOL	Boeing 737-7L9	28004/10	ex OY-MRA	
☐ PR-GOM	Boeing 737-76N	28613/463	ex N312ML	
☐ PR-GON	Boeing 737-76N	30051/436	ex N311ML	

☐ PR-GOO	Boeing 737-76N	30135/1068	ex N135SF			
☐ PR-GOQ	Boeing 737-76N	33417/1215				
☐ PR-GOR	Boeing 737-76N	33380/1231				
☐ PR-GOV	Boeing 737-76N	28580/135	ex N580HE			
☐ PR-GOW	Boeing 737-76N	28584/170	ex N584SR			
☐ PR-GOX	Boeing 737-7K9	28088/19	ex N100UN			
☐ PR-GOY	Boeing 737-7K9	28089/25	ex N101UN			
☐ PR-VBH	Boeing 737-73V	30239/944	ex N239CG			
☐ PR-VBI	Boeing 737-73V	30246/1064	ex N346CL			
☐ PR-VBO	Boeing 737-73V	30247/1066	ex G-EZJL			
☐ PR-VBW	Boeing 737-7BX	30739/758	ex 6V-AHO			
☐ PR-VBY	Boeing 737-73A/W	28499/390	ex N738AL	Varig c/s		
☐ PR-VBZ	Boeing 737-73A/W	28500/414	ex N739AL	Varig c/s		
☐ PR-	Boeing 737-7EH/W					o/o◆
☐ PR-	Boeing 737-7EH/W					o/o◆
☐ PR-GEA	Boeing 737-7EH/W	37595/3026				
☐ PR-GGA	Boeing 737-8EH/W	35063/2476	ex N1787B			
☐ PR-GGB	Boeing 737-8EH/W	35064/2498				
☐ PR-GGD	Boeing 737-8EH/W	34275/2588				
☐ PR-GGE	Boeing 737-8EH/W	35824/2665	ex N1786B			
☐ PR-GGF	Boeing 737-8EH/W	35826/2749				
☐ PR-GGG	Boeing 737-8EH/W	36566/2809				
☐ PR-GGH	Boeing 737-8EH/W	36147/2864	ex N1787B			
☐ PR-GGJ	Boeing 737-8EH/W	35825/2786	ex N1796B			
☐ PR-GGK	Boeing 737-8EH/W	35065/2561				
☐ PR-GGL	Boeing 737-8EH/W	36148/2890				
☐ PR-GGM	Boeing 737-8EH/W	36149/2920	ex N1786B			
☐ PR-GGN	Boeing 737-8EH/W	35827/2991	ex N1786B			
☐ PR-GGO	Boeing 737-8EH/W	35828/3025				
☐ PR-GGP	Boeing 737-8EH/W	35829/3076	ex N1787B			
☐ PR-GGQ	Boeing 737-8EH/W	37596/3103	ex N1786B			
☐ PR-GGR	Boeing 737-8EH/W	36150/3106	ex N1787B			
☐ PR-GGT	Boeing 737-8EH/W	35830/3115				
☐ PR-GGU	Boeing 737-8EH/W	37597/3133				
☐ PR-GGV	Boeing 737-8EH/W	37598/3136				
☐ PR-GGW	Boeing 737-8EH/W	35831/3165	ex PH-GGW			
☐ PR-GGX	Boeing 737-8EH/W	36596/3180	ex N1787B			
☐ PR-GGY	Boeing 737-8EH/W	37599/3191				
☐ PR-GGZ	Boeing 737-8EH/W	37600/3205	ex N1786B			◆
☐ PR-GIE	Boeing 737-8BK/W	33027/1918	ex N1786B			
☐ PR-GIO	Boeing 737-85F/W	30477/976	ex N477GX			
☐ PR-GIP	Boeing 737-85F/W	30571/936	ex N571GX			
☐ PR-GIQ	Boeing 737-86N/W	28616/483	ex TC-SUC			
☐ PR-GIR	Boeing 737-8Q8	28213/50	ex OY-SEA			
☐ PR-GIT	Boeing 737-809	28403/117	ex TC-APM			
☐ PR-GIU	Boeing 737-809	29103/129	ex TC-APZ			
☐ PR-GIV	Boeing 737-86N/W	28578/89	ex VT-JNA			
☐ PR-GIW	Boeing 737-86N/W	28575/91	ex VT-JNB			
☐ PR-GIX	Boeing 737-8Q8	30636/768	ex N330LF			
☐ PR-GOJ	Boeing 737-8CX	32359/1041				[PTY]
☐ PR-GOP	Boeing 737-8BK	30621/1194	ex N461LF	Victoria		
☐ PR-GOT	Boeing 737-8BK	30625/1248				
☐ PR-GTA	Boeing 737-8EH/W	34474/1843	ex N6067U			
☐ PR-GTB	Boeing 737-8EH/W	34475/2020				
☐ PR-GTC	Boeing 737-8EH/W	34277/2028	ex N1786B			
☐ PR-GTE	Boeing 737-8EH/W	34278/2052				
☐ PR-GTF	Boeing 737-8EH/W	34279/2061				
☐ PR-GTG	Boeing 737-8EH/W	34654/2075				
☐ PR-GTH	Boeing 737-8EH/W	34655/2091				
☐ PR-GTI	Boeing 737-8EH/W	34280/2100				
☐ PR-GTJ	Boeing 737-8EH/W	34656/2110				
☐ PR-GTK	Boeing 737-8EH/W	34281/2116				
☐ PR-GTL	Boeing 737-8EH/W	34962/2215	ex N1786B			
☐ PR-GTM	Boeing 737-8EH/W	34963/2240				
☐ PR-GTN	Boeing 737-8EH/W	34267/2311				
☐ PR-GTO	Boeing 737-8EH/W	34964/2332				
☐ PR-GTP	Boeing 737-8EH/W	34965/2341				
☐ PR-GTQ	Boeing 737-8EH/W	36146/2358				
☐ PR-GTR	Boeing 737-8EH/W	34966/2367				
☐ PR-GTT	Boeing 737-8EH/W	34268/2407				
☐ PR-GTU	Boeing 737-8EH/W	34269/2412	ex N1786B			
☐ PR-GTV	Boeing 737-8EH/W	34270/2420				
☐ PR-GTY	Boeing 737-8EH/W	34273/2464				
☐ PR-GTZ	Boeing 737-8EH/W	34274/2468	ex N1795B			
☐ PR-GUA	Boeing 737-8EH/W	37601/3301				◆
☐ PR-GUB	Boeing 737-8EH/W	35832/3309				◆

☐ PR-GUC	Boeing 737-8EH/W	35835/3430	ex N1787B	♦
☐ PR-GUD	Boeing 737-8EH/W	35836/3466		♦
☐ PR-GUE	Boeing 737-8EH/W	35837/3473		♦
☐ PR-GUF	Boeing 737-8EH/W	35838/3508		♦
☐ PR-	Boeing 737-8EH/W			o/o♦
☐ PR-	Boeing 737-8EH/W			o/o♦
☐ PR-	Boeing 737-8EH/W			o/o♦

HELISUL TAXI AEREO — Foz do Iguaçu, PR

☐ PR-HTA	Helibras HS.350B2 Esquilo	AS3523	
☐ PT-HGB	Bell 206B JetRanger III	4298	ex C-FRIN
☐ PT-HMI	Helibras HS.350B Esquilo	1639/HB1046	
☐ PT-HML	Helibras HS.350B Esquilo	1642/HB1049	
☐ PT-HOY	Bell 206B JetRanger III	4171	ex N4171J
☐ PT-HTC	Bell 206B JetRanger III	3449	ex N2113Z
☐ PT-YAP	Bell 206B JetRanger III	3481	ex N215RG
☐ PT-YEL	Bell 206L-4 LongRanger IV	52198	ex N6593X

HELIVIA AERO TAXI — Manaus-Ponta Pelada, AM (PLL)

☐ PT-HVA	MBB Bo.105CBS-4	S-795	ex N5416X
☐ PT-HVB	MBB Bo.105CBS-4	S-792	ex N7062W
☐ PT-HXK	MBB Bo.105CBS-4	S-785	ex N54125
☐ PT-YAW	Aérospatiale SA.330J Puma	1590	ex F-GEQI

INTERAVIA TAXI AEREO

| ☐ PR-JAT | Cessna 208B Caravan I | 208B1193 | ex N13189 |

LITORANEA

| ☐ PR-VLA | LET L-410UVP-E20 | 882101 | ex OK-TDA |

MANAUS AERO TAXI — Manaus-Ponta Pelada, AM (PLL)

| ☐ PR-MPE | Cessna 208 Caravan I | 20800510 | ex N13189 |

META - MESQUITA TRANSPORTES AEREO — Meta (MSQ) — Boa Vista, RR (BVB)

☐ PT-FLY	Embraer EMB.120ER Brasilia	120044	ex PT-SLI
☐ PT-LMZ	Cessna U206F Stationair	U20602184	
☐ PT-LNW	Embraer EMB.110P1 Bandeirante	110346	ex N697RA
☐ PT-LXN	Embraer EMB.120ER Brasilia	120052	ex D-CEMG
☐ PT-OND	Cessna U206G Stationair 6	U20606542	ex N9529Z

MTA CARGO — Master (MST) — Sao Paulo-Viracopos, SP (VCP)

☐ N501TR	Airbus A300B4-203F	053	ex N6254X		<TDX♦
☐ PP-MTA	Douglas DC-10-30CF	47908/215	ex N322FE	Petete IV	
☐ PR-MTC	Douglas DC-10-30F	46540/268	ex N304SP		

NHR TAXI AEREO — Sorocaba, SP (SOD)

☐ PR-ELT	Embraer EMB.110P1 Bandeirante	110412	ex P2-IAL
☐ PR-KIN	Embraer EMB.110P1 Bandeirante	110254	ex P2-IAJ
☐ PR-NHR	Embraer EMB.110P1 Bandeirante	110394	ex P2-IAK
☐ PT-MAL	Embraer EMB.121A1 Xingu	121019	
☐ PT-SHY	Embraer EMB.110P1 Bandeirante	110470	
☐ PT-WAW	Embraer EMB.110 Bandeirante	110122	ex FAB 2189
☐ PT-WCM	Embraer EMB.110 Bandeirante	110041	ex FAB 2148

NHT LINHAS AEREAS — (NHG) — Sorocaba, SP (SOD)

☐ PR-NHA	LET L-410UVP-E20	062636	
☐ PR-NHB	LET L-410UVP-E20	062637	
☐ PR-NHC	LET L-410UVP-E20	072639	
☐ PR-NHD	LET L-410UVP-E20	072640	
☐ PR-NHE	LET L-410UVP-E20	082714	ex OK-2714
☐ PR-	LET L-410UVP-E20		

PANTANAL — Pantanal (P8/PTN) — Sao Paulo-Congonhas, SP (CGH)

☐ PT-MFJ	ATR 42-320	343	ex F-WQHV
☐ PT-MFM	ATR 42-300	376	ex F-GKNH
☐ PT-MFT	ATR 42-320	306	ex G-BXEH
☐ PT-MFU	ATR 42-310	070	ex F-GHJE
☐ PT-MFV	ATR 42-300	043	ex F-GGLR

461

PASSAREDO TRANSPORTES AEREOS		*(PTB)*		*Ribeirao Preto, SP (RAO)*
☐ PR-OAN	Embraer EMB.120RT Brasilia	120051	ex N237AS	
☐ PP-PSA	Embraer EMB.120ER Brasilia	120302		
☐ PP-PSB	Embraer EMB.120ER Brasilia	120303		
☐ PR-PSD	Embraer EMB.120ER Brasilia	120118	ex N507DM	
☐ PT-SLD	Embraer EMB.120ER Brasilia	120147		
☐ PT-SLE	Embraer EMB.120ER Brasilia	120161		
☐ PR-PSF	Embraer ERJ-145EP	145016	ex N826HK	
☐ PR-PSG	Embraer ERJ-145EP	145021	ex N827HK	
☐ PR-PSH	Embraer ERJ-145LR	145597	ex N559MD	
☐ PR-PSK	Embraer ERJ-145LU	145387	ex OH-EBF	◆
☐ PR-PSL	Embraer ERJ-145LR	145269	ex N834HK	◆
☐ PR-PSM	Embraer ERJ-145LR	145281	ex N829HK	◆
☐ PR-PSN	Embraer ERJ-145MP	145407	ex F-GUJA	◆
☐ PR-PSQ	Embraer ERJ-145MP	145244	ex G-CGJR	◆
☐ PR-PSR	Embraer ERJ-145MP	145339	ex G-RJXO	◆
PENTA - PENA TRANSPORTES AEREOS		*Aero Pena (5P/PEP)*		*Santarem, PA (STM)*
☐ PP-ISE	Embraer EMB.120ER Brasilia	120246	ex N6222Z	
☐ PT-LLC	Embraer EMB.110P1 Bandeirante	110427	ex N302EB	
☐ PT-MPB	Cessna 208B Caravan I	208B0630	ex N5263A	
☐ PT-MPD	Cessna 208B Caravan I	208B0644	ex N5267T	
☐ PT-MPG	Cessna 208B Caravan I	208B0645	ex N5268A	
☐ PT-OSG	Cessna 208B Caravan I	208B0300	ex N5516B	
☐ PT-SOF	Embraer EMB.110P1A Bandeirante	110486		
PLATINUM AIR LINHAS AEREAS		*(PLJ)*		*Sao Jose dos Campos (SJK)*
☐ PR-PLH	Boeing 727-225 (Super 27)	22434/1671	ex N770PL	
PUMA AIR LINHAS AEREAS		*Puma Brasil (PLY)*		*Belem, PA (BEL)*
☐ PR-GLK	Boeing 737-322	24668/1905	ex N393UA	
☐ PP-PTB	Embraer EMB.120RT Brasilia	120080	ex F-GFEP	dbr 24Nov06?
☐ PR-PMC	Cessna 208B Caravan I	208B0909	ex N12826	
☐ PT-STN	Embraer EMB.120ER Brasilia	120241		
RICO LINHAS AEREAS		*Rico (C7/RLE)*		*Manaus-Eduardo Gomez, AM (MAO)*
☐ PR-RLA	Boeing 737-241	21009/417	ex PP-VMN	[MAO]
☐ (PR-RLB)	Boeing 737-241	21008/402	ex PP-VMM	[MAO]
☐ (PR-RLC)	Boeing 737-241	21000/378	ex PP-VME	
☐ PT-WDB	Embraer EMB.110C Bandeirante	110051	ex FAB2159	
☐ PT-WJA	Embraer EMB.110P1 Bandeirante	110265	ex PT-OHF	
☐ PT-WJG	Embraer EMB.120ER Brasilia	120064	ex PT-PCA	
☐ PT-WRU	Cessna 208 Caravan I	20800284		FP
☐ PT-WZM	Embraer EMB.120ER Brasilia	120041	ex PP-IAD	
☐		Antonov An-32		o/o
☐		Antonov An-32		o/o
RICO TAXI AEREO				*Manaus-Eduardo Gomez, AM (MAO)*
☐ PT-GJC	Embraer EMB.110E Bandeirante	110055		
☐ PT-MAA	Embraer EMB.121A Xingu II	121001	ex PT-ZCT	
RIO LINHAS AEREAS				
☐ PR-IOA	Boeing 727-214F	21512/1343	ex N750US	◆
☐ PR-IOB	Boeing 727-264F (FedEx 3)	22983/1806	ex N763AT	◆
☐ PR-IOC	Boeing 727-264F (FedEx 3)	22984/1813	ex N764AT	◆
☐ PR-IOD	Boeing 727-264F (FedEx 3)	23014/1816	ex N765AT	◆
☐ PR-IOF	Boeing 727-214F	21692/1479	ex N786AT	◆
☐ PR-IOG	Boeing 727-214F	21691/1480	ex N785AT	◆
☐ PR-RLJ	Boeing 727-214F	21513/1365	ex N751US	◆
SETE TAXI AEREO		*Sete*		*Goiania, GO (GYN)*
☐ PR-MEG	Cessna 208B Caravan I	208B0352	ex N1114N	
☐ PR-MEH	Cessna 208B Caravan I	208B0354	ex N1114W	
☐ PR-MEI	Cessna 208B Caravan I	208B0358	ex N1115P	
☐ PT-MEK	Cessna 208B Caravan I	208B0360	ex N1115W	
☐ PT-MEL	Cessna 208B Caravan I	208B0361	ex N1116G	
☐ PR-STE	Embraer EMB.120ER Brasilia	120295	ex N295UX	◆
☐ PT-EHE	Embraer EMB.820C Navajo	820041		
☐ PT-LHH	Mitsubishi MU-2B-60 Marquise	1508SA	ex N618RT	

462

☐ PT-WST	Mitsubishi MU-2B-36A	711SA	ex N171CA		
☐ PT-WYT	Mitsubishi MU-2B-36A	722SA	ex N722MU		

SIDERAL AIR CARGO

☐ PR-SDL	Boeing 737-3S3F	24060/1519	ex N312AW		♦

SKYLIFT TAXI AEREO · Campinhas, SP (CPQ)

☐ PT-PQD	Short SC.7 Skyvan 3	SH1951	ex C-FSDZ	

SKYMASTER AIRLINES · Skymaster Air (SKC)
Manaus-Eduardo Gomes, AM/Sao Paulo-Viracopos, SP (MAO/VCP)

☐ PR-SKC	Douglas DC-8-63F (BAC 3)	46143/547	ex N959R		
☐ PR-SKI	Douglas DC-8-62F (BAC 3)	46154/554	ex N997CF		
☐ PR-SKM	Douglas DC-8-63F (BAC 3)	46137/527	ex N957R		
☐ PT-MTE	Boeing 707-321C (Comtran 2)	20017/753	ex OB-1716		
☐ PT-MTR	Boeing 707-369C (Comtran 2)	20084/758	ex OB-1699		
☐ PT-WUS	Boeing 707-324C (Comtran 2)	19352/576	ex HK-3604X		[GRU]

TAF LINHAS AEREAS · Tafi (TSD) · Fortaleza, CE (FOR)

☐ PP-SBF	Embraer EMB.110C Bandeirante	110023			[FOR]
☐ PR-MTD	Boeing 727-227F (Raisbeck 3)	21248/1218	ex N76752		
☐ PR-MTG	Boeing 737-217 (AvAero 3)	22255/666	ex N5JY	Gracinha	
☐ PR-MTH	Boeing 737-232 (Nordam 3)	23102/1045	ex N330DL		
☐ PR-MTJ	Boeing 727-2M7F (FedEx 3)	21952/1693	ex N742RW		
☐ PR-MTK	Boeing 727-222F	20037/701	ex N7643U	Adriana	
☐ PR-MTL	Boeing 727-2J7F	20879/1033	ex N128NA		
☐ PT-GJD	Embraer EMB.110EJ Bandeirante	110056			
☐ PT-LBU	Embraer EMB.110C Bandeirante	110033	ex PT-FAE		[FOR]
☐ PT-MTC	Boeing 727-228F (FedEx 3)	20409/845	ex N726DH	Comte Dilsonr	
☐ PT-MTF	Boeing 737-241	21007/400	ex PP-VML		
☐ PT-OGG	Cessna 208A Caravan I	20800041	ex N813FE		
☐ PT-OGL	Cessna 208A Caravan I	20800102	ex N839FE		
☐ PT-OGV	Cessna 208A Caravan I	20800019	ex N805FE		
☐ PT-OQT	Cessna 208B Grand Caravan	208B0314	ex N1018X		
☐ PT-YTF	Helibras AS350B2 Esquilo	AS.3149			

TAM LINHAS AEREAS · TAM (JJ/TAM) · Sao Paulo-Congonhas, SP (GGH)

☐ PR-MAH	Airbus A319-132	1608	ex D-AIJO		
☐ PR-MAI	Airbus A319-132	1703	ex D-AIMM		
☐ PR-MAL	Airbus A319-132	1801	ex D-AVWD		
☐ PR-MAM	Airbus A319-132	1826	ex D-AVWN		
☐ PR-MAN	Airbus A319-132	1831	ex D-AVWR		
☐ PR-MAO	Airbus A319-132	1837	ex D-AVYQ		
☐ PR-MAQ	Airbus A319-132	1855	ex D-AVYA		
☐ PR-MBI	Airbus A319-132	1575	ex N475TA		
☐ PR-MBN	Airbus A319-132	3032	ex D-AVWG		
☐ PR-MBU	Airbus A319-132	3588	ex D-AVYG		
☐ PR-MBV	Airbus A319-132	3595	ex D-AVYC		
☐ PR-MBW	Airbus A319-132	3710	ex D-AVWQ		
☐ PR-MYB	Airbus A319-112	3727	ex D-AVWT		
☐ PR-MYC	Airbus A319-112	3733	ex D-AVWW		
☐ PT-MZA	Airbus A319-132	0976	ex D-AVYI		
☐ PT-MZB	Airbus A319-132	1010	ex D-AVYA		
☐ PT-MZC	Airbus A319-132	1092	ex D-AVYD		
☐ PT-MZD	Airbus A319-132	1096	ex D-AVYR		
☐ PT-MZE	Airbus A319-132	1103	ex D-AVWD		
☐ PT-MZF	Airbus A319-132	1139	ex D-AVYO		
☐ PT-TMA	Airbus A319-132	4000	ex D-AVYA		
☐ PT-TMB	Airbus A319-132	4163	ex D-AVYF		♦
☐ PT-TMC	Airbus A319-132	4171	ex D-AVWJ		♦
☐ PT-TMD	Airbus A319-132	4192	ex D-AVYA		♦
☐ PT-TME	Airbus A319-132	4389	ex D-AVXH		♦
☐ PT-TMF	Airbus A319-132	2467	ex D-ABGB		♦
☐ PT-	Airbus A319-132		ex		o/o♦
☐ PT-	Airbus A319-132		ex		o/o♦
☐ PT-	Airbus A319-132		ex		o/o♦
☐ PR-MAA	Airbus A320-232	1595	ex F-WWBU		
☐ PR-MAB	Airbus A320-232	1663	ex F-WWIE		
☐ PR-MAC	Airbus A320-232	1672	ex F-WWIK	450 anos	
☐ PR-MAD	Airbus A320-232	1771	ex F-WWDD		
☐ PR-MAE	Airbus A320-232	1804	ex F-WWII		

☐ PR-MAG	Airbus A320-232	1832	ex F-WWBD	Sao Paulo 450 Anos	
☐ PR-MAJ	Airbus A320-232	1818	ex F-WWIN		
☐ PR-MAK	Airbus A320-232	1825	ex F-WWIX		
☐ PR-MAP	Airbus A320-232	1857	ex F-WWBZ		
☐ PR-MAR	Airbus A320-232	1888	ex F-WWBS		
☐ PR-MAS	Airbus A320-232	2372	ex F-WWDQ		
☐ PR-MAV	Airbus A320-232	2393	ex F-WWIR		
☐ PR-MAW	Airbus A320-232	2417	ex F-WWDT		
☐ PR-MAX	Airbus A320-232	2602	ex F-WWBO		
☐ PR-MAY	Airbus A320-232	2661	ex F-WWIV		
☐ PR-MAZ	Airbus A320-232	2513	ex F-WWIY		
☐ PR-MBA	Airbus A320-232	2734	ex F-WWBF		
☐ PR-MBB	Airbus A320-232	2737	ex F-WWBH		
☐ PR-MBC	Airbus A320-232	2783	ex F-WWDZ		
☐ PR-MBD	Airbus A320-232	2838	ex F-WWID		
☐ PR-MBE	Airbus A320-232	2859	ex F-WWIU		
☐ PR-MBF	Airbus A320-232	2896	ex F-WWBZ		
☐ PR-MBG	Airbus A320-232	1459	ex OE-LOR		
☐ PR-MBH	Airbus A320-232	2904	ex F-WWDP		
☐ PR-MBJ	Airbus A320-232	2445	ex ZK-OJK		
☐ PR-MBL	Airbus A320-233	2044	ex HC-CDZ		
☐ PR-MBM	Airbus A320-233	1339	ex N463TA		
☐ PR-MBO	Airbus A320-232	3156	ex F-WWDK		
☐ PR-MBP	Airbus A320-232	1215	ex G-TTOA		
☐ PR-MBQ	Airbus A320-232	1652	ex N533JB		
☐ PR-MBR	Airbus A320-232	1802	ex N542JB		
☐ PR-MBS	Airbus A320-232	1835	ex N544JB		
☐ PR-MBX	Airbus A320-232	1591	ex N528JB		
☐ PR-MBY	Airbus A320-232	1891	ex N550JB		
☐ PR-MBZ	Airbus A320-232	1827	ex N546JB		
☐ PR-MHA	Airbus A320-214	2924	ex F-WWDV		
☐ PR-MHB	Airbus A320-214	1692	ex F-GRSN		
☐ PR-MHC	Airbus A320-214	1717	ex EC-ICN		
☐ PR-MHD	Airbus A320-214	1775	ex EC-JHJ		
☐ PR-MHE	Airbus A320-214	3111	ex F-WWIS		
☐ PR-MHF	Airbus A320-214	3180	ex F-WWDT		
☐ PR-MHG	Airbus A320-214	3002	ex F-WWBB		
☐ PR-MHI	Airbus A320-214	3035	ex F-WWDE		
☐ PR-MHJ	Airbus A320-214	3047	ex F-WWDQ		
☐ PR-MHK	Airbus A320-214	3058	ex F-WWDX		
☐ PR-MHM	Airbus A320-214	3211	ex F-WWIR		
☐ PR-MHN	Airbus A320-214	3240	ex F-WWBM		
☐ PR-MHO	Airbus A320-214	3278	ex F-WWDK		
☐ PR-MHP	Airbus A320-214	3266	ex F-WWBS		
☐ PR-MHQ	Airbus A320-214	3284	ex F-WWDQ		
☐ PR-MHR	Airbus A320-214	3313	ex F-WWIQ		
☐ PR-MHS	Airbus A320-214	3325	ex F-WWBF		
☐ PR-MHT	Airbus A320-214	1757	ex EI-DJI		
☐ PR-MHU	Airbus A320-214	3391	ex F-WWDR		
☐ PR-MHV	Airbus A320-214	3540	ex F-WWIO		
☐ PR-MHW	Airbus A320-214	3630	ex F-WWBQ		
☐ PR-MHX	Airbus A320-214	3565	ex F-WWBM		
☐ PR-MHY	Airbus A320-214	3594	ex F-WWDG		
☐ PR-MHZ	Airbus A320-214	3658	ex F-WWDT		
☐ PR-MYA	Airbus A320-214	3662	ex F-WWDV		
☐ PR-MYD	Airbus A320-214	3750	ex F-WWBR		
☐ PR-MYE	Airbus A320-214	3908	ex F-WWIR		
☐ PR-MYF	Airbus A320-214	3972	ex F-WWIQ		
☐ PR-MYG	Airbus A320-214	4320	ex F-WWDJ		♦
☐ PR-MYH	Airbus A320-214	4441	ex F-WWDY		♦
☐ PR-MYI	Airbus A320-214	4446	ex D-AVVY		♦
☐ PR-MYJ	Airbus A320-214	4465	ex D-AVVL		♦
☐ PR-MYK	Airbus A320-214	4544	ex D-AXAN		♦
☐ PR-	Airbus A320-2		ex		o/o♦
☐ PR-	Airbus A320-2		ex		o/o♦
☐ PR-	Airbus A320-2		ex		o/o♦
☐ PR-	Airbus A320-2		ex		o/o♦
☐ PR-	Airbus A320-2		ex		o/o♦
☐ PT-MZG	Airbus A320-232	1143	ex F-WWBG		
☐ PT-MZH	Airbus A320-232	1158	ex F-WWBY		
☐ PT-MZI	Airbus A320-232	1246	ex F-WWIR		
☐ PT-MZJ	Airbus A320-232	1251	ex F-WWIV		
☐ PT-MZK	Airbus A320-232	1368	ex F-WWIJ		
☐ PT-MZL	Airbus A320-232	1376	ex F-WWIN		
☐ PT-MZN	Airbus A320-231	0440	ex ZS-SHG		
☐ PT-MZO	Airbus A320-231	0250	ex ZS-SHC		
☐ PT-MZQ	Airbus A320-231	0335	ex ZS-SHF		

☐ PT-MZR	Airbus A320-231	0334	ex ZS-SHE	
☐ PT-MZT	Airbus A320-232	1486	ex F-WWDV	
☐ PT-MZU	Airbus A320-232	1518	ex F-WWIJ	
☐ PT-MZV	Airbus A320-232	0758	ex N758SL	
☐ PT-MZW	Airbus A320-232	1580	ex F-WWBK	
☐ PT-MZX	Airbus A320-232	1613	ex F-WWDI	
☐ PT-MZY	Airbus A320-232	1628	ex F-WWDO	
☐ PT-MZZ	Airbus A320-232	1593	ex F-WWBT	
☐ PT-MXA	Airbus A321-231	3222	ex D-AVZF	
☐ PT-MXB	Airbus A321-231	3229	ex D-AVZG	
☐ PT-MXC	Airbus A321-231	3294	ex D-AVZE	
☐ PT-MXD	Airbus A321-231	3761	ex D-AZAP	
☐ PT-MXE	Airbus A321-231	3816	ex D-AVZB	
☐ PT-MXF	Airbus A321-231	4352	ex D-AVZC	♦
☐ PT-MXG	Airbus A321-231	4358	ex D-AVZK	♦
☐ PT-	Airbus A321-231		ex	o/o♦
☐ PT-	Airbus A321-231		ex	o/o♦
☐ PT-MVA	Airbus A330-223	232	ex A6-EYX	
☐ PT-MVB	Airbus A330-223	238	ex A6-EYY	
☐ PT-MVC	Airbus A330-223	247	ex F-WWKH	
☐ PT-MVD	Airbus A330-223	259	ex A6-EYB	
☐ PT-MVE	Airbus A330-223	361	ex A6-EYA	
☐ PT-MVF	Airbus A330-203	466	ex F-WWKP	
☐ PT-MVG	Airbus A330-203	472	ex F-WWKQ	
☐ PT-MVH	Airbus A330-203	477	ex F-WWKS	
☐ PT-MVK	Airbus A330-203	486	ex F-WWYL	
☐ PT-MVL	Airbus A330-203	700	ex F-WWKB	
☐ PT-MVM	Airbus A330-223	869	ex F-WWYR	
☐ PT-MVN	Airbus A330-223	876	ex F-WWKE	
☐ PT-MVO	Airbus A330-223	949	ex F-WWKP	
☐ PT-MVP	Airbus A330-223	961	ex F-WWYF	
☐ PT-MVQ	Airbus A330-223	968	ex F-WWYN	
☐ PT-MVR	Airbus A330-223	977	ex F-WWKV	
☐ PT-MVS	Airbus A330-223	1112	ex F-WWYJ	♦
☐ PT-MVT	Airbus A330-223	1118	ex F-WWKS	♦
☐ PT-	Airbus A330-223		ex	o/o♦
☐ PT-	Airbus A330-223		ex	o/o♦
☐ PT-MSL	Airbus A340-541	464	ex C-GKOM	
☐ PT-MSN	Airbus A340-541	445	ex C-GKOL	
☐ PT-MSQ	Boeing 767-33AER	27468/584	ex I-DEID	
☐ PT-MSR	Boeing 767-33AER	27377/561	ex I-DEIC	
☐ PT-MSU	Boeing 767-33AER	27376/560	ex PR-VAG	
☐ PT-MUA	Boeing 777-32WER	37664/727	ex N5573S	
☐ PT-MUB	Boeing 777-32WER	37665/733	ex N6009F	
☐ PT-MUC	Boeing 777-32WER	37666/740		
☐ PT-MUD	Boeing 777-32WER	37667/751		
☐ PT-MQC	Fokker 100	11371	ex PH-JXP	
☐ PT-MRE	Fokker 100	11348	ex PH-LNM	

TAM - TAXI AEREO MARILIA Sao Paulo-Congonhas, SP (GGH)

☐ PP-ITY	Cessna 208B Caravan I	208B0560	ex N1301B
☐ PR-MAU	Cessna 208B Caravan I	208B0621	ex ZP-CAD
☐ PT-MEA	Cessna 208B Caravan I	208B0333	ex N1037L
☐ PT-MEB	Cessna 208B Caravan I	208B0335	ex N1038G
☐ PT-MEC	Cessna 208B Caravan I	208B0342	ex N1045C
☐ PT-MED	Cessna 208B Caravan I	208B0343	ex N1052C
☐ PT-MEJ	Cessna 208B Caravan I	208B0359	ex N1115V
☐ PT-MEM	Cessna 208B Caravan I	208B0405	
☐ PT-MEN	Cessna 208B Caravan I	208B0408	
☐ PT-MEO	Cessna 208B Caravan I	208B0412	
☐ PT-MES	Cessna 208B Caravan I	208B0507	
☐ PT-MEX	Cessna 208B Caravan I	208B0515	ex N50280
☐ PT-MHC	Cessna 208B Caravan I	208B0543	

TASUL - TAXI AEREO SUL Porto Alegre-Salgado Filho, RS (PQA)

☐ PT-JJB	Cessna 402B	402B0399	ex N8063Q
☐ PT-KDA	Cessna 310Q	310Q1087	

TAVAJ LINHAS AEREAS Tavaj (4U/TVJ) Rio Branco, AC (RBR)

☐ PT-GJP	Embraer EMB.110EJ Bandeirante	110065

☐ PT-LRB	Embraer EMB.110P1 Bandeirante	110409	ex N720RA
☐ PT-LRJ	Embraer EMB.110P1 Bandeirante	110384	ex N699RA
☐ PT-LTN	Embraer EMB.110P1 Bandeirante	110418	ex N860AC
☐ PT-OCX	Embraer EMB.110P1 Bandeirante	110316	ex N94PB
☐ PT-LAG	Fokker F.27 Friendship 600	10197	ex PH-FDM
☐ PT-LAH	Fokker F.27 Friendship 600	10178	ex PH-FCS

TAXI AEREO ITAITUBA — Santarem, PA (STM)

☐ PT-GJR	Embraer EMB.110EJ Bandeirante	110070	
☐ PT-GKE	Embraer EMB.110B1 Bandeirante	110096	ex PP-ZKE

TAXI AEREO WEISS — Curitiba, PR (CWB)

☐ PT-EFU	Embraer EMB.820C Navajo	820031	
☐ PT-ELY	Embraer EMB.820C Navajo	820063	
☐ PT-TAW	Embraer EMB.110P1 Bandeirante	110258	ex CX-VIP

TEAM AIRLINES – TEAM TRANSPORTES AEREOS — Team Brasil (TIM) — Rio de Janeiro-Santos Dumont, RJ (SDU)

☐ PR-AIA	LET L-410UVP-E	912611	ex CCCP-67680
☐ PR-IMO	LET L-410UVP-E20	922701	ex OK-XDJ

TOTAL LINHAS AEREAS (TTL)

☐ PR-TTB	Boeing 727-223 (FedEx 3)	22007/1643	ex N891AA
☐ PR-TTO	Boeing 727-2M7F (FedEx 3)	21200/1206	ex N721RW
☐ PR-TTP	Boeing 727-2M7F (FedEx 3)	1339/21502	ex N998PG
☐ PT-TTW	Boeing 727-225F	22438/1685	ex N743DH
☐ PT-MTQ	Boeing 727-243F	22053/1620	ex N198PC
☐ PT-MTT	Boeing 727-243F	22167/1752	ex N270PC

TRIP LINHAS AEREAS (8R) — Sao Paulo-Viracopos, SP (VCP)

☐ PP-ATV	ATR 42-300	298	ex F-WQHA	
☐ PP-PTC	ATR 42-300	035	ex F-ODUD	
☐ PP-PTD	ATR 42-320	091	ex F-WQNS	
☐ PP-PTF	ATR 42-300	072	ex LV-ZNV	
☐ PP-PTG	ATR 42-320	128	ex F-WQNA	
☐ PP-PTI	ATR 42-320	374	ex F-WQNP	
☐ PP-PTJ	ATR 42-320	284	ex CX-PUC	
☐ PP-PTV	ATR 42-500	503	ex F-WNUA	
☐ PP-PTW	ATR 42-500	510	ex F-WNUB	
☐ PR-TKB	ATR 42-500	610	ex I-ADLV	♦
☐ PR-TKC	ATR 42-500	609	ex I-ADLU	♦
☐ PR-TKD	ATR 42-500	604	ex I-ADLP	♦
☐ PR-TKE	ATR 42-500	556	ex F-WKVC	♦
☐ PR-TTE	ATR 42-300	400	ex F-WQNG	
☐ PR-TTF	ATR 42-300	021	ex F-WQNS	
☐ PR-TTG	ATR 42-320	020	ex F-OHOT	
☐ PR-TTH	ATR 42-500	506	ex F-WQNL	
☐ PR-TTK	ATR 42-500	504	ex F-WQNK	
☐ PR-TTM	ATR 42-500	551	ex D-BNNN	
☐ PT-MFE	ATR 42-300	295	ex F-WWLU	
☐ PT-TTL	ATR 42-320	380	ex N988MA	
☐ PP-PTH	ATR 72-202	365	ex F-GMGK	
☐ PP-PTK	ATR 72-202	352	ex F-GKPH	
☐ PP-PTL	ATR 72-212A	773	ex F-WWEL	
☐ PP-PTM	ATR 72-212A	798	ex F-WWEO	
☐ PP-PTN	ATR 72-212A	832	ex F-WWEI	
☐ PP-PTO	ATR 72-212A	837	ex F-WWEO	
☐ PP-PTP	ATR 72-212A	865	ex F-WWEO	
☐ PP-PTQ	ATR 72-212A	874	ex F-WWEZ	
☐ PP-PTR	ATR 72-212A	785	ex F-WWED	
☐ PP-PTT	ATR 72-212A	846	ex F-WWEL	♦
☐ PP-PTU	ATR 72-212A	891	ex F-WWEW	♦
☐ PP-PTX	ATR 72-212A	666	ex F-WKVE	♦
☐ PP-PTY	ATR 72-212A	911	ex F-WWEE	♦
☐ PP-PTZ	ATR 72-212A	918	ex F-WWEP	♦
☐ PR-TKA	ATR 72-212A	926	ex F-WWEB	♦
☐ PR-TTI	ATR 72-212	454	ex N531AS	
☐ PR-TTJ	ATR 72-212	463	ex N534AS	
☐ PR-	ATR 72-212A		ex	o/o♦
☐ PR-	ATR 72-212A		ex	o/o♦

☐ PP-PJA	Embraer ERJ-175LR	17000272	ex PT-SNF			
☐ PP-PJB	Embraer ERJ-175LR	17000277	ex PT-TQD			
☐ PP-PJC	Embraer ERJ-175LR	17000287	ex PT-TQN			
☐ PP-PJD	Embraer ERJ-175LR	17000017	ex D-ALIB			
☐ PP-PJE	Embraer ERJ-175LR	17000291				
☐ PP-PJF	Embraer ERJ-175LR	17000309				♦
☐ PP-PJG	Embraer ERJ-175LR	17000137	ex M-YRGM			♦
☐ PP-PJH	Embraer ERJ-175LR	17000147	ex M-YRGN			♦
☐ PP-PJJ	Embraer ERJ-190LR	19000163	ex HB-JQE			♦
☐ PP-PJK	Embraer ERJ-190LR	19000178	ex HB-JQF			♦
☐ PP-PJL	Embraer ERJ-190LR	19000189	ex HB-JQG			♦
☐ PP-	Embraer ERJ-190LR		ex			o/o♦
☐ PP-	Embraer ERJ-190LR		ex			o/o♦

VARIG   Varig (RG/VRN)   Rio de Janeiro-Galeao, RJ/Porto Alegre-Canoas, RS (GIG/POA)

☐ PP-VNT	Boeing 737-33A	23828/1446			
☐ PP-VNY	Boeing 737-3K9	24864/1918			
☐ PP-VQN	Boeing 737-33A	24098/1783	ex N98NG		
☐ PP-VTA	Boeing 737-3K9	23797/1416	ex PT-TEU	[ROW]	
☐ PP-VTB	Boeing 737-3K9	23798/1429	ex PT-TEV		
☐ PR-VBA	Boeing 737-8AS/W	29916/210	ex EI-CSA		
☐ PR-VBB	Boeing 737-8AS/W	29917/298	ex EI-CSB		
☐ PR-VBC	Boeing 737-8AS/W	29918/307	ex EI-CSC		
☐ PR-VBD	Boeing 737-8AS/W	29919/341	ex EI-CSD		
☐ PR-VBE	Boeing 737-8AS/W	29920/362	ex EI-CSE		
☐ PR-VBF	Boeing 737-8EH/W	34276/2716			
☐ PR-VBG	Boeing 737-8EH/W	35066/2700			
☐ PR-VBJ	Boeing 737-86N/W	36434/2706			
☐ PR-VBK	Boeing 737-8EH/W	34271/2445	ex PR-GTX	<GLO	
☐ PR-VBL	Boeing 737-8EH/W	34272/2449	ex PR-GTW	<GLO	
☐ PR-VBM	Boeing 737-7EA	32406/859	ex N815PG		
☐ PR-VBN	Boeing 737-76N	28577/124	ex N966PG		
☐ PR-VBP	Boeing 737-7EA	32407/904	ex N160CK		
☐ PR-VBU	Boeing 737-76N/W	29905/372	ex N746AL		
☐ PR-VBV	Boeing 737-76N/W	30050/429	ex N748AL		
☐ PR-VBX	Boeing 737-7BX	30738/716	ex 6V-AHN		
☐ PR-VAB	Boeing 767-33AER	27477/337	ex B-2497	[VNF]	
☐ PR-VAC	Boeing 767-27GER	27048/475	ex N48SN		♦
☐ PR-VAF	Boeing 767-38EER	25132/417	ex CC-CIO		
☐ PR-VAN	Boeing 767-328ER	27427/579	ex N801PG	[GIG]	

VARIG LOG   (LC/VLO)   Sao Paulo-Guarulhos, SP/ (GRU)

☐ PP-VQV	Boeing 727-243F	22166/1725	ex PP-SFE		
☐ PR-LGC	Boeing 727-2A1F (FedEx 3)	21342/1256	ex N214UP	Leandra	<Platinum Air
☐ PR-LGH	Boeing 757-225 (PCF)	22211/74	ex N314ST		
☐ PR-LGJ	Boeing 757-225 (PCF)	22210/42	ex N930RD		

WEBJET LINHAS AEREAS   (WEB)   Curitiba (CWB)

☐ PR-WJA	Boeing 737-322	24663/1875	ex N401TZ		
☐ PR-WJB	Boeing 737-341	25050/2125	ex PR-BRG		
☐ PR-WJC	Boeing 737-341	25051/2127	ex PR-BRF		
☐ PR-WJD	Boeing 737-3Y0	23922/1538	ex PT-SSK		
☐ PR-WJE	Boeing 737-33A	25057/2046	ex PT-MNJ		
☐ PR-WJF	Boeing 737-341	24936/1951	ex PP-VOO		
☐ PR-WJG	Boeing 737-322	24452/1728	ex N359UA		
☐ PR-WJH	Boeing 737-341	26856/2321	ex PP-VPB		
☐ PR-WJI	Boeing 737-341	26857/2326	ex PP-VPC		
☐ PR-WJJ	Boeing 737-341	24935/1935	ex PP-VON		
☐ PR-WJK	Boeing 737-33A	23830/1462	ex N238MQ		
☐ PR-WJL	Boeing 737-36N	28590/3097	ex SP-LME		
☐ PR-WJM	Boeing 737-36Q	28660/2883	ex G-THOK		
☐ PR-WJN	Boeing 737-36Q	29327/3023	ex G-THOI		
☐ PR-WJO	Boeing 737-3Q8	26295/2557	ex N295AN		
☐ PR-WJP	Boeing 737-3Q8	26309/2674	ex N309AN		
☐ PR-WJQ	Boeing 737-3U3	28742/2992	ex ZK-FRE		
☐ PR-WJR	Boeing 737-36N	28566/2964	ex PK-GGT		
☐ PR-WJS	Boeing 737-3Y0	24465/1755	ex N465BV		
☐ PR-WJT	Boeing 737-3Y0	24908/2015	ex N908BV		
☐ PR-WJU	Boeing 737-36N	28560/2888	ex SE-RHU		
☐ PR-WJV	Boeing 737-36N	28567/2971	ex N558MS		♦
☐ PR-WJW	Boeing 737-33A	27267/2600	ex N267AN		♦
☐ PR-WJX	Boeing 737-33A	25033/2025	ex LN-KKA		♦

WHITEJETS

| ☐ PR-WTA | Airbus A310-304 | 494 | ex CS-TEJ | ♦ |

PZ- SURINAME (Republic of Suriname)

BLUE WING AIRLINES — Paramaribo-Zorg en Hoop (ORG)

☐ PZ-TGQ	Cessna U206G Stationair 6	U20605917	ex PZ-TAO	
☐ PZ-TLV	Cessna U206G Stationair 6	U20606951		
☐ PZ-TSB	Cessna 208 Caravan I	20800098	ex N207RM	
☐ PZ-TSD	de Havilland DHC-6 Twin Otter 200	117	ex VH-JEA	
☐ PZ-TSH	de Havilland DHC-6 Twin Otter 200	145	ex VH-TZR	
☐ PZ-	Reims Cessna F406 Caravan II	F406-0033	ex VH-JVN	
☐ PZ-TSA	WSK/PZL Antonov An-28	1AJ007-21	ex PZ-TGW	
☐ PZ-TSN	WSK/PZL Antonov An-28	1AJ007-20	ex YV-528C	

GUM AIR — (GUM) — Paramaribo-Zorg en Hoop (ORG)

☐ PZ-TBD	Cessna U206G Stationair	U20603786	ex N8286G	
☐ PZ-TBE	Cessna U206G Stationair 6	U20606776	ex N9959Z	
☐ PZ-TBG	Cessna U206B Super Skywagon	U206-0832	ex N3832G	
☐ PZ-TBH	Cessna 208B Caravan I	208B0923	ex N1132W	Spirit of Pike
☐ PZ-TBL	Britten-Norman BN-2B-26 Islander	2153	ex N633BB	
☐ PZ-TBW	de Havilland DHC-6 Twin Otter 300	601	ex N28SP	
☐ PZ-TBY	de Havilland DHC-6 Twin Otter 300	646	ex N7015A	
☐ PZ-TVC	Cessna 404 Titan	404-0243	ex YV-236CP	
☐ PZ-TVU	Cessna TU206G Stationair 6	U20604783	ex PZ-PVU	

SURINAM AIRWAYS — Surinam (PY/SLM)
Paramaribo-Zanderij International/Zorg en Hoop (PBM/ORG)

☐ PZ-TCM	Boeing 747-306M	23508/657	ex PH-BUW	Ronald Elwin Kappel
☐ PZ-TCN	Boeing 737-36N	28668/2890	ex N668AN	
☐ PZ-TCO	Boeing 737-36N	28669/2897	ex N669AN	
☐ PZ-TCP	Airbus A340-311	049	ex F-GLZG	

P2- PAPUA NEW GUINEA (Independent State of Papua New Guinea)

AIR NIUGINI — Niugini (PX/ANG) — Port Moresby (POM)

☐ P2-ANK	de Havilland DHC-8Q-202	461	ex C-GFBW		
☐ P2-ANL	de Havilland DHC-8-102	153	ex D-BOBO		
☐ P2-ANM	de Havilland DHC-8Q-314	523	ex D-BPAD		
☐ P2-ANN	de Havilland DHC-8-315	401	ex JY-RWB		
☐ P2-ANO	de Havilland DHC-8-311A	252	ex D-BOBU		
☐ P2-ANP	de Havilland DHC-8-102	177	ex D-BOBY		
☐ P2-ANX	de Havilland DHC-8Q-202	463	ex D-BHAL		
☐ P2-ANZ	de Havilland DHC-8Q-201	421	ex N986HA		
☐ P2-PXT	de Havilland DHC-8-402Q	4329	ex C-GNIU		♦
☐ P2-PXU	de Havilland DHC-8-402Q	4316	ex C-GEHE		♦
☐ P2-ANC	Fokker 100	11471	ex PH-MXW		
☐ P2-AND	Fokker 100	11473	ex PT-MRQ		
☐ P2-ANE	Fokker 100	11264	ex PH-THY		
☐ P2-ANF	Fokker 100	11351	ex PH-FDI		
☐ P2-ANH	Fokker 100	11301	ex C-GPNL		
☐ P2-ANQ	Fokker 100	11451	ex PH-ZDJ		
☐ P2-ANI	Fokker F.28 Fellowship 4000	11223	ex PH-RRB		[POM]
☐ P2-ANJ	Fokker F.28 Fellowship 4000	11219	ex PH-RRA		[POM]
☐ P2-ANR	Fokker F.28 Fellowship 4000	11207	ex VH-EWC	W/Cmdr RH (Bobby) Gibbes	[KUL]
☐ P2-ANS	Fokker F.28 Fellowship 4000	11195	ex VH-EWA		[POM]
☐ P2-ANA	Boeing 767-366ER	24541/275	ex TF-LLA		<ICE
☐ P2-ANB	Boeing 757-256	29312/943	ex TF-FIY		<ICE

AIRLINES OF PAPUA NEW GUINEA — (CG/TOK) — Port Moresby (POM)

☐ P2-MCC	de Havilland DHC-6 Twin Otter 200	218	ex VH-IPD
☐ P2-MCD	de Havilland DHC-6 Twin Otter 300	592	ex C-GOVG
☐ P2-MCE	de Havilland DHC-6 Twin Otter 300	673	ex C-GHRB
☐ P2-MCF	de Havilland DHC-6 Twin Otter 300	741	ex C-GRBY

468

☐ P2-MCR	de Havilland DHC-6 Twin Otter 300	219	ex P2-MFY	
☐ P2-MCS	de Havilland DHC-6 Twin Otter 310	516	ex 5W-PAH	
☐ P2-MCG	de Havilland DHC-8-102	6	ex C-GJCB	
☐ P2-MCH	de Havilland DHC-8-102	12	ex C-GPYD	
☐ P2-MCI	de Havilland DHC-8-102	197	ex ZK-NET	
☐ P2-MCJ	de Havilland DHC-8-102	125	ex ZK-NES	
☐ P2-MCL	de Havilland DHC-8-102	27	ex VH-WZJ	
☐ P2-MCP	de Havilland DHC-8-102	33	ex VH-TNX	
☐ P2-MCQ	de Havilland DHC-8-103A	243	ex VH-TNW	
☐ P2-MCT	de Havilland DHC-8-102	135	ex VH-QQH	
☐ P2-MCU	de Havilland DHC-8-102	208	ex VH-QQJ	
☐ P2-CHI	Boeing Vertol 234UT Chinook	MJ-003	ex N237CH	<WCO

ASIA PACIFIC AIRLINES — Tabubil (TBG)

☐ P2-NAX	de Havilland DHC-8-103	229	ex VH-JSI	<NJS
☐ P2-NAZ	de Havilland DHC-8-106	316	ex C-GFUM Spirit of Tabubil	<NJS

CENTRAL AIR TRANSPORT — Port Moresby (POM)

☐ P2-ALM	Britten-Norman BN-2A-26 Islander	124	ex P2-NAA	

EMERALD AIR

☐ P2-EMO	de Havilland DHC-6 Twin Otter 300	726	ex N726JM	

HELI NIUGINI — Madang/Mount Hagen (MAG/HGU)

☐ P2-HBC	Bell 206L-3 LongRanger III	51396	ex VH-SBC	
☐ P2-HBH	Bell 206L-3 LongRanger III	51012	ex SE-HOR	
☐ P2-HBJ	Bell 206L-3 LongRanger III	51373	ex VH-CKP	
☐ P2-HBM	Bell 206L-1 LongRanger III	45241	ex VH-HJL	
☐ P2-HBN	Bell 206L-1 LongRanger III	45487	ex VH-CKU	
☐ P2-HBP	Bell 206L-1 LongRanger III	51042	ex VH-CKI	
☐ P2-JND	Bell 206L-1 LongRanger III	45645	ex VH-MQA	
☐ P2-HBK	Kawasaki/MBB BK-117B-2	1046	ex ZK-HBK	
☐ P2-HBL	Kawasaki/MBB BK-117B-2	1021	ex ZK-HLU	
☐ P2-HBQ	Kawasaki/MBB BK-117B-2	1075	ex ZK-HLI	
☐ P2-RAA	Kamov Ka-32S	8705	ex RA-31583	<VLK
☐ RA-25503	Mil Mi-8MTV-1	95651	ex CCCP-25503	<VLK
☐ RA-27101	Mil Mi-8AMT	59489605182		<VLK
☐ RA-27158	Mil Mi-8AMT	59489611156	ex RA-25755	<VLK
☐ RA-31031	Kamov Ka-32S/T	6106	ex CCCP-31031	<VLK
☐ RA-31032	Kamov Ka-32S	6107	ex CCCP-31032	<VLK
☐ RA-31036	Kamov Ka-32T	6111	ex CCCP-31036	<VLK

HEVI-LIFT (IU) — Mount Hagen/Cairns (HGU/CNS)

☐ P2-HCA	Bell 206L-1 LongRanger II	45337	ex VH-BJX	
☐ P2-HCB	Bell 206L-1 LongRanger II	45404	ex VH-HHS	
☐ P2-HCC	Bell 206L-1 LongRanger III	45427	ex N5019T	
☐ P2-HCD	Bell 206L-1 LongRanger III	45528	ex C-GGHZ	
☐ P2-HCM	Bell 206L-1 LongRanger III	45608	ex P2-NHE	
☐ P2-HCO	Bell 206L-3 LongRanger III	51178	ex N3204K	
☐ P2-HCU	Bell 206L-3 LongRanger III	51416	ex N254EV	
☐ P2-HLT	Bell 206L-3 LongRanger III	51387	ex VH-HQT	
☐ P2-HCJ	Bell 212	30799	ex VH-EMJ	
☐ P2-HCK	Bell 212	30583	ex N212SX	
☐ P2-HCQ	Bell 212	30860	ex JA9528	
☐ P2-HCW	Bell 212	30520	ex PK-EBO	
☐ P2-HLV	Bell 212	30508	ex VH-SYV	
☐ ER-MHL	Mil Mi-8MTV-1	95721	ex RA-25105	
☐ ER-MHM	Mil Mi-8MTV-1	95881	ex RA-27047	
☐ P2-HCA	Bell 407	53054	ex N417AL	♦
☐ P2-HCB	Bell 407	53141	ex N437AL	♦
☐ P2-HCL	Aérospatiale AS350B2 Ecureuil	3374	ex SE-JFO	
☐ P2-HCN	Beech 200C Super King Air	BL-22	ex P2-PJV	
☐ P2-HCS	Bell 412HP	33160	ex VH-HQQ	
☐ P2-	Bell 412EP	36381	ex N413EV	♦
☐ P2-HCV	Bell 412EP	36424	ex N416EV	♦
☐ P2-HCY	Aérospatiale AS350B3 Ecureuil	3242	ex JA6292	
☐ P2-HCZ	Aérospatiale AS350B3 Ecureuil	3634	ex ZK-HRD	
☐ P2-KSF	de Havilland DHC-6 Twin Otter 300	528	ex PK-HCF	

ISLAND AIRWAYS — Madang (MAG)

☐ P2-CBC	Cessna 402B	402B0909	ex VH-LCF

ISLANDS NATIONAIR (CN) — Port Moresby (POM)

☐ P2-IHA	Bell 206L-1 LongRanger II	45333	ex VH-BLV
☐ P2-IHE	Bell 206L-1 LongRanger III	45238	ex N140VG
☐ P2-IHH	Bell 206L-3 LongRanger III	45255	ex P2-NHD

KIUNGA AVIATION — Lae (LAE)

☐ P2-KAA	Cessna 402C	402C0247	ex N2748X

NORTH COAST AVIATION (N9/AOH) — Madang (MAG)

☐ P2-DWA	Britten-Norman BN-2A-26 Islander	113	ex VH-EQE	
☐ P2-IAC	Britten-Norman BN-2A-21 Islander	425	ex P2-KAF	
☐ P2-ISA	Britten-Norman BN-2A-20 Islander	758	ex P2-SWB	
☐ P2-ISB	Britten-Norman BN-2A-20 Islander	709	ex P2-MKW	stored
☐ P2-ISL	Britten-Norman BN-2A-20 Islander	806	ex G-BDYT	
☐ P2-ISM	Britten-Norman BN-2A-20 Islander	227	ex VH-EDI	
☐ P2-NCE	Britten-Norman BN-2A-20 Islander	768	ex P2-IAD	
☐ P2-SAC	Britten-Norman BN-2A-20 Islander	94	ex P2-DNY	
☐ P2-DQU	Cessna U206B Super Skywagon	U206-0892	ex VH-DQU	
☐ P2-GKB	Cessna 402	402-0141	ex VH-GKB	
☐ P2-IDK	Cessna U206G Super Skywagon	U206-1418	ex P2-TNK	
☐ P2-IDM	Cessna U206F Stationair	U20603126	ex P2-SIA	
☐ P2-NCD	Cessna 402B	402B1027	ex VH-USV	
☐ P2-OHS	Cessna P206B Super Skylane	P206-0392	ex P2-HCM	

PACIFIC HELICOPTERS — Goroka (GKA)

☐ P2-PHA	Aérospatiale AS350BA Ecureuil	1181	ex P2-PHU
☐ P2-PHD	Aérospatiale AS350BA Ecureuil	1067	ex 9N-ACQ
☐ P2-PHH	Aérospatiale AS350BA Ecureuil	1608	ex VH-CHO
☐ P2-PHK	Aérospatiale AS350B2 Ecureuil		
☐ P2-PHX	Aérospatiale AS350BA Ecureuil	1817	
☐ P2-PAU	Bell 212	30793	ex A6-BBG
☐ P2-PAV	Bell 212	30913	ex G-GLEN
☐ P2-PAX	Bell 212	30786	ex A6-BBF
☐ P2-PBA	Bell 206L-1 LongRanger III	45642	ex VH-SCV
☐ P2-PBB	Bell 206L-3 LongRanger III	51400	ex N86CE
☐ P2-PBC	Bell 206L-1 LongRanger III	45349	ex N1077N
☐ P2-PBD	Bell 206L-3 LongRanger III	51275	ex VH-CKI

REGIONAL AIR (QT) — Madang (MAG)

☐ P2-KSA	Beech 200 Super King Air	BB-1527	ex N170W	
☐ P2-KSB	de Havilland DHC-6 Twin Otter 300	485	ex VH-RPU	
☐ P2-KSS	de Havilland DHC-6 Twin Otter 300	578	ex N578SA	id not confirmed
☐ P2-KST	de Havilland DHC-6 Twin Otter 300	520	ex YJ-RV5	

SIL AVIATION — Aiyura (AYU)

☐ P2-SIA	Beech B200C Super King Air	BL-39	ex VH-FDR	
☐ P2-SIG	Cessna TU206G Stationair 6	U20606029	ex VH-XAA	Robertson STOL conversion
☐ P2-SIJ	Cessna TU206G Stationair 6	U20605805	ex N5491X	Robertson STOL conversion
☐ P2-SIL	Bell 206B JetRanger III	3498	ex ZK-HTF	
☐ P2-SIT	Cessna TU206G Stationair 6	U20606158	ex N181PK	Robertson STOL conversion
☐ P2-SIV	Britten-Norman BN-2T Islander	2138	ex 9M-TIR	

SOUTHWEST AIR — Mendi (MDU)

☐ P2-SHA	Bell 206L-3 LongRanger III	51533	ex VH-IRE	
☐ P2-SWE	de Havilland DHC-6 Twin Otter 300	480	ex P2-RDL	
☐ P2-SWF	Embraer EMB.110P1 Bandeirante	110237	ex N691RA	[BNE]

TRANSNIUGINI AIRWAYS — Port Moresby (POM)

☐ P2-TND	Britten-Norman BN-2A-21 Islander	813	ex P2-COD

TROPICAIR — Port Moresby (POM)

☐ P2-AMH	Cessna 208B Caravan I	208B0785	ex N785SC
☐ P2-BEN	Cessna 208B Caravan I	208B0424	ex VH-LSA

| ☐ P2-SAH | Cessna 208B Caravan I | 208B1263 | ex N41149 |
| ☐ P2-SMA | Cessna U206G Stationair 6 | U20604227 | ex P2-AAC |

| VAN AIR | | | Vanimo (VAI) |

| ☐ P2-VAB | Britten-Norman BN-2A-20 Islander | 759 | ex P2-MFZ |

P4- ARUBA

| TIARA AIR | | (3P/TNM) | | | Aruba (AUA) |

| ☐ P4-TIA | Short SD.3-60 | SH3619 | ex C-GPCG | |
| ☐ P4-TIB | Short SD.3-60 | SH3621 | ex C-GPCN | [OPF] |

RA- RUSSIA (Russian Federation)

| ABAKAN-AVIA | | Abakan-Avia (ABG) | | Abakan (ABA) |

☐ RA-76457	Ilyushin Il-76T	093421621	ex CCCP-76457	
☐ RA-76509	Ilyushin Il-76T	083413415	ex CCCP-76509	all-white
☐ RA-76780	Ilyushin Il-76T	0013430901	ex CCCP-76780	all-white

| AERO RENT | | Aeromaster (NRO) | | Moscow-Vnukovo (VKO) |

☐ RA-21506	Yakovlev Yak-40KD	9840259	ex CCCP-21506	VIP
☐ RA-42434	Yakovlev Yak-42D	4520424305017		
☐ RA-65557	Tupolev Tu-134A	66380	ex 65557	VIPop for Itera
☐ RA-65790	Tupolev Tu-134A-3	63100	ex UR-65790	VIPop for Stroytransgaz
☐ RA-87397	Yakovlev Yak-40	9410933	ex CCCP-87397	
☐ RA-88306	Yakovlev Yak-40KD	9640651	ex OK-GEL	VIPop for Stroytransgaz

| AERO-KAMOV | | Aerafkam (MSV) | | Moscow-Lyubersty |

☐ RA-31005	Kamov Ka-32T	5701	ex CCCP-31005
☐ RA-31027	Kamov Ka-32S	6102	ex CCCP-31027
☐ RA-31065	Kamov Ka-32A	300048607	ex CCCP-31065
☐ RA-31091	Kamov Ka-32T	8807	
☐ RA-31592	Kamov Ka-32T	8717	

| AEROBRATSK | | Aerobra (BRP) | | Bratsk (BTK) |

☐ RA-22856	Mil Mi-8T	98415350	ex CCCP-22856
☐ RA-24261	Mil Mi-8T	98734147	ex CCCP-24261
☐ RA-88205	Yakovlev Yak-40	9630749	ex CCCP-88205
☐ RA-88215	Yakovlev Yak-40K	9630150	ex CCCP-88215

| AEROFLOT CARGO | Aeroflot Cargo (SU/RCF) | Hahn/Mosvow-Sheremetyevo (HHN/SVO) |

Merged back into Aeroflot, ceased operations 13/May/2010

| AEROFLOT PLUS | | (PLS) | | Moscow-Sheremetyevo (SVO) |

☐ RA-65559	Tupolev Tu-134A	7349909	ex CCCP-65559	VIP
☐ RA-65694	Tupolev Tu-134B-3	63235	ex UN-65694	VIP
☐ RA-65790	Tupolev Tu-134A-3	63100	ex UR-65790	VIP

| AEROFLOT RUSSIAN AIRLINES | | Aeroflot (SU/AFL) | | Moscow-Sheremetyevo (SVO) |

Member of Skyteam

☐ VP-BDM	Airbus A319-111	2069	ex D-AVYJ	A Borodin
☐ VP-BDN	Airbus A319-111	2072	ex D-AVYL	A Dargomyzhsky
☐ VP-BDO	Airbus A319-111	2091	ex D-AVWU	I Stravinsky
☐ VP-BUK	Airbus A319-111	3281	ex D-AVYP	YU Senkevich
☐ VP-BUN	Airbus A319-111	3298	ex D-AVYI	
☐ VP-BUO	Airbus A319-111	3336	ex D-AVYS	
☐ VP-BWA	Airbus A319-111	2052	ex D-AVYA	S Prokofiev
☐ VP-BWG	Airbus A319-111	2093	ex D-AVYE	A Aleksandrov
☐ VP-BWJ	Airbus A319-111	2179	ex D-AVYU	A Shnitke
☐ VP-BWK	Airbus A319-111	2222	ex D-AVYI	S Taneyev
☐ VP-BWL	Airbus A319-111	2243	ex D-AVWV	A Grechaninov
☐ VQ-BBA	Airbus A319-111	3794	ex D-AVXM	S Cheliuskin
☐ VQ-BBD	Airbus A319-111	3838	ex D-AVYP	V Golovnin
☐ VQ-BCO	Airbus A319-111	3942	ex D-AVWR	A Hachaturian

☐ VQ-BCP	Airbus A319-111	3998	ex D-AVYZ	D Mendeleev		
☐ VP-BDK	Airbus A320-214	2106	ex F-WWDR	G Sviridov		
☐ VP-BKC	Airbus A320-214	3545	ex F-WWIT	I Kruzenshtern		
☐ VP-BKX	Airbus A320-214	3410	ex F-WWIJ	G Sedov		
☐ VP-BKY	Airbus A320-214	3511	ex F-WWBZ	M Rostropovich		
☐ VP-BME	Airbus A320-214	3699	ex F-WWBO	N Mikluho-Maklay		
☐ VP-BMF	Airbus A320-214	3711	ex F-WWIV	G Shelihov		
☐ VP-BQP	Airbus A320-214	2875	ex F-WWBJ	A Rublev		
☐ VP-BQU	Airbus A320-214	3373	ex F-WWDG	A Nikitin		
☐ VP-BQV	Airbus A320-214	2920	ex F-WWDY	V Vasnetsov		
☐ VP-BQW	Airbus A320-214	2947	ex F-WWBV	V Vereschchagin		
☐ VP-BRX	Airbus A320-214	3063	ex F-WWDZ	V Surikov		
☐ VP-BRY	Airbus A320-214	3052	ex F-WWDT	K Brulloff		
☐ VP-BRZ	Airbus A320-214	3157	ex F-WWDM	V Serov		
☐ VP-BWD	Airbus A320-214	2116	ex F-WWDY	A Aliabiev		
☐ VP-BWE	Airbus A320-214	2133	ex F-WWDX	N Rimsky-Korsakov		
☐ VP-BWF	Airbus A320-214	2144	ex F-WWBY	D Shostakovich		
☐ VP-BWH	Airbus A320-214	2151	ex F-WWIR	M Balakirev		
☐ VP-BWI	Airbus A320-214	2163	ex F-WWBD	A Glazunov		
☐ VP-BWM	Airbus A320-214	2233	ex F-WWII	S Rackhmaninov		
☐ VP-BZO	Airbus A320-214	3574	ex F-WWBK	V Bering		
☐ VP-BZP	Airbus A320-214	3631	ex D-AVYG	E Haborov		
☐ VP-BZQ	Airbus A320-214	3627	ex F-WWIS	Yu. Lisiansky		
☐ VP-BZR	Airbus A320-214	3640	ex F-WWBR	F Bellinghausen		
☐ VP-BZS	Airbus A320-214	3644	ex F-WWBU	M Lazarev		
☐ VQ-BAX	Airbus A320-214	3778	ex F-WWIM	G Nevelskoy		
☐ VQ-BAY	Airbus A320-214	3786	ex D-AVVL	S Krasheninnikov		
☐ VQ-BAZ	Airbus A320-214	3789	ex F-WWBC	V Obruchev		
☐ VQ-BBB	Airbus A320-214	3823	ex F-WWIT	Yu Gagarin		
☐ VQ-BBC	Airbus A320-214	3835	ex F-WWBI	N Przhevalsky		
☐ VQ-BCM	Airbus A320-214	3923	ex F-WWBN	G Titov		
☐ VQ-BCN	Airbus A320-214	3954	ex F-WWBV	V Chelomey		
☐ VQ-BEH	Airbus A320-214	4133	ex F-WWIS	I Pavlov		
☐ VQ-BEJ	Airbus A320-214	4160	ex D-AVVO	I Kurchatov		
☐ VQ-BHL	Airbus A320-214	4453	ex F-WWIX	S Vavilov	◆	
☐ VQ-BHN	Airbus A320-214	4498	ex D-AUBL	N Lobachevsky	◆	
☐ VQ-	Airbus A320-214		ex			o/o◆
☐ VQ-	Airbus A320-214		ex			o/o◆
☐ VQ-	Airbus A320-214		ex			o/o◆
☐ VQ-	Airbus A320-214		ex			o/o◆
☐ VP-BQR	Airbus A321-211	2903	ex D-AVZD	I Repin		
☐ VP-BQS	Airbus A321-211	2912	ex D-AVZL	I Kramskoi		
☐ VP-BQT	Airbus A321-211	2965	ex D-AVZE	I Shishkin		
☐ VP-BQX	Airbus A321-211	2957	ex D-AVZU	I Ayvazovsky		
☐ VP-BRW	Airbus A321-211	3191	ex D-AVZW	N Rerih		
☐ VP-BUM	Airbus A321-211	3267	ex D-AVZQ	A Deineka		
☐ VP-BUP	Airbus A321-211	3334	ex D-AVZY	M Shagal		
☐ VP-BWN	Airbus A321-211	2330	ex D-AVZR	A Skriabin		
☐ VP-BWO	Airbus A321-211	2337	ex D-AVZS	P Chaikovsky		
☐ VP-BWP	Airbus A321-211	2342	ex D-AVZT	M Musorgsky		
☐ VQ-BEA	Airbus A321-211	4058	ex D-AZAS	I Michurin		
☐ VQ-BED	Airbus A321-211	4074	ex D-AVZT	N Pirogov		
☐ VQ-BEE	Airbus A321-211	4099	ex D-AZAA	I Sechenov		
☐ VQ-BEF	Airbus A321-211	4103	ex D-AZAC	N Zhukovsky		
☐ VQ-BEG	Airbus A321-211	4116	ex D-AZAF	K Tsiolkovsky		
☐ VQ-BEI	Airbus A321-211	4148	ex D-AVZS	S Korelov		
☐ VQ-BHK	Airbus A321-211	4461	ex D-AVZB	M Keldysh	◆	
☐ VQ-BHM	Airbus A321-211	4500	ex D-AVZG	N Vavilov	◆	
☐ VQ-	Airbus A321-211		ex D-			o/o◆
☐ VP-BLX	Airbus A330-243	963	ex F-WWYJ	E. Sveetlanov		
☐ VP-BLY	Airbus A330-243	973	ex F-WWKA	V Vysctsky		
☐ VQ-BBE	Airbus A330-243	1014	ex F-WWKU	I Brodsky		
☐ VQ-BBF	Airbus A330-243	1045	ex F-WWYB	A Griboedov		
☐ VQ-BBG	Airbus A330-243	1047	ex F-WWKD	N Gogol		
☐ VQ-BCQ	Airbus A330-343E	1058	ex F-WWYX			
☐ VQ-BCU	Airbus A330-343E	1065	ex F-WWYJ	V Mayakovsky		
☐ VQ-BCV	Airbus A330-343E	1072	ex F-WWYK	B Pasternak		
☐ VQ-BEK	Airbus A330-343E	1077	ex F-WWKN	A Tvardovskiy		
☐ VQ-BEL	Airbus A330-343E	1103	ex F-WWYR	F Tyutchev	◆	
☐ VQ-B	Airbus A330-343E		ex			o/o◆
☐ VQ-B	Airbus A330-343E		ex			o/o◆
☐ VQ-B	Airbus A330-343E		ex			o/o◆
☐ VQ-B	Airbus A330-343E		ex			o/o◆

☐ VP-BAV	Boeing 767-36NER	30107/761		L Tolstoy
☐ VP-BAX	Boeing 767-36NER	30109/767		F Dostoevsky
☐ VP-BAY	Boeing 767-36NER	30110/775		I Turgenev
☐ VP-BAZ	Boeing 767-36NER	30111/776		N Nekrasov
☐ VP-BDI	Boeing 767-38AER	29618/792	ex N618SH	A Pushkin
☐ VP-BWT	Boeing 767-38AER	29617/741	ex G-OOAL	A Checkov
☐ VP-BWU	Boeing 767-3T7ER	25076/366	ex N601EV	I Bunin
☐ VP-BWV	Boeing 767-3T7ER	25117/370	ex N602EV	A Kuprin
☐ VP-BWW	Boeing 767-306ER	27959/609	ex PH-BZF	
☐ VP-BWX	Boeing 767-306ER	27960/625	ex PH-BZG	
☐ RA-96005	Ilyushin Il-96-300	74393201002	ex CCCP-96005	V Chkalov
☐ RA-96007	Ilyushin Il-96-300	74393201004		A Mayorov
☐ RA-96008	Ilyushin Il-96-300	74393201005		IA Moiseyev
☐ RA-96010	Ilyushin Il-96-300	74393201007		Nikolaj Karpajev
☐ RA-96011	Ilyushin Il-96-300	74393201008		K Kokkinaki
☐ RA-96015	Ilyushin Il-96-300	74393201012		M Gromov
☐ RA-	Ilyushin Il-96-300			o/o
☐ RA-	Ilyushin Il-96-300			o/o
☐ RA-	Ilyushin Il-96-300			o/o
☐ RA-	Ilyushin Il-96-300			o/o
☐ RA-	Ilyushin Il-96-300			o/o
☐ RA-	Ilyushin Il-96-300			o/o
☐ VP-BDP	McDonnell-Douglas MD-11F	48502/520	ex N774BC	
☐ VP-BDQ	McDonnell-Douglas MD-11F	48504/548	ex N702BC	
☐ VP-BDR	McDonnell-Douglas MD-11F	48503/528	ex N725BC	
☐ RA-89001	Sukhoi Superjet 100	95008		M Vodopyanov	o/o♦
☐ RA-89002	Sukhoi Superjet 100	95010			o/o♦
☐ RA-89003	Sukhoi Superjet 100	95011			o/o♦
☐ RA-89004	Sukhoi Superjet 100	95012			o/o♦
☐ RA-	Sukhoi Superjet 100				o/o♦
☐ RA-	Sukhoi Superjet 100				o/o♦
☐ RA-	Sukhoi Superjet 100				o/o♦
☐ RA-	Sukhoi Superjet 100				o/o♦
☐ RA-	Sukhoi Superjet 100				o/o♦
☐ RA-85135	Tupolev Tu-154M	92A922	ex B-2628	
☐ RA-85627	Tupolev Tu-154M	87A756	ex CCCP-85627	
☐ RA-85637	Tupolev Tu-154M	87A767	ex CCCP-85637	
☐ RA-85735	Tupolev Tu-154M	92A917	ex B-2627	
☐ RA-85760	Tupolev Tu-154M	92A942	ex EW-85760	
☐ RA-85765	Tupolev Tu-154M	90A832	ex LZ-HMN	

AEROKUZBASS   Novokuznetsk (NKZ)   Novokuznetsk (NOZ)

☐ RA-85747	Tupolev Tu-154M	92A930	ex EP-EAD	>IRB as EP-MBT
☐ RA-85749	Tupolev Tu-154M	92A931	ex EP-MBM	>IRB as EP-MBQ
☐ RA-22725	Mil Mi-8T	98308700	ex CCCP-22725	
☐ RA-24140	Mil Mi-8T	98841391	ex CCCP-24140	
☐ RA-24430	Mil Mi-8T	98625661	ex CCCP-24430	

AIR BASHKORTOSTAN   (BBT)   Ufa (UFA)

☐ RA-73015	Boeing 757-230	25901/464	ex D-ABNO	<MOV

AIRBRIDGE CARGO   Volga Dnepr (RU/ABW)   MoscowSheremetyevo(SVO)

☐ VP-BIC	Boeing 747-329 (SF)	24837/810	ex TF-ARY	
☐ VP-BIG	Boeing 747-46NERF	35420/1395	ex N5022E	
☐ VP-BII	Boeing 747-281F	24576/818	ex JA8191	
☐ VP-BIJ	Boeing 747-281F	25171/886	ex JA8194	
☐ VP-BIK	Boeing 747-46NERF	35421/1400		
☐ VP-BIM	Boeing 747-4HAERF	35237/1402		
☐ VQ-BFX	Boeing 747-428ERF	33096/1317	ex F-GIUB	
☐ VQ-BGY	Boeing 747-428ERF	33097/1361	ex F-GIUE	♦
☐ VQ-BHE	Boeing 747-4KZF	36784/1411	ex N384NC	♦
☐ VQ-BHZ	Boeing 747-8HVF	37580/1430		o/o♦
☐ VQ-BIA	Boeing 747-4KZF	36785/1418	ex N385NY	♦
☐ VQ-BIM	Boeing 747-446F	33749/1352	ex N402AL	♦
☐ VQ-	Boeing 747-8HVF			o/o♦
☐ RA-64051	Tupolev Tu-204-120C	64051		o/o
☐ RA-64052	Tupolev Tu-204-120C	64052		o/o

AIRSTARS AIRWAYS		**Morozov (PL/ASE)**	**Moscow-Domodedovo (DME)**	
☐ RA-76476	Ilyushin Il-76TD	0043451528	ex CCCP-76476	
☐ RA-76750	Ilyushin Il-76TD	0083485561	ex CCCP-76750	
☐ RA-86523	Ilyushin Il-62M	2241647	ex CCCP-86523	
☐ RA-96002	Ilyushin Il-96-300	74393201001		

AK BARS AERO		**(BGM)**		**Bugulma (UUA)**
☐ VQ-BHF	Canadair CRJ-200LR	7802	ex N510CA	♦
☐ VQ-BHH	Canadair CRJ-200LR	7824	ex N526CA	♦
☐ VQ-BHI	Canadair CRJ-200LR	7809	ex N514CA	♦
☐ VQ-BHJ	Canadair CRJ-200LR	7821	ex N523CA	♦
☐ RA-87209	Yakovlev Yak-40K	9810657	ex CCCP-87209	all-white
☐ RA-87227	Yakovlev Yak-40K	9810559	ex CCCP-87227	all-white
☐ RA-87239	Yakovlev Yak-40	9530643	ex CCCP-87239	
☐ RA-87247	Yakovlev Yak-40	9531543	ex CCCP-87247	
☐ RA-87342	Yakovlev Yak-40	9511139	ex CCCP-87342	Op in Tatneft coloursVIP
☐ RA-87447	Yakovlev Yak-40	9430436	ex CCCP-87447	AK Bars Bank titlesVIP
☐ RA-87462	Yakovlev Yak-40	9430137	ex CCCP-87462	
☐ RA-87505	Yakovlev Yak-40	9510740	ex CCCP-87505	
☐ RA-87517	Yakovlev Yak-40	9521940	ex CCCP-87517	VIP
☐ RA-87588	Yakovlev Yak-40	9222022	ex CCCP-87588	
☐ RA-87849	Yakovlev Yak-40	9331830	ex CCCP-87849	
☐ RA-88165	Yakovlev Yak-40	9611946	ex CCCP-88165	
☐ RA-88182	Yakovlev Yak-40	9620248	ex CCCP-88182	Op in Tatneft colours

ALANIA AIRLINE		**Alania (2D/OST)**	**Vladikavkaz (OGZ)**
☐ RA-42435	Yakovlev Yak-42D	4520424306017 ex ER-YCA	

ALROSA AVIA		**Alrosa (LRO)**	**Moscow-Zhukovsky / Vnukovo**
☐ RA-65693	Tupolev Tu-134B-3	63221	ex YL-LBC	Executive
☐ RA-65907	Tupolev Tu-134A	63996	ex CCCP-65907	Executive

ALROSA AVIATION		**Mirny (6R/DRU)**		**Mirny (MJZ)**
☐ RA-22394	Mil Mi-8T	7296	ex CCCP-22394	
☐ RA-22570	Mil Mi-8T	7816	ex CCCP-22570	
☐ RA-22571	Mil Mi-8T	7817	ex CCCP-22571	
☐ RA-22731	Mil Mi-8T	98308847	ex CCCP-22731	
☐ RA-22744	Mil Mi-8T	98311127	ex CCCP-22744	
☐ RA-22879	Mil Mi-8T	98415832	ex CCCP-22879	
☐ RA-22899	Mil Mi-8T	98417179	ex CCCP-22899	
☐ RA-22902	Mil Mi-8T	98420099	ex CCCP-22902	
☐ RA-24256	Mil Mi-8T	98734114	ex CCCP-24256	
☐ RA-24257	Mil Mi-8T	98734121	ex CCCP-24257	
☐ RA-24435	Mil Mi-8T	98625845	ex CCCP-24435	
☐ RA-24451	Mil Mi-8T	98628263	ex CCCP-24451	
☐ RA-24506	Mil Mi-8T	98520843	ex CCCP-24506	
☐ RA-24536	Mil Mi-8T	98522588	ex CCCP-24536	
☐ RA-24741	Mil Mi-8T	98417837	ex CCCP-24741	
☐ RA-25228	Mil Mi-8T	7763	ex CCCP-25228	
☐ RA-25313	Mil Mi-8T	98203720	ex CCCP-25313	
☐ RA-25333	Mil Mi-8T	98206010	ex CCCP-25333	
☐ RA-25376	Mil Mi-8T	98209062	ex CCCP-25376	
☐ RA-25606	Mil Mi-8T	99150564	ex CCCP-25606	
☐ RA-85654	Tupolev Tu-154M	89A796	ex CCCP-86654	
☐ RA-85675	Tupolev Tu-154M	90A835	ex CCCP-85675	
☐ RA-85684	Tupolev Tu-154M	90A851	ex CCCP-85684	
☐ RA-85728	Tupolev Tu-154M	92A910	ex CCCP-85728	
☐ RA-85757	Tupolev Tu-154M	92A939	ex EP-MHX	
☐ RA-85782	Tupolev Tu-154M	93A966	ex UN-85782	
☐ RA-06036	Mil Mi-26	34001212426	ex CCCP-06036	
☐ RA-06081	Mil Mi-26	34001212471	ex CCCP-06081	
☐ RA-26552	Antonov An-26	3107	ex CCCP-26552	[YKS]
☐ RA-26668	Antonov An-26B-100	8201	ex CCCP-26668	
☐ RA-41904	Antonov An-38-100	4163839010004		
☐ RA-41907	Antonov An-38-100	4163820010007		
☐ RA-46488	Antonov An-24RV	27308106	ex CCCP-46488	
☐ RA-46621	Antonov An-24RV	37308708	ex CCCP-46621	
☐ RA-47272	Antonov An-24B	07306402	ex CCCP-47272	
☐ RA-47694	Antonov An-24B	27307601	ex CCCP-47694	

☐ RA-65101	Tupolev Tu-134A-3	60260	ex CCCP-65101	<ORB
☐ RA-65146	Tupolev Tu-134B-3	61000	ex YL-LBA	
☐ RA-65715	Tupolev Tu-134B-3	63536	ex 4L-AAC	
☐ RA-76357	Ilyushin Il-76TD	1023414467		
☐ RA-76360	Ilyushin Il-76TD	1033414492		
☐ RA-76373	Ilyushin Il-76TD	1033415507		
☐ RA-76420	Ilyushin Il-76TD	1023413446		Jt ops with TIS

AMUR ARTEL STARATELEI AVIAKOMPANIA   Khabarovsk-Novy (KHV)

| ☐ RA-26001 | Antonov An-26 | 9705 | ex CCCP-26001 |
| ☐ RA-26048 | Antonov An-26B | 10901 | ex CCCP-26048 |

AMURSKIE AVIALINII

| ☐ RA-87395 | Yakovlev Yak-40 | 9410733 | |
| ☐ RA-87938 | Yakovlev Yak-40K | 9710153 | ex CCCP-87936 |

ANGARA AIRLINES   Sarma (AGU)   Irkutsk-One (IKT)

☐ RA-26511	Antonov An-26-100	6808	ex CCCP-26511
☐ RA-26655	Antonov An-26-100	7802	ex CCCP-26655
☐ RA-46625	Antonov An-24RV	37308804	ex CCCP-46625
☐ RA-46662	Antonov An-24RV	47309410	ex CCCP-46662
☐ RA-46697	Antonov An-24RV	47309908	ex CCCP-46697
☐ RA-46712	Antonov An-24RV	57310408	ex EK-24408
☐ RA-47818	Antonov An-24RV	17307107	ex CCCP-47818
☐ RA-47848	Antonov An-24B	17307410	ex CCCP-47848

ARKHANGELSK 2ND AVIATION ENT'PRISE   Dvina (5N/OAO)   Arkhangelsk-Vaslearo

☐ RA-67553	LET L-410UVP-E	851430	ex CCCP-67553
☐ RA-67562	LET L-410UVP-E	851602	ex CCCP-67562
☐ RA-67563	LET L-410UVP-E	861603	ex CCCP-67563
☐ RA-67564	LET L-410UVP-E	851604	ex CCCP-67564
☐ RA-67565	LET L-410UVP-E	851605	ex CCCP-67565
☐ RA-67567	LET L-410UVP-E	861607	ex CCCP-67567
☐ RA-67569	LET L-410UVP-E	861609	ex CCCP-67569
☐ RA-22341	Mil Mi-8T	7166	ex CCCP-22341
☐ RA-22762	Mil Mi-8T	98311485	ex CCCP-22762
☐ RA-24012	Mil Mi-8MTV-1	95713	ex CCCP-24012
☐ RA-24485	Mil Mi-8T	98628927	ex CCCP-24485
☐ RA-06039	Mil Mi-26T	34001212429	ex CCCP-06039
☐ RA-06042	Mil Mi-26T	34001212432	ex CCCP-06042
☐ RA-06044	Mil Mi-26T	34001212434	ex CCCP-06044
☐ RA-21077	Mil Mi-6T	7065302B	ex CCCP-21077
☐ RA-21161	Mil Mi-6T	0533	ex CCCP-21161

ARKHANGELSK AIRLINES   Arkhangelsk-Vaslearo

| ☐ RA-46667 | Antonov An-24RV | 47309508 | ex CCCP-46667 |

ASTAIR

| ☐ RA-85031 | Tupolev Tu-154M | 87A751 | ex EX-087 |

ATRAN - AVIATRANS CARGO AIRLINES   Atran (V8/VAS)
Moscow-Domodedovo / Myachkovo (DME/-)

☐ RA-11868	Antonov An-12B	9346310	ex OB-1448	
☐ RA-12990	Antonov An-12B	00347304	ex OB-1449	
☐ RA-26218	Antonov An-26B	5408	ex FAP 363	[Myachkovo]
☐ RA-93913	Antonov An-12B	4342609	ex CCCP-93913	
☐ RA-93916	Antonov An-26	9105	ex CCCP-93916	

AVIACON ZITOTRANS   Zitotrans (ZR/AZS)   Ekaterinburg-Koltsovo (SVX)

☐ RA-76352	Ilyushin Il-76TD	1023411378	ex EP-SFB	Op for UN WFP
☐ RA-76386	Ilyushin Il-76TD	1033418600	ex UK 76386	
☐ RA-76807	Ilyushin Il-76TD	1013405176	ex CCCP-76807	Op for UN WFP
☐ RA-76842	Ilyushin Il-76TD	1033418616		

AVIAENERGO   Aviaenergo (7U/ERG)   Moscow-Sheremetyevo (SVO)

☐ RA-65962	Tupolev Tu-134A-3	3351901	ex CCCP-65962	VIP
☐ RA-85809	Tupolev Tu-154M	94A985		
☐ RA-86583	Ilyushin Il-62M	1356851	ex CCCP-86583	VIP

AVIAL AVIATION CO   New Avial (NVI)   Moscow-Domodedovo (DME)

☐ RA-11113	Antonov An-12TB	01347908	ex CCCP-11113
☐ RA-11115	Antonov An-12BP	01348003	ex CCCP-11115
☐ RA-11372	Antonov An-12BP	401912	ex EW-252TI
☐ RA-11906	Antonov An-12BP	2340802	ex CCCP-11906
☐ RA-69314	Antonov An-12BP	5343004	ex CCCP-69314

AVIALESOOKHRANA VLADIMIR AIR ENTERPRISE   (FFA)   Vladimir

☐ RA-26002	Antonov An-26	07309706	ex CCCP-26002	
☐ RA-26005	Antonov An-26	9809	ex CCCP-26005	
☐ RA-26011	Antonov An-26B	9908	ex CCCP-26011	
☐ RA-26040	Antonov An-26B	10703	ex CCCP-26040	[IKT]
☐ RA-26532	Antonov An-26	7410	ex CCCP-26532	
☐ RA-46480	Antonov An-24RV	27308008	ex CCCP-46480	

AVIANOVA   (AO)

☐ EI-EEI	Airbus A320-232	0661	ex N603AW	
☐ EI-EEL	Airbus A320-232	0543	ex N605AW	
☐ EI-ELD	Airbus A320-232	1918	ex G-TTOF	
☐ EI-ELN	Airbus A320-232	1993	ex G-TTOH	◆

AVIAST AIR   Ialsi (6I/VVA)   Moscow-Vnukovo (VKO)

☐ RA-11756	Antonov An-12BP	4342208	ex CCCP-11756	>SHU
☐ RA-11962	Antonov An-12BP	5343007	ex CCCP-11962	
☐ RA-76843	Ilyushin Il-76TD	1013408269		Op for UN WFP

AVIASTAR – TUPOLEV   Tupolev Air (4B/TUP)   Moscow-Zhukovsky / Domodedovo (-/DME)

☐ RA-64021	Tupolev Tu-204-100C	1450743164021		
☐ RA-64024	Tupolev Tu-204-100C	1450743164024	ex LY-AGT	DHL Colours
☐ RA-64032	Tupolev Tu-204-100C	1450743164032		

BARKOL AVIAKOMPANIA   Moscow-Byokovo/Volgograd-Gurmak (BKA/VOG)

☐ RA-87280	Yakovlev Yak-40	9322025	ex CCCP-87280	Executive
☐ RA-87372	Yakovlev Yak-40	9340332	ex CCCP-87372	Executive
☐ RA-87957	Yakovlev Yak-40K	9821857	ex CCCP-87957	Executive
☐ RA-88229	Yakovlev Yak-40	9641850	ex CCCP-88229	Executive

BURAL   Bural (BUN)   Ulan Ude-Mukhino (UUD)

☐ RA-46408	Antonov An-24B	77304003	ex CCCP-46408
☐ RA-46614	Antonov An-24RV	37308701	ex CCCP-46614

BUSINESS AERO

☐ RA-42344	Yakovlev Yak-42	4520422708295	ex LY-AAQ

BYLINA   Bylina (BYL)   Moscow-Vnukovo (VKO)

☐ RA-88263	Yakovlev Yak-40	9711852	ex CCCP-88263	VIP
☐ RA-88274	Yakovlev Yak-40	9721253	ex CCCP-88274	VIP

CENTER-SOUTH AIRLINES   Center-South (CTS)   Belgorod (EGO)

☐ RA-87655	Yakovlev Yak-40	9211820	ex CCCP-87655
☐ RA-87966	Yakovlev Yak-40	9820958	ex CCCP-87966
☐ RA-88236	Yakovlev Yak-40	9640551	ex CCCP-88236

CENTRE-AVIA AIRLINES   Aviacentre (J7/CVC)   Moscow-Bykovo (BKA)

☐ RA-42325	Yakovlev Yak-42D	4520424402148	ex CCCP-42325	
☐ RA-42341	Yakovlev Yak-42D	4520421706292	ex CCCP-42341	
☐ RA-42353	Yakovlev Yak-42D	4520424711396	ex LY-AAT	
☐ RA-42385	Yakovlev Yak-42D	4520423016309	ex ER-YCC	
☐ RA-42423	Yakovlev Yak-42	4520424216606	ex CCCP-42423	VIP
☐ RA-42542	Yakovlev Yak-42D	11140804	ex CCCP-42542	
☐ RA-87507	Yakovlev Yak-40	9520940	ex LY-AAB	

CHUKOTAVIA   Anadyr (DYR)

☐ RA-26099	Antonov An-26B-100	11905	ex CCCP-26099
☐ RA-26128	Antonov An-26B	12702	ex CCCP-26128
☐ RA-26590	Antonov An-26B	13910	ex CCCP-26590
☐ RA-46616	Antonov An-24RV	37308703	ex CCCP-46616

☐ RA-22728	Mil Mi-8T	98308799	ex CCCP-22728	
☐ RA-24199	Mil Mi-8T	98943825	ex CCCP-24199	
☐ RA-24422	Mil Mi-8T	98625391	ex CCCP-24422	
☐ RA-24497	Mil Mi-8T	98734707	ex CCCP-24497	
☐ RA-24498	Mil Mi-8T	98734729	ex CCCP-24498	
☐ RA-24503	Mil Mi-8T	96520730	ex CCCP-24503	
☐ RA-24531	Mil Mi-8T	98522401	ex CCCP-24531	
☐ RA-24719	Mil Mi-8T	98417340	ex CCCP-24719	
☐ RA-24738	Mil Mi-8T	98417759	ex CCCP-24738	
☐ RA-25158	Mil Mi-8T	99047875	ex CCCP-25158	
☐ RA-25189	Mil Mi-8T	98943829	ex CCCP-25189	
☐ RA-25470	Mil Mi-8MTV-1	95614	ex CCCP-25470	
☐ RA-25988	Mil Mi-8T	7520	ex CCCP-25988	
☐ RA-27014	Mil Mi-8MTV-1	96352		
☐ RA-27025	Mil Mi-8PS	8730		

CONTINENTAL AIRWAYS — Contair (PC/PVV) — Moscow-Sheremetyevo (SVO)

| ☐ RA-85773 | Tupolev Tu-154M | 93A955 | ex EP-TUB | |

DAGHESTAN AIRLINES — Dagal (N2/DAG) — Makhachkala (MCX)

☐ RA-22859	Mil Mi-8T	98415435	ex CCCP-22859	
☐ RA-25760	Mil Mi-8MTV-1	96123		EMS
☐ RA-46654	Antonov An-24RV	47309209	ex CCCP-46654	
☐ RA-65569	Tupolev Tu-134A-3	63340	ex 4L-AAB	
☐ RA-65570	Tupolev Tu-134A-3	66550	ex RA-64451	
☐ RA-85495	Tupolev Tu-154B-2	81A495	ex CCCP-85495	
☐ RA-85756	Tupolev Tu-154M	92A938		
☐ RA-85828	Tupolev Tu-154M	97A1009	Rasul Gamzatov	
☐ RA-85840	Tupolev Tu-154M	98A1011		

DALAVIA — Khabarovsk Air (H8/KHB) — Khabarovsk-Novy (KHV)

☐ RA-46474	Antonov An-24RV	27308002	ex CCCP-46474	
☐ RA-46522	Antonov An-24RV	47310001	ex CCCP-46522	
☐ RA-46529	Antonov An-24RV	57310008	ex CCCP-46529	
☐ RA-46643	Antonov An-24RV	37309001	ex CCCP-46643	
☐ RA-47354	Antonov An-24RV	67310603	ex CCCP-47354	
☐ RA-47367	Antonov An-24RV	77310806	ex CCCP-47367	
☐ RA-86131	Ilyushin Il-62M	4255244	ex CCCP-86131	
☐ RA-86493	Ilyushin Il-62M	4140748	ex CU-T1248	
☐ RA-86525	Ilyushin Il-62M	4851612	ex CCCP-86525	
☐ RA-86560	Ilyushin Il-62M	2153347	ex CCCP-86560	
☐ RA-85114	Tupolev Tu-154M	89A814	ex EP-EAC	
☐ RA-85477	Tupolev Tu-154B-2	81A477	ex CCCP-85477	
☐ RA-85734	Tupolev Tu-154M	86A734	ex B-2608	
☐ RA-85752	Tupolev Tu-154M	92A934	ex EP-MAT	
☐ RA-85797	Tupolev Tu-154M	93A981		
☐ RA-85802	Tupolev Tu-154M	93A961	ex EP-MAN	stored
☐ RA-64502	Tupolev Tu-214	42625002	Yuri Vorob'yoy	
☐ RA-64503	Tupolev Tu-214	43103003		
☐ RA-64507	Tupolev Tu-214	42305007		
☐ RA-64510	Tupolev Tu-214	42305010		
☐ RA-64512	Tupolev Tu-214	42305012		
☐ RA-26000	Antonov An-26	7309604	ex CCCP-26000	
☐ RA-26058	Antonov An-26B	11101	ex CCCP-26058	

DAURIA — Chita-Kadala (HTA)

☐ RA-26053	Antonov An-26B	17310909	ex CCCP-26053	
☐ RA-26543	Antonov An-26	5732709	ex CCCP-26543	[IKT]
☐ RA-47268	Antonov An-24B	07306306	ex CCCP-47268	
☐ RA-47838	Antonov An-24B	17307310	ex CCCP-47838	Avialinii Zabaikalaya titles

DOMODEDOVO AIRLINES — Domodedovo (E3/DMO) — Moscow-Domodedovo (DME)

☐ RA-86519	Ilyushin Il-62M	4140212	ex CCCP-86519	
☐ RA-76799	Ilyushin Il-76TD	1003403075	ex CCCP-76799	>ESL
☐ RA-96006	Ilyushin Il-96-300	74393201003	ex CCCP-96006	
☐ RA-96009	Ilyushin Il-96-300	74393201006		[DME]
☐ RA-96013	Ilyushin Il-96-300	74393202013		[DME]

DONAVIA — Donavia (D9/DNV) — Rostov-on-Don (ROV)

☐ VP-BLF	Boeing 737-528	25232/2231	ex F-GJNG	
☐ VP-BLG	Boeing 737-528	25233/2251	ex F-GJNH	
☐ VP-BVU	Boeing 737-5Q8	25166/2129	ex G-BVZH	
☐ VP-BWY	Boeing 737-528	27305/2574	ex F-GJNO	
☐ VP-BWZ	Boeing 737-528	27304/2572	ex F-GJNN	
☐ VP-BYU	Boeing 737-5Q8	25167/2173	ex G-BVZI	
☐ VP-BYV	Boeing 737-5Q8	25160/2114	ex G-BVZG	
☐ VQ-BAN	Boeing 737-4Q8	25113/2656	ex N782AS	
☐ VQ-BAO	Boeing 737-4Q8	25114/2666	ex N783AS	
☐ VQ-BCS	Boeing 737-43Q	28494/2839	ex SX-BTN	
☐ RA-85149	Tupolev Tu-154M	89A797	ex B-609L	<VARZ
☐ RA-85626	Tupolev Tu-154M	87A753	ex CCCP-85626	
☐ RA-85630	Tupolev Tu-154M	87A759	ex CCCP-85630	
☐ RA-85640	Tupolev Tu-154M	87A772	ex CCCP-85640	
☐ RA-86124	Ilyushin Il-86	51483210092	ex CCCP-86124	[SVO]
☐ RA-86140	Ilyushin Il-86	51483211102	ex CCCP-86140	
☐ RA-86141	Ilyushin Il-86	51483211103		

ELBRUS AVIA — Elavia (NLK) — Nalchik (NAL)

☐ RA-42346	Yakovlev Yak-42D	4520423708311	ex CCCP-42346	<Aviatechnologia Lsg
☐ RA-42371	Yakovlev Yak-42D	4520422914225	ex CCCP-42371	<Aviatechnologia Lsg
☐ RA-42422	Yakovlev Yak-42D	4520424304017	ex ER-YCB	<Aviatechnologia Lsg

EVENKIA AVIA — Tura

☐ RA-26008	Antonov An-26B-100	9902	ex CCCP-26008	
☐ RA-26118	Antonov An-26B-100	12207	ex CCCP-26118	
☐ RA-69354	Antonov An-32	1606	ex CCCP-69354	
☐ RA-87900	Yakovlev Yak-40K	9720254	ex CCCP-87900	VIP

FLIGHT INSPECTIONS & SYSTEMS — Aviaspec (LTS) — Moscow-Bykovo/Khabarovsk-Novy (BKA/KHV)

☐ RA-26571	Antonov An-26	67303909	ex CCCP-26571	Calibrator/Flying laboratory
☐ RA-26631	Antonov An-26ASLK	77305503	ex CCCP-26631	Calibrator/Flying laboratory
☐ RA-26673	Antonov An-26ASLK	97308408	ex CCCP-26673	Calibrator/Flying laboratory
☐ RA-46395	Antonov An-24ALK	07306209	ex CCCP-46395	Calibrator/Flying laboratory

GAZPROMAVIA — Gazprom (4G/GZP) — Moscow-Ostafyevo/Moscow-Vnukovo (-/VKO)

☐ RA-74005	Antonov An-74TK-100C	36547095892	ex CCCP-74005	EMS
☐ RA-74008	Antonov An-74TK-100	36547095900	ex UR-74008	
☐ RA-74012	Antonov An-74D	36547098959	ex UR-74055	VIP, stored
☐ RA-74016	Antonov An-74TK-200	365470991034		
☐ RA-74032	Antonov An-74TK-100	36547098962	ex UR-74032	
☐ RA-74035	Antonov An-74TK-100	36547098963		
☐ RA-74036	Antonov An-74-200	36547098965		
☐ RA-74044	Antonov An-74-200	36547097936	ex UN-74044	
☐ RA-74056	Antonov An-74-200	36547098951		
☐ RA-74058	Antonov An-74-200	36547098956		
☐ RA-21505	Yakovlev Yak-40K	9830159	ex CCCP-21505	
☐ RA-87511	Yakovlev Yak-40	9521340	ex CCCP-87511	
☐ RA-88186	Yakovlev Yak-40K	9620648	ex CCCP-88186	
☐ RA-88300	Yakovlev Yak-40K	9641451	ex OK-GEO	
☐ RA-98113	Yakovlev Yak-40	9710253	ex CCCP-98113	VIP
☐ RA-42425	Yakovlev Yak-42D	4520423303016	ex CU-T1243	
☐ RA-42436	Yakovlev Yak-42D	4520421605018		
☐ RA-42437	Yakovlev Yak-42D	4520423606018		
☐ RA-42438	Yakovlev Yak-42D	4520423609018		VIP
☐ RA-42439	Yakovlev Yak-42D	4520423904019		
☐ RA-42442	Yakovlev Yak-42D	4520421402019		VIP
☐ RA-42451	Yakovlev Yak-42D	4520422708018		VIP
☐ RA-42452	Yakovlev Yak-42D	409016	ex RA-42431	
☐ RA-65045	Tupolev Tu-134A-3	49500	ex CCCP-65045	VIP >KGL
☐ RA-73000	Boeing 737-76N	28630/664	ex VT-JNP	
☐ RA-73004	Boeing 737-76N	28635/734	ex VT-JNQ	
☐ RA-76370	Ilyushin Il-76TD	1033414458		>VDA
☐ RA-76402	Ilyushin Il-76TD	1023413430		>VDA
☐ RA-76445	Ilyushin Il-76TD	1023410330	ex EK-76445	>VDA
☐ RA-76446	Ilyushin Il-76TD	1023412418	ex EK-76446	>VDA

478

☐ RA-85625	Tupolev Tu-154M	87A752	ex CCCP-85625	stored
☐ RA-85751	Tupolev Tu-154M	92A933		[VKO]
☐ RA-85774	Tupolev Tu-154M	93A956		
☐ RA-85778	Tupolev Tu-154M	93A962		

GEODYNAMICA CENTRE — Geo Centre (CGS) — Moscow-Myachkovo

☐ RA-30001	Antonov An-30	1402	ex CCCP-30001	Photo/survey
☐ RA-30006	Antonov An-30	1407	ex CCCP-30006	Photo/survey
☐ RA-30039	Antonov An-30	0710	ex CCCP-30039	Photo/survey

GLOBUS — (GLP)

☐ VP-BTA	Boeing 737-4Q8	25168/2210	ex TF-ELY	
☐ VP-BTH	Boeing 737-42C	24231/1871	ex N60669	
☐ RA-85611	Tupolev Tu-154M	85A715	ex CCCP-85611	
☐ RA-85612	Tupolev Tu-154M	86A721	ex CCCP-85612	
☐ RA-85623	Tupolev Tu-154M	87A749	ex CCCP-85623	[DME]

GROZNYYAVIA — Grozny (GRV)

☐ RA-42379	Yakovlev Yak-42D	4520421014543	ex EP-YAE
☐ RA-42418	Yakovlev Yak-42D	4520423219118	ex CCCP-42418

IFLY

☐ EI-DUA	Boeing 757-256	26247/860	ex N241LF
☐ EI-DUC	Boeing 757-256	26248/863	ex N263LF
☐ EI-DUD	Boeing 757-256	26249/881	ex N271LF

IKAR — Magadan-Sokol (GDX)

☐ RA-28723	WSK-PZL/Antonov An-28	1AJ007-08	ex CCCP-26105
☐ RA-26726	WSK-PZL/Antonov An-28	1AJ007-11	ex CCCP-26105

ILIN AVIAKOMPANIA — Yakutsk-Magan

☐ RA-67623	LET L-410UVP-E	902405	ex CCCP-67623
☐ RA-67664	LET L-410UVP-E	902526	ex CCCP-67664

INTERAVIA AIRLINES — Astair (8D/SUW) — Moscow-Domodedovo (DME)

☐ RA-86533	Ilyushin Il-62M	1343123	ex CCCP-86533	Novowilov
☐ RA-86567	Ilyushin Il-62M	4256314		
☐ RA-86575	Ilyushin Il-62M	1647928	ex UK 86575	
☐ RA-86577	Ilyushin Il-62M	2748552	ex UK 86577	
☐ RA-42339	Yakovlev Yak-42D	4520424606267	ex LY-AAO	
☐ RA-42356	Yakovlev Yak-42D	4520422811400	ex CCCP-42356	
☐ RA-42359	Yakovlev Yak-42D	4520424811417	ex LY-AAW	

IRAERO — Irkutsk-One (IKT)

☐ RA-26051	Antonov An-26B	10906	ex CCCP-26051	
☐ RA-26130	Antonov An-26B	12704	ex CCCP-26130	
☐ RA-26131	Antonov An-26B	12707	ex CCCP-26131	
☐ RA-26692	Antonov An-26	9409	ex CCCP-26692	
☐ RA-46846	Antonov An-24RV	27307504	ex ER-AWC	
☐ RA-47321	Antonov An-24RV	67310507	ex TC-TOR	
☐ RA-47804	Antonov An-24RV	17306903	ex CCCP-47804	
☐ RA-47805	Antonov An-24RV	17306907	ex ER-AWD	♦

IZHAVIA — Izhavia (IZA) — Izhevsk (IJK)

☐ RA-42450	Yakovlev Yak-42	4520424601019	
☐ RA-42524	Yakovlev Yak-42D	11030603	ex EP-TAK
☐ RA-46620	Antonov An-24RV	37308707	ex CCCP-46620
☐ RA-46637	Antonov An-24RV	37308903	ex CCCP-46637
☐ RA-47315	Antonov An-24RV	67310502	ex CCCP-47315
☐ RA-65056	Tupolev Tu-134A-3	49860	ex CCCP-65056

JET 2000

☐ RA-87216	Yakovlev Yak-40	9510440	ex CCCP-87216

JET AIR GROUP — Sistema (JSI) — Moscow-Sheremetyevo (SME)

☐ P4-AIR	McDonnell-Douglas MD-87ER	49412/1424	ex N871DP	Op for Siviera
☐ RA-65723	Tupolev Tu-134A-3M	66440	ex CCCP-65723	Executive
☐ RA-65930	Tupolev Tu-134A-3M	66500	ex CCCP-65930	Executive

479

KAPO		Kazavia (KAO)		Kazan-Bonsoglebskow (KZN)
☐ RA-26597	Antonov An-26B	13310	ex CCCP-26597	
☐ RA-86126	Ilyushin Il-62MF	4154535		
☐ RA-86576	Ilyushin Il-62MF	4546257	ex UK 86576	Frtr
☐ RA-86579	Ilyushin Il-62MF	2951636	ex UK 86579	Frtr Govt of Amur Region
☐ RA-86945	Ilyushin Il-62M	3850145	ex OK-BYV	VIP Govt of Amur Region

KATEKAVIA		Katekavia (KTK)		Sharypovo/Krasnoyarsk-Yernelyanovo (-/KJA)
☐ RA-46491	Antonov An-24RV	27308204	ex 3X-GEB	
☐ RA-46493	Antonov An-24RV	27308206	ex CCCP-46493	
☐ RA-46497	Antonov An-24RV	27308210	ex CCCP-46497	
☐ RA-46520	Antonov An-24RV	37308506	ex CCCP-46520	no titles
☐ RA-46604	Antonov An-24RV	37308601	ex CCCP-46604	
☐ RA-46683	Antonov An-24RV	47309706	ex CCCP-46683	
☐ RA-46689	Antonov An-24RV	47309806	ex CCCP-46689	
☐ RA-46693	Antonov An-24RV	47309904	ex CCCP-46693	
☐ RA-47351	Antonov An-24RV	67310510	ex YL-LCI	
☐ RA-47358	Antonov An-24RV	67310607	ex CCCP-47358	
☐ RA-48102	Antonov An-24RT	1911804	ex CCCP-48102	

KAZAN AIR ENTERPRISES				Kazan Osnovnoi / Khanty Mansisk (KZN/-)
☐ RA-67142	LET L-410UVP	800408	ex CCCP-67142	
☐ RA-67672	LET L-410UVP-E	872013	ex 2013 no titles	
☐ RA-67675	LET L-410UVP-E	882027	ex 2027	[Kazan]
☐ RA-06171	Mil Mi-8T	98420128	ex CCCP-06171	
☐ RA-22674	Mil Mi-8T	8127	ex CCCP-22674	
☐ RA-22679	Mil Mi-8T	8133	ex CCCP-22679	
☐ RA-22734	Mil Mi-8T	98308901	ex CCCP-22734	
☐ RA-22873	Mil Mi-8T	98415711	ex CCCP-22873	
☐ RA-25408	Mil Mi-8T	98233135	ex CCCP-25408	
☐ RA-25519	Mil Mi-8T	9775214	ex CCCP-25519	
☐ RA-25599	Mil Mi-8T	99150362	ex CCCP-25599	
☐ RA-27023	Mil Mi-8T	9754622	ex CCCP-27023	
☐ RA-27176	Mil Mi-8PS	8710	ex TC-HSA	

KHABAROVSK AIRLINES				Nikolaevsk-na-Amure
☐ RA-24532	Mil Mi-8T	98522422	ex CCCP-24532	
☐ RA-24722	Mil Mi-8T	98417398	ex CCCP-24722	
☐ RA-25196	Mil Mi-8T	99047381	ex CCCP-25196	
☐ RA-26174	Antonov An-26B-100	97308304	ex CCCP-26174	
☐ RA-87651	Yakovlev Yak-40	9141220	ex CCCP-87651	Nikolaevsk titles
☐ RA-88251	Yakovlev Yak-40K	9710552	ex CCCP-88251	

KIROV AVIA ENTERPRISE		Vyatka-Avia (KTA)		Kirov (KVX)
☐ RA-46660	Antonov An-24RV	47309307	ex CCCP-46660	
☐ RA-47295	Antonov An-24RV	07306608	ex CCCP-47295	Op as UNO 030
☐ RA-26086	Antonov An-26B	12302	ex CCCP-26086	

KMV MINERALNYE VODY AIRLINES		Air Minvody (KV/MVD)		Mineralnye Vody (MRV)
☐ RA-85380	Tupolev Tu-154B-2	79A380	ex CCCP-85380	
☐ RA-85457	Tupolev Tu-154B-2	80A457	ex CCCP-85457	
☐ RA-85494	Tupolev Tu-154B-2	81A494	ex CCCP-85494	
☐ RA-85715	Tupolev Tu-154M	91A891	ex EP-MAX	
☐ RA-85746	Tupolev Tu-154M	92A929	ex EP-MAV	
☐ RA-85790	Tupolev Tu-154M	93A974	ex EP-CPL	
☐ RA-85792	Tupolev Tu-154M	93A976	ex EP-LAZ	
☐ RA-85826	Tupolev Tu-154M	89A812	ex SP-LCL	
☐ RA-64016	Tupolev Tu-204-100	1450742364016	Alexej Tupolev	
☐ RA-64022	Tupolev Tu-204-100	1450743164022		
☐ RA-	Tupolev Tu-204-300		o/o	
☐ RA-	Tupolev Tu-204-300		o/o	

KNAAPO		Knaapo (KNM)		Komsomolsk na Amur (KXK)
☐ RA-11125	Antonov An-12BP	3341006	ex CCCP-11125	
☐ RA-11371	Antonov An-12BP	00347406	ex 22 red	
☐ RA-11789	Antonov An-12BP	6343905	ex LZ-BFB	

480

KOLAVIA		Kogalym (7K/KGL)		Kogalym (KGP)
☐ RA-22501	Mil Mi-8T	99357415		
☐ RA-26641	Mil Mi-8T	8026	ex CCCP-22641	
☐ RA-22980	Mil Mi-8AMT	59489607603	ex RA-22509	
☐ RA-24588	Mil Mi-8T	98839385	ex CCCP-24588	
☐ RA-25328	Mil Mi-8T	98203998	ex CCCP-25328	
☐ RA-25342	Mil Mi-8T	98206652	ex CCCP-25342	
☐ RA-25761	Mil Mi-8MTV-1	96073		
☐ RA-27066	Mil Mi-8MTV-1	95902	ex CCCP-27066	
☐ TC-KLA	Airbus A320-232	2029	ex N615SA	
☐ TC-KLB	Airbus A320-232	2077	ex N607SA	
☐ RA-65045	Tupolev Tu-134A-3	49500	ex CCCP-65045	VIP <GZP
☐ RA-65943	Tupolev Tu-134A-3	63580	ex (EW-65943)	
☐ RA-65944	Tupolev Tu-134A-3	12096	ex (EW-65944)	
☐ RA-85522	Tupolev Tu-154B-2	82A522	ex CCCP-85522	
☐ RA-85632	Tupolev Tu-154M	87A761	ex CCCP-85632	
☐ RA-85761	Tupolev Tu-154M	93A944		>TBM
☐ RA-85784	Tupolev Tu-154M	93A968		
☐ RA-85829	Tupolev Tu-154M	87A755	ex SP-LCD	

KORYAKAVIA				Tilichiki
☐ RA-28714	WSK-PZL/Antonov An-28	1AJ006-24	ex CCCP-28714	
☐ RA-28715	WSK-PZL/Antonov An-28	1AJ006-25	ex CCCP-28715	
☐ RA-28716	WSK-PZL/Antonov An-28	1AJ007-01	ex CCCP-28716	

KOSMOS AIRLINES		Kosmos (KSM)		Moscow-Vnukovo (VKO)
☐ RA-11025	Antonov An-12TB	6344103	ex CCCP-11025	
☐ RA-65010	Tupolev Tu-134A	46130	ex CCCP-65010	Yelena
☐ RA-65097	Tupolev Tu-134AK	60540	ex CCCP-65097	
☐ RA-65719	Tupolev Tu-134AK	63637	ex CCCP-65719	VIP
☐ RA-65726	Tupolev Tu-134AK	63720	ex CCCP-65726	VIP
☐ RA-65727	Tupolev Tu-134B-3	03564820	ex CCCP-65727	VIP,Bank Moscovski Kapital
☐ RA-65805	Tupolev Tu-134B-3	64775	ex 57	
☐ RA-65935	Tupolev Tu-134A-3	66180	ex CCCP-65935	VIP

KOSTROMA AIR ENTERPRISE				Kostroma (KMW)
☐ RA-26595	Antonov An-26	47313401	ex CCCP-26595	
☐ RA-27210	Antonov An-26-100	5410	ex CCCP-27210	Marshal Novikov

KUBAN AIRLINES		Air Kuban (GW/KIL)	Krasnodar-Pashkovskaya (KRR)	
☐ VQ-BHB	Boeing 737-3Q8	26310/2680	ex G-TOYA	♦
☐ VQ-BHC	Boeing 737-3Q8	26311/2681	ex G-TOYB	♦
☐ VQ-BHD	Boeing 737-3Q8	26312/2693	ex G-TOYC	♦
☐ RA-42331	Yakovlev Yak-42	4520424505128	ex CCCP-42331	
☐ RA-42336	Yakovlev Yak-42	4250422606220	ex CCCP-42336	stored
☐ RA-42342	Yakovlev Yak-42	4520421706302	ex EK-42342	
☐ RA-42350	Yakovlev Yak-42	4520424711372	ex CCCP-42350	
☐ RA-42363	Yakovlev Yak-42D	4520424811438	ex CCCP-42363	
☐ RA-42367	Yakovlev Yak-42D	4520424914133	ex CCCP-42367	
☐ RA-42375	Yakovlev Yak-42D	4520424914410	ex CCCP-42375	
☐ RA-42386	Yakovlev Yak-42D	4520424016310	ex CCCP-42386	
☐ RA-42421	Yakovlev Yak-42D	4520422303017	ex CCCP-42421	
☐ RA-42541	Yakovlev Yak-42	11140704	ex CCCP-42541	

LIPETSK AVIA				
☐ RA-87372	Yakovlev Yak-40	9340332	ex CCCP-87372	
Current status uncertain				

LUKIAVIATRANS			Velikie Luki/Pskov-Kresty (VLU/PKV)	
☐ RA-30042	Antonov An-30	0901	ex CCCP-30042	no titles
☐ RA-30053	Antonov An-30D	1008	ex CCCP-30053	
☐ RA-30067	Antonov An-30	1208	ex CCCP-30067	
☐ RA-46632	Antonov An-30	0201	ex CCCP-46632	

MCHS ROSSII		Sumes (SUM)		Moscow-Zhukovsky
☐ RF-32765	Beriev Be-200ES	768200010101	ex RA-21515	

☐ RF-32766	Beriev Be-200ES	768200010102	ex RA-21516		
☐ RF-32767	Beriev Be-200ES	76820002501	ex RA-21517		
☐ RF-32768	Beriev Be-200ES				
☐ RF-	Beriev Be-200ES				o/o
☐ RA-76362	Ilyushin Il-76TD	1033416533		Anatoliy Lyapidevskiy	
☐ RA-76363	Ilyushin Il-76TD	1033417540		Vasiliy Molokov	
☐ RA-76429	Ilyushin Il-76TD	1043419639			
☐ RA-76840	Ilyushin Il-76TD	1033417553		Nikolay Kamanin	
☐ RA-76841	Ilyushin Il-76TD	1033418601		Mavrikiy Slepnev	
☐ RA-76845	Ilyushin Il-76TDP	1043420696		Mikhail Vodop'yanov	
☐ RA-06075	Mil Mi-26T	34001212465			
☐ RA-06278	Mil Mi-26T	34001212522			
☐ RA-06279	Mil Mi-26T	34001212603			

Above three now believed to be RF-31110, RF-31124 and RF-32821 but order unknown

☐ RF-31122	Antonov An-74P	36547136012	ex RA-74034	Alexander Belyakov	
☐ RF-31350	Antonov An-74P	36547097940	ex RF-31112	Georgl Baidukov	
☐ RA-42441	Yakovlev Yak-42D	4520421402018	ex EP-LAN	Velerij Chkalov	VIP
☐ RA-42446	Yakovlev Yak-42D	4520423308017	ex UN-42446	Vladimir Kokkinaki	
☐ RA-86570	Ilyushin Il-62M	1356344		Mikhail Gromov	

MORDOVIA AIR — Saransk (SKX)

☐ RA-26247	Antonov An-26B-100	4103	ex CCCP-26247		
☐ RA-46505	Antonov An-24RV	37308309	ex CCCP-46505		
☐ RA-46640	Antonov An-24RV	37308908	ex CCCP-46640		>KMV

MOSKOVIA — Gromov Airline (3R/GAI) — Moscow-Zhukovsky

☐ RA-11309	Antonov An-12BP	00347510	ex CCCP-11309	Op for Irkut
☐ RA-11310	Antonov An-12BP	4342601	ex CCCP-11310	Op for Irkut
☐ RA-12162	Antonov An-12BP	3341509	ex CCCP-12162	Op for Irkut
☐ RA-30028	Antonov An-30	0510	ex CCCP-30028	
☐ VQ-BDI	Boeing 737-73A	28497/216	ex N497TF	
☐ VQ-BER	Boeing 737-7L9/W	28006/26	ex N280AG	
☐ VQ-BFR	Boeing 737-883	30468/668	ex SE-DTP	
☐ VQ-BFU	Boeing 737-883	30467/634	ex SE-DTN	
☐ RA-65606	Tupolev Tu-134A-3	46300	ex D-AOBR	Op for Tupolev Design
☐ RA-85615	Tupolev Tu-154M	86A731	ex CCCP-85615	
☐ RA-85736	Tupolev Tu-154M	92A918	ex CCCP-85736	Yuri Morozov
☐ RA-85743	Tupolev Tu-154M	92A926	ex CCCP-85743	Yuri Sheffer

MOSKVA AIR COMPANY — (3G/AYZ) — Moscow-Domodedovo (DME)

☐ RA-	Antonov An-148			o/o♦
☐ RA-	Antonov An-148			o/o♦
☐ RA-	Antonov An-148			o/o♦
☐ RA-	Antonov An-148			o/o♦
☐ RA-	Antonov An-148			o/o♦
☐ RA-	Antonov An-148			o/o♦
☐ RA-	Antonov An-148			o/o♦
☐ RA-	Antonov An-148			o/o♦
☐ RA-	Antonov An-148			o/o♦
☐ RA-	Antonov An-148			o/o♦
☐ RA-	Antonov An-148			o/o♦
☐ VP-BBL	Boeing 737-347	23183/1108	ex N303WA	
☐ VP-BBM	Boeing 737-347	23442/1239	ex N309WA	
☐ VP-BMI	Boeing 737-81Q	29052/557	ex G-XLAD	
☐ VQ-BBR	Boeing 737-8AS/W	32778/1140	ex EI-CSX	♦
☐ VQ-BBS	Boeing 737-8AS/W	32779/1167	ex EI-CSY	♦
☐ VQ-BCH	Boeing 737-8AS/W	32780/1178	ex EI-CSZ	♦
☐ VQ-BDU	Boeing 737-8AS/W	29936/1236	ex EI-CTA	
☐ VQ-BDV	Boeing 737-8AS/W	29937/1238	ex EI-CTB	
☐ VQ-BJY	Boeing 737-8K2/W	28248/1126	ex PH-HZX	♦
☐	Boeing 737-8			o/o♦
☐	Boeing 737-8			o/o♦
☐	Boeing 737-8			o/o♦
☐	Boeing 737-8			o/o♦
☐ RA-	Embraer EMB.120ER Brasilia	120172	ex N365AS	
☐ RA-	Embraer EMB.120ER Brasilia	120133	ex N366AS	
☐ RA-02851	Embraer EMB.120ER Brasilia	120125	ex N363AS	
☐ RA-02852	Embraer EMB.120ER Brasilia	120128	ex N364AS	

☐ RA-02854	Embraer EMB.120ER Brasilia	120136	ex N367AS	
☐ RA-02856	Embraer EMB.120ER Brasilia	120240	ex N203SW	
☐ RA-86109	Ilyushin Il-86	51483208077	ex CCCP-86109	
☐ RA-86123	Ilyushin Il-86	51483210091	ex CCCP-86123	
☐ RA-86125	Ilyushin Il-86	51483210093	ex UR-86125	
☐ RA-86136	Ilyushin Il-86	51483210094		
☐ RA-86138	Ilyushin Il-86	51483210096		
☐ EW-78779	Ilyushin Il-76TD	0083489662	ex CCCP-78779	<TXC
☐ RA-76401	Ilyushin Il-76TD	1023412399	ex CCCP-76401	<UHS
☐ RA-76783	Ilyushin Il-76TD	0093498974	ex CCCP-76783	<UHS
☐ RA-76817	Ilyushin Il-76TD	1023412387	ex CCCP-76817	<ESL
☐ RA-85140	Tupolev Tu-154M	85A716	ex UN-85835	
☐ RA-85709	Tupolev Tu-154M	91A884	ex EP-MAK	
☐ RA-85740	Tupolev Tu-154M	91A895	ex 9XR-DU	VIP
☐ RA-85841	Tupolev Tu-154M	90A858	ex EP-MBG	Jt ops with OMS
☐ RA-85849	Tupolev Tu-154M	89A815	ex B-2620	

NAPO AVIATRANS   Novsib (NPO)   Novosibirsk-Yeltsovka

☐ RA-12193	Antonov An-12BK	9346805	ex CCCP-12193	
☐ RA-12194	Antonov An-12BK	00347203	ex CCCP-12194	
☐ RA-12195	Antonov An-12BK	00347410	ex CCCP-12195	
☐ RA-41900	Antonov An-38-120	4160381607003		>LAY
☐ RA-41902	Antonov An-38-120	4163847010002		>VTK

NORDAVIA REGIONAL AIRLINES   Dvina (5N/AUL)   Arkhangelsk-Talegi (ARH)

☐ VP-BKP	Boeing 737-59D	25065/2028	ex OK-WGD	
☐ VP-BKT	Boeing 737-33R	28871/2900	ex PP-VPY	
☐ VP-BKU	Boeing 737-505	25789/2229	ex G-GFFB	
☐ VP-BKV	Boeing 737-505	27155/2449	ex N215BV	
☐ VP-BOH	Boeing 737-59D	25038/1969	ex G-GFFA	
☐ VP-BOI	Boeing 737-505	24650/1792	ex G-GFFG	
☐ VP-BQI	Boeing 737-5Y0	25186/2236	ex OM-SEA	
☐ VP-BQL	Boeing 737-5Y0	25185/2220	ex OM-SEF	
☐ VP-BRE	Boeing 737-53C	24827/2243	ex OM-SEE	
☐ VP-BRG	Boeing 737-53C	24826/2041	ex OM-SED	
☐ VP-BRI	Boeing 737-5Y0	25289/2288	ex OM-SEG	>AFL
☐ VP-BRK	Boeing 737-5Y0	25288/2286	ex OM-SEC	
☐ VP-BRN	Boeing 737-5Y0	25191/2260	ex OM-SEB	
☐ VP-BRP	Boeing 737-505	24651/1842	ex LN-BRD	
☐ VP-BXM	Boeing 737-59D	24695/1872	ex G-THOD	
☐ VP-BXN	Boeing 737-53A	24754/1868	ex G-GFFF	
☐ RA-65034	Tupolev Tu-134A-3	48565	ex CCCP-65034	
☐ RA-65043	Tupolev Tu-134A-3	49400	ex CCCP-65043	stored
☐ RA-65052	Tupolev Tu-134A-3	49825	ex CCCP-65052	white colours stored
☐ RA-65083	Tupolev Tu-134A-3	60090	ex CCCP-65083	>UTA
☐ RA-65096	Tupolev Tu-134A-3	60257	ex CCCP-65096	
☐ RA-65108	Tupolev Tu-134A-3	60332	ex EW-65108	>UTA
☐ RA-65116	Tupolev Tu-134A-3	60420	ex CCCP-65116	
☐ RA-65564	Tupolev Tu-134A-3	63165	ex CCCP-65564	
☐ RA-26104	Antonov An-26BRL	27312002	ex CCCP-26104	Arctica titles
☐ RA-46528	Antonov An-24RV	47310007	ex CCCP-46528	
☐ RA-46651	Antonov An-24RV	47309202	ex CCCP-46651	

NORDSTAR

☐ VQ-BDN	Boeing 737-8K5/W	32905/1046	ex D-AHLP	
☐ VQ-BDO	Boeing 737-8K5/W	32906/1087	ex D-AHLQ	
☐ VQ-BDP	Boeing 737-8Q8/W	28221/226	ex N282AG	
☐ VQ-BDW	Boeing 737-8K5/W	27977/9	ex D-AHFC	♦
☐ VQ-BDZ	Boeing 737-8K5/W	27978/40	ex D-AHFD	♦

NORDWIND   (N4/NWS)   Moscow-Sheremetyevo (SVO)

☐ VQ-BAK	Boeing 757-2Q8	26332/688	ex N401JS	
☐ VQ-BAL	Boeing 757-2Q8	27351/639	ex N403JS	
☐ VQ-BBT	Boeing 757-2Q8	29443/821	ex N763MX	
☐ VQ-BBU	Boeing 757-2Q8	29442/819	ex N762MX	
☐ VQ-BHR	Boeing 757-2Q8/W	30046/1006	ex OH-LBV	♦
☐ VQ-BJK	Boeing 757-2Q8	29380/836	ex N380RM	
☐ VQ-BKE	Boeing 757-231/W	28484/825	ex N716TW	♦

| ☐ VQ-BOG | Boeing 767-341ER | 30342/774 | ex VP-BWQ | | ◆ |
| ☐ VQ-BRA | Boeing 767-33AER | 27310/545 | ex N310AN | | ◆ |

NOVOSIBIRSK AIR ENTERPRISE — Nakair (NBE) — Novosibirsk-Severny

☐ RA-46642	Antonov An-24RV	37308910	ex CCCP-46642
☐ RA-46659	Antonov An-24RV	47309306	ex CCCP-46659
☐ RA-46682	Antonov An-24RV	47309704	ex CCCP-46682
☐ RA-47306	Antonov An-24RV	57310306	ex CCCP-47306
☐ RA-30007	Antonov An-30D	1408	ex CCCP-30007

ORENAIR — Orenburg (R2/ORB) — Orenburg-Tsentralny (REN)

☐ VP-BEW	Boeing 737-505	26297/2578	ex N371LF		
☐ VP-BGP	Boeing 737-4Y0	24691/1904	ex N691GE		
☐ VP-BGQ	Boeing 737-4Y0	24683/1901	ex N683GE		
☐ VP-BGR	Boeing 737-505	25790/2245	ex ES-ABG		
☐ VP-BPE	Boeing 737-5H6	26445/2327	ex OK-XGV	Aleksandr Kukishev	
☐ VP-BPF	Boeing 737-5H6	26446/2358	ex OK-XGW		
☐ VP-BPG	Boeing 737-8AS/W	29924/578	ex EI-CSI		
☐ VP-BPI	Boeing 737-83N/W	28244/958	ex N308TZ		
☐ VP-BPY	Boeing 737-83N/W	28247/1091	ex N318TZ		
☐ VQ-BCJ	Boeing 737-8AS/W	29932/1030	ex EI-CSS		
☐ VQ-BEM	Boeing 737-85R/W	29036/164	ex N636AC	Michael	
☐ VQ-BEN	Boeing 737-85R/W	29037/177	ex N637AC		
☐ VQ-BFY	Boeing 737-86N/W	29884/1094	ex N117MN		◆
☐ VQ-BFZ	Boeing 737-86N/W	28644/839	ex N116MN		◆
☐ VQ-BJC	Boeing 737-8K5/W	27992/523	ex D-AHFQ		◆

☐ RA-65049	Tupolev Tu-134A-3	49755	ex EW-65049	
☐ RA-65054	Tupolev Tu-134A	49840	ex CCCP-65054	
☐ RA-65090	Tupolev Tu-134A	60185	ex CCCP-65090	>SVR
☐ RA-65101	Tupolev Tu-134A-3	60260	ex CCCP-65101	>DRU
☐ RA-65110	Tupolev Tu-134A-3	60343	ex (HA-LBT)	
☐ RA-65117	Tupolev Tu-134A-3	60450	ex (HA-LBU)	
☐ RA-65136	Tupolev Tu-134A-3	60885	ex CCCP-65136	>UTA

☐ RA-85602	Tupolev Tu-154B-2	84A602	ex CCCP-85602	
☐ RA-85603	Tupolev Tu-154B-2	84A603	ex CCCP-85603	no titles
☐ RA-85604	Tupolev Tu-154B-2	85A604	ex CCCP-85604	
☐ RA-85768	Tupolev Tu-154M	94A949	Konstantine Brexos	

PERM AIRLINES — Perm Air (P9/PGP) — Perm-Bolshoe Savina (PEE)

☐ RA-26520	Antonov An-26-100	87307101	ex CCCP-26520	
☐ RA-26636	Antonov An-26-100	87306306	ex EP-TQB	
☐ RA-47756	Antonov An-24B	79901209	ex CCCP-47756	
☐ RA-65064	Tupolev Tu-134A-3	49886	ex CCCP-65064	
☐ RA-65751	Tupolev Tu-134A-3	61066	ex CCCP-65751	Sverbank titles
☐ RA-65775	Tupolev Tu-134A-3	62530	ex CCCP-65775	

PETROPAVLOVSK-KAMCHATSKY AIR ENTERPRISE — Petrokam (PTK)
Petropavlovsk Kamchatsky-Yelixovo (PKC)

☐ RA-87385	Yakovlev Yak-40K	9411632	ex CCCP-87385	stored
☐ RA-87947	Yakovlev Yak-40K	9621145	ex CCCP-87947	
☐ RA-87949	Yakovlev Yak-40K	9621345	ex CCCP-87949	
☐ RA-87988	Yakovlev Yak-40	9541244	ex CCCP-87988	
☐ RA-88241	Yakovlev Yak-40K	9641351	ex CCCP-88241	

☐ RA-26122	Antonov An-26B	12401	ex CCCP-26122
☐ RA-26251	Antonov An-26-100	9109	
☐ RA-67645	LET L-410UVP-E	902438	ex CCCP-67645
☐ RA-67662	LET L-410UVP-E	902520	ex CCCP-67662

POLAR AIRLINES — Batagai

☐ RA-46333	Antonov An-24B	97305510	ex CCCP-46333
☐ RA-46374	Antonov An-24B	07306005	ex CCCP-46374
☐ RA-47161	Antonov An-24B	89901703	ex CCCP-47161
☐ RA-47260	Antonov An-24B	27307802	ex CCCP-47260

☐ RA-26030	Antonov An-26B	10501	ex CCCP-26030
☐ RA-26061	Antonov An-26B	11108	ex CCCP-26061
☐ RA-26538	Antonov An-26-100	47302102	ex CCCP-26538
☐ RA-26635	Antonov An-26	6305	ex CCCP-26635
☐ RA-26674	Antonov An-26	8506	ex CCCP-26674
☐ RA-26685	Antonov An-26	1307	ex CCCP-26685

484

POLET AVIAKOMPANIA		Polet (YQ/POT)		Voronezh (VOZ)
☐ RA-82010	Antonov An-124-100 Ruslan	9773053616017	ex CCCP-82010	
☐ RA-82014	Antonov An-124-100 Ruslan	9773054732039	ex CCCP-82014	
☐ RA-82024	Antonov An-124 Ruslan	19530502033	ex CCCP-82024	[ULY]
☐ RA-82026	Antonov An-124 Ruslan	19530502127	ex 10 black	[ULY]
☐ RA-82068	Antonov An-124-100 Ruslan	9773051359127	ex RA-82070	
☐ RA-82075	Antonov An-124-100 Ruslan	9773053459147	Boris Naginski	
☐ RA-82077	Antonov An-124-100 Ruslan	9773054459151		
☐ RA-82080	Antonov An-124-100 Ruslan	9773051462161		
☐ RA-	Antonov An-148			o/o♦
☐ RA-	Antonov An-148			o/o♦
☐ RA-	Antonov An-148			o/o♦
☐ RA-	Antonov An-148			o/o♦
☐ RA-	Antonov An-148			o/o♦
☐ RA-	Antonov An-148			o/o♦
☐ RA-	Ilyushin Il-76-90VD			o/o♦
☐ RA-	Ilyushin Il-76-90VD			o/o♦
☐ RA-	Ilyushin Il-76-90VD			o/o♦
☐ RA-96101	Ilyushin Il-96-400T	74393201001		Frtr
☐ RA-96102	Ilyushin Il-96-400T	73439201002		Frtr
☐ RA-96103	Ilyushin Il-96-400T	97693201003		Frtr♦
☐ RA-	Ilyushin Il-96-400T			o/o♦
☐ VQ-BGC	SAAB SF.340B	340B-232	ex N232AE	♦
☐ VQ-BGD	SAAB SF.340B	340B-250	ex N250AE	♦
☐ VQ-BGE	SAAB SF.340B	340B-273	ex N273AE	♦
☐ VQ-BGF	SAAB SF.340B	340B-218	ex N218AE	♦
☐ VP-BPL	SAAB 2000	2000-029	ex HB-IZO	
☐ VP-BPM	SAAB 2000	2000-057	ex HB-IYB	
☐ VP-BPN	SAAB 2000	2000-058	ex HB-IYC	
☐ VP-BPQ	SAAB 2000	2000-060	ex HB-IYE	
☐ VP-BPR	SAAB 2000	2000-061	ex HB-IYF	
☐ RA-30024	Antonov An-30	0502	ex CCCP-30024	
☐ RA-30048	Antonov An-30	0910	ex CCCP-30048	
☐ RA-46676	Antonov An-24RV	47309608	ex CCCP-46676	
☐ RA-46690	Antonov An-24RV	47309901	ex CCCP-46690	Nikolai Pribilov
☐ RA-48096	Antonov An-24RV	57310406	ex CCCP-48096	
☐ RA-88304	Yakovlev Yak-40S2	9510439	ex ST-YAK	

POLYARNYA AVIA				Yakutsk (YKS)
☐ RA-46834	Antonov An-24RV	17306801		

PROGRESS AVIAKOMPANIA		Progress (PSS)		Samara-Bezymyanka (KUF)
☐ RA-26180	Antonov An-26	9737810	ex CCCP-26180	
☐ RA-26192	Antonov An-24RT	1911805	ex CCCP-26192	

PSKOVAVIA		Pskovavia (PSW)		Pskov-Kresty (PKV)
☐ RA-26107	Antonov An-26B	27312008	ex LY-LVR	
☐ RA-26120	Antonov An-26B	27312304	ex CCCP-26120	
☐ RA-26134	Antonov An-26B	12805	ex CCCP-26134	
☐ RA-26142	Antonov An-26B	37312904	ex CCCP-26142	

RED WINGS		Remont Air (VAZ)		Moscow-Vnukovo (VKO)
☐ RA-64018	Tupolev Tu-204-100	1450741964018		
☐ RA-64019	Tupolev Tu-204-100	1450741064019		
☐ RA-64020	Tupolev Tu-204-100	1450743164020		
☐ RA-64043	Tupolev Tu-204-100	64043		o/o
☐ RA-64046	Tupolev Tu-204-100	64046		
☐ RA-64047	Tupolev Tu-204-100	64047		
☐ RA-64049	Tupolev Tu-204-100	64049		
☐ RA-64050	Tupolev Tu-204-100	64050		
☐ RA-64051	Tupolev Tu-204-100	1450743164051		o/o
☐ RA-64053	Tupolev Tu-204-100	1450743164053		o/o

REGIONAL AIRLINES				
☐ VQ-BBX	Embraer EMB.120ER Brasilia	120205	ex N205CA	
☐ VQ-BBY	Embraer EMB.120ER Brasilia	120265	ex N285AS	

☐ VQ-BCB	Embraer EMB.120ER Brasilia	120231	ex N280AS	
☐ VQ-BCL	Embraer EMB.120ER Brasilia	120304	ex N227SW	
☐ VQ-	Embraer EMB.120ER Brasilia	120202	ex N268AS	o/o
☐ VQ-	Embraer EMB.120ER Brasilia	120236	ex N283AS	o/o
☐ RA-28728	WSK-PZL/Antonov An-28	1AJ-007-13	ex CCCP-28728	
☐ RA-28900	WSK/PZL Antonov An-28	1AJ-007-14	ex EX-28729	
☐ RA-28901	WSK/PZL Antonov An-28	1AJ008-01	ex EX-28738	
☐ RA-28903	WSK-PZL/Antonov An-28	1AJ009-19	ex RA-28953	

ROSNEFT-BALTIKA — Rosbalt (RNB) — St Petersburg-Pulkovo (LED)

☐ RA-21500	Yakovlev Yak-40K	9741356	ex CCCP-21500	
☐ RA-87244	Yakovlev Yak-40	9531243	ex CCCP-87244	

ROSSIYA RUSSIAN AIRLINES — Russia (FV/SDM)
Moscow-Vnukovo/St Petersburg-Pulkovo (VKO/LED)

☐ VP-BIQ	Airbus A319-111	1890	ex N917FR	
☐ VP-BIT	Airbus A319-112	1761	ex N909FR	
☐ VP-BIU	Airbus A319-114	0649	ex N574SX	
☐ VQ-BAQ	Airbus A319-111	1560	ex N903FR	
☐ VQ-BAR	Airbus A319-111	1488	ex N901FR	
☐ VQ-BAS	Airbus A319-111	1863	ex N913FR	
☐ VQ-BAT	Airbus A319-112	1876	ex N916FR	
☐ VQ-BAU	Airbus A319-112	1851	ex N915FR	
☐ VQ-BAV	Airbus A319-111	1743	ex N907FR	
☐ EI-DXY	Airbus A320-212	0525	ex D-AKNX	
☐ EI-DZR	Airbus A320-212	0427	ex N265AV	
☐ VQ-BBM	Airbus A320-214	1578	ex EC-HZU	
☐ VQ-BDQ	Airbus A320-214	1767	ex EC-KDD	
☐ VQ-BDR	Airbus A320-214	1130	ex EC-IMU	◆
☐ VQ-BDY	Airbus A320-214	1657	ex EC-KBQ	
☐ VQ-BEY	Airbus A320-212	0426	ex EI-ELK	◆
☐ RA-61701	Antonov An-148-100B	2701504001		
☐ RA-61702	Antonov An-148-100B	2701504002		
☐ RA-61703	Antonov An-148-100B	2701504003		
☐ RA-61704	Antonov An-148-100B	2701504004		
☐ RA-61705	Antonov An-148-100B	2701504005		
☐ EI-CDD	Boeing 737-548	24989/1989	ex EI-BXH	
☐ EI-CDE	Boeing 737-548	25115/2050	ex PT-SLM	
☐ EI-CDF	Boeing 737-548	25737/2232		
☐ EI-CDG	Boeing 737-548	25738/2261		
☐ EI-CDH	Boeing 737-548	25739/2271		
☐ EI-DZH	Boeing 767-3Q8ER	29390/870	ex N101LF	
☐ EI-EAR	Boeing 767-3Q8ER	27616/714	ex N364LF	
☐ EI-ECB	Boeing 767-3Q8ER	27617/722	ex N151LF	
☐ RA-86466	Ilyushin Il-62M	2749316	ex CCCP-86466	
☐ RA-86467	Ilyushin Il-62M	3749733	ex CCCP-86467	VIP
☐ RA-86468	Ilyushin Il-62M	4749857	ex CCCP-86468	VIP
☐ RA-86536	Ilyushin Il-62M	4445948	ex CCCP-86536	
☐ RA-86540	Ilyushin Il-62M	3546548	ex CCCP-86540	VIP
☐ RA-86559	Ilyushin Il-62M	2153258	ex CCCP-86559	VIP
☐ RA-86561	Ilyushin Il-62M	4154842	ex CCCP-86561	VIP
☐ RA-86710	Ilyushin Il-62M	2647646	ex CCCP-86710	
☐ RA-86712	Ilyushin Il-62M	4648339	ex CCCP-86712	VIP
☐ RA-96012	Ilyushin Il-96-300	74393201009		Presidential a/c
☐ RA-96016	Ilyushin Il-96-300PU	74393202010	ex (RA-96013)	Presidential a/c
☐ RA-96018	Ilyushin Il-96-300PU	74393202018		VIP
☐ RA-65093	Tupolev Tu-134A-3	60215	ex UR-65093	
☐ RA-65109	Tupolev Tu-134A-3	60339	ex UR-65109	[LED]
☐ RA-65553	Tupolev Tu-134A-3	66300	ex CCCP-65553	
☐ RA-65555	Tupolev Tu-134A-3	66350	ex CCCP-65555	VIP
☐ RA-65912	Tupolev Tu-134A-3	63985	ex CCCP-65912	
☐ RA-65921	Tupolev Tu-134A-3	63997	ex CCCP-65921	
☐ RA-85187	Tupolev Tu-154M	91A919	ex B-2629	
☐ RA-85629	Tupolev Tu-154M	87A758	ex CCCP-85629	
☐ RA-85645	Tupolev Tu-154M	88A782	ex CCCP-85645	
☐ RA-85658	Tupolev Tu-154M	89A808	ex CCCP-85658	

☐ RA-85659	Tupolev Tu-154M	89A809	ex CCCP-85659	VIP
☐ RA-85739	Tupolev Tu-154M	92A925	ex HA-LGD	
☐ RA-85769	Tupolev Tu-154M	93A951		
☐ RA-85770	Tupolev Tu-154M	93A952		
☐ RA-85771	Tupolev Tu-154M	93A953		
☐ RA-85779	Tupolev Tu-154M	93A963		
☐ RA-85785	Tupolev Tu-154M	93A969		
☐ RA-85800	Tupolev Tu-154M	94A984		
☐ RA-85832	Tupolev Tu-154M	92A908	ex RA-85726	
☐ RA-85834	Tupolev Tu-154M	98A1014	ex OM-AAA	
☐ RA-85835	Tupolev Tu-154M	98A1015	ex OM-AAB	
☐ RA-85836	Tupolev Tu-154M	98A1018	ex OM-AAC	
☐ RA-85843	Tupolev Tu-154M	95A991	ex RA-85811	
☐ RA-64504	Tupolev Tu-214	41203004		
☐ RA-64505	Tupolev Tu-214	42204005		
☐ RA-64506	Tupolev Tu-214	44204006		
☐ RA-64515	Tupolev Tu-214	42305015		
☐ RA-64516	Tupolev Tu-214	42709016		
☐ RA-87203	Yakovlev Yak-40	9741456	ex CCCP-87203	VIP
☐ RA-87969	Yakovlev Yak-40	9831358	ex CCCP-87969	VIP
☐ RA-87971	Yakovlev Yak-40D	9831558	ex CCCP-87971	VIP
☐ RA-88200	Yakovlev Yak-40	9630149	ex CCCP-88200	

RUSAIR   CGI-Rusair (CGI)   Moscow-Sheremetyevo (SVO)

☐ RA-65124	Tupolev Tu-134A	60560	ex ES-AAN	VIP
☐ RA-65566	Tupolev Tu-134A	63952	ex 11+11 GAF	
☐ RA-65771	Tupolev Tu-134A-3	62445	ex CCCP-65771	♦
☐ RA-65908	Tupolev Tu-134A	63870	ex CCCP-65908	VIP Op for VAP Avn Grp
☐ RA-87311	Yakovlev Yak-40	9320629	ex CCCP-87311	VIP, APP titles & logo
☐ RA-87494	Yakovlev Yak-40	9541745	ex CCCP-87494	VIP
☐ RA-87502	Yakovlev Yak-40	9510140	ex CCCP-87502	VIP
☐ RA-42368	Yakovlev Yak-42D	4520422914166	ex EP-LBT	

RUSJET   Moscow-Vnukovo (VKO)

☐ RA-42365	Yakovlev Yak-42D	4520424811447	ex CCCP-42365	
☐ RA-42411	Yakovlev Yak-42D	4520421219043	ex CCCP-42411	VIP
☐ RA-65737	Tupolev Tu-134B-3	64195	ex CCCP-65737	converted Tu-134UBL
☐ RA-87418	Yakovlev Yak-40	9421034	ex CCCP-87418	VIP
☐ RA-88240	Yakovlev Yak-40K	9641151	ex CCCP-88240	Executive

RUSLINE AIR   Rusline Air (RLU)   Moscow-Sheremetyevo (SVO)

☐ RA-65087	Tupolev Tu-134A-3	60155	ex CCCP-65087	VIP
☐ RA-65756	Tupolev Tu-134A	62179	ex CCCP-65756	
☐ RA-65903	Tupolev Tu-134A	63750	ex CCCP-65903	
☐ RA-65934	Tupolev Tu-134A	66143	ex CCCP-65934	
☐ RA-65941	Tupolev Tu-134A-3	60642	ex LZ-TUS	
☐ RA-87248	Yakovlev Yak-40K	9540144	ex CCCP-87248	
☐ RA-87380	Yakovlev Yak-40	9421225	ex 5N-MAR	
☐ RA-87828	Yakovlev Yak-40	9242024	ex CCCP-87828	
☐ RA-87981	Yakovlev Yak-40K	9540444	ex ER-YGA	stored
☐ RA-88308	Yakovlev Yak-40	9230224	ex SP-GEA	
☐ VP-BAO	Canadair CRJ-100	7177	ex F-GPTB	
☐ VQ-BBV	Canadair CRJ-200	7454	ex N654BR	
☐ VQ-BBW	Canadair CRJ-200	7426	ex N651BR	

RUSSIAN SKY AIRLINES   Ruduga (P7/ESL)   Moscow-Domodedovo (DME)

☐ RA-76799	Ilyushin Il-76TD	10034030375	ex CCCP-76799	<DMO
☐ RA-76817	Ilyushin Il-76TD	1023412387	ex CCCP-76817	>AYZ

RYAZANAVIA TRANS   Ryazan Air (RYZ)   Ryazan (RZN)

☐ RA-47359	Antonov An-24RV	67310608	ex UR-47359	
☐ RA-47362	Antonov An-24RV	67310706	ex UR-47362	

S-AIR   S-Air (RLS)   Ermolino

☐ RA-65550	Tupolev Tu-134A-3	66200	ex CCCP-65550	
☐ RA-65692	Tupolev Tu-134A-3	63215	ex YL-LBB	
☐ RA-65721	Tupolev Tu-134A-3M	66130	ex CCCP-65721	

☐ RA-65926	Tupolev Tu-134A-3	66101	ex CCCP-65926	
☐ RA-65932	Tupolev Tu-134A-3	66405	ex 65932	
☐ RA-42402	Yakovlev Yak-42D	4520422116583	ex CCCP-42402	
☐ RA-42427	Yakovlev Yak-42D	4520422305016	Marco Group	

S7 AIRLINES — Siberia Airlines (S7/SBI) — Novosibirsk-Tolmachevo (OVB)

☐ VP-BTJ	Airbus A310-304	520	ex D-AHLA	
☐ VP-BTL	Airbus A310-204	487	ex D-AHLX	
☐ VP-BTM	Airbus A310-204	486	ex F-GYYY	
☐ VP-BHF	Airbus A319-114	1819	ex N350NB	
☐ VP-BHG	Airbus A319-114	1870	ex N356NB	
☐ VP-BHI	Airbus A319-114	2028	ex N367NB	
☐ VP-BHJ	Airbus A319-114	2369	ex N372NB	
☐ VP-BHK	Airbus A319-114	2373	ex N373NB	
☐ VP-BHL	Airbus A319-114	2464	ex N374NB	
☐ VP-BHP	Airbus A319-114	2618	ex N376NB	
☐ VP-BHQ	Airbus A319-114	2641	ex N377NB	
☐ VP-BHV	Airbus A319-114	2474	ex N375NB	
☐ VP-BTN	Airbus A319-114	1126	ex N307NB	
☐ VP-BTO	Airbus A319-114	1129	ex N308NB	
☐ VP-BTP	Airbus A319-114	1131	ex N309NB	
☐ VP-BTQ	Airbus A319-114	1149	ex N310NB	
☐ VP-BTS	Airbus A319-114	1164	ex N311NB	
☐ VP-BTT	Airbus A319-114	1167	ex N312NB	
☐ VP-BTU	Airbus A319-114	1071	ex N303NB	
☐ VP-BTV	Airbus A319-114	1078	ex N304NB	
☐ VP-BTW	Airbus A319-114	1090	ex N305NB	
☐ VP-BTX	Airbus A319-114	1091	ex N306NB	
☐ VP-BCZ	Airbus A320-214	3446	ex F-WWIT	
☐ VP-BCP	Airbus A320-214	3473	ex F-WWBY	
☐ VP-BCS	Airbus A320-214	3490	ex F-WWIS	
☐ VP-BDT	Airbus A320-214	3494	ex F-WWIC	
☐ VQ-BCI	Airbus A320-214	2623	ex EC-JNT	
☐ VQ-BDE	Airbus A320-214	3866	ex F-WWDZ	
☐ VQ-BDF	Airbus A320-214	3880	ex F-WWIL	
☐ VQ-BES	Airbus A320-214	4032	ex F-WWIH	
☐ VQ-BET	Airbus A320-214	4150	ex F-WWBG	
☐ VQ-	Airbus A320-214		ex	o/o
☐ VQ-	Airbus A320-214		ex	o/o
☐ VQ-	Airbus A320-214		ex	o/o
☐ VQ-	Airbus A320-214		ex	o/o
☐ VQ-	Airbus A320-214		ex	o/o
☐ VQ-	Airbus A320-214		ex	o/o
☐ VQ-	Airbus A320-214		ex	o/o
☐ VQ-	Airbus A320-214		ex	o/o
☐ VP-BAN	Boeing 737-4Y0	26071/2361	ex N314PW	
☐ VP-BND	Boeing 737-83N/W	28245/1054	ex N315TZ	
☐ VP-BNG	Boeing 737-83N/W	30640/1035	ex N314TZ	
☐ VP-BQD	Boeing 737-83N/W	28239/847	ex N301TZ	
☐ VP-BQF	Boeing 737-83N/W	28243/984	ex N310TZ	
☐ VP-BQG	Boeing 737-46J	27171/2465	ex EI-DGL	
☐ VQ-	Boeing 737-800		ex	o/o
☐ VQ-	Boeing 737-800		ex	o/o
☐ VQ-	Boeing 737-800		ex	o/o
☐ VQ-	Boeing 737-800		ex	o/o
☐ VQ-	Boeing 737-800		ex	o/o
☐ VP-BVH	Boeing 767-33AER	28495/643	ex N495AN	
☐ VQ-BBI	Boeing 767-328ER	27428/586	ex EC-JJJ	
☐ RA-85610	Tupolev Tu-154M	84A705	ex CCCP-85610	[OVB]
☐ RA-85613	Tupolev Tu-154M	86A722	ex CCCP-85613	
☐ RA-85618	Tupolev Tu-154M	86A737	ex CCCP-85618	SPSR Ekspress titles
☐ RA-85619	Tupolev Tu-154M	86A738	ex CCCP-85619	Yulia Fomina
☐ RA-85620	Tupolev Tu-154M	86A739	ex TC-ACT	[OVB]
☐ RA-85622	Tupolev Tu-154M	87A746	ex CCCP-85622	
☐ RA-85624	Tupolev Tu-154M	87A750	ex CCCP-85624	
☐ RA-85628	Tupolev Tu-154M	87A757	ex CCCP-85628	[OVB]
☐ RA-85633	Tupolev Tu-154M	87A762	ex CCCP-85633	
☐ RA-85635	Tupolev Tu-154M	87A764	ex CCCP-85635	
☐ RA-85652	Tupolev Tu-154M	88A794	ex LZ-LTF	[OVB]
☐ RA-85674	Tupolev Tu-154M	90A834	ex TC-ACI	

488

☐ RA-85687	Tupolev Tu-154M	90A857	ex EP-MAZ	
☐ RA-85688	Tupolev Tu-154M	90A859	ex OM-VEA	
☐ RA-85690	Tupolev Tu-154M	90A861	ex CCCP-85690	
☐ RA-85697	Tupolev Tu-154M	91A870	ex EP-MAQ	[DME]
☐ RA-85699	Tupolev Tu-154M	91A874	ex EP-ITC	
☐ RA-85724	Tupolev Tu-154M	92A906	ex EP-MHD	
☐ RA-85827	Tupolev Tu-154M	87A745	ex SP-LCC	[OVB]
☐ RA-85848	Tupolev Tu-154M	89A804	ex OK-UCE	

SAKHA AVIATION SCHOOL   Moscow-Bykovo (BKA)

| ☐ RA-74003 | Antonov An-74 | 36547070690 | ex CCCP-74003 |
| | Current status uncertain | | |

SAMARA AIRLINES   Beryoza (E5/BRZ)   Samara-Kurumotch (KUF)

☐ RA-65105	Tupolev Tu-134A	60308	ex LY-ABH	
☐ RA-65122	Tupolev Tu-134A-3	60518	ex CCCP-65122	
☐ RA-65753	Tupolev Tu-134A-3	61099	ex CCCP-65753	
☐ RA-65758	Tupolev Tu-134A-3	62230	ex CCCP-65758	
☐ RA-65792	Tupolev Tu-134A-3	63121	ex CCCP-65792	
☐ RA-65797	Tupolev Tu-134A-3	63173	ex CCCP-65797	
☐ RA-85057	Tupolev Tu-154M	07A1001		o/o Op for Samara Oblast
☐ RA-85332	Tupolev Tu-154B-2	79A332	ex ER-85585	
☐ RA-85585	Tupolev Tu-154B-2	83A585	ex CCCP-85585	
☐ RA-85601	Tupolev Tu-154B-2	84A601	ex 85601	Op for Samara Oblast
☐ RA-85707	Tupolev Tu-154M	91A882	ex UR-85707	
☐ RA-85716	Tupolev Tu-154M	91A892	ex EP-MCI	
☐ RA-85723	Tupolev Tu-154M	92A905	ex HA-LGB	
☐ RA-85731	Tupolev Tu-154M	92A913	ex EP-LBH	
☐ RA-85817	Tupolev Tu-154M	95A1007	ex EP-LBM	>KJC
☐ RA-85818	Tupolev Tu-154M	85A719	ex EP-MAJ	AiRUnion colours
☐ RA-85821	Tupolev Tu-154M	89A805	ex SP-LCI	AiRUnion colours
☐ RA-85822	Tupolev Tu-154M	89A806	ex HA-LGC	
☐ RA-85823	Tupolev Tu-154M	88A775	ex HA-LGA	
☐ RA-76475	Ilyushin Il-76TD	0043451523	ex EP-TPV	[KUF] as EP-TPV
☐ RA-76791	Ilyushin Il-76TD	0093497936	ex EP-TPU	[KUF] as EP-TPU

SARATOV AIRLINES   Saratov Air (6W/SOV)   Saratov-Tsentralny (RTW)

☐ RA-42316	Yakovlev Yak-42	4520422202030	ex CCCP-42316	[RTW]
☐ RA-42326	Yakovlev Yak-42D	4520424402154	ex CCCP-42326	
☐ RA-42328	Yakovlev Yak-42	4520421505058	ex CCCP-42328	
☐ RA-42378	Yakovlev Yak-42D	4520421014494	ex TC-FAR	
☐ RA-42389	Yakovlev Yak-42D	4520424016542	ex CCCP-42389	
☐ RA-42432	Yakovlev Yak-42D	4520424410016	ex TC-ALY no titles	
☐ RA-42550	Yakovlev Yak-42D	11140205	ex CCCP-42550	stored
☐ RA-87844	Yakovlev Yak-40	9331330	ex CCCP-87844	

SAT AIRLINES   Satair (HZ/SHU)   Yuzhno-Sakhalinsk Khomutovo (UUZ)

☐ RA-46530	Antonov An-24B	57310009	ex CCCP-46530	
☐ RA-46618	Antonov An-24RV	37308705	ex CCCP-46618	
☐ RA-46639	Antonov An-24RV	37308905	ex CCCP-46639	
☐ RA-47198	Antonov An-24RV	27307702	ex CCCP-47198	
☐ RA-47317	Antonov An-24RV	67310504	ex CCCP-47317	
☐ RA-47366	Antonov An-24RV	77310804	ex CCCP-47366	
☐ RA-67251	de Havilland DHC-8-311	533	ex C-FWFH	
☐ RA-67257	de Havilland DHC-8-201	457	ex C-FJFW	Op for Exxon Neftegas
☐ RA-67259	de Havilland DHC-8-201	459	ex C-FNOP	Op for Exxon Neftegas
☐ RA-67261	de Havilland DHC-8-102	460	ex C-FNOQ	
☐ RA-11364	Antonov An-12V	347601	ex CCCP-11364	
☐ RA-12988	Antonov An-12B	00347206	ex CCCP-12988	
☐ RA-26132	Antonov An-26B	37312708	ex CCCP-26132	
☐ RA-26138	Antonov An-26B	12810	ex CCCP-26138	
☐ RA-48984	Antonov An-12BP	402913	ex UR-48984	
☐ RA-73003	Boeing 737-2J8 (Nordam 3)	22859/890	ex N235WA	
☐ RA-73005	Boeing 737-232 (Nordam 3)	23100/1038	ex N328DL	
☐ RA-73013	Boeing 737-5L9	28721/2856	ex OY-APH	

SATURN AVIAKOMPANIA   Rybmotors (RMO)   Rybinsk-Starosel'ye (RYB)

☐ RA-87225	Yakovlev Yak-40K	9841359	ex CCCP-87225
☐ RA-87936	Yakovlev Yak-40K	9740756	ex CCCP-87936
☐ RA-88289	Antonov An-26B	11804	ex CCCP-88289

489

SEVERSTAL AIRCOMPANY — Severstal (D2/SSF) — Cherepovets (CEE)

☐ RA-87224	Yakovlev Yak-40K	9841259	ex CCCP-87224	VIP Op for Yava Group
☐ RA-87954	Yakovlev Yak-40	9811357	ex CCCP-87954	
☐ RA-88180	Yakovlev Yak-40	9622047	ex CCCP-88180	
☐ RA-88188	Yakovlev Yak-40	9620848	ex CCCP-88188	
☐ RA-88296	Yakovlev Yak-40	9421634	ex VN-A445	VIP

SHAR INK — Sharink (UGP) — Moscow-Ostafyevo

☐ RA-74001	Antonov An-74TK-100	36547070655	ex CCCP-74001	
☐ RA-74014	Antonov An-74-200	36547098968	ex ST-BDA	
☐ RA-74015	Antonov An-74-200	36547098969		
☐ RA-74020	Antonov An-74TK-100	36547195014		
☐ RA-74047	Antonov An-74-200	36547097941		on rebuild
☐ RA-25770	Mil Mi-8PS-11	8709	ex CCCP-25770	VIP

SIBAVIATRANS — Sibavia (5M/SIB) — Krasnoyarsk-Yemelyanovo (KJA)

☐ RA-46674	Antonov An-24RV	47309606	ex CCCP-46674	<OMS
☐ RA-49278	Antonov An-24RV	47309808	ex YR-AMJ	
☐ RA-49279	Antonov An-24RV	17306905	ex YR-AMB	AiRUnion colours
☐ RA-49287	Antonov An-24RV	27307607	ex YR-AME	
☐ RA-65571	Tupolev Tu-134AK	63955	ex EW-63955	
☐ RA-65605	Tupolev Tu-134A	09070	ex EW-65605	
☐ RA-65615	Tupolev Tu-134A-3	4352205	ex D-AOBE	
☐ RA-65881	Tupolev Tu-134A-3	35220	ex CCCP-65881	
☐ RA-65694	Tupolev Tu-134B-3	63235	ex UN-65694	AiRUnion colours
☐ RA-21503	Yakovlev Yak-40K	9820358	ex CCCP-21503	
☐ RA-48113	Antonov An-32	1709	ex CCCP-48113	

SIRIUS AERO — Sirius Aero (CIG) — Moscow-Vnukovo (VKO)

☐ RA-65079	Tupolev Tu-134A-3	60054	ex LY-ASK	VIP
☐ RA-65099	Tupolev Tu-134A-3	63700	ex CCCP-65099	VIP
☐ RA-65604	Tupolev Tu-134AK	62561	ex CCCP-65604	VIP
☐ RA-65722	Tupolev Tu-134A-3M	66420	ex CCCP-65722	VIP
☐ RA-65928	Tupolev Tu-134A-3M	66491	ex CCCP-65928	VIP
☐ RA-65978	Tupolev Tu-134A-3	63357	ex CCCP-65978	Svetlana VIP

SKOL AVIAKOMPANIA — (CDV) — Surgut (SGC)

☐ RA-06033	Mil Mi-26T	34001212423	ex CCCP-06033	
☐ RA-06394	Mil Mi-26T	34001212123		
☐ RA-46848	Antonov An-24RV	27307506	ex CCCP-46848	
☐ RA-87240	Yakovlev Yak-40	9530743	ex CCCP-87240	
☐ RA-87940	Yakovlev Yak-40	9540444	ex CCCP-87940	

SKYEXPRESS — (XW/SXR) — Moscow-Vnukovo (VNO)

☐ VP-BET	Boeing 737-53C	24825/1894	ex D-ACIN	
☐ VP-BFB	Boeing 737-5Y0	26067/2304	ex N606TA	
☐ VP-BFJ	Boeing 737-53A	24859/1919	ex G-THOA	
☐ VP-BFK	Boeing 737-5L9	24928/1961	ex G-THOB	
☐ VP-BFM	Boeing 737-53A	24921/1962	ex N921AW	
☐ VP-BFN	Boeing 737-53A	24922/1964	ex N922AV	
☐ VP-BHA	Boeing 737-529	26538/2298	ex C-GAHB	
☐ VP-BOT	Boeing 737-341	25048/2085	ex N728BC	
☐ VP-BOU	Boeing 737-341	25049/2091	ex N729BC	

SOKOL — Aerosokol (PIV) — Novotitarovskaya Heliport

☐ RA-06025	Mil Mi-26T	34001212401	ex CCCP-06025	
☐ RA-06072	Mil Mi-26T	34001212491	ex CCCP-06072	
☐ RA-06087	Mil Mi-26T	340012112480		
☐ RA-22788	Mil Mi-8T	6201	ex CCCP-22788	

SVERDLOVSK 2ND AIR ENTERPRISE — Pyshma (UKU) — Yekaterinburg-Koltsovo (SVX)

☐ RA-74004	Antonov An-74	36547094890	ex CCCP-74004	VIP
☐ RA-74006	Antonov An-74	36547095896	ex CCCP-74006	
☐ RA-74048	Antonov An-74D	36547098943	all-white, no titles	VIP
☐ RA-87253	Yakovlev Yak-40	9321026	ex CCCP-87253	all-whiteVIP
☐ RA-87503	Yakovlev Yak-40AT	9520240	ex CCCP-87503	VIP. op for Kolsto Ural

490

☐ RA-87524	Yakovlev Yak-40	9520641	ex CCCP-87524	VIP
☐ RA-87974	Yakovlev Yak-40K	9621346	ex CCCP-87974	no titles VIP
☐ RA-88159	Yakovlev Yak-40	9621346	ex CCCP-88159	all-white VIP
☐ RA-88234	Yakovlev Yak-40	9640351	ex CCCP-82834	

TATARSTAN AIR *Air Tatarstan (U9/TAK)* **Kazan-Osnovnoi (KZN)**

☐ VQ-BAP	Boeing 737-322	24665/1889	ex LZ-BOT	
☐ VQ-BBN	Boeing 737-53A	24785/1882	ex LZ-BOY	
☐ VQ-BBO	Boeing 737-548	25165/2463	ex LZ-BOR	
☐ VQ-BDB	Boeing 737-4D7	28702/2978	ex HS-TDL	
☐ VQ-BDC	Boeing 737-341	26852/2273	ex LZ-BOO	
☐ RA-86142	Ilyushin Il-86	51483210097	ex B-2016	[DME]
☐ RA-86143	Ilyushin Il-86	51483210099	ex B-2018	
☐ RA-86926	Ilyushin Il-86	51463210100	ex B-2019	
☐ RA-65065	Tupolev Tu-134A-3	49890	ex CCCP-65065	
☐ RA-65102	Tupolev Tu-134A-3	60267	ex CCCP-65102	
☐ RA-65691	Tupolev Tu-134A	63195	ex CCCP-65691	
☐ RA-65970	Tupolev Tu-134A	3351910	ex CCCP-65970	
☐ RA-65973	Tupolev Tu-134A	3352003	ex LY-ABA	
☐ RA-85101	Tupolev Tu-154M	88A783	ex B-608L	
☐ RA-85109	Tupolev Tu-154M	88A790	ex B-609L	
☐ RA-85136	Tupolev Tu-154M	88A791	ex B-607L	
☐ RA-85798	Tupolev Tu-154M	93A982	ex EP-MBO	
☐ RA-85799	Tupolev Tu-154M	94A983		
☐ RA-42333	Yakovlev Yak-42	4520422606156	ex CCCP-42333	
☐ RA-42335	Yakovlev Yak-42	4520422606204	ex CU-T1274	
☐ RA-42347	Yakovlev Yak-42	4520423711322	ex CCCP-42347	
☐ RA-42357	Yakovlev Yak-42	4520422811408	ex CCCP-42357	[KZN]
☐ RA-42374	Yakovlev Yak-42D	4520423914340	ex CU-T1273	
☐ RA-42380	Yakovlev Yak-42D	4520422014549	ex CU-T1242	
☐ RA-42413	Yakovlev Yak-42D	4520422219066	ex EP-YAB	
☐ RA-42433	Yakovlev Yak-42D	4520421301017		
☐ RA-88287	Yakovlev Yak-40K	9940360	ex CCCP-88287	VIP op for Tatarstan Govt

TOMSKAVIA *Tomsk Avia (TSK)* **Tomsk (TOF)**

☐ RA-26039	Antonov An-26B	10702	ex CCCP-26039	
☐ RA-46679	Antonov An-24RV	47309701	ex CCCP-46679	
☐ RA-47254	Antonov An-24RV	27307706	ex CCCP-47254	
☐ RA-47355	Antonov An-24RV	67310604	ex CCCP-47355	

TRANSAERO AIRLINES *Transoviet (UN/TSO)* **Moscow-Domodedovo (DME)**

☐ EI-CXK	Boeing 737-4S3	25596/2255	ex G-OGBA	
☐ EI-CXN	Boeing 737-329	23772/1432	ex OO-SDW	
☐ EI-CXR	Boeing 737-329	24355/1709	ex OO-SYA	
☐ EI-CZK	Boeing 737-4Y0	24519/1781	ex N519AP	
☐ EI-DDK	Boeing 737-4S3	24165/1720	ex N758BC	
☐ EI-DDY	Boeing 737-4Y0	24904/1988	ex HA-LEV	
☐ EI-DNM	Boeing 737-4S3	24166/1722	ex EC-JHX	
☐ EI-DTU	Boeing 737-5Y0	25175/2150	ex B-2546	
☐ EI-DTV	Boeing 737-5Y0	25183/2218	ex B-2549	
☐ EI-DTW	Boeing 737-5Y0	25188/2238	ex B-2550	
☐ EI-DTX	Boeing 737-5Q8	28052/2965	ex LY-AZX	
☐ EI-EDZ	Boeing 737-8K5/W	27980/45	ex D-AHFF	
☐ EI-EEA	Boeing 737-8K5/W	27989/59	ex D-AHFG	
☐ VP-BPA	Boeing 737-5K5	25037/2022	ex D-AHLI	
☐ VP-BPD	Boeing 737-5K5	25062/2044	ex D-AHLN	
☐ VP-BVQ	Boeing 737-524/W	28915/2993	ex N14654	♦
☐ VP-BYI	Boeing 737-524	28921/3052	ex N14660	
☐ VP-BYJ	Boeing 737-524	28923/3060	ex N14662	
☐ VP-BYN	Boeing 737-524	28924/3063	ex N17663	♦
☐ VP-BYO	Boeing 737-524	28922/3055	ex N23661	♦
☐ VP-BYP	Boeing 737-524	28927/3074	ex N14667	
☐ VP-BYQ	Boeing 737-524	28919/3045	ex N18658	♦
☐ VP-BYT	Boeing 737-524	28928/3077	ex N14668	
☐ EI-XLB	Boeing 747-446	26359/1153	ex N913UN	♦
☐ EI-XLC	Boeing 747-446	27100/1236	ex N919UN	♦
☐ N914UN	Boeing 747-446	26360/1166	ex JA8914	♦
☐ VP-BGU	Boeing 747-346	23482/640	ex N740UN	
☐ VP-BGW	Boeing 747-346	24019/695	ex N742UN	
☐ VP-BGX	Boeing 747-346	24156/716	ex N741UN	

☐ VP-BGY	Boeing 747-346	23640/668	ex N743UN	
☐ VP-BKJ	Boeing 747-444	26638/995	ex N7716Q	
☐ VP-BKL	Boeing 747-444	28468/1162	ex N3508M	
☐ VP-BPX	Boeing 747-267B	22872/566	ex N747VC	
☐ VP-BQC	Boeing 747-219B	22725/563	ex N705TA	
☐ VP-BQE	Boeing 747-219B	22722/523	ex N702TA	
☐ VP-BQH	Boeing 747-219B	22791/568	ex N701TA	
☐ VP-BVR	Boeing 747-444	26637/943	ex (VP-BKG)	
☐ VQ-BHW	Boeing 747-4F6	28959/1158	ex ZS-SBK	◆
☐ VQ-BHX	Boeing 747-4F6	28960/1167	ex ZS-SBS	◆
☐ EI-CXZ	Boeing 767-216ER	24973/347	ex N502GX	
☐ EI-CZD	Boeing 767-216ER	23623/142	ex N762TA	
☐ EI-DBF	Boeing 767-3Q8ER	24745/355	ex F-GHGF	
☐ EI-DBG	Boeing 767-3Q8ER	24746/378	ex F-GHGG	
☐ EI-DBU	Boeing 767-37EER	25077/385	ex F-GHGH	
☐ EI-DBW	Boeing 767-201ER	23899/182	ex N647US	
☐ EI-DFS	Boeing 767-33AER	25346/403	ex ET-AKW	
☐ EI-UNA	Boeing 767-3P6ER	26233/501	ex A4O-GU	
☐ EI-UNB	Boeing 767-3P6ER	26234/538	ex A4O-GY	
☐ EI-UNC	Boeing 767-319ER	29388/785	ex N381LF	◆
☐ EI-UND	Boeing 767-3P6ER	26236/436	ex A4O-GX	
☐ EI-UNF	Boeing 767-3P6ER	26238/440	ex A4O-GT	
☐ EI-UNR	Boeing 777-212ER	28523/239	ex 9V-SRE	◆
☐ EI-UNT	Boeing 777-212ER	28999/150	ex 9V-SRC	◆
☐ EI-UNU	Boeing 777-212ER	28998/149	ex 9V-SRB	◆
☐ EI-UNV	Boeing 777-222ER	28714/205	ex N205UA	◆
☐ EI-UNW	Boeing 777-222ER	30214/254	ex N208UA	
☐ EI-UNX	Boeing 777-222ER	30213/232	ex N207UA	
☐ EI-UNZ	Boeing 777-222	26925/13	ex N770UA	o/o <VTB
☐ RA-64509	Tupolev Tu-214	42305009		
☐ RA-64516	Tupolev Tu-214	42709016		
☐ RA-64517	Tupolev Tu-214	42305017		
☐ RA-64518	Tupolev Tu-214	42305018		
☐ RA-64549	Tupolev Tu-214	42305013	ex RA-64513	

TRANSAVIA GARANTIA
Arkhangelsk-Talagi (ARH)

☐ RA-26024	Antonov An-26B-100	10306	ex CCCP-26024	
☐ RA-26081	Antonov An-26B-100	11703	ex UR-BXU	
☐ RA-26682	Antonov An-26B-100	97308706	ex CCCP-26682	Frtr
☐ RA-26687	Antonov An-26B-100	8902	ex CCCP-26687	
☐ RA-87235	Yakovlev Yak-40	9530143	ex CCCP-87235	
☐ RA-87336	Yakovlev Yak-40	9610539	ex CCCP-87336	

TULPAR AIR (TUL)
Kazan-Osnovnoi / Orenburg-Tsentralny (KZN/REN)

☐ RA-21504	Yakovlev Yak-40K	9831758	ex CCCP-21504		Executive
☐ RA-87496	Yakovlev Yak-40	9541945	ex CCCP-87496		op for Nizhykamsk Petrol
☐ RA-87535	Yakovlev Yak-40	9521941	ex CCCP-87535		Vasili Nesterov
☐ RA-87977	Yakovlev Yak-40	9321128	ex OK-BYH		
☐ RA-88269	Yakovlev Yak-40	9720753	ex LY-AAY		Kamaz titles
☐ RA-42330	Yakovlev Yak-42D	4520422505122	ex UR-42330		
☐ RA-42415	Yakovlev Yak-42D	4520422219089	ex CCCP-42415		
☐ RA-42440	Yakovlev Yak-42D	4520424210018	ex 9L-LDT	all-white	

TUVA AIRLINES
Kyzyl (KYZ)

☐ RA-87425	Yakovlev Yak-40	9420135	ex CCCP-87425	
☐ RA-87925	Yakovlev Yak-40	9731655	ex CCCP-87925	
☐ RA-88212	Yakovlev Yak-40	9631849	ex CCCP-88212	

TYUMENSPECAVIA (TUM)
Tyumen-Roshchino (TJM)

☐ RA-26088	Antonov An-26	17311209	ex CCCP-26088	
☐ RA-26102	Antonov An-26	17311909	ex CCCP-26102	
☐ RA-26662	Antonov An-26	97308101	ex CCCP-26102	all-white

URAL AIRLINES Sverdlovsk Air (U6/SVR) Yekaterinburg-Koltsovo (SVX)

☐ VP-BFZ	Airbus A320-214	0735	ex G-BXKD	
☐ VP-BPU	Airbus A320-211	0220	ex F-GLGH	
☐ VP-BPV	Airbus A320-211	0203	ex F-GLGG	
☐ VP-BQY	Airbus A320-211	0140	ex TS-ING	
☐ VP-BQZ	Airbus A320-211	0157	ex TS-INH	

☐ VQ-BAG	Airbus A320-214	1063	ex EC-KLU		
☐ VQ-BCY	Airbus A320-214	1484	ex EC-HQM		
☐ VQ-BCZ	Airbus A320-214	1777	ex G-OOPW		
☐ VQ-BDJ	Airbus A320-214	2175	ex N268AV		
☐ VQ-BDM	Airbus A320-214	2187	ex N269AV		
☐ VQ-BFV	Airbus A320-214	1152	ex N266AV		♦
☐ VQ-BFW	Airbus A320-214	2327	ex N271AV		♦
☐ VQ-BCX	Airbus A321-211	1720	ex G-OOAV		
☐ VQ-BDA	Airbus A321-211	1012	ex TC-KTY		
☐ RA-46532	Antonov An-24RV	57310101	ex CCCP-46532		
☐ RA-47182	Antonov An-24B	99901907	ex CCCP-47182		
☐ RA-47187	Antonov An-24B	99902002	ex CCCP-47187		
☐ RA-86078	Ilyushin Il-86	51483205049	ex CCCP-86078		
☐ RA-86093	Ilyushin Il-86	51483207064	ex CCCP-86093		
☐ RA-86120	Ilyushin Il-86	51483209088	ex CCCP-86120		
☐ RA-65090	Tupolev Tu-134A	60185	ex CCCP-65090	<ORB	
☐ RA-85337	Tupolev Tu-154B-2	79A337	ex UN-85337		
☐ RA-85374	Tupolev Tu-154B-2	79A374	ex CCCP-85374		
☐ RA-85375	Tupolev Tu-154B-2	79A375	ex CCCP-85375		
☐ RA-85508	Tupolev Tu-154B-2	81A508	ex CCCP-85508		
☐ RA-85807	Tupolev Tu-154M	94A988			
☐ RA-85814	Tupolev Tu-154M	95A994			
☐ RA-85833	Tupolev Tu-154M	01A1020			
☐ RA-85844	Tupolev Tu-154M	03A992			

UTAIR AIRLINES — UTair (UT/UTA) — Tyumen-Roshchino (TJM)

☐ RA-46362	Antonov An-24B	07305903	ex CCCP-46362	
☐ RA-46388	Antonov An-24B	07306201	ex CCCP-46388	
☐ RA-46481	Antonov An-24RV	27308009	ex CCCP-46481	
☐ RA-46509	Antonov An-24RV	37308405	ex CCCP-46509	
☐ RA-46609	Antonov An-24RV	37308606	ex CCCP-46609	
☐ RA-46619	Antonov An-24RV	37308706	ex CCCP-46619	
☐ RA-46828	Antonov An-24B	17306705	ex CCCP-46828	
☐ RA-47271	Antonov An-24RV	07306401	ex BNMAU-47271	
☐ RA-47273	Antonov An-24B	07306403	ex CCCP-47273	
☐ RA-47289	Antonov An-24B	07306509	ex CCCP-47289	
☐ RA-47357	Antonov An-24RV	67310606	ex CCCP-47357	
☐ RA-47827	Antonov An-24B	17307208	ex CCCP-47827	stored
☐ RA-47829	Antonov An-24B	17307210	ex CCCP-47829	
☐ VP-BCA	ATR 42-300	051	ex I-NOWA	
☐ VP-BCB	ATR 42-300	054	ex I-NOWT	
☐ VP-BCD	ATR 42-300	042	ex I-ATRG	
☐ VP-BCF	ATR 42-300	068	ex I-ATRL	
☐ VP-BCG	ATR 42-300	057	ex I-ATRJ	
☐ VP-BLI	ATR 42-300	233	ex D-BCRQ	
☐ VP-BLJ	ATR 42-300	255	ex D-BCRR	
☐ VP-BLN	ATR 42-300	278	ex D-BJJJ	
☐ VP-BLO	ATR 42-300	289	ex D-BCRT	
☐ VP-BLU	ATR 42-300	287	ex D-BCRS	
☐ VP-BPJ	ATR 42-300	165	ex N15823	
☐ VP-BPK	ATR 42-300	166	ex N16824	
☐ VP-BYW	ATR 72-201	174	ex ES-KRE	
☐ VP-BYX	ATR 72-201	251	ex ES-KRK	
☐ VP-BYZ	ATR 72-201	332	ex ES-KRL	
☐ VP-BVL	Boeing 737-524	28926/3069	ex N13665	
☐ VP-BVN	Boeing 737-524	27540/2776	ex N33637	
☐ VP-BVZ	Boeing 737-524	28925/3066	ex N14664	
☐ VP-BXO	Boeing 737-524/W	27314/2566	ex N14601	
☐ VP-BXQ	Boeing 737-524/W	27315/2571	ex N69602	
☐ VP-BXR	Boeing 737-524/W	27316/2573	ex N69603	
☐ VP-BXU	Boeing 737-524/W	27318/2582	ex N14605	
☐ VP-BXV	Boeing 737-524/W	27322/2607	ex N14609	
☐ VP-BXY	Boeing 737-524/W	27328/2640	ex N37615	
☐ VP-BXZ	Boeing 737-524/W	27329/2641	exN52616	
☐ VP-BYK	Boeing 737-524	28918/3026	ex N23657	
☐ VP-BYL	Boeing 737-524	28920/3048	ex N15659	
☐ VP-BYM	Boeing 737-524	28917/3019	ex N11656	
☐ VQ-BAC	Boeing 737-524/W	27321/2597	ex N33608	
☐ VQ-BAD	Boeing 737-524/W	27331/2652	ex N16618	
☐ VQ-BAE	Boeing 737-524/W	27320/2596	ex N16607	

☐ VQ-BIC	Boeing 737-45S	28478/3132	ex OK-FGS			♦
☐ VQ-BID	Boeing 737-45S	28477/3131	ex OK-FGR			♦
☐ VQ-BIE	Boeing 737-45S	28476/3103	ex OK-EGP			♦
☐ VQ-BIF	Boeing 737-45S	28474/3028	ex OK-DGN			♦
☐ VQ-BEY	Boeing 757-2Q8/W	29382/1010	ex OH-LBX			♦
☐ VQ-BEZ	Boeing 757-2Q8/W	29377/857	ex OH-LBU			♦
☐ VQ-BGJ	Canadair CRJ-200LR	7121	ex C-GFNF			♦
☐ VQ-BGK	Canadair CRJ-200LR	7122	ex C-GFNB			♦
☐ VQ-BGL	Canadair CRJ-200LR	7128	ex C-GFNJ			♦
☐ VQ-BGO	Canadair CRJ-200LR	7135	ex D-ACJD			♦
☐ VQ-BGQ	Canadair CRJ-200LR	7200	ex D-ACJF			♦
☐ VQ-BGR	Canadair CRJ-200LR	7220	ex D-ACJG			♦
☐ VQ-BGT	Canadair CRJ-200LR	7266	ex C-GGDQ			♦
☐ VQ-BGU	Canadair CRJ-200LR	7298	ex C-GEDO			♦
☐ VQ-BGV	Canadair CRJ-200LR	7378	ex C-GFMQ			♦
☐ VQ-BGW	Canadair CRJ-200LR	7391	ex C-GFLZ			♦
☐ VQ-BGX	Canadair CRJ-200LR	7394	ex C-GGDR			♦
☐ VQ-	Canadair CRJ-200LR	7165	ex C-GGDO			♦
☐ VQ-	Canadair CRJ-200LR	7114	ex D-ACLW			♦
☐ RA-65005	Tupolev Tu-134A-3	44065	ex CCCP-65005			
☐ RA-65024	Tupolev Tu-134A	48420	ex CCCP-65024			
☐ RA-65033	Tupolev Tu-134A-3	48540	ex CCCP-65033			
☐ RA-65055	Tupolev Tu-134A	49856	ex CCCP-65055			
☐ RA-65127	Tupolev Tu-134A-3	60627	ex EY-65127			
☐ RA-65136	Tupolev Tu-134A-3	60885	ex CCCP-65136			
☐ RA-65148	Tupolev Tu-134A-3	61025	ex CCCP-65148			
☐ RA-65560	Tupolev Tu-134A	60321	ex YU-AJW			
☐ RA-65565	Tupolev Tu-134A-1	63998	ex CCCP-65565			
☐ RA-65572	Tupolev Tu-134AK-3	63960	ex UR-CCG			
☐ RA-65607	Tupolev Tu-134A	48560	ex CCCP-65607		VIP	
☐ RA-65608	Tupolev Tu-134A	38040	ex CCCP-65608		VIP	
☐ RA-65609	Tupolev Tu-134A-3	46155	ex CCCP-65609			
☐ RA-65611	Tupolev Tu-134A-3	3351903	ex CCCP-65611			
☐ RA-65614	Tupolev Tu-134A	4352207	ex CCCP-65614			
☐ RA-65620	Tupolev Tu-134A-3	35180	ex CCCP-65620			
☐ RA-65621	Tupolev Tu-134A-3	48320	ex CCCP-65621			
☐ RA-65622	Tupolev Tu-134A-3	60495	ex CCCP-65622			
☐ RA-65716	Tupolev Tu-134A-3	63595	ex CCCP-65716			
☐ RA-65728	Tupolev Tu-134B-3	49858	ex LZ-TUG			
☐ RA-65755	Tupolev Tu-134A-3	62165	ex CCCP-65755			
☐ RA-65777	Tupolev Tu-134A-3	62552	ex CCCP-65777			
☐ RA-65780	Tupolev Tu-134A-3	62622	ex CCCP-65780			
☐ RA-65793	Tupolev Tu-134A-3	63128	ex CCCP-65793			
☐ RA-65901	Tupolev Tu-134A-3	63731	ex CCCP-65901			
☐ RA-65902	Tupolev Tu-134A-3	63742	ex CCCP-65902			
☐ RA-65916	Tupolev Tu-134A-3	66152	ex CCCP-65916			
☐ RA-65977	Tupolev Tu-134A	63245	ex CCCP-65977			
☐ RA-85013	Tupolev Tu-154M	90A840	ex LZ-MIG			
☐ RA-85016	Tupolev Tu-154M	90A844	ex LZ-MIH			
☐ RA-85018	Tupolev Tu-154M	90A852	ex LZ-MIR			
☐ RA-85056	Tupolev Tu-154M	90A845	ex LZ-MIL			
☐ RA-85069	Tupolev Tu-154M	90A863	ex LZ-MIS			
☐ RA-85595	Tupolev Tu-154B-2	84A595	ex CCCP-85595			
☐ RA-85681	Tupolev Tu-154M	90A848	ex LZ-LTE	Abakan	stored	
☐ RA-85727	Tupolev Tu-154M	92A909	ex ES-LTP			
☐ RA-85733	Tupolev Tu-154M	92A915	ex EP-MAL	Antonina Grigoreva		
☐ RA-85755	Tupolev Tu-154M	92A937		Vasilij Bachilov		
☐ RA-85777	Tupolev Tu-154M	93A959	ex EP-TUA			
☐ RA-85788	Tupolev Tu-154M	93A972	ex EP-ITS			
☐ RA-85789	Tupolev Tu-154M	93A973				
☐ RA-85796	Tupolev Tu-154M	94A980		Victor Muravlenko		
☐ RA-85805	Tupolev Tu-154M	94A986		Farman Salmanov		
☐ RA-85806	Tupolev Tu-154M	94A987				
☐ RA-85808	Tupolev Tu-154M	94A989		Shetr Panov		
☐ RA-85813	Tupolev Tu-154M	95A990				
☐ RA-85820	Tupolev Tu-154M	98A995		Roman Marchenko		
☐ RA-87907	Yakovlev Yak-40	9731254	ex CCCP-87907			
☐ RA-87941	Yakovlev Yak-40	9540545	ex CCCP-87941			
☐ RA-87997	Yakovlev Yak-40	9540145	ex CCCP-87997			
☐ RA-88209	Yakovlev Yak-40K	9730353	ex CCCP-88209			
☐ RA-88227	Yakovlev Yak-40	9641550	ex CCCP-88227		VIP	

494

UTAIR EXPRESS		*Komiinter (UR/KMV)*		*Syktyvkar (SCW)*
☐ RA-13344	Antonov An-24RV	37308310	ex CCCP-13344	
☐ RA-46468	Antonov An-24RV	27307906	ex CCCP-46468	
☐ RA-46494	Antonov An-24RV	27308207	ex CCCP-46494	
☐ RA-46603	Antonov An-24RV	37308510	ex CCCP-46603	
☐ RA-46610	Antonov An-24RV	37308607	ex CCCP-46610	
☐ RA-46640	Antonov An-24RV	37308908	ex CCCP-46640	
☐ RA-46692	Antonov An-24RV	47309903	ex CCCP-46692	
☐ RA-47820	Antonov An-24RV	17307201	ex CCCP-47820	

UVAUGA		*Pilot Air (UHS)*		*Ulyanovsk-Tsentralny (ULY)*
☐ RA-26025	Antonov An-26B	10308	ex CCCP-26025	
☐ RA-26513	Antonov An-26	6810	ex CCCP-26513	
☐ RA-26544	Antonov An-26	2710	ex CCCP-26544	
☐ RA-76401	Ilyushin Il-76TD	1023412399	ex CCCP-76401	>AYZ
☐ RA-76783	Ilyushin Il-76TD	0093498974	ex CCCP-76783	>AYZ
☐ RA-85470	Tupolev Tu-154B-2	81A470	ex CCCP-85470	
☐ RA-85609	Tupolev Tu-154M	84A704	ex CCCP-85609	no titles
☐ RA-87315	Yakovlev Yak-40	9331429	ex CCCP-87315	
☐ RA-87580	Yakovlev Yak-40	9221222	ex CCCP-87580	
☐ RA-42528	Yakovlev Yak-42D	11041003	ex CCCP-42528	[ULY]

VIM AIRLINES		*MovAir (NN/MOV)*		*Moscow-Domodedovo (DME)*
☐ RA-73007	Boeing 757-230	24749/295	ex D-ABNE	
☐ RA-73008	Boeing 757-230	25436/419	ex D-ABNH	
☐ RA-73009	Boeing 757-230	25437/422	ex D-ABNI	
☐ RA-73010	Boeing 757-230	25438/428	ex D-ABNK	
☐ RA-73011	Boeing 757-230	25439/437	ex D-ABNL	
☐ RA-73012	Boeing 757-230	25440/443	ex D-ABNM	
☐ RA-73014	Boeing 757-230	25441/446	ex D-ABNN	
☐ RA-73015	Boeing 757-230	25901/464	ex D-ABNO	>BBT
☐ RA-73016	Boeing 757-230	26433/521	ex D-ABNP returned?	
☐ RA-73017	Boeing 757-230	26434/532	ex D-ABNR	
☐ RA-73018	Boeing 757-230	26435/537	ex D-ABNS	
☐ RA-73019	Boeing 757-230	26436/588	ex D-ABNT	[DME]
☐ RA-42340	Yakovlev Yak-42D	4520424606270	ex CCCP-42340	
☐ RA-42343	Yakovlev Yak-42	4520421708285	ex UR-42343	
☐ RA-42370	Yakovlev Yak-42D	4520422914203	ex CCCP-42370	
☐ RA-42408	Yakovlev Yak-42D	4520422216698	ex EP-YAC	

VLADIVOSTOK AIR		*Vladair (XF/VLK)*		*Vladivostok-Knevichi (VVO)*
☐ VP-BEQ	Airbus A320-212	0422	ex 6Y-JMB	
☐ VP-BRB	Airbus A320-212	0528	ex 6Y-JMA	
☐ VP-BFX	Airbus A320-214	0714	ex G-BXKA	
☐ VP-BFY	Airbus A320-214	0730	ex G-BXKC	
☐ VQ-BCG	Airbus A320-214	1200	ex EC-HGY	
☐ VQ-BCW	Airbus A330-301	070	ex EI-CRK	
☐ VQ-BEQ	Airbus A330-301	086	ex EI-JFK	
☐ VQ-BEU	Airbus A330-301	055	ex EI-DUB	o/o♦
☐ RA-85562	Tupolev Tu-154B-2	82A562	ex CCCP-85562	Dalnerechensk stored
☐ RA-85676	Tupolev Tu-154M	90A836	ex EP-MAM Sayanogorsk	
☐ RA-85685	Tupolev Tu-154M	90A853	ex CCCP-85685	Nakhodka stored
☐ RA-85766	Tupolev Tu-154M	92A923	ex EP-MAP	
☐ RA-85803	Tupolev Tu-154M	89A822	ex EK-85803 Spassk-Dalny	
☐ RA-85837	Tupolev Tu-154M	91A876	ex UR-85701 Khakasia	
☐ RA-64026	Tupolev Tu-204-300	1450743164026		
☐ RA-64038	Tupolev Tu-204-300	1450744464038	Sberbank Rossii titles	
☐ RA-64039	Tupolev Tu-204-300	1450741564039	Sberbank Rossii titles	
☐ RA-64040	Tupolev Tu-204-300	1450744565040		
☐ RA-64044	Tupolev Tu-204-300	1450744564044		
☐ RA-64045	Tupolev Tu-204-300	1450744564045		
☐ RA-87273	Yakovlev Yak-40	9310927	ex CCCP-87273	
☐ RA-87958	Yakovlev Yak-40K	9821957	ex CCCP-87958	
☐ RA-88172	Yakovlev Yak-40K	9611047	ex CCCP-88172	
☐ RA-88216	Yakovlev Yak-40	9630250	ex CCCP-88216	Dveuk

494

495

VOLGA AVIAEXPRESS		Goumrak (WLG)		Volgograd-Goomrak (VOG)
☐ RA-42384	Yakovlev Yak-42D	4520423016230	ex CCCP-42384	
☐ RA-42406	Yakovlev Yak-42D	4520424116683	ex CCCP-42406	stored
☐ RA-42549	Yakovlev Yak-42D	11040105	ex ER-YCD Yevgeni Kucher	
☐ RA-65019	Tupolev Tu-134A	48375	ex CCCP-65019	
☐ RA-65086	Tupolev Tu-134A-3	60130	ex CCCP-65086	
☐ RA-76484	Ilyushin Il-76TD	0063469081	ex CCCP-76484	
☐ RA-88171	Yakovlev Yak-40	9620947	ex EP-LBK	
☐ RA-88228	Yakovlev Yak-40	9641750	ex CCCP-88228	
☐ VP-BMN	Canadair CRJ-200	7179	ex N620BR	
☐ VP-BMR	Canadair CRJ-200	7192	ex N623BR	
☐ VQ-BFA	Canadair CRJ-200ER	7627	ex N466CA	
☐ VQ-BFB	Canadair CRJ-200ER	7637	ex N467CA	
☐ VQ-BFF	Canadair CRJ-200LR	7470	ex N705BR	
☐ VQ-BFI	Canadair CRJ-200ER	7671	ex N478CA	

VOLGA-DNEPR AIRLINES		Volga Dnepr (VI/VDA)		Ulyanovsk-Vostochniy East
☐ RA-82042	Antonov An-124-100	9773054055093	ex CCCP-82042	
☐ RA-82043	Antonov An-124-100	9773054155101	ex CCCP-82043	
☐ RA-82044	Antonov An-124-100	9773054155109	ex CCCP-82044	
☐ RA-82045	Antonov An-124-100	9773052255113	ex CCCP-82045	
☐ RA-82046	Antonov An-124-100	9773052255117	ex RA-82067	
☐ RA-82047	Antonov An-124-100	9773053259121		
☐ RA-82074	Antonov An-124-100	9773051459142		
☐ RA-82078	Antonov An-124-100	9773054559153		
☐ RA-82079	Antonov An-124-100	9773052062157		
☐ RA-82081	Antonov An-124-100M	9773051462165		
☐ EW-76734	Ilyushin Il-76TD	0073476312	ex RA-76734	
☐ EW-78843	Ilyushin Il-76TD	1003403082	ex CCCP-78843	
☐ RA-76370	Ilyushin Il-76TD	1033414458		<GZP
☐ RA-76402	Ilyushin Il-76TD	1023413430		<GZP
☐ RA-76445	Ilyushin Il-76TD	1023410330	ex EK-76445	<GZP
☐ RA-76446	Ilyushin Il-76TD	1023412418	ex EK-76446	<GZP
☐ RA-76483	Ilyushin Il-76TD	0063468042	ex CCCP-76483	
☐ RA-76493	Ilyushin Il-76TD	0043456700	ex CCCP-76493	
☐ RA-76950	Ilyushin Il-76-90VD	2053420697	Vladimir Kokkinaki	
☐ RA-76951	Ilyushin Il-76-90VD	2073421704		
☐ RA-87400	Yakovlev Yak-40	9421233	ex CCCP-87400	
☐ RA-87484	Yakovlev Yak-40	9441238	ex CCCP-87484	<VGV
☐ RA-88231	Yakovlev Yak-40K	9642050	ex CCCP-88231	

VOLOGDA AIR ENTERPRISE		Vologda Air (VGV)		Vologda-Grishino (VGD)
☐ RA-87284	Yakovlev Yak-40	9311927	ex CCCP-87277	
☐ RA-87484	Yakovlev Yak-40	9441238	ex CCCP-87484	
☐ RA-87665	Yakovlev Yak-40	9240925	ex CCCP-87665	no titles
☐ RA-87669	Yakovlev Yak-40	9021760	ex CCCP-87665	no titles
☐ RA-87842	Yakovlev Yak-40	9321030	ex CCCP-87842	
☐ RA-88247	Yakovlev Yak-40	9642051	ex EP-LBJ	

VOSTOK AIRLINES		Vostok (VTK)		Khabarovsk-Novy (KHV)
☐ RA-67634	LET L-410UVP-E	902427	ex CCCP-67634	
☐ RA-67635	LET L-410UVP-E	902428	ex CCCP-67635	
☐ RA-67636	LET L-410UVP-E	902429	ex CCCP-67636	
☐ RA-28920	WSK/PZL Antonov An-28	1AJ008-06	ex CCCP-28920	[KHV]
☐ RA-28929	WSK/PZL Antonov An-28	1AJ008-16	ex CCCP-28929	
☐ RA-28933	WSK/PZL Antonov An-28	1AJ008-20	ex CCCP-28933	
☐ RA-28941	WSK/PZL Antonov An-28	1AJ009-07	ex CCCP-28941	
☐ RA-28942	WSK/PZL Antonov An-28	1AJ009-08	ex CCCP-28942	[KHV]
☐ RA-41901	Antonov An-38-100	4163847010001	Vera	
☐ RA-41903	Antonov An-38-100	4163838010003	Lyubov	

VYBORG AIRLINES		Vyborg Air (VBG)		St Petersburg-Pulkovo (LED)
☐ RA-91014	Ilyushin Il-114	1023823024		
☐ RA-91015	Ilyushin Il-114	1033828025	ex UK 91015	

YAK SERVICE		Yak-Service (AKY)		Moscow-Bykovo (BKA)
☐ RA-42387	Yakovlev Yak-42	4520423016436	ex CCCP-42387	
☐ RA-42412	Yakovlev Yak-42D	4520422219055	ex EP-YAA	

496

☐ RA-87648	Yakovlev Yak-40	9140920	ex CCCP-87648	VIP
☐ RA-87659	Yakovlev Yak-40	9240325	ex CCCP-87659	VIP
☐ RA-88294	Yakovlev Yak-40	9331029	ex UN-88294	VIP
☐ RA-88295	Yakovlev Yak-40	9331329	ex 035	VIP

YAKUTIA AIRLINES — Air Yakutia (K7/SYL) — Yakutsk (YKS)

☐ RA-11354	Antonov An-12BP	401812	ex CCCP-11354	[YKS]
☐ RA-11767	Antonov An-12BP	401909	ex CCCP-11767	[YKS]
☐ RA-46496	Antonov An-24RV	27308209	ex CCCP-47496	
☐ RA-46510	Antonov An-24RV	37308406	ex CCCCP-46510	
☐ RA-46665	Antonov An-24RV	47309506	ex CCCP-46665	
☐ RA-47352	Antonov An-24RV	67310601	ex CCCP-47352	
☐ RA-47353	Antonov An-24RV	67310602	ex CCCP-47353	
☐ RA-47360	Antonov An-24RV	67310704	ex CCCP-47360	
☐ RA-47819	Antonov An-24RV	17307108	ex CCCP-47819	
☐ RA-26105	Antonov An-26B-100	12003	ex CCCP-26105	
☐ RA-26660	Antonov An-26-100	97308008	ex CCCP-26660	
☐ RA-41250	Antonov An-140-100	05A001		stored
☐ RA-41251	Antonov An-140-100	07A012		
☐ RA-41252	Antonov An-140-100	09A014		
☐ RA-41253	Antonov An-140-100	36525305032	ex UR-14008	♦
☐ VQ-BEO	Boeing 737-76Q/W	30293/1496	ex D-ABBN	
☐ VQ-BMP	Boeing 737-86N/W	28617/504	ex SE-RHS	o/o♦
☐ VQ-BOY	Boeing 737-85F	28825/188	ex D-ABBR	♦
☐ VP-BFG	Boeing 757-256/W	26244/616	ex TF-FIT	
☐ VP-BFI	Boeing 757-27B	24838/302	ex TF-FIW	
☐ VQ-BCF	Boeing 757-23N/W	27974/737	ex N518AT	
☐ VQ-BCK	Boeing 757-256/W	26245/617	ex TF-FIS	
☐ VQ-BMW	Boeing 757-23N/W	29330/843	ex N522AT	♦
☐ RA-85007	Tupolev Tu-154M	88A777	ex LZ-HMF	
☐ RA-85700	Tupolev Tu-154M	91A875	ex LZ-HMY	
☐ RA-85791	Tupolev Tu-154M	93A975	ex EP-MBR	
☐ RA-85794	Tupolev Tu-154M	93A978		
☐ RA-85812	Tupolev Tu-154M	94A1005		AirUnion colours

YAMAL AIRLINES — Yamal (YL/LLM) — Salekhard-Nepalkovo (SLY)

☐ VP-BRQ	Boeing 737-528	25230/2191	ex F-GJNE	
☐ VP-BRS	Boeing 737-528	25231/2208	ex F-GJNF	
☐ VP-BRU	Boeing 737-528	25206/2099	ex F-GJNA	
☐ VP-BRV	Boeing 737-528	25227/2108	ex F-GJNB	
☐ VQ-BAB	Boeing 737-56N	28565/2944	ex N565LS	
☐ VQ-BII	Boeing 737-48E	25773/2905	ex N773SJ	♦
☐ RA-65132	Tupolev Tu-134A-3	60639	ex CCCP-65132	
☐ RA-65143	Tupolev Tu-134A	60967	ex CCCP-65143	
☐ RA-65552	Tupolev Tu-134A-3	66270	ex CCCP-65552	
☐ RA-65554	Tupolev Tu-134A-3	66320	ex CCCP-65554	
☐ RA-65906	Tupolev Tu-134A	66175	ex CCCP-65906	Salekhard
☐ RA-65914	Tupolev Tu-134A-3	66109	ex CCCP-65914	
☐ RA-65915	Tupolev Tu-134A-3	66120	ex TC-GRE	
☐ RA-65919	Tupolev Tu-134A-3	66168	ex CCCP-65919	
☐ RA-65983	Tupolev Tu-134A-3	63350	ex CCCP-65983	
☐ RA-87222	Yakovlev Yak-40K	9832058	ex CCCP-87222	
☐ RA-87340	Yakovlev Yak-40	9510939	ex YL-TRA	
☐ RA-87381	Yakovlev Yak-40	9411232	ex CCCP-87381	
☐ RA-87416	Yakovlev Yak-40	9420834	ex CCCP-87416	
☐ RA-88264	Yakovlev Yak-40K	9711952	ex CCCP-88264	
☐ RA-26133	Antonov An-26B	37312709	ex CCCP-26133	
☐ RA-46694	Antonov An-24RV	47309905	ex CCCP-46694	
☐ RA-46695	Antonov An-24RV	47309906	ex UN 46695	
☐ RA-72918	Antonov An-72	36572040548	ex CCCP-72918	
☐ RA-74052	Antonov An-74-200	36547098944		

ZAPOLYARYE AVIAKOMPANIA — Norlisk-Alykel (NSK)

☐ RA-11363	Antonov An-12B	00347505	ex CCCP-11363	
☐ RA-26620	Antonov An-26-100	5104	ex CCCP-26620	
☐ RA-85725	Tupolev Tu-154M	92A907	ex EP-MHB	

497

RDPL- LAOS (Lao People's Democratic Republic)

LAO AIRLINES | Lao (QV/LAO) | Vientiane (VTE)

☐ RDPL-34173	ATR 72-202	870	ex F-WNUD	
☐ RDPL-34174	ATR 72-202	878	ex F-WNUF	
☐ RDPL-34175	ATR 72-202	929	ex F-WKVF	♦
☐ RDPL-34176	ATR 72-202	938	ex F-WKVJ	♦
☐ RDPL-34144	Cessna 208B Caravan I	208B0967	ex VH-KCV	
☐ RDPL-34149	Cessna 208B Caravan I	208B1159	ex N12879	
☐ RDPL-34168	CAIC MA60	0402	ex B-761L	
☐ RDPL-34169	CAIC MA60	0403		
☐ RDPL-34171	CAIC MA60	0507		
☐ RDPL-34172	CAIC MA60	0508		

LAO AVIATION | Lavie (LLL) | Vientiane (VTE)

☐ RDPL-34139		Mil Mi-17 (Mi-8MTV-1)	95946	ex CCCP-27114
☐ RDPL-34140		Mil Mi-17 (Mi-8MTV-1)	95984	ex CCCP-27121
☐ RDPL-34145		Aérospatiale AS350BA Ecureuil	2532	ex D-HLEA
☐ RDPL-34156		Antonov An-12BP	402001	ex LZ-VEF

LAO CAPRICORN AIR

☐ RDPL-34153		Antonov An-12TB	01347907	ex ER-AXA
☐ RDPL-34163	Ilyushin Il-76TD	0053460832	ex UP-I7610	

RP- PHILIPPINES (Republic of the Philippines)

2GO | (BOI) | Manila-Ninoy Aquino Intl (MNL)

☐ RP-C2253	NAMC YS-11-100	2020	ex RP-C1936	[MNL]
☐ RP-C2677	NAMC YS-11A-500	2092	ex JA8717	[MNL]
☐ RP-C2739	NAMC YS-11A-500	2090	ex JA8710	[MNL]
☐ RP-C3389	NAMC YS-11A-213	2078	ex JA8722	stored ?
☐ RP-C3585	NAMC YS-11A-227	2149	ex JA8771	

AIR LINK INTERNATIONAL AIRWAYS | Manila-Sangley Point (SGL)

☐ RP-C180	Cessna 414	414-0402	ex RP.180	
☐ RP-C1102	Beech 88 Queen Air	LP-44	ex RP-94	
☐ RP-C2252	NAMC YS-11A-500	2079	ex RP-C1931	

AIRPHIL EXPRESS | Orient Pacific (2P/GAP) | Manila-Ninoy Aquino Intl (MNL)

☐ RP-C3227	Airbus A320-214	2183	ex OY-VKP	
☐ RP-C3228	Airbus A320-214	2162	ex RP-C3226	
☐ RP-C8388	Airbus A320-214	4415	ex F-WWIZ	♦
☐ RP-C8389	Airbus A320-214	4475	ex D-AUBA	♦
☐ RP-C8390	Airbus A320-214	4504	ex D-AUBM	♦
☐ RP-C8391	Airbus A320-214	4512	ex D-AXAE	♦
☐ RP-C2025	Boeing 737-222	19077/103	ex N9039U	stored
☐ RP-C3011	Boeing 737-2H4	21533/524	ex N52SW	
☐ RP-C3012	Boeing 737-2H4	21448/509	ex N51SW	
☐ RP-C3015	Boeing 737-2H4	21534/526	ex N53SW	
☐ RP-C8001	Boeing 737-2B7 (Nordam 3)	23116/999	ex N283AU	[MNL]
☐ RP-C8002	Boeing 737-2B7 (Nordam 3)	22886/974	ex N274AU	[MNL]
☐ RP-C8003	Boeing 737-2B7 (Nordam 3)	22888/979	ex N276US	[MNL]
☐ RP-C8007	Boeing 737-2B7 (Nordam 3)	22878/921	ex N266AU	
☐ RP-C8009	Boeing 737-201 (Nordam 3)	22879/926	ex N267AU	[MNL]
☐ RP-C8011	Boeing 737-247 (Nordam 3)	23606/1379	ex N379DL	
☐ RP-C8022	Boeing 737-247 (Nordam 3)	23607/1387	ex N380DL	[MNL]
☐ RP-C4007	Boeing 737-332	25996/2488	ex RP-C2000	<PAL
☐ RP-C4011	Boeing 737-3Y0	24770/1941	ex EI-BZN	<PAL
☐ RP-C3016	de Havilland DHC-8Q-314	653	ex C-FNEA	
☐ RP-C3017	de Havilland DHC-8Q-314	657	ex C-FOUN	
☐ RP-C3018	de Havilland DHC-8Q-314	658	ex C-FPDR	
☐ RP-C3030	de Havilland DHC-8-402Q	4064	ex LN-WDD	
☐ RP-C3031	de Havilland DHC-8-402Q	4069	ex LN-WDA	
☐ RP-C3032	de Havilland DHC-8-402Q	4070	ex LN-WDB	
☐ RP-C3033	de Havilland DHC-8-402Q	4071	ex LN-WDC	
☐ RP-C3036	de Havilland DHC-8-402Q	4023	ex LN-RDH	

498

CEBU PACIFIC AIR		Cebu Air (5J/CEB)		Manila-Sangley Point (SGL)
☐ RP-C3189	Airbus A319-111	2556	ex D-AVYG	
☐ RP-C3190	Airbus A319-111	2586	ex D-AVXI	
☐ RP-C3191	Airbus A319-111	2625	ex D-AVYZ	
☐ RP-C3192	Airbus A319-111	2638	ex D-AVWJ	
☐ RP-C3193	Airbus A319-111	2786	ex D-AVYV	
☐ RP-C3194	Airbus A319-111	2790	ex D-AVWN	
☐ RP-C3195	Airbus A319-111	2831	ex D-AVXH	
☐ RP-C3196	Airbus A319-111	2821	ex D-AVXC	
☐ RP-C3197	Airbus A319-111	2852	ex D-AVXL	
☐ RP-C3198	Airbus A319-111	2876	ex D-AVWL	
☐ RP-C3240	Airbus A320-214	2419	ex F-WWID	
☐ RP-C3241	Airbus A320-214	2439	ex F-WWBO	
☐ RP-C3242	Airbus A320-214	2994	ex F-WWIU	
☐ RP-C3243	Airbus A320-214	3048	ex F-WWDR	
☐ RP-C3244	Airbus A320-214	3272	ex F-WWBZ	
☐ RP-C3245	Airbus A320-214	3433	ex F-WWDU	
☐ RP-C3246	Airbus A320-214	3472	ex F-WWBV	
☐ RP-C3247	Airbus A320-214	3487	ex F-WWII	
☐ RP-C3248	Airbus A320-214	3646	ex F-WWBX	
☐ RP-C3249	Airbus A320-214	3762	ex F-WWDI	
☐ RP-C3250	Airbus A320-214	3767	ex F-WWDP	
☐ RP-C3260	Airbus A320-214	4447	ex F-WWII	◆
☐ RP-C3261	Airbus A320-214	4508	ex F-WWBJ	◆
☐ RP-C	Airbus A320-214		ex	o/o◆
☐ RP-C	Airbus A320-214		ex	o/o◆
☐ RP-C	Airbus A320-214		ex	o/o◆
☐ RP-C	Airbus A320-214		ex	o/o◆
☐ RP-C	Airbus A320-214		ex	o/o◆
☐ RP-C	Airbus A320-214		ex	o/o◆
☐ RP-C7250	ATR 72-212A	779	ex F-WWER	
☐ RP-C7251	ATR 72-212A	784	ex F-WWEC	
☐ RP-C7252	ATR 72-212A	820	ex F-WWEJ	
☐ RP-C7253	ATR 72-212A	828	ex F-WWEV	
☐ RP-C7255	ATR 72-212A	842	ex F-WWEH	
☐ RP-C7256	ATR 72-212A	847	ex F-WWEI	
☐ RP-C7257	ATR 72-212A	857	ex F-WWEB	

CHEMTRAD AVIATION				Manila-Sangley Point (SGL)
☐ RP-C28	Britten-Norman BN-2A-21 Islander	409	ex G-BCLF	
☐ RP-C1262	Britten-Norman BN-2A-21 Islander	408	ex G-BCLE	
☐ RP-C2207	Britten-Norman BN-2A-26 Islander	718	ex G-BCAF	

CORPORATE AIR				Subic Bay-Intl (SFS)
☐ RP-C2801	Cessna 208B Caravan I	208B1057	ex N4088Z	

INTERISLAND AIRLINES		(ISN)		Manila-Ninoy Aquino Intl (MNL)
☐ RP-C2639	Antonov An-26	77305509	ex EK-26227	
☐ RP-C2695	Yakovlev Yak-40A	9522041	ex EK-87536	dbr 01Nov06?
☐ RP-C2805	Yakovlev Yak-40	9342031	ex 4L-AVC	
☐ RP-C6868	LET L-410UVP-E	871926	ex 5V-TTG	

ISLAND AVIATION		Soriano (SOY)		Manila-Sangley Point (SGL)
☐ RP-C2282	Dornier 228-202K	8173	ex N23UA	
☐ RP-C2283	Dornier 228-202K	8077	ex F-ODZH	
☐ RP-C22837	Dornier 228-202K	8174	ex VH-YJD	

ISLAND TRANSVOYAGER				Manila-Sangley Point (SGL)
☐ RP-C1008	Dornier 228-212	8193	ex D-CARD	
☐ RP-C2289	Dornier 228-212	8177	ex B-11150	

JANS HELICOPTERS				Guam (GUM)
☐ RP-C2733	Beech 95-B55 Baron	TC-1770	ex N8770R	Frtr
☐ RP-C2324	Learjet 24B	24B-182	ex N155J	Frtr
☐ RP-C2424	Learjet 24B	24B-226	ex N335RY	Frtr
☐ RP-C2702	de Havilland DHC-4A Caribou	98	ex N800NC	Frtr

LIONAIR				
☐ RP-C3988	LET-410UVP-E10	892317	ex 3D-FTY	
☐ RP-C5525	British Aerospace 146 Srs.200	E2031	ex N66LN	>Heritage Air (9M-) ♦

NORTH SOUTH AIRLINES				Manila-Ninoy Aquino Intl (MNL)
☐ RP-C8258	LET L-410UVP-E	882038	ex 3D-RTV	

PACIFIC EAST ASIA CARGO AIRLINES		Pac-East Cargo (Q8/PEC)		Manila-Ninoy Aquino Intl (MNL)
☐ RP-C5353	Boeing 727-23F	19131/218	ex ZS-NPX	
☐ RP-C5354	Learjet 35A	35A-185	ex ZS-SES	
☐ RP-C5355	Boeing 727-223F (FedEx 3)	20185/710	ex PK-YGT	Lsg fr TMG

PACIFIC PEARL AIRWAYS				
☐ RP-C8777	Boeing 737-232 (AvAero 3)	23088/1018	ex N316DL	

PACIFICAIR		Pacific West (GX/PFR)		Manila-Sangley Point (SGL)
☐ RP-C1320	Britten-Norman BN-2A-21 Islander	569	ex PAF-569	
☐ RP-C1321	Britten-Norman BN-2A-21 Islander	547	ex PAF-547	
☐ RP-C1324	Britten-Norman BN-2A-21 Islander	539	ex PAF 538	
☐ RP-C1801	Britten-Norman BN-2A-21 Islander	739	ex G-BCNI	
☐ RP-C2132	Britten-Norman BN-2A-21 Islander	422	ex G-BCSG	
☐ RP-C2137	Britten-Norman BN-2A-21 Islander	443	ex G-BCZU	
☐ RP-C2138	Britten-Norman BN-2A-21 Islander	445	ex G-BCZW	
☐ RP-C1103	Beech H-18	BA-660	ex N638CZ	
☐ RP-C1358	Beech H-18 Tri-Gear	BA-750	ex RP-C1986	
☐ RP-C1611	Cessna 421C Golden Eagle	421C0155	ex N5282J	

PHILIPPINE AIRLINES		Philippine (PR/PAL)		Manila-Ninoy Aquino Intl (MNL)
☐ RP-C3221	Airbus A320-214	0706	ex F-WWIM	
☐ RP-C3223	Airbus A320-214	0745	ex F-WWIR	
☐ RP-C3231	Airbus A320-214	1210	ex N116US	
☐ RP-C8600	Airbus A319-112	2878	ex D-AVWO	
☐ RP-C8601	Airbus A319-112	2925	ex D-AVYP	
☐ RP-C8602	Airbus A319-112	2954	ex D-AVXE	
☐ RP-C8603	Airbus A319-112	3108	ex D-AVYM	
☐ RP-C8604	Airbus A320-214	3087	ex F-WWBV	
☐ RP-C8605	Airbus A320-214	3107	ex F-WWIK	
☐ RP-C8606	Airbus A320-214	3187	ex F-WWDY	
☐ RP-C8607	Airbus A320-214	3205	ex F-WWIH	
☐ RP-C8609	Airbus A320-214	3273	ex F-WWIC	
☐ RP-C8610	Airbus A320-214	3310	ex F-WWIO	
☐ RP-C8611	Airbus A320-214	3455	ex F-WWBH	
☐ RP-C8612	Airbus A320-214	3553	ex F-WWIZ	
☐ RP-C8613	Airbus A320-214	3579	ex F-WWBY	
☐ RP-C8614	Airbus A320-214	3652	ex F-WWDQ	
☐ RP-C8615	Airbus A320-214	3731	ex F-WWDL	
☐ RP-C3330	Airbus A330-301	183	ex F-OHZM	
☐ RP-C3331	Airbus A330-301	184	ex F-OHZN	
☐ RP-C3332	Airbus A330-301	188	ex F-OHZO	
☐ RP-C3333	Airbus A330-301	191	ex F-OHZP	
☐ RP-C3335	Airbus A330-301	189	ex F-OHZQ	
☐ RP-C3336	Airbus A330-301	198	ex F-OHZR	
☐ RP-C3337	Airbus A330-301	200	ex F-OHZS	
☐ RP-C3340	Airbus A330-301	203	ex F-OHZT	
☐ RP-C3430	Airbus A340-313X	173	ex F-OHPJ	
☐ RP-C3431	Airbus A340-313X	176	ex F-OHPK	
☐ RP-C3432	Airbus A340-313X	187	ex F-OHPL	
☐ RP-C3434	Airbus A340-313X	196	ex F-OHPM	
☐ RP-C4007	Boeing 737-332	25996/2488	ex RP-C2000	>GAP
☐ RP-C4011	Boeing 737-3Y0	24770/1941	ex EI-BZN	>GAP
☐ RP-C7471	Boeing 747-4F6	27261/1005	ex N751PR	
☐ RP-C7472	Boeing 747-4F6	27262/1012	ex N752PR	
☐ RP-C7473	Boeing 747-4F6	27828/1039	ex N753PR	
☐ RP-C7475	Boeing 747-469M	27663/1068	ex N754PR	
☐ RP-C8168	Boeing 747-4F6	27827/1038	ex C-FGHZ	
☐ RP-C7776	Boeing 777-36NER	37712/841		
☐ RP-C7777	Boeing 777-36NER	37709/826		

ROYAL STAR AVIATION · Manila-Sangley Point (SGL)

☐ RP-C2812	British Aerospace Jetstream 3217	923	ex N93BA
☐ RP-C8298	British Aerospace Jetstream 4101	41013	ex N302UE
☐ RP-C8299	British Aerospace Jetstream 4101	41080	ex N327UE
☐ RP-C8328	Dornier 328-300 (328JET)	3136	ex N360SK

SOUTH EAST ASIAN AIRLINES · Seair (DG/SRQ)
Manila- Ninoy Aquino Intl/Diosdado Macapagal Intl (MNL/CRK)

☐ RP-C2128	LET L-410UVP-E	882102	ex S9-BOX	
☐ RP-C2328	LET L-410UVP-E3	872004	ex S9-BOY	
☐ RP-C2428	LET L-410UVP-E3	871909	ex 3D-DAM	
☐ RP-C2628	LET L-410UVP-E	871931	ex Russ AF 1931	
☐ RP-C2728	LET L-410UVP-E	861708	ex RA-67588	jungle c/s
☐ RP-C2928	LET L-410UVP-E	871821	ex Russ AF 1821	
☐ RP-C3328	LET L-410UVP-E	872003	ex RP-C528	
☐ RP-C1179	Dornier 28D-2 Skyservant	4127	ex D-IDRH	
☐ RP-C2403	Dornier 24ATT	5345	ex D-CATD	Amphibian
☐ RP-C2814	Dornier 228-200	8019	ex JA8836	
☐ RP-C4328	Dornier 328-120	3042	ex D-CPRT	
☐ RP-C5328	Dornier 328-110	3046	ex D-CPRS	
☐ RP-C6328	Dornier 328-110	3027	ex N653JC	
☐ RP-C7328	Dornier 328-110	3069	ex G-BYML	
☐ RP-C9328	Dornier 328-110	3003	ex D-CDOL	all-white

SPIRIT OF MANILA AIRLINES

☐ RP-C7701	Boeing 737-301	23234/1208	ex HS-AAN
☐ RP-C7702	McDonnell-Douglas MD-83	49939/1787	ex N939MD
☐ RP-C7703	McDonnell-Douglas MD-83	49946/1898	ex N964MD

TRANSGLOBAL AIRWAYS · Diosdado Macapagal IntL (CRK)

☐ RP-C8015	Boeing 737-2B1C	20536/289	ex C9-BAC
☐ RP-C8018	McDonnell-Douglas MD-83	49985/1838	ex PK-ALF

VICTORIA AIR · Manila-Sangley Point (SGL)

☐ RP-C535	Douglas DC-3	15571/27016	ex RP-C95

ZEST AIRWAYS · (6K/EZD) · Manila-Sangley Point (SGL)

☐ RP-C8890	Airbus A319-132	1074	ex SE-RIB	◆
☐ RP-C8897	Airbus A320-232	2141	ex N581JB	
☐ RP-C8988	Airbus A320-232	2147	ex RP-C8898	
☐ RP-C8989	Airbus A320-232	3621	ex F-WWIK	
☐ RP-C8991	Airbus A320-232	4533	ex D-AXAK	◆
☐ RP-C8992	Airbus A320-232	2137	ex G-TTOI	◆
☐ RP-C8892	CAIC MA60	0703	ex B-956L	dam 25Jun09
☐ RP-C8894	CAIC MA60	0710	ex B-956L	
☐ RP-C8895	CAIC MA60	0711	ex B-963L	
☐ RP-C8896	CAIC MA60	0712	ex B-964L	
☐ RP-C2895	de Havilland DHC-7-102	035	ex 7O-ADB	
☐ RP-C2915	de Havilland DHC-7-102	092	ex C-GELY	
☐ RP-C2955	de Havilland DHC-7-102	090	ex SX-BNA	
☐ RP-C2978	de Havilland DHC-7-102	079	ex N67DA	
☐ RP-C2988	de Havilland DHC-7-102	078	ex N60RA	[MNL]
☐ RP-C2996	de Havilland DHC-7-102	018	ex N701AC	
☐ RP-C4000	ITPN CASA CN-235	N020	ex PK-XNV	
☐ RP-C5000	ITPN CASA CN-235	N001	ex PK-MNA	
☐ RP-C2918	LET L-410UVP	902510	ex 9A-BNZ	Fleuris titles
☐ RP-C3880	LET L-410UVP-E	892228	ex RA-67601	Fleuris titles
☐ RP-C3889	LET L-410UVP-E	851511	ex RA-67544	Fleuris titles
☐ RP-C3338	NAMC YS-11A-227	2142	ex JA8766	
☐ RP-C3339	NAMC YS-11A-222	2147	ex JA8768	
☐ RP-C3588	NAMC YS-11A-213	2168	ex JA8787	[MNL]
☐ RP-C3592	NAMC YS-11A-213	2108	ex JA8735	dam 02Jan08

SE- SWEDEN (Kingdom of Sweden)

AIR SWEDEN — (SXN)

☐ SE-DMT	McDonnell-Douglas MD-81	48003/944	ex N480LT
☐ SE-RJM	Airbus A320-212	0289	ex F-WBGE ♦
☐ SE-RJN	Airbus A320-231	0169	ex N196AG ♦
☐ SE-RJP	McDonnell-Douglas MD-82	49209/1191	ex I-DAWS ♦

AMAPOLA FLYG — Amapola (APF) — Stockholm-Arlanda (ARN)

☐ PH-LMA	Fokker 50	20118	ex OY-EBB	<MNL
☐ SE-KTC	Fokker 50	20124	ex OY-MMG	
☐ SE-KTD	Fokker 50	20125	ex OY-MMH	
☐ SE-LIP	Fokker 50	20147	ex PH-PRD	
☐ SE-LJG	Fokker 50	20168	ex LX-LGC	
☐ SE-LJH	Fokker 50	20171	ex LX-LGD	
☐ SE-LJI	Fokker 50	20180	ex LX-LGE	
☐ SE-LJV	Fokker 50	20103	ex VT-CAA	
☐ SE-LJY	Fokker 50	20259	ex OY-PAA	

AVITRANS NORDIC — Extrans (2Q/ETS) — Nyköping (NYO)

☐ SE-ISR	SAAB SF.340A	340A-017	ex LY-ISR
☐ SE-ISY	SAAB SF.340A	340A-080	ex SE-E80
☐ SE-KCS	SAAB SF.340A (QC)	340A-066	ex (SP-KPH)
☐ SE-KCT	SAAB SF.340A (QC)	340A-070	ex OH-FAC
☐ SE-KXE	SAAB SF.340A	340A-111	ex LY-KXE
☐ SE-KXI	SAAB SF.340B	340B-176	ex XA-AFR
☐ SE-LJL	SAAB SF.340A	340A-091	ex N991XK
☐ SE-LJR	SAAB SF.340B	340B-168	ex D-CDAU
☐ SE-LJS	SAAB SF.340B	340B-215	ex D-CDEO
☐ SE-LJT	SAAB SF.340B	340B-221	ex D-CASD

BARENTS AIRLINK — Nordflight (8N/NKF) — Lulea (LLA)

☐ SE-IUX	Beech 200 Super King Air	BB-675	ex N26SD
☐ SE-LTL	Beech 200 Super King Air	BB-582	ex LN-MOA

CITY AIRLINE — Swedestar (CF/SDR) — Gothenburg-Landvetter (GOT)

☐ SE-DZB	Embraer ERJ-145EP	145113	ex PT-SCP
☐ SE-RAA	Embraer ERJ-135ER	145210	ex PT-SFU
☐ SE-RAB	Embraer ERJ-135LR	145453	ex PT-SUY
☐ SE-RAC	Embraer ERJ-145LR	145098	ex N285CD
☐ SE-RAD	Embraer ERJ-145EU	145458	ex G-EMBU ♦
☐ SE-RAE	Embraer ERJ-145EU	145482	ex G-EMBV ♦
☐ SE-RIA	Embraer ERJ-145MP	145320	ex PH-RXB
☐ SE-DMK	McDonnell-Douglas MD-87	53337/1962	ex LN-RMP o/o♦

DIREKTFLYG — Skyreg (HS/HSV) — Borlänge (BLE)

☐ SE-LHB	British Aerospace Jetstream 32EP	844	ex N844JX
☐ SE-LHC	British Aerospace Jetstream 32EP	846	ex N846JX
☐ SE-LHE	British Aerospace Jetstream 32EP	854	ex N854JX
☐ SE-LHF	British Aerospace Jetstream 32EP	855	ex N855JX
☐ SE-LHG	British Aerospace Jetstream 32EP	857	ex N857JX
☐ SE-LHH	British Aerospace Jetstream 32EP	848	ex N848JX
☐ SE-LHI	British Aerospace Jetstream 32EP	841	ex N841JX
☐ SE-LXD	British Aerospace Jetstream 32	977	ex G-BUVD
☐ SE-LXE	British Aerospace Jetstream 32	970	ex G-BUVC

FLY LOGIC SWEDEN — Logic (LOD) — Malmö-Sturup (MMX)

☐ SE-GIN	Piper PA-31 Navajo C	31-7512039	
☐ SE-IDR	Piper PA-31 Navajo C	31-7712085	ex LN-DAB
☐ SE-IKV	Piper PA-31-350 Navajo Chieftain	31-7405148	ex G-BDFN
☐ SE-KCP	Swearingen SA.226TC Merlin	TC-330	ex N7217N

FLYGCENTRUM — (LIQ) — Stockholm-Bromma (BMA)

☐ SE-ITB	Piper PA-31	31-8012059	ex N3585G
☐ SE-ITE	Piper PA-31	31-8012010	ex N3545C
☐ SE-KGH	Piper PA-31-350 Chieftain	31-7305007	ex OY-BVF

GOLDEN AIR		Golden (DC/GAO)		Trollhattan (THN)
☐ OH-FAF	SAAB SF.340B	340B-167	ex SE-F67	<WBA
☐ SE-ISE	SAAB SF.340A	340A-156	ex YL-BAP	
☐ SE-ISG	SAAB SF.340B	340B-162	ex SE-F62	
☐ SE-KTK	SAAB SF.340B	340B-276	ex F-GHVT	
☐ SE-KXG	SAAB SF.340B	340A-164	ex XA-AAO	
☐ SE-LMR	SAAB SF.340A	340A-141	ex OK-UFO	>NTJ
☐ SE-KXK	SAAB 2000	2000-012	ex F-GOZI	
☐ SE-LOM	SAAB 2000	2000-035	ex LY-SBK	
☐ SE-LTU	SAAB 2000	2000-062	ex HB-IYG	
☐ SE-LTV	SAAB 2000	2000-063	ex HB-IYH	
☐ SE-LTX	SAAB 2000	2000-024	ex HB-IZM	
☐ SE-LXH	SAAB 2000	2000-007	ex LY-SBQ	
☐ SE-MDA	ATR 72-212A	778	ex EI-REN	
☐ SE-MDB	ATR 72-212A	822	ex EI-RER	
☐ SE-MDC	ATR 72-212A	894	ex F-WWED	
☐ SE-MDH	ATR 72-212A	917	ex F-WWEO	♦
☐ SE-MDI	ATR 72-212A	930	ex F-WWEF	♦

JONAIR				Umea (UME)
☐ SE-FNE	Piper PA-31-350 Chieftain	31-7405434	ex N54306	
☐ SE-GLE	Piper PA-31 Navajo C	31-7512056		

MALMÖ AVIATION		Scanwing (TF/SCW)	Stockholm-Arlanda/Malmö-Sturup (ARN/MMX)	
☐ SE-DJN	Avro 146-RJ85	E2231	ex HB-IXG	♦
☐ SE-DJO	Avro 146-RJ85	E2226	ex HB-IXF	♦
☐ SE-DJP	Avro 146-RJ70	E1254	ex EI-COQ	♦
☐ SE-DSO	Avro 146-RJ100	E3221	ex N504MM	
☐ SE-DSP	Avro 146-RJ100	E3242	ex N505MM	
☐ SE-DSR	Avro 146-RJ100	E3244	ex N506MM Inga Omvager	
☐ SE-DSS	Avro 146-RJ100	E3245	ex N507MM	
☐ SE-DST	Avro 146-RJ100	E3247	ex N508MM	
☐ SE-DSU	Avro 146-RJ100	E3248	ex N509MM	
☐ SE-DSV	Avro 146-RJ100	E3250	ex N510MM	
☐ SE-DSX	Avro 146-RJ100	E3255	ex N511MM	
☐ SE-DSY	Avro 146-RJ100	E3263	ex N512MM	

NEXTJET		Nextjet (2N/NTJ)	Stockholm-Bromma (BMA)	
☐ SE-KXY	Beech 1900D	UE-236	ex SX-BST	
☐ SE-LEP	SAAB SF.340A	340A-127	ex B-12200	
☐ SE-LJN	SAAB SF.340A	340A-114	ex LY-DIG	
☐ SE-LLO	British Aerospace ATP	2023	ex G-MANP	
☐ SE-LMR	SAAB SF.340A	340A-141	ex OK-UFO	
☐ SE-LCX	Beech 1900D	UE-275	ex N11189	
☐ SE-MAK	British Aerospace ATP	2040	ex G-MANF	
☐ SE-MAL	British Aerospace ATP	2045	ex G-MANE	

NORD-FLYG		Nordex (NEF)		Eskilstuna (EKT)

Ceased operations 01/Apr/2010

NORRLANDSFLYG		Lifeguard Sweden (HMF)	Gallivare/Kiruna (GEV/KRN)	
☐ SE-HAJ	Sikorsky S-76C	760510	ex OH-HCJ	SAR
☐ SE-HAV	Sikorsky S-76C	760377	ex N50KH	SAR
☐ SE-HEJ	Sikorsky S-76C+	760604	ex N71141	SAR
☐ SE-HOJ	Sikorsky S-76C+	760605	ex N8125H	SAR
☐ SE-JEZ	Sikorsky S-76A	760215	ex N72WW	EMS
☐ SE-JUC	Sikorsky S-76A	760219	ex N18KH	EMS
☐ SE-JUS	Sikorsky S-76A	760172	ex N876TC	EMS
☐ SE-JUX	Sikorsky S-76C	760518	ex N552J	SAR♦
☐ SE-JUY	Sikorsky S-76C	760407	ex N154AE	SAR

NOVAIR		Navigator (1I/NVR)	Stockholm-Arlanda (ARN)	
☐ SE-RDN	Airbus A321-231	2211	ex D-AVZK	
☐ SE-RDO	Airbus A321-231	2216	ex D-AVZN	
☐ SE-RDP	Airbus A321-231	2410	ex D-AVZK	

ÖREBRO AVIATION		Bluelight (BUE)	Örebro-Bofors (ORB)	
☐ SE-FNE	Piper PA-31-350 Navajo Chieftain	31-7405434	ex N54306	
☐ SE-GBS	Piper PA-31-310 Navajo	31-7400984	ex OH-MRS	

SCANDINAVIAN AIRLINES SYSTEM Scandinavian (SK/SAS)
Copenhagen-Kastrup/Oslo-Gardermoen/Stockholm-Arlanda (CPH/OSL/ARN)

Member of Star Alliance

☐ OY-KBO	Airbus A319-132	2850	ex D-AVXK	Christian Valdemar Viking	retro c/s
☐ OY-KBP	Airbus A319-132	2888	ex D-AVYG	Viger Viking	
☐ OY-KBR	Airbus A319-131	3231	ex D-AVYV	Sten Viking	
☐ OY-KBT	Airbus A319-131	3292	ex D-AVYC	Ragnvald Viking	
☐ LN-RKI	Airbus A321-232	1817	ex D-AVZK	Gunnhild Viking	
☐ LN-RKK	Airbus A321-232	1848	ex SE-REG	Svipdag Viking	
☐ OY-KBB	Airbus A321-232	1642	ex D-AVZN	Hjörulf Viking	
☐ OY-KBE	Airbus A321-232	1798	ex D-AVZG	Emma Viking	
☐ OY-KBF	Airbus A321-232	1807	ex D-AVZH	Skapti Viking	
☐ OY-KBH	Airbus A321-232	1675	ex D-AVZV	Sulke Viking	
☐ OY-KBK	Airbus A321-232	1587	ex D-AVZK	Arne Viking	
☐ OY-KBL	Airbus A321-232	1619	ex D-AVZB	Gunnbjörn Viking	
☐ LN-RKH	Airbus A330-343X	497	ex F-WWYP	Emund Viking	
☐ OY-KBN	Airbus A330-343X	496	ex F-WWKK	Eystein Viking	
☐ SE-REE	Airbus A330-343X	515	ex F-WWYY	Sigrid Viking	
☐ SE-REF	Airbus A330-343X	568	ex F-WWYS	Erik Viking	Star Alliance c/s
☐ LN-RKF	Airbus A340-313X	413	ex SE-REA	Godfred Viking	[LDE]♦
☐ LN-RKG	Airbus A340-313X	424	ex SE-REB	Gudrod Viking	
☐ OY-KBA	Airbus A340-313X	435	ex F-WWJU	Adalstein Viking	
☐ OY-KBC	Airbus A340-313X	467	ex F-WWJE	Freydis Viking	
☐ OY-KBD	Airbus A340-313X	470	ex F-WWJF	Toste Viking	
☐ OY-KBI	Airbus A340-313X	430	ex F-WWJR	Rurik Viking	
☐ LN-BRE	Boeing 737-405	24643/1860		Hakon V Magnusson	
☐ LN-BRH	Boeing 737-505	24828/1925	ex D-ACBB	Haakon den Gode	
☐ LN-BRI	Boeing 737-405	24644/1938	ex 9M-MLL	Harald Hårfagre	
☐ LN-BRJ	Boeing 737-505	24273/2018	ex YL-BBB	Olav Tryggvason	
☐ LN-BRO	Boeing 737-505	24647/2143		Magnus Haraldsson	
☐ LN-BRQ	Boeing 737-405	25348/2148		Harald Gråfell	
☐ LN-BRV	Boeing 737-505	25791/2351		Hakon Sverresson	
☐ LN-BRX	Boeing 737-505	25797/2434		Sigurd Munn	
☐ LN-BUC	Boeing 737-505	26304/2649		Magnus Erlingsson	
☐ LN-BUD	Boeing 737-505	25794/2803		Inge Krokrygg	[KRS]
☐ LN-BUE	Boeing 737-505	27627/2800		Erling Skjalgsson	
☐ LN-BUF	Boeing 737-405	25795/2867		Magnus den Gode	
☐ LN-BUG	Boeing 737-505	27631/2866		Øystein Haraldsson	
☐ LN-RCN	Boeing 737-883	28318/529	ex SE-DTK	Hedrun Viking	
☐ LN-RCT	Boeing 737-683	30189/303	ex OY-KKF	Fridlev Viking	
☐ LN-RCU	Boeing 737-683	30190/335	ex SE-DNZ	Sigfrid Viking	
☐ LN-RCW	Boeing 737-883	28308/333	ex SE-DNY	Yngvar Viking	
☐ LN-RCX	Boeing 737-683	30196/733	ex SE-DYH	Höttur Viking	
☐ LN-RCY	Boeing 737-883	28324/767	ex SE-DTT	Eylime Viking	
☐ LN-RCZ	Boeing 737-883	30197/798	ex SE-DTS	Glitne Viking	
☐ LN-RNN	Boeing 737-783	28315/464	ex OY-KKI	Borgny Viking	
☐ LN-RNO	Boeing 737-783	28316/476	ex OY-KKR	Gjuke Viking	
☐ LN-RNU	Boeing 737-783/W	34548/3116	ex N1786B		
☐ LN-RNW	Boeing 737-783/W	34549/3210		Granmar Viking	
☐ LN-RPA	Boeing 737-683	28290/100	ex N5002K	Amljot Viking	
☐ LN-RPB	Boeing 737-683	28294/137	ex N1787B	Bure Viking	
☐ LN-RPE	Boeing 737-683	28306/329	ex SE-DOT	Edla Viking	
☐ LN-RPF	Boeing 737-683	28307/330	ex N1784B	Frede Viking	
☐ LN-RPG	Boeing 737-683	28310/255	ex N1787B	Geirmund Viking	
☐ LN-RPH	Boeing 737-683	28605/375		Hamder Viking	
☐ LN-RPJ	Boeing 737-783	30192/486	ex N1786B	Grimhild Viking	
☐ LN-RPK	Boeing 737-783	28317/500	ex N1786B	Heimer Viking	
☐ LN-RPL	Boeing 737-883	30469/673	ex (SE-DYC)	Svanevit Viking	
☐ LN-RPM	Boeing 737-883	30195/696	ex (SE-DYD)	Frigg Viking	
☐ LN-RPN	Boeing 737-883	30470/717	ex (SE-DYG)	Bergfora Viking	
☐ LN-RPS	Boeing 737-683	28298/191	ex OY-KKC	Gautrek Viking	
☐ LN-RPT	Boeing 737-683	28299/193	ex OY-KKD	Ellida Viking	
☐ LN-RPU	Boeing 737-683	28312/407	ex OY-KKP	Ragna Viking	
☐ LN-RPW	Boeing 737-683	28289/92	ex OY-KKA	Alvid Viking	
☐ LN-RPX	Boeing 737-683	28291/112	ex SE-DNN	Nanna Viking	
☐ LN-RPY	Boeing 737-683	28292/116	ex SE-DNO	Olof Viking	
☐ LN-RPZ	Boeing 737-683	28293/120	ex OY-KKB	Bera Viking	
☐ LN-RRA	Boeing 737-783/W	30471/2288	ex (SE-DYD)	Steinar Viking	
☐ LN-RRB	Boeing 737-783/W	32276/2331		Dag Viking	

☐ LN-RRC	Boeing 737-683	28300/209	ex OY-KKG	Sindre Viking	
☐ LN-RRD	Boeing 737-683	28301/227	ex OY-KKH	Embla Viking	
☐ LN-RRE	Boeing 737-85P/W	35706/2586		Knut Viking	
☐ LN-RRF	Boeing 737-85P/W	35707/2610		Froydis Viking	
☐ LN-RRG	Boeing 737-85P/W	35708/2653		Einar Viking	
☐ LN-RRH	Boeing 737-883/W	34546/2898	ex N1786B	Freja Viking	
☐ LN-RRJ	Boeing 737-883/W	34547/2956	ex N5573L	Frida Viking	
☐ LN-RRK	Boeing 737-883/W	32278/1169	ex SE-DYG	Gerud Viking	
☐ LN-RRL	Boeing 737-883/W	28328/1424	ex SE-DYT	Jarlabanke Viking	Star Alliance c/s
☐ LN-RRM	Boeing 737-783	28314/458	ex SE-DTI	Erland Viking	
☐ LN-RRN	Boeing 737-783	30191/404	ex SE-DTG	Solveig Viking	
☐ LN-RRO	Boeing 737-683	28288/49	ex SE-DNM	Bernt Viking	
☐ LN-RRP	Boeing 737-683	28311/382	ex SE-DTU	Vilborg Viking	
☐ LN-RRR	Boeing 737-683	28309/368	ex SE-DTF	Torbjörn Viking	
☐ LN-RRS	Boeing 737-883	28325/1014	ex (SE-DYM)	Ymer Viking	
☐ LN-RRT	Boeing 737-883	28326/1036	ex (SE-DYN)	Lodyn Viking	
☐ LN-RRU	Boeing 737-883	28327/1070	ex (SE-DYP)	Vingolf Viking	
☐ LN-RRW	Boeing 737-883	32277/1554	ex SE-DTR	Saga Viking	
☐ LN-RRX	Boeing 737-683	28296/21	ex SE-DNR	Ragnfast Viking	
☐ LN-RRY	Boeing 737-683	28297/30	ex SE-DNS	Signe Viking	
☐ LN-RRZ	Boeing 737-683	28295/149	ex SE-DNP	Gisla Viking	
☐ LN-TUA	Boeing 737-705	28211/33		Ingeborg Eriksdatter	
☐ LN-TUD	Boeing 737-705	28217/142		Magrete Skulesdatter	
☐ LN-TUF	Boeing 737-705	28222/245		Tyra Haraldsdatter	
☐ LN-TUH	Boeing 737-705	29093/471		Margrete Ingesdatter	
☐ LN-TUI	Boeing 737-705	29094/507	ex N1787B	Kristin Knudsdatter	
☐ LN-TUJ	Boeing 737-705	29095/773		Eirik Blodöks	
☐ LN-TUK	Boeing 737-705	29096/794		Inge Bärdsson	
☐ LN-TUL	Boeing 737-705	29097/1072	ex N1786B	Hakon IV Hakonsson	
☐ LN-TUM	Boeing 737-705	29098/1116		Øystein Magnusson	
☐ OY-KKS	Boeing 737-683	28322/614	ex LN-RPC	Ramveig Viking	
☐ SE-DNX	Boeing 737-683	28304/270	ex G-CDRA	Torvald Viking	
☐ SE-DOR	Boeing 737-683	28305/290	ex G-CDRB	Elisabeth Viking	
☐ SE-DTH	Boeing 737-683	28313/447	ex (OY-KKI)	Vile Viking	
☐ LN-RNL	Canadair CRJ-900	15250	ex C-	Fafner Viking	
☐ OY-KFA	Canadair CRJ-900	15206	ex C-GIAW	Johan Viking	
☐ OY-KFB	Canadair CRJ-900	15211	ex C-	Alfhild Viking	
☐ OY-KFC	Canadair CRJ-900	15218	ex C-	Bertil Viking	
☐ OY-KFD	Canadair CRJ-900	15221	ex C-	Estrid Viking	
☐ OY-KFE	Canadair CRJ-900	15224	ex C-GIBH	Ingemar Viking	
☐ OY-KFF	Canadair CRJ-900	15231	ex C-GZQO	Karl Viking	
☐ OY-KFG	Canadair CRJ-900	15237	ex C-	Maria Viking	
☐ OY-KFH	Canadair CRJ-900	15240	ex C-GZQU	Ella Viking	
☐ OY-KFI	Canadair CRJ-900	15242	ex C-GIAP	Rolf Viking	
☐ OY-KFK	Canadair CRJ-900	15244	ex C-GBSZ	Hardenknud Viking	
☐ OY-KFL	Canadair CRJ-900	15246	ex C-	Regin Viking	
☐ LN-RDA	de Havilland DHC-8-402Q	4013	ex C-GDFT		[NYO]
☐ LN-RDI	de Havilland DHC-8-402Q	4024			[CPH]
☐ LN-RDJ	de Havilland DHC-8-402Q	4010	ex N480DC		[CPH]
☐ LN-RDO	de Havilland DHC-8-402Q	4036	ex C-FDHD		[CPH]
☐ LN-RDP	de Havilland DHC-8-402Q	4012	ex OY-KCA		[NYO]
☐ LN-RDT	de Havilland DHC-8-402Q	4038	ex N382BC		[NYO]
☐ LN-RNC	Fokker 50	20176	ex PH-EXY	Eivind Viking	
☐ LN-RND	Fokker 50	20178	ex PH-EXZ	Inge Viking	
☐ LN-RNE	Fokker 50	20179	ex PH-EXE	Ebbe Viking	
☐ LN-RNG	Fokker 50	20184	ex PH-EXJ	Gudrid Viking	[NWI]♦
☐ LN-RLE	McDonnell-Douglas MD-82	49382/1232		Kettil Viking	
☐ LN-RLF	McDonnell-Douglas MD-82	49383/1236	ex VH-LNJ	Finn Viking	
☐ LN-RLR	McDonnell-Douglas MD-82	49437/1345	ex VH-LNL	Vegard Viking	
☐ LN-RMK	McDonnell-Douglas MD-87	49610/1705		Ragnhild Viking	Sub>JKK
☐ LN-RML	McDonnell-Douglas MD-82	53002/1835		Aud Viking	
☐ LN-RMM	McDonnell-Douglas MD-82	53005/1855		Blenda Viking	
☐ LN-RMO	McDonnell-Douglas MD-82	53315/1947		Bergljot Viking	
☐ LN-RMR	McDonnell-Douglas MD-82	53365/1998		Olav Viking	
☐ LN-RMS	McDonnell-Douglas MD-82	53368/2003		Nial Viking	
☐ LN-RMT	McDonnell-Douglas MD-82	53001/1815	ex OY-KHS	Jarl Viking	
☐ LN-RMU	McDonnell-Douglas MD-87	53340/1967	ex SE-DMC	Grim Viking	[ARN]
☐ LN-RON	McDonnell-Douglas MD-82	53347/1979	ex SE-DMD	Holmfrid Viking	[OSL]
☐ LN-ROP	McDonnell-Douglas MD-82	49384/1237	ex SE-DFS	Bjorn Viking	
☐ LN-ROS	McDonnell-Douglas MD-82	49421/1263	ex SE-DFU	Isulv Viking	
☐ LN-ROT	McDonnell-Douglas MD-82	49422/1264	ex SE-DFR	Ingjald Viking	
☐ LN-ROU	McDonnell-Douglas MD-82	49424/1284	ex SE-DFX	Ring Viking	
☐ LN-ROW	McDonnell-Douglas MD-82	49438/1353	ex SE-DFY	Ottar Viking	[LDE]

☐ LN-ROX	McDonnell-Douglas MD-82	49603/1442	ex SE-DIA	Ulvrik Viking	
☐ OY-KGT	McDonnell-Douglas MD-82	49380/1225	ex N845RA	Hake Viking	
☐ OY-KHC	McDonnell-Douglas MD-82	49436/1303		Faste Viking	
☐ OY-KHE	McDonnell-Douglas MD-82	49604/1456	ex N842RA	Saxo Viking	Star Alliance c/s
☐ OY-KHG	McDonnell-Douglas MD-82	49613/1519		Alle Viking	
☐ OY-KHM	McDonnell-Douglas MD-82	49914/1693		Mette Viking	
☐ OY-KHN	McDonnell-Douglas MD-82	53000/1812		Dan Viking	
☐ OY-KHP	McDonnell-Douglas MD-82	53007/1882		Arild Viking	Star Alliance c/s
☐ OY-KHR	McDonnell-Douglas MD-82	53275/1896		Torkild Viking	[ARN]
☐ OY-KHU	McDonnell-Douglas MD-87	53336/1953		Ravn Viking	[MAD]♦
☐ SE-DIC	McDonnell-Douglas MD-87	49607/1512		Grane Viking	[LDE]
☐ SE-DIK	McDonnell-Douglas MD-82	49728/1553	ex (SE-DIE)	Stenkil Viking	
☐ SE-DIL	McDonnell-Douglas MD-82	49913/1665		Tord Viking	
☐ SE-DIN	McDonnell-Douglas MD-82	49999/1803		Eskil Viking	
☐ SE-DIP	McDonnell-Douglas MD-87	53010/1921	ex N6202D	Margret Viking	
☐ SE-DIR	McDonnell-Douglas MD-82	53004/1846		Nora Viking	
☐ SE-DIS	McDonnell-Douglas MD-82	53006/1869		Adis Viking	
☐ SE-DIU	McDonnell-Douglas MD-87	53011/1931		Torsten Viking	
☐ SE-DMB	McDonnell-Douglas MD-82	53314/1946		Bjarne Viking	

SKYWAYS EXPRESS	Sky Express (JZ/SKX)		Jönköping /Stockholm-Arlanda (JKG/ARN)

☐ SE-LEA	Fokker 50	20116	ex PH-GHK
☐ SE-LEC	Fokker 50	20112	ex VH-FNG
☐ SE-LED	Fokker 50	20111	ex VH-FNF
☐ SE-LEH	Fokker 50	20108	ex VH-FNC
☐ SE-LEL	Fokker 50	20110	ex VH-FNE
☐ SE-LEU	Fokker 50	20115	ex 9M-MGZ
☐ SE-LEZ	Fokker 50	20128	ex PH-PRA
☐ SE-LIO	Fokker 50	20146	ex PH-PRC
☐ SE-LIR	Fokker 50	20151	ex PH-PRE
☐ SE-LIS	Fokker 50	20152	ex PH-PRF
☐ SE-LIT	Fokker 50	20194	ex PH-ZDF

TOR AIR			

☐ SE-RJA	Boeing 737-4Q8	26302/2620	ex EI-CXM

TRANSWEDE	Transwede (5T/TWE)	Gothenburg-Landvetter (GOT)

Ceased operations 28/Feb/2010

TUIFLY NORDIC	Bluescan (6B/BLX)	Stockholm-Arlanda (ARN)

☐ SE-DZK	Boeing 737-804/W	28231/538	
☐ SE-DZN	Boeing 737-804/W	32903/1127	ex PH-AAW
☐ SE-DZV	Boeing 737-804/W	32904/1302	
☐ SE-RFO	Boeing 757-204ER/W	25623/528	ex G-BYAJ
☐ SE-RFP	Boeing 757-204/W	27219/596	ex G-BYAN
☐ SE-RFS	Boeing 767-304ER/W	28040/613	ex G-OBYB

VIKING AIRLINES	Swedjet (4P/VIK)	Athens/Heraklion (ATH/HER)

Suspended operations 14/Oct/2010

WALTAIR EUROPE	Gothic (GOT)	Norrköping (NRK)

☐ SE-KOL	Beech 300LW Super King Air	FA-189	ex N7241V	
☐ SE-LLU	Beech 300 Super King Air	FA-175	ex N1071S	♦

WEST AIR EUROPE	Air Sweden (PT/SWN)	Lidköping (LDK)

☐ SE-KXP	British Aerospace ATP (LFD)	2056	ex G-MANA	
☐ SE-LGU	British Aerospace ATP	2022	ex N853AW	
☐ SE-LGV	British Aerospace ATP	2034	ex N857AW	
☐ SE-LGX	British Aerospace ATP	2036	ex N859AW	
☐ SE-LGY	British Aerospace ATP	2035	ex N858AW	
☐ SE-LHX	British Aerospace ATP	2020	ex LX-WAN	
☐ SE-LNX	British Aerospace ATP	2061	ex OY-SVI	
☐ SE-LNY	British Aerospace ATP	2062	ex OY-SVT	Op for Posten Norge
☐ SE-LPU	British Aerospace ATP	2060	ex LX-WAM	
☐ SE-LPX	British Aerospace ATP	2063	ex OY-SVU	
☐ SE-MAF	British Aerospace ATP	2002	ex G-MAUD	
☐ SE-MAH	British Aerospace ATP	2004	ex G-MANJ	
☐ SE-MAI	British Aerospace ATP (LFD)	2010	ex G-BTPC	<Capital Bank Lsg
☐ SE-MAJ	British Aerospace ATP (LFD)	2038	ex G-BTNI	
☐ SE-MAN	British Aerospace ATP (LFD)	2006	ex G-MANO	
☐ SE-MAP	British Aerospace ATP (LFD)	2037	ex G-CORP	
☐ SE-MAR	British Aerospace ATP	2053	ex G-OBWR	

| □ SE-MEE | British Aerospace ATP | 2019 | ex CS-TGL | ♦ |
| □ SE- | British Aerospace ATP | 2031 | ex CS-TGN | ♦ |

| □ SE-DUX | Canadair CRJ-200F | 7010 | ex C-FJGI | Frtr |
| □ SE-DUY | Canadair CRJ-200F | 7023 | ex C-FJGK | Frtr |

SP-   POLAND (Republic of Poland)

AIR ITALY POLSKA		Polish Bird (4Q/AEI)		Warsaw-Okecie (WAW)
□ EI-EOJ	Boeing 737-8BK/W	33022/1672	ex LN-KHD	
□ EI-IGC	Boeing 757-230	24747/275	ex I-AIGC	

ENTER AIR				Warsaw-Okecie (WAW)
□ SP-ENA	Boeing 737-4Q8	26320/2563	ex HL7592	
□ SP-ENB	Boeing 737-4Q8	26299/2602	ex HL7527	♦
□ SP-ENC	Boeing 737-4Q8	25376/2689	ex EI-DXG	♦
□ SP-ENZ	Boeing 737-85F	28823/174	ex D-ABBM	♦
□ SP-	Boeing 737-4C9	25429/2215	ex YR-BAD	o/o♦

EUROLOT		Eurolot (K2/ELO)		Warsaw-Okecie (WAW)
□ SP-EDA	ATR 42-500	516	ex F-GPYG	
□ SP-EDE	ATR 42-500	443	ex F-WWEZ	
□ SP-EDF	ATR 42-500	559	ex D-BOOO	
□ SP-LFA	ATR 72-202	246	ex F-WWEM	
□ SP-LFB	ATR 72-202	265	ex F-WWEJ	
□ SP-LFC	ATR 72-202	272	ex F-WWEN	
□ SP-LFD	ATR 72-202	279	ex F-WWLD	
□ SP-LFE	ATR 72-202	328	ex F-WWLJ	
□ SP-LFF	ATR 72-202	402	ex F-WWLM	
□ SP-LFG	ATR 72-202	411	ex F-WWEO	
□ SP-LFH	ATR 72-202	478	ex F-WWEK	

EXIN		Exin (EXN)		Katowice-Muchoeiec (KTW)
□ SP-FDP	Antonov An-26B	11903	ex RA-26098	
□ SP-FDR	Antonov An-26B	11305	ex RA-26067	
□ SP-FDS	Antonov An-26B	12205	ex RA-26116	
□ SP-FDT	Antonov An-26B	12102	ex RA-26110	

JET AIR		Jeta (O2/JEA)		Warsaw-Okecie (WAW)
□ SP-KTR	ATR 42-300	092	ex D-BAAA	
□ SP-KWD	British Aerospace Jetstream 3202	847	ex G-BYRM	op for LOT
□ SP-KWE	British Aerospace Jetstream 3201	842	ex G-CBCS	op for LOT
□ SP-KWF	British Aerospace Jetstream 3201	845	ex G-BYRA	op for LOT
□ SP-KWN	British Aerospace Jetstream 3201	856	ex LN-FAC	

LOT - POLISH AIRLINES		LOT (LO/LOT)		Warsaw-Okecie (WAW)

Member of Star Alliance

□ SP-LKC	Boeing 737-55D	27418/2397		
□ SP-LKD	Boeing 737-55D	27419/2401		
□ SP-LKE	Boeing 737-55D	27130/2448	Star Alliance c/s	
□ SP-LKF	Boeing 737-55D	27368/2603		
□ SP-LLA	Boeing 737-45D	27131/2458		
□ SP-LLB	Boeing 737-45D	27156/2492	ex UR-VVH	
□ SP-LLC	Boeing 737-45D	27157/2502		
□ SP-LLE	Boeing 737-45D	27914/2804		
□ SP-LLF	Boeing 737-45D	28752/2874		
□ SP-LLG	Boeing 737-45D	28753/2895	ex SX-BGN	
□ SP-LLK	Boeing 737-4Q8	25740/2461	ex EI-CZG	
□ SP-LLL	Boeing 737-4Q8	25164/2447	ex EI-CXJ	LOT Charter titles
□ SP-LPA	Boeing 767-35DER	24865/322	Warszawa	
□ SP-LPB	Boeing 767-35DER	27902/577	Gdansk	
□ SP-LPC	Boeing 767-35DER	28656/659	Poznan	
□ SP-LPE	Boeing 767-341ER	24843/314	ex N483TC	Star Alliance c/s
□ SP-LPF	Boeing 767-319ER	24876/413	ex ZK-NCF	>AEA
□ SP-LPG	Boeing 767-306ER	26263/592	ex N261LF	
□ SP-	Boeing 787-8			o/o♦
□ SP-	Boeing 787-8			o/o♦

☐ SP-	Boeing 787-8				o/o♦

☐ SP-LGE	Embraer ERJ-145MP	145285	ex PT-SKC		
☐ SP-LGF	Embraer ERJ-145MP	145308	ex PT-SKZ		
☐ SP-LGG	Embraer ERJ-145MP	145319	ex PT-SMK		
☐ SP-LGH	Embraer ERJ-145MP	145329	ex PT-SMV		
☐ SP-LGO	Embraer ERJ-145MP	145560	ex PT-SZV	Pomocy logo	

☐ SP-LDA	Embraer ERJ-170STD	17000023	ex PT-SKQ		
☐ SP-LDB	Embraer ERJ-170STD	17000024	ex PT-SKR		
☐ SP-LDC	Embraer ERJ-170STD	17000025	ex PT-SKS	Star Alliance c/s	
☐ SP-LDD	Embraer ERJ-170STD	17000027	ex PT-SKU		
☐ SP-LDE	Embraer ERJ-170LR	17000029	ex PT-SKW		
☐ SP-LDF	Embraer ERJ-170LR	17000035	ex PT-SUE		
☐ SP-LDG	Embraer ERJ-170LR	17000065	ex PT-SVQ		
☐ SP-LDH	Embraer ERJ-170LR	17000069	ex PT-SVU		
☐ SP-LDI	Embraer ERJ-170LR	17000073	ex PT-SVY		
☐ SP-LDK	Embraer ERJ-170LR	17000074	ex PT-SVZ		

☐ SP-LIA	Embraer ERJ-175LR	17000125	ex PT-SDO		
☐ SP-LIB	Embraer ERJ-175LR	17000132	ex PT-SDV		
☐ SP-LIC	Embraer ERJ-175LR	17000134	ex PT-SDX		
☐ SP-LID	Embraer ERJ-175LR	17000136	ex PT-SDZ		
☐ SP-LIE	Embraer ERJ-175LR	17000153	ex EI-DVW		
☐ SP-LIF	Embraer ERJ-175LR	17000154	ex EI-DVV		
☐ SP-LIG	Embraer ERJ-175LR	17000283	ex PT-TQJ		
☐ SP-LIH	Embraer ERJ-175LR	17000288	ex PT-TQO		
☐ SP-LII	Embraer ERJ-175LR	17000290	ex PT-TQQ		
☐ SP-LIK	Embraer ERJ-175LR	17000303	ex PT-XQC		
☐ SP-LIL	Embraer ERJ-175LR	17000306	ex PT-XQF		♦
☐ SP-LIM	Embraer ERJ-175LR	17000311	ex PT-XQY		♦
☐ SP-LIN	Embraer ERJ-175LR	17000313	ex PT-XUH		♦
☐ SP-LIO	Embraer ERJ-175LR	17000321	ex PT-XUP		♦

☐ SP-	Embraer ERJ-195LR		ex PT-		o/o♦
☐ SP-	Embraer ERJ-195LR		ex PT-		o/o♦
☐ SP-	Embraer ERJ-195LR		ex PT-		o/o♦

SKY TAXI — Iguana (IGA) — Wroclaw (WRO)

| ☐ SP-MRB | SAAB SF.340A (QC) | 340A-100 | ex OE-GIF | all white |
| ☐ SP-MRC | SAAB SF.340A | 340A-143 | ex EC-IRR | |

SPRINT AIR — (SXP) — Warsaw-Okecie (WAW)

☐ SP-KPE	SAAB SF.340A (QC)	340A-130	ex SE-ISL	
☐ SP-KPF	SAAB SF.340A (QC)	340A-135	ex SE-KCU	
☐ SP-KPG	SAAB SF.340A (QC)	340A-065	ex SE-KCR	
☐ SP-KPH	SAAB SF.340A (QC)	340A-015	ex SE-ISP	Op for Farnair
☐ SP-KPK	SAAB SF.340AF	340A-026	ex VH-ZLY	
☐ SP-KPL	SAAB SF.340A	340A-038	ex VH-ZRX	
☐ SP-KPN	SAAB SF.340A	340A-118	ex SE-F18	
☐ SP-KPO	SAAB SF.340A (QC)	340A-010	ex SE-LTI	
☐ SP-KPR	SAAB SF.340A (QC)	340A-139	ex OH-FAE	
☐ SP-KPU	SAAB SF.340AF	340A-145	ex SE-ISD	
☐ SP-KPV	SAAB SF.340A	340A-071	ex SE-LGS	>Direct Fly

WHITE EAGLE GENERAL AVIATION — White Eagle (WEA) — Warsaw-Okecie (WAW)

☐ SP-FES	Mil Mi-8T	99150472	ex UR-25603	
☐ SP-FNS	Beech B300 Super King Air	FL-134	ex N3252V	
☐ SP-KCA	ATR 42-300	085	ex F-WQNY	Frtr

ST- SUDAN (Republic of the Sudan)

ABABEEL AVIATION — Khartoum (KRT)

☐ EX-036	Ilyushin Il-76TD	0093495863	ex RA-76785		<CKW
☐ ST-ARL	Antonov An-26	2606	ex EK-13399		
☐ ST-AWT	Antonov An-26				
☐ ST-WTS	Antonov An-74-200	36547098960	ex UR-74057		

AIR TAXI & CARGO — (WAM) — Khartoum (KRT)

| ☐ ST-TKO | Antonov An-32B | 3110 | ex ER-AWL | Deena | <PXA |

508

AIR WEST CARGO (AWZ) Sharjah (SHJ)

☐ ST-AWH	WSK-PZL/Antonov An-28	1AJ004-07	ex ER-AJH	
☐ ST-AWN	WSK-PZL/Antonov An-28	1AJ004-06	ex ER-AIP	
☐ ST-AWR	Ilyushin Il-76TD	0033447365	ex RDPL-11308	[FJR]
☐ ST-EWC	Ilyushin Il-76TD	0023438129	ex EX-86919	
☐ ST-EWD	Ilyushin Il-76TD	0063466989	ex UR-CAP	
☐ ST-EWX	Ilyushin Il-76TD	1013409282	ex UN-76810	

ALMAJARA AVIATION (MJA)

☐ ST-ATH	Ilyushin Il-76MD	0063472158	ex EK-76705

AYR AVIATION

☐ ST-SMZ	Antonov An-32	3205	ex ER-AFI	AMIS titles

AZZA AIR TRANSPORT Azza Transport (AZZ) Khartoum (KRT)

☐ ST-APS	Ilyushin Il-76TD	1023409316	ex RA-76837	
☐ ST-ARV	Antonov An-12BP	8345310	ex EK-11028	status?
☐ ST-ASA	Antonov An-12	402010	ex RA-11374	
☐ ST-AZN	Antonov An-12	9346808	ex UR-CFC	
☐ ST-AZZ	Ilyushin Il-76TD	1023408265	ex XT-FCB	
☐ ST-DAS	Antonov An-12	7345209	ex ER-AXC	
☐ ST-JAC	Antonov An-26B-100	10203	ex EX-003	
☐ ST-JCC	Boeing 707-384C (Comtran 2)	18948/495	ex P4-JCC	[KRT]

BADR AIRLINES Badr Air (BDR) Khartoum (KRT)

☐ ST-BDE	Ilyushin Il-76TD	1013408252	ex RA-76809	
☐ ST-BDK	Antonov An-72-100	36572060642	ex 4L-SAS	AMIS titles
☐ ST-BDN	Ilyushin Il-76TD	1023413443	ex UK 76448	
☐ ST-BDR	Antonov An-74			
☐ ST-BDT	Antonov An-74	36547097935	ex RA-74046	AMIS titles
☐ ST-BDX	Antonov An-74-200	36547096924	ex RA-7401	AMIS titles
☐ ST-SAL	Antonov An-26B	17311907	ex RA-26100	

BENTIU AIR TRANSPORT Bentiu Air (BNT) Sharjah/Khartoum (SHJ/KRT)

☐ ST-NDC	Antonov An-26	17310908	ex RA-26052
☐ ST-SRA	Antonov An-26	17311807	ex RA-08827

BLUE BIRD AIRLINES Khartoum (KRT)

☐ ST-AFP	de Havilland DHC-6 Twin Otter 300	479	ex C-GDUN-X
☐ ST-AHV	de Havilland DHC-6 Twin Otter 300	765	
☐ ZS-TIL	Beech 1900D	UE-21	ex 5Y-RAE

EL MAGAL AVIATION El Magal (MGG) Khartoum (KRT)

☐ ST-APJ	Antonov An-12BP	2400701	ex RA-11308	
☐ ST-EIB	Antonov An-32B	2903	ex D2-FAP	
☐ ST-ISG	WSK-PZL/Antonov An-28	1AJ005-01	ex EK-28501	
☐ ST-MGD	Ilyushin Il-76TD	1013407230	ex RA-76812	
☐ ST-NSP	Antonov An-32	2109	ex ER-AZW	
☐ S9-PSE	Antonov An-32	2803	ex UR-48053	<GLE

FEEDER AIRLINES (FDD)

☐ ST-NEW	Fokker 50	20138	ex PH-PRB

FORTY EIGHT AVIATION

☐ ST-OHO	Ilyushin Il-62M	1052128	ex UP-I6203	♦

IMAATONG SOUTH SUDAN AIRLINES

☐ 5Y-BTD	Fokker F.27 Friendship 300M	10154	ex TR-LGH	[WIL]

JET Khartoum (KRT)

☐ ST-AWH	WSK/PZL Antonov An-28	1AJ004-07	ex ER-AJH	also reported as operated by TFT

KATA TRANSPORTATION COMPANY Khartoum (KRT)

☐ ST-AZM	Antonov An-12BK	00346907	ex 05 red
☐ ST-HIS	Antonov An-26B	07310310	ex UN-26026

MARSLAND AVIATION		Marslandair (M7/MSL)		Khartoum (KRT)
☐ ST-ARJ	Antonov An-26	5602	ex ER-AZC	
☐ ST-ARP	Antonov An-24RV	37308809	ex EK-46630	
☐ ST-MRL	Yakovlev Yak-42	4520424116690	ex UN-42703	
☐ ST-MRS	Tupolev Tu-134B-3	63333	ex YL-LBG	[FJR]

MID AIRLINES Nile		(7Y/NYL)		Khartoum (KRT)
☐ ST-ARG	Fokker 50	20130	ex LN-BBA	
☐ ST-ARH	Fokker 50	20131	ex LN-BBB	
☐ ST-ARZ	Fokker 50	20134	ex LN-BBC	

NOVA AIRLINES				Khartoum (KRT)
☐ ST-NVA	Fokker F.27 Mk.050 (Fokker 50)	20227	ex PK-AIY	[MST]
☐ ST-NVB	Canadair CRJ-200ER	7807	ex HA-LND	
☐ ST-NVC	Canadair CRJ-200ER	7686	ex HA-LNB	

SACSO AIR LINES				Khartoum (KRT)
☐ ST-ARJ	Antonov An-26	77305602		
☐ ST-ARQ	Antonov An-24B	07305910	ex ST-RAS	

SUDAN AIRWAYS		Sudanair (SD/SUD)		Khartoum (KRT)
☐ ST-ASD	Fokker 50	20201	ex PH-PRI	
☐ ST-ASF	Fokker 50	20155	ex PH-PRG	
☐ ST-ASI	Fokker 50	20247	ex G-UKTB	
☐ ST-ASJ	Fokker 50	20246	ex G-UKTA	
☐ ST-ASO	Fokker 50	20256	ex G-UKTD	
☐ ST-AFA	Boeing 707-3J8C	20897/885	Blue Nile	
☐ ST-ASS	Airbus A300B4-622	252	ex F-ODTK	[CHR]
☐ ST-AST	Airbus A310-322	437	ex SU-BOW	
☐ ST-ATA	Airbus A300B4-622R	775	ex TF-ELC Alqaswa	<ABD
☐ ST-ATB	Airbus A300B4-622R	666	ex TF-ELB Elburag	
☐ D6-CAS	Airbus A320-214	3040	ex EC-KAX	<Comores Isl AW

SUDANESE STATES AVIATION				Khartoum (KRT)
☐ ST-AQW	Boeing 707-336C	20517/854	ex 3D-GFG	[KRT]♦

SUN AIR		(AWZ)		Khartoum (KRT)
☐ ST-SDA	Boeing 737-2T4	23274/1099	ex B-2508	>Nova Air
☐ ST-SDB	Boeing 737-2T4	23273/1097	ex B-2507	>MSL

TRANS ATTICO		Tranattico Sudan (ML/ETC)		Khartoum / Sharjah (KRT/SHJ)
☐ ET-AKZ	de Havilland DHC-8-202	469	ex C-GLOT	<TNW
☐ ST-AQM	Antonov An-26	1404	ex RA-48099 no titles	
☐ ST-AQR	Ilyushin Il-76TD	0043453575	ex 9L-LCX	
☐ ST-AQU	Antonov An-32B	2009	ex RA-69344	
☐ ST-ASX	Ilyushin Il-76	0073479392	ex 5A-DMQ	
☐ ST-CAT	LET L-410UVP-E	902527	ex SP-FGM	
☐ ST-CAU	LET L-410UVP-E	892340	ex RA-67612	

SU- EGYPT (Arab Republic of Egypt)

AIR ARABIA EGYPT				Alexandria (ALY)
☐ SU-AAA	Airbus A320-214	2764	ex A6-ABF	♦
☐ SU-AAB	Airbus A320-214	3152	ex A6-ABN	♦

AIR CAIRO		(MSC)		Cairo-Intl (CAI)
☐ SU-BPU	Airbus A320-214	2937	ex F-WWIJ	
☐ SU-BPV	Airbus A320-214	2966	ex F-WWDC	
☐ SU-BPW	Airbus A320-214	3282	ex F-WWDP	
☐ SU-BPX	Airbus A320-214	3323	ex F-WWBE	

AIR MEMPHIS		Air Memphis (MHS)		Cairo-Intl (CAI)
☐ SU-BME	McDonnell-Douglas MD-83	49628/1582	ex F-GRML	
☐ SU-PBG	Airbus A320-233	1353	ex N464TA	
☐ SU-PBH	Airbus A320-233	1300	ex N461TA	

☐ SU-PBO	Douglas DC-9-31 (ABS 3)	48131/940	ex N928VJ		
☐ SU-YAH	Fokker 50	20123	ex PH-FZJ		♦
☐ SU-YAI	Fokker 50	20143	ex PH-FZI		♦

| *AIR SINAI* | | *Air Sinai (4D/ASD)* | | | *Cairo-Intl (CAI)* |

A wholly owned subsidiary of Egyptair; operates services with aircraft leased from the parent

| *ALEXANDRIA AIRLINES* | | *(ZR/KHH)* | | | *Alexandria* |

| ☐ SU-KHM | Boeing 737-5C9 | 26438/2413 | ex JY-JA1 | | <JAV |

| *ALMASRIA UNIVERSAL AIRLINES* | | *AMC (UJ/LMU)* | | | *Cairo-Intl (CAI)* |

☐ SU-TCA	Airbus A320-232	0932	ex VT-ADX		
☐ SU-TCB	Airbus A320-232	0943	ex VT-ADY		

| *AMC AIRLINES* | | *AMC (YJ/AMV)* | | | *Cairo-Intl (CAI)* |

☐ SU-AYK	Boeing 737-266	21194/455			[CAI]
☐ SU-BOZ	McDonnell-Douglas MD-83	53192/2155	ex N192AJ		>Sham Wings
☐ SU-BPG	Boeing 737-86N/W	32669/1895			
☐ SU-BPZ	Boeing 737-86N/W	35213/2300			
☐ SU-BQA	Boeing 737-86N/W	35220/2406			

| *CAIRO AVIATION* | | *Cairo Air (CCE)* | | | *Cairo-Intl (CAI)* |

☐ SU-EAF	Tupolev Tu-204-120	1450742764027	ex RA-64027		
☐ SU-EAG	Tupolev Tu-204-120S	1450744764028	ex RA-64028 TNT c/s		[CAI]
☐ SU-EAH	Tupolev Tu-204-120	1450744864023			[CAI]
☐ SU-EAI	Tupolev Tu-204-120	1450744964025			
☐ SU-EAJ	Tupolev Tu-204-120S	1450742264029	ex RA-64029 TNT c/s		[CAI]

| *EGYPTAIR* | | *Egyptair (MS/MSR)* | | | *Cairo-Intl (CAI)* |

Member of Star Alliance

☐ SU-BDG	Airbus A300B4-203F	200	ex F-WZMN	Toshki	
☐ SU-GAC	Airbus A300B4-203F	255	ex F-WZMY	New Valley	
☐ SU-GAS	Airbus A300B4-622RF	561	ex F-WWAN	Cheops	
☐ SU-GAY	Airbus A300B4-622RF	607	ex F-WWAB	Seti 1	

☐ SU-GBA	Airbus A320-231	0165	ex F-WWDV	Aswan	
☐ SU-GBB	Airbus A320-231	0166	ex F-WWID	Luxor	
☐ SU-GBC	Airbus A320-231	0178	ex F-WWIQ	Hurghada	
☐ SU-GBD	Airbus A320-231	0194	ex F-WWIZ	Taba	
☐ SU-GBE	Airbus A320-231	0198	ex F-WWDG	El Alamein	
☐ SU-GBF	Airbus A320-231	0351	ex F-WWDM	Sharm El Sheikh	
☐ SU-GBG	Airbus A320-231	0366	ex F-WWDD	Saint Catherine	
☐ SU-GBZ	Airbus A320-232	2070	ex F-WWDJ		
☐ SU-GCA	Airbus A320-232	2073	ex F-WWIO		
☐ SU-GCB	Airbus A320-232	2079	ex F-WWDV		
☐ SU-GCC	Airbus A320-232	2088	ex F-WWBH		
☐ SU-GCD	Airbus A320-232	2094	ex F-WWBX		
☐ SU-GCL	Airbus A320-231	0322	ex SU-RAA		

☐ SU-GBT	Airbus A321-231	0680	ex D-AVZB	Red Sea	
☐ SU-GBU	Airbus A321-231	0687	ex D-AVZR	Sinai	
☐ SU-GBV	Airbus A321-231	0715	ex D-AVZX	Mediterranean	
☐ SU-GBW	Airbus A321-231	0725	ex D-AVZA	The Nileno titles	

☐ SU-GCE	Airbus A330-243	600	ex F-WWYK		
☐ SU-GCF	Airbus A330-243	610	ex F-WWKS		
☐ SU-GCG	Airbus A330-243	666	ex F-WWKQ		
☐ SU-GCH	Airbus A330-243	683	ex F-WWYF		
☐ SU-GCI	Airbus A330-243	696	ex F-WWYR		
☐ SU-GCJ	Airbus A330-243	709	ex F-WWKK		
☐ SU-GCK	Airbus A330-243	726	ex F-WWKP		
☐ SU-GDS	Airbus A330-343X	1143	ex F-WWKQ		♦
☐ SU-	Airbus A330-343X		ex F-		o/o♦
☐ SU-	Airbus A330-343X		ex F-		o/o♦
☐ SU-	Airbus A330-343X		ex F-		o/o♦
☐ SU-	Airbus A330-343X		ex F-		o/o♦

☐ SU-GBM	Airbus A340-212	156	ex F-WWJK	Osiris Express	
☐ SU-GBN	Airbus A340-212	159	ex F-WWJV	Cleo Express	
☐ SU-GBO	Airbus A340-212	178	ex F-WWJD	Hathor Express	

☐ SU-GBH	Boeing 737-566	25084/2019	Karnakno titles	
☐ SU-GBJ	Boeing 737-566	25352/2169	Philae	
☐ SU-GBK	Boeing 737-566	26052/2276	Kalabshano titles	
☐ SU-GBL	Boeing 737-566	26051/2282	Ramesseum	
☐ SU-GCM	Boeing 737-866/W	35558/2054		
☐ SU-GCN	Boeing 737-866/W	35559/2113	ex N1795B	
☐ SU-GCO	Boeing 737-866/W	35561/2369	ex N1795B	
☐ SU-GCP	Boeing 737-866/W	35560/2434	ex N1786B	
☐ SU-GCR	Boeing 737-866/W	35562/2826	ex N1786B	
☐ SU-GCS	Boeing 737-866/W	35563/2695		
☐ SU-GCZ	Boeing 737-866/W	35568/2795		
☐ SU-GDA	Boeing 737-866/W	35565/2999	ex N1796B	
☐ SU-GDB	Boeing 737-866/W	35567/3017	ex N1786B	
☐ SU-GDC	Boeing 737-866/W	35564/3040	ex N1779B	
☐ SU-GDD	Boeing 737-866/W	35566/3061		
☐ SU-GDE	Boeing 737-866/W	35569/3043	ex N1786B	
☐ SU-GDX	Boeing 737-866/W	40757/3409	ex N1786B	♦
☐ SU-GDY	Boeing 737-866/W	40758/3442		♦
☐ SU-GDZ	Boeing 737-866/W	40759/3472		♦
☐ SU-GEA	Boeing 737-866/W	40760/3492	ex N1786B	♦
☐ SU-	Boeing 737-866/W			o/o♦
☐ SU-	Boeing 737-866/W			o/o♦
☐ SU-GBP	Boeing 777-266	28423/71	Nefertiti	
☐ SU-GBR	Boeing 777-266	28424/80	Nefertari	
☐ SU-GBS	Boeing 777-266	28425/85	Tiye	
☐ SU-GBX	Boeing 777-266ER	32629/362	Neit	
☐ SU-GBY	Boeing 777-266ER	32630/368		
☐ SU-GDL	Boeing 777-36NER	38284850		
☐ SU-GDM	Boeing 777-36NER	38285/862		♦
☐ SU-GDN	Boeing 777-36NER	38288/896		♦
☐ SU-GDO	Boeing 777-36NER	38289/907	ex N5023Q	♦
☐ SU-	Boeing 777-36NER			o/o♦

EGYPTAIR EXPRESS (MSE) Cairo-Intl (CAI)

☐ SU-GCT	Embraer ERJ-170LR	17000167	ex PT-SMJ
☐ SU-GCU	Embraer ERJ-170LR	17000169	ex PT-SML
☐ SU-GCV	Embraer ERJ-170LR	17000170	ex PT-SMM
☐ SU-GCW	Embraer ERJ-170LR	17000175	ex PT-SMR
☐ SU-GCX	Embraer ERJ-170LR	17000178	ex PT-SMV
☐ SU-GCY	Embraer ERJ-170LR	17000185	ex PT-SUC
☐ SU-GDF	Embraer ERJ-170LR	17000266	ex PT-SJU
☐ SU-GDG	Embraer ERJ-170LR	17000269	ex PT-SJZ
☐ SU-GDH	Embraer ERJ-170LR	17000274	ex PT-TQA
☐ SU-GDI	Embraer ERJ-170LR	17000276	ex PT-TQC
☐ SU-GDJ	Embraer ERJ-170LR	17000282	ex PT-TQI
☐ SU-GDK	Embraer ERJ-170LR	17000284	ex PT-TQK

FAST LINK Cairo Intl (CAI)

☐ SU-FLE	SAAB SF.340A	340A-146	ex N146SD

KORAL BLUE (KBR) Sharm el Sheikh (SSH)

☐ SU-KBA	Airbus A320-212	0937	ex SU-LBC	
☐ SU-KBB	Airbus A319-112	3171	ex EI-EAF	
☐ SU-KBC	Airbus A320-214	2123	ex EI-EDO	
☐ SU-KBD	Airbus A320-214	1597	ex TS-INP	
☐ SU-KBE	Airbus A320-214	1454	ex EC-HQK	♦

LOTUS AIR Lotus Flower (TAS) Cairo-Intl (CAI)

☐ SU-LBG	Airbus A320-233	0743	ex 9V-VLD
☐ SU-LBH	Airbus A320-233	0739	ex 9V-VLC
☐ SU-LBI	Airbus A320-232	0667	ex OE-LOF
☐ SU-LBJ	Airbus A320-214	1054	ex TC-JLG

MIDWEST AIRLINES EGYPT (MY/MWA) Cairo-Intl (CAI)

☐ SU-MWD	Boeing 737-86N/W	28591/233	ex N112MN	♦
☐ SU-MWE	Boeing 737-8Q8/W	30040/1693	ex G-DLCH	♦
☐ SU-MWF	Boeing 737-8Q8/W	32841/1705	ex EI-EOP	♦

NESMA AIR

☐ SU-NMA	Airbus A320-232	1697	ex G-MIDR	♦

512

NILE AIR		**(NIA)**	

☐ SU-BQB	Airbus A320-232	3183	ex N621SA
☐ SU-BQC	Airbus A320-232	3219	ex N623SA

PETROLEUM AIR SERVICES		**Al Arish / Hurghada (AAC/HRG)**

☐ SU-CAC	Bell 206L-3 LongRanger III	51004	
☐ SU-CAE	Bell 206L-3 LongRanger III	51030	
☐ SU-CAF	Bell 206L-3 LongRanger III	51031	
☐ SU-CAG	Bell 206B JetRanger III	3574	
☐ SU-CAH	Bell 206B JetRanger III	3581	
☐ SU-CAI	Bell 206L-3 LongRanger III	51018	
☐ SU-CAB	Bell 212	31223	
☐ SU-CAJ	Bell 212	31247	
☐ SU-CAL	Bell 212	31215	ex N3889A
☐ SU-CAM	Bell 212	31249	
☐ SU-CAN	Bell 212	31250	
☐ SU-CAO	Bell 212	31260	
☐ SU-CAQ	Bell 212	31262	
☐ SU-CAR	Bell 212	31263	
☐ SU-CAS	Bell 212	31264	
☐ SU-CAU	Bell 212	35036	
☐ SU-CAV	Bell 412HP	36037	ex XA-TNO
☐ SU-CAX	Bell 412HP	36081	ex N2156S
☐ SU-CAY	Bell 412EP	36158	ex N6489P
☐ SU-CAZ	Bell 412EP	36184	ex N55248
☐ SU-CBI	Bell 412EP	36353	ex C-FCSC
☐ SU-CBL	Bell 412EP	36377	ex C-FENJ
☐ SU-CBM	Bell 412EP	36379	ex C-FEON
☐ SU-CBO	Bell 412EP	36410	ex C-FIRW
☐ SU-CBR	Bell 412EP	36432	ex C-FMQV
☐ SU-CBS	Bell 412EP	36468	ex C-FTCJ
☐ SU-CBT	Bell 412EP	36492	ex C-FVDY
☐ SU-CBA	de Havilland DHC-7-102	93	ex C-GFYI
☐ SU-CBB	de Havilland DHC-7-102	96	ex C-GEWQ [CAI]
☐ SU-CBC	de Havilland DHC-7-102	97	ex C-GFQL
☐ SU-CBD	de Havilland DHC-7-102	98	ex C-GEWQ
☐ SU-CBE	de Havilland DHC-7-102	99	ex C-GFBW
☐ SU-CBF	de Havilland DHC-8Q-315	584	ex C-FDHX
☐ SU-CBG	de Havilland DHC-8Q-315	585	ex C-FDHY
☐ SU-CBH	de Havilland DHC-8Q-315	594	ex C-FPJH
☐ SU-CBJ	de Havilland DHC-8Q-315	607	ex C-FBNT
☐ SU-CBN	de Havilland DHC-8Q-315	632	ex C-FIOY
☐ SU-CBP	Eurocopter EC135P2+	0604	
☐ SU-CBQ	Eurocopter EC135P2+	0607	

TRISTAR AIR		**Triple Star (TSY)**	**Cairo-Intl (CAI)**

☐ SU-BMZ	Airbus A300B4-203F	129	ex N825SC

SX-   GREECE (Hellenic Republic)

AEGEAN AIRLINES	**Aegean (A3/AEE)**	**Athens-Eleftherios Venizelos Intl (ATH)**

☐ SX-DGB	Airbus A320-232	4165	ex F-WWBX	
☐ SX-	Airbus A320-232		ex	o/o
☐ SX-	Airbus A320-232		ex	o/o
☐ SX-	Airbus A320-232		ex	o/o
☐ SX-	Airbus A320-232		ex	o/o
☐ SX-	Airbus A320-232		ex	o/o
☐ SX-DVG	Airbus A320-232	3033	ex F-WWBX	Eethos
☐ SX-DVH	Airbus A320-232	3066	ex F-WWIF	Nostos
☐ SX-DVI	Airbus A320-232	3074	ex F-WWIO	Kinesis
☐ SX-DVJ	Airbus A320-232	3365	ex F-WWIS	Exelixis
☐ SX-DVK	Airbus A320-232	3392	ex F-WWDS	
☐ SX-DVL	Airbus A320-232	3423	ex F-WWIV	
☐ SX-DVM	Airbus A320-232	3439	ex F-WWDY	
☐ SX-DVN	Airbus A320-232	3478	ex F-WWDI	
☐ SX-DVQ	Airbus A320-232	3526	ex F-WWDU	

□ SX-DVR	Airbus A320-232	3714	ex D-AVVB	
□ SX-DVS	Airbus A320-232	3709	ex F-WWIT	
□ SX-DVT	Airbus A320-232	3745	ex F-WWIJ	
□ SX-DVU	Airbus A320-232	3753	ex F-WWBS	
□ SX-DVV	Airbus A320-232	3773	ex F-WWDT	
□ SX-DVW	Airbus A320-232	3785	ex F-WWIU	
□ SX-DVX	Airbus A320-232	3829	ex F-WWIZ	
□ SX-DVY	Airbus A320-232	3850	ex F-WWDG	
□ SX-DGA	Airbus A321-231	3878	ex D-AVZP	
□ SX-DVO	Airbus A321-231	3462	ex D-AVZU	Philoxenia
□ SX-DVP	Airbus A321-231	3527	ex D-AVZZ	
□ SX-DVZ	Airbus A321-231	3820	ex D-AVZF	
□ SX-DVA	Avro 146-RJ100	E3341	ex G-6-341	
□ SX-DVB	Avro 146-RJ100	E3343	ex G-6-343	
□ SX-DVC	Avro 146-RJ100	E3358	ex G-6-358	
□ SX-DVD	Avro 146-RJ100	E3362	ex G-6-362	
□ EC-KVI	ATR 72-212A	824	ex F-WWEM	<SWT

AEROLAND AIRWAYS (3S/AEN) Athens-Eleftherios Venizelos Intl (ATH)

□ SX-ARU	Cessna 208B Caravan I	208B1146	ex N1293Z	Isle of Tinos
□ SX-ARW	Cessna 208B Caravan I	208B1174	ex N13080	Isle of Chios
□ SX-ARX	Cessna 208B Caravan I	208B1182	ex N1300G	Isle of Lesvos
□ SX-ARY	Cessna 208B Caravan I	208B1301	ex N2028N	Isle of Paros
□ SX-BVE	de Havilland DHC-8-106	351	ex C-FRIY	Island of Mykonos

ASTRA AIRLINES (A2)

□ SX-DIX	British Aerospace 146 Srs.300	E3193	ex I-ADJF	
□ SX-DIZ	British Aerospace 146 Srs.300	E3206	ex G-JEBE	

AVIATOR AIRWAYS Aviator (AVW) Athens-Eleftherios Venizelos Intl (ATH)

□ SX-APJ	Beech 200 Super King Air	BB-401	ex OY-JAO	
□ SX-BSR	British Aerospace Jetstream 31	718	ex G-OAKI	

BLUEBIRD AIRWAYS

□ SX-DAV	Boeing 737-4Q8	24704/1855	ex N744VA	♦

EPSILON AVIATION Night Rider (GRV) Athens-Eleftherios Venizelos Intl (ATH)

□ SX-BMM	Swearingen SA.227AC Metro III	BC-774B	ex N774MW	Mike
□ SX-BNN	Swearingen SA.227AC Metro III	BC-771B	ex N771MW	Nick

EUROAIR Eurostar (6I/EUP) Athens-Eleftherios Venizelos Intl (ATH)

□ SX-APP	Piper PA-31-350 Chieftain	31-8152171	ex N4093G	
□ SX-BFL	Piper PA-31-350 Chieftain	31-7952171	ex N64TT	
□ SX-BMS	Piper PA-31-350 Navajo Chieftain	31-7752122	ex HP-1049PS	

GAINJET Athens-Eleftherios Venizelos Intl (ATH)

□ SX-RFA	Boeing 757-23N/W	30232/888	ex EI-LTO	

HELLAS JET Hellas Jet (HJ/HEJ) Athens-Eleftherios Venizelos Intl (ATH)

□ SX-BVL	Airbus A320-212	0087	ex N5015G	Pegasus

HELLENIC IMPERIAL AIRWAYS (IMP) Athens-Eleftherios Venizelos Intl (ATH)

□ SX-TIB	Boeing 747-230B	23622/665	ex JY-AUB	
□ SX-TIC	Boeing 747-281B	23501/648	ex AP-BIC	
□ SX-TID	Boeing 747-281B	23502/649	ex (SX-DID)	
□ SX-TIE	Boeing 747-230M	23509/663	ex 5T-AUE	<UVS

OLYMPIC AIRLINES Olympic (OA/OAL) Athens-Eleftherios Venizelos Intl (ATH)

□ SX-OAF	Airbus A319-111	3895	ex D-AHIP	
□ SX-OAG	Airbus A319-112	3950	ex D-AHIQ	
□ SX-OAJ	Airbus A319-112	3905	ex D-AVWS	
□ SX-OAN	Airbus A319-133	1727	ex D-APAC	
□ SX-OAO	Airbus A319-133	1880	ex D-APAD	
□ SX-OAH	Airbus A320-232	3316	ex VT-DNV	
□ SX-OAI	Airbus A320-232	3162	ex VT-DNY	

☐ SX-OAM	Airbus A320-232	3990	ex F-WWBY		
☐ SX-OAP	Airbus A320-232	4065	ex D-AVVL		
☐ SX-OAQ	Airbus A320-232	3748	ex F-WWBQ		
☐ SX-OAR	Airbus A320-232	3812	ex D-AVVE		
☐ SX-OAS	Airbus A320-232	4094	ex D-AVVB		
☐ SX-OAT	Airbus A320-232	4190	ex F-WWII		
☐ SX-OAU	Airbus A320-232	4193	ex F-WWIJ		
☐ SX-BIO	de Havilland DHC-8-102	330	ex C-GZQZ	Katerina Thanou	
☐ SX-BIP	de Havilland DHC-8-102	347	ex C-GZRA	Voula Patoulidou	
☐ SX-BIQ	de Havilland DHC-8-102	361	ex C-GZRD	Kahi Kahiasvili	
☐ SX-BIR	de Havilland DHC-8-102	364	ex C-GZRF	Kostas Kenteris	
☐ SX-BIW	de Havilland DHC-8-102	289	ex OE-HWG		
☐ SX-BIT	de Havilland DHC-8-402Q	4148	ex G-JECV		
☐ SX-BIU	de Havilland DHC-8-402Q	4152	ex G-JECW		
☐ SX-OBA	de Havilland DHC-8-402Q	4267	ex G-PTHA		
☐ SX-OBB	de Havilland DHC-8-402Q	4268	ex G-PTHB		
☐ SX-OBC	de Havilland DHC-8-402Q	4276	ex G-PTHC		
☐ SX-OBD	de Havilland DHC-8-402Q	4311	ex G-PTHD		♦
☐ SX-OBE	de Havilland DHC-8-402Q	4314	ex G-PTHE		♦
☐ SX-OBF	de Havilland DHC-8-402Q	4318	ex G-PTHF		♦
☐ SX-OBG	de Havilland DHC-8-402Q	4321	ex G-PTHG		♦
☐ SX-OBH	de Havilland DHC-8-402Q	4327	ex G-PTHH		♦
☐ SX-DFA	Airbus A340-313X	235	ex F-WWJN	Olympia	[ATH]
☐ SX-DFB	Airbus A340-313X	239	ex F-WWJC	Delphi	[ATH]
☐ SX-DFC	Airbus A340-313X	280	ex F-WWJJ	Marathon	[ATH]
☐ SX-DFD	Airbus A340-313X	292	ex F-WWJB	Epidaurus	[ATH]
☐ SX-BIA	ATR 42-320	169	ex F-WWEW	Plato	[ATH]
☐ SX-BIB	ATR 42-320	182	ex F-WWER	Socrates	[ATH]
☐ SX-BIC	ATR 42-320	197	ex F-WWEE	Aristotle	[ATH]
☐ SX-BID	ATR 42-320	219	ex F-WWEG	Pythagoras	[ATH]
☐ SX-BIE	ATR 72-202	239	ex F-WWED	Thales	[ATH]
☐ SX-BIF	ATR 72-202	241	ex F-WWEA	Democritus	[ATH]
☐ SX-BIG	ATR 72-202	290	ex F-WWLQ	Homer	[ATH]
☐ SX-BIH	ATR 72-202	305	ex F-WWLC	Herodotus	[ATH]
☐ SX-BII	ATR 72-202	353	ex F-WWEK	Hipocrates	[ATH]
☐ SX-BIK	ATR 72-202	350	ex F-WWEG	Archimedes	[ATH]
☐ SX-BIL	ATR 72-202	437	ex F-WWLC	Melina-Eliada	[ATH]
☐ SX-BPA	ATR 42-300	033	ex EI-CVS		[ATH]
☐ SX-BKA	Boeing 737-484	25313/2109		Vergina	[ATH]
☐ SX-BKB	Boeing 737-484	25314/2124		Olynthos	[ATH]
☐ SX-BKC	Boeing 737-484	25361/2130		Philippi	[ATH]
☐ SX-BKD	Boeing 737-484	25362/2142		Amphipoli	[ATH]
☐ SX-BKE	Boeing 737-484	25417/2160		Stagira	[ATH]
☐ SX-BKF	Boeing 737-484	25430/2174		Dion	[ATH]
☐ SX-BLD	Boeing 737-3M8	25071/2039	ex 9M-AAT		[ATH]
☐ SX-BMC	Boeing 737-42J	27143/2457	ex N734AB	City of Alexandroupolis	[CHR]

SKY EXPRESS   *Air Crete (G3/SEH)*   **Heraklion (HER)**

☐ SX-BLL	McDonnell-Douglas MD-83	49933/1837	ex JY-JRC		
☐ SX-BPP	McDonnell-Douglas MD-83	53377/2057	ex JY-JRB		
☐ SX-IDI	British Aerospace Jetstream 32	947	ex N149JH		
☐ SX-DIA	British Aerospace Jetstream 41	41075	ex G-CEYV		
☐ SX-ROD	British Aerospace Jetstream 41	41076	ex G-CEYW		
☐ SX-SEB	British Aerospace Jetstream 41	41070	ex G-MAJK		
☐ SX-SEC	British Aerospace Jetstream 41	41014	ex G-ISAY		♦
☐ SX-	British Aerospace Jetstream 41	41040	ex G-MAJT		o/o♦

SKY WINGS AIRLINES   *(GSW)*   **Heraklion (HER)**

☐ SX-BTF	McDonnell-Douglas MD-83	49857/1687	ex SE-RDE		
☐ SX-BTG	McDonnell-Douglas MD-83	49856/1675	ex SE-RDG		
☐ SX-BTH	Boeing 757-29J	27204/591	ex N410JR		

SWIFTAIR HELLAS   *Med-Freight (MDF)*   **Athens-Eleftherios Venizelos Intl (ATH)**

☐ SX-BGU	Swearingen SA.227AC Metro III	AC-615B	ex EC-HJO		
☐ SX-BKZ	Swearingen SA.227AC Metro III	AC-694B	ex SX-BKW		
☐ SX-BMT	Swearingen SA.227AC Metro III	AC-699B	ex EC-GYB		

VIKING HELLAS AIRLINES

☐ SX-SMT	Airbus A320-231	0393	ex EI-EEX		♦

| ☐ SX-SMU | Airbus A320-231 | 0414 | ex EI-EEY | ◆ |
| ☐ SX-SMS | McDonnell-Douglas MD-83 | 49631/1596 | ex SE-RDI | |

S2- BANGLADESH (People's Republic of Bangladesh)

BEST AIR		Best Air (5Q/BEA)		Dhaka (DAC)
☐ S2-AAT	Hawker Siddeley HS.748 Srs.2A/351	1770	ex ZS-XGE	Frtr
☐ S2-ABE	Hawker Siddeley HS.748 Srs.2A/245	1658	ex F-GODD	Frtr
☐ S2-AEE	Hawker Siddeley HS.748 Srs 2A/242	1647	ex G-ORCP	Frtr

BIMAN BANGLADESH AIRLINES		Bangladesh (BG/BBC)		Dhaka (DAC)
☐ S2-ADF	Airbus A310-325	700	ex F-WWCB	City of Chittagong
☐ S2-ADK	Airbus A310-325	594	ex N594RC	
☐ S2-AFT	Airbus A310-325ET	642	ex N301LF	◆
☐ TC-API	Boeing 737-86N/W	32732/1056		<PGT
☐ S2-AFL	Boeing 737-83N/W	28648/888	ex PR-GOZ	
☐ S2-AFM	Boeing 737-83N/W	28653/948	ex PR-GIA	
☐ CS-TFM	Boeing 777-212ER	28513/144	ex 9V-SRA	<MMZ
☐ S2-AFO	Boeing 777-3E9ER	40122		o/o◆
☐ S2-AFP	Boeing 777-3E9ER	40123		o/o◆
☐ S2-ACO	Douglas DC-10-30	46993/263	ex 9V-SDB	City of Hazrat Shah Makhdoom (RA)
☐ S2-ACP	Douglas DC-10-30	46995/275	ex 9V-SDD	City of Dhaka
☐ S2-ACQ	Douglas DC-10-30	47817/300	ex 9V-SDF	City of Hazrat Shah Jalal (RA)
☐ S2-ACR	Douglas DC-10-30	48317/445		The New Era
☐ S2-ACV	Fokker F.28 Fellowship 4000	11124	ex PK-YPV	
☐ S2-ACW	Fokker F.28 Fellowship 4000	11148	ex PK-YPJ	
☐ S2-ADY	Fokker F.28 Fellowship 4000	11120	ex HS-PBC	
☐ S2-ADZ	Fokker F.28 Fellowship 4000	11123	ex HS-PBA	[DAC]

BISMILLAH AIRLINES		Bismillah (5Z/BML)		Dhaka/Sharjah (DAC/SHJ)
☐ S2-ADW	Hawker Siddeley HS.748 Srs 2A/347	1766	ex G-BGMN	Frtr

EASY FLY				Dhaka (DAC)
☐ S2-AAX	Hawker Siddeley HS.748 Srs.2A/242	1767	ex G-BGMO	[DAK]

GMG AIRLINES		(Z5)		Dhaka (DAC)
☐ S2-AAA	de Havilland DHC-8-102	245	ex N802MA	In memory of Bangabondu
☐ S2-ACT	de Havilland DHC-8-311	307	ex OE-LRW	
☐ S2-ADM	McDonnell-Douglas MD-82	53147/2069	ex PK-LMF	[BKK] <LNI
☐ S2-ADO	McDonnell-Douglas MD-82	53481/2145	ex S7-ASK	
☐ S2-ADP	McDonnell-Douglas MD-83	53044/1776	ex N835NK	
☐ S2-ADX	de Havilland DHC-8Q-311A	464	ex G-BRYZ	In memory of HZT Saha Jalal
☐ S2-AFD	Boeing 767-3Q8ER	30301/762	ex B-2496	◆

REGENT AIRWAYS		(RX)		
☐ S2-AHA	de Havilland DHC-8Q-314	521	ex D-BLEJ	◆
☐ S2-AHB	de Havilland DHC-8Q-314	543	ex D-BEBA	◆

ROYAL BENGAL AIRLINES		(4A)		
☐ S2-AEL	de Havilland DHC-8-102A	225	ex D-BOBL	

UNITED AIRWAYS		United Bangladesh (4H/UBD)		
☐ S2-AER	de Havilland DHC-8-103	366	ex N811WP	
☐ S2-AES	de Havilland DHC-8-103	363	ex N810WP	
☐ S2-AEH	McDonnell-Douglas MD-83	49937/1784	ex YR-HBA	
☐ S2-AEU	McDonnell-Douglas MD-83	49790/1643	ex G-FLTL	
☐ S2-AFF	Airbus A310-325	672	ex M-ABCX	◆

VOYAGER AIRLINES		Voyager Air (V6/VOG)		Dhaka (DAC)

Operates charter flights using aircraft leased from other operators as required

YOUNGONE				
☐ S2-ACU	Cessna 208B Caravan I	208B0612	ex N1215A	

516

ZOOM AIRWAYS	Zed Air (3Z/ZAW)		Dhaka (DAC)
☐ S2-AET	Lockheed L-1011-1F Tristar	193-1012	ex HS-AXF

S5- SLOVENIA (Republic of Slovenia)

ADRIA AIRWAYS	Adria (JP/ADR)		Ljubljana (LJU)

Member of Star Alliance

☐ S5-AAP	Airbus A319-132	4282	ex D-AVWR		♦
☐ S5-AAR	Airbus A319-132	4301	ex D-AVXB		♦
☐ S5-	Airbus A319-132		ex		o/o♦
☐ S5-AAA	Airbus A320-231	0043	ex SX-BAS		[LJU]
☐ S5-AAD	Canadair CRJ-200LR	7166	ex C-FZWS	retd?	
☐ S5-AAE	Canadair CRJ-200LR	7170	ex C-GAIK		
☐ S5-AAF	Canadair CRJ-200LR	7272	ex C-FMND		
☐ S5-AAG	Canadair CRJ-200LR	7384	ex C-FMMT	Star Alliance colours	
☐ S5-AAH	Canadair CRJ-200LR	7032	ex HA-LNX		
☐ S5-AAI	Canadair CRJ-200LR	7248	ex G-DUOH		
☐ S5-AAJ	Canadair CRJ-200LR	8010	ex C-		
☐ S5-AAK	Canadair CRJ-900ER	15128	ex C-		
☐ S5-AAL	Canadair CRJ-900ER	15129	ex C-		
☐ S5-AAN	Canadair CRJ-900ER	15207	ex C-		
☐ S5-AAO	Canadair CRJ-900ER	15215	ex C-		
☐ S5-	Canadair CRJ-1000ER		ex C-		o/o♦

AURORA AIRLINES	(URR)		Ljubljana (LJU)
☐ S5-ACC	McDonnell-Douglas MD-82	48095/1055	ex ZA-ARB	
☐ S5-ACD	McDonnell-Douglas MD-82	49143/1095	ex 9A-CBC	[IST]

SOLINAIR	Solinair (SOP)		Portoroz (POW)
☐ S5-ABS	Airbus A300B4-203F	126	ex TC-MNN		<MNG
☐ S5-BAF	LET L-410UVP-E8C	912540	ex OM-WDA	FedEx colours	Lsd fr/op for ADR
☐ S5-BAM	SAAB SF.340AF	340A-020	ex G-GNTC		
☐ S5-BAO	SAAB SF.340AF	340A-011	ex VH-KEQ		
☐ S5-BAT	SAAB SF.340AF	340A-007	ex S5-BAN		

S7- SEYCHELLES (Republic of Seychelles)

AIR SEYCHELLES	Seychelles (HM/SEY)		Mahe (SEZ)
☐ S7-AAA	Britten-Norman BN-2A-27 Islander	540	ex G-BDZP	Isle of Remire	stored
☐ S7-AAF	de Havilland DHC-6 Twin Otter 300	623	ex S7-AAO	Isle of Praslin	
☐ S7-AAJ	de Havilland DHC-6 Twin Otter 310	499	ex PH-STB	Isle of Desroches	
☐ S7-AAR	de Havilland DHC-6 Twin Otter 300	539	ex PH-STF	Isle of Farquhar	
☐ S7-	de Havilland DHC-6 Twin Otter 400	846	ex C-GLVA		♦
☐ S7-	de Havilland DHC-6 Twin Otter 400		ex		o/o♦
☐ S7-	de Havilland DHC-6 Twin Otter 400		ex		o/o♦
☐ S7-AHM	Boeing 767-37DER	26328/637	ex (S7-AAZ)	Vailee de Mai	
☐ S7-ASY	Boeing 767-3Q8ER	29386/831		Aldabra	
☐ S7-FCS	Boeing 767-306ER	28884/738	ex HA-LHC		
☐ S7-ILF	Boeing 767-205	23057/81	ex N260MY		
☐ S7-PAL	Short SD.3-60	SH3758	ex G-KBAC	Isle de Palme	
☐ S7-PRI	Short SD.3-60	SH3724	ex G-BNMU	Isle of La Digue	
☐ S7-SEZ	Boeing 767-219ER	24150/239	ex N263LF	Isle of Bijoutier	

IDC AIRCRAFT			Mahe (SEZ)
☐ S7-AAI	Reims Cessna F406 Caravan II	F406-0051	ex N7148P	
☐ S7-AAU	Britten-Norman BN-2A-21 Islander	589	ex A2-01M	Op for Coast Guard
☐ S7-IDC	Beech 1900D	UE-212	ex N3217U	

S9- SAO TOME (Democratic Republic of São Tomé & Principe)

GOLFO INTERNATIONAL — São Tomé/Luanda (TMS/LAD)

☐ S9-BAJ	Beech 1900D	UE-357	ex N23598
☐ S9-BAK	Beech 1900D	UE-358	ex N23610

GOLIAF AIR — Goliaf Air (GLE) — São Tomé (TMS)

☐ S9-BOH	Antonov An-32	2108	ex T-256	
☐ S9-BOZ	Antonov An-12A	2340803	ex RA-122375	>Africa West
☐ S9-DAB	Douglas DC-9-32	47313/268	ex LV-YAB	Calypso
☐ S9-DAF	Antonov An-12A	2340606	ex RA-12971	Principe
☐ S9-DBA	Antonov An-12AP	2400802	ex UR-11326	
☐ S9-GAR	Lockheed L-1011-200 Tristar	193U-1201	ex EX-102	
☐ S9-PSB	WSK-PZL/Antonov An-28	1AJ003-07	ex ER-AJA	
☐ S9-PSE	Antonov An-32	2803	ex UR-48053	>MGG
☐ S9-PSO	Antonov An-12BP	5343109	ex EW-11365	
☐ S9-PSV	WSK/PZL Antonov An-28	1AJ008-13	ex ER-AKO	Op for Dallex Air

TRANSAFRIK INTERNATIONAL (TFK) — São Tomé/Luanda (TMS/LAD)

☐ S9-BAE	Boeing 727-31F	18903/147	ex N210NE		
☐ S9-BAG	Boeing 727-30C	19313/411	ex PP-ITP	all-white	[UTN]
☐ S9-BAV	Boeing 727-223 (Raisbeck 3)	21383/1324	ex N871AA	Tanker	
☐ S9-BOC	Boeing 727-23F	18447/127	ex ZS-NMY	all-white	[UTN]
☐ S9-BOD	Boeing 727-25F	18968/223	ex PP-ITA	all-white	[UTN]
☐ S9-BOG	Boeing 727-90C	19170/332	ex N270AX	all-white	[UTN]
☐ S9-CAA	Boeing 727-95F	19836/494	ex HR-AMR		
☐ S9-PAC	Boeing 727-44C (FedEx 3)	20475/854	ex C-GVFA		
☐ S9-TAO	Boeing 727-23F	19390/350	ex N931FT		
☐ 5X-PST	Boeing 727-171C	19859/559	ex S9-PST		
☐ S9-BOF	Lockheed L-382G-32C Hercules	4586	ex N921SJ		
☐ S9-BOR	Lockheed L-382E-20C Hercules	4362	ex N522SJ		
☐ S9-CAV	Lockheed L-382G-11C Hercules	4301	ex N923SJ		
☐ S9-CAW	Lockheed L-382G-13C Hercules	4300	ex N908SJ		
☐ S9-NAL	Lockheed L-382E-25C Hercules	4385	ex 9Q-CHZ		

TRANSLIZ AVIATION — São Tomé (TMS)

☐ S9-KHC	Antonov An-12B	00347306	ex ER-ACY
☐ S9-KHD	Antonov An-12B	01347908	ex ER-ACQ
☐ S9-KHF	Antonov An-12V	00347109	ex ER-ADG
☐ S9-KHL	Antonov An-12B	00347401	ex ER-ACS

Operator Unknown

☐ S9-DBP	Antonov An-12BP	8346201	ex 4K-AZ23
☐ S9-DBS	Antonov An-26	07309504	ex EX-091

TC- TURKEY (Republic of Turkey)

ACT AIRLINES (9T/RUN) — Istanbul-Ataturk (IST)

☐ TC-ACC	Airbus A300B4-203F	147	ex N318FV	
☐ TC-ACD	Airbus A300B4-203F	075	ex N502TA	Op for Empost
☐ TC-ACE	Airbus A300B4-203F	154	ex N320SC	
☐ TC-ACU	Airbus A300B4-203F	183	ex N512TA	
☐ TC-ACY	Airbus A300B4-203F	107	ex N59107	
☐ TC-ACZ	Airbus A300B4-203F	105	ex N317FV	

ANADOLU JET — Ankara/Esenboga International (ESB)

☐ TC-JDT	Boeing 737-4Y0	25261/2258	ex N600SK	Alanya	
☐ TC-JEY	Boeing 737-4Y0	26086/2475		Side	
☐ TC-JEZ	Boeing 737-4Y0	26088/2487		Bergama	
☐ TC-JGA	Boeing 737-8F2/W	29785/544	ex N1786B	Malatya	♦
☐ TC-JGC	Boeing 737-8F2/W	29787/771	ex N1786B	Kocaeli	♦
☐ TC-JGF	Boeing 737-8F2/W	29790/1088	ex N1786B	Ardahan	♦
☐ TC-JHG	Boeing 737-8GJ/W	34958/2688	ex VT-SGD	Pamukkale	
☐ TC-JHH	Boeing 737-8GJ/W	34959/2719		Kemer	
☐ TC-JHI	Boeing 737-8FH/W	35092/2160	ex G-XLAK	Hendek	
☐ TC-JHJ	Boeing 737-86Q	30296/1647	ex VT-AXA		♦
☐ TC-JKF	Boeing 737-76N/W	32684/1889	ex EI-EDT		
☐ TC-JKG	Boeing 737-76N/W	34754/2172	ex OM-NGH	Mugla	

☐ TC-JKH	Boeing 737-76N/W	34757/2241	ex OM-NGL	Ihlara	
☐ TC-JKI	Boeing 737-76N/W	34758/2266	ex EI-EDU	Abant	
☐ TC-JKL	Boeing 737-76N/W	34753/2165	ex OM-NGG	Anamur	
☐ TC-JKM	Boeing 737-76N/W	34755/2187	ex OM-NGJ		
☐ TC-JKS	Boeing 737-73V	32419/1321	ex G-EZJX		◆
☐ TC-JKT	Boeing 737-73V	32420/1341	ex G-EZJY		◆

ATLASJET INTERNATIONAL · Atlasjet (KK/KKK) · Antalya (AYT)

☐ TC-OGI	Airbus A320-232	0640	ex N381LF	
☐ TC-OGJ	Airbus A320-232	0676	ex N391LF	
☐ TC-ETF	Airbus A321-231	1438	ex N585NK	>SVA
☐ TC-ETH	Airbus A321-231	0968	ex TC-IEF	
☐ TC-ETJ	Airbus A321-231	0974	ex TC-IEG	
☐ TC-ETM	Airbus A321-131	0604	ex TC-TUB	
☐ TC-ETN	Airbus A321-131	0614	ex TC-TUC	
☐ TC-ETR	Airbus A321-211	2117	ex TC-KTD	◆
☐ TC-ETV	Airbus A321-221	1950	ex EI-LVA	◆
☐ TC-ETK	Airbus A330-223	358	ex I-EEZA	>SVA
☐ TC-ETL	Airbus A330-223	364	ex I-EEZB	>SVA
☐ TC-ETP	Airbus A330-223	343	ex HB-IQO	◆
☐ TC-ETE	Boeing 757-2Q8	30044/954	ex TC-GLA	◆
☐ TC-ETG	Boeing 757-256	26254/905	ex EC-HDV	>SVA
☐ TC-OGS	Boeing 757-256	29307/924	ex EC-HIQ	>SVA
☐ TC-OGT	Boeing 757-256	29308/935	ex EC-HIR	>SVA

BEST AIR · (5F/BST) · Istanbul-Ataturk (IST)

| ☐ TC-TUA | McDonnell-Douglas MD-82 | 49138/1090 | ex TC-MNO | Tamcelik |

BORAJET

☐ TC-YAB	ATR 72-212A	588	ex G-CGFT
☐ TC-YAC	ATR 72-212A	701	ex OY-EDC
☐ TC-YAD	ATR 72-212A	702	ex OY-EDD

CORENDON AIR · Corendon (7H/CAI) · Istanbul-Sabiha Gokcen Int'l (SAW)

☐ TC-TJB	Boeing 737-3Q8	27633/2878	ex N304FL	Ayhan Saracoglu	
☐ TC-TJC	Boeing 737-4Q8	25374/2562	ex TC-MNL		
☐ TC-TJD	Boeing 737-4Q8	25375/2598	ex TC-MNM		
☐ TC-TJE	Boeing 737-4Y0	26073/2375	ex TC-JER		
☐ TC-TJF	Boeing 737-4Y0	26078/2431	ex TC-JEU		
☐ TC-TJG	Boeing 737-86J/W	29120/202	ex D-ABAT		◆
☐ TC-TJH	Boeing 737-86J/W	29121/239	ex D-ABAU		◆

FREEBIRD AIRLINES · Free Turk (FHY) · Istanbul-Ataturk (IST)

☐ TC-FBE	Airbus A320-212	0132	ex SE-RCG	
☐ TC-FBF	Airbus A320-212	0288	ex 9H-AED	
☐ TC-FBH	Airbus A320-214	4207	ex F-WWBP	◆
☐ TC-FBJ	Airbus A320-232	0580	ex N580CG	
☐ TC-FBR	Airbus A320-232	2524	ex VT-DKZ	
☐ TC-FBG	Airbus A321-231	0771	ex HL7588	
☐ TC-FBT	Airbus A321-231	0855	ex HL7589	

IZMIR AIRLINES · Izmir (4I/IZM) · Izmir (ADB)

☐ TC-IZH	Airbus A319-132	2452	ex N812BR	Goztepe
☐ TC-IZM	Airbus A319-132	2404	ex N809BR	Alsancak
☐ TC-IZR	Airbus A319-132	2414	ex N810BR	Karsiyaka
☐ TC-IZA	Airbus A320-233	2118	ex N488TA	
☐ TC-IZL	Airbus A320-233	1730	ex N486TA	Cesme

KTHY CYPRUS TURKISH AIRLINES · Airkibris (YK/KYV) · Ercan (ECN)

Ceased operations 15/Jul/2010

MARIN AIR · Antalya / Bodrum-Marina / Marmaris-Marina (AYT/-/-)

| ☐ TC-KEU | Cessna 208 Caravan I | 20800317 | ex N52234 | FP |

MNG CARGO AIRLINES — Black Sea (MB/MNB) — Istanbul-Ataturk (IST)

☐ TC-MCA	Airbus A300C4-605R	755	ex TF-ELW			♦
☐ TC-MCB	Airbus A300B4-203F	304	ex N308FV			
☐ TC-MNB	Airbus A300B4-203F	292	ex HL7279			
☐ TC-MNC	Airbus A300B4-203F	277	ex HL7278			
☐ TC-MND	Airbus A300C4-203F	212	ex ZS-SDG		>Ceiba Cargo	
☐ TC-MNJ	Airbus A300B4-203F	123	ex PH-JLH			
☐ TC-MNU	Airbus A300B4-203F	047	ex N740SC			
☐ TC-MNV	Airbus A300C4-605R	758	ex TF-ELG			
☐ TC-MCF	Boeing 737-4K5SF	24126/1697	ex EC-KRD			♦
☐ TC-MNG	Boeing 737-4K5SF	24128/1715	ex N728CF			♦
☐ TC-MBA	Fokker F.27 Friendship 500	10654	ex G-CEXE			
☐ TC-MBF	Fokker F.27 Friendship 600	10405	ex G-BNIZ			
☐ TC-MBH	Fokker F.27 Friendship 500	10550	ex G-CEXB			

ONUR AIR — Onur Air (8Q/OHY) — Istanbul-Ataturk (IST)

☐ TC-OAA	Airbus A300B4-605R	744	ex F-WQRD			
☐ TC-OAB	Airbus A300B4-605R	749	ex F-WQRC	Safuan 1		
☐ TC-OAG	Airbus A300B4-605R	747	ex F-OHLN			
☐ TC-OAH	Airbus A300B4-605R	584	ex S7-RGO		>SVA	
☐ TC-OAO	Airbus A300B4-605R	764	ex D-AIAW			
☐ TC-OAZ	Airbus A300B4-605R	603	ex SX-BEM		>SVA	
☐ TC-ONT	Airbus A300B4-203	138	ex ZS-SDE	Kaptan Bilal Basar		
☐ TC-ONU	Airbus A300B4-203	192	ex ZS-SDF	B Basar		
☐ TC-OBD	Airbus A320-232	0455	ex N11112	Kaspersky		
☐ TC-OBE	Airbus A320-232	0471	ex VT-WAB			
☐ TC-OBH	Airbus A319-132	1492	ex PK-RMJ			♦
☐ TC-OAE	Airbus A321-231	0663	ex F-OHMP			
☐ TC-OAF	Airbus A321-231	0668	ex F-OHMQ			
☐ TC-OAI	Airbus A321-231	0787	ex D-AVZL			
☐ TC-OAK	Airbus A321-231	0954	ex D-ALAI			
☐ TC-OAL	Airbus A321-231	1004	ex D-ALAK			
☐ TC-OAN	Airbus A321-231	1421	ex D-ALAP		>BGH	
☐ TC-OBF	Airbus A321-231	0963	ex OE-IAA		o/o	
☐ TC-ONJ	Airbus A321-131	0385	ex D-AVZG	Kaptan Koray Sahin		
☐ TC-ONS	Airbus A321-131	0364	ex D-AVZD	Funda		
☐ TC-OCA	Airbus A330-322	072	ex EC-IJH			♦
☐ TC-OCB	Airbus A330-342	098	ex B-HYA			♦
☐ TC-ONM	McDonnell-Douglas MD-88	53546/2167		Yasemin		
☐ TC-ONN	McDonnell-Douglas MD-88	53547/2176		Ece		
☐ TC-ONO	McDonnell-Douglas MD-88	53548/2180		Yonca		
☐ TC-ONP	McDonnell-Douglas MD-88	53549/2185		Esra		
☐ TC-ONR	McDonnell-Douglas MD-88	53550/2187		Evren		

PEGASUS AIRLINES — Sunturk (1I/PGT) — Istanbul-Ataturk (IST)

☐ TC-AAD	Boeing 737-5Q8	28201/2999	ex PT-SSF			
☐ TC-AAF	Boeing 737-58E	29122/2991	ex N291SZ			
☐ TC-AAG	Boeing 737-5L9	29234/3068	ex ES-ABI			
☐ TC-APD	Boeing 737-42R	29107/2997				
☐ TC-APR	Boeing 737-4Y0	24685/1859	ex EC-GXR			
☐ TC-AAE	Boeing 737-82R/W	35700/2435		Hayirli		
☐ TC-AAH	Boeing 737-82R/W	35701/2496		Hanim		
☐ TC-AAI	Boeing 737-82R/W	35699/2712				
☐ TC-AAJ	Boeing 737-82R/W	35702/2810	ex N1787B	Ece		
☐ TC-AAK	Boeing 737-8FH/W	35094/2195				
☐ TC-AAL	Boeing 737-82R/W	35984/2937	ex N1786B			
☐ TC-AAN	Boeing 737-82R/W	38173/3011				
☐ TC-AAO	Boeing 737-86N/W	28619/534	ex EI-DJU			
☐ TC-AAP	Boeing 737-86N/W	32736/1113				
☐ TC-AAR	Boeing 737-86N/W	28624/585	ex EI-DGZ			
☐ TC-AAS	Boeing 737-82R/W	40871/3212	ex N1787B			♦
☐ TC-AAT	Boeing 737-82R/W	40872/3227	ex N1786B			♦
☐ TC-AAV	Boeing 737-82R/W	40696/3285	ex N1787B			♦
☐ TC-AAY	Boeing 737-82R/W	40874/3316				♦
☐ TC-AAZ	Boeing 737-82R/W	40875/3325				♦
☐ TC-ABP	Boeing 737-82R/W	40876/3326	ex N1786B			♦
☐ TC-ACP	Boeing 737-82R/W	40697/3354				♦

☐ TC-APH	Boeing 737-8S3/W	29250/792	ex N1787B		
☐ TC-API	Boeing 737-86N/W	32732/1056			>BBC
☐ TC-APJ	Boeing 737-86N/W	32735/1104			
☐ TC-APU	Boeing 737-82R	29344/849	ex N1786B		
☐ TC-	Boeing 737-82R/W				o/o♦
☐ TC-	Boeing 737-82R/W				o/o♦
☐ TC-	Boeing 737-82R/W				o/o♦
☐ TC-	Boeing 737-82R/W				o/o♦
☐ TC-	Boeing 737-82R/W				o/o♦
☐ TC-	Boeing 737-82R/W				o/o♦
☐ TC-	Boeing 737-82R/W				o/o♦

REDSTAR AVIATION — Istanbul-Sabiha Gokcen (SAW)

| ☐ TC-RSA | British Aerospace Jetstream 32EP | 986 | ex G-CBDA | |

SAGA AIRLINES (SGX) — Istanbul-Ataturk (IST)

☐ TC-SGA	Airbus A300B2K-3C	090	ex JA8466	Kemal Kolot	>IRM
☐ TC-SGB	Airbus A310-304	562	ex N351LF	Akçaabat	
☐ TC-SGC	Airbus A310-304	519	ex VT-EVI	Fethiya Kolot	
☐ TC-SGE	Boeing 737-48E	25775/2925	ex VT-JAN	Kalrel Alodolou	
☐ TC-SGF	Boeing 737-83N/W	28249/1123	ex N321TZ		
☐ TC-SGG	Boeing 737-83N/W	30706/929	ex N305TZ		
☐ TC-SGH	Boeing 737-86J/W	28068/36	ex D-ABAN	Vakfikebir	
☐ TC-SGI	Boeing 737-86J/W	28069/42	ex D-ABAO		>AFG
☐ TC-SGJ	Airbus A330-343	407	ex B-HYH	Trabazon	>THY♦

SKY AIRLINES Antalya Bird (SHY) — Antalya (AYT)

☐ TC-SKJ	Airbus A320-211	0138	ex N138LC	Jupiter	
☐ TC-SKK	Airbus A320-211	0148	ex N148LC	Side	
☐ TC-SKT	Airbus A320-232	1194	ex G-MEDE		♦
☐ TC-SKI	Airbus A321-231	0811	ex D-ALAA	Antalya	
☐ TC-SKL	Airbus A321-231	1670	ex HL7712		
☐ TC-SKB	Boeing 737-430	27004/2344	ex EI-CPU	StarAdam+Eve	
☐ TC-SKD	Boeing 737-4Q8	25372/2280	ex TC-JDI	Black Eagle	
☐ TC-SKE	Boeing 737-4Q8	25163/2264	ex VH-TJV	Milky Way	
☐ TC-SKF	Boeing 737-4Q8	26291/2513	ex HL7591	Sugar	
☐ TC-SKG	Boeing 737-4Q8	25371/2195	ex SX-BKK	Gold	
☐ TC-SKH	Boeing 737-8BK	29644/2231	ex N1786B	Rainbow	
☐ TC-SKM	Boeing 737-49R	28882/2845	ex OK-CGI		
☐ TC-SKN	Boeing 737-94XER/W	36086/2910	ex N1787B	Alanya Smile in the Sky	
☐ TC-SKP	Boeing 737-94XER/W	36087/2928	ex N1786B	Kapadokya	
☐ TC-SKR	Boeing 737-83N/W	32576/875	ex PR-GIC		♦
☐ TC-SKS	Boeing 737-83N/W	32348/933	ex PR-GIB		♦
☐ TC-SKU	Boeing 737-883	30194/666	ex EC-IYI		♦

SUNEXPRESS Sunexpress (XQ/SXS) — Antalya (AYT)

☐ TC-SNE	Boeing 737-8HX/W	29684/2539	ex N1786B	
☐ TC-SNF	Boeing 737-8HC/W	36529/2566	ex N1787B	
☐ TC-SNG	Boeing 737-8HC/W	36530/2622	ex N1786B	
☐ TC-SNH	Boeing 737-8FH/W	30826/1732	ex EI-ECD	
☐ TC-SNI	Boeing 737-8FH/W	29671/1700	ex EI-DMZ	
☐ TC-SNJ	Boeing 737-86J/W	30827/1632	ex D-ABBO	
☐ TC-SNL	Boeing 737-86N/W	34251/1817	ex EC-JKZ	♦
☐ TC-SNM	Boeing 737-8BK/W	33023/1682	ex VT-AXB	♦
☐ TC-SNN	Boeing 737-8HC/W	40775/3250		♦
☐ TC-SNO	Boeing 737-8HC/W	40776/3273	ex N1795B	♦
☐ TC-SNP	Boeing 737-8HC/W	40777/3320	ex N1786B	♦
☐ TC-SNR	Boeing 737-8HC/W	40754/3352	ex N1795B	♦
☐ TC-SNT	Boeing 737-8HC/W	40755/3400	ex N1786B	♦
☐ TC-SNU	Boeing 737-8HC/W	40756/3457	ex N1796B	♦
☐ TC-SUG	Boeing 737-8CX/W	32365/1209		
☐ TC-SUH	Boeing 737-8CX/W	32366/1235		
☐ TC-SUI	Boeing 737-8CX/W	32367/1253		
☐ TC-SUJ	Boeing 737-8CX/W	32368/1289		
☐ TC-SUL	Boeing 737-85F/W	28822/166	ex SE-DVO	
☐ TC-SUM	Boeing 737-85F/W	28826/238	ex SE-DVR	
☐ TC-SUO	Boeing 737-86Q/W	30272/824	ex VH-VOE	
☐ TC-SUU	Boeing 737-86Q/W	30274/845	ex VH-VOF	
☐ TC-SUV	Boeing 737-86N/W	30807/829	ex N50089	
☐ TC-SUY	Boeing 737-86N/W	30806/790	ex G-OXLB	
☐ TC-SUZ	Boeing 737-8HXS/W	29649/2515	ex N1786B	

☐ TC-SNB	Boeing 757-2Q8/W	26271/592	ex N804AM		
☐ TC-SNC	Boeing 757-2Q8/W	26273/597	ex N806AM		
☐ TC-SND	Boeing 757-2Q8/W	26268/590	ex N803AM		

TAILWIND AIRLINES   *(TI)*

☐ TC-TLA	Boeing 737-4Q8	25107/2526	ex N774AS		
☐ TC-TLB	Boeing 737-4Q8	25108/2551	ex N775AS		
☐ TC-TLC	Boeing 737-4Q8	25112/2638	ex N780AS	Capt Z Kllic	
☐ TC-TLD	Boeing 737-4Q8	28199/2826	ex N784AS		♦
☐ TC-TLE	Boeing 737-4Q8	27628/2858	ex N785AS		♦

TARHAN AIR   *(TTH)*   *Istanbul-Ataturk (IST)*

| ☐ TC-TTA | McDonnell-Douglas MD-83 | 48096/1057 | ex TC-MNT | Surmeli | [IST] |
| ☐ TC-TTB | McDonnell-Douglas MD-82 | 49144/1096 | ex N800NK | Ufuk | [IST] |

THK-TURK HAVA KURUMU   *Hur Kus (THK)*   *Ankara (ANK)*

☐ TC-CAU	Cessna 208 Caravan I	20800248	ex N1123X	
☐ TC-CAV	Cessna 208 Caravan I	20800256	ex N1249T	
☐ TC-CAY	Cessna 402B	402B1073	ex 10007	
☐ TC-CAZ	Cessna 421C Golden Eagle II	421C0089	ex 10006	
☐ TC-FAH	Piper PA-42-720 Cheyenne IIIA	42-5501033		
☐ TC-THK	Piper PA-42-720 Cheyenne IIIA	42-5501031	ex TC-FAG	
☐ TC-ZTP	Cessna 402B	402B0412	ex N69289	
☐ TC-ZVJ	Cessna 402B	402B1084	ex N1906G	

TURKISH AIRLINES   *Turkair (TK/THY)*   *Istanbul-Ataturk (IST)*

Member of Star Alliance

☐ TC-JCT	Airbus A310-304F	502	ex TF-ELE	Samsun	
☐ TC-JCV	Airbus A310-304F	476	ex F-WWCT	Aras	
☐ TC-JCY	Airbus A310-304F	478	ex F-WWCX	Coruh	
☐ TC-JCZ	Airbus A310-304F	480	ex F-WWCZ	Ergene	

☐ TC-JLM	Airbus A319-132	2738	ex D-AVXN	Sinop	
☐ TC-JLN	Airbus A319-132	2739	ex D-AVXO	Karabuk	
☐ TC-JLO	Airbus A319-132	2631	ex TC-OGU	Ahlat	
☐ TC-JLP	Airbus A319-132	2655	ex TC-OGV	Koycegiz	
☐ TC-JLR	Airbus A319-132	3142	ex SX-OAV		>BON♦
☐ TC-	Airbus A319-132		ex		o/o♦
☐ TC-	Airbus A319-132		ex		o/o♦
☐ TC-	Airbus A319-132		ex		o/o♦

☐ TC-JLJ	Airbus A320-232	1856	ex EI-DIV	Sirnak	
☐ TC-JLK	Airbus A320-232	1909	ex EI-DIW	Kirklareli	
☐ TC-JLL	Airbus A320-232	1956	ex EI-DIX	Duzce	
☐ TC-JPA	Airbus A320-232	2609	ex F-WWBU	Mus	
☐ TC-JPB	Airbus A320-232	2626	ex F-WWDS	Rize	
☐ TC-JPC	Airbus A320-232	2928	ex F-WWDZ	Hasankeyf	
☐ TC-JPD	Airbus A320-232	2934	ex F-WWIC	Isparta	
☐ TC-JPE	Airbus A320-232	2941	ex F-WWIF	Gumushane	
☐ TC-JPF	Airbus A320-232	2984	ex F-WWIE	Yozgat	
☐ TC-JPG	Airbus A320-232	3010	ex F-WWBJ	Osmaniye	
☐ TC-JPH	Airbus A320-232	3185	ex F-WWDX	Kars	
☐ TC-JPI	Airbus A320-232	3208	ex F-WWIS	Dogubevazit	
☐ TC-JPJ	Airbus A320-232	3239	ex F-WWBK	Edremit	
☐ TC-JPK	Airbus A320-232	3257	ex F-WWDI	Erdek	
☐ TC-JPL	Airbus A320-232	3303	ex F-WWIJ	Göreme	
☐ TC-JPM	Airbus A320-232	3341	ex F-WWBN	Harput	
☐ TC-JPN	Airbus A320-232	3558	ex F-WWBE	Sarikamis	
☐ TC-JPO	Airbus A320-232	3567	ex F-WWBP	Kemer	
☐ TC-JPP	Airbus A320-232	3603	ex F-WWDL	Harran	
☐ TC-JPR	Airbus A320-232	3654	ex F-WWDR	Kusadasi	
☐ TC-JPS	Airbus A320-232	3718	ex F-WWBK	Adilcevaz	
☐ TC-JPT	Airbus A320-232	3719	ex D-AVVC	Urgup	
☐ TC-JPU	Airbus A320-214	3896	ex A9C-BAT	Salihli	♦
☐ TC-JPV	Airbus A320-214	3931	ex A9C-BAS	Sisli	♦
☐ TC-JPY	Airbus A320-214	3949	ex A9C-BAP	Beykoz	♦
☐ TC-	Airbus A320-2		ex		o/o♦
☐ TC-	Airbus A320-2		ex		o/o♦
☐ TC-	Airbus A320-2		ex		o/o♦
☐ TC-	Airbus A320-2		ex		o/o♦
☐ TC-	Airbus A320-2		ex		o/o♦
☐ TC-	Airbus A320-2		ex		o/o♦
☐ TC-	Airbus A320-2		ex		o/o♦

☐ TC-	Airbus A320-2		ex			o/o♦
☐ TC-JMC	Airbus A321-231	0806	ex G-MIDA	Aksaray		
☐ TC-JMD	Airbus A321-231	0810	ex G-MIDF	Cankiri		
☐ TC-JME	Airbus A321-211	1219	ex EC-IMA	Burdur		
☐ TC-JMF	Airbus A321-211	1233	ex EC-ILG	Bingol		
☐ TC-JMH	Airbus A321-231	3637	ex D-AVZM	Didim		
☐ TC-JMI	Airbus A321-231	3673	ex D-AVZZ	Milas		
☐ TC-JMJ	Airbus A321-231	3688	ex D-AZAG	Tekirdag		
☐ TC-JMK	Airbus A321-231	3738	ex D-AZAK	Uskudar		
☐ TC-JML	Airbus A321-231	3382	ex G-TTIG	Eminonu		
☐ TC-JRA	Airbus A321-231	2823	ex D-AVZE	Kutahya		
☐ TC-JRB	Airbus A321-231	2868	ex D-AVZI	Sanliurfa		
☐ TC-JRC	Airbus A321-231	2999	ex D-AVZV	Sakarya		
☐ TC-JRD	Airbus A321-231	3015	ex D-AVZX	Balikesir		
☐ TC-JRE	Airbus A321-231	3126	ex D-AVZS	Trabzon		
☐ TC-JRF	Airbus A321-231	3207	ex D-AVZY	Fethiye		
☐ TC-JRG	Airbus A321-231	3283	ex D-AVZZ	Finike		
☐ TC-JRH	Airbus A321-231	3350	ex D-AVZI	Yalova		
☐ TC-JRI	Airbus A321-231	3405	ex D-AVZS	Adiyaman		
☐ TC-JRJ	Airbus A321-231	3429	ex D-AVZC	Corum		
☐ TC-JRK	Airbus A321-231	3525	ex D-AVZY	Batman		
☐ TC-JRL	Airbus A321-231	3539	ex D-AVZB	Tarsus		
☐ G-WWBM	Airbus A330-243	398	ex F-WWKL			<BMA
☐ TC-JDO	Airbus A330-223F	1004	ex F-WWYE	Meric		♦
☐ TC-	Airbus A330-223F		ex			o/o♦
☐ TC-JNA	Airbus A330-203	697	ex F-WWYS	Gaziantep		
☐ TC-JNB	Airbus A330-203	704	ex F-WWKF	Konya		
☐ TC-JNC	Airbus A330-203	742	ex F-WWYF	Bursa		
☐ TC-JND	Airbus A330-203	754	ex F-WWYL	Antalya		
☐ TC-JNE	Airbus A330-203	774	ex F-WWKG	Kayseri		
☐ TC-JNF	Airbus A330-202	463	ex A7-AFN	Canakkale		
☐ TC-JNG	Airbus A330-202	504	ex A7-AFO	Esklsehir		
☐ TC-JNH	Airbus A330-343X	1150	ex F-WWYM	Topkapi		♦
☐ TC-JNI	Airbus A330-343X	1160	ex F-WWKH	Konak		♦
☐ TC-JNJ	Airbus A330-343X	1170	ex F-WWKZ	Kapadokya		♦
☐ TC-JNK	Airbus A330-343X	1172	ex F-WWYK	Sanliurfa		♦
☐ TC-	Airbus A330-343X		ex			o/o♦
☐ TC-	Airbus A330-343X		ex			o/o♦
☐ TC-	Airbus A330-343X		ex			o/o♦
☐ TC-	Airbus A330-343X		ex			o/o♦
☐ TC-	Airbus A330-343X		ex			o/o♦
☐ TC-	Airbus A330-343X		ex			o/o♦
☐ TC-SGJ	Airbus A330-343	407	ex B-HYH	Trabazon		<SGX♦
☐ TC-JDJ	Airbus A340-311	023	ex F-WWJN	Istanbul		
☐ TC-JDK	Airbus A340-311	025	ex F-WWJP	Isparta		
☐ TC-JDL	Airbus A340-311	057	ex F-WWJF	Ankara		
☐ TC-JDM	Airbus A340-311	115	ex F-WWJN	Izmir		
☐ TC-JDN	Airbus A340-313X	180	ex F-WWJU	Adana		
☐ TC-JIH	Airbus A340-313X	270	ex F-WWJP	Kocaeli		
☐ TC-JII	Airbus A340-313X	331	ex F-WWJQ	Aydin		
☐ TC-JIJ	Airbus A340-313X	216	ex 6Y-JMM	Selcuk		
☐ TC-JIK	Airbus A340-313X	257	ex 6Y-JMP	Kas		
☐ TC-JDG	Boeing 737-4Y0	25181/2203		Marmaris		
☐ TC-JDH	Boeing 737-4Y0	25184/2227		Amasra		
☐ TC-JKJ	Boeing 737-752/W	34297/1808	ex N297MD			
☐ TC-JKK	Boeing 737-752/W	34298/1812	ex N298MD			
☐ TC-JKN	Boeing 737-752/W	34299/1829	ex N342CT			♦
☐ TC-JKO	Boeing 737-752/W	34300/1848	ex N343CT			♦
☐ TC-JKR	Boeing 737-7GL/W	34760/2352	ex G-CGFW	Gelibolu		♦
☐ TC-JFC	Boeing 737-8F2/W	29765/80		Diyarbakir		
☐ TC-JFD	Boeing 737-8F2/W	29766/87		Artvin		
☐ TC-JFE	Boeing 737-8F2/W	29767/95	ex N1786B	Hatay		
☐ TC-JFF	Boeing 737-8F2/W	29768/99	ex N1786B	Afyonkarahisar		
☐ TC-JFG	Boeing 737-8F2/W	29769/102	ex N1787B	Mardin		
☐ TC-JFH	Boeing 737-8F2/W	29770/114	ex N1787B	Igdir		
☐ TC-JFI	Boeing 737-8F2/W	29771/228	ex N1795B	Sivas		
☐ TC-JFJ	Boeing 737-8F2/W	29772/242	ex N1786B	Agri		
☐ TC-JFK	Boeing 737-8F2/W	29773/259	ex N1786B	Zonguldak		
☐ TC-JFL	Boeing 737-8F2/W	29774/269	ex N1786B	Ordu		
☐ TC-JFM	Boeing 737-8F2/W	29775/279	ex N1786B	Nigde		
☐ TC-JFN	Boeing 737-8F2/W	29776/308		Bitlis		

☐ TC-JFO	Boeing 737-8F2/W	29777/309		Batman		
☐ TC-JFP	Boeing 737-8F2/W	29778/349	ex N1787B	Amasya		
☐ TC-JFR	Boeing 737-8F2/W	29779/370	ex N1786B	Giresun		
☐ TC-JFT	Boeing 737-8F2/W	29780/454	ex N1787B	Kastamonu		
☐ TC-JFU	Boeing 737-8F2/W	29781/461	ex N1795B	Elazig		
☐ TC-JFV	Boeing 737-8F2/W	29782/490	ex N1786B	Tuncell		
☐ TC-JFY	Boeing 737-8F2/W	29783/497	ex N1786B	Manisa		
☐ TC-JFZ	Boeing 737-8F2/W	29784/539		Bolu		
☐ TC-JGB	Boeing 737-8F2/W	29786/566	ex N1786B	Foca		
☐ TC-JGD	Boeing 737-8F2/W	29788/791	ex N1787B	Nevsehir		
☐ TC-JGG	Boeing 737-8F2/W	34405/1828		Erzincan		
☐ TC-JGH	Boeing 737-8F2/W	34406/1852		Tokat		
☐ TC-JGI	Boeing 737-8F2/W	34407/1873		Siirt		
☐ TC-JGJ	Boeing 737-8F2/W	34408/1880		Aydin		
☐ TC-JGK	Boeing 737-8F2/W	34409/1924	ex N1786B	Kirsehir		
☐ TC-JGL	Boeing 737-8F2/W	34410/1927	ex N1787B	Karaman		
☐ TC-JGM	Boeing 737-8F2/W	34411/1944		Hakkari		
☐ TC-JGN	Boeing 737-8F2/W	34412/1949		Bilecik		
☐ TC-JGO	Boeing 737-8F2/W	34413/1972	ex N1786B	Kilis		
☐ TC-JGP	Boeing 737-8F2/W	34414/1978	ex N1786B	Bartin		
☐ TC-JGR	Boeing 737-8F2/W	34415/1988	ex N1786B	Usak		
☐ TC-JGS	Boeing 737-8F2/W	34416/1996		Kahramanmaras		
☐ TC-JGT	Boeing 737-8F2/W	34417/2009		Avanos		
☐ TC-JGU	Boeing 737-8F2/W	34418/2012		Bodrum		
☐ TC-JGV	Boeing 737-8F2/W	34419/2021	ex N60668	Cesme		
☐ TC-JGY	Boeing 737-8F2/W	35738/2592		Manavgat		
☐ TC-JGZ	Boeing 737-8F2/W	35739/2654		Midyat		
☐ TC-JHA	Boeing 737-8F2/W	35740/2673		Mudanya		
☐ TC-JHB	Boeing 737-8F2/W	35741/2685		Safranbolu		
☐ TC-JHC	Boeing 737-8F2/W	35742/2708		Iskenderun		
☐ TC-JHD	Boeing 737-8F2/W	35743/2717		Serik		
☐ TC-JHE	Boeing 737-8F2/W	357442733	ex N1786B	Burhanlye		
☐ TC-JHF	Boeing 737-8F2/W	35745/2748		Ayvalik		
☐ TC-	Boeing 737-8F2/W					o/o♦
☐ TC-	Boeing 737-8F2/W					o/o♦
☐ TC-	Boeing 737-8F2/W					o/o♦
☐ TC-	Boeing 737-8F2/W					o/o♦
☐ TC-	Boeing 737-8F2/W					o/o♦
☐ TC-JJA	Boeing 777-35RER	35160/653	ex VT-JED	Akdeniz		
☐ TC-JJB	Boeing 777-35RER	35162/666	ex VT-JEF	Marmara		
☐ TC-JJC	Boeing 777-35RER	35164/660	ex VT-JEE	Karadeniz		
☐ TC-JJD	Boeing 777-35RER	35159/650	ex VT-JEC	Anadolu		
☐ TC-JJE	Boeing 777-3F2ER	40707/895	ex N5020K	Dolmabahce		♦
☐ TC-JJF	Boeing 777-3F2ER	40708/899	ex N6009F	Beylerbeyi		♦
☐ TC-JJG	Boeing 777-3F2ER	40791/903	ex N50281	Yildiz		♦
☐ TC-JJH	Boeing 777-3F2ER	40792/906	ex N5016R	Rumeli		♦
☐ TC-JJI	Boeing 777-3F2ER	40709/909	ex N5020K	Ege		♦
☐ TC-	Boeing 777-3F2ER					o/o♦
☐ TC-	Boeing 777-3F2ER					o/o♦
☐ TC-	Boeing 777-3F2ER					o/o♦
☐ TC-	Boeing 777-3F2ER					o/o♦
☐ TC-	Boeing 777-3F2ER					o/o♦
☐ TC-	Boeing 777-3F2ER					o/o♦

TURKUAZ AIR		**(TRK)**			**Istanbul-Ataturk (IST)**
☐ TC-TCE	Airbus A321-211	0666	ex 6Y-JMD		
☐ TC-TCF	Airbus A321-211	0775	ex 6Y-JME		
☐ TC-TCG	Airbus A321-211	1905	ex N361LF		

UENSPED PAKET SERVISI/ UPS		**Unsped (UNS)**			**Istanbul-Ataturk (IST)**
☐ TC-APS	Cessna 340A	340A0247	ex N3964G		
☐ TC-UPS	Swearingen SA.226TC Merlin IVA	AT-044	ex TC-BPS	Beril	Op for UPS

ULS CARGO					**Istanbul-Ataturk (IST)**
☐ TC-ABK	Airbus A300B4-203	101	ex N59101	Adiyaman	
☐ TC-AGK	Airbus A300B4-203F	117	ex G-CEXH	Siirt 5	>AHK
☐ TC-KZU	Airbus A300B4-203	173	ex (TC-ORK)	Siirt 2	>AHK
☐ TC-KZV	Airbus A300B4-103F	041	ex PH-EAN	Siirt 4	
☐ TC-LER	Airbus A310-304F	646	ex A6-EFA		
☐ TC-SGM	Airbus A310-304F	592	ex A6-EFB		
☐ TC-VEL	Airbus A310-304F	622	ex A6-EFC		

TF-   ICELAND (Republic of Iceland)

AIR ATLANTA		Atlanta (CC/ABD)		Keflavik (KEF)
☐ TF-ELF	Airbus A300B4-622RF	529	ex EI-DJN	>TAY
☐ TF-ELK	Airbus A300B4-622RF	557	ex EI-DGU	op for ETD
☐ TF-AAA	Boeing 747-236B (SCD)	22442/526	ex N361FC	>MAS
☐ TF-ALF	Boeing 747-428BCF	25302/884	ex N919CA	o/o♦
☐ TF-AMD	Boeing 747-243M	23476/647	ex N518MC	
☐ TF-AME	Boeing 747-312	23032/603	ex F-GSEA	
☐ TF-AMI	Boeing 747-412 (SF)	27066/940	ex N706RB	>SVA
☐ TF-AMJ	Boeing 747-312	23030/593	ex CP-2525	
☐ TF-AMS	Boeing 747-481BCF	24920/832	ex JA8096	>SVA
☐ TF-AMT	Boeing 747-481	25135/863	ex JA8097	>SVA
☐ TF-AMU	Boeing 747-48EF	27603/1210	ex HL7426	>SVA
☐ TF-AMV	Boeing 747-412	28022/1082	ex 9V-SPI	>SVA
☐ TF-ARH	Boeing 747-230M (SF)	22669/549	ex N531TA	
☐ TF-ARJ	Boeing 747-236M	23735/674	ex G-BDXN	>MAS
☐ TF-ARL	Boeing 747-230B (SF)	22671/574	ex VP-BXE	
☐ TF-ARM	Boeing 747-230B (SF)	22363/490	ex N744SA	
☐ TF-ARN	Boeing 747-2F6B (SF)	22382/498	ex N745SA	>MAS
☐ TF-ARU	Boeing 747-344	22970/577	ex ZS-SAT	>SVA
☐ TF-ATI	Boeing 747-341	24107/702	ex N824DS	[VCV]♦
☐ TF-ATJ	Boeing 747-341	24108/703	ex N420DS	[VCV]
☐ TF-ATZ	Boeing 747-236B (SF)	24088/697	ex G-BDXP	

AIR ICELAND		Iceland (NY/FXI)		Akureyri/Reykjavik (AEY/REK)
☐ TF-JMM	Fokker 50	20214	ex D-AFKM	
☐ TF-JMN	Fokker 50	20223	ex D-AFKN	
☐ TF-JMO	Fokker 50	20205	ex D-AFKK	
☐ TF-JMR	Fokker 50	20243	ex TF-FIR	Asdis
☐ TF-JMS	Fokker 50	20244	ex TF-FIS	Sigdis
☐ TF-JMT	Fokker 50	20250	ex TF-FIT	Freydis
☐ TF-JMA	de Havilland DHC-8-106	335	ex C-FIZE	
☐ TF-JMB	de Havilland DHC-8-106	337	ex C-FHYQ	

BLUEBIRD CARGO		Blue Cargo (BF/BBD)		Keflavik (KEF)
☐ TF-BBD	Boeing 737-3Y0 (SF)	24463/1701	ex OY-SEE	
☐ TF-BBE	Boeing 737-36E (SF)	25256/2123	ex N314FL	
☐ TF-BBF	Boeing 737-36E (SF)	25264/2194	ex N316FL	
☐ TF-BBG	Boeing 737-36E (SF)	25263/2187	ex N317FL	
☐ TF-BBH	Boeing 737-4Y0F	23865/1582	ex N865FC	

ERNIR AIR		Artic Eagle (FEI)		Reykjavik (REK)
☐ TF-ORA	British Aerospace Jetstream 32	925	ex OY-SVR	
☐ TF-ORB	Cessna 207A Stationair 8 II	20700781	ex OY-SUC	
☐ TF-ORC	British Aerospace Jetstream 3212	981	ex OY-SVY	
☐ TF-ORD	Reims Cessna F406 Caravan II	F406-0047	ex D-IAAD	
☐ TF-ORF	Cessna 441 Conquest II	441-0057	ex N441AK	

ICEJET		Icejet (ICJ)		
☐ TF-MIK	Dornier 328-300 (328JET)	3147	ex N402FJ	
☐ TF-MIL	Dornier 328-300 (328JET)	3149	ex N403FJ	
☐ TF-MIO	Dornier 328-300 (328JET)	3181	ex N423FJ	
☐ TF-NPB	Dornier 328-300 (328JET)	3161	ex TF-MIM	

ICELANDAIR		Iceair (FI/ICE)		Keflavik/Reykjavik (KEF/REK)
☐ TF-CIB	Boeing 757-204 (PCF)	26962/440	ex N512NA	
☐ TF-FIA	Boeing 757-256/W	29310/938	ex EC-HIT	Herdubreid
☐ TF-FID	Boeing 757-23A (PCF)	24567/257	ex N757NA	TNT c/s
☐ TF-FIE	Boeing 757-23A (PCF)	24566/255	ex N566AN	
☐ TF-FIG	Boeing 757-23APF	24456/237	ex N571CA	
☐ TF-FIH	Boeing 757-208 (PCF)	24739/273		Hafdis
☐ TF-FII	Boeing 757-208	24760/281		Fanndis
☐ TF-FIJ	Boeing 757-208/W	25085/368	ex G-BTEJ	Surtsey
☐ TF-FIK	Boeing 757-2Y0	26151/472	ex G-ZAPU	♦
☐ TF-FIN	Boeing 757-208/W	28989/780	ex N1790B	Eldborg
☐ TF-FIO	Boeing 757-208/W	29436/859		Krafla
☐ TF-FIP	Boeing 757-208/W	30423/916	ex N1006K	Leifur Eriksson
☐ TF-FIR	Boeing 757-256/W	26242/593	ex EC-FYJ	Askja

☐ TF-FIU	Boeing 757-256/W	26243/603	ex PH-ITA	Hekla
☐ TF-FIV	Boeing 757-208/W	30424/956		Katla
☐ TF-FIX	Boeing 757-308/W	29434/1004	ex N60659	Hengill
☐ TF-FIZ	Boeing 757-256/W	30052/948	ex EC-HIX	Keilir

| ☐ TF-FIB | Boeing 767-383ER | 25365/395 | ex N365SR | |

ICELAND EXPRESS Reykjavik (REK)

| ☐ G-STRF | Boeing 737-76N/W | 29885/1120 | ex EI-CXD |
| ☐ G-STRN | Boeing 737-7L9 | 28007/136 | ex D-AABH |

LOFTLEIDIR ICELANDIC

Operates charter flights and ACMI leases using the AOC of its parent, Icelandair, from whom the *aircraft are leased*

MYFLUG Myflug (MYA) Myvatn (MVA)

☐ TF-MYF	Cessna U206G Stationair 6 II	U20606614	ex TC-FAE
☐ TF-MYX	Beech 200 Super King Air	BB-1136	ex LN-VIZ
☐ TF-MYY	Cessna U206F Stationair	U20602831	ex N35960

NORLANDAIR Akureyri (AEY)

| ☐ TF-NLC | de Havilland DHC-6 Twin Otter 300 | 413 | ex TF-JMC | ♦ |
| ☐ TF-NLD | de Havilland DHC-6 Twin Otter 300 | 475 | ex TF-JMD | ♦ |

WESTMANN ISLANDS AIRLINES Reykjavik (REK)

☐ TF-VEJ	Britten-Norman BN-2B-26 Islander	2209	ex G-BPLR
☐ TF-VEV	Piper PA-31-350 Chieftain	31-8152007	ex N4051Q
☐ TF-VEY	Partenavia P.68B	109	ex G-JVMR

TG- GUATEMALA (Republic of Guatemala)

AEREO RUTA MAYA Guatemala City-La Aurora (GUA)

☐ TG-ARM	Cessna 208B Caravan I	208B0768	ex N5152X
☐ TG-JCA	de Havilland DHC-6 Twin Otter 300	647	ex N300WH
☐ TG-JCB	Cessna 208B Caravan I	20800325	ex N5212M
☐ TG-JCC	Embraer EMB.110P2 Bandeirante	110348	ex N57DA
☐ TG-JCO	Embraer EMB.110P2 Bandeirante	110350	ex N102EB
☐ TG-TJG	LET L-410UVP-E	902419	ex CCCP-67626
☐ TG-TJH	LET L-410UVP-E	902418	ex CCCP-67625

Possibly also trades as Jungle Flying

AVIATECA Guatemala City-La Aurora (GUA)

| ☐ TG-TRA | ATR 42-300 (QC) | 312 | ex 9A-CTS |
| ☐ TG-TRB | ATR 42-300 (QC) | 317 | ex 9A-CTT |

AVCOM Guatemala City-La Aurora (GUA)

☐ TG-JAB	Rockwell 500S Shrike Commander	3303		
☐ TG-JAD	Rockwell 500S Shrike Commander	3123	ex N500MT	
☐ TG-JAM	Aero Commander 500B	1594-205	ex TG-HIA	
☐ TG-JAY	de Havilland DHC-7-102	46	ex C-FYMK	Mundo Maya
☐ TG-JWC	Rockwell 500S Shrike Commander	3209		

DHL DE GUATEMELA (L3/JOS) Guatemala City-La Aurora (GUA)

| ☐ TG-DHP | ATR 42-300 | 052 | ex YV-876C | Operates in DHL colours |

INTER - TRANSPORTES AEREOS INTER Transpo-Inter (9O/TSP) Guatemala City-La Aurora (GUA)

| ☐ TG-MYH | ATR 42-300 | 113 | ex G-ZAPJ | >APP |
| ☐ TG-RMM | Cessna 208B Caravan I | 208B0614 | ex TI-LRV | |

JUNGLE FLYING Guatemala City-La Aurora (GUA)

| ☐ TG-AGY | LET L-410UVP | 851404 | ex HR-IBC |
| ☐ TG-JFT | Cessna 208B Caravan I | 208B0622 | ex N52601 |

RACSA (RUTAS AEREAS CENTRO AMERICANOS) (R6) Guatemala City-La Aurora (GUA)

| ☐ TG-JSG | Nord 262 | 37 | ex HK-3878X |

526

TRANSPORTES AEREOS GUATEMALTECOS (GUM) — Guatemala City-La Aurora (GUA)

☐ TG-BJO	SAAB SF.340A	340A-142	ex N142XJ
☐ TG-JCU	Embraer EMB.110P1 Bandeirante	110218	ex TG-TAY
☐ TG-TAA	Piper PA-23-250 Aztec E	27-7304965	ex TG-PYM
☐ TG-TAB	Bell 206L LongRanger I	45315	ex N2775G
☐ TG-TAJ	LET L-410UVP	800527	ex N26RZ
☐ TG-TAT	Piper PA-31 Turbo Najavo B	31-826	ex N7438L
☐ TG-TAG	Embraer EMB.110P1 Bandeirante	110441	ex VH-LNB
☐ TG-TAK	Embraer EMB.110P1 Bandeirante	110405	ex C-FPCO
☐ TG-TAM	Embraer EMB.110P1 Bandeirante	110220	ex N101RA
☐ TG-TAN	Embraer EMB.110P1 Bandeirante	110342	ex C-GPCQ

TI- COSTA RICA (Republic of Costa Rica)

AEROBELL AIR CHARTER — San José-Tobias Bolanos (SYQ)

☐ TI-BAD	Bell 407	53403	ex N501TH
☐ TI-BAJ	Cessna 208B Caravan I	208B1180	ex N5058J
☐ TI-BAY	Cessna 208B Caravan I	208B1218	

AVIONES TAXI AEREO — San José-Juan Santamaria (SJO)

☐ TI-ABA	Piper PA-23-250 Aztec D	27-4229	ex TI-1089C	stored
☐ TI-ACA	Piper PA-23-250 Aztec C	27-3515	ex TI-1058C	
☐ TI-AST	Piper PA-23-250 Aztec E	27-7554074	ex N54763	
☐ TI-ATZ	de Havilland DHC-6 Twin Otter 200	169	ex N931MA	

NATUREAIR — (5C/NRR) — San José-Tobias Bolanos (SYQ)

☐ TI-AYQ	de Havilland DHC-6 Twin Otter 300	422	ex F-OGJV	
☐ TI-AZC	de Havilland DHC-6 Twin Otter 300	433	ex N239SA	VistaLiner
☐ TI-BBF	de Havilland DHC-6 Twin Otter 300	683	ex N237SA	VistaLiner
☐ TI-BBQ	de Havilland DHC-6 Twin Otter 300	537	ex N147SA	VistaLiner
☐ TI-	de Havilland DHC-6 Twin Otter 300	285	ex N190GC	
☐ TI-BBN	Beech 65-E90 King Air	LW-250	ex N321DM	

PARADISE AIR — San José-Tobias Bolanos (SYQ)

☐ N13AV	Gippsland GA-8 Airvan	GA8-03-028	ex VH-ARW
☐ TI-AZY	Gippsland GA-8 Airvan	GA8-02-021	ex N530AV
☐ TI-BBC	Cessna 208B Caravan I	208B1210	ex N1320U

SANSA REGIONAL — Sansa (RZ/LRS) — San José-Juan Santamaria (SJO)

☐ TI-BAK	Cessna 208B Caravan I	208B0681	ex HP-1355APP
☐ TI-BAN	Cessna 208B Caravan I	208B0710	ex HP-1358APP
☐ TI-BAP	Cessna 208B Caravan I	208B0789	ex HP-1402APP
☐ TI-BAQ	Cessna 208B Caravan I	208B0790	ex HP-1403APP
☐ TI-BCU	Cessna 208B Caravan I	208B2045	ex N5166U
☐ TI-BCV	Cessna 208B Caravan I	208B2050	ex N5148B
☐ TI-BCX	Cessna 208B Caravan I	208B2058	ex N5040E
☐ TI-BCY	Cessna 208B Caravan I	208B2064	ex N5214L
☐ TG-RYM	ATR 42-300	109	ex G-BUPS

TACA COSTA RICA — TACA CostaRica (TI/TAT) — San José-Juan Santamaria (SJO)

☐ TI-BCF	Embraer ERJ-190AR	19000205	ex PT-SGO
☐ TI-BCG	Embraer ERJ-190AR	19000215	ex PT-SGY
☐ TI-BCH	Embraer ERJ-190AR	19000221	ex PT-SHE
☐ TI-BCI	Embraer ERJ-190AR	19000228	ex PT-SHS

TACSA — San José-Tobias Bolanos (SYQ)

☐ TI-ADK	Piper PA-23-250 Aztec C	27-3209	ex TI-1087C
☐ TI-ADT	Piper PA-31 Turbo Navajo	31-403	ex F-OCOE
☐ TI-AML	Cessna TU206G Turbo Stationair 6 II	U20605181	
☐ TI-AOW	Piper PA-34-200 Seneca II	34-7670124	ex N8312C
☐ TI-ATM	Piper PA-23-250 Aztec E	27-7405413	ex N89SL
☐ TI-ATN	Cessna U206G Stationair 6 II	U20604231	ex N756NU
☐ TI-ATT	Piper PA-31 Navajo C	31-7512030	ex N500PM
☐ TI-ATU	Piper PA-31 Navajo C	31-7512011	ex N111MM
☐ TI-ATX	Piper PA-34-200 Seneca II	34-7970150	ex HP-1013JO
☐ TI-AVF	Piper PA-31 Turbo Navajo	31-582	ex N6644L

TJ-   CAMEROON (Republic of Cameroon)

AFRICAN LINES   Douala (DLA)

☐ TJ-ALD   Fokker F.28 Fellowship 4000   11226   ex N477AU
Status uncertain

CAMEROON AIRLINES   Cam-Air (UY/UYC)   Douala (DLA)

☐ TJ-CAC	Boeing 767-33AER	28138/822		Le Dja	[YAO]
☐ TJ-CAD	Boeing 767-231ER	22564/14	ex N601TW		
☐ TJ-CCG	Hawker Siddeley HS.748 Srs.2B/435	1805	ex G-11-11	Menchum	[DLA]

CHC CAMEROON   Douala (DLA)

☐ TJ-ALL	de Havilland DHC-6 Twin Otter 300	572	ex 5N-AKY
☐ TJ-CQD	Aérospatiale SA365N Dauphin 2	6062	ex 5N-ARM
☐ TJ-CQE	de Havilland DHC-6 Twin Otter 300	662	ex 5N-EVS
☐ TJ-SAB	de Havilland DHC-8-311A	276	ex PH-SDT
☐ TJ-SAY	Aérospatiale AS365N3 Dauphin 2	6571	ex PH-SLW

ELYSIAN AIRLINES

☐ ZS-OEN   Embraer EMB.120RT Brasilia   120200   ex N200CD   <NRK

NATIONAL AIRWAYS CAMEROON   (9O)   Yaounde (YAO)

| ☐ ZS-NTT | Beech 200 Super King Air | BB-350 | ex N125MS | |
| ☐ ZS-OLY | Beech 1900D | UE-39 | ex N39ZV | all-white |

TL-   CENTRAL AFRICAN REPUBLIC

AFRICA WEST   Ougadougou (OUA)

| ☐ S9-BOZ | Antonov An-12A | 2340803 | ex RA-122375São Tomé | <GLE |
| ☐ UN-11376 | Antonov An-12BK | 8345805 | ex ER-AXQ | |

CENTRAFRIQUE AIR EXPRESS

| ☐ TL-ADR | Boeing 737-268 | 21281/472 | ex HZ-AGL |
| ☐ TL-ADY | Boeing 727-223 (Raisbeck 3) | 21385/1331 | ex YK-DGL |

LOBAYE AIRWAYS   (LB)   Bangui (BGF)

☐ TL-ADU   Boeing 737-247 (Nordam 3)   23518/1265   ex N244WA

MINAIR   Ormine (OMR)   Bangui (BGF)

☐ ZS-TAS   Cessna 208B Caravan I   208B0378   ex N208SA

TN-   CONGO BRAZZAVILLE (People's Republic of Congo)

AERO FRET BUSINESS   Brazzaville (BZV)

| ☐ EX-124 | Antonov An-12BK | 7345403 | ex TN-AGZ |
| ☐ TN-AHH | Antonov An-24RV | 47309705 | ex 9XR-DB |

AEROSERVICE   Congoserv (BF/RSR)   Brazzaville/Pointe Noire (BZV/PNR)

☐ ER-AZP	Antonov An-24RV	17307002	ex RA-47810	<PXA
☐ TN-ACY	Cessna 402B	402B0810	ex TR-LTN	
☐ TN-ADN	Britten-Norman BN-2A-9 Islander	647	ex TL-AAQ	
☐ TN-ADY	Britten-Norman BN-2A-9 Islander	764	ex TR-LWL	
☐ TN-AEK	Cessna 404 Titan II	404-0132	ex TR-LXI	
☐ TN-AFD	CASA C.212-300	DF72-2-398	ex D4-CBB	

AIR CONGO INTERNATIONAL   Brazzaville (BZV)

☐ TN-AHL	AVIC 1 MA-60	0405	ex B-762L
☐ TN-AHN	AVIC 1 MA-60	0406	ex B-800L
☐ TN-AHO	AVIC 1 MA-60	0408	ex B-800L
☐ ZS-AAG	Embraer EMB.120ER Brasilia	120252	ex TN-AHV

BRAZZA AIRWAYS   Point Noire (PNR)

☐ TN-AHZ   Antonov An-12B   8345507   ex 4R-EXC

CANADIAN AIRWAYS CONGO				Point Noire (PNR)

☐ EX-008	Antonov An-24RV	37308307	ex RA-46502	

COMP AIR MOUENE				

☐ TN-AHF	LET L-410UVP	830922	ex UR-67366	
Status uncertain				

EQUAFLIGHT SERVICE				Brazzaville (BZV)

☐ F-GLPJ	Beech 1900C-1	UC-40	ex OY-BVG	

TRANSAIR CONGO	Trans-Congo (Q8/TSG)		Brazzaville/Pointe Noire (BZV/PNR)	

☐ EX-041	Antonov An-24B	99901908	ex TN-AHB	all-white	
☐ TN-AFZ	Boeing 727-23	19839/542	ex D2-FLZ		<Kirra
☐ TN-AGD	LET L-410MU	781116	ex RA-02155		
☐ TN-AGK	Antonov An-12BP	402006	ex RA-11991		
☐ TN-AHI	Boeing 737-247 (Nordam 3)	23609/1403	ex N328DL		
☐ TN-AIN	Boeing 737-236	23172/1091	ex N843AL		
☐ ZS-XGV	Fokker F.28 Fellowship 4000	11128	ex SE-DGM		

TR-   GABON (Gabonese Republic)

AIR SERVICE GABON		(X7/AGB)		Libreville (LBV)

☐ TR-LFJ	de Havilland DHC-8-311	332	ex N106AV
☐ TR-LGC	de Havilland DHC-8-102	241	ex PH-TTB
☐ TR-LGR	de Havilland DHC-8-102	237	ex PH-TTA
☐ TR-LGS	de Havilland DHC-6 Twin Otter 300	288	ex ZS-OVD
☐ TR-LGU	de Havilland DHC-6 Twin Otter 300	242	ex C-FNAN
☐ TR-LHF	de Havilland DHC-8-102	206	ex C-FHRA

AVIREX		Avirex-Gabon (G2/AVX)		Libreville (LBV)

☐ TR-LEB	Cessna 402B	402B1078	ex TN-AEZ
☐ TR-LEI	Piper PA-31 Turbo Navajo B	31-7300904	ex N4330B
☐ TR-LEQ	Reims Cessna F406 Caravan II	F406-0007	ex LX-LMS
☐ TR-LFG	Cessna 404 Titan II	404-0844	ex TJ-AHY
☐ TR-LGP	Fokker F.28 Fellowship 4000	11126	ex SE-DGL
☐ TR-LHG	Douglas DC-9-32	47198/302	ex 3D-JES
☐ TR-LVR	Cessna 207 Skywagon	20700310	ex N1710U

GABON AIRLINES		(GY/GBK)		Libreville (LBV)

☐ TF-FII	Boeing 757-208	24760/281	Fanndis	<ICE
☐ TR-LHP	Boeing 767-222	21877/46	ex N617UA	
☐ TR-LHQ	Boeing 767-222	21878/48	ex N618UA	[VCV]

LA NATIONALE				Libreville (LBV)

☐ ZS-DOC	Dornier 228-202	8104	ex MAAW-R1
☐ ZS-PMS	SAAB SF.340A	340A-059	ex N327PX

NOUVELLES AIR AFFAIRES GABON		Nouvelle Affaires (NVS)		Libreville (LBV)

☐ PH-JXK	Fokker 50	20233	ex PT-SLK	<DNM
☐ TR-CLB	de Havilland DHC-8Q-314	545	ex D-BDTM	
☐ TR-LEM	Cessna 208B Caravan I	208B0585	ex N1205M	
☐ TR-LFO	Beech 1900D	UE-313	ex ZS-OCW	
☐ TR-LFX	Cessna 208B Caravan I	208B0796	ex N99FX	
☐ TR-LGQ	Fokker 100	11424	ex F-GIOH	

SCD AVIATION				

☐ TR-NRT	Embraer EMB.120ER Brasilia	120184	ex SX-BHW

SKY GABON SA		(GV)		

☐ C-FHNM	Convair 580F	454	ex N583P	<NRL

SOLENTA AVIATION GABON				

☐ TR-LID	Antonov An-26	47302203	ex LZ-MNS
☐ TR-LIE	Antonov An-26	87307504	ex LZ-MNR

TS-   TUNISIA

KARTHAGO AIRLINES		Ka rthago (5R/KAJ)		Tunis-Carthage/Djerba-Zarzis (TUN/DJE)	
☐ TS-IEG	Boeing 737-31S	29116/3005	ex D-ADBS		
☐ TS-IEJ	Boeing 737-322	24655/1814	ex N380UA		

NOUVELAIR		Nouvelair (BJ/LBT)			Monastir (MIB)
☐ TS-INA	Airbus A320-214	1121	ex F-WWBT	Dora	
☐ TS-INB	Airbus A320-214	1175	ex F-WWDO		
☐ TS-INC	Airbus A320-214	1744	ex F-WWBS	Youssef	
☐ TS-IND	Airbus A320-212	0348	ex OY-CNN		>LAA
☐ TS-INE	Airbus A320-212	0222	ex OY-CNC		>LAA
☐ TS-INF	Airbus A320-212	0299	ex G-JDFW		
☐ TS-ING	Airbus A320-214	4347	ex D-AXAT		♦
☐ TS-INI	Airbus A320-212	0301	ex OY-CNM		
☐ TS-INL	Airbus A320-212	0400	ex N346NW		
☐ TS-INN	Airbus A320-212	0793	ex D-AICB		
☐ TS-INO	Airbus A320-214	3480	ex F-WWDK		
☐ TS-	Airbus A320-214		ex		o/o♦
☐ TS-	Airbus A320-214		ex		o/o♦
☐ TS-IQA	Airbus A321-211	0970	ex OO-SUA		
☐ TS-IQB	Airbus A321-211	0995	ex OO-SUB		

SEVENAIR		(UG/TUI)			Tunis-Carthage (TUN)
☐ TS-ISA	Canadair CRJ-900	15091	ex C-	Didon	
☐ TS-	Canadair CRJ-900		ex C-		o/o
☐ TS-LBA	ATR 42-300	245	ex G-BXBV	Alyssa	>MTW
☐ TS-LBC	ATR 72-202	281	ex F-WWLK	Tahar Haddad	
☐ TS-LBD	ATR 72-202	756	ex F-WWEQ	HasdrubalF	
☐ TS-LBE	ATR 72-202	794	ex F-WWEU		
☐ ZS-PYU	Beech 1900D	UE-107	ex N107YV		

TUNISAIR		Tunair (TU/TAR)			Tunis-Carthage (TUN)
☐ TS-IPA	Airbus A300B4-605R	558	ex A6-EKD	Sidi Bou Said	
☐ TS-IPB	Airbus A300B4-605R	563	ex A6-EKE	Tunis	
☐ TS-IPC	Airbus A300B4-605R	505	ex F-OIHB	Amilcar	
☐ TS-IMJ	Airbus A319-114	0869	ex D-AVYW	El Kantaoui	
☐ TS-IMK	Airbus A319-114	0880	ex D-AVYD	Kerkenah	
☐ TS-IMO	Airbus A319-114	1479	ex D-AVYT	Hannibal	
☐ TS-IMQ	Airbus A319-112	3096	ex D-AVWZ	Alyssa	
☐ TS-IMB	Airbus A320-211	0119	ex F-WWIJ	Fahrat Hached	
☐ TS-IMC	Airbus A320-211	0124	ex F-WWIS	7 Novembre	
☐ TS-IMD	Airbus A320-211	0205	ex F-WWDO	Khereddine	
☐ TS-IME	Airbus A320-211	0123	ex F-OGYC	Tabarka	
☐ TS-IMF	Airbus A320-211	0370	ex F-WWIP	Djerba	
☐ TS-IMG	Airbus A320-211	0390	ex F-WWDL	Abou el Kacem Chebbi	
☐ TS-IMH	Airbus A320-211	0402	ex F-WWBN	Ali Belhaouane	>MTW
☐ TS-IMI	Airbus A320-211	0511	ex F-WWDC	Jughurta	
☐ TS-IML	Airbus A320-211	0958	ex F-WWBI	Gafsa El Ksar	
☐ TS-IMM	Airbus A320-211	0975	ex F-WWIR	Le Bardo	
☐ TS-IMN	Airbus A320-211	1187	ex F-WWDU	Ibn Khaldoun	
☐ TS-IMP	Airbus A320-211	1700	ex F-WWIS	La Galite	
☐ TS-IMR	Airbus A320-214	4344	ex D-AXAS	Habib Bourguiba	♦
☐ TS-	Airbus A320-214		ex		o/o♦
☐ TS-	Airbus A320-214		ex		o/o♦
☐ TS-	Airbus A320-214		ex		o/o♦
☐ TS-	Airbus A320-214		ex		o/o♦
☐ TS-	Airbus A320-214		ex		o/o♦
☐ TS-	Airbus A320-214		ex		o/o♦
☐ TS-	Airbus A320-214		ex		o/o♦
☐ TS-IEB	Boeing 737-7L9/W	28015/785	ex OY-MRJ		>MTW
☐ TS-IOG	Boeing 737-5H3	26639/2253		Sfax	
☐ TS-IOH	Boeing 737-5H3	26640/2474		Hammamet	
☐ TS-IOI	Boeing 737-5H3	27257/2583		Mahdia	
☐ TS-IOJ	Boeing 737-5H3	27912/2701		Monastir	
☐ TS-IOK	Boeing 737-6H3	29496/268	ex N1786B	Kairouan	
☐ TS-IOL	Boeing 737-6H3	29497/282	ex N1786B	Tozeur Nefta	
☐ TS-IOM	Boeing 737-6H3	29498/310	ex N1786B	Carthage	

☐ TS-ION	Boeing 737-6H3	29499/510	ex N1786B	Utique
☐ TS-IOP	Boeing 737-6H3	29500/543		El Jem
☐ TS-IOQ	Boeing 737-6H3	29501/563	ex N1787B	Bizerte
☐ TS-IOR	Boeing 737-6H3	29502/816	ex N1786B	Tahar Haddad

TUNISAVIA		*Tunisavia (TAJ)*		*Tunis-Carthage (TUN)*

☐ TS-HSD	Aérospatiale SA365N Dauphin 2	6117	ex F-WXFC
☐ TS-HSE	Aérospatiale SA365N Dauphin 2	6150	ex F-WYMN
☐ TS-LIB	de Havilland DHC-6 Twin Otter 300	716	ex TS-DIB
☐ TS-LSF	de Havilland DHC-6 Twin Otter 300	575	ex TS-DSF

TT- TCHAD (Republic of Chad)

AIR HORIZON AFRIQUE	*Tchad-Horizon (TPK)*	*N'Djamena (NDJ)*

Operates cargo flights with Antonov An-12 Frtrs leased from other operators as required

AMW TCHAD	*(MCW)*	*N'Djamena (NDJ)*

| ☐ TT-DAE | Lockheed L-1011-100 Tristar | 193N-1101 | ex EX-072 |
| ☐ TT-DWE | Lockheed L-1011-100 Tristar | 193N-1093 | ex A8-AAB |

MID EXPRESS TCHAD			*N'Djamena (NDJ)*

| ☐ TT-DAX | Boeing 707-3K1C | 20803/878 | ex S2-ADU |

TOUMAI AIR CHAD	*Toumai Air (9D/THE)*	*N'Djamena (NDJ)*

| ☐ OD-WOL | Boeing 737-232 (AvAero 3) | 23083/1008 | ex N311DL | <WLB |
| ☐ TT-EAS | Fokker F.28 Fellowship 4000 | 11173 | ex TJ-ALC | |

TU- IVORY COAST (Republic of the Ivory Coast)

AIR INTER IVOIRE	*Inter Ivoire (NTV)*	*Abidjan (ABJ)*

☐ TU-TDC	Fairchild FH-227B	558	ex 5N-BCB	
☐ TU-TDM	Grumman G.159 Gulfstream I	20	ex TJ-WIN	[MAD]
☐ TU-TGF	Piper PA-31-350 Navajo Chieftain	31-7305072	ex N74930	
☐ TU-TJF	Piper PA-23-250 Aztec F	27-7654072	ex N62594	
☐ TU-TJN	Beech 58 Baron	TH-776	ex HB-GGE	

AIR IVOIRE	*Air Ivoire (VU/VUN)*	*Abidjan (ABJ)*

☐ F-OIVU	Airbus A321-211	1017	ex G-OOAJ	
☐ TU-TIW	Fokker F.28 Fellowship 4000	11233	ex N483US	all-white
☐ TU-TIX	Fokker F.28 Fellowship 4000	11237	ex N486US	
☐ TU-TSC	Boeing 737-522	25001/1948	ex N394RM	
☐ TU-TSD	Boeing 737-522	25008/1987	ex N384RM	
☐ TU-TSE	Boeing 737-522	25009/1999	ex N374RM	

SOPHIA AIRLINES

| ☐ TU-TBG | LET L-410UVP | 851423 | ex 3D-GAM |
| ☐ TU-TBS | LET L-410UVP | 810724 | ex 3D-BHK |

TY- BENIN (Republic of Benin)

AERO BENIN	*AeroBen (EM/AEB)*	*Cotonou (COO)*

Operates services with Boeing 727 and Boeing 737 aircraft leased from Interair or Aero Africa when required

BENIN GOLF AIR	*Benin Golf (A8/BGL)*	*Cotonou (COO)*

☐ XU-RKA	Boeing 737-2H4 (AvAero 3)	22061/639	ex N63SW	<RKH
☐ XU-RKC	Boeing 737-2H4 (AvAero 3)	22903/905	ex (PK-RIP)	<RKH
☐ XU-RKG	Boeing 727-223F	19475/511	ex N316NE	
☐ 3D-BGA	Boeing 737-2H4	21722/568	ex OM-ERA	<RFC

ROYAL AIR

☐ TY-KEC	Lockheed L-1011-1 Tristar	193C-1225	ex YK-KEC
☐ TY-KEQ	Lockheed L-1011-1 Tristar	193C-1199	ex YK-KEQ
☐ TY-KEU	Lockheed L-1011-1 Tristar	193C-1226	ex YK-KEU

TRANS AIR BENIN	Trans-Benin (N4/TNB)	Cotonou (COO)

Operates services with aircraft leased from Airquarius Aviation or TransAir Congo as required

TZ-   MALI (Republic of Mali)

ASKARI AVIATION

☐ TZ-SGI	Lockheed L1011-250 Tristar	193C-1245	ex EX-044	
☐ TZ-SPA	Lockheed L1011-250 Tristar	193C-1237	ex EX-056	

COMPAGNIE AÉRIENNE DU MALI   Bamako (BKO)

☐ TZ-RCA	Canadair CRJ-200ER	7392	ex N646BR	♦
☐ TZ-RMA	McDonnell-Douglas MD-87	49832/1703	ex I-AFRB	
☐ TZ-RMB	McDonnell-Douglas MD-87	49841/1751	ex EC-EYZ	
☐ TZ-RMK	McDonnell-Douglas MD-83	53463/2089	ex N160BS	
☐ ZS-PML	SAAB SF.340A	340A-034	ex N338BE	

MALI AIR EXPRESS   Avion Express (VXP)   Bamako (BKO)

☐ 3X-GDK	LET L-410UVP	800419	ex RA-67153
☐ 3X-GED	SAAB SF.340A	340A-051	ex ZS-PMN
☐ 3X-GEJ	SAAB SF.340A	340A-136	ex ZK-NLN

MALI AIR TRANSPORT   Bamako (BKO)

☐ TZ-NBA	Boeing 727-2K5/W (Duganair 3)	21853/1640	ex P4-JLI

T3-   KIRIBATI (Republic of Kiribati)

AIR KIRIBATI   (4A)   Tarawa-Bonriki Intl (TRW)

☐ T3-ATI	Harbin Y-12 II	0077	
☐ T3-ATJ	CASA C.212-200	CD67-01-356	ex N398FL

CORAL SUN AIRWAYS

☐ T3-JMR	Britten-Norman BN-2A-21 Islander	494	ex VH-SQS
☐ T3-VIN	Britten-Norman BN-2B-26 Islander	2154	ex VH-YIE

T8A-   PALAU

PACIFICFLYER   (PI/PFL)

☐ CS-TEI	Airbus A310-304	495	ex F-WWCO	<HFY♦

UK   UZBEKISTAN (Republic of Uzbekistan)

AVIALEASING   Twinarrow (EC/TWN)   Tashkent-Vostochny/Miami-Opa Locka, FL (TAS/OPF)

☐ N5057E	Antonov An-26	6101	ex 57 red		based OPF
☐ UK 11418	Antonov An-12B	402504	ex RA-11996		based OPF
☐ UK 12002	Antonov An-12B	402002	ex RA-11373		
☐ UK 26001	Antonov An-26B	67314402	ex UK 26213		[OPF]
☐ UK 26003	Antonov An-26	07310406	ex S9-BOW	The Sky's the Limit	[OPF]

Those based at Opa Locka, FL operate cargo flights for Bahamasair and DHL

QANOT SHARQ   Qanot Sharq (QNT)   Tashkent-Vostochny (TAS)

☐ UK 76353	Ilyushin Il-76TD	102314454	ex 76353

SAMARKAND AIRWAYS   Sogdiana (C7/UZS)   Tashkent-Vostochny (TAS)

Operates services with Antonov An-12/26 and Ilyushin Il-76 aircraft leased from other operators as required

TAPO-AVIA   Cortas (4C/CTP)   Tashkent-Vostochny (TAS)

☐ UK 11807	Antonov An-12BK	00346910	ex CCCP-11807
☐ UK 58644	Antonov An-12BP	2340303	ex CCCP-58644
☐ UK 76375	Ilyushin Il-76TD	1033414496	
☐ UK 76821	Ilyushin Il-76TD	0023441200	ex 4K-AZ62

UZBEKISTAN AIRWAYS · Uzbek (HY/UZB) · Tashkent-Vostochny/Samarkand (TAS/SKD)

☐ UK 31004	Airbus A300B4-622RF	717	ex HL7299	
☐ UK 31005	Airbus A300B4-622RF	722	ex HL7244	
☐ UK 31001	Airbus A310-324	574	ex F-OGQY	Tashkent
☐ UK 31002	Airbus A310-324	576	ex F-OGQZ	Fergana
☐ UK 31003	Airbus A310-324	706	ex F-WWCM	Bukhara
☐ UK 32011	Airbus A320-214	4371	ex D-AVVA	♦
☐ UK 32012	Airbus A320-214	4395	ex D-AVVK	♦
☐ UK 32014	Airbus A320-214	4417	ex F-WWDM	♦
☐ UK 32015	Airbus A320-214	4485	ex D-AUBF	♦
☐ UK 32016	Airbus A320-214	4492	ex D-AUBJ	♦
☐ UK	Airbus A320-214		ex	o/o♦
☐ UK	Airbus A320-214		ex	o/o♦
☐ UK	Airbus A320-214		ex	o/o♦
☐ UK 46223	Antonov An-24B	77303102	ex CCCP-46223	
☐ UK 46360	Antonov An-24B	07305901	ex RA-46360	
☐ UK 46373	Antonov An-24B	07306004	ex CCCP-46373	
☐ UK 46387	Antonov An-24B	07306110	ex 46387	
☐ UK 46392	Antonov An-24B	07306205	ex CCCP-46392	
☐ UK 46573	Antonov An-24B	87304807	ex CCCP-46573	
☐ UK 46594	Antonov An-24B	97305104	ex CCCP-46594	
☐ UK 46623	Antonov An-24RV	37308710	ex CCCP-46623	
☐ UK 46658	Antonov An-24RV	47309304	ex CCCP-46658	
☐ UK 47274	Antonov An-24B	07306404	ex CCCP-47274	
☐ UK 80001	Avro 146-RJ85	E2312	ex G-6-312	VIP a/cop for Govt
☐ UK 80002	Avro 146-RJ85	E2309	ex G-6-309	
☐ UK 80003	Avro 146-RJ85	E2319	ex G-6-319	
☐ UK 75700	Boeing 757-23P	28338/731		Op for Govt
☐ VP-BUB☐	Boeing 757-23P	30060/875	ex UK 75701	Urgench
☐ VP-BUD☐	Boeing 757-23P	30061/886	ex N6066Z	Shahrisabz
☐ VP-BUH	Boeing 757-231	30339/896	ex N726TW	
☐ VP-BUI	Boeing 757-231	28487/878	ex N719TW	
☐ VP-BUJ	Boeing 757-231	28488/884	ex N724TW	
☐ UK 67000	Boeing 767-33PER	35796/958	ex N5014K	VIP a/c op for Govt
☐ UK 67001	Boeing 767-33PER	28370/635	ex VP-BUA	Samarkand
☐ VP-BUE	Boeing 767-3CBER	33469/904	ex N594HA	
☐ VP-BUF	Boeing 767-33PER	33078/928		
☐ VP-BUZ	Boeing 767-33PER	28392/650	ex (UK 76702)Khiva	
☐ UK 76351	Ilyushin Il-76TD	1013408240	ex RA-76351	[TAS]
☐ UK 76358	Ilyushin Il-76TD	1023410339		
☐ UK 76359	Ilyushin Il-76TD	1033414483		
☐ UK 76426	Ilyushin Il-76TD	1043419644		
☐ UK 76428	Ilyushin Il-76TD	1043419648	ex 76428	
☐ UK 76449	Ilyushin Il-76TD	1023403058	ex 76449	
☐ UK 76782	Ilyushin Il-76TD	0093498971	ex CCCP-76782	
☐ UK 76793	Ilyushin Il-76TD	0093498951	ex CCCP-76793	
☐ UK 76794	Ilyushin Il-76TD	0093498954	ex CCCP-76794	[TAS]
☐ UK 76805	Ilyushin Il-76TD	1003403109	ex CCCP-76805	
☐ UK 76811	Ilyushin Il-76TD	1013407223	ex 76811	[TAS]
☐ UK 76813	Ilyushin Il-76TD	1013408246	ex CCCP-76813	[TAS]
☐ UK 76824	Ilyushin Il-76TD	1023410327	ex CCCP-76824	[TAS]
☐ UK 86056	Ilyushin Il-86	51483203023	ex CCCP-86056	[TAS]
☐ UK 86064	Ilyushin Il-86	51483203031	ex CCCP-86064	[TAS]
☐ UK 86090	Ilyushin Il-86	51483207061	ex CCCP-86090	[TAS]
☐ UK 91102	Ilyushin Il-114-100	109380202	ex UK 91009	
☐ UK 91104	Ilyushin Il-114-100	2093800204		
☐ UK 91105	Ilyushin Il-114-100	2063800205	ex 91105	
☐ UK 91106	Ilyushin Il-114-100	2083800206	ex 91106	
☐ UK 85575	Tupolev Tu-154B-2	83A575	ex 85575	[TAS]
☐ UK 85578	Tupolev Tu-154B-2	83A578	ex 85578	[TAS]
☐ UK 85600	Tupolev Tu-154B-2	84A600	ex 85600	[TAS]
☐ UK 85711	Tupolev Tu-154M	91A887	ex 85711	[TAS]
☐ UK 85764	Tupolev Tu-154M	93A947	ex RA-85764	[TAS]
☐ UK 85776	Tupolev Tu-154M	93A958		[TAS]

☐ UK 87923	Yakovlev Yak-40	9741455	ex CCCP-87923	VIP
☐ UK 88194	Yakovlev Yak-40	9621448	ex CCCP-88194	
☐ UK 88217	Yakovlev Yak-40	9630350	ex CCCP-88217	VIP

UP- KAZAKHSTAN (Republic of Kazakhstan)

AEROTRANS — *Bachyt (ATG)* — *Taraz (DMB)*

☐ UN-85521	Tupolev Tu-154B-2	81A521	ex CCCP-85521	
☐ UN-85569	Tupolev Tu-154B-2	82A569	ex LZ-BTV	

AEROTUR AIR — *Diasa (RAI)* — *Astana (TSE)*

☐ UP-T5407	Tupolev Tu-154M	87A754	ex UN-85570	

AIR ALMATY — *Agleb (LMY)* — *Almaty (ALA)*

☐ UP-AN215	Antonov An-12BP	6344305	ex UN-11650	
☐ UP-I7601	Ilyushin Il-76TD	1013409295	ex YL-LAJ	
☐ UP-I7602	Ilyushin Il-76T	0003427796	ex UN-76034	
☐ UP-I7603	Ilyushin Il-76	083414432	ex UN-76023	
☐ UP-I7633	Ilyushin Il-76T	093420594	ex RA-76518	

AIR AKTOBE — *Aktobe*

☐ UP-L4101	LET L-410UVP	841229	ex UN-67464	

AIR ASTANA — *Astanaline(KC/KZR)* — *Astana/Almaty(TSE/ALA)*

☐ P4-YAS	Airbus A319-132	3614	ex D-AVYL	
☐ P4-PAS	Airbus A320-232	2128	ex D-ARFF	
☐ P4-SAS	Airbus A320-232	2016	ex SX-BVC	
☐ P4-TAS	Airbus A320-232	2828	ex F-WWDN	
☐ P4-UAS	Airbus A320-232	2987	ex F-WWIH	
☐ P4-VAS	Airbus A320-232	3141	ex F-WWDO	
☐ P4-WAS	Airbus A320-232	3484	ex F-WWIE	
☐ P4-XAS	Airbus A320-232	3519	ex F-WWDR	
☐ P4-NAS	Airbus A321-231	1042	ex N104AQ	
☐ P4-OAS	Airbus A321-231	1204	ex N120ED	
☐	Embraer ERJ-190LR		ex	o/o♦
☐	Embraer ERJ-190LR		ex	o/o♦
☐ P4-HAS	Fokker 50	20198	ex PH-ZDH	
☐ P4-IAS	Fokker 50	20188	ex PH-ZDD	
☐ P4-JAS	Fokker 50	20195	ex PH-ZDG	
☐ P4-KAS	Fokker 50	20187	ex PH-ZDC	
☐ P4-LAS	Fokker 50	20193	ex PH-ZDE	
☐ P4-EAS	Boeing 757-2G5/W	29488/830	ex D-AMUG	
☐ P4-FAS	Boeing 757-2G5/W	29489/834	ex D-AMUH	
☐ P4-GAS	Boeing 757-2G5/W	28112/708	ex D-AMUI	
☐ P4-MAS	Boeing 757-28A/W	28833/782	ex B-2852	
☐ P4-KCA	Boeing 767-306ER	27612/647	ex PH-BZI	
☐ P4-KCB	Boeing 767-306ER	27614/661	ex PH-BZK	

ASIA CONTINENTAL AIRLINES — *Acid (CID)* — *Almaty (ALA)*

☐ UP-I7617	Ilyushin Il-76TD	0013430890	ex UN-76021	
☐ UP-I7618	Ilyushin Il-76T	0013428831	ex UN-76022	
☐ UP-I7627	Ilyushin Il-76T	0003423699	ex ER-IBV	

ATMA — *(AMA)*

☐ UP-AN211	Antonov An-12B	02348207	ex UN-11017	
☐ UP-AN212	Antonov An-12TB	01347701	ex UN-11019	
☐ UP-AN213	Antonov An-12BP	2340806	ex UN-11015	
☐ UN-76499	Ilyushin Il-76TD	0023441186	ex RA-76499	

ATYRAU AIR WAYS — *Edil (IP/JOL)* — *Atyrau (GUW)*

☐ UP-T3405	Tupolev Tu-134A	40150	ex UN-65610 Bayterek	
☐ UP-T3406	Tupolev Tu-134A	31218	ex UN-65619 Venera	VIP

534

	Reg	Type	c/n	Notes	
☐	UP-T5406	Tupolev Tu-154M	93A965	ex UN-85781	
☐	UN-25358	Mil Mi-8T	98206781	ex CCCP-25388	Jt ops with KAW
☐	UN-27055	Mil Mi-8MTV-1	95889	ex CCCP-27055	
☐	UN-65069	Tupolev Tu-134A-3	49908	ex RA-65069 Kashagan	
☐	UN-65070	Tupolev Tu-134A-3	49912	ex RA-65070 Tungysh	

AVIA JAYNAR — Tobol (SAP) — Kostanay (KSN)

☐	UP-AN401	Antonov An-24B	88901605	ex UN-47153	

BEIBARS

☐	UP-I7625	Ilyushin Il-76TD	0033446350	ex UN-76472	
☐	UP-I7626	Ilyushin Il-76M	1013409303	ex YU-AMJ	

BERKUT AIR — Berkut (BEK) — Almaty (ALA)

☐	UP-Y4003	Yakovlev Yak-40	9632048	ex UN-88198	
☐	UP-Y4023	Yakovlev Yak-40	9411533	ex UN-87403	
☐	UN-87306	Yakovlev Yak-40	9302229	ex CCCP-87306	
☐	UN-88191	Yakovlev Yak-40	9621148	ex CCCP-88191	VIP
☐	UN-88260	Yakovlev Yak-40	9711552	ex CCCP-88260	VIP

BERKUT STATE AIR COMPANY — (BEC) — Almaty (ALA)

☐	UP-AN205	Antonov An-12BP	02348304	ex UN-11373	
☐	UP-B5701	Boeing 757-2M6ER	23454/102	ex P4-NSN	VIP
☐	UP-B6701	Boeing 767-2DXER	32954/861	ex UN-B7601	VIP
☐	UP-I7604	Ilyushin Il-76TD	1033414485	ex UN-76371	
☐	UP-I7605	Ilyushin Il-76TD	1033416520	ex UN-76374	
☐	UP-MI702	Mil Mi-172 (Mi-8MTV-3)	398C01	ex UN-17201	VIP
☐	UP-MI814	Mil Mi-8MTV-1	96275	ex UN-25401	VIP
☐	UP-T5401	Tupolev Tu-154M	91A889	ex UN-85713	
☐	UN-85464	Tupolev Tu-154B-2	80A464	ex 85464	VIP

DETA AIR — Almaty (ALA)

☐	UP-DC101	Douglas DC-10-40F	47823/306	ex VP-BDE	
☐	UP-DC102	Douglas DC-10-40F	47855/349	ex VP-BDF	
☐	UP-I6206	Ilyushin Il-62M	3242321	ex UN-86524 Galina	
☐	UP-I6207	Ilyushin Il-62M	1545951	ex UN-86935	
☐	UP-I6209	Ilyushin Il-62M	3139956	ex RA-86518	

EAST WING — E Wing (EWZ) — Taraz / Fujairah, UAE (DMB/FJR)

☐	UP-I7621	Ilyushin Il-76TD	0013434018	ex UN-76008	
☐	UP-I7622	Ilyushin Il-76T	0003426765	ex UN-76011	
☐	UP-I7623	Ilyushin Il-76TD	0033448404	ex UN-76010	
☐	UP-I7624	Ilyushin Il-76TD	0023442218	ex UN-76033	
☐	UN-76497	Ilyushin Il-76T	043402039	ex 3C-QRA	
☐	UN-B1110	BAC One-Eleven 401AK	078	ex UN-B1111 East Wing titles	
☐	UN-11006	Antonov An-12BP	01347909	ex 3C-QRI	
☐	UN-11008	Antonov An-12B	4342505	ex 18 RED	
☐	UN-11009	Antonov An-12B	53403408	ex 3C-MIR	
☐	UN-11010	Antonov An-12B	53403606		
☐	UN-26087	Antonov An-26	27312601	ex 4L-26087	

EASTERN EXPRESS

☐	UP-I7606	Ilyushin Il-76T	0033446325	ex UN-76026	
☐	UP-I7607	Ilyushin Il-76TD	0033447364	ex UN-76027	
☐	UP-I7612	Ilyushin Il-76T	0003425746	ex UN-76032	
☐	UP-I7628	Ilyushin Il-76TD	0053460790	ex EW-264TH	
☐	UP-I7629	Ilyushin Il-76TD	1013408257	ex HA-TCB	
☐	UN-76029	Ilyushin Il-76TD	1013406294	ex ER-IAS	
☐	UN-11020	Antonov An-12			
☐	UP-AN203	Antonov An-12BK	00347408	ex ER-ACV	
☐	UN-11021	Antonov An-12			

EURO-ASIA INTERNATIONAL — Eakaz (5B/EAK) — Almaty/Sharjah (ALA/SHJ)

☐	UP-Y4026	Yakovlev Yak-40	9510639	ex UN-87337 Aibike titles	VIP
☐	UP-Y4027	Yakovlev Yak-40K	9741856	ex UN-87935	VIP
☐	UP-Y4028	Yakovlev Yak-40K	9710453	ex UN-88266	

EXCELLENT GLIDE

☐ UP-Y4208	Yakovlev Yak-42D	4520423116650	ex UN-42642	

INVESTAVIA | | (TLG) | | Almaty (ALA)

☐ UP-I6210	Ilyushin Il-62M	3255333	ex UN-86130 NRG titles	

KAZ AIR TRANS

☐ UP-B3704	Boeing 737-2H3	22624/758	ex A6-AVE	

KAZAIR WEST | | Kazwest (KAW) | | Atyrau (GUW)

☐ UP-L4104	LET L-410UVP-E	861606	ex UN-67566	
☐ UP-T3402	Tupolev Tu-134B-3	63187	ex UN-65799	VIP
☐ UP-Y4015	Yakovlev Yak-40K	9831958	ex UN-87221	
☐ UN-25358	Mil Mi-8T	98206781	ex CCCP-25358	Jt ops with JOL
☐ UN-25517	Mil Mi-8PS-9	8687	ex CCCP-25517	
☐ UN-67611	LET L-410UVP-E	892339	ex OM-UDX	

KAZAKHMYS

☐ UP-L4102	LET L-410UVP-E	902512	ex UR-SVI	
☐ UP-Y4014	Yakovlev Yak-40K	9732054	ex UN-87912	

KAZZINC

☐ UP-Y4006	Yakovlev Yak-40K	9740556	ex UN-87934	
☐ UP-Y4204	Yakovlev Yak-42	45204223408016	ex UN-42430	VIP

KHOZU AVIA | | Khozavia (OZU) | | Almaty (ALA)

☐ UP-Y4201	Yakovlev Yak-42D	4520423302017	ex UN-42641	VIPop for Govt
☐ UP-Y4202	Yakovlev Yak-42D	4520423402116	ex UN-42323	VIP
☐ UP-Y4204	Yakovlev Yak-42D	4520423408016	ex UN-42430	

KOKSHETAU AIRLINES | | Kokta (KRT) | | Kokchetav (KOV)

☐ UN-86505	Ilyushin Il-62M	1748445	ex UR-86135 no titles	[ALA]
☐ UN-86506	Ilyushin Il-62M	1138234	ex UR-86133	[ALA]
☐ UN-87913	Yakovlev Yak-40	9730255	ex CCCP-87913	
☐ UN-88221	Yakovlev Yak-40	9630750	ex CCCP-88221	
☐ UN-88277	Yakovlev Yak-40	9721953	ex CCCP-88277	

MAK AIR | | (AKM) | | Almaty (ALA)

☐ UP-T5405	Tupolev Tu-154M	89A823	ex UN-85855	

MEGA AIRCOMPANY | | Mega (MGK) | | Almaty (ALA)

☐ UP-B2701	Boeing 727-232 (FedEx 3)	22045/1602	ex UN-B2701	
☐ UP-B2702	Boeing 727-232 (FedEx 3)	21861/1554	ex UN-B2702	
☐ UP-B2703	Boeing 727-232 (FedEx 3)	21584/1478	ex UN-B2703	
☐ UP-I1801	Ilyushin Il-18D	187010204	ex UN-75005	
☐ UP-I1802	Ilyushin Il-18E	185008603	ex UN-75002	
☐ UP-I1803	Ilyushin Il-18V	184006903	ex UN-75003	
☐ UP-I1804	Ilyushin Il-18GrM	186009202	ex UN-75004	
☐ UN-26517	Antonov An-26	7002	ex CCCP-26517	

MIRAS AIR | | Miras (MIF) | | Almaty (ALA)

☐ UP-AN201	Antonov An-12BP	01348007	ex YU-AIA	

SAMAL AIR | | (SAV) | | Almaty (ALA)

☐ UP-T3401	Tupolev Tu-134AK-3	63684	ex UN-65900	[ALA]
☐ UN-86507	Ilyushin Il-62M	4242654	ex RA-86507 Ivan	

SAT AIRLINES | | Satco (SOZ) | | Almaty (ALA)

☐ UP-T3403	Tupolev Tu-134A-3	62545	ex UN-65776	VIP
☐ UP-T3404	Tupolev Tu-134A-3	66212	ex UN-65551	VIP
☐ UN-65720	Tupolev Tu-134B-3	62820	ex CCCP-65720	VIP

SAYAKHAT | | Sayakhat (W7/SAH) | | Almaty (ALA)

☐ UP-I7613	Ilyushin Il-76	1023412395	ex UN-76434	
☐ UP-I7615	Ilyushin Il-76TD	1003401015	ex UN-76384	
☐ UP-T5402	Tupolev Tu-154M	86A726	ex UN-85852	

536

☐ UP-T5403	Tupolev Tu-154M	86A728	ex UN-85853	
☐ UP-T5404	Tupolev Tu-154M	86A729	ex UN-85854	>SXA

SAYAT AIR		**(SYM)**		**Almaty (ALA)**
☐ UP-I6204	Ilyushin Il-62M	4255152	ex UN-86566	
☐ UP-I6205	Ilyushin Il-62M	3357947	ex UN-86586	

SCAT AIRCOMPANY		**Vlasta (DV/VSV)**		**Shymkent**
☐ UP-AN202	Antonov An-12BP	3341201	ex UN-11367	
☐ UP-AN404	Antonov An-24B	17307303	ex UN-26196	
☐ UP-AN405	Antonov An-24B	77303508	ex UN-46265	
☐ UP-AN406	Antonov An-24B	77303604	ex UN-46271	
☐ UP-AN407	Antonov An-24B	87305305	ex UN-46310	
☐ UP-AN408	Antonov An-24B	97305608	ex UN-46340	
☐ UP-AN409	Antonov An-24B	07305909	ex UN-46368	
☐ UP-AN410	Antonov An-24B	07306104	ex UN-46381	
☐ UP-AN411	Antonov An-24B	87304106	ex UN-46421	
☐ UP-AN412	Antonov An-24B	87304309	ex UN-46438	
☐ UP-AN413	Antonov An-24RV	37309305	ex UN-46500	
☐ UP-AN414	Antonov An-24RV	37308305	ex UN-46626	
☐ UP-AN415	Antonov An-24RV	47309505	ex UN-46664	
☐ UP-AN416	Antonov An-24RV	47309604	ex UN-46672	
☐ UP-AN417	Antonov An-24RV	47309910	ex UN-46699	
☐ UP-AN418	Antonov An-24B	89901810	ex UN-47176	
☐ UP-AN419	Antonov An-24RV	27307609	ex UN-47258	
☐ UP-AN420	Antonov An-24B	07306308	ex UN-47270	
☐ UP-AN421	Antonov An-24B	07306407	ex UN-47277	
☐ UP-AN422	Antonov An-24B	07306504	ex UN-47284	
☐ UP-AN423	Antonov An-24RV	67310509	ex UN-47350	
☐ UP-AN424	Antonov An-24RV	27307509	ex UN-47692	
☐ UP-AN425	Antonov An-24B	79901307	ex UN-47763	
☐ UP-AN426	Antonov An-24B	17307406	ex UN-47844	
☐ UP-AN601	Antonov An-26	0503	ex UN-26027	
☐ LY-FLB	Boeing 737-322/W	24667/1893	ex ES-LBA	
☐ UP-B3701	Boeing 737-230 (Nordam 3)	22123/726	ex N123AQ	
☐ UP-B3702	Boeing 737-277 (Nordam 3)	22650/806	ex YA-GAB	
☐ LY-FLG	Boeing 757-204	27237/602	ex G-BYAR	
☐ UP-Y4203	Yakovlev Yak-42D	4250421116567	ex UN-42401	
☐ UP-Y4205	Yakovlev Yak-42D	4520421219029	ex UN-42410	<MSI
☐ UP-Y4210	Yakovlev Yak-42D	4520422306016	ex UN-42428	

SEMEYAVIA		**Ertis (SMK)**		**Semipalatinsk (PLX)**
☐ UP-Y4016	Yakovlev Yak-40K	9810557	ex UN-87208	
☐ UN-87204	Yakovlev Yak-40K	9810157	ex CCCP-87204	

STARLINE KZ				
☐ UP-B2704	Boeing 727-225F (FedEx 3)	22046/1604	ex A6-RSA	

TULPAR AIR SERVICE		**Tulpa (2T/TUX)**		**Qaraghandy-Sary Arka (KGF)**
☐ UP-AN427	Antonov An-24B	97305001	ex UN -46582	
☐ UN-46448	Antonov An-24B	87304410	ex CCCP-46448	
☐ UN-46492	Antonov An-24RV	27305001	ex CCCP-46492	
☐ UN-46611	Antonov An-24RV	37308608	ex CCCP-46611	
☐ UN-26579	Antonov An-26B	13404	ex CCCP-26579	

YUZHNAYA AIRCOMPANY		**Pluton (UGN)**		**Almaty (ALA)**
☐ UN-75001	Ilyushin Il-18D	187009904	ex YR-IMM	
☐ UN-85478	Tupolev Tu-154B-2	81A478	ex EX-017	

ZHETYSU AVIA		**Zhetysu Avia (JTU)**		**Almaty (ALA)**
☐ UP-Y4019	Yakovlev Yak-40K	9741855	ex UN-87927	
☐ UN-87931	Yakovlev Yak-40	9740256	ex CCCP-87931	

ZHEZHAIR		**Ulutau (KZH)**		**Zhezkazgan (DZN)**
☐ UP-Y4012	Yakovlev Yak-40	9742055	ex UN-87929 KCC titles	
☐ UP-Y4013	Yakovlev Yak-40	9731055	ex UN-87920 KCC titles	
☐ UN-24143	Mil Mi-8T	98841441	ex RA-24143	
☐ UN-24262	Mil Mi-8T	98734158	ex CCCP-24262	
☐ UN-67491	LET L-410UVP	841316	ex CCCP-67491	

UR-   UKRAINE

AERO-CHARTER UKRAINE — Charter Ukraine (DW/UCR) — Kiev-Borispol (KBP)

☐ UR-DWA	Antonov An-26	47313905	ex HA-TCS
☐ UR-DWB	Antonov An-26B	6207	ex UR-BXB
☐ UR-DWD	Antonov An-26B	10103	ex ER-AFF
☐ UR-DWF	Antonov An-12BK	8345802	ex LZ-MNK
☐ UR-DWG	Antonov An-12BP	8345710	ex LZ-MNP
☐ UR-CDW	Yakovlev Yak-40	9610546	ex UR-88151
☐ UR-DAP	Yakovlev Yak-40	9521241	ex RA-87530
☐ UR-DWC	Yakovlev Yak-40	9541144	ex UR-87987
☐ UR-LRZ	Yakovlev Yak-40K	9641851	ex LY-ARZ
☐ UR-88290	Yakovlev Yak-40K	9840459	ex CCCP-88290

AEROMOST KHARKOV — Aeromist (HT/AHW) — Kharkov-Osnova (HRK)

☐ UR-14002	Antonov An-140	36525302006

AEROSTAR — Aerostar (UAR) — Kiev-Zhulyany/Kiev-Borispol (IEV/KBP)

☐ UR-AIS	Yakovlev Yak-40	9211821	ex UR-87566

AEROSVIT AIRLINES — Aerosvit (VV/AEW) — Kiev-Borispol (KBP)

☐ UR-46677	Antonov An-24RV	47309609	ex RA-46677	
☐ UR-47294	Antonov An-24RV	07306604	ex RA-47294	<URP
☐ UR-47312	Antonov An-24RV	57310403	ex RA-47312 all-white	
☐ UR-	Antonov An-148-100B			o/o♦
☐ UR-	Antonov An-148-100B			o/o♦
☐ UR-	Antonov An-148-100B			o/o♦
☐ UR-	Antonov An-148-100B			o/o♦
☐ UR-	Antonov An-148-100B			o/o♦
☐ UR-BVY	Boeing 737-2Q8	22760/852	ex F-GEXJ	
☐ UR-VVA	Boeing 737-3Q8	24492/1808	ex N492GD	
☐ UR-VVE	Boeing 737-448	24521/1788	ex EI-BXB	
☐ UR-VVL	Boeing 737-448	25052/2036	ex EI-BXI	
☐ UR-VVM	Boeing 737-448	25736/2269	ex EI-BXK	
☐ UR-VVN	Boeing 737-4Y0	24903/1978	ex M-ABCO	♦
☐ UR-VVP	Boeing 737-4Q8	26290/2482	ex OK-YGA	
☐ UR-VVQ	Boeing 737-5L9	29235/3076	ex OK-DGC	
☐ UR-VVR	Boeing 737-3Q8	24699/1886	ex TC-TJA	
☐ UR-VVS	Boeing 737-5Q8	26324/2735	ex ES-ABC	
☐ UR-VVU	Boeing 737-5Q8	26323/2770	ex ES-ABD	
☐ UR-AAG	Boeing 767-33AER	25532/442	ex V8-RBG	o/o♦
☐ UR-AAH	Boeing 767-33AER	25534/477	ex V8-RBH	o/o♦
☐ UR-AAJ	Boeing 767-33AER	25533/454	ex V8-RBJ	o/o♦
☐ UR-DNM	Boeing 767-322ER	25280/391	ex N202AC	♦
☐ UR-VVF	Boeing 767-383ER	24476/274	ex N4476F	
☐ UR-VVO	Boeing 767-383ER	24475/273	ex XA-MXB	
☐ UR-VVT	Boeing 767-3Q8ER	28132/692	ex B-2493	
☐ UR-VVV	Boeing 767-33AER	25536/504	ex V8-RBK	♦
☐ UR-VVW	Boeing 767-33AER	27189/521	ex V8-RBL	o/o♦

AEROVIS AIRLINES — Aeroviz (VIZ) — Rivnu (RWN)

☐ UR-CBF	Antonov An-12BP	2340507	ex LZ-SFW
☐ UR-CBG	Antonov An-12BP	6343705	ex UR-11302
☐ UR-CCP	Antonov An-12A	2340505	ex LZ-CBM
☐ UR-CEX	Antonov An-12B	4342103	ex RA-93915
☐ UR-CEZ	Antonov An-12B	6344304	ex RA-98118
☐ UR-CFB	Antonov An-12BP	6343802	ex 02 red
☐ UR-CGU	Antonov An-12BK	7345203	ex 09 red

AIR URGA — Urga (3N/URG) — Kirovograd-Khmelyovoye (KGO)

☐ UR-CFU	Antonov An-24RV	7310609	ex RDPL-34005	
☐ UR-ELC	Antonov An-24RV	57310410	ex UR-47313	Op for UN
☐ UR-ELK	Antonov An-24RV	57310203	ex UR-47300 all-white	
☐ UR-ELL	Antonov An-24RV	67310503	ex UR-47316	
☐ UR-ELM	Antonov An-24RV	67310506	ex UR-47319	
☐ UR-ELN	Antonov An-24B	89901607	ex UR-47155	Op for UN as UN-967
☐ UR-ELO	Antonov An-24RV	47309507	ex UR-46666	Op for UNA as UN-628

538

☐ UR-ELT	Antonov An-24RV	27307809	ex XU-054	Op for UN
☐ UR-ELW	Antonov An-24RV	57310109	ex XU-375	stored
☐ UR-46311	Antonov An-24B	97305307	ex LZ-MND	Op for UN as UN-969
☐ UR-46464	Antonov An-24RV	27307810	ex ER-46464	Op for UN
☐ UR-ELB	Antonov An-26B	14005	ex UR-26201	Op for UN as UN-687
☐ UR-ELD	Antonov An-26B	14010	ex UR-26203	
☐ UR-ELE	Antonov An-26B	12108	ex UR-26111	Op for UN
☐ UR-ELF	Antonov An-26B	12204	ex UR-26115	
☐ UR-ELG	Antonov An-26B	12902	ex UR-26140	Op for UN as UN-698
☐ UR-ELH	Antonov An-26B	12908	ex UR-26143	>/ op for Air Boyoma
☐ UR-ELP	Antonov An-26B	47313408	ex UR-26580	
☐ UR-ELR	Antonov An-26B	9807	ex UR-26004	Op for UN as UNO-967

ANTONOV AIRLINES — Antonov Bureau (ADB) — Kiev-Gostomel

☐ UR-82007	Antonov An-124-100	19530501005	ex CCCP-82007	
☐ UR-82008	Antonov An-124-100M-150	19530501006	ex CCCP-82008	
☐ UR-82009	Antonov An-124-100	19530501007	ex CCCP-82009	
☐ UR-82027	Antonov An-124-100	19530502288	ex CCCP-82027	
☐ UR-82029	Antonov An-124-100	19530502630	ex CCCP-82029	
☐ UR-82072	Antonov An-124-100	9773053359136	ex RA-82072	
☐ UR-82073	Antonov An-124-100	9773054359139	ex RA-82073	
☐ UR-09307	Antonov An-22A	043481244	ex CCCP-09307	
☐ UR-11315	Antonov An-12BP	4342307	ex RA-11315	
☐ UR-74010	Antonov An-74T	36547030450	ex CCCP-74010	VIP
☐ UR-82060	Antonov An-225 Mriya	19530503763	ex CCCP-82060	

ARP 410 AIRLINES — Air-Arp (URP) — Kiev-Zhulyany (IEV)

☐ UR-CDY	Antonov An-24RV	47309305	ex ST-SHE	
☐ UR-PWA	Antonov An-24RV	67302608	ex RA-46820	
☐ UR-47256	Antonov An-24RV	27307708	ex TC-MOB	
☐ UR-47294	Antonov An-24RV	07306604	ex RA-47294	>AEW
☐ UR-47297	Antonov An-24RV	07306610	ex CCCP-47297	
☐ UR-BWZ	Antonov An-26B	12208	ex UR-26119	
☐ UR-CBJ	Antonov An-26B	11401	ex UR-26069	
☐ UR-26581	Antonov An-26B	57313503	ex RA-26581	

ARTEM AVIA — Artem Avia (ABA) — Kiev-Zhulyany (IEV)

☐ UR-26094	Antonov An-26B	12706	ex CCCP-26094

AS AVIAKOMPANIA — Kiev-Borispol (KBP)

☐ UR-30036	Antonov An-30	0703	ex CCCP-30036

AVIAEXPRESS AIRCOMPANY — Expressavia (VXX) — Kiev-Zhulyany (IEV)

☐ UR-LAA	LET L-410UVP	851425	ex YL-KAA
☐ UR-67199	LET L-410UVP	790305	ex CCCP-67199

AVIANT — Aviation Plant (UAK) — Kiev-Gostomel

☐ UR-ZYD	Antonov An-124-100	19530502843	ex UR-CCX	>MXU
☐ UR-48023	Antonov An-32B	3409	ex HK-4006X	
☐ UR-48086	Antonov An-32P	2901	ex CCCP-48086	
☐ UR-48087	Antonov An-32B	2904	ex CCCP-48087	

AZOV-AVIA — Azov Avia (AZV) — Melitopol

☐ UR-ZVB	Ilyushin Il-76MD	0053463902	ex UR-76658	Op for UN/WFP
☐ UR-ZVC	Ilyushin Il-76TD	0053463891	ex UR-76656	

CHALLENGE AERO — Sky Challenger (5U/CLO) — Kiev-Zhulyany (IEV)

☐ UR-ECL	Yakovlev Yak-40K	9932059	ex RA-87219
☐ UR-88309	Yakovlev Yak-40	9840859	ex 5R-MUA
☐ UR-88310	Yakovlev Yak-40	9940760	ex 5R-MUB

CONSTANTA AIRLINES — Constanta (UZA) — Zaporozhye (OZH)

☐ UR-ETG	Yakovlev Yak-40	9531143	ex RA-87243	VIP
☐ UR-FRU	Yakovlev Yak-40	9440737	ex RA-87211	VIPop for Sumy Frunze

DNEPR-AIR		*Dniepro (Z6/UDN)*		*Dnepropetrovsk-Kodaki (DNK)*
☐ UR-IVK	Boeing 737-3L9	24571/1815	ex G-IGOT	
☐ UR-KIV	Boeing 737-4Y0	24686/1861	ex F-GQQJ	
☐ UR-DNC	Boeing 737-5L9	28995/2947	ex OY-APK	
☐ UR-DND	Boeing 737-5L9	28722/2868	ex OY-API	
☐ UR-DNH	Boeing 737-5Y0	24696/1960	ex N246ST	
☐ UR-DNJ	Boeing 737-36Q	28659/2680	ex G-THOJ	
☐ UR-DNA	Embraer ERJ-145EU	145088	ex G-EMBF	
☐ UR-DNB	Embraer ERJ-145EU	145094	ex G-EMBG	
☐ UR-DNE	Embraer ERJ-145EU	145357	ex G-EMBS	
☐ UR-DNF	Embraer ERJ-145EU	145404	ex G-EMBT	
☐ UR-DNG	Embraer ERJ-145EP	145394	ex G-ERJG	
☐ UR-DNI	Embraer ERJ-145EP	145325	ex G-ERJF	
☐ UR-DNK	Embraer ERJ-145EU	145039	ex G-EMBD	
☐ UR-DNL	Embraer ERJ-145EU	145042	ex G-EMBE	
☐ UR-DNO	Embraer ERJ-145EP	145237	ex G-ERJB	
☐ UR-DNP	Embraer ERJ-145EP	145290	ex G-ERJD	
☐ UR-DNQ	Embraer ERJ-145EP	145315	ex G-ERJE	
☐ UR-DNV	Embraer ERJ-145LR	145738	ex F-WKXF	◆
☐ UR-BWE	Yakovlev Yak-40	9530943	ex RA-87241	VIP
☐ UR-BWF	Yakovlev Yak-40	9711352	ex RA-88258	VIPop for Privatbank
☐ UR-PIT	Yakovlev Yak-40	9610647	ex RA-88168	VIP
☐ UR-42449	Yakovlev Yak-42D	4520421401018	ex EP-CPC	

DONBASSAERO		*Donbassaero (7D/UDC)*		*Donetsk (DOK)*
☐ UR-DAA	Airbus A320-211	0085	ex EI-CTD	
☐ UR-DAB	Airbus A320-231	0230	ex G-SSAS	
☐ UR-DAC	Airbus A320-233	0733	ex N451TA	
☐ UR-DAD	Airbus A320-233	0747	ex N453TA	
☐ UR-DAF	Airbus A321-231	1869	ex G-TTIC	◆
☐ UR-42327	Yakovlev Yak-42	4520424402161	ex T9-ABF	
☐ UR-42366	Yakovlev Yak-42	4520424814047	ex T9-ABH	no titles
☐ UR-42372	Yakovlev Yak-42D	4520423914266	ex CCCP-42372	no titles
☐ UR-42377	Yakovlev Yak-42D	4520421014479	ex CCCP-42377	
☐ UR-42381	Yakovlev Yak-42D	4520422014576	ex CU-T1705	◆
☐ UR-42383	Yakovlev Yak-42D	4520422016201	ex T9-ABD	

GORLITSA AIRLINES		*Gorlitsa (GOR)*		*Kiev-Zhulyany (IEV)*
☐ UR-BXU	Antonov An-26B-100	17311703	ex UR-26077	
☐ UR-BXV	Antonov An-26B-100	12110	ex UR-26113	
☐ UR-GLS	Antonov An-26B	07310109	ex RA-26017	>TWN
☐ UR-YMR	Antonov An-12BK	9346302	ex UR-11349	non-airworthy; >VPB

ILYICH AVIA				*Marlupol (MPW)*
☐ UR-MMK	Yakovlev Yak-40	9521540	ex RA-87513 Ilyichevets 3	VIP
☐ UR-14007	Antonov An-140-100	36525305029	Ilyichevets 4	stored
☐ UR-14008	Antonov An-140-100	36525305032	Ilyichevets 2	stored

ISD AVIA		*Isdavia (ISD)*		*Donetsk (DOK)*
☐ UR-CAR	Yakovlev Yak-40K	9741756	ex RA-21501	VIP
☐ UR-ISD	Yakovlev Yak-40	9530541	ex RA-88291	VIP stored

KHARKOV AVIATION PRODUCTION ASSOCIATION		*West-Kharkov (WKH)*		*Kharkov-Osnova (HRK)*
☐ UR-NPO	LET L-410UVP-E	871932	ex FLARF-01833	
☐ UR-67472	LET L-410UVP	841237	ex CCCP-67472	

KHORS AIR		*Aircompany Khors (X9/KHO)*		*Kiev-Borispol (KBP)*
☐ UR-CBV	Douglas DC-9-51 (ABS 3)	47772/890	ex OH-LYV	
☐ UR-CBY	Douglas DC-9-51 (ABS 3)	47773/891	ex OH-LYW	>UKM
☐ UR-CCT	Douglas DC-9-51 (ABS 3)	47696/808	ex OH-LYP	>UKM
☐ UR-BXI	McDonnell-Douglas MD-82	53170/2065	ex G-CEPJ	
☐ UR-BXL	McDonnell-Douglas MD-82	49512/1548	ex G-CEPG	
☐ UR-BXN	McDonnell-Douglas MD-83	49569/1405	ex LZ-LDV	>IRK
☐ UR-CBN	McDonnell-Douglas MD-82	49490/1352	ex N72830	
☐ UR-CBO	McDonnell-Douglas MD-82	49483/1314	ex RP-C2986	
☐ UR-CDN	McDonnell-Douglas MD-83	53520/2137	ex TC-OAV	>ATA Air

540

☐ UR-CDP	McDonnell-Douglas MD-83	49769/1559	ex SE-RDF	
☐ UR-CDR	McDonnell-Douglas MD-83	49949/1906	ex SX-BSW	
☐ UR-CDQ	McDonnell-Douglas MD-82	49372/1252	ex SX-BSQ	>IZG
☐ UR-CEL	McDonnell-Douglas MD-83	49390/1269	ex XU-U4D	◆
☐ UR-CHJ	McDonnell-Douglas MD-82	53066/1938	ex N482JC	
☐ UR-CHK	McDonnell-Douglas MD-82	49188/1172	ex N501AM	
☐ UR-CHM	McDonnell-Douglas MD-83	53465/2093	ex TC-OAS	>ATA Air
☐ UR-CHP	McDonnell-Douglas MD-83	53466/2101	ex TC-OAT	>ATA Air
☐ UR-CHQ	McDonnell-Douglas MD-83	53488/2134	ex TC-OAU	>ATA Air
☐ UR-CHS	McDonnell-Douglas MD-83	49572/1468	ex LZ-LDA	>IRK
☐ UR-CHZ	McDonnell-Douglas MD-82	53169/2063	ex G-CEPI	
☐ UR-CJC	McDonnell-Douglas MD-83	53186/2092	ex TC-AKN	◆
☐ UR-	McDonnell-Douglas MD-83	53198/1847	ex N198MD	◆

KIROVOHRADAVIA **Air Kirovograd (KAD)** **Kirovograd-Khmelyovoye (KGO)**

☐ UR-87814	Yakovlev Yak-40	9230524	ex RA-87814	VIP Also reported as Air Kirovograd

KRYM **Crimea Air (KYM)** **Simferopol-Zavodstoye (SIP)**

☐ UR-46833	Antonov An-24RV	17306710	ex CCCP-46833	[SIP]
☐ UR-47265	Antonov An-24RV	27307807	ex CCCP-47265	

LIZINGTEKHTRANS

☐ UR-NTA	Antonov An-148	0101	

LVIV AIRLINES **Ukraine West (5V/UKW)** **Lviv-Snilow (LWO)**

☐ UR-42317	Yakovlev Yak-42	4520422202039	ex 42317	
☐ UR-42369	Yakovlev Yak-42D	4520422914190	ex CCCP-42369	all-white
☐ UR-42403	Yakovlev Yak-42D	4520422116588	ex CCCP-42403	no titles >SAI
☐ UR-42527	Yakovlev Yak-42	11040903	ex CCCP-42527	

MERIDIAN **(MEM)** **Poltava (PLV)**

☐ UR-CAG	Antonov An-12BK	9346904	ex ER-AXY	
☐ UR-CAH	Antonov An-12BK	8345604	ex ER-AXX	
☐ UR-CAJ	Antonov An-12BK	8346106	ex ER-AXZ	
☐ UR-CAK	Antonov An-12BP	6343707	ex ER-ACI	
☐ UR-CGV	Antonov An-12B	6344610	ex EW-266TI	◆
☐ UR-CGW	Antonov An-12B	402410	ex EW-265TI	
☐ UR-CHT	Antonov An-26B	77305901	ex UR-VIV	
☐ UR-MDA	Antonov An-26-100	87307108		
☐ UR-67449	LET L-410UVP	841214	ex CCCP-67449	Avia Soyuz titles

MOTOR SICH AIRLINES **Motor Sich (M9/MSI)** **Zaporozhye (OZH)**

☐ UR-BXC	Antonov An-24RV	37308902	ex UR-46636	
☐ UR-MSI	Antonov An-24RV	27307608	ex UR-47699	
☐ UR-06130	Mil Mi-8T	22686		
☐ UR-06131	Mil-Mi-8T	22688		
☐ UR-11316	Antonov An-12BK	9346810	ex RA-11316	
☐ UR-11819	Antonov An-12B	6344009	ex CCCP-11819	no titles
☐ UR-14005	Antonov An-140	36525305021		
☐ UR-14006	Antonov An-140K	36525305025		
☐ UR-74026	Antonov An-74TK-200	36547096919	ex HK-3810X	Op for UN
☐ UR-87215	Yakovlev Yak-40	9510540	ex OK-FEJ	

MRK AIRLINES **(6V)** **Kiev-Borispol (KBP)**

☐ UR-CGQ	SAAB SF.340A	340A-097	ex N771DF	

ODESSA AIRLINES **Odessa Air (5K/ODS)** **Odessa-Tsentralny (ODS)**

☐ UR-87421	Yakovlev Yak-40	9421734	ex CCCP-87421
☐ UR-14001	Antonov An-140	36535391003	ex UR-PWO

PODILIA AVIA **Podilia (PDA)** **Khmelnitsky-Ruzuchaya (HMJ)**

☐ UR-46397	Antonov An-24B	07306301	ex RA-46397	Op for Istanbul Sabiha Cokcan

RIVNE UNIVERSAL AVIA **Rivne Universal (UNR)** **Rivnu (RWN)**

☐ UR-67084	LET L-410UVP	810721	ex UR-SKD	
☐ UR-67439	LET L-410UVP	841204	ex YL-KAH	based UK
☐ UR-67663	LET L-410UVP-E	902525	ex CCCP-67663	

SEVASTOPOL AVIA		Sevavia (SVL)		Sevastopol
□ UR-TMD	Ilyushin Il-18D	187009903	ex ER-ICL	

SHOVKOVLY SHLYAH		Way Aero (S8/SWW)		Kiev-Zhulyany (IEV)
□ UR-CAF	Antonov An-12BP	3341209	ex 4K-AZ56	
□ UR-CBU	Antonov An-12TBK	9346308	ex 4K-AZ18	
□ UR-CGX	Antonov An-12BP	5343510	ex 4K-AZ60	

SHUTTLE BIRD				Kiev-Borispol (KBP)
□ UR-SEV	LET L-410UVP	851507	ex LY-KAJ	

SOUTH AIRLINES		Southline (YG/OTL)		Odessa-Tsentralny (ODS)
□ UR-MLD	LET L-410UVP	820830	ex UR-87330	
□ UR-SEV	LET L-410UVP	851507	ex YL-KAJ	Shuttle Bird titles
□ UR-TVA	LET L-410UVP	851438	ex ES-PLI	
□ UR-YAM	LET L-410UVP-E	902513	ex UR-67659	
□ UR-67368	LET L-410UVP	830936	ex CCCP-67368	
□ UR-BZY	Tupolev Tu-134A-3	6348565	ex ER-TCH	
□ UR-EEE	Yakovlev Yak-40	9340632	ex 5N-DAN	
□ UR-IMX	SAAB SF.340B	340B-225	ex YR-VGR	

TAVREY AIRCOMPANY		Tavrey (T6/TVR)		Odessa-Tsentralny (ODS)
□ UR-CER	Yakovlev Yak-42D	4520423914323	ex UN-42640	

UKRAINE AIR ALLIANCE		Ukraine Airalliance (UKL)		Kiev-Borispol (KBP)
□ UR-BXQ	Ilyushin Il-76TD	1023410360	ex EX-832	>MXU
□ UR-BXR	Ilyushin Il-76TD	1023411384	ex EX-411	>MXU
□ UR-BXS	Ilyushin Il-76TD	1023411368	ex EX-436	>MXU
□ UR-CAI	Antonov An-26B	7010	ex UR-26519	>TAC
□ UR-CAT	Ilyushin Il-76TD	0053464922	ex UR-76663	
□ UR-CID	Ilyushin Il-76TD	0063465956	ex UP-I7640	
□ UR-26650	Antonov An-26B	87307507	ex UN-26650	all-white
□ UR-48083	Antonov An-32B	3001	ex CCCP-48083	stored
□ UR-	Antonov An-24B	27307903	ex LZ-ASZ	

UKRAINE AIR ENTERPRISE		Enterprise Ukraine (UKN)		Kiev-Borispol (KBP)
□ UR-YVA	Antonov An-74TK-300	36547098984	ex UR-LDK	
□ UR-65556	Tupolev Tu-134A-3	66372	ex 65556	
□ UR-65718	Tupolev Tu-134A-3	63668	ex 65718	
□ UR-65782	Tupolev Tu-134A-3	62672	ex CCCP-65782	
□ UR-86527	Ilyushin Il-62M	4037758	ex 86527	
□ UR-86528	Ilyushin Il-62M	4038111	ex 86528	

UKRAINE FLIGHT STATE ACADEMY		Flight Academy (UFA)		Kirovograd-Khmelyovoye (KGO)
□ UR-47791	Antonov An-24B	67303004	ex LZ-MNF	
□ UR-67357	LET L-410UVP	820917	ex CCCP-67357	
□ UR-67392	LET L-410UVP	831020	ex CCCP-67392	
□ UR-67395	LET L-410UVP	831023	ex CCCP-67395	
□ UR-67411	LET L-410UVP	831039	ex CCCP-67411	
□ UR-67417	LET L-410UVP	831108	ex CCCP-67417	

UKRAINE INTERNATIONAL AIRLINES		Ukraine International (PS/AUI)		Kiev-Borispol (KBP)
□ UR-FAA	Boeing 737-3Y0(SF)	24462/1691	ex N105KH	
□ UR-GAH	Boeing 737-32Q/W	29130/3105	ex N1779B	Mayrni
□ UR-GAJ	Boeing 737-5Y0	25192/2262	ex PT-SSA	
□ UR-GAK	Boeing 737-5Y0/W	26075/2374	ex PT-SLN	
□ UR-GAM	Boeing 737-4Y0	25190/2256	ex HA-LEU	
□ UR-GAN	Boeing 737-36N/W	28569/2996	ex F-GRFC	
□ UR-GAO	Boeing 737-4Z9	25147/2043	ex OE-LNH	
□ UR-GAP	Boeing 737-4Z9	27094/2432	ex OE-LNI	
□ UR-GAQ	Boeing 737-33R/W	28869/2887	ex SX-BLA	
□ UR-GAS	Boeing 737-528/W	25236/2443	ex S5-AAM	
□ UR-GAT	Boeing 737-528/W	25237/2464	ex F-GJNM	Lsd ADR
□ UR-GAU	Boeing 737-5Y0/W	25182/2211	ex N182GE	
□ UR-GAV	Boeing 737-4C9	26437/2249	ex EI-DGM	
□ UR-GAW	Boeing 737-5Y0/W	24898/2079	ex N898ED	

☐ UR-GAX	Boeing 737-4Y0	26066/2301	ex LZ-HVA	
☐ UR-PSA	Boeing 737-8HX/W	29658/2970	ex N1787B	
☐ UR-PSB	Boeing 737-8HX/W	29654/3018		
☐ UR-PSC	Boeing 737-8HX/W	29662/3182	ex N1787B	
☐ UR-PSD	Boeing 737-8HX/W	29686/3259		♦

UKRAINIAN CARGO AIRWAYS — Cargotrans (6Z/UKS) — Zaporozhye (OZH)

☐ UR-UCN	Antonov An-12BK	00347604	ex UR-11303	
☐ UR-UDM	Antonov An-26	0909	ex UR-26241	
☐ UR-UCC	Ilyushin Il-76MD	0083489647	ex UR-78775	Op for UN
☐ UR-UCU	Ilyushin Il-76MD	0073476275	ex UR-76729	
☐ UR-UWA	Mil Mi-8MTV-1	93151	ex LZ-MOT	
☐ UR-UWC	Mil Mi-8MTV-1	95236	ex UR-MOR	
☐ UR-UWD	Mil Mi-8MTV-1	95235	ex UR-MOQ	

UKRAINIAN PILOT SCHOOL — Pilot School (UPL) — Kiev-Chaika

| ☐ UR-28721 | WSK/PZL Antonov An-28 | 1AJ007-06 | ex RA-28721 |

UKTRANSLIZING

| ☐ UR-14004 | Antonov An-140 | 3652530211 |

UM AIR — Mediterranee Ukraine (UF/UKM) — Kiev-Borispol (KBP)

☐ UR-CBY	Douglas DC-9-51 (ABS 3)	47773/891	ex OH-LYW		<KHO
☐ UR-CCS	Douglas DC-9-51 (ABS 3)	47737/829	ex OH-LYS		<KHO
☐ UR-CCT	Douglas DC-9-51 (ABS 3)	47696/808	ex OH-LYP	Diana	<KHO
☐ UR-BHJ	McDonnell-Douglas MD-83	53184/2088	ex TC-AKL		>CPN
☐ UR-CFF	McDonnell-Douglas MD-82	49845/1573	ex N989PG		
☐ UR-CFG	McDonnell-Douglas MD-82	49370/1206	ex N14816		
☐ UR-CHN	McDonnell-Douglas MD-83	49938/1785	ex N938MD		>CPN
☐ UR-CHY	McDonnell-Douglas MD-82	53171/2067	ex G-CEPK		

UTAIR UKRAINE — (UTN)

☐ UR-UTA	ATR 42-320	382	ex VP-BLP	
☐ UR-UTB	ATR 42-320	386	ex VP-BLQ	
☐ UR-UTG	Boeing 737-4Q8	25377/2717	ex EI-ELP	♦

VETERAN AIRLINES — Veteran (VPB) — Simferopol-Zavodstoye (SIP)

☐ UR-CBZ	Antonov An-12BP	402707	ex RA-11117 all-white	
☐ UR-CDB	Antonov An-12BP	401605	ex RA-11766 all-white	
☐ UR-CEM	Antonov An-12BP	3340908	ex RA-11813	>ACP
☐ UR-CEN	Antonov An-12BP	02348203	ex RA-11128 all-white	stored
☐ UR-PAS	Antonov An-12AP	2401105	all-white	op for SDR
☐ UR-YMR	Antonov An-12BK	9346302	ex UR-11349	<GOR

VOLARE AVIATION ENTERPRISE — Ukraine Volare (VRE) — Rivne/Frankfurt-Hahn (RWN/HHN)

| ☐ UR-BWM | Antonov An-12BK | 00347004 | ex 20 blue |
| ☐ UR-76628 | Ilyushin Il-76TD | 0053458741 | ex CCCP-76628 |

WIND ROSE — Wind Rose 7W/WRC — Kiev-Borispol (BPL)

☐ UR-WRH	Airbus A321-231	2462	ex G-TTID		♦
☐ UR-WRI	Airbus A321-231	2682	ex G-TTIE		♦
☐ UR-WRA	Antonov An-24RV	37308709	ex UR-VIK		
☐ UR-WRF	Embraer ERJ-195AR	19000169	ex HZ-NQB		
☐ UR-WRG	Embraer ERJ-195AR	19000157	ex HZ-NQA	Sophia Kylvska Ukraine	
☐ UR-CDI	McDonnell-Douglas MD-82	49279/1230	ex SX-BMP		>IRK
☐ UR-CDX	McDonnell-Douglas MD-82	53119/1956	ex N481JC		
☐ UR-CEW	McDonnell-Douglas MD-82	49634/1419	ex N34838		
☐ UR-WRB	McDonnell-Douglas MD-82	49364/1276	ex N937AS		
☐ UR-WRE	McDonnell-Douglas MD-82	49278/1183	ex UR-CDA		

WIZZ AIR UKRAINE — Wizzair Ukraine (WU/WUA) — Kiev-Borispol (BPL)

| ☐ UR-WUA | Airbus A320-232 | 3531 | ex F-WWDX |
| ☐ UR-WUB | Airbus A319-132 | 3741 | ex F-WWIB |

YAVSON

☐ UR-MAY   Yakovlev Yak-40

YUZMASHAVIA		Yuzmash (2N/UMK)	Dnepropetrovsk-Kodaki (DNK)

☐ UR-78785	Ilyushin Il-76MD	0083489691	ex RA-78785
☐ UR-78786	Ilyushin Il-76TD	0083490693	ex CCCP-78786
☐ UR-87951	Yakovlev Yak-40K	9810957	ex CCCP-87951

VH-   AUSTRALIA (Commonwealth of Australia)

AD-ASTRAL			Perth International, WA (PER)

| ☐ VH-FWA | Beech 1900C | UB-61 | ex N818BE |

ADVANCE AVIAION			Emerald, QLD (EMD)

☐ VH-BCQ	Piper PA-31-350 Chieftain	31-7952134	ex N35265
☐ VH-FWJ	Piper PA-31 Navajo C	31-7712092	ex ZK-PNX
☐ VH-LWW	Piper PA-31 Navajo C	31-8112034	ex VH-NMT
☐ VH-NWN	Piper PA-31-350 Chieftain	31-8152197	ex VH-SAQ
☐ VH-TQC	Cessna 210N Centurion	21063325	ex N44ZP
☐ VH-VJE	Dornier Do.228-202	8041	ex 5N-DOC

AEROLINK AIR SERVICES			Sydney-Bankstown, NSA (BWU)

☐ VH-LJF	Cessna 310R	310R0691	ex N41TV	
☐ VH-OZF	Embraer EMB.110P1 Bandeirante	110201	ex G-EIIO	
☐ VH-UQA	Embraer EMB.110P1 Bandeirante	110245	ex VH-XFL	◆
☐ VH-XMA	Cessna 310R	310R0628	ex N31HS	

AEROPELICAN AIR SERVICES		Aeropelican (OT/PEL)	Newcastle-Belmont, NSW (BEO)

☐ VH-OTD	British Aerospace Jetstream 3202	978	ex G-BZYP	City of Newcastle	
☐ VH-OTE	British Aerospace Jetstream 3202	980	ex G-CBEP	City of Port Stephens	
☐ VH-OTF	British Aerospace Jetstream 3202	982	ex G-CBER	Narrabri Shire	
☐ VH-OTH	British Aerospace Jetstream 32EP	967	ex ZK-ECN		◆
☐ VH-OTP	British Aerospace Jetstream 3202	974	ex G-BURU	Pride of Mudgee	
☐ VH-OTQ	British Aerospace Jetstream 3202	975	ex G-BUTW		
☐ VH-OTR	British Aerospace Jetstream 3202	976	ex G-BUUZ		

AIR FRASER ISLAND			Maryborough, QLD (MBH)

| ☐ VH-BFS | Gippsland GA-8 Airvan | GA8-03-035 |
| ☐ VH-BNX | Gippsland GA-8 Airvan | GA8-03-032 |

AIR FRONTIER			Darwin, NT (DRW)

☐ VH-AKG	Beech Baron 58	TH-1011	ex N2070D	◆
☐ VH-DMD	Beech Baron 58	TH-1294	ex N1839Y	
☐ VH-JBH	Beech 65-B80 Queen Air	LD-443	ex VH-AMQ	
☐ VH-JMD	Piper PA-31 Turbo Navajo B	31-7401260	ex VH-SOW	
☐ VH-MRH	Beech 65-B80 Queen Air	LD-456	ex VH-BQA	
☐ VH-OBI	de Havilland DH.104 Dove 8	04525	ex G-LIDD	
☐ VH-SWP	Beech 65-B80 Queen Air	LD-472	ex VH-MWK	
☐ VH-XGF	Beech Baron 58	TH-379	ex N3078V	◆

AIR LINK		(ZL)	Dubbo, NSW (DBO)

☐ VH-DVR	Piper PA-31-350 Chieftain	31-7952052	ex N27936
☐ VH-DVW	Piper PA-31-350 Chieftain	31-7952011	ex VH-LHH
☐ VH-MWP	Piper PA-31-350 Chieftain	31-8352005	ex N4109C
☐ VH-MZF	Piper PA-31-350 Chieftain	31-8252039	ex N41064

☐ VH-BWQ	Cessna 310R	310R1401	ex N4915A
☐ VH-HSL	Cessna 310R	310R0946	ex N8643G
☐ VH-JMP	Cessna 310R	310R1270	ex N125SP
☐ VH-RUE	Beech 1900D	UE-53	ex ZK-JNG
☐ VH-RUI	Beech 1900D	UE-395	ex N831CA
☐ VH-TDL	Piper PA-39 Twin Comanche C/R	39-152	ex VH-NHC

AIR SOUTH REGIONAL			Adelaide, SA (ADL)

☐ VH-EMP	Beech Baron 58	TH-1491	ex VH-FEK
☐ VH-ENT	Cessna 404 Titan II	404-0818	ex ZK-ECP
☐ VH-EQB	Embraer EMB.110P1 Bandeirante	110214	ex ZK-MAS
☐ VH-SKC	Cessna 404 Titan II	404-0404	ex VH-TWZ
☐ VH-SZP	Cessna 404 Titan II	404-0637	ex ZS-OVU

| ☐ VH-TMP | Cessna 404 Titan II | 404-0125 | ex N37182 | |
| ☐ VH-ZOA | Beech 1900D | UE-85 | ex ZS-SER | |

AIR WHITSUNDAY SEAPLANES   *(RWS)*   *Whitsunday/Airlie Beach, QLD (WSY)*

☐ VH-AQV	de Havilland DHC-2 Beaver	1257	ex N67685		FP stored
☐ VH-AWD	de Havilland DHC-2 Beaver	1066	ex VH-AYS		FP
☐ VH-AWI	de Havilland DHC-2 Beaver	298	ex VH-HQE		FP
☐ VH-AWY	de Havilland DHC-2 Beaver	1444	ex VH-SSG		FP
☐ VH-PGA	Cessna 208 Caravan I	20800312	ex N1127W		FP
☐ VH-PGB	Cessna 208 Caravan I	20800346	ex N209E		FP
☐ VH-PGT	Cessna 208 Caravan I	20800345	ex N208E		FP

AIRLINES OF TASMANIA   *Airtas (FO/ATM)*   *Hobart, TAS (HBA)*

☐ VH-BTD	Piper PA-31 Navajo C	31-7912041	ex VH-ATG
☐ VH-BTI	Piper PA-31 Navajo C	31-8212003	ex ZK-VNA
☐ VH-BTN	Aero Commander 680FL	1695-35	ex D-IBME
☐ VH-CCN	Cessna 404 Titan II	404-0801	ex VH-WZK
☐ VH-LAD	Cessna 404 Titan II	404-0224	ex 9V-BMT
☐ VH-LAM	Cessna 404 Titan II	404-0627	ex VH-ANN
☐ VH-LCD	Cessna U206G Stationair 6	20604523	ex N673AA
☐ VH-MYS	Cessna U206G Stationair 6	20605162	ex N4921U
☐ VH-OBL	Britten-Norman BN-2A-20 Islander	2035	ex ZK-OBL
☐ VH-WZM	Cessna 404 Titan II	404-0837	ex N68075

AIRNORTH REGIONAL   *Topend (TL/ANO)*   *Darwin, NT*

☐ VH-ANK	Embraer EMB.120ER Brasilia	120155	ex VH-YDD		
☐ VH-ANN	Embraer EMB.120ER Brasilia	120203	ex VH-BRP		
☐ VH-ANZ	Embraer EMB.120RT Brasilia	120135	ex VH-XFR		
☐ VH-DIL	Embraer EMB.120ER Brasilia	120153	ex N285UE		
☐ VH-ANO	Embraer ERJ-170LR	17000099	ex B-KXB	Savannah	
☐ VH-ANV	Embraer ERJ-170LR	17000280	ex PT-TQG		
☐ VH-SWO	Embraer ERJ-170LR	17000081	ex B-KXA		♦
☐ VH-ANA	Swearingen SA.227DC Metro 23	DC-871B	ex VH-HCB		
☐ VH-ANW	Swearingen SA.227DC Metro 23	DC-873B	ex N3031Q		
☐ VH-ANY	Swearingen SA.227DC Metro 23	DC-840B	ex N3022L		

ALLIANCE AIRLINES   *Alli (QQ/UTY)*   *Brisbane-International, QLD (BNE)*

☐ VH-FKP	Fokker 50	20161	ex VH-AHX		[ADL]
☐ VH-FKV	Fokker 50	20303	ex B-12273		
☐ VH-FKW	Fokker 50	20306	ex B-12275		
☐ VH-FKX	Fokker 50	20312	ex B-12276		
☐ VH-FKY	Fokker 50	20284	ex B-12271		
☐ VH-FKZ	Fokker 50	20286	ex B-12272		
☐ VH-FKA	Fokker 100	11345	ex N885US		
☐ VH-FKC	Fokker 100	11349	ex P2-ANB		
☐ VH-FKD	Fokker 100	11357	ex N888AU		
☐ VH-FKE	Fokker 100	11358	ex P2-ANA		[BNE]
☐ VH-FKF	Fokker 100	11365	ex N890US		
☐ VH-FKG	Fokker 100	11366	ex N891US		
☐ VH-FKJ	Fokker 100	11372	ex N892US		
☐ VH-FKK	Fokker 100	11379	ex N894US		
☐ VH-FKL	Fokker 100	11380	ex N895US		
☐ VH-FWH	Fokker 100	11316	ex G-BXNF	City of Townsville	based PER
☐ VH-FWI	Fokker 100	11318	ex G-FIOR	City of Rockhampton	based PER
☐ VH-XWM	Fokker 100	11276	ex D-AGPA		♦
☐ VH-XWN	Fokker 100	11278	ex D-AGPB		♦
☐ VH-XWO	Fokker 100	11300	ex D-AGPE		♦
☐ VH-XWR	Fokker 100	11306	ex D-AGPG		♦
☐ VH-XWS	Fokker 100	11314	ex D-AGPL		♦
☐ VH-XWT	Fokker 100	11338	ex D-AGPQ		♦

ALLIGATOR AIRWAYS   *Kununurra, WA (KNX)*

☐ VH-RAS	Cessna 207 Skywagon	20700158	ex N1558U	
☐ VH-WOT	Cessna 207 Skywagon	20700267	ex ZK-DEW	
☐ VH-WOU	Cessna 207 Skywagon	20700099	ex N91164	
☐ VH-WOY	Cessna 207A Stationair 8	20700707	ex N9592M	
☐ VH-NOQ	Gippsland GA-8 Airvan	GA8-00-127	ex VH-WOQ	♦
☐ VH-WOG	Gippsland GA-8 Airvan	GA8-02-012		

☐ VH-WOP	Gippsland GA-8 Airvan	GA8-00-004	ex VH-RYT		
☐ VH-WOS	Gippsland GA-8 Airvan	GA8-00-099	ex VH-AFJ		
☐ VH-WOV	Gippsland GA-8 Airvan	GA8-01-006			
☐ VH-BJN	Piper PA-23-250D Aztec	27-4460	ex F-OCFU		♦
☐ VH-EDE	Cessna 210L Centurion II	21060517	ex (N94140)		
☐ VH-IXE	Partenavia P.68B	178			
☐ VH-KWP	Piper PA-34-220T Seneca	34-8133024	ex ZS-KWN		
☐ VH-OBJ	Britten Norman BN-2A-21 Islander	458	ex ZK-JSB		♦
☐ VH-RDA	Piper PA-31-350 Navajo Chieftain	31-7305032	ex N74903		
☐ VH-WNI	Cessna 210M Centurion II	21062462	ex N761RR		

ARNHEM LAND COMMUNITY AIRLINE — *Cairns, QLD (CNS)*

☐ VH-ASJ	Cessna U206G Stationair 6	U20605867	ex N6402X
☐ VH-KBN	Cessna U206G Stationair 6	U20606630	ex N9731Z
☐ VH-LHQ	Cessna U206G Stationair	U20603773	ex VH-LGN
☐ VH-LHX	Cessna U206G Stationair	U20603555	ex VH-STK
☐ VH-WOC	Cessna U206F Stationair	U20603464	ex N1948C
☐ VH-LHC	Gippsland GA-8 Airvan	GA8-04-057	ex VH-LHH
☐ VH-LHD	Gippsland GA-8 Airvan	GA8-04-051	ex VH-SFX
☐ VH-LHV	Gippsland GA-8 Airvan	GA8-04-045	ex VH-UAF
☐ VH-MFX	Gippsland GA-8 Airvan	GA8-04-053	ex VH-TMN
☐ VH-WRU	Gippsland GA-8 Airvan	GA8-04-048	ex VH-MEX
☐ VH-UBL	Cessna 210N Centurion II	21064712	ex N8148G

AUSTRALIAN AIR EXPRESS — *(XM/XME)* — *Melbourne-Tullamarine, VIC (MEL)*

☐ VH-EEP	Swearingen SA.227AT Expediter	AT-567	ex N565UP	Op by QWA
☐ VH-NJF	British Aerospace 146 Srs.300QT	E3198	ex G-BTLD	Op by NJS
☐ VH-NJM	British Aerospace 146 Srs.300QT	E3194	ex G-BTHT	Op by NJS
☐ VH-NJV	British Aerospace 146 Srs.100QT	E1002	ex G-BSTA	Op by NJS
☐ VH-XMB	Boeing 737-376 (SF)	23478/1251	ex ZK-JNG	Op by EFA
☐ VH-XML	Boeing 737-376 (SF)	23486/1286	ex ZK-JNF	Op by EFA
☐ VH-XMO	Boeing 737-376 (SF)	23488/1352	ex ZK-JNH	Op by EFA
☐ VH-XMR	Boeing 737-376 (SF)	23490/1390	ex ZK-JNA	Op by EFA

AVTEX AVIATION — *Sydney-Bankstown, NSW (BWU)*

Suispended operations 23/Jul/2010

BARRIER AVIATION — *Cairns, QLD (CNS)*

☐ VH-JOH	Cessna 402C	4020486	ex VH-JOC	
☐ VH-LKC	Cessna 402C	4020625	ex N6386X	
☐ VH-THX	Cessna 402C	4020250	ex PK-DCC	
☐ VH-UCM	Cessna 402C	4020472	ex N6838D	
☐ VH-BSO	Britten-Norman BN-2B-26 Islander	2129	ex JA5282	
☐ VH-BWO	Britten-Norman BN-2A-26 Islander	2042	ex T8A-103	
☐ VH-HGO	Cessna 310R II	21061159	ex N2198S	
☐ VH-MDU	Cessna 210M Centurion	21061634	ex (N732NB)	
☐ VH-MHL	Cessna 207 Skywagon	20700059	ex N91076	
☐ VH-SKU	Beech 200 Super King Air	BB-165	ex VH-XRF	♦
☐ VH-URJ	Britten-Norman BN-2A-21 Islander	402	ex VH-OIA	

BRINDABELLA AIRLINES — *(FQ)* — *Canberra, ACT (CBR)*

☐ VH-OZV	Swearingen SA.227AC Metro III	AC-610B	ex VH-TGQ	♦
☐ VH-SEF	Swearingen SA.227AC Metro III	AC-641	ex ZK-SDA	
☐ VH-TAG	Swearingen SA.227AC Metro III	AC-705	ex ZK-NSU	
☐ VH-TAH	British Aerospace Jetstream 41	41084	ex N566HK	
☐ VH-TAI	British Aerospace Jetstream 41	41082	ex N565HK	♦
☐ VH-TAO	Swearingen SA.227AC Metro III	AC-513	ex N513FA	♦
☐ VH-WAL	Piper PA-31 Turbo Navajo B	31-7300943	ex N71TC	

Operates services for Qantas

BRISTOW HELICOPTERS (AUSTRALIA)

Perth-Jandakot/Karratha/Barrow Island, WA / Darwin, NT (-/KTA/BWB/DRW)

☐ VH-BHH	Aérospatiale AS.332L	2059	ex G-TIGW	Nairn
☐ VH-BHK	Aérospatiale AS.332L	2096	ex G-TIGU	
☐ VH-BHX	Aérospatiale AS.332L	2079	ex G-BRWE	City of Albany
☐ VH-BHY	Aérospatiale AS.332L	2129	ex B-HZY	
☐ VH-BWJ	Aérospatiale AS.332L	2023	ex G-TIGB	

546

☐ VH-BXZ	Aérospatiale AS.332L	2078	ex G-TIGT	
☐ VH-BYT	Aérospatiale AS.332L	2083	ex G-CEYJ	
☐ VH-BYV	Aérospatiale AS.332L	2061	ex G-TIGO	
☐ VH-BZB	Aérospatiale AS.332L	2157	ex LN-OND	
☐ VH-BZC	Aérospatiale AS.332L	2036	ex 9M-BEM	
☐ VH-BZF	Aérospatiale AS.332L	2064	ex G-TIGP	
☐ VH-BZU	Aérospatiale AS.332L	2045	ex G-TIGM	
☐ VH-TZD	Aérospatiale AS.332L	2122	ex G-BLPM	
☐ VH-ZFB	Eurocopter EC225LP	2695	ex G-ZZSO	
☐ VH-ZFC	Eurocopter EC225LP	2709	ex G-ZZSP	
☐ VH-ZFD	Eurocopter EC225LP	2724	ex G-CFZE	
☐ VH-ZFE	Eurocopter EC225LP	2726	ex G-CFZY	
☐ VH-ZFH	Eurocopter EC225LP	2723	ex G-ZZSH	
☐ VH-BHI	Sikorsky S-76A+	760118	ex G-BVKS	
☐ VH-BHL	Sikorsky S-76A+	760046	ex G-BHLY	
☐ VH-BHM	Sikorsky S-76A+	760107	ex G-BVKO	
☐ VH-BHQ	Sikorsky S-76A++	760090	ex G-BVKN	
☐ VH-BZR	Sikorsky S-76A++	760132	ex EZ-S704	
☐ VH-BZW	Sikorsky S-76A+	760157	ex G-BITR	
☐ VH-TZI	Sikorsky S-76C++	760774	ex G-CGLS	♦
☐ VH-TZK	Sikorsky S-76A++	760718	ex N2577C	
☐ VH-TZL	Sikorsky S-76C+	760735	ex G-CFPY	
☐ VH-TZN	Sikorsky S-76A	760115	ex G-BVKR	
☐ VH-TZR	Sikorsky S-76C+	760775	ex G-CGLU	♦
☐ VH-ZFJ	Sikorsky S-76C+	760733	ex G-CFPV	
☐ VH-ZFM	Agusta AW139	41233	ex N370SH	♦
☐ VH-ZFN	Agusta AW139	41228	ex N368SH	♦
☐ VH-BHO	Bell 206L-3 LongRanger	51354	ex JA9893	
☐ VH-BKK	Kawasaki/MBB BK-117B-1	1044	ex JA9993	

BROOME AVIATION — Broome, WA (BME)

☐ VH-LWA	Cessna 208B Caravan I	208B1173	ex N208JJ	♦
☐ VH-MOX	Cessna 208 Caravan I	20800227	ex VH-NGD	
☐ VH-NDC	Cessna 208B Caravan I	208B2215	ex N2056W	♦
☐ VH-NGS	Cessna 208B Caravan I	208B0416	ex N1114W	
☐ VH-NTC	Cessna 208B Caravan I	208B0418	ex VH-DEX	
☐ VH-TLD	Cessna 208B Caravan I	208B0339	ex P2-TSJ	
☐ VH-TWX	Cessna 208B Caravan I	208B0648	ex VH-UZF	
☐ VH-DZH	Cessna 210L Centurion II	21061247	ex VH-SJQ	
☐ VH-KDM	Cessna 210N Centurion II	21063041	ex N6467N	
☐ VH-KJL	Cessna 210L Centurion II	21060776	ex N1765C	
☐ VH-RLP	Cessna 210-5 (205)	21050213	ex (N8213Z)	
☐ VH-SJG	Cessna 210L Centurion II	21063529	ex N6450A	♦
☐ VH-SKQ	Cessna 210L Centurion II	21061243	ex N1629C	
☐ VH-TCI	Cessna 210L Centurion II	21060548	ex N94225	
☐ VH-WTX	Cessna 210L Centurion II	21060222	ex (N93025)	
☐ VH-BBU	Cessna U206G Stationair	20604109	ex N756HS	
☐ VH-DAW	Cessna 310R II	310R0148	ex N5028J	
☐ VH-DLF	Cessna 404	404-0683	ex N6763K	
☐ VH-JOR	Cessna 404	404-0642	ex D-IEEE	
☐ VH-SHZ	Cessna U206G Stationair	20603726	ex (N9909N)	

CAIRNS SEAPLANES — Cairns, QLD (CNS)

☐ VH-CXS	de Havilland DHC-2 Beaver	1360	ex N211AW	FP
☐ VH-PCF	de Havilland DHC-2 Beaver	1348	ex VH-CZS	FP

CASAIR — Perth International, WA (PER)

☐ VH-KGX	Swearingen SA.226TC Metro II	TC-326	ex VH-UUK	
☐ VH-NGX	Swearingen SA.226TC Metro II	TC-287	ex VH-WGV	
☐ VH-OGX	Swearingen SA.226TC Metro II	TC-395	ex VH-TFQ	
☐ VH-WGX	Swearingen SA.226TC Metro II	TC-312	ex N1015B	

CHARTAIR (TL) — Alice Springs, NT (ASP)

☐ VH-BYK	Cessna 210L Centurion	21060435	ex N2691W	
☐ VH-IDZ	Cessna 210M Centurion II	21062530	ex N761UN	
☐ VH-JLC	Cessna 210N Centurion II	21063490	ex VH-OKH	
☐ VH-KST	Cessna 210M Centurion II	21062521	ex ZK-KLG	
☐ VH-LTB	Cessna 210N Centurion II	21064679	ex N670A	
☐ VH-NQP	Cessna 210N Centurion II	21064572	ex N9678Y	

☐ VH-OKJ	Cessna 210M Centurion II	21061602	ex VH-FZO	
☐ VH-RDH	Cessna 210N Centurion II	21065374	ex N5427Y	
☐ VH-TFF	Cessna 210N Centurion II	21064277	ex N6169Y	
☐ VH-TFT	Cessna 210N Centurion II	21063448		
☐ VH-TWP	Cessna 210M Centurion II	21061841	ex N1636C	
☐ VH-WMP	Cessna 210M Centurion II	21062731	ex N6278B	
☐ VH-CAJ	Cessna 402C II	402C0026	ex N5717C	
☐ VH-COQ	Cessna 310R	310R1643	ex N2635Y	
☐ VH-FTW	Beech 95-B55 Baron	TC-2123	ex N24097	
☐ VH-HOR	Cessna 402C	402C0108	ex P2-KSR	♦
☐ VH-JJN	Beech Baron 58	TH-1276	ex N3837M	
☐ VH-LGX	Piper PA-31-350 Chieftain	31-8452001	ex N41160	
☐ VH-PBI	Cessna 310R	310R0831	ex N3423G	
☐ VH-SKN	Cessna 310R	310R1681	ex ZK-ETM	
☐ VH-SMW	Beech Baron 58	TH-694	ex N6076S	
☐ VH-TFM	Cessna 402C II	402C0067	ex N2610Y	
☐ VH-TZH	Cessna 402C II	402C0617	ex N6880Y	
☐ VH-UCD	Cessna 402C II	402C0049	ex N5825C	
☐ VH-WZT	Beech Baron 58	TH-642	ex VH-TYR	

CHC HELICOPTERS (AUSTRALIA) — Hems (HEM) — Adelaide, SA (ADL)

☐ VH-LAF	Aérospatiale SA.332L1	2319	ex LN-OBT	<CHC Scotia
☐ VH-LAG	Aérospatiale SA.332L1	2352	ex LN-OBU	<CHC Scotia
☐ VH-LHG	Aérospatiale SA.332L1	2317	ex LN-OBR	
☐ VH-LHH	Aérospatiale AS.332L1	2407	ex 9M-STU	<CHC Intl
☐ VH-LHJ	Aérospatiale AS.332L	2063	ex G-BSOI	
☐ VH-LHK	Aérospatiale AS.332L	2107	ex G-BKZH	<CHC Scotia
☐ VH-LOF	Aérospatiale AS.332L	2058	ex G-CDSV	<CHC Intl
☐ VH-LOJ	Aérospatiale AS.332L	2312	ex C-FWPE	<CHC Intl ♦
☐ VH-LYP	Aérospatiale AS.332L	9008	ex C-GOSA	♦
☐ VH-BZH	Bell 412	33044	ex N18098	
☐ VH-EPH	Bell 412EP	36419	ex N3070R	Op for NSW Air Ambulance
☐ VH-EPK	Bell 412EP	36100	ex N412HH	Op for NSW Air Ambulance
☐ VH-EWA	Bell 412EP	36312	ex C-GUOP	
☐ VH-NSC	Bell 412	33029	ex VH-CRQ	EMS, based CBR
☐ VH-NSP	Bell 412	33091	ex N22976	EMS
☐ VH-NSV	Bell 412	33084	ex VH-AHH	EMS, based MKY
☐ VH-VAA	Bell 412EP	36274	ex C-GLZM	Op for Metropolitan Ambulance Sve
☐ VH-VAB	Bell 412EP	36275		Op for Metropolitan Ambulance Sve
☐ VH-HRP	Sikorsky S-76A+	760122	ex N176CH	based East Sale op for RAAF
☐ VH-LAH	Sikorsky S-76A+	760089	ex RJAF 725	based NTL
☐ VH-LAI	Sikorsky S-76A+	760103	ex RJAF 727	
☐ VH-LHN	Sikorsky S-76A++	760300	ex B-HZE	
☐ VH-LHY	Sikorsky S-76A+	760105	ex RJAF 729	based Pearce
☐ VH-LHZ	Sikorsky S-76A+	760113	ex RJAF 732	RAAF rescue
☐ VH-LYO	Sikorsky S-76A++	760017	ex C-GIML	
☐ VH-LOH	Sikorsky S-92D	920036	ex N8068D	
☐ VH-PVA	Aérospatiale SA365C1 Dauphin 2	5025	ex F-WYMH	based MEN
☐ VH-PVE	Eurocopter EC135T2	0834		based MEN
☐ VH-PVH	Aérospatiale AS365N3 Dauphin 2	6604	ex F-WQDC	based MEN
☐ VH-PVM	Aérospatiale AS350B Ecureuil	2058	ex JA9705	based MEN
☐ VH-SYJ	Agusta AW139	31114		Op for NSW Air Ambulance
☐ VH-SYV	Agusta AW139	31126		Op for NSW Air Ambulance
☐ VH-SYZ	Agusta AW139	31155		Op for NSW Air Ambulance

COBHAM AVIATION SERVICES AUSTRALIA — National Jet (NC/NJS) — Adelaide-International, SA (ADL)

☐ VH-NBK	Avro 146-RJ100	E3365	ex PK-RAZ	♦
☐ VH-NBU	Avro 146-RJ100	E3243	ex PK-RAY	♦
☐ VH-NJC	British Aerospace 146 Srs.100	E1013	ex G-6-013	
☐ VH-NJF	British Aerospace 146 Srs.300QT	E3198	ex G-BTLD	
☐ VH-NJG	British Aerospace 146 Srs.200	E2170	ex G-BSOH	
☐ VH-NJL	British Aerospace 146 Srs.300	E3213	ex G-BVPE	
☐ VH-NJM	British Aerospace 146 Srs.300QT	E3194	ex G-BTHT	
☐ VH-NJN	British Aerospace 146 Srs.300	E3217	ex G-BUHW	
☐ VH-NJP	Avro 146-RJ100	E3354	ex G-BZAW	♦
☐ VH-NJQ	Avro 146-RJ100	E3328	ex G-BZAU	
☐ VH-NJR	British Aerospace 146 Srs.100	E1152	ex G-BRLN	[ADL]♦
☐ VH-NJT	Avro 146-RJ70A	E1228	ex G-OLXX	
☐ VH-NJV	British Aerospace 146 Srs.100QT	E1002	ex G-BSTA	
☐ VH-NJX	British Aerospace 146 Srs.100	E1003	ex EI-CPY	[ADL]

☐ VH-NJY	Avro 146-RJ100	E3331	ex G-BZAV	♦
☐ VH-NJZ	British Aerospace 146 Srs.300QT	E3126	ex G-BPNT	♦
☐ VH-YAD	British Aerospace 146 Srs.200	E2097	ex N293UE	
☐ VH-YAE	British Aerospace 146 Srs.200	E2107	ex N294UE	
☐ VH-JSJ	de Havilland DHC-8-103	170	ex VH-NJD	
☐ VH-LCL	de Havilland DHC-8Q-202	492	ex C-GEOA	Op for RAN
☐ VH-SBJ	de Havilland DHC-8Q-315	578	ex C-FDHI	
☐ VH-ZZA	de Havilland DHC-8-202MPA	419	ex C-FWWU	Op for Custom Coastwatch
☐ VH-ZZB	de Havilland DHC-8-202MPA	424	ex C-FXBC	Op for Custom Coastwatch
☐ VH-ZZC	de Havilland DHC-8-202MPA	433	ex C-FXFK	Op for Custom Coastwatch
☐ VH-ZZE	de Havilland DHC-8Q-315MPA	640	ex C-FHQG	Op for Custom Coastwatch
☐ VH-ZZF	de Havilland DHC-8Q-315MPA	643	ex C-FJKS	Op for Custom Coastwatch
☐ VH-ZZG	de Havilland DHC-8Q-315MPA	644	ex C-FJKU	Op for Custom Coastwatch
☐ VH-ZZI	de Havilland DHC-8-202MPA	550	ex C-GDLD	Op for Custom Coastwatch
☐ VH-ZZJ	de Havilland DHC-8-202MPA	551	ex C-FDHI	Op for Custom Coastwatch
☐ VH-ZZN	de Havilland DHC-8-315	399	ex VH-JSQ	Op for Custom Coastwatch
☐ VH-ZZP	de Havilland DHC-8-202	411	ex VH-JSH	
☐ VH-YZE	Reims Cessna F406 Vigilant	F406-0076	ex VH-ZZE	Op for Custom Coastwatch
☐ VH-YZF	Reims Cessna F406 Vigilant	F406-0078	ex VH-ZZF	[ADL]
☐ VH-YZG	Reims Cessna F406 Vigilant	F406-0079	ex VH-ZZG	[ADL]

CORPORATE AIR — Canberra, ACT (CBR)

☐ VH-VED	Cessna 441 Conquest II	441-0272	ex N394G
☐ VH-VEH	Cessna 441 Conquest II	441-0238	ex N3NC
☐ VH-VEJ	Cessna 441 Conquest II	441-0249	ex N911ER
☐ VH-VEW	Cessna 441 Conquest II	441-0254	ex C-FWCP
☐ VH-VEY	Cessna 441 Conquest II	441-0295	ex N181MD
☐ VH-VEZ	Cessna 441 Conquest II	441-0182	ex VH-AZB
☐ VH-VEA	Cessna 404 Titan II	404-0219	ex VH-ARQ
☐ VH-VEB	Beech Baron 58	TH-399	ex VH-CYT
☐ VH-VEC	Cessna 404 Titan II	404-0217	ex VH-CSV
☐ VH-VEG	Beech Baron 58	TH-822	ex VH-WIM
☐ VH-VEK	Swearingen SA.227DC Metro 23	DC-845B	ex VH-KED
☐ VH-VEU	Swearingen SA.227TC Metro 23	DC-797B	ex VH-KDJ

DE BRUIN AIR — Mount Gambier, SA (MGB)

☐ VH-OAB	British Aerospace Jetstream 32EP	853	ex N853JX
☐ VH-OAE	British Aerospace Jetstream 32EP	851	ex N851JX
☐ VH-OAM	British Aerospace Jetstream 32EP	859	ex N859AE

DENIS BEAHAN AVIATION — Charters Towers, QLD

☐ VH-AMD	Beech 65-B80 Queen Air	LD-504	ex TR-LUU	
☐ VH-BOZ	Cessna 402A	402A0065	ex ZK-DHW	
☐ VH-BPZ	Cessna 402	402-0103	ex N4003Q	
☐ VH-BQL	Beech 65-B80 Queen Air	LD-288	ex DQ-FCQ	
☐ VH-BUS	Cessna 402	402-0198	ex N991SA	
☐ VH-RUU	Beech 65-B80 Queen Air	LC-311	ex N7643N	Excalibur Queenaire 8200 conv
	Current status uncertain			

DIRECT AIR SERVICES

☐ VH-BPI	Cessna 310R	310R0936	ex N8556G
☐ VH-CYT	Cessna 402	402-0293	ex VH-OKZ
☐ VH-OCS	Cessna 441 Conquest II	441-0030	ex N441MM

EASTERN AUSTRALIA AIRLINES (EAQ) — Sydney-Kingsford Smith, NSW (SYD)

A wholly-owned subsidiary of Qantas and operates scheduled services in full colours as QantasLink

EXPRESS FREIGHTERS AUSTRALIA (EFA) — Sydney-Kingsford Smith, NSW (SYD)

☐ VH-XMB	Boeing 737-376 (SF)	23478/1251	ex ZK-JNG	Op for XME
☐ VH-XML	Boeing 737-376 (SF)	23486/1286	ex ZK-JNF	Op for XME
☐ VH-XMO	Boeing 737-376 (SF)	23488/1352	ex ZK-JNH	Op for XME
☐ VH-XMR	Boeing 737-376 (SF)	23490/1390	ex ZK-JNA	Op for XME
☐ VH-	Boeing 767-381F	33510/939	ex JA603F	o/o♦

GAM SERVICES — Melbourne-Essendon, VIC (MEB)

☐ VH-DZC	Rockwell 500S Shrike Commander	3226	ex G-BDAL
☐ VH-KAK	Rockwell 500S Shrike Commander	3269	ex N57163
☐ VH-LET	Rockwell 500S Shrike Commander	3264	ex N70343

☐ VH-LTP	Rockwell 500S Shrike Commander	3323	ex N12RS	
☐ VH-MDW	Rockwell 500S Shrike Commander	3158	ex N801AC	
☐ VH-MEH	Rockwell 500S Shrike Commander	3258	ex N57213	
☐ VH-UJI	Rockwell 500S Shrike Commander	3301	ex VH-TWS	
☐ VH-UJL	Rockwell 500S Shrike Commander	3088	ex N9120N	
☐ VH-UJM	Rockwell 500S Shrike Commander	3117	ex N5007H	
☐ VH-UJN	Rockwell 500S Shrike Commander	3151	ex ZS-NRO	
☐ VH-UJR	Rockwell 500S Shrike Commander	3311	ex VH-PAR	
☐ VH-UJS	Rockwell 500S Shrike Commander	1797-12	ex VH-EXF	
☐ VH-UJU	Rockwell 500S Shrike Commander	3055	ex VH-PWO	
☐ VH-UJV	Rockwell 500S Shrike Commander	3161	ex N712PC	
☐ VH-UJX	Aero Commander 500S Shrike	1839-31	ex VH-EXI	
☐ VH-YJC	Rockwell 500S Shrike Commander	3176	ex VH-ACZ	
☐ VH-YJJ	Rockwell 500S Shrike Commander	3178	ex VH-ACJ	
☐ VH-YJL	Aero Commander 500S Shrike	1875-48	ex VH-ACL	
☐ VH-YJM	Rockwell 500S Shrike Commander	3186	ex RP-C1268	
☐ VH-YJO	Aero Commander 500B	1506-180	ex VH-WRU	
☐ VH-YJR	Rockwell 500S Shrike Commander	3231	ex VH-PCO	
☐ VH-YJS	Rockwell 500S Shrike Commander	3315	ex VH-FGS	
☐ VH-YJU	Aero Commander 500U Shrike	1765-49	ex F-ODHD	
☐ VH-AAG	Rockwell 690 Turbo Commander	11101	ex N57101	
☐ VH-NBT	Rockwell Commander 681B	6047	ex VH-NYE	
☐ VH-NYC	Rockwell 690 Turbo Commander	11026	ex N9226N	
☐ VH-PCV	Rockwell 690ATurbo Commander	11283	ex N57228	
☐ VH-UJA	Aero Commander 680FL	1521-100	ex PK-MAG	
☐ VH-UJG	Rockwell 690 Turbo Commander	11062	ex VH-NEY	
☐ VH-YJA	Aero Commander 680FL	1734-140	ex RP-C699	
☐ VH-YJF	Aero Commander 680FL	1642-122	ex N1414S	
☐ VH-YJG	Rockwell 690A Turbo Commander	11308	ex N99WC	
☐ VH-YJP	Rockwell 690A Turbo Commander	11173	ex N950M	
☐ VH-VJD	Dornier 228-202K	8157	ex D2-EBT	
☐ VH-VJE	Dornier 228-202	8041	ex 5N-DOC	
☐ VH-VJF	Dornier 228-202	8047	ex 5N-ARF	
☐ VH-VJJ	Dornier 228-202	8025	ex 5N-DOA	
☐ VH-IHA	Piper PA-31 Turbo Navajo	31-136	ex N9099Y	
☐ VH-YJZ	Beech 95-B55 Baron	TC-1933	ex VH-ARL	

GOLD COAST SEAPLANES — Coolangatta, QLD (OOL)

☐ VH-IDO	de Havilland DHC-2 Beaver	1545	FP	

GOLDEN EAGLE AIRLINES — Port Hedland, WA (PHE)

☐ VH-AEC	Britten-Norman BN-2B-26 Islander	2164	ex G-BKJO	
☐ VH-AEU	Britten-Norman BN-2B-26 Islander	2130	ex G-BJON	
☐ VH-AEX	Cessna U206G Stationair 6 II	U20606587	ex N9635Z	
☐ VH-EGE	Britten-Norman BN-2A-26 Islander	3015	ex VH-WRM	
☐ VH-FML	Piper PA-31 Navajo C	31-8112015	ex N40540	
☐ VH-KTS	Piper PA-31 Navajo C	31-7912014	ex N27833	
☐ VH-LCK	Piper PA-34-200 Seneca	34-7350236	ex N55663	
☐ VH-NMK	Piper PA-31-350 Chieftain	31-8152163	ex P2-RHA	
☐ VH-NPA	Piper PA-31-350 Chieftain	31-8452016	ex N41171	
☐ VH-PJY	Cessna U206G Stationair 6 II	U20605120	ex N4829U	
☐ VH-UPK	Cessna U206G Stationair 6 II	U20605477	ex (N6399U)	

GOLDFIELDS AIR SERVICES (GOS) — Kalgoorlie, WA (KGI)

☐ VH-ANP	Cessna 404	404-0054	ex N404MP	
☐ VH-LAE	Cessna 402C	402C0097	ex N2614Z	
☐ VH-LNX	Cessna 402	402-0295	ex ZS-LNX	
☐ VH-MFF	Cessna 402B	402B0874	ex N5187J	
☐ VH-OOT	Cessna 310R	310R1635	ex VH-PEE	
☐ VH-SZP	Cessna 404	4040637	ex ZS-OVU	♦
☐ VH-TRC	Cessna 404	4040129	ex HL2013	♦

GREAT WESTERN AVIATION — Brisbane-International, QLD (BNE)

☐ VH-DEH	Piper PA-31 Navajo C	31-7812123	ex N27792	
☐ VH-FMO	Piper PA-31 Navajo C	31-8012052	ex N35574	
☐ VH-FMU	Piper PA-31 Navajo C	31-8212015	ex N41033	
☐ VH-KTU	Piper PA-31 Navajo C	31-7912079	ex N35301	
☐ VH-NAD	Piper PA-31 Navajo C	31-8212004	ex N4099T	
☐ VH-OMM	Piper PA-31-350 Chieftain	31-8152153	ex N4091B	
☐ VH-SGV	Beech 200 Super King Air	BB-718	ex N6728N	

HARDY AVIATION — Darwin, NT (DRW)

	Registration	Type	Serial	Ex	
☐	VH-ANM	Cessna 404 Titan II	404-0010	ex VH-BPM	
☐	VH-ANS	Cessna 210M Centurion II	21062784	ex N784ED	
☐	VH-ARJ	Cessna 402B	402B0629	ex N3784C	
☐	VH-AZW	Cessna 441 Conquest II	441-0028	ex VH-FWA	
☐	VH-BEM	Cessna 402B	404B0590	ex N402HA	
☐	VH-HAZ	Cessna 404 Titan II	404-0046	ex G-BYLR	
☐	VH-HMA	Cessna 404 Titan II	404-0122	ex N37158	
☐	VH-HPA	Cessna U206G Stationair 6	U20605002	ex VH-WIW	
☐	VH-HVR	Cessna 404 Titan II	404-0673	ex N404MT	
☐	VH-JVB	Cessna 441 Conquest	441-0231	ex N441YA	
☐	VH-JZL	Cessna TU206G Stationair 6	U20604721	ex N732TS	
☐	VH-MKS	Swearingen SA.226TC Metro II	TC-262	ex N49GW	
☐	VH-NOK	Cessna 210M Centurion II	21062063	ex N9127M	
☐	VH-RAP	Cessna U206F Stationair	U20602989	ex VH-DXU	
☐	VH-RUY	Cessna 402C	402C0273	ex N1774G	
☐	VH-SGO	Beech 58 Baron	TH-1185	ex N3702D	
☐	VH-SMO	Cessna 441 Conquest	441-0132	ex VH-ANJ	
☐	VH-SQL	Cessna 402C II	402C0326	ex VH-OAS	
☐	VH-TFG	Swearingen SA.227AC Metro III	AC-504	ex N31072	♦
☐	VH-TGD	Swearingen SA.227AC Metro III	AC-667B	ex C-FAFS	
☐	VH-UOP	Cessna 404 Titan II	404-0636	ex N5280J	
☐	VH-XSM	Beech E55 Baron	TE-804	ex P2-COE	

HEAVYLIFT CARGO AIRLINES — HeavyCargo (HN/HVY) — Brisbane-International, QLD (BNE)

	Registration	Type	Serial	Ex
☐	RP-C8017	Boeing 727-51C (FedEx 3)	19289/403	ex 9L-LFJ
☐	RP-C8019	Boeing 727-227F (Raisbeck 3)	21249/1219	ex N76753
☐	RP-C8020	Short SC.5 Belfast	SH1819	ex 9L-LDQ

HINTERLAND AVIATION — Cairns, QLD (CNS)

	Registration	Type	Serial	Ex
☐	VH-CVN	Cessna 208B Caravan I	208B0676	ex N12372
☐	VH-HLJ	Beech 200B Super King Air	BB-945	ex RP-C11577
☐	VH-HLL	Cessna 208B Caravan I	208B0615	ex VH-AGS
☐	VH-JOB	Cessna 310R	310R1236	ex G-BOAT
☐	VH-MRZ	Cessna 208B Caravan I	208B1048	ex N1266V
☐	VH-SKH	Cessna 310R	310R1221	
☐	VH-TFC	Cessna U206G Stationair	U20604576	ex VH-CMT
☐	VH-TFK	Cessna 402C III	402C1011	ex VH-PVU
☐	VH-TFO	Cessna 404 Titan II	404-0076	ex N32L
☐	VH-TFQ	Cessna 208B Caravan I	208B1216	ex N84BP
☐	VH-TFS	Cessna 208B Caravan I	208B1006	ex N1247N
☐	VH-TFU	Cessna 404 Titan	404-0834	ex VH-SZO
☐	VH-TFY	Rockwell 500S Shrike Commander	3057	ex VH-IBY
☐	VH-TFZ	Cessna 402C II	402C0408	ex VH-RMI
☐	VH-TSI	Cessna 402C	402C0492	ex N6841L

ISLAND AIR TAXIS — Hamilton Island, QLD (HTI)

Ceased Trading

JETSTAR AIRWAYS — Jetstar (JQ/JST) — Melbourne-Tullamarine, VIC (MEL)

	Registration	Type	Serial	Ex	
☐	VH-JQG	Airbus A320-232	2169	ex F-WWDQ	
☐	VH-JQL	Airbus A320-232	2185	ex F-WWDB	
☐	VH-JQW	Airbus A320-232	2423	ex TC-OGO	
☐	VH-JQX	Airbus A320-232	2197	ex F-WWDH	
☐	VH-	Airbus A320-232		ex	o/o♦
☐	VH-	Airbus A320-232		ex	o/o♦
☐	VH-	Airbus A320-232		ex	o/o♦
☐	VH-	Airbus A320-232		ex	o/o♦
☐	VH-VGD	Airbus A320-232	4527	ex D-AXAJ	♦
☐	VH-VGF	Airbus A320-232	4497	ex F-WWIK	♦
☐	VH-VGH	Airbus A320-232	4495	ex D-AUBK	♦
☐	VH-VGI	Airbus A320-232	4464	ex F-WWBU	♦
☐	VH-VGJ	Airbus A320-232	4460	ex F-WWBH	♦
☐	VH-VGN	Airbus A320-232	4434	ex D-AVVT	♦
☐	VH-VGO	Airbus A320-232	4356	ex D-AXAV	♦
☐	VH-VGP	Airbus A320-232	4343	ex F-WWBH	♦
☐	VH-VGQ	Airbus A320-232	4303	ex F-WWDY	♦
☐	VH-VGR	Airbus A320-232	4257	ex F-WWIQ	♦
☐	VH-VGT	Airbus A320-232	4178	ex F-WWDZ	♦
☐	VH-VGU	Airbus A320-232	4245	ex F-WWDQ	♦
☐	VH-VGV	Airbus A320-232	4229	ex F-WWBU	♦
☐	VH-VGY	Airbus A320-232	4177	ex D-AVVW	♦

☐ VH-VGZ	Airbus A320-232	3917	ex F-WWBF
☐ VH-VQA	Airbus A320-232	3783	ex F-WWIS
☐ VH-VQB	Airbus A320-232	3743	ex F-WWII
☐ VH-VQC	Airbus A320-232	3668	ex F-WWID
☐ VH-VQD	Airbus A320-232	3547	ex F-WWIV
☐ VH-VQE	Airbus A320-232	3495	ex F-WWIJ
☐ VH-VQF	Airbus A320-232	3474	ex F-WWDE
☐ VH-VQG	Airbus A320-232	2787	ex F-WWBV
☐ VH-VQH	Airbus A320-232	2766	ex F-WWDG Go Roos c/s
☐ VH-VQI	Airbus A320-232	2717	ex F-WWBG
☐ VH-VQJ	Airbus A320-232	2703	ex F-WWIS
☐ VH-VQK	Airbus A320-232	2651	ex F-WWIM
☐ VH-VQL	Airbus A320-232	2642	ex F-WWBZ
☐ VH-VQM	Airbus A320-232	2608	ex F-WWBS
☐ VH-VQN	Airbus A320-232	2600	ex F-WWBK
☐ VH-VQO	Airbus A320-232	2587	ex F-WWDL
☐ VH-VQP	Airbus A320-232	2573	ex F-WWBD Gold Coast Titans c/s
☐ VH-VQQ	Airbus A320-232	2537	ex F-WWIJ Sea World c/s
☐ VH-VQR	Airbus A320-232	2526	ex F-WWDQ
☐ VH-VQS	Airbus A320-232	2515	ex F-WWIE
☐ VH-VQT	Airbus A320-232	2475	ex F-WWDS
☐ VH-VQU	Airbus A320-232	2455	ex F-WWDJ
☐ VH-VQV	Airbus A320-232	2338	ex F-WWIO
☐ VH-VQW	Airbus A320-232	2329	ex F-WWDZ
☐ VH-VQX	Airbus A320-232	2322	ex 9V-VQX
☐ VH-VQY	Airbus A320-232	2299	ex F-WWBV
☐ VH-VQZ	Airbus A320-232	2292	ex 9V-VQZ
☐ VH-VWT	Airbus A321-231	3717	ex D-AVZQ
☐ VH-VWU	Airbus A321-231	3948	ex D-AZAL
☐ VH-VWW	Airbus A321-231	3916	ex D-AVZX
☐ VH-VWX	Airbus A321-231	3899	ex D-AVZW
☐ VH-VWY	Airbus A321-231	1408	ex N584NK
☐ VH-VWZ	Airbus A321-231	1195	ex N583NK
☐ VH-EBA	Airbus A330-202	508	ex F-WWKM
☐ VH-EBB	Airbus A330-202	522	ex F-WWYQ
☐ VH-EBC	Airbus A330-202	506	ex F-WWYU
☐ VH-EBD	Airbus A330-202	513	ex F-WWYV
☐ VH-EBE	Airbus A330-202	842	ex F-WWYV
☐ VH-EBF	Airbus A330-202	853	ex F-WWYU
☐ VH-EBK	Airbus A330-202	945	ex F-WWYV

KAKADU AIR SERVICES — Jabiru, NT (JAB)

☐ VH-JOV	Cessna 402C	4020087	ex VH-JOC ♦
☐ VH-KNA	Gippsland GA-8 Airvan	GA8-04-044	ex VH-IXN
☐ VH-KNB	Gippsland GA-8 Airvan	GA8-07-109	
☐ VH-KNE	Gippsland GA-8 Airvan	GA8-08-133	
☐ VH-KNP	Gippsland GA-8 Airvan	GA8-04-063	ex VH-YAH
☐ VH-LFU	Cessna 207 Skywagon	20700296	ex ZK-DXT
☐ VH-UBW	Cessna 207 Skywagon	20700137	ex N1537U

KARRATHA FLYING SERVICES — Karratha, WA (KTA)

☐ VH-KFF	Piper PA-31-350 Chieftain	31-7952125	ex VH-UOT
☐ VH-KFG	Beech 65-C90 King Air	LJ-777	ex N9AN
☐ VH-KFQ	Piper PA-31 Turbo Navajo B	31-7401250	ex VH-SRZ
☐ VH-KFW	Piper PA-31 Turbo Navajo	31-366	ex VH-WGU
☐ VH-KFX	Beech B200 Super King Air	BB-1862	ex N225WC
☐ VH-ZKF	de Havilland DHC-6 Twin Otter 100	43	ex VH-TZL

KING ISLAND AIRLINES — Melbourne-Moorabbin, VIC (MBW)

☐ VH-KGQ	Embraer EMB.110P1 Bandeirante	110221	ex VH-XFD
☐ VH-KIB	Piper PA-31-350 Navajo Chieftain	31-7305035	ex VH-TXD
☐ VH-KIG	Piper PA-31-350 Chieftain	31-7852146	ex VH-HRL
☐ VH-KIO	Piper PA-31-350 Navajo Chieftain	31-7405487	ex VH-DMV
☐ VH-KIY	Piper PA-31-350 Chieftain	31-7952061	ex VH-KGN

MAROOMBA AIRLINES (KN) — Perth-International, WA (PER)

☐ VH-ITA	Beech B200 Super King Air	BB-1244	ex F-OINC	
☐ VH-LOA	Beech B200 Super King Air	BB-1463	ex ZS-PLK	
☐ VH-MQZ	Beech B200 Super King Air	BB-1961	ex N74061	
☐ VH-QQA	de Havilland DHC-8-102	005	ex P2-MCN	<Skytrans
☐ VH-QQB	de Havilland DHC-8-102	004	ex VH-TQO	<Skytrans

MILITARY SUPPORT SERVICES   Brisbane (BNE)

| ☐ VH-MQD | CASA C.212-200 | CC50-7-272 | ex N433CA |
| ☐ VH-MQE | CASA C.212-200 | CD51-6-318 | ex N7241E |

NETWORK AVIATION AUSTRALIA   Perth-International, WA (PER)

☐ VH-NHA	Embraer EMB.120ER Brasilia	120269	ex N209SW
☐ VH-NHC	Embraer EMB.120ER Brasilia	120152	ex VH-TLZ
☐ VH-NHZ	Embraer EMB.120ER Brasilia	120034	ex N186SW
☐ VH-NIF	Embraer EMB.120ER Brasilia	120054	ex VH-FNQ
☐ VH-TWF	Embraer EMB.120ER Brasilia	120186	ex N197SW
☐ VH-TWZ	Embraer EMB.120ER Brasilia	120266	ex N207SW
☐ VH-NHF	Fokker 100	11398	ex N898US
☐ VH-NHO	Fokker 100	11312	ex D-AGPJ
☐ VH-NHP	Fokker 100	11399	ex D-AGPS

NGAANYATJARRA AIR   Alice Springs, NT (ASP)

| ☐ VH-HXH | Cessna 210N Centurion | 21063847 | ex N6260C |

NORFOLK AIR   Norfolk Island, NSW(NLK)

| ☐ VH-NLK | Boeing 737-33A | 23635/1436 | ex N635AN |

PEARL AVIATION   Perth-International, WA (PER)

☐ VH-FII	Beech 200 Super King Air	BB-653	ex VH-MXK	Op for Flight Inspection Alliance
☐ VH-NTE	Beech 200 Super King Air	BB-529	ex VH-SWP	Op for NT Aerial Medical Services
☐ VH-NTG	Beech 200C Super King Air	BL-9	ex VH-KZL	Op for NT Aerial Medical Services
☐ VH-NTH	Beech 200C Super King Air	BL-12	ex VH-SWO	Op for NT Aerial Medical Services
☐ VH-NTS	Beech 200C Super King Air	BL-30	ex VH-TNQ	Op for NT Aerial Medical Services
☐ VH-OYA	Beech 200 Super King Air	BB-365	ex P2-SML	>RAAF
☐ VH-OYD	Beech 200 Super King Air	BB-1041	ex N200BK	EMS
☐ VH-OYE	Beech 200 Super King Air	BB-355	ex VH-SMB	EMS
☐ VH-OYH	Beech 200 Super King Air	BB-148	ex VH-WNH	Op for Granites Gold Mines
☐ VH-OYT	Beech 200T Super King Air	BT-6/BB-489	ex VH-PPJ	
☐ VH-TLX	Beech 200 Super King Air	BB-550	ex P2-MBM	EMS
☐ VH-PPF	Dornier 328-110	3057	ex N439JS	based PER
☐ VH-PPG	Dornier 328-110	3053	ex D-CIAB	based DRW
☐ VH-PPJ	Dornier 328-110	3059	ex D-CCAD	based CNS
☐ VH-PPQ	Dornier 328-110	3051	ex D-CEAD	based MEB
☐ VH-PPV	Dornier 328-110	3052	ex D-CDAD	based BNE
☐ VH-FIX	Beech 300 Super King Air	FL-90	ex D-CKRA	Calibrator
☐ VH-OYB	Swearingen SA.227DC Metro 23	DC-848B	ex N452LA	
☐ VH-OYG	Swearingen SA.227DC Metro 23	DC-875B	ex VH-SWM	
☐ VH-OYI	Swearingen SA.227DC Metro 23	DC-839B	ex VH-DMI	
☐ VH-OYN	Swearingen SA.227DC Metro 23	DC-870B	ex VH-DMO	

PEL-AIR   Questair (QWA)   Sydney Kingsford-Smith, NSW / Brisbane, QLD (SYD/BNE)

☐ VH-AJG	IAI 1124 Westwind	281	ex N1124F	EMS/Frtr
☐ VH-AJJ	IAI 1124 Westwind	248	ex N25RE	EMS/Frtr
☐ VH-AJK	IAI 1124 Westwind	256	ex 4X-CNB	EMS/Frtr
☐ VH-AJP	IAI 1124 Westwind	238	ex 4X-CMJ	EMS/Frtr
☐ VH-AJV	IAI 1124 Westwind	282	ex N186G	EMS/Frtr
☐ VH-KNR	IAI 1124A Westwind II	340	ex N118MP	Frtr
☐ VH-KNS	IAI 1124 Westwind	323	ex N816H	Frtr
☐ VH-KNU	IAI 1124 Westwind	317	ex VH-UUZ	EMS/Frtr
☐ VH-EEJ	Swearingen SA.227AC Metro III	AC-617	ex VH-SSV	Combi
☐ VH-EEN	Swearingen SA.227AT Expediter	AT-563	ex N563UP	Frtr Jt ops with XME
☐ VH-EEO	Swearingen SA.227AT Expediter	AT-564	ex N564UP	Frtr Jt ops with XME
☐ VH-EEP	Swearingen SA.227AT Expediter	AT-567	ex N565UP	[WGA]
☐ VH-EER	Swearingen SA.227AC Metro III	AC-632	ex VH-SSW	[WGA]
☐ VH-EES	Swearingen SA.227AC Metro III	AC-614	ex VH-SSZ	[WGA]
☐ VH-EEU	Swearingen SA.227AC Metro III	AC-619B	ex VH-OYC	
☐ VH-EEX	Swearingen SA.227AC Metro III	AC-611B	ex VH-NEL	
☐ VH-KAN	Swearingen SA.227DC Metro 23	DC-838B	ex N3021U	
☐ VH-KDO	Swearingen SA.227DC Metro 23	DC-837B	ex N3021N	
☐ VH-KEU	Swearingen SA.227DC Metro 23	DC-846B	ex N30236	
☐ VH-KEX	Swearingen SA.227DC Metro 23	DC-872B	ex N3030X	
☐ VH-EEB	Embraer EMB.120FC Brasilia	120117	ex N1117H	[WGA]
☐ VH-EKD	SAAB SF.340AF	340A-155	ex SE-F55	Frtr

☐ VH-EKT	SAAB SF.340AF	340A-085	ex F-GGBJ		Frtr
☐ VH-KDB	SAAB SF.340AF	340A-008	ex PH-KJK		Frtr
☐ VH-SLD	Learjet 35A	35A-145	ex (N166AG)		Frtr
☐ VH-SLE	Learjet 35A	35A-428	ex N17LH		
☐ VH-SLF	Learjet 36A	36A-049	ex N136ST		
☐ VH-SLJ	Learjet 36	36-014	ex N200Y		Frtr
☐ VH-VAH	Beech 200C Super King Air	BL-156	ex N6388B	Victorian Ambulance Service◆	
☐ VH-VAI	Beech 200C Super King Air	BL-157	ex N6350V	Victorian Ambulance Service◆	
☐ VH-ZKA	Beech 200C Super King Air	BL-154	ex N6354F	Victorian Ambulance Service◆	
☐ VH-ZKB	Beech 200C Super King Air	BL-155	ex N6155S	Victorian Ambulance Service◆	

PIONAIR AUSTRALIA   Sydney-Bankstown, NSW (BWU)

| ☐ VH-PDW | Convair 580F | 86 | ex C-GKFQ |
| ☐ VH-PDX | Convair 580F | 126 | ex C-FIWN |

POLAR AVIATION   Port Hedland, WA (PHE)

☐ VH-BIV	Cessna 210N Centurion II	21063398	ex N5373A
☐ VH-BLW	Beech Baron 58	TH-490	ex N1349K
☐ VH-ILD	Beech 95-E55 Baron	TE-788	ex N4055A
☐ VH-NSM	Beech 58 Baron	TH-1798	ex N1098C
☐ VH-NWT	Cessna 208B Caravan I	208B0733	ex N1269N
☐ VH-YOT	Cessna U206G Stationair	20605045	ex VH-TEO
☐ VH-YSS	Beech 58 Baron	TH-1583	ex N56569

QANTAS AIRWAYS   Qantas (QF/QFA)   Sydney-Kingsford Smith, NSW (SYD)

Member of Oneworld

☐ VH-EBG	Airbus A330-203	887	ex F-WWKD	Barossa Valley	
☐ VH-EBH	Airbus A330-203	892	ex F-WWYT	Hunter Valley	
☐ VH-EBI	Airbus A330-203	898	ex F-WWKM	Yarra Valley	
☐ VH-EBJ	Airbus A330-203	940	ex F-WWKL	Margaret River	
☐ VH-EBL	Airbus A330-203	976	ex F-WWKU	Whitsundays	
☐ VH-EBM	Airbus A330-203	1061	ex F-WWKU	Tamar Valley	
☐ VH-EBN	Airbus A330-203	1094	ex F-WWKM		◆
☐ VH-EBO	Airbus A330-203	1169	ex F-WWKJ		◆
☐ VH-EBP	Airbus A330-203	1174	ex F-WWKS		◆
☐ VH-QPA	Airbus A330-303	553	ex F-WWKS	Kununurra	
☐ VH-QPB	Airbus A330-303	558	ex F-WWYO	Freycinet Peninsula	
☐ VH-QPC	Airbus A330-303	564	ex F-WWYQ	Broken Hill	
☐ VH-QPD	Airbus A330-303	574	ex F-WWYU	Port Macquarie	
☐ VH-QPE	Airbus A330-303	593	ex F-WWKP	Port Lincoln	
☐ VH-QPF	Airbus A330-303	595	ex F-WWKR	Esperance	
☐ VH-QPG	Airbus A330-303	603	ex F-WWYN	Mount Gambier	
☐ VH-QPH	Airbus A330-303	695	ex F-WWYQ	Noosa	
☐ VH-QPI	Airbus A330-303	705	ex F-WWKG	Cairns	
☐ VH-QPJ	Airbus A330-303	712	ex F-WWYM	Port Stephens	
☐ VH-OQA	Airbus A380-842	014	ex F-WWSK	Nancy Bird Walton	
☐ VH-OQB	Airbus A380-842	015	ex F-WWSL	Hudson Fysh	
☐ VH-OQC	Airbus A380-842	022	ex F-WWSR	Paul McGinness	
☐ VH-OQD	Airbus A380-842	026	ex F-WWSX	Fergus McMaster	
☐ VH-OQE	Airbus A380-842	027	ex F-WWSY	Lawrence Hargrave	
☐ VH-OQF	Airbus A380-842	029	ex F-WWSA	Charles Kingsford Smith	
☐ VH-OQG	Airbus A380-842	047	ex F-WWAD	Charles Ulm	◆
☐ VH-OQH	Airbus A380-842	050	ex F-WWAE	Reginald Ansett	◆
☐ VH-OQI	Airbus A380-842	055	ex F-WWAP	David Warren	◆
☐ VH-OQJ	Airbus A380-842	062	ex F-WWAQ	Bert Hinkler	o/o◆
☐ VH-OQK	Airbus A380-842	063	ex F-WWSK	John/Reginald Duigen	o/o◆
☐ VH-OQL	Airbus A380-842	074	ex		o/o◆
☐ VH-OQM	Airbus A380-842	091	ex		o/o◆
☐ VH-TJE	Boeing 737-476	24430/1820		Kookaburra	
☐ VH-TJF	Boeing 737-476	24431/1863		Brolga	
☐ VH-TJG	Boeing 737-476	24432/1879	ex 9M-MLE	Eagle	
☐ VH-TJH	Boeing 737-476	24433/1881		Falcon	
☐ VH-TJI	Boeing 737-476	24434/1912	ex 9M-MLD	Swan	
☐ VH-TJJ	Boeing 737-476	24435/1959		Heron	
☐ VH-TJK	Boeing 737-476	24436/1998		Ibis	
☐ VH-TJL	Boeing 737-476	24437/2162		Swift	
☐ VH-TJM	Boeing 737-476	24438/2171		Kestrel	
☐ VH-TJO	Boeing 737-476	24440/2324		Lorikeet	
☐ VH-TJR	Boeing 737-476	24443/2398		Cockatiel	
☐ VH-TJS	Boeing 737-476	24444/2454		Jabiru	
☐ VH-TJT	Boeing 737-476	24445/2539		Kingfisher	
☐ VH-TJU	Boeing 737-476	24446/2569		Currawong	

☐ VH-TJW	Boeing 737-4L7	26961/2517	ex C2-RN11	Strahan	
☐ VH-TJX	Boeing 737-476	28150/2773		Sharing	
☐ VH-TJY	Boeing 737-476	28151/2785		Trust	
☐ VH-VXA	Boeing 737-838/W	29551/1042	ex (N979AN)	Broome	
☐ VH-VXB	Boeing 737-838/W	30101/1045	ex (N980AN)	Yanani Dreaming	
☐ VH-VXC	Boeing 737-838/W	30897/1049	ex (N981AN)	Gippsland	
☐ VH-VXD	Boeing 737-838/W	29552/1063	ex (N982AN)	Tenterfield	
☐ VH-VXE	Boeing 737-838/W	30899/1071	ex (N983AN)	Coffs Harbour	
☐ VH-VXF	Boeing 737-838/W	29553/1096	ex (N984AN)	Sunshine Coast	
☐ VH-VXG	Boeing 737-838/W	30901/1102	ex (N985AM)	Port Douglas	
☐ VH-VXH	Boeing 737-838/W	33478/1137	ex (N986AM)	Warmambool	
☐ VH-VXI	Boeing 737-838/W	33479/1141	ex (N987AM)	Oonadatta	
☐ VH-VXJ	Boeing 737-838/W	33480/1157	ex (N988AM)	Coober Pedy	
☐ VH-VXK	Boeing 737-838/W	33481/1160	ex (N989AM)	Katherine	
☐ VH-VXL	Boeing 737-838/W	33482/1172		Charleville	
☐ VH-VXM	Boeing 737-838/W	33483/1177	ex N6055X	Mount Hotham	
☐ VH-VXN	Boeing 737-838/W	33484/1180		Freemantle	
☐ VH-VXO	Boeing 737-838/W	33485/1183		Kakadu	
☐ VH-VXP	Boeing 737-838/W	33722/1324		Logan	
☐ VH-VXQ	Boeing 737-838/W	33723/1335		Redlands	
☐ VH-VXR	Boeing 737-838/W	33724/1340		Shepparton	
☐ VH-VXS	Boeing 737-838/W	33725/1352		St Helens	
☐ VH-VXT	Boeing 737-838/W	33760/1412	ex N1787B	Townsville	
☐ VH-VXU	Boeing 737-838/W	33761/1420		Wollongong	
☐ VH-VYA	Boeing 737-838/W	33762/1532		Narooma	
☐ VH-VYB	Boeing 737-838/W	33763/1534		Cape Otway	
☐ VH-VYC	Boeing 737-838/W	33991/1612		Arnhem Land	
☐ VH-VYD	Boeing 737-838/W	33992/1706		Eudunda	
☐ VH-VYE	Boeing 737-838/W	33993/1712		Alice Springs	
☐ VH-VYF	Boeing 737-838/W	33994/1727	ex N1784B	Evandale	
☐ VH-VYG	Boeing 737-838/W	33995/1736		Australind	
☐ VH-VYH	Boeing 737-838/W	34180/1815		Queanbeyan	
☐ VH-VYI	Boeing 737-838/W	34181/1840		Bathurst Island	
☐ VH-VYJ	Boeing 737-838/W	34182/1842	ex N1782B	Cann River	
☐ VH-VYK	Boeing 737-838/W	34183/1846	ex N1784B	Moree	
☐ VH-VYL	Boeing 737-838/W	34184/1854		Wangaratta	
☐ VH-VZA	Boeing 737-838/W	34195/2502	ex N1779B	Port Augusta	
☐ VH-VZB	Boeing 737-838/W	34196/2623	ex N1786B	Lake Macquarie	
☐ VH-VZC	Boeing 737-838/W	34197/2649		Innisfail	
☐ VH-VZD	Boeing 737-838/W	34198/2659		Geelong	
☐ VH-VZE	Boeing 737-838/W	34199/2661	ex N1786B	Bunbury	
☐ VH-OEB	Boeing 747-48E	25778/983	ex HL7416	Phillip Island	
☐ VH-OEC	Boeing 747-4H6	24836/808	ex 9M-MHN	King Island	[VCV]
☐ VH-OED	Boeing 747-4H6	25126/858	ex 9M-MHO	Kangaroo Island	[VCV]
☐ VH-OEE	Boeing 747-438ER	32909/1308	ex N747ER	Nullarbor	
☐ VH-OEF	Boeing 747-438ER	32910/1313	ex N60659	City of Sydney	
☐ VH-OEG	Boeing 747-438ER	32911/1320		Parkes	
☐ VH-OEH	Boeing 747-438ER	32912/1321	ex N5020K	Hervey Bay	
☐ VH-OEI	Boeing 747-438ER	32913/1330		Ceduna	
☐ VH-OEJ	Boeing 747-438ER	32914/1331	ex N60668	Wanula Dreaming	
☐ VH-OJA	Boeing 747-438	24354/731	ex N6046P	City of Canberra	
☐ VH-OJB	Boeing 747-438	24373/746		Mount Isa	
☐ VH-OJC	Boeing 747-438	24406/751		City of Melbourne	
☐ VH-OJD	Boeing 747-438	24481/764		City of Brisbane	
☐ VH-OJE	Boeing 747-438	24482/765		City of Adelaide	
☐ VH-OJF	Boeing 747-438	24483/781		City of Perth	
☐ VH-OJG	Boeing 747-438	24779/801	ex N6009F	City of Hobart	
☐ VH-OJH	Boeing 747-438	24806/807		City of Darwin	
☐ VH-OJI	Boeing 747-438	24887/826	ex N6009F	Longreach	
☐ VH-OJJ	Boeing 747-438	24974/835		Winton	
☐ VH-OJK	Boeing 747-438	25067/857		Newcastle	[VCV]
☐ VH-OJL	Boeing 747-438	25151/865		City of Ballarat	
☐ VH-OJM	Boeing 747-438	25245/875		GoSFord	
☐ VH-OJN	Boeing 747-438	25315/883	ex N6009F	City of Dubbo	
☐ VH-OJO	Boeing 747-438	25544/894	ex N6005C	City of Toowoomba	
☐ VH-OJP	Boeing 747-438	25545/916		City of Albury	
☐ VH-OJQ	Boeing 747-438	25546/924	ex N6005C	Manduran	
☐ VH-OJR	Boeing 747-438	25547/936	ex N6018N	City of Bathurst	
☐ VH-OJS	Boeing 747-438	25564/1230		Hamilton Island	
☐ VH-OJT	Boeing 747-438	25565/1233			
☐ VH-OJU	Boeing 747-438	25566/1239		Lord Howe Island	
☐ VH-OGB	Boeing 767-338ER	24316/242	ex N6005C	City of Kalgoorlie/Boulder	
☐ VH-OGC	Boeing 767-338ER	24317/246	ex N6005C	City of Bendigo	[VCV]
☐ VH-OGD	Boeing 767-338ER	24407/247	ex N6009F	City of Maitland	[VCV]

☐ VH-OGE	Boeing 767-338ER	24531/278		City of Orange
☐ VH-OGF	Boeing 767-338ER	24853/319		City of Lismore
☐ VH-OGG	Boeing 767-338ER	24929/343		City of Rockhampton
☐ VH-OGH	Boeing 767-338ER	24930/344		City of Parramatta
☐ VH-OGI	Boeing 767-338ER	25246/387		City of Port Augusta
☐ VH-OGJ	Boeing 767-338ER	25274/396		Port Macquarie
☐ VH-OGK	Boeing 767-338ER	25316/397	ex N6018N	City of Mackay
☐ VH-OGL	Boeing 767-338ER	25363/402	ex N6018N	Wallabies Rugby World Cup c/s
☐ VH-OGM	Boeing 767-338ER	25575/451		Bundaberg
☐ VH-OGN	Boeing 767-338ER	25576/549		Partnership
☐ VH-OGO	Boeing 767-338ER	25577/550		Unity
☐ VH-OGP	Boeing 767-338ER	28153/615		Forbes
☐ VH-OGQ	Boeing 767-338ER	28154/623		Birdsville
☐ VH-OGR	Boeing 767-338ER	28724/662		City of Corowa
☐ VH-OGS	Boeing 767-338ER	28725/665		Roma
☐ VH-OGT	Boeing 767-338ER	29117/710		Maroochydore
☐ VH-OGU	Boeing 767-338ER	29118/713		Byron Bay
☐ VH-OGV	Boeing 767-338ER	30186/796		
☐ VH-ZXA	Boeing 767-336ER	24337/288	ex G-BNWE	
☐ VH-ZXB	Boeing 767-336ER	24338/293	ex G-BNWF	
☐ VH-ZXC	Boeing 767-336ER	24339/298	ex G-BNWG	
☐ VH-ZXD	Boeing 767-336ER	24342/363	ex G-BNWJ	
☐ VH-ZXE	Boeing 767-336ER	24343/364	ex G-BNWK	
☐ VH-ZXF	Boeing 767-336ER	25203/365	ex G-BNWL	
☐ VH-ZXG	Boeing 767-336ER	25443/419	ex G-BNWP	

QANTASLINK   (QF/QFA)   *various*

☐ VH-NXD	Boeing 717-23S	55062/5031	ex VH-VQD		
☐ VH-NXE	Boeing 717-23S	55063/5034	ex VH-VQE		
☐ VH-NXG	Boeing 717-2K9	55057/5020	ex VH-LAX		
☐ VH-NXH	Boeing 717-2K9	55055/5014	ex VH-IMD		[ADL]
☐ VH-NXI	Boeing 717-2K9	55054/5013	ex VH-IMP		
☐ VH-NXK	Boeing 717-231	55092/5077	ex VH-YQF		
☐ VH-NXL	Boeing 717-231	55093/5083	ex VH-YQG		
☐ VH-NXM	Boeing 717-231	55094/5084	ex VH-YQH		
☐ VH-NXN	Boeing 717-231	55095/5087	ex VH-YQI		
☐ VH-NXO	Boeing 717-231	55096/5093	ex VH-YQJ		
☐ VH-NXQ	Boeing 717-231	55097/5095	ex VH-YQK		
☐ VH-SBB	de Havilland DHC-8Q-315	539	ex C-FDHO		Eastern Australia
☐ VH-SBG	de Havilland DHC-8Q-315	575	ex C-GSAH		Eastern Australia
☐ VH-SBI	de Havilland DHC-8Q-315	605	ex C-FZKU		Eastern Australia
☐ VH-SBT	de Havilland DHC-8Q-315	580	ex C-FDHP		Eastern Australia
☐ VH-SBV	de Havilland DHC-8Q-315	595	ex C-GIHK		Eastern Australia
☐ VH-SBW	de Havilland DHC-8Q-315	599	ex C-GZPN		Eastern Australia
☐ VH-SCE	de Havilland DHC-8Q-315	602	ex C-GZPP		Eastern Australia
☐ VH-SDA	de Havilland DHC-8Q-202	482	ex C-GFQL		Eastern Australia
☐ VH-SDE	de Havilland DHC-8Q-202	453	ex N453DS		Eastern Australia
☐ VH-TQD	de Havilland DHC-8Q-315	598	ex C-GZDO		Eastern Australia
☐ VH-TQE	de Havilland DHC-8Q-315	596	ex C-GDOE		Eastern Australia
☐ VH-TQG	de Havilland DHC-8-201	430	ex C-GDNG		Eastern Australia
☐ VH-TQH	de Havilland DHC-8Q-315	597	ex C-GZDM		Eastern Australia
☐ VH-TQK	de Havilland DHC-8Q-315	600	ex C-GZPO		Eastern Australia
☐ VH-TQL	de Havilland DHC-8Q-315	603	ex C-GZPQ		Eastern Australia
☐ VH-TQM	de Havilland DHC-8Q-315	604	ex C-FZHW		Eastern Australia
☐ VH-TQS	de Havilland DHC-8-202	418	ex 9M-EKB		Eastern Australia
☐ VH-TQX	de Havilland DHC-8-202	439	ex N439SD		Eastern Australia
☐ VH-TQY	de Havilland DHC-8Q-315	552	ex C-FDHP		Eastern Australia
☐ VH-TQZ	de Havilland DHC-8Q-315	555	ex C-GDNK		Eastern Australia
☐ VH-QOA	de Havilland DHC-8-402Q	4112	ex C-FDHG	Gladstone:	Sunstate
☐ VH-QOB	de Havilland DHC-8-402Q	4116	ex C-FERF	Yeppoon	Sunstate
☐ VH-QOC	de Havilland DHC-8-402Q	4117	ex C-FFCD	Mackay	Sunstate
☐ VH-QOD	de Havilland DHC-8-402Q	4123	ex C-FFQL	Emerald	Sunstate
☐ VH-QOE	de Havilland DHC-8-402Q	4125	ex C-FFQE		Sunstate
☐ VH-QOF	de Havilland DHC-8-402Q	4128	ex C-FFQM		Sunstate
☐ VH-QOH	de Havilland DHC-8-402Q	4132	ex C-FGKH	pink colours	Sunstate
☐ VH-QOI	de Havilland DHC-8-402Q	4189	ex C-FNQL	Tamworth	Sunstate
☐ VH-QOJ	de Havilland DHC-8-402Q	4192	ex C-FNZU		Sunstate
☐ VH-QOK	de Havilland DHC-8-402Q	4215	ex C-FQXU		Sunstate
☐ VH-QOM	de Havilland DHC-8-402Q	4217	ex C-FRLL		Sunstate
☐ VH-QON	de Havilland DHC-8-402Q	4218	ex C-FRLP		Sunstate
☐ VH-QOP	de Havilland DHC-8-402Q	4238	ex C-FUOI		Sunstate
☐ VH-QOR	de Havilland DHC-8-402Q	4241	ex C-FUST		Sunstate
☐ VH-QOS	de Havilland DHC-8-402Q	4263	ex C-FXAZ		Sunstate
☐ VH-QOT	de Havilland DHC-8-402Q	4269	ex C-FXYP		Sunstate
☐ VH-QOU	de Havilland DHC-8-402Q	4275	ex C-FYGQ		Sunstate

☐ VH-QOV	de Havilland DHC-8-402Q	4277	ex C-FYIC	Sunstate
☐ VH-QOW	de Havilland DHC-8-402Q	4285	ex C-FZFT	Sunstate
☐ VH-QOX	de Havilland DHC-8-402Q	4287	ex C-FZGC	Sunstate
☐ VH-QOY	de Havilland DHC-8-402Q	4288	ex C-FZGG	Sunstate
☐ VH-	de Havilland DHC-8-402Q		ex C-	o/o♦
☐ VH-	de Havilland DHC-8-402Q		ex C-	o/o♦

REGIONAL PACIFIC AIR — Horn Island, QLD (HID)

| ☐ VH-RPA | Embraer EMB.120RT Brasilia | 120079 | ex DQ-MUM | |

REX – REGIONAL EXPRESS — (ZL/RXA) — Orange, NSW/Wagga Wagga, NSW (OAG/WGA)

☐ VH-EKH	SAAB SF.340B	340B-369	ex SE-C69	
☐ VH-EKX	SAAB SF.340B	340B-257	ex (F-GNVQ)	
☐ VH-KDQ	SAAB SF.340B	340B-325	ex SE-KVO	
☐ VH-KDV	SAAB SF.340B	340B-322	ex SE-KVN	
☐ VH-KRX	SAAB SF.340B	340B-290	ex N361BE	
☐ VH-NRX	SAAB SF.340B	340B-291	ex N362BE	
☐ VH-OLL	SAAB SF.340B	340B-175	ex N143NC	
☐ VH-OLM	SAAB SF.340B	340B-205	ex SE-G05	
☐ VH-ORX	SAAB SF.340B	340B-293	ex N363BE	
☐ VH-PRX	SAAB SF.340B	340B-303	ex N366BE	
☐ VH-RXE	SAAB SF.340B	340B-275	ex N275CJ	
☐ VH-RXN	SAAB SF.340B	340B-279	ex N358BE	
☐ VH-RXQ	SAAB SF.340B	340B-200	ex YR-VGN	
☐ VH-RXS	SAAB SF.340B	340B-285	ex N359BE	
☐ VH-RXX	SAAB SF.340B	340B-209	ex N355BE	
☐ VH-SBA	SAAB SF.340B	340B-311	ex SE-KXA	
☐ VH-TRX	SAAB SF.340B	340B-287	ex N360BE	Kay Hull Plane
☐ VH-XRX	SAAB SF.340B	340B-179	ex N179CT	
☐ VH-YRX	SAAB SF.340B	340B-178	ex N178CT	
☐ VH-ZLA	SAAB SF.340B	340B-371	ex N371AE	
☐ VH-ZLC	SAAB SF.340B	340B-373	ex N373AE	
☐ VH-ZLF	SAAB SF.340B	340B-374	ex N374AE	
☐ VH-ZLG	SAAB SF.340B	340B-375	ex N375AE	
☐ VH-ZLH	SAAB SF.340B	340B-376	ex N376AE	
☐ VH-ZLJ	SAAB SF.340B	340B-380	ex N380AE	
☐ VH-ZLK	SAAB SF.340B	340B-381	ex N381AE	
☐ VH-ZLO	SAAB SF.340B	340B-382	ex N382AE	
☐ VH-ZLQ	SAAB SF.340B	340B-370	ex N370AM	
☐ VH-ZLR	SAAB SF.340B	340B-229	ex SE-KSK	
☐ VH-ZLS	SAAB SF.340B	340B-383	ex N383AE	
☐ VH-ZLV	SAAB SF.340B	340B-386	ex N386AE	
☐ VH-ZLW	SAAB SF.340B	340B-387	ex N387AE	
☐ VH-ZLX	SAAB SF.340B	340B-182	ex ER-SGB	
☐ VH-ZRB	SAAB SF.340B	340B-389	ex N389AE	
☐ VH-ZRC	SAAB SF.340B	340B-390	ex N390AE	
☐ VH-ZRE	SAAB SF.340B	340B-391	ex N391AE	
☐ VH-ZRH	SAAB SF.340B	340B-392	ex N392AE	
☐ VH-ZRI	SAAB SF.340B	340B-394	ex N394AE	
☐ VH-ZRJ	SAAB SF.340B	340B-396	ex N396AE	
☐ VH-ZRK	SAAB SF.340B	340B-397	ex N397AE	
☐ VH-ZRL	SAAB SF.340B	340B-398	ex N398AE	
☐ VH-ZRM	SAAB SF.340B	340B-400	ex N400BR	
☐ VH-ZRN	SAAB SF.340B	340B-393	ex N393AE	
☐ VH-ZRY	SAAB SF.340B	340B-401	ex N901AE	
☐ VH-ZRZ	SAAB SF.340B	340B-388	ex N388AE	

ROSSAIR CHARTER — (RFS) — Adelaide-International, SA (ADL)

☐ VH-NAX	Cessna 441 Conquest II	441-0106	ex VH-HXM	
☐ VH-XBC	Cessna 441 Conquest II	441-0297	ex N441MT	
☐ VH-XMD	Cessna 441 Conquest II	441-0025	ex N441HD	
☐ VH-XMJ	Cessna 441 Conquest II	441-0113	ex N27TA	

ROYAL FLYING DOCTOR SERVICE

☐ VH-FDA	Beech B200 Super King Air	BB-1986	ex N986KA	Queensland
☐ VH-FDB	Beech B200 Super King Air	BB-1977	ex N7317A	Queensland
☐ VH-FDC	Pilatus PC-12/45	426		Queensland
☐ VH-FDD	Beech B200 Super King Air	BB-1697	ex N40483	Queensland
☐ VH-FDE	Pilatus PC-12/45	332		Central Operations
☐ VH-FDF	Beech B200 Super King Air	BB-1696	ex N40481	Queensland
☐ VH-FDG	Beech B200 Super King Air	BB-2012	ex N60312	Queensland
☐ VH-FDI	Beech B200C Super King Air	BL-162	ex N80562	Queensland♦
☐ VH-FDJ	Pilatus PC-12/47	861	ex HB-FST	Central Operations
☐ VH-FDK	Pilatus PC-12/47	466		Central Operations

☐ VH-FDM	Beech B200C Super King Air	BL-161	ex N80761	Queensland♦
☐ VH-FDO	Beech B200 Super King Air	BB-1056	ex VH-RFX	Queensland
☐ VH-FDP	Pilatus PC-12/45	434		Queensland
☐ VH-FDR	Beech B200 Super King Air	BB-1881	ex N36801	Queensland
☐ VH-FDT	Beech B200 Super King Air	BB-1990	ex N990KA	Queensland
☐ VH-FDW	Beech B200 Super King Air	BB-1880	ex N61800	Queensland
☐ VH-FDZ	Beech B200 Super King Air	BB-1882	ex N37082	Queensland
☐ VH-FFI	Beech B200 Super King Air	BB-1037	ex VH-FDI	Queensland♦
☐ VH-FGR	Pilatus PC-12/45	438	ex HB-FRW	Central Operations
☐ VH-FGS	Pilatus PC-12/45	440	ex HB-FRX	Central Operations
☐ VH-FGT	Pilatus PC-12/45	442	ex HB-FRY	Central Operations
☐ VH-FMP	Pilatus PC-12/45	122		Central Operations
☐ VH-FMW	Pilatus PC-12/45	123		Central Operations
☐ VH-FMZ	Pilatus PC-12/45	138		Central Operations
☐ VH-FVB	Pilatus PC-12/47E	1187	ex HB-FTI	Central Operations♦
☐ VH-FVD	Pilatus PC-12/47E	1206	ex HB-FTT	Central Operations♦
☐ VH-FVE	Pilatus PC-12/47E	1221	ex HB-FQQ	Central Operations♦
☐ VH-KWO	Pilatus PC-12/45	363		Western Operations
☐ VH-MSH	Beech B200 Super King Air	BB-1787	ex N44857	South Eastern
☐ VH-MSM	Beech B200 Super King Air	BB-1464	ex N133LC	South Eastern
☐ VH-MSU	Beech B200C Super King Air	BL-48	ex N1860B	South Eastern
☐ VH-MSZ	Beech 200 Super King Air	BB-866	ex ZK-PBG	South Eastern
☐ VH-MVJ	Beech B200 Super King Air	BB-1842	ex N50152	South Eastern
☐ VH-MVL	Beech B200 Super King Air	BB-1333	ex N1101W	South Eastern
☐ VH-MVP	Beech B200 Super King Air	BB-1812	ex VH-AMR	South Eastern♦
☐ VH-MVS	Beech B200 Super King Air	BB-1813	ex VH-AMQ	South Eastern♦
☐ VH-MVW	Beech B200 Super King Air	BB-1980	ex N980KA	South Eastern
☐ VH-MVX	Beech B200C Super King Air	BL-153	ex N3203R	South Eastern
☐ VH-MVY	Beech B200 Super King Air	BB-1324	ex N7087N	South Eastern
☐ VH-MWH	Beech B200 Super King Air	BB-2003	ex N32030	South Eastern
☐ VH-MWK	Beech B200C Super King Air	BL-152	ex N3202W	South Eastern
☐ VH-MWO	Pilatus PC-12/45	379		Western Operations
☐ VH-MWQ	Beech B200 Super King Air	BB-1416	ex N8254H	South Eastern
☐ VH-MWU	Beech B200 Super King Air	BB-1418	ex N131GA	South Eastern
☐ VH-MWV	Beech B200 Super King Air	BB-1814	ex VH-AMS	South Eastern♦
☐ VH-MWX	Beech B200 Super King Air	BB-1424	ex N8236K	South Eastern
☐ VH-MWZ	Beech B200 Super King Air	BB-1430	ex VH-MSM	South Eastern
☐ VH-NQA	Beech B200C Super King Air	BL-68	ex VH-FDS	Queensland♦
☐ VH-NQB	Pilatus PC-12/45	428	ex VH-FDM	Queensland♦
☐ VH-NQC	Cessna 208B Grand Caravan	208B2138		Queensland
☐ VH-NQD	Cessna 208B Grand Caravan	208B2139		Queensland
☐ VH-NWO	Pilatus PC-12/45	396	ex HB-FQQ	Western Operations
☐ VH-OWA	Pilatus PC-12/47E	1115	ex HB-FQR	Western Operations
☐ VH-OWB	Pilatus PC-12/47E	1104	ex HB-FQD	Western Operations
☐ VH-OWD	Pilatus PC-12/47E	1140	ex HB-FRN	Western Operations
☐ VH-OWG	Pilatus PC-12/47E	1155	ex HB-FSV	Western Operations
☐ VH-OWI	Pilatus PC-12/47E	1232	ex HB-FRD	Western Operations♦
☐ VH-OWP	Pilatus PC-12/47E	1032	ex HB-FQL	Western Operations
☐ VH-OWQ	Pilatus PC-12/47E	1052	ex HB-FRF	Western Operations
☐ VH-OWR	Pilatus PC-12/47E	1082	ex HB-FSK	Western Operations
☐ VH-VWO	Pilatus PC-12/45	400	ex HB-FQR	Western Operations
☐ VH-YWO	Pilatus PC-12/45	725		Western Operations
☐ VH-ZWO	Pilatus PC-12/45	467	ex HB-FQM	Western Operations

SEAIR PACIFIC GOLD COAST — Gold Coast, QLD (OOL)

☐ VH-LMD	Cessna 208 Caravan I	20800217	ex 9M-FBA	FP
☐ VH-LMZ	Cessna 208 Caravan I	20800173	ex LN-SEA	FP
☐ VH-LYT	Cessna 208B Caravan I	208B1208	ex N1320B	
☐ VH-MBF	Britten-Norman BN-2A-8 Islander	646	ex P2-MBF	
☐ VH-MBK	Britten-Norman BN-2A Islander	158	ex P2-MBD	
☐ VH-SKG	Britten-Norman BN-2A-9 Islander	609	ex ZK-CRA	

SEAWING AIRWAYS — Sydney Rose Bay, NSW (RSE)

☐ VH-SWB	de Havilland DHC-2 Beaver	1557	ex ZK-CKD	FP

SHARP AIRLINES — Hamilton, VIC (HML)

☐ VH-HWR	Swearingen SA.227DC Metro 23	DC-851B	ex N3025T	
☐ VH-LCE	Piper PA-31-350 Navajo Chieftain	31-7305088	ex N305SP	
☐ VH-MYI	Swearingen SA.227DC Metro 23	DC-869B	ex 9M-APB	♦
☐ VH-SEZ	Swearingen SA.227AC Metro III	AC-637	ex ZK-RCA	
☐ VH-UUN	Swearingen SA.227AC Metro III	AC-686	ex N686AV	
☐ VH-UUB	Swearingen SA.227DC Metro 23	DC-894B	ex N3032F	

SHINE AIR SERVICES   Geraldtown, WA (GET)

☐ VH-ADE	Piper PA-31-325 Navajo C/R	31-7712006	ex N62996
☐ VH-HHX	Beech 58 Baron	TH-270	ex VH-WGS
☐ VH-ITF	Piper PA-31 Navajo C	31-7812014	ex N27435
☐ VH-PGO	Piper PA-31-350 Chieftain	31-7852109	ex VH-SFH
☐ VH-SZD	Cessna 404 Titan II	404-0050	ex 5Y-BGE
☐ VH-VHT	Cessna 404 Titan II	404-0226	ex ZS-OJN
☐ VH-XSY	Beech 58 Baron	TH-425	ex ZK-TWB

SHORTSTOP AIR CHARTER   Melbourne-Essendon, VIC (MEB)

☐ VH-OVC	Swearingen SA.226T Merlin II	T-318	ex OE-FOW	
☐ VH-OVM	Douglas DC-3	16354/33102	ex VH-JXD	Arthur Schutt MBE

SKIPPERS AVIATION   (SY)   Perth-International, WA (PER)

☐ VH-FMQ	Cessna 441 Conquest II	441-0109	ex N26226	
☐ VH-LBX	Cessna 441 Conquest II	441-0091	ex VH-AZY	
☐ VH-LBY	Cessna 441 Conquest II	441-0023	ex VH-TFW	
☐ VH-LBZ	Cessna 441 Conquest II	441-0038	ex VH-HWD	
☐ VH-XFP	de Havilland DHC-8-102A	346	ex VH-TQU	
☐ VH-XFQ	de Havilland DHC-8-106	306	ex VH-TQW	
☐ VH-XFT	de Havilland DHC-8-102	52	ex ZK-NEW	
☐ VH-XFU	de Havilland DHC-8-102	151	ex ZK-NEV	
☐ VH-XFV	de Havilland DHC-8-314A	350	ex D-BMUC	
☐ VH-XFW	de Havilland DHC-8-314A	356	ex D-BKIM	
☐ VH-XFX	de Havilland DHC-8-314A	313	ex D-BHAM	
☐ VH-XFZ	de Havilland DHC-8-314A	365	ex D-BACH	
☐ VH-XUA	Embraer EMB.120ER Brasilia	120045	ex N272UE	
☐ VH-XUB	Embraer EMB.120ER Brasilia	120181	ex VH-XFW	
☐ VH-XUC	Embraer EMB.120ER Brasilia	120208	ex VH-XFV	Pelsaert Princess
☐ VH-XUD	Embraer EMB.120ER Brasilia	120140	ex VH-XFZ	Monket Mia Flyer
☐ VH-XUE	Embraer EMB.120ER Brasilia	120115	ex VH-XFQ	
☐ VH-XUF	Embraer EMB.120ER Brasilia	120207	ex N268UE	
☐ VH-WAI	Swearingen SA.227DC Metro 23	DC-874B	ex N3032L	
☐ VH-WAJ	Swearingen SA.227DC Metro 23	DC-876B	ex N3033U	
☐ VH-WAX	Swearingen SA.227DC Metro 23	DC-877B	ex N30337	
☐ VH-WBA	Swearingen SA.227DC Metro 23	DC-883B	ex N30042	
☐ VH-WBQ	Swearingen SA.227DC Metro 23	DC-884B	ex N30046	Laverton

SKYTRADERS   Melbourne-Tullamarine, VIC (MEL)

☐ VH-VHA	CASA C.212 Srs.400	474		Ginger	Wheels or skis
☐ VH-VHB	CASA C.212 Srs.400	475		Gadget	Wheels or skis
☐ VH-VHD	Airbus A319-115X	1999	ex F-GYAS		

SKYTRANS REGIONAL   (NP)   Cairns, QLD (CNS)

☐ VH-QQA	de Havilland DHC-8-102	5	ex P2-MCN	>Maroomba Air Svs	
☐ VH-QQB	de Havilland DHC-8-102	4	ex VH-TQO	>Maroomba Air Svs	
☐ VH-QQC	de Havilland DHC-8-102	8	ex VH-JSZ		
☐ VH-QQE	de Havilland DHC-8-102	173	ex N821EX	>Aircruising	
☐ VH-QQF	de Havilland DHC-8-102	14	ex P2-MCO	Cairns Taipans colours	
☐ VH-QQG	de Havilland DHC-8-102	36	ex 5W-FAA		
☐ VH-QQI	de Havilland DHC-8-102	67	ex VH-TQF		
☐ VH-QQK	de Havilland DHC-8-102	326	ex N846EX		♦
☐ VH-QQL	de Havilland DHC-8-102A	388	ex N825EX		♦

SKYWEST AIRLINES   (XR/OZW)   Perth-International, WA (PER)

☐ VH-FNA	Fokker 50	20106	ex PH-EXG	City of Albany
☐ VH-FNB	Fokker 50	20107	ex PH-EXF	Shire of Esperance
☐ VH-FND	Fokker 50	20129	ex PH-EXB	
☐ VH-FNE	Fokker 50	20212	ex PH-PRJ	
☐ VH-FNF	Fokker 50	20200	ex PH-PRH	
☐ VH-FNH	Fokker 50	20113	ex PH-EXY	Shire of Carnarvon
☐ VH-FNI	Fokker 50	20114	ex PH-EXZ	City of Geraldton
☐ VH-FNC	Fokker 100	11334	ex D-AGPO	
☐ VH-FNJ	Fokker 100	11489	ex G-BVJA	
☐ VH-FNN	Fokker 100	11326	ex PH-CFD	
☐ VH-FNR	Fokker 100	11488	ex G-BVJB	
☐ VH-FNT	Fokker 100	11461	ex B-12297	
☐ VH-FNU	Fokker 100	11373	ex OO-TUF	

| ☐ VH-FNY | Fokker 100 | 11484 | ex N108ML |
| ☐ VH-FSW | Fokker 100 | 11391 | ex D-AGPR |

SLINGAIR   Kununurra, WA (KNX)

☐ VH-HOC	Cessna 210N Centurion II	21064689	ex N1360U
☐ VH-NLV	Cessna 210N Centurion II	21063093	ex VH-APU
☐ VH-NLZ	Cessna 210N Centurion II	21063769	ex VH-RZZ
☐ VH-OCM	Cessna 210N Centurion II	21064466	ex N9300Y
☐ VH-STB	Cessna 210M Centurion II	21062771	ex N6467B
☐ VH-URX	Cessna 210N Centurion II	21064449	ex N6595Y

☐ VH-BVJ	Gippsland GA-8 Airvan	GA8-07-116	
☐ VH-DER	Piper PA-31 Navajo C	31-7912110	ex N3539D
☐ VH-HAM	Cessna 208	2080296	ex N208MM
☐ VH-IEU	Cessna 207 Skywagon	20700231	ex N69336
☐ VH-JVO	Cessna 310R	310R0539	ex N145FB
☐ VH-KSA	Cessna 208B Caravan I	208B0516	ex N6302B
☐ VH-LNH	Cessna 208B Caravan I	208B0590	ex N590TA
☐ VH-LNN	Cessna 208B Caravan I	208B0801	ex 9M-PMB
☐ VH-LNO	Cessna 208B Caravan I	208B0925	ex N125AR
☐ VH-MZV	Piper PA-31-350 Chieftain	31-8152092	ex N4083C
☐ VH-NLG	Cessna U206G Stationair	U20603930	ex ZS-JGH
☐ VH-RKD	Piper PA-31-350 Chieftain	31-8152048	ex N4076Z
☐ VH-TWY	Cessna 310R	310R0090	ex N69336

STRATEGIC AIRLINES   (VF)

☐ VH-YQB	Airbus A320-211	0279	ex PK-RMA		♦
☐ VH-YQC	Airbus A320-211	0395	ex CS-TNE		♦
☐ YL-LCF	Airbus A320-212	0446	ex N446AN		o/o♦

| ☐ VH-SSA | Airbus A330-223 | 324 | ex HB-IQR | Outback |

SUNSTATE AIRLINES   Sunstate (QF/SSQ)   Brisbane, QLD (BNE)

Wholly owned by Qantas and operates scheduled services in full colours as QantasLink (q.v.)

SYDNEY SEAPLANES   Sydney Rose Bay, NSW

☐ VH-AAM	de Havilland DHC-2 Beaver	1492	ex VH-IMR	FP
☐ VH-AQU	de Havilland DHC-2 Beaver	1544	ex VH-IDN	FP
☐ VH-NOO	de Havilland DHC-2 Beaver	1535	ex VH-IDI	FP
☐ VH-SXF	Cessna 208 Caravan I	20800405	ex N1122Y	FP

TASAIR   Hobart, TAS (HBT)

☐ VH-JVD	Piper PA-31-350 Chieftain	31-7852041	ex N27523
☐ VH-KRR	Cessna U206F Stationair 6	U20603210	ex (N8349Q)
☐ VH-LTW	Piper PA-31-350 Chieftain	31-8152025	ex N40725
☐ VH-MZI	Piper PA-31-350 Chieftain	31-8152131	ex N4087S
☐ VH-SMQ	British Aerospace Jetstream 31	665	ex VH-ESW
☐ VH-TSR	Cessna U206E Stationair	U20601650	ex N9450G
☐ VH-TZY	Piper PA-31-350 Navajo Chieftain	31-7405166	ex N662WR

TASFAST AIR FREIGHT   Melbourne-Moorabin, VIC (MBW)

☐ VH-EDV	Piper PA-31-350 Navajo Chieftain	31-7305025	ex N86568
☐ VH-NLX	Piper PA-31 Navajo C	31-7812055	ex VH-EQX
☐ VH-TBJ	Piper PA-31-350 Navajo Chieftain	31-7552128	ex VH-SAJ

TASMAN CARGO AIRLINES   Freightexpress (HJ/AXF)   Sydney-Kingsford Smith, NSW (SYD)

| ☐ G-BMRJ | Boeing 757-236 (SF) | 24268/214 | | | <DHK♦ |
| ☐ VH-DHE | Boeing 727-2J4F (FedEx 3) | 22080/1598 | ex N729DH | DHL Express c/s | <BCS |

TIGER AIRWAYS   (TT)   Melbourne-Tullamarine, VIC (MEL)

☐ VH-VNB	Airbus A320-232	2906	ex 9V-TAG	
☐ VH-VNC	Airbus A320-232	3275	ex F-WWDE	
☐ VH-VND	Airbus A320-232	3296	ex F-WWDX	
☐ VH-VNF	Airbus A320-232	3332	ex F-WWBI	
☐ VH-VNH	Airbus A320-232	3734	ex F-WWDN	
☐ VH-VNP	Airbus A320-232	2952	ex 9V-TAH	♦
☐ VH-	Airbus A320-232		ex	o/o♦
☐ VH-	Airbus A320-232		ex	o/o♦
☐ VH-	Airbus A320-232		ex	o/o♦

TOLL PRIORITY		(TFR)			Brisbane, QLD (BNE)
☐ ZK-TLA	Boeing 737-3B7 (SF)	23383/1425	ex N508AU		Op by AWK
☐ ZK-TLC	Boeing 737-3B7 (SF)	23705/1497	ex N519AU		Op by AWK
☐ ZK-TLD	Boeing 737-3B7 (SF)	23706/1499	ex N520AU		Op by AWK
☐ VH-HPE	Swearingen SA.227DC Metro 23	DC-823B	ex N823MM		Toll c/s
☐ VH-UUO	Swearingen SA.227AC Metro III	AC-530	ex ZK-NST		
☐ VH-UZA	Swearingen SA.227AT Merlin IVC	AT-502	ex VH-UUA		
☐ VH-UZD	Swearingen SA.227AC Metro III	AC-490	ex N30693		
☐ VH-UZG	Swearingen SA.227AC Metro III	AC-553	ex N220CT		
☐ VH-UZI	Swearingen SA.227AT Expediter	AT-570	ex N570UP		
☐ VH-UZN	Swearingen SA.227DC Metro 23	DC-881B	ex N6BN		The Australian c/s
☐ VH-UZP	Swearingen SA.227AC Metro III	AC-498	ex OY-BPL	David Fell	
☐ VH-UZS	Swearingen SA.227AC Metro III	AC-517	ex VH-UUG		
☐ VH-UZW	Swearingen SA.227AC Metro III	AC-526	ex OY-GAW		Toll c/s
☐ VH-TOQ	ATR 42-300F	079	ex EI-SLB		Toll c/s
☐ VH-TOX	ATR 42-300F	024	ex EI-SLE		Toll c/s

V AUSTRALIA				Brisbane-International, QLD (BNE)
☐ VH-VOZ	Boeing 777-3ZGER	35302/745	Didgeree Blue	
☐ VH-VPD	Boeing 777-3ZGER	37938/756		
☐ VH-VPE	Boeing 777-3ZGER	37939/764		
☐ VH-VPF	Boeing 777-3ZGER	37940/801		
☐ VH-VPH	Boeing 777-3ZGER	37943/898		♦

VINCENT AVIATION (AUSTRALIA)		(BF/VIN)		Darwin, NT (DAW)
☐ VH-EMK	Beech 1900C-1	UC-159	ex N159GL	
☐ VH-VAQ	Beech 1900D	UE-302	ex ZK-VAB	♦
☐ VH-VAZ	Beech 1900D	UE-115	ex ZS-PMD	
☐ VH-VNT	Beech 1900D	UE-91	ex ZS-SEM	
☐ VH-VNV	Beech 1900C	UC-56	ex ZK-VAE	♦
☐ VH-TAZ	Cessna 441 Conquest	4410005	ex N441RZ	

VIRGIN BLUE AIRLINES		Virgin Blue (DJ/VOZ)		Brisbane-International, QLD (BNE)
☐ VH-XFA	Airbus A330-243	365	ex A6-EAB	♦
☐ VH-	Airbus A330-243	372	ex A6-EAC	♦
☐ VH-VBA	Boeing 737-7Q8/W	28238/817	ex N1791B	Brizzie Lizzie
☐ VH-VBB	Boeing 737-7Q8/W	28240/832	ex N1787B	Barossa Babe
☐ VH-VBC	Boeing 737-7Q8	30638/858		Betty Blue
☐ VH-VBD	Boeing 737-7Q8/W	30707/975		Sassy Sydney
☐ VH-VBF	Boeing 737-7Q8/W	30630/1032		Mellie Melbourne
☐ VH-VBH	Boeing 737-7Q8/W	30641/1080		Spirit of Sally
☐ VH-VBI	Boeing 737-7Q8/W	30644/1107		Smurfette
☐ VH-VBJ	Boeing 737-7Q8/W	30647/1159		Perth Princess
☐ VH-VBK	Boeing 737-7Q8/W	30648/1171		Lady Victoria
☐ VH-VBL	Boeing 737-7Q8/W	30633/1220		Victoria Vixen
☐ VH-VBM	Boeing 737-76N/W	32734/1090	ex N734SH	Tassie Tigress
☐ VH-VBN	Boeing 737-76N/W	33005/1134	ex N330SF	Southern Belle
☐ VH-VBO	Boeing 737-76N/W	33418/1226		Tropical Temptress
☐ VH-VBP	Boeing 737-7BX/W	30743/922	ex N368ML	Deja Blue
☐ VH-VBQ	Boeing 737-7BX/W	30744/989	ex N369ML	La Blue Femme
☐ VH-VBR	Boeing 737-7BX/W	30745/1027	ex N370ML	Mackay Maiden
☐ VH-VBU	Boeing 737-7BK/W	30288/1322		Darwin Diva
☐ VH-VBV	Boeing 737-7BK/W	33015/1384		Moulin Blue
☐ VH-VBY	Boeing 737-7FE/W	34323/1751		Virgin-ia Blue50th titles
☐ VH-VBZ	Boeing 737-7FE/W	34322/1777		Maliblue
☐ VH-BZG	Boeing 737-8FE/W	37822/3355	ex N1786B	Brett'sJet	♦
☐ VH-VOB	Boeing 737-8BK/W	30622/1108		Matilda Blue
☐ VH-VOC	Boeing 737-8BK/W	30623/1136		Skye Blue
☐ VH-VOD	Boeing 737-8BK/W	30624/1193	ex N60656	Blue Moon
☐ VH-VOK	Boeing 737-8FE/W	33758/1359		Smoochy Maroochy
☐ VH-VOL	Boeing 737-8FE/W	33759/1364		Goldie Coast
☐ VH-VOM	Boeing 737-8FE/W	33794/1373		Little Blue Peep
☐ VH-VON	Boeing 737-8FE/W	33795/1375		Scarlett Blue
☐ VH-VOQ	Boeing 737-8FE/W	33798/1391		Peta Pan
☐ VH-VOS	Boeing 737-8FE/W	33800/1483		Kimberley Cutie
☐ VH-VOT	Boeing 737-8FE/W	33801/1504		Butterfly Blue
☐ VH-VOU	Boeing 737-8Q8/W	30665/1436		Blue Billie
☐ VH-VOV	Boeing 737-82R	30658/1325		Alluring Alice

Reg	Type	C/n	ex	Name	Notes
VH-VOW	Boeing 737-8Q8/W	32798/1470		Jillaroo Blue	
VH-VOX	Boeing 737-8BK/W	33017/1446	ex ZK-PBC	Missy Mainlander	
VH-VUA	Boeing 737-8FE/W	33997/1559		Bondi Baby	
VH-VUC	Boeing 737-8FE/W	34014/1582		Foxy Rock'sy	
VH-VUE	Boeing 737-8FE/W	34167/1676		Prue Blue	
VH-VUF	Boeing 737-8FE/W	34168/1697		Hobart Honey	
VH-VUG	Boeing 737-8FE/W	34438/1948		Jasmine Tasman	
VH-VUI	Boeing 737-8FE/W	34441/2015		Brandi Blue	
VH-VUJ	Boeing 737-8FE/W	34443/2056		Suzzie Blue	
VH-VUK	Boeing 737-8FE/W	36602/2353		Mackay-be Diva	
VH-VUL	Boeing 737-8FE/W	36603/2356	ex N1782B	Ballina-rina Blue	
VH-VUM	Boeing 737-8BK/W	29675/2414	ex N1786B	Brindabella Blue	>PBN
VH-VUN	Boeing 737-8BK/W	29676/2432		Madelaide	>PBN
VH-VUR	Boeing 737-8FE/W	36606/3059	ex N1786B	Star City	
VH-VUS	Boeing 737-8FE/W	36607/3082		Chitty Chitty Broome Broome	
VH-VUT	Boeing 737-8FE/W	36608/3132		Yabba Dabba Blue	
VH-VUU	Boeing 737-8FE/W	36609/3232	ex N1786B	Lady Blue-tiful	
VH-VUV	Boeing 737-8FE/W	37821/3288	ex N1796B		♦
VH-VUW	Boeing 737-8KG/W	39449/3398			♦
VH-VUX	Boeing 737-8FE/W	37823/3415	ex N1786B		♦
VH-VUY	Boeing 737-8KG/W	39450/3494			♦
VH-	Boeing 737-8				o/o♦
VH-	Boeing 737-8				o/o♦
VH-	Boeing 737-8				o/o♦
VH-	Boeing 737-8				o/o♦
VH-	Boeing 737-8				o/o♦
VH-	Boeing 737-8				o/o♦
VH-	Boeing 737-8				o/o♦
VH-	Boeing 737-8				o/o♦
VH-	Boeing 737-8				o/o♦
VH-ZHA	Embraer ERJ-170LR	17000180	ex PT-SMX	Belle-issimo Blue	
VH-ZHB	Embraer ERJ-170LR	17000187	ex PT-SUG	Braziliant Blue	
VH-ZHC	Embraer ERJ-170LR	17000191	ex PT-SUR	Irresisto Blue	
VH-ZHD	Embraer ERJ-170LR	17000227	ex PT-SFD	Cherry – Belle Blue	
VH-ZHE	Embraer ERJ-170LR	17000247	ex PT-SFY	Bee bop a Blue	
VH-ZHF	Embraer ERJ-170LR	17000255	ex PT-SJH	Little Miss Sunshine Coast	
VH-ZPA	Embraer ERJ-190AR	19000148	ex PT-SAB	Candid Canberra	
VH-ZPB	Embraer ERJ-190AR	19000162	ex PT-SAR	Rio de Gold Coast	
VH-ZPC	Embraer ERJ-190AR	19000170	ex PT-SDF	Jilla Blue	
VH-ZPD	Embraer ERJ-190AR	19000176	ex PT-SDL	Tickled Blue	
VH-ZPE	Embraer ERJ-190AR	19000187	ex PT-SDV	Bluephoria	
VH-ZPF	Embraer ERJ-190AR	19000193	ex PT-SGB	Maiden Brazil	
VH-ZPG	Embraer ERJ-190AR	19000195	ex PT-SGD	Ella E-Jet	
VH-ZPH	Embraer ERJ-190AR	19000199	ex PT-SGD	Hastings Highness	
VH-ZPI	Embraer ERJ-190AR	19000202	ex PT-SGK	Allie Albury	
VH-ZPJ	Embraer ERJ-190AR	19000209	ex PT-SGS	Bambino Blue	
VH-ZPK	Embraer ERJ-190AR	19000218	ex PT-SHB	Aussie Rob	
VH-ZPL	Embraer ERJ-190AR	19000220	ex PT-SHD	Samba Blue	
VH-ZPM	Embraer ERJ-190AR	19000262	ex PT-TLC		
VH-ZPN	Embraer ERJ-190AR	19000312	ex PT-TXA	Kanga Blue	
VH-ZPO	Embraer ERJ-190AR	19000321	ex PT-TXJ	Portia Macquarie	
VH-	Embraer ERJ-190AR				o/o♦
VH-	Embraer ERJ-190AR				o/o♦
VH-	Embraer ERJ-190AR				o/o♦

WEST WING AVIATION — Mount Isa, QLD (ISA)

Reg	Type	C/n	ex
VH-ABP	Beech Baron 58	TH-709	ex N6771S
VH-BAM	Beech Baron 58	TH-478	ex VH-FDC
VH-EZN	Beech 58 Baron	TH-1222	ex N3722P
VH-FBM	Cessna 310R	310R0837	ex VH-HOH
VH-LAP	Beech 58 Baron	TH-646	ex 5N-ATC
VH-RDZ	Cessna 402A	402A0125	ex ZK-CSX
VH-SBM	Beech 200 Super King Air	BB-964	ex VH-HTU
VH-TAN	Cessna 402C	402C1008	ex N1237D
VH-TIA	Cessna 402B	402B0623	ex N3774C
VH-VCB	Beech 200 Super King Air	BB-579	ex P2-MML
VH-WZF	Britten-Norman BN-2A-21 Islander	537	ex 5Y-RAJ
VH-WZI	Aero Commander 500S	1856-38	ex VH-JOG
VH-WZJ	Cessna 208B Caravan I	208B1108	ex N208JJ
VH-WZK	Britten-Norman BN-2A-20 Islander	421	ex VH-UBN
VH-WZP	Britten-Norman BN-2B-20 Islander	2284	ex VH-ZZY
VH-WZQ	Rockwell 500S Shrike Commander	1847-36	ex VH-WPX
VH-WZV	Aero Commander 500U	1656-11	ex N197K
VH-WZY	Cessna 208B Caravan I	208B1035	ex VH-ZGS

☐ VH-XDA	Cessna 404 Titan II	404-0408	ex VH-HOA
☐ VH-XDP	Cessna 404 Titan II	404-0845	ex ZS-PNW
☐ VH-XDV	Beech 200 Super King Air	BB-1100	ex N63971
☐ VH-XDW	Beech 200 Super King Air	BB-1258	ex N2748X
☐ VH-XDY	Beech 1900D	UE-396	ex N838CA

WETTENHALL AIR SERVICES — *Deniliguin, NSW (DNQ)*

☐ VH-MAB	Piper PA-39 Twin Comanche C/R	39-96	ex VH-MED
☐ VH-MAV	Rockwell 500S Shrike Commander	3280	ex N81512
☐ VH-SSL	Swearingen SA.226T Merlin	T-210	ex N173SP

VN-   VIETNAM (Socialist Republic of Vietnam)

AIR MEKONG — *Ho Chi Minh City (SGN)*

☐ VN-A801	Canadair CRJ-900	15102	ex EI-DUU	♦
☐ VN-A802	Canadair CRJ-900	15103	ex EI-DUM	♦
☐ VN-A803	Canadair CRJ-900	15110	ex EI-DUX	♦
☐ VN-A804	Canadair CRJ-900	15112	ex EI-DUY	♦

JETSTAR PACIFIC AIRLINES — *Pacific Airlines (BL/PIC)* — *Ho Chi Minh City (SGN)*

☐ VN-A189	Boeing 737-43Q	28490/2830	ex PK-GWY		
☐ VN-A190	Boeing 737-4H6	27383/2657	ex 9M-MQJ		
☐ VN-A191	Boeing 737-4H6	27306/2685	ex 9M-MQM		
☐ VN-A192	Boeing 737-4Q8	26289/2486	ex OK-YGU	all white	
☐ VN-A195	Airbus A320-232	0990	ex CC-CZB		
☐ VN-A198	Airbus A320-232	4459	ex D-AXAB		♦

SERVICE FLIGHT CORP

☐ VN-8601	Eurocopter EC155B	6645	ex F-WQDF
☐ VN-	Eurocopter EC155B	6647	
☐ VN-8608	Aérospatiale AS.332L2 II	2348	ex F-WTNR
☐ VN-8610	Aérospatiale AS.332L2 II	2380	ex F-WQDD
☐ VN-8614	Aérospatiale AS.332L2 II	2664	ex F-OISY
☐ VN-	Aérospatiale AS.332L2 II	2672	ex F-OISZ
☐ VN-8618	Eurocopter EC225LP	2730	ex F-OKEY
☐ VN-8619	Eurocopter EC225LP	2735	ex F-OKEZ

VASCO — *Vasco Air (0V/VFC)* — *Ho Chi Minh City (SGN)*

☐ VN-B594	Beech 200 Super King Air	BB-1329	ex VH-SWC

VIETNAM AIRLINES — *Vietnam Airlines (VN/HVN)* — *Hanoi-Noi Bal (HAN)*

☐ VN-A301	Airbus A320-214	0590	ex S7-ASA	
☐ VN-A302	Airbus A320-214	0594	ex S7-ASB	
☐ VN-A303	Airbus A320-214	0601	ex S7-ASC	
☐ VN-A304	Airbus A320-214	0605	ex S7-ASD	
☐ VN-A305	Airbus A320-214	0607	ex S7-ASE	
☐ VN-A306	Airbus A320-214	0611	ex S7-ASF	
☐ VN-A307	Airbus A320-214	0617	ex S7-ASG	
☐ VN-A308	Airbus A320-214	0619	ex S7-ASH	
☐ VN-A311	Airbus A320-214	0648	ex S7-ASI	
☐ VN-A322	Airbus A321-231	4311	ex D-AVZU	♦
☐ VN-A344	Airbus A321-231	2255	ex D-AVZH	
☐ VN-A345	Airbus A321-231	2261	ex D-AVZJ	
☐ VN-A347	Airbus A321-231	2267	ex D-AVZL	
☐ VN-A348	Airbus A321-231	2303	ex D-AVZC	
☐ VN-A349	Airbus A321-231	2480	ex D-AVXC	
☐ VN-A350	Airbus A321-231	2974	ex D-AVZN	
☐ VN-A351	Airbus A321-231	3005	ex D-AVZI	>K6
☐ VN-A352	Airbus A321-231	3013	ex D-AVZW	
☐ VN-A353	Airbus A321-231	3022	ex D-AVZY	
☐ VN-A354	Airbus A321-231	3198	ex D-AVZX	
☐ VN-A356	Airbus A321-231	3315	ex D-AVZA	
☐ VN-A357	Airbus A321-231	3355	ex D-AVZB	
☐ VN-A358	Airbus A321-231	3600	ex D-AZAC	
☐ VN-A359	Airbus A321-231	3737	ex D-AZAJ	
☐ VN-A360	Airbus A321-231	3862	ex D-AVZJ	
☐ VN-A361	Airbus A321-231	3964	ex D-AZAW	
☐ VN-A362	Airbus A321-231	3966	ex D-AVZC	
☐ VN-A363	Airbus A321-231	4136	ex D-AZAT	♦

☐ VN-A365	Airbus A321-231	4213	ex D-AVZG	♦
☐ VN-A366	Airbus A321-231	4277	ex D-AZAO	♦
☐ VN-A367	Airbus A321-231	4315	ex D-AVZV	♦
☐ VN-	Airbus A321-231		ex	o/o♦
☐ VN-	Airbus A321-231		ex	o/o♦
☐ VN-A368	Airbus A330-322	087	ex N225LF	
☐ VN-A369	Airbus A330-223	255	ex 9M-MKU	
☐ VN-A370	Airbus A330-223	262	ex 9M-MKT	
☐ VN-A371	Airbus A330-223	275	ex HB-IQG	
☐ VN-A372	Airbus A330-223	294	ex HB-IQJ	
☐ VN-A374	Airbus A330-223	299	ex HB-IQK	
☐ VN-A375	Airbus A330-223	366	ex HB-IQP	
☐ VN-A376	Airbus A330-223	943	ex EI-ELI	♦
☐ VN-A377	Airbus A330-223	962	ex EI-ELJ	♦
☐ VN-A378	Airbus A330-223	1019	ex F-WJKM	♦
☐ VN-B210	ATR 72-212A	678	ex F-WWET	
☐ VN-B212	ATR 72-212A	685	ex F-WWEH	>VAV
☐ VN-B214	ATR 72-212A	688	ex F-WWEK	>VAV
☐ VN-B216	ATR 72-212A	450	ex F-WQNF	
☐ VN-B218	ATR 72-212A	877	ex F-WWEE	
☐ VN-B219	ATR 72-212A	886	ex F-WWEP	
☐ VN-B220	ATR 72-212A	890	ex F-WWEV	
☐ VN-B221	ATR 72-212A	892	ex F-WWEX	
☐ VN-B223	ATR 72-212A	896	ex F-WWEG	
☐ VN-B225	ATR 72-212A	897	ex F-WW	
☐ VN-B227	ATR 72-212A	899	ex F-WWEJ	>VAV♦
☐ VN-B231	ATR 72-212A	906	ex F-WWEW	>VAV♦
☐ VN-B233	ATR 72-212A	912	ex F-WWEG	♦
☐ VN-B236	ATR 72-212A	914	ex F-WWEJ	♦
☐ VN-B237	ATR 72-212A	925	ex F-WWEZ	♦
☐ VN-B239	ATR 72-212A	927	ex F-WWEC	♦
☐ VN-B240	ATR 72-212A	939	ex F-WWEO	♦
☐ VN-A141	Boeing 777-2Q8ER	28688/436		
☐ VN-A142	Boeing 777-2Q8ER	32701/443		
☐ VN-A143	Boeing 777-26KER	33502/450		
☐ VN-A144	Boeing 777-26KER	33503/453		
☐ VN-A145	Boeing 777-26KER	33504/491		
☐ VN-A146	Boeing 777-26KER	33505/486		
☐ VN-A147	Boeing 777-2Q8ER	27607/135	ex VP-BAS	
☐ VN-A149	Boeing 777-2Q8ER	32716/518	ex (VN-A147)	
☐ VN-A150	Boeing 777-2Q8ER	32717/541		
☐ VN-A151	Boeing 777-2Q8ER	27608/164	ex VP-BAU	
☐ VN-A502	Fokker 70	11580	ex PH-EZL	
☐ VN-A504	Fokker 70	11585	ex PH-EZM	

VP-A   ANGUILLA (UK Dependency)

ANGUILLA AIR SERVICES   Anguilla-Wallbake (AXA)

☐ VP-AAS	Britten-Norman BN-2A-26 Islander	206	ex G-ISLA

TRANS ANGUILLA AIRLINES   Anguilla-Wallbake/St Thomas-Cyril E King, VI (AXA/STT)

☐ VP-AAA	Britten-Norman BN-2A-21 Islander	382	ex N361RA
☐ VP-AAF	Britten-Norman BN-2B-21 Islander	2024	ex N21DA

VP-C   CAYMAN ISLANDS (UK Colony)

CAYMAN AIRWAYS   Cayman (KX/CAY)   Georgetown, Grand Cayman (GCM)

☐ VP-CAY	Boeing 737-3Q8	26286/2424	ex N241LF	Spirit of Recovery	
☐ VP-CKW	Boeing 737-36E	26322/2769	ex EI-CRZ		
☐ VP-CKX	Boeing 737-236 (AvAero 3)	23162/1056	ex VR-CKX		[MZJ]
☐ VP-CKY	Boeing 737-3Q8	26282/2355	ex N262KS	The Cayman Islands	
☐ VP-CKZ	Boeing 737-36E	27626/2792	ex EI-CSU		o/o
☐ VP-CYB	Boeing 737-2S2C (Nordam 3)	21929/608	ex N716A	Cayman Brac	[MZJ]

CAYMAN AIRWAYS EXPRESS   Georgetown, Grand Cayman (GCM)

☐ VP-CXA	de Havilland DHC-6 Twin Otter 300	602	ex N602DH
☐ VP-CXB	de Havilland DHC-6 Twin Otter 300	563	ex N563DH

564

ISLAND AIR   (G5)   Georgetown, Grand Cayman (GCM)

| □ VP-CIN | Piper PA-31-350 Chieftain | 31-8152184 | ex VR-CIN | |

VP-F   FALKLAND ISLANDS (UK Dependency)

BRITISH ANTARCTIC SURVEY   Penguin (BAN)   Rothera Base, Antarctica

□ VP-FAZ	de Havilland DHC-6 Twin Otter 300	748	ex (FAP-2029)	Wheels or skis
□ VP-FBB	de Havilland DHC-6 Twin Otter 310	783	ex C-GDKL	Wheels or skis
□ VP-FBC	de Havilland DHC-6 Twin Otter 310	787	ex C-GDIU	Wheels or skis
□ VP-FBL	de Havilland DHC-6 Twin Otter 300	839	ex C-GDCZ	Wheels or skis
□ VP-FBQ	de Havilland DHC-7-110	111	ex G-BOAX	

FIGAS - FALKLAND ISLANDS GOVERNMENT AIR SERVICES   Port Stanley (PSY)

□ VP-FBD	Britten-Norman BN-2B-26 Islander	2160	ex G-BKJK	
□ VP-FBI	Britten-Norman BN-2B-26 Islander	2188	ex G-BLNI	dbr 19Nov06?
□ VP-FBM	Britten-Norman BN-2B-26 Islander	2200	ex G-BLNZ	
□ VP-FBN	Britten-Norman BN-2B-26 Islander	2216	ex G-BRFY	Fishery Patrol
□ VP-FBO	Britten-Norman BN-2B-26 Islander	2218	ex G-BRGA	Fishery Patrol
□ VP-FBR	Britten-Norman BN-2B-26 Islander	2252	ex G-BTLX	

VP-L   BRITISH VIRGIN ISLANDS (UK Colony)

FLY BVI   Beef Island (EIS)

□ N18AU	Cessna 404 Titan II	404-0823	ex ST-AWD	
□ N97AQ	Cessna 404 Titan II	404-0135	ex ST-AJE	
□ N6884A	Piper PA-23-250 Aztec F	27-7954105		
□ N8438F	Cessna 401	401-0286		

VP-M   MONTSERRAT (UK Colony)

AIR MONTSERRAT   Plymouth (MNI)

□ VP-MNI	Britten-Norman BN-2A-27 Islander	0183	ex C-GLOD	
□ VP-MNT	Britten-Norman BN-2B-26 Islander	2186		
□ VP-MON	Britten-Norman BN-2A-26 Islander	82	ex C-GCTZ	

VQ-T   TURKS & CAICOS ISLANDS (UK Colony)

AIR TURKS & CAICOS   Islandways (JY/TCI)   Providenciales (PLS)

□ VQ-TBC	Embraer EMB.120ER Brasilia	120283	ex N639AS	
□ VQ-TDA	Britten-Norman BN-2A-27 Islander	504	ex HI-704CT	
□ VQ-TDG	Embraer EMB.120ER Brasilia	120275	ex N503AS	
□ VQ-TGW	de Havilland DHC-6 Twin Otter 310	414	ex N38535	
□ VQ-TIU	Beech 200C Super King Air	BL-131	ex VH-BQR	
□ VQ-TRS	Beech 200C Super King Air	BL-133	ex VH-BRQ	
□ VQ-TRT	Beech 200C Super King Air	BL-125	ex VH-BRF	
□ VQ-TVG	de Havilland DHC-6 Twin Otter 300	410	ex N974SW	Island Spirit

SKYKING AIRLINES   Skyking (RU/SKI)   Providenciales (PLS)

□ VQ-TBL	Beech 1900C-1	UC-104	ex N104GL	[TPA]
□ VQ-TEB	Beech 1900D	UE-160	ex N160EU	
□ VQ-TGK	Beech 1900C-1	UC-128	ex N15553	[TPA]
□ VQ-TVC	Beech 1900D	UE-222	ex N81553	[TPA]

VT-   INDIA (Republic of India)

AIR INDIA   Airindia (AI/AIC)   Mumbai-Chhatrapatti Shivaji Intl (BOM)

□ VT-AIB	Airbus A310-324	680	ex 9V-STC	Pennan
□ VT-EJG	Airbus A310-304	406	ex F-WWCG	Yamuna
□ VT-EJH	Airbus A310-304F	407	ex F-WWCH	Teesta
□ VT-EJI	Airbus A310-304F	413	ex F-WWCJ	Saraswati

☐ VT-EJJ	Airbus A310-304	428	ex F-WWCR	Beas
☐ VT-EJK	Airbus A310-304	429	ex F-WWCS	Gomati
☐ VT-EJL	Airbus A310-304	392	ex F-WWCB	Sabarmati
☐ VT-EQS	Airbus A310-304F	538	ex F-WWCP	Krishna
☐ VT-EQT	Airbus A310-304F	544	ex F-WWCL	Narmada
☐ VT-SCA	Airbus A319-112	2593	ex D-AVXL	
☐ VT-SCB	Airbus A319-112	2624	ex D-AVYX	
☐ VT-SCC	Airbus A319-112	2629	ex D-AVWC	
☐ VT-SCD	Airbus A319-112	1668	ex C-GJTC	
☐ VT-SCE	Airbus A319-112	1718	ex C-GJVS	
☐ VT-SCF	Airbus A319-112	2907	ex D-AVWT	
☐ VT-SCG	Airbus A319-112	3271	ex D-AVYH	
☐ VT-SCH	Airbus A319-112	3288	ex D-AVWM	
☐ VT-SCI	Airbus A319-112	3300	ex D-AVYN	
☐ VT-SCJ	Airbus A319-112	3305	ex D-AVYO	
☐ VT-SCK	Airbus A319-112	3344	ex D-AVYT	
☐ VT-SCL	Airbus A319-112	3551	ex D-AVWO	
☐ VT-SCM	Airbus A319-112	3620	ex D-AVYN	
☐ VT-SCN	Airbus A319-112	3687	ex D-AVWE	
☐ VT-SCO	Airbus A319-112	3822	ex D-AVYH	
☐ VT-SCP	Airbus A319-112	3874	ex D-AVWF	
☐ VT-SCQ	Airbus A319-112	3918	ex D-AVYY	
☐ VT-SCR	Airbus A319-112	3970	ex D-AVYB	
☐ VT-SCS	Airbus A319-112	4020	ex D-AVYH	
☐ VT-SCT	Airbus A319-112	4029	ex D-AVYJ	
☐ VT-SCU	Airbus A319-112	4052	ex D-AVYQ	
☐ VT-SCV	Airbus A319-112	4089	ex D-AVYY	
☐ VT-SCW	Airbus A319-112	4121	ex D-AVWB	
☐ VT-SCX	Airbus A319-112	4164	ex D-AVYZ	
☐ VT-EDC	Airbus A320-214	4201	ex F-WWBD	♦
☐ VT-EDD	Airbus A320-214	4212	ex F-WWDJ	♦
☐ VT-EDE	Airbus A320-214	4236	ex F-WWDE	♦
☐ VT-EDF	Airbus A320-214	4237	ex F-WWDG	♦
☐ VT-EPB	Airbus A320-231	0045	ex F-WWDY	
☐ VT-EPC	Airbus A320-231	0046	ex F-WWDG	
☐ VT-EPD	Airbus A320-231	0047	ex F-WWDP	
☐ VT-EPF	Airbus A320-231	0049	ex F-WWIA	
☐ VT-EPG	Airbus A320-231	0050	ex F-WWDR	
☐ VT-EPH	Airbus A320-231	0051	ex F-WWIB	
☐ VT-EPI	Airbus A320-231	0056	ex F-WWIC	
☐ VT-EPJ	Airbus A320-231	0057	ex F-WWIF	50 years titles
☐ VT-EPL	Airbus A320-231	0074	ex F-WWIQ	
☐ VT-EPM	Airbus A320-231	0075	ex F-WWIR	50 years titles
☐ VT-EPO	Airbus A320-231	0080	ex F-WWIX	
☐ VT-EPQ	Airbus A320-231	0090	ex F-WWDX	
☐ VT-EPR	Airbus A320-231	0095	ex F-WWDS	
☐ VT-EPS	Airbus A320-231	0096	ex F-WWDU	
☐ VT-ESA	Airbus A320-231	0396	ex F-WWBK	
☐ VT-ESB	Airbus A320-231	0398	ex F-WWDQ	
☐ VT-ESC	Airbus A320-231	0416	ex F-WWBP	
☐ VT-ESD	Airbus A320-231	0423	ex F-WWIT	
☐ VT-ESE	Airbus A320-231	0431	ex F-WWBQ	
☐ VT-ESF	Airbus A320-231	0432	ex F-WWBS	
☐ VT-ESG	Airbus A320-231	0451	ex F-WWIN	
☐ VT-ESH	Airbus A320-231	0469	ex F-WWBD	
☐ VT-ESI	Airbus A320-231	0486	ex F-WWBH	50 years titles
☐ VT-ESJ	Airbus A320-231	0490	ex F-WWDT	50 years titles
☐ VT-ESK	Airbus A320-231	0492	ex F-WWBU	50 years titles
☐ VT-ESL	Airbus A320-231	0499	ex F-WWDO	
☐ VT-EVO	Airbus A320-231	0247	ex N247RX	
☐ VT-EVP	Airbus A320-231	0257	ex N257RX	
☐ VT-EVQ	Airbus A320-231	0327	ex G-OOAC	50 years titles
☐ VT-EVR	Airbus A320-231	0336	ex G-OOAD	50 years titles
☐ VT-EVS	Airbus A320-231	0308	ex EC-GUR	
☐ VT-EVT	Airbus A320-231	0314	ex EC-GLT	
☐ VT-EYB	Airbus A320-231	0386	ex G-MEDD	
☐ VT-EYC	Airbus A320-231	0362	ex G-YJBM	
☐ VT-EYL	Airbus A320-231	0480	ex G-MEDA	
☐ VT-PPA	Airbus A321-211	3130	ex D-AVZT	
☐ VT-PPB	Airbus A321-211	3146	ex D-AVZU	
☐ VT-PPD	Airbus A321-211	3212	ex D-AVZA	
☐ VT-PPE	Airbus A321-211	3326	ex D-AVZW	
☐ VT-PPF	Airbus A321-211	3340	ex D-AVZH	
☐ VT-PPG	Airbus A321-211	3367	ex D-AVZG	

☐ VT-PPH	Airbus A321-211	3498	ex D-AVZG		
☐ VT-PPI	Airbus A321-211	3557	ex D-AVZQ		
☐ VT-PPJ	Airbus A321-211	3573	ex D-AVZC		
☐ VT-PPK	Airbus A321-211	3619	ex D-AVZF		
☐ VT-PPL	Airbus A321-211	3752	ex D-AZAM		
☐ VT-PPM	Airbus A321-211	3792	ex D-AZAR		
☐ VT-PPN	Airbus A321-211	3955	ex D-AZAU		
☐ VT-PPO	Airbus A321-211	4002	ex D-AVZB		
☐ VT-PPQ	Airbus A321-211	4009	ex D-AVZE		
☐ VT-PPT	Airbus A321-211	4078	ex D-AVZU		
☐ VT-PPU	Airbus A321-211	4096	ex D-AVZY		
☐ VT-PPV	Airbus A321-211	4138	ex D-AZAU		
☐ VT-PPW	Airbus A321-211	4155	ex D-AVZZ		
☐ VT-PPX	Airbus A321-211	4280	ex D-AZAP		♦
☐ VT-IWA	Airbus A330-223	353	ex F-WQVY		
☐ VT-IWB	Airbus A330-223	362	ex F-WQVZ		
☐ VT-ESN	Boeing 747-437	27164/1003		Tanjore	
☐ VT-ESO	Boeing 747-437	27165/1009		Khajurao	
☐ VT-ESP	Boeing 747-437	27214/1034		Ajanta	
☐ VT-EVA	Boeing 747-437	28094/1089		Agra	
☐ VT-EVB	Boeing 747-437	28095/1093		Velha Goa	
☐ VT-AIL	Boeing 777-222ER	26935/88	ex N789UA	Kalyani	
☐ VT-AIR	Boeing 777-222	26917/8	ex N766UA	Hamsadhwani	
☐ VT-ALA	Boeing 777-237LR	36300/610	ex N6018N	Andhra Pradesh	
☐ VT-ALB	Boeing 777-237LR	36301/621	ex N5028Y	Arunachal Pradesh	
☐ VT-ALC	Boeing 777-237LR	36302/629	ex N5020K	Assam	
☐ VT-ALD	Boeing 777-237LR	36303/663	ex N5016R	Gujarat	
☐ VT-ALE	Boeing 777-237LR	36304/698		Haryana	
☐ VT-ALF	Boeing 777-237LR	36305/793		Jhardkand	
☐ VT-ALG	Boeing 777-237LR	36306/800		Kerala	
☐ VT-ALH	Boeing 777-237LR	36307/805		Maharashtra	
☐ VT-ALJ	Boeing 777-337ER	36308/643		Bihar	
☐ VT-ALK	Boeing 777-337ER	36309/652		Chattisgarh	
☐ VT-ALL	Boeing 777-337ER	36310/656		Goa	
☐ VT-ALM	Boeing 777-337ER	36311/713		Himachal Pradesh	
☐ VT-ALN	Boeing 777-337ER	36312/719		Jammu and Kashmir	
☐ VT-ALO	Boeing 777-337ER	36313/798		Karnataka	
☐ VT-ALP	Boeing 777-337ER	36314/804		Madhya Pradesh	
☐ VT-ALQ	Boeing 777-337ER	36315/809		Manipur	
☐ VT-ALR	Boeing 777-337ER	36316/814		Meghalaya	
☐ VT-ALS	Boeing 777-337ER	36317/864		Mizoram	♦
☐ VT-ALT	Boeing 777-337ER	36318/871		Nagaland	♦
☐ VT-ALU	Boeing 777-337ER	36319/880		Orissa	♦
☐ VT-ANA	Boeing 787-837	36273/25			o/o♦
☐ VT-ANC	Boeing 787-837	36274/28			o/o♦
☐ VT-AND	Boeing 787-837	36278/29			o/o♦
☐ VT-ANE	Boeing 787-837	36280/30			o/o♦
☐ VT-	Boeing 787-837				o/o♦
☐ VT-	Boeing 787-837				o/o♦
☐ VT-EIO	Dornier 228-201	8037	ex D-IDBG		

AIR INDIA EXPRESS   (AI/AXB)   Mumbai-Chhatrapatti Shivaji Intl (BOM)

☐ VT-AXC	Boeing 737-8BK	33024/1688		dam 11Jly07
☐ VT-AXD	Boeing 737-8Q8/W	30696/1892		
☐ VT-AXE	Boeing 737-8Q8/W	29368/1910		
☐ VT-AXF	Boeing 737-8Q8/W	29369/1939	ex N1787B	
☐ VT-AXG	Boeing 737-8Q8/W	30701/1946	ex N1787B	
☐ VT-AXH	Boeing 737-8HG/W	36323/2108		
☐ VT-AXI	Boeing 737-8HG/W	36324/2132		
☐ VT-AXJ	Boeing 737-8HG/W	36325/2142		
☐ VT-AXM	Boeing 737-8HG/W	36326/2148		
☐ VT-AXN	Boeing 737-8HG/W	36327/2154		
☐ VT-AXP	Boeing 737-8HG/W	36328/2177		
☐ VT-AXQ	Boeing 737-8HG/W	36329/2258		
☐ VT-AXR	Boeing 737-8HG/W	36330/2317		
☐ VT-AXT	Boeing 737-8HG/W	36331/2324		
☐ VT-AXU	Boeing 737-8HG/W	36332/2381		
☐ VT-AXW	Boeing 737-8HG/W	36334/2612		
☐ VT-AXX	Boeing 737-8HG/W	36335/2672		
☐ VT-AXZ	Boeing 737-8HG/W	36336/2782	ex N1786B	
☐ VT-AYA	Boeing 737-8HG/W	36337/2861	ex N6065Y	

☐ VT-AYB	Boeing 737-8HG/W	36338/2962		
☐ VT-AYC	Boeing 737-8HG/W	36339/3039	ex N1786B	

AIR INDIA REGIONAL

☐ VT-ABA	ATR 42-320	390	ex F-WQNK	
☐ VT-ABB	ATR 42-320	392	ex F-WQNL	
☐ VT-ABC	ATR 42-320	315	ex F-WQNB	
☐ VT-ABD	ATR 42-320	356	ex F-WQNF	
☐ VT-ABE	ATR 42-320	333	ex F-WQNF	
☐ VT-ABF	ATR 42-320	351	ex F-WQNC	
☐ VT-ABO	ATR 42-320	406	ex F-WQNE	

ALLIANCE AIR — Allied (CD/LLR) — Delhi-Indira Gandhi Intl (DEL)

☐ VT-EGE	Boeing 737-2A8	22281/679	ex N8291V	[DEL]
☐ VT-EGF	Boeing 737-2A8F	22282/681	ex N8292V	
☐ VT-EGG	Boeing 737-2A8F	22283/689	ex N8290V	
☐ VT-EGH	Boeing 737-2A8	22284/739		
☐ VT-EGI	Boeing 737-2A8F	22285/798		
☐ VT-EGJ	Boeing 737-2A8F	22286/799		
☐ VT-EGM	Boeing 737-2A8C	22473/747		
☐ VT-EHE	Boeing 737-2A8	22860/899	ex K-5011	>Indian AF
☐ VT-EHF	Boeing 737-2A8	22861/902		[DEL]
☐ VT-EHG	Boeing 737-2A8	22862/903		[DEL]
☐ VT-EHH	Boeing 737-2A8F	22863/907		
☐ VT-RJB	Canadair CRJ-700	10217	ex D-ALTE	
☐ VT-RJC	Canadair CRJ-700	10052	ex B-KBB	
☐ VT-RJD	Canadair CRJ-700	10048	ex G-DUOD	
☐ VT-RJE	Canadair CRJ-700	10029	ex N290RB	

BLUE DART AVIATION — Blue Dart (BZ/BDA) — Chennai (MAA)

☐ VT-BDG	Boeing 737-2K9F	22415/702	ex VT-SIE	Vision III
☐ VT-BDH	Boeing 737-25C	24236/1585	ex B-2524	Vision IV
☐ VT-BDI	Boeing 737-2T4F	23272/1093	ex B-2506	Vision V
☐ VT-BDJ	Boeing 757-236 (SF)	24102/179	ex OO-DPI	
☐ VT-BDK	Boeing 757-236 (SF)	24267/211	ex OO-DPL	
☐ VT-BDM	Boeing 757-23N (SF)	27598/692	ex EI-LTA	
☐ VT-BDN	Boeing 757-25CF	25898/475	ex N7273	

DECCAN CARGO — Mumbai-Chhatrapatti Shivaji Intl (BOM)

☐ VT-AIN	Airbus A310-324F	684	ex 9V-STD	Damodar
☐ VT-AIO	Airbus A310-324F	693	ex 9V-STE	Pamba
☐ VT-AIP	Airbus A310-324F	697	ex 9V-STF	Vaigai

FUTURA TRAVELS

☐ VT-ASH	Beech 1900D	UE-361	ex C-GSKQ	

GLOBAL VECTRA HELICORP — Mumbai-Juhu

☐ VT-GVH	Agusta AW139	31074	ex N725TF	♦
☐ VT-AZA	Bell 412SP	33188	ex 9M-SSM	
☐ VT-AZC	Bell 412SP	36161	ex N45169	
☐ VT-AZD	Bell 412SP	33172	ex N63385	
☐ VT-AZE	Bell 412HP	36024	ex N6344X	
☐ VT-AZG	Bell 412SP	33185	ex N9VH	
☐ VT-AZH	Bell 412EP	36371	ex N412GV	
☐ VT-AZI	Bell 412SP	33199	ex I-POPA	
☐ VT-AZJ	Bell 412HP	36027	ex N412HX	
☐ VT-AZK	Bell 412HP	36023	ex N175AR	
☐ VT-AZL	Bell 412HP	36065	ex C-FDDI	
☐ VT-AZM	Bell 412EP	36394	ex N30011	
☐ VT-AZN	Bell 412EP	36397	ex C-FHWW	
☐ VT-AZO	Bell 412EP	36398	ex C-FHWU	
☐ VT-AZP	Bell 412EP	36407	ex N2519A	
☐ VT-AZQ	Bell 412EP	36413	ex N80072	
☐ VT-AZR	Bell 412EP	36415	ex N2086C	
☐ VT-AZS	Bell 412EP	36416	ex N8007U	
☐ VT-AZT	Bell 412EP	36422	ex N8019T	
☐ VT-AZU	Eurocopter EC155B1	6759	ex F-WWOF	

GO AIR   Goair (G8/GOW)   Mumbai-Chhatrapatti Shivaji Intl (BOM)

☐ VT-WAC	Airbus A320-233	1482	ex N482TA	blue
☐ VT-WAE	Airbus A320-214	3256	ex F-WWDF	
☐ VT-WAF	Airbus A320-214	3306	ex F-WWIM	
☐ VT-WAG	Airbus A320-214	3597	ex D-AVVE	
☐ VT-WAH	Airbus A320-214	3616	ex F-WWII	
☐ VT-WAI	Airbus A320-214	3798	ex F-WWBP	
☐ VT-WAJ	Airbus A320-214	3827	ex F-WWIX	
☐ VT-WAK	Airbus A320-214	3900	ex F-WWDU	
☐ VT-WAL	Airbus A320-214	3915	ex F-WWBC	
☐ VT-WAM	Airbus A320-214	4399	ex F-WWBC	♦
☐ VT-WAN	Airbus A320-214	4438	ex F-WWDF	♦

HELIGO CHATERS   Mumbai

☐ VT-HLB	Agusta AW139	31095	ex A6-AWD	
☐ VT-HLC	Agusta AW139	31106	ex A6-AWE	

INDIGO AIRLINES   (6E/IGO)   Bangalore (BLR)

☐ VT-IGH	Airbus A320-232	4008	ex F-WWDZ	
☐ VT-IGI	Airbus A320-232	4113	ex F-WWDV	
☐ VT-IGJ	Airbus A320-232	4156	ex F-WWBM	
☐ VT-IGK	Airbus A320-232	4216	ex F-WWBE	♦
☐ VT-IGL	Airbus A320-232	4312	ex F-WWBD	♦
☐ VT-IGS	Airbus A320-232	4328	ex F-WWIB	♦
☐ VT-IGT	Airbus A320-232	4384	ex F-WWBN	♦
☐ VT-IGU	Airbus A320-232	4488	ex D-AUBH	♦
☐ VT-IGV	Airbus A320-232	4481	ex F-WWDL	♦
☐ VT-IGW	Airbus A320-232	4506	ex D-AUBN	♦
☐ VT-IGX	Airbus A320-232	4518	ex D-AXAH	♦
☐ VT-IGY	Airbus A320-232	4535	ex F-WWDX	♦
☐ VT-IGZ	Airbus A320-232	4552	ex D-AUBR	♦
☐ VT-INA	Airbus A320-232	2844	ex F-WWIH	
☐ VT-INB	Airbus A320-232	2863	ex F-WWIZ	
☐ VT-INC	Airbus A320-232	2883	ex F-WWBR	
☐ VT-IND	Airbus A320-232	2911	ex F-WWDG	
☐ VT-INE	Airbus A320-232	2958	ex F-WWBM	
☐ VT-INF	Airbus A320-232	2990	ex F-WWIO	
☐ VT-INI	Airbus A320-232	3086	ex F-WWBN	
☐ VT-INJ	Airbus A320-232	3159	ex F-WWDQ	
☐ VT-INK	Airbus A320-232	3192	ex F-WWIT	
☐ VT-INL	Airbus A320-232	3227	ex F-WWBC	
☐ VT-INO	Airbus A320-232	3335	ex F-WWBJ	
☐ VT-INP	Airbus A320-232	3357	ex F-WWIH	
☐ VT-INQ	Airbus A320-232	3414	ex F-WWIM	
☐ VT-INR	Airbus A320-232	3453	ex F-WWBF	
☐ VT-INS	Airbus A320-232	3457	ex F-WWBI	
☐ VT-INT	Airbus A320-232	3497	ex F-WWIM	
☐ VT-INU	Airbus A320-232	3541	ex F-WWIP	
☐ VT-INV	Airbus A320-232	3618	ex F-WWIJ	
☐ VT-INX	Airbus A320-232	3782	ex D-AVVK	
☐ VT-INY	Airbus A320-232	3863	ex F-WWDY	
☐ VT-INZ	Airbus A320-232	3943	ex F-WWDT	
☐ VT-	Airbus A320-232		ex	o/o♦
☐ VT-	Airbus A320-232		ex	o/o♦
☐ VT-	Airbus A320-232		ex	o/o♦
☐ VT-	Airbus A320-232		ex	o/o♦
☐ VT-	Airbus A320-232		ex	o/o♦
☐ VT-	Airbus A320-232		ex	o/o♦
☐ VT-	Airbus A320-232		ex	o/o♦
☐ VT-	Airbus A320-232		ex	o/o♦
☐ VT-	Airbus A320-232		ex	o/o♦
☐ VT-	Airbus A320-232		ex	o/o♦
☐ VT-	Airbus A320-232		ex	o/o♦
☐ VT-	Airbus A320-232		ex	o/o♦

JAGSON AIRLINES   Delhi-Indira Gandhi Intl (DEL)

☐ VT-JJC	Avro 146-RJ85	E2289	ex G-CFZM	♦
☐ VT-ESQ	Dornier 228-201	8006	ex A5-RGB	
☐ VT-ESS	Dornier 228-201	8017	ex A5-RGC	
☐ VT-EUM	Dornier 228-201	8096	ex D-CAAL	
☐ VT-JJA	Mil Mi-172	365C157		
☐ VT-JJB	Mil Mi-172	365C158		

JET AIRWAYS		Jet Airways (9W/JAI)		Mumbai-Chhatrapatti Shivaji Intl (BOM)	
☐ VT-JWD	Airbus A330-243	751	ex F-WWKB		
☐ VT-JWE	Airbus A330-243	807	ex F-WWYU		
☐ VT-JWF	Airbus A330-202	825	ex F-WWKE		
☐ VT-JWG	Airbus A330-202	831	ex F-WWKL		
☐ VT-JWH	Airbus A330-202	882	ex F-WWKJ		
☐ VT-JWJ	Airbus A330-202	885	ex F-WWKS		
☐ VT-JWK	Airbus A330-202	888	ex F-WWKL		
☐ VT-JWL	Airbus A330-202	901	ex F-WWKQ		
☐ VT-JWM	Airbus A330-202	923	ex F-WWYZ		
☐ VT-JWN	Airbus A330-202	932	ex F-WWKV		
☐ VT-JWP	Airbus A330-202	947	ex F-WWKM		
☐ VT-JWQ	Airbus A330-202	956	ex F-WWYA		
☐ VT-JCA	ATR 72-212A	572	ex F-WQKD	retd?	
☐ VT-JCB	ATR 72-212A	575	ex F-WQKE		
☐ VT-JCC	ATR 72-212A	593	ex F-WQKP		
☐ VT-JCD	ATR 72-212A	636	ex F-WQMC		
☐ VT-JCF	ATR 72-212A	674	ex F-WQMK	<SFR	
☐ VT-JCG	ATR 72-212A	679	ex F-WQML	<SFR	
☐ VT-JCH	ATR 72-212A	681	ex F-WQMM	<SFR	
☐ VT-JCJ	ATR 72-212A	771	ex F-WWEJ		
☐ VT-JCK	ATR 72-212A	775	ex F-WWEN		
☐ VT-JCL	ATR 72-212A	791	ex F-WWEK		
☐ VT-JCM	ATR 72-212A	793	ex F-WWEN		
☐ VT-JCN	ATR 72-212A	825	ex F-WWEN		
☐ VT-JCP	ATR 72-212A	841	ex F-WWES		
☐ VT-JCQ	ATR 72-212A	843	ex F-WWEJ		
☐ VT-JCR	ATR 72-212A	919	ex F-WWER		♦
☐ VT-JCS	ATR 72-212A	920	ex F-WWES		♦
☐ VT-JCT	ATR 72-212A	924	ex F-WWEX		♦
☐ VT-JCU	ATR 72-212A	928	ex F-WWED		♦
☐ VT-JCV	ATR 72-212A	932	ex F-WWEH		♦
☐ VT-JCW	ATR 72-212A	933	ex F-WWEI		♦
☐ VT-JBB	Boeing 737-8HX/W	36846/2368	ex N846AG		
☐ VT-JBC	Boeing 737-8HX/W	36847/2388	ex N847AG		
☐ VT-JBD	Boeing 737-85R/W	35099/2439			
☐ VT-JBE	Boeing 737-85R/W	35106/2530	ex N1786B		
☐ VT-JBF	Boeing 737-85R/W	35082/2550	ex N1786B		
☐ VT-JBG	Boeing 737-85R/W	35083/2535	ex N1786B		
☐ VT-JBH	Boeing 737-85R/W	35289/2811	ex N1786B		
☐ VT-JBJ	Boeing 737-85R/W	36551/2974	ex N1786B		
☐ VT-JBK	Boeing 737-85R/W	36553/3074	ex N1786B		
☐ VT-JBL	Boeing 737-85R/W	35651/3000			
☐ VT-JBM	Boeing 737-86N/W	36817/3055	ex N1786B		
☐ VT-JBN	Boeing 737-86N/W	36818/3087	ex N1786B		
☐ VT-JBP	Boeing 737-86N/W	36819/3101			
☐ VT-JBR	Boeing 737-85R/W	36695/3281			♦
☐ VT-JBQ	Boeing 737-85R/W	36694/3264	ex N1787B		♦
☐ VT-JBS	Boeing 737-85R/W	36698/3433			♦
☐ VT-JGA	Boeing 737-85R	30410/1228			
☐ VT-JGB	Boeing 737-75R/W	30411/1282	ex N1787B		
☐ VT-JGC	Boeing 737-95R	30412/1314			
☐ VT-JGD	Boeing 737-95R	33740/1350			
☐ VT-JGE	Boeing 737-83N/W	32663/1608	ex EI-DIL		
☐ VT-JGF	Boeing 737-8FH/W	29639/1643	ex EI-DIM		
☐ VT-JGG	Boeing 737-8FH/W	29668/1686	ex EI-DIN		
☐ VT-JGH	Boeing 737-83N/W	32577/973	ex EI-DKX		
☐ VT-JGJ	Boeing 737-83N/W	32578/998	ex EI-DKP		
☐ VT-JGK	Boeing 737-83N/W	32579/1002	ex EI-DKR		
☐ VT-JGL	Boeing 737-76N/W	32738/1392	ex EI-DMD		
☐ VT-JGM	Boeing 737-83N/W	32614/1201	ex EI-DME		
☐ VT-JGN	Boeing 737-83N/W	32616/1212	ex EI-DMF		
☐ VT-JGP	Boeing 737-85R/W	34798/1920			
☐ VT-JGQ	Boeing 737-85R/W	34797/2007			
☐ VT-JGR	Boeing 737-85R/W	34799/2044			
☐ VT-JGS	Boeing 737-85R/W	34800/2085			
☐ VT-JGT	Boeing 737-85R/W	34801/2125			
☐ VT-JGU	Boeing 737-85R/W	34802/2170			
☐ VT-JGV	Boeing 737-85R/W	34803/2209			
☐ VT-JGW	Boeing 737-85R/W	34804/2297			
☐ VT-JGX	Boeing 737-75R/W	34805/2360	ex N1781B		
☐ VT-JGY	Boeing 737-75R/W	34806/2404			
☐ VT-JGZ	Boeing 737-76N/W	35218/2342	ex N1781B		

☐ VT-JLE	Boeing 737-8AS/W	33555/1426	ex EI-DAV			♦
☐ VT-JLF	Boeing 737-8AS/W	33556/1428	ex EI-DAW			♦
☐ VT-JNF	Boeing 737-71Q	29044/152	ex N29887			
☐ VT-JNG	Boeing 737-71Q	29045/169	ex N29975			
☐ VT-JNH	Boeing 737-71Q	29046/181	ex N29976			
☐ VT-JNJ	Boeing 737-85R	29038/297				
☐ VT-JNL	Boeing 737-85R	29039/326				
☐ VT-JNM	Boeing 737-85R	29040/465				
☐ VT-JNN	Boeing 737-85R	29041/489				
☐ VT-JNR	Boeing 737-85R	30403/749	ex N1781B			
☐ VT-JNS	Boeing 737-73A	28498/775	ex N498AW			
☐ VT-JNU	Boeing 737-75R	30404/835	ex N1787B			
☐ VT-JNV	Boeing 737-75R	30405/927				
☐ VT-JNW	Boeing 737-75R	30406/1016	ex N1787B			
☐ VT-JNX	Boeing 737-85R	30407/1073				
☐ VT-JNY	Boeing 737-85R	30408/1146	ex (VT-JGA)			
☐ VT-JNZ	Boeing 737-85R	30409/1185	ex (VT-JGB)			
☐ VT-	Boeing 737-75R					o/o
☐ VT-	Boeing 737-75R					o/o
☐ VT-	Boeing 737-8AL					o/o
☐ VT-	Boeing 737-8AL					o/o
☐ VT-JEA	Boeing 777-35RER	35157/627				
☐ VT-JEB	Boeing 777-35RER	35158/637				
☐ VT-JEG	Boeing 777-35RER	35163/675	ex N1785B			
☐ VT-JEH	Boeing 777-35RER	35166/678	ex N5014K			
☐ VT-JEJ	Boeing 777-35RER	35161/693				
☐ VT-JEK	Boeing 777-35RER	35165/696				

JETLITE — Sahara (S2/RSH) — Delhi-Indira Gandhi Intl (DEL)

☐ VT-JLA	Boeing 737-7Q8	30037/1449	ex EI-DZC		
☐ VT-JLB	Boeing 737-7Q8	28250/1142	ex A4O-BT		
☐ VT-JLC	Boeing 737-71Q	29043/138	ex VT-JNE		♦
☐ VT-SIJ	Boeing 737-81Q	29049/424	ex N8253J		
☐ VT-SIK	Boeing 737-81Q	29050/444	ex N8253V		
☐ VT-SIU	Boeing 737-7K9	28090/205	ex SX-BLT		
☐ VT-SIV	Boeing 737-7K9	28091/223	ex SX-BLU		[DEL]
☐ VT-SIZ	Boeing 737-7BK	33025/1707	ex N325CT		
☐ VT-SJA	Boeing 737-7BK	33026/1715	ex N326CT		
☐ VT-SJE	Boeing 737-7Q8	30727/1005	ex S7-SEZ		
☐ VT-SJF	Boeing 737-86N	28610/449	ex EI-DIS		
☐ VT-SJG	Boeing 737-8Q8/W	30694/1863	ex N164LF		
☐ VT-SJH	Boeing 737-8Q8/W	30695/1891	ex (N201LF)		
☐ VT-SJI	Boeing 737-8K9/W	34399/2030			
☐ VT-SJJ	Boeing 737-8K9/W	34400/2053			
☐ VT-SAQ	Canadair CRJ-200ER	7345	ex G-JECA		
☐ VT-SAR	Canadair CRJ-200ER	7393	ex G-JECB		

KINGFISHER AIRLINES — (IT/KFR) — Mumbai-Chhatrapatti Shivaji Intl / Bangalore (BOM/BLR)

☐ VT-VJK	Airbus A330-223	874	ex F-WWKA		
☐ VT-VJL	Airbus A330-223	891	ex F-WWYO		
☐ VT-VJN	Airbus A330-223	927	ex F-WWKE		
☐ VT-VJO	Airbus A330-223	939	ex F-WWKK		
☐ VT-VJP	Airbus A330-223	946	ex F-WWYX		

KINGFISHER RED — (IT/KFR) — Mumbai-Chhatrapatti Shivaji Intl / Bangalore (BOM/BLR)

☐ VT-KFH	Airbus A319-131	2621	ex D-AVYM		[DEL]
☐ VT-KFI	Airbus A319-131	2634	ex D-AVWG		
☐ VT-KFJ	Airbus A319-131	2664	ex D-AVWW		
☐ VT-VJM	Airbus A319-133X	2650	ex D-AICY	Sidhartha-Leana-Tanya	VIP
☐ VT-ADR	Airbus A320-232	2922	ex F-WWDS		
☐ VT-ADU	Airbus A320-232	2874	ex F-WWBH		
☐ VT-ADV	Airbus A320-232	2366	ex F-WWDN		
☐ VT-ADW	Airbus A320-232	2376	ex F-WWBF		
☐ VT-DKR	Airbus A320-232	2731	ex F-WWBC		
☐ VT-DKS	Airbus A320-232	2747	ex F-WWBQ	Mr Citizen c/s	
☐ VT-DKT	Airbus A320-232	2753	ex F-WWDH		
☐ VT-DKU	Airbus A320-232	2676	ex F-WWIK	Mr Citizen c/s	
☐ VT-DKV	Airbus A320-232	2645	ex F-WWIC		[BOM]
☐ VT-DNZ	Airbus A320-232	3012	ex F-WWBK		
☐ VT-KFA	Airbus A320-232	2413	ex F-WWDH		
☐ VT-KFB	Airbus A320-232	2443	ex F-WWBR		
☐ VT-KFC	Airbus A320-232	2496	ex F-WWIF		

☐ VT-KFD	Airbus A320-232	2502	ex F-WWDI	
☐ VT-KFE	Airbus A320-232	2522	ex F-WWDN	
☐ VT-KFF	Airbus A320-232	2531	ex F-WWIH	
☐ VT-KFG	Airbus A320-232	2576	ex F-WWBI	
☐ VT-KFK	Airbus A320-232	2670	ex F-WWDA	
☐ VT-KFL	Airbus A320-232	2817	ex F-WWDJ	
☐ VT-KFM	Airbus A320-232	2856	ex F-WWIT	
☐ VT-KFT	Airbus A320-232	3089	ex F-WWBY	
☐ VT-KFV	Airbus A320-232	3105	ex F-WWII	
☐ VT-KFX	Airbus A320-232	3270	ex F-WWBX	
☐ VT-	Airbus A320-232		ex F-WW	o/o
☐ VT-	Airbus A320-232		ex F-WW	o/o
☐ VT-	Airbus A320-232		ex F-WW	o/o
☐ VT-	Airbus A320-232		ex F-WW	o/o
☐ VT-	Airbus A320-232		ex F-WW	o/o
☐ VT-KFN	Airbus A321-231	2916	ex D-AVZQ	[BOM]
☐ VT-KFP	Airbus A321-231	2919	ex D-AVZR	
☐ VT-KFQ	Airbus A321-231	2927	ex D-AVZC	
☐ VT-KFR	Airbus A321-231	2933	ex D-AVZS	
☐ VT-KFS	Airbus A321-231	3034	ex D-AVZZ	
☐ VT-KFW	Airbus A321-231	3120	ex D-AVZR	
☐ VT-KFY	Airbus A321-232	3302	ex D-AVZS	
☐ VT-KFZ	Airbus A321-231	3322	ex D-AVZU	
☐ VT-ADJ	ATR 42-500	612	ex N612VX	
☐ VT-ADK	ATR 42-500	613	ex N316VX	
☐ VT-ADN	ATR 42-500	576	ex A4O-AT	<OMA
☐ VT-DKA	ATR 72-212A	718	ex F-WWES	
☐ VT-DKB	ATR 72-212A	720	ex F-WWEA	
☐ VT-DKD	ATR 72-212A	725	ex F-WQNG	
☐ VT-DKE	ATR 72-212A	723	ex F-WWED	
☐ VT-DKH	ATR 72-212A	739	ex F-WWET	
☐ VT-DKI	ATR 72-212A	732	ex F-WWEM	
☐ VT-DKJ	ATR 72-212A	733	ex F-WWEN	
☐ VT-DKK	ATR 72-212A	740	ex F-WWEU	
☐ VT-KAA	ATR 72-212A	699	ex F-WWEV	
☐ VT-KAB	ATR 72-212A	728	ex F-WWEI	
☐ VT-KAD	ATR 72-212A	730	ex F-WWEK	
☐ VT-KAE	ATR 72-212A	737	ex F-WWER	
☐ VT-KAF	ATR 72-212A	738	ex F-WWES	
☐ VT-KAG	ATR 72-212A	743	ex F-WWED	
☐ VT-KAH	ATR 72-212A	746	ex F-WWEG	
☐ VT-KAI	ATR 72-212A	750	ex F-WWEK	
☐ VT-KAJ	ATR 72-212A	754	ex F-WWEO	
☐ VT-KAK	ATR 72-212A	758	ex F-WWES	
☐ VT-KAL	ATR 72-212A	759	ex F-WWEV	
☐ VT-KAM	ATR 72-212A	762	ex F-WWEZ	
☐ VT-KAN	ATR 72-212A	767	ex F-WWEF	
☐ VT-KAO	ATR 72-212A	772	ex F-WWEK	
☐ VT-KAP	ATR 72-212A	776	ex F-WWEO	
☐ VT-KAQ	ATR 72-212A	777	ex F-WWEP	
☐ VT-KAR	ATR 72-212A	782	ex F-WWEX	

MDLR AIRLINES   *Mumbai-Chhatrapatti Shivaji Intl (BOM)*

☐ VT-MDL	Avro 146-RJ70	E1229	ex G-BUFI	
☐ VT-MDM	Avro 146-RJ70	E1230	ex G-CDNB	
☐ VT-MDN	Avro 146-RJ70	E1252	ex G-CDNC	

NORTHEAST SHUTTLE

☐ VT-NES	Cessna 208B Caravan	208B2025	ex N23045	

PAWAN HANS HELICOPTERS   *Pawan Hans (PHE)*   *Mumbai-Juhu*

☐ VT-ELD	Aérospatiale SA365N Dauphin 2	6213	
☐ VT-ELE	Aérospatiale SA365N Dauphin 2	6214	
☐ VT-ELG	Aérospatiale SA365N Dauphin 2	6217	
☐ VT-ELI	Aérospatiale SA365N Dauphin 2	6236	
☐ VT-ELJ	Aérospatiale SA365N Dauphin 2	6239	
☐ VT-ELK	Aérospatiale SA365N Dauphin 2	6245	
☐ VT-ELL	Aérospatiale SA365N Dauphin 2	6246	
☐ VT-ELM	Aérospatiale SA365N Dauphin 2	6248	
☐ VT-ELN	Aérospatiale SA365N Dauphin 2	6254	
☐ VT-ELP	Aérospatiale SA365N Dauphin 2	6260	
☐ VT-ELQ	Aérospatiale SA365N Dauphin 2	6261	
☐ VT-ELR	Aérospatiale SA365N Dauphin 2	6268	

☐ VT-ELS	Aérospatiale SA365N Dauphin 2	6273			
☐ VT-ELT	Aérospatiale SA365N Dauphin 2	6278			
☐ VT-ENW	Aérospatiale SA365N Dauphin 2	6094			
☐ VT-ENZ	Aérospatiale SA365N Dauphin 2	6163			
☐ VT-PHJ	Aérospatiale AS365N3 Dauphin 2	6628			
☐ VT-PHK	Aérospatiale AS365N3 Dauphin 2	6631			
☐ VT-PHL	Aérospatiale AS365N3 Dauphin 2	6682			
☐ VT-PHM	Aérospatiale AS365N3 Dauphin 2	6684			
☐ VT-PHO	Aérospatiale AS365N3 Dauphin 2	6734	ex F-WWOA		
☐ VT-PHP	Aérospatiale AS365N3 Dauphin 2	6736	ex F-WWOU		
☐ VT-PHR	Aérospatiale AS365N3 Dauphin 2	6774			
☐ VT-PHS	Aérospatiale AS365N3 Dauphin 2	6775			
☐ VT-PHA	Bell 206L-4 LongRanger IV	52019	ex N6197Y		
☐ VT-PHD	Bell 206L-4 LongRanger IV	52142	ex N64080	Op for Indian Customs	
☐ VT-PHE	Bell 206L-4 LongRanger IV	52159	ex N9217Z	Op for Indian Customs	
☐ VT-PHF	Mil Mi-172	356C06			
☐ VT-PHG	Mil Mi-172	356C07			
☐ VT-PHH	Bell 407	53210	ex N52263		
☐ VT-PHI	Bell 407	53212	ex N52265		
☐ VT-PHN	Bell 407	53617	ex C-FCBU		
☐ VT-PHQ	Bell 407	53689	ex C-FIAL		

SPICEJET — SpiceJet (SG/SEJ) — Delhi-Indira Ghandi International (DEL)

☐ VT-SGE	Boeing 737-8K2/W	32693/1951	ex PH-HZR	Tamarind	
☐ VT-SGF	Boeing 737-8GJ/W	36367/3218	ex N1786B		
☐ VT-SGG	Boeing 737-8GJ/W	36368/3310			♦
☐ VT-SGH	Boeing 737-8GJ/W	36369/3363			♦
☐ VT-SGI	Boeing 737-8GJ/W	37361/3506	ex N1786B		♦
☐ VT-SGJ	Boeing 737-86J/W	29641/1654	ex G-CGPP		♦
☐ VT-SGK	Boeing 737-8BK/W	33019/1502	ex YR-BIC		♦
☐ VT-SGL	Boeing 737-8AS/W	29925/588	ex YR-BIA		♦
☐ VT-SGO	Boeing 737-8AS/W	29926/722	ex YR-BIB		♦
☐ VT-SPE	Boeing 737-86N	28621/570	ex EI-DIT	Ginger	
☐ VT-SPF	Boeing 737-8GJ/W	34896/1861		Coriander	
☐ VT-SPH	Boeing 737-83N/W	30660/1330	ex N331TZ		
☐ VT-SPJ	Boeing 737-8GJ/W	34897/2069		Mint	
☐ VT-SPK	Boeing 737-8GJ/W	34898/2104		Fennel	
☐ VT-SPL	Boeing 737-8GJ/W	34899/2128		Cardamom	
☐ VT-SPM	Boeing 737-8GJ/W	34900/2167		Pepper	
☐ VT-SPO	Boeing 737-86N/W	35216/2321		Dill	
☐ VT-SPP	Boeing 737-86N/W	35217/2359		Rosemary	
☐ VT-SPQ	Boeing 737-8GJ/W	34903/2335		Basil	
☐ VT-SPR	Boeing 737-8GJ/W	34904/2347	ex N1782B	Thyme	
☐ VT-SPS	Boeing 737-8GJ/W	34905/2392		Mustard	
☐ VT-SPW	Boeing 737-86N/W	32672/1932	ex PH-HSY	Cinnamon	
☐ VT-	Boeing 737-8GJ/W				o/o♦
☐ VT-	Boeing 737-8GJ/W				o/o♦
☐ VT-	Boeing 737-8GJ/W				o/o♦
☐ VT-SGB	Boeing 737-9GJER/W	34956/2608		Oregano	
☐ VT-SGC	Boeing 737-9GJER/W	34957/2639		Fenugreek	
☐ VT-SGD	Boeing 737-9GJER/W	34961/2744	ex N1786B	Sesame	
☐ VT-SPT	Boeing 737-9GJER/W	34952/2426		Clove	
☐ VT-SPU	Boeing 737-9GJER/W	34953/2466		Anise	
☐ VT-	Boeing 737-9GJER/W				o/o♦
☐ VT-	de Havilland DHC-8-402Q				o/o♦
☐ VT-	de Havilland DHC-8-402Q				o/o♦
☐ VT-	de Havilland DHC-8-402Q				o/o♦
☐ VT-	de Havilland DHC-8-402Q				o/o♦
☐ VT-	de Havilland DHC-8-402Q				o/o♦
☐ VT-	de Havilland DHC-8-402Q				o/o♦

UNITED HELICHARTERS — Mumbai-Juhu

☐ VT-HGA	Bell 212	30902	ex A7-HAJ	<Gulf Helicopters	
☐ VT-HGB	Bell 212	31124	ex A7-HAN	<Gulf Helicopters	
☐ VT-HGC	Bell 212	31149	ex A7-HAT	<Gulf Helicopters	
☐ VT-HGF	Bell 412EP	36206	ex A7-HBE	<Gulf Helicopters	
☐ VT-HGG	Bell 412HP	36050	ex VH-CFT	<CHC Helicopters Intl	
☐ VT-HGJ	Bell 212	35103	ex C-FAOC	<CHC Helicopters Intl	

V2- ANTIGUA (State of Antigua and Barbuda)

LIAT - THE CARIBBEAN AIRLINE		LIAT (LI/LIA)		Antigua-VC Bird Intl (ANU)
☐ V2-LCY	de Havilland DHC-8-110	035	ex C-GESR	[ANU]
☐ V2-LDQ	de Havilland DHC-8-102	113	ex EI-BWX	
☐ V2-LDU	de Havilland DHC-8-103	270	ex EI-CBV	
☐ V2-LEF	de Havilland DHC-8-103	144	ex HS-SKH	
☐ V2-LES	de Havilland DHC-8-311B	412	ex C-GETI	
☐ V2-LET	de Havilland DHC-8-311B	416	ex C-GFOD	
☐ V2-LEU	de Havilland DHC-8-311	408	ex C-FWBB	Sir Frank de Lisle
☐ V2-LFF	de Havilland DHC-8-314	410	ex N285BC	
☐ V2-LFM	de Havilland DHC-8-311A	267	ex C-GFPZ	
☐ V2-LFU	de Havilland DHC-8-311	250	ex N802SA	retd?
☐ V2-LFV	de Havilland DHC-8-311A	283	ex PH-SDR	
☐ V2-LGA	de Havilland DHC-8-311A	232	ex C-GZTX	
☐ V2-LGB	de Havilland DHC-8-311A	266	ex C-GZTB	
☐ V2-LGC	de Havilland DHC-8-311	298	ex PH-SDM	
☐ V2-LGG	de Havilland DHC-8-311A	404	ex C-FHFY	
☐ V2-LGH	de Havilland DHC-8-311	242	ex PJ-DHE	
☐ V2-LGI	de Havilland DHC-8-311A	325	ex C-FHXB	
☐ V2-LGN	de Havilland DHC-8-311	230	ex PJ-DHL	

NORMAN AVIATION				Antigua-VC Bird Intl (ANU)
☐ V2-LDN	Piper PA-31-325 Navajo C/R	31-7612017	ex N99910	

V3- BELIZE

MAYA ISLAND AIR		Myland (MW/MYD)		Belize City-Municipal/San Pedro (TZA/SPR)
☐ V3-HFS	Cessna 208B Caravan I	208B0579	ex N52627	for sale
☐ V3-HGD	Cessna 208B Caravan I	208B0910	ex N12522	
☐ V3-HGF	Cessna 208B Caravan I	208B0927	ex N52627	
☐ V3-HGJ	Cessna 208B Caravan I	208B0946	ex N52639	
☐ V3-HGO	Cessna 208B Caravan I	208B0995	ex N1241G	
☐ V3-HGP	Cessna 208B Caravan I	208B0998	ex N5213S	
☐ V3-HGQ	Cessna 208B Caravan I	208B0973	ex N1248G	
☐ V3-HGW	Cessna 208B Caravan I	208B1095	ex N1273Z	
☐ V3-HHA	Cessna 208B Caravan I	208B1292	ex N4117D	
☐ V3-HGE	Britten-Norman BN-2A-26 Islander	911	ex N103NE	
☐ V3-HGI	Gippsland GA-8 Airvan	GA8-01-008	ex VH-AUV	
☐ V3-HGK	Britten-Norman BN-2A-26 Islander	853	ex N271RS	

TROPIC AIR COMMUTER		Tropiser (PM/TOS)		San Pedro (SPR)
☐ V3-HFP	Cessna 208B Caravan I	208B0478	ex N1289Y	
☐ V3-HFQ	Cessna 208B Caravan I	208B0575	ex N52623	on rebuild, dam 15Oct05
☐ V3-HFV	Cessna 208B Caravan I	208B0647	ex N5268M	
☐ V3-HGV	Cessna 208B Caravan I	208B1072		
☐ V3-HGX	Cessna 208B Caravan I	208B1162	ex N5108G	
☐ V3-HIK	Cessna 208B Caravan I	208B0707	ex N23681	
☐ V3-HSS	Cessna 208B Caravan I	208B0407	ex N1116V	
☐ V3-HDT	Cessna 207A Stationair 8	20700716	ex (N9696M)	

V4- ST KITTS & NEVIS (Federation of St Christopher and Nevis)

AIR ST KITTS & NEVIS		Sea Breeze (BEZ)		Basseterre-Golden Rock (SKB)
☐ N785PA	Cessna 208B Caravan I	208B0994	ex C6-NFS	
☐ N910HL	Cessna 208B Caravan I	208B1080	ex N1268R	Frtr, op for DHL

V5- NAMIBIA (Republic of Namibia)

AIR NAMIBIA		Namibia (SW/NMB)		Windhoek-Eros/Hosea Kutako Intl (ERS)
☐ V5-NME	Airbus A340-311	051	ex D-AIMG	
☐ V5-NMF	Airbus A340-311	047	ex D-AIMF	
☐ V5-NDI	Boeing 737-528	25228/2170	ex F-GJNC	
☐ V5-TNP	Boeing 737-528	25229/2180	ex F-GJND	

BAY AIR AVIATION		**Nomad Air (NMD)**		**Walvis Bay (WVB)**

| ☐ V5-FUR | Cessna 310Q | 310Q0456 | ex ZS-FUR | |
| ☐ V5-ODL | Cessna 208B Caravan I | 208B0155 | ex ZS-ODL | |

COMAV AVIATION		**Compion (COX)**		**Windhoek-Eros (ERS)**

☐ V5-CAR	Cessna 208B Caravan I	208B0513	ex ZS-OTU	all-white, no titles
☐ V5-NPR	Cessna 310Q	310Q0985	ex ZS-NPR	
☐ V5-SOS	Cessna 402C	402C0437	ex V5-AAS	EMS International SOS titles
☐ V5-VAN	Cessna 208B Caravan I	208B0544	ex ZS-OWC	no titles
☐ ZS-OUB	Beech 1900C	UB-20	ex V5-MNN	Khomas
☐ ZS-OUD	Beech 1900C	UB-73	ex V5-LTC	Kalahari
☐ ZS-OYA	Beech 1900D	UE-7	ex V5-COY	Kavanga

DESERT AIR				**Windhoek-Eros (ERS)**

☐ V5-AEM	Cessna 210L Centurion II	21061519	ex ZS-NCJ	
☐ V5-MAC	Rockwell 690B Turbo Commander	11557	ex N75WA	
☐ V5-MKR	Cessna T210N Turbo Centurion II	21063060	ex ZS-LAS	
☐ V5-MKS	Cessna T310R II	310R0583	ex N410AS	
☐ V5-SKY	Cessna T210L Turbo Centurion II	21059953	ex ZS-SKY	Sossus Air Taxi titles
☐ V5-TEM	Beech Baron 58	TH-812	ex V5-LZG	

NAMIBIA COMMERCIAL AIRWAYS		**Med Rescue (MRE)**		**Windhoek-Eros (ERS)**

| ☐ ZS-NAT | Britten-Norman BN-2T Turbine Islander | 2158 | ex 7Q-CAV | |
| ☐ V5-NCG | Douglas DC-6B | 45564/1040 | ex GBM112 | Batuleur |

SEFOFANE AIR				**Windhoek-Eros (ERS)**

☐ V5-BAT	Cessna T210N Turbo Centurion II	21064543	ex ZS-MUG	
☐ V5-BUZ	Cessna T210N Turbo Centurion II	21063539	ex ZS-OXI	
☐ V5-ELE	Cessna 208B Caravan I	208B0818	ex N1289Y	
☐ V5-KUD	Cessna 210N Centurion II	21063834	ex ZS-KUD	
☐ V5-MTB	Cessna T210N Turbo Centurion II	21062933	ex ZS-MTB	
☐ V5-RNO	Cessna 208B Caravan I	208B1304	ex N41138	
☐ ZS-ELE	Cessna 208B Caravan I	208B1249	ex 9J-ELE	

WESTAIR WINGS		**Westair Wings (WAA)**		**Windhoek-Eros (ERS)**

☐ V5-AAG	Cessna 210M Centurion II	21062077	ex N9646M	tail magnetometer
☐ V5-DHL	Reims Cessna F406 Caravan II	F406-0062	ex N744C	DHL titles
☐ V5-LWH	Cessna 310R	310R0571	ex ZS-LWH	
☐ V5-LXZ	Cessna 210M Centurion II	21063931	ex ZS-LXZ	
☐ V5-MDY	Cessna 402B	402B1353	ex D2-FFW	
☐ V5-SAC	Cessna 340A	340A0945	ex ZS-KUH	
☐ V5-WAA	Cessna 404 Titan II (RAM)	404-0210	ex N88668	Ghost Rider
☐ V5-WAB	Cessna 310Q	310Q0727	ex N4541Q	
☐ V5-WAC	Cessna 404 Titan II	404-0616	ex ZS-KRJ	
☐ V5-WAD	Cessna 310R	310R1340	ex ZS-KEE	
☐ V5-WAE	Cessna 402C	402C0430	ex ZS-NPA	
☐ V5-WAG	Cessna 310R	310R1668	ex V5-KRK	
☐ V5-WAK	Reims Cessna F406 Caravan II	F406-0048	ex G-FLYN	DHL titles

V6- MICRONESIA (Federated States of Micronesia)

CAROLINE ISLAND AIR			**Pohnpei (PNI)**

☐ V6-01FM	Britten-Norman BN-2A-27 Islander	2014	ex V6-SFM
☐ V6-02FM	Beech 65-80 Queen Air	LC-84	ex N349N
☐ V6-03FM	Britten-Norman BN-2A-21 Islander	660	ex VH-AUN

V7- MARSHALL ISLANDS (Republic of the Marshall Islands)

AIRLINE OF THE MARSHALL ISLANDS		**Marshall Islands (CW/MRS)**		**Majuro Intl (MAJ)**

☐ V7-0210	de Havilland DHC-8-102	218	ex ZK-NEU	[MAJ]
☐ V7-9206	Dornier 228-212	8194	ex D-CAHD	[MAJ]
☐ V7-9207	Dornier 228-212	8201	ex D-CAHE	[MAJ]

V8-   BRUNEI (Negara Brunei Darussalam)

ROYAL BRUNEI AIRLINES		Brunei (BI/RBA)		Bandar Seri Begawan (BWN)
☐ V8-RBP	Airbus A319-132	2023	ex D-AVWW	
☐ V8-RBR	Airbus A319-132	2032	ex D-AVYK	
☐ V8-RBS	Airbus A320-232	2135	ex F-WWIV	
☐ V8-RBT	Airbus A320-232	2139	ex F-WWDO	
☐ V8-RBF	Boeing 767-33AER	25530/414		
☐ V8-BLA	Boeing 777-212ER	30871/378	ex 9V-SVF	♦
☐ V8-BLB	Boeing 777-212ER	30872/398	ex 9V-SVG	♦
☐ V8-BLC	Boeing 777-212ER	28524/350	ex 9V-SVA	♦
☐ V8-BLD	Boeing 777-212ER	28525/353	ex 9V-SVB	♦
☐ V8-BLE	Boeing 777-212ER	28526/355	ex 9V-SVC	♦
☐ V8-BLF	Boeing 777-212ER	30869/366	ex 9V-SVD	♦

XA-   MEXICO (United Mexican States)

AERO BINIZA				Oaxaca (OAX)
☐ XA-UAB	Cessna 208B Caravan I	208B1017	ex XA-TVS	

AERO CALAFIA		Calafia (CFV)		Los Cabos
☐ XA-HVB	Cessna 208B Caravan I	208B1104	ex N4047W	
☐ XA-SFJ	Cessna 208B Caravan I	208B0301	ex N5538B	
☐ XA-TQW	Cessna 206H Stationair	20608072	ex N4002B	

AERO CUAHONTE		Cuahonte (CUO)		Uruapan (UPN)
☐ XA-AIR	Dornier 228-212	8236	ex F-OGVA	
☐ XA-KOC	Cessna 402C	402C0301	ex N3271M	
☐ XA-UNB	Dornier 228-202K	8139	ex F-OGOL	
☐ XA-	Dornier 228-212	8238	ex F-OHQK	♦

AERO DAVINCI INTERNACIONAL				Reynosa (REX)
☐ XA-AFL	Swearingen SA.226TC Metro II			
☐ XA-TGV	Swearingen SA.226TC Metro II	TC-350	ex N4254Y	

AEROCEDROS				Ensenada (ESE)
☐ XA-RYV	Convair 440-0	474	ex XB-CSE	
☐ XA-STJ	Cessna 402B	402B0801	ex N3792C	
☐ XA-TFY	Convair 440-0	472	ex N411GA	
☐ XA-TFZ	Convair 440-94	439	ex N44829	
Operates Convair 440s for Soc Coop Prod Pesque Pescado				

AERODAN				Saltillo (SLW)
☐ XA-YYS	NAMC YS-11A	2071	ex XA-TTY	

AEROFERINCO				Playa del Carmen (PCM)
☐ XA-TFG	LET L-410UVP	851409	ex YL-PAH	Cargo [PCM]
☐ XA-TQC	LET L-410UVP	882030	ex Russ AF 2030	

AEROFUTURO				Mexico City-Toluca (TLC)
☐ XA-UGN	Swearingen SA.226TC Metro II	TC-353	ex XA-SFS	

AEROLAMSA				Playa del Carmen (PCM)
☐ XA-TYL	El Gavilan 358	003	ex TG-TDA	
☐ XA-UBD	Britten-Norman BN-2A Mk.III-2 Trislander	1044	ex YV-2523P	

AEROLINEAS CENTAURO		Centauro (CTR)		Durango (DGO)
☐ XA-JAD	Cessna U206G Stationair 6 II	U20605279		
☐ XA-NAQ	Cessna U206G Stationair 6	U20603880	ex XB-CJQ	
☐ XA-PIQ	Britten-Norman BN-2A-26 Islander	892	ex XC-DUJ	
☐ XA-RNC	Cessna TU206G Stationair 6 II	U20605747	ex XB-CGX	

AEROLINEAS REGIONALES		**(RCQ)**		**Queretaro**	
☐ XA-RCB	Boeing 737-2T4C	23066	ex N306AL		

AEROMAR AIRLINES		**Trans-Aeromar (VW/TAO)**		**Mexico City-Toluca (TLC)**	
☐ XA-SJJ	ATR 42-320	039	ex N71296		
☐ XA-SYH	ATR 42-320	062	ex XA-PEP	Presidente Aleman	
☐ XA-TAH	ATR 42-500	471	ex F-WWLS		
☐ XA-TAI	ATR 42-500	474	ex F-WWLF		
☐ XA-TIC	ATR 42-320	058	ex F-OGNF		
☐ XA-TKJ	ATR 42-500	561	ex F-WWLW		
☐ XA-TLN	ATR 42-500	564	ex F-WWEC		
☐ XA-TPR	ATR 42-500	586	ex F-WWEA		
☐ XA-TPS	ATR 42-500	594	ex F-WWEX		
☐ XA-TRI	ATR 42-500	607	ex F-WWEA		
☐ XA-TRJ	ATR 42-500	608	ex F-WWEB		
☐ XA-UAU	ATR 42-500	462	ex I-ADLF	Edo de Veracruz	
☐ XA-UAV	ATR 42-500	476	ex I-ADLG		
☐ XA-UFA	ATR 42-500	412	ex F-WQNH		
☐ XA-UOZ	Canadair CRJ-200ER	7544	ex N119MN		♦
☐ XA-UPA	Canadair CRJ-200ER	7545	ex N122MN		♦

AEROMEXICO		**AeroMexico (AM/AMX)**		**Mexico City-Benito Juarez Intl (MEX)**	
Member of Skyteam					
☐ EI-DRD	Boeing 737-752/W	35117/2122	ex N1786B		
☐ EI-DRE	Boeing 737-752/W	35787/2111			
☐ N784XE	Boeing 737-752/W	33784/1393	ex XA-BAM		
☐ N788XA	Boeing 737-752/W	33788/1439	ex XA-GAM		
☐ N842AM	Boeing 737-752/W	32842/1814			
☐ N850AM	Boeing 737-752/W	33786/1403	ex XA-DAM		
☐ N851AM	Boeing 737-752/W	29363/1417	ex XA-EAM		
☐ N852AM	Boeing 737-752/W	33787/1421	ex XA-FAM		
☐ N853AM	Boeing 737-752/W	33791/1557	ex XA-JAM		
☐ N855AM	Boeing 737-752/W	33792/1571	ex XA-KAM		
☐ N857AM	Boeing 737-752/W	33793/1597	ex XA-LAM		
☐ N904AM	Boeing 737-752/W	28262/1565	ex N854AM		
☐ N906AM	Boeing 737-752/W	29356/1586			
☐ N908AM	Boeing 737-752/W	30038/1601			
☐ N997AM	Boeing 737-76Q/W	30283/1156	ex G-OSLH		
☐ XA-AAM	Boeing 737-752/W	33783/1381			
☐ XA-AGM	Boeing 737-752/W	35786/2098			
☐ XA-CAM	Boeing 737-752/W	33785/1398			
☐ XA-CTG	Boeing 737-752/W	35123/2374			
☐ XA-CYM	Boeing 737-752/W	35124/2456	ex N1779B		
☐ XA-GMV	Boeing 737-752/W	35118/2151			
☐ XA-GOL	Boeing 737-752/W	35785/2011			
☐ XA-HAM	Boeing 737-752/W	33789/1524			
☐ XA-MAH	Boeing 737-752/W	35122/2348			
☐ XA-NAM	Boeing 737-752/W	33790/1533	ex (XA-IAM)		
☐ XA-PAM	Boeing 737-752/W	34293/1747			
☐ XA-QAM	Boeing 737-752/W	34294/1761	ex N1786B		
☐ XA-VAM	Boeing 737-752/W	34295/1765			
☐ XA-	Boeing 737-752/W				o/o
☐ XA-	Boeing 737-752/W				o/o
☐ XA-	Boeing 737-752/W				o/o
☐ EI-DRA	Boeing 737-852/W	35114/2037	ex N1779B		
☐ EI-DRB	Boeing 737-852/W	35115/2070			
☐ EI-DRC	Boeing 737-852/W	35116/2081			
☐ N359AM	Boeing 737-8CX/W	32359/1041	ex PR-GOJ		♦
☐ XA-JOY	Boeing 737-852/W	35121/2327	ex N1782B		
☐ XA-MIA	Boeing 737-852/W	35119/2273			
☐ XA-ZAM	Boeing 737-852/W	35120/2290	ex N1780B		
☐ XA-AMX	Boeing 767-25DER	24733/261	ex N473AG		♦
☐ XA-APB	Boeing 767-3Q8ER	27618/727	ex (XA-TMG)		
☐ XA-JBC	Boeing 767-284ER	24762/307	ex XA-RVY		
☐ XA-MAT	Boeing 767-3Y0ER	24947/351	ex N942AC		
☐ XA-OAM	Boeing 767-2B1ER	26471/511	ex C9-BAF		
☐ XA-TOJ	Boeing 767-283ER	24727/301	ex PT-TAI		
☐ N745AM	Boeing 777-2Q8ER	32718/554			
☐ N746AM	Boeing 777-2Q8ER	32719/562			

☐ N774AM	Boeing 777-2Q8ER	28689/365	ex N301LF		
☐ N776AM	Boeing 777-2Q8	28692/373	ex N181LF		

☐ XA-TPM	McDonnell-Douglas MD-87	49671/1463	ex PZ-TCG	District of Para	[MEX]

AEROMEXICO CONNECT — Costera (5D/SLI) — Monterrey-Escobedo Intl/Vera Cruz (MTY/VER)

☐ XA-ACA	Embraer ERJ-145LR	145144	ex N261SK	
☐ XA-ACB	Embraer ERJ-145LR	145221	ex N264SK	♦
☐ XA-ALI	Embraer ERJ-145LR	145795	ex PT-SMW	
☐ XA-BLI	Embraer ERJ-145LR	145798	ex PT-SMY	
☐ XA-CLI	Embraer ERJ-145LR	14500803	ex PT-SNG	
☐ XA-DLI	Embraer ERJ-145LR	14500852	ex PT-SQU	
☐ XA-ELI	Embraer ERJ-145LR	14500861	ex PT-SXB	
☐ XA-FLI	Embraer ERJ-145MP	145203	ex N974RP	
☐ XA-GAC	Embraer ERJ-145MP	145406	ex SP-LGL	
☐ XA-GLI	Embraer ERJ-145MP	145444	ex N973RP	
☐ XA-HLI	Embraer ERJ-145MP	145337	ex N975RP	
☐ XA-ILI	Embraer ERJ-145LU	145564	ex D-ACIA	
☐ XA-JLI	Embraer ERJ-145MP	145426	ex N971RP	
☐ XA-KAC	Embraer ERJ-145MP	145322	ex N976RP	
☐ XA-KLI	Embraer ERJ-145MP	145440	ex N972RP	
☐ XA-LLI	Embraer ERJ-145ER	145060	ex PT-SPH	
☐ XA-MLI	Embraer ERJ-145ER	145065	ex PT-SPI	
☐ XA-NLI	Embraer ERJ-145ER	145083	ex PT-SPJ	
☐ XA-OLI	Embraer ERJ-145ER	145089	ex PT-SPK	
☐ XA-PAC	Embraer ERJ-145LR	145498	ex N824HK	
☐ XA-PLI	Embraer ERJ-145ER	145090	ex PT-SPL	
☐ XA-QAC	Embraer ERJ-145LR	145510	ex N825HK	
☐ XA-QLI	Embraer ERJ-145LU	145588	ex HB-JAX	
☐ XA-RAC	Embraer ERJ-145LR	145313	ex N830HK	
☐ XA-RLI	Embraer ERJ-145LU	145559	ex HB-JAS	
☐ XA-SLI	Embraer ERJ-145LU	145580	ex HB-JAW	
☐ XA-TAK	Embraer ERJ-145LR	145475	ex N823HK	
☐ XA-TLI	Embraer ERJ-145LU	145601	ex HB-JAY	
☐ XA-ULI	Embraer ERJ-145LU	145570	ex HB-JAU	
☐ XA-VAC	Embraer ERJ-145LR	145232	ex N831HK	
☐ XA-VLI	Embraer ERJ-145LU	145574	ex HB-JAV	
☐ XA-WAC	Embraer ERJ-145LR	145255	ex N837HK	
☐ XA-WLI	Embraer ERJ-145LU	145434	ex HB-JAN	
☐ XA-XAC	Embraer ERJ-145LR	145128	ex N260SK	
☐ XA-XLI	Embraer ERJ-145LU	145456	ex HB-JAO	
☐ XA-YAC	Embraer ERJ-145LR	145168	ex N262SK	
☐ XA-YLI	Embraer ERJ-145LR	145400	ex HB-JAL	
☐ XA-ZAC	Embraer ERJ-145LR	145199	ex N263SK	
☐ XA-ZLI	Embraer ERJ-145LU	145420	ex HB-JAM	
☐ XA-AAC	Embraer ERJ-190LR	19000121	ex PT-SQP	
☐ XA-BAC	Embraer ERJ-190LR	19000129	ex PT-SQP	
☐ XA-CAC	Embraer ERJ-190LR	19000135	ex PT-SYN	
☐ XA-EAC	Embraer ERJ-190LR	19000145	ex PT-SYX	
☐ XA-FAC	Embraer ERJ-190LR	19000234	ex PT-SIF	
☐ XA-IAC	Embraer ERJ-190LR	19000238	ex PT-SIL	
☐ XA-JAC	Embraer ERJ-190LR	19000248	ex PT-SIS	
☐ XA-	Embraer ERJ-190LR		ex PT-	o/o♦
☐ XA-	Embraer ERJ-190LR		ex PT-	o/o♦
☐ XA-	Embraer ERJ-190LR		ex PT-	o/o♦
☐ XA-	Embraer ERJ-190LR		ex PT-	o/o♦
☐ XA-	Embraer ERJ-190LR		ex PT-	o/o♦
☐ XA-	Embraer ERJ-190LR		ex PT-	o/o♦

AEROMEXICO TRAVEL

☐ XA-TXC	McDonnell-Douglas MD-87	49389/1333	ex EC-GKF	
☐ N583MD	McDonnell-Douglas MD-83	49659/1438	ex YV-39C	
☐ N838AM	McDonnell-Douglas MD-83	49397/1331	ex N830VV	
☐ N848SH	McDonnell-Douglas MD-83	49848/1592	ex SIX-BEU	♦

AEROMEXPRESS CARGO — Aeromexpress (QO/MPX) — Mexico City-Benito Juarez Intl (MEX)

Subsidiary of Mexicana, operates services with Boeing 767-200 (SF)s leased from ABX Air as required.

AERONAVES TSM — Saltilo (SLW)

☐ XA-DCX	Swearingen SA.227AC Metro III	AC-497	ex N98EB
☐ XA-EEE	Swearingen SA.227AC Metro III	AC-503	ex N102GS
☐ XA-EGC	Swearingen SA.227AC Metro III	AC-724	ex N106GS
☐ XA-MIO	Swearingen SA.227AC Metro III	AC-693B	ex N446MA

☐ XA-PNG	Swearingen SA.227AC Metro III	AC-687B	ex N445MA		
☐ XA-SLW	Swearingen SA.227AC Metro III	AC-628B	ex N280EM		
☐ XA-TYX	Swearingen SA.227AC Metro III	AC-627B	ex N799BW		
☐ XA-UKJ	Swearingen SA.227AC Metro III	AC-532	ex N372PH		
☐ XA-UNQ	Swearingen SA.227AC Metro III	AC-565	ex N163WA		♦
☐ XA-ADQ	Swearingen SA.226TC Metro II	TC-409	ex C-FLNG		
☐ XA-ADS	Swearingen SA.226TC Metro II	TC-404	ex C-FGPW		
☐ XA-TSM	Swearingen SA.226TC Metro IIA	TC-412	ex XA-SXB		
☐ XA-UFO	Swearingen SA.226TC Metro II	TC-281	ex N396RY		
☐ XA-UKP	Swearingen SA.226TC Metro II	TC-376	ex N637PJ		
☐ XA-	Swearingen SA.226TC Metro II	TC-337	ex N851LH		
☐ XA-TYF	Convair 600F	101	ex N94279		
☐ XA-	Convair 640	332	ex N640R		♦
☐ XA-UOG	Douglas DC-9-33RC (ABS 3)	47194/324	ex N944F		♦

AEROPACIFICO		**Aero Costa (TAA)**		**Colima (CLQ)**
☐ XA-AFT	Swearingen SA.227AC Metro III	AC-581	ex C-FAFE	Frtr
☐ XA-UAJ	Swearingen SA.227AC Metro III	AC-586	ex N911EJ	Frtr

AEROPACIFICO		**Transportes Pacifico (TFO)**		**Los Mochis (LMM)**
☐ XA-AFE	LET L-410UVP-E	902508	ex N19RZ	
☐ XA-SUS	Swearingen SA.227AC Metro III	AC-430B	ex N430PF	
☐ XA-UEP	British Aerospace Jetstream 31	794	ex N417UE	

AEROPOSTAL	**Postal Cargo (PCG)**		**Mexico City-Benito Juarez Intl (MEX)**
☐ XA-TXS	Douglas DC-8-63CF (BAC 3)	46054/453	ex N796AL

AEROSERVICIOS MONTERREY	**Servimonte (SVM)**	**Monterrey-General Mariano Ecobedo Intl (MTY)**
☐ XA-HAC	Piper PA-31-325 Navajo C/R	31-7912088	ex N3532K

AEROTRON		**Aerotron (TRN)**		**Puerto Vallarta (PVR)**
☐ XA-ADZ	Cessna 402	402-0113	ex N772EA	
☐ XA-TNI	Cessna 208B Caravan I	208B0728		Op for Air Adventure

AEROTUCAN			**Oaxaca (OAX)**
☐ XA-TDS	Cessna 208B Caravan I	208B0559	
☐ XA-UCT	Cessna 208B Caravan I	208B1093	ex N5076J

AEROUNION		**AeroUnion (6R/TNO)**		**Mexico City-Benito Juarez Intl (MEX)**
☐ XA-FPP	Airbus A300B4-203F	247	ex N247AX		♦
☐ XA-LRL	Airbus A300B4-203F	210	ex N2101R		♦
☐ XA-MRC	Airbus A300B4-203F	227	ex N227TN		♦
☐ XA-TVU	Airbus A300B4-203F	074	ex G-HLAC	Nina	
☐ XA-TWQ	Airbus A300B4-203F	045	ex G-HLAB	Tata	

AEROVIAS CASTILLO		**Aerocastillo (CLL)**		**Guadalajara (GDL)**
☐ XA-COJ	Cessna U206G Stationair 6	U20605484	ex XB-ZIC	
☐ XA-IUL	Cessna 402C	402C0091		
☐ XA-JIO	Cessna U206G Stationair 6	U20605330		
☐ XA-JON	Cessna 402C	402C0230	ex N2718R	
☐ XA-KEB	Cessna T207A Stationair 8	20700615	ex N73705	
☐ XA-PEA	Cessna TU206G Stationair 6	U20606379	ex N7590Z	
☐ XA-POM	Cessna 421C Golden Eagle	421C0695	ex N546RP	
☐ XA-RWO	Cessna T210L Turbo Centurion II	21061474	ex N732FE	
☐ XA-SCE	Learjet 24D	24D-271	ex N4305U	

AEROVIAS MONTES AZULES		**Montes Azules (MZL)**		**Tuxtla Gutierrez (TGZ)**
☐ XA-SOG	Piper PA-31-325 Navajo C/R	31-7612056	ex XB-EGX	
☐ XA-TMQ	Cessna TU206G Stationair 6	U20604578	ex N9569E	

ASESA		**Aeroespecial (SVE)**		**Ciudad del Carmen (CME)**
☐ XA-TNF	Bell 412EP	36202	ex N4300Z	
☐ XA-TPG	Bell 412EP	36240	ex N63880	
☐ XA-TPO	Bell 412EP	36221	ex N62355	
☐ XA-TQH	Bell 412EP	36241	ex N6400Z	
☐ XA-TWD	Bell 412EP	36309	ex N24113	

□ XA-TWE	Bell 412EP	36310	ex N2413V
□ XA-UAC	Bell 412EP	36323	ex N80667
□ XA-UAE	Bell 412EP	36325	ex N8067E
□ XA-UBF	Bell 412EP	36331	ex N4537J
□ XA-UBM	Bell 412EP	36335	ex N45391
□ XA-UCC	Bell 412EP	36338	ex N45378
□ XA-UCF	Bell 412EP	36330	ex N45371
□ XA-UGA	Bell 412EP	36402	ex N2077M
□ XA-UGY	Bell 412EP	36427	ex N5075Q
□ XA-UHD	Bell 412EP	36431	ex N9154R
□ XA-UHS	Bell 412EP	36436	ex N3128K
□ XA-AKY	Piper PA-31 Navajo C	31-7712061	ex N27270
□ XA-RTL	Aérospatiale AS365N2 Dauphin 2	6374	ex F-WYMD
□ XA-RUZ	Aérospatiale AS365N2 Dauphin 2	6394	

AVIONES DE SONORA		Sonorav (ADS)		Hermosillo (HMO)

| □ XA-KEA | Cessna 310R | 310R1880 | ex (N3223M) |
| □ XA-KOA | Cessna 340A | 340A0978 | ex YV-1886P |

CLICK MEXICANA		Click Mexicana (QA/CBE)		Mexico City-Benito Juraex Intl (MEX)

Suspended operations 28/Aug/2010

ESTAFETA CARGA AEREA		(E7/ESF)		San Luis Potosi (SLP)

□ XA-AJA	Boeing 737-3Y0 (SF)	23747/1363	ex N331AW
□ XA-ECA	Boeing 737-3M8 (SF)	24024/1689	ex N784DC
□ XA-EMX	Boeing 737-375F	23707/1388	ex N336AW
□ XA-ESA	Canadair CRJ-100ER	7085	ex F-GRJC
□ XA-GGB	Boeing 737-3M8 (SF)	24023/1675	ex N783DC
□ XA-SPO	Canadair CRJ-100ER	7088	ex F-GRJD
□ XA-TWP	Boeing 737-229C (Nordam 3)	21738/576	ex G-BYYF

FLYMEX			

| □ XA-AAS | Dornier 328-300 (328JET) | 3127 | ex N430Z |
| □ XA-FAS | Dornier 328-300 (328JET) | 3125 | ex N410Z |

GLOBAL AIR		Damojh (DMJ)		Mexico City-Benito Juarez Intl (MEX)

□ XA-TWR	Boeing 737-2H4 (AvAero 3)	21812/611	ex N60SW	no titles	>VCV
□ XA-UBB	Boeing 737-291	21750/574	ex N988UA		
□ XA-UMQ	Boeing 737-2Q3	24103/1565	ex N243AG		
□ XA-UNG	Boeing 737-3L9	26441/2550	ex OM-CLD		♦
□ XA-UNW	Boeing 737-3T0	23458/1244	ex N17328		♦

HAWK DE MEXICO		Hawk Mexico (HMX)		Mexico City/Cancun (MEX/CUN)

| □ XA-MVD | Beech 1900D | UE-398 | ex N44118 |

HELI CAMPECHE		Helicampeche (HEC)		Campeche/Mexico City (CPE/-)

□ XA-AAB	Bell 412EP	36253	ex N4217U	<OLOG
□ XA-AAN	Bell 412EP	36254	ex N24171	<OLOG
□ XA-AAR	Bell 412EP	36255	ex N385AL	<OLOG
□ XA-HSD	Bell 412EP	36446	ex N31011	
□ XA-HSG	Bell 412EP	36473	ex N321FB	
□ XA-HSJ	Bell 412EP	36337	ex N45388	
□ XA-HSK	Bell 412EP	36340	ex N45389	
□ XA-HSL	Bell 412EP	36334	ex N45377	
□ XA-HSM	Bell 412EP	36324	ex N8067M	
□ XA-HSN	Bell 412EP	36488	ex N332TB	
□ XA-HSO	Bell 412EP	36489	ex N331AB	
□ XA-SMW	Bell 412HP	36038	ex SU-CAW	
□ XA-SYL	Bell 412HP	36101	ex N87746	
□ XA-TRC	Bell 412HP	36157	ex N389AL	
□ XA-TTL	Bell 412HP	36065	ex D-HHZZ	
□ XA-TXP	Bell 412EP	36311	ex N24129	
□ XA-TXQ	Bell 412EP	36268	ex N61318	
□ XA-TXR	Bell 412EP	36289	ex N2029N	
□ XA-TXV	Bell 412EP	36317	ex N7020C	
□ XA-TXZ	Bell 412EP	36314	ex N7030B	
□ XA-TYA	Bell 412EP	36315	ex N7007Q	
□ XA-UAR	Bell 412	36051	ex D-HHYY	
□ XA-ADL	Bell 407	53447	ex N61201	

☐ XA-HSE	Eurocopter EC135P2+	0591	ex N135TZ		
☐ XA-HSF	Eurocopter EC135P2+	0598	ex N435AL		
☐ XA-JMB	Bell 407	53274	ex XA-TLB		
☐ XA-JOL	Bell 206B JetRanger III	786	ex N31AL		<OLOG
☐ XA-LOC	Bell 206B JetRanger III	3284			<OLOG
☐ XA-SMX	Bell 206L-4 LongRanger IV	52005	ex N2064W		♦
☐ XA-TPC	Bell 407	53313	ex N60664		
☐ XA-TRP	Bell 212	30869	ex N71AL		<OLOG
☐ XA-UEB	Bell 407	53046	ex N416AL		<OLOG

HELIVAN

☐ XA-GFT	Sikorsky S-76C+	760596	ex N71154	
☐ XA-MJV	Sikorsky S-76C+	760581	ex N7113J	
☐ XA-RSY	Sikorsky S-76C+	760598	ex N71026	
☐ XA-RYT	Sikorsky S-76C+	760582	ex N7110U	

INTERJET (4O/INJ)   Toluca (TLC)

☐ XA-ABC	Airbus A320-214	3690	ex F-WWBE	
☐ XA-ACO	Airbus A320-214	1322	ex F-WQUX	
☐ XA-ALM	Airbus A320-214	1308	ex F-WQUU	
☐ XA-IJA	Airbus A320-214	1244	ex F-WQUT	
☐ XA-IJT	Airbus A320-214	1132	ex F-WQUR	
☐ XA-ILY	Airbus A320-214	3123	ex N213MX	♦
☐ XA-INJ	Airbus A320-214	1162	ex F-WQUV	
☐ XA-JCV	Airbus A320-214	3514	ex F-WWDO	
☐ XA-MLR	Airbus A320-214	2227	ex EC-JAB	♦
☐ XA-MTY	Airbus A320-214	1179	ex XA-AIJ	
☐ XA-MXM	Airbus A320-214	3286	ex F-WWDR	
☐ XA-MYR	Airbus A320-214	3021	ex HB-IOV	♦
☐ XA-SOB	Airbus A320-214	2189	ex 9H-AEI	♦
☐ XA-TLC	Airbus A320-214	3312	ex F-WWIP	
☐ XA-UHE	Airbus A320-214	3149	ex F-WWBS	
☐ XA-VAI	Airbus A320-214	3160	ex F-WWDR	
☐ XA-VFI	Airbus A320-214	1780	ex N471LF	♦
☐ XA-VIP	Airbus A320-214	3304	ex XA-MXK	♦
☐ XA-VTA	Airbus A320-214	1259	ex XA-ITJ	
☐ XA-XII	Airbus A320-214	3508	ex F-WWBU	
☐ XA-ZIH	Airbus A320-214	3667	ex F-WWDZ	
☐ XA-	Airbus A320-214		ex	o/o♦
☐ XA-	Airbus A320-214		ex	o/o♦
☐ XA-	Airbus A320-214		ex	o/o♦
☐ XA-	Airbus A320-214		ex	o/o♦
☐ XA-	Airbus A320-214		ex	o/o♦
☐ XA-	Airbus A320-214		ex	o/o♦

MAGNICHARTERS   Grupomonterrey (GMT)   Monterrey-General Mariano Ecobedo Intl (MTY)

☐ XA-MAA	Boeing 737-377	23655/1274	ex N812AR		
☐ XA-MAB	Boeing 737-301	23232/1169	ex N502UW		
☐ XA-MAC	Boeing 737-2C3	21014/397	ex N302AR	damaged 14Sep07	
☐ XA-MAD	Boeing 737-277 (Nordam 3)	22652/831	ex N185AW	Magni titles	
☐ XA-MAE	Boeing 737-277 (Nordam 3)	22648/789	ex N181AW		
☐ XA-MAF	Boeing 737-2K9 (Nordam 3)	22505/815	ex N303AR		
☐ XA-MAI	Boeing 737-322	24537/1774	ex N368UA		
☐ XA-UNA	Boeing 737-322	24248/1636	ex N187AQ		♦
☐ XA-UNL	Boeing 737-322	24532/1754	ex N185AQ		♦

MAS AIR CARGO   Mas Carga (MY/MAA)   Mexico City-Benito Juarez Intl (MEX)

☐ N314LA	Boeing 767-316ERF	32573/848		<LCO
☐ N420LA	Boeing 767-316ERF	34627/948		<LCO

MAYAIR   (MYI)   Mexico City-Benito Juarez Intl (MEX)

☐ XA-MUR	Cessna 208B Caravan I	208B0740	ex XA-TOE	
☐ XA-MYI	Short SD.3-60	SH3602	ex YN-CGF	

MEXICANA   Mexicana (MX/MXA)   Mexico City-Benito Juarez Intl (MEX)

Suspended operations 28/Aug/2010

MEXICANALINK   Link (I6 / MXI)

Suspended operations 28/Aug/2010

NOVA AIR (M4) Mexico City-Benito Juarez Intl (MEX)

☐ XA-OCI	Boeing 737-217 (AvAero 3)	22257/756	ex N2257	[MEX]
☐ XA-OHC	Boeing 737-291 (Nordam 3)	21640/536	ex N982UA	

REPUBLICAIR Republicair (RBC) Mexico City-Benito Juarez Intl (MEX)

☐ XA-RBC	Boeing 737-277 (Nordam 3)	22647/785	ex N180AW	[MEX]
☐ XA-RBD	Boeing 737-277 (Nordam 3)	22649/801	ex N182AW	

SAEMSA Servimex (SXM) Campeche, Tampico & Toluca (CPE/TAM/TLC)

☐ XA-SRL	Aérospatiale SA.330J Puma	1625	ex XC-CME
☐ XA-SRN	Aérospatiale SA.330J Puma	1644	ex XC-FOI
☐ XA-SRO	Aérospatiale SA.330J Puma	1615	ex XC-IMP
☐ XA-SRP	Aérospatiale SA.330J Puma	1616	ex XC-OPS
☐ XA-SRQ	Aérospatiale SA.330J Puma	1613	ex XC-SDE
☐ XA-TFT	Aérospatiale AS365N2 Dauphin 2	6495	ex F-WQDS
☐ XA-TFU	Aérospatiale AS365N2 Dauphin 2	6512	ex F-WQDT
☐ XA-TFV	Aérospatiale AS365N2 Dauphin 2	6513	
☐ XA-TGS	Aérospatiale AS365N2 Dauphin 2	6515	ex F-WWOA
☐ XA-TGY	Aérospatiale AS365N2 Dauphin 2	6516	ex F-WWOB
☐ XA-TGZ	Aérospatiale AS365N2 Dauphin 2	6517	
☐ XA-SSB	Bell 212	30845	ex XC-DAH
☐ XA-SSC	Bell 212	30992	ex XC-DIA
☐ XA-SSD	Bell 212	30988	ex XC-DIF
☐ XA-SSF	Bell 212	30987	ex XC-SER
☐ XA-SSG	Bell 212	30939	ex XC-SET
☐ XA-SSK	Bell 212	30924	ex XC-HFI
☐ XA-SSL	Bell 212	35031	ex XC-HHN
☐ XA-SRF	Cessna U206G Stationair 6	U20605823	ex XC-DOJ
☐ XA-SRG	Cessna U206G Stationair 6	U20604684	ex XC-REX
☐ XA-SRI	Cessna U206G Stationair 6	U20604133	ex XC-MTT
☐ XA-SST	Cessna U206G Stationair 6	U20605820	ex XC-DOI
☐ XA-SRK	Cessna T210M Turbo Centurion II	21062532	
☐ XA-SRW	Sikorsky S-76A	760142	ex XC-FEK
☐ XA-SRX	Sikorsky S-76A	760094	ex XC-FES
☐ XA-SSO	Bell 206B JetRanger	1250	ex XC-GIJ
☐ XA-SSP	Bell 206B JetRanger III	3962	ex XC-HIB

SAINTEX CARGO

☐ XA-MDG	SAAB SF.340A	340A-088	ex N88XW	Frtr

TRANSPORTES AEREOS PEGASO Transpegaso (TPG) Mexico City-Benito Juarez Intl (MEX)

☐ XA-EZM	MBB BK-117C-2	9051	ex D-HMBC
☐ XA-MBB	MBB Bo.105CBS-4	S-676	ex N4573H
☐ XA-NAT	MBB Bo.105LS-A3	2044	ex XA-TTT
☐ XA-THI	MBB Bo.105LS-A3	2046	ex C-GERG
☐ XA-THK	MBB BK-117B-2	7131	ex D-HBCZ
☐ XA-THM	MBB BK-117B-2	7252	ex D-HAEC
☐ XA-UBN	MBB BK-117C-1	7550	
☐ XA-UBO	MBB BK-117C-1	7551	
☐ XA-UBP	MBB BK-117C-1	7555	
☐ XA-UDM	Eurocopter EC135P2	0400	
☐ XA-UDN	Eurocopter EC135P2	0391	
☐ XA-UDO	Eurocopter EC135P2	0389	

VIGO JET Mejets (MJT) Mexico City-Benito Juarez Intl (MEX)

☐ XA-AEG	Lockheed L-188CF Electra	1147	ex HK-3706	[PTY]
☐ XA-MJE	North American NA-265 Sabre 40	282-65	ex XA-GGR	Frtr
☐ XA-UII	Boeing 727-222F (FedEx 3)	19913/672	ex N7640U	
☐ XA-UIJ	Boeing 727-222F (FedEx 3)	19911/668	ex XA-SRC	[MEX]
☐ XA-UIT	SAAB SF.340A	340A-030	ex XA-UGM	

VIVA AEROBUS (VIV) Monterrey-Escobedo Intl (MTY)

☐ XA-TAR	Boeing 737-301	23259/1132	ex HS-AEF
☐ XA-UGL	Boeing 737-3B7	22958/1137	ex N385US
☐ XA-VIA	Boeing 737-3B7	23856/1501	ex N521AU
☐ XA-VIB	Boeing 737-3B7	23378/1339	ex HS-AAU
☐ XA-VIF	Boeing 737-301	23552/1382	ex PK-AWV

☐ XA-VIH	Boeing 737-301	23554/1408	ex PK-AWW	
☐ XA-VIJ	Boeing 737-3Y0	24677/1837	ex 9M-AEC	♦
☐ XA-VIK	Boeing 737-3L9	26442/2277	ex PK-AWN	♦
☐ XA-VIL	Boeing 737-33A	25010/2008	ex TS-IEC	♦
☐ XA-VIM	Boeing 737-33A	25032/2014	ex TS-IED	♦
☐ XA-VIV	Boeing 737-301	23560/1463	ex N573US	
☐ XA-VIX	Boeing 737-3B7	23312/1162	ex N390US	
☐ XA-VIY	Boeing 737-3B7	22959/1140	ex N158VA	

VOLARIS		*(V4/VOI)*		*Toluca (TLC)*
☐ N473TA	Airbus A319-132	1140	ex D-AVYP	Aracely
☐ N474TA	Airbus A319-132	1159	ex D-AVWD	Aline
☐ N501VL	Airbus A319-133	2979	ex D-AVXF	Leopoldo
☐ N502VL	Airbus A319-132	3463	ex D-AVWL	Alejandro
☐ N503VL	Airbus A319-132	3491	ex D-AVYU	Audrey
☐ N504VL	Airbus A319-132	3590	ex D-AVYK	Sebastian
☐ XA-VOA	Airbus A319-132	2771	ex D-AVWP	Alejandro
☐ XA-VOB	Airbus A319-133	2780	ex D-AVYJ	Marco
☐ XA-VOC	Airbus A319-132	2997	ex D-AVXK	Citlali
☐ XA-VOD	Airbus A319-133	3045	ex D-AVWO	Diego
☐ XA-VOE	Airbus A319-133	3069	ex D-AVWT	Francisco
☐ XA-VOF	Airbus A319-133	3077	ex D-AVWQ	Fernando
☐ XA-VOG	Airbus A319-133	3175	ex D-AVXI	Gabriel
☐ XA-VOH	Airbus A319-133	3253	ex D-AVWU	Javier
☐ XA-VOI	Airbus A319-132	2657	ex D-AVYN	Ivetta
☐ XA-VOJ	Airbus A319-133	3279	ex D-AVYM	Jamie
☐ XA-VOK	Airbus A319-133	3450	ex D-AVYT	Veronica
☐ XA-VOL	Airbus A319-132	2666	ex D-AVWX	Loreta
☐ XA-VOO	Airbus A319-133	3705	ex D-AVWK	Andres
☐ XA-VOP	Airbus A319-133	4403	ex D-AVXI	♦
☐ XA-VOQ	Airbus A319-133	4422	ex D-AVXK	♦
☐ XA-VOR	Airbus A319-132	2296	ex F-GXAG	♦
☐ XA-VOS	Airbus A319-132	3252	ex SX-OAL	♦
☐ XA-VOT	Airbus A319-132	3317	ex SX-OAK	♦
☐ XA-	Airbus A319-112	3589	ex D-AHIL	o/o♦
☐ XA-	Airbus A319-132		ex	o/o♦
☐ XA-	Airbus A319-132		ex	o/o♦
☐ XA-VOM	Airbus A320-233	3624	ex F-WWIM	Sara
☐ XA-VON	Airbus A320-232	3672	ex F-WWIN	Isaac
☐ XA-	Airbus A320-232		ex	o/o♦
☐ XA-	Airbus A320-232		ex	o/o♦

XT-   BURKINA FASO (People's Democratic Republic of Burkina Faso)

AIR BURKINA		*Burkina (2J/VBW)*		*Ouagadougou (OUA)*
☐ XT-ABC	McDonnell-Douglas MD-87	49834/1714	ex I-AFRA	
☐ XT-ABD	McDonnell-Douglas MD-87	49839/1739	ex EC-EYX	
☐ XT-ABF	McDonnell-Douglas MD-83	53464/2091	ex N161BS	
☐ XT-FZP	Fokker F.28 Fellowship 4000	11185	ex PH-ZCF	Bonkougou

XU-   CAMBODIA (Kingdom of Cambodia)

CAMBODIA ANGKOR AIR		*(K6/VAV)*		*Phnom Penh-Pochentong (PNH)*
☐ VN-A351	Airbus A321-231	3005	ex D-AVZI	<HVN
☐ VN-B212	ATR 72-212A	685	ex F-WWEH	<HVN
☐ VN-B214	ATR 72-212A	688	ex F-WWEK	<HVN
☐ VN-B227	ATR 72-212A	899	ex F-WWEJ	<HVN♦
☐ VN-B231	ATR 72-212A	906	ex F-WWEW	<HVN♦

IMTREC AVIATION		*Imtrec (IMT)*		*Phnom Penh-Pochentong (PNH)*
☐ RDPL-34155	Ilyushin Il-76T	073411338	ex ER-IBD	
☐ RDPL-34158	Antonov An-32	402437	ex ER-LID	Op for Laotian Army
☐ XU-315	Antonov An-12BP	2400702	ex RA-11131	

KAMPUCHEA AIRLINES		*Kampuchea (E2/KMP)*		*Phnom Penh-Pochentong (PNH)*

Suspended operations but plans to restart, 49% owned by Orient Thai Airlines

PMT AIR		Multitrade (U4/PMT)	Phnom Penh-Pochentong (PNH)	
☐ XU-U4B	Boeing 737-281	20450/262	ex EX-450	
☐ XU-U4E	McDonnell-Douglas MD-83	49395/1286	ex N9305N	[JKT]
☐ XU-U4H	Boeing 727-200			

PRESIDENT AIRLINES		(TO/PSD)	Phnom Penh-Pochentong (PNH)	
☐ XU-881	Fokker F.27 Friendship 100	10168	ex RP-C5888	[PNH]
☐ XU-888	Fokker F.28 Fellowship 1000	11012	ex XU-001	[PNH]

ROYAL KHMER AIRLINES		Khymer Air (RK/RKH)	Phnom Penh-Pochentong (PNH)	
☐ XU-RKA	Boeing 737-2H4 (AvAero 3)	22061/639	ex N63SW	Lsd to/op for BGL
☐ XU-RKB	Boeing 737-2H4 (AvAero 3)	22674/827	ex N74SW	
☐ XU-RKC	Boeing 737-2H4 (AvAero 3)	22903/905	ex (PK-RIP)	Lsd to/op for BGL
☐ XU-RKF	Boeing 727-223F (FedEx 3)	19494/661	ex 4R-SEM	
☐ XU-RKH	Boeing 737-232 (Nordam 3)	23105/1068	ex N334DL	
☐ XU-RKJ	Boeing 727-223 (Raisbeck 3)	20989/1144	ex PK-JGQ Air Dream c/s	abandoned at HAN
☐ XU-RKK	Boeing 737-2H4	23054/969	ex PK-LYA	>IAW

ROYAL PHNOM PENH AIRWAYS		Phnom-Penh-Air (RL/PPW)	Phnom Penh-Pochentong (PNH)	
☐ XU-070	AVIC 1 Y-7-100C	09706	ex B-3448	stored
☐ XU-071	AVIC 1 Y-7-100C	08708	ex B-3449	stored
☐ XU-072	AVIC 1 Y-7-100C	08705	ex B-3494	

SIEM REAP AIR INTERNATIONAL	Siemreap Air (FT/SRH)	Siem Reap (REP)

A wholly owned subsidiary of Bangkok Air and leases aircraft from parent as required – some wear joint titles

XY- MYANMAR (Union of Myanmar)

AIR BAGAN		(W9/JAB)		Yangon (RGN)
☐ XY-AGC	Fokker 100	11327	ex G-BXWE	>MMA
☐ XY-AGD	Airbus A310-222	419	ex B-2303	
☐ XY-AGE	Airbus A310-222	320	ex B-2302	
☐ XY-AGF	Fokker 100	11282	ex N854US	
☐ XY-AIA	ATR 72-212	422	ex F-WQNQ	
☐ XY-AIC	ATR 42-320	159	ex N34820	
☐ XY-AID	ATR 42-300	152	ex N34817	
☐ XY-AIE	ATR 72-212	458	ex F-WQNB	
☐ XY-AIH	ATR 72-212	469	ex F-OHFZ	
☐ XY-AIS	ATR 72-212A	626	ex I-ATPA	♦

AIR MANDALAY		(6T)		Mandalay/Yangon (MDL/RGN)
☐ XY-AEY	ATR 72-212	393	ex F-OHFS	
☐ XY-AIJ	ATR 42-320	268	ex F-OHRN	
☐ XY-AIR	ATR 72-212	467	ex EI-CMJ	♦

MYANMA AIRWAYS		Unionair (UB/UBA)		Yangon (RGN)
☐ XY-ADZ	Fokker F.27 Friendship 600	10574	ex PH-EXF	
☐ XY-AEQ	Fokker F.27 Friendship 400	10294	ex 5Y-BIP	[RGN]
☐ XY-AEW	Fokker F.27 Friendship 600	10352	ex CU-T1290	[RGN]
☐ XY-AEZ	ATR 72-212	475	ex F-OGUO all-white	
☐ XY-AGA	Fokker F.28 Fellowship 4000	11232	ex PH-EZG	
☐ XY-AGB	Fokker F.28 Fellowship 4000	11184	ex YU-AOH	
☐ XY-AGH	Fokker F.28 Fellowship 4000	11161	ex ZS-JAV	♦
☐ XY-AIB	ATR 42-320	178	ex F-WQNM	
☐ XY-AIF	ATR 72-212A	765	ex F-W	
☐ XY-AIG	ATR 72-212A	781	ex F-WWET	

MYANMAR AIRWAYS INTERNATIONAL		Mtanmar (8M/MMA)		Yangon (RGN)
☐ XY-AGC	Fokker 100	11327	ex G-BXWE	<JAB
☐ XY-AGG	Airbus A320-231	0114	ex S5-AAC	
☐ XY-AGI	Airbus A320-231	0113	ex S5-AAB	

YANGON AIRLINES		(HK)		Yangon (RGN)
☐ XY-AIM	ATR 72-212	479	ex F-OIYA	♦
☐ XY-AIN	ATR 72-212	481	ex F-OIYB	♦

YA- AFGHANISTAN (State of Afghanistan)

ARIANA AFGHAN AIRLINES — Ariana (FG/AFG) — Kabul (KBL)

☐ TC-SGC	Airbus A310-304	519	ex VT-EVI	Fethiya Kolot<SGX
☐ TC-SGI	Boeing 737-86J/W	28069/42	ex D-ABAO	<SGX
☐ YA-BAB	Airbus A300B4-203	180	ex VT-EHO	
☐ YA-BAC	Airbus A300B4-203	190	ex VT-EHQ	[FRA]
☐ YA-CAQ	Airbus A310-304	496	ex TC-JDA	Kabul
☐ YA-CAV	Airbus A310-304ER	497	ex TC-JDB	Kandahar
☐ YA-DAL	Antonov An-24RV	57310409	ex UR-48097	
☐ YA-DAM	Antonov An-24RV	57310404	ex YR-BMF	
☐ YA-FAM	Boeing 727-223 (Raisbeck 3)	21088/1255	ex N861AA	
☐ YA-FAN	Boeing 727-227F (FedEx 3)	21245/1202	ex 9L-LFD	
☐ YA-FAS	Boeing 727-223 (Raisbeck 3)	21388/1345	ex N876AA	
☐ YA-FAT	Boeing 727-221/W (Duganair 3)	22542/1799	ex 5N-BFY	
☐ YA-FAY	Boeing 727-228	22289/1719	ex F-GCDH	

KABUL AIR — Kabul (KBL)

☐ YA-KAC	Antonov An-12BP	5343204	ex ER-ACO
☐ YA-KAD	Antonov An-12BP	6343810	ex ER-ACR
☐ YA-KAN	Ilyushin Il-76TD	0043449468	ex RDPL-34146

KAM AIR — Kamgar (RQ/KMF) — Kabul (KBL)

☐ EY-87963	Yakovlev Yak-40K	9831058	ex EP-EAK	<TJK
☐ YA-GAD	Boeing 727-243	22702/1814	ex YU-AKM	
☐ YA-KAM	Boeing 767-222	21879/49	ex N619UA	
☐ YA-KMB	Antonov An-26B	17311802	ex EK-26199	
☐ YA-KMC	Antonov An-24RV	37309008	ex Z3-AAI	
☐ YA-KMF	McDonnell-Douglas MD-82	49704/1490	ex N959U	
☐ YA-KMG	McDonnell-Douglas MD-83	49567/1367	ex N9306T	♦
☐ YA-VIB	Douglas DC-8-63AF (BAC 3)	46034/434	ex A6-HLA	♦
☐ YA-VIC	Douglas DC-8-63F (BAC 3)	46035/438	ex A6-HLB	♦

PAMIR AIR — Pamir (NR/PIR) — Kabul (KBL)

☐ YA-PIB	Boeing 737-4Y0	26077/2425	ex TC-JET	
☐ YA-PID	Boeing 737-4Y0	26085/2468	ex TC-JEV	
☐ YA-PIR	Boeing 737-232 (Nordam 3)	23077/996	ex N305DL	Star of Kabul
☐ EY-538	Boeing 737-4Y0	23980/1667	ex N239DT	

SAFI AIRWAYS — Kabul (KBL)

☐ YA-AQS	Boeing 767-2J6ER	23745/156	ex B-2554	
☐ YA-HSB	Boeing 737-3J6	23303/1237	ex B-2532	City of Mazar
☐ YA-SFL	Boeing 737-3J6	23302/1224	ex B-2531	City of Heart
☐ YA-TTB	Airbus A340-311	015	ex F-WBSR	
☐ YA-TTC	Airbus A320-212	0671	ex 9A-CTM	♦

YI- IRAQ (Republic of Iraq)

AZMAR AIRLINES

☐ C5-JDZ	Douglas DC-9-31	48145/1042	ex N925VJ
☐ C5-LPS	Douglas DC-9-31	48146/1044	ex N926VJ

IRAQI AIRWAYS — Iraqi (IA/IAW) — Baghdad-Al Muthana/Intl (BGW/SDA)

☐ YI-APW	Boeing 737-2B7 (Nordam 3)	22885/966	ex 9L-LEG	Lsd fr/op by TBN
☐ YI-APY	Boeing 737-201 (Nordam 3)	22274/682	ex J2-KCM	Lsd fr/op by TBN
☐ YI-APZ	Boeing 737-201 (Nordam 3)	22354/736	ex JY-JRA	
☐ YI-AQA	Canadair CRJ-900NG	15189	ex C-FULE	
☐ YI-AQB	Canadair CRJ-900NG	15202	ex C-FWPF	
☐ YI-AQC	Canadair CRJ-900NG	15213	ex C-FWZH	
☐ YI-AQD	Canadair CRJ-900NG	15220	ex C-FYED	
☐ YI-AQK	Boeing 737-7BD/W	33935/2315	ex N331AT	
☐ YI-AQL	Boeing 737-7BD/W	35789/2201	ex N317AT	
☐ YI-AQN	Boeing 737-322	24717/1930	ex N202UA	o/o♦
☐ YI-AQO	Boeing 737-322	24673/1920	ex N398UA	
☐ EY-537	Boeing 737-4B7	24550/1793	ex N245DT	
☐ XU-RKK	Boeing 737-2H4	23054/969	ex PK-LYA	<RKH
☐ 9L-LEL	Boeing 727-247 (FedEx 3)	21483/1350	ex N831WA	Lsd fr/op by TBN

KURDISTAN AIRWAYS				Erbil /Beirut (EBL/BEY)

Leases Boeing 737-200 aircraft from Dolphin Air as required

YJ-   VANUATU (Republic of Vanuatu)

AIR VANUATU		Air Van (NF/AVN)		Port Vila (VLI)
☐ YJ-AV1	Boeing 737-8Q8/W	30734/2477	ex N1779B	Spirit of Vanuatu
☐ YJ-AV3	Britten-Norman BN-2A-21 Islander	483	ex F-OCXP	
☐ YJ-AV4	Harbin Y-12 II	028	ex B-958L	
☐ YJ-AV5	Harbin Y-12 II	029	ex B-978L	
☐ YJ-AV6	Harbin Y-12 II	032	ex B-979L	
☐ YJ-AV72	ATR 72-212A	876	ex F-WNUG	
☐ YJ-RV8	de Havilland DHC-6 Twin Otter 300	703	ex F-ODGL	
☐ YJ-RV10	de Havilland DHC-6 Twin Otter 300	679	ex OY-SLI	Melanesian Princess
☐ YJ-RV16	Britten-Norman BN-2A-27 Islander	104	ex ZK-FLU	
☐ YJ-	Britten-Norman BN-2B-207 Islander	2172	ex JA5290	

UNITY AIRLINES				Port Vila (VLI)
☐ YJ-007	Britten-Norman BN-2B-21 Islander	2177	ex H4-WPG	
☐ YJ-009	Britten-Norman BN-2A-26 Islander	65	ex V7-0009	

YK-   SYRIA (Syrian Arab Republic)

CHAM WINGS AIRLINES				Damascus (DAM)
☐ SU-BOZ	McDonnell-Douglas MD-83	53192/2155	ex N192AJ	<AMV

SYRIANAIR		Syrianair (RB/SYR)		Damascus (DAM)
☐ YK-AKA	Airbus A320-232	0886	ex F-WWDH	Ugarit
☐ YK-AKB	Airbus A320-232	0918	ex F-WWIJ	Ebla
☐ YK-AKC	Airbus A320-232	1032	ex F-WWDV	Afamia
☐ YK-AKD	Airbus A320-232	1076	ex F-WWIK	Mari
☐ YK-AKE	Airbus A320-232	1085	ex F-WWIX	Bosra
☐ YK-AKF	Airbus A320-232	1117	ex F-WWBN	Amrit
☐ YK-ANA	Antonov An-24B	87304203		
☐ YK-ANC	Antonov An-26	3007		Govt operated
☐ YK-AND	Antonov An-26	3008		Govt operated
☐ YK-ANE	Antonov An-26	3103		Govt operated
☐ YK-ANF	Antonov An-26	3104		Govt operated
☐ YK-ANG	Antonov An-26B	10907		Govt operated
☐ YK-ANH	Antonov An-26B	11406		Govt operated
☐ YK-AVA	ATR 72-212A	836	ex F-WWEC	♦
☐ YK-AVB	ATR 72-212A	845	ex F-WWEK	♦
☐ YK-AGA	Boeing 727-294	21203/1188		6 Octobre	[DAM]
☐ YK-AGB	Boeing 727-294	21204/1194		Damascus	[DAM]
☐ YK-AGC	Boeing 727-294	21205/1198		Palmyra	[DAM]
☐ YK-AGD	Boeing 727-269	22360/1670	ex 9K-AFB		[DAM]
☐ YK-AGE	Boeing 727-269	22361/1716	ex 9K-AFC		[DAM]
☐ YK-AGF	Boeing 727-269	22763/1788	ex 9K-AFD		[DAM]
☐ YK-AHA	Boeing 747SP-94	21174/284		16 Novembre	[DAM]
☐ YK-AHB	Boeing 747SP-94	21175/290		Arab Solidarity	[DAM]
☐ YK-ATA	Ilyushin Il-76TD	093421613		Govt operated
☐ YK-ATB	Ilyushin Il-76T	093421619		Govt operated
☐ YK-ATC	Ilyushin Il-76T	0013431911		Govt operated
☐ YK-ATD	Ilyushin Il-76T	0013431915		Govt operated
☐ YK-AYA	Tupolev Tu-134B-3	63992		
☐ YK-AYB	Tupolev Tu-134B-3	63994		
☐ YK-AYE	Tupolev Tu-134B-3	66187		
☐ YK-AYF	Tupolev Tu-134B-3	63190		[DAM]
☐ YK-AQA	Yakovlev Yak-40	9341932		Govt operated
☐ YK-AQB	Yakovlev Yak-40	9530443		Govt operated
☐ YK-AQD	Yakovlev Yak-40	9830158		VIP Govt operated

586

☐ YK-AQE	Yakovlev Yak-40K	9830258		Govt operated
☐ YK-AQF	Yakovlev Yak-40	9931859		Govt operated
☐ YK-AQG	Yakovlev Yak-40K	9941959		Govt operated

YL-   LATVIA (Republic of Latvia)

AIR BALTIC — AirBaltic (BT/BTI) — Riga-Spilve (RIX)

☐ YL-BBD	Boeing 737-53S	29075/3101	ex F-GJNU		
☐ YL-BBE	Boeing 737-53S	29073/3083	ex EI-DDT		
☐ YL-BBF	Boeing 737-548/W	24878/1939	ex EI-CDA		
☐ YL-BBG	Boeing 737-548/W	24919/1970	ex EI-CDB		♦
☐ YL-BBH	Boeing 737-548/W	24968/1975	ex EI-CDC		
☐ YL-BBI	Boeing 737-33A/W	27454/2703	ex PT-SSQ		
☐ YL-BBJ	Boeing 737-36Q/W	30333/3117	ex D-ADIA		
☐ YL-BBK	Boeing 737-33V/W	29332/3072	ex HA-LKR		
☐ YL-BBL	Boeing 737-33V/W	29334/3089	ex HA-LKS		
☐ YL-BBM	Boeing 737-522	26680/2366	ex N680MV		
☐ YL-BBN	Boeing 737-522	26683/2368	ex N683MV		
☐ YL-BBP	Boeing 737-522	26688/2404	ex N688MV		
☐ YL-BBQ	Boeing 737-522	26691/2408	ex N691MV		
☐ YL-BBR	Boeing 737-31S	29266/3092	ex G-OTDA		
☐ YL-BBS	Boeing 737-31S	29267/3093	ex G-GSPN		
☐ YL-BBX	Boeing 737-36Q/W	30334/3120	ex D-ADIB		
☐ YL-BBY	Boeing 737-36Q/W	30335/3129	ex D-ADIC		
☐ YL-BDB	Boeing 757-256/W	26251/897	ex EC-HDR		
☐ YL-BDC	Boeing 757-256/W	26253/902	ex EC-HDU		
☐ YL-BAE	de Havilland DHC-8-402Q	4289	ex C-FZGL		
☐ YL-BAF	de Havilland DHC-8-402Q	4293	ex C-GAUI		
☐ YL-BAH	de Havilland DHC-8-402Q	4296	ex C-GBJA		
☐ YL-BAI	de Havilland DHC-8-402Q	4302	ex C-GCKV		♦
☐ YL-BAJ	de Havilland DHC-8-402Q	4309	ex C-GCQG		♦
☐ YL-BAQ	de Havilland DHC-8-402Q	4313	ex C-GDDU		♦
☐ YL-BAX	de Havilland DHC-8-402Q	4324	ex C-GLTI		♦
☐ YL-BAY	de Havilland DHC-8-402Q	4331	ex C-GKLC		♦
☐ LY-BAO	Fokker 50	20189	ex YL-LAO		
☐ LY-BAV	Fokker 50	20190	ex YL-BAV		
☐ LY-BAZ	Fokker 50	20153	ex YL-BAZ		
☐ YL-BAA	Fokker 50	20120	ex SE-LEB		
☐ YL-BAC	Fokker 50	20216	ex SE-LFS		
☐ YL-BAR	Fokker 50	20149	ex PH-LVL	Cesis	
☐ YL-BAS	Fokker 50	20162	ex OY-KAE	Zemgale	
☐ YL-BAT	Fokker 50	20163	ex OY-KAF	Riga	
☐ YL-BAU	Fokker 50	20126	ex PH-AAO		
☐ YL-BAW	Fokker 50	20148	ex OY-MMS		

INVERSIJA — Inver (INV) — Riga-Spilve (RIX)

☐ YL-LAK	Ilyushin Il-76T	0003424707	ex RA-76522 Adagold titles	
☐ YL-LAL	Ilyushin Il-76T	0013433984	ex RA-76755	

KS AVIA — Sky Camel (KSA) — Riga-Spilve (RIX)

☐ YL-KSA	Antonov An-74-200	36547098957	ex RA-74030	
☐ YL-KSB	Antonov An-74	36547136013	ex UR-CAC	

RAF-AVIA — Mitavia (MTL) — Riga-Spilve (RIX)

☐ YL-RAA	Antonov An-26B	97311206	ex RA-26064	
☐ YL-RAB	Antonov An-26B	07310508	ex RA-26032 ACS logo	
☐ YL-RAC	Antonov An-26	07309903	ex CCCP-79169	ACS logo
☐ YL-RAD	Antonov An-26B	47313909	ex RA-26589	
☐ YL-RAE	Antonov An-26B	57314004	ex CCCP-26200	
☐ YL-RAF	Antonov An-74TK-100	36547095905	ex UR-CAE	<CBI
☐ YL-RAG	SAAB SF.340A	340A-052	ex SE-E52	Frtr
☐ YL-RAH	SAAB SF.340A	340A-081	ex EC-IRD	Frtr

SMARTLYNX — (6Y/ART) — Riga-Spilve (RIX)

☐ YL-BBC	Airbus A320-211	0142	ex SX-BVD	
☐ YL-BCB	Airbus A320-211	0726	ex EK-32007	
☐ YL-LCA	Airbus A320-211	0333	ex 4X-ABC	♦

☐ YL-LCB	Airbus A320-211	0384	ex 4X-ABD		♦
☐ YL-LCC	Airbus A320-211	0310	ex C-FKPS		
☐ YL-LCD	Airbus A320-211	0359	ex C-FMSV		
☐ YL-LCE	Airbus A320-211	0311	ex F-HDCE		
☐ YL-LCG	Airbus A320-211	0283	ex N754US		♦
☐ YL-LCH	Airbus A320-212	0814	ex EI-DJH		♦
☐ YL-LCY	Boeing 767-3Y0ER	24952/357	ex C-GGFJ		>BBR
☐ YL-LCZ	Boeing 767-3Y0ER	25000/386	ex C-GHPA		>BBR

YN- NICARAGUA (Republic of Nicaragua)

AIR CHARTER CARGO   Managua (MGA)

☐ YN-CGA	Antonov An-32	3007	ex HP-1217AVL	

Last flown in 2006 but kept in an airworthy state and available for charter

ATLANTIC AIRWAYS   Atlantic Nicaragua (AYN)   Managua (MGA)

☐ YN-CFL	LET L-410UVP-E3	871917	ex OK-SDH	
☐ YN-CFR	LET L-410UVP	861705	ex TG-CFD	

LA COSTENA   Lacostena   Managua (MGA)

☐ YN-CHG	ATR 42-320	323	ex F-OHGL	♦
☐ YN-CFO	Cessna 208B Caravan I	208B0758	ex N5264M	
☐ YN-CGB	Cessna 208B Caravan I	208B0611	ex HP-1407APP	
☐ YN-CGI	Cessna 208B Caravan I	208B0638	ex HR-IBI	
☐ YN-CGU	Cessna 208B Caravan I	208B0607	ex HP-1400	
☐ YN-CGG	Short SD.3-60	SH3612	ex HP-1318APP	<APP

YR- ROMANIA (Republic of Romania)

BLUE AIR   Blue Transport (0B/JOR)   Bucharest-Baneasa (BBU)

☐ YR-BAC	Boeing 737-377	23653/1260	ex ZK-SLA	<AWK
☐ YR-BAE	Boeing 737-4Y0	28723/2886	ex EI-CXL	
☐ YR-BAF	Boeing 737-322F	24453/1730	ex N360UA	
☐ YR-BAG	Boeing 737-5L9	24778/1816	ex N494ST	
☐ YR-BAH	Boeing 737-505	24274/2035	ex LN-BRK	♦
☐ YR-BAI	Boeing 737-4Y0	24314/1680	ex EI-ELU	♦
☐ YR-BAJ	Boeing 737-430	27005/2359	ex EI-COJ	♦
☐ YR-BAK	Boeing 737-430	27003/2328	ex EI-COK	♦
☐ YR-DAA	SAAB SF.340A	340A-116	ex SE-F16	
☐ YR-DAB	SAAB SF.340A	340A-137	ex SE-ISN	

CARPATAIR   Carpatair (V3/KRP)   Timisoara-Giarmata (TSR)

☐ YR-SBA	SAAB 2000	2000-038	ex HB-IZV	<SWR
☐ YR-SBB	SAAB 2000	2000-026	ex HB-IZN	<SWR
☐ YR-SBC	SAAB 2000	2000-039	ex HB-IZW	<SWR
☐ YR-SBD	SAAB 2000	2000-004	ex HB-IZA	<SWR
☐ YR-SBE	SAAB 2000	2000-041	ex HB-IZX	<SWR
☐ YR-SBI	SAAB 2000	2000-052	ex SE-LSH	
☐ YR-SBJ	SAAB 2000	2000-018	ex HB-IZK	<SWR
☐ YR-SBK	SAAB 2000	2000-033	ex HB-IZR	<SWR
☐ YR-SBL	SAAB 2000	2000-013	ex SE-LOT	
☐ YR-SBM	SAAB 2000	2000-014	ex SE-014	
☐ YR-SBN	SAAB 2000	2000-044	ex SE-LSC	
☐ YR-FKA	Fokker 100	11340	ex C-GKZC	
☐ YR-FKB	Fokker 100	11369	ex C-GKZK	
☐ YR-KMA	Fokker 70	11564	ex HA-LMA	
☐ YR-KMB	Fokker 70	11565	ex HA-LMB	♦
☐ YR-KMC	Fokker 70	11569	ex HA-LMC	♦
☐ YR-VGP	SAAB SF.340B	340B-228	ex HB-AKO	

JETRAN INTERNATIONAL AIRWAYS   Air Romania (MDJ)   Bucharest-Baneasa (BBU)

☐ YR-MDJ	McDonnell-Douglas MD-81	48053/986	ex 3D-JET	all-white
☐ YR-MDK	McDonnell-Douglas MD-82	49139/1090	ex N822US	Stage 4 demonstrator

☐ YR-MDL	McDonnell-Douglas MD-82	48079/1016	ex N991PG	[BBU]
☐ YR-MDR	McDonnell-Douglas MD-82	48097/1059	ex TC-MNR	all-white
☐ YR-MDS	McDonnell-Douglas MD-82	48098/1060	ex TC-MNS	
☐ YR-MDT	McDonnell-Douglas MD-82	49570/1440	ex EC-GTO	
☐ YR-OTN	McDonnell-Douglas MD-82	49119/1070	ex YR-MDM	

MEDALLION AIR — HBucharest-Baneasa (BBU)

☐ YR-HBA	McDonnell-Douglas MD-82	49937/1784	ex N983JJ

MIA AIRLINES — Salline (JLA) — Bucharest-Baneasa (BBU)

☐ YR-HRS	BAC One-Eleven 488GH (QTA 3)	259	ex G-MAAH	
☐ YR-MIA	BAC One-Eleven 492GM (QTA 3)	260	ex HR-ATS	Mirjane

ROMAVIA — Aeromavia (WQ/RMV) — Bucharest-Baneasa/Otopeni (BBU/OTP)

☐ EX-115	Ilyushin Il-18	187009904	ex UN-75001		
☐ YR-ABB	Boeing 707-3K1C (Comtran 2)	20804/883		CarpatiRomania titles	VIP

TAROM — Tarom (RO/ROT) — Bucharest-Otopeni (OTP)

☐ YR-ATA	ATR 42-500	566	ex F-WWLF	Dunarea	
☐ YR-ATB	ATR 42-500	569	ex F-WWLH	Bistrita	
☐ YR-ATC	ATR 42-500	589	ex F-WWLR	Mures	
☐ YR-ATD	ATR 42-500	591	ex F-WWLS	Cris	
☐ YR-ATE	ATR 42-500	596	ex F-WWLY	Olt	
☐ YR-ATF	ATR 42-500	599	ex F-WWEB	Arges	
☐ YR-ATG	ATR 42-500	605	ex F-WWLG	Dambovita	
☐ YR-ATH	ATR 72-212	861	ex F-WWEH	Somes	
☐ YR-ATI	ATR 72-212	867	ex F-WWER	Ialomita	
☐ YR-BGA	Boeing 737-38J	27179/2524	ex N5573K	Alba Iulia	
☐ YR-BGB	Boeing 737-38J	27180/2529		Bucuresti	
☐ YR-BGD	Boeing 737-38J	27182/2663		Devaspecial c/s	
☐ YR-BGE	Boeing 737-38J	27395/2671		Timisoara	
☐ YR-BGF	Boeing 737-78J	28440/795		Brâila	
☐ YR-BGG	Boeing 737-78J	28442/827		Craiova	
☐ YR-BGH	Boeing 737-78J	28438/1394		Hunedoara	
☐ YR-BGI	Boeing 737-78J/W	28439/1419		Iasi	♦
☐ YR-BGP	Boeing 737-86J/W	37740/2638	ex D-ABKB	Ploiesti	
☐ YR-BGR	Boeing 737-86J/W	37741/2686	ex D-ABKC		
☐ YR-BGS	Boeing 737-8GJ/W	37360/2783	ex N1787B	Sibiu	o/o
☐ YR-LCA	Airbus A310-325	636	ex F-WQAV	Transilvania	
☐ YR-LCB	Airbus A310-325	644	ex F-WQAX	Moldova	
☐ YR-ASA	Airbus A318-111	2931	ex D-AUAC	Aurel Vlaicu - Aviation Pioneer	
☐ YR-ASB	Airbus A318-111	2955	ex D-AUAE	Traian Vuia - Aviation Pioneer	
☐ YR-ASC	Airbus A318-111	3220	ex D-AUAF	Henri Coanda - Aviation Pioneer	
☐ YR-ASD	Airbus A318-111	3225	ex D-AUAG		

YS- EL SALVADOR (Republic of El Salvador)

TACA INTERNATIONAL AIRLINES — Taca (TA/TAI) — San Salvador-Comalapa Intl (SAL)

☐ N471TA	Airbus A319-132	1066	ex D-AVWE		>TPU
☐ N472TA	Airbus A319-132	1113	ex D-AVWU		>TPU
☐ N476TA	Airbus A319-132	1934	ex D-AVWH		
☐ N477TA	Airbus A319-132	1952	ex D-AVWK		
☐ N478TA	Airbus A319-132	2339	ex D-AVWG	Aviateca titles	
☐ N479TA	Airbus A319-132	2444	ex D-AVWS	Aviateca titles	
☐ N480TA	Airbus A319-132	3057	ex D-AVYV		
☐ N520TA	Airbus A319-132	3248	ex D-AVWH		
☐ N521TA	Airbus A319-132	3276	ex D-AVYK		
☐	Airbus A319-132		ex		o/o♦
☐	Airbus A319-132		ex		o/o♦
☐	Airbus A319-132		ex		o/o♦
☐ EI-TAB	Airbus A320-233	1624	ex N485TA	Mensajero de Esperanza	
☐ EI-TAD	Airbus A320-233	1334	ex N462TA		
☐ EI-TAG	Airbus A320-233	2791	ex (N495TA)		
☐ N490TA	Airbus A320-232	2282	ex F-WWBO		
☐ N491TA	Airbus A320-233	2301	ex F-WWDF		
☐ N492TA	Airbus A320-233	2434	ex F-WWDL		
☐ N493TA	Airbus A320-233	2917	ex F-WWDR		
☐ N494TA	Airbus A320-233	3042	ex F-WWDM		

☐ N495TA	Airbus A320-233	3103	ex F-WWIH		
☐ N496TA	Airbus A320-233	3113	ex F-WWIU		
☐ N497TA	Airbus A320-233	3378	ex F-WWDK		
☐ N498TA	Airbus A320-233	3418	ex F-WWIO		
☐ N499TA	Airbus A320-233	3510	ex F-WWBX		
☐ N680TA	Airbus A320-233	3538	ex F-WWIF		
☐ N681TA	Airbus A320-233	3577	ex F-WWBO		
☐ N682TA	Airbus A320-233	3581	ex F-WWDC		
☐	Airbus A320-233		ex		o/o♦
☐	Airbus A320-233		ex		o/o♦
☐	Airbus A320-233		ex		o/o♦
☐ N564TA	Airbus A321-231	2862	ex D-AVZB		
☐ N566TA	Airbus A321-231	2553	ex D-AVZJ		
☐ N567TA	Airbus A321-231	2610	ex D-AVZM		
☐ N568TA	Airbus A321-231	2687	ex D-AVZE		
☐ N570TA	Airbus A321-231	3869	ex D-AVZO		
☐ N982TA	Embraer ERJ-190AR	19000259	ex PT-STH		
☐ N983TA	Embraer ERJ-190AR	19000265	ex PT-TLF		
☐ N984TA	Embraer ERJ-190AR	19000273	ex PT-TLN		
☐ N985TA	Embraer ERJ-190AR	19000287	ex PT-TZB		
☐ N986TA	Embraer ERJ-190AR	19000360	ex PT-XNB		♦
☐ N987TA	Embraer ERJ-190AR	19000393	ex PT-XNZ		♦
☐ N988TA	Embraer ERJ-190AR	19000399	ex PT-XUE		♦

YU- SERBIA (Republic of Serbia)

AVIOGENEX — Genex (AGX) — Belgrade (BEG)

| ☐ YU-ANP | Boeing 737-2K3 (Nordam 3) | 23912/1401 | | Zadar |

JAT AIRWAYS — JAT (JU/JAT) — Belgrade (BEG)

☐ YU-AND	Boeing 737-3H9	23329/1134		City of Krusevac
☐ YU-ANF	Boeing 737-3H9	23330/1136		
☐ YU-ANH	Boeing 737-3H9	23415/1171	ex TC-CYO	
☐ YU-ANI	Boeing 737-3H9	23416/1175	ex Z3-AAA	
☐ YU-ANJ	Boeing 737-3H9	23714/1305	ex TC-MIO	
☐ YU-ANK	Boeing 737-3H9	23715/1310		
☐ YU-ANL	Boeing 737-3H9	23716/1321	ex Z3-ARF	
☐ YU-ANV	Boeing 737-3H9	24140/1524		
☐ YU-ANW	Boeing 737-3H9	24141/1526	ex TS-IED	
☐ YU-AON	Boeing 737-3Q4	24208/1490	ex N181LF	
☐ YU-AJK	Douglas DC-9-32	47568/689	ex Z3-ARD	
☐ YU-ALN	ATR 72-202	180	ex F-WWEP	
☐ YU-ALO	ATR 72-202	186	ex F-WWEW	
☐ YU-ALP	ATR 72-202	189	ex F-WWED	all-white
☐ YU-ALS	ATR 72-202	140	ex ES-KRB	

KOSMAS AIR CARGO — Kosmas Cargo (KMG) — Belgrade (BEG)

| ☐ YU-AMI | Ilyushin Il-76MD | 0093499982 | ex RA-76822 |

UNITED INTERNATIONAL AIRLINES — (UIL) — Sofia (SOF)

| ☐ YU-UIA | Antonov An-12 | 02348007 | ex LZ-SFA |

YV- VENEZUELA (Bolivarian Republic of Venezuela)

AECA

| ☐ YV211T | Douglas DC-3 | 10201 | ex HK-2666X |
| ☐ YV214T | Douglas DC-6 | 43708/347 | ex HK-4046X |

AERO CARIBE

| ☐ YV1427 | LET L-410UVP | 841224 | ex YV-595C |

AERO EJECUTIVOS — Venejecutiv (VEJ) — Caracas-Simon Bolivar Intl (CCS)

☐ YV1434	LET L-410UVP-E	872014	ex YV-1026CP
☐ YV1854	Douglas DC-3	6135	ex YV-500C
☐ YV201T	Douglas DC-3	11775	ex YV-1179C

☐ YV-426C	Douglas DC-3	4093	ex N10DC	
☐ YV-440C	Douglas DC-3	2201	ex N31PB	Caballo Viejostatus?

AERO FLY MONAGAS

☐ YV1518	LET L-410UVP-E	882022	ex YV-1028CP

AEROBOL - AEROVIAS BOLIVAR   Ciudad Bolivar (CBL)

☐ YV-315C	Cessna U206G Stationair 6	U20604323	ex YV-1465P
☐ YV-387C	Cessna U206G Stationair 6	U20605398	ex YV-1310P
☐ YV-389C	Cessna U206G Stationair 6		
☐ YV-408C	Cessna U206G Stationair 6		
☐ YV-615C	Cessna U206G Stationair 6	U20604759	ex YV-1704P
☐ YV-849C	Cessna U206G Stationair 6		
☐ YV-946C	Cessna U206G Stationair 6		
☐ YV-270C	Britten-Norman BN-2A-20 Islander	573	ex YV-142CP
☐ YV-288C	Cessna 207A Stationair 8	20700708	ex YV-2143P
☐ YV-380C	Cessna 207A Stationair 8		

AEROMED

☐ YV2027	LET L-410UVP	861713	YV-1023CP

AEROPANAMERICANO

☐ YV1674	Beech 1900C-1	UC-47	ex HK-4325
☐ YV1734	Beech 1900	UB-47	ex YV-687CP

AEROPOSTAL   Aeropostal (VH/LAV)   Caracas-Simon Bolivar Intl (CCS)

☐ YV1120	Douglas DC-9-51	47705/842	ex YV-20C	El Guayanes
☐ YV1121	Douglas DC-9-51	47719/845	ex YV-21C	El Zuliano
☐ YV1122	Douglas DC-9-51	47703/841	ex YV-22C	El Margariteno
☐ YV1123	Douglas DC-9-32	47727/848	ex YV-24C	El Falconiano
☐ YV1124	Douglas DC-9-32	47721/847	ex YV-25C	El Andino
☐ YV1126	Douglas DC-9-51	47782/893	ex YV-33C	El Venezolano
☐ YV1127	Douglas DC-9-34CF	47752/872	ex YV-37C	El Llanero
☐ YV135T	Douglas DC-9-51	47712/815	ex YV-35C	El Larense
☐ YV136T	Douglas DC-9-51 (ABS 3)	47738/830	ex YV-14C	
☐ YV137T	Douglas DC-9-51 (ABS 3)	47771/883	ex YV-15C	
☐ YV138T	Douglas DC-9-51	47656/783	ex YV-42C	
☐ YV139T	Douglas DC-9-51	47695/806	ex YV-43C	
☐ YV140T	Douglas DC-9-51	47694/805	ex YV-44C	
☐ YV141T	Douglas DC-9-32	47535/610	ex YV-46C	
☐ YV142T	Douglas DC-9-32	45847/394	ex YV-48C	
☐ YV143T	Douglas DC-9-32	47539/637	ex YV-49C	special colours
☐ YV148T	Douglas DC-9-51	47713/820	ex YV-10C	id not confirmed
☐ N120DL	Boeing 767-332	23279/154		<RYN
☐ (YV1327)	McDonnell-Douglas MD-82	49103/1083	ex YV132T	[MIA]
☐ YV130T	McDonnell-Douglas MD-83	49822/1539	ex YV-01C	[CCS]
☐ YV-40C	Boeing 727-231 (Super 27)	21632/1462	ex N54345	[CCS]

AEROSERVICIOS OK

☐ YV1752	LET L-410UVP-E	861719	ex YV-1776C

AEROSERVICIOS RANGER   Caracas-La Carlota/Lagunillas/Tumeremo (-/LGY/TMO)

☐ YV-429C	Bell 206B JetRanger III	1959	ex N9910K
☐ YV-431C	Bell 206B JetRanger III	2588	
☐ YV-433C	Bell 206B JetRanger II	2106	ex YV-330CP
☐ YV-455C	Bell 206B JetRanger	1481	ex N218AL
☐ YV-457C	Bell 206B JetRanger III	2470	ex N50056
☐ YV-571C	Bell 206B JetRanger	273	ex N59Q
☐ YV-572C	Bell 206B JetRanger	644	ex N7906J
☐ YV1204	Britten-Norman BN-2A-26 Islander	56	ex YV-920C
☐ YV1241	Britten-Norman BN-2A-26 Islander	149	ex YV-921C

AEROTECHNICA   Acarigua (AGV)

☐ YV-101C	Bell 206B JetRanger	459	ex YV-C-GAA
☐ YV-103C	Bell 206B JetRanger III	3211	
☐ YV-104C	Bell 206B JetRanger	467	ex YV-C-GAH
☐ YV-105C	Bell 206B JetRanger	889	ex YV-C-GAL
☐ YV-106C	Bell 206B JetRanger	414	ex YV-C-GAM

☐ YV-108C	Bell 206B JetRanger III	2384				
☐ YV-109C	Bell 206B JetRanger III	2402				
☐ YV-110C	Bell 206B JetRanger	1119	ex N83005			
☐ YV-112C	Bell 206B JetRanger III	3213				
☐ YV-115C	Bell 206B JetRanger II	2099	ex GN-7637			
☐ YV-116C	Bell 206B JetRanger II	2190	ex N103K			
☐ YV-117C	Bell 206B JetRanger III	2692				
☐ YV-118C	Bell 206B JetRanger III	3409				
☐ YV-122C	Bell 206B JetRanger II	1984				
☐ YV-124C	Bell 206B JetRanger III	2215				
☐ YV-251C	Bell 206B JetRanger	1106	ex YV-T-AIN			
☐ YV-254C	Bell 206B JetRanger II	2059	ex N9934K			
☐ YV-320C	Bell 206B JetRanger III	2248				
☐ YV-321C	Bell 206B JetRanger III	2496				
☐ YV-322C	Bell 206B JetRanger III	3359				
☐ YV-323C	Bell 206B JetRanger	874				
☐ YV-325C	Bell 206B JetRanger II	2095	ex GN7635			
☐ YV-326C	Bell 206B JetRanger	1858				
☐ YV-327C	Bell 206B JetRanger	1355	ex YV-235CP			
☐ YV-328C	Bell 206B JetRanger III	3308				
☐ YV-329C	Bell 206B JetRanger III	3336				
☐ YV-333C	Bell 206B JetRanger	1699	ex YV-141CP			
☐ YV-121C	Bell 206L-1 LongRanger II	45501	ex N57480			
☐ YV1465	Beech 65-E90 King Air	LW-234	ex YV-118CP			
☐ YV-730C	Bell 412					

ASAP CHARTER

☐ YV1404	Yakovlev Yak-40	9441137	ex YV-1100CP		VIP

ASERCA AIRLINES — Aserca (R7/OCA) — Caracas-Simon Bolivar Intl (CCS)

☐ YV116T	Douglas DC-9-31	45867/283	ex YV-705C	Virgen del Valle	wfu 2008
☐ YV117T	Douglas DC-9-31	47272/390	ex YV-707C	Virgen de la Coromato	wfu?
☐ YV119T	Douglas DC-9-31	47271/389	ex YV-710C	Virgen de Loreto	
☐ YV122T	Douglas DC-9-31	45875/365	ex YV-706C	Virgen de la Chinita	
☐ YV125T	Douglas DC-9-31	47157/322	ex YV-719C	El Ejecutivas	yellow tail c/s
☐ YV241T	Douglas DC-9-31	48118/942	ex N942AA	San Rafael	all blue c/s
☐ YV298T	Douglas DC-9-31	48147/1048	ex N940AA		dam 12Feb08
☐ YV367T	Douglas DC-9-32	47128/210	ex N614NW	Nuestra Señora del Rosario	
☐ YV368T	Douglas DC-9-32	47518/614	ex N619NW	Madre Teresa de Calcuta	
☐ YV371T	Douglas DC-9-32	47235/436	ex N617NW	San Augustin	
☐ YV372T	Douglas DC-9-32	47575/680	ex N622NW	Santa Teresa de Jesus	
☐ YV1492	Douglas DC-9-31	45864/130	ex YV-708C	Virgen de Socorro	
☐ YV1663	Douglas DC-9-31	48144/1039	ex PJ-SNK	Virgen de La Milagrosa	
☐ YV1879	Douglas DC-9-31	48139/1024	ex YV114T	Virgen del Pilar	
☐ YV1921	Douglas DC-9-31	48154/1046	ex YV111T	Cristo de Jose	
☐ YV1922	Douglas DC-9-31	48138/1021	ex YV115T	Santisima Trinidad	
☐ YV2220	Douglas DC-9-31	48155/1050	ex YV297T	Nuestra Señora de Lourdes	♦
☐ YV2259	Douglas DC-9-31	48120/949	ex YV243T	San Miguel Arcangel	all green c/s
☐ YV2431	Douglas DC-9-31	48119/943	ex YV242T	San Francisco de Asis	
☐ YV2433	Douglas DC-9-31	48141/1030	ex YV244T	San Cristobal	
☐ YV2434	Douglas DC-9-31	47473/598	ex YV286T	San Judas Tadeo	
☐ YV2444	Douglas DC-9-32 (ABS 3)	47282/446	ex YV248T	Espiritu Santo	white c/s
☐ YV2445	Douglas DC-9-32 (ABS 3)	47479/605	ex YV249T	Juan Pablo II	white c/s
☐ YV	Douglas DC-9-32	47129/225	ex N615NW		
☐ YV	Douglas DC-9-31	47249/297	ex N977Z		[ROW]
☐ YV	Douglas DC-9-31	47343/460	ex N979Z		[ROW]

AVIOR AIRLINES — Avior (9V/ROI) — Barcelona (BLA)

☐ YV1364	Beech 1900D	UE-270	ex YV-401C		
☐ YV1365	Beech 1900D	UE-268	ex YV-402C		
☐ YV1366	Beech 1900D	UE-279	ex YV-403C		
☐ YV1367	Beech 1900D	UE-298	ex YV-404C		
☐ YV1368	Beech 1900D	UE-304	ex YV-406C		>ATK
☐ YV1369	Beech 1900D	UE-342	ex YV-438C		
☐ YV1370	Beech 1900D	UE-343	ex YV-466C		
☐ YV1371	Beech 1900D	UE-344	ex YV-503C		
☐ YV1372	Beech 1900D	UE-331	ex YV-660C		
☐ YV1373	Beech 1900D	UE-355	ex YV-663C		
☐ YV1374	Beech 1900D	UE-356	ex YV-664C		
☐ YV1360	Boeing 737-201 (Nordam 3)	21665/534	ex YV-917C		
☐ YV1361	Boeing 737-2H4 (AvAero 3)	22286/878	ex N85SW		
☐ YV187T	Boeing 737-2H4 (AvAero 3)	22964/933	ex N92SW		
☐ YV234T	Boeing 737-2H4 (AvAero 3)	21970/613	ex YV-643C		
☐ YV340T	Boeing 737-232 (Nordam 3)	23079/1003	ex N307DL		

☐ YV342T	Boeing 737-232 (Nordam 3)	23090/1020	ex N318DL		
☐ YV343T	Boeing 737-232 (Nordam 3)	23101/1041	ex N329DL		
☐ YV399T	Boeing 737-2Y5 (Nordam 3)	24031/1523	ex N810AL		
☐ YV1182	Cessna 208B Caravan I	208B0729	ex YV-659C		dam 21Jly07
☐ YV-925C	Cessna 208B Caravan I	208B0793	ex N52627		

CARIBBEAN FLIGHTS   Valencia Intl (VLN)

☐ YV-912C	Douglas DC-3	14506/25951	ex CP-2255	Falcon

CHAPI AIR

☐ YV1996	Britten-Norman BN-2A-7 Islander	242	ex YV178T	

CIACA AIRLINES   Ciudad Bolivar (CBL)

☐ YV-866CP	LET L-410UVP-E	861717	ex HK-4159	
☐ YV-978C	LET L-410UVP	810702	ex CCCP-67066	stored
☐ YV-1097CP	LET L-410UVP	841303	ex YV-981C	
☐ YV-1070CP	Yakovlev Yak-40	9412032	ex RA-87388	

COMERAVIA   (CVV)   Cuidad Bolivar (CBL)

☐ YV1232	LET L-410UVP	810640	ex UR-67064	
☐ YV1233	LET L-410UVP	851427	ex YV-1185C	
☐ YV1332	LET L-410UVP	831028	ex YV-906C	
☐ YV1333	LET L-401UVP-E	861709	ex YV-1108CP	
☐ YV1962	LET L-410UVP	841216	ex YV-1071C	
☐ YV	Short SD.3-60	SH3713	ex G-XPSS	

CONVIASA   Conviasa (V0/VCV)   Caracas-Simon Bolivar Intl (CCS)

☐ YV1005	ATR 42-320	491	ex F-WQNK		
☐ YV1008	ATR 42-320	346	ex F-WQNB		
☐ YV1009	ATR 42-320	487	ex F-WQNL		
☐ YV1850	ATR 72-201	276	ex F-WQNE		
☐ YV2421	ATR 72-212	482	ex F-WQNB		
☐ YV2422	ATR 72-212	486	ex F-WQNA		
☐ XA-TWR	Boeing 737-2H4 (AvAero 3)	21812/611	ex N60SW	no titles	<DMJ
☐ YV1007	Boeing 737-322	23949/1493	ex N317UA		
☐ YV2556	Boeing 737-3G7	24712/1869	ex N311AW		
☐ YV2557	Boeing 737-3G7	24633/1809	ex N306AW		
☐ YV2558	Boeing 737-232 (Nordam 3)	23096/1028	ex XA-UIZ		
☐ YV2559	Boeing 737-232 (Nordam 3)	23097/1029	ex XA-UIY		
☐ YV101T	Boeing 737-291	21747/555	ex HR-ATX		
☐ YV206T	Boeing 737-205	21184/440	ex XA-MAG		
☐ YV398T	Boeing 737-25A (Nordam 3)	23789/1392	ex OB-1799-P		
☐ YV1000	de Havilland DHC-7-102	068	ex YV-1169C		
☐ YV1003	de Havilland DHC-7-102	103	ex C-FEDO		stored
☐ YV1004	Airbus A340-211	031	ex F-WQTN		
☐ YV1115	Canadair CRJ-702NG	10271	ex N628CP		
☐ YV2088	Canadair CRJ-702NG	10274	ex N259CP		
☐ YV2115	Canadair CRJ-702NG	10275	ex N230CP		
☐ YV	Ilyushin Il-96-300	74392302014	ex RA-96014		o/o
☐ YV	Ilyushin Il-96-300	74392302011	ex RA-96017		o/o

HELITEC   Maturin (MUN)

☐ YV171T	Swearingen SA.227AC Metro III	AC-594	ex YV-1000C	
☐ YV256T	Swearingen SA.227DC Metro III	DC-899B	ex N3217P	
☐ YV1412	Swearingen SA.227TT Merlin IIIC	TT-465	ex YV-696CP	
☐ YV-808CP	Swearingen SA.227TT Merlin 300	TT-435	ex N92RC	

ISLAND AIR EXPRESS   Caracas-Simon Bolivar Intl (CCS)

☐ YV-774C	Dornier 28D-2 Skyservant	4111	ex YV-764CP	
☐ YV-776C	Dornier 28D-2 Skyservant	4144	ex YV-765CP	
☐ YV-779C	Dornier 28D-2 Skyservant			

KAVOK AIRLINES   (KVA)

☐ YV2472	British Aerospace Jetstream 32EP	973	ex N973JX	
☐ YV2532	British Aerospace Jetstream 32EP	910	ex N910AE	

LASER · Laser (QL/LER) · Caracas-Simon Bolivar Intl (CCS)

☐ YV1240	McDonnell-Douglas MD-81	49907/1734	ex N228RF	[CCS]
☐ YV1243	McDonnell-Douglas MD-81	49908/1749	ex N908RF	[CCS]
☐ YV1382	Douglas DC-9-14	45745/32	ex YV167T Aldebaran	
☐ YV166T	Douglas DC-9-32	45789/217	ex YV-881C	[CCS]
☐ YV167T	Douglas DC-9-32 (ABS 3)	47281/427	ex YV-1121C	stored
☐ YV231T	Douglas DC-9-32	47133/230	ex HK-4310X	
☐ YV331T	Douglas DC-9-31	48157/1054	ex N934LK	
☐ YV332T	Douglas DC-9-31	48158/1056	ex N935DS	

LINEA AEREA IAACA · Air Barinas (KG/BNX) · Barinas (BNS)

☐ YV1929	ATR 72-212	492	ex YV-1004C

LINEA TURISTICA AEREOTUY · Aereotuy (LD/TUY) · Caracas-Simon Bolivar Intl (CCS)

☐ YV1182	Cessna 208B Caravan I	208B0720	ex YV-659C	
☐ YV1184	de Havilland DHC-7-102	30	ex YV-639C	
☐ YV1185	de Havilland DHC-7-102	5	ex YV-638C	
☐ YV1188	Cessna 208B Caravan I	208B0955	ex YV-863C	
☐ YV382T	ATR 42-320	110	ex LN-FAP	
☐ YV383T	ATR 42-320	206	ex LN-FAR	
☐ YV-640C	de Havilland DHC-7-102	17	ex N47RM	[CCS]

ORIENTAL

☐ YV-594C	Yakovlev Yak-40	9841159	ex CU-T1221
☐ YV-1072C	Yakovlev Yak-40	9841059	ex CU-T1220

PERLA AIRLINES

☐ YV	McDonnell-Douglas MD-83	49232/1178	ex N931AS	[PMV]

RAINBOW AIR · (TZR) · Porlomar

☐ EX-024	Antonov An-26B	11901	ex RA-26096
☐ YV307T	LET L-410UVP	800407	ex CCCP-67141
☐ YV308T	LET L-410UVP	790307	ex CCCP-67111
☐ YV322T	LET L-410UVP	800507	ex LZ-MNO

RUTACA · Rutaca (RUC) · Ciudad Bolivar (CBL)

☐ YV-209C	Cessna U206D Super Skywagon	U206-1338	ex N72247	
☐ YV-210C	Cessna U206G Stationair 6	U20605354		
☐ YV-214C	Cessna U206F Stationair	U20602386	ex YV-138P	
☐ YV-229C	Cessna U206G Stationair	U20603541	ex YV-1153P	
☐ YV-379C	Cessna U206G Stationair 6	U20604150	ex YV-1633P	
☐ YV-785C	Cessna U206G Stationair	U20603889	ex YV-1314P	
☐ YV-786C	Cessna U206G Stationair 6	U20605125	ex YV-1719P	
☐ YV-789C	Cessna U206G Stationair 6	U20604803		
☐ YV-793C	Cessna U206F Stationair	U20603192		
☐ YV1381	Boeing 737-2S3 (Nordam 3)	21774/563	ex YV-216C Vinotinto c/s	
☐ YV169T	Boeing 737-2S3 (Nordam 3)	21776/577	ex YV-1155C	
☐ YV369T	Boeing 737-230 (Nordam 3)	22113/649	ex OB-1837-P	
☐ YV379T	Boeing 737-230 (Nordam 3)	22115/694	ex N215AG	
☐ YV380T	Boeing 737-230 (Nordam 3)	22127/745	ex N227AG	
☐ YV390T	Boeing 737-230 (Nordam 3)	22128/752	ex N128AG	
☐ YV396T	Boeing 737-236	23225/1102	ex N836AL	♦
☐ YV-245C	Embraer EMB.110P1 Bandeirante	110325	ex N103TN	[CBL]
☐ YV-247C	Embraer EMB.110P1 Bandeirante	110293	ex N901A	[CBL]
☐ YV-248C	Embraer EMB.110P1 Bandeirante	110376	ex N61DA	[CBL]
☐ YV-787C	Embraer EMB.110P1 Bandeirante	110403	ex N202EB Curacao	[CBL]
☐ YV-790C	Cessna 208B Caravan I	208B0527	ex N5283S	
☐ YV1950	Cessna 208B Caravan I	208B0555	ex YV-791C	
☐ YV1670	Cessna 208B Caravan I	208B0608	ex YV-792C	
☐ YV-794C	Cessna 208B Caravan I	208B0795	ex N5264U	

SANTA BARBARA AIRLINES · Santa Barbara (S3/BBR) · Maracaibo (MAR)

☐ YV1421	ATR 42-320	300	ex YV-1017C La Immaculada Concepcion
☐ YV1422	ATR 42-320	340	ex YV-1018C Virgen de Coromoto
☐ YV1423	ATR 42-320	360	ex YV-1015C Virgen del Carmen
☐ YV1424	ATR 42-320	368	ex YV-1014C Mi Chinita
☐ YV2314	ATR 42-300	038	ex PR-TTD El Fatima

☐ YV288T	Boeing 757-21B	24402/233	ex N742PA	
☐ YV304T	Boeing 757-21B	24714/262	ex N816PG	
☐ YV2242	Boeing 757-236	24119/167	ex N962PG	
☐ YV2243	Boeing 757-236	24118/163	ex N958PG	
☐ YV	Boeing 757-236	24370/218	ex N580SH	o/o♦
☐ YV	Boeing 757-236	24371/225	ex N579SH	o/o♦
☐ YL-LCY	Boeing 767-3Y0ER	24952/357	ex C-GGFJ	<LTC
☐ YL-LCZ	Boeing 767-3Y0ER	25000/386	ex C-GHPA	<LTC
☐ YV-1038C	Cessna 208B Caravan I	208B0889	ex N52677	
☐ YV-1039C	Cessna 208B Caravan I	208B0901	ex N5267K	
☐ YV-1056C	Boeing 727-2D3 (Super 27)	22269/1701	ex N969PG	
☐ YV153T	McDonnell-Douglas MD-82	49486/1317	ex N486SH	o/o
☐ YV348T	McDonnell-Douglas MD-82	49120/1071	ex N993PG	

SASCA   Porlamar

☐ YV2211	British Aerospace Jetstream 31	645	ex SE-LGC
☐ YV186T	British Aerospace Jetstream 3103	616	ex YV-1163C
☐ YV314T	British Aerospace Jetstream 31	721	ex YV176T
☐ YV315T	British Aerospace Jetstream	697	ex N827JS
☐ YV-1126C	Cessna 208B Caravan I	208B0781	ex N5268A

SERAMI   Cuidad Bolivar (CBL)

☐ YV219T	Beech 1900C-1	UC-118	ex YV-1150C

SOL AMERICA   Solamerica (ESC)   Caracas-Simon Bolivar Intl (CCS)

☐ (YV1415)	Douglas DC-3	16013/32761	ex YV-911C
☐ YV1416	Britten-Norman BN-2A Mk.III-2 Trislander	1034	ex YV-872C
☐ YV2117	Dornier 28D-2 Skyservant		
☐ YV-1120C	LET L-410UVP	841329	ex YV-982C

SOLAR CARGO   Solarcargo (OLC)   Valencia (VLN)

☐ YV1402	Antonov An-26	87307207	ex CU-T1501	<CUB
☐ YV1403	Antonov An-26	17309810	ex YV-1134C	

SUNDANCE AIR

☐ YV1544	LET L-410UVP	831032	ex YV-1114C
☐ YV2063	LET L-410UVP	831010	ex YV-1025C
☐ YV-1029C	LET L-410UVP	831027	ex PZ-TGR
☐ YV	British Aerospace Jetstream 31	909	ex N490UE

TRANACA   Ciudad Bolivar (CBL)

☐ YV-922CP	LET L-410UVP	851426	ex LY-ASB

TRANSAVEN   (VEN)   Caracas-Simon Bolivar Intl (CCS)

☐ YV1417	LET L-410UVP	830939	ex YV-980C
☐ YV1463	LET L-410UVP	861714	ex YV-864C
☐ YV2082	LET L-410UVP-E	902430	ex YV-1175C
☐ YV2083	LET L-410UVP-E	892314	ex YV-1113C
☐ YV-1117C	Britten-Norman BN-2A Mk.III-1 Trislander	1007	ex HP-899PS

TRANSCARGA INTERNATIONAL AIRWAYS   Tiaca (TIW)   Caracas-Simon Bolivar Intl (CCS)

☐ YV1149	Aero Commander 500B	500B-899	ex YV-941C	ex c/n 500A-899-B
☐ YV2546	Embraer EMB.120ER Brasilia	120017	ex N125AM	

TRANSMANDU   Ciudad Bolivar (CBL)

☐ YV1019	British Aerospace Jetstream 32	911	ex N491UE
☐ YV	British Aerospace Jetstream 32	884	ex N476UE

TRANSPORTE AIR IGLESIAS

☐ YV1844	LET L-410UVP	831114	ex YV-953C	no titles

TRANSVALCASA

☐ YV128T	Swearingen SA.226T Merlin II	TT-507

TURISMO AEREO AMAZONAS

☐ YV1157	LET L-410UVP	851412	ex HH-PRT
☐ YV1219	LET L-410UVP	851319	ex YV1147C

VENESCAR INTERNACIONAL — Vecar (V4/VEC) — Caracas-Simon Bolivar Intl (CCS)

☐ YV2308	ATR 42-300F	061	ex YV157T	302		DHL c/s
☐ YV2309	Boeing 727-31F (FedEx 3)	20114/712	ex YV156T			DHL c/s
☐ YV155T	Boeing 727-223F (FedEx 3)	20992/1187	ex YV-905C	408		DHL c/s
☐ YV	Boeing 727-227F (FedEx 3)	21996/1571	ex N781DH			

VENEZOLANA — Venezolana (VNE) — Caracas-Simon Bolivar Intl (CCS)

☐ YV260T	Boeing 737-200				
☐ YV268T	Boeing 737-232 (AvAero 3)	23099/1035	ex N327DL		
☐ YV287T	Boeing 737-217 (AvAero 3)	22728/911	ex N168WP		
☐ YV295T	Boeing 737-217 (AvAero 3)	21717/581	ex N167WP		
☐ YV296T	Boeing 737-2T5 (AvAero 3)	22024/641	ex N166WP		
☐ YV302T	Boeing 737-2T5 (AvAero 3)	23087/1013	ex N315DL		
☐ YV341T	Boeing 737-232 (Nordam 3)	23089/1019	ex N317DL		
☐ YV191T	McDonnell-Douglas MD-83	49392/1272	ex N392AP		
☐ YV179T	British Aerospace Jetstream 31	759	ex YV-1086C		
☐ YV180T	British Aerospace Jetstream 31	770	ex YV-1093C		
☐ YV-1084C	British Aerospace Jetstream 31	734	ex OB-1784-T		
☐ YV-1085C	British Aerospace Jetstream 31	729	ex OB-1785-T		
☐ YV270T	British Aerospace Jetstream 41	41097	ex N329UE		
☐ YV280T	British Aerospace Jetstream 41	41027	ex N314UE		
☐ YV283T	British Aerospace Jetstream 41	41033	ex N315UE		
☐ YV293T	British Aerospace Jetstream 41	41026	ex N313UE		
☐ YV	British Aerospace Jetstream 41	41020	ex N306UE		
☐ YV	British Aerospace Jetstream 41	41029	ex N311UE		o/o
☐ YV	British Aerospace Jetstream 41	41031	ex N317UE		o/o

WYNGS AVIATION

☐ YV1106	Beech 1900D	UE-241	ex YV-1152CP	
☐ YV188T	Beech 1900D	UE-294	ex YV-955CP all-white	

Operator Unknown

☐ YV1275	Antonov An-26	07310607	ex YV-965CP
☐ YV2263	LET L-410UVP	872016	ex YV-1003CP

Z-   ZIMBABWE (Republic of Zimbabwe)

AIR ZIMBABWE — Air Zimbabwe (UM/AZW) — Harare-International (HRE)

☐ Z-WPA	Boeing 737-2N0	23677/1313	ex C9-BAG	Mbuya Nehanda	
☐ Z-WPB	Boeing 737-2N0	23678/1405		Great Zimbabwe	
☐ Z-WPC	Boeing 737-2N0	23679/1415		Matojeni	
☐ Z-WPD	British Aerospace 146 Srs.200	E2065	ex G-5-065	Jongu'e	stored
☐ Z-WPE	Boeing 767-2N0ER	24713/287		Victoria Falls	
☐ Z-WPF	Boeing 767-2N0ER	24867/333		Chimanimani	
☐ Z-WPJ	CAIC MA60	0302	ex B-674L	Nyami-Nyami	
☐ Z-WPK	CAIC MA60	0303		A'sambeni	
☐ Z-WPL	CAIC MA60	0304			

AVIENT AVIATION — Avavia (Z3/SMJ) — Harare-International (HRE)

☐ Z-ALS	Douglas DC-10-30F	46976/254	ex N372BC		
☐ Z-ALT	Douglas DC-10-30F	47818/305	ex 5X-ROY		
☐ Z-ARL	Douglas DC-10-30CF	47907/157	ex N10MB		
☐ Z-AVT	Douglas DC-10-30F	46590/266	ex N401JR	Victor Trimble	
☐ Z-BVT	McDonnell-Douglas MD-11BCF	48410/495	ex N575SH		o/o

DHL AVIATION (ZIMBABWE) — Harare-International (HRE)

☐ Z-KPS	Cessna 208B Caravan I	208B0303	ex N31SE

EXEC-AIR — Axair (LFL) — Harare-Charles Prince

☐ Z-WFP	Cessna 402A	402A0013	ex VP-WFP
☐ Z-WLW	Cessna 210M Centurion II	21061178	ex N732UE
☐ Z-WOR	Piper PA-31 Turbo Navajo	31-35	ex ZS-JWF
☐ Z-WOU	Piper PA-31 Turbo Navajo	31-118	ex ZS-SWA
☐ Z-WRB	Cessna 402B	402B0032	ex N9475P

FALCON AIR   *Harare-Charles Prince*

☐ Z-DDD	Reims Cessna F406 Caravan II	F406-0069	ex F-GIQD	17
☐ Z-DDE	Reims Cessna F406 Caravan II	F406-0068	ex F-GIQC	15
☐ Z-DDF	Reims Cessna F406 Caravan II	F406-0071	ex F-GIQE	16
☐ Z-DDG	Reims Cessna F406 Caravan II	F406-0067	ex F-GEUG	14
☐ Z-WKN	Cessna T207 Skywagon	20700243	ex VP-WKN	

SKY RELIEF   *Harare-Charles Prince*

☐ 9Q-CSR	de Havilland DHC-5 Buffalo	7	ex 5Y-SRD		<ALS, Kenya
☐ 5Y-SRE	de Havilland DHC-5 Buffalo	9	ex Z-SRE	ICRC colours	<ALS, Kenya

SOUTHERN CROSS AVIATION   *Victoria Falls (VFA)*

☐ Z-THL	Cessna U206F Stationair	U20603233	ex N8372Q
☐ Z-WFA	Cessna T207 Staionair 8	20700098	ex VP-WFA

UNITED AIR CHARTERS   *Unitair (UAC)*   *Harare-Charles Prince*

☐ Z-BWK	Cessna U206G Stationair	U20603546	ex N8794Q	
☐ Z-UAC	Beech 58 Baron	TH-211	ex 9J-ADK	
☐ Z-UTD	Britten-Norman BN-2A Mk.III-2 Trislander	1055	ex A2-AGY	
☐ Z-WHG	Beech 95-D55 Baron	TE-761	ex VP-WHG	
☐ Z-WHH	Beech 65-80 Queen Air	LD-101	ex VP-WHH	
☐ Z-WHX	Britten-Norman BN-2A-7 Islander	192	ex VP-WHX	
☐ Z-WKL	Cessna U206F Stationair	U20601707	ex ZS-ILV	
☐ Z-WTA	Cessna U206F Stationair	U20602547	ex OO-SPX	
☐ Z-WTF	Cessna 414A Chancellor	414A0062	ex G-METR	
☐ Z-YHS	Cessna U206C Super Skywagon	U206-1029	ex VP-YHS	

ZA-   ALBANIA (Republic of Albania)

ADA AIR   *Ada Air (ZY/ADE)*   *Tirana (TIA)*

☐ ZA-ADA	Embraer EMB.110P2 Bandeirante	110303	ex F-GCMQ	DHL titles

ALBANIAN AIRLINES   *Albanian (LV/LBC)*   *Tirana (TIA)*

☐ OM-ASE	Boeing 737-306	23545/1343	ex PH-BDK	
☐ ZA-MAK	British Aerospace 146 Srs.100	E1085	ex G-CCLN	
☐ ZA-MAL	British Aerospace 146 Srs.200	E2054	ex G-BZWP	
☐ ZA-MEV	British Aerospace 146 Srs.300	E3197	ex VH-EWS	

BELLE AIR   *(LZ/LBY)*   *Tirana (TIA)*

☐ F-ORAA	ATR 72-212A	879	ex F-WWEH	
☐ F-ORAD	Airbus A320-233	0558	ex F-HBAE	
☐ F-ORAE	Airbus A320-233	0561	ex F-HBAD	
☐ F-ORAF	Airbus A319-132	2335	ex D-ABGD	
☐ F-ORAG	Airbus A319-132	1098	ex M-YVOL	◆
☐ LZ-ATR	ATR 42-300	151	ex F-WQNC	<HMS
☐ ZA-ARD	McDonnell-Douglas MD-82	49104/1085	ex N804NK	

STAR AIRWAYS   *Tirana (TIA)*

☐ ZA-	Airbus A320-211	0112	ex TS-INK	o/o◆
☐ ZA-RED	Airbus A320-231	0415	ex N415MX	[MPL]◆

ZK-   NEW ZEALAND (Dominion of New Zealand)

AIR CHATHAMS   *Chatham (CV/CVA)*   *Chatham Island (CHT)*

☐ ZK-CIA	Beech 65-B80 Queen Air	LD-430	ex N640K	
☐ ZK-CIB	Convair 580	327A	ex C-FCIB	
☐ ZK-CIC	Swearingen SA.227AC Metro III	AC-623B	ex N623AV	Frtr >OGN
☐ ZK-CID	Convair 580F	385	ex HZ-SN11	[PMR]
☐ ZK-CIE	Convair 580	399	ex N565EA	
☐ ZK-CIF	Convair 580	381	ex N566EA	>FAJ
☐ ZK-KAI	Cessna U206G Stationair	U20603711		
☐ ZK-LYP	Britten-Norman BN-2A-27 Islander	821	ex YR-BNO	

AIR FREIGHT NZ — Auckland-Intl (AKL)

☐ ZK-FTA	Convair 580	168	ex C-GKFP	Frtr Op for Parceline
☐ ZK-KFH	Convair 580	42	ex C-FKFL	Frtr
☐ ZK-KFJ	Convair 580	114	ex C-GKFJ	Frtr
☐ ZK-KFL	Convair 580	372	ex C-FKFL	Frtr Op for Parceline
☐ ZK-KFS	Convair 5800	277	ex C-FKFS	Frtr

AIR NAPIER — Air Napier (NPR) — Napier (NPE)

☐ ZK-ELK	Piper PA-32-260 Cherokee Six	32-7600009	ex N8768C
☐ ZK-MSL	Piper PA-34-200T Seneca II	34-7770224	ex N5600V
☐ ZK-NPR	Piper PA-31 Turbo Navajo B	31-777	ex ZK-DOM
☐ ZK-WUG	Piper PA-34-200T Seneca II	34-7970329	ex N2891R

AIR NATIONAL — Auckland-Intl (AKL)

☐ ZK-ECO	British Aerospace 146 Srs.200	E2130	ex C-GRNX
☐ ZK-ECP	British Aerospace Jetstream 32EP	878	ex VH-BAE

AIR NELSON — Link (RLK) — Nelson (NSN)

Wholly owned by Air New Zealand; operates as part of Air New Zealand Link (q.v.).

AIR NEW ZEALAND — NewZealand (NZ/ANZ) — Auckland-Intl/Wellington-Intl (AKL/WLG)

Member of Star Alliance

☐ ZK-OJA	Airbus A320-232	2085	ex F-WWIN		
☐ ZK-OJB	Airbus A320-232	2090	ex F-WWBM		
☐ ZK-OJC	Airbus A320-232	2112	ex F-WWDQ		
☐ ZK-OJD	Airbus A320-232	2130	ex F-WWDK		
☐ ZK-OJE	Airbus A320-232	2148	ex F-WWIH		
☐ ZK-OJF	Airbus A320-232	2153	ex F-WWIS		
☐ ZK-OJG	Airbus A320-232	2173	ex F-WWDJ		
☐ ZK-OJH	Airbus A320-232	2257	ex F-WWDE	Star Alliance c/s	
☐ ZK-OJI	Airbus A320-232	2297	ex F-WWBU		
☐ ZK-OJM	Airbus A320-232	2533	ex F-WWIB		
☐ ZK-OJN	Airbus A320-232	2594	ex F-WWBC		
☐ ZK-OJO	Airbus A320-232	2663	ex F-WWBM	Warner special c/s	
☐ ZK-	Airbus A320-232		ex		o/o♦
☐ ZK-	Airbus A320-232		ex		o/o♦
☐ ZK-	Airbus A320-232		ex		o/o♦
☐ ZK-	Airbus A320-232		ex		o/o♦
☐ ZK-NGD	Boeing 737-3U3	28732/2966	ex N930WA		
☐ ZK-NGE	Boeing 737-3U3	28733/2969	ex N931WA		
☐ ZK-NGF	Boeing 737-3U3	28734/2974	ex N309FL		
☐ ZK-NGG	Boeing 737-319	25606/3123	ex N1795B		
☐ ZK-NGH	Boeing 737-319	25607/3126	ex N1786B		
☐ ZK-NGI	Boeing 737-319	25608/3128	ex N1786B		
☐ ZK-NGJ	Boeing 737-319	25609/3130	ex N1786B	Last 737-300 built	
☐ ZK-NGK	Boeing 737-3K2	26318/2731	ex PH-TSX		
☐ ZK-NGM	Boeing 737-3K2	28085/2722	ex PH-TSY		
☐ ZK-NGO	Boeing 737-37Q	28548/2961	ex G-OAMS		
☐ ZK-NGP	Boeing 737-33A	27459/3007	ex 9H-ADH		
☐ ZK-NGR	Boeing 737-33A	27460/3021	ex 9H-ADI		
☐ ZK-SJB	Boeing 737-33R	28868/2881	ex PP-SFK		
☐ ZK-SJC	Boeing 737-3U3	28738/2988	ex N308FL		
☐ ZK-SJE	Boeing 737-3K2	27635/2721	ex PH-TSZ		
☐ ZK-NBT	Boeing 747-419	24855/815	ex N6018N	Kaikoura	[AKL]
☐ ZK-NBU	Boeing 747-419	25605/933		Rotorua	
☐ ZK-NBV	Boeing 747-419	26910/1180		Christchurch	
☐ ZK-NBW	Boeing 747-419	29375/1228		Wellington	
☐ ZK-SUH	Boeing 747-419	24896/855	ex N891LF	Dunedin	
☐ ZK-SUI	Boeing 747-441	24957/971	ex N821LF	Queenstown	
☐ ZK-SUJ	Boeing 747-4F6	27602/1161	ex N756PR	Auckland	
☐ ZK-NCG	Boeing 767-319ER/W	26912/509			
☐ ZK-NCI	Boeing 767-319ER/W	26913/558	ex N6009F		
☐ ZK-NCJ	Boeing 767-319ER/W	26915/574	ex N6018N		
☐ ZK-NCK	Boeing 767-319ER/W	26971/663			
☐ ZK-NCL	Boeing 767-319ER/W	28745/677			
☐ ZK-OKA	Boeing 777-219ER	29404/534			

☐ ZK-OKB	Boeing 777-219ER	34376/537		
☐ ZK-OKC	Boeing 777-219ER	34377/546		
☐ ZK-OKD	Boeing 777-219ER	29401/550		
☐ ZK-OKE	Boeing 777-219ER	32712/564		
☐ ZK-OKF	Boeing 777-219ER	34378/575		
☐ ZK-OKG	Boeing 777-219ER	29403/591		
☐ ZK-OKH	Boeing 777-219ER	34379/605		
☐ ZK-OKM	Boeing 777-319ER	38405/902		◆
☐ ZK-OKN	Boeing 777-319ER	38406/911		o/o◆
☐ ZK-	Boeing 777-319ER			o/o◆
☐ ZK-	Boeing 777-319ER			o/o◆

AIR NEW ZEALAND LINK — New Zealand (NZ/NZA)
Christchurch-Intl/Nelson/Hamilton (CHC/NSN/HLZ)

☐ ZK-MCA	ATR 72-212A	597	ex F-WQKC	Mount Cook
☐ ZK-MCB	ATR 72-212A	598	ex F-WQKG	Mount Cook
☐ ZK-MCC	ATR 72-212A	714	ex F-WQMV	Mount Cook
☐ ZK-MCF	ATR 72-212A	600	ex F-WQKH	Mount Cook
☐ ZK-MCJ	ATR 72-212A	624	ex F-WQKI	Mount Cook
☐ ZK-MCO	ATR 72-212A	628	ex F-WQKJ	Mount Cook
☐ ZK-MCP	ATR 72-212A	630	ex F-WQKK	Mount Cook
☐ ZK-MCU	ATR 72-212A	632	ex F-WQKL	Mount Cook
☐ ZK-MCW	ATR 72-212A	646	ex F-WQMG	Mount Cook
☐ ZK-MCX	ATR 72-212A	687	ex F-WQMN	Mount Cook
☐ ZK-MCY	ATR 72-212A	703	ex F-WQMR	Mount Cook
☐ ZK-EAA	Beech 1900D	UE-424	ex N2335Y	Eagle
☐ ZK-EAB	Beech 1900D	UE-425	ex N2335Z	Eagle
☐ ZK-EAC	Beech 1900D	UE-426	ex N51226	Eagle
☐ ZK-EAD	Beech 1900D	UE-427	ex N50127	Eagle
☐ ZK-EAE	Beech 1900D	UE-428	ex N3188L	Eagle
☐ ZK-EAF	Beech 1900D	UE-429	ex N50069	Eagle
☐ ZK-EAG	Beech 1900D	UE-430	ex N50430	Eagle
☐ ZK-EAH	Beech 1900D	UE-431	ex N51321	Eagle
☐ ZK-EAI	Beech 1900D	UE-432	ex N5032L	Eagle
☐ ZK-EAJ	Beech 1900D	UE-433	ex N4469Q	Eagle
☐ ZK-EAK	Beech 1900D	UE-434	ex N4474P	Eagle
☐ ZK-EAL	Beech 1900D	UE-435	ex N50815	Eagle
☐ ZK-EAM	Beech 1900D	UE-436	ex N5016C	Eagle
☐ ZK-EAN	Beech 1900D	UE-437	ex N50307	Eagle
☐ ZK-EAO	Beech 1900D	UE-438	ex N4470D	Eagle
☐ ZK-EAP	Beech 1900D	UE-439	ex N50899	Eagle
☐ ZK-EAR	Beech 1900D	UE-388	ex VH-EAS	Eagle
☐ ZK-NEA	de Havilland DHC-8Q-311	611	ex C-FCPO	Air Nelson
☐ ZK-NEB	de Havilland DHC-8Q-311	615	ex C-FDRG	Air Nelson
☐ ZK-NEC	de Havilland DHC-8Q-311	616	ex C-FEDG	Air Nelson
☐ ZK-NED	de Havilland DHC-8Q-311	617	ex C-FERB	Air Nelson
☐ ZK-NEE	de Havilland DHC-8Q-311	618	ex C-FFBY	Air Nelson
☐ ZK-NEF	de Havilland DHC-8Q-311	620	ex C-FFCC	Air Nelson
☐ ZK-NEG	de Havilland DHC-8Q-311	621	ex C-FFOZ	Air Nelson
☐ ZK-NEH	de Havilland DHC-8Q-311	623	ex C-FGAI	Air Nelson
☐ ZK-NEJ	de Havilland DHC-8Q-311	625	ex C-FFPA	Air Nelson
☐ ZK-NEK	de Havilland DHC-8Q-311	629	ex C-FHPZ	Air Nelson
☐ ZK-NEM	de Havilland DHC-8Q-311	630	ex C-FHQB	Air Nelson
☐ ZK-NEO	de Havilland DHC-8Q-311	633	ex C-FIOS	Air Nelson
☐ ZK-NEP	de Havilland DHC-8Q-311	634	ex C-FIOV	Air Nelson
☐ ZK-NEQ	de Havilland DHC-8Q-311	636	ex C-FJKL	Air Nelson
☐ ZK-NER	de Havilland DHC-8Q-311	639	ex C-FJKO	Air Nelson
☐ ZK-NES	de Havilland DHC-8Q-311	641	ex C-FJKP	Air Nelson
☐ ZK-NET	de Havilland DHC-8Q-311	642	ex C-FJKQ	Air Nelson
☐ ZK-NEU	de Havilland DHC-8Q-311	647	ex C-FLTZ	Air Nelson
☐ ZK-NEW	de Havilland DHC-8Q-311	648	ex C-FLUH	Air Nelson
☐ ZK-NEZ	de Havilland DHC-8Q-311	654	ex C-FNPY	Air Nelson
☐ ZK-NFA	de Havilland DHC-8Q-311	659	ex C-FPPN	Air Nelson
☐ ZK-NFB	de Havilland DHC-8Q-311	670	ex C-FVUF	Air Nelson
☐ ZK-NFI	de Havilland DHC-8Q-311	671	ex C-FWGQ	Air Nelson

AIR SAFARIS & SERVICES — Airsafari (SRI) — Lake Tekapo

☐ ZK-FJH	Cessna P206E Super Skylane	P206-0634	ex G-BKSI
☐ ZK-NMC	GAF N24A Nomad	N24A-034	ex VH-DHP
☐ ZK-NMD	GAF N24A Nomad	N24A-060	ex VH-DHU
☐ ZK-NME	GAF N24A Nomad	N24A-122	ex 5W-FAT
☐ ZK-SAE	Gippsland GA-8 Airvan	GA8-04-055	ex VH-VFF

☐ ZK-SAF	Gippsland GA-8 Airvan	GA8-02-017	ex VH-AAP
☐ ZK-SAZ	Gippsland GA-8 Airvan	GA8-05-078	
☐ ZK-SEY	Cessna T207A Stationair 8	20700661	ex N76012
☐ ZK-SRI	Cessna 208B Caravan I	208B0636	ex N208PR

AIR WANGANUI COMMUTER   Wanganui (WAG)

| ☐ ZK-MKG | Beech 65-C90A King Air | LJ-1367 | ex N111MU |
| ☐ ZK-WTH | Piper PA-31P-350 Mojave | 31P-8414003 | ex N9187Y |

AIR2THERE.COM   Paraparaumu (PPQ)

☐ ZK-MYF	Partenavia P.68B	123	ex ZK-ERA
☐ ZK-MYH	Cessna 208B Caravan I	208B0604	ex N64BP
☐ ZK-MYS	Piper PA-31-350 Navajo Chieftain	31-7652032	ex ZK-MCM

AIRWORK NEW ZEALAND   Airwork (AWK)
Auckland-Ardmore/ Christchurch/ Wellington (AMZ/CHC/WLG)

☐ ZK-NQC	Boeing 737-219C (Nordam 3)	22994/928		all-white	
☐ ZK-TLA	Boeing 737-3B7 (SF)	23383/1425	ex N508AU		Op for Toll Logistics
☐ ZK-TLC	Boeing 737-3B7 (SF)	23705/1497	ex N519AU		Op for Toll Logistics
☐ ZK-TLD	Boeing 737-3B7 (SF)	23706/1499	ex N520AU		Op for Toll Logistics
☐ ZK-TLE	Boeing 737-3S1 (SF)	24834/1896	ex N919GF		o/o♦
☐ ZK-LFT	Swearingen SA.227AC Metro III	AC-582	ex ZK-PAA		EMS Op for Life Flight NZ
☐ ZK-NSS	Swearingen SA.227AC Metro III	AC-692B	ex N2707D		EMS
☐ ZK-POB	Swearingen SA.227AC Metro III	AC-606B	ex D-CABG		Op for SkyLink
☐ ZK-POE	Swearingen SA.227CC Metro 23	CC-843B	ex N30228		Op for NZ Post
☐ ZK-POF	Swearingen SA.227CC Metro 23	CC-844B	ex N30229		
☐ ZK-FOP	Piper PA-31-350 Navajo Chieftain	31-7405227	ex N888SG		EMS
☐ ZK-NAO	Fokker F.27 Friendship 500	10364	ex 9V-BFK	all-white	Op for NZ Post
☐ ZK-PAX	Fokker F.27 Friendship 500	10596	ex HB-ILJ	all-white	
☐ ZK-POH	Fokker F.27 Friendship 500	10680	ex VT-NEH	all-white	Op for NZ Post

ASPIRING AIR(OI)   Wanaka (WKA)

| ☐ ZK-EVO | Britten-Norman BN-2A-26 Islander | 785 | ex 5W-FAQ | |
| ☐ ZK-EVT | Britten-Norman BN-2A-26 Islander | 152 | ex YJ-RV19 | Lake Wanaka |

EAGLE AIRWAYS   (EX)   Hamilton (HLZ)

50% owned by Air New Zealand; operates as part of Air New Zealand Link (q.v.)

FLIGHT 2000   Ardmore (AMZ)

| ☐ ZK-DAK | Douglas DC-3 | 15035/26480 | ex VH-SBT | RNZAF colours |

FLIGHT CORPORATION   Flightcorp (FCP)   Nelson (NSN)

| ☐ ZK-SKT | Cessna U206G Stationair 6 II | U20606609 | ex CP-1783 |
| ☐ ZK-TSD | Piper PA-34-200T Seneca II | 34-8070356 | ex ZK-DCQ |

GREAT BARRIER AIRLINES   (AFW)   Auckland-Intl (AKL)

☐ ZK-CNS	Piper PA-32-260 Cherokee Six	32-686	ex N3766W	Stitchbird	
☐ ZK-ENZ	Piper PA-32-260 Cherokee Six	32-1117	ex ZK-DBP	Tomtit	
☐ ZK-FVD	Britten-Norman BN-2A-26 Islander	316	ex G-BJWN	Pigeon	
☐ ZK-KTR	Britten-Norman BN-2A Islander	759	ex PK-VAB		
☐ ZK-LGC	Britten-Norman BN-2A Mk.III-1 Trislander	1042	ex G-RHOP		
☐ ZK-LGF	Britten-Norman BN-2A Mk.III-1 Trislander	1023	ex YJ-LGF		
☐ ZK-LGR	Britten-Norman BN-2A Mk.III-1 Trislander	372	ex VH-BSP		
☐ ZK-LOU	Britten-Norman BN-2A Mk.III-1 Trislander	322	ex VH-MRJ		
☐ ZK-NSN	Piper PA-31 Turbo Navajo	31-687	ex VH-CFP	Bellbird	
☐ ZK-PLA	Partenavia P.68B	86	ex A6-ALO	Tui	
☐ ZK-RDT	Embraer EMB.820C Navajo	820127	ex PT-RDT		
☐ ZK-REA	Britten-Norman BN-2A-26 Islander	43	ex ZK-FWH	Brown Teal	>Soundsair

HELI–HARVEST   Taupo (TUO)

| ☐ ER-MHH | Mil Mi-17 (Mi-8MTV-1) | 96121 | ex RA-25746 | <VLN |
| ☐ ER-MHZ | Mil Mi-17 (Mi-8MTV-1) | 96078 | ex RA-22503 | <VLN |

HELICOPTERS (NZ)   Nelson (NSN)

☐ ZK-HBU	Aérospatiale AS350B2 Ecureuil	2286	ex RP-C2188
☐ ZK-HDE	Aérospatiale AS350BA Ecureuil	1491	ex N5449B
☐ ZK-HDM	Aérospatiale AS350BA Ecureuil	2262	ex N911MV

☐ ZK-HDO	Aérospatiale AS350B2 Ecureuil	2463	ex ZK-HNZ	
☐ ZK-HDQ	Aérospatiale AS350BA Ecureuil	1932	ex VH-BHX	
☐ ZK-HDR	Aérospatiale AS350B2 Ecureuil	2382	ex HB-XJC	
☐ ZK-HFH	Aérospatiale AS350BA Ecureuil	2132	ex VH-WCU	
☐ ZK-HFK	Aérospatiale AS350B2 Ecureuil	1397	ex VH-WCD	
☐ ZK-HJE	Aérospatiale AS350BA Ecureuil	1307	ex N4428V	
☐ ZK-HJQ	Aérospatiale AS350D AStar III	1295	ex C-FBXE	
☐ ZK-HJV	Aérospatiale AS350B2 Ecureuil	2846	ex RP-C1712	
☐ ZK-HJY	Aérospatiale AS350BA Ecureuil	2005	ex JA9463	
☐ ZK-HND	Aérospatiale AS350B Ecureuil	1661	ex VH-HRD	
☐ ZK-HNE	Aérospatiale AS350B2 Ecureuil	2811	ex HB-XLJ	
☐ ZK-HNF	Eurocopter EC130B4	4461	ex C-GECV	
☐ ZK-HNK	Aérospatiale AS350B2 Ecureuil	2349	ex VH-WCS	
☐ ZK-HNQ	Aérospatiale AS350BA Ecureuil	1972	ex JA9450	
☐ ZK-HNX	Aérospatiale AS350BA Ecureuil	1828	ex RP-C2777	
☐ ZK-IBH	Aérospatiale AS350BA Ecureuil	2469	ex JA6067	
☐ ZK-IVZ	Aérospatiale AS350B2 Ecueruil	4256		
☐ ZK-HDA	Bell 412	33066	ex N626LH	
☐ ZK-HDY	Bell 412EP	36099	ex A6-HGS	
☐ ZK-HIU	Agusta-Bell 412	25626	ex I-BRMA	
☐ ZK-HNI	Bell 412SP	33204	ex 9M-AYW	
☐ ZK-HNO	Bell 212	31139	ex VH-BQH	
☐ ZK-HZE	Bell 206B JetRanger	769	ex C-FTPG	
☐ ZK-HNZ	Agusta AW139	31103		
☐ VH-NZE	Agusta AW139	31146	ex ZK-HUL	
☐ VH-NZF	Agusta AW139	31156		

HELIPRO — Helipro (HPR) — Palmerston North (PMR)

☐ ZK-HRS	Bell 206B JetRanger	877	ex JA9087	
☐ ZK-HYD	Aérospatiale AS350D Ecureuil	1258	ex N36079	
☐ ZK-HYE	Kawasaki/MBB BK-117A-3	1008	ex JA9615	
☐ ZK-HYI	Kawasaki/MBB BK-117B-2	1011	ex JA9620	
☐ ZK-HYJ	Aérospatiale AS355F1 Ecureuil 2	5280	ex VT-ERU	
☐ ZK-HYN	Aérospatiale AS355F1 Ecureuil 2	5286	ex JA9588	
☐ ZK-HYD	Aérospatiale AS350D Ecureuil	1186	ex N155EH	
☐ ZK-HYW	Aérospatiale AS350D Ecureuil	1420	ex N5782G	
☐ ZK-HYZ	Kawasaki/MBB BK-117A-3	1010	ex ZK-HRQ	

JETCONNECT — Qantas Jetconnect (QNZ) — Auckland-Intl (AKL)

☐ ZK-JTP	Boeing 737-476	24441/2363	ex VH-TJP	
☐ ZK-JTQ	Boeing 737-476	24442/2371	ex VH-JTQ	
☐ ZK-JTR	Boeing 737-476	24439/2265	ex VH-TJN	
☐ ZK-JTS	Boeing 737-476	28152/2829	ex VH-TJZ	
☐ ZK-ZQA	Boeing 737-838/W	34200/2989	ex VH-VZF	
☐ ZK-ZQB	Boeing 737-838/W	34201/3006	ex VH-VZG	
☐ ZK-ZQC	Boeing 737-838/W	34202/3048	ex VH-VZH	
☐ ZK-ZQD	Boeing 737-838/W	34203/3515		o/o♦
☐ ZK-	Boeing 737-838/W			o/o♦
☐ ZK-	Boeing 737-838/W			o/o♦
☐ ZK-	Boeing 737-838/W			o/o♦

LAKELAND HELICOPTERS — Rotorua (ROT)

☐ ZK-HCH	Bell 206B JetRanger III	2258	ex N16859	
☐ ZK-HIX	Bell 206B JetRanger	869	ex VH-YDA	
☐ ZK-HSP	Bell UH-1H	5352	ex N226MS	
☐ ZK-HZX	Bell UH-1H	11892	ex N3061A	
☐ ZK-LHL	Cessna 425 Conquest I	425-0171	ex N51CU	

MILFORD SOUND FLIGHTSEEING — Queenstown (ZQN)

☐ ZK-DBV	Britten-Norman BN-2A Islander	164	ex VH-EQX	
☐ ZK-MCD	Britten-Norman BN-2A-26 Islander	719	ex G-BCAG	
☐ ZK-MCE	Britten-Norman BN-2A-26 Islander	724	ex G-BCHB	
☐ ZK-MFN	Britten-Norman BN-2B-26 Islander	2168	ex N2407B	
☐ ZK-MSF	Britten-Norman BN-2A-26 Islander	2037	ex OY-PPP	
☐ ZK-TSS	Britten-Norman BN-2A-26 Islander	2043	ex RP-C693	
☐ ZK-ZQN	Britten-Norman BN-2B-26 Islander	2197	ex G-BLNW	

MILFORD SOUND SCENIC FLIGHTS — Queenstown (ZQN)

☐ ZK-DEW	Cessna 207 Skywagon	20700161	ex VH-UBQ	
☐ ZK-DRY	Cessna 207 Skywagon	20700196	ex 5W-FAL	
☐ ZK-LAW	Cessna 207A Stationair 8	20700723	ex N9750M	
☐ ZK-SEW	Cessna T207A Stationair 6	20700584	ex N73394	

| ☐ ZK-SEX | Cessna T207A Stationair 6 | 20700609 | ex N73622 |
| ☐ ZK-WET | Cessna 207A Skywagon | 20700375 | ex VH-SLD |

MOUNT COOK AIRLINE — *Mountcook (NM/NZM)* — *Christchurch-Intl (CHC)*

77% owned by Air New Zealand; operates scheduled services as Air New Zealand Link in full colours using NZ flight numbers

MOUNTAIN AIR — *Taumarunui*

☐ ZK-DLA	Britten-Norman BN-2B-26 Islander	2131	ex VH-ISL	
☐ ZK-DOV	Cessna 206 Super Skywagon	206-0248	ex N5248U	
☐ ZK-PIW	Piper PA-23-250 Aztec E	27-7305089	ex VH-RCI	
☐ ZK-PIX	Piper PA-23-250 Aztec E	27-4738	ex N14174	
☐ ZK-PIY	Britten-Norman BN-2A-20 Islander	344	ex JA5218	
☐ ZK-PIZ	Britten-Norman BN-2B-26 Islander	2012	ex N2132M	Great Barrier Xpress titles
☐ ZK-SFK	Britten-Norman BN-2A-6 Islander	236	ex VH-CPG	

PACIFIC BLUE — *Bluebird (DJ/PBN)* — *Christchurch Intl (CHC)*

☐ VH-VUM	Boeing 737-8BK/W	29675/2414			<VOZ
☐ VH-VUN	Boeing 737-8BK/W	29676/2432			<VOZ
☐ ZK-PBA	Boeing 737-8FE/W	33796/1377	ex VH-VOO	Bonnie Blue	<VOZ
☐ ZK-PBB	Boeing 737-8FE/W	33797/1389	ex VH-VOP	Whitney Sundays	<VOZ
☐ ZK-PBD	Boeing 737-8FE/W	33996/1551	ex (VH-VOY)	Pacific Pearl	<VOZ
☐ ZK-PBF	Boeing 737-8FE/W	33799/1462	ex VH-VOR	Tapu'itea	<VOZ
☐ ZK-PBG	Boeing 737-8FE/W	34015/1594	ex VH-VUD		<VOZ
☐ ZK-PBI	Boeing 737-8FE/W	34440/2003	ex VH-VUH		<VOZ
☐ ZK-PBJ	Boeing 737-8FE/W	34013/1573	ex VH-VUB		<VOZ
☐ ZK-PBK	Boeing 737-8FE/W	36604/2650	ex VH-VUP		<VOZ
☐ ZK-PBL	Boeing 737-8FE/W	36605/2710	ex VH-VUQ		<VOZ
☐ ZK-PBM	Boeing 737-8FE/W	36601/2525	ex VH-VUO		<VOZ

PIONAIR ADVENTURES — *Queenstown (ZQN)*

| ☐ ZK-AMY | Douglas DC-3 | 13506 | ex VH-CAN | Lady Jane |

SALT AIR — *Auckland-Intl (AKL)*

☐ ZK-FOO	Cessna 207 Skywagon	20700075	ex P2-SED
☐ ZK-HBC	Bell 206B JetRanger	2112	ex JA9169
☐ ZK-MJL	Cessna 208B Caravan I	208B0861	ex N861CM
☐ ZK-SAL	Cessna 207 Skywagon	20700171	ex VH-GKZ

SOUNDSAIR — *Wellington (WLG)*

☐ ZK-ENT	Cessna U206G Stationair	U20603667	ex N7551N	
☐ ZK-KLC	Gippsland GA-8 Airvan	GA8-03-040	ex VH-BQR	
☐ ZK-PDM	Cessna 208 Caravan I	20800240	ex N1289N	
☐ ZK-REA	Britten-Norman BN-2A-26 Islander	43	ex ZK-FWH	<AFW
☐ ZK-SAA	Cessna 208B Caravan I	208B0862	ex N208DG	

SOUTH EAST AIR — *Invercargill (IVC)*

☐ ZK-DIV	Piper PA-32-260 Cherokee Six	32-7400015	ex N57306
☐ ZK-FWZ	Britten-Norman BN-2A-26 Islander	52	ex T3-ATH
☐ ZK-FXE	Britten-Norman BN-2A-26 Islander	110	ex F-OCFR
☐ ZK-JEM	Cessna A185E Skywagon	18501780	ex VH-JBM
☐ ZK-RTS	Piper PA-32-300 Cherokee Six	32-7340070	

THE HELICOPTER LINE
Queenstown/Franz Josef Glacier/Fox Glacier/Mount Cook (ZQN/WHO/FGL/MON)

☐ ZK-HKR	Aérospatiale AS350D AStar III	1234	ex N3606X
☐ ZK-HLW	Aérospatiale AS350BA Ecureuil	1524	ex JA9307
☐ ZK-HNG	Aérospatiale AS350BA Ecureuil	2409	ex JA6039
☐ ZK-HKF	Aérospatiale AS355F1 Ecureuil 2	5200	ex VH-HJK
☐ ZK-HKY	Aérospatiale AS355F1 Twin Star	5123	ex N909CH
☐ ZK-HMB	Aérospatiale AS355F1 Twin Star	5016	ex N57812
☐ ZK-HMI	Aérospatiale AS355F1 Twin Star	5029	ex N5775Y
☐ ZK-HML	Aérospatiale AS355F1 Twin Star	5032	ex N5776A
☐ ZK-HPE	Aérospatiale AS355F1 Twin Star	5229	ex N58021
☐ ZK-HPI	Aérospatiale AS355F1 Twin Star	5211	ex N5802N
☐ ZK-HPZ	Aérospatiale AS355F1 Twin Star	5107	ex N87906

VINCENT AVIATION — *Wellington (WLG)*

| ☐ ZK-JSH | British Aerospace Jetstream 31 | 838 | ex G-IBLW |

☐ ZK-VAA	Reims Cessna F406 Caravan II	F4060012	ex ZK-CII	
☐ ZK-VAC	de Havilland DHC-8-102	60	ex ZK-NEZ	
☐ ZK-VAD	Cessna 402C	402C0076	ex VH-COH	
☐ ZK-VAF	Reims Cessna F406 Caravan II	F406-0057	ex F-ODYZ	

ZP- PARAGUAY (Republic of Paraguay)

REGIONAL PARAGUAYA — Asuncion (ASU)

☐ ZP-CAH	Boeing 737-230 (Nordam 3)	22121/720	ex N212AG	Ciudad de Ascuncion
☐ ZP-CAJ	Boeing 737-230 (Nordam 3)	22124/727	ex N214AG	Ciudad de Luque
☐ ZP-CAQ	Boeing 737-201 (Nordam 3)	20211/141	ex 3C-HAC	

SOL DEL PARAGUAY — Asuncion (ASU)

☐ ZP-CAL	Fokker 100	11341	ex XA-TCP	♦

TAM MERCOSUR — Paraguaya (PZ/LAP) — Asuncion (ASU)

☐ ZP-CAR	Cessna 208A Caravan I	20800033	ex PT-OGZ	

Also operates services with Fokker 100 aircraft leased from parent (80% owner), TAM Brasil, as required

ZS- SOUTH AFRICA (Republic of South Africa)

AIR-TEC AFRICA — Bethlehem

☐ ZS-MWM	LET L-410UVP-E20	912613	ex 7Q-YKV	
☐ ZS-OOF	LET L-410UVP-E20	871920	ex 5H-PAJ	Op for Air Express Algeria
☐ ZS-OSE	LET L-420	922729A	ex N420Y	Op for Air Express Algeria
☐ ZS-OUE	LET L-420	012735A	ex OK-GDM	Op for Air Express Algeria
☐ ZS-OXR	LET L-410UVP	972730	ex 5H-HSA	Op for Air Express Algeria
☐ ZS-PNI	LET L-410UVP-E20	871904	ex 5Y-BSV	
☐ 5Y-BRU	LET L-410UVP-E9	912539	ex 5X-UAY	>Aero Kenya
☐ 9G-LET	LET L-410UVP-E20	871922	ex ZS-OOH	>CTQ

AIRLINK — Link (4Z/LNK) — Johannesburg-OR Tambo (JNB)

☐ ZS-ASW	Avro 146-RJ85	E2313	ex N505XJ	<SFR
☐ ZS-ASX	Avro 146-RJ85	E2314	ex N506XJ	<SFR
☐ ZS-ASY	Avro 146-RJ85	E2316	ex N507XJ	<SFR
☐ ZS-ASZ	Avro 146-RJ85	E2318	ex N508XJ	<SFR
☐ ZS-SSH	Avro 146-RJ85	E2285	ex G-CGMT	♦
☐ ZS-SSI	Avro 146-RJ85	E2383	ex G-LCYB	♦
☐ ZS-SSJ	Avro 146-RJ85	E2385	ex G-LCYC	♦
☐ ZS-SSK	Avro 146-RJ85	E2251	ex G-CGSM	♦
☐ ZS-NRE	British Aerospace Jetstream 41	41048	ex G-4-048	
☐ ZS-NRF	British Aerospace Jetstream 41	41050	ex G-4-050	
☐ ZS-NRG	British Aerospace Jetstream 41	41051	ex G-4-051	
☐ ZS-NRH	British Aerospace Jetstream 41	41054	ex G-4-054	
☐ ZS-NRI	British Aerospace Jetstream 41	41061	ex G-4-061	
☐ ZS-NRJ	British Aerospace Jetstream 41	41062	ex G-4-062	
☐ ZS-NRK	British Aerospace Jetstream 41	41065	ex G-4-065	>SZL
☐ ZS-NRL	British Aerospace Jetstream 41	41068	ex G-4-068	
☐ ZS-OEX	British Aerospace Jetstream 41	41103	ex G-4-103	
☐ ZS-OMF	British Aerospace Jetstream 41	41034	ex G-MSKJ	
☐ ZS-OMS	British Aerospace Jetstream 41	41035	ex VH-JSX	
☐ ZS-OMY	British Aerospace Jetstream 41	41036	ex VH-CCJ	
☐ ZS-OMZ	British Aerospace Jetstream 41	41037	ex VH-CCW	
☐ ZS-OTM	Embraer ERJ-135LR	145485	ex PT-SXE	
☐ ZS-OTN	Embraer ERJ-135LR	145491	ex PT-SXK	
☐ ZS-OUV	Embraer ERJ-135LR	145493	ex PT-SXM	Op as Airlink Zimbabwe
☐ ZS-SJW	Embraer ERJ-135LR	145423	ex PT-STU	
☐ ZS-SJX	Embraer ERJ-135LR	145428	ex PT-STZ	
☐ ZS-SNV	Embraer ERJ-135LR	145551	ex N845RP	♦
☐ ZS-SNW	Embraer ERJ-135LR	145720	ex N838RP	♦
☐ ZS-SNX	Embraer ERJ-135LR	145620	ex N844RP	
☐ ZS-SNZ	Embraer ERJ-135LR	145725	ex N840RP	
☐ ZS-	Embraer ERJ-170LR		ex	o/o♦
☐ ZS-	Embraer ERJ-170LR		ex	o/o♦

AIRQUARIUS AVIATION — Quarius (AQU) — Lanseria (HLA)

☐ ZS-SOR	British Aerospace 146 Srs.300	E3155	ex G-BTNU	♦
☐ ZS-GAV	Boeing 737-2L9	22735/825	ex PK-RIR	
☐ ZS-DRF	Fokker F.28 Fellowship 4000	11239	ex 5Y-LLL	Lynne
☐ ZS-JES	Fokker F.28 Fellowship 4000	11236	ex 5H-MVK	Jessica
☐ ZS-SKA	Fokker 70	11559	ex PH-ZFT	♦
☐ ZS-XGW	Fokker F.28 Fellowship 4000	11130	ex SE-DGN	

ALLEGIANCE AIR — Kruger Mpumalanga International

☐ ZS-AAX	British Aerospace 146 Srs.200	E2092	ex TN-AIF	♦
☐ ZS-AAY	British Aerospace 146 Srs.200	E2044	ex TN-AIC	♦
☐ ZS-AAZ	British Aerospace 146 Srs.200	E2039	ex TR-LIQ	♦
☐ ZS-PZY	British Aerospace 146 Srs.200	E2051	ex TN-AHX	♦
☐ ZS-SDX	British Aerospace 146 Srs.200	E2046	ex TN-AIB	♦
☐ ZS-AAD	Embraer EMB.120ER Brasilia	120255	ex N263CA	♦
☐ ZS-OKT	Embraer EMB.120ER Brasilia	120254	ex N261CA	♦
☐ ZS-OTD	Embraer EMB.120ER Brasilia	120230	ex N249CA	♦
☐ ZS-PBT	Embraer EMB.120ER Brasilia	120260	ex N223BD	♦

AWESOME FLIGHT SERVICES — Awesome (ASM) — Lanseria (HLA)

☐ ZS-JAZ	Beech 1900D	UE-6	ex VT-AVJ	
☐ ZS-OYD	Beech 1900D	UE-191	ex VH-IAR	
☐ ZS-PRG	Beech 1900D	UE-90	ex VH-VAU	♦
☐ ZS-SNO	Beech 1900D	UE-96	ex VH-NIA	

BIONIC AIR

☐ ZS-PVU	Boeing 737-2Q8C	21959/610	ex N741AS
☐ ZS-SMO	British Aerospace 146 Srs.300	E3169	ex G-BSNS

BRANSON AIR

☐ ZS-KIS	Boeing 737-291	22743/909	ex CC-CVG

CHC HELICOPTERS (AFRICA) — Cape Town-International (CPT)

☐ ZS-HVJ	Sikorsky S-61N	61493	ex N9119Z	stored
☐ ZS-RDV	Sikorsky S-61N	61716	ex G-BIHH	based SSG
☐ ZS-RLK	Sikorsky S-61N	61772	ex G-BEWM	
☐ ZS-RLL	Sikorsky S-61N	61778	ex G-BFFK	
☐ ZS-RKO	Sikorsky S-76A++	760135	ex VH-LAX	
☐ ZS-RKP	Sikorsky S-76A++	760198	ex VH-LAY	Marine 2
☐ ZS-RNG	Sikorsky S-76A++	760036	ex D2-EXJ	based BSG <CHC Scotia
☐ ZS-RPI	Sikorsky S-76A++	760049	ex G-BHGK	based BSG <CHC Scotia
☐ D2-EVP	Aérospatiale AS.332L2 II	2398	ex F-WQEA	>SOR
☐ ZS-KEI	Convair 580	141	ex N5822	
☐ ZS-LYL	Convair 580	39	ex N511GA	
☐ ZS-RDI	Bell 206L-3 LongRanger III	51392	ex N521EV	
☐ ZS-RGV	Bell 212	30952	ex C-FRUU	
☐ ZS-RNP	Bell 212	30893	ex C-FPKW	based Malabo
☐ ZS-RNR	Bell 212	30829	ex C-FRWL	based Malabo

A member of CHC Helicopter Corp; operates from bases in Equatorial Guinea, Namibia and Angola as well as South Africa

CIVAIR — Civflight (CIW) — Cape Town-International (CPT)

☐ ZS-FWB	Beech 95-D55 Baron	TE-726	ex 9J-FWB
☐ ZS-HGO	Bell 206B JetRanger III	2450	
☐ ZS-HVY	Bell 206B JetRanger	1471	ex N59605
☐ ZS-MUM	Beech 65-B90 King Air	LJ-408	ex N481SA
☐ ZS-RGG	MBB Bo.105C	S-52	ex N291CA
☐ ZS-RGH	Bell 206B JetRanger III	3212	ex N3898P

COMAIR — Commercial (MN/CAW) — Johannesburg-OR Tambo (JNB)

☐ ZS-NNH	Boeing 737-236	21797/653	ex PH-TSD	Kulula special colours
☐ ZS-OAA	Boeing 737-4L7	26960/2483	ex VH-RON	
☐ ZS-OAF	Boeing 737-4S3	25116/2061	ex PP-VTL	Kulula colours
☐ ZS-OAG	Boeing 737-4H6	27168/2435	ex JA737D	Kulula colours
☐ ZS-OAH	Boeing 737-33A	24460/1831	ex N460TF	Kulula colours
☐ ZS-OAI	Boeing 737-33A	24030/1654	ex N240TF	Kulula colours
☐ ZS-OAM	Boeing 737-4S3	24164/1702	ex EI-DFE	Kulula colours

☐ ZS-OAO	Boeing 737-4S3	24163/1700	ex EI-DFD	Kulula colours		
☐ ZS-OAP	Boeing 737-4S3	24167/1736	ex EI-DFF	Kulula colours		
☐ ZS-OAV	Boeing 737-4H6	27086/2426	ex JA737C			
☐ ZS-OKB	Boeing 737-376	23477/1225	ex VH-TAF	BAW colours		
☐ ZS-OKC	Boeing 737-376	23484/1270	ex VH-TAJ	BAW colours		
☐ ZS-OKG	Boeing 737-376	23483/1264	ex VH-TAI	BAW colours		
☐ ZS-OKH	Boeing 737-376	23479/1259	ex VH-TAH	BAW colours		
☐ ZS-OKI	Boeing 737-376	23489/1356	ex VH-TAX	BAW colours		
☐ ZS-OKJ	Boeing 737-376	23487/1306	ex VH-TAV	BAW colours		
☐ ZS-OKK	Boeing 737-376	23485/1277	ex VH-TAK	BAW colours		
☐ ZS-OLA	Boeing 737-236	23163/1058	ex G-BKYE	BAW colours		
☐ ZS-OLB	Boeing 737-236	23167/1074	ex G-BKYI	BAW colours		
☐ ZS-OTF	Boeing 737-436	25305/2147	ex G-DOCC	Kulula colours	<SFR	
☐ ZS-OTG	Boeing 737-436	25840/2197	ex G-DOCJ	BAW colours	<SFR	
☐ ZS-OTH	Boeing 737-436	25841/2222	ex G-DOCK	kulula special colours	<SFR	
☐ ZS-ZWO	Boeing 737-8K2/W	28373/51	ex PH-HZA			
☐ ZS-ZWP	Boeing 737-86N/W	28612/455	ex OK-PIK			
☐ ZS-ZWQ	Boeing 737-8K2/W	28374/57	ex PH-HZB			◆

CTK CITYLINK

☐ ZS-CTK	SAAB SF.340A	340A-068	ex N68XJ	all-white

DHL AVIATION — Worldstar (DHV) — Lanseria (HLA)

Utilises Cessna 208B Caravans and ATR 42 operated by Solenta Aviation in full DHL colours

DODSON INTERNATIONAL CHARTER — Pretoria-Wonderboom (PRY)

☐ ZS-OJJ	AMI Turbo DC-3TP	16213/32961	ex N8194Q	Op for UN / Red Cross
☐ ZS-OJK	AMI Turbo DC-3TP	14165/25610	ex SAAF 6844	
☐ ZS-OJL	AMI Turbo DC-3TP	16565/33313	ex SAAF 6858	[PRY]
☐ ZS-OJM	AMI Turbo DC-3TP	14101/25546	ex N330RD	white colours

EAST COAST AIRWAYS — Eastway (ECT) — Durban-Virginia (VIR)

☐ ZS-LAX	Beech Baron 58	TH-1268	ex G-BMGI	

EGOLI AIR — Johannesburg-Rand (QRA)

☐ ZS-PSO	Antonov An-32B	2808	ex RA-48059	

EXECUTIVE AEROSPACE — Aerospace (EAS) — Johannesburg-OR Tambo (JNB)

☐ ZS-AGB	Hawker Siddeley HS.748 Srs.2B/501	1807	ex 4R-LPV	[JNB]
☐ ZS-LSO	Hawker Siddeley HS.748 Srs.2B/FAA	1783	ex G-BMJU	
☐ ZS-NNW	Hawker Siddeley HS.748 Srs.2B/378	1785	ex G-BOHZ	[DUR]
☐ ZS-NWW	Hawker Siddeley HS.748 Srs.2B/378	1786	ex G-HDBC	[JNB]
☐ ZS-PLO	Hawker Siddeley HS.748 Srs.2B/378	1797	ex G-EMRD	
☐ ZS-TPW	Hawker Siddeley HS.748 Srs.2B/378	1784	ex (ZS-KLC)	[JNB]

EXECUTIVE TURBINE AIR CHARTER — Lanseria (HLA)

☐ ZS-LFM	Beech 200 Super King Air	BB-954	ex N1839S	
☐ ZS-MES	Beech 200 Super King Air	BB-1038	ex N223MH	
☐ ZS-NTL	Beech 200 Super King Air	BB-85	ex V5-CIC	
☐ ZS-PRA	Beech B200 Super King Air	BB-1340	ex OY-GMA	Beech 1300 conversion
☐ ZS-PRC	Beech B200 Super King Air	BB-1341	ex OY-GEU	Beech 1300 conversion
☐ ZS-XGD	Beech 200 Super King Air	BB-286	ex Z-MRS	
☐ ZS-OKU	Beech 1900C-1	UC-50	ex 7Q-NXA	
☐ ZS-OUG	Beech 1900D	UE-14	ex VT-AVI	all-white
☐ ZS-OYF	Beech 1900D	UE-214	ex VH-IMS	
☐ ZS-OYG	Beech 1900D	UE-230	ex 5N-BCQ	all-white
☐ ZS-PHL	Beech 1900C-1	UC-74	ex N374UC	
☐ ZS-PJY	Beech 1900D	UE-204	ex N204GL	
☐ ZS-PKB	Beech 1900D	UE-3	ex N3YV	>TravelMax
☐ ZS-PPI	Beech 1900C	UE-179	ex N179GL	
☐ ZS-PPM	Beech 1900D	UE-150	ex N150GL	UNHS
☐ ZS-ETA	Embraer EMB.120ER Brasilia	120277	ex N213SW	

FEDERAL AIR — Fedair (FDR) — Durban-Virginia (VIR)

☐ ZS-DAT	Pilatus PC-12/45	242	ex HB-FRM	
☐ ZS-FDR	Beech 200 Super King Air	BB-1234	ex N971LE	
☐ ZS-FDL	Cessna 208B Caravan I	208B0896	ex 5Y-TWJ	
☐ ZS-KNL	Cessna 402C II	402C0646	ex N6814D	
☐ ZS-LXO	Beech Baron 58	TH-886	ex N23527	

☐ ZS-NAV	Beech 1900C	UB-62	ex VH-IYP	
☐ ZS-NVH	Cessna 208B Caravan I	208B0473	ex N1287N	
☐ ZS-OJC	Cessna 208B Caravan I	208B0593	ex N1194F	
☐ ZS-OXN	Beech 1900D	UE-83	ex N831SK	all-white
☐ ZS-PUC	Beech 1900D	UE-84	ex N841SK	
☐ ZS-PRH	Beech 1900D	UE-316	ex N21716	all-white
☐ ZS-PWY	Beech 1900D	UE-87	ex N87SK	all-white
☐ 5H-FED	Cessna 208B Caravan I	208B0571	ex ZS-FED	

FUGRO AIRBORNE SURVEYS   Lanseria (HLA)

☐ ZS-AIU	Cessna 404 Titan II	404-0082	ex A2-AIU
☐ ZS-FSA	Cessna 208B Caravan I	208B0877	ex N208LW
☐ ZS-FTA	Cessna 210N Centurion II	21063562	ex VH-JBH
☐ ZS-KRG	Cessna 404 Titan II	404-0676	ex N6761Y
☐ ZS-SSA	Cessna 208B Caravan I	208B0712	ex D-FLIZ

IMPERIAL AIR CARGO   Johannesburg-OR Tambo (JNB)

☐ ZS-IAB	Boeing 737-210C	20917/344	ex N834AL	♦
☐ ZS-IAC	Boeing 727-227F (Raisbeck 3)	21247/1217	ex N73751	<SFR
☐ ZS-SMG	Boeing 737-3Y0F	23499/1242	ex VP-BCJ	
☐ ZS-SMJ	Boeing 737-3Y0F	23500/1243	ex VP-BCN	♦

INTER-AIR   Inline (D6/ILN)   Johannesburg-OR Tambo (JNB)

☐ ZS-IJB	Boeing 767-266ERM	23180/99	ex N573JW	♦
☐ ZS-IJI	Boeing 707-323C (Comtran 2)	19517/614	ex N29AZ	[Pietersburg]
☐ ZS-IJJ	Boeing 737-2H7C	20591/309	ex N24AZ	[Pietersburg]
☐ ZS-IJK	Boeing 727-61 (FedEx 3)	19176/290	ex 3D-ZZN	
☐ ZS-IJN	Fokker F.28 Fellowship 4000	11118	ex 3D-DAW	
☐ ZS-SIH	Boeing 737-244	22587/835		
☐ ZS-SIM	Boeing 737-244	22828/881		<SFR
☐ 3D-ITC	Boeing 727-2F2	21260/1222	ex N103AZ	op by RFC

INTERLINK AIRLINES   Interlink (ID/ITK)   Johannesburg-OR Tambo (JNB)

☐ ZS-OLC	Boeing 737-230	22119/714	ex N219AS
☐ ZS-PVF	Embraer EMB.120RT Brasilia	120261	ex EC-HFZ
☐ ZS-SIC	Boeing 737-244F	22582/805	ex OB-1806-P
☐ ZS-SIN	Boeing 737-236	21802/670	ex CC-CHS
☐ ZS-SIP	Boeing 737-230	22116/701	ex N392AS

KING AIR CHARTER   (RXX)   Lanseria (HLA)

☐ ZS-HFG	Bell 206B JetRanger	1864	
☐ ZS-JSC	Beech B200 Super King Air	BB-1985	ex N71850
☐ ZS-LFW	Beech B200 Super King Air	BB-999	ex 9Q-CPV
☐ ZS-LRS	Beech B200C Super King Air	BL-20	ex 5Y-LRS
☐ ZS-MPC	Cessna 402C II	402C0426	ex C9-MEB
☐ ZS-NHW	Grumman G-159 Gulfstream I	141	ex N800PA
☐ ZS-OED	Beech B200 Super King Air	BB-1149	ex N200HF
☐ ZS-OOW	Beech 1900D	UE-57	ex N57YV
☐ ZS-OZE	Cessna 208B Caravan I	208B0786	ex N208AH
☐ ZS-RFS	Bell 206L-4 LongRanger IV	52116	ex N4252S

KULULA.COM   Johannesburg-OR Tambo (JNB)

Wholly owned low cost, no frills subsidiary of Comair who operate the aircraft

MANGO   (JE)   Johannesburg-OR Tambo (JNB)

☐ ZS-SJG	Boeing 737-8BG/W	32353/711	ex N1786B	<SAA
☐ ZS-SJH	Boeing 737-8BG/W	32354/725	ex PH-HZQ	<SAA
☐ ZS-SJK	Boeing 737-8BG/W	32355/807	ex PH-HZT	<SAA
☐ ZS-SJL	Boeing 737-8BG/W	32356/819	ex PH-HZZ	<SAA

NAC CHARTER   Slipstream (SLE)   Lanseria (HLA)

☐ ZS-NBJ	Beech B200 Super King Air	BB-1070	ex SE-KND	
☐ ZS-OBB	Beech B200 Super King Air	BB-1522	ex N3272E	
☐ ZS-OCI	Beech 200 Super King Air	BB-121	ex TR-LDX	
☐ ZS-ODI	Beech B200 Super King Air	BB-1542	ex N202JT	
☐ ZS-OUI	Beech B200 Super King Air	BB-688	ex 5R-MGH	Catpass 250 conversion
☐ ZS-SMC	Beech B200 Super King Air	BB-1489	ex N1563M	
☐ ZS-OMB	Beech 1900D	UE-81	ex N81SK	all-white

☐ ZS-ORV	Beech 1900D	UE-42	ex N42YV	all-white	
☐ ZS-OSF	Beech 1900D	UE-35	ex N35YV		
☐ ZS-PBZ	Beech 1900C-1	UC-126	ex N139GA		
☐ ZS-PMF	Beech 1900C-1	UC-37	ex N32017		
☐ ZS-SGH	Beech 1900D	UE-263	ex CN-RLB		
☐ ZS-SHH	Beech 1900D	UE-36	ex N136MJ		
☐ ZS-SNJ	Beech 1900D	UE-131	ex N131YV		
☐ ZS-SNK	Beech 1900D	UE-132	ex N132YV		
☐ ZS-SRZ	Beech 1900D	UE-133	ex N133YV		
☐ ZS-SSX	Beech 1900D	UE-143	ex N143YV		♦
☐ ZS-SSY	Beech 1900D	UE-135	ex N135YV		♦
☐ ZS-HKV	Aérospatiale AS350B Ecureuil	1528			
☐ ZS-MKI	Beech 65-C90A King Air	LJ-1099	ex Z-MKI		
☐ ZS-PNN	Beech 95-B55 Baron	TC-1794	ex A2-EAH		
☐ ZS-RDR	Bell 206B JetRanger III	4183	ex Z-RDR		
☐ ZS-RJO	Bell 407	53206			
☐ ZS-RPC	Bell 407	53365	ex C-GAHJ		
☐ ZS-TVT	Beech Baron 58	TH-1962	ex N584j		

NATURELINK CHARTER — Naturelink Southafri (NRK) — Pretoria-Wonderboom (PRY)

☐ ZS-ACS	Beech 200 Super King Air	BB-961	ex A2-AHA		
☐ ZS-KGW	Beech 200 Super King Air	BB-381	ex N4848M		
☐ ZS-PLJ	Beech B200 Super King Air	BB-1401	ex VH-YDH		based Kabul
☐ ZS-PLL	Beech B200 Super King Air	BB-1189	ex VH-KBH		based Kabul
☐ ZS-OEN	Embraer EMB.120RT Brasilia	120200	ex N200CD		>Elysian
☐ ZS-PGY	Embraer EMB.120RT Brasilia	120194	ex N269UE		
☐ ZS-POE	Embraer EMB.120RT Brasilia	120137	ex N137H		
☐ ZS-PPF	Embraer EMB.120RT Brasilia	120156	ex N156CA		Op for UNHCR
☐ ZS-PSB	Embraer EMB.120RT Brasilia	120196	ex N196CA		based Comores >MBN
☐ ZS-PUH	Embraer EMB.120RT Brasilia	120151	ex N196SW		sub>SWX
☐ ZS-PYO	Embraer EMB.120RT Brasilia	120245	ex N256CA		
☐ ZS-SRW	Embraer EMB.120RT Brasilia	120018	ex N95644		
☐ ZS-KMN	Beech 58 Baron	TH-153	ex F-ODMJ		
☐ ZS-OXV	Cessna 208B Caravan I	208B0563	ex N330AK		
☐ ZS-PCC	Beech 1900C-1	UC-143	ex 9J-AFW	all-white	<City Square 526
☐ ZS-PFL	Cessna 208B Caravan I	208B0505	ex N880MA		
☐ ZS-RWN	Aérospatiale AS350BA Ecureuil	1866	ex F-GJAM		

NELAIR CHARTERS & TRAVEL — Nelair (NLC) — Nelspruit (NLP)

☐ ZS-EDG	Cessna U206 Super Skywagon	U206-0382	ex N2182F	
☐ ZS-EVB	Piper PA-30 Twin Comanche 160B	30-1218	ex N8134Y	
☐ ZS-IKZ	Piper PA-32-300 Cherokee Six E	32-7240070	ex ZS-XAS	
☐ ZS-JGW	Cessna 401B	401B0106	ex N7966Q	
☐ ZS-JTX	Piper PA-31-350 Navajo Chieftain	31-7652059	ex N59800	
☐ ZS-JZX	Piper PA-34-200T Seneca II	34-7770269	ex N5911V	
☐ ZS-LTL	Cessna 310Q	310Q0025	ex N8925Z	
☐ ZS-LVR	Douglas DC-3	20475	ex N5000E	
☐ ZS-MHE	Piper PA-31-350 Navajo Chieftain	31-7305096	ex N74950	
☐ ZS-MSO	Piper PA-32-300 Cherokee Six	32-7540083	ex N33050	
☐ ZS-NAO	Cessna T210L Centurion II	21060092	ex N59104	
☐ ZS-NKG	Cessna 208 Caravan I	20800178	ex 5Y-NKG	
☐ ZS-PCN	Cessna U206F Stationair	U20602450	ex N1080V	
☐ ZS-PHI	Grumman G-159 Gulfstream I	164	ex N290AS	
☐ ZS-PHJ	Grumman G-159 Gulfstream I	134	ex 3D-DUE	
☐ ZS-PHK	Grumman G-159 Gulfstream I	025	ex 3D-DLN	
☐ ZS-RAN	Cessna 402B	402B0439	ex ZS-XAV	

NORSE AIR CHARTER — Norse Air (NRX) — Lanseria (HLA)

☐ ZS-PDO	SAAB SF.340B	340B-296	ex 9N-AHM		
☐ ZS-PDP	SAAB SF.340B	340B-289	ex B-3651		
☐ ZS-PDR	SAAB SF.340B	340B-292	ex 9N-AHK		
☐ ZS-PDS	SAAB SF.340B	340B-302	ex B-3654		>Yeti A/l
☐ ZS-PMS	SAAB SF.340A	340A-059	ex N327PX		>Nationale Regionale
☐ ZS-OLU	Beech 1900C-1	UC-116	ex 9G-KFN		
☐ ZS-PBU	Swearingen SA.227DC Metro 23	DC-826B	ex XA-SNF		
☐ ZS-PKM	Beech 200 Super King Air	BB-382	ex N92M		

1TIME AIRLINE — Next Time (1T/RNX) — Johannesburg-OR Tambo (JNB)

☐ ZS-ANX	Douglas DC-9-15	45799/69	ex (5Y-XXD)	no titles	[JNB]
☐ ZS-NNN	Douglas DC-9-32	47516/630	ex N1294L		

☐ ZS-NRA	Douglas DC-9-32	47430/609	ex G-BMAK		[JNB]
☐ ZS-NRB	Douglas DC-9-32	47468/611	ex G-BMAM	O gats	[JNB]
☐ ZS-OBK	McDonnell-Douglas MD-82	49115/1135	ex F-GPZE	kulula colours	<SFR
☐ ZS-OPZ	McDonnell-Douglas MD-83	49617/1464	ex N831NK		<SFR
☐ ZS-SKB	McDonnell-Douglas MD-83	49966/2047	ex G-FLTK		
☐ ZS-TRD	McDonnell-Douglas MD-82	48022/1079	ex PK-LMS	Tjooning You Straight	
☐ ZS-TRE	McDonnell-Douglas MD-82	49387/1288	ex N954AS		
☐ ZS-TRF	McDonnell-Douglas MD-82	49440/1304	ex N135NJ		
☐ ZS-TRG	McDonnell-Douglas MD-87	49830/1684	ex EC-GRN		
☐ ZS-TRH	McDonnell-Douglas MD-87	49831/1688	ex EC-GRO		
☐ ZS-TRI	McDonnell-Douglas MD-83	49707/1487	ex N315FV		
☐ ZS-SIG	Boeing 737-244	22586/829			<SFR

PELICAN AIR SERVICES — Pelican Airways (7V/PDF)   Johannesburg-OR Tambo (JNB)

Also operates services with AMI Turbo DC-3TP and Grumman G-159 Gulfstream leased from Dodson International and Nelair as required. Associated with Ryan Blake Air Charter.

PHOEBUS APOLLO AVIATION — Phoebus (PHB)   Johannesburg-Rand (QRA)

☐ ZS-DIW	Douglas DC-3	11991	ex SAAF 6871		Pegasus
☐ ZS-PAI	Douglas C-54E	27319	ex N4989K	Atlas	
☐ S9-KAZ	Douglas DC-9-32	47368/505	ex ZS-PAK		

PROGRESS AIR — Lanseria (HLA)

☐ ZS-SDM	Swearingen SA.227AC Metro III	AC-756	ex C-FAFW	

QWILA AIR — Q-Charter (QWL)   Lanseria (HLA)

☐ ZS-NUF	Beech 200C Super King Air	BL-4	ex V5-AAL	
☐ ZS-NNZ	Beech 200C Super King Air	BL-8	ex ZS-NAX	
☐ ZS-OKL	Beech 1900D	UE-48	ex 5Y-OKL	
☐ ZS-OMC	Beech 1900D	UE-18	ex N18YV	
☐ ZS-PRE	Beech 1900C	UB-15	ex N715GL	all-white
☐ ZS-SLG	Cessna 208B Caravan I	208B0772	ex N208LT	
☐ ZS-SLT	Cessna 208B Caravan I	208B0459	ex F-OGXK	

ROVOS AIR — Rovos (VOS)   Lanseria (HLA)

☐ ZS-ARV	Convair 340-67	228	ex CP-2237	
☐ ZS-AUA	Douglas DC-4	42934	ex PH-DDS	Flying Dutchman colours
☐ ZS-BRV	Convair 340-67	215	ex CP-2236	
☐ ZS-CRV	Douglas DC-3	13331	ex ZS-PTG	Delaney

RYAN BLAKE AIR — Johannesburg-Rand (QRA)

☐ ZS-OJH	Swearingen SA.227AC Metro III	AC-727	ex N100GS	[George]

SAFAIR — Cargo (FA/(SFR))   Johannesburg-OR Tambo (JNB)

☐ ZS-ASW	Avro 146-RJ85	E2313	ex N505XJ		>LNK
☐ ZS-ASX	Avro 146-RJ85	E2314	ex N506XJ		
☐ ZS-ASY	Avro 146-RJ85	E2316	ex N507XJ		>LNK
☐ ZS-ASZ	Avro 146-RJ85	E2318	ex N508XJ		>LNK
☐ ZS-IAC	Boeing 727-227F (Raisbeck 3)	21247/1217	ex N73751		>Imperial Air Cargo
☐ ZS-PDL	Boeing 727-281F (FedEx 3)	20466/865	ex EI-LCH		
☐ ZS-OTF	Boeing 737-436	25305/2147	ex G-DOCC		>CAW
☐ ZS-OTG	Boeing 737-436	25840/2197	ex G-DOCJ		>CAW
☐ ZS-OTH	Boeing 737-436	25841/2222	ex G-DOCK		>CAW
☐ ZS-SGX	Boeing 737-2T5	22396/730	ex N223AG		
☐ ZS-SID	Boeing 737-244F	22583/809		all-white	>SAA
☐ ZS-SIF	Boeing 737-244F	22585/828		Komati	>SAA
☐ ZS-SIG	Boeing 737-244	22586/829			>RNX
☐ ZS-SII	Boeing 737-244	22588/836			[JNB]
☐ ZS-SIK	Boeing 737-244	22590/854	ex 5N-YMM		
☐ ZS-SIL	Boeing 737-244	22591/859			
☐ ZS-SIM	Boeing 737-244	22828/881			>ILN
☐ ZS-SIT	Boeing 737-236	21790/599	ex V5-AND		
☐ ZS-SPU	Boeing 737-3S3	24059/1517	ex N240AG		♦
☐ ZS-JIZ	Lockheed L-382G-35C Hercules	4695	ex F-GNMM		Op for UN/WFP
☐ ZS-ORA	Lockheed L-382G-7C Hercules	4208	ex S9-CAY		
☐ ZS-ORB	Lockheed L-382G-14C Hercules	4248	ex PK-YRW		
☐ ZS-ORC	Lockheed L-382G-23C Hercules	4388	ex S9-BOQ		
☐ ZS-RSC	Lockheed L-382G-28C Hercules	4475	ex S9-NAD		

☐ ZS-RSF	Lockheed L-382G-31C Hercules	4562	ex S9-CAI	
☐ ZS-RSG	Lockheed L-382G-31C Hercules	4565	ex S9-CAJ	
☐ ZS-RSI	Lockheed L-382G-31C Hercules	4600	ex F-GIMV	>FAB
☐ ZS-OBF	McDonnell-Douglas MD-82	48019/1001	ex F-GPZC	[JNB]
☐ ZS-OBG	McDonnell-Douglas MD-82	48020/1045	ex N823NK	[ROW]
☐ ZS-OBK	McDonnell-Douglas MD-82	49115/1135	ex F-GPZE	>RNX
☐ ZS-OPX	McDonnell-Douglas MD-83	53012/1736	ex N825NK	>RNX
☐ ZS-OPZ	McDonnell-Douglas MD-83	49617/1464	ex N831NK	>RNX

SKY ONE AIR | | | | Lanseria (HLA)

☐ ZS-PWM	Fokker F.28 Fellowship 000	11045	ex PK-RJW	

SKYHAUL | Skyhaul (HAU) | Johannesburg-OR Tambo (JNB)

☐ ZS-SKG	Convair 580	025	ex EC-GDY	
☐ ZS-SKI	Convair 580	186	ex EC-GHN	
☐ ZS-SKK	Convair 580	135	ex EC-GKH	>LAC-SkyCongo
☐ ZS-SKL	Convair 580	458	ex EC-GBF	

SOLENTA AVIATION | | | | Lanseria (HLA)

☐ ZS-MKE	Beech 1900D	UE-44	ex PH-ACY	Op for UN
☐ ZS-NAC	Beech 1900D	UE-28	ex N28YV	
☐ ZS-NPT	Beech 1900C-1	UC-113	ex 5Y-HAC	Op for DHL
☐ ZS-ODG	Beech 1900C-1	UC-158	ex N158YV	Op for DHL
☐ ZS-OHE	Beech 1900C-1	UC-48	ex 9J-AFJ	
☐ ZS-OLY	Beech 1900D	UE-39	ex N39ZV	
☐ ZS-OYC	Beech 1900D	UE-117	ex VH-NTL	
☐ ZS-OYE	Beech 1900D	UE-200	ex VH-IAV	
☐ ZS-OYJ	Beech 1900D	UE-273	ex 5Y-NAC	
☐ ZS-OYK	Beech 1900D	UE-318	ex VH-NBN	all-white
☐ ZS-PJL	Beech 1900C-1	UC-77	ex N77YV	
☐ ZS-PJX	Beech 1900D	UE-102	ex P2-MBX	
☐ ZS-ZED	Beech 1900D	UE-260	ex N260GL	Op for UN
☐ ZS-NIZ	Cessna 208B Caravan I	208B0353	ex 5Y-NIZ	Op for DHL
☐ ZS-SLO	Cessna 208B Caravan I	208B0485	ex F-OGXI	Op for DHL
☐ ZS-SLR	Cessna 208B Caravan I	208B0497	ex N497AC	Op for DHL
☐ ZS-TIN	Cessna 208B Caravan I	208B0261	ex 9J-DHL	Op for DHL
☐ 5Y-OBY	Cessna 208B Caravan I	208B0345	ex ZS-OBY	Op for DHL
☐ 5Y-TLC	Cessna 208B Caravan I	208B0472	ex ZS-TLC	Op for DHL
☐ TR-LII	Antonov An-26			
☐ ZS-PEA	Beech 200C Super King Air	BL-29	ex N500PH	all-white
☐ ZS-ATR	ATR 42-300F	060	ex PH-XLC	Op for DHL
☐ ZS-LUC	ATR 42-320	032	ex PH-RAK	
☐ ZS-OVP	ATR 42-300F	088	ex F-WQNG	Op for DHL
☐ ZS-OVR	ATR 42-300F	116	ex F-WQNB	Op for DHL
☐ ZS-OVS	ATR 42-300F	075	ex F-WQNU	Op for DHL
☐ ZS-XCC	ATR 42-500	528	ex F-WKVI	♦

SOUTH AFRICAN AIRWAYS | Springbok (SA/SAA) | Johannesburg-OR Tambo (JNB)

Member of Star Alliance

☐ ZS-SFD	Airbus A319-131	2268	ex D-AVWW	
☐ ZS-SFE	Airbus A319-131	2281	ex D-AVYK	
☐ ZS-SFF	Airbus A319-131	2308	ex D-AVYE	
☐ ZS-SFG	Airbus A319-131	2326	ex D-AVYT	
☐ ZS-SFH	Airbus A319-131	2355	ex D-AVWC	
☐ ZS-SFI	Airbus A319-131	2375	ex D-AVWR	
☐ ZS-SFJ	Airbus A319-131	2379	ex D-AVWU	
☐ ZS-SFK	Airbus A319-131	2418	ex D-AVYI	
☐ ZS-SFL	Airbus A319-131	2438	ex D-AVWP	
☐ ZS-SFM	Airbus A319-131	2469	ex D-AVYH	
☐ ZS-SFN	Airbus A319-131	2501	ex D-AVWD	
☐ ZS-	Airbus A330-2		ex	o/o♦
☐ ZS-	Airbus A330-2		ex	o/o♦
☐ ZS-	Airbus A330-2		ex	o/o♦
☐ ZS-	Airbus A330-2		ex	o/o♦
☐ ZS-	Airbus A330-2		ex	o/o♦
☐ ZS-SLA	Airbus A340-212	008	ex D-AIBA	
☐ ZS-SLB	Airbus A340-212	011	ex D-AIBC	
☐ ZS-SLC	Airbus A340-212	018	ex D-AIBD	

☐ ZS-SLD	Airbus A340-212	019	ex D-AIBE		
☐ ZS-SLE	Airbus A340-212	021	ex D-AIBH		
☐ ZS-SLF	Airbus A340-212	006	ex D-AIBF		
☐ ZS-SNA	Airbus A340-642	410	ex F-WWCE		
☐ ZS-SNB	Airbus A340-642	417	ex F-WWCG		
☐ ZS-SNC	Airbus A340-642	426	ex F-WWCH	Star Alliance colours	
☐ ZS-SND	Airbus A340-642	531	ex F-WWCX		
☐ ZS-SNE	Airbus A340-642	534	ex F-WWCY		
☐ ZS-SNF	Airbus A340-642	547	ex F-WWCI		
☐ ZS-SNG	Airbus A340-642	557	ex F-WWCG		
☐ ZS-SNH	Airbus A340-642	626	ex F-WWCF		
☐ ZS-SNI	Airbus A340-642	630	ex F-WWCG		
☐ ZS-SXA	Airbus A340-313E	544	ex F-WWJS		
☐ ZS-SXB	Airbus A340-313E	582	ex F-WWJT		
☐ ZS-SXC	Airbus A340-313E	590	ex F-WWJY		
☐ ZS-SXD	Airbus A340-313E	643	ex VT-JWA		
☐ ZS-SXE	Airbus A340-313E	646	ex VT-JWB		
☐ ZS-SXF	Airbus A340-313E	651	ex VT-JWC		
☐ ZS-SXG	Airbus A340-313X	378	ex F-WJKF		♦
☐ ZS-SXH	Airbus A340-313X	197	ex F-WJKP		♦
☐ ZS-SBA	Boeing 737-3Y0F	26070/2349	ex N700JZ		
☐ ZS-SBB	Boeing 737-3Y0F	26072/2369	ex N701JZ		
☐ ZS-SID	Boeing 737-244F	22583/809		all-white	<SFR
☐ ZS-SIF	Boeing 737-244F	22585/828		Komati	<SFR
☐ ZS-SJA	Boeing 737-8S3/W	29248/561			
☐ ZS-SJB	Boeing 737-8S3/W	29249/653	ex N1786B		
☐ ZS-SJC	Boeing 737-85F/W	28828/565	ex N1786B		
☐ ZS-SJD	Boeing 737-85F/W	28829/582			
☐ ZS-SJE	Boeing 737-85F/W	28830/669	ex N1786B		
☐ ZS-SJF	Boeing 737-85F/W	30006/688	ex N1787B		
☐ ZS-SJG	Boeing 737-8BG/W	32353/711	ex N1786B		
☐ ZS-SJH	Boeing 737-8BG/W	32354/725	ex PH-HZQ		
☐ ZS-SJI	Boeing 737-85F/W	30007/746	ex N1787B		
☐ ZS-SJJ	Boeing 737-85F/W	30567/761	ex N1787B		
☐ ZS-SJK	Boeing 737-8BG/W	32355/807	ex PH-HZT		
☐ ZS-SJL	Boeing 737-8BG/W	32356/819	ex PH-HZZ		
☐ ZS-SJM	Boeing 737-85F/W	30476/789	ex N788BA		
☐ ZS-SJN	Boeing 737-85F/W	30569/850	ex N1786B		
☐ ZS-SJO	Boeing 737-8BG/W	32357/918	ex PH-HZS		
☐ ZS-SJP	Boeing 737-8BG/W	32358/955	ex PH-HZU		
☐ ZS-SJR	Boeing 737-844/W	32631/1176	ex N6067U		
☐ ZS-SJS	Boeing 737-844/W	32632/1205			
☐ ZS-SJT	Boeing 737-844/W	32633/1225			
☐ ZS-SJU	Boeing 737-844/W	32634/1383			
☐ ZS-SJV	Boeing 737-844/W	32635/1407	ex N1787B	Star Alliance c/s	
☐ ZS-SAZ	Boeing 747-444	29119/1187		Imonti	stored

| **SOUTH AFRICAN EXPRESS AIRWAYS** | | **Expressways (XZ/EXY)** | **Johannesburg-OR Tambo (JNB)** |

☐ ZS-NBA	Canadair CRJ-200ER	7702	ex N484CA		♦
☐ ZS-NMC	Canadair CRJ-200ER	7225	ex N626BR		
☐ ZS-NMD	Canadair CRJ-200ER	7233	ex N627BR		
☐ ZS-NME	Canadair CRJ-200ER	7240	ex N628BR		
☐ ZS-NMF	Canadair CRJ-200ER	7287	ex N634BR		
☐ ZS-NMG	Canadair CRJ-200ER	7772	ex 5N-BJI		
☐ ZS-NMH	Canadair CRJ-200ER	7787	ex 5N-BJK		
☐ ZS-NMI	Canadair CRJ-200ER	7153	ex C-FZAN		
☐ ZS-NMJ	Canadair CRJ-200ER	7161	ex C-GAUG		
☐ ZS-NMK	Canadair CRJ-200ER	7198	ex C-GBMF		
☐ ZS-NML	Canadair CRJ-200ER	7201	ex C-GBLX		
☐ ZS-NMM	Canadair CRJ-200ER	7234	ex C-FMMT		
☐ ZS-NMN	Canadair CRJ-200ER	7237	ex C-FMMX		
☐ ZS-NBD	Canadair CRJ-701	10033	ex N610QX		♦
☐ ZS-NLT	Canadair CRJ-701	10024	ex N607QX		
☐ ZS-NLV	Canadair CRJ-701	10010	ex N602QX		
☐ ZS-	Canadair CRJ-701ER	10028	ex D-ACSB		♦
☐ ZS-	Canadair CRJ-701ER	10039	ex D-ACSC		♦
☐ ZS-NLW	de Havilland DHC-8-315	338	ex ZS-NLY	301	
☐ ZS-NLX	de Havilland DHC-8-315	348	ex C-GDKL	302	
☐ ZS-NLY	de Havilland DHC-8-315	352	ex ZS-NLW	303	
☐ ZS-NLZ	de Havilland DHC-8-315	354	ex C-GFRP	304	>ATC
☐ ZS-NMA	de Havilland DHC-8-315	358	ex C-GDFT	305	>ATC

☐ ZS-NMB	de Havilland DHC-8-315	368	ex C-GGIU	306
☐ ZS-NMO	de Havilland DHC-8-402Q	4122	ex C-FFCU	
☐ ZS-NMP	de Havilland DHC-8-315B	420	ex ZS-NNJ	307
☐ ZS-NMS	de Havilland DHC-8-402Q	4127	ex C-FFPH	

| **SPRINGBOK CLASSIC AIR** | | *Spring Classic (SPB)* | | *Johannesburg-Rand (QRA)* |

| ☐ ZS-CFC | Beech E-18S | BA-216 | | |

| **STAR AIR CARGO** | | | | *Johannesburg-OR Tambo (JNB)* |

☐ ZS-PUI	Boeing 737-2B7 (Nordam 3)	22890/986	ex 5N-BFJ	>AML
☐ ZS-SFX	Boeing 737-2B7 (Nordam 3)	22889/983	ex 5N-BFH	
☐ ZS-SHL	Boeing 737-247 (Nordam 3)	23520/1329	ex 5H-MVV	
☐ ZS-SKW	Boeing 737-219 (Nordam 3)	23474/1199	ex 9J-KDK	
☐ ZS-SMD	Boeing 737-219 (Nordam 3)	23472/1194	ex N472BC	

| **STARS AWAY AVIATION** | | *(STX)* | | *Cape Town-International (CPT)* |

☐ ZS-DBH	Douglas DC-9-33F (ABS 3)	47384/543	ex N931AX	
☐ ZS-DBL	Hawker Siddeley HS.748 Srs.2B/287 LFD	1737	ex VH-IMK	Frtr
☐ 9G-MKV	Hawker Siddeley HS.748 Srs.2B/287 LFD	1736	ex ZS-DBM	Frtr

| **TRAMON AIR** | | *Tramon (TMX)* | | *Lanseria (HLA)* |

| ☐ ZS-ALX | Grumman G-159 Gulfstream I | 086 | ex N10TB | |
| ☐ ZS-JIS | Grumman G-159 Gulfstream I | 193 | ex PK-TRN | |

| **TRAVELMAX** | | | | *Lanseria (HLA)* |

| ☐ ZS-PKB | Beech 1900D | UE-3 | ex N3YV | <KUS |

| **UTAIR SOUTH AFRICA** | | *(UTR)* | | *Lanseria (HLA)* |

☐ ZS-RUB	Mil Mi-8MTV-1	95960	ex RA-27133	
☐ ZS-RUC	Mil Mi-8MTV-1	95907	ex RA-27071	
☐ ZS-RVE	Mil Mi-8MTV-1	96264	ex RA-25809	
☐ ZS-TUT	Mil Mi-8MTV-1	95151	ex RA-25413	

| **VALAN INTERNATIONAL CARGO** | | *Nalau (VLA)* | | *Johannesburg-Rand (QRA)* |

☐ ZS-OWX	Antonov An-32B	2806	ex ER-AWB	all-white, no titles
☐ ZS-PEL	Antonov An-32B	3004	ex ER-AFG	all-white, no titles
☐ ZS-PHR	Antonov An-32A	2601	ex ER-AEW	o/o
☐ ZS-PSO	Antonov An-32B	2808	ex RA-48059	
Reported to have ceased operations in late 2007				

| **VSA AVIATION** | | | | *Lanseria (HLA)* |

☐ ZS-NRN	Dornier 228-200	8021	ex OY-CHK	Op for UN
☐ ZS-OOU	Cessna 404 Titan II	404-0415	ex 9Q-CMX	>STA Mozambique
☐ ZS-OVM	Dornier 228-201	8056	ex F-GOAH	all-white

Z3- MACEDONIA (Republic of Macedonia)

| **MAT MACEDONIAN AIRLINES** | | *Makavio (IN/MAK)* | | *Skopje (SKP)* |

| ☐ N237MA | Boeing 737-529 | 25249/2145 | ex Z3-AAH | |

| **SKYWINGS INTERNATIONAL** | | *(GSW)* | | |

| ☐ Z3-AAJ | Boeing 737-33A/W | 23827/1444 | ex D-AHIG | |
| ☐ Z3-AAN | Boeing 737-382 | 24365/1695 | ex EI-DJK | ♦ |

| **STAR AIRLINES** | | | | *Skopje (SKP)* |

| ☐ Z3-CAA | Boeing 747-2U3B (SCD) | 22769/562 | ex N923FT | |
| ☐ Z3-CAB | Boeing 747-256B (SF) | 24071/699 | ex TF-ARW | |

3A- MONACO (Principality of Monaco)

| **HELI AIR MONACO** | | *Heli Air (YO/MCM)* | | *Monte Carlo Heliport (MCM)* |

☐ 3A-MAC	Aérospatiale AS350B Ecureuil	1673	ex HB-XBC	
☐ 3A-MAX	Aérospatiale AS350BA Ecureuil	1794	ex F-GMBN	
☐ 3A-MFC	Eurocopter EC130B4 Ecureuil	3768		

☐ 3A-MIL	Aérospatiale AS350BA Ecureuil	1709	ex F-GMBV			
☐ 3A-MJB	Aérospatiale AS350B2 Ecureuil	1988	ex F-GJCM			
☐ 3A-MPJ	Eurocopter EC130B4 Ecureuil	3662				
☐ 3A-MTP	Aérospatiale AS350B2 Ecureuil	1996	ex I-LOLO			
☐ 3A-MTT	Aérospatiale AS350B2 Ecureuil	1967	ex I-LUPJ			
☐ 3A-MCM	Aérospatiale SA365N Dauphin 2	6076	ex N9UW			
☐ 3A-MJP	Aérospatiale SA365C3 Dauphin 2	5015	ex N90049			
☐ 3A-MPG	Eurocopter EC155B1 Dauphin 2	6771				
☐ 3A-MXL	Aérospatiale AS355N Ecureuil 2	5712				

3B- MAURITIUS (Republic of Mauritius)

AIR MAURITIUS — AirMauritius (MK/MAU) — Plaisance (MRU)

☐ 3B-NBF	Airbus A319-112	1592	ex D-AVYX	Mon Choisy	
☐ 3B-NBH	Airbus A319-112	1936	ex D-AVWF	Blue Bay	
☐ 3B-NBL	Airbus A330-202	1057	ex F-WWYF	Nenuphar	
☐ 3B-NBM	Airbus A330-202	883	ex F-WWKK	Trochetia	
☐ 3B-NAU	Airbus A340-312	076	ex F-WWJG	Pink Pigeon	
☐ 3B-NAY	Airbus A340-313X	152	ex F-WWJX	Cardinal	
☐ 3B-NBD	Airbus A340-313X	194	ex F-WWJP	Parakeet	
☐ 3B-NBE	Airbus A340-313X	268	ex F-WWJG	Paille en Queue	
☐ 3B-NBI	Airbus A340-313E	793	ex F-WWJE	Le Flamboyant	
☐ 3B-NBJ	Airbus A340-313E	800	ex F-WWJF	Le Chamarel	
☐ 3B-NBG	ATR 72-212A	690	ex F-WWEM	Port Mathurin	
☐ 3B-NBK	ATR 72-212A	595	ex OY-CIO	Coin de More	<CIM
☐ 3B-NBN	ATR 72-212A	921	ex F-WWET	Ile Aux Aigrettes	♦
☐ 3B-NZD	Bell 206B JetRanger III	4464			
☐ 3B-NZE	Bell 206B JetRanger III	4465			
☐ 3B-NZF	Bell 206B JetRanger III	4496	ex N8152H		

3C- EQUATORIAL GUINEA (Republic of Equatorial Guinea)

CEIBA INTERCONTINENTAL — Malabo (SSG)

☐ TC-MND	Airbus A300C4-203F	212	ex ZS-SDG	[XCR] <MNB
☐ 3C-LLG	ATR 42-300	335	ex F-ODYE	
☐ 3C-LLH	ATR 42-300	671	ex F-WWYE	
☐ 3C-LLI	ATR 72-212A	790	ex F-WWEJ	
☐ 3C-LLM	ATR 72-212A	810	ex F-WWEX	

EUROGUINEANA DE AVIACION — EcuatoGuinea — Malabo (SSG)

Leases Airbus A321s from Spanair as required plus other aircraft when required. Part owned by Spanair.

GEASA — Geasa (GEA) — Malabo (SSG)

☐ RA-87956	Yakovlev Yak-40K	9821757	ex CCCP-87956	

GENERAL WORK AVIACION — Malabo (SSG)

☐ 3C-GWA	Fokker F.28 Fellowship 4000	11240	ex HC-CDG	
☐ 3C-GWB	Fokker F.28 Fellowship 4000	11156	ex 3C-LGP	
☐ 3C-GWC	Fokker F.28 Fellowship 4000	11238	ex TU-TIY	

GETRA — (GET) — Malabo (SSG)

☐ 3C-LLF	Fokker F.28 Fellowship 1000	11073	ex N941TD	

GUINEA EQUATORIAL AIRLINES — (RGE) — Malabo (SSG)

☐ 3C-LGF	Ilyushin Il-76MD	0073479386	ex 3C-HAV	

NATIONAL REGIONAL TRANSPORT — Malabo (SSG)

☐ ZS-DOA	SAAB SF.340A	340A-077	ex C-GQXD	<AAS Leasing

STAR EQUATORIAL AIRLINES

☐ 3C-LLN	Boeing 737-260	23915/1583	ex ET-AJB	

UTAGE		Utage (UTG)		Malabo (SSG)
☐ ER-AZB	Antonov An-24RV	27307507	ex RA-47690	
☐ ZS-OKT	Embraer EMB.120RT Brasilia	120254	ex N261GA	

3D- SWAZILAND (Kingdom of Swaziland)

AERO AFRICA		Aero Africa (RFC)		Johannesburg (JNB)
☐ 3D-AAJ	Boeing 737-222	19075/97	ex 3C-AAJ	op for BGL
☐ 3D-AVC	Boeing 727-251(FedEx 3)	21155/1169	ex 7P-LAA	VIP >MRT
☐ 3D-BGA	Boeing 737-2H4	21722/568	ex OM-ERA	>BGL
☐ 3D-ITC	Boeing 727-2F2	21260/1222	ex N103AZ	op for ILN
☐ 3D-JJM	Boeing 727-231 (Raisbeck 3)	20053/713	ex N64320	[ELP]
☐ 3D-ZZM	Boeing 737-2H7C	20590/304	ex 3C-ZZM all-white	<ILN

EASTERN AIRWAYS				Manzini-Matsapha (MTS)
☐ 3D-AVP	LET L-410UVP	851514	ex LY-AVP	

3X- GUINEA (Republic of Guinea)

AIR GUINEE EXPRESS		Future Express (2U/GIP)		Conakry (CKY)
☐ 3X-GCB	Boeing 737-2R6C	22627/779		[PGF]

EXIM TRADING				
☐ 3X-GEM	Antonov An-12BK	00347005	ex ER-AXK	stored

GUINEE AIR CARGO				Conakry (CKY)
☐ 3X-GEE	Hawker Siddeley HS.748 Srs.2A	1602	ex 3D-POZ	Op Humanitarian flights

4K- AZERBAIJAN (Republic of Azerbaijan)

AZAL CARGO		Azalaviacargo (AHC)		Baku-Bina (BAK)
☐ 4K-AZ16	Ilyushin Il-76TD	1023412411	ex UK 76410	
☐ 4K-AZ26	Ilyushin Il-76TD	1033416525	ex UK 76844	
☐ 4K-26584	Antonov An-26B	13509	ex 26584	[BAK]

AZERBAIJAN AIRLINES		Azal (J2/AHY)		Baku-Bina (BAK)
☐ 4K-AZ01	Airbus A319-115X	2487	ex D-AVWA Baku	Op for Govt [CJ]
☐ 4K-AZ03	Airbus A319-111	2516	ex D-AVWS Ganja	
☐ 4K-AZ04	Airbus A319-111	2588	ex D-AVXJ	
☐ 4K-AZ05	Airbus A319-111	2788	ex D-AVYY Gazakh	
☐ 4K-AZ54	Airbus A320-211	0331	ex 9H-ADZ	[MLA]
☐ 4K-AZ77	Airbus A320-214	2846	ex D-ABDH	
☐ 4K-AZ52	ATR 42-500	667	ex F-WWLA Zagatala	
☐ 4K-AZ53	ATR 42-500	689	ex F-WWLK	
☐ 4K-AZ64	ATR 72-212A	761	ex F-WWEX Gabala	
☐ 4K-AZ65	ATR 72-212A	789	ex F-WWEH Gusar	
☐ 4K-AZ66	ATR 72-212A	799	ex F-WWEP	
☐ 4K-AZ67	ATR 72-212A	818	ex F-WWEH Khankandi	
☐ VP-BBR	Boeing 757-22L	29305/894	ex N6046P Garabagh	
☐ VP-BBS	Boeing 757-22L	30834/947	ex (4K-AZ13)	
☐ 4K-AZ38	Boeing 757-256	26246/620	ex N262CT	
☐ 4K-AZ43	Boeing 757-2M6	23453/100	ex V8-RBB	
☐ 4K-	Boeing 767-3			o/o♦
☐ 4K-	Boeing 767-3			o/o♦
☐ 4K-AZ49	Antonov An-140-100	36525307041		stored
☐ 4K-AZ10	Tupolev Tu-154M	98A1013		
☐ 4K-AZ729	Tupolev Tu-154M	92A911	ex 4K-85729	VIP
☐ 4K-AZ734	Tupolev Tu-154M	92A916	ex 4K-85734 Shusha	
☐ 4K-AZ738	Tupolev Tu-154M	92A921	ex 4K-85738	

IMAIR		Improtex (IK/ITX)		Baku-Bina (BAK)
□ 4K-AZ17	Tupolev Tu-154M	85A718	ex B-2603	
□ 4K-85732	Tupolev Tu-154M	92A914	ex CCCP-85732	

SILK WAY AIRLINES		Silk Line (ZP/AZQ)		Baku-Bina (BAK)
□ 4K-800	Boeing 747-4R7F	29729/1189	ex LX-MCV	♦
□ 4K-AZ19	Ilyushin Il-76TD	0053460820	ex UR-76408	
□ 4K-AZ31	Ilyushin Il-76TD	1013405184	ex RA-76426	
□ 4K-AZ40	Ilyushin Il-76TD	1043419632		
□ 4K-AZ41	Ilyushin Il-76TD	1093420673		
□ 4K-AZ55	Ilyushin Il-76TD	2053420680		
□ 4K-AZ70	Ilyushin Il-76TD	2093421717		
□ 4K-AZ100	Ilyushin Il-76TD-90VD	2073421208		
□ 4K-AZ101	Ilyushin Il-76TD-90VD	2083421716		
□ 4K-AZ23	Antonov An-12BK	8345605	ex 11715	
□ 4K-AZ808	ATR 42-500	673	ex F-WWLG	

SKY WIND		Sky Wind (AZH)		Baku-Bina (BAK)
□ 4K-AZ32	Antonov An-12B	5343006	ex CCCP-11430	
□ 4K-AZ37	Antonov An-12BK	00347506	ex CCCP-11938	
□ 4K-AZ57	Antonov An-26B	9504	ex RA-26693	
□ 4K-78129	Ilyushin Il-76MD	0083489683	ex ER-IBC	
□ 4K-78130	Ilyushin Il-76MD	0043454611	ex UR-78130	

TURANAIR		Turan (3T/URN)		Baku-Bina (BAK)
□ 4K-727	Tupolev Tu-154M	86A727	ex LZ-LCS	[BAK]

4L- GEORGIA (Republic of Georgia)

AIR BATUMI

□ 4L-BTM	Boeing 737-33A	23628/1304	ex N628AG	o/o♦

AIR SIRIN

□ 4L-AFL	Antonov An-26B	17310610	ex UR-AUA	
□ 4L-AFS	Antonov An-26	97308608	ex UR-AFS	

AIR VICTORY

□ 4L-HUS	Antonov An-12BP	6343708	ex LZ-CBE	
□ 4L-IRA	Antonov An-12B	9346510	ex EX-025	
□ 4L-VAL	Antonov An-12BP	9346807	ex LZ-CBH	
□ 4L-VPI	Antonov An-12B	8345510	ex ER-ADY	

AIRZENA – GEORGIAN AIRWAYS		Tamazi (A9/TGZ)			Tbilisi-Lochini (TBS)
□ 4L-TGA	Boeing 737-5Q8	28055/3024	ex B-2110		
□ 4L-TGI	Boeing 737-505	26336/2805	ex B-2973		♦
□ 4L-TGR	Boeing 737-59D	24694/1834	ex G-THOC	Balumi	
□ 4L-TGT	Boeing 737-4Q8	26306/2653	ex N411LF	Tbilisi	
□ 4L-GAE	Canadair CRJ-200ER	7070	ex F-GRJA	all white	
□ 4L-GAF	Canadair CL-600-2B19 (Chal 850)	8046	ex OY-YVI		Op for Government
□ 4L-GAL	Canadair CRJ-200ER	7076	ex F-GRJB		
□ 4L-TGB	Canadair CRJ-200LR	7442	ex OY-MBJ		♦
□ 4L-TGG	Canadair CRJ-200ER	7386	ex OY-MAV		
□ 4L-TGS	Canadair CRJ-200LR	7373	ex EK-20073		
□ 4L-TGN	Yakovlev Yak-40	9611246	ex 4L-88158		

EUREX

□ 4L-KMK	Boeing 747-281F	23139/608	ex N106KZ	

EUROLINE

□ 4L-AJA	Boeing 737-5C9	26439/2444	ex LX-LGP	♦
□ UR-CGR	SAAB SF.340A	340A-124	ex N340JW	
□ 4L-EUI	SAAB SF.340B	340B-163	ex 5Y-FLA	
□ 4L-EUR	Tupolev Tu-134A	63860	ex 4L-AAJ	

614

GLOBAL GEORGIAN AIRWAYS		Global Georgian (GGZ)		Tbilisi-Lochini (TBS)
☐ 4L-12008	Antonov An-12BP	5343103	ex RA-11768	

SAKAVIASERVICE		Sakservice (AZG)		Tbilisi-Lochini (TBS)
☐ 4L-GLG	Antonov An-24RV	27308005	ex UR-4677	
☐ 4L-GLM	Ilyushin Il-76T	093418543	ex EX-117	
☐ 4L-GLN	Antonov An-12BK	9346704	ex EX-131	
☐ 4L-GLR	Ilyushin Il-76T	0013432955	ex UP-I7608	
☐ 4L-GLX	Ilyushin Il-76TD	0033448390	ex EW-263TH	

SKY GEORGIA		National (QB/GFG)		Tbilisi-Lochini (TBS)
☐ 4L-GNL	Douglas DC-9-51 (ABS 3)	48134/980	ex UR-CCK	
☐ 4L-GNN	Douglas DC-9-51	47657/787	ex UR-BYL	
☐ 4L-SKD	Ilyushin Il-76TD	1023410344	ex UP-I7639	♦
☐ 4L-SKY	Ilyushin Il-76TD	0053464934	ex UP-I7638	

TBILAVIAMSHENI		Tbilavia (L6/VNZ)		Tbilisi-Lochini (TBS)
☐ 4L-AAK	Yakovlev Yak-40	9531043	ex 4L-87242	Georgia titles

TRANSAVIA SERVICE		Transavia Service (5I/FNV)		Kutaisi (KUT)
☐ 4L-FAS	Antonov An-72-100	36572020358	ex RA-72901	
☐ 4L-NAS	Antonov An-72	36572020362	ex EK-72902	
☐ 4L-VAS	Antonov An-12BK	7345201	ex EK-12221	

TRADE LINKS AVIATION				
☐ 4L-TAS	Antonov An-24B	89901506	ex EX-004	all-white

VIP-AVIA		VIP Avia (VPV)		Tbilisi-Lochini (TBS)
☐ 4L-VIP	Yakovlev Yak-40	9320129	ex 4L-MGC	VIPop for Government

4O-   MONTENEGRO (Republic of Montenegro)

MONTENEGRO AIRLINES		Motairo (YM/MGX)		Podgorica/Tivat (TGD/TIV)
☐ 4O-AOA	Embraer ERJ-195LR	19000180	ex PT-SDO	
☐ 4O-AOB	Embraer ERJ-195LR	19000283	ex PT-TLX	
☐ 4O-AOC	Embraer ERJ-195LR	19000358	ex PT-PVM	♦
☐ 4O-AOK	Fokker 100	11272	ex YU-AOK	Sveti Petar Cetinjski
☐ 4O-AOL	Fokker 100	11268	ex ZA-ARC	Podgorica
☐ 4O-AOM	Fokker 100	11321	ex YU-AOM	Bar
☐ 4O-AOP	Fokker 100	11332	ex YU-AOP	Boka
☐ 4O-AOT	Fokker 100	11350	ex YU-AOT	

4R-   SRI LANKA (Democratic Socialist Republic of Sri Lanka)

AERO LANKA AIRLINES	AeroLanka (QL/RNL)		Colombo-Bandaranayike Intl/Ratmalana (CMB/RML)	
☐ 4R-SEA	Cessna 404	404-0833	ex N404AM	
☐ 4R-SER	Hawker Siddeley HS.748 Srs.2B/426	1799	ex VH-IMJ	

EXPO AIR	Expoavia (8D/EXV)		Colombo-Bandaranayike Intl/Ratmalana (CMB/RML)	
☐ 4R-EXD	Ilyushin Il-18GrM	187009802	ex YR-IMZ	<RMV
☐ 4R-EXJ	Douglas DC-8-63CF (BAC 3)	46049/479	ex N867BX	

MIHIN LANKA		(MJ/MLR)		Colombo-Bandaranayike Intl (CMB)
☐ 4R-MLA	Fokker F.27 Friendship 500RF	10642	ex 4R-EXH	<EXV
☐ 4R-MRA	Fokker F.27 Friendship 500RF	10631	ex A4O-FC	
☐ 4R-MRB	Airbus A320-232	0977	ex VT-ADZ	
☐ 4R-MRC	Airbus A321-231	3106	ex G-TTIF	♦

SRILANKAN		Srilankan (UL/ALK)		Colombo-Bandaranayike Intl (CMB)
☐ 4R-ABC	Airbus A320-231	0304	ex N304RX	
☐ 4R-ABE	Airbus A320-231	0169	ex G-TICL	
☐ 4R-ABG	Airbus A320-232	2908	ex VT-ADT	

☐ 4R-ABH	Airbus A320-232	2914	ex VT-ADS			
☐ 4R-ABJ	Airbus A320-232	2564	ex VT-DKY			
☐ 4R-ABK	Airbus A320-214	2584	ex 9K-CAB			◆
☐ 4R-ALA	Airbus A330-243	303	ex F-WWYH			
☐ 4R-ALB	Airbus A330-243	306	ex F-WWYL			
☐ 4R-ALC	Airbus A330-243	311	ex F-WWYN			
☐ 4R-ALD	Airbus A330-243	313	ex F-WWYP			
☐ 4R-ALG	Airbus A330-243	404	ex G-WWBB			◆
☐ 4R-ADA	Airbus A340-311	032	ex F-WWJT			
☐ 4R-ADB	Airbus A340-311	033	ex F-WWJU			
☐ 4R-ADC	Airbus A340-311	034	ex F-WWJY			
☐ 4R-ADE	Airbus A340-313X	367	ex F-GTUA			
☐ 4R-ADF	Airbus A340-313X	374	ex F-GTUB			

4X- ISRAEL (State of Israel)

ARKIA ISRAELI AIRLINES   Arkia (IZ/AIZ)   Tel Aviv-Ben Gurion/Sde Dov (TLV/SDV)

☐ 4X-AHM	de Havilland DHC-7-102	73	ex 5N-SKA		[SDV]
☐ 4X-AVT	ATR 72-212A	894	ex F-WWEN		
☐ 4X-AVU	ATR 72-212A	587	ex F-WWES		
☐ 4X-AVW	ATR 72-212A	583	ex F-WWER		
☐ 4X-AVX	ATR 72-212A	656	ex F-WWEJ		
☐ 4X-AVZ	ATR 72-212A	577	ex F-WWEN		
☐ 4X-BAU	Boeing 757-3E7	30178/906	ex N1003M		
☐ 4X-BAW	Boeing 757-3E7	30179/912			
☐ 4X-EMA	Embraer ERJ-195LR	19000172	ex EC-KOZ		

AYEET AVIATION   Ayeet (AYT)   Beer-Sheba (BEV)

☐ 4X-AHP	de Havilland DHC-6 Twin Otter 100	75	ex C-FCSF	
☐ 4X-AYS	Britten-Norman BN-2A-8 Islander	376	ex (G-BJWL)	

CARGO AIR LINES   CAL (5C/ICL)   Tel Aviv-Ben Gurion (TLV)

☐ 4X-ICL	Boeing 747-271C	21964/416	ex N538MC	no titles	<GTI
☐ 4X-ICM	Boeing 747-271C	21965/438	ex N539MC	all-white	<GTI
☐ 4X-ICO	Boeing 747-230F	23348/625	ex TF-ARP		◆

EL AL ISRAEL AIRLINES   ElAl (LY/ELY)   Tel Aviv-Ben Gurion (TLV)

☐ 4X-EKA	Boeing 737-858	29957/204		801 Tiberias	
☐ 4X-EKB	Boeing 737-858	29958/249		802 Eilat	
☐ 4X-EKC	Boeing 737-858	29959/314		803 Beit Shean	
☐ 4X-EKD	Boeing 737-758	29960/327		701 Ashkelon	
☐ 4X-EKE	Boeing 737-758	29961/442		702 Nazareth	
☐ 4X-EKF	Boeing 737-8HX	29638/2766		804 Kinneret	
☐ 4X-EKH	Boeing 737-85P/W	35485/2871		807 Yarden	
☐ 4X-EKI	Boeing 737-86N	28587/192	ex N802NA	812	
☐ 4X-EKJ	Boeing 737-85P/W	35486/2908	ex N1786B		
☐ 4X-EKL	Boeing 737-85P/W	35487/2941	ex N1796B		
☐ 4X-EKO	Boeing 737-86Q/W	30287/1308	ex D-ATUI		
☐ 4X-EKP	Boeing 737-8Q8/W	30639/935	ex 5W-SAO		
☐ 4X-EKS	Boeing 737-8Q8/W	36433/2702	ex N1796B		
☐ 4X-EKT	Boeing 737-8BK/W	33030/1968	ex 5B-DBZ		◆
☐ 4X-AXF	Boeing 747-258C	21594/327		405	
☐ 4X-AXK	Boeing 747-245F	22150/476	ex 9V-SQT		
☐ 4X-AXL	Boeing 747-245F	22151/478	ex 9V-SQU		
☐ 4X-AXM	Boeing 747-2B5B (SF)	22485/513	ex 4X-ICN		
☐ 4X-ELA	Boeing 747-458	26055/1027		201 Tel Aviv-Jaffa	
☐ 4X-ELB	Boeing 747-458	26056/1032	ex N60697	202 Haifa	
☐ 4X-ELC	Boeing 747-458	27915/1062	ex N6009F	203 Beer Sheva	
☐ 4X-ELD	Boeing 747-458	29328/1215		204 Jerusalem	
☐ 4X-ELE	Boeing 747-412	26551/1045	ex 9V-SPB		
☐ 4X-ELF	Boeing 747-412F	26563/1036	ex 9V-SFA		◆
☐ 4X-EBM	Boeing 757-258	23918/156		502	
☐ 4X-EBS	Boeing 757-258ER	24884/325		504	
☐ 4X-EBT	Boeing 757-258ER	25036/356		505	
☐ 4X-EBU	Boeing 757-258	26053/529		506	
☐ 4X-EBV	Boeing 757-258	26054/547		507	

☐ 4X-EAA	Boeing 767-258	22972/62	ex N6066Z	601	
☐ 4X-EAC	Boeing 767-258ER	22974/86	ex N6018N	603	
☐ 4X-EAD	Boeing 767-258ER	22975/89	ex N6046P	604	
☐ 4X-EAE	Boeing 767-27EER	24832/316	ex F-GHGD	605	
☐ 4X-EAF	Boeing 767-27EER	24854/326	ex F-GHGE	606	
☐ 4X-EAJ	Boeing 767-330ER	25208/381	ex N208LS	635	
☐ 4X-EAP	Boeing 767-3Y0ER	24953/405	ex TF-FIA		<ICE
☐ 4X-EAR	Boeing 767-352ER	26262/583	ex VN-A769		
☐ 4X-ECA	Boeing 777-258ER	30831/319		101 Galillee	
☐ 4X-ECB	Boeing 777-258ER	30832/325		102 Negev	
☐ 4X-ECC	Boeing 777-258ER	30833/335		103 Hasharon	
☐ 4X-ECD	Boeing 777-258ER	33169/405		104 Carmel	
☐ 4X-ECE	Boeing 777-258ER	36083/648	ex N5017Q	105 Sderot	
☐ 4X-ECF	Boeing 777-258ER	36084/655	ex N5022E	106	

EL-ROM AIRLINES		**(ELR)**		**Tel Aviv-Sde Dov (SDV)**

☐ 4X-CCD	Piper PA-31-350 Navajo Chieftain	31-7652166	ex N62919
☐ 4X-CCF	Piper PA-31-350 Navajo Chieftain	31-7652169	ex N62921

ISRAIR		**Israir (6H/ISR)**		**Tel Aviv-Ben Gurion (TLV)**

☐ 4X-ABF	Airbus A320-232	4354	ex F-WWDC	♦
☐ 4X-ABG	Airbus A320-232	4413	ex F-WWIR	♦
☐ 4X-ABH	Airbus A320-211	0426	ex EI-ELK	♦
☐ 4X-	Airbus A320-232		ex	o/o♦
☐ 4X-ATM	ATR 42-320	069	ex F-WQFS	
☐ 4X-ATN	ATR 42-320	053	ex F-WQGN	
☐ 4X-ATO	ATR 42-320	064	ex F-GPEC	

MOONAIR AVIATION		**(MOO)**		**Tel Aviv-Sde Dov (SDV)**

☐ 4X-CBY	Piper PA-23-250 Aztec E	27-7304990	ex N405PB
☐ 4X-CCJ	Piper PA-31-350 Navajo Chieftain	31-7405140	ex G-FOEL

SUN D'OR INTERNATIONAL AIRLINES	**Echo Romeo (2R/ERO)**	**Tel Aviv-Ben Gurion (TLV)**

Wholly owned subsidiary of El Al Israel Airlines; leases aircraft from the parent.

TAMIR AVIATION	**(TMI)**	**Haifa (HFA)**

☐ 4X-ANU	Piper PA-31 Turbo Navajo	31-616	ex N6746L

5A- LIBYA (Socialist People's Libyan Arab Jamahiriya)

AFRIQIYAH AIRWAYS	**Afriqiyah (8U/AAW)**	**Tripoli-Ben Gashir Intl (TIP)**

☐ 5A-IAY	Airbus A300B4-620	354	ex TS-IAY	<NVJ
☐ 5A-ONC	Airbus A319-111	3615	ex D-AVYM	
☐ 5A-OND	Airbus A319-111	3657	ex D-AVYS	
☐ 5A-ONI	Airbus A319-111	4004	ex D-AVYC	
☐ S5-AAA	Airbus A320-231	0043	ex SX-BAS	<ADR
☐ 5A-ONA	Airbus A320-214	3224	ex F-WWBY	
☐ 5A-ONB	Airbus A320-214	3236	ex F-WWBI	
☐ 5A-ONJ	Airbus A320-214	4203	ex F-WWBF	♦
☐ 5A-ONK	Airbus A320-214	4330	ex F-WWIJ	♦
☐ 5A-ONL	Airbus A320-214	4489	ex F-WWDV	♦
☐ 5A-ONM	Airbus A320-214	4521	ex F-WWDI	♦
☐ 5A-	Airbus A320-214		ex	o/o♦
☐ 5A-	Airbus A320-214		ex	o/o♦
☐ 5A-ONF	Airbus A330-202	999	ex F-WWYV	
☐ 5A-ONH	Airbus A330-202	1043	ex F-WWKM	
☐ 5A-ONE	Airbus A340-213	151	ex HZ-WBT4	VIPop for Govt

AIR LIBYA	**Air Libya (7Q/TLR)**	**Tripoli-Mitiga/Benghazi (MJI/BEN)**

☐ 5A-	Antonov An-140	o/o
☐ 5A-	Antonov An-140	o/o
☐ 5A-	Antonov An-140	o/o
☐ 5A-	Antonov An-140	o/o
☐ 5A-	Antonov An-140	o/o

☐ EX-87664	Yakovlev Yak-40	9240825	ex CCCP-87664	<AAP
☐ 5A-DKG	Yakovlev Yak-40	9640152	ex 4L-AVP	
☐ 5A-DKI	Yakovlev Yak-40	9331229	ex 9L-LDK	
☐ 5A-DKJ	Yakovlev Yak-40K	9720853	ex EX-88270	
☐ 5A-DKK	Yakovlev Yak-40	9420235	ex EX-87426	
☐ 5A-DKM	Yakovlev Yak-40KD	9841659	ex ST-ARK	Frtr
☐ 5A-DHN	de Havilland DHC-6 Twin Otter 300	712		
☐ 5A-DKQ	British Aerospace 146 Srs.300	E3191	ex G-JEBD	
☐ 5A-DKV	Boeing 727-2D6	22374/1711	ex 7T-VEV	
☐ 5A-DKX	Boeing 727-2D6	22765/1801	ex 7T-VEX	[BEN]
☐ 5A-DKY	Boeing 737-2D6 (Nordam 3)	22766/853	ex 7T-VEY	

AIR ONE NINE   (N6/ONR)   Tripoli-Ben Gashir Intl (TIP)

☐ ZS-GAR	Douglas DC-9-32 (ABS 3)	47132/229	ex 3D-MRO	
☐ 3D-MRL	Douglas DC-9-32	47102/198	ex S9-TGL	
Operates services for its parent, One Nine Petroleum				

AL-AJNIHAH AIRWAYS   (ANH)   Tripoli-Ben Gashir Intl (TIP)

Operates services with Ilyushin Il-76s leased from other operators as required

ALDAWLYH AIR   Aldawlyh Air (IIG)   Tripoli-Ben Gashir Intl/Mitiga (TIP/MJI)

Operates cargo services with Antonov An-124 leased from Libyan Air Cargo as required

ALLEBIA AIR CARGO   Tripoli-Ben Gashir Intl (TIP)

| ☐ 5A-DSH | Antonov An-72 | 36572020337 | ex 9Q-... | |

BURAQ AIR   Buraqair (UZ/BRQ)   Tripoli-Mitiga/Benghazi (MJI/BEN)

☐ J2-KCG	Douglas DC-10-15	48258/346	ex EX-10151	
☐ 5A-DGR	British Aerospace Jetstream 32	945	ex HL5214	
☐ 5A-DMG	Boeing 737-8GK/W	34948/2074	ex N1787B	Tripoli
☐ 5A-DMH	Boeing 737-8GK/W	34949/2106		Benghazi
☐ 5A-DMN	Boeing 727-228	22287/1710	ex TC-JEC	[TIP]
☐ 5A-DMO	Boeing 727-2F2	20983/1088	ex TC-JBJ	[TIP]
☐ 5A-DMP	Boeing 727-2F2	20981/1086	ex TC-JBG	[TIP]
☐ 5A-DMU	Boeing 737-2D6	21212/459	ex 7T-VEO	[TIP]
☐ 5A-DMV	Boeing 737-2D6	21286/482	ex 7T-VER	[TIP]
☐ 5A-DNA	Ilyushin Il-76TD	0023439140		
☐ 5A-MAB	Boeing 737-406	24857/1902	ex PH-BDU	
☐ 5A-MAC	Boeing 737-4B6	26531/2453	ex N563MS	♦

GHADAMES AIR TRANSPORT   (OG/GHT)   Tripoli-Ben Gashir Intl (TIP)

Operates services with British Aerospace 146s and Lockheed L1011 Tristars leased from other operators as required

GLOBAL AIR   (-/GAK)

| ☐ 5A-DQA | Ilyushin Il-76TD | 1003405167 | ex EX-105 | |
| ☐ 5A-DQB | Ilyushin Il-86 | 51483208069 | ex UN-86101 | |

KALLAT EL SAKER AIR   (KES)   Kishinev-Chisinau / Sharjah (KIV/SHJ)

☐ XT-BRK	Lockheed L-1011-500 Tristar	293B-1243	ex OD-JOE	
☐ XT-DMK	Boeing 747-238B	21316/309	ex 3D-NEF	
☐ XT-DMS	Boeing 747-238B	20009/147	ex 3D-NED	stored
☐ XT-RAD	Lockheed L-1011-500 Tristar	193H-1246	ex OD-MIR	

LIBYAN AIR CARGO   Libac (LCR)   Tripoli-Mitiga (MJI)

☐ 5A-DOA	Antonov An-26B	12306	ex LAAF 8207	
☐ 5A-DOB	Antonov An-26B	12307	ex LAAF 8208	
☐ 5A-DOC	Antonov An-26B	12308	ex LAAF 8209	Waddan
☐ 5A-DOD	Antonov An-26B	12406	ex LAAF 8210	
☐ 5A-DOE	Antonov An-26B	13003		
☐ 5A-DOF	Antonov An-26B	13007		
☐ 5A-DOG	Antonov An-26-100	13008		
☐ 5A-DOH	Antonov An-26B	13202	no titles	
☐ 5A-DON	Antonov An-26B	13009	ex LAAF 8304	
☐ 5A-DOU	Antonov An-26B-100	13201T	also reported as c/n 13202T and ex LAAF 8315	
☐ 5A-DOV	Antonov An-26B-100	13109T	ex LAAF	
☐ 5A-DOW	Antonov An-26B	11808	ex LAAF 8203	
☐ 5A-DOZ	Antonov An-26B-100		ex LAAF 8214	

618

☐ 5A-DKS	Ilyushin Il-76TD	1033418584	ex RA-76843		
☐ 5A-DLL	Ilyushin Il-76	0093493799			
☐ 5A-DNC	Ilyushin Il-76TD	0023437084			
☐ 5A-DND	Ilyushin Il-76TD	0033445299			
☐ 5A-DNE	Ilyushin Il-76T	0013432952			
☐ 5A-DNG	Ilyushin Il-76TD	0013432961			
☐ 5A-DNH	Ilyushin Il-76TD	0033446356			
☐ 5A-DNI	Ilyushin Il-76T	0013430878			[FJR]
☐ 5A-DNJ	Ilyushin Il-76T	0013430869			[DME]
☐ 5A-DNK	Ilyushin Il-76T	0013430882			
☐ 5A-DNO	Ilyushin Il-76T	0043451509	ex EX-043		
☐ 5A-DNQ	Ilyushin Il-76TD	0043454641			
☐ 5A-DNT	Ilyushin Il-76TD	0023439141			
☐ 5A-DNU	Ilyushin Il-76TD	0043454651		all-white	
☐ 5A-DNV	Ilyushin Il-76TD	0043454645			
☐ 5A-DRR	Ilyushin Il-76M	083415469			
☐ 5A-DRS	Ilyushin Il-76M	1033414474	ex RA-76367		
☐ 5A-DRT	Ilyushin Il-76TD	1003403063	ex LAAF-110		
☐ 5A-DZZ	Ilyushin Il-76M	093416501			
☐ 5A-DJQ	Lockheed L-382G-40C Hercules	4798	ex N501AK		
☐ 5A-DJR	Lockheed L-382E-15C Hercules	4302	ex RP-C99		
☐ 5A-DKL	Antonov An-124-100 Ruslan	19530502761	ex UR-82066 Susa		
☐ 5A-DKN	Antonov An-124-100 Ruslan	19530502792	ex RA-82003 Sabrata		
☐ 5A-DOM	Lockheed L-382G-62C Hercules	4992	ex N4268M		
☐ 5A-DOO	Lockheed L-382G-64C Hercules	5000	ex N4269M		
☐ 5A-DRC	Antonov An-32P	0703	ex UR-48093		Jt ops with LAAF
☐ 5A-DRD	Antonov An-32P	1306	ex UR-48004		Jt ops with LAAF
☐ 5A-DRF	Antonov An-32P	3602			Jt ops with LAAF
☐ 5A-	Antonov An-72		ex LAAF-721		
☐ 5A-	Antonov An-72		ex LAAF-722		
☐ 5A-	Antonov An-72		ex LAAF-723		
☐ 5A-	Antonov An-72		ex LAAF-724		

LIBYAN AIRLINES   *Libair (LN/LAA)*   **Tripoli-Ben Gashir Intl (TIP)**

☐ 5A-LAH	Airbus A320-214	4405	ex F-WWBX		♦
☐ 5A-LAI	Airbus A320-214	4450	ex F-WWIO		♦
☐ 5A-LAJ	Airbus A320-214	4490	ex D-AUBI		♦
☐ 5A-LAK	Airbus A320-214	4526	ex F-WWDO		♦
☐ 5A-	Airbus A320-214		ex		o/o♦
☐ 5A-	Airbus A320-214		ex		o/o♦
☐ 5A-	Airbus A320-214		ex		o/o♦
☐ 5A-	Airbus A330-2		ex		o/o♦
☐ 5A-LAF	ATR 42-500	691	ex F-WWLM		
☐ 5A-LAG	ATR 42-500	802	ex F-WWLU		
☐ 5A-DIB	Boeing 727-2L5	21051/1109			[TIP]
☐ 5A-DIC	Boeing 727-2L5	21052/1110			[TIP]
☐ 5A-DID	Boeing 727-2L5	21229/1213			[TIP]
☐ 5A-DIE	Boeing 727-2L5	21230/1215			[TIP]
☐ 5A-DIF	Boeing 727-2L5	21332/1257			[TIP]
☐ 5A-DIH	Boeing 727-2L5	21539/1371	ex N1253E		
☐ 5A-DII	Boeing 727-2L5	21540/1386	ex N1261E		
☐ 5A-LAA	Canadair CRJ-900	15120	ex C-FPQO		
☐ 5A-LAB	Canadair CRJ-900	15121	ex C-FPUM		
☐ 5A-LAC	Canadair CRJ-900	15122	ex C-FPUN		
☐ 5A-LAD	Canadair CRJ-900	15214	ex C-		
☐ 5A-LAE	Canadair CRJ-900	15216	ex C-		
☐ 5A-LAL	Canadair CRJ-900	15256	ex C-		♦
☐ 5A-LAM	Canadair CRJ-900	15257	ex C-GZQW		♦
☐ 5A-LAN	Canadair CRJ-900	15258	ex C-GIBO		♦
☐ 5A-DCT	de Havilland DHC-6 Twin Otter 300	627			
☐ 5A-DCV	de Havilland DHC-6 Twin Otter 300	637			
☐ 5A-DCX	de Havilland DHC-6 Twin Otter 300	641			
☐ 5A-DCZ	de Havilland DHC-6 Twin Otter 300	645			
☐ 5A-DDB	de Havilland DHC-6 Twin Otter 300	653			
☐ 5A-DDE	de Havilland DHC-6 Twin Otter 300	677			
☐ 5A-DHY	de Havilland DHC-6 Twin Otter 300	661	ex C-GELZ		
☐ 5A-DJG	de Havilland DHC-6 Twin Otter 300	744	ex (FAP-2029)		
☐ 5A-DJH	de Havilland DHC-6 Twin Otter 300	747			
☐ 5A-DJI	de Havilland DHC-6 Twin Otter 300	757			
☐ 5A-DJJ	de Havilland DHC-6 Twin Otter 300	769			

☐ TS-IND	Airbus A320-212	0348	ex OY-CNN		<LBT
☐ TS-INE	Airbus A320-212	0222	ex OY-CNC		<LBT
☐ 5A-DGC	Cessna 402C II	402C0045	ex N5800C		
☐ 5A-DHG	Cessna 402C II	402C0464	ex N8737Q		
☐ 5A-DHH	Cessna 402C II	402C0444	ex N6790F		
☐ 5A-DHZ	Swearingen SA.226AT Merlin III	T-345	ex OO-HSC		
☐ 5A-DJB	Swearingen SA.226AT Merlin III	T-388	ex OO-XSC		
☐ 5A-DLV	Fokker F.28 Fellowship 4000	11200	ex PH-EXV	Mares	stored
☐ 5A-DLW	Fokker F.28 Fellowship 4000	11194	ex PH-EXZ		
☐ 5A-DLY	Airbus A300B4-622R	601	ex TS-IAX	Al-Gordabia	
☐ 5A-DLZ	Airbus A300B4-622R	616	ex TS-IAZ	Derna	op by NVJ
☐ 5A-DTG	Fokker F.28 Fellowship 4000	11139	ex PK-MSU		
☐ 5A-DTH	Fokker F.28 Fellowship 4000	11140	ex PK-MSV		

LIBYAVIA — *Tripoli-Ben Gashir Intl (TIP)*

☐ 5A-DMX	Airbus A300C4-203F	083	ex TC-ACT	Mersin	Op by RUN

PETRO AIR

☐ 5A-AGR	de Havilland DHC-8-315	601	ex PH-AGR	
☐ 5A-PAA	Embraer ERJ-170LR	17000275	ex PT-TQB	◆
☐ 5A-PAB	Embraer ERJ-170LR	17000279	ex PT-TQF	◆

TOBRUK AIR — *Tobruk Air (7T/TQB)* — *Tripoli-Ben Gashir Intl (TIP)*

Operates cargo flights with leased Douglas DC-10-30F and Ilyushin Il-76 aircraft leased from other operators when required

5B-   CYPRUS (Republic of Cyprus)

CYPRUS AIRWAYS — *Cyprus (CY/CYP)* — *Larnaca (LCA)*

☐ 5B-DBO	Airbus A319-112	1729	ex D-AVWR	Nikoklis
☐ 5B-DBP	Airbus A319-112	1768	ex D-AVWB	Chalkanor
☐ 5B-DCF	Airbus A319-132	2718	ex N518NK	Larnaka
☐ 5B-DBA	Airbus A320-231	0180	ex F-WWIT	Evagoras
☐ 5B-DBB	Airbus A320-231	0256	ex F-WWBH	Akamas
☐ 5B-DBC	Airbus A320-231	0295	ex F-WWIE	Tefkros
☐ 5B-DCG	Airbus A320-232	4197	ex F-WWIU	Aphrodite ◆
☐ 5B-DCH	Airbus A320-232	2359	ex N674AW	Lefkosia ◆
☐ 5B-DCJ	Airbus A320-232	2108	ex LZ-MDT	Amathus ◆
☐ 5B-DCK	Airbus A320-232	2275	ex M-ABDA	Paphos ◆
☐ 5B-DBS	Airbus A330-243	505	ex F-WWKO	Ammochostos
☐ 5B-DBT	Airbus A330-243	526	ex F-WWKY	Keryneia

EUROCYPRIA AIRLINES — *Eurocypria (UI/ECA)* — *Larnaca (LCA)*

Suspended operations 04/Nov/2010

5H-   TANZANIA (United Republic of Tanzania)

AIR EXCEL — *Tinga-Tinga (XLL)* — *Arusha (ARK)*

☐ 5H-AES	LET L-410UVP-E20	871811	ex 5H-PAD
☐ 5H-AXL	Cessna 208B Caravan I	208B0401	ex D-FHEW
☐ 5H-EMK	Cessna TU206G Turbo Stationair 8 II	U20604638	ex 5H-SDA
☐ 5H-SMK	Cessna 208B Caravan I	208B0654	ex VT-TAP
☐ 5H-WOW	Reims Cessna F406 Caravan II	F406-0060	ex PH-GUG

AIR TANZANIA — *Tanzania (TC/ATC)* — *Dar-es-Salaam (DAR)*

☐ 5H-MWF	de Havilland DHC-8-311	474	ex G-BRYW
☐ 5H-MWG	de Havilland DHC-8-311	462	ex G-BRYV

AURIC AIR SERVICES — *Mwanza (MWZ)*

☐ 5H-DTA	Cessna 208B Caravan I	208B2159	ex N62408	◆
☐ 5H-NCS	Cessna 208B Caravan I	208B1311	ex N2123S	
☐ 5H-TWF	Cessna 208B Caravan I	208B1315	ex N21716	
☐ 5H-TWO	Piper PA-34-200T Seneca	34-8170030	ex ZS-KTK	

620

COASTAL AVIATION — Coastal Travel (7I/CSV) — Dar-es-Salaam (DAR)

☐ 5H-BAD	Cessna 208B Caravan I	208B0586	ex N5QP	
☐ 5H-BAT	Cessna 208B Caravan I	208B1030	ex N12554	
☐ 5H-HOT	Cessna 208B Caravan I	208B0677	ex N1256N	
☐ 5H-JOE	Cessna 208B Caravan I	208B0570	ex N9EU	
☐ 5H-MAD	Cessna 208B Caravan I	208B0872	ex N1294K	
☐ 5H-POA	Cessna 208B Caravan I	208B0965	ex N1129Y	
☐ 5H-SUN	Cessna 208B Caravan I	208B0754	ex 5H-PAF	
☐ 5H-VIP	Cessna 208B Caravan I	208B0714	ex N208FK	
☐ 5H-CCT	Cessna TU206G Stationair 6	U20604597	ex ZS-MXV	
☐ 5H-CTL	Cessna TU206F Stationair	U20601988	ex 5H-PBF	
☐ 5H-EXC	Pilatus PC-12/45	220	ex ZS-EXC	dam, repaired?
☐ 5H-GUN	Cessna U206G Stationair 6	U20605223	ex 5H-TGT	
☐ 5H-SRP	Pilatus PC-12/45	317	ex ZS-SRP	
☐ 5H-TOY	Cessna 404 Titan II	404-0668	ex 5Y-MCK	

KILWA AIR

☐ 5H-KLA	Britten-Norman BN-2B-21 Islander	2002	ex 5X-MHB	id not confirmed
☐ ZS-PRL	CASA 212-200	180	ex N160GA	<KUS
☐ 5H-MLB	Cessna T210N Centurion II	21064259	ex ZS-LVC	
Current status uncertain				

NORTHERN AIR — Arusha (ARK)

☐ 5H-NAA	Cessna 208 Caravan I	20800109	ex N9628F
☐ 5H-NAC	Cessna 208B Caravan I	208B0757	ex N1307D
☐ 5H-SJF	Cessna 208B Caravan I	208B0950	ex N1130T

PRECISIONAIR — Precisionair (PW/PRF) — Arusha (ARK)

☐ 5H-PAA	ATR 42-320	308	ex F-WQHB	City of Arusha	
☐ 5H-PAG	ATR 42-320	384	ex F-WQJO		
☐ 5H-PWF	ATR 42-500	819	ex F-WWLA	Bukoba	♦
☐ 5H-PWA	ATR 72-212A	780	ex F-WWES		
☐ 5H-PWB	ATR 72-212A	834	ex F-WWEB		
☐ 5H-PWC	ATR 72-212A	866	ex F-WWEP		
☐ 5H-PWD	ATR 72-212A	880	ex F-WWEI		
☐ 5H-PWE	ATR 72-212A	815	ex F-WWLZ	Kigoma	♦
☐ 5H-PWG	ATR 72-212A	923	ex F-WWEW	Kilimanjaro	♦
☐ 5H-PAY	Reims Cessna 406 Caravan I	F406-0035	ex ZS-OGY		

REGIONAL AIR SERVICES — Regional Services (REG) — Arusha (ARK)

☐ A6-MAR	de Havilland DHC-6 Twin Otter 300	841	ex N9045S
☐ 5H-BMP	de Havilland DHC-7-102	80	ex 5Y-BMP
☐ 5H-KEG	de Havilland DHC-6 Twin Otter 300	799	ex 5Y-KEG

SKY AVIATION TANZANIA — Dar-es-Salaam (DAR)

☐ 5H-SKT	Piper PA-31-350 Chieftain	31-8152058	ex A2-AHP	
☐ 5H-SKX	Cessna 402B	402B-0829	ex 5Y-EAL	
☐ 5H-SKY	Piper PA-32-300 Six	32-770061	ex N3258Q	dbr?

TANZANAIR - TANZANIAN AIR SERVICES — Dar-es-Salaam (DAR)

☐ 5H-GHL	Cessna U206F Stationair II	U20602583	ex 5H-JBJ
☐ 5H-LDS	Cessna 310I	310I0029	ex 5Y-AJN
☐ 5H-TZC	Reims Cessna F406 Caravan II	F406-0028	ex N7037C
☐ 5H-TZE	Reims Cessna F406 Caravan II	F406-0046	ex OY-PED
☐ 5H-TZT	Cessna 208B Caravan I	208B0664	ex ZS-PSR
☐ 5H-TZU	Cessna 208B Caravan I	208B0639	ex ZS-PJJ
☐ 5H-TZX	Beech 200 Super King Air	BB-1196	ex Z-ZLT

TROPICAL AIR — Zanzibar (ZNZ)

☐ 5H-OLA	Cessna 208B Caravan I	208B0384	ex 7T-VIH
☐ 5H-TAR	Piper PA-34-200T Seneca II	34-7970038	ex 5H-MNF
☐ 5H-TZO	Partenavia P.68B	120	ex 5H-AZO
☐ 5H-TZY	Partenavia P.68B	149	ex 5H-AZY

TWIN WINGS AIR — Zanzibar (ZNZ)

☐ 5H-MAY	Cessna 404 Titan II	404-0241	ex 5Y-EDH
☐ 5H-RAY	Cessna 404 Titan II	404-0007	ex N3935C

ZANAIR		Zanair (B4/TAN)		Zanzibar (ZNZ)
☐ 5H-LET	LET L-410UVPE-9	892226	ex 9L-LBK	
☐ 5H-ZAA	LET L-410UVP-E20	982631	ex 5H-PAE	
☐ 5H-ZAP	LET L-410UVPE-9	871824	ex 9L-LBV	
☐ 5H-ZAR	Cessna 404 Titan II	404-0835	ex 5H-AEL	
☐ 5H-ZAY	Cessna 404 Titan II	404-0207	ex N798A	
☐ 5H-ZAZ	Cessna 402C	402C0029	ex 5Y-NNM	

ZANTAS AIR SERVICE				Dar-es-Salaam (DAR)
☐ 5H-FAT	Cessna 206H Stationair	20608168	ex 5H-CWF	
☐ 5H-TAK	Cessna 208B Caravan I	208B0891	ex N1239B	
☐ 5H-TAZ	Cessna 208B Caravan I	208B1186	ex N12998	

5N- NIGERIA (Federal Republic of Nigeria)

AERO CONTRACTORS		Aeroline (AJ/NIG)		Lagos (LOS)
☐ 5N-AQK	Aérospatiale SA365N Dauphin 2	6108		Op for NNPC
☐ 5N-AQL	Aérospatiale SA365N Dauphin 2	6109		Op for NNPC
☐ 5N-BAF	Aérospatiale SA365N2 Dauphin 2	6430	ex F-WYMC	Op for NNPC
☐ 5N-BDA	Aérospatiale SA365N Dauphin 2	6077	ex 8P-PHM	
☐ 5N-BET	Aérospatiale SA365N Dauphin 2	6087	ex TJ-DEM	
☐ 5N-BGF	Aérospatiale SA365N3 Dauphin 2	6593	ex PH-SHH	
☐ 5N-BIX	Aérospatiale AS365N3 Dauphin 2	6657	ex PH-SHI	
☐ 5N-BIY	Aérospatiale AS365N3 Dauphin 2	6738	ex F-WQVR	
☐ 5N-ESO	Aérospatiale SA365N Dauphin 2	6072	ex PH-SSP	
☐ 5N-STO	Aérospatiale SA365N Dauphin 2	6106	ex PH-SSV	
☐ 5N-BIZ	Boeing 737-4B7	24558/1845	ex N436US	
☐ 5N-BJA	Boeing 737-4B7	24873/1931	ex N446US	
☐ 5N-BKQ	Boeing 737-522	26695/2423	ex VP-BSW	
☐ 5N-BKR	Boeing 737-522	26699/2485	ex VP-BSX	
☐ 5N-BLC	Boeing 737-522	26692/2421	ex VP-BSV	
☐ 5N-BLD	Boeing 737-522	26675/2345	ex VP-BSU	
☐ 5N-BLE	Boeing 737-522	26672/2343	ex VP-BSQ	
☐ 5N-BLG	Boeing 737-522	25387/2179	ex VP-BTI	o/o
☐ 5N-BIA	de Havilland DHC-8Q-315	608	ex C-FBOA	
☐ 5N-BIB	de Havilland DHC-8Q-315	609	ex C-FCPM	
☐ 5N-BJO	de Havilland DHC-8Q-311	534	ex C-FLGJ	
☐ 5N-AOA	Aérospatiale AS355F Ecureuil 2	5277	ex F-WZFB	Op for NNPC
☐ 5N-AOB	Aérospatiale AS355F Ecureuil 2	5278	ex F-WZFV	Op for NNPC
☐ 5N-BKG	Eurocopter EC225LP	2681		
☐ 5N-BKH	Eurocopter EC225LP	2688		
☐ 5N-BCX	Sikorsky S-76C+	760466	ex 5N-BCN	
☐ 5N-BHF	Sikorsky S-76C+	760570	ex C-GHRW	
☐ 5N-BHP	Sikorsky S-76C+	760574	ex C-GHRJ	
☐ 5N-BJC	Agusta AW139	31070	ex I-EASY	
☐ 5N-RSN	Agusta AW139	31060	ex 5N-BJB	Op for River States Govt

AFRIJET AIRLINES		Afrijet (6F/FRJ)		Lagos (LOS)
☐ 5N-	ATR 72-500		ex	o/o♦
☐ 5N-	ATR 72-500		ex	o/o♦
☐ 5N-	ATR 72-500		ex	o/o♦
☐ 5N-BCC	Fairchild FH-227D	575	ex HK-1411	[LOS]
☐ 5N-BKO	McDonnell-Douglas MD-83	49855/1728	ex N311FV	
☐ 5N-FRJ	Fairchild F-27J	126	ex 3C-ZZE	Frtr

AIR MIDWEST				Lagos (LOS)
☐ 5N-PVA	Boeing 737-5H6	27354/2637	ex G-GFFH	

AIR NIGERIA		(VK/VGN)		Lagos (LOS)
☐ 5N-VNC	Boeing 737-33V	29338/3114	ex G-EZYN	
☐ 5N-VND	Boeing 737-33V	29337/3113	ex G-EZYM	
☐ 5N-VNE	Boeing 737-33V	29340/3121	ex G-EZYP	
☐ 5N-VNF	Boeing 737-33V	29341/3125	ex G-EZYR	
☐ 5N-VNG	Boeing 737-33V	29342/3127	ex G-EZYS	
☐ 5N-VNJ	Boeing 737-36N	28558/2876	ex N524MS	♦
☐ 5N-VNK	Boeing 737-33A	27469/2864	ex N901AS	♦
☐ 5N-VNL	Boeing 737-33A	27910/2873	ex N902AS	♦

☐ 5N-VNH	Embraer ERJ-190AR	19000210	ex PT-SGT	
☐ 5N-VNI	Embraer ERJ-190AR	19000226	ex PT-SHM	

ALLIED AIR CARGO — Bambi (AJK) — Lagos (LOS)

☐ 5N-BJN	Boeing 727-221F (FedEx 3)	22540/1796	ex 5X-TON	
☐ 5N-BMQ	Boeing 727-2Q6F (FedEx 3)	21971/1540	ex N727WF	
☐ 5N-JNR	Boeing 727-217F (FedEx 3)	21056/1122	ex C-FACK	[MIA]♦
☐ 5N-RKY	Boeing 727-217F (Raisbeck 3)	21055/1117	ex C-FACR	

AMBJEK AIR SERVICES — Abuja (ABV)

☐ 5N-BEA	LET L-410UVP-E	902435	ex OK-VDT	
☐ 5N-BEB	LET L-410UVP-E	882103	ex OK-TDS	

ARIK AIR — Arik Air (W3/ARA) — Lagos (LOS)

☐ 5N-EIA	Airbus A330-223	1002	ex F-WWKP		♦
☐ CS-TFW	Airbus A340-542	910	ex F-WWTK	Our Lady of Perpetual Help	
☐ CS-TFX	Airbus A340-542	912	ex F-WJKI	Captin Bob Hayes, OON	
☐ 5N-MJA	Boeing 737-322	24454/1750	ex N361UA	Eddington	
☐ 5N-MJB	Boeing 737-322	24360/1692	ex N354UA	Augustine	
☐ 5N-MJC	Boeing 737-7BD/W	33932/2234	ex N320AT	Martin	
☐ 5N-MJD	Boeing 737-7BD/W	36073/2248	ex N323AT	Michael	
☐ 5N-MJE	Boeing 737-7GL/W	34761/2401	ex N737AV	McTighe	
☐ 5N-MJF	Boeing 737-7GL/W	34762/2427	ex N737BV	Queen of Angles	
☐ 5N-MJG	Boeing 737-7BD/W	33944/2576	ex N346AT		
☐ 5N-MJH	Boeing 737-7BD/W	36719/2589	ex N347AT		
☐ 5N-MJI	Boeing 737-76N/W	28640/799	ex N740AL		
☐ 5N-MJJ	Boeing 737-76N/W	28641/809	ex N741AL	City of Benin	
☐ 5N-MJK	Boeing 737-76N/W	30830/855	ex N742AL		
☐ 5N-MJN	Boeing 737-86N/W	35638/2789		Eddington	
☐ 5N-MJO	Boeing 737-86N/W	35640/2819	ex N358MT	Augustine	
☐ 5N-MJP	Boeing 737-8JE/W	38970/3030		Sultan of Sokoto	
☐ 5N-MJQ	Boeing 737-8JE/W	38971/3065		City of Calabar	
☐ 5N-	Boeing 737-8JE/W				o/o♦
☐ 5N-	Boeing 737-8JE/W				o/o♦
☐ 5N-	Boeing 737-8JE/W				o/o♦
☐ 5N-	Boeing 737-8JE/W				o/o♦
☐ 5N-	Boeing 737-8JE/W				o/o♦
☐ 5N-	Boeing 777-3				o/o♦
☐ 5N-	Boeing 777-3				o/o♦
☐ 5N-	Boeing 777-3				o/o♦
☐ 5N-	Boeing 777-3				o/o♦
☐ 5N-JEA	Canadair CRJ-900ER	15058	ex C-FHRH	Anthony	
☐ 5N-JEB	Canadair CRJ-900ER	15059	ex C-FHRK	Patrick	
☐ 5N-JEC	Canadair CRJ-900ER	15054	ex C-FGNB		
☐ 5N-JED	Canadair CRJ-900ER	15114	ex C-FMEP	Abraham	
☐ 5N-BKU	de Havilland DHC-8-402Q	4207	ex C-FPPU		
☐ 5N-BKV	de Havilland DHC-8-402Q	4219	ex C-FSRN		
☐ 5N-BKW	de Havilland DHC-8-402Q	4262	ex C-FXAW		♦
☐ 5N-	de Havilland DHC-8-402Q		ex C-		o/o♦
☐ 5N-	de Havilland DHC-8-402Q		ex C-		o/o♦
☐ 5N-	de Havilland DHC-8-402Q		ex C-		o/o♦

ASSOCIATED AIR CARGO — Associated (SCD) — Lagos (LOS)

☐ UR-PAS	Antonov An-12AP	2401105		op by VPB
☐ 5N-BBL	Short SD.3-60	SH3637	ex G-LEGS	
☐ 5N-BHV	Boeing 727-227F (FedEx 3)	21364/1261	ex N86426	
☐ 5N-BJX	Boeing 727-225F (FedEx 3)	20627/947	ex N361KP	
☐ 5N-BJY	Embraer EMB.120ER Brasilia	120174	ex N388JR	
☐ 5N-BJZ	Embraer EMB.120ER Brasilia	120095	ex N788JR	
☐ 5N-	Embraer EMB.120ER Brasilia	120247	ex N258CA	o/o

AXIOM AIR

☐ 5N-BMA	Boeing 737-3Q4 (SF)	24209/1492	ex ZK-TLB	

BELLVIEW AIRLINES — Bellview Airlines (B3/BLV) — Lagos (LOS)

☐ F-GHXK	Boeing 737-2A1	21599/514	ex N171AW	Peace	[LOS]
☐ F-GHXL	Boeing 737-2S3	21775/570	ex G-BMOR		

☐ 5N-BFM	Boeing 737-2L9	22733/812	ex N270FL	Fortitude
☐ 5N-BFX	Boeing 737-291	23024/965	ex CC-CVH	Hope [LOS]

BRISTOW HELICOPTERS (NIGERIA)
Bristow Helicopters (BHN)
Lagos/ Calabar/ Eket/ Port Harcourt/ Warri (LOS/CBQ/-/PHC/-)

☐ 5N-BGO	Aérospatiale AS.332L	2092	ex G-BRXU	
☐ 5N-BGP	Aérospatiale AS.332L	2046	ex G-BWMG	
☐ 5N-BKJ	Aérospatiale AS.332L	2170	ex G-PUMI	
☐ 5N-BNC	Aérospatiale AS.332L2	2500	ex LN-ONI	♦
☐ 5N-AMQ	Bell 206L-1 LongRanger II	45746	ex N31800	
☐ 5N-AQP	Bell 206L-1 LongRanger II	45604	ex N3907E	
☐ 5N-BAS	Bell 206L-1 LongRanger II	45367	ex N1076K	
☐ 5N-BBN	Bell 206L-3 LongRanger III	51005	ex SU-CAD	
☐ 5N-BCW	Bell 206L-3 LongRanger III	51053	ex SU-CAK	
☐ 5N-BFE	Bell 206L-4 LongRanger IV	52272	ex N20796	
☐ 5N-BFF	Bell 206L-4 LongRanger IV	52273	ex N2080C	
☐ 5N-BFG	Bell 206L-4 LongRanger IV	52274	ex N2080W	
☐ 5N-BFH	Bell 206L-4 LongRanger IV	52275	ex N2081K	
☐ 5N-BFV	Bell 206L-4 LongRanger IV	52160	ex 5N-ESC	
☐ 5N-BHH	Bell 206L-4 LongRanger IV	52291	ex N274AL	
☐ 5N-BJR	Bell 206L-4 LongRanger IV	52191	ex N178AL	
☐ 5N-PAA	Bell 206L-1 LongRanger II	45659	ex N39118	
☐ 5N-BEM	Bell 407	53246	ex N567AL	
☐ 5N-BEO	Bell 407	53190	ex N467AL	
☐ 5N-BEP	Bell 407	53107	ex N427AL	
☐ 5N-BFI	Bell 407	53550	ex N2531G	
☐ 5N-BCZ	Bell 412SP	33179	ex B-55521	
☐ 5N-BDZ	Bell 412EP	36278	ex 9Y-ALI	
☐ 5N-BFU	Bell 412EP	36318	ex N7022F	
☐ 5N-BGS	Bell 412SP	33186	ex N464AC	
☐ 5N-BHB	Bell 412EP	36273	ex XA-TTF	
☐ 5N-BHD	Bell 412EP	36354	ex N4202A	
☐ 5N-BIM	Bell 412EP	36373	ex N31195	
☐ 5N-BIO	Bell 412EP	36378	ex N106AL	
☐ 5N-BIP	Bell 412EP	36383	ex N105AL	
☐ 5N-BIR	Bell 412EP	36386	ex N107AL	
☐ 5N-BIS	Bell 412EP	36387	ex N132AL	
☐ 5N-BML	Bell 412EP	36433	ex G-OIBU	
☐ 5N-BDH	Eurocopter EC155B	6591	ex F-WQDQ	Op for Shell Nigeria
☐ 5N-BDI	Eurocopter EC155B	6602		Op for Shell Nigeria
☐ 5N-BDJ	Eurocopter EC155B	6607		Op for Shell Nigeria
☐ 5N-BDK	Eurocopter EC155B	6608		Op for Shell Nigeria
☐ 5N-BDL	Eurocopter EC155B	6610	ex F-WQDA	Op for Shell Nigeria
☐ 5N-BDM	Eurocopter EC155B	6611	ex F-WQDH	Op for Shell Nigeria
☐ 5N-BBO	Sikorsky S-76A++	760114	ex G-BVKP	
☐ 5N-BCT	Sikorsky S-76A++	760109	ex G-BZJT	
☐ 5N-BGC	Sikorsky S-76C+	760481	ex LN-ONY	
☐ 5N-BGD	Sikorsky S-76C+	760540	ex N864AL	
☐ 5N-BGE	Sikorsky S-76C+	760545	ex N20509	
☐ 5N-BIL	Sikorsky S-76C+	760591	ex N869AL	
☐ 5N-BJT	Sikorsky S-76C+	760638	ex N872AL	
☐ 5N-BJU	Sikorsky S-76C+	760640	ex N876AL	
☐ 5N-BKM	Sikorsky S-76C+	760660	ex N45083	
☐ 5N-BMD	Sikorsky S-76C+	760456	ex LN-ONZ	
☐ 5N-BMI	Sikorsky S-76C+	760732	ex G-CFPU	
☐ 5N-BMX	Sikorsky S-76C+	760754	ex G-CFRD	♦
☐ 5N-BLX	Sikorsky S-92A	920082	ex G-CFCA	
☐ 5N-BMN	Sikorsky S-92A	920103	ex G-CGCI	
☐ 5N-BHL	Beech 200 Super King Air	BB-387	ex G-BFOL	
☐ 5N-BJE	Aérospatiale AS365N2 Dauphin 2	6446	ex EP-HCK	
☐ 5N-AMW	Cessna 425 Conquest I	425-0067	ex N6844V	
☐ 5N-BDD	Bell 412	33046	ex N395AL	
☐ 5N-BDY	Bell 412EP	36267	ex N506AL	
☐ 5N-BES	Bell 206B JetRanger III	3216	ex N139H	
☐ 5N-BIQ	Bell 412EP	36385	ex N115AL	♦
☐ 5N-BIW	Cessna 208 Caravan I	20800403	ex N1316N	
☐ 5N-CES	Cessna 208 Caravan I	20800249	ex N1288Y	

CAPITAL AIRLINES		Capital Shuttle (NCP)			Lagos (LOS)
☐ 5N-BLN	Embraer EMB.120RT Brasilia	120191	ex ZS-PGZ		
☐ 5N-CCE	Embraer EMB.120ER Brasilia	120120	ex N194SW		[LOS]
☐ 5N-TUE	Embraer EMB.120ER Brasilia	120109	ex N763BC		[LOS]

CAVERTON HELICOPTERS		(CJR)			Lagos (LOS)
☐ 5N-BHK	Aérospatiale SA365N Dauphin 2	6128	ex CS-HFH		<HeliPortugal
☐ 5N-BHS	Aérospatiale AS350B2 Ecureuil	1871	ex CS-HDK		<HeliPortugal
☐ 5N-BHT	Aérospatiale AS350B2 Ecureuil	1222	ex CS-HEO		<HeliPortugal
☐ 5N-BIK	Aérospatiale SA365N Dauphin 2	6138	ex F-GNVS		<HeliPortugal
☐ 5N-BLJ	de Havilland DHC-6 Twin Otter 300	816	ex HB-LUB		

CHANCHANGI AIRLINES					
☐ 5N-BMB	Boeing 737-3J6	25079/2016	ex B-2536		
☐ 5N-BMC	Boeing 737-3Z0	25089/2027	ex B-2537		

DANA		Dana Air (DAV)			Kaduna (KAD)
☐ 5N-ARP	Dornier 228-201	8013	ex (5N-AOH)		
☐ 5N-AUN	Dornier 228-201	8076	ex D-CEPT		
☐ 5N-DOB	Dornier 228-202	8026	ex N232RP		
☐ 5N-DOD	Dornier 228-202	8048	ex N235RP		for GAM, VH
☐ 5N-DOE	Dornier 228-202	8049	ex N236RP		for GAM, VH
☐ 5N-DOF	Dornier 228-202	8125	ex N245RP		for GAM, VH
☐ 5N-DOI	Dornier 228-202	8137	ex N237RP		for GAM, VH
☐ 5N-DOJ	Dornier 228-202	8138	ex N238RP		for GAM, VH
☐ 5N-DOK	Dornier 228-202	8140	ex N240RP		for GAM, VH
☐ 5N-DOL	Dornier 228-202	8145	ex N241RP		
☐ 5N-DOM	Dornier 228-202	8147	ex N242RP		for GAM, VH
☐ 5N-BCA	Piper PA-23 Aztec 250D	27-4220	ex G-AYZN		
☐ 5N-DOX	Dornier 328-110	3073	ex OE-LKF		
☐ 5N-DOY	Dornier 328-110	3089	ex OE-LKG		
☐ 5N-IEP	Dornier 328-110	3026	ex D-CDHL		
☐ 5N-SAG	Dornier 328-110	3016	ex D-CASU		

DANA AIR					
☐ 5N-JAI	McDonnell-Douglas MD-83	53016/1850	ex N968AS		
☐ 5N-RAM	McDonnell-Douglas MD-83	53019/1784	ex N944AS		
☐ 5N-SAI	McDonnell-Douglas MD-83	53018/1779	ex N943AS		
☐ 5N-SRI	McDonnell-Douglas MD-83	53020/1789	ex N947AS		

EAS AIR LINES		Echoline (EXW)			Lagos (LOS)
☐ 5N-DOZ	Dornier 328-110	3031	ex D-CDXL		

FREEDOM AIR SERVICES		Inter Freedom (FFF)			Lagos (LOS)
☐ 5N-BCY	Boeing 727-235	19461/538	ex N461RD	Hajiya Asmal	

IRS AIRLINES		Silverbird (LVB)			Lagos (LOS)
☐ 5N-AKR	Boeing 727-223A (Raisbeck 3)	20984/1121	ex N843AA	Kalifa Tsitaku	
☐ 5N-BJM	Embraer ERJ-145LR	14500984	ex PT-SKE		
☐ 5N-CEO	Fokker 100	11295	ex N860US	Hajiya Babba	[WOE]
☐ 5N-COO	Fokker 100	11297	ex N861US	Kalifa Junior	
☐ 5N-HIR	Fokker 100	11498	ex G-CFBU		
☐ 5N-SIK	Fokker 100	11286	ex SE-DUU		♦
☐ 5N-SMR	Fokker 100	11291	ex PH-MJN		♦
☐ 5N-NCZ	Fokker F.28 Fellowship 4000	11241	ex ZS-OPS		
☐ 5N-SSZ	Fokker F.28 Fellowship 4000	11190	ex ZS-BAL		

KABO AIR		Kabo (N2/QNK)			Kano (KAN)
☐ 5N-DKB	Boeing 747-251B	23548/644	ex N637US		
☐ 5N-EEE	Boeing 747-243B	19732/134	ex G-VGIN		[MZJ]
☐ 5N-JRM	Boeing 747-251B	23549/651	ex N638US		
☐ 5N-MAD	Boeing 747-251B	23547/642	ex N636US		
☐ 5N-OOO	Boeing 747-136	20952/246	ex G-AWNP		
☐ 5N-PDP	Boeing 747-238B	20842/238	ex G-VJFK	Dr MA Dankabo Jarman Kano	
☐ 5N-PPP	Boeing 747-238B	20921/241	ex G-VLAX		
☐ 5N-RRR	Boeing 747-136	19765/109	ex G-AWNE	Alhaji Ado Bayaro, Emir of Kano	
☐ 5N-LLL	Boeing 727-224 (FedEx 3)	20654	ex N32724		[ADD]

MAXAIR

☐ 5N-BMG	Boeing 747-346	23638/658	ex JA8177
☐ 5N-DBM	Boeing 747-346	23968/693	ex JA8184
☐ 5N-DDK	Boeing 747-346	23967/692	ex JA8183
☐ 5N-MBB	Boeing 747-346	24018/694	ex HS-UTS

MED-VIEW AIRLINES

☐ CS-TEB	Lockheed L-1011-500 Tristar	293A-1240	ex V2-LEO	<MMZ
☐ CS-TFK	Boeing 757-2G5	23983/161	ex N983MQ	<MMZ

OVERLAND AIRWAYS — Overland (OJ/OLA) — Lagos / Abuja (LOS/ABV)

☐ 5N-BCO	Beech 1900D	UE-225	ex N225GL	[HLA]
☐ 5N-BCP	Beech 1900D	UE-116	ex N116YV	
☐ 5N-BCR	ATR 42-300	031	ex F-WQNR	
☐ 5N-BCS	ATR 42-300	025	ex EC-IYE	
☐ 5N-BND	ATR 42-300	363	ex F-WKVD	♦
☐ N340SS	SAAB SF.340A	340A-022	ex SE-C22	

SKYPOWER EXPRESS AIRWAYS — Nigeria Express (EAN) — Lagos (LOS)

☐ 5N-AXR	Embraer EMB.110P1 Bandeirante	110459	ex PT-SHM

TRANSKY AIRLINES — Lagos (LOS)

☐ 5N-TSA	Boeing 737-2H4 (AvAero 3)	23110/1017	ex N104SW

WINGS AVIATION — Lagos (LOS)

☐ 5N-PTL	Beech 1900D	UE-215	ex N850CA

5R-   MADAGASCAR (Democratic Republic of Madagascar)

AEROMARINE — Antananarivo ((TNR)

☐ F-ODQI	Piper PA-31-350 Navajo Chieftain	31-7305065	ex F-BUOI
☐ 5R-MCJ	Piper PA-23-250 Aztec C	27-3644	ex N6449Y
☐ 5R-MCR	Piper PA-31 Turbo Navajo	31-162	ex N9122Y
☐ 5R-MIK	Piper PA-23-250 Aztec B	27-2191	ex TL-ABA
☐ 5R-MKG	Beech 99	U-21	ex F-GFPE
☐ 5R-MLI	Cessna 207A Stationair 7 II	20700496	ex 5R-MVR
☐ 5R-MLJ	Cessna 310R II	310R1372	ex F-GBGB
☐ 5R-MLK	Beech 95-C55 Baron	TE-101	ex F-BOJG
☐ 5R-MLT	Cessna 310R II	310R0328	ex F-BXLT

AIR MADAGASCAR — Air Madagascar (MD/MDG) — Antananarivo (TNR)

☐ 5R-MFG	Boeing 767-383ER	25088/359	ex OY-KDM
☐ 5R-MFJ	Boeing 767-3Y0ER	26200/450	ex N330DF
☐ 5R-MFH	Boeing 737-3Q8	26305/2651	
☐ 5R-MFI	Boeing 737-3Q8	26301/2623	ex N319FL
☐ 5R-MGC	de Havilland DHC-6 Twin Otter 300	328	
☐ 5R-MGD	de Havilland DHC-6 Twin Otter 300	329	
☐ 5R-MGF	de Havilland DHC-6 Twin Otter 300	482	
☐ 5R-MJE	ATR 72-212A	694	ex F-WWEQ
☐ 5R-MJF	ATR 72-212A	698	ex F-WWEU
☐ 5R-MJG	ATR 42-500	649	ex F-WWLG
☐ 5R-MVT	ATR 42-320	044	ex F-WQAD
☐ 5R-MLA	Piper PA-31-350 Chieftain	31-7952076	

MALAGASY AIRLINES — (MLG) — Antananarivo (TNR)

☐ 5R-MDB	Cessna 402B	402B0572	ex ZS-RES
☐ 5R-MHJ	Piper PA-23-250 Aztec	27-409	ex 5R-MVJ
☐ 5R-MKS	Cessna 402B	402B0014	ex 5R-MVC
☐ 5R-MLZ	Cessna TU206G Stationair 6	U20604526	ex F-BVQK
☐ 5R-MVL	Cessna 208 Caravan I	20800001	ex HB-CLD

TIKO AIR — Antananarivo (TNR)

☐ 5R-MJT	ATR 42-320	221	ex (5R-TIK)	
☐ 5R-MRM	Boeing 737-3Z9	24081/1515	ex OE-ILG	Op for Govt

Operator Unknown

☐ 5R-MJL	WSK/PZL Antonov An-28	1AJ005-14	ex ER-AJL

626

5T-   MAURITANIA (Islamic Republic of Mauritania)

COMPAGNIE MAURITANIENNE DE TRANSPORTES – CMT   (CPM)   Nouakchott (NKC)

Operates cargo flights with Antonov aircraft leased from Aerocom and Pskovia when required

MAURITANIA AIRWAYS   (YD/MTW)   Nouakchott (NKC)

☐ TS-IMH	Airbus A320-211	0402	ex F-WWBN		<TAR
☐ TS-LBA	ATR 42-300	245	ex G-BXBV	Alyssa	<TUI
☐ TS-IEB	Boeing 737-7L9/W	28015/785	ex OY-MRJ		<TAR
☐ 5T-CLA	Boeing 737-55S	28469/2849	ex OK-CGH		♦
☐ 5T-CLB	Boeing 737-55S	28470/2861	ex OK-CGJ		♦

5V-   TOGO (Togolese Republic)

AFRICAWEST CARGO   (FK/WTA)   Lome (LFW)

☐ S9-PSA	Antonov An-12BP	6344701	ex UR-TSI

ASKY AIRLINES   (SKK)   Lome (LFW)

☐ ET-ANG	Boeing 737-7K9/W	34401/2216	ex OY-MRP	<ETH♦
☐ ET-ANH	Boeing 737-7K9/W	34402/2270	ex OY-MRR	<ETH♦
☐ ET-AOK	Boeing 737-790/W	33012/1306	ex M-ABDH	<ETH♦
☐ ET-ANW	de Havilland DHC-8-402Q	4320	ex C-GEUN	<ETH♦

ELITE AIR   Elair (EAI)   Lome (LFW)

☐ 5V-TTA	Piper PA-31-350 Navajo Chieftain	31-7405448	ex 9J-JLP
☐ 5V-TTC	Cessna 310Q	310Q0711	ex F-BUFK

5W-   SAMOA (Independent State of Western Samoa)

POLYNESIAN AIRLINES   Polynesian (PH/PAO)   Apia (APW)

☐ 5W-FAV	Britten-Norman BN-2A-8 Islander	42	ex ZK-FMS	Samoa Star	[APW]
☐ 5W-FAW	de Havilland DHC-6 Twin Otter 300	827	ex C-FTLQ	Gogo	
☐ 5W-FAY	de Havilland DHC-6 Twin Otter 300	690	ex VH-UQW	Gillian	

SOUTH PACIFIC EXPRESS

☐ 5W-	Short SD.3-60	SH3693	ex N429AS

5X-   UGANDA (Republic of Uganda)

AIR UGANDA   (U7/UGB)   Entebbe (EBB)

☐ 5X-UGA	McDonnell-Douglas MD-87	49840/1745	ex EC-EYY
☐ 5X-UGB	McDonnell-Douglas MD-87	49837/1730	ex EC-EXT
☐ 5X-UGC	McDonnell-Douglas MD-87	49838/1733	ex EC-EYB
☐ 5X-UGD	Canadair CRJ-100ER	7162	ex F-GRJH
☐ 5X-UGE	Canadair CRJ-200ER	7356	ex N642BR

EAGLE AIR   African Eagle (H7/EGU)   Entebbe (EBB)

☐ 5X-EBZ	Beech 1900C-1	UC-174	ex ZS-PIT
☐ 5X-EIV	LET L-410UVP-E9	962632	ex 5Y-BPX
☐ 5X-GNF	LET L-410UVP-E8	892320	ex OK-UDA
☐ 5X-JNF	LET L-410UVP-E8	861809	ex CCCP-67596

EAST AFRICAN AIRLINES   Crane (QU/UGX)   Entebbe (EBB)

☐ 5X-EAA	Boeing 737-291 (Nordam 3)	22741/871	ex N998UA

RELIANCE AIR   Entebbe (EBB)

☐ 5X-ASI	Cessna 208 Caravan I	20800156	ex N9732F

ROYAL DAISY AIRLINES   Entebbe (EBB)

☐ 5X-TEZ	Embraer EMB.120ER Brasilia	120078	ex ZS-CAE

5Y- KENYA

ACARIZA AVIATION — Nairobi-Wilson (WIL)

☐ 5Y-FWA	Embraer EMB.110P1 Bandeirante	110195	ex ZS-OUM		
☐ 5Y-FWB	Embraer EMB.110P1 Bandeirante	110439	ex ZS-OZJ		

AD AVIATION — Nairobi-Wilson (WIL)

☐ 5Y-JMR	Beech 200C Super King Air	BL-17	ex F-GJMR		

AERO KENYA — Nairobi-Wilson (WIL)

☐ 5Y-BRU	LET L-410UVP-E9	912539	ex 5X-UAY		

AFRICAN EXPRESS AIRWAYS — Express Jet (XU/AXK) — Nairobi-Jomo Kenyatta Intl (NBO)

☐ 5Y-AXB	Boeing 727-231	19565/603	ex 5V-TPB	Garissa	[NBO]
☐ 5Y-AXD	Douglas DC-9-32	47088/180	ex 9L-LDF		
☐ 5Y-AXE	Boeing 727-256	21611/1382	ex 9L-LDV	all-white	>Ishtar
☐ 5Y-AXF	Douglas DC-9-32	47093/237	ex 9L-LDG		
☐ 5Y-AXL	McDonnell-Douglas MD-82	49204/1179	ex I-DAWL		
☐ 5Y-AXN	McDonnell-Douglas MD-82	49207/1189	ex N461LF		

AIRKENYA — (P2/XAK) — Nairobi-Wilson (WIL)

☐ 5Y-BGH	de Havilland DHC-6 Twin Otter 300	574	ex N4226J	
☐ 5Y-BIO	de Havilland DHC-6 Twin Otter 300	579	ex 5H-MRB	
☐ 5Y-BMJ	de Havilland DHC-7-102	83	ex N721AS	[WIL]
☐ 5Y-BPD	de Havilland DHC-7-102	32	ex 7O-ACZ	
☐ 5Y-BTZ	de Havilland DHC-8-102	203	ex VH-TNU	
☐ 5Y-PJP	de Havilland DHC-6 Twin Otter 300	424	ex ZS-LGN	

AIRWORKS KENYA

☐ 5Y-BNH	Cessna 208B Caravan I	208B0385	ex ZS-NYS	
☐ 5Y-EGG	Cessna 208B Caravan I	208B0476	ex ZS-EGG	
☐ 5Y-NFY	Cessna 208B Caravan I	208B0294	ex ZS-NFY	
☐ 5Y-NGO	Cessna 208B Caravan I	208B0322	ex ZS-NGO	
☐ 5Y-NHB	Cessna 208B Caravan I	208B0328	ex ZS-NHB	
☐ 5Y-NKV	Cessna 208B Caravan I	208B0387	ex ZS-NKV	
☐ 5Y-NLM	Cessna 208B Caravan I	208B0375	ex ZS-NLM	
☐ 5Y-TLC	Cessna 208B Caravan I	208B0472	ex ZS-TLC	DHL colours

ALS — Nairobi-Wilson (WIL)

☐ 5Y-BVP	Beech 1900D	UE-136	ex ZS-PHM	op for ICRC
☐ 5Y-BVV	Beech 1900C	UB-29	ex ZS-OUC	
☐ 5Y-BVX	Beech 1900D	UE-101	ex ZS-PJG	
☐ 5Y-DHL	Beech 1900C-1	UC-100	ex N15305	Op for ICRC
☐ 5Y-LKG	Beech 1900C	UB-63	ex C-FUCB	Op for Kenya Airlink
☐ 5Y-SGL	Beech 1900C-1	UC-114	ex V5-SGL	Of for UN Humanitarian Service
☐ 5Y-BVO	de Havilland DHC-8-102	007	ex C-GFQI	
☐ 5Y-BXH	de Havilland DHC-8-102	205	ex C-FLAD	
☐ 5Y-BXI	de Havilland DHC-8-102	376	ex C-GRGQ	
☐ 5Y-BXU	de Havilland DHC-8-102	344	ex C-GFKC	♦
☐ 5Y-PRV	de Havilland DHC-8-102	185	ex C-FGQI	
☐ 5Y-STN	de Havilland DHC-8-102	179	ex C-FCON	
☐ 5Y-BLA	Beech 200C Super King Air	BL-10	ex C-FAMB	
☐ 5Y-HAA	Cessna 208 Caravan I	20800021	ex N9349F	
☐ 5Y-MAK	Cessna 208 Caravan I	20800004	ex HB-CLI	
☐ 5Y-BVY	Embraer ERJ-135LR	145599	ex N843RP	
☐ 5Y-BVZ	Embraer ERJ-135LR	145661	ex N842RP	

ASTRAL AVIATION — Astral Cargo (8V/ACP) — Nairobi-Jomo Kenyatta Intl (NBO)

☐ 5Y-SAN	Douglas DC-9-34CF	47706/821	ex S9-PSR	
☐ UR-CCY	Antonov An-12B	02348106	ex RA-11124	<VPB

BLUEBIRD AVIATION — Cobra (BBZ) — Nairobi -Wilson (WIL)

☐ 5Y-VVN	de Havilland DHC-8-102	62	ex VH-TQN	
☐ 5Y-VVP	de Havilland DHC-8-106	339	ex C-FLPP	
☐ 5Y-VVR	de Havilland DHC-8-102	204	ex VH-TQQ	
☐ 5Y-VVS	de Havilland DHC-8-102A	349	ex VH-TQT	
☐ 5Y-VVT	de Havilland DHC-8-102A	362	ex VH-TQV	

☐ 5Y-VVW	de Havilland DHC-8-402Q	4011	ex LN-RDL	
☐ 5Y-VVX	de Havilland DHC-8-402Q	4018	ex LN-RDB	
☐ 5Y-VVY	de Havilland DHC-8-402Q	4009	ex LN-RDD	♦
☐ 5Y-VVF	Fokker 50	20136	ex N136NM	
☐ 5Y-VVG	Fokker 50	20137	ex N137NM	
☐ 5Y-VVH	Fokker 50	20203	ex N203NM	
☐ 5Y-VVJ	Fokker 50	20133	ex D-AFFZ	
☐ 5Y-VVK	Fokker 50	20213	ex D-AFKL	
☐ 5Y-HHC	LET L-410A	720204	ex OK-DDU	
☐ 5Y-HHF	LET L-410AB	710002	ex OK-ADR	
☐ 5Y-HHL	LET L-410UVP-E9	872018	ex OK-SDA	
☐ 5Y-VVA	LET L-410UVP-E9	962633	ex OK-BDL	dam 23May04
☐ 5Y-VVB	LET L-410UVP-E9	942704	ex OK-BDG	
☐ 5Y-VVC	LET L-410UVP-E20	922728	ex ZS-NIJ	
☐ 5Y-VVE	LET L-410UVP-E20	922726	ex 5Y-YYY	
☐ 5Y-HHE	Beech 200 Super King Air	BB-547	ex ZS-NIP	

BLUE SKY AVIATION · Nairobi-Wilson (WIL)

☐ 5Y-BOD	LET L-410UVP-E20	982727	ex OK-DDF	
☐ 5Y-BSA	LET L-410UVP-E9	892323	ex OK-UDC	
☐ 5Y-BSM	LET L-410UVP-E9	871939	ex 3D-SIG	no titles

CAPITAL AIRLINES · Capital Delta (CPD) · Nairobi Wilson (WIL)

☐ 5Y-JAI	Beech 200 Super King Air	BB-557	ex OY-PAM	
☐ 5Y-SJB	Beech 200 Super King Air	BB-467	ex 5H-MUN	CatPass 250 conversion

DELTA CONNECTION · (Z9/DCP)

☐ 5Y-JAP	Boeing 737-229C	20915/401	ex 5Y-KQN	<EAF

EAST AFRICAN AIR CHARTERS · Nairobi-Wilson (WIL)

☐ 5Y-ALY	Cessna U206F Stationair	U20602266	ex N15588U
☐ 5Y-ART	Cessna 210L Centurion II	21059817	
☐ 5Y-BIX	Reims Cessna F406 Caravan II	F406-0055	ex N65912
☐ 5Y-BLN	Cessna 208B Caravan I	208B0558	ex N50398
☐ 5Y-BMH	Cessna 310R	310R0501	ex N87216
☐ 5Y-BOX	Cessna 208B Caravan I	208B0500	ex 9M-PMV

EAST AFRICAN EXPRESS · (B5/EXZ) · Nairobi-Jomo Kenyatta Intl (NBO)

☐ 5Y-EEE	Fokker F.28 Fellowship 4000	11229	ex 5Y-MNT
☐ 5Y-XXA	Douglas DC-9-14 (ABS 3)	45725/19	ex N600ME
☐ 5Y-XXB	Douglas DC-9-14 (ABS 3)	45711/4	ex N500ME

EXECUTIVE TURBINE KENYA · Nairobi-Wilson (WIL)

☐ 5Y-BSP	Beech 1900D	UE-97	ex N97UX
☐ 5Y-BSS	Beech 1900C-1	UC-88	ex ZS-PJA
☐ 5Y-BTG	Beech 1900C-1	UC-96	ex ZS-PBY
☐ 5Y-BVC	Short SD.3-60	SH3717	ex ZS-PBB

FLY540 · Fly Orange (5H/FFV) · Nairobi-Jomo Kenyatta Intl (NBO)

☐ 5Y-BTN	Beech 1900D	UE-118	ex ZS-PPJ	
☐ 5Y-BUN	ATR 42-320	205	ex ZS-OZX	
☐ 5Y-BUT	ATR 42-320	240	ex ZS-OVL	
☐ 5Y-BUZ	de Havilland DHC-8-102	253	ex C-FOBU	
☐ 5Y-BVD	ATR 42-320	115	ex EI-SLI	
☐ 5Y-BVG	Beech 1900D	UE-62	ex N62ZV	
☐ 5Y-BXB	de Havilland DHC-8-102	213	ex N825PH	
☐ 5Y-	de Havilland DHC-8-102	114	ex C-GRGZ	
☐ 5Y-	ATR 72-212A		ex	o/o♦
☐ 5Y-	ATR 72-212A		ex	o/o♦
☐ 5Y-	ATR 72-212A		ex	o/o♦
☐ 5Y-	ATR 72-212A		ex	o/o♦
☐ 5Y-	ATR 72-212A		ex	o/o♦
☐ 5X-FFD	Fokker F.27 Friendship 500CRF	10530	ex TC-MBC	
☐ 5X-FFN	Fokker F.27 Friendship 500CRF	10531	ex TC-MBD	

GLOBAL AIR CHARTERS

☐ 5Y-BSN	Beech 1900C-1	UC-69	ex OY-GML

JETLINK EXPRESS   Ken Jet (JO/JLX)   Nairobi-Jomo Kenyatta Intl (NBO)

☐ 5Y-JLA	Fokker F.28 Fellowship 4000	11093	ex 5T-CLG	
☐ 5Y-JLB	Canadair CRJ-200	7006	ex XA-UHB	
☐ 5Y-JLC	Canadair CRJ-200	7183	ex F-GPTE	
☐ 5Y-JLD	Canadair CRJ-200	7197	ex F-GPTF	
☐ 5Y-JLE	Canadair CRJ-200	7016	ex XA-UGW	
☐ 5Y-JLG	Canadair CRJ-200	7126	ex F-GPYP	♦
☐ 5Y-JLH	Canadair CRJ-200	7113	ex C-FZGN	

KASKAZI AVIATION   Malindi (MYD)

☐ 5Y-BRX	Dornier 228-100	7004	ex SE-KKX
☐ 5Y-BUV	Dornier 228-201	8050	ex A6-ZYE

KENYA AIRWAYS   Kenya (KQ/KQA)   Nairobi-Jomo Kenyatta Intl (NBO)

Associate member of Skyteam

☐ 5Y-KQA	Boeing 737-3U8	28746/2863		
☐ 5Y-KQB	Boeing 737-3U8	28747/2884		
☐ 5Y-KQC	Boeing 737-3U8	29088/3034		
☐ 5Y-KQD	Boeing 737-3U8	29750/3095	ex N5573L	
☐ 5Y-KQJ	Boeing 737-248	21714/565	ex N1714T	[NBO]
☐ 5Y-KQK	Boeing 737-248	21715/579	ex N1715Z	[NBO]
☐ 5Y-KYN	Boeing 737-306	28720/2957	ex PH-BTI	♦
☐ 5Y-KQE	Boeing 737-76N/W	30133/877		
☐ 5Y-KQF	Boeing 737-76N/W	30136/1145		
☐ 5Y-KQG	Boeing 737-7U8/W	32371/1242	ex N715BA	
☐ 5Y-KQH	Boeing 737-7U8/W	32372/1327		
☐ 5Y-KYB	Boeing 737-8AL/W	35070/2115		
☐ 5Y-KYC	Boeing 737-8AL/W	35071/2138		
☐ 5Y-KYD	Boeing 737-86N/W	35632/2690		
☐ 5Y-KYE	Boeing 737-86N/W	35286/2757	ex N1796B	
☐ 5Y-KYF	Boeing 737-86N/W	35637/2803		
☐ 5Y-KQX	Boeing 767-36NER	30854/844		
☐ 5Y-KQY	Boeing 767-36NER	30841/841		
☐ 5Y-KQZ	Boeing 767-36NER	30853/837		
☐ 5Y-KYW	Boeing 767-319ER	30586/808	ex G-CEOD	♦
☐ 5Y-KYX	Boeing 767-3P6ER	24484/260	ex N244AV	
☐ 5Y-KYY	Boeing 767-3Q8ER	29383/747	ex N171LF	
☐ 5Y-KQS	Boeing 777-2U8ER	33683/522		
☐ 5Y-KQT	Boeing 777-2U8ER	33682/514		
☐ 5Y-KQU	Boeing 777-2U8ER	33681/479	The Pride of Africa	
☐ 5Y-KYZ	Boeing 777-2U8ER	36124/614		
☐ 5Y-KYG	Embraer ERJ-170STD	17000141	ex OH-LEM	♦
☐ 5Y-KYH	Embraer ERJ-170LR	17000230	ex PT-SFG	
☐ 5Y-KYJ	Embraer ERJ-170LR	17000128	ex B-KXD	
☐ 5Y-KYK	Embraer ERJ-170LR	17000111	ex B-KXC	
☐ 5Y-KYL	Embraer ERJ-170STD	17000146	ex OH-LEN	♦
☐ 5Y-KYP	Embraer ERJ-190AR	19000398	ex PT-TYG	♦
☐ 5Y-	Embraer ERJ-190AR		ex PT-	o/o♦

KNIGHT AVIATION   Nairobi-Wilson (WIL)

☐ 5Y-BPH	Embraer EMB.110P2 Bandeirante	110196	ex C9-AUG
☐ 5Y-SRJ	Fokker F.27 Friendship 500F	10372	ex N19XD

MOMBASA AIR SAFARI   Skyrover (RRV)   Mombasa (MBA)

☐ 5Y-NIK	LET L-410UVP-E9	912619	ex OK-WDW
☐ 5Y-UVP	LET L-410UVP-E9	912627	ex OK-WDY

QUEENSWAY AIR SERVICES   Nairobi-Wilson (WIL)

☐ 5Y-BKT	Beech 200 Super King Air	BB-258	ex ZS-NTM
☐ 5Y-BOM	Cessna 208B Caravan I	208B0605	ex ZS-NTM

SAFARI LINKS   Nairobi-Wilson (WIL)

☐ 5Y-BNS	Cessna 208B Caravan I	208B0394	ex N894MA
☐ 5Y-BOP	Cessna 208B Caravan I	208B0642	ex N208GJ
☐ 5Y-NON	Cessna 208 Caravan I	20800036	ex ZS-NON
☐ 5Y-SLA	Cessna 208B Caravan I	208B0574	ex F-OGXY

☐ 5Y-SLC	Cessna 208B Caravan I	208B2091	ex N2234J
☐ 5Y-SLD	de Havilland DHC-8-102	331	ex C-FLPQ

SKYTRAIL	**Skytrail**		**Mombasa (MBA)**
☐ 5Y-AFD	Cessna TU206B Skywagon	U206-0724	ex N3424L
☐ 5Y-SKS	de Havilland DHC-6 Twin Otter 300	682	ex G-BGZP
☐ 5Y-SKT	de Havilland DHC-6 Twin Otter 300	503	ex PH-STC

SKYWAYS KENYA			**Nairobi-Wilson (WIL)**
☐ 5Y-BMB	Douglas DC-3	17108/34375	ex N2025A	stored

SOLENTA AVIATION (KENYA)			**Nairobi-Jomo Kenyatta Intl (NBO)**
☐ 5Y-OBY	Cessna 208B Caravan I	208B0345	ex ZS-OBY	DHL colours

SUPERIOR AVIATION SERVICES		**Skycargo (M7/SUK)**	**Nairobi-Wilson (WIL)**
☐ 5Y-ATH	Piper PA-23-250 Aztec E	27-7305138	
☐ 5Y-PEA	Beech 58 Baron	TH-1067	ex N60664

748 AIR SERVICES	**Sierra Services (IHO)**		**Nairobi-Wilson (WIL)**
☐ 5Y-BSX	Hawker Siddeley HS.780 Andover C.1	Set 20	ex 9Q-COE	
☐ 3C-KKC	Hawker Siddeley HS.780 Andover C.1	Set 18	ex NZ7625	[Lokichoggio]
☐ 5Y-HAJ	Hawker Siddeley HS.748 Srs.2B/371LFD	1776	ex SE-LIB	
☐ 5Y-BVQ	Hawker Siddeley HS.748 Srs.2B/399LFD	1778	ex SE-LIC	
☐ 5Y-EVG	Aérospatiale AS350B2	4439	ex ZK-IHT	♦
☐ 5Y-JGM	de Havilland DHC-8-102A	287	ex N828PH	
☐ 5Y-IHO	de Havilland DHC-8-106	268	ex C-FOEN	

TRACKMARK CARGO			**Nairobi-Wilson (WIL)**
☐ 5Y-TAV	Cessna 208B Caravan I	208B0668	ex ZS-OIH

TRANSWORLD SAFARIS			**Nairobi-Wilson (WIL)**
☐ 5Y-ROH	Piper PA-31-350 Chieftain	31-8152038	ex N217JP	
☐ 5Y-TWA	Beech 200 Super King Air	BB-803	ex G-WPLC	
☐ 5Y-TWC	Beech 200C Super King Air	BL-37	ex G-IFTB	<Aerolite Investments
☐ 5Y-TWG	Cessna 208B Caravan I	208B0674	ex N1286N	
☐ 5Y-TWI	Cessna 208B Caravan I	208B0606	ex 5Y-BNA	

TRIDENT AVIATION			**Nairobi-Wilson (WIL)**
☐ 5Y-MEG	de Havilland DHC-5D Buffalo	62	ex 5V-MAG	Op for UN-WFP
☐ 5Y-OPL	de Havilland DHC-5D Buffalo	84A	ex UAE 310 (1)	Op for UN-WFP
☐ 5Y-TAJ	de Havilland DHC-5E Buffalo	108	ex C-GDOB	Op for UN-WFP
☐ 5Y-TEL	de Havilland DHC-5D Buffalo	68	ex AF-315	Op for UN-WFPdbr?
☐ 5Y-BTP	de Havilland DHC-8-102	104	ex 6Y-JMT	
☐ 5Y-BWG	de Havilland DHC-8Q-311	406	ex C-FTYU	
☐ 5Y-DAC	de Havilland DHC-8-102	251	ex C-GZAN	
☐ 5Y-ENA	de Havilland DHC-8-102	297	ex N836EX	
☐ 5Y-GRS	de Havilland DHC-8-102	355	ex SX-BIS	Echo Flight titles
☐ 5Y-MOC	de Havilland DHC-8-311	374	ex C-FDYW	
☐ 5Y-PTA	de Havilland DHC-8-315	397	ex N788BC	

TROPIC AIR			**Nairobi-Wilson (WIL)**
☐ 5Y-BRT	Cessna 208B Caravan I	208B0682	ex ZS-ELE	
☐ 5Y-BSY	Cessna 208B Caravan I	208B0907	ex N32211	
☐ 5Y-BWV	Aérospatiale AS350B3	4482	ex ZS-RBS	♦

UNITED AIR LINES			**Nairobi-Wilson (WIL)**
☐ 5Y-LAV	Cessna 310R	310R0882	ex N3644G

ZB AIR	**Bosky (ZBA)**		**Nairobi-Wilson (WIL)**
☐ 5Y-OPM	Cessna 208B Caravan I	208B0330	ex N1034S
☐ 5Y-ZBI	Cessna 208B Caravan I	208B0324	ex N1029P
☐ 5Y-ZBL	Cessna 208B Caravan I	208B0338	ex N1042Y
☐ 5Y-ZBR	Cessna 208B Caravan I	208B0446	ex N12922
☐ 5Y-ZBT	Cessna 208B Caravan I	208B1243	ex N1226X
☐ 5Y-ZBW	Cessna 208B Caravan I	208B0409	ex N1115W
☐ 5Y-ZBX	Cessna 208B Caravan I	208B1170	ex N1308N
☐ 5Y-AIS	Beech 95-D55 Baron	TE-680	

☐ 5Y-AUN	Cessna U206F Stationair	U20602531	ex N1244V
☐ 5Y-AYZ	Cessna 310R	310R0121	ex N4940J
☐ 5Y-AZS	Cessna 310R	310R0524	ex N87350
☐ 5Y-SAB	Cessna 404 Titan II	404-0675	ex N6761X
☐ 5Y-ZBK	Beech B200 Super King Air	BB-1714	ex N3214D
☐ 5Y-ZBM	Cessna U206H Stationair 6	U20608114	ex N259ME
☐ 5Y-ZBO	Cessna U206H Stationair	U20608131	ex N373ME
☐ 5Y-ZBZ	Beech 1900	5Y-	

6O- SOMALIA (Democratic Republic of Somalia)

JUBBA AIRWAYS — *Jubba (6J/JUB)* — *Dubai/Sharjah (DXB/SHJ)*

☐ 5Y-BXG	Boeing 737-247 (Nordam 3)	23519/1299	ex YA-GAE

MUDAN AIRLINES — *(MDN)* — *Dubai (DXB)*

☐ ER-46711	Antonov An-24B	99902109	ex RA-46711

STAR AFRICAN AIR — *Starsom (STU)* — *Dubai/Sharjah (DXB/SHJ)*

Operates flights with Antonov An-24 and Ilyushin Il-18 aircraft leased when required

6V- SENEGAL (Republic of Senegal)

AERO SERVICE ASF — *Servo (RSG)* — *Dakar (DKR)*

☐ 6V-AHF	Cessna 208B Caravan I	208B0634	ex N12386
☐ 6V-AHI	Cessna 402C	402C0120	ex F-OHCM

AFRIQUE CARGO SERVICES — *(NFS)* — *Dakar (DKR)*

Operated cargo flights with Antonov An-12 aircraft leased from Tiramavia as required. Current status uncertain as Tiramavia lost their AOC.

AIR SAINT LOUIS — *Air Saint Louis (LOU)* — *Saint Louis (XLS)*

☐ F-BVUN	Bell 206B JetRanger	247	ex D-HAMO
☐ 6V-AHP	Cessna 207 Skywagon	20700209	ex F-GEDM

AIR SENEGAL INTERNATIONAL — *Air Senegal (V7/SNG)* — *Dakar (DKR)*

☐ 6V-AHL	de Havilland DHC-8-315	556	ex C-GDSG	[MST]

ASECNA — *(XKX)* — *Dakar (DKR)*

☐ 6V-AFW	ATR 42-300	117	ex F-WWEN	Calibrator/Pax

SENEGAL AIRLINES — *(SGG)* — *Dakar (DKR)*

☐ 6V-AIH	Airbus A320-214	0799	ex B-2361	♦
☐ 6V-AII	Airbus A320-214	0879	ex B-6258	♦

TURBOT AIR CARGO — *(TAC)* — *Dakar (DKR)*

☐ UR-CAI	Antonov An-26B	7010	ex UR-26519	<UKL
☐ UR-MDA	Antonov An-26	7108	ex Military	<ME

6Y- JAMAICA

AIR JAMAICA — *Jamaica (JM/AJM)* — *Kingston-Norman Manley Intl (KIN)*

☐ 6Y-JAD	Airbus A319-112	3331	ex EI-DZX	201
☐ 6Y-JAI	Airbus A320-214	0628	ex N628AJ	628 Montego Bay
☐ 6Y-JMF	Airbus A320-214	1213	ex EI-DKF	632 Freedom
☐ 6Y-JMG	Airbus A320-214	1390	ex EI-DKG	634 America
☐ 6Y-JMJ	Airbus A320-214	1751	ex B-6266	
☐ 6Y-JMH	Airbus A321-211	1503	ex D-AVZU	515 May Pen

EXEC DIRECT AVIATION

☐ 6Y-JXD	SAAB SF.340A	340A-089	ex SE-LJK	♦

INTERNATIONAL AIRLINK — Kingston-Tinson Peninsula (KTP)

☐ 6Y-JRD	Cessna U206G Stationair 6	U20604522	ex N9019M
☐ 6Y-JRF	Cessna T207A Turbo Skywagon	20700365	ex N1765U
☐ 6Y-JRG	Cessna 208B Caravan I	208B0311	ex YN-CDR

SKYLAN AIRWAYS

☐ 6Y-JIC	British Aerospace Jetstream 32EP	920	ex N920AE

TIMAIR — Montego Bay (MBJ)

☐ 6Y-JLU	Britten-Norman BN-2B-26 Islander	2170	ex 6Y-JLG
☐ 6Y-JNA	Cessna U206G Stationair	U20603837	ex N4515C
☐ 6Y-JNB	Cessna U206G Stationair	U20603615	ex N7332N
☐ 6Y-JNJ	Cessna U206G Stationair 6	U20606359	ex N2447N
☐ 6Y-JNL	Cessna U206G Stationair 6	U20605620	ex N712RS

7O- YEMEN (Republic of Yemen)

FELIX AIRWAYS — Sana'a (SAH)

☐ 7O-FAA	Canadair CRJ-702NG	10267	ex C-	
☐ 7O-FAB	Canadair CRJ-702NG	10268	ex C-	
☐ 7O-	Canadair CRJ-702NG		ex C-	o/o♦
☐ 7O-	Canadair CRJ-702NG		ex C-	o/o♦
☐ 7O-	Canadair CRJ-702NG		ex C-	o/o♦
☐ 7O-	Canadair CRJ-702NG		ex C-	o/o♦
☐ 7O-	Canadair CRJ-702NG		ex C-	o/o♦
☐ 7O-	Canadair CRJ-702NG		ex C-	o/o♦
☐ 7O-FAI	Canadair CRJ-200LR	7307	ex N636BR	
☐ 7O-FAJ	Canadair CRJ-200LR	7308	ex N637BR	

YEMENIA — Yemeni (IY/IYE) — Sana'a (SAH)

☐ 7O-ADR	Airbus A310-324ET	568	ex F-OGYO	Socotra	
☐ 7O-ADV	Airbus A310-325	702	ex F-OHPR	Seiyun	
☐ 7O-ADW	Airbus A310-325	704	ex F-OHPS	Marib	
☐ 7O-	Airbus A320-232		ex		o/o♦
☐ 7O-	Airbus A320-232		ex		o/o♦
☐ 7O-	Airbus A320-232		ex		o/o♦
☐ 7O-	Airbus A320-232		ex		o/o♦
☐ 7O-ADP	Airbus A330-243	625	ex F-WWYD	Sana'a	
☐ 7O-ADT	Airbus A330-243	632	ex F-WWYH	Aden	
☐ 7O-ADX	Airbus A330-243	627	ex EI-EOK		♦
☐ 7O-ADA	Boeing 727-2N8	21842/1512	ex 4W-ACJ		Op for Govt
☐ 7O-ADM	Boeing 737-8Q8/W	28252/1195		Shibam	
☐ 7O-ADN	Boeing 737-8Q8/W	30661/1186		Zabid	
☐ 7O-ADQ	Boeing 737-8Q8/W	30730/2399			
☐ 7O-YMN	Boeing 747SP-27	21786/413	ex A7-AHM		Op for Government
☐ 7O-ADH	de Havilland DHC-6 Twin Otter 310	764	ex G-GBAC		
☐ 7O-ADI	de Havilland DHC-6 Twin Otter 300	664	ex HB-LRT		<FAT
☐ 7O-ADK	de Havilland DHC-6 Twin Otter 310	813	ex A4O-DB		
☐ 7O-ADS	de Havilland DHC-8-102	280	ex C-FMCZ		
☐ 7O-ADU	de Havilland DHC-8-102A	327	ex C-FHLO		
☐ 7O-ADY	de Havilland DHC-8-103	333	ex C-FSID		
☐ 7O-ADF	Ilyushin Il-76TD	1033418578	ex RA-76380		Jt ops with Air Force
☐ 7O-ADG	Ilyushin Il-76TD	1023412402	ex RA-76405		Jt ops with Air Force
☐ 7O-ADD	Lockheed L-382C-86D Hercules	4827	ex 1160		Jt ops with Air Force
☐ 7O-ADE	Lockheed L-382C-86D Hercules	4825	ex 1150		Jt ops with Air Force

7Q-   MALAWI (Republic of Malawi)

AIR MALAWI		Malawi (QM/AML)			Blantyre (BLZ)
☐ ZS-PUI	Boeing 737-2B7 (Nordam 3)	22890/986	ex 5N-BFJ		
☐ 7Q-YKP	Boeing 737-33A	25056/2045		Kwacha	[JNB]
☐ 7Q-YKQ	ATR 42-320	236	ex F-WWES	Shire	
☐ 7Q-YKW	Boeing 737-522	25384/2149	ex N917UA	Sapitwa	[JNB]
☐ 7Q-YKX	Boeing 737-2K9	23405/1178	ex C9-BAI		

7T-   ALGERIA (Democratic & Popular Republic of Algeria)

AIR ALGERIE		Air Algerie (AH/DAH)			Algiers (ALG)
☐ 7T-VJC	Airbus A310-203	291	ex F-WZED		
☐ 7T-VJD	Airbus A310-203	293	ex F-WZEE		
☐ 7T-VJV	Airbus A330-202	644	ex F-WWKD	Tinhinan	
☐ 7T-VJW	Airbus A330-202	647	ex F-WWKF	Lalla Setti	
☐ 7T-VJX	Airbus A330-202	650	ex F-WWKK	Mers el Kebir	
☐ 7T-VJY	Airbus A330-202	653	ex F-WWYK	Monts des Beni Chougrane	
☐ 7T-VJZ	Airbus A330-202	667	ex F-WWKR	Teddis	
☐ 7T-VUI	ATR 72-212A	644	ex F-OHGM		
☐ 7T-VUJ	ATR 72-212A	648	ex F-OHGN		
☐ 7T-VUK	ATR 72-212A	652	ex F-OHGO		
☐ 7T-VUL	ATR 72-212A	672	ex F-OHGP		
☐ 7T-VUM	ATR 72-212A	677	ex F-OHGQ		
☐ 7T-VUN	ATR 72-212A	684	ex F-OHGR		
☐ 7T-VUO	ATR 72-212A	901	ex F-WWEP		◆
☐ 7T-VUP	ATR 72-212A	903	ex F-WWES		◆
☐ 7T-VUQ	ATR 72-212A	909	ex F-WWEB		◆
☐ 7T-VUS	ATR 72-212A	913	ex F-WWEI		◆
☐ 7T-VVQ	ATR 72-212A	676	ex F-WWEA		
☐ 7T-VVR	ATR 72-212A	683	ex F-WWEF		
☐ 7T-VEA	Boeing 727-2D6	20472/850		Tassili	
☐ 7T-VEB	Boeing 727-2D6	20473/855		Hoggar	[ALG]
☐ 7T-VEI	Boeing 727-2D6	21053/1111		Djebel Amour	[ALG]
☐ 7T-VEM	Boeing 727-2D6	21210/1204		Mont du Ksall	
☐ 7T-VEP	Boeing 727-2D6	21284/1233		Mont du Tessala	
☐ 7T-VET	Boeing 727-2D6	22372/1662		Gorges du Rhumel	
☐ 7T-VEU	Boeing 727-2D6 (Raisbeck 3)	22373/1664		Djurdjura	[ALG]
☐ 7T-VEV	Boeing 727-2D6 (Raisbeck 3)	22374/1711	ex N8292V		[ALG]
☐ 7T-VEW	Boeing 727-2D6 (Raisbeck 3)	22375/1723	ex N8295V		[ALG]
☐ 7T-VEX	Boeing 727-2D6 (Raisbeck 3)	22765/1801		Djemila	[ALG]
☐ TC-SKD	Boeing 737-4Q8	25372/2280	ex TC-JDI		<SHY
☐ 7T-VED	Boeing 737-2D6C	20850/311			[ALG]
☐ 7T-VEF	Boeing 737-2D6	20759/332		Saoura	[ALG]
☐ 7T-VEG	Boeing 737-2D6	20884/361		Monts des Oulad Nails	[ALG]
☐ 7T-VEJ	Boeing 737-2D6	21063/407		Chrea	[ALG]
☐ 7T-VEK	Boeing 737-2D6	21064/409		Edough	[ALG]
☐ 7T-VEL	Boeing 737-2D6	21065/416		Akfadou	[ALG]
☐ 7T-VEQ	Boeing 737-2D6	21285/473		Le Zaccar	
☐ 7T-VJQ	Boeing 737-6D6	30209/1115		Kasbah d'Alger	
☐ 7T-VJR	Boeing 737-6D6	30545/1131			
☐ 7T-VJS	Boeing 737-6D6	30210/1150	ex N60559		
☐ 7T-VJT	Boeing 737-6D6	30546/1152			
☐ 7T-VJU	Boeing 737-6D6	30211/1164			
☐ 7T-VJJ	Boeing 737-8D6	30202/610		Jugurtha	
☐ 7T-VJK	Boeing 737-8D6	30203/640	ex N1781B	Mansourah	
☐ 7T-VJL	Boeing 737-8D6	30204/652		Allizi	
☐ 7T-VJM	Boeing 737-8D6	30205/691			
☐ 7T-VJN	Boeing 737-8D6	30206/751		Oued Tafna	
☐ 7T-VJO	Boeing 737-8D6	30207/868	ex N1787B	Tinerkouk	
☐ 7T-VJP	Boeing 737-8D6	30208/896	ex N1787B	Mont Tahat	
☐ 7T-VKA	Boeing 737-8D6/W	34164/1748		Monts Chaboro	
☐ 7T-VKB	Boeing 737-8D6/W	34165/1768	ex N1784B	Mont de l'Assekhrem	
☐ 7T-VKC	Boeing 737-8D6/W	34166/1773			
☐ 7T-VKD	Boeing 737-8D6/W	40858/3406	ex N1786B		◆
☐ 7T-VKE	Boeing 737-8D6/W	40859/3446			◆

634

☐ 7T-VKF	Boeing 737-8D6/W	40860/3471	ex N1787B	♦
☐ 7T-	Boeing 737-8D6/W			o/o♦
☐ 7T-	Boeing 737-8D6/W			o/o♦
☐ 7T-	Boeing 737-8D6/W			o/o♦
☐ 7T-VJG	Boeing 767-3D6ER	24766/310		
☐ 7T-VJH	Boeing 767-3D6ER	24767/323		
☐ 7T-VJI	Boeing 767-3D6ER	24768/332	ex N6009F	
☐ 7T-VIG	Cessna 208B Caravan I	208B0391	ex N1122N	
☐ 7T-VII	Cessna 208B Caravan I	208B0393	ex N1123G	>DTH
☐ 7T-VIL	Cessna 208B Caravan I	208B0601	ex N1247H	
☐ 7T-VIM	Cessna 208B Caravan I	208B0602	ex N1247K	
☐ 7T-VCV	Beech A100 King Air	B-93	ex N9369Q	
☐ 7T-VHL	Lockheed L-382-51D Hercules	4886	ex N4160M	
☐ 7T-VIQ	Beech 1900D	UE-381	ex N31683	VIP
☐ 7T-VRF	Beech A100 King Air	B-147	ex N1828W	

AIR EXPRESS ALGERIA — *Algiers (ALG)*

☐ 7T-VAE	LET L-410UVP-E20	872011	ex OK-SDT	
☐ 7T-VAF	LET L-410UVP-E20	082629	ex CCCP-67698	
☐ ZS-OOF	LET L-410UVP-E20	871920	ex 5H-PAJ	
☐ ZS-OSE	LET L-420	922729A	ex N420Y	
☐ ZS-OUE	LET L-420	012735A	ex OK-GDM	<Air-Tec Africa
☐ ZS-OXR	LET L-410UVP	972730	ex 5H-HSA	
☐ ZS-OYF	Beech 1900D	UE-214	ex VH-IMS	<NAC

STAR AVIATION — *Algiers (ALG)*

☐ 7T-VNA	Pilatus PC-6/B2-H4 Turbo Porter	817	ex HB-FFV	
☐ 7T-VNB	Beech 1900D	UE-305	ex 7T-WRF	
☐ 7T-VND	de Havilland DHC-6 Twin Otter 300	502	ex HB-LRS	
☐ 7T-VNE	de Havilland DHC-6 Twin Otter 300	717	ex HB-LTD	

TASSILI AIRLINES — *Tassili Air (SF/DTH)* — **Hassi Messaoud (HME)**

☐ 7T-VCG	Pilatus PC-6/B2-H4 Turbo Porter	917	ex HB-FLJ	
☐ 7T-VCH	Pilatus PC-6/B2-H4 Turbo Porter	929	ex HB-FLX	
☐ 7T-VCI	Pilatus PC-6/B2-H4 Turbo Porter	933	ex HB-FLY	
☐ 7T-VCJ	Pilatus PC-6/B2-H4 Turbo Porter	934	ex HB-FLZ	
☐ 7T-VCK	Pilatus PC-6/B2-H4 Turbo Porter	930	ex HB-FMA	
☐ 7T-VII	Cessna 208B Caravan I	208B0393	ex N1123G	<DAH
☐ 7T-VIP	Beech 1900D	UE-369	ex N30538	
☐ 7T-	Boeing 737-8			o/o♦
☐ 7T-	Boeing 737-8			o/o♦
☐ 7T-	Boeing 737-8			o/o♦
☐ 7T-	Boeing 737-8			o/o♦
☐ 7T-VCL	de Havilland DHC-8Q-402	4167	ex C-FMIT	
☐ 7T-VCM	de Havilland DHC-8Q-402	4169	ex C-FMIV	
☐ 7T-VCN	de Havilland DHC-8Q-402	4173	ex C-FMKF	
☐ 7T-VCO	de Havilland DHC-8Q-402	4178	ex C-FMTN	
☐ 7T-VCP	de Havilland DHC-8-202	661	ex C-FRIZ	
☐ 7T-VCQ	de Havilland DHC-8-202	664	ex C-FTGX	
☐ 7T-VCR	de Havilland DHC-8-202	665	ex C-FTUE	
☐ 7T-VCS	de Havilland DHC-8-202	666	ex C-FUCF	

8P- BARBADOS

REDJET

☐ 8P-ARB	McDonnell-Douglas MD-82	49469/1410	ex N443AA	♦
☐ 8P-IGB	McDonnell-Douglas MD-82	49471/1418	ex N445AA	♦

TRANS ISLAND AIR 2000 — *Trans Island (TRD)* — **Bridgetown-Grantley Adams (BGI)**

Services performed by Twin Otters operated by SVG Air (J8-)

8Q-   MALDIVES (Republic of Maldives)

ISLAND AVIATION SERVICES		(Q2) (986)		Male (MLE)
☐ 8Q-AMD	de Havilland DHC-8-202	429	ex C-GDKL	
☐ 8Q-IAO	de Havilland DHC-8Q-314	544	ex D-BHOQ	
☐ 8Q-IAP	de Havilland DHC-8Q-315	491	ex LN-WFE	
☐ 8Q-IAQ	de Havilland DHC-8-202	542	ex C-FIKT	
☐ 8Q-IAR	Dornier 228-212	8244	ex D-CBDX	

MALDIVIAN AIR TAXI				Male (MLE)
☐ 8Q-MAA	de Havilland DHC-6 Twin Otter 300	693	ex C-GKCS	FP
☐ 8Q-MAB	de Havilland DHC-6 Twin Otter 300	287	ex C-GKBV	FP
☐ 8Q-MAD	de Havilland DHC-6 Twin Otter 300	273	ex C-FAKB	FP
☐ 8Q-MAE	de Havilland DHC-6 Twin Otter 300	464	ex C-FPOQ	FP
☐ 8Q-MAF	de Havilland DHC-6 Twin Otter 300	449	ex C-FWKQ	FP
☐ 8Q-MAH	de Havilland DHC-6 Twin Otter 300	374	ex C-FMYV	FP
☐ 8Q-MAI	de Havilland DHC-6 Twin Otter 300	279	ex C-GKBM	FP
☐ 8Q-MAJ	de Havilland DHC-6 Twin Otter 300	837	ex C-GJDP	FP
☐ 8Q-MAL	de Havilland DHC-6 Twin Otter 300	321	ex C-GBBU	FP
☐ 8Q-MAM	de Havilland DHC-6 Twin Otter 300	339	ex C-GOKB	FP
☐ 8Q-MAN	de Havilland DHC-6 Twin Otter 300	435	ex C-FWKZ	FP
☐ 8Q-MAO	de Havilland DHC-6 Twin Otter 300	259	ex C-FKBI	FP
☐ 8Q-MAP	de Havilland DHC-6 Twin Otter 300	571	ex C-FKBX	FP
☐ 8Q-MAQ	de Havilland DHC-6 Twin Otter 310	611	ex C-FBKB	FP
☐ 8Q-MAT	de Havilland DHC-6 Twin Otter 200	146	ex 8Q-NTA	FP
☐ 8Q-MAW	de Havilland DHC-6 Twin Otter 300	722	ex C-FWKO	FP
☐ 8Q-MAX	de Havilland DHC-6 Twin Otter 300	755	ex C-FWKX	FP
☐ 8Q-MAZ	de Havilland DHC-6 Twin Otter 300	774	ex C-FWKU	FP
☐ 8Q-MBA	de Havilland DHC-6 Twin Otter 300	691	ex D-IHAI	FP
☐ 8Q-MBB	de Havilland DHC-6 Twin Otter 300	659	ex HB-LUG	FP
☐ 8Q-MBE	de Havilland DHC-6 Twin Otter 300	561	ex OY-ATY	FP♦
☐ 8Q-OEQ	de Havilland DHC-6 Twin Otter 100	44	ex C-FOEQ	FP
☐ 8Q-	de Havilland DHC-6 Twin Otter 400			o/o
☐ 8Q-	de Havilland DHC-6 Twin Otter 400			o/o

MEGA MALDIVES AIRLINES				Male (MLE)
☐ 8Q-MEG	Boeing 767-3P6ER	24496/270	ex N183AQ	♦

TRANS MALDIVIAN AIRWAYS		Hum (TMW)		Male (MLE)
☐ 8Q-TAB	de Havilland DHC-6 Twin Otter 300	582	ex ZS-SAI	FP♦
☐ 8Q-TAC	de Havilland DHC-6 Twin Otter 300	580	ex ZS-PZO	FP♦
☐ 8Q-TMA	de Havilland DHC-6 Twin Otter 100	82	ex 8Q-HIA	FP
☐ 8Q-TMB	de Havilland DHC-6 Twin Otter 300	587	ex C-GASV	FP
☐ 8Q-TMD	de Havilland DHC-6 Twin Otter 310	530	ex 8Q-HIG	FP
☐ 8Q-TME	de Havilland DHC-6 Twin Otter 300	798	ex 8Q-HIH	FP
☐ 8Q-TMF	de Havilland DHC-6 Twin Otter 300	657	ex 8Q-HII	FP
☐ 8Q-TMG	de Havilland DHC-6 Twin Otter 310	597	ex 8Q-HIJ	FP
☐ 8Q-TMH	de Havilland DHC-6 Twin Otter 300	668	ex HK-4194X	FP
☐ 8Q-TMI	de Havilland DHC-6 Twin Otter 300	754	ex N107JM	FP
☐ 8Q-TMJ	de Havilland DHC-6 Twin Otter 300	781	ex N781JM	FP
☐ 8Q-TMK	de Havilland DHC-6 Twin Otter 300	751	ex N710PV	FP
☐ 8Q-TML	de Havilland DHC-6 Twin Otter 300	640	ex N709PV	FP
☐ 8Q-TMN	de Havilland DHC-6 Twin Otter 300	700	ex TJ-OHN	FP
☐ 8Q-TMO	de Havilland DHC-6 Twin Otter 300	234	ex C-FBZN	FP
☐ 8Q-TMP	de Havilland DHC-6 Twin Otter 300	652	ex VH-KZN	FP
☐ 8Q-TMQ	de Havilland DHC-6 Twin Otter 300	753	ex N162AY	FP
☐ 8Q-TMR	de Havilland DHC-6 Twin Otter 300	270	ex N270CM	FP
☐ 8Q-TMS	de Havilland DHC-6 Twin Otter 300	663	ex PK-TWH	FP
☐ 8Q-TMT	de Havilland DHC-6 Twin Otter 300	454	ex C-FNBI	FP
☐ 8Q-TMU	de Havilland DHC-6 Twin Otter 300	467	ex C-FOIM	FP
☐ 8Q-TMV	de Havilland DHC-6 Twin Otter 300	625	ex C-FNBL	FP
☐ 8Q-TMW	de Havilland DHC-6 Twin Otter 300	768	ex C-GDQM	FP
☐ 8Q-ATM	ATR 42-320	194	ex N11835	
☐ 8Q-ATN	ATR 42-300	096	ex PK-VSX	

8R-   GUYANA (Co-operative Republic of Guyana)

AIR GUYANA				Georgetown-Ogle (OGL)
☐ 8R-WAL	Cessna 208B Caravan I	208B0990	ex N208KT	♦

636

AIR SERVICES — Georgetown-Ogle (OGL)

☐ 8R-GAA	Piper PA-34-200T Seneca II	34-7870451	ex 8R-GGJ		
☐ 8R-GAS	Cessna 208B Caravan I	208B0691	ex YN-CFK		
☐ 8R-GER	Britten-Norman BN-2A-27 Islander	478	ex G-BDJX		
☐ 8R-GFI	Britten-Norman BN-2A-9 Islander	677	ex G-AZGU		
☐ 8R-GFM	Cessna U206F Stationair	U20601731	ex N9531G		
☐ 8R-GGE	Cessna U206G Stationair	U20603358	ex N8501Q	FP	
☐ 8R-GHB	Cessna U206G Stationair 6	U20604889	ex 8R-GPF		
☐ 8R-GHE	Britten-Norman BN-2A-6 Islander	269	ex 8R-GHB		
☐ 8R-GYA	Cessna U206G Stationair	U20603654	ex 8R-GGF	R/STOL conv	

RORAIMA AIRWAYS — Roraima (ROR) — Georgetown-Ogle (OGL)

☐ 8R-GRA	Britten-Norman BN-2A-26 Islander	3006	ex N42540	
☐ 8R-GRB	Britten-Norman BN-2B-26 Islander	431	ex N431V	
☐ 8R-GRC	Britten-Norman BN-2B-27 Islander	2114	ex SX-DKA	

TRANS GUYANA AIRWAYS — Trans Guyana (TGY) — Georgetown-Ogle (OGL)

☐ 8R-GGY	Britten-Norman BN-2A-26 Islander	470	ex N81567	
☐ 8R-GHD	Britten-Norman BN-2A-27 Islander	622	ex C-GKES	
☐ 8R-GHM	Britten-Norman BN-2A-27 Islander	216	ex PT-IAS	
☐ 8R-GHR	Cessna 208B Caravan I	208B0519	ex PT-MEZ	
☐ 8R-GHT	Cessna 208B Caravan I	208B0572	ex TI-BBG	
☐ 8R-GTG	Cessna 208B Caravan I	208B0397	ex N397TA	

9A- CROATIA (Republic of Croatia)

CROATIA AIRLINES — Croatia (OU/CTN) — Zagreb (ZAG)

Member of Star Alliance

☐ 9A-CTG	Airbus A319-112	0767	ex D-AVYA	Zadar	
☐ 9A-CTH	Airbus A319-112	0833	ex D-AVYJ	Zagreb	
☐ 9A-CTI	Airbus A319-112	1029	ex D-AVYC	Vukovar	
☐ 9A-CTL	Airbus A319-112	1252	ex D-AVYS	Pula	
☐ 9A-CTF	Airbus A320-212	0258	ex F-OKAI	Rijeka	
☐ 9A-CTJ	Airbus A320-214	1009	ex F-WWDN	Dubrovnik	
☐ 9A-CTK	Airbus A320-214	1237	ex F-WWIK	Split	
☐ 9A-CQA	de Havilland DHC-8-402Q	4205	ex C-FPEL		
☐ 9A-CQB	de Havilland DHC-8-402Q	4211	ex C-FPQD		
☐ 9A-CQC	de Havilland DHC-8-402Q	4258	ex C-FWIJ		
☐ 9A-CQD	de Havilland DHC-8-402Q	4260	ex C-FWZU		
☐ 9A-CQE	de Havilland DHC-8-402Q	4300	ex C-GBKD	Zagorje	♦
☐ 9A-CQF	de Havilland DHC-8-402Q	4301	ex C-GCKE		♦

DUBROVNIK AIRLINE — (DBK) — Dubrovnik (DBV)

☐ 9A-CDA	McDonnell-Douglas MD-83	49602/1435	ex N491GX	Revelin
☐ 9A-CDB	McDonnell-Douglas MD-83	49986/1842	ex PK-ALG	Lovrijenac
☐ 9A-CDC	McDonnell-Douglas MD-82	49112/1068	ex PK-ALI	Minceta
☐ 9A-CDD	McDonnell-Douglas MD-82	49113/1069	ex PK-ALJ	Bokar
☐ 9A-CDE	McDonnell-Douglas MD-82	48066/1019	ex PK-ALH	Sveti Ivan

TRADE AIR — Tradeair (TDR) — Zagreb (ZAG)

☐ 9A-BTB	LET L-410UVP-E3	902506	ex LZ-KLA	
☐ 9A-BTC	LET L-410UVP-E3	902507	ex LZ-KLB	
☐ 9A-BTD	Fokker 100	11407	ex N1424M	Op in Sun Adria colours
☐ 9A-BTE	Fokker 100	11416	ex N1431B	Op in Sun Adria colours

9G- GHANA (Republic of Ghana)

AEROGEM AIRLINES — Aerogem (GCK) — Accra (ACC)

☐ 9G-OAL	Boeing 707-324C (Comtran 2)	19350/537	ex 9G-OLD	all-white

ANTRAK AIR GHANA — Antrak (O4/ABV) — Accra (ACC)

☐ EX-132	Boeing 737-2Q8	21687/554	ex TN-AHK	
☐ 9G-AAB	ATR 42-300	041	ex F-WQCT	

☐ 9G-ANT	ATR 42-300	086	ex ZS-ORE	retd?
☐ 9G-NAN	Douglas DC-9-51	47732/861	ex 5X-TWO	[ACC]
☐ 9G-NIN	Douglas DC-9-51	47746/864	ex 5X-TRE	[SCC]

CITYLINK		*CityLink (CTQ)*		*Accra (ACC)*
☐ 9G-CTL	SAAB SF.340A	340A-044	ex ZS-PMJ	
☐ 9G-LET	LET L-410UVP-E20	871922	ex ZS-OOH	

JOHNSONS AIR		*Johnsonsair (JON)*		*Accra/Sharjah (ACC/SHJ)*
☐ 9G-FAB	Douglas DC-8-63F (BAC 3)	46121/500	ex N786AL	
☐ 9G-LIL	Douglas DC-8-63AF (BAC 3)	46147/549	ex 9G-MKO	>RSE
☐ 9G-PEL	Douglas DC-8-62F (BAC 3)	46085/481	ex 4K-AZ29	[RKT], <ALG Group
☐ 9G-RAC	Douglas DC-8-63PF (BAC 3)	46093/496	ex N816AX	
☐ 9G-SIM	Douglas DC-8-63CF (BAC 3)	46061/480	ex N826AX	
☐ 9G-TOP	Douglas DC-8-63CF (BAC 3)	46151/540	ex 9G-MKN	

MERIDIAN AIRWAYS		*(ACE)*		*Accra (ACC)*
☐ TZ-MHI	Lockheed L-1011-100 Tristar	193B-1221	ex EX-35000	
☐ 9G-AED	Douglas DC-8-62AF	46162/555	ex Z-ALB	
☐ 9G-AXA	Douglas DC-8-63F (BAC 3)	46113/521	ex N811AX	
☐ 9G-AXB	Douglas DC-8-63PF (BAC 3)	46097/503	ex N815AX	
☐ 9G-AXC	Douglas DC-8-63F (BAC 3)	45999/377	ex N828AX	
☐ 9G-AXD	Douglas DC-8-63F (BAC 3)	45927/327	ex N819AX	
☐ 9G-AXE	Douglas DC-8-63F (BAC 3)	46041/439	ex N814AX	

SOBEL AIR				*Accra (ACC)*
☐ 9G-AIR	Fokker F.27 Friendship 100	10266	ex SE-KZF	
☐ 9G-SOB	Fokker F.27 Friendship 100	10287	ex (TL-ADS)	

9H-   MALTA (Republic of Malta)

AIR MALTA		*Air Malta (KM/AMC)*			*Luqa (MLA)*
☐ 9H-AEG	Airbus A319-112	2113	ex C-GAEG	Mdina	
☐ 9H-AEH	Airbus A319-112	2122	ex D-AVWA	Floriana	
☐ 9H-AEJ	Airbus A319-112	2186	ex D-AVWX	San Pawl il-Bahr	
☐ 9H-AEL	Airbus A319-112	2332	ex D-AVYZ	Marsaxlokk	
☐ 9H-AEM	Airbus A319-112	2382	ex D-AVWW	Birgu	
☐ 9H-AEF	Airbus A320-214	2142	ex F-WWBZ	Valletta	
☐ 9H-AEK	Airbus A320-214	2291	ex F-WWBT	San Gijan	
☐ 9H-AEN	Airbus A320-214	2665	ex F-WWBN	Bormia	
☐ 9H-AEO	Airbus A320-214	2768	ex F-WWDK	Isla-Cita'Invicta	
☐ 9H-AEP	Airbus A320-214	3056	ex F-WWDV	Nadur	
☐ 9H-AEQ	Airbus A320-214	3068	ex F-WWIJ	Tarxien	

EFLY		*(LEF)*		*Luqa (MLA)*
☐ 9H-ELE	British Aerospace 146 Srs.300	E3209	ex G-JEBG	

HARBOURAIR		*(HES)*		*Grand Harbour*
☐ 9H-AFA	de Havilland DHC-3 Turbo Otter	406	ex C-FHAH	FP

MEDAVIA		*Medavia (MDM)*		*Luqa (MLA)*
☐ 9H-AAP	CASA C.212-200	9	ex EC-CRV	
☐ 9H-AAR	CASA C.212-200	CC15-1-161		
☐ 9H-AAS	CASA C.212-200	CC15-2-162		
☐ 9H-AET	Dornier 328-110	3117	ex D-COMM	
☐ 9H-AEW	de Havilland DHC-8-102	222	ex PH-SDH	
☐ 9H-AEY	de Havilland DHC-8-315	508	ex G-BRYX	
☐ 9H-AFD	de Havilland DHC-8Q-315	458	ex G-BRYU	>ATW♦
☐ 9H-AFH	Beech 1900D	UE-372	ex PH-RAR	
☐ 9H-AFI	Beech 1900D	UE-31	ex PH-RAH	

9J-   ZAMBIA (Republic of Zambia)

AIRWAVES AIRLINK		*Airlimited (WLA)*		*Lusaka (LUN)*
☐ 9J-CGC	Cessna 208B Caravan I	208B0742	ex N878C	

638

PROFLIGHT AIR SERVICES		Proflight-Zambia (PFZ)		Lusaka (LUN)

☐ 7Q-YMJ	Piper PA-23-250 Aztec D	27-4104	ex ZS-FTO	
☐ 9J-ABD	Cessna P206D Super Skylane	P206-0461	ex ZS-FDA	
☐ 9J-KKN	Piper PA-31-350 Chieftain	31-8052113	ex ZS-KKN	
☐ 9J-PLJ	Britten-Norman BN-2A-21 Islander	799	ex Botswana OA3	
☐ 9J-UAS	Britten-Norman BN-2A Islander	155	ex Z-UAS	
☐ 9J-WEX	Britten-Norman BN-2A Islander	619	ex Z-WEX	

ROYAL AIR CHARTERS				

| ☐ 9J-CID | Cessna 208B Caravan I | 208B1307 | ex N20527 | |

ZAMBEZI AIRWAYS				

☐ 9J-ZJA	Boeing 737-5Y0	26101/2544	ex N611MD	Spirit of Kafue	
☐ 9J-ZJB	Boeing 737-5Y0	26100/2538	ex N610MD	Spirit of Mosi-O-Tunya	
☐ 9J-ZJC	Boeing 737-53S	29074/3086	ex ES-ABH		◆

ZAMBIAN AIRWAYS		Zambian (Q3/MBN)		Lusaka (LUN)

| ☐ 9J-JOY | Boeing 737-244 | 22584/821 | ex ZS-SIE | [JNB] |

9K- KUWAIT (State of Kuwait)

GRYPHON AIRWAYS			Kuwait City (KWI)

| ☐ ZS-GAT | Douglas DC-9-32 | 47797/913 | ex 3D-MRT |
| ☐ ZS-GAU | Douglas DC-9-32 | 47798/914 | ex 3D-MRU |

JAZEERA AIRWAYS		Jazeera (J9/JZR)	Kuwait City (KWI)

☐ 9K-CAA	Airbus A320-214	2569	ex F-WWBF
☐ 9K-CAC	Airbus A320-214	2792	ex F-WWBM
☐ 9K-CAD	Airbus A320-214	2822	ex F-WWDC
☐ 9K-CAI	Airbus A320-214	3919	ex F-WWBH
☐ 9K-CAJ	Airbus A320-214	3939	ex F-WWDR
☐ 9K-CAK	Airbus A320-214	4162	ex F-WWBS

KUWAIT AIRWAYS		Kuwaiti (KU/KAC)		Kuwait City (KWI)

☐ 9K-AHI	Airbus A300C4-620	344	ex PK-MAY	Al-Sabahiya	Op for Govt
☐ 9K-AMA	Airbus A300B4-605R	673	ex F-WWAQ	Failaka	
☐ 9K-AMB	Airbus A300B4-605R	694	ex F-WWAV	Burghan	
☐ 9K-AMC	Airbus A300B4-605R	699	ex F-WWAM	Wafra	
☐ 9K-AMD	Airbus A300B4-605R	719	ex F-WWAB	Wara	
☐ 9K-AME	Airbus A300B4-605R	721	ex F-WWAG	Al-Rawdhatain	
☐ 9K-ALA	Airbus A310-308	647	ex F-WWCQ	Al-Jahra	
☐ 9K-ALB	Airbus A310-308	649	ex F-WWCV	Gharnada	
☐ 9K-ALC	Airbus A310-308	663	ex JY-AGT	Kazma	
☐ 9K-ALD	Airbus A310-308	648	ex F-WWCR	Al-Salmiya	Op for Govt
☐ 9K-AKA	Airbus A320-212	0181	ex F-WWIU	Bubbyan	
☐ 9K-AKB	Airbus A320-212	0182	ex F-WWIV	Kubber	
☐ 9K-AKC	Airbus A320-212	0195	ex F-WWDP	Qurtoba	
☐ 9K-AKD	Airbus A320-212	2046	ex F-WWBG	Al-Mubarakiya	Op for Govt
☐ 9K-ANA	Airbus A340-313	089	ex F-WWJX	Warba	
☐ 9K-ANB	Airbus A340-313	090	ex F-WWJZ	Bayan	
☐ 9K-ANC	Airbus A340-313	101	ex F-WWJE	Meskan	
☐ 9K-AND	Airbus A340-313	104	ex F-WWJJ	Al-Riggah	
☐ 9K-ADE	Boeing 747-469M	27338/1046		Al-Jabariya	Op for Govt
☐ 9K-AOA	Boeing 777-269ER	28743/125		Al-Gurain	
☐ 9K-AOB	Boeing 777-269ER	28744/145		Garouh	

LOADAIR CARGO				Kuwait City (KWI)

| ☐ 9K-DAA | Boeing 747-4HQERF | 37303/1416 | ex N797BA | o/o |
| ☐ 9K-DAB | Boeing 747-4HQERF | 37304/1419 | ex N799BA | o/o |

WATANIYA AIRWAYS			Kuwait City (KWI)

☐ 9K-EAA	Airbus A320-214	3739	ex F-WWIG
☐ 9K-EAB	Airbus A320-214	3791	ex F-WWBF
☐ 9K-EAC	Airbus A320-214	3907	ex D-AVVA

☐ 9K-EAD	Airbus A320-214	4049	ex F-WWIM	
☐ 9K-EAE	Airbus A320-214	4235	ex F-WWDC	♦
☐ 9K-EAF	Airbus A320-214	4304	ex D-AXAJ	♦
☐ 9K-EAG	Airbus A320-214	4411	ex F-WWIJ	♦

9L-   SIERRA LEONE (Republic of Sierra Leone)

AIR RUM — *Air Rum (RUM)* — **Amman (AMM)**

☐ C5-GAE	Boeing 727-51 (FedEx 3)	19124/347	ex HZ-DG1		
☐ 9L-LDV	Lockheed L-1011-1 Tristar	193C-1200	ex 5Y-RUM		WFU
☐ 9L-LFB	Lockheed L-1011-1 Tristar	193P-1156	ex XU-100	Barakah	WFU

BELLVIEW AIRLINES — *O3/ORJ* — **Freetown (FNA)**

Operates services with aircraft leased from Bellview Airlines (5N) as required

PEACE AIR

| ☐ 9Q-CQZ | LET L-410UVP | 851339 | ex 9L-LEM |

9M-   MALAYSIA (Federation of Malaysia)

AIRASIA — *Asian express (AK/AXM)* — **Kuala Lumpur-Sultan Abdul Aziz Shah (KUL)**

☐ 9M-AFA	Airbus A320-214	2612	ex F-WWBV	
☐ 9M-AFB	Airbus A320-214	2633	ex F-WWDY	
☐ 9M-AFC	Airbus A320-214	2656	ex F-WWIO	Manchester United colours
☐ 9M-AFD	Airbus A320-214	2683	ex F-WWIT	
☐ 9M-AFE	Airbus A320-214	2699	ex F-WWDN	
☐ 9M-AFF	Airbus A320-214	2760	ex F-WWDT	
☐ 9M-AFG	Airbus A320-216	2816	ex F-WWIX	
☐ 9M-AFH	Airbus A320-216	2826	ex F-WWDI	
☐ 9M-AFI	Airbus A320-216	2842	ex F-WWIG	
☐ 9M-AFJ	Airbus A320-216	2881	ex F-WWBQ	
☐ 9M-AFK	Airbus A320-216	2885	ex F-WWBS	
☐ 9M-AFL	Airbus A320-216	2926	ex F-WWDX	
☐ 9M-AFM	Airbus A320-216	2944	ex F-WWIN	
☐ 9M-AFN	Airbus A320-216	2956	ex F-WWBY	
☐ 9M-AFO	Airbus A320-216	2989	ex F-WWIK	
☐ 9M-AFP	Airbus A320-216	3000	ex F-WWBC	Special 3000th c/s
☐ 9M-AFQ	Airbus A320-216	3018	ex F-WWBR	Malaysia anniversary c/s
☐ 9M-AFR	Airbus A320-216	3064	ex F-WWIC	
☐ 9M-AFS	Airbus A320-216	3117	ex F-WWBB	
☐ 9M-AFT	Airbus A320-216	3140	ex F-WWDN	
☐ 9M-AFU	Airbus A320-216	3154	ex F-WWDE	
☐ 9M-AFV	Airbus A320-216	3173	ex F-WWIO	
☐ 9M-AFW	Airbus A320-216	3404	ex F-WWBX	ATT & Williams colours
☐ 9M-AFY	Airbus A320-216	3194	ex F-WWIV	
☐ 9M-AFZ	Airbus A320-216	3201	ex F-WWID	
☐ 9M-AHA	Airbus A320-216	3223	ex F-WWBV	
☐ 9M-AHB	Airbus A320-216	3232	ex F-WWBF	
☐ 9M-AHC	Airbus A320-216	3261	ex F-WWDN	
☐ 9M-AHD	Airbus A320-216	3291	ex F-WWDT	
☐ 9M-AHE	Airbus A320-216	3327	ex F-WWBH	
☐ 9M-AHF	Airbus A320-216	3353	ex F-WWIE	
☐ 9M-AHG	Airbus A320-216	3370	ex F-WWDF	Manchester United colours
☐ 9M-AHH	Airbus A320-216	3427	ex F-WWBB	
☐ 9M-AHI	Airbus A320-216	3448	ex F-WWIX	
☐ 9M-AHJ	Airbus A320-216	3477	ex F-WWDH	
☐ 9M-AHK	Airbus A320-216	3486	ex F-WWIH	
☐ 9M-AHL	Airbus A320-216	3521	ex F-WWDS	
☐ 9M-AHM	Airbus A320-216	3536	ex F-WWID	
☐ 9M-AHN	Airbus A320-216	3549	ex F-WWIX	
☐ 9M-AHO	Airbus A320-216	3568	ex F-WWBV	
☐ 9M-AHP	Airbus A320-216	3582	ex F-WWDE	
☐ 9M-AHQ	Airbus A320-216	3628	ex F-WWIU	
☐ 9M-AHR	Airbus A320-216	3701	ex F-WWBP	
☐ 9M-AHS	Airbus A320-216	3776	ex F-WWDX	
☐ 9M-AHT	Airbus A320-216	3997	ex F-WWDH	
☐ 9M-AHU	Airbus A320-216	4070	ex F-WWBK	
☐ 9M-AHV	Airbus A320-216	4079	ex F-WWBP	
☐ 9M-AHW	Airbus A320-216	4098	ex F-WWDJ	

☐ 9M-AHX	Airbus A320-216	4263	ex F-WWBG			♦
☐ 9M-AHY	Airbus A320-216	4293	ex F-WWIY			♦
☐ 9M-AHZ	Airbus A320-216	4361	ex F-WWDP			♦
☐ 9M-AQA	Airbus A320-216	4404	ex F-WWBG			♦
☐ 9M-AQB	Airbus A320-216	4458	ex F-WWBF			♦
☐ 9M-	Airbus A320-216		ex			o/o♦
☐ 9M-	Airbus A320-216		ex			o/o♦
☐ 9M-	Airbus A320-216		ex			o/o♦
☐ 9M-	Airbus A320-216		ex			o/o♦
☐ 9M-	Airbus A320-216		ex			o/o♦
☐ 9M-	Airbus A320-216		ex			o/o♦
☐ 9M-	Airbus A320-216		ex			o/o♦
☐ 9M-	Airbus A320-216		ex			o/o♦

AIR ASIA X (D7 / XAX) Kuala Lumpur-Sultan Abdul Aziz Shah (KUL)

☐ 9M-XAA	Airbus A330-301	054	ex N54AN		
☐ 9M-XXA	Airbus A330-343E	952	ex F-WWKR		
☐ 9M-XXB	Airbus A330-343E	974	ex F-WWKD		
☐ 9M-XXC	Airbus A330-343E	1048	ex F-WWKI		
☐ 9M-XXD	Airbus A330-343E	1066	ex F-WWYI	Soaring Xpectations	
☐ 9M-XXE	Airbus A330-343E	1075	ex F-WWKS	Pioneering Xpedition	♦
☐ 9M-XXF	Airbus A330-343E	1126	ex F-WWYQ		♦
☐ 9M-XXG	Airbus A330-343E	1131	ex F-WWYY		♦
☐ 9M-XXH	Airbus A330-343E	1165	ex F-WWYG		♦
☐ 9M-	Airbus A330-343E		ex		o/o♦
☐ 9M-	Airbus A330-343E		ex		o/o♦
☐ 9M-	Airbus A330-343E		ex		o/o♦
☐ 9M-	Airbus A330-343E		ex		o/o♦
☐ 9M-	Airbus A330-343E		ex		o/o♦
☐ 9M-	Airbus A330-343E		ex		o/o♦
☐ 9M-XAB	Airbus A340-313X	273	ex C-GDVW	Xcalibur	
☐ 9M-XAC	Airbus A340-313X	278	ex C-GDVZ	Xcellence	

AWAN INSPIRASI

☐ 9M-AIG	Sikorsky S-92A	920057	ex C-GOHC	
☐ 9M-AIH	Sikorsky S-92A	920024	ex C-GOHA	
☐ 9M-AIK	Sikorsky S-76C+	760622	ex C-GHRK	
☐ 9M-AIP	Sikorsky S-76C++	760693	ex C-FRSE	

BERJAYA AIR CHARTER Berjaya (J8/BVT) Subang-Sultan Abdul Aziz Shah International (SZB)

☐ 9M-TAG	ATR 72-212A	858	ex F-WWEC	
☐ 9M-TAQ	ATR 72-212A	875	ex F-WWEB	♦
☐ 9M-TAH	de Havilland DHC-7-110	109	ex G-BRYD	
☐ 9M-TAK	de Havilland DHC-7-110	110	ex G-BOAW	
☐ 9M-TAL	de Havilland DHC-7-110	112	ex G-BOAY	

FIREFLY (7E/FFM) Penang (PEN)

☐ 9M-FYA	ATR 72-212A	812	ex F-WWEB	
☐ 9M-FYB	ATR 72-212A	814	ex F-WWED	
☐ 9M-FYC	ATR 72-212A	821	ex F-WWEK	
☐ 9M-FYD	ATR 72-212A	830	ex F-WWEE	
☐ 9M-FYE	ATR 72-212A	840	ex F-WWER	
☐ 9M-FYF	ATR 72-212A	860	ex F-WWEF	
☐ 9M-FYG	ATR 72-212A	868	ex F-WWES	
☐ 9M-FYH	ATR 72-212A	934	ex F-WWEJ	♦
☐ 9M-FYI	ATR 72-212A		ex	o/o♦
☐ 9M-FYJ	ATR 72-212A		ex	o/o♦
☐ 9M-FFA	Boeing 737-8Q8/W	30702/1953	ex 9M-MLA	♦
☐ 9M-FFB	Boeing 737-8Q8/W	30703/1964	ex 9M-MLB	♦
☐ 9M-FZA	Boeing 737-430	27001/2316	ex EI-COH	♦
☐ 9M-MGI	Fokker 50	20175	ex PH-EXB	[SZB]
☐ 9M-MGK	Fokker 50	20248	ex PH-EXR	

HERITAGE AIR

☐ RP-C5525	British Aerospace 146 Srs.200	E2031	ex N66LN	<Lionair ♦

HORNBILL SKYWAYS Koching (KCH)

☐ 9M-BCU	Bell 206L-4 LongRanger IV	52151	ex N337H

☐ 9M-HRM	Bell 430	49018	ex 9M-ATM	
☐ 9M-HSM	Bell 206L-4 LongRanger IV	52295	ex N4204A	
☐ 9M-SGH	Bell 206B JetRanger III	4103	ex N7107Z	
☐ 9M-SGJ	Bell 206B JetRanger III	4059	ex N8129Y	
☐ 9M-WSA	Eurocopter EC135P2	0482	ex D-HECH	
☐ 9M-WSG	Eurocopter EC135P2+	0483	ex D-HECU	

LAYANG-LAYANG AEROSPACE — Layang (LAY) — Miri (MYY)

☐ 9M-LLA	Short SC.7 Skyvan 3	SH1977	ex ZS-LFG	
☐ 9M-LLB	GAF N22C Nomad	N22C-95	ex VH-SNL	
☐ 9M-LLH	Bell 206B JetRanger III	2919	ex VH-WNA	
☐ 9M-LLI	GAF N22C Nomad	N22B-69	ex VH-MSF	
☐ 9M-LLT	Bell 206B JetRanger	969	ex G-TUCH	
☐ 9M-LLU	Bolkow 105C			
☐ RA-41900	Antonov An-38-120	4160381607003		<NPO

MALAYSIA AIRLINES — Malaysian (MH/MAS) — Kuala Lumpur-Sultan Abdul Aziz Shah (KUL)

☐ 9M-MKA	Airbus A330-322	067	ex F-WWKK	
☐ 9M-MKC	Airbus A330-322	069	ex F-WWKM	
☐ 9M-MKD	Airbus A330-322	073	ex F-WWKN	
☐ 9M-MKE	Airbus A330-322	077	ex F-WWKO	
☐ 9M-MKF	Airbus A330-322	100	ex F-WWKZ	
☐ 9M-MKG	Airbus A330-322	107	ex F-WWKV	
☐ 9M-MKH	Airbus A330-322	110	ex F-WWKE	
☐ 9M-MKI	Airbus A330-322	116	ex F-WWKT	
☐ 9M-MKJ	Airbus A330-322	119	ex F-WWKJ	
☐ 9M-MKS	Airbus A330-322	143	ex C-FRAE	
☐ 9M-MKV	Airbus A330-223	296	ex EI-CZS	
☐ 9M-MKW	Airbus A330-223	300	ex EI-CZT	
☐ 9M-MKX	Airbus A330-223	290	ex EI-CZR	
☐ 9M-	Airbus A330-322		ex	o/o♦
☐ 9M-	Airbus A330-322		ex	o/o♦
☐ 9M-	Airbus A330-322		ex	o/o♦
☐ 9M-	Airbus A330-322		ex	o/o♦
☐ 9M-	Airbus A330-322		ex	o/o♦
☐ 9M-	Airbus A330-223F		ex	o/o♦
☐ 9M-	Airbus A330-223F		ex	o/o♦
☐ 9M-MMA	Boeing 737-4H6	26443/2272		
☐ 9M-MMB	Boeing 737-4H6	26444/2308		
☐ 9M-MMC	Boeing 737-4H6	26453/2332		
☐ 9M-MMD	Boeing 737-4H6	26464/2340		
☐ 9M-MME	Boeing 737-4H6	26465/2362		
☐ 9M-MMF	Boeing 737-4H6	26466/2372		
☐ 9M-MMG	Boeing 737-4H6	26467/2378		
☐ 9M-MMH	Boeing 737-4H6	27084/2391		
☐ 9M-MMI	Boeing 737-4H6	27096/2395		
☐ 9M-MMJ	Boeing 737-4H6	27097/2399		
☐ 9M-MMK	Boeing 737-4H6	27083/2403		
☐ 9M-MML	Boeing 737-4H6	27085/2407		
☐ 9M-MMM	Boeing 737-4H6	27166/2410		
☐ 9M-MMN	Boeing 737-4H6	27167/2419		
☐ 9M-MMQ	Boeing 737-4H6	27087/2441		
☐ 9M-MMR	Boeing 737-4H6	26468/2445		
☐ 9M-MMS	Boeing 737-4H6	27169/2450		
☐ 9M-MMT	Boeing 737-4H6	27170/2462		
☐ 9M-MMU	Boeing 737-4H6	26447/2479	ex VT-JAV	
☐ 9M-MMV	Boeing 737-4H6	26449/2491		
☐ 9M-MMW	Boeing 737-4H6	26451/2496		
☐ 9M-MMX	Boeing 737-4H6	26452/2501		
☐ 9M-MMY	Boeing 737-4H6	26455/2507		>UBA
☐ 9M-MMZ	Boeing 737-4H6	26457/2521		
☐ 9M-MQA	Boeing 737-4H6	26458/2525		
☐ 9M-MQB	Boeing 737-4H6	26459/2530		
☐ 9M-MQC	Boeing 737-4H6	26460/2533		
☐ 9M-MQD	Boeing 737-4H6	26461/2536		
☐ 9M-MQE	Boeing 737-4H6	26462/2542		
☐ 9M-MQF	Boeing 737-4H6	26463/2560		
☐ 9M-MQG	Boeing 737-4H6	27190/2568		
☐ 9M-MQI	Boeing 737-4H6	27353/2632	ex 9H-ADJ	
☐ 9M-MQK	Boeing 737-4H6	27384/2673		
☐ 9M-MQN	Boeing 737-4H6	27673/2852	ex 9H-ADK	
☐ 9M-MQO	Boeing 737-4H6	27674/2877	ex 9H-ADL	
☐ 9M-MQP	Boeing 737-46J	28038/2794	ex N380BG	
☐ 9M-MQQ	Boeing 737-4Y0	24915/2055	ex SX-BKL	

☐ 9M-MLC	Boeing 737-8Q8/W	32690/2250	ex G-XLAO		
☐ 9M-MLD	Boeing 737-8GQ/W	35793/2428	ex N793AW		♦
☐ 9M-MLE	Boeing 737-8FH/W	35105/2501	ex N126RB		♦
☐ 9M-MLF	Boeing 737-8FZ/W	29657/3335	ex N1786B		♦
☐ 9M-MLG	Boeing 737-8FZ/W	31779/3395	ex N1787B		♦
☐ 9M-MLH	Boeing 737-8FZ/W	31723/3435	ex N1788B		♦
☐ 9M-MLI	Boeing 737-8FZ/W	31793/3503			♦
☐ 9M-MLJ	Boeing 737-8FZ/W	39319			o/o♦
☐ 9M-MLK	Boeing 737-8FZ/W	39320			o/o♦
☐ 9M-MXA	Boeing 737-8H6/W	40128/3421	ex N1786B		♦
☐ 9M-MXB	Boeing 737-8H6/W	40129/3458			♦
☐ 9M-MXC	Boeing 737-8H6/W	40130/3495	ex N1786B		♦
☐ 9M-	Boeing 737-8H6/W				o/o♦
☐ 9M-	Boeing 737-8H6/W				o/o♦
☐ 9M-	Boeing 737-8H6/W				o/o♦
☐ TF-AAA	Boeing 747-236B (SCD)	22442/526	ex N361FC		<ABD
☐ TF-AAB	Boeing 747-236B (SCD)	22304/502	ex N362FC		
☐ TF-ARJ	Boeing 747-236M	23735/674	ex G-BDXN		op by ABD
☐ TF-ARN	Boeing 747-2F6B (SF)	22382/498	ex N745SA		op by ABD
☐ 9M-MPB	Boeing 747-4H6	25699/965		Shah AlamHibiscus colours	
☐ 9M-MPF	Boeing 747-4H6	27043/1017		Kota Bharu	
☐ 9M-MPH	Boeing 747-4H6	27044/1041	ex N6066B	Langkawi	
☐ 9M-MPK	Boeing 747-4H6	28427/1147		Johor Bahru	
☐ 9M-MPL	Boeing 747-4H6	28428/1150		Penang	
☐ 9M-MPM	Boeing 747-4H6	28435/1152		Melaka	
☐ 9M-MPN	Boeing 747-4H6	28432/1247		Pangkor	
☐ 9M-MPO	Boeing 747-4H6	28433/1290		Alor Setar	
☐ 9M-MPP	Boeing 747-4H6	29900/1296		Putrajaya	
☐ 9M-MPQ	Boeing 747-4H6	29901/1301		Kuala Lumpur	
☐ 9M-MPR	Boeing 747-4H6F	28434/1371			
☐ 9M-MPS	Boeing 747-4H6F	29902/1374			
☐ 9M-MRA	Boeing 777-2H6ER	28408/64	ex N5017V		
☐ 9M-MRB	Boeing 777-2H6ER	28409/74	ex N50217		
☐ 9M-MRC	Boeing 777-2H6ER	28410/78			
☐ 9M-MRD	Boeing 777-2H6ER	28411/84		Freedom of Space c/s	
☐ 9M-MRE	Boeing 777-2H6ER	28412/115			
☐ 9M-MRF	Boeing 777-2H6ER	28413/128			
☐ 9M-MRG	Boeing 777-2H6ER	28414/140			
☐ 9M-MRH	Boeing 777-2H6ER	28415/151			
☐ 9M-MRI	Boeing 777-2H6ER	28416/155			
☐ 9M-MRJ	Boeing 777-2H6ER	28417/222			
☐ 9M-MRK	Boeing 777-2H6ER	28418/231			
☐ 9M-MRL	Boeing 777-2H6ER	29065/329			
☐ 9M-MRM	Boeing 777-2H6ER	29066/336			
☐ 9M-MRN	Boeing 777-2H6ER	28419/394			
☐ 9M-MRO	Boeing 777-2H6ER	28420/404			
☐ 9M-MRP	Boeing 777-2H6ER	28421/496	ex N5016R		
☐ 9M-MRQ	Boeing 777-2H6ER	28422/498			

MASWINGS

☐ 9M-MDK	de Havilland DHC-6 Twin Otter 300	792	ex C-GESR		
☐ 9M-MDL	de Havilland DHC-6 Twin Otter 300	802	ex C-GDFT		
☐ 9M-MDM	de Havilland DHC-6 Twin Otter 300	804	ex C-GDKL		
☐ 9M-MDO	de Havilland DHC-6 Twin Otter 310	629	ex ZK-KHA		
☐ 9M-MGA	Fokker 50	20150	ex PH-EXM		
☐ 9M-MGB	Fokker 50	20156	ex PH-EXP		
☐ 9M-MGD	Fokker 50	20164	ex PH-EXL		
☐ 9M-MGE	Fokker 50	20166	ex PH-EXN		
☐ 9M-MGF	Fokker 50	20167	ex PH-EXO		
☐ 9M-MGG	Fokker 50	20170	ex PH-EXS		[SZB]
☐ 9M-MGJ	Fokker 50	20204	ex PH-EXM		[SZB]
☐ 9M-MWA	ATR 72-212A	817	ex F-WWEG		
☐ 9M-MWB	ATR 72-212A	856	ex F-WWEX		
☐ 9M-MWC	ATR 72-212A	863	ex F-WWEL		
☐ 9M-MWD	ATR 72-212A	873	ex F-WWEX		
☐ 9M-MWE	ATR 72-212A	885	ex F-WWEO		
☐ 9M-MWF	ATR 72-212A	889	ex F-WWET		
☐ 9M-MWG	ATR 72-212A	895	ex F-WWEE		
☐ 9M-MWH	ATR 72-212A	900	ex F-WWEO		
☐ 9M-MWI	ATR 72-212A	904	ex F-WWET	Bario	♦
☐ 9M-MWJ	ATR 72-212A	910	ex F-WWEH		♦

MHS AVIATION — Kerteh/Miri (KTE/MYY)

☐ 9M-SPB	Aérospatiale AS.332L2	2636	ex F-WWOO	
☐ 9M-SPC	Aérospatiale AS.332L2	2639	ex F-WWOJ	
☐ 9M-SPD	Aérospatiale AS.332L2	2646	ex F-WWOO	
☐ 9M-STS	Aérospatiale AS.332L1	2387		
☐ 9M-STV	Aérospatiale AS.332L1	2408		
☐ 9M-STW	Aérospatiale AS.332L1	2312	ex LN-OBQ	<CHC Helicopters Intl
☐ 9M-AIM	Eurocopter EC225LP	2769		◆
☐ 9M-BEG	Sikorsky S-76C+	760568	ex C-GHRY	
☐ 9M-SPP	Sikorsky S-76C+	760661	ex N45067	
☐ 9M-SPQ	Sikorsky S-76C	760662	ex N4507G	
☐ 9M-SPR	Sikorsky S-76C	760663	ex N4508G	
☐ 9M-SPS	Sikorsky S-76C+	760641	ex G-CEKP	
☐ 9M-SPT	Sikorsky S-76C+	760645	ex G-CEKR	
☐ 9M-SPV	Sikorsky S-76C+	760654	ex G-CEOR	
☐ 9M-SPW	Sikorsky S-76C+	760664	ex G-KAZD	
☐ 9M-STA	Sikorsky S-76C	760383		
☐ 9M-STB	Sikorsky S-76C	760384		
☐ 9M-STC	Sikorsky S-76C	760392		
☐ 9M-STD	Sikorsky S-76C	760397		
☐ 9M-STE	Sikorsky S-76C	760398		
☐ 9M-STF	Sikorsky S-76C	760400		
☐ 9M-STG	Sikorsky S-76C	760385	ex ZS-RTC	
☐ 9M-AVP	Sikorsky S-61N	61768	ex G-BEKJ	
☐ 9M-SNA	Aérospatiale AS365N2 Dauphin 2	6246	ex N634LH	
☐ 9M-SSV	Aérospatiale AS355F2 Ecureuil 2	5476		
☐ 9M-SSW	Aérospatiale AS355F2 Twin Star	5467	ex N467CL	
☐ 9M-SSZ	Aérospatiale AS355F2 Ecureuil 2	5292	ex 3A-MVV	
☐ 9M-STL	Beech 1900D	UE-373	ex N31110	
☐ 9M-STM	Beech 1900D	UE-374	ex N31419	

NEPTUNE AIR

☐ 9M-NEA	Boeing 737-210C (Nordam 3)	21822/605	ex PK-YGF
☐ 9M-NEP	Boeing 727-277F (FedEx 3)	22641/1753	ex VH-VLI

PAN-MALAYSIAN AIR TRANSPORT — Pan Malaysia (PMA) — Subang-Sultan Abdul Aziz Shah International (SZB)

☐ 9M-PIH	Short SC.7 Skyvan 3	SH1962	ex G-BFUM

PERFECT AVIATION

☐ N854AA	Boeing 727-223F (FedEx 3)	20995/1192

SABAH AIR — Sabah Air (SAX) — Kota Kinabalu-Intl (BKI)

☐ 9M-AUA	GAF N22B Nomad	N22B-7	
☐ 9M-AWC	Bell 206B JetRanger III	2336	
☐ 9M-AXH	Bell 206B JetRanger III	2480	
☐ 9M-AYN	Bell 206B JetRanger III	3022	ex N5738M
☐ 9M-AZK	Bell 206L-3 LongRanger III	51484	ex N4196G
☐ 9M-KUL	Bell 206L-4 LongRanger IV	52253	ex N9089J
☐ 9M-SAC	Bell 206B JetRanger III	2510	

TRANSMILE AIR SERVICES — Transmile (TH/TSE) — Subang-Sultan Abdul Aziz Shah Intl (SZB)

☐ 9M-TGB	Boeing 727-2F2F/W (Duganair 3)	22998/1810	ex VH-DHF		
☐ 9M-TGE	Boeing 727-247F (FedEx 3)	21697/1471	ex PK-TMA		◆
☐ 9M-TGF	Boeing 727-247F (FedEx 3)	21698/1474	ex N209UP		
☐ 9M-TGG	Boeing 727-247F (FedEx 3)	21699/1485	ex N207UP		
☐ 9M-TGH	Boeing 727-247F (FedEx 3)	21701/1493	ex N208UP		
☐ 9M-TGL	Boeing 727-225F (FedEx 3)	21856/1537	ex N8887Z		
☐ 9M-TGM	Boeing 727-225F (FedEx 3)	22549/1737	ex N902RF		
☐ 9M-PML	Boeing 737-275C	21116/427	ex C-GDPW	DHL colours	Frtr
☐ 9M-PMM	Boeing 737-205C	20458/278	ex RP-C2906	DHL colours	Frtr [KUL]
☐ 9M-PMP	Boeing 737-248C	20220/215	ex PT-MTA		Frtr
☐ 9M-PMQ	Boeing 737-230C	20254/230	ex PT-MTB		Frtr
☐ 9M-PMW	Boeing 737-209F (AvAero 3)	24197/1581	ex PK-TME		◆
☐ 9M-PMZ	Boeing 737-209	23796/1420	ex PK-KAR		◆
☐ 9M-PMA	Cessna 208B Caravan I	208B0800	ex N1278M		

☐ 9M-TGP	McDonnell-Douglas MD-11F	48444/459	ex N625FE	[KUL]
☐ 9M-TGQ	McDonnell-Douglas MD-11F	48446/463	ex N627FE	[KUL]
☐ 9M-TGR	McDonnell-Douglas MD-11F	48485/502	ex N71WF	[KUL]
☐ 9M-TGS	McDonnell-Douglas MD-11F	48486/509	ex N15WF	[KUL]

9N-   NEPAL (Kingdom of Nepal)

AGNI AIR   Kathmandu (KTM)

☐ 9N-AIE	Dornier 228-202K	8165	ex 9M-VAA	
☐ 9N-AIG	Dornier 228-212	8216	ex 9M-VAM	
☐ 9N-AIO	British Aerospace Jetstream 4101	41055	ex N316UE	
☐ 9N-AIP	British Aerospace Jetstream 4101	41058	ex N322UE	
☐ 9N-AIQ	British Aerospace Jetstream 4101	41064	ex N326UE	
☐ 9N-	British Aerospace Jetstream 4101	41081	ex N564HK	o/o

AIR KASTHAMANDAP   Kathmandu (KTM)

☐ 9N-AIZ	Pacific Aerospace 750XL	154	ex ZK-JJH	
☐ 9N-AJB	Pacific Aerospace 750XL	160	ex ZK-KAZ	
☐ 9N-AJF	Pacific Aerospace 750XL	162	ex ZK-KAO	♦

BUDDHA AIR   Buddha Air (BHA)   Kathmandu (KTM)

☐ 9N-AIM	ATR 42-320	388	ex F-WQNF	
☐ 9N-AIN	ATR 42-320	403	ex F-WQNA	
☐ 9N-AIT	ATR 42-320	409	ex F-WKVF	
☐ 9N-AJO	ATR 72-212A	535	ex F-WNUF	♦
☐ 9N-AEE	Beech 1900D	UE-286	ex N11194	
☐ 9N-AEK	Beech 1900D	UE-295	ex N21540	
☐ 9N-AEW	Beech 1900D	UE-328	ex N23179	
☐ 9N-AGH	Beech 1900D	UE-409	ex N4192N	
☐ 9N-AGI	Beech 1900C-1	UC-97	ex N97YV	
☐ 9N-AGL	Beech 1900C-1	UC-108	ex N15856	
☐ 9N-AHZ	Beech 1900D	UE-180	ex N862CA	

COSMIC AIR   Cosmic Air (F5/COZ)   Kathmandu/Pokhara (KTM/PKR)

☐ 9N-AEP	Dornier 228-201	8078	ex D-CBMI	[KTM]
☐ 9N-AGY	Dornier 228-100	7022	ex SE-KTM	[KTM]

GORKHA AIRLINES   (G1)   Pokhara (PKR)

☐ 9N-AHS	Dornier 228-212	8218	ex RP-C2101	

MAKALU AIR   Kathmandu (KTM)

☐ 9N-AJM	Cessna 208B Caravan I	208B0561	ex C-FWAM	♦

NEPAL AIRLINES   Nepal (RA/RNA)   Kathmandu (KTM)

☐ 9N-ACA	Boeing 757-2F8	23850/142		Karnali
☐ 9N-ACB	Boeing 757-2F8C	23863/182	ex N5573K	Gandaki
☐ 9N-ABB	de Havilland DHC-6 Twin Otter 300	302		
☐ 9N-ABM	de Havilland DHC-6 Twin Otter 300	455	ex N302EH	[KTM]
☐ 9N-ABO	de Havilland DHC-6 Twin Otter 300	638		[KTM]
☐ 9N-ABQ	de Havilland DHC-6 Twin Otter 300	655		[KTM]
☐ 9N-ABT	de Havilland DHC-6 Twin Otter 300	812	ex C-GHHI	
☐ 9N-ABU	de Havilland DHC-6 Twin Otter 300	814	ex C-GHHY	
☐ 9N-ABX	de Havilland DHC-6 Twin Otter 300	830	ex C-GIQS	

SHREE AIRLINES   Pokhara/Surkhet (PKR/SKH)

☐ 9N-ADD	Mil Mi-17-1 (Mi-8ATM)	59489607385	ex RA-22160	
☐ 9N-ADL	Mil Mi-17-1 (Mi-8ATM)	59489605283	ex RA-27093	[KTM]
☐ 9N-ADM	Mil Mi-8AMTV-1	95640	ex CCCP-25495	

SITA AIRLINES   Kathmandu (KTM)

☐ 9N-AHA	Dornier 228-202K	8123	ex F-ODZG	
☐ 9N-AHB	Dornier 228-202K	8169	ex F-OGPI	
☐ 9N-AHR	Dornier 228-202	8154	ex C-GSAU	
☐ 9N-AIJ	Dornier 228-212	8239	ex 8Q-IAS	
☐ 9N-AIY	Dornier 228-212	8191	ex F-ODYB	

TARA AIR

☐ 9N-AET	de Havilland DHC-6 Twin Otter 300	619	ex C-GBQA
☐ 9N-AEV	de Havilland DHC-6 Twin Otter 300	729	ex C-FWQF
☐ 9N-AFA	de Havilland DHC-6 Twin Otter 300	665	ex VT-ERV
☐ 9N-AGQ	Dornier 228-202K	8107	ex F-ODZF

YETI AIRLINES (YA) Kathmandu (KTM)

☐ 9N-AHU	British Aerospace Jetstream 41	41072	ex N555HK
☐ 9N-AHV	British Aerospace Jetstream 41	41077	ex N561HK
☐ 9N-AHW	British Aerospace Jetstream 41	41078	ex N562HK
☐ 9N-AHY	British Aerospace Jetstream 41	41066	ex N553HK
☐ 9N-AIB	British Aerospace Jetstream 41	41017	ex G-CDYH
☐ 9N-AIH	British Aerospace Jetstream 41	41085	ex N567HK
☐ 9N-AJC	British Aerospace Jetstream 41	41096	ex G-MAJM

9Q- CONGO KINSHASA (Democratic Republic of Congo)

AEROLIFT SERVICES

☐ 9Q-CJU	Antonov An-32	1408	ex D2-FED

AFRICA ONE Kinshasa-Ndolo (NLO)

☐ 9Q-CAF	Antonov An-32	1703	ex RA-48094 Regd to Business Aviation
☐ 9Q-CFY	WSK-PZL/Antonov An-28	1AJ006-03	ex 9XR-KI

AIR BOYOMA Kisangani (FKI)

☐ UR-ELH	Antonov An-26B	12908	ex UR-26143 <URG

AIR KASAI Kinshasa-Ndolo (NLO)

☐ 9Q-CFD	Antonov An-26B	12901	ex RA-26139	
☐ 9Q-CFL	Antonov An-26B	14003	ex RA-26593	
☐ 9Q-CFM	Antonov An-26B	07310405	ex RA-26235	
☐ 9Q-CFP	Antonov An-26	07310605	ex RA-26237	
☐ 9Q-CJA	Britten-Norman BN-2A-21 Islander	898	ex I-301	
☐ 9Q-CTR	Douglas DC-3	9452	ex ZS-EDX	[FIH]
☐ 9Q-CYC	Douglas DC-3	18977	ex N9984Q	[FIH]
☐ 9Q-CYE	Douglas DC-3	19771	ex 79004	[FIH]

AIR TROPIQUES Kinshasa-Ndolo (NLO)

☐ 9Q-CEJ	Beech 1900C	UB-74	ex ZS-ODR
☐ 9Q-CEM	Beech 100 King Air	B-105	ex ZS-TBS regn also reported as LET L-410UVP
☐ 9Q-CLN	Fokker F.27 Friendship 100	10152	ex ZS-OEH
☐ 9Q-CUZ	Cessna 402B II	402B1358	ex OO-HFC

ALAJNIHAH AIR TRANSPORT

☐ 9Q-CGV	Ilyushin Il-76TD	0033449441	ex UR-76574 Morning Star

ATO - AIR TRANSPORT OFFICE Kinshasa-N'djili (FIH)

☐ 9Q-CTO	Lockheed L-188A Electra	1073	ex 9Q-CRM
☐ 9Q-CVK	Hawker Siddeley HS.780 Andover E.3	Set 17	ex P4-BLL

BRAVO AIR CONGO (BRV)

☐ TN-AHQ	Douglas DC-9-32	48126/951	ex N481SG
☐ 9Q-CDO	Douglas DC-9-32	48125/947	ex N481SF	[FIH]
☐ 9Q-CDT	Douglas DC-9-32	48128/964	ex N128GE
☐ 9Q-CVT	Douglas DC-9-32	48127/961	ex N127GE	[FIH]

BUSINESS AVIATION OF CONGO (4P) Kinshasa-Ndolo (NLO)

☐ 9Q-CBA	Nord 262A-42	57	ex OY-IVA

BUTEMBO Butembo

☐ 9Q-CAX	WZK/PZL Antonov An-28	1AJ002-08	ex EX-28810

CAA – COMPAGNIE AFRICAINE D'AVIATION

☐ 9Q-CSB	Airbus A320-212	0438	ex N190AT ♦

☐ 9Q-CAB	Fokker 50	20276	ex PH-LXP	♦
☐ 9Q-CBD	Fokker 50	20270	ex PH-LXJ	♦
☐ 9Q-CJB	Fokker 50	20196	ex PH-LMS	♦
☐ 9Q-CIB	McDonnell-Douglas MD-82	49394/1285	ex N94EV	

CETRACA AIR SERVICE

☐ 9Q-CAZ	LET L-410UVP	790205	ex UR-67169
☐ 9Q-CKO	Antonov An-26	5210	ex ER-AFW
☐ 9Q-CKT	Antonov An-26B	12001	ex ER-AES
☐ 9Q-CKX	LET L-410UVP	790303	ex ER-LIB

COMAIR

☐ 9Q-CCM	WZK/PZL Antonov An-28	1AJ010-04	ex RA-28957	non-airworthy
☐ 9Q-CKC	WZK/PZL Antonov An-28	1AJ009-18	ex RA-28952	

CO-ZA AIRWAYS — Goma (GOM)

☐ 9Q-CML	Antonov An-26	7408	ex ER-AWN no titles

DOREN AIR CONGO — Goma (GOM)

☐ 9Q-CQZ	LET L-410UVP	851339	ex 9L-LEM
☐ 9Q-CZA	LET L-410UVP	851524	ex OK-PDC

ESPACE AVIATION

☐ 9Q-CTA	Douglas DC-8-54F	45802/247	ex 3D-AFR

ETRAM AIR WING — Kinshasa-N'djili (FIH)

☐ 4K-48136	Antonov An-32B	3103	ex CCCP-48126	
☐ D2-FDZ	Boeing 707-399C (Comtran 2)	19415/601	ex 9Q-FDZ	stored
☐ N56FA	Douglas DC-8-54F	45663/189	ex 3D-ETM	[LAD]

FILAIR — Kinshasa-N'djili (FIH)

☐ 9Q-CDN	LET L-410UVP-E	902422	ex YU-BXX
☐ 9Q-CTR	Antonov An-24RV	77310802	ex 9L-LBQ

GALAXY KAVATSI AVIATION

☐ 9Q-CVE	Antonov An-26	77305301	ex RA-26193 Odessa

HEWA BORA AIRWAYS — Allcongo (EO/ALX) — Kinshasa-N'djili (FIH)

☐ 9Q-CBW	Boeing 707-329C (Comtran 2)	20200/828	ex TL-ADJ	
☐ 9Q-CKK	Boeing 707-366C	20761/867	ex 9Q-CKB Aisha	
☐ 9Q-CKR	Boeing 707-351C	19411/540		
☐ 9Q-CWB	Boeing 707-3B4C	20259/822	ex OD-AFD	
☐ S9-DBM	Boeing 727-22/W (Duganair 3)	18323/136	ex 3D-BOC	VIP
☐ S9-ROI	Boeing 727-30/W (Duganair 3)	18933/185	ex 3D-BOE	VIP
☐ 9Q-CHD	Boeing 727-232 (FedEx 3)	22494/1749	ex N545DA	[FIH]
☐ 9Q-CHE	Boeing 727-232 (FedEx 3)	21310/1298	ex PK-JAE	
☐ 9Q-CHF	Boeing 727-232 (FedEx 3)	22677/1785	ex N546DA	
☐ 9Q-CHG	Boeing 727-232 (FedEx 3)	21586/1488	ex PK-JGX	
☐ 9Q-CHK	Boeing 727-29F/W (Duganair 3)	19401/419	ex N712DH	
☐ 9Q-CRG	Boeing 727-30	18361/28	ex N18477 Ville de Goma	[FIH]
☐ 9Q-CRS	Boeing 727-214	19687/573	ex 5H-ARS	
☐ 9Q-CWA	Boeing 727-227	20775/998	ex N554PE Ville de Bakavu	[FIH]
☐ S9-TOA	McDonnell-Douglas MD-82	49176/11	ex N226AA	
☐ S9-TOB	McDonnell-Douglas MD-82	49178/1122	ex N228AA	
☐ S9-TOP	Boeing 767-266ER	23178/97	ex 9Q-CJD	
☐ 9Q-CKZ	Boeing 737-293	19309/47	ex N464AC	
☐ 9Q-CHL	Douglas DC-8F-55 (QNC 2)	45820/246	ex S9-PSD	
☐ 9Q-CHC	Lockheed L-1011-500 Tristar	193H-1209	ex N767DA	[FIH]

ITAB – INTERNATIONAL TRANS AIR BUSINESS — Lubumbashi-Luano (FBM)

☐ 9Q-CAP	Nord 262A-32	35	ex F-BPNT	
☐ 9Q-CDH	Nord 262C-50P	36	ex XT-OAG	
☐ 9Q-CDP	LET L-410UVP-E	902519	ex 9L-LCL	
☐ 9Q-CJJ	Douglas DC-3	10110	ex ZS-NZA	
☐ (9Q-CON)	BAC One-Eleven 537GF	261	ex 9Q-CDY	
☐ 9Q-CVC	Hawker Siddeley HS.780 Andover C Mk.1	Set 29	ex 3C-KKT	
☐ 9Q-CYA	Britten-Norman BN-2A Islander	617	ex G-AYBB	
☐ 9Q-CYB	Hawker Siddeley HS.780 Andover C Mk.1	Set 22	ex NZ7628	

JETAIR SERVICES — Kinshasa-Ndolo /N'djili (NLO/FIH)

☐ 9Q-CCJ	Partenavia P.68B	163	ex 9Q-CEZ		
☐ 9Q-CCK	Cessna 402B	402B0304	ex TN-ACJ		

LIGNES AERIENNES CONGOLAISES — Congolaise (LCG) — Kinshasa-Ndolo (NLO)

☐ 9Q-CSV Boeing 737-281 20276/231 ex 4X-BAG
Ceased operations in 2005 but believed to have recommenced limited services Aug06. Attempted partnerships with AZW and RKM in 2008 were unsuccessful. Current status unknown.

MALIFT AIR — Malila (MLC) — Kinshasa-N'djili/Khartoum (FIH/KRT)

☐ 9Q-CMD	Antonov An-32B	2210	ex RA-26221	Kevin	[SHJ]
☐ 9Q-CMK	Antonov An-24RV	47309902		Kenzo	
☐ 9Q-CMM	Britten-Norman BN-2A-21 Islander	812	ex 9U-BRV		
☐ 9Q-CMS	Antonov An-26	4206	ex 9U-BNO		non-airworthy

MALU AVIATION — Kinshasa-Ndolo (NLO)

☐ 9Q-CDV	Partenavia P.68B	207		
☐ 9Q-CPM	Nord 262A-32	38	ex F-BPNU	
☐ 9Q-CSP	WSK-PZL/Antonov An-28	1AJ008-09	ex 9Q-CJF	
☐ 9Q-CSD	Short SC.7 Skyvan	SH1831	ex ZS-ORN	
☐ 9Q-	Short SC.7 Skyvan 3	SH1870	ex SE-LDK	id not confirmed

MANGO MAT AIRLINES — Goma (GOM)

☐ S9-PSK	Antonov An-12BK	8345807	ex EX-084	
☐ 9Q-CVM	Antonov An-12B	8345503	ex 9U-BHO	

MIDDLAND — Beni

☐ 9Q-COM WSK-PZL/Antonov An-28 1AJ008-21 ex EX-018

SERVICE AIR

☐ 9Q-	Boeing 727-2S2F	22930/1824	ex N361CW
☐ 9Q-CSV	Boeing 727-2S2F	22924/1818	ex N358PZ

SERVICE COMMUTER — Bukavu (BKY)

☐ 9Q-CFQ WZK/PZL Antonov An-28 1AJ008-05 ex SP-FHW non-airworthy, also a PA-23-250

SOFT TRANS AIR — Kinshasa

☐ 9Q-CYN Antonov An-26 67304001 ex 55 blue non-airworthy

STAG

☐ 9Q-CFB Antonov An-26B 56312909 ex RA-26577

SUCCESS AIRLINES

☐ 9Q-CJI Antonov An-26 6004 ex EL-AHT

SUN AIR SERVICE

☐ 9Q-CMZ PZL/WZK Antonov An-28 1AJ-005-17 ex RA-28784

SWALA AIRLINES — Bukavu (BKY)

☐ 9Q-CXF Short SC.7 Skyvan SH1915 ex (5Y-)

TMK AIR COMMUTER — Goma (GOM)

☐ 9Q-CEL	de Havilland DHC-6 Twin Otter 300	719	ex N719DK	
☐ 9Q-CWP	de Havilland DHC-8-102	105	ex C-FOVR	♦

TOLAZ AVIATION GROUP

☐ 9Q-CGM Antonov An-26B 6401 ex Ukraine AF

TRANSAIR CARGO SERVICE — Kinshasa-N'djili (FIH)

☐ 3X-GEP	Douglas DC-8-62F (BAC 3)	45921/322	ex EC-EMX	
☐ 9Q-CJH	Douglas DC-8-62F (BAC 3)	46023/407	ex 3X-GEN	[JNB]
☐ 9Q-CJL	Douglas DC-8-62F (BAC 3)	45909/307	ex N802BN	
☐ 9Q-CMP	Boeing 727-22C	19892/640	ex 3D-KMJ	
☐ 9Q-CYS	NAMC YS-11A	2051	ex 3D-CYS	

VIRUNGA AIR CHARTER · Goma (GOM)

☐ 9Q-CDD	Dornier 28D-1 Skyservant	4025	ex D-IFAQ
☐ 9Q-CTL	Partenavia P.68B	145	ex 5Y-BCG
☐ 9Q-CTN	Partenavia P.68C-TC	238-04-TC	ex OO-TZT
☐ 9Q-CTX	Dornier 128-6 Turbo Skyservant	6007	ex D-IDOQ

WALTAIR · Kinshasa-N'djili (FIH)

☐ 9Q-CPW	Hawker Siddeley HS.780 Andover C Mk.1	Set14	ex XS607	[FIH]

Believed to be grounded, status uncertain

WIMBI DIRA AIRWAYS · Wimbi Dera (9C/WDA) · Kinshasa-N'djili (FIH)

☐ 9Q-CWD	Boeing 727-231F	19562/576	ex N12305
☐ 9Q-CWE	Douglas DC-9-32 (ABS 3)	47701/822	ex N212ME
☐ 9Q-CWG	Boeing 707-323C	19587/686	ex 3D-ROK
☐ 9Q-CWH	Douglas DC-9-32 (ABS 3)	47744/837	ex N215ME
☐ 9Q-	Douglas DC-9-32	47090/190	ex ZS-NRC
☐ S9-	Douglas DC-9-34CF	47707/823	ex N787CT

9U- BURUNDI (Republic of Burundi)

AIR BURUNDI · Air Burundi (8Y/PBU) · Bujumbura (BJM)

☐ 9U-BHG	Beech 1900C-1	UC-147	ex 9U-BHD

9V- SINGAPORE (Republic of Singapore)

AIRMARK SINGAPORE · Singapore-Seletar (XSP)

Lease aircraft from other operators as required

JETSTAR ASIA AIRWAYS · Jetstar (3K/JSA) · Singapore-Changi (SIN)

☐ 9V-JSA	Airbus A320-232	2316	ex F-WWDR	
☐ 9V-JSB	Airbus A320-232	2356	ex F-WWIQ	
☐ 9V-JSC	Airbus A320-232	2395	ex F-WWIS	
☐ 9V-JSD	Airbus A320-232	2401	ex F-WWIB	
☐ 9V-JSF	Airbus A320-232	2453	ex VH-JQH	
☐ 9V-JSG	Airbus A320-232	2457	ex VH-JQE	
☐ 9V-JSH	Airbus A320-232	2604	ex VH-VQA	
☐ 9V-JSI	Airbus A320-232	4443	ex F-WWIC	♦
☐ 9V-	Airbus A320-232		ex	o/o
☐ 9V-	Airbus A320-232		ex	o/o

JETT 8 AIRLINES CARGO · (JEC) · Singapore-Changi (SIN)

☐ 9V-JEB	Boeing 747-281F	23350/623	ex JA8172	Shogun

SILKAIR · Silkair (MI/SLK) · Singapore-Changi (SIN)

☐ 9V-SBC	Airbus A319-132	1228	ex D-AVYL	
☐ 9V-SBD	Airbus A319-132	1698	ex D-AVYE	
☐ 9V-SBE	Airbus A319-132	2568	ex D-AVXA	
☐ 9V-SBF	Airbus A319-132	3104	ex D-AVYI	
☐ 9V-SBG	Airbus A319-132	4215	ex D-AVYH	♦
☐ 9V-SBH	Airbus A319-132	4259	ex D-AVWO	♦
☐ 9V-SBI	Airbus A319-132		ex D-	o/o
☐ 9V-SBJ	Airbus A319-132		ex D-	o/o
☐ 9V-SLB	Airbus A320-232	0899	ex F-WWDL	
☐ 9V-SLC	Airbus A320-232	0969	ex F-WWBO	
☐ 9V-SLD	Airbus A320-232	1422	ex F-WWBK	
☐ 9V-SLE	Airbus A320-232	1561	ex F-WWBC	
☐ 9V-SLF	Airbus A320-232	2058	ex F-WWBK	
☐ 9V-SLG	Airbus A320-233	2252	ex F-WWBB	
☐ 9V-SLH	Airbus A320-233	2517	ex F-WWIG	
☐ 9V-SLI	Airbus A320-233	2775	ex F-WWDS	
☐ 9V-SLJ	Airbus A320-233	3570	ex F-WWBD	
☐ 9V-SLK	Airbus A320-233	3821	ex F-WWIQ	
☐ 9V-SLL	Airbus A320-232	4118	ex D-AVVU	
☐ 9V-SLM	Airbus A320-232	4457	ex D-AXAA	♦
☐ 9V-	Airbus A320-232		ex	o/o ♦

☐ 9V-	Airbus A320-232		ex	o/o♦
☐ 9V-	Airbus A320-232		ex	o/o♦

SINGAPORE AIRLINES	*Singapore (SQ/SIA)*			**Singapore-Changi (SIN)**

Member of Star Alliance

☐ 9V-STA	Airbus A330-343E	978	ex F-WWKZ	
☐ 9V-STB	Airbus A330-343E	983	ex F-WWYZ	
☐ 9V-STC	Airbus A330-343E	986	ex F-WWKG	
☐ 9V-STD	Airbus A330-343E	997	ex F-WWYM	
☐ 9V-STE	Airbus A330-343E	1006	ex F-WWYB	
☐ 9V-STF	Airbus A330-343E	1010	ex F-WWYF	
☐ 9V-STG	Airbus A330-343E	1012	ex F-WWKA	
☐ 9V-STH	Airbus A330-343E	1015	ex F-WWKV	
☐ 9V-STI	Airbus A330-343E	1085	ex F-WWKA	
☐ 9V-STJ	Airbus A330-343E	1098	ex F-WWKQ	♦
☐ 9V-STK	Airbus A330-343E	1099	ex F-WWYD	♦
☐ 9V-STL	Airbus A330-343E	1105	ex F-WWKR	♦
☐ 9V-STM	Airbus A330-343E	1107	ex F-WWKP	♦
☐ 9V-STN	Airbus A330-343E	1124	ex F-WWYK	♦
☐ 9V-STO	Airbus A330-343E	1132	ex F-WWYL	♦
☐ 9V-STP	Airbus A330-343E	1146	ex F-WWYV	♦
☐ 9V-STQ	Airbus A330-343E	1149	ex F-WWYH	♦
☐ 9V-STR	Airbus A330-343E	1156	ex F-WWKK	♦
☐ 9V-STS	Airbus A330-343E	1157	ex F-WWYX	♦
☐ 9V-SGA	Airbus A340-541	492	ex F-WWTP	
☐ 9V-SGB	Airbus A340-541	499	ex F-WWTR	
☐ 9V-SGC	Airbus A340-541	478	ex F-WWTG	
☐ 9V-SGD	Airbus A340-541	560	ex F-WWTM	
☐ 9V-SGE	Airbus A340-541	563	ex F-WWTU	
☐ 9V-SKA	Airbus A380-841	003	ex F-WWSA	
☐ 9V-SKB	Airbus A380-841	005	ex F-WWSB	
☐ 9V-SKC	Airbus A380-841	006	ex F-WWSC	
☐ 9V-SKD	Airbus A380-841	008	ex F-WWSE	
☐ 9V-SKE	Airbus A380-841	010	ex F-WWSG	
☐ 9V-SKF	Airbus A380-841	012	ex F-WWSI	
☐ 9V-SKG	Airbus A380-841	019	ex F-WWSP	
☐ 9V-SKH	Airbus A380-841	021	ex F-WWSQ	
☐ 9V-SKI	Airbus A380-841	034	ex F-WWSC	
☐ 9V-SKJ	Airbus A380-841	045	ex F-WWSG	
☐ 9V-SKK	Airbus A380-841	051	ex F-WWAH	♦
☐ 9V-SKL	Airbus A380-841	058	ex F-WWSI	o/o ♦
☐ 9V-SKM	Airbus A380-841	065	ex F-WWSM	o/o ♦
☐ 9V-SKN	Airbus A380-841	071	ex F-WWSX	o/o ♦
☐ 9V-SKO	Airbus A380-841	076	ex F-WW	o/o ♦
☐ 9V-SKP	Airbus A380-841	079	ex F-WW	o/o ♦
☐ 9V-SMU	Boeing 747-412	27068/1000		
☐ 9V-SPA	Boeing 747-412	26550/1040		
☐ 9V-SPE	Boeing 747-412	26554/1070		
☐ 9V-SPJ	Boeing 747-412	26556/1084		
☐ 9V-SPM	Boeing 747-412	29950/1241		[VCV]
☐ 9V-SPN	Boeing 747-412	28031/1266		[VCV]
☐ 9V-SPO	Boeing 747-412	28028/1270		
☐ 9V-SPP	Boeing 747-412	28029/1276	Star Alliance c/s	
☐ 9V-SPQ	Boeing 747-412	28025/1289		
☐ 9V-SQA	Boeing 777-212ER	28507/67		
☐ 9V-SQB	Boeing 777-212ER	28508/83		
☐ 9V-SQC	Boeing 777-212ER	28509/86		
☐ 9V-SQD	Boeing 777-212ER	28510/90		
☐ 9V-SQE	Boeing 777-212ER	28511/122		
☐ 9V-SQF	Boeing 777-212ER	28512/126		
☐ 9V-SQG	Boeing 777-212ER	28518/226		
☐ 9V-SQH	Boeing 777-212ER	28519/237		
☐ 9V-SQI	Boeing 777-212ER	28530/390	ex N5023Q	
☐ 9V-SQJ	Boeing 777-212ER	30875/406		
☐ 9V-SQK	Boeing 777-212ER	33368/428		
☐ 9V-SQL	Boeing 777-212ER	33370/451		
☐ 9V-SQM	Boeing 777-212ER	33372/485		
☐ 9V-SQN	Boeing 777-212ER	33373/487		
☐ 9V-SRD	Boeing 777-212ER	28514/153		
☐ 9V-SRF	Boeing 777-212ER	28521/330		
☐ 9V-SRG	Boeing 777-212ER	28522/337		

☐ 9V-SRH	Boeing 777-212ER	30866/343		
☐ 9V-SRI	Boeing 777-212ER	30867/348		
☐ 9V-SRJ	Boeing 777-212ER	28527/372		
☐ 9V-SRK	Boeing 777-212ER	28529/389	ex N5022E	
☐ 9V-SRL	Boeing 777-212ER	32334/409		
☐ 9V-SRM	Boeing 777-212ER	32320/438		
☐ 9V-SRN	Boeing 777-212ER	32318/441		
☐ 9V-SRO	Boeing 777-212ER	32321/447		
☐ 9V-SRP	Boeing 777-212ER	33369/448		
☐ 9V-SRQ	Boeing 777-212ER	33371/449		
☐ 9V-SVE	Boeing 777-212ER	30870/374		
☐ 9V-SVH	Boeing 777-212ER	28532/407	ex N5022E	
☐ 9V-SVI	Boeing 777-212ER	32316/412		
☐ 9V-SVJ	Boeing 777-212ER	32335/415		
☐ 9V-SVK	Boeing 777-212ER	28520/419		
☐ 9V-SVL	Boeing 777-212ER	32336/422		
☐ 9V-SVM	Boeing 777-212ER	30874/430		
☐ 9V-SVN	Boeing 777-212ER	30873/431		
☐ 9V-SVO	Boeing 777-212ER	28533/471		
☐ 9V-SWA	Boeing 777-312ER	34568/586	ex N6018N	
☐ 9V-SWB	Boeing 777-312ER	33377/592		
☐ 9V-SWD	Boeing 777-312ER	34569/600		
☐ 9V-SWE	Boeing 777-312ER	34570/602		
☐ 9V-SWF	Boeing 777-312ER	34571/603		
☐ 9V-SWG	Boeing 777-312ER	34572/604		
☐ 9V-SWH	Boeing 777-312ER	34573/615		
☐ 9V-SWI	Boeing 777-312ER	34574/618		
☐ 9V-SWJ	Boeing 777-312ER	34575/623		
☐ 9V-SWK	Boeing 777-312ER	34576/644	ex N6009F	
☐ 9V-SWL	Boeing 777-312ER	34577/673		
☐ 9V-SWM	Boeing 777-312ER	34578/701		
☐ 9V-SWN	Boeing 777-312ER	34579/703		
☐ 9V-SWO	Boeing 777-312ER	34580/708		
☐ 9V-SWP	Boeing 777-312ER	34581/710		
☐ 9V-SWQ	Boeing 777-312ER	34582/716		
☐ 9V-SWR	Boeing 777-312ER	34583/722		
☐ 9V-SWS	Boeing 777-312ER	34584/729		
☐ 9V-SWT	Boeing 777-312ER	34585/759		
☐ 9V-SYA	Boeing 777-312	28515/180		
☐ 9V-SYB	Boeing 777-312	28516/184		
☐ 9V-SYC	Boeing 777-312	28517/188		
☐ 9V-SYD	Boeing 777-312	28534/192		
☐ 9V-SYE	Boeing 777-312	28531/244	Star Alliance c/s	
☐ 9V-SYF	Boeing 777-312	30868/360		
☐ 9V-SYG	Boeing 777-312	28528/364		
☐ 9V-SYH	Boeing 777-312	32317/420	ex N5020K	
☐ 9V-SYI	Boeing 777-312	32327/484	ex N5028Y	
☐ 9V-SYJ	Boeing 777-312	33374/503	ex N50217	
☐ 9V-SYK	Boeing 777-312	33375/505		
☐ 9V-SYL	Boeing 777-312	33376/515		

SINGAPORE AIRLINES CARGO		*Singapore Cargo (SQ/SQC)*		*Singapore-Changi (SIN)*
☐ 9V-SFC	Boeing 747-412F	26560/1052		>CCA as B-2409
☐ 9V-SFD	Boeing 747-412F	26553/1069		
☐ 9V-SFF	Boeing 747-412F	28026/1105		
☐ 9V-SFG	Boeing 747-412F	26558/1173		
☐ 9V-SFJ	Boeing 747-412F	26559/1285		
☐ 9V-SFK	Boeing 747-412F	28030/1298		
☐ 9V-SFL	Boeing 747-412F	32897/1322	ex N5022E	[VCV]
☐ 9V-SFM	Boeing 747-412F	32898/1333		
☐ 9V-SFN	Boeing 747-412F	32899/1342		
☐ 9V-SFO	Boeing 747-412F	32900/1349		
☐ 9V-SFP	Boeing 747-412F	32902/1364		
☐ 9V-SFQ	Boeing 747-412F	32901/1369		

TIGER AIRWAYS		*(TR/TGW)*		*Singapore-Changi (SIN)*
☐ 9V-TAB	Airbus A320-232	2195	ex F-WWIZ	
☐ 9V-TAC	Airbus A320-232	2331	ex F-WWIF	
☐ 9V-TAD	Airbus A320-232	2340	ex F-WWIY	
☐ 9V-TAE	Airbus A320-232	2724	ex F-WWDO	
☐ 9V-TAF	Airbus A320-232	2728	ex F-WWDU	
☐ 9V-TAM	Airbus A320-232	4181	ex F-WWIA	

☐ 9V-TAN	Airbus A320-232	4210	ex F-WWBR		◆
☐ 9V-TAO	Airbus A320-232	4421	ex F-WWDZ		◆
☐ 9V-TAP	Airbus A320-232	4445	ex F-WWIH		◆
☐ 9V-TAQ	Airbus A320-232	4469	ex F-WWBV		◆
☐ 9V-TAR	Airbus A320-232	4491	ex F-WWIB		◆
☐ 9V-TAS	Airbus A320-232	4493	ex F-WWID		◆
☐ 9V-TAT	Airbus A320-232	4532	ex F-WWDR		◆
☐ 9V-TAU	Airbus A320-232	4561	ex F-WWBB		◆
☐ 9V-	Airbus A320-232		ex		o/o◆
☐ 9V-	Airbus A320-232		ex		o/o◆
☐ 9V-	Airbus A320-232		ex		o/o◆
☐ 9V-	Airbus A320-232		ex		o/o◆
☐ 9V-	Airbus A320-232		ex		o/o◆
☐ 9V-	Airbus A320-232		ex		o/o◆
☐ 9V-TRA	Airbus A319-132	3757	ex D-AVXC		
☐ 9V-TRB	Airbus A319-132	3801	ex D-AVYA		

VALUAIR	**Value (VF/VLU)**	**Singapore-Changi (SIN)**

☐ 9V-VLE	Airbus A320-232	2156	ex 9V-VLA		◆
☐ 9V-VLF	Airbus A320-232	2164	ex 9V-VLB		◆

9XR- RWANDA (Rwanda Republic)

CONGO FRET ESPOIR

☐ 9XR-EF	LET L-410UVP

RWANDAIR EXPRESS	**Rwandair (WB/RWD)**	**Kigali (KGL)**

☐ 9XR-WA	Canadair CRJ-200LR	7439	ex D-ACHG		
☐ 9XR-WB	Canadair CRJ-200LR	7449	ex D-ACHH		
☐ 9XR-WD	Boeing 737-55D	27416/2389	ex SP-LKA		◆
☐ 9XR-WE	Boeing 737-55D	27417/2392	ex SP-LKB		◆
☐ ET-ALX	de Havilland DHC-8-202	475	ex ZK-ECR		<TNW
☐ 7Q-YKW	Boeing 737-522	25384/2149	ex N917UA	Sapitwa	<AML

SILVERBACK CARGO FRTRS	**Silverback (VRB)**	**Kigali (KGL)**

☐ 9XR-SC	Douglas DC-8-62F	46068/463	ex N990CF
☐ 9XR-SD	Douglas DC-8-62F	45956/376	ex N994CF

9Y- TRINIDAD & TOBAGO (Republic of Trinidad & Tobago)

BRIKO AIR SERVICES

☐ 9Y-BKO	British Aerospace Jetstream 31	932	ex N338TE
☐ 9Y-DAS	Aérospatiale AS355F2 Twin Star	5402	ex N227NR
☐ 9Y-JET	British Aerospace Jetstream 31	939	ex N340TE
☐ 9Y-TIY	Cessna 402C	402C0265	ex N3146M

BRISTOW CARIBBEAN				**Port of Spain (POS)**

☐ 9Y-BCO	Bell 412EP	36401	ex N8087N	
☐ 9Y-BHI	Bell 412	33032	ex N418EH	
☐ 9Y-BOB	Bell 412SP	36256	ex N368AL	
☐ 9Y-BRS	Bell 412EP	36396	ex N10269	
☐ 9Y-EVS	Bell 412SP	33212	ex XA-SBJ	<OLOG
☐ 9Y-ONE	Bell 412EP	36421	ex N387AL	
☐ 9Y-REP	Bell 412	33065	ex XA-TUW	
☐ 9Y-SKY	Bell 412EP	36420	ex N8010C	
☐ 9Y-TJM	Bell 412SP	33169	ex PT-HUO	
☐ 9Y-TNT	Bell 412EP	36414	ex N386AL	
☐ 9Y-TSP	Bell 412SP	33169	ex XA-TAM	

CARIBBEAN AIRLINES	**West Indian (BW/BWA)**		**Port of Spain (POS)**

☐ 9Y-ANU	Boeing 737-8Q8/W	28235/697	(ex 9Y-SLU)	
☐ 9Y-BGI	Boeing 737-8Q8/W	28232/547		
☐ 9Y-GEO	Boeing 737-8Q8/W	28225/433	ex PH-HSX	
☐ 9Y-JMA	Boeing 737-8Q8/W	30645/1129	ex 7O-ADL	◆
☐ 9Y-KIN	Boeing 737-8Q8/W	28234/680	(ex 9Y-ANU)	
☐ 9Y-PBM	Boeing 737-8BK/W	29635/2326	ex N810SY	
☐ 9Y-POS	Boeing 737-8Q8/W	28230/506		
☐ 9Y-SLU	Boeing 737-83N/W	28246/1081	ex N317TZ	

☐ 9Y-TAB	Boeing 737-8Q8/W	28233/598	

☐ 9Y-WIL	de Havilland DHC-8Q-311	489	ex C-GFCW
☐ 9Y-WIN	de Havilland DHC-8Q-311	499	ex C-GDSG
☐ 9Y-WIP	de Havilland DHC-8Q-311	538	ex C-FDII
☐ 9Y-WIT	de Havilland DHC-8Q-311	487	ex OE-LSA
☐ 9Y-WIZ	de Havilland DHC-8Q-311	557	ex C-GEMU

EVERGREEN HELICOPTERS INTERNATIONAL (TRINIDAD)

☐ 9Y-DMS	Bell 212	31205	ex N827MS
☐ 9Y-DPB	Bell 212	30886	ex N16974

NATIONAL HELICOPTER SERVICES   *Camden Heliport*

☐ 9Y-THP	MBB Bo.105CBS-4	S-758	ex N725MB
☐ 9Y-TIC	MBB Bo.105CBS-4	S-837	ex N7161N
☐ 9Y-TIW	MBB Bo.105CBS-4	S-671	ex N4573S
☐ 9Y-TJF	MBB Bo.105CBS-4	S-732	ex F-OHQZ
☐ 9Y-MCK	Sikorsky S-76C++	760745	ex N745G
☐ 9Y-NHS	Sikorsky S-76A++	760265	ex N82ES
☐ 9Y-TGW	Sikorsky S-76A	760176	
☐ 9Y-TGX	Sikorsky S-76A	760185	
☐ 9Y-TJJ	Sikorsky S-76A++	760164	ex F-GMIE
☐ 9Y-TJW	Sikorsky S-76A++	760926	ex C-GZIL

JET AND TURBOPROP AIRLINERS IN NON-AIRLINE SERVICE

	Registration	Type	Serial	Operator
☐	5A-IAY	Airbus A300-620	354	Afriqiyah Airways
☐	9K-AHI	Airbus A300-620C	344	Government of Kuwait
☐	F-BUAD	Airbus A300B-B1-100	003	Centre d'Essais en Vol - CEV
☐	YI-APX	Airbus A300B-B4-200	239	Republic of Iraq
☐	A7-AFE	Airbus A310-308	667	Qatar Amiri Flight
☐	EC-HLA	Airbus A310-324ET	489	EADS Military Transport Aircraft Division
☐	HS-TYQ	Airbus A310-324	591	Royal Thai Air Force (Also 60202)
☐	HZ-NSA	Airbus A310-304	431	Al-Atheer Establishment
☐	9K-ALD	Airbus A310-308	648	Government of Kuwait
☐	10+21	Airbus A310-304	498	German Air Force
☐	10+22	Airbus A310-304	499	German Air Force
☐	J-757	Airbus A310-304	473	Pakistan Air Force
☐	T.22-1	Airbus A310-304	550	Spanish Air Force
☐	A6-AAM	Airbus A318 Elite	1599	Dana Executive Jets
☐	A6-AJC	Airbus A318 Elite	3985	AJA - Al Jaber Aviation
☐	B-6186	Airbus A318 Elite	3333	Asia United Business Aviation
☐	B-6188	Airbus A318 Elite	3617	Air China Business Jet
☐	B-6411	Airbus A318 Elite	3886	BAA Jet Management Ltd
☐	LX-GJC	Airbus A318 Elite	3100	Silver Arrows
☐	VP-CKH	Airbus A318 Elite	3530	National Air Services (NAS)
☐	VP-CKS	Airbus A318 Elite	3238	National Air Services (NAS)
☐	VQ-BDD	Airbus A318 Elite	3751	Royal Flight of Jordan
☐	9H-AFL	Airbus A318 Elite	3363	Comlux Aviation Malta
☐	9H-AFM	Airbus A318 Elite	2910	Comlux Aviation Malta
☐	9H-AFT	Airbus A318 Elite	4169	Comlux Aviation Malta
☐	A6-ESH	Airbus A319CJ	0910	Sharjah Ruler's Flight
☐	A7-HHJ	Airbus A319CJ	1335	Qatar Amiri Flight
☐	B-6178	Airbus A319-132	3548	Capital Airlines
☐	CS-TFU	Airbus A319CJ	2440	White
☐	CS-TLU	Airbus A319CJ	1256	White
☐	D-ADNA	Airbus A319CJ	1053	DC Aviation
☐	D-AHAD	Airbus A319CJ	3632	DC Aviation
☐	D-ALEY	Airbus A319CJ	3513	DC Aviation
☐	EK-RA01	Airbus A319-132	0913	Government of Armenia
☐	G-NMAK	Airbus A319CJ	2550	Twinjet Aircraft
☐	G-NOAH	Airbus A319CJ	3826	Acropolis Aviation Ltd
☐	HS-TYR	Airbus A319CJ	1908	Royal Thai Air Force (Also 60221)
☐	HZ-A4	Airbus A319-112	1494	Alpha Star Aviation Services
☐	LZ-AOB	Airbus A319-112	3188	Aviodetachment 28
☐	N3618F	Airbus A319CJ	2748	Frost Administrative Service
☐	OE-LGS	Airbus A319CJ	3046	Triple Alpha
☐	P4-ARL	Airbus A319CJ	2192	System Capital Management
☐	P4-MIS	Airbus A319CJ	3133	Silver Arrows
☐	P4-VNL	Airbus A319CJ	2921	Silver Arrows
☐	TC-ANA	Airbus A319CJ	1002	Government of Turkey
☐	UR-ABA	Airbus A319CJ	3260	Ukraine Air Enterprise
☐	VH-VHD	Airbus A319CJ	1999	Government of Australia
☐	VP-BED	Airbus A319CJ	3073	Planair
☐	VP-BEX	Airbus A319CJ	2706	Planair
☐	VP-BEY	Airbus A319CJ	2675	Planair
☐	VP-CAN	AirbusA319-112	1886	National Air Services (NAS)
☐	VP-CCJ	Airbus A319CJ	2421	Aravco Ltd
☐	VP-CIE	Airbus A319CJ	1589	Mid East Jet
☐	VP-CVX	Airbus A319CJ	1212	VW Air Services
☐	VT-IAH	Airbus A319CJ	2837	Reliance Commercial Dealers Ltd
☐	VT-VJM	Airbus A319CJ	2650	Kingfisher Airlines
☐	4K-AZ01	Airbus A319CJ	2487	Government of Azerbaijan
☐	9H-AFK	Airbus A319CJ	2592	Comlux Aviation Malta
☐	9H-SNA	Airbus A319CJ	3356	Comlux Aviation Malta
☐	9K-GEA	Airbus A319CJ	3957	Government of Kuwait
☐	9M-NAA	Airbus A319CJ	2949	Malaysian Government
☐	0001	Airbus A319CJ	1468	Venezuelan Air Force
☐	2101	Airbus A319CJ	2263	Brazilian Air Force
☐	2801	Airbus A319CJ	2801	Czech Air Force
☐	3085	Airbus A319CJ	3085	Czech Air Force
☐	15+01	Airbus A319CJ	3897	German Air Force
☐	15+02	Airbus A319CJ	4060	German Air Force
☐	MM62174	Airbus A319CJ	1157	Italian Air Force
☐	MM62209	Airbus A319CJ	1795	Italian Air Force
☐	MM62243	Airbus A319CJ	2507	Italian Air Force

☐ A4O-AA	Airbus A320-232	2566	Oman Royal Flight
☐ A6-DLM	Airbus A320-232	2403	Presidential Flight
☐ A6-HMS	Airbus A320-232	3379	Fujairah Amiri Flight
☐ A7-AAG	Airbus A320-232	0927	Qatar Amiri Flight
☐ A7-MBK	Airbus A320-232CJ	4170	Qatar Airways
☐ D-ATRA	Airbus A320-232	0659	DLR Flugbetriebe
☐ F-WWBA	Airbus A320-111	0001	Airbus
☐ HZ-A2	Airbus A320-214X	3164	Alpha Star Aviation Services
☐ HZ-AJ3	Airbus A320-214	0764	Alpha Star Aviation Services
☐ HZ-XY7	Airbus A320-214	2165	National Air Services (NAS)
☐ UP-A2001	Airbus A320-214CJ	3199	Government of Kazakhstan
☐ VP-CSS	Airbus A320-232CJ	3402	SAAD Air Ltd
☐ 9K-AKD	Airbus A320-212	2046	Government of Kuwait
☐ 554	Airbus A320-214CJ	3723	Royal Air Force of Oman
☐ 555	Airbus A320-214CJ	4117	Royal Air Force of Oman
☐ EP-AGB	Airbus A321-231	1202	Government of Iran
☐ A7-HHM	Airbus A330-203	605	Qatar Amiri Flight
☐ A7-HJJ	Airbus A330-202	487	Qatar Amiri Flight
☐ EC-330	Airbus A330-203MRTT	747	EADS Military Transport Aircraft Division
☐ F-RARF	Airbus A330-223	240	French Air Force
☐ F-WWKB	Airbus A330-203	925	Airbus
☐ UP-A3001	Airbus A330-223	863	Government of Kazakhstan
☐ A7-AAH	Airbus A340-313X	528	Qatar Amiri Flight
☐ A7-HHH	Airbus A340-541	495	Qatar Amiri Flight
☐ A7-HHK	Airbus A340-211	026	Qatar Amiri Flight
☐ F-RAJA	Airbus A340-212	075	French Air Force
☐ F-WWAI	Airbus A340-311	001	Airbus
☐ F-WWCA	Airbus A340-642	360	Airbus
☐ HZ-HMS2	Airbus A340-213X	204	Saudi Ministry of Defense and Aviation
☐ SU-GGG	Airbus A340-212	061	Government of Egypt
☐ V8-BKH	Airbus A340-212	046	Government of Brunei
☐ 5A-ONE	Airbus A340-213	151	Government of Libya
☐ 7T-VPP	Airbus A340-541	917	Government of Algeria
☐ 98+47	Airbus A340-313X	274	German Air Force
☐ F-WWDD	Airbus A380-861	004	Airbus
☐ F-WWOW	Airbus A380-841	001	Airbus
☐ UR-30044	Antonov An-30A-100	0906	Kiev City Administration
☐ 3C-CMN	Antonov An-72	36572092858	Government of Equatorial Guinea
☐ 5A-CAA	Antonov An-74TK-300	3654701211080	Libyan DCA
☐ RA-74048	Antonov An-74-200	36547098943	Sverdlovsk 2nd Aviation Enterprise
☐ RDPL-34018	Antonov An-74TK-100	365470991005	Government of Laos
☐ RDPL-34020	Antonov An-74TK-300	36547098982	Government of Laos
☐ UR-YVA	Antonov An-74TK-300	36547098984	Ukraine Air Enterprise
☐ UR-NTN	Antonov An-158	0102	Antonov
☐ 4K-AZ808	ATR 42-500	673	Silk Way Airlines
☐ F-OITQ	ATR 42-500	622	Government of Tahiti
☐ F-WWLY	ATR 42-600	811	ATR
☐ TR-KJD	ATR 42-200	131	Gabon Air Force
☐ F-WWEY	ATR 72-600	098	ATR
☐ HS-GCA	ATR 72-500	872	Royal Thai Air Force (Also 60313)
☐ HS-GCB	ATR 72-500	881	Royal Thai Air Force (Also 60314)
☐ HS-GCC	ATR 72-500	887	Royal Thai Air Force (Also 60315)
☐ HS-GCD	ATR 72-500	893	Royal Thai Air Force (Also 60316)
☐ XY-AIF	ATR 72-500	765	Government of Myanmar
☐ A6-AAB	Avro RJ100	E3387	Presidential Flight
☐ A6-LIW	Avro RJ70	E1267	Presidential Flight
☐ A6-RJ1	Avro RJ85	E2323	Dubai Air Wing
☐ A6-RJ2	Avro RJ85	E2325	Dubai Air Wing
☐ A9C-AWL	Avro RJ100	E3386	Royal Bahrain Air Force
☐ A9C-BDF	Avro RJ85	E2390	Royal Bahrain Air Force
☐ A9C-HWR	Avro RJ85	E2306	Royal Bahrain Air Force
☐ CP-2634	BAE 146-200	E2096	Minera San Christobal
☐ G-OFOA	BAE 146-100	E1006	Formula 1
☐ G-OFOM	BAE 146-100	E1144	Formula 1
☐ G-RAJJ	BAE 146-200	E2108	Cello Aviation Ltd
☐ LZ-TIM	Avro RJ70	E1258	Bulgaria Air
☐ N114M	BAE 146-100	E1068	Moncrief Oil Co

☐ PK-OSP	BAE 146-100	E1124	Airfast Indonesia
☐ PK-PJJ	Avro RJ85	E2239	Pelita Air Service
☐ UK-80001	Avro RJ85	E2312	Uzbekistan Airways
☐ YR-ANJ	BAE 146-200	E2079	Alfa Air Services
☐ ZE700	BAE 146-100	E1021	Royal Air Force
☐ ZE701	BAE 146-100	E1029	Royal Air Force
☐ N161NG	BAC One-Eleven 401AK	067	Northrop Grumman Systems Corp
☐ N162W	BAC One-Eleven 401AK	087	Northrop Grumman Systems Corp
☐ N164W	BAC One-Eleven 401AK	090	Northrop Grumman Systems Corp
☐ N999BW	BAC One-Eleven 419EP	120	Jet Place Inc
☐ TZ-BSA	BAC One-Eleven 492GM	260	Government of Mali
☐ TZ-BSB	BAC One-Eleven 401AK	086	Government of Mali
☐ TZ-BSC	BAC One-Eleven 488GH	259	Government of Mali
☐ UP-BA111	BAC One-Eleven 401AK	078	East Wing
☐ ZH763	BAC One-Eleven 539GL	263	QinetiQ
☐ 9Q-CLL	BAE HS748-Srs 2A	1561	ITAB - International Trans Air Business
☐ 9Q-CYB	BAE Andover C.1	SET 22	Air Katanga
☐ XS646	BAE Andover C.1	SET 30	QinetiQ
☐ G-BWWW	BAe Jetstream 31	614	BAE Systems (Operations) Ltd
☐ G-NFLA	BAe Jetstream 31	637	Cranfield Institute of Technology
☐ HS-DCA	BAe Jetstream 31Super	960	Thai Department of Aviation
☐ N10UP	BAe Jetstream 31	635	Corporate Flight Management
☐ N170PC	BAe Jetstream 31	717	Aerolineas Mas
☐ N646VN	BAe Jetstream 31	646	Air East
☐ N651VN	BAe Jetstream 31	651	Air East
☐ N723CA	BAe Jetstream 31	723	Con Air Charter LLC
☐ N752VN	BAe Jetstream 31	752	Jose Gonzalez Cobian Rodriguez
☐ N831JS	BAe Jetstream 31	716	Small Community Airlines Inc
☐ N865CY	BAe Jetstream 31Super	865	Corporate Flight Management
☐ N888CY	BAe Jetstream 31Super EP	888	Vertical De Aviacion
☐ N903EH	BAe Jetstream 31	605	Sky High Aircraft LLC
☐ N904EH	BAe Jetstream 31	613	Emergency Airlift
☐ XA-UFT	BAe Jetstream 31Super	862	Alternative Air SA de CV
☐ YV	BAe Jetstream 31	668	668 MP Aviation Inc
☐ YV263T	BAe Jetstream 31	645	SASCA
☐ 5A-DGR	BAe Jetstream 31Super	945	Air Kufra
☐ N307UE	BAe Jetstream 41	41021	Sky Limo
☐ N410TJ	BAe Jetstream 41	41038	FABCO Equipment Inc
☐ N680AS	BAe Jetstream 41	41030	Northstar Aviation LLC
☐ ZS-JSM	BAe Jetstream 41	41052	MCC Aviation (Pty) Ltd
☐ ZS-NOM	BAe Jetstream 41	41047	MCC Aviation (Pty) Ltd
☐ RA-21511	Beriev Be-200	7682000002	Beriev TANTK
☐ D2-MAN	Boeing 707-321B	20025	Government of Angola
☐ D2-TPR	Boeing 707-3J6B	20715	Government of Angola
☐ EP-AJD/1002	Boeing 707-3J9C	20832	Iranian Air Force
☐ EP-AJE/1001	Boeing 707-3086C	21396	Iranian Air Force
☐ N707JT	Boeing 707-1038B	18740	John Travolta
☐ N88ZL	Boeing 707-330B	18928	Lowa Ltd
☐ TZ-TAC	Boeing 707-3L6B	21049	Government of Mali
☐ A9C-BA	Boeing 727-2m7RE/W	21824	Bahrain Royal Flight
☐ C5-GAE	Boeing 727-051	19124	Royal Air (Gambia)
☐ FAE-620	Boeing 727-230	21620	Ecuadorian Air Force
☐ FAE-691	Boeing 727-134	19691	Ecuadorian Air Force
☐ HZ-AB3	Boeing 727-2U5RE	22362	Al Anwa Establishment
☐ HZ-SKI	Boeing 727-212RE	21460	Precision International
☐ J2-KBA	Boeing 727-191	19394	Government of Djibouti
☐ M-ETIS	Boeing 727-2X8	22687	Celestial Airways Limited
☐ M-FAHD	Boeing 727-076RE	19254	Flightec International
☐ N25AZ	Boeing 727-030	18370	Inter Air South Africa
☐ N30MP	Boeing 727-021	18998	MP Global Charter LLC
☐ N169KT	Boeing 727-269	22359	Strong Aviation
☐ N289MT	Boeing 727-223	22467	Raytheon Corp
☐ N311AG	Boeing 727-017RE	20512	Gordon P & Ann G Getty
☐ N502MG	Boeing 727-191	19391	RD Aviation LLC
☐ N606DH	Boeing 727-030	18365	Clementine Aviation Services Inc
☐ N615PA	Boeing 727-243	21266	Paradigm Air Operators
☐ N698SS	Boeing 727-223	21369	Paradigm Air Operators
☐ N724CL	Boeing 727-051	19121	Clay Lacy Aviation
☐ N724YS	Boeing 727-281	21474	Fry's Electronics Inc
☐ N727AH	Boeing 727-021	19261	Paxson Communication Management Co

☐ N727NK	Boeing 727-212	21945	FBA Airplane Inc
☐ N727VJ	Boeing 727-044	19318	United Breweries
☐ N794AJ	Boeing 727-227F	21243	Zero Gravity Corp
☐ N800AK	Boeing 727-023	20045	Arabasco
☐ N908JE	Boeing 727-031RE	20115	JEGE Inc
☐ P4-FLY	Boeing 727-022	19148	Aviation Connections
☐ TZ-MBA	Boeing 727-2K5	21853	Government of Mali
☐ VP-BAJ	Boeing 727-030RE	18936	Spectrum Aerospace
☐ VP-BAP	Boeing 727-021	19260	Malibu Consulting Ltd
☐ VP-BDJ	Boeing 727-023	20046	Trump Air
☐ VP-BIF	Boeing 727-1H2RE	20533	New Century Aviation - Oregon LLC
☐ VP-BPZ	Boeing 727-017RE	20327	Enterprise Aviation Bermuda Limited
☐ VP-CJN	Boeing 727-076	20371	Starling Aviation
☐ VP-CML	Boeing 727-2Y4	22968	Government of Afghanistan
☐ VP-CZY	Boeing 727-2P1	21595	Jet Aviation Business Jets
☐ XC-FAD/3501	Boeing 727-014	18912	Mexican Air Force
☐ XT-BFA	Boeing 727-282RE	22430	Government of Burkina Faso
☐ ZS-PVX	Boeing 727-2N6RE	22825	Fortune Air
☐ 4K-8888	Boeing 727-251	22543	SW Business Aviation
☐ 6V-AEF	Boeing 727-2M1RE	21091	Government of Senegal
☐ 7O-ADA	Boeing 727-2N8	21842	Yemenia
☐ 9Q-CBF	Boeing 727-089	19139	Co-Za Airways
☐ 9Q-COP	Boeing 727-030	18933	Hewa Bora Airways
☐ 3505	Boeing 727-264	22661	Mexican Air Force
☐ 3506	Boeing 727-264	22662	Mexican Air Force
☐ 3507	Boeing 727-264	22412	Mexican Air Force
☐ A9C-DAA	Boeing 737-268	22050	Delmun Aviation Services
☐ EP-AGA	Boeing 737-286	21317	Government of Iran
☐ FAP-350	Boeing 737-244	19707	Peruvian Air Force
☐ FAP-352	Boeing 737-244	23042	Peruvian Air Force
☐ HZ-MIS	Boeing 737-2K5	22600	Sheikh M Edress
☐ K2412	Boeing 737-2A8	23036	Indian Air Force
☐ K2413	Boeing 737-2A8	23037	Indian Air Force
☐ K3186	Boeing 737-2A8	20484	Indian Air Force
☐ K-3187	Boeing 737-2A8	20483	Indian Air Force
☐ N165W	Boeing 737-2 200	19605	Northrop Grumman Systems Corp
☐ N370BC	Boeing 737-247	23468	Basic Capital Management Inc
☐ N413JG	Boeing 737-28Q	23148	Westair Aviation
☐ N500VP	Boeing 737-2H4	22062	Sky King
☐ N733PA	Boeing 737-205	23466	Atlantic Richfield Co
☐ N733TW	Boeing 737-2H4	22732	Ameristar Charters
☐ N736BP	Boeing 737-205	23465	Atlantic BP Exploration (Alaska) Inc
☐ N73HK	Boeing 737-2S9	21957	Executive Jet Aviation (Cayman Islands)
☐ N787WH	Boeing 737-2V6	22431	Blair Investors Corp
☐ N902WG	Boeing 737-2H6	22620	Gary 737 LLC
☐ VP-CBA	Boeing 737-2W8	22628	Casbah AG
☐ ZS-IJA	Boeing 737-201	22751	Inter Air South Africa
☐ 5U-BAG	Boeing 737-2N9C	21499	Government of Niger
☐ 0207	Boeing 737-2N1	21167	Venezuelan Air Force
☐ 2115	Boeing 737-2N3	21165	Brazilian Air Force
☐ 2116	Boeing 737-2N3	21166	Brazilian Air Force
☐ 3520	Boeing 737-2B7	23133	Mexican Air Force
☐ C-FPHS	Boeing 737-53A	24970	Global Aerospace Logistics LLC
☐ FAP356	Boeing 737-528	27426	Peruvian Air Force (Also OB-1860)
☐ HS-CMV	Boeing 737-4Z6	27906	Royal Thai Air Force (also 11-111)
☐ N35LX	Boeing 737-330	23528	Lockheed Martin Corp
☐ N37NY	Boeing 737-4YO	23976	Starwood Flight Operations Inc
☐ N444HE	Boeing 737-39A/W	23800	Mirage Aviation Ltd
☐ N731VA	Boeing 737-33A	27456	Premier Aircraft Management Inc
☐ SX-MTF	Boeing 737-3Z9	23774	GainJet Aviation S.A.
☐ XC-LJG	Boeing 737-322	24361	Mexican Air Force (Also TP-03)
☐ XC-UJB	Boeing 737-33A	24095	Mexican Air Force (Also TP-02)
☐ 5R-MRM	Boeing 737-3Z9	24081	Government of Madagascar
☐ 921	Boeing 737-58N	28866	Chilean Air Force
☐ 85101	Boeing 737-3Z8	23152	Republic of Korea Air Force
☐ A36-001	Boeing 737 BBJ1	30829	Royal Australian Air Force
☐ A36-002	Boeing 737 BBJ1	30790	Royal Australian Air Force
☐ A6-AIN	Boeing 737 BBJ1	29268	Royal Jet
☐ A6-AUH	Boeing 737 BBJ2	33473	Presidential Flight
☐ A6-DAS	Boeing 737 BBJ1	29858	Royal Jet
☐ A6-DFR	Boeing 737 BBJ1	30884	Royal Jet
☐ A6-HEH	Boeing 737 BBJ2	32825	Dubai Air Wing
☐ A6-HRS	Boeing 737 BBJ1	29251	Dubai Air Wing
☐ A6-MRM	Boeing 737 BBJ2	32450	Dubai Air Wing

	Registration	Type	Serial	Operator
☐	A6-MRS	Boeing 737 BBJ2	35238	Dubai Air Wing
☐	A6-RJX	Boeing 737 BBJ1	29865	Royal Jet
☐	A6-RJY	Boeing 737 BBJ1	29857	Royal Jet
☐	A6-RJZ	Boeing 737 BBJ1	29269	Royal Jet
☐	B-5266	Boeing 737 BBJ1	29866	Deer Jet
☐	B-LEX	Boeing 737 BBJ1	34683	Silverblatt Ltd
☐	CN-MVI	Boeing 737 BBJ2	37545	Government of Morocco
☐	EW-001PA	Boeing 737 BBJ2	33079	Government of Belarus
☐	EZ-A006	Boeing 737-7GL/W	37236	Government of Turkmenistan
☐	EZ-A007	Boeing 737-7GR/W	37234	Government of Turkmenistan
☐	FAC0001	Boeing 737 BBJ1	29272	Colombian Air Force
☐	HB-JJA	Boeing 737 BBJ1	34303	PrivatAir
☐	HL7227	Boeing 737 BBJ1	35977	Hanwha Chemical Corp
☐	HL7759	Boeing 737 BBJ1	35990	Samsung Techwin Aviation
☐	HL7787	Boeing 737 BBJ1	36852	Hyundai
☐	HL8222	Boeing 737 BBJ1	37660	Korean Air
☐	HS-TYS	Boeing 737-8Z6/W	35478	Royal Thai Air Force (Also 55-555)
☐	HZ-101	Boeing 737 BBJ1	32805	Royal Saudi Arabian Air Force
☐	HZ-102	Boeing 737 BBJ2	32451	Royal Saudi Arabian Air Force
☐	HZ-MF1	Boeing 737 BBJ1	33405	Saudi Ministry of Finance & Economy
☐	HZ-MF2	Boeing 737 BBJ1	33499	Saudi Ministry of Finance & Economy
☐	HZ-TAA	Boeing 737 BBJ1	29188	Prince Talal Bin Abdul Aziz Al Saud
☐	K-5012	Boeing 737 BBJ1	36106	Indian Air Force
☐	K-5013	Boeing 737 BBJ1	36107	Indian Air Force
☐	K-5014	Boeing 737 BBJ1	36108	Indian Air Force
☐	M53-01	Boeing 737 BBJ1	29274	Royal Malaysian Air Force
☐	M-URUS	Boeing 737 BBJ1	34622	Silver Arrows
☐	M-YBBJ	Boeing 737 BBJ1	36027	Silver Arrows
☐	N2TS	Boeing 737 BBJ1	29102	First Virtual Aviation LLC
☐	N43PR	Boeing 737 BBJ1	28581	The Town & Country Food Markets Inc
☐	N50TC	Boeing 737 BBJ1	29024	Tracinda Corp
☐	N90R	Boeing 737 BBJ1	32775	Occidental Petroleum Corp
☐	N92SR	Boeing 737 BBJ1	37111	Essar Shipping & Logistics Ltd
☐	N108MS	Boeing 737 BBJ1	33102	YONA Aviation II LLC
☐	N111VM	Boeing 737 BBJ1	36090	MWWMMWM Ltd (BVI)
☐	N162WC	Boeing 737 BBJ1	30329	WCA Holdings III LLC
☐	N164RJ	Boeing 737 BBJ1	30328	Akira Investments Ltd
☐	N315TS	Boeing 737 BBJ1	30772	Tudor-Saliba Corp
☐	N371BC	Boeing 737 BBJ2	32971	Mid East Jet
☐	N500LS	Boeing 737 BBJ1	29054	Limited Stores
☐	N720MM	Boeing 737 BBJ1	33010	MGM Mirage
☐	N737AG	Boeing 737 BBJ1	30496	Funair Corp
☐	N737CC	Boeing 737 BBJ1	29135	Mid East Jet
☐	N737ER	Boeing 737 BBJ1	30754	Boetti Air Inc
☐	N737L	Boeing 737 BBJ1	30751	Legatum Aviation Ltd
☐	N737M	Boeing 737 BBJ2	33361	EIE Eagle Inc Establishment
☐	N737WH	Boeing 737 BBJ1	29142	Victory Aviation
☐	N742PB	Boeing 737 BBJ1	29200	Chartwell Partners
☐	N796BA	Boeing 737 BBJ1	30327	Boeing
☐	N800KS	Boeing 737 BBJ1	30782	Clay Lacy Aviation
☐	N835BA	Boeing 737 BBJ1	30572	ShareJet
☐	N836BA	Boeing 737 BBJ1	30756	Boeing
☐	N888TY	Boeing 737 BBJ1	29749	TY Corp
☐	N888YF	Boeing 737 BBJ1	33036	Evergreen International SA
☐	N889NC	Boeing 737 BBJ1	30070	News America Inc
☐	N88WR	Boeing 737 BBJ1	29441	Las Vegas Jet LLC
☐	N920DS	Boeing 737 BBJ1	28579	Delaware Global Operations LLC
☐	N7600K	Boeing 737 BBJ1	32628	SAS Institute Inc
☐	N8767	Boeing 737 BBJ1	32807	Avjet Corp
☐	N79711	Boeing 737 BBJ1	30547	Dallah Avco
☐	OE-ILX	Boeing 737 BBJ2	32777	Global Jet Austria GmbH
☐	P4-AFK	Boeing 737 BBJ1	36493	PremierAvia
☐	P4-ASL	Boeing 737 BBJ1	29791	Arabasco
☐	P4-KAZ	Boeing 737 BBJ1	32774	Prime Aviation JSC
☐	P4-LIG	Boeing 737 BBJ1	37592	Petroff Air Ltd
☐	P4-NGK	Boeing 737 BBJ1	37583	Itera Holdings
☐	PR-BBS	Boeing 737 BBJ1	32575	Banco Safra
☐	TS-IOO	Boeing 737 BBJ1	29149	Government of Tunisia
☐	TT-ABD	Boeing 737 BBJ1	29136	Government of Chad
☐	VP-BBJ	Boeing 737 BBJ1	29273	Picton II Ltd
☐	VP-BBW	Boeing 737 BBJ1	30076	GAMA Aviation
☐	VP-BEL	Boeing 737 BBJ1	29139	Orient Global
☐	VP-BFT	Boeing 737 BBJ1	36714	Jet Aviation Business Jets
☐	VP-BHN	Boeing 737 BBJ2	32438	Saudi Oger
☐	VP-BIZ	Boeing 737 BBJ1	34477	Siva Air Limited
☐	VP-BJJ	Boeing 737 BBJ1	30330	Avenair Worldwide (BBJ) Ltd
☐	VP-BNZ	Boeing 737 BBJ1	35959	Gazpromavia

☐ VP-BRM	Boeing 737 BBJ1	28976	Zeem Corp
☐ VP-BRT	Boeing 737 BBJ1	32970	Jet Aviation Business Jets
☐ VP-BWR	Boeing 737 BBJ1	29317	Usal Ltd
☐ VP-BYA	Boeing 737 BBJ1	29972	Saudi Oger
☐ VP-BZL	Boeing 737 BBJ2	32915	Lowa Ltd
☐ VP-CBB	Boeing 737 BBJ2	32806	A S Bugshan & Bros
☐ VP-CLR	Boeing 737 BBJ1	34865	Lukoil Avia
☐ VP-CPA	Boeing 737 BBJ1	30031	Mid East Jet
☐ VP-CSK	Boeing 737 BBJ2	34620	Nafo Aviation
☐ VQ-BOS	Boeing 737-8GQ/W	35792	Bayham Ltd
☐ ZS-RSA	Boeing 737 BBJ1	32627	South African Air Force
☐ 3C-EGE	Boeing 737 BBJ1	33367	Government of Equatorial Guinea
☐ 5N-FGT	Boeing 737 BBJ1	34260	Nigerian Air Force
☐ 9H-BBJ	Boeing 737 BBJ1	30791	Privajet Ltd
☐ 3701	Boeing 737-8AR/W	30139	Republic of China Air Force
☐ 05-4613	Boeing 737 BBJ1	34809	US Air Force
☐ 01-0015	Boeing 737 BBJ1	32916	US Air Force
☐ 01-0040	Boeing 737 BBJ1	29971	US Air Force
☐ 01-0041	Boeing 737 BBJ1	33080	US Air Force
☐ 02-0042	Boeing 737 BBJ1	33500	US Air Force
☐ 02-0201	Boeing 737 BBJ1	30755	US Air Force
☐ 02-0202	Boeing 737 BBJ1	30753	US Air Force
☐ 02-0203	Boeing 737 BBJ1	33434	US Air Force
☐ 05-0730	Boeing 737 BBJ1	34807	US Air Force
☐ 05-0932	Boeing 737 BBJ1	34808	US Air Force
☐ A4O-OMN	Boeing 747-430	32445	Oman Royal Flight
☐ A4O-SO	Boeing 747-SP27	21785	Oman Royal Flight
☐ A6-COM	Boeing 747-433	25074	Dubai Air Wing
☐ A6-HRM	Boeing 747-422	26903	Dubai Air Wing
☐ A6-MMM	Boeing 747-422	26906	Dubai Air Wing
☐ A6-UAE	Boeing 747-48E	28551	Presidential Flight
☐ A6-YAS	Boeing 747-4F6	28961	Presidential Flight
☐ A9C-HAK	Boeing 747-SPP6	23610	Bahrain Royal Flight
☐ A9C-HMK	Boeing 747-4P8	33684	Bahrain Royal Flight
☐ HL7465	Boeing 747-4B5	26412	Republic of Korea Air Force
☐ HZ-AIF	Boeing 747-SP68	22503	Government of Saudi Arabia
☐ HZ-AIJ	Boeing 747-SP68	22750	Government of Saudi Arabia
☐ HZ-HM1A	Boeing 747-3G1	23070	Government of Saudi Arabia
☐ HZ-HM1B	Boeing 747-SP68	21652	Government of Saudi Arabia
☐ HZ-WBT7	Boeing 747-4J6	25880	Kingdom Holding
☐ N5017Q	Boeing 747-8KZF	36136	Boeing
☐ N747A	Boeing 747-SP27	21992	Fry's Electronics Inc
☐ N747GE	Boeing 747-121F	19651	General Electric Company
☐ N787RR	Boeing 747-267B	21966	Rolls-Royce North America Inc
☐ N911NA	Boeing 747-SR46	20781	NASA
☐ P4-FSH	Boeing 747-SP31	21963	Ernest Angley Ministries
☐ V8-ALI	Boeing 747-430	26426	Government of Brunei
☐ VP-BAT	Boeing 747-SP21	21648	Worldwide Aircraft Holding Co (Bermuda) Ltd
☐ VP-BLK	Boeing 747-SP31	21961	Interface Operations Bermuda Ltd
☐ VQ-BMS	Boeing 747-SP21	21649	Interface Operations Bermuda Ltd
☐ 7O-YMN	Boeing 747-SP27	21786	Government of Yemen Arab Republic
☐ 9K-ADE	Boeing 747-469	27338	Kuwait Airways
☐ 00-0001	Boeing 747-YAL-1	30201	Boeing Integrated Defense Systems
☐ 20-1101	Boeing 747-47C	24730	Japan Air Self Defence Force
☐ 20-1102	Boeing 747-47C	24731	Japan Air Self Defence Force
☐ 82-8000	Boeing 747 VC-25A	23824	US Air Force
☐ 92-9000	Boeing 747 VC-25A	23825	US Air Force
☐ HB-IEE	Boeing 757-23A/W	24527	PrivatAir
☐ N757A	Boeing 757-200	22212	Boeing Logistics Spares Inc
☐ N757HW	Boeing 757-225	22194	Honeywell International Inc
☐ N757LL	Boeing 757-23N/W	27972	Talos Aviation Ltd
☐ N757MA	Boeing 757-24Q	28463	Mid East Jet
☐ N757SS	Boeing 757-236	22176	Luxury Air LLC
☐ N770BB	Boeing 757-2J4/W	25220	The Yucaipa Companies LLC
☐ N801DM	Boeing 757-256	26240	North American Airlines
☐ N1757	Boeing 757-23A/W	24923	Vulcan Inc
☐ SX-RFA	Boeing 757-23N/W	30232	GainJet Aviation S.A.
☐ T-01	Boeing 757-23A	25487	Argentine Air Force
☐ UK-75700	Boeing 757-23P	28338	Uzbekistan Airways
☐ UP-B5701	Boeing 757-2M6	23454	Government of Kazakhstan
☐ XC-UJM	Boeing 757-225/W	22690	Mexican Air Force (Also TP-01)
☐ 98-0001	Boeing 757 C32A	29025	US Air Force
☐ 98-0002	Boeing 757 C32A	29026	US Air Force
☐ 99-0003	Boeing 757 C32A	29027	US Air Force
☐ 99-0004	Boeing 757 C32A	29028	US Air Force

☐ 985	Boeing 767-3YOER	26205	Chilean Air Force
☐ EZ-A700	Boeing 767-32KER	33968	Government of Turkmenistan
☐ J2-KBE	Boeing 767-216ER	23624	Government of Djibouti
☐ N673BF	Boeing 767-238ER	23402	Polaris Aviation Solutions LLC
☐ N767A	Boeing 767-2AXER	33685	ARAMCO Associated Co
☐ N767KS	Boeing 767-24QER	28270	Mid East Jet
☐ N767MW	Boeing 767-277	22694	Swift Air
☐ N804MS	Boeing 767-3P6ER	27255	Interface Operations LLC
☐ N2767	Boeing 767-238ER	23896	Google
☐ P4-MES	Boeing 767-33AER	33425	Silver Arrows
☐ UK-67000	Boeing 767-33PER	35796	Government of Uzbekistan
☐ UP-B6701	Boeing 767-2DXER	32954	Government of Kazakhstan
☐ V8-MHB	Boeing 767-27GER	25537	Government of Brunei
☐ VP-BKS	Boeing 767-3P6ER	27254	Kalair Ltd
☐ VP-CME	Boeing 767-231	22567	Sheikh M Edress
☐ ZS-SOF	Boeing 767-259	24835	Government of Djibouti
☐ A6-ALN	Boeing 777-2ANER	29953	Presidential Flight
☐ N777AS	Boeing 777-24Q	29271	Mid East Jet
☐ N787BA	Boeing 787-881	40690	Boeing
☐ N787BX	Boeing 787-800	40692	Boeing
☐ N787EX	Boeing 787-83Q	40691	Boeing
☐ N787FT	Boeing 787-800	40694	Boeing
☐ N787ZA	Boeing 787-800	40695	Boeing
☐ N7874	Boeing 787-800	40693	Boeing
☐ B-1110L	CAIC ARJ21-700	104	China Aviation Industry Corp
☐ B-970L	CAIC ARJ21-700	101	China Aviation Industry Corp
☐ B-991L	CAIC ARJ21-700	102	China Aviation Industry Corp
☐ B-992L	CAIC ARJ21-700	103	China Aviation Industry Corp
☐ 4L-GAF	Canadair Challenger 850	8046	AirZena - Georgian Airways
☐ 5A-UAD	Canadair Challenger 850	8087	United Aviation
☐ 9H-AFU	Canadair Challenger 800	7176	Carre Aviation Ltd
☐ A6-BNH	Canadair Challenger 850	8069	GAMA Aviation FZC
☐ B-4005	Canadair Challenger 800	7138	People's Liberation Army Air Force
☐ B-4006	Canadair Challenger 800	7149	People's Liberation Army Air Force
☐ B-4007	Canadair Challenger 800	7180	People's Liberation Army Air Force
☐ B-4010	Canadair Challenger 800	7189	People's Liberation Army Air Force
☐ B-4011	Canadair Challenger 800	7193	People's Liberation Army Air Force
☐ B-4701	Canadair Challenger 800	7639	China Ocean Aviation Group
☐ B-4702	Canadair Challenger 800	7455	China Ocean Aviation Group
☐ B-7695	Canadair CRJ200ER	7268	ZYB Lily Jet Business Aviation Ltd
☐ B-7697	Canadair Challenger 850	8089	ZYB Lily Jet Business Aviation Ltd
☐ C-FUQY	Canadair Challenger 850	8095	Bombardier Inc
☐ C-FWEZ	Canadair Challenger 850	8092	Chartright Air
☐ C-GDTD	Canadair Challenger 800	8067	Flightexec
☐ C-GSLL	Canadair Challenger 850	8103	Image Air Charter Inc
☐ C-GSUW	Canadair Challenger 800	8047	Suncor Energy Inc
☐ D-AAIJ	Canadair Challenger 850	8065	Imperial Jet
☐ D-AANN	Canadair Challenger 850	8073	ExecuJet Europe GmbH
☐ D-ACRN	Canadair CRJ200LR	7486	FAI rent-a-jet
☐ D-ATRI	Canadair Challenger 850	8081	Fly Independence
☐ EI-EEZ	Canadair Challenger 850	8085	Airlink Airways
☐ EW-301PJ	Canadair Challenger 850	8057	Belavia
☐ G-GJMB	Canadair Challenger 850	8055	Corporate Jet Management Ltd
☐ G-IGWT	Canadair Challenger 850	8078	Ocean Sky Aviation Ltd (UK)
☐ G-SHAL	Canadair Challenger 850	8066	TAG Aviation (UK) Ltd
☐ HB-IDJ	Canadair Challenger 800	7136	TAG Aviation
☐ M-ANTA	Canadair Challenger 850	8094	Miklos Services Corp
☐ M-FZMH	Canadair Challenger 850	8068	ExecuJet Middle East
☐ M-ISLA	Canadair Challenger 850	8080	Excellence Aviation Services
☐ M-TAKE	Canadair Challenger 850	8079	Prime Aviation JSC
☐ N135BC	Canadair Challenger 800	7075	DJ Burrell & Burrell Professional Labs et al
☐ N155MW	Canadair CRJ200LR	7021	Dog Leg Transportation Co LLC
☐ N500PR	Canadair Challenger 800	7846	Penske Racing Inc
☐ N501LS	Canadair Challenger 800	7584	Boston Enterprises LLC
☐ N529DB	Canadair Challenger 800	7152	Solarius Aviation
☐ N601LS	Canadair Challenger 800	7008	Directional Visions LLC
☐ N711WM	Canadair Challenger 800	7140	Gaughan Flying LLC
☐ N888AU	Canadair CRJ200 Phoenix	7211	Jet Asia
☐ N888GY	Canadair CRJ200 ExecLiner	7471	GY CRJ Leasing LLC
☐ N888WU	Canadair CRJ200 ExecLiner	7481	Wu Air Corp
☐ OD-AMR	Canadair CRJ200ER	7255	Med Airways
☐ OD-TAL	Canadair CRJ200 ExecLiner	7086	Easy Fly S.A.L.
☐ OE-IKG	Canadair Challenger 850	8063	MAP Executive Flightservice

☐ OE-ILI	Canadair Challenger 850	8048	VistaJet Luftfahrtunternehmen
☐ OE-ILV	Canadair Challenger 850	8082	VistaJet Luftfahrtunternehmen
☐ OE-ILY	Canadair Challenger 850	8076	VistaJet Luftfahrtunternehmen
☐ OE-ILZ	Canadair Challenger 850	8086	VistaJet Luftfahrtunternehmen
☐ OE-ISA	Canadair Challenger 850	8043	Avcon Jet AG
☐ OH-SPB	Canadair Challenger 850	8056	Jetflite
☐ OY-NAD	Canadair Challenger 850	8052	ExecuJet Europe A/S
☐ OY-VEG	Canadair Challenger 850	8075	ExecuJet Europe A/S
☐ OY-VGA	Canadair Challenger 850	8077	ExecuJet Europe A/S
☐ P4-AST	Canadair Challenger 850	8054	Comlux KZ
☐ P4-GAZ	Canadair CRJ Regional Jet	200	Renaissance 7159 Flight Test Consultants
☐ P4-GJL	Canadair Challenger 850	8053	Silver Arrows
☐ P4-VIP	Canadair CRJ200 Renaissance	7158	Flight Test Consultants
☐ PH-AAG	Canadair CRJ200 Hemisphere	7763	Solid Air
☐ RA-67218	Canadair Challenger 850	8074	Kolavia
☐ RA-67219	Canadair Challenger 850	8090	Kolavia
☐ RA-67220	Canadair Challenger 850	8091	Kolavia
☐ RP-C6226	Canadair Challenger 850	8088	Subic International Air Charter
☐ UP-C8502	Canadair Challenger 850	8049	Comlux KZ
☐ UP-C8503	Canadair Challenger 850	8093	Euro-Asia Air
☐ UR-ICD	Canadair Challenger 850	8072	ISD Avia
☐ UR-OAM	Canadair Challenger 850	8084	ISD Avia
☐ UR-RUS	Canadair CRJ200LR	7990	ISD Avia
☐ VH-LEF	Canadair Challenger 850	8060	Air National Australia Pty Ltd
☐ VP-BCC	Canadair Challenger 800	7717	S & K Bermuda Limited
☐ VP-BSD	Canadair Challenger 850	8051	Arabian Support and Services Co Ltd (ASASCO)
☐ VP-BVJ	Canadair Challenger 850	8071	Vacuna Jets Ltd
☐ VP-CON	Canadair Challenger 850	8083	Lukoil Avia
☐ VT-ARE	Canadair CRJ200 ExecLiner	7163	Club One Air
☐ VT-IBP	Canadair Challenger 850	8070	Airmid Aviation Services Private Ltd
☐ VT-KML	Canadair Challenger 800	7351	Span Air (India) Pvt
☐ C-FNXG	Canadair CRJ1000 NextGen	19001	Bombardier Inc
☐ C-FRJX	Canadair CRJ1000ER NextGen	19991	Bombardier Inc
☐ B-4060	Canadair Challenger 870	10164	People's Liberation Army Air Force
☐ B-4061	Canadair Challenger 870	10183	People's Liberation Army Air Force
☐ B-4062	Canadair Challenger 870	10187	People's Liberation Army Air Force
☐ B-4063	Canadair Challenger 870	10204	People's Liberation Army Air Force
☐ B-4064	Canadair Challenger 870	10206	People's Liberation Army Air Force
☐ N1RL	Canadair Challenger 870	10004	Indycar Aviation LLC
☐ N602LJ	Canadair CRJ701	10002	Northrop Grumman Systems Corp (Delaware)
☐ N870DC	Canadair Challenger 870 NG	10314	Dow Chemical Co
☐ UP-CL001	Canadair Challenger 870 NG	10289	Euro-Asia Air
☐ VP-BCL	Canadair Challenger 870	10247	S & K Bermuda Limited
☐ C-GSUA	Canadair Challenger 890 NG	15182	Suncor Energy Oil Sands Limited
☐ C-GSUM	Canadair Challenger 890	15158	Suncor Energy Oil Sands Limited
☐ 5V-TGF	Douglas DC-8-62	46071	Government of Togo
☐ N817NA	Douglas DC-8-72	46082	NASA
☐ VP-BHM	Douglas DC-8-62	46111	Brisair Ltd
☐ F-GVTH	Douglas DC-9-21	47308	Thales
☐ N120NE	Douglas DC-9-15	45731	Aircraft Guaranty Holdings & Trust LLC
☐ N45NA	Douglas DC-9-33RC	47410	National Nuclear Security Adminstration
☐ N697BJ	Douglas DC-9-32	47799	Blue Jackets Air LLC
☐ N880DF	Douglas DC-9-32	47635	Detroit Pistons
☐ N8860	Douglas DC-9-15	45797	Scaife Flight Operations LLC
☐ N932ML	Douglas DC-9-31	47547	US Government - Department of Navy
☐ ZS-MNT	Douglas DC-9-15	45740	Government of South Africa
☐ N910SF	Douglas DC-10-10	46524	US Air Force
☐ N168CF	McDonnell-Douglas MD-87	49670	Sunrider International
☐ N287KB	McDonnell-Douglas MD-87	49768	KEB Aircraft Sales Inc
☐ N789BV	McDonnell-Douglas MD-83	49789	Dugan Kinetics NV LLC
☐ N880DP	McDonnell-Douglas MD-83	49504	Detroit Pistons
☐ SX-IFA	McDonnell-Douglas MD-83	49809	Amjet Executive
☐ TT-ABC	McDonnell-Douglas MD-87	49888	Government of Chad
☐ VP-CBH	McDonnell-Douglas MD-82	53577	Mineralogy Pty Ltd
☐ VP-CNI	McDonnell-Douglas MD-87	49767	Corporate Aviation Holdings Corp
☐ VP-CTF	McDonnell-Douglas MD-87	49777	AMAC Aerospace
☐ C-GVWD	De Havilland DHC-7-102	108	Trans Capital Air
☐ C-FBCS	De Havilland DHC-8-202B	413	Bombardier Inc
☐ C-FJJA	De Havilland DHC-8-Q401	4001	Bombardier Inc
☐ C-FXAW	De Havilland DHC-8-Q402	4262	Bombardier Inc
☐ D2-EWT	De Havilland DHC-8-315	563	Government of Angola
☐ N308RD	De Havilland DHC-8-102A	265	Presidential Airways

☐ N637CC	De Havilland DHC-8-202	637	Northrop Grumman Systems Corp
☐ N646CC	De Havilland DHC-8-202	646	Northrop Grumman Systems Corp
☐ N649CC	De Havilland DHC-8-202	649	Northrop Grumman Systems Corp
☐ P4-TCO	De Havilland DHC-8-202	484	Prime Aviation JSC
☐ PP-EIX	Embraer EMB-110P1 Bandeirante	110468	State Government of Amapa
☐ PP-FFV	Embraer EMB-110B Bandeirante	110284	INPE - Instituto Nacide Pesquisas Espaciais
☐ PT-SHN	Embraer EMB-110P1 Bandeirante	110460	GENSA
☐ PT-SHO	Embraer EMB-110P1 Bandeirante	110461	Furnas Centrais Electricas SA
☐ PT-SHP	Embraer EMB-110P1 Bandeirante	110462	Hidroelectrica Sao Francisco
☐ PT-SHR	Embraer EMB-110P1 Bandeirante	110464	Furnas Centrais Electricas SA
☐ PT-SHU	Embraer EMB-110P1 Bandeirante	110466	Amazonaves Taxi Aereo
☐ PT-WTL	Embraer EMB-110P1 Bandeirante	110104	Taxi Aereo Itaituba
☐ D2-FFY	Embraer EMB-120 Brasilia	120171	Diexim Expresso
☐ N109EM	Embraer EMB-120 Brasilia	120195	Evernham Motorsports LLC
☐ N289YV	Embraer EMB-120ER Brasilia	120289	Charter Air Transport
☐ N650CT	Embraer EMB-120 Brasilia	120198	Charter Air Transport
☐ N651CT	Embraer EMB-120 Brasilia	120197	Charter Air Transport
☐ N653CT	Embraer EMB-120ER Brasilia	120243	Charter Air Transport
☐ N707TG	Embraer EMB-120 Brasilia	120182	Gordon Air
☐ N919EM	Embraer EMB-120ER Brasilia	120160	Evernham Motorsports LLC
☐ N16731	Embraer EMB-120 Brasilia	120190	MWR Racing LLC
☐ PP-IAS	Embraer EMB-120 Brasilia	120111	Imetame Metalmechanica
☐ PT-SOK	Embraer EMB-120ER Brasilia	120358	Companhia Vale do Rio Doce
☐ PT-SXP	Embraer EMB-120ER Brasilia	120323	Embraer
☐ T-500	Embraer EMB-120ER Brasilia	120359	Angolan Peoples Air Force
☐ A6-AJA	Embraer Legacy 600	14501089	AJA - Al Jaber Aviation
☐ A6-AJB	Embraer Legacy 600	14501098	AJA - Al Jaber Aviation
☐ A6-DPW	Embraer Legacy 600	14500955	Prestige Jet
☐ A6-FLL	Embraer Legacy 600	14501051	Falcon Aviation Services
☐ A6-FLO	Embraer Legacy 600	14501096	Falcon Aviation Services
☐ A6-MAZ	Embraer Legacy 600	14500978	Unconfirmed UAE Operator
☐ A6-NKL	Embraer Legacy 600	14500944	Empire Aviation Group FZCO
☐ A6-NLA	Embraer Legacy 600	14501075	Prestige Jet
☐ A6-PJE	Embraer Legacy 600	14500972	Prestige Jet
☐ A6-SSV	Embraer Legacy 600	14501041	Empire Aviation Group FZCO
☐ A6-SUN	Embraer Legacy 600	14501001	Empire Aviation Group FZCO
☐ A6-UGH	Embraer Legacy 600	14500993	DAS Holding
☐ A6-VVV	Embraer Legacy 600	14501057	GAMA Aviation FZC
☐ A9C-MTC	Embraer Legacy 600	14500975	MAE Aircraft Management WLL
☐ CE-01	Embraer ERJ-135ER	145449	Belgian Air Force
☐ CE-02	Embraer ERJ-135LR	145480	Belgian Air Force
☐ CN-MBP	Embraer Legacy 600	14501117	Dalia Air
☐ D-ADCP	Embraer Legacy 600	14501067	Flugbereitschaft GmbH
☐ D-AKAT	Embraer Legacy 600	14501038	KamAvia Handels Gmbh
☐ D-ARTN	Embraer Legacy 600	14500941	DC Aviation
☐ D-AVIB	Embraer Legacy 600	14501109	Vibro Air Flugservice
☐ EC-IIR	Embraer Legacy 600	145540	Audeli
☐ EC-KHT	Embraer Legacy 600	14500863	Aerodynamics Malaga
☐ EC-LGG	Embraer Legacy 600	14501025	Aerodynamics Malaga
☐ FAE-051	Embraer Legacy 600	14501082	Ecuadorian Air Force
☐ G-CFJA	Embraer Legacy 600	14501045	TAG Aviation (UK) Ltd
☐ G-CGSE	Embraer Legacy 600	14500995	GE Capital Corporation (Leasing) Ltd
☐ G-CJMD	Embraer Legacy 600	14500994	Corporate Jet Management Ltd
☐ G-CMAF	Embraer Legacy 600	14501011	TAG Aviation (UK) Ltd
☐ G-HUBY	Embraer Legacy 600	14500854	London Executive Aviation
☐ G-IRSH	Embraer Legacy 600	14501048	London Executive Aviation
☐ G-LALE	Embraer Legacy 600	14501017	London Executive Aviation
☐ G-OGSK	Embraer Legacy 600	14501074	TAG Aviation
☐ G-PGRP	Embraer Legacy 600	14501102	GAMA Aviation
☐ G-RBNS	Embraer Legacy 650	14501121	London Executive Aviation
☐ G-RHMS	Embraer Legacy 600	14501072	International Jet Club Ltd
☐ G-RUBE	Embraer Legacy 600	14501100	London Executive Aviation
☐ G-SHSI	Embraer Legacy 600	14501114	TAG Aviation (UK) Ltd
☐ G-SUGA	Embraer Legacy 650	14501128	Titan Airways
☐ G-SYLJ	Embraer Legacy 600	14500937	TAG Aviation
☐ G-THFC	Embraer Legacy 600	14500954	London Executive Aviation
☐ G-WCCI	Embraer Legacy 600	145505	London Executive Aviation
☐ HB-JED	Embraer Legacy 600	145644	Nomad Aviation AG
☐ HB-JEL	Embraer Legacy 600	14500933	G5 Executive
☐ HP-1A	Embraer Legacy 600	14501066	SENAN - Servicio Nacional Aeronaval
☐ JY-CMC	Embraer Legacy 650	14501126	Arab Wings
☐ JY-KME	Embraer Legacy 600	14501055	Arab Wings
☐ K3601	Embraer Legacy 600	14500867	Indian Air Force
☐ K3602	Embraer Legacy 600	14500880	Indian Air Force

☐	K3603	Embraer Legacy 600	14500910	Indian Air Force
☐	K3604	Embraer Legacy 600	14500919	Indian Air Force
☐	LX-NVB	Embraer Legacy 600	14501002	Silver Arrows
☐	LX-RLG	Embraer Legacy 600	14500967	Silver Arrows
☐	M-AKAK	Embraer Legacy 600	14500970	AA Kassar Sal
☐	M-DSCL	Embraer Legacy 600	14500851	Legacy Aviation Limited
☐	M-ESGR	Embraer Legacy 600	14501016	Hermes Executive Aviation Limited
☐	M-KPCO	Embraer Legacy 600	14500973	National Legacy for Aircraft Management
☐	M-NATH	Embraer Legacy 600	14501021	Barbedos Group Limited
☐	M-OLEG	Embraer Legacy 600	14500991	Club 17 SA
☐	M-RCCG	Embraer Legacy 600	14501113	RMK Group
☐	M-YNJC	Embraer Legacy 600	14500961	Hermes Executive Aviation Limited
☐	N6GD	Embraer Legacy 600	14500983	Elite Air Inc
☐	N10SV	Embraer Legacy 600	14500974	Siva Air Limited
☐	N53NA	Embraer Legacy 600	145770	Aero Air LLC
☐	N63AG	Embraer Legacy 600	14501061	ACM Aviation
☐	N89FE	Embraer Legacy 600	14501058	FirstEnergy Solutions Corp
☐	N89LD	Embraer ERJ-135SE	145648	McKee Foods Transportation LLC
☐	N124LS	Embraer Legacy 600	14500948	Executive Jet Management
☐	N135SK	Embraer Legacy 600	14500989	United Aviation
☐	N135SL	Embraer Legacy 600	145711	United Aviation
☐	N226HY	Embraer Legacy 600	14501014	Executive Flightways Inc
☐	N227WE	Embraer Legacy 600	14501018	United States Aviation Co
☐	N325JF	Embraer ERJ-135SE	145499	Intel Air Shuttle Aircraft
☐	N357TE	Embraer Legacy 600	14501079	BUA Delaware Inc
☐	N373RB	Embraer Legacy 600	14500957	RBGT LLC
☐	N386CH	Embraer ERJ-135SE	145467	Intel Air Shuttle Aircraft
☐	N451DJ	Embraer Legacy 600	145789	Universal Jet Aviation Inc
☐	N486TM	Embraer ERJ-135SE	145364	Intel Air Shuttle Aircraft
☐	N494TG	Embraer Legacy 600	145678	Sentient Flight Group
☐	N503JT	Embraer Legacy 600	14501032	ExcelAire Service Inc
☐	N515JT	Embraer Legacy 600	14500950	Excelaire LLC
☐	N580ML	Embraer Legacy 600	14500990	Stone Tower Air
☐	N600YC	Embraer Legacy 600	14501069	Rimbaka Forestry Corp Sdn Bhd
☐	N605WG	Embraer Legacy 600	14500980	Wings West Aircraft
☐	N615PG	Embraer Legacy 600	14501004	Pacific Gas & Electric Company
☐	N617WA	Embraer Legacy 600	14500884	Administaff Inc
☐	N642AG	Embraer Legacy 600	145642	Swift Air
☐	N676TC	Embraer Legacy 600	145699	Alpine Cascade Corp
☐	N678RC	Embraer Legacy 600	14501064	Financial Business Concepts Inc
☐	N702DR	Embraer Legacy 600	14500925	SCSM Aviation LLC
☐	N728PH	Embraer Legacy 600	14500985	ExcelAire Service Inc
☐	N730BH	Embraer Legacy 600	145730	Swift Air
☐	N806D	Embraer Legacy 600	14501095	Dominion Resources Services Inc
☐	N809TD	Embraer Legacy 600	14500809	Swift Air
☐	N818HR	Embraer Legacy 600	14501105	HR INV LLC
☐	N827TV	Embraer Legacy 600	14500971	Pinnacle Aviation Inc
☐	N829RN	Embraer ERJ-135SE	145361	Intel Air Shuttle Aircraft
☐	N865LS	Embraer Legacy 600	14501080	Leon Advertising and Public Relations Inc
☐	N888ML	Embraer Legacy 600	14500818	New Macau Landmark Management Ltd
☐	N898JS	Embraer Legacy 600	14501071	The LaLit Hotels
☐	N900DP	Embraer Legacy 600	14500903	Business Aviation/Del Inc
☐	N900EM	Embraer Legacy 600	14500976	Air By Jet LLC
☐	N904FL	Embraer Legacy 600	145780	Nextant Aircraft LLC
☐	N905FL	Embraer Legacy 600	145775	Flight Options
☐	N909LX	Embraer Legacy 600	14500942	Flight Options
☐	N909TT	Embraer Legacy 600	14501044	Transcon International Inc
☐	N910LX	Embraer Legacy 600	14500952	Flight Options
☐	N912JC	Embraer Legacy 600	14501015	Vitesse Aviation Services
☐	N913LX	Embraer Legacy 600	14501007	Flight Options
☐	N924AK	Embraer Legacy 600	14501034	Talon Air Inc
☐	N925FL	Embraer Legacy 600	14500825	Flight Options
☐	N926FM	Embraer ERJ-135SE	145466	Intel Air Shuttle Aircraft
☐	N939AJ	Embraer Legacy 600	14500939	Orfro LLC & Ares Technical Administration
☐	N948AL	Embraer ERJ-135SE	145450	Intel Air Shuttle Aircraft
☐	N966JS	Embraer Legacy 600	14500966	Pebuny LLC
☐	N983JC	Embraer ERJ-135LR	14500977	Johnson Controls Inc
☐	N1023C	Embraer ERJ-135SE	145550	ConocoPhillips Co
☐	OE-IBK	Embraer Legacy 600	14501110	Avcon Jet AG
☐	OE-IBR	Embraer Legacy 600	14500960	Global Jet Austria GmbH
☐	OE-IDB	Embraer Legacy 600	14500999	Avcon Jet AG
☐	OE-IDH	Embraer Legacy 600	14501026	EUROP STAR Aircraft GmbH
☐	OE-IRK	Embraer Legacy 600	14500916	Avcon Jet AG
☐	OK-GGG	Embraer Legacy 600	14500986	ABS Jets
☐	OK-JNT	Embraer Legacy 600	14501087	ABS Jets
☐	OK-KKG	Embraer Legacy 600	14500873	Grossmann Air Service
☐	OK-ROM	Embraer Legacy 600	14501039	ABS Jets

☐	OK-SLN	Embraer Legacy 600	145796	ABS Jets
☐	OK-SUN	Embraer Legacy 600	14500963	ABS Jets
☐	P4-AEG	Embraer Legacy 600	14501111	AEG Air AVV
☐	P4-IVM	Embraer Legacy 600	145686	RusJet
☐	P4-MIV	Embraer Legacy 600	14501031	RusJet
☐	P4-MSG	Embraer Legacy 600	14500913	PremierAvia
☐	P4-PAM	Embraer Legacy 600	14500982	Petroff Air Ltd
☐	P4-SIS	Embraer Legacy 600	145586	PremierAvia
☐	P4-SMS	Embraer Legacy 650	14501123	Petroff Air Ltd
☐	P4-SVM	Embraer Legacy 600	14501060	Petroff Air Ltd
☐	P4-VVP	Embraer Legacy 600	145549	Petroff Air Ltd
☐	PK-DHK	Embraer Legacy 600	14501046	Premiair
☐	PK-OME	Embraer Legacy 600	145516	Airfast Indonesia
☐	PK-RJG	Embraer Legacy 600	14500969	Premiair
☐	PK-RJW	Embraer Legacy 600	14501106	Premiair
☐	PK-RSS	Embraer Legacy 600	14501020	Enggang Air Service
☐	PP-VVA	Embraer ERJ-135LR	145702	Companhia Vale do Rio Doce
☐	PP-VVV	Embraer Legacy 600	14501099	JBS SA
☐	PR-AVX	Embraer Legacy 600	14501037	Grupo EBX Participacoes Ltda
☐	PR-BEB	Embraer Legacy 600	14501035	Dedalus Administracao e Participacoes Ltda
☐	PR-LTC	Embraer Legacy 600	14501091	Macbens Patrimonial Ltda
☐	PR-NIO	Embraer Legacy 600	14501012	CBMM-Compania Brasileira de Metalurgia e Mineracao
☐	PR-ODF	Embraer Legacy 600	14501054	Global Taxi Aereo Ltda / Reali Taxi Aereo Ltda
☐	PR-ORE	Embraer Legacy 600	145625	Companhia Vale do Rio Doce
☐	PR-RIO	Embraer Legacy 600	145717	Unibanco Leasing
☐	PT-SCR	Embraer Legacy 600	14500946	Sao Conrado Taxi Aereo
☐	PT-SKM	Embraer Legacy 600	14501090	Embraer
☐	PT-SKW	Embraer Legacy 600	14501006	Sao Conrado Taxi Aereo
☐	PT-TKI	Embraer Legacy 650	14501115	Embraer
☐	PT-TKV	Embraer Legacy 650	14501119	Embraer
☐	S5-ABL	Embraer Legacy 600	14501008	Linxair Business Airlines
☐	S5-ALA	Embraer Legacy 600	14501029	Linxair Business Airlines
☐	SE-DJG	Embraer Legacy 600	14501042	EFS European Flight Service
☐	SX-CDK	Embraer Legacy 600	14500998	K2 SmartJets
☐	SX-DGM	Embraer Legacy 600	14501023	Interjet
☐	T-501	Embraer Legacy 600	14500981	Angolan Peoples Air Force
☐	VH-VLT	Embraer Legacy 600	14501107	Southern Cross Jets
☐	VP-CFA	Embraer Legacy 600	145637	SAMCO Aviation
☐	VP-CHP	Embraer Legacy 600	14500802	JBJE
☐	VP-CLL	Embraer Legacy 600	14501052	Titan Aviation
☐	VP-CMK	Embraer Legacy 600	14501083	Comoro Gulf Aviation
☐	VP-CUP	Embraer Legacy 600	145555	Fort Aero
☐	VQ-BFP	Embraer Legacy 600	14501049	Planair
☐	VQ-BFQ	Embraer Legacy 600	14501062	Planair
☐	VQ-BLU	Embraer Legacy 600	14501086	Air Mercury Ltd
☐	VT-BSF	Embraer Legacy 600	14500901	Indian Border Security Force
☐	VT-CKP	Embraer Legacy 600	14501094	Krishnapatnam Port Company Ltd
☐	5N-RSG	Embraer Legacy 600	14500891	Government of River State of Nigeria
☐	209	Embraer ERJ-135ER	145209	Greek Air Force
☐	484	Embraer Legacy 600	145484	Greek Air Force
☐	1124	Embraer ERJ-135LR	14501124	Royal Thai Army
☐	2113	Embraer ERJ-135LR	14501125	Royal Thai Navy
☐	2560	Embraer ERJ-135LR	145600	Brazilian Air Force
☐	2561	Embraer ERJ-135LR	145608	Brazilian Air Force
☐	2580	Embraer Legacy 600	145412	Brazilian Air Force
☐	2581	Embraer Legacy 600	145462	Brazilian Air Force
☐	2582	Embraer Legacy 600	145495	Brazilian Air Force
☐	2583	Embraer Legacy 600	145528	Brazilian Air Force
☐	2584	Embraer Legacy 600	14500997	Brazilian Air Force
☐	2585	Embraer Legacy 600	14501078	Brazilian Air Force
☐	1084/HS-AMP	Embraer ERJ-135LR	14501084	Royal Thai Army
☐	2112/HS-NVA	Embraer ERJ-135LR	14501077	Royal Thai Navy
☐	2524	Embraer ERJ-145EP	145034	Brazilian Air Force
☐	3C-QQH	Embraer ERJ-145EP	145076	Government of Equatorial Guinea
☐	CE-03	Embraer ERJ-145LR	145526	Belgian Air Force
☐	CE-04	Embraer ERJ-145LR	145548	Belgian Air Force
☐	N138DE	Embraer ERJ-145LR	145129	Champion Air LLC
☐	N500DE	Embraer ERJ-145LR	145084	Champion Air LLC
☐	PR-DPF	Embraer ERJ-145EP	145127	Brazilian Federal Police Force
☐	PR-PFN	Embraer ERJ-145LR	145002	Brazilian Federal Police Force
☐	PT-SPM	Embraer ERJ-145EP	145114	Companhia Vale do Rio Doce
☐	PP-XJB	Embraer 170	17000003	Embraer
☐	PP-XJD	Embraer 175	17000014	Embraer
☐	SP-LIG	Embraer 175LR	17000283	Polish Air Force
☐	SP-LIH	Embraer 175LR	17000288	Polish Air Force

☐ 2590	Embraer 190LR	19000214	Brazilian Air Force
☐ 2591	Embraer 190LR	19000277	Brazilian Air Force
☐ A6-AJH	Embraer Lineage 1000	19000140	AJA - Al Jaber Aviation
☐ A6-AJI	Embraer Lineage 1000	19000261	AJA - Al Jaber Aviation
☐ A6-ARK	Embraer Lineage 1000	19000109	Prestige Jet
☐ A6-HHS	Embraer Lineage 1000	19000296	Falcon Aviation Services
☐ A6-KAH	Embraer Lineage 1000	19000236	Al Habtoor Group
☐ G-RBNB	Embraer Lineage 1000	19000203	Hangar 8 Ltd
☐ M-SBAH	Embraer Lineage 1000	19000225	Flemming House
☐ PP-XMA	Embraer 190	19000001	Embraer
☐ PP-XMI	Embraer 190	19000003	Embraer
☐ PP-XTF	Embraer Lineage 1000	19000159	Embraer
☐ PT-SDD	Embraer Lineage 1000	19000177	Embraer
☐ XA-AYJ	Embraer Lineage 1000	19000243	Grupo Omnilife Sa de CV
☐ MT-216	Fairchild FH-227D	578	Mexican Navy
☐ PH-NLZ	Fairchild (Swearingen) Metro II	TC-277	Stichting Nationaal Lucht en Ruimtevaart Lab.
☐ D-CNEU	Fairchild/Dornier 228-200NG	8206	RUAG Aerospace Ltd
☐ D-CATZ	Fairchild/Dornier 328-100	3090	Private Wings Flugcharter
☐ D-CPWF	Fairchild/Dornier 328-100	3112	Private Wings Flugcharter
☐ N28CG	Fairchild/Dornier 328-100	3024	Corning Inc
☐ N38CG	Fairchild/Dornier 328-100	3034	Corning Inc
☐ OB2	Fairchild/Dornier 328-100	3083	Botswana Defence Force
☐ OO-ELI	Fairchild/Dornier 328-100	3060	ASL - Air Service Liege
☐ PH-EVY	Fairchild/Dornier 328-100	3095	Solid Air
☐ C-GCPW	Fairchild/Dornier 328JET	3129	Pratt & Whitney Canada
☐ D-BGAS	Fairchild/Dornier 328JET	3139	DC Aviation
☐ D-BJET	Fairchild/Dornier 328JET	3207	Private Wings Flugcharter
☐ HB-AEU	Fairchild/Dornier 328JET Envoy 3	3199	Swiss Jet
☐ N38VP	Fairchild/Dornier 328JET	3174	Vision Airlines
☐ N57TT	Fairchild/Dornier 328JET	3205	Thompson Tractor Co Inc
☐ N117LM	Fairchild/Dornier 328JET	3167	Livemercial Aviation Holding LLC
☐ N131BC	Fairchild/Dornier 328JET	3168	International Bank of Commerce
☐ N328WW	Fairchild/Dornier 328JET Envoy 3	3116	Ultimate Jetcharters Inc
☐ N359SK	Fairchild/Dornier 328JET	3202	Ultimate Jetcharters Inc
☐ N406FJ	Fairchild/Dornier 328JET	3156	Ultimate Jetcharters Inc
☐ N804CE	Fairchild/Dornier 328JET	3184	Cummins Inc
☐ N807LM	Fairchild/Dornier 328JET	3099	Air Force Research Laboratory
☐ N821MW	Fairchild/Dornier 328JET	3160	JHK Development LLC
☐ OE-HMS	Fairchild/Dornier 328JET	3121	Tyrolean Jet Service
☐ OE-HRJ	Fairchild/Dornier 328JET	3206	Icejet
☐ OE-HTJ	Fairchild/Dornier 328JET	3114	Tyrolean Jet Service
☐ UR-AER	Fairchild/Dornier 328JET	3176	Aerostar
☐ UR-WOG	Fairchild/Dornier 328JET	3118	Aerostar
☐ VP-CJD	Fairchild/Dornier 328JET Envoy 3	3221	Easy Aviation
☐ XC-LLS	Fairchild/Dornier 328JET	3197	Procuraduria General de la Republica Nacional
☐ ZS-IOC	Fairchild/Dornier 328JET	3219	Sishen Iron Ore Co
☐ A-2701	Fokker F.27-400M	10536	Indonesian Air Force
☐ G-525	Fokker F.27-400M	10520	Ghana Air Force
☐ J-752	Fokker F.27-200	10281	Pakistan Air Force
☐ 7T-VRN	Fokker F.27-600	10527	Government of Algeria
☐ 10669	Fokker F.27-500RF	10669	Philippine Air Force
☐ 59-0259	Fokker F.27-200	10115	Philippine Air Force
☐ 1250	Fokker F.28-3000	11153	Government of Philippines
☐ A-2801	Fokker F.28-1000	11042	Indonesian Air Force
☐ FAC0002	Fokker F.28-1000	11992	Colombian Air Force
☐ FAC1041	Fokker F.28-3000C	11162	Colombian Air Force
☐ G-530	Fokker F.28-3000	11125	Ghana Air Force
☐ M28-01	Fokker F.28-1000	11088	Royal Malaysian Air Force
☐ T-02	Fokker F.28-4000	11203	Argentine Air Force
☐ T-03	Fokker F.28-1000	11028	Argentine Air Force
☐ T-50	Fokker F.28-1000	11048	Argentine Air Force
☐ TJ-ALG	Fokker F.28-4000	11227	Air Leasing Cameroon
☐ 5A-DSO	Fokker F.28-2000	11110	Petro Air
☐ 5H-CCM	Fokker F.28-3000	11137	Government of Tanzania
☐ 5V-TAI	Fokker F.28-1000	11079	Government of Togo
☐ 5001	Fokker 50	20229	Republic of China Air Force
☐ 5002	Fokker 50	20238	Republic of China Air Force
☐ 5003	Fokker 50	20242	Republic of China Air Force

☐ 27228	Fokker 50	20228	Royal Thai Border Police
☐ 5H-TGF	Fokker 50	20231	Government of Tanzania
☐ KAF308	Fokker 70	11557	Government of Kenya
☐ PH-KBX	Fokker 70	11547	Dutch Royal Flight
☐ OE-IIB	Fokker 100	11403	Moscow Sky
☐ OE-IIC	Fokker 100	11406	Moscow Sky
☐ OE-IID	Fokker 100	11368	Moscow Sky
☐ PK-RJI	Fokker 100	11328	Premiair
☐ N49	General Dynamics (Convair) 580	479	FAA / US DoT
☐ N580HW	General Dynamics (Convair) 580	2	Honeywell Inc
☐ N730RS	Gulfstream Aerospace Mallard	J-50	Richard Sugden
☐ VP-CLK	Gulfstream Aerospace Mallard	J-34	Mallard Aviation Corporation
☐ B-3826	Harbin Y-12 IV	H5005	Harbin Aircraft Manufacturing Corporation
☐ B-610L	Harbin Y-12 E	YUN12E001	Harbin Aircraft Manufacturing Corporation
☐ 1907	Hawker Beechcraft 1900C-1	UC-7	Republic of China Air Force
☐ 5N-MPA	Hawker Beechcraft 1900D	UE-149	Mobil Producing Nigeria Ltd
☐ 5N-MPN	Hawker Beechcraft 1900D	UE-77	Mobil Producing Nigeria Ltd
☐ C-FJDF	Hawker Beechcraft 1900C	UB-68	Courtesy Air
☐ C-FJTF	Hawker Beechcraft 1900C	UB-39	Courtesy Air
☐ HC-CBC	Hawker Beechcraft 1900D	UE-17	SAEREO
☐ N27NG	Hawker Beechcraft 1900D	UE-382	Northrop Grumman Systems Corp
☐ N121WV	Hawker Beechcraft 1900C-1	UC-78	Warbelow's Air Ventures
☐ N1883M	Hawker Beechcraft 1900D	UE-354	Meijer Stores Limited Partnership
☐ N1900R	Hawker Beechcraft 1900D	UE-64	Hawker Beechcraft Corp
☐ N191CS	Hawker Beechcraft 1900D	UE-392	Freeport-McMoran Corp
☐ N196NW	Hawker Beechcraft 1900D	UE-362	Red Line Air LLC
☐ N470MM	Hawker Beechcraft 1900D	UE-394	Schwan's Shared Services LLC
☐ N640MW	Hawker Beechcraft 1900C-1	UC-1	Marvin Lumber & Cedar Co
☐ N655MW	Hawker Beechcraft 1900D	UE-377	Marvin Lumber & Cedar Co
☐ N83413	Hawker Beechcraft 1900D	UE-25	Hawker Beechcraft Corp
☐ PK-OCY	Hawker Beechcraft 1900D	UE-393	Airfast Indonesia
☐ TT-ABB	Hawker Beechcraft 1900D	UE-406	Government of Chad
☐ VH-EMI	Hawker Beechcraft 1900C-1	UC-109	Defence Science & Technology Organisation
☐ VT-ASH	Hawker Beechcraft 1900D	UE-361	Futura Travels Ltd
☐ YV1106	Hawker Beechcraft 1900D	UE-241	Wings Aviation (Venezuela)
☐ YV1894	Hawker Beechcraft 1900D	UE-157	Toyota of Venezuela
☐ VT-XSD	Hindustan Aeronautics Saras	PT-1	National Aerospace Laboratories
☐ RA-91003	Ilyushin Il-114	2053800109	Russian Navy
☐ RA-75454	Ilyushin Il-18D	187010104	Rossiya Special Flight Detachment
☐ RA-75903	Ilyushin Il-18 (Il-22)	0393610235	Russian Air Force
☐ P-618	Ilyushin Il-62M	2546624	Air Koryo
☐ RA-86467	Ilyushin Il-62M	3749733	Rossiya Special Flight Detachment
☐ RA-86468	Ilyushin Il-62M	4749857	Rossiya Special Flight Detachment
☐ RA-86539	Ilyushin Il-62M	2344615	223rd State Airline Flight Unit
☐ RA-86540	Ilyushin Il-62M	3546548	Rossiya Special Flight Detachment
☐ RA-86555	Ilyushin Il-62M	4547315	223rd State Airline Flight Unit
☐ RA-86559	Ilyushin Il-62M	2153258	Rossiya Special Flight Detachment
☐ RA-86561	Ilyushin Il-62M	4154842	Rossiya Special Flight Detachment
☐ RA-86579	Ilyushin Il-62M	2951636	KAPO - Gorbunova
☐ RA-86583	Ilyushin Il-62M	1356851	Aviaenergo
☐ ST-PRA	Ilyushin Il-62M	2357711	Government of Sudan
☐ UR-86527	Ilyushin Il-62M	4037758	Ukraine Air Enterprise
☐ UR-86528	Ilyushin Il-62M	4038111	Ukraine Air Enterprise
☐ RA-96012	Ilyushin Il-96-300	74393201009	Rossiya Special Flight Detachment
☐ RA-96016	Ilyushin Il-96-300	74393202010	Rossiya Special Flight Detachment
☐ RA-96018	Ilyushin Il-96-300	74393202018	Rossiya Special Flight Detachment
☐ RA-96019	Ilyushin Il-96-300	74393202019	Rossiya Special Flight Detachment
☐ TJ-AAS	Israel Aerospace Industries Arava	081	Government of Cameroon
☐ 5501	Kawasaki Heavy Industries P-1	PROTO001	Japan Maritime SDF
☐ 5502	Kawasaki Heavy Industries P-1	PROTO002	Japan Maritime SDF
☐ 08-1201	Kawasaki Heavy Industries XC-2 (C-X)	001	Japan Air Self Defence Force
☐ N44KS	Saab 340A	050	JMJ Flight Services LLC
☐ N541BC	Saab 340A	029	IBC Airways

☐ N632RF	Saab 340A	042	Pegasus Air Limited
☐ N702RS	Saab 340B	233	SST Aero Services
☐ N703RS	Saab 340B	252	SST Aero Services
☐ N727DL	Saab 340A	036	Club SAAB 340
☐ N508RH	Saab 2000	027	Hendrick Motorsports LLC
☐ N509RH	Saab 2000	030	Hendrick Motorsports LLC
☐ N511RH	Saab 2000	020	Hendrick Motorsports LLC
☐ N519JG	Saab 2000	017	Joe Gibbs Racing Inc
☐ SE-045	Saab 2000AEW	045	Saab Aircraft AB
☐ 82911	Sukhoi SU-80GP	0102	Sukhoi Design Bureau
☐ 97003	Sukhoi Superjet 100-95LR	95003	Sukhoi Design Bureau
☐ 97004	Sukhoi Superjet 100-95LR	95004	Sukhoi Design Bureau
☐ 97005	Sukhoi Superjet 100-95LR	95005	Sukhoi Design Bureau
☐ 63957	Tupolev Tu-134A	63957	Ukrainian Air Force
☐ 65098	Tupolev Tu-134Sh	73550815	MIR Scientific Industrial Enterprise
☐ 65606	Tupolev Tu-134A	46300	Tupolev Design Bureau
☐ 65738	Tupolev Tu-134A	2351507	SIBNIA
☐ 03 RED	Tupolev Tu-134Sh	ZR105	Russian Air Force
☐ 100 BLUE	Tupolev Tu-134A	63780	Russian Navy
☐ 34 BLUE	Tupolev Tu-134Sh	83550970	Russian Air Force
☐ 4K-65496	Tupolev Tu-134A	63468	Azerbaijan Defence Ministry
☐ RA-63757	Tupolev Tu-134A	1363757	Russian Navy
☐ RA-63769	Tupolev Tu-134A	63769	SpetsTrans Servis
☐ RA-64454	Tupolev Tu-134A	66140	Gromov Flight Research Institute (LII)
☐ RA-65079	Tupolev Tu-134A	60054	Sirius Aero
☐ RA-65124	Tupolev Tu-134A	60560	Rusair
☐ RA-65127	Tupolev Tu-134A	60627	UTair Express
☐ RA-65132	Tupolev Tu-134A	60639	Yamal Airlines
☐ RA-65550	Tupolev Tu-134A	66200	Meridian Air
☐ RA-65557	Tupolev Tu-134A	66380	Kosmos Airlines
☐ RA-65559	Tupolev Tu-134A	49909	JetAlliance East
☐ RA-65570	Tupolev Tu-134A	66550	SE Airlines
☐ RA-65574	Tupolev Tu-134B	64748	Kosmos Airlines
☐ RA-65576	Tupolev Tu-134B	63285	Rusair
☐ RA-65604	Tupolev Tu-134A	62561	Sirius Aero
☐ RA-65608	Tupolev Tu-134A	38040	UTair Express
☐ RA-65692	Tupolev Tu-134B	63215	Center-South Airlines
☐ RA-65700	Tupolev Tu-134B	64783	Center-South Airlines
☐ RA-65719	Tupolev Tu-134A	63637	Kosmos Airlines
☐ RA-65721	Tupolev Tu-134A	66130	JetAlliance East
☐ RA-65722	Tupolev Tu-134A	66420	Sirius Aero
☐ RA-65723	Tupolev Tu-134A	66440	Jetair Group
☐ RA-65724	Tupolev Tu-134A	66445	Meridian Air
☐ RA-65727	Tupolev Tu-134B	64820	RusJet
☐ RA-65733	Tupolev Tu-134B	64425	223rd State Airline Flight Unit
☐ RA-65737	Tupolev Tu-134B	64195	RusJet
☐ RA-65747	Tupolev Tu-134B	64715	RusJet
☐ RA-65756	Tupolev Tu-134A	62179	Rusline
☐ RA-65790	Tupolev Tu-134A	63100	Rusair
☐ RA-65798	Tupolev Tu-134A	63179	Meridian Air
☐ RA-65805	Tupolev Tu-134B	64775	Kosmos Airlines
☐ RA-65830	Tupolev Tu-134A	12093	Unconfirmed Russian Operator
☐ RA-65903	Tupolev Tu-134A	63750	Rusline
☐ RA-65904	Tupolev Tu-134A	63953	Rossiya Special Flight Detachment
☐ RA-65905	Tupolev Tu-134A	63965	Rossiya Special Flight Detachment
☐ RA-65908	Tupolev Tu-134A	63870	Rusair
☐ RA-65911	Tupolev Tu-134A	63972	Rossiya Special Flight Detachment
☐ RA-65917	Tupolev Tu-134A	63991	Meridian Air
☐ RA-65921	Tupolev Tu-134A	63997	Rossiya Special Flight Detachment
☐ RA-65926	Tupolev Tu-134A	66101	Meridian Air
☐ RA-65927	Tupolev Tu-134A	66198	Russian Air Force
☐ RA-65930	Tupolev Tu-134A	66500	Jetair Group
☐ RA-65932	Tupolev Tu-134A	66405	Center-South Airlines
☐ RA-65934	Tupolev Tu-134A	66143	Rusline
☐ RA-65941	Tupolev Tu-134A	60642	Kosmos Airlines
☐ RA-65945	Tupolev Tu-134B	64010	Unconfirmed Russian Airline
☐ RA-65965	Tupolev Tu-134A	2351803	Russian Air Force
☐ RA-65978	Tupolev Tu-134A	63357	Sirius Aero
☐ RA-65979	Tupolev Tu-134A	63158	Russian Air Force
☐ RA-65984	Tupolev Tu-134A	63400	Russian Air Force
☐ RA-65995	Tupolev Tu-134A	66400	Rossiya Special Flight Detachment
☐ RA-65996	Tupolev Tu-134A	63825	236th State Airline Flight Unit
☐ UN-65683	Tupolev Tu-134A	62199	Kazakhstan Ministry of Defence

☐ UP-T3402	Tupolev Tu-134B	63187	Kazair West
☐ UP-T3409	Tupolev Tu-134B	62820	Euro-Asia Air
☐ UR-65556	Tupolev Tu-134A	66372	Ukraine Air Enterprise
☐ UR-65718	Tupolev Tu-134A	63668	Ukraine Air Enterprise
☐ YK-AYA	Tupolev Tu-134B	63992	Syrianair
☐ YK-AYB	Tupolev Tu-134B	63994	Syrianair
☐ 102	Tupolev Tu-154M	862	Polish Air Force
☐ 4K-85729	Tupolev Tu-154M	911	Government of Azerbaijan
☐ B-4028	Tupolev Tu-154M	967	People's Liberation Army Air Force
☐ B-4138	Tupolev Tu-154M	712	People's Liberation Army Air Force
☐ EW-85815	Tupolev Tu-154M	1010	Government of Belarus
☐ OM-BYR	Tupolev Tu-154M	1012	Slovakian Government Flying Service
☐ RA-85001	Tupolev Tu-154M	820	Rossiya Special Flight Detachment
☐ RA-85019	Tupolev Tu-154M	1019	Federal Security Service
☐ RA-85084	Tupolev Tu-154M	1004	Federal Security Service
☐ RA-85155	Tupolev Tu-154M	1000	Russian Air Force
☐ RA-85360	Tupolev Tu-154B	360	Russian Air Force
☐ RA-85510	Tupolev Tu-154B	510	Russian Air Force
☐ RA-85565	Tupolev Tu-154B	565	Russian Ministry of the Interior
☐ RA-85614	Tupolev Tu-154M	723	Russian Navy
☐ RA-85686	Tupolev Tu-154M	854	Rossiya Special Flight Detachment
☐ RA-85712	Tupolev Tu-154M	888	Aero Rent
☐ RA-85740	Tupolev Tu-154M	895	Moskva Air Company
☐ UN-85464	Tupolev Tu-154B	464	Government of Kazakhstan
☐ RA-64010	Tupolev Tu-204-300 (Tu-234)	1450743164010	Biznes Aero
☐ RA-64150	Tupolev Tu-204-100SM	145074##64150	Aviastar-SP
☐ RA-64517	Tupolev Tu-204-214	41709017	Rossiya Special Flight Detachment
☐ 94005	Tupolev Tu-334-100	01005	Tupolev Design Bureau
☐ RA-94001	Tupolev Tu-334-100	01001	Tupolev Design Bureau
☐ D-ADAM	VFW614	G17	DLR Flugbetriebe
☐ SP-DDF	WSK-PZL Mielec M28 Skytruck (P&W)	1ANJP10-03	WSK-PZL MIELEC
☐ B-3489	Xian Y-7-100	07708	Peoples Republic of China Navy
☐ B-3493	Xian Y-7-100	08704	Peoples Republic of China Navy
☐ 4L-EUN	Yakovlev Yak-40	9530541	Georgian International Airlines
☐ 5A-DKK	Yakovlev Yak-40	9420235	Air Libya
☐ EW-88187	Yakovlev Yak-40	9620748	Government of Belarus
☐ OM-BYE	Yakovlev Yak-40	9440338	Slovakian Government Flying Service
☐ OM-BYL	Yakovlev Yak-40	9940560	Slovakian Government Flying Service
☐ RA-21500	Yakovlev Yak-40K	9741356	Rosneft Baltika
☐ RA-21504	Yakovlev Yak-40K	9831758	Jetair Group
☐ RA-21506	Yakovlev Yak-40K	9840259	Unconfirmed Russian Operator
☐ RA-87203	Yakovlev Yak-40	9741456	Rossiya Special Flight Detachment
☐ RA-87216	Yakovlev Yak-40	9510440	Jet 2000
☐ RA-87224	Yakovlev Yak-40K	9841459	Severstal Aircompany
☐ RA-87226	Yakovlev Yak-40K	9841259	Tulpar Air
☐ RA-87227	Yakovlev Yak-40K	9841559	UTair
☐ RA-87244	Yakovlev Yak-40	9531243	Rosneft Baltika
☐ RA-87253	Yakovlev Yak-40	9321026	Sverdlovsk 2nd Aviation Enterprise
☐ RA-87280	Yakovlev Yak-40	9322025	Barkol Aviakompania
☐ RA-87286	Yakovlev Yak-40	9310128	Vladikavkaz Air Enterprise
☐ RA-87342	Yakovlev Yak-40	9511139	AK Bars Aero
☐ RA-87353	Yakovlev Yak-40	9330231	Lukoil Avia
☐ RA-87397	Yakovlev Yak-40	9410933	Aerobratsk
☐ RA-87429	Yakovlev Yak-40	9420535	Rusline
☐ RA-87447	Yakovlev Yak-40	9430436	AK Bars Aero
☐ RA-87496	Yakovlev Yak-40	9541945	Aerolimousine
☐ RA-87499	Yakovlev Yak-40	9610246	Saratov Aviation Plant
☐ RA-87503	Yakovlev Yak-40	9520240	Sverdlovsk 2nd Aviation Enterprise
☐ RA-87517	Yakovlev Yak-40	9521940	AK Bars Aero
☐ RA-87524	Yakovlev Yak-40	9520641	Sverdlovsk 2nd Aviation Enterprise
☐ RA-87535	Yakovlev Yak-40	9521941	Jet Express
☐ RA-87569	Yakovlev Yak-40D	9220222	Alliance Avia
☐ RA-87655	Yakovlev Yak-40	9211820	Center-South Airlines
☐ RA-87669	Yakovlev Yak-40	9021760	Unconfirmed Russian Operator
☐ RA-87807	Yakovlev Yak-40D	9231723	Estar Avia
☐ RA-87828	Yakovlev Yak-40	9242024	Bylina
☐ RA-87900	Yakovlev Yak-40K	9720254	KrasAvia
☐ RA-87908	Yakovlev Yak-40	9721354	Aerolimousine
☐ RA-87938	Yakovlev Yak-40K	9710153	Amur Regional Government
☐ RA-87953	Yakovlev Yak-40K	9811157	AIST M Airclub

☐ RA-87966	Yakovlev Yak-40	9820958	Center-South Airlines
☐ RA-87968	Yakovlev Yak-40	9841258	Rossiya Special Flight Detachment
☐ RA-87969	Yakovlev Yak-40	9831358	Rossiya Special Flight Detachment
☐ RA-87971	Yakovlev Yak-40	9831558	Rossiya Special Flight Detachment
☐ RA-87977	Yakovlev Yak-40	9321128	Tulpar Air
☐ RA-87983	Yakovlev Yak-40	9540644	AIST M Airclub
☐ RA-88227	Yakovlev Yak-40K	9641550	Khanty-Mansi Autonomous District
☐ RA-88240	Yakovlev Yak-40	9641151	RusJet
☐ RA-88293	Yakovlev Yak-40	9510138	TGK-9 - Territorial Generating Company No 9
☐ RA-88294	Yakovlev Yak-40	9331029	Unconfirmed Russian Operator
☐ RA-88295	Yakovlev Yak-40	9331329	Yak Service
☐ RA-88296	Yakovlev Yak-40	9421634	Severstal Aircompany
☐ RA-88297	Yakovlev Yak-40	9530142	Lukoil Avia
☐ RA-88298	Yakovlev Yak-40K	9930160	Vostotsnaya Neftyanaya Kompaniya
☐ RA-88306	Yakovlev Yak-40K	9640651	Aviakompaniya SKOL
☐ RA-88308	Yakovlev Yak-40	9230224	Yak Service
☐ RF-88301	Yakovlev Yak-40K	9641251	Russian Ministry of the Interior
☐ UN-87213	Yakovlev Yak-40K	9641050	Unconfirmed Kazakhstan Operator
☐ UN-87488	Yakovlev Yak-40	9441638	Government of Kazakhstan
☐ UN-87533	Yakovlev Yak-40	9541741	Unconfirmed Kazakhstan Operator
☐ UN-87816	Yakovlev Yak-40	9230724	Government of Kazakhstan
☐ UN-87850	Yakovlev Yak-40	9441738	Kazakhstan Border Guards
☐ UP-Y4015	Yakovlev Yak-40	9530842	TOO Gamma
☐ UP-Y4025	Yakovlev Yak-40K	9831958	Kazair West
☐ UR-87215	Yakovlev Yak-40	9510540	Motor Sich Aviakompania
☐ UR-87964	Yakovlev Yak-40	9820758	Ukraine Air Enterprise
☐ UR-88310	Yakovlev Yak-40	9940760	Challenge Aero
☐ UR-BWF	Yakovlev Yak-40	9711352	Privatbank
☐ UR-CAR	Yakovlev Yak-40K	9741756	ISD Avia
☐ UR-CDW	Yakovlev Yak-40	9610546	ACR Aero Charter
☐ UR-CLH	Yakovlev Yak-40	9530642	Challenge Aero
☐ UR-DAP	Yakovlev Yak-40	9521241	ACR Aero Charter
☐ UR-DWC	Yakovlev Yak-40	9541144	ACR Aero Charter
☐ UR-ECL	Yakovlev Yak-40K	9932059	Challenge Aero
☐ UR-ETG	Yakovlev Yak-40	9531143	Constanta Airlines
☐ UR-FRU	Yakovlev Yak-40	9440737	Constanta Airlines
☐ UR-LRZ	Yakovlev Yak-40K	9641851	ACR Aero Charter
☐ UR-PVS	Yakovlev Yak-40	9331430	Mostobud
☐ UR-UAS	Yakovlev Yak-40	9420835	ACR Aero Charter
☐ YK-AQB	Yakovlev Yak-40	9530443	Government of Syria
☐ YV-1070CP	Yakovlev Yak-40	9412032	CAICA
☐ YV161T	Yakovlev Yak-40	9441137	ASAP Charters CA
☐ B-4012	Yakovlev Yak-42D	4520424914375	Peoples Republic of China Navy
☐ B-4013	Yakovlev Yak-42D	45204249144##	Peoples Republic of China Navy
☐ EK-42470	Yakovlev Yak-42D	4520424116677	Armavia
☐ RA-42330	Yakovlev Yak-42D	4520422505122	Tulpar Air
☐ RA-42344	Yakovlev Yak-42D	4520422708295	Rusair
☐ RA-42365	Yakovlev Yak-42D	4520424811447	JetAlliance East
☐ RA-42368	Yakovlev Yak-42D	4520422914166	Rusair
☐ RA-42402	Yakovlev Yak-42D	4520422116583	Rusair
☐ RA-42411	Yakovlev Yak-42D	4520421219043	RusJet
☐ RA-42412	Yakovlev Yak-42D	4520422219055	United Aircraft Corporation
☐ RA-42415	Yakovlev Yak-42D	4520422219089	RusJet
☐ RA-42423	Yakovlev Yak-42D	4520424216606	RusJet
☐ RA-42424	Yakovlev Yak-42D-100 (Yak-142)	4520421502016	Lukoil Avia
☐ RA-42427	Yakovlev Yak-42D	4520422305016	JetAlliance East
☐ RA-42438	Yakovlev Yak-42D	4520423609018	Gazpromavia
☐ RA-42440	Yakovlev Yak-42D	4520424210018	Tulpar Air
☐ RA-42441	Yakovlev Yak-42D	4520421402018	MChS Rossii - Emercom
☐ RA-42442	Yakovlev Yak-42D	4520421402019	Gazpromavia
☐ RA-42445	Yakovlev Yak-42D	4520424116669	Tulpar Air
☐ RA-42451	Yakovlev Yak-42D	4520422708018	Gazpromavia
☐ UP-42721	Yakovlev Yak-42D	4520423310017	Kazakhstan Air Force
☐ UP-Y4201	Yakovlev Yak-42D	4520423302017	Fly Jet Kz
☐ UP-Y4202	Yakovlev Yak-42D	4520423402116	Avia Jaynar

IATA TWO-LETTER DESIGNATORS

0B	Blue Air	YR		4Y	Flight Alaska	N
0D	Darwin Airline	HB		4Z	Airlink	ZS
0V	Vasco	VN				
				5A	Alpine Air Express	N
1I	Novair	SE		5B	Euro Asia Intl	UP
1I	Pegasus Airlines	TC		5C	Air Tahoma	N
1T	1Time Airline	ZS		5C	Natureair	TI
				5C	Cargo Air Lines	4X
2B	Bahrain Air	A9C		5D	Aeromexico Connect	XA
2D	Alania Airline	RA		5E	SGA Airlines	HS
2E	AVE.com	A6		5F	Arctic Circle Air Service	N
2E	Smokey Bay Air	N		5F	Best Air	TC
2F	Payim Intl Air	EP		5H	Fly540	5Y
2F	Frontier Flying Service	N		5I	Transavia Service	4L
2G	Cargoitalia	I		5J	Cebu Pacific Air	RP
2G	Northwest Seaplanes	N		5K	Hi Fly	CS
2G	San Juan Airlines	N		5K	Odessa Airlines	UR
2I	Star peru	OB		5L	Aerosur	CP
2J	Air Burkina	XT		5M	National Airlines	N
2K	Aerogal	HC		5M	Sibaviatrans	RA
2L	Helvetic Airways	HB		5N	Arkhangelsk 2nd Aviation Enterprise	RA
2M	Moldavian Airlines	ER		5N	Nordavia Regional Airlines	RA
2N	NAS Air	HZ		5O	Europe Airpost	F
2N	Nextjet	SE		5P	PENTA - Pena Transportes Aereos	PP
2N	Yuzmashavia	UR		5Q	Best Air	S2
2O	Island Air Service	N		5R	Custom Air Transport	N
2P	Puerto Rico Air Management Services	N		5R	Karthago Airlines	TS
2P	AirPhil Express	RP		5S	Sapair	HI
2Q	Air Cargo Carriers	N		5T	Canadian North	C
2Q	Avitrans Nordic	SE		5U	LADE	LV
2R	Sud D'Or Intl Airlines	4X		5U	Challenge Aero	UR
2T	Tulpar Air Service	UP		5V	Lviv Airlines	UR
2U	Air Guinee Express	3X		5W	Astraeus	G
2W	Welcome Air	OE		5X	UPS Airlines	N
				5Y	Isles of Scilly Skybus	G
30	Peau Vava'u Air	A3		5Y	Atlas Air	N
3B	Central Connect Airlines	OK		5Z	Bismillah Airlines	S2
3F	Pacific Airways	N				
3G	Moskva Air Company	RA		6B	Tuifly Nordic	SE
3H	Air Inuit	C		6D	Pelita Air	PK
3K	Everts Air Cargo	N		6E	Indigo Airlines	VT
3K	Jetstar Asia Airways	9V		6F	Ufly Airways	N
3L	Intersky	OE		6F	Afrijet Airlines	5N
3M	Gulfstream Intl	N		6H	Israir	4X
3N	Air Urga	UR		6I	Aviast Air	RA
3O	Air Arabia Maroc	CN		6I	Euroair	SX
3P	Tiara Air	P4		6J	Skynet Asia Airways	JA
3R	Moskoviya	RA		6J	Jubba Airways	6O
3S	Air Antilles Express	F		6K	Zest Airways	RP
3S	Air Guyane Express	F		6M	Air Minas	PP
3S	Aeroland Airways	SX		6N	Aerosucre	HK
3T	Turanair	4K		6O	Air Satellite	C
3U	Sichuan Airlines	B		6R	Alrosa Aviation	RA
3V	TNT Airways	OO		6R	Aerounion	XA
3X	Japan Air Commuter	JA		6S	Star Air Intl	AP
3Y	Kartika Airlines	PK		6T	Air Mandalay	XY
3Z	Everts Air Alaska	N		6U	Air Cargo Germany	D
3Z	Zoom Airways	S2		6V	MRK Airlines	UR
				6W	Saratov Airlines	RA
4A	Air Kiribati	T3		6Y	Smartlynx	YL
4B	Perimeter Aviation	C		6Z	Panavia Cargo Airlines	HP
4B	Aviastar - Tupolev	RA		6Z	Van Air Europe	OK
4C	Click Airways	EX		6Z	Ukrainian Cargo Airways	UR
4C	Aires	HK				
4C	Tapo-Avia	UK		7A	Air Next	JA
4D	Air Sinai	SU		7C	Jeju Air	HL
4E	Tanana Air Service	N		7D	Donbassaero	UR
4G	Gazpromavia	RA		7E	Aeroline	D
4H	United Airways	S2		7E	Evergreen Helicopters	N
4I	Izmir Airlines	TC		7E	Firefly	9M
4K	Kenn Borek Air	C		7F	First Air	C
4M	LAN Argentina	LV		7G	Starflyer	JA
4N	Air North	C		7H	Era Aviation	N
4O	Interjet	XA		7H	Corendon Air	TC
4P	Business Aviation of Congo	9Q		7I	Insel Air Intl	PJ
4T	Belair Airlines	HB		7I	Coastal Aviation	5H
4U	Germanwings	D		7J	Tajik Air	EY
4U	Tavaj Linhas Aereas	PP		7K	Kolavia	RA
4W	Warbelow's Air	N		7L	Aerocaribbean	CU
4Y	Airbus Transport Intl	F		7M	Air Atlantique	G

7N	Inland Aviation Services	N		AS	Alaska Airlines	N
7P	Batavia Air	PK		AT	Royal Air Maroc	CN
7Q	Pan Am Dominica	HI		AU	Austral Lineas Aereas	LV
7Q	Air Libya	5A		AV	Avianca	HK
7S	Arctic Transportation Services	N		AW	CHC Airways	PH
7T	Air Glaciers	HB		AW	Dirgantara Air Service	PK
7T	Trans Am	HC		AX	American Connection	N
7T	Wind Rose	UR		AY	Finnair	OH
7T	Tobruk Air	5A		AZ	Alitalia	I
7U	Aviaenergo	RA				
7V	Pelican Air Services	ZS		B2	Belavia Belarussian Airlines	EW
7Y	Flying Carpet Air Transport Services	OD		B3	Bellview Airlines	5N
7Y	Mid Airlines	ST		B4	Bankair	N
				B4	Zanair	5H
8A	Atlas Blue	CN		B5	East African Express	5Y
8A	Arrow Panama	HP		B6	Jetblue Airways	N
8C	ATI - Air Transport Intl	N		B7	Uni Air	B
8D	Interavia Airlines	RA		B8	Botir-Avia	EX
8D	Expo Air	4R		B8	Eritrean Airlines	E3
8E	Bering Air	N		B9	Iran Air Tour Airline	EP
8J	Jet4You	CN		BA	British Airways	G
8K	K-Mile Air	HS		BB	Seaborne Airlines	N
8L	Lucky Airlines	B		BC	Skymark Airlines	JA
8M	Myanmar Airways Intl	XY		BD	BMI	G
8N	Barents Skylink	SE		BD	BMI Regional	G
8O	West Coast Air	C		BD	Servant Air	N
8P	Pacific Coastal Airlines	C		BE	FlyBe	G
8Q	Baker Aviation	N		BF	Bluebird Cargo	TF
8Q	Onur Air	TC		BF	Aeroservice	TN
8R	SOL Lineas Aereas	LV		BF	Vincent Aviation (Australia)	VH
8R	Trip Linhas Aereas	PP		BG	Biman Bangladesh Airlines	S2
8T	Air Tindi	C		BH	Hawkair Aviation Service	C
8U	Afriqiyah Airways	5A		BI	Royal Brunei Airlines	V8
8V	Wright Air Service	N		BJ	Nouvelair	TS
8V	Astral Aviation	5Y		BK	OK Airways	B
8W	Private Wings	D		BL	Jetstar Pacific Airlines	VN
8Y	China Postal Airlines	B		BP	Air Botswana	A2
8Y	Air Burundi	9U		BR	EVA Airways	B
8Z	Wizz Air Bulgaria	LZ		BS	British Intl	G
				BT	Air Baltic	YL
9D	Toumai Air Chad	TT		BV	Blu Express.com	I
9H	Dutch Antilles Express	PJ		BV	Blue Panorama Airlines	I
9K	Cape Air	N		BW	Caribbean Airlines	9Y
9L	Colgan Air	N		BX	Air Busan	HL
9M	Central Mountain Air	C		BY	Thomsonfly.com	G
9N	Satena	HK		BZ	Keystone Air Service	C
9N	JP Express	JA		BZ	Blue Dart Aviation	VT
9O	Inter - transportes Aereos Inter	TG				
9O	National Airways Cameroon	TJ		C4	Zimex Aviation	HB
9S	Spring Airlines	B		C6	Canjet	C
9S	Southern Air	N		C7	Rico Linhas Aereas	PP
9T	Transwest Air	C		C7	Samarkand Airways	UK
9T	ACT Airlines	TC		C8	Cargolux Italia	I
9U	Air Moldova	ER		C9	Cirrus Airlines	D
9V	Avior Airlines	YV		CA	Air China	B
9W	Jet Airways	VT		CA	Air China Cargo	B
9X	Itali Airlines	I		CB	Scotairways	G
				CC	Air Atlanta	TF
A2	Cielos Airlines	OB		CD	Alliance Air	VT
A2	Astra Airlines	SX		CF	City Airline	SE
A3	Aegean Airlines	SX		CG	Airlines of Papua New Guinea	P2
A5	Airlinair	F		CH	Bemidji Airlines	N
A6	Air Alps Aviation	OE		CI	China Airlines	B
A8	Benin Golf Air	TY		CJ	BA Cityflyer	G
A9	Airzena - Georgian Airlines	4L		CK	China Cargo Airlines	B
AA	American Airlines	N		CL	Lufthansa Cityline	D
AB	AirBerlin	D		CM	Copa Airlines	HP
AC	Air Canada	C		CN	Grand China Airlines	B
AE	Mandarin Airlines	B		CN	Islands Nationair	P2
AF	Air France	F		CO	Expressjet Airlines	N
AG	Air Contractors	EI		CU	Cubana de Aviacion	CU
AH	Air Algerie	7T		CV	Cargolux Airlines Intl	LX
AI	Air India	VT		CV	Air Chathams	ZK
AI	Air India Express	VT		CW	Airline of the Marshall Islands	V7
AJ	Aero Contactors	5N		CX	Cathay Pacific Airways	B
AK	Airasia	9M		CY	Cyprus Airways	5B
AL	Trans Avia Export Cargo Airlines	EW		CZ	China Southern Airlines	B
AL	Alsair	F				
AI	Midwest Connect	N		D0	DHL Air	G
AM	Aeromexico	XA		D2	Severstal Aircompany	RA
AO	Avianova	RA		D3	Daalo Airlines	J2
AR	Aerolineas Argentinas	LV		D4	Alidaunia	I

Code	Airline		Code	Airline	
D5	DHL Aero Expresso	HP	G4	Allegiant Air	N
D6	Inter-Air	ZS	G5	China Express Airlines	B
D9	Donavia	RA	G5	Island Air	VP-C
DB	Brit'Air	F	G8	Go Air	VT
DC	Golden Air	SE	G9	Air Arabia	A6
DD	Nok Air	HS	GA	Garuda Indonesia	PK
DE	Condor	D	GB	ABX Air	N
DG	South East Asian Airlines	RP	GD	Granstar Cargo Airlines	B
DJ	Virgin Blue Airlines	VH	GD	Air Alpha Greenland	OY
DJ	Pacific Blue	ZK	GE	Transasia Airways	B
DK	Thomas Cook Scandinavia	OY	GF	Gulf Air	A9C
DL	Delta Airlines	N	GI	Itek Air	EX
DL	Delta Connection	N	GL	Air Greenland	OY
DO	Air Vallée	I	GR	Aurigny Air Services	G
DQ	Coastal Air Transport	N	GS	Tianjin Airlines	B
DS	Easyjet Switzerland	HB	GV	XL Airways Germany	D
DT	TAAG Angola Airlines	D2	GV	Grant Aviation	N
DU	Hemus Air	LZ	GW	Kuban Airlines	RA
DV	Scat Aircompany	UP	GX	Pacificair	RP
DW	Aero-Charter Ukraine	UR	GY	Tri-MG Intra-Asia Airlines	PK
DX	Danish Air Transport	OY	GY	Gabon Airlines	TR
DY	Norwegian	LN	GZ	Air Rarotonga	E5
E3	Eagle Airlines	I	H2	Sky Airline	CC
E3	Domodedovo Airlines	RA	H3	Harbour Air Seaplanes	C
E5	Samara Airlines	RA	H6	Hageland Aviation Services	N
E7	Estafeta Carga Aerea	XA	H7	Eagle Air	5X
E9	Boston-Maine Airways	N	H8	Dalavia	RA
EC	Avialeasing	UK	HA	Hawaiian Airlines	N
ED	AirBlue	AP	HD	Air Do	JA
EF	Strategic Airlines	VH	HE	LGW - Luftfahrtgesellschaft Walter	D
EH	Air Nippon Network	JA	HG	Niki	OE
EI	Aer Lingus	EI	HI	Papillon Grand Canyon Airways	N
EJ	New England Airlines	N	HJ	Hellas jet	SX
EK	Emirates	A6	HJ	Tasman Cargo Airlines	VH
EL	Air Nippon	JA	HK	Four Star Air Cargo	N
EM	Aero Benin	TY	HK	Yangon Airlines	XY
EN	Air Dolomiti	I	HM	Air Seychelles	S7
EO	Hewa Bora Airways	9Q	HN	Heavylift Cargo Airlines	VH
EP	Iran Aseman Airlines	EP	HO	Juneyao Airlines	B
EQ	TAME	HC	HS	Direktflyg	SE
ER	Astar Air Cargo	N	HT	Aeromost Kharkov	UR
ES	DHL Intl Aviation	A9C	HU	Chang An Airlines	B
ET	Ethiopian Airlines	ET	HU	China Xinhua Airlines	B
EU	Chengdu Airlines	B	HU	Hainan Airlines	B
EW	Eurowings	D	HV	Transavia Airlines	PH
EX	Air Santo Domingo	HI	HW	North Wright Airways	C
EY	Etihad Airways	A6	HW	Hello	HB
EZ	Evergreen Intl Airlines	N	HX	Hong Kong Airlines	B
EZ	Sun-Air of Scandinavia	OY	HX	Trans North Aviation	N
			HY	Uzbekistan Airways	UK
F3	Sky King	N	HZ	SAT Airlines	RA
F4	Shanghai Cargo	B			
F5	Cosmic Air	9N	I6	Sky Eyes Aviation	HS
F7	Baboo	HB	I9	Air Italy	I
F9	Frontier Airlines	N	IA	Iraqi Airways	YI
FA	Safair	ZS	IB	Iberia	EC
FB	Bulgaria Air	LZ	ID	Interlink Airlines	ZS
FC	Falcon Express Cargo Airlines	A6	IE	Solomons	H4
FC	Finncomm Airlines	OH	IF	Islas Airways	EC
FD	Thai Airasia	HS	IG	Meridiana Fly	I
FG	Ariana Afghan Airlines	YA	II	IBC Airways	N
FI	Icelandair	TF	IJ	Great Wall Airlines	B
FJ	Air Pacific	DQ	IK	Imair	4K
FK	Keewatin Air	C	IN	MAT Macedonian Air Transport	Z3
FK	Kivalliq Air	C	IP	Atyrau Air Ways	UP
FL	Airtran Airways	N	IQ	Augsburg Airways	D
FM	Shanghai Airlines	B	IR	Iran Air	EP
FN	Regional Air Lines	CN	IS	Island Airlines	N
FO	Airlines of Tasmania	VH	IT	Kingfisher Airlines	VT
FP	Freedom Air	N	IT	Kingfisher Red	VT
FQ	Thomas Cook Airlines Belgium	OO	IU	Hevi-Lift	P2
FQ	Brindabella Airlines	VH	IV	Windjet	I
FR	Ryanair	EI	IW	Wings Air	PK
FV	Rossiya Russian Airlines	RA	IY	Yemenia	7O
FW	Ibex Airlines	JA	IZ	Arkia Israeli Airlines	4X
FX	Federal Express	N			
FZ	FlyDubai	A6	J0	Jetlink Express	5Y
			J2	Azerbaijan Airlines	4K
G1	Gorkha Airlines	9N	J3	Northwestern Air	C
G2	Avirex	TR	J4	Buffalo Airways	C
G3	Gol Transportes Aereos	PP	J4	Jordan Intl Air Cargo	JY
G3	Sky Express	SX	J5	Donghai Airlines	B

J5	Alaska Seaplane Service	N		LX	Swiss Intl Airlines	HB
J6	Cruiser Taxi Aero Brasil	PP		LY	El Al Israel Airlines	4X
J7	Centre-Avia Airlines	RA		LZ	Belle Air	ZA
J8	Berjaya Air Charter	9M				
J9	Jazeera Airways	9K		M3	North Flying	OY
JA	BH Airlines	E9		M3	ABSA Cargo	PP
JB	HeliJet Intl	C		M4	Nova Air	XA
JC	JAL Express	JA		M5	Kenmore Air	N
JD	Capital Airlines	B		M6	Amerijet Intl	N
JE	Mango	ZS		M7	Marsland Aviation	ST
JF	LAB Flying Service	N		M7	Superior Aviation Services	5Y
JH	Fuji Dream Airlines	JA		M9	Motor Sich Airlines	UR
JI	Jade Cargo Intl	B		MA	Malev	HA
JI	Eastern Caribbean Air	N		MB	MNG Cargo Airlines	TC
JJ	TAM Linhas Aereas	PP		ME	Middle East Airlines	OD
JK	Spanair	EC		MF	Xiamen Airlines	B
JL	J-Air	JA		MG	Midex Airlines	A6
JL	Japan Airlines	JA		MH	Malaysia Airlines	9M
JM	Air Jamaica	6Y		MI	Silkair	9V
JP	Adria Airways	S5		MJ	Mihin Lanka	4R
JQ	Jetstar Airways	VH		MK	Air Mauritius	3B
JS	Air Koryo	P		ML	Trans Attico	ST
JT	Lion Airlines	PK		MM	Euro Atlantic Airways	CS
JU	JAT Airways	YU		MM	SAM Colombia	HK
JV	Bearskin Airlines	C		MN	Comair	ZS
JY	Air Turks & Caicos	VQ-T		MO	Calm Air	C
JZ	Skyways Express	SE		MP	Martinair	PH
				MQ	American Eagle	N
K2	EuroLot	SP		MS	Egyptair	SU
K3	Taquan Air Service	N		MT	Thomas Cook Airlines	G
K4	Kalitta Air	N		MU	China Eastern Airlines	B
K5	Wings of Alaska	N		MW	Maya Island Air	V3
K6	Cambodia Angkor Air	XU		MX	Manx2 Airlines	G
K7	Yakutia Airlines	RA		MY	Midwest Airlines Egypt	SU
KA	Dragonair	B		MY	MAS Air Cargo	XA
KB	Druk Air	A5		MZ	Merpati Nusantara Airlines	PK
KC	Air Astana	UP				
KE	Korean Air	HL		N2	Daghestan Airlines	RA
KF	Blue1	OH		N2	Kabo Air	5N
KG	Aerogaviota	CU		N4	Trans Air Benin	TY
KG	Linea Aerea Iaaca	YV		N5	Skagway Air Service	N
KK	Atlasjet Intl	TC		N6	Air One Nine	5A
KL	KLM Royal Dutch Airlines	PH		N9	Nordic Solutions Air Services	LY
KM	Air Malta	9H		N9	North Coast Aviation	P2
KN	China United Airlines	B		NA	North American Airlines	N
KN	Maroomba Airlines	VH		NC	Northern Air Cargo	N
KO	Alaska Central Express	N		NC	Cobham Aviation Services Australia	VH
KQ	Kenya Airways	5Y		NF	Air Vanuatu	YJ
KR	Comores Aviation	D6		NH	ANA - All Nippon Network	JA
KR	Kitty Hawk Aircargo	N		NI	Portugalia Airlines	CS
KS	Penair	N		NK	Spirit Airlines	N
KU	Kuwait Airways	9K		NL	Sheheen Air Intl	AP
KV	KMV Mineralnye Vody Airlines	RA		NN	Vim Airlines	RA
KW	Kelowna Flightcraft Air Charter	C		NO	Neos	I
KX	Cayman Airways	VP-C		NP	Skytrans Regional	VH
KY	Kunming Airlines	B		NQ	Air Japan	JA
KZ	Nippon Cargo Airlines	JA		NR	Pamir Air	YA
				NS	Hebei Airlines	B
L2	Lynden Air Cargo	N		NT	Binter Canarias	EC
L3	DHL de Guatemala	TG		NU	Japan Transocean Air	JA
L5	CHC Helikopter Service	LN		NV	Air Central	JA
L5	Lufttransport	LN		NX	Air Macau	B
L6	Tbilaviamsheni	4L		NY	Air Iceland	TF
LA	LAN Airlines	CC		NZ	Air New Zealand	ZK
LB	LAB Airlines	CP		NZ	Air New Zealand Link	ZK
LB	Lobaye Airways	TL				
LC	Varig Log	PP		O2	Jet Air	SP
LD	Air Hong Kong	B		O3	Bellview Airlines	9L
LD	Linea Turistica Aereotuy	YV		O4	Antrak Air Ghana	9G
LG	Luxair	LX		OA	Olympic Airways	SX
LH	Lufthansa	D		OB	Boliviana de Aviacion	CP
LH	Lufthansa Cargo	D		OC	Omni - Aviacao e Tecnoligia	CS
LI	LIAT - The Caribbean Airline	V2		OF	Air Finland	OH
LJ	Jin Air	HL		OG	One-Two Go	HS
LL	Miami Air Intl	N		OG	Ghadames Air Transport	5A
LN	Libyan Airlines	5A		OI	Aspiring Air	ZK
LO	LOT - Polish Airlines	SP		OJ	Overland Airways	5N
LP	LAN Peru	OB		OK	CSA Czech Airlines	OK
LS	Jet2	G		OL	OLT - Ostfriesische Lufttransport	D
LU	LAN Express	CC		OM	MIAT - Mongolian Airlines	JU
LV	Albanian Airlines	ZA		ON	Our Airline	C2
LW	Pacific Wings	N		OO	Skywest Airlines	N

OQ	Chongqing Airlines	B		R8	Kyrghyzstan Airlines	EX
OR	Arkefly	PH		RA	Nepal Airlines	9N
OS	Austrian Airlines	OE		RB	Syrianair	YK
OT	Aeropelican Air Services	VH		RC	Atlantic Airways	OY
OU	Croatia Airlines	9A		RD	Ryan Intl Airlines	N
OV	Estonian Air	ES		RE	Aer Arann	EI
OV	Estonian Air Regional	ES		RF	Florida West Intl Airlines	N
OX	Orient Thai Airlines	HS		RG	Varig	PP
OY	Omni Air Intl	N		RH	Robin Hood Aviation	OE
OZ	Asiana Airlines	HL		RH	RPX Airlines	PK
				RI	Mandala Airlines	PK
P2	Airkenya	5Y		RJ	Royal Jordanian	JY
P4	Aerolineas Sosa	HR		RK	Royal Khmer Airlines	XU
P5	Aerorepublica Colombia	HK		RL	Royal Phnom Penh Airways	XU
P6	Transair	N		RO	Tarom	YR
P7	Russian Sky Airlines	RA		RQ	Kam Air	YA
P8	Pantanal	PP		RT	Rak Airlines	A6
P9	Perm Airlines	RA		RU	Airbridge Cargo	RA
PA	Florida Coastal Airlines	N		RU	Skyking Airlines	VQ-T
PB	Provincial Airlines	C		RV	Caspian Airlines	EP
PC	Air Fiji	DQ		RX	Regent Airways	S2
PC	Continental Airways	RA		RY	Royal Wings Airlines	JY
PD	Porter Airlines	C		RZ	Sansa Regional	TI
PF	Primera Air Scandinavia	OY				
PG	Bangkok Airways	HS		S0	Slok Air Intl	C5
PH	Transavia Denmark	OY		S2	Jetlite	VT
PH	Polynesian Airlines	5W		S3	Santa Barbara Airlines	YV
PI	Pacific Sun	DQ		S4	SATA Internacional	CS
PI	Pacificflyer	T8A		S5	Trast Aero	EX
PJ	Air St Pierre	F		S5	Shuttle America	N
PK	Pakistan Intl Airlines	AP		S6	Salmon Air	N
PL	Southern Air Charter	C6		S6	Star Air	OY
PL	Airstars Airways	RA		S7	S7 Airlines	RA
PM	Tropic Air Commuter	V3		S8	Shovkovly Shlyah	UR
PN	West Air	B		SA	South African Airways	ZS
PO	Polar Air Cargo	N		SB	Aircalin	F
PR	Philippine Airlines	RP		SC	Shandong Airlines	B
PS	Ukraine Intl Airlines	UR		SD	Sudan Airways	ST
PT	Capital Cargo Intl Airlines	N		SE	XL Airways France	F
PT	West Air Europe	SE		SF	Tassili Airlines	7T
PU	Pluna Lineas Aereas Uruguayas	CX		SG	Spicejet	VT
PV	Panair Lineas Aereas	EC		SI	Sierra Pacific Airlines	N
PV	St Barth Commuter	F		SJ	Sriwijaya Air	PK
PW	Precisionair	5H		SK	Scandinavian Airline System	SE
PX	Air Niugini	P2		SO	Superior Aviation	N
PY	Surinam Airways	PZ		SP	SATA Air Acores	CS
PZ	TAM Mercosur	ZP		SQ	Singapore Airlines	9V
				SQ	Singapore Airlines Cargo	9V
Q2	Island Aviation Services	8Q		SS	Corsair	F
Q3	Zambian Airways	9J		ST	Germania	D
Q5	40 Mile Air	N		SU	Aeroflot Russian Airlines	RA
Q6	Aerocondor	OB		SV	Saudi Arabian Airlines	HZ
Q8	Pacific East Asia Cargo Airlines	RP		SW	Air Namibia	V5
Q8	Transair Congo	TN		SY	Sun Country Airlines	N
QB	Sky Georgia	4L		SY	Skippers Aviation	VH
QD	Air Class	CX				
QE	Air Moorea	F		T0	TACA Peru	OB
QF	QANTAS Airways	VH		T2	Nakina Outpost Camps and Air	C
QF	Qantaslink	VH		T3	Eastern Airways	G
QH	Kyrgyzstan	EX		T5	Turkmenistan Airlines	EZ
QI	Cimber Air	OY		T6	Tavrey Aircompany	UR
QK	Air Canada Jazz	C		T7	Twin Jet	F
QL	Laser	YV		TA	TACA Intl Airlines	YS
QL	Aero Lanka Airlines	4R		TB	Jetairfly	OO
QM	Air Malawi	7Q		TC	Air Tanzania	5H
QN	Air Armenia	EK		TF	Malmo Aviation	SE
QQ	Alliance Airlines	VH		TG	Thai Airways	HS
QR	Qatar Airways	A7		TH	Transmile Air Services	9M
QS	Smartwings	OK		TI	Tolair Services	N
QS	Travel Service Airlines	OK		TI	TACA Costa Rica	TI
QT	Tampa Airlines	HK		TK	Turkish Airlines	TC
QT	Regional Air	P2		TL	Airnorth Regional	VH
QU	East African Airlines	5X		TL	Chartair	VH
QV	Lao Airlines	RDPL		TM	LAM - Linhas Aereas de Mocambique	C9
QX	Horizon Air	N		TN	Air Tahiti Nui	F
QZ	Indonesia Airasia	PK		TO	Transavia France	F
				TO	President Airlines	XU
R0	Royal Airlines	AP		TP	TAP Air Portugal	CS
R2	Orenair	RA		TR	Tiger Airways	9V
R5	Jordan Aviation	JY		TS	Air Transat	C
R6	Danu Oro Transportas	LY		TT	Tiger Airways	VH
R6	RACSA	TG		TU	Tunisair	TS
R7	Aserca Airlines	YV		TV	Brussels Airlines	OO

TX	Air Caraibes	F	WI	Skylease Air Cargo	N
TX	Air Caraibes Atlantique	F	WJ	Air Labrador	C
TY	Iberworld Airlines	EC	WK	Edelweiss Air	HB
TY	Air Caledonie	F	WL	Aeroperlas	HP
			WM	Winair	PJ
U2	Easyjet Airlines	G	WN	Southwest Airlines	N
U3	Avies Air Company	ES	WO	World Airways	N
U4	PMT Air	XU	WP	Island Air	N
U5	USA 3000 Airlines	N	WQ	Romavia	YR
U6	Ural Airlines	RA	WS	Westjet	C
U7	Air Uganda	5X	WT	Wasaya Airways	C
U8	Armavia	EK	WU	Wizz Air Ukraine	UR
U9	Tatarstan Air	RA	WW	BMIBaby	G
UA	United Air Lines	N	WX	City Jet	EI
UA	United Express	N	WY	Oman Air	A4O
UB	Myanma Airways	XY			
UC	LAN Cargo	CC	X3	Tuifly	D
UD	Hex'Air	F	X7	Air Service Gabon	TR
UF	Um Air	UR	X8	Icaro Express	HC
UG	Sevenair	TS	X9	Khors Air	UR
UJ	Almasria Universal Airlines	SU	XA	Blue Islands	G
UL	Srilankan	4R	XC	KD Air	C
UM	Air Zimbabwe	Z	XF	Vladivostok Air	RA
UN	Transaero Airlines	RA	XK	Air Corsica	F
UO	Hong Kong Express Airways	B	XL	LAN Ecuador	HC
UO	Sky Shuttle Helicopters	B	XM	Alitalia Express	I
UP	Bahamasair	C6	XM	Australian Air Express	VH
UR	Utair Express	RA	XN	Xpress Air	PK
US	US Airways	N	XP	Xtra Airways	N
UT	Utair Airlines	RA	XQ	Sunexpress	TC
UU	Air Austral	F	XR	Skywest Airlines	VH
UV	Helisuretse	EC	XT	Skystar Airways	HS
UW	Uni-Top Airlines	B	XU	African Express Airways	5Y
UX	Air Europa	EC	XW	Skyexpress	RA
UY	Cameroon Airlines	TJ	XZ	South African Express Airways	ZS
UZ	Buraq Air	5A			
			Y5	Pace Airlines	N
V0	Conviasa	YV	Y8	Yangtze River Express	B
V3	Carpatair	YR	Y9	Kish Air	EP
V4	Volaris	XA	YA	Yeti Airlines	9N
V4	Venescar Intl	YV	YD	Gomelavia	EW
V5	Danube Wings	OM	YD	Mauritania Airways	5T
V6	VIP - Vuelos Internos Privados	HC	YE	Eram Air	EP
V6	Voyager Airlines	S2	YG	South Airlines	UR
V7	Air Senegal Intl	6V	YI	Air Sunshine	N
V8	Air Mikisew	C	YJ	AMC Airlines	SU
V8	Iliamna Air Taxi	N	YL	Yamal Airlines	RA
V8	Atran - Aviatrans Cargo Airlines	RA	YM	Montenegro Airlines	4O
VC	Voyageur Airways	C	YN	Air Creebec	C
VD	Henan Airlines	B	YO	Heli Air Monaco	3A
VF	Valuair	9V	YQ	Polet Aviakompania	RA
VG	VLM Airlines	OO	YR	Scenic Airlines	N
VH	Aeropostal	YV	YS	Régional	F
VI	Volga-Dnepr Airlines	RA	YV	Mesa Airlines	N
VJ	Jatayu Air	PK	YW	Air Nostrum	EC
VK	Air Nigeria	5N	YX	Midwest Airlines	N
VL	VIA - Air Via	LZ			
VN	Vietnam Airlines	VN	Z3	Promech Air	N
VQ	Vintage Prop and Jets	N	Z3	Avient Aviation	Z
VR	TACV – Transp. Aer. de Cabo Verde	D4	Z5	GMG Airlines	S2
VS	Virgin Atlantic Airways	G	Z6	Dnepr-Air	UR
VT	Air Tahiti	F	Z8	Amaszonas Transportes Aereos	CP
VU	Air Ivoire	TU	Z9	Delta Connection	5Y
VV	Aerosvit Airlines	UR	ZB	Monarch Airlines	G
VW	Aeromar Airlines	XA	ZD	Dolphin Air	A6
VX	Virgin America	N	ZE	Arcus Air	D
VY	Vueling Airlines	EC	ZF	Atlantic Airlines	HR
			ZH	Shenzhen Airlines	B
W3	Arik Air	5N	ZI	Aigle Azur	F
W4	M & N Aviation	N	ZK	Great Lakes Airlines	N
W5	Mahan Air	EP	ZL	Air Link	VH
W6	Wizz Air	HA	ZL	REX - Regional Express	VH
W7	Sayakhat	UP	ZM	Cityline Hungary	HA
W8	Cargojet Airways	C	ZN	Naysa Aerotaxis	EC
W9	Air Bagan	XY	ZP	Air St Thomas	N
WA	KLM Cityhopper	PH	ZP	Silk Way Airlines	4K
WB	Rwandair Express	9XR	ZR	Aviacon Zitotrans	RA
WC	Islena Airlines	HR	ZR	Alexandria Airlines	SU
WE	WDL Aviation	D	ZT	Titan Airways	G
WE	Centurion II Air Cargo	N	ZV	Air Midwest	N
WF	Wideroe's Flyveselskap	LN	ZX	Air Georgian	C
WG	Sunwing Airlines	C	ZY	Ada Air	ZA

ICAO THREE-LETTER DESIGNATORS

AAF	Aigle Azur	F	AKF	Anikay Air	EX
AAG	Air Atlantique	G	AKM	Mak Air	UP
AAG	Atlantic Reconnaissance	G	AKN	Alkan Air	C
AAL	American Airlines	N	AKY	Yak Service	RA
AAP	Aerovista Airlines	EX	ALG	Bristows US	N
AAQ	Copterline	OH	ALK	Srilankan	4R
AAR	Asiana Airlines	HL	ALX	Hewa Bora Airways	9Q
AAW	Afriqiyah Airways	5A	ALZ	Alta Flights	C
AAY	Allegiant Air	N	AMA	ATMA	UP
ABA	Artem Avia	UR	AMC	Air Malta	9H
ABD	Air Atlanta	TF	AMF	Ameriflight	N
ABF	Scanwings	OH	AMK	Amerer Air	OE
ABG	Abakan-Avia	RA	AML	Air Malawi	7Q
ABJ	Abaete Linhas Aereas	PP	AMP	Aero Transporte	OB
ABK	Alberta Citylink	C	AMU	Air Macau	B
ABL	Air Busan	HL	AMV	AMC Airlines	SU
ABO	APSA - Aeroexpreso Bogota	HK	AMW	Air Midwest	N
ABQ	AirBlue	AP	AMX	Aeromexico	XA
ABR	Air Contractors	EI	ANA	Air Nippon Network	JA
ABS	Transwest Air	C	ANA	ANA - All Nippon Network	JA
ABV	Antrak Air Ghana	9G	ANE	Air Nostrum	EC
ABW	Airbridge Cargo	RA	ANG	Air Niugini	P2
ABX	ABX Air	N	ANH	Al-Ajnihah Aiways	5A
ABY	Air Arabia	A6	ANK	Air Nippon	JA
ABZ	ATA Brasil	PP	ANO	Airnorth Regional	VH
ACA	Air Canada	C	ANQ	ADA - Aerolineas de Antioquia	HK
ACD	Academy Airlines	N	ANS	Andes Lineas Aereas	LV
ACE	Meridian Airways	9G	ANT	Air North	C
ACI	Aircalin	F	ANU	Starlink Aviation	C
ACL	Itali Airlines	I	ANX	Canadian North	C
ACP	Astral Aviation	5Y	ANZ	Air New Zealand	ZK
ACT	Flight Line	N	AOG	Aero VIP	LV
ACX	Air Cargo Germany	D	AOH	North Coast Aviation	P2
ADB	Antonov Airlines	UR	APC	Airpac Airlines	N
ADE	Ada Air	ZA	APF	Amapola Flyg	SE
ADI	Audeli	EC	APP	Aeroperlas	HP
ADO	Air Do	JA	APT	LAP - Lineas Aéreas Petroleras	HK
ADR	Adria Airways	S5	AQU	Airquarius Aviation	ZS
ADS	Aviones de Sonora	XA	ARA	Arik Air	5N
AEA	Air Europa	EC	ARE	Aires	HK
AEB	Aero Benin	TY	ARG	Aerolineas Argentinas	LV
AEE	Aegean Airlines	SX	ARL	Airlec Air Espace	F
AEK	Aerocon	CP	ARR	Air Armenia	EK
AEN	Aeroland Airways	SX	ART	Smartlynx	YL
AER	Alaska Central Express	N	ASA	Alaska Airlines	N
AEU	Astraeus	G	ASB	Air-Spray	C
AEW	Aerosvit Airlines	UR	ASD	Air Sinai	SU
AEY	Air Italy	I	ASE	Airstars Airways	RA
AFE	Airfast Indonesia	PK	ASH	Mesa Airlines	N
AFG	Ariana Afghan Airlines	YA	ASJ	Air Satellite	C
AFL	Aeroflot Russian Airlines	RA	ASM	Awesome Flight Services	ZS
AFR	Air France	F	ATC	Air Tanzania	5H
AFW	Great Barrier Airlines	ZK	ATG	Aerotrans	UP
AGB	Air Service Gabon	TR	ATM	Airlines of Tasmania	VH
AGO	Angola Air Charter	D2	ATN	ATI - Air Transport Intl	N
AGU	Angara Airlines	RA	ATU	Atlant Hungary	HA
AGV	Air Glaciers	HB	AUA	Austrian Airlines	OE
AGX	Aviogenex	YU	AUB	Augsburg Airways	D
AHA	Air Alpha Greenland	OY	AUI	Ukraine Intl Airlines	UR
AHC	Azal Cargo	4K	AUL	Nordavia Regional Airlines	RA
AHF	Aspen Helicopters	N	AUR	Aurigny Air Services	G
AHK	Air Hong Kong	B	AUT	Austral Lineas Aereas	LV
AHT	HTA Helicopters	CS	AVA	Avianca	HK
AHU	ABC Air Hungary	HA	AVJ	Avia Traffic Company	EX
AHW	Aeromost Kharkov	UR	AVN	Air Vanuatu	YJ
AHX	Amakusa Airlines	JA	AVW	Aviator Airways	SX
AHY	Azerbaijan Airlines	4K	AVX	Avirex	TR
AIA	Avies Air Company	ES	AWC	Titan Airways	G
AIC	Air India	VT	AWK	Airwork New Zealand	ZK
AIE	Air Inuit	C	AWQ	Indonesia Airasia	PK
AIP	Alpine Air Express	N	AWU	Aeroline	D
AIQ	Thai Airasia	HS	AWZ	Air West Cargo	ST
AIT	Airest	ES	AWZ	Sun Air	ST
AIZ	Arkia Israeli Airlines	4X	AXB	Air India Express	VT
AJI	Ameristar Air Charter	N	AXF	Tasman Cargo Airlines	VH
AJK	Allied Air Cargo	5N	AXK	African Express Airways	5Y
AJM	Air Jamaica	6Y	AXM	Airasia	9M
AJT	Amerijet Intl	N	AXQ	Action Airlines	N
AJV	JP Express	JA	AYN	Atlantic Airways	YN
AJX	Air Japan	JA	AYT	Ayeet Aviation	4X

AYZ	Moskva Air Company	RA	BRG	Bering Air	N
AZA	Alitalia	I	BRP	Aerobratsk	RA
AZE	Arcus Air	D	BRQ	Buraq Air	5A
AZF	Air Zermatt	HB	BRU	Belavia Belarussian Airlines	EW
AZG	Sakaviaservice	4L	BRV	Bravo Air Congo	9Q
AZH	Sky Wind	4K	BRZ	Samara Airlines	RA
AZQ	Silk Way Airlines	4K	BSK	Miami Air Intl	N
AZS	Aviacon Zitotrans	RA	BSL	Air Brasil Cargo	PP
AZU	Azul	PP	BST	Best Air	TC
AZV	Azov-Avia	UR	BTA	Expressjet Airlines	N
AZW	Air Zimbabwe	Z	BTI	Air Baltic	YL
AZZ	Azza Air Transport	ST	BTL	Baltia Airlines	N
			BTR	Botir-Avia	EX
BAB	Bahrain Air	A9C	BTV	Batavia Air	PK
BAJ	Baker Aviation	N	BUC	Bulgarian Air Charter	LZ
BAN	British Antarctic Survey	VP-F	BUE	Orebro Aviation	SE
BAW	British Airways	G	BUN	Bural	RA
BBC	Biman Bangladesh Airlines	S2	BVT	Berjaya Air Charter	9M
BBD	Bluebird Cargo	TF	BWA	Caribbean Airlines	9Y
BBO	Baboo	HB	BXH	Bar XH Air	C
BBR	Santa Barbara Airlines	YV	BXR	Redding Aero Enterprises	N
BBT	Air Bashkortostan	RA	BYA	Berry Aviation	N
BBZ	Bluebird Aviation	5Y	BYL	Bylina	RA
BCI	Blue Islands	G	BZH	Brit'Air	F
BCS	EAT Leipzig	D			
BCY	City Jet	EI	CAI	Corendon Air	TC
BDA	Blue Dart Aviation	VT	CAJ	Air Caraibes Atlantique	F
BDI	Benair Air Service	OY	CAL	China Airlines	B
BDR	Badr Airlines	ST	CAO	Air China Cargo	B
BEA	Best Air	S2	CAT	Copenhagen Airtaxi	OY
BEC	Berkut State Air Company	UP	CAV	Calm Air	C
BEE	FlyBe	G	CAW	Comair	ZS
BEK	Berkut Air	UP	CAY	Cayman Airways	VP-C
BER	AirBerlin	D	CBC	Caribair	HI
BET	Beta Cargo Air	PP	CBT	Catalina Flying Boats	N
BEZ	Air St Kitts & Nevis	V4	CCA	Air China	B
BFC	Basler Airlines	N	CCE	Cairo Aviation	SU
BFF	Air Nunavut	C	CCG	Central Connect Airlines	OK
BFL	Buffalo Airways	C	CCI	Capital Cargo Intl Airlines	N
BGA	Airbus Transport Intl	F	CCM	Air Corsica	F
BGH	BH Air	LZ	CCQ	Capital City Air Carrier	N
BGK	British Gulf Airlines	EX	CCY	Cherry-Air	N
BGL	Benin Golf Air	TY	CDG	Shandong Airlines	B
BGM	AK Bars Aero	RA	CDN	Canadian Helicopters	C
BGT	Bergen Air Transport	LN	CDP	Aerocondor	OB
BHA	Buddha Air	9N	CDV	Skol Aviakompania	RA
BHL	Bristow Helicopters	G	CEB	Cebu Pacific Air	RP
BHN	Bristow Helicopters (Nigeria)	5N	CEM	Central Mongolian Airlines	JU
BHP	Belair Airlines	HB	CES	China Eastern Airlines	B
BHR	Bighorn Airways	N	CFA	China Flying Dragon Co	B
BHS	Bahamasair	C6	CFE	BA Cityflyer	G
BID	Binair	D	CFG	Condor	D
BIE	Air Mediterrannée	F	CFV	Aero Calafia	XA
BIG	Big Island Air	N	CFZ	Zhongfei Airlines	B
BKA	Bankair	N	CGI	Rusair	RA
BKP	Bangkok Airways	HS	CGK	Click Airways	EX
BLE	Blue Line	F	CGN	Chang An Airlines	B
BLF	Blue1	OH	CGS	Geodynamica Centre	RA
BLM	Blue Sky	EK	CHB	West Air	B
BLS	Bearskin Airlines	C	CHC	CITIC Offshore Helicopters	B
BLV	Bellview Airlines	5N	CHG	Challenge Aero	UR
BLX	Tuifly Nordic	SE	CHH	Hainan Airlines	B
BMI	BMI	G	CHI	Cougar Helicopters	C
BMI	BMIBaby	G	CHN	Channel Island Aviation	N
BMJ	Bemidji Airlines	N	CIB	Condor Berlin	D
BML	Bismillah Airlines	S2	CID	Asia Continental Airlines	UP
BMM	Atlas Blue	CN	CIG	Sirius Aero	RA
BMR	BMI Regional	G	CII	Cityfly	I
BMY	Bimini Island Air	N	CIM	Cimber Air	OY
BND	Bond Offshore Helicopters	G	CIR	Arctic Circle Air Service	N
BNT	Bentiu Air Transport	ST	CIU	Cielos Airlines	OB
BNX	Linea Aerea Iaaca	YV	CIW	Civair	ZS
BOI	2Go	RP	CJA	Canjet	C
BOL	TAB Cargo	CP	CJC	Colgan Air	N
BON	BH Airlines	E9	CJR	Caverton Helicopters	5N
BOS	Open skies	F	CJT	Cargojet Airways	C
BOT	Air Botswana	A2	CKK	China Cargo Airlines	B
BOV	Boliviana de Aviacion	CP	CKM	BKS Air	EC
BOX	Aerologic	D	CKS	Kalitta Air	N
BPA	Blu Express.com	I	CLG	Chalair Aviation	F
BPA	Blue Panorama Airlines	I	CLH	Lufthansa Cityline	D
BPS	Budapest Air Services	HA	CLL	Aerovias Castillo	XA

CLX	Cargolux Airlines Intl	LX
CME	Prince Edward Air	C
CMN	Cimarron Aire	N
CMP	Copa Airlines	HP
CMS	Aviation Commercial Aviation	C
CMV	Calima Aviacion	EC
CNB	Cityline Hungary	HA
CNI	Aerotaxi	CU
CNK	Sunwest Aviation	C
COX	Comav Aviation	V5
COZ	Cosmic Air	9N
CPA	Cathay Pacific Airways	B
CPB	Corporate Express Airline	C
CPD	Capital Airlines	5Y
CPJ	Corpjet	N
CPM	Comp. Mauritanienne de Transportes	5T
CPN	Caspian Airlines	EP
CPT	Corporate Air	N
CQH	Spring Airlines	B
CQN	Chongqing Airlines	B
CRC	Conair Aviation	C
CRF	Air Central	JA
CRG	Cargoitalia	I
CRK	Hong Kong Airlines	B
CRL	Corsair	F
CRN	Aerocaribbean	CU
CRQ	Air Creebec	C
CRT	Caribintair	HH
CSA	CSA Czech Airlines	OK
CSC	Sichuan Airlines	B
CSH	Shanghai Airlines	B
CSJ	Castle Aviation	N
CSN	China Southern Airlines	B
CSQ	IBC Airways	N
CSV	Coastal Aviation	5H
CSY	Shuangyang Aviation	B
CSZ	Shenzhen Airlines	B
CTA	Aero Charter	N
CTL	Central Air Southwest	N
CTN	Croatia Airlines	9A
CTP	Tapo-Avia	UK
CTQ	Citylink	9G
CTR	Aerolineas Centauro	XA
CTS	Center-South Airlines	RA
CTT	Custom Air Transport	N
CUA	China United Airlines	B
CUB	Cubana de Aviacion	CU
CUO	Aero Cuahonte	XA
CVA	Air Chathams	ZK
CVC	Centre-Avia Airlines	RA
CVE	Cabo Verde Express	D4
CVU	Grand Canyon Airlines	N
CVV	Comeravia	YV
CWC	Centurion II Air Cargo	N
CWY	Woodgate Executive Air Services	G
CXA	Xiamen Airlines	B
CXH	China Xinhua Airlines	B
CXI	Shan Xi Airlines	B
CXP	Xtra Airways	N
CXS	Boston-Maine Airways	N
CXT	Coastal Air Transport	N
CYP	Cyprus Airways	5B
CYZ	China Postal Airlines	B
DAE	DHL Aero Expresso	HP
DAG	Daghestan Airlines	RA
DAH	Air Algerie	7T
DAL	Delta Airlines	N
DAL	Delta Connection	N
DAO	Daalo Airlines	J2
DAP	Aerovias DAP	CC
DAT	Brussels Airlines	OO
DAV	Dana	5N
DBH	Hebei Airlines	B
DBK	Dubrovnik Airlines	9A
DCD	Air 26	D2
DCL	Transportes Aereos Don Carlos	CC
DCP	Delta Connection	5Y
DCT	Direct Flight	G
DES	CC Helicopters	C
DHE	DAP Helicopteros	CC
DHK	DHL Air	G
DHL	Astar Air Cargo	N

DHX	DHL Intl Aviation	A9C
DIR	Dirgantara Air Service	PK
DKH	Juneyao Airlines	B
DKT	Business Aviation Courier	N
DLA	Air Dolomiti	I
DLH	Lufthansa	D
DMJ	Global Air	XA
DMO	Domodedovo Airlines	RA
DNL	Dutch Antilles Express	PJ
DNU	Danu Oro Transportas	LY
DNV	Donavia	RA
DOC	Norsk Luftambulance	LN
DRA	Capital Airlines	B
DRK	Druk Air	A5
DRU	Alrosa Aviation	RA
DRY	Deraya Air Taxi	PK
DSM	LAN Argentina	LV
DST	Aex Air	N
DTA	TAAG Angola Airlines	D2
DTH	Tassili Airlines	7T
DTR	Danish Air Transport	OY
DVR	Divi Divi Air	PJ
DWT	Darwin Airline	HB
DYL	Seair Airways	C6
EAA	Eastok Avia	A6
EAI	Elite Air	5V
EAK	Euro Asia Intl	UP
EAN	Skypower Express Airways	5N
EAS	Executive Aerospace	ZS
EAV	Kyrghyz Airways	EX
ECN	Euro Continental Air	EC
ECT	East Coast Airways	ZS
EDJ	Edwards Jet Centre of Montana	N
EDO	Elidolomiti	I
EDW	Edelweiss Air	HB
EEX	Avanti Air	D
EEZ	Meridiana Fly	I
EFA	Express Freighters Australia	VH
EFG	Elifriula	I
EGS	Eagle Airlines	I
EGU	Eagle Air	5X
EIA	Evergreen Intl Airlines	N
EIN	Aer Lingus	EI
ELH	Elilario Italia	I
ELL	Estonian Air	ES
ELL	Estonian Air Regional	ES
ELO	EuroLot	SP
ELR	El-Rom Airlines	4X
ELY	El Al Israel Airlines	4X
EMT	Emetebe Taxi Aero	HC
ENI	Enimex	ES
ENJ	Enerjet	C
EPA	Donghai Airlines	B
EPS	Epps Aviation Charter	N
EQA	Elilombarda	I
EQF	American Eagle	N
ERG	Aviaenergo	RA
ERH	Era Aviation	N
ERO	Sud D'Or Intl Airlines	4X
ERT	Eritrean Airlines	E3
ESC	Sol America	YV
ESD	Essen Air	EX
ESF	Estafeta Carga Aerea	XA
ESJ	Eastern Skyjets	A6
ESL	Russian Sky Airlines	RA
ETC	Trans Attico	ST
ETD	Etihad Airways	A6
ETH	Ethiopian Airlines	ET
ETS	Avitrans Nordic	SE
EUP	Euroair	SX
EVA	EVA Airways	B
EWG	Eurowings	D
EWZ	East Wing	UP
EXN	Exin	SP
EXS	Jet2	G
EXT	Nightexpress	D
EXV	Expo Air	4R
EXW	EAS Air Lines	5N
EXY	South African Express Airways	ZS
EXZ	East African Express	5Y
EZA	Enzis Airways	JU
EZE	Eastern Airways	G

Code	Airline	Prefix
EZS	Easyjet Switzerland	HB
EZY	Easyjet Airlines	G
FAB	First Air	C
FAH	Farnair Hungary	HA
FAJ	Air Fiji	DQ
FAM	FAASA Aviacion	EC
FAO	Ufly Airways	N
FAT	Farnair Switzerland	HB
FCL	Florida Coastal Airlines	N
FCP	Flight Corporation	ZK
FCR	Flying Carpet Air Transport Services	OD
FDA	Fuji Dream Airlines	JA
FDD	Feeder Airlines	ST
FDE	Federico Helicopters	N
FDN	Dolphin Air	A6
FDR	Federal Air	ZS
FDX	Federal Express	N
FEI	Ernir Air	TF
FFA	Avialesookhrana Vladimir Air Enterprise	RA
FFF	Freedom Air Services	5N
FFG	Flugdienst Fehlhaber	D
FFM	Firefly	9M
FFT	Frontier Airlines	N
FFV	Fly540	5Y
FHE	Hello	HB
FHY	Freebird Airlines	TC
FIF	Air Finland	OH
FIN	Finnair	OH
FJI	Air Pacific	DQ
FKI	FLM Aviation	D
FLE	Flair Airlines	C
FLI	Atlantic Airways	OY
FLX	Flight Express	N
FNT	Flight Intl Aviation	N
FNV	Transavia Service	4L
FPO	Europe Airpost	F
FRE	Freedom Air	N
FRG	Freight Runners Express	N
FRJ	Afrijet Airlines	5N
FSC	Four Star Air Cargo	N
FTA	Frontier Flying Service	N
FTL	Flightline	EC
FTR	Finist'Air	F
FVS	Falcon Express Cargo Airlines	A6
FWI	Air Caraibes	F
FWL	Florida West Intl Airlines	N
FXI	Air Iceland	TF
FYA	Saicus Air	EC
FZB	FlyDubai	A6
GAE	Tricoastal Air	N
GAI	Moskoviya	RA
GAK	Global Air	5A
GAL	Galaxy Airlines	EX
GAO	Golden Air	SE
GAP	AirPhil Express	RP
GBK	Gabon Airlines	TR
GBX	GB Airlink	N
GCK	Aerogem Airlines	9G
GCR	Tianjin Airlines	B
GDC	Grand China Airlines	B
GEA	Geasa	3C
GEC	Lufthansa Cargo	D
GEN	Gensa	PP
GET	Getra	3C
GFA	Gulf Air	A9C
GFG	Sky Georgia	4L
GFT	Gulfstream Intl	N
GGL	Gira Globo	D2
GGN	Air Georgian	C
GGZ	Global Georgian Airways	4L
GHS	Gatari Air Service	PK
GHT	Ghadames Air Transport	5A
GHY	German SkyAirlines	D
GIA	Garuda Indonesia	PK
GIP	Air Guinee Express	3X
GLA	Great Lakes Airlines	N
GLE	Goliaf Air	S9
GLG	Aerogal	HC
GLL	Air Gemini	D2
GLO	Gol Transportes Aereos	PP
GLP	Globus	RA
GLR	Central Mountain Air	C
GMI	Germania	D
GMT	Magnicharters	XA
GOA	Province of Alberta	C
GOM	Gomelavia	EW
GOR	Gorlitsa Airlines	UR
GOS	Goldfields Air Services	VH
GOT	Waltair Europe	SE
GOW	Go Air	VT
GRL	Air Greenland	OY
GRV	Epsilon Aviation	SX
GSC	Granstar Cargo Airlines	B
GSS	Global Supply Systems	G
GSW	Sky Wings	SX
GSW	Skywings Intl	Z3
GTI	Atlas Air	N
GTV	Aerogaviota	CU
GUM	Gum Air	PZ
GUM	Transportes Aereos Guatemaltecos	TG
GUN	Grant Aviation	N
GUY	Air Guyane Express	F
GWI	Germanwings	D
GWL	Great Wall Airlines	B
GWY	USA 3000 Airlines	N
GXL	XL Airways Germany	D
GZA	Excellent Air	D
GZP	Gazpromavia	RA
HAD	Dragonair	B
HAG	Hageland Aviation Services	N
HAL	Hawaiian Airlines	N
HAX	Benair	LN
HBI	CHC Denmark	OY
HCW	Star1 Airlines	LY
HEC	Heli Campeche	XA
HEJ	Hellas jet	SX
HEL	Helicol	HK
HEM	CHC Helicopters (Australia)	VH
HER	Hex'Air	F
HES	Harbourair	9H
HET	TAF Helicopters	EC
HFY	Hi Fly	CS
HHA	Atlantic Airlines	HR
HHH	Helicsa Helicopteros	EC
HHK	Sky Shuttle Helicopters	B
HIB	Helibravo Aviacao	CS
HIS	Heliswiss	HB
HIT	Heli-Italia	I
HKA	Superior Aviation	N
HKE	Hong Kong Express Airways	B
HKN	Jim Hankins Air Service	N
HKR	Hawk Air	LV
HKS	CHC Helicopter Service	LN
HLF	Tuifly	D
HLG	Helog	HB
HLR	Heli Air	LZ
HLU	Heli-Union	F
HLW	Heliworks	CC
HMA	Air Tahoma	N
HMF	Norrlandsflyg	SE
HMS	Hemus Air	LZ
HMX	Hawk de Mexico	XA
HPL	Heliportugal	CS
HPR	Helipro	ZK
HSE	Helisuretse	EC
HSS	Transportes Aereos del Sur	EC
HSU	Helisul	CS
HSV	Direktflyg	SE
HSW	Heliswiss Iberica	EC
HTA	Helitrans	LN
HTG	Grossmann Air Transport	OE
HVL	Heavylift Intl	A6
HVN	Vietnam Airlines	VN
HVY	Heavylift Cargo Airlines	VH
HXA	China Express Airlines	B
HYD	Hydro-Quebec	C
IAR	Iliamna Air Taxi	N
IAW	Iraqi Airways	YI
IBB	Binter Canarias	EC
IBE	Iberia	EC

IBX	Ibex Airlines	JA		JTU	Zhetysu Avia	UP
ICD	Icaro Express	HC		JTY	Jatayu Air	PK
ICE	Icelandair	TF		JUB	Jubba Airways	6O
ICJ	Icejet	TF		JUS	USA Jet Airlines	N
ICL	Cargo Air Lines	4X		JZA	Air Canada Jazz	C
ICV	Cargolux Italia	I		JZR	Jazeera Airways	9K
IDA	Indonesia Air Transport	PK				
IGA	Sky Taxi	SP		KAC	Kuwait Airways	9K
IGO	Indigo Airlines	VT		KAD	Kirovohradavia	UR
IIG	Aldawlyh Air	5A		KAE	Kartika Airlines	PK
IKA	Itek Air	EX		KAJ	Karthago Airlines	TS
ILF	Island Air Charters	N		KAL	Korean Air	HL
ILN	Inter-Air	ZS		KAO	Kapo	RA
IMP	Hellenic Imperial Airways	SX		KAP	Cape Air	N
IMT	Imtrec Aviation	XU		KAW	Kazair West	UP
IMX	Zimex Aviation	HB		KBA	Kenn Borek Air	C
INC	Insel Air Intl	PJ		KBR	Koral Blue	SU
INJ	Interjet	XA		KDC	KD Air	C
INL	Intal Air	EX		KEE	Keystone Air Service	C
INV	Inversija	YL		KEN	Kenmore Air	N
IOS	Isles of Scilly Skybus	G		KES	Kallat el Saker Air	5A
IRA	Iran Air	EP		KFA	Kelowna Flightcraft Air Charter	C
IRB	Iran Air Tour Airline	EP		KFR	Kingfisher Airlines	VT
IRC	Iran Aseman Airlines	EP		KFR	Kingfisher Red	VT
IRG	Naft Air	EP		KFS	Kalitta Charters II	N
IRI	Navid Air	EP		KFS	Kalitta Flying Services	N
IRK	Kish Air	EP		KGA	Kyrghyzstan Airlines	EX
IRM	Mahan Air	EP		KGL	Kolavia	RA
IRP	Payim Intl Air	EP		KHA	Kitty Hawk Aircargo	N
IRQ	Qeshm Air	EP		KHB	Dalavia	RA
IRR	Tara Airlines	EP		KHH	Alexandria Airlines	SU
IRU	Chabahar Air	EP		KHO	Khors Air	UR
IRX	Aria Air	EP		KIL	Kuban Airlines	RA
IRY	Eram Air	EP		KIS	Contact Air	D
IRZ	Saha Airline	EP		KKK	Atlasjet Intl	TC
ISA	Island Airlines	N		KLC	KLM Cityhopper	PH
ISD	ISD Avia	UR		KLM	KLM Royal Dutch Airlines	PH
ISK	Intersky	OE		KMF	Kam Air	YA
ISN	Interisland Airways	RP		KMG	Kosmas Air Cargo	YU
ISR	Israir	4X		KMI	K-Mile Air	HS
ISV	Islena Airlines	HR		KMV	Utair Express	RA
ISW	Islas Airways	EC		KMZ	Comores Aviation	D6
ITK	Interlink Airlines	ZS		KNA	Kunming Airlines	B
ITX	Imair	4K		KNE	NAS Air	HZ
IWD	Iberworld Airlines	EC		KNM	Knaapo	RA
IYE	Yemenia	7O		KOP	Copters	CC
IZA	Izhavia	RA		KOR	Air Koryo	P
IZG	Zagros Airlines	EP		KPA	Henan Airlines	B
IZM	Izmir Airlines	TC		KQA	Kenya Airways	5Y
				KRE	Aerosucre	HK
JAB	Air Bagan	XY		KRP	Carpatair	YR
JAC	Japan Air Commuter	JA		KRT	Kokshetau Airlines	UP
JAE	Jade Cargo Intl	B		KSA	KS Avia	YL
JAF	Jetairfly	OO		KSM	Kosmos Airlines	RA
JAI	Jet Airways	VT		KSP	SAEP	HK
JAL	J-Air	JA		KST	PTL Luftfahrtunternehmen	D
JAL	Japan Airlines	JA		KTA	Kirov Avia Enterprise	RA
JAT	JAT Airways	YU		KTC	Kyrgyz Trans Air	EX
JAV	Jordan Aviation	JY		KTK	Katekavia	RA
JBA	HeliJet Intl	C		KVA	Kavok Airlines	YV
JBU	Jetblue Airways	N		KYM	Krym	UR
JCI	Jordan Intl Air Cargo	JY		KZH	Zhezhair	UP
JCK	Jackson Air Services	C		KZR	Air Astana	UP
JEA	Jet Air	SP				
JEC	Jett 8 Airlines Cargo	9V		LAA	Libyan Airlines	5A
JET	Windjet	I		LAB	LAB Flying Service	N
JEX	JAL Express	JA		LAL	Air Labrador	C
JFU	Jet4You	CN		LAM	LAM - Linhas Aereas de Mocambique	C9
JJA	Jeju Air	HL		LAN	LAN Airlines	CC
JKK	Spanair	EC		LAO	Lao Airlines	RDPL
JLA	Mia Airlines	YR		LAP	TAM Mercosur	ZP
JLX	Jetlink Express	5Y		LAU	Lineas Aéreas Sudamericanas	
JNA	Jin Air	HL			Colombia	HK
JOL	Atyrau Air Ways	UP		LAV	Aeropostal	YV
JON	Johnsons Air	9G		LAV	Alba Star	EC
JOR	Blue Air	YR		LAY	Layang-layang Aerospace	9M
JOS	DHL de Guatemala	TG		LBC	Albanian Airlines	ZA
JSA	Jetstar Asia Airways	9V		LBT	Nouvelair	TS
JSI	Jet Air Group	RA		LBY	Belle Air	ZA
JSJ	JS Focus Air	AP		LCB	LC Burse	OB
JST	Jetstar Airways	VH		LCG	Lignes Aeriennes Congolaises	9Q
JTA	Japan Transocean Air	JA		LCN	Lineas Aereas Canedo	CP
JTG	Jettime	OY		LCO	LAN Cargo	CC

LCR	Libyan Air Cargo	5A
LDE	LADE	LV
LER	Laser	YV
LFL	Exec-Air	Z
LGL	Luxair	LX
LGW	LGW - Luftfahrtgesellschaft Walter	D
LIA	LIAT - The Caribbean Airline	V2
LID	Alidaunia	I
LIQ	Flygcentrum	SE
LKE	Lucky Airlines	B
LLB	LAB Airlines	CP
LLC	Small Planet Airlines	LY
LLL	Lao Aviation	RDPL
LLM	Yamal Airlines	RA
LLR	Alliance Air	VT
LMU	Almasria Universal Airlines	SU
LMY	Air Almaty	UP
LNE	LAN Ecuador	HC
LNI	Lion Airlines	PK
LNK	Airlink	ZS
LOD	Fly Logic Sweden	SE
LOF	American Connection	N
LOG	Loganair	G
LOT	LOT - Polish Airlines	SP
LOU	Air Saint Louis	6V
LPE	LAN Peru	OB
LPV	Air Alps Aviation	OE
LRA	Little Red Air Service	C
LRB	LR Airlines	OK
LRO	Alrosa Avia	RA
LRS	Sansa Regional	TI
LSE	Lassa - Lineas de Aeroservicios	CC
LSK	Aurela	LY
LSR	Alsair	F
LSY	Lindsay Aviation	N
LTR	Lufttransport	LN
LTS	Flight Inspections & Systems	RA
LUZ	Luzair	CS
LVB	IRS Airlines	5N
LVR	Aviavilsa	LY
LXF	Lynx Air Intl	N
LXP	LAN Express	CC
LYC	Lynden Air Cargo	N
LYD	Lydd Air	G
LYM	Key Lime Air	N
LYN	Kyrgyzstan	EX
LYT	Apatas	LY
LZB	Bulgaria Air	LZ
LZT	Lanzarote Aircargo	EC
MAA	MAS Air Cargo	XA
MAC	Air Arabia Maroc	CN
MAH	Malev	HA
MAK	MAT Macedonian Air Transport	Z3
MAL	Morningstar Air Express	C
MAS	Malaysia Airlines	9M
MAU	Air Mauritius	3B
MAW	Mustique Airways	J8
MAX	Max Aviation	C
MBB	Air Manas	EX
MBC	Aerojet	D2
MBI	Salmon Air	N
MBM	Starjet	JY
MBN	Zambian Airways	9J
MBV	Aeriantur-M Airlines	ER
MCM	Heli Air Monaco	3A
MCW	AMW Tchad	TT
MDA	Mandarin Airlines	B
MDC	Mid-Atlantic Freight	N
MDF	Swiftair Hellas	SX
MDJ	Jetran Intl Airways	YR
MDL	Mandala Airlines	PK
MDM	Medavia	9H
MDN	Mudan Airlines	6O
MDS	McNeely Charter Service	N
MDV	Moldavian Airlines	ER
MEA	Middle East Airlines	OD
MEM	Meridian	UR
MEP	Midwest Airlines	N
MGE	Asia Pacific Airlines	N
MGG	El Magal Aviation	ST
MGK	Mega Aircompany	UP

MGL	MIAT - Mongolian Airlines	JU
MGX	Montenegro Airlines	4O
MHS	Air Memphis	SU
MIF	Miras Air	UP
MIX	Midex Airlines	A6
MJA	Almajara Aviation	ST
MJT	Vigo Jet	XA
MKU	Island Air	N
MLA	40 Mile Air	N
MLC	Malift Air	9Q
MLD	Air Moldova	ER
MLG	Malagasy Airlines	5R
MLR	Mihin Lanka	4R
MMA	Myanmar Airways Intl	XY
MMZ	Euro Atlantic Airways	CS
MNA	Merpati Nusantara Airlines	PK
MNB	MNG Cargo Airlines	TC
MNG	Aero Mongolia	JU
MNL	Miniliner	I
MON	Monarch Airlines	G
MOO	Moonair Aviation	4X
MOV	Vim Airlines	RA
MPH	Martinair	PH
MPJ	Mapjet	OE
MPT	Miapet Avia	EK
MRA	Martinaire	N
MRE	Namibia Commercial Airways	V5
MRR	Northwest Seaplanes	N
MRR	San Juan Airlines	N
MRS	Airline of the Marshall Islands	V7
MSA	Mistral Air	I
MSC	Air Cairo	SU
MSE	Egyptair Express	SU
MSI	Motor Sich Airlines	UR
MSL	Marsland Aviation	ST
MSM	Aeromas	CX
MSQ	META - Mesquita Transportes Aero	PP
MSR	Egyptair	SU
MST	MTA Cargo	PP
MSV	Aero-Kamov	RA
MTL	RAF-Avia	YL
MTN	Mountain Air Cargo	N
MTW	Mauritania Airways	5T
MUA	National Airlines	N
MUI	Transair	N
MVD	KMV Mineralnye Vody Airlines	RA
MWA	Midwest Airlines Egypt	SU
MWT	Midwest Aviation	N
MXE	Mocambique Expresso	C9
MXU	Maximus Air Cargo	A6
MYA	Myflug	TF
MYD	Maya Island Air	V3
MYI	Mayair	XA
MZL	Aerovias Montes Azules	XA
NAC	Northern Air Cargo	N
NAL	Northway Aviation	C
NAO	North American Airlines	N
NAX	Norwegian	LN
NAY	Naysa Aerotaxis	EC
NBE	Novosibirsk Air Enterprise	RA
NCA	Nippon Cargo Airlines	JA
NCB	North Cariboo Air	C
NCH	Phillips Air Charter	N
NCP	Capital Airlines	5N
NCS	Simpson Air Commuter Canada	C
NDN	Transportes Aereos Cielos Andinos	OB
NEA	New England Airlines	N
NFA	North Flying	OY
NFS	Afrique Cargo Services	6V
NGK	Oriental Air Bridge	JA
NHG	NHT Linhas Aereas	PP
NIG	Aero Contactors	5N
NJS	Cobham Aviation Services Australia	VH
NKF	Barents Skylink	SE
NKS	Spirit Airlines	N
NKZ	Aerokuzbass	RA
NLC	Nelair Charters & Travel	ZS
NLF	Westair Aviation	C
NLK	Elbrus Avia	RA
NLY	Niki	OE
NMB	Air Namibia	V5

NMD	Bay Air Aviation	V5		PGL	Premiair Aviation Services	G
NMI	Pacific Wings	N		PGP	Perm Airlines	RA
NOF	Fonnafly	LN		PGT	Pegasus Airlines	TC
NOK	Nok Air	HS		PGX	Paragon Air Express	N
NOR	Bristow Norway	LN		PHA	Phoenix Air	N
NOS	Neos	I		PHB	Phoebus Apollo Aviation	ZS
NOT	Linea Aerea Costa Norte	CC		PHE	Pawan Hans Helicopters	VT
NPO	Napo Aviatrans	RA		PHM	PHI - Petroleum Helicopters	N
NPR	Air Napier	ZK		PHW	AVE.com	A6
NPT	West Atlantic	G		PHY	Phoenix Avia	EK
NRG	Ross Aviation	N		PIA	Pakistan Intl Airlines	AP
NRK	Naturelink Charter	ZS		PIC	Jetstar Pacific Airlines	VN
NRL	Nolinor Aviation	C		PIR	Pamir Air	YA
NRO	Aero Rent	RA		PIV	Sokol	RA
NRR	Natureair	TI		PKW	Sierra West Airlines	N
NRX	Norse Air Charter	ZS		PLC	Police Aviation Services	G
NSE	Satena	HK		PLJ	Platinum Air Linhas Aereas	PP
NTA	NT Air	C		PLM	Pullmantur Air	EC
NTC	Heartland Aviation	N		PLR	Northwestern Air	C
NTH	Hokkaido Air System	JA		PLS	Aeroflot Plus	RA
NTJ	Nextjet	SE		PLY	Puma Air Linhas Aereas	PP
NTV	Air Inter Ivoire	TU		PMA	Pan-Malaysian Air Transport	9M
NVD	Nordic Solutions Air Services	LY		PMS	Planemasters	N
NVI	Avial Aviation Co	RA		PMT	PMT Air	XU
NVR	Novair	SE		PNA	Universal Airlines	N
NVS	Nouvelles Air Affaires Gabon	TR		PNP	Pineapple Air	C6
NWL	North Wright Airways	C		PNR	Panair Lineas Aereas	EC
NXA	Air Next	JA		PNS	Penas	PK
NYL	Mid Airlines	ST		POE	Porter Airlines	C
NZA	Air New Zealand Link	ZK		POT	Polet Aviakompania	RA
				PPG	Phoenix Airtransport	N
OAE	Omni Air Intl	N		PPK	Ramp 66	N
OAL	Olympic Airways	SX		PPW	Royal Phnom Penh Airways	XU
OAO	Arkhangelsk 2nd Aviation Enterprise	RA		PRF	Precisionair	5H
OAV	Omni - Aviacao e Tecnoligia	CS		PRG	Empressa Aero - Servicios Parrague	CC
OAW	Helvetic Airways	HB		PRN	Pirinair Express	EC
OBS	Orbest	CS		PRO	Propair	C
OCA	Aserca Airlines	YV		PRY	Priority Air Charter	N
ODS	Odessa Airlines	UR		PSC	Pascan Aviation	C
OEA	Orient Thai Airlines	HS		PSD	President Airlines	XU
OHY	Onur Air	TC		PSS	Progress Aviakompania	RA
OKA	OK Airways	B		PST	Air Panama	HP
OKS	Slok Air Intl	C5		PSV	Sapair	HI
OLA	Overland Airways	5N		PSW	Pskovavia	RA
OLC	Solar Cargo	YV		PTG	Privatair	D
OLS	SOL Lineas Aereas	LV		PTI	Privatair	HB
OLT	OLT - Ostfriesische Lufttransport	D		PTK	Petropavlovsk-Kamchatsky	
OMA	Oman Air	A4O			Air Enterprise	RA
OMR	Minair	TL		PTN	Pantanal	PP
ONE	Avianca Brazil	PP		PUA	Pluna Lineas Aereas Uruguayas	CX
ONR	Air One Nine	5A		PVG	Privalege Style	EC
ORB	Orenair	RA		PVI	Panavia Cargo Airlines	HP
ORJ	Bellview Airlines	9L		PVU	Peau Vava'u Air	A3
ORZ	Zorex	EC		PVV	Continental Airways	RA
OST	Alania Airline	RA		PWF	Private Wings	D
OTL	South Airlines	UR		PYZ	Players Air	N
OVA	Aeronova	EC				
OZU	Khozu Avia	UP		QAT	Air Quasar	C
OZW	Skywest Airlines	VH		QCL	Air Class	CX
				QFA	QANTAS Airways	VH
PAC	Polar Air Cargo	N		QFA	Qantaslink	VH
PAG	Perimeter Aviation	C		QNK	Kabo Air	5N
PAL	Philippine Airlines	RP		QNT	Qanot Sharq	UK
PAO	Polynesian Airlines	5W		QNZ	Jetconnect	ZK
PAS	Pelita Air	PK		QTG	One-Two Go	HS
PBN	Pacific Blue	ZK		QTR	Qatar Airways	A7
PBU	Air Burundi	9U		QUE	Government of Quebec	C
PCE	Pace Airlines	N		QWA	Pel-Air	VH
PCG	Aeropostal	XA		QWL	Qwila Air	ZS
PCO	Pacific Coastal Airlines	C		QXE	Horizon Air	N
PCP	Aerolinea Principal Chile	CC				
PDA	Podilia Avia	UR		RAC	Ryukyu Air Commuter	JA
PDF	Pelican Air Services	ZS		RAD	Alada	D2
PDG	PDG Helicopters	G		RAE	Régional	F
PEA	Pan Européenne Air Service	F		RAG	Regio-Air	D
PEC	Pacific East Asia Cargo Airlines	RP		RAI	Aerotur Air	UP
PEL	Aeropelican Air Services	VH		RAM	Royal Air Maroc	CN
PEN	Penair	N		RAX	Royal Air Freight	N
PEP	PENTA - Pena Transportes Aereos	PP		RBA	Royal Brunei Airlines	V8
PFL	Pacificflyer	T8A		RBC	Republicair	XA
PFR	Pacificair	RP		RBW	Rainbow Jet	B
PFZ	Profilght Air Services	9J		RCQ	Aerolineas Regionales	XA
PGA	Portugalia Airlines	CS		RCT	Arctic Transportation Services	N

Code	Airline	Country
RDS	Rhoades Intl	N
REA	Aer Arann	EI
REG	Regional Air Services	5H
REU	Air Austral	F
REX	RAM Air Freight	N
RFC	Aero Africa	3D
RFS	Rossair Charter	VH
RGE	Guinea Equatorial Airlines	3C
RGE	Star Equatorial Airlines	3C
RGL	Regional Air Lines	CN
RGN	Gestair Cargo	EC
RHA	Robin Hood Aviation	OE
RHD	Bond Air Services	G
RHL	Air Archipels	F
RIT	Zest Airways	RP
RIU	Riau Airlines	PK
RJA	Royal Jordanian	JY
RKH	Royal Khmer Airlines	XU
RKM	Rak Airlines	A6
RLA	Airlinair	F
RLE	Rico Linhas Aereas	PP
RLR	Airnow	N
RLS	S-Air	RA
RLU	Rusline Air	RA
RMO	Saturn Aviakompania	RA
RMV	Romavia	YR
RMX	Air Max	LZ
RNA	Nepal Airlines	9N
RNB	Rosneft-Baltika	RA
RNG	Orange Aircraft Leasing	PH
RNL	Aero Lanka Airlines	4R
RNV	Armavia	EK
RNX	1Time Airline	ZS
ROE	Aeroeste	CP
ROI	Avior Airlines	YV
RON	Our Airline	C2
ROR	Roraima Airways	8R
ROT	Tarom	YR
ROX	Roblex Aviation	N
RPB	Aerorepublica Colombia	HK
RPC	Aeropacsa	HC
RPH	RPX Airlines	PK
RPK	Royal Airlines	AP
RPX	HD Air	G
RRV	Mombasa Air Safari	5Y
RSB	Rubystar	EW
RSE	SNAS Aviation	HZ
RSG	Aero Service ASF	6V
RSH	Jetlite	VT
RSI	Air Sunshine	N
RSR	Aeroservice	TN
RSU	Aerosur	CP
RTM	Trans Am	HC
RUC	Rutaca	YV
RUM	Air Rum	9L
RUN	ACT Airlines	TC
RUS	Cirrus Airlines	D
RVE	Airventure	OO
RVL	Air Vallée	I
RVT	Veteran Airline	EK
RWD	Rwandair Express	9XR
RWG	C&M Airways	N
RWS	Air Whitsunday Seaplanes	VH
RXA	REX - Regional Express	VH
RYN	Ryan Intl Airlines	N
RYR	Ryanair	EI
RYW	Royal Wings Airlines	JY
RYZ	Ryazanavia Trans	RA
RZO	SATA Internacional	CS
RZZ	Anoka Air Charter	N
SAA	South African Airways	ZS
SAB	Sky Way Air	EX
SAH	Sayakhat	UP
SAI	Sheheen Air Intl	AP
SAM	SAM Colombia	HK
SAP	Avia Jaynar	UP
SAS	Scandinavian Airline System	SE
SAT	SATA Air Acores	CS
SAV	Samal Air	UP
SAX	Sabah Air	9M
SAY	Scotairways	G
SBF	SB Air	N
SBI	S7 Airlines	RA
SBM	Sky Bahamas	C6
SBU	St Barth Commuter	F
SBX	North Star Air Cargo	N
SCD	Associated Air Cargo	5N
SCE	Scenic Airlines	N
SCH	CHC Airways	PH
SCU	Air Scorpio	LZ
SCW	Malmo Aviation	SE
SCX	Sun Country Airlines	N
SDK	SADELCA	HK
SDL	Skysouth	G
SDM	Rossiya Russian Airlines	RA
SDO	Air Santo Domingo	HI
SDR	City Airline	SE
SE H	Sky Express	SX
SEE	Sheheen Air Cargo	AP
SEJ	Spicejet	VT
SEQ	Sky Eyes Aviation	HS
SEV	Serair	EC
SEY	Air Seychelles	S7
SFF	Safewing Aviation	N
SFJ	Starflyer	JA
SFN	Safiran Airlines	EP
SFR	Safair	ZS
SGB	Sky King	N
SGD	Skygate Intl	JY
SGG	Senegal Airlines	6V
SGS	Saskatchewan Government Northern Air Operations	C
SGX	Saga Airlines	TC
SGY	Skagway Air Service	N
SHQ	Shanghai Cargo	B
SHU	SAT Airlines	RA
SHY	Sky Airlines	TC
SHZ	CHC Scotia Helicopters	G
SIA	Singapore Airlines	9V
SIB	Sibaviatrans	RA
SJY	Sriwijaya Air	PK
SKC	Skymaster Airlines	PP
SKI	Skyking Airlines	VQ-T
SKK	Asky Airlines	5V
SKS	Sky Service	OO
SKT	Skystar Airways	HS
SKU	Sky Airline	CC
SKW	Skywest Airlines	N
SKX	Skyways Express	SE
SKY	Skymark Airlines	JA
SKZ	Skyway Enterprises	N
SLD	Silver Air	OK
SLE	NAC Charter	ZS
SLI	Aeromexico Connect	XA
SLK	Silkair	9V
SLM	Surinam Airways	PZ
SMC	Sabang Merauke Raya Air Charter	PK
SMH	Smithair	N
SMJ	Avient Aviation	Z
SMK	Semeyavia	UP
SMX	Alitalia Express	I
SNC	Air Cargo Carriers	N
SNG	Air Senegal Intl	6V
SNJ	Skynet Asia Airways	JA
SOA	Southern Air Charter	C6
SOL	Solomons	H4
SOO	Southern Air	N
SOP	Solinair	S5
SOR	Sonair	D2
SOV	Saratov Airlines	RA
SOY	Island Aviation	RP
SOZ	SAT Airlines	UP
SPA	Sierra Pacific Airlines	N
SPB	Springbok Classic Air	ZS
SPM	Air St Pierre	F
SPP	Sapphire Aviation	N
SPR	Provincial Airlines	C
SQC	Singapore Airlines Cargo	9V
SRC	Searca Colombia	HK
SRF	Transportes Aereos San Rafael	CC
SRI	Air Safaris & Services	ZK
SRK	Skywork Airlines	HB
SRO	SAEREO	HC

SRQ	South East Asian Airlines	RP
SRR	Star Air	OY
SRU	Star peru	OB
SSC	Southern Seaplane	N
SSF	Severstal Aircompany	RA
SSG	Slovak Government Flying Service	OM
SSS	SAESA	EC
STH	South Airlines	EK
STI	Sontair	C
STT	Air St Thomas	N
STU	Star African Air	6O
STX	Stars Away Aviation	ZS
SUB	Suburban Air Freight	N
SUD	Sudan Airways	ST
SUF	Pacific Sun	DQ
SUK	Superior Aviation Services	5Y
SUM	MCHS Rossii	RA
SUS	Sun-Air of Scandinavia	OY
SUW	Interavia Airlines	RA
SVA	Saudi Arabian Airlines	HZ
SVD	SVG Air	J8
SVE	Asesa	XA
SVH	Sterling Aviation	G
SVJ	Silver Air	J2
SVL	Sevastopol Avia	UR
SVM	Aeroservicios Monterrey	XA
SVR	Ural Airlines	RA
SVT	748 Air Services	5Y
SWA	Southwest Airlines	N
SWG	Sunwing Airlines	C
SWH	Adler Aviation	C
SWN	West Air Europe	SE
SWR	Swiss Intl Airlines	HB
SWT	Swiftair	EC
SWU	Swiss European Air Lines	HB
SWW	Shovkovly Shlyah	UR
SXM	Saemsa	XA
SXN	Air Sweden	SE
SXP	Sprint Air	SP
SXR	Skyexpress	RA
SXS	Sunexpress	TC
SYJ	Slate Falls Airways	C
SYL	Yakutia Airlines	RA
SYM	Sayat Air	UP
SYR	Syrianair	YK
SYX	Midwest Connect	N
TAA	Aeropacifico	XA
TAC	Turbot Air Cargo	6V
TAE	TAME	HC
TAH	Air Moorea	F
TAI	TACA Intl Airlines	YS
TAJ	Tunisavia	TS
TAK	Tatarstan Air	RA
TAM	TAM Linhas Aereas	PP
TAN	Zanair	5H
TAO	Aeromar Airlines	XA
TAP	TAP Air Portugal	CS
TAR	Tunisair	TS
TAS	Lotus Air	SU
TAT	TACA Costa Rica	TI
TAY	TNT Airways	OO
TBM	Taban Air	EP
TBN	Teebah Airlines	J2
TBQ	Tobruk Air	5A
TCF	Shuttle America	N
TCI	Air Turks & Caicos	VQ-T
TCV	TACV - Transportes Aereos de Cabo Verde	D4
TCW	Thomas Cook Airlines Belgium	OO
TCX	Thomas Cook Airlines	G
TCY	Twin Cities Air Service	N
TDK	Transavia Denmark	OY
TDR	Trade Air	9A
TDX	Skylease Air Cargo	N
TEB	Tenir Airlines	EX
TET	Tepavia Trans Airline	ER
TFK	Transafrik Intl	S9
TFL	Arkefly	PH
TFO	Aeropacifico	XA
TFR	Toll Priority	VH
TFT	Thai Flying Service	HS
TGN	Trigana Air Service	PK
TGW	Tiger Airways	9V
TGY	Trans Guyana Airways	8R
TGZ	Airzena - Georgian Airlines	4L
THA	Thai Airways	HS
THE	Toumai Air Chad	TT
THK	THK - Turk Hava Kurumu	TC
THT	Air Tahiti Nui	F
THU	Thunder Airlines	C
THY	Turkish Airlines	TC
TIM	TEAM Airlines – Team Transportes Aereos	PP
TIW	Transcarga Intl Airways	YV
TJK	Tajik Air	EY
TJS	Tyrolean Jet Service	OE
TJT	Trast Aero	EX
TJT	Twin Jet	F
TLB	Atlantique Air Assistance	F
TLG	Investavia	UP
TLR	Air Libya	5A
TLT	Turtle Airways	DQ
TLX	Telesis Transair	N
TLY	Top-Fly	EC
TMG	Tri-MG Intra-Asia Airlines	PK
TMI	Tamir Aviation	4X
TMS	Temsco Helicopters	N
TMW	Trans Maldivian Airways	8Q
TMX	Tramon Air	ZS
TNA	Transasia Airways	B
TNB	Trans Air Benin	TY
TNL	Sky Horse Aviation	JU
TNM	Tiara Air	P4
TNO	Aerounion	XA
TNR	Tanana Air Service	N
TNT	Trans North Helicopters	C
TNV	Transnorthern Aviation	N
TNW	Trans Nation Airways	ET
TOK	Airlines of Papua New Guinea	P2
TOL	Tolair Services	N
TOM	Thomsonfly.com	G
TOS	Tropic Air Commuter	V3
TPA	Tampa Airlines	HK
TPC	Air Caledonie	F
TPG	Transportes Aereos Pegaso	XA
TPK	Air Horizon Afrique	TT
TPS	Tapsa Aviacion	LV
TPU	TACA Peru	OB
TRA	Transavia Airlines	PH
TRD	Trans Island Air 2000	8P
TRG	Tragsa Medios Aereos	EC
TRI	Ontario Ministry of Natural Resources Aviation Services	C
TRN	Aerotron	XA
TRS	Airtran Airways	N
TSC	Air Transat	C
TSD	TAF Linhas Aereas	PP
TSE	Transmile Air Services	9M
TSG	Transair Congo	TN
TSH	Regional 1 Airlines	C
TSK	Tomskavia	RA
TSO	Transaero Airlines	RA
TSP	Inter - transportes Aereos Inter	TG
TSU	Gulf and Caribbean Air	N
TSY	Tristar Air	SU
TTA	TTA - Sociedade de Transportes e Trabalho Aereo	C9
TTC	Transteco	D2
TTH	Tarhan Air	TC
TTL	Total Linhas Aereas	PP
TUA	Turkmenistan Airlines	EZ
TUI	Sevenair	TS
TUL	Tulpar Air	RA
TUM	Tyumenspecavia	RA
TUP	Aviastar - Tupolev	RA
TUR	Atur	HC
TUS	ABSA Cargo	PP
TUX	Tulpar Air Service	UP
TUY	Linea Turistica Aereotuy	YV
TVF	Transavia France	F
TVH	Tavasa	EC
TVJ	Tavaj Linhas Aereas	PP
TVL	Travel Service Hungary	HA
TVR	Tavrey Aircompany	UR
TVS	Smartwings	OK

TVS	Travel Service Airlines	OK
TWM	Transairways	C9
TWN	Avialeasing	UK
TXC	Trans Avia Export Cargo Airlines	EW
TXU	Atesa	HC
TZR	Rainbow Air	YV
UAC	United Air Charters	Z
UAE	Emirates	A6
UAK	Aviant	UR
UAL	United Air Lines	N
UAR	Aerostar	UR
UBA	Myanma Airways	XY
UCR	Aero-Charter Ukraine	UR
UDC	Donbassaero	UR
UDN	Dnepr-Air	UR
UFA	Ukraine Flight State Academy	UR
UGB	Air Uganda	5X
UGN	Yuzhnaya Aircompany	UP
UGP	Shar Ink	RA
UGX	East African Airlines	5X
UHS	Uvuaga	RA
UIA	Uni Air	B
UIL	United Intl Airlines	YU
UKL	Ukraine Air Alliance	UR
UKM	Um Air	UR
UKN	Ukraine Air Enterprise	UR
UKS	Ukrainian Cargo Airways	UR
UKU	Sverdlovsk 2nd Air Enterprise	RA
UKW	Lviv Airlines	UR
UMK	Yuzmashavia	UR
UNF	Union Flights	N
UNR	Rivne Universal Avia	UR
UNS	Uensped Paket Servisi / UPS	TC
UPL	Ukrainian Pilot School	UR
UPX	UPS Airlines	N
URG	Air Urga	UR
URJ	Star Air Intl	AP
URN	Turanair	4K
URP	ARP 410 Airlines	UR
URR	Aurora Airlines	S5
USA	US Airways	N
USC	Airnet Systems	N
USX	US Airways Express	N
UTA	Utair Airlines	RA
UTG	Utage	3C
UTR	Utair South Africa	ZS
UTY	Alliance Airlines	VH
UYA	Flight Alaska	N
UYC	Cameroon Airlines	TJ
UZA	Constanta Airlines	UR
UZB	Uzbekistan Airways	UK
UZS	Samarkand Airways	UK
VAA	Van Air Europe	OK
VAL	Voyageur Airways	C
VAS	Atran - Aviatrans Cargo Airlines	RA
VAT	Vision Air	EI
VAZ	Red Wings	RA
VBG	Vyborg Airlines	RA
VBW	Air Burkina	XT
VCV	Conviasa	YV
VDA	Volga-Dnepr Airlines	RA
VEA	Cargo Air	LZ
VEC	Venescar Intl	YV
VEJ	Aero Ejectivos	YV
VEN	Transaven	YV
VES	Vieques Air Link	N
VFC	Vasco	VN
VGN	Air Nigeria	5N
VGV	Vologda Air Enterprise	RA
VIM	VIA - Air Via	LZ
VIN	Vincent Aviation (Australia)	VH
VIR	Virgin Atlantic Airways	G
VIS	Vision Air Intl	AP
VIV	Viva Aerobus	XA
VIZ	Aerovis Airlines	UR
VKG	Thomas Cook Scandinavia	OY
VLA	Valan Intl Cargo	ZS
VLG	Vueling Airlines	EC
VLK	Vladivostok Air	RA
VLM	VLM Airlines	OO

VLO	Varig Log	PP
VLU	Valuair	9V
VMM	Vuelos Mediterrano	EC
VNE	Venezolana	YV
VNZ	Tbilaviamsheni	4L
VOG	Voyager Airlines	S2
VOI	Volaris	XA
VOS	Rovos Air	ZS
VOZ	Virgin Blue Airlines	VH
VPB	Veteran Airlines	UR
VPV	Vip-Avia	4L
VRA	British Intl	G
VRB	Silverback Cargo Freighters	9XR
VRD	Virgin America	N
VRE	Volare Aviation Enterprise	UR
VRN	Varig	PP
VSO	Aerolineas Sosa	HR
VSV	Scat Aircompany	UP
VTA	Air Tahiti	F
VTE	Corporate Flight Management	N
VTK	Vostok Airlines	RA
VTS	Everts Air Cargo	N
VTS	Everts Air Alaska	N
VUN	Air Ivoire	TU
VUR	VIP - Vuelos Internos Privados	HC
VVA	Aviast Air	RA
VXP	Mali Air Express	TZ
VXX	Aviaexpress Aircompany	UR
VZR	Air Loyauté	F
WAA	Westair Wings	V5
WAB	Aero Industries	N
WAE	Western Air Express	N
WAK	Wings of Alaska	N
WAM	Air Taxi & Cargo	ST
WAP	Arrow Panama	HP
WAV	Warbelow's Air	N
WBA	Finncomm Airlines	OH
WBR	Air Choice One	N
WCO	Columbia Helicopters	N
WDL	WDL Aviation	D
WEA	White Eagle General Aviation	SP
WEB	Webjet Linhas Aereas	PP
WEW	Express Air	C
WEW	West Wind Aviation	C
WFR	Alwafeer Air	HZ
WHT	White	CS
WIA	Winair	PJ
WIF	Wideroe's Flyveselskap	LN
WIG	Wiggins Airways	N
WJA	Westjet	C
WKH	Kharkov Aviation Production Association	UR
WLA	Airwaves Airlink	9J
WLB	Wings Of Lebanon Aviation	OD
WLC	Welcome Air	OE
WLG	Volga Aviaexpress	RA
WLX	West Air Europe	LX
WOA	World Airways	N
WON	Wings Air	PK
WOW	Air Southwest	G
WRC	Wind Rose	UR
WRT	Wright Air Service	N
WSG	Wasaya Airways	C
WST	Western Air	C6
WTV	Western Aviators	N
WUA	Wizz Air Ukraine	UR
WVL	Wizz Air Bulgaria	LZ
WZZ	Wizz Air	HA
XAK	Airkenya	5Y
XAR	Xpress Air	PK
XKX	Asecna	6V
XLF	XL Airways France	F
XLL	Air Excel	5H
XME	Australian Air Express	VH
YZR	Yangtze River Express	B
ZAQ	Zoom Airways	S2
ZBA	ZB Air	5Y

685

AIRPORT THREE-LETTER CODES

Code	Airport	Code	Airport	Code	Airport
AAC	Al-Arish, SU	AMS	Amsterdam-Schiphol, PH	BBJ	Bitburg, D
AAH	Aachen-Merzbrück, D	AMZ	Auckland-Ardmore, NZ	BBP	Bembridge, G
AAL	Aalborg, OY	ANC	Anchorage Intl, AK	BBU	Bucharest-Baneasa, YR
AAN	Al Ain (A6)	ANE	Angers-Marce, F	BBX	Blue Bell-Wing Field, PA
AAR	Aarhus-Tirstrup, OY	ANF	Antofagasta-Cerro Moreno	BBZ	Zambezi, 9J
ABA	Abakan,RA		Intl, CC	BCN	Barcelona-le Prat, EC
ABD	Abadan- Boigny Intl, EP	ANG	Angouleme /	BCS	Belle Chase, LA
ABI	Abilene Regional, TX		Brie-Champniers, F	BCT	Boca Raton, FL
ABJ	Abidjan-Felix Houphouet	ANI	Aniak, AK	BDA	Bermuda Intl Hamilton, VP-B
	Boigirly, TU	ANK	Ankara-Etimesgut, TC	BDB	Bundaberg, Qld
ABQ	Albuquerque Intl, NM	ANR	Antwerp-Deurne, OO	BDG	Blanding-Municipal, UT
ABS	Abu Simbel, SU	ANU	Saint Johns/VC Bird, V2	BDJ	Banjarmasin-
ABV	Abuja-Intl, 5N	AOC	Altenburg-Nobitz, D		Syamsuddin Noor, PK
ABX	Albury, NSW	AOG	Anshun, B	BDL	Windsor Locks-Bradley
ABZ	Aberdeen-Dyce, G	AOI	Ancona-Falconara, I		Intl, CT
ACA	Acapulco-Gen.Alvarez Intl, XA	AOR	Alor Setar, 9M	BDO	Bandung-Husein
ACC	Accra-Kotoka Intl, 9G	AOT	Aosta-Corrado Gex, I		Sastranegara, PK
ACE	Arrecife, Lanzarote, EC	APA	Denver-Centennial, CO	BDQ	Vadodora, VT
ACH	Altenrhein, HB	APF	Naples-Municipal, FL	BDR	Bridgeport-
ACI	Alderney-The Blaye, G	APS	Anapolis, PP		Sikorsky Memorial, CT
ACK	Nantucket Memorial, MA	APV	Apple Valley, CA	BDS	Brindisi-Papola Casale, I
ACO	Ascona, HB	APW	Apia-Faleolo, 5W	BDU	Bardufoss, LN
ACS	Achinsk, RA	AQJ	Aqaba, JY	BEB	Benbecula, G
ACT	Waco Regional, TX	ARA	New Iberia-Acadiana, LA	BEC	Wichita-Beech Field, KS
ACY	Atlantic City Intl, NJ	ARG	Walnut Ridge, AR	BED	Bedford-Hanscom Field, MA
ADA	Adana-Sakirpasa, TC	ARH	Arkhangelsk-Talagi, RA	BEG	Belgrade Intl, YU
ADB	Izmir-Adnan Menderes, TC	ARK	Arusha, 5H	BEL	Belem-Val de Caes, PP
ADD	Addis Ababa-Bole Intl, ET	ARN	Stockholm-Arlanda, SE	BEN	Benghazi-Benina, 5A
ADE	Aden Intl, 7O	ASB	Ashgabat/Ashkhabad, EZ	BEO	Newcastle-Belmont, NSW
ADL	Adelaide, SA	ASF	Astrakhan-Narimanovo, RA	BES	Brest-Guipavas, F
ADM	Ardmore Municipal, OK	ASH	Nashua-Boise Field, NH	BET	Bethel, AK
ADQ	Kodiak, AK	ASJ	Amami O Shima, JA	BEV	Beer-Sheba-Teyman, 4X
ADS	Dallas-Addison, TX	ASM	Asmara Intl, E3	BEW	Beira, C9
ADZ	San Andres-	ASP	Alice Springs, NWT	BEY	Beirut Intl, OD
	Sesquicentenario, HK	ASU	Asuncion-	BFE	Bielefeld, D
AEH	Abecher, TT		Silvio Pettirossi, ZP	BFF	Scottsbluff-Western
AEP	Buenos Aires Aeroparque	ASW	Aswan, SU		Nebraska Regional, NE
	Jorge Newbery, LV	ATH	Athens-Eleftherios Venizelos	BFI	Seattle-Boeing Field, WA
AER	Sochi-Adler, RA		Intl, SX	BFM	Mobile Downtown, AL
AES	Aalesund-Vigra, LN	ATL	Atlanta-William B Hartsfield	BFN	Bloemfontein-
AET	Allakaiket, AK		Intl, GA		JBM Hertzog, ZS
AEX	Alexandria-Intl, LA	ATW	Appleton-Outagamie Co, WI	BFP	Beaver Falls, PA
AEY	Akureyri, TF	AUA	Oranjestad-	BFS	Belfast-Intl, G
AFW	Fort Worth Alliance, TX		Reina Beatrix, P4	BGA	Bucaramanga, HK
AGA	Agadir-Inezgane, CN	AUF	Auxerre-Branches, F	BGF	Bangui-M'Poko, TL
AGB	Augsburg-Mühlhausen, D	AUH	Abu Dhabi Intl, A6	BGI	Bridgetown-Grantley
AGC	Pittsburgh-Allegheny Co, PA	AUR	Aurillac, F		Adams Intl, VP-B
AGF	Agen-La Gareenne, F	AUS	Austin-Bergstrom Intl, TX	BGO	Bergen-Flesland, LN
AGP	Malaga, EC	AUZ	Aurora-Municipal, IL	BGR	Bangor, ME
AGR	Agra-Kheria, VT	AVB	Aviano, I	BGW	Baghdad-Al Muthana, YI
AGV	Acarigua Oswaldo	AVN	Avignon-Caumont, F	BGY	Bergamo-Orio al Serio, I
	Guevera Mujica, YV	AVP	Scranton-Wilkes	BHB	Bar Harbor-Hancock Co, ME
AID	Anderson Municipal, IN		Barre Intl, PA	BHD	Belfast-City, G
AJA	Ajaccio-Campo Dell'Oro, F	AVV	Avalon, VIC	BHE	Blenheim, ZK
AKC	Akron-Fulton Intl, OH	AVW	Marana-Regional, AZ	BHM	Birmingham ,AL
AKL	Auckland Intl, ZK	AWK	Wake Island, V6	BHQ	Broken Hill, SA
AKN	King Salmon, AK	AWM	West Memphis-Municipal, AR	BHX	Birmingham Intl, G
AKT	Akrotiri, 5B	AWZ	Ahwaz,EP	BIA	Bastia-Poretta, F
AKX	Aktobe/Aktyubinsk, UN	AXA	Anguilla-Wallblake, VP-A	BIK	Biak-Frans Kaiieppo, PK
ALA	Almaty, UN	AYK	Arkalyk, UN	BIL	Billings-Logan Intl, MT
ALB	Albany-County, NY	AYT	Antalya, TC	BIM	Bimini Intl, C6
ALC	Alicante, EC	AYU	Aiyura, P2	BIO	Bilbao, EC
ALF	Alta, LN	AZI	Abu Dhabi-Bateen, A6	BIQ	Biarritz-Parme,F
ALG	Algiers-	AZP	Mexico City-Atizapan, XA	BIR	Biratnagar, 9N
	Houari Boumediene, 7T			BJI	Bemidji, MN
ALW	Walla Walla Regional, WA	BAH	Bahrain Intl, A9C	BJL	Banjul-
ALY	Alexandria, SU	BAK	Baku-Geidar Aliev Intl, 4K		Yundum Intl, C5
AMA	Amarillo Intl, TX	BAQ	Barranquilla-Ernisto	BJM	Bujumbura Intl, 9U
AMD	Ahmedabad, VT		Cortissoz, HK	BJS	Beijing-Metropolitan, B
		BAX	Barnaul-Mikhailovka, RA	BJY	Belgrade-Batajnica, YU
AMM	Amman-Queen Alia Intl, JY	BBF	Burlington, MA	BKA	Moscow-Bykovo, RA

686

BKI	Kota Kinabalu Intl, 9M
BKK	Bangkok Suvarnabhumi, HS
BKO	Bamako-Senou, TZ
BKV	Brooksville-Pilot Co, FL
BKY	Bukavu-Kavumu, 9Q
BLA	Barcelona-Gen Anzoategui Intl, YV
BLD	Boulder City, NV
BLI	Bellingham-Intl, WA
BLK	Blackpool, G
BLL	Billund, OY
BLQ	Bologna-Guglielmo Marconi, I
BLR	Bangalore-Hindustan, VT
BLX	Belluno, I
BLZ	Blantyre-Chileka, 7Q
BMA	Stockholm-Bromma, SE
BME	Broome, WA
BNA	Nashville Intl, TN
BND	Bandar Abbas, EP
BNE	Brisbane Intl, Qld
BNI	Benin City, TY
BNK	Ballina, NSW
BNS	Barinas, YV
BNX	Banja Luka, T9
BOD	Bordeaux-Merignac, F
BOG	Bogota-Eldorado, HK
BOH	Bournemouth Intl, G
BOI	Boise Air Terminal (Gowen Field), ID
BOM	Mumbai Intl, VT
BON	Kralendijk-Flamingo Int, Bonaire, PJ
BOO	Bodo, LN
BOS	Boston-Logan Intl, MA
BPN	Balikpapan-Sepinggan, PK
BQH	Biggin Hill, UK
BQK	Brunswick-Glynco Jetport, GA
BQN	Aguadilla-Rafael Hernandez, PR
BQS	Blagoveschensk-Ignatyevo, RA
BRE	Bremen, D
BRN	Bern-Belp, HB
BRO	Brownsville, TX
BRQ	Brno-Turany, OK
BRS	Bristol-Lulsgate, G
BRU	Brussels-National, OO
BRV	Bremerhaven, D
BRW	Barrow-Wiley Post / Will Rogers Memorial, AK
BSB	Brasilia Intl, PP
BSG	Bata, 3C
BSL	Basle-Mulhouse EuroAirport, HB
BSR	Basrah Intl, YI
BTK	Bratsk, RA
BTR	Baton Rouge, LA
BTS	Bratislava-MR Stefanik, OM
BTV	Burlington Intl, VT
BTZ	Bursa, TC
BUD	Budapest-Ferihegy, HA
BUF	Buffalo-Greater Buffalo Intl, NY
BUG	Benguela, D2
BUQ	Bulawayo, Z
BUR	Burbank-Glendale Pasadena, CA
BUS	Batumi-Chorokh, 4L
BVA	Beauvais-Tille, F
BVB	Boa Vista Intl, PP
BVO	Bartlesville, OK
BVX	Batesville-Municipal, AR
BWB	Barrow Island, WA
BWE	Braunschweig, D
BWI	Baltimore-Washington Intl, MD
BWN	Bandar Seri Begawan / Brunei Intl, V8
BWO	Balakovo, RA
BWS	Blaine, WA
BWU	Sydney-Bankstown, NSW
BXJ	Burundai, UN
BYG	Buffalo-Municipal, WY
BZE	Belize City-Philip SW Goldson Intl, V3
BZG	Bydgoszcz, SP
BZK	Bryansk, RA
BZV	Brazzaville Maya-Maya, TN
BZZ	Brize Norton, G
CAE	Columbia Metropolitan, SC
CAG	Cagliari-Elmas, I
CAI	Cairo Intl, SU
CAK	Akron-Canton Regional, OH
CAN	Guangzhou-Baiyun, B
CAP	Cap Haitien Intl, HH
CAS	Casablanca-Anfa, CN
CAY	Cayenne-Rochambeau, F-O
CBB	Cochabamba-Jorge Wilsterman, CP
CBG	Cambridge, G
CBL	Cuidad Bolivar, YV
CBQ	Calabar, 5N
CBR	Canberra, ACT
CCL	Chinchilla, Qld
CCP	Concepcion-Carriel Sur, CC
CCS	Caracas-Simon Bolivar Intl, YV
CCU	Calcutta-Chadra Bose Intl, VT
CDB	Cold Bay, AK
CDC	Cedar City-Municipal, UT
CDG	Paris-Charles de Gaulle, F
CDU	Camden, NSW
CDW	Caldwell-Essex Co, NJ
CEB	Cebu-Lahug, RP
CEE	Cherepovets, RA
CEJ	Chernigov-Shestovitsa, UR
CEK	Chelyabinsk-Balandino, RA
CEQ	Cannes-Mandelieu, F
CER	Cherbourg-Maupertun, F
CEW	Crestview-Bob Sikes, FL
CFE	Clermont-Ferrand, F
CFN	Donegal-Carrickfin, EI
CFR	Caen-Carpiquet, F
CFS	Coffs Harbour, NSW
CFU	Corfu: Kerkira-Ioannis Kapodidtrias, SX
CGH	Sao Paulo-Congonhas, PP
CGK	Jakarta-Soekarno Hatta Intl, PK
CGN	Cologne-Bonn, D
CGO	Zhengzhou, B
CGP	Chittagong Intl, S2
CGQ	Changchun, B
CGR	Campo Grande Intl, PP
CHA	Chattanooga, TN
CHC	Christchurch Intl, ZK
CHD	Chandler-Williams AFB, AZ
CHR	Chateauroux-Deols, F
CHS	Charleston Intl, SC
CHT	Chathams Island-Karewa, ZK
CIA	Rome-Ciampino, I
CIC	Chico, CA
CIH	Changzhi, B
CIX	Chiclayo-Cornel Ruiz, OB
CJB	Coimbatore-Peelamedu, VT
CJJ	Cheongju City, HL
CJN	El Cajun, CA
CJU	Cheju Intl, HL
CKC	Cherkassy, UR
CKG	Chongqing, B
CKY	Conakry-Gbessia, 3X
CLD	Carlsbad, CA
CLE	Cleveland-Hopkins Intl, OH
CLO	Cali-Alfonso Bonilla Aragon, HK
CLQ	Colima, XA
CLT	Charlotte-Douglas Intl, NC
CLU	Columbus-Municipal, IN
CMB	Colombo-Bandaranayike Intl, 4R
CMD	Cootamundra, NSW
CME	Cuidad del Carmen, XA
CMF	Chambery/Aix les Bains, F
CMH	Columbus-Port Intl, OH
CMN	Casablanca-Mohammed V, CN
CMR	Colmar-Houssen, F
CMU	Kundiawa-Chimbu, P2
CMV	Coromandel, ZK
CND	Constanta-Kogalniceanu, YR
CNF	Belo Horizonte-Neves Intl, PP
CNI	Shanghai, B
CNL	Sindal, OY
CNS	Cairns, Qld
CNW	Waco-James Connolly, TX
COA	Columbia, CA
COE	Coeur d'Alene, ID
CON	Concord-Municipal, NH
COO	Cotonou-Cadjehoun, TY
COR	Cordoba-Pajas Blancas, LV
COS	Colorado Springs Memorial, CO
COU	Columbia Regional, MO
CPE	Campeche-Intl, XA
CPH	Copenhagen-Kastrup, OY
CPQ	Campinhas-Viracopos Intl, PP
CPR	Casper-Natrona County Intl, WY
CPT	Cape Town-DF Malan Intl, ZS
CRD	Comodoro Rivadavia / Gen Mosconi, LV
CRE	Myrtle Beach-Grand Strand, SC
CRK	Diosdado Macapagal Intl, RP
CRL	Brussels-Charleroi, OO
CRU	Carriacou Island, J3
CRZ	Chardzhev, EZ
CSE	Crested Butte, CO
CSL	San Luis Obispo-O'Sullivan, CA
CSM	Clinton, OK
CSN	Carson City, NV
CSY	Cheboksary, RA
CTA	Catania-Fontanarossa, I
CTC	Catamarca, LV
CTG	Cartagena-Rafael Nunez, HK
CTM	Chetumal, XA
CTN	Cooktown, Qld
CTS	Sapporo-New Chitose, JA
CTU	Chengdu-Shuangliu, B
CUB	Columbus-Owens Field, SC
CUD	Caloundra, Qld
CUE	Cuenca, EC
CUG	Cudal, NSW
CUH	Cushing-Municipal, OK
CUM	Cumana-Antonio Jose de Sucre, YV
CUN	Cancun Intl, XA
CUR	Curacao-Willemstadt, YV
CUU	Chihuahua / Gen Villalobos Intl, XA
CUZ	Cuzco-Velaazco Astete, OB
CVF	Courchevel, F
CVG	Cincinnati-Covington Intl, OH
CVJ	Cuernavaca, XA
CVN	Clovis-Municipal, NM
CVQ	Carnarvon, G
CVR	Culver City, CA
CVT	Coventry-Baginton, G
CWA	Mosinee Central, WI
CWB	Curitiba-Alfonso Pena, PP
CWC	Chernovtsy, UR
CWF	Chenault Airpark, AK

GLO	Gloucester, G	HKD	Hakodate, JA	IOM	Ronaldsway, M
GLS	Galveston-Scholes Field, TX	HKG	Hong Kong Intl, B-H	IQQ	Iquique-Diego Aracena, CC
GLZ	Gilze-Rijen, PH	HKT	Phuket Intl, HS	IQT	Iquitos-Coronel Vignetta, OB
GME	Gomel-Pokalubishi, EW	HLA	Lanseria, ZS	IRK	Kirksville-Regional, MO
GMN	Greymouth, ZK	HLF	Hultsfred, SE	ISA	Mount Isa, Qld
GNB	Grenoble-St Geoirs, F	HLP	Jakarta-	ISB	Islamabad-Chaklala, AP
GOA	Genoa-Cristoforo Colombo, I		Halim Perdanakusuma, PK	ISM	Kissimmee Municipal, FL
GOH	Godthaab-Nuuk, OY	HLT	Hamilton, VIC	ISO	Kinston-Stalling Field, NC
GOI	Goa-Dabolim, VT	HLZ	Hamilton, ZK	IST	Istanbul-Ataturk, TC
GOJ	Nizhny Novogorod-	HME	Hassi Messaoud, 7T	ITB	Itaituba, PP
	Streigino, RA	HMJ	Khmelnitsky-Ruzichnaya, UR	ITM	Osaka-Itami Intl, JA
GOM	Goma, 9Q	HMO	Hermosillo-	ITO	Hilo Intl, HI
GON	Groton-New London, CT		Gen Garcia Intl, XA	IVC	Invercargill, ZK
GOT	Gothenburg-Landvetter, SE	HMT	Hemet-Ryan Field, CA	IWA	Ivanovo-Zhukovka, RA
GOV	Gove-Nhulunbuy, NWT	HND	Tokyo-Haneda Intl, JA		
GPT	Gulfport-Biloxi Regional, MS	HNL	Honolulu Intl, HI	JAA	Jalalabad, YA
GRO	Gerona-Costa Brava, EC	HNS	Haines Municipal, AK	JAB	Jabiru, NT
GRQ	Groningen-Eelde, OY	HOH	Hohenems-Dornbirn, OE	JAN	Jackson Intl, MS
GRR	Grand Rapids-Kent County, MI	HOM	Homer, AK	JAV	Ilulissat-Jakobshavn, OY
GRU	Sao Paulo-Guarulhos, PP	HOT	East Hampton, NY	JAX	Jacksonville Intl, FL
GRV	Grozny, RA	HOU	Houston-Hobby, TX	JDP	Paris-Heliport, F
GRZ	Graz-Thalerhof, OE	HRB	Harbin-Yanjiagang, B	JED	Jeddah-King Abdul Aziz
GSE	Gothenburg-Save, SE	HRE	Harare Intl, Z		Intl, HZ
GSO	Greensboro-Piedmont	HRG	Hurghada, SU	JER	Jersey, G
	Triad Intl, SC	HRK	Kharkiv-Osnova, UR	JFK	New York-JFK Intl, NY
GTR	Columbus-	HSH	Las Vegas-Henderson, NV	JGC	Grand Canyon Heliport, AZ
	Golden Triangle Regional, GA	HSM	Horsham, VIC	JHB	Johor Bahru-Sultan Ismail
GUA	Guatemala City-La Aurora, TG	HST	Homestead, FL		Intl, 9M
GUB	Guerrero Negro, XA	HTA	Chita-Kadala, RA	JHE	Helsingborg Heliport, SE
GUM	Guam-	HTI	Hamilton Island, Qld	JHW	Jamestown-Chautauqua Co, NY
	Ab Won Pat Intl, N	HTO	East Hampton, NY	JIB	Djibouti-Ambouli, J2
GUP	Gallup-	HUF	Terre Haute-	JIL	Jilin, B
	Sen Clark Municipal, NM		Hulman Regional, IN	JJN	Jinjiang, B
GUW	Akyrau, UN	HUM	Houma-Terrebonne, LA	JKG	Jonkoping-Axamo, SE
GVA	Geneva-Cointrin, HB	HUV	Hudiksvall, SE	JNB	Johannesburg-
GVL	Gainsville, GA	HUY	Humberside, G		OR Tambo Intl, ZS
GVQ	Coyhaique-Teniente Vidal, CC	HVB	Hervey Bay, Qld	JNU	Juneau Intl, AK
GVT	Greenville-Majors Field, TX	HVN	New Haven-Tweed, CT	JST	Johnstown-Cambria County, PA
GWO	Greenwood-le Floor, MS	HWO	Hollywood-North Perry, FL	JUB	Juba, ST
GWT	Westerland-Sylt, D	HYA	Hyannis-	JVL	Janesville-Rock County, WI
GWY	Galway-Carnmore, EI		Barnstable Municipal, MA		
GXQ	Coyhaique-Teniente Vidal, CC	HZB	Mervilel-Calonnel, F	KAD	Kaduna, 5N
GYE	Guayaquil-Simon Bolivar, HK			KAN	Kano Mallam Aminu
GYN	Goiania-Santa Genoveva, PP	IAB	Wichita-McConnell AFB, KS		Intl, 5N
GYR	Goodyear-Litchfield, AZ	IAD	Washington-	KBL	Kabul-Khwaja Rawash, YA
GZA	Gaza-Yasser Arafat		Dulles Intl, DC	KBP	Kiev-Borispol, UR
	Intl, SU-Y	IAG	Niagara Falls-Intl, NY	KCH	Koching, 9M
GZM	Gozo, 9H	IAH	Houston-	KDH	Kandahar, YA
			George Bush Intl, TX	KDK	Kodiak Municipal, AK
HAH	Moroni-Prince Said Ibrahim, D6	IBA	Ibadan, 5N	KEF	Keflavik Intl, TF
HAJ	Hannover, D	IBE	Ibague-Perales, HK	KEH	Kenmore Air Harbor, WA
HAK	Haikou-Dayingshan, B	IBZ	Ibiza, EC	KEJ	Kemorovo, RA
HAM	Hamburg-Fuhlsbüttel; D	ICN	Seoul-Incheon, HL	KEP	Nepalgunj, 9N
HAN	Hanoi-Gialam, VN	ICT	Wichita-Mid Continent, KS	KER	Kerman, EP
HAO	Hamilton, OH	IEV	Kiev-Zhulyany, UR	KGC	Kingscote, SA
HAU	Haugesund, LN	IFJ	Isafjordur, TF	KGD	Kaliningrad-Khrabovo, RA
HAV	Havana-	IFN	Isfahan, EP	KGF	Qaragandy-Sary Arka, UN
	Jose Marti Intl, CU	IFO	Ivano-Frankivsk, UR	KGI	Kalgoorlie, WA
HBA	Hobart, TAS	IFP	Laughlin-Bullhead Intl, AZ	KGL	Kigali-
HDD	Hyderabad, VT	IGM	Kingman, AZ		Gregoire Kayibanda, 9XR
HEL	Helsinki-Vantaa, OH	IJK	Izhevsk, RA	KGO	Kirovograd-Khmelyovoye, UR
HEM	Helsinki-Malmi, OH	IKI	Iki, JA	KGP	Kogalym, RA
HER	Heraklion, SX	IKT	Irkutsk, RA	KHH	Kaoshiung Intl, B
HEX	Santo Domingo-la Herrara, HI	ILG	Wilmington-Newcastle, DE	KHI	Karachi Jinnah Intl, AP
HFA	Haifa U Michaeli, 4X	ILI	Iliamna, AK	KHV	Khabarovsk-Novy, ra
HGH	Hangzhou-Jianqio, B	ILN	Wilmington-	KIH	Kish Island, EP
HGL	Helgoland-Dune, D		Airborne Airpark, OH	KIN	Kingston-Norman Manley
HGR	Hagerstown, MD	ILR	Ilorin, 5N		Internatonal, 6Y
HGU	Mount Hagen-Kagamuga, P2	IMT	Iron Mountain-Ford, MI	KIV	Kishinev-Chisinau, ER
HHN	Hahn, D	IND	Indianapolis Intl, IN	KIW	Kitwe-Southdowns, 9J
HHR	Hawthorne, CA	INI	Nis, YU	KIX	Osaka-Kansai Intl, JA
HID	Horn Island, Qld	INN	Innsbruck-Kranebitten, OE	KJA	Krasnoyarsk-Yemelyanovo, RA
HIG	Highbury, Qld	INT	Winston-Salem-	KJK	Kortrijk-Wevelgem, OO
HII	Lake Havasu City-Municipal, AZ		Smith Reynolds, NC	KKJ	Kitakyushu-Kokura, JA
HIK	Honolulu-Oahu Island, HI	INU	Nauru Island Intl, C2	KLF	Kaluga, RA
HIR	Honiara-Henderson, H4	INV	Inverness-Dalcross, G	KLU	Klagenfurt, OE

Code	Location	Code	Location	Code	Location
KMG	Kunming-Wujiaba, B	LEJ	Leipzig-Halle, D	MAH	Menorca-Mahon, EC
KMI	Miyazaki, JA	LEN	Leon, EC	MAJ	Majuro-Amata Kabua
KMJ	Kumamoto, JA	LEQ	Lands End-St Just, G		Intl, V7
KMW	Kostroma, RA	LEW	Lewiston-Auburn Municipal, ME	MAN	Manchester Intl, G
KNX	Kununurra, WA	LEY	Lelystad, PH	MAO	Manaus-Eduardo Gomes, PP
KOA	Kailua Kona, HI	LFT	Lafayette-Regional, AL	MAR	Maracaibo-
KOV	Kokhshetan, UN	LFW	Lome-Tokoin, 5V		La Chinita Internatonal, YV
KOW	Ganzhou, B	LGA	New York-La Guardia, NY	MAW	Malden, MO
KRB	Karumba, Qld	LGB	Long Beach-	MBA	Mombasa-Moi Intl, 5Y
KRH	Redhill, G		Daugherty Field, CA	MBD	Mmbatho Intl, ZS
KRK	Krakow Intl, SP	LGG	Liege-Bierset, OO	MBH	Maryborough, Qld
KRN	Kiruna, SE	LGW	London Gatwick, G	MBJ	Montego Bay-
KRO	Kurgan, RA	LGY	Lagunillas, YV		Sangster Internatonal, 6Y
KRP	Karup, OY	LHD	Anchorage-	MBW	Melbourne-Moorabin, VIC
KRR	Krasnodar-Pashkovskaya, RA		Lake Hood SPB, AK	MBX	Maribor, S5
KRS	Kristiansand-Kjevik, LN	LHE	Lahore Allama Iqbal	MCI	Kansas City Intl, MO
KRT	Khartoum-Civil, ST		Intl, AP	MCM	Monte Carlo Heliport, 3A
KSC	Kosice-Barca, OM	LHR	London-Heathrow, G	MCO	Orlando Intl, FL
KSD	Karlstad, SE	LHW	Lanzhou, B	MCP	Macapa-Intl, PP
KSF	Kassel-Calden, D	LIG	Limoges-Bellegarde, F	MCT	Muscat-Seeb Intl, A4O
KSK	Karlskoga, SE	LIL	Lille-Lesquin, F	MCW	Mason City Municipal, IA
KSM	St Mary's Bethel, AK	LIM	Lima-Jorge Chavez Intl, OB	MCX	Makhachkala-Uytash, RA
KSN	Kustanay, UN	LIN	Milan-Linate, I	MCY	Sunshine Coast, Qld
KSZ	Kotlas, RA	LIS	Lisbon, CS	MDE	Medellin-Olaya Herrera, HK
KTA	Karratha, WA	LIT	Little Rock-Adams Field, AR	MDL	Mandalay, XY
KTE	Kerteh-Petronas, 9M	LJU	Ljubljana-Brnik, S5	MDT	Harrisburg Intl, PA
KTM	Kathmandu-	LKE	Seattle-Lake Union, WA	MDU	Mendi, P2
	Tribhuvan Intl, 9N	LKO	Lucknow-Amausi, VT	MDW	Chicago-Midway, IL
KTN	Ketchikan Intl, AK	LKP	Lake Placid, NY	MEA	Macae & Sao Tome, PP
KTP	Kingston-Tinson Peninsula, 6Y	LLA	Lulea-Kallax, SE	MEB	Melbourne-Essendon, VIC
KTR	Katherine-Tindal, NWT	LLC	Valdez, AK	MEL	Melbourne-Tullamarine, VIC
KTW	Katowice-Pyrzowice, SP	LLW	Lilongwe-	MEM	Memphis Intl, TN
KUF	Samara-Kurumoch, RA		Tilange Intl, 7Q	MER	Merced-Castle AFB, CA
KUL	Kuala Lumpur Intl, 9M	LME	Le Mans-Arnage, F	MES	Medan-Polonia, PK
KUN	Kaunus-	LMM	Los Mochis, XA	MEV	Minden-Douglas Co, NV
	Karlelava Intl, LY	LNA	West Palm Beach-	MEX	Mexico City-
KUT	Kutaisi, 4L		Lantana Co Park, FL		Juarez Intl, XA
KVB	Skovde, SE	LNX	Smolensk, RA	MFE	McAllen-Miller, TX
KVX	Kirov, RA	LNZ	Linz-Hoersching, OE	MFM	Macau Intl, B-M
KWE	Guiyang, B	LOS	Lagos-Murtala Mohammed, 5N	MFN	Milford Sound, ZK
KWI	Kuwait Intl, 9K	LPA	Las Palmas-Gran Canaria, EC	MGA	Managua-Sandino, YN
KXK	Komsomolsk, RA	LPB	La Paz-El Alto, CP	MGB	Mount Gambier, VIC
KYZ	Kyzyi, RA	LPI	Linkoping-Malmen, SE	MGL	Mönchengladbach, D
KZN	Kazan-Bonsoglebskow, RA	LPK	Lipetsk, RA	MGQ	Mogadishu Intl, 6O
KZO	Kzyl-Orda, UN	LPL	Liverpool-	MHB	Auckland-Mechanics Bay, ZK
			John Lennon Intl, G	MHD	Mashad-Shahid Hashemi
LAD	Luanda-4 de Fevereiro, D2	LPP	Lappeenranta, OH		Nejad Intl, EP
LAE	Lae-Nadzab, P2	LPY	Le Puy-Loudes, F	MHG	Mannheim-Neu Ostheim, D
LAF	Lafayette-Purdue University, IN	LRD	Laredo Intl, TX	MHH	Marsh Harnour, C6
LAJ	Lages, PP	LRE	Longreach, Qld	MHP	Minsk 1 Intl, EW
LAL	Lakeland Regional, FL	LRH	La Rochelle-Laleu, F	MHQ	Mariehamn, OH
LAO	Laoag Intl, RP	LRR	Lar, EP	MHR	Sacramento-Mather, CA
LAP	La Paz	LSI	Sumburgh, G	MHV	Mojave-Kern Co, CA
	Gen Leon Intl, XA	LST	Launceston, TAS	MIA	Miami Intl, FL
LAS	Las Vegas-	LTN	London-Luton, G	MID	Merida, XA
	McCarran Intl, NV	LTX	Latacunga, HC	MIE	Newcastle, IN
LAW	Lawton, OK	LUG	Lugano, I	MIR	Monastir-Habib Bourguiba
LAX	Los Angeles Intl, CA	LUK	Cincinatti Municipal, OH		Intl, TS
LBA	Leeds-Bradford, G	LUN	Lusaka Intl, 9J	MIU	Maiduguri, 5N
LBB	Lubbock, TX	LUX	Luxembourg, LX	MJI	Mitiga, 5A
LBD	Khudzhand, EY	LWB	Lewisburg-	MJM	Mbuji Mayi, 9Q
LBE	Latrobe-Westmoreland Co, PA		Greenbrier Valley, WV	MJZ	Mirny, RA
LBG	Paris-le Bourget, F	LWO	Lviv-Snilow, UR	MKC	Kansas City Downtown, MO
LBH	Sydney-Palm Beach SPB, NSW	LWR	Leeuwarden, PH	MKE	Milwaukee-Mitchell Field, WI
LBV	Libreville-Leon M'Ba, TR	LXA	Lhasa, B	MKY	MacKay, Qld
LCA	Larnaca Intl, 5B	LXR	Luxor, SU	MLA	Malta-Luqa, 9H
LCE	La Ceibe-	LXT	Latacunga, HC	MLB	Melbourne-Cape Kennedy, FL
	Goloson Intl, TG	LYN	Lyon-Bron, F	MLC	McAlester-Regional, OK
LCH	Lake Charles-Regional, LA	LYP	Faisalabad, AP	MLE	Male Intl, 8Q
LCK	Columbus-Rickenbacker, OH	LYS	Lyon-Satolas, F	MLH	Basle-Mulhouse EuroAirport, F
LCY	London-City, G	LYT	Lady Elliott Island, Qld	MLU	Monroe-Regional, LA
LDB	Londrina, PP	LYX	Lydd Intl, G	MLW	Monrovia-Spriggs Payne. A8
LDE	Tarbes-Ossun-Lourdes, F			MMK	Murmansk, RA
LDH	Lord Howe Island, NSW	MAA	Chennai, VT	MML	Marshall-Ryan Field, MN
LDK	Lidkoping-Hovby, SE	MAC	Macon-Smart, GA	MMX	Malmo-Sturup, SE
LED	St Petersburg-Pulkovo, RA	MAD	Madrid-Barajas, EC	MNI	Plymouth-WH Bramble (VP-M)
LEH	le Havre-Octeville, F	MAG	Madang, P2	MNL	Manila-

	Nino Aquino Intl, RP	NIM	Niamey-Diori Hamani, 5U	OTS	Anacortes, WA
MNZ	Manassas, VA	NKC	Nouakchott, 5T	OTZ	Kotzebue-Wien Memorial, AK
MOB	Mobile-Regional, AL	NKG	Nanjing, B	OUA	Ouagadougou, XT
MOL	Molde, LN	NKM	Nagoya-Komaki AFB, JA	OUL	Oulu, OH
MON	Mount Cook, ZK	NLK	Norfolk Island, NSW	OVB	Novosibirsk-Tolmachevo, RA
MOR	Morristown, TN	NLO	Kinshasa-N'dolo, 9Q	OVD	Castrillón-Asturias (EC)
MPB	Miami-Watson Island SPB, FL	NLP	Nelspruit, ZS	OWD	Norwood Memorial, MA
MPL	Montpellier-Mediterranean, F	NNK	Naknek, AK	OXB	Bissau Vieira Intl, J5
MPM	Maputo, C9	NNR	Connemara, EI	OXC	Oxford-Waterbury, CT
MPR	McPherson, KS	NOA	Nowra, NSW	OXR	Oxnard, CA
MPW	Marlupol, UR	NOE	Norden-Norddeich, D	OYS	Mariposa-Yosemite, CA
MQF	Magnitogorsk, RA	NOU	Noumea-La Tontouta, F-O	OZH	Zaporozhye-Mokraya, UR
MQL	Mildura, VIC	NOZ	Novokuznetsk, RA		
MQS	Mustique Intl, J8	NPE	Napier, ZK	PAC	Albrook-Marcos A Gelabert
MQT	Marquette-Sawyer, MI	NQA	Millington, TN		Panama City, HP
MQY	Smyrna, TN	NQN	Neuquen, LV	PAD	Paderborn-Lippstadt, D
MRI	Anchorage-Merrill Field, AK	NQY	Newquay-St Mawgan, G	PAE	Everett-Paine Field, WA
MRO	Masterton, ZK	NRK	Norrkoping, SE	PAP	Port-au-Prince
MRS	Marseille-Marignane, F	NRT	Tokyo-Narita Intl, JA		Intl, HH
MRU	Plaisance Intl, 3B	NSI	Yaounde, TJ	PAQ	Palmer Municipal, AK
MRV	Mineralnye Vody, RA	NSK	Norilsk, RA	PAZ	Poza Rica, XA
MRX	Morristown Nexrad, TN	NSN	Nelson, ZK	PBG	Plattsburgh, NY
MSC	Mesa-Falcon Field, AZ	NSO	Scone, NSW	PBH	Paro, A5
MSE	Manston-Kent Intl, G	NTB	Notodden, LN	PBI	Palm Beach Intl, FL
MSO	Missoula Johnson-Bell Field, MT	NTE	Nantes-Atlantique, F	PBM	Paramaribo-
MSP	Minneapolis-	NTL	Newcastle-Williamstown, NSW		Pengel Interntional, PZ
	St Paul Intl, MN	NTY	Sun City-Pilansberg, ZS	PCB	Pondok Cabe, PK
MSQ	Minsk 2 Intl, , EW	NUE	Nurenburg, D	PCL	Pucalipa-Rolden, OB
MST	Maastricht-Aachen, PH	NVA	Neiva-La Marquita, HK	PCM	Playa del Carmen, XA
MSU	Maseru-Moshoeshoe, 7P	NVR	Novgorod, RA	PDC	La Verne-Bracketts Field, CA
MSY	New Orleans Intl, LA	NWI	Norwich, G	PDK	Atlanta-Peachtree, GA
MTM	Metlakatla, AK	NYM	Nadym, RA	PDL	Ponta Delgada, CS
MTN	Baltimore-Glenn L Martin, MD	NYO	Nykoping-Skavsta, SE	PDV	Plovdiv, LZ
MTS	Manzini-Matsapha, 3D	NZC	Jackonsville Cecil Field, FL	PDX	Portland Intl, OR
MTY	Monterey-Gen Escobedo			PEE	Perm-Bolshoe-Savino, RA
	Intl, XA	OAG	Orange, NSW	PEK	Beijing-Capital, B
MUB	Maun, A2	OAJ	Jacksonville, NC	PEN	Penang-Intl, 9M
MUC	Munich-Franz Joseph Straus, D	OAK	Oakland Intl, CA	PER	Perth Intl, WA
MUN	Maturin, YV	OAX	Oaxaca-Xoxocotlan, XA	PEZ	Penza, RA
MVA	Myvatn-Rykiahlid, TF	OBF	Oberpfaffenhofen, D	PFO	Paphos Intl, 5B
MVD	Montevideo-	OBN	Oban, G	PGA	Page, AZ
	Carrasco Intl, CX	OBO	Obihiro, JA	PGD	Punta Gorda-Charlotte Co, FL
MVQ	Mogilev, EW	OCF	Ocala-Taylor Field, FL	PGF	Perpignan-Rivesaltes, F
MVY	Martha's Vineyard, MA	ODB	Cordoba-Palma del Rio, EC	PGX	Periguex-Brassillac, F
MWO	Middletown-	ODE	Odense-Beldringe, OY	PHC	Port Harcourt, 5N
	Hook Field Memorial, OH	ODS	Odessa-Tsentralny, UR	PHE	Port Hedland, WA
MWZ	Mwanza, 5H	ODW	Oak Harbor, WA	PHF	Newport News, VA
MXE	Maxton, NC	OEL	Orel, RA	PHL	Philadelphia Intl, PA
MXN	Morlaix-Ploujean, F	OGG	Kahului-Intl, HI	PHS	Phitsanulok-Sarit Sena, HS
MXP	Milan-Malpensa, I	OGL	Georgetown-Ogle, 8R	PHX	Phoenix-Sky Harbor Intl, AZ
MXX	Mora-Siljan, SE	OGZ	Vladivkavkaz-Beslan, RA	PHY	Phetchabun, HS
MYD	Malindi, 5Y	OKA	Okinawa-Naha, JA	PIE	St Petersburg-
MYL	McCall, ID	OKC	Oklahoma City-Will Roger, OK		Clearwater Intl, FL
MYR	Myrtle Beach, SC	OKD	Sapporo-Okadama, JA	PIK	Prestwick, G
MYV	Marysville-Yuba Co, CA	OLB	Olbia-Costa Smeralda, I	PIR	Pierre-Regional, SD
MYY	Miri, 9M	OLM	Olympia, WA	PIT	Pittsburgh Intl, PA
MZJ	Marana-Pinal Airpark, AZ	OMA	Omaha-Eppley Field, NE	PKC	Petropavlovsk Kamchatsky-
		OME	Nome, AK		Yelizovo, RA
NAG	Nagpur-Sonegaon, VT	OMS	Omsk-Severny, RA	PKR	Pokhara, 9N
NAL	Nalchik, RA	ONT	Ontario Intl, CA	PKU	Pekanbaru-Simpang Tiga, PK
NAN	Nadi Intl, DQ	OOL	Coolangatta, Qld	PKV	Pskov, RA
NAP	Naples-Capodichino, I	OPF	Opa Locka, FL	PLB	Plattsburg-Clinton Co, NY
NAS	Nassau Intl, C6	OPO	Porto, CS	PLH	Plymouth, G
NAY	Beijing-Nan Yuan, B	ORB	Orebro-Bofors, SE	PLL	Manaus-Ponta Pelada, PP
NBO	Nairobi-Jomo Kenyatta	ORD	Chicago-O'Hare Intl, IL	PLS	Providenciales Intl, VQ-T
	Intl, 5Y	ORG	Paramaribo-Zorg en Hoop, PZ	PLU	Belo Horizonte-Pampulha, PP
NCE	Nice-Cote d'Azur, F	ORK	Cork, EI	PLV	Poltava, UR
NCL	Newcastle, G	ORL	Orlando-Executive, FL	PLX	Semipalatisnk, UN
NDJ	N'djamena, TT	ORY	Paris-Orly, F	PMB	Pembina, ND
NEV	Nevis-Newcastle, V4	OSC	Oscoda-Wurtsmith AFB, MI	PMC	Puerto Montt, CC
NEW	New Orleans-Lakefront, LA	OSH	Oshkosh-Wittman Field, WI	PMD	Palmdale, CA
NFG	Nefteyugansk, RA	OSL	Oslo Intl, LN	PMF	Parma, I
NGO	Nagoya-Chubu, JA	OSR	Ostrava-Mosnov, OK	PMI	Palma de Mallorca, EC
NGS	Nagasaki, JA	OSS	Osh, EX	PMO	Palermo-Punta Raisi, I
NHT	RAF Northolt, G	OST	Ostend, OO	PMR	Palmerston-North, ZK
NIC	Nicosia, 5B	OTP	Bucharest-Otopeni Intl, YR	PNA	Pamplona, EC

PNE Philadelphia-Northern, PA
PNH Phnom Penh-Pochentong, XU
PNI Pohnpei-Caroline Islands, V6
PNK Pontianak-Supadio, PK
PNR Pointe Noire, TN
PNS Pensacola-Regional, FL
PNX Sherman-Denison, TX
POA Porto Alegre-Canoas, PP
POC La Verne-Brackett Field, CA
POG Port Gentil, TR
POM Port Moresby, P2
POP Puerto Plata Intl, HI
POS Port of Spain-Piarco, 9Y
POW Portoroz, S5
POX Pontoise-Cormeilles, F
PPB Presidente Prudente, PP
PPG Pago Pago Intl, N
PPK Petropavlovsk, UN
PPQ Paraparaumu, ZK
PPT Papeete-Faaa, , F-O
PQQ Port Macquarie, NSW
PRA Parana, LV
PRC Prescott-
    Ernest A Love Field, AZ
PRG Prague-Ruzyne, OK
PRN Pristina, YU
PRV Prerov, OK
PRY Pretoria-Wonderboom, ZS
PSA Pisa-Galileo, I
PSM Portsmouth-Pease Intl, NH
PSR Pescara, I
PSY Port Stanley, VP-F
PTA Port Alsworth, AK
PTG Pietersburg-Gateway, ZS
PTI Port Douglas, Qld
PTK Pontiac-Oakland, MI
PTN Ptterson-HPW Memorial, LA
PTP Pointe a Pitre-Le Raizet, F-O
PTY Panama City-Tocumen Intl, HP
PUF Pau-Pyrenees, F
PUG Port Agusta, SA
PUQ Punta Arenas, CC
PUU Puerto Asi, HK
PUY Pula, 9A
PVG Shanghai-Pu Dong Intl, B
PVH Porto Velho, PP
PVR Puerto Vallarta-Lic Gustavo
    Dias Ordaz Intl, XA
PVU Provo-Municipal. UT
PWK Chicago-Pal Waukee, IL
PWM Portland Intl Jetport, ME
PWQ Pavlodar, UN
PYL Perry Island SPB, AK
PZE Penzance, G

QKC Karaj-Payam, EP
QLA Lasham, G
QPG Paya Lebar, 9V
QPI Palmira, CP
QRA Johannesburg-Rand, ZS
QRC Rancagua-
    de la Independence, CC
QSC San Carlos, PP
QSM Utersen, D
QTK Rothenburg, D

RAB Rabaul, P2
RAI Praia-Mendes, D4
RAK Marrakesh-Menara, CN
RAO Ribeirao Preto, PP
RAR Rarotonga, E5
RAS Rasht, EP
RBA Rabat-Sale, CN
RBR Rio Branco-Medici, PP
RBY Ruby-Municipal, AK
RCM Richmond, Qld
RDD Redding-Municipal, CA

RDG Reading-Gen Spaatz Field, PA
RDM Redmond-Roberts Field, OR
RDU Raleigh-Durham Intl, NC
REC Recife-Guararapes, PP
REK Reykjavik, TF
REN Orenburg-Tsentralny, RA
REP Siem Reap, XU
REX Reynosa-Gen Lucio Blanco
    Intl, XA
RFD Rockford, IL
RGN Yangon Intl, XY
RHE Reims Champagne, F
RHI Rhinelander-Oneida Co, WI
RHO Rhodes-Diagoras, SX
RIC Richmond-Byrd Intl, VA
RIX Riga-Skulte Intl, YL
RJK Rijeka, 9A
RKD Rockland-Knox County, ME
RKE Roskilde, OY
RKT Ras al Khaimah Intl, A6
RLG Rostock-Laage, D
RMA Roma, Qld
RMI Rimini, I
RML Colombo-Ratmalana, 4R
RNC McMinnville-Warren Co, OR
RNO Reno-Cannon Intl, NV
RNS Rennes-St Jacques, F
RNT Seattle-Renton, WA
ROB Monrovia Roberts Intl, A8
ROK Rockhampton, IL
ROM Rome Urbe, I
ROR Koror-Airai, T8A
ROS Rosario-Fisherton, LV
ROT Rotorua, ZK
ROV Rostov-on-Don, RA
ROW Roswell-
    Industrial Air Center, NM
RPM Ngukurr, NT
RSE Sydney-Au Rose, Qld
RTM Rotterdam, PH
RTW Saratov-Tsentrainy, RA
RUH Riyadh-
    King Khalid Intl, HZ
RUN St Denis-Gilot, F-O
RVH St Petersburg-Rzhevka, RA
RWN Rivnu, UR
RYB Rybinsk-Staroselye, RA
RZN Ryazan, RA

SAH Sana'a Intl, 7O
SAL San Salvador-
    Comalapa Intl, YS
SAN San Diego-Lindbergh Intl, CA
SAT San Antonio Intl, TX
SAW Instanbul-Sabiha Gokcen
    Intl, TC
SBA Santa Barbara Municipal, CA
SBD San Bernadino-Norton AFB, CA
SBH St Barthelemy, F-O
SBP San Luis Obispo, CA
SBY Salisbury-Wicomico, MD
SCC Prudhoe Bay, AK
SCH Schenectady County, NY
SCI San Cristobal-Paramilio, YV
SCK Stockton Metropolitan, CA
SCL Santiago-Merino Benitez
    Intl, CC
SCN Saarbrucken-Ensheim, D
SCU Santiago de Cuba, CU
SCW Syktyvkov, RA
SDA Damascus- Intl, YK
SDF Louisville-Standiford Field, KY
SDJ Sendai, JA
SDQ Santo Domingo Intl, HI
SDU Rio de Janeiro-
    Santos Dumont, PP
SDV Tel Aviv-Sde Dov, 4X

SEA Seattle-Tacoma Intl, WA
SEL Seoul-Kimpo Intl, HL
SEN Southend, G
SEZ Mahe-Seychelles Intl, S7
SFB Sanford Regional, FL
SFC St Francois, F-O
SFD San Fernando de Apure, YV
SFG St Martin-Esperance, F-O
SFJ Kangerlussuaq-
    Sondre Stromfjord, OY
SFO San Francisco Intl, CA
SFS Subic Bay Intl, PR
SFT Skelleftea, SE
SGC Surgut, RA
SGD Sondeberg, OY
SGF Springfield-
    Branson Regional, MO
SGH Springfield-Beckley, OH
SGL Manila-Sangley Point, RP
SGN Ho Chi Minh City-
    Tansonnhat, VN
SGU St George Municipal UT
SGW Saginaw Bay, AK
SGY Skagway Municipal, AK
SGZ Songkhla, HS
SHA Shanghai-Hongqiao, B
SHE Shenyang, B
SHJ Sharjah Intl, A6
SHR Sheridan County, WY
SIA Xi'an-Xiguan, B
SID Sal-Amilcar Cabral Intl, D4
SIG San Juan-Isla Grande, PR
SIN Singapore-Changi, 9V
SIP Simferopol, UR
SIR Sion, HB
SIT Sitka, AK
SIX Singleton, NSW
SJC San Jose Intl, CA
SJJ Sarajevo-Butmir, T9
SJK Sao Jose dos Campos, PP
SJO San Jose-Juan Santamaria
    Intl, YS
SJU San Juan-Luis Munoz
    Marin Intl, PR
SJY Deinajoki-Ilmajoki, OH
SKB Basseterre-Golden Rock, V4
SKD Samarkand, UK
SKE Skien-Geiteryggen, LN
SKF San Antonio-Kelly AFB, TX
SKH Surkhet, 9N
SKP Skopje, Z3
SKX Saransk, RA
SKY Sandusky, OH
SLA Salta Intl, LV
SLC Salt Lake City Intl, UT
SLM Salamanca Matacan, EC
SLU Castries, J6
SLW Saltillo, XA
SLY Salekhard, RA
SMA Santa Maria-Vila do Porto, CS
SMF Sacramento-Metropolitan, CA
SML Stella Maris, C6
SMN Salmon, ID
SMO Santa Monica, CA
SMX Santa Maria-Public, CA
SNA John Wayne-Orange Co, CA
SNN Shannon, EI
SNR St Nazaire-Montoir, F
SOD Sorocaba, PP
SOF Sofia-Vrazhdebna Intl, LZ
SOU Southampton Intl, G
SOW Show Low-Municipal, AZ
SPB St Thomas Seaplane, VI
SPI Springfield Capital, IL
SPN Saipan Island Intl, N
SPR San Pedro, V3
SPU Split, 9A

692

SPW	Spencer Municipal, IA	THF	Berlin-Tempelhof, D	ULY	Ulyanovsk, RA
SPZ	Springdale, AR	THN	Trolhattan-Vanersborg, SE	UME	Umea, SE
SRG	Senerang, PK	THR	Teheran-Mehrabad Intl, EP	UNK	Unalakleet Municipal, AK
SRN	Strahan, Tas	TIA	Tirana-Rinas, ZA	UNU	Juneau-Dodge Co, AK
SRQ	Sarasota-Bradenton Intl, FL	TIF	Taif, HZ	UPG	Ujang Pendang, PK
SRZ	Santa Cruz-El Trompillo, CP	TIJ	Tijuana-Rodriguez Intl, XA	UPN	Uruapan, XA
SSA	Salvador-Dois de Julho, PP	TIP	Tripoli Intl, 5A	URA	Uratsk, UN
SSG	Malabo, 3C	TIS	Thursday Island, Qld	URC	Urumqi-Diwopou, B
SSH	Sharm el Sheikh, SU	TIV	Tivat, YU	URS	Kursk, RA
SSQ	La Sarre, QU	TJM	Tyumen-Roschino, RA	UTN	Upington, ZS
STA	Stauning, OY	TKA	Talkeetna, AK	UTP	Utapao, HS
STI	Santiago Intl, HI	TKJ	Tok, AK	UTT	Umtata, ZS
STL	St Louis-Lambert Intl, MO	TKU	Turku, OH	UUA	Bugulma, RA
STM	Santarem-Gomez Intl, PP	TLC	Toluca-Alfonso Lopez, XA	UUD	Ulan Ude-Mukhino, RA
STN	London-Stansted, G	TLL	Tallinn-Ylemiste, ES	UUS	Yuzhno-Sakhalinsk, RA
STR	Stuttgart, D	TLR	Tulare-Mefford Field, CA		
STS	Santa Rosa-Sonoma, CA	TLS	Toulouse-Blagnac, F	VAI	Vanimo, P2
STT	St Thomas-Cyril E King, VI	TLV	Tel Aviv-Ben Gurion Intl, 4X	VAR	Varna Intl, LZ
STU	Santa Cruz, V3	TMB	Miami-New Tamiami, FL	VBS	Brescia, I
STW	Stavropol-Shpakovskoye, RA	TML	Tamale, 9G	VCE	Venice-Marco Polo, I
STX	St Croix -Hamilton Airport, VI	TMO	Tumeremo, YV	VCP	Sao Paulo-Viracopos, PP
SUA	Stuart-Witham Field, FL	TMP	Tampere-Pirkkala, OH	VCT	Victoria-Regional, TX
SUB	Surabaya-Juanda, PK	TMS	Sao Tome Intl, 9L	VCV	Victorville, CA
SUI	Sukhumi, 4L	TMW	Tamworth-Westdale, NSW	VDM	Viedma-Castello, LV
SUS	St Louis-Spirit of St Louis, MO	TNA	Jinan, B	VDZ	Valdez-Municipal, AK
SUV	Suva-Nausori, DQ	TNF	Toussus-le-Noble, F	VER	Vera Cruz-Jara Intl, XA
SVD	Kingstown-ET Joshua , V8	TNN	Tainan, B	VFA	Victoria Falls, Z
SVG	Stavanger-Sola, LN	TNR	Antananarivo, 5R	VGD	Vologda, RA
SVH	Statesville Municipal, NC	TOA	Torrance, CA	VGT	Las Vegas-North, NV
SVO	Moscow-Sheremetyevo, RA	TOE	Tozeur-Nefta, TS	VIE	Vienna-Schwechat, OE
SVQ	Seville-San Pablo, EC	TOF	Tomsk, RA	VIH	Vichy-Rolla National, MO
SVU	SavuSavu, DQ	TOL	Toledo-Express, OH	VIR	Durban-Virginia, ZS
SVX	Yekaterinburg-Koltsovo, RA	TOM	Tombouctu, TZ	VIS	Visalia-Municipal, CA
SWA	Shantou, B	TPA	Tampa Intl, FL	VKO	Moscow-Vnukovo, RA
SWF	Newburgh-Steward-Hudson Valley Intl, NY	TPE	Taipei-Chiang Kai Shek Intl, B	VLC	Valencia, EC
		TPQ	Tepic, XA	VLE	Valle-J Robidoux , AZ
SWH	Swan Hill, Vic	TPS	Trapani, I	VLI	Port Vila-Bauerfield, YJ
SXF	Berlin-Schönefeld, D	TRD	Trondheim-Vaernes, LN	VLK	Volgodonsk, RA
SXM	St Maarten-Philipsburg, PJ	TRG	Tauranga, ZK	VLL	Volladolid, EC
SXQ	Soldotna, AK	TRN	Turin-Caselle, I	VLN	Valencia Intl, YV
SYD	Sydney-Kingsford Smith Intl, NSW	TRS	Trieste, I	VLU	Velikie Linki, RA
		TRW	Tarawa, T3	VNC	Venice, FL
SYR	Syracuse-Hancock Intl, NY	TSA	Taipei-Sung Shan, B	VNE	Vannes-Meucon, F
SYQ	San Jose-Tobias Bolanos Intl, YS	TSE	Astana, UN	VNO	Vilnius Intl, LY
		TSM	Taos-Municipal, NM	VNY	Van Nuys, CA
SYX	Sanya-Fenghuang, B	TSN	Tianjin, B	VOG	Volgograd-Gumrak, RA
SYY	Stornoway, G	TSR	Timisoara-Giarmata, YR	VOZ	Voronezh-Chertovtskye, RA
SYZ	Shiraz Intl, EP	TSV	Townsville, Qld	VPC	Cartersville, GA
SZB	Subang-Sultan Abdul Aziz Shah Intl, 9M	TTD	Portland-Troutdale, OR	VQS	Vieques, PR
		TTN	Mercer-County, Trenton, NJ	VRN	Verona-Villafranca, I
SZG	Salzburg, OE	TUL	Tulsa Intl, OK	VSG	Lugansk, UR
SZO	Shanzhou, B	TUN	Tunis-Carthage, TS	VTE	Vientiane-Wattay, RDPL
SZX	Shenzhen-Huangtian, B	TUO	Taupo, ZK	VTG	Vung Tau, VN
SZZ	Szczecin-Goleniow, SP	TUS	Tucson Intl, AZ	VVC	Villavicencio-La Vanguardia, HK
		TWB	Toowomba, Qld		
TAB	Scarborough-Crown Point, 9Y	TWF	Twin Falls, Joslin Field-Sun Valley Regional, ID	VVI	Santa Cruz-Viru Viru Intl, CP
TAM	Tampico-Gen Francisco Javier Mina Intl, XA	TXK	Texarkana Municipal, AR	VVO	Vladivostock-Knevichi, RA
TAR	Taranto-Grottaglie, I	TXL	Berlin-Tegel, D	WAG	Wanganui, ZK
TAS	Tashkent-Yuzhny, UK	TYA	Tula, RA	WAT	Waterford, EI
TAT	Tatry-Poprad, OM	TYF	Torsby-Frylanda, SE	WAW	Warsaw-Okecie, SP
TBG	Tabubil, P2	TYN	Taiyuan-Wusu, B	WDH	Windhoek-Hosea Kutako Intl, V5
TBS	Tbilisi-Novo Alexeyevka, 4L	TYS	Knoxville-McGhee Tyson, TN		
TBU	Tongatapu-Fua'Amotu Intl, A3	TYZ	Taylor, AZ	WDR	Winder-Barrow Co, GA
TBZ	Tabriz, EP	TZA	Belize-Municipal, V3	WFB	Ketchikan Waterfront SPB, AK
TBW	Tambov, RA			WGA	Wagga Wagga, NSW
TEB	Teterboro, NJ	UAO	Aurora-State, OR	WHO	Franz Josef Glacier, ZK
TED	Thisted, OY	UBS	Columbus-Lowndes Co, MS		
TER	Lajes-Terceira Island, CS	UCT	Ukhta, RA	WHP	Los Angeles-Whiteman Field, CA
TFN	Tenerife-Norte los Rodeos, EC	UES	Waukesha, WI		
TFS	Tenerife-Sur Reine Sofia, EC	UFA	Ufa, RA	WIL	Nairobi-Wilson, 5Y
TGD	Podgorica, YU	UIK	Ust-Ilimsk, RA	WIR	Wairoa, ZK
TGR	Touggourt, 7T	UIO	Quito-Mariscal Sucre, HC	WKA	Wanaka, ZK
TGU	Tegucigalpa-Toncontin Intl, HR	UKK	Ust-Kamenogorsk, UN	WLG	Wellington Intl, ZK
TGZ	Tuxtla-Gutierrez, XA	UKX	Ust-Kut, RA	WMX	Wamena, PK
THE	Terresina, PP	ULN	Ulan Bator, JU	WOE	Woensdrecht, PH

WOW	Willow, AK	
WRO	Wroclaw-Strachowice, SP	
WST	Westerly State, RI	
WSY	Airlie Beach-Whitsunday, Qld	
WUH	Wuhan, B	
WVB	Walvis Bay, V5	
WVL	Waterville-Lafleur, ME	
WVN	Wilhelmshaven-Mariensiel, D	
WWA	Wasilla, AK	
WYA	Whyalla, SA	
WYN	Wyndham, WA	
XBE	Bearskin Lake, ON	
XCM	Chatham, ON	
XCR	Vatry, F	
XFW	Hamburg-Finkenwerder, D	
XIY	Xi'an Xianyang, B	
XLS	Saint Louis, 6V	
XLW	Lemwerder, D	
XMN	Xiamen-Gaoqi, B	
XPK	Pukatawagan, MB	
XSP	Singapore-Seletar, 9V	
YAG	Fort Frances Municipal, QC	
YAM	Sault Ste Marie, ON	
YAO	Yaounde, TJ	
YAW	Halifax-Shearwater CFB, NS	
YBC	Baie Comeau, QC	
YBL	Campbell River, BC	
YBW	Calgary Springbank, AL	
YBX	Lourdes-de-Blanc Sablon, QC	
YCA	Courtenay, BC	
YCB	Cambridge Bay, NT	
YCD	Nanaimo-Cassidy, BC	
YCE	Centralia, ON	
YCH	Miramichi, NB	
YCL	Charlo, NB	
YCN	Cochrane-Lillabelle Lake, ON	
YCR	Cross Lake-Sinclair Memorial, MB	
YCW	Chilliwack, BC	
YDF	Deer Lake, NL	
YDL	Dease Lake, BC	
YDQ	Dawson Creek, BC	
YDT	Vancouver-Boundary Bay, BC	
YDU	Kasba Lake, NT	
YEG	Edmonton-Intl, AB	
YEL	Elliott Lake-Municipal, ON	
YEV	Inuvik-Mike Zubko, NT	
YFB	Iqaluit, NT	
YFC	Fredericton, NB	
YFO	Flin Flon, MB	
YFS	Fort Simpson, NT	
YGG	Ganges Harbour, AK	
YGH	Fort Good Hope, NT	
YGL	La Grande Riviere, QC	
YGM	Gimli, MB	
YGR	Iles de la Madelaine, QC	
YGV	Havre St Pierre, QC	
YGX	Gillam, MB	
YHF	Hearst, ON	
YHM	Hamilton, ON	
YHN	Homepayne, ON	
YHR	Chevery, QC	
YHS	Sechelt-Gibson, BC	
YHT	Haines Junction, YK	
YHU	Montreal-St Hubert, QC	
YHY	Hay River, NT	
YHZ	Halifax Intl, NS	
YIB	Atikokan Municipal, ON	
YIP	Detroit-Willow Run, MI	

YJF	Fort Liard, NT	
YJN	St Jean, QC	
YKA	Kamloops, BC	
YKE	Knee Lake, MB	
YKF	Kitchener-Waterloo, ON	
YKL	Schefferville, QC	
YKS	Yakutsk, RA	
YKZ	Toronto-Buttonville, ON	
YLB	Lac la Biche, AB	
YLJ	Meadow Lake, SK	
YLL	Lloydminster, AB	
YLP	Mingan, QC	
YLQ	La Tuque, QC	
YLT	Alert, NT	
YLW	Kelowna, BC	
YMM	Fort McMurray, AB	
YMO	Moosonee, ON	
YMP	Port McNeil, BC	
YMT	Chibougamau-Chapais, QC	
YMX	Montreal-Mirabel Intl, QC	
YNA	Natashquan, QC	
YNC	Wemindji, QC	
YND	Ottawa-Gatineau, QC	
YNF	Corner Brook, NL	
YNR	Arnes, MB	
YOJ	High Level/Footner Lake, AB	
YOO	Oshawa, ON	
YOW	Ottawa-McDonald Cartier Intl, QC	
YPA	Prince Albert, SK	
YPB	Port Alberni-Sproat Lake, BC	
YPD	Parry Sound, ON	
YPE	Peace River, AB	
YPL	Pickle Lake, ON	
YPQ	Peterborough	
YPR	Prince Rupert-Digby Island, BC	
YPZ	Burns Lake, BC	
YQA	Muskoka, ON	
YQB	Quebec-Jean Lesage Intl, QC	
YQD	The Pas, MB	
YQF	Red Deer, AB	
YQH	Watson Lake, YT	
YQK	Kenora, ON	
YQN	Nakina, ON	
YQR	Regina, SK	
YQS	St Thomas, ON	
YQT	Thunder Bay, ON	
YQU	Grande Prairie, AB	
YQV	Yorkton, SK	
YQX	Gander Intl, NL	
YRB	Resolute Bay, NT	
YRJ	Roberval, QC	
YRL	Red Lake, ON	
YRO	Ottawa-Rockcliffe, ON	
YRP	Carp, ON	
YRT	Rankin Inket, NU	
YSB	Sudbury, ON	
YSE	Squamish, BC	
YSF	Stony Rapids, SK	
YSJ	Saint John, NB	
YSM	Fort Smith, NT	
YSN	Salmon Arm, BC	
YSQ	Atlin-Spring Island, BC	
YTA	Pembroke, ON	
YTF	Alma, QC	
YTH	Thompson, MB	
YTP	Tofino SPB, BC	
YTZ	Toronto-City Centre, ON	
YUL	Montreal-Pierre Elliot Trudeau, QC	
YUY	Rouyn-Noranda, QC	

YVA	Moroni-Iconi, D6	
YVC	La Ronge, SK	
YVG	Vermillion Bay, AB	
YVO	Val d'Or/La Grande, QC	
YVP	Kuujjuaq, QC	
YVQ	Norman Wells, NT	
YVR	Vancouver Intl, BC	
YVT	Buffalo Narrows, SK	
YVV	Wiarton, ON	
YWF	Halifax-Waterfront Heliport, NS	
YWG	Winnipeg Intl, MB	
YWH	Victoria-Inner Harbour, BC	
YWJ	Deline, NT	
YWK	Wabush, NL	
YWR	White River, ON	
YWS	Whistler, BC	
YXD	Edmonton Municipal, AB	
YXE	Saskatoon-John D Diefenbacker, SK	
YXH	Medicine Hat, AB	
YXJ	Fort St John, BC	
YXK	Rimouski, QC	
YXL	Sioux Lookout, ON	
YXS	Prince George, BC	
YXT	Terrace, BC	
YXU	London, ON	
YXX	Abbotsford, BC	
YXY	Whitehorse, YT	
YXZ	Wawa-Hawk Junction, ON	
YYB	North Bay, ON	
YYC	Calgary-Intl, AB	
YYD	Smithers, BC	
YYE	Fort Nelson, BC	
YYF	Penticton, BC	
YYG	Charlottetown, PE	
YYJ	Victoria-Intl, BC	
YYL	Lynn Lake, MB	
YYQ	Churchill, MB	
YYR	Goose Bay, NL	
YYT	St Johns, NL	
YYW	Armstrong, ON	
YYZ	Toronto-Lester B Pearson Intl, ON	
YZF	Yellowknife, NT	
YZH	Slave Lake, AB	
YZT	Port Hardy, BC	
YZU	Whitecourt, AB	
YZV	Sept-Iles, QC	
ZAG	Zagreb-Pleso, 9A	
ZAM	Zamboanga Intl, RP	
ZAZ	Zaragoza, EC	
ZFD	Fond du Lac, SK	
ZFM	Fort McPherson, NT	
ZIH	Ixtapa-Zihuatanejo Intl, XA	
ZJN	Swan River, MB	
ZNQ	Ingolstadt, D	
ZNZ	Zanzibar-Kisuani, 5H	
ZPB	Sachigo Lake , ON	
ZQN	Queenstown-Frankston, NZ	
ZQS	Queen Charlotte, BC	
ZRH	Zurich-Kloten, HB	
ZRJ	Weagqmow-Round Lake, ON	
ZSJ	Sandy Lake, ON	
ZSW	Price Rupert-Seal Cove, BC	
ZTH	Zante-Zakinthos, SX	
ZTR	Zhitomyr, UR	
ZUC	Ignace, ON	
ZUH	Zhuhai-Jiuzhou, B	

NATIONALITY INDEX

This index lists the world's current registration prefixes and is a guide to their location in the main part of this book.

5N-	Nigeria	621		ZS-	South Africa	602
LN-	Norway	254		EC-	Spain	146
				4R-	Sri Lanka	614
A4O-	Oman	9		ST-	Sudan	507
				PZ-	Suriname	467
AP-	Pakistan	7		3D-	Swaziland	612
T8A	Palau	531		SE-	Sweden	501
SU-Y	Palestine	-		HB-	Switzerland & Liechtenstein	207
HP-	Panama	224		YK-	Syria	585
P2-	Papua New Guinea	467				
ZP-	Paraguay	602		EY-	Tajikistan	175
OB-	Peru	424		5H-	Tanzania	619
RP-	Philippines	497		TT-	Tchad	530
SP-	Poland	506		HS-	Thailand	226
CS-	Portugal	121		5V-	Togo	626
				A3-	Tonga	9
A7-	Qatar	16		9Y-	Trinidad & Tobago	651
				TS-	Tunisia	529
YR-	Romania	587		TC-	Turkey	517
RA-	Russia	470		EZ-	Turkmenistan	176
9XR-	Rwanda	651		VQ-T	Turks & Caicos Islands	564
				T2-	Tuvalu	-
VQ-H	St Helena	-				
V4-	St Kitts Nevis	573		5X-	Uganda	626
J6-	St Lucia	-		UR-	Ukraine	537
J8-	St Vincent & Grenadines	253		A6-	United Arab Emirates	10
5W-	Samoa	626		G-	United Kingdom	188
T7-	San Marino	-		N	United States of America	264
S9-	Sao Tome	517		CX-	Uruguay	125
HZ-	Saudi Arabia	229		UK-	Uzbekistan	531
6V-	Senegal	631				
YU-	Serbia	589		YJ-	Vanuatu	585
S7-	Seychelles	516		YV-	Venezuela	589
9L-	Sierra Leone	639		VN-	Vietnam	562
9V-	Singapore	648				
OM-	Slovak Republic	433		7O-	Yemen	632
S5-	Slovenia	516				
H4-	Solomon Islands	232		9J-	Zambia	637
6O-	Somalia	631		Z-	Zimbabwe	595

OPERATOR INDEX

Afrijet Airlines	5N	621	
Afriqiyah Airways	5A	616	
Afrique Cargo Services	6V	631	
Agni Air	9N	644	
Aigle Azur	F	177	
Air 26	D2	143	
Air Aktobe	UP	533	
Air Aland	OH	429	
Air Algerie	7T	633	
Air Almaty	UP	533	
Air Alpha Greenland	OY	436	
Air Alps Aviation	OE	427	
Air America	N	265	
Air Antilles Express	F	187	
Air Arabia	A6	11	
Air Arabia Egypt	SU	509	
Air Arabia Maroc	CN	118	
Air Archipels	F	186	
Air Arctic	N	265	
Air Armenia	EK	164	
Air Armenia Cargo	EK	164	
Air Asia X	9M	640	
Air Astana	UP	533	
Air Atlanta	TF	524	
Air Atlantique	G	188	
Air Austral	F	186	
Air Bagan	XY	583	
Air Baltic	YL	586	
Air Bashkortostan	RA	472	
Air Batumi	4L	613	
Air Botswana	A2	8	
Air Boyoma	9Q	645	
Air Brasil Cargo	PP	456	
Air Bravo	C	55	
Air Burkina	XT	582	
Air Burundi	9U	648	
Air Busan	HL	220	
Air Cab	C	55	
Air Cairo	SU	509	
Air Caledonie	F	186	
Air Canada	C	55	
Air Canada Jazz	C	58	
Air Caraibes	F	187	
Air Caraibes Atlantique	F	187	
Air Cargo Carriers	N	265	
Air Cargo Germany	D	128	
Air Central	JA	240	
Air Charter Cargo	YN	587	
Air Chathams	ZK	596	
Air China	B	19	
Air China Cargo	B	23	
Air Choice One	N	266	
Air Class	CX	125	
Air Colombia	HK	215	
Air Congo International	TN	527	
Air Contractors	EI	159	
Air Corsica	F	177	
Air Creebec	C	60	
Air Cuenca	HC	211	
Air Direct	N	266	
Air Do	JA	240	
Air Dolomiti	I	233	
Air Dolphin	JA	241	
Air Engiadina	HB	207	
Air Europa	EC	146	
Air Evac	N	266	
Air Excel	5H	619	
Air Express Algeria	7T	634	
Air Fiji	DQ	142	
Air Finland	OH	429	
Air Flamenco	N	267	
Air France	F	177	
Air Fraser Island	VH	543	
Air Freight NZ	ZK	597	
Air Frontier	VH	543	
Air Gemini	D2	143	
Air Georgian	C	60	
Air Glaciers	HB	207	
Air Grand Canyon	N	267	
Air Greenland	OY	436	
Air Guinee Express	3X	612	
Air Guyana	8R	635	
Air Guyane Express	F	187	
Air Hamburg	D	128	
Air Highnesses	EK	164	
Air Hong Kong	B	47	
Air Horizon Afrique	TT	530	
Air Iceland	TF	524	
Air India	VT	564	
Air India Express	VT	566	
Air India Regional	VT	567	
Air Inter Ivoire	TU	530	
Air Inuit	C	60	
Air Italy	I	233	
Air Italy Polska	SP	506	
Air Ivanhoe	C	61	
Air Ivoire	TU	530	
Air Jamaica	6Y	631	
Air Japan	JA	241	
Air Kasai	9Q	645	
Air Kasthamandap	9N	644	
Air Katafanga	DQ	142	
Air Kipawa	C	61	
Air Kiribati	T3	531	
Air Koryo	P	439	
Air Labrador	C	61	
Air Libya	5A	616	
Air Link	VH	543	
Air Link International Airways	RP	497	
Air Loyauté	F	186	
Air Macatina	C	61	
Air Macau	B	51	
Air Madagascar	5R	625	
Air Majoro	OB	424	
Air Malawi	7Q	633	
Air Maleo	PK	444	
Air Malta	9H	637	
Air Manas	EX	173	
Air Mandalay	XY	583	
Air Mark Indonesia Aviation	PK	444	
Air Mauritius	3B	611	
Air Max	LZ	262	
Air Mediterrannée	F	181	
Air Mekong	VN	562	
Air Melancon	C	61	
Air Memphis	SU	509	
Air Methods	N	268	
Air Midwest	N	269	
Air Midwest	5N	621	
Air Mikisew	C	61	
Air Minas	PP	456	
Air Moldova	ER	170	
Air Mont-Laurier	C	61	
Air Montmagny	C	62	
Air Montserrat	VP-M	564	
Air Moorea	F	106	
Air Namibia	V5	573	
Air Napier	ZK	597	
Air National	ZK	597	
Air New Zealand	ZK	597	
Air New Zealand Link	ZK	598	
Air Next	JA	241	
Air Nigeria	5N	621	
Air Nippon	JA	241	
Air Nippon Network	JA	242	
Air Niugini	P2	467	
Air Nootka	C	62	
Air North	C	62	
Air Nostrum	EC	148	
Air Nunavut	C	62	
Air One Nine	5A	617	
Air Optima	C	62	
Air Pacific	DQ	142	
Air Panama	HP	224	
Air Quasar	C	62	
Air Rarotonga	E5	176	
Air Roberval	C	62	
Air Rum	9L	639	
Air Safaris & Services	ZK	598	
Air Saguenay	C	62	
Air Saint Louis	6V	631	
Air Santo Domingo	HI	213	
Air Satellite	C	63	
Air Scorpio	LZ	262	
Air Senegal International	6V	631	
Air Service Berlin	D	128	

Air Service Gabon	TR	528	Airzena - Georgian Airlines	4L	613
Air Service Liege	OO	433	AK Air	N	274
Air Service Wildgruber	D	128	AK Bars Aero	RA	473
Air Services	8R	636	Alada	D2	143
Air Seychelles	S7	516	Alajnihah Air Transport	9Q	645
Air Sinai	SU	510	Al-Ajnihah Aiways	5A	617
Air Sirin	4L	613	Alania Airline	RA	473
Air South Regional	VH	543	Alas Del Sur	CP	120
Air Southwest	G	188	Alaska Airlines	N	274
Air St Kitts & Nevis	V4	573	Alaska Central Express	N	275
Air St Pierre	F	187	Alaska Seaplane Service	N	276
Air St Thomas	N	269	Alaska West Air	N	276
Air Sunshine	N	269	Alba Star	EC	148
Air Sweden	SE	501	Albanian Airlines	ZA	596
Air Tahiti	F	186	Alberta Central Airways	C	64
Air Tahiti Nui	F	186	Alberta Citylink	C	65
Air Tahoma	N	269	Aldawlyh Air	5A	617
Air Tango	LV	259	Alexandria Airlines	SU	510
Air Tanzania	5H	619	Aliansa	HK	215
Air Taxi & Cargo	ST	507	Alidaunia	I	233
Air Tejas	N	269	Alitalia	I	233
Air Tindi	C	63	Alitalia Express	I	236
Air Transat	C	63	Alkan Air	C	65
Air Tropiques	9Q	645	Allebia Air Cargo	5A	617
Air Tunilik	C	64	Allegiance Air	ZS	603
Air Turks & Caicos	VQ-T	564	Allegiant Air	N	276
Air Uganda	5X	626	Allen Airways	C	65
Air Urga	UR	537	Alliance Air	VT	567
Air Vallée	I	233	Alliance Airlines	VH	544
Air Vanuatu	YJ	585	Allied Air Cargo	5N	622
Air Victory	4L	613	Alligator Airways	VH	544
Air Wakaya	DQ	142	Allwest Freight	N	277
Air Wanganui Commuter	ZK	599	Almajara Aviation	ST	508
Air West Cargo	ST	508	Almasria Universal Airlines	SU	510
Air Whitsunday Seaplanes	VH	544	Aloha Air Cargo	N	277
Air Zermatt	HB	208	Alpen Helicopters	C	65
Air Zimbabwe	Z	595	Alpine Air Express	N	277
Air2there.com	ZK	599	Alpine Aviation	C	65
Airasia	9M	639	Alpine Helicopters	C	65
Airawak	F	187	Alrosa Avia	RA	473
AirBerlin	D	128	Alrosa Aviation	RA	473
AirBlue	AP	7	ALS	5Y	627
Airborne Energy Solutions	C	64	Alsair	F	182
Airborne Support	N	270	Alta Flights	C	66
Airbridge Cargo	RA	472	Alwafeer Air	HZ	230
Airbus Transport International	F	181	Amakusa Airlines	JA	242
Aircalin	F	186	Amapola Flyg	SE	501
Airco Aircraft Charters	C	64	Amaszonas Transportes Aereos	CP	120
Air-Dale Flying Service	C	60	Amazon Sky	OB	424
Aires	HK	215	Amazonaves Taxi Aero	PP	456
Airest	ES	170	Ambjek Air Service	5N	622
Airexplore	OM	433	AMC Airlines	SU	510
Airexpress Ontario	C	64	Amerer Air	OE	427
Airfast Indonesia	PK	444	American Airlines	N	277
Airgo Airlines of Sofia	LZ	262	American Connection	N	286
Airkenya	5Y	627	American Eagle	N	287
Airlec Air Espace	F	181	American Jet	LV	259
Airlift	LN	254	Ameriflight	N	291
Airlinair	F	181	Amerijet International	N	293
Airline of the Marshall Islands	V7	574	Ameristar Air Charter	N	293
Airlines of Papua New Guinea	P2	467	Amigo Airways	C	66
Airlines of Tasmania	VH	544	Amsterdam Airlines	PH	439
Airlines Tonga	A3	9	Amur Artel Staratelei Aviakompania	RA	474
Airlink	ZS	602	Amurskie Avialinii	RA	474
Airlink Arabia	ER	170	AMW Tchad	TT	530
Aimet Systems	N	270	ANA - All Nippon Network	JA	242
Aimorth Regional	VH	544	Anadolou Jet	TC	517
Airnow	N	271	Andalus Lineas Aereas	EC	148
Airpac Airlines	N	271	Andes Lineas Aereas	LV	259
AirPhil Express	RP	497	Andrew Airways	N	294
Airquarius Aviation	ZS	603	Angara Airlines	RA	474
Airserv International	N	272	Angola Air Charter	D2	143
Airspan Helicopters	C	64	Angolan Airservices	D2	143
Air-Spray	C	63	Anguilla Air Services	VP-A	563
Airstars Airways	RA	473	Anikay Air	EX	173
Air-Tec Africa	ZS	602	Anoka Air Charter	N	294
Airtran Airways	N	272	Antonov Airlines	UR	538
Airventure	OO	433	Antrak Air Ghana	9G	636
Airwaves Airlink	9J	637	Apatas	LY	262
Airwing	LN	254	APSA - Aeroexpreso Bogota	HK	215
Airwork New Zealand	ZK	599	Apui Taxi Aero	PP	456
Airworks Kenya	5Y	627	Aqua Airlines	I	236

Best Air	TC	518
Best Air	S2	515
Beta Cargo Air	PP	457
BH Air	LZ	263
BH Airlines	E9	177
BHS -		
Brazilian Helicopter Services Taxi Aero	PP	457
Big Island Air	N	298
Big Salmon Air	C	67
Bighorn Airways	N	298
Biman Bangladesh Airlines	S2	515
Bimini Island Air	N	298
Binair	D	131
Binter Canarias	EC	148
Bionic Air	ZS	603
Bismillah Airlines	S2	515
BKS Air	EC	148
Black Sheep Aviation	C	68
Black Tusk Helicopter	C	68
Blackcomb Helicopters	C	68
Blu Express.com	I	236
Blue Air	YR	587
Blue Bird Airlines	ST	508
Blue Dart Aviation	VT	567
Blue Islands	G	188
Blue Line	F	182
Blue Panorama Airlines	I	236
Blue Sky	EK	165
Blue Sky Aviation	5Y	628
Blue Water Aviation Services	C	68
Blue Wings Airlines	PZ	467
Blue1	OH	429
Bluebird Airways	SX	513
Bluebird Aviation	5Y	627
Bluebird Cargo	TF	524
BMI	G	189
BMI Regional	G	189
BMIBaby	G	189
Boliviana de Aviacion	CP	120
Bolton Lake Air Services	C	68
Bond Air Services	G	190
Bond Offshore Helicopters	G	190
Borajet	TC	518
Borinquen Air	N	298
Bosques Arauco	CC	114
Boston-Maine Airways	N	298
Botir-Avia	EX	173
BQB Lineas Aereas	CX	125
Branson Air	ZS	603
Bravo Air Congo	9Q	645
Bravo Airlines	N	298
Brazza Airways	TN	527
BremenFly	D	1263
Briko Air Services	9Y	651
Brindabella Airlines	VH	545
Bristow Caribbean	9Y	651
Bristow Helicopters	G	190
Bristow Helicopters (Australia)	VH	545
Bristow Helicopters (Nigeria)	5N	623
Bristow Norway	LN	254
Bristows US	N	298
Brit'Air	F	182
British Airways	G	191
British Antarctic Survey	VP-F	564
British Gulf Airlines	EX	173
British International	G	194
Brooks Aviation	N	300
Broome Aviation	VH	546
Brroks Fuel	N	300
Brucelandair International	C	68
Brussels Airlines	OO	434
Budapest Air Services	HA	206
Buddha Air	9N	644
Buffalo Airways	C	68
Bulgaria Air	LZ	263
Bulgarian Air Charter	LZ	263
Bural	RA	475
Buraq Air	5A	617
Bushland Airways	C	69
Business Aero	RA	475
Business Air	HS	226
Business Aviation Courier	N	300
Business Aviation of Congo	9Q	645
Businesswings	D	131
Butembo	9Q	645
Butler Aircraft	N	300
Bylina	RA	475
C&M Airways	N	300
CAA - Compagnie Africane D'Aviation	9Q	645
Cabo Verde Express	D4	145
Cairns Seaplanes	VH	546
Cairo Aviation	SU	510
Calima Aviacion	EC	148
Calm Air	C	69
Cambodia Angkor Air	XU	582
Cameron Air Service	C	69
Cameroon Airlines	TJ	527
Campbell Helicopters	C	69
Canadian Air Crane	C	69
Canadian Airways Congo	TN	528
Canadian Helicopters	C	69
Canadian North	C	71
Canjet	C	71
Can-West Corporate Air Charter	C	71
Cape Air	N	301
Capital Airlines	B	23
Capital Airlines	5Y	628
Capital Airlines	5N	624
Capital Cargo International Airlines	N	301
Capital City Air Carrier	N	302
Caravan Airlines	C	72
Cardig Air	PK	445
Cargair	C	72
Cargo Air	LZ	263
Cargo Air Lines	4X	615
Cargoitalia	I	237
Cargojet Airways	C	72
Cargolux Airlines International	LX	261
Cargolux Italia	I	237
Caribair	HI	213
Caribbean Airlines	9Y	651
Caribbean Flights	YV	592
Caribbean Sun Airlines	N	302
Caribintair	HH	212
Caroline Island Air	V6	574
Carpatair	YR	587
Carson Air	C	72
Carson Helicopters	N	302
Casair	VH	546
Cascade Air	N	302
Caspian Airlines	EP	166
Castle Aviation	N	303
Cat Island Air	C6	126
Catalina Flying Boats	N	303
Cathay Pacific Airways	B	48
Caverton Helicopters	5N	624
Cayman Airways	VP-C	563
Cayman Airways Express	VP-C	563
CC Helicopters	C	72
CDF Aviation	N	303
Cebu Pacific Air	RP	498
Cegisa	EC	149
Ceiba Intercontinental GE	3C	611
Center-South Airlines	RA	475
Central Air Southwest	N	304
Central Air Transport	P2	468
Central Airways	EK	165
Central American Airways	HR	226
Central Charter Airlines Slovakia	OM	433
Central Connect Airlines	OK	431
Central Flyway Air	C	72
Central Mongolian Airlines	JU	251
Central Mountain Air	C	73
Centralafrique Air Express	TL	527
Centre-Avia Airlines	RA	475
Centurion II Air Cargo	N	304
Cetraca Air Service	9Q	646
Chabahar Air	EP	166
Chalair Aviation	F	183
Challenge Aero	UR	538
Cham Wings Air	YK	585
Champlain Air	N	304
Chanchangi Airlines	5N	624

Chang An Airlines	B	24
Channel Island Aviation	N	304
Chapi Air	YV	592
Chartair	VH	546
CHC Airways	PH	439
CHC Cameroon	TJ	527
CHC Denmark	OY	437
CHC Helicopters (Africa)	ZS	603
CHC Helicopters (Australia)	VH	547
CHC Helicopters International	C	73
CHC Helicopters Netherlands	PH	439
CHC Helikopter Service	LN	255
CHC Ireland	EI	160
CHC Scotia Helicopters	G	194
Chemtrad Aviation	RP	498
Chengdu Airlines	B	24
Cherokee Air	C6	126
Cherry-Air	N	304
Chimo Air Service	C	73
China Airlines	B	51
China Cargo Airlines	B	24
China Eastern Airlines	B	24
China Express Airlines	B	28
China Flying Dragon Co	B	28
China Postal Airlines	B	29
China Southern Airlines	B	29
China United Airlines	B	34
China Xinhua Airlines	B	35
Chongqing Airlines	B	35
Chukotavia	RA	475
Ciaca Airlines	YV	592
Cielos Airlines	OB	425
Cimarron Aire	N	305
Cimber Air	OY	437
Cimber Sterling	OY	437
Cirrus Airlines	D	131
Cirrus Middle East	OD	426
CITIC Offshore Helicopters	B	35
Citilink	PK	445
City Airline	SE	501
City Jet	EI	160
Cityfly	I	237
Cityline Hungary	HA	206
Citylink	9G	637
Civair	ZS	603
Classic Norway Air	LN	255
Clearwater Airways	C	73
Click Airways	EX	174
Coastal Air Transport	N	305
Coastal Aviation	5H	620
Coastal Helicopter	N	305
Cobham Aviation Services Australia	VH	547
Cochrane Air Services	C	73
Colgan Air	N	305
Columbia Helicopters	N	305
Comair	ZS	603
Comair	9Q	646
Comav Aviation	V5	574
Comeravia	YV	592
Comores Air Service	D6	146
Comores Aviation	D6	146
Comores Island Airways	D6	146
Comp Air Mouene	TN	528
Compagnie Aérienne du Mali	TZ	531
Compagnie Mauritanienne de Transportes	5T	626
Conair Aviation	C	74
Condor	D	132
Condor Berlin	D	132
Congo Fret Espoir	9XR	651
Constanta Airlines	UR	538
Contact Air	D	132
Continental Airways	RA	476
Conviasa	YV	592
Copa Airlines	HP	224
Copenhagen Airtaxi	OY	437
Copterline	OH	430
Copters	CC	115
Coral Sun Airways	T3	531
Corendon Air	TC	518
Corilar Charters	C	74
Corpjet	N	306
Corpo Forestale Dello Stato	I	237
Corporate Air	N	306

Corporate Air	RP	498
Corporate Air	VH	548
Corporate Express Airline	C	75
Corporate Flight Management	N	306
Corsair	F	183
Cosmic Air	9N	644
Cosmos Air Cargo	HK	216
Cougar Helicopters	C	75
Coulson Aircrane	C	75
Courtesy Air	C	75
Co-Za Airways	9Q	646
Croatia Airlines	9A	636
Cruiser Taxi Aero Brasil	PP	458
CSA Czech Airlines	OK	431
CTK Citylink	ZS	604
Cubana de Aviacion	CU	124
Custom Air Transport	N	306
Custom Helicopters	C	75
Cyprus Airways	5B	619
Czech Charter Airlines	OK	432
Daalo Airlines	J2	253
Daghestan Airlines	RA	476
Daily Air	B	52
Dalavia	RA	476
Dana	5N	624
Dana Air	5N	624
Dancopter	OY	437
Danish Air Transport	OY	437
Danu Oro Transportas	LY	262
Danube Wings	OM	433
DAP Helicopteros	CC	115
Darwin Airline	HB	208
Dauria	RA	476
De Bruin Air	VH	548
Deccan Cargo	VT	567
Delta Air	A2	8
Delta Airlines	N	306
Delta Connection	N	317
Delta Connection	5Y	628
Delta Helicopters	C	76
Denis Beahan Aviation	VH	548
Deraya Air Taxi	PK	445
Desert Air	N	326
Desert Air	V5	574
Destination Air	HS	226
Deta Air	UP	534
DHL Aero Expresso	HP	225
DHL Air	G	195
DHL Aviation (Zimbabwe)	Z	595
DHL de Guatemala	TG	525
DHL International Aviation	A9C	18
Diexim Express	D2	144
Direct Air Services	VH	548
Direct Flight	G	195
Direktflyg	SE	501
Dirgantara Air Service	PK	445
Divi Divi Air	PJ	443
Dnepr-Air	UR	539
Dodita Air Cargo	N	326
Dodson International Charter	ZS	604
Dolphin Air	A6	11
Domodedovo Airlines	RA	476
Donavia	RA	477
Donbassaero	UR	539
Donghai Airlines	B	35
Donghua Airlines	B	36
Doren Air Cargo	9Q	646
Dragonair	B	50
Druk Air	A5	10
Dubnica Air	OM	433
Dubrovnik Airlines	9A	636
Dutch Antilles Airlines	PJ	443
Dutch Antilles Express	PJ	443
Dynamic Airways	N	326
Dynamic Flight Services	C	76
Eagle Air	5X	626
Eagle Air Services	C	76
Eagle Airlines	I	237
Eagle Copters	C	76
Eagle Copters	CC	115
EAS Air Lines	5N	624

East African Air Charters	5Y	628
East African Airlines	5X	626
East African Express	5Y	628
East Air	EY	175
East Coast Airways	ZS	604
East Wing	UP	534
Eastarjet	HL	221
Eastern Airways	G	196
Eastern Airways	3D	612
Eastern Caribbean Air	N	326
Eastern Express	UP	534
Eastern Skyjets	A6	11
Eastindo	PK	446
Eastok Avia	A6	12
East-West Transportation	C	76
Easy Fly	S2	515
Easyfly	HK	216
Easyjet Airlines	G	196
Easyjet Switzerland	HB	208
EAT Leipzig	D	133
Eco Express	CP	120
Edelweiss Air	HB	208
Edwards Jet Centre of Montana	N	326
Efly	9H	637
EG & G	N	327
Egoli Air	ZS	604
Egyptair	SU	510
Egyptair Express	SU	511
El Al Israel Airlines	4X	615
El Magal Aviation	ST	508
Elbafly	I	237
Elbow River Helicopters	C	76
Elbrus Avia	RA	477
Elidolomiti	I	237
Elifriula	I	237
Elilario Italia	I	237
Elilombarda	I	238
Elite Air	5V	626
El-Rom Airlines	4X	616
Elysian Airlines	TJ	527
Emerald Air	P2	468
Emetebe Taxi Aero	HC	211
Emirates	A6	12
Empire Airlines	N	327
Empressa Aero - Servicios Parrague	CC	115
Enerjet	C	77
Enimex	ES	171
Enter Air	SP	506
Enterprise Air	C	77
Enzis Airways	JU	251
Epps Aviation Charter	N	327
Epsilon Aviation	SX	513
Equaflight Service	TN	528
Era Aviation	N	327
Era Helicopters	N	327
Eram Air	EP	166
Erickson Air Crane	N	329
Eritrean Airlines	E3	176
Ernir Air	TF	524
Espace Aviation	9Q	646
Essen Air	EX	174
Estafeta Carga Aerea	XA	579
Estonian Air	ES	171
Estonian Air Regional	ES	171
Ethiopian Airlines	ET	172
Etihad Airways	A6	14
Etram Air Wing	9Q	646
Eurex	4L	613
Euro Asia International	UP	534
Euro Atlantic Airways	CS	121
Euro Continental Air	EC	149
Euroair	SX	513
Euroline	4L	613
EuroLot	SP	506
Europe Airpost	F	183
Eurowings	D	133
EVA Airways	B	52
Evenkia Avia	RA	477
Evergreen Helicopters	N	329
Evergreen Helicopters Intl (Trinidad)	9Y	652
Evergreen International Airlines	N	330
Everts Air Alaska	N	330

Everts Air Cargo	N	331
Everts Air Fuel	N	331
Exact Air	C	77
Excellent Air	D	133
Excellent Glide	UP	535
Exec Direct Aviation	6Y	631
Exec-Air	Z	595
Executive Aerospace	ZS	604
Executive Turbine Air Charter	ZS	604
Executive Turbine Kenya	5Y	628
Exim Trading	3X	612
Exin	SP	506
Exploits Valley Air Service	C	77
Expo Air	4R	614
Express Air	C	77
Express Freighters Australia	VH	548
Expressjet Airlines	N	331
FAASA Aviacion	EC	149
Falcon Air	Z	596
Falcon Express Cargo Airlines	A6	15
Far West Helicopters	C	77
Farnair Hungary	HA	206
Farnair Switzerland	HB	208
Fars Air	EP	166
Fast Air	C	77
Fast Link	SU	511
Federal Air	ZS	604
Federal Express	N	331
Federico Helicopters	N	331
Feeder Airlines	ST	508
Felix Airways	7O	632
FIGAS	VP-F	564
Filair	9Q	646
Finist'Air	F	183
Finnair	OH	430
Finncomm Airlines	OH	431
Firefly	9M	640
Fireweed Helicopters	C	77
First Air	C	77
Flair Airlines	C	78
Flamingo Air	C6	126
Fleet Air International	HA	206
Flight 2000	ZK	599
Flight Alaska	N	340
Flight Corporation	ZK	599
Flight Express	N	341
Flight Inspections & Systems	RA	477
Flight International Aviation	N	342
Flight Line	N	342
Flightline	EC	149
FLM Aviation	D	133
Florida Air Cargo	N	342
Florida Air Transport	N	342
Florida Coastal Airlines	N	342
Florida West International Airlines	N	342
Flugdienst Fehlhaber	D	134
Fly BVI	VP-L	564
Fly Logic Sweden	SE	501
Fly540	5Y	628
FlyBe	G	199
FlyDubai	A6	15
Flygcentrum	SE	501
Flying America	LV	260
Flying Bulls	OE	428
Flying Carpet Air Transport Services	OD	426
FlyLal Charters Esti	ES	171
Flymex	XA	579
Flysur	EC	149
Fonnafly	LN	255
Forde Lake Air Services	C	78
Forest Patrol	C	78
Forest Protection	C	78
Fort Francis Sportsmen Airways	C	78
Forty Eight Aviation	ST	508
Four Seasons Aviation	C	78
Four Star Air Cargo	N	343
Freebird Airlines	TC	518
Freedom Air	N	343
Freedom Air Services	5N	624
Freight Runners Express	N	343
Fretax Taxi Aereo	PP	458

Name	Code	Page
Frisia Luftverkehr	D	134
Frontier Airlines	N	343
Frontier Flying Service	N	344
Fugro Airborne Surveys	ZS	605
Fugro Aviation Canada	C	78
Fuji Dream Airlines	JA	245
Futura Travels	VT	567
Gabon Airlines	TR	528
Gading Sari Aviation Services	PK	446
Gainjet	SX	513
Galaxy Airlines	EX	174
Galaxy Kavatsi Aviation	9Q	646
Gallup Flying Services	N	345
GAM Services	VH	548
Garinco Airways	EX	174
Garuda Indonesia	PK	446
Gatari Air Service	PK	447
Gateway Helicopters	C	79
Gazpromavia	RA	477
GB Airlink	N	345
Geasa	3C	611
Geffair Canada	C	79
Gemini Helicopters	C	79
General Work Aviacon	3C	611
Genex	EW	172
Gensa	PP	458
Geo Air	N	345
Geodynamica Centre	RA	478
Geographic Air Survey	C	79
Georgian Bay Airways	C	79
German SkyAirlines	D	134
Germania	D	134
Germanwings	D	134
Gestair Cargo	EC	149
Getra	3C	611
Ghadames Air Transport	5A	617
Gillam Air Services	C	79
Gira Globo	D2	144
Girassol Aerotaxi	PP	458
Global Air	XA	579
Global Air	5A	617
Global Air Charters	5Y	628
Global Georgian Airways	4L	614
Global Supply Systems	G	200
Global Vectra Helicopter	VT	567
Globus	RA	478
GMG Airlines	S2	515
Go Air	VT	568
Go!	N	345
Gogal Air Services	C	79
Gol Transportes Aereos	PP	458
Gold Coast Seaplanes	VH	549
Goldak Airborne Surveys	C	79
Golden Air	SE	502
Golden Eagle Airlines	VH	549
Goldfields Air Services	VH	549
Golfo International	S9	517
Goliaf Air	S9	517
Gomelavia	EW	173
Gorkha Airlines	9N	644
Gorlitsa Airlines	UR	539
Government of Quebec	C	79
Grand Canyon Airlines	N	345
Grand China Airlines	B	36
Granstar Cargo Airlines	B	36
Grant Aviation	N	345
Great Barrier Airlines	ZK	599
Great Lakes Airlines	N	345
Great Northern Air	N	346
Great Slave Helicopters	C	80
Great Wall Airlines	B	36
Great Western Aviation	VH	549
Great Wing Airlines	B	53
Green Airways	C	81
Griffin Flying Service	N	346
Grixona	ER	170
Grizzly Mountain Aviation	N	346
Grondair	C	81
Grossmann Air Transport	OE	428
Groznyavia	RA	478
Gryphon Airways	9K	638
GT Air	PK	448
Guardian Air	N	346
Guardian Helicopters	C	81
Guinea Equatorial Airlines	3C	611
Guinee Air Cargo	3X	612
Gulf Air	A9C	18
Gulf and Caribbean Air	N	346
Gulf Helicopters	A7	16
Gulfstream International	N	346
Gum Air	PZ	467
Hageland Aviation Services	N	347
Hainan Airlines	B	36
Halcyon Air	D4	146
Hanair	HH	212
Hangar Uno	LV	260
Happy Air	HS	227
Harbour Air Seaplanes	C	81
Harbourair	9H	637
Hardy Aviation	VH	550
Hauts-Monts	C	82
Hawaiian Airlines	N	347
Hawk Air	LV	260
Hawk Air	C	82
Hawk de Mexico	XA	579
Hawkair Aviation Service	C	82
HD Air	G	200
Hearst Air Service	C	82
Heartland Aviation	N	348
Heavy Lift Helicopters	N	348
Heavylift Cargo Airlines	VH	550
Heavylift International	A6	15
Hebei Airlines	B	38
Hebridean Air Services	G	200
Hegedus	HA	206
Heli Air	LZ	263
Heli Air Monaco	3A	610
Heli Campeche	XA	579
Heli Duero	EC	150
Heli Express	C	82
Heli Niugini	P2	468
Heliand	C3	126
Heliandes	HK	217
Helibol	CP	120
Helibravo Aviacao	CS	121
Helicargo	HK	217
Helicol	HK	217
Helicopter Services	EP	166
Helicopter Transport Services	C	83
Helicopter Transport Services	N	348
Helicopteros Del Pacifico	CC	115
Helicopteros Mercosur	OB	425
Helicopters (NZ)	ZK	599
Helicopters Chile	CC	115
Helicraft 2000	C	83
Helicsa Helicopteros	EC	150
Heli-Excel	C	82
Heliflight	N	348
Heli-Flite	N	348
Helifor Industries	C	84
Heligo Charters	VT	568
Heli-Harvest	ZK	599
Heli-Inter	C	83
Heli-Italia	I	238
Heli-Jet	N	348
HeliJet International	C	84
Heli-Lift International	C	83
Helimar	EC	150
Heliportugal	CS	121
Helipro	ZK	600
Heliqwest Aviation	C	84
Helisul	CS	122
Helisul Taxi Aereo	PP	460
Helisur	OB	425
Helisuretse	EC	151
Heliswiss	HB	209
Heliswiss Iberica	EC	152
Helitaxi Services	OB	425
Helitec	HK	217
Helitec	YV	592
Helitrans	LN	255
Helitrans	C3	126
Heli-Union	F	183
Helivalle	HK	217

Helivan	XA	580
Helivia Aero Taxi	PP	460
Heliworks	CC	115
Hellas jet	SX	513
Hellenic Imperial Airways	SX	513
Hello	HB	209
Helog	HB	209
Helog Lufttransport	D	135
Helvetic Airways	HB	209
Hemus Air	LZ	263
Henan Airlines	B	38
Heritage Air	9M	640
Heritage Aviation	D6	146
Hevi-Lift	P2	468
Hewa Bora Airways	9Q	646
Hex'Air	F	184
Heyes Helicopter Services	C	82
Hi Fly	CS	122
Hicks & Lawrence	C	84
Highland Helicopters	C	85
Hinterland Aviation	VH	550
HM Airways	D2	144
Hokkaido Air System	JA	245
Homer Air	N	348
Hong Kong Airlines	B	50
Hong Kong Express Airways	B	50
Horizon Air	N	348
Hornbill Skyways	9M	640
Horne Air	C	85
HTA Helicopters	CS	122
Huron Air and Outfitters	C	85
Hydro-Quebec	C	85
IBC Airways	N	349
Iberia	EC	152
Iberworld Airlines	EC	154
Ibex Airlines	JA	245
ICAR	E9	177
Icaro Express	HC	211
Icarus Flying Service	C	85
Icejet	TF	524
Iceland Express	TF	525
Icelandair	TF	524
IDC Aircraft	S7	516
Ifly	RA	478
Ignace Airways	C	86
Ikar	RA	478
Iliamna Air Taxi	N	350
Ilin Aviakompania	RA	478
Ilyich Avia	UR	539
Imaatong South Sudan Airlines	ST	508
Imair	4K	613
Imperial Air Cargo	ZS	605
Imtrec Aviation	XU	582
Inaer Helicopter Chile	CC	115
Indigo Airlines	VT	568
Indonesia Air Transport	PK	448
Indonesia Airasia	PK	448
Infinity Flight Services	C	86
Inland Air Charters	C	86
Inland Aviation Services	N	350
Insel Air International	PJ	443
Intal Air	EX	174
Integra Air	C	86
Inter - transportes Aereos Inter	TG	525
Inter Island Air	N	350
Inter-Air	ZS	605
Interavia Airlines	RA	478
Interavia Taxi Aero	PP	460
Interisland Airways	RP	498
Interjet	XA	580
Interlink Airlines	ZS	605
Intermountain helicopters	N	350
International Air Link	6Y	632
International Air Response	N	350
Intersky	OE	428
Inversija	YL	586
Investavia	UP	535
Iraero	RA	478
Iran Air	EP	167
Iran Air Tour Airline	EP	167
Iran Aseman Airlines	EP	168

Iraqi Airways	YI	584
Irish Helicopters	EI	160
IRS Airlines	5N	624
ISD Avia	UR	539
Island Air	VP-C	564
Island Air	N	350
Island Air Charters	N	350
Island Air Express	YV	592
Island Air Service	N	350
Island Airlines	N	351
island Airways	N	351
Island Airways	P2	469
Island Aviation	RP	498
Island Aviation Services	8Q	635
Island Seaplane Service	N	351
Island Seaplanes	PK	448
Island Transvoyager	RP	498
Island Wings	C6	126
Island Wings Air Service	N	351
Islands Nationair	P2	469
Islas Airways	EC	154
Islena Airlines	HR	226
Isles of Scilly Skybus	G	200
Israir	4X	616
ITAB - International Trans Air Business	9Q	646
Itali Airlines	I	238
Italiatour Airlines	I	238
Itek Air	EX	174
Izhavia	RA	478
Izmir Airlines	TC	518
Jackson Air Services	C	86
Jade Cargo International	B	38
Jagson Airlines	VT	568
J-Air	JA	246
JAL Express	JA	246
Janes Aviation	G	200
Jans Helicopters	RP	498
Japan Air Commuter	JA	246
Japan Airlines	JA	247
Japan Transocean Air	JA	250
JAT Airways	YU	589
Jatayu Air	PK	448
Jazeera Airways	9K	638
Jeju Air	HL	221
Jet	ST	508
Jet 2000	RA	478
Jet Air	SP	506
Jet Air Group	RA	478
Jet Airways	VT	569
Jet2	G	200
Jet4You	CN	118
Jetair Services	9Q	647
Jetairfly	OO	434
Jetblue Airways	N	351
Jetconnect	ZK	600
Jetlink Express	5Y	629
Jetlite	VT	570
Jetran International Airways	YR	587
Jetstar Airways	VH	550
Jetstar Asia Airways	9V	648
Jetstar Pacific Airlines	VN	562
Jett 8 Airlines Cargo	9V	648
Jettime	OY	438
Jiangnan Universal Aviation	B	38
Jim Hankins Air Service	N	353
Jin Air	HL	221
Johnny May's Air Charters	C	86
Johnsons Air	9G	637
Jonair	SE	502
Jordan Aviation	JY	252
Jordan International Air Cargo	JY	252
JP Air Cargo	ES	171
JP Express	JA	250
JS Focus Air	AP	7
Jubba Airways	6O	631
Juneyao Airlines	B	38
Jungle Flying	TG	525
K2 Aviation	N	356
Kabeelo Airways	C	86
Kabo Air	5N	624

Kabul Air	YA	584		L and A Aviation	C	88
Kachina Aviation	N	353		La Costena	YN	587
Kakadu Air Services	VH	551		La Nationale	TR	528
Kalahari Air Services & Charter	A2	8		LAB Airlines	CP	120
Kalitta Air	N	353		LAB Flying Service	N	356
Kalitta Charters II	N	354		Labrador Air Safari	C	88
Kalitta Flying Services	N	354		Lac la Croix Quetico Air Service	C	88
Kallat el Saker Air	5A	617		Lac Seul Airways	C	89
Kalstar	PK	448		LADE	LV	260
Kalusair	C	86		Lake & Peninsula Airlines	N	357
Kam Air	YA	584		Lake Clark Air	N	357
Kamaka Air	N	355		Lakeland Airways	C	89
Kapo	RA	479		Lakeland Helicopters	ZK	600
Karratha Flying Services	VH	551		Lakelse Air	C	89
Karthago Airlines	TS	529		Lakes District Air Services	C	89
Kartika Airlines	PK	449		LAM - Linhas Aereas de Mocambique	C9	127
Kasaba Air Service	C	86		LAN Airlines	CC	115
Kaskazi Aviation	5Y	629		LAN Argentina	LV	260
Kata Transport Company	ST	508		LAN Cargo	CC	117
Katekavia	RA	479		Lan Cargo Colombia	HK	217
Katmai Air	N	355		LAN Ecuador	HC	212
Kavok Airlines	YV	592		LAN Express	CC	117
Kayair	C	86		LAN Peru	OB	425
Kaz Air Trans	UP	535		Lanzarote Aircargo	EC	154
Kazair West	UP	535		Lao Airlines	RDPL	497
Kazakhmys	UP	535		Lao Aviation	RDPL	497
Kazan Air Enterprises	RA	479		Lao Capricorn Air	RDPL	497
Kazzinc	UP	535		LAP - Lineas Aéreas Petroleras	HK	217
KD Air	C	86		Las Vegas Helicopters	N	357
Kechika Valley Air	C	86		Laser	YV	593
Keewatin Air	C	86		Lassa - Lineas de Aeroservicios	CC	117
Kelowna Flightcraft Air Charter	C	86		Latina de Aviacon	HK	217
Kenmore Air	N	355		Lauzon Aviation	C	89
Kenn Borek Air	C	87		Lawrence Bay Airways	C	89
Kenora Air Service	C	87		Layang-layang Aerospace	9M	641
Kenya Airways	5Y	629		LC Burse	OB	425
Key Lime Air	N	355		Leair Charter Services	C6	126
Keystone Air Service	C	88		Leuenberger Air Service	C	89
Khabarovsk Airlines	RA	479		LGW - Luftfahrtgesellschaft Walter	D	135
Kharkov Aviation production Association	UR	539		Liard Air	C	89
Khors Air	UR	539		LIAT - The Caribbean Airline	V2	573
Khozu Avia	UP	535		Libyan Air Cargo	5A	617
Kilwa Air	5H	620		Libyan Airlines	5A	618
King Air Charter	ZS	605		Libyavia	5A	619
King Airelines	N	356		Lignes Aeriennes Congolaises	9Q	647
King Flying Service	N	356		Lindsay Aviation	N	357
King Island Airways	VH	551		Linea Aerea Costa Norte	CC	117
Kingfisher Airlines	VT	570		Linea Aerea Iaaca	YV	593
Kingfisher Red	VT	570		Linea Turistica Aereotuy	YV	593
Kirov Avia Enterprise	RA	479		Lineas Aereas Canedo	CP	120
Kirovohradavia	UR	540		Lineas Aéreas Sudamericanas Colombia	HK	217
Kish Air	EP	168		Lion Airlines	PK	449
Kississing Air	C	88		Lionair	RP	499
Kitty Hawk Aircargo	N	356		Lipetsk Avia	RA	480
Kiunga Aviation	P2	469		Litoranea	PP	460
Kivalliq Air	C	88		Little Red Air Service	C	89
KLM Cityhopper	PH	440		Lizingtekhtrans	UR	540
KLM Royal Dutch Airlines	PH	441		Loadair Cargo	9K	638
Kluane Airways	C	88		Lobaye Airways	TL	527
K-Mile Air	HS	227		Loch Lomand Seaplanes	G	201
KMV Mineralnye Vody Airlines	RA	479		Lockhart Air Services	C	89
Knaapo	RA	479		Loganair	G	201
Knight Aviation	5Y	629		Logistic Air	N	357
Kokshetau Airlines	UP	535		LOT - Polish Airlines	SP	506
Kolavia	RA	480		Lotus Air	SU	511
Kolob Canyons Air Services	N	356		LR Airlines	OK	432
Koral Blue	SU	511		Lucky Airlines	B	39
Korean Air	HL	221		Lufthansa	D	135
Koryakavia	RA	480		Lufthansa Cargo	D	139
Kosmas Air Cargo	YU	589		Lufthansa Cityline	D	139
Kosmos Airlines	RA	480		Lufthansa Italia	I	239
Kostroma Air Enterprise	RA	480		Lufttransport	LN	256
Krym	UR	540		Luftverkehr Friesland Harle	D	140
KS Avia	YL	586		Lukiaviatrans	RA	480
Kuban Airlines	RA	480		Luxair	LX	261
Kunming Airlines	B	39		Luzair	CS	122
Kura Kura Aviation	PK	449		Lviv Airlines	UR	540
Kuwait Airways	9K	638		Lydd Air	G	201
Kyrghyz Airways	EX	174		Lynden Air Cargo	N	357
Kyrghyzstan Airlines	EX	174		Lynx Air International	N	357
Kyrgyz Trans Air	EX	174				
Kyrgyzstan	EX	174		M & N Aviation	N	357
				Macair Jet	LV	260

Mack Air	A2	8
Magnicharters	XA	580
Mahan Air	EP	168
Major's Air Services	C6	127
Mak Air	UP	535
Makalu Air	9N	644
Malagasy Airlines	5R	625
Malaysia Airlines	9M	641
Maldivian Air Taxi	8Q	635
Malev	HA	206
Mali Air Express	TZ	531
Mali Air Transport	TZ	531
Malift Air	9Q	647
Malmo Aviation	SE	502
Malu Aviation	9Q	647
Manaus Aero Taxi	PP	460
Mandala Airlines	PK	450
Mandarin Airlines	B	53
Mango	ZS	605
Mango Mat Airlines	9Q	647
Manitoba Government Air Services	C	89
Manunggal Air	PK	450
Manx2 Airlines	G	201
Mapjet	OE	428
Marin Air	TC	518
Maritime Air Charter	C	90
Maroomba Airlines	VH	551
Marsland Aviation	ST	509
Martinair	PH	442
Martinaire	N	358
Martini Aviation	C	90
MAS Air Cargo	XA	580
Maswings	9M	642
MAT Macedonian Air Transport	Z3	610
Mauritania Airways	5T	626
Maverick Helicopters	N	358
Max Aviation	C	90
Maxair	5N	625
Maximus Air Cargo	A6	15
Maya Island Air	V3	573
Mayair	XA	580
McCall Aviation	N	359
MCHS Rossii	RA	480
McMurray Aviation	C	90
McNeely Charter Service	N	359
MDLR Airlines	VT	571
Meadow Air	C	90
Medallion Air	YR	588
Medavia	9H	637
Med-View Airlines	5N	625
Mega Aircompany	UP	535
Mega Maldives Airlines	8Q	635
Melaire	C	90
Meridian	UR	540
Meridian Airways	9G	637
Meridiana Fly	I	239
Merpati Nusantara Airlines	PK	450
Mesa Airlines	N	359
META - Mesquita Transportes Aero	PP	460
MHS Aviation	9M	643
Mia Airlines	YR	588
Miami Air International	N	359
Miami Air Lease	N	359
Miapet Avia	EK	165
MIAT - Mongolian Airlines	JU	251
Mid Airlines	ST	509
Mid Express Tchad	TT	530
Mid-Atlantic Freight	N	359
Middland	9Q	647
Middle East Airlines	OD	426
Midex Airlines	A6	15
Midwest Airlines	N	359
Midwest Airlines Egypt	SU	511
Midwest Aviation	N	360
Midwest Connect	N	360
Midwest Helicopter Airways	N	360
Mihin Lanka	4R	614
Milford Sound Flightseeing	ZK	600
Milford Sound Scenic Flights	ZK	600
Military Support Services	VH	552
Minair	TL	527
Minden Air	N	360
Miniliner	I	239
Minipi Aviation	C	90
Mint Airways	EC	154
Miras Air	UP	535
Missinippi Airways	C	90
Missionair	C	90
Mistral Air	I	239
MNG Cargo Airlines	TC	519
Mocambique Expresso	C9	128
Mokulele Airlines	N	360
Moldavian Airlines	ER	170
Molson Air	C	90
Mombasa Air Safari	5Y	629
Monarch Airlines	G	201
Montair Aviation	C	90
Montenegro Airlines	4O	614
Moonair Aviation	4X	616
Mordovia Air	RA	481
Moremi Air Services	A2	8
Morgan Air Services	C	91
Morningstar Air Express	C	91
Moskoviya	RA	481
Moskva Air Company	RA	481
Motor Sich Airlines	UR	540
Mountain Air	ZK	601
Mountain Air Cargo	N	360
Mountain West Helicopters	N	360
MRK Airlines	UR	540
MTA Cargo	PP	460
Mudan Airlines	6O	631
Mustang Helicopters	C	91
Mustique Airways	J8	253
Myanma Airways	XY	583
Myanmar Airways International	XY	583
Myflug	TF	525
NAC Charter	ZS	605
NAC Executive Charter	A2	9
Naft Air	EP	169
Nakina Outpost Camps and Air	C	91
Namibia Commercial Airways	V5	574
Napo Aviatrans	RA	482
NAS Air	HZ	230
Nas Air	E3	176
Nation Air	HH	212
National Airlines	N	360
National Airways Cameroon	TJ	527
National Helicopter Services	9Y	652
National Helicopters	C	91
National Regional Transport	3C	611
Native American Air Services	N	361
Natureair	TI	526
Naturelink Charter	ZS	606
Navair	N	361
Navid Air	EP	169
Navigator Airlines	EK	165
Naysa Aerotaxis	EC	154
Nelair Charters & Travel	ZS	606
Neos	I	240
Nepal Airlines	9N	644
Neptune Air	9M	643
Neptune Aviation Services	N	361
Nesma Air	SU	511
Nestor Falls Fly-in Outposts	C	91
Network Aviation Australia	VH	552
New Central Aviation	JA	250
New England Airlines	N	361
New Mexico Airlines	N	361
Newfoundland & Labrador Air Services	C	92
Nextjet	SE	502
Ngaanyatjarra Air	VH	552
NHR Taxi Aereo	PP	460
NHT Linhas Aereas	PP	460
Nightexpress	D	140
Niki	OE	428
Nile Air	SU	512
Nippon Cargo Airlines	JA	250
Nok Air	HS	227
Nolinor Aviation	C	92
Noordzee Helikopters Vlaanderen	OO	435
Nord Aviation	N	361
Nordair Quebec 2000	C	92

Airline	Code	Page
Nordavia Regional Airlines	RA	482
Nordic Solutions Air Services	LY	262
Nordplus	C	92
Nordstar	RA	482
Nordwind	RA	482
Norfolk Air	VH	552
Norlandair	TF	525
Norman Aviation	V2	573
Norrlandsflyg	SE	502
Norse Air Charter	ZS	606
Norsk Luftambulance	LN	256
North American Airlines	N	361
North Cariboo Air	C	92
North Coast Aviation	P2	469
North Flying	OY	438
North Pacific Seaplanes	C	93
North South Airlines	RP	499
North Star Air Cargo	N	361
North Star Aviation	N	362
North Wright Airways	C	93
Northeast Shuttle	VT	571
Northern Air	A2	9
Northern Air	5H	620
Northern Air Care	C	93
Northern Air Cargo	N	362
Northern Air Charter	C	93
Northern Air Services	DQ	142
Northern Air Solutions	C	93
Northern Lights Air	C	93
Northstar Air	C	93
Northward Air	C	93
Northway Aviation	C	93
Northwest Flying	C	94
Northwest Helicopters	N	362
Northwest Seaplanes	N	362
Northwestern Air	C	94
Norwegian	LN	256
Nouvelair	TS	529
Nouvelles Air Affaires Gabon	TR	528
Nova Air	XA	581
Nova Airlines	ST	509
Novair	SE	502
Novosibirsk Air Enterprise	RA	483
NT Air	C	94
Nueltin Lake Air Service	C	94
Nusantara Air Charter	PK	451
OCA International	D	140
Odessa Airlines	UR	540
OK Airways	B	39
OLT - Ostfriesische Lufttransport	D	140
Olympic Airways	SX	513
Oman Air	A4O	9
Omega Air	C	94
Omni - Aviacao e Tecnoligia	CS	122
Omni Air International	N	362
Omniflight Helicopters	N	362
One-Two Go	HS	227
Ontario Ministry of Natural Resources Aviation Services	C	94
Onur Air	TC	519
Ootsa Air	C	95
Open skies	F	184
Orange Aircraft Leasing	PH	443
Orbest	CS	122
Orca Air	C	95
Orebro Aviation	SE	502
Orenair	RA	483
Orient Thai Airlines	HS	227
Oriental	YV	593
Oriental Air Bridge	JA	250
Ornge	C	95
Osnaburgh Airways	C	96
Osprey Wings	C	95
Ostseeflug	D	141
Our Airline	C2	125
Overland Airways	5N	625
Pace Airlines	N	363
Pacific Airways	N	363
Pacific Blue	ZK	601
Pacific Coastal Airlines	C	96
Pacific Eagle Aviation	C	96
Pacific East Asia Cargo Airlines	RP	499
Pacific Helicopters	N	363
Pacific Helicopters	P2	469
Pacific Island Air	DQ	143
Pacific Pearl Airways	RP	499
Pacific Sun	DQ	143
Pacific Western Helicopters	C	96
Pacific Wings	N	363
Pacific Wings Airlines	C	96
Pacificair	RP	499
Pacificflyer	T8A	531
Pakistan International Airlines	AP	7
Pamir Air	YA	584
Pan Am Dominica	HI	213
Pan Européenne Air Service	F	184
Panair Cargo	HP	225
Panair Lineas Aereas	EC	154
Panavia Cargo Airlines	HP	225
Pan-Malaysian Air Transport	9M	643
Panorama Helicopters	C	96
Pantanal	PP	460
Papillon Grand Canyon Airways	N	363
Paradise Air	TI	526
Paragon Air Express	N	364
Paramount Jet	N	364
Pascan Aviation	C	97
Passaredo Transportes Aereos	PP	461
Patagonia Airlines	CC	117
Pawan Hans Helicopters	VT	571
Payim International Air	EP	169
PDG Helicopters	G	202
Peace Air	9L	639
Pearl Airlines	VH	552
Peau Vava'u Air	A3	9
Pegasus Airlines	TC	519
Pel-Air	VH	552
Pelican Air Services	ZS	607
Pelican Narrows Air Services	C	97
Pelita Air	PK	451
Penair	N	364
Penas	PK	452
PENTA - Pena Transportes Aereos	PP	461
Perfect Aviation	9M	643
Perimeter Aviation	C	97
Perla Air	YV	593
Perm Airlines	RA	483
Peruvian Airlines	OB	425
Petra Airlines	JY	252
Petro Air	5A	619
Petroleum Air Services	SU	512
Petropavlovsk-Kamchatsky Air Enterprise	RA	483
PGA Express	CS	122
PHI - Petroleum Helicopters	N	365
Philippine Airlines	RP	499
Phillips Air Charter	N	368
Phoebus Apollo Aviation	ZS	607
Phoenix Air	N	368
Phoenix Airtransport	N	368
Phoenix Avia	EK	165
Phoenix Heli-Flight	C	97
Phuket Airlines	HS	227
Pineapple Air	C6	127
Pionair Adventures	ZK	601
Pionair Australia	VH	553
Pirinair Express	EC	155
Planemasters	N	369
Platinum Air Linhas Aereas	PP	461
Platinum Airlines	N	369
Players Air	N	369
Pluna Lineas Aereas Uruguayas	CX	125
PMT Air	XU	583
Podilia Avia	UR	540
Polar Air Cargo	N	369
Polar Airlines	RA	483
Polar Aviation	VH	553
Polet Aviakompania	RA	484
Police Aviation Services	G	202
Polyarnya Avia	RA	484
Polynesian Airlines	5W	626
Ponderosa Airlines	N	369
Porter Airlines	C	97
Portugalia Airlines	CS	122
Precisionair	5H	620

Premiair	PK	452
Premiair Aviation Services	G	202
Premier Helicopters	EI	160
President Airlines	XU	583
Presidential Airways	N	369
Primera Air Scandinavia	OY	438
Prince Edward Air	C	98
Priority Air	N	369
Priority Air Charter	N	369
Privalege Style	EC	155
Privatair	D	141
Privatair	HB	209
Private Wings	D	141
Professional Air Charter	N	369
Profilght Air Services	9J	638
Progress Air	ZS	607
Progress Aviakompania	RA	484
Promech Air	N	370
Pronair Airlines	EC	155
Propair	C	98
Province of Alberta	C	98
Provincial Airlines	C	98
Provincial Helicopters	C	99
Pskovavia	RA	484
PTL Luftfahrtunturnehmen	D	141
Puerto Rico Air Management Services	N	370
Pullmantur Air	EC	155
Puma Air Linhas Aereas	PP	461
Qanot Sharq	UK	531
QANTAS Airways	VH	553
Qantaslink	VH	555
Qatar Airways	A7	16
Qeshm Air	EP	169
Quantum Helicopters	C	99
Queensway Air Services	5Y	629
Quick Air	N	370
Qwest Helicopters	C	99
Qwila Air	ZS	607
RACSA	TG	525
RAF-Avia	YL	586
Rainbow Air	YV	593
Rainbow Airways	C	99
Rainbow Jet	B	39
Rak Airlines	A6	16
RAM Air Freight	N	370
Ram Air Services	N	370
Ramp 66	N	370
Rapid Air	N	371
Rayyan Air	AP	7
RCMP	C	99
Red Sucker Lake Air Services	C	100
Red Wings	RA	484
Redding Aero Enterprises	N	371
RedJet	8P	634
Redstar Aviation	TC	520
Regent Airways	S2	515
Regio-Air	D	141
Régional	F	184
Regional 1 Airlines	C	100
Regional Air	P2	469
Regional Air	C6	127
Regional Air Lines	CN	118
Regional Air Services	5H	620
Regional Airlines	RA	484
Regional Pacific Air	VH	556
Regional Paraguaya	ZP	602
Regourd Aviation	F	185
Reliance Air	5X	626
Remote Helicopters	C	100
Republicair	XA	581
Resource Helicopters	C	100
REX - Regional Express	VH	556
Rhoades International	N	371
Riau Airlines	PK	452
Rico Linhas Aereas	PP	461
Rico Taxi Aereo	PP	461
Rio Linhas Aereas	PP	461
River Air	C	100
Rivne Universal Avia	UR	540
Robin Hood Aviation	OE	429

Roblex Aviation	N	371
Roc Aviation	B	53
Rogers Helicopters	N	371
Rollins Air	HR	226
Romavia	YR	588
Roraima Airways	8R	636
Rosneft-Baltika	RA	485
Ross Air	C	100
Ross Air Service	C	100
Ross Aviation	N	372
Rossair Charter	VH	556
Rossiya Russian Airlines	RA	485
Rotorcraft	N	372
Rovos Air	ZS	607
Royal Air	TY	530
Royal Air Charters	9J	638
Royal Air Freight	N	373
Royal Air Maroc	CN	118
Royal Airlines	AP	8
Royal Bengal Airlines	S2	515
Royal Brunei Airlines	V8	575
Royal Daisy Airlines	5X	626
Royal Falcon	JY	252
Royal Flying Doctor Service	VH	556
Royal Jordanian	JY	252
Royal Khmer Airlines	XU	583
Royal Phnom Penh Airways	XU	583
Royal Star Airlines	RP	500
Royal Wings Airlines	JY	253
RPX Airlines	PK	452
Rubystar	EW	173
Rus Aviation	EY	175
Rusair	RA	486
Rusjet	RA	486
Rusline Air	RA	486
Russian Sky Airlines	RA	486
Rusts Flying Service	N	373
Rusty Myers Flying Service	C	101
Rutaca	YV	593
Rwandair Express	9XR	651
Ryan Blake Air	ZS	607
Ryan International Airlines	N	373
Ryanair	EI	160
Ryazanavia Trans	RA	486
Ryjet	EC	155
Ryukyu Air Commuter	JA	250
S7 Airlines	RA	487
Sabah Air	9M	643
Sabang Merauke Raya Air Charter	PK	452
Sabourin Lake Lodge	C	101
Sacso Airlines	ST	509
SADELCA	HK	218
SADI	HK	218
Saemsa	XA	581
SAEP	HK	218
SAEREO	HC	212
SAESA	EC	155
Safair	ZS	607
Safari Air	A2	9
Safari Links	5Y	629
Safat Airlines	EP	169
Safewing Aviation	N	374
Safi Airways	YA	584
Safiran Airlines	EP	169
Saga Airlines	TC	520
Saha Airline	EP	169
Saicus Air	EC	155
Saint Louis Helicopter	N	374
Saintex Cargo	XA	581
S-Air	RA	486
Sakaviaservice	4L	614
Sakha Aviation School	RA	488
SAL - Sociedade de Aviacao Ligeira	D2	144
Salamis Aviation	C6	127
Salmon Air	N	374
Salt Air	ZK	601
Salt Spring Air	C	101
Saltwater West Enterprises	C	101
SAM Colombia	HK	218
Samal Air	UP	535
Samara Airlines	RA	488

Samarkand Airways	UK	531
San Juan Airlines	N	374
Sandy Lake Seaplane Service	C	101
Sansa Regional	TI	526
Santa Barbara Airlines	YV	593
Sapair	HI	213
Sapawe Air	C	101
Sapphire Aviation	N	374
Saratov Airlines	RA	488
Sarpa	HK	218
Sasair	C	101
SASCA	YV	594
Saskatchewan Government Northern Air Operations	C	101
SAT Airlines	RA	488
SAT Airlines	UP	535
SATA Air Acores	CS	122
SATA Internacional	CS	123
Satena	HK	218
Saturn Aviakompania	RA	488
Saudi Arabian Airlines	HZ	230
Sayakhat	UP	535
Sayat Air	UP	536
SB Air	N	374
Scandinavian Airline System	SE	503
Scanwings	OH	431
Scat Aircompany	UP	536
SCD Aviation	TR	528
Scenic Airlines	N	374
Scenic Aviation	N	374
Scotairways	G	203
Seaborne Airlines	N	374
Seair Airways	C6	127
Seair Pacific Gold Coast	VH	557
Seair Seaplanes	C	102
Searca Colombia	HK	219
Seawing Airways	VH	557
Seawings	A6	16
Securité Civile	F	185
Sefofane Air	V5	574
Sefofane Air Charter	A2	9
Selkirk Air	C	102
Selva	HK	219
Semeyavia	UP	536
Senegal Airlines	6V	631
Sequoia Helicopters	C	102
Serair	EC	155
Serami	YV	594
Servant Air	N	375
Service Air	9Q	647
Service Commuter	9Q	647
Service Flight Corp	VN	562
Servicios Aereos de Los Andes	OB	425
Servisair	D2	144
Setco	HR	226
Sete Taxi Aereo	PP	461
Sevastopol Avia	UR	541
Sevenair	TS	529
Severstal Aircompany	RA	489
SF Airlines	B	39
SGA Airlines	HS	227
Shan Xi Airlines	B	39
Shandong Airlines	B	39
Shanghai Airlines	B	40
Shanghai Cargo	B	41
Shar Ink	RA	489
Sharp Airlines	VH	557
Sharp Wings	C	102
Sheheen Air Cargo	AP	8
Sheheen Air International	AP	8
Shenzhen Airlines	B	41
Shine Air Services	VH	558
Shortstop Air Charter	VH	558
Shovkovly Shlyah	UR	541
Showalter's Fly-In Service	C	102
Shree Airlines	9N	644
Shuangyang Aviation	B	43
Shuttle America	N	375
Shuttle Bird	UR	541
Sibaviatrans	RA	489
Sichuan Airlines	B	43
Sichuan Aolin General Aviation	B	44
Sideral Air Cargo	PP	462
Sierra Pacific Airlines	N	375
Sierra West Airlines	N	375
Sifton Air Yukon	C	102
Sil Aviation	P2	469
Silk Way Airlines	4K	613
Silkair	9V	648
Siller Aviation	N	375
Silver Air	OK	432
Silver Air	J2	253
Silver Air	A6	16
Silverback Cargo Freighters	9XR	651
Silverwing	HZ	232
Simpson Air Commuter Canada	C	102
Singapore Airlines	9V	649
Singapore Airlines Cargo	9V	650
Sioux Air	C	102
Sioux Narrows Airways	C	102
Sirius Aero	RA	489
Sita Airlines	9N	644
Skagway Air Service	N	375
Skippers Aviation	VH	558
Skol Aviakompania	RA	489
Sky Airline	CC	117
Sky Airlines	TC	520
Sky Aviation Tanzania	5H	620
Sky Bahamas	C6	127
Sky Castle Aviation	N	375
Sky Express	SX	514
Sky Eyes Aviation	HS	227
Sky Gabon SA	TR	528
Sky Georgia	4L	614
Sky Horse Aviation	JU	252
Sky King	N	375
Sky One Air	ZS	608
Sky Regional Airlines	C	103
Sky Relief	Z	596
Sky Service	OO	435
Sky Shuttle Helicopters	B	50
Sky Taxi	SP	507
Sky Way Air	EX	174
Sky Wind	4K	613
Sky Wings	SX	514
Skybridge Airops	I	240
Skydive & Air Service	OK	432
Skyexpress	RA	489
Skygate International	JY	253
Skyhaul	ZS	608
Skyking Airlines	VQ-T	564
Skylan Airways	6Y	632
Skylease Air Cargo	N	375
Skylift Taxi Aereo	PP	462
Skyline Helicopters	C	103
Skylink Arabia	A6	16
Skymark Airlines	JA	251
Skymaster Airlines	PP	462
Skynet Asia Airways	JA	251
Skynorth Air	C	103
Skypower Express Airways	5N	625
Skysouth	G	203
Skystar Airways	HS	227
Skytraders	VH	558
Skytrail	5Y	630
Skytrans Regional	VH	558
Skyway Enterprises	N	376
Skyways Express	SE	505
Skyways Kenya	5Y	630
Skywest Airlines	N	376
Skywest Airlines	VH	558
Skywings International	Z3	610
Skywork Airlines	HB	209
Slate Falls Airways	C	103
Slingair	VH	559
Slok Air International	C5	126
Slovak Government Flying Service	OM	433
Small Planet Airlines	LY	262
Smartlynx	YL	586
Smartwings	OK	432
Smithair	N	376
Smokey Bay Air	N	376
SNAS Aviation	HZ	232
Snow Aviation	N	376
Sobel Air	9G	637
Soft Trans Air	9Q	647

Sokol	RA	489
Sol America	YV	594
Sol Del Paraguay	ZP	602
SOL Lineas Aereas	LV	261
Solar Cargo	YV	594
Solenta Aviation	ZS	608
Solenta Aviation Gabon	TR	528
Solenta Aviation Kenya	5Y	630
Solinair	S5	516
Solitaire	JY	253
Solomons	H4	232
Somon Air	EY	175
Sonair	D2	144
Sontair	C	103
Sophia Airlines	TU	530
Sorem	I	240
Soundsair	ZK	601
South Aero	N	376
South African Airways	ZS	608
South African Express Airways	ZS	609
South Airlines	UR	541
South Airlines	EK	165
South East Air	ZK	601
South East Asian Airlines	RP	500
South Morseby Air Charters	C	103
South Pacific Express	N	376
South Pacific Express	5W	626
Southeast Aviation	N	376
Southern Air	N	376
Southern Air Charter	C6	127
Southern Aviation	C	103
Southern Cross Aviation	Z	596
Southern Seaplane	N	377
Southwest Air	P2	469
Southwest Airlines	N	377
Spanair	EC	155
Spernak Airways	N	384
Spicejet	VT	572
Spirit Airlines	N	384
Spirit of Manila Airlines	RP	500
Spring Airlines	B	44
Springbok Classic Air	ZS	610
Sprint Air	SP	507
Spur Aviation	N	385
Srilankan	4R	614
Sriwijaya Air	PK	452
St Barth Commuter	F	187
STA - Spciedade de Transport Aereos	C9	128
Stag	9Q	647
Star African Air	6O	631
Star Air	OY	438
Star Air Cargo	ZS	610
Star Air International	AP	8
Star Airlines	Z3	610
Star Airways	ZA	596
Star Aviation	7T	634
Star Equatorial Airlines	3C	611
Star peru	OB	425
Star1 Airlines	LY	262
Starflyer	JA	251
Starjet	JY	253
Starline KZ	UP	536
Starlink Aviation	C	103
Stars and Stripes Air Tours	N	385
Stars Away Aviation	ZS	610
Stella Maris Aviation	C6	127
Stenberg Aviation	OY	438
Sterling Aviation	G	203
Strait Air	C	103
Strategic Airlines	VH	559
Suburban Air Freight	N	385
Success Airlines	9Q	647
Sud D'Or International Airlines	4X	616
Sudan Airways	ST	509
Sudanese States Aviation	ST	509
Sudbury Aviation	C	103
Summit Air Charters	C	103
Sun Air	ST	509
Sun Air Service	9Q	647
Sun Country Airlines	N	385
Sun-Air of Scandinavia	OY	438
Sundance Air	YV	594
Sunexpress	TC	520
Sunwest Aviation	C	104
Sunwing Airlines	C	104
Superior Airways	C	104
Superior Aviation	N	386
Superior Aviation Services	5Y	630
Superior Helicopters	C	104
Superior Helicopters	N	386
Surinam Airways	PZ	467
Susi Air	PK	453
Sustut Air	C	104
Suvarnabhumi Airlines	HS	227
Sverdlovsk 2nd Air Enterprise	RA	489
SVG Air	J8	254
Swala Airlines	9Q	647
Swanberg Air	C	104
Swiftair	EC	156
Swiftair Hellas	SX	514
Swiss European Air Lines	HB	209
Swiss International Airlines	HB	209
Sydney Seaplanes	VH	559
Syrianair	YK	585
TAAG Angola Airlines	D2	145
TAB Cargo	CP	120
Taban Air	EP	170
TACA Costa Rica	TI	526
TACA International Airlines	YS	588
TACA Peru	OB	426
Tacsa	TI	526
TACV -		
Transportes Aereos de Cabo Verde	D4	146
TAF Helicopters	EC	156
TAF Linhas Aereas	PP	462
Tailwind Airlines	TC	521
Tajik Air	EY	175
Take Air Lines	F	187
Talkeetna Air Taxi	N	386
TAM - Taxi Aereo Marilia	PP	464
TAM - Transportes Aereo Militar	CP	121
TAM Linhas Aereas	PP	462
TAM Mercosur	ZP	602
TAME	HC	212
Tamir Aviation	4X	616
Tampa Airlines	HK	219
Tanana Air Service	N	386
Tanzanair - Tanzanian Air Services	5H	620
TAP Air Portugal	CS	123
TAP Lineas Aereas	HK	219
Tapo-Avia	UK	531
Tapsa Aviacion	LV	261
Taquan Air Service	N	386
Tara Air	9N	645
Tara Airlines	EP	170
Tarhan Air	TC	521
Tarom	YR	588
Taron Avia	EK	166
TAS - Transporte Aereo de Santander	HK	219
TAS Transportes Aereos del Sur	EC	157
Tasair	VH	559
Tasfast Air Freight	VH	559
Tasman Cargo Airlines	VH	559
Tasman Helicopters	C	104
Tassili Airlines	7T	634
TASUL - Taxi Aereo Sul	PP	464
Tatarstan Air	RA	490
Tavaj Linhas Aereas	PP	464
Tavasa	EC	157
Tavrey Aircompany	UR	541
Taxi Aereo Cusiana	HK	219
Taxi Aereo Itaituba	PP	465
Taxi Aereo Weiss	PP	465
Taxi Air Fret	F	185
Tbilaviamsheni	4L	614
TBM	N	386
TEAM Airlines -		
Team Transportes Aereos	PP	465
Teebah Airlines	J2	253
Telesis Transair	N	386
Temsco Helicopters	N	386
Tenir Airlines	EX	175
Tepavia Trans Airline	ER	170

Universal Airlines	N	407	Wahkash Contracting	C	110
Universal Helicopters	C	108	Walsten Air Service	C	110
UPS Airlines	N	407	Waltair	9Q	648
Ural Airlines	RA	491	Waltair Europe	SE	505
US Airways	N	410	Wamair Service & Outfitting	C	110
US Airways Express	N	415	Warbelow's Air	N	422
US Forest Service	N	420	Ward Air	N	422
US Helicopters	N	420	Wasaya Airways	C	110
USA 3000 Airlines	N	420	Wataniya Airways	9K	638
USA Jet Airlines	N	420	Watson's Skyways	C	111
Utage	3C	612	WDL Aviation	D	142
Utair Airlines	RA	492	Weagamow Air	C	111
Utair Express	RA	494	Webjet Linhas Aereas	PP	466
Utair South Africa	ZS	610	Welcome Air	OE	429
UTAir Ukraine	UR	542	West Air	B	46
Utin Lento	OH	431	West Air Europe	SE	505
Uvuaga	RA	494	West Air Europe	LX	261
Uzbekistan Airways	UK	532	West Atlantic	G	205
			West Coast Air	C	111
V Australia	VH	560	West Coast Helicopters	C	111
Valan International Cargo	ZS	610	West Wind Aviation	C	111
Valhalla Helicopters	C	108	West Wing Aviation	VH	561
Valley Helicopters	C	108	Westair Aviation	C	111
Valuair	9V	651	Westair Wings	V5	574
Van Air	P2	470	Western Air	C6	127
Van Air Europe	OK	433	Western Air Express	N	422
Vancouver Island Air	C	108	Western Air Express	N	422
Varig	PP	466	Western Aviators	N	422
Varig Log	PP	466	Westjet	C	112
Vasco	VN	562	Westland Helicopters	C	113
Venescar International	YV	595	Westman Islands Airlines	TF	525
Venezolana	YV	595	Westwind Aviation	N	422
Vertical de Aviacion	HK	219	Wettenhall Air Services	VH	562
Vertir	EK	166	Whistler Air Services	C	113
Veteran Airline	EK	166	White	CS	124
Veteran Airlines	UR	542	White Eagle General Aviation	SP	507
VIA - Air Via	LZ	263	White River Air	C	113
Viarco	HK	220	Whitejets	PP	467
Victoria Air	RP	500	Wideroe's Flyveselskap	LN	257
Vieques Air Link	N	421	Wiggins Airways	N	423
Vietnam Airlines	VN	562	Wildcat Helicopters	C	113
Vigo Jet	XA	581	Wilderness Air	C	113
VIH Helicopters	C	108	Wilderness Helicopters	C	113
Viking Hellas Airlines	SX	514	Williston Lake Air Services	C	113
Villiers Air Services	C	109	Willow Air	N	423
Vim Airlines	RA	494	Wimbi Dira Airways	9Q	648
Vincent Aviation	ZK	601	Winair	PJ	443
Vincent Aviation (Australia)	VH	560	Wind Rose	UR	542
Vintage Prop and Jets	N	421	Windjet	I	240
VIP - Vuelos Internos Privados	HC	212	Windward Air Services	C	113
Vip-Avia	4L	614	Windward Express Airways	PJ	444
Virgin America	N	421	Wings Air	PK	454
Virgin Atlantic Airways	G	205	Wings Aviation	5N	625
Virgin Blue Airlines	VH	560	Wings of Alaska	N	423
Virunga Air Charter	9Q	648	Wings Of Lebanon Aviation	OD	426
Vision Air	EI	164	Wings Over Kississing	C	113
Vision Air	C6	127	Wizz Air	HA	207
Vision Air	HH	213	Wizz Air Bulgaria	LZ	264
Vision Air International	AP	8	Wizz Air Ukraine	UR	542
Vision Airlines	N	421	Wolverine Air	C	114
Viva Aerobus	XA	581	Woodgate Executive Air Services	G	206
Vladivostok Air	RA	494	World Airways	N	423
VLM Airlines	OO	436	Wright Air Service	N	424
Vol Air	HI	213	Wyngs Aviation	YV	595
Volare Aviation Enterprise	UR	542			
Volaris	XA	582	Xiamen Airlines	B	46
Volga Aviaexpress	RA	495	Xinjiang General Aviation	B	47
Volga-Dnepr Airlines	RA	495	XL Airways France	F	185
Voliamo	I	240	XL Airways Germany	D	142
Vologda Air Enterprise	RA	495	Xpress Air	PK	454
Vostok Airlines	RA	495	Xtra Airways	N	424
Voyage Air	C	109	Xunaga Air	A2	9
Voyager Airlines	S2	515			
Voyageur Airways	C	109	Yak Service	RA	495
VSA Aviation	ZS	610	Yakutia Airlines	RA	496
Vueling Airlines	EC	157	Yamal Airlines	RA	496
Vuelos Mediterrano	EC	158	Yangon Airlines	XY	583
Vyborg Airlines	RA	495	Yangtze River Express	B	47
			Yas Air	EP	170
Waasheshkun Airways	C	110	Yavson	UR	543
Wabakimi Air	C	110	Yellowhead Helicopters	C	114
Wabusk Air Service	C	110	Yemenia	7O	632

Yeongnam Air	HL	223
Yeti Airlines	9N	645
Youngone	S2	515
Yukon Aviation	N	424
Yuzhnaya Aircompany	UP	536
Yuzmashavia	UR	543
Zagros Airlines	EP	170
Zambezi Airways	9J	638
Zambian Airways	9J	638
Zanair	5H	621
Zantas Air Service	5H	621
Zapolyarye Aviakompania	RA	496
ZB Air	5Y	630
Zest Airways	RP	500
Zhetysu Avia	UP	536
Zhezhair	UP	536
Zhongfei Airlines	B	47
Zimex Aviation	HB	210
Zimmer Air Services	C	114
Zoom Airways	S2	516
Zorex	EC	158

NOTES:

NOTES:

NOTES:

NOTES:

NOTES:

AIR-BRITAIN MEMBERSHIP
Join on-line at www.air-britain.co.uk

If you are not currently a member of Air-Britain, the publishers of this book, you may be interested in what we have on offer to provide for your interest in aviation.

About Air-Britain
Formed 63 years ago, we are the world's most progressive aviation society, and exist to bring together aviation enthusiasts with every type of interest. Our members include aircraft historians, aviation writers, spotters and pilots - and those who just have a fascination with aircraft and aviation. Air-Britain is a non-profit organisation, which is independently audited, and any financial surpluses are used to provide services to the world-wide membership which currently stands at around 4,000, some 700 of whom live overseas.

Membership of Air-Britain
Membership is open to all. A basic membership fee is charged and every member receives a copy of the quarterly house magazine, Air-Britain Aviation World, and is entitled to use all the Air-Britain specialist services and buy **Air-Britain publications at discounted prices**. A membership subscription includes the choice to add any or all of our other three magazines, News &/or Archive &/or Aeromilitaria. Air-Britain also publishes 10-20 books per annum (around 70 titles in stock at any one time). Membership runs January - December each year, but new members have a choice of options periods to get their initial subscription started.

Air-Britain Aviation World is the quarterly 52-page house magazine containing not only news of Air-Britain activities, but also a wealth of features, illustrated substantially in colour, on many different aviation subjects, contemporary and historical, contributed by our members. Extra colour Photo News pages are now included.

Air-Britain News is the world aviation news monthly, containing data on aircraft registrations worldwide and news of Airlines and Airliners, Business Jets, Local Airfield News, Civil and Military Air Show Reports, and International Military Aviation News. An average 160 pages of lavishly-illustrated information for the dedicated enthusiast.

Air-Britain Archive is the quarterly 48-page specialist journal of civil aviation history. Packed with the results of historical research by Air-Britain specialists into aircraft types, overseas registers and previously unpublished facts about the rich heritage of civil aviation. Up to 100 photographs per issue, some in colour.

Air-Britain Aeromilitaria is the quarterly 48-page unique source for meticulously researched details of military aviation history edited by the acclaimed authors of Air-Britain's military monographs featuring British, Commonwealth, European and U.S. Military aviation articles. Illustrated in colour and black & white.

Other Benefits
Additional to the above, members have exclusive access to the Air-Britain e-mail Information Exchange Service (ab-ix) where they can exchange information and solve each other's queries, and to an on-line UK airfield residents database. Other benefits include numerous Branches, use of the Specialists Information Service; Air-Britain trips; and access to black & white and colour photograph libraries. During the summer we also host our own popular FLY-IN. Each autumn, we host an Aircraft Recognition Contest.

Membership Subscription Rates - from £20 per annum.
Membership subscription rates start from as little as £20per annum (2011), and this amount provides a copy of 'Air-Britain Aviation World' quarterly as well as all the other benefits covered above. Subscriptions to include any or all of our other three magazines vary between £25 and £57 per annum (slightly higher to overseas).
Join in 2011 for two years (2011-2012) and save £5 off the total subscription

Join on-line at www.air-britain.co.uk or write to 'Air-Britain' at 1 Rose Cottages, 179 Penn Road, Hazlemere, High Wycombe, Bucks HP15 7NE, UK. Alternatively telephone/fax on 01394 450767 (+44 1394 450767 from outside UK) or e-mail membenquiry@air-britain.co.uk and ask for a membership pack containing the full details of subscription rates, samples of our magazines and a book list.

AIR-BRITAIN SALES

Companion publications to this AIRLINE FLEETS 2011 are also available by post-free mail order from:

Air-Britain Sales Department (Dept AF11)
41 Penshurst Road, Leigh,
Tonbridge, Kent TN11 8HL

Orders may also be placed by Answerphone/Fax 01732 835637 or by e-mail to
sales@air-britain.co.uk

For a full list of current titles and details of how to order, visit our e-commerce site at www.air-britain.co.uk Visa credit / Visa debit / Mastercard / Solo / Maestro accepted - please give full details of card number and expiry date.

AIRLINE FLEETS QUICK REFERENCE - AFQR 2011

Contains 240 pages of airline fleet lists of all the major national and international carriers likely to be seen in Western Europe and in major airports world wide. The companion A5 size volume to Airline Fleets, AFQR includes types, c/ns, fleet numbers, lease data and easy-to-use tick boxes.
Price £8-95 (or £6-95 to Air-Britain members)

BUSINESS JETS & TURBOPROPS QUICK REFERENCE– BizQR 2011

Contains 160 A5-pages listing all currently active civil or military business jets and corporate airliners by country in registration/serial order. Now expanded to include Business Turboprops. Correct to January 5th 2011 and also includes US reserved registrations. *Price £8-95 (or £6-95 to Air-Britain members)*

UK/IRELAND CIVIL/MILITARY REGISTERS QUICK REFERENCE– UKQR 2011

Around 180 A5-size pages giving the regns and types of all current UK, Irish and foreign-registered aircraft based in the UK, serials and types of all current military aircraft, and lists of which aircraft are based at all of the major and many of the minor UK/Ireland civil airfields and microlight strips.
Price £8-95 (or £6-95 to Air-Britain members)

UK/IRELAND CIVIL REGISTERS 2011

The 47th annual edition of our longest-running title lists all current G-, M- and EI- allocations, plus overseas-registered aircraft based in the UK, alphabetical index by type, military-civil marks de-code, full BGA and microlight details, museum aircraft etc. At over 600 pages this is the UK civil aircraft register bible.
Publication scheduled for April 2011

BUSINESS JETS INTERNATIONAL 2011

The only publication that gives full production lists for all biz-jets in c/n order with details of all regns/serials carried, model numbers and fates, plus a 65,000+ index of biz-jet regns, now in its 26th edition at around 600 pages. *Publication scheduled for May 2011*

EUROPEAN REGISTERS HANDBOOK 2011

Now in combined book/CD format for the 26th edition, ERH contains the current civil aircraft registers of all 45 European countries lying to the west of Russia except the UK. The book is in A5 quick-reference format while the searchable CD contains all the c/ns with full previous identities and additional data including balloons, gliders and microlights. Many colour images of selected 2010 European civil flying events are also featured.
Publication scheduled for May 2011

IMPORTANT NOTE - Members receive substantial discounts on prices of all the above Air-Britain publications, as shown, together with many other direct benefits. Remember to quote your Membership number when ordering.
**For details of membership see previous page or visit our website at
http://www.air-britain.co.uk**